W9-BMZ-124

THE Rolling Stone ALBUM GUIDE

COMPLETELY NEW REVIEWS: EVERY ESSENTIAL ALBUM, EVERY ESSENTIAL ARTIST

EDITED BY

ANTHONY DECURTIS AND JAMES HENKE

WITH HOLLY GEORGE-WARREN

REVIEWERS: MARK COLEMAN, J. D. CONSIDINE, PAUL EVANS, DAVID McGEE

RANDOM HOUSE/NEW YORK

This work was originally published
in different form as *The* ROLLING STONE *Record Guide*
in 1979 by Random House, Inc. A revised and
updated edition was published in 1983
by Random House, Inc.

Library of Congress Card Cataloging-in-Publication Data

The Rolling Stone album guide: completely new reviews: every
essential album, every essential artist/ edited by Anthony DeCurtis
and James Henke with Holly George-Warren: reviewers, Mark Coleman
. . . [et al.].
p.   cm.
ISBN 0-679-73729-4
1. Popular music—Discography.   2. Sound recordings—Reviews.
I. DeCurtis, Anthony.   II. Henke, James.   III. George-Warren, Holly.
IV. Rolling Stone.
ML156.4.P6R62   1992   781.66′026′6—dc20   92-50156
CIP
MN

Manufactured in the United States of America
6897

INTRODUCTION BY ANTHONY DeCURTIS

This completely new version of *The* ROLLING STONE *Album Guide* is the product of two complementary aspirations. The first is to provide a first-rate consumer guide for fans who want knowledgeable assistance as they explore styles of music or the work of artists with whom they are wholly or partially unfamiliar. The second is to provide, in addition to recommendations of specific albums, a critical overview of artists' careers, so that a rich understanding of the music can become part of the listener's enjoyment.

That second goal means that, as they flip through the pages of the *Album Guide*, readers will hopefully find unanticipated pleasures, signposts that will send them off in directions they otherwise might not have taken. Unlike so much critical writing about rock & roll these days, the entries in this book assume that readers are intelligent and interested, that music and ideas about music are important elements in their lives. The book also takes a broad-minded approach to the worth of—and the ability of all people to appreciate—all types of music. If fans of My Bloody Valentine find themselves absorbed in the essay about Dinah Washington, or if fanatic Beatlemaniacs are gripped by the Public Enemy piece, the most idealistic purposes of the *Album Guide* will have been fully realized.

Astonishingly, the entire *Album Guide* was written by four critics, the hardest-working men in show business: Mark Coleman, J. D. Considine, Paul Evans and David McGee. All longstanding contributors to ROLLING STONE's record review section, they bring to the *Guide* both specific areas of expertise and the ability to write in informed and sympathetic ways about many types of music. Broadly speaking, their assignments were based on decades: McGee handled artists of the Fifties and earlier; Evans tackled the Sixties; Coleman concentrated

on the Seventies; and Considine covered the period from the Eighties to the present. Beyond that chronological breakdown, each writer took on subjects outside his focus, either to make a point about certain artists and their relation to particular period styles—or for the sheer fun of it.

The decision to have four writers do the entire *Guide*—as opposed to the more than fifty who contributed to the earlier versions—resulted from a desire to achieve a greater consistency of voice and tone in the book, thereby making it more valuable as a critical reference. The idea is that even casual readers will eventually establish a relationship with each of the four critics and develop a feel for their perspectives. That will better enable readers to determine how completely they abide the writers' opinions. One person's classic may well be another's disaster, after all, and knowing what a critic's criteria are makes it easier to know when that's the case.

Some general guidelines should be kept in mind when reading the *Guide*. In all instances, the book attempts to focus on albums that are in print and possible to find (as of Spring 1992). In some cases, usually at the discretion of the individual writer, out-of-print albums are listed in the discography or discussed in the accompanying essay. When that happens, the album will be referred to in the text as "out of print" or "deleted." Readers should be aware that out-of-print albums are sometimes possible to find in secondhand shops or even regular record stores; that a company has stopped producing an album does not mean that every copy of it has disappeared from the market. Also, in the age of CD reissues, innumerable albums are being brought back into print. If a description of a deleted album catches your eye, it may well be worth your time to seek it out.

Some mail-order houses offer catalogues that may prove helpful in tracking down hard-to-find albums:

Mosaic Records, 204 Fairview Avenue, Stamford, CT 06902 (203-327-7111): Vintage jazz and blues.

Rhino Mail Order, 2225 Colorado Avenue, Santa Monica, CA 90404 (800-432-0020): Vintage rock & roll, R&B, country and novelty reissues.

Roots & Rhythms, 6921 Stockton Avenue, El Cerrito, CA 94530 (415-525-1494): Vintage rock & roll, R&B and country, as well as folk and world music.

Rounder Records, P.O. Box 154, North Cambridge, MA 02140 (800-443-4727): Folk, blues, vintage rock, R&B.

Shanachie Records, 37 East Clinton Street, Newton, NJ 07860 (201-579-7763): World music, reggae, Celtic, vintage blues and gospel.

The *Guide*'s chapters are organized alphabetically by artist, with separate chapters included for soundtracks and anthologies. The discography for each artist consists of chronological entries for individual albums, including the album's title, the label on which the album is available and the year in which the album was released. In the case of reissues, the original release date precedes the label on which the album is currently available; the reissue date then follows. When no release date is available, the indication "NA" follows the label.

Take the following entry as an example:

★ ★ ★ ★ **Back in the USA (1970; Rhino, 1992)**
The entry indicates that *Back in the USA*, a four-star album originally released in 1970, was reissued by Rhino in 1992.

For all of the factual information and critical rankings it makes available, *The* ROLLING STONE *Album Guide* stands as a resounding tribute to the accomplishments of popular music. The staggering array of artists who have devoted their lives to writing, playing and singing—the brash experiments and the crass commercial one-offs, the aesthetic breakthroughs and serviceable run-throughs, the masterpieces and the embarrassments—all blend into a compelling vision of the world rendered in sound. Good fortune on your travels through that world.

RATINGS

★ ★ ★ ★ ★

Classic: Albums in this category are essential listening for anyone interested in the artist under discussion or the style of music that artist's work represents.

★ ★ ★ ★

Excellent: Four-star albums represent peak performances in an artist's career. Generally speaking, albums that are granted four or more stars constitute the best introductions to an artist's work for listeners who are curious.

★ ★ ★

Average to Good: Albums in the three-star range will primarily be of interest to established fans of the artist being discussed. This mid-range, by its very nature, requires the most discretion on the part of the consumer.

★ ★

Fair to Poor: Albums in the two-star category either fall below an artist's established standard or are, in and of themselves, failures.

★

Disastrous: Albums in the range of one star or less are wastes of vital resources. Only masochists or completists need apply.

CONTRIBUTORS

Reviewers

MARK COLEMAN (M.C.) began reviewing albums when they were still called records. Since 1980 his articles have appeared in ROLLING STONE, *Details, Musician*, the *Los Angeles Times, Newsday, Star Hits*, the *Village Voice, New York Rocker* and other assorted periodicals. Currently the pop music critic for *Us* magazine, he lives in New York City with his wife, Susan.

J. D. CONSIDINE (J.D.C.) has been writing about music since 1977. In addition to his duties as pop music critic at the *Baltimore Sun* and *Evening Sun*, he is a contributing editor at *Musician* and writes regularly for ROLLING STONE; his work has also appeared in a variety of other publications, including *Playboy*, the *Village Voice*, the *Washington Post, Request* and numerous now-defunct magazines. He is the author of *Van Halen!*, and lives in Baltimore with his wife, Susanne, and cat, Miles.

PAUL EVANS (P.E.) is an Atlanta-based free-lance writer who regularly contributes album reviews to ROLLING STONE. He has written about Prince for *The* ROLLING STONE *Illustrated History of Rock & Roll* (Random House, 1992), and his fiction has been published by *Puerto del Sol* and *South Atlantic Quarterly*.

DAVID MCGEE (D.M.) is the senior editor and Nashville bureau chief for the recording industry trade publication *Pro Sound News* and a free-lance writer specializing in music, sports, travel and men's health and fitness. He was formerly assistant managing editor of the music industry trade publication *Record World*, editor of *Record* magazine and managing editor of *Spin*. As a journalist, he has been published by ROLLING STONE, *New Musical Express, BMI*

Music World, Video, Healthy Man and *Men's Health*. In addition, he has written scripts for the 1987 highlight films of the Milwaukee Brewers and Los Angeles Dodgers, for four volumes of *SPORT Baseball Video Magazine* and for an instructional baseball video, *The Inner Game of Baseball*, starring major league veterans Dave Parker and Mark McGwire. He is currently at work on a biography of rock & roll pioneer Carl Perkins.

Editors

ANTHONY DECURTIS is a senior features editor at ROLLING STONE, where he oversees the record review section, and the pop music critic for *Weekend All Things Considered* on National Public Radio. He edited *Present Tense: Rock & Roll and Culture* (Duke University Press, 1992), and his liner notes for the Eric Clapton retrospective *Crossroads* won a Grammy in 1988. He holds a Ph.D. in American literature from Indiana University.

JAMES HENKE has been an editor at ROLLING STONE since 1977. Currently the magazine's music editor, he has interviewed numerous artists over the years, including U2, Bruce Springsteen and Eric Clapton. He is also the author of *Human Rights Now!*, a journal of the 1988 Amnesty International tour.

HOLLY GEORGE-WARREN is the coauthor of *Musicians in Tune: Seventy-Five Contemporary Musicians Discuss the Creative Process* (Fireside/Simon & Schuster, 1992), and has contributed to many magazines and books, including the essay "Women in Revolt" for *The* ROLLING STONE *Illustrated History of Rock & Roll* (Random House, 1992).

A

ABBA

★★★★   **Greatest Hits (Atlantic, 1976)**
  ★★★   **Greatest Hits, Vol. 2 (Atlantic, 1979)**
  ★★★   **I Love Abba (Atlantic, 1984)**
  ★★★   **Abba Live (Atlantic, 1986)**

ANNI-FRIDA LYNGSTAD (FRIDA)

  ★★★½   **Something's Going On (Atlantic, 1982)**

Like a certain ubiquitous fast-food chain, the Swedish conglomerate Abba sold millions of its plastic-wrapped pop songs during the '70s and early '80s—in all four corners of the globe. Agnetha Faltskog and Anni-Frida Lyngstad chirp and coo in bland English, while studio-meisters Bjorn Ulvaeus and Benny Andersson achieve a sort of musical Esperanto. Abba is the purest expression of Euro-pop: a synthesized, easy-listening gloss on the Beatles' lighter moments. Abba's calculated inoffensiveness still offends people.

Abba's *Greatest Hits* lurks in bargain bins, so beware: its guilty pleasures have reduced many otherwise "serious" listeners to gibbering fools. Deceptively simple, Abba's cheerful ditties have a way of wearing down all sensible objections; the telegraphic chorus of "S.O.S.," the galloping charge of "Waterloo," the merry-go-round twirl of "I Do I Do I Do I Do I Do," the oh-so-grave sappiness of "Fernando"—these aren't the kind of hooks one argues with. The scarcer *Greatest Hits, Vol. 2* picks up Abba's singles trail in 1977; with the notable exception of "Dancing Queen," many of the same songs are available on 1984's longer (and more satisfying) *I Love Abba*. The strange, surprisingly exciting live album stands out in a singularly odd career; apparently, Abba didn't invent lip-synching after all. It's recommended to fanatics, but then, Abba tends to inspire total devotion or nothing at all.

Despite all those bouncy worldwide million-sellers—and partially *because* of 'em—Abba's star quickly faded in 1981. That's a shame because singer Anni-Frida Lyngstad, better known as Frida, released a sharp, rock-oriented, delightfully eclectic solo album (*Something's Going On*) in 1982. The LP packs a surprising guitar punch: a heightened appreciation of Abba's smooth Euro-pop voicings is definitely not required here. Teaming up with then-fledgling producer Phil Collins, Frida proves to be conversant with a range of material that looks odder than it sounds. She finds an emotional center in offbeat songs by Bryan Ferry, Giorgio Moroder and Stephen Bishop, and even pulls off a Dorothy Parker poem set to music. Like many out-of-print major-label albums, *Something's Going On* frequently crops up in the discount bins. It's worth the search. — M.C.

PAULA ABDUL

  ★★   **Forever Your Girl (Virgin, 1988)**
   ★   **Shut Up and Dance (The Dance Mixes) (Virgin, 1990)**
 ★★½   **Spellbound (Virgin, 1991)**

Former Laker Girl and perennial MTV diva, Paula Abdul made the most successful debut in history (!) with an album featuring an embarrassment of hits. "Forever Your Girl," "Cold Hearted," "Opposites Attract," "Straight Up," etc., etc.—aerobicized rhythm tracks and sex-chipmunk singing, this was Madonna-cloning at its most plastic. The things did, however, pound out of your radio; and if Abdul's genius was packaging, it only made her CD exactly right for its moment. Her followup, of course, was dance mixes of her hits—a move brilliant in its obviousness. Her next full-length album, *Spellbound*, showed little advance. — P.E.

ABC

 ★★★   **The Lexicon of Love (Mercury, 1982)**
 ★★½   **Beauty Stab (Mercury, 1983)**

★ ★ ★   **How to Be a . . . Zillionaire!**
(**Mercury, 1983**)
★ ★ ★½ **Alphabet City (Mercury, 1985)**
★ ★ ★   **Up (Mercury, 1989)**
★ ★ ★ ★ **Absolutely (Mercury, 1990)**
Vocalist Martin Fry and keyboardist Mark
White are the debonair duo behind ABC,
and their pop smarts are undisputable. After
a while, all ABC sounds samey, so relentless
is the band's instrumental professionalism
and so apt (predictable?) its hooks. *Beauty
Stab* features more guitar than *The Lexicon
of Love*; *Alphabet City* is more
straightforward in its lyrics than *Zillionaire!*
But those are fine distinctions. Roxy Music
without Ferry's tortured romanticism seems
to be ABC's aspiration—and they pull it off
in spades. — P.E.

ACCEPT
★ ★ ★   **Restless & Wild (Portrait, 1983)**
★ ★ ★   **Balls to the Wall (Portrait, 1984)**
★ ★ ★½ **Metal Heart (Portrait, 1985)**
★ ★ ★   **Russian Roulette (Portrait, 1986)**
★ ★ ★   **Accept (Portrait, 1986)**
  ★ ★   **Eat the Heat (Epic, 1989)**
★ ★ ★ ★ **Staying a Life (Epic, 1990)**
Fronted by Udo Dirkschneider, a leather-
lunged singer whose sound could best be
described as a cross between the strident
tenor of Judas Priest's Rob Halford and the
throat-shredding howl of AC/DC's Brian
Johnson, this German heavy-metal outfit
never had a mass following in the U.S. But
in Europe, Accept's uncompromising sound
and unmistakable passion helped make it
the hottest metal act on the Continent. It
wasn't simply that Accept's sound hit hard,
backing Dirkschneider's guttural shrieks
with ear-searing guitar and bone-crunching
rhythm work; what put Accept over the top
was the way it used that fiery sound to forge
melodic steel.

Although several Accept albums (in
various packages) had been released in this
country before Portrait picked up *Restless &
Wild*, the band's sound had been uneven
and unfocused. *Restless* is a step in the right
direction, matching its hell-for-leather attack
with a sturdy set of melodies, but it's *Balls
to the Wall* that really put Accept on the
map. Both the title tune and "Fight It
Back" show how easily Accept can chain
instrumental aggression to a stirring metal
melody, but the real interest lies with the
likes of "London Leatherboys," which goes
well beyond the usual limits of the
heavy-metal song form. (All but three songs
from *Restless & Wild* and one song from
Balls to the Wall are included on *Accept*).

With *Metal Heart*, Accept entered its
prime. In addition to the title tune, which
manages to work bits of "Marche Slave"
and "Für Elise" into its sonic assault, its
offerings range from the frothing fury of
"Dogs on Leads" to the surprisingly
pop-friendly "Screaming for a Love-Bite."
Russian Roulette, though, sacrifices pop
sense for aural impact; although "Aiming
High" and "Man Enough to Cry" boast
many of the same strengths as *Metal Heart*'s
best, most of the album is mere sound and
fury, signifying nothing. That was to be
Accept's last hurrah, however; both
Dirkschneider and guitarist Jörg Fischer
were gone by the time of *Eat the Heat*, and
though the album delivers much of the
punch of its predecessors, the songs seem
flat by comparison. Fortunately, the
live-in-Japan *Staying a Life* catches the
band at its best. — J.D.C.

AC/DC
  ★ ★   **High Voltage (Atlantic, 1976)**
  ★ ★½ **Let There Be Rock (Atlantic,
1977)**
  ★ ★½ **Powerage (Atlantic, 1978)**
  ★ ★ ★ **If You Want Blood, You've Got It
(Atlantic, 1978)**
  ★ ★ ★ **Highway to Hell (Atlantic, 1979)**
★ ★ ★ ★ **Back in Black (Atlantic, 1980)**
  ★ ★ ★ **Dirty Deeds Done Dirt Cheap
(Atlantic, 1981)**
  ★ ★ ★½ **For Those About to Rock, We
Salute You (Atlantic, 1981)**
  ★ ★½ **Flick of the Switch (Atlantic,
1983)**
  ★ ★½ **'74 Jailbreak (Atlantic, 1984)**
  ★ ★½ **Fly on the Wall (Atlantic, 1985)**
★ ★ ★ ★ **Who Made Who (Atlantic, 1986)**
  ★ ★½ **Blow Up Your Video (Atlantic,
1988)**
  ★ ★ ★ **The Razor's Edge (Atco, 1990)**
AC/DC rose during the second half of the
'70s, but this veteran Australian quintet
forged the metal archetype of the '80s with
its turn-of-the-decade release *Back in Black*.
Perhaps AC/DC's most crucial innovation
is the way its lyrics make plain the boys'
locker-room conception of sexuality that
had previously bubbled just under the
surface of most heavy-duty rock.
Shamelessly sexist panderers or refreshingly
frank entertainers? AC/DC fits both
descriptions, but the truth is, none of it
would matter if guitarist Angus Young
wasn't such a gargantuan riff-monger
equipped with a Godzilla-like rhythm
section to boot. Learn to laugh with or at
lead singer Brian Johnson's shrieking

depictions of those hormonal surges, and AC/DC's thundering musical charge will sweep you up like a riptide.

Before *Back in Black*, the band could never quite harness its sound and fury. Original lead singer Bon Scott pioneered the raunchy, high-pitched style that Johnson later perfected; he died shortly after AC/DC's belated American breakthrough, *Highway to Hell*. Produced by pop-metal maven Robert John "Mutt" Lange, that album actually sharpens the band's impact by refining some of its rougher edges. "You Shook Me All Night Long," from *Back in Black*, the Lange-produced platinum followup, epitomizes AC/DC's streamlined attack: a ringing, near-melodic chorus is welded onto a granite-shattering beat. "Rock and Roll Ain't Noise Pollution" insists the climactic final cut, but overall *Back in Black* proves that noise pollution, when properly deployed, can qualify as rock & roll.

Predictably, AC/DC hasn't changed a whit since then. Angus Young still stalks the stage in a schoolboy's uniform, tossing off riffs and abbreviated solos while his brother Malcolm strokes a propulsive rhythm guitar and Brian Johnson shakes the roof. *For Those About to Rock* almost measures up to the heft of *Back in Black*, but successive albums quickly become rote. AC/DC's macho posturing is unspeakably dull when it is not supported by killer hooks. (*Dirty Deeds Done Dirt Cheap* compiles the best of Bon Scott–era AC/DC; the title cut is a trashy, irresistible revenge fantasy.) A quickie soundtrack album, *Who Made Who* nevertheless works as an effective introduction to the group: previous triumphs ("You Shook Me All Night Long") contrast with reclaimed later efforts ("Sink the Pink," from *Fly on the Wall*) and a completely out-of-character '70s blooze number called "Ride On." Of course, AC/DC returns to business-as-usual with *Blow Up Your Video*, where even the hottest riffs ("Heatseeker") don't seem to detonate with the same gratifying crunch. But after girding its loins for a few years, AC/DC confidently stalked back into the metal arena with *The Razor's Edge*—loud and proud. "Money Talks" makes the prospect of AC/DC's eventual hits collection seem all the more enticing to non-metalheads.
— M.C.

JOHNNY ACE
★ ★ ★ ★ **The Johnny Ace Memorial Album (MCA, 1974)**

Born John Alexander in Memphis, Johnny Ace was the piano player in a band dubbed the Beale Streeters that often backed B. B. King and Bobby Bland in the late '40s. But Ace, blessed with a smooth, sturdy baritone voice, had no intention of remaining a faceless backing musician. Signed to Duke Records, he proceeded to cut several R&B hits that showed him comfortable delivering a blues ballad ("So Lonely") as well as uptempo material ("Don't You Know"). He didn't have great range, and sometimes he wobbled slightly off-key, but Ace did have presence and personality. Among the 12 cuts here is "Pledging My Love," the ballad that hit the Top Twenty and might have made him a crossover star if it hadn't made him a legend first. When it was released in 1955, Ace was dead, having expired on Christmas Eve of 1954 after losing a game of Russian roulette backstage before a Christmas Eve show at the City Auditorium in Houston, Texas. *Memorial Album*'s hyperbolic liner notes lack any references to backing musicians or recording dates, but those familiar with some of the early Sun blues sessions will want to check out the scorching, distorted guitar solo on "How Can You Be So Mean," in title and atmosphere a bow to B. B. King. — D.M.

WILLIAM ACKERMAN
★ ★ ★   **In Search of the Turtle's Navel (Windham Hill, 1976)**
★ ★½ **It Takes a Year (1977; Windham Hill, 1986)**
★ ★½ **Childhood and Memory (Windham Hill, 1979)**
★ ★ ★   **Passage (Windham Hill, 1981)**
★ ★½ **Past Light (Windham Hill, 1983)**
★ ★ ★   **Conferring With the Moon (Windham Hill, 1986)**
★ ★½ **Imaginary Roads (Windham Hill, 1988)**
★ ★½ **The Opening of Doors (Windham Hill, 1992)**

If only for having founded Windham Hill, Ackerman would be guaranteed a place in the new acoustic pantheon. But the fact is, he's also a pretty good guitarist—a better colorist than a composer, granted, but quite a listenable player nonetheless. His debut, the solo guitar *In Search of the Turtle's Navel*, offers a nice compromise between traditional folkie finger-picking and fashionable new age atmospherics, but on the whole, his most interesting albums stress ensemble playing. Of these, *Passage* offers a pleasant approximation of chamber ensemble interplay, and *Conferring With the*

Moon plays off of some inspired instrumental combinations (the cello choir on "The Last Day at the Beach" is particularly striking). — J.D.C.

ROY ACUFF

★★ **The Best of Roy Acuff (1963; Capitol, 1989)**
★★★★ **Greatest Hits (Columbia, 1970)**
★★★★ **Roy Acuff: Columbia Historic Edition (Columbia, 1985)**
★★★ **American Originals (Columbia, 1990)**

It's hard to pinpoint what might be most amazing about Roy Acuff's career. He peaked as a recording artist in the 1940s, but the songs he did to that point are among the most celebrated in country music history, and unquestionably broadened the audience for country music at a time when its boundaries were limited to the southern United States. He is not technically a gifted singer, but he has mastered several different styles and his rough-hewn mountain voice carries incredible emotional wallop, even in his late 80s. He is not the best fiddler to come down the pike, yet he is forever linked with the instrument. Family, trains and church are about all he has ever sung about, but he has taken these themes and made them and himself about as big as America. He was the first nationally recognized Grand Ole Opry star, an immediate sensation following his first appearance in 1938. A nervous Acuff destroyed his live and national radio audience with a stirring version of "The Great Speckled Bird," a mysterious religious tune written in part by Acuff himself; over 50 years later he remains the Opry's star attraction, hosting two segments a night every Friday and Saturday, and a Sunday matinee, where he invariably performs "The Great Speckled Bird" and his other signature song, "The Wabash Cannonball."

Columbia's *Greatest Hits* and *Historic Edition* albums offer the most complete overview of Acuff's critical recordings. The former includes "The Great Speckled Bird" and "Wabash Cannonball," as well as other items from Acuff's early repertoire, notable among them being an awesome rendition of "Were You There When They Crucified My Lord" that sounds like an on-the-scene report. *Historic Edition* is in many ways the more interesting of the two collections, owing to its inclusion of rare sides that offer a broad perspective of the many styles Acuff explored in his heyday. "Freight Train Blues" and "Steel Guitar Blues," for

example, show Acuff's familiarity with blues structures; "Ida Red" finds Acuff and his band stepping lively into the realm of the hoe-down; "When I Lay My Burden Down" and "Drifting Too Far From the Shore" are gospel evocations of guilt and redemption; "You're the Only Star (in My Blue Heaven)" could easily have landed on the pop Hit Parade of its time. *Historic Edition* gets the nod over the *American Originals* set for its extensive liner notes, as compared to none on the latter. The Capitol *Best of* collection contains new recordings of most of Acuff's classic songs, none as satisfying as the originals. — D.M.

ADAM AND THE ANTS

★★ **Dirk Wears White Sox (1979; Epic, 1983)**
★★★½ **Kings of the Wild Frontier (Epic, 1980)**
★★ **Prince Charming (Epic, 1981)**

ADAM ANT

★★★½ **Friend or Foe (Epic, 1982)**
★ **Strip (Epic, 1983)**
★★ **Vive le Rock (Epic, 1985)**
★★★ **Manners & Physique (MCA, 1989)**
★★★½ **Antics in the Forbidden Zone (Epic, 1990)**

Pirouetting onstage in Jolly Roger drag and Apache war paint, Adam Ant was the campiest figurehead of the New Romantic moment that also enlisted Bow Wow Wow and Duran Duran. Fashioning himself as a sort of ironic teen idol from Mars, Adam parlayed snappy '50s-derived rock cut with B-movie kitsch—Tarzan conga drums meet twanging guitars, chants and echoey production. Adam had the pop dash that hits big in England, but coaxes snickers stateside. *Kings of the Wild Frontier* was the first cohesive version of the Adam "vision"; leering, self-mythologizing and driven by the Duane Eddy guitar of Adam's crown flunky, Marco Pirroni, the record broadcast loopy, faux-teen fun.

Adam's first solo bit was better. Buoyed by slap-dash brass, *Friend or Foe*'s "Goody Two Shoes" and "Crackpot History and the Right to Lie" were gasping, sighing pop-rock. More of a face than a voice, Adam has made trash as often as he's mined gold. He came back strong with *Manners & Physique* in 1989. More mainstream than his fetchingly odd Antmusic, it traded on the skills of ex-Prince cohort André Cymone, whose production helped it work as a mix of British glamour-pop and Minneapolis R&B. *Antics in the Forbidden Zone* (1990) compiles all the Ant worth having. — P.E.

BRYAN ADAMS
★ ★ ★   Bryan Adams (A&M, 1980)
  ★ ★   You Want It, You Got It (A&M, 1981)
★ ★ ★   Cuts Like a Knife (A&M, 1983)
★ ★ ★½ Reckless (A&M, 1984)
  ★ ★   Into the Fire (A&M, 1987)
★ ★ ★   Waking Up the Neighbours (A&M, 1991)

As a singer, Adams can't quite master Paul Rodgers's clenched passion or Rod Stewart's tender gruffness. As a writer, he falls more than a few notches short of Bob Seger's small-town mythologizing. But, in the early '80s, Adams tried valiantly to match these strengths—and, on his singles, at least, came close to delivering an easier, radio-perfect version. Beginning as a songwriter for Bachman-Turner Overdrive, Kiss and Bob Welch, the harmlessly leather-jacketed Canadian embodied the rock-as-career-choice approach of his moment; he was crafty, modest, competent, likable. And sometimes inspired. "Cuts Like a Knife" (1983) and "Summer of '69" (1985) were perfect as bright, chunky singles. Otherwise, he comes on like a true professional—he makes few mistakes; he makes even fewer risky, significant songs. "(Everything I Do) I Do It for You," off *Waking Up the Neighbours*, sold in stratospheric amounts, but it was Adams at his slickest, not his best. — P.E.

FAYE ADAMS
★ ★ ★   Golden Classics (Collectables, 1988)
Blues belter Adams was the lead singer in Joe Morris's Blues Cavalcade when that group was signed to Atlantic Records in the early '50s, then went solo after the Cavalcade broke up without ever recording a side. Signed to the Herald label, she cut three major hits out of the box: "Shake a Hand," "I'll Be True" and "Hurts Me to My Heart," each one a performance of both power and subtlety, the vocals at once angry and aggressive, dry and cynical. This set comprised of two of the hits ("Hurts Me to My Heart" is missing) and such interesting obscurities as "Witness to the Crime" and "The Hammer (Keeps A-Knockin)" shows off her versatility to good effect. — D.M.

JOHNNY ADAMS
★ ★ ★½ From the Heart (Rounder, 1984)
★ ★ ★½ After Dark (Rounder, 1986)
  ★ ★   Christmas in New Orleans With Johnny Adams (Maison De Soul, NA)

★ ★ ★ ★   Room With a View of the Blues (Rounder, 1988)
★ ★ ★ ★   Walking on a Tightrope (Rounder, 1989)
★ ★ ★½ Johnny Adams Sings Doc Pomus: The Real Me (Rounder, 1991)

A fine New Orleans soul singer, tending toward jazz rather than funk, Adams radiates subtlety and class. After hitting haphazardly in the late '60s with the country-ish "Release Me" and "Reconsider Me" on the small SSS label, the smooth-voiced performer began releasing tasty, powerful records in the 1980s. *From the Heart* had strong material by Doc Pomus, Dr. John and Sam Cooke; *After Dark* continued along those lines, adding numbers by John Hiatt and Paul Kelly as well as an assertive reading of the R&B classic, "Do Right Woman—Do Right Man." *Room With a View of the Blues* is Adams's leanest, highlighting the sweet slow blues of Percy Mayfield and making the most of Adams's ace collaborator, guitarist Walter "Wolfman" Washington. *Walking on a Tightrope* is total Mayfield, and it's horn-driven, elegant and durable stuff. On *The Real Me*, a set of tunes written by Doc Pomus, Adams turns in a customary first-rate performance. — P.E.

KING SUNNY ADE
★ ★ ★ ★   "Juju Music" (Mango, 1982)
★ ★ ★ ★   Synchro System (Mango, 1983)
★ ★ ★ ★   Ajoo (Makossa, 1983)
★ ★ ★ ★½ Aura (Mango, 1984)
★ ★ ★ ★   Return of the Juju King (Mercury, 1987)
★ ★ ★½ Live Live Juju (Rykodisc, 1988)

A genuine superstar in his native Nigeria since the late '60s, juju musician King Sunny Ade was introduced to audiences in Europe and the U.S. in 1982 as "the next Bob Marley"—a sales pitch aimed more at stoking the engines of hype than accurately describing Ade's music. Granted, juju (as Ade plays it) is a catchy and exotic sound, but far more foreign to Western ears than reggae ever was. Instead of being centered around the vocal line, juju accords equal or greater importance to its guitars and drums, with episodic melodic development instead of regular verse-chorus structures. Moreover, the fact that Ade sang only in Yoruba meant that his lyrics were largely unintelligible to non-Nigerians.

Even so, Ade's Western recordings are surprisingly accessible. Well-versed in musical technology even before signing with Mango, Ade's African Beats had no difficulty absorbing the synths and drum machines added by producer Martin Meissonnier to *Juju Music* and *Synchro System*; indeed, the sound of those albums isn't all that different from what Ade offers his old audience on *Ajoo* (a Nigerian recording licensed for American release). There's even a Stevie Wonder cameo on *Aura*, which adds sparkle to the music but did little to improve sales; shortly thereafter, Ade was dropped from the label, and disbanded the African Beats.

In 1986, he returned to recording with a new group, whose sound—as evinced on *The Return of the Juju King*, a distillation of three Nigerian recordings—is somewhat more techno-intense and percussive. *Live Live Juju* gives a reasonable approximation of that group's concert sound. — J.D.C.

AEROSMITH

★ ★ ★½ **Aerosmith (Columbia, 1973)**
★ ★ ★ **Get Your Wings (Columbia, 1974)**
★ ★ ★ ★ **Toys in the Attic (Columbia, 1975)**
★ ★ ★ ★ **Rocks (Columbia, 1976)**
★ ★ ½ **Draw the Line (Columbia, 1977)**
★ ★ ½ **Live Bootleg (Columbia, 1978)**
★ ★ **A Night in the Ruts (Columbia, 1979)**
★ ★ ★ ★ **Aerosmith's Greatest Hits (Columbia, 1980)**
★ **Rock in a Hard Place (Columbia, 1982)**
★ ★ **Classics Live (Columbia, 1984)**
★ ★ ★ **Done With Mirrors (Geffen, 1985)**
★ ★ ★ **Classics Live II (Columbia, 1987)**
★ ★ ½ **Permanent Vacation (Geffen, 1987)**
★ ★ ½ **Gems (Columbia, 1988)**
★ ★ ★ ½ **Pump (Geffen, 1989)**

Aerosmith clarifies the distinction between hard rock and heavy metal. Loudly. Where Black Sabbath distills Led Zeppelin's mystical side into a bubbling crude, this Boston quintet drenches its arena-filling sound in the rhythmic essence of the blues. Lead singer Steven Tyler's quick lips and guitarist Joe Perry's anthemic riffs drew endless comparisons to the Rolling Stones during their peak; today, thanks to Run-D.M.C.'s revealing "Walk This Way" and the comeback success of *Pump* (1989), Aerosmith stands as a true original. *Toys in the Attic* and *Rocks* accelerate the Stones' initial hard-driving abandon, meeting the demands of an even more hedonistic audience.

Aerosmith establishes the band's swaggering control: the rapid-spinning musical dialogue between Tyler and Perry pushes every limit, while the rhythm section (second guitarist Brad Whitford, bassist Tom Hamilton and drummer Joey Kramer) plays it right on the money every time. The slow-building, "Stairway to Heaven"–derived mellotron ode "Dream On" became an FM radio staple upon *Aerosmith*'s release in 1973, though it didn't become a pop hit until after the success of *Rocks* three years later.

"Same Old Song and Dance" sums up the problems with *Get Your Wings*; the song and album both are better than that title suggests—but not by much. *Toys in the Attic* and *Rocks* are where Aerosmith really gets off the ground, harnessing the melodic pop thrust of "Dream On" into the band's roaring jet-engine live sound. Decadence, both real and implied, brings Aerosmith crashing down to earth on *Draw the Line* and *Live Bootleg*. By the time of the aptly titled *A Night in the Ruts*, Joe Perry had left to form his own group. (None of the Joe Perry Project's just-okay Epic albums remain in print.) Despite its huge influence in the early '80s, Aerosmith's resurgence from beyond the grave seems like a miracle. *Permanent Vacation* and the trashy, irrepressible single "Dude Looks Like a Lady" prove that the electric juice still flows through Aerosmith's collectively cleaned-up systems; *Pump* and the startling "Janie's Got a Gun" suggest that these 40-plus hard-rockers are still capable of creative growth. — M.C.

AFRIKA BAMBAATAA

★ ★ ★ ★ ★ **Planet Rock—The Album (Tommy Boy, 1986)**
★ ★ ★½ **Beware (The Funk Is Everywhere) (Tommy Boy, 1986)**
★ ★ ★½ **The Decade of Darkness (1990-2000) (EMI, 1991)**

Even if Afrika Bambaataa had never recorded a note, his place in rap history would have been assured. As leader of the Zulu Nation, this DJ-philosopher held dances, preached peace, organized break-dance competitions and generally helped promote hip-hop culture. But Bambaataa did make records, including "Planet Rock," one of the most influential dance singles of the early '80s. Essentially a gloss on Kraftwerk's "Trans-Europe Express," the single combined throbbing electrobeats (programmed by beatmasters Arthur Baker and John Robie) with enthusiastic call-and-response rapping from Bambaataa and Soulsonic Force. That single can be found on *Planet Rock—The Album*, an essential compilation collecting the Soul Sonic Force's best-known singles.

Although Afrika Bambaataa and Family's *Beware (The Funk Is Everywhere)* isn't quite as spectacular, it's far more typical of Bambaataa's album-making process. Recorded with producer Bill Laswell, it's well focused yet impressively eclectic, with material ranging from the "Atomic Dog" spoof "Bionic Kats" to an energetic take on the MC5's "Kick Out the Jams." Bambaataa tried to expand that approach with the musical "family" assembled for the unsuccessful (and since deleted) *The Light*, but bounced back with a surprisingly strong album entitled *The Decade of Darkness*. As with most of his work, the music borrows freely from other sources, but Bambaataa's ability to transform even the most familiar grooves keeps the album sounding fresh, from "Sweat" (a rewrite of Prince's "Head") to an inspired and timely update of James Brown's "Say It Loud (I'm Black, I'm Proud)." — J.D.C.

AFTER 7
★★★ **After 7 (Virgin, 1989)**
Solid if unexceptional New Jack Swing, After 7 benefits more from the ingenuity of producers L.A. Reid and BabyFace than from the skill of singers Melvin and Kevon Edmonds. Fun, but forgettable. — J.D.C.

AFTER THE FIRE
★★ **ATF (Epic, 1983)**
Tepid, arty new wave by an overblown U.K. quartet whose only claim to fame is an English-language version of "Der Kommissar." — J.D.C.

A-HA
★★ **Hunting High and Low (Warner Bros., 1985)**
★½ **Scoundrel Days (Warner Bros., 1986)**
★★½ **Stay on These Roads (Warner Bros., 1988)**
★★ **East of the Sun, West of the Moon (Warner Bros., 1990)**
Norwegian pretty boys whose first album was optioned more on the basis of the group's looks than its sound, a-ha is probably best remembered for the cartoon-style video that accompanied "Take on Me" (from *Hunting High and Low*). Musically, a-ha comes off like a lighter-weight Duran Duran (assuming such a thing is possible), the only difference being Morten Harket's excruciating falsetto. Stick with the posters. — J.D.C.

THE ALARM
★★½ **Declaration (I.R.S., 1984)**
★★½ **Strength (I.R.S., 1985)**
★★½ **Eye of the Hurricane (I.R.S., 1987)**
★★½ **Electric Folklore Live (I.R.S., 1988)**
★★½ **Change (I.R.S., 1989)**
★★★ **Standards (I.R.S./MCA, 1990)**
★★½ **Raw (I.R.S., 1991)**
With deafening acoustic guitars and electro-shock haircuts, the Alarm was mildy arresting when it came along in the mid-Eighties. And even while it shuddered with battlefield metaphors and hoarse sincerity in such obvious ways that the band seemed like clumsy copycats of the Clash, *Declaration* was promising. *Strength*, however, found the group still confused about its identity; "Spirit of '76" was a tough elegy of the kind Mott the Hoople delivered with such grace; the rest of the record still echoed Mick Jones and Joe Strummer whenever it didn't sound like U2. Oddly enough, even as the Alarm became less interesting in terms of ideas or influence, they started sounding more competent. *Eye of the Hurricane* seemed like an odd cross of U2 and Power Station: big, echoing vocals meeting crunching arena rock. *Change* also had little to say, but said it powerfully, as did *Raw*. *Standards* is the best-of; that it's not very cohesive only proves its faithfulness in rendering the Alarm's long personality crisis. — P.E.

ALICE COOPER
★★ **Pretties for You (1969; Engima Retro, 1989)**
★★★ **Easy Action (1970; Enigma Retro, 1989)**
★★★★ **Love It to Death (Warner Bros., 1971)**
★★★★ **Killer (Warner Bros., 1971)**
★★★ **School's Out (Warner Bros., 1972)**
★★ **Billion Dollar Babies (Warner Bros., 1973)**
★ **Muscle of Love (Warner Bros., 1974)**
★★★★½ **Alice Cooper's Greatest Hits (Warner Bros., 1974)**
★★★ **Welcome to My Nightmare (Atco, 1975)**
★ **Alice Cooper Goes to Hell (Warner Bros., 1976)**
★ **Lace and Whiskey (Warner Bros., 1977)**
★★ **The Alice Cooper Show (Warner Bros., 1977)**
★ **From the Inside (Warner Bros., 1978)**

★   **Flush the Fashion (Warner Bros., 1980)**
★   **Special Forces (Warner Bros., 1981)**
★½ **Poison (Epic, 1989)**
★ ★ **Trash (Epic, 1989)**
★ ★ **Hey Stoopid (Epic, 1991)**

Rock, especially the heftier variety, lost the ability to shock so long ago that Alice Cooper's original impact is hard to fathom now. A true early '70s anti-hero, Alice bridged the old generation gap and defined a new one: concerned older siblings and parents alike couldn't fathom what young teenagers *saw* in the scrawny cross-dressing geek and the simplistic blare his band passed off as music. These days, the only shocking thing about these records is just how perfect the early ones still sound. *Love It to Death* and *Killer* flesh out Alice's theatrical fantasy trip with sublime, straight-ahead rock & roll: punchy guitar riffs, roadworthy rhythms, defiant melodies, and, yes, memorable lyrics.

Vince Furnier became Alice Cooper sometime after his high-school garage band had moved to Los Angeles from Phoenix, Arizona. Frank Zappa recorded the group on his fledgling Straight label in 1969 and '70. The first album (*Pretties for You*) was strictly inept psychedelia, but the Cooper persona and a collective songwriting prowess emerged on the second (*Easy Action*). Alice Cooper moved to Detroit in 1970, where the band had been well-received on the burgeoning Midwestern heavy-metal circuit. Taking cues from the MC5's *Back in the U.S.A.* and Iggy Pop's maniacal stage approach, Alice Cooper simultaneously became tighter and even more outrageous. Caked with makeup, wrapped in a live boa constrictor, prime-time Alice was both repellent and somehow reassuring. His late-night horror-show act dramatized his fans' barely spoken fears: no matter how sexually uncertain or generally flipped out you might have felt, it was nothing compared to the Coop.

Producer Bob Ezrin provided a crisp, dynamic sound on *Love It to Death, Killer* and *School's Out.* That title track was Alice Cooper's moment: a liberating gust of pure adolescent rebellion. Unfortunately, the corny *West Side Story* quotes on "Gutter Cats Vs. the Jets" pointed toward Alice's imminent future—pure show biz. The original band departed after the sagging *Muscle of Love,* though Cooper held his ground by hiring the guitar tag-team of Steve Hunter and Dick Wagner for *Nightmare.* "Only Women Bleed" came out

of left field to become a pop hit in 1975, but Alice failed to expand on its slightly more mature tone. Golfing with George Burns, goofing on *Hollywood Squares,* Alice Cooper started making wan, lazy albums that sadly reflected his shifting priorities. *The Alice Cooper Show* featured the able Hunter-Wagner band pummeling the early classics—nostalgia, already. Alice Cooper bottomed out with the mercifully deleted *Flush the Fashion,* a half-hearted new-wave makeover from the early '80s. Subsequent MCA albums (*Constrictor, Prince of Darkness,* and *Raise Your Fist and Yell*) barely registered on the metal meter. Produced by songsmith Desmond Child, the ballyhooed 1989 comeback, *Poison,* placed a defanged Alice Cooper in the uncomfortable position of power balladeer. But *Hey Stoopid* contained a flash or two of the old reprobate's wit and wisdom, mostly on the cautionary title track: "Hey, bro, take it slow, you ain't livin' in a video." *Greatest Hits* collects all his hard-rock battle cries from the decadent days of yore—"Eighteen," "Under My Wheels," "School's Out," "No More Mr. Nice Guy"—in one irresistible, timeless album.   — M.C.

LEE ALLEN
★ ★½ **Walkin' With Mr. Lee (Collectables, NA)**

A New Orleans session player, Lee Allen alternated with Herb Hardesty as the featured saxophonist on numerous Fats Domino recordings. He had his moment in the sun in 1958 with the struttin' instrumental, "Walkin' With Mr. Lee." He rode that train for a year, making frequent appearances on the concert circuit and on television shows, particularly "American Bandstand." Later in '58, his single "Tic Toc" made it onto the lower regions of the charts, but Allen was pretty well played out as a solo artist. *Walkin' With Mr. Lee* shows off his exuberant sax style and offers a good helping of Crescent City rock & roll, circa the late '50s.   — D.M.

DUANE ALLMAN
★ ★ ★ ★ **An Anthology (Capricorn, 1972)**
★ ★ ★ ★ **An Anthology, Volume II (Capricorn, 1974)**

Both volumes of *Anthology* collect sterling examples of Duane Allman's session work, and are highly recommended to guitar students and Southern soul buffs alike. His famous solo on Aretha Franklin's "The Weight," on Volume One, is worth the price of admission alone.   — M.C.

GREGG ALLMAN

★ ★ ★ **Laid Back (Capricorn, 1974)**
★ ★ ★½ **Playin' Up a Storm (Capricorn, 1977)**
★ ★ ★ **I'm No Angel (Epic, 1987)**
★ ★ ★ **Just Before the Bullets Fly (Epic, 1988)**

Never a prolific songwriter, Gregg Allman re-cast some of his Allman Brothers tunes as moody blue pop on his 1974 solo debut (*Laid Back*) and scored a surprise hit. *Playing Up a Storm*, his harder-hitting 1977 followup, actually eclipsed most of the Allmans' work of the same period. A decade later, Gregg made a few tentative steps back in the right direction with *I'm No Angel* (1987), followed by *Just Before the Bullets Fly* (1988); the title track of the former presents a battle-scarred veteran with a surprising amount of fire left in his bones.
— M.C.

ALLMAN BROTHERS BAND

★ ★ ★ ★ **The Allman Brothers Band (Capricorn, 1969)**
★ ★ ★ ★ **Idlewild South (Capricorn, 1970)**
★ ★ ★ ★ **At Fillmore East (Capricorn, 1971)**
★ ★ ★ ★ **Eat a Peach (Capricorn, 1972)**
★ ★ ★ ★ ★ **Beginnings (Capricorn, 1973)**
★ ★ ★ ★ **Brothers and Sisters (Capricorn, 1973)**
★ ★ ★ **Win, Lose or Draw (Capricorn, 1975)**
★ ★ ★½ **The Road Goes on Forever (Capricorn, 1975)**
★ ★½ **Wipe the Windows, Check the Oil, Dollar Gas (Capricorn, 1976)**
★ ★ ★ **Enlightened Rogues (Capricorn, 1979)**
★ ★ ★ **Best of the Allman Brothers Band (Polydor, 1981)**
★ ★ ★ ★½ **Dreams (Polydor, 1989)**
★ ★ ★½ **Live at Ludlow Garage, 1970 (Polydor, 1990)**
★ ★ ★ **Seven Turns (Epic, 1990)**
★ ★ ★½ **Shades of Two Worlds (Epic, 1991)**
★ ★ ★½ **Decade of Hits (1969–79) (Polydor, 1991)**

Don't be fooled by the two lead guitars, the two drummers, the legendary concerts that only kicked into gear around the two-hour mark: boogie-til-you-puke overkill really isn't a part of the Allman Brothers' recorded legacy. Guitarist Duane and singer-organist Gregg Allman knocked around Los Angeles in the late '60s, polishing their chops in third-billed psychedelic ballroom bands such as the Hourglass and Allman Joys. Moving back to Macon, Georgia, in 1968, the Allmans put together a powerhouse outfit of similarly inclined players: second guitarist Dickie Betts, bassist Berry Oakley, drummers Butch Trucks and Jai Johanny Johanson. At the same time, Duane Allman began doing session work at the Muscle Shoals studio in Alabama—where this skinny white hippie quickly earned a reputation as a stinging, soulful accompanist. Duane and Gregg both exhibited a natural feel for black music that the much-hyped British "blues masters" of the period couldn't begin to match. Growing up in the South, they absorbed gutbucket R&B and sanctified gospel along with the more common influences of soul and freedom jazz, and came up with an unprecedented sound: a searching, polyrhythmic extension of rock. Duane and Dickie Betts shied away from distortion and over-amplified special effects; instead, they stroked clean, precise lines out of their Gibsons. On a good night, they seemed to nudge and push each other toward new heights, supported by a massive, rock-solid wall of rhythms. And Gregg's capacity as a blues belter—already startling when he was in his early 20s—grows deeper and more resonant with time.

The "Don't Want You No More"/"It's Not My Cross to Bear" medley kicks off the debut in definitive style. After a fluid jazzy intro ("Don't Want You") the band explodes into a slow blues ("Not My Cross") where Duane's guitar and Gregg's voice join in a beautifully anguished duet—wailing from the very depths of their souls. The bittersweet, organ-drenched "Dreams" showcases the band's easy-rolling melodic punch, while "Whipping Post" draws up a sturdy blueprint for the cathartic concert extrapolations that would become the Brothers' signature. *Idlewild South* is way too skimpy time-wise, but the musical development is stunning. The bible-thumping "Revival" emphasizes a crucial country music influence and the haunting, melancholy "Midnight Rider" fully asserts Gregg's identity as a singer. Once again, "In Memory of Elizabeth Reed" presents the blueprint of a concert warhorse, capturing the Allmans at their most adventurous. This is what jazz-rock fusion groups of the mid-'70s should have aspired toward.

Some would say *At Fillmore East* is the peak achievement of the band. Certainly, it communicates all the excitement and drama of the group's concert explorations. The blues standards sound grittier and more rockin' than anything on the first two albums, and after "Whipping Post" builds to its shuddering peak, that long spacey fade-out provides sheer post-orgasmic bliss. Nevertheless, *Beginnings* (the debut album and *Idlewild* packaged together) gets the nod over *Fillmore* since it takes account of the Brothers' considerable pop-song potential as well as its instrumental prowess. But rock jamming just doesn't get any better than *Fillmore East*.

Just a few months after that landmark was recorded, Duane Allman died in a motorcyle accident. He was 24. The stop-gap *Eat a Peach* extracts even more magic from the historic Fillmore stand. Perhaps the live "Mountain Jam" (almost 3/4 of an hour long) loses something in the translation to disc, but the snarling cover of Sonny Boy Williamson's "One Way Out" and the devastatingly pretty studio tracks like "Blue Sky" add quite a bit to the legend.

Bassist Berry Oakley was killed in similar circumstances in '72, just a little more than a year to the day after Duane's accident. Miraculously, the remaining group bounced back strong with *Brothers and Sisters*, wisely adding a pianist, Chuck Leavell (rather than trying to replace Duane with another guitarist), and emphasizing Dickie Betts's country-tinged picking and singing. The Brothers' refurbished, slightly twangier sound soon became the flagship model of a new genre—"southern rock." The instrumental "Jessica" isn't quite up to the standard of "Elizabeth Reed," but the liquid guitar leads on the hit single "Ramblin' Man" introduced the pop mainstream to a tangy, intoxicating regional delight.

Hard touring (and the resultant hard living) took an inevitable toll on the band, though. *Win, Lose or Draw*, a lackluster live album (*Wipe the Windows, Check the Oil, Dollar Gas*) and a passable best-of (*The Road Goes on Forever,* now deleted) show further signs of strain. *Enlightened Rogues,* from 1979, has its moments, though the presence of guest star Bonnie Bramlett on the best cut ("Crazy Love") doesn't bode well for this proudly self-contained band. The band reached its low point with a pair of rudderless albums on Arista (*Reach for the Sky* and *Brothers of the Road*, both mercifully out of print) and seemed to break up for good in the early '80s.

Inevitably, the Brothers re-convened during the nostalgic summer of '89, but the group's live shows quickly laid to rest any accusations of reputation-pimping. Gregg's voice emerges with a fresh, whiskey-ruined authority on the respectable *Seven Turns* (1990), and somehow the 1991 followup actually expands on that renewed promise. Gregg fills his sobriety songs with the shaky conviction of lived experience on *Shades of Two Worlds*: he's been to the "End of the Line" and back. But finally, it's the timeless, soaring improvisations of "Desert Blues" and "Kind of Bird" that reassert the Allman Brothers Band's unique, enduring brand of blues power. *Dreams* (1989) is a model boxed set; the surprisingly listenable, early-days selections and the carefully picked recent outings complete a picture of the band, rather than damage it with unflattering details. — M.C.

HERB ALPERT

★★½ **The Lonely Bull (A&M, 1962)**
★★★ **Whipped Cream & Other Delights (A&M, 1965)**
★★★ **Going Places (A&M, 1965)**
★★★½ **Greatest Hits (A&M, 1970)**
★★★ **Greatest Hits Vol. 2 (A&M, 1973)**
★★ **Four Sider (A&M, 1973)**
★★★ **Rise (A&M, 1979)**
★★½ **Keep Your Eye on Me (A&M, 1987)**
★★★½ **Classics Volume 20 (A&M, 1987)**
★★ **Under a Spanish Moon (A&M, 1988)**
★★ **My Abstract Heart (A&M, 1989)**
★★ **North on South Street (A&M, 1991)**
★★½ **Midnight Sun (A&M, 1992)**

Though not a particularly great trumpeter, Herb Alpert has always been a consummately tuneful player, and that, more than anything else, explains how he came to be the last of the great pop instrumentalists while fronting the Tijuana Brass. It wasn't his taste in material, which ran the gamut from big-band oldies ("Tangerine," "Getting Sentimental Over You") to gimmicky novelty numbers ("Zorba the Greek," "Tijuana Taxi") to a sort of proto-Muzak rock ("Love Potion #9," "Lemon Tree"). Nor was it his band's ostensibly Mexican sound, which was to mariachi music what Chi-Chi's is to Mexican food; after *The Lonely Bull,* the TJB's "South of the Border" sound rarely amounted to more than two-part trumpet harmony and the occasional burbling marimba. Alpert's real draw was his lyrical tone and understated delivery, and the lean, rhythmically focused arrangements he fashioned around each melody only intensified that strength.

Alpert recorded more than a dozen

albums with the TJB, of which only a selection remain in print. *The Lonely Bull* is mostly Mexicali instrumentals, although it does stretch its arrangements enough to include the likes of "Never on Sunday" and "Desafinado." But it's *Whipped Cream & Other Delights* that shows the real pop potential of Alpert's sound, building the groundwork for the singles collected on *Greatest Hits, Greatest Hits Vol. 2* and *Classics.*

After spending most of the '70s running A&M Records, the label he founded with Jerry Moss, Alpert returned with a more contemporary sound. *Rise*, for instance, took a jazz-funk approach, and gave Alpert one of the biggest singles of his career, the melancholy, bass-driven title track. *Keep Your Eye on Me* tried to up the ante by bringing in Jimmy Jam and Terry Lewis as producers on four tracks; one, "Diamonds," went Top Ten, but more on the strength of Janet Jackson's guest vocal than anything Alpert played on trumpet. Chastened since then, Alpert has tended more toward light jazz than instrumental pop.   — J.D.C.

ALTERED IMAGES
★ ★ ★½ **Happy Birthday (Portrait, 1981)**
   ★½ **Pinky Blue (Portrait, 1982)**
  ★ ★   **Bite (Portrait, 1983)**
★ ★ ★   **Collected Images (Epic UK, 1984)**
Imagine a young Shirley Temple fronting Siouxsie and the Banshees, and that's Altered Images. An acquired taste, to be sure, but not without its charms, most of which can be heard on the giddy, goofy *Happy Birthday*. Claire Grogan's chirpy vocals may seem overly precious at times, but the engagingly forthright melodic quality of songs like "Insects" and "Happy Birthday" are compensation enough. Sadly, that's not the case with the other albums. *Pinky Blue* pushes the group's youthful charm to the point of self-parody, as the inadvertently hysterical version of "Song Sung Blue" makes plain. *Bite* abandons the group's guitar-based approach entirely, opting for an ostensibly adult dance pop sound which, though it yielded a few hits—notably "Don't Talk to Me About Love"—now seems hopelessly dated. Highlights of all three can be found on the U.K. best-of, *Collected Images*, along with the group's endearingly childish debut, "Dead Pop Stars."   — J.D.C.

DAVE ALVIN
★ ★ ★   **Romeo's Escape (Epic, 1987)**
  ★ ★½ **Blue Blvd (Hightone, 1991)**

Like a lot of rock songsmiths, Dave Alvin is better at writing 'em than singing 'em, and while that hardly mattered when he was in the Blasters (since he could always rely on the golden throat of his brother, Phil), it makes quite a difference with his solo recordings. It isn't as if he's a bad singer; he can carry a tune well enough, and has no trouble handling simple C&W mannerisms. But because he's unable to add much in the way of subtlety or shading to his delivery, all we get are the bare bones of his songs—and frankly, that's not enough. *Romeo's Escape*, for instance, includes remakes of some of the Blasters' best songs, including "Border Radio" and "Long White Cadillac," but they gain nothing from the revival; even Alvin's best singing—on the honky-tonk lament "Every Night Around This Time," for instance—seems only to hint at the riches his melodies hold. *Blue Blvd* attempts to sidestep the problem by scaling back the melodies and emphasizing the lyrics, but frankly, that sort of camouflage doesn't strengthen the performance—it just weakens the songs.   — J.D.C.

PHIL ALVIN
★ ★ **Un "Sung Stories" (Slash, 1986)**
As an act of tribute, this collection of classic jazz and blues tunes is certainly a testament to Alvin's love for American music. But as a performance, it suggests that the former Blasters lead singer needs to be reminded that there's a difference between preserving a style of music, and embalming it.
— J.D.C.

AMBITIOUS LOVERS
★ ★ ★   **Envy (Editions EG, 1984)**
★ ★ ★   **Greed (Virgin, 1988)**
★ ★ ★½ **Lust (Elektra, 1991)**
Ambitious? Absolutely—these titles are the first in a planned seven-album cycle organized around the Seven Deadly Sins (although just how each album relates to its title is, frankly, difficult to discern). Lovers? Well, it's hard to tell. They certainly seem to like noise—no surprise, considering that the group's taste in session players runs to new music whiz kids like John Zorn and Bill Frisell—but there's also an obvious feeling for Brazilian pop and arty, oblique funk in the music.

However it comes together, though, the music created by this duo—guitarist-vocalist Arto Lindsay and keyboardist-producer Peter Scherer—is unlike anything else in American popular music. Whether that's a good thing depends upon your musical palate, since there's plenty of melodic interest for anyone who can hear through the abrasive textures and occasionally arcane structures. *Envy* (which is available only in Japan) is the edgiest of the three, although "Let's Be Adult" compensates through its surprisingly insinuating dance beat; *Greed* also has its noisy bits ("Too Far," which takes it there), but ups the Brazilian content considerably, especially in the engagingly egomaniacal "King." *Lust*, though, almost seems like a bid for the mainstream, thanks to near-accessible funk numbers like "Slippery" and "Monster," as well as a soulful rethink of Jorge Ben's "Ponta de Lanca Africano (Umbabarauma)." Noise junkies, however, will be relieved by the well-balanced dissonance of "Half Out of It." — J.D.C.

AMERICA
* ★ **America (Warner Bros., 1972)**
* ★ **Homecoming (Warner Bros., 1972)**
* ★ **Hat Trick (Warner Bros., 1973)**
* ★ **Holiday (Warner Bros., 1974)**
* ★ **Hearts (Warner Bros., 1975)**
* ★★½ **History: America's Greatest Hits (Warner Bros., 1976)**
* ★ **Hideaway (Warner Bros., 1976)**
* ★ **Harbor (Warner Bros., 1976)**
* ★ **America Live (Warner Bros., 1977)**
* ★ **Silent Letter (Warner Bros., 1979)**
* ★ **Alibi (Capitol, 1980)**
* ★ **View from the Ground (Capitol, 1982)**
* ★★ **Encore! More Greatest Hits (Rhino, 1990)**

You can hear the entire catalogue of America's wimpy hits recycled any night of the week by hapless folk duos in hotel bars—there's no reason to endure the originals. Beginning in 1972 by ripping off the spare, soft sound of Neil Young's lesser efforts for "Horse With No Name," this pandering California threesome made a career of diluting the style of CSN&Y—"Ventura Highway," "Sister Golden Hair," "I Need You" were humongous '70s hits, and each one was boring, earnest and ingratiating. Thinly produced (probably as a result of a mistaken faith in sounding "natural"), every one of America's albums sounds weak; with "Muskrat Love," off of *Hat Trick*, the group reached an early nadir in cuteness. Without exception, all of America's records are lame. — P.E.

ERIC ANDERSEN
* ★★★½ **The Best of Eric Andersen (1970; Vanguard, 1988)**
* ★★★★ **Blue River (1972; Columbia, 1988)**
* ★★★½ **Ghosts Upon The Road (Gold Castle, 1989)**
* ★★★★ **Stages: The Lost Album (Columbia, 1991)**

A seminal '60s folkie who'd hopped freight trains in true Woody Guthrie–Jack Kerouac fashion, Eric Andersen remained throughout the decade a figure of eternal promise who never quite caught on. While hyped early on as Dylan's successor, this very literate songwriter and graceful singer soon proved himself an artist of a very different stripe—if Bob was chameleon-like, remote and ingenious, Eric was open, receptive and the very soul of sensitivity. In time, his style (at its softest) would suggest Harry Chapin's; his country songs suggested the world-weariness of the Kristofferson to come; and his endearing sex appeal and wounded romanticism forecast those of Jackson Browne.

The title track and "Dusty Box Car Wall" from *Today Is the Highway* (1965, out of print) echoed Woody Guthrie's open-air Americana in the same reverent way that "Plains of Nebrasky-o" recalled Pete Seeger—but with "Come to My Bedside" and "Everything Ain't Been Said," it was already apparent that love songs would be Andersen's forte. *'Bout Changes and Things* (out of print) did boast his best "ramblin' boy" anthem, "Thirsty Boots," but "Close the Door Lightly When You Go" and the astonishing "Violets of Dawn" displayed deeper, more idiosyncratic gifts: By the time of his second album, Andersen had already found his theme—the ambiguous beauty and fierceness of desire. The now-deleted *'Bout Changes and Things, Take 2* merely transformed the previous set into a tentative electric version; it was less musically significant a maneuver than a mark of the singer's hipness—while others among the folk crowd looked askance at Dylan's desertion from acoustic-only fare, Andersen smartly followed suit.

Beatles' manager Brian Epstein then courted Andersen for a while, but died before cementing any alliance. Possibly as a result of that encounter, however, *More Hits From Tin Can Alley* (out of print) featured unconvincing *Sgt. Pepper*–style embellishments. Plainly, Andersen's early promise had not paid off by this time (*The Best of Eric Andersen* was an unmerited collection), and he continued to flounder with the soft-country songs of *A Country Dream* (out of print). *Blue River* (1972) was his overdue breakthrough. An album of gentle, highly crafted love songs woven together by a thread of melancholy, it remains, along with Carole King's *Tapestry*, Joni Mitchell's *Blue*, Jackson Browne's *Late for the Sky* and James Taylor's debut, the best example of the '70s singer-songwriter movement.

Then occurred an "accident" that soon came to be read as emblematic of Andersen's bad luck—the tapes to *Blue River*'s eagerly awaited follow-up mysteriously vanished. Understandably devastated by the bizarre turn of events, the singer loss momentum, and the rest of his work throughout the decade was marked by confusion and fitfulness. Unearthed and released nearly 20 years later, *Stages*, the legendary "lost album," reveals itself indeed as a masterwork. While more assured than *Blue River*, it retains that album's grace— and with all-star help from Leon Russell, Joan Baez and Dan Fogelberg, the playing is superb throughout. "Time Run Like a Freight Train" is Andersen's best song; "Baby I'm Lonesome" is leaner than he'd sounded in years; and "Wild Crow Blues," a valentine to Patti Smith, shows that he was certainly beginning to outgrow singer-songwriter preciousness—and seeking a harder, deeper sound. On the 1991 release, Andersen includes strong new material as well; backed by Rick Danko and Garth Hudson, "Dream to Rimbaud" is the standout.

It wasn't until *Ghosts Upon the Road* (1989) that Andersen truly returned to form—the record marked an outstanding return. "Irish Lace," "Too Many Times (I Will Try)" and "Six Senses of Darkness" are music of rare intelligence and finesse; the autobiographical ten-minute title track is narrative songwriting at its richest—and the entire set stands as one of the best albums of the 1980s. — P.E.

JOHN ANDERSON

★★★   **John Anderson (Warner Bros., 1980)**
★★★   **2 (Warner Bros., 1981)**
★★★   **I Just Came Home to Count the Memories (Warner Bros., 1981)**
★★★   **Wild and Blue (Warner Bros., 1982)**
★★★   **All the People Are Talkin' (Warner Bros., 1983)**
★★★   **Eye of a Hurricane (Warner Bros., 1984)**
★★★★½ **Greatest Hits (Warner Bros., 1984)**
★★★   **Tokyo, Oklahoma (Warner Bros., 1985)**
★★½ **Countrified (Warner Bros., 1986)**
★★★½ **Greatest Hits, Vol. II (Warner Bros., 1990)**

★★½ **Blue Skies Again (MCA, 1988)**
★★½ **10 (MCA, 1988)**
★★★   **Seminole Wind (BNA, 1992)**

A consistently good—and occasionally great—country singer, Anderson was one of the brighter lights in country's "new traditionalist" movement of the early '80s. As a ballad singer, he's generally at the mercy of the lyric, meaning that he only shines when the words do. While that hasn't kept him from having hits with a few slow ones, most notably "I Just Came Home to Count the Memories" (from the album of the same name), Anderson's best work is on the uptempo tunes like "Black Sheep" (from *All the People Are Talkin'*), on which his drawlin' delivery and soulful inflection intensify the groove without ever seeming to push it.

All that remains in print of Anderson's Warner Bros. recordings are his two *Greatest Hits* albums, which may miss a few memorable LP tracks but also save the listener from a whole mess of filler; if you're interested in full albums from this period, seek out either *John Anderson*, the best moments of which still seem fresh a dozen years later, or *Tokyo, Oklahoma*, which shows what Anderson can do when he puts his mind to rocking. His MCA albums, on the other hand, get by mostly on craft (although "If It Ain't Broke Don't Fix It" from *10* has its charms). *Seminole Wind* is solid enough to suggest that Anderson has life in him yet. — J.D.C.

LAURIE ANDERSON

★★★   **Big Science (Warner Bros., 1982)**
★★★½ **Mister Heartbreak (Warner Bros., 1984)**
★★★   **United States Live (Warner Bros., 1984)**
★★★   **Home of the Brave (Warner Bros., 1986)**
★★★½ **Strange Angels (Warner Bros., 1989)**

Performance artists are entertainers as much as they are artists, and in that context, the skills Laurie Anderson most relies upon tend to be comedic, not musical: timing; inflection; a sense of character that allows her to slip out of her normal deadpan and into a believable secondary voice; and, of course, the ability to distill an idea in the fewest and most effective words possible. That's not to slight her music, mind you, for though Anderson isn't much of a singer (or, at least, wasn't until *Strange Angels*), she does know how to delegate. She fleshes out her compositions with craftily arranged, meticulously produced rhythm beds, backing vocals and instrumental hooks. In other words, her albums are competent and listenable—but are they worth hearing? Yes and no. Sure, Anderson's shtick is inventive and funny, and her wry observations and revealing non sequiturs can be illuminating. In the end, though, what you're left with is closer to theater than to music, and frankly, theater isn't the sort of thing that can be listened to as readily or repeatedly as mere music.

Even so, what got Anderson's recording career going was, ironically enough, a hit single: "O Superman." Granted, it was only a hit in Britain, and owed its success mostly to the way its hypnotic strangeness transformed the mundane (an answering machine message) into the surreal, but it fits in perfectly with the rest of *Big Science.* On that album, Anderson's speech is the focus, and her musical support—keyboards, percussion and occasional saxophone or bagpipes—is skeletal and hypnotic. All of its selections came from Anderson's massive theater piece *United States,* which is offered in its entirety on *United States Live,* a four-and-a-half-hour marathon that heaps pronouncements, gags, epigrams and shaggy-dog stories into an amiable, enigmatic statement on America's inscrutability. Despite its epic sprawl, the set (five LPs, four CDs or four cassettes) moves along nicely—although it's doubtful many listeners will want to plough through it more than twice.

Anderson's other albums aren't quite as ambitiously conceptual, which makes for somewhat easier listening. *Mister Heartbreak* has the patina of pop, thanks to Bill Laswell's production on "Sharkey's Day" and "Sharkey's Night," and to "Excellent Birds," a witty collaboration with Peter Gabriel. The soundtrack *Home of the Brave* remakes the Sharkey songs and features some attractive guitar work by Adrian Belew, although the Nile Rodgers–produced "Language Is a Virus" is more clever than successful. With *Strange Angels,* though, Anderson sings more than she talks, and while that doesn't entirely turn her words-and-music constructions into songs, their cheerful melodies and flowing, Caribbean cadences make this the most approachable of Anderson's albums. — J.D.C.

LEE ANDREWS & THE HEARTS
★ ★ ★ **Gotham Recording Sessions**
   (Collectables, NA)
★ ★ ★ **Lee Andrews & the Hearts Featuring**
   Their Biggest Hits (Collectables, NA)

Lee Andrews had one sweet tenor voice, and he employed it to great effect with the Hearts in 1957 and 1958, when the group hit the Top Forty twice with, respectively, "Tear Drops" and "Try the Impossible." These tearjerkers (and another enduring track, "Long Lonely Nights") gave Andrews a chance to use his voice's highest, most fragile register to suggest a singer on the verge of a crying jag, as the Hearts glided in easily to support him with close, delicate harmony patterns. Andrews's heartfelt explications of a heart at odds with itself remind us that while the world has changed, certain human feelings apply to any place, any time when love is the issue. Andrews even acquits himself well with stirring interpretations of "Bells of St. Mary," a song Clyde McPhatter gave a near-definitive reading of with the Drifters, and "White Cliffs of Dover," a standard that was a hit for the Five Keys. And lest it be forgot, this is great slow-dancing music. *Gotham Recording Sessions* represents some of the group's earliest recorded efforts, after it had left the Rainbow label following three unsuccessful singles. Group members Andrews and Roy Calhoun were both working at Gotham pressing records when Andrews & the Hearts signed with the label. Of note among the 13 cuts from these 1956 sessions are previously unissued versions of "Long Lonely Nights," "Try the Impossible" and "Why Do I," all of which have different arrangements than the hit versions released in later years. — D.M.

AN EMOTIONAL FISH
★ ★ ★½ **An Emotional Fish (Atlantic, 1990)**
Poetic fervor and strong, beautiful playing enliven the Celtic soul of this accomplished foursome. There are hints of Lou Reed's artful disillusionment in the lyrics, and Enda Wyatt's assertive bass playing recalls the great underground Athens, Georgia, dance group, Pylon—otherwise this is an idiosyncratic music. Gerard Whelan is a passionate singer whether he's brooding or rocking, and the group isn't leery of the big themes—loneliness, anger, compassion, identity. "Lace Virginia," "Blue" and "Julian" are the standouts, but all the songs are intense and provocative. — P.E.

THE ANGELS
★ ★ **My Boyfriend's Back (Collectables, NA)**
This female trio had a Number One record in 1963 with "My Boyfriend's Back," one of the signal moments in the history of girl groups and a signal moment in the Angels'

history too, because it was the one instance in their career where the trio projected personality. Otherwise they got over solely on the strength of the songs they sang, which usually were syrupy sweet and blandly romantic. Lacking the Ronettes' panache or the Shangri-Las' attitude, the Angels opted for the safe center. "My Boyfriend's Back," then, is more like a glitch on their resume; more typical of their taste are mainstream pop songs like "Sentimental Journey," "Thank You and Goodnight" and, from 1961, "Till," the group's first hit. — D.M.

THE ANIMALS

> ★ ★ ★½ **The Animals (MGM, 1964)**
> ★ ★ ★   **The Animals on Tour (MGM, 1965)**
> ★ ★ ★ ★ **Animal Tracks (MGM, 1965)**
> ★ ★ ★ ★ ★ **The Best of the Animals (MGM, 1966)**
> ★ ★ ★ ★½ **Animalization (MGM, 1966)**
> ★ ★ ★½ **Animalism (MGM, 1966)**
> ★ ★ ★ ★ **The Best of Eric Burdon and the Animals, Vol. 2 (Polygram, 1967)**
> ★ ★ ★½ **Before We Were So Rudely Interrupted (United Artists, 1977)**
> ★ ★ ★   **Ark (I.R.S., 1983)**
> ★ ★ ★   **Rip It to Shreds: Greatest Hits Live (I.R.S., 1984)**

Monstrously talented, the Animals were second only to the Rolling Stones as British purveyors of R&B in the '60s. But internal divisiveness dogged them from the start, and while popular during their short peak, they never mustered the survivalist smarts of the Stones, and their songwriting fell consistently short of Jagger and Richards'. England never produced a finer singer, however, than Eric Burdon at his best. Hailing, as did his bandmates, from Newcastle upon Tyne, Burdon was the archetypal working-class hero, a short, boozing scrapper gifted improbably with an amazing voice. Blues and R&B perfectly suited his skills and sensibility; the U.K. equivalent of Mitch Ryder, he sang black music with almost eerie assurance. Searching for a singer, the Alan Price Combo (Price: keyboards, Hilton Valentine: guitar, Chas Chandler: bass, John Steel: drums) enlisted Burdon, guaranteeing themselves success, but also tension—Price would soon prove no match for the charismatic Burdon. So frantic were the group's early stage shows that they renamed themselves the Animals, and in their reworking of the blues standard

off Dylan's first album, "House of the Rising Sun," they gained a Number One hit with only their second single. The band then scored with a brilliant cover of Nina Simone's "Don't Let Me Be Misunderstood" and with Mann-Weill's "We Gotta Get Out of This Place," both songs making *Animal Tracks* an exceptional album. *Animalization*, however, remains their most fully realized album— effects-heavy and menacing, the guitar work on Goffin-King's "Don't Bring Me Down" is Valentine at his toughest; "Gin House Blues" is Burdon singing with frightening authority; "Inside—Looking Out" builds to a ferocious climax. Although Price left in 1965, the substitution of classically trained Dave Rowberry ensured that organ and piano would contribute heavily to the group's distinction—and the playing of the other Animals was always first-rate. But Burdon was the ace. Remarkable phrasing and unwavering focus characterized all of his work with the band; *The Best of the Animals* covers most of the essential stuff, from the anthemic "It's My Life," to their snappy last single, "See See Rider"—but the compilation isn't really extensive enough to do them justice.

In September 1966, the original Animals fell apart. Burdon was becoming enraptured with nascent psychedelia and gobbling acid; so LSD-addled had Valentine become that he began believing he was Jesus; and the rest of the group was simply exhausted. A new band, Eric Burdon and the Animals, was the result: taking along only drummer Barry Jenkins (replacing Steel, who had left in '66), Burdon moved to California and left R&B behind. The original Animals got back together in 1977 on *Before We Were So Rudely Interrupted*. A better reunion album than most, its highlight is Burdon's tortured version of "Many Rivers to Cross." Another comeback bid, *Ark*, from 1983, was less successful, and a live greatest hits package, *Rip It to Shreds*, released the next year, didn't take off, either. — P.E.

PAUL ANKA

> ★ **Diana and Other Hits (1963; RCA, 1990)**
> ★ **Paul Anka, His Best (RCA, 1978)**
> ★ ★ **30th Anniversary Collection (Rhino, 1989)**

Creepily fascinating, Paul Anka made 53 hit singles, virtually defined the Vegas sensibility and became synonymous with schlock. Johnny Carson's "Tonight Show" owed him its theme; Sinatra owes him "My Way."

While he's plundered whole continents of genres—fake Mariachi ("My Home Town," 1960), fake bossa nova ("Eso Beso [That Kiss]," 1962), and fake gospel ("Jubilation," 1972)—Anka first came to late-'50s fame penning such teen mush as "Diana," "Lonely Boy" and "Put Your Head on My Shoulder." He plumbed early depths with "The Teen Commandments"; it warned against "impure thoughts."

A singer of the worst sort—he insists on adding vibrato to his thin delivery; he can't resist verbal winking and cajoling—Anka, as a writer, bases most of his songs on generic chord progressions and verbal tropes. Starting off as a sort of diluted Bobby Darin, he only got oilier—"(You're) Having My Baby" (1974) was another low point in a career of commercial Matterhorns and aesthetic canyons. Anka is the Anti-rocker, whose notions of "class," "professionalism" and "sincerity" are why rock & roll was not only musically, but politically and spiritually, necessary. — P.E.

ANTHRAX
   ★★   **Fistful of Metal (Caroline/Megaforce, 1984)**
   ★★★   **Armed and Dangerous (Caroline/Megaforce, 1985)**
   ★★★½   **Spreading the Disease (Island, 1985)**
   ★★★   **Among the Living (Island, 1987)**
   ★★★★   **I'm the Man (Island, 1987)**
   ★★★★   **State of Euphoria (Island, 1988)**
   ★★★★   **Persistence of Time (Island, 1990)**
   ★★★★½   **Attack of the Killer B's (Island, 1991)**

Up until *I'm the Man,* Anthrax seemed like a perfectly typical thrash act. After all, not only does *Fistful of Metal* (recorded with original lead singer Neil Turbin) underscore the band's debt to conventional metal, but the version of "God Save the Queen" on *Armed and Dangerous* (featuring subsequent vocalist Joe BellaDonna) points up its debt to punk. *Spreading the Disease* shows off its chops (check the "Theme From *Masterpiece Theatre*" quote in "Gung-Ho"), while *Among the Living* emphasizes its ferocity ("Caught in a Mosh," "Efilnikufesin") and *State of Euphoria* its uncompromising point of view ("Make Me Laugh," "Schism"). But *I'm the Man* not only features a rap tune—"I'm the Man"—that outdoes the Beastie Boys at their own game, but augments that bit of hip-hop hipness with a couple of killer live tracks and a Black Sabbath cover. In other words, not only was the group down with rap, but it refused to recognize a difference between rap and thrash—a powerful gesture.

Anthrax expands in other directions with *Persistence of Time,* adding an epic sweep to songs like "Blood" and "H8 Red," while expanding its social commentary with the likes of "Keep It in the Family" and "In My World." It even has a Joe Jackson cover ("Got the Time")! Yet *Attack of the Killer B's* tops even that, boasting a version of "Bring the Noise" recorded with Public Enemy's Chuck D and Flavor Flav, as well as a nasty country-style attack on record labeling ("Startin' Up a Posse") and a deliciously deadpan ballad parody called "N.F.B. (Dallabnikufesin)." — J.D.C.

APOLLONIA
   ★½   **Apollonia 6 (Warner Bros., 1984)**
   ★   **Apollonia (Warner Bros., 1988)**
As Prince's co-star in *Purple Rain,* Patty "Apollonia" Kotero was more fun to watch than to listen to, a quality she has carried into her recording career. *Apollonia 6* is an offshoot of the *Purple Rain* soundtrack, in which Kotero is backed (and upstaged) by the non-Vanity members of Vanity 6; Apollonia swaddles her expressionless voice in a variety of dance pop styles, but still can't hide its essential vacuity. — J.D.C.

ARCADIA
   ★★   **So Red the Rose (Capitol, 1985)**
This Duran Duran spin-off project retains all the group's pretensions, but little of its approachability. Arch and arty, it's enough to make you wish Roxy Music had never happened. — J.D.C.

ARGENT
   ★★½   **Anthology (A Collection of Greatest Hits) (Epic, 1976)**
Rod Argent's keyboards cast a spell over the Zombies' oddly enduring '60s hits; in his early-'70s incarnation, he opts for all-conquering *heaviness.* Typically, the group quickly sinks under its own weight. Argent's early albums—all eight originals are out of print—concoct a promising formula. Guitarist Russ Ballard pumps out pounding, mock-anthemic hooks, with Rod Argent applying touches of color and shade on the quieter verses. The FM radio staples "Hold Your Head Up" and "Liar" are vastly appealing period-pieces. Unfortunately, the bare-bones *Anthology* does little more than reflect Argent's subsequent descent into undistinguished pummeling: from the lingering simplicity of "Hold Your Head Up" and "Liar" to the

born-again bombast of "God Gave Rock & Roll to You" and a hammer-headed live version of "Time of the Season," all in just under 40 minutes! Maybe an extensive reissue drawn from *Argent, Ring of Hands* and *All Together Now* could rehabilitate this group's fading reputation; maybe not. Argent's sole remaining document does capture a transitory moment in rock's evolution, though; the roots of arena rock lie here, if anybody's interested. — M.C.

JOAN ARMATRADING

★★ **Whatever's for Us (A&M, 1974)**
★★½ **Back to the Night (A&M, 1975)**
★★★★ **Joan Armatrading (A&M, 1976)**
★★★★ **Show Some Emotion (A&M, 1977)**
★★★½ **To the Limit (A&M, 1978)**
★★★½ **Me, Myself, I (A&M, 1980)**
★★★½ **Walk Under Ladders (A&M, 1981)**
★★★½ **The Key (A&M, 1983)**
★★★★ **Track Record (A&M, 1983)**
★★★ **Secret Secrets (A&M, 1985)**
★★★ **Sleight of Hand (A&M, 1986)**
★★★½ **The Shouting Stage (A&M, 1988)**
★★★★ **Classics, Volume 21 (A&M, 1988)**
★★★ **Hearts and Flowers (A&M, 1990)**

Between her calmly expressive vocals and impeccable ear for confessional nuance, this West Indian–born, English-bred singer-songwriter has quietly assembled quite an impressive catalogue. While none of Joan Armatrading's albums will reach out and grab you at first hearing, her best songs have a way of settling in long after the disc stops spinning. After releasing two tentative folk-pop efforts, Armatrading struck up a stimulating partnership with producer Glyn Johns. He lends just the right supportive touch to *Joan Armatrading* and *Show Some Emotion*: adding tasteful orchestrations when required, allowing Joan's subtle voice-and-guitar blend sufficient room to shine on signature compositions like "Love and Affection" and "Down to Zero" (from *Joan Armatrading*) or the title track of *Show Some Emotion*. Both albums are required listening for Tracy Chapman fans, and recommended to everybody else.

Though Armatrading doesn't vary her songwriting approach, her successive albums hop around the musical map. *To the Limit* adds chunky rock guitar and a beguiling touch of reggae ("Bottom to the Top"). Armatrading resolutely holds her own against the new-wave ministrations of producers Richard Gottehrer (*Me, Myself, I*) and Steve Lillywhite (*Walk Under*

Ladders), eventually responding to the change of pace. On *The Key*, her second album with Lillywhite, she adjusts her ever-ambiguous focus to fit the jumpy synthed-up musical backing ("Call Me Names"). *Track Record* is a near-flawless summary of her career up to this point. Strangely, after the hard-earned triumphs of the early '80s, Armatrading more-or-less coasts through the austerely tuneless *Secret Secrets* and the featherweight *Sleight of Hand*. Maybe she felt like she'd already proven that all Joan Armatrading albums really don't sound alike. *The Shouting Stage* contains her most sombre meditations, yet the vaguely jazzy music pulls you into the slowly unfolding story of a stunted relationship. *Hearts and Flowers* offers more of the usual well-crafted fare, with overt spiritual—and synthesized—overtones. — M.C.

LOUIS ARMSTRONG

★★★ **Louis Armstrong Plays W.C. Handy (1954; Columbia, 1986)**
★★★ **Satch Plays Fats (Columbia, 1955)**
★★★ **Ella & Louis (Verve/Polygram, 1956)**
★★★ **Hello, Dolly! (MCA, 1964)**
★★★★ **The Best of Louis Armstrong (1965; MCA, 1980)**
★★★ **What a Wonderful World (1968; MCA, 1988)**
★★★★★ **Louis Armstrong & King Oliver (1974; Milestone, 1992)**
★★ **Mostly Blues (Olympic, 1974)**
★★ **The Essential Louis Armstrong (1976; Vanguard, 1987)**
★★★ **An Evening with Louis Armstrong and His All Stars (GNP Crescendo, 1977)**
★★ **Satchmo at Symphony Hall (MCA, 1977)**
★★★ **Louis and the Big Bands, 1928–30 (1987; Disques Swing, 1990)**
★★★★ **Pops (Bluebird/RCA, 1987)**
★★★★★ **The Hot Fives, Volume I (Columbia, 1988)**
★★★★★ **The Hot Fives & Hot Sevens, Volume II (Columbia, 1988)**
★★★ **Stardust (Portrait Masters/CBS, 1988)**
★★★★ **The Best of the Decca Years, Vol. One: The Singer (Decca Jazz/MCA, 1989)**
★★★★★ **The Hot Fives & Hot Sevens, Volume III (Columbia, 1989)**
★★★★ **Louis Armstrong & Earl Hines (Columbia, 1989)**

★ ★ ★ ★ **Pops: The 1940s Small Band Sides (Bluebird/RCA, 1989)**
★ ★ ★ ★ **The Best of the Decca Years, Vol. Two: The Composer (Decca Jazz/MCA, 1990)**
★ ★ ★ ★ **Louis Armstrong of New Orleans (Decca Jazz/MCA, 1990)**
★ ★ ★ **Mack the Knife (Pablo, 1990)**
★ ★ ★ ★ **Louis Armstrong's Greatest Hits (Curb, 1990)**
★ ★ ★ ★ ★ **St. Louis Blues (Columbia, 1991)**
★ ★ ★ **Ella & Louis Again (Verve/Polygram, NA)**

Biographers, critics and annotators have spent years debunking the myths surrounding Louis Armstrong's birth and impoverished childhood in New Orleans, even as they have agreed on other basic facts: "The whole vocabulary of mature jazz was based on Armstrong's phrases, Armstrong rhythms, Armstrong transformations," according to jazz authority Dan Morgenstern. Armstrong was born and raised in New Orleans by his mother in a district outside the notorious Storyville red-light zone; his schooling was erratic, and at an early age he was making money playing dice games on the street. After his mother moved herself and her son to the Black Storyville section, Armstrong and three of his young friends formed a vocal quartet and began singing on street corners.

On New Year's Eve in 1912 the Armstrong quartet took to the street to celebrate. It was customary for people to mark the incoming year by firing blank pistols into the air. Armstrong took a real .38 pistol belonging to his mother's boyfriend. When a boy fired a blank cartridge in Armstrong's direction, Louis fired off a .38 round in retaliation. He was arrested and given an indeterminate sentence in the Colored Waif's Home, beginning, by most estimates, in 1912. The Home was dedicated to discipline through instruction. It was the first completely structured experience of Armstrong's life.

Equally important, the Home had a band. Armstrong joined, first playing tambourine, then drum, then alto horn, and finally the instrument of his choice, the cornet. The stars of brass bands then popular in the United States were the cornet and trumpet soloists. In Armstrong's case, a major influence was the cornetist "King" Oliver. Released from the Waif's Home in 1914, Armstrong began playing in blues bands in Black Storyville's honky tonks. Although Buddy Bolden appears to have been a crucial figure in this stage of Armstrong's development, it was King Oliver who became the young cornetist's sponsor and mentor. In 1917 New Orleans closed down the Storyville district, and the great musicians who played there migrated to other towns where work was more plentiful. Among these was King Oliver, who accepted an offer to join a band of New Orleans musicians in Chicago. Before he left New Orleans, Oliver recommended to Kid Ory that Armstrong replace him in Ory's band, then the best in town. This association lasted about a year, at which point Ory moved to California. Armstrong began playing on riverboats. In 1922, Armstrong left for Chicago; King Oliver had invited him to join his Creole Jazz Band as second cornetist. Chicago became Armstrong's base for the better part of the next seven years. In the spring of 1923 the Oliver band was extended an offer to record under the auspices of the Gennett Record Company in Richmond, Indiana. In addition, 1923 saw the Oliver band recording for Okeh, Columbia and Paramount.

Louis Armstrong & King Oliver would have to rank with Jelly Roll Morton's Gennett sides, also cut in 1923, as the most important documents in early jazz. Oliver's music was typical of the time in that it was primarily of the ensemble variety with solos few and far between. The tempo is easy, the feel lighthearted, the edges reined in, although the musical passages weaving in and out are deceiving in their rhythmic complexity. It is ebullient, happy music.

Oliver's band at this juncture included Armstrong, Honoré Dutrey on trombone, Johnny Dodds on clarinet, Lil Hardin (later Mrs. Louis Armstrong) on piano, Stump Evans and Charlie Jackson on saxophones, Bill Johnson and Johnny St. Cyr on banjos, and Baby Dodds on drums. On this outing their work is ragged. Armstrong's role is dicey. He does little more than support Oliver's leads and offer a passing commentary when given an opportunity. In the 40-plus sides Armstrong cut with Oliver's band, he took four solos; three of them are included, "Chimes Blues," "Froggie Moore" and "Riverside Blues." As well he is heard on a few breaks, in duets with Oliver, and in a lead role on occasion, in each case standing out from the crowd by virtue of the clarity and warmth of his playing. The Armstrong solo on Jelly Roll Morton's "Froggie Moore" is considered one of the most important in jazz history in the complex ways it points both Armstrong and the music toward the future.

As history records it, Lil Hardin's mission became to assist Armstrong in finding fame. She bought new clothes for him, and prodded him to lose 50 pounds, take control of his own finances (which had been handled by Oliver), and finally, to marry her. Also, Oliver's band was falling apart. In 1924, Fletcher Henderson, whose band was then installed at the Roseland Ballroom in New York City, offered the Armstrongs work, so off they went to Manhattan. There they met Clarence Williams, a bandleader who used both Armstrongs on recordings made in 1924 by his Blue Five and Red Onion Jazz Babies. The latter are the most famous of these sessions, and are issued on *Louis Armstrong & King Oliver*. The key instrumentalist in the Red Onions contingent, apart from Armstrong himself, was Sidney Bechet on soprano saxophone on three cuts, including the smoking version of "Cake Walking Babies From Home." Bechet's bold style is overpowering. Bechet and Armstrong drive "Cake Walking" with relentless propulsion; even a tossed-off vocal chorus by Josephine Beatty (better known as Alberta Hunter) doesn't diminish the forcefulness and energy of these two giants' playing. "Terrible Blues" shows Armstrong's untutored mastery of theme and variation and stands as one of his most compelling solos on record. Yet another facet of his artistry is revealed on "Texas Moaner Blues," when his accompaniment of Hunter's vocal displays the great sensitivity he brought to his work in support of blues vocalists, which would reach full flower the next year when he went into the studio to back Bessie Smith on sides now available on Columbia's Smith retrospective, *The Complete Recordings, Vol. 1*. The Blue Five recordings featuring Armstrong are almost impossible to find, although two cuts are included on a currently unavailable (while the label is converting its catalogue to CD) Biograph release, *The Great Soloists featuring Louis Armstrong*.

By 1925 Armstrong was paramount among New Orleans musicians, an artist both envied and emulated. His time in New York had broadened his music, and he had given something back to the music as well, in the form of a new path that other musicians were then traversing as jazz continued its development. Lil Armstrong had gone back to Chicago and began asking Louis to return to the Windy City. In November 1925 he returned to Chicago's

Okeh studio with a band assembled to play music New Orleans style—Kid Ory, Johnny Dodds, Johnny St. Cyr, Lil Armstrong, and Louis himself: The Hot Five.

Strictly a studio group, the Hot Five recorded approximately 60 sides that were issued variously as Louis Armstrong and His Hot Five, Louis Armstrong and His Hot Seven, Louis Armstrong and His Orchestra, Louis Armstrong and His Savoy Ballroom Five, with the Hot Five constituting the bulk of these releases. Their recordings changed not only jazz, but 20th century music as well. For one, the Hot Five, while rooted in New Orleans ensemble jazz traditions, emphasized solos; and in Armstrong, clarinetist Dodds and trombonist Ory the group had three of the preeminent players of the time. But Armstrong himself is the story. Armstrong exudes confidence, strutting out on his solos, engaging other musicians in easy banter, and approaching the song less as a set form than as a blueprint anchored only by chord changes. One can hear, especially on *Louis Armstrong & Earl Hines*, the full spectrum of human emotion played out in passages of searing beauty and profound melancholy. On *The Hot Fives, Volume I and II* we hear him introduce scat singing in the band's first hit, "Heebie Jeebies"; pioneer the stop-time chorus in "Cornet Chop Suey"; and build a song on breaks and use his own voice as an instrument on "Skid-Dat-De-Dat."

The cuts on side two of this disc are from a later session of Hot Five recordings, done in September and December of 1927, bookending the Hot Seven sessions. Ory was back in the fold at this time, and a new addition was the blues guitarist Lonnie Johnson, who stands out on "I'm Not Rough," a tough performance in which the Mississippi Delta meets the Crescent City. The key track, considered one of the greatest in jazz history, is "Hotter Than That," wherein Armstrong musters all his techniques and invents some new ones in scatting and soloing his way through this scorcher. A duet with Johnson, with Armstrong scatting in response to Johnson's straight-ahead guitar lines, is a breathtaking display of intuition.

The initial Hot Seven sessions, cut in May of 1927, brings drummer Baby Dodds and tuba player Pete Briggs into the Hot Five, with trombonist John Thomas subbing for Ory, who was away playing with the King Oliver band; St. Cyr also doubles on guitar and banjo on these dates. Armstrong continues to blaze new trails, soloing with an inventiveness unparalleled at that time and virtually unequalled since. In one startling solo, at the end of "Willie the Weeper," Armstrong in effect discards the past and signals a new standard in jazz artistry, which he then proceeds to define anew on the extraordinary "Potato Head Blues."

In June, July and December of 1928 Armstrong made his final Hot Five recordings, some of which were issued as Louis Armstrong and his Savoy Ballroom Five. The key player in this group was Earl Hines, one of the revered figures in jazz piano, who had revolutionized his instrument as Armstrong had his. Although Dodds and Ory are absent and their replacements, Jimmy Strong and Fred Robinson, are hardly in the same league, Armstrong still produced some of his best music with this group. Armstrong and Hines engaged in a spirited duet on the acclaimed "Weather Bird," which finds the two musicians egging each other on with chase choruses and other conceits, with the end result being a rousing summit of the highest order. *Louis Armstrong & Earl Hines* is the critical document from these sessions, including as it does "Weather Bird," "St. James Infirmary," "Basin Street Blues," "Tight Like This" and "West End Blues," the latter regarded by many critics as Armstrong's finest performance.

Louis and the Big Bands, 1928–30 chronicles the first uncertain time in Armstrong's recorded history. After the Hot Five and Hot Seven recordings had brought him to national attention, he embarked on a busy schedule of club dates and recording sessions, often stretching himself thin artistically. Nevertheless his stature was growing. Armstrong returned to New York and began fronting a band led by a pianist of little note, Luis Russell, which contained several top-flight instrumentalists, including Lonnie Johnson, as well as some from New Orleans. One of the songs on this set, "I Can't Give You Anything but Love," signals the direction Armstrong's career would take. Armstrong's vocal finds him playing with the tempo, unable to resist adding some zest to an ordinary tune with his vocal flourishes. Eight tracks with the Russell group are included on this set.

Before being hooked up with the Russell band, Armstrong landed a part in the Broadway musical *Hot Chocolates*, starring and featuring songs by Fats Waller. Singing "Ain't Misbehavin'," he received rave reviews, and Armstrong found himself on

solid footing in New York, with club owners clamoring for his services. After he would finish his night on Broadway, he would hustle uptown, to Connie's Inn in Harlem, where, backed by Carroll Dickerson's band (which included Pete Briggs on tuba and Earl Hines on piano), he would reprise his numbers from *Hot Chocolates*. Several of these are found on *Louis and the Big Bands*; conspicuous by their absence are several excellent sides Armstrong cut with a band led by Les Hite.

In the early 1930s Armstrong made some of the best music of his life. *Stardust* captures some of the peak performances from the period 1930–32, when Armstrong was further refining his singing and playing, producing some gems along the way. "Stardust" and "Between the Devil and the Deep Blue Sea" are the acknowledged classics from this time, but a fine version of "All of Me" features one of Armstrong's most sensitively rendered vocals. On a lesser note, but still of interest, is the rare Olympic issue, *Mostly Blues*, a 1938 return, albeit fleeting, to a pure jazz format. For a radio show in 1938, disc jockey Martin Block assembled an all-star lineup for a jam session. The musicians included Armstrong, Fats Waller, Jack Teagarden, Bud Freeman, Al Casey and George Wettling. As promising as this sounds, it was a disaster; what we are left with is a record showing Armstrong at his most self-involved, engaging in pointless vocal and instrumental histrionics, although Teagarden's inspired playing nearly saves the day.

In 1935 Armstrong began his fruitful association with Decca Records, when his work with big bands produced numerous high points, but also showed him falling back on gimmickry of the sort that mars the *Mostly Blues* session. This era was once tracked thoroughly and quite wonderfully in MCA's Jazz Heritage series, but the Jazz Heritage titles have been pulled off the market and are being reconfigured for CD reissues. From the '30s the new representative title is Volume Two of *The Best of the Decca Years*, subtitled *The Composer*, although only four of its tracks date from the 1930s. As the title indicates, the focus is on Armstrong's underappreciated songwriting, and includes the rare "Satchel Mouth Swing" from 1938, and a 1957 reworking of "Potato Head Blues." *Louis Armstrong of New Orleans* is another broad overview, spanning from 1927 to 1950. The big band sides from the '30s include "Dipper Mouth Blues," a track from 1936 teaming Armstrong with the Jimmy Dorsey Orchestra. There's also two Hot Five tracks here, "Georgia Bo Bo" and "Drop That Sack," although the band is billed as Lil's Hot Shots.

The '40s constituted a period of retrenchment for Armstrong, who, no longer the innovator, was floundering in his efforts to keep pace with the times. A resurgence of interest in Dixieland in the late '30s left him cold, and then the militancy of the early bebop artists and fans placed him outside the loop of hip music for the first time in his career. The end of World War II in 1945 marked the beginning of the end of the big band era, which would be dead before the decade was out. In 1946 he signed with RCA and returned to the small band lineup—the Louis Armstrong All-Stars—featured on *Pops* and *Pops: The 1940s Small Band Sides*. At various times the group included some of the outstanding veteran names. Though Armstrong himself had lost some physical strength, he was up to delivering some incandescent moments.

Satchmo at Symphony Hall, a concert recording from 1947, shows the strengths and weaknesses of the All-Stars lineup. There are some wonderful solos by Armstrong, but he also sits out many numbers, his famous lip having very nearly been worn out from the years of playing long and hard. From the time he began playing back at the Waif's home, Armstrong had formed his embouchure incorrectly, and over time had caused considerable distress to his upper lip, resulting in his playing less and less as he got older. Near the end of his life the trumpet was little more than a prop, although he generally had enough left to produce a scintillating moment or two. Velma Middleton, a 250-pound singer whom critics despised, had joined Armstrong in the early '40s, and is heard on three numbers; minus the visual impact of her comic jiving onstage, she comes off well, particularly on a nice duet with Armstrong, "That's My Desire."

The sense of an artist in decline was hardly diminished by a rote set captured in *An Evening with Louis Armstrong and His All-Stars*. Nevertheless, Armstrong was cutting some interesting records on other labels apart from RCA and Decca, notably the fine duets with Ella Fitzgerald. The MCA reissue *The Singer* fits in here, volume one of the label's *Best of the Decca Years* series. It's appropriate for this period, because Armstrong's voice had taken on the weight of age. There is a track from 1937, a duet with the Mills Brothers on "In the Shade of the Old Apple Tree," but otherwise the remaining 12 cuts are all from 1950s sessions. Of note: a duet with Louis Jordan, the stylistic bridge between Armstrong and Ray Charles with his Tympanny Five, on "You Rascal You" in which two outsized egos get it together for some boisterous fun; an interpretation of "La Vie en Rose" that compares favorably with the immortal Edith Piaf recording; and the touching "It's All in the Game," a 1951 track recorded with Gordon Jenkins's orchestra.

Armstrong's '60s work can be summed up in two words: "Hello, Dolly!" It was one of the musical phenomena of the decade, this Broadway show tune album coming out of the blue to bump the Beatles' second American album from its chart-topping position in May 1964. It was good enough to keep him in the public eye for the rest of the decade, though he had no further hits. A session in 1968, though, produced the timeless, bittersweet version of "What a Wonderful World." *What a Wonderful World* features the original take of the song. In the greatest-hits category, both the Columbia and MCA titles offer updated versions of songs dating back to the Hot Five days. Armstrong died on July 6, 1971.

The titles listed represent only a portion of Louis Armstrong's recordings, but cover the most essential titles. An exhaustive overview of Armstrong's Decca years is available in the 30-volumes-plus MCA Jazz Heritage titles, which still show up in stores in cassette form minus any liner information. — D.M.

EDDY ARNOLD

★★★   **One More Time (1962; RCA, 1990)**
★★★½ **The Best of Eddy Arnold (RCA, 1967)**
★★★   **Pure Gold (RCA, 1975)**
★★★   **Collector's Series (RCA, 1987)**
  ★★   **Christmas With Eddy Arnold (RCA, 1990)**
  ★★   **Hand-Holdin' Songs (RCA, 1990)**
  ★★   **You Don't Miss a Thing (RCA, 1991)**

In terms of record sales and popular appeal, Eddy Arnold was once the king of country music, particulary in the late '40s and early '50s, when many of his self-composed songs ruled the country and pop charts. He was almost alone among country artists crossing over to pop in those days, but then he was almost alone in having a voice virtually free of country inflections as well. Warm and mellow seem to have been terms coined with Arnold's singing style in mind, and as the years progressed Arnold remained a country artist in name only. His records, cut with the cream of Nashville's session musicians, were squarely in the middle of the road. When something interesting does happen—such as the snarling electric guitar solo on "That's How Much I Love You" (from *Pure Gold*)—it seems out of place, because Arnold continues to sing as if he's sitting in a rocking chair on a lazy summer afternooon.

Still, the man has had a raft of hits, though his current catalogue only hints at his enormous output. *The Best of Eddy Arnold* contains 12 cuts, five of which never charted; nevertheless, it does contain such Arnold classics as "Cattle Call" and "Make the World Go Away," as well as one of Roger Miller's most clever songs, "The Last Word in Lonesome Is Me," which was a Top Forty pop record in 1966, 19 years after Arnold's first hit single, "I'll Hold You in My Heart," also included on *Best of. Pure Gold* and *Collector's Series* are truncated greatest-hits albums, the latter having only eight cuts; stick with *Best of. Hand-Holdin' Songs* and *You Don't Miss a Thing* are well-produced MOR fare, with Arnold's voice still in fine shape, although his material's hurting. *Hand-Holdin' Songs* (the title alone is bad news) does feature a nice version of the '40s hit, "It's Been a Long, Long Time" that offers a glimpse of the sensitive touch Arnold applies so well in investing a good lyric with a sense of longing. Arnold's 1962 album, *One More Time,* a set of personable mood music with bluesier intent than most of the artist's recordings, was reissued in 1990, and shows the singer at his soothing best. *Christmas With Eddy Arnold* is entertaining fare owing to Arnold's warm voice being well-suited to the material; also recommending it is the inclusion of Boudleaux Bryant's seldom-heard "Christmas Can't Be Far Away." — D.M.

STEVE ARRINGTON
★★★½ **Steve Arrington's Hall of Fame I (Atlantic, 1983)**
★★½ **Positive Power (Atlantic, 1984)**
★★★★ **Dancin' in the Key of Life (Atlantic, 1985)**
★★★ **The Jammin' National Anthem (Atlantic, 1986)**
★★★ **Jam Packed (Manhattan/EMI, 1987)**

What happened to Steve Arrington's promising solo career in the mid-'80s? The key lies buried in the credits on *Positive Power*: "Brothers and Sisters, In the middle of this album, a change came over me. I found God. So this album shows where I've been and where I'm going." Where he ended up—commercial limbo—is a typical, disappointing pop conversion story. But before that, for one glorious moment, Steve Arrington achieved his lofty goal. *Dancin' in the Key of Life* strikes a miraculous balance between faith and the funk; it's a down-to-earth gospel album, as well as a sanctified modern R&B record. Lead singer and bassist for the hard-hitting funk troupe Slave from 1979 to 1981, Arrington took Bootsy Collins's wildly exaggerated, "cartoon vocal" style and turned it into actual singing. His initial solo work builds on that animated approach; unforgettable R&B chart singles like "Nobody Can Be You" and "Weak at the Knees" (from *Hall of Fame I*) add a vague spiritual dimension to the stomping groove. But even a written warning can't quite prepare listeners for the reborn Arrington. Along with the power of God, a stronger command of melody uplifts every song on his third album—no boogie-down vamps here. The vocal acrobatics are more firmly rooted, and the words carry that weight. Besides celebrating his beliefs, Arrington also acknowledges the real world of "Gasoline" and even delivers his message about abortion ("Willie Mae") with a sensitivity to other points of view. You don't have to agree with him to be moved by *Dancin' in the Key of Life.* What makes Arrington's later work a come-down is his preachiness. Still, amid some heavy moralizing, *The Jammin' National Anthem* and *Jam-Packed* both contain solid examples of Arrington's heavenly realism. It comes as no surprise that snatches of his best-known songs—that voice and those bass lines—often crop up as hip-hop samples. — M.C.

ARROW
★★★★ **Best of Arrow (Red Bullet, 1987)**
★★★ **Knock Dem Dead (Mango, 1988)**
★★★½ **O La Soca (Mango, 1990)**
★★★ **Soca Dance Party (Mango, 1990)**

Along with David Rudder and Charlie's Roots, Sparrow, Shadow and Becket, Arrow is one of the leading lights of the Trinidadian soca scene. A perennial favorite in Trinidad's annual Carnival song competition, Arrow is best known in this country for "Hot, Hot, Hot," which became a hit for Buster Poindexter (the original, which smokes Poindexter's cover, can be found on *Best of Arrow*). Like most soca performers, Arrow has always borrowed from American R&B—"soca" is itself a combination of the words "soul" and "calypso"—but his Mango recordings are unusually eclectic, dabbling in rap ("Hey Pocky-a-Way," from *O La Soca*), house (an acid remix of "Groove Master" appears on the CD version of *Knock Dem Dead*) and zouk ("Zouk Me," from *Soca Dance Party*). Yet no matter how far afield his music goes, Arrow never loses sight of his soca roots, retaining the style's rolling rhythms and vibrant energy even as he expands upon it. — J.D.C.

DANIEL ASH
★★½ **Coming Down (Beggars Banquet, 1991)**
Coming Down is an eclectic solo effort by Love and Rockets singer-guitarist Daniel Ash. Though some tracks—the jaunty, danceable "This Love," or the crunchy "Coming Down Fast"—would sound perfectly at home on an L&R album, others go surprisingly far afield. Among the oddest are the Latin-tinged "Walk This Way," a quirky, country-ish "Closer to You" and a version of "Me and My Shadow" that sounds like it was intended for a David Lynch movie. — J.D.C.

ASHFORD & SIMPSON
★★ **Gimme Something Real (Warner Bros., 1973)**
★★ **I Wanna Be Selfish (Warner Bros., 1974)**
★★½ **Come As You Are (Warner Bros., 1976)**
★★★½ **So So Satisfied (Warner Bros., 1977)**
★★★½ **Send It (Warner Bros., 1977)**
★★★★ **Is It Still Good to Ya? (Warner Bros., 1978)**
★★★½ **Stay Free (Warner Bros., 1979)**
★★★ **Musical Affair (Warner Bros., 1980)**
★★★ **Performance (Warner Bros., 1981)**
★★★½ **Solid (Capitol, 1984)**
★★★ **Real Love (Capitol, 1986)**
Nickolas Ashford and Valerie Simpson were one of Motown's most distinctive songwriting units; this husband-and-wife team is best known for steamy Marvin Gaye and Tammi Terrell duets like "Ain't No Mountain High Enough" and "You're All I Need to Get By." Branching off on a solo career in the early '70s, Ashford & Simpson expanded on those elegant romantic themes. It took a while for their style to cohere, but

the duo's late '70s hits helped establish the "adult" orientation of post-soul R&B. Ashford & Simpson examine the pitfalls and highs of monogamy from a complex, shifting perspective. Though the music is often plush, even luxurious, a mellow fire illuminates the introspective lyrics and subtle rhythmic hooks. Believe it: Ashford & Simpson's finely distilled passion can scorch an unsuspecting listener. Even at their most content, they rarely sound complacent.

So So Satisfied is where Ashford & Simpson's mature approach clicks into place. Overall, it's a more consistent album than *Send It*, but that LP kicked off a successful run on the R&B charts with its irresistible title track and "Don't Cost You Nothin'." *Is It Still Good to Ya?* captures Ashford & Simpson at their peak, mixing sensitivity (the title track) and sensuality ("It Seems to Hang On") in carefully measured doses. Along with Chic's "Good Times," Ashford & Simpson's "Found a Cure," from *Stay Free* (1979), brought a solid sense of melody to bear on disco. Even though "Found a Cure" points the way toward a dance floor–bedroom fusion, Ashford & Simpson retreat to more familiar musical trappings on the disappointingly mild *A Musical Affair*. Since there's no greatest-hits album, the overblown *Performance* will have to suffice as a summary of Ashford & Simpson's salad days. Needless to say, a one- or two-CD retrospective seems long overdue. (All the original Warner albums are deleted.)

Ashford & Simpson moved to Capitol in the early '80s, releasing several unexceptional albums and producing several gorgeous hits for Gladys Knight (especially "Landlord"). *Solid* came rolling out of left field in late 1984, re-establishing the duo's suave dynamics in a bracing, hip-hop-influenced mix. "Solid" may well be their most convincing declaration of marital faith, while "Babies" introduces a bold topical spin without undercutting the album's emotional framework. *Real Love* follows up in a similiar electro-mode, though the songwriting is nowhere near as striking. — M.C.

ASIA
★★ **Asia (Geffen, 1982)**
★ **Alpha (Geffen, 1983)**
★ **Astra (Geffen, 1985)**
★ **Then and Now (Geffen, 1990)**
★ **Asia: Live in Moscow (Rhine, 1992)**
One of the last of the art-rock supergroups, Asia matched John Wetton (King Crimson,

UK), Steve Howe (Yes) and Carl Palmer (ELP) with pseudo-new waver Geoff Downes (Buggles). Although Downes's glib melodicism lent a veneer of pop accessibility, the group's tendency to instrumental self-aggrandizement invariably overwhelmed its material. By *Then and Now*, a comeback-cum–greatest hits package, Howe had been replaced by assorted studio hacks. — J.D.C.

ASLEEP AT THE WHEEL
★★★★   Comin' Right at Ya (U.A., 1973)
★★★   Asleep at the Wheel (Epic, 1974)
★★★★   The Wheel (Capitol, 1977)
★★★   Collision Course (Capitol, 1978)
★★★   Framed (MCA, 1980)
★★★½   Asleep at the Wheel (MCA, 1985)
★★★   Asleep at the Wheel: 10 (Epic, 1987)
★★★   Western Standard Time (Epic, 1988)
★★★   Keepin' Me Up Nights (Arista, 1990)

Led by smooth-voiced guitarist Ray Benson, this band of western swing revivalists moved from its native home (West Virginia) to its spiritual one (Texas) in the early '70s. Asleep at the Wheel mastered the jazzed-up country hybrid pioneered by Bob Wills and His Texas Playboys—without sterilizing or nostalgizing it. Unfortunately, Asleep at the Wheel's best albums (such as its debut on U.A., *Comin' Right at Ya*) are out of print. *Asleep at the Wheel* (1974) features the band's original lineup: Benson is balanced by the considerable talents of female singer Chris O'Connell, songwriter-guitarist Leroy Preston and pedal-steel player Lucky Oceans. *The Wheel* (out of print) features some highly memorable originals ("My Baby Thinks He's a Train"), as well as hot ensemble playing. Asleep at the Wheel stretched into more eclectic territory on *Collision Course* (1978) and *Framed* (1980), with mixed results. Several members of Dan Hicks and the Hot Licks appear on the latter record, lending a decidedly whimsical air to the proceedings. The late '80s LPs find Benson helming a new lineup, but indistinct material keeps *10* and *Keepin' Me Up Nights* in a predictable groove. The snazzy cover versions on *Western Standard Time*, however, firmly support Asleep at the Wheel's reputation as a rug-cutting live act. — M.C.

THE ASSOCIATION
★★   Greatest Hits (Warner Bros., 1968)
★   Songs That Made Them Famous (Pair, 1986)

White-bread, saccharine, fake flower-power shmaltz. Atop elevator-music instrumentation, the Association crooned. While hits like "Windy" and "Along Comes Mary" convey the daffy zing of toothpaste ads, and "Cherish" tingles as a makeout classic, the band bombed on anything more ambitious, like, for example, the anti-war dirge "Requiem for the Masses" or the Pepsi Generation anthem, "Enter the Young." — P.E.

RICK ASTLEY
★★★   Whenever You Need Somebody (RCA, 1988)
★★   Hold Me in Your Arms (RCA, 1989)
★★½   Free (RCA, 1991)

Sounding like a cross between Michael McDonald and Jim Nabors, Astley began his career as a cog in the Stock/Aitken/ Waterman hit machine, mindlessly delivering melodies over a booming disco beat. *Free* replaces the SAW sound with an attempt at soul, but to little avail. — J.D.C.

CHET ATKINS
★★½   The Atkins-Travis Traveling Show (RCA, 1975)
★★★   Chester and Lester (RCA, 1976)
★★½   The Best of Chet and Friends (RCA, 1976)
★★★   A Legendary Performer (RCA, 1977)
★★½   Reflections (RCA, 1980)
★★★   Collector's Series (RCA, 1985)
★★★   Stay Tuned (Columbia, 1985)
★★½   Tennessee Guitar Man (Pair, 1986)
★★★   Guitar for All Seasons (Pair, 1986)
★★★   Street Dreams (Columbia, 1986)
★★★½   Sails (Columbia, 1987)
★★★½   Chet Atkins, C. G. P. (Columbia, 1989)
★★★   Country Gems (Pair, 1990)
WITH MARK KNOPFLER
★★★★   Neck and Neck (Columbia, 1990)

Like Nashville's other ace instrumentalists (Floyd Cramer, Boots Randolph, Charlie McCoy), guitarist Chet Atkins spent a long time releasing albums that showcased remarkable skill—in contention with syrupy string arrangements, babytalk back-up vocalizing and mediocre material. He began recording in the late '50's, and he's amassed oceans of such product; the Pair reissues compile the more tolerable cuts—the rest can be found on at least 30 albums that show up with some frequency at garage sales.

A Legendary Performer is a fair collection of Atkins at his solo best, but his more exciting works are collaborations. *Chester and Lester* pairs him with Les Paul, and a sweet fire gets going between the two old masters; Merle Travis drives *The Atkins-Travis Traveling Show* (now out of print); and the concept album, *The Night Atlanta Burned*, is an intriguing novelty—an orchestral piece on which Atkins is accompanied by mandolin and violin. The rest of his '70's output is pleasant hokum.

In a welcome turn, Atkins revived in the next decade. Helped out by bassist David Hungate and keyboardist Darryl Dybka, he released a series of albums that, for all their jazz-lite glossiness, surrounded him with very accomplished players. A guitar conclave, *Stay Tuned* joins him with Earl Klugh, Steve Lukather, George Benson and Dire Straits mainman Mark Knopfler, and, while the tunes are formulaic, the playing is impressive. A follow-up, *Sails* is easy-listening raised to an artform. *Neck and Neck* is irresistible—with Atkins and Knopfler as equal partners, this labor of love ranges in style from Stephane Grapelli to Don Gibson. Its strength, however, are its country numbers—on a few of which Atkins actually sings (quite credibly).
— P.E.

BRIAN AUGER
★★½ Befour (RCA, 1970)
★★ Oblivion Express (RCA, 1971)
★★★ A Better Land (RCA, 1971)
★★ Second Wind (RCA, 1972)
★★ Closer to It (RCA, 1973)
★★½ Straight Ahead (RCA, 1974)
★★ Live Oblivion, Vol. 1 (RCA, 1974)
★★½ Reinforcements (RCA, 1975)
A jazz organist whose early live work featured Rod Stewart, Long John Baldry and the cool-voiced Julie Driscoll, Auger hit his stride with *Befour*, from 1970. While the classical playing on the record was tasty (it suffered from none of the overblown pretensions of, say, Keith Emerson), it was the swinging material that kicked: influenced by Jimmy Smith and Herbie Hancock, Auger's fusion had little of the strain or schlock such horn-based contemporaries as Blood, Sweat and Tears displayed in abundance. His next three albums were kicky stuff, too—but before long Auger had lost much of his interest in either rocking hard or jazzing fiercely. Most of his work now sounds pretty tepid. — P.E.

HOYT AXTON
★★★ Life Machine (A&M, 1974)
★★★ Southbound (A&M, 1975)
★★★ Fearless (A&M, 1976)
★★★ Snowblind Friend (MCA, 1977)
★★★ Never Been to Spain (1977; MCA, 1987)
★★★½ Road Songs (A&M, 1977)
★★★ Free Sailin' (MCA, 1978)
★★★ Spin of the Wheel (D.P.I., 1990)
Hoyt Axton's mother penned "Heartbreak Hotel," and while it's obvious that nothing her boy ever wrote had the earth-shaking effect of that classic, he came up with his share of hits. The Kingston Trio covered "Greenback Dollar" and made it a folkie standard; Steppenwolf shook heavy-metal thunder from "The Pusher"; Three Dog Night, among its other crimes, scored a noxious smash with Hoyt's insufferably cutesy "Joy to the World." While obviously a versatile writer, Axton never really broke through on his own. *Life Machine*'s "When the Morning Comes" did well on the country charts; with the out-of-print *Southbound*'s "No No Song" he might have found pop success, but Ringo Starr's remake fared much better. Almost all of Axton's records are capable—he's an engaging, gruff-voiced singer, and his backup musicians are generally top-notch—but the only essential album remains *Road Songs*. A two-disc set would have served as a truer "best-of," but *Road* contains a fair selection of his prime cuts: James Burton's guitar work is, as always, impeccable, and Linda Ronstadt's duet vocals sound great. — P.E.

ALBERT AYLER
★★★½ Witches and Devils (1964; Freedom, 1988)
★★★ Lorrach/Paris 1966 (Hat Art, 1986)
Most of avant-garde jazzer Albert Ayler's peripetically dazzling recordings are now out of print, on obscure labels or on imports—a truly unfortunate situation. Because at his strongest—*Prophecy* (ESP, 1964), *Spiritual Unity* (ESP, 1964), *Spirits Rejoice* (ESP, 1965) and *Music Is the Healing Force of the Universe* (Impulse, 1969)—this saxophonist was a wonder. The 1964 sets feature his boldest backing (Gary Peacock on bass, Sonny Murray on drums), and they are music of a fierce, free abandon. *Witches and Devils* flourishes Ayler's distinctive playing—whether on soprano, alto or, primarily, tenor, the man was a marvel of speed and intensity. *Lorrach/Paris* came slightly later; once more it's a record of such

urgency that it helps explain Ayler's rep—some critics thought him a jazz messiah; others simply dismissed him as mad. His death, in 1970, remains shrouded in mystery; his body was found in New York's East River. — P.E.

AZTEC CAMERA
★ ★ ★½ **High Land, Hard Rain (Sire, 1983)**
★ ★ ★½ **Knife (Sire, 1984)**
  ★ ★½ **Love (Sire, 1987)**
★ ★ ★½ **Stray (Sire, 1990)**
A kind of post-punk Ray Davies, Roddy Frame writes folk-pop vignettes: very British tales of bed-sit listlessness and hope, his songs mix telling snapshots, smart wordplay and high emotionalism—and they're pretty great. *High Land* is an accomplished debut; its acoustic guitar–based power is effortless,

and Frame comes off as a precocious wise child. On *Knife*, the sound is stronger, and Frame's voice drops lower—a new assurance underlies the long and gorgeous title track. The boy is capable of hubris: on "Just Like the U.S.A." he compares his own malaise to the state of an entire nation, but he's often witty. And the sincerity of a ballad like "The Birth of the True" is touching. *Love* was a strange misstep. A tribute to the spirit of Philadelphia soul, it was music far too glossy for Frame's idiosyncratic vocalizing and intriguing ideas. Leaner and more melodic, *Stray* found Frame collaborating to great effect with Mick Jones ("Good Morning Britain" has some of the power of *Combat Rock*–period Clash) and going in for fine jazz-inflected numbers. — P.E.

B

BABYFACE

★ ★½ **Lovers (1986, Solar/Epic, 1989)**
★ ★ ★½ **Tender Lover (Solar, 1989)**
★ ★ ★½ **A Closer Look (Solar, 1991)**

Along with Antonio "L.A." Reid, Kenneth "Babyface" Edmonds has produced perky, R&B-inflected pop hits for Paula Abdul, Bobby Brown, Whitney Houston and a host of others. Although his solo albums aren't quite as intensely accessible, they do boast many of the same virtues. *Lovers*, recorded after L.A. and Babyface had left the Deele, is competent but predictable, with the singer lavishing his light tenor on slow, soulful ballads like the Stylistics' "You Make Me Feel Brand New" or the title tune. Unsurprisingly, *Tender Lover* also includes a few powerhouse ballads, the best of which ("Whip Appeal," for instance) capture the insinuating cadences of a lover's pillow talk. It's not all slow jams, though, and uptempo numbers like "It's No Crime" and "My Kinda Girl" drive their hooks home. *A Closer Look* provides highlights from both albums, as well as two live tracks and duets Babyface recorded for albums by Karyn White and Pebbles. — J.D.C.

BURT BACHARACH

★ ★½ **Burt Bacharach's Greatest Hits (A&M, 1974)**
★ ★ ★ **Woman (A&M, 1979)**
★ ★ ★½ **Classics, Vol. 23 (A&M, 1987)**

Classically trained and phenomenally industrious, Burt Bacharach began writing hits in the '50s for performers as various as Perry Como, Marty Robbins and Gene Pitney, after having honed his arranging skills as conductor for Marlene Dietrich. With lyricist Hal David, he went on to deliver an astonishing series of '60s pop singles for Dionne Warwick—music whose effervescence has withstood the vagaries of fashion and the carping of cynics. Combining Tin Pan Alley craft,

Gershwinesque jazz flourishes, and daring offbeat rhythms, his songs became Muzak staples—a sad but inevitable fate.

On his own, he made albums that featured lush, symphonic versions of his work for other artists. He sometimes sang (very poorly); more often, he assembled dreadful choirs who crooned like jingle hacks. If you can get beyond this, his arrangements still pack punch and surprise. Over-fond of whimsical instrumentation (harpsichords, bossa nova guitars), he still comes off as a distinctive musical intelligence—he does "light" with more class than almost any other AOR composer. *Woman* (1979, out of print), a semi-classical epic, is his most ambitious work, but *Classics* contains the sweeter candy: "Alfie," "I Say a Little Prayer for You," "Promises, Promises," "What the World Needs Now Is Love," and more. — P.E.

BACHMAN-TURNER OVERDRIVE

★ ★ ★ **Bachman-Turner Overdrive (Mercury, 1973)**
★ ★ ★ **Bachman-Turner Overdrive II (Mercury, 1974)**
★ ★ ★ **Not Fragile (Mercury, 1974)**
★ ★ **Four Wheel Drive (Mercury, 1975)**
★ ★ **Head On (Mercury, 1975)**
★ ★ ★½ **Best of Bachman-Turner Overdrive (So Far) (Mercury, 1976)**
★ ★ **Freeways (Mercury, 1977)**
★ **Street Action (Mercury, 1978)**
★ **Rock 'n' Roll Nights (Mercury, 1978)**

Bachman-Turner Overdrive launched a million bad jokes about spare tires and hefty metal in its prime, but this Canadian band's ambling power-hooks still motor past all tasteful objections. Toughening his old group's approach with a big guitar sound, ex-Guess Who member Randy Bachman hit the ground running in his '70s vehicle. "Let It Ride," "Roll on Down the Highway" and

"You Ain't Seen Nothing Yet" all sound like they rolled off the same assembly line—on purpose. B.T.O maintains a fairly high standard of quality across its initial releases, pumping out tuneful filler alongside the aforementioned hits. However, the optimistically titled *Best of (So Far)* is all the B.T.O any general listener needs to hear. Tossing in the FM standard "Gimme Your Money Please" (about a mugging) and the ambitious "Blue Collar Lookin' Out for #1," this one qualifies as essential if your car has a tape deck. The later albums sputter and eventually stall. — M.C.

BAD BRAINS
★ ★½ **Bad Brains (ROIR, 1982)**
★ ★ ★ **Rock for Light (1983; Caroline, 1991)**
★ ★ ★½ **I Against I (SST, 1986)**
★ ★ **Live (SST, 1988)**
★ ★ ★½ **Quickness (Caroline, 1989)**
★ ★ ★ **The Youth Are Getting Restless (Caroline, 1990)**

What originally made the Bad Brains so unusual wasn't that this quartet was as adept at the slo-mo skank of reggae as it was at the hi-speed roar of hardcore, but that it made both approaches seem equally intense. Granted, *Rock for Light* does it better than the debut, *Bad Brains*, and not just because it boasts songs as ferocious and tuneful as "Sailin' On." Part of the reason is that *Rock for Light* is better recorded, but mostly it's because the reggae tunes on *Bad Brains* aren't as brutally uncompromising as the hardcore numbers (like, for instance, "Pay to Cum").

With *I Against I,* the reggae numbers are gone, and the rockers slow down almost to the point that the Brains could be mistaken for a mainstream metal act. Nor is that a complaint, as tunes like "She's Calling You" and "Secret 77" expand upon the melodic potential hinted at on *Rock for Light*. Apart from a reggae rendition of "Day Tripper," *Live* merely reaffirms those advances. But *Quickness* brings the fast stuff back into the band's repertoire, and does so without compromising straight-up metal tunes like "Soul Craft" or "Yout' Juice." As for *The Youth Are Getting Restless,* consider it a live best-of, and count its version of "Banned in D.C." as superior both in sound and fury to the original. — J.D.C.

BAD COMPANY
★ ★ ★½ **Bad Company (Swan Song, 1974)**
★ ★ ★ **Straight Shooter (Swan Song, 1975)**
★ ★½ **Run With the Pack (Swan Song, 1976)**
★ ★½ **Burnin' Sky (Swan Song, 1977)**
★ ★ ★ **Desolation Angels (Swan Song, 1979)**
★ ★½ **Rough Diamonds (Swan Song, 1982)**
★ ★ **Fame & Fortune (Atlantic, 1986)**
★ ★ **Dangerous Age (Atlantic, 1988)**
★ ★ ★ ★ **10 From 6 (Atlantic, 1988)**
★ ★ **Holy Water (Atco, 1990)**

This mid-'70s supergroup picks up precisely where lead singer Paul Rodgers' old band left off. Bad Company coarsens and distorts Free's economical blooze attack just enough to put it across to a howling, smoke-filled arena. Compared to his shrieking competition, Rodgers is a remarkably musical hard-rock frontman. And former Mott the Hoople guitarist Mick Ralphs proves an able foil; his stuttering riffs and clipped solos boldly copy Free guitarist Paul Kossoff's signature, while ex-Free drummer Simon Kirke provides thundering foursquare rhythms. Bad Company came as a breath of fresh air amid heavy metal's increasing stench, but this particular breeze quickly turned into a gust of hot air. Rodgers & Co never could get beyond the "Baby I'm a bad man" stance of "Bad Company." The no-bullshit minimalism and rhythmic thrust of the debut becomes a rut by the third album. That said, there's not a bum riff or bogus groan to be found on Bad Company's greatest hits package. *10 From 6* mixes full-bore earthquakes ("Can't Get Enough") and half-acoustic lust ballads ("Shooting Star") along with musings on the road ("Movin' On") and the music ("Rock & Roll Fantasy"). It's essential to any survey of '70s rock. The later albums find Ralphs and Kirke keeping company with an unfortunate Rodgers clone called Brian Howe. *Holy Water* isn't bad enough to be an abomination—or shameless enough to be a success. — M.C.

BAD ENGLISH
★ **Bad English (Epic, 1989)**
★½ **Backlash (Epic, 1991)**
In which John Waite helps Neil Schon and Jonathan Cain relive the worst of Journey's excesses. Both albums are predictable and pandering, sounding as if concocted by programming consultants, but *Backlash* is easily the more spirited, from the feisty "So This Is Eden" to their "Life in the Fast Lane" ripoff, "Life at the Top." — J.D.C.

BADFINGER
★ ★ ★ **Magic Christian Music (1970; Capitol, 1991)**

★★★ No Dice (1970; Capitol, 1992)
★★★½ Straight Up (Apple, 1971)
★★ The Best of Badfinger Vol. 2 (Rhino, 1989)
★★½ Badfinger Day After Day (Rykodisc, 1990)

Receiving the Beatles imprimatur cut two ways for Badfinger: this British quartet would have been accused of outright imitation even if its records didn't come out on Apple, the recently retired moptops' fledgling label. But the association also underscored how precise the imitation was: Badfinger perfectly replicates the *Beatles '65* three-minute rush on "No Matter What," beefing up the guitar sound only slightly. On the rest of *No Dice*, Badfinger recycles familiar riffs and harmonies in far less striking configurations. Paul McCartney helped the group out on its debut, *Magic Christian Music,* by penning the hit "Come and Get It." Produced by George Harrison, "Day after Day" (from *Straight Up*) is a far more affecting trifle; a gently weeping guitar line pulls along the dumbstruck, in-love-by-gosh vocal hook. "Baby Blue," the Todd Rundgren–produced followup single, brings a touch of *Revolver* to the Badfinger mix. "Perfection" comes close, though the rest of *Straight Up* devolves into competent genre exercises. You could argue that Badfinger was ahead of its time, promoting the concise pop-song verities while rock bloated beyond recognition. Except the group's subsequent out-of-print Warner Bros. albums—collected on *The Best of Badfinger Vol. 2*—are comprised of totally clueless arena-rock moves. At least the live *Day After Day*, recorded in '74, doesn't include many guitar solos. — M.C.

JOAN BAEZ

★★★★ Joan Baez (1960; Vanguard, 1987)
★★★★ Joan Baez 2 (1961; Vanguard, 1987)
★★★★ In Concert/Part One (1963; Vanguard, 1988)
★★★½ In Concert/Part Two (Vanguard, 1963)
★★★★ Joan Baez 5 (Vanguard, 1964)
★★★★ Farewell Angelina (Vanguard, 1965)
★★★ Noel (1966; Vanguard, 1987)
★★★ Portrait (Vanguard, 1966)
★★½ Joan (Vanguard, 1967)
★★★½ Baptism (Vanguard, 1968)
★★★ Any Day Now (Songs of Bob Dylan) (1968; Vanguard, 1987)
★★½ David's Album (Vanguard, 1969)
★★½ One Day at a Time (Vanguard, 1970)
★★★★ The First Ten Years (1970; Vanguard, 1987)
★★★ Blessed Are (Vanguard, 1971)
★★½ Carry It On (Vanguard, 1972)
★★ Come From the Shadows (A&M, 1972)
★★ Where Are You Now, My Son? (Vanguard, 1973)
★★★ Hits, Greatest and Others (Vanguard, 1973)
★★★★ Ballad Book (1974; Vanguard, 1987)
★★★ Gracias a la Vida (Here's to Life), (A&M, 1974)
★★★½ Diamonds and Rust (A&M, 1975)
★★ Live In Japan (Vanguard, 1975)
★★★ Lovesong Album (1976; Vanguard, 1987)
★★★ From Every Stage (A&M, 1976)
★★ Gulf Winds (A&M, 1976)
★★★ Blowing Away (Portrait, 1977)
★★★ Best of Joan Baez (A&M, 1977)
★★½ Honest Lullaby (Portrait, 1979)
★★★½ Country Music Album (1979; Vanguard, 1987)
★★★★ The Night They Drove Old Dixie Down (1979; Vanguard, 1985)
★★★½ Very Early Joan Baez (1982; Vanguard, 1987)
★★★ The Contemporary Ballad Book (Vanguard, 1987)
★★★½ Recently (Gold Castle, 1987)
★★★½ Speaking of Dreams (Gold Castle, 1989)
★★★½ Diamonds and Rust in the Bullring (Gold Castle, 1989)
★★★ Brothers in Arms (Gold Castle, 1991)

With Joan Baez, musical and political significance so fuse that it's hard to assess her importance solely on aesthetic grounds. Throughout her career she's been resolutely committed, and often at great cost, to thoughtful humanitarianism that's manifested itself in resistance, feminist critique and an ongoing fight for human rights. A leading participant in the '60s cultural revolution, she lent intelligent credibility to radical ideas; and not only did her perfectly enunciated versions of Bob Dylan and Tim Hardin songs win high-brow listeners over to the new music, but her chaste—if sometimes overbearing—seriousness made the message of that music appear all the more critical and "legitimate." In the '70s, long after many of her peers had given up on the notion of music as message, Baez persevered. By the time of the U.S.A. for Africa revival of social consciousness a decade later, she had become a figure largely ignored, dismissed as unhip. The '80s triumph of intelligent, strong female folk singers, however, testifies, no matter how indirectly, to Baez's spiritual influence—Tracy Chapman and Suzanne Vega are as certainly her pyschic daughters as they are Joni Mitchell's.

Gathered together on a dizzying array of repackagings, Baez's early work is traditional folk ("Man of Constant Sorrow," "Streets of Laredo," "Silver Dagger") of the most pristine variety. Baez's high, resonant, vibratoed delivery is sometimes more musically satisfying than interpretively acute; her acoustic guitar playing can be equally hyper-precise, and, too often, the songs sound like a folklorist's reverent guide to the form rather than a singer comfortably emoting. But *Very Early* and *In Concert* are strong collections of Scots/Irish traditionals; and *Ballad Book*, *Lovesong Album* and *Country Music Album* remain admirable.

Joan Baez 5 sees the singer branching out. Delivered with light-operatic grace, an impressive Villa-Lobos classical piece shows off her soprano to its best advantage; and with Richard Farina's "Birmingham Sunday," Phil Ochs's "There but for Fortune" and Bob Dylan's "It Ain't Me Babe," she begins crusading for contemporary songwriters. Paired romantically with Dylan during the early '60s as the "King and Queen of Folk," she concentrated throughout the decade on reverent readings of his songs. Championing his genius proves to be one of her most endearing gestures—but as her Dylan collection, *Any Day Now*, attests, it's exactly by handling his lyrics as Holy Writ that Baez betrays her signal weakness. As a singer she triumphs when rendering dignified pathos; the ambivalence of Dylan eludes her. *Baptism* is mid-period Baez at her most ambitious. Having nearly exhausted standard folk music, she tries out sung and spoken readings of Welsh ballads, spirituals and poems by Garcia Lorca, Yevtushenko, Whitman and e. e. cummings. With orchestral arrangements by Peter Schikele (*P.D.Q. Bach*), the record has its gorgeous moments, but it's an effortful listen; like a PBS special, it's too apparently "good for you."

In the early '70s, Baez turned out artful covers of Kristofferson and Beatles songs, hit a high point with her version of the Band's "The Night They Drove Old Dixie Down," and on *Hits, Greatest and Others* shows herself to be an artful, if not very revealing interpreter of high-end pop. She

begins, too, to write more of her own material—and *Gulf Winds*, *Come From the Shadows* and *Diamonds and Rust* are certainly smarter than most singer-songwriter albums of the time. But her best work (*From Every Stage*) remains her less obviously personal—"Swing Low, Sweet Chariot" and "Joe Hill" are strong and effortless, betraying none of the fretful quality that sometimes weakens her autobiographical songs.

Generating no interest on the part of record companies, Baez was absent from the scene in the early '80s. When she finally returned, however, her work had gained in assurance. *Recently* and *Speaking of Dreams* are graceful sets; working with the Gipsy Kings, Paul Simon and a host of studio aces, her delivery more casual than in her heyday, she sings about old loves and current causes—and she sounds not only wise but comfortable.   — P.E.

PHILIP BAILEY

★ ★ ★	**Chinese Wall** (Columbia, 1984)
★ ★ ★	**The Wonders of His Love** (Myrrh, 1984)
★ ★ ★ ★	**Inside Out** (Columbia, 1986)
★ ★ ★½	**Triumph** (Myrrh, 1986)
★ ★ ★	**Family Affair** (Myrrh, 1989)
★ ★ ★ ★	**The Best of Philip Bailey: A Gospel Collection** (Word/Epic, 1991)

At first, Philip Bailey's solo career seemed like a dispiriting adjunct to the mighty Earth, Wind and Fire saga. The 1983 debut, *Continuation* (now deleted), never got off the ground, artistically or commercially. Although the Phil Collins–produced *Chinese Wall* yielded a hit duet, "Easy Lover" strongly recalls the Brit popmeister's vague funk excursions. Try as he might, Bailey can't overcome Collins's nagging chorus with his gliding falsetto. On his next album, Bailey and producer Nile Rodgers form a tight, responsive bond. *Inside Out* doesn't sound like EW&F—or Chic. Contemporary dance grooves ("Welcome to the Club"), strutting funk-rock ("Back It Up"), pulsating ruminations ("State of the Heart"), eloquent heartbreak ("Don't Leave Me Baby"): somehow, this remarkably well-balanced album—and now out of print—got lost in the mid-80s shuffle. Philip Bailey then turned to a higher purpose, putting his secular experience to great use on a series of bright pop-gospel albums. *The Best of Philip Bailey: A Gospel Collection* culls the divine hooks from those three records; the synthesized punch and heaven-sent melodies of songs like "I Am Gold," "All Soldiers" and "Thank You" could provide inspiration for legions of frustrated Earth, Wind and Fire fans. — M.C.

ANITA BAKER

★ ★½ **The Songstress (1983; Elektra, 1991)**
★ ★ ★ ★ **Rapture (Elektra, 1986)**
★ ★ ★ **Giving You the Best That I Got (Elektra, 1988)**
★ ★½ **Compositions (Elektra, 1990)**

Blessed with a warm, resonant alto and a vocal style that effectively adapts the fluid phrasing of Sarah Vaughan to the soulful sound of quiet storm, Anita Baker became a pop sensation on the strength of her sultry *Rapture* album. And no wonder; few albums expressed the sensual pleasures of grown-up love as convincingly as Baker does in "You Bring Me Joy," "Been So Long" or "Sweet Love."

Baker didn't pull this sound out of thin air, of course; her gentle glissandi and slurred, jazzy phrasing was also evident on *The Songstress*, though the material is less than inspiring. Once Baker found her groove, however, she wasn't about to abandon it. *Giving You the Best That I Got* proceeds apace from *Rapture,* leaning heavily on slow, supple grooves and cool, jazzy keyboard coloring, but the songwriting is nowhere near as strong, relying more on mood than melody to carry the day. And even that would be an improvement over the mush on *Compositions*, an album so devoid of cogent songwriting that one wonders if the title wasn't meant ironically. — J.D.C.

LaVERN BAKER

★ ★ ★ ★ **LaVern Baker Sings Bessie Smith (1958; Atlantic, 1988)**

Those who remember the powerful voice that fueled mainstream R&B hits like "Jim Dandy," "Tweedlee Dee" and "Voodoo Voodoo" will hardly be surprised that LaVern Baker bows to no one, not even Bessie Smith, when it comes to a low-down, cagey delivery of the real blues. Still, Smith's sensibility informs Baker's approach, and there are other parallels as well: both were physically prepossessing, both suffered too many raw deals personally and professionally and both were great singers. At least Smith, despite her tragic death, was justly acclaimed in her lifetime; Baker's fame in the '50s and early '60s, though well-earned, stemmed from songs that barely hinted at her depth and versatility. *LaVern*

Baker Sings Bessie Smith corrects this problem. Here she is by turns bawdy ("Baby Doll"), forceful and independent ("I Ain't Gonna Play No Second Fiddle," "Young Woman's Blues"), vulnerable ("Empty Bed Blues," "After You've Gone") and bowed but proud ("Nobody Knows You When You're Down and Out"). Among a stellar supporting cast of players, Buck Clayton on trumpet and Vic Dickenson on trombone stand out with solo turns that buttress Baker's testifying with potent instrumental commentaries. In asserting her heritage, Baker tells anyone who will listen that this music defines her. Indeed, she sings Bessie Smith, and in grand style. But the control, the phrasing and the attitude are all LaVern Baker. — D.M.

MARTY BALIN

★ ★ **Balince: A Collection (Mirror Music, 1990)**

Balin's Jefferson Airplane ballads were some of the highlights of that pioneering band's early records, but with the Jefferson Starship's massive 1975 single, "Miracles," he'd assumed the lounge-act style that his subsequent solo work seldom departed from. His rock numbers sound like Toto (great chops in service of pablum), and his slow songs are mushy. A strong singer, he's also a very mannered one (generally after a heavily seductive fashion), and his choice of material is almost uniformly bad. *Balince* represents him well enough: there's "Miracles," along with the hits off his debut ("Atlanta Lady," "Hearts") and five schlocky unreleased cuts. — P.E.

MARCIA BALL

★ ★ ★ **Soulful Dress (Rounder, 1984)**
★ ★ **Hot Tamale Baby (Rounder, 1986)**
★ ★ ★ **Gatorhythms (Rounder, 1989)**

One of the *grande dames* of the Austin scene, along with Angela Strehli and Lou Ann Barton, Marcia Ball seems at once the most self-conscious of the three honky-tonk legends and the most free-swinging. It's an odd combination. Physically attractive, Ball favors slinky, below the knee dresses that accent her figure, which is noteworthy only because it's yet another contradiction: all dressed up for the Ritz but booked at the Armadillo. Ball makes all of this work in her favor. The clarity of her singing and the preciseness of her diction keep the focus on the message, not the messenger. And Ball isn't at all shy about letting us inside her world. On the opening cut of her first album, *Soulful Dress*, she announces, "I'm going to put on my dress/that's got those slits up both the sides/it's got a tight-fittin' waist/and a low neckline." She then moves on through ten songs that describe the emotional roller coaster she's been riding in trying to come to grips with this thing called love. Selected song titles tell the tale: "Made Your Move Too Soon," "My Mind's Made Up," "Soul on Fire," "Don't Want No Man." Blues ballads and contemporary honky-tonk stylings further recommend an album that is both personally revealing and musically swinging. *Hot Tamale Baby* follows in its predecessor's footsteps, both in theme and style. No questioning the forcefulness of Ball's singing—the lady can put over a lyric—but there's little to distinguish this effort from *Soulful Dress*, except that the band seems to be pumping at about twice the volume.

Gatorhythms, on the other hand, finds Ball exploring the rhythms of her native Louisiana while remaining in a Lone Star state of mind. She's also credited as co-producer, and writes seven of the ten songs on the album—encouraging signs. Ball continues to lay her soul bare; two ballads, "The Power of Love" and "Find Another Fool," find the singer admitting vulnerability, even insecurity, in her search for a significant other. She's always got time to rock, too, and does so convincingly on "How You Carry On" and the zydeco-flavored "Daddy Said." For Ball, *Gatorhythms* is a record documenting growth, both personal and professional. It's one to build on. — D.M.

BANANARAMA

   ★ ★½   **Deep Sea Skiving (London, 1983)**
   ★ ★ ★   **Bananarama (London, 1984)**
   ★ ★½   **True Confessions (London, 1986)**
   ★ ★ ★   **Wow! (Polydor, 1987)**
★ ★ ★ ★   **Greatest Hits Collection (Polydor, 1988)**
   ★ ★   **Pop Life (London, 1991)**

A girl group in the old-fashioned sense of the term, Bananarama started out with more enthusiasm than talent, but found stardom anyway. As in the old days, most of the credit for that success belongs with the group's producers, in this case the teams of Swain/Jolley and Stock/Aitken/Waterman. *Deep Sea Skiving* is an agreeable hodge-podge that flaunted Bananarama's amateurishness but came up with a few decent singles, most notably the mock-exotic "Aie a Mwana" and the chipper, Swain/Jolley-produced "Shy Boy." Not wishing to mess with a winning formula, Swain/Jolley

produced all of *Bananarama* and most of *True Confessions*, although with somewhat diminishing returns; their embrace of unison vocal lines pulls a certain poignancy from the B-girls' voices (as "Cruel Summer," from *Bananarama* demonstrates), but diminishes their overall pop appeal.

Enter SAW, a neo-disco production team that was in 1986 just coming into its ascendancy. Not only did SAW hand the trio its biggest U.S. hit with an impossibly upbeat remake of the Shocking Blue hit, "Venus," but it gave the group backing tracks so irrepressibly tuneful that Bananarama's vocal strengths (or lack thereof) were essentially beside the point. As such, *Wow!* was a perfect pop bon-bon, from hook-heavy dance tunes like "I Heard a Rumour" and "I Can't Help It" to relatively low-key confections like "Nathan Jones." No wonder *The Greatest Hits Collection*—track for track, the group's best album—relies so heavily upon this period.

Siobhan Fahey left just before *Hits*, and Jacquie O'Sullivan was brought in as B-girl No. 3, a change more noticeable in the album art than the sound of the music. The absence of Stock-Aitken-Waterman on *Pop Life*, however, was much more noticeable; although ex-Killing Joke bassist–turned–disco producer Youth tries to add some edge to the girls' sound, their meringue-like voices seem largely unaffected by his efforts. As a result, *Pop Life* lacks both. — J.D.C.

THE BAND

★ ★ ★ ★   **Music From Big Pink (Capitol, 1968)**
★ ★ ★ ★ ★   **The Band (Capitol, 1969)**
★ ★ ★ ★   **Stage Fright (1970; Capitol, 1990)**
   ★ ★½   **Cahoots (Capitol, 1971)**
★ ★ ★ ★   **Rock of Ages (Capitol, 1972)**
★ ★ ★   **Moondog Matinee (Capitol, 1973)**
★ ★ ★   **Northern Lights—Southern Cross (Capitol, 1975)**
★ ★ ★   **The Best of the Band (Capitol, 1976)**
★ ★ ★   **Islands (Capitol, 1977)**
★ ★ ★ ★   **Anthology (Capitol, 1978)**
★ ★ ★   **Rock of Ages, Vol. 1 (Capitol, 1982)**
★ ★ ★   **Rock of Ages, Vol. 2 (Capitol, 1982)**
★ ★ ★ ★   **The Last Waltz (Warner Bros., 1978)**
★ ★ ★ ★   **To Kingdom Come: The Definitive Collection (Capitol, 1990)**

Astonishing instrumental prowess makes the Band one of the strongest musical forces in rock & roll history—but what elevates the group to greatness is the power and clarity of its vision. Exercises in elegiac Americana that work as metaphors for very modern states of mind, Robbie Robertson's songs fuse folklore and history into a mythology of moonlit cornfields and small-town dreaming, of fading natural beauty and the immediate anxiety of individual souls. Rock has its lyric poets in Dylan and Van Morrison; Robertson commands vernacular detail and narrative force, however, in ways that more closely echo literature's short-story masters.

Together for nearly a decade before releasing *Big Pink*, the Band began by providing back-up for rockabilly pioneer Ronnie Hawkins. Then, serving as Bob Dylan's band, they provoked the fury of folk purists who couldn't abide Dylan's switch to rock. After the motorcycle wreck that caused Dylan's brief late-'60s retirement, the Band retreated to a communal home in Woodstock named Big Pink. *Music From Big Pink* was the group's tour de force debut: Robertson's "The Weight" and Dylan's "I Shall Be Released" encapsulated the Band's strengths—the lean grace of Robertson's guitar, the understated drive of Levon Helm's drumming, and, especially, the solo and ensemble brilliance of the group's three singers. With Helm handling the grittier numbers, bassist Rick Danko the steadier fare and keyboardist Richard Manuel the more soulful songs, *Big Pink* introduced vocalists of distinct capabilities; and Robertson's remarkable skill at matching the singer to the song set a pattern for all of the group's subsequent work.

The organ majesty of "Chest Fever" unleashed the Band's secret weapon: Garth Hudson. And Hudson's amazing arsenal of textures—carousel motifs, ragtime piano, a wah-wah clavinet that sounded like crickets—was then featured heavily on *The Band*, one of the richest and deepest records in rock history. The autumnal beauty of "King Harvest Has Surely Come," the sly country funk of "Up on Cripple Creek," the slow dignity of "The Night They Drove Old Dixie Down" reveal breathtaking sweep. Nearly all the songs boasted tricky metrical changes and shifts in style, and the playing was that of musicians so assured that their skill never overwhelmed their passion.

Stage Fright wasn't quite so commanding, but "All the Glory" and "Daniel and the

Sacred Harp" were Robertson at his most haunting, and "The Shape I'm In," as well as the title track, displayed writing of a penetrating psychological acuity. With *Cahoots*, strain began showing. Allen Toussaint's horn arrangements on "Life Is a Carnival" and a guest appearance by Van Morrison on "4% Pantomime" were great highlights, but the record was uncertain, murky and unsatisfying—Dylan's "When I Paint My Masterpiece" being the only song that rivaled the Band's earlier depth.

Notable mainly for the excellent addition of horns (again by Toussaint), *Rock of Ages* was a massive 1972 live set (later purposely re-released in two volumes), and a fond look back on past glory. Making that spirit more emphatic, the Band then released *Moondog Matinee*, an album of muted, if expert, covers of the early rock & roll that formed the group's roots (Clarence "Frogman" Henry's "Ain't Got No Home" was rollicking; Elvis's "Mystery Train" was a subtle, inventive remake).

Northern Lights and *Islands* showed the band shifting slightly toward a less complicated sound. Hudson's work, in particular, was remarkable on both records, but glossiness and ennui infected *Islands*— and Robertson's songs seemed pale, easier versions of his classics. A grand summing up, the three-LP *The Last Waltz* was the record of the Band's final concert and the soundtrack for a fine, elegiac film by Martin Scorsese. This late in the group's career, a heavy reverence surrounded them; adulated for years, the musicians seemed exhausted, overburdened by their own history. *Waltz*, however, remains a very lively farewell— Dylan, Neil Young, Van Morrison, Eric Clapton, Muddy Waters and Joni Mitchell all joined in, and the album remains a moving testimony not only to a band, but to an era of resolute musical independence. Even though the group played throughout the '70s, the Band, in retrospect, seemed one of the last great '60s outfits in spirit: absolute artists, uncompromising players, and a true, uneasy brotherhood.   — P.E.

THE BANGLES
★★★   **All Over the Place (Columbia, 1984)**
★★★   **Different Light (Columbia, 1985)**
★★★   **Everything (Columbia, 1988)**
★★★½ **Greatest Hits (Columbia, 1990)**
Mining the early Beatles for rock & roll catchiness and the Mamas and the Papas for vocal harmonies, this self-conscious L.A. girl group began with '60s revivalism of an earnest, unexamined sort and ended up with

lush radio-perfect pop. Extremely capable practitioners of hitcraft, the band played tightly and chose their songs well—and achieved gigantically the dubious triumph of sound over significance. With "Going Down to Liverpool" and "Hero Takes a Fall," *All Over the Place* presented a quartet of British Invasion fans well-versed in the chiming guitars and brisk melodies of a competent second-string act of that era (the Bangles were hardly fake Kinks, for example; more like fake Searchers). *Different Light* reaped hits aplenty, in Prince's "Manic Monday," the funky novelty "Walk Like an Egyptian," and Jules Shear's lovely "If She Knew What She Wants." Rhythm guitarist Susanna Hoffs mastered a singing style that combined pep, coy sweetness and an occasional plaintive resonance; bassist Michael Steele's "Following" featured tough-talk vocalizing that nicely leavened the band's tendency toward a cloying, somewhat arch delivery. Off *Everything*, Hoffs's "In Your Room" caught definitively the Bangles' gift for pastiche—its strings recalled the Stones' "2,000 Light Years From Home," its organ riffs echoed the Detroit Wheels, its guitar was crunchy like sanitized punk. "Eternal Flame" was a wide-screen, fairly bathetic ballad, its orchestral sweep connoting a new, unwelcome "seriousness." Predictably, *Greatest Hits* is the best Bangles—no real thematic consciousness enlivened their individual albums, and on the compilation there's the nice addition of two sharp singles, Simon and Garfunkel's "Hazy Shade of Winter" and the Grassroots' "Where Were You When I Needed You." Far more authentic an enterprise than, say, the Monkees, the Bangles put out smart, clean pop—it's a drag, though, that underneath the lustre lurks the cold glint of calculation, professionalism and a very '80s-style careerism. — P.E.

BOBBY BARE
★★★★ **This Is Bobby Bare 1963–1969 (RCA, 1970)**
  ★★★ **As Is (Columbia, 1981)**
    ★★ **Greatest Hits (1981; RCA, 1987)**
    ★★ **Encore (Columbia, 1982)**
    ★★ **Biggest Hits (Columbia, 1984)**

Bobby Bare's recording career began in 1958 when he subbed for an absent Bill Parsons and recorded the novelty song "All American Boy," a sendup of a popular rock & roll star who gets drafted into the Army (guess who?). The record remained credited to Parsons, but it was Bare's voice that told the tale that rose to Number Two on the

pop charts. Bare went on to carve out an interesting career in rock and country that is predictable only in its unpredictability. In the '60s he cut a string of Top Forty singles that were grounded as much in folk and country as they were in pop. "Detroit City" and "500 Miles Away From Home" were Top Twenty singles in 1963 that Bare rendered powerfully in a languorous, world-weary voice. Bare's work in the '60s seems impervious to time and changing tastes—the aforementioned hits as well as other folk-flavored singles from that period (notably "Streets of Baltimore," "Four Strong Winds," and "Long Black Veil") are powerfully rendered tales of longing and loss. This period is well chronicled in RCA's now-deleted two-record set, *This Is Bobby Bare, 1963–1969*. All that's left of Bare's RCA catalogue is the scandalous eight-track set, *Greatest Hits*. This has a couple of Bare's wry commentaries in "Rosalie's Good Eats Cafe" and "Lullabys, Legends and Lies," but eight tracks, even at a budget price, is a sad way to represent an artist with so much more to offer.

In the '70s and '80s Bare's work on Columbia was strictly in the country field and remained unusual and often compelling. As with his RCA catalogue, most of Bare's Columbia recordings are now deleted. *Biggest Hits* and *Encore* at least give some small sampling of work that was interesting either for the performances themselves or the choice of material. The former showcases more straight-ahead country songs; *Encore* emphasizes novelty items from a period (1978–1981) when the artist's albums were uneven at best. From this latter period the Bare album to track down is *As Is*, from 1981. Now deleted, this Rodney Crowell–produced session finds Bare turning in one stellar reading after another on a host of compelling songs. — D.M.

BAR-KAYS
  ★★★ **Soul Finger (1967; Rhino/Atlantic, 1992)**
  ★★★ **Coldblooded (1974; Stax, 1981)**
  ★★★ **Money Talks (1978; Stax, 1991)**
   ★★½ **In Joy (Mercury, 1979)**
  ★★★ **As One (Mercury, 1980)**
  ★★★ **The Best of the Bar-Kays (1988; Stax, 1990)**
  ★★½ **Banging the Walls (Mercury, 1985)**
  ★★½ **Contagious (Mercury, 1987)**
  ★★★ **Animal (Polygram, 1989)**

The Bar-Kays hit the charts in 1967 with "Soul Finger" (on the band's debut album, *Soul Finger*). Four of the six original

Bar-Kays died with Otis Redding in his 1967 plane crash, thus ending the band's brush with greatness. Together with new members, the survivors embarked upon a long and fairly successful career—albeit one marked more by skillful playing than imagination. *The Best of the Bar-Kays* captures their early '70s funk—"Son of Shaft" and "Don't Stop Dancing" remain capable, bassy, horn-heavy dance fare, notable primarily for a fusion of soul rhythm and rock guitar.

By the end of the '80s, reduced to a nucleus of lead singer Larry Dodson, keyboardist Winston Stewart and saxophonist Harvey Hendersen, they continued to sound like a very efficient bar band. Every album they've produced is serviceable—but from *Money Talks* (1978) to *Animal* (1989) their best cuts resemble lite pastiches of other bands' refinements (Sly, P-Funk, Kool and the Gang). Basically, they've never quite lived up to their promise. — P.E.

SYD BARRETT
★ ★ ★½ **The Madcap Laughs (1970; Capitol/EMI, 1990)**
★ ★ ★½ **Barrett (1970; Capitol/EMI, 1990)**
★ ★ ★½ **The Madcap Laughs/Barrett (1974; Capitol/EMI, 1990)**
★ ★ ★ **Opel (Capitol/EMI, 1989)**
★ ★ ★ **The Peel Sessions (Dutch East India/Strange Fruit, 1991)**

Pink Floyd's troubled founder didn't shuffle off into obscurity the way most acid burnouts do; Syd Barrett fell apart on record, his personality dissolving in a multicolored wash of sound. Moments of weird beauty and warm humor pop up all over his two solo albums, but *The Madcap Laughs* and *Barrett* can be pretty tough going, too. Reissued as two-fer in 1974, these albums have spawned a somewhat ghoulish cult—true believers who regard Syd's every halting sigh and painful stutter as "pure" artistic utterances. Ordinary listeners may find the flubs and false starts more than a little depressing; compared to the quirky songcraft, verbal wit and lingering melodies on fully realized songs like "Wined and Dined," "Dark Globe" and "Octopus," these lapses portend a tragic waste of talent. Though the songs document an emotional roller-coaster ride, producer David Gilmour constructs a musical support system that actually reins in Syd's swirling vision for minutes at a time. In fact, *The Madcap Laughs* and *Barrett* can be heard as a more human analogue to Pink

Floyd's chilly, cerebral work of the early '70s. The later albums contain some previously unavailable gems—*Opel*'s title track, the live "Two of a Kind" on *The Peel Sessions*—along with the expected breakdown-period acoustic shambles. — M.C.

BARRY & THE REMAINS
★ ★ ★ ★ **Barry & the Remains (1966; Epic/Legacy, 1991)**

One of the best American bands of the British Invasion era, the Remains (dubbed Barry & the Remains on this reissue in tribute to front man Barry Tashian) were big stars in Boston, but unknown almost everywhere else. Which, as this collection suggests, was an incredible injustice, for not only did the Remains have great material— "Don't Look Back," "Say You're Sorry" and "Why Do I Cry" are as good as anything Manfred Mann or the Pretty Things ever recorded—but the band's playing was both soulful and exciting. — J.D.C.

LOU ANN BARTON
★ ★ ★ ★ **Read My Lips (Antone's, 1989)**

When her now-deleted debut album, *Old Enough*, was released by Asylum in 1982, it appeared to signal the start of a career that would find Texas native Lou Ann Barton eventually being hailed as one of the greatest blues and country singers of her generation. Personal and professional problems promptly ensued, though, and Barton retreated to the Lone Star state, into a marriage and largely out of the public eye. Another album, *Forbidden Tones* (now out of print), surfaced in 1986, even as Barton maintained her low profile. And so it is today with Barton, who came back again in 1989 on the Austin-based Antone's label with a set of scorching performances that remind us not of what she might have been, but what she is—a natural-born singer who's learned hard lessons by living them. Every vocal nuance is tinged with blue, every lyric is read as if she wrote it. Her version of Barbara Lynn's "You'll Lose a Good Thing" is a wonder of self-assurance. Jimmy Reed's "Shake Your Hips" offers Barton a chance to deliver some low-down blues in her most suggestive voice, while "It's Raining," a signature song for Irma Thomas, becomes a masterpiece of loss and longing when Barton's throaty delivery is augmented by David "Fathead" Newman's mournful sax lines. "Rocket in My Pocket" and "Let's Have a Party" are served up as the forceful rockers they are.

So commanding is Barton's presence that she almost overshadows her uniformly first-rate instrumental support from a host of Austin-based musicians. Of particular note is Jimmie Vaughan, who gets the record off to a blazing start with his stinging lead work on "Sugar Coated Love" and also offers some wry commentaries in support of Barton's playful rendition of Slim Harpo's "Te Ni Nee Ni Nu." Remarkable in every way, *Read My Lips* requires no interpreter. — D.M.

BASIA

★★★ Time and Tide (Epic, 1987)
★★★★ London Warsaw New York (Epic, 1989)
★★★ Brave New Hope (EP) (Epic, 1991)

Like Everything but the Girl's Tracey Thorn or Swing Out Sister's Corrine Drewery, Basia Trzetrzelewska started out with a sound that evoked the slick sophistication of the jazz-pop stylists like Nancy Wilson or Astrud Gilberto. Unlike the others, though, Basia managed to recast that sophistication in completely contemporary terms, without falling back on camp affectation or ironic distance. That's why "Promises" or "From Now On," from *Time and Tide*, can play off samba rhythms without seeming mannered or imitative. *London Warsaw New York* takes that a step further by reinforcing the music's jazzy undertow with supple, soulful dancebeats, an approach that not only allows her to work wonders with the Aretha Franklin hit "Until You Come Back to Me (That's What I'm Gonna Do)" but adds extra allure to the likes of "Cruising for Bruising" and "Baby You're Mine." The *Brave New Hope* EP makes the dance influence even more explicit, pairing rhythm-driven songs like "Give Me That" and "Masquerade" with house-style remixes of "Cruising for Bruising" and "Until You Come Back to Me." — J.D.C.

COUNT BASIE

★★★★½ One O'Clock Jump (1937; Decca/MCA, 1990)
★★★★ Brand New Wagon (1947; Bluebird, 1990)
★★★★ April in Paris (Verve, 1955)
★★★★★ At Newport (1957; Verve, 1989)
★★★★½ Sing Along with Basie (1958; Roulette, 1991)
★★★★ Kansas City Suite (1960; Roulette, 1990)
★★★½ Count Basie and the Kansas City 7 (1962; MCA/Impulse, 1986)

★★★★ Basie in Sweden (1962; Roulette, 1991)
★★★½ Li'l Ol' Groovemaker . . . Basie! (Verve, 1963)
★★★½ Jazzfest Masters (1969; Scotti Bros., 1992)
★★★ Basic Basie (Verve/MPS, 1970)
★★★ High Voltage (Basic Basie, Vol. 2) (1970; Verve/MPS, 1975)
★★★ Basie Jam (1973; Pablo, 1975)
★★★★★ The Best of Count Basie (1937–39) (MCA, 1973)
★★★ For the First Time (1974; Pablo, 1987)
★★★ Basie Big Band (Pablo, 1975)
★★★ Fun Time (1975; Pablo, 1991)
★★★ I Told You So (Pablo, 1976)
★★★½ Prime Time (1977; Pablo, 1987)
★★★ Montreux '77 (1977; Pablo Live, 1989)
★★★½ Count Basie Jam: Montreux '77 (1977; Pablo Live, 1989)
★★★★ The Best of Count Basie (1980; Pablo, 1987)
★★★½ Kansas City Shout (1980; Pablo, 1987)
★★★ On the Road (Pablo, 1980)
★★½ Kansas City 6 (1981; Pablo, 1990)
★★★ 88 Basie Street (1983; Pablo, 1987)
★★½ Fancy Pants (1983; Pablo, 1987)
★★½ Me and You (1983; Pablo, 1987)
★★★ Mostly Blues . . . and Some Others (1983; Pablo, 1987)
★★★★ The Essential Count Basie, Volume 1 (1936–39) (Columbia, 1987)
★★★★★ The Essential Count Basie, Volume 2 (1939–40) (Columbia, 1987)
★★★ Live in Japan '78 (Pablo, 1987)
★★★ Get Together (1979; Pablo, 1987)
★★★★½ The Essential Count Basie, Volume 3 (1940–41) (Columbia, 1988)
★★½ Basie and Friends (1974–81) (Pablo, 1988)
★★★½ The Standards (1963–70) Verve, 1989)
★★★★ One More Time (1958–59) (Roulette, 1991)
★★★★★ The Complete Roulette Live Recordings of Count Basie and His Orchestra (1959–62) (Mosaic, 1991)
★★★★★ The Essence of Count Basie (Columbia Legacy, 1991)

★ ★ ★ ★   **Basie's Basement (Bluebird/
RCA, 1992)**
★ ★ ★ ★ ★   **The Complete Decca Recordings
(1937–1939) (Decca/GRP, 1992)**
WITH ROY ELDRIDGE
    ★ ★½   **Loose Walk (1972; Pablo, 1988)**
WITH OSCAR PETERSON
★ ★ ★ ★   **"Satch" and "Josh" (1974;
Pablo, 1988)**
    ★ ★ ★   **Satch and Josh . . . Again
(1977; Pablo, 1987)**
    ★ ★½   **The Timekeepers (1978; Pablo,
1983)**
    ★ ★½   **Yessir, That's My Baby (1978;
Pablo, 1987)**
WITH ZOOT SIMS
    ★ ★ ★   **Basie & Zoot (Pablo, 1976)**
WITH JOE WILLIAMS
★ ★ ★ ★ ★   **Count Basie Swings and Joe
Williams Sings (Verve, 1955)**
    ★ ★ ★½   **The Greatest! (Verve, 1957)**

One of the few big-band leaders to remain a
vital force in jazz long after the big-band era
itself had become a memory, William
"Count" Basie was a pivotal figure in
American popular music. Where other
bands in the '30s seemed to place most of
their emphasis on melody and ensemble
work, Basie's band stressed rhythm and
solos. To that extent, the Basie ensemble
operated more like a combo than a big
band, often relying on riff-based
arrangements that provided a launching pad
for improvisation. Moreover, the kind of
material the Basie band specialized in—lean,
blues-based songs powered by an aggressive,
hard-swinging backbeat—set the stage for
jump blues outfits like those led by Louis
Jordan, Big Joe Turner and Eddie
"Cleanhead" Vinson.

What led Basie to that sound was luck as
much as anything else. Born in Red Bank,
New Jersey, in 1904, Basie was playing
organ in a touring vaudeville show when he
found himself stranded in Kansas City.
Working his way into that city's jazz scene,
he played first with the Blue Devils, before
joining up with Bennie Moten's Kansas City
Orchestra. It was with Moten that Basie
made his first recordings, although the
playing tends mostly to the "stomp" style
popular in the midwest at that time, it's easy
to hear the origins of the Basie sound,
particularly in the insistent, bass-driven
pulse of "Moten Swing."

Moten died in 1935, and Basie put
together his own band, drawing on some of
his old Moten bandmates (alto saxophonist
Jack Washington, trombonist Dan Minor,
bassist Walter "Big Un" Page) as well as
some hot new players (most notably tenor
saxophonist Lester Young, trumpeter Buck
Clayton and drummer Jo Jones). Instead of
the fancy ensemble writing that was the
norm then, the Basie band often worked
from "head arrangements"—loose, casually
organized charts with parts worked out
cooperatively among the band
members—letting the groove do most of the
work. And work it did. When critic and
talent scout John Hammond heard the band
during a radio broadcast in early 1936, he
was instantly smitten, and rushed to get the
Basie band signed. Unfortunately, he only
got a quintet performance of "Oh, Lady Be
Good" on wax for Columbia (it's on *The
Essential Count Basie, Vol. 1*) before Basie,
short on cash, signed the band with Decca.
Financially, it was a bum deal (it took the
intervention of the musicians' union for
Basie to earn any royalties), but musically,
it's hard to argue with the results. *The
Complete Decca Recordings* offers eloquent
testimony to how great this early Basie band
was. Casual listeners, however, may want to
settle for *One O'Clock Jump* that includes
the classic riff tune "One O'Clock Jump,"
which became the band's signature, as well
as "Topsy," "Good Morning Blues" (with
Jimmy Rushing on vocals) and the fiery
"John's Idea," but it lacks the breadth of
MCA's *The Best of Count Basie*, a 24-tune
compilation comprised of such classics as
"Cherokee," "Every Tub," "Jumpin' at the
Woodside," "You Can Depend on Me" and
"Swinging at the Daisy Chain." An
absolutely essential collection, but not, at
this point, available on compact disc.

In 1939, Basie finally got free of his Decca
deal, and went over to Columbia, where he
cut the material assembled on the three
volumes of *The Essential Count Basie*.
Although the tunes lack the pop appeal of
the Decca material, the playing is far more
exciting, as the band's soloists—particularly
Lester Young—truly come to the fore. All
three volumes are good, but *Vol. 2* is
especially fine, featuring a classic pair of
performances by Count Basie's Kansas City
Seven ("Dickie's Dream," featuring
trombonist Dickie Wells, and "Lester Leaps
In," one of Young's most memorable
recordings) as well as such full-band classics
as "Tickle Toe," "Blow Top" and "Super
Chief."

From there, Basie went to RCA in 1947,
but with a much different band. Young and
Clayton were gone and Washington was
dead, and though the rhythm section
retained its flavor, the horn arrangements

grew brash and brassy, adding tremendous kick to tunes like the red-hot "House Rent Boogie." *Brand New Wagon* offers a fair sampling of this period in the band's development, but doesn't include any of the band's popular novelty numbers, like its chart-topping cover of Jack McVea's "Open the Door, Richard" or the topical "Did You See Jackie Robinson Hit That Ball?"

Basie folded his band in 1950, and—except for a big-band engagement at the Apollo in 1951—worked strictly with small ensembles for the next two years before assembling a new band to record for Verve (of the albums he recorded during this period, only a handful are now in print). Again, it's the rhythm section that determined the character of the band, and new drummer Sonny Payne puts real punch into the familiar Basie groove. Payne is admirably explosive on the title track of *April in Paris*, but he shines even brighter on *Count Basie Swings and Joe Williams Sings*, on which his forthright backbeat helps this collection of blues pack a wallop that rivals even Joe Turner's finest (the Basie/Williams version of "Every Day I Have the Blues" actually went to No. 2 on the R&B charts). Unfortunately, the Basie-Williams album *The Greatest!* has nowhere near the sizzle of its predecessor, but *At Newport* more than makes up, flanking Williams with such all-star alumni as Lester Young, Roy Eldridge and Jo Jones.

In 1957, Basie moved to Roulette Records, where he and arranger Neal Hefti (who, at this point, is probably better known for the "Batman" TV theme than for his stunning big-band writing) immediately showed their versatility through the lovely ballad "Li'l Darling" (from *The Atomic Mr. Basie*, now out of print). Basie recorded fairly extensively for Roulette, cutting everything from thematically focused albums like *Kansas City Suite* to one-off collaborations with such singers as Tony Bennett (on the wonderful *Basie Swings, Bennett Sings*) and Sarah Vaughan (*Basie, Vaughan*, now out of print). Perhaps the most unusual of these is *Sing Along With Basie*, in which Basie and Williams are joined by Lambert, Hendricks and Ross for vocalized versions of Basie classics like "Tickle Toe" and "Every Tub." But the best of the Roulette recordings were the live albums culled from performances at Miami's Americana Hotel in 1959, New York's Birdland in 1961, and the Grona Lund amusement park in Stockholm, Sweden, in 1962. Of the original albums, only *Count*

Basie in Sweden is in print, but even if the others are brought back into print, *The Complete Roulette Live Recordings* is still preferable, both for its completeness (its six CDs offer over six-and-a half hours of music) and its ability to convey a sense of what this band was like in concert.

In many senses, the Roulette years were the Basie band's high water mark, for the group would never again attain such a consistent level of greatness. That's not to say the Basie band didn't have its moments, but after 1962, they didn't always come when expected. For instance, the Quincy Jones charts on *Li'l Ol' Groovemaker . . . Basie* are certainly nothing to sneeze at, but frankly the band at that period seemed to have more snap when backing Frank Sinatra on albums like *Sinatra-Basie* and *It Might as Well Be Swing*.

Perhaps the most problematic of Basie's recordings, though, are the ones he made for Pablo, the label Verve-founder Granz launched in the early '70s. The problem is sheer volume, as Granz recorded 30-odd albums worth of Basie material in the 12 years before his death in 1984. Naturally, not every note is golden. Granz did have some good ideas, and some of the small group recordings—particularly the trio album *For the First Time*, the lively *Basie Jam* and *"Satch" & "Josh,"* the first of the Oscar Peterson collaborations—are pleasant surprises. His big band albums, however, are a mixed lot, with the feisty *Prime Time* and the nostalgic *Montreux '77* being the only standouts. — J.D.C.

THE BEACH BOYS

★★★½ **Surfin' Safari/Surfin' USA (1962/63; Capitol, 1990)**

★★★½ **Surfer Girl/ Shut Down Volume 2 (1963/64; Capitol, 1990)**

★★★★ **Little Deuce Coupe/All Summer Long (1963/64; Capitol, 1990)**

★★★ **Beach Boys Christmas Album (Capitol, 1964)**

★★★★★ **Today/Summer Days (and Summer Nights) (1965; Capitol 1990)**

★★½ **Concert/Live in London (1964/1976; Capitol 1990)**

★★★★★ **Pet Sounds (1966; Capitol, 1990)**

★★★ **Best of the Beach Boys (Capitol, 1966)**

★★½ **Party!/Stack O Tracks (1966; Capitol, 1968)**

★★★ **Smiley Smile/Wild Honey (1967; Capitol, 1990)**

★★ Friends (1968)/20/20 (1968/1969; Capitol, 1990)

★★★ Sunflower (1970; Caribou/Epic, 1991)

★★★½ Surf's Up (1971; Caribou/Epic, 1991)

★★½ Holland (1973; Caribou/Epic, 1991)

★,★ Carl and the Passions—So Tough (1972; Caribou/Epic, 1991)

★★½ The Beach Boys in Concert (1973; Caribou/Epic, 1991)

★★★★★ Endless Summer (Capitol, 1974)

★★★★ Spirit of America (Capitol, 1975)

★★½ 15 Big Ones (1976; Caribou/Epic, 1991)

★★★★ Beach Boys Love You (1977; Caribou/Epic, 1991)

★ M.I.U. (1978; Caribou/Epic, 1991)

★ L.A. (Light Album) (Caribou/Epic, 1979)

★ Keepin' The Summer Alive (1980; Caribou/Epic, 1991)

★★★ Ten Years of Harmony (1979; Caribou/Epic, 1991)

★★ Made in the USA (Capitol, 1986)

★ Still Cruisin' (Capitol, 1989)

★★★★★ California Girls (Capitol, 1990)

BRIAN WILSON

★★½ Brian Wilson (Sire, 1988)

DENNIS WILSON

★★½ Pacific Ocean Blue (1977; Caribou/Epic, 1991)

MIKE LOVE

★ Looking Back With Love (Boardwalk, 1981)

Growing up in suburban southern California, Brian Wilson could look out of his bedroom window and see the perfect world Chuck Berry envisioned in the lyrics of his rock & roll classics. Writing songs about this booming adolescent culture was a natural move for a creatively inclined teenager. And Brian Wilson turned out to be much more than another talented kid with "the knack." He formed the Beach Boys at the start of the '60s with his younger brothers Carl (guitar) and Dennis (drums), their cousin Mike Love (vocals) and their neighbor Alan Jardine (guitar). (Jardine left before the group started making records, and was replaced by David Marks; he rejoined in 1963, after Marks was fired.) Brian played bass and, most importantly, masterminded the stunning vocal harmonies and subtle arrangements that soon became the group's calling card.

Capitol's exemplary CD reissue series of the original Beach Boys albums, including a number of "two-fers" and bonus tracks, chart the development of a genius—step by fascinating step. Brian Wilson expands and deepens the Beach Boys' musical frame of refenence without deserting the commercial formulas that made the group a success. Until *Pet Sounds*, anyway, and that's quite a run. Even on the good timin' early albums, flashes of Brian's musical ambition and emotional turmoil surface: "In My Room" on *Surfer Girl* introduces his devastatingly insightful quiet side and suggests unlimited future possibilities for those five fresh voices. *Little Deuce Coupe* documents the drag-strip mentality with a participant's enthusiasm and eye for detail.

All Summer Long is where the Beach Boys as-we-know-them arrive. "I Get Around," "Wendy" and the title track represent incredible leaps in terms of melody, production and verbal sophistication. Just consider the way "I Get Around" underlines its celebration of teen freedom with creeping ambivalence: "I get bugged driving up and down the same old strip."

Today and *Summer Days (and Summer Nights)* are the Beach Boys' peak performances. Perhaps *Pet Sounds* really is the masterpiece it's supposed to be, perhaps not. However, the preceding two albums exhibit the full range—and pop immediacy—of Brian Wilson's achievement: not just the exquisite hit singles "Help Me Rhonda" and "California Girls" but perfectly sculpted, equally catchy songs like "Please Let Me Wonder," "She Knows Me Too Well," "Girl Don't Tell Me" and "Let Him Run Wild." Brian Wilson became increasingly obsessed with studio-craft; having improved on Phil Spector's wall-of-sound methods, he had to out-do the Beatles and Motown, too. Some listeners think the shiver-inducing 1966 single "Good Vibrations" (included on *Smiley Smile*, a truncated version of the aborted *Smile* project and the last Beach Boys album Brian produced until 1977) is his pinnacle; others swear by the pristine, complex melancholia of *Pet Sounds*. For all its painstaking sonic accomplishment, the most influential thing about *Pet Sounds* may be its self-obsessed tone.

Wild Honey is the Beach Boys' most underrated album. The scruffy R&B influence takes some getting used to, but it buffets the Boys' voices. Similarly, the loopy sense of humor that emerges on that album goes a long ways toward erasing some post-*Pet Sounds* gloom. The Beach Boys' subsequent albums sport a winning song or two: "Do It Again" and "I Can Hear Music," from *20/20*, for example, amid oceans of intemperate, slight experimentation.

Frustrating is the kindest way to characterize the rest of the Beach Boys' recording career. The group doesn't appear to have had much fun during the '70s—let alone "Fun, Fun, Fun." *Sunflower* shies away from avant noodling and sticks to songs. Suprisingly, it sounds sweet and strangely indistinct; "Deirdre" could be Beach Boys–influenced anybody. *Surf's Up* features strong contributions from the other members: Al Jardine and Mike Love's "Don't Go Near the Water," Carl Wilson and manager Jack Rieley's "Long Promised Road." Carl also contributed a pleasant mood piece called "Feel Flows," while Brian collaborates with Van Dyke Parks on the murky title suite, which was originally intended for *Smile*. Sadly, *Holland* is far more typical of this period: one fantastic track ("Sail On Sailor," soulfully sung by Blondie Chaplin, who was in the band for this album alone) and a veritable shit-load of meditative drivel. Slowly but surely, the Beach Boys begin to fall back on those crowd-pleasing golden oldies; *In Concert* captures the group just before it degenerated into a shameless nostalgia act.

Capitol's *Endless Summer* package sparked a full-fledged Beach Boys revival in the mid-'70s, augmented by the group's seemingly endless summer tours. Of course, filling up a second double-record volume (*Spirit of America*) is absolutely no problem with these guys. Since the band had been poorly served by inferior Capitol reissues in the '70s, these two greatest hits sets originally came as a godsend. But after years of party- and radio-play, the Beach Boys' classics can sound shopworn. With their revelatory "filler" cuts, the reissued original albums are probably a better investment at this point, for fans and neophytes alike.

Beach Boys Love You is Brian Wilson's last gasp of brilliance. It mines a warm, slightly funky vein, adding a markedly adult horniness and out-there sense of humor. Those once-innocent voices are now ragged, even ravaged, but somehow still right. After that, the trapdoor opens and boom! The cover illustration of the wan *Keepin' The Summer Alive* album, from 1980, says more than words ever could: the Beach Boys play

under a heated bubble, plying those sunny hits in the middle of a blizzard—oblivious. *Ten Years of Harmony* offers a random, disappointing sampler of the group's '70s output. Collecting the joyless ditties (like "Kokomo") that have become the Beach Boys' '80s refuge, *Still Cruisin'* is the absolute pits. And even completists might have trouble coming to terms with the various solo albums: Brian's ballyhooed 1988 comeback is a bland tangle of psycho-babble and automaton melodies, while Dennis's 1977 outing is a lukewarm attempt at emulating his older brother's orchestral sweep. Mike Love's *Looking Back With Love*, now out of print, is notable only for its title track: an egregious "salute" to those crazy ol' '60s that would probably make a dandy Republican campaign jingle. No matter. As long as America, automobiles and adolescents exist in some recognizable form, the Beach Boys' best records will remain essential. — M.C.

THE BEASTIE BOYS
★ ★ ★½ **Licensed to Ill (Def Jam/Columbia, 1986)**
★ ★ ★ ★ **Paul's Boutique (Capitol, 1989)**
★ ★ ★ ★ **Check Your Head (Capitol, 1992)**

Elvis covered Big Boy Crudup and remade American music and politics; Pat Boone diluted Little Richard and merely made dollars and mush. With white players mining the black motherlode, the difference between homage-solidarity and pandering-theft is a matter of spirit. And with *Licensed to Ill*, from 1986, three white New York homeys nailed the rap spirit flat. Run-D.M.C. producer Rick Rubin delivered maximum boom; Adam "Ad-Rock" Horovitz, Adam "MCA" Yauch and Michael "Mike D" Diamond beer-stoked rhymes with the zest of drive-by Dead End Kids. The samples and references were nutty and ranging—Led Zepplein, War and the theme to "Mr. Ed"—and for good measure, Rubin mixed in AC/DC-style metal guitar. All this was fantasy, of course—no more authentic than, say, California's Creedence Clearwater Revival and that group's Deep South swamp rock—but "Posse in Effect," "She's Crafty" and "Time to Get Ill" were charming fantasy: not since the '50s Kerouac hipster myth had white boys tried so damn hard to be bad. Rubin and the Beasties showed smarts, too: their rap didn't strain too hard for true street credibility—it was a high-school version, and with "Fight for Your Right (to Party)," *Licensed* boasted a behavior-disorder anthem that was right up there with Brownsville Station's "Smokin' in the Boys' Room," Alice Cooper's "School's Out" and Kiss's "Rock and Roll All Nite." In a perfect world, N.W.A would have gone megaplatinum before the Beasties, but the Boys' success still was nicely subversive. All of mall America suddenly got hip to high tops, malt liquor, baseball caps and at least an introductory version of rap's astonishingly inventive lexicon.

Remarkably, *Paul's Boutique* revealed the Beasties as not merely die-hard assimilators, but rap auteurs. A riotous epic cartoon, chockful of allusions not only to Ed Koch and "hand me down Pumas," but to Isaac Newton, *Clockwork Orange* and the Old Testament, this was heady, ambitious stuff. Among its other triumphs, it caught New York with as much grit and detail as did Spike Lee or Lou Reed. And—talk about Rainbow Coalition—there's even a few country music sound-bites thrown in. *Check Your Head*, recorded after the Beasties had relocated to California, perfectly displays the bands' roots in thrash and hip-hop without compromising either genre. Also, for the first time, the Beasties play their own instruments—bass, drums, guitar. — P.E.

THE BEATLES
★★★★★ Please Please Me (1963; Capitol, 1987)
★★★★★ With the Beatles (1963; Capitol, 1987)
★★★★★ Meet the Beatles (Capitol, 1964)
★★★★★ The Beatles' Second Album (Capitol, 1964)
★★★ The Beatles' Story (Capitol, 1964)
★★★★½ Something New (Capitol, 1964)
★★★★★ A Hard Day's Night (1964; Capitol, 1987)
★★★★★ Beatles '65 (Capitol, 1964)
★★★★★ Beatles for Sale (1964; Capitol, 1987)
★★★★★ Early Beatles (Capitol, 1965)
★★★★½ Beatles VI (Capitol, 1965)
★★★★½ Help! (1965; Capitol, 1987)
★★★★★ Rubber Soul (1965; Capitol, 1987)
★★★★★ Yesterday . . . And Today (Capitol, 1966)
★★★★★ Revolver (1966; Capitol, 1987)
★★★★★ Sgt. Pepper's Lonely Hearts Club Band (Capitol, 1967)
🎔★★★★ Magical Mystery Tour (Capitol, 1967)
★★★★★ The Beatles (Apple, 1968)
★★★ Yellow Submarine (Apple, 1969)
★★★★★ Abbey Road (Apple, 1969)
★★★★½ Hey Jude (Apple, 1970)
★★★★★ Let It Be (Apple, 1970)
★★★★★ The Beatles 1962–1966 (Capitol, 1973)
★★★★★ The Beatles 1967–1970 (Capitol, 1973)
★★★★★ Rock 'n' Roll Music (Capitol, 1976)
★★★★ Love Songs (Capitol, 1977)
★★★★ Live at the Hollywood Bowl (Capitol, 1977)
★★★ Live! at the Star Club in Hamburg, Germany, 1962 (Capitol, 1977)
★★★ Rarities (Capitol, 1980)
★★★½ Reel Music (Capitol, 1982)
★★★★★ Rock 'n' Roll Music, Vol. II (Capitol, 1980)
★★★ The Early Tapes of the Beatles (The Beatles/The Beatles With Tony Sheridan/Tony Sheridan and the Beat Brothers) (Polydor, 1986)
★★★★★ Past Masters, Volume 1 (Capitol, 1988)
★★★★★ Past Masters, Volume 2 (Capitol, 1988)
★★★★★ The Ultimate Box Set (Capitol, 1989)

The importance of the Beatles cannot be overstated. Transforming rock & roll from a rebel yell and a lover's whisper into the most comprehensive music of the century, they blazed through a breathtaking succession of creative periods whose ultimate end was the severing of the line between high art and popular entertainment. As the world's best-loved band, they determined, too, that the sensibility of their period would mirror their own—and, indeed, the rock & roll of the '60s was predominantly Beatles-spirited: celebratory, omnivorous in its appetite for diverse influence, politically expansive and spiritually open. The interchange of their personalities created the perfect band—John Lennon (rebel genius), Paul McCartney (perfectionist craftsman), George Harrison (mystic) and Ringo Starr (clown). Finally, the Beatles were arguably the last band that everyone from Leonard Bernstein to school children embraced. Theirs is the final, great consensus in popular music—not liking them is as perverse as not liking the sun.

Through 1966, confusing record company strategies produced U.K. and U.S. albums whose differing contents were mainly a matter of song selection. In 1987 Capitol released on CD the Beatles' original 12 albums in their British formats, relegating the original American album versions to cassette and whatever vinyl remains. (The reissues of the British albums are those with two release dates in the discography above. British singles and EP cuts not found on American albums were reissued on Volumes One and Two of *Past Masters.*) American Beatlemania began with Capitol's *Meet the Beatles* in 1964. "I Want to Hold Your Hand," of course, was the keynote—the song screamed, but nicely—and with the urgent "It Won't Be Long" and the softer "All My Loving" the fertile John-Paul tension of bitter and sweet was introduced. This record was quintessential "Merseybeat"—deft, sweet rocking patterned on a mix of the Beatles' primary influences, R&B and Buddy Holly. (On CD, "Hand" is on *Past Masters, Volume One*; the other two songs are on *With the Beatles.*) The soul cover tunes on *The Second Album* proved how hard the band could rock: John's version of Barrett Strong's "Money" (also on *With the Beatles*) ranks alongside the greatest rock & roll singing ever recorded, and with "Long Tall Sally" (CD: *Past Masters, Volume One*), Paul nearly rivals Little Richard. *A Hard Day's Night* wasn't helped by producer-arranger George Martin's sappy string filler, but in the title track John debuted the wordplay cleverness that was soon a Beatles trademark. Not at all incidentally, *A Hard Day's Night*, the movie, with its jump-cut editing and exhilarating atmosphere of speed would become the standard rock film style: every video derives from it.

After *Something New*, inflated by a German version of "I Wanna Hold Your Hand" but boasting the rockabilly charm of Carl Perkins's "Matchbox" (both on *Past Masters, Volume One*) and Paul's great fusion of folk and bossa nova, "And I Love Her" (on *A Hard Day's Night* CD), *Beatles '65* showed the band beginning to think in terms of albums, not singles. As songwriters, Lennon and McCartney had outgrown their puppy-love anthems; "I'm a Loser" (CD: *Beatles for Sale*) and "She's a Woman" (CD: *Past Masters, Volume One*) revealed a new complexity of emotion. Fortuitously released three months later, *The Early Beatles* made it possible to see how far the band had come instrumentally as well. McCartney's stature as a remarkably melodic bassist was confirmed; Harrison's bell-like electric lead guitar work had gained in subtlety; Ringo had proved himself by

now the steadiest drummer in rock. As a rhythm guitarist, Lennon would remain a minimalist, but the interpretive depth of his singing had become manifest.

Beatles VI carried on consistently, and "Help!," the title song to the group's second movie soundtrack, featured John's best songwriting yet. *Rubber Soul*, however, was a real breakthrough. By now, Lennon and McCartney had absorbed the music of Bob Dylan—their greatest influence after the classic early rockers—and the record was a folk-rock masterpiece. On "Norwegian Wood," George's sitar and John's lyrics made for music of intense longing and regret; "Michelle" saw Paul achieving a new sophistication.

On *Yesterday . . . And Today*, "Day Tripper" (CD: *Past Masters, Volume Two*) gave the Beatles their strongest rocker in quite some time, and Paul's "Yesterday" (CD: *Help!*) triumphed even over "Michelle." But it was with *Revolver* that the group left virtually all their contemporaries behind. George Martin provided arranging assistance, but Paul's idea for the string quartet that undergirded "Eleanor Rigby" was all his own. Tape loops, a new cryptic bent to his lyrics, and soaring, chanting vocals made John's "Tomorrow Never Knows" a pioneering piece of studio music. Harrison's tabla-and-sitar "Love You To" offered up the possibilities not only of Indian music but of Eastern religion. And *Revolver* was only the prelude to *Sgt. Pepper.*

By 1967, exhaustion, death threats and fan hysteria had forced the Beatles to stop touring entirely. Straight rock & roll has always been primarily a live artform, and with the group's retreat into the studio—as well as the direction they'd taken since *Rubber Soul*—it made sense that the sound they'd emerge with would not be rock. It was, instead, the most astonishing single record of popular music ever released. Its cover-art portraits of icons from Dylan to Marilyn to Oscar Wilde hinted at the range of styles inside, and with Madame Toussaud's wax figurines of the Fab Four also adorning the sleeve, the record bade farewell to the Beatles as anyone's idea of mere teenybop idols. Adamant auteurs by now, they fused the orchestral and electronic arts in unprecedented ways; if "She's Leaving Home" was a song as structurally sound as any Schubert leider, "A Day in the Life" was music that only studio technology made possible. While thematically unified by its general air of wonder, the album, however, foretold disharmony—*Sgt. Pepper* was chiefly McCartney's triumph, even if Lennon's singing on "A Day in the Life" provided its most moving moment.

Magical Mystery Tour, a hodgepodge, sounded like *Pepper* outtakes and, indeed, "Strawberry Fields Forever" and "Penny Lane" were recorded early in the sessions that eventually produced *Sgt. Pepper*. Lennon's "Strawberry Fields Forever" and "I Am the Walrus" displayed not only his Joycean language gifts, but their music—a kind of symphonic-high-tech balance—was the most distinctive sound he'd make until his first solo album. McCartney's "Penny Lane" featured a clarion, baroque trumpet motif.

That Lennon and McCartney now were a partnership in name only was proven by *The Beatles*—or "The White Album," in common parlance. The double-album wasn't really a group effort at all. McCartney's "Blackbird" was Paul at his simplest and most melodic; "Why Don't We Do It in the Road" found him rocking so desperately that he verged on parody. The primal rock of John's "Yer Blues" negated the spirit of *Sgt. Pepper*, while his lovely elegy for his mother, "Julia," was soul-bearing of a distinctively private sort. "While My Guitar Gently Weeps" was Harrison's best Beatles' song and Ringo soldiered on with characteristic good humor, but the Beatles now were four different men, their remarkable synergy had exploded. *Yellow Submarine* reunited them in truly cartoon form. The record's best songs were Harrison's ("Only a Northern Song" and "It's All Too Much").

Fittingly, the Beatles' end came with the end of the decade whose zeitgeist had in significant part been their creation. On *Abbey Road*, Lennon reasserted his rock & roll soul with "Come Together"; on side two, McCartney assembled a song-suite of a variety and sweep the band hadn't displayed since *Sgt. Pepper*. This was pop music of a matchless assurance, with all of the band's signal virtues—grace, humor, wordplay, unrivaled melodies—resolutely intact. Their swan song, *Let It Be*—released after, but recorded before *Abbey Road*—more faithfully captured the spirit of the group's last days. With some songs overproduced (by Phil Spector) and others sounding nearly unfinished, it betrayed exhaustion. Paul's best numbers (the title track and "Get Back") and John's best singing ("I've Got a Feeling," "Don't Let Me Down") are the sounds of two different bands—and the

most poignant moment is provided by the pair's vocals on the melodically simple, but spiritually overwhelming, "Two of Us."

Of the Beatles' many compilations, *The Ultimate Box Set* indeed lives up to its name—it includes all the individual albums, plus *Past Masters I and II*. Greatest-hits packages obviously don't do this band justice, but a Martian who had never heard the Beatles might want to start with *Hey Jude*. *Live at the Hollywood Bowl* explains what Beatlemania was all about; the pre-Fab Four work, on *The Early Tapes*, *The Decca Tapes* and *Live! at the Star Club*, is certainly of historical interest, but the sound quality is wretched. *The Beatles Story*, a 1964 documentary record released only to cash in on fan frenzy, is of interest to collectors only. — P.E.

BEATS INTERNATIONAL
★★★ **Let Them Eat Bingo (Elektra, 1990)**
★★★½ **Excursion on the Version (Elektra, 1992)**

An English house-music outfit fronted by former Housemartin Norman Cook, the Beats are hardly innovators. They do show a flair for creative larceny: "Dub Be Good to Me," for instance, grounded the S.O.S. Band's "Just Be Good to Me" with a bass line swiped from the Clash's "Guns of Brixton." There are even more reggae-house interminglings on *Excursion on the Version*, though the album's most affecting selection is a fairly straightforward reading of "In the Ghetto." Ephemeral but fun. — J.D.C.

THE BEAU BRUMMELS
★★★ **Introducing the Beau Brummels (1965; Rhino, 1982)**
★★★½ **The Best of the Beau Brummels (Rhino, 1987)**

Touching in their heartfelt bid to copy the Beatles, the Beau Brummels succeeded uncannily at putting an American spin on Merseybeat. "Laugh Laugh" and "Just a Little" are flawless singles; an insinuating harmonica, Sal Valentino's clear, radio-perfect vocals and the band's deft playing make for pop that's immediate and memorable. San Francisco popsters copping their title from a 19th-century English rake, the lads not only had the look but the smarts to serve as a legitimate proto-Monkees—"Don't Talk to Strangers," "Sad Little Girl" and "Still in Love with You Baby" rival the best of Herman's Hermits, Gerry and the Pacemakers and the like. The later material, reflecting the folkish turn of their Liverpool idols (with *Rubber*

Soul) and Bob Dylan (with *John Wesley Harding*), isn't as catchy. But in its melody and charm, it's well worth a listen. — P.E.

BEAUSOLEIL

★ ★ ★	The Spirit of Cajun Music (Swallow, 1977)	
★ ★ ★½	Zydeco Gris Gris (1980; Swallow, 1985)	
★ ★ ★	Parlez-Nous à Boire (1981; Arhoolie, 1990)	
★ ★ ★	Bayou Boogie (Rounder, 1986)	
★ ★ ★½	Allons à Lafayette (Arhoolie, 1986)	
★ ★ ★	Belizaire the Cajun (Arhoolie, 1986)	
★ ★ ★ ★	Hot Chili Mama (Arhoolie, 1987)	
★ ★ ★	Live! From the Left Coast (Rounder, 1989)	
★ ★ ★½	Bayou Cadillac (Rounder, 1989)	
★ ★ ★½	Déjà Vu (Swallow, 1990)	
★ ★ ★ ★	Cajun Conja (RNA, 1991)	

It would be tempting to describe Beausoleil as the Cajun equivalent to Fairport Convention, except that while Fairport sought to bring a traditional folk sensibility to rock & roll, Beausoleil fusion moves in the opposite direction. In fact, Beausoleil's first album, *The Spirit of Cajun Music,* is traditional almost to the point of purism; only occasional experiments with instrumentation like the saxophones on "Blues á Bébé" distinguish the group's sound from that of old-timers like the Balfa Brothers. Beausoleil's sound broadens a bit with *Zydeco Gris Gris*—note Michael Doucet's bluesy fiddling in "Valse à Beausoleil," and the conga-driven backbeat on "Zydeco Gris-Gris"—but sticks closer to Cajun tradition for *Parlez-Nous à Boire.* Some of that seems to stem from marketing considerations; Rounder, which released *Zydeco Gris Gris,* seemed to see Beausoleil as a Cajun crossover band, while Arhoolie, which did *Parlez-Nous à Boire,* preferred to present the band as hardcore traditionalists. As such, the group bounces back and forth, adding even more rock influence on *Bayou Boogie,* with its Bo Diddley–beat remake of "Zydeco Gris Gris" and a gutsy electric slide guitar on "Fais Pas Ça," while *Allons à Lafayette* gets no funkier than a touch of dobro on "Mon Vieux Wagon."

Beausoleil finally resolves its split-personality problems with *Hot Chili Mama,* which finds the band doing to Cajun music what Clifton Chenier did to zydeco—bring in a strong blues influence (like Pat Breaux's sax solo in "Les Bons Temps Rouler Waltz") without appreciably changing the old-style beat. *Bayou Cadillac* mostly continues in that vein, although it does find room for such unexpected touches as "Hey Baby, Quoi Ça Dit?" and the "Bayou Cadillac" medley, which uses a Bo Diddley groove to combine "Not Fade Away" with "Bo Diddley" and "Iko Iko." By *Cajun Conja,* Beausoleil's transformation into real rock & roll Cajuns is complete—even to the point of bringing in guitarist Richard Thompson for a pair of gracefully played cameos. *Déjà Vu* is a compilation that draws from Beausoleil's mostly traditional recordings for Swallow, while *Belizaire the Cajun* is the soundtrack from Glen Pitre's 1986 film. — J.D.C.

THE BEAUTIFUL SOUTH

★ ★½	Welcome to the Beautiful South (Elektra, 1990)	
★ ★	Choke (Elektra, 1990)	
★ ★½	0898 (Elektra, 1992)	

Gratingly polemical agit-pop, the Beautiful South is only occasionally redeemed by the sweet-voiced singing of former Housemartin Paul Heaton. Ideal for those who like the idea of popular music but wouldn't be caught dead enjoying it. — J.D.C.

JEFF BECK

★ ★ ★½	Truth (Epic, 1968)	
★ ★½	Beck-Ola (Epic, 1969)	
★ ★ ★	Rough and Ready (Epic, 1971)	
★ ★	Jeff Beck Group (Epic, 1972)	
★ ★	Beck Bogert Appice (Epic, 1973)	
★ ★ ★ ★	Blow by Blow (Epic, 1975)	
★ ★½	Wired (Epic, 1976)	
★	Jeff Beck with the Jan Hammer Group Live (Epic, 1977)	
★ ★½	There & Back (Epic, 1980)	
★ ★ ★½	Flash (Epic, 1985)	
★ ★½	Jeff Beck's Guitar Shop (Epic, 1989)	
★ ★ ★ ★	Beckology (Epic, 1991)	

Probably the greatest guitarist in rock never to have made a great album (or even many good ones), Jeff Beck has forged a solo career that is testimony to the fact that it takes more than guitar heroics to make memorable rock & roll. Between his virtuosic command of the fretboard and his daredevil feel for feedback and distortion, Beck's playing is rarely less than astonishing. But he lacks the vision and determination necessary to convert that instrumental intensity into any viable group chemistry, a weakness that has kept his solo career from amounting to much more than a few dazzling moments scattered through a lot of disappointing music.

Perhaps the closest he's ever come to fronting a band that could balance and enhance his strengths as a soloist was with the group he formed after leaving the Yardbirds. Because both singer Rod Stewart and bassist-guitarist Ron Wood had enough presence and confidence to hold their own ground against Beck, the music they made together was often as cohesive as it was exciting. *Truth*, despite a tendency to confuse showboating with ambition, is an excellent example of the heights Beck and his bandmates could achieve; had they continued in this vein, they could in time have eclipsed even the mighty Zeppelin. Unfortunately, it was not to be; although *Beck-Ola* features a couple of amusingly energized Elvis covers ("Jailhouse Rock," "All Shook Up"), the group's attempt to add a heavier edge to its sound only succeeds in making its music more lugubrious.

After losing Stewart and Wood to the Faces, Beck opted for a funkier approach, built around jazz-oriented keyboardist Max Middleton and David Clayton-Thomas imitator Bob Tench. It wasn't an ideal match; *Rough and Ready* stumbles whenever faced with a ballad but otherwise offers a passable gloss on the sort of jazzy white soul Traffic made popular. But *Jeff Beck Group* pushes the band's mannerisms to the point of self-parody. Beck then tried the power-trio approach, but the results, as embodied by *Beck Bogert Appice*, aren't much better, offering all the self-indulgence of Cream but none of the focus or pop appeal. (A concert recording from this period, *Beck Bogert Appice Live*, is even more embarrassing, but was released only in Japan.)

By rights, Beck's next attempt at re-invention—this time as a fusion jazz star—ought to have been just as disastrous as the last three, but thanks to producer George Martin, the all-instrumental *Blow by Blow* emerges as one of the most listenable and consistent albums of the guitarist's career. Beck isn't much of a jazzman, but Martin works around his limitations, elegantly framing the solos with sympathetic rhythm arrangements and lush string orchestrations. With *Wired*, Beck leaps into the deep end, abandoning all his *Blow by Blow* playmates except Middleton to work with Mahavishnu Orchestra alumni Jan Hammer and Narada Michael Walden. Beck plays gamely, but it's really Hammer's album, since his synth solos are what ultimately galvanize the group. *Jeff Beck*

With the Jan Hammer Group Live would seem a natural outgrowth from this collaboration, but the results are a mess, with Beck getting by on feedback and flash while Hammer's group tries to hold the music together. *There & Back* returns Beck to the studio with a more sympathetic set of collaborators (Hammer, drummer Simon Phillips, keyboardist Tony Hymas), but still goes nowhere.

Astonishingly, Beck's next album, *Flash*, was a pop outing with Wet Willie alumnus Jimmy Hall singing on most tracks. Thanks to producers Nile Rodgers and Arthur Baker, it's consistent and accessible, but sparks flew only when the guitarist reunited with Rod Stewart for a version of "People Get Ready." Bored, Beck went back to fusion and the empty acrobatics of *Jeff Beck's Guitar Shop*. Although not quite a career summation, the boxed set *Beckology* includes highlights from the above, as well as Beck's first recordings (with the Tridents), a good sampling of his Yardbirds material and a smattering of arcana. It's not perfect, but then, no collection representative of Beck's solo career could be. — J.D.C.

THE BEE GEES

★★½ Bee Gees 1st (1967; Polydor, 1988)
★½ Horizontal (1968; Polydor, 1988)
★½ Idea (1968; Polydor, 1989)
★★★ Odessa (1969; Polydor, 1987)
★★★ Best of Bee Gees (1969; Polydor, 1987)
★½ Cucumber Castle (1970; Polydor, 1989)
★★½ Trafalgar (1971; Polydor, 1989)
★½ 2 Years On (1971; Polydor, 1989)
★½ To Whom It May Concern (Atco, 1972)
★★ Best of the Bee Gees, Vol. 2 (1973; Polydor, 1987)
★½ Life in a Tin Can (RSO, 1973)
★½ Mr. Natural (RSO, 1974)
★★★½ Main Course (1975; Polydor, 1988)
★★★ Children of the World (1976; Polydor, 1989)
★★★½ Bee Gees Gold, Vol. 1 (RSO, 1976)
★★★½ Greatest Hits (RSO, 1979)
★★★ Here at Last . . . Live (1977; Polydor, 1990)
★★★ Spirits Having Flown (1979; Polydor, 1989)
★★★½ Bee Gees Greatest (1979; Polydor, 1988)
★★½ Living Eyes (RSO, 1981)

★ ★ **E.S.P. (Warner Bros., 1987)**
★ ★ **One (Warner Bros., 1989)**
★ ★ ★ ★ **Tales From the Brothers Gibb: A History in Song, 1967–1990 (Polydor, 1990)**
★ ★ **High Civilization (Warner Bros., 1991)**

Nothing if not professional, the Aussie Brothers Gibb—leader Barry and twin followers, Maurice and Robin—enjoyed two mega-careers playing two sorts of music: lush, Beatles-like pop and high-gloss disco. Milking the pop sensibility that prizes gesture over authenticity, they made remarkable Sixties jukebox love songs, their trademark warbling conveying genuine passion about as accurately as Hollywood kisses capture the mess and tangle of real love. The trick, however, to "Holiday," "Words," "I Started a Joke" and "To Love Somebody" was that the Bee Gees understood their teenage make-out audience. So what if the lyrics didn't make sense? Who cared, when everything sounded so "emotional"?

After *Odessa*, the *Sgt. Pepper's* copy all '60s headliners felt driven to attempt (the Bee Gees' wasn't bad; faulting it for pretentiousness makes absolutely no sense), the Bee Gees faded, resurfacing occasionally with such ace radio balladry as "How Can You Mend a Broken Heart." Then, with the out-of-nowhere timing of melodrama, they returned in the '70s with brilliant, plastic R&B. Pumped by finger-popping bass and swishing high-hat cymbals, *Main Course*, *Spirits Having Flown* and, most spectacularly, their contributions to *Saturday Night Fever* (for review, see "Soundtracks" section), didn't create disco but mainstreamed it with stunning craft. They had gigantic hits, of course. A third bid at stardom seemed to risk the ire of even the most indulgent of gods. The '80s Bee Gees appeared tentative and flailing. Who can say, though, that they won't resurrect again? — P.E.

HARRY BELAFONTE
★ ★ ★ **Calypso (RCA, 1956)**
★ ★ ★ ★ **Belafonte at Carnegie Hall (RCA, 1959)**
★ ★ ★ ★ **To Wish You a Merry Christmas (1962; RCA, 1990)**
★ ★ ★ **Pure Gold (RCA, 1975)**
★ ★ ★ **A Legendary Performer (RCA, 1978)**
★ ★ ★ ★ **All-Time Greatest Hits, Vol. 1 (1978; RCA, 1988)**
★ ★ ★ ★ **All-Time Greatest Hits, Vol. 2 (RCA, 1988)**

★ ★ ★ ★ **All-Time Greatest Hits, Vol. 3 (RCA, 1989)**
★ ★ **Belafonte '89 (EMI, 1989)**
★ ★ ★ **Day-O & Other Hits (RCA, 1990)**

To his credit, Harry Belafonte's well-honed commitment to social activism hasn't waned with age, as his participation in U.S.A. for Africa indicated. Nor is Belafonte the type to sing his song and walk away as if there weren't many more rivers to cross. He supported the civil-rights movement in its earliest days, and his repertoire has always reflected his vision of the global community.

RCA, which once had over 20 Belafonte albums in its catalogue, has pared that total down to nine; Belafonte is more fortunate than many of his RCA labelmates in that the remaining titles at least do justice to the scope of his career. This is due almost totally to the three *All-Time Greatest Hits* collections, which comprise a breathtaking overview of his most important studio work, and to the continued availability of *Belafonte at Carnegie Hall*, a spectacular live performance from 1959. What has been deleted is almost too painful to contemplate, but includes an album recorded with Miriam Makeba (*An Evening With Belafonte/Makeba*), a second Carnegie Hall album (*Belafonte Returns to Carnegie Hall*), *Porgy and Bess* with Belafonte and Lena Horne, an album of spirituals (*My Lord What a Mornin'*) . . . Is it necessary to suggest that these belong in any essential Belafonte collection? Or to mourn their demise?

As this list of deleted albums indicates, Belafonte's music came from everywhere and embraced everyone. To the general public his fame may stem from introducing calypso to the American mainstream with the hit singles "Jamaica Farewell" in 1956 and "Mama Looka Boo Boo" and "Banana Boat Song (Day-O)" in 1957; his albums, though, survey musical styles ranging from pop to folk (from Europe, Africa and South America, as well as North America) to gospel, blues and rock. His husky baritone isn't an impressive instrument technically, but Belafonte compensates with great expressiveness and an emphasis on precise diction and elegance of manner that translates to impressive style—class, in short. The three volumes of *All-Time Greatest Hits* contain a total of 53 songs, the earliest being recorded in 1952 (a delicate version of "Scarlett Ribbons"), the latest in 1973 (the least impressive tracks on the set). An almost total absence of liner notes is the only criticism that can be leveled at this collection.

Carnegie Hall includes the hits, of course, but adds some interesting touches on songs unavailable on any of the greatest hits albums, like, for example, a gentle, longing interpretation of that old warhorse "Danny Boy," performed not as pop schmaltz but as the Irish folk song that it is; a good-natured romp through "Hava Nageela"; and a near five-minute rendition of Leadbelly's prisoner's lament, "Sylvie," a complex song that juxtaposes harsh images of prison life with tender recollections of a woman's love. *Calypso* was Belafonte's third album and one that deserves the superlative of "monster." It was Number One for 31 weeks in 1956, an amazing feat doubtless aided by the inclusion of "Banana Boat Song" and "Jamaica Farewell" among its 11 tracks. Being the record that sparked a calypso craze in America, and having great, good spirit and compelling songs to recommend it, *Calypso* belongs in the Belafonte pantheon. Belafonte's Christmas album, *To Wish You a Merry Christmas*, can surely be appreciated by anyone who treasures exquisite interpretive singing. Wrapped around traditional seasonal fare such as "Silent Night" and "The Twelve Days of Christmas" are lesser-known gems like "Mary, Mary," "Where the Little Jesus Sleeps" and "Jehovah the Lord Will Provide." The other RCA albums—*Pure Gold*, *A Legendary Performer*, and *Day-O & Other Hits*—are various permutations of greatest hits (each one begins with "Day-O") and non-hits, with the 12-track *Legendary Performer* being the longest-running of the three. *Belafonte '89*, a live album cut in Ravensburg, West Germany, finds the artist a tad short on inspiration and charging hard for the secure middle ground, his music now nestled in strings and synths. — D.M.

ADRIAN BELEW

★★★★ Lone Rhino (Island, 1982)
★★ Twang Bar King (Island, 1983)
★★★ Desire Caught by the Tail (Island, 1986)
★★★½ Mr. Music Head (Atlantic, 1989)
★★ Young Lions (Atlantic, 1990)
★★★ Desire of the Rhino King (Island, 1991)
★★★★ Inner Revolution (Atlantic, 1992)

A gifted guitarist with a one-of-a-kind sound, Belew's searing, quicksilver leads and quirky, sci-fi sound effects made him much sought after as a sideman, and his playing has added fire to albums by David Bowie, King Crimson, Talking Heads and others. But his own projects don't always provide a

suitable framework for his sonic excursions, too often emphasizing instrumental texture over melodic structure. *Desire Caught by the Tail* is perhaps the most extreme example of his fondness for abstraction, offering idiosyncratic guitar etudes instead of conventional rock songs. *Lone Rhino* and *Mr. Music Head*, on the other hand, balance Belew's instrumental ingenuity with a genuine pop sensibility, but only *Inner Revolution*, in which the emphasis is squarely on his strengths as a writer, actually succeeds on a song-by-song basis. *Desire of the Rhino King* is a compilation album drawing from his three Island recordings. — J.D.C.

WILLIAM BELL

★★★★½ The Soul of a Bell (1967; Atlantic, 1991)
★★★★ The Best of William Bell (Stax, 1990)

Nothing flashy or facile undercuts the singing of William Bell—which may be why this great soul singer remains underrated and largely unheard. Compared to the hyper-urgency of Otis Redding, the baroque idiosyncracies of James Brown or the vocal acrobatics of Aretha Franklin, Bell's subtlety is hardly so immediately riveting. But it grows on you. One of the pillars of Stax Records, Bell turned out near flawless Memphis soul singles for the label for 15 years. Often co-writing with Booker T. Jones, he distinguished himself by adhering particularly closely to the melodies of his material, and by the strong tenderness of his ballad singing. With Bell, Booker T. tried out novel instrumentation (an occasional harmonica, sometimes vibes), that didn't always work, but underscored his awareness that the singer wasn't cut from quite the same raw cloth as other Southern soul stars. So smooth, in fact, was Bell that he could've had considerable pop impact. But the understated fervor of such numbers as "Everybody Loves a Winner," "You Don't Miss Your Water" (both on *The Soul of a Bell*), "Lonely Soldier," "My Whole World Is Falling Down" and "A Smile Can't Hide (a Broken Heart)" (all three on *The Best of*) makes for music that isn't at all easy or reassuring. Bell is soul in all its romantic agony; he just insinuates, rather than declaims. — P.E.

BELL BIV DEVOE

★★★½ Poison (MCA, 1990)
★★★ WBBD—Bootcity! (MCA, 1991)

This New Edition spin-off is fronted by Ricky Bell, Michael "Biv" Bivins and

Ronnie DeVoe. Although the trio's "nasty" songs are often nastier than need be, BBD's canny incorporation of rap-style rhythm tracks in what are otherwise traditional R&B songs makes this "Poison" unusually easy to swallow. That formula gets repeated, with minor variations, on the remix collection *WBBD*. Annoying as the album's "on the air" conceit can be, the beefed up beats are generally a plus, but the New Edition mini-reunion on "Word to the Mutha!" is disappointing. — J.D.C.

REGINA BELLE
★ ★ ★ **All by Myself (Columbia, 1987)**
★ ★ ★ ★ **Stay With Me (Columbia, 1989)**
Because her rich, resonant voice and luxuriant phrasing seem tailor-made for sultry ballads and sexy slow-jams, Belle's singing has all the best qualities of Anita Baker—but without Baker's pretensions to jazz. That's particularly true of *Stay With Me*, where the material really showcases her strengths. — J.D.C.

THE BELOVED
★ ★ ★ **Happiness (Atlantic, 1990)**
At its best, the Beloved comes across as a darker, less ironic Pet Shop Boys, and though that doesn't happen often enough to make *Happiness* a complete success, it does give the group a minor classic in "Hello." — J.D.C.

JESSE BELVIN
★ ★ ★ ★ **Yesterdays (RCA, 1975)**
★ ★ ★ ★ ★ **Jesse Belvin: The Blues Balladeer (Specialty, 1990)**
At a time when American record companies have found a market for reissues, thus justifying the re-release of many priceless but long out of print performances by important roots artists, Jesse Belvin remains an innovator whose rich legacy has been only partially restored to the public domain. One can speculate that had Belvin survived an automobile accident in 1960 and gone on to produce the ambitious work that seemed the logical progression of his career path, his name might today be as well known as that of his contemporary Sam Cooke, who picked up more than a few notions from Belvin's singing style and masterful control of audiences. Belvin the vocalist had the sensuous, smoky voice and precise enunciation associated with Nat King Cole and Billy Eckstine, but his musical roots ran deeper into gospel. As his career evolved, Belvin explored not only rhythm & blues, but pop (with a jazz influence), traditional

group harmony and even doo-wop, both as a performing and recording artist, and as a prolific songwriter on his own and in collaboration with Marvin Phillips, a compadre of the teenage Belvin in the Big Jay McNeely Band's vocal group, 3 Dots & a Dash. Without question his two most famous songs remain "Earth Angel," a collaboration that became a million-seller for the Penguins in 1954, and "Goodnight My Love," a Top Ten R&B hit for Belvin in 1956.

The Specialty disc collects 24 Belvin tracks, some solo, some recorded with Phillips as the duo Jesse & Marvin (who had a Top Ten R&B hit of their own in 1953 with their self-penned "Dream Girl," included here); also included are seven tracks Belvin cut for the Dolphin label in Los Angeles in the early '50s. Dolphin was a record store–record label operation whose in-house recordings were given away free to every customer who bought one major label record. That these "freebies" survived in any form is a fortuitous development that helps clarify the evolution of Belvin's artistry. Among these cuts is an exquisite solo version of "Dream Girl." In addition to Belvin's Specialty tracks, *The Blues Balladeer* contains a number of previously unissued, undated demos. One of the apparent problems in getting a handle on dates is that Belvin had complete disregard for legal niceties such as contracts, and showed up on numerous labels in various guises. The liner notes here indicate that he recorded as the Sheiks and the Californians with Johnny Otis as his producer; as the Gassers for Dolphin; as the Cliques for Modern; and supplied an uncredited vocal part in the Shields' 1958 hit, "You Cheated." Every so often he would drop in at Specialty, cut a wonderful track or two, and hit the road. Regardless, everywhere he went he left behind one enthralling performance after another.

RCA was Belvin's last label stop and site of his only major pop hit when "Guess Who" peaked at Number 13 in 1959. Comprised of a dozen tracks Belvin recorded in the months preceding his death (five of which are released here for the first time), *Yesterdays* hints at what may have been ahead for Belvin, particularly the new tracks that find him working with top jazz instrumentalists such as Mel Lewis, Red Callender, Howard Roberts, Shelly Manne, Barney Kessel and others. As an example of what he was up to, Belvin took some of these players in and had them work out on a smoky gospel blues called "It Could've Been Worse," which features one of Belvin's most measured vocals; in the end, this cut busts all the barriers, being a little of everything—jazz, blues, gospel, pop— without settling squarely in any one camp. Indicative of the range of moods and attitudes Belvin was exploring at this transitional stage, consider the inclusion in his repertoire of pop standards by Johnny Mercer–Harold Arlen ("Blues in the Night") and Cole Porter ("In the Still of the Night," "It's All Right With Me"), and then consider that one of Belvin's two original contributions, the ballad "Guess Who," begs comparison to the sophisticated offerings Belvin chooses as cover versions. Ultimately one thinks of Buddy Holly, Ritchie Valens, Sam Cooke—men who, like Belvin, seemed destined to create truly groundbreaking music, if only they had lived. The evidence here suggests Belvin may well have outdistanced them all—if only. — D.M.

PAT BENATAR
★ ★½ **In the Heat of the Night (Chrysalis, 1979)**
★ ★½ **Crimes of Passion (Chrysalis, 1980)**
★ ★ **Precious Time (Chrysalis, 1981)**
★½ **Get Nervous (Chrysalis, 1982)**
★½ **Live From Earth (Chrysalis, 1983)**
★½ **Tropico (Chrysalis, 1984)**
★ ★ **Seven the Hard Way (Chrysalis, 1985)**
★½ **Wide Awake in Dreamland (Chrysalis, 1988)**
★ ★ ★ **Best Shots (Chrysalis, 1989)**
½ ★ **True Love (Chrysalis, 1991)**

Just as there are a lot of songwriters who have no business singing, there are a lot of singers who would really be better off not writing. Like Pat Benatar. As a singer, her ability was obvious from the first, for not only did *In the Heat of the Night* do more with John Mellencamp's "I Need a Lover" than he ever did, but its emphasis on metallic, Suzi Quatro–style rockers like "Heartbreaker" and the title tune gave Benatar a workable image and a sound that made the most of her full-throated delivery. *Crimes of Passion* follows much the same pattern, thanks to tough-but-tuneful offerings like "Treat Me Right" and "Hit Me With Your Best Shot." But Benatar wanted more than cover-song success; she wanted to prove her mettle as a writer, and actually does so with "Hell Is for Children," an anti–child abuse song written by Benatar and bandmates Neil Geraldo and Roger Capps (from *Crimes*).

Trouble is, "Hell" was a fluke, as *Precious Time* proves. Apart from "Fire and Ice," a transparent attempt at duplicating the sound of "Heartbreaker" and "Treat Me Right," the album's original songs are silly or cliched, sometimes both. *Get Nervous* continues the decline, while *Live From Earth* (eight concert recaps of earlier hits, plus two studio tracks) perks up only when it gets to "Love Is a Battlefield"—a song Benatar and band didn't write.

Tropico shifts gears slightly as the band moves away from arena-rock clichés and toward a more intricately arranged sound, but only Lowen and Navarro's "We Belong" does anything with the approach. Tellingly, *Seven the Hard Way* is loaded with outside material, and Benatar soars through the likes of "Sex as a Weapon" and "Invincible."

About the only thing on *Wide Awake in Dreamland* that's worth hearing is "All Fired Up," and it—along with most of Benatar's hits—can be found on *Best Shots*. As for *True Love*, Benatar's painfully earnest bout with the blues, it seems to be the product of a misunderstanding; traditionally, one must suffer to sing the blues, not suffer listening to them. — J.D.C.

TONY BENNETT
★ ★ ★ ★ **Basie Swings, Bennett Sings: Count Basie/Tony Bennett (Roulette, 1959)**
★ ★ ★ ★ **I Left My Heart in San Francisco (Columbia, 1962)**
★ ★ ★ **The Movie Song Album (Columbia, 1966)**
★ ★ ★ **Snowfall/The Tony Bennett Christmas Album (Columbia, 1969)**
★ ★ ★ ★ **Tony Bennett's All-Time Greatest Hits (Columbia, 1972)**
★ ★ ★ ★ **The Tony Bennett/Bill Evans Album (1975; Fantasy, 1990)**
★ ★ ★ **The Rodgers and Hart Songbook (1976; DRG, 1987)**
★ ★ ★ ★ **Together Again: Tony Bennett & Bill Evans (1977; DRG, 1986)**
★ ★ ★ **The Special Magic of Tony Bennett (1979; DRG, 1988)**
★ ★ ★ ★ **16 Most Requested Songs (Columbia, 1986)**
★ ★ ★ ★ **The Art of Excellence (Columbia, 1986)**
★ ★ ★ ★ **Bennett/Berlin (Columbia, 1987)**
★ ★ ★ ★ ★ **Jazz (Columbia, 1987)**
★ ★ ★ ★ **Astoria: Portrait of an Artist (Columbia, 1990)**
★ ★ ★ ★ ★ **40 Years of Artistry (Columbia, 1991)**

In the category of long time coming, Tony Bennett, who Frank Sinatra said is the best all-time classic pop singer, is finally getting his due. The title of a 1991 retrospective, *40 Years of Artistry*, suggests the magnitude of the man's achievement. Even when saddled with Mitch Miller's overblown arrangements in the '50s, Bennett cut through to create magic: it was the voice, a warm baritone, exuding character and personality, alternately swinging and caressing, coming on like an old and treasured friend whose counsel is cherished for its wisdom. Age has not only brought greater dignity to Bennett, it has pushed him to refine his vocal skills by toning down the sometimes-offputting extroverted quality of the early uptempo performances in favor of a measured approach that adds depth by revealing subtext. Using more head and throat tones, in turn, has resulted in Bennett's voice having an expanded range of colors, both muted and bright, that allow him to cut closer to the bone of his own experience.

Bennett's first single after being signed to Columbia Records was "The Boulevard of Broken Dreams," a minor hit in 1950; then he came back strong in 1951 with two chart-topping singles only a month apart: "Because of You," one of his best-known songs, and a cover of Hank Williams's "Cold, Cold Heart," the first significant pop venture into country music and one that opened the door for country and pop artists to borrow from each other's idioms. When rock & roll began pushing his generation off the charts, Bennett resisted taking the easy road to the mainstream and clung to the sophisticated songs he'd been singing all along. A staple in the Top Forty before rock & roll arrived, Bennett stayed there through the late '50s, even scoring a Top Ten hit in 1957 with "In the Middle of an Island." In '62 he recorded the bittersweet "I Left My Heart in San Francisco," which peaked at Number 19 on the pop chart but has since been one of the most enduring songs in pop history. He followed that song with two more stellar singles, "The Good Life" and "I Wanna Be Around."

Bennett has recorded almost continuously throughout his career, save for a brief period in the mid-'70s. Many of the albums are out of print, but those remaining offer an overview that is at least representative of his work over the years. Topping the list is *40 Years of Artistry*, a four-CD box set of career highlights ranging from "Boulevard of Broken Dreams" to his most recent single, "When Do the Bells Ring for Me,"

released in 1989 and included on the autobiographical song cycle, *Astoria*. *40 Years* should whet anyone's appetite for more Bennett, and indeed, to leave off there would be to miss many exquisite moments. *Astoria* is a special entry in the Bennett catalogue owing to the songs being carefully chosen to reflect the ideas and moods of the singer's formative years. That Bennett is at his most tender and reflective on this album is indicative of the degree to which this material reaches into his marrow as he takes stock of a world long passed but lovingly recalled.

I Left My Heart in San Francisco (1962) peaked at Number Five and remained on the Top Forty album chart for 83 weeks, largely on the strength of the title song, of course, but not at the expense of other noteworthy performances: "Tender Is the Night," "Smile," "The Best Is Yet to Come" are all top-flight. While *Astoria* provides perspective on a life, *Jazz* does so on a career. Though a pop singer by definition, Bennett has recorded with some of the top jazz players of his day; two of his finest albums, *Cloud 7* and *The Beat of My Heart* (both now deleted), make a case for him as a jazz singer. *Jazz* supplants these titles by surveying an assortment of nominal jazz sides cut between 1954 and 1967. Bridging jazz and pop, Bennett recorded two wonderful, after-hours-ish albums with the late jazz pianist Bill Evans, *The Tony Bennett/Bill Evans Album* and *Together Again*, as well as *The Rodgers and Hart Songbook*, on which he is accompanied by the Ruby Braff–George Barnes Quartet, and the scintillating *Basie Swings, Bennett Sings* with Count Basie and His Orchestra. Taken together these albums render moot the question of whether Bennett is or is not a jazz singer; better to regard him simply as a great singer whose stylistic range cuts across genres.

Bennett/Berlin teams the master interpreter with a set of Irving Berlin tunes less obvious than one might imagine, despite the inclusion of "White Christmas." Focusing on several melancholy entries in the Berlin canon, Bennett in effect delivers a concept album quite moving in its depictions of shattered love. A 1986 album, *The Art of Excellence*, finds Bennett ruminating over aspects of love in a low-key, almost dispassionate manner; the performance is enlivened by a humorous, topical give-and-take duet with Ray Charles on "Everybody Has the Blues." — D.M.

GEORGE BENSON

★ ★ ★½ **The New Boss Guitar of George Benson With the Brother Jack McDuff Quartet (1964; Prestige, 1990)**

★ ★   **Beyond the Blue Horizon (1970; Columbia, 1987)**

★ ★   **Body Talk (1974; Columbia, 1989)**

★ ★   **Bad Benson (1974; Columbia, 1988)**

★ ★½ **Benson and Farrell (1976; Columbia, 1988)**

★ ★ ★   **Good King Bad (1976; Columbia, 1989)**

★ ★½ **Breezin' (Warner Bros., 1976)**

★ ★   **George Benson in Concert: Carnegie Hall (1977; Columbia, 1988)**

★ ★   **In Flight (Warner Bros., 1977)**

★ ★   **Weekend in L.A. (Warner Bros., 1978)**

★ ★   **Livin' Inside Your Love (Warner Bros., 1979)**

★ ★½ **Give Me the Night (Warner Bros., 1980)**

★ ★ ★½ **The George Benson Collection (Warner Bros., 1981)**

★ ★   **In Your Eyes (Warner Bros., 1983)**

★ ★   **20–20 (Warner Bros., 1984)**

★ ★   **While the City Sleeps (Warner Bros., 1986)**

★ ★   **Twice the Love (Warner Bros., 1988)**

★ ★   **Tenderly (Warner Bros., 1989)**

★ ★½ **Big Boss Band Featuring the Count Basie Orchestra (Warner Bros., 1990)**

George Benson began his career as a promising jazz guitarist. Brother Jack McDuff pulled him from his native Pittsburgh in the '60s and made his funky organ trio a quartet. *The New Boss Guitar of George Benson* is a loose, soulful blowing session; Benson pursues a cool blue attack very reminiscent of Wes Montgomery. In the late '60s, Benson recorded several adventurous tracks with Miles Davis. His clean, cutting lines can be deciphered—fleetingly—in the ethereal, just-pre-fusion mists of *Miles in the Sky* (Columbia). Moving to producer Creed Taylor's then-flourishing CTI label, Benson released a series of lushly appointed, barely swinging jazz-fusion albums: the prototype of what we think of as "quiet storm" soundtracks today, only with weirdly strident arrangements and odd cover versions. ("White Rabbit" is one thing, but "Last Train to Clarksville"? At least Wes Montgomery had the taste to pick "A Day in the Life.") Benson left behind those strained jazz ties when he jumped to Warner

Bros. *Breezin'* established him as a "pretty" and not-unlistenable MOR instrumentalist (the title track) and a halting, awkward singer ("This Masquerade"). This embarrassing performance of an already-mawkish Leon Russell ballad somehow made it into the Top Ten; Benson's subsequent albums proved it was no fluke, sales-wise at least. His voice improved enough by the time of "Give Me the Night" (1980) and "Turn Your Love Around" (1981) that you could hum along with the peppy pop-soul choruses he was negotiating. *The George Benson Collection* adds a couple of CTI-period oddities ("White Rabbit" and "Last Train to Clarksville," of course) to the easy-listening hits, resulting in a pleasantly mixed, if completely innocuous, summation of a now-distant phenomenon. — M.C.

BROOK BENTON

★ ★ ★ ★ **The Brook Benton Anthology (Rhino, 1986)**

★ ★   **This Is Brook Benton (RCA, 1989)**

After honing his chops in the Golden Gate gospel quartets in the early '50s, Brook Benton ventured into the pop realm and proceeded to cut a wide swath through it: four gold records and a baker's dozen of Top Twenty singles between 1959 and 1970. Sam Cooke had taken a similar path with equally spectacular results, but Cooke remained firmly rooted in gospel and R&B; Benton's warm, smooth style was pop-oriented, in the vein of Nat King Cole and Billy Eckstine. Benton was also a formidable songwriter who in 1958 collaborated with Clyde Otis on two hit singles, "Looking Back" for Nat King Cole and "A Lover's Question" for Clyde McPhatter. In 1959 he landed a recording contract with Mercury and broke from the gate with a Number Three single, "It's Just a Matter of Time," that established the romantic style that informed his best recordings. In 1960 he established a short-lived but fruitful association with labelmate Dinah Washington; her sassiness and bluesy attitude meshed well with Benton's relaxed approach, resulting in two Top Ten singles that year, "Baby (You've Got What It Takes)" and "A Rockin' Good Way (to Mess Around and Fall in Love)." Benton's tenure at Mercury ended in the mid-'60s, and he ventured to RCA, where he cut a number of interesting but unsuccessful sides, as he would continue to do at the end of the decade after being signed to Reprise Records. In 1970 Benton came roaring back one last time with an interpretation of Tony Joe White's "Rainy Night in Georgia" for the Cotillion label. It peaked at Number Four, but Benton's attempts at a followup failed, and he went through the decade label-hopping without producing anything significant.

Rhino's *Brook Benton Anthology* is the essential Benton album, comprising the best-known Mercury sides, as well as choice items from the later years, including "Rainy Night in Georgia" and another Benton reading of a White gem, "Don't It Make You Want to Go Home." RCA's *This Is Brook Benton* is fair-to-middling, lacking much of the bite of Benton's best work earlier in the decade. Part of the problem may have been that Benton was writing less of his own material by this time—only one song, the unremarkable "Mother Nature, Father Time," is a Benton-Otis collaboration. Otherwise he surveys songs that could be said to have been sung once too often—"Love Is a Many Splendored Thing," for example. Stick with *Anthology* to get the biggest bang for the buck.
— D.M.

BERLIN
  ★½ **Pleasure Victim (Geffen, 1982)**
  ★ **Love Life (Geffen, 1984)**
  ★★½ **Count Three and Pray (Geffen, 1986)**
  ★★½ **Best of Berlin 1979–1988 (Geffen, 1988)**
Perhaps the greatest difference between modernism and trendiness is that the modern endures, while the trendy ends up seeming tacky, silly and dated. Take, as an example, the clean, uncluttered lines of the Barcelona chair, which more than half a century later leave it looking just as futuristic as when it was new; take, as another, the pulsing synth-beats and borrowed Bowie-isms of Berlin, which in less than a decade have taken the band from the cutting edge of club culture to the clearance section of the oldies bin.

Granted, Berlin seemed like a pretty good idea at the time. When *Pleasure Victim* first made its appearance, the arch, synth-driven sound of songs like "Tell Me Why" and "The Metro" owed enough to the electronic angst-rock of Bowie and Ultravox to win over America's anglophilic new-wavers, while the heavy-breathing "Sex (I'm a . . .)" —sort of a cross between Donna Summer's "I Feel Love" and *Penthouse Forum*— earned the band an easy berth on AOR radio. *Love Life*, though, is hopelessly muddled, trying everything from mannered,

Giorgio Moroder–produced dance music ("No More Words," "Dancing in Berlin") to tepid sex talk ("When We Make Love," "Touch") to imitation Pat Benatar ("In My Dreams").

Ironically, that last wound up being the band's future, as Berlin abandoned its new-wave cool for strict commerciality with *Count Three and Pray*. Sure, the album has its share of sleaze, as "Sex Me, Talk Me" and "Pink and Velvet" make plain, but that's just a sideline. This time, the band puts most of its energy into straight-ahead rockers, such as "Like Flames" or "Will I Ever Understand You." But the album's best moment is its corniest: "Take My Breath Away," a predictably formulaic movie theme (from *Top Gun*) that nonetheless makes the most of Terri Nunn's warm, throaty alto. As for *The Best of Berlin*, it includes three cuts from *Love Life*, as well as virtually everything anyone would want to hear from *Pleasure Victim* and *Count Three*. Nothing more was heard from the band, but Nunn eventually released a solo album, *Moment of Truth* (DGC, 1992); though most of the music is fatuous and forgettable, connoisseurs of camp will doubtless enjoy hearing her "rap" in "80 Lines." — J.D.C.

CHUCK BERRY
  ★★★★ **Chuck Berry Is on Top (1959; Chess/MCA, 1987)**
  ★★★★ **Rockin' at the Hops (1960; Chess/MCA, 1987)**
  ★★★★ **New Juke Box Hits (Chess, 1961)**
  ★★★★★ **From St. Louis to Liverpool (Chess, 1964)**
  ★ **Chuck Berry's Golden Hits (Mercury, 1967)**
  ★★ **The London Chuck Berry Sessions (Chess/MCA, 1972)**
  ★★★ **Rockit (Atco, 1979)**
  ★★★★★ **The Great Twenty-Eight (1982; Chess/MCA, 1984)**
  ★★★★ **Rock 'n' Roll Rarities (Chess/MCA, 1986)**
  ★★★★ **More Rock 'n' Roll Rarities (Chess/MCA, 1986)**
  ★★★ **Hail! Hail! Rock 'n' Roll (MCA, 1987)**
  ★★★★★ **The Chess Box (Chess/MCA, 1988)**
  ★★★★ **Missing Berries: Rarities, Volume 3 (Chess/MCA, 1990)**
WITH BO DIDDLEY
  ★★ **Two Great Guitars: Bo Diddley & Chuck Berry (1964; MCA/Chess, 1987)**

By now it's easy to see that rock & roll was an inevitable outgrowth of all the seemingly disparate musics emerging in the postwar years, rather than something that fell out of the sky whole cloth on the day Elvis Presley walked into the Memphis Recording Service. All the early rock & roll giants occupied distinctive niches defined by their musical approach. Chuck Berry was the first important writer-performer-instrumentalist in the rock & roll style, a man whose immediately identifiable playing and powers of observation and eloquence have remained touchstones for succeeding generations of artists, one of the standards by which great rock is measured. Had he been only a profound influence on Bob Dylan, the Beatles and the Rolling Stones he would merit distinction; but Berry's signature shows up frequently in contemporary rock as well.

At a time when critics discounted rock & roll as adolescent caterwauling, Berry was not only defining a subculture, he was providing running commentary on a country in the midst of change, more mobile, more affluent, more restless, free for the moment from the spectre of war but bitterly divided internally over racial issues. Aiming his messages unequivocally at the younger generation, Berry made poetry of the seemingly mundane complexities of adolescent life. His was folk music for teens, with references to a world with its own language, symbols and customs.

But as much as he was a chronicler of young American culture, so was Berry given to deeper ruminations. "Too Much Monkey Business" is a vivid depiction of the drudgery and ennui of the working life. If you can get by the clever images spicing "Brown-Eyed Handsome Man" the story becomes one of black men overcoming the strictures of segregation. A touching memory of love lost and love renewed is rendered in mellow, bluesy fashion in "Time Was." The force and sincerity behind "I've Changed" will move anyone familiar with Berry's checkered history with the law. At a time when American families are breaking up in record numbers, the story of a divorced father's desperate search for his daughter in "Memphis" takes on new relevance. He also wrote the greatest songs *about* rock & roll in "Sweet Little Sixteen," "Around and Around," "Rock and Roll Music" and "Roll Over, Beethoven."

The Chess Box will satisfy the requirements of anyone seeking classic Berry in one place, as will *The Great Twenty-Eight*. The *Box*, though, not only takes the listener into the early '70s with two first-rate cuts from the artist's final Chess album, *Bio* (1973), but also offers the pleasure of side trips into Berry's lesser-known work, much of it in a blues vein, and some of it instrumental. When he arrived at Chess in 1955, Berry was familiar with a number of styles. In his long-time pianist Johnnie Johnson he had an accompanist equally at home in blues, boogie-woogie, R&B and rock & roll, and at Chess he worked with the sterling players populating the label's studio: Willie Dixon, Fred Below, Jimmy Rogers; even Bo Diddley and his maraca man Jerome Green sit in on a few cuts. Completists, then, are advised to add to their collections the three *Rarities* issues, particularly Volume 3, which has the best sampling of blues-oriented material.

Also noteworthy are *Chuck Berry Is on Top*, *Rockin' at the Hops*, and *New Juke Box Hits*. These show how Berry was wedging in what might be called alternative material amidst his rock & roll—check out Berry's steel guitar on the instrumental "Blues for Hawaiians" from *Berry Is on Top*, the deeply felt covers of Jay McShann's "Confessin' the Blues" and Charles Brown's timeless "Driftin' Blues" on *Rockin' at the Hops*, and a stirring treatment of B.B. King's "Sweet Sixteen" on *New Juke Box Hits*. *St. Louis to Liverpool* is a title that only barely hints at the range of Berry's influence, although in 1964, when this album was released, it was clear that the Beatles, the Rolling Stones and lesser British rockers were deeply indebted to the man. In addition to classic tracks—"Little Marie," "Promised Land," "You Never Can Tell" and "No Particular Place to Go"—the album includes one of the best cover versions of the Charles Brown classic, "Merry Christmas, Baby," a tough rendition of Guitar Slim's "Things I Used to Do" and a searing instrumental, "Liverpool Drive"; then Berry calms down with a mellow, after-hours blues, "Night Beat." *The London Chuck Berry Sessions* (1972) is notable for producing Berry's only Number One single, "My Ding-a-Ling," about which the less said the better. *Hail! Hail! Rock 'n' Roll* is the soundtrack from the like-titled film, with Berry running through his hits supported by an all-star band comprised of Keith Richards, Chuck Leavell, Bobby Keys, Steve Jordan and NRBQ's Joey Spampinato, with guest appearances by Eric Clapton, Robert Cray and others.

Berry left Chess to record for Mercury between 1966 and 1969, producing nothing of note. *Chuck Berry's Golden Hits* consists of reworkings of some of the great Chess sides, plus one new track, the unremarkable "Club Nitty Gritty." Accept no substitutes for the originals. Apart from the Chess material, the other Berry album of note is the now-deleted *Rockit*, released on Atco in 1979. No gem this, but an exemplary return to good rockin' form. Guitar aficionados may find something of interest in the teaming of Berry and Bo Diddley on two of the four extended instrumental tracks on *Two Great Guitars*, but for these two masters, the workouts are fairly routine.
— D.M.

RICHARD BETTS
★★½ Highway Call (Capricorn, 1974)
★★½ Pattern Disruptive (Epic, 1988)
Allman Brothers guitarist Dickie Betts's bluegrass-flavored 1974 solo debut follows the Allmans' hit "Ramblin' Man" to its logical conclusion. Unfortunately, his hesitant vocals can't match the pace of his lightning fingers. The same holds true on his second solo outing. — M.C.

THE B-52'S
★★★   The B-52's (Warner Bros., 1979)
★★★½ Wild Planet (Warner Bros., 1980)
★★★★   Party Mix (Warner Bros., 1981)
  ★½ Mesopotamia (EP) (Warner Bros., 1982)
  ★★   Whammy! (Warner Bros., 1983)
  ★★   Bouncing off the Satellites (Warner Bros., 1986)
  ★★½ Cosmic Thing (Warner Bros., 1989)
★★★½ Party Mix/Mesopotamia (Warner Bros., 1991)
  ★★   Good Stuff (Warner Bros., 1992)
A party band in the truest sense of the term, the B-52's, who hailed from Athens, Georgia, were one of the first pop acts to pick up on the ironic attitude of the post-punk underground. *The B-52's* is obsessed with the detritus of hip, embracing such trash icons as lava lamps and beehive hairdos (the latter having in fact inspired the band's name). Yet for all its playful sarcasm, the album manages to avoid the usual pitfalls of camp, never daring to act as if the band was somehow superior to its material. Even so, that attitude would likely wear thin were it not for the band's other strength—its music. Applying the amateurism of New York punk to the abandon of beach music (the soulful Carolina kind, not the twangy California

stuff), the band came up with a sound unlike anything else on the scene. It wasn't Ricky Wilson's idiosyncratic guitar lines or the simple stomp of Keith Strickland's drumming that did it, so much as the way their jerry-rigged groove reinforced the campy quality of Fred Schneider's declamations and Cindy Wilson and Kate Pierson's B-girl harmonies. This was the chemistry that made "Rock Lobster" so oddly arresting, and that spirit carries over to the rest of the album, from the sci-fi silliness of "Planet Claire" to the fevered insistence of "Dance This Mess Around."

Wild Planet improves on the formula by fleshing out the musical mannerisms with actual songs, offering everything from the dark, enigmatic groove of "Private Idaho" to the near-pathos of Cindy Wilson's "Give Me Back My Man." That triumph was short-lived, however. After *Party Mix*, a collection of club-oriented remixes of the most danceable songs from the first two albums, *Mesopotamia* found the band out of its element as it tried to swap its fun-loving frivolity for the arch art-rock of bands like Talking Heads (whose David Byrne produced the album). Never had the group's music sounded so boring or pretentious. (Both EPs have since been combined on a single CD). *Whammy!* is an attempt to return to the silliness of the first albums, but is unable to overcome either its self-conscious songs (which range from the mock-utopian "Song for a Future Generation" to the pseudo-Southern culture of "Butterbean") or the stiffness of its drum machine–driven rhythm tracks. With the death of Ricky Wilson in 1985, the B-52's were thrown even further into disarray, having not only to augment the band's lineup with session players, but to virtually reinvent its sound. No wonder *Bouncing off the Satellites* flops miserably; it sounds hollow and contrived. So the band went back to its roots, and hit the jackpot. Commercially, *Cosmic Thing* was far and away the band's most successful effort, producing two Top Five singles and spending nearly a year in the Top Forty. Artistically, though, it's less heartening. Despite their no-nonsense melodicism, most of the songs here reprise the band's early sound without any edge or ambiguity. Thus, "Love Shack," instead of sending up beach music dance parties, becomes a straight-up tribute—an act of imitation, not transcendence. And while the slicker production doesn't stop the band from generating a simulacrum of its original groove on the likes of "Channel Z" and

"Deadbeat Club," the B-52's end up seeming mere caricatures, an impression cemented by the formulaic sound of *Good Stuff.* — J.D.C.

BIG AUDIO DYNAMITE
★ ★ ★ **This Is Big Audio Dynamite (Columbia, 1985)**
★ ★ ★ ★ **No. 10, Upping St. (Columbia, 1986)**
★ ★ ★ ★ **Tighten Up, Vol. 88 (Columbia, 1988)**
★ ★ ★ **Megatop Phoenix (Columbia, 1989)**
BIG AUDIO DYNAMITE II
★ ★ ★ **The Globe (Columbia, 1991)**

Formed by guitarist Mick Jones after his split with the Clash, Big Audio Dynamite was an early and prescient attempt to reconcile guitar-based rock with the electrobeats and sonic manipulation of hip-hop. Although the band's initial experiments were more gimmicky than illuminating, by *No. 10, Upping St.* its use of samples was no longer simply a matter of sonic special effects. "C'Mon Every Beatbox," for instance, used its electronics to create a common ground between hip-hop, rock and reggae, while *Tighten Up, Vol. 88* expanded the music's base even further to include ska, rockabilly and even country music. Yet even as B.A.D. was laying the groundwork for later work by Jesus Jones, the Farm and EMF, the group's refusal to embrace dance music outright, combined with Jones's predilection for predictable, singsong melodies, has kept it from ever topping its early successes. — J.D.C.

BIG BLACK
★ **Lungs (EP) (Ruthless, 1983)**
½ ★ **Bulldozer (EP) (Ruthless-Fever, 1984)**
★ ½ **Racer-X (EP) (Homestead, 1984)**
★ ½ **Atomizer (Homestead, 1986)**
★ ½ **The Hammer Party (Homestead, 1986)**
★ ½ **Headache (EP) (Touch and Go, 1987)**
★ ½ **The Rich Man's Eight-Track Tape (Homestead, 1987)**
★ ★ **Songs About Fucking (Touch and Go, 1987)**

Outrageousness for its own sake becomes a tiresome exercise after a while, and Big Black's one-two punch of white noise and white rage is no exception. Sure, the band's bile-spewing lyrics can be shocking, disgusting or outright offensive, but then, they're meant to be. Big Black's music is also supposed to be ear-searingly intense, but to be honest, it's just noisy. Guitarists Steve Albini and Santiago Durango certainly understand how to make the most of electronically tweaked distortion—check the exquisitely shaped squeals and squawks that introduce "Cables," from *Atomizer*—but take away their stomp-boxes and all you're left with are pro forma punk licks backed by breakneck drum machine beats. *Songs About Fucking* ups the intensity some, but not enough to make the music as scary as it so obviously wants to be.

Racer-X is the EP that made the group's reputation, thanks to the ostensible sarcasm of "The Ugly American" and a brittle, unfunky version of James Brown's "The Big Payback." It, along with all of *Lungs* and *Bulldozer*, can be found on the CD edition of *The Hammer Party* (the LP and cassette include only *Lungs* and *Bulldozer*). Big Black's other CD compilation, *The Rich Man's Eight Track Tape,* combines *Atomizer* with *Headache,* with three additional tracks. — J.D.C.

BIG BOPPER
★ ★ ★ ½ **Hellooo Baby! The Best of the Big Bopper 1954–1959 (Rhino, 1989)**

By now everyone surely knows that the Big Bopper, born J. P. Richardson, died in the same plane crash that claimed the lives of his fellow Texan Buddy Holly and 17-year-old nascent rock & roll star Ritchie Valens. What is less well known is that Richardson cut many more sides beyond the oft-programmed "Chantilly Lace." Some of these traded on the lascivious, fun-loving, forever put-upon Bopper character Richardson created ("Big Bopper's Wedding," "Bopper's Boogie Woogie," "Little Red Riding Hood"), but others showed the Bopper, who wrote most of his material, to have more serious intent than his comedic image suggested. "Someone Watching Over You" and "Strange Kisses" are strong ballads with sensitive, bluesy vocals inspired by the Presley style, while "Crazy Blues" has pure rockabilly soul recommending it. Also included here is the Bopper's version of "White Lightning," his self-penned ode to the joys of moonshine, with which George Jones kick-started his career in 1959. For those who remember and for those who were unaware, this collection restores much-needed perspective to the Big Bopper's recorded legacy. — D.M.

BIG BROTHER AND THE HOLDING COMPANY
★ ★ **Big Brother and the Holding Company (1967; Columbia, 1971)**
★ ★ ★ **Cheap Thrills (Columbia, 1968)**

★★ **Big Brother and the Holding Company**
   Live (Rhino, 1985)
Complete with R. Crumb cover art, endless,
warped guitar solos and clunky, hippie
homages to "da blooze," *Cheap Thrills* sums
up acid rock. Even the group's name was an
underground pun—"holding" being doper's
slang for possessing drugs. What makes the
record more than a period piece is, of
course, its singer, Janis Joplin. While her
more-focused work came later, Joplin
already thrills like a force of nature: "Piece
of My Heart" and Big Mama Thornton's
"Ball and Chain" unleash a vocalist whose
urgency finds no equal in mainstream rock.
From her ripest beginnings, Joplin comes on
as an archetypal desperado, her passion
ripped from the same inner source as that of
the timeless bluesmasters, Ma Rainey,
Howlin' Wolf and the like.   — P.E.

BIG COUNTRY
★★★★ **The Crossing (Mercury, 1983)**
   ★★★ **Steeltown (Mercury, 1984)**
   ★★ **The Seer (Mercury, 1986)**
   ★★★ **Peace in Our Time (Reprise, 1988)**
As much as any group of its generation, Big
Country placed itself in a tradition that
dates back to politically committed music
and has its rock roots in '60s guitar-based
bands like the Byrds and Buffalo
Springfield. Guitarist-songwriter Stuart
Adamson, a native of Scotland, seems
indebted further to Bob Dylan and Robbie
Robertson, both in terms of his social
consciousness and in his sense of nature as a
force that can destroy or heal. When Big
Country—Adamson, guitarist Bruce
Watson, and the redoubtable rhythm section
of Tony Butler (bass) and Mark Brzezicki
(drums)—emerged in 1983 with the Steve
Lillywhite–produced *The Crossing*, they were
a breath of fresh air in a scene increasingly
dominated by techno-pop. Adamson's
anthems and ballads evinced an awareness
of a world gone awry. Adamson's husky,
keening vocals conveyed urgency, and he
and the other musicians powered their
messages with searing efficiency. Lillywhite
gave it a dense ambience through which the
guitars cut clearly—ringing, chiming,
soaring—and the solid bottom hammered
out a warning. In the midst of all this
thunder, it was in a haunting ballad,
"Chance," that Adamson stated his position
most succinctly: "Oh Lord where did the
feeling go?"
   The Crossing rose into the Top Twenty
and established Big Country as one of the
bright new hopes of the '80s. An EP

followed, the now-deleted *Wonderland*,
featuring the rousing title track, a single
mixed by Jimmy Iovine, and three other
cuts, including "The Crossing," which was
not included on the group's first album. On
the next full-length album, *Steeltown*,
Lillywhite and the band hewed to the big
sound and bold arrangements that had
energized *The Crossing*, while Adamson
turned his attention to the post-industrial
decline he was witnessing in Scotland. Yet
despite the grim nature of the topic,
Adamson managed to come out of his songs
with hope intact, his optimism buoyed by
love and by pride. This was all well and
good, but the album did not fare well
commercially.
   Enter Peter Wolf as producer, attemping
to put some glide in Big Country's stride.
On *Peace in Our Time* the sound is stripped
down, made rawer, with Adamson's voice
mixed way out front; the rhythm section
was boosted, the heavy guitar attack diluted
in favor of more ensemble give-and-take. A
cow bell—heretofore unthinkable in a Big
Country context—even shows up in the
opening cut, "King of Emotion," and a
mandolin on "Broken Heart (Thirteen
Valleys)" softens the texture as it adds
dimension to the song. Evenly dividing his
text between observations on love
alternately touching and cutting, and
musings about peace and love for
humankind in general, Adamson continued
to demonstrate admirable inner growth
while avoiding empty sloganeering.   — D.M.

BIG DADDY KANE
★★★ **Long Live the Kane (Cold Chillin',
   1988)**
★★★½ **It's a Big Daddy Thing (Cold
   Chillin', 1989)**
★★★½ **Taste of Chocolate (Cold Chillin',
   1990)**
★★★½ **Prince of Darkness (Cold Chillin',
   1991)**
What made Big Daddy Kane a rap sex
symbol was the way his debut, *Long Live
the Kane,* allowed him to play it both tender
and tough, waxing romantic on "The Day
You're Mine" but showing his strengths
with the ultra-macho "Raw." What made
the Kane more than just a ladies' man,
though, was the way his smooth, hard
delivery played off the dense grooves
producer Marley Marl set up behind him,
particularly on noise-edged funk like "Ain't
No Half-Steppin'." *It's a Big Daddy Thing*
ups the ante on both fronts, but only pays
off on the musical end, as the stripped-

down funk of "I Get the Job Done" and well-layered samples in "It's a Big Daddy Thing" bring more to his raps than the free-floating fantasies of "Pimpin' Ain't Easy," one of the clearest cases of testosterone poisoning on record.

To his credit, the Kane makes up for "Pimpin' Ain't Easy" with "Big Daddy Vs. Dolemite," a comic duet with Rudy Ray Moore on *Taste of Chocolate,* an album that also features a few Afrocentric raps, of which only "Dance With the Devil" merits pursuing. Kane changes his style with *Prince of Darkness,* on some tracks augmenting his usually measured delivery with bursts of tongue-tripping wordplay, but what ultimately puts the album over are the deeply soulful grooves behind raps like "T.L.C." and "I'm Not Ashamed." — J.D.C.

BIG STAR

- ★ ★ ★ ★   #1 Record (Ardent, 1972)
- ★ ★ ★ ★   Radio City (Ardent, 1974)
- ★ ★ ★ ★ ★   Sister Lovers (Rykodisc, 1992)
- ★ ★ ★ ★   Big Star Live (Rykodisc, 1992)
- ★ ★ ★ ★   #1 Record/Radio City (Stax, 1992)

CHRIS BELL

- ★ ★ ★¹⁄₂   I Am the Cosmos (Rykodisc, 1992)

Alex Chilton belted out "The Letter" and "Cry Like a Baby" as lead singer of the Box Tops in the '60s; you'd never guess that grits-and-butter voice emanated from a Memphis teenager. Chilton stopped singing that way as soon as he got out on his own, however, ditching the blue-eyed studio soul for a delightfully rough take on Beatles- and Brian Wilson–derived popcraft with Big Star. Complex and catchy three-minute songs weren't exactly hip in the early '70s; Big Star's cult status came after the punk revolution. Recorded for Ardent, an offshoot of Stax, the group's two proper albums garnered good reviews and few sales when they were initially released. Big Star founder and guitarist Chris Bell balances out Chilton's mercurial fits of inspiration on *#1 Record*; he left the group soon after, and Big Star became Chilton's baby. *Radio City* captures the budding genius at an accessible peak: The beautifully tortured choruses of "September Gurls" and "Back of a Car" actually fulfill some of the inflated claims made about their author. Chilton can't be blamed for all of Big Star's shallow power-pop imitators: once he invented and perfected the formula, he certainly didn't repeat it. (The first two albums were reissued on one CD in 1992.)

This is where the path gets twisted. Recorded in 1974, the next Big Star album (*Third*) didn't come out until 1978. *Third* illuminates what must've been a dark and depressed period in Chilton's life with lucid songwriting and quietly assured melodies. Retitled *Sister Lovers,* the album has been re-released several times with added tracks. The current Rykodisc version carries two more—presumably the last—unreleased tunes from the same sessions. *Big Star Live* is a flashback to a 1974 live radio broadcast, in which the three-piece Big Star (performing songs from the first two LPs) split the bill with Chilton performing solo acoustic versions of such gems as "The Ballad of El Goodo" and Loudon Wainwright's "Motel Blues." *I Am the Cosmos* compiles tracks from Bell's erratic (but borderline brilliant) recording legacy; Bell died in a car accident in 1978. — M.C.

ACKER BILK

- ★   Best of Acker Bilk, Vol. I (GNP/Crescendo, 1978)
- ★   Best of Acker Bilk, Vol. II (GNP/Crescendo, 1984)
- ★ ★   Acker Bilk Plays Lennon & McCartney (GNP/Crescendo, 1987)

A leader of the trad jazz movement in England in the late '50s with his Paramount Jazz Band, clarinetist Acker Bilk had the Number One song in the U.S. in 1962 with the instrumental "Stranger on the Shore," barely dented the charts in '62 and '63 and dropped out of sight thereafter. The 1978 *Best of* collection includes a re-recording of "Stranger on the Shore" that is far inferior to the original. Bilk's clarinet solo, so stark and lonesome in the '62 take, sort of meanders through a weak string arrangement, in search of the brooding tone that made "Stranger" an outstanding pop instrumental. But then, it's not as if Bilk is Benny Goodman, or even Pete Fountain. His playing has a friendly, comforting tone, and he's supported by cloying strings at every turn. This is MOR fodder for diehards. Give him credit, though, on the *Lennon & McCartney* album—his choice of songs is interesting, as he assays Lennon ("Imagine," "Woman"), McCartney ("Mull of Kintyre," "Pipes of Peace"), and Lennon-McCartney ("World Without Love," "Here, There & Everywhere,"). Otherwise, zippo. — D.M.

THE BIRTHDAY PARTY

- ★ ★ ★¹⁄₂   The Birthday Party (import) (Missing Link, 1980)

★ ★ ★½ **Drunk on the Pope's Blood (EP, import) (4AD, 1982)**
★ ★ ★½ **Junkyard (4AD, 1982)**
★ ★ ★½ **A Collection (1985; Suite Beat, 1986)**

Most of its catalogue (6 EPs, 5 LPs, listed either under "The Birthday Party" or under the group's original name "Boys Next Door") is on hard-to-find Aussie or other import labels. And that's a drag, because this Melbourne-based outfit made some of the sharpest post-punk music ever recorded. *A Collection* highlights *Prayers on Fire* (1981) and *Junkyard* (1982)—it sets great ominous lyrics against a backdrop of hellacious noise. Singer Nick Cave, fixated equally on God, rockabilly and gothic visions that are distinctly his own, wails and bellows; guitarist Rowland Howard hurls sound around like a musical abstract expressionist. It's not a bad intro to the band, but worth seeking out as well are the debut (*The Birthday Party*, on Australian Missing Link, 1980) and the riotous, live *Drunk on the Pope's Blood* EP (on 4AD, 1982).

What makes the Birthday Party much more than sheer mania, however, is the depth of the band's obsessiveness. Imagine a crew of Dostoevski's mad truth-seekers wielding electric guitars. You get the picture. — P.E.

ELVIN BISHOP

★ ★½ **The Best of Elvin Bishop: Crabshaw Rising (Epic, 1972)**
★ ★ ★ **Let It Flow (Capricorn, 1974)**
★ ★ ★½ **Juke Joint Jump (Capricorn, 1975)**
★ ★ ★½ **Struttin' My Stuff (Capricorn, 1976)**
★ ★½ **Hometown Boy Makes Good (Capricorn, 1977)**
★ ★ ★½ **Raisin' Hell (Capricorn, 1977)**
★ ★ ★½ **Hog Heaven (Capricorn, 1978)**
★ ★ ★½ **Big Fun (Alligator, 1988)**
★ ★ ★½ **Don't Let the Bossman Get You Down (Alligator, 1991)**

His spaced hayseed persona—Pigboy Crabshaw—slightly obscures Elvin Bishop's cunning slide guitar and natural grasp of the blues. He cut his teeth with the groundbreaking Butterfield Blues Band in the late '60s, alongside the more-heralded Mike Bloomfield. Going solo in 1969, Bishop cut a series of albums for Bill Graham's fledgling Fillmore label. Later summarized on *The Best of Elvin Bishop*, this boogie stew never quite rises to a boil. Moving to Capricorn in the '70s, Bishop found a comfortable home at the citadel of Southern rock. The gently prodding groove of his new band proved to be the perfect medium for Elvin's casually charged guitar attack and sixpack-fueled sense of humor. *Let It Flow* is almost too laid-back for its own good, but *Juke Joint Jump* gains good-time velocity on the very first track. Bishop and second guitarist Johnny "V" Vernazza mesh rolling lines over the lightly syncopated backbeat of "Juke Joint Jump," while keyboardist Phil Aaberg lays a funky clavinet cackle over the piano-and-organ base. The tentative quaver and raw breaks in Bishop's voice can grate at times, though his impact is effectively softened—not dulled—by female backups on "Sure Feels Good" and the reggae-flavored "Hold On." Still, John Lee Hooker's "Crawling King Snake" receives appropriately rough-handed treatment. *Struttin' My Stuff* leavens the salty boogie instincts with pop sweetening. Adding vocalist Mickey Thomas to the crew, Bishop scored a hit single with the gloriously bathetic "Fooled Around and Fell in Love" in 1975. It was a tenuous balance, though; *Hometown Boy Makes Good* gets stuck between rock and a softer place, and the cosmic rube routine can quickly turn into shuck 'n' jive. Surprisingly, *Raisin' Hell,* the inevitable double-live album, catches Bishop's offhand charm and low-slung chops in full swing.

With a little session-playing help, Bishop nailed a comfortable R&B groove on *Hog Heaven*. Bolstered by soulful horns, he tightens up his vocal style to good effect. Maria Muldaur assists on "It's a Feelin' " and "Let's Breakdown"; she pretty much walks away with "True Love." *Hog Heaven* is a varied and suitably low-key career capper for Elvin Bishop's '70s. While not as diverse stylistically, Bishop's gratifying late '80s return sounds just as lazily assured as his earlier highlights. The blues-drenched riffing on *Big Fun* totally benefits his new, Chicago-based label. *Don't Let the Bossman Get You Down* offers another generous helping of that "Devils' Slide" while also indicating that Bishop's eyes and ears are open. "You Got to Rock 'Em" neatly lays out his hard-won philosophy over a bracing shuffle beat. The half-funky drum kicks and Bishop's drawling rap actually hint at some ungodly hick-hop fusion—no anti-sampling rants here. He can relate *everything* back to the blues! His regally burning solos and carnival-barker tributes to the immortal Kings (B.B., Freddie and Albert) illuminate the steady-moving "Rollin' With My Blues." — M.C.

BIZ MARKIE
★ ★   Goin' Off (Cold Chillin', 1988)
★ ★½ The Biz Never Sleeps (Cold
     Chillin'/Warner Bros., 1989)
★ ★½ I Need a Haircut (Cold Chillin', 1991)
There are basically two ways of looking at
the collected works of Biz Markie: Either
he's kidding, in which case his amateurish
delivery, unflinching body-function raps and
hopelessly off-key singing are the work of a
demented genius; or he's serious, in which
case his work is simply demented. Either
way, it's the sort of thing more likely to be
loved by seventh graders than responsible
adults. *Goin' Off* opens up with "Pickin'
Boogers," and goes downhill from there.
Musically, it's damned catchy, thanks to
Marley Marl's beat-savvy production, but
conceptually, well . . . if you haven't started
laughing by the third track, you should quit
while you're ahead. Astonishingly, *The Biz
Never Sleeps* actually parlayed Markie's
peculiarities into a pop hit, the
poignant-yet-tuneless "Just a Friend."
Consider it a fluke; the rest of the album
tends more to stuff like "The Dragon," a
meditation on the evils of bad-breath, and
"Spring Again," a goofy (and appallingly
sung) homage to Barry White. Mercifully,
Markie sticks to rapping for most of *I Need
a Haircut*, although he does add a "c" for
"T.S.R. (Toilet Stool Rap)." — J.D.C.

CLINT BLACK
★ ★ ★ ★ Killin' Time (RCA, 1989)
★ ★ ★ ★ Put Yourself in My Shoes (RCA,
     1990)
Exhibiting both style and substance, Clint
Black's first two albums demonstrate his
sure grasp of a wide variety of traditional
country and pop forms. *Killin' Time* traffics
in western swing, honky tonk, country blues
and dabbles in folk as well, while the
follow-up, *Put Yourself in My Shoes*, adds
to the mix a cowboy ballad and some lilting
country pop of the Jimmy Buffett variety.
Co-writing with guitarist Hayden Nicholas,
Black also delivers some impressive depth in
his lyrics. "A Better Man," from *Killin'
Time*, surveys the honorable emotions of a
man walking away from a broken
relationship thankful for the lessons learned
rather than crying in his beer. On *Shoes*,
"One More Payment" purports to comment
on the tyranny visiting the financially
overextended worker, then suggests in one
line ("Ain't that the way the heart
goes/Seems they just attack without a sign")
that this reality serves as metaphor for the
ways of the heart as well. Time and again

Black and Nicholas find the extraordinary
within the ordinary, and then express it in
unusual and unexpected terms. Disdaining
melisma for straightforward readings that
bolster the message of his stories, Black
proves himself a thoughtful singer who
understands that less often equals more. His
band's solid instrumental support and James
Stroud's no-frills production further
recommend the work of an artist whose
integrity and intelligence speak louder than
his considerable sex appeal. He's the
standard-bearer for his generation, the one
whose music honors tradition as it points
the way to the future. — D.M.

BLACK BOX
★ ★ ★ Dreamland (RCA, 1990)
   ★ ★ Remixed Reboxed Black Box (RCA,
     1991)
This Italian house-music outfit with a talent
for strong and tuneful hooks has the bad
habit of inadequately crediting its vocalists.
Hence, its biggest hits—"Ride on Time" and
"Everybody Everybody"—both sparked
lawsuits, as Loleatta Holloway and Martha
Wash respectively demanded proper credit
for their contributions. *Remixed Reboxed* is
more of the same in different mixes.
— J.D.C.

BLACK CROWES
★ ★ ★½ Shake Your Money Maker (Def
     American, 1990)
★ ★ ★½ The Southern Harmony and Musical
     Companion (Def American, 1992)
Tough and funky, "Hard to Handle" was
the 1990 hit off this exceptional debut, but it
only hinted at the power and finesse of the
rest of the album. An Atlanta quintet
headed by the brothers Robinson (Chris on
vocals, Rich on guitars), the Crowes
successfully recreate the sound of Brit '70s
guitar glory. Every song on *Money Maker*
kicks—these guys are masters of swagger,
and they know about tunefulness as well.
   The band's second effort proved that its
debut was no fluke. The sound basically
remained the same, as did the strategy: They
substituted a Bob Marley song for the Otis
cover that had given the band its first big
hit. Originals, such as "Hotel Illness" and
"Black Moon Creeping," continue to
impress. — P.E.

BLACK FLAG
     ★ ★½ Jealous Again (EP) (SST, 1980)
★ ★ ★ ★   Damaged (SST, 1981)
     ★ ★½ Everything Went Black (SST,
     1982)

★ ★ ★ ★   The First Four Years (SST, 1983)
★ ★¹/₂ My War (SST, 1983)
★ ★   Family Man (SST, 1984)
★ ★ ★   Slip It In (SST, 1984)
★¹/₂ Live '84 (SST, 1984)
★ ★   Loose Nut (SST, 1985)
★ ★¹/₂ The Process of Weeding Out (EP) (SST, 1985)
★ ★¹/₂ In My Head (SST, 1985)
★ ★ ★   Who's Got the 10 1/2? (SST, 1986)
★ ★ ★ ★¹/₂ Wasted . . . Again (SST, 1987)

Lords of the Huntington Beach surf punk scene and pioneers of the California hardcore aesthetic, Black Flag was an enormously influential band in its day, and made a handful of indisputably great records—as well as an unconscionable number of mediocrities. Granted, a good bit of that had to do with the near-insane rate at which the band churned out new albums, but far more damaging was its fondness for poetry readings and dissonant, self-indulgent instrumental recordings.

Perhaps the best place to start is *Damaged,* a stunning display of suburban disaffection. Black Flag's writing is cuttingly sharp, and the band makes some telling points in consumer-culture parodies like "Gimmie Gimmie Gimmie" and "TV Party." But the group's greatest strength is guitarist Greg Ginn, whose slash-and-burn rhythm work and short, searing solos recall the classic cacophony of Johnny Thunders.

Beyond that, the band's discography becomes a minefield of missteps, spotty albums and ramshackle reissues. Both *The First Four Years,* which recaps the band's early singles and EPs, and the career-spanning best-of *Wasted . . . Again* are worth owning, but *Everything Went Black,* a collection of early studio sessions and outtakes, is for collectors only. *My War, Slip It In, Loose Nut* and *In My Head* all have their moments, but only *Slip It In* is justifiably a full album. *Live '84* is rambling and chaotic, but *Who's Got the 10 1/2?* cuts through its self-indulgence with intense playing. And though almost every solo on *The Process of Weeding Out* goes on too long, at least it spares us the poetic recitations that make *Family Man* so hard to bear. — J.D.C.

BLACKFOOT
★ ★ ★   No Reservations (Island, 1975)
★ ★¹/₂ Flyin' High (Epic, 1976)
★ ★ ★¹/₂ Strikes (Atco, 1979)
★ ★¹/₂ Tomcattin' (Atco, 1980)
★ ★¹/₂ Marauder (Atco, 1981)
★ ★ ★   Vertical Smiles (Atco, 1984)

Heavier than Loverboy and cruder than Foreigner, this Jacksonville, Florida, crew delivers high-end arena rock. A bluesy touch enlivens Blackfoot's early work, and "Train, Train," off *Strikes,* is a truly tough guitar workout. On *Vertical Smiles,* by covering Tim Rose's folk classic "Morning Dew," Blackfoot displays a bit of class rare for the group's genre; and on much of the band's material powerhouse singer Rick Medlocke delivers the goods with surprising—for hard rock—restraint. Blackfoot's lyrics recycle endless macho cliches, but in terms of sheer sonic boom, Blackfoot dependably delivers. — P.E.

BLACK SABBATH
★ ★   Black Sabbath (Warner Bros., 1970)
★ ★ ★¹/₂ Paranoid (Warner Bros., 1971)
★ ★ ★   Master Of Reality (Warner Bros., 1971)
★ ★   Volume 4 (Warner Bros., 1972)
★ ★ ★¹/₂ Sabbath Bloody Sabbath (Warner Bros., 1973)
★ ★¹/₂ Sabotage (Warner Bros., 1975)
★ ★ ★   We Sold Our Soul for Rock 'n' Roll (Warner Bros., 1976)
★ ★   Technical Ecstasy (Warner Bros., 1976)
★ ★   Never Say Die (Warner Bros., 1978)
★ ★   Heaven and Hell (Warner Bros., 1980)
★ ★   Mob Rules (Warner Bros., 1981)
★ ★   Born Again (Warner Bros., 1983)
★ ★   Live Evil (Warner Bros., 1983)
★   The Eternal Idol (Warner Bros., 1987)
★   Headless Cross (I.R.S., 1989)

Black Sabbath broke new ground with its grave-digging debut album. Stoned-out, dumb, clumsy, soulless, overamplified and ugly: surely rock was sinking to an all-time low with this satanic claptrap. Well, maybe the critics of the day were onto something there. Black Sabbath slogs along at an unbearable pace—like a brontosaurus in a tar pit—and the rudimentary guitar solos on side two barely provide relief. Ozzy Osbourne's ruptured wail is the stuff of nightmare, without a doubt. All that makes *Paranoid* hard to explain: the title track will either give you goose bumps or trigger nausea. On the heavy-metal mountain, "Paranoid" is a teetering two-ton boulder. Tony Iommi teases with a fuzzy guitar lick, and then applies the classic power-chord slam to Ozzy's shrieking declaration of insanity: "Finished with my woman cause she couldn't help me with my mind." From the murky depths comes "Iron Man," where Osbourne intones a la Boris Karloff over a turgid, all-encompassing roar. Like the love scenes in a horror movie, acoustic interludes and moments of instrumental repose provide breathing space between *Paranoid*'s cartoon thrills 'n' chills. If heavy makes you happy, this just might be heaven.

Master of Reality is cut from the same cloth, minus the killer hooks of "Paranoid" and "Iron Man." And it's important to note that for all the gloomy decadence this group seems to promote, "Sweet Leaf" points out the discomforting effects of marijuana and "Children of the Grave" insists that too much death-obsession is a fatal bummer. *Volume 4* demonstrates just how easily Black Sabbath can slip into dull self-parody. When they're bad, they're numbing. Which makes *Sabbath Bloody Sabbath* a red herring; just a dash of synthesizer and some sharper arrangements result in an appreciable difference. An honest-to-Lucifer tune such as "No Time to Live" suggests that Sabbath can expand its range while staying true to form. Of course, that didn't happen: it's been a downhill slide for these troupers ever since.

There have been plenty of subsequent Sabbath albums bought and sold in the meantime, though. The post-Ozzy records (beginning with *Heaven and Hell* and featuring lead yelper Ronnie James Dio) are simply impossible to tell apart—unless you're a recent convert, of course. Connoisseurs of occult headbanging are directed to Ozzy Osbourne's solo career for any further indulgence. — M.C.

BLACK UHURU

★★★ **Love Crisis (Third World, 1977)**
★★★½ **Showcase (Heartbeat, 1979)**
★★★½ **Sinsemilla (Mango, 1980)**
★★★ **Black Sounds of Freedom (1981; Shanachie, 1990)**
★★★★★ **Red (Mango, 1981)**
★★½ **Tear It Up (Mango, 1982)**
★★★ **Chill Out (Mango, 1982)**
★★★½ **Guess Who's Coming to Dinner (1983; Heartbeat, 1987)**
★★★½ **The Dub Factor (Mango, 1983)**
★★★ **Anthem (Mango, 1984)**
★★★★ **Reggae Greats (Mango, 1984)**
★★★★ **Brutal (RAS, 1986)**
★★★½ **Brutal Dub (RAS, 1986)**
★★★ **Positive (RAS, 1987)**
★★★½ **The Positive Dub (RAS, 1987)**
★★★ **Now (Mesa, 1990)**
★★★ **Now Dub (Mesa, 1990)**
★★★ **Iron Storm (Mesa, 1991)**

Although this reggae trio had been doing consistently strong work up until then, it wasn't until the release of *Red* in 1981 that

Black Uhuru was recognized as the most important group to have emerged from the reggae scene since Bob Marley's Wailers first splashed down in the U.S. Like its predecessors, *Red* made ample use of lead singer Michael Rose, whose elaborately ornamented phrasing at times has more in common with cantorial singing than with typical reggae vocal style; likewise, the album's rhythm work—by producers Sly Dunbar and Robbie Shakespeare and their cohorts—is flawless and enticing. But the writing is what really makes this album sizzle, from the spiritual wisdom of "Youth of Eglington" and "Carbine" to the sensual pleasures of "Sponji Reggae" and "Puff She Puff."

Black Uhuru's output up to *Red* was solid, if hard to track. Its debut, *Love Crisis* (later remixed and reissued as *Black Sounds of Freedom*) has many of the same vocal and instrumental strengths as *Red*, but suffers from overly conventional material; *Showcase*, a collection of singles that was later repackaged as *Guess Who's Coming to Dinner*, is much stronger, thanks to militant numbers like "Abortion" and "Guess Who's Coming to Dinner." *Sinsemilla* consolidates these strengths, and makes somewhat better use of singer Puma Jones (who joined during the period covered by *Showcase*).

Regrettably, the group's live album, *Tear It Up*, doesn't, but that poor showing may simply reflect the changes Black Uhuru was going through as the group developed a more cosmopolitan approach. Certainly *Chill Out* is far more urban (and far less doctrinaire) than its predecessors, but even that album seems cautious and conservative when compared to the techno-intense sound of *Anthem*. *Anthem* is one of the group's most insinuating efforts, but apart from tunes like "Party Next Door" and a version of Steve Van Zandt's "Solidarity," the songwriting is less than convincing.

Rose left the group at this point, and was replaced on *Brutal* by Junior Reid. Reid's performance isn't terribly distinctive, but the songs and production more than make up the difference, particularly on the Arthur Baker–remixed "Great Train Robbery." Reid takes more of a leading role with *Positive* (Jones's last album with the group), although the dub version almost outclasses the original. But he, too, left the group soon after, leaving founding member Duckie Simpson to recruit Don Carlos and Garth Dennis (both of whom had sung in Black Uhuru's very first lineup) for the polished-but-pedestrian *Now*, *Now Dub* and *Iron Storm*. — J.D.C.

RUBÉN BLADES

★ ★ ★　Bohemio y Poeta (Fania, 1979)
★ ★ ★　Maestra Vida, Primera Parte (Fania, 1980)
★ ★ ★　Maestra Vida, Segunda Parte (Fania, 1980)
★ ★ ★　El Que la Hace la Paga (Fania, 1982)
★ ★ ★ ★　Mucho Mejor (Fania, 1984)
★ ★ ★ ★ ★　Buscando America (Elektra, 1984)
★ ★ ★ ★ ★　Escenas (Elektra, 1985)
★ ★ ★　Crossover Dreams (Elektra, 1986)
★ ★ ★½ Doble Filo (Fania, 1986)
★ ★ ★ ★　Agua de Luna (Elektra, 1987)
★ ★ ★ ★½ Antecedente (Elektra, 1988)
★ ★ ★　Nothing But the Truth (Elektra, 1988)
★ ★ ★ ★　Y Son del Solar . . . Live! (Elektra, 1990)
★ ★ ★ ★　Caminando (Sony Discos International, 1991)

Born in Panama, educated at Harvard Law and well respected in Hollywood, Blades would have been a success even if he hadn't gone into music. But it is as a singer, songwriter and bandleader that he has made his greatest mark, and deservedly so. After a period of apprenticeship at the Fania record label, Blades linked up with veteran bandleader Willie Colon in 1975. Colon and Blades collaborated on several albums: *Willie Colon Presents Rubén Blades: Metiendo Mano!, Siembra*, the Grammy-winning *Canciones del Solar de los Aburridos* and a soundtrack called *The Last Fight*. Colon also produced the ambitious *Maestra Vida* albums; augmenting dramatic, character-oriented songs with slice-of-life dialogue, the albums were conceptually a step forward from the more conventional salsa of *Bohemia y Poeta*, but the bloated, cinematic orchestration blunts the music's power.

It wasn't until *Buscando America* that Blades fully realized the greatness that *Maestra Vida* hinted at. Although it was his first major-label effort, the only concession it made to the Anglo market was to include English translations of the Spanish lyrics; otherwise, Blades's perspective was unchanged. This time, though, the power of the music matched the potency of the lyrics, so as Blades went "searching for America" (to translate the title), what he found were ways of working rock devices (doo-wop harmonies, singer-songwriter narratives) into his music without watering it down. *Escenas*, which featured cameos by Linda

Ronstadt and Joe Jackson, went even further, thanks to sharper songwriting and the increasing agility of Blades's band, Seis del Solar.

Crossover Dreams reverted to a more traditional salsa approach, but, being a soundtrack, at least had an excuse. That wasn't the case with *Nothing But the Truth*, Blade's first all-English album; not only didn't this crossover dream deliver him a mainstream Anglo audience, but its standard-issue rock arrangements robbed the songs of impact and originality. Unfortunately, its failure sealed Blades's fate with the Anglo market, and after fulfilling his obligation to Elektra, he moved to Sony Discos International, a label where the focus is primarily on the Hispanic market. Even so, *Caminando* maintains the attitude and flavor of his Elektra recordings, from the forthright melodic appeal of songs like "Tengan Fe" and "Prohibido Olvidar," right down to the bilingual lyric sheet.
— J.D.C.

BLAKE BABIES

★ ★ ★　Earwig (Mammoth, 1989)
★ ★ ★½ Sunburn (Mammoth, 1990)
★ ★ ★½ Rosy Jack World (EP) (Mammoth, 1991)

While recalling the wide-eyed wonder of early R.E.M. or 10,000 Maniacs, Blake Babies are a looser outfit—and a completely charming one. Juliana Hatfield sings like a knowing waif, her high, delicate vocals contrasting effectively with her assertive bass guitar work. And drummer Freda Boner and guitarist-vocalist John Strohm flesh out the gorgeous sound with deft, spare playing that allows Hatfield room to move. "Lament," "Don't Suck My Breath" and "Rain" make *Earwig* a strong debut, but the fuller production of *Sunburn* and such standouts as "Sanctify" and "Gimme Some Mirth" show the band gaining in edge as well as grace. The 1991 EP, *Rosy Jack World*, with its college-radio hit, "Temptation Eyes," was, if anything, craftier. — P.E.

BOBBY "BLUE" BLAND

★ ★ ★ ★ ★　The Best of Bobby Bland (1972; MCA, 1974)
★ ★ ★ ★　Two Steps From the Blues (1973; MCA, 1989)
★ ★ ★　Ain't Nothing You Can Do (MCA, 1974)
★ ★ ★　Here's the Man (MCA, 1974)
★ ★ ★ ★　The Soul of the Man (MCA, 1974)

★ ★ ★ ★ **The Best of Bobby Bland, Volume 2** (MCA, 1974)
★ ★ ★ **Call on Me** (MCA, 1974)
★ ★ ★ **Introspective of the Early Years** (MCA, 1974)
★ ★ ★ **Reflections in Blue** (MCA, 1977)
★ ★ ★ **I Feel Good, I Feel Fine** (MCA, 1979)
★ ★ ★ **Members Only** (Malaco, 1985)
★ ★ ★ **After All** (Malaco, 1986)
★ ★ ★ **Blues You Can Use** (Malaco, 1987)
★ ★ ★ ★ **First Class Blues** (Malaco, 1987)
★ ★ ★ ★ **Midnight Run** (Malaco, 1989)
★ ★ ★ ★ **Portrait of the Blues** (Malaco, 1991)
WITH B.B. KING
★ ★ ★ ★ **B.B. King & Bobby Bland: Together for the First Time Live** (MCA, 1974)
★ ★ **B.B. King & Bobby Bland: Together Again . . . Live** (MCA, 1976)

Born into the church and mesmerized by the young B.B. King (he was once his valet and chauffeur), Tennessee native Bobby Bland is one of the cornerstones of modern R&B, a distinction earned on the strength of his extraordinary recordings for the Duke label beginning in the '50s and emphasized by his still-strong work for the Malaco label today. The Dixie Hummingbirds' Ira Tucker, one of the most important gospel singers in history, was the first influence on the young Bland, who began singing regularly as a child in his church in Memphis; it was the early recordings of B.B. King that helped crystallize Bland's own synthesis of gospel and blues into a distinctive stance.

Like King, Bland comes on with great dignity and composure, which makes his emotional explosions all the more exciting. However much he took from gospel and blues in fashioning his own style, so did Bland adopt the urbane, stand-up vocalist style of Joe Turner and Jimmy Rushing, along with those singers' big band approach. Flashy, cool, Bobby "Blue" Bland is the whole package, style personified.

Most of Bland's essential work remains in print. Out of print but less important are Bland's recordings for ABC in the mid- to late-'70s (with the exception of two live albums recorded with B.B. King, now on MCA); there's not much to chew on from this period, though. The choice parts are still out there, and still compelling.

Signed to Duke Records in 1954, Bland produced R&B hits steadily into the early '70s; a number of these are now considered standards. Most of the Duke albums are now on MCA, but recommending one over another is difficult. Bland was at his best during these years, and to say one album is better than another is to be accused of downgrading some classic performance or two on an otherwise solid set of performances. That said, *The Best of Bobby Bland* contains *all* classic performances and justifies its title. *The Soul of the Man* is a nice sampling of the gospel-oriented, minor key blues at which Bland has few peers; the first cut alone, "I Can't Stop," is one of the singer's most heartbreaking performances. *Introspective of the Early Years* is Bland in a raw mode, backed by a small combo, the horn section less prominent than it became later on, and offering up a collection of songs considerably darker in mood than his usual fare.

Like King, Bland has aged well. His Malaco recordings are in-the-pocket gospel-soul, and the song selection remains exemplary. A good starting point for this period of Bland's career is *First Class Blues*, a kind of greatest hits package containing several tracks from Bland's first two Malaco albums, *After All* and *Members Only*, as well as a couple of Bland classics, "Two Steps from the Blues" and "St. James Infirmary." A wrenching version of "In the Ghetto" is soul on ice, Bland's slow, deliberate reading driving home the overwhelming desperation of inner city life.

Midnight Run and *Portrait of the Blues* are further displays of a great vocalist in peak form. — D.M.

THE BLASTERS
★ ★ ★ ½ **The Blasters** (Slash/Warner Bros., 1981)
★ ★ ★ **Over There: Live at the Venue, London** (EP) (Slash/Warner Bros., 1982)
★ ★ ½ **Non Fiction** (Slash/Warner Bros., 1983)
★ ★ ½ **Hard Line** (Slash/Warner Bros., 1985)
★ ★ ★ ★ **The Blasters Collection** (Slash/Warner Bros., 1990)

Briefly the brightest light of the roots-rock movement, the Blasters typify the limits of rock classicism. Although their first album, a raucous bit of neo-rockabilly called *American Music*, barely caused a ripple outside of collectors' circles (where it is prized as much for its rarity as for its music), the group's major-label debut, *The Blasters*, made quite a splash. Reprising two of *American Music*'s titles—"Marie, Marie," which was a massive hit for the English rockabilly star Shakin' Stevens, and "American Music" itself—it presented a band that was aggressive and accomplished, as at home with the New Orleans–style roll of "Hollywood Bed" as with the rockabilly kick of "No Other Girl." As if to cement the group's reputation as devoted revivalists, *The Blasters* was followed by a live EP, *Over There*, which offered one original and five rip-roaring covers, including the piano-fired "High School Confidential" and "Roll 'Em Pete."

But the Blasters wanted to be more than just a revival act, and so began to expand their vision with *Non Fiction*. What songwriter Dave Alvin came up with was impressive enough on paper, but seemed wordy and overwrought when tied to the band's energetic-but-unimaginative trad-rock arrangements. *Hard Line* tries to remedy that overreach by bringing in such musical allies as the Jordanaires, but that just makes the songs more complex, not more convincing.

As of early 1992, all of those albums were out of print, leaving only *The Blasters Collection*, an overview that includes the first seven songs from *The Blasters* as well as highlights from the other three albums, plus three previously unreleased tracks— which, to be honest, is about all the Blasters most rock fans would need, anyway.

— J.D.C.

CARLA BLEY

★★★★★   **Escalator Over the Hill (JCOA, 1972)**
★★★½   **Tropic Appetites (Watt, 1973)**
★★★½   **Dinner Music (Watt, 1977)**
★★★½   **European Tour, 1977 (Watt, 1978)**
★★★★   **Musique Mecanique (Watt, 1979)**
★★★★★   **Social Studies (ECM, 1980)**
★★★★   **Live! (ECM, 1982)**
★★★½   **Heavy Heart (Watt, 1984)**
★★★½   **Night-Glo (Watt, 1985)**
★★★½   **Sextet (Watt, 1987)**
★★★½   **Duets (1988)**
★★★½   **Fleur Carnivore (Watt, 1989)**
★★★★   **Orchestra Jazz Siciliana Plays the Music of Carla Bley (xtraWATT, 1990)**
★★★★   **The Very Big Carla Bley Band (Watt, 1991)**

WITH MICHAEL MANTLER

★★★½   **13 & 3/4 (Watt, 1975)**

One of the outstanding musical events of the '70s, Carla Bley's *Escalator Over the Hill* took several years to record, clocked in at more than the length of three conventional albums, and stands as a sort of avant-garde partner to *Sgt. Pepper's*. That is, it dips nimbly into all manner of styles, gracefully flaunts its ambitiousness and repays constant listening. But it's considerably more difficult than the Beatles' triumph. Pianist-organist Bley, after all, flashes intimidating, high-art credentials— co-founder of the Jazz Composers Orchestra Association (JCOA), she'd played with Pharoah Sanders, wrote music for vibraphonist Gary Burton—and had built up a reputation as one of the more interesting post-Ornette Coleman jazzers even before she released *Escalator*. Uniting such diverse figures as Gato Barbieri and Linda Ronstadt, Warhol star Viva and John McLaughlin, Jack Bruce and Don Cherry, the epic is jazz-fusion that sounds nothing like either the African and blues-derived menace of Miles's *Bitches Brew*, nor the smarmy dilutions of such popularizers as Chuck Mangione or Jean-Luc Ponty. Instead, with its libretto by poet Paul Haines, its virtuosic playing and its cryptic humor, *Escalator* is postmodern opera— difficult, intense, often abstract. And gorgeous.

Nothing Bley has done since has flourished such Olympian power—but every record she's made is provocative. Whether working out dense, majestic brass arrangements with her big band or recording austerely lovely duets with bassist Steve Swallow, she combines a jazz player's sense of freedom with the complex intelligence of a modern classical composer. *Sextet* features some of her nicer melodies; *Musique Mecanique*, with its standout 12-minute "Jesus Maria and Other Spanish Strains" combines the graceful ambience of chamber music with the heat of jazz (bassist Charlie Haden, a regular contributor, contributes outstanding work, as does guitarist Eugene Chadbourne). *Tropic Appetites* highlights the exceptional vocals of Julie Tippetts (formerly Julie Driscoll, whose early fame came with Brian Auger in the '60s); with husband Michael Mantler, *13 & 3/4* is brilliant large-ensemble music, its intricacy and sweep emblematic of much of the music Bley-Mantler offer on their Watt record label. Bley at her most approachable can be found on 1991 versions of her "greatest hits" performed by the Orchestra Jazz Siciliana, and *Social Studies* (1980) comes closest to *Escalator* in artistic derring-do.

Frank Zappa (without the sophomoric smutty humor) or Laurie Anderson are performers who meet Bley on the ground of avant-pop synthesis—but Bley is very nearly sui generis as a musician; consistently, she astonishes. — P.E.

BLIND FAITH
★ ★ ★ ★ **Blind Faith (1969; Polydor, 1986)**
Rock's first supergroup, Blind Faith combined Eric Clapton and Ginger Baker (from the recently dissolved Cream), Steve Winwood (on hiatus from Traffic) and Rick Grech (from Family, which was a big deal in Britain, at least). Like almost every supergroup since then, Blind Faith was never quite the sum of its parts; although its one album had some incredible moments, the ethereal "Presence of the Lord" and "Can't Find My Way Home" among them, too much of the album was given over to directionless jamming. And, like almost every supergroup since then, the band barely lasted a year, breaking up after a single album and tour. — J.D.C.

BLONDIE
★ ★ ★ ★   **Blondie (1976; Private Stock/Chrysalis, 1977)**
★ ★ ★   **Plastic Letters (Chrysalis, 1977)**
★ ★ ★ ★½ **Parallel Lines (Chrysalis, 1978)**
★ ★ ★½ **Eat to the Beat (Chrysalis, 1979)**
★ ★ ★   **Autoamerican (Chrysalis, 1980)**
★ ★ ★ ★   **Best of Blondie (Chrysalis, 1981)**
★ ★   **The Hunter (Chrysalis, 1982)**
"Blondie Is a Group!" announced the ads for this New York combo's first album, somewhat defensively. For once, the hype was correct, though lead singer and focal point Deborah Harry certainly had the ability to steal a spotlight—and hold on to it. One of the earliest punk bands, Blondie was pretty much a second-string act at CBGB until its debut album came out in late '76. Harry, guitarist Chris Stein (later Harry's husband) and cohorts flaunt an enthusiasm for pop-effluvia that's absolutely contagious. Surf music, girl groups, Motown, bubblegum, glitter rock, even a touch of heavy metal—everything gets boiled down into sweet little concoctions that release surprisingly complex, lasting pleasures. Eventually, Stein and Harry's devotion to the Bowie/Eno/Roxy Music school of art rock overwhelmed their pure pop impulses. But for a while, Blondie's stylistic experiments yielded impressive results. While Debbie Harry was hardly a punk anti-star like Patti Smith, her sex symbolism exuded street smarts and a

knowing sense of humor. Clearly, this woman was nobody's bimbo.

Blondie revels in the trashiest strains of '60s pop, adding a dry Manhattan twist to "X Offender" and "Rip Her to Shreds." *Plastic Letters*, the followup, sounds rushed and hollow, though the catchy singles "Denis" and "(I'm Always Touched by Your) Presence, Dear" both tap into Harry's emotional reserves. *Parallel Lines*, recorded with an expanded lineup, represents a huge leap in musicianship and overall conception. From the dynamite rock & roll opener ("Hangin' on the Telephone") to the rock-disco crossover "Heart of Glass," Blondie keep the hooks—and ideas—coming fast. *Eat to the Beat* strives for the same natural balance, and comes suprisingly close.

You have to admire Blondie's artistic gumption. However, by the time of *Autoamerican*, the band's eclecticism begins to diffuse. "Rapture" and "The Tide Is High" were satisfying singles, but Blondie's grasp of hip-hop and reggae (respectively) wasn't nearly as strong as its hold on good ol' rock & roll. The end came in the early '80s during Chris Stein's prolonged illness with a rare disease (he's since recovered): Blondie's last tour and album (*The Hunter*) were distracted, painful affairs. — M.C.

BLOODROCK
★ ★½ **D.O.A. (Capitol, 1989)**
Nowhere near as morbid as its name or best-known song might suggest, Bloodrock is a fairly typical band of second-stringers from the early '70s concert circuit. Over the course of a half-dozen albums, the group went from reproducing its sweaty live sound—exuberantly dumb, metalized southern rock—to experimenting with R&B and, gulp, jazz. This budget-line compilation is all that remains in print. *D.O.A.* does include some laughable art-rock noodling: "Stilled by Whirlwind Tongues," indeed. But the cuts produced by Grand Funk maestro Terry Knight boogie along with an agreeable lope; an organ drones the power chords while Jim Rutledge's stinging guitar leads float high above the sludge. "Jessica" and "You Gotta Roll" almost sound funky. Bloodrock slows down to a crawl on the signature title track, however. "D.O.A." is a portentous deathbed epic, a druggy, fuzz-toned update of J. Frank Wilson's immortal early '60s weeper "Last Kiss." It's worth hearing, but the deleted double-record set *Live* (1972) will satisfy any further curiosity—and then some. Anyone intrigued

by the drawling rock sounds of the South might instead seek out the long-lost Capitol albums by Bloodrock collaborator John Nitzinger. His eponymous power trio pumped out a succinct strain of high-energy boogie, prefiguring Lynyrd Skynyrd by several years. The scorching 1972 debut *Nitzinger* leaves Bloodrock lumbering behind. — M.C.

BLOODSTONE

★ ★ ★ **Greatest Hits (CBS, 1985)**

This Kansas City soul quintet changed its name—from the Sinceres—when it began recording for Decca's London imprint, in London. Bloodstone couldn't sound more American, though. "Natural High" was the group's first single and biggest hit; this ethereal declaration of love floated into the pop Top Ten at the end of 1973. Bloodstone's *Greatest Hits* ignores the group's later, funkier efforts on the Isley Brothers' T-Neck label (all out of print), concentrating instead on "Natural High" and its less successful followups. Like the Trammps or the Commodores, Bloodstone mines the turf between funk and disco. Humorous uptempo workouts ("Traffic Cop," "Do You Wanna Do a Thing") provide a breather between keening heartbreak ballads ("Outside Woman," "My Little Lady"). Lead singer Charles McCormick strains occasionally, but the snappy, Philadelphia-inspired string arrangements provide all the support he needs. Bloodstone's *Greatest Hits* is far from essential. But if you can get off on "Natural High," the rest of the album sure won't bring you down. — M.C.

BLOOD, SWEAT AND TEARS

★ ★ ★ ★   **Child Is Father to the Man (Columbia, 1968)**
  ★ ★½ **Blood, Sweat and Tears (Columbia, 1969)**
  ★ ★½ **Blood, Sweat and Tears 3 (1970; Columbia, 1986)**
  ★ ★ ★ **Greatest Hits (Columbia, 1972)**
    ★ **New Blood (Columbia, 1972)**
    ★ **No Sweat (Columbia, 1973)**
  ★ ★ ★ **Live & Improvised (Columbia, 1991)**

Frighteningly pretentious, BS&T were fired by the same questionable impulse to fuse rock and jazz that compromised Miles Davis and nearly killed off Jeff Beck. Convinced that rock & roll just wasn't too bright, these high-culture bullyboys figured that what was missing was brass. Horns, of course, had been a brilliant mainstay for Little Richard and James Brown, but what BS&T had in

mind was fat Big Band—Woody Herman, Glenn Miller, et al. Soon staging a saxophone shootout with contemporary rivals, Chicago, BS&T delivered hits that indeed featured breathtaking arrangements and playing—but virtuosity this misbegotten hadn't been heard since the more extreme Liszt.

Dylan sideman and ex-Blues Project member Al Kooper founded BS&T, but held on only long enough for their first, and best, record. Featuring such classy writers as Harry Nilsson and Randy Newman, *Child Is Father to the Man* showed a band not yet gripped by terminal condescension; it's an elegant, ambitious record. Then came David Clayton-Thomas. Bearish, amiable and deeply desirous of the chintz mantle earned by being "a great entertainer," C-T was a scenery chewer of a singer, radiating bogus black soul and arrogant "chops." Bellowing "And When I Die," "Spinning Wheel" and "You've Made Me So Very Happy," he made their second album hit-heavy and hollow—and primed them for a career of unintended Vegas-aspiring. BS&T is best represented by an album of 1975 concerts, *Live & Improvised* (currently out of print). Again, on material like the Cannonball Adderley–tribute blues "Unit Seven" there are passages of crack playing as expert as, say, "The Tonight Show" orchestra. — P.E.

LUKA BLOOM

★ ★ ★½ **Riverside (Reprise, 1990)**
★ ★ ★½ **The Acoustic Motorbike (Reprise, 1992)**

Piercingly lovely, "This Is for Life," is Bloom at his best. From his debut, *Riverside*, it's a lament of sweethearts separated by English prison bars, and Bloom sings it with erotic Celtic soul. Taking his first name from Suzanne Vega's song about child abuse and his surname from the hard-hit Leopold Bloom, hero of James Joyce's *Ulysses*, Bloom is a folk singer of literate high purpose. "Gone to Pablo" elegizes the lover's suicide of Picasso's second wife; "The Man Is Alive" is packed with bittersweet autobiographical vignettes. Artful as well as earnest, *Riverside* is a noteworthy first album, a lean, mature reflection on the wants of the body and the needs of the soul. *The Acoustic Motorbike* also impresses with its melodicism and Celtic-inflected instrumentation. — P.E.

MIKE BLOOMFIELD

★ ★ ★ **Super Session (With Al Kooper, Stephen Stills) (Columbia, 1968)**

★★★ It's Not Killing Me (Columbia, 1969)

★★★ The Live Adventures of Mike Bloomfield and Al Kooper (Columbia, 1969)

★★½ Try It Before You Buy It (Columbia, 1973)

★★★ Triumvirate (Columbia, 1973)

★★★ Analine (Takoma, 1977)

★★★ Mill Valley Session (Polydor, 1976)

★★★ If You Love These Blues, Play 'Em As You Please (Guitar Player, 1977)

★★★ Mike Bloomfield (Takoma, 1978)

★★½ Between a Hard Place and the Ground (Takoma, 1980)

★★½ Living in the Fast Lane (Waterhouse, 1981)

★★★½ Cruisin' for a Bruisin' (Takoma, 1981)

★★★½ Bloomfield (Columbia, 1983)

A brilliant blues player, critically acclaimed and commercially a failure, Bloomfield remains a cult figure—a musician, not a showman, he's essentially a guitarist's guitarist. Finding early renown with the Paul Butterfield Blues Band, he mastered a style of hard Chicago blues, urban, quick and very electric. With a style based on the stinging attack of B.B. King, he was capable, too, of very fluid runs and fills, and his solos were breathtakingly precise. The Electric Flag provided him his best backdrop; their innovative synthesis of blues rock and horn-driven jazz provoked some of his tastiest playing, but he left the band a year after he'd joined them. From then on, he never found exactly the right vehicle for his talents. His work with Al Kooper was graceful and exciting, but Kooper couldn't really keep up with him, and Triumvirate, a collaboration with John Hammond and Dr. John, was highly professional blues—but the one-shot band took few risks. On his own, he made solid, sharp records—the best being It's Not Killing Me and Cruisin' for a Bruisin'—but they lacked the fire he'd found when playing with musicians of equal stature. If You Love These Blues, an instructional guide to blues guitar, earned him a well-deserved Grammy in 1977, and yet it served, too, to remind listeners that here was an awesome player in search of a band.

The 1983 Bloomfield compilation, released two years after his tragic, fatal drug overdose, provides the best intro; collecting the best of his work with Butterfield, the Electric Flag and Kooper, as well as some previously unreleased gems, it serves as a fine memorial. — P.E.

KURTIS BLOW

★★★ Kurtis Blow (Mercury, 1980)

★★ Deuce (Mercury, 1981)

★★ Tough (Mercury, 1982)

★★★½ Party Time? (Mercury, 1983)

★★ Ego Trip (Mercury, 1984)

★★★ America (Mercury, 1985)

★★ Kingdom Blow (Mercury, 1986)

★★ Back by Popular Demand (Mercury, 1988)

Blow was the first rapper to cut albums for a major label, a breakthrough that would have been more impressive had Blow actually been an album artist. But he was essentially a singles act, meaning that while his albums have their moments—"The Breaks" on Kurtis Blow, say, or "Basketball" from America—moments are usually all they offer. The exception is Party Time? (which, at five songs, is actually an EP rather than an album), on which Blow's temporary alliance with EU produces the first meaningful rap-hip-hop fusion. — J.D.C.

BLUE ANGEL

★★★ Blue Angel (Polydor, 1980)

Cyndi Lauper's original band, Blue Angel, consisted of four cute boys and the cartoon diva herself, all making cute on new-wave originals that traded heavily on the Phil Spector Wall of Sound. Nothing substantial, but a whole lot of fun. Cyndi was great as an ersatz Ronette, and the rest of the crew doo-wopped credibly. — P.E.

BLUEBELLS

★★★½ Sisters (Sire, 1984)

Given a full, gorgeous production by Elvis Costello, Sisters is highly accomplished and truly smart pop. Acoustic guitar riffs provide the basis for ten songs by Robert Hudgens—a writer with a brilliant way with a hook. Mandolins and strings fill out the sound, which varies from an updated Merseybeat to tuneful, slow numbers. "Cath" and the "The Patriot Game" are the standouts, but every number is a gem. — P.E.

BLUE CHEER

★★ Louder than God: The Best of Blue Cheer (Rhino, 1986)

Gleefully ugly mega-noise, the raw romp of these late-'60s San Francisco guitar thugs now sounds prescient—if not good. Unwittingly providing a prototype for thrash and speed metal, bassist-vocalist-mastermind Dickie Peterson mangled Eddie Cochran's "Summertime Blues" and Mose Allison's "Parchment

Farm" by subjecting them to the same trademark treatment this band offered to such original material as "Magnolia Caboose Babyfinger" and "Fruit and Icebergs"—white noise and screaming. A true-life Spinal Tap, Blue Cheer were bad taste of an almost surreal intensity. — P.E.

BLUE MAGIC
★ ★ ★½ **Greatest Hits (Omni/Atlantic, 1986)**
★ ★ ★ **From Out of the Blue (OBR/Columbia, 1989)**

Even though this quartet was a second-string outfit at the Philly Soul sound factory, there's nothing second-rate about Blue Magic. The group may not scale the peaks attained by the Spinners and O'Jays, but producer Norman Harris orchestrates their romantic despair to great dramatic effect on "Sideshow," "Three Ring Circus" and "Stop to Start" (from *Greatest Hits*). *From Out of the Blue* is a medium-voltage lightning bolt. It goes a long way toward rewiring the vocal-group sound with some hip-hop juice—not to mention rescuing Blue Magic from the oldies circuit. — M.C.

THE BLUE NILE
★ ★ ★½ **A Walk Across the Rooftops (A&M, 1983)**
★ ★ ★½ **Hats (A&M, 1989)**

This impressive Scots threesome digs the challenge of tight, self-imposed limits. *A Walk Across the Rooftops* and *Hats* are seven-song keyboard quasi-suites; no song speeds past mid-tempo; all lyrics are imagistic; and the psychic state remains nearly unvaried—muted, ecstatic yearning, the overspill of musings on fated romance. In the Blue Nile's case, such tactics don't produce boredom, but entrancing intensity. From the debut, "Easter Parade" and its spare, acoustic piano, achieves a Zen beauty. Unusually subtle synthesizer players, they seemed fueled by an almost classical impulse in pursuing string textures and fields of pure tonality. *Hats* maintains that standard, with the plus of featuring their finest song, "The Downtown Lights," a glimmering tone poem. — P.E.

BLUE ÖYSTER CULT
★ ★ ★ ★ **Blue Öyster Cult (Columbia, 1972)**
★ ★ ★ ★ **Tyranny and Mutation (Columbia, 1973)**
★ ★½ **Secret Treaties (Columbia, 1974)**
★ ★½ **On Your Feet or on Your Knees (Columbia, 1975)**
★ ★ ★½ **Agents of Fortune (Columbia, 1976)**
★ ★½ **Spectres (Columbia, 1977)**
★ ★ **Some Enchanted Evening (Columbia, 1978)**
★ ★ **Mirrors (Columbia, 1979)**
★ ★ **Cultosaurus Erectus (Columbia, 1980)**
★ ★ **Fire of Unknown Origin (Columbia, 1981)**
★ **Extraterrestrial Live (Columbia, 1982)**
★ **Revolution by Night (Columbia, 1983)**
★ **Club Ninja (Columbia, 1984)**
★ ★½ **Imaginos (Columbia, 1987)**
★ ★ **Career of Evil (Columbia, 1990)**

In 1971, a third-string psychedelic rock band called Soft White Underbelly changed its name and devised a new attack plan: louder and heavier, with guitars and drums wound tight. Blue Öyster Cult wrapped its arcane verbal conceits in a whip-cracking leather 'n studs image. What saves the Cult from becoming a smug parody of the early metal scene—at first, anyway—is lead guitarist Donald "Buck Dharma" Roeser. Buck Dharma couples an understanding of raw chord power with a sense of melody and restraint. His stinging riffs and floating solos lift *Blue Öyster Cult* and *Tyranny & Mutation* above the ordinary—a powerhouse one-two punch. But the flashes of wit quickly turn into schtick, amid all the absurd S&M trappings. *Secret Treaties* buries the Cult's best song—"Dominance and Submission," not at all what you think—in petrifying hard-rock clichés. The fluke hit "Don't Fear the Reaper" arrested the band's inevitable slide; that ringing, bittersweet guitar line bids the '60s a fond, lingering adieu. Buck Dharma continued to plumb killer licks for a spell (check out "Godzilla" on *Spectres*). By the time the Cult got around to covering MC5's "Kick Out the Jams" on the live *Some Enchanted Evening*, however, punk had rendered its brand of heaviness old-fashioned —if not irrelevant. Certainly, the band's subsequent efforts support that judgment, though *Imaginos* is a bizarre, almost-interesting mess of sci-fi concepts and that familiar "stun guitar." The haphazard *Career of Evil* contains later, inferior live versions of some of the group's better-known songs. Blue Öyster Cult deserves better; at its peak, the band brought a rare sophistication to heavy metal. — M.C.

THE BLUES BROTHERS
★ **Briefcase Full of Blues (Atlantic, 1978)**
★ **Made in America (Atlantic, 1980)**

★ ★ The Blues Brothers—Original Soundtrack (Atlantic, 1980)
★ Best of the Blues Brothers (Atlantic, 1981)

Once *Saturday Night Live* turned them into TV superstars, John Belushi and Dan Aykroyd acted out a long-running musical fantasy. Christening themselves Jake and Elwood Blues, this comedy duo hired a crack band of soul session vets and released an album of lame-to-insulting cover versions. Of course, *Briefcase Full of Blues* went straight to Number One, and the Brothers parlayed their tasteless schtick into another album and a feature film. Credit the pair for giving James Brown and Aretha Franklin cameo parts in their movie, and urging fans to "buy all the blues albums you can." But they deserve a lot of blame, too: for reducing this emotionally resonant music into a blaring frat-boy party soundtrack, and for reaping sizable profits off it.
— M.C.

BODEANS
★ ★½ Love & Hope & Sex & Dreams (Slash/Warner Bros., 1986)
★ ★ Outside Looking In (Slash/Reprise, 1987)
★ ★ Home (Slash/Reprise, 1989)
★ ★ Black and White (Slash/Reprise, 1991)

Sammy Llanas and Kurt Neumann—a.k.a. Sammy and Beau BoDean—are terrific singers, and have a real flair for injecting a touch of soul into the most mundane harmony arrangements. As songwriters, however, the two are if not quite hacks then certainly not very far removed, specializing in the sort of roots-rock twaddle beloved by those who like having new albums to buy but desperately hate new music. — J.D.C.

MICHAEL BOLTON
★½ Michael Bolton (Columbia, 1983)
★ ★ The Hunger (Columbia, 1987)
★ ★ Soul Provider (Columbia, 1989)
★ Time, Love and Tenderness (Columbia, 1991)
★½ The Early Years (1974–76) (RCA, 1991)

If you'd like a quick way to chart the course of Michael Bolton's career, simply look at the covers he's recorded. On *The Early Years* (compiled from two solo albums recorded in the mid '70s), he moans through the Guess Who's "These Eyes" in an attempt at Top Forty credibility, but adds a credibly soulful edge to the Stones' "Time Is on My Side"—in other words, he's a rocker with R&B roots. *Michael Bolton* comes

closer to balancing the two, but falls short as the singer pushes too hard through an overburdened rendition of the Supremes' "Back in My Arms Again." *The Hunger* finds Bolton turning to Otis Redding's "(Sittin' On) The Dock of the Bay," which gets a reading so faithful to the original you'd think Bolton had begun doing impressions. Unfortunately, he pushes that a bit too far with the version of "Georgia on My Mind" on *Soul Provider*. He goes completely overboard on *Time, Love and Tenderness*, turning in a version of "When a Man Loves a Woman" that seems almost a parody of soul singing.

All of which is a shame, really, because when Bolton is left to his own material, the results can be stunning. Songs like "Walk Away" and "That's What Love Is All About" (from *The Hunger*) may seem like pro forma rock ballads, but Bolton understands how to play off their inner dynamics to add drama to their heartbreak sentiment. Sure, that can easily lead to schmaltz, but performances like "How Am I Supposed to Live Without You" or "How Can We Be Lovers" (both from *Soul Provider*) suggest that Bolton could be capable of greatness. — J.D.C.

GRAHAM BOND
★ ★ ★ Solid Bond (Warner Bros., 1970)
★ ★ ★ Live at Klook's Kleek (Decal/Charly, 1990)

A gruff and burly presence on the English pop scene in the early '60s, Graham Bond was instrumental in spurring British interest in R&B. Beginning as a jazz saxophonist with a special devotion to Charles Mingus, he switched to organ and vocals when joining together with drummer Ginger Baker, double-bassist Jack Bruce and guitarist John McLaughlin (all three, graduates of Alexis Korner's Blues Incorporated) as the Graham Bond Organisation. *Solid Bond* (now out of print) features Bond on alto and piano as well as organ, playing in 1963 at Klook's Kleek, an ultra-hip nightclub of the period. The extended jazz cuts (Sonny Rollins's "Doxy," Bond-McLaughlin's "The Grass Is Greener") are only capable, but the R&B stuff kicks—as their later careers obviously proved, Bond's musicians were first-rate, and their promise is readily apparent even at this early date.

Live at Klook's Kleek (1990), a 1965 club date, is even stronger. The album's production values are primitive, but the crude sound and smoke-and-ale ambience only add atmosphere to a session of fierce blues and jazz-tinged soul. Baker, in particular, comes across as a monster, and Bond's deep voice thunders. Always a catalyst and cult figure, never a star, Bond suffered through heroin addiction in the '60s and then, in 1971, formed Holy Magick with his wife, singer Diane Stewart. Divorce soon followed, and Bond's preoccupation with the occult reached the point of obsession (he began believing he was the son of black magician Aleister Crowley). In 1973, he died mysteriously, under the wheels of a (parked) subway train. — P.E.

JOHNNY BOND
★★★ **The Best of Johnny Bond (Starday, NA)**
★ **How I Love Them Old Songs (Lamb & Lion, NA)**
Though nominally considered a country artist, the late Johnny Bond resists easy categorization. He was a backup singer for Gene Autry, but his own material leaned toward honky-tonk, rockabilly and blues. His claim to fame is a 1960 Top Thirty hit, "Hot Rod Lincoln," that had a second life a decade later when recorded by Commander Cody. That song and another minor hit from '65, "10 Little Bottles," were recitations set to a big beat; in both, alcohol played a prominent thematic role, as it does in "Sick, Sober, and Sorry," and "Three Sheets to the Wind." *The Best of Johnny Bond* lays out the whole boozy saga; a more repentant Bond shows his spiritual side on *How I Love Them Old Songs.* — D.M.

GARY U.S. BONDS
★★★ **Dedication (EMI, 1981)**
★★★ **Best of Gary U.S. Bonds (Rhino, 1990)**
Some of the best singles of the early '60s, pre-Beatles period in rock came via the team of Gary U.S. Bonds and his producer-mentor Frank Guida. In 1960 Guida bought a recording studio that was about to go out of business, and his first record out of the new facility was "New Orleans," featuring local singer Gary Bonds as a last-minute substitute for a singer whose bad attitude cost him the recording date. "New Orleans" peaked at Number Six on the pop chart, and established, once and forever, the Bonds-Guida sound. Ironically, Bonds is almost the least important element in the mix. Lacking much subtlety or even timbre, Bonds offered instead exuberance and an ingratiating personality. A party atmosphere recommended Bonds's records, along with the singer's quaint projection of

the idea that he and he alone *was* the party.
Around Bonds's shouting, Guida produced a wall of sound, with instruments meshing indistinguishably (save for a honking sax) into a rock & roll juggernaut. Bonds's third single, "Quarter to Three," was the monster that secured for him an important niche in rock history, influencing not only the artists of his day, but a number of important artists of succeeding generations, including Bruce Springsteen, who once made the song a regular part of his repertoire; Springsteen later wound up producing some singles (and writing one, "This Little Girl") that fueled Bonds's short-lived comeback in the early '80s. In addition to the usual hyperkinetic Bonds vocal, "Quarter to Three" featured 14 children whooping it up in the studio and sounding for all the world like the most debauched human beings on the planet at that moment. To this Guida added five more overdubs of party ambience, and voila! A Number One record in '61. Succeeding singles—"School Is Out," "School Is In," "Dear Lady Twist"—were less successful variations on the formula, always lively but none as transcendent as "Quarter to Three." Bonds's last charted single, "Copy Cat," barely made it into the Top 100 in 1962; from that time until his re-emergence as a recording act nearly 20 years later, Bonds tirelessly worked the oldies circuit. It's a living.

Best of charts the high and low points of the Bonds-Guida axis, and also includes three previously unreleased tracks. The CD version contains four bonus tracks of little note, three being justifiably obscure singles, one the B side of "Dear Lady Twist." Bonds's 1981 album, *Dedication*, was co-produced by Springsteen and then–E Street Band guitarist Steve Van Zandt. — D.M.

BON JOVI
★★ **Bon Jovi (Mercury, 1984)**
★½ **7800° Fahrenheit (Mercury, 1985)**
★★★½ **Slippery When Wet (Mercury, 1986)**
★★ **New Jersey (Mercury, 1988)**
JON BON JOVI
★½ **Blaze of Glory (Mercury, 1990)**
Hard-rock hackwork of the most banal sort, Bon Jovi's output fused the crass popcraft of Journey and Starship with the average-Joe populism of Bruce Springsteen for a sound that hinted at rock & roll grandeur but delivered little more than empty flash. *Bon Jovi* and *7800° Fahrenheit* understand the basic formula, but offer little in the way of memorable material, sticking close to pop conventions like heartbreak lyrics and

strident, minor-key choruses. Bon Jovi is nearly redeemed by *Slippery When Wet*, an album that in its better moments—"You Give Love a Bad Name," "Wanted Dead or Alive"—delivers enough razzle-dazzle to make the band's shameless posturing semi-forgivable. Unfortunately, the band's massive sales instilled an even greater need in frontman-songwriter Jon Bon Jovi (born Bongiovi) to show how little success had changed him—hence the bombastic and overblown "street" sentiment of *New Jersey*. Bon Jovi the band went on hiatus after its fourth album, during which time Bon Jovi the singer released the solo album-cum-soundtrack *Blaze of Glory* (for the film *Young Guns II*), which updates "Wanted Dead or Alive" with its title tune but otherwise makes the Wild West sound suspiciously like East Jersey. — J.D.C.

THE BONZO DOG BAND
★★★½ **Best of the Bonzo Dog Band (Rhino, 1990)**
Before Monty Python, there was Bonzo. A remarkably inventive gang of wits, this late-'60s London quintet did twisted vaudeville, delivering custard-pie funny bits with an acid-era sense of the absurd. Lord Buckley and Lenny Bruce were among their influences; the satirical pieces of the Mothers of Invention provided an American parallel (although the Bonzos were far more cheery). Keeping close watch on the zeitgeist, the Bonzos sent up hippie preoccupations on "Kama Sutra" and "Can Blue Men Sing the Whites?"; Paul McCartney produced their 1968 hit, "I'm the Urban Spaceman." As is true of most comedy acts, the Dog Band's routines were uneven, but the Rhino anthology scores with surprising consistency. For one thing, the boys could really play their saxes, guitars and assorted devices; for another, their sheer intelligence transcends their period concerns. — P.E.

BOOGIE DOWN PRODUCTIONS
★★★ **Criminal Minded (1987; Sugar Hill, 1992)**
★★★ **By All Means Necessary (Jive, 1988)**
★★★★ **Ghetto Music: The Blueprint of Hip Hop (Jive/RCA, 1989)**
★★★½ **Edutainment (Jive/RCA, 1990)**
★★★★ **Live Hardcore Worldwide: Paris, London & NYC (Jive/RCA, 1991)**
★★★★ **Sex and Violence (Jive/RCA, 1992)**
For all their emphasis on education, BDP's albums tend to teach more about rap style and strategy than about history or politics.

That's not to demean rapper KRS-One's message or ideas, mind you, for he has a nimble mind. But what makes his raps worth hearing isn't what he has to say, so much as how he says it.

The independently released *Criminal Minded*, which paired KRS-One with DJ Scott LaRock, who was shot to death after the album's release, was a seminal album in the development of gangsta rap. It highlighted LaRock's eclectic scratching and sampling and sold 500,000 copies. "My Philosophy," from *By All Means Necessary*, plays off the aggressive, braggadocio of New York hardcore to pump power into its message, and ends up arguing that hardcore's glorification of violence is for chumps—a classic case of having-your-cake-and-eating-it-too, but effective nonetheless. Still, what's most interesting about the album isn't the way KRS-One spins variations on that theme, but the agility with which he incorporates rock and reggae influences into the music.

Even so, the album seems amateurish compared to *Ghetto Music*. Not only is the sound more inclusive, with tracks like "Breath Control" drawing on everything from jazz scratches to old-style "human beatbox" grooves, but the lyrics are more pointed, particularly the anti-brutality rap of "Who Protects Us From You?" *Edutainment*—the title combines "education" and "entertainment"—continues in that vein. But as strong and inventive as the beats are, KRS-One's proselytizing becomes the group's chief priority, a shift that adds fire to some tracks but leaves others sounding like sermons. Fortunately, *Live Hardcore Worldwide* avoids that problem, in part because the music emphasizes BDP's reggae roots, but mostly because KRS-One puts so much energy into engaging his audiences that the listener can't help but be drawn in.

And while *Sex and Violence* finds KRS-One devoting as much time to pugnacious putdowns as social criticism, the underlying wit of raps like "13 and Good" or "Who Are the Pimps?" keeps his harangues from becoming overbearing. — J.D.C.

JAMES BOOKER
★★★★ **New Orleans Piano Wizard: Live! (Rounder, 1981)**
★★★★ **Classified (Rounder, 1982)**
A classically trained pianist, the late James Booker bears a name spoken in New Orleans with the reverence reserved for native sons such as Louis Armstrong and Professor Longhair. Booker moved away

from classical and into gospel and blues by the time he was 12, when he landed his own radio program on New Orleans' WMRY; he made his first record when he was 14, for the Imperial label, with producer Dave Bartholomew. That led to an increasingly hectic schedule of session work for Crescent City artists, among them Fats Domino, some of whose recordings feature Booker's piano supporting Domino's vocal. After he graduated from high school, Booker began working on the road with Joe Tex, who was signed to Ace Records. Regular gigs as a sideman on Ace recordings ensued, as did a demanding touring schedule which at one point found Booker impersonating Huey "Piano" Smith because the latter hated to travel but had contractual commitments to play concerts outside of New Orleans. In 1960 Booker, recording for the Duke label, had a Top Ten R&B single with the instrumental "Gonzo," but didn't pursue a solo career; instead, he hit the road and stayed there for most of the next 15 years, working with a stellar cast of important R&B artists. In 1977 a promoter convinced Booker to perform a series of solo concerts in Europe. He was an instant success, and proceeded to cut three live albums and a studio album for the European market.

A heroin addict for many years, Booker was given to strange behavior that fueled his legend here and abroad. One night he is reputed to have pulled a gun onstage and threatened to shoot himself if customers didn't start filling up the tip jar. He was also known to interrupt his sets to lecture the audience about the evils of the C.I.A. He was so petulant about recording his *Classified* album that his producer and sax player finally forced him to sit at his instrument by lifting him bodily and placing him on his piano bench. Two days later he began playing.

Two Booker albums were released before his death from intestinal bleeding and heart and lung failure in November of 1983. In 1981 Rounder issued *New Orleans Piano Wizard: Live!*, recorded in Zurich, Switzerland, and originally released in Germany on the Gold Records label. Booker was as mischievous in performance as he was in private. Here, for instance, he offers "Something Stupid"—yes, the Frank and Nancy Sinatra song—as a march, but injects a quote from "Tea for Two" at the end before closing it out with a bombastic cadenza. But he could also get deep into material that touched him on a more fundamental level. His pained vocal on the

Percy Mayfield blues, "Please Send Me Someone to Love," has the feel of something pulled from a part of himself that outsiders rarely were allowed to see.

Given the tumultuous circumstances of its recording, *Classified*, Booker's first album for an American label, comes highly recommended for its intelligence and humor. Booker, the product of a long line of great New Orleans pianists, shows off the full panoply of styles at his command. Longhair in specific is honored with a "Professor Longhair Medley" comprised of "Bald Head"and "Tipitina"; the playing is jaunty, bluesy, evocative, searching; the medley itself is short, as Booker walked out in mid-song so that he could cash a check before the local bank closed. "King of the Road" may seem an unlikely choice, but Booker gives it an original spin. Reaching into the Sinatra canon again, Booker offers a poignant instrumental version of "Angel Eyes" that is a smooth melding of blues and classical influences. In another lifetime Booker might have been Jelly Roll Morton, pimp turned piano legend, and left a legacy as extensive as it is influential. These two albums will assure that Booker's influence extends to future generations, and there may be enough tall tales to turn him into a folk hero as well. — D.M.

BOOKER T. AND THE MG'S

★ ★ ★½ **Green Onions (1962; Atlantic, 1991)**

★ ★ ★ **Soul Dressing (1965; Atlantic, 1991)**

★ ★ ★ **And Now! Booker T. and the MG's (1966; Rhino/Atlantic, 1992)**

★ ★ ★½ **Back to Back (Stax, 1967)**

★ ★ ★ ★ **The Best of Booker T. and the MG's (Atlantic, 1968)**

★ ★ ★ **Doin' Our Thing (1968; Rhino/Atlantic, 1992)**

★ ★ ★½ **Hip Hug-Her (1968; Rhino/Atlantic, 1992)**

★ ★ ★ **Soul Limbo (Stax, 1968)**

★ ★ ★ **Uptight (Stax, 1968)**

★ ★ ★ **The Booker T. Set (Stax, 1969)**

★ ★ ★ **McLemore Avenue (Stax, 1970)**

★ ★ ★ **Melting Pot (Stax, 1971)**

★ ★ ★ ★ **Booker T. and the MG's Greatest Hits (Atlantic, 1974)**

★ ★ ★ **Memphis Sound (Warner Bros., 1975)**

★ ★ ★ **Union Extended (Warner Bros., 1976)**

★ ★ ★½ **Time Is Tight (Warner Bros., 1976)**

★ ★ ★ **Universal Language (Asylum, 1977)**
★ ★½ **Try and Love Again (A&M, 1978)**
Backing up Otis Redding and a host of Stax all-stars, Booker T. and the MG's were among the prime movers behind the Memphis Sound. Adamant in their insistence that less is more, each of the quartet's players was a virtuoso of a lean and startling efficiency. One of the inventors of funk guitar, Steve Cropper flourished rhythm work that formed a deft series of trebly, swift riffs; his lead lines were telegraphic and never flashy. An unorthodox player, Donald "Duck" Dunn seldom relied on the blues patterns of most R&B players—his bass, instead, provided essential punctuation. Drummer Al Jackson's spare drumming was soul music's counterpart to that of Rolling Stone Charlie Watts. Only Booker T. Jones himself, a teenage wunderkind when he started out at Stax, was a more expansive talent—and the eloquence of his organ lent the band's records an insinuating grace.

The MG's' '60s instrumentals are the band's masterworks. "Green Onions," "Hip Hug-Her," "Groovin' " and "Soul Limbo" are singles that can't be improved upon. All of the Stax records have worthwhile cuts; and each of the best-of compilations is timeless, elegant funk. — P.E.

BOOK OF LOVE
★ ★ ★½ **Book of Love (Sire, 1986)**
★ ★½ **Lullaby (Sire, 1988)**
★ ★ ★ **Candy Carol (Sire, 1991)**
With song titles like "Modigliani (Lost in Your Eyes)" and "Die Matrosen" and a sound that was equal parts Philip Glass and Giorgio Moroder, *Book of Love* was a promising idea that never quite panned out; it's really only worth owning on CD, on which its songs are fleshed out by club-savvy remixes that put some punch into the band's ideas. And though subsequent efforts had their moments—like *Lullaby*'s version of "Tubular Bells," or the childlike "Alice Everyday" from *Candy Carol*—Book of Love never quite understood that dance music is meant to move the body, not merely engage the mind. — J.D.C.

BOOMTOWN RATS
★ ★ ★ **A Tonic for the Troops (Columbia, 1978)**
★ ★½ **The Fine Art of Surfacing (Columbia, 1979)**
★ ★ **Mondo Bongo (Columbia, 1980)**
★ ★ ★ **Greatest Hits (Columbia, 1987)**
The Boomtown Rats were a decidedly middle-of-the-road Irish band that got caught up in the punk-rock media swirl of 1977. At least the group's deleted U.S. debut album, *The Boomtown Rats*, sports a couple of throat-grabbing rockers. In fact, the sardonic anti-anthem "Lookin' After No. 1" stands as lead singer and songwriter Bob Geldof's most penetrating (and catchiest) outburst. Switching record labels and hooking up with pop-metal producer "Mutt" Lange on *A Tonic for the Troops*, the Rats come off as Springsteen wannabes with a ominous bent for Queen-ly pomp overkill. Still, "Rat Trap" and "Joey's on the Street Again" (a repeat from the debut) kick up an acceptable head of steam, while "She's So Modern" should delight fans of the Elvis Costello–Joe Jackson school of manners. A former music journalist, Geldof does possess a striking way with words as well as a thin, nasal voice. On *Tonic*, he pulls off sarcastic ditties about Howard Hughes and Adolf Hitler without lapsing into cheap "punk" tastelessness.

"I Don't Like Mondays," a pointed ballad from the otherwise confused *The Fine Art of Surfacing*, does commit that lapse, however. It's hard to say what's more offensive about this 1979 FM novelty hit: the lyric's glib depiction of senseless violence (based on a then-contemporary incident in Los Angeles) or the cloying, string-laden orchestration. With the exception of the sprightly "Elephant Walk" from *Mondo Bongo*, the Rats were never quite able to follow up the flukey success of "Mondays" with another surefire hook. Two more tuneless stylistic grab bags followed: both *V Deep* (1982) and *In the Long Grass* (1985) are out of print. — M.C.

PAT BOONE
★ ★ **Best of Pat Boone (MCA, 1982)**
★ **Greatest Hits (Curb, 1990)**
It's difficult to work up much bile toward Pat Boone because he did make some good records and he's not nearly as loathsome as some '50s teen idols. But at no time has he ever been a rock & roll singer. This was apparent at the outset of his career when he recorded versions of "Ain't That a Shame," "At My Front Door (Crazy Little Mama)," "Tutti Frutti," "I Almost Lost My Mind" and "Long Tall Sally" that are so spectacularly awful they can only be considered novelty songs. What Boone could do passably was put over a ballad. He had a placid, smooth baritone voice, and given lush production he could hit his own

limited groove. "Love Letters in the Sand" has a certain *je ne sais quoi*, "April Love" is one of pop's grandest mushy moments and "Moody River" is a marvelous teenage death song. Even the theme song from the album *Friendly Persuasion* has an engaging sincerity to recommend it.

Those in need of a Pat Boone fix are advised to go for the MCA album, which contains the original versions of many of Boone's hits. The Curb record has one side of originals, and one side of dismal re-recordings. Boone has also cut a dozen-plus spiritual albums for the Lamb & Lion label. Wade into these at your own risk. — D.M.

BOO-YAA T.R.I.B.E.

★½ **New Funky Nation (4th & Broadway/Island, 1990)**

"Boo-yaa" is L.A. street slang for the sound a shotgun makes, and the Boo-Yaa T.R.I.B.E. is a Samoan rap sextet who like to boast that they've got "lyrics like a 12-gauge." Maybe so, but their aim needs work—apart from "Pickin' up Metal," which grounds its genre-joining rap with some metal funk, their scattershot attack is wide of the mark. — J.D.C.

BOSTON

★★★½ **Boston (Epic, 1976)**
★★½ **Don't Look Back (Epic, 1978)**
★★½ **Third Stage (MCA, 1987)**

After painstakingly experimenting in his basement studio for years, Boston guitarist and MIT-trained engineer Tom Scholz channeled his frustrations into a song called "More Than a Feeling." This 1976 pop Top Ten ushers in the long, cold winter of arena rock; Boston's soaring combination of high-tech metal guitar punch and smooth pop vocal hooks quickly became the cornerstone of Album Oriented Radio. But as slick as it sounds, "More Than a Feeling" also strikes an uncommonly resonant emotional note.

In retrospect, it's a classic one-shot-to-glory tale. Only problem is, Boston went on to make two far less distinctive and even more popular albums. *Boston* itself sports two satisfying, if similar followups ("Peace of Mind" and "Hitch a Ride"), alongside a couple of cleaned-up boogie crowd-pleasers ("Smokin' " and "Rock & Roll Band"). The title track of *Don't Look Back* would hold its own on the debut, but Boston's formulaic virtuosity dulls rather quickly. Perhaps Scholz realized this; he retired for nine years after the second album. When the

long-delayed *Third Stage* finally saw the light of day, the Boston concept seemed a little musty. That didn't stop "Amanda" from climbing to the top of the charts, of course. — M.C.

ANNE RICHMOND BOSTON

★★★½ **The Big House of Time (DB, 1991)**

Songwriter-guitarist Jeff Calder's gothic humor and impressive craft made the albums of Atlanta's Swimming Pool Q's a rare delight—but the most richly musical of that band's pleasures was Anne Richmond Boston's singing. With a precision recalling that of Fairport Convention's Sandy Denny (mixed with some of Grace Slick's power), Boston flourished a genuine interpretive skill. On her solo debut, that skill is lavished on remarkable material—Boston's take on John Sebastian's "Darling Be Home Soon" rivals Joe Cocker's contrasting version of that fine ballad (Anne's elegance exactly counters Joe's fever); her remake of Neil Young's "When You Dance I Can Really Love" soars. Helped out by guitarist-writer-coproducer Rob Gal (an Atlanta alternative-scene hero), Boston is also commanding on the album's orginals ("The Soul Side of Your Mind" is cosmic mood music that is all the stronger for its absolute lack of irony)—she comes on, in fact, as a veteran so assured that both force and subtlety fall easily within her grasp. — P.E.

DAVID BOWIE

★★ **David Bowie (Mercury, 1967)**
★★½ **Space Oddity (1970; Rykodisc, 1990)**
★★★ **The Man Who Sold the World (1970; Rykodisc, 1990)**
★★★★ **Hunky Dory (1971; Rykodisc, 1990)**
★★★½ **The Rise and Fall of Ziggy Stardust and the Spiders From Mars (1972; Rykodisc, 1990)**
★★★½ **Aladdin Sane (1973; Rykodisc, 1990)**
★★★ **Pin Ups (1973; Rykodisc, 1990)**
★★ **Diamond Dogs (1974; Rykodisc, 1990)**
★★½ **David Live (1974; Rykodisc, 1990)**
★★½ **Young Americans (1975; Rykodisc, 1990)**
★★★★ **Station to Station (1976; Rykodisc, 1990)**
★★★★ **Changesonebowie (1976; Rykodisc, 1990)**
★★★½ **Low (1977; Rykodisc, 1991)**
★★★★ **Heroes (1978; Rykodisc, 1991)**
★★★ **Stage (1978; Rykodisc, 1991)**

★ ★ ★ ★   **Lodger (1979; Rykodisc, 1991)**
★ ★ ★½   **Scary Monsters (1980; Rykodisc, 1991)**
★ ★ ★   **Changestwobowie (RCA, 1981)**
★ ★½   **Let's Dance (EMI America, 1983)**
★ ★   **Tonight (EMI America, 1983)**
★ ★   **Never Let You Down (EMI America, 1987)**
★ ★ ★ ★   **Sound + Vision (Rykodisc, 1989)**
★ ★ ★ ★   **Changesbowie (Rykodisc, 1990)**
★ ★ ★   **David Bowie: Early On (1964–1966) (Rhino, 1991)**

TIN MACHINE

★ ★½   **Tin Machine (EMI America, 1989)**
★ ★½   **Tin Machine II (EMI America, 1991)**

David Bowie's imagination, impact and influence changed the face of rock & roll in the '70s. His actual music is only part of the story, though. Bowie perfected the pop art of image-brokering, while introducing a brazen theatrical element and exaggerated fashion sense to the dowdy, pot-dazed counterculture. "Turn and face the strange ch-ch-changes," he insists at the outset of *Hunky Dory* (1971). "Changes" plots the trajectory of a fascinatingly inconsistent career; until the '80s, at least, David Bowie's ambitious output was never boring. When rock needed a shove in a fresh direction, this *agent provocateur* somehow managed to be in the right place at the right time.

The young David Jones played in a couple of mod-era bands before changing his name; the first two albums contain his earliest attempts at a Dylanesque stance—"man of words, man of music" (the original title for *Space Oddity*). Recorded several years before the title track became a hit, *Space Oddity* marks the emergence of a different beast, a slippery rock & roll chameleon. Aside from the alien resonance of "Space Oddity," the album flounders amid indistinct writing and playing. *The Man Who Sold the World* suffers from a murky overall sound (even on CD), but guitarist Mick Ronson's power-chord sting connects with Bowie's emerging persona(s) on the title track, "Black Country Rock" and the perverse epic "Width of a Circle."

Hunky Dory takes Bowie's sexual ambiguity and runs with it. He hasn't completely donned the entertainer's mask yet; there are flashes of humanity, like "Kooks" (a touching song for his son) on this breathlessly eclectic whirlwind. Bowie tips his hat to forefathers Lou Reed ("Queen Bitch") and Andy Warhol ("Andy Warhol"), while "Changes" and "Oh, You Pretty Things" herald the coming of a confused, flamboyant post-hippie style glitter.

Next: An alien being comes to earth and forms a rock band, in order to warn the humanoids that self-immolation is nigh. The plot from some forgotten made-for-TV movie? No, it's *The Rise and Fall of Ziggy Stardust and the Spiders From Mars*! Like most rock concept albums, *Ziggy* is burdened by its pretensions. When the Mick Ronson–propelled band gets to ride the throttle, Bowie reveals an ironic flair for flat-out rockers like "Suffragette City" and "Hang on to Yourself." But too often, his melodramatic crooning sounds mannered and blank. The grueling set piece "Rock 'n' Roll Suicide" suggests the cabaret hack Anthony Newley gone glam-decadent.

Aladdin Sane proves David Bowie isn't a total poseur; the gut-bucket guitar riffs on "Panic in Detroit" and "The Jean Genie" kick in with vicious urgency. The churning Keith Richards–style rhythms of "Watch That Man" almost make up for the fey excesses of "Cracked Actor" and "Time." *Pin Ups* picks up where *Aladdin Sane*'s cover of "Let's Spend the Night Together" leaves off; if Bowie's mostly faithful versions of British Invasion classics pale in comparison with the originals, his mostly teenage cult was too young to know or care about the difference. For many, *Pin Ups* was an invaluable history lesson.

Save for the electrifying "Rebel Rebel," *Diamond Dogs* represents the leaden nadir of Bowie's science-fiction trip. Without Mick Ronson's tuneful interaction, his anti-utopian vision turns ugly and exhausting. *David Live* catches the fakir in a rare transitory phase, on the move from swinging London to Soulful Philadelphia. "Young Americans" gracefully completes that journey; the naive, celebratory lyrics seem gushingly heartfelt by Bowie's previous standards. Somewhat predictably, the accompanying album gets bogged down by uncertain singing and stiff grooves. But once again, Bowie's basic instincts turned out to be provocative—Ziggy fanatics were *pissed*—and also prescient. By the time the disco fad hit full-force, just a couple of years later, Bowie was already doing something completely different.

Station to Station ushers in Bowie's most fecund and increasingly less commercial period. If the title track's chilly grandeur hasn't aged well, the eerie, compelling man-machine groove of "TVC15" has only deepened with time. Gradually dropping the stagey emphasis, Bowie now approaches the serious, rarefied level of art-rock with consuming intensity. Collaborating with self-schooled technology maven Brian Eno, Bowie fashions a complex, yet somehow organic-sounding trilogy with *Low, Heroes* and *Lodger*. The first two albums evenly divide between shimmering pop-song experiments and rambling "ambient" instrumentals, but fully realized tracks like *Low*'s "Sound and Vision" and the title track from *Heroes* calmly bridge the chasm between rock's old avant-garde and its bold new wave.

Lodger puts Eno's minimalistic strategies to work on perhaps the most personal songs Bowie has ever recorded. *Lodger* isn't a concept album per se, but nearly every song reflects an utterly believable restlessness of spirit. A perceptive sensibility forever caught between creeping alienation and the seductive allure of the open road: *Lodger*'s fascinating thumbnail sketch is as close to the real David Bowie as we're likely to get.

Scary Monsters summarizes Bowie's progress through the decade he helped to define. Some of the lesser numbers are surprisingly standard, but the resonantly cynical "Ashes to Ashes" neatly updates "Space Oddity" and brings Bowie's strange saga to a satisfying conclusion. Ah, if only . . . the transition from maverick to elder statesman has been a particularly difficult one for David Bowie. Perhaps it's an impossible makeover; Bowie's '80s albums echo with automatic, hollow professionalism. They're devoid of even camp appeal. The functional *Let's Dance* gets over thanks to producer Nile Rodgers's funky touch and Iggy Pop's bittersweet "China Girl." And at least Bowie bothers to go through the motions; *Tonight* sounds like a computer simulation of *au courant* Bowie product, while *Never Let You Down* stoops to lazy self-cannibalization. And while Bowie's current guitar-dominated "band project" rebounds from his witless mid-'80s alliance with Peter Frampton, nothing on Tin Machine's two albums will surprise anybody who's paid even marginal attention to the last ten years of "edgy" rock; both albums are long on thunder and short on actual tunes. Guitarist Reeves Gabrels is an adept but humorless guitar technician. On *Tin Machine II*, every track builds to a flat anti-climax. There are no killer riffs or stuttering choruses here, just gentlemanly avant-garde competence. Bowie imitations have become so commonplace that Bowie himself can't get away with it anymore.

Rykodisc's reissues of the RCA albums are models of historical accuracy and technological care; many include timely archival tracks and B sides. Bowie's various albums are matters of individual taste, but the flawless greatest-hits package *Changesonebowie* is essential to any rock & roll collection both as '70s documentary and '80s blueprint. The more expensive *Sound + Vision* package is a must for Bowie-philes. — M.C.

BOW WOW WOW

★★★ **Your Cassette Pet (EMI Harvest, 1980)**
★★½ **See Jungle! See Jungle! Go Join Your Gang Yeah, City All Over! Go Ape Crazy! (RCA, 1981)**
★★ **The Last of the Mohicans (EP) (RCA, 1982)**
★½ **I Want Candy (RCA, 1982)**
★★★ **12 Original Recordings (Capitol, 1982)**
★ **When the Going Gets Tough the Tough Get Going (RCA, 1983)**

This being Malcolm McLaren's first big project after the Sex Pistols finally imploded, the erstwhile media manipulator made sure Bow Wow Wow bounded onto the scene with a whole gaggle of gimmicks. The first was Annabella Lwin, a 14-year-old Burmese immigrant McLaren found working in a laundry and decided to remake into a post-punk goddess. Then there was what used to be Adam's Ants, the trio of Matthew Ashman (guitar), Leroy Gorman (bass) and Dave Barbarossa (drums), whom McLaren introduced to African music—specifically, the sound of Burundi tribal drumming—then induced to dump Adam and follow him.

But it was the product that ultimately pulled the package together. Bow Wow Wow's cassette-only first single, a home-taping anthem called "C-30, C-60, C-90 Go!," had little going for it musically—a basic Burundi beat groove topped with a chant-along vocal—but made quite a stink when it hit the charts smack in the middle of the British Phonograph Industry's "Home taping is killing music" campaign. No surprise, then, that the group's first album, *Your Cassette Pet* (on cassette only), was almost pure provocation, filled with such nudge-wink nasties as "Uomo Sex al Apache" (say it real fast) and "Sexy Eiffel Towers" (a tribute to the famous Gallic phallic symbol). But between the boys' vigorous rhythm work and Annabella's charming vocals, even the likes of "Louis Quatorze"—in which Annabella breathily recounts her ravishings by the beastly Louis—seems more silly than scandalous.

Much the same can be said for the impossibly titled *See Jungle! See Jungle!*, which introduced the group to this country. But American pop radio proved less-than-enamored of McLaren's recastings of Rousseau ("Go Wild in the Country") and McLuhan ("[I'm a] T.V. Savage"), so RCA turned the Bows over to a proven hitmaker: Kenny Laguna, who converted the band's Burundi beat into a jazzy Bo Diddley groove and gave it a near-hit single with a remake of the Strangeloves' "I Want Candy." *The Last of the Mohicans* includes the single and three others, but since all four tracks also appear on *I Want Candy*, the only reason to seek it out is its cover photo, which finds an unclothed Annabella posed with the rest of the band in McLaren's last art-school joke: A recreation of Manet's "Le Déjeuner sur l'herbe."

I Want Candy did well enough to encourage Capitol to issue *12 Original Recordings*, an LP-edition of *Your Cassette Pet* and the band's first British singles. But *Candy*'s lack of material—half its tracks are remakes of earlier recordings—and spiritless performances marked the beginning of the end for the band. By the time the McLaren-less group got around to cutting the slick, empty *When the Going Gets Tough*, smart listeners knew to get going.   — J.D.C.

THE BOX TOPS

★ ★ ★ ★ **Greatest Hits (Rhino, 1982)**
The Box Tops' three late-'60s mega-smashes were recipes for radio glory. "The Letter" crossed thumping bass and bubblegum organ with nifty jet sound effects; "Cry Like a Baby" featured fake sitar; "Soul Deep" was straight, simple, white R&B. Behind them all was the Memphis band's main ingredient: the gruff perfection of Alex Chilton's voice. Elevating even strange pap like "I Met Her in Church," breathing an air of intimacy into "Neon Rainbow" or meaning into "Sweet Cream Ladies," Chilton was best at going broke for drama (his version of Dylan's "I Shall Be Released" fails due to its curious restraint). After three years of spotty success, the Box Tops broke up—and Chilton became a cult legend (especially for his subsequent work with Big Star). As a singles band, the Tops' appeal is presented ably on Rhino's greatest-hits set.   — P.E.

BOY GEORGE

★ **Sold (Virgin, 1987)**
★ **High Hat (Virgin, 1989)**
★ **The Martyr Mantras (Virgin, 1991)**

Perhaps the only thing worse than a washed-up pop star is one who tries to make a career of being washed up, a situation that pretty well sums up the post-Culture Club recordings of Boy George. Still, as annoying as his "poor, poor, pitiful me" act gets through *Sold*—which, with "Where Are You Now" and "Next Time," blames his troubles on the press—or *High Hat*, which finds him coyly alluding to his drug problems with "You Are My Heroin," at least the music—a club-savvy gloss on contemporary R&B grooves—is semi-bearable. Not so *The Martyr Mantras*, which offers a version of acid house so obtuse that any hint of melody is probably a hallucination.
   — J.D.C.

BILLY BRAGG

★ ★ ★ ★   **Back to Basics (Elektra, 1987)**
★ ★ ★ ★   **Talking With the Taxman About Poetry (Elektra, 1986)**
★ ★ ★   **Help Save the Youth of America (Elektra, 1988)**
★ ★ ★½   **Workers Playtime (Elektra, 1988)**
★ ★ ★½   **The Internationale (Elektra, 1990)**
★ ★ ★ ★   **Don't Try This at Home (Elektra, 1991)**

Don't call Bragg a folk singer unless you understand that the term says less about his musical roots (the Clash) than his principal interest: that is, average folk like you and me. Indeed, it's his overriding sense of humanity that puts the heart in his love songs, the sparkle in his social sketches, and keeps even his most stridently ideological material from turning into harangues.

These qualities can be found in their rawest form on *Back to Basics*, a 21-song album compiling all of Bragg's first three U.K. releases *(Life's a Riot With Spy Vs. Spy, Brewing Up With Billy Bragg* and *Between the Wars)*. Recorded for the most part with little more than Bragg's electric guitar behind his rough-hewn vocals, the best of these songs—"The Milkman of Human Kindness," "A New England," "Love Gets Dangerous," "Which Side Are You On"—are tuneful and affecting. Nor does *Talking With the Taxman About Poetry* add much in the way of accompaniment, but that hardly keeps Bragg from pulling a sense of drama from "Levi Stubbs' Tears" or lending "Ideology" the sort of power-chord majesty associated with bands like the Who.

Bragg begins to move toward a full-band sound with *Workers Playtime*, an album that bears the subtitle "Capitalism Is Killing Music." (If you think Bragg doesn't see the joke in having such a legend on a major-label release, you underestimate his sense of humor.) As usual, the love songs are well-drawn and emotionally involving, but the political tunes—particularly the country-ish "Rotting on Remand"—have the edge melodically. That's also the case with *The Internationale,* although Bragg can't take credit, since most of these songs are well-known anthems. *Don't Try This at Home* is easily the most accessible of Bragg's albums, with love songs ("Moving the Goalposts," "You Woke Up My Neighbourhood," "Sexuality") that are winning and witty, and issue songs ("God's Footballer," "North Sea Bubble") that suck the listener in with melody before springing their message.   — J.D.C.

THE BRAINS

★ ★ ★　The Brains (Mercury, 1980)
★ ★　Electronic Eden (Mercury, 1981)
★ ★ ★ ★　Dancing Under Streetlights (EP)
　　(Landslide, 1982)

"Money Changes Everything," the indie single that earned this Atlanta quartet its reputation and recording contract, is a classic new-wave single, full of anger, resignation and insight, not to mention great hooks. Cyndi Lauper cleaned the song up and nearly got a hit out of it, but it's the version on *The Brains*—raw, rapturous and murderously intense—that truly captures its spirit. And though little else on the album quite matches that burst of melodic inspiration, the mood evoked by the band's synth-and-guitar sound manages to convey whatever the songs themselves forget to say. With *Electric Eden,* singer-keyboardist Tom Gray pushes his synths further up in the mix, and while that might have seemed suitably modern at the time, it leaves the album sounding dated while underscoring the weakness of the writing. Mercury pulled the plug soon after, but the Brains made one last stand anyway. Ironically, *Dancing Under Streetlights* is probably the group's best (although least-heard) work, featuring four songs that maintain a sense of thematic unity while summarizing everything that was admirable about the band's sound. Worth hearing if only for the hauntingly urgent "Tanya."   — J.D.C.

BRAND NUBIAN

★ ★　One for All (Elektra, 1990)

When James Brown pleads "take it to the bridge," it's a do-or-die situation. That expert display of tension-and-release defines the funk. Brand Nubian displays a knack for tasty sampling on its debut, latching on to some slippery, bass-thumping grooves. But *One for All* is bogged down by pedantic rapping ("Dance to My Ministry") and a complete absence of musical resolution. *One for All* clocks in at just under an hour; it only feels like forever.   — M.C.

BRAVE COMBO

★ ★½　Musical Varieties (Rounder, 1987)
★½　Polkatharsis (Rounder, 1987)
★ ★　Humansville (Rounder, 1988)
★ ★　A Night on Earth (Rounder, 1990)

Why is it that whenever musical wiseguys want to prove how funny they are, they play a polka? In the case of Brave Combo, "camp" seems to be the answer. Like 3 Mustaphas 3, the Combo has a weakness for worldbeat arcana, and *Musical Varieties* (which compiles selections from the group's earliest albums) goes for guffaws with stunts like a version of the Doors' "People Are Strange" done as a "psychedelic hora," as well as something called "O Holy Night Cha Cha Cha." Ironically, the group's one attempt at polka legitimacy, *Polkatharsis,* is flatter than day-old beer.   — J.D.C.

ANTHONY BRAXTON

★ ★ ★ ★ ★　Three Compositions of New
　　　　Jazz (1968; Delmark, 1989)
★ ★ ★ ★　For Alto (1969; Delmark, 1990)
★ ★ ★ ★　In the Tradition, Vol. 1 (Inner
　　　　City, 1974)
★ ★ ★ ★　In the Tradition, Vol. 2 (Inner
　　　　City, 1976)
★ ★ ★ ★ ★　Creative Orchestra Music 1976
　　　　(1976; Bluebird, 1987)
★ ★ ★ ★　Anthony Braxton Live (1976;
　　　　Bluebird, 1988)
★ ★ ★ ★　Alto Saxophone Improvisations
　　　　(Arista, 1979)
★ ★ ★½　Open Aspects '82 (Hat Art,
　　　　1982)
★ ★ ★½　Six Compositions for Quartet
　　　　(Antilles, 1982)
★ ★ ★ ★　Composition 113 (PolyGram
　　　　Imports, 1984)
★ ★ ★ ★　Seven Standards 1985, Vol. I
　　　　(Magenta/Windham Hill, 1985)
★ ★ ★ ★　Seven Standards 1985, Vol. II
　　　　(Magenta/Windham Hill, 1986)
★ ★ ★ ★　Six Monk's Compositions (1987;
　　　　Black Saint, 1988)

While Anthony Braxton's expert readings of Clifford Brown and Paul Robeson pieces on *Seven Standards, Vol. I* and of John Coltrane, Thelonious Monk and Charlie Parker works on *Vol. II* demonstrate unequivocally his mastery of jazz that's recognizable to the conventional listener, this saxophonist is best known as a monster of the avant-garde. Unabashedly intellectual, Braxton has committed his daunting musical theories to print—the combined eight volumes of *Tri-Axium Writing* and *Composition Notes*—and the sounds those texts explicate has generally been just as challenging as his prose.

The double-album *For Alto* (1969) is early Braxton, unaccompanied, intense and, for all but the most fearless "free jazz" follower, well-nigh inscrutable. By the time of *The Complete Braxton* (a 1971 Arista recording, now out of print), the composer, in league with Chick Corea, Barry Altschul and Dave Holland, had incorporated the influence of such modern European titans as Stockhausen, Schoenberg and Varése—and was beginning to work in the orchestral idiom. *Creative Orchestra Music 1976* is the triumph of that style; it's sweeping, colorful and overwhelmingly ambitious. Both *Six Compositions for Quartet* (1982) and *Open Aspects '82* offer pieces that can be enjoyed by non-musicologists—but it's important to note that Braxton is always demanding: his fusion of post-Ornette Coleman jazz and contemporary classical music finds a rough match in the sensibility of the equally intimidating Cecil Taylor, and it's not for audiophiles wedded to any traditional understanding of melody or rhythm.
— P.E.

BREAD
★ ★　 **Bread (Elektra, 1969)**
★ ★　 **On the Water (Elektra, 1970)**
★ ★½ **Manna (Elektra, 1971)**
★ ★½ **Baby I'm A-Want You (Elektra, 1972)**
★ ★ ★　 **Guitar Man (Elektra, 1972)**
★ ★ ★½ **The Best of Bread (Elektra, 1973)**
Middle-of-the road schlock for hippies, right? Well, no. Those easy-listening hits—"Baby I'm-A-Want You," "Make It With You" and "Everything I Own"—dig in their hooks quietly and effectively. Singer-songwriter David Gates wields a true studio craftsman's touch, but what really sets Bread apart is his choice of subject matter. The above-mentioned songs trace the steady pressures and rewards of a marriage with sensitive, steady hands. *The Best of Bread* flags badly after its first half, and that's telling: the original albums fill out great singles with awkward-sounding rock attempts. *Guitar Man* contains this group's last sweet gasp before "trucking" (as one song puts it) off toward golden-oldies oblivion. A graft of that title track, "Aubrey" and "Sweet Surrender" would improve *Best of Bread* considerably. At its best, though, Bread celebrates the simplest pleasures of Top Forty pop in a manner that's both adult and contemporary.
— M.C.

BREATHE
★½ **All That Jazz (A&M, 1987)**
★　 **Peace of Mind (A&M, 1990)**
If you ever have trouble understanding why the English think George Michael is a great soul singer, simply give this stuff a listen. *All That Jazz*, which, astonishingly, produced three Top Ten singles, is pleasantly inoffensive, specializing in a pallid balladry that puts a limp gloss of soul mannerisms over an easy-listening melody ("Hands to Heaven" is typical). The result is to real R&B as Cheez Whiz is to Cheddar. Still, at least *All That Jazz* had hits, such as they were; *Peace of Mind* tries to get by merely on mood, and ends up sounding like Wham! if Andrew Ridgely been the group's creative genius. — J.D.C.

EDIE BRICKELL AND NEW BOHEMIANS
★ ★ ★　 **Shooting Rubberbands at the Stars (Geffen, 1988)**
★ ★ ★½ **Ghost of a Dog (Geffen, 1990)**
An archetypal college-radio band, New Bohemians woke up in the big leagues with the 1988 success of "What I Am," an engagingly loping single that highlighted Brickell's coy vocals and wide-eyed musings. Their first album was self-conscious folk-rock, with jazzy guitar riffs and twists adding ambitious touches of class. *Ghost of a Dog* grooves a bit harder, with a number like "Black & Blue" sounding semi-tough, but the songs remain canvases for Brickell's aural versions of winsome finger painting. Her tentative voice swoops over the material with a fetching daring, but too often her cuteness catches up with her—on "Oak Cliff Bra" she displays such a sticky-sweet persona that she makes Melanie, Brickell's true flower-power precursor, sound as deep and dark as Schopenhauer. — P.E.

BRINSLEY SCHWARZ
★ ★ ★　 **Brinsley Schwarz (Capitol, 1970)**
★ ★ ★½ **Despite It All (Capitol, 1970)**
★ ★ ★½ **Silver Pistol (1971; Edsel, 1986)**
★ ★ ★½ **Nervous on the Road (United Artists, 1972)**
★ ★ ★　 **Please Don't Ever Change (United Artists, 1973)**

★ ★ ★ ★ **Original Golden Greats (United Artists, 1974)**
★ ★ ★ ★ **Fifteen Thoughts of Brinsley Schwarz (United Artists, 1978)**

Named after its lead guitar player, Brinsley Schwarz was a London-based band that emulated a Hollywood band (the Byrds) who were busy trying to sound like Nashville cats. Go figure: It actually works, more often than not. Lots of other styles float around on the murky debut, *Brinsley Schwarz*, but the band's blend of unlikely country roots and solid folk & roll momentum takes hold on the next three albums. "Surrender to the Rhythm," in this case, isn't just an empty command. Though the acoustic-based buzz is a mellow one, the group's economical attack and bassist Nick Lowe's wry melodic edge prefigured some of the decade's more adventurous musical activities. (Lowe went on to produce Graham Parker and Elvis Costello, while Schwarz and keyboardist Bob Andrews later founded Parker's backing band, the Rumour.) These deserving, if low-key records went largely unnoticed in the United States. Both hits collections (*Golden Greats* or *15 Thoughts*) come highly recommended.
— M.C.

GARTH BROOKS

★ ★ ★ **Garth Brooks (Capitol, 1989)**
★ ★½ **No Fences (Capitol, 1990)**
★ ★ **Ropin' the Wind (Capitol, 1991)**

Oklahoma native Garth Brooks, whose mother was one of the singers on Red Foley's TV show in the mid-'50s, has achieved a degree of popular appeal rivalled only by older, established artists such as Johnny Cash and Willie Nelson—but Cash and Nelson never sold records like Garth Brooks sells records, nor have they been the across-the-board concert draw Brooks has been. In fact, his meteoric rise and staggering record sales are beginning to evoke comparisons to Elvis Presley and the Beatles.

Would that Brooks warranted such raves. As a writer (or co-writer, most often) he's shown only minor progress. *Garth Brooks* promises a great deal: "If Tomorrow Never Comes" is moving because it expresses important feelings and does so without gratuitous adornment. Time has shown this to be a glitch in an otherwise unremarkable portfolio. And then there's the matter of Brooks's singing, which has grown calculated to the point where some of his songs are unlistenable. The tics—the catch in the throat, the way he moves up and

down within his limited register, the clipped words that fall away into sadness—came across as sincere and heartfelt on the two best songs from his first album, "If Tomorrow Never Comes" and "The Dance"; but by the time *No Fences* came around, Brooks was sounding like a self-pitying parody of Ernest Tubb, the overrated "Friends in Low Places" being a prime example of vocal schtick run amuck.

Stylistically Brooks comes from many places, but mostly from the marketplace. He folds in a little honky-tonk, a little rock & roll, bows to wimpy '70s singer–songwriters like Dan Fogelberg, adds some pedal steel and calls it country. But Brooks's music is an approximation of the real thing. On aesthetic and historical grounds, these records must be deemed risky business.
— D.M.

BIG BILL BROONZY

★ ★ ★ ★ **Feelin' Low Down (GNP Crescendo, 1973)**
★ ★ ★ ★ ★ **Good Time Tonight (Columbia, 1990)**
★ ★ ★ ★ ★ **The Young Big Bill Broonzy 1928–1935 (Yazoo, 1991)**

An important transitional link between acoustic country blues and electrified urban blues, Big Bill Broonzy made first-rate recordings in both modes and wrote over 300 songs before his death in 1958. Sharecropping and music were his mealtickets when he was growing up in the rural South, but he relocated in the '20s to Chicago where he pursued music full time, although he continued to move back and forth between country and city over the years. In Chicago he began recording, and almost immediately became one of the Windy City's best-known blues artists. National recognition came in 1938, when Broonzy appeared at New York's Carnegie Hall as a replacement for Robert Johnson, who had died of poisoning, on John Hammond's "From Spirituals to Swing" concert. He worked steadily around Chicago through the 1940s before being discovered by a newly emerging folk audience in lower Manhattan and being embraced as an authentic country blues man, despite his years of recordings made with small combos.

A laid-back vocalist whose rich voice moved easily from a world-weary moan to a mellow, sanguine tone, Broonzy supported his singing with a guitar style that was less rhythmically complex than that of his Delta peers but packed plenty of emotion in its spare commentary. More than any guitarist of his time, Broonzy made effective use of silence as a dramatic device in his music, sometimes using only a few strong, angular retorts to punctuate key lyric sections. His peak years are well-documented on the Yazoo and Columbia collections. The former features primarily solo acoustic or duet recordings from 1928 to 1935, while the latter offers both acoustic and combo recordings spanning the years 1930 to 1940. Those who doubt that the line between country music and country blues is exceedingly thin need listen to Broonzy's "I Can't Be Satisfied," a 1930 recording (available on the Yazoo and Columbia albums) that is the model for one of Ernest Tubb's best-known early hits, "You Nearly Lose Your Mind," recorded in 1942. GNP Crescendo's *Feelin' Low Down* is a set of acoustic sides, raw and potent, but lacking any dates or session information. Apart from that oversight, the record's 14 cuts are vintage Broonzy in many moods on songs ranging from his own moving originals (notably "Big Bill Blues" and "Lonesome Road Blues") to stirring covers of the traditional folk song "John Henry" and Leroy Carr's "In the Evening." — D.M.

BROTHERS FOUR
★ ★ **Greatest Hits (Columbia, 1962)**
The members of this clean-cut quartet from Seattle met as fraternity brothers at the University of Washington, started performing together at campus clubs, and landed a recording contract. Their 1960 debut single, the melancholy "Greenfields," was their biggest hit, but they remained prolific in the studio through the mid-'60s and were popular with apolitical hootenanny crowds. Though nominally folk artists, the Brothers disdained the sort of social commentary being advanced by Bob Dylan, Joan Baez, Tom Paxton, Phil Ochs and other Woody Guthrie acolytes; they were, in fact, an extension of the bland, white '50s pop quartets, although even the Ames Brothers and the Four Aces could summon genuine feeling from time to time and had better material to boot. — D.M.

BOBBY BROWN
★ ★½ **King of Stage (MCA, 1986)**
★ ★ ★ ★½ **Don't Be Cruel (MCA, 1988)**
★ ★ ★ **Dance . . . Ya Know It! (MCA, 1989)**
Brown was the first member of New Edition to go solo, and the first to find the path

from New Jack cool to crossover stardom, but his success has been less a matter of personal vision than finding the right production team. After all, *King of Stage* relies on many of the same elements that drove *Don't Be Cruel*, from the rap interlude in "Baby, I Wanna Tell You Something" to the scratch-heavy hip-hop rhythms of the title tune, yet none of the selections have any of the second album's spark. Why not? A lot of it had to do with the production. *Stage*, for instance, relied on the likes of Larry Blackmon and John Luongo to provide its street credibility, and though those two delivered the groove, they left the melody to Brown—who, lamentably, has neither the power nor personality to add much to their tunes. *Cruel*, on the other hand, completely envelops Brown in the production. For instance, "My Prerogative" (produced by Gene Griffin) pumps its Teddy Riley groove to the max, pushing Brown's vocals into place with effortless efficiency; likewise, the L.A. and Babyface tunes—"Every Little Step," "Roni," "Don't Be Cruel"—use Brown's voice as just a well-oiled cog in a pop-savvy machine. In both cases, though Brown's singing is superb, it's invariably the backing tracks that carry the day—an impression the remix album *Dance! . . . Ya Know It!* simply reinforces. — J.D.C.

BUSTER BROWN
★ ★ ★½ **New King of the Blues (Collectables, NA)**
Georgia-born Buster Brown began his career playing the harmonica and singing the blues in Southern backwoods joints in the early '50s. Later that decade he moved to New York City and started working the club circuit, which led to a recording contract with Fire Records. His first single, a raucous, wall of sound blowout called "Fannie Mae," hit the Top Fifty. That was his only hit, but it has remained a staple of oldies radio. Contrary to the title of this album, Buster Brown was never the king of the blues, but he had a husky, gospel shouter's voice and an unfailing sense of humor. And he played drop-dead harmonica. This record is nothing if not lively great and timeless bar band music. — D.M.

CHARLES BROWN
★ ★ ★ ★ **One More for the Road (1986; Alligator, 1989)**
★ ★ ★ ★ **All My Life (Bullseye Blues/ Rounder, 1990)**

Late night, lights down low, bottle of wine at hand, someone to dream with, and Charles Brown, blues elegance personified—now there's a scenario suitable for any true romantic. Blues and R&B have had any number of outstanding boudoir vocalists, but Charles Brown has always brought a special warmth and engaging personality to his efforts, and thus carved for himself an exalted place among his peers, if not among the general public. He had his first hit in 1945, while a member of Johnny Moore and the Three Blazers; the song, "Driftin' Blues," which Brown wrote in high school, catapulted the group to fame. He also wrote and recorded a seasonal standard, "Merry Christmas, Baby," which is delivered in a verbal slow burn that is as cutting as it is pained. It too is a blues classic, but to many tastes the definitive version was cut by Elvis Presley. Nevertheless, Brown's approach to a lyric has influenced some of the most important singers of succeeding generations, including Sam Cooke, Ray Charles, and Little Richard. Brown has recorded sporadically over the years, despite continuing to perform regularly in night clubs throughout the States. *One More for the Road* is Alligator's 1989 reissue of a 1986 album released on the Blue Side label. Here Brown explores a typical potpourri of songs, not the least being a couple of his own (the album's slow grooving opener, "I Cried Last Night," is particularly strong) as well as songs otherwise associated with Frank Sinatra, Charlie Rich and Nat King Cole. Whatever the source material, it all comes out blues, and Brown has few rivals when it comes to making a listener feel a lyric. Brown's 1990 release, *All My Life,* is another smooth, assured effort showing the artist's interpretive powers not only undiminished by time, but more resonant, more nuanced, more informed by harsh experience.

Fans should also look for the now-deleted *Driftin' Blues* album issued on Mainstream. In addition to "Driftin' Blues," it contains moving, low-key interpretations of "Our Day Will Come," "Days of Wine and Roses," "More," and—get this—"Go Away Little Girl." — D.M.

JAMES BROWN

★ ★ ★   Please Please Please (King, 1959)
★ ★½   Try Me (King, 1959)
★ ★ ★ ★   Think (King, 1960)
★ ★½   The Amazing James Brown (King, 1961)

★ ★ ★ ★   James Brown Presents His Band (King, 1961)
★ ★ ★½   Excitement Mr. Dynamite (King, 1962)
★ ★½   James Brown and His Famous Flames Tour the U.S.A. (King, 1962)
★ ★ ★ ★ ★   Live at the Apollo (King, 1963)
★ ★ ★   Prisoner of Love (King, 1963)
★ ★ ★ ★   Pure Dynamite! (King, 1964)
★ ★½   Showtime (Smash, 1964)
★ ★½   Grits and Soul (Smash, 1964)
★ ★ ★ ★   Papa's Got a Brand New Bag (King, 1965)
★ ★½   James Brown Plays James Brown Today and Yesterday (Smash, 1966)
★ ★ ★ ★   I Got You (I Feel Good) (King, 1966)
★ ★ ★   Mighty Instrumentals (King, 1966)
★ ★ ★   James Brown Plays New Breed (The Boo-Ga-Loo) (Smash, 1966)
★ ★ ★½   It's a Man's, Man's, Man's World (King, 1966)
★ ★   Christmas Songs (King, 1966)
★ ★ ★   Handful of Soul (Smash, 1966)
★ ★   The James Brown Show (Smash, 1967)
★ ★ ★ ★   James Brown Sings Raw Soul (King, 1967)
★ ★ ★   James Brown Plays the Real Thing (Smash, 1967)
★ ★ ★   Live at the Garden (King, 1967)
★ ★ ★ ★   Cold Sweat (King, 1967)
★ ★½   James Brown Presents His Show of Tomorrow (King, 1968)
★ ★ ★   I Can't Stand Myself (When You Touch Me) (King, 1968)
★ ★ ★   I Got the Feelin' (King, 1968)
★ ★ ★   James Brown Plays Nothing But Soul (King, 1968)
★ ★ ★ ★ ★   Live at the Apollo, Vol. II (1968; Rhino, 1985)
★ ★ ★½   Thinking About Little Willie John and a Few Nice Things (King, 1968)
★ ★   A Soulful Christmas (King, 1968)
★ ★ ★ ★   Say It Loud, I'm Black and I'm Proud (King, 1969)
★ ★   Gettin' Down to It (King, 1969)
★ ★ ★   The Popcorn (King, 1969)
★ ★ ★   It's a Mother (King, 1969)
★ ★½   Ain't It Funky (King, 1970)
★ ★½   Soul on Top (King, 1970)
★ ★ ★ ★½   It's a New Day—Let a Man Come In (King, 1970)

★ ★ ★ ★½ Sex Machine (King, 1970)
★ ★ ½ Hey, America (King, 1970)
★ ★ ★ Super Bad (King, 1971)
★ ★ Sho Is Funky Down Here (King, 1971)
★ ★ ★½ Hot Pants (Polydor, 1971)
★ ★ ★½ Revolution of the Mind (Live at the Apollo, Vol. II (Polydor, 1971)
★ ★ ★ ★½ There It Is (Polydor, 1972)
★ ★ ★½ Get On the Good Foot (Polydor, 1972)
★ ★ Black Caesar (Polydor, 1973)
★ ★ Slaughter's Big Rip-Off (Polydor, 1973)
★ ★ ★ The Payback (Polydor, 1974)
★ ★ ★ ★ Hell (Polydor, 1974)
★ ★ ½ Reality (Polydor, 1975)
★ ★ Sex Machine Today (Polydor, 1975)
★ ★ Everybody's Doin' the Hustle and Dead on the Double Bump (Polydor, 1975)
★ ★ ★ Hot (Polydor, 1976)
★ ★ ★ Get Up Offa That Thing (Polydor, 1976)
★ ★ Bodyheat (Polydor, 1976)
★ ★½ Mutha's Nature (Polydor, 1977)
★ ★ ★ ★ ★ Solid Gold (Polydor UK, 1977)
★ ★½ Jam 1980's (Polydor, 1978)
★ ★ ★ Take a Look at Those Cakes (Polydor, 1979)
★ ★ ★ The Original Disco Man (Polydor, 1979)
★ ★ ★ People (Polydor, 1980)
★ ★ ★ Hot on the One (Polydor, 1980)
★ ★ ★ ★ Soul Syndrome (1980; Rhino, 1991)
★ ★ ★ Nonstop! (Polydor, 1981)
★ ★½ The Greatest Hits Live in Concert (1981; Sugar Hill, 1991)
★ ★ ★½ Bring It On! (Churchill/Augusta, 1983)
★ ★ ★ ★½ The Federal Years, Part One (Solid Smoke, 1984)
★ ★ ★ ★ The Federal Years, Part Two (Solid Smoke, 1984)
★ ★ ★ ★½ Ain't That a Groove (Polydor, 1984)
★ ★ ★ ★ ★ Doing It to Death (Polydor, 1984)
★ ★ ★½ Gravity (Scotti Bros., 1986)
★ ★ ★ The CD of JB (Sex Machine and Other Soul Classics) (Polydor, 1985)
★ ★ ★ ★½ James Brown's Funky People (Polydor, 1986)
★ ★ ★ ★½ In the Jungle Groove (Polydor, 1986)

★ ★ ★ ★ The CD of JB II (Cold Sweat and Other Soul Classics) (Polydor, 1987)
★ ★ ★½ I'm Real (Scotti Bros., 1988)
★ ★ ★ ★ James Brown's Funky People (Part 2) (Polydor, 1988)
★ ★ ★ Soul Session Live (Scotti Bros., 1989)
★ ★ ★ ★ Motherlode (Polydor, 1988)
★ ★ ★ ★½ Roots of a Revolution (Polydor, 1989)
★ ★ ★ ★ Messing With the Blues (Polydor, 1990)
★ ★ ★ ★ ★ Star Time (Polydor, 1991)
★ ★ ★ ★ Love Over-Due (Scotti Bros., 1991)
★ ★ ★ ★ ★ 20 All-Time Greatest Hits! (Polydor, 1991)
★ ★ ★½ The Greatest Hits of the Fourth Decade (Scotti Bros., 1992)

James Brown may never have captured the zeitgeist as Elvis Presley or the Beatles did, nor can he be said to have dominated the charts like Stevie Wonder or the Rolling Stones, but by any real measure of musical greatness—endurance, originality, versatility, breadth of influence—he towers over them all. Brown has been astonishingly productive over the first 36 years of his recording career, churning out more than 85 albums (give or take a few anthologies) as a singer, bandleader or instrumentalist; many are great, and nearly all are worth hearing. And even though none of the 44 singles he put into the Billboard Top Forty ever made it to Number One—indeed, only two cracked the Top Five—in retrospect, that reflects worse on the pop audience than it does on his music.

Indeed, Brown has long boasted that his best ideas were years ahead of their time, and history has borne him out. Hip-hop borrowed freely from his catalog, as rappers like Rob Base, Kool Moe Dee, Eric B. & Rakim and Hammer all powered singles with beats Brown produced as much as 20 years earlier. Nor were they the only ones, for by the early '90s the churning fatback pattern immortalized in Brown's "Funky Drummer" (1969) was a staple among club-savvy alternative rock acts. Even Michael Jackson's celebrated moonwalk was little more than an update of a Brown move called the camel walk.

Dealing with a body of work so wide-ranging and important is not easy, particularly for those starting from scratch. Certainly, there are greatest hits albums available, of which *20 All-Time Greatest Hits!* is the best buy (the two *CD of JB* collections offer a slightly wider range of hits between them, but often in truncated versions; the "Sex Machine" on the first *CD of JB*, for example, lacks the original single's spoken introduction, which is included on the *20 All-Time Greatest Hits!* track). Those interested in some of the lesser hits, particularly from his funk-fueled late-'60s and early-'70s work, may want to augment *20 All-Time Greatest Hits!* with either or both *Ain't That a Groove* and *Doing It to Death*. But the single best introduction to Brown's work is *Star Time*, a wonderfully annotated, admirably representative four-CD/four-cassette box set that follows Brown's career from "Please Please Please," his 1956 debut, to "Unity," a 1984 collaboration with hip-hop godfather Afrika Bambaataa. In addition to including all the intervening hits, it restores some singles to their full-length versions, offers a fair amount of non-LP material, and includes several illuminating rarities, among them the previously unreleased original version of "Papa's Got a Brand New Bag." Five stars is barely enough to describe its greatness.

Apart from such compilations, however, much of Brown's original catalog remains out of print. That's not to say these titles are unavailable; some can be had as Japanese or German imports, and others may still be found (although often at a premium) on the used album market. Moreover, a fair number are likely to be brought back into circulation in the coming years as Polygram, which currently controls the rights to Brown's back catalog on King, Smash and Polydor, implements its reissue program.

Curiously, Brown's early recordings— though far from being his best work—have been the most easily obtainable. Perhaps the best overview of this period can be had from Solid Smoke's now-deleted albums, *The Federal Years, Part One* and *Part Two*, which include all of Brown's hits from the years 1956–60, plus a representative slice of his other work from that time. Greater depth can be had from the 43-song *Roots of a Revolution* (focusing on 1956–62, with two songs each from '63 and '64), but this set purposely excludes Brown's best-known titles, under the assumption that serious fans would already have them.

Then there are the original albums themselves. Of these, *Think* is by far the best, in part because it has the highest hit quotient ("Think," "I'll Go Crazy," "Good

Good Lovin' "), but mostly because it offers Brown's most distinctive work to that point, particularly in its chugging title tune. *Please Please Please,* despite including Brown's first single, the raw, gospel-inflected "Please Please Please" and his first R&B chart-topper, the more-traditional R&B tune "Try Me," is mostly given over to derivative material like "Chonnie-on-Chon" and "Let's Make It." *Try Me*, which was reissued in 1964 as *The Unbeatable James Brown*, repeats "Try Me" but otherwise leans more toward the blues, thanks to songs like "I Want You So Bad" and "Messing With the Blues," while *The Amazing James Brown* shows off the increasing proficiency of his band through gritty titles like "Dancin' Little Thing" and "Come Over Here." With *Presents His Band*, Brown moves into the instrumental realm and delivers his epochal remake of Jimmy Forrest's "Night Train," but *Excitement Mr. Dynamite* (which has also been available as *Shout and Shimmy*) returns Brown and company to the hard-hitting vocal approach of *Think*, even to the point of repeating "Good Good Lovin'."

At that point, though, Brown was still better-known for his live show than for his recordings, a fact that explains the somewhat misleading title to the studio album *James Brown and His Famous Flames Tour the U.S.A.* Incredibly, King Records president Syd Nathan felt there was no market for a real James Brown live album, so the singer went ahead and recorded *Live at the Apollo* on his own; it turned out to be the album that finally put him on the map. And no wonder. An astonishing document, it doesn't just present the hits, but shows off the incredible precision of Brown's band as well as the uncanny bond he had with his audience. *Pure Dynamite!*, an even more energetic set recorded before a raucously appreciative crowd at Baltimore's Royal Theatre, followed a year later, and Brown would release eight more live albums after that, including two more recorded at the Apollo: *Live at the Apollo, Vol. II*, with its itchy, intense rendition of "There Was a Time"; and *Revolution of the Mind: Live At the Apollo, Vol. III*. Because Brown toured with an entire revue, *The James Brown Show* puts its emphasis on the other players in the show, including his band; likewise, *James Brown Presents His Show of Tomorrow* features only two tracks by Brown, with the rest given over to members of the revue. Brown also put out a couple of "faked" live albums—studio recordings with audience noise dubbed in later. Perhaps the most notorious of these was *Showtime* (fortunately, its best tunes appear without embellishment on *Messing With the Blues*), but *Super Bad* repeats the ruse, as does the first half of the double-album *Sex Machine*, although the loping, hypnotic groove generated by his band on "Give It Up or Turnit a Loose" makes such fakery almost forgivable.

Brown later admitted that his model for *Live at the Apollo* was Ray Charles's concert recording *In Person*. That wasn't his only nod to Brother Ray; *Prisoner of Love*, with its string sweetening and choral cushioning, is self-consciously in the vein of Charles's ABC recordings—although Brown remains far too raw a singer to seem much at home in these MOR arrangements. No matter; the direction Brown takes with *Papa's Got a Brand New Bag* would soon leave Charles in the dust, at least from an R&B perspective. This, in effect, is the birth of funk, as Brown's songs grow lean and repetitious, with fewer and fewer chord changes and a greater emphasis on rhythmic tension. Granted, nothing else on the album takes that idea quite as far as its two-part title tune, but that was more than enough. The revolution truly had begun.

Actually, Brown suggests in his autobiography that the revolution had actually begun with *Out of Sight*, an album he recorded for Smash shortly before *Brand New Bag*, but a legal battle between Brown, King Records and Smash resulted in a court order withdrawing the album shortly after its release (the single "Out of Sight" can be found on *Star Time*). Part of the loss when *Out of Sight* was put out of the picture was a track entitled "I Got You (I Feel Good)," but Brown, typically, turned the situation to his advantage and recut the song with a harder groove; both versions of the song can be found on *Star Time*, but the funkier and more familiar of the two is the centerpiece of *I Got You (I Feel Good)*. Brown didn't cut down on his balladry during this period, however. *It's a Man's, Man's, Man's World* certainly has its share of funk, including the two-part "Ain't That a Groove," but there's room enough for the slow ones, including the title track and a tearfully intense number called "The Bells." Likewise, *James Brown Sings Raw Soul* alternates rhythmically intense tunes like "Money Won't Change You" and "Let Yourself Go" with soppy ballads along the lines of "Tell Me That You Love Me." Even the unstoppable groove of "Cold Sweat"—which, with its

driving, monolithic bass pulse and exquisite Maceo Parker sax break, was a milestone almost as important as "Papa's Got a Brand New Bag"—is flanked on *Cold Sweat* by MOR numbers like "Mona Lisa" and "Nature Boy" as well as a smattering of rock & roll oldies.

Of course, some of that was simply a reflection of Brown's determined eclecticism. Like Ray Charles, Brown refused to see himself as a one-dimensional musician, and regularly fleshed out his albums with material that ranged far afield from the sound of his singles. Sometimes, he did whole albums of such songs, like *Thinking About Little Willie John and a Few Nice Things*, a tribute to the seminal R&B stylist that boasts a touching cover of John's "Talk to Me!" He also flirted with jazz, trying his hand at lounge singing with the Dee Felice Trio on *Gettin' Down to It* and recording *Soul on Top* with the Louis Bellson big band.

But Brown's most consistent sideline was playing organ, piano and even vibraphone. Although Brown is by no means a master technician, his solos are remarkably fluid, and at their best compare well with the work of jazz funk players like Les McCann and Ramsey Lewis. In all, Brown released 11 all-instrumental albums between 1961 and '71; some, like *James Brown Plays the New Breed*, *James Brown Plays the Real Thing* or *James Brown Plays James Brown Today and Yesterday* feature his funky, Jimmy McGriff-style organ solos; others, like *Mighty Instrumentals*, *The Popcorn* and *Ain't It Funky* put the emphasis on his band. Most have been written off as inconsequential, but the music is often quite good, particularly on rhythmically centered tunes like "Peewee's Groove in 'D'," from *Real Thing*, or "Soul Pride," from *Popcorn*. Nor should we forget the albums he produced for his backing band, the JBs, and their various spin-offs, a sampling of which is spread between *James Brown's Funky People* and *James Brown's Funky People (Part 2)*.

With *Say It Loud, I'm Black and I'm Proud* Brown states what had long been implicit in his music; the black power sentiment of the title tune generated a certain amount of controversy at the time, but the album isn't all politics, as the loping "Licking Stick—Licking Stick" makes clear. Brown's band was getting funkier with each passing month; even his outtakes are astonishing, as evidenced by the selection on *Motherlode*. *It's a New Day So Let a Man*

Come In is especially strong, thanks to "Give It Up or Turnit a Loose," a mesmerizing workout with interlocking guitar and bass patterns, as well as such lesser greats as "It's a New Day" and "Let a Man Come in and Do the Popcorn." But many of Brown's hottest singles from this period—"Funky Drummer," for instance—didn't make it to album until Brown began to be anthologized in the '80s and '90s. Some of these tracks turn up in remixes on *In the Jungle Groove*, a DJ-oriented release that augments "Funky Drummer" with a three-minute "Bonus Beat Reprise." Still, *Star Time* offers the choicest selection as well as the most complete versions of these tracks, an important consideration when dealing with singles like "Mother Popcorn," which fades out during Maceo Parker's tenor solo on *The CD of JB* but appears in its full glory on *Star Time*. Beware—neither *Sex Machine* or *Super Bad* contains the single versions of their title tunes, offering faux live renditions instead.

Fortunately, that changes with *Hot Pants*, which does indeed include the salacious "Hot Pants," and gets better with *There It Is* (both "I'm a Greedy Man" and the marvelously kinetic "Talkin' Loud & Sayin' Nothing," plus the dark message number "King Heroin"). After the double-album *Get on the Good Foot*, Brown released several soundtracks before getting on track with *The Payback*; from there, he went straight to *Hell*, a somewhat mixed double-album that includes the Nixon-inspired "Funky President (People It's Bad)." By this point, Brown was losing his edge, and as he tried to cope with the disco era, his albums grew increasingly spotty. Some, like the remake-oriented *Sex Machine Today* or the uncharacteristically mellow *Everybody's Doin' the Hustle and Dead on the Double Bump*, are conceptual failures, while others—*Body Heat*, *Mutha's Nature*, *Jam 1980's* or *People*—are uninspired. Still, he had his moments: *Hot*, on which Brown copied David Bowie's "Fame" for "Hot (I Need to Be Loved, Loved, Loved)"; *Get Up Offa That Thing*, with its insistent title tune; "For Goodness Sakes, Look at Those Cakes," on *Take a Look at Those Cakes*. With *The Original Disco Man*, he even came to terms with disco itself, and proved on *Soul Syndrome* that he could imitate the Miami sound as well as anyone.

By the early '80s, Brown was in limbo, with no label and a waning audience. He recorded a live album at Studio 54; entitled *Live in Concert* (originally *Live in New York*), it isn't even as good as the live-in-Japan *Hot on the One*, recorded a year earlier. He tried going independent, releasing the pleasantly retro *Bring It On!* through the tiny Churchill/Augusta label; a good album heard by almost no one. He even went Hollywood for a time, appearing in and contributing to the soundtracks of *The Blues Brothers* and *Dr. Detroit*; the latter has the more interesting musical performance ("Get Up Offa That Thing/Dr. Detroit" can also be found on *Greatest Hits of the Fourth Decade*.). But it wasn't until he cut "Living in America" for the soundtrack to *Rocky IV* that Brown was able to re-establish himself. Ironically, part of the reason "Living in America" works is that it plays off the clichéd James Brown-isms that had come back into vogue; in a sense, Brown was just imitating himself, as he is through the rest of *Gravity*. *I'm Real* takes the opposite approach, with Brown complaining about rappers ripping him off, over rhythm tracks largely built around—ahem—sampled James Brown records. *Soul Session Live* is the soundtrack from a Cinemax special that offers more stars (Aretha Franklin, Joe Cocker, Wilson Pickett) than memorable music, but *Love Over-Due*, recorded after Brown's release from prison, is a return to form that boasts a sharp new band and a classic sense of material. — J.D.C.

JULIE BROWN

★★★★ **Goddess in Progress (Rhino, 1984)**
  ★★★ **Trapped in the Body of a White Girl (Sire/Warner Bros., 1987)**

More a singing comic than a comical singer, Brown is generally only as good as her material. Which, in the case of *Goddess in Progress*, is pretty damn fine, thanks to her deft send-ups of sex roles (" 'Cause I'm a Blond") and California culture ("The Homecoming Queen's Got a Gun"). *Trapped in the Body of a White Girl* has its moments—including a remake of "I Like 'Em Big and Stupid" and "Girl Fight Tonight!," the ultimate Shangri-Las parody—but ultimately overdoses on Madonna-style dance pop. — J.D.C.

MAXINE BROWN

★★★ **Golden Classics (Collectables, NA)**

Though she's had only three hits of any magnitude, Maxine Brown must be considered one of the truly gifted singers of her generation who, with the right breaks, might have established herself in the same rank as Nancy Wilson in terms of versatility and depth. Clearly she had the wherewithal to adapt almost any type of song to her sultry style, and then put an individual spin on it. Pop with an R&B base was her forte, and it was her style to float lightly over the beat, delivering the lyrics with a sly twist or a mock-throwaway turn that peeled away layers of feeling, especially pain. Her 1961 hit "Funny" is the Maxine Brown song most often programmed these days, although "All In My Mind," from earlier that same year, was her only Top Twenty single. Her last hit came in late '64 with "Oh No, Not My Baby." These are all here, as well as three stirring duets with Chuck Jackson, whose fervent delivery is the perfect complement to Brown's deceptive sangfroid. Woulda been, coulda been, shoulda been: Maxine Brown's career is a testimony to the advisability of being in the right place at the right time. — D.M.

NAPPY BROWN
★★★ Tore Up (1984; Alligator, 1990)
★★★ Something Gonna Jump Out the Bushes (Black Top, 1988)

Hailing from Charlotte, North Carolina, Nappy Brown made his mark as an urban-style blues singer with a series of fierce singles for the Savoy label in the mid-'50s, most of them written by Rose Marie McCoy, one of the prolific black writers of that era. Typical of the fate befalling most black artists in the '50s, two of Brown's best efforts, "Don't Be Angry" and "Piddily Patter Patter," received more exposure when covered by white artists (the Crew-Cuts and Patti Page, respectively), although Brown's version of "Don't Be Angry" did rise to Number 25 on the pop charts before being undercut by the Crew-Cuts' cover, which peaked at Number 14. Brown's best shot at the charts had passed, but he has continued working and recording. On *Something Gonna Jump Out the Bushes*, from 1987, Brown is in great, gruff voice—a tinge of B.B. King here, Howlin' Wolf there—and good humor to boot. He's also backed by some terrific musicians, most notably Anson Funderburgh, whose serpentine, razor-sharp guitar lines are one of this album's constant pleasures. Never a major artist, Brown is an engaging performer and ebullient presence, qualities that recommend both his live shows and the two albums that remain in print. — D.M.

ROY BROWN
★★★★ Good Rockin' Tonight (Quicksilver, 1982)

Perhaps the late Roy Brown isn't a name that springs to mind quickly when rock pioneers are enumerated, but his influence on the genre was profound and far-reaching. Born in New Orleans, relocating to Los Angeles as a teenager, Brown was a blues singer at heart (his idol was the estimable Wynonie Harris, who would later cut a wonderful version of Brown's "Good Rockin' Tonight"), although his vocal style was also shaped by white crooners of his youth, such as Bing Crosby; that such a voice should catch the attention of a young Elvis Presley in thrall with the same wide spread of music is as logical as Presley's decision to record "Good Rockin' Tonight" for Sun Records and add a country feel to it. Returning to New Orleans in the late '40s, Brown's use of big bands played a formative role in the development of Crescent City rock & roll; moving on, he also influenced the post-war blues scene during a tenure in Memphis in the early '50s, his eclectic approach informing the work of both B.B. King and Bobby "Blue" Bland. All reports indicate Brown was a flamboyant showman as well, and this too must be taken into account when considering how long a shadow he cast over the music of his time. Writer, singer, performer— Brown had all the bases covered. *Good Rockin' Tonight* is a live performance from the early '70s that cooks from beginning to end. All Brown's children are in the grooves here: the soulful cries that punctuate the opener, "Travelin' Blues," lead us to Bobby Bland; "Love for Sale," a tender, mournful blues, features the clear, precise, pained diction common to B.B. King; the macho swagger of "Good Rockin' Tonight"— indeed, the falsetto cries throughout the album—reveal a deep root of Presley's style. Reissues of Brown's early recordings are unavailable at present, but one import retrospective is worth seeking out: *Good Rockin' Tonight* on the British Route 66 label. Rhino Records' *Best of New Orleans Rhythm & Blues, Vol. 1* also includes Brown's 1957 studio recording of "Let the Four Winds Blow," co-written by Fats Domino and Dave Bartholomew. Brown died of a heart attack in 1981. — D.M.

RUTH BROWN
★★★ Gospel Time (1963; Lection/Mercury, 1989)
★★★ Have a Good Time (Fantasy, 1988)
★★★★ Blues on Broadway (Fantasy, 1989)
★★★★ Miss Rhythm (Greatest Hits and More) (Atlantic, 1989)

To say that Ruth Brown put Atlantic Records on the map after being signed in 1948 is to be guilty of understatement. Her first hit, "So Long," released in 1949, was only the second hit for the nascent Atlantic label; over the course of the next decade Brown racked up 23 more R&B hits, leading one wag to dub Atlantic "the house that Ruth built." In all, she recorded over 80 songs between 1949 and 1962, and left the label in 1963 as the best-selling artist in its history. Brown's style is rooted in gospel and legitimate swing. Growing up in Portsmouth, Virginia, she worked in the fields by day, and by night sang at church. Her professional career began in 1947 as a vocalist with Lucky Millinder's Big Band, and a year later she went solo when Atlantic co-founders Ahmet Ertegun and Herb Abramson offered her a contract following a roof-raising performance at the Crystal Cavern in Washington, D.C. In those days, and on her early Atlantic recordings, her vocal timbre is light and airy, but the blues inflections and impeccable sense of phrasing are already evident. Age and experience deepened her voice and brought out the lusty belter in her. This evolution is dramatically illustrated on the 40-track, two-CD Atlantic retrospective, *Miss Rhythm*, which includes not only her best-known songs (e.g., "[Mama] He Treats Your Daughter Mean," "5-10-15 Hours," "Wild, Wild Young Men," "Lucky Lips," "This Little Girl's Gone Rockin' "), but lesser-known—but no less inspired—singles (notably "Have a Good Time," the gospel-influenced "I Can See Everybody's Baby," and "As Long As I'm Moving"), and three previously unreleased tracks, including a swinging performance on "It's All for You." Obviously, *Miss Rhythm* is essential for anyone interested in the work of one of the finest R&B singers this country has ever produced.

However, the Brown saga doesn't end with her tenure at Atlantic. She left Atlantic and cut two albums for Philips; one of these, *Gospel Time*, is currently back in the catalogue on Mercury's gospel label, Lection. In 1963, producer Shelby Singleton recorded Brown in Nashville with some of Music City's top session players. She sounds transported, declaiming and testifying as if she were back at church. *Gospel Time* turns out to be an object lesson in the point at which gospel intersects R&B, as Brown puts new spins on such well-worn items such "Just a Closer Walk with Thee" and "Peace in the Valley."

Brown eventually fell on hard times and dropped out of the business. Spurred by Miles Davis's support, though, she resumed her career to greater achievement than she had known in the '50s. She is no longer simply a recording artist, but an actress as well, with a Tony Award presented to her in 1989 for her performance in the Broadway musical *Black and Blue*. This new phase of Brown's career is aptly summarized on disc with a live recording, *Have a Good Time*, and a 1989 studio album, *Blues on Broadway*. Among the first-rate performances on the former are updates of three of her Atlantic gems, "5-10-15 Hours," "Have a Good Time," and "(Mama) He Treats Your Daughter Mean." *Blues on Broadway* is even more imposing. The Ruth Brown of the '50s could never have delivered a version of "Good Morning Heartache" that compares favorably to Billie Holiday's; but the older Ruth Brown is on intimate terms with every deep cut inflicted by the song's lyrics, and she tells it without flinching. This is a woman who describes a life lived full measure every time she sings. And it ain't over yet. — D.M.

SHIRLEY BROWN
★★★★ **Woman to Woman** (1974; Stax, 1979)

On the hit title track of her debut, Shirley Brown lays it on the line—the telephone line. Dropping a dime on her two-timing man, she dials the number on a matchbook. "Hello, Barbara? This is Shirley." As the Stax house band puts down a slinky groove, Shirley's steady rap builds to a head of indignation: "That car he drives? I pay the note every month." And then she slides into the sweet singing on the chorus: "I just love that man." While it's not exactly a feminist tract, "Woman to Woman" reflects the new outspokenness of early '70s soul. Talk about tellin' it like it is: neither bitter nor bitchy, Brown simply states her case and moves on. Nothing else on the album is quite that compelling, but Shirley Brown's voice—with its subtle range, sanctified roots and salty tone—holds your interest even when the songs don't. "Ain't No Fun" features a listen-up-sisters rap digression, and overall the sound is leaner and spicier—more Southern—than most concurrent psychedelic soul and proto-disco competition. Shirley Brown never equalled the debut on her subsequent Stax releases, which are out of print, but her one-shot hit really is a wonder. — M.C.

JACKSON BROWNE
★★★½ **Jackson Browne** (Asylum, 1972)
★★★★   **For Everyman** (Asylum, 1973)

★ ★ ★ ★   Late for the Sky (Asylum, 1974)
★ ★ ★½   The Pretender (Asylum, 1976)
★ ★ ★ ★ ★   Running on Empty (Asylum, 1978)
★ ★ ★½   Hold Out (Asylum, 1980)
★ ★ ★   Lawyers in Love (Asylum, 1983)
★ ★ ★   Lives in the Balance (Asylum, 1986)
★ ★ ★   World in Motion (Elektra, 1989)

Co-written by Jackson Browne and the Eagles' Glenn Frey, "Take It Easy" pinpoints the attitudinal and musical changes taking place at the start of the '70s: "Don't even try to understand/Just find a place to make your stand/And take it easy." While the Eagles pursued the more hedonistic implications of that agenda, "trying to understand" is what Jackson Browne has always been about. Though he's focused on events in the world around him since the mid-'80s, Browne refined and perfected the role of singer-songwriter in the '70s. He took the autobiographical charge of Joni Mitchell's early transmissions and raised the voltage. His philosophical slant endeared Browne to a generation of smart teenagers who'd read a bit and were asking Big Questions, too. Along with Mitchell, Jackson Browne served as a combination bard–sex symbol–intellectual mentor. Though both these L.A. troubadours also commanded sizable audiences among adults, their formative influence on current singers and songwriters—not to mention people—can't be overstated. Browne's debut lays the groundwork for future heart-and-soul excavations. "Doctor My Eyes," an early hit single, communicates the subdued, subtle power of his half-spoken melodies, while "Rock Me on the Water" and "Song for Adam" foreshadow the free-ranging contemplation to come. *For Everyman* strikes a remarkable balance, though; the cool introspection of "I Thought I Was a Child" and "Sing My Song to Me" is leavened by the warm humor of "Ready or Not" and "Redneck Friend." David Lindley's loping slide guitar and arsenal of stringed instruments buoys Jackson's occasional slides into melancholy. "These Days," an FM-radio hit for Gregg Allman, stands as one of Browne's most intricately detailed emotional scenarios.

Late for the Sky strengthens and solidifies Browne's approach; it's the quintessential Browne album, if not quite the best. The metaphorical complexity of "Fountain of Sorrow" and the clear-eyed poignancy of "For a Dancer" would be a tough act to

follow; unsurprisingly, "The Fuse" and "Sleep's Dark and Silent Gate" (both from *The Pretender*) aren't quite as eloquent. They are effective, though; Browne's once-hesitant singing improves with each album. But even when his songwriting is sharp, the mellowing trend in his music dulls the impact. Browne eerily predicts the rise of the yuppie on *The Pretender*'s title track, only to have his point undercut by a creeping string section.

Just when it seemed that mellow inevitably turned to mush, Browne made good on all the singer-songwriters' claims to confessional integrity. At a time when the overdub-enhanced live double album was a rock commonplace, Browne released a real concert document. *Running on Empty* collects new material, unrecorded cover versions, motel jams, loose ends, rough edges, mistakes and unexpected moments of triumph. *Running on Empty* exudes intimacy, revealing the empathetic, flexible bond between Browne and his audience.

Hold Out returns to the pop-ification program begun on *The Pretender*, though even the catchiest ruminations (the title track and "Hold On Hold Out") don't sink in over time like the thoughtful hooks of old. *Lawyers in Love* marks Jackson's transition from the personal to the political. The title track is a cutting slice of social observation, but the remainder of the album is muddled. For the first time, Browne seems unsure of himself. Interestingly, both Browne and Mitchell started writing topical songs in the mid-'80s. Browne has stuck with it. The subsequent albums convey his passion and commitment, though the well-intentioned broadsides and liberation anthems never quite connect with the musical setting: tasteful state-of-the-art L.A. studiocraft. Little Steve Van Zandt's "I Am a Patriot," from *World in Motion*, is the only truly memorable song on Browne's trilogy of protest albums.   — M.C.

DAVE BRUBECK
★ ★ ★ ★   Jazz at the College of the Pacific (1953; Fantasy, 1987)
★ ★ ★ ★   Stardust (1953; Fantasy, 1990)
★ ★ ★½ Jazz Goes to College (1954; Columbia, 1989)
★ ★ ★   The Last Set at Newport (1958; Atlantic, 1973)
★ ★ ★½ Gone With the Wind (1959; Columbia, 1987)
★ ★ ★ ★½ Time Out (Columbia, 1960)
★ ★ ★ ★½ A la Mode (Fantasy, 1960; Fantasy, 1985)

★★★½ Brubeck/Mulligan/Cincinnati
(1971; MCA, 1990)
★★★ Two Generations of Brubeck
(Atlantic, 1973)
★★★½ We're All Together for the First
Time (Atlantic, 1973)
★★★ Brubeck and Desmond—1975: The
Duets (Horizon, 1975)
★★★ All the Things We Are (Atlantic,
1976)
★★★ 25th Anniversary Reunion (A&M,
1977)
★★½ Concord on a Summer Night
(Concord, 1982)
★★★½ Dave Brubeck/Paul Desmond
(1982; Fantasy, 1990)
★★★★ Twenty-Four Classic Original
Recordings (1982; Fantasy, 1990)
★★★ Reflections (Concord, 1986)
★★★★ The Dave Brubeck Quartet
Featuring Paul Desmond in
Concert (Fantasy, 1986)
★★★½ Music from "West Side Story"
and . . . (Columbia, 1986)
★★★ Blue Rondo (Concord, 1987)
★★★ Moscow Night (Concord, 1988)
★★★★ The Great Concerts (Columbia,
1988)
★★★½ Jazz Impressions of New York
(Columbia, 1990)
★★★ Quiet as the Moon
(MusicMasters, 1991)

The fiercer among jazz purists often quibble about Dave Brubeck's braininess—having studied theory with Darius Milhaud, the pianist was as influenced by classical music as he was by the jazz tradition, and it's apparent that he thinks when he swings. But he was smart enough, too, to collaborate in his essential outfit, the Dave Brubeck Quartet, with a highly intuitive alto saxophonist, Paul Desmond, whose introspective style lent airy grace to Dave's often highly technical compositions. And the Quartet blazed trails. At the forefront of the "West Coast" school (musicians who prized a "cool" style, in contrast to bebop's frenzy), they were among the first to experiment with novel time signatures. Desmond's "Take Five," off the breakthrough *Time Out* (1960), was played in 5/4, a rhythm today's braver jazzers might take for granted; Brubeck's "Blue Rondo à la Turk" was done in 9/8—yet while Max Roach and Benny Carter, among others, had tried out off-kilter rhythms, the Brubeck Quartet was popular enough that its movement beyond traditional 4/4 had broad and lasting impact.

The Quartet's college gigs, in fact, were enormously influential in turning white-bread Americans into finger-snapping cultists; Brubeck was, for many, the first experience of any jazz beyond Dixieland. Fantasy has reissued good volumes of early Dave: *Stardust, Twenty-Four Classic Original Recordings*, and especially *Jazz at the College of the Pacific* and anything featuring Paul Desmond, hold up well. Columbia's reissues, *Music From "West Side Story"* and *The Great Concerts* present representative sets of the Quartet at its finest; along with *Jazz Impressions of New York*, they show off, too, Dave's gift for melody. *All the Things We Are* finds Brubeck contending with avant-gardiste Anthony Braxton; *We're All Together for the First Time* and *Brubeck/Mulligan/Cincinnati* congenially pair the pianist with saxist Gerry Mulligan; the later Brubeck, primarily on Concord, continues in the very tasteful style of his early work. — P.E.

JACK BRUCE
★★★★ Songs for a Tailor (1969; Polydor,
1989)
★★★ Things We Like (1970; Polydor,
1989)
★★★ Harmony Row (1971; Polydor,
1989)
★★★ Out of the Storm (Polydor, 1974)
★★ How's Tricks (1977; Polydor, 1989)
★★★★ Will Power (Polydor, 1989)
★★★ A Question of Time (Epic, 1989)

After leaving Cream, bassist Jack Bruce cut several underrated solo albums. His debut *Songs for a Tailor* offers a surprisingly pungent taste of jazz-rock fusion. That rambling bass and rumbling voice are buoyed by punchy horn lines and weirdly memorable songs—complex little ditties with legible melodies and impenetrable titles. *Out of the Storm* edges back toward the power-trio rock that Bruce helped invent; even some quicksilver licks from Detroit guitarist Steve Hunter can't disguise his lack of enthusiasm for re-covering old ground. Bruce's *How's Tricks* is a journeyman effort hardly worth dredging up. *Will Power* compiles the quirky highlights of Bruce's early, experimental period into an eye-opening set. Despite the presence of various hotshot guitar soloists and P-Funk alumni, however, *A Question of Time* (1989) doesn't provide any convincing answers about Bruce's future—or current—musical direction. — M.C.

ROY BUCHANAN

★ ★½ **Roy Buchanan (Polydor, 1972)**
★ ★½ **Second Album (1973; Polydor, 1988)**
★ ★ ★ **That's What I Am Here For (Polydor, 1974)**
★ ★ ★ **In the Beginning (1974; Polydor, 1988)**
★ ★½ **Live Stock (1975; Polydor, 1988)**
★ ★ ★ **A Street Called Straight (Atlantic, 1976)**
★ ★ ★ **Loading Zone (Atlantic, 1977)**
★ ★½ **You're Not Alone (Atlantic, 1978)**
★ ★½ **My Babe (Waterhouse, 1980)**
★ ★½ **Dancing on the Edge (Alligator, 1986)**
★ ★ ★ **When a Guitar Plays the Blues (Alligator, 1985)**
★ ★ **Hot Wires (Alligator, 1988)**

Three unaccompanied notes from Roy's Telecaster, sustained like muted trumpet blasts, introduce the first song on his debut—and serve notice that Buchanan's primary interest and appeal will lie exclusively in his playing. And he was, indeed, a remarkable guitarist. Chiefly a blues stylist, he based his approach on the stinging clarity of Albert and B.B. King, but then extended into a demonic virtuosity of jazz flourishes and lightning runs—he was ultra-precise, but almost always a very passionate interpreter. His passion, however, was a private, almost hermetic one—unlike Jeff Beck, he didn't have much of a sense of humor; unlike Jimmy Page, was neither a rhythmic innovator or a crowd-pleaser; and he seldom approached the raw fury Hendrix was master of. He was, essentially, a guitarist's guitarist—subtle, concentrated, intense.

Beginning by providing backup for the great rockabillies Dale Hawkins and Ronnie Hawkins, Buchanan then did sessions before going solo. And he retained a sideman's mentality—playing, not vision, remained his strength. His first album set a pattern from which he only later departed—blues, countryish rockers, and the occasional spiritual number (Roy's father was a preacher). Nearly all of the lengthy instrumental passages are smart and exciting, but until the arrival of blue-eyed soulster Bill Sheffield, on *In the Beginning*, he worked with truly mediocre vocalists, and he never found a good drummer until he switched over to Atlantic. While Buchanan himself sang on only a couple of songs per record, his efforts were painfully embarrassing; his monotonous blues delivery only proved how demanding that superficially simple style can be; when he

tried for a ballad, he was generally off-key. On "The Messiah Will Come Again" from *Roy Buchanan*, he settled for simply talking, and even that didn't work (his speaking voice oddly recalls a dour Elvis's).

That's What I Am Here For, with its Hendrix tribute ("Hey Joe") and its varied song selection, holds up well, as does *In the Beginning*, on which a full horn section lends interest. Arif Mardin's production helps fill out the sound on *A Street Called Straight*, and *Loading Zone*, produced by Stanley Clarke, is probably the most ambitious Buchanan—he ranges from a jazz-like density to a swooning grace (although the inclusion of unimaginative strings and harp glissandos gets in the way). Much more straightforward, the Alligator albums are Buchanan returning to his metier—the blues. — P.E.

LINDSEY BUCKINGHAM

★ ★ ★½ **Law & Order (1981; Warner Bros., 1987)**
★ ★ ★ **Go Insane (1984; Warner Bros., 1987)**
★ ★ ★ ★ **Out of the Cradle (Warner Bros., 1992)**

The best Fleetwood Mac song of the '80s ("Trouble") appears on guitarist Lindsey Buckingham's first solo album (*Law & Order*). With a firm rhythmic assist from Mick Fleetwood on drums, Buckingham wraps an artfully strummed melody line around a seductive, breathless reverie. It's like listening to a long, sweet sigh. The rest of *Law & Order* is less transcendent: "Bwana" and the doo-wop version of "September Song" stumble, while "Shadow of the West" (with Christine McVie harmonies) and the deliciously mean "That's How We Do It in LA" soar away. *Go Insane* smoothly updates *Tusk*-style experimentation for the CD-computer era, though it doesn't necessarily make catchy choruses or hooks any easier to find. Buckingham officially left Fleetwood Mac in 1987; with *Out of the Cradle*, Buckingham leaps out of semi-retirement. Armed with his strongest hooks since *Rumours*, he focuses his studio-obsessive flair this time. On catchy song after song, the sonic details flesh out the deceptively simple melodies. — M.C.

THE BUCKINGHAMS

★ ★ ★ **Mercy, Mercy, Mercy: A Collection (Columbia/Legacy, 1991)**

With their late-'60s hits, "Kind of a Drag," "Don't You Care" and "Hey Baby (They're Playing Our Song)," the Buckinghams made sprightly, insignificant frat-boy pop distinguished by John Poulos's jazzy (for AM radio) drumming, and a heavy non-R&B reliance on horns. These tastes were those of producer James William Guercio, who went on to indulge them with Chicago. — P.E.

TIM BUCKLEY
★★★ Tim Buckley (Elektra, 1967)
★★★★ Goodbye and Hello (Elektra, 1967)
★★★★ Happy/Sad (Elektra, 1969)
★★★ Lorca (Elektra, 1970)
★★★★ Blue Afternoon (1970; Enigma/Retro, 1989)
★★★★ Starsailor (1971; Enigma/Retro, 1989)
★★★ Greetings from L.A. (1972; Enigma/Retro, 1989)
★ Sefronia (1974; Enigma/Retro, 1989)
★ Look at the Fool (1974; Enigma/Retro, 1989)
★★★ Dream Letter (Live in London, 1968) (Enigma/Retro, 1990)

Dreamily handsome, possessed of a genuine, if eccentric, poetic gift, capable of singing a veritable choir of voices, and brandishing an archetypally romantic sensibility, Tim Buckley was a sort of late-'60s folkie Coleridge—overwhelmed by the gods with too many gifts. His work was as ambitious as any of his contemporaries: it was also a commercial disaster. His fatal overdose in 1975, however metaphorically apt, was a true tragedy—and for a long time even the Buckley myth was an obscure one, as most of his records had gone out of print.

With such curious instrumentation as bottleneck guitar, harmonium, kalimba and the vibes that would become a Buckley trademark, *Goodbye and Hello* drew critical raves for its meandering beauty, willful vision and strange grace. Somewhat psychically akin to Van Morrison's *Astral Weeks* and Leonard Cohen's earliest work, this was orphic, amorphously lovely stuff. With titles like "Phantasmagoria in Two" and "I Never Asked to Be Your Mountain," the record's lyrics recalled Wallace Stevens, and Buckley's voice seemed almost a little mad in its dramatic versatility (he sounds alternately like a child, a crone and a straightforwardly expert folk singer). With his tone poems extending to ten and twelve minutes on *Happy/Sad*, the songs soared past any verse-chorus-verse structure; this was abstract expressionism of a rare bravery. So were Buckley's next three albums, with the jazzy *Starsailor* being that

cluster's standout. Perhaps frustrated with his cultic status, Buckley then veered wildly—*Greetings From L.A.* was rock, of a sort, and *Look at the Fool* was desperate (his voice sounds like a croaking Al Green, and the record funks around to no purpose). In his glory hour, however, Tim Buckley embodied all the virtue of grace. — P.E.

BUCKWHEAT ZYDECO
★★ Take It Easy Baby (Blues Unlimited, 1980)
★★★ 100% Fortified Zydeco (Black Top, 1983)
★★ Turning Point (Rounder, 1984)
★★½ Waitin' for My Ya Ya (Rounder, 1985)
★★★ Zydeco Party (Rounder, 1987)
★★★★ On a Night Like This (Island, 1987)
★★★½ Taking It Home (Island, 1988)
★★★★ Where There's Smoke, There's Fire (Island, 1990)
★★★½ On Track (Charisma, 1992)

One of several pretenders to Clifton Chenier's throne, Stanley "Buckwheat" Dural Jr. is a journeyman blues player and competent zydeco accordionist whose recordings, though seldom exceptional, are rarely less than entertaining. He actually began his professional career as an R&B organist, and is a fair soloist in the Jimmy McGriff mold, as "Jasperoux" (from *100% Fortified Zydeco*) attests. As a zydeco accordionist, though, he's an oddity. Though he clearly knows the repertoire (no surprise, considering the time he spent as part of Chenier's Red Hot Louisiana Band), Buckwheat's approach to the traditional material is considerably less convincing than his creole-style takes on pop tunes, as he shows with his version of Mungo Jerry's "In the Summertime" (*100% Fortified Zydeco*).

Unfortunately, it was a while before this truth dawned on any of his producers. Hence, *Take It Easy, Baby* attempts to re-create the blues-based sound of Chenier's early recordings; *Turning Point* meanders from bayou funk (the title tune) to half-hearted rock ("Tutti Frutti"); and *Waitin' for My Ya Ya* alternates between the classic New Orleans rhythms of "My Feet Can't Fail Me Now" or "Tee Nah Nah" and such oddities as a reggae-style version of Lee Dorsey's "Ya Ya." (*Zydeco Party* combines the best moments of *Turning* and *Waitin'* with a fiery performance of "Hot Tamale Baby.")

On a Night Like This, however, solves most of Buckwheat's problems. Not only does producer Ted Fox wisely emphasize the resilient groove of Buckwheat's rhythm section, which creates a pulse that puts plenty of punch into "Ma 'Tit Fille," but he also matches Buckwheat with a handful of stunningly appropriate covers, including the Blasters' "Marie Marie," Booker T.'s "Time Is Tight" and the Dylan title tune. Both *Taking It Home* and *Where There's Smoke, There's Fire* continue in that vein, although the mostly traditional *Home* offers but a single cover, a version of Derek and the Dominos' "Why Does Love Got to Be So Sad." *Smoke*, on the other hand, not only pairs Buckwheat with Los Lobos' David Hidalgo, it even brings in Dwight Yoakam for an inspired "Hey, Good Lookin'." But *On Track* is neither as ambitious nor as successful, despite a sterling rendition of "The Midnight Special." — J.D.C.

BUFFALO SPRINGFIELD

★ ★ ★½ **Buffalo Springfield (Atco, 1966)**
★ ★ ★ ★ ★ **Buffalo Springfield Again (Atco, 1967)**
★ ★ ★ **Last Time Around (Atco, 1968)**
★ ★ ★ **Retrospective (Atco, 1969)**
★ ★ ★ ★ ★ **Buffalo Springfield (Atco, 1973)**

Creative tension between Stephen Stills, the highly proficient craftsman, and Neil Young, the erractic, extreme genius, produced, in Buffalo Springfield, one of America's best '60s bands. Simultaneously more of a mainstream musical pro and more of an unexamined hippie than the idiosyncratic Young, Stills sang declamatory vocals and played tremolo guitar on "For What It's Worth," a 1967 Top Ten hit decrying the Sunset Strip riots in which flower children faced off the police. Young's standout from the debut was the characteristically ambitious "Nowadays Clancy Can't Even Sing" with its surreal poetry and keening vocals.

Potentially nearly an American Beatles, the supergroup employed orchestral arrangements, four-part vocals, Wild West mythmaking, unrivaled instrumental prowess—and a fertile internal explosiveness along the lines of the Who's. Stills's finest hour came with the band; "Bluebird" and "Rock & Roll Woman" find him a stronger singer and more versatile guitarist than he's ever been since. And in Buffalo Springfield, Young tried out not only such bravura cinematic fare as "Broken Arrow," but premiered the artful naivete of "I Am a Child," its resonant simplicity paving the way for his solo hits.

The other members were hardly slouches.

Rhythm guitarist Richie Furay's "Kind Woman" served as a blueprint for the refined country rock he'd later make with Poco. Bassist Jim Messina would join Furay in Poco, and then pair with Kenny Loggins in one of the '70s biggest soft-rock acts. The band's twin peaks, of course, would fitfully collaborate again in Crosby, Stills, Nash and Young—an inflated Springfield that, for all its musical achievement and countercultural significance, lacked the buoyancy of its prototype.

Only two years after its dazzling start, the Springfield was just a memory. But a memory that lingers: rock & roll this expert and melodic would prove hard to find in the years to come. — P.E.

JIMMY BUFFETT

★ ★ ★½ **A White Sport Coat & a Pink Crusteacean (MCA, 1973)**
★ ★ ★½ **Living and Dying in 3/4 Time (MCA, 1974)**
★ ★ ★½ **A1A (MCA, 1974)**
★ ★ ★ **Havana Daydreamin' (MCA, 1976)**
★ ★ ★ **Changes in Latitudes, Changes in Attitudes (MCA, 1977)**
★ ★½ **Son of a Son of a Sailor (MCA, 1978)**
★ ★ **Volcano (MCA, 1979)**
★ ★½ **Coconut Telegraph (MCA, 1981)**
★ ★ **Somewhere Over China (MCA, 1981)**
★ ★ **Last Mango in Paris (MCA, 1985)**
★ ★ **Off to See the Lizard (MCA, 1989)**
★ ★ ★ **Boats Beaches Bars & Ballads (Margaritaville/MCA, 1992)**

Success turned Jimmy Buffett into a human tourist attraction; surprisingly, this Southern singer-songwriter's early albums have a lot more to offer than escape fantasies and drinking songs. Never a strong singer, Buffett nonetheless displays a subtle, winning touch with country love songs. The beautiful "Come Monday" (from *Living and Dying in 3/4 Time*) established him on the pop charts, and that plainspoken ache and quiet melody still cut deep. A former journalist and history major, Buffett unassumingly puts his literate background to good use: his story-songs resonate with sharp observations, his travelogues include a strong sense of time and place, his shaggy-dog tales stay on the leash. And most importantly, he applies his wry sense of humor to counterculture hedonism, even as he celebrates it. At his best, Jimmy Buffett casts a musical spell that's as intoxicating as the quirky characters and situations he describes.

Living & Dying and *A White Sport Coat & a Pink Crustacean* mix chunky little bits of honky-tonk and Western swing into Buffett's defiantly left-of-center sensibility, preventing him from becoming too ironic. *A1A* (named after Florida's coastal highway) introduces the seafaring theme on cuts like "Trying to Reason With Hurricane Season," "A Pirate Looks at Forty" and "Nautical Wheelers." Buffett captures the lazy serenity of a steamy late summer day on "Life Is Just a Tire Swing"—effortless, graceful and damn near impossible to repeat.

That didn't stop him from trying, of course. As his musical approach turns slick and more pop-oriented, Jimmy Buffett begins to sound routine. *Changes in Latitudes* made him a superstar, briefly, but only the breakthrough hit "Margaritaville" exudes the pungent, evocative air of the old albums. The sound is breezy soft rock, but the self-recriminating edge is pure country: "Some people say there's a woman to blame/but I know it's my own damn fault." After that flash of insight, Jimmy Buffett retreats to his own personal "Margaritaville"—at least he knew what he was getting into.

The rest of Buffett's ouevre—including a half-dozen '80s albums not reviewed—exists solely for his cult: the "Parrotheads," who flock to his annual tours. Presumably, they're too juiced and/or buzzed to notice the curdling synths on *Last Mango in Paris* (1985) or the fact that Jimmy sounds like a waterlogged James Taylor impersonator on *Off to See the Lizard.* The overly generous four-CD boxed set, *Boats Beaches Bars & Ballads,* plays up the party atmosphere *ad nauseum.* — M.C.

BULLETBOYS

★ ★½ **BulletBoys (Warner Bros., 1989)**
★ ★½ **Freakshow (Warner Bros., 1991)**
Imitation Van Halen, with all the hormones but only half the musicality. — J.D.C.

ERIC BURDON

★ ★ ★ **The Greatest Hits of Eric Burdon and the Animals (MGM, 1969)**
★ ★½ **Eric Burdon Declares War (1970; Rhino, 1992)**
★ ★ ★ **Wicked Man (GNP, 1988)**
After singing top-notch R&B with the original Animals, the brilliant, brawling Eric Burdon moved to Californa and reconstructed himself as an ultra-hippie. His new band, Eric Burdon and the Animals, were nothing like the original crew—they

made novelty singles, albums awash in psychedelic clichés, and strange, overheated epics. Their out-of-print albums are hard to find, but *Greatest Hits* covers the essentials. It's a strange collection, but in some ways compelling—Burdon is so fervent a vocalist that he makes even a slight single like "Sky Pilot," with its phase-shifter effects and clunky anti-war message, sound almost significant, and when he goes for broke on an operatic treatment of the Bee Gees' "To Love Somebody" or Ike and Tina Turner's "River Deep, Mountain High," he achieves the thrilling, almost surreal melodrama of a mad, latter-day Gene Pitney.

Frenzied in his passion for black music, Burdon began working with a California funk outfit in 1970. "Spill the Wine" was the first, and very infectious single, released by Eric Burdon and War, and found on *Declares War.* A followup double-album, *Black Man's Burdon* (out of print), however, was embarrassingly inflated, and the exhausted singer left War to its own devices. War flourished; he floundered. Recording with one of his idols, blues legend Jimmy Witherspoon, he turned in a credible performance on *Guilty!* (now out of print)—but the '70s as a whole were a wasteland for the singer.

The Eric Burdon Band was basically a wash-out. Burdon reunited with the original Animals and flourished briefly in the early '80s, and then put out the solo album *Wicked Man* (1988). Recorded with a cast of nobodies, the record features solid, undistinguished playing—but Burdon's voice sounds, as always, remarkable. A certain pathos attends his remake of the Animals' classic "House of the Rising Sun"—that of a brilliant talent, lost and nearly forgotten. — P.E.

SOLOMON BURKE

★ ★ ★ ★ **The Best of Solomon Burke (1965; Atlantic, 1989)**
★ ★ ★ **Into My Life You Came (Savoy, NA)**
★ ★ ★ **Lord, We Need a Miracle (Savoy, NA)**
★ ★ ★ ★ **Soul Alive (Rounder, 1984)**
★ ★ ★ **A Change Is Gonna Come (Rounder, 1986)**
★ ★ ★½ **Home Land (Bizarre/Straight, 1991)**
★ ★ ★ ★ **Home in Your Heart: The Best of Solomon Burke (Rhino/Atlantic, 1992)**
Whether Solomon Burke is the first true soul artist may be a matter of dispute; that

he is a pioneer of the form is unquestioned. His first hit, "Just Out of Reach (of My Two Open Arms)," was a country song to which Burke gave an R&B spin with his smooth, crooning style. That's typical: Burke's music—not only his hits for Atlantic in the '60s, but his gospel and secular work over the decades—shows his deep affinity for gospel, country and R&B. While his hits were few—five in the Top Forty—and hardly monstrous (the easy-rocking "Got to Get You Off My Mind," from 1965, was his highest charting single at Number 22), Burke was a profound influence on '60s soul singers. Not only is his music steeped in varied traditions, he is as convincing a balladeer as he is a shouter. Atlantic's *The Best of Solomon Burke* is an excellent overview of his most important recordings, most of which he had a hand in writing; in addition, the CD version contains seven tracks unavailable on other configurations. The wonderful two-CD anthology *Home in Your Heart* includes "Got to Get You Off My Mind" and 39 other classic recordings from 1962–68.

Burke has continued recording and performing, and he's stayed close to his gospel roots. The Savoy albums are by turns fire and brimstone and soothing and meditative, with the message coming through loud and clear whatever the approach. Burke's two Rounder releases bring him back to the secular world. *Soul Alive* is a live album that catches him in one of his feistier moods, ranging across a broad spectrum of material that includes several of his Atlantic sides and stirring interpretations of songs identified with other legends, such as "Send Me Some Lovin' " (Little Richard), "He'll Have to Go" (Jim Reeves), "I Almost Lost My Mind" (Nat King Cole) and "I Can't Stop Loving You" (Ray Charles). *A Change Is Gonna Come*, a studio album, is a spotty attempt at updating Burke's sound. When it works, it's startling—his take on "A Change is Gonna Come" is given added resonance by the sadness, almost resignation, in his delivery; there's a world of pain in his voice. His 1991 release, *Home Land*, shows Burke in fine form, singing with conviction on the hard-hitting "Baby Please Don't Cry" and a powerful version of Otis Redding's "Try a Little Tenderness." — D.M.

T-BONE BURNETT

★★★ Truth Decay (Takoma, 1980)
★★★½ Trap Door (Warner Bros., 1982)
★★ Proof Through the Night (Warner Bros., 1983)
★★★ T Bone Burnett (Dot, 1986)
★★★★ The Talking Animals (Columbia, 1988)
★★★★ The Criminal Under My Own Hat (Columbia, 1992)

A terrific songwriter but a terrible sermonizer, T-Bone Burnett makes albums that offer an intriguing, sometimes maddening mixture of roots-oriented rock and high-minded rant. His first album, *Truth Decay*, is a solidly melodic, rockabilly-based outing that gets a little ham-fisted with its message (as in his the-devil-is-an-adman number, "Madison Avenue") but keeps the music light and lithe. Amazingly, *Trap Door* uses the same band but offers a completely different sound, which at its best—"Hold On Tight," say, or "I Wish You Could Have Seen Her Dance"—has all the chiming effervescence of a latter-day Byrds album. The production values are even higher on *Proof Through the Night*, which brings in a passel of high-profile guest musicians (Ry Cooder, Mick Ronson, Richard Thompson, Pete Townshend), but the high-gloss sound doesn't much help the material, which ultimately collapses under the weight of its bitterly pedantic lyrics.

Burnett throws a curve ball with *T Bone Burnett*, a more-or-less conventional country album that's wonderfully well sung but a tad too low-key. *The Talking Animals*, on the other hand, not only finds him returning to rock & roll, but regaining the ground lost with *Proof Through the Night* through wickedly funny songs like "Image," a tango in four languages, or the dementedly Pirandellian "The Strange Case of Frank Cash and the Morning Paper." *The Criminal Under My Own Hat* continues in that vein, offering such sonically delicious concoctions as the dense Bo Diddley groove powering "Tear This Building Down" and the slide-guitar-and-string-quartet combination that brightens "Every Little Thing." — J.D.C.

JOHNNY BURNETTE & THE ROCK N' ROLL TRIO

★★★★ Tear It Up (Solid Smoke, 1976)

Splendid, often inspired pop-rockabilly. The influence of this Memphis-based trio (brothers Johnny and Dorsey Burnette and Paul Burlison), whose success was mostly regional, has been long-standing and widespread. Particularly notable is guitarist Burlison, who perfected a fuzz-tone sound by loosening a tube in his amp. Until MCA decides to reactivate its Rock n' Roll Trio catalogue, this out of print Solid Smoke reissue from 1976 will have to suffice.

The Trio seemed always to be imitating rather than anticipating Elvis Presley's next move, and the band's recordings are rife with that most sincere form of flattery. Still, Johnny Burnette's vocals have a fire about them that cuts through the heavy echo of strong efforts such as "Honey Hush," "Lonesome Train" and "Tear It Up." That the Trio was also adept at boogie and uptempo blues is indicated by their takes on "Drinkin' Wine Spo-Dee-O-Dee" and "Train Kept a-Rollin'." As success eluded them, the brothers became disenchanted with their music and with each other, and in the fall of 1957 the Trio, which had been recording for only a year, disbanded. Dorsey went on to cut a hit single in 1960, "Tall Oak Tree," and Johnny carved out a couple of major pop hits for himself that same year in "Dreamin' " and "You're Sixteen." Johnny's in particular were fine pop performances, but the material was far softer than the tough stuff the Trio had dealt. Both Burnette brothers are now dead, Johnny having drowned in 1964, Dorsey having suffered a fatal heart attack in 1979.
— D.M.

BURNING SPEAR

★★★★   **Marcus Garvey (Island, 1976)**
★★★½   **Garvey's Ghost (Island, 1976)**
★★★★   **Man in the Hills (1976; Mango, 1989)**
★★★★   **Dry and Heavy (1977; Mango, 1992)**
★★★   **Live (1978; Mango, 1991)**
★★★★½ **Harder Than the Rest (1979; Mango, 1991)**
★★★   **Far Over (Heartbeat, 1982)**
★★★   **Fittest of the Fittest (Heartbeat, 1983)**
★★★   **Resistance (Heartbeat, 1984)**
★★★★   **Reggae Greats (1984; Mango, 1991)**
★★★   **Mistress Music (Slash, 1988)**
★★★   **Live in Paris: Zenith, 1988 (Slash, 1989)**
★★★★   **Marcus Garvey/Garvey's Ghost (Mango, 1990)**
★★½   **Mek We Dweet (Mango, 1991)**
★★½   **Jah Kingdom (Mango, 1991)**

While Bob Marley brought reggae to worldwide attention, Burning Spear struck at the heart of the music's roots consciousness. Winston Rodney's deep, steamy vocal streams lull and hypnotize, yet repetition renders his messages crystal clear.

"Do you remember the days of slavery?" he wonders, sadly, on *Marcus Garvey*'s "Slavery Days." The graceful force of his voice makes that catchy chorus a subtly insistent reminder, rather than a rhetorical question. Through its thick rhythms and crisp horn charts Burning Spear's debut asserts the Rastafarian tenet that black identity and liberation can only be achieved through an understanding of history. *Garvey's Ghost* was one of the first instrumental "dub" albums released outside of Jamaica, and it's still one of the most listenable examples of this ganja-fuelled artform: a real must for connoisseurs of modern scratch 'n' sample dance music. (Though the first two albums fell out of print, they were reissued together by Mango in 1990.)

Man in the Hills posits Rodney as a rural mystic and the Jamaican equivalent of a country singer; as his singing reaches after cloud-dappled transcendence, his words frequently evoke the hard-scrabble day-to-day family life in those mountains. *Dry and Heavy* counterbalances the anger and dread of the early albums by displaying a downright optimistic side; the stunning anti-war anthem "Throw Down Your Arms" proves Rodney isn't some cranky, dreadlocked prophet of doom.

Drawing from those albums and the import-only *Social Living* (1980), Burning Spear's greatest-hits collection is indeed *Harder Than the Rest*. Along with Bob Marley and the Wailers' breakthough albums, *Harder* provides a key to the rich Jamaican musical kingdom. The later *Reggae Greats* set—which duplicates many tracks—serves as a passable substitute.

After releasing several albums on his own label, Winston Rodney re-emerged on Slash in the late '80s with a sharp, rangy new band. Mushy songwriting sinks the impeccable performances on Burning Spear's recent releases, though; the *Live in Paris* album sounds exciting on the surface, but Rodney never fully connects with these old-fashioned love songs. While Burning Spear's original Rasta-fied groove deepens with time, its latter-day romantic glow quickly fades. — M.C.

KATE BUSH

★★½   **The Kick Inside (EMI America, 1978)**
★★   **Lionheart (EMI America, 1978)**
★★½   **Never for Ever (EMI America, 1980)**
★★★   **The Dreaming (EMI America, 1982)**

★★½ **Kate Bush (EP) (EMI America, 1983)**

★★★½ **The Hounds of Love (EMI America, 1985)**

★★★★ **The Whole Story (EMI America, 1986)**

★★★★ **The Sensual World (Columbia, 1989)**

Eccentric and idiosyncratic, this woman's work is an odd offshoot of English art rock, capturing much of its spirit while avoiding the worst of its instrumental indulgences. Despite an occasional flash of pop accessibility, her early efforts are easily dismissed. *The Kick Inside*, with its effusive arrangements and parade of dead lovers, seems almost a parody of rock romanticism; *Lionheart* was a rush-job, and sounds it; *Never for Ever*, though stylistically adventurous, is undercut by uneven arrangements. Eventually, Bush discovered digital synthesis, and with it constructed a universe better suited to her songs. Unlike her early albums, the sound of *The Dreaming* and *The Hounds of Love* is as focused as it is fantastic, lending credibility to her witches, sorcerers and demon lovers. After *The Whole Story*, a greatest hits collection, Bush jettisoned such juvenalia altogether; though her music maintained its sense of aural adventure, she addressed herself to more mature (and markedly feminine) material in *The Sensual World*. — J.D.C.

JERRY BUTLER

★★ **Love's on the Menu (Motown, 1976)**

★★ **Suite for the Single Girl (Motown, 1977)**

★★★★★ **Only the Strong Survive (The Legendary Philadelphia Hits) (Mercury, 1984)**

★★★½ **The Best of Jerry Butler (Rhino, 1987)**

Jerry Butler founded the Impressions in 1957 with fellow choir member Curtis Mayfield. He sang lead on "For Your Precious Love," the Chicago-based vocal group's 1958 breakthrough, and then promptly went solo. Recording for the local Vee Jay label, Butler scored several R&B chart hits in the '60s: most notably the Top Tenners "He Will Break Your Heart" and "Let It Be Me" (a duet with Betty Everett). But the lightning didn't really strike until he hitched up with fledgling producers Kenny Gamble and Leon Huff in the late '60s. Zap! What would later be dubbed "the Sound of Philadelphia" first arises on Butler's magnificent string of Mercury singles: "Never Give You Up," "Hey, Western Union Man," "Only the Strong Survive," "Moody Woman." This is the sound of Gamble and Huff arriving: the full arrangements are razor-sharp, each instrument crystal-clear in the dynamic mix. Butler's burnished voice—sleek but gutsy—is a natural complement to Gamble and Huff's orchestral ambitions and uplifting lyrics. His two great Mercury albums (*Ice on Ice* and *The Iceman Cometh*) are both out of print, but *The Legendary Philadelphia Hits* will more than suffice. The Motown albums are failed disco accommodations. *The Best of Jerry Butler* on Rhino collects the pre-Philly hits; unfortunately, some dated early '60s filler ("Moon River") is included as well. — M.C.

THE PAUL BUTTERFIELD BLUES BAND

★★★★ **The Paul Butterfield Blues Band (Elektra, 1965)**

★★★★ **East-West (Elektra, 1966)**

★★★★ **The Resurrection of Pigboy Crabshaw (1968; Elektra, 1989)**

★★★ **In My Own Dream (Elektra, 1968)**

★★★ **The Butterfield Blues Band Live (Elektra, 1971)**

★★★★ **Golden Butter: The Best of the Paul Butterfield Blues Band (Elektra, 1972)**

PAUL BUTTERFIELD

★★★ **It All Comes Back (1973; Rhino, 1987)**

★★★ **Better Days (1973; Rhino, 1987)**

★★ **Put It in Your Ear (1976; Rhino, 1987)**

★★ **North South (1981; Rhino, 1987)**

The Rolling Stones and Led Zeppelin toyed brilliantly with the blues, thus broadcasting versions of that deep music to middle-class teens who wouldn't have heard it otherwise. Chicago's Paul Butterfield played the blues straight—but not soberly. One of rock's truly honorable figures, it was Butterfield in fact who introduced the magic of Otis Rush, Little Walter, Buddy Guy and others into the mainstream and, in the process, helped mold Mike Bloomfield and Elvin Bishop into premier guitarists. Modesty and zeal marked his approach—a strong harpist, he was a reverent aspirant to the singing of his black mentors, not an original stylist—and while his mission at times seemed more instructive than creative, he didn't play like any professor. With standout solos by Bloomfield and Bishop, *East West* (1966) showed early skill and confidence. Even with Bloomfield departed, *The Resurrection of Pigboy Crabshaw* was even stronger—and more relaxed. On the epic nine minutes of "Driftin' and Driftin'," a fine horn section highlighted by David Sanborn gets down grittily, but tastefully; "Born Under a Bad Sign" kicks, and on "Pity the Fool," Butterfield sounds more uninhibited than he ever would again. The record's R&B pep shows a progress away from the very careful attack of the first two albums—and a casual verve the singer would never quite recover.

It All Comes Back and *Better Days* were post-Blues Band projects: each was steady, sure and unremarkable. Only by the time of *Put It In Your Ear* and *North South,* however, did Butterfield appear to be running out of steam. The first was an incoherent crossover attempt, chockful of bad strings and big-name sidemen (Levon Helm, Eric Gale, Bernard Purdie); the second was an idea that should've worked—a partnership with Al Green's legendary Memphis producer, Willie Mitchell. Instead, it backfires, embarrassing Butterfield in its clumsy funk. — P.E.

BUTTHOLE SURFERS

★ ★ ★ ★ **Butthole Surfers (Alternative Tentacles, 1983)**
★ ★ ★ ★ **Live PCPPEP (Alternative Tentacles, 1984)**
★ ★ ★ **Psychic . . . Powerless . . . Another Man's Sac (Touch and Go, 1984)**
★ ★ **Cream Corn From the Socket of Davis (EP) (Touch and Go, 1985)**
★ ★ ★½ **Rembrandt Pussyhorse (Touch and Go, 1986)**
★ ★ **Locust Abortion Technician (Touch and Go, 1987)**
★ ★ **Hairway to Steven (Touch and Go, 1988)**
★ ★ **piouhgd (Rough Trade, 1991)**

Unlike most shock rock, which uses gross-out tactics as a cynical means to guarantee a reaction, the Butthole Surfers' early albums are shocking not as a result of their content (which starts with the tasteless and goes downhill) but because the group is so genuine in its depravity. Take, as an example, "The Shah Sleeps in Lee Harvey's Grave" from *Butthole Surfers;* as horribly funny as Gibby Haynes's demented rhymes are, what gives the performance its disquieting power is the way it ends, with Paul Leary's ear-shredding guitar noise shuddering to a stop over the anguished screams of someone yelling "Shut up!" Like

many of the album's other tracks, the weirdness is much too real to qualify as mere dadaist showmanship. Scarier still, the music is often catchy, with a surprisingly strong sense of melody and structure.

Much of the debut's material is repeated on the *Live PCPPEP,* which lacks some of its predecessor's intensity but makes the most of Leary's grunge-and-grind. But *Psychic . . . Powerless . . . Another Man's Sac* finds the Buttholes hitting new lows in vulgarity (early copies were pressed on piss-colored vinyl), while maintaining their musical standards through efforts like the dirtball boogie tune "Lady Sniff."

Things decline sharply, though, as the group begins to cater to the thrill-seeking pseudo-bohemians that made up the bulk of its audience. With *Locust Abortion Technician,* the electronic effects that had shaped the guitar noise on *Creamed Corn From the Socket of Davis* had come to dominate the group's sound, much to the music's detriment; by *pioughd,* it had degenerated to third-rate electro-noise, with material no more shocking than the average WaxTrax band, and a lot less imaginative. — J.D.C.

THE BUZZCOCKS

★ ★ ★ ★ ★ **Singles Going Steady (I.R.S., 1979)**
★ ★ ★½ **A Different Kind of Tension (I.R.S., 1980)**
★ ★ ★ **Lest We Forget (ROIR, 1988)**
★ ★ ★ ★ **Product (Restless Retro, 1989)**
★ ★ ★ **The Peel Sessions Album (Strange Fruit/Dutch East India, 1991)**
★ ★ ★ ★ **Operators Manual (I.R.S., 1991)**

Hurtling along at an uncommon velocity, this Manchester, England, quartet went against the grain of punk in several ways. Guitarist Pete Shelley wrote pointed, pungent lyrics about sex and, yes, romance. And the best Buzzcocks songs—a series of eight English import singles—are grounded by stong rhythms, tightly wound choruses and firm melodies. From "Orgasm Addict" (1977) onward, the band issued a flow of evocative three-minute eruptions. Lead singer Shelley is a perfectly capable and affecting howler. *Singles Going Steady,* the group's U.S. debut, follows as the Buzzcocks leap from peak to peak: "Ever Fallen in Love," covered by Fine Young Cannibals ten years later, is barely the tip of the iceberg. *A Different Kind of Tension,* the followup, includes another jagged gem

("You Say You Don't Love Me") as well as the Buzzcocks' inevitable attempts to expand their influential power-pop formula. The results are mixed, though bassist Steve Diggle proves an able songwriter and Shelley's seven-minute opus ("I Believe") is a stunner. The gleeful way he shouts that bleak chorus—"there is no love in this world anymore"—indicates that he'll keep searching for it anyway. After releasing several disastrously arty singles in Britain, the Buzzcocks broke up in 1981. Neither of the subsequent live albums—*Lest We Forget* and *The Peel Sessions*—supplants the original versions, though both communicate the band's surprisingly raw in-concert buzz. *Product* is a soup-to-nuts collection: just about everything the band ever cut in the studio, plus some live tracks. Unfortunately, it's become quite scarce. *Operators Manual* is an extremely acceptable, easier-to-find alternative. Briefer and cheaper, this single-disc compilation taps the tune-heavy bulk of *Singles Going Steady* along with later highlights like "I Believe." Shelley released three solo albums in America: *Homosapien* (Arista, 1982), *XL1* (Arista, 1983) and *Heaven and the Sea* (Mercury, 1986) are all deleted. The title track of the former, a dance-floor hit in 1982, shocked a lot of old Buzzcocks fans with its scintillating synth-pop bubble beat and sexually ambiguous hook. But the rest of *Homosapien* will delight anyone taken with sweetly spaced-out choruses. Shelley reformed the Buzzcocks for a tour in 1990–91; an album seems inevitable. — M.C.

THE BYRDS
★ ★ ★ ★ ★   Mr. Tambourine Man (Columbia, 1965)
★ ★ ★ ★ ★   Turn! Turn! Turn! (Columbia, 1966)
★ ★ ★½   Fifth Dimension (Columbia, 1966)
★ ★ ★ ★   Younger Than Yesterday (Columbia, 1967)
★ ★ ★ ★ ★   Byrds' Greatest Hits (Columbia, 1967)
★ ★ ★ ★   The Notorious Byrd Brothers (Columbia, 1968)
★ ★ ★ ★½   Sweetheart of the Rodeo (Columbia, 1968)
★ ★ ★   Dr. Byrds & Mr. Hyde (Columbia, 1969)
★ ★ ★ ★½   Preflyte (1969; Columbia, 1973)
★ ★ ★ ★½   The Ballad of Easy Rider (1970; Columbia, 1989)
★ ★ ★ ★   (Untitled) (Columbia, 1970)
★ ★ ★   Byrdmaniax (Columbia, 1971)
★ ★ ★   Farther Along (Columbia, 1971)
★ ★ ★ ★ ★   The Best of the Byrds (Greatest Hits, Volume 2) (1972; Columbia, 1987)
★ ★   Byrds (Asylum, 1973)
★ ★ ★ ★   The Byrds Play Dylan (Columbia, 1980)
★ ★ ★ ★ ★   The Original Singles, 1965-1967 (Columbia, 1981)
★ ★ ★ ★   The Very Best of the Byrds (Pair, 1986)
★ ★ ★   Never Before (Reflyte, 1988)
★ ★ ★   In the Beginning (Rhino, NA)
★ ★ ★ ★ ★   The Byrds (Columbia, 1990)
★ ★ ★ ★   20 Essential Tracks From the Boxed Set: 1965–1990 (Columbia, 1992)

Roger McGuinn paid homage to the pop power of the Beatles in many ways: the anglophile spelling of "Byrds," the mod whimsy of his trademark granny sunglasses, basing his group's sound on infectious vocal harmonies and the fundamental rock & roll lineup of heavy bass, assertive drums and electric guitars. He also rewrote the Bob Dylan songbook in radio-speak, tightening arrangements and embellishing the new, catchy versions with his signature 12-string guitar. From this West Coast synthesis developed one of America's best bands and the folk-rock that few of the form's many later proponents would grace with anything near the elegance of the original version by the Byrds.

In short order, *Mr. Tambourine Man* and *Turn! Turn! Turn!* revolutionized American pop. In McGuinn, David Crosby and Gene Clark, the Byrds boasted a vocal ensemble nearly as inventive as the Beach Boys; in Chris Hillman, they had a bassist powerful enough to ground the celestial singing in a sure backbeat; and, with McGuinn's tastes predominating, the band flourished a sophisticated musical sensibility and a rare songwriting talent. Employing Dylan covers as their craftiest vehicle, they charged the AM airwaves with meaningful lyrics and melodies that challenged the standard three chords of radio pop.

With the uneven but ambitious *Fifth Dimension* came another progression, "Eight Miles High" and its pioneering psychedelia. Exuberant mind-warp lyrics met freer musical structures borrowed from Indian ragas and modal jazz; even while the record provoked other bands into flower-power paeans that often dwindled into fuzz-tone noodling, the Byrds' prototype featured playing of a characteristic precision. "Mr. Spaceman" was a hippie-ish tease of the country music the band soon would embrace more seriously; "John Riley" exemplified the folk fare that loomed large in the Byrds' repertoire, and the song's subtle strings typified the group's growing maturity.

Perhaps the Byrds' finest Dylan cut, "My Back Pages," joined the McGuinn/Hillman original "So You Want to Be a Rock 'n' Roll Star" in stamping *Younger Than Yesterday* as the work of a band gaining in thematic toughness; Crosby's "Everybody's Been Burned" also veered away from the Byrd's early sunniness. Personnel changes that soon became dizzying initiated the shift away from the congenial experimentation of the Byrds' first efforts; with both Gene Clark and Crosby departed, *The Notorious Byrd Brothers* seemed more the product of individuals than a band. "Draft Morning," "Wasn't Born to Follow" and "John Robertson" are all fine songs, but little stylistic unity shows through on the album.

Southern-born singer-songwriter Gram Parsons was a Byrd for only five months, but his influence was decisive. The same year Dylan returned to roots music on *John Wesley Harding*, the Byrds released *Sweetheart of the Rodeo*, an album of purist country that began the group's long spell of absorbing Nashville influence with more faith and less irony than did any other rock band, with the possible exception of the *American Beauty*–period Grateful Dead or the Flying Burrito Brothers (formed in 1968 by Parsons and Hillman). Penning beauties like "Hickory Wind" and "One Hundred Years from Now," and introducing traditional fare like the Louvin Brothers' "The Christian Life," Parsons was the driving force behind this shift in taste and, for a moment, a rival to McGuinn. Even after Parsons left, soon followed by Hillman, the Byrds retained their country graces boosted considerably by the subtleties of new guitarist Clarence White.

By this juncture, the country material had assumed a self-conscious, mythologized dimension best captured by "Chestnut Mare" and other songs off *Untitled* that McGuinn had hoped to form into a folk-opera he'd begun writing with psychologist Jacques Levy—and White's passionate playing couldn't be constrained by the severe style of pure country (check out *Untitled*'s "Lover of the Bayou").

Its title track, along with the rousing "Jesus Is Just Alright" and Woody Guthrie's "Deportee," made the *The Ballad of Easy Rider* the Byrds' last great studio album, but both *Byrdmaniax* and *Farther Along* would be considered stellar efforts if released by bands with a lesser history. *Preflyte* consists of excellent samplings from the early Byrds; most of its material had not been released previously. *Never Before* also exhumes great buried treasures. The boxed set, *The Byrds*, is a marvel, providing an exhaustive overview, fine outtakes (particularly of Parsons's and White's contributions) and smart notes by critic David Fricke. Tom Petty, R.E.M. and countless others have learned from the Byrds, and the musical uplift and spiritual verve of McGuinn and company remain remarkably fresh. — P.E.

DAVID BYRNE
★★★★ **The Complete Score From the Broadway Production of *The Catherine Wheel* (Sire, 1981)**
★★★★ **Music for *The Knee Plays* (ECM, 1985)**
★★½ **Rei Momo (Luaka Bop/Sire, 1989)**
★★½ **The Forest (Luaka Bop/Sire, 1991)**
★★★ **Uh-Oh (Warner Bros., 1992)**
WITH RYUICHI SAKAMOTO AND CONG SU
★★★½ **The Last Emperor (Virgin Movie Music, 1988)**

Most of David Byrne's diverse solo projects have been soundtracks for film, theater and dance projects; surprisingly, each one stands up on its own as an album. Good or bad, perhaps—but never indifferent. Credit the Talking Heads' frontman for pushing himself, even if his fidgety experiments don't always yield coherent results. He tends to nail a musical concept in several bold strokes, or miss it by a gaping margin. Byrne's first venture away from the Heads was a collaboration with Brian Eno, *My Life in the Bush of Ghosts. Music from "The Catherine Wheel"*—the accompanying score to a Twyla Tharp dance performance—sounds like a logical, stripped-down companion piece to the Heads' *Remain in Light*. Eno's influence is felt in the evocative electronic textures, but the haunting instrumentals get prodded along by Byrne's funk guitar. On a handful of actual songs, his compellingly stark vocals add vital contrast. "Big Blue Plymouth (Eyes Wide Open)" could stand with Talking Heads' very best, and the rest of *The Catherine Wheel* is far from incidental.

Music for "The Knee Plays," the spoken and sung score of an experimental theater piece by Robert Wilson, is earthier than its description could ever suggest. Smoothly incorporating the brass band struts and funeral marches of New Orleans into his downtown New York sensibility, Byrne proves that his intuitive musical skills cut deeper than those of the average world-music voyeur.

Given the general success of Byrne's African ventures and his astute series of compilation albums (*Brazil Classics*, Volumes One through Four), *Rei Momo*'s flat-footed attempt at duplicating salsa and other Latin American rhythms comes as a puzzling, unpleasant surprise. The lineup of musicians and singers is impeccable and Byrne's weird voice is more nimble than ever, yet even the solid melodies and sure rhythms of original compositions like "Make Believe Mambo" and "Dirty Old Town" never take hold. There's something about the words—urban distance and ironic angles, maybe—that doesn't fit with the music's organic, unaffected swing. On his 1992 outing, *Uh-Oh*, however, Byrne successfully mixes the Latin-Caribbean influences with Talking Heads-ish funk and pop, improving the sound. Along with co-composers Ryuichi Sakamoto and Cong Su, Byrne won the Best Soundtrack Oscar in 1989 for *The Last Emperor*. Perhaps inspired by that (deserved) prize, Byrne composed and conducted a fully orcestrated score for a 1991 film, *The Forest*. While it's by no means embarrassing or inept, *The Forest*'s demi-classical impressions don't come close to matching the dramatic ambience of *The Catherine Wheel* or *The Knee Plays*. — M.C.

C

CABARET VOLTAIRE
- ★★ **Mix-Up (1979; Mute, 1990)**
- ★★ **Live at the YMCA 27-10-79 (1979; Restless/Mute, 1990)**
- ★★ **Three Mantras (1980; Restless/Mute, 1990)**
- ★★ **The Voice of America (1980; Restless/Mute, 1990)**
- ★★½ **3 Crépuscule Tracks (EP) (Rough Trade, 1981)**
- ★★★½ **Red Mecca (1981; Restless/Mute, 1990)**
- ★★ **Johnny YesNo (1981; Restless/Mute, 1990)**
- ★★★★ **2x45 (1982; Restless/Mute, 1990)**
- ★★½ **Hai! (1982; Restless/Mute, 1990)**
- ★★½ **The Crackdown (Some Bizzare/Virgin, 1983)**
- ★★★½ **Micro-Phonies (Some Bizzare/Virgin, 1984)**
- ★★★ **The Drain Train (EP) (1986; Restless/Mute, 1990)**
- ★★★½ **Drinking Gasoline (Caroline, 1985)**
- ★★★½ **The Covenant, the Sword and the Arm of the Lord (Caroline, 1985)**
- ★★★ **Listen Up With Cabaret Voltaire (Restless/Mute, 1990)**
- ★★★★ **Code (EMI Manhattan, 1987)**
- ★★ **The Living Legends . . . (Restless/Mute, 1990)**
- ★★★ **Groovy, Laidback and Nasty (EMI Parlophone UK, 1990)**
- ★★★ **Body and Soul (Crépuscule, 1991)**
- ★★★½ **Colours (Mute/Plastex, 1991)**

Part of the problem with pioneering electronic acts is that the music they produce is often more influential than it is listenable. Take Cabaret Voltaire as an example. This duo was among the first rock acts to tie electronic dissonance to trance-like rhythms, and also to lead the way in the use of "found sound"—that is, taped snippets of TV preachers or police announcements that would later be incorporated as ironic commentary into the group's recordings. In fact, most of what has since been done to death by avant-garde dance music groups like Revolting Cocks or Front 242 was done first by Cabaret Voltaire.

So why are so many of Cabaret Voltaire's albums so excruciatingly dull? Part of the problem is that the Cabs were frequently more interested in musical method than compositional content, meaning that the "how" of their music frequently outweighed the "why." As such, most of the group's early output, from the primitive singles and live tracks collected on *The Living Legends* . . . to the densely layered textures of *3 Crépuscule Tracks*, is gratingly monotonous; *Three Mantras* is interesting for its Eastern influences and *Voice of America* has a few intriguing soundbites, but that's about as far as it goes. Things begin to change with *Red Mecca*, on which the interplay between the synths and the percussion lends an exotic flavor to the music on "A Touch of Evil" and its ilk. There are also some interesting touches on *2x45*, particularly the sparring saxophones on "Protection" and the subtle Middle Eastern groove behind "Get Out of My Face."

Still, it isn't until *Micro-Phonies* that Cabaret Voltaire is able to convert its interest in static structures into anything resembling conventional dance music. Although the melodic interest remains fairly limited, there's a surprising amount of pop appeal in the way Stephen Mallinder's vocals play off Richard H. Kirk's churning electronics on "Do Right" and the slow-churning "Spies in the Wires." Both *Drinking Gasoline* and *The Covenant, the Sword and the Arm of the Lord* further the advances made by *Micro-Phonies*, but it isn't until the hard, mechanical pulse of *Code* that Cabaret Voltaire finds the ideal balance between accessibility and menace; between the hard-edged funk of "Sex,

Money, Freaks" and the clanking pulse powering "Here to Go," this is perhaps the duo's most exhilarating work. Strangely, from there the Cabs coast into predictability with the house-influenced *Groovy, Laidback and Nasty*, which sounds almost pop-friendly on tunes like the buoyant "Keep On (I Got This Feeling)." But *Body and Soul* returns the group to the brittle minimalism of yore, while the nastier moments of *Colours* manage to turn the beat-driven colorism of acid house into the musical equivalent of a bad trip. — J.D.C.

THE CADILLACS
★ ★ ★½ **The Best of the Cadillacs (Rhino, 1990)**

A group that went through numerous personnel changes and produced a host of splinter groups billing themselves as the Cadillacs is represented on this collection by its best-known recordings featuring the *sine qua non* by which all Cadillacs must be measured: lead singer Earl "Speedy" Carroll, whose smooth-as-silk tenor proved a most malleable instrument over the years. On the group's first hit, "Gloria," he struck a blow for the soaring, plaintive lead vocal that set a standard for all group harmony contingents aspiring to the pantheon. Conversely, on the group's signature song, "Speedoo," he adopted a singsong conversational patter that was itself a hilarious comment on the pretense and braggadocio of his self-proclaimed finesse with women. Carroll could also deliver a straight-ahead lyric with sensitivity and feeling, minus any gimmicks or comedic turns, as he does here on such mellow Cadillacs' entries as "Zoom," "You Are" and "Tell Me Today," the latter showing the 1960 version of the group (only Carroll remained of the original members) moving toward the middle of the road, softening its sound with strings and orchestral backgrounds. Nevertheless, Carroll's vocal is all nuance and control, caressing the high notes just so at the right moment, coming back soft and tender in other passages. Carroll continues to work with yet another configuration of Cadillacs and also performs for his favorite audience—children at school assemblies at P.S. 87 in Manhattan, where he works as the head custodian. He's still got it, too. — D.M.

JOHN CAFFERTY AND THE BEAVER BROWN BAND
★ ★ **Eddie and the Cruisers (Scotti Bros., 1983)**
★ **Tough All Over (Scotti Bros., 1985)**
★ **Eddie and the Cruisers II: Eddie Lives! (Scotti Bros., 1989)**
½ ★ **Eddie and the Cruisers: Unreleased Tapes (Scotti Bros., 1991)**
★ **Live in Concert (Scotti Bros., 1992)**

A *New York Times* headline once suggested that "If There Hadn't Been a Bruce Springsteen, Then the Critics Would Have Made Him Up," but that's utter nonsense. If rock critics had tried to invent a Springsteen, this is what they would have come up with—a singer who understands rock's drama and tradition but lacks the vision necessary to transform them into something greater. In other words, John Cafferty.

Cafferty's Springsteen-style raps and Jersey Shore backing band suit the *Eddie and the Cruisers* soundtrack well enough, particularly when left to oldies like "Runaround Sue." But Cafferty's writing is as obvious as it is contrived, and though some of the music's silliness can be blamed on the script (particularly the Rimbaud-without-a-clue "Season in Hell"), that excuse does not apply to the grandiloquent claptrap of *Tough All Over*. As for *Eddie* and *the Cruisers II*, it's no better a soundtrack than it was a movie, while *The Unreleased Tapes* should have stayed that way. — J.D.C.

J.J. CALE
★ ★ ★   **Really . . . J.J. Cale (1972; Mercury, 1990)**
★ ★½ **Naturally . . . J.J. Cale (1972; Mercury, 1987)**
★ ★   **Okie (1974; Mercury, 1990)**
★ ★   **Troubadour (1976; Mercury, 1987)**
★ ★   **5 (1979; Mercury, 1990)**
★ ★   **Shades (1980; Mercury, 1991)**
★ ★   **Grasshopper (Mercury, 1982)**
★ ★   **8 (Mercury, 1983)**
★ ★ ★   **Special Edition (Mercury, 1988)**

This Tulsa-based white country-blues stylist is best remembered through a pair of cover versions: his "After Midnight" got a jolt of slowhand power from Eric Clapton, while Lynyrd Skynyrd applied a rhythmic goose to "Call Me the Breeze." J.J. Cale's original versions (both on the debut, *Really*) dribble along like molasses. Any more laid-back and he'd be snoring. Subsequent albums emphasize the country end of his equation; if *emphasize* isn't too forceful a word, that is. — M.C.

JOHN CALE
★ ★ ★½ **Vintage Violence (1970; Columbia, 1990)**

★ ★ ★   **Church of Anthrax (Columbia, 1971)**
★ ★ ★   **The Academy in Peril (Reprise, 1972)**
★ ★ ★ ½   **Paris 1919 (Reprise, 1973)**
★ ★ ★ ★   **Fear (Island, 1974)**
★ ★ ★ ★   **Slow Dazzle (Island, 1975)**
★ ★ ★ ½   **Helen of Troy (Island import, 1975)**
★ ★ ★ ★ ½ **Guts (Island, 1977)**
★ ★ ★   **Sabotage Live (Spy/I.R.S., 1979)**
★ ★ ★   **Honi Soit (A&M, 1981)**
★ ★ ★   **Music for a New Society (ZE/Island/Passport, 1982)**
★ ★ ½   **Caribbean Sunset (Island, 1984)**
★ ★ ★ ½   **Words for the Dying (Warner Bros., 1989)**

At the outset of his solo career, John Cale completely turned away from the Velvet Underground's imposing rock assault, a sound his crying viola and throbbing bass helped to define. Despite its title, *Vintage Violence* exhibits Cale's quiet, melodic side. His Welsh accent and enigmatic-at-best lyrics aren't for everyone, but Cale's a gifted producer and arranger as well as a total eccentric. On this album he blends those quirks, rough edges and pretensions into a gentle, glossy folk-rock groove.

Cale explored his classical roots on *Church of Anthrax* (with minimalist composer-keyboardist Terry Riley) and *The Academy in Peril* (with the Royal Philharmonic). *Paris 1919* returns to the song-oriented structure of *Vintage Violence*; this time, Cale is accompanied by some members of Little Feat and some L.A. session players. "Andalucia" perfectly captures the tone Cale had been striving for: a beautiful setting infused with a troubling, vaguely mysterious air.

With a firm nudge from Roxy Music guitarist Phil Manzanera and keyboard theorist Brian Eno, *Fear* bring backs the Velvet Underground's aggressive stance, and then some. Cale works himself into an awesome lather on the title track and "Gun," but what makes his shock-rock so scary is that trigger-finger control he never quite cracks. *Slow Dazzle* reintroduces Cale's melodic skills and skewed pop sense to his new love of "Dirtyass Rock & Roll." He adresses an apt, catchy tribute to the lost Beach Boy ("Mr. Wilson") and exorcises Mr. Presley's ghost on a compelling creepshow version of "Heartbreak Hotel." *Helen of Troy* carries on in that vein; the vinegary-sweet "Leaving It All Up to You" and the pissed-off stomp through "Pablo Picasso" are both definitive Cale.

"Unpredictable" doesn't begin to describe the next phase in Cale's career. After a 1975 incident in which he allegedly decapitated a chicken onstage, Cale earned a reputation (only half-deserved) as a rock showman, sort of an Alice Cooper for the punk set. *Sabotage* documents his tour with a raggedy young band drawn from the CBGB scene in New York; there are some charged moments, though several tracks dunder on for many more minutes than necessary. *Honi Soit* coupled the near-impenetrable "political" ramblings of *Sabotage* with the ministrations of a slick young studio band; if there were such a thing as left-wing AOR stations, this would have been a playlist staple. *Music for a New Society* is a half-successful avant-comeback; at least it's listenable, which is more than can be said for the distracted, empty *Caribbean Sunset*.

Cale and Eno's 1990 return raised a lot of hopes, especially since Eno had stopped making pop records around 1980. *Wrong Way Up* doesn't radiate the mad brainiac immediacy of either artist's classic work, but the sombre melodies and sparse electronics eventually prove insinuating to the sympathetic ear. Less consistent and more intriguing is Cale's 1989 solo, *Words for the Dying*: after an extended symphonic score to a Dylan Thomas poem (which is better than it sounds in description), Cale pounds out a trance-inducing pair of solo piano pieces and then joins Eno for a refreshingly full, album-closing finale. The Andy Warhol tribute-elegy *Songs for Drella* is dominated by Lou Reed's writing and strumming, though Cale's viola, piano and occasional vocals serve to shape and stimulate his former bandmate's trademark three-chord attack. With another run of successful collaborations under his belt, John Cale seems about ready to kick-start his solo career into full gear. — M.C.

RANDY CALIFORNIA
★ ★ ★ ★ **Kapt. Kopter & the (Fabulous Twirly-Birds) (1972; Epic/Edsel import, 1986)**

After leaving the experimental pop band Spirit, guitarist Randy California dropped this mega-watt garage bomb on an unsuspecting public. A shameless devotee of Jimi Hendrix, he plays fast and loose with that mind-expanding vocabulary on his solo debut. *Kapt. Kopter* rounds up a pack of mongrel cover versions; California treats gems by the Beatles ("Rain," "Day Tripper") and Paul Simon ("Mother and Child Reunion") with rough, affectionate hands—no cheap irony or hot-dog tricks. For all its instrumental fluency, though, *Kapt. Kopter* also foreshadows punk's irreverent spirit and sonic immediacy. The vaunted psychedelic revival of the early '80s never came close to producing an album as funny and adventurous as this one. — M.C.

CAMEO

★ ★ ★   **Cameosis (Casablanca, 1980)**
★ ★ ★   **She's Strange (Atlanta Artists, 1984)**
★ ★ ★½   **Single Life (Atlanta Artists/ Polygram, 1985)**
★ ★ ★ ★   **Word Up! (Atlanta Artists/ Polygram, 1986)**
★ ★ ★   **Machismo (Atlanta Artists/Polygram, 1988)**
★ ★ ★   **Real Men . . . Wear Black (Atlanta Artists/Polygram, 1990)**
★ ★ ★   **Emotional Violence (Reprise, 1992)**

Cameo has been funking around since the mid-'70s, expanding from a six- to a 12-piece, P-Funk-styled R&B band and ending up, some 14 albums later, as a three-piece, techno-intense studio act. *Cameosis* is the sole early title still in print—and not without cause; only a hardcore funk fiend would find much interesting in the derivative grooves fueling *Ugly Ego* (1978), *Secret Omen* (1979) or *Alligator Woman* (1982).

She's Strange is another story entirely. Although most of the album is given over to run-of-the-mill funk tunes, "Talkin' Out the Side of Your Neck" is brash, brassy and angrily politicized, while "She's Strange" augments its groove with dreamy, atmospheric synths and vocals that manage to walk the line between rap and soul singing. With its title tune, *Single Life* expands impressively on the synth-and-rhythm combination "She's Strange" introduced, constructing the verse around a tension-building, six-note bass riff and grounding the chorus with a whistling synth hook swiped from Ennio Morricone's "The Good, the Bad & the Ugly." From there it's just a simple step to *Word Up!* and "Word Up," which uses a strikingly similar rhythmic strategy—another bass-driven verse, the same Morricone lift—but ups the impact by tying it to a stronger melodic idea. More importantly, *Word Up!* doesn't come off as one good single surrounded by an album's worth of B sides; between the rap-flavored "She's Mine" and the jazzy "Back and Forth," the album is listenable from beginning to end.

That's not quite the case with *Machismo*. Despite its admirable ambition—grounding "I Like the World" with crunchy, metallic guitars, adding a Miles Davis solo to "In the Night"—the songs seem too concerned with production techniques to deliver much in the way of melody. Interesting, but hardly essential. And though *Real Men . . . Wear Black* and *Emotional Violence* find the band getting back to basics, there isn't enough melodic interest to make their beefed-up grooves worth celebrating. — J.D.C.

GLEN CAMPBELL

★ ★   **Gentle on My Mind (Capitol, 1967)**
★ ★   **By the Time I Get to Phoenix (Capitol, 1967)**
★ ★   **Wichita Lineman (Capitol, 1968)**
★ ★   **That Christmas Feeling (Capitol, 1968)**
★ ★   **Galveston (Capitol, 1969)**
★ ★   **"Live" (Capitol, 1969)**
★ ★   **Try a Little Kindness (Capitol, 1970)**
★ ★½   **Glen Campbell's Greatest Hits (Capitol, 1971)**
★ ★   **The Last Time I Saw Her (Capitol, 1971)**
★ ★   **Arkansas (Capitol, 1975)**
★ ★½   **Rhinestone Cowboy (Capitol, 1975)**
★ ★ ★   **The Best of Glen Campbell (Capitol, 1976)**
★ ★   **Bloodline (Capitol, 1976)**
★ ★   **Southern Nights (Capitol, 1977)**
★ ★½   **It's the World Gone Crazy (Capitol, 1981)**
★ ★ ★   **The Very Best of Glen Campbell (Capitol, 1987)**
★ ★ ★   **Walkin' in the Sun (Capitol, 1990)**
★ ★ ★   **Greatest Country Hits (Curb, 1990)**
★ ★ ★½   **Classics Collection (Capitol Nashville, 1990)**

Sour memories of his ingratiating late-'60s network variety show linger, and Campbell's glad-handing personality can be off putting. But he does have talent. A session guitarist for everyone from Dean Martin to the Mamas and the Papas, and having served a brief stint as a Beach Boy, the blond from Delight, Arkansas, gained late-'60s country crossover success doing Jimmy Webb songs—"By the Time I Get to Phoenix," "Wichita Lineman" and "Galveston." However syrupy the arrangements, Campbell's guitar was skillful, and his careful singing conveyed lyrics that faithfully rendered suburban heartbreak in detail-rich vignettes. He also scored with John Hartford's "Gentle on My Mind"—which took narrative detail to absurd lengths and confused tongue-twisters for poetry.

In the '70s, the coy "Rhinestone Cowboy" was Campbell's big smash (and the basis for constant ridiculing skits by Johnny Carson). More MOR than country, Campbell's oeuvre is either remarkably formulaic or consistent, depending on one's taste for polished pleasantry. Of his super abundance of greatest-hits packages, *Classics Collection* is the best.   — P.E.

CAMPER VAN BEETHOVEN
★★★ **Telephone Free Landslide Victory (Independent Project/Rough Trade, 1985)**
★★★★ **II & III (Pitch a Tent/Rough Trade, 1986)**
★★★½ **Camper Van Beethoven (Pitch a Tent/Rough Trade, 1986)**
★★★ **Vampire Can Mating Oven (EP) (Pitch a Tent/Rough Trade, 1987)**
★★★★½ **Our Beloved Revolutionary Sweetheart (Virgin, 1988)**
★★★★ **Key Lime Pie (Virgin, 1989)**
Fond of unexpected juxtapositions, arcane musical styles and lyrical non sequiturs, Camper Van Beethoven stands as proof that a band can get away with almost anything, provided it has a sense of humor and a way with melody. Granted, the Campers' initial success had more to do with the former than the latter, thanks to the wacky "Take the Skinheads Bowling," from *Telephone Free Landslide Victory*. But what kept the group from succumbing to the sort of novelty-act status accorded the Dead Milkmen or Mojo Nixon was its ability to surround its punchlines with artful, intriguing numbers like "Vladivostock" and "Balalaika Gap."

II & III, the group's second album, sharpens the music's focus by more tightly integrating the various influences, leading to a sound one song aptly describes as "ZZ Top Goes to Egypt." Again, there's plenty of wit in the writing, as in the suburban satire of "(Don't You Go to) Goleta," but the Campers' obvious affection for country and folk idioms keeps things from getting too glib. That doesn't help much with *Camper Van Beethoven*, however, a more audacious outing that adds multi-instrumentalist Eugene Chadbourne to the lineup, and augments relatively conventional tunes like "(The) History of Utah" with experimental efforts like "Stairway to Heavan (sic)," a combination that, unfortunately, isn't quite as interesting as it sounds. (Camper Van Beethoven, or

members thereof, collaborated with Chadbourne on two albums for Fundamental records, *Camper Van Chadbourne* and the live *Eugene Van Beethoven's 69th Sin Funny*. Both alternate between arty deconstructions of country music and seemingly directionless free improvisation.)

After an EP's worth of odds and ends (*Vampire Can Mating Oven*), CVB moved to the majors, signing with Virgin and releasing the best of its albums, *Our Beloved Revolutionary Sweetheart*. Because these songs make the most of the band's melodic instincts while somehow finding room for its stylistic quirks, the album is an ideal showcase for the Campers' strengths. *Key Lime Pie* falls short of that mark, but not by much; although the album's mood is much darker, there's still plenty of sparkle to the likes of "When I Win the Lottery" and "All Her Favorite Fruit." Sadly, the band broke up soon after; singer David Lowery is pursuing a solo career with his own group, Cracker, while guitarist Greg Lisher, bassist Victor Krummenacher and drummer Chris Pedersen continue with their side project, the Monks of Doom.   — J.D.C.

CANNED HEAT
★★ **Canned Heat (Liberty, 1967)**
★★ **Boogie With Canned Heat (Liberty, 1968)**
★★★ **Living the Blues (Liberty, 1969)**
★★½ **Hallelujah (Liberty, 1969)**
★ **Vintage Heat (Janus, 1970)**
★★½ **Canned Heat Live in Europe (Liberty, 1970)**
★★★ **Future Blues (Liberty, 1970)**
★★★ **Cookbook (1970)**
★★★ **Hooker 'n' Heat (Springboard, 1970)**
★★½ **Live at the Topanga Corral (Wand, 1971)**
★★ **Historical Figures and Ancient Heads (United Artists, 1972)**
★★ **New Age (United Artists, 1973)**
★★★ **One More River to Cross (Atlantic, 1974)**
★★★½ **The Best of Canned Heat (EMI, 1987)**
★★★ **Reheated (Dali, 1990)**
Former record store manager Bob "The Bear" Hite and renowned amateur blues scholar Al "Blind Owl" Wilson founded this California outfit in 1966 to spread the gospel of country blues. While feverish in their passion for their music, they were more engaging as popularizers than as purists—hence, their best songs are their

hits, the Wilson-penned "On the Road Again" (1968) and a cover of Wilbert Harrison's "Let's Work Together" (1970). A sprawling two-record affair, *Living the Blues* was their magnum opus—and while their zeal is evident on all 40 minutes of "Refried Boogie, Parts I and II," as well as on another very long jam entitled "Partenogenesis," it's the lighter fare—and the neat horn arrangements by Dr. John—that holds up. With its engaging flute riff, Wilson's "Going Up the Country" remains the Heat's snappiest number—a crowd pleaser at Woodstock, it served as one of the essential theme songs for the movie made of the festival. *Future Blues* took a tougher approach, and the record is a strong one; *Hooker 'n' Heat* nicely pairs these ardent fans with one of their absolute idols—John Lee Hooker. A deft guitarist and very distinctive high-voiced singer, Wilson died in 1970—and the quality of the band's work suffered greatly after his departure. *One More River to Cross* was fairly accomplished, however, with Hite's gruff vocalizing carrying the day. The well-edited 1987 *Best of*—supplanting the earlier *Cookbook* compilation—contains all the essential Canned Heat, and it provides a fitting memorial for two engaging zealots (Hite died in 1981). The giants are missing, of course, but *Reheated* (1990) represents a commendable comeback bid.   — P.E.

FREDDY CANNON
★★★ 14 Booming Hits (Rhino, 1982)
Great fun, this "Boom Boom" man, who parlayed a fierce style of singing, a big beat and a penchant for exclaiming "Whoo!" at every opportunity into seven years of chart successes between 1959 and 1966. "Tallahassee Lassie" (his first hit, co-written by Bob Crewe, who would go on to co-write and produce many of the Four Seasons' most important records), "Palisades Park," "Way Down Yonder in New Orleans" and "Abigail Beecher" hardly changed the face of rock & roll, but they were pop records with irresistible spirit and some tough playing and singing at a time when the music needed exactly those qualities. All the hits are here, including his last Top Twenty single, "Action," the theme from Dick Clark's "Where the Action Is" TV show, released in 1965. To this there is little to add save . . . whoo!   — D.M.

THE CAPRIS
★★½ There's a Moon Out Tonight (Collectables, NA)

This doo-wop quintet from Ozone Park, New York, almost topped the chart in '61 with "There's a Moon Out Tonight," written by lead singer Nick Santo and featuring his soaring falsetto parts over the close, driving harmonies of his mates in what has become a romantic standard of the genre. Follow-ups "Where I Fell in Love" and "Girl in My Dreams" were dreamy enough efforts, but failed to strike a responsive chord with the masses, and the Capris were history. In 1982 a reconfigured Capris, with Santo still on lead, cut a new LP, *There's a Moon Out Again*, for the now-defunct Ambient Sound label. It sank without a trace, but doo-wop fans might be interested to hear Santo sounding every bit the spry, young whippersnapper on a credible update of the group's signature song.   — D.M.

CAPTAIN BEEFHEART
★★★ The Legendary A&M Sessions (EP) (1965; A&M, 1984)
★★★★ Safe as Milk (1967; Buddah, 1985)
★★½ Strictly Personal (Blue Thumb, 1968)
★★★½ Trout Mask Replica (1969; Reprise, 1970)
★★★★ Lick My Decals Off, Baby (1970; Rhino, 1991)
★★★ Mirror Man (1965; One Way, 1990)
★★★½ The Spotlight Kid/Clear Spot (1972; Reprise, 1991)
★★½ Unconditionally Guaranteed (1974; Blue Plate/Caroline, 1990)
★★ Bluejeans & Moonbeams (1974; Blue Plate/Caroline, 1990)
★★★★ Shiny Beast (Bat Chain Puller) (1978; Rhino, 1991)
★★★★½ Doc at the Radar Station (Virgin, 1980)
★★★★ Ice Cream for Crow (1982; Blue Plate/Caroline, 1990)
Even though he turned his back on music a decade ago, Captain Beefheart (born Don Van Vliet) still casts a long shadow across rock & roll's avant garde. Although his albums have never sold well, their influence has been enormous, and his work has been a touchstone for bands ranging from Devo to Pere Ubu to the Clash. Yet Beefheart's music is often misunderstood even by his fans, who seem dazzled by its virtuosic weirdness without understanding any of its underlying structure or stylistic discipline.
    Beefheart's musical roots are in blues and R&B, and fairly conventional fare at that.

He made his first recordings for A&M, and enjoyed some popular success through a raucous remake of the Bo Diddley hit "Diddy Wah Diddy." A&M didn't see much commercial potential in his subsequent work, however, and quickly dropped him; "Diddy Wah Diddy" and five other tunes were later released with the oddly self-congratulatory title *The Legendary A&M Sessions*. Reorganizing his Magic Band, Beefheart added 19-year old Ry Cooder to the line-up and cut *Safe as Milk*, an astonishing combination of soulful conventionality and audacious invention. Cooder's playing is especially engaging, blessed with a fluidity that grounds the music in the blues even while pulling it away from the predictability of most white blues bands. But the most startling thing about this album is its range, which stretches from the doo-wop-derived harmonies of "I'm Glad" to the throbbing, trance-like "Abba Zaba" and the snarling roar of "Electricity." With *Strictly Personal*, Beefheart—this time without Cooder—tried to expand on *Milk*'s approach, but the album was remixed and cuted-up while he was on tour in Europe, enraging Beefheart (justly so). As such, only the live *Mirror Man* presents his post-Cooder band in its unvarnished prime; though the playing is first-rate, the performances ramble interminably.

Refusing to relinquish artistic control ever again, Beefheart brought in his old friend Frank Zappa (the two had met in their teens) to produce the overrated *Trout Mask Replica*. Musically, much of what Beefheart does on the album is stunning, merging the melodic plasticity of early Delta blues with the disjointed interplay of free-form improvisation. But Zappa's production undoes much of that, both by working to reveal the inherent artifice of the recording process (for instance, the mistakes-and-all intro to "Pena," in which Beefheart is heard coaching one of his cohorts through a piece of poetry), and mixing Beefheart's voice so high that it almost obscures the magic his band is working (as on "Dachau Blues"). Thus, despite occasionally amazing moments, like "Sugar 'N Spikes" and "Dali's Car," the album's superficial weirdness overwhelms the band's brilliantly warped take on the blues.

Beefheart restores the music's balance on the self-produced *Lick My Decals Off, Baby*, on which the music is often just as challenging as on *Replica* but far easier to follow. Here, every move the band makes

stands out—the vocal wit of "The Smithsonian Institute Blues," the gnarled instrumental interplay of "Peon," the free-blowing dissonance of "Flash Gordon's Ape." On *The Spotlight Kid* the chemistry between his rhythm section and guitarists remains as volatile as ever, but the melodic structure verges almost on hard rock normalcy, particularly on "I'm Gonna Booglarize You Baby" and "Alice in Blunderland." *Clear Spot* continues Beefheart's move toward the mainstream, but doesn't quite coalesce, despite engaging moments like the New Orleans–style "Nowadays a Woman's Gotta Hit a Man." Still, even that seems brilliant compared to *Unconditionally Guaranteed* and *Bluejeans & Moonbeams*, on which his increasingly watered-down sound robs his music of its essential energy.

Fortunately, Beefheart is back on course with *Shiny Beast (Bat Chain Puller)*. Thanks to the jazz-schooled assurance of his sidemen, the album includes some of Beefheart's most eloquent instrumental work ("Ice Rose") while still finding room for such pop-friendly titles as "Harry Irene." *Doc at the Radar Station* isn't quite as easy-going, what with the anxious stop-start pulse of "Dirty Blue Gene" and the ominously grinding "Making Love to a Vampire with a Monkey on My Knee," though the music remains disarmingly approachable, even hooky at times. Beefheart's last album, *Ice Cream for Crow*, brings him full circle, as his final Magic Band returns to the blues-based sound of *Safe as Milk*. Granted, there's still quite a lot of jazz in the mix (check the confident swing of the instrumental "Semi-Multicoloured Caucasian"), but the gritty slide guitar riffs roiling beneath the title tune rank among his most memorable. — J.D.C.

IRENE CARA
★★ **What a Feelin'** (Geffen, 1983)
Mediocre Donna Summer impression redeemed only by the campy exuberance of the title tune. — J.D.C.

MARIAH CAREY
★★★ **Mariah Carey** (Columbia, 1990)
★★½ **Emotions** (Columbia, 1991)
Given the colossal success of Whitney Houston, radio predictably insisted on a Whitney II. With "Vision of Love" and "I Don't Wanna Cry," on her debut album, Carey fits the bill nicely—even utilizing, in producer Narada Michael Walden, the

single intelligence behind the Whitney juggernaut. She has, of course, one helluva voice—a force of nature capable of swoops, sighs and flourishes, all squandered on pop-psych love songs played with airless, intimidating expertise. Like billion-dollar naugahyde, this ersatz soul music is breathtaking in its wrongheadedness—skill and passion slaving over piffle. *Emotions* offers more of the same, with less interesting material. — P.E.

BELINDA CARLISLE

★ ★½ Belinda Carlisle (IRS, 1986)
★ ★ ★ Heaven on Earth (MCA, 1987)
★ ★ ★ Runaway Horses (MCA, 1989)
★ ★ Live Your Life Be Free (MCA, 1991)

Forget the giddy enthusiasm of her work with the Go-Go's—on her own, Carlisle's singing is strictly generic girl pop, flanking pro forma rockers with tepid power ballads. Apallingly, "Heaven Is a Place on Earth," a transparent rewrite of Bon Jovi's "You Give Love a Bad Name," from *Heaven on Earth*, actually topped the pop charts in 1988. That was an aberration, though; not even the most gullible pop fans were fooled by the flat, forgettable *Runaway Horses*, and by *Live Your Life Be Free*, Carlisle's increasingly wobbly vibrato left her sounding like a flabby imitation of Cher. — J.D.C.

WENDY (WALTER) CARLOS

★ ★ ★ Digital Moonscapes (Columbia, 1984)
★ ★ ★ Beauty in the Beast (Audion, 1986)
★ ★ ★ Secrets of Synthesis (Columbia, 1987)
★ ★ ★ Switched-On Brandenburg Concertos, Vol. 1 (Columbia, 1987)
★ ★ ★ Switched-On Brandenburg Concertos, Vol. 2 (Columbia, 1987)

Walter Carlos caused a stir in the late '60s with *Switched-On Bach*, a sort of Johann's "greatest hits" played exclusively on synth. Classical purists balked, but the record was trail-blazing—no longer could the Moog machine be relegated to the role of a special effect; it could deliver "Jesu, Joy of Man's Desiring" as music, not as a series of squawks. Choosing Bach was smart; while the dynamics and tone of the music certainly lost something in translation to the language of blips and bleeps, the mathematical precision of the composer's style lent itself to the fastidiousness of the electronic approach. And Carlos was a dazzling technician—he proved the capabilites of the new instrument in ways that proved influential for years to come.

After his '60s heyday, Walter, through means of a sex-change operation, became Wendy—and experimented with original music. Much less satisfying than that of such avant-gardists as Terry Riley, her work flashed more technique than imagination. *Beauty in the Beast* and *Digital Moonscapes* might now be filed under "New Age"—and they're pleasant. The Brandenburg sets, obviously, are Bach, and they remain intriguing. Of interest primarily to musicians, *Secrets of Synthesis* features Wendy demonstrating and discussing tricks of the keyboardist's trade. — P.E.

KIM CARNES

★ ★ ★ ★ Sailin' (A&M, 1976)
★ ★½ Romance Dance (EMI, 1980)
★ ★ ★ Mistaken Identity (EMI, 1981)
★ ★½ Voyeur (EMI, 1982)
★ ★ ★ The Best of You (A&M, 1982)
★ ★½ Cafe Racers (EMI, 1983)
★ ★ ★ ★ A View from the House (MCA, 1988)

In another time and place Kim Carnes might have been recognized as a great singer. No question about the voice: it's worn, aged, soulful, defiant, utterly lacking smooth edges—an enormously compelling instrument to anyone enamored of blue-eyed soul. But the lady can't catch a break. Her story is one of great records that nobody hears. In 1976 she cut a classic for A&M, *Sailin'*, with producers Jerry Wexler and Barry Beckett at Muscle Shoals Sound, and all the superb Muscle Shoals players behind her. It didn't have a bad song on it, and many of the songs were written or co-written by Carnes: yes, she does that too. The album sank. So did everything else she did for A&M.

A label change to EMI in 1979 almost righted things. *Romance Dance* (1980) at least made it to Number 57. The next year she went all the way. *Mistaken Identity* hit Number One in large part on the strength of a marvelous single, "Bette Davis Eyes." It was pop production of the highest caliber by Val Garay, who surrounded Carnes's vocals in a swirl of high-tech machinery and rock-solid drums. Finally the rest of the world knew what Carnes's fans had known all along. But Carnes seemed to be straining to assert her identity on other tracks. *Mistaken Identity* was a one-shot. Her '82 follow-up, *Voyeur*, barely dented the Top 50, and the ill-conceived *Cafe Racers* (1983) peaked at 97.

In 1988 she headed south again, to Nashville, and co-produced with Jimmy

Bowen a minor masterpiece in *View From the House*. It even begins with one of the most probing songs Carnes has ever written: "Brass & Batons" (co-written with Donna Weiss), a meditation on the tyranny of memory. Later she turns in one of her most complex vocals on a John Prine song, "Speed of the Sound of Loneliness," with a reading that communicates equal parts pain and acceptance. — D.M.

THE CARPENTERS
★　Close to You (A&M, 1970)
★　Carpenters (A&M, 1971)
★　Ticket to Ride (A&M, 1971)
★　A Song for You (A&M, 1972)
★　Now and Then (A&M, 1973)
★★★　The Singles: 1969–73 (A&M, 1973)
★　Horizon (A&M, 1975)
★　A Kind of Hush (A&M, 1976)
★　Passage (A&M, 1977)
★　Christmas Portrait (A&M, 1978)
★★　Lovelines (A&M, 1989)
★★½ From the Top (A&M, 1991)

The Carpenters are the very definition of clean-cut, inoffensive pop. Karen and Richard Carpenter offered a healthy alternative—if not the antidote—to the excesses of the early '70s. Karen's crystal-clear phrasing and immaculate tone are matched by Richard's chaste arrangements and crystalline production; there's barely a hint of rock influence on the Carpenters' records. "Close to You" kicked off a five-year chart run. There's a real note of longing in Karen's sweet daydream, despite the antiseptic musical backing. This tendency is even more pronounced on "Superstar" and "Rainy Days and Mondays," both from *Carpenters*. Underneath the easy-listening veneer, you can sense creeping panic in the former and deeply subsumed desire in the latter. These disarming singles can still catch a listener totally unawares.

Those tracks highlight *The Singles: 1969–73*, the closest thing to a consistently listenable Carpenters album. Even on that collection, however, saccharine simplicity ("Sing") and florid nostalgia ("Yesterday Once More") set the rule. The second half of *Now and Then* cements the duo's Vegas aspirations: it's a medley of rock & roll oldies, narrated by a DJ. Karen Carpenter's voice deepened and improved over the years, though her material grew even more shallow and emotionally undemanding. Sales eventually slipped in the late '70s. The group drifted apart, and Karen Carpenter later died of anorexia in 1982. *Lovelines*, a

posthumously released solo album, mixes some Carpenters outtakes with various stylistic experiments. It's intriguing, though not a revelation.

Even the legions of Carpenters cultists—ironic or not—may be daunted by the group's four-disc box set. They should be: *From the Top* contains a whole lotta cotton candy: consume the whole thing and you'll be sorry. The presence of so many also-rans and outright misses turns this career summary into a directionless ordeal. — M.C.

PAUL CARRACK
★★½　Suburban Voodoo (Epic, 1982)
★★½　One Good Reason (Chrysalis, 1987)
★★★　The Carrack Collection (Chrysalis, 1988)
★★★　Groove Approved (Chrysalis, 1989)

Better known as a sideman than a solo artist, Carrack sang on several Top Ten hits, including "How Long" with Ace and both "Living Years" and "Silent Running (On Dangerous Ground)" with Mike + the Mechanics, and was the voice behind "Tempted," Squeeze's best-known single. On his own, though, Carrack's career is less stellar. *Suburban Voodoo*, recorded with what was then Nick Lowe's band, is a passable showcase for Carrack's soulful tenor, but rarely delivers the kind of material that makes his singing shine; smart as the songs often are, only "I Need You" and "Lesson in Love" repay repeated listens. (Both can be found, along with "Tempted," "How Long" and "Silent Running," on *The Carrack Collection*.)

Carrack abandoned that approach on *One Good Reason*, and wound up with an album that's just as unsatisfying. Though the songs seem tailored to exploit the aching beauty of Carrack's voice, only "Don't Shed a Tear" manages any emotional credibility—the rest come across as manipulative fluff. *Groove Approved*, then, is a retrenchment of sorts, maintaining the production standards of *One Good Reason* while returning to the rootsy feel of *Suburban Voodoo*. And if nothing on the album sounds quite like a hit, neither is any of it boring or condescending. — J.D.C.

JOE "KING" CARRASCO AND THE CROWNS
★★　Joe "King" Carrasco & the Crowns (Hannibal/Stiff, 1981)
★★　Party Safari (Hannibal, 1981)
★★　Tales From the Crypt (The Basement Tapes 1979) (ROIR, 1984)

★★ **Bandido Rock (Rounder, 1987)**
★★ **Tex-Mex Rock-Roll (ROIR, 1989)**
Out of Austin, Texas, by way of Dumas, Texas, Joe "King" Carrasco and his band the Crowns gained their first measure of national attention in 1980, when they ventured into lower Manhattan and injected some desperately needed humanism into a scene that was terminally nihilistic. They had life, they had verve, they even had a sense of humor. Carrasco's music is many things and no one thing: it's rooted in Tex-Mex (hence the horns and marimba) and rock without ever being firmly in either camp. The Sir Douglas Quintet is an obvious point of reference (Sir Doug's keyboardist Augie Meyers sat in on sessions for the band's first album, available now on the cassette-only ROIR label as *Tex-Mex Rock-Roll*), but not exactly a very good one. Like Sir Doug, Carrasco enjoys the sound of a cheesy Farfisa organ, but unlike Sir Doug, Carrasco has little personality as a vocalist. His thin, colorless voice gets the job done, and little more, when the band is in a rocking mode, but give him a more somber tune, such as "Tears Been Falling" on *Tales From the Crypt* (these being glorified demo recordings from 1979), and Carrasco can't even get close. Ultimately this limitation is the band's undoing. All the Farfisas, marimbas and horns, the witty excursions into rockabilly and polka ("One More Time" and "Federales" on *Joe "King" Carrasco and the Crowns*) and the entire garage band ethos of ragged-but-right playing can't substitute for emotional texture. — D.M.

JIM CARROLL
★★★★ **Catholic Boy (Atco, 1980)**
★★ **Dry Dreams (Atco, 1982)**
★★½ **Praying Mantis (Giant, 1991)**
A teenage junkie and a wunderkind street-talk writer, Jim Carroll published poetry and bad-boy memoirs (*The Basketball Diaries*) not too long after he'd started shaving—and New York avant-garde literary critics justifiably took notice. Great expectations attended his rock & roll debut; remarkably, *Catholic Boy* delivered. Brandishing brain power and a Lou Reed fixation, Carroll bashed his way through gripping songs derived from the Velvet Underground and Patti Smith, climaxing in the remarkable "People Who Died." A page of mythologized autobiography, the song recorded the sad fates of tough guys and misfits, its bitter but elegiac spirit owing more than a little to Jean Genet. *Dry*

Dreams, however, was a serious letdown. After the colloquial power of *Catholic Boy*, the pretentious lyrics of *Dry Dreams* were particularly disappointing—and the record's bullshit air of high, serious danger overwhelmed even Lenny Kaye's sharp guitar. *Praying Mantis* is a recording of Carroll reading his cryptic poetry. — P.E.

THE CARS
★★★★ **The Cars (Elektra, 1978)**
★★★½ **Candy-O (Elektra, 1979)**
★★★ **Panorama (Elektra, 1980)**
★★★ **Shake It Up (Elektra, 1981)**
★★★½ **Heartbeat City (Elektra, 1984)**
★★★★ **Greatest Hits (Elektra, 1985)**
★★½ **Door to Door (Elektra, 1987)**
The Cars' debut album triggered the new-wave deluge. This Boston quintet was too musically experienced—and too old—to qualify as punks, though their hook-filled distillation of Roxy Music and Iggy Pop exudes a similar, all-pervasive sense of alienation. Polished pop irony quickly became the MO for dozens of clueless skinny-tie outfits with enticing names, but *The Cars* never approaches that sort of distanced smirk. Lead singer and songwriter Ric Ocasek uncovers raw nerve endings and tangled emotional states beneath every leather facade, while the band hurtles along its sleek, technologically enhanced path. *The Cars* blends a rich electronic atmosphere with spare guitar lines and driving (as in AM radio) rhythms; the synthesizer textures rival those of any art-rockers you'd care to mention. "Just What I Needed" and "My Best Friend's Girl" still jump out of the speakers like natural-born hit singles, but the rest of the debut achieves a sheer, seamless quality: each cut blends into the next, raising or lowering the pulse without losing the underlying groove.

The Cars' subsequent albums quickly settled into an unsurprising pattern: one or two surefire hit vehicles surrounded by inconsistent experiments and brooding, cryptic meditations on doomed romance. Even the singles begin to sound robotic: "Let's Go" (from *Candy-O*) ascends to the level of the debut with ease, but *Panorama*'s "Touch and Go" and *Shake It Up*'s title track merely punch the obvious pleasure buttons. Just as obsolescence threatened, the Cars overhauled their approach with *Heartbeat City* and scored three refreshing Top Forty singles. "You Might Think" and "Magic" soften Ocasek's tone, keeping just enough of his trademark bite. Bassist Ben Orr steps out with "Drive."

But a mellow middle age wasn't in the cards. The Cars broke up, somewhat acrimoniously, not long after the muddled, joyless *Door to Door* (1987). Ocasek releases intermittent solo albums, while Ben Orr's out-of-print 1986 debut, *The Lace,* sports a winning Top Forty seduction fantasy in the "Drive" mode ("Stay the Night"). *Greatest Hits* presents a consistently catchy overview of the group. Compared to the fluid acceleration of *The Cars,* however, this sort of nonstop roller coaster can leave you feeling queasy and overstimulated. — M.C.

CARLENE CARTER
★ ★ ★ ★ **I Fell in Love (Reprise, 1990)**
In the late '70s and early '80s Carlene Carter seemed like she might be the one to achieve the most powerful fusion of rock & roll and traditional country styles. Daughter of June Carter, granddaughter of Maybelle Carter, Carlene has her mother's strong but lonesome voice. It carries weight and feeling, and projects strength of character as well. Carter's early records tried hard to be all things to all people, and ended up satisfying no one. Nick Lowe, to whom Carter was once married, lent his skill as a producer and player (and backed Carter with fellow pub rockers Brinsley Schwarz and members of Graham Parker's band the Rumour), but the result was an unsatisfying hybrid. Carter sounded adrift.

These problems were corrected in spectacular fashion when Carter came back in 1990 with *I Fell in Love.* Produced by Howie Epstein, the album leaned on Carter's country roots but rocked hard when appropriate. It didn't hurt that Carter had written or co-written a batch of songs that addressed in honest terms some of the triumphs and torments she had suffered over the years, and also reconciled her feelings regarding her august lineage. A jaunty cover of A.P. Carter's "My Dixie Darlin' " acknowledges the timeless quality of her forebears' music, but real healing occurs on "Me and Wildwood Rose." Here Carter recounts in loving detail memories of her grandmother's house as a place of music and laughter where the elders wrapped their children in song "sweet and low." These songs are indicative of the entire album's personal nature: everything sounds pulled from hard experience. Compared to *I Fell in Love,* Carter's earlier albums are irrelevant (they're also out of print). This is where the story begins. — D.M.

CLARENCE CARTER
★ ★ ★ ★ **Snatching It Back: The Best of Clarence Carter (Rhino/Atlantic, 1992)**
He cuts a comparatively minor figure among the giants of soul music, but Clarence Carter projects a sassy elan that's all his own. Pulling together a string of R&B singles from the late '60s, *The Best of Clarence Carter* presents a solid sampler of the Muscle Shoals sound—a slightly breezier variant on Stax-Volt's gritty rhythms. The scintillating "Slip Away" and the country-tinged tale of "Patches" carried Carter over to the pop charts, though he really shines on funky, lover-spurned numbers like "I Smell a Rat" and "Snatching It Back." Hearing his horny laugh ricochet against those horn riffs is alone worth the price of admission. There really isn't a slack track to be found on *The Best of Clarence Carter.* — M.C.

THE CARTER FAMILY
★ ★ ★ ★ ★ **20 of the Best of the Carter Family (RCA International, 1984)**
★ ★ ★ **Wildwood Flower (Mercury, 1988)**
★ ★ ★ ★ ★ **The Carter Family: Country Music Hall of Fame Series (MCA, 1991)**
The history of modern country music begins with the original Carter Family (A.P. Carter, his wife Sara, and Sara's cousin, Maybelle Addington, who later married A.P.'s brother, Ezra) and Jimmie Rodgers, whose 1927 recordings made in Bristol, Tennessee, brought the music out of the mountains and rural backwaters into the commercial market. Unlike the eclectic, charismatic Rodgers, who made blues and blues variations a part of his repertoire, the dour, proper Carters were the repository of the old-time mountain, folk and gospel styles common to the Clinch Mountain area of Virginia where they were raised. A.P. was a diligent folklorist—for lack of a better term—who not only had great affection for the songs he heard in his own small part of the world, but who would tap any source, including family, friends, passing strangers or the public domain, for ideas. Their popularity aside, the early Carter Family recordings take on the aspect of monuments, both in the commitment and authority of the musicians' performances and in terms of the repertoire's rich history. A.P. often credited himself as songwriter, but in fact many of the Carter Family standards were built on found material from ages past.

Prior to the Bristol sessions, country records were largely instrumental. But in 1927 the advances in microphones were such that for the first time the subtle harmonies of mountain singers such as the Carters were distinguishable, and the piercing alto of an untutored but instinctively gifted singer such as Sara Carter could be heard with a clarity impossible to achieve in earlier years. That the Carters' singing was more rhythmic than many of their contemporaries' resulted from a freedom rooted in the complex guitar playing of Maybelle Carter, who picked the melody lines on the bass strings at the same time as she strummed the rhythm on the treble strings. Her technique was immediately emulated, and remains one the foundations of country guitar.

As of this writing, RCA, which once had numerous Carter Family albums available on its Camden label, shows nothing in print in its current catalogue. The Country Music Foundation has filled the gap somewhat with its Carter Family entry, which is excellent by any standard, but essential given the absence of other easily available recordings. The 16 tracks on the CMF collection date from the Family's Decca years, 1936–38, which followed their most productive era, 1927–34, on RCA. Still, there is notable work to be found on the CMF release, work that is indicative of the scope of the Carters' repertoire. "Hold Fast to the Right" is an old gospel song; "Young Freda Bolt" comes from a 1930 Victor recording, "The Story of Frieda Bolt" by the Floyd County Ramblers; "Just a Few More Days" comes out of the black gospel tradition. As usual, the CMF provides a well-researched pamphlet of information about the group's history. Until a domestic release covers the waterfront, the import *20 of the Best of the Carter Family* assembles the most important songs in the Carter's catalogue in one place. "Keep on the Sunny Side," "Wildwood Flower," "My Clinch Mountain Home," "I'm Thinking Tonight of My Blue Eyes," "Worried Man Blues" and "I Never Will Marry" are only a handful of the songs that hold a hallowed place in country music history. The Carter Family tradition is being carried on today by Maybelle's daughters Helen, Anita and June (the latter married to Johnny Cash) and June's daughter, Carlene Carter, who together recorded the 1988 LP *Wildwood Flower*. Nothing really compares to Sara Carter's stark rendering of "Wildwood Flower," recorded in 1928, but the version

included on this set does justice to the original. Other performances of original Carter Family material such as "Worried Man Blues, "Dixie Darlin'," and "Church in the Wildwood" are similarly moving. Produced by Jack Clement, *Wildwood Flower* is an honorable extension of a proud legacy. — D.M.

PETER CASE
★★★½ **Peter Case (Geffen, 1986)**
★★★★ **The Man With the Blue Postmodern Fragmented Neo-traditionalist Guitar (Geffen, 1989)**
★★★½ **Six Pack of Love (Geffen, 1992)**
Former frontman of the Plimsouls, whose best work can be found on Rhino's 1992 compilation *The Plimsouls . . . Plus,* Case traded garage-influenced new wave for a folkier sound when he went solo. As the title of his second album suggests, Case is sometimes too clever for his own good, but his best songs, like "Steel Strings" from *Peter Case* or "Poor Old Tom" from *Blue Guitar,* show both a solid sense of roots and a deep-seated melodicism. *Six Pack of Love* rocks much harder than its predecessors but otherwise maintains their tone; particularly noteworthy are the Lennonesque "Dream About You'" and the droll "Déjà Blues."
— J.D.C.

JOHNNY CASH
★ **Hymns by Johnny Cash (Columbia, 1959)**
★★★ **Ride This Train (Columbia, 1960)**
★ **Hymns From the Heart (Columbia, 1962)**
★★★ **Blood, Sweat and Tears (Columbia, 1963)**
★★★ **Ring of Fire (Columbia, 1963)**
★★ **I Walk the Line (Columbia, 1964)**
★★ **Johnny Cash Sings the Ballads of the True West (Columbia, 1965)**
★★★ **Orange Blossom Special (Columbia, 1965)**
★ **Mean as Hell! (Columbia, 1966)**
★ **Everybody Loves a Nut (Columbia, 1966)**
★★★ **Greatest Hits, Vol. 1 (Columbia, 1967)**
★★★★★ **Johnny Cash at Folsom Prison (Columbia, 1968)**
★ **The Holy Land (Columbia, 1968)**
★★★ **Johnny Cash at San Quentin (Columbia, 1969)**
★★★ **Original Golden Hits, Vol. 1 (Sun, 1969)**
★★★ **Original Golden Hits, Vol. 2 (Sun, 1969)**

★ ★ Story Songs of the Trains and
Rivers (Sun, 1969)
★ ★ ★ Get Rhythm (Sun, 1969)
★ ★ Showtime (Sun, 1969)
★ ★ ★ ★ Hello, I'm Johnny Cash (Columbia,
1970)
★ ★ ★ ★ The Rough-Cut King of Country
Music (Sun, 1970)
★ ★ The Singing Story Teller (Sun,
1970)
★ ★ ★ ★ The Legend (Sun, 1970)
★ ★ ★ ★ The World of Johnny Cash
(Columbia, 1970)
★ ★ Original Golden Hits, Vol. 3 (Sun,
1971)
★ ★ ★ The Man, the World, His Music
(Sun, 1971)
★ ★ Man in Black (Columbia, 1971)
★ ★ Johnny Cash & Jerry Lee Lewis
Sing Hank Williams (Sun, 1971)
★ ★ ★ His Greatest Hits, Vol. 2
(Columbia, 1971)
★ ★ ★ ★ Johnny Cash Sings Precious
Memories (Columbia, 1971)
★ ★ ★ Christmas: The Johnny Cash Family
(Columbia, 1972)
★ Any Old Wind That Blows
(Columbia, 1973)
★ Sunday Morning Coming Down
(Columbia, 1973)
★ The Gospel Road (Columbia, 1973)
★ ★ ★ Johnny Cash and His Woman (with
June Carter Cash) (Columbia, 1973)
★ Ragged Old Flag (Columbia, 1974)
★ ★ ★ Five Feet High and Rising
(Columbia, 1974)
★ The Junkie and the Juicehead Minus
Me (Columbia, 1974)
★ ★ ★ ★ Johnny Cash at Folsom Prison and
San Quentin (1968, 1969; Columbia,
1975)
★ ★ ★ John R. Cash (Columbia, 1975)
★ ★ Johnny Cash Sings Precious
Memories (Columbia, 1975)
★ ★ Look at Them Beans (Columbia,
1975)
★ ★ ★ Strawberry Cake (Columbia, 1976)
★ ★ ★ One Piece at a Time (Columbia,
1976)
★ ★ ★ The Last Gunfighter Ballad
(Columbia, 1976)
★ ★ Superbilly (Sun, 1977)
★ ★ Golden Souvenirs (Plantation, 1977)
★ ★ ★ ★ The Rambler (Columbia, 1977)
★ ★ ★ ★ Gone Girl (Columbia, 1978)
★ ★ ★ Greatest Hits, Vol. 3 (Columbia,
1978)
★ ★ ★ I Would Like to See You Again
(Columbia, 1978)
★ ★ ★ Silver (Columbia, 1979)

★ ★ ★ Rockabilly Blues (Columbia, 1980)
★ ★ ★ Classic Christmas (Columbia,
1980)
★ ★ ★ Encore (Greatest Hits, Vol. 4)
(Columbia, 1981)
★ ★ ★ The Baron (Columbia, 1981)
★ ★ A Believer Sings the Truth (1979;
Columbia, 1982)
★ ★ ★ Biggest Hits (1982; Columbia,
1987)
★ ★ ★ The Adventures of Johnny Cash
(Columbia, 1982)
★ ★ ★ Rainbow (Columbia, 1985)
★ ★ ★ Believe in Him (Word, 1986)
★ ★ ★ Johnny Cash Is Coming to Town
(Mercury, 1987)
★ ★ ★ ★ Johnny Cash—Columbia Records
1958–1986 (Columbia, 1987)
★ ★ ★ ★ The Vintage Years (1955–1963)
(Rhino, 1987)
★ ★ ★ Classic Cash/Hall of Fame Series
(Mercury, 1988)
★ ★ ★ ★ ★ Water From the Wells of Home
(Mercury, 1988)
★ ★ ★ ★ ★ The Sun Years (Rhino, 1990)
★ ★ Patriot (Columbia, 1990)
★ ★ ★ I Walk the Line and Other Big
Hits (Rhino, 1990)
★ ★ ★ The Mystery of Life (Mercury,
1991)
★ ★ ★ Johnny Cash Country Christmas
(Laserlight, 1991)
★ ★ ★ ★ ★ The Essential Johnny Cash
(1955–1983) (Columbia/Legacy,
1992)
**WITH JERRY LEE LEWIS AND CARL
PERKINS**
★ ★ ★ ★ The Survivors: Johnny Cash, Jerry
Lee Lewis, Carl Perkins
(Columbia, 1982)
WITH WAYLON JENNINGS
★ ★ ★ Heroes (Columbia, 1986)
Now closing in on 40 years of recording,
Johnny Cash has stepped into the late John
Wayne's boots as a near-mythical figure
who embodies all that's good, bad and
contradictory about America. He's a
born-again Christian whose gospel albums
thunder with righteous indignation over
humankind's sinful ways; he's a recidivist
drug addict whose bad habit has landed him
in jail and rehab centers more than once;
he's a solid establishment figure of
ambiguous politics who on *Man in Black*
(1971) criticized the Vietnam war in "Singin'
in Viet Nam Talkin' Blues," embraced
Richard Nixon's favorite evangelist, Billy
Graham, in a duet, "The Preacher Said,
'Jesus Said,' " and, in the title song,
launched a missile at the government in

declaring his intention to protest poverty, prejudice and the rest of society's many ills by adorning himself in black until things change.

However puzzling and contradictory his public behavior and stances, when Johnny Cash has stepped into a recording studio, wonderful things have happened, repeatedly. Looking over the entirety of his career on record one can see some utter follies—*Man in Black* and the even weirder *The Junkie and the Juicehead Minus Me* (1974)—but the overall impression is one of admiration, even awe, at the way he has evolved instead of coasting on his early hits. That he cut one of the best albums of his career with *Water From the Wells of Home* (1988) is commendable; that it came 32 years after his first hit single is stunning. Cash has stayed hungry.

Signed to Sun Records in 1955, Cash was the most dedicated country artist of the label's original rockabilly class, and many of his Sun sides are claimed by both country and rock fans. The Cash sound was set with "I Walk the Line": Marshall Grant slapping away at his bass, guitarist Luther Perkins picking out simple lead lines on the bass strings and Cash strumming insistent rhythm. It endures to this day. Never a versatile or flexible instrument, Cash's low baritone (now lower) nonetheless was powerful and expressive. Its raggedness and ofttimes wobbly nature worked in Cash's favor, giving him the appearance of being only a little more talented than the average guy. He also happened to sing great songs, many of which he wrote himself. Some of his best Sun sides came from the fertile imagination of the label's house producer–talent scout Jack Clement. Invariably the topics were prison, love, trains, but Cash's flair for striking imagery and the cutting phrase elevated his material to the level of poetry. And when he got hold of Clement's songs—"Ballad of a Teenage Queen," "Guess Things Happen That Way"—he gave them definitive interpretations. Considering the magnitude of his Sun recordings, it's sometimes difficult to believe he was with the label only two years before splitting for Columbia in 1958.

The *Original Golden Hits* series will do for the most complete overview of Cash's work at Sun, including non-hits. These discs, as well as Rhino's *The Sun Years*, demonstrate the evolution of Cash's sound from the spare trio arrangements of the early sides to the use of background choruses and additional instruments (piano, drums, fiddle, pedal steel) on the later ones. Despite its title Rhino's *The Vintage Years (1955–1963)* is mostly Sun material, repeated from *The Sun Years*.

Throughout the '60s Cash came on like the title of one of his Sun albums, *The Rough-Cut King of Country Music*. This was the God-fearing, Bible-quoting, populist folk singer period of Cash's career, and he's pretty much carried that stance into the '90s, notwithstanding some of his slick, countrypolitan outings in the '70s. *Ring of Fire* reprises some of the Sun songs, but also finds Cash coming on tough and embattled on June Carter's title song, which featured an inventive use of horns unlike anything that had been done in the genre to that time. *Blood, Sweat and Tears* introduced a Harlan Howard classic, "Busted," and has more of a country-blues slant than any of the other albums from this period. *Orange Blossom Special* is notable for Cash's interpretations of three Bob Dylan songs ("It Ain't Me, Babe," "Don't Think Twice," "Mama, You Been on My Mind"). By far the best album of this period was *Folsom Prison*, recorded live at the California penal institution. Cash, accompanied by June Carter and his band, gives a powerhouse performance. The songs are first-rate: "25 Minutes to Go" details the final moments of a convict on Death Row to chilling effect; "Give My Love to Rose," a song from the Sun days about a dying man asking that a stranger send a final request to his wife, has special poignance in this setting; Cash's and Carter's duet on "Jackson" is sassy and sexy; "Folsom Prison Blues" roars mightily as Cash and band deliver a thinly disguised excoriation of the prison system. Cash's other prison album, *Johnny Cash at San Quentin*, is a disappointing attempt to re-create *Folsom Prison*: good concept, uninspired execution. Two good songs come out of it, though, in Shel Silverstein's "A Boy Named Sue" and Cash's forceful interpretation of Bob Dylan's "Wanted Man." These albums are now packaged as a two-fer cassette. Of the three gospel albums—*Hymns by Johnny Cash, Hymns from the Heart, The Holy Land*—the first two are fairly uninspired outings; *The Holy Land*, a travelogue of Cash's trip to Israel, does serve up the Carl Perkins gem "Daddy Sang Bass."

With *Hello, I'm Johnny Cash* the '70s got off to a strong start, with Cash in one of his strongest grooves, writing good songs, finding good songs by other writers, and connecting with his material as well as he ever had or has since. *Hello* has more of a country-folk feel than many of Cash's records, thanks in part to the inclusion of Tim Hardin's "If I Were a Carpenter," Kris Kristofferson's "To Beat the Devil" and Cash's own folk-flavored "Southwind." After the weirdness of *Man in Black*, Cash came back strong with *Precious Memories*, a stately reading of several well-known country hymns. The mid-'70s was a less productive period, and is marked more by collections than by new studio recordings. Of these, *Five Feet High and Rising* is the strongest, although a duet album with June Carter Cash, *Johnny Cash and His Woman*, has its share of pleasures. Musts to avoid: *The Junkie and the Juicehead Minus Me*, *Any Old Wind That Blows*, *Sunday Morning Coming Down*.

Cash hit his stride again in the second half of the decade, beginning with a top-notch live album recorded in London, *Strawberry Cake*. Of special interest is the presence of June Carter Cash and her sister Helen; they perform a medley of Carter Family songs. Those high, keening mountain harmonies are simply exquisite, and one of the treats of this album is that the Carters return at the end to sing "Destination Victoria Station." *The Last Gunfighter Ballad* is a half-baked concept album saved by the Carter Family's harmonizing on the extraordinary "Far Side Banks of Jordan," "You're So Close to Me," "Cindy, I Love You," "That Silver Haired Daddy of Mine" and "I Will Dance With You." Another concept album, *The Rambler* (1977) intersperses dialogue with songs concerned with travel, and it works to spectacular effect. All the songs are written by Cash, and some—"Hit the Road and Go," "Lady," "If It Wasn't for the Wabash River," "My Cowboy's Last Ride"—are among his best.

Gone Girl is Cash's best album of the decade. Produced by Larry Butler, this is the first album on which Cash seems to be looking back and taking stock of his life, and the wistful mood of the record is moving. His ragged cover of Jagger-Richards's "No Expectations" tells a story in itself; Cash's own "It Comes and Goes" paints a picture of a man hopelessly bored with his station in life but lacking motivation to change it; and the final, devastating track is an interpretation of Rodney Crowell's "A Song for the Life," which finds Cash giving muted thanks for having learned to "listen to a sound like the sun going down," after a life spent in hard drinking. *Silver* continued the pattern set with *Gone Girl*: strong tunes revelatory of Cash's inner feelings, promoting no cause save that of unburdening his soul. Tom T. Hall's opener, "The L&N Don't Stop Here Anymore" speaks to the sad state of rail travel, but might also be read as a statement about Cash's frame of mind. That he follows this unsettling tale with his own "Lonesome to the Bone" only underscores the double-edged nature of the material. There's a nice duet with George Jones on "I'll Say It's True," and the record closes out with Cash asserting "I'm Gonna Sit on the Porch and Pick On My Old Guitar."

Throughout the '80s Cash focused on reconciliation as a theme. It began with the Jack Clement–produced *Rockabilly Blues*—not a rockabilly album, but a hard country album with rockabilly overtones. Nice touches: Nick Lowe's "Without Love," with Lowe and his buddy Dave Edmunds playing along; a cover of a wise, witty Steve Goodman–John Prine song, "The Twentieth Century Is Almost Over"; and Cash's title song, which recounts life on the road in Texas circa 1955. *The Survivors* captures a concert performance in Stuttgart, Germany, when Cash's Sun labelmates Carl Perkins and Jerry Lee Lewis showed up to juice up the show. Cash and Perkins get it together pretty good on "Goin' Down the Road Feelin' Bad," and the trio comes up a winner on "Peace in the Valley." *The Adventures of Johnny Cash* and *Rainbow* team Cash with, respectively, producers Clement and Chips Moman, which is usually a sign of good things to come, and so it was. The former's outstanding songs include John Prine's "Paradise," Billy Joe Shaver's "Georgia on a Fast Train" and Merle Haggard's "Good Old American Guest." *Rainbow* is enlived by a moving treatment of John Fogerty's "Have You Ever Seen the Rain" and a tender version of "Love Me Like You Used To."

Cash ended his long association with Columbia in 1986 and moved over to Mercury. The 20-song retrospective, *Johnny Cash—Columbia Records 1958–1986*, hardly does justice to so much work over so long a time, but it still hits a good many highlights (and includes Cash's version of Bruce Springsteen's "Highway Patrolman"). The three-CD *Essential Johnny Cash (1955–1983)* box set hits the mark squarely, however. At Mercury Cash has been produced almost exclusively by Jack Clement, and the partnership has produced strong results. The one must-have album out of this group is *Water From the Wells of Home*, a towering effort. It's tender, romantic, nostalgic, tough and moving, with traditional instrumentation and crisp arrangements. A sleeper is the 1986 gospel album, *Believe in Him*, on which majestic country hymns are given, in most cases, spare, acoustic arrangements, creating the intimate effect of a bunch of pickers bringing their guitars, mandolins, and banjos over to Cash's place for a singing service. — D.M.

ROSANNE CASH
* ★ ★ ★ **Right or Wrong (Columbia, 1980)**
* ★ ★ ★ **Seven Year Ache (Columbia, 1981)**
* ★ ★ ★ **Somewhere in the Stars (Columbia, 1982)**
* ★ ★ ★ **Rhythm and Romance (Columbia, 1985)**
* ★ ★ ★ ★ **King's Record Shop (Columbia, 1987)**
* ★ ★ ★ ★ **Hits 1979–1989 (Columbia, 1989)**
* ★ ★ ★ ★½ **Interiors (Columbia, 1990)**

Rosanne Cash has pretty much cleared the field of any writers who would pretend to challenge her eloquence, brutal honesty and revealing insight in dissecting the duplicitous games men and women play. What Cash is engaged in is self-discovery; sometimes, as she revealed on *Interiors*, other people get in the way of that, and the resulting pain cuts deep. Since the outset of her career (discounting a half-baked, self-titled and long out-of-print debut album released by Ariola in 1978), Cash has evinced a clouded view of relationships, seeing them not as winding up in the happily-ever-after realm but in complete moral, philosophical and physical disintegration. Marriage (to Rodney Crowell) and motherhood seemed to have only deepened her conviction that anything put together will fall apart. If all this sounds deadly serious, it is. Nevertheless, until *Interiors* she always found a way to leaven her dark internal monologues with a dash of humor.

As much as Cash's albums have been literary events, so have they been compelling musical statements. Credit goes to Crowell, Cash's producer-songwriter on several albums—and the subject of an unmerciful skewering on her self-produced *Interiors*, where the awful details of their coming apart are laid out against a stark background. But in 1980, with *Right or Wrong*, Crowell showed amazing facility for blending rock and country styles into a seamless whole with the sonic focus kept

simple and Cash's husky voice prominent. He didn't make a false move on that outing; on succeeding albums he showed judiciousness in upgrading Cash's sound with rock-based arrangements and strings creeping in only when the mood justified their use. The only album Crowell hasn't produced in toto, apart from *Interiors*, is *Rhythm and Romance*, Cash's boldest effort yet to move onto the rock charts. Although *R and R* contains some of Cash's best songs—"Hold On," "I Don't Know Why You Don't Want Me," a reconciliation with her father on "My Old Man" and the first intimate, wrenching rumblings of a relationship on shaky ground in "Closing Time"—Crowell's productions overshoot the mark in going full-tilt rock & roll. In retrospect *Rhythm and Romance* appears as an experiment in style; what Crowell and Cash were aiming for is realized on *King's Record Shop* where the rock is fiery but not boisterous ("Rosie Strike Back") and the country has a pop lilt that sounds natural and fresh (most striking in a graceful cover of John Hiatt's "The Way We Make a Broken Heart").

The key new ingredient at this point is lead guitarist Steuart Smith. Smith's lead lines are the fire to Cash's ice. His always impeccable choices are so original that it's impossible to anticipate what he'll play next. On *Interiors*, his insinuating grace notes and concise commentaries stretch the songs, adding a torrent of notes or a forlorn, quiet phrase. All along Cash has suggested trouble in paradise, in her own songs and those by other writers, one of the most revealing being Crowell's "I Don't Have to Crawl" on *King's Record Shop*, where Smith's tortured lead lines strike a hard contrast to Cash's almost detached reading of the lyric, "I don't have to crawl/I'll just walk away."

That would seem to be the starting point for *Interiors*, where the first words we hear from Cash are, "We crawled night and day through the tears and debris." Having thus established her theme, Cash proceeds to lay waste to the unexamined life and to the quaint notion that complete self-expression and fulfillment are possible in a close, committed relationship. Ultimately the pain of betrayal ("Paralyzed") produces movement toward a goal dimly seen but deeply felt, with the promise of a whole human being emerging complete at journey's end. Cash rages in terms both blunt and graphic, sparing no one a thorough accounting. — D.M.

THE CASTELLES
★★ **The Sweet Sound of the Castelles**
(Collectables, NA)
This California quartet did indeed have a
sweet harmony sound, comparable to the
Lettermen, but was about three bricks shy
of a load when it came to soul, again,
comparable to the Lettermen. The Castelles
got it together for one great, overblown love
song, though, in the form of their 1962 hit,
"So This Is Love." Unfortunately, it's not
on this collection, nor is the group's first
AM hit, 1961's "Sacred." What's here is
sweet, but not popular. — D.M.

C+C MUSIC FACTORY
★★★ **Gonna Make You Sweat (Columbia,**
1990)
CLIVILLÉS AND COLE
★★★½ **Greatest Remixes, Vol. I (Columbia,**
1992)
Less a performing entity than a producers'
project, C+C Music Factory is the work of
mixmasters Robert Clivillés and David Cole,
who hired the singers, chose the samples,
programmed the beats and designed the
package. It's also proof that dance music,
like any other commodity, can be mass-
produced without a significant loss in product
integrity. With *Greatest Remixes*, Clivillés
and Cole round out their best C+C work
with reconfigured versions of singles the duo
produced for Seduction, Sandee and Lisa
Lisa & Cult Jam, as well as a rethink of the
house classic "Do It Properly." — J.D.C.

NICK CAVE
★★★ **From Her to Eternity (1984;**
Restless/Mute, 1990)
★★★ **The Firstborn Is Dead**
(Mute/Homestead, 1985)
★★★½ **Kicking Against the Pricks**
(Homestead, 1986)
★★★ **Your Funeral . . . My Trial**
(Mute/Homestead, 1986)
★★★ **Tender Prey (Enigma/Mute, 1988)**
★★★★ **The Good Son (Mute/Elektra,**
1990)
★★★½ **Henry's Dream (Mute/Elektra,**
1992)
In the early '80s, brilliant Australian
eccentric Nick Cave fronted the Birthday
Party, an intense outfit dedicated to gloom,
grandeur and noise. Leaving the band in the
mid-'80s, he continued to delve deeply into
his romantic obsessions—death, desire, Elvis
mythology and the Old Testament. This
time his vehicle was subtler: the Bad Seeds
were spare and atmospheric players—ex-
Birthday Party drummer Mick Harvey, ex-

Magazine bassist Barry Adamson, and
Einstürzende Neubauten guitarist Blixa
Bargeld provided Cave with chilling, almost
abstract backdrops for his rich, allusive tone
poems. On *The Firstborn Is Dead*, Cave
wails and moans, often achieving the
haunted fervor of a postmodern John Lee
Hooker. His dense lyrics are rife with
symbols, and he sings them with a
compelling desperation.
 The Good Son is just as arresting, but far
more mature. With ex-Gun Club guitarist
Kid Congo Powers aboard, the sound is
fuller, and with Harvey adding deft
vibraphone touches, the songs take on a
new grace. Best of all are the string
arrangements—somber and idiosyncratic,
they allow Cave the epic sweep he's always
aspired to. *Son* features Cave's music at its
most stately, and the lyrics to "Sorrow's
Child," the title track and "The Weeping
Song" take on the authority of the most
primal kind of myth. *Henry's Dream*
continues Cave's apocalyptic vision,
presented more aggressively than on his
previous issue. — P.E.

EXENE CERVENKA
★ **Old Wives' Tales (Rhino, 1989)**
★½ **Running Sacred (RNA, 1990)**
When you get right down to it, Exene
Cervenka is one lousy singer. Her voice is
thin, she has trouble with pitch, her
phrasing is erratic—and those are her good
points. But because she was once part of the
legendary L.A. punk group X, Cervenka has
been deemed worthy of a solo career, and so
has inflicted two albums upon us. Wordy
and pretentious, the quasi-folk songs that
litter *Old Wives' Tales* are annoying, but not
half as much as jazz-'n'-poetry numbers like
"Famous Barmaid." Mercifully, she reads
no poems on *Running Sacred*, and even
manages to include a fair amount of rock &
roll. But being not-entirely-annoying is still
a long way from being good. — J.D.C.

CHAD AND JEREMY
★ **The Best of Chad & Jeremy (Capitol,**
1966)
½★ **Of Cabbages and Kings (Columbia,**
1967)
½★ **Yesterday's Gone (World Artists, 1967)**
Strictly easy listening, somewhat dandified
by British accents, this posh duo,
distinguished by breathy enunciation and
cute jawlines, scored in 1964 with "A
Summer Song" and "Yesterday's
Gone"—limp exercises in string-laden,
folksy wistfulness. *Of Cabbages and Kings*

ventured in psychedelia. Everything else they did was (even) worse. — P.E.

CHAIRMEN OF THE BOARD
★ ★ ★ ★ **Greatest Hits (HDH/Fantasy, 1990)**
General Norman Johnson isn't the most commanding of soul singers, but the quavering, confessional edge in his tenor voice has the power to devastate or inspire. Long before Holland-Dozier-Holland convened the Chairmen of the Board at their Invictus/Hot Wax hit factory, General Johnson earned his place in history by singing lead on the Showmen's immortal "It Will Stand." The Showmen cut more than a dozen sides for Allen Toussaint's Minit label, but "It Will Stand" was the group's only hit—it charted twice, in 1961 and '64. By the late '60s, the Showmen had returned home, to the nurturing Southern club circuit: the Carolinas' legendary "beach scene." When General Johnson arrived in Detroit a few years later, the former H-D-H Motown songwriting team was just kicking its own label into gear. Chairmen of the Board's "Give Me Just a Little More Time" put the new hit factory on the map; General Johnson's pleading intensity cuts through the dense, layered production like a sharp knife. Increasingly, Holland-Dozier-Holland pursued an intricate version of psychedelic soul in the early '70s, but the Chairmen's subsequent records toe a somewhat straighter R&B line. *Greatest Hits* taps worthy vocal contributions from Board members Danny Woods ("Pay to the Piper") and Harrison Kennedy ("Chairmen of the Board"), along with General Johnson's original version of the sentimental, but heartfelt "Patches" (a hit for Clarence Carter in 1970. And on "Finders Keepers," from 1973, sideman Bernie Worrell steals that delicious clavinet line from "Superstition" outright, ending the Chairmen of the Board saga on an audaciously funky note. Back at the beach, General Johnson still records and performs regularly on the local level. — M.C.

THE CHAMBERS BROTHERS
★ ★ ★ **The Time Has Come (Columbia, 1968)**
★ ★ ★ ½ **Greatest Hits (Columbia, 1971)**
★ ★ ★ **Best of the Chambers Brothers (Fantasy, 1973)**
Sloppy, overheated, but gifted haphazardly with prophetic instinct, Mississippi's four Chambers Brothers began as a gospel quartet and ended up in the late '60s doing funk/hippie-fusion psychedelized soul that

hinted at such (significantly stronger) later talents as Sly Stone and Prince. The Brothers hit big in 1968 with "Time Has Come Today." Driven by the most engaging cowbell this side of the Stones' "Honky Tonk Women" or Mountain's "Mississippi Queen," the epic jam had a rude, weird power; gruff Baptist-revival chants led into instrumental quotes from "The Little Drummer Boy" and climaxed with a guitar freak-out that almost sounds like punk, of the droning, Velvet Underground–derived variety. The raw pep of "I Can't Turn You Loose" and the gospel restraint of "People Get Ready" were the Chambers' stylistic poles: they tended toward the former. While perhaps chiefly of political significance in opening pathways for crossover followers, their music still retains its sweaty verve. The 1971 *Greatest Hits* collection is pretty fine. — P.E.

GENE CHANDLER
★ ★ ★ **Stroll on With the Duke (Solid Smoke, 1984)**
★ ★ ★ **The Duke of Soul (Chess, 1984)**
Best-remembered for his 1962 chart-topper "Duke of Earl," Gene Chandler (nee Eugene Dixon) came out of the Chicago R&B/doo-wop scene in the late '50s and carved out a consistent, productive career for himself into the early '70s. Apart from "Duke of Earl," Chandler's most productive years were in the mid-to-late '60s, when fellow Chi-towner Curtis Mayfield produced and wrote a succession of first-rate singles that kept Chandler's name prominent in R&B circles and in the Top Forty of the pop charts. Chandler's pose was that of the vulnerable, searching soul man, a bit desperate, but strong nonetheless. His style was to bite off phrases in macho declamation, then swoop into a falsetto shriek, and finally bring it all back home softly and tenderly.

The out-of-print *Stroll on With the Duke* documents in fine detail the Chandler-Mayfield collaboration on the Constellation label, as well as Chandler's pre-Mayfield recordings (such as "Duke of Earl") for Vee Jay with his group the Dukays. Notable among these efforts are a spectacular live version of Mayfield's "Rainbow '65," recorded at the Regal Theater in Chicago; a handful of velvet-smooth soul stirrings with the Impressions; and two collaborations with the Dells from 1964. *The Duke of Soul*, also out of print, duplicates much of the material on *Stroll on*, but adds a few interesting cuts unavailable on the former, such as "Rainbow in My Heart," the exquisite Mayfield-penned predecessor to "Rainbow '65," and "You Threw a Lucky Punch," Chandler's answer to Mary Wells's "You Beat Me to the Punch."

As the '60s neared an end, Chandler retreated to producing, and in 1969 delivered a Top Ten single for Mel and Tim, "Backfield in Motion." Moving to Mercury in 1970, he cut what remains his last major pop hit, "Groovy Situation." Through the '70s he recorded several albums for 20th Century Records in a futile effort to crack the disco market. These are deservedly out of print. — D.M.

THE CHANTELS
★★★★ Best of the Chantels (Rhino, 1990)

The liner notes refer to the Chantels as "the first great rock 'n' roll girl group," and there's no reason to argue with this assessment. Lead singer Arlene Smith had few peers when it came to putting over a song—if heartbreak has a sound, it's Smith's voice. Her melismatic touches and the raw passion she pours into her delivery were as individual a sound as any rock has ever produced, and no one could cut her when it came time for that soprano to soar off into the stratosphere. To say Arlene Smith gave it her all is to diminish the lady, because there was always more to give, another passion to plumb, another open wound that demanded she raise her voice to heaven and cry, cry, cry. *Best of* charts the Chantels' history from 1957 to 1961, when they were guided by Richard Barrett, one of the most prolific behind-the-scenes operators (songwriter-producer-player-manager) in rock history. Smith left the group in 1959, but Barrett managed to squeeze a couple more hits out of the girls, the Top Twenty "Look in My Eyes," a lightweight piece of pop, and "Well, I Told You," which reached Number 29. The key tracks feature Smith—including, especially, the group's first hit, "He's Gone" (co-written by Smith and Barrett); the immortal *cri de coeur*, "Maybe"; a scorching cameo vocal on Willie Smith and the Tunemasters' "I've Lied"; and the relentless, driving "I Love You So." Actually, whenever her voice comes on, you'll stop and listen—every performance has its riveting moment, one that'll take your breath away. — D.M.

HARRY CHAPIN
★★ Verities & Balderdash (Elektra, 1974)
★★ Portrait Gallery (Elektra, 1975)
★★ Greatest Stories—Live (Elektra, 1976)

★★ On the Road to Kingdom Come (Elektra, 1976)
★★ Dance Band on the Titanic (Elektra, 1977)
★★ Living Room Suite (Elektra, 1978)
★★ Legends of the Lost & Found (Elektra, 1979)
★★ Anthology of Harry Chapin (Elektra, 1985)

The late Harry Chapin brought the issue of world hunger to the forefront in the cozy mid-'70s, when Bob Geldof was still singing stuff like "Looking After No. 1" with the Boomtown Rats. Truly, his dedicated activism helped pave the way for Live Aid, but as a singer-songwriter, well . . . Chapin is best remembered as a social activist. It's tempting merely to cite the title of his most popular album, *Verities & Balderdash*, as being completely accurate, and move on. However, Chapin's banal homilies and awkward love songs apparently struck a chord with many listeners. (And what DJ or radio programmer could be expected to resist the maudlin self-justification of 1973's "W.O.L.D"? Few did.) The FM radio staple "Taxi" established Chapin's hangdog narrative style in 1972, while the 1974 Top Ten hit "Cat's in the Cradle" exhibits his utter dependence on heavy-handed, moralistic payoffs. Chapin and his fans often described these songs as folksy short stories, but folkie sermons—and they're not especially short—falls a lot closer to the truth. *Anthology* collects Chapin's best-known work; including the already mentioned singles, the first half sustains mild historical interest, but Harry's awkward talk-singing and dated, overbaked "pop" productions pull the second half into the mire. When he pulls out all the stops at the end of "Better Place to Be," the effect is more depressing than all the lyric's boozy hard-luck tales combined. Harry Chapin's heart was in the right place; sadly, that doesn't make him any easier to hear at this late date. — M.C.

TRACY CHAPMAN
★★★★½ Tracy Chapman (Elektra, 1988)
★★★★ Crossroads (Elektra, 1989)
★★★ Matters of the Heart (Elektra, 1992)

One of those rare talents who seem to have sprung full-grown, Chapman found instant success with her 1988 debut. For a while, singers like Suzanne Vega and Rickie Lee Jones had been making the world safe for sharp, no-nonsense women singers, and the climate was right for Chapman's arrival.

Still, no one was prepared for the depth and breadth of the album—for its dignity, seasoned musicality and thematic reach.

"Fast Car" was the first marvel, a folk song real enough to acknowledge the existence of convenience stores and a woman's thirst for speed. And it sounded great, too: drum heavy and tough, its efficiency allowed Chapman's voice to glide and slur. Then there was "Talkin' 'Bout a Revolution," its '60s spirit revamped by a Reagan-era urgency (and by the fact that Chapman was no counter-cultural vet, but a young black woman). "For My Lover" showed that she could also handle the intimate revolution—a hip defense of loving however you want to love, it alluded both to a Virginia jail and psychoanalysis, encapsulating Chapman's neat blending of archetypal folk references and the talk of today.

Chapman's followup, *Crossroads*, was also fine. Again, she offered folk's perennial philosophy—working-class solidarity, a yearning for independence and release—alongside newer ways of thinking: womyn power, African-American pride and self-help stubbornness. With its violin played by ex-Dylan accompanist Scarlet Rivera, "This Time" revealed the writer's new capacity for elegance; Neil Young, reprising the childlike piano of "Helpless," added grace to "All That You Have Is Your Soul." And throughout the record, Chapman's knowing vocals sounded wise beyond her years. *Matters of the Heart*, an introspective album, doesn't break any new ground; none of its atmospheric songs really stand out. — P.E.

CHARLATANS U.K.
★ ★ Some Friendly (Beggars Banquet/RCA 1990)

Along with such Manchester outfits as Inspiral Carpets and Happy Mondays, the Charlatans U.K. pulled off the improbable feat of returning the organ to lead instrument status—a position it hasn't held since the bad old days of ELP or Lee Michaels. Droning but insinuatingly memorable, "The Only One I Know" wasn't bad, but there's little else that's intriguing about this Brit quintet—except for the fact that they might become the Manfred Mann (tedious and overrated) of their generation. — P.E.

RAY CHARLES
★ ★½ The Early Years (NA; King/Highland, 1990)

★ ★ ★½ The Great Ray Charles (1956; Atlantic, 1987)
★ ★ ★ ★ Ray Charles (Atlantic, 1957)
★ ★ ★ Yes Indeed!! (Atlantic, 1958)
★ ★ ★ ★ What'd I Say (Atlantic, 1959)
★ ★ ★ ★½ The Genius of Ray Charles (Atlantic, 1959)
★ ★½ The Genius Hits the Road (ABC, 1960)
★ ★ ★ The Genius After Hours (1961; Atlantic, 1985)
★ ★ ★ ★ The Genius Sings the Blues (Atlantic, 1961)
★ ★ ★ ★ The Greatest! (Atlantic, 1961)
★ ★ ★ Dedicated to You (ABC, 1961)
★ ★ ★ ★½ Genius + Soul = Jazz (1961; DCC, 1988)
★ ★ ★ ★ Ray Charles and Betty Carter (1961; DCC, 1988)
★ ★ ★ ★ ★ Modern Sounds in Country and Western Music (1962; Rhino, 1988)
★ ★ ★ ★ ★ Greatest Hits (ABC, 1962)
★ ★ ★ ★ ★ Modern Sounds in Country and Western Music, Vol. 2 (ABC, 1963)
★ ★ ★ ★ Ingredients in a Recipe for Soul (1963; DCC, 1990)
★ ★ ★½ Sweet and Sour Tears (ABC, 1964)
★½ Have a Smile with Me (ABC, 1964)
★ ★ ★ ★ Live in Concert (ABC, 1965)
★ ★ ★ Together Again (ABC, 1965)
★ ★ ★½ Crying Time (ABC, 1966)
★ ★ ★ Ray's Moods (ABC, 1966)
★ ★ Ray Charles Invites You to Listen (ABC, 1967)
★ ★ ★ A Portrait of Ray (ABC, 1968)
★ ★½ I'm All Yours, Baby (ABC, 1969)
★ ★ ★ ★ Doing His Thing (ABC, 1969)
★ ★½ Love Country Style (ABC, 1970)
★ ★ ★ My Kind of Jazz (Tangerine, 1970)
★ ★ ★½ The Best of Ray Charles (1956–58) (Atlantic, 1970)
★ ★ ★ Volcanic Action of My Soul (ABC, 1971)
★ ★ ★ ★ ★ 25th Anniversary in Show Business Salute (ABC, 1971)
★ ★ ★ ★ A Message From the People (ABC, 1972)
★ ★½ Through the Eyes of Love (ABC, 1972)
★ ★ ★ Jazz Number II (Tangerine, 1972)
★ ★½ Come Live With Me (Crossover, 1974)

★★★★ Renaissance (Crossover, 1975)
★★ My Kind of Jazz, Part 3 (Crossover, 1975)
★★★ True to Life (Atlantic, 1977)
★★½ Love & Peace (Atlantic, 1978)
★★★ Ain't It So (Atlantic, 1979)
★★★ Brother Ray Is at It Again (Atlantic, 1980)
★★★★ A Life in Music (1956–59) (Atlantic, 1982)
★★★ Wish You Were Here Tonight (Columbia, 1983)
★★ Do I Ever Cross Your Mind (Columbia, 1984)
★★½ Friendship (Columbia, 1984)
★★ The Spirit of Christmas (Columbia, 1985)
★★ From the Pages of My Mind (Columbia, 1986)
★★★★ Ray Charles Live (1958–59) (Atlantic, 1987)
★★★½ His Greatest Hits, Vol. 1 (1960–71) (DCC, 1987)
★★★★ His Greatest Hits, Vol. 2 (1960–72) (DCC, 1987)
★★★★★ Greatest Country & Western Hits (1962–65) (DCC, 1988)
★★★★ Greatest Hits, Volume 1 (1960–67) (Rhino, 1988)
★★★★ Greatest Hits, Volume 2 (1960–72) (Rhino, 1988)
★★★★★ Anthology (Rhino, 1989)
★★½ Just Between Us (Columbia, 1988)
★★ Seven Spanish Angels and Other Hits (Columbia, 1989)
★½ Would You Believe? (Warner Bros., 1990)
★★★★★ Ray Charles 1954–1966 (Time Life Music, 1991)
★★★★★ The Birth of Soul (1952–59) (Atlantic, 1991)

WITH MILT JACKSON
★★★ Soul Brothers (Atlantic, 1958)
★★½ Soul Meeting (Atlantic, 1962)
★★★ Soul Brothers/Soul Meeting (1957–58) (Atlantic, 1989)

WITH CLEO LAINE
★★★★★ Porgy & Bess (1976; RCA, 1989)

One of popular music's most protean talents, Ray Charles has tried almost every imaginable style in his 40-odd years as a recording artist, building a body of work that includes not only classic R&B and rock numbers, but also forays into country, jazz and even middle-of-the-road pop. His heartfelt eclecticism has resulted in some astonishing music, but it has also led to enough misguided and mediocre work to make even the most sympathetic listener wish that the singer's judgment was as sterling as his talent.

Charles made his first recordings in 1947–48, and began releasing singles on the Downbeat label (it eventually became Swingtime) in '49. These sides have been assembled in low-cost packages of varying content and quality; to that extent, *The Early Years* is typical, offering minimal fidelity and little or no recording information, although habitués of bargain bins and used record stores will surely find others. Musically, the value of these collections is marginal, as Charles's earliest singles owe much to the sound of Charles Brown or Nat "King" Cole. But the singer's maturity is immediately apparent, even if his future greatness is not.

As such, the Ray Charles story begins, for all intents and purposes, in 1952, when his contract with Swingtime was purchased by Atlantic Records. Atlantic was where Charles's sound finally came into focus, and where he recorded his first—and in many ways, most influential—R&B hits, although it took a few years for him to build up to that point. Those interested in a chronological view of his progress should proceed directly to the triple-album *The Birth of Soul*, which finds the young singer-pianist starting with more or less conventional blues (e.g. "The Sun's Gonna Shine Again") and jump tunes ("Mess Around," "Jumpin' in the Morning") before hitting on the formula that would beget "I Got a Woman," "Hallelujah I Love Her So" and other breakthrough singles. What makes these singles so affecting is the way they fuse jump-blues rhythm work to a gospel-inflected vocal, an approach that electrified pop fans (but scandalized church-goers, who felt its marriage of secular and spiritual was nothing short of sacrilege). "I Got a Woman," "Mess Around" and "Hallelujah I Love Her So" are all on *Ray Charles*, although lesser tunes like "Funny but I Still Love You" and "Losing Hand" are just as interesting, if only for Mickey Baker's growling guitar work. *Yes Indeed!!* adds Charles's first Top Forty hit, "Swanee River Rock (Talkin' Bout That River)," as well as the similarly soulful "Leave My Woman Alone" and "Lonely Avenue," while *What'd I Say* delivers the singer's first Top Ten pop hit, the supercharged call-and-response number "What'd I Say," as well as the churchy "Tell All the World About You" and a surprisingly swinging version of the Scots folk song "My Bonnie." 'I Believe to My Soul" and "Hard Times" are the highlights of *The Genius Sings the Blues*, but the album flanks those performances with lesser numbers from Charles's earliest sessions for the label. (*The Birth of Soul* includes everything on these four albums, which have been deleted but are widely available on import). *Live* augments the 1958 recording *Ray Charles at Newport* with six selections recorded a year later (and originally released on *Ray Charles in Person*), and is a stunning testament to the power of Charles's live band, particularly Margie Hendrix of the Raeletts.

Even though his commercial success was strictly with R&B tunes, Atlantic considered Charles as much a jazz musician as a pop star; indeed, his Atlantic discography contains almost as much instrumental work as vocal. Unfortunately, his Atlantic jazz sessions have been packaged and repackaged so many times over the years that it takes some work to sort it all out. Take, for instance, *The Great Ray Charles*, which is available both in its original format—a soulful, small-band session featuring his horn players, particularly alto saxophonist David "Fathead" Newman—and in a CD version that not only changes the track order but adds three trio performances and two full-band tracks that had originally been issued on *The Genius After Hours* (which itself remains in print). Two more tunes from *After Hours* have been added to the Ray Charles–Milt Jackson double-CD *Soul Brothers/Soul Meeting*, although the individual albums *Soul Brothers* and *Soul Meeting* are available only on cassette.

Whether it's worth sifting through these titles is, of course, another issue entirely. Charles isn't a bad jazz pianist, but neither is he an especially inspiring one, being generally more adept at rhythm work and accompaniment than strict improvisation. Then again, these aren't terribly demanding jazz dates, either, tending more toward the sort of soul-jazz groovesmanship of Ramsey Lewis or Ahmad Jamal, with only the Milt Jackson collaborations managing to push the playing beyond the pedestrian. Some of that can be chalked up to the fact that *Soul Brothers* and *Soul Meeting* find Charles playing with a better class of musician (Oscar Pettiford, Connie Kay, Kenny Burrell), but it helps that both feature Charles on alto saxophone, an instrument that brings out much of the same soulful passion that informs his singing.

Perhaps the the most important of his

albums for Atlantic is *The Genius of Ray Charles*—not because it's full of hits (it isn't) or contains his best work for the label (it doesn't), but because it introduces the musical approach he would follow for much of the '70s. Although *The Genius of Ray Charles* puts him in front of a big band, the sound he pursues is nothing like that of the swing-era bands, or even the jazzy, large-ensemble sound singers like Frank Sinatra or Dean Martin went for; instead, what Charles comes up with is a curious hybrid of the brassy R&B of his pop-oriented recordings and the showy schmaltz favored by the era's middle-of-the-road acts. Hence, Charles bounces from the powerhouse blues of "Let the Good Times Roll" or "Two Years of Torture" to overblown and gimmicky renditions of fare like "Alexander's Ragtime Band," although at times—"Come Rain or Come Shine" comes to mind—he's able to incorporate elements of both. (Be aware, however, that the album is abysmally recorded, with frequent overmodulation muddying its brasher moments).

By the dawn of the '60s Charles had jumped to ABC Records, negotiating a deal that gave him, among other things, full ownership of the master tapes of the recordings he made for the label. Ironically, Charles's control of these recordings is part of the reason most of his albums from this era have been out of print for years—despite the fact that this period produced his biggest hits, including such singles as "Hit the Road Jack" and "Unchain My Heart." Granted, most (but not all) of Charles's Top Forty hits from this period have been collected on the two DCC CDs, *His Greatest Hits, Vol. 1* and *Vol. 2*, but considering that this was when Charles first began to think in terms of albums instead of singles and planned his recordings with that in mind, serious listeners have little choice but to seek out the used record market.

Still, it helps to shop carefully, for in the early '60s Charles had an unfortunate fondness for conceptually organized albums, an approach that often led to trouble. His first album, for instance, was a collection of place-name songs called *The Genius Hits the Road*, which on the one hand boasts "Georgia on My Mind," perhaps his greatest ballad performance ever, and on the other drags in such dreck as "Moon Over Miami" and an appallingly gimmicky "Deep in the Heart of Texas." *Dedicated to You* focuses on songs featuring women's names in their titles; *Sweet and Sour Tears* offers songs about crying; *Have a Smile With Me* goes for allegedly funny songs like "Two Ton Tessie" and "The Man with the Weird Beard"; and so on. Most seem a trifle forced, but when Charles gets ahold of a theme that grabs him musically—say, the various shades of blue on *Crying Time*, particularly "Let's Go Get Stoned"—the results are amazing.

Nowhere is that more the case than on *Modern Sounds in Country and Western Music*, an album of country songs performed Ray Charles–style. This wasn't unknown territory for the singer, as he'd grown up listening to country music and even played piano in a hillbilly band, but what makes the album work is his ability to transform these songs. Consider, for instance, the way he turns Floyd Tillman's twangy "It Makes No Difference Now" into a jaunty, horn-driven blues or adds a jazzy edge to Hank Williams's "Hey, Good Lookin'." But it was his sturdily straightforward reading of the Don Gibson hit "I Can't Stop Loving You" that struck the strongest chord with the pop audience. Even more stunning is his soulful take on "You Are My Sunshine," from *Modern Sounds in Country and Western Music, Vol. 2* (and added as a bonus track to Rhino's CD version of *Modern Sounds in Country and Western Music*), which treats it as a groove tune, with solid rhythm work and scintillating interplay with the Raeletts. But then, Charles's second *Modern Sounds* album is generally superior to the first, both because its balladry is smoother (as with his version of Williams's "Your Cheatin' Heart") and because the blues tunes rock harder (check his smouldering rendition of Gibson's "Don't Tell Me Your Troubles"). Highlights from both albums can be found on DCC's *Greatest Country & Western Hits*, but, curiously, nothing from *Together Again*, his third country-style album; certainly his funky approach to Buck Owens's "I've Got a Tiger by the Tail" or Bill Monroe's "Blue Moon of Kentucky" are well worth hearing.

As he did at Atlantic, Charles continued to make jazz albums. *Genius + Soul = Jazz* is by far the best of the lot, since its big band-and-organ arragements retain much of the sound of his pop albums, but the low-key and swinging *Ray Charles and Betty Carter* also shines, particularly when the two genially spar through "Baby, It's Cold Outside." There are also a few jazzy moments on *Live in Concert*, much as there were on his Newport album for Atlantic. But his self-indulgent '70s jazz albums are easily ignored, apart from the funkier moments of *My Kind of Jazz* (in particular, "Booty Butt").

By the mid-'60s, much of Charles's output was solidly middle-of-the-road, with a heavy emphasis in his albums on string-laden ballads. That's not to say he'd abandoned the soul side of his sound, just that it grew ever more compartmentalized, as with *A Portrait of Ray*, which is split into separate slow and uptempo sides. Still, Charles doesn't get significantly funky again until *Doing His Thing*, an album that's long on groove but short on songs (although the interplay between Charles and Jimmy Lewis on "If It Wasn't for Bad Luck" is delightful). *A Message from the People* pushes even further toward a progressive soul sound, thanks to its playful treatment of the New Seekers' "Look What They've Done to My Song, Ma" and John Denver's "Take Me Home, Country Roads." But the album's real strength is its approach to social issues, and it's hard not to be moved by his performances of "America the Beautiful" or "Abraham, Martin, and John." It's a tough album to top, though *Renaissance*, with its gospel-ized renditions of both Stevie Wonder's "Livin' for the City" and Randy Newman's "Sail Away," certainly comes close.

By the mid-'70s, Charles was better known for what he'd done than what he was doing. That didn't stop him from making good records, of course—the *Porgy and Bess* he recorded with Cleo Laine is easily one of the best pop performances those songs have seen, at times surpassing even the legendary Louis Armstrong/Ella Fitzgerald version—but the good ones were becoming increasingly rare. He returned to Atlantic in 1977 and released four albums, none of which particularly demand hearing, though they have their moments: His "Oh, What a Beautiful Morning" from *True to Life*, for instance; the quasi-disco "You 20th Century Fox" from *Love & Peace*, a genuine hoot; the way he rephrases the Dobie Gray hit "Drift Away" on *Ain't It So*.

There was worse to come, however. Charles jumped to Columbia in 1983, where he proceeded to turn himself into a country singer. It wasn't a complete transformation, of course; *Just Between Us* is mostly blues and features a rollicking "Save the Bones for Henry Jones," recorded with Lou Rawls and Milt Jackson, while *The Spirit of Christmas* reverts to the MOR + R&B formula that served him so well in the '60s. When Charles did sing country for

Columbia, though, he sang it straight, without any of the R&B overtones that marked his first C&W experiments. And frankly, the music gains nothing from his fidelity. If anything, the reverse is true, as most of these albums are indistinguishable from the Music Row hackwork Charles's producer, Billy Sherrill, churned out for his other clients. Granted, the singer does occasionally rise above the production-line predictability of his material, as when he breathes life into "3/4 Time" on *Wish You Were Here Tonight*, or joins Merle Haggard in savoring the loneliness of a "Little Hotel Room" on *Friendship*. Still, saying that these albums aren't entirely bad hardly counts as a recommendation. *Would You Believe*, Charles's first Warner Bros. release, isn't much cause for hope, since it sounds less like a finished album than a collection of demos, but considering that the singer followed it with a Pepsi commercial that was more popular than any of his recent recordings, it seems far too early to count him out for good.

Given the breadth of Charles's output, it might seem that the best introduction would be a well-balanced best-of album. *A 25th Anniversary in Show Business Salute* is perhaps the best single package ever assembled, inasmuch as its 35-song selection draws upon both his Atlantic and ABC recordings; trouble is, the set is so far out of print that desperate fans have resorted to ultra-expensive Japanese imports. Of the Atlantic collections, while *The Greatest Ray Charles* delivers the basic hits, *The Best of Ray Charles* has none, tending to showcase his jazz side; *A Life in Music* tries for a better overview of his Atlantic tenure, but has little depth despite its 50-song length, and seems at times ashamed of Charles's pop proclivities. That's certainly not the case with the way DCC's two-volume *His Greatest Hits* represents his ABC years, for these albums avidly embrace his MOR side. But even though they're each 50 percent longer than their Rhino counterparts (while covering the same period), they're not as well organized, jumping from hit to hit without any real logic. Rhino's *Anthology* is an excellent collection, including the ABC hits and other recordings of interest.

— J.D.C.

CHEAP TRICK

★ ★ ★½ Cheap Trick (Epic, 1977)
★ ★ ★ ★ In Color (Epic, 1977)
★ ★ ★½ Heaven Tonight (Epic, 1978)
★ ★ ★ ★ Live at Budokan (Epic, 1979)

★ ★ ★ Dream Police (Epic, 1979)
★ ★ ★½ All Shook Up (Epic, 1980)
★ ★ ★½ Found All the Parts (EP) (Epic, 1980)
★ ★ One on One (Epic, 1982)
★ ★ Next Position Please (Epic, 1983)
★ ★ Standing on the Edge (Epic, 1985)
★ ★ The Doctor (Epic, 1986)
★ ★ Lap of Luxury (Epic, 1988)
★ ★ ★ Busted (Epic, 1990)

When its first album came out, Cheap Trick had already reached legendary status among disaffected Midwestern rock & rollers. During the darkest days before punk, this Chicago-based quartet bucked the ruling rock-club system. Rather than reproduce letter-perfect hit cover versions, Cheap Trick played three sets of original material every night, filling out its loopy metalized Beatlemania with the occasional Roy Wood or Terry Reid obscurity. Contrasting the traditional rock-star smolder of singer Robin Zander and bassist Tom Petersson with guitarist Rick Nielsen's geeky theatricality and drummer Bun E. Carlos's avuncular inscrutability, Cheap Trick gave paying customers an eyeful as well as an earful.

The image is important: Cheap Trick pioneered the videogenic, stage-conscious metal stance of today. But this band's primary impact is musical. *Cheap Trick*, *In Color* and *Heaven Tonight* all draw from the incredible backlog of songs from the group's early days, mostly penned by Rick Nielsen. His writing echoes his guitar playing: concise and witty, crammed with quotes, allusions, outright ripoffs, corny jokes, bent-out-of-shape riffs and heart-rending hooks. Aerosmith producer Jack Douglas brings a gratifyingly raw edge to the debut, but Tom Werman's sonic polishing on the following two albums puts a gleam on those pure pop melodies without correcting their overbite. "Surrender" from *Heaven Tonight* exemplifies Cheap Trick's raffish charm, though *In Color* captures the seamless energy and sustained invention of the band's live sets. "Ready to rock" at the drop of a hat, Cheap Trick could roll, too—not exactly a common attribute in the late '70s.

Somehow, Cheap Trick went on to become the very thing those initial albums rebelled against. After the commercial breakthrough of *Live at Budokan*, years of slogging the arena circuit gradually dulled the group's edge. A soggy, conceptual title cut nearly sinks the otherwise-snappy *Dream Police*, and the hotly contemplated match-up with Beatle producer George

Martin (*All Shook Up*) misfires almost completely. The following records document a descent into the Stygian AOR nether regions, culminating with *Lap of Luxury* and its depressing Number One power-ballad, "The Flame." However, Cheap Trick's irreverent spark may not be totally extinguished. Definite flickers of life emerge on *Busted* amid the expected radio-ready ringers; if Cheap Trick ever throws commercial caution to the wind and returns to its gleefully twisted roots, current-day bands like Extreme and Enuff Z'Nuff might learn a thing or two about making metal go pop. — M.C.

CLIFTON CHENIER

★★★★ **Louisiana Blues and Zydeco (1965; Arhoolie, 1990)**
★★★½ **Black Snake Blues (Arhoolie, 1967)**
★★★ **Sings the Blues (1969; Arhoolie, 1988)**
★★★ **Live at St. Mark's (1971; Arhoolie, 1990)**
★★★★ **Bayou Blues (Specialty, 1971)**
★★★½ **Out West (1972; Arhoolie, 1991)**
★★★★★ **Bogalusa Boogie (1975; Arhoolie, 1990)**
★★★½ **The King of Zydeco Live at Montreux (1975; Arhoolie, 1990)**
★★★ **Boogie in Black and White (Jin, 1976)**
★★★★ **Boogie 'N' Zydeco (Maison de Soul, 1977)**
★★★ **And His Red Hot Louisiana Band (Arhoolie, 1978)**
★★★ **New Orleans (GNP Crescendo, 1978)**
★★★ **King of Zydeco (Home Cooking, 1980)**
★★★★ **Classic Clifton (Arhoolie, 1980)**
★★★ **The King of Zydeco (Arhoolie, 1981)**
★★★★½ **I'm Here! (Alligator, 1982)**
★★★ **Country Boy Now Grammy Award Winner 1984! (Maison de Soul, 1984)**
★★★ **Live at the San Francisco Blues Festival (Arhoolie, 1985)**
★★★½ **60 Minutes With the King of Zydeco (Arhoolie, 1988)**
★★★ **Clifton Chenier & Rockin' Dupsee (Flyright, 1989)**
★★★½ **Bon Ton Roulet (Arhoolie, 1990)**
★★★★ **Bayou Soul (Maison de Soul, NA)**

Clifton Chenier wasn't just the king of zydeco—he pretty much invented zydeco as we know it. Although he came up playing the same Creole party music as his father and grandfather, the young accordionist began to incorporate blues elements into his sound in the mid-'50s, and in so doing redefined zydeco. Although Chenier made his first recordings for the tiny Elko label in 1954, his earliest works in print are his 1955 sessions for Specialty, collected on *Bayou Blues*; tracks like "I'm on My Way" and "Eh, Petite Fille" are typical of his blues-fueled style. His only other recordings from this period to have made the transition to digital can be found on the first eight tracks of *Clifton Chenier & Rockin' Dupsee*, but as much as these sessions capture the sweaty enthusiasm of his playing, their heavily distorted sound makes them of interest only to dedicated fans.

Chenier's recordings thereafter simply refined the style he'd developed in the '50s. *Bon Ton Roulet* and *Bayou Soul* show how well he could rock, while the solidly traditional two-steps and waltzes included on *Louisiana Blues & Zydeco* are proof that Chenier was by no means just a rocker. Still, perhaps the best of Chenier's albums is *Bogalusa Boogie*, a near-flawless recording that vividly captures the accordion-and-washboard interplay between Clifton and his brother Cleveland, as well as the solidly soulful groove of their Red Hot Louisiana Band.

Due to diabetes, Chenier's health began to fail in 1979, but that hardly slowed his recording schedule; if anything, it increased. Unfortunately, of the albums recorded between 1979 and his death in 1987, only *I'm Here* manages any consistent degree of quality; the rest, though generally superior to most of his competition, lack the sparkle of his earlier output. — J.D.C.

CHER

★★ **Gypsies, Tramps and Thieves (Kapp/MCA, 1971)**
★★½ **Greatest Hits (MCA, 1974)**
★ **I Paralyze (Columbia, 1982)**
★★ **Cher (Geffen, 1987)**
★★ **Heart of Stone (Geffen, 1989)**
★★½ **Bang Bang (My Baby Shot Me Down): The Best of Cher/Legendary Masters Series (EMI, 1990)**
★★½ **Love Hurts (Geffen, 1991)**

No surprise, really, that Cher graduated to television and movies; her dramatic flair (and pancake-flat voice) are evident on her hits from the '60s, both with first husband–producer Sonny Bono and (nominally) on her own. *Bang Bang: The Best of Cher* spirals off into undistinguished covers of "Alfie" and the like, though Cher's breathy determination brings to life the canned domestic scenarios of "Bang Bang (My Baby Shot Me Down)" and "You Better Sit Down, Kids." By the early '70s, *The Sonny and Cher Show* made the couple a household name.Though her recording career continued to find some success, Cher left behind whatever minute rock & roll influence she'd once possessed. Hyperbolic production numbers like "Half-Breed," "Dark Lady" and "Gypsies, Tramps and Thieves"—wickedly dubbed her "swarthy trilogy" by critic Robert Christgau—established Cher as an utterly campy, but somehow compelling presence on the pop charts. However, those three glorious howlers can't rescue Cher's *Greatest Hits* from the gaping clutches of dispassionate shlock like "The Way of Love." Splitting up with Sonny in the midst of their televised heyday, Cher seemed to embark on an express journey to Palookaville. It's hard to say which album is more misbegotten: her shamelessly transparent disco come-on (*Take Me Home*, 1979) or her post-Gregg Allman metal gross-out with boyfriend Les Dudek at the helm (*Black Rose*, 1980). Thankfully, both those albums are out of print.

In the wake of her '80s film stardom, Cher jump-started her singing career once again. Unsurprisingly, the overwrought power ballads and metal-lite sounds of the Bon Jovi generation are right up her alley. The title track of *Love Hurts* pays appropriate (and annoying) tribute to Nazareth's screechy 1976 rendition, not the Everly Brothers original. And only Cher—primed from years of aerobics and weight training—could pump up the pro-crafted hook of "Love and Understanding" until it actually appears to mean something. There's an enjoyable one-disc *Best Of* spread out over Cher's spotty twenty-year career, but the number of record companies involved will probably stop it from ever being compiled. On the bright side, perhaps we'll also be spared a Cher boxed set. — M.C.

NENEH CHERRY

★ ★ ★½ **Raw Like Sushi (Virgin, 1989)**
Raw Like Sushi proved a refreshing novelty: dance music with subject matter outside itself. Sure, "Buffalo Stance" and the rest of this texture-fest have grooves and sly aural

percolations aplenty, but this is hip-hop you can actually think to. The stepdaughter of jazz trumpeter Don Cherry, Neneh snarls and dishes and wails snappy message songs—"Manchild" wrestles the male animal (but compassionately); "Next Generation" sweetly and toughly contemplates the future; "Inna City Mama" does New York with a sort of James Baldwin mix of fear and fascination. "Kisses on the Wind" boasts a neat Spanish intro, and the wordplay of "Outre Risque Locomotive" is just as zesty as the song's rhythmic mimicking of foreplay. Not just a personal victory for Cherry, *Raw Like Sushi* also elevates the genre by appealing to the whole body, brain included. — P.E.

CHIC

★ ★	**Chic (Atlantic, 1978)**
★ ★½	**C'est Chic (Atlantic, 1978)**
★ ★ ★ ★	**Risqué (Atlantic, 1979)**
★ ★ ★ ★ ★	**Les Plus Grands Succès de Chic (Chic's Greatest Hits) (Atlantic, 1979)**
★ ★ ★ ★	**Real People (Atlantic, 1980)**
★ ★ ★ ★	**Take It Off (Atlantic, 1981)**
★ ★ ★½	**Tongue in Chic (Atlantic, 1982)**
★ ★ ★	**Believer (Atlantic, 1983)**
★ ★ ★ ★	**Dance Dance Dance: The Best of Chic (Atlantic, 1991)**
★ ★ ★	**Chicism (Warner Bros., 1992)**

Chic bridged the great divide between rock and disco. The brainchild of guitarist Nile Rodgers and bassist Bernard Edwards, Chic broke out of the studio with two booty-shaking novelty hits. "Le Freak" and "Dance, Dance, Dance (Yowsah Yowsah Yowsah)" distill the essence of post-*Saturday Night Fever* dance music: both songs are sophisticated-sounding, a little silly and irresistibly *alive*. The albums *Chic* and *C'est Chic* succumb to fluff and filler, but the group's third Top Ten single uncovered deep emotional and melodic resources. "I Want Your Love" is subtle and haunting, yet the rhythmic pulse never lets up. Along with drummer Tony Thompson, Rodgers and Edwards forged a funky power-trio groove beneath the sweet soul singing and succinct string arrangement. On "Good Times," Chic's next single, they took this formula to the bank. A stirring hedonist anthem tinged with melancholy, "Good Times" climbed to Number One just as disco fever started to backfire in mid-'79. The collections *Les Plus Grands Succès de Chic (Chic's Greatest Hits)* and *Dance Dance Dance* argue in favor of a maligned musical era. They are essential.

Risqué and *Real People* diversify Chic's signature sound, pointing toward rock without abandoning the boudoir or the dance floor. Vocalists Alfa Anderson, Luci Martin and sessionman supreme Fonzi Thornton continue to make solid contributions, but Rodgers's innovative guitar work and bold rhythms come to dominate the later albums. While the complex, knotty funk of *Take It Off* holds up to repeated listening, only a contortionist could dance to it. No wonder the hit parade stopped cold. As the '80s wore on, Edwards and (especially) Rodgers were in constant demand as producers; finally, Chic's once-boundless energy began to sound taxed. Even so, the slightly wan, over-synthesized *Believer* holds some indelible moments. *Chicism*, Rodgers and Edwards's 1992 return, doesn't catch fire until the very last track "M.M.F.T.C.F. (Make My Funk the Chic Funk)." — M.C.

CHICAGO

★ ★ ★   **Chicago Transit Authority (Columbia, 1969)**
★ ★ ★   **Chicago II (Columbia, 1970)**
★ ★ ★   **Chicago III (Columbia, 1971)**
★ ★   **At Carnegie Hall Volumes I–IV (Columbia, 1971)**
★ ★ ½ **Chicago V (Columbia, 1972)**
★ ★ ½ **Chicago VI (Columbia, 1973)**
★ ★ ½ **Chicago VII (Columbia, 1974)**
★ ★   **Chicago VIII (Columbia, 1975)**
★ ★ ★ ½ **Chicago's Greatest Hits (Columbia, 1975)**
★ ★   **Chicago X (Columbia, 1976)**
★ ★   **Chicago XI (Columbia, 1977)**
★ ★   **Hot Streets (Columbia, 1978)**
★ ★   **Chicago 13 (Columbia, 1979)**
★   **Chicago XIV (Columbia, 1980)**
★ ★ ½ **Chicago's Greatest Hits Volume II (Columbia, 1981)**
★   **Chicago 16 (Warner Bros./Full Moon, 1982)**
★ ★ ★ ½ **If You Leave Me Now (Columbia, 1983)**
★   **Chicago 17 (Warner Bros./Full Moon, 1984)**
★   **Chicago 18 (Warner Bros., 1986)**
★   **Chicago 19 (Reprise, 1988)**
★ ★   **Chicago's Greatest Hits 1982–89 (Reprise, 1989)**
★ ★ ★ ½ **Group Portrait (Columbia/Legacy, 1991)**

Originally known as Chicago Transit Authority, this long-running "horn band" could never lay claim to the jazz pedigree of Blood, Sweat and Tears. Chicago began life as a hard-working show band; musically adept young men with more nightclub gigs than rock festivals under their belts. Lacking the focus of a dynamic frontman, the group turned its anonymous, professional air into a virtue—and a marketing strategy. Chicago could boast several gifted commercial tunesmiths: guitarist Terry Kath, keyboardist Robert Lamm and bassist Peter Cetera all exhibit the knack at various points. Chicago seemed to be a constant presence on the pop charts during the '70s, one Top Ten blending into the next. Gradually, the pumped-up hippie pep rallies give way to gentle falsetto romance; occasionally, one of those creamy vocal hooks or pesky horn lines can stick. But how do you actually find "Saturday in the Park" among Chicago's numerous and unimaginatively titled albums?

Group Portrait points the way, while bravely arguing in favor of Chicago's historical importance. Spanning four stuffed-full discs, this 1991 box set communicates the full range of Chicago's ambitions. (*Chicago II* and *Chicago III* are double albums on vinyl; the whopping four-record solo fest *Live at Carnegie Hall* is overkill.) Presenting the failed protest suites and botched disco-era efforts along with oodles of golden oldies is accurate, but unflattering. The music on *Group Portrait* undercuts the eloquently stated claims of the liner notes; Chicago's boundary-pushing instrumentals conjure up visions (memories?) of a high school marching band wigging out on pot. For the less studious, the first Chicago's *Greatest Hits* album will suffice. *If You Leave Me Now* is a tight, beguiling mix of punchy early '70s fare ("25 or 6 to 4," "Does Anybody Really Know What Time It Is?") and borderline-saccharine late '70s love songs (like the title track). This is the Chicago album to get if you're only buying one, and a budget-line item at that.

Unfortunately, the '80s Chicago doesn't even have the horns going for it, really. Bland synthesized orchestration and an overreliance on sugary-sweet vocal harmonies completely ruins *Chicago's Greatest Hits 1982–89*. These surging, gutless power ballads make Peter Cetera and company sound like the Bee Gees with severe head colds. Watch out: the latter-day, post-Cetera edition of Chicago is on its way to becoming a Beach Boys–style presence on the nostalgia circuit. Ask for "Old Days," from good old *Chicago VIII*—definitely, a band ahead of its times. — M.C.

CHICKASAW MUDD PUPPIES
★ ★ ★ **White Dirt (Polygram, 1990)**
★ ★ ★ **8-track Stomp (Polygram, 1991)**
Laying out all the fixings for delightful, warped hoedown, the Chickasaw Mudd Puppies are two Athens, Georgia, faux-yokels, Brant Slay (vocals, "stomp board" and harmonica) and Ben Reynolds (vocals, guitar, bass). While both of their records feature heavy input from R.E.M.'s Michael Stipe and other college-radio guest stars, the duo's weirdness—made apparent by such song titles as "Shannon Love Biscuit" and "Omaha (Sharpless)"—is certainly their own. There do seem to be indirect precedents (the funkier efforts of Captain Beefheart come to mind), but the Puppies are a pretty distinct crew—imagine the sound of field hollerin' rednecks after they'd come upon a cache of B-52's records, and then incorporated that Martian party mood into backwoods blues. — P.E.

THE CHIEFTAINS
★ ★ ★   **1 (1964; Shanachie, 1987)**
★ ★ ★   **2 (1969; Shanachie, 1987)**
★ ★ ★½ **3 (1971; Shanachie, 1987)**
★ ★ ★ ★ **4 (1973; Shanachie, 1988)**
★ ★ ★½ **5 (1975; Shanachie, 1987)**
★ ★ ★½ **6 Bonaparte's Retreat (1976; Shanachie, 1988)**
★ ★ ★   **Live (Island, 1977)**
★ ★ ★   **7 (Columbia, 1978)**
★ ★ ★½ **8 (Columbia, 1978)**
★ ★ ★ ★ **9 Boil the Breakfast Early (Columbia, 1979)**
★ ★ ★   **10 Cotton Eyed Joe (Shanachie, 1981)**
★ ★ ★½ **The Year of the French (Shanachie, 1983)**
★ ★ ★   **The Ballad of the Irish Horse (Shanachie, 1985)**
★ ★ ★   **In China (Shanachie, 1985)**
★ ★ ★½ **Celtic Wedding (BMG Classics/RCA, 1987)**
★ ★ ★   **In Ireland (with James Galway) (BMG Classics/RCA, 1987)**
★ ★ ★ ★ **A Chieftains Celebration (BMG Classics/RCA, 1989)**
★ ★ ★   **Over the Sea to Skye (with James Galway) (RCA Victor, 1991)**
★ ★ ★½ **"Reel Music"/The Filmscores (RCA Victor, 1991)**
★ ★ ★ ★ **The Bells of Dublin (RCA Victor, 1991)**
★ ★ ★½ **The Best of the Chieftains (Columbia/Legacy, 1992)**
★ ★ ★ ★ **An Irish Evening: Live at the Grand Opera House, Belfast (RCA Victor, 1992)**

Not the first of the Irish folk revivalists but by far the most influential, the Chieftains have done more to further the spread of Irish traditional music than anything since the potato famine. Although leader Paddy Moloney had played with Sean O Riada's Celtic chamber orchestra, Ceoltoiri Cualann, his approach was more casual than classical; his ensemble arrangements were ingenious, but they so cleverly showcased each soloist that they almost seemed invisible. With *4*, the group gained both harpist Derek Bell and its first hit, "Women of Ireland" (from the film *Barry Lyndon*); *6 Bonaparte's Retreat* features its most ambitious arranging; and *9 Boil the Breakfast Early* its most well-rounded material. In the late Eighties, the group began to broaden its base, both through film scores like *The Year of the French* and cross-cultural experiments like *In China*. Be advised: *The Best of the Chieftains*, though admirable enough, draws only from *7, 8* and *9*. There's also an astonishing array of collaborations scattered through the group's output. In addition to the two albums with classical flutist James Galway, the group recorded the spirited *Irish Heartbeat* with Van Morrison, and *An Irish Evening* brings in both Roger Daltrey (who sings "Behind Blue Eyes" and "Raglan Road") and Nanci Griffith. But the group's most determinedly eclectic offering would have to be *The Bells of Dublin*, a collection of Christmas-themed music ranging from versions of "I Saw Three Ships a Sailing" with Marianne Faithfull and a medley of "Il est né/Ca berger" sung by Kate and Anna McGarrigle to performances of original songs by Elvis Costello and Jackson Browne. — J.D.C.

THE CHIFFONS
★ ★½ **Golden Classics (Collectables, NA)**
A key entry in the annals of the girl-group sound, the Chiffons hailed from the Bronx, had a forceful, distinctive lead singer in Judy Craig, and were blessed with good material and blistering production in their brief but productive career. The classics are "He's So Fine," a Number One record for four weeks in 1963; the Gerry Goffin–Carole King masterwork, "One Fine Day"; and the group's final Top Ten hit, "Sweet Talkin' Guy," from 1966. As produced by the Tokens (of "The Lion Sleeps Tonight" fame), the Chiffons were always working in a cauldron of instrumental support that bore some resemblance in its hugeness to Phil Spector's Wall of Sound. "He's So Fine" may have been the chart-topper, but

few moments in rock history match the ferocity of the piano chording that kicks off and reappears throughout "One Fine Day." Beyond these, the "Golden Classics" of the title were mostly that for other artists; you don't really get anything out of the Chiffons covering "Da Doo Ron Ron," "My Boyfriend's Back," "It's My Party" or "Will You Still Love Me Tomorrow?" while the other Chiffons originals are unremarkable on every level. But those three Chiffons hits are so fine, doo-lang, doo-lang, doo-lang. — D.M.

JANE CHILD
★★★ **Jane Child (Warner Bros., 1989)**
On "Don't Wanna Fall in Love," Child's synth-heavy dance pop sounds agreeably like early Prince; elsewhere, it sounds as if she has too much technique, and too little idea of what to do with it. — J.D.C.

THE CHI-LITES
★★★★½ **The Chi-Lites Greatest Hits (Rhino, 1992)**
Like most of their brethren in the early '70s vocal-group boom, the Chi-Lites had been harmonizing together since the late '50s. The quintet didn't possess much of a track record when it arrived at Chicago's Brunswick Records in the late '60s: a small-label single here and there. Tenor singer Eugene Record connected his falsetto with his songwriting muse not long after that, however—and the rest is history, or at least *Greatest Hits.* "(For God's Sake) Give More Power to the People" gets its billboard message across via rolling fuzz-toned rhythms, while the super-produced 1971 Top Ten hits "Have You Seen Her" and "Oh Girl" articulate a breadth of emotion that's still heart-stopping. Drawing on the group's Brunswick volumes, *Greatest Hits* never sags. Even lesser-known tracks—the oddly sensitive "Homely Girl"—showcase Record's social awareness and the group's probing vocal exchanges. Record left before the Chi-Lites began recording for Mercury in 1976; he rejoined four years later, to little avail. None of the group's subsequent records remain in print; aside from a 1983 neo-funk hit on the Larc label ("Bottoms Up"), the latter-day Chi-Lites haven't enjoyed much commercial success, either. Still, you never know what may happen: nobody expected this sound to come back the first time. — M.C.

CHILLS
★★ **The Lost EP (1985; Homestead, 1988)**
★★★ **Kaleidoscope World (1986; Homestead, 1989)**
★★ **Brave Words (1987; Homestead, 1988)**
★★★½ **Submarine Bells (Slash/Warner Bros., 1990)**
A low-key but pleasantly tuneful alternative band from New Zealand, the Chills first proved their pop potential in a series of earnestly melodic, occasionally edgy singles and EPs, most of which are collected on *Kaleidoscope World.* But the group doesn't really hit its stride until *Submarine Bells,* on which Gary Smith's sympathetic production gives songs like "Heavenly Pop Hit" the high-gloss finish they need to shine. — J.D.C.

ALEX CHILTON
★★★ **High Priest (Big Time, 1987)**
★★★★ **19 Years: A Collection of Alex Chilton (Rhino, 1991)**
After stints as lead singer of best-selling blue-eyed soulmen the Box Tops and visionary songmeister of cult pop idols Big Star, Alex Chilton took a turn for the worse—stumbling through recordings of covers (the Seeds' "Can't Seem to Make You Mine," Jimmy C. Newman's "Alligator Man") and originals ("My Rival"). These tracks found their way to a hodgepodge of indie and import labels, on such titles as *Like Flies on Sherbert, Bach's Bottom, Alex Chilton's Lost Decade* and *Singer Not the Song. 19 Years: A Collection of Alex Chilton* dredges up some surprisingly listenable cuts from those years, presenting the hillbilly punk of "Bangkok" (a 1978 single) and the southern-fried skronk of "Rock Hard" (from *Flies*) alongside several gold nuggets from *Sister Lovers* and some bracing later work. Sober but unbowed, Chilton continued to defy expectations when he re-emerged in the mid-'80s. *19 Years* pulls some keepers from Chilton's two hit-or-miss EPs *Feudalist Tarts* (1985) and *No Sex* ('86). "Tee Ni Nee Ni Noo/Tip On In" points out just how deeply buried his R&B roots remain, but the topical ditties "Lost My Job" and "No Sex" both hurl their pissed-off hooks into your flesh parts. *High Priest* features Chilton and a rough 'n' ready band veering all over the stylistic map—from "Volare" to "Raunchy." True believers will swallow it whole, of course, while agnostics should be satisfied by the four *High Priest* cuts included on *19 Years.* — M.C.

THE CHIPMUNKS
★ ★ **Christmas With the Chipmunks (1962; EMI, 1980)**
★ ★ **Christmas With the Chipmunks, Vol. 2 (1963; EMI, 1974)**
★ ★ **Very Best of the Chipmunks (EMI, 1975)**

David Seville, nee Ross Bagdasarian, created the fictional Chipmunk characters by speeding up tape recordings of his voice. He then named the individual critters after executives at Liberty Records (Al Bennett, Si Waronker, and Ted Keep) at the session that produced "The Chipmunk Song," now a Christmas standard, and a Number One single for four weeks in 1958. Under his own name Seville had a Number One novelty hit, "Witch Doctor," in April of '58, before hatching the Chipmunks later in the year. Between December of '58 and December of '62, the Chipmunks had eight Top Forty singles, three of them being "The Chipmunk Song," which was re-released in '61 and '62. The two Christmas albums are replete with the most popular standards of the season, warbled in true Chipmunk style, with bratty Alvin doing his best to be uncooperative except under extreme duress. Volume 1 contains "The Chipmunk Song." *Very Best* contains other charted items and miscellany. For kids of all ages, obviously.
— D.M.

THE CHORDETTES
★ ★ **Best of the Chordettes (Rhino, 1989)**
Beginning their career as a female barbershop quartet in Sheboygan, Wisconsin, in 1947, the quartet known as the Chordettes adapted their intricate harmony style to the modern pop sound developing in the early '50s and became mainstays in the Top Thirty between 1956 and 1961, when they disbanded rather than replace their lead singer, who retired to take care of her ailing mother. Listeners might want to forget that Manhattan Transfer has named the Chordettes as a major influence, and instead remember the smooth blend of voices that was one of the signature sounds of mainstream music in America in the 1950s, and, at that, one of the sounds that rock & roll was pushing under the carpet. Tough it's not; sweet, yes; unthreatening, yes; lively, sometimes. Eighteen cuts back-to-back, though? Boring. There's simply not enough variety or surprise in these tracks to sustain one's interest over the long haul. That said, it should be added as well that the Chordettes' hits retain a certain charm of days gone by. "Mr. Sandman,"

"Born to Be With You," "Lay Down Your Arms," "Teen Age Goodnight," the effervescent "Lollipop," even "Zorro" are all sweetness and light, most with bounce to spare. There's no reason to dislike the Chordettes, and indeed, much to admire about the quality of their group harmonies. They found their formula, mined it, called it a day at the right moment, and left behind some solid MOR pop, before anyone ever heard of MOR. Good work, albeit static.
— D.M.

CHARLIE CHRISTIAN
★ ★ ★ ★ **The Genius of the Electric Guitar (Columbia, 1987)**
Charlie Christian was not the first practitioner of the amplified electric guitar—that distinction belongs to Eddie Durham, who played in bands headed by Benny Moten, Jimmie Lunceford and Count Basie—but he was its most important adherent, its visionary. Recording with Benny Goodman's band between 1939 and 1942 (he died of tuberculosis in 1942, at the age of 23), Christian used the electric guitar's sonic possibilities to redefine the instrument's role in the band context, and, indeed, pretty much spelled the end of the acoustic guitar in the jazz ensemble. Inspired and influenced by tenor saxophonist Lester Young's lyricism, Christian, who played tenor sax as well, adopted a similar style in constructing a singular approach to technique, melody and harmony that was then in opposition to the guitar's traditional role as a supporting player. That is to say, Christian approached the electric guitar as a solo instrument. Sustained legato phrases; improvisations based on the passing chords played between a song's root harmonies; a tonal style that rendered the guitar's sound comparable to that of a reed instrument were innovations pioneered by Christian that propelled jazz music into the modern age. What remains of Christian's recordings is this 16-song CD of tracks cut with the Goodman band, plus five live cuts on Vanguard's *From Spirituals to Swing* two-CD set. *Genius of* does its job well—"Rose Room" and "Waiting for Benny" (the latter cut during a rehearsal when the musicians were waiting for the late-arriving leader) are especially strong indicators of where Christian was taking his instrument—and the live cuts recorded in 1939 are stirring in their way. But fans are advised to search diligently for the double album 1972 release on Columbia, *Solo Flight—The Genius of Charlie Christian*. It

has 28 cuts, notable among these being three credited to the Charlie Christian Quintet, recorded privately in Minneapolis in 1939. Here Christian is allowed ample opportunity to develop his solo ideas, and the results are striking. On "I Got Rhythm," Christian turns the melody inside out, then backtracks, alternating between the staccato style that was common among guitar players before he arrived on the scene and the legato style that became his signature. "Stardust" shows Christian at his most lyrical, stretching out long, yearning lines with the gentlest of touches. "Tea for Two" takes the Quintet back into the uptempo mode of "I Got Rhythm," with Christian fashioning an elegant, angular solo in support of Jerry Jerome's Young-style voicings on tenor sax. So little of Christian's artistry being available in the first place means *The Genius of* becomes an indispensable record; *Solo Flight*, however, best demonstrates the wide scope of that genius. — D.M.

LOU CHRISTIE
★★★ **Enlightnin'ment: The Best of Lou Christie (Rhino, 1988)**

There was a time when Lou Christie was big. His five Top Twenty-Five hits between 1963 and 1969 were sexually charged melodramas fueled by his striking voice, which would build from a soft, almost drab tenor to an orgasmic explosion of falsetto shrieks. One of his 1966 hits, "Rhapsody in the Rain," was exceedingly brazen in likening sexual intercourse to the rhythm of a car's windshield wipers; this, plus references to such dalliance occurring on a first date, had some bluenoses in a huff, forcing a change in the lyrics to make the song safe for airplay. Christie co-wrote almost all of his material with a Bohemian Gypsy named Twyla Herbert, who claimed to have mystic powers and the ability to predict all of her compadre's hits. Whatever she, and they, had, it worked to the tune of four multi-million-selling singles. Producers played a critical role in Christie's legend, too, as his most successful recordings were done with Charles Calello behind the board at a time when Calello was also writing some spectacular arrangements for most of the Four Seasons' mid-'60s hits; Jack Nitzsche, who learned from Phil Spector, also figures in Christie's history, having produced a couple of Christie sides. *Enlightnin'ment*'s 18 tracks get to the heart of the matter, beginning with Christie's first hit, "The Gypsy Cried" (1963) and

concluding with "I'm Gonna Make You Mine," a Top Ten single from 1969. These plus the other three essential Christie singles —"Lightnin' Strikes," "Two Faces Have I" and "Rhapsody in the Rain"—comprise some of the most individual pop records of the '60s. Christie works the oldies circuit nowadays, although his appearances are infrequent. He did surface for one splendid performance in 1989, singing the country-tinged "Beyond the Blue Horizon" for the *Rain Man* soundtrack. Looking back, one can say this about Lou Christie: He kept it lively. — D.M.

THE CHURCH
★★ **Of Skins and Heart (1981; Arista, 1988)**
★★★ **The Blurred Crusade (1982; Arista, 1988)**
★★★ **Seance (1983; Arista, 1988)**
★★★★ **Remote Luxury (1984; Arista, 1988)**
★★★ **Heyday (1985; Arista, 1988)**
★★★½ **Starfish (Arista, 1988)**
★★★★ **Gold Afternoon Fix (Arista, 1990)**
★★★★ **Priest = Aura (Arista, 1992)**

With its murmured melodies and atmospheric instrumental arrangements, this Sydney quartet sounds little like such Oz-rock contemporaries as Midnight Oil, Divinyls or the Angels, having far more in common with the sound of Liverpool neo-psychedelic acts like Echo and the Bunnymen or Paisley Underground groups like L.A.'s Rain Parade. The resemblance isn't entirely coincidental; *Of Skins and Heart* introduces the Church as a typical early-'80s new-wave outfit, replete with adenoidal vocals (courtesy Steve Kilbey) and jittery melodies.

But *The Blurred Crusade*, recorded after the first wave of the psychedelic revival had washed ashore, shows the Churchmen to have been eager converts, softening the contours of the band's sound, replacing jagged rhythm riffs with jangly, Byrds-like guitar vamps, and bringing out the croon in Kilbey's voice. It's not pop, exactly, but as "When You Were Mine" and "Secret Corners" indicate, it is a step in the right direction. *Seance* further refines the approach, adding depth and texture, but *Remote Luxury* is where the Church's change in direction really pays off. Credit Kilbey's writing for most of the difference, because the songs are concise, accessible and memorable, from the brassy chorus of "Maybe These Boys" to the quiet tug of the verses in "Violet Town."

Heyday doesn't quite measure up, in part because it seems a bit more experimental than its predecessor, but *Starfish* more than compensates. It isn't just that the band applies the arranging expertise of *Heyday* to more deserving melodies; it's that the Church comes across as a genuine pop act without having to compromise its sound. As songs like "Spark" or "Under the Milky Way" make plain, it's the band's way with a song that matters, and that strength carries through even into the dark, hypnotic textures of *Gold Afternoon Fix*, where the dramatic dynamics of "You're Still Beautiful" or the mock-orchestral flourishes of "Metropolis" only intensify the music's appeal. Likewise, the dolorous cadences of *Priest = Aura* not only helps flesh out the sense of melancholy that haunts its songs, but adds resonance to tunes like "Aura" and "Witch Hunt." — J.D.C.

CINDERELLA

★★½ **Night Songs (Mercury, 1986)**
★½ **Long Cold Winter (Mercury, 1988)**
★★★½ **Heartbreak Station (Mercury, 1990)**

With a voice somewhere between Steven Tyler's yowl and the sound of fingernails on a blackboard, Cinderella frontman Tom Keifer is definitely an acquired taste. But you've got to admire the spirit of a guy who can cop Stones licks as shamelessly as Keifer does on *Heartbreak Station*, on which he delivers the obviously derivative "Shelter Me" and "Sick for the Cure" with such conviction you'd think he thought them up himself. The band's earlier efforts are rather less remarkable; *Night Songs* is OK if you're a sucker for boogie-by-numbers hard rock, but *Long Cold Winter* is a hapless jumble of half-assed rockers and irritating power ballads. — J.D.C.

ERIC CLAPTON

★★★½ **Eric Clapton (RSO/Polydor, 1970)**
★★★ **Eric Clapton's Rainbow Concert (Polydor, 1973)**
★★★★★ **461 Ocean Boulevard (RSO/Polydor, 1974)**
★★★ **There's One in Every Crowd (RSO/Polydor, 1974)**
★★½ **E.C. Was Here (RSO/Polydor, 1975)**
★★★ **No Reason to Cry (RSO, 1976)**
★★★★★ **Slowhand (RSO/Polydor, 1977)**
★★★½ **Backless (RSO/Polydor, 1978)**
★★★½ **Just One Night (RSO, 1980)**
★★★ **Another Ticket (RSO/Polydor, 1981)**
★★★★ **Timepieces (The Best of Eric Clapton) (RSO/Polydor, 1982)**
★★★½ **Timepieces Vol. II: Live in the Seventies (RSO/Polydor, 1983)**
★★★★ **Money and Cigarettes (Duck/Warner Bros., 1983)**
★★★½ **Behind the Sun (Duck/Warner Bros., 1985)**
★★★ **August (Duck/Warner Bros., 1986)**
★★★★★ **Crossroads (Polydor, 1988)**
★★★ **Homeboy (Virgin, 1989)**
★★★★ **Journeyman (Reprise, 1989)**
★★★ **24 Nights (Reprise, 1991)**
★★★½ **Rush (Reprise, 1992)**

Eric Clapton may have earned his reputation with his guitar, but he owes his solo career to his voice. It's his singing, after all, that has carried his best work, from the frenetic gospel groove of "After Midnight" to the pointed melancholy of "Old Love." In fact, his least interesting recordings tend to be those which most emphasize his solos—an irony, perhaps, but also a testament to the fact that Clapton today is more than just another guitar hero.

Eric Clapton, the album that launched his solo career, was recorded with musicians he'd met while a part of Delaney & Bonnie and Friends (he was a featured player on the duo's 1970 release, *On Tour*), and boasts similar blues-and-gospel overtones. Although his lithe, understated vocals make the most of "Blues Power" and a cover of J.J. Cale's "After Midnight," Clapton seems somewhat overwhelmed by the size of the band; perhaps that's why he grabbed the rhythm section—Bobby Whitlock, Carl Radle and Jim Gordon—and ran off to form Derek and the Dominos. But that band fell apart in 1971, and Clapton, beset by depression and a heroin problem, wasn't heard from until 1973, when Pete Townshend organized the star-studded (but generally forgettable) *Eric Clapton's Rainbow Concert*.

Joining forces with producer Tom Dowd, Clapton went to Florida to record *461 Ocean Boulevard*, the album that first showed his pop star potential. Although the material isn't obviously commercial, being given mainly to blues (Robert Johnson's "Steady Rollin' Man"), oldies (Johnny Otis's "Willie and the Hand Jive") and reggae ("I Shot the Sheriff," by the little-known Bob Marley), Clapton's affectless delivery is almost irresistible, cutting to the heart of the blues while avoiding the sort of guttural mannerisms most pop listeners found off-putting. The album was a massive success, but its standard wasn't easy to maintain. *There's One in Every Crowd*, for instance, virtually duplicates its predecessor's approach, but with considerably less success, and the difference was mostly a matter of writing. After all, no amount of reggae groove is going to make Clapton's "Don't Blame Me" as memorable a song as "I Shot the Sheriff."

After a passable live album, *E.C. Was Here*, Clapton returned to the studio in search of a new direction. *No Reason to Cry* wasn't quite it; despite a duet with Bob Dylan ("Sign Language") and a backing band that includes Ron Wood, Robbie Robertson and Georgie Fame, the only track that really works is the amiable, calypso-tinged "Hello, Old Friend." So Clapton ditched the all-star approach, and took a low-key approach to his next recording, *Slowhand*. Bingo—the best album of his career. Working with his own band and once again relying more on the songs than the groove, Clapton seems utterly at home, from the wistful balladry of "Wonderful Tonight" to the stoned shuffle of "Cocaine" (yet another Cale composition). And though there's plenty of blowing room on the album—check the slide work on his version of Arthur Crudup's "Mean Old Frisco"—the fact that the writing is so strong always leaves him with a strong foundation from which to build.

Backless tries hard to recreate that balance, but falls short in spite of a few lovely songs ("Tell Me That You Love Me" in particular) and some inspired rhythm work (especially on the Marcy Levy feature, "Roll It"). As had by then become customary, it was time for another live album, but *Just One Night* improves on the usual, thanks to a crack new band that keeps Clapton on his toes through the extended versions of "Double Trouble" and "Cocaine." Unfortunately, that dynamic didn't quite translate to the studio, and apart from the quietly dramatic title tune, *Another Ticket* is a disappointment.

Clapton changed labels soon after, a switch that prompted a predictable round of best-ofs. Apart from a non-LP version of "Knockin' On Heaven's Door," *Timepieces* boasts few surprises; *Timepieces Vol. II: Live in the Seventies* is easily ignored.

Meanwhile, Clapton's new deal was already producing impressive changes. Although *Money and Cigarettes* was something of a let-down commercially, it's

anything but a disappointment musically, thanks to a comfortable collection of songs and a backing band that includes slide virtuoso Ry Cooder and Stax session man Duck Dunn. Charmingly unassuming, it's classic Clapton. *Behind the Sun*, on the other hand, is perhaps the guitarist's most daring effort, a (mostly) Phil Collins–produced project that finds him gamely trying everything from guitar synthesizer (on "Never Make You Cry") to what can only be described as 12-bar art rock (on "Same Old Blues"). Unfortunately, not everyone appreciated such risk-taking, and Warner Bros. honchos Ted Templeman and Lenny Waronker later added three tracks— including "Forever Man"—to increase the album's commercial appeal. Perhaps that's why *August*, also partially produced by Collins, backs off a bit from its predecessor's innovations and does nothing more radical than adding a layer of synths to its version of Robert Cray's "Bad Influence." (It does, however, include "Tearing Us Apart," a stunning duet with Tina Turner that ranks among Clapton's finest vocal performances.)

Any such failings, however, were completely forgotten with *Crossroads*, a career-spanning, 73-song retrospective that included all of Clapton's most memorable recordings, from his days with the Yardbirds to the *August* sessions. It's an absolutely stunning collection—so monumental, in fact, that Clapton himself probably felt at a loss to follow it. Tellingly, *Journeyman* seems by the very nature of its title to shrug off any implications of greatness, and as such turns out to be a remarkably relaxed and satisfying album. But Clapton's work with composer-arranger Michael Kamen on the *Homeboy* soundtrack, coming on the heels of similarly symphonic contributions to the *Lethal Weapon II* score, opens yet another direction for the guitarist, one which he pursues on his own with his score to *Rush*. Fascinating as it is on a formal level, though, Clapton's orchestral work can't quite match the pop appeal of his songs, as the achingly lovely "Tears in Heaven" plainly proves. Perhaps that's why Clapton's contributions to the *Lethal Weapon III* soundtrack included songs with both Sting ("It's Probably Me") and Elton John ("Runaway Train").

Where he'll go from there is hard to say, but judging from the multi-ensemble live album, *24 Nights*—in which the guitarist performs with a quartet, a nonet, a blues

band and a Kamen-conducted orchestra—
Clapton isn't ruling out any possibilities.
— J.D.C.

DEE CLARK
★ ★ ★ **Hey Little Girl (Vee Jay, NA)**
Dee Clark, whose biggest hit was
"Raindrops" (1961), which featured some of
the most lonesome guitar lines (courtesy Phil
Upchurch) on any record ever recorded,
may well have been too talented for his own
good. *Hey Little Girl* shows Clark in endless
pursuit of an individual voice. Actually he
had quite a good voice—soulful, smooth,
strong, clear—but many of his best records
sound like someone else's best record.
"Your Friends," for example, finds Clark
emoting in Sam Cooke style. On a 1958
track, "Wondering," Clark summons a high,
quavering tenor voice reminiscent of Clyde
McPhatter. What's interesting is Clark's
evolution from the crooning style of early
R&B vocal groups—as can be heard on
several tracks Clark cut in the mid- to
late-'50s with the Kool Gents—to
harder-edged, Southern soul of the sort
featured on the 1963 track, "I'm Going
Home," written by Don Covay. A steady
hitmaker between '59 and '61, Clark's most
productive years show far more good work
than most of the general public ever knew
existed. — D.M.

PETULA CLARK
★ ★ ★ **Greatest Hits (GNP, NA)**
In a flourish of threatened, institutional
anti-hipness, the Grammy award committee
voted Pet Clark's "Downtown" Best Rock
and Roll Recording of 1965. The ditty's nice
bounce, of course, had nothing to do with
Elvis or Little Richard—but Clark's Brit
appeal, coinciding with the Beatles' advent,
together with the relative assertiveness of the
song's drum track, must have tricked fogies
into thinking that this wasn't merely MOR
given a mild Phil Spector-ish production.
Actually, Petula's cool, clipped delivery
proved that while she was no Dionne
Warwicke, her orchestral fare wasn't retread
Doris Day either. A showbiz pro from age
11, Clark was canny enough to read the
signs of the times, and her choice of
material carefully avoided the
ultra-sunniness of pre-'60s pop. "The Other
Man's Grass Is Always Greener," "Don't
Sleep in the Subway" and "I Know a
Place," all included on *Greatest Hits,* gave
her fairly spirited hits nearly into the
'70s—and they remain enjoyable. — P.E.

STANLEY CLARKE
★ ★ ★ ★   **Stanley Clarke (1974; Epic, 1980)**
   ★ ★½ **Journey to Love (1975; Epic, 1980)**
   ★½ **School Days (1976; Epic, 1980)**
   ★ **Rocks, Pebbles and Sand (Epic, 1980)**
   ★ ★ **Modern Man (Epic, 1978)**
   ★ **Let Me Know You (Epic, 1982)**
   ★ ★½ **Time Exposure (Epic, 1984)**
   ★ ★½ **Find Out! (Epic, 1985)**
   ★ ★ **Hideaway (Epic, 1986)**
★ ★ ★   **If This Bass Could Only Talk (Portrait/Epic, 1988)**
   ★ ★ ★½ **Live 1976–1977 (Epic, 1991)**
WITH GEORGE DUKE
   ★ ★½ **The Clarke/Duke Project (Epic, 1981)**
   ★ ★½ **The Clarke/Duke Project (Epic, 1983)**
★ ★ ★   **Stanley Clarke–George Duke 3 (Epic, 1990)**
Perhaps the most gifted bassist of his
generation, Stanley Clarke is as adept on
double bass as on electric, something which
marks him as a more versatile (if not quite
as influential) player than Jaco Pastorius, his
closest rival. Like Pastorius, who made
several noteworthy recordings with Joni
Mitchell, Clarke has also made inroads into
rock & roll, playing with both Jeff Beck and
Keith Richards's New Barbarians. But
where Pastorius merely flirted from afar,
Clarke actively courted the pop market, and
that made for a very different sort of
recording career. His early albums, in fact,
painted him as a serious jazzbo—both
Stanley Clarke and *Journey to Love* include
compositions for double bass and string
section (*Journey*'s offering is even
pretentiously titled "Concerto for Jazz/Rock
Orchestra")—but what sets *Stanley Clarke*
above the rest is the quality of its lineup,
which includes Jan Hammer, Bill Connors
and Tony Williams. With *School Days,*
Clarke moves closer to rock, but his belief
in bass as a lead instrument keeps him from
having much success with the style; as
Rocks, Pebbles and Sand makes plain,
Clarke is a mediocre rocker and an abysmal
singer. Fortunately, he's a terrific
collaborator; his work with George Duke is
funkier by far. *The Clarke/Duke Project,* for
instance, may not have much in the way of
hits, but it does have the right attitude
(loose, loopy and on the one) and a killer
version of "Louie Louie," while *3* delivers a
pleasant P-Funk tribute with the
"Mothership Connection" medley. Even
without Duke, Clarke had his moments; for

instance, *Find Out!* is daring enough to try "Born in the U.S.A." as rap (and it works, too).

Still, Clarke's most satisfying recordings are those that forget commercial considerations and simply let him blow. *If This Bass Could Only Talk* is full of such star turns, from the stirring rendition of "Goodbye Pork Pie Hat" to the Gregory Hines collaboration on the title tune. And though *Live 1976–1977* reprises much of the material found on *Stanley Clarke*, *Journey to Love* and *School Days*, the playing is superior to most of the studio recordings. — J.D.C.

THE CLASH

★ ★ ★ ★ ★   **The Clash (1977; Epic 1979)**
★ ★ ★½   **Give 'Em Enough Rope (Epic, 1978)**
★ ★ ★ ★ ★   **London Calling (Epic, 1979)**
★ ★½   **Sandinista! (Epic, 1980)**
★ ★ ★   **Black Market Clash (Epic, 1980)**
★ ★ ★½   **Combat Rock (Epic, 1982)**
★½   **Cut the Crap (Epic, 1985)**
★ ★ ★ ★½   **The Story of the Clash, Vol. 1 (Epic, 1988)**
★ ★ ★ ★   **Clash on Broadway (Epic/Legacy, 1991)**

Though the Sex Pistols were English punk's premier singles band, it was the Clash who most successfully translated the style's anything-goes, do-it-yourself aesthetic to albums. That's not to say the group didn't make great singles—indeed, what sets *The Clash* apart from its import precursor is the substitution of such English singles as "Clash City Rockers," "I Fought the Law" and the immortal "White Man in Hammersmith Palais" for several of the original album's weaker cuts. But unlike punk's other three-minute heroes, the Clash also knew how to keep its fires burning over the long haul. Moreover, it never made a fetish of punk's preference for harder-and-faster rock; in addition to an impressive facility for reggae, the group tried everything from rockabilly to rap.

Still, there's a difference between versatility and malleability, which may be why *Give 'Em Enough Rope* (produced by Blue Oyster Cult manager Sandy Pearlman) never lived up to the potential of its material. *London Calling*, on the other hand, was as close to perfect as punk got. From the exuberant melodicism of "Train in Vain" to the menacing reggae of "Guns of Brixton" to the anthemic refrain of the title tune, it was as if the group was capable of

achieving anything it attempted. *London Calling* was an intoxicating album, but its success went to the band's head; by *Sandinista!* the Clash tried anything and everything, releasing songs whether they worked or not. Of the album's 36 selections, less than a dozen are worth hearing; even the B sides and obscurities collected on *Black Market Clash* made a more coherent statement.

Chastened, the band sharpened its focus for *Combat Rock*. Although still daringly experimental, apart from the poetic flotsam of "Ghetto Defendant," it rarely drifted into the ether, and gave the band its first and only Top Ten single, the oil-crisis satire "Rock the Casbah." Sadly, such triumphs were short-lived; Mick Jones, responsible for many of the band's most melodic moments, was pushed out of the group (he later formed his own band, Big Audio Dynamite), and *Cut the Crap* found the Clash sounding like a parody of its former self. Consequently, the last Clash albums are all retrospectives, from the simple, efficacious *Story of the Clash* to the beautifully packaged but somewhat bloated box set, *Clash on Broadway*. Though *The Story of the Clash* is hopefully subtitled "Vol. 1," it's doubtful we'll ever see this band's likes again. — J.D.C.

THE CLASSICS IV

★ ★   **The Very Best of the Classics IV (EMI-USA, 1975)**

Quintessential lounge-rockers of the mid-'60s, Atlanta's Classics IV featured Dennis Yost's breathy vocals and smarmy charm, and, in Buddy Buie, a songwriter who went on to star in the very boring Atlanta Rhythm Section. "Stormy" and "Traces" were mandatory furtive-grope numbers at proms of the period; they later became elevator music standards. — P.E.

ANDREW DICE CLAY

½ ★   **Andrew Dice Clay (Def American, 1989)**
½ ★   **The Day the Laughter Died (Def American, 1990)**
½ ★   **Dice Rules (Def American, 1991)**

A fatuous defense of the comedy of Andrew Dice Clay might suggest that this crap is cathartic, that by strutting like a wildman while spewing shit, the Diceman releases some repressed demon inside our selves and exposes it to the light. Maybe. Shock comedy can indeed be liberating, an act of rebellion and release that forces us to confront uncomfortable truths. But its truly radical proponents (Jonathan Swift, Lenny Bruce) used outrage to champion the world's misfits; Dice uses it exactly to trash anyone "different." In so doing, he's the ultra-conformist, the playground bully grown up into the normalcy police.

Taking swipes at every conceivable ethnic group, verbally assaulting the elderly and the physically impaired, using the voice of Edith Bunker when imitating any woman, Dice is funny only in the way that psychopathology and self-loathing are "funny." The quintessential record is *Dice Rules*: smutty nursery rhymes, tit jokes and a monologuist's equivalent of belching. This stuff is boring. — P.E.

THE CLEFTONES
★★★ **Best of the Cleftones (Rhino, 1990)**
Best known for their driving rendition of "Heart and Soul," a song that dates back to 1931 when it was a Number One hit for Larry Clinton and His Orchestra, the Cleftones are notable for being among the first generation of group harmony outfits whose sensibilities and approach were informed by the blues ballad style of the early '50s and transformed by the big beat of rock & roll. In addition to the exuberance of the group's singers, the Cleftones' recordings were further enlivened by the honking tenor sax of Jimmy Wright, who bowed to no one—not King Curtis, not Herb Hardesty—when it came to goosing a song into high gear with a pointed solo. Although "Heart and Soul," from 1961, was the group's only substantial hit (a Top Twenty record, it was), the Cleftones cut several gems in the years ('55 to '62) covered in this retrospective. A 1956 track, "Can't We Be Sweethearts," prefigures the sort of harmony and lead arrangements that worked so well years later for Dion and the Belmonts—lead singer Herb Cox's vocal on this track is also a dead ringer for Dion's voice both in timbre and in its insouciant swagger; "See You Next Year," from 1957, features an unusual dual lead vocal that's rooted in gospel, the deepest source of doo-wop's genesis; also from '57, "Why You Do Me Like You Do" finds an orchestra hitting a solid groove that will sound familiar to anyone who's listened to Chicago soul, circa the mid-'60s; "Heart and Soul," the Cleftones' enduring statement, finds the group reaching the apotheosis of its style: a personable, urgent tenor lead jumping in and out of unison harmony backgrounds, with a rock band pumping away mightily in support. "Heart and Soul"

is a classic track, to be sure, but this set brings into sharp focus the multitude of innovative sounds the Cleftones purveyed in their heyday. This is a smart, well-annotated, thoroughly pleasing disc. — D.M.

JOHNNY CLEGG AND SAVUKA
★★★ **Third World Child (Capitol, 1987)**
★★½ **Shadow Man (EMI-Capitol, 1988)**
★★ **Cruel, Crazy, Beautiful World (EMI-Capitol, 1989)**
Chapter two in the Johnny Clegg story, Savuka (Zulu for "We have awakened, or risen") was assembled after Juluka co-founder Sipho Mchunu decided to return to farming in 1985. Although its blend of rock and mbaqanga is similar to that of Juluka, Savuka seems far more interested in the international market than its predecessor, and as such puts a greater emphasis on maintaining standard Western song structure than on incorporating Zulu elements into the music.

That's not a problem for *Third World Child*, thanks in large part to the strength of the songs. "Asimbonanga (Mandela)" is an especially fine piece of work, thanks to its poetic imagery and memorable melody, while its reworking of the Juluka track "Scatterlings of Africa" speaks well for the group's instrumental strengths. *Shadow Man* ups the pop content somewhat, swathing the arrangements in synths and underscoring the rhythm section's grounding in funk, and though some songs benefit from the treatment ("Take My Heart Away"), others don't. "Siyayilanda," another borrowing from the Juluka songbook, sounds particularly silly in its new setting, as Clegg's clipped vocals come across at points as a bad attempt at rapping. Still, that's better than the overstuffed *Cruel, Crazy, Beautiful World*, which opens with a bad Earth, Wind & Fire imitation—"One (Hu)'Man, One Vote"—and never fully recovers. — J.D.C.

REV. JAMES CLEVELAND
★★★ **This Sunday in Person: James Cleveland with the Angelic Gospel Choir (Savoy, 1961)**
★★★ **Rev. James Cleveland with the Angelic Choir, Vol. 2 (Savoy, 1962)**
★★★★★ **Peace Be Still: Rev. James Cleveland and the Angelic Choir, Vol. 3 (Savoy, 1963)**
★★★ **Songs of Dedication (Savoy, 1968)**

★ ★ ★ ★ I Stood on the Banks of Jordan: Rev. James Cleveland with the Angelic Choir, Vol. 4 (Savoy, 1970)

★ ★ ★ In the Ghetto: Rev. James Cleveland and the Southern California Community Choir (Savoy, 1973)

★ ★ ★ Give It to Me: Rev. James Cleveland and the Southern California Community Choir (Savoy, 1973)

★ ★ ★ Tomorrow (with the Charles Fold Singers) (Savoy, 1978)

★ ★ ★ ★ Lord Let Me Be an Instrument: James Cleveland with the Charles Fold Singers, Vol. 4 (Savoy, 1979)

★ ★ ★ ★ ★ James Cleveland Sings With the World's Greatest Choirs (Savoy, 1980)

★ ★ ★ ★ This Too Will Pass: James Cleveland, Charles Fold and the Charles Fold Singers (Savoy, 1983)

★ ★ ★ Jesus Is the Best Thing That Ever Happened to Me (with the Charles Fold Singers) (Savoy, 1990)

★ ★ ★ ★ ★ Touch Me (with the Charles Fold Singers) (Savoy, 1990)

★ ★ ★ ★ Give Me My Flowers: James Cleveland with the Angelic Choir, Vol. 5 (Savoy, NA)

★ ★ ★ ★ James Cleveland and the Angelic Choir, Vol. 8—Part 2: Recorded Live (Savoy, NA)

★ ★ ★ ★ Merry Christmas from James Cleveland and the Angelic Choir (Savoy, NA)

★ ★ ★ ★ ★ James Cleveland with the Gospel Chimes (Savoy, NA)

While the above listings indicate only a portion of the Rev. James Cleveland's extensive Savoy catalogue, these selections limn the most important era of his long career. Inspired and influenced by the singing of Mahalia Jackson, the forthright poetry of the Rev. Thomas Dorsey's songs and the inventive, genre-jumping piano stylings of Roberta Martin, Cleveland, a third generation modern gospel singer born in 1932, absorbed the music that preceded him, took what he liked, and then re-created it to address the changing times.

Cleveland jumped around from group to group in the '50s, his stature growing within the gospel community on the strength of his powerhouse singing, blues-tinged arrangements and eloquent songwriting. His most important early association was with the Gospel Chimes, who already boasted

three of the top young singers in the field in Jessy Dixon, Lee Charles and Claude Timmons. Dixon was a formidable figure, well-versed in pop and R&B mannerisms, with a physical presence to match Cleveland's. Listening to their aggressive give-and-take on *James Cleveland and the Gospel Chimes*, one hears gospel melding into soul and the roots of a new male duo style that would reach full flower with the emergence of Sam and Dave in Memphis a decade later. (At the same time, his full-bore gospel shouting on "Walking With the King" prefigures the Wilson Pickett style.)

In 1960 Cleveland joined the Voices of Tabernacle, a progressive Detroit choir, with whom he ushered in the modern gospel sound via a recording of the Soul Stirrers' "The Love of God" that became a gospel best-seller. Signed to Savoy, Cleveland had moderate success with the Gospel Chimes and the Gospel All Stars, but finally hit his stride when teamed with the Angelic Choir. Cleveland brought with him an organist from his previous group, the Cleveland Singers, one Billy Preston, whose soulful accompaniment moved Cleveland to his most possessed performances. Volume 3 of the Angelic Choir recordings proved to be a breakthrough record. Propelled by the stunning title song, "Peace Be Still," the album catapulted Cleveland into the gospel pantheon where he achieved a measure of wealth and fame virtually without parallel in the black gospel music world.

For a minute Cleveland thought he might transform himself into a pop singer, but he quickly retreated back to the music he knew and loved. It has been his practice to record before live church audiences, and though some of these efforts leave much to be desired in sound quality, they also add compelling context to the performances. *James Cleveland Sings with the World's Greatest Choirs* is an apt summation of the master's breadth. It includes a selection with the Voices of Tabernacle, one each with 15 others, including the Southern California Community Choir, the Angelic Choir and the Voices of Christ—in essence, an overview of the modern choir movement.

The recordings with the Charles Fold Singers are recommended without qualification. All live recordings, these performances have moments of tenderness (on "Lord Let Me Be an Instrument" Cleveland gives a controlled, deeply felt reading that would be the envy of Jerry "The Iceman" Butler), but the dominant mode is fire. Cleveland is relentless in pushing the emotional envelope, and the choir gives it right back. And whoever finds the name of the unidentified female soloist on *Touch Me* should sign her up: she closes out the service with a scalding treatment of "If You Have the Faith" with a force rivaled only by Aretha Franklin. No exaggeration—she's that good. — D.M.

JIMMY CLIFF

★ ★ ★½ Wonderful World, Beautiful People (A&M, 1970)
★ ★½ In Concert: The Best of Jimmy Cliff (Reprise, 1976)
★ ★ ★ Give Thanx (Warner Bros., 1978)
★ ★ I Am the Living (MCA, 1981)
★ ★ Give the People What They Want (MCA, 1981)
★ ★ Special (Columbia, 1982)
★ ★½ The Power and the Glory (Columbia, 1984)
★ ★ Cliff Hanger (Columbia, 1985)
★ ★ Hanging Fire (Columbia, 1988)

Jimmy Cliff's two best performances—both groundbreaking reggae classics—are included on the soundtrack of *The Harder They Come*. Twice. Apart from "You Can Get It If You Really Want It" and "The Harder They Come" the rest of Cliff's career has been devoted to a frustrated, one-sided affair with the American pop-soul mainstream. *Wonderful World, Beautiful People* contains his only other true contender: "Vietnam," a searingly melodic and rhythmically bold interpretation of the reluctant draftee blues. But the title track of this 1970 album exhibits the shallow sentimentality that sinks his subsequent efforts. At least "Wonderful World, Beautiful People" is catchy enough to get your attention for three minutes; with the exception of the pleasantly breezy *Give Thanx* (1978), Jimmy Cliff's later albums don't even get that far. Avoid the slick remakes of earlier material on *In Concert: The Best of Jimmy Cliff*, and stick with *The Harder They Come*. — M.C.

PATSY CLINE

★ ★ ★ Patsy Cline (1957; MCA, 1988)
★ ★ ★ Showcase (1961; MCA, 1988)
★ ★ ★ Sentimentally Yours (1962; MCA, 1988)
★ ★ ★ ★ The Patsy Cline Story (1963; MCA, 1988)
★ ★ ★ ★ A Portrait of Patsy Cline (1964; MCA, 1988)
★ ★ ★ ★ A Portrait of Patsy Cline/Country Great (1964, 1973; MCA, 1983)

★ ★ ★ ★ Patsy Cline's Greatest Hits (1967; MCA, 1973)
★ ★ ★ Always (1980; MCA, 1988)
★ ★ ★ 20 Golden Pieces of Patsy Cline (Bulldog, 1981)
★ ★ ★ Remembering: Patsy Cline & Jim Reeves (1982; MCA, 1988)
★ ★ ★ Try Again (Quicksilver, 1982)
★ ★ ★ ★ Songwriters' Tribute (1982; MCA, 1986)
★ ★ ★ Sentimentally Yours/Showcase (MCA, 1983)
★ ★ ★ Today, Tomorrow & Forever (MCA, 1985)
★ ★ ★ Stop, Look & Listen (MCA, 1986)
★ ★ ★ Here's Patsy Cline (MCA, 1988)
★ ★ ★ ★ The Last Sessions (MCA, 1988)
★ ★ ★ ★ 12 Greatest Hits (MCA, 1988)
★ ★ ★ ★ Live at the Opry (MCA, 1988)
★ ★ ★ ★ Live, Volume Two (MCA, 1990)
★ ★ ★ ★ ★ Walkin' Dreams: Her First Recordings, Volume One (Rhino, 1989)
★ ★ ★ ★ ★ Hungry for Love: Her First Recordings, Volume Two (Rhino, 1989)
★ ★ ★ ★ ★ Rockin' Side: Her First Recordings, Volume Three (Rhino, 1989)
★ ★ ★ ★ ★ The Patsy Cline Collection (MCA, 1991)

However accurate, terming Patsy Cline the greatest female singer in country music history doesn't quite cut it. In a brief recording career that began in 1957 and ended abruptly in 1963 when she died in a plane crash, Cline expanded the boundaries of country music by making records that bled into pop and R&B territory, and she also paved the way for a new breed of female country artist who projected an image of strength and self-sufficiency.

Listen to any of the earliest recordings featuring Cline with a small band and no strings, and her affinity becomes apparent for country blues, swing, and traditional country as well. But Cline's producer, Owen Bradley, envisioned her developing into an important pop singer, and numerous critics have compared her singing style and vocal timbre to that of Kay Starr, Jo Stafford, Patti Page and other notable female pop vocalists who came to prominence in the '40s and '50s. Bradley has been criticized for his liberal use of strings on Cline's recordings, but his perception of her versatility was accurate. Moreover, Cline preferred material that challenged her interpretive skill; thus her preference for songs by the likes of Willie Nelson, Don Gibson, Hank Williams, Cole Porter and Bob Wills.

Whatever gains women had made in other genres, in country music they were second-class citizens at the time Cline cut her first hit in 1957, "Walkin' After Midnight." Kitty Wells had retreated to less controversial ground after her 1952 hit "It Wasn't God Who Made Honky-Tonk Angels" had found a sizable audience for its distaff point of view; Cline, on the other hand, was a bulwark of feminine fortitude to the end of her life. Combining this forceful attitude with forthright expressions of vulnerability, longing, and desire created a new model for female country singers that remains a touchstone for contemporary artists like K. T. Oslin, Reba McEntire, Rosanne Cash, and Lorrie Morgan.

Rating Cline's catalogue is difficult, because even lesser titles feature first-rate vocal performances. The obvious place to begin, though, is with the 1991 four-CD box set, *The Patsy Cline Collection*. Produced by the Country Music Foundation, this set includes all of Cline's Decca recordings from 1960 to 1963, as well as several tracks cut prior to her signing with Decca, and ten previously unreleased performances from recording sessions and live radio performances. Which means you get "I Fall to Pieces," "Crazy," "Walkin' After Midnight," "She's Got You," "Back in Baby's Arms" and Cline's other signature songs in their original versions. There's more than four hours of music, over 100 songs, an excellent book with complete discography and session information, and a concise, intelligent biography of Cline by Paul Kingsbury.

Rhino's three-CD volumes of early Cline recordings are excellent in their own right. These are comprised of original recordings of songs cut between 1955 and 1959, with each disc representing (more or less) a specific aspect of Cline's art: honky-tonk (Vol. 1), rock & roll (Vol. 2), and pop-rock-country love songs (Vol. 3). Few of the big hits are here—"Walkin' After Midnight" and its flip side, "A Poor Man's Roses," are the best-known—but some inspired minor tracks recommend each individual volume.

The two live albums include one volume of songs recorded at the Grand Ole Opry between 1956 and 1962 that shows Cline every bit as ingratiating a performer as she was a singer; *Live, Volume Two* is actually a series of studio cuts (with canned applause) recorded in 1956 and transcribed for radio broadcast on shows sponsored by the Armed Forces.

For completists, *Patsy Cline*, *Showcase*, and *Sentimentally Yours* are the only studio albums released in Cline's lifetime; the Bulldog and Quicksilver albums are early tracks recorded when Cline was under contract to 4 Star, which was licensing her singles to Coral, and then Decca. Almost all of these recordings are included on *The Patsy Cline Collection* and the three Rhino CDs. The numerous titles left in the Cline catalogue are various reworkings on the greatest hits concept; all have their virtues—great singing foremost among them, of course—but *Collection* comes close to rendering everything else superfluous.
— D.M.

GEORGE CLINTON

★ ★ ★ ★ **Computer Games (Capitol, 1982)**
★ ★ ★ ★ **You Shouldn't-Nuf Bit Fish (Capitol, 1983)**
★ ★ ★ ½ **Some of My Best Jokes Are Friends (Capitol, 1985)**
★ ★ ★ **R&B Skeletons in the Closet (Capitol, 1986)**
★ ★ ★ **The Mothership Connection (Live From Houston) (Capitol, 1986)**
★ ★ ★ ½ **The Best of George Clinton (Capitol, 1986)**
★ ★ ★ ½ **The Cinderella Theory (Paisley Park/Warner Bros., 1989)**

As his Parliament-Funkadelic empire reached its zenith, George Clinton started to spread himself a little too thin, between all the side projects, splinter groups and off-shoots. Around 1980, the records began to sound a little peaked, too. Perhaps economics forced Clinton to focus his wild creative energies on a subsequent solo deal; anyway, the move did his music a world of good. All the Capitol albums contain trademark moments of beauty and booty-stomping grooves; the addition of stark, unsettling synth textures and angry, politicized lyrics forms Clinton's response to the Reaganite mindset.

Computer Games re-wires the idea of electro-pop dance music, grounding it in the rhythmic and vocal traditions of soul. The hit "Atomic Dog" stands as one of Clinton's masterworks: it's a philosophical treatise on tail-chasing with an inescapable howl-along chorus. *You Shouldn't-Nuf Bit Fish* plugs Funkadelic-style guitar fire ("Quickie") and unforgettable meldodies ("Last Dance") back into the socket, and the juice connects. Thomas Dolby joins the always-expanding cast on *Some of My Best Jokes Are Friends*; the sweetened electronic sound is used to convey an embattled, but proud anti-war message on simmering tracks like "Double Oh-Oh." *R&B Skeletons in the Closet* just sounds embittered. Though the title track scores a strong point off the crossover trend and "Do Fries Go With That Shake" proves George hasn't completely lost his sense of humor, it also gets a little repetitive. So does the live album, which includes a handful of greatest hits from the preceding records. *The Best of George Clinton* offers a more acceptable selection from these years, but in terms of overall coherence and vision, *Computer Games* and *Fish* will both go cut-for-cut with any classic rock album you'd care to name.

The Cinderella Theory finds Clinton outside Minneapolis, throwing down with a crew of old cronies and blazing young guns (including Public Enemy's Chuck D and Flavor Flav). Prince opened the door to his Paisley Park studio, and wisely left the man alone to do his own thing. *The Cinderella Theory* reminds us that many of the recent advances in pop music are things Clinton has been messing around with for years. Whatever the latest technology, be it electric guitars or computer samples, he always takes it to the max—and the next stage. After more than 25 years, Clinton's ongoing career proves one of his own oft-repeated verities: "The Funk Is Its Own Reward."
— M.C.

ROSEMARY CLOONEY

★ ★ ★ **Everything's Coming Up Rosie (Concord Jazz, 1977)**
★ ★ ★ **Rosie Sings Bing (Concord Jazz, 1978)**
★ ★ ★ **Here's to My Lady (Concord Jazz, 1979)**
★ ★ ★ ★ **Rosemary Clooney Sings the Lyrics of Ira Gershwin (Concord Jazz, 1980)**
★ ★ ★ **With Love (Concord Jazz, 1981)**
★ ★ ★ ★ **Rosemary Clooney Sings the Music of Cole Porter (Concord Jazz, 1982)**
★ ★ ★ **My Buddy (Concord Jazz, 1983)**
★ ★ ★ **Rosemary Clooney Sings the Music of Harold Arlen (Concord Jazz, 1983)**
★ ★ ★ ★ **Rosemary Clooney Sings the Music of Irving Berlin (Concord Jazz, 1984)**
★ ★ ★ ★ **Rosemary Clooney Sings Ballads (Concord Jazz, 1985)**
★ ★ ★ **Rosemary Clooney Sings the Music of Jimmy Van Heusen (Concord Jazz, 1986)**
★ ★ ★ ★ **Rosemary Clooney Sings the Lyrics of Johnny Mercer (Concord Jazz, 1987)**
★ ★ ★ **Show Tunes (Concord Jazz, 1989)**
★ ★ ★½ **16 Most Requested Songs (Columbia, 1989)**
★ ★ ★ ★ **Rosemary Clooney With the L.A. Jazz Choir Sings Rodgers, Hart & Hammerstein (Concord Jazz, 1990)**
★ ★ ★ ★ **For the Duration (Concord Jazz, 1991)**
★ ★ ★ **Girl Singer (Concord Jazz, 1992)**

Rosemary Clooney's story of triumph, tragedy and comeback is every bit as stirring as the music she's made. In the '50s she was one of America's most popular singers while recording for Columbia Records. However successful those records—and successful they were, with 24 Top Forty singles between 1951 and 1954—producer Mitch Miller's insistence that Clooney record songs with novelty appeal obscured the singer's tremendous gift as an interpreter. Fluff such as "Come On-A My House" (a Number One single in 1951), "Botch-A-Me" and "Mambo Italiano" helped define Clooney's public image, despite her success with more sophisticated songs on the order of "You'll Never Know," a Top Twenty single in 1953, and "Hey There," a Number One in 1954.

Clooney's career came undone as rock & roll pushed popular music off the charts. Forgotten, Clooney became increasingly dependent on pills and alcohol. In 1968, a singing engagement in Reno ended prematurely when Clooney launched into an onstage tirade directed at the audience. A medical team took Clooney in restraints to a Los Angeles hospital, where she was remanded to the psychiatric ward for four weeks. Upon her release, she began a long recovery that was aided by Bing Crosby, who added her as an opening act on every concert he played during the last year and a half before his death in 1977. Her story was dramatized in the 1978 TV movie, *Escape from Madness*, based on her 1977 autobiography, *This for Remembrance*.

That year (1977) also marked her return to recording with a set of standards, *Everything's Coming Up Rosie*, for the Concord Jazz label. She has since concentrated on the jazz and pop songs that are her natural *metier*, and in the process has made a case for herself as a peerless vocalist. Her voice retains its airy,

conversational quality, but her impeccable articulation and timing are even more impressive. Clooney also gets deeper into her songs' emotional shadings than she did in her younger days. You don't have to know much of her background to appreciate the sense of renewal she brings to her reading of "Ding Dong! the Witch is Dead," of all things, on *Rosemary Clooney Sings the Music of Harold Arlen*; that feeling of a new day being born is well-understood by anyone who's made enormous changes. By the same token, the dark clouds hanging over her clipped, terse reading of the opening lines of the Johnny Mercer–Victor Schertzinger standard "I Remember You" (on *Rosemary Clooney Sings the Lyrics of Johnny Mercer*) bespeaks a moving sense of time lost. Describing the highlights of Clooney's Concord Jazz catalogue is a book unto itself. Suffice it to say that the *Rosemary Clooney Sings* albums are required listening. This is not to dismiss the other albums, though. *For the Duration* includes readings of "I'll Be Seeing You" and Cole Porter's "You'd Be So Nice to Come Home To" that stand up to any other singer's. On *Here's to My Lady*, she pays stirring tribute to Billie Holiday, but places her individual stamp on the Holiday repertoire. At a time when most artists of her generation have long passed their peak, Clooney sounds like she's beginning anew.
— D.M.

THE CLOVERS
★ ★ ★ ★ **Their Greatest Recordings—The Early Years (Atco, 1975)**
★ ★ ★ ★ **Down in the Alley (Atlantic; 1991)**
★ ★ ★ **The Best of the Clovers—Love Potion No. 9 (EMI, 1991)**
Antedating the Ink Spots, predating the Coasters, the Clovers, out of Washington, D.C., can lay claim to being the first rock & roll vocal group, although much of their best work was done before the term rock & roll was ever applied to a musical genre. However much dispute ensues from being acclaimed "the first," the Clovers are one of the most important vocal groups in the music's history. The 21 tracks on Atlantic's reissue prove the point and restore to the catalogue the work of one of the label's vital group harmony contingents, whose 1971 retrospective, *Their Greatest Recordings*, has long been out of print. The EMI set covers the group's final productive years.
Signed to Atlantic in 1950, the quintet came under the studio guidance of label founders Ahmet Ertegun and Herb

Abramson (and soon, Jerry Wexler), who fashioned a hard-driving rhythmic style to support the group's blues and gospel leanings. The release of the Clovers' first single in 1951, a two-sided Number One R&B hit, "Don't You Know I Love You" b/w "Fool, Fool, Fool," heralded the decline of the Ink Spots and their acolytes, who favored romantic ballads and fast novelty tunes. The Clovers' music was something young people identified as theirs, because it did not sound like the music preferred by adults who had grown up on the mellow group harmony sounds of the '40s. In John "Buddy" Bailey the Clovers also had that *sine qua non*, the versatile tenor lead who could handle a sentimental pop ballad, a hard blues, a blues ballad, even a novelty song with consummate ease.
From 1951 through 1956 the Clovers were omnipresent near the top of the R&B charts, then broke through to the pop charts in the late '50s with "Love, Love, Love," which went Top Thirty in 1956, and the enduring "Love Potion No. 9" (the Clovers' most successful pairing with producers-writers Jerry Leiber and Mike Stoller, who were then doing wondrous things with the Coasters), which peaked at Number 23 in 1959—and is included on the EMI set. One of history's unanswerable questions is whether the Clovers' original versions of "Devil or Angel" and "Blue Velvet"(both from 1955) might be better known today than Bobby Vee's or Bobby Vinton's cover versions, had the Clovers been granted access to the pop charts during their most productive years. Neither of those singers could even contest Bailey's delicate, swaying lead, nor are the pop records blessed with the same captivating rhythms that provide such an elegant touch to the Clovers' performances. In addition to the albums listed here, Clovers' hits remain available on anthologies, notably Volumes 1–3 of *Atlantic Rhythm and Blues, 1947–1974*. — D.M.

CLUB NOUVEAU
★ ★ ★ ★ **Life, Love & Pain (Warner Bros., 1986)**
★ ★ ½ **Listen to the Message (Warner Bros., 1988)**
★ ★ **Under a Nouveau Groove (Warner Bros., 1989)**
What makes this club so nouveau is that its principal members—singer-producer Jay King, keyboardist-programmer Alex Hill and singer Valerie Watson—were originally part of the Timex Social Club (along with

singer Michael Marshall and keyboardist Marcus Thompson), which had a massive R&B hit with "Rumors." Unfortunately, shortly after that, the club members had a massive falling out, with King, Hill and Watson striking off on their own. It should hardly come as a surprise, then, that *Life, Love & Pain* opens with the fang-baring, vengeful "Jealousy." Don't get the wrong idea, though. This album isn't about settling the score; it's about making one. With the team of Thomas McElroy and Denzil Foster on hand to sharpen the hooks and beef up the beats, *Life, Love & Pain* is irresistibly entertaining, whether goofing through the technobeats of "Promise Promises," redefining the blues with "Why You Treat Me So Bad" or bouncing happily through a gleefully kinetic remake of Bill Withers's "Lean On Me."

Club Nouveau never lost sight of that formula, but without McElroy and Foster on hand to husband the grooves, the group's subsequent efforts fell flat. By the time of *Under a Nouveau Groove*, the Club's sound was as tired as it was old. — J.D.C.

THE COASTERS
★ ★ ★ ★ **Their Greatest Recordings: The Early Years (Atco, 1971)**
★ ★ ★ ★ **Greatest Hits (1958; Atco, 1989)**
★ ★ ★ ★ ★ **50 Coastin' Classics: The Coasters Anthology (Rhino/Atlantic, 1992)**

In Carl Gardner and bass singer Will "Dub" Jones, who replaced original bass Bobby Nunn in 1958, the Coasters had two of the most dominant vocal personalities of the early R&B groups that made the transition to rock & roll. Formed by Gardner and Nunn after they had left the Robins to move to Atco with their writers-producers Jerry Leiber and Mike Stoller, the Coasters brought mini-vaudeville skits to rock & roll with Gardner and Jones as comic leads. Using the Coasters as their laboratory, Leiber and Stoller gave the Coasters both witty material and steady production, and took care to back them with such gifted players as guitarist Mickey Baker and, most prominent of all, saxophonist King Curtis, whose stuttering solos instantly defined the classic rock & roll sax break. Skilled writers in the blues idiom, Leiber and Stoller didn't write down to the teenage audience they wanted to reach with the Coasters. Rather, they used their verbal gifts and flair for striking imagery in the service of material that spoke directly to the experiences familiar to their young listeners: "Yakety Yak" is the beleaguered teen

perspective on overbearing parents; "Charlie Brown" limns the hopeless antics of the class clown; at other times, the songs were more adult in attitude, more ominous in point of view, more adventurous in structure ("Down in Mexico," "Riot in Cell Block No. 9," "Shopping for Clothes"). No matter the scope of the task at hand, Gardner in particular always rose to the occasion—he could be swinging, loose and bemused, or he could be brooding, and deliver his vocals in a tremulous voice that suggested anything but good times ahead. It's easy to think of the Coasters as comedians only; in fact, Leiber and Stoller were streetwise, socially conscious writers who gave the group a number of songs that were, in fact, ruminations on some of the inequities they saw in America in the 1950s.

The Coasters' most productive years were 1957 to 1959, when they scored six consecutive Top Ten hits, including one Number One with "Yakety Yak." *The Early Years* is mistitled, seeing as how its 14 tracks span the years from 1954 (the Robins material) to 1961, when "Little Egypt" was the group's last Top Thirty single. Still, the two discs extant, despite duplications in programming, offer an adequate if incomplete historical overview of the Coasters' history. Lesser hits such as "I'm a Hog for You," "Run Red Run," "One Kiss Led to Another" (the Coasters' first single to make the pop charts, in 1956) and "Love Potion No. 9" (the group's final chart record, in 1971, a song that had been a hit previously for the Clovers in 1959 and the Searchers in 1964) are nowhere to be found on either of these two collections. The Rhino/Atlantic two-CD retrospective is the thorough overview the group deserves, a bona-fide five-star album. A must-have set, it replaces the 1982 Atco compilation, *Young Blood*, with an additional 26 tracks. — D.M.

EDDIE COCHRAN
★ ★ ★ **Legendary Masters Series, Volume 1 (EMI, 1990)**
★ ★ ★ **Greatest Hits (Curb, 1990)**

Acknowledged as one of the most gifted of the early rock & roll artists, Eddie Cochran died in a car accident in 1960, leaving unsettled his standing in relation to other first-generation rockers. Between 1957 and 1959, he had only three Top Forty hits, the biggest being the classic "Summertime Blues," which peaked at Number Eight in 1958. While Buddy Holly and Ritchie Valens had established strong individual

identities at the time of their deaths, leaving open to speculation only the question of how their careers would have evolved, Cochran died having released some spirited sides without establishing a point of view distinctively his own. On balance, the tracks on the EMI and Curb sets simply don't measure up to the best work of Cochran's peers. "Summertime Blues" and "Twenty Flight Rock" remain among the very best singles of the '50s, and have proven to be inspirational touchstones for succeeding generations of unreconstructed rockers who find in Cochran the essence of early rock & roll's rebel spirit. But many of Cochran's recordings sound more like blueprints made by an artist searching for his voice.
— D.M.

BRUCE COCKBURN

★★½ Bruce Cockburn (True North, Can., 1970)
★★½ High Winds, White Sky (1971; Columbia, 1991)
★★½ Sunwheel Dance (True North, Can., 1972)
★★★ Night Vision (True North, Can., 1973)
★★½ Salt, Sun & Time (True North, Can., 1974)
★★★½ Joy Will Find a Way (True North, Can., 1975)
★★½ In the Falling Dark (True North, Can., 1977)
★★½ Circles in the Stream (True North, Can., 1977)
★★★ Further Adventures Of (True North, Can., 1978)
★★★½ Dancing in the Dragon's Jaws (1979, Columbia, 1991)
★★★½ Humans (1980; Columbia, 1992)
★★★ Inner City Front (1981; Columbia, 1992)
★★★★ Mummy Dust (True North, Can., 1981)
★★★ The Trouble With Normal (1983; Columbia, 1992)
★★★★ Stealing Fire (1984; Columbia, 1991)
★★★½ World of Wonders (1986; Columbia, 1992)
★★★★ Waiting for a Miracle (True North, Can., 1987)
★★★ Big Circumstance (1989; Columbia, 1991)
★★★ Bruce Cockburn Live (True North, Can., 1990)
★★★★ Nothing But a Burning Light (Columbia, 1991)

Bruce Cockburn is nothing if not prolific. Granted, his productivity hasn't earned him a mass audience in this country—indeed, his only American Top Forty hit is "Wondering Where the Lions Are," from Dancing in the Dragon's Jaws—but his tuneful intelligence and passionate commitment make for rewardingly consistent listening. Cockburn started out with a basic acoustic-guitar-and-vocals approach to recording, which lends a strong folk-rock flavor to his debut and High Winds, White Sky. Cockburn's acoustic instrumentation doesn't limit him to folk, however. Night Vision, for instance, takes a fairly jazzy approach to the blues in tunes like "Déjà Vu" and "Mama Just Wants to Barrelhouse All Night Long," and there's a similar jazziness to Further Adventures; the arrangements on Dancing in the Dragon's Jaws, on the other hand, have a much more exotic feel, evoking the music of Africa and South America through its use of dulcimer, marimba and hand percussion.

With Humans, though, Cockburn's work takes a sudden turn to the left, addressing such diverse issues as capitalist manipulation of public policy ("Grim Travellers"), populist insurgencies ("Guerilla Betrayed") and environmental abuse ("Fascist Architecture"). This wasn't the first time Cockburn's work had addressed social issues, as plenty of his early songs are pointedly political, from the ominous generalizations of "It's Going Down Slow" (from Sunwheel Dance) to the angry particulars of "Burn" (from Joy Will Find a Way). But by making this the focus of his work, Cockburn significantly sharpened his songwriting, and his next few albums seem energized by the shift. Stealing Fire is particularly good in this respect, not only by affording Cockburn the righteous indignation of "If I Had a Rocket Launcher" but allowing for both the generalized compassion of "Lovers In a Dangerous Time" and the haunting specificity of "Peggy's Kitchen Wall." On the other hand, the mythic weight of Nothing But a Burning Light is just as impressive, particularly when Cockburn applies the power of allegory and legend to make his point on songs like "Soul of a Man" and "Kit Carson."

Both Mummy Dust (which has also been available under the title Resumé) and Waiting for a Miracle are best-ofs; the former shows off his songwriting skills and draws heavily on his folk-oriented work, while the latter merely compiles his singles through 1987. — J.D.C.

JOE COCKER

★★★½ With a Little Help From My
          Friends (A&M, 1969)
★★★★   Joe Cocker! (A&M, 1969)
★★★½ Mad Dogs and Englishmen
          (A&M, 1970)
  ★★½ Joe Cocker (A&M, 1972)
  ★★★ I Can Stand a Little Rain (A&M,
          1974)
★★★★   Greatest Hits (A&M, 1977)
★★★½ Sheffield Steel (Island, 1982)
    ★★   Civilized Man (Capitol, 1984)
    ★★   Cocker (Capitol, 1986)
★★★★   Classics Volume 4 (A&M, 1987)
    ★★   Unchain My Heart (Capitol,
          1987)
    ★★   One Night of Sin (Capitol, 1989)
  ★★½ Joe Cocker Live (Capitol, 1990)

Joe Cocker perfectly describes his vocals in
one of the titles from his debut LP:
"Sandpaper Cadillac." He can rub your skin
raw with hoarse soul shouts, or comfortably
cruise through a roughhewn ballad. *With a
Little Help From My Friends* taps a stellar
late-'60s cast led by Jimmy Page and Stevie
Winwood, but that voice absolutely
dominates the proceedings. Never a subtle
interpreter, Cocker makes Traffic's "Feeling
Alright" entirely his own possession and
leaves a lasting mark on Dylan's "I Shall Be
Released" and the Beatles' "With a Little
Help From My Friends." *Joe Cocker!* marks
the singer's true arrival. Co-producer Leon
Russell proves a valiant foil; he supplies the
Brit belter with a custom-made swamp rock
howler ("Delta Lady") and a looser 'n'
livelier ensemble sound. When Cocker
bombastically erupts amid the taut piano-led
arrangements of "Hitchcock Railway" and
"She Came in Through the Bathroom
Window," the band effortlessly kicks into
higher gear. *Mad Dogs and Englishmen*, a
circus-like double-LP concert set from the
following year, documents the downside of
this friendly supersession approach. Too
many cooks (and solos) spoil the soup,
though Cocker's urgent reading of "The
Letter" (a Top Ten hit) gets carried along
by a swift, beefy horn section.
    Larded with undistinguished originals, *Joe
Cocker* is a surprisingly drab follow-up to
Mad Dogs. I Can Stand a Little Rain returns
Cocker to the role of bloozy interpreter,
though the choice of songwriters is far less
astute than before: the melodic ironies of
Randy Newman, Jimmy Webb and Harry
Nilsson aren't exactly up Joe's stylistic alley.
He fares better with the title track and
"You Are So Beautiful," though the
bathetic tone of the latter (a Top Five hit)

sadly points the way for Cocker's future
efforts. With the notable exception of the
reggae-flavored (by Sly & Robbie) *Sheffield
Steel*, subsequent Cocker albums languish in
the torpid MOR zone. "Up Where We
Belong," his 1982 soundtrack duet with
Jennifer Warnes, is the catchiest thing he's
rasped in years. Consider that a warning:
Joe Cocker Live reveals the torn and frayed
underpinnings of a once-mighty voice.
 — M.C.

COCTEAU TWINS

  ★★★ Garlands (1982; Capitol, 1991)
   ★★ Lullabies (EP) (1982; Capitol,
        1991)
  ★★★ Head Over Heels (1983; Capitol,
        1991)
  ★★½ Peppermint Pig (EP) (1983;
        Capitol, 1991)
★★★★ Sunburst and Snowblind (EP)
        (1983; Capitol, 1991)
★★★½ Pearly-Dewdrops' Drops (EP)
        (1984; Capitol, 1991)
★★★½ Treasure (1984; Capitol, 1991)
★★★★½ The Pink Opaque (1985; Capitol,
        1991)
  ★★★ Aikea-Guinea (1985; Capitol,
        1991)
  ★★★ Tiny Dynamite (EP) (1985;
        Capitol, 1991)
  ★★★ Echoes in a Shallow Bay (EP)
        (1985; Capitol, 1991)
★★★★ Victorialand (1986; Capitol, 1991)
★★★½ Love's Easy Tears (EP) (1986;
        Capitol, 1991)
★★★½ The Moon & the Melodies (1986;
        Capitol, 1991)
★★★★ Blue Bell Knoll (4AD/Capitol,
        1988)
 ★★½ Iceblink Luck (EP) (4AD/Capitol,
        1990)
★★★★½ Heaven or Las Vegas
        (4AD/Capitol, 1990)
★★★★½ Cocteau Twins (4AD/Capitol,
        1991)

Punk's embrace of inspired amateurism has
been responsible for many musical surprises,
but none so delightful as the Cocteau Twins.
This Scots combo—Robin Guthrie,
Elizabeth Fraser and, eventually, Simon
Raymonde—doesn't write songs so much as
shape sounds into some semblance of a
verse-chorus construction, after which
Fraser appends her otherworldly melodies
and inscrutable lyrics. It's not the most
musicianly way of doing things, and the
band's early efforts, *Garlands* and the EP
Lullabies, flail more than they fly. But when
the Cocteaus hit their mark, as they do on

Garlands' "Wax and Wane," the result is deliriously tuneful, like a snippet from some faerie melody or a song heard in a dream.

That's the sort of magic the Cocteaus excelled at; trouble is, it took them—that is, Fraser and Guthrie—a while to get good at it. Apart from the strident "Musette and Drums" and the rattletrap "When Mama Was Moth," *Head Over Heels* is too noisily primitive to cast much of a spell, while *Peppermint Pig* presents an unseemly brusqueness. Then, almost unexpectedly, comes the luscious, shimmering beauty of *Sunburst and Snowblind*, which includes a much-improved "Sugar Hiccup" (a coarser cousin can be found on *Head Over Heels*) and the gorgeous, moody "From the Flagstones." Raymonde joins up in time for *Pearly-Dewdrops' Drops*, which introduces the tasty title song. *Treasure* continues the Twins' ascent into aural bliss, thanks to such infectious concoctions as "Lorelei" or the hauntingly sibilant "Aloysius." Highlights from those records, along with the otherwise-unavailable "Millimillenary," can be found on the compilation *The Pink Opaque*.

With *Aikea-Guinea*, the degree of craft that went into the group's soundscapes began to increase while the melodic content declined. That doesn't exactly work against *Aikea-Guinea, Tiny Dynamite* or *Echoes in a Shallow Bay*, as each eloquently conveys its own, individual sense of atmosphere, but it does diminish the band's pop appeal. *Victorialand*, recorded without Raymonde, goes even further in its pursuit of the ineffable, as the aptly titled "Lazy Calm" and "Fluffy Tufts" make clear. Yet the duo could still summon its melodic gifts if so moved, as demonstrated by the slippery refrain to "Whales Tails," as well as the classic lines of "Love's Easy Tears" and the quirky choruses of "Orange Appled," both from the *Love's Easy Tears* EP. Even *The Moon and the Melodies*, a collaboration with minimalist composer Harold Budd, manages to deliver tuneful gems like "Sea, Swallow Me" and the slow, deliberate "She Will Destroy You."

Blue Bell Knoll inaugurated the group's association with Capitol Records in the U.S., and though the album can hardly be considered "commercial," it does boast an added sense of sparkle, from the giddy arabesques of Fraser's vocal on "Carolyn's Fingers" to the implied funk of "A Kissed Out Red Floatboat." *Iceblink Luck* enhances that sense of groove to near dance-single strength, offering a prelude of sorts to

Heaven or Las Vegas, wherein the Cocteaus ground their soft-focus soundscapes with low-key, bass-driven rhythm tracks, a strategy that nicely enhances the music's appeal. *Cocteau Twins* is a boxed collection of the group's EPs, plus a bonus disc containing several non-LP and previously-unreleased tracks. — J.D.C.

DAVID ALLAN COE
- ★★ **Penitentiary Blues (SSS, 1970)**
- ★ **Mysterious Rhinestone Cowboy (Columbia, 1974)**
- ★★ **Once Upon a Rhyme (Columbia, 1975)**
- ★★ **Long-haired Redneck (Columbia, 1976)**
- ★ **David Allan Coe Rides Again (Columbia, 1977)**
- ★ **Tattoo (Columbia, 1977)**
- ★★ **Texas Moon (Plantation, 1977)**
- ★★ **Family Album (Columbia, 1978)**
- ★★ **Human Emotions (Columbia, 1979)**
- ★ **I've Got Something to Say (Columbia, 1980)**
- ★ **Invictus Means Unconquered (Columbia, 1981)**
- ★★ **D.A.C. (Columbia, 1982)**
- ★ **Castles in the Sand (Columbia, 1983)**
- ★★★ **For the Record: The First 10 Years (Columbia, 1984)**

One of country music's most unfettered souls, David Allan Coe, wise in the ways of self-promotion, came on the scene in the early '70s with boasts of having served prison time for murdering another man. As it turned out, he was indeed in prison, but the murder conviction turned out to be a product of Coe's imagination. Undaunted by this revelation, Coe maintained a rough and rugged public persona and aligned himself with the outlaw movement (as explained in his song "Willie, Waylon & Me"). While he is hardly in the same league with Nelson and Jennings, Coe did deliver some good early songs that received their best treatment by other artists, notably Tanya Tucker ("Would You Lay With Me [in a Field of Stone]"). While this song shows Coe's sensitive side, this quality—along with a sense of humor—is largely lacking on his own self-indulgent recordings. Stick with *For the Record: The First 10 Years* and delve into the rest of the catalogue at your own risk. — D.M.

LEONARD COHEN
- ★★★★½ **The Songs of Leonard Cohen (Columbia, 1968)**
- ★★★½ **Songs From a Room (1969; Columbia, 1990)**

★ ★ ★½ **Songs of Love and Hate
(Columbia, 1971)**
★ ★ ★½ **New Skin for the Old Ceremony
(Columbia, 1974)**
★ ★ ★ ★ **Best of Leonard Cohen (Columbia,
1976)**
★ ★ **Death of a Ladies Man (1977;
Columbia, 1988)**
★ ★ ★ **Recent Songs (Columbia, 1979)**
★ ★ ★ **Various Positions (PVC, 1985)**
★ ★ ★½ **I'm Your Man (Columbia, 1988)**

Canadian poet, novelist (*Beautiful Losers,*
1966) and haute monde cult figure, Cohen
crafts elegant, bittersweet mood music for
dark nights of the soul. While
hyper-romantic at heart, he avoids
mushiness by cultivating a veneer of
Europeanized world-weariness a la Jacques
Brel or Brecht-Weill. Like Bob Dylan, he's a
deft non-singer, his ragged delivery
compensated for by cinematic
arrangements—on early work, his huskiness
and offhand acoustic guitar jostle film-noir
strings; later (*Recent Songs,* from 1979) he
played with a mariachi band, and was
accompanied by such non-pop surprises as
the Middle Eastern oud and the English
horn.

The Songs of Leonard Cohen (1968)
remains his finest hour—his themes of love,
death, betrayal and the conflict of flesh and
spirit conveyed hauntingly through simple,
repetitive melodies (Cohen understandably
favors minor chords, and his lyrics stress
suggestion over statement). *Death of a
Ladies Man* paired him with Phil Spector in
an odd bid to join Spector's pop-orchestral
Wall of Sound bravado with Cohen's
high-art seriousness and occasional mystic
concerns. He's also experimented with
French Canadian song structures and,
effectively, with duets with Jennifer Warnes
(on *Recent Songs* and *Various Positions*): her
bell-like singing sets off his dry-voiced
pleading like gilt framing an abstract
artwork.

Judy Collins and Joe Cocker ably covered
Cohen ("Suzanne," from *Songs of Leonard
Cohen,* and "Bird on a Wire," from *Songs
From a Room,* respectively), and, continuing
with such gems as *I'm Your Man* (1988),
Cohen exerts considerable influence on the
folk-poet revival of Suzanne Vega and
others. — P.E.

COLDCUT
★ ★ ★½ **What's That Noise (Tommy
Boy/Warner Bros., 1989)**

Consisting of English DJs Matt Black and
Jonathan More, Coldcut started out as just

another acid-house remix act, but eventually
coalesced into an impressively eclectic
production team. Here, the duo tries
everything from the straight-up retro-disco
of "People Hold On," featuring the
then-unknown Lisa Stansfield, to the dense,
industrial funk of "(I'm) In Deep," with
vocals by Mark E. Smith of the Fall.
— J.D.C.

LLOYD COLE AND THE
COMMOTIONS
★ ★ ★½ **Rattlesnakes (1984; Capitol, 1988)**
★ ★ ★½ **Easy Pieces (1985; Capitol, 1988)**
★ ★ ★ **Mainstream (Capitol, 1987)**
★ ★ ★ ★ **1984–1989 (Capitol, 1989)**
LLOYD COLE
★ ★ ★½ **Lloyd Cole (Capitol, 1990)**
★ ★ ★ ★ **Don't Get Weird On Me, Babe
(Capitol, 1991)**

Lloyd Cole's specialty is unconventional
love songs, compositions that can take a few
telling details and a certain cast of melody
and somehow paint a vivid picture of a
woman or a relationship. At their best, his
songs recall the subtle depth and disarming
simplicity of Leonard Cohen's work—a high
compliment, indeed.

Opening with the jangly "Perfect Skin,"
Rattlesnakes works out of the same musical
vocabulary as the buoyant neo-pop of Scots
bands like Orange Juice and the Bluebells.
But the unblinking honesty of songs like
"Forest Fire" or "Are You Ready to Be
Heartbroken?" keeps the band from
tumbling into the melodic glibness that
made the other acts seem so superficial.
There's an even richer sense of melancholy
to the songs on *Easy Pieces,* but there's
enough humor in the wry "Why I Love
Country Music" or the jaunty "Lost
Weekend" to keep the album's mood from
seeming oppressive. *Mainstream,* though, is
something of a disappointment, having
much the same sound as its predecessors but
little of their wit or vivacity (although "Sean
Penn Blues" has its moments).

Cole canceled the Commotions in
1989—the retrospective *1984–1989* includes
most of the highlights from the band's three
albums, plus the non-LP tracks "Her Last
Fling" and "You Will Never Be No
Good"—and commenced upon a solo career
almost immediately. As far as the
songwriting goes, *Lloyd Cole* is blessed with
many of the same strengths as his earlier
albums, thanks to hauntingly melodic
numbers like "No Blue Skies" and
"Downtown," but the playing is much
stronger, thanks to a studio band built

around guitarist Robert Quine, bassist Matthew Sweet and drummer/co-producer Fred Maher. Much the same crew is on hand for *Don't Get Weird On Me, Babe,* but the writing is brighter and more upbeat, from the low-key sarcasm of "She's a Girl and I'm a Man" to the snarling guitars of "To the Lions." — J.D.C.

NATALIE COLE

★ ★ ★ ★ **Inseparable (Capitol, 1975)**
★ ★ ★ ★ **Natalie . . . Live! (Capitol, 1978)**
★ ★ ★ **The Natalie Cole Collection (Capitol, 1984)**
★ **Dangerous (Modern, 1985)**
★ ★ **Everlasting (EMI, 1987)**
★ ★ **Good to Be Back (EMI, 1989)**
★ ★ ★ ★ **Unforgettable (Elektra, 1991)**

When she made her debut in 1975, Natalie Cole seemed headed for great things. For one, she was determined to carve her own niche without reference to her beloved father, Nat "King" Cole. For another, she was possessed of enormous ability as a vocalist, was comfortable in a wide range of styles (blues, gospel, soul, rock, pop) and moods, and projected a strong, independent streak. She also hooked up with the producing-writing team of Chuck Jackson (not the Chuck Jackson of "Any Day Now" fame) and Marvin Yancy, who were prolific and polished in every way, and conscious of the art of understatement in their lyrics and arrangements.

At the outset the Jackson-Yancy-Cole triumvirate worked spectacularly. Cole's first single, "This Will Be," was a little bit funk, a little bit soul, a little bit rock and as radio-ready as any record could be. Cole gave it a fiery, assertive reading, and it and her career went into overdrive. The single peaked on the pop charts at Number Six, and Cole was a star. She continued to do well on the black music charts, but it would be almost two years before she returned to the pop Top Ten, with "I've Got Love on My Mind," followed the next year by another pop hit, "Our Love." By that time Jackson and Yancy were working at less than full inspiration, and Cole's records and performances took on a rote quality.

Drug-dependent and mired in mediocrity, Cole spent most of the '80s in a futile effort to recapture the spirit of her early recordings. Toward the end of the decade, she had cleaned up, cut a couple of promising albums for EMI, and was dazzling again in concert (her now-deleted *Natalie . . . Live!* album from 1978 is powerful testimony to her onstage

pyrotechnics). What she needed, though, was a hit. She got it, and more, in 1991 with *Unforgettable.* It was the album she refused to do for so many years—a collection of her father's songs—but it made her a major star again. Cole sings with conviction, sensitivity and gusto as the occasion demands—a real virtuoso display. Having found her bearings, Cole would seem to have a handle on her direction in the '90s. *Unforgettable* and Capitol's *The Natalie Cole Collection* (greatest hits, for short) make splendid bookends. *Inseparable* remains in print, though, and belongs right there with *Unforgettable* among Cole's best efforts. And look high and low for *Natalie . . . Live!* — D.M.

NAT KING COLE

★ ★ ★ ★ ★ **Jumpin' at Capitol: The Best of the Nat King Cole Trio (1950; Capitol, 1992)**
★ ★ ★ ★ **Unforgettable (1953; Capitol, 1990)**
★ ★ ★ ★ **The Christmas Song (1954; Capitol, 1990)**
★ ★ ★ ★ **Just One of Those Things (1957; Capitol, 1991)**
★ ★ ★ ★ **After Midnight (1957; Capitol, 1978)**
★ ★ ★ ★ **Love Is the Thing (1957; Capitol, 1991)**
★ ★ ★ ★ **The Very Thought of You (1958; Capitol, 1991)**
★ ★ ★ **Cole Espanol (1958; Capitol, 1991)**
★ ★ ★ ★ **Ramblin' Rose (1962; Capitol, 1991)**
★ ★ ★ **Nat "King" Cole Sings/George Shearing Plays (1962; Capitol, 1991)**
★ ★ ★ **More Cole Espanol (1962; Capitol, 1991)**
★ ★ ★ **Love Is Here to Stay (Capitol, 1974)**
★ ★ ★ ★ **Nat King Cole Sings for Two in Love (Capitol, 1987)**
★ ★ ★ ★ ★ **Hit That Jive, Jack (Decca/MCA, 1990)**
★ ★ ★ ★ **Cole, Christmas & Kids (Capitol, 1990)**
★ ★ ★ ★ **Capitol Collector's Series (Capitol, 1990)**
★ ★ ★ ★ ★ **The Nat King Cole Story (Capitol, 1991)**

Nat King Cole was a true superstar (even before the word was coined) whose enormous appeal transcended boundaries of race, age, gender and musical preference. The record shows 86 singles and 17 albums in the Top Forty between 1943 and 1964 (he died of lung cancer in 1965). He recorded ballads, jazz instrumentals, foreign language songs, Christmas carols, pop standards and what might now be termed pop-rock. But Cole's legacy is far more substantial than is suggested by his impressive sales figures or by his imposing reputation as a vocalist *non pareil*.

Cole came out of the gospel world, having played organ and piano at his father's church in Chicago, where the family had lived since moving from Montgomery, Alabama, when Cole was four. Despite his grounding in gospel, Cole was infatuated with jazz, in particular with the forward-thinking approach being pioneered by the great Windy City pianist Earl "Fatha" Hines. Cole incorporated many of Hines's techniques into his own approach, added a strong but subtle left hand, and became a link between Hines and later giants of jazz piano, notably Bud Powell.

Cole formed his first group, a trio, in the late '30s; joined by the inventive guitarist Oscar Moore and bassist Wesley Prince, Cole opened at L.A.'s Swanee Inn. Signed to Decca in 1940, the trio cut 16 sides, all unsuccessful commercially, but important signposts to Cole's future. As collected on *Hit That Jive, Jack,* these sides showcase the trio's instrumental approach—the swinging conversations among the instruments collectively setting up solos that are models of economy—as well as the range of material Cole was capable of handling as a vocalist. The title song has a jump feel and is a stylistic precursor to Cole's definitive 1946 recording of "Get Your Kicks on Route 66"; "That Ain't Right" is a straight blues number; "Sweet Lorraine," the first song Cole ever recorded as a vocalist, and "This Will Make You Laugh" are aching, lovely ballads.

Leaving Decca, the trio signed with Capitol in 1943, and there Cole would remain for the rest of his career, his reputation growing with each new, warm, personable vocal performance. Soft, but possessed of backbone, Cole's airy baritone was easy on ballads, ebullient but controlled on uptempo numbers, the diction always precise, the phrasing smart. He so stamped material with his signature reading that it's impossible to imagine any contemporary singer being able to work meaningful changes on Cole's songs. *Jumpin' at Capitol* surveys the trio's early years at Capitol up to 1950, beginning with its first single, "All for You" (1943). Cole's delicate reading of

George Gershwin's "Embraceable You" points toward the style of his later years, while the original take of "Get Your Kicks on Route 66" shows off the lilting, good-time swing in Cole's voice.

Jazz purists will beg off Cole after these two discs, protesting that as the artist moved more into the pop vein (and attendant orchestral arrangements) his music lost its intimate quality and Cole lost his distinctiveness as a performer. This insular viewpoint insults three of the finest arrangers in popular music of the '50s and '60s: Billy May, Nelson Riddle and Gordon Jenkins, each of whom produced significant sides with Cole. The two-CD *Nat King Cole Story*, originally released as a multiple-album package in the early '60s, offers a wide-ranging survey of Cole's recordings in different veins dating from his early efforts on the label. Several of Cole's defining hits are included—"Mona Lisa," "Nature Boy," "The Christmas Song," "Unforgettable," "Walkin' My Baby Back Home"—in addition to some interesting, lesser-known sides, such as the Brook Benton–penned "Looking Back" and the gospel-styled "Oh, Mary, Don't You Weep" (arranged by Jenkins). *Story* plus the Capitol Collector's Series album covers the key entries from Cole's pop years, with nothing of note omitted and several top-flight album tracks buttressing the better-known titles.

At this point the hits and the formative years are well in hand. But there is much more to treasure in this catalogue. *After Midnight* (1956) teams Cole with a sterling jazz trio and a small cast of guest artists, including the great Harry "Sweets" Edison on trumpet. Cole's final effort in the small combo vein, this set has a loose, jam session feel, with spirited instrumental interplay, and Cole, naturally, being the essence of cool. One of Cole's sustained efforts of vocal mastery is heard on *The Christmas Song*. If ever a man was born to sing of the Yuletide it was Cole, who approaches the material with both dignity and good humor. Both *The Christmas Song* and *Cole, Christmas & Kids* are inspiring and timeless classics of their kinds. Finally, Cole's work with May, Jenkins, and Riddle needs to be mentioned. With these arrangers-conductors Cole cut moments of pop splendor rivaled only by Sinatra's great Capitol recordings with Riddle. It's advised, then, that any Cole collection include three great exercises in American popular song: *Just One of Those Things* (with Billy May), the extraordinary Gordon Jenkins–arranged *The*

Very Thought of You, and the wistful look at love, *Nat King Cole Sings for Two in Love* (with Nelson Riddle). — D.M.

ORNETTE COLEMAN

★ ★ ★ ★   **Something Else!!** *(*1958; Contemporary, 1988)

★ ★ ★ ★ ★   **The Shape of Jazz to Come** (Atlantic, 1959)

★ ★ ★ ★   **Tomorrow Is the Question** (1959; Contemporary, 1988)

★ ★ ★ ★ ★   **This Is Our Music** (Atlantic, 1960)

★ ★ ★ ★ ★   **Free Jazz** (Atlantic, 1961)

★ ★ ★ ★½   **At the "Golden Circle" Stockholm** (1965; Blue Note, 1987)

★ ★ ★ ★½   **At the "Golden Circle" Stockholm, Vol. 2** (1965; Blue Note, 1987)

★ ★ ★ ★   **Ornette on Tenor** (Atlantic, 1966)

★ ★ ★ ★   **New York Is Now!** (1968; Blue Note,1990)

★ ★ ★ ★   **The Art of the Improvisers** (1970; Atlantic Jazz, 1988)

★ ★ ★ ★   **Ornette Coleman/Twins** (1971; Atlantic, 1981)

★ ★ ★ ★ ★   **Skies of America** (Columbia, 1972)

★ ★ ★ ★ ★   **Dancing in Your Head** (1977; A&M, 1988)

★ ★ ★ ★½   **Ornette Coleman in All Languages** (Caravan of Dreams, 1987)

★ ★ ★ ★   **Virgin Beauty** (Portrait, 1988)

Alto saxophonist Ornette Coleman discovered a personal style of astonishing expressiveness—paying no heed to rules, the genius founded an entire school of jazz, and he continues to delight, befuddle and challenge.

Ultimately a fairly straightforward melodist (the intricacy either of Mingus or Ellington lies beyond Ornette's grasp), Coleman in the late '50s soared out of a firm grounding in the blues to revolutionize jazz through "harmolodics"—his own term for a radical style of playing that disregarded the chord changes of any given piece of music and abandoned the soloist to pure melodic improvisation. *Free Jazz* was the triumph of the maneuver, and it remains to jazz what the Sex Pistols' *Never Mind the Bollocks* was to rock & roll: an album whose burst of desperate, raw power provides a litmus test for just how much intensity a listener can take.

The early Coleman, *Something Else!!*, *Tomorrow Is the Question*, *The Shape of*

Jazz to Come, is straighter fare—but not by much. At the time, Ornette confounded purists by often playing a plastic alto; his daring counterpart, Don Cherry, used a pocket trumpet—and the duo, with the expert backing of bassist Charlie Haden and drummer Billy Higgins, came on like mad, brilliant kids. The post-*Free Jazz* work of the middle '60s (the two *Golden Circle* sets, primarily) refined the gains Ornette had made with his forays into unchained melody; the early '70s masterwork, out of print at this point, was *Skies of America* (1972), a vast, 21-part symphonic piece that introduced harmolodics in an orchestral setting. *Dancing in Your Head* (1977) brought another breakthrough, as Ornette turned himself loose on a very funky version of rock-jazz fusion; he continued to experiment throughout the '80s with an electric ensemble, Prime Time (the toughest tracks are on *Virgin Beauty*, from 1988, an album that features good guest work from Jerry Garcia). — P.E.

ALBERT COLLINS

★ ★ ★ ★ ★   **Truckin' With Albert Collins** (1969; MCA, 1991)

★ ★ ★ ★½   **Ice Pickin'** (Alligator, 1978)

★ ★ ★½   **Frostbite** (Alligator, 1980)

★ ★ ★   **Frozen Alive!** (Alligator, 1981)

★ ★ ★   **Don't Lose Your Cool** (Alligator, 1983)

★ ★ ★   **Cold Snap** (Aligator, 1986)

★ ★ ★   **Iceman** (Charisma/Point Blank, 1991)

★ ★ ★ ★   **The Complete Imperial Recordings** (EMI, 1991)

The stinging sub-zero blitz of his Fender Telecaster earned Albert Collins his "Iceman" moniker. Like all Texas guitarists, he came up in the massive shadow of T-Bone Walker. However, Collins forged a unique finger-picking attack on a series of independently released singles in the '60s, puncturing funky instrumentals like "Frosty" and "Icy Blue" with jabbing leads and eerie tone clusters. *Truckin' With Albert Collins* is a welcome reissue of these long-unavailable sides, fleshed out with a few vocal numbers: barely clocking in at half an hour, it leaves you itchin' for more. *The Complete Imperial Recordings* documents Collins's next few years a little too closely, perhaps, but the loose let's-jam atmosphere triggers some wonderful excursions into second-line New Orleans funk and organ-drenched soul jazz, along with the requisite, terse 12-bar blowouts. After a long silence, Collins emerged with a sackful of striking songs to go along with his deep-six string mastery. *Ice Pickin'* burrows down to the real nitty gritty of urban existence, tapping veins of humor ("Master Charge," "Honey Hush") as well as regret ("When the Welfare Turns Its Back on You," "Cold, Cold Feeling")—it's one of the best '70s blues albums. Collins's razor-sharp style is so pointed and precise, however, that it can easily settle into formula. His subsequent albums vary the domestic themes and horn-sparked arrangements of *Ice Pickin'*; the results gradually become formulaic, if not utterly predictable. Though his cool-blue playing is always sharp, Collins's vocals—and songwriting—are less consistent. *Iceman* isn't bad, especially if you're a newcomer. But either one of those reissues could reduce these riff-blocks to warm puddles. — M.C.

BOOTSY COLLINS
★★★★   **Stretchin' Out in Bootsy's Rubber Band (Warner Bros., 1976)**
★★★½   **Ahh . . . The Name Is Bootsy, Baby! (Warner Bros., 1977)**
★★★½   **Bootsy? Player of the Year (Warner Bros., 1978)**
★★½   **This Boot Is Made for Fonk'n (Warner Bros., 1979)**
★★★½   **Ultra Wave (Warner Bros., 1980)**
★★★   **The One Giveth, the Count Taketh Away (Warner Bros., 1982)**
★★★★   **What's Bootsy Doing? (Columbia, 1988)**

James Brown recruited Cincinnati-born bassist William "Bootsy" Collins (and his guitarist brother Phelps "Catfish" Collins) into the JBs' fold in 1969. Still a teenager, Bootsy didn't serve all that long in the mercurial Brown's backing band—about two years. Yet he left an indelible mark on the emergent new sound. Along with Family Stone bassist Larry Graham, Bootsy is responsible for the plunking, nimbly polyrhythmic bass attack that makes up the cornerstone of funk. Hooking up with P-Funk overlord George Clinton in '72, Bootsy was a key player in the traveling Parliament/Funkadelic circus. Clinton's acid-stoked inspiration brought this gangly prodigy out of his shell, both as a musician and a theatrical "concept." Bootsy became Caspar: a friendly black ghost with star-shaped glasses, a star-shaped bass, a spacey demeanor and one randy chuckle of a deep voice.

Bootsy's Rubber Band was the first of many P-Funk sidetrips, though it's hardly a mere figment of Clinton's overactive imagination. With the Horny Horns (including Maceo Parker and Fred Wesley) and sweet-lipped soul singer Gary "Mudbone" Cooper on board, the Rubber Band backs up Bootsy's occasionally loopy digressions with rock-solid grooves. *Stretchin' Out in Bootsy's Rubber Band* carves out its own little niche in the Clinton game plan: it's sparser than the free-ranging Funkadelic, tangier than the pop-conscious Parliament. Heart-stopping seduction scenarios bump up against bottom-heavy funk vamps highlighting Bootsy's extraterrestrial sense of humor. *Stretchin' Out* is actually a super-tight, directed session for this crew; the real fun 'n' games begin on Bootsy's second album.

Ah . . . The Name Is Bootsy, Baby! expounds "The Pinocchio Theory" and expands P-Funk's audience to include the pre-teen "Geepies." Bootsy makes a genial host for this kiddie show. On the slightly more tuneful *Bootsy? Player of the Year*, the former Caspar re-emerges as "Bootzilla"—the first "rhinestone monster rockstar doll, baby brothah." Sometimes this loose atmosphere obscures some astounding musical moves. "Hollywood Squares," from *Player*, glides through jazz-fusion and neo-classical segments before it locks into an almighty bass-driven strut. That sort of thing doesn't happen quite often enough to counter some of the excessive silliness, though. Bootsy albums are not for the sober-sided. In fact, the giggles and hi-jinks get laid on a bit thick during the tuneless *This Boot Is Made for Fonk'n*. Collins (and Clinton) snapped back with *Ultra Wave*; a regulation-strength dose of adult P-Funk. *The One Giveth, the Count Taketh Away* sounds automatic, but Bootsy released a soaring one-off single ("Body Slam") in late '82. After that, he kept a low profile for the next five years or so. A series of session gigs with the likes of Keith Richards and Sly and Robbie prompted *What's Bootsy Doing?* With Catfish, Mudbone and the Horny Horns behind him, Bootsy drops his most consistent album since the debut. It's a (relatively) straightforward set of songs. Bootsy seems to have outgrown the comic-book jams of old without losing his sense of adventure. The trademark humor and horniness are now communicated through cunning vocal hooks, snarling guitar lines, and—of course—those awesome double-jointed bass lines. — M.C.

JUDY COLLINS

- ★★★ **A Maid of Constant Sorrow** (Elektra, 1962)
- ★★★ **Golden Apples of the Sun** (Elektra, 1963)
- ★★★ **Judy Collins #3** (Elektra, 1963)
- ★★½ **The Judy Collins Concert** (Elektra, 1964)
- ★★★★ **Judy Collins' Fifth Album** (Elektra, 1965)
- ★★★★ **In My Life** (Elektra, 1967)
- ★★★★ **Wildflowers** (Elektra, 1968)
- ★★★ **Who Knows Where the Time Goes** (Elektra, 1968)
- ★★★½ **Recollections** (Elektra, 1969)
- ★★★★ **Whales and Nightingales** (Elektra, 1971)
- ★★★½ **Living** (Elektra, 1972)
- ★★★★ **Colors of the Day/The Best of Judy Collins** (Elektra, 1972)
- ★★★ **True Stories and Other Dreams** (Elektra, 1973)
- ★★★ **Judith** (Elektra, 1975)
- ★★½ **Bread and Roses** (Elektra, 1976)
- ★★★★ **So Early in the Spring: The First Fifteen Years** (Elektra, 1977)
- ★★½ **Hard Times for Lovers** (Elektra, 1979)
- ★★½ **Running for My Life** (Elektra, 1980)
- ★★½ **Times of Our Lives** (Elektra, 1982)
- ★★½ **Trust Your Heart** (Gold Castle, 1987)
- ★★½ **Sanity and Grace** (Gold Castle, 1987)
- ★★★ **Fires of Eden** (Columbia, 1990)

Particularly in its middle register, Collins's voice is a true wonder—and chaste power and intelligence characterize her delivery. A subtle reader of almost any kind of ballad, she came into her own in the mid-'60s with a series of stunning albums featuring art songs of an austere grace. Verging on easy listening, her later work remains lovely, but weak material and obvious arrangements reduce this remarkable interpreter to the status of just another (very fine) singer.

The excellent *Fifth Album* marks Collins's movement away from traditional folk: "Lord Gregory" and Billy Edd Wheeler's "The Coming of the Roads" are beautiful, spare renderings of simple songs, but with Eric Andersen's "Thirsty Boots" and three Dylan covers, Collins starts moving toward denser material. On *In My Life* and *Wildflowers*, Joshua Rifkin's orchestral settings are gorgeous and artful, and the song selection shows real ambition. Lennon-McCartney's "In My Life," Dylan's "Tom Thumb's Blues" and Donovan's

"Sunny Goodge Street" get fresh, lovely treatments; on material by Leonard Cohen, Randy Newman, Jacques Brel and Brecht/Weill, Collins sings with absolute command. In this context, her biggest hit, Joni Mitchell's "Both Sides Now," sounds a bit trite. With the subsequent *Who Knows Where the Time Goes*, Collins falters slightly—the mild rock arrangements by Stephen Stills (her boyfriend at the time) are dated, and, while the autobiographical "My Father" may be her best original song, the record's ingratiating pop is a disappointing step down from the demanding elegance she'd previously mustered.

In Flemish and French, Jacques Brel's "Marieke" is the standout of *Whales and Nightingales*; a Scots traditional ("Farewell to Tarwathie"), songs by Dylan and Pete Seeger, and a powerful "Amazing Grace" show Collins returning to form (Rifkin's reappearance helps considerably). The Cohen songs on *Living* are brilliantly handled, and "Secret Gardens," from *True Stories*, nearly equals "My Father." On the latter album, however, Collins seems uncertain: her "Che" is didactic and wordy, and Valerie Carter's "Cook With Honey" is the rare example of Collins coming off cute. *Bread and Roses* is also tentative: the Mimi Fariña, Duke Ellington and Victor Jara songs are great—tunes by Andrew Gold and Elton John don't hold up in this company.

Judith may be her most accessible and varied album—Sondheim's "Send in the Clowns," Jagger/Richards's "Salt of the Earth," Steve Goodman's "City of New Orleans"—but it marks a turn toward the mere niceness of the records to come. All of those have their moments, but by relying on lesser writers (Henry Gross, Marvin Hamlisch, Harry Chapin), Collins never recaptures her earlier, fiercer loveliness. *Recollections*, *Colors of the Day* and *So Early in the Spring* are all best-of albums, and they're all fine—the best is *Colors*.
— P.E.

PHIL COLLINS

- ★★★ **Face Value** (Atlantic, 1981)
- ★★½ **Hello, I Must Be Going** (Atlantic, 1982)
- ★★★★ **No Jacket Required** (Atlantic, 1985)
- ★★½ **12'ers** (Atlantic, 1988)
- ★★½ **Buster (soundtrack)** (Atlantic, 1988)
- ★★½ **. . . But Seriously** (Atlantic, 1989)
- ★★★½ **Serious Hits Live!** (Atlantic, 1990)

Collins is in many ways the perfect mainstream rock star. His voice is light but soulful, his songs are tuneful without resorting to formula, and, thanks to his tenure in Genesis and his ubiquity as a sideman, he's damn near inescapable on the radio. All of which has gone a long way toward making him enormously popular with the listening public, and an obvious target for critics. Despite his lumpen-pop appeal, however, Collins is an incisive songwriter and resourceful musician whose work is far more subtle than its accessibility would suggest.

Of all his albums, *Face Value* sounds most like his work with Genesis; "I Missed Again" and "If Leaving Me Is Easy" carry the same mournfulness of *Duke*, while "In the Air Tonight" condenses *Wind and Wuthering*'s musical dramatics to a five-minute mini-epic. With *Hello, I Must Be Going*, Collins begins to find his own voice, flirting with soul (although soul didn't always flirt back, as his remake of "You Can't Hurry Love" demonstrates) and sharpening his skills at ballad-writing (although that wouldn't pay off until 1984, with "Against All Odds (Take a Look at Me Now)," from the *Against All Odds* soundtrack). Collins pulled it all together with the aggressively likeable *No Jacket Required*, which had solid rockers, great ballads and a pleasantly silly rewrite of Prince's "1999" ("Sussudio").

Unfortunately, the peripatetic Collins was unable to sustain that momentum. *12'ers* was an unconvincing collection of dance remixes, the *Buster* soundtrack squandered "Two Hearts" (co-written with Motown auteur Lamont Dozier) on what was otherwise an oldies album, and . . . *But Seriously* put more emphasis on its message than its music. *Serious Hits Live!*, however, is a delightful surprise, a live album that actually improves on its material.
— J.D.C.

JOHN COLTRANE
★ ★ ★½ Coltrane (1957; Fantasy, 1987)
★ ★ ★½ Traneing In (1957; Fantasy, 1985)
★ ★ ★ Dakar (1957; Fantasy, 1989)
★ ★ ★ ★ ★ Blue Train (1957; Blue Note, 1985)
★ ★ ★½ Bahia (1958; Fantasy, 1989)
★ ★ ★½ Black Pearls (1958; Fantasy, 1989)
★ ★ ★½ The Stardust Session (Prestige, 1958)
★ ★ ★ ★ ★ Soultrane (1958; Fantasy, 1987)
★ ★ ★ ★ ★ John Coltrane (Prestige, 1958)
★ ★ ★ ★ ★ Lush Life (1958; MCA/Impulse, 1987)

★ ★ ★ ★ Standard Coltrane (1958; Fantasy, 1990)
★ ★ ★ ★ Settin' the Pace (1958; Fantasy, 1987)
★ ★ ★ ★ ★ Coltrane Jazz (Atlantic, 1960)
★ ★ ★½ Africa/Brass (1960; MCA/Impulse, 1988)
★ ★ ★½ Africa/Brass, Vol. 2 (1960; MCA/Impulse, 1988)
★ ★ ★ ★ ★ Giant Steps (Atlantic, 1960)
★ ★ ★ Countdown (1960; Atlantic, 1986)
★ ★ ★ ★ Olé Coltrane (1961; Atlantic, 1989)
★ ★ ★ ★ ★ My Favorite Things (Atlantic, 1961)
★ ★ ★ ★ ★ Live at the Village Vanguard (1961; MCA/Impulse, 1990)
★ ★ ★ ★ Coltrane (1962; MCA/Impulse, 1987)
★ ★ ★ ★½ John Coltrane and Johnny Hartman (Atlantic, 1963)
★ ★ ★ ★ Crescent (1964; MCA/Impulse, 1987)
★ ★ ★ ★ ★ A Love Supreme (1964; MCA/Impulse, 1986)
★ ★ ★ ★ ★ Meditations (1965; MCA, 1990)
★ ★ ★ ★ ★ Ascension (Impulse, 1965)
★ ★ ★ ★ Om (1965; MCA/Impulse, 1987)
★ ★ ★ ★ The Last Trane (1965; Fantasy, 1989)
★ ★ ★ ★ ★ The Best of John Coltrane, His Greatest Years (1961–1966) (1972; MCA/Impulse, 1982)
★ ★ ★ ★ ★ The Best of John Coltrane, His Greatest Years, Vol. 2 (1961–1967) (1972; MCA/Impulse, 1982)
★ ★ ★½ Paris Concert (1979; Pablo, 1987)
★ ★ ★½ The European Tour (1980; Pablo, 1988)
★ ★ ★ ★ ★ The Art of John Coltrane (The Atlantic Years) (1983; Pablo, 1991)
★ ★ ★ ★ ★ The Coltrane Legacy (Atlantic, NA)

A sort of existentialist saint, gentle, enigmatic and plagued throughout his 41 years with piercing inner agony, jazz genius John Coltrane offered up his suffering in music that, at its height, achieves a nearly harrowing power, an exhausting beauty. *A Love Supreme* (1964) is Coltrane at his peak: the saxophonist whose technical prowess freed him to play as many as a thousand notes a minute turns in dazzling variations on a simple four-note theme. Backed by the best of his regular quartets (pianist McCoy Tyner, drummer Elvin Jones, bassist Jimmy Garrison) with help from Archie Shepp on tenor, Coltrane is working the modal style he encountered first as a sideman for Miles Davis; it's the innovator experimenting with "polytonality"—playing in two keys simultaneously. He recorded *Ascension* (1965) with a powerhouse of horn players (Shepp, Pharoah Sanders, John Tchicai, Marion Brown, Freddie Hubbard, Dewey Johnson); the entire record is one long cut of post-Ornette Coleman "free jazz"—the soloists periodically erupt from an intensity of sheer rhythm, then return to passages of free ensemble blowing. Incredibly demanding, these albums are musical abstract expressionism—they offer very little to hold on to except absolute soul power— and they make real the prayer Coltrane wrote for the liner notes of *A Love Supreme*, "ELATION-ELEGANCE-EXALTATION/ All from God."

Achieving these fearsome heights, of course, took time, pain and work. And the early career of John Coltrane was notable for its quality of blazing: a junkie and a compulsive overeater, addicted to, among other things, the Life Savers that rotted his teeth, causing him extreme irritation whenever he played, this was a musician whose aesthetic discipline was equally obsessive—'Trane simply couldn't stop practicing, refining his aggressive tenor and sweeter alto sax work first with Dizzy Gillespie and then Miles Davis. Starting as a hard bop player after the school of Charlie Parker, he perfected in the late '50s (*Giant Steps*, *John Coltrane*, *Lush Life*) a jagged, lightning-fast delivery that came to be termed as "sheets of sound." *Giant Steps*, with its gorgeous ballad playing on "Naima" (named for his first wife), was the saxophonist's breakthrough; while Sonny Rollins continued for a while as a rival instrumentalist, Coltrane emerged as a powerfully individual creator. With its beautiful extended soprano playing on the title cut, *My Favorite Things* brought him a mass audience as well as critical acclaim—it was a following that he would very soon outdistance.

Next came 'Trane's modal work. With alto titan Eric Dolphy beside him on such albums as *Olé* and *Live at the Village Vanguard*, he explored the possibilities of anchoring his solos on a given single scale rather than on chord changes; this is trance music, even if the trance-state it induces is one of a whirling, dizzying variety. Heading toward his mid-'60s summit, Coltrane had evolved into what poet LeRoi Jones termed

"a scope of feeling." If Louis Armstrong's keynote was very human joy, Ellington's a bittersweet nostalgia, Parker's a rush of exhilaration, Coltrane had become a player whose every musical gesture was one of the soul in turmoil—the archetypal seeker, he kept pushing harder, diving deeper. *Meditations*, with its spare and lovely song titles ("The Father and the Son and the Holy Ghost," "Love" "Consequences," "Serenity," "Compassion") and the solid half-hour single piece that makes up *Om* were the music 'Trane made after *A Love Supreme* and *Ascension*.

Again, they're albums of a very difficult grace. And, drawn from the core of the man's hurt, sweet character, they are— like evey note he played—deserving of close attention and great respect.
— P.E.

SHAWN COLVIN
★ ★ ★½ Steady On (Columbia, 1989)
Suzanne Vega and Bruce Hornsby lend a hand, but *Steady On* is very much Colvin's record, and it's a truly accomplished debut. "Shotgun Down the Avalanche," a song about love, despair and release, highlights her gift for poetic imagery; "Something to Believe In" testifies without tears to the human need for faith; "Another Long One" combines psychological acuity and sure melodic sense. Very intelligent modern folk music, these songs are gems—and Colvin's strong, graceful voice lends them careful polish. — P.E.

COMMANDER CODY AND HIS LOST PLANET AIRMEN
★ ★ ★   Lost in the Ozone (Paramount/ MCA, 1971)
★ ★ ★½ Hot Licks, Cold Steel and Trucker's Favorites (Paramount/ MCA, 1972)
★ ★ ★   Country Casanova (Paramount/ MCA, 1973)
★ ★ ★ ★ Live From Deep in the Heart of Texas (Paramount/MCA, 1974)
★ ★   Commander Cody and His Lost Planet Airmen (Warner Bros., 1975)
★   Tales From the Ozone (Warner Bros., 1976)
★ ★   We've Got a Live One Here! (Warner Bros., 1976)
★ ★ ★   Too Much Fun—The Best of Commander Cody (MCA, 1990)
Country rockers tend to take an overly earnest tack, and that's one reason this

inconsequential bar band still sounds so *necessary*. Commander Cody and His Lost Planet Airmen barrel on down that lost highway, ponytails and flannel shirts a-flappin'. These seven space cowboys don't exactly qualify as virtuoso musicians, but they've got an enthusiastic handle on a half-dozen older styles: Texas swing, boogie-woogie piano, honky-tonk heartbreak, rockabilly, jump blues, hell, even truck-driving songs. The first four albums are all recommended: *Ozone* has the breakthrough hit "Hot Rod Lincoln," *Trucker's Favorites* delivers on the promise of its title, *Country Casanova* tightens up and swings hard, while *Live* captures the band at peak intoxicating power. *Too Much Fun* pretty much sums it up. Later efforts are surprisingly bland, and a little bleary-eyed. Commander Cody still turns up on the club circuit, though, pounding those '88s behind a crew of aging Airmen like there's no morning after. — M.C.

COMMODORES
★★★★ Greatest Hits (1978; Motown, 1991)
★★★ In the Pocket (Motown, 1981)
★★★ Nightshift (Motown, 1985)
Formed at the Tuskegee Institute in Alabama, this versatile septet signed to Motown in the early '70s—just as the funk movement began to gather steam. The Commodores brought a graceful southern lilt to its plunking bass lines and sharp horn punctuations. Balancing that party-hearty attack with lead singer Lionel Richie's penchant for soft-soul balladry, the Commodores rode out the '70s on a hot crossover streak. Now out of print, *Caught in the Act* (1975), *Movin' On* (1975), *Hot on the Tracks* (1976), *Commodores* (1977) and *Natural High* (1978) all feature seductive après-disco moods along with the overheated dance-floor attitudes. *Greatest Hits* sums up the group's heyday quite well; it begins with the flawless thumper "Brick House" and ends with the borderline-unctious "Three Times a Lady." In between those extremes come equally funky throwdowns and considerably less cloying love songs. Just compare the Commodores' sweet, soothing "Easy" to one of Lionel Richie's solo bubble baths—if you dare. *In the Pocket* includes Lionel Richie's last one-two punch with the Commodores: the soaring "Lady (You Bring Me Up)" and the schlocky "Oh No." *Nightshift* is the best Commodores album with replacement singer J. D. Nicholas, mostly due to its hit title track: "Night Shift" is a subtly synthesized,

beautifully understated tribute to the late Marvin Gaye. — M.C.

COMMUNARDS
★★½ Communards (MCA, 1986)
★★★½ Red (MCA, 1987)
Formed by pop falsetto Jimmy Somerville after he left Bronski Beat and pursuing a similar musical strategy, the Communards offer essentially only two kinds of song: Either pensive, impassioned love ballads, or buoyant, Hi-NRG remakes of disco classics. That's not to say they play them quite so narrowly as the Bronskis did; on *Communards*, for instance, the slow stuff ranges from the synthesized arabesques of "So Cold the Night" to a heartfelt (though unsuccessful) piano-and-voice remake of the Billie Holiday classic "Lover Man (Oh, Where Can You Be?)." But it's their cover of the Thelma Houston hit "Don't Leave Me This Way" that gives the album its kick.

Red isn't quite as much fun, but that's intentional. The ballads are far more forward in their approach to gay issues, and Somerville's occasionally grating falsetto takes on new warmth as it upends traditional notions of romance in "T.M.T.L.T.B.M.G." (that is, "there's more to love than boy-meets-girl"), asks for understanding in the anti-prejudice lyrics of "Matter of Opinion" and evokes the fear and loneliness of a person with AIDS in "Victims." And though they do include the requisite disco cover—a version of "Never Can Say Goodbye" modeled on the Gloria Gaynor single—it doesn't overshadow the rest of the album. — J.D.C.

ARTHUR CONLEY
★★★ Sweet Soul Music (Atco, 1967)
★★ More Sweet Soul (Atco, 1969)
Conley's "Sweet Soul Music," co-written with Sam Cooke and Otis Redding, was a massive 1967 hit, and it deserved to be. With its snappy horn lines and its role call of great soul stars—Conley sung the praises of James Brown and Wilson Pickett with incredible zest—the song was radio perfection. But despite his talent, and the generous mentoring he received from Redding, Conley never really caught on. His remake of Big Joe Turner's "Shake, Rattle and Roll" was a minor follow-up; he hit the Top Twenty with "Funky Street" (1968) and then Conley faded fast. — P.E.

THE CONNELLS
★★★ Darker Days (TVT, 1987)
★★★½ Boylan Heights (TVT, 1987)

★★★ **Fun and Games (TVT, 1989)**
★★★½ **One Simple Word (TVT, 1990)**
A Raleigh, North Carolina, college-radio
dream team, the Connells craft smart
minor-key pop charged with elusive,
affecting lyrics. Insinuating stuff, their
records recall the infectious introspection of
such Brit bands as Aztec Camera and the
Housemartins as easily as they do
R.E.M.—and the guitar-bass team of
Connell brothers Mike and David is as tight
as their blood bond might suggest. Seldom
does this quintet outright rock, but the
strength of their melodies makes virtually
every song memorable. — P.E.

HARRY CONNICK, JR.
★★★½ **Harry Connick, Jr. (Columbia,
1987)**
★★★ **20 (Columbia, 1988)**
★★★★ **When Harry Met Sally
(Columbia, 1989)**
★★ **We Are In Love (Columbia, 1990)**
★★★½ **Lofty's Roach Souffle (Columbia,
1990)**
★★ **Blue Light, Red Light (Columbia,
1991)**
The Marsalis clan might have paved the way
for jazz's youth movement, but it was
Connick who most blatantly capitalized on
it. *Harry Connick, Jr.*, recorded when the
pianist was just 19, shows tremendous
promise; despite obvious debts to
Thelonious Monk and James Booker,
Connick clearly had a voice of his own
(although, as *Lofty's Roach Souffle* would
later suggest, he hasn't a clue how to
develop it). With *20*, Connick adds a
Sinatra-style croon to his repertoire, but it's
When Harry Met Sally that makes the most
of it, fleshing out his café society piano-and-
vocals act with lush, Gershwinesque
orchestration. Both *We Are in Love* and
Blue Light, Red Light try the same trick but
with Connick writing the tunes; Cole Porter
he ain't. — J.D.C.

THE CONTOURS
★★★ **Do You Love Me? (Motown, 1981)**
Not one of the star groups in the Motown
universe, but an interesting anomaly in that
the quintet had a raw sound more
appropriate to Memphis than to Detroit.
But it was 1962 and Motown productions
hadn't yet become as stylized as they would
become as the decade progressed. So you
get the incendiary "Do You Love Me?," a
Number Three pop hit, and a succession of
all-stops-out dance numbers that achieved
varying degrees of chart success, none

greater than the first hit. "Do You Love
Me?" was also a hit in a cover version by
the Dave Clark Five; another Contours
tune, "First I Look at the Purse," was a
mainstay of the J. Geils Band's live show
for years. In both instances, the original is
still the greatest. — D.M.

TOMMY CONWELL AND THE YOUNG RUMBLERS
★★½ **Rumble (Columbia, 1988)**
★★★½ **Guitar Trouble (Columbia, 1990)**
Tommy Conwell built his reputation playing
the same mid-Atlantic bar circuit that
produced George Thorogood, and like
Thorogood, he has an affection and affinity
for simple, blues-based rock & roll. But
that's not all there is to Conwell's music; he
also wants to transcend that sound, to push
beyond the boundaries of tradition and pull
something larger from the music. The only
question is, how? *Rumble*'s answer—turn
Conwell into a low-budget Springsteen—is
certainly not the answer. There's obviously
pop appeal to material as ebulliently
melodic as "I'm Not Your Man" and
"Walkin' on the Water," but the
arrangements simply weigh the songs down,
rendering them awkward and overstuffed.
Fortunately, *Guitar Trouble* avoids that
trap, keeping the production spare and the
arrangements to the point. As a result, all
the fun of the funky "She's Got It All" or
the boogie-based title tune comes through
unscathed, and the blunt insistence of "I'm
Seventeen," perhaps Conwell's most sharply
drawn song to date, is preserved. With luck,
Conwell may yet reach his potential—not to
mention the mass audience he deserves.
— J.D.C.

RY COODER
★★½ **Ry Cooder (Reprise, 1970)**
★★★ **Into the Purple Valley (Reprise,
1972)**
★★★½ **Boomer's Story (Reprise, 1972)**
★★★ **Paradise and Lunch (Reprise,
1974)**
★★★★ **Chicken Skin Music (Reprise,
1976)**
★★½ **Jazz (Warner Bros., 1978)**
★★½ **Bop Till You Drop (Warner Bros.,
1979)**
★★ **Borderline (Warner Bros., 1980)**
★★★ **The Long Riders (Warner Bros.,
1980)**
★★★½ **The Border (Backstreet, 1981)**
★★ **The Slide Area (Warner Bros.,
1982)**
★★★ **Paris, Texas (Warner Bros., 1984)**

★ ★ ★½ **Alamo Bay (Slash, 1985)**
  ★ ★   **Blue City (Warner Bros., 1986)**
  ★ ★   **Crossroads (Warner Bros., 1986)**
★ ★½ **Get Rhythm (Warner Bros., 1987)**
★ ★ ★½ **Johnny Handsome (Warner Bros., 1989)**

To say that Ry Cooder is an extremely gifted musician is not only an understatement, but misleading as well. Certainly, Cooder has achieved an extraordinary level of technical proficiency in his playing, but what truly makes his music exceptional is the degree of stylistic expertise he has attained. Simply put, Ry Cooder can play damn near anything, from slide guitar to mandolin to banjo, saz or tiple, or any style, be it gospel, folk, blues, calypso, Tex-Mex or Hawaiian slack-key guitar. But if Cooder's ability is unquestionable, his taste is not. Despite credentials that include studio work with Taj Mahal, the Rolling Stones, Captain Beefheart and Eric Clapton, Cooder's own work ranges in quality from the intriguingly experimental to the utterly embarrassing.

Why this is the case isn't entirely clear, but it must have to do with the guitarist's willingness to try anything. That seems to be the undoing of his debut, *Ry Cooder*. Although the album has its moments, including Randy Newman's acrid "Old Kentucky Home" and a delightfully unadorned mandolin version of Sleepy John Estes's "Goin' to Brownsville," it also ends up lumbered with the overwrought arrangements of "One Meatball" and Leadbelly's "Pig Meat." Fortunately, Cooder scales back for *Into the Purple Valley*, and the music improves immensely. Cooder still can't help tinkering with the arrangements, but this time around, the unexpected touches—for instance, the celesta in "Denomination Blues"—work in his favor. But the best moments, like the traditional "Billy the Kid" or his slide-guitar rendition of Woody Guthrie's "Vigilante Man," are generally straightforward, presenting each song with minimal ornamentation.

Both *Boomer's Story* and *Paradise and Lunch* proceed in a similar vein, with minor variations and occasional cameos. Cooder brings in Sleepy John Estes for a version of "President Kennedy" on *Boomer's Story*, although that album's highlight is probably Cooder's slide guitar treatment of "Dark End of the Street." For *Paradise and Lunch*, Earl "Fatha" Hines is on hand to add stride piano flourishes to "Ditty Wah Ditty." But *Chicken Skin Music* takes this guest-star strategy to new levels by bringing in two exceptional and distinctive players: Tex-Mex accordion legend Flaco Jimenez and Hawaiian slack-key guitar whiz Gabby Pahinui. It's marvelous enough when the music is geared to their specialties, but when Cooder changes the context—by using Jimenez for a rendition of Ben E. King's "Stand By Me," say—the results are stunning. Sadly, *Jazz* (1978) doesn't quite meet *Chicken Skin Music*'s standard. Even though it includes tunes by "Jellyroll" Morton and Bix Beiderbecke, *Jazz* isn't a jazz album. Nor does Cooder intend it to be, since he's far more interested in showing parallels between Morton's *habañiera* and the Bahamanian guitar style of Joseph Spence. And it makes for a fascinating lesson, if a tad too pedantic to be truly entertaining.

With *Bop Till You Drop*, Cooder makes a serious wrong turn, applying his rootsy eclecticism to material culled from rock and R&B. It's not a particularly novel approach for him—*Purple Valley*, for instance, included a version of the Drifters' "Money Honey"—but it brings out the worst in his music. *Bop*, at least, is able to balance its excesses with refreshingly rootsy instrumentals like "I Think It's Going to Work Out Fine"; *Borderline*, on the other hand, goes completely off the deep end. "Down in the Boondocks," "634-5789" and "Crazy 'Bout an Automobile (Every Woman I Know)" are songs that barely needed to be remade, much less reinvented as false nostalgia. Cooder downplays that tendency on *The Slide Area*, offering a blues shuffle treatment of "Blue Suede Shoes" but otherwise sticking with more modern material like the Little Feat-ish "I'm Drinking Again" or "UFO Has Landed in the Ghetto." But *Get Rhythm* finds him fiddling with the oldies again, slogging through an overblown boogie makeover of "All Shook Up" and a version of Johnny Cash's "Get Rhythm" done as imitation doo-wop.

Uneven as those albums are, Cooder was still making great music during this period—he just happened to be doing it for movie studios instead of record companies. Cooder was no stranger to soundtrack work, having contributed to both *Performance* and *Candy* before cutting his first solo album, but it wasn't until he provided some Southwestern atmosphere for Walter Hill's *The Long Riders* that his soundtrack career truly got into gear. Ironically, Cooder actually wound up

making better rock records for movies than he did for himself; compare *The Border* to *The Slide Area* or *Get Rhythm*, and it's obvious that the focused demands of film-scoring bring out the best in his playing. *Alamo Bay* is impressively protean, with selections ranging from the sweetly harmonized "Quatro Vicios" (featuring David Hidalgo and Cesar Rosas from Los Lobos) to the punkish "Gooks on Mainstreet," while *Paris, Texas* is eloquently atmospheric, conveying a palpable sense of the town's barren landscape. Neither *Blue City*, which tends to predictable rock & roll, nor *Crossroads*, which is too heavy on overstuffed blues, are terribly impressive, but *Johnny Handsome* gets everything right, from the ominous quiet of the "Main Theme" to the jaunty good mood of "Clip Joint Rhumba."
— J.D.C.

SAM COOKE

★ ★ ★ ★ **The Best of Sam Cooke, Vol. 1 (RCA, 1962)**
★ ★ ★ ★ **The Best of Sam Cooke, Vol. 2 (RCA, 1965)**
★ ★ ★ ★ ★ **The Gospel Soul of Sam Cooke With the Soul Stirrers, Vol. 1 (Specialty, 1969)**
★ ★ ★ ★ **The 2 Sides of Sam Cooke (1970; Specialty, 1984)**
★ ★ ★ ★ ★ **The Gospel Soul of Sam Cooke With the Soul Stirrers, Vol. 2 (Specialty, 1970)**
★ ★ ★ ★ **That's Heaven to Me: Sam Cooke With the Soul Stirrers (Specialty, 1972)**
★ ★ ★ ★ **Sam Cooke Interprets Billie Holiday (RCA, 1975)**
★ ★ ★ ★ **One Night Stand: Sam Cooke Live at the Harlem Square Club, 1963 (RCA, 1985)**
★ ★ ★ **Forever (Specialty, 1986)**
★ ★ ★ ★ ★ **The Man and His Music (RCA, 1986)**
★ ★ ★ ★ ★ **Sam Cooke With the Soul Stirrers (Specialty, 1991)**

Sam Cooke, who emerged from gospel stardom to help create soul music and then bring to it a political dimension inherent in gospel's shouts of struggle, peace and freedom, is one of the towering figures in postwar popular music. A prolific and eloquent songwriter, Cooke left behind important songs in both the gospel and soul fields, standards that continue to be played, sung and recorded. Alone among black artists in a white-dominated industry, Cooke took control of his career on the business side, owning his own record label (Sar/ Derby), music publishing firm (Kags Music), and management company.

But it is the music that has lived on and grown more resonant since Cooke's death under tragic (and, some contend, suspicious) circumstances in 1964, when he was shot to death in a Los Angeles motel by a woman who claimed Cooke had attacked her.

In the gospel world he became the star attraction of the genre's most popular group, the Soul Stirrers, whose venerable lead singer R. H. Harris took the young Cooke under his wing and helped him develop an original style. Young (he was 20 when he joined the Stirrers) and handsome, with an athlete's grace, Cooke's impassioned performances drew hordes of adoring teenage girls to the Soul Stirrers' shows and soon made his name the best-known on the gospel circuit.

Cooke's work in the gospel field is now well-documented on record. The broadest overview is available on the Specialty CD, *Sam Cooke With the Soul Stirrers*, which includes 20 of his finest outings for the Soul Stirrers as well as his first five solo recordings, made when he was still under contract to Specialty and moving into the pop field. From the earliest cut, a tender version of Thomas Dorsey's "Peace in the Valley," from 1951, the Cooke style is in full evidence: the cautious approach to a lyric that quickly evolves into forthright commands or plaintive cries; the superior control of diction, dynamics, nuance, phrasing and drama; the vocal flourishes.

Unlike other CD retrospectives, this Specialty disc doesn't render irrelevant other albums of Soul Stirrers material. *That's Heaven to Me*, *The Two Sides of Sam Cooke*, and the two volumes of *The Gospel Soul of Sam Cooke With the Soul Stirrers* all contain material that won't be found on other releases. (See also *The Soul Stirrers Featuring Sam Cooke* and *The Original Soul Stirrers Featuring Sam Cooke*, compilations that include a few Cooke tracks.) There are observers who feel Cooke was never better than in his gospel days, and indeed, it's hard to argue—"Touch the Hem of His Garment," a Cooke original, is two minutes of perfection, with an interpretation of the old Baptist hymn "Were You There" and James Cleveland's "One More River" falling close behind.

In 1956 Cooke entered the pop world with his recording of "Lovable" (available on *Sam Cooke With the Soul Stirrers*) released under the name Dale Cook so as not to offend the gospel audience. It did offend Specialty owner Art Rupe, however, who released Cooke from his Specialty contract. Cooke and producer Bumps Blackwell took some of the demos they'd been working on at Specialty and signed with the tiny Keen label. The first of these, "You Send Me," had a three-week run atop the pop charts in 1957; from then until 1965 Cooke recorded 28 Top Forty pop hits and 30 Top Forty R&B hits.

At Keen from '57 through mid-1960, Cooke recorded material that was light and upbeat, rooted more in pop than in any form of gospel or R&B. When he signed to RCA in 1960, Cooke reached back to his gospel roots and to blues for inspiration; he built many of these later songs on the base of experience he knew as a black man and spoke nearly as directly to his audience as he had back in the gospel years. There was always room for a bright love song such as "Cupid" or a double-edged dance tune on the order of "Having a Party," but Cooke also covered Willie Dixon's "Little Red Rooster." His first significant record in this vein was "Bring It On Home to Me" (1962), a soulful plea enlivened by an urgent call-and-response section featuring Cooke sparring with his backup vocalist, Lou Rawls, as if he were back in the church. His penultimate moment, the one most keyed to the temper of the times, came after his death, when RCA released "A Change Is Gonna Come," a song whose message resonates with the hope of a new day dawning even as Cooke's world-weary vocal communicates suspicions of a long, hard journey ahead.

RCA's *The Man and His Music* offers the necessary sweeping overview of Cooke's Keen and RCA sides (and includes as well three Specialty tracks, including "Touch the Hem of His Garment"). Specialty's *Forever* includes the pop sides cut for the label before Cooke's departure and some early RCA sides. Two RCA releases complete a broader picture of Cooke. *One Night Stand*, recorded live at the Harlem Square Club in 1963, finds Cooke working the crowd in gritty, get-down fashion in contrast to the urbane singer we know from the studio recordings. *Sam Cooke Interprets Billie Holiday*, on the other hand, connects Cooke to a tradition of jazz singing seemingly far afield from his taste. In fact, he delivers the material with impeccable feel and admirable restraint, adding dimension to his work as he honors the spirit of Holiday's definitive interpretations. — D.M.

LES COOPER
★ ★ "Wiggle Wobble": Golden Classics (Collectables, NA)

More prominent as an arranger and manager (for the Charts, who had one hit, "Desirie,"in 1957), Les Cooper was a one-hit wonder as an artist. His 1962 instrumental "Wiggle Wobble" is otherwise notable for an infectious, strutting bass line that has since been heard too many times to count on other recordings. This album surveys Cooper's other non-golden classics, many of them ill-fated efforts at dance songs. — D.M.

JULIAN COPE
★ ★ ★ World Shut Your Mouth (Mercury U.K., 1983)
★ ★ ½ Fried (Mercury U.K., 1984)
★ ★ ★ ★ Saint Julian (Island, 1987)
★ ★ ★ ½ My Nation Underground (Island, 1988)
★ ★ ★ ½ Peggy Suicide (Island, 1991)

After piloting the Teardrop Explodes through two albums of occasionally brilliant neo-psychedelia, Julian Cope abruptly broke camp and, with Teardrop drummer Gary Dwyer, recorded *World Shut Your Mouth*. Yet though Cope's melodic instincts are generally sure, the album's exquisite sense of sonic detail is undercut by Cope's occasional self-indulgence and often impenetrable wordplay ("Kolly Kibber's Birthday"? "Metranil Vavin"?). *Fried* is even more bizarre, as Cope steamrollers down a variety of musical culs de sac. But rather than go completely over the top, Cope goes in the opposite direction on the masterful *Saint Julian*. Extravagant as the arrangements sometimes are, there's no denying Cope's songcraft, and that makes the album unexpectedly pop-friendly. From the triumphant powerchords driving the chorus to "World Shut Your Mouth" to the insinuating melodic line within "Eve's Volcano," Cope's unwavering tunefulness is nearly irresistible. *My Nation Underground* isn't quite as effervescent, but its best songs—"5 O'Clock World," "Charlotte Anne"—are winning. With *Peggy Suicide*, however, Cope outdoes himself, turning in a double-length album that is at once stunningly ambitious and hopelessly silly. Although the music is eloquent, Cope's convoluted, crackpot lyrics are better left unheard. — J.D.C.

CHICK COREA
★ ★ ★ ★ ★ Now He Sings, Now He Sobs (1968; Blue Note, 1988)

★ ★ ★ ★½ The Song of Singing (1970; Blue Note, 1985)
★ ★ ★ ★ ★ Piano Improvisations, Vol. 1 (1971; ECM, 1987)
★ ★ ★ ★ ★ Piano Improvisations, Vol. 2 (1972; ECM, 1987)
★ ★ ★ ★ Inner Space (1974; Atlantic, 1988)
★ ★ ★ ★½ Chick Corea (Blue Note, 1975)
★ ★ ★ ★ My Spanish Heart (Polydor, 1977)
★ ★½ Friends (1978; Polydor, 1991)
★ ★ ★½ Delphi 1 (Polydor, 1979)
★ ★ ★½ Chick Corea and Gary Burton: In Concert, Zurich, October 28, 1979 (1980; ECM, 1987)
★ ★ ★ ★ ★ Trio Music (ECM, 1982)
★ ★ ★½ Again and Again (Elektra/Musician, 1983)
★ ★ ★ ★ Children's Songs (ECM, 1984)
★ ★ ★ ★ Chick Corea and Steve Kujala Voyage (ECM, 1985)
★ ★ ★ ★ ★ Works (ECM, 1985)
★ ★ ★ ★½ Trio Music, Live in Europe (ECM, 1986)
★ ★ ★½ Early Days (Denon, 1986)
WITH RETURN TO FOREVER
★ ★ ★ ★½ Return to Forever (1972; ECM, 1988)
★ ★ ★ ★ Light as a Feather (Polydor, 1972)
★ ★ ★ ★ ★ Hymn of the Seventh Galaxy (1972; Polydor, 1991)
★ ★ ★ Where Have I Known You Before (Polydor, 1974)
★ ★ No Mystery (Polydor, 1975)
★ ★ ★½ The Leprechaun (Polydor, 1976)
★ ★ ★ Romantic Warrior (1976; Columbia, 1990)
★ ★ ★ ★ The Best of Return to Forever (Columbia, 1980)
WITH THE AKOUSTIC BAND
★ ★ ★ Chick Corea Akoustic Band (GRP, 1989)
★ ★ ★ Akoustic Band: Alive (GRP, 1991)
WITH THE ELEKTRIC BAND
★ ★ ★ The Chick Corea Elektric Band (GRP, 1986)
★ ★ Light Years (GRP, 1987)
★ ★ ★ Eye of the Beholder (GRP, 1988)
★ ★ ★ Inside Out (GRP, 1990)
★ ★ Beneath the Mask (GRP, 1991)

Following the 1970 release of Miles Davis's *Bitches Brew*, jazz-rock fusion exploded—very often with hapless results. But among its stronger proponents (players who sacrificed neither the inventiveness of jazz nor the straight-out wham of rock) during the form's '70s heyday were the Mahavishnu Orchestra, Weather Report, Soft Machine, Herbie Hancock—and Chick Corea's Return to Forever. A keyboard prodigy, Corea began with Mongo Santamaria and Herbie Mann, playing Latin-inflected jazz on acoustic piano before recording a breakthrough 1968 set: *Now He Sings, Now He Sobs*. With Miroslav Vitous on bass and Roy Haynes on drums, *Sings* was dazzling. He then took up with bassist Dave Holland and Barry Altschul for music of a more cerebral turn (*The Song of Singing*), before adding avant-garde saxophonist Anthony Braxton to the lineup (becoming known as Circle, the group released trail-blazing work in the late '60s, such as *Circle Paris* and *Circulus*, none of which is now in print). At the start of the '70s, Corea recorded two volumes of solo *Piano Improvisations*: lovely albums, they stand as his classics.

Return to Forever saw Corea, fresh from a tenure with Miles, unleashing his skills on electric keyboards (Fender Rhodes, Mini-Moog, etc.). With its primary personnel consisting of drummer Lenny White, bassist Stanley Clarke and guitarist Bill Connors (later, Al DiMeola), the group was a monster. *Hymn of the Seventh Galaxy* is fusion as it was intended to be, polytechnical but exuberant—and while their breezier work (usually with Brazilian vocalist Flora Purim) hasn't remained as enjoyable as the scorching stuff, *Return to Forever* and *Light as a Feather* were pathfinding examples of the new hybrid.

In the late '70s and early '80s, Corea's group sets alternated between expert fluff (*Friends*) and significant excitement (*My Spanish Heart*); his solo piano *Delphi 1*, while featuring a nice side of tributes to Art Tatum, hadn't quite the freshness of the *Piano Improvisations*. He came back strong, however, with *Trio Music* and its in-concert counterpart, *Trio Music, Live in Europe*; reunited with Vitous and Haynes, he again swung with a powerful grace, and solidified his relationship with ECM Records, the label that released his best '80s music.

More recently, the keyboardist, recording with frenzy, has come up with two outfits, the Elektric Band and the Akoustic Band, that divide his time and reveal both his strengths and weaknesses. The Elektric stuff is corny compared to RTF at its toughest; the Akoustic fare is more kopacetic. — P.E.

ELVIS COSTELLO

★ ★ ★ ★ ★ My Aim Is True (Columbia, 1977)
★ ★ ★ ★ ★ This Year's Model (Columbia, 1978)

★★★★ Armed Forces (Columbia, 1979)
★★★★ Get Happy!! (Columbia, 1980)
★★★ Taking Liberties (Columbia, 1980)
★★★½ Trust (Columbia, 1981)
★★ Almost Blue (Columbia, 1981)
★★★½ Imperial Bedroom (Columbia, 1982)
★★★½ Punch the Clock (Columbia, 1983)
★★★ Goodbye Cruel World (Columbia, 1984)
★★★½ The Best of Elvis Costello and the Attractions (Columbia, 1985)
★★★ King of America (CBS, 1986)
★★★ Blood & Chocolate (CBS, 1986)
★★½ Spike (Warner Bros., 1989)
★★★ Girls Girls Girls (Columbia, 1990)
★★½ Mighty Like a Rose (Warner Bros., 1991)

Just as rumors of British punk rock began to hurtle across the sea, *My Aim Is True* found its mark in America. Lumped in with the torn T-shirt crowd because of his angry bent, Elvis Costello's subsequent career proves he's a classic singer-songwriter. On his first four albums, Costello upends the intimate '70s confessional mode by re-emphasizing raw musical impact. His voice emerges fully formed on the debut. Perhaps the most versatile and adept of rock's many literate non-singers, Costello employs a wide range of peculiar inflections and punning emphases. His tricky adenoidal ploys twist and turn the lyrics, which are driven by tight writing and clear melodies. Underneath the churning, impatient veneer lurks a fan-turned-musician with a startling command of roots.

Recorded with the San Francisco bar band Clover, *My Aim Is True* establishes Costello's great themes: media omniscience ("Watching the Detectives"), political and emotional fascism ("Less Than Zero"), unrequited and/or misunderstood love ("Alison"). *This Year's Model* introduces the Attractions. Pumping piston-beats underline Costello's raging insight; versatile keyboardist Steve Nieve applies bold, primary colors, smoothing out Costello's raggedy edges without softening the overall effect. "Radio Radio" isn't merely the tuneful outcry of a professionally alienated rebel: "anesthetized" described the pop landscape pretty well. As an antidote, *This Year's Model* retains full potency. Producer Nick Lowe sweetens the sound of *Armed Forces*, though Costello's politicized bent is loudly pronounced on "Accidents Will Happen" and "Oliver's Army." They're the catchiest songs on a hook-laden pop album—next to Lowe's guileless ("What's So Funny 'Bout) Peace Love and

Understanding," of course. *Get Happy!!* captures the tumbling, catch-us-if-you-can energy of punk: not every one of the 20 short tracks is perfect—the Stax-Volt influence doesn't completely wash—but it's hard not to get swept up by the whirlwind. Heartbreak songs like "Motel Matches" signal a confident country influence, though *Get Happy!!*'s eclecticism barely hints at the direction Elvis Costello would take in the next decade. *Taking Liberties* collects some of his prolific early period's B sides and outtakes, most notably "Girls Talk" and "Stranger in the House." *Trust* attempts a return to the sound of *Armed Forces*, but this time the Attractions lag behind Elvis's verbal sprints and guilt marathons. Unfortunately, that sets the pattern for future albums.

From this point on, following Elvis Costello requires work. Badly mangling an album of country standards (*Almost Blue*), Costello continues to draw on Nashville and Tin Pan Alley sources with wildly mixed results. The problem lies in his vocal limitations; Costello writes songs that he's physically incapable of singing. *Imperial Bedroom* finesses this lapse with rich production, highlighting some of Costello's most telling meditations on love with consistent, subtle musical detailing. Producers Clive Langer and Alan Winstanley favor a sort of rococco pop, and both *Punch the Clock* and *Goodbye Cruel World* are burdened by clutter. But the former contains several of Costello's very best performances ("Everyday I Write the Book," "Shipbuilding"), while the latter boasts a few worthy, overlooked ones ("Peace in Our Time").

Considered by some to be Costello's vindication as a roots rocker, *King of America* also can be heard as a bloated, overreaching mess. Dropping the Attractions in favor of accomplished L.A. studio pros, Elvis lards his country-rock groove with top-heavy metaphors and leaden irony. Despite the Attractions' return, *Blood & Chocolate* sounds just about as congruent as its title. True believers achieve spiritual release in the vitriol of "I Want You." Old fans may find it oppressive, and most ordinary listeners understandably couldn't be bothered.

Spike represents a further widening of Costello's musical scope—Mardi Gras parades, collaboration with Paul McCartney, nods to Broadway and Memphis—and reveals a loss of focus. *Spike* recalls the sort of genteel pop indulgence that led to punk in the first place. *Girls,*

Girls, Girls jumbles Costello's '70s classics and '80s adventures into a big ball of angst. What should be an utter mess turns out to be an appropriately twisted summation of his restless career. *Mighty Like a Rose* recaps a couple of vintage riffs and seems like a pleasing comeback effort at first. Eventually, its surfeit of tuneless, over-arranged mid-tempo numbers releases a troubling air of decay. Elvis rasps and crows his way through "All Grown Up," and the chorus is painful to hear: "But look at yourself/You'll see you're still so young/You haven't earned the weariness/That sounds so jaded upon your tongue." Physician, heal thyself. — M.C.

COUNTRY JOE AND THE FISH

★ ★ **Electric Music for the Mind and Body (Vanguard, 1967)**
★ ★ ★ **I-Feel-Like-I'm-Fixin'-To-Die (Vanguard, 1967)**
★ **Together (Vanguard, 1968)**
★ **Here We Go Again (Vanguard, 1969)**
★ ★ **The Best of Country Joe and the Fish (Vanguard, 1979)**
★ **C.J. Fish (Vanguard, 1970)**
★ ★ **Life and Times of Country Joe and the Fish (Vanguard, 1971)**
★ **Reunion (Fantasy, 1977)**
★ ★ ★½ **The Collected Country Joe and the Fish (Vanguard, 1987)**

The political significance of this happy Haight-Ashbury crew is undeniable. Sixties agitators of the prankster variety, they aimed blows against the empire by developing a famous F-U-C-K cheer (gimme an "F") to be bellowed at demonstrations and concerts, they starred at Woodstock—they summed up hippie rebellion. Named after Joseph Stalin, Country Joe was to the leftist manner born, and he continued his politicking throughout his career: touring with Jane Fonda in a revue called FTA (Fuck The Army) and, later, fighting to save the whales.

But the music the Fish made now demands the indulgence of nostalgia. Guitarist Barry Melton is a feverish, bluesy player, and Country Joe a zesty, if not good, singer, but the band's songs are loose, jamming statements, and the haphazard mixture of styles—folk, rock, jug band—that may once have seemed eclectic now comes off as confused. *Electric Music* offers the mild tunefulness of "Not So Sweet Martha Lorraine." Their second album features the famous anti-Vietnam ditty, "I Feel Like I'm Fixin' to Die," and *Together* has, in "Rock and Soul Music," their only rave-up. The *Collected Country Joe* is a fine overview—its notes offer intelligent perspective, its song selection is thorough, and it's hard to imagine that listeners would now need the rest of the Fish catalogue. — P.E.

COWBOY JUNKIES

★ ★ ★ **Whites Off Earth Now (1986; RCA, 1990)**
★ ★ ★ ★ **The Trinity Session (RCA, 1988)**
★ ★ ★½ **The Caution Horses (RCA, 1990)**
★ ★ ★ ★ **Black-Eyed Man (RCA, 1992)**

Any band that gets the psychic connection of the Velvet Underground to Patsy Cline to Hank Williams is an extraordinarily knowing one—and *The Trinity Session* (1988) proved the Cowboy Junkies to be exactly that. A remarkable live set, it joins "Sweet Jane," "Walking After Midnight" and "I'm So Lonesome I Could Cry" to traditional folk and riveting Junkies orginals. A family affair, siblings Michael, Peter and Margo Timmins come off as faithful hipsters—their songs drenched in a smoke of late-night regret, stoic soulfulness and a few fond memories.

Brighter, more open, but no less fine, *The Caution Horses* finds Michael crafting elegant, stark songs for his sister—"Cause Cheap is How I Feel" and "Sun Comes Up, It's Tuesday Morning" are filled with the colloquial heartbreak only country writers generally master. Neil Young's great "Powderfinger" is one smart cover, and "You Will Be Loved Again" by the Cowboys' Canadian compatriot Mary Margaret O'Hara is naked soul. With fiddle and pedal steel played wholly without cutes or condescension, this is prime, late-model American folk music. *Whites Off Earth Now* (the band's 1986 debut, reissued in 1990) tackles some of the most demanding blues around—Robert Johnson, Bukka White, Lightnin' Hopkins. Again, the Junkies pull it off. *Black-Eyed Man* is the best since *Trinity Session*; the standout track is Margo's duet with John Prine on "If You Were the Woman, and I Was the Man." — P.E.

THE COWSILLS

★ ★½ **The Best of the Cowsills (1969; Polydor, 1988)**

Four brothers, plus Mom and Sis, the Cowsills—the inspiration for the Partridge Family TV show—were a tuneful family harmony group in the mid-'60s. "The Rain, the Park and Other Things," "We Can Fly" and a version of "Hair" were their hits.

They called themselves "America's First Family of Song," and though they weren't by any means rock & rollers, they wrote and played their own songs, in addition to well-chosen covers. In 1990 they regrouped (Bob, Paul, John and Susan Cowsill), and as of this writing were performing again on the West Coast club scene. — P.E.

FLOYD CRAMER

★ ★ **The Best of Floyd Cramer (1964; RCA, 1987)**
★ **Collector's Series (1974; RCA, 1988)**
★ **Piano Masterpieces, 1900–1975 (1975; RCA, 1990)**
★ **Great Country Hits (RCA, 1981)**

A session pianist whose work has graced hundreds of country and pop albums recorded in Nashville over the past three decades plus, Floyd Cramer had a national pop hit in 1960 with the instrumental "Last Date." Cramer attacks his repertoire straight-on, with little or no point of view. "Last Date" is the exception to this rule, its lonesome melody and crying strings speaking volumes about a romance's end. In 1961 Cramer had two more Top Ten singles, "On the Rebound" and "San Antonio Rose." The more you listen to his solo work, though, the more ordinary he sounds. Of Cramer's in-print albums, *The Best of Floyd Cramer* contains the original recordings of his hits; *Collector's Series* contains a "live" version of "Last Date" (the applause sounds grafted on) that's tepid compared to the original. For all the grandiosity of its title, *Piano Masterpieces, 1900–1975* contains only ten tracks, hardly a representative sampling. *Great Country Hits* is a snoozeathon. — D.M.

THE CRAMPS

★ ★ ★½ **Gravest Hits (EP) (Illegal, 1979)**
★ ★ ★½ **Songs the Lord Taught Us (I.R.S., 1980)**
★ ★½ **Psychedelic Jungle (IRS, 1981)**
★ ★½ **Smell of Female (Enigma, 1983)**
★ ★ ★ ★ **Bad Music for Bad People (IRS, 1984)**
★ ★ ★ **A Date With Elvis (1986; Enigma, 1990)**
★ ★½ **Stay Sick! (Enigma, 1990)**
★ ★ ★½ **Look Mom No Head! (Restless, 1991)**

Holding forth at the intersection between rockabilly raunch and sick psychedelia, the Cramps are the incarnation of early rock's sleaziest impulses. Their first release, *Gravest Hits* (which has since been combined on CD with *Psychedelic Jungle*), contrasts the itchy anxiety of "Human Fly" against an earnest cover of the Trashmen classic "Surfin' Bird." A similar dichotomy can be found on *Songs the Lord Taught Us*, on which Lux Interior's Gene Vincent–meets–Fred Schneider delivery generates maximum friction against the brittle edges of the band's punkabilly instrumental attack. (*Bad Music for Bad People* combines the best of *Songs the Lord Taught Us* with highlights from *Gravest Hits* and *Psychedelic Jungle*). Sadly, neither the low-key *Psychedelic Jungle* nor the live *Smell of Female* are able to match that edgy chemistry, but the unrepentant sexism of *A Date With Elvis* almost makes up the difference; after all, where else are you likely to hear songs as tastelessly titled as "The Hot Pearl Snatch" or "Can Your Pussy Do the Dog?" *Stay Sick!* adds a few kinks to the Cramps' lyrics (e.g. "Journey to the Center of a Girl"), but musically, the group seems pretty well stagnated, as the album's only original move is the rheumy cover of "Muleskinner Blues." But *Look Mom No Head!* not only picks up the tempo on most tunes, but brings in Iggy Pop for the thoroughly demented "Miniskirt Blues," then one-ups it with the single-entendre rocker "Bend Over, I'll Drive." — J.D.C.

ROBERT CRAY BAND

★ ★ ★ **Who's Been Talking (1980; Tomato, 1988)**
★ ★ ★ ★ **Bad Influence (High Tone, 1983)**
★ ★ ★ **False Accusations (High Tone, 1985)**
★ ★ ★ **Strong Persuader (Mercury, 1986)**
★ ★ ★ **Don't Be Afraid of the Dark (Mercury, 1988)**
★ ★ ★ ★ **Midnight Stroll (Mercury, 1990)**
WITH ALBERT COLLINS AND JOHNNY COPELAND
★ ★ ★ ★ **Showdown! (Alligator, 1985)**

Now nearing 40, Robert Cray, along with Stevie Ray Vaughan, spearheaded a group of young artists who came of age in the '80s and were determined to prove blues a viable force. That both succeeded in grand style says as much about the compelling honesty of blues itself as it does about the integrity of these new artists' music. Beginning with his little-known Tomato debut, and kicking in mightily on his first High Tone LP, *Bad Influence*, Cray has propagated a form of blues that finds its basis in southern soul music and hard-edged Texas blues. Memphis predominates, though, and the point is emphasized on the Mercury albums, on which the Cray quartet is augmented by the robust Memphis Horns.

Apart from their acknowledged

instrumental prowess, Cray and Vaughan separate themselves from the pack with their songwriting. Cray's own songs, and those by other writers he covers, disdain the stereotypical bluesman's pose of being forever put-upon by conniving women. His blues stem from harsh assessments of his own fallibility. Cray brings it all home with stinging Stratocaster lead lines underpinning his smooth-but-plaintive vocal style.

Cray's albums are all satisfying. The High Tone recordings are stripped-down, basic band affairs in comparison to the Mercury albums, when the Memphis Horns come aboard and add dimension to the blues attack. Of note to blues guitar enthusiasts is the Alligator *Showdown!* summit teaming Cray with Albert Collins ("The Master of the Telecaster") and Johnny Copeland ("The Texas Twister"). On one cut, "T-Bone Shuffle," each wizard takes a vocal and guitar solo, and when they've finished their thundering, they have reclaimed the past and put the present in new perspective. Cray fans can't afford to miss this one.
— D.M.

THE CRAZY WORLD OF ARTHUR BROWN
★ The Crazy World of Arthur Brown (1968; Polydor, 1991)

Basically a rock footnote, ex-philosophy student Arthur Brown anticipated Alice Cooper in his use of mondo bizarro stage-gear (a flaming helmet) and earned a 1968 flash of notoriety with one single, "Fire." Heavy with organ, sound effects, and theatrical "I-am-Lucifer" vocalizing, the song was a curio. English eccentricity at its most daft. — P.E.

CREAM
★★★ Fresh Cream (Polydor, 1966)
★★★½ Disraeli Gears (Polydor, 1967)
★★★★ Wheels of Fire (Polydor, 1968)
★★★ Goodbye Cream (Polydor, 1969)
★★ Live (Polydor, 1970)
★★ Live, Volume 2 (Polydor, 1972)
★★★★½ Strange Brew: The Very Best of Cream (Polydor, 1983)

From a historical standpoint, it's nearly impossible to exaggerate the importance of Cream. This was rock's first power trio, its first significant psychedelic blues band, and the first to make a fetish of instrumental virtuosity. Its success catapulted Eric Clapton, Jack Bruce and Ginger Baker to superstardom, and inspired several generations of hard-rock heroes, from Grand Funk to Van Halen. More than two

decades after the trio called it quits, Cream remains a staple of AOR radio. For all that, it's also quite easy to overestimate the value of Cream's recorded output. Sure, the group cut some astonishing singles—"Badge," "Sunshine of Your Love," "White Room"—but it also made some incredibly misdirected and embarrassing live albums. It was almost as if Cream existed with two distinct identities, one a pithy singles act, and the other a self-indulgent jam band.

Although neither side completely emerges on *Fresh Cream*, it's easy enough to see the shape of things to come. "I Feel Free" and "I'm So Glad" were slick and tuneful, handily showing off the group's ability to pull pop from the blues, while "Toad" and "Rollin' and Tumblin' " bore witness to the trio's propensity for showboating. Things on the pop side tightened up considerably when producer Felix Pappalardi came aboard; not only did he dress up *Disraeli Gears* with odd instruments and exotic sounds, but he kept the band's instrumental interplay in check, so that even a song as seemingly heavy as "Sunshine of Your Love" came across as singles fodder.

Wheels of Fire brought further refinements in Pappalardi's pop eclecticism. It added such exotic sounds as cello, marimba and tonette, extended Pappalardi's studio role from producer to player, and offered the first recorded example of Cream's concert approach; from the focused fury of "White Room" to the rambling, 16-minute version of "Toad," it remains the most representative slice of the Cream legacy. Sadly, things went downhill soon after, and *Goodbye*, recorded in the band's death throes, balances some of the band's most exquisite studio work ("Badge," in particular) with so-so concert recordings; it barely seems a complete album. *Strange Brew* is essentially a singles compilation and holds up well to repeated listenings, but the two volumes of *Live Cream* are muddled leftovers released solely to cash in on the band's enduring popularity. — J.D.C.

CREEDENCE CLEARWATER REVIVAL
★★★★ Creedence Clearwater Revival (Fantasy, 1968)
★★★★ Bayou Country (Fantasy, 1969)
★★★★★ Green River (Fantasy, 1969)
★★★★★ Willy and the Poor Boys (Fantasy, 1969)
★★★★ Cosmo's Factory (Fantasy, 1970)
★★★★ Pendulum (Fantasy, 1970)
★★★ Mardi Gras (Fantasy, 1972)
★★★★ Creedence Gold (Fantasy, 1972)

★ ★ Live in Europe (Fantasy, 1973)
★ ★ ★ More Creedence Gold (Fantasy, 1973)
★ ★ ★ ★ ★ Chronicle (Fantasy, 1976)
★ ★ ★ ★ ★ Creedence 1969 (Fantasy, 1978)
★ ★ ★ ★ ★ Creedence 1970 (Fantasy, 1978)
★ ★ ★ ★ Royal Albert Hall Concert (Fantasy, 1981)
★ ★ ★ Creedence Country (Fantasy, 1981)

The artful product of John Fogerty's desperate romance with a mythic American South, Northern California's CCR demonstrated, the way Zeppelin did with the blues, the triumph of imagination over literalism—America's best basic rock band, theirs was the victory of a true believer's fantasy. While Creedence came of age during flower power, nothing remotely psychedelic infected them. Instead, Fogerty delved back into Sun Records and swamp-thick bayou mystery to fetch up fresh boogie that kicked like a heavier rockabilly or a tuneful funk—the first singles off their self-titled debut were Dale Hawkins's "Suzie Q." and a Screamin' Jay Hawkins tune. No dusty archivist, Fogerty was faithful to the spirit, not the law, of his roots sources. Soon he was writing music as "commercial" as early rock & roll: hard, hooky songs, which during the band's short glory days (1969–70), made their six albums masterworks—and made the radio a wonderland.

From *Bayou Country* came "Proud Mary," the group's biggest hit. *Green River* served up "Lodi," the definitive journeyman rocker's anthem, and the darkly oracular "Bad Moon Rising." *Willy and the Poor Boys* was CCR's best—a kind of anti-*Sgt. Pepper's,* its only concept being the band's poetic redneck myth, and its emphasis wholly on singles rather than suites. "Fortunate Son" and "Don't Look Now (It Ain't You or Me)" was the most convincing political rock & roll done before the Clash; "Down on the Corner" and "Cotton Fields" celebrated both the town and country of Fogerty's dream Dixie.

At its time (1970), *Pendulum* seemed weaker. Maybe—but any record that encompasses the nearly punk starkness of "Molina" and the gorgeous yearning of "Have You Ever Seen the Rain" is none too shabby. *Cosmo's Factory* rocked hard with the slide guitar workout "Up Around the Bend" and produced "Who'll Stop the Rain"—in its deep, simple language and epic questioning, the latter had the condensed power of a parable. Creedence's

players, drummer Doug "Cosmo" Clifford, bassist Stu Cook and, until *Mardi Gras,* John's brother, Tom, on second guitar, were straightforwardly effective, but it was basically John's songs, guitar and singing that made the band. Like Joe Cocker's, Fogerty's voice was an amazing creation—a hoarse soulful thing that, borrowing from great past belters, insistently sacrificed intelligibility to emotion, and caution to sheer, hoarse expressiveness. — P.E.

MARSHALL CRENSHAW

★ ★ ★ Marshall Crenshaw (Warner Bros., 1982)
★ ★ ★ Field Day (Warner Bros., 1983)
★ ★ ★ Downtown (Warner Bros., 1985)
★ ★ ★ Good Evening (Warner Bros., 1989)
★ ★ ★ Life's Too Short (Paradox/MCA, 1991)

Marshall Crenshaw's albums all contain catchy, well-constructed, melodic tunes. *Good Evening* and *Life's Too Short* show stronger melodies and sharper lyrics than the earlier material—but still sound derivative. Though Crenshaw is a master of rock song forms, his music is unremarkable in terms of attitude. — D.M.

THE CRESTS

★ ★ ★ The Crests (Collectables, NA)
★ ★ ★ ★ Best of the Crests (Rhino, 1990)

An anomaly of sorts in their day, a multiracial group in an era when this was a rarity, the Crests cut five genuinely inspired hit singles that have retained all their luster over the years. This is due in part to the exhilarating backup work of J. T. Carter, Harold Torres and Talmadge Gough, whose doo-wop harmonies betray the trio's deep roots in and familiarity with gospel music. Over this soared one of the most distinctive tenors of the day, Johnny Maestro, whose fascination with great R&B singers taught him something about the perfectly modulated performance. Both of these collections showcase the group's best-known recordings—"16 Candles," "Six Nights a Week," "Trouble in Paradise," "Step by Step" and "The Angels Listened In"—as well as obscure but no less impressive Crests recordings such as "Young Love" and "I Thank the Moon." The story really is Maestro's voice, as pure and plaintive an instrument as ever emerged from the group harmony scene. Of the two collections, the Rhino package is highly recommended, owing to the detailed liner notes and sessionography by Bob Hyde. — D.M.

THE CRICKETS
½ ★ **The Liberty Years (EMI, 1991)**
After leaving Buddy Holly in 1958, the Crickets continued recording on their own with little success in the States, although they had three hit singles in England in the early '60s. This is one time when our English brethren were wrong: they have been staunch in their support of rock & roll pioneers, but what they found in the Crickets is a mystery as yet unsolved. On their own the Crickets had nothing to say. *The Liberty Years* is one of the least essential retrospectives ever released.
— D.M.

JIM CROCE
★ ★ ★½ **Photographs and Memories: His Greatest Hits (21 Records/Atlantic, 1974)**
★ ★ ★ **Time in a Bottle: Jim Croce's Greatest Love Songs (21 Records/Atlantic, 1977)**
Compared to the more sensitive singer-songwriters of his time, Jim Croce possessed an appealing, humorous edge. The goony word-slinging swagger of "You Don't Mess Around With Jim" (1972) and "Bad, Bad Leroy Brown" ('73) offered a welcome respite from Cat Stevens–style cosmic FM mewling, and Croce's firm sense of melody fit him right into the AM Top Forty, too. He followed up "You Don't Mess Around With Jim" with a bittersweet, folky ballad called "Operator"; here Croce zeroes in on the lonely detail of a telephone booth with the accuracy of a country tunesmith. "Time in a Bottle" floats along on an even prettier chorus, but the lyrics drift toward sentimentality and nostalgia. If that trend is solidified with the blustery "I Got a Name" and the unctuous "I'll Have to Say I Love You in a Song," well, so was Croce's popularity. His death in a 1973 plane accident rendered those last two hits—and most of his acclaim—a largely posthumous phenomenon, however. *Photographs and Memories* collects the sharpest snapshots from his three out-of-print albums; *Time in a Bottle* sure could stand a boisterous story-song or two. — M.C.

DAVID CROSBY
★ ★½ **If I Could Only Remember My Name (Atlantic, 1971)**
★ ★½ **Oh Yes I Can (A&M, 1989)**
Neil Young, Jerry Garcia, Grace Slick, Joni Mitchell and half, it seems, of the population of California sit in on *If I Could Only Remember My Name*—but it still

sounds like nothing but ex-Byrd, CSN stalwart, David Crosby. That is, the overlong tunes meander; the vocals are gorgeous; an overabundance of songs ("What Are Their Names," "I'd Swear There Was Somebody Here," "Song With No Words [Tree With No Leaves]") are meditations on bewilderment. This is boring music, performed with infuriating craft. Crosby can set a mood—but it's always the same one: woozy, waterlogged, uncertain. The 1989 album was released after Crosby's much-publicized bout with drug addiction, but it doesn't mark much of an improvement musically. — P.E.

DAVID CROSBY AND GRAHAM NASH
★ ★½ **Crosby and Nash (Atlantic, 1972)**
★ ★ ★ **Wind on the Water (ABC, 1975)**
★ ★ **Whistling Down the Wire (ABC, 1976)**
★ ★ **Live (ABC, 1977)**
★ ★ ★ **Best of Crosby and Nash (MCA, 1978)**
Even if they're the less intellectually interesting half of Crosby, Stills, Nash and Young, they still manage great, effortless harmonies and distinctive sonic delights. Crosby's free-form writing style is interesting in its avoidance of verse-chorus-verse structure; a typical Crosby song drifts and swirls, and there's spacey pleasure to be found in "Carry Me" and "Bittersweet" (both from *Wind on the Water*). Nash works often with minor keys and heavy rhythms; "Love Work Out" (from *Wind*) is characteristic, but the sprightly "Southbound Train" (off *Crosby and Nash*) is his best song.
Wind is their only record that holds up consistently; *Whistling Down the Wire* suffers from saccharine orchestral arrangements; *Live* isn't very exciting; *Best of Crosby and Nash* concentrates on recycling *Wind*. — P.E.

CROSBY, STILLS AND NASH
★ ★ ★ ★ **Crosby, Stills and Nash (Atlantic, 1969)**
★ ★ ★ **CSN (Atlantic, 1977)**
★ ★ ★ **Replay (Atlantic, 1980)**
★ ★ **Daylight Again (Atlantic, 1982)**
★ **Live It Up (Atlantic, 1990)**
★ ★ ★ ★ **CSN (Atlantic, 1991)**
While dominated instrumentally by Stephen Stills, founder of the pioneering folk rockers Buffalo Springfield, CSN's impressive debut album reflected three distinct sensibilities. Enraptured at the time with Judy Collins, Stills led with "Suite: Judy Blue Eyes"—the

seven-minute mini-epic conveyed his easy mastery of a number of styles (folk ballad, light rock, Latin-inflected rhythm), highlighted his sharp guitar work and introduced the soaring ensemble harmonies that would become the group's trademark. Nash's slight but charming "Marrakesh Express" extended from the fluid pop he'd perfected with the Hollies. Ex-Byrd David Crosby turned in the loosely structured ballad "Guinevere"—all drifty atmosphere and wide-eyed poetry, it exemplified his hippie mysticism. Of as much sociological as musical interest, the album exactly captured the spirit of the last high moment of the American '60s. Exhausted by Vietnam, embarked upon mind expansion and lifestyle rebellion, the CSN generation found in the band both spokesmen and representatives— the singers' slightly weary utopianism, their bucolic fantasies and their songs about love and its losses reflected the inward turning of an aging youth culture, the movement away from public struggle to self-examination.

By the time of *CSN*, the moment that lent intensity and credibility to the trio's songs had passed—and their music had become nice, bland and comfortable. Perhaps unsurprisingly, Nash's simple popcraft produced the most dependable of *CSN*'s mild pleasures. *Daylight Again* was no great shakes, either, even if Crosby's voice sounded stronger than his years of highly publicized hard living might suggest. "Might As Well Have a Good Time" underscored the album's air of drastically lowered expectations—and the song wasn't even an original. *Live It Up* was an embarrassment—over-reliant on outside writers for inspiration, the group sounded tired and confused—and a techno-happy production, full of synthesizer rhythm tracks, didn't help.

Replay is a compilation of material from the debut and the singers' solo projects. With 25 of its 77 selections being alternate takes or previously unreleased rarities, the *CSN* boxed set not only documents the group's history thoroughly but it unearths quite a few pleasant surprises. — P.E.

CROSBY, STILLS, NASH AND YOUNG
★★★★ Déjà Vu (Atlantic, 1970)
★★½ 4 Way Street (Atlantic, 1971)
★★★ So Far (Atlantic, 1974)
★★★ American Dream (Atlantic, 1988)

Enlisting the aid of Stephen Stills's Buffalo Springfield collaborator (and rival), Neil Young, proved a risky move on the part of Crosby, Stills and Nash—Young's urgency and depth would make any CSN record that featured him gain immensely in power; his absences from their other albums, however, would equally resound. Contributing "Helpless," one of his loveliest and leanest ballads, as well as the gorgeous three-song suite, "Country Girl," to *Déjà Vu*, Young also added jagged guitar work that counterbalanced Stills's more technical grace—and his keening, wise-child vocals lent haunting dimension to the trio's harmonies. Though Young's songs were the strongest, the other band members rose to his challenge.

Released in 1970, it is the juxtaposition of CSN&Y's individual styles, in fact, that makes *Déjà Vu* an even more accurate time capsule than *Crosby, Stills and Nash*—the tension of the band's fitful union reflects the restlessness that pervaded the end of the '60s, and each member's songs capture a facet of the countercultural experience. With Crosby's melodramatic "Almost Cut My Hair," the communal rebellion of the protest era is reduced to an individual, symbolic gesture; Nash's "Teach Your Children" and "Our House" express the urge toward domesticity on the part of former rebels; Stills's strong, electric reworking of Joni Mitchell's "Woodstock" takes on in retrospect the air of a last hurrah. The Stills-Young collaboration, "Everybody I Love You," is so sweeping as to now sound a bit desperate; and Crosby's reincarnation-saga, "Déjà Vu," hints at the New Age e-z mysticism that would eventually preoccupy many survivors of the CSN generation.

Unsurprisingly, CSN&Y soon came apart —Young's forward-looking vision being antithetical to the air of comfort that inflated *CSN*. The live *4 Way Street* distinctly lacked team spirit; and a best-of set, *So Far*, seemed perfunctory. *American Dream* was still stronger than any Crosby, Stills and Nash record—even if Young's four songs were hardly standouts, the trio sounded more vital with Neil on board. The record's most touching number, however, was Crosby's "Compass," an apologia for his years of substance abuse. On that graceful note of redemption, this edgy brotherhood— at least temporarily—retired. — P.E.

CROWDED HOUSE
★★★★ Crowded House (Capitol, 1986)
★★★ Temple of Low Men (Capitol, 1988)
★★½ I Feel Possessed (EP) (Capitol, 1989)
★★★ Woodface (Capitol, 1991)

When Neil Finn, the former Split Enz guitarist and Crowded House frontman, is at his peak, the songs he produces are Beatlesque in the very best sense of the term. Trouble is, he peaked too early; *Crowded House* was a near-perfect piece of popcraft, sparkling brilliantly from the buoyant abandon of "Now We're Getting Somewhere" to the melodic melancholy of "Don't Dream It's Over." But *Temple of Low Men* merely sputtered, recalling the glory of its predecessor on "Better Be Home Soon" and "I Feel Possessed," but offering little more than mood elsewhere; the *I Feel Possessed* EP recapitulates that single, and adds three lukewarm Byrds covers recorded with Roger McGuinn. By the time *Woodface* got recorded, Finn's brother Tim had turned the trio into a quartet, an addition that added bite to the group's material. — J.D.C.

RODNEY CROWELL

★ ★ ★ ★   **Ain't Living Long Like This (Warner Bros., 1978)**
   ★ ★ ★ ½ **Street Language (Columbia, 1986)**
★ ★ ★ ★ ½ **Diamonds & Dirt (Columbia, 1988)**
★ ★ ★ ★ ½ **Keys to the Highway (Columbia, 1989)**
★ ★ ★ ★   **The Rodney Crowell Collection (Warner Bros., 1989)**
   ★ ★ ½ **Life Is Messy (Columbia, 1992)**

Though he's nominally a country artist, Rodney Crowell's point of reference seems to be *Rubber Soul*: beginning with his early songs written for and recorded by Emmylou Harris (Crowell was a member of Harris's Hot Band at the time he started recording solo) to his own solo albums of the late '80s, Crowell has displayed an eloquence and sense of song-as-confession that has as much to do with Lennon-McCartney as it does Hank Williams and Merle Haggard; as a producer, he has fashioned a sound, centered on a basic band lineup and liberal use of acoustic instruments, that underscores the introspective nature of his material. Silence is another of Crowell's most effective devices. In some of his best songs—"After All This Time" from *Diamonds & Dirt*, "Many a Long & Lonesome Highway" from *Keys to the Highway*, for example—his consciously tentative vocals and stark productions pack as much emotional wallop as his lyrics.

It was genuinely amusing to find Crowell nominated for a best new country artist award by the Academy of Country Music for his 1988 *Diamonds & Dirt* album. By that time Crowell had ten years of solo albums under his belt. His debut album, *Ain't Living Long Like This*, was about as good as any nominally country record released in 1978. In addition to the rocking title song, the album included Crowell's own lilting version of "Voila! An American Dream," later a Top Twenty single for the Dirt Band; a wondrous remake of "A Fool Such as I" that was equal parts Elvis Presley and Hank Snow; and a devastating bit of self-flagellation, "Song for the Life." It was an audacious debut, but it went nowhere. He explained it best on "Ballad of Fast Eddie" from the *Street Language* album: "I hung the moon too soon to be respected." Two more Warners albums followed, then Crowell moved over to Columbia. His Warners catalogue is now down to one album, the 1989 *Rodney Crowell Collection*, that features Crowell's own versions of some of his best-known songs (among them, "Ashes by Now," "Shame on the Moon," a hit for Bob Seger, "Voila! An American Dream," "Leaving Louisiana in the Broad Daylight," a hit for the Oak Ridge Boys). It's an excellent overview of Crowell's early work.

At Columbia Crowell has continued his remarkable growth as a writer-singer-producer, but has also been selling records. His terrific but overlooked label debut, *Street Language*, paired him as co-producer with Booker T. Jones in what has been his strongest foray into rock and soul. By this time Crowell was married to Rosanne Cash, and their tumultuous relationship was leading him into some often painful truths about his life. Among the songs on *Street Language*, none hits harder than "Past Like a Mask," when Crowell sings, "I was told to be a man was build defenses strong/Keep your woman in her place and she'll keep hangin' on/Now I've grown to realize my life's been filled with lies/The thread that I've been hangin' on has broken in her eyes." This song, along with "Ballad of Fast Eddie," "When the Blue Hour Comes" and "When I'm Free Again" constructed a foundation of brutal truth on which Crowell has since built his songs.

A commercial breakthrough came with *Diamonds & Dirt*. Co-produced by Crowell and Tony Brown, the album yielded five Number One country singles. The honor was justified, as Crowell came up with the strongest range of songs he had ever put on disc (including a deft reading of Harlan Howard's "Above and Beyond"), from knowing but humorous observations on a rocky relationship ("She's Crazy for Leavin' ") to tender but tortured love songs ("After All This Time"). *Diamonds & Dirt*, Crowell's look at men and women together and apart, is open, warm, pained, tender, searching—a stirring treatise on the quest for understanding and balance in a relationship.

Crowell went in another direction on *Keys to the Highway*. While he still attempted to resolve male-female conundrums, his best songs on this album were born of tragedy. The death of his father moved Crowell to an acute examination of his life as a man, to his worthiness as a son, and then to lay out his observations in telling detail. "Things I Wish I'd Said" is explicitly about his father's final hours and Crowell's coming to terms with the inevitable. "Many a Long & Lonesome Highway," the album's best song, makes reference to his father's wisdom in describing a man determined to be self-sufficient. Crowell seems to have come out of this a tougher man, or at least expressing a tougher attitude in his songs. On "Soul Searchin'," "The Faith Is Mine," "Now That We're Alone," "Tell Me the Truth" and especially "I Guess We've Been Together for Too Long" he's defined himself in unequivocal terms.

Life Is Messy (wherein Brown is supplanted by three producers, none of whom seem to have his high regard for the integrity of the song) continues Crowell's introspective odyssey, with a few more rock touches than in the past. The songwriting level isn't up to the standard Crowell has set for himself—some of the lyrics are forced and silly—but even a subpar performance such as this contains moments of beauty and insight.

As a whole, Crowell's work shows growth both as music and as personal statement. He's come out on the other side of a career that started with the announcement *Ain't Livin' Long Like This*. On *Keys to the Highway* he sings of his father, "your journey's just begun." And so it is with Rodney Crowell. — D.M.

ARTHUR "BIG BOY" CRUDUP

★ ★ ★ ★ **Mean Ole Frisco (1957; Collectables, 1990)**
   ★ ★ ★ **Look On Yonder's Wall (Delmark, 1968)**
   ★ ★ ★ **Crudup's Mood (Delmark, 1970)**

Born in Forest, Mississippi, in 1905, Arthur "Big Boy" Crudup spent his early life working a variety of manual labor jobs, before deciding at age 32 to take up the guitar and play the country blues that had become his passion. Even at his best Crudup the player can sound amateurish—he was given to striking the wrong notes, playing in the wrong key—but Crudup the vocalist had a brooding authority that could not be denied. Signed to Bluebird in 1941, he cut more than 80 songs over the next 15 years, and was a consistent chart presence on the R&B side. His fame remained regional, though. Crudup entered into legend in 1954 when Elvis Presley cut his song "That's All Right" as his first single for Sun Records, inaugurating what the critic Robert Palmer has termed a dynasty. After moving to RCA in 1956, Presley cut two more Crudup songs, "So Glad You're Mine" and "My Baby Left Me."

All three of Crudup's in-print albums have commendable virtues. The absolute must-have is Collectables' *Mean Ole Frisco*, which is a reissue of an album Crudup cut for the Fire label in 1957. The 12 tracks are remakes of songs Crudup wrote (excluding the title song) and recorded for Bluebird, including "That's All Right," "So Glad You're Mine" and "Rock Me Baby." While not peak Crudup the two Delmark albums have a loose, easy ambience. *Look on Yonder's Wall* finds Crudup reprising "That's All Right" in fine, understated fashion. For a sampling of Crudup's Bluebird recordings, look for the deleted 1971 LP on RCA, *Father of Rock 'n' Roll*. — D.M.

JULEE CRUISE

★ ★ **Floating into the Night (Warner Bros., 1989)**

With a voice that rarely rises above a whisper and a songbook (lyrics by David Lynch, music by Angelo Badalamenti) wreaking of camp and irony, Cruise comes across as a sort of post-modern Claudine Longet—an amusing concept, to be sure, but hardly worth an entire album. — J.D.C.

THE CULT

   ★ ★ **Dreamtime (Beggars Banquet, 1984)**
   ★ ★½ **Love (Sire, 1985)**
★ ★ ★½ **Electric (Sire, 1987)**
   ★ ★ ★ **Sonic Temple (Sire, 1989)**
   ★ ★ ★ **Ceremony (Sire, 1991)**

Essentially a heavy-metal band for folks who think they're above such things, the Cult built its sound out of equal parts post-punk guitar aggression and neo-hippy mysticism, a combination that quite naturally results in some of the most pompous and silly music rock has seen since the heyday of the Doors. Typically, it was some time before the band got even that good, as the import-only *Dreamtime* never quite gets up a head of steam while the frenzied, unfocused playing on *Love* squanders the melodic potential of its best songs ("She Sells Sanctuary" and the overlong "Brother Wolf, Sister Moon").

With producer Rick Rubin on hand to tighten and toughen the group's sound, *Electric* manages to kick ass even when its lyrics make no sense, as on the relentless "Love Removal Machine." (Note to the band: There's a difference between "trippy" and "stupid.") But having found its formula, the Cult wasted no time in hammering it into the ground. *Sonic Temple* may attempt an epic sweep on some songs while *Ceremony* tries a sort of hard rock transcendentalism, but neither adds enough difference to the music to make further distinctions worthwhile. — J.D.C.

CULTURE

★★★★★   **Two Sevens Clash (1978; Shanachie, 1987)**
★★★★   **Cumbolo (1979; Shanachie, 1988)**
★★★★   **International Herb (1979; Shanachie, 1988)**
★★★   **Lion Rock (Heartbeat, 1982)**
★★★   **Culture in Culture (1986; Heartbeat, 1991)**
★★★½   **Culture at Work (Shanachie, 1986)**
★★★½   **Nuff Crisis! (Shanachie, 1988)**
★★★½   **Three Sides to My Story (Shanachie, 1991)**

While Bob Marley and the Wailers brought reggae to international pop attention in the late '70s, Culture deepened and refined the music's roots on a groundbreaking triple-play of complex, yet completely accessible albums. Centered on Joseph Hill's commanding and flexible lead singing, this vocal trio expounds its Rastafarian creed and decries racist oppression in a seductively tuneful, rhythmically urgent context. Widely acknowledged as a reggae classic, *Two Sevens Clash* lays down an indelible blueprint for later works: Hill's mysterioso chants and incantations mesh with the soulful harmonies of Kenneth Dayes and Albert Walker amid taut, bristling horn-and-keyboard arrangements. Though he sticks to tried-and-true subject matter, Hill is an estimable songwriter as well. There really isn't a weak cut on the album; *Cumbolo* continues Culture's natural-flowing buoyancy. For every dreadlock-shaking plaint about injustice ("Poor Jah People,"

"They Never Love in This Time"), there's a stirring call-to-arms ("Natty Dread Naw Run," "Natty Never Get Weary"). *International Herb* flaunts Hill's relaxed virtuosity; he gracefully moves from the buzzed-out, delightful celebrations of the title track to the piercing, disconsolate cries of "I Tried" and "It a Guh Dread" without upsetting the fluid musical groove. After a spell of nearly impenetrable, somewhat rote Rasta preaching on *Lion Rock* and *Culture in Culture*, the group returns to more approachable form on the three recent Shanachie releases. Addressing current concerns in both music ("Dance Hall Style" from *Culture at Work*) and subject matter ("Crack in New York" from *Nuff Crisis!*), Culture stands poised to bring its roots reggae attack into the future. *Three Sides to My Story* reasserts the trio's proven strengths, while admitting a refreshing taste of relevant new influences: a jolting shot of synthesizer juice here, a rich sliver of African-inflected guitar lead there. Tasty, if not quite as mind-boggling as *Two Sevens Clash*. But then, the apocalypse only comes once. — M.C.

CULTURE CLUB

★★★   **Kissing to Be Clever (Virgin, 1982)**
★★★   **Colour By Numbers (Virgin, 1983)**
★½   **Waking Up with the House On Fire (Virgin, 1984)**
★   **From Luxury to Heartache (Virgin/Epic, 1986)**

Should anyone ever doubt the amount of personal charisma Boy George once exuded, the fact that Culture Club was able to generate such extraordinary popularity on the basis of such utterly ordinary music ought to be proof enough. Listening to them now, it seems incredible that these albums produced six Top Ten singles (eight in Britain). Yet it wasn't delusion, really—it was charm, pure and simple. Just listen to George's tremulous tenor imploring, "Do You Really Want to Hurt Me" on *Kissing to Be Clever*; how could anyone resist a voice so guileless? Never mind that the rest of the album is chock-a-block with bleached funk and bland reggae, offering only the denatured carnival rhythms of "I'll Tumble 4 Ya" as inducement; sheer force of personality was what carried the day back then. And the same goes for *Colour by Numbers*; outré as the metaphor in "Miss Me Blind" might have been, outright silly as the chorus to "Karma Chameleon" truly was, the point remains that Boy George made us believe, if only for a moment.

So what happened? Well, sad to say, the

Boy turned serious. *Waking Up with the House on Fire* opens with the overwrought "message" of "Dangerous Man," and goes straight downhill from there, through the insufferable sanctimony of "The War Song" to the sheer inanity of "Crime Time" and "Mistake No. 3." By *From Luxury to Heartache*, the slide into irrelevance was so complete that the album's only real virtue was George's voice—an obvious case of too little, too late. — J.D.C.

THE CURE

★ ★ ★ ★   **Boys Don't Cry (1980; Elektra, 1988)**
★ ★ ★½   **Seventeen Seconds (1980; Elektra, 1988)**
★ ★ ★   **Faith (1981; Elektra, 1988)**
★ ★½   **Pornography (1982; Elektra, 1988)**
★ ★ ★ ★   **Japanese Whispers (Sire, 1983)**
★ ★   **The Top (Sire, 1984)**
★ ★ ★   **The Head on the Door (Elektra, 1985)**
★ ★ ★ ★   **Standing on the Beach: The Singles (Elektra, 1986)**
★ ★ ★ ★   **Kiss Me, Kiss Me, Kiss Me (Elektra, 1987)**
★ ★ ★ ★   **Disintegration (Elektra, 1989)**
★ ★ ★   **Integration (Elektra, 1990)**
★ ★½   **All Mixed Up (Elektra, 1990)**
★ ★ ★ ★   **Wish (Elektra, 1992)**

Never a lighthearted outfit, the Cure began its torturous path by bashing out tight, tuneful three-minute treatises on subjects ranging from Camus ("Killing an Arab") to new-wave trendiness ("Jumping Someone Else's Train"). Originally a trio, this continually evolving group orbited around guitarist and lead singer Robert Smith right from the git-go. His seemingly limitless capacity for brooding, claustrophobic melodrama isn't immediately apparent; *Boys Don't Cry*, an expanded version of the Cure's 1979 British debut (*Three Imaginary Boys*), subsumes its melancholy edge in an avalanche of punched-up melodies and angular riffs. Despite the group's subsequent mass popularity, this is still the most direct and accessible Cure album. Arguably, *Boys Don't Cry* marks the transition from punk to post-punk, the switch from late '70s anarchy to early '80s artiness.

Adding lush electronic keyboards and paring down its guitar buzz to skeletal connecting lines, the Cure moves into mope-rock territory (first defined by Joy Division) on its next two albums. *Seventeen Seconds* retains more of *Boys*' hooky impact than first seems apparent: if you can deal with the placid exterior and Smith's wailing,

such sombre meditations as "A Forest" and "Play for Today" leave a lasting, unsettling impression. The same cannot be said of *Faith*: clearly, Smith doesn't let the absence of memorable choruses or compelling song structures get in the way of venting his obsessions. Though *Pornography* is revered by Cureheads as a masterstroke, normal listeners will probably find it impenetrable. By this time, the Cure had started to become a vehicle for Smith and whomever he gathers in the studio. *Japanese Whispers* collects some singles and odd tracks; "Let's Go to Bed" asserts Smith's pop knack as well as his hard-to-fathom seductive appeal. It's a natural, but indulgences like "The Love Cats" suggest this budding autuer needs an editor—or a real band—to rein him in every once in a while. Otherwise, every successive Cure album would resemble *The Top*, on which flighty, disjointed noodlings hide the one catchy track ("The Caterpillar"). After a spell with Siouxsie and the Banshees in 1983–84, Robert Smith reactivated the Cure as a working group. Bassist Simon Gallup (an on-again, off-again member) chairs the new lineup, centering Smith's increasingly psychedelic explorations with a foursquare rock sensibility. Hanging on the engagingly sweet single "In Between Days" and not a whole lot else, *The Head on the Door* accomplished the unlikely task of breaking the Cure in America. The excellent singles compilation *Standing on a Beach* (retitled *Staring at the Sea* and expanded on CD) cemented the group's breakout status. For a sub-generation weaned on Duran Duran, discovering the Cure's angst-ridden soundtracks constitutes a major mind-blowing experience.

Smith manages to have it both ways on the Cure's next album. A rambling double-album set, *Kiss Me, Kiss Me, Kiss Me* positions the group's first bona fide hit single (the aching "Why Can't I Be You") alongside its most adventurous—and accomplished—actual ensemble playing since the debut. Under Smith's guiding presence, the Cure plows through wah-wah encrusted garage band raveups, suicidally bummed-out set pieces and thumping rock-disco grooves with equal assurance. Appropriately, *Disintegration* can be heard as the Cure's career-summing peak or an epic art-rock snooze-athon. The songs flow at their own leisurely speed, carefully piling layer after intricate layer of synthesized demi-classical textures on top of Smith's now-familiar plaintive cries and troubled love songs. Just when *Disintegration* does threaten to collapse under its own weight, Smith signs off with a sparse, hauntingly melodic confession. Perhaps the most emotionally direct and revealing song this professional enigma has yet delivered, it's called "Untitled." Of course. — M.C.

CUTTING CREW
★ **Broadcast (Virgin, 1987)**
★ **The Scattering (Virgin, 1989)**
"(I Just) Died in Your Arms," from *Broadcast*, a pallid imitation of Asia's pompous synth pop, is this band's musical masterstroke. You can imagine what the rest is like. — J.D.C.

CYMANDE
★ ★ ★½ **Cymande (Janus, 1972)**
★ ★ ★ **Second Time Around (Janus, 1973)**
Cymande played world-beat music long before there was a name for it. "Nyah-rock" is what this eight-man West Indian band called its polyglot boogie. Recorded in London, Cymande's out-of-print albums achieve a comfortable, cosmopolitan fusion, merging Africa's deep rhythms and folk melodies with the American tradition of soul and R&B. *Cymande* includes the 1973 R&B chart hits "The Message" and "Dove," and both tracks can still motivate a dance floor. *Second Time Around* drifts into spaciness at times, but a pulsing rhythmic undercurrent pulls Cymande back from the brink of mellow. Musical exploration of the Third World has become widespread, but, decades later, Cymande still sounds fresh and invigorating. — M.C.

THE CYRKLE
★ ★½ **Red Rubber Ball: A Collection (Columbia/Legacy, 1991)**
Although the song is certainly tuneful, it's hard to believe that the Cyrkle's 1966 proto-bubblegum hit, "Red Rubber Ball" was written by Paul Simon. It's also hard to believe that Beatles manager Brian Epstein thought these guys had potential. Their stuff is likable—but fluff. — P.E.

D

DICK DALE & HIS DEL-TONES
  ★ ★ ★   **Greatest Hits (1975; GNP Crescendo, 1986)**
★ ★ ★ ★½ **King of the Surf Guitar: The Best of Dick Dale & His Del-Tones (Rhino, 1989)**

For once, someone claiming royal blood isn't deluding himself or others. Dick Dale is indeed the one, true king of the surf guitar, the *ne plus ultra*, the *sine qua non*, Alpha and Omega, everyone else pack it up and go home. With the release of his first single in 1961, "Let's Go Trippin'," he created an entire genre, surf music, as well as one of the most unique and influential guitar styles in the history of rock & roll. The latter point is critical, for Dale was almost exclusively an instrumentalist. He did offer up a vocal here and there in a rugged voice much akin to Ronnie Hawkins's. (Unfortunately, Dale's hard-charging rendition of "Greenback Dollar"—by far his most engaging singing on record—is available only on the out-of-print *King of the Surf Guitar* album recorded for Capitol in 1963, which is not to be confused with the like-titled 1989 hits collection on Rhino.) But Dale's stock in trade was the whiplash, razor-sharp, trebly guitar line, double-picked and heavily-reverbed—"wet," as the cognoscenti say. Dale was on top of technology, too, being among the first featured guitarists to use Fender's portable electronic reverb unit, which went a long way toward establishing his signature sound. Dale's association with Fender extended to testing prototypes of the company's new gear on the road before the pieces went into mass production. Legend has it that he blew up 40 amplifiers before Fender perfected its popular Showman model.

While groups such as the Beach Boys and Jan and Dean focused on the surfing lifestyle rather than the sport itself, Dale's *modus operandi* was to recreate in his music the physical sensation of riding the waves. Lyrics, then, were the least of Dale's concern; he came on snarling and muscular in his guitar solos, the better to conjure the feeling of riding the wild surf. To say Dick Dale's music is high energy to the hilt is to diminish it. It's a relentless, unforgiving assault, all reverb, war whoops, and rock-solid drumming with wailing sax solos by Steve Douglas very nearly matching Dale's in-your-face attack. The 1989 Rhino package is the one to own, as it contains the original recordings of Dale's masterpieces. The GNP/Crescendo album contains 1975 re-recordings of many of the songs on the Rhino set; all display Dale in his usual aggressive form, but they are hollow-sounding and poorly produced (because his voice isn't miked properly, Dale's cries can barely be heard in the background). In addition to showcasing much of Dale's best work, Rhino's *King of the Surf Guitar* also offers newcomers to the Dale legacy a nice taste of the artist's interest in exotica—"Misirlou," one of his greatest performances and still breathtaking today, is drawn from a Greek pop standard of the 1940s; a year after "Misirlou" 's release, Dale cut a rollicking but respectful version of "Hava Nagila"; "The Victor," a 1964 track, features finger cymbals, a droning beat, and a heavy Middle Eastern accent in the melody.

As a technician, Dale steps out most profoundly on the aforementioned "Misirlou," which features his extraordinary double-picking technique at breakneck speed almost from first note to last; "Surf Beat," recorded six months after "Misirlou" in 1962, is all reverb run amock, with Dale cutting and slashing his way through the melody line. As a plus, the Rhino set closes with a version of the surf classic, "Pipeline" (originally done by the Chantay's), that Dale recorded with the late Stevie Ray

Vaughan in 1987 for the *Back to the Beach* soundtrack. This cut has to be heard to be believed. It's yet another reminder that Vaughan will not easily be replaced; it's also certifiable proof that the tiger that is Dick Dale is still loose. Pray for surf; the King lives. — D.M.

ROGER DALTREY

★★ **Daltrey (MCA, 1973)**
★ **Ride a Rock Horse (MCA, 1975)**
★★★ **One of the Boys (MCA, 1977)**
★★★ **Under a Raging Moon (Atlantic, 1985)**
★★★ **The Best of Rockers and Ballads (Polydor, 1991)**

Players in bands with impressive histories often like to flex their independence on their solo debuts: *Daltrey* is an extreme example. Nothing on this genial, mediocre album sounds at all like the Who. Russ Ballard of Argent performs a guitar freakout on one song's coda, but otherwise these generally slow songs are driven either by piano or lush strings. What really sets it apart, however, from the teenage-god vocal style Daltrey patented with Pete Townshend's songs, is the modesty of Roger's vocalizing. He gets up to old, glorious strength on the seven minutes of a fine nostalgia epic, "Hard Life/Giving It All Away"—otherwise he sounds tired or too relaxed. "One Man Band," a trite, vaudeville number, was Daltrey's minor hit; the rest of the material, by Adam Faith and Leo Sayer, is tasteful and bland. And Daltrey displays hardly any personal vision.

With *Ride a Rock Horse*, he puts himself in Ballard's hands for another, if slightly tougher, mediocrity; *One of the Boys* finds him at last rocking out. While it's hardly an original statement, *Under a Raging Moon* is much more assured. Townshend provides the charging "After the Fire," and a pair of Bryan Adams songs are capable arena rock. What makes the record work, however, is an echoing production that gets Daltrey sounding dramatic once again—and he even tries for some shifts in style ("Fallen Angel" oddly mimics Billy Idol; "It Don't Satisfy Me" is Robert Plant-ish). Daltrey remains more of a voice than a mind, and the relative strength of his material completely determines his music's success. — P.E.

DAMN YANKEES

★★ **Damn Yankees (Warner Bros., 1990)**
In which Ted Nugent, Styx's Tommy Shaw and Night Ranger's Jack Blades combine forces to remind us why people hated '70s hard rock in the first place. — J.D.C.

THE DAMNED

★★★½ **Damned Damned Damned (1977; Frontier, 1989)**
★★ **Music for Pleasure (1977; Demon import, 1986)**
★★★ **Machine Gun Etiquette (1979; Emergo, 1991)**
★★ **The Black Album (I.R.S., 1980)**
★ **Phantasmagoria (MCA, 1985)**
★ **Anything (MCA, 1986)**
★★½ **The Light at the End of the Tunnel (MCA, 1987)**
★★ **Final Damnation (Restless, 1989)**
★★½ **The Best of the Damned (Emergo, 1991)**

Damned Damned Damned is historically significant on three counts: this quartet's chaotic debut is the first proper album by a British punk unit, the first release on Stiff Records and the home of a single head-banging classic—"New Rose." Lead shouter Dave Vanian mutters a spoken quote from the Shangri-Las (by way of Doll-Heartbreaker Johnny Thunders) "Is she really going out with him," and then they're off. The group sprints through an exuberant three-chord bash-up in pursuit of fleeting beauty. Produced by Nick Lowe, barely, the album only comes close to "New Rose" on "Neat Neat Neat"—the opener. As more accomplished and intense bands arose, this groundbreaking unit seemed notable mostly for its assumed monikers: who could top Rat Scabies (drums) and Captain Sensible (bass)? Until recently, *Damned Damned Damned* and its follow-ups were available only as British imports. *Music for Pleasure* is a caterwauling dud, even by punk standards, but *Machine Gun Etiquette* zeroes in on a handful of actual tunes. "I Just Can't Be Happy Today" and "Love Song" reveal some pop aspirations, while "Noise Noise Noise" and "Smash It Up" revel in that good ol' anarchy. *The Black Album*, the Damned's better-late-than-never U.S. debut, is a failed mainstream-accommodation move: it sounds like the group couldn't decide between AOR and power pop. *The Best of the Damned* attempts to sum up these years, though extremely spotty song selection renders it useless. After a string of personnel changes, the Damned became a vehicle for Dave Vanian's wailing descent into goth-rock hell. *Phantasmagoria* and *Anything* totally lack the doomy musical wallop and lyrical concentration required to put over this kind of mock-horror fantasy trip; it would have been appropriate for the band to change its name to the Darned at this point.

The Light at the End of the Tunnel is an overgenerous career-long Damned retrospective. *Final Damnation* documents the inevitable reunion tour of the Damned's original lineup—just the sort of nostalgic gig that punk rock originally set out to destroy forever. — M.C.

DANA DANE
★ ★ ★½ **Dana Dane With Fame (Profile, 1987)**
★ ★ ★ **Dana Dane 4-Ever (Profile, 1990)**
With his fey delivery and fake English accent, Dane sounds like a cut-rate Slick Rick, but that hardly diminishes the wit and imagination of his best raps. "Cinderfella Dana Dane," from *Dana Dane With Fame*, establishes the pattern, but "What Dirty Minds U Have," from *Dana Dane 4-Ever*, is probably his best, a blithe burlesque of risqué rap that ribs both 2 Live Crew and its critics. — J.D.C.

CHARLIE DANIELS BAND
★ ★ ★ **Fire on the Mountain (1974; Epic, 1976)**
★ ★ **Night Rider (1975; Epic, 1977)**
★ ★ ★ **Saddle Tramp (1976; Epic, 1977)**
★ ★ **High Lonesome (Epic, 1977)**
★ ★ **Midnight Wind (Epic, 1977)**
★ ★ ★ **Million Mile Reflections (Epic, 1979)**
★ ★ ½ **Full Moon (Epic, 1980)**
★ ★ ★ **Windows (Epic, 1982)**
★ ★ ★ ★ **A Decade of Hits (Epic, 1983)**
★ ★ **Me & the Boys (Epic, 1985)**
★ ★ **Powder Keg (Epic, 1987)**
★ ★ ½ **Homesick Heroes (Epic, 1988)**
★ ★ ½ **Simple Man (Epic, 1989)**
★ ★ **Renegade (Epic, 1991)**
A veteran Nashville session player, Charlie Daniels started his band during the '70s. Tipping their hats to the Allman Brothers, Charlie and the boys rode in on the first wave of Southern rock. They aren't the most accomplished jammers in the pack, but Daniels's humorous good ol' hippie boy demeanor sparked a series of novelty hits. "Uneasy Rider," from the deleted LP of the same name, established the Charlie Daniels Band as FM radio stalwarts. *Fire on the Mountain* tightens the band's attack and Daniels lays on that fiddle, pushing his agenda ("The South's Gonna Do It" and "Long Haired Country Boy") smack into the listener's face. A tendency toward flaccid instrumental sections and automatic rabble-rousing mars most CDB albums, though. *Million Mile Reflections* adds a coating ot two of pop varnish, resulting in

Daniels's biggest hit: "The Devil Went Down to Georgia." Unlike his Southern rock peers, Daniels regularly crossed over to the country chart, and his '80s albums reflect that growing shift. "In America" (from *Full Moon*) is pure bumper-sticker sloganeering, while "Still in Saigon" (from *Windows*) offers a devastating and believable look at a Vietnam vet's inner turmoil.
A Decade of Hits peaks with the latter song—and perhaps Charlie Daniels's career does, too. Trimming away the excess fat of the preceding albums, *Decade* provides a surprisingly nourishing platter of boogie anthems and shaggy dog stories. For fans of unreconstructed Southern rock, it's a treat. Since then, Charlie Daniels has scored an occasional country chart hit with the likes of "Drinkin' My Baby Goodbye" (1985) and "Boogie Woogie Fiddle Country Blues" (1988). But his recent albums could sure use a shot of that old juice : the tastefully strummed version of Eric Clapton's "Layla" (from *Renegade*) quietly conforms to the polite dictates of current country radio. And that just doesn't seem right. — M.C.

DANZIG
★ ★ ★ **Danzig (Def American, 1988)**
★ ★ ★½ **Danzig II: Lucifuge (Def American, 1990)**
No matter how hard it tries for shock value or sacrilege, most "Satanic" rock is too silly to be scary. But that works to Danzig's advantage, because this is one of the few acts in devil rock that's actually in on the joke. Not that Danzig's material is particularly parodic; songs like "I Am Demon" (from *Danzig*) and "Long Way Back From Hell" (from *Lucifuge*) manage to play off both the malevolent power of their subjects and the ironic glee the band takes in embracing them. But between the band's good-natured grunge and (ex-Misfits frontman) Glenn Danzig's Elvis-from-hell delivery, it's obvious that irony wins every time. — J.D.C.

TERENCE TRENT D'ARBY
★ ★ ★½ **Introducing the Hardline According to Terence Trent D'Arby (Columbia, 1987)**
★ ★ ★ ★ **Neither Fish nor Flesh (Columbia, 1989)**
Initially gaining notoriety as much for his big mouth as for his music, Terence Trent D'Arby's "I-am-a-genius" posturing turned off a lot of listeners. Which is a drag—as Muhammad Ali proved, boasting doesn't mean you don't have the goods. *Introducing*

the Hardline delivered goods aplenty—an ambitious debut about family, heaven, love and pride, it was state-of-the-art postmodern R&B. Terence proved himself an encyclopedic vocalist; from gentle to gruff, he conveyed soul history. "Wishing Well" and its perky keyboard riff, set amidst stark rhythm, drew inevitable parallels to Prince; the sinuous "Sign Your Name" flashed D'Arby's skills as a multi-instrumentalist.

Neither Fish nor Flesh proved astonishing. Again, the singing managed to cover bases from Wilson Pickett to Roberta Flack, but it was the realized grandiosity of the project that was truly gripping. Trying for a *Sgt. Pepper's* on only his second time out, TTD gives up raga references, Stax/Volt horns, kiddie jingles, and gospel. "Billy Don't Fall" is gay-straight bonding that's lovely and strong; "You Will Pay Tomorrow" is relentlessly real in its ethic, no matter how showy its lyrics; and "I Don't Want to Bring Your Gods Down" reads like some strange version of William Blake. That the record, subtitled "A Soundtrack of Love, Faith, Hope & Destruction," tries way too hard is only a tribute to D'Arby's drive—he seems congenitally incapable of playing it safe. — P.E.

BOBBY DARIN

- ★★ **Darin at the Copa (1961; Bainbridge, 1981)**
- ★ **Bobby Darin 1936–1974 (Motown, 1974)**
- ★★★ **Capitol Collector's Series (Capitol, 1989)**
- ★★★ **The Bobby Darin Story (1961; Atco, 1989)**
- ★★★ **Splish Splash: The Best of Bobby Darin, Vol. 1 (Atco, 1991)**
- ★★★ **Mack the Knife: The Best of Bobby Darin, Vol. 2 (Atco, 1991)**

WITH JOHNNY MERCER

- ★★★ **Two of a Kind: Bobby Darin & Johnny Mercer (1961; Atco, 1990)**

Bobby Darin is one of popular music's sadder stories, one of a talented, often inspired singer who might have been a great stylist had he been less concerned with his hipness quotient. This led to artistic schizophrenia as he rushed from one image to another, according to his perception of what the times were demanding. In his heart he was a classic popular singer; indeed, his early hits included "Mack the Knife" and the lilting "Beyond the Sea," as well as nominal rock & roll songs that were believably done: "Splish Splash," the 1958 Top Ten single that jump-started Darin's career; "Queen of the Hop"; and especially the yearning ballad, "Dream Lover." His tenure at Atco was one of constant flip-flop between these two styles; similarly, he performed regularly in Vegas to adult audiences (*Darin at the Copa*), but was also written up in the rock & roll teen books of the '50s.

At Capitol in the early '60s he moved close to a folk-rock style; as the decade wore on he grew his hair long, sported a moustache and beard on occasion and made some embarrassing appearances on talk shows bedecked in jeans, paisley shirts and beads. And yet he cut some credible records: "18 Yellow Roses" is a masterful depiction of dread and devastation over losing someone you love. The Capitol Collector's Series entry demonstrates how easily and successfully Darin shifted gears after the first rock era.

Throughout these changes, Darin remained on the charts, often in the Top Twenty. In the early '70s he ditched the hippie garb and retreated into pop when he signed with Motown, where he remained without a hit until his death during heart surgery in 1973. He left behind some wonderful records, one of the liveliest being his jaunty duet album with Johnny Mercer, *Two of a Kind*, on which Darin's skill in the classic pop vein is evident and admirable. The Atco reissues contain what might be termed the essential Bobby Darin in two volumes; *The Bobby Darin Story* encompasses the early hits only ('58 through '61). The Motown record is the least interesting of all the titles, remarkable only as a document of an artist who had almost completely lost his way. — D.M.

THE DARLING BUDS

- ★★★½ **Pop Said . . . (Columbia, 1988)**
- ★★★★ **Crawdaddy (Columbia, 1990)**

Vocals as flirtatiously fine as prime Debbie Harry, songs prickly with hooks and ferocious playing make the Darling Buds' *Crawdaddy* (1990) a masterpiece of '60s revivalism. Their debut, *Pop Said*, was snazzy, too, but their second album reveals a Welsh band that has not only done its homework—specifically, they seem to study ambitious, orchestral, flawed stuff like *Magical Mystery Tour*, *Their Satanic Majesties Request*, and the Move—but that thunders ahead like it's doing something new. Wah-wahs, churning strings and full-kit drumming have seldom proved so engaging. — P.E.

DAVID AND DAVID
★★★★ Boomtown (A&M, 1986)

Davitt Sigerson's pristine production helps, as does great percussion work by Paulinho Da Costa, but it's the musical intelligence of David Baerwald and David Ricketts that makes *Boomtown* a triumph. Obviously at home in the studio, these boys deploy all manner of technical cunning as they go about making remarkably mature fare: they're smart lyricists, too—and great singers. Atmospheric, intense and memorable, their songs add rock's hard edge to pop's craftiness; every cut on the album is sharp and satisfying. — P.E.

MILES DAVIS

★★★ Bopping the Blues (1946; Black Lion, 1987)

★★★ Miles Davis and the Lighthouse All-Stars (1953; Fantasy, 1985)

★★★★ Bag's Groove (1954; Prestige, 1987)

★★★★ Walkin' (1954; Prestige, 1987)

★★★½ Blue Moods (1955; Debut, 1990)

★★★½ Musings of Miles (1955; Prestige, 1989)

★★★★ The New Miles Davis Quintet (1955; Prestige, 1982)

★★★★★ Round About Midnight (Columbia, 1955)

★★★★ Green Haze (1955; Prestige, 1976)

★★★★★ Steamin' With the Miles Davis Quintet (1956; Prestige, 1989)

★★★★★ Relaxin' With the Miles Davis Quintet (1956; Prestige, 1987)

★★★★★ Miles Davis (1956; Prestige, 1972)

★★★★★ Workin' (1956; Prestige, 1987)

★★★★½ Steamin' (1956; Prestige, 1989)

★★★★★ Workin' and Steamin' (1956; Prestige, 1974)

★★★★ Miles Davis, Volume 1 (1956; Blue Note, 1988)

★★★★½ Miles Davis, Volume 2 (1956; Blue Note, 1990)

★★★★½ Miles Ahead (Columbia, 1957)

★★★★ L'Ascenseur pour L'échafaud (1958; Philips, 1989)

★★★★ Milestones (Columbia, 1958)

★★★ Miles and Monk at Newport (1958; Columbia, 1964)

★★★★ Porgy and Bess (Columbia, 1958)

★★★★ '58 Sessions (1958; Columbia, 1991)

★★★★★ Kind of Blue (Columbia, 1959)

★★★½ Live in Stockholm (with Sonny Stitt) (1960; Secret, 1989)

★★★★★ Sketches of Spain (Columbia, 1960)

★★★★ Someday My Prince Will Come (1961; Columbia, 1990)

★★★★ In Person: Friday Night at the Blackhawk (1961; Columbia, 1988)

★★★★ In Person: Saturday Night at the Blackhawk, Volume 2 (1961; Columbia, 1988)

★★★★½ At Carnegie Hall (Columbia, 1961)

★★★★ Live Miles: More Music from Carnegie Hall (1961; Columbia, 1987)

★★½ Quiet Nights (Columbia, 1962)

★★★★ Seven Steps to Heaven (Columbia, 1963)

★★★★ Miles Davis in Europe (Columbia, 1963)

★★★½ My Funny Valentine (Columbia, 1964)

★★★★½ "Four" & More (Columbia, 1964)

★★★★ Miles in Tokyo (CBS Jap., 1964)

★★★★ Miles in Berlin (CBS Ger., 1964)

★★★★ Heard 'Round the World (1964; Columbia, 1983)

★★★★½ E.S.P. (1965; Columbia, 1991)

★★★★ Live at the Plugged Nickel (1965; Columbia, 1982)

★★★½ Cookin' at the Plugged Nickel (1965; Columbia, 1987)

★★★★ Miles Smiles (Columbia, 1966)

★★★½ Sorcerer (Columbia, 1967)

★★★★★ Nefertiti (Columbia, 1967)

★★★½ Miles in the Sky (Columbia, 1968)

★★★★½ Filles de Kilimanjaro (Columbia, 1968)

★★★★★ In a Silent Way (Columbia, 1969)

★★★★½ Greatest Hits (Columbia, 1969)

★★★★★ Bitches Brew (Columbia, 1969)

★★★★★ A Tribute to Jack Johnson (Columbia, 1970)

★★★ At the Fillmore (Columbia, 1970)

★★★★½ Live-Evil (Columbia, 1970)

★★★★½ In Concert (1972; Columbia, 1973)

★★★½ On the Corner (Columbia, 1972)

★★★★ Tallest Trees (Prestige, 1972)

★★★★½ Facets (Columbia, 1973)

★★★★½ Basic Miles: Classic Performances (Columbia, 1973)

★★★ Big Fun (Columbia, 1974)

★ ★ ★ ★   **Get Up With It (Columbia, 1974)**

★ ★ ★ ★½ **Agharta (1976; Columbia, 1991)**

★ ★ ★ ★ ★ **Pangaea (1976; Columbia, 1990)**

★ ★ ★½ **Water Babies (Columbia, 1976)**

★ ★ ★ ★   **Circle in the Round (Columbia, 1979)**

★ ★ ★ ★   **Directions (Columbia, 1981)**

★ ★ ★½ **The Man With the Horn (Columbia, 1981)**

★ ★ ★ ★   **We Want Miles (Columbia, 1982)**

★ ★ ★½ **Star People (Columbia, 1983)**

★ ★ ★ ★½ **Aura (1984; Columbia, 1989)**

★ ★ ★ ★   **Decoy (Columbia, 1984)**

★ ★ ★   **You're Under Arrest (Columbia, 1985)**

★ ★ ★ ★   **Tutu (Warner Bros., 1986)**

★ ★ ★ ★½ **And the Jazz Giants (Prestige, 1986)**

★ ★ ★ ★½ **Siesta (Warner Bros., 1987)**

★ ★ ★ ★½ **Collector's Items (Prestige, 1987)**

★ ★ ★ ★ ★ **Chronicle: The Complete Prestige Recordings (Prestige, 1987)**

★ ★ ★ ★½ **The Columbia Years 1955–1985 (Columbia, 1988)**

★ ★ ★ ★   **Ballads (Columbia, 1988)**

★ ★ ★ ★   **Blue Haze (Prestige, 1988)**

★ ★ ★   **Amandla (Warner Bros., 1989)**

★ ★ ★½ **First Miles (Savoy, 1989)**

★ ★ ★½ **Modern Jazz Giants (Prestige, 1989)**

★ ★ ★ ★ ★ **Birth of the Cool (Capitol, 1989)**

★ ★ ★ ★   **Dingo (with Michel Legrand) (Warner Bros., 1991)**

★ ★ ★ ★½ **The Essence of Miles Davis (Columbia, 1991)**

★ ★ ★ ★   **Doo Bop (Warner Bros., 1992)**

★ ★ ★ ★   **The Complete Concert: 1964 (Columbia, 1992)**

One of the two or three most important jazz musicians ever, Miles Davis started out at the top and managed to stay there for the rest of his 46-year career. As a soloist, his ideas were startlingly original and his tone utterly unmistakable; as a leader, he often recognized talent well before anyone else, and knew how to get the most out of almost any sideman. But it was as a stylist that Davis had his greatest impact. Most jazzmen are lucky if they can be linked to even a single formal breakthrough; Davis can be credited with several. After the teenage trumpeter graduated from Charlie Parker's groundbreaking quintet, he turned bebop's frenetic virtuosity on its head with a series of small-group recordings introducing what came to be known as "cool" jazz. A few years later, he and his quintet had swapped cool's languid lyricism for a tougher, more intense sound, and were acknowledged leaders in the hard bop movement. Next came his embrace of modality, which shifted his improvisational emphasis from chord changes and harmonic structure to a scale-based approach that gave soloists a whole new musical vocabulary. And then, after being among the first to incorporate electric instruments in a jazz rhythm section, he abandoned the music's traditional dependence on swing and began working with rock- and funk-based rhythms, in the process setting the groundwork for such fusion bands as Weather Report, Return to Forever and the Mahavishnu Orchestra.

Davis, like most jazzmen, began his career as a sideman, and had played in Billy Eckstine's big band and Charlie Parker's quintet before making his recording debut in 1945 with saxophonist Herbie Fields, a session that would have been quickly forgotten had Davis not become so famous later. Those tunes are included on *First Miles*, along with the first recordings actually issued under Davis's own name. Cut with Parker and a rhythm section featuring John Lewis and Max Roach, its basic form is straight bebop, but the young trumpeter's voice can already be heard in its adventurous writing and measured phrasing. It's far preferable to *Bopping the Blues*, a sideman date finding Davis blowing blues obbligati behind singers Earl Coleman and Ann Baker.

Still, the sessions that made Davis's reputation as a leader are the ones collected under the title *Birth of the Cool*. Using either an octet or nonet, Davis and arranger Gil Evans generate a sound that conveys the coloristic range of a big band while maintaining a chamber music sense of dynamics; moreover, because the playing manages to employ all the harmonic sophistication of bebop while trading its instrumental flash for more leisurely, contemplative soloing, it produced jazz that was far closer to the depth and consideration of art music than anything that had gone before. And though these recordings hardly stand as a commercial breakthrough, their influence is incalculable, as groups ranging from the Modern Jazz Quartet to the Gerry Mulligan/Chet Baker quartet to the Stan Kenton Orchestra all learned from them.

Ironically, the Davis nonet existed only for the *Cool* project, which, like most of his early-'50s output, was the product of one-off recording sessions. The same is true of the boppish Blue Note dates compiled as *Volume One* and *Volume Two*, and the deliciously unconventional *Blue Haze*, recorded with Charles Mingus for Debut. Even Davis's recordings for Prestige, the label for which he most frequently recorded during this period, were varied and episodic. Admittedly, that had its advantages, as a session with Thelonious Monk (included, variously, on *Bag's Groove*, *Tallest Trees* and *Miles Davis and the Jazz Giants*) makes plain. *Chronicle* traces Davis's days with Prestige admirably, including all his sessions as a leader as well as four tunes recorded under Lee Konitz's name, and is a boon to anyone who wants a comprehensive overview of the period without having to endure the inevitable redundancies caused by 30 years of repackaging.

Those interested only in the highlights, however, should skip ahead to 1955, when Davis introduces saxophonist John Coltrane into his hard-bop quintet. Although Coltrane's contributions are relatively low-key on *The New Miles Davis Quintet*, his aggressive, questing solos offer a dynamic contrast to the acerbic economy of Davis's playing. Add in the wry elegance of the rhythm section (Red Garland, Paul Chambers and the incomparable Philly Joe Jones), and these albums—*Cookin'*, *Relaxin'*, *Workin'* and *Steamin'* (which also are collected on the two-fers *Miles Davis* and *Workin' and Steamin'*)—constitute the best of his work for that label.

This version of the quintet followed Davis when he moved to Columbia Records, and can be heard on the lovely *Round About Midnight*. But the album that truly introduces Davis's Columbia period is *Miles Ahead*, which featured a large ensemble under the direction of Davis's old *Birth of the Cool* collaborator, Gil Evans. Theirs was an uncommonly sympathetic pairing, for Evans's coloristic approach to arranging brought out the best in Davis's dark, warm tone (particularly when the trumpeter switched to flugelhorn), while Evans's inventive voicings seemed to inspire Davis to ever more brilliant improvisations. Together, they produced material for a half dozen albums, and, apart from the half-hearted bossa nova of *Quiet Nights*, it's uniformly excellent. *Porgy and Bess*, a setting of selections from the Gershwin opera, was particularly popular in its time, but their masterwork is undoubtedly *Sketches of Spain*, a work of unparalleled grace and lyricism. (A concert rendition of its "Concierto de Aranjuez" appears on *Live Miles*.)

Davis continued his small group work, of course, adding alto saxophonist Cannonball Adderley on *Milestones* and the Miles side of *Miles and Monk at Newport*, and replacing Garland and Jones with, respectively, pianist Bill Evans and drummer James Cobb for the '58 Sessions. (Davis also appears as a sideman on Adderley's *Somethin' Else* at this time.) Good as these albums are, they're minor work when compared to *Kind of Blue*. On that album Davis introduces the concept of modal improvisation, in which the soloist works from a predetermined set of scales instead of extrapolating a line from a song's chord changes, but it isn't the theoretical breakthrough that makes this worth hearing—it's the charged spontaneity of the performances that makes the album so continually rewarding. Even after a thousand replays, this music remains startlingly vital.

Coltrane would spend the rest of his life refining the concepts introduced on that album, but he'd do it without Davis's help; the swinging and incisive *Someday My Prince Will Come* is his last album with the trumpeter, as Hank Mobley is added on tenor at that point (he is the only saxophonist on the two *In Person* albums). In addition to George Coleman, yet another new tenor man, *Seven Steps to Heaven* introduces what is widely considered to be Davis's greatest rhythm section: pianist Herbie Hancock, bassist Ron Carter and drummer Tony Williams. Although much younger than Davis's previous cohorts (Hancock was 23, Carter 25 and Williams just 17), this trio played with astonishing energy and insight, and the sheer physicality of their live work—as heard on *Miles in Europe*, *My Funny Valentine* and *"Four"* & *More*—is breathtaking. (*My Funny Valentine* and *"Four"* & *More* have since been combined as *The Complete Concert, 1964*.)

Coleman's input is somewhat more irregular, although his best work (as on much of *"Four"* & *More*, his last album with the group) recalls the fire of Coltrane. Saxophonist Sam Rivers adds an interesting twist to *Live in Tokyo*, but it's not until Art Blakey alumnus Wayne Shorter joins, on *Live in Berlin*, that Davis finds a saxophonist whose harmonic imagination matches his own. (Both the Tokyo and Berlin dates have been collected on *Heard 'Round the World*). From there, the music grows ever more daring, from the angularity of *E.S.P.* through the moody eloquence of *Nefertiti*, until it seems to tug at the very seams of mainstream jazz.

For Davis, however, those albums marked the end of an era, for with *Miles in the Sky* and *Filles de Kilimanjaro* he begins to move away from swing-based rhythms and toward the electric, backbeat-driven sound of rock and funk. He wasn't entirely a pioneer in this regard, as Williams had already been toying with rock rhythms in his own group, Lifetime. But by grafting those rock influences to the same sort of harmonically demanding jazz he'd been playing, Davis devised an entirely new sound. *In a Silent Way* pushes this approach even further, relying on more amplification, a larger ensemble (including guitarist John McLaughlin, on loan from Williams's Lifetime, and keyboardists Joe Zawinul and Chick Corea) and a rambling, riff-based approach to composition. It was quite a departure; only the album's relative quiet kept jazz purists from considering it complete apostasy.

There was no ignoring the implications of *Bitches Brew*, however. Where *In a Silent Way* merely flirts with funk, *Bitches Brew* openly courts its rhythmic insistence; naturally, the jazz community was in an uproar over the album. Yet this is by no means a pop record, for Davis's compositions remained harmonically challenging, while his ensemble (which augmented the electric guitar, keyboards and Fender bass with soprano sax and bass clarinet) seems to have been assembled mostly for its coloristic range. Even so, the die was cast, and Davis's subsequent albums draw more and more obviously from rock reference points, from the bluesy guitar of *Jack Johnson* to the spacey, Sly Stone–style funk of *On the Corner*.

It wasn't just the sound of the music that changed. Davis had also taken a cue from rock's approach to record-making, and began to assemble his albums from cleverly spliced snippets instead of whole performances; the results could be jarringly kaleidoscopic, but nonetheless produced their share of gems, like the Keith Jarrett electric piano solo in "Funky Tonk" (from *Live Evil*) or the searing guitar solo in "Maiysha" (from *Get Up With It*). Any doubts about Davis's vision as a leader were quickly quelled by *Agharta* and *Pangaea*, two live albums culled from a single day's performance in Osaka, Japan. Alternately audacious, poetic, hypnotic and abrasive,

these albums (particularly *Pangaea*) captured the risk-taking genius of Davis's band in riveting detail, and have worn better over time than any of his '70s albums.

They were also his last recordings of the decade, thanks to an auto accident that sent him on a downward spiral of ill-health and chemical dependence. Not that his absence kept Columbia from releasing new albums, as the vault-scrounging *Circle in the Round* and *Directions* make plain. Nor was his return to action, in the form of *The Man With the Horn*, much cause for hope, inasmuch as it overly relies on hackneyed attempts at commerciality like the title tune. Still, Davis soon found his footing; the live *We Want Miles* is a considerable improvement, and thanks to his unfailing taste in bright young sidemen, Davis's output through *You're Under Arrest* is solid and consistent. Still, only *Aura*—an adventurous big band suite conceived by Danish jazzman Palle Mikkelborg—offers anything in the way of revelation.

Davis left Columbia for Warner Bros. in 1985; Columbia's response (or was it revenge?) was to issue *The Columbia Years*, a 30-year retrospective that culls most of the obvious highlights, but shortchanges both Davis's electric period and his Evans albums. *Tutu*, his first Warners album, is a one-on-one pairing with producer/multi-instrumentalist Marcus Miller (who played bass in Davis's comeback band); it's good, but not as impressive as their second outing, a soundtrack album called *Siesta* that marvelously updates the Iberian groove of *Sketches of Spain*. Davis's other Warners soundtrack, *Dingo*, released shortly after his death in 1991, is also intriguing—in part because it includes his first attempts at traditional, bop-derived jazz in 23 years, but mostly because its plot, which features Davis as a jazz legend who inspires a young trumpeter, makes an eerily appropriate coda to his career. Still, it's hard not to wonder what else he could have done, given the astonishing jazz-rap synthesis of *Doo Bop*.
— J.D.C.

SKEETER DAVIS
★ ★ ★ **The Best of Sandy Posey and Skeeter Davis (Highland Music, NA)**
★ ★ ★ **Best of the Best of Skeeter Davis (Highland Music, NA)**
★ **Heart Strings (Tudor, 1983**

Skeeter Davis (nee Mary Frances Penick) has been recording sporadically for nearly 40 years but will always be remembered for two 1963 hits that are among the finest examples of early '60s pop, "The End of the World" and Carole King's "I Can't Stay Mad at You." Her producer Chet Atkins said it best when he observed that Davis's voice, thin and keening with little color, was wholly unremarkable until he rolled the tape. What happened then was, Atkins said, "magic." Davis sings with appealing warmth and humanity, turning vulnerability into an asset. She hasn't repeated that success, but has continued performing in Nashville on the Grand Ole Opry. Hers has been a long career, dating to the early '50s, when, teamed with the late Betty Jack Davis as the Davis Sisters, she posted one of the top country hits of 1953 with "I Forgot More Than You'll Ever Know." The flip side of that single, "Rock-a-Bye Boogie," is available in its original version on Rounder's collection of female rockabilly recordings, *Wild, Wild Young Women*, and in a barely-updated version on Davis's *Heart Strings* (1983) album. An energetic, delightful boogie, it's the best moment on an otherwise dreary album that finds Davis struggling to stay in tune. She earns points, though, for reviving Native American Marvin Rainwater's 1957 Top Twenty country-pop hit, "Gonna Find Me a Bluebird," a pretty song seldom heard anymore. — D.M.

THE SPENCER DAVIS GROUP
★ ★ ★½ **The Best of the Spencer Davis Group (Rhino, 1987)**

Two triumphant singles, "Gimme Some Lovin'" (1966) and "I'm a Man" (1967), featuring Steve Winwood's earliest (and some of his best) singing, made this Birmingham quartet one of Britain's classiest and toughest R&B outfits. A trad blues fan, Davis had the luck to discover the 16-year-old Winwood, and the smart modesty basically to hand over the band to the precocious soulster. Steve obviously came through—had the rest of this band been even half so tough, they would've rivaled the Animals. The band's original albums are out of print, but Rhino's greatest hits album is a good summing-up of the band's high points. — P.E.

TYRONE DAVIS
★ ★ ★ **Tyrone Davis' Greatest Hits (1972; Columbia, 1983)**
★ ★ ★½ **The Best of Tyrone Davis (Rhino, 1992)**

Mississippi-born, Tyrone Davis achieved black radio success in the mid-'60s after he'd moved to Chicago and signed with the now-defunct Dakar Records. His warm baritone voice could stretch to handle almost any form of soul, but it was best suited to rich, seductive ballads of a kind that seemed outdated in the disco '70s. Smashes like "Can I Change My Mind" and "Turn Back the Hands of Time" (included on *Greatest Hits* and *The Best of*) made him a talent ripe for major-label interest, and in 1977 he joined up with Columbia. There he tried grappling with the disco beast—and floundered. In 1992 Rhino released a new best-of compilation; it brings to the fore an overlooked talent. — P.E.

BOBBY DAY
★ ★ ★½ **Golden Classics (Collectables, NA)**

Although his legend rests almost exclusively on his 1958 hit, "Rockin' Robin" (and Lord knows there's a couple of generations that probably think Michael Jackson cut the original version), Bobby Day was one of the more interesting figures from rock's early era. A compelling singer with a voice equally suited to rough-edged, blues-oriented material as well as smooth, R&B-styled ballads, Day was also a clever songwriter with a feel for ingratiating melodies and lyrics with unexpected poetic turns. Unfortunately, one of his most vivid lyrics, "Buzz Buzz Buzz," which he wrote and recorded while a member of the Hollywood Flames in 1957, isn't on this collection. What's here is choice, nonetheless. "Rockin' Robin," of course, remains a classic; Thurston Harris had a Top 10 hit in 1957 with Day's "Little Bitty Pretty One," which Day had recorded that same year as a member of the Satellites; the Dave Clark Five topped the charts with their 1965 version of Day's "Over and Over," but for Day it was a minor hit as the B side of "Rockin' Robin." Of note among the other songs in this collection are "That's All I Want," a minor chart triumph for Day in 1959 that appears to have been the inspiration for some of the production flourishes that energized Gary U.S. Bonds's "New Orleans" hit a year later; and a cryptic but intriguing B side, "Three Young Rebs from Georgia." — D.M.

MORRIS DAY
★ ★ **Color of Success (Warner Bros., 1985)**
★ ★½ **Daydreaming (Warner Bros., 1987)**

Like a comedian who can't get a laugh without somebody to play off, Morris Day never seemed to catch his stride without Prince or the Time to support him. As a result, no matter how much manic energy he poured into his solo albums, the best he could do with either was surround a couple of fair singles ("The Oak Tree" on *Color of Success*, "Fishnet" on *Daydreaming*) with a lot of overwrought filler. — J.D.C.

TAYLOR DAYNE
★★½ **Tell It to My Heart (Arista, 1987)**
★★½ **Can't Fight Fate (Arista, 1989)**
Taylor Dayne looks hot, sings with a highly trained "soulfulness," almost never writes her own music and works up a sultry sweat on MTV. All of her fast tunes sound like Madonna or the peppier Whitney Houston; the slow ones sound like Mariah Carey or the slower Whitney Houston. Synths and percussion all over the place, lyrics alternating self-assertion or "I'm-a-love-victim" bathos, these records are state-of-the-art late '80s AOR. And they serve as a reminder that that was a very sorry state. — P.E.

THE DB'S
★★★★ **Stands for deciBels (1981; I.R.S. 1989)**
★★★½ **Repercussion (1982; I.R.S., 1989)**
★★★★ **Like This (1984; Rhino/Bearsville, 1987)**
★★★½ **The Sound of Music (I.R.S., 1987)**
Had the dB's arrived 15 years earlier, their ability to blend arty invention with Beatlesque melodies would have made them a sensation. Instead, it took two albums before this North Carolina quartet even managed to land an American record deal (*Stands for deciBels* and *Repercussion* were originally released on the British Albion label). A miscarriage of musical justice? Maybe. But, as the career of Marshall Crenshaw also demonstrates, there's a fairly limited market for pop-rock classicism— particularly when it's as brainy as this. *Stands for deciBels* was an audacious start, and its best songs—"Bad Reputation," "I'm In Love" and "Dynamite"—sound as strong today as when they were recorded. The writing is often as good on *Repercussion*, but the playing lacks focus; it's almost as if the band were afraid of sounding too pop. Chris Stamey, one of the band's chief writers, left just before *Like This* was recorded, but that only seems to sharpen front man Peter Holsapple's melodic instincts, as "Love Is for Lovers" and "A Spy in the House of Love" prove. But even the surviving line-up couldn't withstand the strain of consistent commercial indifference, and the dB's called it quits after the polished (but not entirely convincing) *The*

Sound of Music. Holsapple and Stamey regrouped as a duo in 1990. — J.D.C.

DEACON BLUE
★★★½ **Raintown (Columbia, 1988)**
★★★★ **When the World Knows Your Name (Columbia, 1989)**
★★★ **Ooh Las Vegas (CBS UK, 1990)**
★★★★ **Fellow Hoodlums (Columbia, 1991)**
Like Prefab Sprout, this Scots sextet combines a sense of Celtic melancholy with the cool jazziness of Steely Dan. But where the Sprouts exploit that sound for poetic atmosphere, Deacon Blue plays it as straight pop, making its albums more consistent, and more consistently enjoyable. There's a soulful undercurrent to some of the songs on *Raintown* that adds pop appeal to "When Will You (Make My Telephone Ring)" and "Chocolate Girl," but such trappings lack the emotional sweep of "Love's Great Fears" and the title tune.

Perhaps that's why there's a more pronounced rock feel to *When the World Knows Your Name*, which ranges from the mannered crunch of "This Changing Light" to the elegiac quiet of "Sad Loved Girl." In any case, the writing is impressive throughout, with "Real Gone Kid" and "Fergus Sings the Blues" being particularly catchy. The U.K.-only *Ooh Las Vegas* is an odds-and-ends collection of interest only to completists (though the Deacons' take on Julian Cope's "Trampoline" is interesting enough), but *Fellow Hoodlums* picks up where *World* left off, playing off the vocal chemistry between main man Ricky Ross and secondary singer Lorraine McIntosh in emotionally charged performances like "Your Swaying Arms" and the rollicking Celtic rocker "One Day I'll Go Walking." — J.D.C.

DEAD BOYS
★★ **Young Loud and Snotty (Sire, 1977)**
★★ **We Have Come for Your Children (Sire, 1978)**
So much loutish behavior and public indecency has been committed in the name of punk during the last 15 years that it's now impossible to gauge the Dead Boys' historical import. It can't be purely musical: compared to the piranha bite of vintage Sex Pistols or the Ramones' goony joie de vivre, these two out-of-print albums sound like borderline-competent heavy metal hammered out with a nasty, vicious attitude.

Before they became Dead Boys, Cheetah Chrome (guitar) and Johnny Blitz (drums) were in the groudbreaking Cleveland proto-punk band Rocket From the Tombs, along with Pere Ubu founders Peter Laughner and David Thomas. Tellingly, the best cuts on both Dead Boys albums are Rocket holdovers: *Young Loud & Snotty*'s rousing anti-anthem "Sonic Reducer" is co-written by Thomas, while *We Have Come for Your Children*'s morose and compelling "Ain't It Fun" is the late Peter Laughner's unsparing elegy for himself (co-written with Chrome). Otherwise, these records are distinguised mostly by gross sexism ("Caught With the Meat in Your Mouth" on *Snotty*) and tabloid sensationalism ("Son of Sam" on *Children*). Live, lead sniveller Stiv Bators took Iggy Pop's daredevil stage antics three cocky steps forward into utter anarchy. For anybody who witnessed Bators's simulation of hanging himself while broken glass rained down onstage, his snarling tag-line on the Stooges soundalike "All This and More" (on *Snotty*) was no joke. "I'll die for you if you want me to." Bators did, in fact, meet his maker after being hit by a bus in Paris in 1990. — M.C.

DEAD KENNEDYS
- ★ ★ ★½ **Fresh Fruit for Rotting Vegetables (I.R.S., 1981)**
- ★ ★ ★½ **In God We Trust, Inc. (Alternative Tentacles, 1981)**
- ★ ★ ★ **Plastic Surgery Disasters (Alternative Tentacles, 1982)**
- ★ ★ ★ **Frankenchrist (Alternative Tentacles, 1985)**
- ★ ★ ★ **Bedtime for Democracy (Alternative Tentacles, 1986)**
- ★ ★ ★ ★ **Give Me Convenience or Give Me Death (Alternative Tentacles, 1987)**

Their confrontational politics and total scorn for the status quo led many to consider this pioneering California hardcore band the only American punk act on a par with the Sex Pistols, but that's confusing social significance with musical power. As often as the Dead Kennedys gave the establishment a poke in the eye, the impact derived from the inspired vitriol of Jello Biafra's lyrics, not the music behind him. Indeed, while the Pistols semi-metal roar seems threatening even when Johnny Rotten isn't singing, the DKs' frenetic rave-ups offer little more than cluttered cacophony, substituting speed for power, noise for intensity.

As a result, the most lasting material on *Fresh Fruit for Rotting Vegetables* is its most conventional—post-Ramones rockers like "Kill the Poor" or "California Über Alles" —although there is a certain nasty glee to be found in the likes of "Let's Lynch the Landlord." There's even more righteous rage (or is it rage against righteousness?) on *In God We Trust, Inc.*, but even the ferociously catchy "Nazi Punks Fuck Off" sacrifices some of its musical power to the lyrics' occasionally awkward cadences. Much the same can be said of *Plastic Surgery Disasters*, *Frankenchrist* and *Bedtime for Democracy*, on which the group's increasingly didactic material seems to exist more as political commentary than as rock & roll. In that respect, it's almost ironic that the group's undoing wasn't its often scabrous assault on the establishment, but an obscenity suit prompted by a poster (of H. R. Giger's "Penis Landscape") included in *Frankenchrist*. Although the band eventually won that battle, it lost the war, disbanding not long after *Bedtime for Democracy*; its final release, *Give Me Convenience or Give Me Death* is a compilation album collecting many of the Dead Kennedys' most listenable songs.
 — J.D.C.

DEAD OR ALIVE
- ★ **Sophisticated Boom Boom (Epic, 1984)**
- ★ ★½ **"Youthquake" (Epic, 1985)**
- ★ ★ **Mad, Bad and Dangerous to Know (Epic, 1986)**
- ★ ★ ★ **Rip It Up (Epic, 1988)**
- ★ **Nude (Epic, 1989)**

Although its cross-dressing frontman, Pete Burns, had his roots in the Liverpool psychedelic scene, Dead or Alive found its metier in the trashy Hi-NRG sound that replaced the New Romantic movement in London clubs. In fact, a certain amount of New Romantic detritus bobs up throughout *Sophisticated Boom Boom*, something that might explain the too-stiff synthbeats but hardly excuses the painfully un-funky remake of K.C. and the Sunshine Band's "That's the Way (I Like It)." With *"Youthquake"* came the Stock-Aitken-Waterman production team, and that not only put a much higher gloss on the band's sound, but gave Dead or Alive its most enduring hit, the giddily kinetic "You Spin Me Round (Like a Record)." *Mad, Bad and Dangerous to Know* safely repeats the formula, but lacks the campy edge that put its predecessor over the top. Still, the most listenable of the SAW collaborations is *Rip It Up*, which not only offers all of the group's British hits to that point, but ups

the ante with danceably insistent remixes. *Nude*, its follow-up, finds Burns laboring under the misapprehension that he's an artiste, a delusion which quickly robs the album of any amusement potential.
— J.D.C.

JIMMY DEAN
★★ **Jimmy Dean's Greatest Hits (Columbia, 1966)**
★★ **American Originals (Columbia, 1989)**
Jimmy Dean has an ingratiating, avuncular presence and once had a bold swagger in his voice that suggested he was capable of delivering tougher material than the mainstream country fare he was purveying. He latched onto his hit formula in 1961 with the saga song "Big Bad John," which topped the pop charts for five weeks. In 1962 he returned to the Top Ten again with "P.T. 109," which portrayed John F. Kennedy as the hero he apparently wasn't in World War II. These oddities are entertaining for their macho bluster. As his career progressed, Dean occupied the safe ground in the middle of the road and produced nothing of note. — D.M.

DEBARGE
★★★ **The DeBarges (Gordy, 1981)**
★★★ **All This Love (Gordy, 1982)**
★★ **In a Special Way (Gordy, 1983)**
★★ **Rhythm of the Night (Gordy, 1985)**
★★ **Greatest Hits (Motown, 1986)**
What began with such promise at the outset of the '80s ended by the middle of the decade in total predictability. The DeBarges (four brothers and a sister), out of Grand Rapids, Michigan, were in the forefront of a young generation of black artists who demonstrated an affinity for updating classic Motown pop-soul arrangements with harder, electronically powered dance floor grooves and then laying on silky ensemble harmonies to support—in this instance, El DeBarge's pleading vocals (much in the vein of *Off The Wall*–era Michael Jackson). The siblings were signed to Motown subsidiary Gordy after an audition arranged by two other DeBarge brothers, Bobby and Tommy, whose own band, Switch, was one of Motown's rising young groups.

DeBarges' first album generated little action, but *All This Love* yielded two Top Forty singles in "I Like It" and the dreamy title song. But while the El DeBarge–produced *In a Special Way* produced a Top Twenty hit in "Time Will Reveal," the songs were growing more clichéd, the arrangements more static. Chaos ensued on *Rhythm of the Night* when the group employed four

different producers and brought in outside writers to bolster the tune stack. Resorting to corporate pop from Diane Warren was the surest sign that the end was near. El's ensuing solo career iced DeBarges' fadeout. Neither he nor they have ever recovered.
— D.M.

EL DEBARGE
★ **El DeBarge (Gordy, 1986)**
★★½ **Gemini (Motown, 1989)**
As a solo artist El DeBarge has gone all over the map without creating much memorable music, though he gets points for at least trying to stretch into some new areas. In making this effort, though, he's stretched himself so thin there's little personality left. Consider his 1986 debut: four, count 'em, four producers are credited, always the first sign of trouble. Peter Wolf and Robbie Buchanan presumably supply the album's rock credentials, Jay Graydon brings pop-jazz chops, and the Burt Bacharach–Carole Bayer Sager team lends a mainstream—read MOR—sheen. That such a mish-mosh should translate into a misguided album is hardly surprising. *Gemini* at least has some focus, being concerned with smooth, heartfelt ballads and some sharp pop-soul dance tunes. Apart from two tracks produced by Graydon, El produced this one himself and he turns out to have been the right man for the job—this one has all the conceptual and sonic unity his first solo outing lacked. And while "Real Love," "Broken Dreams" and "Turn the Page" have a degree of emotional depth greater than anything he did with DeBarge, whether El sees himself as the next great Love Man or the dreaded all-around entertainer remains unanswered. — D.M.

CHRIS DE BURGH
★★ **Far Beyond These Castle Walls (A&M, 1975)**
★★ **Spanish Train and Other Stories (A&M, 1976)**
★★ **End of a Perfect Day (A&M, 1977)**
★★½ **Crusader (A&M, 1979)**
★★½ **Eastern Wind (A&M, 1980)**
★★½ **The Getaway (A&M, 1982)**
★★★ **Man on the Line (A&M, 1984)**
★★★½ **Into the Light (A&M, 1986)**
★★★ **Flying Colours (A&M, 1988)**
In the '70s, Ireland's Chris De Burgh penned castles 'n' candlelight love lyrics that had all the subtlety of Harlequin romances— and his tunes resembled those of a tranquilized Moody Blues. Painstaking musicianship and a beguiling voice, however, kept his career alive until he

became a star in, of all places, Norway. (*Eastern Wind* was sufficiently brooding, it seems, that it thrilled listeners in the land of deep introspection). Working with producer-arranger Rupert Hine, he continued putting out glossy fare (*Crusader*, *The Getaway*) that throbbed and gushed—as a writer of straight ballads, he progressed considerably, but still was fatally enraptured with anything vaguely mythic, medieval or otherwise arcane. In the '80s, he finally found the style that suited him—lush, synth-driven AOR of the sort Steve Winwood and Phil Collins parlay. His best album, *Into the Light*, boasts the playing of crack studio musicians (Pino Palladino, Danny McBride), and in "The Lady in Red" he achieves a schmaltzy grandeur: his singing is gorgeous, and if you ignore the ghost of Gino Vannelli hovering in the wings, the album is satisfying in a make-out music sort of way. *Flying Colours* repeats the formula. — P.E.

JOEY DEE AND THE STARLITERS

★★ Hey, Let's Twist! The Best of Joey Dee and the Starliters (Rhino, 1990)

Notable as the house band at New York's Peppermint Lounge in the early '60s, the buttoned-down Joey Dee and the Starliters were the society crowd's idea of chic. By any standards their stage shows were flamboyant and they brought a new kind of dance music to a generation otherwise dispossessed by rock & roll. "The Peppermint Twist" put them on the map in 1961 and remains by far the best-known Joey Dee song. As this record shows, there wasn't much else to hang your hat on with these fellows, so conservative and lukewarm was the remainder of their work. Of historical note: Johnny Nash, who had a Top Five hit with the reggae-influenced "Hold Me Tight" in 1968 and a Number One record in 1972 with "I Can See Clearly Now," found an early outlet for his songs with Joey Dee. Three Nash tunes ("What Kind of Love Is This," "I Lost My Baby" and "Help Me Pick Up the Pieces") are included in this collection, though the vocalist's wooden interpretations do an injustice to some good lyrics. — D.M.

DEEE-LITE

★★★★ World Clique (Elektra, 1990)
★★★★ Infinity Within (Electra, 1992)

Deceptively frothy dance pop, with deep grooves and a strong sense of soul tucked away beneath the lighthearted lyrics and kitchen-sink samples. Because Deee-Lite's music emphasizes song structure as much as rhythm tracks, the album has more pop appeal than most dance records. But it's the group's combination of campy humor and wholly unironic optimism that makes *World Clique* utterly irresistible. *Infinity Within* continues in much the same vein, intensifying the trio's muddle-headed politics while updating the rhythm approach to include techno and ambient grooves.
— J.D.C.

DEEP PURPLE

★★★ Deep Purple in Rock (Warner Bros., 1970)
★★½ Fireball (Warner Bros., 1971)
★★★★ Machine Head (Warner Bros., 1972)
★★★ Who Do We Think We Are! (Warner Bros., 1973)
★★½ Made in Japan (Deep Purple/Warner Bros., 1973)
★★★ Burn (Deep Purple/Warner Bros., 1974)
★★½ Stormbringer (Warner Bros., 1974)
★★½ Come Taste the Band (Warner Bros., 1975)
★★½ Made in Europe (Warner Bros., 1976)
★★★ When We Rock, We Rock and When We Roll, We Roll (Warner Bros., 1978)
★★★ Deepest Purple (Deep Purple/Warner Bros., 1980)
★★½ Perfect Strangers (Mercury, 1984)
★★½ Nobody's Perfect (Mercury, 1986)
★★ Slaves & Masters (RCA, 1990)

Deep Purple scored a memorable Top Ten hit in 1968 with its proto-metal demolition of Neil Diamond's "Hush." But the British quintet's early albums (on the defunct Tetragrammaton label) get stuck somewhere between keyboardist Jon Lord's classical aspirations and a cruder, bar-band sensibility. With the addition of lead shrieker Ian Gillan and bassist Roger Glover, *Deep Purple in Rock* stakes the band's claim in the heavy-duty musical territory of a new decade. "Speed King" tumbles out with all the subtlety of a landslide; the combination of Lord's thundering organ runs and guitarist Ritchie Blackmore's lightning-fingered solos can rattle teeth even at half-volume.

If Deep Purple's next LP (*Fireball*) never quite achieves ignition, *Machine Head* blazes from start to finish. The molten three-chord riff of "Smoke on the Water" became a garage-band classic. "Space Truckin' " and "Highway Star" chug along at a comparatively rapid pace, propelled by the kind of mindless energy that punk rock later claimed as its birthright. On "Lazy," Lord and Blackmore flash their chops; unlike most metal jams, at least it won't put you to sleep.

Who Do We Think We Are! fires off another irresistibly goofy single ("Woman From Tokyo") amid the increasingly dull Purple haze. *Burn* is notable mostly for the addition of lead singer David Coverdale; the jumpy title track and "Might Just Take Your Life" are somehow listenable despite the future Whitesnake's slithery presence. On *Come Taste the Band*, cult guitar hero Tommy Bolin replaces Blackmore, to little avail. Even the compilations *When We Rock* and *Deepest Purple* can't compare to *Machine Head*'s seamless headbanging. Deep Purple reconvened its most successful lineup in 1984, but the Mercury albums turned out to be stolid rehashing of former glories. The American yelper Joe Lynn Turner takes Ian Gillan's place on *Slaves & Masters*; at best, his bloozy Paul Rodgers imitations clash with Deep Purple's rumbling power-boogie signature. At worst, Deep Purple's ready-made power ballads can't be distinguished from the similarly faceless efforts of the latter-day Bad Company. What's the world coming to?
— M.C.

DEF LEPPARD
★ ★ ★½ **On Through the Night (Polydor, 1980)**
★ ★ ★ **High 'n' Dry (Polydor, 1981)**
★ ★ ★ ★½ **Pyromania (Polydor, 1983)**
★ ★ ★ ★ ★ **Hysteria (Polydor, 1987)**
★ ★ ★ ★ **Adrenalize (Mercury, 1992)**
Arguably the world's most popular heavy metal band and certainly the best-selling, Def Leppard owes its success not to attitude or virtuosity (the usual strengths of heavy metal heroes) but to songwriting and studio craft—attributes more commonly associated with pop acts. That's not to suggest there's anything wimpy about the band's sound; indeed, the Leps are as fond of mega-watt crunch as any old-time headbangers. But unlike such contemporaries as Iron Maiden and Saxon—products all of the "new wave of British heavy metal"—Def Leppard has always seen its sound as a means, not an end, and as such seems willing to try anything in the interests of furthering a song or sharpening a hook.

Initially, of course, the band's efforts were fairly modest. The vocal harmonies fleshing out *On Through the Night* may lend color to the likes of "Hello America," but hardly count as formal breakthroughs. Nor did *High 'n' Dry* alter the formula, though as

"Bringin' on the Heartbreak" demonstrates, the writing grew far more intricate and involved. With *Pyromania*, though, the rules changed for good. Not only is the band's traditional guitars-bass-drums instrumentation augmented by digital keyboards and state-of-the-art special effects, but that sound-shaping technology often becomes part of the songs themselves. Consequently, the backwards snare and carefully contoured backing vocals don't just add depth and texture to "Photograph" —they actually change the way the music flows and the melody develops. And that's equally true of "Rock of Ages," "Foolin' " and most of the other songs on the album.

Hysteria is even more techno-intense, yet the obviously fussy arrangements and production never seem to get in the way of the music. If anything, the opposite is true; from the processed vocals in "Animal" to the multiple layers of echo sheathing the groove in "Pour Some Sugar On Me," the overload of aural detail seems to enhance the album's melodic allure, underscoring the material's pop appeal without dulling its metallic edge. The perfect Def Leppard album, *Adrenalize* finds the band moving closer to pop than on its previous outings, but without losing its metallic edge.
— J.D.C.

DESMOND DEKKER
★ ★ ★½ **Rockin' Steady: The Best of Desmond Dekker (Rhino, 1992)**
In 1969, straight out of Kingston, Desmond Dekker scored a Top Ten hit with the reggae single "Israelites," paving the way for stronger talents like Bob Marley. Although in the U.S. Dekker remained a one-hit wonder, his influence in Britain was more substantial. Championing the outlaw ethic ("Rude Boy Train"), Dekker's early work was low-tech and punchy; but even with such slicker fare as his cover of Jimmy Cliff's "You Can Get It If You Really Want," his sly vocal style cuts through.
— P.E.

DEL AMITRI
★ ★ ★½ **Del Amitri (Chrysalis, 1985)**
★ ★ ★½ **Waking Hours (A&M, 1989)**
While sometimes the dash and power of this Glasgow outfit's lyrics recall the elegant anger of Elvis Costello's earliest albums, the music is closer in pop spirit to the Housemartins or Squeeze. With deft, brisk folk guitars bolstered by snappy electric riffs, the songs are expertly crafted slice-of-life vignettes. Nothing showy, but very satisfying. — P.E.

DELANEY AND BONNIE

★ ★ ★½ **Accept No Substitute: The Original Delaney and Bonnie (Elektra, 1969)**
★ ★ ★ ★ ★ **On Tour (With Eric Clapton) (Atco, 1970)**
★ ★ ★ **To Delaney From Bonnie (Atco, 1970)**
★ ★ ★½ **Motel Shot (Atco, 1971)**
★ ★½ **Genesis (GNP, 1971)**
★ ★ ★ **The Best Of Delaney and Bonnie (Atco, 1973)**
★ ★ ★ ★½ **The Best Of Delaney and Bonnie (Rhino, 1990)**

In its toughest, 1969 incarnation—an 11-piece revue—this was Southern soul-rock of a scorching expertise. Honing her R&B chops as history's only white Ikette, powerhouse vocalist Bonnie Bramlett and husband, Delaney, an ace picker and country-tinged singer, had the talent and charisma to attract breathtaking sidemen: Leon Russell, Bobby Keys, Carl Radle, Rita Coolidge, Jim Keltner—and, at various times, Eric Clapton and Duane Allman. As one of the best bands in rock & roll, they make *On Tour* a triumph: Clapton tears up Steve Cropper's "Things Get Better," D&B exult the funk on "I Don't Want to Discuss It." The acoustic "Motel Shot" is another kind of wonder: traditionals like "Going Down the Road Feeling Bad" and "Will the Circle Be Unbroken" played with a casual, loving freedom. *To Delaney From Bonnie* (currently out of print) captures some of the same spirit. The duo's first record, *Accept No Substitute* (also deleted) formulated the synthesis of Stax/Volt, gospel and hard country that created the D&B sound. It remains exciting—as do most of their records. The musicians they introduced are featured on Clapton's first solo album and on Joe Cocker's *Mad Dogs and Englishmen.* The closest rock has come to a true big band untainted by pomposity, they radiate the joy of playing. — P.E.

DE LA SOUL

★ ★ ★ ★ **3 Feet High and Rising (Tommy Boy, 1989)**
★ ★ ★ ★ **De La Soul Is Dead (Tommy Boy, 1991)**

If Public Enemy consists of rap's bad-boy geniuses, De La Soul provides their good-guy counterparts. Tricked out in day-glo colors and peace-symbol neck chains, this trio comes on like very merry pranksters—and while the pose alone is a relief from the usual gangsta stance, De La Soul's relentlessly positive force is even more so. Especially because these guys are hardly wimps. Instead, they're probably the most musically inventive power in rap. With even their inscrutably daffy monikers (Posdnuos, Trugoy, and The Big Ban/Baby Huey Maseo) suggesting that they've learned more than a little from R&B's great surrealists, Parliament/Funkadelic, De La Soul's albums rival prime George Clinton in their textural density, inside-joke madness, and bonkers energy. *3 Feet High and Rising* and *De La Soul Is Dead* mix in truly bizarre soundbites with furious James Brown samplings, and the band's sense of concept is breathlessly original. Masters of the studio, they craft epic aural cartoons—filled with street-talk wordplay, extra-terrestrial humor and inspired lunacy. Brave and witty enough not only to make first-class rap, but to comment, criticize and challenge the form—they're b-boy auteurs, and makers of some of the most inventive pop music available, bar genre. — P.E.

THE DELFONICS

★ ★ ★ **Best of the Delfonics (Arista, 1985)**

A bridge between the romantic soul style of the late '60s and the lushly produced extravaganzas that evolved at Philadelphia International in the '70s, the Delfonics were the vehicle that brought arranger Thom Bell into prominence before he teamed with Kenny Gamble and Leon Huff to create the sound known as Philly soul. The roots of that sound, which dominated black music through most of the '70s the way Motown dominated the '60s, are to be found in the string-laden, sensuous arrangements that cushion the Delfonics' high-pitched harmonies. The trio was blessed in having a lead singer whose baritone could ease on up to a yearning falsetto—not unlike the Temptations' Eddie Kendricks—and stay there as his mates fell in step and the strings laid on the sweetness. Their grandest moments came in 1968, with the soothing "La-La Means I Love You," and in 1970, with "Didn't I (Blow Your Mind This Time)," both Top Ten singles. This album has the two big hits as well as other minor gems such as "Trying to Make a Fool of Me" and "Ready or Not Here I Come (Can't Hide From Love)." — D.M.

DELLS

★ ★ ★½ **There Is (1968; Chess/MCA, 1989)**
★ ★ ★½ **The Dells Vs. the Dramatics (1974; Chess/MCA, 1984)**
★ ★ ★ ★ **The Dells (Chess/MCA, 1984)**
★ ★ ★½ **Music From the Motion Picture: The Five Heartbeats (Virgin, 1991)**

★ ★ ★ ★ ★ **On Their Corner: Best of the Dells (Chess/MCA, 1992)**
In 1956, this Chicago harmony quintet scored with the elegant, sexy "Oh, What a Night." The Dells' follow-up hit came twelve years later; "Stay in My Corner" is a standard-issue lover's plea lifted by its dynamic vocal arrangement and Marvin Junior's warm baritone. When the group re-emerged on Chess later in the '60s, after knocking around on several independents, its bold new sound left that classic street-corner casualness far behind. A full quotient of strings and horns contrast and emphasize the play of voices. When everything falls into place, as it does on the heaven-bound "There Is," the Dells' harmonies rumble and flash like an approaching storm. *There Is* duplicates the original Cadet LP; both its title track and an extended remake of "Stay in My Corner" repeat on the sterling *Dells* collection. The leaner sound of early '70s soul nuggets like "Give Your Baby a Standing Ovation" and "Bring Back the Love of Yesterday" offsets the re-made earlier hits: *The Dells* explains doo-wop to people too young to remember the real thing.

For a pick-up match, *The Dells Vs. the Dramatics* never lapses into hot-dog tricks. Sensitive arrangements carry the day: "Love Is Missing From Our Lives" is clearly a duet between two harmony groups, not two lead singers. Dramatics main man Ron Banks erupts with gruff, joyous Stax soul on "Choosing Up On You," but the Dells' Marvin Junior invests "Strung Out Over You" with tragic, helpless beauty. This battle royale comes out to a draw—everyone's a winner. The Dells' more recent and far less necessary efforts on Mercury and Private have fallen out of print. But once again, this veteran group rebounded: "A Heart Is a House for Love," taken from *The Five Heartbeats* soundtrack, sounds comfortable and assured on the 1991 R&B charts. *On Their Corner* is a luminous single-disc collection. The deliciously orchestrated mid-'70s ballads ("I Wish It Was Me You Loved" and "My Pretending Days Are Over") shimmer alongside the Dells' earlier, better-known hits. Seventy minutes of soul vocal group heaven.
— M.C.

THE DELL VIKINGS
★ ★ ★ ★ **1956 Audition Tapes (Collectables, NA)**
★ ★ ★ ★ **The Dell Vikings (Collectables, NA)**

One of the first biracial groups in rock history, the Dell Vikings assembled in 1955 when all five of its original members were stationed at the same Air Force base in Pittsburgh. Signed to the local Fee Bee label, the group cut two Top Ten hits in 1957 with "Come Go With Me" and "Whispering Bells," both featuring complex vocal parts, imaginative production and strong lead vocals by Kripp Johnson. The Air Force's habit of transferring personnel overseas contributed to numerous changes within the Dell Vikings (one of the latter configurations included Chuck Jackson), and in late '57 the group lost Johnson when he was bound by contract to remain with Fee Bee while the other group members jumped to Mercury. Johnson formed a new Dell Vikings (including Jackson), but had no more success than did Mercury's version of the group, which is to say none. *The Dell Vikings* duplicates an original Fee Bee cover and logo and contains "Come Go With Me" and "Whispering Bells," two great songs that only improve with time; also included are some of the Mercury sessions featuring fine singing but sluggish production. The curious item remaining in print is Collectables' *1956 Audition Tapes*, which lacks even a scintilla of liner information to indicate the circumstances or time of the recordings. Whether it is a true audition, or demo, tape is open to question. But even demo tapes are expected to show some professional polish, and this one does: the voices are smooth and mature, neither a ragged edge nor a false note anywhere, and the vocal arrangements are all worked out to final form. A disc jockey who identifies himself as Barry Kay of WJAS in Pittsburgh introduces the tape and crops up between songs with brief commentary on the next song's origins; at the end of the tape he advises that "this is just an audition tape; we used only drums and electric guitar. Now it's up to you."

Well, if there are drums and electric guitar, they're buried so low that the Dell Vikings sound like they're performing a cappella. But this tape does show the group's roots in a close, sweet harmony sound that is far less percussive than that of their Fee Bee recordings. The *1956 Audition Tapes* isn't the Holy Grail of doo-wop, but it's a fascinating document that shows the Dell Vikings stripped down and still wonderful, even without the rock & roll backdrop that enlivened their two big hits. For those who prefer the rock & roll backdrop, *Dell Vikings* is a must. — D.M.

THE DELMORE BROTHERS
★ ★ ★ **Brown's Ferry Blues 1933–41 Recordings (Country, NA)**
★ ★ ★ **The Best of the Delmore Brothers (Starday, NA)**

Duly acknowledged as being among the groups that refocused the Grand Ole Opry from a showcase for string bands to one for singers, Alton and Rabon Delmore, a couple of unassuming lads born in Alabama after the turn of the century, have only recently been given credit for broadening the scope of the country music of their time. The Brothers' two hard-to-find albums document two distinct periods of their history. *Brown's Ferry Blues*, on the obscure Country label, showcases the country-blues with which they made their name in the '30s, while *The Best of* reflects their move toward a more rhythmically driving, black-influenced style. Beyond these notable achievements, the Delmores were also prolific songwriters, whose "Blues Stay Away From Me" and "Beautiful Brown Eyes" have become country standards. — D.M.

CATHY DENNIS
★ ★ ★½ **Move to This (Polydor, 1990)**

Dennis first made a splash singing D-Mob's perky "C'Mon and Get My Love" (included here), but proved she was no producer's plaything by flanking that track with dance hits of her own devising. Well-crafted and soulfully sung, it's an impressive (if lightweight) debut. — J.D.C.

SANDY DENNY
★ ★ ★   **Fotheringay (Island, 1970)**
★ ★ ★½ **The North Star Grassman and the Ravens (1971; Hannibal, 1987)**
★ ★ ★ ★ **Sandy (A&M, 1972)**
★ ★ ★   **Rendezvous (1973; Hannibal, 1986)**
★ ★ ★½ **Like an Old Fashioned Waltz (Island, 1977; Hannibal, 1986)**
★ ★ ★ ★ **The Best of Sandy Denny (Hannibal, 1987)**
★ ★ ★½ **Sandy Denny and the Strawbs (Hannibal, 1991)**
★ ★ ★ ★ **Who Knows Where the Time Goes? (Hannibal, 1991)**

One of the finest singers England has ever produced, Sandy Denny was a linchpin of the original Fairport Convention. Delivering, alongside Richard Thompson and Ian Matthews, a radical mixture of Dylan covers and Renaissance music, she helped make Fairport leaders (in company with Pentangle) of Britain's '60s Olde Musik revival.

Denny had been a member, first, of a sort of lesser Fairport, the Strawbs, and Hannibal's *Sandy Denny and the Strawbs*, a 1991 reissue of their unreleased 1967 tapes, captures exactly her early promise—on assured folk numbers by Dave Cousins, she sings with unerring precision, her bell-like delivery coming across as a very natural gift. *The Best of Sandy Denny* includes selections from her Fairport work—and while the individual albums represented (*Unhalfbricking, Liege and Lief*) remain essential listening in their entirety—the compilation's choices do her justice. After Fairport, she formed Fotheringay, whose style continued along the lines of lutes 'n' flutes. *The North Star Grassman and the Ravens* is her final triumph of the style, making way for the fine modern folk of *Sandy* and *Like an Old Fashioned Waltz* (the latter features a deft remake of Cahn-Chaplin's "Until the Real Thing Comes Along," suggesting a jazz direction that Denny never fully developed).

Casting her as a pop singer didn't quite work on *Rendezvous*—despite its all-star cast (Steve Winwood, Richard Thompson), the album is dogged by a busy "Candle in the Wind" and a merely capable "Silver Threads and Golden Needles." The three-CD retrospective, *Who Knows Where the Time Goes?*, is an excellent collection of Denny's work with the Strawbs, Fairport, and Fotheringay, as well as her solo recordings (including live performances and outtakes).

In a tragic accident, Denny died in 1978 after falling down a flight of stairs. Today's neo-folkies owe her a debt, and a wider audience would certainly benefit from a Sandy Denny revival. — P.E.

JOHN DENVER
★ ★   **Poems, Prayers and Promises (RCA, 1971)**
★ ★   **Rocky Mountain High (RCA, 1972)**
★ ★½ **Greatest Hits (RCA, 1973)**
★   **Greatest Hits, Volume 2 (RCA, 1977)**

Why John Denver? Twenty years later, his superstar ascension is tough to figure. Of all the earnest strummers who followed in Bob Dylan's bootprints, Denver purveyed sentimental lyrics and slight vocals that barely distinguished him. "Leaving on a Jet Plane" (a hit for Peter, Paul and Mary) and "Goodbye Again" both have a surprisingly bittersweet folkie twang, but Denver quickly turned his homegrown "Rocky Mountain High" buzz into a hokey nature-boy media schtick. Where "Poems, Prayers and

Promises" ('71) waxes rhapsodic about the insight gained by passing the pipe around a campfire, "Rocky Mountain High" ('72) could be natural (maybe not) and that line in "Sunshine on My Shoulders" ('73) about "gets me high" comes across as wholesome and innocent as a Christmas special. *Greatest Hits* offers those tracks, and it should be all the Denver any sentient adult needs to hear. *Hits, Volume 2* charts his decline into sheer caricature. The ersatz-rural jive talk on "Thank God I'm a Country Boy" is insulting, the rest is just dull. — M.C.

DEPECHE MODE
★ ★   **Speak & Spell** (Sire, 1981)
★ ★   **A Broken Frame** (Sire, 1982)
★ ★   **Construction Time Again** (Sire, 1982)
★ ★   **People Are People** (Sire, 1984)
★ ★ ★½ **Some Great Reward** (Sire, 1985)
★ ★ ★   **Catching Up With Depeche Mode** (Sire, 1985)
★ ★ ★   **Black Celebration** (Sire, 1986)
★ ★½   **Music for the Masses** (Sire, 1987)
★ ★ ★½ **101** (Sire, 1989)
★ ★ ★½ **Violator** (Sire, 1990)

At the start of the Eighties, Depeche Mode was one more New Romantic synth-band, less arrogant but less amusing than Visage or Spandau Ballet. But by the decade's end, the Modes had soared beyond fad status—they were gigantic, the kings of arena techno-pop. Given that their robotic dance-fare is much less tuneful than OMD, and that they don't have even the highly distinctive, if morbid, charm of the Cure, their success remains baffling. Certainly, they'd mastered the very Eighties art of clever marketing, with ultra-designer CD covers and lots of attitude, and they worked like maniacs (an output of an album a year recalls Sixties popsters, not late-model artistes). Basically, the band concentrated on singles, and on winning the hearts of disaffected, artsy teens. Like Kraftwerk, the granddaddy of the genre, Depeche Mode insisted on a synthesizers-only sound; this technophile purism resulted, of course, in an overall atmosphere of airlessness and chilly perfection.

Vince Clarke's "Just Can't Get Enough" was the snappy confection that sold *Speak & Spell*—it's catchy, as is most of the debut. Clarke departed and left Martin Gore very much in charge, but *A Broken Frame* and *Construction Time Again* are *Speak* remakes, even if the latter flashes a new seriousness in its lyrics. With *Some Great Reward*,

Depeche made its first strong album. The palette of textures is more varied, and the album grapples with interesting themes—the dominance/submission politics of "Master and Servant" and the iconoclasm of "Blasphemous Rumours." Slow and portentous, *Black Celebration* finds the boys brooding—and singer David Gahan attempting emotion. *Music for the Masses* is cheerier, but slighter. *Violator* features "Personal Jesus," by far the band's best single (it even swings, slightly), and it's the strongest Depeche Mode album since *Reward*.

A massive in-concert package, *101* may be the most palatable Depeche for all but cultists. Crowd noises add a touch of humanity, and the live ambience helps the band sound marginally less mechanical. *Catching Up* is a decent greatest-hits collection of early work. — P.E.

DEREK AND THE DOMINOS
★ ★ ★ ★ ★ **Layla and Other Assorted Love Songs** (RSO, 1970)
★ ★ ★½   **In Concert** (RSO, 1973)
★ ★ ★½   **The Layla Sessions/20th Anniversary Edition** (Polydor, 1990)

An astonishing evocation of unrequited love, "Layla" is almost as celebrated for its real life circumstances as for its emotionally involving sound. Written for the most part by Eric Clapton and inspired by the classical Persian love poem "The Story of Layla and Majnun," the song sprung from a love triangle between Clapton, his best friend (George Harrison) and the best friend's wife (Pattie Boyd). Heavy stuff, to be sure; indeed, Clapton later admitted that, "being Derek was a cover for the fact that I was trying to steal someone else's wife." Of course, everyone knew Derek was Eric, just as they knew that the Dominos were the rhythm section Clapton had picked up through his association with Delaney and Bonnie. But it was just as obvious that the pain and longing expressed in the single was real, and that genuine show of emotion puts an edge on Clapton's vocals and fire in his guitar playing, helping his churning rhythm work throw sparks against the tart counterpoint of Duane Allman's slide. But it's Jim Gordon's stately, pastoral piano figure that has the final word, adding an air of hope and transcendence that seems almost to answer the pleas of the opening verses. Rarely do love songs provide such a sense of redemption.

That isn't the only place such anguish

comes across on *Layla and Other Assorted Love Songs*—"Have You Ever Loved a Woman" and "Why Does Love Got to Be So Sad" spring to mind—but the album isn't just an exploration of love denied. Instead, *Layla* is ultimately about the transformation of the blues. "Bell Bottom Blues," for instance, distills the pop blues approach of Blind Faith and Cream; "Tell the Truth" brings the white soul groove Clapton mastered with Delaney and Bonnie to its fruition; while the exquisitely arranged "Little Wing" pulls a pathos from the song that even Hendrix missed.

As with any masterpiece, it wasn't easy achieving such clarity of vision, and anyone wishing to hear just how much mediocre music had to be thrown away in making the album need only listen through the almost two-and-a-quarter hours of outtakes and jam sessions included in *The Layla Sessions*. Although this 20th-anniversary-issue box set will doubtless be of interest to guitar fiends (thanks to more than an hour's worth of Clapton-Allman jams) and Clapton collectors, the sheer volume of material seems almost to lessen the original album's achievement. *In Concert* at least has the advantage of a slightly different set list, including Blind Faith's "Presence of the Lord" and three songs from Clapton's first solo album. — J.D.C.

RICK DERRINGER

★★½ **All American Boy (Blue Sky, 1973)**
★★½ **Derringer (Blue Sky, 1976)**
★★★ **Live (Blue Sky, 1977)**

A wunderkind at 15, Indiana's Rick Derringer formed the McCoys and had a great frat-rock hit in 1965 with "Hang On Sloopy." By the late '70s, the cute guitarist was dueling with Johnny Winter on a series of albums—and nearly holding his own, if not on the blues, then certainly on the rockers. But with his solo career, he proved, like Ron Wood or Mick Ronson, unsteady when straining beyond his capacity as a very strong sideman. *All American Boy* reprised "Rock 'n' Roll Hoochie Koo," the bar-band hit he penned for Winter (Rick's guitar sounded great; sadly missing were Winter's slurs and yelling), but on anything other than boogie, Derringer's vocals were thin and his ambitions confused by fusion-style instrumentals and MOR-ish ballads. *Live* shows Derringer at his most rockin'. *Spring Fever* (now out of print) featured a neat update of "Sloopy." In 1976, forming the band "Derringer" with the tough rhythm section of Kenny Aronson and Vinny

Appice, he focused on rock & roll—but with surprisingly iffy results. Due largely to a muscular production by Mike Chapman that overturned the glossiness of the group's other records (now deleted), *If I Weren't So Romantic, I'd Shoot You* was the crunchiest: "It Ain't Funny" swaggered fine, a cover of Warren Zevon's "Lawyers, Guns and Money" was credible—plus, there was the novelty of the (awful) lyrics to the title track, dreamed up by the odd pairing of Alice Cooper and Bernie Taupin. — P.E.

JACKIE DESHANNON

★★★ **Laurel Canyon (Imperial, 1968)**
★★½ **Jackie (Atlantic, 1972)**
★★★★ **The Best of Jackie DeShannon (Rhino, 1991)**

Jackie DeShannon scored massive hits in 1965 and 1969 with Burt Bacharach's "What the World Needs Now is Love" and her own "Put a Little Love in Your Heart"—but despite possessing a terrific, sexy-hoarse singing style and releasing a number of instrumentally impressive albums (which have all fallen out of print), she has remained a behind-the-scenes wonder, best known for her songwriting. Kentucky-born, DeShannon moved to L.A. when she was 16, and began churning out hits for Brenda Lee and collaborating with Randy Newman and Phil Spector cohort Jack Nitzsche. Her early singles were orchestral-rock gems—"When You Walk in the Room" and "Needles and Pins," both hits for the Searchers. For a while she turned out note-perfect Supremes homages ("Love Is Leading Me," "Are You Ready for This") before going the singer-songwriter route in the late '60s. A solid concept album, *Laurel Canyon*, featured her best work of this period.

Playing with members of Elvis's touring band, she put out the country-tinged *Jackie*, and in 1975 co-wrote "Bette Davis Eyes," the song that made Kim Carnes a star. DeShannon's solo albums aren't easy to find. Luckily, the Rhino collection is very strong—it features pop craft of the very highest order. — P.E.

DEVO

★★★★ **Q: Are We Not Men? A: We Are Devo (Warner Bros., 1978)**
★★★ **Duty Now For the Future (Warner Bros., 1979)**
★★★½ **Freedom of Choice (Warner Bros., 1980)**
★ **Devo Live (EP) (Warner Bros., 1981)**

★★★ New Traditionalists (Warner Bros., 1981)
★★ Oh No! It's Devo (Warner Bros., 1982)
★ Shout (Warner Bros., 1984)
★ E-Z Listening Disc (Rykodisc, 1987)
★★ Total Devo (Enigma, 1988)
★★ Now It Can Be Told (Enigma, 1989)
★ Smooth Noodle Maps (Enigma/Capitol, 1990)
★★ Hardcore, Vol. 1 (Rykodisc, 1990)
★★★★ Greatest Hits (Warner Bros., 1991)
★★★½ Greatest Misses (Warner Bros., 1991)

Devo was a highly elaborate, and pretty good, joke. Embarking upon a furious, mystic mission to redeem rock of its signature "excesses"—passion, rhythm, tunefulness and aspirations to meaning—these '80s postmodernists dubbed themselves "suburban robots here to entertain corporate life-forms." The product of a sensibility spun-off from William Burroughs, Warhol, Kraftwerk and drive-in sci-fi, Devo's vigorous embrace of technology paid off in hilarious, deadpan videos, daffy futuristic uniforms and a neat mythology—with its mascot/idol the kewpie-freak Booji Boy, the Devo shtick celebrated "de-evolutionized" blankness, with the corporation replacing love and family, and the microchip filling in for the soul.

Like most radical gestures, Devo was best in its first flexing—*Q: Are We Not Men? A: We Are Devo* was a brilliant hoot, with the fearsome five clinically deconstructing the Stones' "Satisfaction" and, in "Mongoloid" and "Jocko Homo," penning anthems to hail the victory of "aliens" over "animals." The group's snappiest single was *Freedom of Choice's* "Whip It"; its danceability seemed almost to subvert the tight-hipped Devo ideology—or to suggest that even androids sometime like to funk it up. "Through Being Cool," off *New Traditionalists*, is swift; it celebrates sheer wimpery. The album also boasts one of their patented, debunking covers—Lee Dorsey's "Working in the Coalmine" done with an assembly-line sense of swing. The rest of Devo is the same gestalt. Funny but monochromatic. — P.E.

HOWARD DEVOTO
★★ Jerky Versions of the Dream (I.R.S., 1983)

LUXURIA (HOWARD DEVOTO AND NOKO)
★★★½ Unanswerable Lust (Beggars Banquet/RCA, 1988)
★★★½ Beast Box (Beggars Banquet/RCA, 1990)

In the late '70s, Howard Devoto played smart, tough pop with the Buzzcocks; he then formed Magazine and spent most of the '80s churning out humming synth-trance music, heavy with melodramatic angst. With Magazine alumni Barry Adamson and Formula, he produced more of the same painstaking, overweening stuff on *Jerky Versions of the Dream*—vignettes of urban alienation, loss of soul, ennui, etc., etc. In 1988, Devoto joined up with a multi-instrumentalist going by the novel name of Noko: the pair became Luxuria—a ruthlessly artful aggregation. Actually, Devoto began making the most interesting music of his career by pushing the pedal to the metal—where once he was simply pretentious, he now was well-nigh operatic, his songs assuming a heady, if inscrutable grandeur. *Unanswerable Lust* sounds like pop dreamed up by Cocteau; Howard quotes Proust (in French), gleefully employs words like "nyktomorphic" in his cryptic-gorgeous lyrics, builds up by means of brass and string arrangements an air of exhaustion—and manages to pull the whole thing off. His voice, hectoring or whining, remains problematic, but the music is stunning.

Beast Box is equally unrelenting. Ranging from meditations on Kennedy and Monroe, Elvis's corpse, "my prick," "Winnie the Obscure," and the "funerary nakedness" of some object of his desire, Devoto pulls out all the stops—he raves, he trembles. With Noko joining in on violin and "banjolin," he actually makes decadence interesting again—a feat that hasn't been managed since early Roxy Music. — P.E.

NEIL DIAMOND
★★ Sweet Caroline (MCA, 1969)
★★ Touching You, Touching Me (MCA, 1969)
★★ Tap Root Manuscript (MCA, 1970)
★★ Stones (MCA, 1971)
★★½ Neil Diamond/Gold (MCA, 1971)
★★ Moods (MCA, 1972)
★★★ Hot August Night (MCA, 1972)
★★ Rainbow (MCA, 1973)
½★ Jonathan Livingston Seagull (Columbia, 1973)
★ Serenade (Columbia, 1974)

★ ★ ★ ★   His Twelve Greatest Hits (MCA, 1974)
★ ★¹/₂ Beautiful Noise (Columbia, 1976)
★ ★   Love at the Greek (Columbia, 1977)
★   I'm Glad You're Here With Me Tonight (Columbia, 1977)
★ ★   You Don't Bring Me Flowers (Columbia, 1978)
★   September Morn (Columbia, 1979)
★ ★   The Jazz Singer (Capitol, 1980)
★   On the Way to the Sky (Columbia, 1981)
★ ★ ★¹/₂ Greatest Hits, Volume II (Columbia, 1982)
★   Heartlight (Columbia, 1982)
★ ★ ★ ★¹/₂ Classics/The Early Years (Columbia, 1983)
★   Primitive (Columbia, 1984)
★   Headed to the Future (Columbia, 1986)
★   Hot August Night II (Columbia, 1987)
★   The Best Years of Our Lives (Columbia, 1988)
★   Lovescape (Columbia, 1991)
★ ★ ★   The Greatest Hits (1966–1992)

This Brooklyn native worked at the Brill Building in the '60s, writing hits for a variety of performers before striking out on his own. Once you've heard Neil Diamond apply that ripe baritone to "I'm a Believer," well, the Monkees' version just won't sound the same. Though he eventually descends into sensitive MOR schmaltz for the bulk of his career, once upon a time Diamond rocked Top Forty AM radio. Dependably. Produced by fellow Brill Building vets Jeff Barry and Ellie Greenwich, Diamond's string of hit singles (originally released on the Bang label) winds tight rhythm tracks around hooky, folk-flavored choruses. *Classics/The Early Years* (1983) grabs all of his essential sides in one succinct, exciting package: "Kentucky Woman," "Cherry, Cherry," "Red, Red Wine."

In the '70s, Diamond tried to position himself as a "serious" singer-songwriter—being a good pop singer and songwriter just wasn't enough. His MCA albums are windy bores, mostly, though each one spawned an indelible hit single or two. Even while pursuing his creative muse, Diamond still wields the knack for crafting catchy tunes. His *Twelve Greatest Hits* contains guilty pleasures galore: honestly, who can resist singing along with such wedding classics as "Sweet Caroline" or "Song Sung Blue"? *Hot August Night* is a convincingly sweaty live set—closer to Elvis-in-Vegas than

Engelbert Humperdinck, anyway. From the proto–new age mush of *Jonathan Livingston Seagull* onward, it's all downhill. *Beautiful Noise*, produced by Robbie Robertson, is a muddled-sounding, much-hyped attempt to realign Diamond with the rock audience. *Twelve Greatest Hits, Vol. II* culls the best tracks from that incongruous album, along with a Barbra Streisand duet ("You Don't Bring Me Flowers") and several tracks from the soundtrack to *The Jazz Singer*. Diamond flirted with rock—or something—on the clueless *The Best Years of Our Lives* (1988). But neither that album nor the pallid *Lovescape* can erase the indelible memory of "Solitary Man" (from *Classics*) or "Cracklin' Rosie" (from *Tap Root Manuscript* and *His Twelve Greatest Hits*). *The Greatest Hits (1966–1992)* isn't nearly as definitive as its title suggests. The early rockers and "You Don't Bring Me Flowers" are the original versions, but "Sweet Caroline" and '70s hits are represented by live in 1992 renditions.
— M.C.

THE DIAMONDS

★ ★¹/₂ Best of the Diamonds (Rhino, 1984)
This white quartet from Canada established itself in 1956 with a string of cover versions of songs originally recorded by black vocal groups, including "Why Do Fools Fall in Love," the Willows' "The Church Bells May Ring" and the G-Clefs' "Ka-Ding-Dong." They hit the big time in early '57 with "Little Darlin'," which went to Number Two on the pop charts and remains one of the most popular singles on oldies radio today. In its original version, "Little Darlin' " was an R&B hit for the Gladiolas, whose lead singer, Maurice Williams, also wrote the song. Williams went on to found the Zodiacs; another of his songs, "Stay," was a national hit and also oft-covered by white groups. The Diamonds' version of "Little Darlin' " deserves its place of honor in early group harmony annals: the record opens with castanets chattering away, a cowbell clanging, and then a falsetto voice shrieking, "Ay-yi-yi-yi-yi-yi-yi-yi-yi/ yi-yi-yi-yi." It's a classic. Lead vocalist Dave Somerville delivers a frenetic, but controlled, reading of Williams's lyrics, and the recitative by bass singer Bill Reed walks a fine mock-serioso line that plays well against the other singers' urgent wailing.

Other than this, the Diamonds have left behind precious little, especially if one has access to the original versions of their more popular singles. To their credit, they didn't butcher the black style to the same degree as Pat Boone, and most of the cuts on *Best of* are agreeable examples of middle-of-the-road, doo-wop harmonizing. But the Diamonds only got it together once, for "Little Darlin' "; the work showcased here makes a case for them as spirited but shallow crooners, and nothing more. — D.M.

THE DICTATORS
★ ★ ★ ★   Go Girl Crazy (1975; Epic/Sony Special Products, 1991)
★ ★ ½ Manifest Destiny (Asylum, 1977)
★ ★ ½ Bloodbrothers (Asylum, 1978)
★ ★ ½ Live—Fuck 'Em If They Can't Take a Joke (ROIR, 1981)

The Dictators really couldn't play or sing very well, but that didn't stop these Bronx bombers from tackling the Beach Boys' harmonies and Lou Reed's *Rock & Roll Animal* head on. *Go Girl Crazy* takes classic rock & roll subject matter ("I Live for Cars & Girls"), and drags it down to an exciting new level of tasteless guitar-riff excess ("Teengenerate"). There's a pronounced self-consciousness to the Dictators' goony stance, though it doesn't spill over into contempt for the audience; most of the jokes have hooks, and that sure doesn't hurt. "California Sun" lands squarely between the surf-rock original and the Ramones' speedy 1977 version: heard in that light, the Dictators provide a missing link between suburban metal and urban punk. The out-of-print Asylum albums regress to a more traditional, heavier sound. And by the time of the live reunion album (a cassette-only release), all the recycled power chords and pro wrestling references started to sound shopworn. You can't stay "young, fast and scientific" forever. But for *Go Girl Crazy*'s 30-plus minutes, anyway, the Dictators still rule. — M.C.

BO DIDDLEY
★ ★ ★ Bo Diddley (1958; Chess/MCA, 1986)
★ ★ ★ ★ Bo Diddley/Go Bo Diddley (1958, 1959; Chess/MCA, 1987)
★ ★ ★ In the Spotlight (1960; Chess/MCA, 1987)
★ ★ ★ ★ Bo Diddley Is a Gunslinger (1963; Chess/MCA, 1989)
★ ★ Two Great Guitars: Bo Diddley & Chuck Berry (1964; MCA/Chess, 1986)
★ ★ The London Bo Diddley Sessions (1973; Chess/MCA, 1989)

★ ★ ★ ★ The Super Super Blues Band: Bo Diddley, Muddy Waters & Howlin' Wolf (Chess/MCA, 1986)
★ ★ ★ ★ Superblues: Bo Diddley, Muddy Waters and Little Walter (Chess/MCA, 1986)
★ ★ ★ ★ His Greatest Sides (MCA/Chess, 1986)
★ ★ ★ ★ ★ The Chess Box (Chess/MCA, 1990)

Bo Diddley is a man who took a simple shave-and-a-haircut-six-bits rhythm and added to it layer upon rhythmic layer, courtesy of Jerome Green's maracas and his own heavily-tremeloed guitar on which he played two different rhythms simultaneously. Add in the myriad harmonic and textural approaches Diddley employed as a guitarist, and it's easy to see why both guitarists *and* percussionists are still coming to grips with the elements of his sound. Beyond this, Diddley was in control of his studio recordings, even if he wasn't credited as a producer, and he also built his own home studio and recorded in primitive stereo by locking together two-track and three-track machines. As a prolific songwriter he locked together gospel and blues and spiced the blend with quotes from black street-corner culture ("Say Man" being an early example of Diddley's use of "the dozens," or ritualized insults, boasts and dares, in song). Add to this an instantly identifiable voice and a view begins to form of the fellow born Ellas McDaniel in McComb, Mississippi, as "500 percent more man," as he asserted in one of his most memorable lyrics.

The logical place to begin assessing McDaniels's work is *The Chess Box*, two CDs containing 45 Diddley tracks recorded between 1955 and 1968, including all the best-known songs—"Who Do You Love," "I'm a Man/Bo Diddley," "Mona," "Say Man," an extended version of "Signifying Blues"—as well as a host of alternate takes, B sides and previously unreleased tracks. In the accompanying booklet, critic Robert Palmer offers a complex, authoritative dissection of Diddley's music that demands the artist's *oeuvre* be considered anew.

The Chess Box may be the Alpha and Omega of the Diddley catalogue, but in between are some interesting entries that should pique the curiosity of anyone inspired by Palmer's essay to look for further justification of Diddley's genius. *Bo Diddley Is a Gunslinger* is highly recommended for its uniform first-rate performances, notable among them being

"Ride On Josephine," which finds Diddley doing Berry (Chuck, that is) and opening with a riff copped by Lonnie Mack for his own take on Berry's "Memphis." Diddley's steamroller version of "Sixteen Tons," coupling the famous beat to an angry, menacing vocal, is a classic. Also on the A list is *The Super Super Blues Band* teaming Diddley with Muddy Waters and Howlin' Wolf on a fabulous set of raw, electric blues, with all three participants toasting each other at every turn. For sheer drive, few albums approach the jiving, juking, incendiary summit meeting heard on *Superblues*. Diddley, Waters and Little Walter Jacobs play like men with hellhounds on their trail, talking trash, spurring each other to more resonant performances. The version of Diddley's "Who Do You Love" included is the model for the raging, near-meltdown performance of the tune that Diddley delivers on the *La Bamba* soundtrack. Jacobs blows low and mean behind Diddley and Waters on "I'm a Man," as the two guitarists spar instrumentally and verbally. The other super session here, *Two Great Guitars*, teams Diddley and Chuck Berry on four extended instrumental tracks that are pretty much in the sound-and-fury-signifying-nothing category. Diddley's first two album releases, *Bo Diddley* and *Go Bo Diddley* are now available in a two-fer CD and represent in 24 tracks prime early Diddley; this is a good alternative to the more expensive *Chess Box* for anyone on a limited budget or with only a casual interest in Diddley's work, as it contains a number of hit sides ("Bo Diddley," "I'm a Man," "Who Do You Love," "Say Man") as well as scintillating items such as "Diddy Wah Diddy" and "Before You Accuse Me." *The London Bo Diddley Sessions*, recorded in 1973 (six of its nine tracks were actually recorded in London, with bassist Roy Wood being the most prominent guest artist), finds Diddley addressing different styles of music— Memphis soul, reggae, Sly Stone–style funk—without a great deal of success, although "Get Out of My Life" is a nice dip into soul music's mellow division. Diddley's fourth album for Chess, *In the Spotlight*, includes "Road Runner," as well as a lesser-known gem, "Signifying Blues." — D.M.

DIFFORD & TILBROOK
★ ★ ★ **Difford & Tilbrook (A&M, 1984)**
Although the writing has its merits, the performances on this solo (duo?) album by

the Squeeze writing team are too flat and lifeless for these songs to seem anything more than clever. Consequently, though its better moments—"Love's Crashing Waves," "Man for All Seasons"—come across well enough, the rest of the album reeks of wasted potential. — J.D.C.

THE DILLARDS
★ ★ ★ **Back Porch Bluegrass (Elektra, 1963)**
★ ★½ **Live . . . Almost! (Elektra, 1964)**
★ ★ ★ **Pickin' and Fiddlin' (Elektra, 1965)**
★ ★ ★½ **Wheatstraw Suite (Elektra, 1968)**
★ ★ ★ **Copperfields (Elektra,1970)**
★ ★ ★ **Roots and Branches (Anthem, 1972)**
★ ★ **The Dillards Vs. the Incredible Flying L.A. Time Machine (Flying Fish, 1977)**
★ ★ **Decade Waltz (Flying Fish, 1979)**
★ ★ ★ **Homecoming and Family Reunion (Flying Fish, 1981)**
★ ★ ★ **Let It Fly (Vanguard, 1990)**
DOUG DILLARD
★ ★ ★½ **Heaven (Flying Fish, 1979)**
★ ★ ★ **Jackrabbit! (Flying Fish, 1980)**
★ ★ ★ **What's That (Flying Fish, 1986)**
★ ★ ★½ **Heartbreak Hotel (Flying Fish, 1988)**
RODNEY DILLARD
★ ★½ **Rodney Dillard at Silver Dollar City (Flying Fish, 1985)**
DILLARD HARTFORD DILLARD
★ **Permanent Wave (Flying Fish, 1980)**
Originally an orthodox bluegrass outfit from the Ozark Mountains, the Dillards achieved a folk-country-rock synthesis by hanging out with Roger McGuinn, leavening their own trad repertoire with Dylan songs, and touring relentlessly. Giving concerts that highlighted their ingratiating aw-shucks humor—these boys had none of the remoteness that sometimes dogs folk purists—they won over a pop audience, while conceding nothing in the way of instrumental finesse or authentic spirit. Headed in their early days by the brothers Dillard–Rodney on vocals and guitar, Doug playing banjo and singing–the group went through many personnel changes during its long career, but its vision remained intact.
Featuring a very early version of "Duelin' Banjos," the band's debut was stone-cold bluegrass; *Live . . . Almost!* was almost a comedy album, so light-hearted was the Dillards' approach to stage work. With *Pickin' and Fiddlin'* they began a sporadic alliance with ace fiddler Byron Berline—and the album remains one of their most solid sets of old-time music.

Doug then departed, and the group began branching out. *Wheatstraw Suite* was their most successful foray into country rock; its versions of Lennon/McCartney and Tim Hardin songs don't sound at all jarring alongside Rodney Dillard originals. *Copperfields* was a kind of *Wheatstraw* II, less satisfying, but still energetic.

From *Roots and Branches* through *Decade Waltz*, the Dillards strayed farthest from their bluesgrass roots: these records, then, aren't quite so effective. The live *Homecoming* finds them back on more familiar turf; the banjo contributions by paterfamilias, Homer "Pop" Dillard, are especially charming. *Let It Fly* was a trifle smooth, but given the fact that it was released more than 30 years after the Dillards started out, the freshness of the group's playing is impressive.

Of the Dillard spinoffs, the only one that doesn't really work is Dillard Hartford Dillard's *Permanent Wave*; a slick collaboration with John "Gentle on My Mind" Hartford, the record is bland when it isn't bizarre (a banjo band doing Stevie Wonder's "Boogie On Reggae Woman"?). Doug's *Heaven* is a fine album of country spirituals, and *Heartbreak Hotel,* boast the strong, sometimes scrappy, vocalist Ginger Boatwright (her singing on the title track to *Heartbreak Hotel* is particularly sassy). — P.E.

DINO

★★ 24/7 (4th & B'way/Island, 1989)
★★ Swingin' (Island, 1990)

For all the musical merit of his songs, from the K.C.-quoting wit of "I Like It" (from *24/7*) to the slick, Latin hip-hop beats behind "Romeo" (from *Swingin'*), the treacly teen-love lyrics make it unlikely that anyone over 13 could take this twaddle seriously. — J.D.C.

DINOSAUR JR

★★ Dinosaur (Homestead, 1985)
★★ You're Living All Over Me (SST, 1987)
★★ Bug (SST, 1988)
★★★★ Green Mind (Sire, 1991)

After getting it together on three explosive but uneven indie records and five years of touring, Massachusetts's Dinosaur Jr released a bang-up masterpiece in 1991: *Green Mind.* For guitar maniacs only, this crunching, thunderous happy stuff recalls Neil Young at his Crazy Horse rawest; at other times, the ghost of Hendrix grins. Mainly, however, it's to the early

Replacements that Dinosaur owes a heavy nod. Mastermind vocalist-axman J Mascis writes raveups with the amphetamine melodies of the Replacements; his voice doesn't sound dissimilar to Paul Westerberg's—and even the persona behind his songs is reminiscent of Westerberg in its bad-boy-with-a-big-heart charm. Giddily entertaining, Dinosaur can even redeem a title like "Puke + Cry," and "How'd You Pin That One on Me" is the glorious noise every garage band dreams of. — P.E.

DIO

★½ Holy Diver (Warner Bros., 1983)
★½ Last in Line (Warner Bros., 1984)
★ Sacred Heart (Warner Bros., 1985)
★★ Dream Evil (Warner Bros., 1987)
★½ Lock Up the Wolves (Warner Bros., 1990)

A real traditionalist, Ronnie James Dio makes heavy-metal albums the old-fashioned way, with plenty of sludgelike guitar, dime-store satanism and the sort of vocal vibrato usually found in aging Salvation Army workers. Granted, none of that offers enough to make *Holy Diver*, *Last in Line* or *Sacred Heart* distinguishable from one another (although *Heart* was recorded live, and therefore has somewhat flatter sound). But if foolish consistency is your favorite heavy-metal hobgoblin, they should be right up your alley. Astonishingly, *Dream Evil*— recorded after guitarist Vivian Campbell had left to join Whitesnake—alters the formula, as "Sunset Superman" possesses an almost-catchy melody. But that would soon pass—*Lock up the Wolves* merely reinvents the old sound with (apart from Dio himself) an entirely new cast of players. Guess you can't teach an old devil new tricks. — J.D.C.

DION

★★★ Presenting Dion and the Belmonts (1960; Collectables, 1983)
★★ When You Wish Upon a Star (1960; Collectables, 1983)
★★★ Runaround Sue (1961; Collectables, 1983)
★★★★ Dion Sings His Greatest Hits (Laurie, NA)
★★★★ Everything You Always Wanted to Hear by Dion and the Belmonts (Laurie, 1973)
★★★ Reunion: Dion & the Belmonts (1973; Rhino, 1989)
★★★ Dion's Greatest Hits (Columbia, 1973)
★★ Streetheart (Warner Bros., 1976)

★ ★ ★ **Return of the Wanderer (Lifesong, 1978)**

★ ★ ★ **Inside Job (DaySpring/Word, 1980)**

★ ★ ★ **Only Jesus (DaySpring/Word, 1981)**

★ ★ ★ **I Put Away My Idols (DaySpring/Word, 1983)**

★ ★ ★ ★ ★ **24 Original Classics (Arista, 1984)**

★ ★ ★ ★ **Seasons (DaySpring/Word, 1984)**

★ ★ ★ **Kingdom in the Streets (Myrrh/Word, 1985)**

★ ★ ★ **Velvet & Steel (DaySpring/Word, 1986)**

★ ★ ★ **Yo Frankie (Arista, 1989)**

★ ★ ★ **Bronx Blues: The Columbia Recordings (Columbia, 1990)**

★ ★ ★ ★ **20 Golden Classics (Collectables, NA)**

Exhibit A in defense of rock & roll in the years post-1958 and pre-1964: Dion DiMucci. The kid from the Bronx ranks with the greatest singers rock & roll has ever produced. Of Italian heritage, Dion was raised in the doo-wop era, and came out of a Neapolitan singing tradition that, like that of the black doo-wop singers whose roots were in gospel, elevated the ability to project personality, style and point of view to a plateau equal to technical facility. Consider that Vito and the Salutations, the Capris, the Crests, the Duprees, the Skyliners, and the Elegants all had compelling lead singers who created some of the '50s most memorable singles, and then understand that Dion closed out every one of them. Purists decry his early ballad-oriented material with the Belmonts (Fred Milano, Angelo D'Aleo, Carlo Mastrangelo), but in fact songs such as "Where or When" and "Teenager in Love" are performed with gripping commitment and sensitivity and stand up to any of the decade's best slow songs. On the other hand, it is also beyond dispute that nothing in Dion and the Belmonts' repertoire approached the magnitude of Dion's work as a solo artist.

Considering how the very mention of their name causes hearts to flutter among doo-wop aficionados, Dion and the Belmonts had only a brief fling together on record. Not that it wasn't memorable: seven Top Forty hits between 1958 and 1960 before Dion went solo. The first of these was "I Wonder Why," which mated the Belmonts' rousing group harmony support to Dion's soaring vocal in creating one of the decade's finest singles; it remains energizing to this day. Their breakthrough came in 1959, with a Doc Pomus–Mort

Shuman song that asked the eternal question, "Why must I be a teenager in love?" The group followed up with an interpretation of Rodgers and Hart's "Where or When" done in the style of early '50s vocal groups. It peaked at Number Three, and Dion opted to go it alone thereafter.

Out of the box he hit the Top Twenty in late 1960 with "Lonely Teenager." What happened next created a rock & roll legend. On his first single release in 1961, "Runaround Sue," Dion unleashed the persona that had only been suggested in his work with the Belmonts. Over the next three years he cut a succession of singles that reinforced the image of the tender-tough street kid. These records sounded great too —and such invention: "Little Diane" is enlivened by a kazoo solo that cooks. Backed mostly by an uncredited vocal group called the Del-Satins, Dion's lessons in self-assertiveness were further buttressed by hand claps and feisty arrangements that gave the singer some room to maneuver vocally against the grain of the song's momentum. This period is heavily documented on the Laurie, Collectables and out-of-print Arista albums (Arista's *24 Original Classics* also is the only one with annotation). FYI: the Collectables titles are repackages of original album releases complete with original cover art and in the case of *Runaround Sue*, original liner notes.

With 1963 came a move to Columbia Records, resulting in three Top Ten singles, and a total of five altogether in the Top Forty, including the bluesy "Ruby Baby," and a bit of rocking doo-wop in "Donna the Prima Donna." Following a Top Ten single in late '63, "Drip Drop," Dion was absent from the charts for five years. He'd had a drug problem since his teens, and it worsened as he became more famous. When he could work, he was moving in a different direction, into blues, folk, folk rock, but his new label, Columbia, declined at that juncture to release any of the sides he cut (these are now available on *Bronx Blues*). In 1968 he returned to the Laurie label, where he had begun his career with the Belmonts and as a solo artist. His first release captured the tenor of the times. "Abraham, Martin and John," a solemn, folk-based tribute to three slain leaders, was a temporary balm to a country beset by strife. Commercially it was the peak of this third phase of Dion's career. His song selection reflected the growth of his social consciousness: *Dion*, now out of print, included material by Bob Dylan, Joni Mitchell and Jimi Hendrix, as well as "Abraham, Martin and John."

Upon signing with Warner Bros. in 1969 Dion went full-tilt into folk rock with a series of low-key, introspective albums (now out of print), and an in-your-face anti-drug single, "Clean Up Your Own Back Yard." This period, however, was unfruitful commercially—a dream project with producer Phil Spector was such a dud that Warners declined even to issue the album Stateside (England got it instead). On the other hand, a one-shot reunion with the Belmonts at Madison Square Garden in 1972 produced *Reunion*, now available on Rhino. It shows Dion and the Belmonts all in fine voice, working some changes on their old material, and having the time of their lives.

Following the commercial debacle of his 1976 album, *Streetheart*, Dion resurfaced in 1978 on Lifesong, where his first and only release, *Return of the Wanderer*, was an aesthetic triumph. A single, "I Used to Be a Brooklyn Dodger," is one of Dion's most poignant vocals, finding him looking back, in fondness and in sorrow, at his younger life and what he had lost over time. Finding no audience for his music in the rock field, Dion turned to gospel, and without fanfare recorded several excellent albums extolling his newfound faith in God. These are best appreciated by true believers—in Dion and in God, one should add—but the persuasiveness of Dion's vocals often is mesmerizing.

But the journey Dion embarked on in 1960 continues today. He returned to the secular world following the publication of his autobiography in the late '80s and in '89 teamed up with producer Dave Edmunds on the inspired *Yo Frankie*. Edmunds keeps Dion front and center, while surrounding him with a guitar-heavy wall of sound and lush backup vocals. True, the album trades some on Dion's nostalgia value with "King of the New York Streets" and "Written on the Subway Wall Little Star," but its new-old ambience pushes Dion to some of his most impassioned performances. With body and soul intact, Dion serves notice here that his work remains unfinished.
— D.M.

DIRE STRAITS
★★★½ Dire Straits (Warner Bros., 1978)
★★★ Communiqué (Warner Bros., 1979)
★★★ Making Movies (Warner Bros., 1980)
★★★★ Love Over Gold (Warner Bros., 1982)
★★★ Twisting By the Pool (Warner Bros. EP, 1983)
★★★ Alchemy (Warner Bros., 1984)
★★★★½ Brothers in Arms (Warner Bros., 1985)
★★★ Money for Nothing (Warner Bros., 1988)
★★★★ On Every Street (Warner Bros., 1991)

Because Dire Straits are essentially the dominion of Mark Knopfler, an acerbic tunesmith and virtuoso guitarist, it's easy to assume that the band's greatest virtue would be its songwriting or fancy picking. But the truth is that those elements are generally more ornamental than essential; at bottom, Dire Straits is nothing if not a groove band. That's not the same thing as calling the Straits a funk band or soul act, mind you, for this group's notion of groove has far more in common with the low-key, country blues rhythms favored by J.J. Cale and later Eric Clapton. All of which ought to have been obvious from the quartet's first success, an insinuatingly bluesy bit of bar-band myth-making called "Sultans of Swing." As well as Knopfler's lyrics paint his picture of an under-appreciated pub combo, what ultimately sells the listener on the Sultans' unassuming greatness is the laid-back insistence of Dire Straits' rhythm work, a quality that carries through the rest of *Dire Straits*, from the Dylanesque flavor of "Wild West End" to the galloping groove of "Down to the Waterline."

Communiqué continues in that fashion, but expands the scope of Knopfler's storytelling through the moody, elegiac "Once Upon a Time in the West." With the departure of rhythm guitarist David Knopfler (Mark's brother), the band's size is scaled down, but the music on the aptly-titled *Making Movies* moves in the opposite direction, toward sprawling story-songs like the sweet, Springsteen-like "Romeo and Juliet," although, as "Skateaway" indicates, the band's pursuit of musical drama sometimes comes at the expense of melody. Fortunately, the band regains its focus for *Love Over Gold*, on which the Straits—now a quintet—easily sustain the mood and melodic structure of a 14-minute megawork like "Telegraph Road." Even better, they're able to augment such epics with material as sharply funny as the wry "Industrial Disease" or the lighthearted title tune from *Twisting by the Pool*.

Alchemy, a long-winded live album, focuses almost exclusively on the band's larger works, offering some flashes of instrumental brilliance but little insight into the songs, something that makes the pop-friendly brevity of the songs on *Brothers in Arms* all the more surprising. It may be easy to find parallels to the album's biggest hits in the band's early output—for instance, the way "Walk of Life" seems to cross "Sultans of Swing" with "Twisting by the Pool," or how "Money for Nothing" taps the same satiric vein as "Industrial Disease"—but the reality is that *Brothers* is an exception to Dire Straits' sound. A delightful exception, to be sure, and one that turned the band into a multi-platinum superact, but an exception nonetheless.

Perhaps that's why Knopfler and company waited so long to deliver that album's follow-up, *On Every Street* (*Money for Nothing* is simply a best-of collection). Although the album has its lighter moments, such as the dead-Presley "Calling Elvis" or the consumerist sarcasm of "Heavy Fuel," the bulk of its songs find Dire Straits doing what they do best, stretching dry, reflective words and tunes over moody, effortlessly maintained grooves. — J.D.C.

DIRTY DOZEN BRASS BAND
★★★ My Feet Can't Fail Me Now (George Wein Collection, 1984)
★★★½ Live: Mardi Gras in Montreux (Rounder, 1986)
★★★½ Voodoo (Columbia, 1989)
★★★★ The New Orleans Album (Columbia, 1990)
★★★★ Open Up: Whatcha Gonna Do for the Rest of Your Life? (Columbia, 1992)

A brass band in the most genuine sense, the only members of this octet who don't have to blow into their instruments are its drummers—one of whom plays snare, the other bass drum. Yet the band's sound seems traditional only if you accept the notion that progress is itself a tradition with such New Orleans outfits. Hence, the group emerges with a sound as likely to draw upon George Clinton as Bunk Johnson, and which performs Thelonious Monk tunes as if they were a bit of both. *My Feet Can't Fail Me Now* is perhaps the closest the group comes to straight jazz, and admittedly, it isn't all that close; *Mardi Gras in Montreux* covers some of the same territory, but with more humor and greater

energy (not to mention a killer revision of the theme from "The Flintstones"). *Voodoo*, though, is much more ambitious, augmenting the group's usual groove with occasional cameos (including bits by Dizzy Gillespie, Dr. John and Branford Marsalis). And though *The New Orleans Album* seems to continue in that vein with an Elvis Costello feature, its best moments actually come from lesser-known (outside of New Orleans, that is) guests like Dave Bartholomew and Eddie Bo. But *Whatcha Gonna Do for the Rest of Your Life?* needs no outside help to stretch the limits of the band's sound—the Dozen do it themselves, through the sassy funk of "Use Your Brains" and the eloquent laments of "The Lost Souls (of Southern Louisiana)." — J.D.C.

DIXIE DREGS
★★ Free Fall (Capricorn, 1977)
★★★½ What If (Capricorn, 1978)
★★★ Night of the Living Dregs (Capricorn, 1979)
★★★ The Best of the Dixie Dregs (Grand Slamm, 1988)
★★★½ Divided We Stand/The Best of The Dregs (Arista, 1989)

It's impossible to assess the Dregs outside of their chosen context—fusion, that misguided synthesis of jazz's time signatures, pretense and instrumental gunslinging and rock's volume and marketability. A horrid idea during its '70s flash, most of it sounds even worse now. But this Georgia quintet boasted some of the sharper players in a genre crammed with virtuosos, and, in guitarist Steve Morse, featured a composer capable of wit. Steering clear of the schmaltz of a Spyro Gyra, heading, in fact, closer to the Mahavishnu Orchestra, the Dregs joined the tightness of fusion to a certain happy thunder, best captured on *What If*. Violinist Allen Sloan provided novelty and sweep; bassist Andy West's demonic technique still left room for funking. "Sleep," from *Free Fall*, is a nice, Gothic lullaby; "Hand Jig" charmingly shows off Sloan's fiddle. "Punk Sandwich," from *Night of the Living Dregs*, is almost metal-fusion, a fitting sub-genre. — P.E.

DIXIE HUMMINGBIRDS
★★★★★ The Best of the Dixie Hummingbirds (Peacock, NA)
★★★★ In the Morning (Peacock, NA)
★★★★ A Christian Testimonial (Peacock, NA)

★ ★ ★ ★ **Dixie Hummingbirds Live (1977; MCA, 1991)**

From the first sung note of this outstanding live set, you understand why the Dixie Hummingbirds are first among equals in the pantheon of modern gospel quartets. Guitarist Howard Carroll comes on sweet and stinging, circling around the quintet's robust harmonies before lead singer Ira Tucker breaks out into a stomping declaration of spiritual fervor on "Doing All the Good I Can." The Birds then proceed to work the audience into a frenzy of redemption and renewal on 14 other tracks, all recorded live at a New Jersey church in 1976.

Though James Walker and James Davis are recognized as outstanding singers, it is Tucker who is the Birds' symbol and guiding light, one of the greatest vocalists and writers in gospel history. It was his style to move around on stage as the spirit dictated, or to stroll the aisles and mingle with the crowd as he delivered his testimony. As a writer he has brought country and gospel sensibilities together in his songs, several of which have found their way into the repertoires of white quartets.

Beginning in 1945 the Birds began a long association with Duke/Peacock Records, but this material is now out of print. *Live* and some albums made for a small Southern label, Atlanta International, are the only Birds albums in print. A good place to start, *Live* captures the group on a strong night, when all the singers make significant solo contributions and the audience plugs into the energy. They perform Paul Simon's "Loves Me Like a Rock," one of their fleeting moments of national acclaim as a result of having backed Simon's version on *There Goes Rhymin' Simon*. All in all, a rousing evening, and a good introduction to what the Hummingbirds do best.

Live is one of the initial entries in MCA's gospel reissue program of material recorded on the Peacock label. The Hummingbirds had a long association with Peacock beginning in 1952, and presumably more of their voluminous catalogue will be coming back onto the market in the years ahead. Until then, cutout titles to look for include *The Best of the Dixie Hummingbirds*, *In the Morning* and *A Christian Testimonial*.

— D.M.

WILLIE DIXON
★ ★ ★ ★ **Willie's Blues (1959; Bluesville/Prestige, 1990)**
★ ★ ★ ★ **I Am the Blues (Columbia, 1970)**

★ ★ **Hidden Charms (Bug/Capitol, 1988)**
★ ★ ★ ★ ★ **The Chess Box (Chess/MCA, 1988)**
★ ★ ★ **The Big Three Trio (Columbia, 1990)**

Without ever establishing a style of his own as distinctive as that of the artists with whom he has worked, Willie Dixon became one of the architects of urban blues on the strengths of his skills as a songwriter, bandleader, musician, arranger, producer and diplomat. In these roles Dixon reigned supreme at Chess Records in the 1950s and early '60s, when he worked in one capacity or another with every significant artist on the label. Even a cursory listing of his many songwriting credits indicates the breathtaking scope of his contributions to American music and to the language of the blues: "My Babe," "You Shook Me," "Back Door Man," "Little Red Rooster," "Spoonful," "Wang Dang Doodle," "I Can't Quit You Baby," "Seventh Son," "I Just Want to Make Love to You." Muddy Waters, Howlin' Wolf, Little Walter, Bo Diddley, Lowell Fulson, and Jimmy Witherspoon are only the most prominent of the musicians in Dixon's debt. They and others are heard on the two-CD boxed set from Chess/MCA, which is as essential a blues overview as any on the market. It's impossible to listen to the 36 tracks here and be complacent about Dixon's stature— even the overused term "giant" seems insufficient.

Oddly, Dixon failed to achieve great success as a solo artist. One can observe that Dixon the vocalist never sounded as transported as, for instance, Muddy Waters and Howlin' Wolf. Certainly there is nothing to quibble with in regards to the musicianship and production of his records, nor are Dixon's vocals totally bereft of inspiration. But the zone Waters and Wolf were in, where passion, pain and technique all blended into one explosive package, is one Dixon visited in other capacities, but not on his own releases.

That said, it should be added that Dixon's recordings all have their stirring moments. The earliest of these, Columbia's *Big Three Trio*, finds Dixon near the start of his career, joined by Leonard Caston and Ollie Crawford in a trio purveying blues-tinged popular music in the style of the Mills Brothers. Among the interesting tracks here is the Dixon-Caston–penned "If the Sea Was Whiskey," the first verse of which has shown up in countless songs, most notably

"Rollin' and Tumblin'." Bluesville/Prestige has re-released Dixon's first album as a bandleader, *Willie's Blues*, recorded in 1959 and featuring the redoubtable Memphis Slim on piano. Imbued with a dark, after-hours ambience, the album is Dixon's strongest solo recording. Dixon on standup bass and Gus Johnson on drums make a formidable rhythm section, which gives Slim, guitarist Wally Richardson and tenor sax man Al Ashby a solid foundation for their soloing. Dixon's stuttering vocal on "Nervous" is one of his most effective on record, and one of the better tracks is the loping "Youth to You," a thinly disguised reworking of "I Just Want to Make Love to You." *I Am the Blues* features Dixon's own interpretations of nine of his best-known songs, and for this reason alone becomes a good companion volume to the Chess box. Dixon's most recent effort, the T-Bone Burnett-produced *Hidden Charms*, is a solid if unspectacular outing.   — D.M.

D.J. JAZZY JEFF AND THE FRESH PRINCE
★★ **Rock the House (Jive/RCA, 1987)**
★★ **He's the D.J., I'm the Rapper (Jive/RCA, 1988)**
★★ **And in This Corner . . . (Jive/RCA, 1989)**
This stuff isn't the ersatz rap of Vanilla Ice or New Kids on the Block—but its market is pretty much the same as theirs. Clean-cut and ingratiating, D.J. Jazzy Jeff and the Fresh Prince are a less eccentric Kid 'N Play, turning out credible grooves for the pre-teen set. No tales of O.G's, bitches, ho's, and nines—and for that, this rap has almost a novelty value, but after a while its sheer innocuousness gets grating. It makes sense that the Fresh Prince gained a sitcom after his over-exposure on MTV: all his rhymes are rated "G."   — P.E.

DJAVAN
★★★ **Seduzir (1981, World Pacific, 1990)**
★★★★ **Bird of Paradise (1987; Columbia, 1988)**
★★★½ **Puzzle of Hearts (1989; Columbia, 1990)**
★★★½ **Alumbramento & Djavan (World Pacific, 1992)**
Djavan's jazzy vocal style and irresistibly melodic material have earned him quite a few admirers among American musicians; the Manhattan Transfer, for example, devoted much of its *Brasil* album to his

songs. Nor is it hard to understand why after hearing the languorous, insinuating *Bird of Paradise*. Produced by Ronnie Foster and featuring a mostly American rhythm section, it offers a delightful balance between Brazilian and American pop elements; even when he's singing in Portuguese, Djavan's delivery is wonderfully affecting. Though recorded in Brazil, *Puzzle of Hearts* reprises that approach, from the percolating percussion of "Amazon Farewell" to the sophisticated samba cadences of "Being Cool." *Seduzir* and the double album *Alumbramento & Djavan*, on the other hand, are more in the vein of Milton Nascimento or Gilberto Gil, and though they have some strong songs to their credit, they lack the immediate appeal of his later albums.   — J.D.C.

D-MOB
★★★ **A Little Bit of This, A Little Bit of That (London, 1989)**
One of Britain's original acid house outfits, D-Mob caused a minor sensation with the loopily infectious "We Call It Acieed." But as with most house music combos, D-Mob's real roots are in R&B, and that's what colors most of this album.   — J.D.C.

THE D.O.C.
★★★ **No One Can Do It Better (Ruthless, 1989)**
Actually, a lot of rappers can do it better, but the D.O.C. does it well enough. Vocally, this is pretty much generic gangsta stuff, enlivened only by clean diction and occasional nods to reggae. But the production, by N.W.A's Dr. Dre, is inventive and exciting, giving the D.O.C. a definite edge on the competition.   — J.D.C.

DR. BUZZARD'S ORIGINAL SAVANNAH BAND
★★★★ **Dr. Buzzard's Original Savannah Band (RCA, 1976)**
★★½ **Dr. Buzzard Meets King Pennett (RCA, 1978)**
★★★½ **Dr. Buzzard Goes to Washington (Elektra, 1979)**
★★ **Calling All Beatnicks! (Passport, 1984)**
Only in New York. Dr. Buzzard's Original Savannah Band made some of the most adventurous and satisfying dance music of the late '70s: a sizzling, upscale hash scraped together from the Broadway stage, the dance floor at Studio 54 and a closet full of old salsa and merengue records up in Spanish Harlem. These hit-or-miss albums

are a carefully acquired taste. Lead singer Cory Daye girds her sexy tone with a streetwise resilience, and when bandleaders August Darnell and Stony Browder connect their songwriting and arranging skills with their ambitious concepts, Dr. Buzzard soars above the disco competition. Steering well clear of campy self-parody, *Original Savannah Band* is one of the few cogent, satisfying albums to emerge from the disco years. There's a storyline involved, and you can actually dance to most of it. *King Pennett* sounds a bit rushed and joyless in comparison, but *Washington* recaptures the insouciant buzz of the debut—and adds a dose of social reality. *Calling All Beatnicks!* represents a failed comeback attempt by Daye and Browder; Darnell and sideman Andy Hernandez continue to record as Kid Creole and the Coconuts. — M.C.

DR. FEELGOOD
★½ **Down by the Jetty (United Artists, 1975)**
★★★ **Malpractice (United Artists, 1975)**
★★ **Sneakin' Suspicion (United Artists, 1977)**
★★★ **Be Seeing You (United Artists, 1977)**

Impassioned purveyors of hard R&B and rock & roll, the members of Dr. Feelgood were quintessential '70s English pub rockers of the kind whose authenticity and sweat could only be captured truly in concert. Wilko Johnson attempted to recreate the Telecaster fury of Mick Green, the trailblazing guitarist for Johnny Kidd and the Pirates; the sound was lean, spiky and intense. Along with shouter Lee Brilleaux and an engagingly forthright drummer called "The Big Figure," they favored a mix of Willie Dixon, Bo Diddley and revivalist originals. All their records are punchy and fun, if a little too thinly produced. The standouts remain *Malpractice* and its great cover of "Riot in Cell Block #9" and the Nick Lowe–produced *Be Seeing You*, with its pub anthem, "Milk and Alcohol."
— P.E.

DR. JOHN
★★½ **Gris-Gris (1968; Alligator, 1987)**
★★ **Babylon (Atco, 1968)**
★★ **Remedies (Atco, 1970)**
★★ **The Sun, Moon, & Herbs (Atco, 1971)**
★★★★ **Gumbo (1972; Alligator, 1986)**
★★★½ **In the Right Place (1973; Atco, 1990)**
★★★½ **Desitively Bonnaroo (Atco, 1974)**
★★½ **Hollywood Be Thy Name (United Artists, 1975)**
★★★ **City Lights (Horizon, 1978)**
★★ **Tango Palace (Horizon, 1979)**
★★★★ **Dr. John Plays Mac Rebennack (Clean Cuts, 1981)**
★★★★ **The Brightest Smile in Town (Clean Cuts, 1983)**
★★★★ **The Ultimate Dr. John (Warner Special Products, 1987)**
★★★½ **In a Sentimental Mood (Warner Bros., 1990)**

Mac Rebennack began his musical career as a guitarist and pianist on the New Orleans R&B scene of the '50s, and eventually followed Earl Palmer, Harold Battiste and other N.O. session players to the Los Angeles studio scene in the mid-'60s. And in a very real way, the musical persona Rebennack assumed for his solo career— that of Dr. John Creaux, the Night Tripper—was a product of the collision between Louisiana creole funk and West Coast hippie mysticism. Take, for instance, the way *Gris Gris* parlays the imagery of voodoo magic (the historical Dr. John Creaux was acclaimed as the King of Voodoo in 19th-century New Orleans) into the hallucinatory groove of "Walk on Gilded Splinters," ending up with a sound that draws equally on Creole soul and psychedelic rock.

That fusion didn't always take, of course. *Babylon*, for instance, quickly dissolves into the hippie foolishness of "Glowin' " and "The Patriotic Flag-Waiver" (sic), and while *Remedies* has its moments—the joyful "Mardi Gras," say—its moments just aren't enough. In truth, Dr. John didn't really hit his stride until he returned to roots with *Gumbo*, which offers funky updates of classic New Orleans R&B numbers like "Iko Iko," "Junko Partner," Professor Longhair's classic "Tipitina" and a medley of Huey Smith hits. From there it's an easy jump to the second-line funk of *In the Right Place*, which was recorded with the Meters and produced by Allen Toussaint; it contains Dr. John's only Top Ten single, "Right Place Wrong Time." There's more of the same on *Desitively Bonnaroo*, thanks to the irresistible rhythms of "(Everybody Wanna Get Rich) Rite Away" and "Quitters Never Win." *The Ultimate Dr. John* compiles highlights from *Gris Gris, Gumbo, Remedies* and *Desitively Bonnaroo*, but not necessarily the tunes every fan would have chosen.

Apparently tiring of the voodoo shtick, Dr. John tries a bit of straight-up rock &

roll revivalism with *Hollywood Be Thy Name*, a mostly live album that offers mildly spiced renditions of oldies like "The Way You Do the Things You Do" and "Yesterday" along with a few Dr. John originals; it's second-rate rock despite the first-rate band. With *City Lights*, he makes a bid for light-jazz respectability, but not even the sympathetic backing of New York studio aces Steve Gadd, Will Lee and Richard Tee can completely overcome the pedestrian nature of the material; perhaps that's why *Tango Palace* resorts to the jivey insincerity of "Disco-Therapy" and "Fonky Side."

Yet just when it seemed Dr. John had exhausted all his options, he brought his skills back into focus with *Dr. John Plays Mac Rebennack*, a solo piano session that brings him back home to the New Orleans piano stylings he cut his teeth on; essential listening, if only for "Memories of Professor Longhair." *The Brightest Smile in Town* not only maintains its predecessor's momentum but actually broadens the music's scope with a few standards like "Come Rain or Come Shine." But *In a Sentimental Mood*, though it boasts a coy "Makin' Whoopee" recorded with Rickie Lee Jones, wastes too much energy on large-scale arrangements that overwhelm both the singer and the songs. — J.D.C.

JOHN DOE

★★★½ **Meet John Doe (DGC, 1990)**
Without the rest of X to back him up, John Doe sounds . . . well, pretty much the same as ever. Which, funnily enough, is why the album doesn't quite work. Had a song like "Take #52" been rendered with the sort of ragged semi-competence for which X was known, its ironic self-awareness would have come off as a post-modern send-up of country sincerity; instead, the all-too-competent accompaniment leaves it sounding like the work of a singer too clever for his own good. — J.D.C.

THOMAS DOLBY

★★★★½ **The Golden Age of Wireless (1981; EMI America, 1983)**
★★★★ **The Flat Earth (Capitol, 1984)**
★★★ **Aliens Ate My Buick (EMI Manhattan, 1988)**
A perfect product of the synthesizer age, Dolby's compositional skills seem as much attuned to the finer points of electronic sound-shaping as to mundane matters like melody and harmony. To be honest, that's something of an advantage for Dolby,

though, since it often provides his songs with a second layer of hook-potential. On *The Golden Age of Wireless*, for example, he grounds the airy imagery of "Windpower" with whooshing, whispering synths and eerily sampled backing vocals, while "Europa and the Pirate Twins" fleshes out its basic Bo Diddley beat with all sorts of electronically altered accents. It's an attractive sound, but not an inherently commercial one, which may explain why the album was reconfigured in '83 to include the extraordinarily catchy novelty number "She Blinded Me with Science."

Still, he sticks with atmospherics for the bulk of *The Flat Earth*, building an otherworldly soundscape for "White City" and evoking the loneliness of longing in "I Scare Myself," while still providing "Dissidents" and (especially) "Hyperactive" with plenty of rhythmic pep. Dolby then seemed to lose interest in pop as such, turning instead to the world of cinema; in '86, he produced a set of (hopefully parodic) pop songs for the megaflop *Howard the Duck*, and a year later contributed to the overwrought atmosphere of *Gothic*. There's also a certain amount of cinematic influence in *Aliens Ate My Buick* (credited to Thomas Dolby and the Lost Toy People), but by this point Dolby's witticisms are too trite to seem funny, and apart from the perkily percolating "Airhead," the album lacks much in the way of pop smarts. — J.D.C.

ERIC DOLPHY

★★★★★ **Outward Bound (1960; Fantasy, 1987)**
★★★★★ **Out There (1960; Fantasy, 1982)**
★★★★½ **Eric Dolphy In Europe, Vol. 1 (1963; Prestige, 1989)**
★★★★★ **Out to Lunch (1964; Blue Note, 1987)**
★★★½ **Last Date (1964; Fontana, 1986)**
★★★★ **Eric Dolphy In Europe, Vol. 2 (1965; Prestige, 1989)**
★★★★ **Eric Dolphy in Europe, Vol. 3 (1965; Prestige, 1989)**
★★★★ **Vintage Dolphy (GM Recordings, 1987)**
★★★½ **Other Aspects (Blue Note, 1987)**
★★★½ **The Berlin Concerts (Enja, 1989)**
★★★★ **Candid Dolphy (Candid, 1990)**
★★★½ **Stockholm Sessions (Enja, 1990)**
WITH BOOKER LITTLE
★★★★ **Memorial Album: Recorded Live at the Five Spot (1964; Fantasy, 1989)**

★ ★ ★ ★ **Far Cry (1961; Fantasy, 1989)**
★ ★ ★ ★ **At the Five Spot, Vol. 1 (Prestige, 1991)**

Dying at age 36 in 1964, jazz impressionist Eric Dolphy left behind recordings of an intense, haunting loveliness. An intellectual, introspective player, his solos—on alto saxophone, flute, and, in particular, bass clarinet—were careful, intricate work, his sensibility recalling high European romanticism (Debussy, the modern classical composers) nearly as easily as very cerebral bebop.

Starting out with Chico Hamilton and then playing with Charles Mingus, Dolphy debuted as a leader on *Outward Bound* (1960); the title track was solidly grounded in the blues, but a version of "Glad to Be Unhappy" suggested Dolphy's capacity for a subtler lyricism. With his sidemen including Freddie Hubbard on trumpet and Jackie Byard on piano, Dolphy drew comparison to Ornette Coleman—but while the young player's style was indeed marked by the "free" approach that was Ornette's chief contribution to jazz, Dolphy was hardly the wildman Coleman was. *Out There*, with phenomenal cello work by Ron Carter, emphasized Dolphy's finesse; the album's last cut, "Feathers," exemplifies his profound delicacy.

He collaborated next with Booker Little, a trumpet prodigy whose best work came close to paralleling Dolphy's in its lucid drive (Little died, three years before Dolphy, at age 23). *Far Cry, Memorial Album* and *At the Five Spot* feature the fruit of the alliance; the former's "Mrs. Parker of K.C. (Bird's Mother)" and "Ode to Charlie Parker" are reflective gems. With *Out to Lunch*, Dolphy swung harder and more freely—on such standouts as the title track and the Thelonious Monk tribute, "Hat and Beard," he tests to the utmost the awesome talents of Freddie Hubbard, Bobby Hutcherson on vibes, bassist Richard Davis and a very young Tony Williams on drums. Feeling unappreciated in this country, Dolphy left for Europe shortly after *Out to Lunch*. A few years before, with a somewhat naive Danish rhythm section, he'd played the series of 1961 Copenhagen concerts that ended up as the three volumes of *Eric Dolphy in Europe*—and had found a very receptive audience. Dying in Berlin of a diabetes-related heart seizure, Dolphy was cut down before he'd had a chance to develop fully his remarkable gifts. The essence of the man's art can be found on an unaccompanied bass clarinet version of

Billie Holiday's "God Bless the Child," from *Eric Dolphy in Europe, Vol. 1.* Staggering. — P.E.

FATS DOMINO

★ ★ ★ **Fats Domino—His Greatest Hits (MCA, 1986)**
★ ★ ★ **Live at Montreux (Atlantic, 1987)**
★ ★ ★ ★ **My Blue Heaven—The Best of Fats Domino (EMI, 1990)**
★ ★ ★ ★ ★ **They Call Me the Fat Man—Antoine "Fats Domino": The Legendary Imperial Recordings (EMI, 1991)**

Conservative of dress, mild of manner and unfailingly polite, Fats Domino, alone among the first generation of important rock & roll artists, stood as the strongest argument in defense of the music. Critics could rail against Presley's gyrations, and scorn the flamboyant behavior of Chuck Berry, Little Richard and Jerry Lee Lewis—but Fats . . . Fats was *only* about music, without a hint of scandal onstage or off to feed the naysayers' crusade.

That rock & roll was here to stay may not have been obvious to those horrified by its emergence in the mid-'50s, but it was old news to Fats, who had been cutting hit records since 1949 ("The Fat Man," a hit in 1950, is another candidate for the title of First Rock & Roll Record).

Domino's influences were many and varied, encompassing all the important names in New Orleans music in the '40s and R&B stars of his youth. Artists such as Professor Longhair and Champion Jack Dupree shaped his approach to the piano; powerful vocalists such as Big Joe Turner, Roy Brown and Amos Milburn taught him a thing or two about feeling and attitude. Of all these the most important would seem to be Louis Jordan, whose music rocked well ahead of its time and was further enlivened by an unfettered sense of humor and good will towards all—an apt description of Fats Domino's music as well. Even on his few melancholy singles—1960's "Walking to New Orleans" being a prime example— Domino's delivery held the promise of sunshine over the horizon.

Having been dominant on the R&B charts since the release of "The Fat Man," Domino cracked the pop chart in 1952 with "Goin' Home" and stayed there through 1963. Among rock & roll's founding fathers, only Presley rivals Domino in terms of sales. An ambassador for New Orleans, he was backed in the studio by the Crescent City's best musicians and guided by a genius of a producer-composer in Dave Bartholomew.

In Domino's music, they distilled the spirit and style of the city's multicultural heritage and imbued it with propulsion. Like all great music, Domino's best recordings—"Blueberry Hill," "I'm Walkin'," "Whole Lotta Lovin'," "Walking to New Orleans"—still sound vital.

If the advent of the compact disc has done nothing else, it has given us access again to many long out-of-print or difficult-to-locate recordings. Domino's greatest hits were always around in one form or another, but EMI's late-'91 release of a four-CD boxed set, *They Call Me the Fat Man,* tells the whole glorious story in one superior package. Domino is reported to have recorded some 260 sides for Imperial, and 100 of those are here, dating from 1949 through 1962, all of them terrific, and a good number of them hits. Only one track, "Darktown Strutter's Ball," from 1958, is previously unreleased; only three tracks are alternate versions. The set also comes with an entertaining and informative biography by New Orleans music critic Jeff Hannusch that is further buttressed by complete discographical and session details as well as by notes from the producer and compiler explaining the project's genesis and development. A great American artist has finally been given his due.

The box set leaves little to say about EMI's *My Blue Heaven* CD, except that its 20 tracks and accompanying annotation are outstanding. It's the low-cost alternative to the boxed set. *His Greatest Hits* and *Live at Montreux* are live recordings, the Montreux set dating from 1978, and *His Greatest Hits* from 1986. Nothing wrong with either of these, as Fats gives his all and seems not to have aged a bit. Of note on the '86 album is the presence in Domino's band of a couple of key figures from his early days, one being the redoubtable Dave Bartholomew on trumpet, the other being Herb Hardesty on tenor sax. Fats continued recording after he left Imperial, but the records he cut for ABC, Mercury and Reprise are now out of print. The Reprise sessions were produced by Richard Perry and resulted in one terrific single, a hilarious interpretation of "Lady Madonna," that is as good as any of the Imperial tracks. — D.M.

DONOVAN
★★★½ **Catch the Wind (1965; DCC, 1988)**
★★★½ **Sunshine Superman (1966; Epic, 1990)**
★★★½ **A Gift From a Flower to a Garden (Epic, 1968)**
★★★ **Donovan in Concert (Epic, 1968)**
★★★½ **Hurdy Gurdy Man (1968; Epic, 1986)**
★★★ **Barabajagal (1969; Epic, 1987))**
★★★★★ **Donovan's Greatest Hits (Epic, 1969)**
★★★½ **Open Road (Epic, 1970)**
★★½ **Essence to Essence (Epic, 1974)**
★★★ **7 Tease (Epic, 1974)**
★★½ **Slow Down World (Epic, 1976)**

Epitomizing flower power, Donovan's trippy musings are redeemed from '60s nostalgia not only by his belief that there's nothing funny about peace, love and understanding, but by the sheer pop charm of his songs. Coming on as the breathlessly sincere Scots twin to Bob Dylan, Donovan was a quintessential folkie—acoustic guitar, harmonica, story songs, benign rebellion and, making him distinctive, a Celtic romanticism. Dewy with hope, confident and ambitious, the title track of *Catch the Wind,* now out of print, and "Ramblin' Boy" radiated mythic, wide-eyed yearning.

As Dylan had, Donovan then went electric. But if Bob's rock was tough and bluesy, Donovan's was pop, spun off from the sassy tunefulness of his mod peers. And it was psychedelic. Indeed, "Sunshine Superman" bounced along as a wry, ultra-hip manifesto, its winking delivery hinting at all manner of illicit pleasures. "Mellow Yellow" (supposedly about the arcane high of smoking banana peels) outright broadcast the theme of blow-your-mind wisdom.

With its cover shot of the Maharishi and swooning ditties like "Wear Your Love Like Heaven," *A Gift From a Flower to a Garden* delivered the Donovan persona to the max—a troubadour St. Francis, filling his lyrics with exotic poetry that promoted a bliss straight out of William Blake's *Songs of Innocence.* After a string of late-'60s hits celebrating a private wonderland—"Jennifer Juniper," "Hurdy Gurdy Man" and "Barabajagal" (with Jeff Beck), Donovan's moment passed. Such later work as *Open Road* and *Cosmic Wheels,* both now deleted, showed occasional strength, but, compared to the golden-hour singles, the music was less distinctive. — P.E.

THE DOOBIE BROTHERS
★★★ **Toulouse Street (Warner Bros., 1972)**
★★½ **The Captain and Me (Warner Bros., 1973)**
★★½ **What Were Once Vices Are Now Habits (Warner Bros., 1974)**

★★ Stampede (Warner Bros., 1975)
★★★ Takin' It to the Streets (Warner
Bros., 1976)
★★★½ Best of the Doobies (Warner Bros.,
1976)
★★½ Livin' on the Fault Line (Warner
Bros., 1977)
★★★ Minute by Minute (Warner Bros.,
1978)
★★★½ Best of the Doobies, Volume 2
(Warner Bros., 1981)
★★ Brotherhood (Capitol, 1991)

Named after the ass end of a joint, the
Doobie Brothers yielded a succession of hits
in the mid-'70s. Moving from mellow boogie
to slick blue-eyed soul, this long-running
group actually managed to improve along
the way. The Doobies began as a bar band
in Northern California. After the group's
now-deleted 1971 debut album, *The Doobie
Brothers*, floated away to oblivion, the
Brothers honed a couple of sharp hooks on
Toulouse Street and bagged a winner. The
toe-tapping power chords of "China Grove"
and the strum-along buzz of "Listen to the
Music" both sink in far deeper than the
singing or, God knows, the songwriting.
Laid-back to the point of appearing blank,
the Doobies come on like a slightly heavier
Eagles—or a slimmed-down Bachman
Turner Overdrive. *The Captain and Me*
belies the extent of the group's vision.
"Rockin' Down the Highway" and "Long
Train Runnin' " are virtual clones of the
above-mentioned songs; of course, that
didn't stop them from becoming just as
popular.

By the fourth album, lead guitarist and
chief composer Tom Johnston starts to seem
tapped-out. Rhythm guitarist Patrick
Simmons supplies the ersatz country-rock
hit "Black Water," but the rest of *Vices*
barely stays afloat. *Stampede* is led by
studio guitarist Jeff "Skunk" Baxter:
centered around a sluggish Motown cover
("Take Me in Your Arms"), the thundering
charge never quite gains sufficient
momentum. Exit Baxter, enter singer
Michael McDonald—another Steely Dan
alumni. His luxurious tone and grain of
soulfulness turned the Doobie Brothers' beat
around. The 1976 hit "Takin' It to the
Streets" steers clear of the funky gutter,
reaching instead for a loftier veneer:
MOR&B. "Takin' It to the Streets" also
revolves around McDonald's vocals, electric
piano and a mildly syncopated beat—the
guitars and mellow country-rock gait are
conspicuously absent. The Doobies quickly
became Michael McDonald's franchise.

Founder Tom Johnston left in 1978, and the
Brothers went on to release their best album
since *Toulouse Street*. *Minute by Minute*'s
title cut and the hit single "What a Fool
Believes" flaunt McDonald's suave vocal
mastery quite effectively, though this elegant
penthouse heartbreak certainly is a far cry
from the group's origins. Surprisingly, this
stylistic contrast strengthens *The Best of the
Doobies*, resharpening some rather
well-worn classic rock choruses. *Brotherhood*
reunites the group's original lineup; in
typical '90s fashion, however, the Doobies
can't find the sparks required to re-ignite
their flame. — M.C.

THE DOORS

★★★★ The Doors (Elektra, 1967)
★★★½ Strange Days (Elektra, 1967)
★★★½ Waiting for the Sun (Elektra,
1968)
★★★ The Soft Parade (Elektra, 1969)
★★★★★ Morrison Hotel (Elektra, 1970)
★★½ Absolutely Live (Elektra, 1970)
★★★½ Thirteen (Elektra, 1970)
★★★★ L.A. Woman (Elektra, 1971)
★★★★★ Weird Scenes Inside the Gold
Mine (Elektra, 1972)
★★★★ Best of the Doors (Elektra,
1973)
★★½ American Prayer (Elektra,
1978)
★★★★ The Doors Greatest Hits
(Elektra, 1980)
★★ Alive, She Cried (Elektra, 1983)
★★★½ In Concert (Elektra, 1991)
★★★½ The Doors/An Oliver Stone
Film (Elektra, 1991)

Three great American '60s bands rendered
versions of the California myth. For the
Beach Boys, it was sun, surf and teenage
blondes. The Grateful Dead embodied
hippie utopianism, the acid love-in and the
endless, mystic jam. The Doors' California
was a construct of the darker psyche; it was
L.A. crash pads and needle fever,
Hollywood bungalows and film-noir threat.
At its far limits were the surrounding
hills—rich with the threat and promise of
Indian burial grounds and natural
mysteries—and the ocean, surging deep into
oblivion and release. The Doors were
originals—Robbie Krieger, a competent
guitarist who sounded best when he kept
things either elegant or bluesy; the steady
John Densmore on drums; and Ray
Manzarek, an organist and electric piano
player whose semi-classical turns added a
touch of the baroque.

The Doors ultimately, however, were Jim Morrison. Except for Jimi Hendrix, there hadn't been since Elvis an American rock star of such raw immediacy. The Lizard King, Dionysus-beautiful in black leather, he was also the prototype of the rocker in desperate search for transcendence through self-destruction; liquor-ridden, abusive and hurling himself fascinated toward death, he was in the end both tragic and pathetic.

A genuine poet, Morrison turned to the French Symbolists: Rimbaud, Baudelaire and those Orphic voices who captured the heady fragrances of the flowers of evil. At their best, his suggestive lyrics were clipped and cinematic, either bursts of street talk or snatches at myth. Calling himself an "erotic politician," Morrison was preoccupied with urge, rebellion and release—if some of his work now sounds melodramatic or forced, his intensity remains compelling, and his acknowledgment of night, pain and loneliness comes off as riveting and real.

Although the abbreviated, 45 version hit harder, "Light My Fire" neatly introduced the Doors' effect: vocals alternately powerful and langorous, swirling keyboards and the message that sex could mean deliverance. "Break on Through," however, is the debut album's better song and the essential Doors statement. "The End" attempted an epic—the song served notice that this band was going deep. With the exception of the hard blues, "Love Me Two Times," and the rock tango, "Moonlight Drive," *Strange Days* didn't have the power of *The Doors*; it sounded instead like twilit, ominous carnival music. "People Are Strange," "Strange Days" and "I Can't See Your Face in My Mind" obsessively examined disconnection and the sense of drifting; "Horse Latitudes" was an early example of sheer atmosphere.

Waiting for the Sun featured "Hello I Love You," a jagged Kinks' rip-off in which Morrison comes on like a rapist; "Five to One" was revolutionary sloganeering. The rest of the record was considerably subtler: Krieger's flamenco guitar on "Spanish Caravan" is stirring, "Summer's Almost Gone" is remarkably tender, and the chanted "My Wild Love," with its affecting, cracked-voice vocal, works well at re-creating an air of primitive folk power.

The Door's shakiest album, *The Soft Parade*, was cluttered with horns and strings. While not at all music for the band's hard-rock followers, Krieger's "Touch Me" and "Tell All the People" are intriguing; they're pop songs, basically, but sifted

through the Doors' sensibilities, they take on a surreal quality. "Wild Child" is Morrison parodying himself, and the long concept title song doesn't work.

A return to form, *Morrison Hotel* was the most cohesive record; aside from the throwaway grunter "Maggie McGill," every song was masterful—and the band swings tougher and easier than it ever had before. Morrison's voice is almost shot, but its strain lends grit to the rockers ("Roadhouse Blues," "You Make Me Real") and poignancy to the ballads ("Blue Sunday," "Indian Summer"). The lyrics are some of Morrison's finest; "Queen of the Highway," in particular, neatly fuses contemporary reference and myth.

"Riders on the Storm," "Love Her Madly," "L'America" and the title track were the standouts of the final album, *L.A. Woman*. Inventive playing characterizes every song, but so does a heavy air of psychic exhaustion. Morrison's voice is a ghost of its former glory—doom, heartbreak and frustration sound in his every note. Difficult and sad, the record has some of the power of Neil Young's *Tonight's the Night*: it's a straining for catharsis.

Probably over-represented by compilations and live albums, the Doors are best served by the tight *Greatest Hits* and the fuller *Weird Scenes*. *In Concert* compiles material from all previous live records, and makes them redundant. The band could be pretty sloppy onstage, but *In Concert* has exciting passages. *An American Prayer* is Morrison reading his poetry over moody accompaniment by the Doors; it's intriguing but suitable mainly for Morrison fanatics; Oliver Stone's excellent movie features a soundtrack that's not a bad Doors overview.
— P.E.

JIMMY DORSEY

★★★ **Jimmy Dorsey's Greatest Hits (1971; MCA, 1980)**
★★★ **Uncollected Jimmy Dorsey & His Orchestra, 1939–1940 (Hindsight, NA)**
★★★ **Uncollected Jimmy Dorsey & His Orchestra, 1942–1944 (Hindsight, NA)**
★★ **Uncollected Jimmy Dorsey & His Orchestra, 1949–1951 (Hindsight, NA)**
★★ **Uncollected Jimmy Dorsey & His Orchestra, 1950 (Hindsight, NA)**
★★ **Uncollected Jimmy Dorsey: The Dorseyland Band, 1950 (Hindsight, NA)**

A respected clarinet player and a more respected alto saxophonist, Jimmy Dorsey, with and apart from his brother Tommy, headed one of the most popular big bands of the '30s and '40s, and worked steadily into the '50s as well. Like Tommy, Jimmy's bands were distinguished by first-rate vocalists, though none to compare to Tommy's lineup of Frank Sinatra, Jo Stafford and the Pied Pipers. Still, Bob Eberly and Helen O'Connell did okay fronting the Orchestra: together and solo they sang on ten Number One singles between 1936 and 1944. Kitty Kallen, who had a brief stint with Dorsey in the mid-'40s, later had three Top Forty pop hits, the last coming in 1963, "My Coloring Book," which peaked at Number 18. The Dorsey Brothers are also remembered for their 1956 replacement show for Jackie Gleason, on which they introduced to the nation a new singer from the South named Elvis Presley. In '57 Dorsey made the charts again with an instrumental, "So Rare," which sold over a million copies and spent four weeks at Number Two on the pop charts, shortly after which Dorsey passed away.

MCA's *Greatest Hits* features several of Dorsey's best-known numbers, both instrumental and with vocals, including "Tangerine," "Amapola," "Green Eyes" and "Brazil," all but the latter being Number One singles. The Hindsight series offers the broadest perspective, although the last two volumes are slow going. — D.M.

DOUG E. FRESH
★ ★ ★　　Oh, My God! (Reality, 1986)
★ ½　The World's Greatest Entertainer
　　(Reality, 1988)
After getting his career off to a tenuous start by claiming to be "The Original Human Beatbox," Doug E. Fresh managed to deliver one of the biggest rap hits of 1985, a loopy tour de force called "The Show." With co-MC Ricky D (a.k.a. Slick Rick) providing hilarious anecdotes while Fresh shows off his sound effects, it sounded like nothing else in rap (though imitations, like Salt-N-Pepa's "The Showstopper," soon sprouted like weeds). Unfortunately, it's also like no other rap on *Oh, My God!*, as Fresh found Jesus and lost Slick Rick between making the single and cutting the album. And despite a minor comeback with "Keep Risin' to the Top," *The World's Greatest Entertainer* is just as bad, offering empty boasts and hackneyed philosophizing in place of witty rhymes and rhythmic energy. — J.D.C.

DOUG LAZY
★ ★ ★　Doug Lazy Gettin' Crazy (Atlantic,
　　1990)
Lazy's no slouch as a producer, and his approach to rhythm neatly blends hip-hop's raucous dynamism with the repetitious pulse of house music. But as a performer, Lazy never does any more than he has to, and while that sometimes makes his tunes bracingly minimal, it can also leave them seeming irritatingly thin. — J.D.C.

NICK DRAKE
★ ★ ★ ★　　Five Leaves Left (1969; Hannibal,
　　　　1986)
★ ★ ★ ★　　Bryter Later (1970; Hannibal,
　　　　1986)
★ ★ ★ ★　　Pink Moon (1972; Hannibal,
　　　　1986)
★ ★ ★ ½　Time of No Reply (Hannibal,
　　　　1986)
★ ★ ★ ★　　Fruit Tree: The Complete Works
　　　　of Nick Drake
　　　　(Hannibal/Rykodisc, 1986)
Music of a melancholy, twilit beauty, Drake's three albums *Five Leaves Left*, *Bryter Later* and *Pink Moon* echo, in muted intensity, Van Morrison's *Astral Weeks*; they are suites of gemlike songs urged on by Drake's nimble guitar, set against arrangements whose finesse recalls chamber music. *Pink Moon* is the sparest; some of its lyrics read like Zen koans. Everything Drake wrote—and sang in a haunting, sometimes chilling near-whisper—is pervaded by a fragile hypersensitivity, and while his mood seldom varies, it has its dark, resonant magic. Dead of a drug overdose in 1974, Drake was sudden like lightning—and the afterglow still shimmers. *Time of No Reply* is a collection of outtakes and fine unreleased tracks. *Fruit Tree* beautifully packages all of Drake's recordings and includes a comprehensive biographical booklet. — P.E.

THE DRAMATICS
★ ★ ★ ½　Whatcha See Is Whatcha Get
　　　　(1972; Stax, 1978)
★ ★ ★ ½　A Dramatic Experience (Stax,
　　　　1972)
★ ★ ★　　Dramatically Yours (1974; Stax,
　　　　1983)
★ ★ ★ ★　　Best Of the Dramatics (Stax,
　　　　1981)
★ ★ ★　　Dramatics Live (Stax, 1981)
★ ★ ★　　Positive State of Mind (Stax,
　　　　1989)
★ ★ ★　　Stone Cold (Stax, 1990)

Lead singer Ron Banks has piloted this Detroit vocal quintet since the '60s. The Dramatics hit a successful stride at Stax in the early '70s, working with such Motown-based producers as Tony Hester. The Top Ten breakthrough "Whatcha See Is Whatca Get," from the Stax debut album, helped establish the psychedelically enhanced sound of baroque soul: a loping fuzztone guitar underlines the vocal parts, while the horns and string section hover without intruding.

The Dramatics can be a little melodramatic at times, playing up that startling bass-tenor contrast as often as possible. "In the Rain" pours on the special effects, but those heated voices cut through the storm every time. *A Dramatic Experience* is a solid follow-up to the debut, sporting wah-wah-drenched production numbers ("The Devil Is Dope") alongside sweetly updated doo-wop ("Hey You! Get Off My Mountain"). While some of the embellishments and topical references may sound a bit dated, the spirted harmonies (and the lyrics' underlying concerns) have barely aged at all.

The Dramatics have weathered several personnel and label changes over the years, without ever quite returning to that level of artistic—or commercial—success. Long out of print, the ABC albums *Drama V* (1976) and the discofied *Shake It Well* (1977) dropped satisfying jams onto the R&B charts, but didn't cross over. Recent efforts on Fantasy's revived Stax imprint show that Ron Banks still has a good ear for what's happening, though the rigid synthesized grooves don't alway mesh with the Dramatics' fluid vocal dynamics. — M.C.

THE DREAM ACADEMY

★ ★½ **The Dream Academy (Warner Brothers, 1985)**
★ ★ **Remembrance Days (Reprise, 1987)**
★ ★ **A Different Kind of Weather (Reprise, 1990)**

On its first album, posing in Nehru jackets and Afros amidst a sunlit sylvan setting, and offering up titles like "The Love Parade" and "The Edge of Forever," the Dream Academy seemed a parody of psychedelic revivalism. A gooey confection of cellos, tympani, "Penny Lane"-like lyrics and swooning vocalizing, "Life in a Northern Town," proved, however, that the group was damned earnest in recreating a cross between the Moody Blues and, say, the orchestral ambitions of the Move. Exactly why the Academy wanted to do that

remains puzzling, but the nifty throwback worked, resulting in 1985 chart success. *Remembrance Days*, with help from Lindsey Buckingham, was almost the same record, with the '60s shtick toned down a bit. But, minus a hit, it came off as merely painstakingly tasteful aural wallpaper.

A Different Kind of Weather, another skillful, bland, well-intentioned effort, is notable mainly for a cover of John Lennon's "Love" that is conflated with a Hare Krishna chant. Talk about gilding the lily. — P.E.

THE DRIFTERS

★ ★ ★ ★ ★ **Let the Boogie Woogie Roll: Greatest Hits 1953–1958 (Atlantic, 1988)**
★ ★ ★ ★ ★ **1959–1965 All-Time Greatest Hits and More (Atlantic, 1988)**

For sustained quality and influence, the Drifters have few if any parallels in vocal group history. Not only is their longevity remarkable, but the consistent high quality of their music over the years is almost miraculous. The Drifters were forever losing great lead singers—and replacing them with other great singers. These vocalists emerged from long shadows and cast substantial ones of their own: Clyde McPhatter links Claude Jeter to Smokey Robinson and Al Green; Ben E. King is the bridge between Julius Cheeks and Wilson Pickett.

On the production side, the Drifters were guided by the most important producer-songwriters of the '50s, Jerry Leiber and Mike Stoller, who used the group as a laboratory for attempts at more sophisticated productions, just as they had used the Coasters as a vehicle to express their comical observations about popular culture. Between 1959 and 1963 Leiber and Stoller framed great songs provided largely by Doc Pomus and Mort Shuman with string-laden orchestrations and arrangements heavy on Latin influences, all perfect touches to underscore the poetry of Pomus-Shuman's urban romances. Theirs was the first big blast of modern soul music. And when Leiber and Stoller ended their run with the Drifters in 1963 to find and produce artists on the Red Bird label, in stepped producer Bert Berns, a songwriter of note whose credits included "Twist and Shout." And the hits kept on coming.

The group's history dates back to 1953, shortly after Clyde McPhatter had left Billy Ward's Dominoes and signed to the fledgling Atlantic label. He assembled the first group of Drifters, and sang lead on the group's fabled early sides, including "Money Honey," "Such a Night," "White Christmas," "Honey Love" and "Whatcha Gonna Do," before being drafted into the army in 1954. A succession of lead singers followed McPhatter, but without much success. McPhatter embarked on a solo career after his army stint, and in 1958 the original Drifters disbanded, with manager George Treadwell retaining rights to the name. Treadwell then recruited a Harlem R&B group, the Five Crowns, and their lead singer Ben E. King, to be the new Drifters. This reconstituted quartet was an immediate success, its first single, "There Goes My Baby," reaching Number Two on the pop charts in 1959. Thus began a run of 16 Top Forty singles that lasted through 1964. Come 1960, King exited for a solo career shortly after the group hit Number One with Pomus-Shuman's "Save the Last Dance for Me." Enter, by way of gospel (he had been with the Clara Ward Singers), Rudy Lewis. Three more years of hits followed, including two Top Ten entries, "Up on the Roof," in 1962, and "On Broadway," in 1963. Mid-1964 produced both tragedy and beauty, when Lewis died suddenly on the day of a Drifters recording session. Johnny Moore, who had been with the Drifters from 1955-57 following McPhatter's departure, had rejoined the group in 1963; he assumed lead vocal duties on the recording of "Under the Boardwalk." What he laid down that day stands as one of rock & roll's most tender and most wistful performances. Two more Top Forty hits followed in '64. The group continued working through the '60s, but was commercially dead, except in England.

This extraordinary history is thoroughly chronicled on the double-CD sets, *Let the Boogie Woogie Roll* and *All-Time Greatest Hits and More*, which cover, respectively, the years 1953-1958, and 1959-1965. These all-inclusive collections are well-annotated, too. — D.M.

DRIVIN' N' CRYIN'

★ ★ ★ Scarred But Smarter (Island, 1986)
★ ★ ★ ½ Whisper Tames the Lion (Island, 1988)
★ ★ ★ ½ Mystery Road (Island, 1989)
★ ★ ★ ★ Fly Me Courageous (Island, 1990)

What raises this Atlanta combo above most Big Star wannabes is that Drivin' n' Cryin' has always favored power over pop. The band goes for crunch, and doesn't worry whether the full-throttle roar of the guitars

will overwhelm the melodic side of the songs. Of course, it never does, not even when faced with the lo-fi production of *Scarred but Smarter*, the sound quality of which is barely above demo level. Its songs, though, are something else again, matching feisty, semi-metal riffs with resilient, pop-friendly melodies; "Saddle on the Side of the Road" and "Count the Flowers" are particularly fine. *Whisper Tames the Lion* improves the sound quality and broadens the music's scope, augmenting the power-chord punch of "Can't Promise You the World" and "Whisper Tames the Lion" with the cheery guitar pop of "The Friend Song" or the country-rock balladry of "Check Your Tears at the Door."

There's even more range to *Mystery Road*, which not only cranks up the rockers —check out the Aerosmith-on-speed intro to "Malfunction Junction"—but highlights the country and folk elements in quieter tunes like "With the People" or "Peacemaker." *Fly Me Courageous*, on the other hand, is solid rock and strikingly consistent, from the Bo Diddley groove of "Look What You've Done to Your Brother" to the breakneck pace of "Lost in the Shuffle." — J.D.C.

GEORGE DUKE

★ ½ Reach for It (1977; Epic, 1991)
★ Don't Let Go (Epic, 1978)
★ ★ A Brazilian Love Affair (1979; Epic, 1990)
★ Dream On (Epic, 1982)

Once a fairly inventive jazz pianist, George Duke sleepwalked through a string of forgettable fusion albums before devoting himself to production and session-player duties. Of the four titles in print, only *A Brazilian Love Affair* is worth hearing in its entirety, although *Reach for It* has a few interesting electronic interludes. — J.D.C.

KEVIN DUNN AND THE REGIMENT OF WOMEN

★ ★ ★ ½ The Judgment of Paris (DB Recs, 1981)

KEVIN DUNN

★ ★ ★ ½ C'est toujours la meme guitare (Press, 1984)
★ ★ ★ ½ Tanzfeld (Press, 1986)

A dazzling Frippertronics-styled guitarist and a songwriter with a brain on overdrive, Atlanta's Kevin Dunn makes demanding, deconstructed pop—you have to think when listening to this stuff, but the effort pays off. All techno-guitars, synths and treated

vocals, Dunn's songs ambitiously employ the harmonic structures of high classical music, with the wit and occasional pop catchiness of '70s British pop (a band like Sparks comes to mind). The lyrics to "Nam," "Giovanezza," and "20,000 Years in Sing Sing" flourish an idiosyncratic humor; Dunn's singing style is often wryly arch. He has, too, a real gift for truly arresting cover versions—from "Burning Love" to "Louie, Louie" to an oddly lovely instrumental take on "Somewhere Over the Rainbow." Art music of a genuine cleverness, all of Dunn's albums are worthwhile—keep in mind, though, that each is the antithesis of easy listening.
— P.E.

THE DUPREES
★ ★ ★ **Best of the Duprees (Collectables, NA)**
One of the outstanding examples of the pop-based white group harmony sound, the Duprees chalked up one Top Ten hit, two Top Twenty hits and one Top Forty single in 1962-63. Their first and biggest hit, "You Belong to Me," from 1962, had been done in a definitive pop version ten years earlier by the estimable Jo Stafford (and covered that year by both Patti Page and Dean Martin), but the Duprees cut theirs a bit hotter with stratospheric harmonies that played well behind Joe Vann's urgent but controlled lead. Thus was the mold cast for the follow-up hit in '62, a wrenching version of "My Own True Love" (also known as "Tara's Theme," from *Gone With the Wind*). A certain amount of bombastic background was the ideal complement to the smidgen of heartbreak the Duprees served up in their smooth vocal blend. In '63 the group had a minor hit with the unremarkable "Why Don't You Believe Me," but came back strong toward the end of that year with "Have You Heard," which was even higher and more insistent in its performance than "You Belong to Me." The Duprees' run was brief, but the group left behind a notable legacy: theirs are the rare records that serve both as great make-out music and as cathartic balms to young hearts newly broken. — D.M.

DURAN DURAN
★ ★ ★   **Duran Duran (Capitol, 1981)**
★ ★ ★   **Rio (Capitol, 1982)**
  ★½ **Seven and the Ragged Tiger (Capitol, 1983)**
½ ★   **Arena (Capitol, 1984)**
★ ★ ★½ **Notorious (Capitol, 1986)**
  ★ ★   **Big Thing (Capitol, 1988)**

★ ★ ★½ **Decade (Capitol, 1989)**
½ ★   **Liberty (Capitol, 1990)**
In its prime, Duran Duran was a true creature of MTV, a band whose enormous popularity had more to do with its videogenic image than anything it did on record. Granted, the albums aren't total rubbish, since the singles were often catchy enough to bear under repeated listenings, but neither are they wrongfully dismissed classics; Duran Duran had a decent rhythm section and a good ear for hooks, but that's about it.

Duran Duran introduces the group in a swirl of synthesizers and secondhand attitude (borrowed mostly from Bryan Ferry and Bowie); although the post-disco gloss of "Planet Earth" hasn't aged particularly well, "Girls On Film" holds up, thanks to its dramatic chorus and driving, rock-edged rhythm arrangement. Mass success had already set in by the time *Rio* was recorded, which, perhaps, explains its propensity for disposable dance grooves and extravagant, pulp-novel lyrics, though even that can't quite sink the insinuating "Hungry Like the Wolf." Not so *Seven and the Ragged Tiger*; this silly bit of self-indulgence was apparently intended as a concept album, but since the group never actually got around to formulating a concept, it instead limps by on trifles like "Union of the Snake" (oooh, how symbolic!). Still, it's a better buy than *Arena*, a lifeless live album augmented by the group's most-pretentious-ever single, "The Wild Boys."

As its popularity began to recede, Duran Duran went on hiatus, with two members (John Taylor and Andy Taylor) joining up with Robert Palmer and two members of Chic (Bernard Edwards and Tony Thompson) to form the Power Station, while the other three Durannies (singer Simon LeBon, keyboardist Nick Rhodes and drummer Roger Taylor) recorded under the name Arcadia. By 1986, however, Duran Duran had regrouped (minus Roger Taylor, and with Andy Taylor on only four songs) to deliver its most mature album, the stylish, sassy *Notorious*. Taking what had been learned from the side projects, Duran Duran was finally able to ground its songs with a credible blend of funk rhythm and rock attitude, a combination that lent impressive punch to "Meet El Presidente" and the title tune.

It was not to last, though. *Big Thing* is utterly lacking in melodic interest, while the trend-mongering *Liberty* isn't even that good. But, as *Decade* demonstrates, by that point Duran Duran had already passed into nostalgia. — J.D.C.

BOB DYLAN

★ ★ ★ ★½ Bob Dylan (Columbia, 1962)
★ ★ ★ ★½ The Freewheelin' Bob Dylan (Columbia, 1962)
★ ★ ★ ★ The Times They Are a-Changin' (Columbia, 1964)
★ ★ ★ ★ ★ Another Side of Bob Dylan (Columbia, 1964)
★ ★ ★ ★ ★ Bringing It All Back Home (Columbia, 1965)
★ ★ ★ ★ ★ Highway 61 Revisited (Columbia, 1965)
★ ★ ★ ★ ★ Blonde on Blonde (Columbia, 1966)
★ ★ ★ ★ ★ Bob Dylan's Greatest Hits (Columbia, 1967)
★ ★ ★ ★ ★ John Wesley Harding (Columbia, 1968)
★ ★ ★ ★ Nashville Skyline (Columbia, 1969)
★ ★ Self-Portrait (Columbia, 1970)
★ ★ ★ ★ New Morning (Columbia, 1970)
★ ★ ★ ★ Bob Dylan's Greatest Hits, Vol. 2 (Columbia, 1971)
★ ★ ★ ★ Pat Garrett and Billy the Kid (Columbia, 1973)
★ Dylan (Columbia, 1973)
★ ★ ★½ Planet Waves (Asylum, 1974)
★ ★ ★½ Before the Flood (Asylum, 1974)
★ ★ ★ ★ ★ The Basement Tapes (Columbia, 1975)
★ ★ ★ ★ ★ Blood on the Tracks (Columbia, 1975)
★ ★ ★ ★ Desire (Columbia, 1975)
★ ★ ★ Hard Rain (Columbia, 1976)
★ ★ ★ Street Legal (Columbia, 1978)
★ Dylan at Budokan (Columbia, 1978)
★ ★ ★ Slow Train Coming (Columbia, 1979)
★ ★ ★ Saved (Columbia, 1980)
★ ★ ★½ Shot of Love (Columbia, 1981)
★ ★ ★½ Infidels (Columbia, 1983)
★ ★ ★ Real Live (Columbia, 1984)
★ ★ ★ Empire Burlesque (Columbia, 1985)
★ ★ ★ ★ ★ Biograph (Columbia, 1985)
★ ★ ★ Knocked Out Loaded (Columbia, 1986)
★ ★ ★ Down in the Groove (Columbia, 1988)
★ ★ ★ ★ Oh Mercy! (Columbia, 1989)
★ ★ Dylan & the Dead (Columbia, 1989)
★ Under the Red Sky (Columbia, 1990)
★ ★ ★ ★ ★ The Bootleg Series (Columbia, 1991)

The most significant American rocker since Elvis, Bob Dylan ranks alongside the Beatles as a '60s cultural revolutionary, transforming the world not only musically, but politically and spiritually. His greatest achievement, however, may lie in inventing an entirely new language for popular music. Dylan flourished the sensibility of an actual poet—drawing from Whitman, the Beats and the French Symbolists, he employed words provocatively, often cryptically, and with a surreal, dreamlike power. And those words served a range of emotion—irony, prophecy, anger, anxiety and private jubilation—that had by and large gone unspoken in mainstream pop. Fittingly, the voice delivering the new language was a startling one—absolutely unschooled, Dylan's singing struck some of the radio-ears of his moment as ugly or funny, but as an interpretive vehicle it soon became understood as a revelation: Dylan sang with the immediacy of talking, of sharing secrets and conveying intimate truths.

With his first four albums, it was already apparent that Dylan was Woody Guthrie's heir. Not only had a sweet connection been formed when the Minnesota youth traveled to visit the aging bard in his sickbed, but *Bob Dylan*'s "Song to Woody" and "Talkin' New York" already showed a precocious grasp of the veteran's idiom. "Blowin' in the Wind" and "A Hard Rain's a-Gonna Fall," from *Freewheelin'*, were protest anthems whose popular appeal outdistanced any Guthrie song other than "This Land Is Your Land," and *The Times They Are a-Changin'* solidified the singer's status as the leader of a new folk music boasting broader impact than any attempted before or since. With *Another Side*, he delved deeper into his individual soul; "Spanish Harlem Incident," "My Back Pages" and "I Don't Believe You" were free-form autobiography, and Dylan began moving away from the explicit to the suggestive, from prose toward poetry. Acoustic guitar and harmonica (the latter employed as a punctuational aside) were Dylan's lean folk-singer instrumentation, bringing his language into accessible relief.

With *Bringing It All Back Home*, Dylan went electric for the first time. The jaunty, plugged-in rhythms of "Subterranean Homesick Blues" and the hallucinatory folk music of "Mr. Tambourine Man" showed Dylan progressing in every conceivable way. Rock & roll with an assertive mind, the music coaxed the Beatles and Stones into writing more reflective songs, and folk-rock outfits sprang up everywhere. *Highway 61*

Revisited was an even more dramatic development. Coupling the power of Little Richard with that of Woody Guthrie, he further cranked up the electricity—with Al Kooper playing remarkable organ and Mike Bloomfield turning in blazing B.B. King guitar, "Like a Rolling Stone" was phenomenal rock & roll. For the mythic backroads that had inspired his early work, Dylan now substituted the street—from the album's cover, he stares slightly menacingly; in a motorcycle T-shirt, silk jacket and pompadour, he comes off as nobody's folkie, but an updated James Dean. The 11-minute epic "Desolation Row" showed him working out his new surrealism, and the entire record wasn't only that of a new Dylan, it was music and words of a force seldom heard in pop music ever before.

Blonde on Blonde is Dylan's absolute masterpiece. The two-record set featured the stoned celebration of "Rainy Day Women #12 & 35" and the sweetly engaging "I Want You," but it was for its ballads—"Visions of Johanna," "Just Like a Woman" and the side-long "Sad Eyed Lady of the Lowlands"—that he drew forth the most dense, hypnotic music of his career, and poetry that overflowed not only with inventive wordplay but a depth of mood that language rarely can convey. Played by guitarist Robbie Robertson, the future leader of the Band, as well as by a group of ace Nashville studio musicians, the songs were hardly country songs, but the recording milieu certainly was—and it suggested the next turn Dylan might take.

A notorious 1966 motorcyle wreck, however, intervened, and Dylan retreated. Holing up with Robertson and those players who would become the Band, Dylan worked in secrecy on the prescient country-rock fusion that he'd release nine years later as *The Basement Tapes*. Discursive, fragmentary, experimental, the material ranged from amazing ("This Wheel's on Fire") to merely amusing throwaways—had it been released at the time of its making, however, it not only would have anticipated the ruralist turn of such contemporary bands as the Byrds and the Grateful Dead, but it would have placed Dylan's next record, *John Wesley Harding*, in some understandable context.

As it was, *Harding* came as a real surprise. If not quite a country album, it was a folksy turning inward. Even on such a visionary song as "All Along the Watchtower," Dylan sounded muted, mysterious. With instrumentation pared down to the essential, this was a record that

haunted and insinuated, whose force was that of an urgent whisper. *Nashville Skyline*, with its pedal steel and Johnny Cash duets on "Girl From the North Country," was outright country music; "Lay Lady Lay" showed Dylan writing with absolute simplicity. While no classic, *Skyline* still flourished enough power that the next record, *Self-Portrait*, seemed all the weaker. Its title alone was inscrutable: this was a double record that relied heavily on the lesser efforts of lesser talents (Gordon Lightfoot, Paul Simon)—and it was a strange Dylan album indeed that featured as its best song the almost wordless "All the Tired Horses." And *Dylan*, a collection of outtakes released against the singer's will, was even worse.

New Morning and the movie soundtrack *Pat Garrett and Billy the Kid* were marginal returns to form. Al Kooper reappeared on *Morning*, and the almost jazzy "Sign on the Window" was promising; "Knockin' on Heaven's Door," from *Garrett*, was by far the strongest Dylan in years, but the songs still betrayed tentativeness and confusion. The Band sounded strong on *Planet Waves*, but Dylan didn't—from any other writer, "Forever Young" would've been impressive, but Dylan's preoccupation with memory and family life during this period sparked little resonance.

The live *Before the Flood* collaboration with the Band showed Dylan fighting nostalgia by reworking his catalogue in almost vengefully startling ways. Due perhaps to that catharsis, his next pair of records were nearly of the quality of his best work. From *Blood on the Tracks*, "Idiot Wind" was Dylan at his most angrily eloquent since "Positively 4th Street," and "Tangled Up in Blue" was completely lovely. *Desire* didn't have quite the same assurance—and Dylan's reliance on lyricist Jacques Levy was unsettling—but the ambition of its two outlaw epics, "Joey" and "Hurricane," seemed a sign of assurance regained. The end of the decade, however, marked another time of confusion. The live *Hard Rain* was unrevealing, and *Street Legal*, with its dabblings in reggae and R&B, lacked focus. And *Dylan at Budokan* was even more pitiful than *Self-Portrait*.

Focus, of the most adamant sort, is exactly what Dylan found with *Slow Train Coming*. Born again as a fundamentalist Christian, the Jewish-born singer seemed, however, less the servant of a merciful Jesus than of wrathful Jehovah on such jeremiads as "When You Gonna Wake Up" and

"Gotta Serve Somebody." *Saved* was *Slow Train* doubled, and doubly worse. *Shot of Love* was a considerable improvement; the record rocked, and the self-righteousness was leavened with appropriate compassion. With help from guitarists Mark Knopfler and Mick Taylor, *Infidels* set the standard for the competence of Dylan's '80s records. *Empire Burlesque* was almost slick, with its ill-fitting state-of-the-art production and backup singers, and the singer sounded nothing but professional. Tom Petty helped make *Knocked Out Loaded* sound almost reckless, and *Down in the Groove* retained a certain crude power. But it wasn't until *Oh Mercy!*, from 1989, that Dylan made an album of anything near his earlier grace. Produced by Daniel Lanois, and featuring great New Orleans players, such standouts as "Where Teardrops Fall" and "Political World" found Dylan in much less churlish form than he had been. Released the same year, *Dylan and the Dead* wasn't the embarrassment that some of his live sets had been, but it wasn't Dylan and the Band by a long shot.

Dylan's first album of the '90s, *Under the Red Sky*, was his worst studio set since *Self-Portrait*; its misguided attempt to recover an earlier simplicity of style resulted in lyrics with all the depth of doggerel. Luckily, it was overshadowed by the release of *The Bootleg Series*, a dazzling boxed-set collection of 58 outtakes and surprises from Dylan's earliest days on through *Oh Mercy!*. Excluding Dylan's first greatest-hits album, best-of collections don't really work in Dylan's case, although *Biograph*, with its outtakes and early live recordings—and because its 53 selections at least scratch the surface—is the best. — P.E.

THE DYNATONES
★ ★ ★ **Live It Up! (Rounder, 1985)**
★ ★ ★ **Tough to Shake (Rounder, 1985)**
★ ★ ★ **Shameless (Warner Bros., 1988)**
★ ★ ★ **Chopped & Channeled (Rhino, 1991)**
In order to pull off this '60s revivalist rock-soul revue routine, you've got to have (a) some interesting vision that transcends your influences, whether Otis, the Rascals or the Detroit Wheels; (b) an incredible band; (c) a phenomenal singer. The Dynatones pull off two out of three. A powerhouse rhythm section and great sax work boost capable original material into a controlled frenzy that could pass at least for good Sam & Dave outtakes—but the crucial soul is delivered by Chip "C.C." Miller's vocals. From grit to velvet, he's got the style down; he makes Southside Johnny, for example, sound forced. What the crew lacks, however, is its own sensibility. — P.E.

EAGLES

★ ★ ★   **Eagles (Asylum, 1972)**
★ ★ ★   **Desperado (Asylum, 1973)**
★ ★ ★½ **On the Border (Asylum, 1974)**
★ ★ ★   **One of These Nights (Asylum, 1975)**
★ ★ ★ ★ **Their Greatest Hits, 1971–1975 (Asylum, 1975)**
★ ★ ★ ★ **Hotel California (Asylum, 1976)**
★ ★ ★   **The Long Run (Asylum, 1979)**
★ ★½   **Eagles Live (Asylum, 1980)**

Reviled and revered with equal intensity, the Eagles epitomize the L.A. wing of rock's early-'70s grass-roots movement. The hippie-cowboy pose that so angered East Coast rock critics attracted legions of suburban record buyers. The members of the Eagles weren't boy scouts, of course, but they did emit a certain jock-ish All-American wholesomeness. No mistaking these guys for a clan of transvestite fashion plates or emaciated metal shock-rockers. In retrospect, the Eagles' music hasn't aged as well as that of Jackson Browne, say. Today, many of the album cuts that surround those fondly recalled hits sound indistinguishable from the work of Eagles imitators. If nothing else, the Eagles remain one of the most influential bands to arise during the '70s.

The band started off squarely in the folk-rock mold set down by Buffalo Springfield. "Take It Easy," co-written with Jackson Browne, outdistances everything else on the debut; "Peaceful Easy Feeling" is an outright sequel, while "Witchy Woman" and "Train Leaves Here This Morning" nod to Springfield founders Neil Young and Stephen Stills, respectively. *Desperado* is too laid-back for its own good; the funereally paced title track runs its outlaws-with-six-string-shooters metaphor into the ground.

Bassist Randy Meisner had been a founding member of Poco, but the Eagles blended pedal steel and banjo picking into a pop context instead of striving for folk (or rock) authenticity. Drummer Don Henley and guitarist Glenn Frey wound up as the group's primary singing (and writing) voices. The sharper, slightly more rock-oriented production of *On the Border* underscores their strengths: "James Dean" captures Frey's rowdy enthusiasm, while "Best of My Love" displays Henley's sure, steady hand with ballads. Not incidentally, the latter song became the Eagles' first Number One hit.

One of These Nights turned the group into superstars, spawning three Top Ten singles. The title track builds up an acceptable level of guitar tension behind the sexy, pleading lyrics, but the sugar-coated vitriol of "Lyin' Eyes" and "Take It to the Limit" still leaves a sour aftertaste. If the mere mention of those titles whets your appetite, though, *Their Greatest Hits* will satisfy the most ravenous nostalgic cravings.

Former James Gang leader Joe Walsh joined the Eagles in 1976; his relatively aggressive arena-rock guitar riffing and goony midwestern sensibility bolster *Hotel California*. Far and away, this is the Eagles' most consistent album, the one that still holds up. The title track and "Life in the Fast Lane" bring an illuminating flash of insight—and humor, finally—to the group's traditional subject matter. *Hotel California* comments on the passing scene as it cautions of the excesses yet to come. After that artistic (and commercial) triumph, *The Long Run* comes off sounding a trifle smug and self-justifying. Well, the Eagles prevailed at the time: "The Long Run" itself is enduringly catchy. We found out in the long run, too: only Don Henley has gone ahead to record anything of equal significance during the '80s. In fact, the Eagles' albums would fit into a time-capsule—perfectly. Maybe after another ten years.   — M.C.

SNOOKS EAGLIN
★ ★ ★   **Possum up a Simmon Tree (Arhoolie, 1971)**
★ ★ ★   **Baby, You Can Get Your Gun! (Black Top, 1987)**
★ ★ ★½   **Out of Nowhere (Black Top, 1989)**
A very appealing New Orleans blues and rock & roll guitarist, Eaglin's strength is his sense of humor—and his total saturation in the roots music that formed him. With Fats Domino's rhythm section along for the ride, *Baby, You Can Get Your Gun!* is tough and rollicking; *Out of Nowhere*, featuring Smiley Lewis's "Playgirl," is even zestier. A very nimble player, Snooks also sings up a storm.
— P.E.

STEVE EARLE
★ ★ ★½   **Guitar Town (MCA, 1986)**
★ ★ ★½   **Exit O (MCA, 1987)**
★ ★ ★ ★½   **Copperhead Road (Uni/MCA, 1988)**
★ ★ ★ ★   **Shut Up and Die Like an Aviator (MCA, 1990)**
★ ★ ★   **The Hard Way (MCA, 1991)**
Conversant with rockabilly, blues, country and rock & roll, Steve Earle has made remarkable growth over the course of five years to become one of the most trenchant songwriters of his generation. *Guitar Town* displayed his ease with all those styles, and, along with *Exit O*, established an image of Earle as an outsider dancing on danger's edge, always on the move, quick to defend what he loves, and foursquare in favor of individual liberty. Earle's nasally growl of a voice is a keen, cutting instrument, lacking range but loaded with feeling. As well, the music has been helped along by excellent band work—a powerhouse rhythm section, slashing and jangly guitars, and on *Copperhead Road* and *The Hard Way*, intelligent and dynamic vocal support from Maria McKee.

Even so, who could have predicted *Copperhead Road*? This masterwork resonates with history. Earle details an anti-authoritarian legacy handed down to him by his grandfather, who is identified as a bootlegger in the album's title song; this leads the narrator—a Vietnam Vet damaged physically and spiritually by his experience—into chicanery ("Snake Oil"), gunplay ("The Devil's Right Hand"), isolation and paranoia ("Back to the Wall") and finally, disillusionment ("Johnny Come Lately"). Earle's band comes roaring out of "Copperhead Road" like a wild animal, attacking everything in sight. The writing is pithy, dramatic, disturbing.

On *The Hard Way* Earle is again involved in politics and history. But where *Copperhead Road* had the feel of an epic, *The Hard Way* is more akin to a secret diary describing a solitary man's travails in an America largely devoid of mercy, justice and love. *Shut Up and Die Like an Aviator*, a live album released late in 1991, is an explosive affair comprised of familiar songs, save for cover versions of "She's About a Mover" and "Dead Flowers." Earle also offers up a tasty version of Jimmie Rodgers's "Blue Yodel #9" in acknowledgement of an artist whose influence on his work is inestimable. It's a good live album (a rarity, that), and it feels like the end of a chapter.   — D.M.

EARTH, WIND AND FIRE
★ ★½   **Earth, Wind and Fire (Warner Bros., 1970)**
★ ★½   **The Need of Love (Warner Bros., 1972)**
★ ★½   **Last Days and Time (Columbia, 1972)**
★ ★ ★   **Head to the Sky (Columbia, 1973)**
★ ★ ★ ★   **Open Our Eyes (Columbia, 1974)**
★ ★ ★ ★   **That's the Way of the World (Columbia, 1975)**
★ ★ ★½   **Gratitude (Columbia, 1975)**
★ ★ ★½   **Spirit (Columbia, 1976)**
★ ★ ★   **All 'n All (Columbia, 1977)**
★ ★ ★ ★½   **The Best of Earth, Wind and Fire Vol. 1 (ARC/Columbia, 1978)**
★ ★ ★   **I Am (ARC/Columbia, 1979)**
★ ★½   **Faces (ARC/Columbia, 1980)**
★ ★ ★   **Raise! (ARC/Columbia, 1981)**
★ ★ ★   **Powerlight (Columbia, 1983)**
★ ★½   **Electric Universe (Columbia, 1983)**
★ ★ ★   **Touch the World (Columbia, 1987)**
★ ★ ★ ★   **The Best of Earth, Wind and Fire Vol. II (Columbia, 1988)**
★ ★½   **Heritage (Columbia, 1990)**
Earth, Wind and Fire didn't merely popularize the Parliament-Funkadelic clan's approach; this Chicago-based groove conglomerate presented its own wholesome parallel to George Clinton's whacked-out game plan. Even though it could be argued that *The Best of Earth, Wind and Fire* portrays the best singles band of the '70s, EWF's eclectic impulses and killer pop instincts eventually coalesced on a pair of bracingly consistent and diverse albums: *Open Our Eyes* (1974) and the crossover smash *That's the Way of the World* (1975).

EWF founder Maurice White had been a session drummer at the Chess studios in

Chicago during the '60s; he forged a pack of young local players into the new group in 1969. The Warner Bros. albums, now deleted, lean toward the softer end of jazz-rock fusion, peppered by the occasional R&B-flavored horn chart; the initial Columbia albums are caught in the same muddle, although White had assembled a new band.

Gradually, singer Philip Bailey emerges as the point man for White's cosmic vision and commercial ambition. The soaring vocal hooks, hip platitudes and indelible melodies that became the group's calling card start to peek out from under the spacey jams and African spiced percussion on *Head to the Sky*. But those nascent songs—"Evil" and "Keep Your Head to the Sky"—are scant preparation for *Open Our Eyes*: newly focused songwriting and the ensemble's responsive playing result in uplifting dance strokes ("Mighty Mighty"), convincing soul testimony ("Devotion"), sweet mid-tempo melancholy ("Feelin' Blue") and an intriguing whiff of the Third World ("Kalimba Story").

That's the Way of the World boils that down to a potent, nourishing pop formula. "Shining Star" and the title track launched EWF's run on the pop charts; Philip Bailey's heart-stopping "Reasons," the funky "Yearnin', Learnin' " and "Africano" add balance and depth to a landmark album, the soundtrack to a forgotten film about the music-biz hustle. *Gratitude* devotes three sides to EWF live, and the band lives up to its onstage rep, and tosses in a handful of hits and ringers. *Spirit* keeps it up, pretty much, though the tone of party anthems like "Saturday Nite" is noticeably light. So is the beat. Slowly but surely, super-efficient disco rhythms and automatic-pilot song material weakened EWF's impact. Though the group's golden knack remained in place, the subsequent albums are strictly hit or miss. Perhaps *Raise!* and *Powerlight* could be better represented, but nonetheless *Best of EWF Vol. II* remains the only necessary album from the group's later days. *Touch the World* marked a very encouraging re-grouping. With the signature sound discretely modernized by way of glossy synths and hip-hop beats, the other basic elements shine through, especially Bailey's intimate vocals and the topicality and clear-eyed optimism of "System of Survival." Surprisingly, *Heritage* is dragged down by an unnecessary reliance on hammy guest appearances by currently hot rappers. — M.C.

EASTERHOUSE
★ ★ ★ **Contenders (Columbia, 1986)**
★ ★ ★ **Waiting for the Redbird (Columbia, 1989)**

With Andy Perry's deep-toned, dramatic vocals echoing Jim Morrison or Ian McCulloch and playing whose trance-rock kick recalls the Psychedelic Furs or a harder Simple Minds, this Manchester crew is a sharp, capable outfit. The band's hardline leftist politics, however, are about the only thing that makes them distinctive (they're hardly the musical innovators the Clash were)—and the unvarying fatalism of the lyrics gets a bits tiresome. — P.E.

SHEENA EASTON
★ ★ **Sheena Easton (EMI America, 1981)**
★ **You Could Have Been with Me (EMI America, 1981)**
★ **Madness, Money and Music (EMI America, 1982)**
★ ★ **Best Kept Secret (EMI America, 1983)**
★ ★½ **A Private Heaven (EMI Manhattana, 1984)**
★½ **Do You (EMI Manhattan, 1985)**
★ ★½ **No Sound but a Heart (EMI America, 1987)**
★ ★ ★ **The Lover in Me (MCA, 1988)**
★ ★ ★ **The Best of Sheena Easton (EMI America, 1989)**
★ ★½ **What Comes Naturally (MCA, 1991)**

Starting out in the middle of the road, Sheena Easton began her career as a sort of latter-day Olivia Newton-John, dividing her time between semi-liberated fluff like "Morning Train (Nine to Five)" and "Modern Girl" (both from *Sheena Easton*) and traditional MOR treacle like "Wind Beneath My Wings" (from *Madness, Money and Music*). She began to change gears on *Best Kept Secret*, bouncing between the demure country-pop of "Almost Over You" and the trendy techno-groove of tunes like "Telefone (Long Distance Love Affair)," but it's *A Private Heaven* that finds her truly taking her career in a new direction. "Strut" adds a sassy flirtatiousness to the danceable synth beat "Telefone" presaged, but "Sugar Walls" (penned by Prince under the pseudonym "Alexander Nevermind") goes even further, building its entire lyric around a vaginal metaphor.

"Sugar Walls" expanded Easton's audience considerably, even earning her some R&B airplay, but EMI seems to have seen its success as an anomaly; hence, *Do*

You returns to the comfortable predictability of her previous work. Easton, though, seems to have had other ideas about her pop potential, and *No Sound But a Heart* offers an interesting compromise, backing its songs with solid, R&B grooves but, in an apparent sop to her MOR following, keeping the focus on soul balladry. After moving to MCA, she began courting the R&B crossover audience even more actively. With production by L.A. & Babyface, Jellybean and (on "101") Prince, *The Lover in Me* is slick, sexy and, at times, soulful; *What Comes Naturally* repeats the formula, but with lesser producers and less success. *Best of* compiles all her EMI hits, including the James Bond theme "For Your Eyes Only."
— J.D.C.

THE EASYBEATS
★ ★ ★½ **The Best of the Easybeats (Rhino, 1985)**
"Friday on My Mind" was a terrific 1967 hit. The Aussies behind its cheerful thunder were the Easybeats' mainmen, Harry Vanda and George Young (brother of AC/DC's Angus and Malcolm). Never a great Stateside success, and defunct by 1970, the Easybeats, on the strength of a crack rhythm section and consistently sharp songs, wear better than much British Invasion pop. Their late-'60s work sounds like the big-ballad Bee Gees. Which isn't bad. Even there, however, an intriguing oddness peeks through. — P.E.

EAZY-E
★ ★ **Eazy-Duz-It (Ruthless/Priority, 1988)**
This solo album by the foulmouthed mastermind of N.W.A. suggests his real talent lies in marketing, not rapping.
— J.D.C.

ECHO AND THE BUNNYMEN
★ ★ ★   **Crocodiles (Sire, 1980)**
★ ★   **Heaven Up Here (Sire, 1981)**
★ ★ ★½ **Porcupine (Sire, 1983)**
★ ★ ★½ **Ocean Rain (Sire, 1984)**
★ ★ ★½ **Songs to Learn and Sing (Sire, 1986)**
★ ★½ **Echo and the Bunnymen (Sire, 1987)**
★ ★½ **Reverberation (Sire, 1990)**
Starting on the '80s as leaders of the "New Psychedelia," Echo consisted of working-class Liverpudlians hellbent on a mission— to reclaim the musical ambitiousness of '60s rock, while conceding nothing in the way of punk anger. Fronted by Ian McCulloch, a sour, cute moptop with a Jim Morrison fetish, and flourishing the jagged expertise of

guitarist Will Sergeant, the foursome's debut was impressive: a title like "Happy Death Men" caught Echo's propensity for dark whimsy, and the material overall displayed an instrumental ferocity that would soon develop into a juggernaut.

From *Heaven Up Here*, the bass-orgy of "A Promise" was almost catchy and "All My Colours" worked as a slice of Ingmar Bergman-like atmosphere, but the album proved tough going in its adolescent pessimism. Although failing to solidify any stateside following, *Porcupine* was Echo's musical breakthrough. Few records begin with the adrenaline rush of "The Cutter," "Back of Love" and "My White Devil"— boosted by the Mideastern fiddle-freakouts of new collaborator, Shankar, this was frantic stuff: gothic in its literate gloominess (McCulloch even had the smarts or hubris to refer to obscure Elizabethan playwright John Webster), but overheatedly baroque in its dense grandeur. *Ocean Rain* wasn't necessarily better, but it did show the band reaching maturity. Finally giving itself, and the audience, a break, the record isn't quite as relentless as the previous work. Strings drench the songs, but, for Echo, the orchestral heaviness works—this is a band for whom lush exaggeration is a raison d'etre.

Songs to Learn and Sing gathered up Echo's "hits"; it also featured the closest Echo has come to pop, in the semi-buoyant "Bring on the Dancing Horses." With *Echo and the Bunnymen*, the band lost some cult aficionados, but gained new listeners through the strategy of playing more leanly: the record is sharply focused, and neat keyboard work by Ray Manzarek nicely acknowledges Echo's debt to the Doors, but it misses something of the old Wagnerian thunder. After McCulloch left to pursue a solo career, Echo returned on *Reverberation*. By then, only two of the original Bunnymen were on hand, but the record surprisingly captures Echo's threatrical sound. — P.E.

DUANE EDDY
★ ★ **Have "Twangy" Guitar Will Travel (1958; Jamie/Motown, 1987)**
★ ★ **$1,000,000 Dollars of Twang (1960; Jamie/Motown, 1987)**
★ ★ ★ **16 Greatest Hits (1961; Jamie/Motown, 1987)**
★ ★ ★ **The Vintage Years (Sire, 1975)**
"Twang" is the word most closely associated with guitar legend Duane Eddy,

and certainly that sound best summarizes his personality on record. But Eddy wasn't all lower register melodies, liberal tremolo and omnipresent whammy bar. His instrumentals were the original music-minus-one exercises—only the vocalist was missing. This emphasis on song construction separated Eddy from inspired '50s primitives such as Link Wray and set a standard for the rock instrumental that flowered in the '60s when the Ventures came on the scene, and later with the advent of surf music. As well as his overpowering lyricism—evident from his first hit single, "Rebel Rouser," from 1958—Eddy was supported by outstanding musicians. The sax especially was a key element of Eddy's sound, and on songs such as "Ramrod" and the "Peter Gunn Theme," Eddy's twanging was clearly subservient to the impassioned honking that gave both songs a rugged edge.

Eddy was consistently in the Top Forty between '58 and '63, making it as high as Number Four in 1960 with the lush theme to the film *Because They're Young*, a vehicle designed to make Eddy a movie star. It bombed and he kept on twanging. His best recordings were on the Jamie label, which were reissued by Motown in 1987, and at this writing are being negotiated with another distributor. *16 Greatest Hits* gets you the important work. The best Eddy collection is the out-of-print *Vintage Years* two-record retrospective issued on Sire in 1975, with extensive liner notes by Greg Shaw. — D.M.

DAVE EDMUNDS

★ ★ ★½ **Rockpile (MAM, 1972)**
★ ★ ★ **Subtle as a Flying Mallet (RCA, 1975)**
★ ★ ★½ **Get It (Swan Song, 1977)**
★ ★ ★½ **Dave Edmunds, Rocker: Early Works 1968–72 (EMI/Parlophone, 1977)**
★ ★ ★ ★ **Tracks on Wax 4 (Swan Song, 1978)**
★ ★ ★ ★ **Repeat When Necessary (Swan Song, 1979)**
★ ★ ★ **Twangin' (Swan Song, 1981)**
★ ★ ★ **The Best of Dave Edmunds (Swan Song, 1981)**
★ ★ ★½ **D.E. 7th (Columbia, 1982)**
★ ★½ **Information (Columbia, 1983)**
★ ★½ **Riff Raff (Columbia, 1984)**
★ ★ ★ **I Hear You Rockin'—Live (Columbia, 1988)**
★ ★½ **Closer to the Flame (Capitol, 1990)**

Dave Edmunds helped bring back some of the roll to rock, long after it had fallen out of fashion. He didn't revive rockabilly, he reasserted its rhythmic pulse—revealing his suprisingly twisted roots in country, the blues, Chuck Berry and the Beatles. "I Hear You Knockin'," from *Rockpile*, entered the U.S. Top Ten in early '71, sounding nothing at all like the competition. Drenching Smiley Lewis's New Orleans R&B oldie in quavering slide guitar, Edmunds turns his British accent into a naturally affecting twang. Rather than just imitiating a Yank, he captures some of American music's spirit and applies it to his own experience.

Rockpile establishes Edmunds as low-key, but effective interpreter with a canny eye for material; he successfully covers James Burton ("Down, Down, Down"), Neil Young ("Dance, Dance, Dance") and the semi-ubiquitous "It Ain't Easy." The 1977 double album, *Dave Edmunds, Rocker*, available as an import only, pairs the Rockpile sessions with material by Love Sculpture, Edmunds's late-'60s band. *Subtle as a Flying Mallet*, long out of print, suffers from more predictable song selection.

Dave Edmunds found a kindred soul in former Brinsley Schwarz bassist Nick Lowe, whose composing skills and pop touch complemented Edmunds's instrumental verve and tunefulness. Their collaboration is kick-started on *Get It* ("I Knew the Bride," "Here Comes the Weekend"), then settles into a comfortable groove with *Tracks On Wax 4* and *Repeat When Necessary*. Those two albums feature the band Rockpile: Edmunds, Lowe, second guitarist Billy Bremner and drummer Terry Williams earned a solid reputation as a volatile, no-bullshit rock & roll band. They could play rings around the punks even on a bad night, yet Rockpile is powered by the same energy source.

The Best of Dave Edmunds presents an adequate summary of these years, though *Tracks* and *Repeat* are both succint, well-balanced albums. After a nasty split with Lowe, Edmunds bounds back with the solid *D.E.7th*. It doesn't quite provide the slap-in-the-face urgency of prime Rockpile, though Edmunds puts his indelible stamp on Bruce Springsteen with "From Small Things (Big Things One Day Come)" and wheels out some winning originals. *Riff Raff* and *Information* mark a strained collaboration with ELO-meister Jeff Lynne; presumably, this is where Lynne ironed the wrinkles out of the Wilburys' traveling suits. The live *I Hear You Rockin'* finds Edmunds running through a '70s-vintage hit list with a young, audibly enthused backing band. For a rent gig, not bad.

Shockingly, *Closer to the Flame* never catches fire; it's the first time in 20 years that Edmunds has sounded tired. But he turned around and produced his old mate Nick Lowe's sterling *Party of One* comeback right after that. — M.C.

808 STATE
★★★½ **Utd. State 90 (Tommy Boy, 1990)**
★★★ **Ex:El (Tommy Boy, 1990)**
This idiosyncratic Manchester act's coloristic approach to house music verges on a sort of danceable new age sound. "Pacific 202," with its dreamy synths and jazzy sax floating over an agreeably insistent beat, established the group's sound, and most of *Utd. State 90* proceeded in kind, although the raucous "Cubik" did add some bite to the album. *Ex:El* not only toughened the instrumental attack, but incorporated vocals, with mixed results; although Sugarcube Björk Gudmundsdottir's vocals complement the 808 groove, Bernard Sumner's contributions to "Spanish Heart" reduce the track to warmed-over New Order. — J.D.C.

EL DORADOS
★★★ **Crazy Little Mama (Vee Jay, 1989)**
This Chicago quintet has one group harmony classic, from 1955, to its credit, "At My Front Door" (which is often referred to by its opening lyric, "Crazy little mama"—witness this album's title). They followed that song with a lovely mating of doo-wop and pop, "I'll Be Forever Loving You," a song that was covered gloriously by the Persuasions on their *Street Corner Symphony* album in 1972. Singer Pirkle Moses had a thin but plaintive tenor and was always given rousing backup support by the other singers. A 1956 cut, "A Fallen Tear," is one of the more adventurous records of its time, as it has no single lead voice, but about three voices singing together and around each other, with one being heavily echoed and soaring over the harmony choruses. The group disbanded in 1957 after failing in several attempts to duplicate the success of "At My Front Door"—not even a clone song, "Bim Bam Boom" (1956) could reignite interest in the El Dorados. *Crazy Little Mama* indicates the group deserved better, but history declared otherwise. — D.M.

ELECTRIC FLAG
★★★½ **Long Time Comin' (Columbia, 1968)**
★★ **The Electric Flag (Columbia, 1969)**

★★★ **The Best of the Electric Flag (Columbia, 1970)**
Formerly of the Butterfield Blues Band, blues guitarist Mike Bloomfield was the Electric Flag's ace player—but bassist Harvey Brooks, saxist Herbie Rich and drummer Buddy Miles were no slouches (the band's other mainstay, Nick Gravenites, was an earnest singer, but a better writer). A short-lived supergroup, the Flag debuted at the Monterey Pop Festival in June of 1967 with the jazz-rock sound that made the band's first album a minor classic. The group's blues were mainly Bloomfield's show—and a great one. But it was with mid-tempo numbers that the band sounded most distinctive; experimenting with an aggressive horn section, the Flag succeeded, where Blood, Sweat and Tears and Chicago failed, at creating a new kind of swing that lost no rock power. Soul music fanatics (the group dedicated a song "with great respect" to Steve Cropper and Otis Redding), the Flag's stellar technique never overwhelmed its passion. Without Bloomfield, the band's second record, *The Electric Flag*, is weak, as is their *Best of.* — P.E.

ELECTRIC LIGHT ORCHESTRA
★★★ **No Answer (1972; Jet/Epic, 1977)**
★★ **ELO II (1973; Jet/Epic, 1977)**
★★★ **On the Third Day (1973; Jet/Epic, 1977)**
★★★½ **Eldorado (1974; Jet/Epic, 1977)**
★★★ **Face the Music (Jet/Epic, 1975)**
★★★ **Ole' ELO (Jet/Epic, 1976)**
★★★ **A New World Record (Jet/Epic, 1976)**
★★★ **Out of the Blue (Jet/Epic, 1977)**
★★½ **Discovery (Jet/Epic, 1979)**
★★★★ **Greatest Hits (Jet/Epic, 1979)**
★★½ **Time (Jet/Epic, 1981)**
★★ **Secret Messages (CBS Associated, 1983)**
★★ **Balance of Power (CBS Associated, 1986)**
★★★ **Afterglow (Epic, 1990)**
★ **Part Two (Scotti Brothers, 1991)**
★★★★ **ELO Classics (Sony Music Special Products, 1990)**
An unabashed late-period Beatlemaniac, Jeff Lynne turned his *Sgt. Pepper's* fixation into a workable pop formula for the '70s. The aspiring guitarist-singer-composer-producer founded Electric Light Orchestra with Birmingham homeboy Roy Wood, who'd led the Move through a similiar Fab Four infatuation during the late '60s. When Lynne joined the Move in 1970, the seeds for ELO were germinated. Their debut, *No*

Answer, strives for an unlikely fusion of rock & roll and classical music; unsurprisingly, only the haunting "10538 Overture" really takes hold. That single sounds more like the Move's dense rock studiocraft than ELO's subsequent hits; Wood soon left ELO to pursue his own eccentric orchestral muse. Though it was a commercial success, *ELO II* didn't bode well for Lynne's artistic future; with its snatches of Beethoven and ham-handed Berry-isms, "Roll Over Beethoven" quickly became an FM radio irritant—like hearing a one-line joke over and over.

Lynne continued to hone his approach, and on *On the Third Day* his knack for hummable tunes and subtle hooks is revealed. Oh, there's still a Grieg-inspired tune to deal with, but the vaguely funky and overtly catchy "Showdown" indicates that Lynne was still keeping an ear trained on the competition. *Eldorado* sustains the group's glossy Beatles hommage over the course of an entire album—ELO's most consistent and cohesive. Nevertheless, for all the band's ambitions, the evidence insists that ELO is at heart one hell of a singles band.

Hits off *Face the Music* ("Strange Magic," "Livin' Thing") and *New World Record* ("Telephone Line") mark Lynne's creative and commerical apex. *Olé ELO* is an acceptable though incomplete compilation, while the superlative *Greatest Hits* delivers the goods. (Watch out for the Sony Music Special Products ELO package *Classics*, a brief budget repackaging of the '79 collection.) *Out of the Blue* shows Lynne's expansiveness clouding ELO's vision once again; its two discs map incredible peaks ("Turn to Stone") and bottomless valleys (the sidelong "Concerto for a Rainy Day"). After that, the ELO spark fades to an occasional flicker: "Hold on Tight" (from *Time*) and "Rock 'n' Roll Is King" (from *Secret Messages*) foreshadow the sleek roots-rock groove Lynne later perfected with the Traveling Wilburys, Roy Orbison's final sessions and his own 1989 solo album.

Led by veteran Move-ELO drummer Bev Bevan, the latter-day ELO "comeback" is a robotic simulation of the original group's sound: it's not even campy, just depressing. And the indisputable glow of ELO's best shots is dimmed somewhat by the overlong *Afterglow*: instead of three CDs, two—or even one gem-packed killer—would have made a much stronger case. As it is, this box set helps explain how Jeff Lynne got to where he is today, but not why it took him so long. — M.C.

ELECTRONIC

★ ★ ★½ **Electronic (Warner Bros., 1991)**
Considerably more organic than its title might indicate, Electronic pools the talents of Manchester lads Bernard Sumner (Joy Division, New Order) and Johnny Marr (the Smiths). Synthesized melodies and programmed drum beats set the blue mood, though Marr's crisp strumming and subtle bursts of guitar fire certainly enliven Sumner's emotionally hesitant talk-singing. When he's pushed by strongly focused material, Sumner can project an enticing vulnerability. And Pet Shop Boy Neil Tennant's contributions manage to push him just the right way: "The Patience of a Saint" and "Getting Away With It" are perfect vehicles for Sumner's tuneful neuroticism. If the rest of the album doesn't quite keep up, it does move along at a brisk pace. Even the two rap-flavored tracks get over. Electronic poses no threat to Public Enemy or N.W.A, but surely "Idiot Country" and "Feel Every Beat" make better sense than "Ice Ice Baby." Maybe there is life after mope-rock? — M.C.

ELEVENTH DREAM DAY

★ ★ ★ **Beet (Atlantic, 1989)**
★ ★ ★ **Lived to Tell (Atlantic, 1991)**
This brainy Chicago foursome comes up with lyrics that are sometimes subtle and provocative ("North of Wasteland)" and sometimes clever ("Bomb the Mars Hotel"). "I Could Be Lost" and "Daedalus," however, are obtuse and over-ambitious; they read like the musings of grad students. Luckily, the sonic pleasures of Rick Rizzo's and Baird Figi's guitars shake loose of most of Eleventh Dream Day's pretentions— echoing Neil Young's work with Crazy Horse, this music is smart faux-primitivism. Rizzo's a genial, offhand vocalist; he sounds best with drummer (and wife) Janet Beveridge Bean joining in. Visionaries in the making, the band's poetic sensibility is apparent on both albums—and while a little amorphous, it's rich with suggestion. — P.E.

DUKE ELLINGTON

★ ★ ★ ★   **Hi-Fi Ellington Uptown (Columbia, 1953)**
★ ★ ★ ★½ **Black, Brown and Beige (Columbia Special Products, 1958)**
★ ★ ★ ★ ★ **Duke Ellington and His Orchestra at Newport (1956; Columbia, 1987)**
★ ★ ★ ★ ★ **Four Symphonic Works (MusicMasters, 1989)**

★★★★★ Ellington Indigos (1957; Columbia, 1989)

★★★★★ Ellington Jazz Party (1959; Columbia, 1987)

★★★½ Ellington/Basie—First Time! The Count Meets the Duke (Columbia, 1961)

★★★★ Duke Ellington and His Orchestra Featuring Paul Gonsalves (1962; Fantasy, 1991)

★★★½ Latin American Suite (1970; Fantasy, 1990)

★★★★ Ellington/Brewer—It Don't Mean a Thing . . . (1973; Columbia, 1981)

★★★½ The Duke's Big 4 (1974; Pablo, 1988)

★★★½ Yale Concert (1973; Fantasy, 1991)

★★★½ The Pianist (Fantasy, 1974)

★★★★★ Second Sacred Concert (1974; Prestige, 1990)

★★★★ The Ellington Suites (1976; Pablo, 1990)

★★★½ The Intimate Ellington (Pablo, 1977)

★★★★★ The Duke Ellington Carnegie Hall Concerts—January, 1943 (Prestige, 1977)

★★★★★ The Duke Ellington Carnegie Hall Concerts—December, 1944 (Prestige, 1977)

★★★★★ The Duke Ellington Carnegie Hall Concerts—January, 1946 (Prestige, 1977)

★★★½ The Duke Ellington Carnegie Hall Concerts—December, 1947 (Prestige, 1977)

★★★½ The Best of Duke Ellington (1980; Pablo, 1991)

★★★★ The All-Star Road Band (1983; CBS Special Products, 1989)

★★★★ The All-Star Road Band, Vol.2 (1983; Columbia Special Products, 1989)

★★★★ New Mood Indigo (1985; CBS Special Products, 1989)

★★★★ Harlem (Pablo, 1985)

★★★★ Duke Ellington/Happy Reunion (Sony Music Special Products, 1985)

★★★★ The Intimacy of the Blues (1986; Fantasy, 1991)

★★★★★ Duke Ellington: The Blanton-Webster Band (Bluebird, 1986)

★★★★ And His Mother Called Him Bill (Bluebird, 1987)

★★★½ In the Uncommon Market (Pablo, 1987)

★★★★★ Black, Brown and Beige (Bluebird, 1988)

★★★★ Back Room Romp (Portrait, 1988)

★★★★ Blues in Orbit (Columbia, 1988)

★★★★ The Best of Duke Ellington (CBS Special Products, 1989)

★★★★★ Braggin' in Brass—The Immortal 1938 Year (Portrait, 1989)

★★★★ Duke Ellington Live! (Emarcy, 1989)

★★★★ The Brunswick Era, Vol. 1 (MCA, 1990)

★★★★ Three Suites (Columbia, 1990)

★★★★★ The Okeh Ellington (Columbia, 1991)

★★★★★ The Essence of Duke Ellington (Columbia/Legacy, 1991)

★★★★★ Small Groups, Vol. 1 (Columbia/Legacy, 1991)

★★★½ Hot Summer Dance (Red Baron/Sony, 1991)

WITH RAY BROWN

★★★★½ This One's For Blanton (1975; Pablo, 1991)

WITH BILLY STRAYHORN

★★★★½ Piano Duets: Great Times! (Riverside, 1984)

WITH JOHNNY HODGES

★★★★★ Side by Side (Verve, 1959)

★★★★★ Back to Back: Duke Ellington and Johnny Hodges Play the Blues (Verve, 1963)

WITH JOHN COLTRANE

★★★★★ Duke Ellington and John Coltrane (1962; MCA/Impulse, 1988)

WITH COLEMAN HAWKINS

★★★★★ Duke Ellington Meets Coleman Hawkins (1962; MCA/Impulse, 1986)

With over 2,000 compositions and scads of recordings to his credit, Duke Ellington was to 20th-century American music what Picasso was to modern art. Unlike the archetypal jazz-genius-as-extremist (Bix Beiderbecke, Charlie Parker), Ellington didn't burn out in his brilliant youth, but continued into a vigorous old age, innovating, experimenting, refining. Using the broadest of musical canvases (the big band, the orchestra), Duke and composer-arranger Billy Strayhorn, his partner ever since the late '30s, worked large ensembles with the precision that great soloists bring to a single instrument—the Ellington sound combined staggering musical intelligence with intuitive character study: Duke wrote not for generic instrumentalists but for his specific, long-time stars, exacting from such giants as alto saxophonist Johnny Hodges, trumpeter Cootie Williams and clarinetist Barney Bigard their greatest work. Grounded in the blues, Ellington extended into all but the most passing or outre forms of jazz; he was unintimidated, as well, by the European classical tradition and, as his career progressed, he concentrated more heavily on longer pieces whose form extended far beyond jazz structure. The loveliest of jazz melodists, Ellington wrote music that, however exuberant and elegant, had almost always in it a quality of dignified pathos or yearning—the man himself was a regal personality, careful, somewhat aloof, highly romantic, restless and complex.

Getting a grip on Ellington takes work, not because his music was ever inaccessible (Duke's motto, of course, was "It don't mean a thing, if it ain't got that swing"), but because there's simply so much of it. Neophytes wouldn't do at all badly by starting with any number of "best-of" packages: combining *The Best of Duke Ellington*, on CBS Special Products, with Columbia/Legacy's *The Essence of Duke Ellington* nets a nice, brisk intro—"Sophisticated Lady," "Solitude," "Don't Get Around Much Anymore" "Dimuendo and Crescendo in Blue (The Wailing Interval)" span music from the '30s to the '50s, and as short pieces, they flourish equally the composer's melodic gifts and his remarkable concision—nobody either naps or indulges himself on these sessions, and the sound is efficiency itself. Verve's *Duke Ellington and Friends* is nice, too—this is Duke a little later on, with Ella Fitzgerald, Billy Strayhorn on piano, tenor saxophonist Ben Webster and drummer Louis Bellson turning in late '50s–early '60s versions of the Ellington classics. Both volumes of *The All-Star Road Band* series (CBS Special Products) are copacetic: with the Ellington heavyweights blowing in a dance setting, "Perdido," "Take the A Train" and other hits come across with an assured, easy grace. Romantics might find the best entry into the elegiac Ellington with *Ellington Indigos* (Columbia): from 1957, these are wonderful moody vignettes of great tenderness and charm—"Solitude," "Autumn Leaves," "Willow Weep for Me" and the album's other cuts often bring Duke's piano uncharacteristically to the fore, and Johnny Hodges plays like a dream. Columbia's *It Don't Mean a Thing* (1973) is a fine Ellington for non-jazzers—a

collaboration with ace vocalist Teresa Brewer, it captures an essential mood of the master for listeners scared off by long solos. Braver sorts then might want to dive into *Ellington at Newport*. His best-selling album, it captures a ground-breaking live performance in which tenor saxophonist Paul Gonsalves set the crowd afire by blazing through 27 choruses of "Dimuendo and Crescendo in Blue"—it's roughly the jazz equivalent of Hendrix at Woodstock. At the opposite end from the introductory work are the Ellington monuments. Duke's own favorites were his *Sacred Concerts* of the late '60s, of which only the second remains in print. Some jazz purists don't dig these works, but the combination of some of Ellington's strongest sidemen, gospel choirs and stellar solo vocalists remains inspiring. Portrait's *Braggin' in Brass—The Immortal 1938 Year* includes among its 32 gems a strong "Black and Tan Fantasy"—first recorded in 1927, the piece was an early example of Ellington's trailblazing incorporation of the jazz player's improvisational skills within a completely structured piece. Ellingtonians often argue that his orchestra reached the peak of its power in the '40s when such long-form landmarks as "Liberian Suite" and "Ko-Ko" were unveiled—and Prestige's four volumes of the ensemble's four *Carnegie Hall Concerts* make the claim hard to refute. The 1943 set is the most impressive, debuting "Black, Brown and Beige," the first of Duke's massive, extended pieces. MusicMasters' *Four Symphonic Works* includes a version of that milestone, as well as "Harlem," "New World a-Comin" and "Three Black Kings," works that may not rank among Duke's greatest, but help point out his mastery of the orchestral idiom. Another impressive collection of the Ellington orchestra at its height is Bluebird's *Black, Brown and Beige*, with its 58 selections from the 1944–1946 period.

For the early work, check out MCA's *The Brunswick Years, Vol. 1*, along with *The Okeh Ellington* and its 50 cuts of embryonic (1927–30) greatness; as counterpoint, *The Duke's Big 4* (1974) presents the lion in winter—recorded with only three other remarkable players (Joe Pass on guitar, Ray Brown on bass, Louis Bellson on drums), it highlights Ellington's often overlooked playing. The amazing thing about Ellington is that all of his creative periods bore remarkable fruit, and virtually any of his recordings bears the stamp of genius.
— P.E.

RAMBLIN' JACK ELLIOTT

★ ★ ★ **Ramblin' Jack Elliott Sings Woody Guthrie and Jimmie Rodgers (MTR, 1962)**

★ ★ ★ **The Essential Ramblin' Jack Elliott (Vanguard, 1976)**

★ ★ ★ **Hard Travelin' (Fantasy, 1989)**

Companion to Woody Guthrie on the latter's mythmaking rambles across America, Elliott was an engaging folk presence—a dharma bum of the kind Kerouac celebrated. Born in Brooklyn, he fled city life to join the rodeo, and then ended up spinning yarns in Greenwich Village. One early Elliott fan was Bob Dylan, who paid back his psychic debt by bringing the old hipster cowboy along on his 1975 Rolling Thunder tour.

Worn and frayed, Elliott's voice is perfect for Guthrie's songs—and for the Leadbelly, Jimmy Driftwood and traditional material that's represented best on *The Essential*. *Hard Travelin'*, a compilation that pairs two classic '60s albums—*Jack Elliott Sings the Songs of Woody Guthrie* and *Ramblin' Jack Elliott*—is also fine and gritty folk. — P.E.

JOE ELY

★ ★ ★ ★   **Joe Ely (1977; MCA, 1991)**

★ ★ ★ ★½ **Honky Tonk Masquerade (1978; MCA, 1991)**

★ ★ ★ ★   **Down on the Drag (1979; MCA, 1991)**

★ ★ ★½ **Musta Notta Gotta Lotta (1981; MCA, 1991)**

★ ★ ★½ **Live Shots (MCA, 1981)**

★ ★ ★½ **High-Res (MCA, 1984)**

★ ★ ★½ **Lord of the Highway (Hightone, 1987)**

★ ★ ★   **Dig All Night (Hightone, 1988)**

★ ★ ★   **Live at Liberty Lunch (MCA, 1990)**

"Tennessee's Not the State I'm In," Joe Ely declares on his 1977 debut album. Of course, Texas is the only state that could nurture such an idiosyncratic and resilient country sound. Like his forebears Buddy Holly and Waylon Jennings, Ely hails from the dusty towns of Amarillo and Lubbock. Along with compadres Butch Hancock and Jimmie Dale Gilmore, Ely was part of a hippie trio called the Flatlanders in the early '70s. Their brand of spacey, folk-tinged balladry (as evidenced on the Rounder reissue *More a Legend Than a Band*) offers scant preparation for the rollicking honky-tonk eclecticism of Ely's solo work, however. Armed with powerful songs by Hancock and Gilmore as well as his own material, Ely mounted a formidable challenge to the mellow country-rock hierarchy.

Actually, Joe Ely consistently evades the country-rock brand. Blues, R&B, rockabilly, Tex-Mex and western swing: the currents flow together on his first four albums, merging into a deep, easy-flowing stream. Though songwriting is this singer's secret weapon, Ely also helms a crackerjack roadhouse band: Jesse Taylor on lead guitar, Lloyd Maines on pedal steel and Ponty Bone on accordion all assert their individual strengths without overplaying. Rather than self-consciously trying to re-create traditional influences, Ely and crew jumble their diverse musical heritage into a natural-sounding melange.

Joe Ely is a rangy and confident debut album, but *Honky Tonk Masquerade* cuts deeper. There's a telling new touch of gravel in Ely's plain voice, and he breathes a gritty realism into ten distinct songs. He howls at a "Cornbread Moon" and chortles when those "Fingernails" click on the piano, floats the idea of Gilmore's "Tonight I'm Gonna Go Downtown" and glides through Hancock's "West Texas Waltz." The haunting small-town lament "Boxcars" is about watching trains go past, not riding them into the sunset. And the ultra-seductive "Jericho (Your Walls Must Come Tumbling Down)" could test the resistance of a saint—or a country-hating atheist.

Down on the Drag suffers from muddy production and slightly less inspired songwriting, though most of its tracks sink in over time. *Musta Notta Gotta Lotta* cranks up the rockabilly and R&B quotient; some of the rhythm fever sounds rushed, but Gilmore's swinging "Dallas" and Ely's pointed "I Keep Getting Paid the Same" anchor this transitional album. The out-of-print *Live Shots* documents the beginning of Ely's hard-rock push; it was recorded right around the time Joe toured with the Clash and dropped his pedal steel guitar in favor of honking saxophone.

The synthsizer-laden *High-Res* offended the coterie of Ely fanatics and underwhelmed the Brit-pop–crazed general public. "Cool Rockin' Loretta" flashes the expected mettle, but elsewhere the metal grunts and heavy gloss rub against Ely's rootsy grain. Re-emerging on the independent label Hightone, Ely spikes the more familiar-sounding *Lord of the Highway* with his best composition to date: "Me & Billy the Kid" is a compelling and convincingly weird narrative, a story song that deepens the more you listen to it. The rowdy *Dig All Night* could use a "Me &

Billy the Kid"—not to mention a Jimmie Dale Gilmore or Butch Hancock contribution. *Live at Liberty Lunch* could use some pedal steel or accordion; though Ely's vocal chops are in effect and the energy level stays high, the steady-chugging bar band accompaniment obscures the musical unpredictability that made Ely so special in the first place. — M.C.

EMERSON, LAKE AND PALMER

★ ★ ★   **Emerson, Lake and Palmer (Atlantic, 1971)**

★ ★½   **Tarkus (Atlantic, 1971)**

½ ★   **Pictures at an Exhibition (Atlantic, 1972)**

★ ★ ★   **Trilogy (Atlantic, 1972)**

★ ★ ★   **Brain Salad Surgery (Atlantic, 1973)**

★ ★   **Welcome Back My Friends to the Show That Never Ends (Manticore/Atlantic, 1974)**

★ ★   **Works Volume 1 (Atlantic, 1977)**

★ ★   **Works Volume 2 (Atlantic, 1977)**

★   **In Concert (Atlantic, 1979)**

★ ★ ★   **The Best of ELP (Atlantic, 1980)**

Emerson, Lake and Palmer wreaked havoc on the classics, exacting revenge for a generation of involuntary piano pupils. Keyboard flash Keith Emerson developed his flamboyant, showy attack in a '60s combo misnamed the Nice; teaming up with original King Crimson vocalist Greg Lake on bass and drummer Carl Palmer at the turn of the decade, he pioneered the bombastic pretensions of art rock. ELP's debut album balances Emerson's lengthy instrumental screeds ("The Barbarian") with Lake's legitimately catchy, Moody Bluesian vocal showcases ("Lucky Man"). *Tarkus* spells out the trio's fondess for brutally synthesized overkill—it's almost unlistenably crude by today's electronic standards. *Pictures at an Exhibition* submits Mussorgsky's work to a pummeling: this particular musical museum tour crashes into a dead end. That didn't stop ELP from pursuing its ill-advised fusion on a slightly smaller scale. The next two albums mix Emerson's ponderous suites with more straightforward fare from Greg Lake: *Trilogy*'s "From the Beginning" is ELP's most captivatingly mellow moment, while "Karn Evil 9" coheres as well as any other side-long epic you'd care to name. After that, indulgence rules: *Welcome Back* is a three-record live set, and *The Works* albums collect a hodgepodge of solo efforts, outtakes and even an Aaron Copland composition (on *II*). Though Emerson, Lake and Palmer set out to demystify classical music's tradition of virtuosity, the group ended up inspiring the kill-your-idols attitude of punk. Forget rolling over: Beethoven never so much as budged. — M.C.

EMF

★ ★ ★ **Schubert Dip (EMI, 1991)**

So slick, predictably and robotically feverish is most late-'80s model dance music that describing any of its purveyors as raw or rowdy seems impossible. But this Brit quintet are indeed that. With "Unbelievable," "Child" and "I Believe" they manage to synthesize techno-funk's blips and noises with a nearly rocking power. And their lyrics aren't the usual "Let's Party" fluff. — P.E.

THE EMOTIONS

★ ★ ★   **Flowers (Columbia, 1976)**

★ ★ ★   **Rejoice (Columbia, 1977)**

★ ★ ★   **Sunshine (Stax/Fantasy, 1977)**

★ ★ ★½ **Chronicle: Greatest Hits (Stax/Fantasy, 1979)**

Sometimes the Emotions' exquisite three-part harmonies sound a little too pure; the spun-sugar high notes on *Flowers* and *Rejoice* can cause blinding toothaches. Produced by Earth, Wind and Fire's Maurice White, those two albums established this long-running soul trio with a mainstrean audience in the late '70s. "Best of My Love" (from *Rejoice*) is one of the few believably romantic songs to come out of disco: it's simple and satisfying. *Flowers* is the stronger of the two, but both albums are undercut by White's feel-good slogans and surprisingly bland arrangements.

Chronicle displays the Emotions' full range. "So I Can Love You" is haunted by merging voices and Isaac Hayes's looming orchestration; "My Honey and Me" seems to prefigure Prince with its itchy rhythm. On "Runnin Back and Forth," the foxy interplay between lead singer Wanda Hutchinson, her sister Sheila and Teresa Davis is tied to a grinding riff. That sexy direction turned out to be the road not taken. The Emotions joined Earth, Wind and Fire for an enjoyably lightweight dance hit in 1978—"Boogie Wonderland." Everybody knows Earth, Wind and Fire accomplished much more than that; so did the Emotions. — M.C.

ENGLAND DAN AND JOHN FORD COLEY

★   **Nights Are Forever (Big Tree, 1976)**

★½   **Best of England Dan and John Ford Coley (Big Tree, 1979)**

In 1976, this duo's "I'd Really Love to See You Tonight," like the terrible, tacky rust-colored shag carpet laid down in every apartment complex of the period, was everywhere. A massive hit, the song summed up the soft-rock lifestyle of swingles tentatively on the make—it was ingratiating, smug and coy. Truly repellent, England Dan and John Ford Coley's entire product line is bland and timid; its offensiveness, however, is due to its wheedling quality—these guys managed always to sound like oafish bores breaking their backs to be "sensitive." — P.E.

ENGLISH BEAT

★★★★½ **I Just Can't Stop It (1980; I.R.S., 1983)**
★★★ **Wha'ppen? (1981; I.R.S., 1983)**
★★★★ **Special Beat Service (I.R.S., 1982)**
★★★★ **What Is Beat? (I.R.S., 1983)**
★★★½ **The Beat Goes On (I.R.S., 1991)**

To call the English Beat a ska band would be like calling the Beatles a Merseybeat act—accurate as far as it goes, but hardly going far enough. One of the few bands in the two-tone movement to extend its integrationist approach to matters of musical style, the Beat (as the band was known in Britain) drew equally from Motown, '60s rock, music hall and punk, in the process developing a sound that was rich and allusive, but which always put the songs first.

All of which makes *I Just Can't Stop It* irresistible. It isn't just the ease with which the band recasts "Tears of a Clown" as insinuatingly supple ska, or fills its remake of "Can't Get Used to Losing You" with sweet regret; what pushes the album over the top is its authority and ingenuity. Despite the lyric's sarcastic wit, the true power of "Mirror in the Bathroom" is its snaky, obsessive groove, a sound that says more about narcissism than words ever could. But that sort of aural authority is typical of the album, filling in the bluster behind "Hands Off . . . She's Mine" and adding a sense of withering contempt to the anti-Thatcher "Stand Down Margaret."

After such a strong start, *Wha'ppen?* is a good question; although the band's musical skills are still strong, the songs are forgettable. But *Special Beat Service* returns the group to form, escalating the Caribbean influence from the retro-skank of ska to dub-wise reggae, as "Pato and Roger a Go Talk" (with Pato Banton) illustrates, and adding instrumental lustre to pop gems like "I Confess." But it's the writing that cinches it, from the catchy "Jeanette" to the irrepressible "Save It for Later," the Beat's music is always seductive. *What Is Beat?* collects most of the group's hits, as well as two live tracks and a couple of non-LP singles, while *The Beat Goes On* augments a smattering of hits ("Mirror in the Bathroom," "I Confess," the dub "Stand Down Margaret") with samplings from the bands formed by the Beat's alumni: General Public, Fine Young Cannibals, the International Beat and solo artists Dave Wakeling and Ranking Roger. — J.D.C.

BRIAN ENO

★★★★ **Here Come the Warm Jets (EG Records, 1973)**
★★★★ **Taking Tiger Mountain (By Strategy) (EG Records, 1974)**
★★★★½ **Another Green World (EG Records, 1975)**
★★★ **Discreet Music (EG Records, 1975)**
★★★★★ **Before and After Science (EG Records, 1977)**
★★★ **Music for Films (EG Records, 1978)**
★★★★ **Ambient 1/Music for Airports (EG Records, 1978)**
★★★ **Ambient 4/On Land (EG Records, 1982)**
★★★ **Apollo (Atmosphere and Soundtracks) (EG Records, 1983)**
★★★ **Thursday Afternoon (EG Records, 1985)**
★★★★ **More Blank Than Frank (EG Records, 1986)**
★★★★½ **Desert Island Selection (EG Records, 1986)**
WITH DAVID BYRNE
★★★½ **My Life in the Bush of Ghosts (Sire, 1981)**
WITH JOHN CALE
★★★★ **Wrong Way Up (Opal/Warner Bros., 1990)**

A brilliant conceptualist, a self-described "non-musician" and a founding member of Roxy Music, Brian Eno is probably better-known for the music he has coaxed out of others, as producer for albums by U2, Talking Heads and David Bowie, than for anything he recorded himself. And that's too bad, really, for Eno's albums can be delightful, full of entrancing tunes and ingenious countermelodies. But melody has never quite been as interesting to Eno as sound itself, and that's why his solo albums—particularly the later efforts—can seem airy, empty and maddeningly diffuse.

His first solo releases, however, were

pop-smart despite their arty bite. Though it's easy to hear both an anticipation of punk and an echo of Roxy Music in the arch clangor of *Here Come the Warm Jets*, what lingers is the offhand accessibility of Eno's melodies. It hardly matters whether he's playing with style (for instance, the doo-wop undercurrent to "Cindy Tells Me") or fooling with form (the portmanteau construction of "Dead Finks Don't Talk"); his verses, hooks and choruses shine through. Listening to it now, the album seems almost a blueprint for the pop experiments Bowie (with Eno producing) would conduct with *Low*.

Taking Tiger Mountain (By Strategy) is just as tuneful and eclectic, but shies away from the abrasive textures of its predecessor, swapping distortion and dissonance for blurred edges and open-ended harmonies. Not that the album is entirely without teeth, for there's an itchy aggression to the breathless "Third Uncle," and an ominous urgency to the latter half of "The True Wheel." But Eno keeps such snarls on a tight leash; far more typical is the dry wit of "Back in Judy's Jungle." Eno pushes that approach even further with the well-pruned textures of *Another Green World*. He uses the studio itself as an instrument, molding directed improvisation, electronic effects and pop-savvy melodies into perfectly balanced aural ecosystems like "Sky Saw" or "St. Elmo's Fire." It doesn't even matter if there's a vocal; even the background noises seem tuneful. Still, it isn't until *Before and After Science* that it all comes into focus. Combining the pop instincts of *Here Come the Warm Jets* with the exquisite soundcraft of *Another Green World*, it's a nearly perfect piece of work, framing Eno's melodic instincts in every imaginable way, from the chilly funk of "No One Receiving," to the irrepressible vigor of "King's Lead Hat" (a tribute to Talking Heads, by way of anagram), to the dreamy cadences of "Here He Comes."

Unfortunately, Eno never made another album like it—although the brittle, uneven *Wrong Way Up*, recorded with John Cale, is a good try—choosing instead to pursue a sort of high-concept mood music. Initially, he referred to these quiet soundscapes as "discreet" music, and on *Discreet Music* demonstrates his basic tools: minimal melodies, subtle textures and variable repetition. *Music for Airports* codifies that into an aesthetic, and even provides a label for the sound: ambient music. But as much as Eno understands about psycho-acoustics

and the relationship between what is heard and what is merely sensed, the largely functional (and mostly tuneless) nature of the music limits the listening pleasure of *On Land, Apollo* and *Thursday Afternoon*. (Eno also produced albums by other artists for his ambient series: Harold Budd's rich, moody *The Plateaux of Mirror* and Laraaji's shimmering *Day of Radiance*, both of which are slightly more energetic than Eno's own efforts.)

My Life in the Bush of Ghosts, which takes its title from Amos Tutuola's novel, was recorded in collaboration with David Byrne, and offers some insight into the cut-and-paste approach to groove the two applied while making Talking Heads' *Remain in Light*. But its "found art" approach to vocals (however scrupulously the two document their sources) is an acquired taste. *More Blank Than Frank* and *Desert Island Selection* are best-of albums emphasizing material from *Warm Jets* through *Science*. Of the two, the CD version (*Desert Island*) is preferable, since it offers a slightly more balanced overview. — J.D.C.

JOHN ENTWISTLE

★★★   **Smash Your Head Against the Wall (MCA, 1971)**
★★★★   **Whistle Rhymes (MCA, 1972)**
★★½ **Rigor Mortis Sets In (1973)**
★★½ **Mad Dog (MCA, 1975)**
★★½ **Too Late the Hero (Atco, 1981)**

According to Pete Townshend, Jimi Hendrix once claimed that John Entwistle's "Boris the Spider" was his favorite Who song. One hopes that Jimi was only having his bit of fun because, while Entwistle's contributions to the Who were notable, they were properly subsidiary—his dark whimsy provided counterpoint to Pete's achingly empathetic teen angst anthems and breathlessly mystic turn, but even John's best numbers ("My Wife," "Whiskey Man") had boasted little of the melodic assurance that Townshend flourished so easily.

On his own, the Who bassist is free to indulge his impressive instrumental expertise (trumpet, French horn, keyboard)—and all his solo work features outstanding playing. His voice, however, is limited, and his composing skills are haphazard. *Smash Your Head Against the Wall* nicely mixes extremely heavy rock with pop ballads, and it's a commendable debut. *Whistle Rhymes* represents a quantum leap forward; some of Peter Frampton's best guitar work enlivens the record, and its ten songs are masterpieces of painstaking craft. *Rigor*

Mortis is Entwistle's lighthearted homage to early rock; snappy, if unsurprising, covers of "Lucille" and "Hound Dog" balance doo-wop–derived originals. Recorded with his short-lived spinoff group, Ox, *Mad Dog* rocks capably, as does *Too Late the Hero*, an Entwistle-Joe Walsh collaboration.
— P.E.

ENUFF Z'NUFF
★★★½ **Enuff Z'Nuff (Atco, 1989)**
★★★★ **Strength (Atco, 1991)**
This is smart, savvy hard rock with a good sense of melody and strong psychedelic undertones. Although front man Chip Z'Nuff seems to carry most of the weight on record, it's Donnie Vie's convention-shredding songwriting that gives the band its edge; his "Kiss the Clown" and "Fly High Michelle" highlighted the band's debut, while his collaborations with Z'Nuff on *Strength* (particularly "In Crowd" and "Holly Wood Ya") suggest what might have happened had Elvis Costello wound up fronting Cheap Trick. — J.D.C.

EN VOGUE
★★★ **Born to Sing (Atlantic, 1990)**
★★★ **Remix to Sing (East-West, 1991)**
★★★½ **Funky Divas (East-West, 1992)**
As the titles suggest, this female foursome knows how to harmonize, handling everything from standard soul to close-harmony jazz parts with ease. But however much those voices may soar, it's the New Jack groove of producers Denzil Foster and Thomas McElroy that gets the album off the ground. *Remix to Sing* consists of remixed versions of *Born to Sing*'s best, as well as the seasonal special "Silent Nite (Happy Holiday Mix)." It's *Funky Divas*, though, that fully establishes the group's pop stature, making the most of its lustrous harmonies while pumping up the predictable-yet-catchy pulse of Foster and McElroy's rhythm arrangements. — J.D.C.

ENYA
★★★ **Enya (Atlantic, 1988)**
★★★★ **Watermark (Geffen, 1988)**
★★★½ **Shepherd Moons (DGC, 1991)**
Postmodern Gaelic music, strong and lovely, *Enya* consists of pleasures perhaps too arcane for all but Yeats fanatics or the most catholic followers of world music. *Watermark*, however, is marginally more accessible—and it's a remarkable record. Some of the songs are still sung in Irish (and one in Latin), but the pristine strength of Enya Ni Bhraonain's voice—and the cinematic sweep of her songs' arrangements—translates in an aural landscape of spare ecstasy that carries you away. "Storms in Africa," "Evening Falls" and "Orinoco Flow" achieve nearly mythic resonance—and her startling fusion of passion and severity make Enya a true original. *Shepherd Moons*, however, is a bit of a comedown.
— P.E.

EPMD
★★★½ **Strictly Business (Fresh, 1988)**
★★½ **Unfinished Business (Priority, 1990)**
★★½ **Business as Usual (RAL/Columbia, 1991)**
Eric "E" Sermon and Parrish "P" Smith are EPMD ("Eric and Parrish Making Dollars"), and while their breakout singles, "You Gots to Chill" and "So What Ya Sayin,' " also managed to make statements—"Sayin' " is one of the toughest declarations of pride that rap's produced—the pair generally comes off as more canny than creative. That is to say that the follow-ups to their impressive debut hardly gained new ground. While their no-nonsense approach has its merits (dependability, primarily), EPMD needs tracks as risky as its subject matter. Instead, too often the duo play it safe. — P.E.

ERASURE
★★½ **Wonderland (Sire, 1986)**
★★★ **Circus (Sire, 1987)**
★★½ **The Two Ring Circus (Sire, 1987)**
★★½ **The Innocents (Sire, 1988)**
★★ **Crackers International (EP) (Sire, 1988)**
★★ **Wild! (Sire, 1989)**
★★½ **Chorus (Sire, 1991)**
Formed by Vince Clarke after the demise of Yaz (and the even shorter-lived Assembly), Erasure initially seemed something of a Yaz Mk. II, thanks to its techno-soul arrangements and Andy Bell's Alison Moyet-ish vocals. But because the group avoided the artsy excess of Yaz's more experimental efforts, the frothy dance pop of "Who Needs Love Like That" (from *Wonderland*) or "Victim of Love" (from *The Circus*) tended to be typical of the group's pop-friendly output. (*The Two Ring Circus* combines remixed versions of singles from *Circus* with a half-dozen pointless live tracks.)

To their credit, Clarke and Bell did attempt to widen their musical palette. *The Innocents* augments dance fodder like "Chains of Love" with odd novelty numbers like "Sixty-Five Thousand" and an ill-advised remake of Ike & Tina Turner's "River Deep, Mountain High," while *Wild!* relies on lush atmospherics (the instrumental "Piano Song") and campy attempts at nostalgia ("Blue Savannah"). Neither approach was especially satisfying, however, which may explain why the duo returned to a more conventional take on synth-pop with the pleasantly pedestrian *Chorus.* — J.D.C.

ERIC B. AND RAKIM
★★   Paid in Full (4th & Broadway/Island, 1987)
★★★   Follow the Leader (UNI, 1988)
★★★½   Let the Rhythm Hit 'Em (MCA, 1990)

Singularly focused from the start, rapper Rakim and DJ Eric B. have eschewed anything cute or clever in conveying basic street politics—they make rap free of pop crossover strategizing, and at their finest, they're deadly. Hitting in 1987 with the propulsive "Paid in Full," they gathered strength on *Follow the Leader*; on cuts like "Lyrics of Fury" and "No Competition," they came on with a gruff grandeur, Eric B.'s manipulations of funk and synth riffs never undercutting Rakim's deep-voiced menace. *Let the Rhythm Hit 'Em*, however, represented a quantum leap forward. Sticking close to James Brown funk, Eric B. provided backing lean and strong enough for Rakim's most pointed rhymes—"In the Ghetto" and "No Omega" are songs of hard-fought pride, leagues beyond the adolescent boasting of the genre's poseur gangstas. — P.E.

ROKY ERICKSON
★★★½   The Evil One (1981; Pink Dust, 1987)
★★★½   I Think of Demons (Edsel UK, 1987)
★★★   Don't Slander Me (Pink Dust, 1986)
★★   Gremlins Have Pictures (Pink Dust, 1986)
★★★★   You're Gonna Miss Me: The Best of Roky Erickson (Restless, 1991)
VARIOUS
★★★★   Where the Pyramid Meets the Eye (Sire, 1990)

As with Syd Barrett, Roky Erickson's reputation has as much to do with his acid-casualty notoriety as with the flashes of brilliance that run through his music. As a member of the 13th Floor Elevator, Erickson is widely credited with having invented psychedelic rock—indeed, the quintet's 1966 debut, *The Psychedelic Sounds of the 13th Floor Elevator*, predates both Grateful Dead and Pink Floyd's *The Piper at the Gates of Dawn*—but his personal interest in mind-expansion took its toll. Erickson was arrested for marijuana possession in 1968; pleading insanity, he spent almost four years ensconced at the Hospital for the Criminally Insane in Rusk, Texas.

Erickson resumed his musical career in the late '70s, cutting a couple of singles before forming the Aliens, with whom he recorded an album's worth of demented material in 1980; originally released as *Roky Erickson and the Aliens* on CBS UK in 1980, expanded versions of the album have since been released under the titles *The Evil One* and *I Think of Demons*. Unlike the showbiz satanism heavy-metal bands dabble in, this is truly disturbing material, as Erickson delivers the likes of "Don't Shake Me Lucifer," "Night of the Vampire" and "Two Headed Dog" with the creepy conviction of one whose demons are a little too real.

Apart from the paranoid title tune, *Don't Slander Me* doesn't seem quite so deranged, returning Erickson to the blues-based grooves that were the Elevator's meat-and-potatoes, but *Gremlins Have Pictures*, recorded in haphazard sessions with various lineups, is merely a document of Erickson's musical deterioration. *You're Gonna Miss Me: The Best of Roky Erickson* draws from all of the above as well as a smattering of concert recordings, and offers the most representative overview of his solo career.

In 1990 a surprisingly diverse group of Erickson fans—including ZZ Top, Doug Sahm, R.E.M., Julian Cope, Primal Scream and the Jesus & Mary Chain—participated in a tribute album entitled *Where the Pyramid Meets the Eye*, a collection offering eloquent tribute to the enduring strength of Erickson's songwriting. — J.D.C.

GLORIA ESTEFAN
★★★½   Let It Loose (Epic, 1987)
★★½   Cuts Both Ways (Epic, 1989)
★★★   Exitos de Gloria Estefan (CBS Discos, 1990)
★★   Into the Light (Epic, 1991)

Although the Miami Sound Machine was pretty much finished even before Estefan took top billing, *Let It Loose* is a classic piece of Latin-influenced pop, from the lovelorn "Can't Stay Away From You" to the steamy "Rhythm Is Gonna Get You." But *Cuts Both Ways*, though it doesn't much deviate from the group's formula, does water things down, reducing Estefan's sound to bland ballads and mildly spicy salsa. Still, that lack of adventure is preferable to *Into the Light*'s incompetent experiments, which range from tepid funk to the least soulful gospel singing this side of Amy Grant. *Exitos de Gloria Estefan*, by the way, purports to offer versions of her solo and Sound Machine hits in Spanish, but somehow neglects to translate "Dr. Beat" and "Conga." Still, the ballads are wonderfully affecting. — J.D.C.

MELISSA ETHERIDGE
★★ **Melissa Etheridge (Island, 1988)**
★½ **Brave and Crazy (Island, 1989)**
★ **Never Enough (Island, 1992)**
With her big, blues-mama voice and confessional folkie persona, Melissa Etheridge draws from a range of bar-band clichés, and manages to make all of them seem equally cheap and manipulative. A specialist in the wronged-lover school of songwriting, her material—which runs the gamut from why-don't-you-want-me? to you-used-to-want-me, why-don't-you-want-me-now?—is moderately melodic and unfailingly melodramatic, a combination that may go over well in nightclubs but proves almost unbearable on album. *Melissa Etheridge* tends more toward anger than poetry, and therefore is at least emotionally credible, but the over-ambitious *Brave and Crazy* finds the singer so overwhelmed by her writing ability that she actually sings stuff like "Shame, shame but I love your name/And the way you make the buffalo roam." Whether that counts as bravery or craziness is up to you. In any case, by *Never Enough* she'd abandoned semi-poetic sentimentality in favor of semi-slick guitar rock, an approach that leaves her sounding like bad-imitation Rod Stewart. — J.D.C.

EU
★★½ **Future Funk (Galaxy, 1982)**
★★ **2 Places at the Same Time (Island, 1986)**
★★★ **Go Ju Ju Go (E. Unlimited, 1987)**
★★★★ **Livin' Large (Virgin, 1989)**
★★½ **Cold Kickin' It (Virgin, 1990)**
One of the oldest of the D.C. go-go bands, EU (originally Experience Unlimited) is a singles band by nature. Many of the band's best early efforts have never been available on album, apart from compilations like Island's *Go-Go Crankin'*, and the original version of its biggest hit—the funky, infectious "Da Butt"—can only be found on the soundtrack from *School Daze*. That's not to say that EU's album output is

therefore a waste of time, just that it doesn't always represent the band at its best. *Future Funk*, for instance, works a bit of "Ooh La La La" into the side-long "Crankin' at the Go-Go," but it conveys neither the snap of the actual single nor the percussive power of EU live, coming off as a well-meaning but inept compromise. Still, given the band's reputation as a live act, it makes sense to try and capture some of that EU concert magic on tape; too bad *2 Places at the Same Time* goes about it the wrong way, settling for a live-in-the-studio simulacrum instead of an actual go-go throwdown. *Go Ju Ju Go* (named for EU drummer William "Ju Ju" House) comes closer to getting that groove on wax, particularly on the drum-driven second side, but comes no closer to memorable songwriting than "Shake It Like a White Girl."

With *Livin' Large*, EU's fortunes change drastically. In addition to remakes of "Shake It" (hotter than the original) and "Da Butt," the band strikes gold with both the raucous rhythms of "Buck Wild" and the hip-hop-inflected title tune. Apart from a pair of unconvincing falsetto ballads ("Taste of Your Love" and "Don't Turn Around"), *Livin' Large* gets it all right. So what happened between that album and *Cold Kickin' It*? Blame it on misplaced ambition if you like, but this calculated, automated attempt at R&B normalcy robs EU of everything that made it interesting in the first place. — J.D.C.

EUROPE
★½ **Europe (1983; Epic, 1989)**
★½ **Wings of Tomorrow (Epic, 1984)**
★★ **The Final Countdown (Epic, 1986)**
★★ **Out of This World (Epic, 1988)**
★★★ **Prisoners in Paradise (Epic, 1991)**
Why do bands with continent-sized names always prove so colossally bad? These Swedish hard-rockers may not sound as absurdly overblown as their colleagues in Asia, but it's not for lack of trying. Joey Tempest, for instance, possesses a voice as suited to heavy metal as to light opera, and he sings the former as if it were the latter; guitarist John Norum, meanwhile, is the sort of player who will never play two notes if he thinks there's room for 20. Between them, they make both *Europe* and *Wings of Tomorrow* tiresome in the extreme. By *The Final Countdown*, Tempest's interest in melody had matured to the point that some songs, like "Rock the Night," ended up listenable in spite of their arrangements. Apparently, this was too much for Norum

to bear, and he left the group, leaving *Out of This World* overflowing with power ballads and silly-but-hummable rockers like "Superstitious." *Prisoners in Paradise*, though, puts more emphasis on boogie licks than bombast—a transparent attempt to broaden the band's American audience, perhaps, but one which greatly improves its overall sound.   — J.D.C.

EURYTHMICS
★ ★½ **In the Garden (RCA UK, 1981)**
★ ★ ★½ **Sweet Dreams (Are Made of This) (RCA, 1983)**
★ ★ ★½ **Touch (RCA, 1983)**
★ ★ **1984 (RCA, 1984)**
★ ★ ★ ★ **Be Yourself Tonight (RCA, 1985)**
★ ★½ **Revenge (RCA, 1986)**
★ ★ **Savage (RCA, 1987)**
★ ★ **We Too Are One (Arista, 1989)**
★ ★ ★ ★ **Greatest Hits (Arista, 1991)**

On one level, the Eurythmics were a perfect musical marriage, balancing the full-throated passion of singer Annie Lennox with the studio-savvy pop craft of guitarist-keyboardist-producer Dave Stewart. But at the same time, what worked best about the duo's musical chemistry wasn't necessarily in line with what the two most wanted to do, meaning that their best albums were inevitably based on compromise. That certainly is the case with *Sweet Dreams (Are Made of This)*, the group's first American album. Although its predecessor, the import-only *In the Garden*, used its electronics mainly as a means of fleshing out its standard-issue new-wave arrangements, *Sweet Dreams* built a significant portion of its sound around synthesizers. But while that added poignancy to "Love Is a Stranger" and the title tune, Lennox truly cuts loose on the duo's cover of the Sam and Dave hit "Wrap It Up." Nonetheless, *Touch* not only reprises *Sweet Dreams*' synths-plus-voice formula, but one-ups it with "Here Comes the Rain Again." Unfortunately, *1984*, their soundtrack for Michael Radford's film of the George Orwell novel, uses its musical technology almost too well, lending an oppressive chill to the music.

With *Be Yourself Tonight*, the Eurythmics expand from duo to full band, and while that shift doesn't entirely displace the group's electronics—"There Must Be an Angel (Playing with My Heart)," for instance, still relies heavily on synths—it does shift the emphasis. Indeed, "It's Alright (Baby's Coming Back)," "Would I Lie to You?" and the Aretha Franklin duet

"Sisters Are Doin' It for Themselves" take a soulful tack that makes the most of Lennox's delivery. Lennox aside, though, the Eurythmics' credibility as R&B stylists is fairly limited, and cracks begin to show in their facade as early as *Revenge*, where the bluesy bluster of "Missionary Man" sounds dishearteningly hollow. Chastened, the Eurythmics return to the techno-intense sound of *Sweet Dreams* on *Savage*, but by this point the duo's sound is too mannered to have much impact; at best, songs like "I Need a Man" and "Beethoven (I Love to Listen To)" come across as little more than academic exercises. Still, that's better than *We Too Are One*, which is unable to eke even the slightest melodic interest from the band's empty professionalism.   — J.D.C.

THE EVERLY BROTHERS
★ ★ ★ ★ **The Everly Brothers (1958; Rhino, 1988)**
★ ★ ★ ★ **The Fabulous Style of the Everly Brothers (1960; Rhino, 1988)**
★ ★ ★ ★ **The Golden Hits of the Everly Brothers (Warner Bros., 1962)**
★ ★ ★ ★ **Christmas With the Everly Brothers and the Boys Town Choir (Warner Bros., 1962)**
★ ★ ★ ★ **Songs Our Daddy Taught Us (1964; Rhino, 1988)**
★ ★ **The Very Best of the Everly Brothers (Warner Bros., 1964)**
★ ★ ★ ★ **The Reunion Concert (Mercury, 1983)**
★ ★ ★ ★ **EB 84 (Mercury, 1984)**
★ ★ ★ ★ ★ **Cadence Classics (Their 20 Greatest Hits) (Rhino, 1985)**
★ ★ ★ ★ **The Best of the Everly Brothers (Rhino, 1985)**
★ ★ ★ **Some Hearts (Mercury, 1988)**
★ ★ ★ ★ **All They Had to Do Was Dream (Rhino, 1988)**

Raised in Kentucky by parents who were successful folk and country artists, Don and Phil Everly were one of early rock & roll's most direct links to Appalachian folk music and traditional country and bluegrass; their keening harmonies continue to show up in country music, and made an impact on second-generation rockers such as the Beatles, the Hollies, Simon and Garfunkel, and certainly on lesser lights such as Peter and Gordon and Chad and Jeremy.

Their first professional experience outside their family shows came in 1955 when the teenage brothers were hired as songwriters by Roy Acuff's music publishing company in Nashville. One of Don's songs, "Thou Shalt Not Steal," became a hit for Kitty

Wells, but the brothers' own attempts at recording fell flat. But in 1957 their fortunes changed when Cadence Records president Archie Bleyer brought them a song written by Nashville writers Felice and Boudleaux Bryant, "Bye Bye Love." Thirty acts had passed on the song, but Bleyer, who had originally declined to sign the Everlys but had given them an introduction at Columbia, thought them the right act to give Cadence rock & roll credibility. With the Everlys' pleading harmonies soaring high over an insistent, acoustic-guitar-driven beat, "Bye Bye Love" peaked at Number Two on the pop chart, and was followed in short order by the first of three Number One singles, "Wake Up Little Susie," another Bryant-Bryant song. Largely on the strength of the Bryants' well-observed commentaries on teen feelings, the Everlys were one of the dominant groups in rock & roll in the late '50s with 11 singles in the Top Thirty from '57 through '59, with "All I Have to Do Is Dream" and "Bird Dog" following "Wake Up Little Susie" to the top of the pop charts. In allowing room for the playful ("Bird Dog," "Problems") and the poignant ("Devoted to You," "Take a Message to Mary") the Bryants' songs offered the Everlys a broad palette of colors mirroring their audience's most extreme emotions.

The brothers continued to develop as songwriters as well, and soon were having hits with their original compositions—Don checking in with a Top Ten single in 1959, " 'Til I Kissed You," Phil in 1960 with "When Will I Be Loved," also a Top Ten single. In 1960, the brothers began a productive association with Warner Bros. that was marked by a reflective turn in the Everlys' material. Don's "So Sad (to Watch Good Love Go Bad" and the Greenfield-King tearjerker "Crying in the Rain" were indicative of the brothers' journey into love's darker recesses, and with that came deeper, more cutting lyrics.

In 1968 the brothers released *Roots* (currently out of print), a moving look back at the sources of their music, which is somewhat of a companion volume to an excellent album they cut in 1958, *Songs Our Daddy Taught Us*, with a repertoire comprised of an Irish ballad, a cowboy song, folk songs and traditional country songs. A year after *Roots*, a celebration of family, the family split apart when Phil stalked off stage in mid-concert and left Don to announce the group's breakup. Years of personal animosity and

unsuccessful solo albums followed, until finally the brothers reunited for a concert at London's Royal Albert Hall in September of 1983. Captured on record (*The Reunion Concert*) and filmed for HBO, the concert was a complete triumph, proceeding from a deeply felt and telltale opening song, "The Price of Love," through all the group's hits and other chestnuts from rock's first golden era.

Succeeding years have found the Everlys working regularly, and recording again, but without notable chart success. Still, *EB 84* was a strong return to the studio, with one of their grandest singles coming out of it in the form of the soaring "On the Wings of a Nightingale," written and produced by Paul McCartney. But in songs such as "The Story of Me," "You Make It Seem So Easy," and, especially, the tender "Asleep," the brothers work out their reconciliation in forceful detail, in the process delivering their strongest studio effort to date. *Some Hearts* continued in a self-revelatory vein on the strength of Don's poignant title song and a cover of John Hiatt's too-true take on love's fleeting nature, "Any Single Solitary Heart."

As for the classic early tracks, any number of releases offer broad retrospectives. Beware *The Very Best of the Everly Brothers*—it's comprised of re-recordings of the Cadence hits done when the brothers switched to Warners. *Golden Hits* is in fact the very best of the Warners years, while *The Everly Brothers* and *The Fabulous Style of the Everly Brothers* are repackages (with original art) of the duo's first and third albums, respectively. *Cadence Classics* is what it claims to be, the original recordings, 20 tracks' worth, with a truncated version available as *The Best of the Everly Brothers*. Everlys completists will enjoy *All They Had to Do Was Dream*, outtakes from the Cadence sessions complete with the musicians' between-songs patter. — D.M.

THE EXCITERS
★★★ Tell Him (EMI, 1991)
While the Exciters are remembered primarily for their Number Four single from 1962, "Tell Him," this 20-track chronicle sets the record straight on a couple of points. For one, lead singer Brenda Reid was as fine a female voice as pop has produced; the intensity of her delivery, the emotion redolent in her readings, brooks comparison with the incendiary fury of the Chantels's Arlene Smith and the husky sensuality of the Shirelles's Shirley Alston. For another,

the Exciters cut many more fine tracks than ever achieved hit status. Working almost exclusively with producers Jerry Leiber and Mike Stoller, the group has left behind a host of interesting productions and powerful performances, including the original recording of Jeff Barry-Ellie Greenwich's "Do-Wah-Diddy," released in early 1964 and brought to the top of the charts later that year in a cover version by Manfred Mann. Greenwich also co-wrote (with Tony Powers) another great Exciters track, the relentless "He's Got the Power," included here in both edited and unedited versions. Rock archaeologists will want to dig the two different versions of "Tell Him" included here, one being the unedited stereo mix, with Reid blowing some lyrics, that was released by mistake as the original single.

The Exciters went on to record for years for other labels without notable success. This latter period is represented here by a 1985 track, "All Grown Up," released on a U.K.-only album, with Reid supported by some uncredited and wholly unremarkable background singers. — D.M.

EXPOSE
★ ★ ★ **Exposure (Arista, 1987)**
★ ★½ **What You Don't Know (Arista, 1989)**
Expose's classic Miami dance pop boasts tough, Latin-tinged grooves, brash, insistent instrumental arrangements and slick, semi-anonymous singing. Although the label promoted the three vocalists as personalities once the act broke pop, the real star of the group is producer Lewis Martinee, who parlayed the club hit "Point of No Return" into a multi-platinum pop group. — J.D.C.

F

THE FABULOUS THUNDERBIRDS
★ ★ ★½ The Fabulous Thunderbirds
(Takoma, 1979)
★ ★ ★ What's the Word (Chrysalis,
1980)
★ ★ ★½ Butt Rockin' (Chrysalis, 1981)
★ ★ ★ T-Bird Rhythm (Chrysalis, 1982)
★ ★ ★½ Tuff Enuff (Columbia, 1986)
★ ★ ★ Hot Number (Epic, 1987)
★ ★ ★ Powerful Stuff (Epic, 1989)
★ ★ ★ Walk That Walk, Talk That Talk
(Columbia, 1991)
★ ★ ★ ★ The Essential Fabulous
Thunderbirds Collection (Epic,
1991)

Solid, sometimes spectacular, always
rousing, the Fabulous Thunderbirds have
produced remarkably consistent albums
since debuting on the Takoma label in 1979.
It was *Tuff Enough* (1986) that brought
them their first substantial hit in its title
track, but long before that the T-Birds were
working their own interesting changes on
the Texas blues tradition.

Truth be told, the T-Birds may live and
work in Austin, and carry the flag of Austin
music to the rest of the world, but the
musicians draw inspiration from sources
both in and outside the Lone Star State.
Jimmie Vaughan, brother of Stevie Ray,
might quote T-Bone Walker one minute,
and in the next dig out an old quote from
B.B. King or Muddy Waters. Lead singer
Kim Wilson rumbles and roars through the
songs, then will go to the harmonica and rip
a solo straight out of Little Walter.

The T-Birds typically mix in blues
chestnuts with original songs written
primarily by Wilson. Chrysalis has
assembled a good cross-section of T-Birds
highlights on *The Essential Fabulous
Thunderbirds Collection*, but that shouldn't
keep anyone from going deeper into the
catalogue and checking out the pleasures of
The Fabulous Thunderbirds or *Butt Rockin'*.

Nick Lowe came on board as producer for
T-Bird Rhythm and polished up the sound
without undercutting the band's attack. *Tuff
Enuff* is a hard-polished, mature bit of work
that has a bit of a darker edge than the
other albums. The challenge ahead, as it has
always been, is for the band to find
interesting avenues of expression within the
stylistic parameters of the blues they were
born into. *Walk That Walk, Talk That Talk*
doesn't always respond to that challenge,
but even when treading water the Fabulous
Thunderbirds find something interesting to
say if you hang with them. — D.M.

THE FACES
★ ★ ★½ First Step (Warner Bros., 1970)
★ ★ ★ Long Player (Warner Bros., 1971)
★ ★ ★½ A Nod Is as Good as a Wink to a
Blind Horse (Warner Bros., 1971)
★ ★½ Ooh La La (Warner Bros., 1973)
★ ★ Overture/Coast to Coast (Mercury,
1974)
★ ★ ★½ Snakes and Ladders: The Best of
Faces (Warner Bros., 1976)

In 1969, the Small Faces lost its lead singer
to Humble Pie. Small Faces organist Ian
McLagan, drummer Kenney Jones and
bassist Ronnie Lane were soon joined by the
roistering tag-team of Rod Stewart and Ron
Wood—and the Faces were born. Having
slaved as singer and bassist for control-freak
Jeff Beck, Stewart and Wood were eager for
their new band's boozy camaraderie. *First
Step* was nifty, with Stewart doing raw rock
on Dylan's "Wicked Messenger," Wood's
guitar aping Beck pyrotechnics on "Around
the Plynth" and the whole band bashing
away on "Shake, Shudder, Shiver." It also
featured Stewart-McLagan's sweet "Three
Button Hand Me Down"—the kind of
working-class fight-song Stewart would
champion on his first solo work (and later
shamefully betray). *Long Player* had Stewart
making holy hell of Paul McCartney's

"Maybe I'm Amazed," and, in the process, investing the song with a grit Paul never dreamed of. *A Nod Is as Good as a Wink* gave the Faces their one hit in the cartoon-brutish road-life saga, "Stay With Me" and found them zestfully chugging away at Chuck Berry's "Memphis"; it also had one of Lane's nicer numbers, the populist ballad, "Debris." By the time of *Ooh La La* (1973), the fun was wearing thin. "Cindy Incidentally" is snappy; "Borstal Boy" rocks out, and Lane's "Just Another Honky" captures his rare modesty, but "Silicone Grown" presages the leering and snickering Rod would later make millions with. *Overtures/Coast to Coast* was their live album; they sound about to drop from partying.

The Faces' sloppiness now sounds prescient. Certainly there was no happier band. And with Rod's vocals naked of big-production echo, he was the rocker he's never been since. More so, perhaps, even than the Stones, the Faces are the nudge behind such latter-day avengers as the Black Crowes, Georgia Satellites and the London Quireboys.   — P.E.

DONALD FAGEN
★ ★ ★ ★ **The Nightfly (Warner Bros., 1982)**
WITH THE NEW YORK ROCK & SOUL REVUE
 ★ ★ ★ **Live at the Beacon (Giant, 1991)**
Unsurprisingly, *The Nightfly* sounds like Steely Dan. Donald Fagen doesn't try to disassociate himself from his former group—as if he could. He's stuck with that voice. Without Walter Becker at his side, however, Fagen opts for a more direct style of songwriting. His lone solo album is an intimate recollection of suburban adolescence circa 1960: post-Beat, pre-Beatles. The music swings and glides; unabashed pop melodies flirt with sophisticated jazz rhythms. The lyrics probe and poke around behind the happy facade, but Fagen avoids both baby-boom nostalgia and post-hippie cynicism. There's a warm tone to his recollections, whether he's drinking beer with his buddies in Dad's fallout shelter, dreaming of Manhattan with the distant "Maxine" or discovering Miles and Monk on the title track's late-night radio show. *The Nightfly* conveys the squeaky-clean optimism of the Kennedy era, and drops hints about the funky, liberating confusion that followed. It's one of the few rock concept albums that actually holds up. The "superstar" get-together Fagen organized under the heading of the New

York Rock & Soul Revue—featuring Michael McDonald, Phoebe Snow, Boz Scaggs, Charles Brown and the Brigati brothers—is inconsistent. R&B chestnuts like "Knock on Wood," "Shakey Ground" and "Lonely Teardrops" falter, but the individual singers shine on performances of their own material.   — M.C.

JOHN FAHEY
 ★ ★ ★½ **Death Chants, Breakdowns and Military Waltzes (Takoma, 1962)**
 ★ ★ ★½ **Dance of Death and Other Plantation Favorites (Takoma, 1964)**
 ★ ★ ★½ **John Fahey Guitar (Takoma, 1967)**
 ★ ★ ★½ **Blind Joe Death (Vanguard, 1967)**
 ★ ★ ★ **The Yellow Princess (Vanguard, 1969)**
 ★ ★ ★ **The New Possibility (Xmas Album) (Takoma, 1969)**
 ★ ★ ★½ **Fare Forward Voyagers (1973; Shanachie, 1992)**
 ★ ★ ★½ **The Transfiguration of Blind Joe Death (Takoma, 1973)**
 ★ ★ ★½ **Essential John Fahey (Vanguard, 1974)**
 ★ ★ ★½ **John Fahey/Leo Kottke/Peter Lang (Takoma, 1974)**
 ★ ★ ★½ **Old Fashioned Love (Takoma, 1975)**
 ★ ★ ★ **Christmas With John Fahey (Takoma, 1975)**
 ★ ★ ★ ★ **Best of John Fahey (1959–1977) (Takoma, 1977)**
 ★ ★ ★½ **Live in Tasmania (Takoma, 1981)**
 ★ ★ ★½ **Christmas Guitar, Vol. 1 (Varrick, 1982)**
 ★ ★ ★½ **Popular Songs of Christmas and New Years (Varrick, 1983)**
 ★ ★ ★½ **Let Go (Varrick, 1985)**
 ★ ★ ★½ **Rain Forests, Oceans and Other Themes (Varrick, 1985)**
 ★ ★ ★½ **I Remember Blind Joe Death (Varrick, 1987)**
 ★ ★ ★½ **God, Time and Causality (Shanachie, 1990)**
 ★ ★ ★½ **Old Fashion Love (Shanachie, 1990)**
No matter that John Fahey's album titles (*Death Chants, Breakdowns and Military Waltzes, Blind Joe Death*) suggest either a dark private humor or a truly scary death fixation, this Maryland guitarist's forte is music of an exhilarating, almost rapturous beauty. Either uplifting or soothing, his sets of country blues, Scots-Irish folk or classically derived melodies are acoustic guitar work that's almost always dazzling.

Generally unaccompanied and relying on no overdubs, he crafts complex weaves of sound; his virtuosity is less a matter of speed or jazzy convolution than tone—and Fahey's guitar resounds like no other. Big, bell-like, immediate, helped out by very clear productions, his tone comes through, like a signature, on all his albums. A very consistent artist—the assured delivery of "Old Southern Medley" off *The Transfiguration of Blind Joe Death*, from 1973, isn't dissimilar to his rousing take on Eric Clapton's "Layla" (*Let Go*)—he's kept to a very high standard throughout his 30-year career. Gorgeous mood music that can indeed provoke a trance of reverie, his albums might appeal to New Age listeners—but they're denser and smarter than anything in that genre. — P.E.

FAIRPORT CONVENTION

★ ★ ★ ★ ★   **Fairport Convention (1968; Polydor, 1990)**
★ ★ ★ ★ ★   **Unhalfbricking (1969; Hannibal, 1986)**
  ★ ★ ★ ★   **What We Did On Our Holidays (1968; Hannibal, 1987)**
    ★ ★ ★   **Heyday (1968; Hannibal, 1987)**
  ★ ★ ★½   **Liege and Lief (A&M, 1969)**
  ★ ★ ★½   **Full House (1970; Hannibal, 1986)**
    ★ ★ ★   **Angel Delight (A&M, 1971)**
    ★ ★ ★   **Babbacombe Lee (A&M, 1972)**
  ★ ★ ★ ★   **The History of Fairport Convention (Island, 1972)**
    ★ ★ ★   **Rosie (Island, 1973)**
    ★ ★ ★   **Nine (A&M, 1974)**
  ★ ★ ★½   **Live Convention (A Moveable Feast) (Island, 1974)**
    ★ ★ ★   **Rising for the Moon (Island, 1975)**
    ★ ★ ★   **House Full (1976; Hannibal, 1986)**
    ★ ★ ★   **Live at the L.A. Troubadour (Island, 1976)**
    ★ ★ ★   **Gottle o' Geer (Island, 1976)**
★ ★ ★ ★ ★   **Fairport Chronicles (A&M, 1976)**
  ★ ★ ★½   **Gladys' Leap (Varrick, 1986)**
  ★ ★ ★½   **Expletive Delighted (Varrick, 1987)**
    ★ ★ ★   **In Real Time (Island, 1987)**

A remarkable debut, *Fairport Convention* (1968) introduced a band whose instrumental prowess and eclectic repertoire qualified them as a nascent supergroup. Dizzying personnel shifts and haphazard commercial success, however, would dog the band throughout its long career, making Fairport ultimately more a style and a vision than a cohesive aggregation. Whatever the lineup, Fairport's players managed a union of Scots-Irish folk, rock & roll rhythm, and cunning, elliptical lyrics. *Unhalfbricking* featured a legendary cast: angel-voiced Sandy Denny and guitarist Richard Thompson were as potent a pair of singers as the Jefferson Airplane's Grace Slick and Marty Balin, and Dave Swarbrick's violin playing grounded the band in the Celtic tradition; drummer Dave Mattacks kept things swinging. Whether soaring through the 11 minutes of "A Sailor's Life" or rendering Dylan's "If You Gotta Go, Go Now" the group came off as daunting, witty virtuosos. *Liege and Lief* completed Fairport's first chapter, establishing the group at the forefront of experimental late-'60s British bands.

By the time of *Angel Delight* both Thompson and Denny had departed—and the band's foray even further into traditional music seemed limiting. *Angel* and *Babbacombe Lee* were mainly Swarbrick's shows, and the band suffered from the lack of an outstanding vocalist. The pleasant, if unremarkable *Rosie* featured none of Fairport's original players; *Live Convention* brought back Sandy Denny for a very brief stay—and the album was one the band's last true highlights.

Fairport kept on going, however. All the albums after *Gottle o' Geer* (1976) are worth a listen, but they only echo the long-past glory of the group's first three records. *Fairport Chronicles* compiles the best of that period, and it's masterful. *Expletive Delighted* (1987) is a fair example of the group's later work; it's an interesting fusion of jazzy licks and Celtic reels. — P.E.

MARIANNE FAITHFULL

      ★ ★   **Marianne Faithfull's Greatest Hits (1969; Abkco, 1988)**
    ★ ★½   **Faithless (1978; Immediate, 1989)**
  ★ ★ ★ ★   **Broken English (Island, 1979)**
    ★ ★ ★   **Dangerous Acquaintances (Island, 1981)**
    ★ ★ ★   **A Child's Adventure (Island, 1983)**
    ★ ★ ★   **Strange Weather (Island, 1987)**
  ★ ★ ★ ★   **Blazing Away (Island, 1990)**

As Mick Jagger's mod-period squeeze, Marianne Faithfull played the archetypal Brit rock star girlfriend, pale, blond, regal, hip. And this daughter of an Austrian noble could sing—notably, at 17, Jagger-Richard's lovely "As Tears Go By." A few other hits followed, but by 1966, she was finished as a soft-voiced popster. *Greatest Hits* chronicles this period; *Faithless* is a reissue of her '70s pop—her voice is strong, the material is not.

By the dawn of the '80s, experience, in the stark form of heartbreak, drug busts, press notoriety and suicide attempts, had made Marianne Faithfull an artist. As a demimonde chanteuse, Faithfull is now undisputably the real thing—wised-up, courageous, notably bullshit-free. *Broken English*, with a song about cock-sucking and a dramatic reading of Lennon's "Working Class Hero," was her startling adult entrance, unleashing a Gauloise-rich voice and an intelligence few had suspected. *Dangerous Acquaintances* insinuated its power more softly, its Steve Winwood collaboration, "For Beauties Sake," taking a wary look at obsession. *A Child's Adventure* found her in stronger, but still uningratiating voice; while a fine record, especially for the wounded strength of "Falling From Grace," it just missed the cracked accomplishment of her debut. With *Strange Weather*, Faithfull darkly covered work by Dylan, Leadbelly and Jerome Kern. And, in *Blazing Away*, she commemorates her life-lessons; a sharp live album, it serves as a loose "Best of."
— P.E.

FAITH NO MORE
★★★ **Introduce Yourself (Slash, 1987)**
★★★★ **The Real Thing (Slash/Reprise, 1989)**
★★★ **Live at the Brixton Academy (Slash/London Import, 1991)**

Fusionists in the most literal sense, Faith No More weaves the disparate threads of punk rock, heavy metal, rap, funk and jazz into a single fabric. It's a difficult balance to maintain, of course, and it is achieved only sporadically on *Introduce Yourself*. Most of the basic elements are there—Jim Martin's crunching power guitar churning through "Faster Disco," Bill Gould's slap-and-pop bass lines percolating beneath "Anne's Song"—but the overall sound is too monolithic to make the interplay of influences stand out. Worse, Chuck Mosley's whiny vocals blunt whatever momentum the rest of the band generates. Mosley left before the band began work on *The Real Thing*, with the result that much of the album was written without vocals. Surprisingly, this worked to Faith No More's advantage; not only do the tracks leave more room for the group's influences to make themselves heard, but they also leave greater latitude for new vocalist Mike Patton. Hence, the stomping groove and

symphonic refrains of "Epic" somehow end up as rap, "The Real Thing" moves easily between jazzy tension and metallic fury, and the swirling maelstrom of sound in "Falling to Pieces" comes across as straight rock & roll. Though the concert portions of *Live at the Brixton Academy* adds little to the basic approach, they do have a loose wit and charming irreverence. It also includes two moderately interesting leftovers from *The Real Thing*. — J.D.C.

FALCO
★★½ **Einzelhaft (A&M, 1982)**
★★ **Junge Roemer (A&M, 1984)**
★★★ **Falco 3 (A&M, 1985)**
★½ **Emotional (Sire, 1986)**
★ **Wiener Blut (Sire, 1988)**
★★★ **The Remix Hit Collection (Sire, 1991)**

Born Johann Holzel, this Austrian singer is best known for "Rock Me Amadeus," a loopy Mozart tribute that was the first (and, so far, only) German-language rap song ever to top the U.S. pop charts. Not that Falco is a rapper in any real sense of the term; although rap elements have been heard on his albums since "Der Kommissar," from *Einzelhaft*, Falco's roots are actually in new wave. There's a pronounced bent toward Bowie in his work, with echoes of "Fame" turning up in "Tut-Ench-Amon," from *Junge Roemer*, but that aspect of his sound is downplayed somewhat on *3*, *Emotional* and *Wiener Blut*, where producers Rob and Ferdi Bolland favor a gimmicky, dance-oriented approach. That works well enough on *3*, with "Rock Me Amadeus" and the quirky "Vienna Calling" (and survives the studio tinkering of *The Remix Hit Collection* with ease), but grows tedious with the campy excess of *So Emotional* and *Wiener Blut*. — J.D.C.

THE FALL
★★★½ **Live at the Witch Trials (Step-Forward/I.R.S., 1979)**
★★★ **Dragnet (Step-Forward UK, 1979)**
★★½ **Totale's Turns (Rough Trade UK, 1980)**
★★ **Grotesque (After the Gramme) (Rough Trade, 1980)**
★★½ **Early Years 77–79 (Faulty Products, 1981)**
★★½ **Hex Enduction Hour (Kamera UK, 1982)**
★★★ **Room to Live (Kamera UK, 1982)**
★★★ **Perverted By Language (Rough Trade UK, 1983)**

★★★½ **The Wonderful and Frightening World of the Fall** (PVC/Beggars Banquet, 1984)
★★½ **Hip Priest and Kamerads** (Situation Two UK, 1985)
★★★★½ **This Nation's Saving Grace** (PVC/Beggars Banquet, 1985)
★★★★ **The Fall (EP)** (PVC, 1986)
★★★★½ **Bend Sinister** (Beggars Banquet UK, 1986)
★★★★ **The Domesday Pay-Off Triad—Plus!** (Big Time, 1987)
★★½ **The Peel Sessions (EP)** (Strange Fruit, 1987)
★★★ **In: Palace of Swords Reversed** (Rough Trade, 1987)
★★★★½ **The Frenz Experiment** (Beggars Banquet, 1988)
★★★★ **I Am Kurious Oranj** (Beggars Banquet, 1988)
★★★ **Seminal Live** (Beggars Banquet, 1989)
★★★★★ **458489 A Sides** (Beggars Banquet, 1990)
★★★½ **458489 B Sides** (Beggars Banquet UK, 1990)
★★★½ **Extricate** (Cog-Sinister/Fontana, 1990)
★★★ **Shiftwork** (Fontana, 1991)
★★★ **Code: Selfish** (Fontana, 1991)

A cult band in the purest sense of the term, the Fall is prolific because it has to be. Like many whose music is too idiosyncratic or demanding to attract a mass audience, these Britons realized early on that they would never sell albums to a lot of people, and so proceeded to make a lot of albums in hopes that the fans they had would buy them all. Fortunately for the rest of us, the Fall has largely managed to justify its output, delivering albums that are consistently challenging, and occasionally great.

With its churning rhythmic interplay and simple, repetitious melodies, *Live at the Witch Trials* is fairly typical post-punk material with the corrosive commentary of frontman Mark E. Smith (the only Fall member to appear on all of the group's albums) being the band's chief distinguishing characteristic. Their sound changes, along with the lineup, on *Dragnet*, getting denser and more dissonant, and it continues that approach through *Grotesque (After the Gramme)* as well as the concert recordings *Totale's Turns* and, to a lesser extent, *Hex Enduction Hour*.

By *Room to Live*, the Fall's interest in aural aggression begins to wane, and a taste for churning, cyclical rhythmic patterns replaces it. Although this shift in strategy doesn't make the music noticeably more accessible, it does have structural advantages, affording the band plenty of room to play while providing a framework durable enough to sustain workouts like the six-minute "Hard Life in Country." *Perverted By Language* and *The Wonderful and Frightening World of the Fall* each push the idea a bit further, but it isn't until *This Nation's Saving Grace* that it really begins to bear fruit, matching the Fall's brittle rhythms with edgy, brash melodies. Guitarist Brix Smith—Mark E.'s missus—deserves credit for much of this, and indeed, her influence is audible in *Wonderful and Frightening* tracks like "Elves" and "God-Box" (on CD reissue of LP). But even those oddly catchy numbers lack the genuinely tuneful charm of *This Nation*'s "L.A." and "Cruiser's Creek." Even better, the Fall maintain this balance through *Bend Sinister* (highlights of which include "Terry Waite Sez" and a cover of the Other Half's garage rock chestnut, "Mr. Pharmacist"), *The Frenz Experiment* (which boasts a version of the Kinks' "Victoria") and *I Am Kurious Oranj* (a ballet, believe it or not, inspired by the career of William of Orange).

After the Smiths' marriage collapsed in 1989, Brix left the band to devote herself full-time to the Adult Net, which she had formed in 1985. Her absence is obvious on *Extricate*, which lacks the melodic cogency of its predecessors, but to its credit, the Fall does offer some interesting substitutions, including the sequencer-fueled dance groove of "Telephone Thing" (produced by Coldcut). Unfortunately, neither *Shiftwork* nor *Code: Selfish* follow that effort with similarly imaginative experiments. The Fall also issued a host of compilation albums, among them *Early Years 77–79*, *Hip Priest and Kamerads*, *In: Palace of Swords Reversed*, *Domesday Pay-Off*, *458489 A Sides* and *458489 B Sides*; of these, only *458489 A Sides*, which compiles the A sides of all the band's singles during the Brix period, is essential listening. — J.D.C.

THE FAMILY STAND
★★★ **Chain** (Atlantic, 1990)
★★★½ **Moon in Scorpio** (East-West, 1991)
Nodding to Sly Stone and winking at Prince, this Brooklyn trio juggles hip-hop beats, hot guitar lines, cool synthesizers and coed gospel harmonies—without flinching. For that reason, the Family Stand's debut album is precariously balanced. But the

standout tracks—"Ghetto Heaven," "Sweet Liberation," "Little White, Little Black Lies"—pulse with ideas, and a distinct musical personality emerges. *Moon in Scorpio* is a tripped out explosion of talent; the Family Stand vaults all over the place, but at times the production sounds unfocused and the metal influence a little too heavy. However, the good bits— "Shades of Blue" and "Winter in My Heart"—are very good indeed. — M.C.

RICHARD AND MIMI FARIÑA
★ ★ ★ **Celebrations for a Grey Day**
   (Vanguard, 1965)
★ ★ ★ **Reflections in a Crystal Wind**
   (Vanguard, 1966)
   ★ ★ **Memories (Vanguard, 1968)**
★ ★ ★ **The Best of Richard and Mimi Fariña**
   (Vanguard, 1971)

Erudite early '60s folkies, the Fariñas began as members of the resolutely activist and anti-commercial circle who hoped to wrest college listeners away from the pap they perceived pop to be—and convert them to traditional black and Scots-Irish fare. A political as well as musical crusade, the effort was intended not only to win a new audience for the songs, but to encourage an appreciation of folk music's empathy with outsiders and the unconventional. Joan Baez's sister, Mimi, was married to Richard, an aspiring literary figure (his 1966 novel, *Been Down So Long It Looks Like Up to Me,* became a countercultural manifesto).

By their second album, however, the pair began moving toward a richer, more personal sound—a fusion of poetry and atmospheric melody, somewhat along the lines of the free-form music Tim Buckley would develop with much greater intensity. A celesta, instead of an acoustic guitar, might carry a tune, and a rock rhythm section added texture.

The Fariñas' first two records now sound a bit dated, but they're very enjoyable; the 26 songs off the best-of compilation offer an overview that's a bit too exhaustive, but the strongest work ("Pack Up Your Sorrows," "Bold Marauder," "V" and "Raven Girl") remains impressive. — P.E.

FASTER PUSSYCAT
★ ★ ★¹/₂ **Faster Pussycat (Elektra, 1987)**
★ ★ ★¹/₂ **Wake Me When It's Over (Elektra,**
   1989)

Emerging from the same club scene that produced Guns n' Roses, L.A. Guns and Poison, Faster Pussycat (the name comes from a Russ Meyer film) specializes in an endearingly trashy variety of glam rock, one which owes more to the raucous raunch of the New York Dolls than the snake-hipped groove of R&B hounds like Aerosmith. *Faster Pussycat* is the wittier of the two albums, thanks in large part to songs like "Bathroom Wall" (sample lyric: "Got your number off the bathroom wall/Boy am I lucky I didn't use the other stall"). But *Wake Me When It's Over* packs more punch, thanks to edgy, amphetamine boogie tunes like "Little Dove" and "Pulling Weeds." — J.D.C.

FEAR
★ ★ **The Record (Slash, 1982)**
   ★ **More Beer (Restless, 1985)**

One of the lower points in the L.A. punk movement, Fear reveled in its combination of cheap nihilism, sexist posturing and shock-value politics, as if the band had somehow thought "asshole" and "punk" were synonymous. Better-than-average chops keep *The Record* from being a complete waste of time, lending ferocious glee to "Let's Have a War," but you've got to wonder about a band that sneers at New York punk's artiness in one song ("New York's All Right If You Like Saxophones"), then apes it in another (a self-consciously dissonant cover of "We Got to Get Out of This Place"). As for *More Beer*, it has less taste and is less fulfilling—unless, of course, your idea of wit runs to songs about rape and dismemberment. — J.D.C.

CHARLIE FEATHERS
★ ★ ★ **Charlie Feathers (Elektra, 1991)**

Charlie Feathers was one of the most eccentric in a stable full of eccentric artists at Sun Records in the mid-'50s. That he was talented is a fact no one disputes, particularly when the discussion turns to what he could do when he got hold of a country song and gave it a blues feeling. His pure rockabilly sides for Sun were minor records at best, although Sun freaks regard them as being only a few notches below those cut by Presley, Perkins, Cash and Lewis. What was honest and heartfelt in his country songs was corrupted into kitsch when he raged into rockabilly with an unchecked arsenal of hiccups, stutters and stilted phrasing—he never seemed to know when the gimmick had lost its novelty. Finally he became his own greatest creation, with wild, unsubstantiated claims of having coached Presley, of having written a number of songs without being properly credited (on one he apparently did co-write and Presley recorded, "I Forget to Remember to Forget," Feathers embellished the story to identify himself as the person who taught Presley the vocal licks and arrangement) and of having functioned as a Sun staff producer. Ultimately, his tenure at Sun is marked by one top-notch rockabilly recording, "Tongue-Tied Jill," a handful of other rousing sides, and tall tales.

Feathers remained in Memphis after he left Sun, playing in clubs and polishing his legend. In the late '70s he hooked up with some Cincinnati studio people and formed his own label, Feathers Records, and cut a series of hellacious singles and two albums, *Charlie Feathers* and *Charlie Feathers, Volume 2*, both of them searing blasts of rockabilly and country with Feathers singing straight-ahead and hard. And then silence. Come 1991 and Elektra digs up Feathers for its American Explorers series. Lo and behold, like so many of the original rockabilly artists, Feathers comes on with body and soul intact, hiccuping and growling his way through more country and rockabilly, as unpredictable as ever. He even reprises "You're Right, I'm Left, She's Gone," a song written for Presley during the Sun years by Stan Kesler, with whom Feathers did or did not write "I Forget to Remember to Forget." Kesler shows up on this disc playing bass and steel guitar, while another of Feathers's Sun cronies, Roland Janes, is featured on guitar. Feathers shows what he can do with a country song when he starts probing Hank Williams Sr.'s "(I Don't Care) If Tomorrow Never Comes," and scorches some of the rockabilly entries as well. But others ("Defrost Your Heart," "When You Come Around," "Mean Woman Blues," "Oklahoma Hills") are only middling. However fleeting, it's an interesting comeback that enables Feathers to add another chapter to his oddball history. — D.M.

THE FEELIES

★★★★ Crazy Rhythms (1980; A&M, 1990)
★★★★ The Good Earth (Coyote/Twin/Tone, 1986)
★★★½ Only Life (Coyote/A&M, 1988)
★★★★ Time for a Witness (Coyote/A&M, 1991)

Among the formal breakthroughs managed by the Velvet Underground was something called the drone strum. As perfected by Lou Reed, this strum didn't syncopate to emphasize the backbeat the way rock

rhythm guitar usually did—in fact, it barely syncopated at all, tending more toward chopped, evenly-accented eighth notes dropped squarely on the beat. And it was this nervous chink-chink-chink-chink-chink-chink-chink-chink that gave the likes of "I'm Waiting for the Man" or "White Light/White Heat" their anxious edge. That same strum is at the heart of the Feelies' sound on *Crazy Rhythms*. Yet as much as it defines the band's groove, it doesn't limit the band's rhythmic vocabulary; indeed, songs like the briskly tuneful "Fa Cé-La" or the slow-building "The Boy With Perpetual Nervousness" augment the basic pulse with a second line of overdubbed percussion. Moreover, this strictly disciplined approach to rhythm makes even the slightest variations, like the lengthy breakdown on the title tune, stand out in bold relief.

Six years later, the Feelies—this time sporting a new bassist and drummer as well as a full-time percussionist—returned for round two, *The Good Earth*. This time around, the band's groove is more conventional (note the standard folk-rock strum of the acoustic guitars on "On the Roof") but still heavily indebted to Reed and the Velvets. If anything, the group has added a few Velvet-isms to its repertoire—in particular, the "Heroin"-style acceleration and explosion of "Slipping (Into Something)." *Only Life* can't quite match that growth (though it does include a cover of Reed's "What Goes On"), though it doesn't backslide, either. But *Time for a Witness* pushes beyond mere imitation as the band refines its sound into something that's at once evocative of its influences and yet stylistically distinct, especially on the plangent, bluesy "What She Said" or the moody "Find a Way." — J.D.C.

JOSE FELICIANO

★★ Feliciano! (RCA, 1968)
★ Feliciano/10 to 23 (RCA, 1969)
★★ Alive, Alive-0! (RCA, 1969)
★ Encore! (RCA, 1971)
★ Jose Feliciano (RCA, 1971)
★ Jose Feliciano Sings (RCA, 1972)
★ Compartments (RCA, 1973)
★ And the Feeling's Good (RCA, 1974)
★ Just Wanna Rock 'n' Roll (RCA, 1975)
★ Sweet Soul Music (Private Stock, 1976)
★ Jose Feliciano (Motown, 1981)
★★ His Hits & Other Classics (Pair, 1986)
★★½ All Time Greatest Hits (RCA, 1988)
★ I'm Never Gonna Change (EMI, 1989)

It's hard to forgive this amiable guitarist for his 1968 slaughter of "Light My Fire." Feliciano seemed to have believed that the song was only a weirder version of "Girl from Ipanema." His slighter material, "Hi-Heel Sneakers" and "Hey Baby," doesn't suffer from such misguided ambitiousness—but it's tame stuff. A 1969 cover of Dale Hawkins's "Suzie Q" is all contrived "sexiness." His theme for TV's "Chico and the Man" is about as pleasant as Feliciano gets (there's none of his straining after passion). His Latin records are considerably better. — P.E.

FREDDY FENDER

★ ★ ★½ **Before the Next Teardrop Falls (MCA, 1974)**

★ ★ ★ ★ **The Best of Freddy Fender (Dot, 1977)**

Baldemar Huerta recorded as Freddy Fender in the mid-'50s, releasing Tex-Mex rockabilly singles in Spanish *and* English. The world caught up with him in 1975. "Before the Next Teardrop Falls" and "Wasted Days and Wasted Nights" reached the Top Ten that summer, saturating the airwaves with quavering barrio heartbreak. In between, Fender had worked as a migrant farmer and a mechanic, survived a hitch in the Marines and served a stretch in Louisiana's infamous Angola State Prison (for marijuana possession). By the early '70s, he'd retired from music. Then, rocker Doug Sahm (who covered "Wasted Days" with his Sir Douglas Quintet) recommended Fender to the veteran Houston-based producer Huey Meaux. It turned out to be a perfect match. Meaux provides an appropriately spare setting for this eclectic traditionalist, sweetening Freddy's roots just enough for a broad-based audience. Conveniently, the very best of their work is all that's left in print. Both albums contain the breakthrough hits, "I Love My Rancho Grande" and a mind-blowing, bilingual version of the honky-tonk milestone "Wild Side of Life." *Before the Next Teardrop Falls* emphasizes hard-country cheating songs, while *Best Of* peppers the mix with strong R&B and Cajun influences. Freddy Fender's "overnight" success story may be a fading bit of trivia now, but his low-key country soul still sounds timeless. — M.C.

BRYAN FERRY

★ ★ ★ ★ **These Foolish Things (Reprise, 1973)**

★ ★ ★ **Another Time, Another Place (Reprise, 1974)**

★ ★ ★½ **Let's Stick Together (Reprise, 1976)**

★ ★ ★½ **In Your Mind (Reprise, 1977)**

★ ★ ★½ **The Bride Stripped Bare (Reprise, 1978)**

★ ★ ★½ **Boys and Girls (Warner Bros., 1985)**

★ ★½ **Bete Noire (Reprise, 1988)**

Bryan Ferry's solo career can be heard as a codicil to Roxy Music—even after that innovative band's presumed demise in the early '80s. His debut followed Roxy's glitter phase with more arty outrage: *These Foolish Things* contains radical—downright sacreligious—cover versions of Bob Dylan ("A Hard Rain's a-Gonna Fall") and the Stones ("Sympathy for the Devil") alongside "It's My Party" and the torchy title track. The clipped intensity of Ferry's vocal style takes some getting used to, but he treats these chestnuts with a compelling mixture of skepticism and respect. *Another Time, Another Place* offers a disappointing second helping. On *Let's Stick Together*, Ferry remakes some of his own compositions from the first Roxy Music album as well as the title track, an R&B anthem by Wilbert Harrison. Guitarist Chris Spedding lends a spry hard-rock feel, throwing new emphasis on Ferry's deepened, earthier tone. His "Let's Stick Together" isn't a bit ironic.

In Your Mind strives for the windswept, bracing impact of Roxy Music's 1975 classic *Siren*. The surfeit of Ferry compositions is gratifying, though even the hookiest ("Tokyo Joe," "Party Doll") merely restate Roxy's familiar romantic and musical themes. *The Bride Stripped Bare* is more adventurous; many listeners thought it was foolhardy. Bryan Ferry recording in L.A. with session veterans? Well, guitarist Waddy Wachtel pulls out some surprisingly ripe riffs, while Ferry croons both Al Green's "Take Me to the River" and the Velvet Underground's "What Goes On" without showing signs of strain. Recent Roxy Music converts might begin their Ferry appreciation course with this undervalued and very accessible item.

After a long silence from both Ferry and Roxy Music, *Boys and Girls* appeared in 1985. Set in the richly synthesized mode of *Avalon* (Roxy's 1982 swan song), Ferry's sixth album envelopes the listener in emotional subtleties and sonic nuance. Then it's over, like a pleasant dream. *Boys and Girls* could stand a couple of more tunes along the memorable lines of "Slave to Love" or "Don't Stop the Dance." On the other hand, *Bete Noire* could use one solid melody. As hushed and haunted as ever, Ferry's deeply evocative voice nevertheless gets lost amid the grandiose and antiseptic musical trappings of the digital recording era. *Bete Noire* is depressingly tasteful and restrained—state-of-the-art rock wallpaper. — M.C.

THE FIFTH DIMENSION
★★½ **Greatest Hits on Earth (Arista, 1972)**
★★★ **Anthology (Rhino, 1986)**
"Up, Up and Away," "Wedding Bell Blues," "Aquarius/Let the Sunshine In," "One Less Bell to Answer"—the Fifth Dimension's many hits are the stuff that provides inspiration for sitcom theme songs. Hugely successful in the late '60s, the vocal quintet covered painstakingly crafted, surefire MOR by the genre's high-end songwriters (Burt Bacharach, Jimmy Webb) and helped mainstream the breathlessly ambitious work of Laura Nyro (a fairly interesting choice of writer—and an outre one, given 5D's characteristic fare). Buffed to a blinding sheen, their hits were carried by the oh-so-smoothness of Marilyn McCoo's ingratiating vocals (the group's second lead, Billy Davis, functioned mainly as McCoo's echo). Exhaustively comprehensive, containing all the hits mentioned and more, *Anthology* proves that, as Muzak with voices, this stuff engenders a pleasant, soporific mood; the Motown albums, however, don't even work well as tranquilizers. — P.E.

FINE YOUNG CANNIBALS
★★★½ **Fine Young Cannibals (I.R.S., 1986)**
★★★★½ **The Raw & the Cooked (I.R.S./MCA, 1988)**
★★★ **The Raw & the Remix (I.R.S./MCA, 1990)**
After leaving the English Beat, guitarist Andy Cox and bassist David Steele hooked up with singer Roland Gift to form the Fine Young Cannibals (which took its title from the 1960 Robert Wagner-Natalie Wood feature *All the Fine Young Cannibals*). Although the mannered soul approach favored by the trio's debut, *Fine Young Cannibals*, has its moments—most notably "Johnny Come Home" and a cover of the Elvis Presley hit "Suspicious Minds"—it wasn't until *The Raw & the Cooked* that the Cannibals found their milieu. Part of the difference is simply a matter of material, as the group moves easily from the classic '60s soul lines of "Good Thing" to the inspired revisionism of "Ever Fallen in Love," a richly expressive remake of the Buzzcocks

single. But the group's stylistic range is just as much a factor, from the dry, mechanical pulse of "She Drives Me Crazy" to the itchy, post-modern James Brown sound of "I'm Not the Man I Used to Be." Moreover, the album was such a tremendous success that an album of dance-club remixes, *The Raw & the Remix*, followed. Unfortunately, this project reduced the Cannibals to bit players, as these tracks have less to do with the songs or even the performances than with whatever tricks the remixers—a cast that includes such dance club deities as Soul II Soul's Jazzie B & Nellee Hooper, Monie Love, Smith & Mighty and Matt Dike—bring to the music. — J.D.C.

TIM FINN
★★ **Big Canoe (1986; Virgin, 1988)**
★★★ **Tim Finn (Capitol, 1989)**
Finn's strengths as a melodist notwithstanding, there's something basically disappointing about this Split Enz vet's solo albums. It isn't that his songs aren't tuneful (although some of the examples offered on *Big Canoe* come distressingly close to meeting that description), just that he rarely seems to know what to do with the melodic momentum his songs generate. As a result, even his best efforts—like "How'm I Gonna Sleep" from *Tim Finn*—seem underdeveloped. — J.D.C.

FIREHOSE
★★★ **Ragin', Full-On (SST, 1986)**
★½ **if'n (SST, 1987)**
★★★ **fROMOHIO (SST, 1989)**
★★★½ **flyin' the flannel (Columbia, 1991)**
★★★ **The Live Totem Pole EP (EP) (Columbia, 1992)**
Literally raised from the ashes of the Minutemen, fIREHOSE began after D. Boon's death when surviving Minutemen Mike Watt and George Hurley were contacted by raging fan Ed Crawford (a.k.a. Ed fROMOHIO). *Ragin', Full On* presents a faithful recreation of the brittle, aggressive punk funk that was the Minutemen's calling card, and overcomes its generally spotty writing with impassioned playing. But the utter fizzle of *if'n* suggests too much enthusiasm and too little focus, and though *fROMOHIO* puts the band back on course, only the likes of "In My Mind" and "If'n" offer any real sense of the band's potential. Fortunately, *flyin' the flannel* steers clear of the band's worst indulgences, wisely using its instrumental strengths to bring more out of songs like "Can't Believe" and "Too

Long," though the raucous *The Live Totem Pole EP*—which alternates oddball covers like Public Enemy's "Sophisticated Bitch" with so-so originals—finds the band backsliding a bit. — J.D.C.

THE FIRM
★★½ **The Firm (Atlantic, 1985)**
★★ **Mean Business (Atlantic, 1986)**
Five years after Led Zeppelin split up, interest in the band still hadn't abated. The re-emergence of Jimmy Page couldn't have come at a better time than 1985: people were primed, especially after Page, Robert Plant and John Paul Jones played a one-off set at the Live Aid concert. And what better henchman than former Bad Company-Free belter Paul Rodgers? The most soulful hard-rock shouter of the '70s needed a career boost himself. Pity that the Firm duly lived up to its dull moniker: brusque and businesslike, the supergroup plunks out some incredibly mundane metallic blooze. Dated isn't the word. Page's guitar riffs and Rodgers's macho strut sound positively decayed, ossifying before your very ears. There's a brief flash of the old firepower at the end of Page's solo on "Radioactive" (from *The Firm*). Watch his face light up during that part of the video clip—he's glad to be back. Otherwise, skip these depressing exercises and try *Outrider*, Page's 1988 solo album instead. — M.C.

FISHBONE
★★½ **Fishbone (EP) (Columbia, 1985)**
★★★ **In Your Face (Columbia, 1986)**
★★½ **It's a Wonderful Life (Gonna Have a Good Time) (EP) (Columbia, 1987)**
★★★½ **Truth and Soul (Columbia, 1988)**
★★★★ **The Reality of My Surroundings (Columbia, 1991)**
Boasting an acerbic sense of social commentary and a sound almost too eclectic for its own good, Fishbone's reach frequently exceeds its grasp. But at its best, the group transforms the breakneck intensity of post-hardcore ska into something far more soulful and resonant. Granted, it took some time for the band to work up to that level. Though admirably energetic, both *Fishbone* and *In Your Face* are more noteworthy for their high-octane performances than for the songs (although "When Problems Arise" and "Cholly," from *In Your Face*, have their moments), while the sour Christmas songs on *It's a Wonderful Life* are just seasonal oddities. *Truth and Soul* broadens the band's sound,

incorporating everything from a searing, speed-metal take on Curtis Mayfield's "Freddie's Dead" to the brittle funk of "Ghetto Soundwave," but that ambition doesn't really pay dividends until *The Reality of My Surroundings*, which finally molds the group's diverse interests into a single, cohesive sound. — J.D.C.

ELLA FITZGERALD
★★★★★ **Ella Fitzgerald Sings the Cole Porter Songbook, Vol. 1 (Verve, 1956)**
★★★★★ **Ella Fitzgerald Sings the Cole Porter Songbook, Vol. 2 (Verve, 1956)**
★★★★★ **Ella Fitzgerald Sings the Rodgers and Hart Songbook (Verve, 1957)**
★★★★★ **The Duke Ellington Songbook (1957; Verve, 1988)**
★★★½ **Jazz at the Philharmonic: Lady Be Good! (1957; Verve, 1985)**
★★★★ **Ella Fitzgerald at the Opera House (1957; Verve 1986)**
★★★★★ **The Best of Ella Fitzgerald (1958; MCA, 1973)**
★★★★★ **The Best of Ella Fitzgerald, Vol. 2 (1958; MCA, 1977)**
★★★½ **Ella in Rome (1958; Verve, 1988)**
★★★★½ **The Irving Berlin Songbook, Vol. 1 (1958; Verve, 1986)**
★★★★½ **The Irving Berlin Songbook, Vol. 2 (1958; Verve, 1986)**
★★★★½ **Ella Fitzgerald Sings the George and Ira Gershwin Songbook (1959; Verve, 1978)**
★★★★ **Mack the Knife: Ella in Berlin (1960; Verve, 1985)**
★★★½ **Ella Returns to Berlin (1961; Verve, 1991)**
★★★★ **The Harold Arlen Songbook, Vol. 1 (1961; Verve, 1988)**
★★★★ **The Harold Arlen Songbook, Vol. 2 (1961; Verve, 1988)**
★★★★ **The Jerome Kern Songbook (1964; Verve, 1985)**
★★★½ **Brighten the Corner (1967; Capitol, 1991)**
★★★½ **Ella Fitzgerald and Louis Armstrong (1972; Verve, 1984)**
★★★½ **Ella in London (1974; Pablo, 1987)**
★★★ **Take Love Easy (1974; Pablo, 1987)**
★★★½ **Montreux, 1975 (1975; Pablo, 1987)**
★★★★ **Ella & Oscar (1975; Pablo, 1987)**

★★★½ **Fitzgerald and Pass . . . Again (1976; Pablo, 1988)**
★★★½ **Ella Fitzgerald With the Tommy Flanagan Trio (1977; Pablo, 1989)**
★★★½ **Lady Time (1978; Pablo, 1988)**
★★★½ **Dream Dancing (1978; Pablo, 1987)**
★★★½ **A Classy Pair (1979; Pablo, 1982)**
★★★½ **Fine and Mellow (1979; Pablo, 1987)**
★★★★ **A Perfect Match: Ella & Basie (1980; Pablo, 1987)**
★★★★ **Digital III at Montreux (Pablo, 1980)**
★★★★ **Ella Abraça Jobim (1981; Pablo, 1991)**
★★★ **The Best Is Yet to Come (Pablo Today, 1982)**
★★★½ **Speak Love (1983; Pablo, 1987)**
★★★½ **Ella à Nice (1983; Pablo Live, 1990)**
★★★½ **Nice Work If You Can Get It (1983; Pablo, 1987)**
★★★½ **Easy Living (Pablo, 1986)**
★★★★½ **The Best of Ella Fitzgerald (Pablo, 1988)**
★★★½ **Ella: Things Ain't What They Used to Be (and You Better Believe It) (Reprise, 1989)**
★★★½ **Jazz 'Round Midnight (Polydor, 1990)**
★★★½ **All That Jazz (Pablo, 1990)**
★★★ **The Intimate Ella (Polygram, 1990)**

The surest and steadiest of all jazz singers, Ella Fitzgerald earned the title "First Lady of Song" by remaining unshakably subservient to her material. Billie Holiday and Sarah Vaughan, among the titans, were the genre's ace interpreters, vocalists who bent and shaped melodies and lyrics to conform to their own mercurial inspiration. Compared to them, Ella remains a rock—she sings with a singular fidelity, letting the song pass untampered through the vehicle of her unsurpassingly clear voice. A peerless scat singer, Ella obviously can breathtakingly improvise (the essential talent of any jazz great), but her essential genius lies in holding steadfast to the mood of any of the awesome number of classic songs she's delivered. She comes across, then, as a remarkably selfless artist—one through whom the song itself comes always and unerringly to life.

Born and orphaned just after World War I, Ella hooked up in the 1930s with Chick Webb, big-band leader and volcanic drummer. The husband-and-wife team scored a gigantic hit in 1938 with "A-Tisket, A-Tasket," making Ella an instant star—

and, unusual for that time, the band became a crossover success, its style appealing not only to the black audience they'd gained at New York's famous Savoy Ballroom, but to whites as well. After Webb's death, the strongwilled if affable Fitzgerald kept the band together for a couple years before going solo—and then working with almost all of the greatest of her peers.

On Decca Records, up until the mid '50s, Ella could be considered at least as much a pop singer as a jazz one; she never let go of her capacity to swing, but the broad range of her material and her warm way with it transcended the confines of "hipness." In 1955, moving over to Verve, the label founded by her manager and "Jazz at the Philharmonic" impressario, Norman Granz, she began sharpening her jazz edge—while simultaneously embarking on a series of definitive recordings of Broadway material that earned her lasting critical and popular success.

Continuing to perform with unabated vigor throughout the '60s, Ella sat out a while in the early '70s due to eye surgery, but soon returned in full force. Whether singing with Count Basie or longtime cohort Oscar Peterson on piano, with ultra-smooth guitarist Joe Pass, with a full orchestra or the excellent Tommy Flanagan Trio, Fitzgerald maintained her poise and elegance—her classicism made human, however, through her zest, charm and exemplary ease.

The two MCA *Best of* sets aren't a bad place to start when tackling the singer's voluminous catalog: They feature her Decca work with Chick Webb ("A-Tisket, A-Tasket") and the other early hits—already Fitzgerald sounds like the soul of confidence. But the essential Ella remains the "songbooks"—the monumental late-'50s Verve series that covers the work of the classic writers of American song. Cole Porter, Rodgers and Hart, Duke Ellington, Jerome Kern, the Gershwins and Harold Arlen all get treated with a respect that raises even their slighter songs to a level of irresistible enjoyment; the orchestras, whether led by Buddy Bregman or Nelson Riddle, really cook—and Ella's exuberance is a thing of wonder. All of the sets are worth checking out—as is a later followup, the Jobim "songbook," *Ella Abraça Jobim* (1981)—but, for sheer, stunning grace, the Cole Porter, Rodgers and Hart, and Ellington records have the edge.

A strong intro to the later Ella is provided by the Pablo *Best of:* A representative sample of her '70s period, it features orchestral settings and small combo work, as well as nice examples of her collaborations with Joe Pass (Pass fans should also check *Speak Love, Fitzgerald and Pass . . . Again* and *Digital III at Montreux*). *Nice Work If You Can Get It* (1983) is an assured Gershwin set with Andre Previn that shows Fitzgerald still delivering in her later years; with Benny Carter on alto sax and Clark Terry on trumpet, *All That Jazz* (1989) is the music of a lion in winter: Ella's voice has obviously aged, but her skill and zest are unassailable. — P.E.

THE FIVE KEYS
★ The Five Keys (King, 1978)
★ ★ ★ The Five Keys: Capitol Collector's Series (Capitol, 1989)
★ ★ ★ The Five Keys: The Aladdin Years (EMI, 1991)

Inspired by the mellow harmonies of the Ink Spots and the Ravens, building on the rhythmic pulse brought to group harmony singing by the Orioles, the Five Keys stand as one of the earliest legitimate R&B vocal groups. Make no mistake, though: the smooth ballad was the Five Keys' stock in trade. Lead tenor Rudy West ranks as one of the most influential ballad singers in group harmony annals, adding his own plaintive cry to a style otherwise beholden to the precision and clarity of the Ink Spots' remarkable lead singer, Bill Kenny. Much of the Five Keys' recorded history remains available, thanks to the reissue programs at EMI and Capitol. *The Aladdin Years* showcases the group at its creative peak between the years 1951 and 1953. Its material was a mix of standards and original songs, but West made everything sound newly written especially for him. There's elegance in wistful songs of lost love ("With a Broken Heart," "Can't Keep From Crying"), but Hit Parade staples such as "The Glory of Love," "Red Sails in the Sunset" and "White Cliffs of Dover" shine like new money when West's silk-smooth tenor glides in over his mates' close harmonies. This disc also contains eight previously unreleased tracks uncovered by a collector in 1971 and originally issued surreptitiously on a fake Aladdin label. One of these happens to be an outstanding track, "(I Don't Stand a) Ghost of a Chance." The *Capitol Collector's Series* disc hits the high points of the group's 1954-1962 tenure at the label, including a venture into rock & roll with "Ling Ting Tong," a percussive song originally recorded by the Charms (a black group covering a black group was

virtually unheard of, but the Keys did it). West was in the army when the group switched labels in August of that year, so the lead chores were handled by Ulysses K. Hicks. In October 1954, though, West returned, Hicks departed, and the group forged ahead, cutting several consecutive hit singles.

King was the Keys' next stop after leaving Capitol, but they arrived without West, who had gone into semi-retirement. New lead singer Dick Threatt sounded uncannily like West, but he had neither the soulful tone nor the generous attitude of his predecessor. Thus *The Five Keys* is interesting only as a document of a group in decline. — D.M.

THE FIVE SATINS
★ ★ ★ The Five Satins Sing (Collectables, 1982)

In 1956, Fred Parris wrote a song for the doo-wop group he was fronting, the Five Satins, and recorded it in the basement of a church in the group's native New Haven, Connecticut, using a two-track machine. The song, "In the Still of the Night," featured Parris's heartfelt tenor soaring high over a turgid beat and brooding "shoo-do-shoo-be-do" background chants. Released on the Standard label, the song hit the Top Thirty of the pop charts, and was followed a year later by another Top Thirty single, "To the Aisle," featuring Bill Baker on lead in place of Parris, who was in the army. Parris returned, but the Five Satins were finished as a commercial entity. "In the Still of the Night," however, remained very much alive, showing up in regular rotation on oldies stations, and continuing to sell.

The Five Satins Sing kicks off with "In the Still of the Night," but also turns into a showcase for some fine, under-acknowledged recordings, some with Parris on lead, others with Baker. Of special note are "Shadows," with Baker delivering great feeling and conviction, and a moving interpretation of Bing Crosby's 1944 chart-topper, "I'll Be Seeing You." — D.M.

THE FIXX
★ ★ Shuttered Room (MCA, 1982)
★ ★ ½ Reach the Beach (MCA, 1983)
★ ★ Phantoms (MCA, 1984)
★ ★ Walkabout (MCA, 1986)
★ ★ React (MCA, 1987)
★ ½ Calm Animals (RCA, 1988)
★ ★ ½ Greatest Hits: One Thing Leads to Another (MCA, 1989)
★ ½ Ink (Impact, 1991)

One in a seemingly endless string of pop-savvy new-wave acts, the Fixx crafted a sound that is typical of the early '80s. Musically, the group took the middle ground, being neither quite as glib as Duran Duran nor as pompous as Ultravox, and that approach helped the Fixx gain a toe-hold in the American charts, particularly with *Reach the Beach* and its designated hit "One Thing Leads to Another." At this point, however, that album (like most of the band's output) is interesting only as a matter of nostalgia—and even then is likely to leave you feeling as if you've just stumbled onto the aural equivalent of a Nehru jacket. — J.D.C.

ROBERTA FLACK

★★★ **First Take (Atlantic, 1969)**
★★★ **Chapter Two (Atlantic, 1970)**
★★ **Quiet Fire (Atlantic, 1971)**
★★½ **Killing Me Softly (Atlantic, 1973)**
★★ **Blue Lights in the Basement (Atlantic, 1977)**
★★★ **The Best of Roberta Flack (Atlantic, 1981)**
★★ **I'm the One (Atlantic, 1982)**
★★ **Oasis (Atlantic, 1988)**
★★½ **Set the Night to Music (Atlantic, 1991)**

WITH DONNY HATHAWAY

★★ **Roberta Flack & Donny Hathaway (Atlantic, 1972)**
★★★ **Roberta Flack Featuring Donny Hathaway (Atlantic, 1980)**

WITH PEABO BRYSON

★★ **Live and More (Atlantic, 1981)**
★★½ **Born to Love (Capitol, 1983)**

While Aretha Franklin was busy pushing soul into the mainstream, the classically trained Roberta Flack brought a taste of pop refinement to the booming post-R&B black music scene. Flack's disciplined power and precise phrasing are a far cry from the fevered shout-and-shimmy of her gospel-trained peers. *First Take* is marked by the hushed, folkish accompaniment of "The First Time Ever I Saw Your Face" and Leonard Cohen's "Hey, That's No Way to Say Goodbye." *Chapter Two* is somewhat spunkier, especially "Reverend Lee"—this is probably Flack's most soulful set, next to her duets with the late Donny Hathaway. "Where Is the Love," frothy and pungent, captures both singers at their least mannered and most appealing. On their 1972 album, Roberta and Donny blithely hop from "Be Real Black for Me" to "You've Got a Friend," and beyond. Flack's *Quiet Fire* barely sparks at all, but "The First Time" became a belated Number One in 1972.

Her career off and running, Roberta

Flack sweetened her melancholy sound just enough to stay contemporary. Though "Killing Me Softly With His Song" followed "The First Time" to the top of the charts in '73, it's nowhere near as stark or affecting as the breakthrough hit. *Killing Me Softly* and the deleted *Feel Like Makin' Love* (1974) continue this inocuous vein. Flack scored regular crossover hits with the likes of "The Closer I Get to You" (from *Blue Lights in the Basement*) but her genteel romantic fantasies tend to fade into background music. A dalliance with sub-Pendergrass love man Peabo Bryson produced one memorable cooing session ("Tonight I Celebrate My Love," from *Born to Love*) and a lot of hot air. After several low-profile years, Flack tested the waters with *Oasis*—a tentative session that is barely kept afloat by an all-star studio crew. *Set the Night to Music*, produced by R&B legend Arif Mardin, is clearly meant to be a career-capper and second start. It's about half-successful; a slew of cover versions demonstrates Flack's strengths and weaknesses. Her stately reading of the Stylistics' "You Are Everything" feels all wrong, and then a funky update of Nat King Cole's "Unforgettable" works, somehow. "Summertime," co-written by Leonard Cohen, strikes another refreshing contemporary groove. Too bad about the hit title track: "Set the Night to Music," a duet with pop-reggae crooner Maxi Priest, is yet another faceless slab of danceable program music. — M.C.

FLAMIN' GROOVIES

★★★ **Supersnazz (1969; Epic/CBS Special Products, 1991)**
★★★½ **Flamingo (Kama Sutra, 1970)**
★★★ **Teenage Head (Kama Sutra, 1971)**
★★★½ **Shake Some Action (Sire, 1976)**
★★★ **Now! (Sire, 1978)**
★★★ **Jumpin' in the Night (Sire, 1979)**
★★★½ **The Flamin' Groovies' Greatest Grooves (Sire, 1989)**

Resolutely behind its times, this San Francisco quintet nevertheless prefigured a fair amount of punk and new-wave activity. At the height of psychedelia, the Flamin' Groovies revelled in the crude verities of '50s rock & roll; when the '70s were in full gear, the band reverted to a mop-top Merseybeat sound. No wonder obsessed record collectors have always revered these guys—and most casual listeners have never heard of 'em. Like East Coast virtuosos NRBQ and Midwest gonzos Brownsville Station, the Groovies brought a needed roots perspective to the late '60s–early '70s scene. Recently reissued, the Groovies' somewhat fey debut (*Supersnazz*) hardly lives up to its reputation as a long-lost classic. The rockin' *Flamingo* and the bluesy *Teenage Head*—both long out of print—come on a bit rougher, capturing the band's hangover-bound boogie in full stumble. After the departure of rockabilly-crazed lead singer Roy Loney in 1972, guitarist Cyril Jordan pointed the Groovies' musical direction toward Liverpool. *Groovies' Greatest Grooves* combines most of the Dave Edmunds–produced gem *Shake Some Action* (1976) with standout cuts from the uneven follow-ups: *Now!* (1978) and *Jumpin' in the Night* (1979). Even if the later-day Flamin' Groovies must be held responsible for the Knack and its followers, the jangly hooks on "Shake Some Action" and "Jumpin' in the Night" haven't begun to rust. — M.C.

THE FLAMINGOS

★ ★ ★ ★ **Flamingos (Chess, 1984)**
★ ★ ★ ★ **Best of the Flamingos (Rhino, 1990)**
The sweet science of close harmony includes few greater practitioners than the Flamingos, whose career began in 1953 and continues today, albeit without a recording contract. Two names dominate the Flamingos' history, those being cousins Zeke and Jake Carey, who founded the group and guided it through numerous changes in personnel and musical styles. Black men raised in the Hebrew faith, the Careys' musical sensibilities were virtually untouched by the sanctified and jubilee styles of gospel singing that were having such a profound impact on the popular black music of the early Fifties. Control and precision were the Flamingos' trademarks; even uptempo tunes such as "Shilly Dilly" did not feature flamboyant testifying of the sort passing into the secular world through the popularity of gospel singers such as R.H. Harris of the Soul Stirrers and Archie Brownlee of the Five Blind Boys of Mississippi. Along with the Harptones, the Orioles and the Five Keys, the Flamingos epitomized the cool school of group harmony. Their strength was Nate Nelson, the best of several Flamingos lead singers, who joined the group in 1954 and for the next six years lent his high, clear tenor to a wealth of sensitive ballads and gently swinging love songs. Only one of these, "I Only Have Eyes for You," became a national hit of any magnitude, peaking at Number 11 on the pop chart and remaining the group's most identifiable song today.

However, there is more to the Flamingos than that tune, as the selections on two excellent records attests. Intricate harmonizing, deeply-felt lead vocals, and the often-mesmerizing minimalist guitar work of Terry "Buzzy" Johnson characterize the group's recordings throughout its history, as is borne out by the performances from the various eras represented on the two albums left in print. Start with Rhino's *Best of*, notable both for its literate liner notes and for its comprehensiveness in covering selected high points from the years 1953 to 1960, by far the most productive and most important in a recording career that extended into the early Seventies. Chess's *Flamingos* is a must-have as well, though it lacks liner notes of any kind. Still, in covering the group's years on the Parrot-Checker label ('53–'56), the collection offers 12 songs not available on the Rhino set, as well as vintage Nate Nelson. *Flamingos* is further recommended for the inclusion of "Would I Be Crying," a tortured account of love gone wrong, that the group performed in the 1957 film *Rock, Rock, Rock* with such authority that their moment almost wiped out strong cameos by the likes of Chuck Berry and Frankie Lymon and the Teenagers. — D.M.

FLAT DUO JETS

★ ★ ★ **Flat Duo Jets (Dog Gone, 1989)**
★ ★ ★ ½ **Go Go Harlem Baby (Sky, 1991)**
★ ★ ★ **In Stereo (EP) (Sky, 1992)**
Flat Duo Jets founder-singer-guitarist Dexter Romweber is a happy minimalist—and a furiously rocking one. Backed by a drummer (occasionally joined by a bassist), Romweber turns out a kind of punkabilly that manages to incorporate some of the swagger of such Sun stars as Billy Lee Riley with an almost-thrash attack. Suicide's Alan Vega and early Nick Cave tried out something sort of like the Jets; but where they verged on the portentous or the obscure, this crew is fierce, funky fun. — P.E.

THE FLATLANDERS

★ ★ ★ ★ ½ **More a Legend Than a Band**
        (1972; Rounder, 1990)
What becomes a legend most? How about one monumental record, released in a configuration (8-track) that assures its immediate consignment to history and rumor, as the artists who made it go on to sort-of glory apart from each other? Meet the Flatlanders.

The group came together haphazardly in

Lubbock, Texas, in 1970, when Jimmie Dale Gilmore, Joe Ely, and Butch Hancock, having nothing better happening in their loosely defined careers, and sharing similar wide-ranging tastes in music, decided maybe they had a plan. So they did, and they pursued it together, Gilmore and Hancock contributing their own well-observed songs describing an unfriendly world closing in on them, supporting musicians coming and going like sunrise and sunset. One day the triumvirate that coalesced out on the flat land of west Texas found its music striking a deep vein inside them, being beholden on one hand to the entire sweep of country and mountain folk music of an Appalachian nature, on the other to nothing save the sort of brutal honesty that cuts into souls in the dark heart of a lonesome night.

In 1972 the triumvirate-plus-four found itself in a Nashville recording studio cutting what was to be an album for a label headed by Shelby Singleton, notable now for having bought up the Sun catalogue when Sam Phillips decided to bid adieu to the business. Gilmore's haunting meditation on "Dallas" was released as a promo single, garnered zippo response, and the entire project crashed and burned. Some time later an album by the Flatlanders, as the group came to be known, was issued as an 8-track and died an ignominious but predictable death before anyone had a clue as to what had been loosed upon the unsuspecting public. *More a Legend Than a Band*, as it turns out, is a great record. This is real outlaw music, years ahead of its time and years behind; it is the first blow of the new traditionalist movement, sharper and more penetrating than the anguished (and justly acclaimed) sides the late Gram Parsons produced in 1973.

Why do Gilmore's tremulous vocals seem so innocent while also suggesting a premonition of impending, overwhelming tragedy? Why is every romantic metaphor delivered so wistfully, in surrender to a truth that dictates love never works out in the end? Why does the eerie, mournful wail of Steve Wesson's musical saw seem to float free and clear in the room, a ghostly presence at once apart from and part of the strange parade of blasted souls described in these songs?

In the end, there may be no satisfactory explanation for the Flatlanders. Their record exists now for all to hear and to judge; inevitably, some will say "Good, not great." And they will be wrong. *More a Legend Than a Band* may be only a moment in

time, but what an extraordinary moment, bringing with it wonder, amazement, laughter, tears, horrors, exultations. Their moment may have passed, but the Flatlanders' time is forever.   — D.M.

BELA FLECK

★★★★ Crossing the Tracks (Rounder, 1979)
★★★ Natural Bridge (Rounder, 1982)
★★★★ Double Time (Rounder, 1984)
★★★ Deviation (Rounder, 1985)
★★★★ In Roads (Rounder, 1986)
★★★★ Daybreak (Rounder, 1987)
★★★★ Places (Rounder, 1987)
★★★½ Drive (Rounder, 1988)
★★★★ Bela Fleck and the Flecktones (Warner Bros., 1990)
★★★★ Flight of the Cosmic Hippo (Warner Bros., 1991)

Fleck is a banjo virtuoso, and that in itself is a singular achievement. But what truly makes his music exceptional is the way he has applied his astonishing ability to such unlikely ends. Sure, he plays bluegrass, and is a wizard at fleet-fingered Scruggs-style picking. But he's equally at home in bebop, fusion or any of the hybrid folk styles that have grown up around the new acoustic movement.

As such, though many of his albums start off with what might be considered a traditional bluegrass sound, where they end up is often impossible to predict. *Crossing the Tracks*, for instance, seems relatively straightforward when Fleck is left to the likes of "Dear Old Dixie" or "Texas Barbecue," but heads into uncharted territory when Fleck and his playmates rip through the jazzy changes of Chick Corea's "Spain." It's an astonishing bit of playing, but hardly prevents Fleck from ending the album with a wonderful old-timey tune called "Ain't Gonna Work Tomorrow." And though the music isn't quite as audacious on *Natural Bridge*, the musicians on hand—including David Grisman, Mark O'Connor and Ricky Scaggs—keep the music from getting dull. (Selections from these albums, as well as from a trio album with Tony Trischka and Bill Keith called *Fiddle Tunes for Banjo*, can be found on the CD compilation *Daybreak*.)

Double Time finds Fleck moving into the new acoustic camp with a set of ingenious, genre-hopping duets. Some, like "Sweet Rolls," with fellow picker John Hartford, are fairly traditional, while others—for instance, the electronically embellished "Light Speed"—are anything but. Still, the most interesting tracks are those like "Ladies and Gentlemen" (with cellist Darol Anger) that draw from traditional styles but take a wholly unique approach. In fact, Fleck's playing is so exciting in such circumstances that it's almost a disappointment to hear him revert to the relatively traditional sound of *Deviation*— almost, but not quite. *Deviation* may be more like a bluegrass album than *Double Time* is, but because Fleck cut the album with his then-bandmates in the New Grass Revival, there's plenty of experimentation. But *In Roads* more than makes up, for though it maintains a strong sense of roots, it pushes Fleck in a variety of new directions, from the quiet Celtic melancholy of "Ireland" to the jazzy interplay of the vibes-driven "Perplexed." (Highlights from these three albums can be found on the CD compilation *Places*.)

Fleck's last album for Rounder, *Drive*, is also something of a farewell to bluegrass. Masterfully played and featuring such stalwart soloists as Mark O'Connor, Jerry Douglas and Tony Rice, it neatly sums up Fleck's past, but offers not a clue about his future. No wonder. *Bela Fleck and the Flecktones* is built around one of the oddest ensembles in improvised music, a quartet that includes Howard Levy on harmonica and keyboards, Victor Wooten on electric bass, and Roy "Future Man" Wooten on Synth-axe/Drumitar, an electronic gizmo that's part guitar, part synth and part drum machine. Given the unorthodox nature of the instrumentation, it follows that the music would be similarly singular—and it is. Fleck may touch on many of the same sources he's always drawn from, but the music invariably pushes in an unexpected direction. "Half Moon Bay," for instance, starts out as a lovely neo-folk waltz but somehow sidesteps into a bit of bebop; "The Sinister Minister" flirts with funk even as Fleck finger-picks Scruggs-style arpeggios; and "Reflections of Lucy" is a jazzy reverie that somehow backs into "Lucy in the Sky with Diamonds." And, as the adventurous *Flight of the Cosmic Hippo* suggests, this band is just warming up. — J.D.C.

FLEETWOOD MAC

★★★★   **Then Play On (Warner Bros., 1970)**
★★★★   **Kiln House (Warner Bros., 1970)**
★★★   **Future Games (Warner Bros., 1971)**
★★★½   **Bare Trees (Warner Bros., 1972)**
★★½   **Penguin (Warner Bros., 1973)**

★★★   **Mystery to Me (Warner Bros., 1973)**
★★   **Heroes Are Hard to Find (Warner Bros., 1974)**
★★★★   **Fleetwood Mac (Reprise, 1975)**
★★★★★   **Rumours (Warner Bros., 1977)**
★★★½   **Tusk (Warner Bros., 1979)**
★★½   **Fleetwood Mac Live (Warner Bros., 1980)**
★★★   **Mirage (Warner Bros., 1982)**
★★★   **Tango in the Night (Warner Bros., 1987)**
★★★½   **Greatest Hits (Warner Bros., 1988)**
★★½   **Behind the Mask (Warner Bros., 1990)**

Fleetwood Mac began life as a blues band, named after its rhythm section: drummer Mick Fleetwood and bassist John McVie. The group's calling card, however, was its triple-guitar frontline: Peter Green, Jeremy Spencer and Danny Kirwan. Unlike the bulky mass of late '60s British boogie merchants, Fleetwood Mac wields a sure, sensitive hand with its oft-abused source material. The band's deleted early albums (*Fleetwood Mac* and *English Rose*) revolve around Peter Green's economical lead lines and Spencer's Elmore James–style slide attack; Carlos Santana plucked "Black Magic Woman" from *English Rose*, solo nearly intact.

Then Play On isn't the bloozy guitarfest that title might suggest. Emphasizing Danny Kirwan's folk-rock leanings and Mick Fleetwood's adventurous rhythmic sense alongside Green's virtuosity, Fleetwood Mac conjures a sparse, propulsive sound that's more reminiscent of California than Chicago or the Mississippi Delta. On the epic "Oh Well," an itchy electric-acoustic shuffle turns into a stately semi-classical fade; more compact cuts like "Coming Your Way" and "Before the Beginning" pack the tangled guitar lines into clear melodic structures. "Rattlesnake Shake" proves those strings can still sputter and burn, when required. After *Then Play On*, Green split for a brief solo career (*End of the Game*) and early retirement. It was only the first of many personnel changes.

With Kirwan and Spencer in control, *Kiln House* is a low-key charmer. The gently rockin' tributes to Buddy Holly (all three of 'em!) point out the difference between loose and sloppy, while the orgasmic guitar workouts (all three of 'em!) build to lazy, quivering peaks. Not long after that album came out, Spencer left, and Fleetwood Mac was down to one guitarist. However, the addition of Christine McVie (nee Perfect) on keyboards and vocals turned out to be a key choice. Replacement guitarist Bob Welch never quite gelled with the rest of the band, though, despite years of trying. Flashes of Fleetwood Mac's latter-day pop sound can now be detected on the band's transitional albums: Christine's disarming "Show Me a Smile" on *Future Games*, the smooth-talking title track of *Bare Trees*. Taken individually, however, these fair-to-middling LPs are too scattershot to hold much interest. Danny Kirwan left the group after *Bare Trees*, and then Fleetwood Mac floundered for several years—split between homogenized heaviness (Bob Welch) and a quieter mainstream approach (Christine McVie). The group nearly splintered for good at one point; when Welch left in 1974 the McVies and Mick Fleetwood went back to square one.

Stevie Nicks and Lindsey Buckingham were a young folk-rock duo with one unremarkable album (*Buckingham-Nicks*, now deleted) under their belts when they joined Fleetwood Mac. Her sultry voice and his songwriting knack provided a focus for the group's fledging pop ambitions; Nicks and Buckingham not only fit in, they stimulated the core trio. Christine McVie responded with a brace of catchy songs, while John McVie and Mick Fleetwood remained prominent in the smoothed-out mix; this is easy-listening music with a definite kick. *Fleetwood Mac* went to Number One in 1976, easily outdistancing all the band's previous efforts. "Rhiannon" establishes Nicks's seductive sirenlike presence, while "Say You Love Me" unfurls Christine McVie's wry melodic edge. Unlike many blockbusters, however, the surrounding songs nearly equal the hits here. The bouncy opener "Monday Morning" and the heavy centerpiece "World Turning" let Buckingham strut his tuneful stuff, though overall the pace never really slacks.

Rumours is even better: this album not only went to Number One, it stayed there 31 weeks. Fleetwood Mac's cast of voices cuts even deeper when you consider that the two couples in the group were breaking up as the album went down. Buckingham's "Go Your Own Way" and Nicks's "Dreams" spell out two clear takes on a romantic dilemma. *Rumours* can be heard as a dialogue between a loose circle of estranged lovers, culminating with "The Chain" (written by the entire group). After striking such a perfect match between self-expression and commerciality,

Fleetwood Mac succumbed to artiness. The double LP *Tusk* reveals Lindsey Buckingham's secret fixation: to become Brian Wilson, perhaps with a touch of Brian Eno thrown in. "Sara" maintains the pop profile, but the bulk of *Tusk* sounds cold and fussy next to the emotional heat of *Rumours*. Returning to simple pleasures on *Mirage*, Fleetwood Mac seems to have lost its spirit. Reconvening again on *Tango in the Night* (1987), Fleetwood Mac carries on as if it was still 1982—or 1977. The hits "Big Love" and (especially) Christine McVie's "Little Lies" surge with all the relaxed soft-rock grace of yore but none of the quiet fire, hinting at a premature nostalgia. Buckingham quit the band prior to a 1987 tour; in retrospect, that last straw may have broken this band's back. Buckingham's L.A. cowboy replacements (Rick Vito and Billy Burnette) add little to the washed-out *Behind the Mask*. A band that practically became a brand-name franchise in the late '70s, Fleetwood Mac set a standard of quality that's proven tough to maintain—or equal. — M.C.

THE FLEETWOODS
★★★ Best of the Fleetwoods (Rhino, 1990)
The trio of Gary Troxel, Barbara Ellis and Gretchen Christopher formed while in high school in Olympia, Washington, and quickly perfected the art of close, soft harmony in support of tearjerk love songs ("The Great Imposter," "Tragedy," "Mr. Blue") and great makeout love songs ("Come Softly to Me," "Outside My Window"). There was nothing deep about the Fleetwoods, but their voices blended in a sound singularly elegant and pristine, singularly fragile and compelling. Among all the vocal groups of their time purveying tender ballads, the Fleetwoods' consistency was impressive: nine Top Forty hits between 1959 and 1963, two Number Ones (their first single, "Come Softly to Me," and "Mr. Blue," both in 1959), and another Top Ten with their cover version of Thomas Wayne's 1959 hit, "Tragedy." Frighteningly square in appearance—the girls draped in crinoline, the boy in the most conservative of suits—and by all accounts statues onstage, the trio functioned most effectively as a studio entity, where their often intricate vocal blends were supported by some of the best studio musicians in Los Angeles—Glen Campbell and Leon Russell are on many of the group's '60s sides, as well as Billie Holiday's bassist, Red Callendar. That their songs hold up better today than those of,

say, the Chordettes, who were mining much the same turf, is a tribute to the persuasive powers of those voices in putting over good material, particularly the original contributions from such writers as Hal David ("Outside My Window") and Jackie DeShannon ("[He's] The Great Imposter"). The Fleetwoods staggered into the mid-'60s trying to adapt their sound to better suit the era; alas, these efforts failed, but are documented here via the trio's woeful version of "Before and After" (which became a hit when recorded by Chad and Jeremy in 1965), and a conventional reading of the Toys' hit, "A Lover's Concerto," that is sorely missing the original's quirky lead vocal. A final, unsuccessful stab at a hit came in the form of "Climb Ev'ry Mountain," from *The Sound of Music* soundtrack. Again the voices are there, but the concept didn't fly. Only time had flown, leaving the Fleetwoods behind. — D.M.

THE FLESHTONES
  ★ ★   **Up-Front (EP) (I.R.S., 1980)**
  ★ ★½ **Roman Gods (I.R.S., 1981)**
  ★ ★   **Blast Off (ROIR, 1982)**
★ ★ ★   **Hexbreaker! (I.R.S., 1983)**
  ★ ★   **Speed Connection (Fr. I.R.S., 1985)**
★ ★ ★   **Speed Connection II (I.R.S., 1985)**
  ★ ★½ **Fleshtones Vs. Reality (Emergo, 1987)**
  ★ ★½ **Living Legends: Best of the Fleshtones (I.R.S., 1989)**
Good-hearted but basically mediocre garage revivalists, the Fleshtones understood the music's basic chemistry—what settings to use on a Farfisa, how much surf guitar is needed to flesh out a hook, when to use fuzztone and when to break out the maracas—but never seemed to find a formula that worked. That's not to say the group didn't have its moments, but the sad fact is that the Fleshtones only got close to album-length quality twice: In the studio with *Hexbreaker!*, thanks to songs like "Screamin' Skull" and "New Scene"; and live on *Speed Connection II* (be sure to avoid the import-only *Speed Connection*, which offers inferior renditions of nearly the same songs). — J.D.C.

FLIPPER
  ★ ★ ★½ **Album—Generic Flipper (1981; Def American, 1992)**
★ ★ ★ ★ **Gone Fishin' (Subterranean, 1984)**
  ★ ★½ **Blow'n Chunks (ROIR, 1984)**
★ ★ ★   **Public Flipper Limited Live 1980– 1985 (Subterranean, 1986)**

★ ★ ★ ★ **Sex Bomb Baby! (Subterranean, 1988)**
Few things sum up the Flipper aesthetic as neatly as this slogan, which is spray-painted across the side of Flipper's van (as pictured on the cover of *Gone Fishin'*): "Flipper suffered for their music—now it's your turn." Born out of the San Francisco punk scene and conceived as a reaction against the lockstep rebellion of California hardcore, Flipper's sound was a mass of contradictions. Flipper could be astonishingly noisy, with feedback, distortion and outright dissonance competing in the cacophony, yet at the same time there was always a strong sense of melody and structure to its songs. And though the pace rarely moved beyond a mid-tempo trot, there was more rhythmic energy to the typical Flipper dirge than could be found on a half-dozen hardcore albums.

Album—Generic Flipper establishes the band's sound as well as its sense of humor, and is noteworthy both for "Ever," a sneeringly funny send-up of punk nihilism, and "Sex Bomb," a one-line riff rocker so gleefully simplistic it makes "Louie Louie" seem like Mahler's Ninth. It's fun, but nowhere near as consistent as *Gone Fishin'*, which boasts smarter jokes, tighter songs and a more richly anarchic spirit. *Blow'n Chunks* and *Public Flipper Limited* are both live albums, the former being the lo-fi document of a 1983 CBGB show, the latter a warts-and-all collection of highlights from five years of tour tapes. *Sex Bomb Baby!* is a more-or-less greatest hits set, and includes the landmark early singles "Love Canal" and "Ha Ha Ha." — J.D.C.

A FLOCK OF SEAGULLS
★ ★ ★   **A Flock of Seagulls (Jive, 1982)**
  ★ ★½ **Listen (Jive, 1983)**
  ★½ **The Story of a Young Heart (Jive, 1984)**
  ★   **A Dream Come True (Jive, 1986)**
★ ★ ★   **The Best of a Flock of Seagulls (Jive, 1987)**
In its prime, Liverpool's A Flock of Seagulls was essentially a two-gimmick band, the first being its blend of minor-key melodies and low-tech electronics, the second being singer Mike Score's hair, an astonishingly ambitious bit of pompadour that spilled over his forehead like a breaking wave. Score's look, along with the arty urgency of the Bill Nelson-produced "Telecommunication," managed to lend *A Flock of Seagulls* a certain cutting-edge sheen at the time, but it

was the old-fashioned hooks of "I Ran" that earned the group an audience. With *Listen*, the Gulls pretty much repeat that approach, although with considerably less pizzazz; the album's most melodic number, "Wishing (If I Had a Photograph of You)," drags, while the attempts at techno-cool— "(It's Not Me) Talking" and its ilk—now seem laughably dated. Things begin to go downhill fast with *The Story of a Young Heart,* a totally clueless concept album packed with quasi-romantic piffle like "The More You Live, the More You Love," and finally reach rock-bottom with *A Dream Come True*, which lacks focus, hits or even a reason for existing. *The Best of a Flock of Seagulls* is exactly what it claims to be— which is to say, not much. — J.D.C.

FLYING BURRITO BROTHERS

★ ★ ★ ★ ★   **The Gilded Palace of Sin (A&M, 1969)**
★ ★ ★½   **Burrito Deluxe (A&M, 1970)**
★ ★ ★   **The Flying Burrito Brothers (1971; A&M/Mobile Fidelity Sound Lab, 1991)**
★ ★ ★   **Last of the Red-Hot Burritos (A&M, 1972)**
★ ★ ★½   **Close Up the Honky Tonks (A&M, 1972)**
★ ★ ★ ★   **Farther Along: The Best of the Flying Burrito Brothers (A&M, 1988)**

After a brief stint with the Byrds, resulting in the country-flavored *Sweetheart of the Rodeo,* Gram Parsons took his vision of "cosmic American music" and joined forces with Texas bassist Chris Ethridge and like-minded ex-Byrd Chris Hillman to form the Flying Burrito Brothers. Their first—and most satisfying—effort, *The Gilded Palace of Sin* (now, unfortunately, deleted) strives for a deep understanding of the honky-tonk tradition, striking beyond the good-timin' Saturday night veneer at hard-core country's emotional depths. The sound is a true fusion: volatile, shaky at times, but always stimulating. The band enlisted Sneeky Pete Kleinow on pedal steel, who blended the instrument's characteristic whine with fuzzy rock guitar riffs. Songs mix traditional country themes with contemporary specifics. At times it's pleasantly effective, other times it's enticingly weird. That psychedelic riff at the end of "Hippie Boy" creeps along like a longhair walking past a church parking lot on Sunday morning, while "My Uncle" is a twangy draft-dodger's road anthem. Parsons's breaking tenor voice isn't a powerful instrument, but his matter-of-fact tone and affectless delivery speak of the

personal commitment that's so central to country singing. Covering the Southern soul classics "Dark End of the Street" and "Do Right Woman" in high honky-tonk fashion, Parsons and the Burritos unearth some deeply buried roots. The emotional high points, however, lie within originals, "Hot Burrito #1" and "Hot Burrito #2."

Burrito Deluxe, also out of print, jacks up the rock quotient, and includes the addition of future Eagle Bernie Leadon. The results are far less intriguing, though the cover of the Stones' "Wild Horses" may well be definitive. The best tracks from *Deluxe* are included on the *Farther Along* set; so is most of the debut, though "Hippie Boy" and "My Uncle" are inexplicably absent. The deleted anthology *Close Up the Honky Tonks* does include these songs along with cuts from the first two albums and outtakes.

After Parsons split from the Burritos in 1970, guitarist Rick Roberts joined in with Chris Hillman. *The Flying Burrito Brothers* hints at the encroaching blandness that would later dog both Roberts and Hillman. However, *Last of the Red Hot Burritos* is a fiery farewell from this edition of the group. Bolstered by bluegrass fiddler Byron Berline on several cuts, the Hillman-led Burritos charge through a program of mostly Parsons-era material with a verve that's entirely missing from their other work. — M.C.

DAN FOGELBERG

★ ★   **Home Free (Columbia, 1972)**
★ ★ ★   **Souvenirs (Full Moon/Epic, 1974)**
★ ★   **Captured Angel (Full Moon/Epic, 1975)**
★ ★   **Netherlands (Full Moon/Epic, 1977)**
★ ★   **Phoenix (Full Moon/Epic, 1979)**
★ ★½   **The Innocent Age (Full Moon/Epic, 1981)**
★ ★½   **Greatest Hits (Full Moon/Epic, 1981)**
★ ★   **Windows And Walls (Full Moon/Epic, 1984)**
★ ★½   **High Country Snows (Full Moon/Epic, 1985)**
★ ★   **Exiles (Full Moon/Epic, 1987)**
★ ★   **The Wild Places (Full Moon/Epic, 1990)**
★ ★   **Dan Fogelberg Live—Greetings From the West (Full Moon/Epic, 1991)**

WITH TIM WEISBERG

★ ★   **Twin Sons Of Different Mothers (Full Moon/Epic, 1978)**

Dan Fogelberg's debut album, *Home Free*, got lost in the first glut of singer-songwriter releases. The Colorado-based bard bounced back with the soft-rocking *Souvenirs*, produced by Joe Walsh. Fogelberg's hushed, breathy delivery suits the unhurried catchiness of "Part of the Plan," but the lyrics are pure mellowspeak. The album-closing opus ("There's a Place in the World for a Gambler") portends the pomp to come.

Fogelberg possesses a mean neoclassical streak. String-laden cuts like "Promises Made" (from *Netherlands*) resemble some bizarre hybrid of the Moody Blues and early James Taylor. Many listeners find Fogelberg reassuring, though. He racked up fairly consistent hit singles through the early '80s, beginning with "Power of Gold" from *Twin Sons of Different Mothers* (a 1978 collaboration with lite-jazz flutist Tim Weisberg). His artistic and commercial peak is *The Innocent Age*. Banal and overblown, this autobiographical concept album also spawned three Top Ten singles: "Hard to Say," "Same Olde Lang Syne" and "Leader of the Band." *Greatest Hits* covers the basics.

Fogelberg is often cited as an influence by country singers like Garth Brooks and Clint Black, but a latter-day crossover seems unlikely: There's barely a trace of twang in his entire catalogue, and the all-star bluegrass backing on *Snows* doesn't do much more for his sensitive murmur than the orchestral maneuvers of yore. *The Wild Places* resembles a late-'70s Linda Ronstadt session: there's a slick vintage cover version (The Cascades' "Rhythm of the Rain"), a borrowed gem from an unknown songwriter (Bruce Cockburn's "Lovers in a Dangerous Time"), an efficent band of studio heavies. But the six-minute epic ("The Spirit Trail") turns out to be a hackneyed attempt at "modern rock," not a symphonic excursion into Fogelberg's restless soul. Still, his most popular albums have endured beyond all critical predictions. — M.C.

JOHN FOGERTY

★ ★½ **Blue Ridge Rangers** (1973; Fantasy, 1991)
★ ★ ★ **John Fogerty** (Asylum, 1975)
★ ★ ★ **Centerfield** (Warner Bros., 1985)
★ ★½ **Eye of the Zombie** (Warner Bros., 1986)

John Fogerty's solo albums prove decisively that Creedence Clearwater Revival was a phenomenal band. While his own raw guitar and rawer vocals clearly dominated America's best straight rock outfit of the early '70s, the ramshackle grace of CCR's rhythm section provided crucial, spontaneous verve. Urgency, in fact, was

Creedence's hallmark—the band responded to its fitful times with songs crammed with messages and metaphors of tumult and apocolypse—Vietnam, America's own civil war, and the crashing end of the utopian '60s provoked remarkable songwriting from Fogerty, and great, ragged playing from the group.

While crafty and sometimes entertaining, Fogerty's own records are missing exactly the spontaneity that comes with inspired collaboration—and the edge of his lyrics is gone. No longer confronted with high-profile upheaval, he hasn't much to say about America's subtler, ongoing crisis—he trades mainly in nostalgia or writes "good time" stuff. A well-meaning attempt to pay tribute to Hank Williams, Jimmie Rodgers, Merle Haggard and trad country music, *Blue Ridge Rangers* is actually Fogerty alone in the studio, playing everything. Such hermeticism, of course, is the antithesis of the familial spirit of classic country—and while Fogerty's playing is impressive, it's a cold virtuosity. Even more unfortunate are his vocals. With Creedence, Fogerty expertly mimicked blues belters (Screamin' Jay Hawkins), but steered wisely clear of its subtler interpreters (Muddy Waters, Robert Johnson). *Blue Ridge* finds him deaf to the complex grace of country singing—he hits all the notes; he misses all the nuance. On *John Fogerty*'s "Rockin' All Over the World" and "Almost Saturday Night" he returns, thankfully, to rock & roll. A solid set, if a little too heavy on (pro forma) oldies, it's Creedence-lite. Hailed at the time as a return to form, *Centerfield* (1985) no longer holds up. "The Old Man Down the Road" is functional swamp rock; "Rock and Roll Girls" is charming, but slight; and the attempts at significance of the sort Fogerty once managed so effortlessly fall flat—the title track's baseball-player/journeyman-rocker metaphor leads nowhere, as does the baby-boom elegy "I Saw It on TV." That the music at times tries to extend beyond Fogerty's trad rock limits bespeaks commendable ambition—but the syn-drum break on "Vanz Kant Danz" is the kind of thing a Spandau Ballet roadie could handle with more panache. The lovely "Sail Away" from *Eye of the Zombie* features Fogerty's best singing in years; the rest of the record, however—all studio gloss and labored funking—only marks the highpoint of his professionalism. And for this soulful artist, "professionalism" should be a dirty word. — P.E.

FOGHAT

★ ★   Foghat (1972; Bearsville/Rhino, 1987)
★   Foghat (1973; Bearsville/Rhino, 1987)
★   Energized (1974; Bearsville/Rhino, 1987)
★ ★   Rock and Roll Outlaws (1974; Bearsville/Rhino, 1987)
★ ★½ Fool for the City (1975; Bearsville/Rhino, 1987)
★ ★   Night Shift (1976; Bearsville/Rhino, 1987)
★ ★   Live (1977; Bearsville/Rhino, 1987)
★ ★   Stone Blue (1978; Bearsville/Rhino, 1987)
★ ★½ The Best of Foghat (Rhino, 1988)
★ ★½ The Best of Foghat, Volume 2 (Rhino, 1992)

Lumbering blooze and lunk-headed boogie from the ex-lead singer and slide guitarist (Dave Peverett) of Savoy Brown—breeding always tells. Foghat is even more metallic and unswinging than Savoy Brown, if that's possible. The group's one great moment—and that's about how long it lasts—occurs during the brontosaurus-stomping "Slow Ride" (from *Fool for the City*, 1975). Out of nowhere comes a thumping, finger-popping funk bass line, cutting through those sinewy power chords like a butcher's knife. Apart from that, Foghat tends to latch onto a barking, primieval rock riff—strictly one per song, please—and ride the sucker into the mud. If that sounds like something you'd dig, two volumes of *The Best of Foghat* await. Don't forget galoshes. — M.C.

RED FOLEY

★ ★ ★ Beyond the Sunset (MCA, 1981)
★ ★ ★ ★ Red Foley: Country Music Hall of Fame Series (MCA, 1991)

An expressive, personable baritone voice, good looks and ingratiating way with an audience won Red Foley a loyal, devoted following from the time of his first hit in 1941, "Old Shep" (a wrenching memorial to his dog that the young Elvis Presley sang to win a talent contest; Elvis recorded "Old Shep" on his second RCA album, as well), up to his death in 1968. He was also an important figure in the birth of the Nashville recording industry, being among the first artists to record exclusively in Music City. As his appeal grew and he branched out beyond radio and records into television, he helped country music gain exposure in urban areas outside the South. Foley drew upon a variety of music for inspiration, and in his career ranged far and wide in his selections of material. *Beyond the Sunset* is a collection of hymns, sung in a stately, reserved manner, with lush strings and a choir supporting Foley's readings. No question that he's cloying in his testimonials—the spoken sections of some of these songs are tough to take if you have a limited capacity for the sort of appeals you might hear from a TV evangelist—but when Foley sings he brings authority to his material. This set includes his version of Thomas Dorsey's magisterial "Peace in the Valley," another Foley recording that served as a model for a Presley cover, and a syncopated arrangement of "Just a Closer Walk With Thee."

The Country Music Hall of Fame set is more representative of the scope of Foley's work. It, too, includes "Old Shep" and "Peace in the Valley," but adds some of his significant sides cut in the late '40s and early '50s. Notable among these are "Tennessee Saturday Night," a 1949 recording informed by R&B; "Sugarfoot Rag," also from 1949, featuring a spectacular guitar solo by Hank Garland; "Chattanoogie Shoe Shine Boy," from 1950, which stands in all its rhythmic propulsion as one of the first country records to cross over to the pop charts with great success; "Deep Blues" and "Midnight," which make clear to doubters the impact that blues artists had on Foley's style. When country's sound hardened into honky-tonk in the early '50s, Foley was there in fine shape with labelmate Kitty Wells on the duet "One by One." Foley had no hits after 1959, but he remained a popular figure in country music up to his death. The songs collected here show why. — D.M.

STEVE FORBERT

★ ★ ★ Alive on Arrival (Nemperor/Epic, 1978)
★ ★½ Jackrabbit Slim (Nemperor/Epic, 1979)
★ ★½ Little Stevie Orbit (Nemperor/Epic, 1980)
★ ★½ Steve Forbert (Nemperor/Epic, 1982)
★ ★ ★ Streets of This Town (Geffen, 1988)
★ ★ ★ The American in Me (Geffen, 1992)

An observant songwriting style and a bristling solo-acoustic attack distinguish *Alive on Arrival*, Steve Forbert's critically lauded debut album. Rising out of the punk-dominated New York scene of the late '70s, this young singer-songwriter couldn't afford to be too sensitive. The oft-cited "New Dylan" tag hangs on Forbert as well as anybody, though his source material seems to be the sparser *Freewheelin' Bob*

Dylan rather than the full-blown rock & roll *Highway 61 Revisited*. Unfortunately, Forbert's wryly reported narratives and thumbnail sketches never quite add up to memorable songs; *Alive on Arrival* is more notable for its form than its content. Producer John Simon, who orchestrated Leonard Cohen's groundbreaking debut album, steers Forbert in more varied stylistic directions on *Jackrabbit Slim*. "Romeo's Tune" provided Forbert with a Top Twenty hit in 1979, but it also revealed his cloying self-conscious side. What sounds like a promising raw talent on the debut turns into a crippling lack of focus on *Slim* and its scattershot follow-ups *Little Stevie Orbit* and *Steve Forbert*. After a long silence, Forbert quietly re-emerged with *Streets of This Town*. Produced by Garry Tallent (of E Street Band fame), *Streets* matches Forbert's still-developing writing voice—now more assured, more mature and more cynical— with a foursquare traditional rockbeat. If that album leans toward obvious Springsteen derivations, *The American in Me* fitfully lurches into the land of John Mellencamp and pre-Hollywood Bob Seger. The title track is a little too obvious, perhaps. But overall, country-rock producer Pete Anderson proves to be the best collaborator Forbert's had to date. He frames some carefully carved reflections on thirtysomething rebellion ("Born Too Late," "If You're Waiting on Me," "Responsibility") in firm, jangle-free acoustic-electric settings. Forbert strips down to just-acoustic on the centerpiece "You Cannot Win 'Em All." It's suprisingly effective, at least until a honking nostalgic harmonica solo reminds you where Steve Forbert's roots lie. — M.C.

FORCE M.D.'S
★★   Love Letters (Tommy Boy, 1984)
★★½ Chillin' (Tommy Boy, 1986)
★★   Touch and Go (Tommy Boy, 1987)
★★   Step to Me (Tommy Boy/Reprise, 1990)
★★½ For Lovers and Others (Tommy Boy, 1992)
Along with Planet Patrol, the Force M.D.'s were one of the first hip-hop harmony groups, a gimmick the group virtually runs into the ground on *Love Letters* (although the playful "Itchin' for a Scratch" redeems its worst excesses). *Chillin'* gives the group its most enduring hit with the Jimmy Jam/ Terry Lewis ballad "Tender Love," but the group was unable to manage a follow-up, and as the subsequent albums show,

gradually deteriorated into soul-harmony mediocrity. Still, the ballad-based best-of, *For Lovers and Others*, does have its moments. — J.D.C.

LITA FORD
★★★   Lita (RCA, 1988)
★★½ Stilleto (RCA, 1990)
★★   Dangerous Curves (RCA, 1991)
Produced by glam-pop meister Mike Chapman, the former Runaways guitarist's solo debut fulfills the closet metal fanatic's wildest daydream. From an opener called "Back to the Cave" to a speedy rave co-written with Motörhead's Lemmy ("Can't Catch Me"), from a full-force power ballad ("Kiss Me Deadly") to a horror-movie duet with Ozzy Osbourne ("Close My Eyes Forever"): *Lita* is stacked with sinful treats and guilty pleasures. The inevitable airbrushing and sonic polishing begins with the next album; the totally staid treatment given Alice Cooper's oh-so-ripe "Only Women Bleed" reveals *Stilleto*'s dull edge. *Dangerous Curves* is straightforward pop-metal formula; everything's in place except for a couple of hooks. It's a pity: Lita Ford's first album hinted that she understood the difference between trashy fun and the usual garbage. — M.C.

TENNESSEE ERNIE FORD
★★★ Hymns (Capitol, 1957)
★★★★ Spirituals (Capitol, 1957)
★★★ He Touched Me (Word, 1977)
★★★ There's a Song in My Heart (Word, 1982)
★★★ Keep Looking Up (Word, 1985)
★★★ 16 Tons of Boogie/ The Best of Tennessee Ernie Ford (Rhino, 1989)
★★★★ All-Time Greatest Hymns (Curb, 1990)
★★★ Capitol Collectors Series (Capitol, 1991)
★★★ Country Gospel Classics, Vol. 1 & 2 (Capitol, 1991)
There was a time in the mid-'50s when Tennessee Ernie Ford was among the most popular entertainers in America, with a top-rated TV show and records that sold in the millions. It was his foreboding reading of Merle Travis's "Sixteen Tons" in 1955 that ensured Ford's legend: the song was Number One for eight weeks and remains one of the best-selling singles in history.

Long before "Sixteen Tons," Ford had been cutting interesting singles for Capitol Records in a country-boogie style that had its genesis in mid-'40s recordings by Red Foley, Johnny Bond and the Delmore

Brothers. Eighteen of these tracks, recorded between 1949 and 1953 ("Sixteen Tons" being the lone cut to fall outside this period), are collected on *16 Tons of Boogie*; the Capitol Collectors Series entry takes him from the late '40s to the late '50s (one cut, "Hicktown," dates from 1965), and includes several unreleased tracks. Together these two albums flesh out the scope of this artist's history. Ford worked his deep baritone voice and careful diction to good effect on songs ranging from beat-heavy material such as "Shotgun Boogie" and cover versions of R&B-based songs on the order of Willie Mabon's "I Don't Know."

But Ford was preeminent in the area of country gospel. On his best-sellers *Hymns* (1957) and *Spirituals* (also from 1957), Ford swings and gets into some lively call-and-response with the background chorus. Capitol has reissued these recordings on its 1991 release, *Country Gospel Classics*. Curb Records put some of the tracks off these two albums and other of Ford's spiritual recordings on *All-Time Greatest Hits*. Ford's Word albums are also comprised of religious music, but are routine in comparison to his Capitol releases. — D.M.

JULIA FORDHAM

★★★½ **Julia Fordham (Virgin, 1988)**
★★★½ **Porcelain (Virgin, 1989)**
★★★½ **Swept (Virgin, 1991)**

Fordham's records reveal a singer-songwriter driven intriguingly berserk by hypersensitivity and high jazz aspirations. Enraptured by Sarah Vaughan and every other power-voiced diva, Fordham sings elegantly, carefully and coldly, squeezing her every song in a stranglehold of taste. All sly chord arrangements and studied textures, her musings on love and pain cross feverish poetasting with New Age wisdom. Few writers since Laura Nyro have labored so hard for quivering significance. The overall atmospheric effect, however, is fairly gorgeous. Expert session players lay down lush carpets of sound, and Fordham's force of personality is persuasive. On every number, she pulls out all the stops. — P.E.

FOREIGNER

★★★½ **Foreigner (Atlantic, 1977)**
★★★½ **Double Vision (Atlantic, 1978)**
★★★ **Head Games (Atlantic, 1979)**
★★★½ **4 (Atlantic, 1981)**
★★★★ **Records (Atlantic, 1982)**
★★★½ **Agent Provocateur (Atlantic, 1984)**
★★★ **Inside Information (Atlantic, 1987)**
★★★½ **Unusual Heat (Atlantic, 1991)**

Boston, Heart and Styx, among others, deserve equal credit for inventing '70s arena-rock, but no band has parlayed the sound of the stadiums with such dependable smarts as Foreigner. Mainman Mick Jones is the key to the band's success. A battle-scarred, hit-savvy veteran who played with the artful organ-rock outfit Spooky Tooth before going platinum by founding Foreigner, Jones is not only a master of the hook, but a guitarist of unerring efficiency. In Foreigner's early days, former King Crimson multi-instrumentalist Ian McDonald added a touch of class, but Jones's passion for a streamlined sound meant that the band was soon reduced to a smarter, trimmer rhythm section core.

And, of course, there's ace vocalist Lou Gramm. Not quite a stylist on the order of Paul Rodgers, Gramm was still one of the finest singers in all of pop metal. In Foreigner, Gramm's gift lay in roughening up Jones's shimmering grooves; Gramm brought an R&B, almost bluesy style to bear on the band's rockers, and in time became the Pavarotti of the power ballad.

Foreigner's catalogue of car-stereo hits is nearly unrivaled: "Feels Like the First Time," "Cold as Ice" (*Foreigner*); "Hotblooded" (*Double Vision*); "Dirty White Boy" (*Head Games*); "Waiting for a Girl Like You" (*4*). The canny Jones keeps the sound fresh by working with different producers on each album—and he's got a knack for adding exactly the surprising flourish (Junior Walker's sax coda on "Urgent," for example) that makes a song take off. Foreigner's high point came with the release of *Agent Provocateur*'s "I Want to Know What Love Is"—backed by a gospel choir, Gramm belted away with commendable anguish. *Inside Information* also displayed his growth as a vocalist, and the record's synth-work saw Foreigner keeping pace with the times. By the time of *Unusual Heat*, however, Jones had asked Gramm to depart. New singer Johnny Edwards was ultra-competent, but he hadn't yet developed a distinctive style. *Heat*, as a whole, marked a return to full-out rocking of Foreigner's reliable standard. *Records* is the group's greatest hits collection. Every bar band in the world has burned through several copies. — P.E.

THE FOUR ACES

★★★ **Best of the Four Aces (MCA, 1974)**

Among the first of the Four groups (Four Coins, Four Deuces, Four Freshmen, Four Lads, Four Preps, and others) that proliferated throughout the '50s, the Four

Aces hailed from Chester, Pennsylvania, and set the standard for smooth quartet harmonizing over swinging orchestral arrangements and lush, string-laden productions. The Aces' vocals were invariably light (they were practicing the politics of joy before the term had been coined), impeccably enunciated, and indicative of a world hungry for happy endings. Even a song as inherently wistful as "Maybe You'll Be There" was rendered almost cheerily, with cloying strings providing only the slightest hint of sadness clouding the Aces' happy-face ambience.

That said, it's also true that the Four Aces' smooth pop sound, however unchallenging, epitomized the apex of Hit Parade offerings in the early '50s. They defined middle of the road, and were rewarded in kind with consistent Top Ten and Top Twenty singles between 1951 and 1954, including a Number One single in '54 with the theme to *Three Coins in the Fountain*. In fact, movie themes and sentimental love songs found the quartet at its best, when baroque arrangements provided the emotional pull lacking in the vocals. This *Best of* package highlights many of the Four Aces hits, including "Tell Me Why," a Number Two single in 1951 that was a Top Twenty hit for Bobby Vinton in 1964; Vinton had an even bigger hit—a Number One—in 1963 with another Aces tune on this set, "There! I've Said It Again." Also of note here is the song "It's a Woman's World," the theme from a fascinating but obscure Hollywood film of 1954 that depicted the female of the species in charge of everything from the home to the corporate board room. — D.M.

THE FOUR FRESHMAN
★ **The Four Freshmen Live at Butler University With Stan Kenton and His Orchestra (Creative World, 1972)**
★ ★ **Capitol Collectors Series (Capitol, 1991)**
Two of the original members remain from the quartet that formed at Butler University in Indiana in 1947, and two of the group's 30-plus albums remain in print. A little bit of the Four Freshmen goes a long way, though. In the Freshmen's close harmonies and in the nasally high tenor lead are the roots of the Beach Boys' sound, but its hard to get through material as unrelievedly sweet and cloying as theirs. They have their champions, though, particularly devotees of light jazz who admire the quartet for its various members' facility on several instruments, a quality that sets them apart from most other vocal groups of the Fifties.

Capitol Collectors Series serves up the group's best-known songs, including its only Top Twenty hit, the saccharine "Graduation Day," from 1956.

You'd think being back on campus might inspire the Freshmen to break out "Graduation Day" for one more lap, but such is not the case. Instead the quartet, self-accompanied and with the Stan Kenton Orchestra, serves up pleasant harmonies, spirited instrumental work and stale jokes, and reduces one of the few good songs here, Bacharach-David's "Walk On By," to an academic exercise. Not much to hang your hat on. — D.M.

THE FOUR PREPS
★ ★ ★ **Capitol Collector's Series (Capitol, 1989)**
In the spirit of the Four Aces, the Four Lads and the Four Freshmen, the Four Preps offered close, four-part harmonizing on largely sentimental songs concerning the vagaries of love—real moon-spoon-June kind of stuff. Relentlessly upbeat, the quartet had two Top Five singles out of the box in 1958, and stayed in the Top Forty through 1961 before finally tapping out in 1964 with "A Letter to the Beatles"—like the Beatles needed advice from the Four Preps. The Capitol Collector's Series includes all the essential Preps tracks—"Big Man," "26 Miles," "Down by the Station." — D.M.

THE FOUR SEASONS
★ **The Four Seasons Sing Big Hits by Burt Bacharach/Hal David/Bob Dylan (1965; Rhino, 1988)**
★ ★ ★ **Working My Way Back to You (1966; Rhino, 1988)**
★ ★ ★ ★ **25th Anniversary Collection (Rhino, 1987)**
★ ★ ★ ★ ★ **Anthology (Rhino, 1988)**
★ ★ **Rarities, Volume 1 (Rhino, 1990)**
★ ★ **Rarities, Volume 2 (Rhino, 1990)**
With the Four Seasons, the more they recorded, the worse they got. And the drop was a long one, because in the '60s, the Four Seasons were about as good a band as any in rock & roll. Blessed with intelligent material from outstanding songwriters such as Bob Gaudio (who joined the group in 1961 after a stint with the Royal Teens, for whom he wrote the hit "Short Shorts"), Bob Crewe and Sandy Linzer; adventurous arrangements by Charlie Callelo; grand, Spector-style production courtesy of Crewe, who would use handclaps, tambourines, foot stomps and, it seemed, any gadget he could

get his hands on to create a percussive effect; and a vocal blend that had its roots in street-corner harmony, early R&B, and classic American pop, the Four Seasons were omnipresent on the charts from 1962 to 1967, racking up worldwide sales of 80 million copies of extraordinary records.

In 1975, however, a new configuration of the group assembled around lead singer Frankie Valli and proceeded to turn out some execrable pop. Worse still, someone convinced Frankie Valli he had the makings of a Vegas crooner, which resulted in a clutch of loathesome, virtually unlistenable singles—half-baked love songs like "My Eyes Adored You"; a putrid, assembly-line disco effort, "Swearin' to God"; the annoying title song from the equally annoying film Grease. Gaudio and Crewe were among the driving forces behind this second generation Seasons-Valli revival. They should've known you can't go back.

It was Valli, though, who separated the Seasons from every other pretender to the throne. His voice was a natural tenor, but he could soar effortlessly into a falsetto and stay there forever; his technique, particularly on the essential '60s recordings, is strictly scorched earth—once he was into a lyric, and the falsetto took over, he seemed possessed. Valli had honed his style in the '50s, fronting a number of vocal groups that played the lounge circuit in his native New Jersey. In 1956 Valli's group the Four Lovers recorded some sides for RCA and generated enough attention to garner an appearance on The Ed Sullivan Show. Their RCA success was short-lived, though their records for that label remain interesting portents of the Four Seasons to come (they also remain virtually impossible to find). Jumping from one label to another produced nothing for the group except a name change, to the Four Seasons (also the name of a famous New Jersey bowling alley of the day) and shifting personnel. In 1962 the Seasons—now numbering Valli, Gaudio, guitarist Tom DeVito and bassist Nick Massi—signed with Philadelphia producer Crewe and cut his song "Sherry" in their first session. It went to Number One. So did their next two singles, "Big Girls Don't Cry" and "Walk Like a Man." It's not surprising that the Four Seasons did so well at a time when rock songwriters were expressing themselves in sophisticated, complex terms—the Seasons invariably had something interesting to say about love in its many permutations, and the forcefulness of their presentations demanded that attention be paid.

Anthology is the place to start. The Rhino set collects virtually all the essential sides from the '60s, and also charts the beginning of Valli's solo career with the inclusion of his '67 hit, "Can't Take My Eyes Off You." 25th Anniversary is a four-cassette boxed tribute to the band, with an informative, concise history included as well. Two albums from the group's '60s catalogue remain in print. Working My Way Back to You features the title hit and 11 other rather interesting non-hit songs by Crewe, Gaudio, Linzer and others; The Four Seasons Sing Big Hits by Burt Bacharach/Hal David/Bob Dylan is to be avoided at all cost. Every performance is ill-conceived, poorly arranged, dreadfully executed. The two Rarities albums collect B sides, obscure singles (some of which were only released overseas) and promo-only cuts ("Cousin Brucie Go Go") recorded between 1964 and 1977. There are some interesting things here—"No Surfin' Today," the B side of "Dawn," may be the only song in rock history that would qualify for inclusion in both an anthology of surfing songs and an anthology of teenage death songs (the girl drowns in the ocean in this one). Rumors abound of yet another incarnation of the Four Seasons. In light of the band's underwhelming '70s output, and considering its otherwise awesome legacy to rock & roll, the words of Lennon-McCartney come to mind: Let it be. — D.M.

FOUR TOPS

★ ★ ★½ **Four Tops (1965; Motown, 1989)**
★ ★ ★½ **Second Album (1966; Motown, 1989)**
★ ★ ★ **On Top (Tamla, 1966)**
★ ★ ★ **Live (Tamla, 1967)**
★ ★ ★½ **Reach Out (1967; Motown, 1991)**
★ ★ ★½ **On Broadway (Tamla, 1967)**
★ ★ ★ ★ **Greatest Hits (Tamla, 1967)**
★ ★ ★½ **Yesterday's Dreams (Tamla, 1968)**
★ ★ ★ **Four Tops Now (1969; Motown, 1989)**
★ ★ ★ **Soul Spin (Tamla, 1969)**
★ ★½ **Still Waters Run Deep (1970; Motown, 1982)**
★ ★½ **Changing Times (1970; Motown, 1990)**
★ ★ ★ **Greatest Hits, Volume 2 (Tamla, 1971)**
★ ★ ★½ **Nature Planned It (1972; Motown, 1989)**
★ ★ ★ **Keeper of the Castle (1972; Motown, 1987)**
★ ★ ★ ★ **Four Tops Story (Tamla, 1973)**
★ ★½ **Main Street People (Dunhill, 1973)**

★★ **Live and in Concert** (Dunhill, 1974)

★★ **Night Lights Harmony** (Dunhill, 1975)

★★ **Catfish** (ABC, 1976)

★★ **The Show Must Go On** (ABC, 1977)

★★ **At the Top** (MCA, 1978)

★★★ **Four Tops Tonight** (Casablanca, 1981)

★★ **One More Mountain** (Casablana, 1982)

★★½ **Back Where I Belong** (Motown, 1983)

★★★ **Indestructible** (Arista, 1988)

★★★★★ **Anthology** (Motown, 1989)

As George Jones is to country, and Roy Orbison to early rock & roll, so is Levi Stubbs to '60s soul—its baroque expressionist. The other three Tops (Lawrence Payton, Renaldo Benson, Abdul Fakir) are fine, strong singers, but the fire of the most dramatic of all Motown groups remains Stubbs.

With the Tops, the writing-production team of Holland-Dozier-Holland found the perfect vehicle for their symphonic aspirations—nothing outside of Phil Spector's epic work for the Righteous Brothers and Ike and Tina Turner rivals the sweep of "Baby I Need Your Loving," "It's the Same Old Song," "I Can't Help Myself" or, especially, "Reach Out I'll Be There" and "Standing in the Shadows of Love." On the last two numbers, both released in 1966, the Tops and Motown came of age—cinematic orchestral arrangements, lyrics of an utmost poetic immediacy, and the straining of Stubbs's voice toward a pitch of just-short-of-transcendent frustration make for music of spine-tingling intensity. Gothic soul, of a sort.

So perfectly embodying the spirit of Motown's heyday, the Four Tops conformed to poetic justice by becoming has-beens (if decent sellers) in the years that followed. Neither disco nor funk suited this most operatic of soulsters—the drop-off of quality from *Greatest Hits, Vol. 1* to *Vol. 2* demonstrates the demise. Stick with the classics, best represented on *Anthology*.

— P.E.

PETER FRAMPTON
★★★ **Wind of Change** (A&M, 1972)

★★★ **Frampton's Camel** (A&M, 1973)

★★ **Something's Happening** (A&M, 1974)

★★ **Frampton** (A&M, 1975)

★★★ **Frampton Comes Alive!** (A&M, 1976)

★ **I'm in You** (A&M, 1977)

★ **Where I Should Be** (A&M, 1979)

★ **Breaking All the Rules** (A&M, 1981)

The "overnight success" of *Frampton Comes Alive*—over 8 million copies sold, ten weeks at Number One—came as the payoff from four years of touring. Guitarist Peter Frampton and his band must have played hundreds of arena concerts in the mid-'70s, gradually building up a strong word-of-mouth reputation as a crowd-pleasing opening act. Releasing a double live album was also something of a desperate move, though. None of the four preceding Frampton albums captured the impact of his live show, and they sold poorly. First tagged for stardom in a late '60s British band called the Herd, Frampton had always seemed to be a natural. He combined teen idol wholesomeness with an unflashy instrumental dexterity. He earned his heavy chops as lead guitarist in Humble Pie: moving from the obtuse blooze of *Rockin' the Fillmore* to the genial singalongs of *Frampton Comes Alive!* is one hell of a mellowing-out process. *Frampton's Camel* is the most tuneful and assured of the pre–*Comes Alive* albums: there's fire behind the catchy choruses of "White Sugar," "Do You Feel Like We Do" and "Lines on My Face," enough to let you ignore the sappy sentiments of the lyrics. Those last two songs repeat on the live album, and the difference is instructive. Frampton's chatty guitar solos gather some cheers in concert—like the sonic equivalent of his flashing smile. But the surefire hook of both songs—and the key to the album's success—is audience participation. *Frampton Comes Alive* resembles an audio souvenir of the concert experience—better than the T-shirts of today because you could actually listen to it.

The Frampton phenomenon ushered in the rock journeymen era, when veteran roadrats like REO Speedwagon and Journey finally triumphed over good taste, and newcomers like Heart and Foreigner succeeded in sounding like they'd been around forever. Frampton wound up being a harbinger of Album Oriented Radio rather than one of its masters, however. His fall from grace was brutal and swift. A paucity of decent material and Frampton's somewhat cloying vocal tone ruin the hotly anticipated follow-up, *I'm in You*: without a hook to hang it on, all the eager-to-please charm starts to seem a little smarmy. Tellingly, all of Frampton's indistinct '80s albums on Atlantic have fallen out of print. — M.C.

CONNIE FRANCIS

★ ★ ★ ★ **The Very Best of Connie Francis (Polydor, 1986)**
   ★ ★ **The Very Best of Connie Francis, Volume Two (Polydor, 1987)**
   ★ ★ **Rocksides (1957–1964) (Polydor, 1987)**
   ★ ★ ★ **Christmas in My Heart (Polydor, 1988)**

Although the British Invasion of 1963 pretty much spelled the end of Connie Francis's reign as a teen queen, by that time she had logged five consecutive years of hit singles. However lacking in depth her material may have been—and it was drippy—Francis boasted an extraordinary voice that could wring the last teardrop out of the most saccharine tune. She sounded less comfortable on uptempo songs, although one of these, "Everybody's Somebody's Fool," became her first Number One single in 1960. Some credit must go to the variety of producers she worked with, all of whom nestled her voice in a thick layer of strings and orchestral arrangements, but in the end it's Francis's unerring instincts as an interpreter that render her material palatable today.

Of her remaining in-print albums, the one to own is *The Very Best of Connie Francis*, which collects most of the hit singles in its 21 tracks, beginning with the 1958 track "Who's Sorry Now" and concluding with the Top Twenty "Follow the Boys" from 1963. *The Very Best of, Volume Two* is tougher to get through, since it contains no major hits and includes a number of overproduced tracks from the late '60s. The well-annotated *Rocksides* includes some previously unreleased tracks and, as its title suggests, showcases Francis in a more uptempo groove, which, as noted above, is hardly her forte. *Christmas in My Heart*, on the other hand, is Francis's voice at its most heart-rending and powerful on 12 traditional Yuletide songs (the CD version has a bonus track). Her readings of "The First Noel" and "Ave Maria" alone will make you forgive her for recording "Where the Boys Are." — D.M.

FRANKIE GOES TO HOLLYWOOD

★ ★ **Welcome to the Pleasuredome (ZTT/Island, 1984)**
½ ★ **Liverpool (ZTT/Island, 1986)**

One-hit wonders who verged on being one-hype wonders, Frankie Goes to Hollywood was supposed to represent the arty upside to the Reagan era's wretched excess; sadly, the only upside evident in the sprawling *Welcome to the Pleasuredome* was that Trevor Horn's high-gloss production periodically overcame the group's utter incompetence. Like most of the era's one-hit wonders, the group did make a second album, though God only knows why anyone would want to hear it. — J.D.C.

ARETHA FRANKLIN

★ ★ ½ **Aretha (Columbia, 1961)**
★ ★ ★ **The Electrifying Aretha Franklin (Columbia, 1962)**
★ ★ ★ **Laughing on the Outside (Columbia, 1963)**
★ ★ ½ **The Tender, the Moving, the Swinging Aretha Franklin (Columbia, 1963)**
★ ★ ½ **Running Out of Fools (Columbia, 1964)**
★ ★ ½ **Yeah! Aretha Franklin in Person (Columbia, 1965)**
★ ★ ★ **Soul Sister (Columbia, 1966)**
★ ★ ★ **Greatest Hits (Columbia, 1967)**
★ ★ ★ ½ **Unforgettable (Columbia, 1964)**
★ ★ ★ ★ **Songs of Faith (Checker, 1964)**
★ ★ ★ ★ ★ **I Never Loved a Man (the Way I Love You) (Atlantic, 1967)**
★ ★ ★ **Aretha Arrives (Atlantic, 1967)**
★ ★ ★ ★ ★ **Lady Soul (Atlantic, 1968)**
★ ★ ★ ½ **Aretha Now (Atlantic, 1968)**
★ ★ ★ **Aretha in Paris (Atlantic, 1968)**
★ ★ ★ ½ **Soul '69 (Atlantic, 1969)**
★ ★ ★ ★ **Aretha's Gold (Atlantic, 1969)**
★ ★ ★ ½ **This Girl's in Love With You (Atlantic, 1970)**
★ ★ ★ ½ **Spirit in the Dark (Atlantic, 1970)**
★ ★ ★ ½ **Greatest Hits (Atlantic, 1971)**
★ ★ ★ **Live at Fillmore West (Atlantic, 1971)**
★ ★ ★ ½ **Young, Gifted and Black (Atlantic, 1972)**
★ ★ ★ ★ ★ **Amazing Grace (Atlantic, 1972)**
★ ★ ★ **The Great Aretha Franklin: The First 12 Sides (Columbia, 1972)**
★ ★ ★ ½ **All-Time Greatest Hits (Columbia, 1972)**
★ ★ ½ **Hey Now Hey (The Other Side of the Sky) (Atlantic, 1973)**
★ ★ ★ **Best of Aretha Franklin (Atlantic, 1973)**
★ ★ ★ **Let Me in Your Life (Atlantic, 1974)**
★ ★ ★ **With Everything I Feel in Me (Atlantic, 1974)**
★ **You (Atlantic, 1975)**
★ ★ **Sparkle (Atlantic, 1976)**
★ ★ ★ **Ten Years of Gold (Atlantic, 1976)**
★ ★ **Sweet Passion (Atlantic, 1977)**

★★   **Almighty Fire (Atlantic, 1978)**
★★   **La Diva (Atlantic, 1979)**
★★   **Aretha (Arista, 1980)**
★★★   **Love All the Hurt Away (Arista, 1981)**
★★★   **Jump to It (Arista, 1982)**
★★½   **Sweet Bitter Love (Columbia, 1982)**
★★★½   **Get It Right (Arista, 1983)**
★★★½   **Aretha's Jazz (Atlantic, 1984)**
★★★½   **Who's Zoomin' Who (Arista, 1985)**
★★★   **Aretha Sings the Blues (Columbia, 1985)**
★★★★★   **30 Greatest Hits (Atlantic, 1985)**
★★½   **Aretha (Arista, 1986)**
★★★   **After Hours (Columbia, 1987)**
★★★★   **One Lord, One Faith, One Baptism (Arista, 1987)**
★★★   **Through the Storm (Arista, 1989)**
★★★   **What You Get Is What You Sweat (Arista, 1991)**
★★★★★   **The Queen of Soul (Rhino/ Atlantic, 1992)**

A supple mezzo-soprano of astonishing range, Aretha Franklin's voice is a force of nature. What makes her one of the great singers in the history of popular music, however, is the knowing command with which she deploys that force. So artful is her approach to her instrument that she might've chosen any genre within which to triumph—daughter of Rev. C. L. Franklin, a preacher whose many albums of sermons had earned him the name "The Million Dollar Voice," Aretha could've inherited Mahalia Jackson's crown as the queen of gospel. Equally, she might've followed after Billie Holiday, conquering the blues, or Sarah Vaughan, mastering jazz. In fact, all of these strains find rich expression in Franklin's work—but her signal passion made her "Lady Soul."

Discovered by John Hammond, the unerring Columbia talent scout who'd also mentored Bob Dylan, Franklin was first forced into the mold of a pop singer covering such easy fare as "Over the Rainbow." Her work for that label—now best represented on *The First 12 Sides* and a trio of '80s reissues—in no way approaches her coming glory, even if her brilliant piano playing and innate vocal power can't quite be buried by glossy arrangements.

Pairing up, in 1966, with Atlantic Records vice president Jerry Wexler and the famed Muscle Shoals, Alabama, studio players, Franklin found her true voice: against a backdrop of surging rhythm and punching horns, she turned loose her gospel piano, and began singing with such graceful abandon that she became recognized very soon as one of the handful of inventors of hard-core soul. Motown was making R&B with a symphonic sweep and sweet melodicism; Aretha's music—boosted greatly by production assists from Wexler, Tom Dowd and Arif Mardin—would be consistently tougher, rawer and, arguably, much deeper.

I Never Loved a Man debuted the new Aretha—and it was a staggering introduction. Her version of Otis Redding's "Respect" knocked cold even his amazing original; and with the title track, "Do Right Woman—Do Right Man," "Dr. Feelgood" and "Save Me," this was music of absolute, fluid assurance. The record may stand as the greatest single soul album of all time.

"Baby I Love You" enlivened the capable *Aretha Arrives*, but *Lady Soul* was another masterpiece, producing the hits, "(You Make Me Feel Like) A Natural Woman," "(Sweet Sweet Baby) Since You've Been Gone," and, most significantly, "Chain of Fools." With Aretha singing with infectious swagger and its background vocals recalling the Staple Singers, the song encapsulated the Franklin soul style—while as catchy as any early rock & roll number, it resounded with a much wiser force.

On *Aretha Now*, the singer showed that she could transform pop songs into soul numbers; infusing Burt Bacharach's "I Say a Little Prayer" with swing, she added edge to the delicate melody. And *Soul '69* proved her to be a jazz singer of rare intelligence and dimension. With its great takes on Sam Cooke's "Bring It On Home to Me" and Big Maybelle Smith's "Ramblin' " and its tight brass section featuring King Curtis, *Soul '69*'s highlights can now be found on *Aretha's Jazz*. That compilation also presents the better work from Franklin's later orchestral jazz set with Quincy Jones, *Hey Now Hey (The Other Side of the Sky)*.

The early '70s marked the end of Aretha's titanic period. *Greatest Hits* featured "Spanish Harlem," a gospel "Bridge Over Troubled Water" and Ashford/Simpson's "You're All I Need to Get By"; *Young, Gifted and Black* presented the spare, urgent "Rock Steady" and the lovely "Day Dreamin' "; *Live* found Aretha collaborating with Ray Charles. All of these records are confidant and immediate; none, however, matches the majesty of her contemporaneous two-album gospel magnum opus, *Amazing Grace*. Featuring James Cleveland and the Southern California Community Choir, *Grace* is Franklin transcendent, returning to the source of her own—and soul music's—earliest inspiration.

In 1981, Aretha came back from a series of bland, sometimes discofied albums in which she often sounded bored or exhausted, with *Love All The Hurt Away*—a funky pop near-triumph. While it wasn't music of the caliber of the best Atlantic sides, the record showed off her newly energized singing—and its success paved the way for her commercial re-emergence with *Who's Zoomin' Who*. In many ways a rock record—there's a duet with the Eurythmics, a Carlos Santana guitar solo and sax work by Clarence Clemons—*Zoomin'* may be lyrically slight, but it kicks aplenty. With help from the Mighty Clouds of Joy, Jesse Jackson and Mavis Staples, *One Faith* reasserted Aretha's gospel prowess—predictably, it was the best record she'd made in over a decade.

While incapable of turning in a vocal performance that doesn't catch fire, Aretha has truly shone only in company with sympathetic producers (Wexler/Dowd/Mardin)—and she's sometimes been overwhelmed by less congenial ones (Van McCoy, Luther Vandross). Occasionally willfull, reticent or inscrutable, she has the tortured personality of a very private soul, and her career has sometimes suffered from lack of direction. She remains, however, the spirit of soul—a singer of genius. Nearly all of her 1967–72 releases are essential R&B records; the excellent *Queen of Soul*, a four-CD boxed set, presents Aretha Franklin at her finest. — P.E.

MICHAEL FRANKS

★★½ **The Art of Tea (Reprise, 1976)**
★★½ **Sleeping Gypsy (Warner Bros., 1977)**
★★ **Burchfield Nines (Warner Bros., 1978)**
★★ **Tiger in the Rain (Warner Bros., 1979)**
★★ **One Bad Habit (Warner Bros., 1980)**
★★½ **Skin Dive (Warner Bros., 1985)**
★★ **The Camera Never Lies (Warner Bros., 1987)**
★★ **Previously Unavailable (DRG, 1989)**
★★ **Blue Pacific (Reprise, 1990)**
While technological advances have lent Michael Franks increasingly hygienic versions of the ultra-clean studio sound he favors, he has seldom strayed from his formula—jazz lite, with soft, mildly seductive vocals. Working primarily with

session vets and fusion stalwarts, Franks puts out tasteful fare that's not quite Muzak, but not much more spirited. The very limitations of his nice-guy singing save him from the histrionics of Gino Vannelli, but he's hardly as cool as even the slightest Boz Scaggs. He featured the Crusaders on *The Art of Tea* and its cutesy, minor hit "Popsicle Toes," played with Brazilian musicians on *Sleeping Gypsy* and with Brenda Russell and Ron Carter on *Skin Dive*—but his casts of guest players don't alter his sound. Or the attitude his music is intended to provoke—which is invariably: Dim the lights, get out the Chardonnay, cuddle up. — P.E.

STAN FREBERG

★★ **Capitol Collectors Series (Capitol, 1990)**
Capitol once had several Stan Freberg titles in its catalogue, but these have been deleted in favor of this single-disc summary of his work in the '50s and '60s. Actually the best work Freberg did was in the realm of television commercials and ad campaigns, one of the most memorable featuring the actress Ann Miller dancing atop a soup can. On record he came across as bitter and spiteful much of the time, although this could work to good effect when he inveighed against the commercialism of the Christmas season in "Green Christmas," a minor hit in 1959. He also evinced a mean streak when it came to rock & roll and the culture around it. His 1956 satire, "Heartbreak Hotel," ranks with Steve Allen's recitation of the lyrics of "Be Bop a Lula" as one of the most wrongheaded attacks on the music. On the other hand, "The Old Payola Roll Blues" (1960) was a proper skewering of what Freberg termed "pay radio." His best effort was a 1961 album, *Stan Freberg Presents the United States of America*, that found Freberg punning his way through the major events in this country's history in a thick Jewish accent. Subtle and incisive, his text prefigured the artful commentary purveyed a decade later by the Firesign Theatre. — D.M.

FREE

★★ **Tons of Sobs (A&M, 1969)**
★★★ **Free (A&M, 1970)**
★★★★ **Fire and Water (A&M, 1970)**
★★★ **Highway (A&M, 1970)**
★★½ **Free Live (A&M, 1971)**
★★ **Free at Last (A&M, 1972)**
★★ **Heartbreaker (Island, 1973)**
★★★½ **Best of Free (A&M, 1975)**

This is where Paul Rodgers earns his reputation as England's premier hard-rock vocalist. The late guitarist Paul Kossoff matches Rodgers's control and sharp phrasing, riff after shivery riff, while bassist Andy Fraser and drummer Simon Kirke form a taut rhythmic backbone. Conveniently, the band's most telling efforts—the smoking breakthrough *Fire and Water*, the inevitable *Live*, and a slightly sloppy *Best of* collection—are also the only Free albums still in print. All three records include the Top Ten hit "All Right Now"; this tense three-chord stomp compresses its power into three explosively catchy minutes. Culling memorable moments from the spotty later period, *Best of Free* skips a few from the early days: the wah-wah moan of "I'll Be Creeping" (from *Free*) and the extended centerpiece "Mr. Big" (from *Fire and Water* or *Live*) might have provided more balance. There's plenty of taut, strutting cock-rock on *Best of Free*, though; cuts like "The Stealer" and a live cover of Albert King's "The Hunter" suggest that a well-considered reissue of this group could put many current practitioners to shame. After Free broke up, Paul Rodgers and Simon Kirke merged with Bad Company. — M.C.

FRENCH FRITH KAISER THOMPSON
★★★ Live, Love, Larf & Loaf (Rhino, 1987)
★★★½ Invisible Means (Windham Hill, 1990)

A genuinely motley crew, this quartet brings together three leading lights of the experimental rock world—avant-guitar guru Henry Kaiser, Henry Cow's Fred Frith (playing bass), and former Captain Beefheart drummer John French—and one ringer, folk-rock hero Richard Thompson. Amazingly, the foursome not only finds plenty of common ground (improvisationally on *Live, Love, Larf & Loaf*, compositionally on *Invisible Means*), but end up producing music that's far more accessible than what their individual resumes would leave you expecting. — J.D.C.

GLENN FREY
★★ No Fun Aloud (Asylum, 1982)
★★ The Allnighter (MCA, 1984)
★½ Soul Searchin' (MCA, 1988)

After the Eagles split up, guitarist-singer Glenn Frey cut a predictably slick solo debut in his old band's party-boy mode; *No Fun Aloud* is like a Joe Walsh album with

(slightly) better singing. Not songs, though; apparently that was Don Henley's department. *The Allnighter* glistens with synthesized oomph, but the sugar-coating doesn't sit well on Frey's mannered white R&B loveman act. The set piece "Smuggler's Blues" was utilized in an episode of the television show *Miami Vice* (Frey had a small role), jump-starting *The Allnighter* on the charts. "Smuggler's Blues," the catchiest tune on the album by far, was a lot more intesting to watch—like a dramatized video clip—than it is to listen to, however. By the time *Soul Searchin'* came out, Frey could be spotted working as a pitchman on television commercials; too bad those pump-your-body gym ads display more sweat and effort than his last album. — M.C.

KINKY FRIEDMAN
★★½ Sold America (Vanguard, 1973)
★★½ Lasso from El Paso (Epic, 1976)

Kinky Friedman deserves credit for shaking up the country music scene in the '70s—certainly tunes like "They Ain't Making Jews Like Jesus Anymore" and "Asshole From El Paso" and a band dubbed the Texas Jewboys were guaranteed to raise some Nashville eyebrows. But Friedman's schtick (and, in particular, his voice) have not worn well. While this comedy fare isn't quite so dated as, say, the hippie humor of the Holy Modal Rounders, it has not ripened with age. — P.E.

FRIENDS OF DISTINCTION
★½ Grazin' (RCA, 1969)
★½ Golden Classics (Collectables, NA)

With its endless high-speed repetitions of the lyric, "Can you dig it?" "Grazin' in the Grass" was a zippy bit of MOR funk, and a big hit in 1969. Everything else the group did, however, was boring easy-listening versions of '70s soul, complete with congas, bad strings, and wah-wah guitars. Because they're less slick than the 5th Dimension, they may seem more authentic. They're not (and the 5D sing better). — P.E.

ROBERT FRIPP
★★★★ Exposure (Polydor/EG, 1979)
★★½ God Save the Queen/Under Heavy Manners (Polydor/EG, 1980)
★★★½ Let the Power Fall (1981; Editions EG, 1989)
WITH BRIAN ENO
★★★½ No Pussyfooting (1973; Editions EG, 1981)

★ ★ ★ ★   Evening Star (1976; Editions EG, 1981)
WITH THE LEAGUE OF GENTLEMEN
★ ★ ★   The League of Gentlemen (Polydor; 1981)
★ ★ ★   God Save the King (Editions EG, 1985)
WITH ANDY SUMMERS
★ ★ ★ ★   I Advance Masked (A&M, 1982)
★ ★ ★   Bewitched (A&M, 1984)
WITH THE LEAGUE OF CRAFTY GUITARISTS
★ ★ ★   Live! (1986; Editions EG, 1989)
★ ★ ★½   Show of Hands (Editions EG, 1991)

For a guy intent on maintaining a solo career, King Crimson founder Robert Fripp certainly hates being left alone. Of the 11 albums listed, only three are credited to Fripp alone, the rest being either duo albums or group collaborations. Yet this chronic need for shared credit is hardly the product of artistic modesty, for Fripp easily dominates these albums; instead, the shared billing seems to be an acknowledgment that his best work is usually in reaction to the efforts of others. His work with Brian Eno, for instance, takes a simple idea— "Frippertronics," a tape-loop system that allows Fripp to build layers of humming, buzzing guitar phrases into a shimmering mass of sound—and exploits Eno's talents for tape manipulation to push it one step further. Moving out on his own, *Exposure* finds Fripp making a (typically obtuse) stab at conventional pop as he alternates Frippertronic instrumentals and odd snatches of conversation with surprisingly accessible songs performed by Peter Gabriel, Daryl Hall, Terre Roche and others; at its best, as on Gabriel's rendition of "Here Comes the Flood," the music is wonderfully affecting. *God Save the Queen/Under Heavy Manners* finds him returning to Frippertronics, with three pleasantly pastoral instrumentals on the *Queen* side, and something called "discotronics"—that is, Frippertronics with an overdubbed rhythm section—on the *Manners* side. An interesting concept, but discotronics on the whole sounds like a wallflower's notion of dance music. Following this was Fripp's only totally non-collaborative effort, a sleepily elegiac album of Frippertronics called *Let the Power Fall*.

With *The League of Gentlemen*, Fripp returns to the role of bandleader with a sort of minimalist King Crimson called the League of Gentlemen. Despite some interesting noises from former XTC keyboardist Barry Andrews and some stalwart rhythm work, the League's music is stiff and overly mannered. *The League of Gentlemen* has since been reissued, along with the discotronic portion of *God Save the Queen/Under Heavy Manners* as *God Save the King*, thereby allowing canny consumers to avoid two mediocrities at once.

Somehow, Fripp also found time to record two instrumental albums with Police guitarist Andy Summers. *I Advance Masked* is an impressively even match, with Summers's adventurous harmonic ideas and sophisticated tonal palette spurring Fripp to new heights, while Fripp's tricks with echo and repetition provide Summers with a challenging melodic framework to work against; *Bewitched*, though, seems too obsessed with electronic effects and guitar synthesis for the improvisations to be completely satisfying. Perhaps that's what pushed Fripp to the opposite extreme with his *League of Crafty Guitarists* albums. A by-product of a series of guitar craft seminars Fripp organized in the mid-'80s, these albums find the master and his acolytes fashioning an acoustic simulacrum of Frippertronics' coloristic drones. *Show of Hands* is the more satisfying of the two, no doubt due to the more stringently structured nature of the material.

Fripp completists should also note that he accompanies his wife, singer Toyah Willcox, on the now-deleted *The Lady or the Tiger* (Editions EG, 1986), a presentation of two short stories by Frank R. Stockton. Fripp and Willcox are also half of Sunday All Over the World, a short-lived rock ensemble whose sole album, *Kneeling at the Shrine* (EG, 1991), offers all the complexity of a King Crimson release, but none of the pleasure. — J.D.C.

BILL FRISELL
★ ★ ★ ★   In Line (ECM, 1983)
★ ★ ★½   Rambler (ECM, 1985)
★ ★ ★ ★   Lookout for Hope (ECM, 1988)
★ ★ ★ ★½   Works (ECM, 1988)
★ ★ ★½   Before We Were Born (Elektra Musician, 1989)
★ ★ ★   Is That You? (Elektra Musician, 1990)
★ ★ ★ ★   Where in the World? (Elektra Musician, 1991)
WITH VERNON REID
★ ★ ★   Smash & Scatteration (1985; Rykodisc, 1986)

Being a capable technician and resourceful improvisor isn't enough for jazz guitarists these days; in addition to providing the right notes, they must also have a handle on all the right sounds. But that's one of the things Bill Frisell does best, shaping his tone with such skill that it almost seems three-dimensional. That's part of the reason he's such a sought-after sideman, and it's no accident that half of the selections on *Works* are taken from other leaders' recordings (interested listeners should definitely seek out any of the recordings by Bass Desires, the Marc Johnson-led quartet that uses Frisell in tandem with guitarist John Scofield). Still, Frisell's output as a leader is nothing to sniff at. *In Line*, a lusciously reflective collection of solos and duets (the latter with bassist Arild Andersen), offers perhaps the clearest view of his playing, followed by *Smash & Scatteration*, a wittily coloristic collaboration with Living Colour guitarist Vernon Reid. On the other end of the spectrum is *Rambler*, which finds Frisell flanked by trumpeter Kenny Wheeler, tubist Bob Stewart, drummer Paul Motian and bassist Jerome Harris; impressive as the interplay often is, it can be hard to get past the occasionally odd ensemble textures.

Frisell records most frequently with quartets, though. His own Bill Frisell Band—cellist Hank Roberts, bassist Kermit Driscoll and drummer Joey Baron—is featured on *Lookout for Hope*, *Where in the World?* and parts of *Before We Were Born*, with *Lookout* being the most approachable and *Where?* the most daring. *Is That You?*, recorded with Wayne Horvitz, is not as dynamic or consistent as the albums with Frisell's own band. — J.D.C.

LEFTY FRIZZELL
    ★ ★ **Lefty Frizzell's Greatest Hits (Columbia, 1966)**
★ ★ ★ ★ **Columbia Historic Edition (Columbia, 1982)**
   ★ ★ ★ **American Originals (Columbia, 1990)**
★ ★ ★ ★ **The Best of Lefty Frizzell (Rhino, 1991)**

When Lefty Frizzell died at 47 of a stroke in 1975, country music lost one of its most original singers and most literate writers. In his voice one hears the plaintive tones of Jimmie Rodgers's style; Frizzell's own warm tenor and distinctive phrasing have pervaded the singing styles of Merle Haggard, Willie Nelson, John Anderson and particularly Randy Travis, who often sounds like Frizzell resurrected. As a writer Frizzell was deceptively tough—even at his most sentimental, his readings were so strong you

instantly understood the depth and sincerity of his feelings.

Rhino's *Best of* restores some of the gloss on Frizzell's soiled recorded legacy by virtue of giving us the man's work in its original glory, both hits and interesting non-hits as well. Otherwise, only the Columbia Historic Edition shows any degree of sensitivity, with a good thumbnail sketch of Frizzell's career, and a song selection including both the well-known ("I Love You a Thousand Ways," "Always Late [With Your Kisses]") and the otherwise unavailable. If it contained only "No One to Talk to (but the Blues)," a burning country blues, this album would rank as an essential addition to the Frizzell catalogue. *American Originals*, like most of the titles in this series, seems to have been thrown together without much thought, but it does collect ten sterling Frizzell performances, including his last Number One record, the brooding "Saginaw, Michigan," from 1964. Avoid *Greatest Hits*: most of these selections are poor re-recordings or have sloppy overdubs tacked onto the original recordings.
— D.M.

FUGAZI
★ ★ ★ ★ **13 Songs (Dischord, 1989)**
  ★ ★ ★½ **Repeater (Dischord, 1990)**
   ★ ★½ **Steady Diet of Nothing (Dischord, 1991)**

In the early '80s, when Washington, D.C.'s hardcore scene was second only to California's, Ian MacKaye's Minor Threat was the last word in harder-faster-purer punk. But unlike many punk icons, MacKaye has been able to maintain the ideals that drew him into the music without holding blindly onto the stylisms that were current when he started. And that, perhaps more than anything else, explains why Fugazi sounds the way it does. On *13 Songs*, for instance, this quartet makes no secret of its musical might—just listen to the raveup that introduces "Burning Too"—but neither does it restrict itself to such devices. Instead, the best moments on this album (which actually combines two EPs, *Fugazi* and *Margin Walker*) are more like "Bulldog Front" or "Provisional," making excellent use of tempo shifts and changes in dynamics.

There's a similar diversity to the sound of *Repeater*, as Fugazi moves easily from the mid-tempo thrash of "Break-In" to the stop-and-start groove of "Greed," to the chugging, feedback-tinged pulse of "Repeater." Here, however, the lyrics begin to take on an irritating ideological stiffness as the band's holier-than-thou attitudes lead to such glib profundities as "We are all bigots" (from "Styrofoam") or "You are not what you own" (from "Merchandise"). But that preachiness is nothing compared to the sermonizing on *Steady Diet of Nothing*, on which the lyrics are filled with apocalyptic paranoia and the music reverberates with buzzsaw guitar chords and anxiously churning rhythm work. Yet for all its urgent dread, *Steady Diet* delivers nothing of substance, until Fugazi seems subsumed by the very attitude-mongering the band's anti-rockstar stance argues against. — J.D.C.

BOBBY FULLER

★ ★ ★½ **The Best of the Bobby Fuller Four (Rhino, 1987)**
Though it would take a blistering cover by the Clash to transform "I Fought the Law" into a true rebel anthem, Bobby Fuller's theme song was a fabulous 1965 single. It was one of the rare American rockers that held its own against the British Invasion. El Paso's Fuller didn't make many records (for the tiny label, Mustang) before his presumed suicide in 1966 but most of them rock steady. Wholly unoriginal, Fuller instead was gifted with a love so passionate for his idols (Buddy Holly, Ritchie Valens) that his songs have the desperate grace and charming modesty of a rock & roll true believer—no prima donna, but a total fan. "It's Love, Come What May" is lovely ersatz Holly; "Saturday Night" buoyantly rips off Eddie Cochran's "C'mon Everybody." Sort of a Tommy Roe with a genuine heart, Fuller holds up just fine. — P.E.

FULL TIME MEN

★ ★ ★½ **Full Time Men (EP) (Coyote, 1985)**
★ ★ ★½ **Your Face My Fist (Coyote, 1988)**
A side project of Fleshtone guitarist Keith Streng, Full Time Men make glorious garage rock. A host of college radio gods and underground celebs (R.E.M.'s Peter Buck, Smithereen mainman Pat DiNizio, ex-Dead Boy Stiv Bators, and Fleshtone Peter Zaremba) collaborate on *Your Face My Fist*—the kind of party record Humble Pie might've made had those hardy troglodytes been gifted with more than the most elementary sense of humor. Streng wails righteously on his slambam originals; on his R&B covers, he pits a skilled horn section against the power-pop talents of his guest stars—and every one kicks. An earlier,

eponymously titled Full Time Men EP is also worth checking out; basically a Streng/Buck duo recording, it sounds very similar to early R.E.M., with Streng singing more heartily (if less interestingly) than Michael Stipe. — P.E.

FUNKADELIC

★ ★ ★½ **Funkadelic (Westbound, 1970)**
★ ★ ★ **Free Your Mind and Your Ass Will Follow (Westbound, 1970)**
★ ★ ★ ★ **Maggot Brain (Westbound, 1971)**
★ ★ ★ **America Eats Its Young (Westbound, 1972)**
★ ★ ★½ **Cosmic Slop (Westbound, 1973)**
★ ★ ★½ **Standing on the Verge of Getting It On (Westbound, 1974)**
★ ★ ★ ★ **Let's Take It to the Stage (Westbound, 1975)**
★ ★ ★ ★ **Funkadelic's Greatest Hits (Westbound, 1975)**
★ ★ ★ **Tales of Kidd Funkadelic (Westbound, 1976)**
★ ★ ★½ **Hardcore Jollies (Warner Bros., 1976)**
★ ★ ★ ★ ★ **The Best of the Funkadelic Early Years (Westbound, 1977)**
★ ★ ★ ★ ★ **One Nation Under a Groove (Warner Bros., 1978)**
★ ★ ★½ **Uncle Jam Wants You (Warner Bros., 1979)**
★ ★ **Connections and Disconnections (LAX, 1981)**
★ ★ ★ ★ **The Electric Spanking of War Babies (Warner Bros., 1981)**
The name says it all: Funkadelic equals high-energy, mind-expanding black rock & roll, a soulful psychotic reaction. It couldn't have happened anywhere but Detroit; funkmeister George Clinton, a former Motown staff writer, was also the leader of a long-running vocal quintet. When a legal wrangle forced the Parliaments to change names and record labels in the late '60s, Clinton concocted the perfect handle for his radical new sound. (Parliament resumed recording several years later.) *Funkadelic* runs the group's R&B roots into a head-on collision with psychedelic rock. Smokey vocal lines and sure rhythms smack up against wailing walls of feedback-drenched guitar. The supertight "I'll Bet You" twists a shivery solo around a heart-searing doo-wop love pledge, while the ramblin' raps on "Mommy What's a Funkadelic" and "What Is Soul?" provide flashes of bone-tickling wit. "I Got a Thing, You Got a Thing, Everybody's Got a Thing" lays

down this band's open-minded creed in both words and music.

Free Your Mind and Your Ass Will Follow doesn't quite live up to its magnificent billing; the elongated title track of this brief follow-up is the talkiest of Funkadelic's philosophical treatises. "Funky Dollar Bill" and "I Wanna Know If It's Good to You?" are more like it: heat-seeking Hendrixoid riffs tied to provocative critiques of capitalism and sexual liberation, respectively. Begininning with an ear-bending Eddie Hazel guitar workout ("Maggot Brain") and concluding with a crackpot Satanic boogie meltdown ("Wars of Armageddon"), *Maggot Brain* contains the nasty, ooozing essence of Funkadelic. "Super Stupid" could lift the head off an average Black Sabbath or Metallica fan, while "Can You Get to That" wraps unbelievably sweet vocals and acoustic guitar around Clinton's disillusioned musings on the counterculture.

America Eats Its Young gets bogged down in polticized anger and a temporary absence of redemptive grooves. Funkadelic soon got over its funk: *Cosmic Slop* and *Standing on the Verge of Getting It On* mix relatively straight-ahead songs and experimental jams in a stimulating jumble. A growing cast of musicians—including keyboarist Bernie Worrell, guitarist Glen Goins, guitarist Gary Shider—offer strong contributions under Clinton's omniscient leadership. Cartoonist Pedro Bell began designing album covers with *Cosmic Slop*. His bugged-out illustrations and inscriptions perfectly reflect the music's wild spirit, making Funkadelic a true "self-contained packaging-marketing concept." *Let's Take It to the Stage* evokes the spontaneous combustion of a Funkadelic concert; the 1975 *Greatest Hits* is eclipsed by the definitive *Best of the Funkadelic Early Years*. If ever an album deserved to be called ahead of its time, this catchy and challenging funk-rock raveup definitely qualifies. *Tales of Kidd Funkadelic* collects odds and sods from the Westbound years (including the delectable "I'm Never

Gonna Tell It" and the cautionary "Take Your Dead Ass Home!"). *Hardcore Jollies* marks a move to a much larger record company; fresh guitar recruit Mike Hampton earns his stripes on "Comin' Round the Mountain" and a remake of "Cosmic Slop." That hardly signals a retrenchment; two years (and two Parliament albums) later, Funkadelic returned with its most ambitious—and accesible—album to date.

One Nation Under a Groove provides an eloquent answer to its own musical question. "Who Says a Funk Band Can't Play Rock?"—nobody who's heard Funkadelic in full flight on this uplifting, loose-limbed party masterpiece. Vocals and keyboards are slightly more prominent than before, but the singers' steamy R&B leanings are offset by the snappy guitar parts and those feet-itching rhythms. Dismiss this milestone as mere "disco" and you risk missing some of the very best music the '70s produced. On the other hand, the bulk of *Uncle Jam Wants You* suspiciously resembles mundane dance-floor fodder; only the hit "(Not Just) Knee Deep" really gets off the ground. By this time, the P-Funk colony had mutated into so many branches (Boosty's Rubber Band, Parlet, Brides of Funkenstein, et al.) that the main creative stream eventually dried up. *Connections and Disconnections* is a dispirited effort by some of the original Parliaments (led by Fuzzy Haskins) to trade in on their former gigs—Clinton and crew are nowhere to be heard on this bland slab. *The Electric Spanking of War Babies* is the bona fide Funkadelic swan song; the title track introduces a thick, satisyfing synth-based attack while "Funk Get Stronger" wheels out guest Sly Stone for a surprisingly convincing performance. Ending the saga on an appropriately gross note, "Icka Prick" attaches its outrageously funny stream of "equal-opportunity nasties" to a sinus-clearing guitar lick and a stomach-churning beat. — M.C.

G

PETER GABRIEL

   ★ ★ ★   Peter Gabriel (Atco, 1977)
   ★ ★ ★½ Peter Gabriel (Atlantic, 1978)
   ★ ★ ★ ★ Peter Gabriel (Geffen, 1980)
   ★ ★ ★ ★½ Security (Geffen, 1982)
   ★ ★ ★   Plays Live (Geffen, 1983)
   ★ ★ ★½ Music from the Film "Birdy"
             (Geffen, 1984)
★ ★ ★ ★ ★ So (Geffen, 1986)
   ★ ★ ★½ Passion: Music for "The Last
             Temptation of Christ" (Geffen,
             1989)
★ ★ ★ ★½ Shaking the Tree: Sixteen
             Golden Greats (Geffen, 1990)

Without question, Peter Gabriel's metamorphosis from pointy-headed, theatrical cult artist to canny, minimalist pop star is one of the most impressive transformations pop music has seen. Take, for instance, the first of his *Peter Gabriel* albums (the one with the car cover). Although it avoids the sort of mock-symphonic pomp that lurked around the edges of many Genesis albums, its sound hardly constitutes a clean break from his old group, what with the sophomoric grotesqueries of "Moribund the Burgermeister" and the overblown whimsy of "Excuse Me." None of which undercuts the album's melodic appeal, of course, or diminishes the majesty of songs like "Solsbury Hill" or "Here Comes the Flood." But a redefinition of his sound it isn't.

For that, you'd need to look toward the second *Peter Gabriel* album (with the fingernails cover). Blessed with a less intensely commercial producer (Robert Fripp instead of Bob Ezrin) and boasting a leaner, more aggressive sound, it marks Gabriel's discovery of punk—or, more accurately, the punk aesthetic, as "D.I.Y." put it. Although some carry-overs from his art-rock days remain—for instance, the woodwinds and strings on "Indigo"—most

of the songs have an edgy, pared-down sound that ranges from the guitar rage of "On the Air" to the spare, abstract groove of "Exposure." It's the third *Peter Gabriel* album (with the melting face cover), though, that finally pushes his sound into uncharted ground. Some of that difference had to do with his embrace of the Fairlight CMI, a computer-controlled digital synthesizer that gave him unparalleled control over the sounds in his songs, but mostly it had to do with a shift in the writing itself. For the first time, Gabriel is writing from rhythm tracks instead of chord patterns, and that adds an unexpected power to his songs, whether the mood is urgent, as on "Intruder" and "No Self Control," or blissfully transcendent, as on "Games Without Frontiers" and "Biko."

Security elaborates on its predecessor's approach by adding world music elements into the mix. Granted, Gabriel made moves in this direction on "Biko," which opens with a brief mbube chorale, but that's nowhere near as dramatic as his use of the Ekome Dance Company in "The Rhythm of the Heat." Yet it isn't simply exoticism that makes the song (or the similarly flavored "San Jacinto" and "The Family and the Fishing Net") so intriguing; it's the way Gabriel incorporates such touches into his melodic structures, generating a kind of magic that's as applicable to the boisterously tuneful "Shock the Monkey" as the moody, mysterious "I Have the Touch."

Gabriel's new musical strategy didn't particularly translate to live performance, at least not on the evidence of *Plays Live* (although *P.O.V.*, a 1991 concert video shot with a different band and repertoire, isn't quite so flat). But it does make excellent soundtrack source material. In fact, several selections on the all-instrumental *Music From the Film "Birdy"* simply revamp tracks from *Security*, emphasizing mood over melodic content.

Still, the most impressive use Gabriel found for his new musical strategy can be found on *So*, on which he plays it as pop. Amazingly, he does so without compromising the ambition or adventurousness of his previous efforts; apart from the funk-inflected "Sledgehammer" and "Big Time" (both of which serve up a fair amount of sarcasm with their big-beat arrangements), the songs are astonishingly wide-ranging, drawing upon everything from Shona mbira themes (alluded to in Tony Levin's bass line for "Don't Give Up") to Senegalese mbalax singing (as represented by Youssou N'Dour's cameo on "In Your Eyes"). What makes them pop isn't their concessions (if any) to the marketplace, but the sheer ingenuity of Gabriel's songcraft.

There isn't much of that to be found on *Passion*, a soundtrack album (for Martin Scorsese's *The Last Temptation of Christ*) that takes its inspiration almost from a variety of folk music styles (specific examples of which are offered on the compilation album *Passion—Sources*). But his greatest-hits collection, *Shaking the Tree*, more than compensates, culling the most accessible tracks from his solo albums, plus a collaboration with Youssou N'Dour (the title tune) and a new version of "Here Comes the Flood." — J.D.C.

GALAXIE 500
★ **Today (Rough Trade, 1988)**
★ **On Fire (Rough Trade, 1989)**
★ **This Is Our Music (Rough Trade, 1990)**
It would be tempting to say that Galaxie 500 plays music in the tradition of the Velvet Underground—songs full of slow, muffled drones, affectless vocals and occasional squawks of feedback—except for the fact that had the Velvets been this pointless and self-indulgent, nobody would have remembered them long enough for there to be a tradition. By *This Is Our Music*, this feckless trio had improved to the point of including shreds of melody in its songs, although given Dean Wareham's difficulties with pitch, this may have been entirely accidental. — J.D.C.

GANG OF FOUR
★ ★ ★ ★½ **Entertainment! (Warner Bros., 1979)**
★ ★½ **Gang of Four (EP) (Warner Bros., 1980)**
★ ★ ★ **Solid Gold (Warner Bros., 1981)**
★ ★ ★ ★ **Another Day, Another Dollar (EP) (Warner Bros., 1981)**

★ ★ ★ **Songs of the Free (Warner Bros., 1982)**
★ ★ **Hard (Warner Bros., 1983)**
★ ★ ★ ★ **A Brief History of the Twentieth Century (Warner Bros., 1990)**
★ ★ **Mall (Polydor, 1991)**
Oh, the burden of a university education! Gang of Four sprang up around England's Leeds University about the same time as the Mekons, the Au Pairs and Delta 5, exhibiting a marked fondness for brittle, simplistic funk riffs, jagged, post-Hendrix guitar noise and, in the lyrics, a blunt, post-Marxist dialectic. But what kept the Gang of Four from slipping—at least at first—into the sort of postgraduate tedium such a formula suggests was a flair for propulsive, approachable pop and an understanding that the band's ideology should never supersede its musical values. (Even its radicalism had its lighter side, since the band name was as much a pun on the band's four-piece lineup as a reference to Mme. Jiang Qing and her counterrevolutionary cohorts.) *Entertainment!* draws most of its energy from Andy Gill's slash-and-burn rhythm guitar, which uses feedback-singed shards of sound to cauterize the beat, making the music as abrasive as any punk act without sacrificing its rhythmic agility. Earlier versions of this approach can be found on the *Gang of Four* EP, but *Solid Gold* downplays Gill, making it a disappointment despite the rhythm section's valiant efforts. *Another Day, Another Dollar* pumps up the rhythm section even further, while restoring Gill to his primacy; as a result, "To Hell with Poverty" stands as the group's finest moment. Unfortunately, bassist Dave Allen—the disco cover band vet who first gave the Gang its funk—left soon thereafter, and things quickly fell apart. Although *Songs of the Free* and *Hard* have their moments, they are few and far between, as the Gang's efforts to spruce up its sound with slick production merely highlights the vocal inadequacies of front man Jon King. *A Brief History* is a choppy but well-chosen best-of; *Mall* is a comeback attempt that finds the Gang of Two (Gill and King) plying its old formula amidst house beats and painfully didactic samples. — J.D.C.

THE GAP BAND
★ ★ **The Gap Band (Mercury, 1979)**
★ ★½ **The Gap Band II (Mercury, 1979)**
★ ★ ★ **The Gap Band III (Mercury, 1980)**

★★★★ Gap Band IV (Total Experience, 1982)
★★★ The Gap Band V-Jammin' (Total Experience, 1983)
★★★★ Gap Gold; Best of the Gap Band (Mercury, 1985)
★★ Gap Band VI (Total Experience, 1985)
★½ Gap Band VII (Total Experience, 1986)
★½ Gap Band VIII (Total Experience, 1986)
★★★ The 12" Collection (Mercury, 1986)
★½ Straight From the Heart (Total Experience, 1987)
★★ Round Trip (Capitol, 1989)

So what if the Gap Band's best ideas are generally just P-Funk rip-offs? Originality has always played second-fiddle to groove in dance music, and that goes double for this crew. Consisting of brothers Ronnie, Charles and Robert Wilson, the Gap Band had a handful of solid (if slightly goofy) funk hits spread across its first three albums, including "I Don't Believe You Want to Get Up and Dance (Oops!)" from *The Gap Band II*, and "Burn Rubber On Me (Why You Wanna Hurt Me)" from *The Gap Band III*, which also includes the Isley-style ballad "Yearning for Your Love." But it was *Gap Band IV* that made the group's reputation, stretching as it does from the rhythmic insistence of "Early in the Morning" and "You Dropped a Bomb On Me" to slow and soulful songs like "Stay With Me" (a thinly veiled rewrite of the Orleans hit "Dance With Me") and "Outstanding."

Unfortunately, the group pretty much peaked there. *The Gap Band V* does deliver a workable groove with "Party Train," but *Gap Band VI* begins to fall back on stuff like "Beep a Freak," which seems derivative even by this band's standards. *Gap Gold* collects all the hits to this point (meaning, in other words, all the hits), and includes five of *Gap Band IV*'s eight selections. Subsequent albums, however, merely chronicle the Gap-sters' slow march to irrelevance. — J.D.C.

JERRY GARCIA
★★½ Garcia (Warner Bros., 1972)
★★ Compliments (Grateful Dead, 1974)
★★½ Garcia (Round, 1974)
★★ Merl Saunders, Jerry Garcia, John Kahn, Bill Vitt: Live at the Keystone (Fantasy, 1973)
★★½ Reflections (Round, 1976)
★★★½ Cats Under the Stars (Arista, 1978)

★★★ Run for the Roses (Arista, 1982)
★★★ Almost Acoustic (Grateful Dead, 1988)
★★★½ Jerry Garcia Band (Arista, 1991)
WITH DAVID GRISMAN
★★★½ Jerry Garcia/David Grisman (Acoustic Disc, 1991)

Sounding very much like the mellower Grateful Dead, Jerry Garcia's solo work is pleasant and unremarkable. In combination with Dead lyricist Robert Hunter, he turns out well-crafted fare; his vocals are capable, his guitar, as always, understated and stunning. The Arista records are the glossiest but also the best. On *Cats Under the Stars*, the vocal ensemble of Garcia, Keith Godchaux and Donna Godchaux shines on the lovely "Down Home"—and "Palm Sunday," too, is graceful. *Run for the Roses* features laid-back keyboardist Merl Saunders, unerring drummer Ron Tutt and other expert players on competent originals and fairly mild covers (a midtempo reading of the Beatles' "I Saw Her Standing There," a reggaeish twist on Dylan's "Knockin' on Heaven's Door" and a remake of Clyde McPhatter's "Without Love" that boasts excellent singing by Garcia). On the Dead's label, the live *Almost Acoustic* is delightful; a folk quintet tackles such Dead classics as "Casey Jones" and "Ripple." Two of Garcia's strongest sets are his most recent— the acoustic gem, *Jerry Garcia/David Grisman*, is a fine collaboration between the guitarist and a legendary mandolinist; *Jerry Garcia Band* is a live double-album that features Jerry's expert dueling with organist Melvin Seals. — P.E.

ART GARFUNKEL
★★½ Angel Clare (Columbia, 1973)
★★★ Breakaway (Columbia, 1975)
★★★½ Watermark (Columbia, 1977)
★★ Fate for Breakfast (Columbia, 1979)
★½ Scissors Cut (Columbia, 1981)
★ Lefty (Columbia, 1988)
★★★ Garfunkel (Columbia, 1988)

On his own, Garfunkel exhibits many of the same strengths that marked his work with Simon—an angelic tenor, a fine sense of subtlety, and a genius for harmony vocals. Unfortunately, that's not enough to support a solo career, and without a strong creative voice to play off, Garfunkel's albums end up seeming as empty as they are pretty. *Angel Clare* is all too typical. When given good material, like Randy Newman's "Old Man" or Van Morrison's "I Shall Sing," Garfunkel is in his element, but when the material slips, as on "Mary Was an

Only Child," so does his performance. Fortunately, *Breakaway* maintains standards high enough to keep that from being a problem; he soars on oldies like the Flamingos' "I Only Have Eyes for You" and Stevie Wonder's "I Believe (When I Fall In Love With You It Will Be Forever)," while "99 Miles from L.A." and the Gallagher and Lyle title tune give him ample opportunity to show off his gift for longing. There's even a Simon and Garfunkel reunion in "My Little Town." But it's *Watermark*, built around a Jimmy Webb song cycle, that highlights Garfunkel's solo career. The album's combination of innocence and loss makes it the perfect vehicle for Garfunkel's voice, even though the cover of Sam Cooke's "(What a) Wonderful World," cut with Simon and James Taylor, was the only hit.

From there, it's pretty much straight downhill. *Fate for Breakfast*, an indigestible attempt at mainstreaming Garfunkel's sound, invests too much in slick sound and not enough in songwriting; *Scissors Cut* returns to Webb and Gallagher and Lyle, but is too dull to leave a mark; and *Lefty* strikes out, whether with the emptily dramatic "I Have a Love" or the pallid attempt at "When a Man Loves a Woman." *Garfunkel* proves that a greatest-hits package is not necessarily the same thing as a best-of album. — J.D.C.

JUDY GARLAND

★★★★ **Judy (1956; Capitol, 1989)**
★★★★★ **Judy at Carnegie Hall (Capitol, 1961)**
★★★★ **Miss Show Business (1963; Capitol, 1989)**
★★★★ **Judy Garland Live! (Capitol, 1989)**
★★★ **The Best of the Decca Years, Vol. One—Hits! (MCA, 1989)**
★★★★ **All-Time Greatest Hits (Curb, 1991)**
★★★★ **The One & Only (Capitol, 1991)**

The quintessential diva of desperate emotionalism, Judy Garland perfected that style of melodramatic yearning and big-production "heart" that survives not only in the work of Bette Midler, Barbra Streisand and Garland's own daughter, Liza Minnelli, but also figures, however indirectly, in the outsized deliveries of Madonna and Anita Baker.

Born Frances Ethel Gumm (George Jessel supplied her with her stage name), Garland sang in vaudeville hallls with her two sisters before scoring a solo contract with MGM

in 1935. Starring, with Mickey Rooney, as America's sweetheart in the Andy Hardy films of the late '30s, she cemented her persona of "little girl lost" with the colossal success of *The Wizard of Oz* and its Harold Arlen-penned theme, "Somewhere Over the Rainbow." The song's note of wide-eyed wonder set the tone for her subsequent work—no matter how sophisticated the later Garland's material became, her signature mood was always one of longing.

Garland's notorious insecurity (manifested in bouts of drinking, pill-taking and general despair) was classically that of the child star forced always to confront the demons of precocious celebrity—the adult Garland, however, proved to be a powerhouse talent. The strongest evidence of both her impressive vocal skill and almost eerie capacity for emotional outpouring remains *Judy at Carnegie Hall.* With Mort Lindsey leading a crack orchestra in this 1961 set, it presents the mature performer in front of her absolutely adoring public—and Garland storms through her hits ("The Trolley Song," "For Me and My Gal," "That's Entertainment"). By turns brash and winsome, she's engaging on anything uptempo, but it's the ballads, "Alone Together" and "The Man That Got Away," among others, that are the real revelation—Judy sings about loss in a way, that for all its theater, remains harrowing in its intensity. A lush box set, *The One & Only* is primarily for Garland maniacs; however, if *Carnegie Hall* wins you over, the three CDs of studio and stage work are well worth checking out. Strong solo work from the late '50s and early '60s, *Judy* and *Miss Show Business* are Garland doing what she did best—interpreting, with trembling verve, the work of classic American songwriters. Recently unearthed, *Judy Garland Live!* rescues 1962 performances the singer had made as a follow-up to the Carnegie Hall recordings; at the time, studio execs had considered that her voice had coarsened to the point of embarrassment and refused to put out the disc. *Live!* proves them half-way wrong: indeed, Judy sounds strained at times—but the passion of her delivery lends her songs, if anything, an even greater measure of pathos. — P.E.

MARVIN GAYE

★★★½ **That Stubborn Kind of Fellow (Tamla, 1963)**
★★★½ **M.P.G. (Tamla, 1969)**
★★★★ **Superhits (Tamla, 1970)**
★★★★★ **What's Going On (Tamla, 1971)**

★★½ **Trouble Man Soundtrack (Tamla, 1972)**
★★★★ **Let's Get It On (Tamla, 1973)**
★★★★★ **Anthology (Tamla, 1974)**
★★½ **I Want You (Tamla, 1976)**
★★★ **Live at the London Palladium (Tamla, 1977)**
★★★½ **Here, My Dear (Tamla, 1978)**
★★★ **In Our Lifetime (Tamla, 1981)**
★★★★ **Midnight Love (Columbia, 1982)**
★★½ **Dream of a Lifetime (Columbia, 1985)**
★★ **Romantically Yours (Columbia, 1985)**
★★★★ **Motown Remembers Marvin Gaye (Tamla, 1986)**
★★★½ **I Heard It Through the Grapevine (Motown, 1986)**
★★★ **The Marvin Gaye Collection (Tamla/Motown, 1990)**
★★★ **The Last Concert Tour (Giant, 1991)**

Marvin Gaye is the original love man. His suave, effortless delivery carries a warming blast of blues fire. As the '60s progressed, this Motown pioneer excelled at both ultra-romantic duets and forward-looking R&B tracks like "I Heard It Through the Grapevine." By the early '70s, Gaye had absorbed the expansive spirit of Bob Dylan and the Beatles; between its pointedly topical lyrics and rich orchestration, *What's Going On* revolutionized the sound of soul music. Returning to the love songs that made him famous on later albums, Gaye continued to challenge himself musically until his death in 1984.

Simply put, Marvin Gaye made some of the very best records to come out of Berry Gordy's hit factory. Like all Motown artists, he was geared toward singles, and like all Motown artists, his classics from the '60s are best consumed on greatest hits or best-of anthologies. There are dozens of inferior collections and competing reissues available on most Motown artists; in Marvin Gaye's case, all his definitive works are still in print too. Proceed with caution. Though Motown's filler-to-hit ratio is notorious, *That Stubborn Kind of Fellow* ("Pride and Joy," "Hitch Hike,") and the later *M.P.G.* ("Too Busy Thinking About My Baby," "That's The Way Love Is") are better than average albums, reflecting Marvin's range. *Superhits* barely skims the surface of those years; *Anthology* delivers the cream of Marvin Gaye. It collects Gaye's solo hits from "Stubborn Kind of Fellow" on through *What's Going On* and the funky *Trouble Man* movie theme from '72. Also

included are heavenly vocal matchups with Mary Wells ("What's the Matter With You Baby"), Kim Weston ("It Takes Two") and most spectacularly, Tammi Terrell ("Ain't No Mountain High Enough"). Primo soul, from start to finish.

Beginning with *What's Going On*, Gaye made albums, not singles. Though there's overlap between the two, *What's Going On* fits on the shelf right next to *Anthology*. The hopeful concern of "Mercy Mercy Me (The Ecology)" and "Inner City Blues (Makes Me Wanna Holler)" gains weight from the solid gospel underpinnings and lush overall sound. The sexy rhythmic grind on *Let's Get It On* anticipates disco, but Gaye's voice exudes a warm R&B sophistication that reaches beyond the dance floor. Even his sweet nothings ("You Sure Love to Ball," "Keep Gettin' It On") leap out of the ever-shifting groove. *I Want You* is a considerably less urgent follow-up.

Live at the London Palladium is far from the definitive concert album, though it's almost worth getting for the full studio version of "Got to Give It Up." This 1977 Number One qualifies as a full-fledged disco hit—and one of the very best, with Marvin's sweet falsetto floating around a rump-bumping rhythm that doesn't give up for 12 minutes. *Here, My Dear* is Gaye's musical farewell to his departing wife Anna Gordy; it's a rambling, jazz-influenced double-record concept album about their divorce. Occasionally bitter lyrics are more than offset by the music's supple touch and Gaye's own tuneful instinct. However painful its subject matter, *Here, My Dear* is always listenable and occasionally ("A Funky Space Reincarnation") danceable.

In Our Lifetime folds traces of reggae and African grooves into a gently simmering stew that never quite bubbles over into a sweet funk. *Midnight Love* scored a Number Three with the gorgeous "Sexual Healing," reasserting Gaye's command of both the sensual and spiritual sides of soul music. Fresh Caribbean rhythms enliven the rest of the album; as on *Let's Get It On*, the hypnotic vocal variations never grow repetitious. Gaye's death in 1984 prompted a flood of vault-emptying at both his surviving record companies. His new label dropped two forgettable ones: *Dream of a Lifetime* (1985) boasts some randy X-rated outtakes that should have stayed in the closet. *Romantically Yours* (1986) is awash in gloopy strings. *Motown Remembers Marvin Gaye*, on the other hand, does its subject proud: these outtakes and should-have-beens, mostly from the '60s, hold up quite well against Gaye's best known. A real find, this album must be recommended over the spotty, overlong box set. *The Marvin Gaye Collection* gets bogged down by the kind of song selection that drove Gaye to rebel with *What's Going On* in the first place. — M.C.

CRYSTAL GAYLE

★★★★ Classic Crystal (EMI, 1979)
  ★★ These Days (Columbia, 1980)
  ★★ Hollywood, Tennessee (1981; Capitol/Nashville, 1990)
  ★★ Crystal Gayle's Greatest Hits (Columbia, 1983)
  ★★ A Crystal Christmas (Warner Bros., 1986)
  ★ What If We Fall in Love (Warner Bros., 1987)
  ★★ Best of Crystal Gayle (Warner Bros., 1987)
  ★★ Nobody's Angel (Warner Bros., 1988)
  ★★★ Ain't Gonna Worry (Capitol/Nashville, 1990)
  ★★★ All-Time Greatest Hits (Curb, 1990)

Crystal Gayle has avoided comparisons with her older sister Loretta Lynn by steering her career away from hard country into country-pop with a tinge of blue. The tremble in her voice and its occasional weepy quality betray the influence of Tammy Wynette, with whom Gayle also shares a penchant for melodrama. *Classic Crystal* summarizes her early years on United Artists, and includes the hit single that put her on the pop map in 1977, "Don't It Make My Brown Eyes Blue," as well as its Number One follow-up, "Talking in Your Sleep." The Columbia years found Gayle adrift, mostly for lack of good material and a seeming uncertainty as to whether she should move more in a pop direction, or more into country. A move to Warner Bros. was a step in the right direction, and these albums—save for the horrendous duets with Gary Morris on *What If We Fall in Love*—find Gayle in a country vein. Another label change, to Capitol, resulted in *Ain't Gonna Worry* (1990), which finds her teamed with a first-rate producer in Allen Reynolds and the strongest set of songs she's had since the UA days. Vocally, she sounds warmer and more open as she moves from the gentle pleading of "Everybody's Reaching Out for Someone" to the forceful passion of "Just Like the Blues." This is the album she needed to make after leaving UA, but better late than never. — D.M.

GLORIA GAYNOR

★★★½ Never Can Say Goodbye (MGM, 1975)
  ★★ Experience Gloria Gaynor (MGM, 1975)
  ★★ I've Got You (Polydor, 1976)
  ★★ Glorious (Polydor, 1977)
  ★★ Gloria Gaynor's Park Avenue Sound (Polydor, 1978)
★★★½ Love Tracks (Polydor, 1979)
  ★★★ I Have a Right (Polydor, 1979)
  ★★ Gloria Gaynor (Polydor, 1982)
★★★½ Gloria Gaynor's Greatest Hits (Polydor, 1988)

Unrivalled by anyone other than Donna Summer as the quintessential disco diva, Gaynor belts and wails credibly enough—but it's the team of Tony Bongiovi, Meco Monardo and Jay Ellis which proves beyond question that disco was mainly a producer's art form. Congas, swirling strings, muted wah-wah guitars and swishing hi-hat cymbals elevate the trailblazing suite of "Honey Bee," "Never Can Say Goodbye," "Reach Out I'll Be There," off Gaynor's debut, into campy funk glory. *Love Tracks*, with the "Me Decade" anthem, also cooks—but her *Greatest Hits* is probably the only other essential Gloria for all but connoisseurs of this still-dubious genre. — P.E.

THE J. GEILS BAND

★★★½ The J. Geils Band (Atlantic, 1970)
  ★★★ The Morning After (Atlantic, 1971)
★★★½ Full House (Atlantic, 1972)
  ★★½ Bloodshot (Atlantic, 1973)
  ★★★ Ladies Invited (Atlantic, 1973)
  ★★½ Nightmares . . . and Other Tales From the Vinyl Jungle (Atlantic, 1974)
  ★★½ Hotline (Atlantic, 1975)
  ★★½ Blow Your Face Out (Atlantic, 1976)
★★★½ Monkey Island (Atlantic, 1977)
  ★★★ Sanctuary (EMI America, 1978)
  ★★★ The Best of the J. Geils Band (Atlantic, 1979)
  ★★★ Love Stinks (EMI America, 1980)
★★★½ Freeze-Frame (EMI America, 1981)
  ★★★ The Best of the J. Geils Band, Volume 2 (Atlantic, 1982)
  ★★★ Showtime! (EMI America, 1982)
  ★★½ You're Getting Even While I'm Getting Odd (EMI America, 1984)
★★★★ Flashback: The Best of the J. Geils Band (EMI America, 1985)

The lead guitarist lent this Boston sextet its name. And the hyperactive lead singer— former R&B DJ Peter Wolf—was the living, jive-talking embodiment of the phrase "impossible to ignore." But the J. Geils Band really was a band; that's what sets this roots-stoking crew apart from its blooze & boogie competition. Rather than jam and solo till the cows came home, they could catch a collective groove and ride it. On a good night, that is, onstage. On record, the J. Geils Band remained a dicey, inconsistent pick until the early '80s. Finally adding a needed touch of pop refinement to their ragged bamalama raveup formula, the band scored its biggest hits and then broke up.

The J. Geils Band mixes scorching R&B covers ("Homework," "First I Look at the Purse") with like-minded originals: the group's grasp is deceptively loose, sloppy but sure. After a less distinctive second helping (*The Morning After*), J. Geils weighed in with an industrial-strength live album. Recorded in front of a typically rabid Detroit audience, *Full House* captures the band's musical strengths—harpist Magic Dick blows a furious blues called "Whammer Jammer"—and also its weaknesses. Over the next few albums, in fact, the Geils Band let its party-cartoon image overshadow its chops and commitment. *Ladies Invited* marks a small return to soulfulness, but "Must of Got Lost"—a huge step forward in terms of rhythm and emotion—gets buried amid a pile of greasy Stones rips on the 1974 *Nightmares* outing.

The Geils Band was flirting with self-parody by the time of *Blow Your Face Out*; tellingly, its second live album is almost twice as long and not half as exciting as *Full House*. Things turned around quickly, though. *Monkey Island* shows the group focusing on songwriting and arrangement to a far greater degree than before, while maintaining the expected breakneck energy level most of the time. Everything but the pretentious title track works, even—especially—the quasi-autobiographical "Wreckage." The development continues on *Sanctuary* ("One Last Kiss," the title track) and *Love Stinks* ("Just Can't Wait," the title track), though inane filler-jokes like "No Anchovies, Please" (from *Love Stinks*) persist. *Freeze-Frame* jettisons that adolescent silliness in favor of the sardonic "Centerfold" and the haunting "Angel in Blue," adding synthesizers and a bit of cheeky new-wave irrereverence. Well, there is a track called

"Piss on the Wall" too. EMI's posthumous *The Best of the J. Geils Band* is consistent from soup to nuts. When Peter Wolf left for a solo career in 1983, the remaining members went on to release the lackluster *You're Getting Even While I'm Gettin' Odd*.
— M.C.

BOB GELDOF
★ ★ **Deep in the Heart of Nowhere (Atlantic, 1986)**
★ ★ **The Vegetarians of Love (Atlantic, 1988)**
By the time Bob Geldof set about organizing the historic Band Aid concerts in 1984, his original band, the Boomtown Rats, was fizzling out. Though it would be nice to report that Geldof's exemplary battle against world hunger inspired a satisfying solo career, such is not the case. Both his solo albums are torturously ponderous, musically bankrupt affairs. *Deep in the Heart of Nowhere* taps an incongruous electro-pop groove for his ameliorative musings, while *The Vegeterians of Love* cooks up a folk-laced acoustic backing for the numbing likes of "Chains of Pain" and "The End of the World." Instead, try reading Geldof's lucidly written, anecdote-stuffed 1987 autobiography.
— M.C.

GENERAL PUBLIC
★ ★   **. . . All the Rage (I.R.S., 1984)**
★ ★½ **Hand to Mouth (I.R.S., 1986)**
With both Dave Wakeling and Ranking Roger in the front line, General Public has no trouble duplicating the English Beat's vocal sound. But without Andy Cox and David Steele, GP lacks the Beat's drive and fluidity, and that makes all the difference. Despite the occasional buoyancy provided by "Never You Done That" or "As a Matter of Fact," the songs on . . . *All the Rage* are all craft and no soul. *Hand to Mouth* improves matters slightly, thanks to the high dudgeon of "Forward As One."
— J.D.C.

GENERATION X
★ ★ ★½ **Generation X (Chrysalis, 1978)**
 ★ ★½ **Valley of the Dolls (Chrysalis, 1979)**
 ★ ★   **Kiss Me Deadly (Chrysalis, 1981)**
Even his nom de punk sets the former William Broad apart from his class of '77 peers: Billy Idol doesn't have quite the same ring as Johnny Rotten or Joe Strummer. Idol never hid his pop aspirations, but the band he fronted, Generation X, achieved credibility as well as a fair amount of commercial acceptance with hooky

slam-fests like "Your Generation," "Ready Steady Go" and "Wild Youth." A snarling, provocative cover version of John Lennon's "Truth" rounds out *Generation X*, but the Ian Hunter-produced *Valley Of the Dolls* sounds stale. Generation X released one more album, *Kiss Me Deadly*, before Idol skipped the country with its best cut "Dancing With Myself," which he recut to jump-start his stateside solo career. Gen X, without Idol, died a quick death. — M.C.

GENESIS

★ ★½ **From Genesis to Revelation (1969; DCC, 1990)**
★ ★½ **Trespass (1970; MCA, 1980)**
★ ★ **Nursery Cryme (Atlantic, 1971)**
★ ★½ **Foxtrot (Atlantic, 1972)**
★ ★ ★ **Genesis Live (Atlantic, 1973)**
★ ★ **Selling England by the Pound (Atlantic, 1973)**
★ ★ ★½ **The Lamb Lies Down on Broadway (Atco, 1974)**
★ ★ ★½ **A Trick of the Tail (Atco, 1976)**
★ ★ ★ **Wind and Wuthering (Atco, 1977)**
★ ★ ★ **Seconds Out (Atlantic, 1977)**
★ ★ ★½ **. . . And Then There Were Three (Atlantic, 1978)**
★ ★ ★ ★ **Duke (Atlantic, 1980)**
★ ★ ★½ **Abacab (Atlantic, 1981)**
★ ★½ **Three Sides Live (Atlantic, 1982)**
★ ★ ★ ★ **Genesis (Atlantic, 1983)**
★ ★ ★½ **Invisible Touch (Atlantic, 1986)**
★ ★ ★½ **We Can't Dance (Atlantic, 1991)**

Like Rodney Dangerfield, Genesis has had a hard time getting respect. In the early '70s, when the group specialized in ambitious, theatrical story songs, it attracted an avid cult following but was largely ignored by the rock press and the public at large. Later in the decade, lead singer Peter Gabriel was finally recognized as a major talent—but only after he'd left the band, which was at this point being derided as middlebrow throwbacks still in thrall to the pomposities of art rock. Even in the early '80s, when Genesis did finally shed its art-rock inclinations and moved toward pop, becoming international stars in the process, the press was unimpressed, dismissing the group as easy-listening lightweights. By the '90s, even the solo success of members Phil Collins and Mike Rutherford was being held against the group, by then one of the best-known rock acts in the world.

All of which has been grossly unfair. Granted, Genesis has made its share of mediocre albums—perhaps even more than its share, considering how long the band has been around. But bad albums? None to

speak of. In fact, the worst that can be said of the group's early albums is that they sound dated, almost quaint. *From Genesis to Revelation* seems laughably "mod" at points—for instance, the jazzy, bongo-spiked intro to "The Serpent"—but that hardly takes away from the genuinely tuneful quality of the songs. Genesis was hardly a band when this was recorded, however, and it isn't until *Trespass* that we get any real sense of what the group has to offer. Unfortunately, it's something of a mixed bag. At their best, the lyrics are grippingly mythic, but too often Gabriel's wordplay loses its way in a forest of puns and self-conscious allusions; likewise the music, although often potently melodic and making nice use of Tony Banks's semi-orchestral approach to keyboards, is frequently sidetracked by too-busy arrangements and needlessly ornate embellishments.

That was pretty much the pattern for the band's early albums, though. *Nursery Cryme*, for instance, offers Mother Goose tales in the ten-minute "The Musical Box," while *Foxtrot* concludes with the marathon "Supper's Ready," an ambitious, inscrutable 23-minute suite built around such titles as "Apocalypse in 9/8 (co-starring the delicious talents of Gabble Ratchet)." Stilted as this stuff sometimes sounded in the studio, it did have an edge in concert; indeed, the performances on *Genesis Live* are enough to make even the most skeptical listener reconsider the value of "The Return of the Giant Hogweed." But "edge" wasn't really what this band was looking for, and so *Selling England by the Pound* continues Genesis's journey into the conceptual, flanking blissfully melodic material like "I Know What I Like (in Your Wardrobe)" with the self-consciously clever "Dancing with the Moonlit Knight" and its ilk. No wonder, then, that the group's masterpiece move—an intensely abstruse double album entitled *The Lamb Lies Down on Broadway*—is both brilliant and overblown, with moments of genuine majesty and long stretches of pointless obscurantism.

Gabriel left in 1975, and Genesis auditioned hundreds of singers before finally deciding on Collins, who had been drumming with the group since *Trespass* (and who, in fact, had already sung lead on "More Fool Me," from *Selling England*). It was a canny choice, for Collins, though obviously possessing a voice of his own, sounds enough like Gabriel to ensure a smooth transition for the band. Even so, it isn't Collins's voice that makes *A Trick of the Tail* a turning point for the band—it's the writing. Instead of showcasing the band's cleverness, this album puts the emphasis on the music, unveiling an unexpected gift for close-harmony singing in "Entangled." *Wind & Wuthering* expands the band's musical palette further; typical is the droll clockwork effect that crops up during an instrumental segment of "One for the Vine." More telling, though, is the ballad "Your Own Special Way," a gorgeously lilting love song that seems a harbinger of the band's pop-friendly future.

Indeed, after *Seconds Out*—a concert double album apparently intended to prove that Collins and company could handle the band's back catalog—Genesis made a genuine pop breakthrough with . . . *And Then There Were Three*. With guitarist Steve Hackett gone, Genesis's studio lineup is reduced to just Collins, Banks and Rutherford, and while that doesn't noticeably affect the instrumental mix, it does hone the playing so that there's less empty flash and wasted energy. At this point, the songs are the focus, and while that doesn't prevent the band from showing off (note the odd-metered rhythms of "Down and Out"), it does add power to character songs like "Say It's Alright Joe," and it gave the band its first U.S. pop success, through the winsome, upbeat "Follow You, Follow Me." *Duke* and *Abacab* further enhance the group's pop reputation—the former through "Misunderstanding," a simple, poignant broken-heart song that brings Collins to the fore as a writer, and the latter through "No Reply at All," a surprisingly complex composition that leaves the band plenty of playing room yet maintains strong melodic content. Unfortunately, these pop-oriented efforts are followed by *Three Sides Live*, a double album that's mostly live and totally tedious.

It hardly mattered, though, for by this point the band's superstar status had been established beyond the shadow of a doubt, and both *Genesis* and *Invisible Touch* merely seemed to confirm its popularity. And not without reason, either, as both are sublimely melodic, producing hits as effortless and idiosyncratic as "That's All" (from *Genesis*) and "Tonight, Tonight, Tonight" (from *Invisible Touch*). But *We Can't Dance*, despite its strong pop inclinations, finds the band trying to reclaim some of its old turf, a move that works surprisingly well,

thanks to tuneful but extended numbers like "Driving the Last Spike" and "Fading Lights." — J.D.C.

BOBBIE GENTRY
★★★ Ode to Billy Joe (Capitol, 1967)
★★★½ Bobbie Gentry's Greatest (Capitol, 1967)

Hitting massively in 1967 with "Ode to Billy Joe," Mississippi's Bobbie Gentry was soon swallowed by easy-listening radio and a soft-country audience. Perhaps her Dolly-clone bouffant and fake lashes caused others not to pay her much mind—a mistake. It's hard to ignore the power of "Ode," a folk epic about Deep South love and suicide—its depiction of rural life rendered in compelling detail—backed by a slow, Tony Joe White-ish swampy syncopation, and sung with Gentry's characteristic precision. But the rest of her best is almost as fine. With its celebration of "chigger bites" and "scuppernongs," "Mississippi Delta" catalogues regionalist pleasures with care, and Gentry's vocal is fine soul. A sort of novelty number, "Ace Insurance Man," includes a country bumpkin voice-over that's a bit daft. "Glory Hallelujah, How They'll Sing" and "Sweet Peony" are slight. When she's working other people's material, or dueting with Glen Campbell on "All I Have to Do Is Dream" (1970), she's never less than competent. — P.E.

THE GENTRYS
★★ Keep On Dancing (MGM, 1965)

With its tight snare sound, funky trumpet lines and slick organ riffs, "Keep On Dancing" was a great prom hit in 1965. Singers Jimmy Hart and Larry Raspberry were right for radio and the rest of this Memphis garage band were snappy players. But they never delivered anything as delightful as their one hit. — P.E.

BARBARA GEORGE
★★★ I Know (You Don't Love Me No More) (Collectables, NA)

New Orleans–born Barbara George was one of the more versatile Crescent City pop singers, whose only substantial hit, "I Know (You Don't Love Me No More)," from 1961, only partially illustrated her depth as a singer. This re-release of her first album for the A.F.O. label shows her equally at home with R&B, New Orleans–style rock & roll and blues ballads; she was only 19 when she cut "I Know" and the other songs here, but she is one of those remarkable female singers of the time who seemed mature well

beyond her years. Unlike most of her female contemporaries, though, George wrote and performed her own material, including her big hit. Among the 12 cuts here the only dud is George's pedestrian cover of the Lenny Welch hit, "Since I Fell for You."
— D.M.

THE GEORGIA SATELLITES
★★★½ **The Georgia Satellites (Elektra, 1986)**
★★★½ **Open All Night (Elektra, 1988)**
★★★½ **In the Land of Salvation and Sin (Elektra, 1989)**

"Keep Your Hands to Yourself," from *The Georgia Satellites* roughed up the pop Top Ten in 1986; between its bramble-patch guitar charge and no-nonsense take on the travails of lust, this Atlanta bar band seemed refreshingly out-of-touch. Apparently, nobody told the Satellites that the neo-Stones thing wasn't happening. If there isn't an obvious follow up single to "Hands" on *Open All Night*, well, the blooze on tap never runs flat, either. Lead singer Dan Baird puts across his randy tales with verve and a beguiling humility. Good-time purists might be offended by his singer-songwriter moves on the next Satellites album; while uneven and a little overwrought, *In The Land of Salvation and Sin* shows promise. The Satellites are recommended to devotees of thoughtful boogie in the Little Feat-Lowell George mode. — M.C.

GERARDO
★★ **Mo' Ritmo (Interscope/Atlantic, 1991)**

This red-hot crossover rapper is a pure product of music video. Gerardo's appeal on the small screen seems as well-defined as his pectorals. Turn off the tube, though, and his album sounds calculated and empty. Gerardo credits Parliament for his "We Want the Funk," at least. Baldly recycling that groove, he also manages to flatten George Clinton's high spirits. No great shakes as a rapper, Gerardo deserves some credit: his delivery is smooth. The way he hip-hops from English to Spanish in every song holds your attention. Sadly, Gerardo brings a swaggering, old-school machismo to his stance. Pumping the pleasures of promiscuity, he revives a string of tired cliches about "loving 'em and leaving 'em." Gerardo isn't downright offensive; he's just immature. Growing up on MTV won't be easy. — M.C.

GERRY AND THE PACEMAKERS
★★½ **The Best of Gerry and the Pacemakers, the Definitive Years (EMI, 1991)**

Baby boomers overcome by nostalgia for Merseybeat might still find merit in Gerry and the Pacemakers, one of the original groups to hit big with that plucky early '60s sound—but these Liverpool lads make even the early Beatles' sweetest tunes sound ferocious. The Pacemakers' pop was mawkish—with their sappy strings and crooning vocals, "Don't Let the Sun Catch You Crying" and "Ferry Cross the Mersey" are really bathetic. Their upbeat hits, "I Like It" and "How Do You Do It" come across as almost idiotically cheery—and as for their rock & roll credibility, it helps to remember that one of their biggest hits was a cover of Rodgers and Hammerstein's "You'll Never Walk Alone." — P.E.

GETO BOYS
★★½ **The Geto Boys (Def American, 1990)**
★★★ **We Can't Be Stopped (Def American, 1991)**

While there's no denying the visceral impact of this Houston-based crew's gangsta rapping, there's also precious little to recommend on its debut album. Musically speaking, Bushwick Bill and the lads specialize in crude rhymes and rudimentary-at-best beats. But music surely isn't what attracted national attention to the group; it's hard to even think about giving up the funk when you're bombarded by gruesomely detailed porno-violence ("Gangster of Love"), rape and dismemberment fantasies ("Mind of a Lunatic") or just the seemingly endless, soul-numbing rounds of "fuck you!" Any sort of dramatic distance or telling irony seems to be well beyond the Boys' grasp; unlike horror movie directors, rappers pride themselves on striking a note of realism and immediacy above all else. Whatever hard-earned insight the group has gleaned from inner city life—"Life in the Fast Lane" and "City Under Seige" both have solid points to make—gets snuffed by the pervasive air of sensationalism.

We Can't Be Stopped is an even less-imaginative sequel, save for one stone killer of a track: "Mind Playing Tricks on Me." Clean enough to get played on the radio (and become a hit), funky enough to rivet your attention without curses or murder threats, "Mind" paints a chilling portrait of the the personal cost of drug addiction. If the Geto Boys ever decide to pursue this sharpened mainstream angle full-time—leaving the sick thrills to Freddie Kreuger, "Chuckie" and other filmic slashers—it could become truly dangerous: a positive hip-hop force, rather than a First Amendment–protected media hype. — M.C.

DEBBIE GIBSON

★ ★½ **Out of the Blue (Atlantic, 1987)**
★ ★ **Electric Youth (Atlantic, 1989)**
★ **Anything Is Possible (Atlantic, 1990)**
However you stretch it, bubblegum eventually loses its snap. For a shameless Madonna wannabe, though, Debbie Gibson displayed a certain precocious talent right off the bat. Writing all the songs on *Out of the Blue*, producing the Top Ten hit "Foolish Beat" herself, the 17-year-old Long Islander came on like a young Carole King. If Gibson's peppy dance hits "Shake Your Love" and "Out of the Blue" sound prepackaged to adult ears, they do project an appealing, almost preteen innocence. Problem is, Gibson can't seem to escape that puppy-love phase of development. *Electric Youth* grasps at Significance. Attempting to speak for her generation, Debbie commits one of the most empty-headed anthems of all time. At least the mindless zeal of "Electric Youth" is catchy: the rest of the album lumbers into Tin Pan Alley. *Anything Is Possible* stands in blatant contradiction of its title: strained, "adult" funk numbers coexist rather uneasily with chaste heartbreak ballads. In her own parlance, Debbie Gibson went for it—only she left her fans behind. Or perhaps they'd already moved on. — M.C.

DON GIBSON

★ ★ ★ **Collector's Series (1985; RCA, 1987)**
★ ★ ★ ★ ★ **All-Time Greatest Hits (RCA, 1990)**
For an artist whose influence as a writer, singer and guitarist is felt almost across the entire spectrum of American popular music, Don Gibson has been woefully served by his record label. Only these two greatest-hits collections remain in print; one, *Collector's Series*, contains only seven tracks—seven superb tracks, but only seven nonetheless. *All-Time Greatest Hits* is more like it, with 20 of the songs on which Gibson's reputation rests. Gibson's first hit as a writer came via Faron Young's 1956 version of "Sweet Dreams," a song Patsy Cline would cover in 1963 and with which she would forevermore be identified. Working

with producer Chet Atkins in 1958, Gibson established himself as a solo artist with a double-sided hit, "Oh Lonesome Me" and "I Can't Stop Loving You," the latter being the song Ray Charles would make the cornerstone of his pioneering effort to fuse R&B and country styles on his 1962 chart-topping album, *Modern Sounds in Country and Western Music*. Each side of his first hit established certain Gibson trademarks. "Oh Lonesome Me" is propelled by a quickly strummed acoustic guitar and a shuffling rhythm that has the feeling of rockabilly, making Gibson unique among his Nashville peers in acknowledging a debt to anything that happened in Sam Phillips's Sun Studios 200 miles to the west. "I Can't Stop Lovin' You," on the other hand, marries piano and guitar ostinatos to create a simple but effective instrumental hook as Gibson steps forward with a deep, melancholy vocal to bring home the lyric in dramatic fashion. In Atkins Gibson found his perfect studio complement, someone who shared his taste for adventurous arrangements and unconventional recording techniques. It's hardly an accident that Gibson's records have atmosphere to burn, that everything going on in support of Gibson's vocal is there for the specific reason of augmenting the pain in the singer's voice.

Gibson approached record making in a distinctive, identifiable way, and his records are anything but formulaic. The only constant in his work is the unbearable pain of loneliness that is his subject matter. Even the few non-originals in his repertoire take long, hard looks at broken hearts and shattered dreams. The best of these, and in many ways Gibson's finest hour on record, was "Sea of Heartbreak," a Number Two single in 1961. But Gibson's every performance has some magic moment when all the elements come together to render the emotion overpowering. A vision lonely and dark, described in beautiful, moving detail: Don Gibson's music ranks with the most personally revealing ever produced by a country artist. — D.M.

GILBERTO GIL

★ ★ ★½ **Um Banda Um (WEA Latina, 1982)**
★ ★ ★ ★ **Extra (WEA Latina, 1983)**
★ ★ ★ ★ **Raça Humana (WEA Latina, 1984)**
★ ★ ★ ★ **Dia Dorim Noite Neon (WEA Latina, 1985)**

★★★ **Personalidade: Gilberto Gil**
(Philips, 1987)
★★★½ **Soy Loco por Ti America**
(Braziloid, 1988)
★★★★½ **O Eterno Deus Mu Dança**
(Tropical Storm, 1989)
Perhaps the most soulful of Brazil's pop
stars, Gilberto Gil was, along with Caetano
Veloso, one of the guiding forces of
tropicalismo, the ferociously eclectic style
that dominated Brazilian pop in the late '60s
and '70s. As with Veloso, Gil's obliquely
political lyrics were considered seditious by
Brazil's military government, and the two
were jailed in the late '60s, and later released
into exile. While living in London, Gil
became enamored of Bob Marley and the
Wailers, and began to incorporate reggae
elements into his music; a subsequent trip to
Africa widened his musical vocabulary
further.

As of this writing, Gil had recorded more
than 25 albums for the Brazilian market,
but only a handful are readily available in
this country. *Personalidade* compiles some of
his best work from the '70s, much of
which—like the samba-based "Aquele
Abraço" or the bossa nova "Chiclete com
Banana"—is conventionally Brazilian in
flavor. Still, some American pop influence is
evident in the boogaloo beat given "Back in
Bahia" or the Santana-style chorus to
"Maracatu Atomicô." Gil's later work is far
more eclectic: *Extra* includes the R&B-based
"Funk-Se Quem Puder" as well as
something called "Punk Da Periferia,"
which translates as "Periphery Punk"; *Raça
Humana* evinces a strong African influence
as well as some surprisingly heavy guitar on
"O Roque Do Segurança"; *Dia Dorim Noite
Neon* ranges from the reggae-inflected
"Abertura: Minha Ideologia, Minha
Religião" to the bossa-nova beat of "Seu
Olhar"; while *O Eterno Deus Mu Danca*
indulges in everything from the title tune's
Michael Jackson–style funk to the brassy
carnival groove of "De Bob Dylan a Bob
Marley Um Samba Provocação." Each is
well worth hearing, and don't worry about
not understanding Portuguese—Gil's voice
needs no translation. — J.D.C.

JOHNNY GILL
★½ **Johnny Gill (Atlantic, 1983)**
★★★ **Chemistry (Atlantic, 1985)**
★★★★ **Johnny Gill (Motown, 1990)**
Blessed with a powerful baritone voice, Gill
sounds considerably older than his years,
something his debut exploits by having the
16-year-old take on Sam & Dave's "When

Something Is Wrong with My Baby." Gill
does well enough with that, but seems
ill-suited to the lightweight production
elsewhere on the album. *Chemistry*, with its
deeper grooves and larger sound, provides a
much better balance, and though the songs
tend toward the forgettable, Gill's singing is
rarely less than excellent.

Still, it wasn't until the second *Johnny
Gill*, recorded after he had replaced Bobby
Brown in New Edition, that the singer got
the acclaim he deserved. It helps, of course,
that its songs were produced by either Jam
& Lewis or L.A. & Babyface, but what
ultimately carries the album is the singing,
from the impassioned growl of "Rub You
the Right Way" to the sexy, soulman croon
of "Feels So Much Better." — J.D.C.

DIZZY GILLESPIE
★★★ **A Portrait of Duke Ellington**
(1960; Verve, 1984)
★★★ **Dizzy on the French Riviera**
(1962; Philips, 1986)
★★★½ **Swing Low, Sweet Cadillac**
(Impulse, 1967)
★★½ **The Trumpet Kings Meet Joe**
Turner (1975; Pablo, 1990)
★★½ **Dizzy's Big 4 (1975; Pablo,**
1990)
★★ **The Trumpet Kings at**
Montreux (1975; Pablo, 1990)
★★★½ **Dizzy Gillespie Y Machito:**
Afro-Cuban Jazz Moods (1976;
Pablo, 1990)
★★★ **Dizzy Gillespie Jam (1977;**
Pablo, 1989)
★★½ **The Trumpet Summit Meets the**
Oscar Peterson Big Four (1980;
Pablo, 1990)
★★★½ **The Best of Dizzy Gillespie**
(1980; Pablo, 1987)
★★ **The Alternate Blues (Pablo,**
1982)
★★★½ **Dee Gee Days (1951–52)**
(Savoy, 1985)
★★★★★ **Groovin' High (1945–46)**
(Musicraft, 1986)
★★★★★ **One Bass Hit (1945–46)**
(Musicraft, 1986)
★★★★★ **Dizziest (1946–49) (RCA, 1987)**
★★★★½ **Compact Jazz (1954–64)**
(Mercury, 1987)
WITH STAN GETZ
★★★ **Diz and Getz (Verve, 1955)**
**WITH SONNY ROLLINS AND SONNY
STITT**
★★★½ **Duets (1958; Verve, 1988)**
★★★ **Sonny Side Up (1958; Verve,**
1986)

WITH THE DOUBLE SIX OF PARIS
★ ★ ★ **Dizzy Gillespie & the Double Six of Paris (Philips, 1963)**

Mention John Birks "Dizzy" Gillespie, and the association that immediately comes to mind is Charlie "Yardbird" Parker—as in Bird and Diz, bebop's most famous and photogenic pairing. They first worked together as members of the Earl Hines Orchestra in 1943, and from there went to Billy Eckstine's legendary (and short-lived) proto-bop big band. Like Parker, Gillespie had already been building a reputation for musical audacity, and the adventurous harmonies he essayed on *"Pickin' Up the Cabbage"*—which he wrote for and recorded with Cab Calloway's band—show that he was moving beyond the boundaries of swing as early as 1940.

But it wasn't until Parker and Gillespie joined the coterie of like-minded nonconformists on the 52nd St. jazz scene that the two truly came into their own. Gillespie was the first to land a recording contract, and in 1945 he and a small group featuring Parker cut some sides for Guild, including "Groovin' High," "Shaw Nuff," "Hot House" and "Salt Peanuts." These sessions, included on *Groovin' High,* typify the inspired abandon of the bebop style, and Gillespie seemed uniquely suited to its demands. It wasn't just his technique that did it, although his range, dexterity and precision never ceased to amaze; it was also the strength of his ideas, the way his quicksilver phrases and daredevil flourishes suggested a world of rhythmic and harmonic possibility.

Gillespie also had bandleader ambitions, and as bebop's star began to rise, he assembled an orchestra of his own to try and pick up where Eckstine's big band left off. Its legacy was enormous—this, for example, was where Milt Jackson, John Lewis, Percy Heath and Kenny Clarke coalesced into what would become the Modern Jazz Quartet—but despite the artistic achievement of its recordings (collected on *One Bass Hit*), the Gillespie band was unable to make a go of it commercially. Fortunately, Gillespie was not one to give up, and by 1947 had assembled yet another big band, which found him working to incorporate Afro-Cuban rhythms into the bop vocabulary. Again, Gillespie's band hardly racked up major-league sales, but its music was first-rate, particularly on such classic sides as "Manteca," "Cubana Be" and "Cubana Bop" (all of which can be found on *Dizziest*).

By 1950, though, Gillespie had been shown the door by RCA. Finding himself without a deal, he took matters into his own hands, and formed a label of his own, Dee Gee, whose output is collected on *Dee Gee Days.* Gillespie's recordings during this phase of his career were nowhere near as audacious as his earlier efforts; indeed, his increasing reliance on vocals (mostly by Joe Carroll, although Freddy Strong, Melvin Moore and Diz himself contributed at times) suggests a growing awareness of audience expectations. Even so, Gillespie generally maintained his artistic standards, whether with the vigorous bop workout on "Tin Tin Deo" or the playful Louis Armstrong impression of "Confessin' (Pop's)."

Eventually, Gillespie signed with Normah Granz's Verve label, where he experimented with everything from Latin jazz to straight blowing sessions. Unfortunately, much of the best material, including a 1957 big band gig at the Newport Jazz Festival and his small combo recordings with pianist Lalo Schifrin, is out of print at this writing (though some stunners remain, like the big-band *A Portrait of Duke Ellington*). Most of the Verve material runs to straight-ahead blowing sessions, such as the Sonny Rollins—Sonny Stitt albums *Duets* and *Sonny Side Up,* and while little of the music is as revelatory as the trumpeter's early work, he's a nimble enough improvisor to keep things interesting throughout. Still, the quintessential Gillespie album from this period has to be *Swing Low, Sweet Cadillac,* a concert recording with a blend of wit, groove and virtuosity that is typical of his live act.

After a few deservedly forgotten attempts at jazz pop in the early '70s, Gillespie rejoined Granz, who by then had founded Pablo. Sadly, the majority of what he recorded for the label is disappointingly slapdash, tending toward extremely casual jam session recordings. *Afro-Cuban Jazz Moods* is a notable exception, however, with Gillespie and percussionist Machito offering a credible recreation of the great 1947 big band sessions. — J.D.C.

MICKEY GILLEY
★ ★ ★½ **Gilley's Greatest, Hits Vol. 1 (Playboy/Epic, 1976)**
★ ★ ★½ **Greatest Hits, Vol. II (Playboy/Epic, 1977)**
★ ★ ★ **Mickey Gilley Live at Gilley's (Epic, 1979)**
★ ★ **Encore (Epic, 1981)**
★ ★ **Biggest Hits (Epic, 1982)**
★ ★ **Ten Years of Hits (Epic, 1984)**

The brief *Urban Cowboy* craze made Mickey Gilley a household name around 1980, though you can't really accuse this piano-pounding saloon proprietor of musical trend-hopping. Both preceding *Greatest Hits* volumes emit the raw, rangy spirit of Jerry Lee Lewis's later phase: just as the Killer's country career started to bottom out, Mickey stepped into his first cousin's shoes—and damn near filled 'em. Striving to become the "Number One rock & roll C&W boogie bluesman" during the mid-'70s heyday of countrypolitan pop, Gilley fashioned a string of rough-hewn hits with simpatico producer Eddie Kilroy. Rampant originality may not be his hallmark, but Gilley displays a sensitive touch with tear-in-my-beer heartbreak songs (*Vol. 1*) and roadhouse stompers (*Vol. 2*) alike. *Biggest Hits* and the subsequent collections chart Gilley's commercial ascent and transition from iconoclast to icon. After "The Power of Positive Drinkin'," it's a quick, cruel slide into Music City mush. Sighing string sections replace wailing fiddle players, and slightly mildewed R&B covers such as "Stand By Me" (from the *Urban Cowboy* soundtrack) come to dominate Gilley's repertoire. Still, those initial *Greatest Hits* packages might blow the cowboy hat off any current honky-tonker you'd care to name. — M.C.

DAVID GILMOUR

★ ★½ David Gilmour (Columbia, 1978)
★ ★ About Face (Columbia, 1984)
These two albums are typical sideman-steps-out projects from the lead guitarist of Pink Floyd. The languid wallop of his playing guarantees a certain listenability, but the unfocused material doesn't sustain much interest. Perhaps the absence of Waters's overweening ego and conceptual bent has too much of a liberating effect on Gilmour: like hollow meteors, his own records float off into the progressive-rock cosmos. — M.C.

ALLEN GINSBERG

★ ★ ★ First Blues (John Hammond Records, 1982)
★ ★ ★ ★ The Lion for Real (Island, 1989)
Allen Ginsberg's excellent spoken-word albums of his poetry, *Howl* (Fantasy, 1959) and *Kaddish* (Atlantic, 1963), are out of print, as is his musical debut, *William Blake, Songs of Innocence and Experience* (Verve/Forecast, 1970). And *First Blues*, a sharp long set of words and music, is notoriously hard to find. Luckily, then, there's *The Lion for Real*, a 1989

collaboration between the Beat Generation's seraphic living legend and some of the leading lights of avant-garde pop. Producer Hal Willner headed up the project—and it's a splendid one. Ginsberg intones ecstatic verses written as early as 1948 and then reaches into the mid-'80s; on record he sounds exactly like a wise, genial, if still-rebellious, force. Arto Lindsay and Steve Swallow are among the cast of musicians who provide suitably atmospheric backing for "Gregory Corso's Story," "Cleveland, the Flats," "Stanzas: Written at Night in Radio City" and other visionary poems. From the high, Zen-like beauty of "Guru" to the homoerotic smut-talk of "C'Mon Jack," this is Ginsberg as always, mixing, like the most human of mystics, the sacred and profane. — P.E.

GIPSY KINGS

★ ★ ★ Allegria (1982; Elektra/Musician, 1990)
★ ★½ Gipsy Kings (Elektra/Musician, 1988)
★ ★ Este Mundo (Elektra/Musician, 1991)
As the name suggests, this is gypsy music—but it's nothing like the strolling violin stuff most Americans associate with the genre, owing more to the flamenco tradition of Andalusia. As such, it would hardly seem the sort of thing likely to make a splash with American pop fans. But "Bamboleo," a catchy, minor-key tune from *Gipsy Kings*, managed to become a minor hit, doubtless due to its sturdy chorus and persuasively percussive arrangement. Little else on the album measures up, however. Though the guitar playing is admirable, most selections depend more on mood than melody to make their point (and it's hard to believe that even the French would fall for a version of "My Way" as fatuous as this one). Drawing from recordings made in the early '80s, *Allegria* serves as a sort of roots album; it's pleasant enough, but not nearly as percussive or pop-friendly as *Gipsy Kings*. *Este Mundo*, on the other hand, is clearly meant to help the Kings claim a larger piece of the international market, for not only are most tracks augmented with additional percussion, some go so far as to include horns, synths and strings. How well does this upgraded production work? Those who enjoyed the raw passion of "Bamboleo" may resent the way these arrangements soften the group's sound, while those who didn't get it the first time are unlikely to be convinced by such sweetening. — J.D.C.

GARY GLITTER

★★★½ **Greatest Hits (Rhino, 1991)**
It could only have happened in Britain.
Gary Glitter came on like the Fonz in Ziggy
Stardust drag: ducktail pompadour,
platform shoes, luminescent jumpsuit, visible
paunch—totally over the top. Glitter's
mid-'70s hits all vibrate to the same beat, a
ricocheting tattoo broken by snarling guitar
riffs and the man's own inimitable vocal
style. Rather than sing, he leads halftime
chants: "Rock and Roll Part One" ("Rock
and Roll!"), "Rock and Roll Part 2"
("Hey!"), "Do You Want to Touch Me?"
("There-Where?"), "I Didn't Know I Loved
You ('Til I Saw You Rock and Roll)" (you
guessed it). Glittermania barely caught on
outside of Britain; only "Rock and Roll
Part 2" met with much success here. Surely
Adam Ant and Bow Wow Wow derived
their "tribal rhythms" schtick from the
moldie oldies re-packaged on this album.
And Glitter's "Leader of the Gang" revs the
numbing beat up to punk pace, several years
before the Ramones and Sex Pistols stepped
on the accelerator. One of Gary Glitter's
loopy, propulsive hits belongs on every
party tape; Rhino's comprehensive
anthology contains them all—plus some.
— M.C.

THE GO-BETWEENS

★★½ **Send Me a Lullaby (Rough Trade UK, 1981)**
★★★½ **Before Hollywood (Rough Trade UK, 1983)**
★★★★ **Spring Hill Fair (Sire UK, 1984)**
★★★★★ **Liberty Belle and the Black Diamond Express (Big Time, 1986)**
★★★★ **Tallulah (Big Time, 1987)**
★★★★½ **16 Lovers Lane (Capitol, 1988)**
★★★½ **The Peel Sessions (Strange Fruit, 1989)**
★★★★½ **1978–1990 (Capitol, 1990)**

ROBERT FORSTER

★★★★ **Danger in the Past (Beggars Banquet, 1991)**

G.W. MCLENNAN

★★★★½ **Watershed (Beggars Banquet/RCA, 1991)**
Like a lot of punk-era bands, the
Go-Betweens were always better songwriters
than they were musicians. But what
separates this Australian combo from its
competition is that the Go-Betweens
eventually managed to play almost as well
as they wrote—and that's "almost" only
because few tunesmiths can top Robert

Forster and Grant McLennan when it
comes to capturing an emotion in melody.
Send Me a Lullaby introduces the
Go-Betweens as a trio (drummer Lindy
Morrison was the third member), and
though there are flashes of brilliance—"The
Girls Have Moved," for example, or the
vivid depiction of jealousy in "Eight
Pictures"—the album's overall sound is too
amateurish and intellectualized to be entirely
convincing. There's a marked improvement
in the playing on *Before Hollywood*,
although the band hasn't entirely shed its
influences (note how clearly "On My Block"
recalls the sound of early Talking Heads).
Still, the songs are marvelous, with Forster
and McLennan capturing an impressive
range of emotions, from the resigned anger
of "A Bad Debt Follows You" to the
melancholic nostalgia of "Cattle and Cane."
With *Spring Hill Fair*, however, the
band's execution begins to catch up with its
conception. This album's sound is
surprisingly polished, and it isn't simply the
addition of Robert Vickers (whose
assumption of bass-playing duties allows
McLennan to concentrate on guitar) that
does the trick. Instead, what ultimately
makes this album such a step forward is the
way its wholehearted embrace of melody is
furthered by better vocals and suitably
ambitious production values; between them,
songs like "Bachelor Kisses," "Draining the
Pool for You" and the dramatic "Slow Slow
Music" have the feel of classics. But even
that achievement pales when compared to
*Liberty Belle and the Black Diamond
Express*, perhaps the Go-Betweens' finest
album. As with *Spring Hill Fair*, the
production is lush and supportive, but keyed
to the demands of each individual song; as
such, there's a wonderful richness to "Spring
Rain," a vivid sense of atmosphere to "The
Wrong Road" and a lithe locomotion to the
sound of "Head Full of Steam." And the
songs themselves are nothing less than
magnificent.
Adding a fifth member (multi-
instrumentalist Amanda Brown) for
Tallulah, the Go-Betweens broaden their
stylistic vocabulary still further, even to the
point of incorporating funk elements on
"Cut It Out." But despite several standout
songs—the intoxicating "Someone Else's
Wife" and the mournful "The Clarke
Sisters," among them—the album is
something of a let-down. Fortunately, *16
Lovers Lane* more than makes up for it,
thanks to the ebullient arrangements and

confident performances lent "Love Is a Sign," the charming "Streets of Your Town" and the joyous "Love Goes On!"

Lamentably, that was the group's swan song. Capitol did release a retrospective entitled *1978–1990*; it culls the most representative (though not necessarily the most memorable) tracks from *Before Hollywood*, *Spring Hill Fair*, *Liberty Belle*, *Tallulah* and *16 Lovers Lane*, and augments them with an assortment of B sides and rarities. (An earlier best-of, *Metal and Shells*, had been issued in 1985 on the PVC label but is out of print.) In addition, four delightful performances recorded for John Peel's BBC One radio program were issued as *The Peel Sessions*.

Since disbanding, Forster and McLennan have both embarked on solo careers. Forster's *Danger in the Past* is very much in the vein of the Go-Betweens' later work, full of thoughtfully melodic numbers like "Leave Here Satisfied." But McLennan's *Watershed*, though just as consistently tuneful, is far more adventurous stylistically, adding extra interest to such songs as "Haven't I Been a Fool" and the funk-edged "Putting the Wheels Back On." McLennan also collaborated with drummer Pryce Surplice and the Church's Steve Kilbey on *Jack Frost* (Arista, 1991), an edgy, eclectic outing that's far more experimental than either McLennan's or Kilbey's usual work, but no less listenable. — J.D.C.

THE GO-GO'S

★ ★ ★½ **Beauty and the Beat (I.R.S., 1981)**
★ ★½ **Vacation (I.R.S., 1982)**
★ ★ ★ **Talk Show (I.R.S., 1984)**
★ ★ ★ ★ **Greatest (I.R.S., 1990)**

Although the Go-Go's came out of the same L.A. underground that produced X, Fear and the Germs, you wouldn't know it from the group's sound, which was tuneful, perky and decidedly listener-friendly. But the Go-Go's, despite their roots, were punk only in attitude; musically, they owed more to beach music and girl groups than to the Stooges and Sex Pistols. *Beauty and the Beat* played up those roots admirably, from Gina Shock's surf-rock drumming behind "We Got the Beat" to the itchy innocence of Belinda Carlisle's vocal on "Lust to Love." Much to everyone's surprise, the album was a hit, which may be why things suddenly got slicker with *Vacation*; the album was overproduced and, apart from the title tune and "Beatnik Beach," easily forgettable. *Talk Show* brought things back into focus, but by then the band was splintering;

despite a reunion rendition of "Cool Jerk" on *Greatest*, the Go-Go's were gone-gone. — J.D.C.

THE GOLDEN PALOMINOS

★ ★ ★ ★ **The Golden Palominos (OAO-Celluloid, 1983)**
★ ★ ★ ★½ **Visions of Excess (Celluloid, 1985)**
★ ★ ★½ **Blast of Silence (Celluloid, 1986)**
★ ★ ★ **A Dead Horse (Celluloid, 1989)**
★ ★ ★ ★ **Drunk with Passion (Charisma, 1991)**

Essentially the dominion of drummer Anton Fier, the Golden Palominos started out as a New York avant-funk outfit, with a cast of contributors that, on *The Golden Palominos*, includes Fred Frith, John Zorn, Arto Lindsay, Bill Laswell and Jamaaladeen Tacuma. Yet what makes the record work isn't a matter of who plays, but how; by building these pieces around accessible rhythmic ideas, even the sonic arcana of Zorn and Frith has enough context to make sense to pop fans.

Even so, Fier veers away from experimental music with *Visions of Excess*. Working with an eclectic combination of rockers—Richard Thompson, Jack Bruce, Michael Stipe, Chris Stamey, John Lydon, P-Funk's guitarist Mike Hampton and keyboardist Bernie Worrell—Fier pulls both depth and breadth from his band. "Omaha," a version of the Moby Grape tune featuring Stipe on vocals, was released as a single, but its familiarity isn't quite as impressive as the blues fusion of "Silver Bullet," which balance Bruce's singing against Thompson's guitar fills, or the dark resonance of "Boy (Go)."

With *Blast of Silence*, Fier and company put yet another twist on their sound, this time moving in the general direction of country rock—although theirs is probably the only country rock in history to blend pedal-steel licks with Indian hand percussion, as the Pals do behind Syd Straw on "I've Been the One." Unexpected juxtapositions like that are common, though, as with the funk-meets-country groove of "Faithless Heart," or when guitarist Nicky Skopelitis cuts through the folk-rock prettiness of "Something Becomes Nothing" with a searing, acid-rock wah-wah solo.

After such excitement, the relative calm of *A Dead Horse* seems almost out of character, but at least Fier has a good excuse—the music is less diverse because the band is becoming more stable. That's not to say that the Palominos' lineup is set in stone (it isn't) or that the band doesn't still rely on special guests (it does), but with Skopelitis, Laswell and singer Amanda Kramer making regular appearances throughout the album, the songs seem more consistent than ever. But this more focused approach doesn't really start paying off until *Drunk with Passion*, on which the music's passionate energy is obvious whether the songs are as genial as the Stipe-sung "Alive and Living Well," or as fiery as the Bob Mould feature, "Dying From the Inside Out." — J.D.C.

BOBBY GOLDSBORO
★ **All-Time Greatest Hits (Curb, 1990)**
Even soap operas seldom stoop so low as did Goldsboro's massive 1968 hit, "Honey." A lugubrious story song, it's "plot," you may recall, goes something like this: Boy meets girl who's "kinda smart and kinda dumb"; boy gives girl puppy: girl gets misty-eyed watching late-night TV; girl wrecks car; boy says it's OK; out of nowhere girl dies. Lush strings, angelic choirs and Goldsboro's repellently sincere vocal make this one of the sappiest songs in history. But wait . . . remember "Watching Scotty Grow"? — P.E.

LESLEY GORE
★★★★½ **The Lesley Gore Anthology (Rhino, 1986)**
At a certain time in the history of American teenage pop music, Lesley Gore was as fine a singer and conscience for her peer group as anyone around. For one, she was a teenager herself—she was 17 at the time of her first Number One record, "It's My Party," from 1963, which was also her first single; by the time her chart run ended in 1967 with the dreamy "California Nights," she was only 21. But she was finished as a pop star, because her peers had grown up and moved on to more sophisticated music, while Gore wandered label-less, unable to find an outlet that might allow her to grow up as an artist. A Motown subsidiary, Mowest, finally gave her a shot in 1972, but the resulting album, *Someplace Else Now*, whose title told the story of where she was at, had some fine performances to recommend it but lacked a song anywhere near as attuned to her generation's feelings as those of her younger days. A jump to A&M in 1978 yielded another album, *Love Me by Name*, which again showed Gore in fine voice while failing to ignite any interest with fans or radio stations, even though it re-teamed her with producer Quincy Jones,

who had discovered her and produced most of her hits. At the end of the '70s, Gore was playing cabarets in New York City and co-writing songs with her brother Michael, one of which ended up on his soundtrack for the movie *Fame*.

Once, though, she was great. The songs she sang dealt almost exclusively with the wildly unpredictable emotions of teen love, and Gore's audience in the early '60s knew she was singing about them. In 1963 she declared unabashed petulance in "It's My Party" and followed it a couple of months later with unabashed gloating in "Judy's Turn to Cry," the text detailing her rival's having been dumped by the same beau who dumped her in the earlier song; but by 1964 she was saying to any male who would listen, "You Don't Own Me." She even extended this position on a minor hit from 1965 (co-written by Lesley and Michael), "I Won't Love You Anymore (Sorry)," which is included here and shows her taking an even more resolute stand against a duplicitous male. Not that straying females were spared Gore's wrath—in "She's a Fool," Gore rages against the girl who's cheating on the boy Gore feels is to die for.

But all of this would not amount to much if Gore had not been blessed with good material throughout her career. She also had the voice to pull it off—hers was just this side of husky, but smooth, warm, and ageless in the sense that she could deliver a wide spectrum of material convincingly. *Anthology* is a 26-song overview of Gore's Mercury years, including all the hits, some good B sides and lesser-known but interesting album tracks. The double-cassette package lacks any liner information, a most unusual oversight for Rhino Records. Still, this set will do fine, thank you, as a reminder that it was Lesley Gore who brought to bear most forcefully on teen pop the advanced idea that women could be self-reliant. — D.M.

GRAND FUNK RAILROAD
★★ **On Time (Capitol, 1969)**
★★ **Grand Funk Railroad (Capitol, 1969)**
★★½ **Closer to Home (Capitol, 1970)**
★★ **Live Album (Capitol, 1970)**
★★½ **Survival (Capitol, 1971)**
★½ **E Pluribus Funk (Capitol, 1971)**
★★★ **Mark, Don and Mel, 1969-1971 (Capitol, 1972)**
★½ **Phoenix (Capitol, 1972)**
★★★ **We're An American Band (Capitol, 1973)**

★ **All the Girls in the World Beware!**
   (Capitol, 1974)
★ **Shinin' On (Capitol, 1974)**
★ **Caught in the Act (Capitol, 1975)**
★★★ **Hits (Capitol, 1976)**
★★ **Good Singin', Good Playin' (MCA,**
   1976)
★ **Grand Funk Lives (Full Moon/Warner**
   Bros., 1981)
★ **What's Funk (Full Moon/Warner**
   Bros., 1983)
★★★ **Collector's Series (Capitol, 1991)**
★★ **More of the Best (Rhino, 1991)**

Grand Funk Railroad is the '70s prototype of today's crowd-pleasing pop-metal. Reviled by critics and hippies alike, this Flint, Michigan, power trio connected with a younger audience: newly freaky 12- to 15-year-olds, who viewed the group as true messengers of the revolution. They weren't: guitarist Mark Farner added a slight chicken-scratch stutter to his heavy riffs, but nobody ever accused drummer Don Brewer and bassist Mel Schacher of actually playing funk. Beyond nostalgia, there's not much reason to exhume this group's sodden, clockwork studio albums. The best-of collections help explain Grand Funk Railroad's massive popularity, though; at its sweat-dripping best, the band emits a surging, elemental blast of hard-rock heat.

Mark, Don and Mel is a legitimate period piece: a double-album document of Grand Funk's meteoric rise from free festivals in '69 to Madison Square Garden in '71. Adding keyboardist Craig Frost and dropping "Railroad," Grand Funk began a pop phase with the Todd Rundgren-produced *We're an American Band*. That album's title track inaugurated a run of crudely irresistible singles, which are collected on *Hits*. A commercial rut followed soon after, though the group soldiered on for quite a spell. *Collector's Series* summarizes the strange-but-true saga of Grand Funk's monstrous popularity, leaving out some of the gorier details. Even though nobody wants to hear about it now, Grand Funk Railroad shaped the tastes of a generation. — M.C.

AMY GRANT

★★★ **My Father's Eyes (Myrrh/Reunion,**
   1979)
★★★ **Never Alone (Myrrh/Reunion, 1980)**
★★★★ **In Concert (Myrrh/Reunion, 1981)**
★★★★ **In Concert Volume Two**
   (Myrrh/Reunion, 1981)
★★★★ **Age to Age (Myrrh/Reunion, 1982)**
★★★★ **Straight Ahead (A&M, 1984)**
★★★ **Unguarded (A&M, 1985)**
★★★★ **The Collection (Myrrh/Reunion,**
   1986)
★★★ **Lead Me On (A&M, 1988)**
★★★ **Heart in Motion (A&M, 1991)**

A contemporary gospel phenomenon whose move into the pop world paid off in platinum in 1991, Amy Grant has used pop rock as a medium for communicating her well-crafted expressions of faith and devotion. These songs make their point so subversively you don't always realize that her spiritual orientation informs every lyric. Even the high-gloss electronics that propelled her 1991 album, *Heart in Motion*, into the Top Thirty hardly signaled a turn away from heavenly concerns. Where it's not obvious—as, say, on the Top Ten single, "That's What Love Is For"—it's usually the subtext. Most everything she sings is good, too. Her clear, dry voice projects a forceful personality, and her command of vocal dynamics is impressive. Grant's success in the secular world is testimony to the power of her message, the persuasiveness of her performance, the quality of her songs and the credibility of her stance.

So it is that her Myrrh/Reunion albums are of a piece with her A&M releases. All have their virtues. *The Collection* is a good place to start, as it contains a powerful sampling of some of her finest tracks from 1979 through 1986; one song, "Angels," from 1984, is a first-rate piece of pop drama. *Age to Age*, containing one of her most moving songs in "Raining on the Inside," also holds the distinction of being the first certified gold album by a solo gospel artist. The two concert albums are alternately rousing and meditative, showcases for the full scope of Grant's art. Of the A&M albums, *Straight Ahead* is straight gospel, while *Unguarded*, which yielded a minor hit in "Find a Way," is her first foray into the pop market. *Lead Me On* is a holding pattern, albeit an interesting one that sets the stage for her breakthrough with *Heart in Motion*. — D.M.

EARL GRANT

★★★ **The Best of Earl Grant (MCA, 1983)**

Although known primarily as a pianist and organist, classically trained Earl Grant hit the Top Ten in 1963 for the first and only time in his career with "The End," a single without a trace of keyboards on it. However, it did have a moving vocal performance by Grant. Why he didn't sing more is a bit of a mystery. While "The End" is done in the smooth, low-key

crooning style of Nat "King" Cole, another
song, "A Closer Walk," shows him equally
at home in a gospel mode. In addition to
these tracks this set is rounded out with
several lush organ instrumentals, as well as
some blue-tinged piano solos. — D.M.

EDDY GRANT
★★★   Living on the Front Line (Epic, 1979)
★★★½ Walking on Sunshine (Epic, 1979)
★★★   Killer on the Rampage (Epic, 1982)
 ★★½ Going for Broke (Epic, 1984)
 ★★½ Born Tough (Epic, 1986)
 ★★   File Under Rock (Enigma, 1990)
 ★★   Barefoot Soldier (Enigma, 1990)

Born in Guyana, Eddy Grant moved to
London and wound up in a rock-soul band
called the Equals. Ten years after the band's
single "Baby Come Back" hit on both sides
of the Atlantic in 1968, Eddy Grant came
riding back on top of a supple, poppy
reggae sound. As a multi-instrumentalist
and producer, he deftly mixed bits of soca
and calypso into *Living on the Front Line*'s
synthesized curry. Serious reggae heads
probably won't cotton to Grant's strong
taste for funk and disco, though. The title
cut from *Walking on Sunshine* bounced
around dance clubs for years: the Eddy
Grant original, Bill Summers & Summers
Heat's fusion-lite reading and an electro
hip-hop version by Rockers Revenge all
combined to blur the distinction between the
city beat and the island groove. *Killer on the
Rampage* added a pungent rock influence to
the mix, and Grant's perseverence paid off
when the single "Electric Avenue" strutted
into the Top Ten. — M.C.

GRATEFUL DEAD
 ★★½ Grateful Dead (Warner Bros., 1967)
★★★   Anthem of the Sun (Warner Bros., 1968)
★★★   Aoxomoxoa (Warner Bros., 1969)
★★★★ Live Dead (Warner Bros., 1970)
★★★★★ Workingman's Dead (Warner Bros., 1970)
★★★★★ American Beauty (Warner Bros., 1970)
★★★   The Grateful Dead (Warner Bros., 1971)
★★★   Europe '72 (Warner Bros., 1972)
★★★   History of the Grateful Dead, Volume 1—Bear's Choice (Warner Bros., 1973)
★★★   Wake of the Flood (Grateful Dead, 1973)
★★★★ Best of the Grateful Dead—Skeletons From the Closet (Warner Bros., 1974)
★★★   The Grateful Dead From the Mars Hotel (Grateful Dead, 1974)
★★★   Blues for Allah (Grateful Dead, 1975)
 ★★   Steal Your Face (Grateful Dead, 1976)
★★★½ Terrapin Station (Arista, 1977)
★★★★ What a Long Strange Trip It's Been (Warner Bros., 1977)
 ★★   Shakedown Street (Arista, 1978)
★★★★ The Grateful Dead Go to Heaven (Arista, 1980)
★★★   Dead Reckoning (1981; Arista, 1990)
★★★★ Dead Set (Arista, 1981)
★★★★ In the Dark (Arista, 1987)
★★★   Built to Last (Arista, 1989)
★★★½ Without a Net (Arista, 1990)

As much a phenomenon as a band, the
Grateful Dead have over the last
quarter-century gathered together the
far-flung members of their massive cult for
live shows that function less as musical
events than love-ins. The group for a while
toured six months a year and boasted a
23-ton sound system, and it's never been the
album, but rather the concert that forms the
essential Dead document—a fittingly
momentary one for a band whose
characteristic mood is that of drifting into
ether, spacing out on good vibes.
Deadheads—ex-hippies or tie-dye
wannabes—celebrate the Dead's myth of
genial counterculturalism. The songs provide
an excuse for the revelry—and they remain
songs whose appeal is all but inscrutable to
non-initiates.

House band for the famous acid tests that
transformed San Francisco into one large
freakout, the original group was comprised
of ex-jug band guitarist/singer Jerry Garcia,
electronic music fancier Phil Lesh on bass,
rocker Bob Weir on rhythm guitar,
keyboardist "Pigpen" McKernan and
drummer Bill Kreutzmann. In time they'd
add Mickey Hart as a second drummer;
unlike the two-kit Allman Brothers,
however, the Dead's rhythm section never
sounded powerful, but instead went in for
polyrhythmic subtleties. Recorded in three
days, *Grateful Dead* sounds about as
carefully thought out as a scattershot jam:
the ten minutes of "Viola Lee Blues"
foretold endless improvisations to come—
the remainder balanced undistinguished trad

rockers ("Good Morning Little School Girl") and woolyheaded originals ("The Golden Road [to Unlimited Devotion]").

Then taking half a year to come up with *Anthem of the Sun*, the band pulled out all the stops. A suite, "That's It (for the Other One)," featured such mystifying segments as "Cryptical Envelopment" and "Quadriplet for Tender Feet"; "Alligator" clocked in at 15 minutes, and the musicians employed such exotica as finger cymbals, a John Cage-ish "prepared piano," celesta and crotales in service of a puzzling experimentalism. *Aoxomoxoa* was somewhat more tuneful, but it was only with *Live Dead* that the band found its style. Lyricist Robert Hunter provided free-form musings, and with the delicate "Saint Stephen" and the 24-minute moodiness of "Dark Star," the Dead arrived at music whose effect was very much like jazz. If rock & roll had been built on intensity and concision, the Dead's new sound was the antithesis of that. Neither Garcia nor Lesh was at all an urgent singer, and Garcia's ruminative, single-note, discursive guitar playing alluded more to Charlie Christian than Chuck Berry.

For all but fanatics, the next pair of albums, *Workingman's Dead* and *American Beauty*, comprised the band's irrefutable high point. Hippie country music, complete with Jerry on pedal steel, both albums featured carefully arranged songs and tight playing. "Ripple," "Casey Jones," "Sugar Magnolia" and "Truckin' " were alternately witty or lovely, and the Dead's signal strength—its casual, loping swing—found its best vehicle. Until the band switched record labels, the Dead contented itself mainly with live albums, with *Europe '72* being the standout. *Blues for Allah* found the Dead trying out jazz riffs, and with the addition of pianist Keith Godchaux and his wife Donna on vocals, the band's late-'70s sound was fuller. *Terrapin Station* and its long title track song-suite was the last of the Dead's studio epics; the band concentrated henceforth on shorter numbers. *Shakedown Street* hinted at disco in its drumming and wah-wah guitar and it stands as a low point. With *Go to Heaven*, from 1980, however, and a strong production by Gary Lyons, the Dead came up with its most accessible set of songs in quite some time, and on "Alabama Getaway" they came very close to rocking.

Throughout the '80s the band busied itself with massive, live sets and scanty studio ones. Of the latter, *In the Dark* finally gained the group a chart hit in the sweet "Touch of Grey." *Built to Last* was also late-model, newly accessible Dead—an aggregation of polished players making pleasant, unthreatening music. Much more characteristic were the concert albums: *Dead Set* recycled the group's classics in standard electric versions; *Reckoning*, an all-acoustic look backward proved that the band's country and folk sides were its more effective ones.

The Dead kicked off the '90s with—what else?—a two-CD live extravaganza, *Without a Net*. The group's obsessive reworkings of its own history will no doubt continue—delighting its rabid following, and puzzling the rest of the world. The retrospective *What a Long Strange Trip It's Been* isn't a bad place for the uninitiated to begin.
— P.E.

DOBIE GRAY
★★ **Dobie Gray Sings for In Crowders That Go 'Go-Go' (Collectables, NA)**
★★ **Drift Away (MCA, 1973)**
★★ **New Ray of Sunshine (Capricorn, 1975)**
★★ **Midnight Diamond (Infinity, 1978)**
★★ **Dobie Gray (Infinity, 1979)**
Texas-born Gray scored big in 1965 with "The 'In' Crowd," an elegantly hip bit of jive-talk soul. Better by far than anything else he recorded during the early part of his career, the single showed him more capable of wit than urgency; he was an R&B sophisticate. Lying low for the rest of the decade, he emerged in 1973 with "Drift Away" and its much more passionate sound. A stirring rock & roll anthem, later covered with flair by Rod Stewart, the song was followed by the sweeping "Loving Arms." Gray then turned toward mild disco on the bland *New Ray of Sunshine*, and the rest of his output was passable country soul.
— P.E.

GREAT WHITE
★½ **On Your Knees (1982; Capitol, 1987)**
★½ **Great White (Capitol/EMI USA, 1984)**
★½ **Shot in the Dark (Capitol, 1986)**
★★ **Once Bitten (Capitol, 1987)**
★½ **Recovery: Live! (Capitol, 1987)**
★★ **Twice Shy (Capitol, 1989)**
★★½ **Hooked (Capitol, 1991)**
An essentially pedestrian hard-rock act, there are two things that set Great White apart from the pack. The first is Jack Russell's voice, which by the time of *Twice Shy* had blossomed into a fairly impressive Robert Plant impression; the second is the band's taste in cover material, which by

Hooked included a classic Ian Hunter tune ("Once Bitten, Twice Shy," on *Twice Shy*) and two tunes from Australia's the Angels ("Face the Day," on *Shot in the Dark*, and "Can't Shake It," on *Hooked*). Neither makes the band especially worth listening to, but when dealing with music this prosaic even the slightest distinctions help.
— J.D.C.

BORIS GREBENSCHEKOV
★★½ **Radio Silence (Columbia, 1989)**
Boris Grebenschekov was an underground rock star in the Soviet Union (this was back when there was a Soviet Union), and his American debut may have lost something in translation—though not enough to be considered a failure. Unlike Western rockers, whose work derives from rhythmic ideas implicit in the music, Grebenschekov's songs take their sense of direction from the sound of the words—an odd notion by American standards, but very Russian in spirit. Consequently, a fair amount of the album has a moody, almost mystical feel to it. That's not to say Grebenschekov doesn't rock; "Radio Silence" is urgent and tuneful in the tradition of Lou Reed and early Springsteen, while "Young Lions" offers proof that you can rock it in Russian.
— J.D.C.

AL GREEN
★★★★	**Al Green Gets Next to You (Hi, 1970)**
★★★★	**Let's Stay Together (1972; Motown, 1983)**
★★★★	**I'm Still in Love With You (1972; Motown, 1982)**
★★★★★	**Call Me (1973; Motown, 1982)**
★★★★	**Livin' for You (1973; Motown, 1983)**
★★★★	**Al Green Explores Your Mind (1974; Motown, 1982)**
★★★★★	**Greatest Hits, Volume 1 (1975; Motown, 1982)**
★★★½	**Al Green Is Love (Hi/Motown, 1975)**
★★★½	**Full of Fire (Hi/Motown, 1976)**
★★★	**Have a Good Time (Hi, 1976)**
★★★★½	**The Belle Album (1977; Motown, 1983)**
★★★★½	**Greatest Hits, Volume 2 (1977; Motown, 1983)**
★★★★	**Truth 'n' Time (1978; Motown, 1983)**
★★★★	**The Lord Will Make a Way (Myrrh, 1980)**
★★★★	**Tokyo . . . Live (Cream import, 1981)**
★★★★	**Higher Plane (Myrrh, 1981)**
★★★	**Precious Lord (Myrrh, 1982)**
★★★★	**I'll Rise Again (Myrrh, 1983)**
★★★	**Al Green Sings the Gospel (Motown, 1983)**
★★★	**Trust in God (Myrrh, 1984)**
★★★½	**He Is the Light (A&M, 1985)**
★★★½	**Soul Survivor (A&M, 1987)**
★★★★½	**Love Ritual: Rare & Previously Unreleased 1968-76 (MCA, 1989)**
★★★½	**I Get Joy (A&M, 1989)**
★★★★	**One in a Million (Word/Epic, 1991)**

Al Green's blazing streak of hit singles sweetened the sound of Memphis soul just enough to suit the changing times; he reasserted the music's gospel base without losing that identifying grit. Even though he returned to the church halfway through the decade, Green is the preeminent soul man of the '70s—hands down. And given the proper motivation, he can still move mountains. He'd already been performing gospel in public for several years when his secular debut, "Back Up Train" by Al Green and the Soul Mates, reached the R&B Top Ten during the soul-saturated year of 1967. Moving from Grand Rapids down to Memphis a couple of years later, Green hooked up with producer and bandleader Willie Mitchell—the creative mainman at Hi Records, Stax/Volt's crosstown rival. *Green Is Blues*, now out of print, made for a rather tentative (if mostly uptempo) debut. But *Al Green Gets Next to You*, released later that same year and also out of print, acomplishes its stated goal. Here, Green finds the intimate tone that will become his calling card and Willie Mitchell finally defines a Hi house sound: slower and sweatier than the bristling Booker T.–Bar-Kays groove, but fully capable of the same supercharged emotional impact. Together, they reshape the Temptations' chesty Motown classic "I Can't Get Next to You" into something fresh—no small feat.

"Tired of Being Alone" and "Let's Stay Together" brought Al Green to the pop charts in 1971, introducing his lush, electrifying romanticism to an apparently ballad-starved general public. Sliding from a gravy-thick lower register to an ethereal, heart-stopping falsetto, Al Green makes his seductive pleading hard to resist throughout *Let's Stay Together*. Hi's house band hits its stride right alongside the label's new star: former MG's drummer Al Jackson, Jr. pumps up a subtle pulse, while guitarist "Teenie" Hodges plucks uncommon, jazz-flavored chord progressions against

Mitchell's bittersweet horn and string arrangements.

I'm Still in Love With You refines that approach on the title cut and "Look What You Done for Me," while indicating Green's wide-ranging tastes with cover versions of Roy Orbison's "Oh, Pretty Woman" and Kris Kristofferson's "For the Good Times." If those interpretations are a bit forced, Green breathes natural fire into the Memphis-Nashville connection on his next album, *Call Me*. His readings of "I'm So Lonesome I Could Cry" (Hank Williams) and "Funny How Time Slips Away" (Willie Nelson) merge the country heart-tugging of the originals with some R&B sinew-flexing—magnificent. *Call Me* captures Green at a dizzying peak: the hit title track sums up his preceding achievements, while "Jesus Is Waiting" suggests his future destination.

In retrospect, you can hear Al Green inching closer and closer to the Lord on each subsequent record: "Sweet Sixteen" and "My God Is Real" stand out on the spacey, string-laden *Livin' for You*, while "Take Me to the River" is the testifying centerpiece of the funkier, more direct *Explores Your Mind*. The flawless *Greatest Hits* concludes his superstar run, but he's far from finished.

After releasing two increasingly sketchy albums in 1976, Al Green stopped working with Willie Mitchell—and radically changed his tune. Around this time, Green's singles quit crossing over to the pop charts. *The Belle Album* explains just what he'd been going through: a difficult, often painful reassessment of his faith and its relation to his art. Picking up an acoustic guitar, Green began to write and sing about his transformation, about his belief and his nagging doubts. "It's you that I want," he tells his lover on the title track, "but it's Him that I need." Perhaps because of Green's up-front uncertainty, *The Belle Album*'s gently funky heat can melt the coldest, most atheistic resolve. *Truth 'n' Time* plugs this best-of-both-worlds approach back into Green's traditional mix of originals and cover versions; "Say a Little Prayer" and, yes, "To Sir With Love" lend themselves to the task quite well. Al Green's next move comes as no surprise, then: in 1980 he began recording straight-up gospel for the Myrrh label. The import-only live album captures a good-sized chunk—but not all—of Green's seductive stage presence and thrill-a-minute virtuosity, while the outtakes and rarities on *Love Ritual*

soar above his official mid-'70s releases (especially the wild, African-influenced mix of the title track).

Expectations of a return to secular music sabotaged these albums for many Al Green devotees at the time of their release. In retrospect, the very best ones (*The Lord Will Make a Way*, *Higher Plane* and *I'll Rise Again*) weave a delicious spell all their own; they're not as robust as '70s Green, but just as musically complex and soul-satisfying. Though he's shifted his lyric focus to pure spread-the-word proselytizing, Al Green (now a reverend and preacher with his own church in Memphis) has never really lost his knack for crafting dramatic, catchy pop songs—or his ability to make the most unlikely cover versions sound utterly natural. Take *Higher Plane* as an example; "Amazing Grace" is as good as you'd hope, but nobody else on earth could pull off "The Battle Hymn of the Republic" quite the way Green does. *Precious Lord* is a little too soft, and not all the lightweight pop covers on *Trust in God* get over—he is human, after all. The long-awaited reunion with Willie Mitchell (*He Is the Light*) sounds bracingly familiar, and yet a curiously uninspired batch of songs (save for the Clark Sisters' "You Brought the Sunshine") makes it something less than a magic moment. To his credit, Green didn't linger at this nostalgic crossroads; *Soul Survivor* and especially *I Get Joy* tastefully integrate some contemporary rhythms and synth textures into his ongoing testimony. *One in a Million* is a frustrating, brutally truncated summary of Al Green's Myrrh period; still, those 38 minutes (including "Amazing Grace") should be enough to convince any skeptic. With Al Green, hearing is believing.   — M.C.

NANCI GRIFFITH
- ★★★ **There's a Light Beyond These Woods (1978; Philo/Rounder, 1986)**
- ★★★ **Poet in My Window (1982; Philo/Rounder, 1986)**
- ★★★ **Once in a Very Blue Moon (Philo/Rounder, 1985)**
- ★★★★ **Last of the True Believers (Philo/Rounder, 1986)**
- ★★★★ **Lone Star State of Mind (MCA, 1987)**
- ★★★★ **Little Love Affairs (MCA, 1988)**
- ★★★★ **One Fair Summer Evening (MCA, 1988)**
- ★★★★ **Storms (MCA, 1989)**
- ★★★★ **Late Night Grande Hotel (MCA, 1991)**

Texan Nanci Griffith has delivered nine albums of clear-eyed songs in which she looks mostly at love, but also at a world turning cold. She has termed her music "folkabilly," and has conceived each album as a novella or series of short stories centered on a theme born of life on the road. Thus *Late Night Grande Hotel* and its songs of leaving home and loved ones, and of longing to return to the sanctuary home provides. Thus *Storms*, about turbulent relationships. Thus *Little Love Affairs* with people, with places, with the past. Griffith's songs, based in folk and traditional country, with pop overtones, find her characters overwhelmed by forces massive, uncontrollable and unseen, but moving them to act in a manner sometimes thoughtless and at other times wise.

Having co-produced her first four Philo albums, then working with one of Nashville's best producers in Tony Brown, and moving on to Glyn Johns (*Storms*) and Peter Van Hooke and Rod Argent (*Late Night Grande Hotel*), Griffith has updated her sound in subtle ways via the discreet use of synthesizers and, on *Late Night*, strings, while keeping the focus on acoustic stringed instruments. Singing in a clear, reedy voice that recalls Judy Collins and Emmylou Harris, she displays on *Late Night* a huskier, bluesier tone akin to that of K.T. Oslin; it's appealing and unexpected, given the lightness of her voice otherwise. Quietly, she has constructed one small classic after another, limning turf where love is hard-won at best, and memory weighs heavily on the heart. — D.M.

GRIN

★ ★ ★   Grin (Spindizzy/Columbia, 1971)
★ ★ ★ ½ 1 + 1 (1972; Columbia, 1992)
  ★ ★ ½ All Out (Spindizzy/Columbia, 1972)
★ ★ ★   Gone Crazy (A&M, 1973)
★ ★ ★ ½ Best of Grin (1976; Epic, 1985)

Still a teen when he formed Grin with bassist-vocalist Bob Gordon and drummer Bob Berberich, Nils Lofgren was a wunderkind tunesmith, a crack powerhouse guitarist and a protege of Neil Young. His commitment to basic rock & roll appeared almost reactionary in the singer-songwriter early '70s; now, of course, it seems prophetic. Veteran producer David Briggs gave Grin a little too clean a sound on the band's four albums—luckily, the polish doesn't obscure the band's energy. Singing sweetly on ballads that are gems of popcraft, Nils makes *Grin* an engaging debut; and if his hoarse-voiced bellowing

gets a tad annoying on the rockers, it's redeemed by his Fender pyrotechnics and exuberant faith in a hard backbeat. Grin's best, *1 + 1* is considerably more accomplished: nifty strings boost the sappy-wonderful "Just a Poem"; the wistful, slow songs are lovely and the dance tunes kick. Nils's brother Tom adds good rhythm guitar work to *All Out*, but the songs are tepid and cautious, and it's the group's only weak set. *Gone Crazy* recovers impressively—"Beggar's Day" and the rest of its rockers are the toughest and most assured the band ever produced; the ballads are shaky, but still worth a listen.

Moving on to a haphazard solo career, Lofgren has made some fine music since Grin; hardly any of it, however, has quite the freshness—or boasts the desperate ambition—of his first efforts. — P.E.

GTR

½ ★ GTR (Arista, 1986)
Pointless, pompous guitar wank-a-rama, featuring Steve Hackett (formerly of Genesis) and Steve Howe (periodically of Yes). Ttl Sht. — J.D.C.

VINCE GUARALDI

  ★ ★ Modern Music From San Francisco (1955; Fantasy, 1987)
  ★ ★ ★ Vince Guaraldi Trio (1956; Fantasy, 1987)
  ★ ★ ★ A Flower Is a Lovesome Thing (Fantasy, 1957)
  ★ ★ ★ Jazz Impressions (Fantasy, 1962)
★ ★ ★ ★ Jazz Impressions of "Black Orpheus" (1965; Fantasy, 1990)
★ ★ ★ ★ A Charlie Brown Christmas (1965; Fantasy, 1988)
  ★ ★ Oh, Good Grief! (Warner Bros., 1968)
  ★ ★ ★ A Boy Named Charlie Brown (1969; Fantasy, 1989)
★ ★ ★ ★ Greatest Hits (1980; Fantasy, 1989)
★ ★ ★ ★ Live at El Matador (Fantasy, 1987)

Along with Bill Evans and Ramsey Lewis, the late Vince Guaraldi helped define a school of jazz piano that emphasized melodic improvisation and a heightened concern for the lyric line. He was less an innovator than an explorer rooting around in pop songs for some new way to express an emotion. His records are distinguished not only by impeccable choices of material—including his own Impressionistic compositions—but also by easy conversation between the various instruments (he most often worked with a trio). Although not highly regarded by jazz critics, Guaraldi suffered no such indignities among his peers. His lyricism and graceful, swinging style—honed during his years with the Woody Herman and Cal Tjader groups—were well-suited to exotica, and throughout his career he was associated with and championed gifted and important artists such as Mongo Santamaria and Bola Sete. He appears with Tjader on one key cut of Santamaria's *Afro Roots* album, and recorded two acclaimed albums with Sete.

Two events brought Guaraldi's music out of the jazz world into the popular marketplace. One was his self-penned single "Cast Your Fate to the Wind," an instrumental tinged with melancholy that hit the Top Forty in 1963; the other was his scores for several Charlie Brown TV specials. These latter provided the sympathetic underpinning to the Peanuts characters' endless quest for truth and meaning, played easy on the ears, but were challenging in their ever-changing emotional colors. None was more perfectly conceived than the score for *A Charlie Brown Christmas*. Here were melodies and insinuating rhythms that captured the spirit of the holiday season.

At the time of his death in 1976, Guaraldi was far better known to the general public for his Charlie Brown scores than for any of the estimable work he'd done in the '50s and early '60s. Nothing wrong with that, except that it ignores his stirring *Jazz Impressions of "Black Orpheus,"* four tracks from the score of the film *Black Orpheus* that bring Guaraldi back to his twin interests of American jazz and Latin music, and the African influence shared by both. This album also marks the first appearance on record of "Cast Your Fate to the Wind," and includes as well a heartbreaking rendition of Henry Mancini's "Moon River." For sheer lyricism, Guaraldi was at his peak on *A Flower Is a Lovesome Thing*. In addition to Billy Strayhorn's beautiful title song, Guaraldi also assays a Gershwin tune ("Looking for a Boy"), Bobby Troup's "Lonely Girl," Romberg-Hammerstein's "Softly, as in a Morning Sunrise," and "Willow Weep for Me," in addition to offering a fine tune of his own, "Like a Mighty Rose." *Live at El Matador*, the only remaining in-print album of the two he made with Bola Sete, is essential listening for anyone interested not only in the legendary Brazilian guitarist, but also in the inspired interplay of ideas from disparate cultures. Apart from these, *Greatest Hits* guides the listener around Guaraldi's palette,

which includes standards, movie themes, a couple of the *Black Orpheus* tracks, "Cast Your Fate to the Wind," and Charlie Brown music. The final and most eloquent testimony to Guaraldi's artistry comes by way of the late jazz critic Ralph J. Gleason, who wrote in his liner notes to *A Flower Is a Lovesome Thing*: "I know a number of pianists whose impact on the jazz world will be greater than Vince's in terms of trend-setting and as an influence on others. But I don't know one of them—with the exception of Red Garland and Erroll Garner—whose LPs are as suitable for day in day out listening in whatever mood you're in."
— D.M.

GUITAR SLIM
★ ★ ★ ★ **The Things That I Used to Do** (1970; Specialty, 1988)
★ ★ ★ ★ **The Atco Sessions** (Atlantic, 1987)
★ ★ ★ ★ ★ **Sufferin' Mind** (Specialty, 1991)
Only 32 years old when he died in 1959, Guitar Slim (nee Eddie Jones) had all the tools: his songwriting was literate, insightful, and brutally honest, sparing no one, least of all himself; his singing was a marvel of expressiveness, his rough voice capable of unusual emotional impact whether he was exploring a down-and-dirty blues or working out in an uptempo groove; his guitar playing was fired by emotion and infallible instincts. And on his one indisputably great cut, "The Things I Used to Do," from 1953, he had the services of the young Ray Charles as a piano player and arranger, which produced a masterpiece of self-recrimination as well as a forerunner of Charles's groundbreaking work later in the decade. "The Things I Used to Do" spent six weeks in the Number One spot on the R&B chart and remains one of the genre's finest moments.

Specialty's *Sufferin' Mind* collects all the tracks from its previous release, *The Things I Used to Do*, adds 13 more, and becomes in 26 tracks (cut between 1953 and 1955) an important document in tracing the blues roots of R&B and the R&B roots of rock & roll. In his Specialty work one hears tradition honored and new standards set, especially in the hyperkinetic vocal delivery that would later characterize rock & roll artists such as Little Richard (who owes Slim no small debt) and Jerry Lee Lewis. "The Things That I Used to Do," "Story of My Life" and "Sufferin' Mind" paint a picture of a tortured soul doomed to live his life alone.

After being released by Specialty in 1956,

Slim moved over to Atlantic and recorded extensively in New Orleans and New York in 1956–58. Atlantic subsidiary Atco released only four singles on Slim prior to his death; those, plus the remaining unissued sides comprise the stunning *Atco Sessions*. You can feel his pain in the gruff shouts and stinging guitar lines on "I Won't Mind at All," and then be knocked senseless by the man's equanimity when he croons plaintively in "If I Had My Life to Live Over." — D.M.

GUN CLUB
* ★ ★   **Fire of Love** (Ruby, 1981)
* ★ ★½ **Miami** (Animal, 1982)
* ★ ★   **Sex Beat 81** (Lolita, 1983)
* ★ ★ ★½ **The Las Vegas Story** (Animal, 1984)
* ★ ★ ★½ **Mother Juno** (Fundamental, 1987)

The brainchild of basement-voiced Jeffrey Lee Pierce, L.A.'s Gun Club flailed gleefully away at grunge-rock in the early '80s—the band's initial efforts, *Fire of Love* and *Miami*, were unremarkable except when betraying Pierce's passion for fierce blues of the Howlin' Wolf variety. Fervor, however, too seldom met skill. Blondie's Chris Stein produced *Miami* and Debbie Harry sang pseudonymous backup, but the sound had yet to coalesce. The breakthrough came with *The Las Vegas Story*, whose music parallels the strange luminosity of black velvet artwork—Pierce prays to the ghost of Elvis and is rewarded with great gothic stuff like "Walkin' With the Beast" and "The Stranger in Our Town"; The Blasters' Dave Alvin guests on guitar; the band tackles such composers as Pharoah Sanders and Gershwin; credited properly for "excessive feedback," Kid Congo Powers rocks without mercy on guitar; and the entire sloppy affair is an almost-triumph. In more streamlined fashion, *Mother Juno* builds upon *Las Vegas*—it's swamp music for thinking people. — P.E.

GUNS N' ROSES
* ★ ★ ★ ★ ★ **Appetite for Destruction** (Geffen, 1987)
* ★ ★ ★   **GNR Lies** (Geffen, 1988)
* ★ ★ ★ ★   **Use Your Illusion I** (Geffen, 1991)
* ★ ★ ★ ★½   **Use Your Illusion II** (Geffen, 1991)

A band as widely reviled as it is revered, Guns n' Roses embodies many of the contradictions of contemporary rock culture. On the one hand, the band's music can be sublimely affecting, synthesizing the second-hand strains of '70s hard rock (post-Zep metal, Aerosmith-style boogie) into a sound as emotionally eloquent as what the Rolling Stones drew from the blues and country music on *Let It Bleed* and *Exile on Main Street*. On the other hand, the Gunners can be just as nasty as they wanna be, reveling in xenophobia, class resentment and violent misogyny, and as much as that bad attitude puts some listeners off, the eagerness with which this band has been unquestioningly embraced by hard rock's core audience has left commentators on the left and right shaking their heads in disgust.

But what the band's critics either don't get or won't accept is that Guns n' Roses' emphasis on ugliness and anger is not celebratory but cathartic, a way of taking at least temporary control over the demons that threaten them and their audience in real life. That much is obvious in the first notes of *Appetite for Destruction*, as the interlocking guitar lines gain momentum beneath the police-siren wail of Axl Rose's voice. Alternately terrifying, seductive and inspiring, the songs on this album are nothing short of stunning, from the dark sarcasm of "It's So Easy" to the romantic sincerity of "Sweet Child o' Mine." Nor is it just what the songs have to say that impresses; the music is magnificent, too, exhibiting an admirable degree of structural complexity and a stylistic range that stretches from the funk-fueled rhythm riffs of "Mr. Brownstone" to the thrashlike intensity of "You're Crazy."

GNR Lies is less an album than a double EP, combining the band's 1986 mini-album *Live?!*@ Like a Suicide* with four semi-acoustic tracks of more recent vintage. "Patience," a melancholy love song with heavy Rolling Stones overtones, was a hit for the band, but "I Used to Love Her," a joke song whose chorus continues its title with the words " . . . but I had to kill her," further angered feminists already appalled by the casual sexism of the band's debut, while "One in a Million" got the band branded as bigots, thanks to lyrics like "Police and niggers—that's right!—get outta my way," and "Immigrants and faggots, they make no sense to me." Ironically, the song as a whole focuses more on self-loathing than on hatred of others, but that point was easily overlooked in the rush to condemn the group.

Guns n' Roses' next project was somewhat less controversial, but only barely. *Use Your Illusion I* and *Use Your Illusion II*, though released simultaneously, were presented as separate entities, a gimmick some dismissed as little more than a ploy to get the band's fans to shell out for two albums instead of one. Maybe so, but it's worth noting that *Illusion II* is darker and more despairing than *Illusion I*—and, not coincidentally, a stronger collection of songs. That's not to say *Illusion I* is particularly lighthearted, inasmuch as it opens with the full-throttle fury of "Right Next Door to Hell" and closes with the near-death reveries of "Coma." But on *I*, the band tempers its aggression with a surprising amount of pop content, whether in the form of a straightforward reading of Paul McCartney's "Live and Let Die" or the Elton John-ish balladry of "November Rain." *Illusion II*, by contrast, offers little respite, raging on from the take-no-prisoners recriminations of "Get in the Ring" to the peculiar private hell described in "My World," a song that sounds like an unholy cross between "Me So Horny" and "They're Coming to Take Me Away." Yet the band's refusal to capitulate, to give any opponent the satisfaction of seeing its spirit crumble, is the album's real triumph, audible in everything from the quiet majesty of "Civil War" to the chugging momentum of "Locomotive." — J.D.C.

ARLO GUTHRIE

★★★½ **Alice's Restaurant (Reprise, 1967)**
★★ **Arlo (1968; Rising Son, 1988)**
★★★ **Running Down the Road (1969; Rising Son, 1988)**
★★★ **Washington County (1970; Rising Son, 1988)**
★★★ **Hobo's Lullaby (1972; Rising Son, 1987)**
★★★ **Last of the Brooklyn Cowboys (1973; Rising Son, 1987)**
★★★ **Arlo Guthrie (1974; Rising Son, 1988)**
★★★★ **Amigo (1976; Rising Son, 1986)**
★★★ **The Best of Arlo Guthrie (Warner Bros., 1977)**
★★ **One Night (1978; Rising Son, 1988)**
★★★★ **Outlasting the Blues (1979; Rising Son, 1986)**
★★★ **Power of Love (1981; Rising Son, 1986)**
★★★ **Someday (Rising Son, 1986)**
★★★ **All Over the World (Rising Son, 1991)**
★★★ **Son of the Wind (Rising Son, 1992)**

As sons of titanic fathers go, Arlo has acquitted himself pretty well. The 20 minutes of "Alice's Restaurant"—the draft protest that thrust him to fame at the 1967 Newport Folk Festival—don't hold up to repeated listening, but Guthrie's comfortable, slightly wiggy persona remains welcome. Contending not only with the potent ghost of Woody (whose simple, prophetic songs form America's definitive folk music), but with Woody's disciple, Bob Dylan, Arlo has opted generally for easier music. As resolutely anti-authoritarian as his forebears, he champions personal and political rebellions, but he's nostalgic in ways they never were, and his humor has little of their bite.

As a vocalist, however, his sunniness lends his delivery charm. "Coming Into Los Angeles," a doper's gleeful apologia, was a big hit at Woodstock and the best thing off *Running Down the Road*; *Hobo's Lullaby* featured Arlo's other mass exposure, in a cover of Steve Goodman's sweet "City of New Orleans." *Last of the Brooklyn Cowboys* is an ambitious crazy-quilt of all kinds of American music, from country to Latino; *Amigo* was stronger, and perhaps Arlo's best.

Best of isn't very intelligently compiled. Definitely worth seeking out is *Outlasting the Blues*; it's popular music at its most honest. A rigorous self-examination, spurred on by Guthrie's conversion to Catholicism, it meditates deeply on love, faith and death. — P.E.

WOODY GUTHRIE

★★★★ **Songs to Grow On (Folkways, 1951)**
★★★★ **Songs to Grow On, Vol. 2 (Folkways, 1958)**
★★★★ **Songs to Grow On, Vol. 3 (Folkways, 1961)**
★★★★ **Woody Guthrie Sings Folk Songs (1962; Smithsonian/Folkways, 1990)**
★★★★ **Dust Bowl Ballads (1964; Rounder, 1988)**
★★★★ **Woody Guthrie Sings Folk Songs, Vol. 2 (Folkways, 1964)**
★★★★ **This Land Is Your Land (Folkways, 1967)**
★★★★★ **A Legendary Performer (RCA, 1977)**
★★★★ **Woody Guthrie (Warner Bros., 1977)**
★★★★★ **The Greatest Songs of Woody Guthrie (Vanguard, 1988)**
★★★★ **Columbia River Collection (Rounder, 1987)**
★★★★ **Library of Congress Recordings (Rounder, 1988)**

★ ★ ★ ★ **Struggle (Smithsonian/Folkways, 1990)**
★ ★ ★ ★ **Worried Man Blues (Collectables, 1990)**
★ ★ ★ ★ **Immortal Woody Guthrie (Collectables, 1990)**

Weathered, lean, kindly and hurt, Woody Guthrie's face is the face of American folk music. Born in 1912, this astonishingly prolific composer is to the gritty, acoustic story song what Louis Armstrong is to jazz and Little Richard and Elvis are to rock & roll—the clearest, deepest source. Writing, according to his friend Pete Seeger, a thousand songs in the years between 1936 and 1954, he recorded with absolute fidelity, wit and grace the struggles and celebrations of the working class. An Okie leftist (his guitar bore the legend, "This machine kills fascists"), he was an activist whose politics were the furthest thing from theoretical—he'd suffered the wrongs he strove so passionately to correct. Outlaws from Jesus Christ to Pretty Boy Floyd, from debtors and prisoners to hobos, formed the misfit pantheon from whom he took inspiration—and his hard, but ecstatic life was an act of protest and of prayer, of anger and healing.

Influenced by Jimmie Rodgers and the Carter Family, Guthrie also absorbed the strains of cowboy music, country blues and the music-hall pop of his day; from that tangled yarn he wove his own bardic, simple, music, with each song featuring only a few chords but entire, condensed volumes of wisdom. His voice was flat, clear, somewhat trebly and unerringly direct: he sang like a casually chatting prophet. So profound was his effect not only on American music, but on the American character, that it's not only Dylan, Springsteen and every single folk musician who owes him a debt, but writers like Kerouac and the rest of the Beats, as well as naturalist filmmakers, vernacular poets and populist politicians. Alongside Walt Whitman, Guthrie remains a national poet laureate.

While all his records are worth owning, the best place to start is with either the fine single-album, *Legendary Performer*, or the much fuller *The Greatest Songs* (its 23 selections are the crucial Guthrie: "This Land Is Your Land," "So Long, It's Been Good to Know Yuh," "Deportee," "Hard Travelin'," and so on). *Library of Congress Recordings* is an epic three-record set, featuring a good handul of Guthrie's dust-bowl ballads and laconically witty spoken intros to the songs. *Folk Songs* pairs

him with his friends Leadbelly, Cisco Houston, Sonny Terry and Bess Lomax Hawes; *Struggle* concentrates on the political work. *Columbia River Collection* is an excellent round of 1941 songs that had been lost for 40 years. Also essential for full appreciation of the man is his 1943 autobiography, *Bound for Glory*. — P.E.

GUY
★ ★ ★ **Guy (Uptown/MCA, 1988)**
★ ★ ★ ½ **The Future (MCA, 1990)**

With Guy, production's the thing. The songs and the singing are ultra-pro on these albums, but it's the sound—a percolating, hip-hop feast of slamming percussion and floating keyboard textures—that grabs the listener. This makes sense, as one-third of the trio Guy is producer Teddy Riley, virtually the creator of New Jack Swing. New Jack, of course, added new musicality and sonic surprise to all manner of rap—and Guy was a proving ground for the form. Michael Jackson hired Riley to produce *Dangerous* (1991), and to take the Gloved One to hipper ground. — P.E.

BUDDY GUY
★ ★ ★ ★   A Man and the Blues (Vanguard, 1968)
★ ★ ★ ★   This Is Buddy Guy (Vanguard, 1968)
★ ★ ★ ★   I Was Walkin' Through the Woods (1970; Chess/MCA, 1989)
★ ★ ★ ½   Hold That Plane (1972; Vanguard, 1987)
★ ★ ★ ½   Stone Crazy! (Alligator, 1981)
★ ★ ★ ½   I Left My Blues in San Francisco (Chess/MCA, 1987)
★ ★ ★ ½   Damn Right, I've Got the Blues (Silvertone, 1991)
★ ★ ★ ★   The Very Best of Buddy Guy (Rhino, 1992)
★ ★ ★ ★   The Complete Chess Studio Recordings (Chess/MCA, 1992)
WITH JUNIOR WELLS
★ ★ ★ ★   Buddy Guy & Junior Wells Play the Blues (1972; Rhino, 1992)
★ ★ ★ ½   Drinkin' TNT and Smokin' Dynamite (Blind Pig, 1982)
★ ★ ★ ½   Alone and Acoustic (Hightone, 1991)

Slash-and-burn guitar solos are the specialty of this Chicago blues mainstay. Emerging in the late '60s, Buddy Guy staked his claim with a series of string-sizzling sides for Chess. *I Was Walkin' Through the Woods* collects his best-known hailstones and firestorms, like "My Time After Awhile" and "Stone Crazy." *A Man and the Blues* gets similairly drenched in flames, while *This Is Buddy Guy* is a live set. Touring with harmonica player Junior Wells in the '70s, Guy added R&B licks and chunks of rock to his trick bag. *Buddy Guy & Junior Wells Play the Blues* features indebted guests along the lines of Eric Clapton, while *Drinkin' TNT and Smokin' Dynamite* catches the duo's act at the 1974 Montreux Jazz Festival. Guy has recorded less and less frequently as the years slip by—though when he does, his stun-power is undiminished. Even with its requisite superstar walk-ons (Clapton and Jeff Beck this time), *Damn Right I've Got the Blues* administers the most satisfying dose of pure Buddy Guy fretwork since the righteously wailin' *Stone Crazy!*, from 1981. Rhino's 1992 anthology is a wonderful retrospective of Guy's career. — M.C.

H

SAMMY HAGAR
★ ★½ Standing Hampton (Geffen, 1981)
★ ★   Three Lock Box (Geffen, 1982)
★ ★   VOA (Geffen, 1984)

After making his name as the voice behind
Montrose, Sammy Hagar launched his own
band in 1976, and spent most of the next
decade churning out unmemorable
assemblages of raucous, glandular hard
rock. At this writing, all but three of his ten
solo albums are out of print, and the world
is none the worse for it. Nor is Hagar (who
has since replaced David Lee Roth in Van
Halen), inasmuch as the remaining albums
are the least embarrassing remnants of his
solo career.

Although *Standing Hampton* has the
veneer of hard rock—loud guitars, loud
drums, loud everything else—the writing is
surprisingly pop-friendly, and includes two
of Hagar's finest: "There's Only One Way
to Rock" and the tuneful, touching "I'll Fall
In Love Again." *Three Lock Box* pursues
that approach into full-blown pop rock, and
ends up sounding like bad-imitation
Journey, but *VOA*—which includes the
got-a-fast-car anthem, "I Can't Drive 55"—
returns him to the chest-thumping sound of
yore, with predictably tedious results.
— J.D.C.

MERLE HAGGARD
    ★ ★ ★ Strangers (Capitol, 1965)
      ★ ★ Just Between the Two of Us
            (Capitol, 1965)
    ★ ★ ★ Swinging Doors (Capitol, 1966)
  ★ ★ ★ ★ I'm a Lonesome Fugitive (Capitol,
            1967)
  ★ ★ ★ ★ Branded Man (Capitol, 1967)
  ★ ★ ★ ★ Sing Me Back Home (Capitol,
            1968)
    ★ ★ ★ The Legend of Bonnie & Clyde
            (Capitol, 1968)
★ ★ ★ ★ ★ The Best of Merle Haggard
            (Capitol, 1968)
    ★ ★ ★ Mama Tried (Capitol, 1968)

      ★ ★ Pride in What I Am (Capitol,
            1969)
  ★ ★ ★ ★ Same Train, a Different Time
            (Capitol, 1969)
    ★ ★ ★ Close-Up Merle Haggard
            (Capitol, 1969)
    ★ ★ ★ Okie from Muskogee (Capitol,
            1970)
    ★ ★ ★ Introducing My Friends—The
            Strangers (Capitol, 1970)
    ★ ★ ★ The Fightin' Side of Me (Capitol,
            1970)
  ★ ★ ★ ★ Tribute to the Best Damn Fiddle
            Player in the World: My Salute to
            Bob Wills (Capitol, 1970)
    ★ ★ ★ High on a Hilltop (Capitol, 1971)
    ★ ★ ★ Sing a Sad Song (Capitol, 1971)
    ★ ★ ★ Hag (Capitol, 1971)
  ★ ★ ★ ★ Someday We'll Look Back
            (Capitol, 1971)
    ★ ★ ★ Land of Many Churches (Capitol,
            1971)
    ★ ★ ★ Let Me Tell You About a Song
            (Capitol, 1972)
★ ★ ★ ★ ★ The Best of the Best of Merle
            Haggard (Capitol, 1972)
    ★ ★ ★ It's Not Love (but It's Not Bad)
            (Capitol, 1972)
    ★ ★ ★ Totally Instrumental, With One
            Exception (Capitol, 1973)
  ★ ★ ★ ★ I Love Dixie Blues (Capitol,
            1973)
  ★ ★ ★ ★ Merle Haggard's Christmas
            Present (Something Old,
            Something New) (Capitol, 1973)
  ★ ★ ★ ★ If We Make It Through December
            (Capitol, 1974)
    ★ ★ ★ My Love Affair With Trains
            (Capitol, 1974)
  ★ ★ ★ ★ Merle Haggard Presents His 30th
            Album (Capitol, 1974)
    ★ ★ ★ Keep Moving On (Capitol, 1975)
      ★ ★ It's All in the Movies (Capitol,
            1976)
  ★ ★ ★ ★ The Roots of My Raising
            (Capitol, 1976)

★ ★ ★ ★ ★ **Songs I'll Always Sing (Capitol, 1976)**
★ ★ ★ ★ **A Working Man Can't Get Nowhere Today (Capitol, 1977)**
★ ★ ★ **Eleven Winners (Capitol, 1977)**
★ ★ ★ **Ramblin' Fever (MCA, 1977)**
★ ★ **My Farewell to Elvis (MCA, 1977)**
★ ★ **I'm Always on a Mountain When I Fall (MCA, 1978)**
★ ★ ★ **The Way It Was in '51 (Capitol, 1978)**
★ ★ ★ ★ **Serving 190 Proof (MCA, 1979)**
★ ★ ★ **The Way I Am (MCA, 1980)**
★ ★ **Back to the Barrooms (MCA, 1980)**
★ ★ **Back to the Barrooms/The Way I Am (MCA, 1980)**
★ ★ ★ ★ **Rainbow Stew/Live at Anaheim Stadium (MCA, 1981)**
★ ★ ★ **Songs for the Mama That Tried (MCA, 1981)**
★ ★ ★ **Big City (Epic, 1981)**
★ ★ ★ **Merle Haggard's Greatest Hits (MCA, 1982)**
★ ★ ★ **Goin' Home for Christmas (Epic, 1982)**
★ ★ ★ **Going Where the Lonely Go (Epic, 1982)**
★ ★ ★ **That's the Way Love Goes (Epic, 1983)**
★ ★ ★ **The Epic Collection (Recorded Live) (Epic, 1983)**
★ ★ ★ **It's All in the Game (Epic, 1984)**
★ ★ ★ ★ **His Epic Hits—The First 11 to Be Continued (Epic, 1984)**
★ ★ ★ ★ **His Greatest and His Best (MCA, 1985)**
★ ★ ★ **His Best (MCA, 1985)**
★ ★ **Amber Waves of Grain (Epic, 1985)**
★ ★ ★ **Kern River (Epic, 1985)**
★ ★ ★ **Out Among the Stars (Epic, 1986)**
★ ★ **A Friend in California (Epic, 1986)**
★ ★ ★ **Chill Factor (Epic, 1987)**
★ ★ ★ ★ **5:01 Blues (Epic, 1989)**
★ ★ ★ **More of the Best (Rhino, 1990)**
WITH WILLIE NELSON
★ ★ ★ **Poncho and Lefty (Epic, 1982)**
★ ★ ★ **Seashores of Old Mexico (Epic, 1987)**
WITH GEORGE JONES
★ ★ ★ **A Taste of Yesterday's Wine (Epic, 1982)**

Merle Haggard is both a guardian of the country music tradition and one of that tradition's most important artists. It's tempting, but dangerous, to dismiss most of the Hag's recent work as inferior to the great Capitol albums from the '60s, and some of the interesting titles he released on MCA and Epic in the '70s and early '80s. He's not as consistently brilliant as he was in his younger days, but on sporadic occasions, he's as good as anyone out there. Both *5:01 Blues*, another entry addressing the drudgery of the working life, and *Kern River* have moments of grandeur, and Hag's world-weary delivery brings a cutting edge. Moreover, time has tempered a self-righteous streak in Hag's makeup. Considered as a whole, the body of work Haggard has created is stunning in its stylistic range, historical resonance, and flinty observations on the forces that bring people together and then tear them apart.

Haggard's affinity for the working class is bred in the bone. His family fled from the Oklahoma dust bowl in the early '30s and settled in Bakersfield, California. Born in 1937, Haggard saw his life become unhinged at age nine, when his father died. From that point through his teens he became familiar with the insides of reform schools and jails, where he was often confined on charges of breaking and entering, petty theft and other minor offenses. In 1957 he hit rock bottom when he was sentenced to a maximum of 15 years in San Quentin on a robbery charge. Upon his release in 1960 he headed for the Bakersfield club scene, where he found work as a sideman in various local bands. He began recording in 1963 for the small Tally label, and his second single, "Sing a Sad Song," written by Wynn Stewart, who was heading a band for which Haggard was playing, hit the Top Twenty on the country chart. After a Top Ten single in 1965, "(All My Friends Are Gonna Be) Strangers," Capitol bought out the Tally label, and with it Haggard's contract.

Every aspect of Haggard's earliest work indicates his debt to the plainspoken eloquence of Jimmie Rodgers and the plaintive but solid vocal style of Lefty Frizzell. He has also named Bing Crosby as an influence, and indeed, some of his bluesier phrasings recall Der Bingle's subtle touch. Always there was the spirit of Bob Wills hovering over Haggard's eclectic approach. Fittingly, Haggard assembled a band, the Strangers, that could move easily between folk, country, and western swing; its members included lead guitarists James Burton and Roy Nichols, rhythm guitarist Glen Campbell, Glen D. Hardin on piano and the estimable Ralph Mooney on pedal steel.

After establishing himself with some standard drinking and cheating songs, Haggard dug into deeper material beginning in 1966, when he recorded Liz and Casey Anderson's "I'm a Lonesome Fugitive." He also made public his own sordid past, and began mining it, immediately penning one of his most poignant songs, "Sing Me Back Home," reportedly written for a friend on San Quentin's Death Row. These two songs brought an implicit political dimension to Haggard's work that would become more pronounced in the following years when songs such as "Okie from Muskogee" (written, Haggard insists, as a goof) and "The Fightin' Side of Me" (a conscious blast aimed at Vietnam War protesters) were embraced first as anthems by Nixon-era right-wingers and shortly thereafter as inspired satires by a younger generation at odds with the president's agenda. This seemed to amuse Haggard, who had taken note of the changing times during a visit to Sunset Strip in the late '60s, when he saw "hippies running down the street with Bibles under their arms and pencils up their asses." Always a thoughtful man, Haggard understood that the line between right and wrong was now blurred almost beyond his comprehension; rather than play into the reactionary fervor his songs generated, he did a 360 and released *A Tribute to the Best Damn Fiddle Player in the World*, an album honoring the artistry of Bob Wills (a concept that had also worked to grand effect on a Jimmie Rodgers salute, *Same Train, a Different Time*, in 1969). Hag's fiddle work here is a bit ragged, but he'd only been playing the instrument for three months at the time he recorded the Wills tribute; more to the point, when he dug into Tommy Duncan's treasured "Time Changes Everything," he seemed to be speaking in the most personal terms about the need for understanding in a society becoming increasingly polarized.

However much of a hero he became to the right wing, Haggard rarely let politics intrude so blatantly on his music again. His best songs from the Capitol years were autobiographical gems on the order of "Mama Tried" and "Hungry Eyes," deeply felt and often tragic adult love songs ("The Emptiest Arms in the World," "Someday We'll Look Back," "It's Not Love [but It's Not Bad]"), and observations on the struggles of the working class. *A Working Man Can't Get Nowhere Today* (1977) is the most sustained statement of policy from this period, and it's also as tough a set of country blues as was released in the '70s. (There is, however, no excusing the racist sentiments of "I'm a White Boy.") Three

collections—*The Best of Merle Haggard*, *The Best of the Best of Merle Haggard* and *Songs I'll Always Sing*—represent the highlights of the Capitol years, but boiling down Haggard's work to "hits" ignores much of what is essential about the man. All of the above-mentioned albums are worth the price of admission, as are a tribute to Hank Williams and Lefty Frizzell, *The Way It Was in '51*; *High on a Hilltop*; and the laconic *30th Album*, which finds Hag dipping into blues, western swing and traditional country in spare settings.

The MCA and Epic years represent periods of retrenchment, consolidation, and, of late, renewal. Boozing and broken hearts are the dominant themes, save for a recent return to social commentary. If you sift through these selections, a few treasures emerge. *Ramblin' Fever* contains in the title song one of Haggard's acutely observed ruminations on wanderlust, while "If We're Not Back in Love by Monday" depicts in moving detail a couple's efforts to salvage their relationship. On "When My Blue Moon Turns to Gold Again," Hag does Hank Snow better than Hank Snow was doing himself in those days. By far his best from the MCA years is *Serving 190 Proof*. Cut in the midst of a mid-life crisis, Hag's contradictory feelings about his life and career produce some mesmerizing, if unsettling, moments; enigmatic and moving, it's a first-rate effort. Apart from these two albums, the MCA years are aptly summarized in several collections, the best of the lot being *His Best* and *His Greatest and His Best*. *Rainbow Stew/Live* captures the star and his band at their peak.

His music having taken on a darker shade of blues, Haggard has remained introspective on his Epic albums. *Going Where the Lonely Go* (1983) is one of the best of this ilk, although its follow-up, *That's the Way Love Goes*, finds him at his contradictory best on "What Am I Gonna Do (With the Rest of My Life)" and the album's closer, "I Think I'll Stay." Three duet albums, *A Taste of Yesterday's Wine* with George Jones, and *Poncho and Lefty* and *Seashores of Old Mexico*, both with Willie Nelson, team Haggard with vocalists who can challenge him; the results, though spotty, are always interesting. Rhino's *More of the Best* is a representative overview of Haggard's key songs from the Capitol and MCA years.

Though he's sounding more weary than ever, Haggard remains remarkably in command of his phrasing and inflection. He sounds like he knows a little bit more than he's letting on; his great art is in suggesting you better beware of what's coming and get strapped in for a bumpy ride. With Hag, it's take it day to day, make your stand, and hope the sun comes up tomorrow. — D.M.

HAIRCUT 100
★★ **Pelican West (Arista, 1982)**
Tuneful, fey dance pop of the sort which might have seemed reasonable at one time but now appears utterly ridiculous. Docked one star for singer Nick Heyward, who sounds like a prepubescent Joe Jackson.
— J.D.C.

BILL HALEY AND HIS COMETS
★ **Rock Around the Country (GNP Crescendo, 1976)**
★★ **Greatest Hits (MCA, 1980)**
★★★ **Bill Haley and His Comets—From the Original Master Tapes (MCA, 1985)**
Time has been good to Bill Haley. Once dismissed as an aging country artist who stumbled upon beat music in an effort to sustain an unremarkable career, the Michigan-born rock & roll pioneer is now properly viewed as having had an interest in folk, country & western, swing, and blues and incorporated elements of all these musics in his own cauldron. There's no question that his retooling as a rock & roll star took his career off life support—he'd been recording without notable success in the country field for eight years when he cut a cover version of Jackie Brenston's "Rocket 88" in 1951 and became convinced that there was a large and hungry audience of young people lying in wait for some kind of new music. In 1952 he changed the name of his group from the Saddlemen to Bill Haley and His Comets, and cut another uptempo side, "Rock the Joint," that sold 75,000 copies, and was followed the next year by a Haley original, "Crazy Man Crazy," which spoke the lingo and also made the charts. A label change to Decca in 1954 proved to be the most fortuitous event in Haley's career. His first record, a cover of a 1952 single by Sunny Dae, "Rock Around the Clock," was only a modest success, but its follow-up, a sanitized cover of Joe Turner's "Shake, Rattle and Roll," was a Top Ten record both here and in England, and a million-seller to boot. In 1955 "Rock Around the Clock" was re-released and went to Number One; a rebel image also accrued to the rather square Haley as a result of the song being used as the theme for *Blackboard Jungle*, a stark depiction of

urban juvenile delinquency. In '55 and '56 he cut 11 Top Forty singles and was the best-known rock & roll artist in the world. Elvis Presley's breakthrough in 1956, followed by the emergence of a host of other young, handsome, and musically dynamic artists, stole Haley's thunder. He hit the Top Forty one more time, with "Skinny Minnie" in 1958, remained active on the concert circuit—his popularity never ebbed in Europe—and resurfaced in the late '60s in rock revival shows. He recorded a final album, *Rock Around the Country*, in Nashville in 1976, with some of the original Comets and a host of stalwart session players. A stiff, uninspired effort, it went nowhere, and Haley went into retirement. He died at his home in Harlingen, Texas, in 1981.

The two MCA titles remaining in Haley's catalog adequately tell the story of his most noteworthy years. *From the Original Master Tapes* is a compelling collection of tracks from 1955 and 1956 that includes most of Haley's hits with the exception of "Skinny Minnie." *Greatest Hits* does contain "Skinny Minnie" as well as a solid interpretation of Louis Jordan's timeless "Choo Choo Ch'Boogie." However quickly he ran out of ideas, Haley still commands respect for seeing the potential of the new music he heard down South and supporting it while he commanded an international platform. — D.M.

DARYL HALL
★★★½ **Sacred Songs (RCA, 1980)**
★★½ **Three Hearts in The Happy Ending Machine (RCA, 1986)**
John Oates's contribution to Hall and Oates's hit-making skills have been questioned over the years, but Hall's solo work suggests that Oates's presence is a key ingredient. Interestingly, both *Sacred Songs* and *Three Hearts* are dominated by outside producers: Robert Fripp and Dave Stewart, respectively. Of the two, Fripp's studious art rock proves to be far more stimulating than Stewart's cluttered high-tech psychedelia.
— M.C.

HALL AND OATES
★★ **Whole Oats (Atlantic, 1972)**
★★★· **Abandoned Luncheonette (Atlantic, 1973)**
★★ **War Babies (Atlantic, 1974)**
★★½ **Daryl Hall and John Oates (RCA, 1975)**
★★½ **Bigger Than Both of Us (RCA, 1976)**

★ ★ ★ **Beauty on a Back Street (RCA, 1977)**
★ ★ ★½ **Along the Red Ledge (RCA, 1978)**
★ ★½ **Livetime (RCA, 1978)**
★ ★½ **X-Static (RCA, 1979)**
★ ★ ★ **Voices (RCA, 1981)**
★ ★ ★ **Private Eyes (RCA, 1981)**
★ ★ ★ **H₂O (RCA, 1982)**
★ ★ ★ ★ **Rock 'n' Soul, Part 1 (RCA, 1983)**
★ ★ ★½ **Big Bam Boom (RCA, 1984)**
★ ★ ★ **Live at the Apollo With David Ruffin & Eddie Kendricks (RCA, 1985)**
★ ★½ **Ooh Yeah! (Arista, 1988)**
★ ★½ **Change of Season (Arista, 1990)**

The tall blond guy is the one with the voice. Daryl Hall started singing soul songs around Philadelphia in the late '60s, often with singer-guitarist John Oates accompanying. When the two men signed to Atlantic in the early '70s, they were juggling blue-eyed urban R&B and spacey suburban folk rock—somewhat uncomfortably. "She's Gone" (from *Abandoned Luncheonette*) proved to be the first of a long line of hits, though it was around for several years before it reached the Top Ten in 1976. "Sara Smile" (from *Daryl Hall and John Oates*) and "Rich Girl" (from *Bigger Than Both of Us*) established the duo's knack for catchy melodies that same year, but the accompanying albums were less satisfying.

Still stuck between rock and soul at this point, Hall and Oates gradually merged their conflicting interests over the next few (out-of-print) albums. *Beauty on a Back Street* and (especially) *Along the Red Ledge* infuse classic formulas with contemporary elements: a touch of hard-rock guitar here, a burst of new-wave nervous energy there. These albums didn't produce hits, but their emphasis on cohesion and stronger rhythms laid the groundwork for the grand fusion yet to come.

Beginning with *Voices*, Hall and Oates finally hit their synthesized stride—and enlivened the otherwise-moribund Top Forty for the next couple of years. Conversant in trendy technology and traditional love-man emoting, Daryl Hall puts his best lines across with indelible melodies. He's got your "Kiss on My List" and a team of "Private Eyes" watching your ev-ery move. All he wants is a game of "One On One" tonight, but ask him to lie and it's "I Can't Go for That (No Can Do)." There are a couple of lost gems on the albums from this peak period, such as *Voices'* "Everytime You Go Away" (later a

hit for Paul Young). But for the most part, *Private Eyes* and *H₂O* helped to reassert Hall and Oates's status as an awesomely consistent singles machine. The greatest hits collection *Rock 'n' Soul Part 1* goes a long way toward fulfilling the title's promise. A troubling streak of nastiness also emerges here, running from "Rich Girl" to "Maneater," though Hall and Oates's soulful virtues outweigh their occasional macho lapses.

Big Bam Boom adds a dollop of dance-music thud to Hall and Oates's already melodramatic big sound, and it turns out to be a comfortable fit. "Out of Touch" and "Method of Modern Love" continue in the rock & soul vein, and stronger than usual material rounds out the album. *Live at the Apollo* acknowledges a long-standing debt to the Temptations; sadly, Daryl Hall and John Oates are in top form but David Ruffin and Eddie Kendricks are not. Regrouping after a brief split, Hall and Oates seemed to have misplaced that magic touch. The Arista albums sound blandly generic. What made the early hits so compelling was their facile blend of happening influences; now Hall and Oates strain to sound like "classic" Hall and Oates. — M.C.

TOM T. HALL
★ ★ ★ ★½ **In Search of a Song (Mercury, 1971)**
★ ★ ★½ **Tom T. Hall's Greatest Hits (Mercury, 1972)**
★ ★½ **Greatest Hits, Volume 2 (Mercury, 1975)**
★ ★ ★ **Greatest Hits, Volume 3 (Mercury, 1978)**
★ ★ ★ **Greatest Hits, Volumes 1 & 2 (Mercury, 1983)**
★ ★ ★ ★½ **The Essential Tom T. Hall: Twentieth Anniversary Collection/The Story Songs (Mercury, 1988)**

Just when rock songwriters started to fling their concepts around, country tunesmith Tom T. Hall had an idea that bit him like a bug. What if he put his gift for musical narrative to work on the road? Setting out with a guitar, notepad, tape recorder and an iron stomach, Tom T. Hall came back with a remarkable album. *In Search of a Song* unfolds like a conversation: Hall introduces himself with a revealing tale from his own past ("The Year Clayton Delaney Died"), and then relates the highlights of an accidental odyssey. He's not the rangiest country singer by far, though his dry inflections and raconteur's sense of pace maintain an even flow. His observations and descriptions are often startling: "Trip to Hyden" depicts the grim beauty and pervasive dread of Kentucky's coal-mining hills, while "L.A. Blues" takes a look at city life—and shrugs it off with a sardonic laugh. Hall tells a good one on himself in the hangover romance of "Tulsa Telephone Book," but "A Million Miles to the City" and "Who's Gonna Feed Them Hogs" both indicate that he's a sharp listener.

Greatest Hits includes "Clayton Delaney" and a handful of similarly beguiling yarns from deleted albums like *Homecoming* and *I Witness Life*. Hall's soft-hearted (and soft-headed) streak is revealed on "One Hundred Children" and "Me and Jesus," however, and *Vol. 2* is a repository for the sloppy sentiments of "I Like Beer," "I Love," "Country Is" and "(Old Dogs, Children and) Watermelon Wine." *Vol. 3* rebounds somewhat, mostly due to the inclusion of some early-'70s tracks. The *Essential* collection taps Hall's peak period.
— M.C.

STUART HAMM
★ ★ ★½ **Radio Free Albemuth (Relativity, 1988)**
★ ★ ★ ★ **Kings of Sleep (Relativity, 1989)**
★ ★ ★½ **The Urge (Relativity, 1991)**

Like guitarist Joe Satriani (with whom he sometimes tours), bassist Stuart Hamm is a musician first, and a virtuoso second. That is, for all their prodigious displays of technique, what holds Hamm's albums together is their musicality. Granted, he's not entirely averse to showing off, as with the bass-on-top renditions of Beethoven's "Moonlight Sonata" and Debussy's "Dr. Gradus ad Parnasum" on *Radio Free Albemuth*, but his best work shows a deep understanding of the bassist's role in an ensemble, and finds him moving easily between flashy lead work and solidly supportive rhythm playing.

Radio Free Albemuth takes a fairly standard fusoid approach, alternating the above-mentioned classical showcases with fast and furious jazz-rock workouts with soloists Satriani and Allan Holdsworth. *Kings of Sleep*, however, brings Hamm's virtuosity into focus. As his slap-and-pop performance on "Black Ice" shows, he knows how to push a rock rhythm section, and has no trouble fueling the fires of guitarist Harry K. Cody. But he's equally adept at jazzy lyricism, as "I Want to Know" demonstrates.

The Urge includes a gentle, raga-influenced number called "As Children" and an astonishing live solo composition called "Quahogs Anyone?" But the increasing emphasis on rock sidemen—in addition to Cody, the players include guitarist Eric Johnson and Mötley Crüe's Tommy Mars—has Hamm emphasizing the heavy-riff aspects of his writing, and even trying to sing on a few tunes (Jack Bruce he ain't).
— J.D.C.

HAMMER
★ ★ ★½ **Let's Get Started (Capitol, 1988)**
★ ★ ★ **Please Hammer Don't Hurt 'Em (Capitol, 1990)**
★ ★ **Too Legit to Quit**

Because his success owes more to hard work and showmanship than to originality, Hammer (who called himself M.C. Hammer on his first two albums) is frequently reviled in the hip-hop community as a sellout, a fake. Which is a bum rap. True, his music beds not only borrow from the most obvious sources—Queen's "Another One Bites the Dust" for "Let's Get Started," Rick James's "Superfreak" for "U Can't Touch This," James Brown's "Superbad" for "Here Comes the Hammer"—but often act as straight-up covers, like *Please Hammer*'s embarrassing remake of the Chi-Lites' "Have You Seen Her." But he does understand the value of a strong beat (particularly on *Let's Get Started*), and knows how to wring every ounce of energy from a dance groove. But the relentless criticism took its toll as *Too Legit to Quit* finds the rapper avoiding sample-based grooves and hedging his bets by moving toward a more explicitly R&B sound, an approach that works passably on "This Is the Way We Roll" and the album's title tune, but fizzles elsewhere. (Consumers should note that his "Addams Groove" appears only on the cassette version of *Too Legit*). This stumble is a shame, really, for Hammer may not be one of rap's finest, but he's far from the worst. — J.D.C.

JOHN HAMMOND
★ ★ **John Hammond (Vanguard, 1963)**
★ ★ **Big City Blues (Vanguard, 1964)**
★ ★ **So Many Roads (Vanguard, 1965)**
★ ★ **Country Blues (Vanguard, 1965)**
★ ★ **Mirrors (Vanguard, 1968)**
★ ★½ **I Can Tell (Atlantic, 1968)**
★ ★ **Sooner or Later (Atlantic, 1968)**
★ ★ ★½ **The Best of John Hammond (Vanguard, 1970)**

★ ★ ★½ Southern Fried (Atlantic, 1970)
★ ★ ★½ Source Point (Columbia, 1971)
★ ★ ★ I'm Satisfied (Columbia, 1972)
★ ★½ When I Need (Columbia, 1973)
★ ★ ★ Triumvirate (Columbia, 1973)
★ ★½ Spirituals to Swing (Vanguard, 1973)
★ ★½ Can't Beat the Kid (Capricorn, 1975)
★ ★½ John Hammond: Solo (Vanguard, 1976)
★ ★ Footwork (Vanguard, 1978)
★ ★½ Hot Tracks (Vanguard, 1978)
★ ★½ Frogs for Snakes (Rounder, 1982)
★ ★ ★ John Hammond Live (Rounder, 1984)
★ ★½ Nobody But You (Rounder, 1987)

A powerful, distinctive voice, fine acoustic guitar work (with a special emphasis on bottleneck), tasteful song selection and tireless industry characterize this journeyman blues player. Son of industry legend John Hammond, Sr.—the man who discovered Bob Dylan and Aretha Franklin, among others—the younger Hammond has for years recorded poor-selling, but very faithful covers of country blues. So consistent is his approach that the energetic take on, say, Muddy Waters's "Sail On" off *Nobody but You* (1987) hardly differs at all in spirit from his early '60s renderings of Robert Johnson and Blind Willie McTell. *Southern Fried* and *Source Point* remain his best and most electric albums; *Live* kicks, too. (A frequent quest on "Austin City Limits," Hammond is an engaging, very earnest performer.) *Triumvirate*, a collaboration with Dr. John and Mike Bloomfield, is solid but unspectacular. For a while, Hammond fulfilled the role of a blues popularizer, along the lines of the Butterfield Blues Band, if not with as much flair. But with blues revivals occurring, however halfheartedly, every ten years or so anyway, Hammond's pedagogical purpose is moot. He simply seems to play now for his own enjoyment, and he does so with relish.
— P.E.

HERBIE HANCOCK

★ ★ ★ ★½ Takin' Off (1962; Blue Note, 1987)
★ ★ ★ ★ My Point of View (1963; Blue Note, 1987)
★ ★ ★ Inventions & Dimensions (1963; Blue Note, 1988)
★ ★ ★ ★ Empyrean Isles (1964; Blue Note, 1985)
★ ★ ★ ★½ Maiden Voyage (1965; Blue Note, 1986)

★ ★ ★½ Speak Like a Child (Blue Note, 1968)
★ ★ ★½ The Prisoner (1969; Blue Note, 1987)
★ ★ ★ ★ Mwandishi (Warner Bros., 1971)
★ ★ ★ ★½ Crossings (Warner Bros., 1972)
★ ★ ★ ★ ★ Sextant (Columbia, 1973)
★ ★ ★ ★½ Headhunters (Columbia, 1974)
★ ★ ★ Thrust (Columbia, 1974)
★ ★ ★ ★ Man-Child (Columbia, 1975)
★ ★ ★ Secrets (Columbia, 1976)
★ ★ ★½ The Quintet (1977; Columbia, 1988)
★ ★½ Feets Don't Fail Me Now (Columbia, 1979)
★ ★ ★ ★ The Best Of Herbie Hancock (1979; Columbia, 1986)
★ ★ Monster (1980; Columbia, 1986)
★ ★ ★½ Mr. Hands (Columbia, 1980)
★½ Lite Me Up (Columbia, 1982)
★ ★ ★ ★ Future Shock (Columbia, 1983)
★ ★ ★ ★½ Sound-System (Columbia, 1984)
★ ★ ★½ Round Midnight (soundtrack) (Columbia, 1986)
★ ★ ★ ★ Perfect Machine (Columbia, 1988)
★ ★ ★ ★ ★ The Best of Herbie Hancock (Blue Note, 1988)
★ ★ ★½ A Jazz Collection (Columbia, 1991)

WITH FODAY MUSA SUSO
★ ★ ★ ★ Village Life (Columbia, 1985)
★ ★ ★ ★½ Jazz Africa (1987; Verve, 1990)

Jazz purists tend to see Herbie Hancock as having a split personality. Put him on piano with an acoustic rhythm section, and he's a jazz classicist, blessed with the same genius that fired the legendary Miles Davis Quintet of the mid-'60s. Surround him with electronic instruments, on the other hand, and he immediately becomes Mr. Sellout, a gadget-obsessed pop wannabe who'll willingly prostitute his talent for a few minutes on the charts.

Needless to say, the truth is somewhat less extreme. For one thing, although Hancock's acoustic work can, indeed, be brilliant, it's also true that his traditional playing has a tendency to rely more on competence than inspiration. Likewise, though some of his electronic albums can push their dance-driven rhythms past the point of monotony, others find him at his most resourceful and creative, and easily rank these recordings with the best of his work.

But the bottom line is simply that Hancock has always had an equal fondness for both funk and straight jazz. That much is evident in the sound of *Takin' Off*, his first solo outing. Recorded before he joined the Davis quintet, most of the album is given over to standard-issue hard bop. "Watermelon Man," however, finds Hancock and his sessionmates playing the sort of funky jazz Horace Silver was known for (though even Silver rarely got this soulful); it wasn't pop, exactly, but it showed potential.

"Blind Man, Blind Man," from *My Point of View*, is in some ways an extension of the "Watermelon Man" groove and benefits from the inclusion of guitarist Grant Green in the ensemble. But Hancock, no doubt influenced by his association with Davis (whose quintet he joined in 1963), grew more interested in toying with form than playing to a mass audience, and his subsequent sessions for Blue Note are far less pop-friendly. That doesn't mean they aren't tuneful; the dreamy "Maiden Voyage," for instance, quickly became something of a jazz standard. But *Inventions and Dimensions* (which was briefly available under the title *Succotash*) proffers loosely structured experiments with Latin rhythms; *Empyrean Isles* and *Maiden Voyage* are Davis-influenced small-group sessions with Freddie Hubbard on trumpet; while *Speak Like a Child* and *The Prisoner* use slightly larger ensembles to extend the coloristic possibilities of his music. *The Best of Herbie Hancock* highlights the best of his Blue Note recordings.

Hancock went electric after leaving Blue Note, and his sound changed radically, recalling the rock-influenced sound of Davis's *Bitches Brew* but augmenting it with the sort of instrumental arrangements heard on *The Prisoner*. It wasn't exactly jazz rock and neither was it traditional jazz, yet it captured the strengths of both. *Mwandishi* is dark and dreamy, all rolling rhythms and swirling electronics, while the sonic tapestry of *Crossings* conveys an almost otherworldly sense of atmosphere, particularly on the haunting, synth-colored "Quasar." But *Sextant* is the standout, thanks to its richly detailed sound and intricate interplay. Appallingly, all three albums are out of print.

Those albums may have introduced changes in Hancock's sound, but it was the stripped-down sound of *Headhunters*—or, more accurately, the pop credibility he earned through the success of "Chameleon" —that changed the course of his career. *Headhunters* isn't an R&B album per se, but clearly the die was cast, as each subsequent

album got funkier and funkier. *Thrust* plays down the more abstract elements that rounded out *Headhunters*, emphasizing the music's pulse, while *Man-Child* introduced R&B sessionmen to the mix, adding depth to the groove without compromising the improvised content. (These are the albums emphasized in Columbia's *The Best of Herbie Hancock*.)

Yet despite his pop success (*Headhunters*, *Thrust* and *Man-Child* all cracked the Top Forty), Hancock wasn't about to divorce himself from jazz. *Secrets* sought to strike a balance between the two, but it was with *The Quintet* that Hancock truly tried to turn back the clock. Recorded with his old Davis bandmates—Wayne Shorter, Ron Carter and Tony Williams, plus Hubbard on trumpet—it featured much the same sound as the Davis Quintet's classic recordings, though little of their fire or daring. Still, the album went over well enough with jazz traditionalists that Hancock began to live a musical double life, recording acoustic albums (the rest of which have since been deleted, although *A Jazz Collection* offers a fair sampling) and electric albums simultaneously.

Unfortunately, that separation led Hancock to believe that his non-acoustic albums ought to be more like real R&B sessions. Big mistake. It isn't so bad when *Feets Don't Fail Me Now* rounds out its arrangements with background vocals, and much of *Mr. Hands* seems a throwback to the *Headhunters* era. But the quasi-pop approach of *Monster* and *Lite Me Up!* is hopelessly hokey.

Mercifully, hip-hop and high technology eventually saved the day. With *Future Shock*, Hancock uses drum machines, digital synths and DJ Grandmixer D.ST. to conjure the sound of the urban jungle, an approach that turned "Rockit" into a club-level hit. *Sound-System* adds a worldbeat flavor to the mix, thanks to Hancock's use of Gambian griot Foday Musa Suso (with whom he later recorded the wonderfully exotic *Village Life* and a somewhat more predictable live album, *Jazz Africa*), while *Perfect Machine* relies on P-Funk bassist Bootsy Collins and Ohio Player Leroy "Sugarfoot" Bonner for its edge.

In addition to his solo career, Hancock has also been doing soundtrack work since 1966, when he scored Michelangelo Antonioni's *Blow Up* (though pop fans are more likely to remember the Yardbirds' performance of "Stroll On"). His contributions can be heard in films ranging from *Death Wish* to the elegiac *Round Midnight*, a score that's just as jazz-soaked and moody as the film itself. — J.D.C.

KIP HANRAHAN

★ ★½ **Coup de Tete (American Clave, 1981)**
★ ★ ★ ★½ **Desire Develops an Edge (American Clave, 1983)**
★ ★ ★½ **Vertical's Currency (American Clave, 1985)**
★ ★ **A Few Short Notes From the End Run (EP) (American Clave, 1986)**
★ ★ ★½ **Days and Nights of Blue Luck Inverted (Pangea, 1987)**
★ ★ ★ **Tenderness (American Clave, 1990)**

Hanrahan describes himself not as a bandleader or producer, but as the musical equivalent of a film director, and odd as that job description might seem, it fits. Like a director, Hanrahan expresses himself not through personal action, but by choosing those who will carry each part; also, like a director, Hanrahan uses these other people to bring a distinctly personal vision into being. Music isn't film, however, nor is improvising jazz the same thing as acting from a script, which perhaps explains why Hanrahan's albums seem so tempestuous. Despite an impressively eclectic group of players, *Coup de Tete* never quite comes together; part of the problem is the too-sketchy compositions, part of it is Hanrahan's hopeless attempts at singing. But *Desire Develops an Edge* is a real stunner, an album that bridges jazz, rock and Caribbean music without seeming to strain; it also boasts one of the best vocal performances Jack Bruce has ever given. *Vertical's Currency* can't quite sustain the achievement, but it's easy to hear a similar brilliance in its brightest moments. With *A Few Short Notes*, all that comes to an end in a maudlin fit of self-examination from which *Days and Nights of Blue Luck Inverted* doesn't entirely recover; fortunately, the album is well-enough cast (particularly on the jazz end) that the performance easily overcomes any weaknesses in the script. — J.D.C.

HAPPY MONDAYS

★ ★ **Squirrel and G-Man (Factory, 1987)**
★ ★ **Bummed (Elektra, 1989)**
★ **Hallelujah (EP) (Elektra, 1989)**
★ ★½ **Pills 'n' Thrills and Bellyaches (Elektra, 1990)**
★ ★½ **Live (Elektra, 1991)**

A bewildering U.K. success when their records emerged from Manchester's house music scene, the Mondays assemble dance noise by lifting elements piecemeal from an entire arsenal of kitsch. *Shaft*-soundtrack wah-wah, congas, discofied bass, and cheapo organ meld with Shaun Ryder's tuneless shouts in creating one big throb. John Cale produced *Squirrel and G-Man* (1987); it soon was followed by their English breakthrough, *Bummed*. "Fat Lady Wrestlers," "Brain Dead," "Lazy Itis"— such were the band's themes; the sound was big, bold, blurry. With *Pills 'n' Thrills 'n' Bellyaches*, they cleaned up the mix, took on the police ("God's Cop"), and flower power ("Donovan") and tried out a kind of non-rap smut-funk on "Bob's Yer Uncle." Leering, mean-spirited, and "experimental." — P.E.

TIM HARDIN

★ ★ ★½ **Tim Hardin I (MGM, 1966)**
★ ★ ★½ **Tim Hardin II (MGM, 1967)**
★ ★ ★ **This Is Tim Hardin (Atco, 1967)**
★ ★ **Tim Hardin III Live in Concert (Verve, 1968)**
★ ★ ★ **Tim Hardin IV (Verve, 1969)**
★ ★½ **Suite for Susan Moore and Damian (Columbia, 1970)**
★ ★ ★ **The Best of Tim Hardin (Verve, 1970)**
★ ★ **Bird on a Wire (Columbia, 1971)**
★ ★ ★ **Painted Head (Columbia, 1973)**
★ ★½ **Archetypes (MGM, 1973)**
★ ★ ★ **Nine (Antilles, 1973)**
★ ★ ★ ★ **The Tim Hardin Memorial Album (Polygram, 1981)**
★ ★ ★ ★ **Reason to Believe: The Best of Tim Hardin (Polydor, 1987)**

Few musicians ever mustered the honesty and poetic precision Tim Hardin did in his hard career; and his fatal 1980 heroin overdose only makes his brief '60s glory moment all the more poignant. A remarkable, jazz-inflected vocalist, Hardin sang with singular directness, his voice cracking slightly at appropriate instances of stress or inspiration—and the vehicle that provoked that emotional nakedness was his small but highly charged body of work. "If I Were a Carpenter," "Black Sheep Boy" "Don't Make Promises" and "Reason to Believe" all come from his first two records—and they're music of an almost austere beauty. Accompanied by acoustic guitar and deep, subtle string arrangements (cellos predominate), Hardin's penetrating singing is a form of revelation that comes insinuatingly—he never evades sometimes embarrassing epiphanies, but he never cajoles or preaches, either.

Except for the live set that he never wanted released, there are moments of beauty on all of Hardin's records, but he begins to sound exhausted by around the time of *Bird on a Wire*. Never himself a popular performer, his greatness was recognized by the score of other singers who covered his songs; standout versions of Hardin remakes range from Rod Stewart's spare "Reason to Believe" to ex-Zombie Colin Blunstone's lovely orchestral "Misty Roses." Hardin remains, however, his own best interpreter. Nearly interchangeable, *Memorial* and *Reason to Believe* are excellent best-ofs that concentrate on the early material. The slight advantage goes to *Reason* for including the very fine "Red Balloon." — P.E.

JOHN WESLEY HARDING

★★★ It Happened One Night (1988; Rhino, 1991)
★★★ God Made Me Do It The Christmas EP (Sire, 1989)
★★★★ Here Comes the Groom (Sire, 1990)
★★★½ The Name Above the Title (Sire, 1991)

"Bob Dylan is my father, Joan Baez is my mother/And I'm their bastard son," sings the improbably named John Wesley Harding at the end of *Here Comes the Groom*, but it's obviously a lie; if this guy has any rock-star relatives, it would have to be uncles Nick Lowe, Billy Bragg and Elvis Costello. It would have been Lowe, of course, who passed down the wit that led to *God Made Me Do It*'s "Talking Christmas Goodwill Blues" and the hysterically earnest folk version of Madonna's "Like a Prayer," while Bragg seems the most likely source of songs like the sarcastic "July 13th, 1985," a Live-Aid song on *It Happened One Night* (Harding's English debut) or the revisionist "Cathy's New Clown" and the didactic "Scared of Guns" from *Here Comes the Groom*. But Uncle Costello, though he probably passed down the genes responsible for *Groom*'s "The Devil in Me," must also bear the blame for the excessive cleverness that mars *The Name Above the Title*. — J.D.C.

SLIM HARPO

★★★★ The Best of Slim Harpo (Rhino, 1989)

Amid the current blues revival, Slim Harpo seems a forgotten figure, his name rarely evoked, his songs rarely played. Yet Harpo (nee James Isaac Moore) casts a long shadow over rock & roll, particularly the generation of artists who came of age in the '60s. The Rolling Stones, the Kinks, Van Morrison and Them, Dave Edmunds (in Love Sculpture), the Jeff Beck–era Yardbirds all recorded Harpo's songs; the Moody Blues took their name from one of them. This collection offers a good sampling of Harpo's prolific output between 1955 and 1968, and there's not a bad cut on it. That so many rock bands have covered Harpo's songs is unsurprising in light of the evidence: the man had a homegrown, stone natural feel for the big beat in his blues. That combination conspired to lift him out of obscurity, as both "Rainin' in My Heart" and "Baby Scratch My Back" were chart hits, peaking at Number 34 and Number 16, respectively. It's easy to get caught up in the smoky ambience of Harpo's recordings without realizing you're falling victim to an infectious vocal style. With only the slightest twist, his laconic delivery can mutate from playful but devilish one moment ("Baby Scratch My Back," "I'm a King Bee") to pleading and pain-wracked the next ("Rainin' in My Heart"). He has to be considered one of the most subversive singers ever. Slim Harpo was an original; this collection does him proud. — D.M.

EMMYLOU HARRIS

★★★½ Pieces of the Sky (Reprise, 1975)
★★★ Elite Hotel (Reprise, 1976)
★★★★ Luxury Liner (Warner Bros., 1977)
★★★ Quarter Moon in a Ten Cent Town (Warner Bros., 1978)
★★★★ Profile: The Best of Emmylou Harris (Warner Bros., 1978)
★★★½ Blue Kentucky Girl (Warner Bros., 1980)
★★★★ Roses in the Snow (Warner Bros., 1980)
★★★ Light of the Stable (Warner Bros, 1981)
★★★ Evangeline (Warner Brothers, 1981)
★★★ Cimarron (Warner Bros., 1982)
★★★½ White Shoes (Warner Bros., 1983)
★★★★ Profile: The Best of Emmylou Harris, Volume II (Warner Bros., 1984)
★★★ The Ballad of Sally Rose (Warner Bros., 1985)

★★★½ Thirteen (Warner Bros., 1986)
★★★ Angel Band (Warner Bros., 1987)
★★★ Bluebird (Reprise, 1987)
★★★★ Duets (Reprise, 1990)
★★★ Brand New Dance (Reprise, 1990)
★★★★ At the Ryman (Reprise, 1992)

Emmylou Harris adds unmistakably sad soprano harmonies to Gram Parsons's pair of solo albums (*GP* and *Grievous Angel*). Stepping out on her own, she forged a soft country-rock sound that appeals to fans of both styles. Her immaculate tone and gentle phrasing may not sit well with a purist (rock or country), but it's hard to argue with her taste in material—or her execution. Harris's albums are inconsistent up until the deft *Luxury Liner*, on which she tackles the Louvin Brothers ("When I Stop Dreaming") and Townes Van Zandt ("Pancho and Lefty") with striking results. Although it could be longer by half, *Profile: The Best of Emmylou Harris* leaves a lasting impression: especially her reading of Dolly Parton's proto-feminist missive "To Daddy" (originally on *Quarter Moon in a Ten Cent Town*).

Sparked by the bluegrass accompaniment of Ricky Skaggs, Harris makes a convincing roots move on *Blue Kentucky Girl* and *Roses in the Snow*. The latter album, largely acoustic and resolutely traditional, may be her best overall. To her credit, Harris kept "Movin' On" when the new traditionalist movement—which she'd prefigured by a decade—hit Nashville in the '80s. Turning to pop with the same measured grace she brought to folk and bluegrass, Harris fills her 1983 live album (*White Shoes*) with some boggling cover selections and boldly flirts with rock on her lucky *Thirteen*. The second *Profile* album, from 1984, nearly equals the first in terms of quality—and length, unfortunately. *Duets* is a definitive selection of what some listeners feel is Emmylou Harris's true calling: harmony. But that's far from the whole story. *At the Ryman* is a wide-ranging assortment of covers performed at the original home of the Grand Ole Opry, with the all-acoustic Nash Ramblers. — M.C.

RICHARD HARRIS

★★½ A Tramp Shining (Dunhill, 1968)
★ Slides (ABC, 1972)
★ The Prophet (Atlantic, 1974)

After his hammy triumph as King Arthur in Broadway's *Camelot*, Harris attempted to transfer his regal presence from the stage to the recording studio. The most notable result was *A Tramp Shining* (now out of print) and its centerpiece "MacArthur Park"—seven and a half minutes of melodramatic kitsch. Contending with lush, eccentric string arrangements, Harris's grainy, "sensitive" actor's voice is only one more texture; certainly the greeting-card-surrealist lyrics make little sense, and Harris doesn't sing so much as he orates. His air of grandiosity, however, perfectly suits Jimmy Webb's breathless tour de force—a songwriter whose best work was the skillful fluff he produced for the Fifth Dimension, he aims for pop symphonic glory on *A Tramp Shining* but achieves only the effect of a mildy hipper Mantovani. A few year later, Harris "sang" again on *Slides* (also deleted), a set of easy-listening music and ersatz poetic lyrics. Lacking even the intriguing pomposity of the Webb collection, the album is absolutely forgettable. Harris's recording career drew to a close with Arif Mardin's "musical interpretation" of Kahlil Gibran's schmaltz-mysticism classic, *The Prophet*. Needless to say, the album is dreck. — P.E.

GEORGE HARRISON

★★★★ All Things Must Pass (Apple, 1971)
★★★ Concert for Bangladesh (1972; Capitol, 1991)
★★½ Living in the Material World (Apple, 1973)
★ Dark Horse (Apple, 1974)
★★★ The Best of George Harrison (1976; Capitol, 1981)
★★½ 33⅓ (Dark Horse/Warner Bros., 1976)
★★ George Harrison (Dark Horse/Warner Bros., 1979)
★★ Somewhere in England (Dark Horse/Warner Bros., 1981)
★★★½ Cloud Nine (Dark Horse/Warner Bros., 1987)
★★★ Best of Dark Horse (Dark Horse, 1989)
★★ Live in Japan (Dark Horse/Warner Bros., 1992)

"While My Guitar Gently Weeps," "Don't Bother Me," "Something," "Here Comes the Sun," "Within You, Without You": George Harrison's Beatles songs may not have been among the Fab Four's finest, but in their sure sense of melody they didn't seem jarring—even set alongside songs by the best writers in the history of rock. Without John and Paul's support (and editing), however, George has floundered. With the staggering exception of *All Things Must Pass*, he's made a middling career with nice-guy records—pleasant, professional product enlivened occasionaly by the happenstance of a nifty single. While consistently a fine guitarist, his singing is weak, his lyrics chidingly or cheerfully banal. His music is passionless and disengaged; it captures little of his Beatles-period inventiveness, and conveys hardly any of the ecstasy or spiritual fire his longtime devotion to Eastern religion presumably might have provoked. He may be a visionary, but he's a closed one—tight-lipped and curiously inexpressive.

All Things Must Pass, though, remains intriguing. Fueled perhaps by songwriting ambition pent up during his long time as the most stellar of sidemen, this six-sided would-be epic sprawls and swoops unevenly, but its very giganticism now seems thrilling: here's Harrison, for once (and never after) going for broke. Psychically, Phil Spector and his massive Wall of Sound is the perfect production choice, and Spector lays it on thick—enveloping George, Ringo and a cast of crack players (Bobby Keys, Gary Brooker, Dave Mason, Jim Gordon) in a cathedral air of echo. George later was slammed with a lawsuit for "unknowingly" ripping off the Chiffons' "He's So Fine" for "My Sweet Lord," but his lovely slide guitar propels the tune far above its oldies basis. "Wah-Wah" is thunderous, as is "What Is Life" and, for all their philosophical straining, "Art of Dying" and "Beware of Darkness" retain a certain haunting grace.

With that last, long-ago bang resounding, George's remainder seems especially a whimper. *Concert for Bangladesh* is better Dylan than Harrison; "Give Me Love" (off *Living in the Material World*) is tuneful but preachy; *Dark Horse* is unremittingly disastrous; "All Those Years Ago" (a 1981 eulogy for John Lennon, from *Somewhere in England*) is oddly distanced. *Cloud Nine*, produced by ELO mainman (and Beatle maniac) Jeff Lynne is relatively peppy, but "When We Was Fab" seems a strangely offhand reminiscence—more like the work of a desultory fan than an actual Beatle.

Live in Japan was recorded during Harrison's 1991 tour of Japan, with Eric Clapton. — P.E.

JERRY HARRISON
★★½ **Casual Gods (Sire, 1987)**
★★½ **Walk on Water (Sire, 1990)**
The utility player and secret weapon of Talking Heads, guitarist-keyboardist Jerry Harrison has markedly improved as a singer and songwriter since *The Red and the Black*,

his deleted and undistinguished 1981 solo debut. But not enough. Pumping out vague art-funk constructs that echo the work of his currently dormant old band, Harrison still sounds a little too casual to qualify as a viable solo entity—let alone a deity. If these albums don't quite stand up on their own, however, they do make an impressive sampler of Harrison's production skills. — M.C.

DEBORAH HARRY
★★½ **KooKoo (Chrysalis, 1981)**
★★★½ **Def, Dumb & Blonde (Sire/Warner Bros., 1989)**
Blondie vocalist Debbie Harry's 1981 matchup with Chic's Nile Rodgers seemed promising, but her solo debut (*KooKoo*) never quite gets off the ground. After a long layoff, Harry shook off the cobwebs with *Rockbird* (from 1986 and already out of print), and proceeded to bounce back with the tuneful *Def, Dumb & Blonde* in 1989. Moving comfortably from punk to funk and back again, *D, D & B* recaptures Blondie's musical flair and flexibility—while steadfastly avoiding new-wave nostalgia. — M.C.

GRANT HART
★★★½ **Intolerance (SST, 1989)**
A solo album in the truest sense, *Intolerance* finds the former Hüsker Dü drummer covering all bases himself, an approach that works better than you'd think. Hart isn't quite the singer that one-time bandmate Bob Mould is, but he writes just as well, and the best songs—particularly "All of My Senses" and "Twenty-Five Forty-One"—are emotionally engaging and powerfully catchy. *Intolerance* also includes two of the three songs on Hart's solo EP, *2541*. — J.D.C.

JOHN HARTFORD
★★½ **Aero-Plain (Warner Bros., 1971)**
★★½ **Tennessee Jubilee (Flying Fish, 1975)**
★★½ **Mark Twang (Flying Fish, 1976)**
★★½ **Nobody Knows What You Do (Flying Fish, 1976)**
★★½ **Glitter Grass From the Nashwood Hollyville Strings (Flying Fish, 1976)**
★★½ **All in the Name of Love (Flying Fish, 1977)**
★★½ **Headin' Down Into the Mystery (Flying Fish, 1978)**
★★½ **Slumberin' on the Cumberland (Flying Fish, 1979)**
★★½ **You and Me at Home (Flying Fish, 1981)**

★★★ Catalogue (Flying Fish, 1981)
★★½ Gum Tree Canoe (Flying Fish, 1984)
★★★ Me Oh My, How the Time Does Fly: A John Hartford Anthology (Flying Fish, 1987)
★★ Down on the River (Flying Fish, 1989)
★★★ Hartford and Hartford (Flying Fish, 1991)

With album titles like *Mark Twang* and *Gum Tree Canoe*, this lanky guitarist-banjo-player's mild wit and winsomeness have become his trademark. A deft instrumentalist, Hartford makes no bones about not being a singer—his aw-shucks talking delivery has the charm of a folkie Jimmy Stewart. Gaining early fame for penning the pleasant "Gentle on My Mind" for Glen Campbell, Hartford went on to develop the persona of a hippie Mississippi riverboat mythologizer; his records are all sweet Americana, given a slightly loopy countercultural twist (from *Nobody Knows*, "Granny Wontcha Smoke Some Marijuana" exemplifies the routine).

All of Hartford's albums are versions of the same genial hoedown: *Catalogue* and *Me Oh My* are sufficiently exhaustive compilations for all but cornball fanatics. *Hartford and Hartford* is the most mature album; on this collaboration with his mandolin-playing son, Hartford sings and plays straightforwardly—and the cover material, from Johnny Bond to Howlin' Wolf, is solid. Ultimately, Hartford is a prototype of every genial nice-guy musician who haunts arts 'n' crafts fairs in college towns. Unambitious and pleasant. — P.E.

DAN HARTMAN
★★★ Instant Replay (Blue Sky/Epic, 1978)

Fresh from a stint with Edgar Winter's group, bassist Dan Hartman assembled a disco LP that actually stands up as an album. The thumpathon title cut provides *Instant Replay* with its requisite hit, while unsubtle rock-funk moves ("Chocolate Box," "Double-O-Love") and a string-sweetened dance ballad ("Love Is a Natural") provide some unexpected variety. All the slick studio help can't quite hide Hartman's vocal deficiencies, however; the cosmic "Time and Love" painfully drags on and on. Hartman followed up with *Relight My Fire* in 1979, now deleted; an extended, percolating remix of the title cut is included on the high-quality *Let's Dance: D.J.'s Collection of Dance Club Classics* (Columbia, 1987).

Dan Hartman worked as a producer during the '80s, charting again in 1984 with "I Can Dream About You." That flickering soft-rock flame is far removed from any kind of disco heat, though his voice is probably better suited to such mellow pursuits. Hartman landed his best-known production job in 1986, but his dance music pedigree is barely in evidence on James Brown's cluttered, show-bizzy *Livin' in America*. Disco fanatics should seek out Hartman's *Instant Replay*, though; it's like finding a sequined skeleton in some respectable person's closet. — M.C.

HAVANA 3 A.M.
★★½ Havana 3 a.m. (I.R.S., 1991)

New wave recycling effort by ex-Clash bassist Paul Simonon and former Figure Gary Myrick. Raw, rootsy and more than a little hackneyed, it's the music of professionals, not artists. — J.D.C.

RICHIE HAVENS
★★★½ Mixed Bag (Verve/Polydor, 1967)
★★★ Something Else Again (1967; Verve/Forecast, 1988)
★★★★ Richard P. Havens, 1983 (1968; Verve/Forecast, 1988)
★★★ Alarm Clock (Stormy Forest, 1971)
★★★ Richie Havens on Stage (Stormy Forest, 1972)
★★ Portfolio (Stormy Forest,1973)
★★ Mixed Bag II (Polydor, 1974)
★★ End of the Beginning (A&M, 1976)
★★ Mirage (A&M, 1977)
★★★ Richie Havens Sings the Beatles and Dylan (Rykodisc, 1987)
★★★½ Collection (Rykodisc, 1987)
★★½ Now (1991)

Strumming holy hell out of his E-chord open-tuned acoustic guitar and bellowing, entranced, like a shaman, Richie Havens was a hit at Woodstock. Singing "Freedom" in a dashiki, he was a hip black presence radiating a perceived authenticity—somewhat like a patchouli Paul Robeson. Two years later, he did well on the radio with a remake of George Harrison's "Here Comes the Sun." Other than those moments, however, his career has been more ebb than flow.

After releasing two records on the small Douglas label, he put out the excellent *Mixed Bag* in 1967. The blueprint for most of his work for the next 15 years, it featured tasteful takes on eclectic material ("Just Like a Woman," "Eleanor Rigby") not often covered by black artists. Not quite folk, the sound was meditative and artful, his remarkable voice lending significance to even the slighter pieces. His range was very narrow, but his grainy tone and, primarily, his air of great authority made him a riveting interpreter.

Two years later he released a masterwork that's remained underrated ever since. The double album *Richard P. Havens, 1983* was dark, introspective stuff—a sort of highly serious psychedelic melange of Beatles, Dylan, Donovan and Leonard Cohen covers and Havens originals. Colin Walcott played sitar and tabla, Steve Stills helped out on bass, Weldon Myrick did good work on pedal steel, and the entire set was smart mood music.

Throughout the '70s, Havens continued putting out capable records, even while that decade's emphasis on entertainment didn't jibe with his earnestness. By the start of the '90s, he'd settled for AOR, perhaps hoping to achieve the kind of success another harsh-voiced singer, Joe Cocker, had gained by going the synths-and-strings route. *Now* forces Havens to sing in a more conventional manner: it doesn't work.
— P.E.

EDWIN HAWKINS

★★★½ Oh Happy Day (1969; Fixit, 1991)
★★★ Mass Choir (1983; Fixit, 1991)
★★★ Imagine Heaven (1989; Fixit, 1991)
★★★½ Music and Arts Seminar Chicago
   Mass Choir (1990; Fixit, 1991)
★★★ Face to Face (1990; Fixit, 1991)

As the '60s waned, God rock for a while was a mini-phenomenon. The Edwin Hawkins Singers, bona fide gospel wailers, rode the wave with "Oh Happy Day" (1969) and managed to pull off an unheard-of coup—a chart-topping gospel-pop crossover hit. The times were right. Hawkins then played around with glitzier gospel, before coming back in the '80s to choral arrangements of a more orthodox power. *Music and Arts Seminar Chicago Mass Choir* (1990) is the strongest exemplar of his return to form—the singing is gorgeous. — P.E.

RONNIE HAWKINS

★★★½ Best of Ronnie Hawkins and the
   Hawks (Rhino, 1990)

In Colin Escott's entertaining and detailed liner notes to this 18-cut guide through Ronnie Hawkins's career, he tells us that Morris Levy, major domo of Roulette Records, once claimed Hawkins "moved better than Elvis, he looked better than Elvis and he sang better than Elvis." As a rock critic, Levy made a great disreputable

label chief. Hawkins indeed had a lot going for him in all the critical departments, save that of vision. Hawkins was a self-styled, rough-cut rockabilly born to solid, middle-class parents in Huntsville, Arkansas. Emerging in 1959 with a Top Thirty hit in "Mary Lou," he can lay legitimate claim to carrying the rockabilly banner into the '60s when its leading practitioners from the '50s were moving on to country or mainstream rock & roll in the new decade. All of the '50s sides in this collection showcase the trademark Hawkins growl to good effect, although there is precious little variety from one track to the next. Still, there's some hot stuff here—the driving, previously unreleased "Forty Days," Hawkins's rewrite of Chuck Berry's "Thirty Days"; the moody "One of These Days"; a taste of struttin', New Orleans–influenced rock in "Odessa." Any of these could have been hits, but weren't. Thus the luck of the draw.

Not the least of the legends associated with Hawkins is that of his band, the Hawks, who are heard in three incarnations on this collection, the last one featuring the musicians who would ascend to rock's pantheon as the Band. By any standard, all the various Hawks provided redoubtable support to Hawkins, with the latter-era version no more or less fiery than its predecessors. The album closes with a cut off Hawkins's 1970 comeback album, recorded in Muscle Shoals with some of the finest session players in the South. "Down in the Alley" is a languid, resigned blues; Hawkins's voice has by this time taken on a deeper timbre, his phrasing characterized by a deceptively casual air that betrays the regret in his attitude. This stunning performance is further augmented by one of Duane Allman's finest moments on record, a slide guitar commentary darting all around the singer, laying on hurt after hurt. Allman's playing is so rich, so imbued with the lived-in pain of deep blues, that it is a virtual aural definition of soul. If Hawkins leaves us with this, and is remembered for nothing else (which is not likely), he will have made an unassailable contribution to the music he loves. — D.M.

SCREAMIN' JAY HAWKINS

★★★ Voodoo Jive: The Best of Screamin'
   Jay Hawkins (Rhino, 1990)
★★★ Cow Fingers and Mosquito Pie
   (Epic/Legacy, 1991)

Although he had only one major hit, Screamin' Jay Hawkins has left his mark on rock & roll by way of a wildman persona quite unlike anything anyone had ever seen in the '50s. Little Richard was weird, Chuck Berry had his duckwalk, the Big Bopper favored loud suits, but Screamin' Jay was in his own league. Carried onstage in a coffin, he would emerge decked out in a suit of the unlikeliest color and pattern, with a silk cape around his shoulders and in his hand a human skull.

His only major hit, "I Put a Spell On You," retains its luster today, and Hawkins has done a good job of riding that one hit from 1956 into legend. Apart from this, the cuts on *Best of* and Epic-Legacy's newer *Cow Fingers and Mosquito Pie* show him to be a marginal R&B singer who was at his best when he didn't really have to sing: "I Put a Spell On You," recorded when Hawkins and his backing band were drunk, is mostly ominous growl and ghostly laugh. *Best of* also includes two of Hawkins's rare recordings done pre-"Spell"—"(She Put The) Wamee (On Me)" and "This Is All"—that show him playing it straight. He might have made a name for himself as an R&B vocalist had he stayed on this early path; after "Spell," he seemed in relentless pursuit of the bizarre, which resulted in one other minor hit, Leiber and Stoller's "Alligator Wine," a 1958 single that is fairly unremarkable. Among *Cow Fingers*'s oddities are a version of Cole Porter's "I Love Paris" and of "There's Something Wrong with You," which may be much funnier than Hawkins intended. — D.M.

ISAAC HAYES

★ ★ ★ ★   Hot Buttered Soul (Stax, 1969)
  ★ ★½ The Isaac Hayes Movement (1970, Stax, 1989)
  ★ ★½ To Be Continued (Stax, 1971)
  ★ ★½ Shaft (Stax, 1971)
  ★ ★   Black Moses (1971; Stax, 1989)
  ★ ★½ Joy (Stax, 1973)
  ★ ★½ Live at the Sahara Tahoe (Stax, 1975)
★ ★ ★½ Best of Isaac Hayes, Volume 1 (Stax, 1986)
  ★ ★ ★ Best Of Isaac Hayes, Volume 2 (Stax, 1986)
  ★ ★   U Turn (Columbia, 1984)
  ★ ★½ Love Attack (Columbia, 1988)

Shades, dashiki, gleaming bald pate: Isaac Hayes cut an imposing figure during his early-'70s heyday. Hard to believe that the hulking auteur behind the ultra-funky "Theme From Shaft" was actually a Barry White prototype, given to steamy bedroom raps and lush orchestrations. Or maybe it isn't: the remainder of the *Shaft* soundtrack is rather mundane action-movie music,

spiced by the occasional burst of streetwise syncopation or vocal color. A far cry from Curtis Mayfield's *Superfly*, to say the least. However, Hayes shouldn't be written off as a period oddity. His rambling soundtracks and full-blown cover versions had a big effect on soul music in general, broadening and softening the instrumental palate. Hayes paved the way for disco; whether he deserves credit or blame is a matter of taste.

Hayes and David Porter comprised one of the most successful songwriting and production teams at Stax/Volt. When they started to drift apart in the late '60s, Hayes began to record under his own name. *Presenting Isaac Hayes*, his now-deleted 1967 debut, is a loose and bluesy after-hours jam session. *Hot Buttered Soul*, the 1969 follow-up, must have seemed like the eccentric vanity project of a brilliant behind-the-scenes man—until it reached the pop Top Ten, anyway.

Elongated and embellished to the point of sonic overkill, "Walk on By" and "By the Time I Get to Phoenix" saunter through full-blown rearrangements. The former song entered the Top Forty as an edited single, though the full-length version of the latter (*Soul*'s entire second side on vinyl) establishes the Hayes game plan. Using the basic melody as theme and springboard, Hayes ruminates on the vagaries of romance in a spoken intro that takes up nearly half the song. His words aren't cued to the rhythm like a modern rapper's, but the contrast between the smoothly spoken and haltingly sung sections adds a delicate tension. *Hot Buttered Soul* is a landmark album.

Spread across two hour-long CDs, *The Best of Isaac Hayes* conveys the maddening expansiveness of his Stax records. *Volume 1* holds "Theme From 'Shaft' " and "Walk on By," along with all 19 minutes of the rote "Do Your Thing." *Volume 2* includes a delicious silk 'n' molasses crawl through "Never Can Say Goodbye" and the full version of "By the Time I Get to Phoenix." A collection of single edits—a distillation album—would be less authentic, but more approachable. Several of Hayes's biggest hits are included on a dynamite series of Stax samplers: *Original Big Hits Volume 1–4*.

Though he occasionally dented the charts in the mid-to-late '70s, Hayes sounds like he's playing catch-up on his disco period entries. (Albums such as *Disco Connection*, *Chocolate Chip* and *Don't Let Go* are all out of print.) Even the bubbly "Don't Let

Go," from 1980, has nowhere near the commanding presence of earlier Hayes concoctions. And "Ike's Rap," from the otherwise forgettable *Love Attack*, lays claim to hip-hop over a soupy, unsympathetic beat. Perhaps modern technology makes Hayes and his bodacious sense of scale seem anachronistic, but then again, *Shaft*'s stuttering wah-wah rhythm has launched many a rap jam. — M.C.

OFRA HAZA
★ ★ ★ ★   Fifty Gates of Wisdom (Shanachie, 1987)
   ★ ★ ★   Shaday (Sire, 1988)
   ★ ★½   Desert Wind (Sire, 1989)

On *Fifty Gates of Wisdom*, Ofra Haza shucks the pop-disco conventions that made her a star in Israel and offers up a performance of the devotional music traditionally sung by Yemenite Jews. Though it was recorded as an act of tribute to her parents, the passion she put into these songs makes the album irresistible. It was also—given the lean, percussive nature of the music—natural fodder for dance remixes. You can hear bits of "Im Nin 'Alu" in both Eric B. & Rakim's "Paid In Full" and "Pump Up the Volume" by M/A/R/R/S, but if you want to hear the official remix, look to *Shaday*, which also funks up a few other tracks from *Fifty Gates*. Unfortunately, the rest of the album leaves Haza sounding like an Israeli Gloria Estefan, and the same goes for *Desert Wind*. — J.D.C.

JEFF HEALEY BAND
   ★ ★ ★   See the Light (Arista, 1988)
   ★ ★ ★½   Hell to Pay (Arista, 1990)

A gifted, idiosyncratic player, Healey, who is blind, not only taught himself blues guitar, but developed a lap-based technique giving him astonishing control over his phrasing and vibrato. Not that such virtuosity always translates into memorable music; *See the Light*, for instance, is technically dazzling, but too often descends into bar-band theatrics. *Hell to Pay* is more consistent, though the celebrity cameos—like George Harrison's appearance on an overwrought "While My Guitar Gently Weeps"—detract from straight-up rockers like "Something to Hold On To." Ironically, some of Healey's best playing can be found on the soundtrack of an otherwise forgettable Patrick Swayze film called *Road House*, though it's questionable whether hearing Healey's take on "Hoochie Coochie Man" is worth suffering through the tunes Swayze himself sings. — J.D.C.

HEART
   ★ ★ ★½   Dreamboat Annie (Mushroom, 1976)
   ★ ★ ★   Little Queen (Portrait, 1977)
   ★ ★   Magazine (Mushroom, 1978)
   ★ ★½   Dog and Butterfly (Portrait, 1978)
   ★ ★ ★   Bebe Le' Strange (Epic, 1980)
   ★ ★ ★   Greatest Hits—Live (Epic, 1980)
   ★ ★½   Private Audition (Epic, 1982)
   ★ ★½   Passionworks (Epic, 1983)
   ★ ★½   Heart (Capitol, 1985)
   ★ ★½   Bad Animals (Capitol, 1987)
   ★ ★   Brigade (Capitol, 1990)
   ★ ★½   Rock the House "Live" (Capitol, 1991)

Along with debut albums from Foreigner and Boston, Heart's *Dreamboat Annie* ushered in the era of arena rock and Album Oriented Radio. Nancy and Ann Wilson shrewdly pulled off a Led Zep role-reversal. Lead singer Ann can shift from pop-thrush blandness to piercing shrieks with the stroke of a power chord, as she does on "Crazy on You" and "Magic Man." "Barracuda" upped the heavy quotient with satisfying results, though murky folk-rock filler like "Dream of the Archer" cuts away at *Little Queen*'s overall power. Some aspects of Led Zeppelin's legacy are better left alone, as the clunky *Dog and Butterfly* attests. *Magazine* was a rush-job release of demo tapes, perpetrated when Heart skipped from the Canadian label Mushroom over to Epic.

Bebe Le' Strange shows strong signs of development. On "Even It Up" Ann's vocals are bolstered by a snappy horn chart and firm beat. *Greatest Hits—Live* kicks off well, pulling together the obvious highpoints—and promptly falls apart, concluding with a turgid cover of Zeppelin's "Rock & Roll." *Private Audition* is a failed attempt at regaining *Bebe*'s relatively adventurous spirit. *Passionworks* introduces the Wilsons' latter-day approach on cuts like "Allies" and "How Can I Refuse"—super-charged bathos encased in a glossy production. Another label change jump-started Heart's career a second time. *Heart* and *Bad Animals* are the repositories for half-a-dozen interchangeable power ballad smashes, any one of which could break your heart or turn your stomach. Oddly enough, *Rock the House "Live"* is not the second-time-around summation fans might have expected. It's a realistic tour documentary, at best: a hodgepodge of minor album cuts and several resounding non-hits from the middling *Brigade*. — M.C.

THE HEARTBEATS/SHEP & THE LIMELITES

★ ★ ★ ★ **The Best of the Heartbeats including Shep & the Limelites (Rhino, 1990)**

Preeminent practitioners of New York–style group harmony, the Heartbeats were blessed with one of the most distinctive and versatile lead singers in the field, James "Shep" Sheppard, whose baritone-tenor could deliver the most salacious tension-and-release on slow ballads, or soar high and plaintive on love songs. Before Sheppard joined the group, baritone Robby Tatum and tenor Vernon Seavers had already proved themselves gifted arrangers in constructing a smooth, uncluttered sound, with unusual vocal changes, that set the group apart from its many New York competitors. Sheppard brought with him not only a fabulous voice and mesmerizing stage presence, but the soul of a writer and the eloquence of a poet. It all came together for him on the late-'56 release, "A Thousand Miles Away," Sheppard's heartfelt lamentation over a girlfriend who had moved away. As the decade wore on, the Heartbeats continued to cut some good singles—"Everybody's Somebody's Fool," "Down on My Knees," "I Found a Job"—and upgrade their sound to suit the changing times. There were no more hits, though, and in 1961 Sheppard left to form a new group, Shep & the Limelites. At the outset it appeared Sheppard would pick up where "A Thousand Miles Away" left off, with "Daddy's Home," a thinly disguised sequel to the Heartbeats' big hit. It was one of the biggest records of '61, peaking at Number Two. In all, six of the group's 13 singles recorded for the Hull label made the Top 100, cementing Sheppard's reputation as one of the most important figures to come out of the group harmony scene. "Daddy's Home" was the first in a series of related songs Sheppard turned out that charted the course of a seesaw relationship, the others documenting marriage ("Three Steps from the Altar"), remembrance ("Our Anniversary"), conflagration ("What Did Daddy Do"), and reflection ("Remember Baby"). Thinking conceptually was a highly irregular pursuit among pop groups in the early '60s, but Sheppard always seemed a few steps ahead of the pack anyway. This Rhino set is a stirring tribute to two groups, and one man, who sang not only for the moment, but also for the future.
— D.M.

THE HEART THROBS

★ ★ ★ **Cleopatra Grip (Elektra, 1990)**

While the Heart Throbs suffer from cutesiness (lyrics sometimes are gushing nonsense), they're capable of strong melodies, irresistible hooks and gorgeous noise. Echo and the Bunnymen's mixer, Gil Norton, assists in the production—and the band does the big, lush sound proud. If you don't strain hard after meaning, the songs work a neat, drifting magic. — P.E.

HEAVEN 17

★ ★ ★   **Heaven 17 (Arista, 1982)**
★ ★ ★ ½ **The Luxury Gap (Arista, 1983)**
 ★ ★ ½ **How Men Are (Arista, 1984)**
★ ★ ★   **Pleasure One (Arista, 1986)**
★ ★ ★ ½ **Teddy Bear, Duke & Psycho (Virgin, 1988)**

This Brit synth trio (their name a quote from Anthony Burgess's *A Clockwork Orange*) pursued a deliberately less commercial direction than the Human League, the band from which two of its members departed. While still a remarkably catchy collection of techno-funk dance-fare, their American debut, *Heaven 17*, was notable also for its verbal sophistication—and for the fact that, in Glenn Gregory, Heaven 17 boasted a singer whose interpretive skills were considerably broader than the range common to the genre. *The Luxury Gap* fused slick production and prole sentiments—and throughout the record, Ian Craig Marsh and Martyn Ware kept the Fairlight textures crisp and surprising. *How Men Are* fell victim to hubris; it was the sound of smart guys trying far too hard. *Pleasure One*, despite a superabundance of outside players, found Heaven 17 back on the mark, the record's assurance preparing the way for the band's most accomplished set, *Teddy Bear, Duke and Psycho*. With that 1988 release—a number of whose songs feature subtle, atmospheric jazzy intros that give way to crunching, irresistible funk—Heaven 17 made music with real smarts and a sharp bite. — P.E.

HEAVY D. AND THE BOYZ

★ ★ ★ ½ **Living Large (MCA, 1987)**
★ ★ ★ ½ **Big Tyme (MCA, 1989)**
★ ★ ★ ½ **Peaceful Journey (MCA, 1991)**

Dismiss "Da Heavster" as a novelty artist at your own risk. Each of these albums offers more than the obvious laughs—though, Lord knows, this outsized rapper loves to draw attention to his appearance. "Mr. Big Stuff," "Chunky but Funky," "The

Overweight Lovers in the House": *Living Large* strikes a liberating blow, because Heavy D. sees his girth as a unique advantage. His rumbling, boom-box baritone voice—friendly but fierce—rolls over most objections.

An early Teddy Riley production, *Living Large* marches to the harsh, compelling drumbeats of old-school New York funk; only the remixed "Chunky but Funky" hints at the synthesized melodies of New Jack Swing tracks to come. Riley's sound emerges fully formed on Heavy D.'s elegantly insistent 1989 album-opener, "We Got Our Own Thang." The rest of *Big Tyme* hops between different producers, and when Marley Marl ups the musical ante on three cuts, Heavy D. takes his rap attack to the next phase. He finesses the slippery phrasing of "EZ Duz It Do It EZ," adds a touch of reggae toasting to "Gyrlz, They Love Me," bounces words against the beat like a dribbling basketball on "Here We Go, Again, Y'all." *Peaceful Journey* continues the progression. If the title track and the all-star centerpiece "Don't Curse" inveigh a little too piously, "Now That We Found Love" and "Let It Rain" are every bit as seductive—and "deep"—as this love man intends them to be. Heavy D. calmly holds his own against Guy's swooping lead singer Aaron Hall on the former tune, successfully negotiating a New Jack update of this pro-monogamy Philly Soul classic. And the latter cut just might be the smoothest, most enticing come-hither rap this side of Barry White. Let the skinny guys eat their hearts out. — M.C.

RICHARD HELL

★ ★ ★ ★ **Blank Generation (Sire, 1977)**
★ ★ ★ ★ **Richard Hell/Neon Boys (EP) (Shake, 1980)**
★ ★ ★ **Destiny Street (Red Star, 1982)**
★ ★ ★½ **R.I.P. (R.O.I.R., 1984)**

The sullen, punked-out *Blank Generation* stings like a casual insult. "Love Comes in Spurts"—if you're lucky. Behind the sliced T-shirts and ear-scorching amplification, however, lurks an underrated band: the Voidoids focus Richard Hell's boundless alienation into bold, innovative rock & roll. Lead guitarist Robert Quine spikes the angry rush of sound with quick runs and sudden explosions; Quine milks each tender electric nerve of his Fender for all its worth. Hell's no more a poet than he is a bass player, but his snarl-to-a-croak vocal range sounds downright affecting here, not affected. His snarling indictments of society

(and himself) are propelled by his band's headlong attack: there's not a wasted growl or gust of feedback on *Blank Generation*.

Hell deserves credit (or blame) for originating much of the punk imagery and style associated with the London scene. Musically, though, the Voidoids resemble Captain Beefheart's Magic Band much more than the Sex Pistols. And Hell has never managed to capitalize on his early notoriety. During the long lay-off between *Blank Generation* and *Destiny Street*, his creative momentum froze; the latter album sounds testy, a little hedging—not exactly what you'd expect from the author of scathing raveups like "Betrayal Takes Two" and "New Pleasures." *R.I.P.* bookends some Voidoids-era outtakes with an odd 1984 New Orleans session and some crude, compelling demos from Hell's howling tenure with Johnny Thunders and the Heartbreakers. The hard-to-find seven-inch EP *Neon Boys* includes some of Hell's pre-Television work with Tom Verlaine as well as his best Voidoids composition: a parched, lingering ballad called "Time." It's one hell of an epitaph. — M.C.

JIMI HENDRIX

★ ★ ★ ★ ★ **Are You Experienced? (Reprise, 1967)**
★ ★ ★ ★ ★ **Axis: Bold as Love (Reprise, 1968)**
★ ★ ★ ★ ★ **Electric Ladyland (Reprise, 1968)**
★ ★ ★ ★ ★ **Smash Hits (Reprise, 1969)**
★ ★ ★ ★ **Band of Gypsys (Capitol, 1970)**
★ ★ ★ ★ **Otis Redding/Jimi Hendrix Experience: Historic Performances Recorded at the Monterey International Pop Festival (Reprise, 1970)**
★ ★ ★ ★ **The Cry of Love (Reprise, 1971)**
★ ★ ★½ **Rainbow Bridge (Reprise, 1971)**
★ ★ ★½ **Hendrix in the West (Reprise, 1972)**
★ ★ ★ **War Heroes (Reprise, 1972)**
★ ★ ★ **Soundtrack From the Film, *Jimi Hendrix* (Reprise, 1973)**
★ ★ ★ **Crash Landing (Reprise, 1975)**
★ ★ ★ **Midnight Lightnin' (Reprise, 1976)**
★ ★ ★ ★ **The Essential Jimi Hendrix, Vol. 1 (Reprise, 1978)**
★ ★ ★ ★ **The Essential Jimi Hendrix, Vol. 2 (Reprise, 1979)**
★ ★ ★½ **Nine to the Universe (Reprise, 1980)**
★ ★ ★½ **The Jimi Hendrix Concerts (Warner Bros., 1982)**

★★★½ **Band of Gypsys 2 (Capitol, 1986)**
★★★½ **Jimi Plays Monterey (Reprise, 1986)**
★★★½ **Johnny B. Goode (Capitol, 1986)**
★★★★ **Live at Winterland (Rykodisc, 1987)**
★★★★ **Radio One (Rykodisc, 1988)**
★★★½ **Lifelines (The Jimi Hendrix Story) (Reprise, 1990)**
★★★★ **Stages 1967–1970 (Reprise, 1991)**

Aside from Bob Dylan, no other rock titan rivals Jimi Hendrix in complexity of achievement—the dimensions of his legitimate myth seem nearly inexhaustible. As only classical or jazz players had done before him, Hendrix defined his music's instrument: fully exploring the possibilities of the amplified six-string, he confirmed beyond question its status as rock's essential vehicle—as Pablo Casals was to the cello and Charlie Parker to the saxophone, so was Jimi Hendrix to the electric guitar. Psychic successor to Elvis Presley, Hendrix also embodied the politics of rock & roll as a black-white fusion—the twin pillars of his music were the earthiness of the blues and the ethereality of jazz (obviously, the great aesthetic motherlodes of African-American experience), but his primary contemporary audience was white rock fans, and the psychedelic subgenre that provided the context for his particular triumph was a white one. Finally, through lyrics heavily influenced by Bob Dylan, he delivered a message of universal emancipation. A personality large enough to thrive on apparently contradictory impulses, he was both the painstaking artist and the unabashed cock-rocker, a showman whose act presaged the melodrama both of glitter and of punk, a player explosive enough to influence equally jazz perfectionists and heavy-metal thunderers, an erotic liberator and a spiritual force. Sly Stone and Prince obviously learned much from Hendrix; so did Pete Townshend, Gil Evans and Bob Marley.

The Seattle-born ex-paratrooper began his career, with mythic appropriateness, backing up such originators as B.B. King and Little Richard. Significantly, however, he only hit his stride in England—where someone who possessed both Hendrix's looks and talent could pass for an exotic god; Animals' bassist Chas Chandler hooked him up with bassist Noel Redding (a former lead guitarist whose playing would subsequently, and felicitously, betray its grounding in melody) and jazz-styled drummer Mitch Mitchell. The interracial Jimi Hendrix

Experience was born—ready to come on like monsters (already Jimi sometimes soloed with his teeth, and the band's freak-out garb was an acidhead's dream). *Are You Experienced?* was the Summer of Love debut, and it sounded like divine madness— "Purple Haze," "I Don't Live Today," "Manic Depression" and "Fire" were all feedback finesse and arrogant virtuosity wrapped around lyrics sprung from primal wondering, lust and fear.

Axis: Bold as Love plunged deeper. Ballads ("Little Wing") met mind-warp blues—the songs blurred together, metaphorically implying the fact of Hendrix's creative impatience (and prefiguring his later ventures into jazz freedom). Psychedelia's triumph came next: a double-album manifesto featuring contributions from Steve Winwood, Buddy Miles and Jack Casady, *Electric Ladyland* showed Hendrix serving notice of his unstoppable ambition. The chord progressions of "Burning of the Midnight Lamp" echoed Bach (and featured perhaps the only example of a wah-wah pedal employed elegantly); "Crosstown Traffic" was the Experience at its most rocking; "All Along the Watchtower" became Hendrix's classic Dylan cover; and, with "Voodoo Child (Slight Return)," the songwriter reached back into gris-gris mythology to fashion a mock-cosmic persona. Like the sounding of a gigantic gong, the album reverberated across the airwaves; it also sounded the death-knell for the Experience.

Mitchell held on long enough to join Jimi and new bassist Billy Cox for an appearance at Newport, but the legendary Woodstock gig (including the famous, fiery "Star Spangled Banner") was performed by an ad hoc group called the Electric Sky Church, and by the time of the live *Band of Gypsys*, the drummer's post had been taken by the bombastic Buddy Miles. For once playing with a black band, Hendrix tackled funk. "Machine Gun" and "Message of Love" were *Gypsy*'s fearsome highlights, yet while the power-trio achieved the essence of force, they lacked melody—and aesthetic fullness suffered as a result.

Hendrix died in 1970, choking on vomit following barbiturate and alcohol intoxication, at a period of seeming creative transition. He'd been moving farther away from rock, alternately returning to blues, delving deeper into funk and studying jazz-fusion. *The Cry of Love* (1971), however, showed the master, playing with Cox and Mitchell, at his most confident:

"Ezy Rider" and "Angel" are the tough and tender faces of the genius at his most appealing.

A deluge of posthumous albums then began. Of the live work, *Radio One*, *Live at Winterland*, the Hendrix side of the Otis Redding/Jimi Hendrix Monterey set, and the four-CD *Stages*, a fine concert retrospective, are the most exciting. *Crash Landing* and *Midnight Lightnin'* represent a faintly bizarre endeavor on the part of Hendrix curator Alan Douglas to celebrate the legacy—using studio players, he overdubbed new tracks atop unreleased late-period Hendrix originals to come up with something like "Jimi Does Fusion." The ethics of the maneuver remain questionable, but Hendrix sounds great (the Douglas-produced *Nine to the Universe*, a record of the guitarist jamming with jazz organist Larry Young on two tracks is rawer, but more vital). Most of the rest of the re-issues, rarities and novelty packagings of the cannon are fodder for devotees: *Smash Hits* remains the tightest best-of; *The Essential Hendrix* is messily compiled; the four-CD *Lifelines* is an intriguing documentary crammed with standards and alternate takes, but the inclusion of Hendrix interviews is problematic—they're interesting, but they impede the music's flow. — P.E.

DON HENLEY

★ ★ ★ ★ I Can't Stand Still (Asylum, 1982)
★ ★ ★ ★ ★ Building the Perfect Beast (Geffen, 1984)
★ ★ ★ ★ The End of the Innocence (Geffen, 1989)

Don Henley's first solo album (*I Can't Stand Still*) sounds like a leaner, meaner update of the Eagles' *Hotel California*. The rhythms are gripped tight, the guitars tend to be electric, the singing is rarely wimpy, the barbed observations sink in later: a subtle, but definite improvement. Henley recites the cynical media blitz on "Dirty Laundry" with just the right mix of disgust and fascination, while "You Better Hang Up" rocks with an earthy gusto the Eagles could never have mustered.

Building the Perfect Beast releases Henley from his old band's reputation; the key ingredients for perfection include an arsenal of synthesized keyboards and a newly flexible command of words. The electronic layers buffer the bittersweet May-December illusions of "The Boys of Summer," making for an unusually resonant Top Ten single. Henley's savvy musical sense of what's

happening in the marketplace grounds his restless outlook on songwriting. "All She Wants to Do Is Dance" rises to just the right peak, "Sunset Grill" lopes along like all the regulars do, "You're Not Drinking Enough" kicks up an L.A.-style honky-tonk mess, "Land of the Living" closes on a note of hope. Damn near a perfect pop album—and a popular one to boot.

"End of the Innocence," the title track and lead single from Henley's next album, ties a mercilessly clearheaded assessment of the '80s to an understated but indomitable melody. Slowly but surely, *End of the Innocence* backs off a bit from the overt pop thrust of *Beast*. When Henley declares that he won't go quietly, the measured flow of the music somewhat undermines his point. Maybe not quietly, but certainly controlled. — M.C.

HERMAN'S HERMITS

★ ★½ Their Greatest Hits (1973; Abkco, 1988)

With their de rigeur identical suits and moptops, Herman's Hermits boasted an outrageous adorability quotient—and the songs of this Manchester quintet were equally sticky sweet. "I'm Into Something Good," "Silhouettes," "I'm Henry VIII, I Am," "There's a Kind of Hush" and especially "Mrs. Brown You've Got a Lovely Daughter," with Herman (Peter Noone) working his English accent for all that it was worth, were Brit Invasion smashes of the most juvenile sort. These puppets of mod Svengali Mickie Most were certainly pre-fab, but not very fab for real. — P.E.

BOO HEWERDINE AND DARDEN SMITH

★ ★ ★ ★ Evidence (Ensign/Chrysalis, 1989)

Hewerdine is the brains behind the Bible (the English rock act, not the religious document), Smith is an Austin-based singer-songwriter, and this get-together was originally meant as a sort of busman's holiday. Instead, it resulted in 13 exquisite collaborations, songs that were neither rock nor new country, but a hybrid as unique and distinctive as the voices that deliver them. Whether through the exultant chorus of the poppy "All I Want (Is Everything)" or the considered quiet of "The First Chill of Winter," this is an album that captures the unpretentious joy of music made for fun, not profit. — J.D.C.

HOWARD HEWETT

★ ★½ **I Commit to Love (Elektra, 1986)**
★ ★½ **Forever and Ever (Elektra, 1988)**
★ ★ ★½ **Howard Hewett (Elektra, 1990)**

After giving up the ghost of Shalamar, Howard Hewett outfitted himself as a pop-soul loveman—closer to Luther Vandross than Teddy Pendergrass. He scored R&B chart hits from his first two solo albums, though neither one quite breaks out of its lush romantic rut. *Howard Hewett* comes as a surprise, then. Producer Leon Sylvers lends a hand on two shimmering, fresh cuts and ex-Scritti Politti synthmaster David Gamson fashions a pair of melodic thumpers. Finally, Hewett's versatility and verve carry the day; he makes the ultra-seductive "Let Me Show You How to Fall in Love" sound as natural as his proudly announced love for "Jesus." And that's what a good pop-soul record is all about. — M.C.

HEX

★ ★ ★ **Hex (First Warning, 1989)**
★ ★ ★½ **Vast Halos (Rykodisc, 1990)**

Hex is an arty, atmospheric collaboration between ex-Game Theory singer-guitarist Donnette Thayer and Church singer-guitarist Steve Kilbey that combines the heady experimentation of art rock with the interplay of chamber music. *Vast Halos* is particularly worth hearing, inasmuch as it retains all the intimacy of the first album while introducing a sly, insinuating pop sensibility. — J.D.C.

JOHN HIATT

★ ★ ★½ **Hangin' Around the Observatory (Epic, 1974)**
★ ★ ★ **Overcoats (Epic, 1975)**
★ ★ ★ ★ **Slug Line (MCA, 1979)**
★ ★ ★ **Two Bit Monsters (MCA, 1980)**
★ ★ ★ **All of a Sudden (Geffen, 1982)**
★ ★ ★ ★ **Riding With the King (Geffen, 1983)**
★ ★ ★ **Warming up to the Ice Age (Geffen, 1985)**
★ ★ ★½ **Bring the Family (A&M, 1987)**
★ ★ ★ ★ **Slow Turning (A&M, 1988)**
★ ★ ★ **Stolen Moments (A&M, 1990)**

He stood right at the brink of something bigger for so damn long that you can't really blame John Hiatt for finally sitting back and relaxing on his last couple of records. This Indiana-born singer-songwriter has a plethora of slightly neurotic gems sprinkled throughout his bumpy career: witty 'n' warm love songs that have provided hits for Three Dog Night ("Sure As I'm Sittin' Here," from *Hangin' Around the Observatory*) to Bonnie Raitt ("Thing Called Love," from *Bring the Family*). Stylistic uncertainity and a wavering vocal attack marred even the best of Hiatt's own albums, though several have much to recommend them and none (save the Tony Visconti-produced synth-pop disaster *All of a Sudden*) are outright duds. The Epic albums (*Observatory* and *Overcoats*) are his most country-oriented, though Hiatt would return to Nashville in the mid-'80s after a new-wave-inspired spell. *Slug Line* failed to establish Hiatt as the American Elvis Costello, but the rangier, nervously rockin' accompaniment accentuates the slightly twisted hooks of "You're My Love Interest," "Radio Girl" and the title track. Despite his flair for sardonic rockers, Hiatt also evinces a talent for disarmingly pretty ballads on "Washable Ink" (exquisitely covered by the Neville Brothers a few years later). *Two Bit Monsters* is a somewhat pallid follow-up in the same mode; "Pink Bedroom" (later claimed by Rosanne Cash) is the only true keeper in the pile. Hiatt's wicked sense of humor comes to the fore on the confident *Riding With the King*, bolstered by the producing and bass-thumping presence of Nick Lowe. The double-edged title track and "She Loves the Jerk" cut far beyond the surface yucks.

Typically, Hiatt follows up this artistic turning point with another shakey holding-pattern album: on *Warming Up to the Ice Age*, a heavy-handed AOR mix sabotages sterling heartbreak sagas like "The Usual" and "She Said the Same Things to Me." Recorded with a band consisting of Lowe, Ry Cooder and drummer Jim Keltner, *Bring the Family* greatly benefits from their loose, spacious tone and bluesy input. Not quite the breakthrough impatient fans and critics hyped it as, *Bring the Family* is still one of Hiatt's most consistent efforts. Hiatt reaches a mature peak on *Slow Turning*, recorded with his tight regular road band; the heartfelt hearth-and-home scenarios ("Georgia Rae," "Is Anybody There?") lend contrast and depth to the gleefully perverse stompers ("Drive South," "Trudy & Dave," "Tennessee Plates"). But when Hiatt kicks off the too-satisfied *Stolen Moments* by declaring himself "unworthy" of his woman's "Real Fine Love," his self-deprecating gift starts to resemble a glib automatic reaction. — M.C.

AL HIBBLER

★ ★ ★ ★ **For Sentimental Reasons (Open Sky, 1984)**

★ ★ ★ ★ **After the Lights Go Down Low (Atlantic, 1989)**

Not to take anything away from the Righteous Brothers, but back in 1956 Al Hibbler cut the original version of "Unchained Melody" (the theme song of the film *Unchained*), and staked a claim on it that he has never relinquished. In 1955–56 he had two Top Twenty singles and three Top Tens, and was one of the major players of the nascent rock & roll era. While chart success eluded him after '56, Hibbler continued performing and recording. There are times when Hibbler's gruff, growling style brings to mind Louis Armstrong, and like Armstrong, Hibbler always cut the growl with sly humor. He also shared his contemporary and fellow bass-baritone Billy Eckstine's sense of grandeur when delivering a tender lyric. At his rollicking best, he was totally unpredictable—swooping, growling, moving freely up and down his vocal range, uncovering multiple personalities in the most straightforward material. Hibbler was said to have been an ardent Spike Jones fan, and when he got hold of something like "Gee Baby, Ain't I Good to You" or the pair of Fats Waller songs he weaves into a gut-busting medley on *For Sentimental Reasons*, he gave a good impression of a one-man Spike Jones–style attack on melody, harmony, rhyme and reason.

Hibbler wasn't a novelty vocalist, though: every flourish had a purpose. Often he simply played it straight. At those moments he was the crooner's crooner, an elegant stylist who could caress and coax a lyric with deeply felt understanding. He honed his chops as the singer in Duke Ellington's band in the 1940s before embarking on a solo career in 1950. In the ensuing decade he recorded for RCA, Columbia, Atlantic, and Decca, the latter being the home port of his mid-'50s hits (Atlantic bought the masters of "After the Lights Go Down Low," a Top Ten hit for Hibbler in 1956, and it's included on the 1989 album that bears its name). Hibbler's career as a recording artist hit the skids briefly in 1963 after he was arrested while participating in a civil rights march in Birmingham, Alabama, where he led protesters in singing "You'll Never Walk Alone." Frank Sinatra brought him back into the fold by making him the first signing to Sinatra's newly formed Reprise label. He had no further hits, but Sinatra's gesture allowed Hibbler to reestablish himself on the club circuit.

After the Lights Go Down Low is vintage early Hibbler, fronting four different orchestras in sessions recorded in 1950 and 1951. Material runs the gamut from soft ballads ("Dedicated to You"), slow, grinding love songs (the title track, "Autumn Winds") and some rugged blues ("Blues Came Falling Down"). *For Sentimental Reasons* is latter-day Hibbler, circa 1982, when his voice was still mellifluous but far more low-down than it was in his younger days. Hibbler works it like the seasoned pro he is, investing the lyrics with humor, heartache, and a certain elevated perspective born of advancing years. He's accompanied by the aptly named Hank Jones All-Stars, who are Jones on piano, Buddy Tate on tenor sax and clarinet, Milt Hinton on bass and Oliver Jackson on drums. Their versatility is well-suited to Hibbler's individual style. Unfortunately, "Unchained Melody" is nowhere to be found on either of these albums, which are all that remain in print of Hibbler's recordings. No matter. Both are splendid outings, one capturing a great singer in his restless youth, honing his style; the other revelatory of the subtle adjustments he made with age. — D.M.

SARA HICKMAN

★ ★ ★ **Equal Scary People (Elektra, 1989)**

★ ★ ★ **Shortstop (Elektra, 1990)**

Tuneful, clever and carefully observed, Sara Hickman's material has all the strengths expected of a contemporary Texas songwriter, plus one more—whimsy. And though sometimes she sells her songs short by going for the obvious gag, her best work combines the puckish wit of Christine Lavin with the true-to-life warmth of cartoonist Lynda Barry. — J.D.C.

DAN HICKS AND HIS HOT LICKS

★ ★½ **Original Recordings (Epic, 1969)**

★ ★ ★ **Where's the Money (Blue Thumb/MCA, 1971)**

★ ★½ **Striking It Rich (Blue Thumb/MCA, 1971)**

★ ★ ★½ **Last Train to Hicksville . . . The Home of Happy Feet (Blue Thumb/MCA, 1973)**

★ ★ ★ **It Happened One Bite (Warner Bros., 1978)**

Dan Hicks got his start as drummer for the Charlatans, a pioneering San Francisco folk-rock band that predates even the Dead and the Airplane. By the time psychedelia caught on nationwide, just a few years later, Hicks was busy taking an ironic stab at pre-rock nostalgia in front of his acoustic

Hot Licks. *Original Recordings* succumbs to the blandishments of the "canned music" that Hicks both loves and loathes, but the subsequent addition of Sid Page's swinging fiddle and the distinctive voice of Maryanne Price (along with Naomi Eisenberg) puts meat on the bones of this scrawny stoner's concept. *Where's the Money* is an entertaining live set, marred somewhat by its total lack of a beat (not even a finger snap) and dated "hip" attitude; Hicks's satirical sense of humor—alternately surreal and observant, witty and snide—is captured in full. *Last Train to Hicksville* shines a light on the group's musical dexterity, and the players support Hicks's wry raps with fluid takes on the jazzy flow of western swing. Along with Commander Cody and His Lost Planet Airmen and Asleep at the Wheel, Dan Hicks and His Hot Licks are a "starter" band; their loose approximations can't hold a candle to the originals, but these longhairs turned on a generation of young rebels to some of country music's deepest, most enduring roots. Out of those three acts just mentioned, however, Hicks's recordings probably hold the least interest for modern listeners. — M.C.

THE HIGHWAYMEN
★ ★ **Highwayman (Columbia, 1985)**
★ **Highwayman 2 (Columbia, 1990)**
Willie Nelson, Johnny Cash, Waylon Jennings and Kris Kristofferson team for a country version of Blind Faith but come up short in the way of energy and inspiration. Kristofferson doesn't belong here—his diminishing reputation rests on a handful of songs he wrote some two decades ago, and as a performer he is a wonder of somnambulistic splendor. On the other hand, his cohorts here have remained important artists, Jennings and Cash on the strength of some tough-minded original songs and interesting selections of outside material, Nelson on the strength of his having turned into the interpreter extraordinaire after drying up as a songwriter in the late '70s. Jennings, Cash and Nelson have isolated moments of grandeur on the two Highwaymen albums, Kristofferson wobbles through both affairs a distant fourth, and producer Chips Moman hits all the right notes in terms of ambience and mix. Of the two albums in question, *The Highwaymen* has a better song selection, and a Jimmy Webb title song replete with metaphor, historical sweep, and suggestions of mystical retribution for past sins. Cash brings it all home in sinister fashion on the

last verse. Unfortunately, the title track is so strong it diminishes the good but less ambitious songs in its wake. — D.M.

JESSIE HILL
★ ★ ★½ **Golden Classics (Collectables, NA)**
With all its material taken from 1960–1962 singles released on obscure labels, this collection does a great job of catching the absolute urgency of Jessie Hill. An R&B belter of the most primal kind—he sometimes summons enough juice to rival Wilson Pickett—Hill favors zesty novelty numbers ("Ooh Poo Pah Doo," "Oogsey Moo") over ballads and slower blues, and nearly all of his songs feature great swaggering interplays of sax and piano. "Whip It on Me" is the standout, but all these sides really kick. — P.E.

Z.Z. HILL
★ ★ ★½ **The Rhythm and the Blues (Malaco, 1982)**
★ ★ ★½ **Greatest Hits (Malaco, 1990)**
An R&B vocalist whose easy swing put him in the stylistic camp of William Bell and Bobby "Blue" Bland rather than, say, Otis Redding or James Brown, Z.Z. Hill was more a master of consistency and taste than of a raw, emotional delivery. Out of print, his *Down Home* album had an astonishingly successful run on the R&B charts in 1984, but his crossover appeal remained limited. The greatest-hits collection is a strong set; even where the arrangements are less than inventive, Hill's subtle singing triumphs. — P.E.

PETER HIMMELMAN
★ ★ ★½ **This Father's Day (Island, 1986)**
★ ★ ★ **Gematria (Island, 1987)**
★ ★ ★ ★ **Synesthesia (Island, 1989)**
★ ★ ★½ **From Strength to Strength (Epic, 1991)**
An intelligent and inventive songwriter, Peter Himmelman fronted the Minneapolis new-wave band Sussman Lawrence (whose long-out-of-print *Pop City* is well worth hearing) before deciding on a solo career in 1985. Ironically, *This Father's Day* was recorded with three out of his four Sussman Lawrence bandmates, but it's easy to hear why Himmelman decided to break away, for these low-key, folkish songs sound nothing like Sussman Lawrence's energetic Elvis Costelloisms—though their tuneful resilience pays big dividends on the reflective "Eleventh Confession." *Gematria* maintains a similar mood, though it lacks its predecessor's melodic sparkle. *Synesthesia*

more than makes up the difference, however, emphasizing Himmelman's pop smarts without compromising the intelligence or integrity of his material. Consequently, the album is a delight, with Himmelman addressing himself with equal ardor to such diverse topics as romantic bliss (the jovial "Surrender"), disillusionment (the regretful "Difficult to Touch") and social stagnation (the ominous, angry "Babylon").

Unfortunately, *From Strength to Strength* doesn't quite go that way. Although there's much to be said for the passionate conviction and melodic invention of "Love of Midnight," "Only Innocent" or the touchingly romantic "Mission of My Soul," Himmelman too often stumbles on overreaching lyrics like those to "Woman With the Strength of 10,000 Men" (which, appallingly, actually uses its near-unsingable title as part of the chorus). — J.D.C.

HINDU LOVE GODS
★ ★½ **Hindu Love Gods (Giant/Reprise, 1990)**
A busman's holiday for Warren Zevon and R.E.M.'s three instrumentalists, the Hindu Love Gods maul a handful of (mostly) blues covers with rough, slapdash affection. Robert Johnson and Muddy Waters have withstood far less sensitive treatment, but the Gods' revamp of Prince's "Raspberry Beret" isn't really sacreligious enough to grab your attention. Even though guitarist Peter Buck, bassist Mike Mills and drummer Bill Berry form a flexible, well-versed rock ensemble, the tricky New Orleans syncopations of "Junko Partner" escape them. So does the soul shuffle of Albert King's "Crosscut Saw," for that matter. On the other hand, the country song, "I'm a One Woman Man" (a hit for George Jones), and Woody Guthrie's "Vigilante Man" are right up the Gods' alley. Too bad those two tracks conclude the album; like many vacations, *Hindu Love Gods* ends just as things start to get interesting. — M.C.

ROBYN HITCHCOCK
★ ★ ★½ **Black Snake Diamond Role (1981; Relativity, 1986)**
★ ★½ **I Often Dream of Trains (1984; Relativity, 1986)**
★ ★½ **Groovy Decoy (Relativity, 1986)**
★ ★ ★ **Eaten By Her Own Dinner (EP) (Midnight Music, 1986)**
★ ★½ **Invisible Hitchcock (Relativity, 1986)**
★ ★ ★½ **Eye (Twin/Tone, 1990)**

ROBYN HITCHCOCK AND THE EGYPTIANS
★ ★ ★ ★ **Fegmania! (Slash, 1985)**
★ ★ ★ ★½ **Gotta Let This Hen Out! (Relativity, 1985)**
★ ★ ★ **Exploding in Silence (Relativity EP, 1986)**
★ ★ ★ ★½ **Element of Light (Relativity, 1986)**
★ ★ ★ **Globe of Frogs (A&M, 1988)**
★ ★ ★ ★ **Queen Elvis (A&M, 1989)**
★ ★ ★ ★½ **Perspex Island (A&M, 1991)**
One of rock & roll's most gifted eccentrics, Robyn Hitchcock makes music that evokes much of the same benign insanity that marked John Lennon's most whimsical moments—and, at times, displays even a similar sense of melody. His first solo album, *Black Snake Diamond Role* (umlaut) picks up pretty much where his work with the Soft Boys left off, even to the point of employing most of his former bandmates. Still, this suits the material, particularly the manic "Brenda's Iron Sledge" and the lovely, semi-psychedelic "Acid Bird."

After a three-year hiatus, Hitchcock returned with the drolly-titled *I Often Dream of Trains.* Recorded without a band, its lean, guitar and/or piano arrangements leave it sounding less like a finished album than a collection of song demos. Thus, though the songs—particularly "Sounds Great When You're Dead" and the barbershop harmony number "Uncorrected Personality Traits"—are wonderful, the performances rarely do them justice. Working with a pick-up band, Hitchcock then recorded *Groovy Decay,* using ex-Gong guitarist Steve Hillage as producer. Dissatisfied with the result, Hitchcock eventually withdrew the album, substituting a revamped version entitled *Groovy Decoy;* although some of the songs are agreeably melodic (especially "America" and "The Cars She Used to Drive"), neither the Hillage recordings nor the Matthew Seligman–produced remakes are in any way essential.

Eventually, Hitchcock got tired of being alone and recruited the Soft Boys' original rhythm team of Morris Windsor and Andy Metcalfe (plus keyboardist Roger Jackson) for a new band, the Egyptians. That this was the right thing to do becomes obvious with the first notes of *Fegmania!,* which showcases Hitchcock's cheerful insanity through authoritatively played, tunefully surreal numbers like "Egyptian Cream" (a perverse fertility song) and "The Man With the Lightbulb Head" (a loopy monster-movie send-up). Even better, Hitchcock and band followed *Fegmania!* with the spirited concert album *Gotta Get This Hen Out*, which not only righted some of the wrongs done by *I Often Dream of Trains* and *Groovy Decay* by remaking "Sometimes I Wish I Was a Pretty Girl" and "America," but also reclaims the Soft Boys' "Leppo & the Jooves." But Hitchcock and the Egyptians don't really begin to show their true potential until *Element of Light*, which augments the usual verbal whimsy with well-crafted, insinuating melodies, like those to "Winchester," "Lady Waters & the Hooded One" and the whimsically homoerotic "Ted, Woody and Junior."

Obviously, others sensed the group's potential, for with *Globe of Frogs*, Hitchcock and the Egyptians made the leap to the majors. Unfortunately, the album doesn't quite live up to the inspired standards of *Element of Light*, for despite the appealing lunacy of "Balloon Man" and the raucous "Sleeping With Your Devil Mask," the album fizzles where it should sizzle. Hitchcock bounces back, though, with *Queen Elvis*, which includes the expected flashes of insanity (for instance, the wicked wit of "The Devil's Coachman"), but puts the bulk of its energy into tuneful tidbits like "Wax Doll" or the chiming, Byrds-like "Madonna of the Wasps." Hitchcock hadn't gone completely commercial, however, and had by this point assembled enough musical oddities to fill an album; hence, *Eye*, which takes the same stripped-down approach as *I Often Dream of Trains* though without its predecessor's lo-fi sound. It's not a great album, but Hitchcock does seem to need an outlet for his apparently relentless creativity. After all, up to this point he had been regularly releasing occasional collections like *Eaten By Her Own Dinner* or *Exploding in Silence*; indeed, *Invisible Hitchcock* compiles more than a dozen songs from such projects.

Still, Hitchcock more than makes up the difference with *Perspex Island*, his most accessible effort. Yet what makes this such a delight isn't that its conventional love songs—"So You Think You're in Love," for instance—are irresistibly infectious, but that Hitchcock's melodic standards are the same regardless of what he is writing about. Meaning, in other words, that everything from "Birds in Perspex" to "Child of the Universe" is equally enjoyable. — J.D.C.

BILLIE HOLIDAY
★ ★ ★ ★ **Lady in Satin (1958; Columbia, 1986)**

★ ★ ★ ★ **Last Recording (1959; Verve, 1988)**
★ ★ ★ ★½ **Greatest Hits (MCA, 1968)**
★ ★ ★ ★ ★ **God Bless the Child (Columbia, 1972)**
★ ★ ★ ★ **The Original Recordings (Columbia, 1973)**
★ ★ ★ ★ ★ **Billie Holiday's Greatest Hits (Columbia, 1984)**
★ ★ ★ ★½ **The Silver Collection (Verve, 1984)**
★ ★ ★ ★ ★ **The Complete Billie Holiday on Verve (1946-1959) (Verve, 1985)**
★ ★ ★ ★ ★ **The Quintessential Billie Holiday, Vol.1 (1933–1935) (Columbia, 1987)**
★ ★ ★ ★ ★ **The Quintessential Billie Holiday, Vol. 2 (1936) (Columbia, 1987)**
★ ★ ★ ★½ **The Billie Holiday Songbook (Verve, 1987)**
★ ★ ★ ★½ **Lady's Decca Days, Vol. 1 (MCA, 1988)**
★ ★ ★ ★½ **Lady's Decca Days, Vol. 2 (MCA, 1988)**
★ ★ ★ ★½ **Billie's Blues (MCA, 1988)**
★ ★ ★ ★ ★ **The Quintessential Billie Holiday, Vol. 3 (1936–1937) (Columbia, 1988)**
★ ★ ★ ★ ★ **The Quintessential Billie Holiday, Vol. 4 (1937) (Columbia, 1988)**
★ ★ ★ ★ ★ **The Quintessential Billie Holiday, Vol. 5 (1937–1938) (Columbia, 1988)**
★ ★ ★ ★½ **Lover Man (Zeta, 1989)**
★ ★ ★ ★ ★ **The Quintessential Billie Holiday, Vol. 6 (1938) (Columbia, 1990)**
★ ★ ★ ★ ★ **The Quintessential Billie Holiday, Vol. 7 (1938–1939) (Columbia, 1990)**
★ ★ ★ ★ **Billie Holiday Live (Verve, 1990)**
★ ★ ★ ★ ★ **The Quintessential Billie Holiday, Vol. 8 (1939–1940) (Columbia, 1991)**
★ ★ ★ ★ ★ **The Quintessential Billie Holiday, Vol. 9 (1940–1942) (Columbia, 1991)**
★ ★ ★ ★½ **Lady in Autumn: The Best of the Verve Years (Verve, 1991)**
★ ★ ★ ★ ★ **The Legacy (1933–1958) (Columbia, 1991)**
★ ★ ★ ★ ★ **The Complete Decca Recordings (GRP, 1991)**

Epitomizing as absolutely as does Charlie Parker the saga of the jazz genius as tragic soul, Billie Holiday's biography reads like a Dostoevski novel: raped at ten years old by a neighbor (some accounts say "cousin"), she was sent to a home for wayward girls; in her teens she spent four months in jail for prostitution. Starting as a singer in New York's rough and tumble speakeasies of the early '30s, she was famous by mid-decade. Heroin and a hard-luck love life began wearing her down in the '40s; with her success, too, came the pressures of song pluggers and aesthetic compromise—all of Tin Pan Alley's hack songwriters dogged Holiday to sing their tunes. Her personality a tense mix of the rebel and the victim, Holiday's life was wholly struggle; self-destructive, incandescent, she died at 44. And she left music that, at its finest, continues to work like a depth charge—few singers of any genre can approach its emotional intensity; few singers, either, command her skill.

Remarkably, Holiday's voice wasn't the natural force that some stars (Sarah Vaughan, Aretha Franklin, even Dionne Warwick) have been given. Instead, her greatness lies in how she deployed it; by 1937, she was in full control of her style, hitting notes against the beat the way all jazz horn players do (an early influence was Louis Armstrong's trumpet), she shaped rhythmic lines ingeniously—and interpreted lyrics with intuitive savvy. Humor, sass, toughness and yearning all formed part of her staggering emotive repertoire; Holiday was expert both at laying bare the essence of a great lyric or, alternately, at tossing off a mediocre one with such happy virtuosity that the words were elevated into pure swinging sound.

Two massive, worthwhile compilations cover Holiday. Columbia's *Quintessential* series chronicles her work from 1933–1942 heyday; her sessions are grounded on the elegant piano work of Teddy Wilson, and her range of sidemen extends to such legends as clarinetist Artie Shaw and saxophonist Lester Young; she cuts a few sides, too, with the orchestras of both Benny Goodman and Count Basie. *Volumes 3, 4* and *5* are the crème de la crème; Billie at the peak of her powers. *Legacy* does a good job of condensing the nine sets of the *Quintessential* series, including such standouts as "I Must Have That Man," "Having Myself a Time," "God Bless the Child," "Summertime" and "Long Gone Blues." Holiday's later work continues to divide listeners—some jazz purists scorn her experiments with string arrangements, others consider her interpretive approach occasionally melodramatic or strained, and some fans of Billie's early, clearer tone find disturbing the roughness that comes into

her voice in the mid-1940's. Listen to *The Complete Billie Holiday on Verve*, a ten-record collection that documents her 1946-1959 period, however, and discover remarkable music that, for all its hit-and-miss technique (sometimes poorly chosen material, sometimes overwhelming instrumentation), is an astonishing spiritual autobiography—at times, Holiday's singing is the very voice of pain, loss and hard experience. *Lady in Autumn* encapsulates the Verve years, and it's a bittersweet triumph; in fact, it's often against the lush backdrop of a full orchestra that she achieves her most eerie effect—her singing is acid splashed against velvet. Those who appreciate the fearsome, agonized Holiday might also check out *Lady in Satin* and *The Last Recording*; Ray Ellis's somewhat soupy arrangements serve (who knows how intentionally?) to set off Lady Day's singing in ways that can provoke feelings of real terror.

Of Holiday's live work, fine examples can be found on Zeta's *Lover Man* (featuring such greats as Basie, Art Tatum, Coleman Hawkins and others, the set spans the years from 1937 to 1958) and Verve's *Billie Holiday Live*. Another good studio compilation is MCA's two-volume *Lady's Decca Days*; with its selections recorded between 1944 and 1950, it's Holiday in her middle period—not quite so swaggering as during her late-'30s reign, nor so powerfully desperate as she became later on.
— P.E.

THE HOLLIES
★ ★ ★   **Hollies' Greatest (Capitol, 1980)**
★ ★ ★   **More Great Hits (EMI America, 1986)**
★ ★ ★   **Later Hits (EMI America. 1987)**
★ ★ ★½ **The Hollies: The Best, Vol. 1 (EMI Manhattan, 1988)**
★ ★ ★½ **The Hollies: The Best, Vol. 2 (EMI Manhattan, 1988)**
★ ★ ★   **All Time Greatest Hits (Curb, 1990)**
★ ★ ★½ **Epic Anthology (Epic, 1990)**
Sweet-voiced, ultra-crafted, lyrically undemanding and upbeat, the Hollies' early '60s hits were British Invasion pop of the cute school. Chipper vocalists Allan Clarke and Graham Nash cornered the market on teenage love fare. Later to form 10cc, Graham Gouldman provided such valentines as "Here I Go Again," "Look Through Any Window" and "Bus Stop" as perfect backdrops for harmonies that provided a sheerly sonic celestial rush. The band made massive singles, but couldn't stretch enough for albums, and bombed

when trying anything difficult (an album of Dylan covers, for example). Nash departed, glow intact, for Crosby, Stills and Nash in 1968, but the Hollies, with ex-Swinging Blue Jean Terry Sylvester added on second lead vocal, persevered. The '70s found them scoring big with "Long Cool Woman," "He Ain't Heavy, He's My Brother" and "The Air That I Breathe." — P.E.

BUDDY HOLLY

★ ★ ★ ★ ★ **The Chirping Crickets (1957; MCA, 1987)**
★ ★ ★ ★ ★ **Buddy Holly (1958; MCA, 1989)**
★ ★ ★ ★ ★ **20 Golden Greats (MCA, 1978)**
★ ★ ★ ★ ★ **The Complete Buddy Holly (MCA, 1981)**
★ ★ ★ ★ ★ **Legend (MCA, 1985)**

From once having one of the most abysmal catalogues of any major rock & roll figure, Buddy Holly now has one of the very best. Until the mid-'80s stateside fans hungering for even a taste of Holly's prolific output had to search the import bins, where treasures abounded; otherwise the options were limited to a dozen-plus albums, all but a couple having been released after Holly's death in 1959, almost all altered and patched together haphazardly without sensitivity to Holly's art. In 1978, a film version of Holly's life reignited interest in the music, and MCA responded with *20 Golden Greats*, all original performances, no overdubs, no slicing and dicing of half-finished tapes. If it's the hits pure and simple you're after, you can't go wrong with this album, or with *Legend*, which is much the same program with a couple of differences, one significant one being the inclusion of "True Love Ways," which is not on *20 Golden Greats*. *Legend* marked the beginning of the Holly catalogue reclamation project on MCA, which has provided the domestic market with Holly's complete history on record. The choice now is down to how complete a fan wants his or her Holly collection to be, because everything—alternate takes, home recordings, radio interviews—is out there.

Each of the Holly albums confirms the artist's reputation as one of the most original musicians this country has ever produced. From the outset of his career, Holly had a sense of how to present his music—he wrote or co-wrote virtually everything he recorded—and fought to gain the sort of control over his work that was denied virtually all '50s artists, major and otherwise. His death came at the moment he was looking to a future when he would

produce his own recordings, as well as those of other artists.

In addition to the above-mentioned albums, MCA has also reissued Holly's first two albums, *The Chirping Crickets* and *Buddy Holly*. There's a temptation to distinguish these from the collected hits and essential boxed set by awarding four stars instead of five, but that would imply there's some dross on these records. No. On the latter, Holly can't cut Elvis's version of "You're So Square (Baby I Don't Care)," but he does a serviceable take on "Valley of Tears," which was a hit for Fats Domino, and his version of "Ready Teddy" is a soulful raveup powerful enough to make Holly's friend Little Richard say "Shut up!" *Buddy Holly* also contains the immortal "Peggy Sue"; "Everyday," with its chiming, charming celesta filigrees setting off a remarkable Holly vocal; "Rave On," one of the great rock & roll songs; "Words of Love," one of Holly's most tender lyrics, and the subject of a superb cover version by the Beatles; the rambunctious "I'm Gonna Love You Too," a minor hit in '65 for the Hullabaloos; and "Listen to Me," an extraordinary tender-tough ballad, one of Holly's best-conceived efforts. *The Chirping Crickets* is the only album Holly made with his band before he was given headline billing (Holly recorded for three labels: Decca and Coral, as a solo artist; Brunswick, as a member of the Crickets). A partial list of the song selection here: "Oh Boy," "Not Fade Away," "Maybe Baby," "That'll Be The Day," rock classics all. There's also a Holly cover of R&B legend Chuck Willis's "It's Too Late" that is so forceful that the song is sometimes attributed to Holly's own pen; a nice turn on "Send Me Some Lovin'," recorded originally by Little Richard; and a cover of "An Empty Cup (and a Broken Date)," one of Roy Orbison's early entries in the tear-stained ballad category.

The ultimate Buddy Holly is the boxed set, *The Complete Buddy Holly*. First available as an import in 1969, the six-record set was released domestically in 1981 and answered all the questions about this remarkable artist. All of Holly's music is included, beginning with the country & western and rockabilly sides he cut in Lubbock, Texas, while teamed with his friend Bob Montgomery in a popular duo that billed itself as purveyors of "Western & Bop." The early sides show the influence of Hank Williams on the duo's style; side two of the record shows rockabilly and R&B

taking over the pair, with rousing cover versions of early classics such as "Blue Suede Shoes," "Shake, Rattle & Roll" and "Good Rockin' Tonight," as well as an early Holly original, "Holly Hop." Record Two documents Holly's ill-fated sojourn to Nashville where, under the aegis of Patsy Cline's producer Owen Bradley, Holly cut some hard-rocking rockabilly sides patterned after Presley's style both in Holly's phrasing and in Bradley's use of the echo chamber on Holly's voice. This set includes a version of "That'll Be the Day" that differs considerably from the version cut a year later with the Crickets. Here Holly's voice is thinner and his phrasing more clipped than it would be in 1957, the arrangement a bit more ragged; when Holly sang the song in 1957 with Norman Petty producing, he served up the lyrics, particularly the threat implied in the title sentiment, in a voice far more self-assured than the one he displayed in Nashville. Still, Holly is finding his groove as a writer at this juncture, at least in terms of reconciling his feelings for the sentimental side of country music and the raucous, celebratory nature of the emerging rock & roll.

The next three records, subtitled, respectively, "Clovis, New Mexico," "Clovis, New Mexico, and on to New York," and "New York, N.Y.—Planning for the Future," are the heart and soul of Holly's legacy. Here are the hits, the B sides, and the experiments Holly was engaged in as he attempted to move his music forward. The word "experiments" may be too radical a description of what Holly was up to, given that he seemed intent on making the lushest records he could when he got to slower material, which translated to laying on the string sections. The "New York, N.Y." set is interesting primarily because it shows Holly's writing losing some of its wide-eyed innocence and taking on a darker hue. The final record in the collection, "The Collectors Buddy Holly," begins with six demos Holly recorded in his New York apartment in January of 1959, only a month before his death in the plane crash that also claimed the lives of Ritchie Valens and the Big Bopper. Accompanying himself on guitar, Holly works out a hesitating version of "Slippin' & Slidin'," a "Words of Love" clone called "Dearest," a cover of Mickey and Sylvia's "Love Is Strange," "Peggy Sue Got Married," "That Makes It Tough" and "Learning the Game," one of Holly's deepest lyrics. Also included are both sides of Cricket Jerry Allison's 1958 single release;

Holly productions of New York singer Lou Giordano's Brunswick single, "Stay Close to Me" (the only song Holly wrote that he never recorded, even on a home demo) backed with "Don't Cha Know," written by Phil Everly, and Waylon Jennings's first single, "Jole Blon" b/w "When Sin Stops Love Begins"; and a number of radio and TV interviews supplemented by live takes from Holly's appearances on Ed Sullivan's and Dick Clark's TV shows. One doesn't think of record companies as having the interest to correct its atrocities, but MCA has, and has done right by Buddy Holly. The music is here, in agreeable form at last.
— D.M.

THE HOLMES BROTHERS
★★★★ In the Spirit (Rounder, 1990)
★★★★ Where It's At (Rounder, 1991)
When Wendell and Sherman Holmes made their recording debut in 1990, they had been playing without fanfare in the New York City area for 20 years. That music this powerful could escape attention for so long is one of the mysteries of life. The easiest classification for the music the Brothers purvey is classic soul with a strong spiritual base. Their self-composed songs betray deep roots in gospel, but the scope of their material shows them equally at home with classic Stax-Volt ("When Something Is Wrong With My Baby," from In the Spirit), Sam Cooke ("That's Where It's At," from Where It's At), Jimmy Reed ("Baby, What You Want Me to Do," from In the Spirit) and Hank Williams ("I Saw the Light," from Where It's At). Wendell Holmes is also showing considerable growth as a songwriter.

The other factor in the mix is the Brothers' longtime partner, drummer Popsy Dixon. His is the unearthly falsetto that plays so well against his cohorts' aggressive vocal stylings, adding tenderness and delicacy to the more boisterous outings and a smooth edge to their ensemble singing. His lead vocal on In the Spirit's "The Final Round" finds him declaiming a la Otis Redding and soaring a la Curtis Mayfield.

Both In the Spirit and Where It's At are highly recommended. If in doubt, buy both.
— D.M.

PETER HOLSAPPLE AND CHRIS STAMEY
★★★ Mavericks (RNA, 1991)
No matter how much this reunion of the dB's brain trust might promise tuneful and

intelligent alternative pop, the fact is that neither Holsapple nor Stamey seems especially inspired by the get-together. As such, this album is low-key, low-watt, and decidedly disappointing. — J.D.C.

THE HOLY MODAL ROUNDERS

★★ **The Holy Modal Rounders: Stampfel and Weber (Fantasy, 1972)**
★★ **Alleged in their Own Time (Rounder, 1976)**
★★ **Stampfel & Weber (Fantasy; Rounder, 1981)**
★★ **Have Moicy (Rounder, 1981)**

Perhaps you had to have been there—lounging blissfully zonked at some outdoor festival with the sounds of this acidhead comedy folk music wafting through the incensed air. But, heavens, this stuff sounds dismal now. Playwright Sam Shepard played drums in an early incarnation of the Holy Modal Rounders, but the group's resident "brains" were guitarist-singer Steve Weber and Peter Stampfel on fiddle, banjo and vocals. Basing their shtick on jug music and countryish blues, the duo provided inanely hardy-har-har off-key vocals and lyrics either ribald or sophomorically surreal. *The Holy Modal Rounders* compiles the early '60s LPs, *Holy Modal Rounders,* Volumes One and Two, a pair of albums that provided a blueprint for the hi-jinks from which the group seldom varied. *Alleged in Their Own Time* and *Stampfel and Weber* are more of the same, featuring such gigglesome fare as "Shoot That Turkey Buzzard" and "When the Iceworms Nest Again." People say that humor sometimes doesn't translate across space (as, for example, the stupid silliness of Benny Hill that the English find riotous). The Rounders prove that the same holds true for time—this hippie hilarity is now nearly unlistenable. — P.E.

HONEY CONE

★★★½ **Greatest Hits (HDH/Fantasy, 1990)**

Revenge of the Girl Groups! Edna Wright, Shellie Clark and Carolyn Willis were experienced background singers when Brian Holland, Lamont Dozier and Eddie Holland signed them to the fledgling Hot Wax label in 1969. Honey Cone boldly asserts its position, right from the start. The R&B chart hits "Girls, It Ain't Easy" and "While You're Out Looking for Sugar" reflect the everyday changes wrought by the sexual revolution; women could suddenly say things to men that they'd thought about for years. Of course, these songs were mostly written by a pool of men; so were Laura

Lee's even tougher feminist funk anthems on the same label. If H-D-H's post-Motown hit factory became trapped by new formulas after a while, the Honey Cone sides must have been cut while the mold was still fresh. The pop crossover hit "Want Ads"—Number One in '71—telegraphs its appeal in a deftly arranged break: "Extra, extra . . . read all about it/WANTED: YOUNG MAN, SINGLE AND FREE." Quite literally, the follow-up single begins precisely where "Want Ads" leaves off; "Stick-Up" gleefully reprises its predecessor, nicking a Sly and the Family Stone hook along the way. For assembly-line soul, Honey Cone's *Greatest Hits* maintains a high standard of quality. — M.C.

HOODOO GURUS

★★½ **Stoneage Romeos (Big Time/A&M, 1984)**
★★★★ **Mars Needs Guitars! (Elektra, 1985)**
★★★ **Blow Your Cool (Elektra, 1987)**
★★★ **Magnum Cum Louder (RCA, 1989)**
★★★★ **Kinky (RCA, 1991)**

Brash and quirky, the Hoodoo Gurus epitomize all that is admirable in Australian pub rock, from the over-amped roar of their pop-savvy hooks to the warped wit of their off-center lyrics. *Stoneage Romeos* wasn't a particularly promising debut, since much of the material seemed eccentric to the point of derangement, but *Mars Needs Guitars!* was practically perfect, balancing enthusiastic raveups ("Like Wow—Wipeout" and the title tune) with classically constructed guitar pop ("Bittersweet," "Death Defying"). Although both *Blow Your Cool* and *Magnum Cum Louder* had their moments, neither could match *Mars* for its melodic imagination or consistency. *Kinky,* on the other hand, not only found the band returning to form, but even displayed a few new wrinkles, like the Hendrix-derived psychedelia adorning "Miss Freelove '69." — J.D.C.

JOHN LEE HOOKER

★★★★ **House of the Blues (1959; Chess/MCA, 1987)**
★★★★★ **John Lee Hooker Plays & Sings the Blues (1961; Chess/MCA, 1989)**
★★★★ **Boogie Chillun (1962; Fantasy, 1972)**
★★★★ **The Real Folk Blues (1968; Chess/MCA, 1987)**
★★★★★ **Alone (1970; Tomato, 1989)**

★★★★★ **Goin' Down Highway 51**
(Specialty, 1971)

★★★★ **Mad Man Blues (Chess/MCA,**
1971)

★★★ **Hooker 'N' Heat: Canned Heat**
and John Lee Hooker (1971;
EMI, 1991)

★★★ **Never Get Out of These Blues**
Alive (Crescendo, 1972)

★★★★ **Black Snake (Fantasy, 1977)**

★★★ **The Cream (Tomato, 1978)**

★★★★ **That's Where It's At (1979;**
Stax/Fantasy, 1990)

★★★★ **Sad and Lonesome (Muse, 1979)**

★★★★ **Lonesome Road (MCA, 1983)**

★★★ **Infinite Boogie: John Lee Hooker**
and Canned Heat (Rhino, 1986)

★★★ **John Lee Hooker and Canned**
Heat Recorded Live at the Fox
Venice Theatre (Rhino, 1986)

★★★★★ **The Best of John Lee Hooker**
(GNP Crescendo, 1987)

★★★★ **Gotham Golden Classics**
(Collectables, 1989)

★★★★ **The Healer (Chameleon, 1989)**

★★★★ **Detroit Blues 1950–1951: John**
Lee Hooker/Eddie Burns
(Collectables, 1991)

★★★★ **Mr. Lucky (Charisma/PointBlank,**
1991)

★★★★★ **The Ultimate Collection:**
1948-1990 (Rhino, 1991)

Though he was born in the Mississippi Delta, John Lee Hooker learned blues from his stepfather Will Moore, a popular guitarist around the Clarksdale area who was raised in Louisiana and played a style of blues built on a one-chord droning tone, relentless vamping, and stinging, lower-strings punctuations. Blind Lemon Jefferson, Blind Blake and Charley Patton often visited Moore at his house, but their effect on Hooker was virtually nil—Moore's music possessed him and is the most direct influence on a style that became one of the touchstones of blues-based rock & roll. In fact, Hooker is now at that point in life when all his "children" are paying homage to their inspiration. In two excellent recent releases, *The Healer* and *Mr. Lucky*, Hooker is joined by Bonnie Raitt, Albert Collins, Robert Cray, Keith Richards, Carlos Santana, Los Lobos, George Thorogood, Booker T. Jones, Johnnie Johnson, John Hammond, Charlie Musselwhite, a new incarnation of Canned Heat, Ry Cooder, Johnny Winter, and others in what amounts to Hooker's whistlestop tour through 25-plus years of rock music bearing his signature in the voices of other players.

The Hooker signature, though, isn't easily

copied because its only pattern is no pattern at all. Vamping and droning are the constants of his sound, but Hooker regularly breaks down the 12-bar structure in order to extend his story to a conclusion only he envisions, his fingering and chording follow no discernible logic, and time is without question a moving thing almost from bar to bar in Hooker's songs. If there is a constant it is Hooker's low-down, dark-hued singing style, hinting at danger even in its brightest moments. Like Muddy Waters's, Hooker's sound is the deepest of deep blues.

After working odd jobs and playing music as a sideline in Memphis and Cincinnati in the late '30s and early '40s, Hooker moved to Detroit and cut his first records with a local distributor, who leased the first master to the Modern label. That song, "Boogie Chillun," remains one of the most important blues songs in history. Hooker's masters were leased to a variety of labels with Hooker identified by a different name on each title (Delta John, Texas Slim, the Booker Man, even John Lee Booker). But while the name changed, the music remained the same—Hooker accompanied only by his electric guitar and his own foot-stomping.

Apart from *The Healer* and *Mr. Lucky*, Hooker's most noted band sessions are those he cut in 1970 with blues revivalists Canned Heat, now reissued in a two-CD set by EMI, *Hooker 'N' Heat,* and on Rhino's *Infinite Boogie* (same albums, different titles). Rhino also has available a live album, *John Lee Hooker and Canned Heat*, featuring Hooker, Canned Heat, and, providing backup vocals, the Chambers Brothers. In its original incarnation with 300-pound lead singer Bob Hite and ace guitarist-vocalist Al Wilson (both now deceased), Canned Heat was the foremost exponent of Hooker-style boogie in a blues-rock setting.

Nothing, however, supplants Hooker solo or with minimal backing. His finest records through the years have benefited from a stark approach that elevates the mood of his often personal stories. *The Ultimate Collection: 1948–1990* supports this theory even as it shows Hooker sometimes effective in a broader setting. Guitarist Eddie Kirkland, who provided exemplary support on several Hooker sessions, is heard here in good form on "Think Twice Before You Go," and again on a 1968 track, "Back Biters and Syndicators," which also features Louis Myers on harmonica, Eddie Taylor on bass and Al Duncan on drums. Similarly, a track from Hooker's first-rate

The Real Folk Blues album, "You Know, I Know," finds him backed by one of his early accompanists, guitarist Eddie Burns, as well as Lafayette Leake on piano, Willie Dixon on bass and the incomparable Fred Below on drums.

You don't have to be a purist, though, to appreciate the power of Hooker's earliest sides cut in Detroit and issued on Chess, Vee Jay and Specialty. These represent the darkest tales in the artist's literature as well as his most acerbic slants on life as black Americans knew it in the immediate post-War years. Some of these have the feel of having been carefully prepared and worked out, others are ragged and improvisatory.

Rather than get into album-by-album critiques of Hooker's many recordings, suffice it to say that Detroit years (1948–1952) present the rawest blues Hooker ever recorded. The key titles here are *Detroit Blues 1950–1951*, featuring solo recordings by Hooker and Eddie Burns (Hooker's tracks are also available separately in Collectables' *Gotham Golden Classics*); Specialty's *Alone* and *Goin' Down Highway 51*; *That's Where It's At*; Chess's *John Lee Hooker Plays and Sings the Blues, House of the Blues, Mad Man Blues;* and MCA's Jazz Heritage selection, *Lonesome Road*. An overview that takes Hooker from his solo accompaniment into his first band sides is available via GNP Crescendo's well-done *The Best of John Lee Hooker*.

The development of Hooker's style within a band context is demonstrated on the sides dating from the late '50s forward. Not that the style developed all that much—Hooker is resolutely Hooker to this day; what's interesting is how other musicians respond to the challenge posed by Hooker's unorthodox sense of song structure. *Black Snake, Boogie Chillun, Sad and Lonesome* and *The Real Folk Blues* move Hooker from the late '50s into the late-'60s. *Black Snake*, in particular, is an imposing title, being a two-fer reissue of two early Hooker albums, one consisting of Hooker solo, another featuring Hooker with solid support from bassist Sam Jones and drummer Louis Hayes.

Payback time begins in the '70s with the Canned Heat sessions. Additionally, *Never Get Out of These Blues Alive* teams Hooker with a band whose numbers are bolstered on several cuts by Elvin Bishop on slide guitar, Canned Heat's Mark Naftalin on piano, and, on the title track, Naftalin, Bishop and Van Morrison, the latter sharing lead vocals with Hooker. *The Cream* is four

sides of live, prime Hooker, recorded in 1977 with a band featuring Charlie Musselwhite on harmonica. Put these recordings up against *The Healer* and *Mr. Lucky*, and feel how vital Hooker's blues remain over four decades after he first sat down in front of a recording mike. Monumental; simply monumental. — D.M

THE HOOTERS
★ ★ ★½ **Nervous Night (Columbia, 1985)**
★ ★ ★   **One Way Home (Columbia, 1987)**
★ ★ ★   **Zig Zag (Columbia, 1989)**

Because the Hooters are so good at making big noises, it's tempting to assume that the band's music is empty and glib. But the songs on *Nervous Night* are just as good as the band's arrangements, meaning that there's more to "And We Danced" than its chirping mandolins and jubilant harmony vocals, and more to "All You Zombies" than its deep-thudding bass and itchy reggae groove. *One Way Home* is nearly as catchy, thanks to "Satellite," "Karla With a K" and the charmingly traditional "Graveyard Waltz." But *Zig Zag* finds the band forsaking its flash for a darker, less ebullient sound, and while the message songs are sometimes guilty of overstatement (particularly on the likes of "Give the Music Back" and "Brother, Don't You Walk Away"), this newfound seriousness adds resonance to "500 Miles" and "Don't Knock It 'Til You Try It." — J.D.C.

LIGHTNIN' HOPKINS
★ ★ ★ ★ ★ **Lightnin' Hopkins (1959;**
          Smithsonian/Folkways, 1990)
★ ★ ★ ★ **Autobiography (Tradition, 1960)**
★ ★ ★ ★ **The Best of Lightnin' Hopkins**
          (Prestige, 1960)
★ ★ ★ ★ **Lightnin' (1960; Bluesville, 1990)**
★ ★ ★ ★ **Blues in My Bottle (1961;**
          Prestige/Bluesville, 1990)
★ ★ ★ ★ **How Many More Years I Got**
          (1962; Fantasy, 1989)
★ ★ ★   **Goin' Away (1963;**
          Prestige/Bluesville, 1990)
★ ★ ★ ★ **Soul Blues (1964; Prestige, 1991)**
★ ★ ★ ★ **Double Blues (1964; Fantasy,**
          1989)
★ ★ ★   **Hootin' the Blues (Prestige, 1964)**
★ ★ ★   **The Legacy of the Blues, Vol. 12:**
          Lightnin' Hopkins (GNP
          Crescendo, 1976)
★ ★ ★ ★ **Mojo Hand/Golden Classics**
          (Collectables, 1987)
★ ★ ★   **An Anthology of the Blues, Part**
          1: Drinkin' in the Blues
          (Collectables, 1988)

★ ★ ★ **An Anthology of the Blues, Part 2: Prison Blues (Collectables, 1988)**

★ ★ ★ **An Anthology of the Blues, Part 3: Mama and Papa Hopkins (Collectables, 1988)**

★ ★ ★ **An Anthology of the Blues, Part 4: Nothin' but the Blues (Collectables, 1988)**

★ ★ ★ ★ **The Herald Recordings—1954 (Collectables, 1988)**

★ ★ ★ ★ ★ **Texas Blues (Arhoolie, 1989)**

★ ★ ★ **The Lost Texas Tapes, Volume 1 (Collectables, 1989)**

★ ★ ★ **The Lost Texas Tapes, Volume 2 (Collectables, 1989)**

★ ★ ★ **The Lost Texas Tapes, Volume 3 (Collectables, 1989)**

★ ★ ★ ★ **The Lost Texas Tapes, Volume 4 (Collectables, 1989)**

★ ★ ★ **The Lost Texas Tapes, Volume 5 (Collectables, 1989)**

★ ★ ★ ★ ★ **The Gold Star Sessions—Vol. 1 (Arhoolie, 1990)**

★ ★ ★ ★ ★ **The Gold Star Sessions—Vol. 2 (Arhoolie, 1990)**

★ ★ ★ ★ ★ **The Complete Prestige/Bluesville Recordings (Prestige/Bluesville, 1991)**

★ ★ ★ **Lightnin' Strikes Back (Collectables, 1991)**

Sam "Lightnin'" Hopkins, who died in 1982, left behind a voluminous collection of country blues as personal and topical as any artist of his time. Born in the small Texas farming community of Centerville in 1912, Hopkins spent most of his life in and around Houston, making money playing on the streets (sometimes with Blind Lemon Jefferson) or wherever else he could be paid. One of his earliest associations was as an accompanist for Texas Alexander, a Texas folk poet inclined toward improvising his extremely personal blues while performing, necessitating that any guitarist playing behind him be quick enough to execute the proper changes without warning. The dexterity Hopkins developed would later lead a recording engineer to nickname him "Lightnin'," and the autobiographical, improvisational style favored by Alexander came to be Hopkins's style as well.

In the late 1940s Hopkins recorded a series of duets for the Los Angeles–based Aladdin label with pianist-vocalist Thunder Smith. Those sides generated little interest, so Hopkins returned to Houston, where he recorded as a solo artist for the Gold Star label. A 1947 single, "Short Haired Woman" b/w "Big Mama Jump" sold 40,000 copies, a follow-up single, "Baby Please Don't Go," sold twice that number, and Hopkins was off on a recording career that found him leaving many children with many labels. By some accounts he is the most frequently recorded blues artist in history.

Women figure prominently in Hopkins's songs, although they are generally regarded with derision. But Hopkins was also something of a social commentator in that his songs observed the events unfolding in the world around him. "Tim Moore's Farm" describes in explicit detail the hard life of a black field hand; the song became a local hit and led Mr. Moore to show up at one of Hopkins's shows and demand he cease singing the number whenever he was in the area. "Bud Russell Blues" is a scalding account of the chief transfer agent (who is also immortalized in Leadbelly's "Midnight Special") for the Texas State Prison system whose job it was to transfer convicts to a central location from which they would be assigned to work camps; having spent some time working on the Houston Prison Farm's road gang, Hopkins knew whereof he sang. In later songs he limned the hazards of the approaching Jet Age in "DC-7," and celebrated in "Happy John Glenn Blues" the personal triumph of the Clean Marine's triple orbit of the earth. With his gift for meter and rhyme, Hopkins was also known to make up songs on the spot from ideas supplied by his audience.

The albums listed are by no means the complete Hopkins legacy. He is said to have recorded for over 20 labels in his lifetime, and much has fallen out of print. Still, these titles are all choice, easily available, and representative of Hopkins's approach, which varied hardly at all from his Gold Star recordings forward. Arhoolie's *Early Recordings* and *The Gold Star Sessions* document the beginning of Hopkins's career (1947–1950) and the wide variety of material he was singing at that early juncture. For example, in the midst of more or less traditional folk blues on Volume 1 of *The Gold Star Sessions*, Hopkins rendered "Zolo Go," which in fact is a phonetic misspelling of zydeco, and the song itself, with Hopkins on organ, one of the first recorded examples of zydeco.

From the 1950s, Hopkins is represented by a set of recordings made for the Herald label now issued as *The Herald Recordings— 1954*, and by *Lightnin' Hopkins*, recorded in 1959 when Hopkins's career was revitalized after he was rediscovered by blues scholar Samuel Charters, who produced these sessions. The Prestige/Fantasy/Bluesville titles represent Hopkins's work from 1960 to 1964, most easily obtained in *The Complete Prestige/Bluesville Recordings*, a seven-CD set that includes an in-depth audio interview conducted by Charters. *Double Blues* is a single-CD reissue of *Soul Blues* and the currently-deleted *Down Home Blues*; *Hootin' the Blues* is a live album featuring among its cuts an etiology of the blues ("Blues Is a Feeling") and an instrumental dialogue of Hopkins's creation depicting a musical interchange between himself and Ray Charles ("Me and Ray Charles"). One of the more interesting entries in the Hopkins catalogue is Tradition's *Autobiography in Blues*. Consciously designed to show the different aspects of the artist's approach to songs, its tracks include traditional fare such as "Trouble in Mind" that Hopkins personalized to express his own point of view; songs he wrote himself that became staples of his repertoire ("Short Haired Woman," "75 Highway"); and a group of songs without defined structure or lyrics that Hopkins would re-create anew with each playing ("Get Off My Toe").

The four-volume *Anthology of the Blues* series on Collectables is culled from the Everest label's vaults and takes Hopkins from the late '50s into the early '60s. Another Collectables title, *Mojo Hand*, features some of Hopkins's most searing guitar work, close-miked and violent in its intensity, produced by Bobby Robinson, whose Fire and Fury labels were home to some of the greatest blues and R&B artists of the '50s.

From Hopkins's later years comes the GNP Crescendo *Legacy of the Blues* entry, which reunited Hopkins with Samuel Charters in 1976 for what proved to be one of Hopkins's final recording sessions. Collectables also chips in with an intriguing five-volume series called *The Lost Texas Tapes*, which may be (there's no annotation whatsoever) recordings Hopkins made in Houston in the '70s. Volumes 1 through 3 are Hopkins solo; 4 and 5 bring on guest artists. Volume 4 is a live recording, a true down-home effort done not in a club but most likely in a restaurant—patrons are heard conversing in the background, and on one track a cash register rings as Hopkins plays. He's accompanied by Curley Lee, who blows mean and low harmonica throughout and engages Hopkins in some humorous but cutting between-songs banter. — D.M.

BRUCE HORNSBY AND THE RANGE
★★★ **The Way It Is (RCA, 1986)**
★★½ **Scenes From the Southside (RCA, 1988)**
★★★ **A Night on the Town (RCA, 1990)**
Craft, earnestness and musical talent make Bruce Hornsby a hard guy to knock. His mid-'80s singles were almost aggressively tasteful: ultra-professional piano pastiches, Americana and MOR-ready hooks. But "The Way It Is" and "Mandolin Rain" suffered from a curious defeatism in their lyrics, an air of wistfulness that passed, on first listen, for melancholy but left a "Well-then-who-gives a-damn?" aftertaste. *Scenes From the Southside* continued in the same vein, producing, in "The Valley Road," another stainless hit. Hornsby enlisted such diverse talents as Jerry Garcia and Wayne Shorter to help make *A Night on the Town* his most direct, almost bluesy record. Not that far a departure from the Range's earlier sound, it garnered a predictable response: critical encouragement, no big hits. — P.E.

JOHNNY HORTON
★★★ **Greatest Hits (Columbia, 1960)**
★★★ **American Originals (Columbia, 1990)**
Johnny Horton was only 33 when he died in a car wreck in 1960, and by that time he had recorded three Top Ten singles in little more than a year. His first single, "The Battle of New Orleans," topped the singles chart for six weeks in 1959, and its follow-ups, "Sink the Bismarck" and "North to Alaska," peaked at Numbers Three and Four, respectively. Clearly Horton had established himself supreme in the realm of song-based historical narratives, but these were in essence novelties. Before his death he had released two more singles, "Honky-Tonk Man" and "Sleepy-Eyed John," that were not hits, but were more adventurous than his recorded work to that point. Horton was moving into hard country, and he had the rough-edged, blues-tinged voice to pull it off. He proved that on *Honky-Tonk Man*, a long out-of-print album released in 1962. *American Originals*, while heavy on the hits, at least gives some indication of where the man might have taken his music; *Greatest Hits* collects all the above-mentioned singles, as well as items like "Johnny Reb" and "Johnny Freedom." — D.M.

HOTHOUSE FLOWERS
★★★½ **People (Polydor, 1988)**
★★★½ **Home (Polydor, 1990)**

Beating out even U2 and Sinéad O'Connor, Hothouse Flowers' 1988 debut was the best-selling in the history of Irish pop. Sounding neither like the guitar-and-bellow jubilee of Bono and crew nor the artful gorgeousness of the Bald One, *People* instead mixed Celtic soul with epic rock in a way that recalled a cross between the Waterboys and Bruce Springsteen. Like U2 and Sinéad, however—and artists as diverse as Van Morrison, Enya, Kevin Rowland and An Emotional Fish—the Dublin band's hallmark was its fierce urge toward transcendence, a spiritual force that seems almost endemically Irish.

Employing such arcane instrumentation as bouzouki and bodhran along with regular rockers' gear, the band's two albums forefront the dramatic vocals and piano of leader Liam Ó Maonlai and feature lyrics filled with rapturous poetry. While a certain blithe '60s love 'n' peace sensibility informs the songs, the Flowers steer clear of the musical clichés of neo-psychedelia—their power is both earthier and more intense. Ranging from covers of "I Can See Clearly Now" to standout originals such as "Love Don't Work This Way" and "Don't Go," the group has, in a very short time, established itself as offhand virtuosos—and as visionaries. — P.E.

HOT TUNA
    ★ ★½ **Hot Tuna (RCA, 1970)**
    ★ ★½ **First Pull Up, Then Pull Down (RCA, 1971)**
    ★ ★ ★ **Burgers (Grunt, 1972)**
    ★ ★ ★½ **The Phosphorescent Rat (Grunt, 1973)**
    ★ ★ ★ **America's Choice (Grunt, 1973)**
    ★ ★ ★ **Yellow Fever (Grunt, 1975)**
    ★ ★ ★½ **Hoppkorv (Grunt, 1976)**
    ★ ★ ★ **Double Dose (Grunt, 1977)**
    ★ ★ ★½ **Final Vinyl (Grunt, 1979)**
    ★ ★ ★ **Pair a Dice Found (Epic, 1991)**
Originally begun as a side project, Hot Tuna was formed by Jefferson Airplane's instrumental powerhouse, guitarist Jorma Kaukonen and bassist Jack Casady. The two went in for laid-back "authenticity" with the blues, the opposite approach from the Airplane's other spinoff, the glossy Jefferson Starship. Kaukonen and Casady deserve credit for exposing the work of the Rev. Gary Davis to a larger public, for proselytizing for country blues as a whole, and for generating an in-concert atmosphere of funky geniality and casual virtuosity. But they suffered, after a while, from too coy a modesty in their approach. With the

Airplane, Casady and Kaukonen were dangerous, risky players; as Hot Tuna, they grinned and boogied, but seldom blazed. Kaukonen's vocals, for one, were rarely more than a diffident mumble, and the structure of blues itself offered little to encourage Casady's capacity for experimentation. After an acoustic self-titled debut, they added ex-Airplane violinist, Papa John Creach, and cranked up the amps. Both maneuvers helped greatly in terms of creating a more varied sound; Jorma began writing more (if somewhat shapeless) songs—and *The Phosphorescent Rat* and *Hoppkorv* were solid. Their blues, however, virtually never had the soul or bite of the original versions. — P.E.

SON HOUSE
    ★ ★ ★ **Father of the Folk Blues (Columbia, 1965)**
    ★ ★ ★ ★ ★ **Son House (Arhoolie, 1973)**
    ★ ★ ★ ★ **The Real Delta Blues (Blue Goose, 1979)**
    ★ ★ ★ ★ ★ **Son House and Blind Lemon Jefferson (Biograph, NA)**
    ★ ★ ★ ★ **Son House and Robert Pete Williams (Roots, NA)**
    ★ ★ ★ ★ **The Vocal Intensity (Roots, NA)**
    ★ ★ ★ ★ ★ **Delta Blues: The Original Library of Congress Sessions From Field Recordings 1941–1942 (Biograph, 1991)**
Before anyone gets too rapturous about all the important artists whose vintage work is being returned to print via compact disc, take a minute to consider that as of late 1991, all of Son House's recordings had gone out of print. This is the same Son House who as a young man growing up in the Mississippi Delta was taken under the wing of Charley Patton; the same Son House immortalized in blues lore as an early mentor of Robert Johnson. More important, the same Son House whose 1941–42 recordings for Paramount are widely regarded as providing a showcase for blues singing that is virtually without parallel in terms of vocal authority and emotional commitment. Before he ever got around to recording, though, House had had time to take up preaching (as a 15-year-old in Lyon, Mississippi), only to have to surrender his pulpit and leave town in disgrace after marrying his 32-year-old neighbor; and he'd had time to be sent to prison for two years for shooting a man. One of his songs, "My Black Mama," provided the foundation for Robert Johnson's "Walkin' Blues" and for

Muddy Waters's "Country Blues" and "Feel Like Goin' Home."

Arhoolie's *Son House*, Biograph's *Son House and Blind Lemon Jefferson* and *Delta Blues* are the key entries in House's early and most important work. The out-of-print Blue Goose album, *The Real Delta Blues*, is comprised of some private recordings House made in 1964, when he was rediscovered in Rochester, New York. Though in ill health at the time, House's performances don't hurt for fire, and in fact are quite compelling on numbers such as "Pony Blues" and "Mississippi County Farm Blues." Blue Goose is long out of business, and with it went *The Real Delta Blues*. It seems inconceivable that the masters won't make their way to some other label, but until that day comes, anyone who manages to track down a copy of this album will be richly rewarded for the time spent. — D.M.

HOUSEMARTINS

★ ★ ★ ★   London 0 Hull 4 (Elektra, 1986)
★ ★ ½ The People Who Grinned
         Themselves to Death (Elektra,
         1987)

Odd birds even by English rock standards, the Housemartins were a sweet-voiced quartet whose albums blended gloriously melodic guitar pop with stridently moralistic lyrical invective; imagine being harangued by a Christian-Marxist Everly Brothers, and you're getting there. *London 0 Hull 4* (so-named because the quartet hailed from the provincial English town of Hull) sheathes its political agenda in an almost irresistible string of melodies, casting the songs in such energetically tuneful terms that you almost don't notice the pro-temperance message of "Happy Hour" or the anti-conformity diatribe hidden within the lush harmonies of "Sheep." Apparently, even the 'Martins themselves thought the approach too subtle, for *The People Who Grinned Themselves to Death* delivers its message with all the subtlety of a flying mallet. Even so, the glorious vocal work on a capella bonus tracks like "Caravan of Love" almost redeems the album. — J.D.C.

HOUSE OF LOVE

★ ★ ★   The House of Love (Fontana, 1990)
★ ★ ½ A Spy in the House of Love
         (Fontana, 1990)

Between frontman Guy Chadwick's dark, deadpan vocals and the band's understated but expressive rhythm arrangements, this London band definitely knows how to do a lot with a little, and the better moments of *The House of Love*—"Shine On," say, or "I Don't Know Why I Love You"—exploit that to the fullest, delivering a sound that's somewhere between the chiming colorism of the Church and the mordant drone of Bauhaus. *A Spy in the House of Love* isn't quite as impressive, but then, being a collection of outtakes and B sides, it isn't meant to be. — J.D.C.

WHITNEY HOUSTON

★ ★ ★   Whitney Houston (Arista, 1985)
★ ★ ½ Whitney (Arista, 1987)
   ★ ½ I'm Your Baby Tonight (Arista,
         1990)

Whitney Houston has one of the most powerful and polished voices in popular music, an instrument exquisitely capable of balladic intimacy, gospel exuberance and soulful expression, and she uses it to sell some of the blandest pap on the planet. Imagine if Andrew Wyeth had abandoned oil painting on the assumption that there was more money to be had drawing Garfield cartoons, and you'll have a sense of the waste in Houston's career. For all its audience targeting, *Whitney Houston* does have its moments, particularly when Houston leans toward R&B, as on "You Give Good Love." *Whitney*, on the other hand, was an outright attempt to capitalize on her growing Top Forty following; as a marketing move, it was genius, but as music it's not much. Oddly, *I'm Your Baby Tonight* found the singer trying to recapture an increasingly alienated R&B audience, to little avail; tellingly, a non-LP single of "The Star Spangled Banner" earned almost as much attention as the album's designated hits. — J.D.C.

MIKI HOWARD

   ★ ★   Come Share My Love (Atlantic,
         1986)
★ ★ ★   Love Confessions (Atlantic, 1987)
★ ★ ★ ½ Miki Howard (Atlantic, 1989)

Like Anita Baker and Regina Belle, Miki Howard is a soul singer whose roots lean toward gospel but whose taste runs to jazz—a potent combination, and one put to fine use on *Love Confessions* and *Miki Howard*. Despite its attempts at R&B currency and a spark-throwing duet with Gerald Levert on "That's What Love Is," *Love Confessions* works best when Howard emphasizes the jazzier side of her sound; because she works on the song instead of the groove, her reading of Earth, Wind and Fire's "Reasons" is tasteful and nuanced, while "You've Changed" shows she can handle the standards with confidence and aplomb. Even so, *Miki Howard* does all that and manages to shine on the R&B numbers. Granted, it doesn't hurt that the song list emphasizes balladry over groove, but both the perky "Love Under New Management" and her New Jack remake of the Aretha Franklin hit "Until You Come Back to Me (That's What I'm Gonna Do)" show that Howard can ride the beat as impressively as she can shape a slow, soulful phrase.

— J.D.C.

HOWLIN' WOLF

★ ★ ★ ★ ★ **Howlin' Wolf (1958; Chess/MCA, 1987)**
★ ★ ★ ★ ★ **Moanin' in the Moonlight (1964; Chess/MCA, 1986)**
★ ★ ★ ★ ★ **Howlin' Wolf/Moanin' in the Moonlight (1958, 1964; Chess/MCA, 1987)**
★ ★ ★ ★ **Poor Boy (Chess, 1965)**
★ ★ ★ ★ ★ **Real Folk Blues (Chess, 1966)**
★ ★ ★ ★ ★ **Evil (Chess, 1967)**
★ ★ ★ ★ ★ **More Real Folk Blues (1967; Chess/MCA, 1988)**
★ ★ ★ ★ **The London Sessions (1971; Chess/MCA, 1989)**
★ ★ ★ ★ **The Back Door Wolf (Chess, 1973)**
★ ★ ★ ★ **Change My Way (1977; Chess/MCA, 1990**
★ ★ ★ ★ ★ **His Greatest Sides, Vol. 1 (MCA/Chess, 1986)**
★ ★ ★ ★ **Cadillac Daddy: Memphis Recordings, 1952 (Rounder, 1987)**
★ ★ ★ ★ ★ **The Chess Box (Chess MCA, 1991)**

Along with his lifetime rival, Muddy Waters, Howlin' Wolf became the archetypal Chicago bluesman—raw, electric, deep and continually astonishing. Born Chester Burnett in 1910, the singer-guitarist was raised in Mississippi, there absorbing the country-blues tradition of Robert Johnson and Charley Patton. Picking up on the harmonica style of Sonny Boy Williamson, he formed his first band in Memphis with James Cotton and Junior Parker in the 1930s; he'd go on to play with Ike Turner, Willie Dixon and other genre greats. While seldom recording as a guitarist, he gripped listeners with his voice in the early '50s—moving to Chicago, he recorded a series of seminal electrified singles whose powerful appeal, particularly to Brit rock legends (the Stones, Yardbirds, Led Zeppelin), was their sheer visceral power. A performer known for keening like

his namesake, for cavorting onstage on all fours, and for his intimidating physical presence, the gigantic Wolf was indeed a force of nature.

The Chess Box is, by far, the best collection. Not only is it comprehensive—extending from 1951 to 1973, its three CDs feature 71 songs—but its roster, not only of rarities, but of all Wolf's hits (most of them written by Willie Dixon) makes it indispensable. "How Many More Years," "Smokestack Lightning," "I Ain't Superstitious," "Killing Floor" and "Back Door Man" are preternaturally moving music, by turns sly and terrifying, spooky, profane and wise. *The London Sessions* is a good late collaboration with Eric Clapton, Stevie Winwood, Charlie Watts and Bill Wyman; *Cadillac Daddy* collects hard-to-find gems from Wolf's earliest recording career; with the exception of *Live and Cookin'* and *Message to the Young* (both out of print) all of the Chess records are worth seeking out. *The Box*, however, is so thorough (and nicely annotated) that it serves as more than a mere introduction.

— P.E.

HUGO LARGO

★ ★ ½ **Drum (1987; Opal 1988)**
★ ★ ★ **Mettle (Opal, 1989)**

If assembling a rock band with no guitars and no drums—just two bass players, a violinist and a singer—strikes you as the sort of thing a rock critic would dream up on his off hours, well, you'd be right. Hugo Largo was the brainchild of New York critic (and eventual MTV personality) Tim Sommer, and for the most part, its sound is pretty much what might be expected of such an ensemble—lots of dark, droning interplay between the basses, topped with vocals and the periodic, moaning swoop of violin. From a melodic standpoint, violinist Hahn Rowe generally carries the group, lightening the heavy burden of the basses' rumbling conversation, but it's ultimately singer Mimi Goese who saves the group. Although Goese isn't much of a singer—her background, tellingly, was in performance art—she's quite a talker, and the chatty, near-poetic quality of her lyrics can be riveting. Even so, *Drum* is a tad too pretentious to survive repeated listenings. *Mettle* is better; even though the music remains ephemeral, Goese's "Turtle Song" and "Four Brothers" are wonderful.

— J.D.C.

HUMAN LEAGUE

★½ Reproduction (1979; Virgin, 1988)
★★ Travelogue (1980; Virgin, 1988)
★★★ Dare (A&M, 1981)
★★½ Love and Dancing (A&M, 1982)
★★ Fascination! (EP) (A&M, 1983)
★½ Hysteria (A&M, 1984)
★★½ Crash (A&M, 1986)
★★★½ Greatest Hits (A&M, 1988)
★½ Romantic? (A&M, 1990)

When the Human League started out, synth-pop was a daringly futuristic idea, and this group seemed on the cutting edge of technology. A dozen years and millions of microchips later, synths were cheap and ubiquitous, and the Human League had become a none-too-extraordinary vocal group. Such are the perils of progress. Needless to say, the League's early recordings sound pretty dated at this point. With its buzzing, clanking synths and dour "post-industrial" perspective, *Reproduction* sounds less like a rock album than an art-school project gone awry; even its nod to the mainstream—a cover of the Righteous Brothers' "You've Lost That Loving Feeling"—seems studied and self-conscious. The League loosens up some with *Travelogue*. But as much as that adds in pop appeal, particularly through tunes like "Life Kills" and "Being Boiled," the still-primitive synth programming leaves the arrangements seeming clunky and mechanical.

Between *Travelogue* and *Dare* two unexpected developments changed the Human League's sound. One was the departure of Martyn Ware and Ian Marsh, the band's original synth wizards; the other was the introduction of the Linn drum, a computerized drum machine that used digitally sampled drum sounds instead of synthesized equivalents. Original singer Phil Oakey recruited a new lineup, including ex-Rezillo Jo Callis plus singers Joanne Catherall and Susanne Sulley, and delivered the first true synth-pop album. In truth, the most radical thing about *Dare* was its instrumentation, since the songs—particularly "Love Action (I Believe in Love)" and the melodramatic "Don't You Want Me"—were fairly conventional pop numbers. But in 1981, drum machines and sequencers were novelty enough, and helped make *Dare* a smash.

The League immediately cashed in on its newfound success, releasing an amusing album of dance-oriented remixes entitled *Love and Dancing,* which is credited, in a nod to Barry White, to the League Unlimited Orchestra. An amusing trifle, it's a prelude of sorts to *Fascination!,* a somewhat thinner slice of dance pop whose principal point of interest is the flirtatious "(Keep Feeling) Fascination." Apparently afraid of falling into a rut, the Human League tried to turn serious again with *Hysteria.* Unfortunately, it doesn't work, as pompous message-heavy numbers like "The Lebanon" end up seeming as ridiculous as dance fluff like "Rock Me Again and Again and Again and Again and Again and Again."

Just when the League was beginning to seem irrelevant, the group decamped for Minneapolis and the studios of Jimmy Jam and Terry Lewis. *Crash* is a schizo affair, with some songs ("Money") sounding like the League of yore, and others ("Swang") coming across like contemporary R&B. Fortunately, "Human," a classic Jam and Lewis ballad, finds the perfect middleground, thus rescuing the album as well as the group.

"Human," along with the rest of the group's singles, can also be found on *Greatest Hits,* which is the group's most consistent album. And though the League returns to its old tricks with *Romantic?,* only "Heart Like a Wheel" justifies the effort.
— J.D.C.

HUMBLE PIE

★★★ As Safe as Yesterday Is (1969; CBS Special Products, 1991)
★★★ Town and Country (1969; CBS Special Products, 1991)
★★★ Humble Pie (A&M, 1970)
★★★ Rock On (A&M, 1971)
★★ Performance: Rockin' the Fillmore (A&M, 1971)
★ Smokin' (A&M, 1972)
★ On to Victory (Atco, 1980)
★ Go for the Throat (Atco, 1980)
★★ The Best (A&M, 1982)
★★½ Humble Pie Classics (A&M, 1987)

At the peak of the Pie's inscrutably monstrous success—*Performance: Rockin' the Fillmore* (1971)—amiable maniac Steve Marriott brandished one of the most annoying voices in rock: a hectoring, sandpaper parody of black authenticity. With the group's platform boots and troglodyte riffing crushing the subtlety out of blues standards, *Fillmore* featured a 16-minute slaughter of Muddy Waters's "Rollin' Stone" that typified the band's "appeal." Now unlistenable, this stuff then was considered soulful, perhaps as a populist headbanging antidote to the smarmy "good taste" of the singer-songwriters who dominated radio.

For Marriott, at least artistically, such

tripe was a bringdown. Having begun as a snappy popster with Small Faces, he formed Humble Pie in 1968 as a progressive outfit whose first two albums weren't bad, no matter how fawning in their homage to the Band. *Humble Pie* and *Rock On* hit harder, but still nodded toward taste. Peter Frampton helped keep things tuneful. Formerly of the Herd and later to find mega-stardom as a heartthrob, Frampton on guitar balanced Marriott like sweet does sour. Soon enough, though, Humble Pie headed for the boogie wastelands, never to return. — P.E.

ENGELBERT HUMPERDINCK

★ **Release Me (London, 1967; London, 1987)**
★ **A Man Without Love (Parrot/ London, 1968)**
★★ **Greatest Hits (Polydor, 1987)**
★ **Live in Concert/All of Me (Epic, 1989)**

Born Arnold George Dorsey in Madras, India, this Vegas god-to-be was singled out for stardom by Tom Jones's manager, Gordon Mills. Ripping off an obscure German opera composer for his client's name, Mills groomed Hump to bookend Tom. Jones would be tease and histrionic belting (big band rock, tamed R&B and lush country); Eng would croon, seldom stain his tux, and smile. Jones was rape-fantasy; Humperdinck, seduction. Needless to say, the shtick went over big. Serving up a glossy take on Ray Price's "Release Me" in 1967, Humperdinck went on to become the sultan of love-schmaltz, with big, quivery hits like "The Last Waltz," "A Man Without Love" and "There Goes My Everything." Predictable orchestral arrangements add the veneer of "class" to his records; a nice-guy persona and a buttery voice keep things smooth. This former idol is the kind of singer who makes Dean Martin seem interesting. — P.E.

ALBERTA HUNTER

★★½ **Blues Serenaders (Fantasy, 1961)**
★★★★ **Amtrak Blues (Columbia, 1980)**

One of the most acclaimed blues singers of the '20s and '30s, Alberta Hunter made her recording debut in 1921 with the Fletcher Henderson orchestra, and as her career gathered momentum, recorded with Louis Armstrong, appeared with Paul Robeson in the 1928 production of *Showboat*, and toured widely through Europe, Africa and Asia. Then, in 1956, she retired from music to work as a practical nurse, recording only sporadically until her second retirement— this time from nursing—in 1977.

Hunter's comeback officially began with her contributions to the soundtrack of *Remember My Name* in 1978, but *Amtrak Blues* (the only recording from this period in print) more accurately captures the sassy strength of her singing. *Blues Serenaders*, recorded during her nursing days, is rather less impressive, tending more toward Chicago jazz nostalgia than bluesy vitality. — J.D.C.

IAN HUNTER

★★★½ **Ian Hunter (1975; Columbia, 1990)**
★★½ **All American Alien Boy (1976; Columbia, 1990)**
★★★★ **Shades of Ian Hunter (1978; Chrysalis, 1989)**
★★★ **You're Never Alone With a Schizophrenic (Chrysalis, 1979)**
★★★ **Short Back and Sides (Chrysalis, 1981)**

WITH MICK RONSON

★★★½ **Y U I Orta (Mercury, 1990)**

Seldom seen without sunglasses, Ian Hunter was the literate dandy behind the almost-legendary glam stars Mott the Hoople. Apostolic in his love for basic rock & roll boosted by knowing, Dylan-ish lyrics, Hunter ushered in his first and finest solo album with the quintessential rocker, "Once Bitten Twice Shy"—later covered, with zero subtlety and mucho success, by Great White. The brooding, hiply poetic "Boy" reflected Hunter's flip side. A nine-minute, widescreen ballad, it honored the "dudes"— the young male fans Mott had cultivated with perhaps even more fervor than the Who expended in insisting that its followers, "the kids," were "alright." Mick Ronson, ex-Bowie sideman and occasional Mott ally, played some of his best guitar on the album —power chords giving way to soaring, high-register melodies.

Hunter's subsequent records continued the balance of punchy rockers and overblown ballads. *All American Alien Boy* is sharp, but lacks the cohesiveness of *Ian Hunter*. *You're Never Alone With a Schizophrenic* and *Short Back and Sides* (with cool guitar by Mick Jones of the Clash) are straightforward in their rock attack, but less ambitious musically than Hunter's debut. *Shades* is a fair best-of package. *Y U I Orta* placed Hunter and Ronson on equal footing, and it's a terrific Stones-like raver. With the big time strangely eluding him, Hunter remains the best kind of rocker, combining a journeyman's integrity with a veteran's hard-won faith. — P.E.

IVORY JOE HUNTER
★ ★ ★ ★ **I'm Coming Down With the Blues
(Home Cooking, 1989)**

A rhythm & blues singer who moved easily
in country and pop circles, Ivory Joe Hunter
was one of the distinctive voices of the '40s
and '50s. Though his renown has
diminished, Hunter's recordings remain
special events. His plaintive voice with a
hint of a rasp was comforting, even when
Hunter was into his deepest blues, and his
fluid, stride-influenced piano playing was
guaranteed to please and surprise. He was
also one of the first black entrepreneurs in
the music business, founding his own Ivory
label in 1944, before moving on to record
for King, 4 Star and other labels. His first
national success came in 1949, with "Guess
Who" and "Jealous Heart," followed in
1950 by two singles, "I Need You So" and
"I Almost Lost My Mind," that played
around in the upper reaches of the chart. ("I
Almost Lost My Mind" was later given a
lugubrious cover treatment by Pat Boone.)
Some of his most productive years were
spent with Atlantic. One of his most famous
sides, "Since I Met You Baby," peaked at
Number 12 on the pop chart in 1956. His
affinity for country music landed him a
regular spot on the Grand Ole Opry in the
late '60s, leading to an attempted pop
comeback in 1971 with the Epic album *The
Return of Ivory Joe Hunter.*

In 1968 Hunter returned to his native
Texas and cut the sides that comprise *I'm
Coming Down With the Blues.* Most of the
tracks are Hunter originals written for this
album, in addition to new versions of "I
Almost Lost My Mind" and "Empty
Arms." Hunter's in good form, his voice
sounding strong and his performances
inspired. As evidence of his versatility, he
offers a new country song, "The Cold Gray
Light of Dawn," as well as a classically
constructed pop song, "The Masquerade Is
Over." In-the-pocket '50s-style R&B is the
rule, though, and it sounds as if a good time
was had by all. Hunter's Atlantic albums
are now out of print, but his original
versions of "Since I Met You Baby" and
"Empty Arms" can be found on the
historical collection, *Atlantic Rhythm &
Blues, Volume 3: 1955–1958.* — D.M.

HUNTERS AND COLLECTORS
★ ★ ★½ **World of Stone (EP) (White Label
Aus., 1981)**
★ ★ ★ ★ **Hunters and Collectors (White
Label Aus., 1982)**
★ ★ ★ ★ **Payload (EP) (White Label Aus.,
1982)**
★ ★ ★ ★½ **Hunters and Collectors (A&M,
1982)**
★ ★ ★ **The Fireman's Curse (EP) (White
Label Aus., 1983)**
★ ★ ★ ★ **The Jaws of Life (Slash, 1984)**
★ ★ ★ ★ **The Way to Go Out (White Label
Aus., 1985)**
★ ★ ★ ★ **Human Frailty (I.R.S., 1986)**
★ ★ ★ **Living Daylight (EP) (I.R.S.,
1987)**
★ ★ ★ ★ **Fate (I.R.S., 1988)**
★ ★ ★ ★½ **Ghost Nation (Atlantic, 1989)**
★ ★ ★ ★½ **Collected Works (I.R.S., 1990)**

Like Gang of Four or the Red Hot Chili
Peppers, Australia's Hunters and Collectors
specialize in a brittle, rhythm-driven
approach that's often described as "white
funk" but in fact derives from something
quite different. In this case, H&C owe less
to R&B than to a sort of punkish tribalism,
the principal difference being that this band,
unlike most punk acts, built its pulse on the
soulful give-and-take of bass and drums, not
the aggressive clangor of rhythm guitar and
drums. As expressed in the murky
collectivism of the *World of Stone* EP, the
band's sound was just one more variation
on the bass-heavy drone of PiL, but by the
time of "Talking to a Stranger" (from
Hunters and Collectors) and "Towtruck"
(from the *Payload* EP), it had evolved into
something utterly unique. Instead of trying
to write great groove tunes, the group wrote
tunes that used bits of melody—whether
from Mark Seymour's vocals or the band's
three-piece brass section—to frame the
groove, reconciling the rhythm section's
propulsive energies with the band's need for
structure and focus. (All of the *Payload* EP,
plus "Talking to a Stranger" and two other
tracks from *Hunters and Collectors* were
released in the U.S. as *Hunters and
Collectors.*)

Having found its sound, the band
discovered that it wasn't entirely sure what
to do with it, and turned to German
producer Conny Plank for direction. Plank's
first impulse, communal improvisation, was
a mistake, leading to the conceptual
dead-end of *The Fireman's Curse.* But *The
Jaws of Life,* also recorded with Plank, finds
the band back on course, ripping through
the brutal cadences of "The Way to Go
Out" and "Betty's Worry" or "The Slab,"
and even delivering a credible version of
Ray Charles's "I Believe." Best of all, Plank
managed to capture all the chaos and
aggression of the band's live sound, a fact

borne out by the in-concert *The Way to Go Out.*

Still, the fact that the band's songbook relied more on compromise than composition kept H&C from realizing its potential. That began to change with *Human Frailty,* which balances the rhythmic energies of "Is There Anybody in There" and "The 99th Home Position" with the melodic focus of "Everything's On Fire" and "Throw Your Arms Around Me"; the *Living Daylight* EP ices the cake with the memorable melancholy of "January Rain" (included, along with the rest of the EP, on the *Human Frailty* CD). *Fate* (which had been released in Australia in slightly different form as *What's a Few Men?*) continues in that vein, thanks to the urgent "Do You See What I See?" and the poignant "Back on the Breadline," but *Ghost Nation* ups the ante once again, blurring the distance between the band's ballads and groove tunes, and delivering an almost unassailable blend of melody and rhythm with the likes of "When the River Runs Dry," "Crime of Passion" and "The Way You Live." *Collected Works* is, as its title suggests, a best-of, but though the Australian version spans the group's output up to *Ghost Nation,* the American album only goes as far as *Fate.* —J.D.C.

MICHAEL HURLEY

★★★ **Long Journey (Rounder, 1976)**
★★★ **Snockgrass (Rounder, 1980)**
★★ **Blue Navigator (Rooster, 1984)**
★★★ **Watertower (Fundamental, 1989)**
A cheerfully idiosyncratic singer and songwriter, Hurley specializes in a sort of off-brand country music that lacks both the slick sophistication of Nashville product and the offhand virtuosity of bluegrass and its variants. In other words, it's the country market's equivalent to alternative rock, meaning that unless whimsical songwriting and rough-hewn arrangements hold special appeal, these hardly qualify as essential listening. —J.D.C.

HÜSKER DÜ

★ **Land Speed Record (New Alliance, 1981)**
★★ **Everything Falls Apart (Reflex, 1982)**
★★★ **Metal Circus (EP) (SST, 1983)**
★★★½ **Zen Arcade (SST, 1984)**
★★★½ **New Day Rising (SST, 1984)**
★★★★ **Flip Your Wig (SST, 1985)**
★★★★½ **Candy Apple Grey (Warner Bros., 1986)**

★★★★★ **Warehouse: Songs and Stories (Warner Bros., 1987)**
A pop band with roots in an anti-pop movement, Hüsker Dü gave no quarter in any direction. Its material could be gratingly aggressive or endearingly tuneful, and was often both at once. But instead of hobbling Hüsker Dü's sound, this collision of melody and noise actually enhanced it, giving it an exuberance that lifts the band's best recordings above the usual limits of either hardcore or pop.

None of this is evident on *Land Speed Record,* a sloppy, lo-fi live recording from 1981 that presents the Hüskers as a by-the-numbers hardcore act, nor does the studio setting of *Everything Falls Apart* significantly improve things. But the *Metal Circus* EP presents the first glimmerings of pop potential in "It's Not Funny Anymore," an engaging rocker that maintains its sense of melody no matter how loudly the band rages. But that's one small step compared to the giant leap of *Zen Arcade,* a double album boasting 23 songs (which were recorded and mixed in a mere 85 hours). Although it's as much a testament to the band's energy and endurance as to its musical growth, it's hard to deny the strength of these songs, whether as breathlessly insistent as "Whatever" and "I'll Never Forget You," or as haunting as "The Tooth Fairy and the Princess." Of course, *Zen Arcade* might have been even more amazing had its manic sprawl been better focused, and the same goes for the relatively more compact *New Day Rising.* Even though this album avoids mantric marathons like *Zen Arcade's* 14-minute "Recurring Dreams," songs like "Plans I Make" or "New Day Rising" do linger long after they've made their point. But both of the band's songwriters—guitarist Bob Mould and drummer Grant Hart—continue to exhibit an awesome degree of musical ingenuity, and pieces like "I Apologize," "Powerline" and "Celebrated Summer" more than make up for the occasional overindulgence. There's even less flab on *Flip Your Wig,* thanks to tightly arranged and tuneful compositions like "Flexible Flyer" and the irrepressible "Makes No Sense at All."

Flip Your Wig was the band's last indie album, but the Hüskers' jump to Warner Bros. with *Candy Apple Grey* didn't cause half as much consternation among its fans as acoustic tunes like "Too Far Down" and "Hardly Getting Over It." A pity, since the only thing that separates those songs from the band's usual sound is a lack of amplifier overdrive. Besides, it's not as if the rest of the album is wanting in that department, for there's plenty of clangor to the likes of "Dead Set on Destruction" and "I Don't Know for Sure." The Hüskers had learned their lesson, however, and *Warehouse: Songs and Stories* is as raucous as it is tuneful, approaching the breadth of *Zen Arcade* but far surpassing it in depth. Indeed, this is probably the band's most consistent album, moving from strength to strength as it roars from the buoyant "Charity, Chastity, Prudence and Hope" to the dark "Ice Cold Ice," to the jazzy "She Floated Away," to the classic chorus of "She's a Woman (and Now He Is a Man)." — J.D.C.

BRIAN HYLAND
★★ **Greatest Hits (Rhino, 1987)**
In terms of advanced thinking, how about Brian Hyland singing way back in 1961, "Tie me down/make me behave," in his hit, "Let Me Belong to You"? Seems like he was onto the seamy side of human behavior well ahead of Lou Reed. Be that as it may, Hyland was a legitimate teen idol with an impressively engineered, grease-laden pompadour, and a somewhat bland delivery.

His strength was in being surrounded by good producers and players; however trivial the material—and it's hard to find anything more trivial than "Itsy Bitsy Teenie Weenie Yellow Polka Dot Bikini"—Hyland's records always sounded good. He lives mostly on the strength of one bona fide summer classic, "Sealed With a Kiss," which is all atmosphere and feeling, both on the part of the players and of Hyland, whose singing here achieves a degree of subtlety and feeling uncommon to most of his other cuts. Which is not to suggest he had nothing going for him: his problem was consistency. Early songs such as "Ginny Come Lately" and "Sealed With a Kiss," and later efforts, such as his cover of Curtis Mayfield's "Gypsy Woman," show real depth; indeed, Hyland's delicate treatments of the tender lyrics in the country-inflected "Warmed Over Kisses (Left Over Love)" and "I'm Afraid to Go Home" indicate he might have been able to make a transition to the mainstream of that genre after he was beached as a teen idol. But then other entries—"Let Me Belong to You," "Hung Up in Your Eyes"—are so insubstantial that a short-lived career seems inevitable.
— D.M.

JANIS IAN

★★   Janis Ian (Polydor, 1967)
★   Present Company (Capitol, 1971)
★★   Stars (Columbia, 1974)
★★★½ Between the Lines (Columbia, 1975)
★★★   Aftertones (Columbia, 1975)
★★½ Miracle Row (Columbia, 1977)
★★   Night Rains (Columbia, 1979)
★★   Restless Eyes (Columbia, 1981)

Janis Ian's white-knuckled grasping for significance and big statements can wear at times, but her heart is so obviously in the right place—with the misfits and ugly ducklings—that it's hard not to find her hyper-seriousness touching. Causing a stir in 1967 with the interracial love song "Society's Child" (off *Janis Ian*), she hit big nearly a decade later with the high-school confessional "At Seventeen." The centerpiece of her only solid album, *Between the Lines*, the song is dogged by wordiness, and its strained attempts at poetry make it formally clumsy—but it conveys with total empathy the ache of adolescent alienation. The painstaking arrangements of the rest of the songs and the anguished quaver of Ian's tiny voice may be off-putting to cynics, but she often manages a very fine and telling image, and some of her melodies are haunting. *Aftertones* is a lesser *Between the Lines*, and it's fairly good. The rest are only for those won over by "At Seventeen."
   — P.E.

IAN AND SYLVIA

★★★   Ian and Sylvia (Vanguard, 1962)
★★★½ Northern Journey (1964; Vanguard, 1990)
★★★   Four Strong Winds (Vanguard, 1964)
★★★   Early Morning Rain (Vanguard, 1965)
★★★   Play One More (Vanguard, 1966)
★★½ So Much for Dreaming (Vanguard, 1967)
★★½ Ian and Sylvia (Columbia, 1967)
★   Nashville (Vanguard, 1968)
★★   Full Circle (Vanguard, 1968)
★★½ The Best of Ian and Sylvia (Vanguard, 1968)
★★★   Greatest Hits, Vol. 1 (1970; Vanguard, 1987)
★★★   Greatest Hits, Vol. 2 (Vanguard, 1971)
★★   You Were on My Mind (Columbia, 1972)
★★   The Best of Ian and Sylvia (Columbia, 1973)

On guitar and autoharp, Ian and Sylvia began in the early '60s as very engaging folk singers covering traditional Scots-English fare, spirituals, Gordon Lightfoot songs and Tommy Makem tunes. Indeed, their early Vanguard liner notes are curious for their shuddering disdain of anything pop—these two Canadians were hardly protest singers, but they were adamantly artists with a cause. Rock & roll was in its pre-Beatles doldrums, and Ian and Sylvia (along with the Clancy Brothers, Joan Baez and the Kingston Trio) crusaded against all forms of commercialism with an intensity that now seems a bit quaint. Soon, however, the duo relaxed enough to attempt clear-voiced, reverent versions of Dylan (the approach pays off with "Tomorrow Is a Long Time," but doesn't work with their brittle remake of "The Mighty Quinn").

Their first four albums are their strongest, especially *Four Strong Winds*, with its heartfelt versions of "Spanish Is a Loving Tongue" and "Poor Lazarus." But the virtues of their style—careful taste, severe accompaniment, and an air of muted exuberance—are period ones; Ian and Sylvia were very pleasant, but not very exciting (Sylvia's "You Were on My Mind" was done much more snappily, for instance, by We Five). Their greatest-hits packages could benefit from editing; the ballads ("Four

Strong Winds," "Un Canadien Errant") are almost always lovely, but the happier, more rousing fare ("Little Beggarman," "When I Was a Cowboy") are strictly for hootenanny addicts. — P.E.

ICE CUBE
★ ★ ★½ **AmeriKKKa's Most Wanted (Priority, 1990)**
★ ★ ★ ★ **Kill at Will (EP) (Priority, 1990)**
★ ★½ **Death Certificate (Priority, 1991)**

An alumnus of N.W.A and responsible for many of the toughest and best rhymes on *Straight Outta Compton*, Ice Cube approached *AmeriKKKa's Most Wanted* with all the bad attitude you'd expect. Boasting that he was "The Nigga Ya Love to Hate," he played the role to the hilt, but despite his fondness for 9mm bang-bang, there are flashes of brilliance on the album, particularly "It's a Man's World," in which Ice Cube spouts the testosterone party line only to take a few from ferociously articulate female rapper Yo-Yo. Such give-and-take is rare in the hyper-competitive world of gangsta rap, where anything less than a "fuck you" is taken as a sign of weakness, and suggests that Ice Cube may grow beyond the genre. "Dead Homiez" and "The Product," both from *Kill at Will*, recast the gangsta style with a view to its consequences, but *Death Certificate* turns that one step forward into two steps back as Cube's pleas against social self-destruction are undone by the violent vehemence of his gangsta rap rhetoric. His relentless disparagement of Asians, gays, white "devils" and bourgeois blacks far outweigh his scorn for drug dealers, gang-bangers and easy women. As a result, neither the raw wit of "Robin Lench" nor the considerable musicality of "Steady Mobbin' " and "True to the Game" is enough to redeem *Certificate*. — J.D.C.

ICEHOUSE
★ ★½ **Icehouse (Chrysalis, 1981)**
★ ★ **Primitive Man (Chrysalis, 1982)**
★ ★ **Sidewalk (Chrysalis, 1984)**
★ ★½ **Measure for Measure (Chrysalis, 1986)**
★ ★ **Man of Colours (Chrysalis, 1987)**
★ ★½ **Great Southern Land (Chrysalis, 1989)**

Professional and pleasant, these Aussie swoon-rockers are remarkable only for their narrow range of influences—and how slight the distance they ever stray from them. When frontman Iva Davies isn't mimicking Bryan Ferry with early Icehouse, he's aping David Bowie on the later stuff. The

Roxy-ish "Hey Little Girl," off *Primitive Man* is engaging; *Measure for Measure* features Eno all over the place; most of Icehouse's records, however, are interchangeable. *Great Southern Land* is the best-of, although it's really no stronger an album than any of the others. — P.E.

ICE-T
★ ★ ★ **Rhyme Pays (Sire, 1987)**
★ ★½ **Power (Sire, 1988)**
★ ★ ★ **The Iceberg/Freedom of Speech . . . Just Watch What You Say (Sire, 1989)**
★ ★ ★ ★ **O.G. Original Gangster (Sire, 1991)**
★ ★ ★½ **Body Count (Sire, 1992)**

Ice-T wasn't the first gangsta rapper (Schoolly D was the head of that class), nor was he the first West Coast rapper of note (Too Short beat him on that one). But Ice-T put L.A. rap on the map and established the sound of West Coast hard core, and that makes him a major player in the rap world. *Rhyme Pays* establishes his M.O. with an Uzi-illustrated logo on the cover and a set of crime-but-no-punishment raps inside. Although much of his tough talk simply seemed a matter of establishing his bona fides, the album's standout, "6 'N the Morning," demonstrates a narrative sense that gives the track far more edge than his sing-song delivery and the drum-driven groove. With *Power*, he upgrades his musical content—stronger beats, funkier samples—and backs off a bit from the criminal-minded perspective of his debut. Trouble is, his ambition often outstrips his ideas; "Drama" is a nicely sarcastic morality tale, but it's hard to be impressed by the anti-drug sermonizing of "I'm Your Pusher." *Power* also included a nasty little number called "Girls L.G.B.N.A.F." which created a minor furor when the P.M.R.C. discovered that the initials stood for "Let's Get Butt Naked and Fuck." No big deal, really, but it did prompt Ice-T to consider the issues of free speech and censorship, subjects that loom large on *The Iceberg/ Freedom of Speech . . . Just Watch What You Say*. Naturally, Ice-T's take on the subject is mostly pure defiance, but his awareness of such issues puts a different edge on his sex and violence raps, one which notes, as "Lethal Weapon" puts it, that brain power is more potent than any armament. How Ice-T uses that brain, however, isn't likely to win him too many friends on the left or right. As much as his anti-authoritarian viewpoint insists on absolute free speech, what he says may strike some listeners as offensive in the extreme, as with *O.G. Original Gangster*, on which the rapper tries to justify his use of the words "bitch" and "nigger." Even so, what *O.G.* lacks in politesse it makes up in power, delivering tough talk and hard beats with uncompromising intensity.

Interestingly, *O.G.* also found Ice-T dabbling with thrash, a pursuit he takes up in full with *Body Count*. Intensely political, exultantly provocative, it manages to be as hard as speed metal, as soulful as the best rap, and funnier than either. — J.D.C.

BILLY IDOL

★ ★½ **Don't Stop (EP) (Chrysalis, 1981)**
★ ★ ★ **Billy Idol (Chrysalis, 1982)**
★ ★½ **Rebel Yell (Chrysalis, 1983)**
★ ★½ **Whiplash Smile (Chrysalis, 1986)**
★ ★ ★½ **Vital Idol (Chrysalis, 1987)**
★ ★ ★ **Charmed Life (Chrysalis, 1990)**

When Billy Idol left the British punk band Generation X and moved to New York for a solo career, he took one key Gen X track with him. Re-recorded with a jumpy robo-disco pulse, "Dancing With Myself" suited the early-'80s club scene to a tee—a guaranteed, enduring floor-filler. The *Don't Stop* EP backs up "Dancing" with a grating cover of Tommy James's "Mony Mony" and a couple of throwaways.

Idol became an early proponent of rock video; his sneering leather 'n peroxide punk pose was custom-made for the new medium. Still, he retains the knack for crafting obvious, but unforgettable hit singles; there's usually one stone-cold knockout punch per album. Teaming up with guitarist Steve Stevens, Idol struck platinum with his *Billy Idol* and *Rebel Yell*. "White Wedding" (from *Billy Idol*) stands as his crowning moment of hard-rock glory, a snarling Doors update. The MTV "classics" on *Rebel Yell* lose their walloping impact without the visuals, however: "Flesh for Fantasy" sounds wan and jaded, while "Eyes Without a Face" barely registers. After a layoff, Idol snapped back in 1986 with his most ambitious record: saturated with the essence of Presley, "I Forgot to Be Your Lover" is actually a hopped-up cover of a William Bell Stax/Volt nugget. Unsuprisingly, the rest of *Whiplash Smile* flattens out immediately after that audacious opening cut. *Charmed Life,* from 1990, is only a marginal improvement: the hit "Cradle of Love" adds a knowing wink to Idol's trademark sneer, and "Trouble With the Sweet Stuff" burns all the way down.

But a roaming, desperately uninspired version of "L.A. Woman" irrevocably points Billy Idol toward a familiar destination. "All right, Las Vegas, are you ready to rawk and roll?!!" The overblown remixed-hits package says it all; *Vital Idol* is both a cynical recycling ploy and the essential Billy Idol album. Catch it before he falls. — M.C.

JULIO IGLESIAS

★ ★½ **Hey! (Columbia, 1980)**
★ ★½ **From a Child to a Woman (Columbia, 1981)**
★ ★ **Moments (Columbia, 1982)**
★ **In Concert (Columbia, 1983)**
★½ **Julio (Columbia, 1983)**
★½ **1100 Bel Air Place (Columbia, 1984)**
★ ★ **Libra (Columbia, 1985)**
★ ★ **NonStop (Columbia, 1988)**
★ ★ ★ **Starry Night (Columbia, 1990)**

Arguably the most popular singer on Earth, Julio Iglesias is a megastar in Latin America and a major draw in Europe. In the U.S., however, he's a cult figure at best, something that says less about his strengths as a singer than America's taste in pop music. Although he is frequently described as a crooner, Iglesias's singing style is more subtle than that; instead of employing the mellifluous understatement of a Bing Crosby, his approach relies on a light, lyric tenor and liberal use of vibrato that lends an almost bel canto glow to his singing. As a result, he manages to caress a melody with such tenderness that it's easy to understand why the women in his audience react with such swooning adoration.

Iglesias makes admirable use of that sound throughout his first three albums, which combine breathy balladry with occasional upbeat numbers like "Ron Y Coca Cola (Rum and Coca Cola)" from *Hey!* or "Volver a Empezar (Begin the Beguine)," from *From a Child to a Woman*. All three albums are listenable, although the cheesy disco arrangements on *Moments* can be trying; *In Concert*, on the other hand, is recommended only to those dying to hear his rendition of "Feelings." *Julio*, which draws heavily from his first three albums, marks Iglesias's first play for the American market. It's a mixed effort, though; his English is passable, but the music doesn't really translate, particularly when he tries oddball stuff like the disco-mariachi "Oú Est Passée Ma Bohéme?" So with *1100 Bel Air Place*, Iglesias begins to Americanize his sound. He's on fairly solid ground when he can count on guests like Diana Ross ("All of You") or Willie Nelson (the charming "To All the Girls I've Loved Before"), but sounds like an interloper otherwise. It isn't that Iglesias has no feel for American pop idioms—he just doesn't have the voice. Take his treatment of the Hollies hit "The Air That I Breathe." Though Iglesias has a good sense of how to phrase the song, his ethereal tenor lacks the oomph of Allan Clarke's vocal on the original, making this version sound wimpy and ineffectual. No wonder his next album, *Libra*, found him returning to the relative safety of Spanish and Portuguese pop. As with *1100 Bel Air Place*, much of the music on *NonStop* seems calculated to appeal to American tastes. Some tracks are painfully transparent attempts at chart success, but the duet with Stevie Wonder offers some genuine musical sparks instead of the usual celebrity bonding. The Albert Hammond-produced *Starry Night* finally puts Iglesias on the right course, finding material ("Can't Help Falling in Love," "Mona Lisa," "Yesterday, When I Was Young") more palatable to American tastes, but better suited to Iglesias's delivery. — J.D.C.

THE IMPRESSIONS
★ ★ ★ ★ ★ **The Impressions' Greatest Hits (MCA, 1989)**
Beginning with "Gypsy Woman," from 1961, *The Impressions' Greatest Hits* defines the sweet inspiration of soul music. This Chicago-based harmony group amplifies its gospel conviction ("Amen," "Meeting Over Yonder") through a lush, orchestral pop approach ("It's All Right," "You Must Believe Me"). Working with arranger Johnny Pate, group leader Curtis Mayfield constructs a supple wall of sound: his dynamic string arrangements underline, rather than undercut, the urgency of his messages. "People Get Ready" and "Keep On Pushing" reflect and reinforce the hard-earned optimism of the civil rights movement. These two spiritual pleas sound more relevant—and necessary—than ever. Original lead singer Jerry Butler left after an initial hit, "For Your Precious Love," in 1958, and was replaced by Fred Cash. (It's no accident that Butler later achieved solo success with producers Gamble and Huff; the precise richness of Curtis Mayfield's songwriting and production strongly foreshadows the Sound of Philadelphia.) Mayfield, Cash and Sam Gooden carried on together until 1970, when Mayfield departed to pursue a solo career. While Motown hits

of the mid-60's go for your gut, *The Impressions' Greatest Hits* aims a little higher—and never misses. — M.C.

THE INCREDIBLE STRING BAND
★ ★	**The Incredible String Band (Elektra, 1966)**
★ ★ ★	**The 5000 Spirits or the Layers of the Onion (Elektra, 1967)**
★ ★ ★ ★ ★	**The Hangman's Beautiful Daughter (1967; Hannibal, 1986)**
★ ★ ★½	**Wee Tam (Elektra, 1968)**
★ ★ ★½	**The Big Huge (Elektra, 1968)**
★ ★ ★½	**Changing Horses (Elektra, 1969)**
★ ★ ★½	**I Looked Up (Elektra, 1970)**
★ ★ ★½	**Relics (Elektra, 1970)**
★ ★ ★½	**U (Elektra, 1971)**
★ ★ ★	**Liquid Acrobat as Regards the Air (Elektra, 1972)**
★ ★ ★	**Earth Span (Island, 1972)**
★ ★ ★	**No Ruinous Feud (Island, 1973)**
★ ★ ★	**Hard Rope and Silken Twine (Island, 1974)**
★ ★ ★	**Seasons They Change (Island, 1974)**

Garbed in ragtag cloaks like Breughel peasants and disporting themselves on sitar, guitar, oud, gimbri, fiddle and anything else that can be strummed or plucked, the Incredible String Band consisted of arcane '60s concept-folksters—hippies masquerading as medieval mummers. Only a few degrees odder, perhaps, than the Stones mimicking Delta bluesmen, the conceit was yet a remarkably quaint and precious one. Through dauntless zeal, however, ISB mainmen Robin Williamson and Mike Heron brought it off intriguingly in the band's early days—and continued gamely through a dozen albums. Occupying a middle ground between the straighter Olde English revival of peers like Fairport Convention or John Renbourn and the cosmic winsomeness of Donovan, the group became a monster among English counterculturalists by feeding an appetite for theater, ruralist Utopianism and acid romance.

With their third album, *The Hangman's Beautiful Daughter*, the Incredibles achieved their finest synthesis of curiosities—a fusion of pre-Renaissance and Mideastern riffs coupled with references to Gilbert and Sullivan and church music. Their lyrics—as indicated by such titles as "Koeeoaddi There," "Mercy I Cry City" and "The Minotaur's Song"—seemed like Joseph Campbell run amok. But the intensity of the duo's lovely singing invested their private mythologies with a sort of free-form spiritual buzz, even if there's just no telling what it signified.

Wee Tam, The Big Huge and *Changing Horses* all contain flashes of idiosyncratic delight: the group sings about Oliver Twist, Hitler, caterpillars and love, supported by two regular backup singers named, with militant whimsy, Licorice and Rose. The longer songs (10- and 12-minute pastiches), however, show the band beginning to nod. By the time of *No Ruinous Feud* and *Hard Rope and Silken Twine*, the ensemble had doffed its jester regalia and settled for bell-bottoms. The fashion shift was telling: they'd moved (as close as they'd get) to more mainstream music. While the instrumentation remained as eclectic as ever, the material had lost much of its early, lunar grace. *Relics* is the group's greatest hits collection; it doesn't hang together, and *The Hangman's Beautiful Daughter* remains definitive. — P.E.

INDIGO GIRLS

★ ★ ★½ **Indigo Girls (Epic, 1989)**
★ ★ ★ **Strange Fire (Epic, 1989)**
★ ★ ★ **Nomads Indians Saints (Epic, 1990)**
★ ★ ★½ **Back on the Bus, Y'all (Epic, 1991)**
In the wake of Tracy Chapman, Suzanne Vega and the other strong forces behind the late-'80s folk revival, this Atlanta duo found a readily receptive audience for its accomplished acoustic fare. "Closer to Fine," off *Indigo Girls,* became a college-radio standard, and the Girls' Dylan-derived lyrics, occasional nod to R.E.M. and constant touring made them stars. With a sensibility incorporating feminism, New Age self-assertion, environmental awareness and the remnant spirituality of their native South, Amy Ray and Emily Saliers were right for their moment. Their singing an engaging bittersweet blend, they also rocked catchily at times—and if a song like "Southland in the Springtime" from *Nomads Indians Saints* sounded a tad too glossy, the handcrafted feel of most of their material capitalized instead on the earnestness that is their signal strength. The live *Back on the Bus, Y'all* is the Indigos at their rawest—and their best. — P.E.

INFORMATION SOCIETY

★ ★ ★½ **Information Society (Tommy Boy, 1988)**
★ ★ ★ ★ **Hack (Tommy Boy, 1990)**

Considering their art-rock influences and technological inclinations, it would be fair to expect these former Minneapolitans to end up with a sound that's somewhere between Ultravox and Figures On a Beach. Instead, their strongest songs are pure Latin hip-hop—an unexpected turn, but a pleasure to hear, particularly given the dark spin Kurt Valaquen's tart voice lends the upbeat melodies. *Hack* is particularly noteworthy, if only for finding (through sampling) the common ground between James Brown and Kraftwerk. — J.D.C.

JAMES INGRAM

★ ★ **It's Your Night (Qwest, 1983)**
★ ★ **It's Real (Warner Bros., 1989)**
★ ★ ★ **The Power of Great Music (Warner Bros., 1991)**
As a vocal stylist, James Ingram is capable of handling almost any kind of material, from the funkiest dance tune to the schlockiest ballad. Trouble is, he handles them all the same way—with flawless technique and minimal emotional involvement. Granted, that's less of a problem with the dance material, and on "It's Real" (from *It's Real*), he rides the rhythm section's New Jack groove with such assurance you'd almost think he was working up a sweat. But Ingram's true specialty is the sort of sappy, theatrical showpieces found on soundtracks and celebrated at Grammy ceremonies. Meaning, in other words, that *The Power of Great Music*—a best-of including "One Hundred Ways," the General Hospital theme "Baby, Come to Me," and the movie theme "Somewhere Out There"—is about as good as his albums are ever going to get. — J.D.C.

THE INK SPOTS

★ ★ ★ ★ ★ **The Best of the Ink Spots (MCA, 1980)**
★ ★ **Just Like Old Times (Open Sky, 1982)**
★ ★ ★ ★ **Greatest Hits (MCA, 1989)**
Founded in 1934, the Ink Spots developed a pop-oriented group harmony style that kept them on the charts from 1939 through 1951 and influenced many of the most important vocal groups of the Fifties. The group's trademark was the contrasting voices of lead tenor Bill Kenny and bass singers Orville Jones and Herb Kenny (the latter joining in 1944 after Jones's death). Kenny, in particular, with his impeccable control and diction in the highest register of his tenor, became the singer's singer, a master of

technique with a peerless sense of drama. Of the pre-rock era vocal groups, only the Ravens exerted an influence comparable to that of the Ink Spots.

MCA's *Best of* is the most complete overview of the Ink Spots remaining in print. At 24 tracks, it has nine more songs than the otherwise-excellent *Greatest Hits* album, and these are nine tracks that must be heard. "We'll Meet Again," "Until the Real Thing Comes Along," "I Cover the Waterfront" and "It Is No Secret" are among the songs unavailable on *Greatest Hits* that are classic performances. Both sets include the original versions of songs that were hits in the Fifties and Sixties for the Platters—"My Prayer," "To Each His Own," "If I Didn't Care" and "I'll Never Smile Again"—and one that has become a staple of the Manhattan Transfer's repertoire, "Java Jive." Unfortunately, the cassette version of *Best of* contains no liner or biographical information, while *Greatest Hits* offers the briefest of biographies, songwriter credits and release dates.

Just Like Old Times features a latter-day version of the Ink Spots formed by original member Ivory "Deek" Watson. The harmonies are smooth, the material passable, but lead singer Gene Miller's attempts at Kenny-style vocals miss the mark. Accept no substitutes. — D.M.

INNER CITY
★ ★ ★½ **Big Fun (Virgin, 1989)**
★ ★ **Fire (Virgin, 1990)**
When Inner City burst onto the club scene with "Good Life," the duo's genuinely soulful approach to house music seemed a breath of fresh air, and most of *Big Fun* carries the same spirit (especially later versions of the album, which also included the luscious "Whatcha Gonna Do With My Lovin' "). Unfortunately, *Fire* found I.C. mastermind Kevin Saunderson moving toward a colder, techno-intense sound; though it still delivered big beats, the lack of pop content greatly reduced its appeal. — J.D.C.

INSPIRAL CARPETS
★ ★½ **Life (Mute/Elektra, 1990)**
★ ★ ★ **The Beast Inside (Mute/Elektra, 1991)**
Musical ambitiousness, strong melodies and a striving after greatness make this quintet more than a flicker of the lava lamp that flashed on Manchester's ecstatic dance floors. *Life* was a strong debut, inspiring an avid cult. *The Beast Inside* (1991) marked a

leap forward—"Sleep Well Tonight" recalled the Velvets at their most Teutonically romantic; "Grip" pounded fiercely; the piano work on "Mermaid" was nifty, like Rod Argent with the Zombies. Plainly the Carpets' centerpiece, Clint Boon's keyboards sounded both B-movieish and Voice-of-God-like. You never knew if he was trying for Bach or "In-a-Gadda-Da-Vida." Intriguing, no matter what. — P.E.

THE INTRUDERS
★ ★ ★ **Intruders Super Hits (1969; Gamble/CBS, 1973)**
★ ★ ★ ★ **Save the Children (Gamble/CBS, 1973)**
This long-running Philadelphia vocal quartet served as a laboratory for producers Kenny Gamble and Leon Huff. The Philly International masterminds developed their precisely defined sound on the Intruders' late-'60s singles. The pop crossovers "Cowboys to Girls" and "(Love Is Like a) Baseball Game" attach dramatic arrangements to novel "hook" metaphors, while R&B chart singles such as "Together" and "Sad Girl" revert to a more traditional ballad style. *Super Hits* is only an adequate summary, though; it includes the aforementioned cuts but skips over such invigorating uptempo jaunts as "Give Her a Transplant" and "(Win, Place or Show) She's a Winner." And the Intruders' true "super hit" comes from the out-of-print album that followed: "I'll Always Love My Mama" is peak-period Philly Soul. Maximizing the warm crack in lead singer Sam "Little Sonny" Brown's drawling tenor, Gamble and Huff expertly mix heartfelt sentiments with clear-eyed realism and an irresistible beat. Arguably, disco begins here: the fleet guitar-and-horn stroke that ignites "Mama" points the way toward a new, non-rock dance groove. Historical considerations aside, *Save the Children* also qualifies as one of the few consistently satisfying albums to come from the Philly factory: for once, even the cover versions (Gil Scott Heron's title track and Paul Simon's "Mother and Child Reunion") fit into a coherent overall picture. — M.C.

INXS
★ ★½ **INXS (Atco, 1980)**
★ ★½ **Underneath the Colours (1981; Atco, 1984)**
★ ★ ★ **Shabooh Shoobah (Atco, 1982)**
★ ★ ★ **The Swing (Atco, 1984)**
★ ★ ★ ★½ **Listen Like Thieves (Atlantic, 1985)**
★ ★ ★ ★½ **Kick (Atlantic, 1987)**

★ ★ ★½ **X (Atlantic, 1990)**
★ ★ ★½ **Live Baby Live (Atlantic, 1991)**
With singer Michael Hutchence exuding a
classic star's bravado and the three Farriss
brothers providing the essential instrumental
muscle for this Aussie sextet, INXS had
become an irresistible rock force by the end
of the '80s. Finding a cohesive style, though,
took them a while.

INXS was all busy new-wave urgency;
Hutchence's Jaggeresque vocal style was
already very developed, but the non-R&B
fusion of sax and a big beat (somewhat
along the lines of early Graham Parker)
didn't quite come off, and the wordy songs
were unfocused. By the time of *Shabooh
Shoobah*, however, the band had begun
working out the kinks; they'd arrived,
through the agency of producer Mark Opitz,
at the big production sound that suited
them—and they'd started paring down their
songs to thick riffs and crunchy rhythms.
On a few numbers, Hutchence introduced
the deep Jim Morrison-like delivery that
would become a mainstay of his repertoire.
And on "Old World New World," he
debuted his interesting—and very
postmodern—trick of gathering together
potent sound-bite phrases (the song alludes
to everything from Shambala to "talking
digital") and shuffling them up with
haphazard, sometimes provocative results.

On *The Swing* INXS found direction. Nile
Rodgers produced the driving "Original
Sin," and with it the band began formatting
spare, elegant funk. "Burn for You" and
"All the Voices" also made much of
high-tech textures, as INXS began using the
studio as its weapon of choice. *The Swing*
was the first hint that the power of this
band lay less in melody or even in hooks
than in atmospheres—either of a dense,
glossy beauty or of a very physical release.
Listen Like Thieves built on these strengths:
"What You Need" was a saxy workout;
"Shine Like It Does" was airy and majestic;
"This Time" borrowed from U2 a
trance-rock momentum. With "Biting
Bullets" and "Red Red Sun," INXS came
on as full-out rockers, a pose that their
customary precision had tended to preclude.

Given the band's new assurance, the
massive success of *Kick* was unsurprising.
Hutchence's telegraphic lyrical style found
strong vehicles in the punchy "New
Sensation" and "Devil Inside," and, with
"Never Tear It Apart" and its gorgeous
synth-cello undergirding, INXS proved
themselves capable of delivering a truly
lovely ballad. Again, Hutchence wrote

songs, mainly about self-assertion or an
inchoate hunger for transcendence, that
tended to suggest or wonder rather than to
state—a posture that allowed for almost any
kind of interpretation. *X* was a sort of *Son
of Kick:* rather than breaking ground, INXS
solidified its position: the sound was crafty,
spacious and inviting, the meaning remained
a teasing mystery. — P.E.

IRON BUTTERFLY
★ **Heavy (Atco, 1968)**
★ ★ **In-a-Gadda-Da-Vida (Atco, 1968)**
★ **Ball (Atco, 1969)**
Purveyors of halfwit mysticism and
pompous noise, Iron Butterfly was notable
among psychedelic groups for forefronting
organ and bass in its sound—and for its
massive, baffling success. With the live
version clocking in at 19 minutes,
"In-a-Gadda-Da-Vida" established Iron
Butterfly as kings of baroque heaviness.
Keyboardist Doug Yule bellowed like Zeus
and noodled away at the Hammond; the
rest of the band followed clangorous suit,
and for a while the band was the
biggest-selling group in Atlantic Records
history. Other than as a curio, Iron Butterfly
is now unlistenable. — P.E.

IRON MAIDEN
★ ★ ★½ **Iron Maiden (Capitol, 1980)**
★ ★½ **Killers (Capitol, 1981)**
★ ★ **Maiden Japan (EP) (Capitol, 1981)**
★ ★ ★ **The Number of the Beast (Capitol,
1982)**
★ ★ **Piece of Mind (Capitol, 1983)**
★ ★½ **Powerslave (Capitol, 1984)**
★ ★ **Live After Death (Capitol, 1985)**
★ ★½ **Somewhere in Time (Capitol, 1986)**
★ ★ ★½ **Seventh Son of a Seventh Son
(Capitol, 1988)**
★ ★ ★½ **No Prayer for the Dying (Epic, 1990)**
★ ★ **Fear of the Dark (Epic, 1992)**
Although the band rode in on the "new
wave of British heavy metal," Iron Maiden
never made any claims to rock & roll
revisionism. Indeed, rather than spurn the
excesses of '70s HM, the band's early output
embraces them, and though *Iron Maiden*
and *Killers* are chockablock with hyperdrive
blues riffs and wankarama guitar solos,
they're offered with such unabashed passion
that even the band's most obvious moves
somehow avoid seeming clichéd.

After *Maiden Japan*, a live EP released
mostly to satisfy fan demand, original
frontman Paul Di'anno was replaced by
former Samson singer Bruce Dickinson, and
the band began moving toward a more

song-oriented approach. Although *The Number of the Beast* is by no means pop-metal, it does move the band further toward the mainstream, thanks to cunningly tuneful numbers like "The Prisoner" and, especially, "Run to the Hills." (The album's references to the anti-Christ also earned the band an undeserved reputation as Satanists.) Both *Piece of Mind* and *Powerslave* proceed in kind, albeit with diminished melodic interest, and *Live After Death* is a lengthy-but-predictable concert document (there's also a video version for those who miss the band's elaborate stage props).

With *Somewhere in Time*, the band begins to vary its sonic palette, augmenting its galloping bass lines and wide-vibrato vocals with occasional quiet bits, apparently in an attempt to make the songs more dramatic (note the slow, "Bolero"-like build-up given "Alexander the Great"). *Seventh Son of a Seventh Son* goes even further, adding synth sequences, acoustic guitars, even—gasp!—a ballad of sorts ("Infinite Dreams"), while fleshing out the vocal line with unexpectedly pop-friendly vocal harmonies on "Can I Play With Madness." More of the same can be found on the intricately arranged *No Prayer for the Dying*, which also boasts the band's all-time-silliest song title: "Public Enema Number One." — J.D.C.

CHRIS ISAAK
★★★   Silvertone (Warner Bros., 1985)
★★★   Chris Isaak (Warner Bros., 1987)
★★★½ Heart Shaped World (Warner Bros., 1989)

There's not a whole lot of variety here. Moody, vibrato-drenched blue rockabilly is what Chris Isaak *does*, though he does work at it. If you've heard "Wicked Game," well, the rest of his repertoire won't exactly come as a shock. Long on atmosphere, these albums lack a distinctive songwriting voice. Isaak has developed into a fairly compelling singer, though: a dreamy cross between his idols Roy Orbison (grand heartbreak) and Chet Baker (offhanded tragedy). That belated 1991 breakout hit (from *Heart Shaped World*) also happens to be his most perfectly realized performance. "Wicked Game" slowly builds to a haunting, forlorn climax: Isaak sighs "love don't love nobody" into the wind. — M.C.

ERNIE ISLEY
★★★½ High Wire (Elektra, 1990)

If imitating Jimi Hendrix were illegal, Ernie Isley would be serving time. In the early '70s, he acted out every rock guitarist's

fantasy—and not only with the sweet, searing solos on "Who's That Lady." Draped in scarves and playing left-handed, he paid howling tribute to Jimi at every Isley Brothers concert. But Isley is no common wannabe; he comes by the influence honestly. Hendrix toured and recorded with the Isleys during the mid-'60s, and evidently their teenage brother was taking notes. Long after his notoriety died down, in fact, Isley rocketed back from oblivion with this solo debut: minus the clone look, with Fender Strat in complete working order. *High Wire* suggests that Ernie has been listening to his brothers' harmonies and ballad-craft over the years; his guitar workouts—more agile than ever—support a range of material. He can be a halting, tentative-sounding singer, though a giving melody (and those six strings) actually makes that sound expressive on "Fare thee Well, Fair-Weather Friend." There are delicious strains of country and vocal R&B amid all the psychedelic probing and chugging drum-machine rhythms here. But be forewarned: when the opportunity to play a solo presents itself, Ernie Isley usually winds up playing two or three. If that sounds like a recommendation, *High Wire* won't let you down. — M.C.

THE ISLEY BROTHERS
★★★½ 3 + 3 (T-Neck/CBS, 1973)
★★★   The Heat Is On/Featuring "Fight the Power" (T-Neck/CBS, 1975)
★★★   Go for Your Guns (T-Neck/CBS, 1977)
★★★   Winner Takes All (T-Neck/CBS, 1979)
★★★   Between the Sheets (T-Neck/CBS, 1983)
★★★★ Greatest Hits, Volume 1 (T-Neck/CBS, 1984)
★★★   Smooth Sailin' (Warner Bros., 1987)
★★★   The Complete UA Sessions (EMI, 1990)
★★★★ The Isley Brothers Story/ Volume 1: The Rockin' Years (1959–68) (Rhino, 1991)
★★★★★ The Isley Brothers Story/ Volume 2: T-Neck Years (1968–85) (Rhino, 1991)

ISLEY BROTHERS FEATURING RONALD ISLEY
★★½ Spend the Night (Warner Bros., 1988)
★★★   Tracks of Life (Warner Bros., 1992)

Ronald, Rudolph and O'Kelly Isley came roaring out of Cincinnati with "Shout Part 1 & 2"; this 1959 rock & roll hit climaxes with a gospel-powered explosion that still gives goose bumps. The Isley Brothers jumped from label to label in the '60s, recording a handful of soul nuggets and a lot of filler (see *The Complete UA Sessions* for ample evidence). Lead singer Ronald—a raw, rangy tenor—and his harmonizing brothers only connected twice during their Tamla residency, but "This Old Heart of Mine (Is Weak for You)" and "I Guess I'll Always Love You" number among the great lost Motown songs. *Volume 1* of the Rhino series summarizes this period fairly well, leaving in some ragged edges along with galvanizing soul workouts like "Twist & Shout," "Respectable" and "Nobody But Me."

In retrospect, the turning point for the Isley Brothers was a young sideman they employed in the mid-'60s: Jimi Hendrix. Though he's barely noticeable on a couple of *UA Sessions* tracks, Hendrix and his probing psychedelic spirit inspired younger brother Ernie Isley. When guitarist Ernie and bass-plucking Marvin joined the clan in the late '60s, the Isley Brothers constructed a bold, funky new sound to match—a grandly appointed soul castle built on solid rock.

"It's Your Thing" established the Isleys' T-Neck label by crossing over to the pop charts. This horny blast of Stax/Volt–style swagger doesn't hint at the new direction, but subsequent R&B hits like "Lay Away," "Work to Do" and "Pop That Thang" (all from 1972) introduce fresh rhythms and stinging lead guitar lines to the elder Isleys' rough-hewn harmony attack. And talk about cover versions! At least Stephen Stills's "Love the One You're With" and Dylan's "Lay Lady Lay" are in the Isleys' thematic ballpark; resuscitating Seals and Crofts' "Summer Breeze" qualifies as a miracle. *3 + 3* and the sweet summer single "That Lady" (a funkadelicized re-reading of an earlier track) brought the Isley Brothers mainstream success in 1973. Here the group settles into a comfortable—if increasingly predictable—game plan, splitting its albums between extended party-jam throwdowns and surprisingly tight, satisfying sex ballads. Over the course of two CDs, Rhino's second Isleys volume collects the cream of the '70s crop. The first disc mines the deep funk vein of "That Lady," peaking with the politicized throb of "Fight the Power." The second reflects the lusty glow of the group's later

years, after beginning with the plaintive "Harvest for the World." Alongside Funkadelic and Earth, Wind and Fire, the Isley Brothers led a crucial musical movement that we've only recently begun to appreciate. Steeped in R&B tradition, *The T-Neck Years* also recalls today's metal-funk cutting edge at times but *never* when the Isley Brothers are singing.   — M.C.

ISLEY JASPER ISLEY
★★★   **Broadway's Closer to Sunset Boulevard (CBS Associated, 1984)**
★★★½ **Caravan of Love (CBS Associated, 1985)**
★★★½ **Different Drummer (CBS Associated, 1987)**

The younger siblings in this soul clan stepped out with longtime sideman Chris Jasper in the early '80s, releasing three solid albums of rock-enhanced romantic funk that somehow escaped notice. The rough and supple harmonies of the elder Isley Brothers are missed, of course—especially on the love-me-all-over slow numbers. But Isley Jasper Isley compensate with a rich, deliciously synthesized groove that's further enhanced by Ernie Isley's slinky psychedelic guitar leads (Marvin Isley plays drums). Ernie and keyboardist Jasper both grow into their newfound roles as vocalists. The debut bounces between "Sex Drive" and "Love Is Gonna Last Forever," then finally arrives with the perfectly balanced "Look the Other Way." *Caravan of Love* is more assured; its title track transmits the socially conscious vibe of the Isley Brothers' "Harvest of the World." The best tunes on *Different Drummer* ("Brother to Brother," the title track) add a touch of today's nervous machine beat to the fuzzy-but-inspiring late-'60s optimism.   — M.C.

BURL IVES
★★★   **The Wayfaring Stranger (1947; Stinson, NA)**
★★   **The Best of Burl Ives (MCA, 1965)**
★★   **The Best of Burl's for Boys and Girls (MCA, 1980)**
★★   **Burl Ives Sings (Columbia, 1981)**

A contemporary of Pete Seeger and Woody Guthrie, Burl Ives was far less didactic than either of his colleagues, and far more popular. Working solo and with the Almanac Singers in the 1940s, he played a major role in popularizing folk music; in the 1950s he turned to acting and landed choice film roles and regular appearances on network TV. His was an avuncular presence, soothing and gentle and jolly, his soft voice and wide girth lending him a huggy bear aspect. However beloved by audiences, though, Ives earned the enmity of many musical artists when, in 1951, he testified on subversion in folk music before the House Un-American Activities Committee (HUAC) headed by Joseph McCarthy. Writing in the folk-music publication *Sing Out*, Seeger denounced Ives in the strongest terms for "fingering, like any common stool pigeon, some of his radical associates," which Seeger claimed Ives did for the sake of preserving "his lucrative contracts."

The American public seemed not to care, and continued to buy Ives's recordings. In 1962 he had two Top Ten singles, "A Little Bitty Tear" and "Funny Way of Laughin' "; a Top 20 single, "Call Me Mr. In-Between"; and a Top Forty single, "Mary Ann Regrets." *Burl Ives Sings* and *The Wayfaring Stranger* are solid overviews of some of the traditional folk songs that helped earn Ives his large following. The latter, edited by musicologist Alan Lomax from 78-rpm recordings, shows a considerably rawer Ives accompanied only by his acoustic guitar; it has a stark grandeur absent from the studio recordings of the artist's later years. Oddly, the remaining in-print MCA titles feature none of the hit singles from the Sixties; instead, both *The Best of Burl Ives* and *The Best of Burl's for Boys and Girls* offer chestnuts such as "Blue Tail Fly," "Big Rock Candy Mountain" and "Down in the Valley," with Ives again accompanying himself on acoustic guitar. There's no edge to these songs; they are often pretty, sweet in a way, but light as marshmallow Fluff. Post-HUAC, it would appear that the only line Ives walked was down the side of the road. — D.M.

CHUCK JACKSON
★ ★ ★ **Golden Classics (Collectables, NA)**
After singing lead for the Del-Vikings from
1957 to 1959, Chuck Jackson set out on a
solo career. A tour with Jackie Wilson
landed him a contract with Wand Records,
a subsidiary of the Scepter label, and
Jackson used his forceful baritone to good
effect on his first single, "I Don't Want to
Cry," which hit the Top Forty in 1961.
Heavy on strings and orchestral backings,
Jackson's recordings anticipated the style of
mainstream black pop that would reach full
flower in the best work of Dionne Warwick
later in the decade. Jackson's biggest hit
came in 1962, a Top Thirty item written by
Burt Bacharach called "Any Day Now,"
which the singer delivered in a more
blues-based style than he had evinced on "I
Don't Want to Cry." After leaving Wand in
the late '70s, Jackson roamed from label to
label without notable success, although his
records were often interesting for the singing
alone. *Golden Classics* explores the Wand
years, and is the cream of Jackson's
— D.M.

FREDDIE JACKSON
★ ★ ★ **Rock Me Tonight (Capitol, 1985)**
★ ★ **Just Like the First Time (Capitol, 1986)**
★ ★ **Don't Let Love Slip Away (Capitol, 1988)**
★ ★ ★ **Do Me Again (Capitol, 1989)**
Having grown up singing in Harlem
churches, Love Man supreme Freddie
Jackson brings to bear on his boudoir soul a
style influenced by Jackie Wilson and
Marvin Gaye, with a few tricks learned
from his contemporary and fellow Love
Man supreme Luther Vandross. Jackson
today is much the same smooth, soulful
singer he was on his 1985 debut, save for
exhibiting a greater concern for dynamics
and nuance than he did in his younger days.

There's nothing groundbreaking about his
music, though, and his theme remains
unwavering: love and sex, particularly the
latter when it lasts all night long. At least
he's an agreeable cocksman who wraps his
explicitly stated desire in a high-tech sheen
of synths and silky background vocals. That
his first and most recent albums are his best
hardly seems accidental: these feature
Jackson's early mentor Paul Laurence in
more than a secondary role. While
producer-songwriter Barry Eastman's work
in Jackson's service has been admirable,
Laurence's sense of the artist seems more
keenly developed. Jackson might produce a
genuinely great album with Laurence in tow.
— D.M.

JANET JACKSON
★ ★   **Janet Jackson (A&M, 1982)**
★ ★½   **Dream Street (A&M, 1984)**
★ ★ ★ ★ **Control (A&M, 1986)**
★ ★ ★   **Janet Jackson's Rhythm Nation 1814 (A&M, 1989)**
Even Janet Jackson must have been
surprised when her third solo album shot to
the top of the pops in 1986. *Janet Jackson*
and *Dream Street* sound like bland
dance-music ready-mades; perhaps she'd
give brother Jermaine a run for his money
someday, but Michael's hallowed level of
success seemed well beyond Janet's grasp at
that point. Then she took a trip to
Minneapolis, hooking up with Jimmy Jam
and Terry Lewis.

With a scintillating shrug of her shoulder,
Jackson asserted her newfound *Control*—
quite convincingly. She's not completely
autonomous, of course; *Control* is also
where Jam and Lewis perfect their melodic,
full-blown funk attack. Not a commanding
vocal presence by any means, Jackson fills
each track with a breathy, believable
presence: romantically yearning on the
bittersweet "When I Think Of You,"

seductively relishing the slinky hook on "Nasty." Cynics accused her of filling in the gap for her brother Michael and/or rifling through Madonna's cast-off closet, but *Control* developed a blockbuster momentum all its own. Two years later, a new crop of female singers (like Paula Abdul and Karyn White) were charged with imitating Janet.

Rather than following up with an obvious sequel, Jackson continued to stretch. Predictably, *Janet Jackson's Rhythm Nation 1814* is more than a little strained and self-conscious. Heartfelt pleas for racial unity and cloudy musings on the "State of the World" can't quite obscure the pulsating beat of "Miss You Much," "Rhythm Nation" or "Black Cat." The Jackson-Jam-and-Lewis troika can still work wonders: when they're not trying too damn hard to be meaningful, anyway. Though you've got to admire Jackson for pursuing her ambitions, all the pseudo-intellectual clutter and some windy arrangements compromise *Rhythm Nation*'s underlying groove thang. No matter: A series of exquisitely choreographed video clips helped to cement *Rhythm Nation*'s multi-platinum sales. — M.C.

JERMAINE JACKSON

★ ★ ★   **Let's Get Serious** (Motown, 1980)
★ ★½   **Superstar Series, Volume 17** (Motown, 1981)
★ ★ ★   **Jermaine Jackson** (Arista, 1984)
★ ★   **Don't Take It Personal** (Arista, 1989)
★ ★   **You Said** (La Face/Arista, 1991)

Jermaine's initial solo releases in the '70s—sampled on *Superstars Series Volume 17*—catered to someone's idea of "adult" tastes. His cloying cover of Shep and the Limelite's "Daddy's Home" hit the Top Ten in early '73, when Jackson 5 fever was just about cresting. Since Jermaine had married Hazel Gordy (Berry's daughter), he stayed at Motown when the other four Jacksons left for Epic. On *Let's Get Serious*, Jermaine finally did, albeit briefly. The Stevie Wonder penned-and-produced title track is a winning piece of romantic dance-floor boogie. "Dynamite" (from *Jermaine Jackson*) packs a considerable synth-pop charge, but subsequent efforts have fizzled (and fallen out of print). "Word to the Badd!" an "unauthorized" alternate version from *You Said*, caused a controversy when it was leaked to radio stations in 1991. The sharply worded bit of brotherly advice is just the hook that the baby-skin smooth *You Said* cries out for in vain. — M.C.

JOE JACKSON

★ ★ ★ ★   **Look Sharp!** (A&M, 1979)
★ ★ ★   **I'm the Man** (A&M, 1979)
★ ★ ★   **Beat Crazy** (A&M, 1980)
★ ★ ★½   **Jumpin' Jive** (A&M, 1981)
★ ★ ★   **Night and Day** (A&M, 1982)
★ ★ ★   **Body and Soul** (A&M, 1984)
★ ★½   **Mike's Murder** (A&M, 1983)
★ ★   **Big World** (A&M, 1986)
★ ★   **Will Power** (A&M, 1987)
★ ★½   **Live 1980/86** (A&M, 1988)
★ ★   **Blaze of Glory** (A&M, 1989)
★ ★ ★   **Laughter & Lust** (A&M, 1991)

Joe Jackson cut a striking figure on his debut album: *Look Sharp!* portrays an angry young tunesmith, a messenger of the new wave who sends stinging telegrams to former lovers ("Is She Really Going Out With Him?") and the world at large ("Sunday Papers"). Less literate than Elvis Costello and less soulful than Graham Parker, Jackson wields a light-fingered pop touch that's entirely his own. Ironically, the borderline-nasty wit and unchecked exuberance of *Look Sharp!* quickly give way to self-seriousness and a middlebrow disdain of rock itself. Jackson turned into a bigger crank than his two old rivals put together—and that's saying a mouthful! Apart from the heart-opening "It's Different For Girls," *I'm the Man* feels like a nervous, rushed sequel to the debut. *Beat Crazy* is a bit more consistent; bassist Graham Maby propels Jackson's tight road band through its paces, while Joe cooly dissects casual sex on the ultra-catchy "Biology." Posing the question "Why did we try?" in *Beat Crazy*'s liner notes, however, Jackson flaunts the condescending culture-snob attitude that has marred all his subsequent musical adventures.

Jumpin' Jive is the best of Jackson's stylistic jaunts; he doesn't really have the pipe for '40s R&B, but he does a fair job of conjuring up the horny "Saturday Night Fish Fry" spirit of Louis Jordan and His Tympani Five. *Night and Day* takes a dance-floor spin through Spanish Harlem, but Jackson's respectful attempt at salsafied disco catches fire just once—on "Steppin' Out," his only Top Ten single. *Body and Soul* blends elements of jazz and even musical theater in another polite matchup; "Happy Ending" and "Be My Number Two" hark back to the incisive cynicism of Jackson's breakthrough albums. Jackson intended *Big World* to be a big deal: three sides of all-new material, recorded live in front of a New York audience, with a solid-rocking quartet sound. Problem is, this glory shot backfires; none of Jackson's awkward topical missives finds its target, despite the crisp musical accompaniment. Turning away from pop singing altogether on the *Will Power*, Jackson busied himself with orchestral fantasies and piano suites.

After the dismal autobiographical concept album *Blaze of Glory* fizzled, Jackson switched labels and laid down some of his punchiest, most pungent work since the '70s on *Laughter & Lust*. Too bad he feels compelled to title the two most striking tunes "Hit Single" and "Obvious Song," though. For masochists who just can't get enough, Joe Jackson is the man. — M.C.

MAHALIA JACKSON

★ ★ ★ **Bless This House (Columbia, 1963)**
★ ★ ★ **Mahalia Jacksons: Greatest Hits (Columbia, 1963)**
★ ★ **Sings the Best-Loved Hymns of Dr. Martin Luther King, Jr. (Columbia, 1968)**
★ ★ **Christmas With Mahalia (Columbia, 1968)**
★ ★ **Sings America's Favorite Hymns (Columbia, 1971)**
★ ★ **The Great Mahalia Jackson (Columbia, 1972)**
★ ★ ★ ★ **How I Got Over (Columbia, 1976)**
★ ★ ★ **Gospels, Spirituals & Hymns (Legacy/Columbia, 1991)**

Inspired by Bessie Smith, Mahalia Jackson is regarded as the singer who brought blues into the gospel field and then brought gospel to a secular audience with greater success than any other artist in the field. Stubborn, contentious and not altogether a model of propriety, Jackson seemed to use her singing performances to transport herself to more sanctified ground: her majestic contralto voice could handle a wide range of material, and her gift as an interpreter allowed her to work a lyric with such conviction you sensed someone unburdening her soul in powerful terms.

Born in New Orleans in 1911, she moved to Chicago in 1927, and in 1936 married a man who wanted her to sing jazz and classics; she even auditioned for *The Jazz Mikado*, but bowed out before the audition was completed. The marriage ended, and Jackson went back on the gospel circuit and began to build a following. In 1937 she recorded a few sides for Decca, all of them wonderful, but another nine years elapsed before she recorded again. Signed to the Apollo label, she made her most important records in the late '40s and early '50s. These

are out of print now, but lest any show up in cut-out bins, the titles to latch onto are *The Best of Mahalia Jackson* and *1911–1972*.

In the years after her move to Columbia in 1954 and prior to her death in 1972, Jackson was by most estimations the most popular gospel artist in America. But at the same time she was experiencing all this fame, her music was suffering. Columbia saw an opportunity to reach a mass audience and saddled Jackson's arrangements with strings and sometimes a full orchestra (the most egregious example being the out-of-print *The Power and the Glory*, with arrangements by Percy Faith, the very model of the corporate studio hack). It is a testament to her consummate artistry that Jackson surmounts most every obstacle placed in her path; each of the Columbia albums has profound moments, even if none are totally successful or representative of the breadth and depth of the woman's power.

Bless This House features her with a small rhythm section, but the inspired accompaniment of her longtime pianist Mildred Falls comes through loud and clear. A male quartet—sounding for all the world like something cooked up by Mitch Miller—disrupts some otherwise ebullient performances, but these miscalculations are more than offset by powerhouse vocals on "God Knows the Reason Why," "Trouble of the World" and "Precious Lord." A 1976 release, *How I Got Over*, is the best of the Columbia titles precisely because it's culled from 1954 radio performances plus some songs from a 1963 television appearance and captures Jackson close to the form she displayed on her best Apollo sides. A loyal friend and supporter of Dr. Martin Luther King, Jr., her album devoted to his memory includes a powerful reading of "We Shall Overcome," as well as "Precious Lord," King's last request of Jackson. Beware of *Greatest Hits*, as it contains re-recordings of some of the Apollo sides as well as newer material. *The Great Mahalia Jackson* is a worst-case example of Columbia's mishandling of this great artist, rife as it is with pop fluff such as "Danny Boy," "Sunrise, Sunset," and "What the World Needs Now Is Love." The set, *Gospels, Spirituals & Hymns*, is a good summary of Jackson's Columbia catalogue, but a summary is all it amounts to: its 36 tracks represent only a small portion of her output in nearly two decades with the label. The definitive Mahalia Jackson, and along with it a proper appreciation of her artistry, is yet to come. —D.M.

MICHAEL JACKSON

★★★   **Got to Be There (Motown, 1972)**
★★   **Ben (Motown, 1972)**
★★★½ **The Best of Michael Jackson (Motown, 1975)**
★★★   **Anthology (1976; Motown, 1986)**
★★★★★ **Off the Wall (Epic, 1979)**
★★★★★ **Thriller (Epic, 1982)**
★★★★ **Bad (Epic, 1987)**
★★★★ **Dangerous (Epic, 1991)**

Michael Jackson has been criticized for effectively bleaching his roots in soul and R&B. Musically speaking, however, a spin through *The Best of Michael Jackson* (1975) should be enough to remind anyone of this video-age icon's long-standing crossover ambitions. The funky, precocious strut of "Rockin' Robin" (from *Got to Be There*) aside, he's always cultivated a downright schmaltzy aspect. (Take "Ben," his cloying 1972 ode to a cinematic rat.) The Jackson 5 was an awesomely telegenic act right from the start, too; they scored with the "Goin' Back to Indiana" TV special and a Saturday morning cartoon series. One of the many wondrous things about Jackson's coming of age on *Off the Wall* is how smoothly he and producer Quincy Jones absorbed those disparate influences and show-biz impulses into a whole. Drawing room balladry, dramatic production number, dance-floor boogie: it all comes together in a seamlessly orchestrated groove. Eventually, a dash of rock guitar completes the picture on *Thriller*. Simply put, superstar product doesn't come any better than this.

Unfortunately, Jackson's Motown solo career went the route of *Got to Be There*'s daydreamy title track rather than the sprightly "Rockin' Robin." *Best of* should satiate all but the most devoted fans: show tunes from *Lady Sings the Blues* and *Pippin* round out the hits. The Holland-Dozier-Holland produced "We're Almost There" places Michael—somewhat tentatively—in a contemporary (1974) sleek-soul setting.

Off the Wall is where the reborn Michael Jackson arrives, both artistically and commercially. A former jazz arranger and bandleader who had composed for movies and television, Quincy Jones proves to be the perfect lightning rod for Jackson's creative thunderstorm. He provides a smooth, yet bristling pulse—so the dancing machine doesn't have to stop until we all get enough. "She's Out of My Life" reveals

Michael's mature ballad style, while "Rock With You" achieves an incredibly sensual roll. *Off the Wall* argues that a dance groove can only be improved by a few solid melodies and one fantastically equipped singer. When Michael announces that living off the wall ain't so bad at all, his steamy conviction is reassuring—rock-solid. Even he couldn't guess just how weird things would get.

Thriller widens the stylistic net further; it's mainstream in the very best sense of the word. Snarling metal guitar (Eddie Van Halen guesting on "Beat It") and silly love songs (Paul McCartney dueting on "The Girl Is Mine") comfortably flow alongside those chunky video-funk blockbusters. "Thriller" sums up and celebrates Jackson's now larger-than-life appeal, while "Billie Jean" hauntingly examines its psychosexual toll on this former child star.

Bad is better than you may remember. Overexposure hurt many of the mid-'80s pop explosion's guiding lights, but it crippled Michael Jackson. Radically changing his appearance didn't seem to help much, and a familar-sounding, "Q"-produced musical backdrop got *Bad* tagged as a disappointing sequel. However obvious their antecedents, these tracks do sink in over time—even "Dirty Diana" hits home after the videos and dance routines fade.

Surprisingly, Jackson didn't play it all that safe on the long-awaited *Dangerous*. Collaborating with writer-prouder Teddy Riley on seven of its fourteen cuts, Jackson attempts to make his peace with modern dance music. His eccentric charisma permeates the package, of course, from the cosmic banalities inscribed in the liner notes to a note-perfect rewrite of USA for Africa's "We Are the World" titled "Heal the World." But it turns out that New Jack Swing—the melodic electro-groove patented by Riley—fits the thirtysomething Jackson like a glove. Some of Jackson's most assured and probing vocals rise out of the melancholy synth-and-sample settings on "Why You Wanna Trip on Me," "She Drives Me Wild" and especially "In the Closet." If the rest of *Dangerous* is less adventurous, at least the risk-taking Riley tracks suggest Michael Jackson hasn't totally retreated into his private twilight zone. — M.C.

RONALD SHANNON JACKSON

★★★★   **Mandance (Antilles, 1982)**
★★★   **Barbeque Dog (Antilles, 1983)**
★★★½ **Decode Yourself (Island, 1985)**

★ ★ ★ Live at the Caravan of Dreams
(Caravan of Dreams, 1986)
★ ★ ★ Taboo (Caroline, 1990)
★ ★ ★ ★½ Red Warrior (Axiom, 1990)
Ronald Shannon Jackson was the drummer
in Prime Time, Ornette Coleman's first
electric "harmolodic" ensemble, and has
spent most of his solo career spinning
variations on the funk-oriented free jazz he
played with Coleman. That's not to say
Jackson's work merely clones Coleman's, for
Jackson's albums with his Decoding Society
(a group that for many years included
Living Colour guitarist Vernon Reid) are as
a rule more rigorously arranged, with a
greater emphasis on composition than on
collective improvisation. Jackson's writing
particularly stands out on *Mandance*, which
makes excellent use of instrumental textures,
and *Decode Yourself*, though the latter owes
much to producer Bill Laswell. Apparently,
though, the balance between cogent song
structures and open improvisation is not an
easy one to maintain, as *Taboo* seems stifled
by its over-involved arrangements, while the
too-loose *Live at the Caravan of Dreams* at
times degenerates into pretentious funk. On
the other hand, the guitar-crazed *Red
Warrior* offers an inspired blend of
organization and anarchy, and is easily the
most visceral of these albums. — J.D.C.

STONEWALL JACKSON
★ ★ American Originals (Columbia, 1990)
Stonewall Jackson has become something of
a country music legend by virtue of his
having made it to the Grand Ole Opry
without benefit of a major-label affiliation.
In fact, the story goes, Jackson had no label
affiliation at all when he drove to Nashville
from Georgia in 1956, auditioned for the
Opry, and was brought on board
immediately. He's a straight-ahead country
singer who has adapted his style to suit the
times, and has a bit more rock & roll in him
than he's given credit for. *American
Originals* restores some interesting tracks to
the marketplace, not the least of which is his
sole crossover hit, "Waterloo," a Number
Four pop single from 1959. — D.M.

WANDA JACKSON
★ ★ ★ ★ Rockin' in the Country: The Best of
Wanda Jackson (Rhino, 1990)
One of the coolest women in rock history,
Wanda Jackson came roaring out of
Oklahoma City in the mid-'50s singing
rockabilly, rock & roll and hard country in
a constricted, razor-sharp, red-hot voice that
was an attitude monster. A tough,

independent, no bullshit sort, Jackson was
cut from the same cloth as the robust,
earthy blues singers of the '20s and '30s, like
Ma Rainey, Bessie Smith and Ethel Waters.
Rockin' in the Country surveys Jackson in a
variety of modes, from full-throttle rock
("Let's Have a Party," originally recorded
by Elvis Presley and featured in the film
Loving You) to rockabilly ("Honey Bop,"
with a heavily echoed, maximum glottal
stop vocal that is right out of the Gene
Vincent stylebook) to traditional country
(the weeper "Why I'm Walkin' " gets over
via a vocal imbued with the profound
sadness so characteristic of Patsy Cline's
great tearjerkers). Eighteen cuts spanning
1956 through 1970 show that Jackson didn't
broaden her turf so much as stake it out
and protect it with a vengeance; even the
softer, more mainstream material from the
later years after Jackson had become a
born-again Christian is delivered with a lilt
that is positively nasty and clearly
subversive. — D.M.

THE JACKSON 5
★ ★ ★ Diana Ross Presents the Jackson
5 (1970; Motown, 1981)
★ ★ ★ ABC (1970; Motown, 1981)
★ ★ ★ Third Album (1970; Motown,
1981)
★ ★½ Maybe Tomorrow (1971; Motown,
1981)
★ ★ ★ ★ Greatest Hits (1971; Motown,
1981)
★ ★ ★½ Dancing Machine (Motown, 1974)
★ ★ ★ ★ Anthology (1976; Motown, 1986)
THE JACKSONS
★ ★ ★ The Jacksons (Epic, 1976)
★ ★ ★ Goin' Places (Epic, 1977)
★ ★ ★ ★ Destiny (Epic, 1978)
★ ★ ★ ★ Triumph (Epic, 1980)
★ ★ ★ The Jacksons Live (Epic, 1981)
★ ★ ★½ Victory (Epic, 1984)
★ ★½ 2300 Jackson Street (Epic, 1989)
This Gary, Indiana–based family act was
already legendary in black music circles
when Motown scooped them up in 1968; the
mighty mite in front of the Jackson 5 left an
indelible impression on people, right from
the start. Eleven-year-old Michael and his
brothers (Jackie, Tito, Jermaine and
Marlon) had already been touring and
performing around the country when Diana
Ross "discovered" them. Depending on
your perspective, the Jackson 5 were either
Motown's last classic gasp or the
standard-bearers of a second generation that
never quite took over. Either way: the
confident kiddie-soul of "I Want You Back"
(from the debut), "ABC" and "The Love

You Save" (from *ABC*) still carries an emotional depth charge.

Like every Motown act before them, the Jackson 5 were positioned as a singles act. Nightclub-bound shlock and obvious cover versions pad these hits-plus-filler albums. "I'll Be There" (from *Third Album*) demonstrates the swelling, overweening ballad treatment favored by Berry Gordy and his production-songwriting team (tellingly credited as the Corporation). The similarly paced "Never Can Say Goodbye" (also from *Third Album*) is a big improvement: the disarming warmth of Michael's voice obviates through the strings and cooing backup vocals.

The flurry of Jackson 5 releases in the first years of the '70s shows the brothers bumping up against the limits of Motown formula. "Sugar Daddy" (from *Maybe Tomorrow*) feels like "ABC" revisted—already. After several more uneven LPs (now deleted), the Jackson 5 confronted the emergent disco animal on what would be its finest overall Motown effort: *Dancing Machine*—especially its percolating title track—is where the Michael Jackson we know today first emerges. When the group split for Epic Records in 1975, Jermaine stayed behind (he'd married Berry Grody's daughter Hazel in 1973) and was replaced by younger sibling Randy. *The Jacksons* and *Goin' Places* brought the renamed quintet to Philadelphia, though the expansive Gamble and Huff groove has a leveling effect on their newfound dance sound. Moving from one hit factory to another didn't exactly provide the artistic freedom that the Jacksons—especially Michael—craved. Despite somewhat rote songwriting, you can spot Michael developing by leaps and bounds. The 1977 R&B hit "Show You the Way to Go," from *The Jacksons*, wraps his deepening vocal twists and turns in a creamy-rich double-tracked chorus; singing rings around himself, Michael sounds like nobody else on earth.

His brothers' contributions shouldn't be completely discounted; *Destiny* and *Triumph* hold up quite well against *Off the Wall* and *Thriller*. Finally producing themselves, the Jacksons and a coterie of sessionmen (led by keyboardist Greg Phillinganes) fashioned a glossy, yet progressive pop-soul sound on *Destiny*; they plowed right through the late '70s rock-disco barricade without thinking about it. Michael's skittering, intense vocal workouts on "Blame It on the Boogie" and "Shake Your Body (Down to the Ground)" made dancing seem like very serious

business, indeed. *Triumph* is where the Jacksons reach an audible peak; "Can You Feel It" and "Heartbreak Hotel" are so all-encompassing they teeter on the brink of sonic overkill—without caving in. That air of melodrama adds something, but it's a bit ominous, too. The super-nova phase of Michael's solo career soon overshadowed the Jacksons. *Victory* suffered unjustly from the fallout surrounding the group's last tour in 1984. It's not up to the level of the last two, but Jermaine's return signals a consistent, communal effort—and Michael's somewhat restrained presence never hurts. Unfortunately, the post-Michael *2300 Jackson Street* is nowhere near that assured. The remaining Jacksons perform competent takes on current R&B modes, slipping into an unctious kiddie chorus on the gaudy "autobiographical" title track.

The Jackson 5's classics can be found amid very mixed company on the extremely brief *Greatest Hits*, while the even-spottier *Anthology* adds "Dancing Machine" and Michael Jackson's earliest smashes. — M.C.

LITTLE WALTER JACOBS

★★★★★ **The Best of Little Walter (1958; Chess/MCA, 1986)**
★★★★★ **Hate to See You Go (1969; Chess/MCA, 1990)**
★★★★ **Boss Blues Harmonica (1973; Chess/MCA, 1984)**
★★★★ **The Blues World of Little Walter (Delmark, 1983)**
★★★★ **The Best of Little Walter, Volume Two (Chess/MCA, 1989)**
★★★★ **Little Walter and Otis Rush: Live in Chicago (Quicksilver, NA)**

The title of the late Little Walter Jacobs's Chess/MCA release, *Boss Blues Harmonica*, couldn't be more appropriate. Acknowledged by blues scholars as the greatest blues harmonica player in history, Jacobs's fame rests on the twin poles of skill and invention.

Born near Marksville, Louisiana, Jacobs began playing professionally at age 12 in clubs and on the streets of New Orleans and Monroe. By age 14 he had gravitated to the growing blues community in Helena, Arkansas. His playing at that time was redolent with the influences of John Lee Williamson and Rice Miller (both of whom recorded as Sonny Boy Williamson), but he was also studying the jump blues of Louis Jordan. Jacobs began imitating Jordan's saxophone solos on his harmonica, and soon his peers were imitating Jacobs. But Jacobs's skill was virtually unrivaled—as he developed, his incorporation of various jazz and jump blues quotations combined with his sheer command of intricate melodic patterns placed him well ahead of other blues harmonica players of his time. In the mid-'40s he joined the exodus of Delta blues musicians to Chicago, and hooked up with Muddy Waters's first electric band, the standard-bearer of post-War urban blues.

Jacobs's solo career began incidentally, when at the end of a Waters session for Chess Records in 1952 he and the band recorded an instrumental, "Your Cat Will Play," that Waters had been using as a theme song. Label co-owner Leonard Chess issued it under Jacobs's name and retitled it "Juke." It reached Number One on the R&B charts and stayed there for eight weeks; more important, it blazed a new trail when Jacobs amplified his harmonica, which served to heighten his mastery of inflection and tone. Having the biggest hit ever recorded by any of the Delta or Chicago bluesmen, Jacobs went out on his own, taking over a band called the Aces (later renamed the Jukes) that had been fronted by another harmonica player, Junior Wells, who moved over to replace Jacobs in Waters's band. Between 1952 and 1958 Jacobs recorded 14 Top Ten R&B hits, a number matched only by Muddy Waters during the same period. Beyond being the master of the blues harp, Jacobs was also a terrific singer; some of his vocals are so overpowering it's easy to forget that the man is known primarily as an instrumentalist.

In recent years a healthy domestic catalogue of Jacobs's work has been released, and every title is worth owning. The two Chess/MCA *Best of* collections spotlight his work for the label, with Volume Two being heavy on Jacobs's vocals, including such enduring tracks as "Oh Baby," "Key to the Highway" and "Boom Boom (Out Go the Lights)," as well as two rare entries, "Boogie" and "I Don't Play." *Hate to See You Go* encompasses recordings from 1952 to 1960 featuring Jacobs with the stellar musicians who supported him in the studio over those years: Muddy Waters, Jimmy Rogers, Elgin Evans, Willie Dixon, Fred Below, Robert Jr. Lockwood, Luther Tucker, Fred Robinson—a real Chicago blues all-star jam. Even Bo Diddley makes an appearance on his own composition, "Roller Coaster." For sheer drive, few albums approach the incendiary summit meeting heard on *Superblues*. Muddy Waters, Bo Diddley and

Jacobs play like men with hellhounds on their trail, talking trash, spurring each other to more resonant performances. The version of Diddley's "Who Do You Love" approaches meltdown, and is the model for the raging performance Diddley delivered on the *La Bamba* soundtrack. Jacobs blows low and mean behind Diddley and Waters on "I'm a Man," as the two guitarists spar verbally and instrumentally. Delmark's *Blues World of Little Walter* contains some of Jacobs's earliest Chicago recordings, made for the Parkway label in January of 1950. The eight tracks feature Jacobs (excelling on both guitar and harmonica), Muddy Waters, and another Delta bluesman who was part of Waters's first steady band, Baby Face Leroy Foster, billed as the Baby Face Trio (which became the Little Walter Trio when some of these recordings were released later on the Regal label). Tracks include "I Just Keep Loving Her" and two pounding versions of "Rollin' and Tumblin'." *Live in Chicago* features one side of first-rate performances by Little Walter, and another side of Otis Rush in concert. Certainly no serious blues fan can afford to be without any of the albums listed here, but even the marginal fan will find little repetition from title to title, and great excitement from all.
— D.M.

MICK JAGGER
★ ★ ★ **She's the Boss** (Columbia, 1985)
★ ★ ★ **Primitive Cool** (Columbia, 1987)
Away from the Stones, Jagger settles for fashion, the adamant grasping of the aging hipster for whatever is au courant. On *She's the Boss*, he puts himself in the hands of ultra-producer Bill Laswell, and comes up with glossy rock, heavy with all kinds of percolating percussion and studio texturalism. "Just Another Night" is a fine, if hardly, profound single, enlivened by a tasty acoustic guitar motif; the rest of the record is crunchy funk, intriguing chiefly for the title track and "Hard Woman." Odd (ironic?) defenses of strong women, both songs are perhaps intended as late-in-the-day correctives to the Stones' exaggerated reputation as misogynists. Big names and studio aces—Jeff Beck, Pete Townshend, Nile Rodgers, Robbie Shakespeare and Sly Dunbar—help craft the record, and with Mick flourishing the soul of a die-hard professional, the sound he gets is nothing if not accomplished.

With *Primitive Cool*, this time with Eurythmic Dave Stewart as collaborator, he takes more risks in style and lyrics; it's a commendable effort, but the results are haphazard. The title song finds Jagger in the role of "daddy" and doing nostalgia—a sentiment that doesn't suit him at all. "Let's Work" is an odd, but telling paen to the Protestant ethic, its championing of honest toil comes off as yuppie gospel. But the rocker "Shoot Off Your Mouth" is fine, vintage bad boyism; "Say You Will" is a lovely ballad; "Peace for the Wicked" is neat, Prince-ish R&B; and "War Baby," for all its clunkiness, is a heartfelt political meditation. Mick even returns to country for the charming "Party Doll," and throughout the record, he sounds more human than he has in some time. The playing, again by a studio outfit led by Beck, is predictably assured. — P.E.

THE JAM

★ ★ ★ ★   In the City (Polydor, 1977)
★ ★ ★½   This Is the Modern World (Polydor, 1977)
★ ★ ★   The Peel Sessions (1977; Strange Fruit, 1991)
★ ★ ★   All Mod Cons (Polydor, 1978)
★ ★ ★½   Setting Sons (Polydor, 1979)
★ ★ ★ ★   Sound Affects (Polydor, 1980)
★ ★ ★   The Gift (Polydor, 1982)
★ ★ ★   Dig the New Breed (Polydor, 1982)
★ ★ ★ ★   Snap! (Polydor, 1983)
★ ★ ★ ★   Greatest Hits (Polydor, 1991)

The Jam stood out from the class of '77—what with its sharp suits, supercharged Merseybeat quotes, taut arrangements and guitarist-songwriter Paul Weller's thoughtful flashes. *In the City* barrels along at a pogo pace; though bassist Bruce Foxton and drummer Rick Buckler don't exactly swing the martial rhythms, they do interact much more than your average slam-happy punk rhythm. Weller's affecting melodic side emerges on "Away From the Numbers," while articulate pounders like "Sounds From the Street" and "Non Stop Dancing" fully live up to their titles. *This Is the Modern World* is a hit-or-miss sequel. After brazenly cribbing riffs from Pete Townshend, Paul Weller takes several pages from the Ray Davies book of songwriting on the transitional *All Mod Cons*: he covers the Kinks' "David Watts" and tries his own hand at social observation on "Mr. Clean" and "In the Crowd." *Setting Sons* is an altogether more successful attempt to mine this vein; the crisp, yet sombre music matches the lyrics' fretful outlook. "Eton Rifles" is the first—and best—of Weller's explicitly left-leaning anthems. On *Sound*

Affects the Jam shakes free of the baggage of punk ideology once and for all, adding horn lines ("Start!") and guitar solos (all over the place), tossing in happy love songs ("I'm Different Now") alongside the critiques of capitalism ("Pretty Green"). Two of the strongest tunes, "That's Entertainment" and "Going Underground," seem to predict the band's breakup in 1982. First came *The Gift*, on which Paul Weller's white soul aspirations—later pursued full-time in the Style Council—come bubbling to the surface. Though *Sound Affects* made the Jam virtual superstars at home, they never made much of a dent in America. The live album *Dig the New Breed* is a fairly marginal moemento; when the group prides itself on a rough, spontaneous studio sound, isn't a concert album kind of beside the point? *Snap!* encapsulates the Jam's mercurial career in a stirringly breathless rush of tunes; taken together, *In the City* and *Sound Affects* make an even stronger case for this undervalued British export. — M.C.

ELMORE JAMES

★ ★ ★ ★   Elmore James/John Brim: Whose Muddy Shoes (1969; Chess/MCA, 1991)
★ ★ ★ ★   Street Talkin' (1975; Muse, 1988)
★ ★ ★ ★   Golden Classics: Guitars in Orbit (Collectables, NA)
★ ★ ★ ★ ★ Red Hot Blues (Quicksilver, 1982)
★ ★ ★ ★   Let's Cut It: The Very Best of Elmore James (Flair/Virgin, 1987)
★ ★ ★ ★ ★ The Complete Fire and Enjoy Sessions Part 1 (Collectables, 1989)
★ ★ ★ ★ ★ The Complete Fire and Enjoy Sessions Part 2 (Collectables, 1989)
★ ★ ★ ★ ★ The Complete Fire and Enjoy Sessions Part 3 (Collectables, 1989)
★ ★ ★ ★ ★ The Complete Fire and Enjoy Sessions Part 4 (Collectables, 1989)
★ ★ ★ ★   Dust My Broom (Tomato, 1991)
★ ★ ★ ★ ★ The Complete Elmore James Story (Capricorn/Warner Bros., 1992)

There are few sounds in music more distinctive than Elmore James's wailing slide guitar. James's style shows up in the playing of virtually every important British blues guitarist and in great American blues guitarists such as Roy Buchanan, Duane Allman and Dickie Betts, to name but three prominent examples.

Born in Mississippi and reared on Delta blues, James learned to play the guitar at age 12; in his teens he began traveling around the region in the company of Rice Miller (Sonny Boy Williamson #2) and Robert Johnson. James's first hit, recorded surreptitiously in 1951, was a version of Johnson's "Dust My Broom." By 1939 James had begun playing dances with a lineup including another guitarist, a trumpet player, a drummer and a saxophonist, marking one of the earliest attempts by any of the Delta blues players to expand into a band context. After a stint in the Navy, James came back to Mississippi and again hooked up with Rice Miller for dances and occasional appearances on Miller's local radio show. By this time James was playing electric guitar, but he stayed with what he knew best: the slide guitar as a cry of the soul. As a writer, he was fast becoming eloquent and incisive, his songs replete with startling descriptions of torment, desire and mean mistreaters.

After moving to Chicago in 1952, James and his band the Broomdusters began recording for the Meteor label, as well as a variety of other labels, as he traveled back and forth from Mississippi to Chicago until his death from a heart attack in 1963. The ferocity of this music is equal to any of the rock & roll recorded during this era, and much of it is now available domestically. *Whose Muddy Shoes* is a good starting point, as it contains tracks recorded for Chess in 1953 and again seven years later in 1960. Among these is another version of "Dust My Broom" (James recorded this classic several times), and an homage to one of James's principal influences, T-Bone Walker, via a singed interpretation of "Stormy Monday." Six tracks are devoted to the underrated Chicago bluesman John Brim, whose band included Robert Jr. Lockwood, Willie Dixon and, on a couple of cuts, Little Walter Jacobs. *Red Hot Blues* and *Golden Classics: Guitars in Orbit* are both highly recommended compendiums of James's best-known recordings—chief among them "Look on Yonder Wall," "The Sky Is Crying," "It Hurts Me Too" and "I Believe." Muse's *Street Talkin'* divides 14 tracks between James and Eddie Taylor, with Taylor's being of more import owing to the presence in his band of guitarists Jimmy Reed and Hubert Sumlin. A 1987 collection, *Let's Cut It*, is in the vein of a greatest-hits album, but does feature an alternate take of "Hawaiian Boogie." *Dust My Broom* (1991) collects fifteen splendid

tracks that James recorded between 1959 and his death in 1963.

Between 1960 and 1962 James cut over 50 sides for the Fire and Enjoy labels; these were originally collected in a four-volume set by Collectables, and have since been issued by Capricorn in one extraordinary package. Among the incredible tracks is James's overpowering "Something Inside of Me." This is the track you'd play for someone who wanted to know about blues: not only does it display a master's touch in its crafting, but it's also covered in blood. Elmore James taught some hard lessons in his music, and the most important ones are contained in this essential collection.

— D.M.

ETTA JAMES

★★★★ **At Last (1961; Chess/MCA, 1987)**
★★★★ **The Second Time Around (1961; Chess/MCA, 1989)**
★★★ **Etta James Rocks the House (1963; Chess/MCA, 1986)**
★★★★ **Tell Mama (1968; Chess/MCA, 1988)**
★★ **Come a Little Closer (1974; Chess/MCA, 1986)**
★★★ **Deep in the Night (Warner Bros., 1978)**
★★★ **Her Greatest Sides, Vol. 1 (Chess/MCA, 1986)**
★★★ **Blues in the Night, Vol. 1: The Early Show (Fantasy, 1986)**
★★★★ **Blues in the Night, Vol. 2: The Late Show (Fantasy, 1986)**
★★★★ **R&B Dynamite (1986; Flair/Virgin, 1991)**
★★★★ **The Sweetest Peaches (Chess/MCA, 1988)**
★★★★★ **The Sweetest Peaches: The Chess Years, Vol. One (1960–1966) (Chess/MCA, 1988)**
★★★★★ **The Sweetest Peaches: The Chess Years, Vol. Two (1967–1975) (Chess/MCA, 1988)**
★★★ **Seven Year Itch (Island, 1989)**
★★★ **Stickin' to My Guns (Island, 1990)**
★★★ **The Gospel Soul of Etta James (AJK, 1990)**

Born in 1938 to parents of Italian and African-American descent, Etta James came by her blues naturally and remains, over three decades after her first hit, one of the most moving singers of the postwar era. She began singing professionally at age 15 in a vocal trio with two female friends; together they had written an answer record to Hank Ballard's early R&B sagas "Work With Me

Annie" and "Annie Had a Baby." Johnny Otis heard the girls sing "Roll With Me Henry" during one of his dates in San Francisco, took Etta down to Los Angeles, and recorded the song. Released on the Modern label as "The Wallflower" (radio stations shied away from the original title), the single rose to Number Two on the R&B chart and was also successful in a sanitized pop version by Georgia Gibbs retitled again as "Dance With Me Henry." A follow-up single, "Good Rockin' Daddy," reached the Top Twenty of the R&B charts, but was shorter-lived than its predecessor and faded quickly. So did James's career at Modern, despite her having cut several other first-rate sides as the '50s progressed. James's Modern recordings are now available on the reissue *R&B Dynamite*. James relocated to Chicago in 1959 and signed with the Chess label, where one of the A&R men was Harvey Fuqua, founder of the Moonglows and a solo recording artist who had cut a duet with James on Modern ("I Hope You're Satisfied").

It was at Chess that James produced the performances on which her legend rests. James's work was so personal it would be painful if it weren't so beautiful; she cried out in song, as illustrated by Volume One of *The Sweetest Peaches*. The 12 cuts on this volume are among the best R&B singles of the '60s. A sampling of titles maps out James's barren emotional landscape: "All I Could Do Was Cry," "Fool That I Am," "I Wish Someone Would Care," "Pushover." Her song, "Stop the Wedding," was a Top Forty pop hit in 1962, enabling James to plunge into the good life; ultimately, though, she yielded to the temptations of drugs. Her music assumed a near-bitter edge (it's a long road from "All I Could Do Was Cry" to a tough cover version of Jimmy Reed's unapologetic "Baby What You Want Me To Do") as her life fell into disarray. Though 1963 produced a rocking live album, *Etta James Rocks the House*, recorded at a small club in Nashville with a band whose members are unidentified, the singer was in a tailspin. Eventually she headed back to California, went into rehab, and came out clean. Looking to reinvigorate her music, she went south, to Muscle Shoals Sound. Soul music was the order of the day, and some of the best was coming out of the northern Alabama facility where Aretha Franklin and Wilson Pickett had cut some of their best work. *Tell Mama* and four tracks on Volume Two of *The Sweetest Peaches* reveal the wisdom of this move: *Tell Mama* is one of the decade's exceptional albums; it produced two Top Thirty hits in the title song and the Otis Redding-penned "Security," as well as other deeply felt performances.

The early '70s found James moving into a blues-rock mode under the auspices of producer Gabriel Mekler, who had worked with Three Dog Night, Janis Joplin and Steppenwolf. *Come a Little Closer* (along with cuts on Vol. Two of *The Sweetest Peaches*) was the result of this unsuccessful association. James's wizened vocals were as potent as ever, but Mekler's glossy arrangements weren't a good fit with the singer's intense approach. After another near-disastrous bout with drugs and another rehab program, James left Chess. In 1978 she was signed to Warner Bros. and delivered the Jerry Wexler–produced *Deep in the Night* (currently out of print), which pointed her in the right direction again professionally.

James came all the way back with her live album *Blues in the Night*, recorded in Los Angeles in 1986 with a band that included alto saxophonist Eddie "Cleanhead" Vinson. Her version of "At Last" is as smoky and affecting as the original, and on "Misty" she shows she can deliver a pop standard as well. A companion volume, *The Late Show*, is even better, with a rollicking version of "Baby What You Want Me to Do," and impassioned renditions of "Sweet Little Angel" and "I'd Rather Go Blind" that are further enlivened by blues soloing from guitarist Shuggie Otis. Of her two Island albums, *Stickin' to My Guns* best shows her adapting a hard R&B approach to a contemporary funk-rock sound. Produced by Barry Beckett, who played on James's Muscle Shoals sessions, the album's song selection runs the gamut from rock to country-soul. James sounds at home throughout, albeit harder than on any of her recent albums—but then, it's been that kind of life. — D.M.

RICK JAMES

★★★   Come Get It! (Gordy, 1978)
★★½   Bustin' Out of L Seven (Gordy, 1979)
★★½   Fire It Up (Gordy, 1979)
★★   In 'n' Out (Gordy, 1980)
★★   Garden of Love (Gordy, 1980)
★★★★ Street Songs (Gordy, 1981)
★★★½ Throwin' Down (Gordy, 1982)
★★★½ Cold Blooded (Gordy, 1983)
★★★★ Reflections: All the Great Hits (Gordy, 1984)
★★   Glow (Gordy, 1985)
★½   The Flag (Gordy, 1986)

★ ★ ★ ★   **Greatest Hits (Motown, 1986)**
★ ★½ **Wonderful (Reprise, 1988)**
When you get right down to it, Rick
James's greatest strengths as a pop star
weren't musical, but entrepreneurial. He
knew, for instance, that positioning himself
in-between rock and R&B—as the avatar of
punk funk, his own personal brand of funk
& roll—that he'd end up with a bigger
audience than if he pursued either
individually. He also recognized how much
Parliament/Funkadelic's sex-and-freakiness
message appealed to the mass pop audience,
and built his own sound around a cleaned-
up version of that George Clinton groove.

But the main thing he understood was
image. On his album covers and in his
music, James dressed like a rocker, sang like
a soul man and strutted like a Mack Daddy.
Although there was nothing particularly
"street" about his sound, he knew enough
buzzwords and inserted enough nudge-wink
innuendo—particularly drug references like
"Mary Jane" from *Come Get It!*, "Cop'n'
Blow" from *Bustin' Out of L Seven* or
"South American Sneeze" from *In 'n' Out*—
to convince most of the kids back in the
'burbs. And for a while, it worked like a
dream.

Musically, James was slick but shallow.
His best albums, *Street Songs* and *Throwin'
Down*, owe more to production values than
to any sort of originality (although, in
fairness, *Street Songs'* "Super Freak" and
"Give It to Me Baby" had terrific hooks
even if they aren't great songs). Elsewhere,
he relies on everything from secondhand
Bootsy Collins (*Fire It Up*) to third-rate
Larry Graham (*In 'n' Out*), with varying
degrees of success.

James pretty much ran out of ideas by
1982, and though *Cold Blooded* is a passable
attempt at synthesizing the funk & roll
chemistry of *Street Songs*, his subsequent
albums for Gordy are a waste. Nor is
Wonderful, his 1988 comeback attempt,
much better, although Roxanne Shanté's
cameo on "Loosey's Rap" is worth hearing.
— J.D.C.

SKIP JAMES
★ ★ ★ ★ ★ **Skip James Today! (1966;
        Vanguard, 1991)**
★ ★ ★ ★ ★ **Devil Got My Woman (1968;
        Vanguard, 1991)**
One of the most distinctive of the Delta
blues artists, Skip James sang in a high,
pained, near-falsetto voice and developed an
intricate style of guitar playing that
influenced folk, bluegrass and country blues
artists; contemporary disciples include guitar

virtuosos such as Leo Kottke and John
Fahey. In his own time James had an
impact on Robert Johnson via such songs as
the frightening "22-20 Blues," which
Johnson transformed into an equally
disturbing "30-20 Blues"; James's
monumental "Devil Got My Woman"
shows up in the melody and guitar
accompaniment of Johnson's "Hellhound on
My Trail," and one verse is incorporated
into Johnson's "Come on in My Kitchen."

The two Vanguard albums showcase Skip
James in fine form, and obviously, *Devil Got
My Woman* is a must-have on the strength
of the title track alone. Among the excellent
tracks on *Skip James Today!* is "I'm So
Glad," a James song from the '30s later
covered by Cream. No one sounded quite
like James, whose gentleness produced a
music that is more reflective than that of
many of his peers. Another essential Skip
James title is *Early Blues Recording—1931*,
released on Yazoo in CD form. It includes
the sides James cut for Paramount
(including the original version of "Devil Got
My Woman") that had such profound
impact on other blues artists.   — D.M.

SONNY JAMES
★ ★ ★ **The Best of Sonny James (Capitol,
        1966)**
★ ★ ★ **American Originals (Columbia, 1989)**
Until recent years, Sonny James, "the
Southern Gentleman," was a fixture on the
country charts with his comforting tenor
employed in the service of soothing,
romantic, and ofttimes sentimental, material.
Nevertheless his sincerity is endearing, and
even at his most cloying he comes across as
a man who walks it like he talks it. He was
one of the first country artists to have a
major pop hit in the early days of rock &
roll, when his stark, passionately delivered
ballad "Young Love" topped the chart in
1957. A follow-up single, "First Date, First
Kiss, First Love," played on the same theme
and was James's last entry in the Top
Thirty. As a country artist, though, he has
had numerous Number One singles. "When
the Snow Is on the Roses," remains a
moving evocation of home and hearth that
serves as James's equivalent of deep blues.
Both of the albums are recommended as
examples of Nashville-style mainstream
country done with feeling and dignity.
— D.M.

TOMMY JAMES & THE SHONDELLS
★ ★ ★½ **Crimson & Clover/Cellophane
        Symphony (1969, 1969; Rhino,
        1991)**

★ ★ ★½ **Anthology (Rhino, 1989)**
★ ★ **Tommy James: The Solo Years (1970–1981) (Rhino, 1991)**

Trash pop made in heaven. Crunching staccato bass, cricket sound effects, the best weirdo keyboard riff since Del Shannon's "Runaway," and Tommy panting away at his sexiest, "I Think We're Alone Now" may be the best of the Shondells. Or there's "Crimson and Clover," with its loopy wah-wah vocals, and a guitar break about as dramatic as the one in Cream's "Badge." Or "Crystal Blue Persuasion," its lounge-act rim-shots and chord changes elevated by Tommy's wetly earnest urge for transcendence. The point is, the Shondells made '60s radio fluff of a remarkable catchiness, employing theatrical studio trickery, irresistible instrumental flourishes and a talent for hooking the listener. Genuine, this crew wasn't. But they constructed shimmering pop surfaces with unerring instinct.

Born to be a teen idol, Michigan's Tommy James possessed a voice of absolute adolescent yearning, and a passion for sublime nonsense. He hit the Top Forty 15 times in five years. Obviously a singles artiste, James made albums that were crammed with filler. Any of his greatest hits sets are nifty. After the Shondells, he made the neatly thudding "Draggin' the Line," but his solo oeuvre doesn't stick in the mind with quite the bubblegum grip of his work with the band. — P.E.

JAMES GANG
★ ★ ★ **Yer Album (1969; One Way/MCA, 1991)**
★ ★ ★ ★ **Rides Again (MCA, 1970)**
★ ★ ★½ **Thirds (1970; One Way/MCA, 1990)**
★ ★ ★ **Live in Concert (1971; Mobile Fidelity/MCA, 1990)**
★ ★ ★ **16 Greatest Hits (MCA, 1973)**
★ ★½ **Bang (1973; Atco, 1990)**
★ ★½ **Miami (1974; Atco, 1990)**

This Cleveland power trio caught Pete Townshend's ear in 1969, and no wonder. Guitarist Joe Walsh mounts a dramatic, slashing rhythm attack clearly patterned after the Who. Rather than soloing forever like Eric Clapton's legions of followers, Walsh lets the power chords do the talking interrupting the flow with brief, stinging leads. *Rides Again*, James Gang's second and best album, showcases Walsh's keen pop sense on its more melodic second half. The first side lays on those riffs with a satisfyingly heavy touch. "Funk #49" ends

up much closer to Grand Funk than James Brown, but it moves. After flashing his chops with "The Bomber," Walsh unveils a talent for surging keyboard melodies ("Tend My Garden") and a taste for mild-mannered country rock ("There I Go Again"). Those two tracks neatly predict Walsh's subsequent solo career and stint with the Eagles. His leaping sense of ambition, not to mention a little *variety*, makes *James Gang Rides Again* an enduring hard-rock landmark.

Drummer Jim Fox and bassist Dale Peters kept the band going after Walsh departed in 1971. Initially, they recruited two Canadians, singer Roy Kenner and guitarist Dominic Troiano, and recorded two fairly tepid albums, *Straight Shooter* and *Passin' Thru*. Troiano then left, and Walsh recommended his former bandmates hire Tommy Bolin, a talented Jimmy Page devotee. Previously with the Denver-based group Zephyr, Bolin stayed around for two albums, *Bang* and *Miami*, then went on to play with Deep Purple and record two solo albums (now out of print) before he died in 1977. Cult fanatics and guitar students can up *Bang*'s grade a notch: Bolin's slow-burning sonic wallop rises out of these mundane rock-star fantasies like exotic smoke. Fans of songs and singing can live without it. — M.C.

JAN AND DEAN
★ **The Best of Jan and Dean (EMI, 1987)**
★ ★ ★ ★ **Surf City: The Best of Jan and Dean–The Legendary Masters Series (EMI, 1990)**

High-school buddies in Los Angeles, Jan Berry and Dean Torrance had experienced only minor success with a handful of mainstream, ineffectual rock singles in the early '60s before fate intervened and teamed them on a show with the Beach Boys in 1963. Brian Wilson began collaborating on songs with Berry, and the duo immediately produced a Number One single in May of '63, "Surf City." Jan and Dean had lithe bodies and surfer-boy good looks, but until Wilson came on the scene they were hurting for material that mapped into their culture and their image. Turnabout being fair play, Jan and Dean often popped into Beach Boys recording sessions. Dean, for instance, sang the uncredited lead vocal on the Boys' hit cover version of "Barbara Ann." The Wilson-Berry team (often with Wilson collaborator Roger Christian in on the action) produced a steady stream of hits for

Jan and Dean through the mid-'60s, most all of them trading on a Holy Trinity of themes—surfing, drag racing and girl chasing. Along the way Berry became a strong producer, fashioning a sound that packed layer after layer of detail beneath crisply-recorded vocals.

In '64 Jan and Dean's finest hour on record occurred in the form of "Dead Man's Curve." Detailing a horrible car wreck, the song makes its terrifying point both in the lyrics and in all-stops-out production flourishes such as screeching tires, breaking glass, a deadpan spoken-word bridge ("Well, the last thing I remember, Doc, I started to swerve . . . ") and a full-bore instrumental blast as J&D's multi-tracked voices shout, "Won't come back from Dead Man's Curve!" A similar approach was used on "Ride the Wild Surf." Of the 22 tracks on *Surf City*, 18 are Berry productions, most of them models of inspired choices behind the board. In addition to the hit singles, the album also contains some rather obscure but nonetheless commendable Jan and Dean efforts, most notably "She's My Summer Girl" and "Meet Batman."

Where Jan and Dean were headed artistically became a moot point in April of 1966 when Berry's Corvette crashed into a parked truck near the real Dead Man's Curve in Los Angeles. After being in a coma for a month, Berry regained consciousness; but he had suffered severe aphasia as a result of his head injuries, and it would be another seven years before he performed again. Even so, he had difficulty speaking—and for all intents and purposes could not sing with any degree of professional polish or even amateur enthusiasm—and remained partially paralyzed on his right side.

The Best of Jan and Dean is an atrocity—ten cuts of barely in-tune pseudo doo-wop/rock with the duo attempting to insert the bomp-a-bomp in as many songs as possible. All that's of interest on this set are "Jennie Lee," the Jan and Arnie hit from 1958 that teamed Berry with his friend Arnie Ginsberg on a recording made in Berry's garage; and Jan and Dean's first hit, "Baby Talk," an inexplicable omission from the *Surf City* set. — D.M.

JANE'S ADDICTION

★★★½ Jane's Addiction (Triple X, 1987)
★★★ Nothing's Shocking (Warner Bros., 1988)
★★★★ Ritual de lo Habitual (Warner Bros., 1990)

By far the most distinctive band to bubble up out of the L.A. rock underground in the late '80s, Jane's Addiction fashioned a dense, churning sound that captured both the droning intensity of alternative-rock faves like Siouxsie and the Banshees as well as the dramatically shifting dynamics that made mainstream rockers like Led Zeppelin so popular. On top of which the group also had helium-voiced Perry Farrell, one of the few front men of his generation who could genuinely be considered provocative. Getting this act on vinyl was easier said than done, however; *Jane's Addiction*, recorded live, conveys a sense of the band's ferocity but its mid-fi sound doesn't offer much detail. Though the sound problems were easily remedied with *Nothing's Shocking*, the music sounds stilted, as if the band lost sight of the songs in its eagerness to make neat sounds. Which may be why *Ritual de lo Habitual* emphasizes groove over almost everything else, for that allows Farrell and guitarist Dave Navarro plenty of room to play with dynamics while maintaining a sense of structure—something which no doubt explains the extraordinary wallop of songs like "STOP!" and "Been Caught Stealing." — J.D.C.

BERT JANSCH

★★★½ Jack Orion (Vanguard, 1970)
★★★½ Sketches (Temple, 1990)
★★★½ The Ornament Tree (Gold Castle, 1991)

As a member of Pentangle, guitarist Bert Jansch helped pioneer the late-'60s Brit folk renaissance—an eclectic movement that relied as heavily on medieval influence as it did on blues and Scots-Irish traditional music. His classic solo album remains *Jack Orion*; his finger-picking style is polytechnically impressive but, more importantly, soulful. In the '80s, a number of small labels released Jansch albums—*Rare Conundrum and Thirteen Down* (Kicking Mule), *Strolling Down the Highway* (Transatlantic), *Heartbreak* (Hannibal). They're out of print and hard to find but worth seeking out as examples of powerful, subtle acoustic guitar work. In 1990, Jansch came on strong with *Sketches*, a sterling collection of British Isles folk. — P.E.

AL JARREAU

★★★ We Got By (Reprise, 1975)
★★ Glow (Reprise, 1976)
★½ Look to the Rainbow: Live in Europe (Warner Bros., 1977)

★½ **All Fly Home (Warner Bros., 1978)**
★★★ **This Time (Warner Bros., 1980)**
★★★ **Breakin' Away (Warner Bros., 1981)**
★★★ **Jarreau (Warner Bros., 1983)**
★★ **High Crime (Warner Bros., 1984)**
★★½ **In London (Warner Bros., 1985)**
★★★ **L Is for Lover (Warner Bros., 1986)**
★★★ **Heart's Horizon (Reprise, 1988)**

Al Jarreau isn't a jazz singer, just a jazzy one, a soul stylist whose taste in vocal ornamentation runs not to the usual range of gospel-derived melisma but to a sort of scat-style improvisation. It's an odd sound, and definitely something of an acquired taste, particularly since Jarreau's choice in scat syllables runs mostly to "oing," "enngh" and "baoww," as if he'd modeled his sound on the twanging of rubber bands. That's not a problem on *We Got By*, on which the songs (written by Jarreau) provide enough of a framework to keep his vocalisms in check. But the cover-packed *Glow* is another matter, for Jarreau's renditions of "Fire and Rain" and "Your Song" shed no light on the songs themselves, instead emphasizing the peculiarity of his sound. Still, it's nowhere near the annoyance *Look to the Rainbow* is, as Jarreau's mannerisms run amok through these live versions of Paul Desmond's "Take Five" and his own "We Got By." By *All Fly Home*, Jarreau's aesthetic is so muddled that "She's Leaving Home" is played as soul while "Sittin' on the Dock of the Bay" is treated with the antiseptic respect of art rock.

Fortunately, producer Jay Graydon comes aboard for *This Time* and straightens things out. Rather than jettison Jarreau's jazziness, Graydon focuses the singer's approach so the album ends up stressing tuneful material like Chick Corea's "Spain (I Can Recall)" and Jarreau's own "Never Givin' Up." But it's *Breakin' Away* that pays the biggest dividends, for this album finds Jarreau strutting his stuff through a demanding (but listenable) version of Dave Brubeck's "Blue Rondo a la Turk," but making the most of his pop smarts on "We're in This Love Together." All told, it's probably the singer's most balanced album, though both *Jarreau* and *High Crime* have their points, particularly when the singer stresses his pop side.

Although the live *In London* makes up a bit for the indulgences of *Look to the Rainbow*, it adds little to the singer's catalog. *L Is for Lover* is another story, though, for this Nile Rodgers–produced album rounds out its funky foundation with melodies intricate enough to give Jarreau something to chew on, an approach that's

more inventive and just as listenable as the kind of conventional funk dispensed by *Heart's Horizon.* — J.D.C.

JASON AND THE SCORCHERS
★★★ **Thunder and Fire (A&M, 1989)**

Jason and the Scorchers came out of the South—Nashville, specifically—in the early '80s pushing searing, razor-sharp guitar-based rock informed by traditional country, urban blues, Southern soul, and the first generation of Southern rock as exemplified by Lynyrd Skynyrd. In Jason Ringenberg the band had a forceful, personable lead singer and frontman, and in Warner Hodges it had a lead guitarist as conversant with Keith Richards as he was with the Duane Allman–Dickie Betts–Rossington-Collins axis (with frequent nods to Eddie Van Halen as well). Good press and strong live shows didn't translate to record sales, and despite a promising start with the EMI releases *Fervor* and *Lost and Found* (both now out of print) the band never quite clicked. In 1989 they resurfaced on A&M with *Thunder and Fire*, a strong effort that shows some of Steve Earle's influence in its hard-edged approach. In fact, Earle's involvement (he co-wrote the album's richest song, "Bible and a Gun") points up a problem with Jason and the Scorchers. Where Earle's music has grown by quantum leaps since his *Guitar Town* debut, Jason and the Scorchers were still singing about girls and driving in pretty much the same basic terms. Ringenberg released a solo album, *One Foot in the Honky Tonk* (Liberty), in 1992. — D.M.

JAY AND THE AMERICANS
★★ **All-Time Greatest Hits (Rhino, 1986)**
★ **Greatest Hits (EMI, 1988)**

A change in lead singers following this Brooklyn quintet's first hit, "She Cried," from 1962, set the stage for a string of hit singles through the '60s featuring Jay Black's booming tenor and arrangements often so bombastic that the rest of the vocalists tended to disappear in the mix. The great rock songwriting team of Jerry Leiber and Mike Stoller provided the reconstituted group with its first hit of '63, "Only in America," originally cut by the Drifters and then rejected by Atlantic Records because the label felt it was wrong for a black group to be singing a song suggesting anyone "could grow up to be President," when all available evidence indicated this theory applied only to people with white skin. That intrusion of politics into the career of Jay and the Americans may be the most interesting fact in the group's history. Their hits never pretended to relevance, but instead were good if unchallenging pop songs that operated a couple of notches above standard fare owing to the power and emotion of Black's singing. Rhino's set collects all the group's hits and is hands down the title to own. EMI's *Greatest Hits* set is missing "Let's Lock the Door (and Throw Away the Key)" and "Livin' Above Your Head," a couple of Jay the Americans' best tracks. On the other hand, two major miscalculations are absent from *Greatest Hits*, one being a cover of the Drifters' "This Magic Moment" that is completely lacking the original's sense of romance and wonder; and a cover of the Ronettes' "Walking in the Rain" that is ill-conceived in every respect. — D.M.

BLIND LEMON JEFFERSON

★ ★ ★ ★ ★ **Blind Lemon Jefferson (Milestone, 1974)**
★ ★ ★ ★ ★ **King of the Country Blues (Yazoo, 1988)**
★ ★ ★ **Penitentiary Blues (Collectables, 1989)**

Among the influential blues guitarists of the 1920s, only Lonnie Johnson's stature compares to that of Blind Lemon Jefferson, the first in a long line of great blues guitarists hailing from Texas. His unpredictable riffs and irregular rhythms seemed to have sprung organically from his own genius, free from any easily pinpointed influence. At once amazed and baffled by Jefferson's difficult style, his peers began working variations on it, but ultimately no one sounded like the master himself. As a songwriter, Jefferson was given to the dark, brooding tales common among country blues artists, but he was also a wise and often witty observer of his own life and the follies he saw all around him. "See That My Grave Is Kept Clean" and "Easy Rider Blues" are among the songs he wrote that have become blues classics, and another song, "Matchbox," was retooled by Carl Perkins into a rockabilly raveup, and was later covered by the Beatles. Jefferson recorded steadily between 1926 until his death in 1929 or 1930, an indication of his popularity, as blues artists of this period found themselves unwelcome in recording studios as soon as their record sales fell off.

The Yazoo and Milestone albums are highly recommended, with little duplication between them. Both are also well-annotated. By comparison, the nine-track *Penitentiary*

Blues duplicates a few of the songs on the Milestone set, and its generic annotation fails to provide any information about the album itself. Aficionados, however, will find the two versions of "Black Snake Moan" interesting, as well as the starkly rendered title song. — D.M.

JEFFERSON AIRPLANE

★ ★ ★ **Takes Off (1966; RCA, 1989)**
★ ★ ★ ★ **Surrealistic Pillow (RCA, 1967)**
★ ★ ★ ★ **After Bathing at Baxter's (1967; RCA, 1989)**
★ ★ ★ ½ **Crown of Creation (RCA, 1968)**
★ ★ ★ ★ **Bless Its Pointed Little Head (1969; RCA, 1989)**
★ ★ ★ ★ ½ **Volunteers (RCA, 1969)**
★ ★ ★ **The Worst of the Jefferson Airplane (RCA, 1970)**
★ ★ ★ **Bark (Grunt, 1971)**
★ ★ ★ **Long John Silver (Grunt, 1972)**
★ ★ ½ **Thirty Seconds Over Winterland (Grunt, 1973)**
★ ★ ★ **Early Flight (Grunt, 1974)**
★ ★ ★ ★ ★ **2400 Fulton Street (RCA, 1987)**
★ ★ ★ **White Rabbit and Other Hits (RCA, 1990)**
★ ★ ½ **Jefferson Airplane (Epic, 1989)**

Even though the group adhered faithfully to the tribal ethic that sparked the Summer of Love and its resultant psychedelic explosion, the Jefferson Airplane couldn't help distinguishing themselves from the rest of their fellow tie-dyed pioneers. For one thing, the band boasted a lineup none of its peers could match—both Marty Balin and Grace Slick were remarkable singers, Jorma Kaukonen a ferocious guitarist, and Jack Casady the most dexterous American rock bassist. For another, all of them wrote: while rhythm guitarist Paul Kantner's contributions came to dominate, it was the fertile exchange of diverse styles and ideas among the members that produced a vison darker and deeper than any other in acid rock.

Jokingly dubbing themselves after the mythic bluesman "Blind Thomas Jefferson Airplane," the group was formed by Balin in 1965. Sturdy folk rock, the first album, *Jefferson Airplane Takes Off*, highlighted Balin's rich, sensuous singing and ballad writing, but the band's distinctiveness came from featuring a strong second vocalist, Signe Anderson. It wasn't until her departure, however, and the release of *Surrealistic Pillow*, that the group hit its stride. New member Grace Slick's "Somebody to Love" and "White Rabbit" became Airplane anthems, their soaring melodies coaxing inventive arrangements and a new instrumental assertiveness from the rest of the band. And Slick's singing made her the counterpart of San Francisco's other reigning diva, Janis Joplin. Where Janis was raw blues urgency, her persona combining the toughness of biker's mama with the pathos of a strayed waif, Slick was queenly, stentorian, her voice an instrument of almost operatic authority and her beauty dark, mysterious and remote. *Surrealistic Pillow* was a record commanding enough that the band couldn't be ignored—and by dint of its sheer melodicism it cracked open AM radio. Acid rock insinuated itself into the mainstream.

By contrast, *After Bathing at Baxter's* flipped out into experimentalism of a kind baffling to all but the trippiest of the Airplane's fans. Melody still held on in Kantner's "The Ballad of You and Me and Pooneil" and "Won't You Try/Saturday Afternoon," but such inside jokes as "A Small Package of Value Will Come to You, Shortly" and an overall air of maniacal weirdness made for strange, adventurous music more admirable than likable—and more than a little forbidding. Relative accessibility, at least in terms of the Airplane's music, returned with *Crown of Creation*. By now the group's playing had evolved into a compelling mastery, but the band's thematic concerns were becoming more abstruse—Kanter had become obsessed with sci-fi; drummer Spencer Dryden turned woozily mystical with an odd ditty entitled "Cushingura"; and Slick was working her own sex-as-liberation trip with a version of David Crosby's ménage à trois ode, "Triad." A blistering live set, *Bless Its Pointed Little Head*, removed the band from the hothouse environment the studio had become; and when the group returned to record, it emerged with a masterpiece, *Volunteers*. A summing up of psychedelia, the record featured a host of hippie royalty—Jerry Garcia, David Crosby, Stephen Stills—and the Airplane's most cohesive set of songs. Crosby-Kantner-Stills's "Wooden Ships" blended sci-fi and a bittersweet utopianism; the title track, "We Can Be Together" and the rest of the record rocked with more assurance than the Airplane had ever summoned before. With Balin departed, neither *Bark* nor *Long John Silver* flourished the tradmark Airplane sound, and while the addition of violinist Papa John Creach affirmed that the band's experimental edge had not been blunted entirely, neither record was much more than

pleasant. *Thirty Seconds Over Winterland*, a live album, hardly packed as much punch as *Pointed Head*, and it served as a fairly uninteresting swan song. The Airplane came together in 1989 for a reunion album—but the synergy could not be recovered. Because the Airplane was a conceptual band, none of the greatest-hits albums really works, but, sheerly on the grounds of thoroughness, *2400 Fulton Street* is the best. — P.E.

JEFFERSON STARSHIP

★★★½ Blows Against the Empire (1970; RCA, 1988)
★★★½ Dragon Fly (1974; RCA, 1988)
★★★½ Red Octopus (Grunt, 1975)
★★★ Spitfire (Grunt, 1976)
★★★ Earth (Grunt, 1978)
★★★★ Gold (Grunt, 1979)
★★ Freedom at Point Zero (Grunt, 1979)
★★ Modern Times (RCA, 1981)
★★ Winds of Change (Grunt, 1982)
★★ Nuclear Furniture (RCA, 1984)
★★★ Knee Deep in the Hoopla (RCA, 1985)
★★ No Protection (RCA, 1987)
★★★ Love Among the Cannibals (RCA, 1989)
★★★ Greatest Hits (Ten Years and Change, 1979–1991) (RCA, 1991)

Divisive, extreme and visionary, the Jefferson Airplane was a band of absolute artists—Jefferson Starship, at its best, became nothing but a band of hitmakers. While the Grateful Dead evolved into a ritual celebration of nostalgic utopianism, and the rest of the acid-rock pioneers simply vanished, those members of the Airplane who formed Jefferson Starship chose survival by means of sheer commercialism. The transformation of Paul Kantner and Grace Slick into crafty corporate rockers, of course, took a while, but by the mid-'70s the changeover had become concrete. Occasionally (and infuriatingly), their music echoed their former adventurousness, but in general they manufactured glossy zombie stuff—faceless, expert and bland.

A Kantner project starring Slick and members of the Grateful Dead, "Jefferson Starship" was originally a one-off assemblage responsible for *Blows Against the Empire* (1970), a sci-fi song suite that now suffers from concept-album creakiness but at its time boasted an experimental edge. In 1974 Kantner and Slick put together Jefferson Starship, the actual working group. Their proven songwriting skills and Slick's vocal expertise made the new band appear promising—but the seeds of mediocrity had already been sown. Exhausted by working alongside difficult virtuosos in the Airplane, Slick and Kantner traded down when picking new players— Pete Sears (a Rod Stewart session man) and David Freiberg (ex-Quicksilver) on keyboards and bass were unthreateningly competent; guitarist Craig Chaquico substituted '70s flash for '60s soul. Papa John Creach, the Airplane's violinist, provided spark for a while but soon dropped out; Grace's old singing partner, Marty Balin, would periodically (and fitfully) collaborate throughout Jefferson Starship's career—almost all of his appearances garnering the band a skillful, hollow hit.

"Caroline" and "Ride the Tiger," from *Dragon Fly*, and "Play on Love" and "Fast Buck Freddie," from *Red Octopus*, defined the early Starship sound—smooth instrumental work, strong singing and occasionally interesting lyrics. But with Balin's "Miracles," *Octopus*'s massive hit, the band began shifting toward the schmaltz that would characterize almost all of its following hits. Balin now sounded like a lounge singer, and on *Spitfire* and *Earth*, smarmy expertise ruled, resulting in a passel of hits ("With Your Love," "Count on Me," "Love Too Good" and "Runaway") that quivered with the ersatz "sexiness" typical of '70s AOR fare. Balin departed on the advent of *Freedom at Point Zero*, his place taken by ex–Elvin Bishop Group singer Mickey Thomas. A vocalist with all of the arena-rock aspirations to become another Steve Perry, Thomas perfectly suited Jefferson Starship in its relentless descent into mediocrity.

The hits kept on a-comin'—"Jane" (*Freedom*), "Sara," "We Built This City" (both from *Knee Deep in the Hoopla*), "Nothing's Gonna Stop Us Now" (*No Protection*). By 1985, the band had dropped "Jefferson" from its name—thus ditching painful memories of a glorious past. *Gold* is Jefferson Starship's greatest hits, and it's entertaining. *Starship* is the Starship best-of, and it's embarrassing. — P.E.

GARLAND JEFFREYS

★★★½ **Garland Jeffreys (Atlantic, 1973)**
★★★★ **Ghost Writer (A&M, 1977)**
★★★ **One-Eyed Jack (A&M, 1978)**
★★★½ **American Boy and Girl (A&M, 1979)**
★★★★ **Escape Artist (Epic, 1981)**
★★★ **Rock 'n' Roll Adult (Epic, 1981)**

★★½ **Guts for Love (Epic, 1983)**
★★★★ **Don't Call Me Buckwheat (RCA, 1992)**

A literate biracial rocker with a streetwise flair and a taste for reggae, Garland Jeffreys remains one of the best-kept secrets of the '70s. *Ghost Writer* is his most inspired stroke; "Wild in the Streets," previously released as a single, is a cruising chant-anthem that outguns the Jersey boardwalk bard himself. "I May Not Be Your Kind" and "Why-O" typify Jeffreys' frank, tuneful jabs at racism and other social issues; "35 Millimeter Dreams" bears down on a haunting image—and chorus. "Cool Down Boy" exults in Garland's street corner doo-wop roots. *One-Eyed Jack* is a somewhat confused, less-than-catchy concept album. *American Boy and Girl* comes closer to sustaining that narrative form: Jeffreys's compassion for the street kids he chronicles is audible, and the orchestrated set piece "Matador" landed him a European hit. *Escape Artist* is foursquare meat-and-potatoes "R.O.C.K." for the most part—and a guaranteed good time. Count on Garland to supply "True Confessions" and a couple of sneaky reggaefied love songs, too. After a nine-year layoff, Jeffreys was inspired to re-enter the fray after a thoughtless epithet landed on him. *Don't Call Me Buckwheat* is an eloquent, enraged response. Jeffreys reveals more of himself than ever before on tracks like "I Was Afraid of Malcolm," laying bare the double-edged impact of everyday language on "Racial Repertoire," "Spanish Blood" and the title track. All this musically underdeveloped album needs is a surefire melody or ripping rhythm track to put the message across. Garland Jeffreys deserves to be heard. — M.C.

JELLYBEAN

★★★ **Wotupski!?! (EP) (EMI America, 1984)**
★★★ **Just Visiting This Planet (Chrysalis, 1987)**
★★★★ **Jellybean Rocks the House (Chrysalis, 1988)**
★★½ **Spillin' the Beans (Atlantic, 1991)**

After making his name as a DJ, remix artist and producer, John "Jellybean" Benitez built up such an impressive catalog of hits that he eventually landed a record deal of his own. Like Quincy Jones, Jellybean's role on his own albums is largely supervisory, but his creative vision alone is enough. *Wotupski!?!*, for instance, includes two dance classics, "The Mexican" and the

Madonna-penned "Sidewalk Talk," while *Just Visiting This Planet* offers "Who Found Who." Good as these albums are, they don't quite deliver the punch of *Jellybean Rocks the House*, which features full-blown dance remixes of songs from both. Jellybean tries to get the best of both worlds with the CD version of *Spillin' the Beans* (which also features his singing debut) by augmenting the album with remixes of its best tracks. Unfortunately, the songs lack the melodic sparkle of his earlier hits, leaving the album long on beats but short on hooks. — J.D.C.

WAYLON JENNINGS

  ★ ★ ★ ★½ **The Taker–Tulsa/Honky Tonk Heroes (1971; 1973; Mobile Fidelity Sound, 1991)**
  ★ ★ ★ ★ **This Time (RCA, 1974)**
  ★ ★ ★ ★ **Dreamin' My Dreams (RCA, 1975)**
    ★ ★ ★ **Are You Ready for the Country (RCA, 1976)**
    ★ ★ ★ **I've Always Been Crazy (RCA, 1977)**
★ ★ ★ ★ ★ **Greatest Hits (RCA, 1979)**
    ★ ★ ★½ **It's Only Rock & Roll (RCA, 1983)**
    ★ ★ ★ ★ **Will the Wolf Survive (MCA, 1986)**
    ★ ★ ★ **The Best of Waylon (RCA, 1986)**
    ★ ★ ★ **Full Circle (MCA, 1988)**
    ★ ★ ★ **The Early Years (RCA, 1989)**
    ★ ★ ★ **New Classic Waylon (MCA, 1989)**
    ★ ★ ★ **The Eagle (Epic, 1990)**

WITH WILLIE NELSON

    ★ ★ ★½ **Waylon and Willie (RCA, 1978)**
    ★ ★½ **Waylon and Willie II (RCA, 1982)**
    ★ ★½ **Clean Shirt (Epic, 1991)**

WITH WILLIE NELSON, JESSI COLTER AND TOMPALL GLASER

    ★ ★ ★ **Wanted: The Outlaws (RCA, 1976)**

This plainspoken Texas troubadour began his career as Buddy Holly's bass player, though the Chet Atkins–produced *Early Years* (released in 1989) hardly makes that obvious. Waylon Jennings's rock & roll background does creep up in the sly rhythms of his country songs, however; just listen to the suave version of Chuck Berry's "Brown Eyed Handsome Man" on *Early Years*. Straining against Nashville slickness, Jennings asserts his rough-hewn sensibility with the taut, rollicking "The Only Daddy That'll Walk the Line."

Teaming up with producer–singer–studio owner Tompall Glaser in the early '70s, Jennings started making country records his way. The music gets stripped down to its honky tonk and western swing roots, while the lyrics reach for complexity and often achieve it. Most of these albums are out of print; the Mobile Fidelity CD matches a good one (*The Taker–Tulsa*) with a great one (*Honky Tonk Heroes*). The latter is a near-perfect set of songs (many written by Billy Joe Shaver); the title track, "Old Five and Dimers Like Me," "Black Rose" and "We Had It All" all define the Outlaw stance at its best, before self-awareness turned to self-consciousness.

For a while, however, Waylon Jennings jumped from strength to strength. *This Time* accentuates his quiet side, and introduces the first of many genial collaborations with Willie Nelson. *Dreamin' My Dreams* captures the full range of Jennings's talent, from the reflective title cut to the full-tilt rebellion of "Are You Sure Hank Done It This Way" and "Bob Wills Is Still the King." *Wanted: The Outlaws* and *Waylon and Willie* are of mostly historical interest now; the best songs on these breakthrough packages appear on other, superior albums by both Jennings and Nelson. In fact, Waylon's first *Greatest Hits* album offers a superb introduction to Jennings and the Outlaws as a whole, moving from "The Only Daddy That'll Walk the Line" on through to the Waylon and Willie trilogy: "Mamas Don't Let Your Babies Grow Up to Be Cowboys," "Good Hearted Woman" and the heart-shattering "Luckenbach, Texas."

By the early '80s, Jennings's eclectic approach had long since become inconsistent (except for two anthologies, his RCA albums have fallen out of print). His Neil Young cover (from *Are You Ready for the Country*) and Buddy Holly medley (from *I've Always Been Crazy*) are well worth searching out. But of his later RCA albums, only the sardonic, touchy *It's Only Rock & Roll* coheres in the way that those seemingly effortless '70s albums do.

Will The Wolf Survive confidently reasserts Jennings's presence on the country scene without his stooping to a new traditionalist makeover. The overall sound is appropriately terse, and Jennings's weatherbeaten voice cuts a little deeper than before, if that's possible. "Working Without a Net" might be the most realistic sobriety song of recent years, while the mid-life crisis of "Suddenly Single" and Los Lobos' rockin' title track both seem custom-made for Waylon's warm, questioning tone. He's been dogged by inferior, rote songwriting ever since, though. *The Eagle* contains some passable approximations of past glories, but Waylon Jennings can still lift up a piece of ready-made radio-fluff like "Gone" and send it soaring away. This semi-retired Outlaw may well have another card trick or two up his sleeve. — M.C.

THE JESTERS
★★½ **The Best of the Jesters (Collectables, NA)**

The Jesters were a mid-'50s New York quintet with a towering reputation among doo-wop aficionados that made *The Paragons Meet the Jesters* one of the genre's most sought-after recordings. Like the Jesters, the Paragons were a local group, and the two were often teamed in live mock-competitions. On record the Jesters were largely ineffectual from a sales standpoint, but left behind some good singles. One of these, "Love No One But You," was a New York R&B hit in 1957 and is in this collection. Not the best doo-wop group, the Jesters, but a cut above the average nonetheless. — D.M.

JESUS JONES
★★½ **Liquidizer (SBK, 1989)**
★★★ **Doubt (SBK, 1991)**

Acolytes of this British group suggest there's a postpunk/hip-hop fusion at work, but the actual sound of Jesus Jones doesn't exactly give up the funk. You've really got to dig through the pseudo-psychedelic clutter to get at any sort of groove; the use of sampling gives Jesus Jones a herky-jerky forcebeat that only the most sedentary Cure or Siouxsie fan could mistake for rap. *Liquidizer* resembles a Jell-O mold: a hodgepodge of stale ingredients in a bland, if colorful, casing. Jesus Jones latches onto an effective vehicle, an old-fashioned song, with *Doubt*'s "Right Here, Right Now," and drives it home. In years to come, Jesus Jones's brand of future schlock will be recalled as a weird, jumbled dream or maybe a particularly vicious hangover from the '80s. Set the alarm. — M.C.

JESUS AND MARY CHAIN
★★★½ **Psychocandy (Reprise, 1985)**
★★★½ **Darklands (Warner Bros., 1987)**
★★★ **Barbed Wire Kisses (Warner Bros., 1988)**
★★½ **Automatic (Warner Bros., 1989)**
★★★ **Honey's Dead (Def American, 1992)**

A "Be My Baby" drum riff kicks off *Psychocandy* and the entire album's 14 songs contain rock quotes—the Velvet Underground's dark, trancelike power, distorted jangling guitars that sound like fuzztone Byrds, deep vocals that recall Jim Morrison or Echo and the Bunnymen's Ian McCulloch. No matter how derived the sound, though, the record has its own intensity—Glasgow brothers Jim and William Reid make brooding hypnotic noise that captures the ambiance of a black-and-white underground movie.

With *Darklands*, the Chain cleans up the atmosphere considerably—"Darklands" wouldn't be out of place on a Psychedelic Furs record; "April Skies" doesn't sound dissimilar to R.E.M.'s postmodern pop. But the ominous beauty remains. *Barbed Wire Kisses* is mainly B sides, but some of it is irresistible—a deconstruction of the Beach Boys' "Surfin' U.S.A." and the Chain's own priceless "Bo Diddley Is Jesus." The Reid brothers recorded *Automatic* as a duo, and the album seems sketchy and solipsistic. A move to Def American brought an improved effort, *Honey's Dead*, in 1992. — P.E.

REVEREND CLAUDE JETER
★★★★ **Yesterday and Today (Spirit Feel/Shanachie, 1988)**

To pop listeners, Jeter may be of primary interest as an influence on Al Green's singing style (indeed Green's phrasing at times almost eerily recalls Jeter's), but the Reverend is a powerhouse all on his own. Forming the Harmony Kings in the late 1930s, the Alabama-born gospel singer in time became one of the form's true stars; his innovative falsetto was his trademark. In 1942, the Kings changed their name to the Swan Silvertones and evolved into a quartet so accomplished that their fame transcended gospel circles. Their a capella work remains astonishing, and it's Jeter's voice that truly soars. *Yesterday and Today* (1988) is Jeter live with the Silvertones and other gospel stars. Remarkable and urgent music, the collection proves the continuing vitality of gospel—and the song selection is so irresistible that even heathens should be able to groove. — P.E.

JETHRO TULL
★★★ **This Was (Chrysalis, 1969)**
★★★½ **Stand Up (Chrysalis, 1969)**
★★★½ **Benefit (Chrysalis, 1970)**
★★★½ **Aqualung (Chrysalis, 1971)**
★ **Thick as a Brick (Chrysalis, 1972)**

★ ★ ★ ★   **Living in the Past (Chrysalis, 1972)**
★   **Passion Play (Chrysalis, 1973)**
★ ★   **War Child (Chrysalis, 1974)**
★ ★ ★   **Minstrel in the Gallery (Chrysalis, 1975)**
★ ★ ★   **M.U./The Best of Jethro Tull (Chrysalis, 1976)**
★ ★   **Too Old to Rock 'n' Roll, Too Young to Die (Chrysalis, 1976)**
★ ★ ★   **Songs from the Wood (Chrysalis, 1977)**
★ ★   **Heavy Horses (Chrysalis, 1978)**
★ ★   **Bursting Out/Jethro Tull Live (Chrysalis, 1978)**
★ ★   **Storm Watch (Chrysalis, 1979)**
★ ★ ★   **A (Chrysalis, 1980)**
★ ★ ★   **Broadsword and the Beast (Chrysalis, 1982)**
★   **Walk Into Light (Chrysalis, 1983)**
★   **Under Wraps (Chrysalis, 1984)**
★ ★ ★   **Crest of a Knave (Chrysalis, 1987)**
★ ★ ★ ½   **20 Years of Jethro Tull (Chrysalis, 1988)**
★ ★   **Rock Island (Chrysalis, 1989)**
★ ★ ★   **Catfish Rising (Chrysalis, 1991)**

Jethro Tull isn't his name, of course, but it might as well be. At the mere mention of this venerable British art-rock outfit, most people flash on the image of flute-wielding Tull frontman Ian Anderson. *This Was* and *Stand Up*, both from 1969, present the group as jazz- and folk-influenced progressives; Anderson's rasping, meldodramatic style of play takes off from Rashaan Roland Kirk's multi-reed explorations. Guitarist Martin Barre contributes heavy, hooky riffs to accompany Anderson's burgeoning songwriting voice on *Stand Up*. And then, Tull clicked with young American audiences. *Aqualung* combines heaving melodies and moralistic liberal diatribes against church and state: you know the rest. Thanks to twenty years of radio rotation, heavy-handed manifestos like "Aqualung" and "Wind Up" rank right up there with "Stairway to Heaven" on the over-familiarity meter. *Living in the Past,* which ably documents Tull to this point, is recommended over the later compilations.

The immediate success of *Aqualung* spurred Anderson to indulge his artistic whims, resulting in two virtually unlistenable theatrical concept albums: *Thick as a Brick* (quite) and *Passion Play*. After that strategy backfired, Jethro Tull returned to traditional song structure on *War Child* and the acoustic-flavored *Minstrel in the Gallery*. Things were never quite the same again, though. Anderson's bizarre stage presence and the band's back catalogue made Tull a popular live act throughout the '70s—long after its records had ceased to hold much interest for anyone but hard-core fans. After the excessively snide 1976 hit *Too Old to Rock 'n' Roll, Too Young to Die,* Tull retreated into a sylvan glade of arty Elizabethan folk rock. This latter-day approach is best captured on *A,* on which former members of Fairport Convention and Roxy Music add crucial support. After releasing a pair of electronic stinkers (*Walk Into Light* and *Under Wraps*) in the '80s, Anderson retired the Tull moniker for several years. The 1988 box-set retrospective (*20 Years of Jethro Tull*) is a maddening, overstuffed hodgepodge—representative, but mighty tough for the average listener to wade through. Jethro Tull released the folkish *Crest of a Knave* in 1987; *Catfish Rising* contains the most rock-oriented—and catchy—songs Anderson has committed to disc since the '70s. — M.C.

THE JETS

★   **The Jets (MCA, 1985)**
½ ★   **Christmas with the Jets (MCA, 1986)**
★ ½   **Magic (MCA, 1987)**
★   **Believe (MCA, 1989)**
★ ★   **Best of the Jets (MCA, 1990)**

Tonga's answer to the Osmonds, the eight Wolfgramm children who comprise the Jets are wholesome, talented and apparently incapable of making music with any kind of edge at all. Not that it kept them from cracking the charts; indeed, the group's catchily vapid singles infested the Top Forty on a regular basis in the late '80s. When devoting themselves to upbeat material like "Crush On You" (from *The Jets*) or "Cross My Broken Heart" (from *Magic*), the Jets are almost bearable, but it takes a fistful of Dramamine to get through their ballads. As such, *Best of the Jets* is the only album worth bothering with, keeping in mind, of course, that "best" is a relative term. — J.D.C.

JOAN JETT

★ ★ ★ ★   **Bad Reputation (1981; Blackheart, 1992)**
★ ★ ★ ★   **I Love Rock 'n' Roll (1981; Blackheart, 1992)**
★ ★ ★ ½   **Album (1983; Blackheart, 1992)**
★ ★ ★   **Glorious Results of a Misspent Youth (1984; Blackheart, 1992)**
★ ★ ★   **Good Music (Blackheart, 1986)**
★ ★ ★   **Up Your Alley (Blackheart, 1988)**
★ ★ ★   **The Hit List (Blackheart, 1990)**
★ ★ ★   **Notorious (Blackheart, 1991)**

Liberated from the Kim Fowley–ruled Runaways, lead guitarist Joan Jett took off on a confident solo flight. Applying the punky "do it yourself" philosophy to the Gary Glitter-Sweet school of pop-metal, Jett aimed a killer one-two punch at the complacent gut of Album Oriented Radio. Her first and second albums are brilliantly summarized by their titles: No, Joan Jett doesn't give a damn 'bout her bad reputation and yes, she loves rock & roll with every fibre of her being. Mixing inspired cover versions and wide-eyed originals, *Bad Reputation* and *I Love Rock 'n' Roll* rocket along at a fleet-footed pace. But that fast 'n' loose go-for-what-you-know ambience—at first a source of strength—becomes a stylistic drawback on subsequent Jett outings.

Album, despite its generic title, finds Jett stretching her self-imposed boundaries a bit. A foursquare run-through of Sly's "Everyday People" feels heartfelt, but the song's underlying funky uplift gets plowed over by power chords. *Good Music* begins her retrenchment; the title track is a backward-gazing Beach Boys tribute, nostalgic harmonies included. A cover of "Fun, Fun, Fun" fares better, though the best tracks are originals this time: "This Means War," "Just Lust." "Black Leather" takes on the Aerosmith–Run-D.M.C. notion of rock-rap with a wink and a hot guitar riff, but the overall tone of *Good Music* is staunchly conservative. In three short years, Joan moves from defiant celebration to defending the verities.

Predictably, *Up Your Alley* brings the chartwise song doctor Desmond Child into the picture. Less predicably, Joan Jett connects with several of the infamous Bon Jovi collaborator's meaty hooks. She turns a by-the-numbers heartbreak anthem ("I Hate Myself for Loving You") into a rocking therapy session, imbuing clichéd lyrics with a howling sense of emotional turmoil. Chuck Berry's "Tulane" and the Stooges' "I Wanna Be Your Dog"—obvious but gratifying choices—round out a solid first volley, though *Alley*'s second half never regains that momentum.

The Hit List is entirely comprised of cover versions: newly recorded, if not exacly fresh, the selection ranges from AC/DC to ZZ Top. There are no surprises, and no letdowns; typical Joan Jett, in other words. *Notorious* could use a few *Hit List* leftovers. "Backlash" is a tangy, bittersweet matchup between Jett and Replacement Paul Westerberg. Truth be told, though, the Jett-Child-Diane Warren bombshell ("The

Only Good Thing [You Ever Said Was Goodbye]") blows that one away with its explosive chorus. "Machismo" flashes some of Jett's expected feisty spirit, though "Treading Water" turns out to be a little too apt. By the end of this competent-but-dull set, most listeners will be craving a classic rock snack—something along the lines of "Wipe Out" or "Kick Out the Jams." — M.C.

THE JIVE BOMBERS
★ ★ ★ ½ **Bad Boy** (Savoy Jazz, 1984)
The Jive Bombers' history dates back to the mid-'40s, when a configuration of the group, featuring the redoubtable lead singer Clarence Palmer, was a popular attraction in New York City nightclubs. Palmer, one of the outstanding voices and comedic singers in popular music, had been performing since the mid-'20s, when he and his two brothers, billed as the Palmer Brothers, developed an innovative style of vocal harmony that earned them top billing around Manhattan and praise from their peers in the jazz world. They recorded with Duke Ellington, and in 1941 joined the Cab Calloway Orchestra for a few years before Clarence's two brothers retired. Near the end of the decade, Palmer hooked up with a group of show business veterans that included the Tinney Brothers, Allen and Pee Wee; as the Sparrows, this lineup backed Al Sears on a recording of Lil Armstrong's "Brown Boy" (Armstrong, ex-wife of Louis Armstrong, had titled the song "Brown Gal" and recorded it herself in 1936) that was released on the Coral label in 1949. The Jive Bombers proceeded to endure numerous personnel changes over the years, but came up with a winning combination in 1956 when tenor saxophonist and vocalist Earl Johnson joined the group. "Brown Boy" was changed to "Bad Boy" when the Bombers recorded the song for Savoy Records, and Palmer, his voice sharp and echoic, produced one of his most rousing vocal performances.

"Bad Boy" vaulted the Jive Bombers into the Top Forty in early '57, and the group suddenly found itself sharing concert bills with a host of young upstart doo-wop and R&B vocal groups, some of whose members weren't even born when Palmer began his career. A follow-up single, "Cherry" (dusted off from 1928), failed to generate much interest, though, and Palmer took this as his cue to go solo. Neither he nor the reconstituted Jive Bombers had any further success.

Bad Boy is quintessential Jive Bombers,

sometimes funny, sometimes tender, sometimes in a blue mood. Two takes of "Bad Boy" are included, as well as "Cherry" and terrific renditions of "Stardust," "The Blues Don't Mean a Thing" and "All of Me." Palmer's is an unforgettable voice, and *Bad Boy* a tribute to a vocalist who stood toe-to-toe with the very best R&B singers of his time. — D.M.

JIVE BUNNY & THE MASTERMIXERS
½ ★ **Jive Bunny & the Mastermixers—The Album (Atco, 1989)**
It has been said that history repeats itself twice; first as comedy, then as tragedy. Jive Bunny, on the other hand, suggests that history repeats itself like a bad Mexican dinner. This collection of "mastermixes" burps up bits of rock and swing hits in an attempt to demonstrate a pop continuum stretching from "In the Mood" to "Rock Around the Clock," but ends up reducing everything to the level of semi-digested pap. In short, the sort of album that makes sampling seem like a hanging crime. — J.D.C.

THE JIVE FIVE
★ ★ ★½ **Greatest Hits (Collectables, NA)**
You find the makings of the Jive Five's stellar lead vocalist Eugene Pitt in history: in the brooding of the Five Blind Boys of Alabama's Clarence Fountain; in the ecstatic leaps of the soul common to Claude Jeter of the Swan Silvertones; in the sturdy machismo of Bobby "Blue" Bland; in the sensitivity of the Harptones' Willie Winfield. In effect, his style is a bridge connecting the last commercial gasp of Fifties doo-wop with the pop-oriented soul music of the early '60s. He has never been judged an innovator, and indeed he isn't, in the sense that Ray Charles is an innovator. But he is a great singer, and maybe that's enough. In 1961 he and his mates put it all together in grand fashion with the confessional "My True Story," as fine an account of faithless love as anyone put on record in the pre-Beatles era. Pitt's vocal is the true story, the real deal. He invests a simple, innocuous lyric like "She's a wonderful girl" with the destructiveness of a nine-pound hammer by delivering it almost as an aside, an afterthought, while putting a sorrowful twist on it that tells you all you need to know about the song's desperate characters. A nondescript R&B hit, "These Golden Rings," followed in 1962, along with a minor pop hit, the portentous "What Time Is It?" but it would be 1965 before the

group tasted true pop success again, with "I'm a Happy Man," a pop-soul entry that features an upbeat lyric playfully rendered by Pitt in a soaring, carefree style. By the end of the '60s the Five was down to four and had renamed itself the Jyve Fyve, but the quartet and its spelling belonged to another era. "I'm a Happy Man" is an egregious omission from this collection, but otherwise there's ample evidence here to prove Pitt's superiority in the vocal category. His reading of "The Girl with the Wind in Her Hair" is exquisitely delicate and worth the price of admission alone. In 1982 the group cut a new album, *Here We Are!*, for the now-defunct Ambient Sound label; it's worth scouting out, both for Pitt's potent vocals and for an interpretation of Steely Dan's "Hey Nineteen" that will bring tears. — D.M.

J.J. FAD
★ ★ ★ **Supersonic (Ruthless/Atco, 1988)**
★½ **Not Just a Fad (Ruthless/Atco, 1990)**
J.J. Fad is a rap one-hit wonder, and with a fairly unoriginal hit at that—"Supersonic," a low-budget rewrite of Salt-N-Pepa's "Push It" put together by N.W.A.'s production team. As for *Not Just a Fad*, I beg to differ. — J.D.C.

BILLY JOEL
★ ★ **Cold Spring Harbor (1971; Columbia, 1984)**
★ ★½ **Piano Man (Columbia, 1973)**
★ ★ ★ **Streetlife Serenade (Columbia, 1974)**
★ ★ ★½ **Turnstiles (Columbia, 1976)**
★ ★ ★ ★ **The Stranger (Columbia, 1977)**
★ ★ ★ **52nd Street (Columbia, 1978)**
★ ★ ★ **Glass Houses (Columbia, 1980)**
★ ★½ **Songs in the Attic (Columbia, 1981)**
★ ★ ★½ **The Nylon Curtain (Columbia, 1982)**
★ ★ ★½ **An Innocent Man (Columbia, 1983)**
★ ★ ★ ★ **Greatest Hits, Volumes 1 & 2 (Columbia, 1985)**
★ ★ ★½ **The Bridge (Columbia, 1986)**
★ ★ ★ **Kohuept (In Concert) (Columbia, 1987)**
★ ★ ★ ★ **Storm Front (Columbia, 1989)**
With Billy Joel, a light touch is everything. A sense of melody and song structure after the manner of Tin Pan Alley, the Brill Building, Burt Bacharach and Paul McCartney is Joel's most apparent gift; the

closer he keeps to it, the surer his approach. When he tries anything harder, he often comes off forced. He's best when he's most tuneful and relaxed.

"She's Got a Way" from *Cold Spring Harbor* set the pattern for the ballads Joel would soon turn out effortlessly on almost every album. "Everyone Loves You Now" was tougher, its note of sarcasm one he'd continue through the years. Already, on his first album, Joel showed himself a graceful pianist; his singing was harder to assess—an error in the record's mix (corrected in the 1984 re-release) sped up the vocal track and he sounds trebly. The title track of *Piano Man* gave Joel his first hit; it also introduced a trademark theme that he's since treated with alternate grace and bitterness—the pathos of the performer. Filled with ambitious story songs ("Captain Jack," "The Ballad of Billy the Kid"), the record provoked comparisons to Elton John and Harry Chapin.

The narrative vignettes off *Streetlife Serenade* ("Los Angelenos," "The Mexican Connection") strained too hard to be clever; "Roberta," a ballad, was more solid, and "The Last of the Big Time Spenders," with its rollicking jazzy piano was fun. Both the title song and "The Entertainer" again semi-ironically celebrated journeymen musicians. *Turnstiles* shows Joel writing with assurance and loveliness about family and memory ("I've Loved These Days," "Summer, Highland Falls"). "Say Goodbye to Hollywood" was a neat Phil Spector tribute, and "New York State of Mind" was Joel reaching an early acme. This new assurance paid off with *The Stranger*, Joel's commercial breakthrough. "Just the Way You Are" and "She's Always a Woman to Me" boasted strong and memorable melodies, and Joel's singing was elegant. "Only the Good Die Young" was more bouncy than rocking, but its words were interesting, and the overall atmosphere of the record was confident.

52nd Street, however, was too overbearing. The sweet music of "Honesty" was sabotaged by trite lyrics; "Big Shot" was bombastic, though the swagger of "My Life" was a good epitaph for the Me Decade. "Until the Night" was vast and romantic. *Glass Houses* displayed Billy in a black leather jacket on its cover, but the album's best track was the modest "Don't Ask Me Why" and the brassy "All for Leyna." On *The Nylon Curtain*, "Allentown" dealt with unemployment and "Goodnight Saigon" with Vietnam.

Examinations of domestic strife and modern-day pressures completed the record—along with the strong melody and philosophizing of "Scandinavian Skies."

Innocent Man—a spiritual tribute to doo-wop, the Four Seasons, the Drifters and the sound of early rock & roll ("Uptown Girl," "The Longest Time," "Leave a Tender Moment Alone")—is Joel's most likeable album. *The Bridge* echos *Innocent*'s lightness, if not in quite so breezy a fashion; its standout remains Billy's fond duet with Ray Charles on "Baby Grand." *Storm Front* found Joel in the unlikely guise of a stadium rocker. "We Didn't Start the Fire" kicked heartily, as did "I Go to Extremes." With a streamlined production helping out, Joel found a way to sound tough without seeming overwrought. Of Joel's live work, *Kohuept*, a record of his 1987 Leningrad concert, is sharper and more comprehensive than *Songs in the Attic*. His *Greatest Hits* is a fine overview of Joel's career to that point. — P.E.

DAVID JOHANSEN
★★★★ **David Johansen (1978; Razor & Tie, 1992)**
★★★½ **In Style (1979; Razor & Tie, 1992)**
★★ **Here Comes the Night (1981; Razor & Tie, 1992)**
★★★ **Live It Up (1982; Razor & Tie, 1992)**
★★★ **Sweet Revenge (Passport, 1984)**
BUSTER POINDEXTER
★★★ **Buster Poindexter (RCA, 1987)**
★★½ **Buster Goes Berserk (RCA, 1989)**

After his tenure with the New York Dolls and his zesty try at lipstick metal or glamor punk, Johansen settled down briefly in the late '70s for his most convincing mainstream rock. A singer engagingly in love with the sound of his own voice, Johansen vocalized big on his solo debut, *David Johansen*. All nine songs are brilliant guitar-stoked Stonesish rock: an ode to thrift shopping, "Funky but Chic" kicked butt, but giggled; "Donna" is the ultimate mythic teenage jukebox love lament. Critics loved the disc, and it sank like a stone.

Having always worked with Mick Ronson wannabes, Johansen decided to team up with real Mick on *In Style*. Another remarkable record, it may not have the songs the previous album boasted, but it has—in vast, thundering echos—the sound. Faltering briefly with *Here Comes the Night*, Johansen came back with *Live It Up*, an onstage raver that boasts a first-rate Animals medley.

With none of his rock & roll selling

much, it's hard to fault Johansen for manufacturing his next incarnation, the early R&B revue-cum-comedy act, Buster Poindexter—hard to fault, but pretty sad. (Johansen also began spending time as a character actor in several films.) As a white boy in psychic blackface on snappy numbers like the tropical "Hot Hot Hot," which appears on the first album in his new guise, *Buster Poindexter,* Johansen is fairly expert. And the gig is, in a pandering way, "fun," landing Poindexter in venues as diverse as *Saturday Night Live* and schmaltzy suburban lounges. But it's as a full-out rocker that he coulda been a contender.
— P.E.

ELTON JOHN

★★★★   Elton John (MCA, 1970)
★★★   Tumbleweed Connection (MCA, 1971)
★★½   11-17-70 (MCA, 1971)
★★★   Madman Across the Water (MCA, 1971)
★★★★   Honky Chateau (MCA, 1972)
★★★   Don't Shoot Me I'm Only the Piano Player (MCA, 1973)
★★★½   Goodbye Yellow Brick Road (MCA, 1973)
★★★½   Caribou (MCA, 1974)
★★★½   Greatest Hits (MCA, 1974)
★★★½   Captain Fantastic and the Brown Dirt Cowboy (MCA, 1975)
★★★½   Empty Sky (MCA, 1975)
★★★½   Rock of the Westies (MCA, 1975)
★★½   Blue Moves (MCA, 1976)
★★   Here and There (MCA, 1976)
★★★½   Elton John's Greatest Hits, Volume 2 (MCA, 1977)
★★½   A Single Man (MCA, 1978)
★   Victim Of Love (MCA, 1979)
★★½   The Thom Bell Sessions (1979; MCA, 1989)
★★   21 at 33 (MCA, 1980)
★★   The Fox (Geffen, 1981)
★★½   Jump Up! (Geffen, 1982)
★★★   Too Low for Zero (Geffen, 1983)
★★½   Breaking Hearts (Geffen, 1984)
★★½   Live in Australia (With Melbourne Symphony Orchestra) (MCA, 1987)
★★★   Elton John's Greatest Hits, Volume III (Geffen, 1987)
★★½   Reg Strikes Back (MCA, 1988)
★★½   Sleeping With the Past (MCA, 1989)
★★★★   To Be Continued (MCA, 1990)
★★½   The One (MCA, 1992)

Elton John's U.S. debut quickly established him as Britain's leading entry in the singer-songwriter sweepstakes: even though *Elton John* was a breakthrough success, it barely hints at the flamboyant, piano-pounding Top Forty wunderkind lurking behind those sensible spectacles. "Your Song" ties a casual, folkie sense of intimacy to a carefully plotted pop melody—without sounding overly calculated. There are flashes of the rocker to come on "Take Me to the Pilot," but Bernie Taupin's mystifying lyrics and Paul Buckmaster's portentous string arrangements eventually pull this tune—and the rest of the album—in a more sensitive direction. Taupin has taken a lot of knocks for his writing over the years; still, his chemistry with John is immediately apparent. Right from the start, Elton's undeniable skills as a stage performer weren't all he had going for him.

Of course, that unlikely-at-first charisma surely didn't hurt. The live *11-17-70* was rushed out to capitalize on the buzz; as hasty as it sounds, at least there's no mistaking the hyper-animated John for James Taylor or Cat Stevens. *Tumbleweed Connection* and *Madman Across the Water* both suffer from uncertain melodies and Buckmaster's hollow-sounding orchestrations; somehow, he manages to make a real violin section sound like a Mellotron! But the lovely "Country Comfort" stands out amid *Tumbleweed*'s less pleasing downhome experiments, and memorable character sketches like "Levon" and "Tiny Dancer" (from *Madman*) document further songwriting development. (The first CD of the *To Be Continued* box set does a marvelous job of summarizing this gestation period, adding early efforts and worthy obscurities for detail.)

Honky Chateau bares the hooks and a wicked sense of humor: "Honky Cat" effectively sends up the hippie rusticism of *Tumbleweed Connection*, while "I Think I'm Gonna Kill Myself" can still sting parents' ears. On *Honky Chateau*, John also masters his pop chameleon act: "Honky Cat" kicks up a beguiling faux R&B groove to offset its sarcasm, "Rocket Man" compacts the atmosphere of the earlier productions into an evocative, catchy chorus, and the ballad "Mona Lisas & Mad Hatters" displays Elton's vastly underrated vocal prowess. You can tell he was listening to the competition—from Philly Soul singles to triple bills at the Fillmore—and learning from it.

For all his subsequent chart success, Elton John is very much an album artist. In his case, a volume of greatest hits or even two probably won't be enough. If you enjoy a certain hit, you should try the accompanying LP. Not everything works, but Elton always manages to set an overall tone for his records, so the hits and misses cohere into a messy, compelling gestalt. Unfortunately, CD reissues only tell part of the story: prime-period Elton records were elaborately packaged with color booklets, foldout sleeves and tons of pix—heavy on the wacky glasses and huge shoes. Today the music has to suffice, and suprisingly, it does just that.

Don't Shoot Me I'm Only the Piano Player introduces nostalgia, bubblegum and MOR into Elton's arsenal ("Crocodile Rock," "Teacher I Need You," "Daniel"). Yes, he was willing to try anything. The double album *Goodbye Yellow Brick Road* proves that with a vengeance. It's typical of John's catch-as-catch-can spirit; the smash "Bennie and the Jets" might be his most annoying moment, while lesser-known album cuts like "Grey Seal," "All the Young Girls Love Alice" and "The Ballad of Danny Bailey (1909–34)" rank with his best. *Caribou* contrasts hard-rock strut ("The Bitch Is Back") with unashamed swoon-crooning ("Don't Let the Sun Go Down on Me").

Captain Fantastic and the Brown Dirt Cowboy is a concept album that traces Bernie and Elton's working relationship up to that point. As expected, several excerpts stand up quite well on their own ("[Gotta Get a] Meal Ticket," "Someone Saved My Life Tonight"). *Rock of the Westies* starts off sounding slapdash and winds up rocking harder than any other Elton album: "Hard Luck Story" and "Street Kids" add considerable weight to the ironic spin of "Island Girl" and "Grow Some Funk of Your Own." *Empty Sky* is the American issue of Elton's 1969 British debut; for fans, anyway, the epic, eight-minute title track itself is worth the price of admission.

Elton John's superstar roll came to a grinding halt with *Blue Moves*. The reason why is plainly audible: two albums and nary a hook to be found—not even a pinpoint. *Greatest Hits Volume II* collects Elton's last couple of catchy gasps ("Philadelphia Freedom" and the featherweight "Don't Go Breaking My Heart"), before he sinks in a sea of musical confusion. What remains amazing is not Elton's fall from grace, but the sustained amount of time he stayed on top of the zeitgeist.

John reached his nadir with *Victim of Love* (1979): there were plenty of misconceived records during this era, but, really, a disco "Johnny B. Goode" is beyond the pale. Surprisingly, *Victim* is the only down-period Elton album that's out of print. There is nothing much to recommend until *Too Low For Zero* (1983). "I'm Still Standing" neatly reasserted Elton's melodic pizzazz; he made his point and his comeback without copping to the ususal show-biz "survivor" clichés. "I Guess That's Why They Call It the Blues" and "Sad Songs (Say So Much)" (*Breaking Hearts*) demonstrate Elton still knew his way around slow ones; however, the sly edge of his '70s work has been replaced by bland, feel-good sentiments. Even *The Thom Bell Sessions* fails to set off John's spark. He's still in fine voice, however; the 1987 live version of "Candle in The Wind," from the otherwise windy *Melbourne Symphony* album, cuts the original (from *Yellow Brick Road*) to shreds. But the title of his box-set overview *To Be Continued*—comes across as defensive rather than defiant, revealing Elton's touchy post-stardom position. Despite a disappointing fourth disc, though, *To Be Continued* accurately measures the breadth of a remarkable career. — M.C.

LITTLE WILLIE JOHN
★★★★★ **Free at Last (King, 1976)**
One of the strangest, most tortured yet curiously buoyant voices in the history of rhythm & blues belongs to Little Willie John, who lived fast, died young (at 30 of pneumonia while serving time on a manslaughter charge), and left an extraordinary legacy. His hits began when he signed with King Records at the age of 18 and released a single, "All Around the World," that owed much to the Kansas City boogie-woogie style and served notice that this young man knew a lot more about the ways of the world than his tender years would indicate. Beyond this, he left the impression that something terrible was gaining on him, that he was always, as he declared in one of his most moving performances, "suffering with the blues."

Thus, virtually everything John cut is double-edged. "Talk to Me, Talk to Me," a Top Twenty single in 1958, evolves from a gentle nudge to a desperate plea; "Sleep," his last hit, in 1960, juxtaposes a bright melody and bouncing rhythm against lyrics that suggest that only in dreams can comfort be found; "It Only Hurts a Little While" means to say that it hurts forever. *Free at Last* is 23 cuts worth of vintage Little Willie John, including the above-mentioned songs and other first-rate recordings, such as John's original 1956 version of "Fever"; the tortured "Big Blue Diamonds"; and a blues-rock raveup with Hank Ballard, "I Like to See My Baby." The album cover shows a prison cell with the words "Free at Last" written on the wall and the song titles listed below it. There is nothing, though, in Little Willie John's disposition on record to indicate he ever knew the feeling of freedom. This was a man with hellhounds on his trail to his dying day. — D.M.

BLIND WILLIE JOHNSON
★ ★ ★ ★ ★ Praise God I'm Satisfied (Yazoo, 1976)
★ ★ ★ ★ ★ Sweeter as the Years Go By (Yazoo, 1990)

Born in Texas in 1900, Blind Willie Johnson led a life that reads like pure blues legend. Learning his craft on a cigar-box guitar, he became a country blues evangelist and a "race records" giant, spreading the Gospel by means of bottleneck guitar and a singing style of absolute directness. In 1950, after his house burned down, Johnson caught pneumonia. A hospital turned him away (because of his blindness!), and he died after a long, remarkable career.

Both albums featuring material recorded between 1927 and 1930, the Yazoo collections are extraordinary; each boasts exemplary notes. *Praise God I'm Satisfied* concentrates on Johnson's slide guitar work; *Sweeter as the Years Go By* features his finger-picking style. His playing would influence musicians for years to come, but it's his singing that's truly riveting. "John the Revelator," "If I Had My Way I'd Tear the Building Down" and "Can't Nobody Hide From God" reveal the agony and joy of a soul given over completely to struggle with things divine. — P.E.

DON JOHNSON
★ ½ Heartbeat (Epic, 1986)
★ ★ ★ Let It Roll (Epic, 1989)

In the '60s, TV stars made albums all the time. Vocal ability wasn't an issue—fame was. And so a host of famous-but-unmusical actors ended up putting out albums, from Sebastian Cabot to Jack Webb to William Shatner. But Don Johnson, being a hip, late-'80s TV star, didn't start making records simply because he was famous. No, he made them because he was a frustrated rock singer who just happened to star in an enormously popular TV show (*Miami Vice*, in case you'd forgotten). Unlike the previous

generation of TV stars, Johnson could, in fact, carry a tune; trouble is, he couldn't carry it very well. Sounding at best like an anemic Don Henley, Johnson does his damnedest to sound like he knows what he's doing on *Heartbeat*, but not even the help of ringers like Bonnie Raitt, Willie Nelson and Stevie Ray Vaughan can cover for his anoretic tenor. To his credit, *Let It Roll* is a marked improvement. His voice is stronger, and his phrasing more assured—though not quite enough to warrant an attempt at "Tell It Like It Is"—and the cameos are kept to a minimum. Not that the music is any more listenable, but for a TV star, mere competence is achievement enough. — J.D.C.

LINTON KWESI JOHNSON
★ ★ ★ ½ Dread Beat an' Blood (1978; Frontline, 1991)
★ ★ ★ ★ ★ Forces of Victory (Mango, 1979)
★ ★ ★ ★ Bass Culture (Mango, 1980)
★ ★ ★ ½ LKJ in Dub (Mango, 1980)
★ ★ ★ ★ Making History (Mango, 1984)
★ ★ ★ ★ Reggae Greats (Mango, 1984)
★ ★ ★ ½ In Concert With the Dub Band (Shanachie, 1985)
★ ★ ★ ★ Tings an' Times (Shanachie, 1991)

Dub poetry is what Linton Kwesi Johnson calls it: a pulsating mixture of topical commentary, passionate observation and reasoned analysis set to a vibrant, adventurous reggae groove. A Briton of Jamaican descent, Johnson trains a sociologist's eyes and a musician's ears on black London; his portrait is acutely politicized, though never doctrinaire or self-righteous. Producer-keyboardist Dennis Bovell designs a distinct and accessible soundtrack, matching Johnson's clearheaded insights with punchy horn charts and John Kpiaye's jazzy guitar lines. Bovell deploys the spacey techniques of dub-style reggae to revealing effect; the eerie silences and jarring shifts underline the rhythmic lilt in Johnson's spoken-word flow. After a while, you sense the organic connection between music and subject matter. Once LKJ's messages and melodies sink in, they have a tendency to stick around.

Released under the moniker Poet and the Roots, *Dread Beat an' Blood* is an early sketch of the sound to come. The backdrop is much sparser, the tone choked with outrage at racial mistreatment. *Forces of Victory* doesn't back off from that anger so much as bolster it with hooky choruses and heated instrumental dialogues. "Fite Dem Back," "Independent Intavenshan," "Forces of Viktry": LKJ peppers his erudition with patois and street slang, without ever sounding like a slumming intellectual. On "Sonny's Lettah (Anti-Sus Poem)," he reads a prisoner's missive to his worried mother with a startling, personal immediacy. Rather than distancing a listener from the dramatic situation, LKJ employs this literary device as a means of entry—he puts you inside Sonny's head.

Bass Culture examines the power of music as well as political power struggles on cuts like "Reggae Sounds." There's even a love song ("Loraine"). "Street 66," "Reggae Fi Peach," and the title track continue the ongoing political discussions, to the accompanying tune of Bovell and the crack Dub Band. The overall thrust—beats meshed with ideas—prefigures the progressive wing of rap. After an extended silence, *Making History* finds Johnson's social consciousness developing alongside his musical confidence. Either *Reggae Greats* or the somewhat talky *In Concert With the Dub Band* can serve as an LKJ primer. His original albums stand tall as coherent entities, however, and they definitely pose a stronger bet. Anyway, Johnson just gets better: *Tings an' Times* steps beyond *Making History* with grace and assurance. Accordion and violin solos expand the music well beyond its Jamaican roots, while LKJ continues to extract "Sense Outa Nonsense." He even exhumes the ghost of communism on "Mi Revalueshanary Fren," questioning his own socialist faith at the same time. Though the seven-cut album is far too brief, there's plenty to digest.
— M.C.

LONNIE JOHNSON
★ ★ ★ ★ **Idle Hours (1961; Bluesville/Prestige, 1987)**
★ ★ ★ ★ **Losing Game (1961; Bluesville/Prestige, 1991)**
★ ★ ★ **Blues by Lonnie Johnson (Bluesville/Prestige, NA)**
★ ★ ★ ★ ★ **Steppin' on the Blues (Columbia, 1990)**

New Orleans–born Lonnie Johnson has been called the first great guitarist of the 20th century, and there's plenty of evidence to back up such a grandiose claim. Like his contemporary Jelly Roll Morton, Johnson began working professionally at an early age in the Storyville section of New Orleans. By the time he made his first recordings in 1925, Johnson had a growing reputation as

a guitarist without peer. Although blues was his medium of choice, Johnson worked comfortably in many styles, particularly jazz. In the '20s and '30s he recorded with Louis Armstrong's bands, including the Hot Five, one of the most influential outfits in jazz history, and his performances with the guitar virtuoso Eddie Lang from the same period rank among the most important and influential jazz recordings ever made. The style Johnson developed—aggressive single-string solos being a dominant feature of his playing—resonates in the work of some of the most celebrated guitarists in the jazz and blues idioms. In their harmonic sophistication, superb lyricism, and technical grace, Django Rheinhardt, Charlie Christian, Robert Johnson, Robert Jr. Lockwood, and B.B. King are only the most obvious heirs to the Johnson tradition.

However brilliant his guitar work, Johnson's greatness rests as well on his prolific output as a songwriter. From the time he began recording in 1925 until his death in 1970, he wrote hundreds of original songs that testify both to the sophistication he gained growing up in an urban environment and to his familiarity with country lore; these have added immeasurably to the language of the blues. Along with his contemporaries Big Bill Broonzy and Blind Lemon Jefferson, Johnson's records found a large audience, thus establishing the commercial viability of the blues. As well as recording on his own, he played numerous sessions with other artists—Chippie Hill, Victoria Spivey and Duke Ellington among them.

Johnson's in-print catalogue leaves something to be desired, considering his enormous output. The titles listed here, however, will provide interested listeners an earful of Johnson's genius. Columbia's *Steppin' on the Blues* captures Johnson at his peak in cuts dating from 1925 through 1932. Two Johnson-Lang duets are here ("Have to Change Keys [to Play These Blues]" and "Guitar Blues"), as well as two tracks featuring vocalist Texas Alexander and two with Johnson and Spivey in duet with Clarence Williams on piano. Apart from these the album is pure, undiluted Lonnie Johnson blues, with the man accompanying himself on guitar and sometimes with a piano player sitting in.

Prestige/Bluesville's *Idle Hours* teams Johnson with Spivey more than three decades after they had made their first recordings together. The two are wonderful together: Spivey's spunk is the perfect complement to Johnson's mellow singing, and some of Johnson's acoustic solos are among the tastiest he ever recorded. Though both were old warriors at the time of this 1961 recording, Spivey and Johnson sound revitalized when they spar and flirt their way through two Spivey-composed tunes, "Idle Hours" and "Long Time Blues." This is far from the trailblazing material Johnson recorded earlier in his career, but the authority and power of his work on *Idle Hours* is still worth cherishing. *Losing Game* and *Blues by Lonnie Johnson* are further examples of Johnon's artistry in peak form even in his later years. — D.M.

ROBERT JOHNSON
★★★★★ **King of the Delta Blues Singers (Columbia, 1961)**
★★★★★ **King of the Delta Blues Singers, Vol. 2 (Columbia, 1970)**
★★★★★ **The Complete Recordings (Columbia, 1990)**

It doesn't take a great leap of the imagination to declare Robert Johnson the winner of the 1990 comeback of the year award. Who could have foreseen that a two-CD boxed set of 41 recordings, 12 of them alternate takes, cut over the course of four days in 1936 and 1937 by a troubled blues man now dead 53 years would knock on the gold standard's door, selling over 350,000 copies and still counting? Is it blues being rediscovered? Is it simply cool to have Robert Johnson on CD? Or some way, somehow is his music moving the masses in ways heretofore unimagined? Whatever the answer, Robert Johnson is in people's lives again. This is a blessing.

Born out of wedlock on May 8, 1911 in Hazlehurst, Mississippi, Johnson learned the blues by studying and incorporating stylistic elements of the great Delta bluesmen all around his part of the state: Charlie Patton, the acknowledged father of the Delta blues and a riveting, relentlessly rhythmic guitarist whose exploration of the instrument's tonal possibilities opened new avenues of expression to every musician who heard him play; Son House, possibly the most gifted of the Delta guitarists, whose bottleneck technique enabled him to shape the instrument's sound into another voice, as Johnson would do later to stunning effect; Willie Brown, House's friend and also a superior guitarist, whom Johnson undoubtedly learned from as well, and indeed, even refers to as "my friend-boy Willie Brown" in "Cross Road Blues"; Lonnie Johnson, whose single-string style

Johnson quotes from liberally on "Malted Milk" and "Drunken Hearted Man." The list of influences is lengthy and somewhat overpowering, given the variety of styles Johnson ate up. His singular genius was to take this multitude of approaches, assimilate them, and create something that seemed to have been constructed out of whole cloth.

It's not Johnson's playing alone that's so remarkable, though. Breathtaking it is, but it's the playing in service of Johnson's anguished, bedeviled tales that elevates his work to a rarefied plateau. Rarely has an artist opened a vein and bled so profusely, admitting to visions of the hounds of hell chasing him ("Hellhound on My Trail"), of the torments of the flesh ("Terraplane Blues," "Phonograph Blues"), of the loneliness and pain of the drifter's life. Johnson's women aren't symbolic figures. He names names—Beatrice, Willie Mae, Bernice, Thelma, Ida Belle—and, love-starved, makes promises he sounds like even he doesn't believe. There is in his lyrics a desperation and sense of the moment that can transport a listener into the deep heart of Johnson's darkness, where the hurt and isolation become palpable. The songs have been widely covered and credibly so, by Muddy Waters, Elmore James, Big Joe Williams, Johnny Shines, Cream, the Rolling Stones, and others; as good as their versions are, Johnson's are much better, if only for the degree of tension and drama he brings to his own performances.

The Columbia two-CD boxed set includes a handsome book with priceless photos and a complete sessionography and discography. Keith Richards and Eric Clapton submit short appreciations of Johnson's influence on their own music, and music historian Stephen C. LaVere details specifics of Johnson's recording sessions in convincing fashion. LaVere's biography of Johnson is problematic, however. He offers an account of Johnson's death by poisoning that is the most detailed ever to reach print. Yet he cites no sources for this information, which is specific enough to include an account of a conversation between Johnson and Sonny Boy Williamson II that occurred only moments before Johnson drank bad whiskey. LaVere has reportedly spent several years researching Johnson's life and has a book in the works; the curious, though, are advised to turn to Robert Palmer (*Deep Blues*) and/or Samuel Charters (*Robert Johnson*) for more trustworthy portraits and appraisals. On the other hand, the cassette versions of the

original *King of the Delta Blues Singers*
releases contain no liner information
whatsoever, for those who wish to be
unburdened of context and history.
Scavengers should be on the lookout for the
vinyl version of *Vol. 2*, as it contains a
sensible essay on Johnson by blues authority
Pete Welding.

Finally, consider this: In one momentous
session Johnson cut "Cross Road Blues,"
"Walkin' Blues," "Last Fair Deal Gone
Down," "Preachin' Blues" and "If I Had
Possession Over Judgment Day." Has there
been any other single recording session that
produced music so beautiful, so tortured, so
insular and obsessive in its concerns with sin
and certain damnation, so historically
resonant? No. Nothing can match the
vividness of Johnson's explications of a
world where all options have been closed
out, where the last fair deal has gone down.
Recorded over half a century ago, this
music is ageless. — D.M.

GEORGE JONES

   ★ ★ ★½ The Best of George Jones (Epic,
         1975)
   ★ ★ ★ ★ All Time Greatest Hits Volume
         1 (Epic, 1977)
   ★ ★ ★½ My Very Special Guests (Epic,
         1979)
   ★ ★ ★ ★ I Am What I Am (Epic, 1980)
   ★ ★ ★½ Still the Same Ol' Me (Epic,
         1981)
  ★ ★ ★ ★ ★ Anniversary—Ten Years of Hits
         (Epic, 1982)
   ★ ★ ★½ Jones Country (Epic, 1983)
   ★ ★ ★ By Request (Epic, 1984)
   ★ ★ ★½ George Jones Salutes Hank
         Williams (Mercury, 1984)
   ★ ★ ★ Rockin' the Country (Mercury,
         1985)
   ★ ★ ★ First Time Live (Epic, 1985)
   ★ ★ ★½ Wine Colored Roses (Epic,
         1986)
   ★ ★ ★ Super Hits (Epic, 1987)
   ★ ★½ Too Wild Too Long (Epic,
         1987)
  ★ ★ ★ ★ One Woman Man (Epic, 1989)
   ★ ★ ★ You Oughta Be Here With Me
         (Epic, 1990)
   ★ ★½ Hallelujah Weekend (Epic,
         1990)
   ★ ★ ★½ And Along Came Jones (MCA,
         1991)
  ★ ★ ★ ★ ★ The Best of George Jones
         1955–67 (Rhino, 1991)

WITH TAMMY WYNETTE

   ★ ★ ★ ★ Greatest Hits (Epic, 1977)

If the late Hank Williams established the
honky-tonkin' sound of modern country
music, George Jones mastered and expanded
it. Wedding an awesome technical ability to
an intuitive emotional grasp, Jones is a
peerless singer. When he's on, you can
forget about the "country" qualification. Of
course, his recording career (and his
recordings) mirror some severely bumpy ups
and downs: epic battles with the bottle, a
failed picture-book marriage to fellow
superstar Tammy Wynette, more booze,
drugs, bankruptcy, missed concerts,
backslides and comebacks. Just when he
appeared to bottom out for the last time,
Jones turned himself (and his fading
reputation) around with the cathartic *I Am
What I Am* (1980). Amazingly, the musical
highs keep on coming.

Even by the conservative standards of
country, Jones has remained resolutely
traditional. He's never really strayed from
the type of romantic material he sang in the
'50s, opting to elevate and refine his
approach rather than alter it to reflect
current trends. Born in 1931, Jones started
performing in beer joints around the Texas
town of Beaumont in the late '40s. Like
many country singers his age, Jones tried his
hand at rockabilly in the wake of Elvis. He
scored his first Number One on the country
charts in 1959 with "White Lightning," but
in general those jumpy rhythms didn't suit
his more measured, melancholy vocal style.
(*Rockin' the Country* fully accounts for this
period, though *Salutes Hank Williams* gives
a more accurate view of Jones's roots and
future direction.) "Why Baby Why," the
indignant plaint that introduced Jones to a
national audience in 1955, epitomizes his
heartbroken barroom eloquence. Moving
from the tiny Starday label to Mercury,
Jones continued to issue complex,
devastating reports from the love-wars front:
"Window Up Above," "Tender Years,"
"She Thinks I Still Care," "A Girl I Used
to Know."

Rhino's *The Best of George Jones* collects
all these gems and more—plus a generous
serving of the uptempo novelties ("The Race
Is On," "Love Bug") that George always
throws in for relief. Overall, it's a sterling
effort: the only complaint is that this
single-disc collection could easily be twice as
long without suffering any loss of quality.
Jones's late-'60s work on the defunct
Musicor label is given short shrift:
predictably, the jokey "I'm a People" gets
the nod over heartrending slow songs like
"Take Me" and "Things Have Gone to

Pieces." Still, this is the perfect place to start any country appreciation course (after Hank Sr.), or to fill in the gaping holes in an existing Jones collection.

Signing with Epic in 1971, Jones began a long and fruitful collaboration with house producer Billy Sherrill. Over the years, Sherrill has been accused of overwhelming his charges with gloppy string sections and bland vocal choruses, extracting the twang from their voices in hopes of pop crossover. OK, guilty as charged. But the orchestrated fullness of his countrypolitan (the name says it all) approach can't mask the dramatic complexities of Jones's mature delivery. In fact, it often complements the singer's revealing swoops and telling eye for detail. Sherrill made some damn good records in the early '70s—especially with Jones, his then-wife Tammy Wynette and rockabilly veteran Charlie Rich. Many of the original Jones-Sherrill albums are out of print, but *Anniversary—Ten Years of Hits* renders them (and the 1975 *Best of George Jones*) irrelevant. *All Time Greatest Hits Volume 1* contains surprisingly unslick remakes of Jones's pre-Sherrill classics.

It's possible to hear *Anniversary* as the chronicle of George and Tammy's ill-starred union: from the swelling hope of "We Can Make It" to the sensual ecstasy of "Loving You Could Never Be Better," from the impending gloom of "Once You've Had the Best" to the down-and-out misery of "These Days (I Barely Get By)." And it's impossible to hear George and Tammy's duets on their wonderful *Greatest Hits* as anything but autobiography: from the supportive harmonies of "We're Gonna Hold On" to the estranged monologues of "Southern California." (Recording your wedding vows, as George and Tammy do on "The Ceremony," may be asking for trouble.) After their 1975 divorce, George enters his most dissolute and inconsistent period. *Anniversary* culls the best from these years: the devastating "I'll Just Take It Out in Love" and laugh-to-keep-from-crying novelties like "Her Name Is . . . " (where the steel guitar provides the punch line). *My Very Special Guests* matches a somewhat under-the-weather Jones with duet partners from Waylon 'n' Willie to James Taylor and Elvis Costello: the results are mixed, to say the least.

Jones emerges from a hospital stay—weathered and wiser—on *I Am What I Am*, from 1980. "He Stopped Loving Her Today" looms as his tragic masterpiece, while "I'm Not Ready Yet" displays fresh

resolution and "I've Aged Twenty Years in Five" glows with pitiless self-recognition. Sherrill provides a slightly harder-edged honky-tonk backdrop, making *I Am What I Am* their best regular-issue album by a country mile. Though its core tracks appear on *Anniversary*, this album easily stands on its own.

It's been hit or miss for George Jones ever since. Appropriately, his most satisfying album of recent years is the odds 'n' sods hodgepodge *One Woman Man*. But when he connects with a good song, you'll forgive him the next half-dozen washouts and walk-throughs. Try *Wine Colored Roses* from 1986: "The Right Left Hand" and "Don't Leave Without Taking Your Silver" fully measure up to Jones's better-known milestones. Avoid quickie repackaging jobs like *By Request, Super Hits* and *Hallelujah Weekend*.

Hooking up with new traditionalist producer Kyle Lehning simply gives Jones another chance to quietly show the young bucks how it's done. On *And Along Came Jones*, this veteran singer reasserts his interpretive power without making a big fuss about it. Nobody but Jones could read such profound meanings into those "little yellow Post-It notes" scattered throughout "You Couldn't Get the Picture." Now that it's too late, he can't forget his departed lover's final missives—so he makes sure that you won't, either. More than three decades after he first recorded a song called "Ragged But Right," George Jones still fits the bill.
— M.C.

GRACE JONES

★	**Portfolio (Island, 1977)**
★	**Fame (Island, 1978)**
★	**Muse (Island, 1979)**
★★★½	**Warm Leatherette (Island, 1980)**
★★★½	**Nightclubbing (Island, 1981)**
★★★	**Living My Life (Island, 1982)**
★★★	**Island Life (Island, 1985)**
★★½	**Slave to the Rhythm (Manhattan/Island, 1985)**
★★½	**Inside Story (Manhattan, 1986)**
★★	**Bulletproof Heart (Capitol, 1989)**

Grace Jones's early recorded efforts support every popular misconception about disco; in other words, they suck. A towering former fashion model intones decadent banalities over a fluffy Studio 54 foxtrot: not the kind of thing that ages well. Though Grace hails from Jamaica, hooking up with the hotshot reggae rhythm section of Sly Dunbar and Robbie Shakespeare wasn't exactly an obvious move for her in 1980. Drummer Sly and bassist Robbie were emerging as a production team at this time, and Grace Jones albums became their pop testing ground. They devised a much more sensible—not to mention sensual—backdrop for Grace's haughty talk-singing. Leavening their sprung riddims with a salty dash of funk, Sly and Robbie hipped Jones to rock's new wave on *Warm Leatherette* and *Nightclubbing.* Throbbing polyrhythmic cover versions of current anti-heroes—Iggy Pop's "Nightclubbing," Roxy Music's "Love Is the Drug," the Pretenders' "Private Life"—turned out to be more her speed than the Edith Piaf-meets-Barry White routines of yore.

Living My Life contains "My Jamaican Guy," which might be the best single track to come out of this fruitful collaboration. But the original material on this album lacks the hooky snap of those half-familiar cult favorites. Split between Grace's sublime and ridiculous periods, *Island Life* is a disappointing summary. Away from Sly and Robbie, Jones hasn't been able to find another groove. Though "Slave to the Rhythm" is a haunting single, the Trevor Horn–produced album is a conceptual mess: jumbled, overblown, tough to sit through. *Inside Story* benefits from an urbane Nile Rodgers production, though Grace's songwriting is totally unremarkable when it's not inscrutable. *Bulletproof Heart* is a routine late '80s thumpathon; Jones's dry humor and quirky vocal phrasing are all but lost in swelling, generic mixes. — M.C.

HOWARD JONES

★ ★ ★　Human's Lib (Elektra, 1984)
★ ★ ★　Dream Into Action (Elektra, 1985)
★ ★ ½　Action Replay (EP) (Elektra, 1986)
★ ★ ½　One to One (Elektra, 1986)
★ ★ ★　Cross That Line (Elektra, 1989)
★ ★ ½　In the Running (Elektra, 1992)

Now that the electronics are no longer the novelty they once were, synth-pop turns out to be just plain pop, with all its attendant virtues and vulnerabilities. So it hardly matters that Howard Jones is an able technician and imaginative synth programmer; what his albums ultimately live or die by are melodies, and his ability to bring them to life.

On the first count, Jones acquits himself admirably. *Human's Lib* is filled with engaging pop tunes, only one of which— "New Song"—depends overly on synth gimmickry; at their best, as on "What Is Love?" the melodies soar. Unfortunately, the same cannot be said of Jones's voice, an

adenoidal tenor that recalls the Thompson Twins' Tom Bailey at his most congested. Jones doesn't have any trouble hitting the notes, mind you, just in making them fly, but that's enough to limit the appeal of the otherwise charming "Things Can Only Get Better," which opens *Dream Into Action.* To his credit, Jones is canny enough to let his rhythm arrangements take some of the weight off his voice, which works well enough with the coy calypso of "Life in One Day," and even better on the remixed version of "No One Is to Blame" (originally on *Dream Into Action*, then remixed on the dance EP *Action Replay*, and later added to the CD version of *One to One*).

With *One to One*, Jones's songs take on a reflective cast, which neither helps their melodies nor enhances his singing, but *Cross That Line* is more-or-less a return to form, thanks to the tuneful simplicity of songs like "Everlasting Love" or the melancholy "Last Supper." *In the Running* finds him changing his sound somewhat, augmenting his synth-based sound with rippling, Bruce Hornsbyish piano flourishes, but on the whole his material smacks more of calculation than craft. — J.D.C.

MARTI JONES

★ ★ ★ ½　Unsophisticated Time (A&M, 1985)
★ ★ ★　Match Game (A&M, 1986)
★ ★ ★ ★　Used Guitars (A&M, 1988)
★ ★ ★ ½　Any Kind of Lie (RCA, 1990)

Jones is sometimes described as the alternative-rock Linda Ronstadt, and though that is an accurate enough assessment of some of her work—she does as much for Peter Holsapple and John Hiatt as Ronstadt did for Warren Zevon and J.D. Souther—it severely shortchanges the rest. *Unsophisticated Time* and *Match Game* are perhaps most guilty of Ronstadtism, both because of the quality of the cover material and the way producer (later, husband) Don Dixon framed Jones's warm, rich voice, but it's hard to argue with the performances. But *Used Guitars*, despite sterling renditions of Hiatt's "The Real One" and Janis Ian's "Ruby," also features strong originals, in particular "Tourist Town," while *Any Kind of Lie* avoids covers almost entirely. — J.D.C.

QUINCY JONES

★ ★ ★　Body Heat (A&M, 1974)
★ ★ ★　Mellow Madness (A&M, 1975)
★ ★ ★　Roots (A&M, 1977)
★ ★ ★ ½　The Dude (A&M, 1981)

★ ★ ★ **The Quintessence (MCA/Impulse, 1986)**
★ ★ ★ **Compact Jazz: Quincy Jones (Phillips/PolyGram, 1989)**
★ ★ ★ ★ **Back on the Block (Qwest, 1990)**
Trumpeter Quincy Jones was 15 years old when he was befriended by an older musician on the late-'40s Seattle jazz club scene. That 17-year-old piano player was Ray Charles. Both these legends-to-be developed a remarkable gift for musical arrangement—and for absorbing various styles into a reshaped whole. Having paid his dues with Lionel Hampton and others, Jones prospered in Hollywood during the '60s. Judging from his colorful, if somewhat unadventurous jazz compilations (*Quintessesnce* and *Compact Jazz*), movies and television soundtracks are more suited to his flashy dramatic style. Jones gradually worked his way into the pop market during the mid-'70s, grafting various guests vocalists onto his orchestrated funk concoctions. *Mellow Madness*, from 1975, introduced the Brothers Johnson with an R&B hit called "Is It Love That We're Missin'." Producing Michael Jackson's *Off the Wall* in 1979 must have jump-started Quincy's nascent song sense. *The Dude* struts some much catchier material: mellow pop-soul embers from vocalists James Ingram and Patti Austin. It's lightweight stuff, but highly enjoyable. Perhaps the U.S.A. for Africa "We Are the World" extravaganza—which he helped to organize—triggered his next brainstorm. Only Jones could have pulled off *Back on the Block*: an African-American musical history tour with input from just about everybody on the block but Michael J. Q's got the connections down, both social and musical. Throwing down skittery bebop rhythms behind Big Daddy Kane's free-flowing raps, to cite just one example, Jones deftly shows where he's coming from—and where black music is going—without showing off. — M.C.

RICKIE LEE JONES
★ ★ ★ ★   **Rickie Lee Jones (Warner Bros., 1979)**
★ ★ ★ ★   **Pirates (Warner Bros., 1981)**
★ ★ ★   **Girl at Her Volcano (EP) (Warner Bros., 1983)**
★ ★ ★ ½ **The Magazine (Warner Bros., 1984)**
★ ★ ★ ★   **Flying Cowboys (Geffen, 1989)**
★ ★   **Pop Pop (Geffen, 1991)**
Skittering and strutting her way down the lazy folkie-bop avenue with "Chuck E.'s In Love," Rickie Lee Jones scored an unlikely Top Ten hit in 1979. Her debut album firmly established that Jones is more than a novelty artist, though her vocal swoops and gushy Beat sensibility make *Rickie Lee Jones* a love-it-or-hate-it affair. If you can swing with her somewhat mannered approach, *Pirates* may be an even better album; from the surefire melody of "We Belong Together" to impressionistic cuts like "Traces of the Western Slopes," it's certainly more consistent than her platinum predecessor. *Girl at Her Volcano*, an EP-length compendium of live cuts and cover versions, stopped the gap between proper albums. On *The Magazine*, Rickie Lee goes way over the top, but, despite the synthesized art-rock trappings, even Jones's flightiest excursions are grounded by solid musical ability. *The Magazine* is far more listenable than you'd expect for an album centered on a pop-psych suite ("Rorschachs Theme for the Pope") to be. "Juke Box Fury" and "It Must Be Love" rank as some of Rickie Lee's most accessible and direct moments.

Producer (and post-Steely Dan recluse) Walter Becker gracefully coaxes Jones back down to earth on *Flying Cowboys*. The enlivened rhythmic pulse—especially a sweet reggae influence on several cuts—makes a crucial difference; a return to traditional song structures doesn't hurt, either. This overlooked, career-summing album is strong enough to convert a rock & roll skeptic to Jones's fold. Unfortunately, *Pop Pop* confirms many listeners' worst instincts about this mercurial singer. Reveling in her most precious excesses, this torchy covers package is a flat-out annoyance. Jones commits breathless, vague interpretations of incongruent standards; "Up From the Skies" (Jimi Hendrix) and "Comin' Back to Me" (Jefferson Airplane) don't fare any better than pre-rock favorites like "Second Time Around" and "Bye Bye Blackbird." *Pop Pop* fizzles out. — M.C.

SPIKE JONES
★ ★ ★ ★ **Dinner Music . . . for People Who Aren't Very Hungry (1957; Rhino, 1988)**
★ ★ ★ ★ ★ **Spike Jones Is Murdering the Classics (RCA, 1971)**
★ ★ ★ ★ **Best of Spike Jones (RCA, 1975)**
★ ★ ★ ★ **Best of Spike Jones, Vol. 2 (RCA, 1981)**
★ ★ ★ **It's a Spike Jones Christmas (Rhino, 1990)**
Along with the Harry Partches, the John Cages and the Roland Kirks of the world, Spike Jones deserves an honored place

among the visionaries who approached music and instruments in totally unconventional terms. Consider, for example, a partial list of the instruments Jones and his band, the City Slickers, employ on *Dinner Music*: garbage disposal, grinding violin, .38 calibre pistol, ratchet, 1911 Blackhawk Stutz, pneumatic pile driver breaking pavement, anvil, Paris taxi horns, burpaphone, and yes, the infamous poontangaphone. One must question whether Partch, Cage and Kirk had anything at all on Jones, or whether the Master of Musical Mayhem is in a class by himself, a founding father of the avant-garde. What might be lost in reading over Jones's instrument list is that he never forgot to be musical. Jones used all his tricks to support the song. Jones even extended his special effects into the realm of editorial commentary. In 1945, his version of "Cocktails for Two" (which had been a Number One record in 1934 for Duke Ellington) followed a tender reading of the lyric "as we enjoy a cigarette" with the sound of a hacking cough.

Jones came by his calling honorably, as a Hollywood studio drummer who knew there was a better world out there somewhere and proceeded to assemble a band consisting of players whose comedic skills were on a par with their considerable facility as musicians. His first record, released on the Bluebird label in 1942 and now unavailable on any of the albums still in print, featured vocalist Mel Blanc (the voice of Bugs Bunny, Daffy Duck and most of the other Warner Bros. cartoon characters) on "Clink, Clink, Another Drink." Through 1953 Jones was a mainstay on the pop charts, chalking up nine Top Ten hits; one of these, "All I Want for Christmas Is My Two Front Teeth," featuring George Rock's unparalleled toothless, whistling vocal, occupied the Number One position for three weeks in 1948. "Cocktails for Two" climbed to Number Four on the strength of its juxtaposition of Jones's pointed sound effects against a quite smooth vocal by Carl Grayson (Jones seemed to have an endless supply of first-rate singers; he was not among them, having described himself as a graduate of Juilliard, "*Magna Cum Louder*"). His first million-seller came in 1942, with a timely scorching of Adolf Hitler and his henchmen in "Der Fuehrer's Face" that went to Number Three.

What remains of the Jones *oeuvre* are two essential *Best of* collections that span the range of Jones's disciplines, from pop songs ("That Old Black Magic") to novelties

(everything) to classical (a must on Volume I: Ponchielli's "Dance of the Hours," interrupted in mid-flight by Doodles Weaver calling a horse race, a schtick worked to even greater effect on "The William Tell Overture"). *Dinner Music* is Rhino's re-release of the first Spike Jones album, circa 1957. In his song-by-song liner descriptions, Jones refers to the track "Ramona" as being "probably the only time in musical history that the snare drum almost carried the melody"; of "The Black and Blue Danube Waltz," he advises, "if you listen closely, you can hear the recording engineer throw a brick through the window of the recording booth"; "Memories Are Made of This," a lovely pop song, features the Canine 9 on lead vocals. You get the idea? *Spike Jones Is Murdering the Classics* features the master's convoluted interpretations of 12 works from or inspired by great composers. Otherwise the record goes its dignified way offering what might be called "alternative" music spiced with gargles, coughs, wheezes, sneezes and hiccups punctuated by shots from Jones's Smith & Wesson .22.

It's a Spike Jones Christmas isn't for anyone looking for musical mayhem, although two of its songs are sung in Pig Latin. Spike constructed a solid, middle-of-the-road celebration of the season. Employing a 25-voice choir on most of the repertoire, Jones keep things cheerful on breezy readings of traditional Christmas fare, and appropriately solemn on a moving medley of hymns. The choir offers a stately version of "Silent Night," followed by a jaunty take on Leroy Anderson's "Sleigh Ride." These two comprise a wonderful moment and speak well of the great heart that always informed Jones's work. A remarkable American artist. — D.M.

TOM JONES

★★½ **What's New Pussycat (1965; Polydor, 1987)**
★★★ **Green, Green Grass of Home (Decca/Parrot, 1967)**
★★½ **Delilah (1968; London, 1987)**
★★½ **Tom Jones Live in Las Vegas (Parrot, 1969)**
★★½ **What a Night (Epic, 1977)**
★★★ **The Greatest Hits (London, 1980)**
★★½ **Darlin' (Mercury, 1981)**
★★½ **Tender Loving Care (Mercury, 1985)**
★★★ **Move Closer (Jive, 1988)**
★★½ **Things That Matter Most to Me (Mercury, 1988)**

His name synonymous with soft-porn shlock, Tom Jones remains a phenomenon of pandering and a marketing triumph. Gifted with an eerily astonishing voice—in terms of volume alone, it's staggering, and its rich tone makes it an erotic instrument of almost cartoon power—the singer was lifted up from Welsh obscurity by show-biz Svengali (and, later, Englebert Humperdinck manager) Gordon Mills. Finding in Jones a performer with the physique and oily charisma of Elvis in his overripe prime, Mills deployed his new charge in chart wars against the legitimate English rockers of the mid-'60s. It was a combat of styles: the slick, tuxedoed hunk versus the scruffy artistes. Predictably, Jones scored big with an older demographic: the bouffant crowd melted. Cannily, his early singles, Mills's "It's Not Unusual" and Bacharach-David's "What's New Pussycat?" combined sassy pop brass parts and a rock & roll rhythm section: this was titillating music, the aural equivalent of a beefcake striptease.

Attempting also to market "earnestness," Mills and Jones turned toward country music and its vast catalogue of heartache songs and yearning weepers. *Green, Green Grass of Home* was the result: a baroque soap opera. Inevitably, Vegas beckoned and *Tom Jones Live in Las Vegas* found the singer gleefully enacting self-parody. He pulled out all the stops: Latin horn parts underscored the sweaty appeal that reached back to Rudolph Valentino; he got funky like a sex machine; he charmed with the subtlety of a steamroller.

Throughout the '70s, Jones kept up a relentless pace, and then settled, in the next decade, for country success. In 1988, he updated the act with a new (and fairly adventurous) form of pop—*Move Closer* featured a credible version of Prince's "Kiss" with, of all people, the ultra-aesthete synth band, Art of Noise, as well as a take on "Satisfaction." As much of a symbol as a singer, Tom Jones made Chippendale's possible—he's the prototype of the manufactured male sex-toy, leering and grinding (and chuckling to himself). — P.E.

JANIS JOPLIN
★ ★ ★ ★ **I Got Dem Ol' Kozmic Blues Again Mama! (Columbia, 1969)**
★ ★ ★ ★ **Pearl (Columbia, 1971)**
★ ★ ★ **Joplin in Concert (Columbia, 1972)**
★ ★ ★ **Janis Joplin's Greatest Hits (Columbia, 1973)**
★ ★ ★ **Anthology (Columbia, 1980)**
★ ★ **Farewell Song (Columbia, 1982)**
★ ★ ★ **Pearl/Cheap Thrills (Columbia, 1986)**

Equal parts Southern Comfort, honey and gall, Janis Joplin's voice made her the greatest white female blues singer. And with a hard history of unhappy loves, angst and a talent so huge that it weighed too heavy, she died, at 27 of a heroin OD, ready-made for myth. Her deserved legend began at the 1967 Monterey Pop Festival—redefining grace, sex appeal and popular singing, the Texas vagabond shrieked and staggered over fevered but formless blues riffing by Big Brother and the Holding Company, whom she'd soon outgrow. With its horns and tight soulsters, *I Got Dem Ol' Kozmic Blues Again Mama!* provided intriguing context: her raw delivery shocked even more effectively when backed by crack players. Adding quivering heart to the sturdy pop skeleton of the Bee Gees' "To Love Somebody" and thunder to Jerry Ragovoy's "Try," she was now balancing a Big Mama Thornton fervor with an Aretha Franklin sense of timing.

Released posthumously, *Pearl*, the album that bore her nickname, found her moving easily and naturally into country, with the definitive take on Kris Kristofferson's "Me & Bobby McGee"; she also dripped blood on Ragovoy's "Cry Baby," and mustered an unintentional epitaph in "Buried Alive in the Blues." The 1968 album Joplin recorded with Big Brother, *Cheap Thrills*, was reissued with her most successful solo album, *Pearl*, on one CD in 1986. Joplin survives not only as a singer, but as a sympathetic, if harrowing, archetype. Too rushed to develop the casual confidence of Billie Holiday or Bessie Smith, she remains the all-time singer of the desperate blues.
— P.E.

LOUIS JORDAN
★ ★ ★ ★ **The Best of Louis Jordan (1975; MCA, 1989)**
★ ★ ★ **I Believe in Music (Classic Jazz, 1980)**
Born in Brinkley, Arkansas, Louis Jordan got his start playing alto saxophone with Chick Webb's band in 1936; in 1939 he formed his own group, the Tympany Five, and set out laying the foundation for R&B. Between 1944 and 1949, Jordan was omnipresent on both the black and pop charts with a succession of swinging, blues-oriented singles. Jordan's big voice and driving arrangements fueled some of the decade's best novelty and dance songs, most of which have retained their appeal over the years. The MCA collection presents 20 tracks of Jordan in prime form. Despite the absence of classics such as "G.I. Jive"

(1944) and "Is You or Is You Ain't (My Baby)" (1944), these tracks will do the job early in the morning or late at night. Check out the nodding vocal on "What's the Use of Getting Sober (When You Gonna Get Drunk Again)," and the smooth blues crooning on "Don't Let the Sun Catch You Crying" (not the Gerry and the Pacemakers single) for an idea of Jordan's stylistic versatility; a later track, "I Want You to Be My Baby," written by Jon Hendricks, requires more complex, jazz-based phrasing, and Jordan pulls it off with ease and humor. At the same time, he could get deep inside himself for a straight blues rendering of Jimmie Cox's chestnut, "Nobody Knows You When You're Down and Out." Important and influential, Jordan's work here cries out for additional volumes. The 1980 Classic Jazz sessions, issued as *I Believe in Music* (now out of print), were among Jordan's last, and consist of several updates of classic material such as "Caldonia," "I'm Gonna Move to the Outskirts of Town" and "Is You or Is You Ain't My Baby." Older and wiser, Jordan invests each reading with his singular point of view. The supporting band (especially tenor sax man Irv Cox) is solid throughout.
— D.M.

JOURNEY
★★   Journey (Columbia, 1975)
★★   Look Into the Future (Columbia, 1976)
★★   Next (Columbia, 1977)
★★   Infinity (Columbia, 1978)
★★   Evolution (Columbia, 1979)
★★   In the Beginning (Columbia, 1979)
★★   Departure (Columbia, 1980)
★★   Captured (Columbia, 1981)
★★½   Escape (Columbia, 1981)
★★   Dream After Dream (Columbia, 1982)
★★½   Frontiers (Columbia, 1983)
★★   Raised on Radio (Columbia, 1986)
★★★   Greatest Hits (Columbia, 1988)

Give 'em this much: Journey has progressed over the years. This post-hippie Bay Area unit moved from faceless art-rock competence to annoying AOR omnipotence. With the addition of leather-lunged lead singer Steve Perry on *Infinity*, Journey sprouted hooks and quickly became unavoidable on the radio. Guitarist Neal Schon and original keyboardist Gregg Rolie had both played with Santana, but their jamming impulses were easily roped in by Perry's pop focus. Chrome synthesizer plating, super-charged vocal capacity, dependable rhythmic drive, white-wall guitar flash: Journey's slick, comfortable sound is custom-built for the expressway.

There's a unifying blandness to Journey's work; the individual albums are largely interchangeable. *Greatest Hits* doesn't exactly redeem the group's critical status as the rock anti-Christ, but it does reclaim some pleasurable moments from radio's middle-of-the-road twilight zone: "Lovin', Touchin', Squeezin' " and "Only the Young" bracket a handful of similarly overwrought confections. But despite the group's popularity and undeniable influence, the memory of Journey quickly faded as the next generation of bands took up its mantle.
— M.C.

JOY OF COOKING
★★★★   Retro Rock #3: The Best of Joy of Cooking (Capitol, 1990)

Joy of Cooking didn't have to play loud and posture with electric guitars: singers Toni Brown and Terri Garthwaite grasped the essence of classic blues and applied it to their early-'70s countercultural milieu. This eclectic, sexually integrated Berkeley quintet steers clear of leftist stridency and folkie mellowdom. The group's trademark piano-and-acoustic-guitar combination jumps to the beat of a steady drummer, while the warm contrast between Brown and Garthwaite's voices adds tension and depth to the music's easy flow. Unlike 99% of the "Retro Rock" competition, Joy of Cooking hardly sounds dated. If anything, a pragmatic and propulsive call-to-arms like "Closer to the Ground" makes even better sense after 20 years. *The Best of Joy of Cooking* draws from all three of the band's original albums (*Joy of Cooking, Closer to the Ground, Castles*), and its quality never falters. Fans of Bonnie Raitt will find an embarrassment of riches inside this budget-line quickie. — M.C.

JOY DIVISION
★★★½   Unknown Pleasures (1979; Qwest, 1985)
★★★★   Closer (1980; Qwest, 1985)
★★★   Still (1981; Qwest, 1985)
★★★★   Substance 1977–1980 (Qwest, 1988)
★★★   The Peel Sessions (Strange Fruit/Dutch East India, 1990)

Perhaps the most influential British group of the '80s, Joy Division inspired a subgeneration of dolorous poseurs. Blaming mope rock on this Manchester quartet is a mistake, though: Joy Division's brief recorded legacy towers over the subsequent efforts of its imitators. The suicide of lead singer Ian Curtis in 1980 guarantees that the group always will be misunderstood, or stupidly romanticized; for all the harrowing detail of Curtis's obsessed monotone, Joy Division breathes fresh musical ideas into punk rock. *Unknown Pleasures* and *Closer* obliquely acknowledge the demon disco: deploying space and silence around Steven Morris's (barely) syncopated beat, emphasizing Peter Hook's melodic bass lines and reducing Bernard Albrecht's guitar to a textural metal blur. When Ian Curtis's inner vision gets claustrophobic, the music opens up a window. "Love Will Tear Us Apart" (on *Substance* and *The Peel Sessions*) epitomizes Joy Division's austere psychedelia, tying on a pointed hook that's custom-designed for the dance floor. "Love Will Tear Us Apart" also points toward the direction Joy Division's surviving members would follow in New Order. *Still* combines surprisingly compelling outtakes from the first two albums with various live cuts—including a cruder-than-crude pummeling of the Velvet Underground's "Sister Ray." Unlike most bands that came roaring out of the 1977 revolution, Joy Division ends up somewhere quite different from where it begins. — M.C.

JUDAS PRIEST
- ★★ **Rocka Rolla (RCA, 1975)**
- ★★ **Sad Wings of Destiny (RCA, 1976)**
- ★★½ **Sin After Sin (Columbia, 1977)**
- ★★½ **Best of Judas Priest (RCA, 1978)**
- ★★½ **Stained Class (Columbia, 1978)**
- ★★½ **Hell Bent for Leather (Columbia, 1979)**
- ★★ **Live—Unleashed in the East (Columbia, 1979)**
- ★★★ **British Steel (Columbia, 1980)**
- ★★ **Point of Entry (Columbia, 1981)**
- ★★ **Screaming for Vengeance (Columbia, 1982)**
- ★★★ **Defenders of the Faith (Columbia, 1984)**
- ★★½ **Turbo (Columbia, 1986)**
- ★★½ **Priest . . . Live (Columbia, 1987)**
- ★★½ **Ram It Down (Columbia, 1989)**
- ★★½ **Painkiller (Columbia, 1990)**

Judas Priest is the elder prophet of the metal tribes. This English quintet didn't invent a single move, mind you; falling squarely between Led Zep and Black Sabbath, their mid-'70s sound codified the previous five years or so of metallic developments. Since then, Judas Priest has refined its attack with a nearly religious zeal. Lead singer Rob Halford can match the range and sharp impact of Robert Plant, but his shrieks and moans aren't nearly as deep. No matter: Glenn Tipton and K. K. Downing trade off solos in a duelling guitar approach, and their best tandem riffs give the Priest a hooky, driving momentum that's usually missing from the doomy end of heavy metal. And make no mistake, these guys are doom-oriented; Judas Priest pumped out apocalyptic epics like "Island of Domination" (from the RCA best-of collection) and "Dissident Aggressor" (from *Sin After Sin*) when Metallica and its followers were still in junior high. Both of those albums contain the group's mincing desecration of Joan Baez's "Diamonds and Rust," in case anybody thought this music completely lacks a sense of humor. With its exaggerated leather 'n' studs theatrical bent and polished musical consistency, Judas Priest encapsulates the metal experience for true believers—many of whom will be listening to something else in five years. Every Columbia album sports at least one tuneful surefire drivetime rocker, though—some two or three. "Breaking the Law" and "Living After Midnight" enliven *British Steel*, while *Screaming for Vengeance* maxes out with "Freewheel Burning" (catchy, whatever the hell it means) and the campy send-ups that raised Tipper Gore's foolish ire: "Eat Me Alive" and "Love Bites." *Turbo* finds Priest backing off just a touch, adding guitar synthesizers, but the speed-metal-refreshed *Painkiller* defies the current power-ballad trend. As long as there's heavy metal, Judas Priest will continue to administer the rites of passage to an eager audience. — M.C.

THE JUDDS
- ★★ **The Judds: Wynonna & Naomi (Curb/RCA, 1984)**
- ★★★ **Why Not Me (Curb/RCA, 1984)**
- ★★★ **Rockin' With the Rhythm (Curb/RCA, 1985)**
- ★★ **Heart Land (Curb/RCA, 1987)**
- ★★★ **Christmas Time with the Judds (Curb/RCA, 1987)**
- ★★★★ **Greatest Hits (Curb/RCA, 1988)**
- ★★★★ **River of Time (Curb/RCA, 1989)**
- ★★★★ **Love Can Build a Bridge (Curb/RCA, 1990)**
- ★★★ **Collector's Series (Curb/RCA, 1990)**
- ★★★★ **Greatest Hits Volume Two (Curb/RCA, 1991)**

WYNONNA JUDD
- ★★★½ **Wynonna (Curb/RCA, 1992)**

You have to go back a ways to find a female duo of any significance in country

music. Certainly there are men working
behind the scenes supporting the Judds, but
it's mother Naomi and daughter Wynonna
whose sensibilities have shaped this career.
On the creative side, the only male of note
is producer Brent Maher, whose
contributions are hardly minor in terms of
helping craft a sound and approach that is
beholden to the past and firmly grounded in
the present.

Questions of gender aside, the Judds have
clung tight to a distinctive sound: acoustic
based, it is never far from country blues and
wouldn't be entirely out of place in Los
Angeles in the early '70s. Maher and the
Judds have remained firm in their
commitment to a natural sound centered on
the Judds' impassioned harmonies and solos
supported by a basic band; strings and
background choruses are foreign elements.
When guests show up, it's people on the
order of Dire Straits' Mark Knopfler, who
contributes some typically pungent soloing
on a cover version of his "Water of Love"
on the *River of Time* album, or Bonnie
Raitt, whose slide guitar is featured on a
screed against a faithless male in "Rompin'
Stompin' Blues," from *Love Can Build a
Bridge*.

Another standard characteristic of the
duo's music is its hard focus on love.
There's virtually nothing else these ladies
sing about, and they can address it from all
angles. *Why Not Me*, the duo's second
release, is concerned with male-female
relationships; five years later they deliver
River of Time, and follow it with *Love Can
Build a Bridge*, two albums that have their
share of blues, but are recommended more
for the moving explorations of love between
friends ("River of Time") and family
("Guardian Angels," from *Love Can Build a
Bridge*). Wynonna's 1992 solo album,
Wynonna, extends the spirit of the duo's
recordings while demonstrating her pop
leanings. If Wynonna and Naomi never
record together again (ill health has forced
Naomi to retire from performing), theirs will
always be a history worth savoring. — D.M.

JULUKA
★ ★ ★ African Litany (1982; Rhythm
Safari, 1991)
★ ★ ★ Ubuhle Bemvelo (1982; Rhythm
Safari, 1991)
★ ★ ★½ Scatterlings (Warner Bros., 1983)
★ ★½ Stand Your Ground (Warner Bros.,
1984)
★ ★ ★ Musa Ukungilandela (1984; Rhythm
Safari, 1992)

★ ★ ★ Universal Men (1984; Rhythm
Safari, 1992)
★ ★ ★ ★ The Best of Juluka (Rhythm Safari,
1991)
Contrary to popular belief, Paul Simon was
not the first white musician whose
multi-racial blend of rock and traditional
Zulu pop styles both delighted pop fans and
enraged the South African establishment.
Juluka's founders, Johnny Clegg and Sipho
Mchunu, began playing together in the
'70s—quite a feat in apartheid-ruled South
Africa, considering that Mchunu is a Zulu
and Clegg is white—and eventually formed
a band, which they dubbed Juluka ("sweat"
in Zulu). The group was enormously
popular in South Africa, and released
several albums of mbaqanga-flavored rock—
including *African Litany* and the wonderful
Ubuhle Bemvelo—before dissolving in 1985.

Juluka went international in 1983 with
Scatterlings, which nicely showcased the
contrast between Clegg's light, folk-inflected
tenor and Mchunu's gruff, Zulu-style vocals.
"Scatterlings" itself is particularly striking.
Juluka moved toward a more Western
sound on *Stand Your Ground*, with mixed
results; "Kilimanjaro," for instance, sounds
eerily like the Men at Work hit "Down
Under," while the conventional rock-style
chord changes behind "Bye Bye December
African Rain" don't quite mesh with the
arrangement's Zulu flavor. But *The Best of
Juluka*, which includes a fair sampling of the
group's South African releases, keeps such
missteps to a minimum. — J.D.C.

THE JUNGLE BROTHERS
★ ★ ★ Straight Out the Jungle (Warlock,
1988)
★ ★ ★ ★ Done by the Forces of Nature
(Warner Bros., 1989)
Part of the Native Tongues Posse, the
Jungle Brothers share the low-key humor
and Afrocentric positivity of De La Soul, A
Tribe Called Quest and Queen Latifah.
What separates the J.B.s from the rest of
that crew, though, is their sense of musical
tradition; *Done by the Forces of Nature*, in
particular, does an excellent job
underscoring the continuity between early
rap and classic R&B. — J.D.C.

JUNKYARD
★ ★ ★½ Junkyard (Geffen, 1989)
★ ★ ★½ Sixes, Sevens and Nines (Geffen,
1991)
Call it what you want—metal-flaked
suburban blues, the new honky-tonk blooze
or just a gloss on the same old noise—

Junkyard delivers the goods. This double-guitar quintet (rooted in hardcore punk, of all things) came roaring out of the glitter-heavy L.A. metal scene with a straight ahead hard-rock debut. Produced by veteran Tom Werman, *Junkyard* is more reminiscent of his snappy albums with Cheap Trick than his more routine work for Mötley Crüe. Lead singer David Roach occasionally crosses over into high-pitched metal hysteria, but Chris Gates's raunchy slide guitar runs and a razor-strapping rhythm section keep him aloft. The songs examine dissolution with a stark morning-after perspective that's always frank, and often downright alarming. *Sixes, Sevens and Nines* delves even deeper into this territory, cataloguing the toll taken on young lives by bad luck and the bottle. If that sounds like country music, rest assured that Junkyard kicks out its latter-day barroom laments with Stones-style swagger. — M.C.

BILL JUSTIS
★★★½ **Raunchy** (Sun, 1969)
One of Sam Phillips's ablest sessionmen during Sun Records' early days, Bill Justis is a prime example of a rock & roll saxophonist whose melodiousness is tempered by a craftsman's precision. Nowhere is this better demonstrated than on "Raunchy," a single that peaked at Number Two in 1957 and remains one of the most incendiary rock instrumentals ever, truly a landmark effort and a model for a host of inspired instrumentals that followed in its wake. It's also the cornerstone of this lively album. — D.M.

K

KALEIDOSCOPE

★★½ **Greetings From Kartoonista . . . We Ain't Dead Yet (Gifthorse/Curb, 1988)**
★★★ **Egyptian Candy: A Collection (Legacy/Sony, 1991)**

As the most versatile among Jackson Browne's sidemen, and as leader of his own band, El Rayo-X, David Lindley has produced all manner of magic from nearly any stringed instrument imaginable. It figures, then, that his first group, the somewhat zany late-'60s obscurantists Kaleidoscope, would have brandished an eclectic battery of sounds. And it did—so eclectic, in fact, that the quintet garnered a few critical raves, gigged in desultory fashion and very soon disappeared. While others among its trippy peers experimented with ragas, this crew absorbed a heavy Middle Eastern influence—Lindley's guitar, violin and mandolin work was augmented by that of Solomon Feldthouse, Kaleidoscope's main man and master of such arcane instruments as vina, saz and oud. Album titles like *Side Trips* and *A Beacon From Mars* (both out of print) underscore the band's psychedelic sensibility—but its sound was anything but acid rock. At its most accessible, Kaleidoscope favored a sort of funky folk rock—even if its incorporation of Cajun, R&B, gypsy and jazz influences made the group almost unclassifiable. Such aesthetic derring-do deserves kudos, but, at this late date, it doesn't make Kaleidoscope any more approachable. Neither Lindley nor Feldthouse was much of a singer, and while their chops remain obvious, their tunes seldom hold up. Kaleidoscope was an oddity during its brief existence and remains a curio. — P.E.

KANSAS

★★½ **Kansas (Kirshner/CBS, 1974)**
★★½ **Song for America (Kirshner/CBS, 1975)**
★★ **Masque (Kirshner/CBS, 1975)**
★★½ **Leftoverture (Kirshner/CBS, 1976)**
★★½ **Point of Know Return (Kirshner/CBS, 1977)**
★★ **Two for the Show (Kirshner/Epic, 1978)**
★★ **Monolith (Kirshner/Epic, 1979)**
★★ **Audio-Visions (Kirshner/Epic, 1980)**
★★ **Vinyl Confessions (Kirshner/Epic, 1982)**
★★ **Drastic Measures (CBS Associated, 1984)**
★★★ **The Best of Kansas (CBS Associated, 1984)**

Kansas was America's answer to Yes and King Crimson. While this Midwestern septet can seem unbearably corny today, the group's homespun variation on the classical-gas motif retains a certain power because it sounds more organic—and less imperious—than the British model. The earnest blowhard quality of hit singles like "Carry on Wayward Son" (from *Leftoverture*) and "Dust in the Wind" (from *Point of Know Return*) drives those soaring choral hooks under the toughest skin; Kansas's string-enhanced musical melodrama magnifies the lyrics' shopworn "insights" to epic proportions.

On its most effective albums, Kansas blends a couple of outright catchy numbers with a rambling fusionoid suite or two: beginning with "Can I Tell You" and "Death of Mother Nature Suite" on the debut, peaking with "Carry On" and "Magnum Opus Suite" on *Leftoverture*. Listeners with a taste for this particular strain of '70s indulgence will find those albums as satsifying as *The Best Of Kansas*. To anybody else, this dusty, windblown territory is best left unexplored. — M.C.

KAOMA

★ ★½ **World Beat (Epic, 1989)**
This world-beat group was created by
French producers Jean-Claude Bonaventure
and Olivier Lorsac to promote the lambada
craze (well, it was a craze in France,
anyway). "Lambada" itself is pretty catchy,
but by the time they get to "Lambareggae"
and the zouk-style "Lamba Caribe," its
appeal wears pretty thin. — J.D.C.

KASSAV'

★ ★ ★ ★ **Vini Pou (Columbia, 1988)**
  ★ ★ ★ **Majestik Zouk (Columbia, 1989)**
Zouk is the dominant pop style of the
French Antilles, an inspired blend of
African pop, R&B, Eurodisco and native
Caribbean styles that has enjoyed
tremendous popularity in Europe and the
Caribbean, and Kassav' virtually invented it.
Of course, that was some albums before the
group signed with Epic, meaning that its
sound was already quite cosmopolitan
before even the first American Kassav'
album had been pressed. Not that the
music's modernity or sophistication takes
away from its charm; indeed, *Vini Pou* is as
charmingly exotic as it is rhythmically
vibrant, thanks to the irresistible "Syé
Bwa," "Souf' Zouk" and "Zót Vini Pou."
But *Majestik Zouk*, though slicker and
sumptuously arranged, lacks its
predecessor's rhythmic vitality, even if it
does boast slightly better singing. — J.D.C.

KATRINA AND THE WAVES

★ ★ ★ ★   **Walking on Sunshine (Attic Can.,
       1983)**
  ★ ★ ★   **2 (Attic Can., 1984)**
★ ★ ★ ★   **Katrina and the Waves (Capitol,
       1985)**
  ★ ★½   **Waves (Capitol, 1986)**
  ★ ★   **Break of Hearts (SBK, 1989)**
A Canadian quartet made up of expatriate
Americans and Englishmen, Katrina and the
Waves are an unfortunately apt example of
what happens when a band starts out with a
successful formula and then tries to change
it. Their first Canadian album, *Walking on
Sunshine*, is a masterpiece of guitar pop,
playing off the conventions of classic '60s
rock but with the detachment of post-punk
pros and the affection of true fans. Between
the powerhouse vocals of frontwoman
Katrina Leskanich and the melodic
ingenuity of songwriter (and former Soft
Boy) Kimberley Rew, the album is almost
irresistibly tuneful, from the melancholy
"Going Down to Liverpool" to the exotic
"Que Te Quiero," to the exuberant

"Walking on Sunshine." That blend still
holds for most of *2*, thanks to songs like
"Do You Want Crying?" and "Red Wine
and Whisky," but the R&B elements
introduced in "Cry for Me" and "The
Game of Love" don't entirely work. Rather
than simply license the group's Canadian
recordings, *Katrina and the Waves* offers the
best songs from the first two albums in
remixed or re-recorded versions that adjust
the scale of the arrangements to U.S.
proportions. But *Waves* finds the group
continuing to broaden its stylistic base, a
move that would be more impressive if it
worked. Instead, stilted, overreaching songs
like the mock-soulful "Is That It?" or the
formulaic riff-rocker "Lovely Lindsey" leave
the group sounding shallow. Nor does
Break of Hearts improve matters, as the
writing is just as empty and mannered.
— J.D.C.

JORMA KAUKONEN

★ ★ ★½ **Quah (1975; Relix, 1984)**
★ ★ ★   **Jorma (RCA, 1979)**
  ★ ★½ **Barbecue King (RCA, 1981)**
★ ★ ★   **Too Hot To Handle (Relix, 1985)**
★ ★ ★   **Magic (Relix, 1987)**
Exhausted by the blazing experimentalism of
Jefferson Airplane, ace guitarist Jorma
Kaukonen chilled out for a long while in the
'70s with Hot Tuna, a genial blues outfit
he'd formed with bassist extraordinaire and
fellow Airplane alum, Jack Casady. If
anything, his initial solo outing, *Quah*, was
even more laid-back—he still drew
inspiration from the country blues of Rev.
Gary Davis and other giants of the genre,
but concentrated on his own folk-derived
love songs. Shorn of the bluesy affectations
that had verged on the parodistic in the
context of Tuna, his vocals were some of the
best in his career, and his acoustic guitar
work delivered dependable pleasure. On
Jorma, he cranked up the amps, and while
the blues-rock record kicked, the total
absence of a rhythm section seemed a bit
perverse. *Barbecue King* found him making
competent, if hardly trailblazing power pop;
Too Hot to Handle returned him to the
acoustic-only format of early Hot Tuna. A
true electric guitar dazzler with Jefferson
Airplane, Kaukonen has since that time
made fine music, but of a more muted and
less ambitious sort. — P.E.

JOHN KAY

★ ★ ★ **Forgotten Songs and Unsung Heroes
      (Dunhill, 1972)**
★ ★ ★ **Lone Steppenwolf (MCA, 1987)**

Growling lead singer for Steppenwolf and mastermind of their biker poetics, John Kay did credible bluesman imitations on their great garage-band classics, "Born to Be Wild" and "Magic Carpet Ride." On his own, he bombed. With the *Forgotten Songs and Unsung Heroes* (now out of print), he managed to score one mild hit in a cool remake of Hank Snow's "I'm Movin' On." His only currently in-print album, *Lone Steppenwolf*, is competent, unspectacular blooze-rock, but the best of his solo work can be found on the 1991 double-CD anthology, *Born to Be Wild/A Retrospective (1966–1990)*. — P.E.

KC & THE SUNSHINE BAND
★ ★ ★ ★ **The Best of KC & the Sunshine Band (Rhino, 1989)**
Keyboardist H.W. Casey ("KC") and bassist Rick Finch worked their way into the house band at TK Records, a fledgling Miami-based R&B label of the early '70s. Before mounting KC & the Sunshine Band, they wrote and produced "Rock Your Baby" for George McRae. This 1974 pop Number One pumped the refreshing Miami sound to a national audience: swaying Caribbean breeze, shifting rhythmic pulse, sweetly suggestive soul voice, silly-sexy nonsense words. "Rock Your Baby" isn't quite disco, though it's clear just where all that gentle back-and-forth action will lead—straight to the dance floor. Pushing Casey's giddy chants right up front, KC & the Sunshine Band rode this effervescent groove all the way to the bank in 1975–76. Surprisingly, the killer hooks are still mighty sharp: it takes superhuman strength to resist come-ons like the salacious "uh-huh, uh-huh" in "That's the Way (I Like It)," the shimmering surfside rhythm guitar on "Get Down Tonight," the salt-spray-in-the-face horn line during "I'm Your Boogie Man." Admittedly, all the high-stepping spirit gets a bit single-minded over the course of an hour-long CD, but the handful of actual hits really is great. While the inevitable decline-period material doesn't exactly broaden this bubble machine's one-trick reputation, the beefed-up "Let's Go Rock & Roll" (from 1980) isn't nearly as grotesque as you might expect. Hard-core discophiles will find a treasure trove of delectable trivia on *The Best of KC & the Sunshine Band*, but casual partygoers will probably be satisfied by the KC inclusions on Rhino's *The Disco Years, Volume 1*. — M.C.

KEEDY
★ ★ ★ **Chase the Clouds (Arista, 1991)**
The synthesizers hum, the rhythm machines percolate. Keedy makes high-gloss dance music that skirts formula sheerly through the bubblegum appeal of the singer's wise-waif voice and the irresistible catchiness of her tunes. More reminiscent of Abba than Madonna, this is guilty-pleasure pop—completely insubstantial, but oodles of fun. — P.E.

TOMMY KEENE
★ ★ ½ **Strange Alliance (Avenue, 1983)**
★ ★ ★ ★ **Places That Are Gone (EP) (Dolphin, 1984)**
★ ★ ★ **Back Again (Try . . .) (EP) (Dolphin, 1984)**
★ ★ ★ **Songs From the Film (Geffen, 1986)**
★ ★ ½ **Run Now (EP) (Geffen, 1986)**
★ ★ ★ ½ **Based On Happy Times (Geffen, 1989)**
Had Tommy Keene been blessed with blond hair and a soaring, tenor voice, he'd surely have been a star. His songs, after all, would have been perfect for radio, what with their ringing guitars, catchy choruses and vivid descriptions of romantic angst. But Keene is neither a blond nor a tenor, which is probably why his audience never stretched much beyond the reach of college radio. Too bad. *Places That Are Gone* is an indie classic, thanks to should-have-been hits like "Back to Zero" and the title tune, which sparkle despite Keene's limited vocal ability. There's also a version of "Places That Are Gone" on *Songs From the Film*, this time with stronger singing but less sizzle; although the rest of Keene's sound was finally coming into focus, his rhythm section had begun to fizzle. *Based On Happy Times* brings in an entirely new band, and at its best sounds like a happier version of the Replacements; "Highwire Days" is particularly fine. — J.D.C.

PAUL KELLY AND THE MESSENGERS
★ ★ ★ ½ **Gossip (A&M, 1987)**
★ ★ ★ ½ **Under the Sun (A&M, 1988)**
★ ★ ★ ½ **So Much Water So Close to Home (A&M, 1989)**
Aussie vocalist and acoustic guitarist Paul Kelly pens quick, tight, slice-of-life vignettes, and the Messengers rock like sleek, sharp furies—the question, then, remains: why hasn't this group garnered the respect it deserves? The answer may lie in the relative subtlety of its approach. While the combo plays with the precision of such fine late-'70s

Brit pub rockers as Ducks Deluxe or Brinsley Schwartz, and their mainman's gruff vocals aren't at all dissimilar from those of the star of that scene, Graham Parker. Kelly hasn't the outsized rage of Parker, nor does he flourish the polysyllabic poetry of another writer with whom he shares sensibility, Elvis Costello. Instead, Kelly's lyrics are the vernacular verse of a songwriter whose emotional range is generous and nuanced—his very lack of flash may have kept him from finding an easy audience. This is, however, rock & roll for grown-ups, and it's clear, memorable and strong. — P.E.

EDDIE KENDRICKS
★ ★ ★½ **Superstar Series, Volume 19 (Motown, 1981)**
★ ★ ★½ **At His Best (Motown, 1990)**
Rail-thin and ultra-elegant, Eddie Kendricks lent his strong tenor voice to the Temptations for more than ten years—his sly use of falsetto juxtaposing effectively against David Ruffin's gruff delivery. In 1971, he broke from the group and soared solo throughout the early part of the decade. His foxy, high-voiced hits of 1973, "Keep on Truckin'," and 1974, "Boogie Down," demonstrated deft pop flair. His career faltered, however, after he signed with Arista in 1978; two reunion albums with his former Temps bandmate, *Live at the Apollo with David Ruffin and Eddie Kendricks* (with Hall and Oates) and *David Ruffin and Eddie Kendricks*, found him in steady form, but he never truly recovered his earlier distinction. — P.E.

CHRIS KENNER
★ ★ ★ ★ **I Like It Like That (Collectables, NA)**
Chris Kenner's only pop hit, "I Like It Like That, Part 1" in 1961, has assured him a spot on most oldies radio rotations, but this album shows off the chops of a singer and writer who was much more than a one-hit wonder. Yet another of New Orleans' stellar voices, Kenner marries the steady-rolling Crescent City groove to material that has deep roots in gospel, even when addressing secular concerns such as dancing and mean-woman blues. Those who think "Land of 1000 Dances" originated with Cannibal & the Headhunters are in for a shock—Kenner wrote the song, and he delivers it here as if he were rebuking a backsliding congregation. Elsewhere, he employs his husky, brooding baritone to great effect on the blues-gospel lament "Never Reach

Perfection" and on the previously unissued "I Found Peace," another gospel-based gem. It's the rare Kenner song, in fact, that lacks some kind of reference, be it oblique or forcefully stated, to the dire consequences of serving God and Mammon. Coming by way of Clarence Fountain of the Five Blind Boys of Alabama and Julius Cheeks of the Sensational Nightingales, Kenner delivers some of the edgiest, darkest pop ever produced in New Orleans—or anywhere else. — D.M.

KENNY G
★½ **Kenny G (Arista, 1982)**
★ **G Force (Arista, 1983)**
★ **Gravity (Arista, 1985)**
★½ **Duotones (Arista, 1986)**
★ ★ **Silhouette (Arista, 1988)**
★ **Live (Arista, 1989)**
½ ★ **Dying Young: Original Soundtrack Album (Arista, 1991)**
Although reviled by jazz fans as a featherweight and fake, what saxophonist Kenny G plays would be best described as "fuzak"—that is, a combination of fusion and Muzak, which at its worst manages to be more soporific than either individually. Apparently, it took a while for him to work up to this breakthrough; *Kenny G* is given to light jazz in a Grover Washington vein, while *G Force* and *Gravity* are feckless, funkless attempts at an R&B identity. But *Duotones* makes the most of the G-man's melodic instincts, particularly on slower tunes like "Songbird" and "Don't Make Me Wait for Love," a formula *Silhouette* exploits to the fullest. It's not a bad album, really, particularly when G gets to play off Smokey Robinson's silken phrasing in "We've Saved the Best for Last." But it's all downhill from there, as *Live* barely shows a pulse and *Dying Young* turns out to be dead on arrival. — J.D.C.

THE KENTUCKY COLONELS
★ ★ ★½ **Clarence White and the Kentucky Colonels (Rounder, NA)**
★ ★ ★½ **Onstage (Rounder, NA)**
★ ★ ★½ **The Kentucky Colonels (1976; Rounder, 1987)**
★ ★ ★½ **The White Brothers: The New Kentucky Colonels Live in Sweden, 1973 (1977; Rounder, 1988)**
★ ★ ★½ **Long Journey Home (Vanguard, 1991)**
Joining the Byrds in 1968, Clarence White not only sparked new life with the furious precision of his electric playing on such songs as "Lover of the Bayou" and "This

Wheel's on Fire," but he encouraged the direction toward country music the band had taken during its brief alliance with Gram Parsons. Born in Maine and raised in California, White was neither a good old boy nor a cowboy, but his country credentials were impeccable. Ever since 1962, he'd honed his remarkably dextrous acoustic guitar skills with the Kentucky Colonels, a classic bluegrass outfit he'd founded with his brother Roland, a mandolin player. On such standards as "I Am a Pilgrim" and "Wildwood Flower" (from *Clarence White and the Kentucky Colonels*) the White Brothers played and sang with grace, total conviction and no irony whatsoever. The group's vitality saved its respectful performances from tipping over into archivist reverence—and all its material sounds fresh today. *Long Journey Home* (1991) documents a 1964 performance at the Newport Folk Festival, showing the group in excellent form. Killed by a drunk driver in 1973, White is remembered mainly for his work with the Byrds—the Colonels' music, however, forms a significant and delightful part of his legacy. — P.E.

THE KENTUCKY HEADHUNTERS
★ ★ ★½ Pickin' on Nashville (Mercury, 1989)
★ ★ ★½ Electric Barnyard (Mercury, 1991)
Had they emerged in the '70s, the HeadHunters would've been labeled "Southern rock"; a decade later, they wouldn't have seemed misfit alongside Jason and the Scorchers and other cowpunk contenders. But, coming out in the '90s, they were marketed country for redneck hippies raised on Hank Jr. or fans of the later Allman Brothers—longhairs who just can't get enough guitar.

And the Heads deliver. Voted Country Music Association Album of the Year in 1990, the band's debut was country of a kind—but its nose-tweaking title, *Pickin' on Nashville,* warned that this Stratocaster blaze through chestnuts (Don Gibson's "Oh Lonesome Me), cornpone ("Skip a Rope") and '50s-ish rock originals wasn't no Minnie Pearl. The follow-up continued the winning formula: sporting fringed jackets, coonskin caps and hair as long as Berry Oakley's, the Heads pounded the hell out of "The Ballad of Davy Crockett," Norman Greenbaum's Jesus-boogie "Spirit in the Sky" and the self-explanatory "Kickin' Them Blues Around." Good old boys whose woodsheddin' time reaped thunder, the

HeadHunters are the shitkickers that, say, Black Oak Arkansas always wanted to be. — P.E.

JACK KEROUAC
★ ★ ★ ★ The Jack Kerouac Collection (Rhino, 1989)
The music that inspired Jack Kerouac and the rest of the late-'50s loose confederacy of rebel mystics and road scholars who called themselves the Beats was Charlie Parker's hard bop. Borrowing from Parker a faith in untrammelled improvisation, they wrote word-music, language drunk on rhythm. Their poetry derived from Blake and from the French symbolists (Baudelaire, Rimbaud) who'd later find disciples in Dylan and Jim Morrison. And their urge to wander reflected an American restlessness that reached back to Woody Guthrie, Walt Whitman, and ultimately the original pioneers. These methods and impulses, fired by the spiritual poverty and conformism of Eisenhower America, paved the way for rock & roll. Published at the moment of Elvis's ascent, Kerouac's *On the Road* (1957) was the novel that delivered the Beat message with the truest of pop power—its irresistible prose celebrated appetite (food, sex, drink, drugs) while insisting, too, that the spirit must be fed. With their fellow hipsters (James Dean and Marlon Brando, Miles Davis and the cool jazz players, Jackson Pollack and the Abstract Expressionists), the Beats were rock & roll in embryo—their struggle was the birth throes of cultural revolt.

A beautiful three-CD set, gloriously annotated and filled with tributes, *The Jack Kerouac Collection* presents the writer reading verse that lauds trains, the moon, Mexico, and Charlie Parker, delivering thoughts on "The Beat Generation," and scatting riffs from *On the Road.* The affable Steve Allen comps piano as Jack moans and declaims; elsewhere, jazzers Al Cohn and Zoot Sims accompany him as he turns out American haikus and short "blues" poetry. Producers Bob Thiele and Bill Randle leave the tape going during the sessions—and some of Kerouac's offhand comments are nearly as appealing as his poems. What emerges is the soul of the man—expansive, errant and desperately alive. — P.E.

DOUG KERSHAW
★ ★½ The Cajun Way (Warner Bros., 1969)
★ ★ Spanish Moss (Warner Bros., 1970)
★ ★ Doug Kershaw (Warner Bros., 1971)
★ ★ Swamp Grass (Warner Bros., 1972)

★★½ **Devil's Elbow (Warner Bros., 1972)**
★★ **Douglas James Kershaw (Warner Bros., 1973)**
★★½ **Mama Kershaw's Boy (Warner Bros., 1974)**
★★ **Alive and Pickin' (Warner Bros., 1975)**
★★★ **The Ragin' Cajun (Warner Bros., 1976)**
★★½ **Louisiana Man (Warner Bros., 1978)**
★★★½ **The Best of Doug Kershaw (Warner Bros., 1989)**

Doug Kershaw played rollicking Cajun music eons before the late-'80s revival. Kershaw, however, sometimes passed for a novelty act; a furious fiddler, he was also an irrepressible ham, and for every fine song he played, he turned out ten that were schlock. More of an enthusiastic vocalist than a good one, he was best at delivering the aural equivalent of winking. *Ragin' Cajun* is his only solid album; the better bet is his best-of compilation. Containing his breakthrough early-'60s hits, "Louisiana Man" and "Diggy Diggy Lo," as well as zesty takes on Hank Williams's "Jambalaya (On the Bayou)" and Fats Domino's "I'm Walkin,' " it's great party music. While too idiosyncratic a figure to be credited for sparking appreciation for Louisiana music as a whole, Kershaw remains a commendable eccentric. — P.E.

CHAKA KHAN
★★★ **Chaka (Warner Bros., 1978)**
★★★ **Naughty (Warner Bros., 1980)**
★★★ **What Cha' Gonna Do for Me (Warner Bros., 1981)**
★★★½ **Chaka Khan (Warner Bros., 1982)**
★★★ **I Feel for You (Warner Bros., 1984)**
★★½ **Destiny (Warner Bros., 1986)**
★★★ **CK (Warner Bros., 1988)**
★★ **Life Is a Dance/The Remix Project (Warner Bros., 1989)**

Chaka Khan's albums often sound downright frustrated—and frustrating. Khan opts for a contemporary R&B sound in her solo work, toning down the rock influence of her ex-band, Rufus. When she connects with strong material, there's no stopping her. But a surfeit of tasteful filler and half-successful jazz excursions weigh down even the best of these albums. The dance-floor classics and chart hits can be riveting: "I'm Every Woman" and "Life Is a Dance" from *Chaka*; "Clouds" from *Naughty*. *What Cha' Gonna Do for Me* stakes her claim to the '80s, blithely folding

some of Chaka's scatty vocal finesse into a fidgety, synthesized dance track. *Chaka Khan* is probably her best overall solo album, though. She smolders on "Slow Dancin' " and pulls off a "Be Bop Melody" without breaking a sweat. "I Feel for You," with its electro hip-hop beats and Melle Mel's guest rap, ruled the airwaves in 1984. Over the course of an entire album, that keyboard-dominated approach drowns out Khan's nuanced singing style. On the overproduced and underwritten *Destiny*, Khan sounds a bit distanced. *CK* is a big improvement; Prince's production provides an audible spark, but the album still falls short. Avoid *The Remix Project* at all costs: a pointless, ugly reshuffling of Chaka's classic dance anthems. — M.C.

KID CREOLE AND THE COCONUTS
★★ **Off the Coast of Me (Antilles, 1980)**
★★½ **Fresh Fruit in Foreign Places (Sire, 1981)**
★★★ **Wise Guy (Sire, 1982)**
★★ **Doppelganger (Sire, 1983)**
★★ **In Praise of Older Women and Other Crimes (Sire, 1985)**
★½ **I, Too, Have Seen the Woods (Sire, 1987)**
★★½ **Private Waters in the Great Divide (Columbia, 1990)**
★★ **You Shoulda Told Me You Were . . . (Columbia, 1991)**
★★★ **Kid Creole Redux (Sire, 1992)**

Simply as a matter of style, it's hard not to admire August "Kid Creole" Darnell's chutzpah. Here, after all, is a guy who thinks it's the height of fashion to hit the stage looking like a cross between Cab Calloway and Desi Arnaz. Admittedly, it wasn't such a bad bit of shtick when Darnell and cohort "Sugar-Coated" Andy Hernandez were part of Dr. Buzzard's Original Savannah Band, just as the pan-Caribbean big-band groove he whipped up for *Off the Coast of Me* seemed amusing for an album or two. But his songwriting flagged after *Wise Guy*, while his conceptual indulgences grew ever more baroque. As such, the singles-only collection, *Kid Creole Redux* is far more consistent than any of the albums from which it draws. To his credit, Darnell manages to coax some new life from the formula by funking it up on *Private Waters in the Great Divide*, which is enjoyable in spite of its version of "Lambada." But *You Shoulda Told Me You Were . . .* offers little evidence that this is a permanent improvement. — J.D.C.

KID 'N PLAY

★ ★ ★½ **2 Hype (Select, 1988)**
★ ★   **Kid 'N Play's Funhouse (Select, 1990)**
★ ★   **Face the Nation (Select, 1991)**

Witty and entertaining, *2 Hype* puts Kid 'N Play in the good-natured company of D.J. Jazzy Jeff & the Fresh Prince; although little on the album lives up to the go-go-powered groove of "Rollin' With Kid 'N Play," its amiable energy never disappoints. *Kid 'N Play's Funhouse* is little more than a spin-off from the duo's appearance in the film *House Party*; the raps are so-so, and the between-tracks chatter is downright annoying. Still, the album must have worked on some level, since the two were given their own Saturday morning (short-lived) cartoon show shortly thereafter. But by *Face the Nation*, Kid 'N Play make the mistake of many rap has-beens, lecturing other rap acts without realizing how laughable their own sound has become; perhaps *Smell the Coffee* would have been a more appropriate title. — J.D.C.

GREG KIHN

★ ★½ **Greg Kihn (Beserkley, 1976)**
★ ★ ★ **Greg Kihn Again (Beserkley, 1977)**
★ ★½ **Next of Kihn (Beserkley, 1978)**
★ ★ ★ **With the Naked Eye (Beserkley, 1979)**
★ ★½ **Glass House Rock (Beserkley, 1980)**
★ ★ ★ ★ **Rockihnroll (Beserkley, 1981)**
★ ★ ★ **Kihntinued (Beserkley, 1982)**
★ ★ ★ ★ **Kihnspiracy (Beserkley, 1983)**
★ ★ ★½ **Kihntagious (EMI Beserkley, 1984)**
★ ★½ **Citizen Kihn (EMI America, 1985)**
★ ★ **Love and Rock and Roll (EMI America, 1986)**
★ ★ ★ **Unkihntrollable (Rhino, 1989)**
★ ★ ★ ★ **Kihnsolidation: The Best of Greg Kihn (Rhino, 1989)**

Combining the earnest melodies of Buddy Holly with the lean, classic sound of the Beau Brummels, Greg Kihn's best work is so honest and straightforward it's almost hard to believe that he's a product of the new-wave '70s. That's not to say he wrote and recorded in a time warp; indeed, his "Jeopardy" (from *Kihnspiracy*) is pure early-'80s dance pop. But Kihn's best tended to rise above pop trends, and his most memorable work—songs like "The Breakup Song (They Don't Write 'Em)" from *Rockihnroll*, "Reunited" from *Kihntagious*, "Testify" from *Kihntinued*—boasts the same rootsy enthusiasm and tuneful economy that mark Steve Miller's finest. — J.D.C.

KILLING JOKE

★ ★ ★ **Killing Joke (EG, 1980)**
★ ★ ★ **what's THIS for . . . ! (EG, 1981)**
★ ★½ **Revelations (EG, 1982)**
★ ★ ★ ★ **Fire Dances (EG, 1983)**
★ ★ ★ **Night Time (EG, 1985)**
★ ★ ★ **Brighter Than a Thousand Suns (EG, 1987)**
★ ★ ★ **Outside the Gate (EG, 1988)**
★ ★ ★ **Extremities, Dirt & Various Repressed Emotions (Noise/RCA, 1990)**

Everything about early Killing Joke was jagged—power-drill guitars, foghorn synths, militantly unswinging drums, and shouted vocals. Spearheaded by singer-keyboardist Jaz Coleman and guitarist Geordie, these Londoners were men with a mission: to bring forward into the '80s an unphased punk anger. What made them more than noise-mongers, however, was the efficiency of their assault—while *Killing Joke* and *what's THIS for . . . !* were hardly hook-heavy, such songs as "Wardance," "Bloodsport," "The Fall of Because" and "Tension" were well-constructed ideology machines; their political outrage was obvious, but the tunes didn't fall apart under the weight of their anger.

A distancing production buffed the edge off *Revelations*, but sharper playing almost compensated for the loss, and the bitterness of "We Have Joy" and "The Pandys Are Coming" proved that complacency had hardly settled in. With *Fire Dances*, the tentative experiments with polish embarked upon with *Revelations* bore full, ripe fruit; Killing Joke's best album, it kicks into funkier rhythms, embraces melody, and suggests, in its lyrics, action rather than despair—all this, without conceding an inch in power. *Night Time* capitalized on *Fire*'s advances, delivering these determined outsiders a successful single (of all things!) in the romantic-agony anthem, "Love Like Blood."

With *Brighter Than a Thousand Suns*, however, Killing Joke began upsetting the fine tension of rage and outreach it had achieved in its maturity. This synth-driven mood music isn't quite that of Depeche Mode, but it comes at times perilously close. *Outside the Gate* is new-model Joke as well, and while the dance-music grooves sound more assured this time and the lyrics are hardly nursery rhymes, the old, pure

vehemence is M.I.A. *Extremites, Dirt &
Various Repressed Emotions* marks a
marginal return to toughness. — P.E.

ALBERT KING

★★★★★ **Born Under a Bad Sign
(Atlantic, 1967)**

★★★★ **King of the Blues Guitar (1968;
Atlantic, 1977)**

★★★ **Live Wire Blues Power (1968;
Stax/Fantasy, 1979)**

★★★ **Jammed Together: Albert King,
Steve Cropper, Pop Staples
(1969; Stax/Fantasy, 1988)**

★★★★ **Years Gone By (1969;
Stax/Fantasy, 1982)**

★★★★ **Lovejoy (1970; Stax/Fantasy,
1990)**

★★★ **I'll Play the Blues for You
(1972; Stax/Fantasy, 1987)**

★★★ **I Wanna Get Funky (1973;
Stax/Fantasy, 1987)**

★★★★ **Albert Live (Utopia, 1977)**

★★★ **The Pinch (Stax/Fantasy, 1977)**

★★★ **New Orleans Heat (Tomato,
1979)**

★★★ **Montreux Festival
(Stax/Fantasy, 1979)**

★★½ **Blues for Elvis (Stax/Fantasy,
1981)**

★★ **The Lost Session (Stax/Fantasy,
1986)**

★★★ **The Best of Albert King
(Stax/Fantasy, 1986)**

★★★ **Blues at Sunrise (Stax/Fantasy,
1988)**

★★★★★ **Let's Have a Natural Ball
(Modern Blues, 1989)**

★★★ **Wednesday Night in San
Francisco (Live at the Fillmore)
(Stax/Fantasy, 1990)**

★★★ **Thursday Night in San
Francisco (Live at the Fillmore)
(Stax/Fantasy, 1990)**

★★★★★ **Masterworks (Atlantic, NA)**

Born in 1923 in Indianola, Mississippi,
Albert King (no relation to B.B.) shaped a
style of stinged blues guitar that echoed
Elmore James and Robert Nighthawk but
was also distinguished by steely single-string
lead lines and muscular phrasing that
borrowed from Lonnie Johnson and T-Bone
Walker. Tuning to an open E-minor chord,
King, a lefty, played the guitar as strung for
a right-handed player, but upside down, and
executed the most amazing string bending
known to man by pulling down across the
fretboard until he reached the right note.
But King relied less on flash than on
solidity; basic, straight ahead, unrelenting

drive minus filigree or ostentatious displays
of technique.

Though he first recorded in the early '50s
for the Parrot label, King remained fairly
obscure until he signed with the St.
Louis-based Bobbin label in 1959 and began
turning out some first-rate sides that found
him blazing away on guitar in front of a
jump band outfitted with a saxophone
section. A 1961 single, "Don't Throw Your
Love on Me So Strong," became a national
R&B hit, but little happened in its wake.
Then in 1966 King signed with the Stax
label and made his mark.

Backed by Booker T. and the MG's and
the redoubtable Memphis Horns, King
delivered a series of strong albums—one,
Born Under a Bad Sign (1967), the peak of
King's recording career and a classic by any
standard—that displayed the full range of
his interests and his ability to recast the
unlikeliest material into ringing personal
statements. "Crosscut Saw" and the title
song are legendary tracks from *Born Under
a Bad Sign*. For a man whose style is often
defined in harsh terms, King had a tender
streak a mile wide, and he made the most of
his engaging but limited voice when he
ventured into left field. His not-altogether-
successful tribute to Elvis Presley, *Blues for
Elvis*, is a case in point: King is defeated by
"Jailhouse Rock" and "Heartbreak Hotel,"
but he gives "All Shook Up" a rousing
jump-blues treatment and elevates "Love
Me Tender" by playing it as gospel-soul.
Blues, however, remained the bedrock of
King's repertoire; nothing could supplant his
downright dangerous takes on Howlin'
Wolf's "Killing Floor" (on *Years Gone By*)
or T-Bone Walker's "Call It Stormy
Monday" (on *Thursday Night in San
Francisco*, the second volume of a
sensational two-volume live collection;
volume one is, naturally enough, *Wednesday
Night in San Francisco*). No single Stax
album is definitive King in the way the out-
of-print *Born Under a Bad Sign* is definitive
King, but each one has its virtues.

The Lost Session stands as an interesting
but failed experiment teaming King with
John Mayall in a halfhearted move toward
jazz. The rocking *Lovejoy* finds King
journeying to Muscle Shoals for five tracks
of greasy North Alabama soul. From King's
post-Stax years, the out-of-print Tomato
release, *New Orleans Heat*, takes King to
the Crescent City and to producer Allen
Toussaint for a flawed but fascinating
melding of jazz and blues. *Let's Have a
Natural Ball*, on Modern Blues, is the

absolutely essential work from King's early career, comprised of King's initial releases on the Bobbin and King labels. The most concise overview of King's later work is the out-of-print Atlantic *Masterworks* two-record set, which takes King through the high points of his Stax years and into the late '70s. — D.M.

B.B. KING

★ ★ ★ ★ The Unexpected . . . Instrumental B.B. King . . . Just Sweet Guitar (Kent, NA)

★ ★ ★ ★ Blues Is King (MCA, 1967)

★ ★ ★ ★ Lucille (Bluesway/ABC, 1968)

★ ★ ★ ★ The Electric B.B. King—His Best (MCA, 1968)

★ ★ ★ ★ Live & Well (Bluesway/ABC, 1969)

★ ★ ★ ★ Completely Well (Bluesway/ABC, 1969)

★ ★ ★ ★ Incredible Soul of B.B. King (1970; Kent, 1987)

★ ★ ★ ★ Indianola Mississippi Seeds (MCA, 1970)

★ ★ ★ Live in Cook County Jail (MCA, 1971)

★ ★ ★ ★ ★ Live at the Regal (MCA, 1971)

★ ★ ★ B.B. King in London (ABC, 1971)

★ ★ ★ ★ Back in the Alley: The Classic Blues of B.B. King (ABC, 1973)

★ ★ ★ ★ The Best of B.B. King (1973; MCA, 1987)

★ ★ ★ ★ To Know You Is To Love You (ABC, 1973)

★ ★ ★ Friends (ABC, 1974)

★ ★ ★ ★ B.B. King & Bobby Bland: Together for the First Time Live (MCA, 1974)

★ ★ ★ ★ Lucille Talks Back (1975; MCA, 1990)

★ ★ B.B. King & Bobby Bland: Together Again . . . Live (1976; MCA, 1990)

★ ★ ★ ★ King Size (ABC, 1977)

★ ★ ★ Midnight Believer (ABC, 1978)

★ ★ ★ Take It Home (MCA, 1979)

★ ★ ★ ★ Live "Now Appearing" at Ole Miss (MCA, 1980)

★ ★ ★ ★ Great Moments with B.B. King (MCA, 1981)

★ ★ ★ ★ ★ There Must Be a Better World Somewhere (MCA, 1981)

★ ★ ★ ★ Love Me Tender (MCA, 1982)

★ ★ ★ ★ Blues 'N' Jazz (MCA, 1983)

★ ★ ★ Six Silver Strings (MCA, 1985)

★ ★ ★ King of the Blues 1989 (MCA, 1989)

★ ★ ★ ★ Live at San Quentin (MCA, 1990)

★ ★ ★ ★ ★ The Best of B.B. King, Volume One (1986; Flair/WEA, 1991)

★ ★ ★ ★ There Is Always One More Time (MCA, 1991)

One eventually runs out of superlatives in attempting to catalogue B.B. King's accomplishments. He is a great singer; a list of the most influential guitarists in history would include his name near the top; whether fronting a small combo or full-blown orchestra, his instincts are infallible, his leadership compelling; as a songwriter he has penned several blues classics, including "Paying the Cost to Be the Boss," "Why I Sing the Blues," "Sweet Sixteen" and "Sweet Little Angel."

In arriving at an individual voice, King proved to be a great consolidator of styles. Born in Itta Bena, Mississippi, he sang in gospel quartets and on street corners; in the '40s, while he was playing at a cafe in West Memphis, Arkansas, he often worked with a group of musicians that included singer Bobby Bland and pianist Johnny Ace. His guitar technique at that time was largely unformed, being derivative of both Blind Lemon Jefferson and T-Bone Walker. His attempts to master the single string soloing techniques pioneered by Walker, Lonnie Johnson, Eddie Lang and Charlie Christian led him to Robert Jr. Lockwood, who was playing a less ornate style of Delta blues on the electric guitar. The combination of Lockwood's instruction and King's fortuitous landing of a job as a disc jockey with Memphis's WDIA (which in the late '40s became the first U.S. radio station to feature an all-black format) were the signal events in his development as an instrumentalist. At WDIA King gained a reputation for playing the hippest records in town. As an added "bonus" for listeners, King would play along with the records, in effect going to school on the air.

King also performed regularly at the theaters on Beale Street, the black Mecca of the South, and it was at one of these shows that he was spotted by Sam Phillips, who had been an engineer at station WREC and was in charge of the ballroom sound system at the opulent Peabody Hotel in downtown Memphis. King's performance convinced Phillips that there was a future in recording the wealth of black talent in and around Memphis. In 1950 he opened the Memphis Recording Service at 706 Union Avenue in a converted radiator shop. One of the first artists contacted by Phillips, King was in the studio by the summer of '50, recording for the Bihari brothers of Modern Records in

Los Angeles, who leased the masters from Phillips. Success came quickly. In 1951 King covered Lowell Fulsom's "Three O'Clock Blues" and it became a national R&B hit; his guitar playing was strongly redolent of T-Bone Walker, but his pleading, forceful singing voice was undeniably his own.

Until recently, King's recordings for Modern's Kent subsidiary have been long out of print, or available only on hard-to-find imports. However, England's Ace Records has struck a deal with WEA Distribution to release a series of titles Stateside. Among the first batch of releases is *The Best of B.B. King, Volume One*, 20 tracks from King's Kent era. The importance of this record should be obvious, particularly since it includes some previously unreleased tracks. The liner notes promise more to come, and if the remaining discs are equal to Volume One, King's history on record will be even more satisfying than it is now. *The Unexpected . . . Instrumental B.B. King . . . Just Sweet Guitar* is a marvelous all-instrumental album. *Incredible Soul* makes an interesting contrast to King's latter-day recordings, particularly in the almost throwaway treatment he gives "I've Got Papers On You Baby," for years a staple in King's concert repertoire. Also, the vocals are, by blues standards, innocent. *Unexpected* is of interest to anyone wishing a capsule lesson in the development of King's guitar technique. In its eight tracks one hears King quoting all of his influences, but also making his instrument sing in the quintessential B.B. King manner. Some of the languorous passages prefigure King's "boudoir soul" albums (*Midnight Believer*, *Love Me Tender*) of the late '70s and early '80s. Where to find the Kent albums is another issue entirely: I purchased them at a truck stop in Lyman, Wyoming. A subsequent search in legitimate retail record stores and in blues specialty shops produced only puzzlement.

King is also well-represented by several live albums. His performances have been consistently pleasing over the years, and all of the live recordings have their splendid moments. Most essential of the many titles is the extraordinary 1964 set from the Regal in Chicago, *Live at the Regal*, on which King demonstrates his superior musicianship as well as his exemplary rapport with his audience. Stirring performances of "Every Day I Have the Blues," "Sweet Little Angel" and "Woke Up This Mornin' " key the show, but the highlight is the hilarious "Help the Poor."

Also, King's first album with Bobby Bland, *Together for the First Time . . . Live* is spectacular: Two towering figures of American music burn their way through a repertoire that includes "Three O'Clock Blues," "Driftin' Blues," "Goin' Down Slow" and a medley comprised in part of "Rock Me Baby," "Driving Wheel" and "Chains of Love." The second King-Bland summit is less fiery, but King and Bland shine throughout.

King also released a steady stream of good studio albums in the late '60s and early '70s, one of which, *Completely Well*, gave him his lone Top Twenty pop hit, "The Thrill Is Gone," in 1970. Producer Bill Szymczyk, who went on to produce most of the Eagles' albums, was behind the board on *Completely Well* and *Indianola Mississippi Seeds*, and these recordings show a stylistic breadth that points the way to King's later years. In 1971 King teamed up with some of the most respected white blues and rock artists of the day on *B.B. King in London*. Ringo Starr, Peter Green, Alexis Korner, Jim Keltner, Jim Gordon, Bobby Keys, and Mac Rebennack are among the supporting cast that produces some rousing moments.

King remained true to his style as the '70s wore on, but he upset purists with his 1978 collaboration with the Crusaders on *Midnight Believer*, which by King standards amounts to cocktail-lounge fare, being all soft edges and mellow moods; he returned to the gentle sound on *Love Me Tender* (1982). But in between these albums he produced a genuine masterpiece in *There Must Be a Better World Somewhere*. *Live at San Quentin* got King off to a good start in the '90s with another first-rate performance. More encouraging, King's first studio album of the decade, *There Is Always One More Time*, finds him singing with renewed vigor and conviction. The poignant title song, one of the most emotional performances of King's long career, was the last song written by Doc Pomus before his death.

It's the rare artist who won't allow his legend to let him relax. *There Is Always One More Time* shows that the only predictable fact about B.B. King's career right now is that he's going to deliver more good music in the years ahead. Makes you glad that some things never change. — D.M.

BEN E. KING
★★★ **Stand By Me: The Best of Ben E. King (Atlantic, 1986)**
★★★★ **The Ultimate Collection: Ben E. King (Atlantic, 1987)**

Ben E. King rates as one of the most important soul singers in history. In his short stint with the Drifters (1959 and part of 1960), he redefined the group from one built around the sweet, plaintive stylings of Clyde McPhatter to a more brusque, harder-edged blend of pop and R&B. That much of the Drifters' best-known work coincides with King's Drifters years is recommendation enough, given the strength of the group's vocalists throughout their long history. Apart from his singing, which hearkens back to the emotional explosions of the Sensational Nightingales' Julius Cheeks, King also made a couple of noteworthy contributions as a songwriter. "There Goes My Baby," the first hit he sang with the Drifters, was King's own composition, and remains one of the group's signature songs. His finest effort, though, was his Number Four hit in 1961, "Stand By Me," a stark, moving love song that is as unsettling as it is uplifting.

With the Drifters and as a solo artist, King worked with the dominant producer-songwriters of the '50s, Jerry Leiber and Mike Stoller, and was the recipient of some of the finest songs ever written by Doc Pomus and Mort Shuman. That duo delivered smart, unsentimental urban romanticism incorporating Latin rhythms; Leiber-Stoller brought it all home with arrangements that boosted the emotional impact of the vocal performances. The 20-track *Ultimate Collection* set spans King's most productive years (solo and with the Drifters), and also includes his wonderful 1975 comeback single, "Supernatural Thing (Part 1)." *Stand by Me* contains only ten tracks, all of which can be found on *Ultimate Collection*. Neither set is well annotated. — D.M.

CAROLE KING

★ ★ ★	Writer (Ode, 1970)	
★ ★ ★ ★¹⁄₂	Tapestry (Ode, 1971)	
★ ★ ★	Music (Ode, 1971)	
★ ★ ★	Rhymes and Reasons (Ode, 1972)	
★ ★ ★	Fantasy (Ode, 1973)	
★ ★ ★	Wrap Around Joy (Ode, 1974)	
★ ★ ★	Thoroughbred (Ode, 1976)	
★ ★	Simple Things (Capitol, 1977)	
★ ★	Welcome Home (Capitol, 1978)	
★ ★ ★ ★	Her Greatest Hits (Ode/Columbia, 1978)	
★ ★	Touch the Sky (Capitol, 1979)	
★ ★	Pearls (Capitol, 1980)	
★ ★	One to One (Atlantic, 1982)	

Carole King and her husband, Gerry Goffin, were one of the most successful songwriting teams that worked out of New York's legendary Brill Building. Goffin and King co-wrote four Number One hits while Carole was still in her teens and early 20s: The Shirelles' "Will You Love Me Tomorrow," Bobby Vee's "Take Good Care of My Baby," Little Eva's "The Loco-Motion," and "Go Away Little Girl"—a song that went all the way for both Steve Lawrence and Donny Osmond. After a fallow period and a divorce in the late '60s, King emerged as a solo artist in 1970, adding an experienced voice to the blossoming singer-songwriter movement.

Her debut (*Writer*) sounds tentative, but the equally reflective follow-up couldn't be more self-assured. *Tapestry* became the biggest-selling album in history up to that point, and the reasons why are still audible. Carole King brought an arresting intimacy to mainstream pop—she managed to grow without losing her youthful melodic knack. "It's Too Late" evaluates a stale relationship with startling clarity. Rather than strain for a folkie-soul effect à la Laura Nyro, King opts for a plainspoken vocal style that's perfectly suited to her lyrics. She reinvigorates tired images ("I Feel the Earth Move"), boldly recasts a couple of her earlier compositions ("Will You Love Me Tomorrow" and "A Natural Woman [You Make Me Feel Like]") and even rescues "Beautiful" from the sentimental deep end.

King's post-*Tapestry* albums—*Music, Rhymes and Reasons, Fantasy, Wrap Around Joy*—are well represented on *Greatest Hits*. Hits like "Sweet Seasons," "Been to Canaan," "Corazon" and "Jazzman" hold their own alongside the *Tapestry* classics, but "Believe in Humanity" is all most people need to know about Carole King's pop-psych meanderings. *Thoroughbred*, featuring the return of Gerry Goffin and a crew of L.A. session heavies, is probably the most consistent of King's later efforts. "Only Love Is Real" echoes the simple insight and strength of "It's Too Late," effectively bringing King's search to a logical and satisfying conclusion. — M.C.

CLAUDE KING

★	American Originals (Columbia, 1990)

A country singer from Shreveport, Louisiana, Claude King is best known for his Top Ten pop hit in 1962, "Wolverton Mountain," about a man's determination to woo the "pretty young daughter" of mountain man Clifton Clowers. King's performance recommends the song as a dark novelty, but otherwise there's little to hang

your hat on when it comes to the art, such
as it is, of Claude King. — D.M.

FREDDIE KING
★★★ **Freddie King Sings (1961; Modern
Blues, 1989)**
★★★½ **Getting Ready (1972; DCC, 1989)**
★★★½ **The Texas Cannonball
(1934–1976) (1972; DCC, 1990)**
★★★½ **The Best of Freddie King (1977;
DCC, 1990)**
★★★★ **Just Pickin' (Modern Blues, 1989)**
Mixing country and urban blues with a
genuine feeling for country music, Freddie
King, who died in 1976, was one of the
touchstones of modern blues, particularly as
practiced by a generation of English blues
guitarists led by Eric Clapton and Jeff Beck.
King's reference points as an instrumentalist
were pioneering electric blues guitarists
Muddy Waters, B.B. King and T-Bone
Walker. His style was forceful and
aggressive, blues picked hard on
heavy-gauge strings, but King also had a
keen sense of phrasing and the proper use of
space to heighten the effect of his solos.

In 1960 King signed with Cincinnati's
King label; a year later he hit the Top
Thirty with his rocking instrumental,
"Hideaway," which was based on a Hound
Dog Taylor boogie and incorporated quotes
from Jimmy McCracklin's "The Walk" and
"The Peter Gunn Theme." The song has
long been a blues standard, and has been
recorded numerous times. King recorded
frequently from 1968 until his death in 1976.
Selected tracks from three albums cut with
Leon Russell's bunch at Shelter have been
compiled by DCC on *The Best of Freddie
King. Just Pickin'* contains all the tracks
from King's two all-instrumental albums for
the King label, including "Hideaway" and
"San-Ho-Zay." Although known primarily
as an instrumentalist, King had an easy,
friendly vocal style that he used to good
effect on uptempo numbers; he was less
convincing on slower numbers, but his
pained reading of "Have You Ever Loved a
Woman" is a marvel of quiet agony. *Freddie
King Sings* set the record straight regarding
King's skill as a vocalist. *Getting Ready* and
The Texas Cannonball are reissues of two
early-'70s albums. — D.M.

KING CRIMSON
★★★½ **In the Court of the Crimson King
(1969; EG, 1989)**
★★½ **In The Wake of Poseidon (1970;
EG, 1989)**
★★ **Lizard (1970; EG, 1989)**
★½ **Islands (1971; EG, 1989)**
★½ **Earthbound (Editions UK, 1972)**
★★★★★ **Larks' Tongues in Aspic (1973;
EG, 1989)**
★★★½ **Starless and Bible Black (1974;
EG, 1989)**
★★★½ **Red (1974; EG, 1989)**
★★★½ **USA (Editions EG, 1975)**
★★★½ **Discipline (Warner Bros./EG,
1981)**
★★★★ **Beat (Warner Bros./EG, 1982)**
★★★★ **Three of a Perfect Pair (Warner
Bros./EG, 1984)**
★★★½ **The Compact King Crimson
(1986; EG, 1989)**
★★★★★ **Frame by Frame (Editions EG,
1991)**
★★★★ **The Abbreviated King Crimson:
Heartbeat (Caroline, 1991)**
One of the first art-rock bands and arguably
the most consistently interesting, King
Crimson is a creature of guitarist Robert
Fripp. That's not quite the same thing as
being a Fripp solo project, for despite his
reputation as a less-than-democratic
bandleader, Fripp recognizes that Crimson's
musical identity has always been more the
product of collaboration than direction.
That the group started out as a collective
operation ought to be evident from the
chamber music dynamics found in most of
the playing on *In the Court of the Crimson
King*. Although best remembered for the
sci-fi fury of "21st Century Schizoid Man,"
the other songs find the band operating in
the semi-classical mode favored by early art
rockers; apart from occasional Mellotron
overkill and singer Greg Lake's tendencies
to pomposity, it remains quite listenable.
That's not quite the case with *In the Wake
of Poseidon*, on which the band's sound
grows more complicated, with jazzy rhythms
and knotty, dissonant instrumental lines
flavoring "Pictures of a City" and "Cat
Food," while lengthy, obtuse improvisations
dominate "The Devil's Triangle." *Lizard*
pushes those elements even harder, although
with considerably less success; apart from
the "Bolero" section of the 24-minute
"Lizard," most of the improvisational
sections eventually degenerate into showy
self-indulgence.

A new rhythm section and singer Boz
Burrell debut on *Islands*, but apart from
"Ladies of the Road," which sets its
groupie-adoration lyric to a lean, edgy
blues, the songs rank among the group's
most pretentious. Nor was this version of
Crimson particularly long-lasting, as the
other members abandoned Fripp the

following year. (*Earthbound*, a live album featuring this lineup, was released in Europe; it has since been deleted). Fripp's next incarnation of King Crimson was on many counts its best ever. In addition to being enormously capable players, this band—violinist David Cross, bassist-vocalist John Wetton, drummer Bill Bruford and percussionist Jamie Muir—was disciplined enough to keep the improvisational passages sharp and lean. As such, *Larks' Tongues in Aspic* alternates between crisply played, dramatically paced instrumentals like the two-part title tune, and quirky vocal numbers like "Book of Saturday" and the clankingly catchy "Easy Money." Never before had Crimson's music been so daring and focused. After reaching such heights, *Starless and Bible Black* is a let-down; although "The Great Deceiver" and "Starless and Bible Black" both have their moments, the material is generally too fragmented to cohere. But *Red* more than makes up. With Crimson reduced by this point to a power-trio, the chemistry between Fripp, Wetton and Bruford is intensely dynamic, and that puts added bite into works like "Fallen Angel" or the electrifying "Red." *U.S.A.*, a live album recorded with the Cross-Fripp-Wetton-Bruford lineup, is further testimony to this group's abilities, but is out-of-print.

King Crimson called it quits in 1975, but Fripp, never one to say never, brought the band back into existence in 1981 with *Discipline*. Bruford and Fripp were the only carry-overs from the last incarnation; joining them were bassist Tony Levin and guitarist Adrian Belew. On a musician-by-musician basis, this was by far the most virtuosic Crimson, and the quartet's ferocious technique is more than obvious on knottily rhythmic, harmonically demanding workouts like "Thela Hun Ginjeet," "Elephant Talk" and "Discipline." *Beat*, this crew's sophomore effort, is a little less rigorous, with Belew's melodic instincts adding a pop sheen to the snakily complex instrumental lines beneath "Neal and Jack and Me" and "Waiting Man." Sometimes, as with "Heartbeat," that even spilled over into something approaching pop accessibility, but this Crimson was far from being a pop group, as the gordian cadences of "Requiem" and the raging "Two Hands" drove home. Nor is *Three of a Perfect Pair* any more pop-friendly, though it does introduce funk elements (a first!) to the band's rhythmic repertoire, as well as making a nod to the band's past in "Larks'

Tongues in Aspic Part III." Then, after a 1984 tour, King Crimson disbanded yet again.

Of the available anthologies, *The Compact King Crimson* is perhaps the least useful, drawing only from *In the Court of the Crimson King*, *Discipline*, *Beat* and *Three of a Perfect Pair*. The boxed anthology *Frame By Frame* is considerably more inclusive, offering one disc's worth of music for each of the band's three periods of development, plus a fourth live disc. Fripp himself claims it represents "all you need to know" about the group—not the most objective opinion, to be sure, but pretty much on the mark. *The Abbreviated King Crimson* reduces *Frame by Frame*'s bulk to a single, judiciously edited CD. — J.D.C.

KING CURTIS

★ ★ ★ **The New Scene of King Curtis (New Jazz/Prestige, 1960)**
★ ★ ★ **King Soul (Prestige, 1960)**
★ ★ ★ **Soul Meeting (Prestige, 1960)**
★ ★ ★ **Trouble in Mind (1961; Prestige, 1987)**
★ ★ ★ ★ **Live at the Fillmore West (Atco, 1971)**
★ ★ ★ **Jazz Groove (Prestige, 1973)**
★ ★ ★ ★ **King Curtis & Champion Jack Dupree: Blues at Montreux (Atlantic, 1973)**
★ ★ ★ ★ **Soul Twist (Collectables, 1988)**
★ ★ **The Best of King Curtis (Collectables, 1989)**

As a sought-after session player in the '50s, King Curtis helped define the spirit of early rock & roll-R&B with his honking, stuttering tenor saxophone solos. The Coasters' "Yakety Yak" is only the most notable of Curtis's many inspired moments, but as the leader of Aretha Franklin's backup band he figured in some of the greatest soul sessions in history. As a solo artist Curtis stayed close to his blues, R&B and gospel roots and delivered several pleasing if hardly monumental albums. *The New Scene of King Curtis*, *King Soul* and *Soul Meeting* (the latter two were combined as the 1973 reissue *Jazz Groove*), found him leading a combo that included Wynton Kelly, Paul Chambers, Nat Adderley, and Oliver Johnson. These fairly tame sides have their moments—the ballad "Willow Weep for Me" and the gospel-rooted "Little Brother Soul" on *The New Scene* are standouts—but on the whole are considerably less than earth-shaking. *Soul Twist* is a fine sampling of Curtis's lesser-known but still exemplary work fronting his own group the Noble Knights (whose "Soul Twist" is a genuinely great instrumental) and backing other artists.

Live at the Fillmore West is Curtis the bandleader at his absolute best on a night when his extraordinary band included Bernard Purdie, Jerry Jemmott and Cornell Dupree. The powerful communication these players had with each other produces a set that is a model of intelligent choices made without sacrificing spontaneity and fire. The same could be said for the live album, *Blues at Montreux*, which teams Texan Curtis with the great New Orleans piano player Champion Jack Dupree on six original songs, five co-written by the two principals. Another side of Curtis gets ample exposure on *Trouble in Mind*, a reissue of an album originally recorded for the Tru-Sound label in 1961. Instead of tenor, Curtis played alto sax on most of the cuts; more significant, he made an impressive debut as a vocalist and showed an agile, personable touch on material ranging from the low-down "Trouble in Mind" to the spirited "But That's Alright." There's a bit of Ray Charles in his voice (emphasized by the background vocals of three former Raelettes), but a bit of Freddie King as well. He even gets down as a guitarist on "Ain't Nobody's Business." On the strength of *Trouble in Mind* it's possible to see the full dimension of Curtis's talent, although nothing can supplant the roar of that sax. — D.M.

KINGDOM COME

★★½ Kingdom Come (Polydor, 1988)
★ In Your Face (Polydor, 1989)
★ Hands of Time (Polydor, 1991)

With Lenny Wolf's keening, Robert Plant–derived tenor and a full set of color-by-numbers Zeppelin riffs fleshing out its songbook, *Kingdom Come* is an astonishing bit of classic-rock wish-fulfillment—an album that sounded "old" even when it was new. Trouble is, once you get past the cover-band cleverness of "Get It On" and its ilk, *Kingdom Come* is appallingly pedestrian. But *In Your Face*, on which the band stressed its "originality," isn't even that good—which may explain why *Hands of Time* (recorded by Wolf as a virtual solo album), finds him resurrecting the insta-Zep approach for the title tune. — J.D.C.

THE KINGSMEN

★ The Best of the Kingsmen (Rhino, 1985)

The Kingsmen's "Louie, Louie" remains the definitive trash-rock single—stomping, cheerfully stupid and, because of its mangled vocal, supposedly obscene. And, as you might imagine, nothing else this Oregon bunch did was quite as "good." — P.E.

THE KINGSTON TRIO

★★★ Capitol Collectors Series (Capitol, 1990)
★★ Best of the Best (Proarté, 1986)
★★★ Greatest Hits (Curb, 1991)
★★★ Make Way/Goin' Places (Capitol, 1992)
★★★ Sold Out/String Along (Capitol, 1992)

Their staid, traditional performances may seem quaint by today's standards, but in the late '50s and early '60s the Kingston Trio made an important contribution to American popular music of the folk variety by reviving a scene that was moribund commercially following the demise of the Weavers and the blacklisting of Pete Seeger in the early '50s. In the process they paved the way for other folk artists—notably Peter, Paul and Mary and the Chad Mitchell Trio—who in turn opened doors for young songwriters (Bob Dylan among them) lacking other avenues of popular exposure.

The Trio (Bob Shane, Nick Reynolds, and Dave Guard were the original members; John Stewart replaced Guard in 1961) came out of the gate with a Number One single in '58, "Tom Dooley," and five of its first six albums had extended runs atop the album chart as well. Updates of traditional folk songs ("Worried Man Blues," from the Carter Family canon) as well as original material from contemporary songwriters such as Bob Dylan and Pete Seeger comprised the Trio's repertoire. The *Capitol Collectors Series* and *Greatest Hits* albums contain a good helping of the Trio's most popular songs in their original versions, including "Tom Dooley," "Reverend Mr. Black," "Where Have All the Flowers Gone," and the timeless memorium to after-hours languor, "Scotch and Soda." In addition, Capitol has begun reissuing the group's original studio albums as two-fer CDs. Proarté's *Best of the Best* is a recently recorded live album featuring only one original Trio member, Bob Shane. *Caveat emptor*: This too is a compendium of greatest hits, albeit performed in a more casual manner than the studio recordings available on the Capitol and Curb sets. This is not the Kingston Trio of yore, only a pale imitation. — D.M.

KING'S X

★ ★¹/₂ Out of the Silent Planet
    (Megaforce/Atlantic, 1988)
★ ★ ★ ★ Gretchen Goes to Nebraska
    (Megaforce/Atlantic, 1989)
★ ★ ★ ★ Faith Hope Love
    (Megaforce/Atlantic, 1990)
★ ★ ★ ★ King's X (Atlantic, 1992)

King's X started out with a great sound: a
lean, meaty power-trio roar topped with
complex, Beatlesque vocal harmonies, an
approach that was neither art pop nor hard
rock, but both. And even though there's not
much more to *Out of the Silent Planet* than
that sound (the songwriting never quite
takes full advantage of the band's ability) it
augured great things. Nor did *Gretchen Goes
to Nebraska* disappoint. Even as the band's
arrangements grow more lavish—
interlocking vocal lines, dramatically shifting
dynamics, an almost orchestral use of
overdubs—the songwriting became sharper,
more focused. The band feels free to try
almost anything. Thus, where "Everybody
Knows a Little Bit of Something" withholds
its chorus, teasing the listener along, "Out
of the Silent Planet" luxuriates in its layers
of melody, leaving the listener drunk with
song. But it's "Over My Head," with its
recurring chorus, dreamlike imagery and
powerful allusions to a traditional spiritual,
that ultimately reveals the strength of the
band's vision, and the transcendence of its
Christianity. *Faith Hope Love* pushes that
vision to its next plateau. The songs
continue to explore the band's Christianity,
but avoid the obviousness of *Gretchen*'s
"Mission" or "Over My Head" in favor of
the more generalized messages of songs like
"It's Love" and "We Are Finding Who We
Are." Even so, it's the music that remains
most impressive. With this album, King's X
expands its approach to include such
experiments as the semi-psychedelic "Mr.
Wilson" and the hell-for-leather
"Moanjam," as well as more typical touches
like the slow-grinding "Faith Hope Love"
or the dizzying chorale of "It's Love."
King's X provides similar scope, ambling
easily from the anthemic "Black Flag" to
the dense harmonies of "Lost in Germany."
And the scary thing is, this seems only the
beginning for King's X. — J.D.C.

THE KINKS

★ ★ ★ Kinks (Pye, 1964)
★ ★ ★¹/₂ You Really Got Me (1964; Rhino, 1988)
★ ★ ★¹/₂ Kinks-Size (1965; Rhino, 1988)
★ ★ ★¹/₂ Kinda Kinks (1966; Rhino, 1988)
★ ★ ★ Face to Face (Reprise, 1966)
★ ★ ★ The Live Kinks (Reprise, 1967)
★ ★ ★¹/₂ Kinkdom (1967; Rhino, 1988)
★ ★ ★ ★ Greatest Hits (1968; Rhino, 1989)
★ ★ ★ ★ ★ Something Else (Reprise, 1968)
★ ★ ★ ★¹/₂ The Kinks Are the Village Green Preservation Society (Reprise, 1969)
★ ★ ★ ★ Arthur (Reprise, 1969)
★ ★ ★¹/₂ Lola Versus Powerman and the Moneygoround (Reprise, 1970)
★ ★ ★ ★ Muswell Hillbillies (1971; Rhino; 1990)
★ ★ ★ ★ ★ Kink Kronikles (Reprise, 1972)
★ ★ ★ Everybody's in Showbiz, Everybody's a Star (1972; Rhino, 1990)
★ ★¹/₂ Preservation, Act One (RCA, 1973)
★ ★¹/₂ Preservation, Act Two (RCA, 1974)
★ ★¹/₂ Soap Opera (1975; Rhino, 1990)
★ ★ ★ Schoolboys in Disgrace (1975; Rhino, 1990)
★ ★ ★ Greatest Hits—Celluloid Heroes (RCA, 1976)
★ ★¹/₂ Sleepwalker (Arista, 1977)
★ ★¹/₂ Misfits (Arista, 1978)
★ ★ ★ Low Budget (Arista, 1979)
★ ★¹/₂ One for the Road (Arista, 1980)
★ ★ Second Time Around (RCA, 1980)
★ ★ ★¹/₂ Give the People What They Want (Arista, 1981)
★ ★ ★¹/₂ State of Confusion (Arista, 1983)
★ ★¹/₂ Word of Mouth (Arista, 1984)
★ ★ ★ ★ Come Dancing With the Kinks (Arista, 1986)
★ ★ ★ Think Visual (MCA, 1987)
★ ★ ★ Live: The Road (MCA, 1988)
★ ★ ★ U.K. Jive (MCA, 1989)

Singer/guitarist Ray Davies, lead guitarist
Dave Davies and drummer Mick Avory are
the Kinks' mainstays, and they've been
together for thirty years. Beginning as rock
revolutionaries and ending up trading in
rock nostalgia, the Kinks remain the most
adamantly British of the Brit Invasion
bands—a vanishing, romanticized world of
village greens, pubs and public schools is the
elegiac source of Ray's sometimes fearsome
defense of traditional values; he contrasts
the faded charms of an ended Empire to the
dole queues and dark skies of today's
collapsed England, and he's alternately
bitter and paralyzed with pathos.

Throughout their long career, neither musical skill nor range have carried the Kinks; instead they've served to catalogue Davies's moods and obsessions. Early on, Ray sang about lust, loneliness and need; in his middle period, he began the pop Proustian enterprise of crafting a mythologized England and dealing, as well, with the psychic dilemmas of outsiders (dreamers, transvestites, failures). Of late, when not perplexed or made bitter by politics, he's been preoccupied with memory; a great deal of the Kinks' later work aches of loss. Irony remains the characteristic Davies defense, but it's one he's very ambivalent about: The Kinks remain true rockers, above all, because they sing so often about the high hope and real difficulty of breaking free.

In 1964, "You Really Got Me" exploded. Dave's crunching riffs set the pattern for all heavy rock, from metal to punk; Ray's odd, fey vocals stamped him as the kind of vocalist he'd always be—whether preaching, acting or camping it up, he assumes roles, rather than sings songs. Mod dandies dripping with cavalier attitude, the Kinks tore through ravers on their first half-dozen albums—"All Day and All of the Night" is the power-rock twin of "You Really Got Me"—but Davies could also turn tender with finesse ("Tired of Waiting for You," "I Need You," "Stop Your Sobbing").

As the '60s waned, Davies began musing: stamped with yearning, envy and regret, Something Else is his strongest collection of songs—"Waterloo Sunset" may be the loveliest ballad in the history of rock. Village Green, the Kinks' quietest record, was a transfixing exercise in conveying a sense of place—a rural town of lawns and steeples, its citizens enduring, with hard-bitten grace, the joy and heartbreak of humdrum life. The subtitle to Arthur, the "Decline and Fall of the British Empire," summed up Davies's nostalgic state at the time; but with the Chuck Berryish delight, "Victoria," the lads began rocking again.

"Lola," about a guy who digs wearing girls' clothes, was a much-needed hit—and it underlined the band's growing professionalism. "Get Back in Line" and "A Long Way From Home" were standout ballads from Lola Vs. Powerman; the rest of the record was snappy, but a bit slight. Muswell Hillbillies, the tougher counterpart to the wistful Village Green, was another triumphant round of Ray's story songs, although their mood seemed increasingly bleak. With Everybody's in Show Biz, Davies assumed the persona of a tired cabaret artiste—"Celluloid Heroes" was a sad paean to Hollywood—and the album showed signs of strain.

A penchant for drama dominated the next records—the Preservation set and Soap Opera were full-blown theatrical affairs. Concept albums burdened with the task of making narrative sense, they're as weak as most musicals and, during Soap's tour, the band was reduced to such hammy schtick as wearing multicolored Afro wigs. Schoolboys was at least a step away from this vaudeville; it was the beginning, however, of the new hit-oriented Kinks—from then on, their albums would be haphazard mixes of fine songs and facile product. Sleepwalker boasts the excellent "Juke Box Music," but Ray's voice sounds ravaged; "A Rock 'n' Roll Fantasy" and the title track to Misfits are near-classic Kinks, and Dave's "Trust Your Heart" features some of his best guitar, but a "Lola" remake, "Out of the Wardrobe," captures the record's spirit—the Kinks aren't doing self-parody, but they're repeating themselves. "(I Wish I Could Fly Like) Superman" was indeed a new sound—but a wrongheaded one; a big, silly discofied hit off Low Budget, it was surrounded by the Kinks' defensive, forced rocking on songs featuring lyrics by Ray at his most churlish.

Very late in the game, the Kinks revived remarkably on Give the People What They Want and State of Confusion. Give recycles their early-'60s sound a bit dopily, but the record rocks and "Better Things" is prime, self-confident Ray; State isn't so tough, but it's a finer album—"Come Dancing," "Long Distance" and "Don't Forget to Dance" all may be exercises in nostalgia, but they're sure and moving songs. The MCA records aren't as accomplished, but they're hardly embarrassing.   — P.E.

KEVN KINNEY
★★★ MacDougal Blues (Island, 1990)
Recorded while on hiatus from his regular band, Drivin' n' Cryin', MacDougal Blues is less a folk album than an album about folk, in which Kinney and his acoustic guitar play with the myths and mannerisms of the contemporary folk scene. As with Drivin' n' Cryin', Kinney's material is charming, tuneful and perceptive, but it's Peter Buck's understated production—not Kinney's self-deprecating singing—that ultimately brings the album into focus.   — J.D.C.

RAHSAAN ROLAND KIRK

★★★½ Introducing Roland Kirk (1960; Chess, 1990)

★★★½ Kirk's Works (1961; Fantasy, 1990)

★★★★ We Free Kings (1961; Mercury, 1986)

★★★ Domino (1962; Mercury, 1986)

★★★★ The Case of the 3 Sided Dream in Audio Color (Atlantic, 1975)

★★★★ The Inflated Tear (Atlantic, 1982)

★★★★★ "Rahsaan": The Complete Mercury Recordings of Roland Kirk (Mercury, 1990)

★★★★ The Man Who Cried Fire (Virgin, 1991)

Of the many great portraits of Rahsaan Roland Kirk, a series stands out: the big, blind woodwind master splendiferous in the raffish top hat and tails of those New Orleans players whose sad, ecstatic funeral marches hark back to the earliest days of jazz. Kirk, while never ranking as one of the titans of the music, embodied the tradition—so over-brimming was his musical energy that the image of the man blowing three instruments simultaneously has come to encapsulate his combination of happy virtuosity and furious zeal. But Kirk was hardly a reverent archivist. Whether experimenting with a post-Ornette Coleman free-style, turning in a graceful arrangement of a Villa-Lobos piece, or swinging hard on a version of "Peter Gunn" with the Quincy Jones Orchestra, Kirk's jazz was an accessible, engaging music; he crammed his sound full with surreal humor, wasn't afraid at times to be perceived as pop, and played with a visceral power. While his standard instrument was tenor sax, some fans preferred his breathy flute work—and his arsenal included English horn, trumpet, clarinet, manzello and stritch. *Rahsaan*, Mercury's excellent ten-CD compilation, is Kirk at his 1961–1965 prime; his quartet work, particulary when the lineup included Wynton Kelly on piano and Elvin Jones on drums, was tough, smart and engaging. While Kirk's hard-bop background ensured that his music never would lack for drive, he was a great, raunchy player on (relatively) straightforward blues, and his ballad work cuts deep. *The Man Who Cried Fire* is assertive live fare recorded in the '70s; also on Atlantic is the nifty curio-piece, *The Case of the 3-Sided Dream in Audio Color*—along with its strange diversity of cover material ("The Entertainer," "High Heel Sneakers," "Bye Bye Blackbird"), it highlights Kirk's humor ("Echoes of Primitive Ohio and Chili Dogs") and incorporates weirdo interludes comprised of spoken dreams and sound effects. — P.E.

KISS

★★★ Kiss (Casablanca, 1974)

★★ Hotter Than Hell (Casablanca, 1974)

★★★ Dressed to Kill (Casablanca, 1975)

★★★½ Alive (Casablanca, 1975)

★★★ Destroyer (Casablanca, 1976)

★★ Rock and Roll Over (Casablanca, 1977)

★★ Love Gun (Casablanca, 1977)

★★ Alive II (Casablanca, 1977)

★★ Double Platinum (Casablanca, 1978)

★★ Dynasty (Casablanca, 1979)

★ Unmasked (Casablanca, 1980)

★★½ Music From the Elder (Casablanca, 1981)

★ Creatures of the Night (Casablanca, 1982)

★ Lick It Up (Mercury, 1983)

★ Animalize (Mercury, 1984)

★★ Asylum (Mercury, 1985)

★ Crazy Nights (Mercury, 1987)

★★★½ Smashes, Thrashes & Hits (Mercury, 1988)

★ Hot in the Shade (Mercury, 1989)

SOLO ALBUMS

★★ Ace Frehley (Casablanca, 1978)

★ Paul Stanley (Casablanca, 1978)

★ Peter Criss (Casablanca, 1978)

★ Gene Simmons (Casablanca, 1978)

Cartoon characters or crankin' metal band? In its mid-'70s heyday, Kiss was a bit of both. This costumed New York quartet utilized image and packaging with a shrewdness that belies the lunk-headed crudeness of its musical attack. Kiss turned the campy, low-budget excesses of glitter rock into a high-tech (for the '70s) circus of horrors, right down to the fire-breathing and tongue-rolling sideshow antics. And while the music could be almost unlistenably raw (especially on the poorly produced first three albums), the group also managed to concoct some undeniably catchy teen-rebellion anthems. Stumbling across a ripe riff or pungent chorus, this crew knew exactly where to put it—right in your face.

Kiss weighs in with a handful of crass classics ("Deuce," "Strutter," "Black Diamond"), while *Dressed to Kill* offers the gloriously forthright "Rock and Roll All Nite." But muddy sound sinks these albums; *Alive* is a much brighter document of the band's (literally) explosive impact on the arena circuit. Produced by former Alice

Cooper guiding light Bob Ezrin, *Destroyer* is where Kiss makes its sophistication move. A proto-power ballad if there ever was one, "Beth"—lovingly mewled by drummer Peter Criss, over a string section—reached the Top Ten in 1976. Elsewhere on *Destroyer*, Kiss refines its party-hearty stance, glossing over some of its trademark exuberance in the process. Only "Detroit Rock City" and "Shout It Out Loud" carry the electro-shlock jolt of *Alive*. After *Destroyer*, however, Kiss settled for just dishing out the shlock to ever-younger audiences. Another double-live album; a record titled *Unmasked,* where the band members weren't; four woefully indulgent and over-hyped solo albums: by the end of the decade, Kiss seemed like a marketing phenomenon that had outstayed its welcome.

Retreating to the heavy metal sub-strata, the band soldiered on throughout the '80s. Drummer Peter Criss left the fold in 1980, followed by guitarist Ace Frehley in 1982. When remaining guitarist Paul Stanley and bassist Gene Simmons finally did drop their masks, on the self-descriptive *Lick It Up*, from 1983, Kiss still had problems getting noticed. Amazingly, the 1988 album *Smashes Thrashes & Hits* culls some scorching rockers from the group's dire later days—like the sinful "Heaven's on Fire" from *Animalize*. This career-spanning grab bag also contains some goofy inclusions— like replacement drummer Eric Carr's retooled version of "Beth." But overall, it's the most consistently listenable Kiss album by far, and the only one that most people need to own. — M.C.

KIX
★ ★ ★ ★   **Kix (Atlantic, 1981)**
  ★ ★ ★   **Cool Kids (Atlantic, 1983)**
  ★ ★ ★   **Midnight Dynamite (Atlantic, 1985)**
★ ★ ★ ★ ½ **Blow My Fuse (Atlantic, 1988)**
★ ★ ★ ★   **Hot Wire (East/West, 1991)**
Gutsy, aggressive and hearteningly tuneful, Kix is the nice-guy answer to AC/DC, being just as fond of hyperactive boogie but nowhere near as mindlessly macho. *Kix*, in fact, is downright innocent in its enthusiasms, from the '50s-style formalism of "Heartache" to the euphemistic passion of "The Itch," not that it diminishes the megawatt wallop of rockers like "Kix Are for Kids" or the Kinks-style "The Kid." *Cool Kids* augments that sound with unseemly techno flourishes like the synth and claptrack on "Body Talk," but offers enough overdriven punch through songs like

"Love Pollution" and "Nice On Ice" to keep it from seeming a total misstep. With *Midnight Dynamite*, the group returns to hard-rock basics, but it's *Blow My Fuse* that makes the move pay off. Not only is the album packed with hooky, hard-hitting rockers ("Red Lite, Green Lite, TNT," "She Dropped Me the Bomb," "No Ring Around Rosie"), but it also provides the group with its first great ballad, "Don't Close Your Eyes." *Hot Wire* offers a similar blend, but scores most of its points through adrenaline rockers like "Girl Money" and "Bump the La La." — J.D.C.

KLF
  ★ ★ ½ **Chill Out (Wax Trax, 1990)**
  ★ ★ ★   **The White Room (Arista, 1991)**
★ ★ ★ ½ **Justified & Ancient (EP) (Arista, 1992)**
Clever, conceptual dance music from James Cauty and Bill Drummond, the same pop pranksters responsible for both the Justified Ancients of Mu Mu and the Timelords. As with the duo's earlier efforts, KLF depends as much upon judicious borrowing as melodic ingenuity, but that hardly takes away from the music's appeal. *Chill Out* is quiet and atmospheric, and fuctions better as background. But the best moments on *The White Room* are aggressive and insistent, with a sturdy dance beat driving the likes of "What Time Is Love?" or "3 A.M. Eternal." Still the group doesn't really show its genius for the unexpected until the *Justified & Ancient* EP, which offers five takes on the group's signature song, "Justified & Ancient," the best of which features crunchy, metallic guitar, throbbing house bass, sweet Zulu harmonies and—wonder of wonders!—a lead vocal by Tammy Wynette. — J.D.C.

THE KNACK
★ ★ ½ **Get the Knack (Capitol, 1979)**
  ★ ★   **. . . But the Little Girls Understand (Capitol, 1980)**
   ★   **Round Trip (Capitol, 1981)**
   ★   **Serious Fun (Charisma, 1991)**
The Knack got under people's skin. Using the Ping-Pong powerchord hook of "My Sharona" as an entree, this boorish Los Angeles quartet topped the charts during the summer of 1979. Packaged as outright Beatles clones, the Knack managed to offend '60s believers and new-wave converts alike. The kids who thought of Paul McCartney as the bass player in Wings couldn't have cared less, of course. Although the easy pleasures of "My

Sharona" are impossible to resist on a cranked car radio, *Get the Knack* reveals a crippling lack of imagination. Lead singer and songwriter Doug Fieger knocks off catchy chorus after catchy chorus, but cuts like "She's So Selfish" exhibit a decided nasty streak. From its title on down, the follow-up album does little to dispel that sexist image. In the total absence of a "Sharona"-esque sureshot, the Knack's hormone-pumping harmonies sound pinched and unnatural. The bloodless *Round Trip* sealed the group's fate as a one-hit wonder.

Ten years later, the Knack's reunited. The lumbering arena-rock on *Serious Fun*— "tastefully" produced by Don Was—wouldn't raise the hackles of an REO Speedwagon fanatic. Hard to believe this band once inspired "Knuke the Knack" T-shirts. — M.C.

GLADYS KNIGHT AND THE PIPS
 ★ ★ ★ **Everybody Needs Love (1967; Motown, 1989)**
 ★ ★ ★ **Silk 'n' Soul (1969; Motown, 1990)**
 ★ ★ ★ ★ **Greatest Hits (Soul, 1970)**
 ★ ★ ★ **Standing Ovation (1972; Motown, 1990)**
 ★ ★ ★ ★ **Neither One of Us (Soul, 1972)**
 ★ ★ ★ ★ **Imagination (Buddah, 1973)**
 ★ ★ ★ ★ **Anthology (Motown, 1974)**
 ★ ★ ★ **Claudine (Buddah, 1974)**
 ★ ★ ½ **Knight Time (Soul, 1974)**
 ★ ★ ★ ½ **I Feel a Song (Buddha, 1974)**
 ★ ★ ★ **Second Anniversary (Buddah, 1975)**
 ★ ★ ★ ★ **The Best of Gladys Knight and the Pips (Buddah, 1976)**
 ★ ★ **Miss Gladys Knight (Buddah, 1978)**
 ★ ★ **Gladys Knight (Columbia, 1979)**
 ★ ★ ★ **Touch (Columbia, 1982)**
 ★ ★ ★ **Visions (Columbia, 1983)**
 ★ ★ ★ **Life (Columbia, 1985)**
 ★ ★ ★ **All Our Love (MCA, 1987)**
 ★ ★ ★ ½ **The Best of Gladys Knight and the Pips: The Columbia Years (Columbia, 1988)**
 ★ ★ ★ ½ **Every Beat of My Heart: The Greatest Hits (Chameleon, 1989)**
 ★ ★ ★ ★ **Soul Survivors: The Best of Gladys Knight and the Pips (Rhino, 1990)**
 ★ ★ ★ ½ **Good Woman (MCA, 1991)**

Not possessing the headstrong genius of Aretha Franklin, the eccentric brilliance of Dionne Warwick, or the cartoon charisma of Diana Ross, Gladys Knight instead has evolved into the most dependable of soul

divas—she's neither a visionary, nor a truly distinctive stylist, but, consistently, she delivers. With both of her parents gospel performers, Gladys began singing at age four; while still in her teens she assembled her male backup group, dubbing them the Pips after the nickname of her cousin and manager. Her first record, Johnny Otis's doo-wop "Every Beat of My Heart" (1960) was pleasant enough, but only after Knight signed with Motown in 1966 did the hits begin. And they were tremendous—"I Heard It Through the Grapevine" "The Nitty Gritty," "The End of the Road" and "You Need Love Like I Do (Don't You)" carried her into the '70s, establishing her gritty, gospel-derived delivery as one of the strongest in R&B.

By 1973, the Pips had switched labels to Buddah and released their strongest album, *Imagination*, featuring the landmark "Midnight Train to Georgia." Soon, however, their style changed; like Diana Ross, Knight embraced AOR. She did so with customary class, but over the next 15 years or so, her only great albums were *I Feel a Song* (1974) and *All Our Love* (1987). The Pips-less *Good Woman* (1991), featuring a neat ensemble piece with Patti LaBelle and Dionne Warwick, is representative of her later style—ultra-professional, and a tad too flawless. — P.E.

MARK KNOPFLER
 ★ ★ ½ **Local Hero (Warner Bros., 1983)**
 ★ ★ ★ ½ **Cal (Mercury, 1984)**
 ★ ★ ★ **The Princess Bride (Warner Bros., 1987)**
 ★ ★ **Last Exit to Brooklyn (Warner Bros., 1989)**

Unlike some rock musicians, whose soundtracks are virtually identical to their usual work, Mark Knopfler takes his film-scoring seriously—so much so, in fact, that Dire Straits fans are likely to be disappointed by these albums. There are elements in common, of course. *Local Hero*, for instance, is recorded with Alan Clark, John Illsley and Terry Williams, and at times evokes much the same mood as the quieter bits of *Love Over Gold*. *Cal* also uses a few Straitsmen in the rhythm section (Illsley, Williams and Guy Fletcher), but pulls more of its color from the Irish folk contributions of Paul Brady and Liam O'Flynn. There's also a wonderfully stinging backward guitar solo on "In a Secret Place." But *The Princess Bride* is straight-up movie scoring. With Guy Fletcher helping out on the orchestral end, this soundtrack features all sorts of suspense-building strings and swashbuckling flourishes, as well as a wonderfully sentimental vocal by Willie DeVille on "Storybook Love." Fun, but not as idiomatically convincing as Randy Newman's film work. Knopfler wrote and produced *Last Exit to Brooklyn*, and also played a bit of guitar on the album, but leaves most of the recording to Fletcher. It's just as well, though, since this is movie music at its most mechanical—a nice exercise in mood manipulation, but meaningless without the visuals. — J.D.C.

BUDDY KNOX

★★½ **The Best of Buddy Knox (Rhino, 1990)**

The sweet side of Texas rock & roll is represented by Happy, Texas, native Buddy Knox, whose soft, heavily echoed voice fueled five Top Forty singles between 1957 and 1961. Ironically, Knox, who was most credible singing lilting love songs on the order of "Whenever I'm Lonely," scored his biggest hits with a couple of rockabilly-inspired songs, "Party Doll," his debut single and a Number One record in 1957, and "Hula Love," another 1957 release that proved to be his final Top Ten hit. Before switching from the Roulette label to Liberty in 1960, he had one more minor hit, the rather disturbing "I Think I'm Gonna Kill Myself," which some radio stations refused to play.

At the same session that produced "Party Doll," Jimmy Bowen, a member of Knox's band the Rhythm Orchids, sang lead on a song called "I'm Stickin' With You." Roulette released it under Bowen's name and hit the Top Twenty the same month "Party Doll' topped the chart. Bowen moved into production in the '60s and cut albums with Frank Sinatra, Dean Martin and a slew of pop artists; in 1984 he became the head of MCA's country division, and revolutionized album production in Nashville by increasing recording budgets and embracing digital technology.

For his part, Knox moved around to several labels in the '60s without success. He resurfaced in 1978 on an English import, *Four Rock 'n' Roll Legends*, recorded live in London in 1977, and sounded pretty much the same after all those years. It's a good, lively performance that compares favorably to other strong efforts on the album by Charlie Feathers, Jack Scott and Warren Smith. *The Best of Buddy Knox* contains all the hits and more from the Roulette years, as well as his final charting singles cut for Liberty in the early '60s. — D.M.

KOOL & THE GANG

★★★   **Wild and Peaceful (De-Lite, 1973)**
★★★½ **Spin Their Top Hits (De-Lite, 1978)**
★★½ **Ladies' Night (1979; Mercury, 1984)**
★★   **Celebrate! (1980; Mercury, 1984)**
★★   **Something Special (1981; Mercury, 1984)**
★★   **As One (1982; Mercury, 1984)**
★★   **In the Heart (1983; Mercury, 1984)**
★★   **Emergency (Mercury, 1984)**
★★   **Forever (Mercury, 1986)**
★★★   **Everything's Kool & the Gang (Mercury, 1988)**
★★   **Sweat (Mercury, 1989)**

Bass player Robert "Kool" Bell leads this veteran black pop troupe. The Gang began as a potentially devastating funk band; "Funky Stuff," "Jungle Boogie" and "Hollywood Swinging" (all included on *Spin Their Top Hits*) broke new rhythmic ground in 1973–74—and continue to fill dance floors today. Mellowing a bit during the disco years, Kool & the Gang landed "Open Sesame" on the block-busting *Saturday Night Fever* soundtrack in 1977. With the arrival of lead singer James "JT" Taylor on *Ladies' Night* (1979), the group makes a beeline for the middle of the road. And, for quite a while, the Top Ten. "Ladies Night" and "Celebration" (from *Celebrate!*) pump up the fake enthusiasm of a car commercial, but a long string of flaccid ballads in the early-to-mid-'80s positioned Taylor as an ersatz Lionel Richie. The occasional beguiling hook (like "Joanna" from *In the Heart* or "Misled" from *Emergency*) gets totally overwhelmed by the unctuous sugar-sappy production. *Everything's Kool & the Gang* collects the '80s hits as well as hip-hop-style remixes of the vintage '70s funkathons; ironically, those original plunking "Kool" bass lines helped inspire rap in the first place. — M.C.

KOOL MOE DEE

★★★★ **Kool Moe Dee (Rooftop-Jive, 1986)**
★★★★ **How Ya Like Me Now (Rooftop-Jive, 1987)**
★★★★ **Knowledge Is King (Jive/RCA, 1989)**
★★★ **Funke, Funke Wisdom (Jive, 1991)**

Outspoken exemplar of rap's "old school," Kool Moe Dee has actually progressed quite a bit since he pioneered hip-hop with the Treacherous Three. Though he holds true to the classic boasting format, the former Mohandas Dewase also delivers uplifting messages and pumps knowledge as well as any of his would-be successors. On *Kool Moe Dee*, he knows when to put a humorous spin on his point ("Go See the

Doctor," "Dumb Dick") and when to let the horrible truth—reality—speak for itself ("Monster Crack," "Little Jon"). Credited as one of several co-producers, Teddy Riley makes a contribution that is now immediately apparent. His distinctive, swinging synths and electronic percussion are all over this New Jack milestone. Dissing L.L. Cool J on the cover of *How Ya Like Me Now*, Kool Moe Dee lays down an equally defiant—and stone cold funky—groove on the inside. Outrageous and imaginative, his self-promotion campaign is coupled to fearsomely deep sampled beats. When Kool Moe Dee lets loose on "Wild Wild West" or "Way Way Back," well, his claims to legendary status are rather convincing. The feistiness threatens to turn into defensiveness (at times) on *Knowledge Is King*, but Riley reaches a new peak, supplying breathtaking (at times) musical support. And Moe Dee closes *Knowledge* with a wide-ranging, propulsive street manifesto called "Pump Your Fist." Overly severe and slightly less driven-sounding, *Funke, Funke Wisdom* could sure use a shot of the wit Kool Moe Dee displayed back on his debut. — M.C.

AL KOOPER

★ ★½ **Super Session (Columbia, 1968)**
★ ★ **I Stand Alone (Columbia, 1969)**
★ ★ **You Never Know Who Your Friends Are (Columbia, 1969)**
★½ **The Live Adventures of Al Kooper and Mike Bloomfield (Columbia, 1969)**
★ ★ **Kooper Session (Columbia, 1970)**
★ ★½ **Unclaimed Freight (Columbia, 1975)**
★ ★ ★ **Al's Big Deal (Columbia, 1989)**
Adding superb organ to Dylan's "Like a Rolling Stone," Kooper was a strong sideman. He also formed Blood, Sweat and Tears and produced Lynyrd Skynyrd. His own work is problematic. Dylanesque balladry, gushing homages to R&B, Harry Nilsson-like pop, John Prine and James Taylor covers—Kooper has tried out a ton of formats and can be faulted neither for lack of dexterity nor for puny ambition. But his quavering, sometimes off-key voice gets grating; inflated production and overblown arrangements smother his better intentions; and, too often, his singing persona is an odd mix of cutesy and swell-headed.
Super Session is Kooper's best-known: the side featuring Stephen Stills is tripe; Mike Bloomfield, however, and his blues guitar have never sounded better than on side two (a followup, *The Live Adventures of Al Kooper and Mike Bloomfield* is notable only

for its cover art: the rare example of Norman Rockwell doing rock star portraits). *I Stand Alone* has some pretty good poppy stuff; *You Never Know Who Your Friends Are* sounds like BS&T before David Clayton-Thomas. His only LPs currently in print are the mediocre *Unclaimed Freight* and *Al's Big Deal,* a retrospective that Kooper himself helped compile.
A smart guy—and, God knows, a hardworking one—Kooper is interesting primarily as a reference point. His albums' personnel credits read like a roster of late '60s–early '70s talent—everyone from Charlie Daniels, jazzer Don Ellis, Rita Coolidge and the Atlanta Rhythm Section—and his range of styles is a fair index of the musical preoccupations of his time. — P.E.

ALEXIS KORNER
★ ★ ★ **Bootleg Him! (Warner Bros., 1972)**
Alexis Korner braved the opposition of Britain's trad jazz followers by setting up the Ealing Rhythm & Blues Club in London in 1962—and, to various degrees, virtually all of England's later blues enthusiasts, from the Rolling Stones and the Animals to Manfred Mann and Cream, owe him a debt. *Bootleg Him!* includes work by all the major incarnations of Korner's Blues Incorporated—among whose alumni are Charlie Watts, members of Pentangle and the Graham Bond Organisation, and Jack Bruce. There's also music by less notable names that carry over into the '70s—versions of Mance Lipscomb and Curtis Mayfield tunes, and capable Korner originals. Because much of the playing is that of big names before their stardom, there's a nice lack of pretension; Korner's singing and guitar work is credible, too, and the historical interest of these recordings is significant. While the package is mainly for archivists, it provides a fine overview of the very earliest beginnings of British R&B.
— P.E.

LEO KOTTKE
★ ★ ★ ★ **Leo Kottke (Chrysalis, 1976)**
★ ★ ★ **Burnt Lips (Chrysalis, 1978)**
★ ★ **Balance (Chrysalis, 1979)**
★ ★ ★½ **Guitar Music (Chrysalis, 1982)**
★ ★ ★ ★ **Time Step (Chrysalis, 1983)**
★ ★ ★ **A Shout Towards Noon (Private Music, 1986)**
★ ★ ★ ★ **Regards From Chuck Pink (Private Music, 1988)**
★ ★ ★ **My Father's Face (Private Music, 1989)**

★ ★ ★   That's What (Private Music, 1990)
★ ★ ★½ Great Big Boy (Private Music, 1991)
★ ★ ★½ Essential Leo Kottke (Chrysalis, 1991)

Considering that Leo Kottke made his name on an album of old-timey guitar instrumentals called *6- and 12-String Guitar* (originally on Takoma; now out of print), it might be tempting to think of him as a folk instrumentalist like John Fahey. But "folk eccentric" is actually closer to it, for Kottke is the sort of player whose music follows no set course, heeds no particular style, and at its best sounds like nothing else in popular music.

Kottke's earliest recordings, *12-String Blues* and *Circle 'Round the Sun* (both out of print), were reflections of his coffeehouse act, as was *6- and 12-String Guitar*. But after he moved to Capitol Records in 1971, Kottke's albums gradually became more adventurous, adding vocals—despite his voice, described in the liner notes to the Takoma album as sounding like "geese farts on a muggy day"—as well as occasional rhythm sections. Kottke cut six albums for Capitol; all, as well as the two best-ofs subsequently assembled, are out of print, but *Mudlark* (1971) and the live *My Feet Are Smiling* (1973) include some of his best guitar work, while *Ice Water* (1974) shows just how engaging his deep, deadpan voice can be.

Moving to Chrysalis in 1976, Kottke immediately redefined his sound. Recorded with a variety of ensembles and making full use of electronic effects and multitrack recording, *Leo Kottke* shows the full range of the guitarist's genius; from the ragtime-meets-rock of "Hayseed Suede" to the orchestra-and-slide guitar "Range," Kottke seems capable of playing just about anything. Typically, he followed this star turn with *Burnt Lips*, an unassuming collection of songs that, for the most part, could as easily have fit on his early Capitol recordings; still, his version of Nick Lowe's "Endless Sleep" is a pleasant surprise. Kottke followed this yo-yo pattern for the rest of his stay on Chrysalis: *Balance* is a none-too-successful attempt at pop credibility that finds Kottke fronting a country-rock ensemble and occasionally playing electric guitar; *Guitar Music* returns him to the solo-instrumental format; *Time Step* puts him back in front of a band, although with considerably more success, thanks to sympathetic production by T-Bone Burnett and cameos by Albert Lee and Emmylou Harris.

By the time he switched labels again, Kottke had finally settled into . . . well, not a sound, exactly, but an approach: The Kottke-ization of American music. *Regards From Chuck Pink*, for instance, does an astonishing job of translating Kottke's stylistic quirks into a variant on new acoustic music; not quite jazz, not quite folk, it gives Kottke an interesting set of playmates (as well as some stunning string arrangements) and plenty of solo space. On the other hand, *My Father's Face* alternates between quirky vocal numbers along the lines of "Why Can't You Fix My Car," and jazzy instrumentals like "B.J.," and includes "Everybody Lies," one of Kottke's loveliest songs, with harmony vocals by David Hidalgo. *Great Big Boy* even goes as far afield as funk (well, Kottke's version, anyway) on "The Other Day (Near Santa Cruz)," although the sardonic, mariachi-flavored "Pepe Hush," a duet with Cowboy Junkie Margo Timmins, is more typical of the album.   — J.D.C.

KRAFTWERK

★ ★ ★   Autobahn (1974; Elektra, 1988)
★ ★   Radio Activity (Capitol, 1975)
★ ★ ★½ Trans-Europe Express (Capitol, 1977)
★ ★ ★½ The Man Machine (Capitol, 1978)
★ ★ ★   Computer World (1981; Elektra, 1988)
★ ★   Electric Cafe (1986; Elektra, 1988)
★ ★ ★   The Mix (Elektra, 1991)

Kraftwerk—the cleanest-sounding and most minimalistically inclined practitioners of Teutonic electronic trance music—captured the attention of American listeners with *Autobahn*'s hypnotic title track. Sighing synth winds rise and fall around a chanted robot refrain, enveloping your senses like an eventless five-hour trip on the expressway. *Radio Activity* emits a wide range of analog groans and cross-wired giggles that dissolve into the atmosphere without leaving much of an impression. *Trans-Europe Express* and *The Man Machine* spice the mechanical lull with genuine melodies, sly humor and a firmer rhythmic pulse. Though these albums shaped the future course of both dance music and hip-hop, Kraftwerk faded from the vanguard almost as quickly and silently as it had arrived. On *Computer World* and (especially) *Electric Cafe*, the group stops weaving repetitious spells and starts merely to repeat itself. Appropriately enough, *The Mix* juggles and jumbles some of Kraftwerk's best-known "numbers" into nearly unrecognizable (though not-unlistenable) forms.   — M.C.

LENNY KRAVITZ
★★★ **Let Love Rule (Virgin, 1989)**
★★★ **Mama Said (Virgin, 1991)**
Lenny Kravitz is the personification of
Classic Rock. His backward-gazing musical
vision takes in soul and funk along with
Jimi and the Beatles, however, and that may
be his saving grace. Ultimately, both these
albums get over on sheer conviction and
articulate rhythms. But this nouveau
hippie's reliance on bell-bottom platitudes
and recycled hooks can get old pretty fast.
The baroque extremes of high-'60s
psychedelia color the debut album. Kravitz
ignites a Princely groove on "Mr. Cab
Driver," though, making a sharp point
about racial identity in the process. No
matter how natural his takes on "white"
rock & roll may sound, our society won't let
Lenny Kravitz forget that he's black.
Kravitz doesn't let it slow him down. He
bulldozes his way through the hooky title
track, turning a dippy plea into an
optimist's anthem. "Let Love Rule" is his
moment of glory—almost good enough to
make you forget "Flower Child."
   The singing and playing sound much
more assured on *Mama Said*. While no
single performance quite matches up to "Let
Love Rule," Kravitz deepens his funk with
catchy appropriations of Curtis Mayfield
("What Goes Around Comes Around") and
Earth, Wind and Fire ("It Ain't Over 'Til
It's Over"). — M.C.

KRIS KRISTOFFERSON
★★ **Me and Bobby McGee (Columbia, 1971)**
★★ **The Silver Tongued Devil and I (Columbia, 1971)**
★★ **Jesus Was a Capricorn (1972; Sony Music, 1991)**
★★ **A Star Is Born Soundtrack (Columbia, 1976)**
★★ **Songs of Kristofferson (Columbia, 1977)**
★★ **Third World Warrior (Mercury, 1990)**
★★★★ **Singer/Songwriter (Columbia Legacy, 1991)**
WITH RITA COOLIDGE
★★ **Breakaway (1974; Sony Music, 1991)**
An Army veteran and Rhodes Scholar, Kris
Kristofferson changed the course of country
music with his literate, witty songwriting. He
didn't do it single-handedly, of course.
Unique tunesmiths like Roger Miller ("King
of the Road") and Tom T. Hall ("Harper
Valley P.T.A.") were already shaking up

Nashville when Kristofferson arrived in the
mid-'60s. Kris was influenced by Bob Dylan
as well as the ghost of Hank Williams. Only
one problem with Kristofferson's own
albums, most of which are out of print: the
songwriter can barely sing. His halting,
talky delivery makes Willie Nelson sound
like Frank Sinatra (or better yet George
Jones). None of Kristofferson's readings
come close to the cover versions of his
material. *Singer/Songwriter* finesses the
dilemma by including one disc devoted to
each; it's perhaps the smartest packaging
ploy to come out of the box set reissue glut.
Listen to the second disc first: between Janis
Joplin's comfortably ragged "Me and Bobby
McGee" and Ray Price's tuxedo-smooth
"For the Good Times," just for starters,
you'll be fully prepared for Kristofferson's
flawed, but affecting performances. Needless
to say, Nashville could use some of
Singer/Songwriter's iconoclastic viewpoints
and incisive melodies these days. Judging
from the liberal pieties of the recent *Third
World Warrior*, so could Kris Kristofferson.
— M.C.

FELA ANIKULAPO KUTI
★★★½ **Music of Fela (1972; Makossa International, 1975)**
★★★ **Music of Fela, Volume 2 (1974; Makossa International, 1975)**
★★★ **Upside Down (1976; Celluloid, 1990)**
★★★ **Unnecessary Begging (1976; Makossa International, 1982)**
★★★★ **Zombie (Mercury, 1977)**
★★★½ **No Agreement (1977; Celluloid, 1985)**
★★★ **Shuffering and Shmiling (1978; Celluloid, 1985)**
★★★★ **Black President (1981; Capitol, 1984)**
★★★★ **Original Sufferhead (1981; Capitol, 1984)**
★★★★★ **Original Sufferhead (1984; Shanachie, 1991)**
★★★½ **Live in Amsterdam (Capitol, 1984)**
★★★½ **Army Arrangement (Celluloid, 1985)**
★★★★ **Army Arrangement: Original Version (Celluloid, 1985)**
★★★★ **Teacher Don't Teach Me Nonsense (Mercury, 1986)**
★★★ **Beasts of No Nation (Shanachie, 1989)**
★★★★ **O D O O (Shanachie, 1990)**
WITH GINGER BAKER
★★★ **Live With Ginger Baker (1971, Celluloid, 1985)**

WITH ROY AYERS
★★★ **Music of Many Colours (1980, Celluloid, 1986)**

A lot of pop singers fancy themselves threats to the establishment, but few can claim to be the genuine annoyance Fela Anikulapo Kuti has been to various Nigerian regimes over the last two decades. In 1977, for instance, his personal compound outside Lagos was attacked and razed by troops acting on orders of the nation's military government; in 1984, he was imprisoned (by a subsequent military government) on spurious currency charges, and languished in jail for two years until yet another government freed him. And the source of his troubles, almost without exception, has been his music—specifically, his bitingly political lyrics, and the insistently hypnotic beat that has carried those words to his audience over more than 50 albums.

For listeners outside Nigeria, Fela's political harangues aren't always easy to follow, particularly since he sings in a combination of English and patois. But his sound—a blend of highlife, jazz and American soul which he dubbed "Afrobeat"—needs no translation. Indeed, his reputation among rockers is surprisingly strong; Ginger Baker recorded with him in 1971, Paul McCartney described Fela's live show as one of the most astonishing performances he'd ever seen, and Talking Heads cited his band as an inspiration for *Remain in Light*.

With so much to choose from (even given the limited U.S. release of his albums), it's hard to know where to start. Few of Fela's albums offer more than two songs—which is not as miserly as it seems, considering that the average Fela tune clocks in at 15 minutes or longer—meaning that most of his albums emphasize a single groove. His output is surprisingly consistent, meaning that almost any Fela title will be worth hearing. *Zombie* is a particularly fine example of his '70s band, boasting sharp horn work and a loping, muscular pulse; the feisty *Original Sufferhead* and *Black President* (which features the catchy "I.T.T.") are also recommended. Of his more recent material, both versions of *Army Arrangement* are good, but the original version has a little more edge than Bill Laswell's beefed-up remix. And though *Beasts of No Nation* is a bit spotty, the brutally relentless *O D O O* is one of his strongest albums to date.

Still, the best buys at this point tend to be CD compilations like Shanachie's reissue of *Original Sufferhead*, which includes "Original Sufferhead" itself as well as all of the Capitol album, *Black President*, thereby delivering a sizeable serving of prime Afrobeat. Also worth seeking are any of the four-volume Fela series on the French Baya label, which packages much of his '70s output in double-length CDs. — J.D.C.

PATTI LABELLE
★★★   **Patti LaBelle (Epic, 1977)**
★★★   **The Best of Patti LaBelle (1974; Epic, 1982)**
★★★   **I'm in Love Again (Philadelphia International, 1984)**
★★★   **Winner in You (MCA, 1986)**
★★½   **Be Yourself (MCA, 1988)**
★★★   **Starlight Christmas (MCA, 1990)**
★★★½   **Burnin' (MCA, 1991)**

After parting ways with LaBelle, this veteran soul singer gradually dropped the spacey rock-funk regalia. Her Epic albums—only *The Best of Patti LaBelle* remains in print—veer between disco and a softer place, never quite touching down on solid ground. *The Best of* tosses in several LaBelle ringers, but the group's album *Nightbirds* (Epic, 1974) is still the way to go. Moving to Philadelphia International in its final days, Patti found more suitable musical accommodations. The orchestral grandness of late-period Philly Soul matches LaBelle's towering intensity peak for peak. "If Only You Knew" and "Love, Need and Want You" re-established Patti as an R&B chart presence in 1983–84. There's a seductive warmth to those hits; for all her showy command, LaBelle almost comes on like a female Teddy Pendergrass.

That may come as a shock to people who only know Patti LaBelle from her over-the-top television performances—her Live Aid extravaganza is a classic. Patti strutted a synthed-up "New Attitude" and scored a corporate-pop hit on the *Beverly Hills Cop* soundtrack LP. *Winner in You* captures some of the aforementioned overkill, especially on the title cut. There are more subtle moments, though: the vague uplift of "Oh People" is pleasant enough, a spliced duet with Michael McDonald ("On My Own") succeeds in spite of itself, several of the dancey tracks (like "Something Special") find a flexible groove.

If *Be Yourself* is a disappointingly obvious followup to *Winner*, then *Burnin'* is the power-packed sampler album that Patti LaBelle's fans have patiently waited for. Ranging from rap-flavored funk to soaring potential show tunes, this R&B diva leaps from strength to strength. Producer match-ups with Prince ("I Hear Your Voice") and Philly vet Bunny Siegler ("Burnin'") yield memorable results. Even the LaBelle reunion ("Release Yourself") catches a spark, while avoiding outright nostalgia. And "We're Not Making Love Anymore"—a cutting contest with the soulless yelper Michael Bolton—becomes downright listenable in this refreshingly varied context.   — M.C.

LADYSMITH BLACK MAMBAZO
★★★½   **Ulwandle Oluncgwele (1977; Shanachie, 1985)**
★★★   **Umthombo Wamanzi (1982; Shanachie, 1988)**
★★★½   **Induku Zethu (1983; Shanachie, 1984)**
★★★½   **Inala (1986; Shanachie, 1986)**
★★★½   **Shaka Zulu (Warner Bros., 1987)**
★★★★   **Journey of Dreams (Warner Bros., 1988)**
★★★   **How the Leopard Got His Spots (with Danny Glover) (Windham Hill, 1989)**
★★★★   **Classic Tracks (Shanachie, 1990)**
★★★★   **Two Worlds One Heart (Warner Bros., 1990)**

Best known in the U.S. for its work with Paul Simon on *Graceland*, Ladysmith Black Mambazo is one of the foremost mbube choirs in South Africa. On the Shanachie recordings—straightforward repackagings of the group's African releases—it's easy to hear why; not only are the a capella harmonies gorgeous and the vocal effects astonishing, but leader Joseph Shabalala sings with such dramatic eloquence that not even the language barrier can stop him from putting his point across. By contrast, the Warner Bros. albums attempt, to varying degrees, to Americanize the group. *Shaka Zulu*, produced by Simon, uses some English but leaves the music unmolested; *Journey of Dreams* tries a Simon-arranged version of "Amazing Grace" and succeeds nicely (thanks in part to the religiosity of the other tracks); *Two Worlds One Heart* adds rhythm to the mix, with one track produced by fellow *Graceland* alum Ray Phiri and a surprisingly successful collaboration with George Clinton. *How the Leopard Got His Spots*, a setting of the Rudyard Kipling tale, won't do much for African music fans, but their kids may like it. — J.D.C.

FRANKIE LAINE
★★★½ **Frankie Laine's Golden Hits (Mercury, 1961)**
★★★ **Greatest Hits (Columbia, NA)**
One of the most popular pop singers of the post–World War II era, Frankie Laine's distinctive voice stood out even in an era rife with distinctive voices. His was a big, booming instrument, full of melodrama and passion, ideally suited to booming orchestral accompaniment but also with a tender side capable of investing a ballad's lyrics with great feeling. Laine had productive years on both the Mercury and Columbia labels, although with the latter his recordings often became overblown production numbers, courtesy of producer Mitch Miller, and post-Mercury he failed to hit the top of the charts again, as he had done three times in 1949–50. Ironically, Laine may well be best-remembered for the movie themes he recorded at Columbia, notable among them being "High Noon" (1952). *Greatest Hits* is an adequate document of his Columbia period, and includes his first hit for the label, "Jezebel," which made it to Number Two in 1951, and the powerful "Moonlight Gambler" from 1956. *Frankie Laine's Golden Hits*, on the other hand, shows him at the beginning of his career working with someone (there is no liner information) who downplayed the accompaniment and let Laine's voice carry the day. On many of these cuts he is backed by a small combo, and the effect is striking. Of note among these dozen cuts are "That Lucky Old Sun," "Mule Train" and "The Cry of the Wild Goose." A Top Twenty single from 1950, "Music, Maestro, Please," is one of Laine's finest moments on record. In this lilting blues the singer is accompanied only by a piano as he gives a measured, anguished

reading of the downcast lyric. Laine isn't often mentioned as one of the great stylists of his generation, but his recorded legacy indicates that he could deliver the goods. Those who remember him only as the guy who sang "High Noon" or "Blazing Saddles" ought to seek out the Mercury set. It's startling. — D.M.

MAJOR LANCE
★★★ **Um, Um, Um, Um, Um, Um—The Best of Major Lance (Epic, 1976)**
Relentlessly swinging, always impassioned, a bit salacious, Major Lance was one of the architects of the Chicago soul sound of the '60s. Along with Jerry Butler, Curtis Mayfield, Gene Chandler and others, Lance rode that deep, horn-laden R&B groove into chart prominence from 1963 to 1965 when he was recording for the Windy City–based Okeh label. Following a short stint as a professional boxer, Lance met Mayfield, who gave the aspiring singer a song, "The Monkey Time," that landed Mayfield and Lance contracts with Okeh, the former as staff producer, the latter as a recording artist. "The Monkey Time" peaked at Number Eight in '63, set off a dance craze (the Monkey), and kicked off a productive two-year period for both Mayfield and Lance. *Um, Um, Um* shows the evolution of Lance's sound—and the sound of Chicago—as the decade wore on, and includes both "The Monkey Time" and another Mayfield-penned Top Ten hit, "Um, Um, Um, Um, Um, Um," from 1964. Eight of Lance's songs can also be found on the 1982 Epic release, *Okeh Soul*, now out of print. — D.M.

K.D. LANG
★★★ **A Truly Western Experience (Bumstead, 1984)**
★★★★ **Angel With a Lariat (Sire, 1987)**
★★★ **Shadowland (Sire, 1988)**
★★★★ **Absolute Torch and Twang (Sire, 1989)**
★★★★ **Ingénue (Sire, 1992)**
k.d. lang deals in post-modern country sounds, music that applies a genuine affection for C&W tradition to a thoroughly contemporary musical sensibility. And though that may read like an overly intellectualized approach, it never sounds that way, for lang—being both connected enough to feel the music with a fan's fervor, yet distanced enough to recognize Nashville hokum for what it is—often does for country what the Band did for rock & roll.
Angel With a Lariat, for instance, is as at home with the Cajun two-step of "Got the

Bull By the Horns" as with the upscale swing of "Rose Garden," because lang can accommodate both styles without noticeably modifying her affectionately indulgent delivery. Moreover, it seldom plays these styles for novelty value, as *A Truly Western Experience* sometimes does. And though she sometimes verges on the wiseacre—note the glee with which she dispatches the off-balance cadences in "Watch Your Step Polka"—there's never a sense that she's looking down at the material. Still, even a little bit of quirkiness can be hard for the country audience to overcome, which may be why lang felt inclined to prove her bona fides with *Shadowland*, a painstakingly pure tribute to Patsy Cline. Not content with merely singing her heroine's songs, lang recruited Cline's original producer, Owen Bradley, and his presence lends an authority to the project no mere re-creation could match. Yet for all her obvious enthusiasm, lang's performance is more impressive as devotion than interpretation, for she too often loses her own identity in an attempt to seem authentic.

Fortunately, *Absolute Torch and Twang* brings the focus back to lang herself. She has wondrous fun with the uptempo tunes, whether homegrown (the cool-rocking "Didn't I") or borrowed (her sly, swinging remake of "Full Moon Full of Love"). But the slow songs are where she really proves her mettle, for between the bluesy inflection of "Three Days" and the melancholy yodel tugging at "Trail of Broken Hearts," lang shows herself to be one of the most gifted—and certainly the most unique—song stylists in country music today. No wonder, then, that *Ingénue* makes genre distinctions all but irrelevant as lang fuses her influences into a unique and distinctive sound encompassing everything from the torch-song sophistication of "Miss Chatelaine" to the Patsy Cline–meets–Joni Mitchell lament, "Save Me." — J.D.C.

DANIEL LANOIS
★★★★ Acadie (Opal/Warner Bros., 1989)
Having lent his supple production skills to such heavyweights as Bob Dylan and U2, it's fitting that Lanois would craft his own record, *Acadie*, with the care that makes it sonically gorgeous—warm, immediate, bell-like. Eno is Lanois's collaborator and secret weapon, the avant-garde experimentalist adding subtle, effective oddities—cello sounds, whistling synthesizers—that transform the folk-based melodies into textured mood-music that's more self-consciously distinct. New Orleans

provides the spiritual home for the project: "O Marie" is sung in French, "Jolie Louise" has a soft, Cajun lilt. Fascinating in its mix of high technology and rootsy integrity, *Acadie* is artful without being precious, studied but still passionate. — P.E.

CYNDI LAUPER
★★★★ She's So Unusual (Portrait, 1984)
★★ True Colors (Portrait, 1986)
★★ A Night to Remember (Epic, 1989)
A brilliant debut, Cyndi Lauper's *She's So Unusual* kicked off with a quartet of songs ("Money Changes Everything," "Girls Just Want to Have Fun," "When You Were Mine," "Time After Time") that revealed her as a genre-bending sharpie—mistress of styles varying from post-punk rock to neo-'50s pop to sex funk to balladry. With a voice that combined the cartoon soul of Little Eva and the happy naughtiness of Betty Boop, Lauper may have backed away a bit from the depth or urgency of the writers whose work she mainstreamed (among them, Prince, Jules Shear and Tom Gray of Atlanta's Brains), but her transformation of their power into sheer pop was ultimately subversive—giggling all the way, she incited legions of mall rats into orange-hair rebellion and a measure of self-assertion. A homely-pretty, good-bad girl, Lauper proved that the woman singer need be neither "sensitive" nor agonized nor "artful" nor conventionally sexy nor a male imitator.

What a drag, then, that her subsequent career was a bust. Turning far too soon toward self-parody, she became a figure about as radical and liberating as a Muppet. Cuddly, "talented" and redundant. — P.E.

LEADBELLY
★★★★ Leadbelly's Last Sessions, Vol. 1 (Folkways, 1953)
★★★★ Leadbelly's Last Sessions, Vol. 2 (Folkways, 1953)
★★★★ Leadbelly Memorial, Volume 1 (Stinson, NA)
★★★★ Leadbelly Memorial, Volume 2 (Stinson, NA)
★★★★ Leadbelly Memorial, Volume 3 (Stinson, NA)
★★★★ Leadbelly Memorial, Volume 4 (Stinson, NA)
★★★ Leadbelly Sings and Plays (Stinson, NA)
★★★ Leadbelly Sings Folk Songs (1968; Smithsonian/Folkways, 1989)
★★★★ Alabama Bound (RCA, 1989)
★★★ Bourgeois Blues (Collectables, 1989)

★ ★ ★ ★ **King of the Twelve-String Guitar (Columbia/Legacy, 1991)**
★ ★ ★ ★ ★ **Midnight Special (Rounder, 1991)**
★ ★ ★ ★ ★ **Gwine Dig a Hole to Put the Devil In (Rounder, 1991)**
★ ★ ★ ★ ★ **Let It Shine on Me (Rounder, 1991)**

Huddie Ledbetter, better known as Leadbelly, rose from penitentiary prisoner to beloved folk troubadour in the 1930s, when his influence spread far and wide. It was remarkable enough that a black man achieved such widespread popular acclaim at a time when crossover was a near-nonexistent phenomenon. His songs are even more remarkable and enduring. Americans who would otherwise draw a blank at the mention of Leadbelly's name will recognize "Goodnight Irene" and "Rock Island Line," to name but two of his best-known songs.

Leadbelly was discovered in 1933 by folklorist John Lomax and his son Alan, who were touring the south, recording blues, work and folk songs for the Library of Congress. In the course of their travels the Lomaxes often set up their recording gear in prisons, which were a limitless source of the music they were seeking. In 1933, at Louisiana State Penitentiary, they found Leadbelly, who had been convicted of attempted homicide. The Lomaxes recorded him, then brought him to New York in 1935 after his release (he was pardoned after writing a song for the governor of Louisiana). Leadbelly was an instant hit playing in New York clubs and throughout the Northeast, but by the decade's end he was back in prison on an assault charge.

Upon his release in the spring of 1940, he took an apartment in lower Manhattan and soon joined the Headline singers, whose members included Woody Guthrie, Sonny Terry and Brownie McGhee. At that time he began to record his songs for various labels and even made one short film, *Three Songs by Leadbelly*, in 1945. His touring intensified after World War II, but he fell ill in 1949, was diagnosed with Lou Gehrig's Disease, and died late in the year. But he left behind a wealth of recordings.

Stinson's four-volume *Memorial* set features the artist, his bold voice and 12-string guitar in a variety of contexts encompassing virtually every type of song Leadbelly played: Volume 1 is a program of work songs, blues and spirituals; Volume 2 is more of the same with Leadbelly playing piano concertina as well as 12-string;

Volume 3 is a collection of previously unreleased masters and rare tracks, including "In the Evening When the Sun Goes Down" and a tribute to a great blues artist, "Blind Lemon"; Volume 4 finds Leadbelly telling his life story by way of song, traveling from the cotton fields to prison to the big city (some of this material is duplicated on Collectables' *Bourgeois Blues* CD).

The Folkways *Last Sessions* albums constitute recordings done in an apartment occupied by Leadbelly's friend and folk music enthusiast-scholar Frederic Ramsey, Jr. Over the course of three nights Leadbelly played and, with Ramsey's encouragement, offered anecdotes about his life and the songs. This is the fullest picture of Leadbelly on record, and along with the Columbia/ Legacy and Stinson titles the most important of Leadbelly's recordings extant. Another recommended cross-section of work comes via RCA's *Alabama Bound*, which features eight tracks recorded in 1940 with the Golden Gate Jubilee Quartet, one of the '40s most important gospel groups. As always, the quality and variety of material and of Leadbelly's own performances is spellbinding. Columbia/Legacy's excellent entry, *King of the Twelve-String Guitar*, restores to print Leadbelly's first commercial sessions, recorded in 1935. *Leadbelly Sings and Plays* and *Leadbelly Sings Folk Songs* both find Leadbelly whooping it up with other artists, including Woody Guthrie, Cisco Houston, Sonny Terry and, on *Sings and Plays*, Josh White. Unavailable for many years, the three Rounder CDs released in 1991 are must-haves for anyone even remotely interested in the roots of folk and blues in 20th-century America. Recorded by Alan Lomax for the Library of Congress between the years 1934 and 1942, these early recordings contain many of Leadbelly's most powerful performances. Indispensable.
— D.M.

LED ZEPPELIN
★ ★ ★ ★ **Led Zeppelin (Atlantic, 1969)**
★ ★ ★ ★ **Led Zeppelin II (Atlantic, 1969)**
★ ★ ★ ★ **Led Zeppelin III (Atlantic, 1970)**
★ ★ ★ ★ ★ **Untitled (Atlantic, 1971)**
★ ★ ★ ★ ★½ **Houses of the Holy (Atlantic, 1973)**
★ ★ ★ ★ **Physical Graffiti (Swan Song, 1975)**
★ ★ ★ ½ **Presence (Swan Song, 1976)**
★ ★ ½ **The Song Remains the Same (Swan Song, 1976)**

★ ★ ★   **In Through the Out Door (Swan Song, 1979)**

★ ★½ **Coda (Swan Song, 1982)**

★ ★ ★ ★½ **Led Zeppelin (Atlantic, 1990)**

Let's give the legions of Led Zeppelin imitators a little credit: ten years' worth of fossilized heavy rock throws the originators into bold relief. Listening to Zeppelin albums now, you notice everything the macho metallers haven't been able to photo-copy: complexity, subtlety, idiosyncracy, vision.

Of all the British "guitar heroes" of the late '60s, perhaps Jimmy Page is the one who truly assimilated black American influences and forged a new style. Surely he fathered heavy metal with the thundering blues reductions of *Led Zeppelin II*; but just as important, the group didn't let the impact of "Whole Lotta Love" impede its musical progress. The debut, *Led Zeppelin*, maps its range of intent: later albums expand on the acoustic grace of "Babe I'm Gonna Leave You," the heaving inevitability of "Communication Breakdown," the enveloping roar of Robert Plant's vocals on "Dazed and Confused," the pop flavoring of "Your Time is Gonna Come."

Page and bassist-keyboardist John Paul Jones capitalized on their extensive studio experience during London's swingin' mid-'60s, but Zeppelin became the very definition of a rock & roll *band*. Each element is clearly pronounced, yet never overbearing. Instead of the expected indulgences, Page offers melodic, sharply focused invention: he's the master of contrasts, shading, texture, dynamics. For all his ham-hock power, drummer John Bonham echoes Page's exquisite sense of timing; as time went on, Zeppelin's puncturing rhythms took a gradual, inexorable turn toward funk.

After the *I-II* punch, *Led Zeppelin III* was a commercial disappointment. Split down the middle between steam-shovel rockers and largely acoustic, folkish material, this underrated album presents a rough blueprint for Zeppelin's towering monument. *Untitled* synthesizes this mix, adding a needed dose of unrestricted "Rock & Roll" to the growing pomp and circumstance. Robert Plant tempers his flair for melodrama with a new directness; he delivers his hippie encomiums and medieval fantasies with such heart-on-the-sleeve passion that they're hard to resist. "Stairway to Heaven" blends the electric-acoustic dual identities into a seamless whole. But the Mississippi mud–drenched "When the Levee Breaks"

just might be Zeppelin's *real* crowning glory: over an oceanic beat, Plant's slippery voice and Page's slide guitar cry out as one.

Houses of the Holy is a satisfying and ambitious followup. "Over the Hills and Far Away" and "Dancing Days" elegantly restate established themes, while the James Brown tribute ("The Crunge") and reggae attempt ("D'Yer Maker") extend the band's reach. Perhaps *Physical Graffiti* reaches too far: one resounding ten-minute epic per album is *plenty*. "Kashmir" achieves its exotic, mesmerizing effect without losing the beat, but the bulky remainder of *Graffiti* drags a bit; only the haunting "Custard Pie" and the swinging "Houses of the Holy" represent advances. Recorded quickly during a period of personal turmoil for the group, *Presence* sounds rushed and uncertain, especially by Zeppelin's meticulous standards. Hard-charging cuts like "Nobody's Fault but Mine," "Candy Store Rock" and "For Your Life" benefit from that looseness, though. And "Achilles' Last Stand" holds up as well as any other mythic guitar-demolition set piece. If nothing else, Page goes down fighting.

In Through the Out Door indicates that punk had unsettled rock's reigning dinosaurs: while "Hot Dog" and "I'm Gonna Crawl" go looking for inspiration in the grunge, the hit "Fool in the Rain" relies on keyboards and vocals to an unprecedented degree. At times, Page sounds like a Steely Dan sideman here, weighing in with a tasteful comment on the proceedings. After John Bonham's unexpected death in 1980, Zeppelin loyally called it a day. *Coda* collects some unspectacular outtakes; its best tracks are included on the Atlantic box set. The idea of anthologizing Led Zeppelin—stubborn champions of the album-as-art-form argument—on CD seems wildly inappropriate. Of course, Page's selection and remixing are hard to argue with: this expertly pieced-together set reconsiders the early milestones and redeems some of the later work. Technically, it's got everything you need, but the essential magic of Led Zeppelin still emanates from those original releases. — M.C.

ALVIN LEE

★ ★½ **On the Road to Freedom (Columbia, 1973)**

★ ★ ★   **In Flight (Columbia, 1974)**

★ ★   **Pump Iron (Columbia, 1975)**

★ ★   **Rocket Fuel (RSO, 1978)**

★ ★   **Alvin Lee (Columbia, 1978)**

★ ★ ★ **Ride On (RSO, 1979)**
★ ★ **Free Fall (Avatar, 1980)**
★ ★ ★ **Detroit Diesel (21 Records/Atco, 1986)**

All blazing fingers and nifty shag haircut, Lee was a quintessential late-'60s guitar stud who astounded Woodstock audiences by churning out boogie riffs at breakneck speed. Ten Years After, his somewhat turgid blues-rock band, capitalized on that success; the group toured maniacally, playing to the same crowds as did Humble Pie, Foghat and Savoy Brown—and sold a fair number of records. Without Ten Years After (in particular, the moody organ work of Chick Churchill), Lee faltered. *On the Road to Freedom* paired him with Georgia gospel rocker Mylon LeFevre and a big-name cast (George Harrison, Steve Winwood, Ron Wood), yet it's a somnolent set. *Pump Iron* was standard boogie fare; and while the presence of ex–King Crimson saxophonist Mel Collins and drummer Ian Wallace enlivened *In Flight*, the double-album live set of competent originals and oldies ("Money Honey," "Mystery Train") offered few surprises. Giving Lee plenty of room for pyrotechnics, the power trio Ten Years Later recaptured his early basic-rock sound—*Ride On* stands as the guitarist's best post–Ten Years After album, its live work ("Hey Joe," "Going Home") retaining a sassy, headbanging appeal. Basically a strong instrumentalist and an undependable songwriter, Lee remains a talent who haphazardly dazzles, but more often parlays only expertise. — P.E.

BRENDA LEE
★ ★ ★ **Merry Christmas From Brenda Lee (MCA, 1964)**
★ ★ ★½ **The Brenda Lee Story—Her Greatest Hits (1973; MCA, 1991)**
★ ★ **Greatest Country Hits (MCA, 1990)**
★ ★ ★ ★ **The Brenda Lee Anthology, Volume One 1956-1961 (MCA, 1991)**
★ ★ ★ ★ **The Brenda Lee Anthology, Volume Two 1962-1980 (MCA, 1991)**

Checking in at four-feet, eleven inches tall, Brenda Lee was dubbed "Little Miss Dynamite" early on in her career. The reference, though, was as much to her singing style as her height. When she was ruling the pop charts in the '60s, she could be convincing with an almost straight pop approach to a heartbreaking ballad, then swing into an uptempo number that would

reveal a deep streak of blues and honky-tonk in her style. A protégé of Patsy Cline's producer, Owen Bradley, Lee recorded her first pop hit in 1960—"Sweet Nothin's," which peaked at Number Four—and then set about becoming one of the dominant female vocalists of the decade. Pop hit after pop hit ensued, all charting the rocky course of love and its accompanying *angst*. Bradley, who has been criticized for his extravagant use of strings on Cline's recordings, found a more appropriate vehicle for his lush arrangements in Lee; in fact, he can be said to have made all the right moves in the studio in terms of his decisions to lay on the strings or to let Lee wail with only a basic rock band pushing the beat. The two-volume *Anthology* series collects Lee's most essential sides in their original form (Bradley had a habit of having his artists re-record their hits for album releases). In particular, "All Alone Am I," "As Usual," "Thanks a Lot," "Break It to Me Gently," "Sweet Nothin's" and "Johnny One Time" are superb examples of the different styles Lee employed in getting a lyric across. Among female pop artists in the '60s, Lee, Lesley Gore, and Dionne Warwick are pretty much alone in terms of their ability to affix an individual stamp to first-rate material.

Unlike *The Brenda Lee Story*, *Anthology* includes not only the hits but the early, less successful recordings Lee made with Bradley in the mid- to late-'50s, beginning with the first single from her first session, "Jambalaya" and "BIGELOW 6-200," recorded when Lee was 11 years old. *Anthology* also distinguishes itself by offering a smattering of Lee's country recordings, made in the '70s and '80s after her reign on the pop charts had ended. Among its many virtues, *Anthology* corrects one of *Story*'s major oversights in listing session and release dates as well as personnel, and adds detailed liner notes by Diana Haig.

Merry Christmas From Brenda Lee kicks off with "Rockin' Around the Christmas Tree" and continues in good rockin' seasonal fashion with ebullient takes on "Jingle Bell Rock," "A Marshmallow World" and "Winter Wonderland." But it's not all fun here: "Christmas Will Be Just Another Lonely Day" and "Blue Christmas" offer a reminder that absent friends make the holidays horrific for some. Unfortunately, Lee's segue into mainstream country has failed to produce distinctive work. The deleted *Greatest Country Hits*, a collection of tracks dating back to 1973, is marred mostly by mediocre songs. Strictly for hard-core fans. — D.M.

LAURA LEE

★ ★½ **That's How It Is: The Chess Years (Chess/MCA, 1990)**
★ ★ ★ ★ **Greatest Hits (HDH/Fantasy, 1991)**

Sassy and saucy, Laura Lee's records on the Hot Wax label epitomize the bold soul sister stance of the early '70s. Lobbying for "Women's Love Rights," proclaiming "Wedlock Is a Padlock," "setting up" her unfaithful man for a grand "Rip Off"—this young gospel veteran didn't mince words on her funky secular sermons. Though these sexual protests became Laura Lee's signature songs (and biggest hits), she hardly conforms to the old man-hating "Women's Libber" stereotype. "Crumbs Off the Table" and "Two Lonely Pillows" are yearning, enticing R&B torch songs: she appreciates what her man has to give—she just wants her fair share, that's all. On the latter song's climax, Laura Lee starts to testify for all the lonely people out there. When *Greatest Hits* throws in a straight-up gospel song ("You've Got to Save Me") for contrast, you barely notice the mention of Jesus. Laura Lee brings a fervent conviction and easy authority to Holland-Dozier-Holland's colossal psychedelia-enhanced funkscapes; neither wah-wah pedal nor orchestra can still her voice. Laura Lee believes what she's singing about on many of those *Greatest Hits*, and believe me, it shows. The Chess set culls some far less distinctive material from the mid-to-late '60s. — M.C.

PEGGY LEE

★ ★ ★ **Miss Peggy Lee (Columbia, 1957)**
★ ★ ★ **Let's Love (Atlantic, 1974)**
★ ★ ★ **Mirrors (A&M, 1975)**
★ ★ ★ **Close Enough for Love (DRG, 1979)**
★ ★ ★ ★ **The Best of Peggy Lee (MCA, 1980)**
★ ★ ★ ★ **Capitol Collectors Series: The Early Years (Capitol, 1990)**
★ ★ ★ **The Peggy Lee Songbook: There'll Be Another Spring (Musicmasters, 1990)**
★ ★ **Peggy Lee Sings With Benny Goodman (Columbia Special Products, NA)**
★ ★ ★ **All-Time Greatest Hits (Curb, 1990)**

To say that Peggy Lee has done it all is to be guilty of understatement. As well as being one of the major popular singers of her generation, Lee is also a songwriter of note whose work includes both pop songs and film scores, and she was a persuasive enough actress to have been nominated for an Academy Award. She was also one of the few singers of the '40s whose popularity remained undiminished through the '50s after the emergence of rock & roll. In light of a tortured personal history that includes four failed marriages, a childhood marred by parental abuse and debilitating health problems, Lee's professional accomplishments are all the more impressive.

A singular, highly compelling style accounts for the public's ongoing affection for Lee's music. Her calm purr of a voice, soft and delicate, commands attention; even more so when she starts cuddling up to a lyric or affects an easy, sensuous swagger that adds a touch of blue to her phrasing. Always sensual, always passionate, Lee projects high romance, stylish living and the allure of sustained desire. Her break came in 1941 when Benny Goodman signed her to sing in his band after hearing her at a small club in Chicago. A 1943 release, "Why Don't You Do Right?," brought Lee her first national attention, but it was a 1945 single, "Waitin' for the Train to Come In," that started an incredible run of hit singles that lasted until 1969, with her distracted reading of Leiber and Stoller's odd "Is That All There Is." The song most identified with Lee is her sultry 1958 interpretation of Little Willie John's "Fever."

The first of Lee's two productive tenures at Capitol Records is given a wide overview on the Capitol Collectors Series entry *The Early Years*, which takes her from 1945 to 1950. When her Capitol contract lapsed she signed with Decca and picked up where she had left off, comfortably ensconced in the Top Thirty until she returned to Capitol in 1958 and cut "Fever." The Decca years are aptly summarized on *The Best of Peggy Lee*. Until the next volume of the Capitol Collectors Series surfaces, those desiring "Fever" on CD are directed to the Curb release, *All-Time Greatest Hits*, which also includes "Is That All There Is." Lee recorded for several labels in the '70s, without hits but not without interesting moments. Her 1974 Atlantic album, *Let's Love*, marked a short-lived—as in one song—teaming with Paul McCartney, who wrote and produced the title track. Strangest of the lot is *Mirrors*, a full-blown Leiber-Stoller production with a massive orchestra and an offbeat repertoire of Leiber-Stoller quasi-art songs written especially for Lee. The theme is encapsuled in the title of the album's final song, "Longings for a Simpler Time." (*Mirrors* would seem to be the prototype for Lee's ill-fated 1983 autobiographical Broadway musical, *Peg*, which closed soon after opening. Its most memorable number: a childhood reminiscence titled "One Beating a Day [Maybe More].") Plagued by diabetes, a respiratory ailment so severe she requires an oxygen tank wherever she travels, a bad heart, and wheelchair-bound since falling on a Las Vegas stage, Lee continues to write, record and perform. In 1990 she released *The Peggy Lee Songbook: There'll Be Another Spring:* new interpretations of some of her personal favorites among the songs she's recorded. Future volumes are promised. Despite her infirmities, Lee's voice is still a thing of beauty. — D.M.

THE LEFT BANKE
★ ★ ★   The History of the Left Banke (Rhino, 1985)
★ ★ ★ ½   There's Gonna Be a Storm: The Complete Recordings, 1966–1969 (Mercury, 1992)

With its charming pseudo-chamber music harpsichord and violins, the Left Banke's "Walk Away Renee" sprang from the same mid-'60s pop impulse urge toward elegance that sparked "Eleanor Rigby" and Procol Harum's "A Whiter Shade of Pale." "Renee" was hardly of that order—but it wasn't silly, either. Written by singer Michael Brown at the ripe age of 16, the 1966 smash introduced a style from which the band seldom varied—"Pretty Ballerina," "Desiree" and "Love Songs in the Night" were sweet romance for misty-eyed teens. A two-hit wonder, the Left Banke collapsed after Brown's departure. — P.E.

LEMONHEADS
★ ★ ★ ½   Lick (Taang!, 1989)
★ ★ ★ ½   Lovey (Atlantic, 1990)

Like Dinosaur Jr, Lemonheads are alternative rockers with strong roots in (or, at least, an unironic appreciation of) '70s-style hard rock. In other words, these guys know all the moves but never bought the Marshall amps, sticking instead to the garage-band racket expected of college radio acts. *Lick* makes the most of its low-budget sound, working up an impressive lather on songs like "Glad I Don't Know" and "Circle of One," and is most memorable for its earnest, balls-out rendition of Suzanne Vega's "Luka."

By the time the 'Heads got around to *Lovey*, only Evan Dando remained from the original lineup (although guitarist Corey Loog Brennan turns up for two tracks); perhaps as a consequence, the rockers there are augmented by occasionally introspective ballads, the best of which are disarmingly tuneful, and surprisingly moving. No surprise, then, that this album's cover tune—Gram Parsons's "Brass Buttons"—is served straight-up and country style. Dando continues to soften his sound on *It's a Shame About Ray,* stressing acoustic guitars and bassist Juliana Hatfield's breathy harmony vocals until the songs seem more power pop than punk. Nor is that necessarily a bad idea, particularly when they result in melodies as strong as "Confetti" or "Alison's Starting to Happen." — J.D.C.

LE MYSTÈRE DES VOIX BULGARES
★ ★ ★ ★ ½   Le Mystère des Voix Bulgares (Nonesuch, 1987)
★ ★ ★ ★   Le Mystère des Voix Bulgares, Vol. 2 (Nonesuch, 1988)
★ ★ ★ ★   Le Mystère des Voix Bulgares, Vol. 3 (Verve, 1990)
★ ★ ★ ★   A Cathedral Concert (Verve World, 1992)

Bulgarian choral music may not be the kind of rock & roll touchstone doo-wop and gospel singing are, but a surprising number of rock stars swear by this odd, entrancing music. It wasn't *Le Mystère des Voix Bulgares* that first made Bulgarian folk music hip, though; credit for that belongs with three earlier Nonesuch albums: *Music of Bulgaria*, *Village Music of Bulgaria* and *In the Shadow of the Mountain*, all of which were released in the mid-'60s. Back then, it was essentially a cult interest, but its adepts proved influential. David Crosby claims the odd intervals and impossibly close harmonies of Bulgarian choral music inspired the Crosby, Stills & Nash vocal blend; David Lindley drew from Bulgarian folk idioms while a member of Kaleidoscope; and Robert Plant was so impressed by the vocal styles that he actually considered taking lessons.

Even so, Bulgarian folk music didn't get the American audience it deserved until 1987 and *Le Mystère des Voix Bulgares* (literally, "the mystery of Bulgarian voices"). Assembled by Swiss musicologist Marcel Cellier (and originally released on his own label, Disques Cellier, in 1979) this exquisite collection has several advantages over Nonesuch's earlier Bulgarian albums.

Like *Music of Bulgaria*, it relies upon the performances of a well-established choral group—in this case, the Bulgarian State Radio and Television Female Vocal Choir (a.k.a. Choir RTB)—but unlike that earlier album, it draws upon a wide range of performances, an approach that lends the album the consistency of a greatest-hits collection. But Cellier's song selection revels in the sensual pleasures of Bulgarian choral singing, something which brings an almost otherworldly charm to the music. From the urgent beauty of "Svatba" to the tender cadences of "Polegnala e Todora," these recordings combine the warmth and lustre of Slavic choral music with the brash virtuosity of Islamic sacred singing. It's hard to imagine a listener who wouldn't be captivated by this album.

Le Mystère des Voix Bulgares, Vol. 2 continues much in the same vein even as it broadens its sources to include other choirs, including the groups Trakia, Pirin and a choir led by Philip Koutev, whose Ensemble of the Bulgarian Republic was heard on *Music of Bulgaria*. There's a corresponding expansion in the musical range as well, with selections running the gamut from the dramatic dynamics of "Di-Li-Do" to the ghostly restraint of "Dragaba I Salvei" to the vigorous rhythms of "Ovdoviala Lissitchkata." By the time *Vol. 3* arrived, not only had "Le Mystère des Voix Bulgares" become near-synonymous with Bulgarian folk music, but the Choir RTB was deemed mainstream enough to appear on "The Tonight Show." Ironically, the group only appears on three of *Vol. 3*'s 12 tracks; most of the album is performed by Trakia. But the material is much the same, though somewhat more energetic than the earlier albums, and even includes a male soloist on one selection. *A Cathedral Concert* was recorded by the Women's Choir and soloists during a 1987 concert in Bremen, Germany; it's wonderfully sung, but breaks no new ground. — J.D.C.

JOHN LENNON

★ ★ ★ ★ ★   **John Lennon/Plastic Ono Band (Apple/Capitol, 1970)**
★ ★ ★ ★   **Imagine (Apple/Capitol, 1971)**
★ ★ ★ ½   **Mind Games (Apple/Capitol, 1973)**
★ ★ ★   **Walls and Bridges (Apple/Capitol, 1974)**
★ ★ ★ ½   **Rock 'n' Roll (Apple/Capitol, 1975)**
★ ★ ★ ★   **Shaved Fish (Apple/Capitol, 1975)**

★ ★ ★   **Menlove Avenue (Capitol, 1986)**
★ ★ ★   **John Lennon Live in New York City (Capitol, 1986)**
★ ★ ★ ½ **The John Lennon Collection (Capitol, 1990)**
★ ★ ★ ★   **Lennon (Capitol, 1990)**
WITH YOKO ONO
★ ★ ½   **Some Time in New York City (Apple, 1972)**
★ ★ ★ ★   **Double Fantasy (Geffen, 1980)**
★ ★ ★ ½ **Milk and Honey (Geffen, 1984)**

The shorthand assessment of Lennon as the tough rock genius and McCartney as the sweet pop craftsman has always seemed facile (and unfair to Paul). But with *John Lennon/Plastic Ono Band*, Lennon brutally, brilliantly and definitively underlined the differences between himself and his ex-Beatle brother. "Love" is one of John's prettiest songs and "Look at Me" is all fragile yearning, but the rest is anti-pop; rather, it's rock & roll as Lennon always understood it: anger, catharsis, deliverance. One of the most demanding albums ever made, *Plastic Ono Band* is also one of the finest—singing with more verve than he'd mustered since the Beatles' "Money," his urgency encouraged by primal scream therapy with Arthur Janov, Lennon bares his soul. The trio lineup—John on guitar and piano, Ringo on drums, and longtime Beatles ally Klaus Voorman on bass—keeps the playing fierce, spare and commanding; the force is helped greatly by Phil Spector's vast, echoing production. "God," "Remember" and "Isolation" find John unburdening himself of an exhausting, mythic past, and seeking—through harsh, nihilistic exhilaration—release. "Well, Well, Well" and "I Found Out" are tougher rock than nearly anything released before the Sex Pistols; "Mother" is painful, lovely and spine-chilling. And with "Working Class Hero" Lennon shucks off his gigantic stardom and reclaims the black-leather spirit of his Liverpool youth.

After the focused intensity of *Plastic Ono Band* came the much steadier *Imagine*. The title track is perhaps Lennon's most popular song, but there are other great songs on the record : "I Don't Wanna Be a Soldier Mama I Don't Wanna Die" is blistering trance-rock; "Gimme Some Truth" is furious. The famous savaging of Paul, "How Do You Sleep?," however, is John at his nastiest.

Some Time in New York City is a not-bad rocking collaboration with the capable band, Elephant's Memory; the lyrics, about the Attica prison riots, feminism and Angela

Davis, are far below Lennon's standard. On *Mind Games*—distinguished primarily by its sweeping, Spector-ish title track—John rocked tough in places, but it's mainly a holding-pattern disc. From *Walls and Bridges*, "Whatever Gets You Through the Night," a duet with Elton John, gained Lennon his only Number One hit; even better is "#9 Dream," a heavily atmospheric number boasting cool cellos and fine singing.

Critically derided as a step backward, *Rock 'n' Roll* in fact offers delights for those true believers who share Lennon's lifelong insistence that early rock is the only music that really matters. Another Spector production, its standouts include takes on "Ain't That a Shame," "Just Because" and "Stand By Me." Its lack of forced fever ultimately only makes the record stronger—John lends dignity to these classics; his singing is tender, convincing and fond.

Lennon had been adamant throughout his life in maintaining that he and Yoko were artistic equals. While Yoko had achieved distinction on her own as an avant-gardist, *Double Fantasy* comes close to redeeming Lennon's claim on the pop front. John's "Starting Over," with its easy, Fats Domino-like roll, and the music and vocals of "Watching the Wheels" and "Woman" are the highlights, and Yoko sounds better than she ever did. Lennon's posthumous work—the six Lennon songs off *Milk and Honey*, the raucous 1972 concert that makes up *Live* and the *Rock 'n' Roll* and *Walls and Bridges* pieces on *Menlove Avenue*—is good, but unspectacular. *Shaved Fish* is a good best of; the 74 songs that make up the Lennon boxed set comprise a comprehensive summary. — P.E.

JULIAN LENNON
★★ **Valotte (Atlantic, 1984)**
★★ **The Secret Value of Daydreaming (Atlantic, 1986)**
★★ **Mr. Jordan (Atlantic, 1989)**
★★★ **Help Yourself (Atlantic, 1991)**
To be commended for daring even to whisper after the echo of his formidable father, Julian settles for clean but modest stuff—high-end MOR. More a record-maker than a songwriter, he assembles crack studio vets (Michael Brecker, Barry Beckett, Ralph MacDonald) and, through the almost clinical packaging of their playing, turns out compositions that vaguely resemble backing tracks to Steely Dan. Genes make sounding like John inevitable, and Julian does so,

eerily, on his first album's not-bad title ballad, and, from his second outing, the haunting "Want Your Body." *Valotte* gave Lennon his one Top Ten hit, in the pale reggae "Too Late for Goodbyes." *Mr. Jordan* found him, for some odd reason, uncannily recreating David Bowie's vocals. Lennon's records are pervaded with a sort of listlessness, a free-floating pathos. The one thing he hasn't done is rock, and, given the standard he's inevitably compared to, that's one wise move. — P.E.

LET'S ACTIVE
★★★ **Afoot (EP) (IRS, 1983)**
★★½ **Cypress (IRS, 1984)**
★½ **Big Plans for Everybody (IRS, 1986)**
★★★★ **Every Dog Has His Day (IRS, 1988)**
Mitch Easter—the man behind Let's Active—helped midwife the first few R.E.M. albums, and it shows, from the carefully layered overdubs to the fondness for intricate, arpeggiated rhythm guitar parts. Where the two part company, though, is mood. Unlike R.E.M.'s albums, which can be dark, murky and full of resonant depths, Let's Active's output is generally more upbeat and pop-friendly. That's certainly the case with *Afoot*, which almost outdoes the Beatlesque buoyancy of the dB's on tunes like "Room With a View" and "Every Word Means No." Sadly, the songs on *Cypress* seem much more labored, as the tuneful exuberance of "Blue Line" and "Waters Part" is undercut by the arty indulgence of "Crows on a Phone Line" and its ilk. With drummer Sara Romweber gone and bassist Faye Hunter mostly on the sidelines, *Big Plans for Everybody* is almost an Easter solo project, and though the arrangements are considerably tighter, the album's glibness makes touches like the retro-psychedelia of "Writing the Book of Last Pages" almost unbearable.

Every Dog Has His Day, though, offers a fresh start for Easter and pals, with a new lineup (Hunter is gone, and there are guys in the rhythm section), a new sound (muscular drumming and raucous powerchords now augment the jangly guitar of yore) and songs running the gamut from loud-and-catchy ("Sweepstakes Winner," "Every Dog Has His Day") to low-key-and-tuneful ("Mr. Fool," "Forty Years"). — J.D.C.

THE LETTERMEN

★ ★ ★ **Best of the Lettermen (Capitol, 1966)**
★ ★ **Best of the Lettermen, Vol. 2 (Capitol, 1969)**
★ ★ ★ **All Time Greatest Hits (Capitol, 1974)**

Rising to popularity on the college circuit in the early '60s, the three Lettermen advanced the art of romantic balladeering popularized by white vocal quartets of the '50s. That they advanced this in the '60s when rock & roll was closing out this type of group says something about the Lettermen's appeal and, early on at least, the quality of their material. What was once an extensive catalogue has now been boiled down to three greatest-hits albums. The one to own is *Best of the Lettermen*, which contains the group's initial hits, including 1961 updates of Jerome Kern's "The Way You Look Tonight," a Top Twenty single, and "When I Fall in Love," a remake of Doris Day's 1952 hit. *Best of, Vol. 2* consists of mediocre performances of mediocre songs. *All Time Greatest Hits* reprises moments from both the *Best of*s; better to stick with the original. — D.M.

LEVEL 42

★ ★ **Level 42 (Polydor, 1981)**
★ ★ **The Pursuit of Accidents (1982; Polydor, 1985)**
★ ★ ★ ★ **Standing in the Light (Polydor, 1983)**
★ ★ ★ **True Colours (Polydor, 1984)**
★ ★ **A Physical Presence: Part 1 (1985; Polydor, 1987)**
★ ★ **A Physical Presence: Part 2 (1985; Polydor, 1987)**
★ ★½ **A Physical Presence (Polydor, 1985)**
★ ★ ★½ **World Machine (Polydor, 1985)**
★ ★ ★ **Running in the Family (Polydor, 1987)**
★ ★ **Staring at the Sun (Polydor, 1988)**
★ ★ ★½ **Level Best (Polydor, 1989)**
★ ★½ **Guaranteed (RCA, 1992)**

Level 42 is a fusoid funk band fronted by British bassist Mark King. On its early albums, the group's tepid grooves and semi-jazzy instrumental flourishes left it sounding like a Below-Average White Band, but with "Micro Kid," from *Standing in the Light*, Level 42's pop instincts came to the fore. *True Colours* stumbles somewhat in its attempts at Eurofunk (as with the groove behind "The Chant Has Begun"), and the concert album *A Physical Presence* squanders too much playing time on pointless noodling (the CD omits two songs included on cassette-only *Part 1*, "Turn It On" and "Mr. Pink," and one, "88," from *Part 2*, although it's hard to imagine why this would matter to anyone not related by blood to one of the band members). "Something About You," the group's biggest hit (and most alluring pop number), is on *World Machine*, though the album on the whole isn't quite as consistently tuneful as *Standing in the Light*. Both *Running in the Family* and *Staring at the Sun* repeat *World Machine*'s approach, but with steadily diminishing success. — J.D.C.

LEVERT

★ ★½ **Bloodline (Atlantic, 1986)**
★ ★ ★ **The Big Throwdown (Atlantic, 1987)**
★ ★ ★ ★ **Just Coolin' (Atlantic, 1988)**
★ ★½ **Rope a Dope Style (Atlantic, 1990)**

As the sons of O'Jay Eddie Levert, Gerald and Sean Levert (who, with Marc Gordon, make up Levert) have a better claim to the soul harmony tradition than most singers their age. And it shows, from Gerald's gritty, impassioned leads to the satiny sound of their ensemble work. So it's only natural that *Bloodline* should consist of songs as well harmonized as "Let's Go out Tonight" or the exquisitely smooth "(Pop, Pop, Pop, Pop) Goes My Mind." Pleasant as it is, though, the approach doesn't do much for the few groove tunes (like the Cameo-derived "Pose") the band bothered to include. Fortunately, *The Big Throwdown* finds a neat way around that. Although most of the album is given over to the same sort of richly arranged harmony numbers that powered *Bloodline*, "Casanova" and "Temptation" play off a New Jack groove that pumps the beat while leaving plenty of room for the trio's vocal blend.

A Heavy D. rap on the title tune is just one of the ways LeVert shows off its newfound street sensibility on *Just Coolin'*. It's not as if the group has abandoned balladry, since that's virtually all there is on the second half of the album. But the beats are bigger, the funk is deeper, and LeVert seems in the process of reinventing its whole sound. Sure enough, *Rope a Dope Style* finds the trio doing its own raps, playing with samples and doing the whole hip-hop thing. As a show of hipness, it's pretty impressive, but Bell Biv DeVoe these guys aren't, and apart from the old-style slow songs, most of *Rope a Dope Style* is forgettable. Better to seek out Gerald Levert's solo album, *Private Line* (EastWest, 1991), which offers a much more comfortable blend of old soul and New Jack beats. — J.D.C.

BARBARA LEWIS

★★★ **Golden Classics (Collectables, 1987)**
She didn't have the voice of her Atlantic labelmates LaVern Baker and Ruth Brown, but Barbara Lewis could caress a lyric with the best of them, even at the tender age of 19 when her first single, "Hello Stranger," climbed to Number Three in 1963. That wisdom-beyond-her-years quality played well in the mid-'60s, when she had five Top Forty singles. Forever in search of love ("Hello Stranger") and forever offering love ("Make Me Your Baby," "Baby, I'm Yours," "Make Me Belong to You"), Lewis had all the right neuroses for her time and beyond. This set collects all but one of her hits ("Puppy Love," from 1964, is missing), and some inspired non-hits, notably a swinging version of "Someday We're Gonna Love Again," a hit for the Searchers in 1964. — D.M.

EARL LEWIS AND THE CHANNELS

★★★ **New York's Finest (Collectables, NA)**
Legendary among New York doo-wop fans, Earl Lewis and the Channels cut some quintessential group harmony hits in the mid-'50s for the local Whirlin' Disc, Fire, and Fury labels. *New York's Finest* is not too far off the mark as a title describing the group's standing in the doo-wop pantheon, and the 13 tracks here prove the point. Whether gracing a ballad or an uptempo song, Earl Lewis's lead tenor is as pliant and evocative as they come. "The Closer You Are," from 1956, is the cut on which the group's reputation is based. Released on Whirlin' Disc, the original single remains among the most prized and most sought-after collector's items on the market. A splendid example of the New York school of doo-wop, *New York's Finest* gives just due to a group whose work maintained a consistent level of quality. — D.M.

GARY LEWIS

★★ **Greatest Hits (Rhino, 1985)**
★★½ **The Best of Gary Lewis and the Playboys: The Legendary Masters Series (EMI, 1989)**
With material and direction provided by Bobby Vee producer Snuff Garrett and a pre-hip Leon Russell, Jerry Lewis's genially nerdy kid scored a Number One hit with his very first record, "This Diamond Ring"— and followed it with a mini-career of toe-tapping tripe. Drumming with the skills of a high-school band second-stringer and singing with the soul of a dutiful cue-card reader, Gary was harmless and zealous; his mid-'60s smashes, "Count Me In," "Everybody Loves a Clown" and "Green Grass" sounded like sitcom rock & roll— bright and absolutely vacant. For a real strange gas, check out "Time Stands Still," on the Rhino *Greatest Hits* compilation. Understandably never released during the lad's glory days, it's Gary (goofily? vengefully?) imitating his Pop. — P.E.

HUEY LEWIS AND THE NEWS

★★ **Huey Lewis and the News (Chrysalis, 1980)**
★★ **Picture This (Chrysalis, 1982)**
★★★ **Sports (Chrysalis, 1983)**
★★ **Fore! (Chrysalis, 1986)**
★★ **Small World (Chrysalis, 1988)**
★★½ **Hard at Play (EMI, 1991)**
Huey Lewis found gargantuan mid-'80s success by masquerading as a rock & roller. Due to the News's bar-band competence, the hits were letter-perfect versions of fundamental rock, but Lewis's remarkably un-nuanced vocals and jockish sensibility were such that the songs missed the spirit by miles. After a desultory debut, the Bay Area sextet—originally named American Express—scored with "Workin' for a Livin' " and "Hope You Love Me Like You Say You Do" from *Picture This*. It was an album of blueprints for the generic fare that would soon endear the News to millions. Almost everything off *Sports* was swallowed up by radio. "Bad Is Bad" pretended to be blues; "I Want a New Drug" sounded naughty; "The Heart of Rock 'n' Roll" pandered to everyone who didn't like any music past 1977. The entire record— predictable, polished, inert—could have passed for the soundtrack of a TV commercial. With *Fore!*, Lewis was actually getting people to believe that "It's Hip to Be Square." *Small World* and *Hard at Play* were more of the same. — P.E.

JERRY LEE LEWIS

★★★★ **Jerry Lee Lewis (1958; Rhino, 1989)**
★★★ **Jerry Lee's Greatest! (1961; Rhino, 1989)**
★★★★ **The Greatest Live Show on Earth (Smash, 1964)**
★★ **The Golden Rock Hits of Jerry Lee Lewis (1967; Smash, 1987)**
★★★★★ **Jerry Lee Lewis' Original Golden Hits, Vol. 1 (Sun, 1969)**
★★★★★ **Jerry Lee Lewis' Original Golden Hits, Vol. 2 (Sun, 1969)**

★ ★ ★ ★	Jerry Lee Lewis' Rockin' Rhythm and Blues (Sun, 1969)
★ ★ ★	Jerry Lee Lewis' Golden Cream of the Country (Sun, 1969)
★ ★ ★ ★	A Taste of Country (Sun, 1970)
★ ★ ★ ★	Sunday Down South (Sun, 1970)
★ ★ ★	Ole Tyme Country Music (Sun, 1970)
★ ★ ★	There Must Be More to Love Than This (Mercury, 1970)
★ ★ ★ ★ ★	Monsters (Sun, 1971)
★ ★ ★ ★ ★	Jerry Lee Lewis' Original Golden Hits, Vol. 3 (Sun, 1971)
★ ★ ★ ★	The "Killer" Rocks On (Mercury, 1972)
★ ★ ★	The Session (Mercury, 1973)
★ ★ ★	Odd Man In (Mercury, 1975)
★ ★ ★	Boogie Woogie Country Man (Mercury, 1975)
★ ★ ★	Country Class (Mercury, 1976)
★ ★ ★ ★	Best of Jerry Lee Lewis, Vol. 2 (Mercury, 1978)
★ ★ ★	Jerry Lee Lewis (Elektra, 1979)
★ ★ ★ ★	Killer Country (Elektra, 1980)
★ ★ ★	When Two Worlds Collide (Elektra, 1980)
★ ★ ★	The Best of Jerry Lee Lewis (Featuring 39 and Holding) (Elektra, 1982)
★ ★ ★ ★ ★	18 Original Sun Greatest Hits (Rhino, 1984)
★ ★ ★ ★ ★	Milestones (Rhino, 1985)
★ ★ ★	Ferriday Fireball (Sun, 1986)
★ ★ ★ ★	20 Classic Jerry Lee Lewis Hits (Original Sound, 1986)
★ ★ ★ ★	Rare and Rockin' (Sun, 1987)
★ ★ ★	The Original Jerry Lee Lewis (Sun, 1988)
★ ★ ★	Rocket '88 (Tomato, 1989)
★ ★ ★	Heartbreak (Tomato, 1989)
★ ★ ★½	Live (Pair, 1989)
★ ★ ★ ★	Rare Tracks (Rhino, 1989)
★ ★ ★½	Killer: The Mercury Years, Volume One, 1963-1968 (Mercury, 1989)
★ ★ ★½	Killer: The Mercury Years, Volume Two, 1969-1972 (Mercury, 1989)
★ ★ ★½	Killer: The Mercury Years, Volume Three, 1973-1977 (Mercury, 1989)
★ ★ ★ ★ ★	Classic Jerry Lee Lewis (Bear Family import, 1989)
★ ★ ★	Best of Jerry Lee Lewis (Curb, 1991)

While Jerry Lee Lewis's behavior throughout his career has created the impression that what was sprung from Memphis by way of Ferriday, Louisiana, in 1956, was something unholy and vile, time has been Lewis's ally. Time hasn't tamed his image, of course, but it has allowed the record to be rolled back via the issuing of all of his nearly 300 Sun tracks, which reveal an artist of enormous stylistic range. His bedrock Sun recordings make the progression of his career seem logical; even if he hadn't been forced into it after becoming the scourge of mainstream America by marrying his 13-year-old cousin, torpedoing his rock & roll career in the process, Lewis's natural evolution would have been into country music. If there's anything surprising about Jerry Lee the country artist, it's that the basic rugged concept of his personality hasn't been altered by the trouble he's seen: the furor over his cradle-robbing; a puzzling tendency of his wives to die under mysterious circumstances; a battle with the bottle; unstable health; a hair-trigger temper that's landed him in one jam after another; and the ghost of Elvis hovering to remind the Killer that the one true King of Rock & Roll lived on Elvis Presley Boulevard in Memphis, Tennessee. He remains, as he said recently in a TV interview, "an old country boy, mean as hell."

The Sun recordings are available in various configurations encompassing greatest hits collections, original albums and rare tracks. For completists, the import Bear Family box, *Classic Jerry Lee Lewis*, is the *ne plus ultra* of Lewis retrospectives. Issued in 1989, and retailing for nearly $200, it encompasses 246 songs, virtually everything Lewis cut in the Sun studio. As a measure of Lewis's artistic reach, this set is staggering in showing the ease with which the artist handled any type of music that came his way. Traditional country ("Deep Elem Blues"), R&B ("Sixty Minute Man"), Dixieland ("When the Saints Go Marchin' In"), pop ("That Lucky Old Sun"), traditional Southern gospel (collected on the 1970 Sun album *Sunday Down South*), folk ("Goodnight Irene"), even minstrels ("Carry Me Back to Old Virginia"). Nearly everything is played with authority, and sung with utter conviction.

As an alternative to the big-ticket box set, numerous greatest-hits collections, as well as assemblages of rare tracks, dot the market. It's important to key in on the authentic single releases rather than remakes of the originals or album tracks of hit titles. The best place to begin is Rhino's *18 Original Sun Greatest Hits*, on which the pumping piano and wild voice are present in all their raucous glory. Similarly, any of the Sun hits packages are worthwhile investments. The must-to-avoid is Smash's *Golden Rock Hits* of *Jerry Lee Lewis*, which consists of remakes of "Whole Lotta Shakin' Goin' On," "Great Balls of Fire," "Breathless," "High School Confidential" and the rest that pale in comparison to the glorious Sun takes. *Jerry Lee Lewis* and *Jerry Lee's Greatest!* are reissues of Lewis's two long-playing Sun albums; in truncated form these demonstrate the Killer's versatility early on: the former includes among its tracks "Jambalaya," "Matchbox" and "Goodnight Irene," as well as "High School Confidential" and "Whole Lotta Shakin' Goin' On"; the latter wraps Fats Domino's "Hello Josephine," Hank Williams's "Cold, Cold Heart" and Barrett Strong's "Money (That's What I Want)" around "Great Balls of Fire" and other rockers. *Rare Tracks* is what it says it is.

In the '60s, a transition into country revived Lewis's career. Melancholy creeped in, but he made it cathartic ("What Made Milwaukee Famous [Has Made a Loser Out of Me]"), and he would often slip back into the rocker's mode ("Boogie Woogie Country Man"). One hesitates to give blanket approval to a body of work as substantial as Lewis's country recordings, but in fact the Mercury sides are solid and ingratiating. Three volumes of *Killer: The Mercury Years* anthologizes the best cuts from this period. The various live albums demonstrate that the Killer bowed to no one when it came to proving it all night. Rhino's *Milestones* is a must-have set that starts with Lewis's first Sun recording, "The End of the Road," hits all of the Sun highlights, and summarizes in concise fashion the Mercury years, concluding with "Middle Age Crazy." Excellent annotation provides essential background on Lewis's career through the years, and, whether by accident or design, the programming demonstrates the minor adjustments Lewis made in retooling himself for the country audience's consumption.

The Elektra years are spotty (those albums are currently out of print), but when Lewis gets it together he's hard to beat. *The Best of Jerry Lee Lewis (Featuring 39 and Holding)* is a good overview, but *Jerry Lee Lewis* is the most essential of these titles, and one of the best in Lewis's career. The tune selection runs from Arthur Alexander's "Every Day I Have to Cry" to the Dylan-Jacques Levy collaboration "Rita Mae" to Charlie Rich's "Who Will the Next Fool Be" to Lloyd Price's "Personality." Challenged by this material, Lewis digs with more zeal than he'd mustered since the Sun

days—his salacious, growling version of Jesse Stone's "Don't Let Go" opens the album in a rocking good way and things improve from there.

Have we need of mad men, that this fellow has been brought to play the mad man in our presence? Why yes, of course.
— D.M.

RAMSEY LEWIS
★★★½ The In Crowd (Columbia, 1965)
★★★ Blues for the Night Owl (1972; Columbia, 1981)
★★★½ The Best of Ramsey Lewis (1973; Columbia, 1981)
★★★ Golden Hits (Columbia, 1973)
★★★ Sun Goddess (Columbia, 1974)
★★★ Tequila Mockingbird (Columbia, 1977)
★★★ Les Fleurs (Columbia, 1979)
★★★ Three-Piece Suite (Columbia, 1981)
★★★½ Reunion (Columbia, 1982)
★★★ Keys to the City (Columbia, 1987)
★★★ Classic Encounter (Columbia, 1988)
★★★ The Greatest Hits of Ramsey Lewis (Chess, 1988)
★★★ Urban Renewal (Columbia, 1989)
★★★ Live at the Savoy (Columbia, 1982)
★★★ Electric Collection (Columbia, 1991)
WITH NANCY WILSON
★★★ The Two of Us (Columbia, 1984)
WITH BILLY TAYLOR
★★★ We Meet Again (Columbia, 1989)

Keyboardist Ramsey Lewis's jazz-pop hybrid is never as challenging as real jazz, and it's seldom as appealing as the pop songs he's enjoyed massive success in covering (Dobie Gray's "The In Crowd," the McCoys' "Hang On Sloopy," Stevie Wonder's "Living for the City")—but in its mix, it offers dependable, mild pleasure. Starting off as pianist in a standard jazz trio, Lewis demonstrated ultra-competent technique and commercial savvy, scoring hits with a pop audience few trad players managed to connect with (he was sort of the jazz counterpart to country's Floyd Cramer); Chess's *Greatest Hits* collects his early acoustic period (1962–1967), and it's nice, if unsurprising, music. Collaborating with Earth, Wind and Fire on *Sun Goddess* (1974), Lewis tackled fusion, making a sort of gentleman's agreement with unthreatening funk. *Tequila Mockingbird* found the player deeper into the fuzak bag—the record hit big, even if his electronic keyboard work was hardly ever inventive. Lewis continued along these lines for a very long time, only to emerge in 1989 with his strongest album since *Reunion* (with his original rhythm section): a fine acoustic collaboration with Billy Taylor, *We Meet Again* is two players turning in a no-frills set of jazz standards. — P.E.

GORDON LIGHTFOOT

★ ★ ★½ **If You Could Read My Mind (Reprise, 1970)**
★ ★ ★   **Sundown (Reprise, 1974)**
★ ★ ★   **Gord's Gold (Reprise, 1975)**
★ ★ ★   **Summertime Dream (Reprise, 1976)**
★ ★ ★   **East of Midnight (Warner Bros., 1986)**
★ ★½   **Gord's Gold, Volume II (Warner Bros., 1988)**

This Canadian songwriter first gained notice when several American artists successfully covered his material in the late '60s. Lightfoot's deep, easy voice and melodic knack made him a natural commercial crossover; he really didn't have to change much to attract a mass audience. *If You Could Read My Mind* is his best pop shot; the slight sentiments attached to the title song are offset by straight-up folksongs like "Sit Down Young Stranger"—Lightfoot's welcoming message to Canada's influx of Vietnam draft resisters. *Sundown*'s title track communicates the same romantic tang as "If You Could Read My Mind," but Lightfoot's reassuring tone sounds a little pat on the hit followup, "Carefree Highway." *Gord's Gold* packages his '70s hits with glossy remakes of folkier '60s songs like "Canadian Railroad Trilogy," and it's only partially satisfying. Perhaps "The Wreck of the Edmund Fitzgerald," from *Summertime Dream*, best captures Gordon Lightfoot in his role of Top Ten troubadour. As the string sections swell and crash, Lightfoot details the sinking of a Great Lakes freighter. By picking an event from the year before rather than a history book, he reasserted folk music's original, communicative function. Unfortunately, Lightfoot's second anthology is almost entirely given over to remakes. Even the version of "Edmund Fitzgerald" on *Volume II* floats by in a soupy, laid-back haze. — M.C.

LIL LOUIS

★ ★ ★ **From the Mind of Lil Louis (Epic, 1989)**

Back before the English turned "acid house" into a synonym for ecstacy-fueled self-indulgence, what the term referred to was a sense of sonic experimentalism that would push house music beyond the usual boundaries of soul-derived dance music.

Which is pretty much the approach taken by Lil Louis, whose aural exercises run the gamut from low-key balladry to Prince-style mysticism. Be advised, however, that the version of "French Kiss" included on *From the Mind of Lil Louis* is not the exquisitely minimal single version, which stretched a two-beat rhythm pattern into a ten-minute masterpiece, but a tricked-up remake that pads out the original groove with unnecessary vocals and corny saxophone obbligatos. — J.D.C.

DAVID LINDLEY

★ ★ ★ ★ **El Rayo X (Asylum, 1981)**
★ ★ ★   **Win This Record (Asylum, 1982)**
★ ★ ★   **Very Greasy (Elektra, 1988)**

Jackson Browne fans are well aware of his longtime lead guitarist's multi-instrumental knack; for anybody else, David Lindley's wildly diverse solo debut, *El Rayo X*, will come as a leftfield delight. He tosses blues and reggae into the mix alongside the expected folk and country influences, casually dispensing his virtuosity like an even-spacier Ry Cooder. The followup albums add tastes of New Orleans and funk, impeccably executed, but the obscure cover versions and unfocused vocalizing make all the fun sound a bit contrived after a while. — M.C.

LINEAR

★ ★ **Linear (Atlantic, 1990)**

Linear is unlike most Miami-sound bubblegum acts in that it relies upon photogenic young guys (not photogenic young women) to fill in the vocal parts. Unfortunately, that's the only difference. — J.D.C.

MANCE LIPSCOMB

★ ★ ★½ **Texas Sharecropper and Songster (Arhoolie, 1960)**
★ ★ ★   **Texas Songster, Vol. 2 (Arhoolie, 1964)**
★ ★ ★   **Mance Lipscomb, Texas Songster, Vol. 3 (Arhoolie, 1964)**
★ ★ ★   **Texas Songster in a Live Performance (Arhoolie, 1966)**
★ ★ ★   **Mance Lipscomb, Texas Songster, Vol. 4 (Arhoolie, 1967)**
★ ★ ★   **Mance Lipscomb, Texas Songster, Vol. 5 (Arhoolie, 1970)**
★ ★ ★   **Mance Lipscomb, Texas Songster, Vol. 6 (Arhoolie, 1974)**
★ ★ ★   **You'll Never Find Another Man Like Mance (Arhoolie; 1978)**
★ ★ ★ ★ **Texas Songster (Arhoolie, 1989)**

With its 22 selections combining Mance
Lipscomb's debut album and a portion of
the classic *Vol. 3, Texas Songster*, from
1989, provides the best introduction to this
classic bluesman. Born in 1895, the
guitarist-singer not only chronicled the myth
of the blues, but lived it—he took time for
his music only after 12 hours a day of
sharecropper's field work. In the 50 years
before he first entered a studio, however,
he'd amassed a vast canon of ballads and
jubilees, traditional country blues and
vintage period pieces. "Sugar Babe," "Ella
Speed," "Angel Child" and "I'm Looking
for My Jesus" reveal with particular
effectiveness the subtlety of his
conversational singing style and slide guitar
work, but all of his albums are very strong.
Almost always, Lipscomb recorded with no
accompaniment other than his guitar—and
the music he made, whether witty, racy,
haunting or rocking, retains the power of
utter directness. — P.E.

LISA LISA & CULT JAM
  ★ ★ **Lisa Lisa & Cult Jam with Full
     Force (Columbia, 1985)**
  ★ ★ ★ **Spanish Fly (Columbia, 1987)**
  ★ ★ ★ **Straight to the Sky (Columbia,
     1989)**
  ★ ★ ★ ★ **Straight Outta Hell's Kitchen
     (Columbia, 1991)**
Lisa Lisa got her break the old-fashioned
way—an outstanding indie record that
sounded unlike anything else on the radio.
In her case, the hit was "I Wonder If I Take
You Home," a single more noteworthy for
its lyrics (a club-conscious update of "Will
You Love Me Tomorrow") than for the
perfunctory Latin hip-hop groove or Lisa
Lisa's engagingly amateurish vocal.
Fortunately, *Lisa Lisa & Cult Jam with Full
Force* is more polished than the single;
though the material is ephemeral, the
performances are solid, with Lisa Lisa
showing unexpected vocal power on the
ballad "All Cried Out." The songwriting
improves significantly on *Spanish Fly*,
particularly with "Head to Toe," a canny
update of '60s girl-group conventions, and
the effervescent "Lost in Emotion." But it's
Straight to the Sky that finds the group
truly coming into its own. Not only is Lisa
Lisa's singing stronger and more soulful,
capably handling the funk feel of "Just Git
It Together," but the songs are also a step
forward, offering everything from the
hard-core street sound of "U Never Nu
How Good U Had It" to the
semi-psychedelic "Little Jackie Wants to Be

a Star." *Straight Outta Hell's Kitchen*
maintains that strategy, but changes tactics
somewhat by bringing in club heroes David
Cole and Robert Clivillés to produce half
the album (Full Force, as usual, does the
rest). Predictably, the C+C tracks are
danceably insistent, but what ultimately
carries the likes of "Let the Beat Hit 'Em"
and "Something 'Bout Love" are the vocals,
which find Lisa Lisa cutting loose with the
full-throated fury of a true diva. — J.D.C.

LITTLE ANTHONY AND THE
IMPERIALS
  ★ ★ ★ **Best of Little Anthony and the
     Imperials (Rhino, 1989)**
In a business where even the best groups
have a limited lifespan, Little Anthony and
the Imperials have the distinction of having
had not one, but two lives. Coming out of
the fertile Brooklyn doo-wop scene, the
group began life as the Duponts and
recorded a few sides with a superb backing
band that included Mickey Baker on guitar,
Sam Taylor on sax, Panama Francis on
drums, and Dave "Baby" Clowney on
piano. When the Duponts' records flopped,
lead singer Anthony Gourdine sailed off for
more promising shores. He joined the
Chesters, who auditioned for and were
signed to End Records, and then had their
name changed to the Imperials. In 1958
their first session produced a million-selling
single, "Two People in the World" b/w
"Tears on My Pillow," featuring Gourdine's
high, trembling, feminine voice singing lead.
Disc jockey Alan Freed broke the record on
his New York radio show, and began
crediting it to Little Anthony and the
Imperials. A followup was hard to come by,
though. The group cut a new song that Neil
Sedaka had brought to them, "The Diary,"
but when End delayed releasing it, Sedaka
cut it himself. It became his first hit single,
while the group's version, hastily released as
Sedaka's climbed the charts, was DOA. A
year later a bopping novelty song, "Shimmy
Shimmy Ko-Ko-Bop," hit the Top Thirty
and seemed to breathe new life into the
quartet (the song is also a historical
footnote in rock history as the last record
Alan Freed played before announcing his
resignation on the air in 1960, at the height
of the payola scandal hearings). Instead,
more hard times followed.
  In 1961, Little Anthony and the Imperials
went their separate ways, but also failed to
find success apart from each other. Enter
Teddy Randazzo, one of the most vacuous
of the '50s teen idols who sang lead in a pop

monstrosity called the Three Chuckles and acted, if you can call it that, in several of the cheapo rock jukebox musicals of the time. But he also learned his way around a recording studio, and along the way became an adept songwriter to boot. When Gourdine reunited with the Imperials under Randazzo's aegis, the results were stupendous. On the strength of four successive Randazzo-penned and -produced Top Twenty singles, Little Anthony and the Imperials were propelled to hard-earned stardom at a time when British bands had taken over the charts. The songs were real weepers, but Gourdine used his unusual voice to impart pain even as he struck a cool stance that abrogated self-pity. Those four songs—"I'm on the Outside (Looking In)," "Goin' Out of My Head," "Hurt So Bad," "Take Me Back"—remain among the most identifiable of the decade, and Randazzo's ornate production techniques provided a bridge between R&B and the slicker soul sound evolving at Motown. This package has all the hits mentioned above, some miscalculations ("The Diary"), some flops, as well as a rare track co-written by Gourdine and Sam Cooke, "I'm Alright"— in short, all you need to know about Little Anthony and the Imperials.   —D.M.

LITTLE FEAT

★★★★ **Little Feat (Warner Bros., 1971)**
★★★★½ **Sailin' Shoes (Warner Bros., 1972)**
★★★★★ **Dixie Chicken (Warner Bros., 1973)**
★★★★ **Feats Don't Fail Me Now (Warner Bros., 1974)**
★★★½ **The Last Record Album (Warner Bros., 1975)**
★★★ **Time Loves a Hero (Warner Bros., 1977)**
★★★★ **Waiting for Columbus (Warner Bros., 1979)**
★★★ **Down on the Farm (Warner Bros., 1979)**
★★★★ **Hoy Hoy (Warner Bros., 1981)**
★★★ **Let It Roll (Warner Bros., 1988)**
★★★ **Representing the Mambo (Warner Bros., 1989)**
★★★ **Shake Me Up (Morgan Creek, 1991)**

Lowell George dominates the earliest Little Feat albums; his nimble slide-guitar runs and honey-in-the-sludge vocals run over patches of blues, country, beatnik poetry and rock. At a time when most rockers were busy cultivating eccentricities and sub-dividing into strict genres, Little Feat melted its various influences into a big, lazy-rolling ball of wax. Though the band isn't at all "country rock," in musical terms, George does address some traditional subject matter on *Little Feat*—from a slightly skewed hippie perspective. "Willin'," "Truck Stop Girl" and "Brides of Jesus" all testify to George's haltingly tender way with a slow one; the Howlin' Wolf medley ("Forty-Four Blues/How Many More") features a guitar showdown between George and Ry Cooder. *Sailin' Shoes* pits clearer melodies against more focused songwriting; "Easy to Slip" and the beefed-up "Willin' " are catchy enough to be pop songs, with no appreciable loss of passion. Even the rootsy rave-ups are blunter, more focused: "Apolitical Blues" and "Teenage Nervous Breakdown" reveal a gleaming sardonic edge. Both the title track and "Trouble" assert George's reflective power, while "Cold, Cold, Cold" and "Tripe Face Boogie" show some of the band's propulsive flair.

A lineup change right before *Dixie Chicken* resulted in a fortified, funkified Litte Feat. The addition of bassist Kenny Gradney, conga player Sam Clayton and guitarist Paul Barrère expanded the band's rhythmic base, freeing George to pursue his elusive lyrics and snakey solos. On the title track and "Fat Man in the Bathtub," Lowell rocks on top of a mountainous groove; "Two Trains" is pulled along by a haunting guitar echo. The version of Allen Toussaint's "On Your Way Down" hits a deep stride; the Little Feat of previous albums probably couldn't have pulled off this graceful, melancholic strut.

Feats Don't Fail Me Now exhibits all the benefits and detriments of heavy touring. Tight as a high-tension wire by this point, Little Feat detonates the revamped "Cold, Cold, Cold/Tripe Face Boogie" showstopper. Their reputation as a live band was well-earned; see *Waiting for Columbus*, recorded a couple of years later, for further proof. The downside comes on tracks like "Rock and Roll Doctor," "The Fan" and "Oh Atlanta," where salty-fresh instrumental riffs are paired with stale "life on the road" lyrics. Pianist Bill Payne lays down supple, jazzy patterns on *Feats'* delectable "Skin It Back," but the band's subsequent move toward the danceable end of jazz-rock fusion proved to be a serious misstep.

George's gradual retreat from the singing and songwriting frontline didn't help, either.

He contributes two gems to *The Last Record Album* ("Down Below the Borderline" and "Long Distance Love"), though Paul Barrère's "All That You Dream" may be this inconsistent album's best cut. *Time Loves a Hero* piles on the synthesizer-enhanced fusion jams; at least "Old Folks Boogie" gets there, soon enough. Lowell George died in 1979; his tunes ("Kokomo," "Six Feet of Snow" and "Be One Now") are heartbreaking standouts on *Down on the Farm*. It's hard to say what direction George might have pursued outside Little Feat. *Thanks I'll Eat It Here* is a genial, if directionless solo debut; Lowell's burly voice shines on the Ann Peebles and Rickie Lee Jones covers, however. He thrived on making apparent contradictions sound completely natural, right up 'til the end.

Hoy Hoy offers a meaty sampler of Little Feat's prime cuts, though the first four albums constitute a better value for the boogie-hungry classic-rock consumer. Replacing George with former collaborator Fred Tackett and Pure Prairie League founder Craig Fuller, the latter-day Little Feat pumps out a cheerfully forgettable stew consisting of Southern rock and New Orleans R&B ingredients. If nothing else, Little Feat is still a reliable live act; those old George-penned chestnuts are damn near indestructible. — M.C.

LITTLE RICHARD

★★★★ **Here's Little Richard (1957; Specialty, 1991)**
★★★ **Little Richard (1958; Specialty, 1991)**
★★★ **The Fabulous Little Richard (1959; Specialty, 1991)**
★★★★★ **His Biggest Hits (1959; Specialty, 1991)**
★★★★★ **Little Richard's Grooviest 17 Original Hits (1959; Specialty, 1991)**
★★★ **It's Real (Lection/Polygram, 1962)**
★★★ **Well Alright! (1970; Specialty, 1991)**
★★★★ **The Essential Little Richard (Specialty, 1985)**
★★★★★ **18 Greatest Hits (Rhino, 1985)**
★★★ **Shut Up! A Collection of Rare Tracks (1951–1964) (Rhino, 1988)**
★★★★★ **The Specialty Sessions (Specialty, 1990)**
★★★ **Little Richard/Roy Orbison/Rock Legends (RCA, 1990)**
★★★★★ **The Georgia Peach (Specialty, 1991)**

★★★ **The Second Coming (Reprise, NA)**
★★★★ **The Rill Thing (Reprise, NA)**

By this time the basic facts and claims about Little Richard Penniman are well known and, on record, now well documented, thanks to an ambitious reissue program on Specialty's part. All of Little Richard's Specialty albums are now available in their original packaging—vinyl even—and original song selection. So are numerous collections of the songs that form one of the foundations of rock & roll—"Rip It Up," "Long Tall Sally," "Keep A-Knockin'," "Lucille," "Jenny Jenny," "Tutti Frutti," "Good Golly, Miss Molly" and "Ready Teddy." Pause and consider that the Quasar of Rock recorded these Olympian moments, which have influenced each succeeding generation of rock artists and will continue doing so until the planet destroys itself, in a two-year period dating from September 1955 to October 1957, when Penniman had a religious conversion and retired from rock & roll to study for the ministry. Ranking these collections is something of a problem, because in any setting the hits retain their emotional pull and historical resonance. Those so inclined will find in these tracks more fuel for the argument that New Orleans was the birthplace of rock & roll, as many of Penniman's sessions were cut in the Crescent City with then-unknown musicians who were inventing something new virtually every time they picked up their instruments. So indeed, consumers will get their money's worth from *His Biggest Hits*, *Little Richard's Grooviest 17 Original Hits*, *The Essential Little Richard*, *18 Greatest Hits*, and *The Georgia Peach*, with the latter having an edge over the other titles because of its splendid annotation by Billy Vera. Still the music carries the day, and all are legitimate classics.

If that is the case, there should be an extra star for *The Specialty Sessions*, because it is the rare box set that can be enjoyed by completists, historians, and casual fans alike. This is, as the title suggests, everything Penniman put on tape for the Specialty label, from previously unreleased demo sessions in February of 1955 before he was signed, to sessions cut in 1964 when Penniman was making the first of his many comebacks. In between are all the famous songs, alternate takes, demos, false starts, the movie version of "The Girl Can't Help It," even commercials Penniman cut for Gene Nobles's "Royal Crown Hairdressing." In addition, each disc in this three-CD collection comes with a well-researched booklet explaining the who, what, why, when, where, and how of the sessions, as well as keeping track of Penniman's career as limned by the disc in question. To say this is the most important work Penniman has done in his long career is to state the obvious; to say that it ranks with the most important work by any of rock's pioneers may also be stating the obvious, but it needs to be said anyway simply to emphasize the long shadow these songs cast.

What has happened in recent years, though, is the release of material Penniman cut before he ever convinced Specialty owner Art Rupe to take him seriously as well as some of the material he recorded after leaving Specialty. Penniman did not come out of a vacuum in Macon, Georgia, and help create the style and sound of early rock & roll. His career began in 1951, while he was still in his teens, traveling with B. Brown's band and various minstrel shows. On the style front, Penniman, who often performed in drag or in pancake makeup, found his models in Billy Wright, a Savoy recording artist who favored makeup, mascara and a multi-level pompadour; and in a strange character named Esquerita, he of the mile-high pompadour and unconventional piano technique. In October of 1951 and January of 1952 Penniman made his first recordings, eight tracks cut in Atlanta for RCA Victor with producer Steve Sholes, who would go on to produce Elvis Presley's first RCA sessions. After being out of print almost from the time of their release, these sides are once again available, on RCA's *Rock Legends* disc, along with seven tracks from Roy Orbison's brief stay at the label. Favoring jump blues and blues ballads, Penniman reveals a forceful, emotional vocal style; the problem was, it wasn't *his* vocal style. On the jump blues he's a dead ringer for Roy Brown; on the slower material, he affects the nasal tone of Esther Phillips.

When his RCA recordings flopped, Penniman headed to Houston and joined the Tempo Toppers, with whom he recorded one session for the Peacock label. Three of the tracks featured Johnny Otis's band, and found Penniman approaching the distinctive voice he would spring on the unsuspecting public in 1955. Also long out of print, four of the Peacock tracks are available on Rhino's *Shut Up!* collection, which also includes one of the RCA tracks, as well as sessions cut in the early '60s for Mercury, Atlantic, Little Star and Vee Jay. As for the latter label, the two cuts represented, "Hound Dog" and "Whole Lotta Shakin' Goin' On," include Jimi Hendrix (then known as Maurice James) on guitar.

From the gospel years comes the out-of-print Lection release, *It's Real*, which finds Penniman back to his Roy Brown voice for the most part; when he's not sounding like Brown, he's a dead ringer for Mahalia Jackson or Smokey Robinson. In the mid-'60s Penniman mounted another comeback, but these years are, unfortunately, lost to history at the moment. Enterprising souls should be on the alert for two out-of-print Reprise albums, *The Rill Thing* and *The Second Coming*. The former, recorded in Muscle Shoals and produced by Penniman, features the rousing "Freedom Blues," which put Penniman back on the charts briefly in 1970. A genuinely great moment—impassioned, wailing, relentless—it compares favorably to the classic Specialty sides. *The Second Coming* encapsules Penniman's many incarnations in songs that reflect his grounding in gospel, R&B, and New Orleans. Teamed with his Specialty producer "Bumps" Blackwell as well as many of the New Orleans stalwarts who played on his incendiary sides, Penniman extends '50s traditions into '70s music. When it's all said and done, one must conclude that the Quasar of Rock was quite a singer, period. Shut up! . . . and listen. — D.M.

LITTLE RIVER BAND

    ★★   **Little River Band (Capitol, 1976)**
    ★★½ **Diamantina Cocktail (Capitol, 1977)**
    ★★½ **Sleeper Catcher (Capitol, 1978)**
    ★★   **First Under the Wire (Capitol, 1979)**
    ★½ **Backstage Pass (Capitol, 1980)**
    ★★   **Time Exposure (Capitol, 1981)**
★★★½ **Little River Band/Greatest Hits (Capitol, 1982)**
    ★½ **The Net (Capitol, 1983)**
    ★   **Playing to Win (Capitol, 1985)**
    ★   **No Reins (Capitol, 1986)**
    ★½ **Monsoon (MCA, 1988)**
    ★½ **Get Lucky (MCA/Curb, 1990)**
    ★½ **Worldwide Love (Curb, 1991)**

Combining the country-ish close harmonies of the Eagles with a tuneful, light-rock instrumental approach, the Little River Band produced a sound that had tremendous commercial potential but only minimal artistic value. With Glenn Shorrock singing lead and Graham Goble doing most of the writing, both *Little River Band* and *Diamantina Cocktail* take what could be described as a diet cola approach to country rock—it's a little too sweet and has no nutritional value, but it goes down easy and tastes almost like the real thing. *Sleeper Catcher*, *First Under the Wire* and *Time Exposure* find the band creeping ever closer to an MOR sound, which makes the songs seem sappier than ever, but made the band a massive success in the U.S. "Reminiscing" (from *Sleeper*), a lush ballad in which the band waxes nostalgic over an era none of its members are old enough to remember, is typical. The *Greatest Hits* album covers most of this era's highlights with minimal fuss; *Backstage Pass* is live, but not terribly lively.

Shorrock left to pursue a solo career in 1982, and the band recorded three drearily forgettable albums—*The Net*, *Playing to Win* and *No Reins*—with singer John Farnham. By '87 and *Monsoon*, Shorrock was back, Farnham was out, and the band had regained much of its old sound. But without anything resembling hit material, there's little to recommend it or its successors, the marginally catchier *Get Lucky* and *Worldwide Love*. — J.D.C.

LITTLE VILLAGE
★ ★ ★ **Little Village (Reprise, 1992)**
Little Village, released at the onset of 1992, reunites the band that recorded John Hiatt's *Bring the Family* album. Ry Cooder, Nick Lowe, Jim Keltner and Hiatt run through a far less distinct set of songs than on the previous work. — M.C.

LIVING COLOUR
★ ★ ★ ★½ **Vivid (Epic, 1988)**
★ ★ ★ ★½ **Time's Up (Epic, 1990)**
★ ★ ★ ★ **Biscuits (EP) (Epic, 1991)**
A lot of hard-rock acts imitate Led Zeppelin, but Living Colour is one of the few that has managed to emulate the group. Instead of slavishly copping licks from the Zep catalog, what Living Colour appropriates is the band's eclecticism and eagerness to experiment, a combination that keeps it from falling victim to the clichés that make most metal so predictable.

After all, how many other hard-rock acts would open an album with a soundbite from Malcolm X? But that's exactly how *Vivid* begins, and not only does the quote fit neatly into the sound and sensibility of "Cult of Personality," it nicely balances the song-ending samples of JFK and FDR. More interesting than the song's message, however, is its method, for "Cult of Personality" happily augments its bluesy power-riffing with modal asides that augment the melody without diminishing the aural impact. Of course, it helps that the band's founder, Vernon Reid, built his reputation as a jazz guitarist, and that the rhythm section is as at home with funk beats as metal stomps. But *Vivid* is full of unexpected left turns, from the Beach Boys bridge in "I Want to Know" to the James Brownisms of "What's Your Favorite Color?" to the furious, fusion-style intro to "Desperate People." Best of all, the band backs its musical vision with insight, offering pointed, perceptive social commentary through songs like "Funny Vibe" and "Open Letter (To a Landlord)."

With *Time's Up*, Living Colour doesn't just maintain its initial momentum, but actually picks up speed. Musically, the band casts an even wider net, opening the album with a nod to the Bad Brains ("Time's Up") and bringing in such guests as Little Richard, Maceo Parker and Queen Latifah. Accordingly, its best moments are absolutely stunning: "Elvis Is Dead" is a meditation on the Lord of Graceland; "Type" is a thought-provoking attack on the power of image over substance; while "Love Rears Its Ugly Head" is a modern blues, a song about sex and fear and desire that's as real as life itself. And though there's nothing new on *Biscuits*—a live "Desperate People," a leftover original from *Time's Up* and three covers—it's worth hearing if only for the band's crunchy remake of Al Green's "Love and Happiness" and Reid's incendiary take on Hendrix's "Burning of the Midnight Lamp." — J.D.C.

L.L. COOL J
★ ★ ★½ **Radio (Def Jam/Columbia, 1985)**
★ ★½ **Bigger and Deffer (Def Jam/Columbia, 1987)**
★ ★ ★ **Walking With a Panther (Def Jam/Columbia, 1989)**
★ ★ ★ ★ **Mama Said Knock You Out (Def Jam/Columbia, 1990)**
Following fast on Run-D.M.C.'s trail, James Todd Smith roared out of Queens, New York, with a Kangol brim and his *Radio* cranked to 10. "I Can't Live Without My Radio" establishes his rap persona: L.L. Cool J is cocksure and quick-witted, but he also comes equiped with disarming frankness and a winning sense of humor. He freely admits the boom box drives pedestrians nuts—even if he wouldn't dream of turning it down. His debut pumps nonstop; "Reduced by Rick Rubin" reads the cover, and that's about right. *Radio* boils funk and heavy-metal riffs down to a

potent essence, and L.L. capitalizes on it. Raps like the withering "That's a Lie" display a verbal flair and inventiveness that's still uncommon.

Bigger and Deffer collapses under the sophomore strain—Busier and Dumber might be closer to the truth—though the crossover hit "I Need Love" represents the first, and most satisfying, example of "ballad rap." ("L.L. Cool J," after all, is short for "Ladies Love Cool James.") *Walking With a Panther* pares down the cartoon samples and toughens the funk. L.L. reasserts himself with some feisty assaults, though his incessant boasting grates after a while. It's hard to tell if "Big Ole Butt" celebrates or lampoons macho sexuality; L.L.'s expertly paced narrative flow and the seductive rhythm track don't give you much chance to think. Two steps forward, one step back: overall, *Panther* is a little frustrating.

Mama Said Knock You Out lands a whopping blow. Once again, L.L. extends his range—and even displays a certain amount of maturity. He exhibits a hard-earned self-awareness on cuts like the devastating "Cheesy Rat Blues" and the hilarious "The Boomin' System," though there are no lectures or sermons here—not even on "The Power of God." Producer Marley Marl constructs firm musical support as L.L. revisits the scene of rap's past triumphs, acknowledges its present state of affairs and points to possible futures. Most concurrent pop and rock albums aren't nearly as ambitious—or as consistently satisfying—as *Mama Said Knock You Out*. — M.C.

RICHARD LLOYD
★★★★ **Alchemy (Elektra, 1979)**
   ★★★ **Field Of Fire (Mistlur import/Moving Target, 1986)**
Television's often self-effacing second guitarist set out in a notably different direction on his solo debut. *Alchemy* melds wistful, sometimes nostalgic romantic daydreams with rangy, taut electric guitar rhythms; this long-deleted minor gem prefigures every self-conscious, slightly off-key '80s "pop" band from the dB's and early R.E.M. on down. Lloyd fleshes out his own snaky playing with not one but two more strummers, though the band's layered attack never gets too cluttered. Rather than capitalize on the emerging new-wave scene he'd helped create, Richard Lloyd got into trouble with drugs and watched his career quickly bottom out. Happily, his bracing

clean-and-sober comeback, the 1986 independent release *Field of Fire*, alternates the expected mellow guitar heat with a folkier "heartland" sound somewhere between Tom Petty and Bryan Adams. Since then, Lloyd has made a number of appearances as a session guitarist for like-minded alternative rockers. They owe him. — M.C.

LOBO
   ★ **Lobo's Greatest Hits (Curb, 1990)**
  ★★ **Best of Lobo (Rhino, 1992)**
Lobo's "Me and You and a Dog Named Boo" and "I'd Love You to Want Me" were early-'70s saccharine piffle by a singer-songwriter who apparently thought Bread were the Beatles. Avoid the Curb compilation; if you're a fan, the Rhino anthology compiles all the hits (and misses). — P.E.

HANK LOCKLIN
  ★★ **Golden Hits (Plantation, 1977)**
Hank Locklin, a Florida-born country singer with a quintessential nasal whine of a voice, made a name for himself in the late '50s with a string of hit singles, one of which, "Please Help Me I'm Falling," is something of a country standard. Other than that, his best-known songs remain "Geisha Girl" (1957) and the 1958 tearjerker "Send Me the Pillow That You Dream On," which became a pop hit in 1962 when covered by Johnny Tillotson. Hardly an innovator, Locklin cut a sturdy presence on record; they don't make voices like his anymore. — D.M.

ROBERT JUNIOR LOCKWOOD
  ★★★ **Steady Rollin' Man (Delmark, 1973)**
  ★★★ **Hangin' On (Rounder, 1980)**
  ★★★ **Mr. Blues Is Back to Stay (Rounder, 1981)**
Born and bred in Delta blues, Robert Junior Lockwood is most easily identified as Robert Johnson's stepson and pupil. But Lockwood learned from Johnson and moved on to develop his own style and voice. Inspired by the single-string technique of Lonnie Johnson and the innovations of electric guitar pioneer Charlie Christian, Lockwood enlarged the blues he learned in Mississippi, explored jazz and charted new paths for the generation following him. His songs betrayed a less bedeviled, more resilient soul than was common among Delta bluesmen, but he delivered his stories in a full, deep voice with enough darkness in it to indicate Lockwood had overcome more than a few stones in his passway.

Steady Rollin' Man, recorded in 1973 with a trio backing Lockwood, has the feel of the Delta about it, and the sound of the urban blues Lockwood took up after moving to Chicago in 1950 and becoming a top session player. Of particular note is Lockwood's version of Robert Johnson's "Rambling on My Mind." It honors the original's sense of the moment, while striking a more languid pace that allows Lockwood time to develop some interesting single-string commentaries. *Hangin' On* and *Mr. Blues Is Back to Stay* team Lockwood with fellow Delta bluesman and former Johnson sideman Johnny Shines for two memorable albums that show both musicians taking the blues in all sorts of directions, south included. — D.M.

NILS LOFGREN

★ ★ ★ ★   **Nils Lofgren (1975; Rykodisc, 1988)**
★ ★ ½   **Cry Tough (A&M, 1976)**
★ ★ ★   **Back It Up!! (A&M, 1976)**
★ ★   **I Came to Dance (A&M, 1977)**
★ ★   **Night After Night (A&M, 1977)**
★ ★ ★   **Nils (A&M, 1979)**
★ ★   **Night Fades Away (MCA/Backstreet, 1981)**
★ ★ ★   **Wonderland (MCA/Backstreet, 1983)**
★ ★ ½   **Flip (Columbia, 1985)**
★ ★ ★   **The Best of Nils Lofgren (A&M, 1985)**
★ ★ ★ ★   **Classics Volume 13 (A&M, 1989)**
★ ★ ★   **Silver Lining (Rykodisc, 1991)**

A tiny dynamo, Nils Lofgren has been called "The Original Punk"—but he's hardly nasty enough for that. Instead, he's an adamant high-spirited rock & roller—his guitar style a direct spinoff of classic Chuck Berry—and a songwriter whose pop sense saves him from sounding like a roots revivalist. Barely 17 when he formed Grin, a pop-rock outfit whose critical success never paid off commercially, Lofgren gained early renown by playing piano on mentor Neil Young's brilliant *After the Goldrush* and by writing a few songs for Crazy Horse. At that time, however, Grin remained his chief concern, and he fronted that band throughout the course of its rocky career.

With Aynsley Dunbar on drums, Lofgren's self-titled debut was an absolute delight: solid rock delivered with infectious energy and great self-confidence. "Keith Don't Go," a paean to his idol, Rolling Stone Keith Richards, was bouyant and tough; "Back It Up" was a jukebox-perfect pop song—and the general strength of the entire album suggested a glorious future for Nils.

But he faltered. Enlisting Al Kooper as producer for *Cry Tough*, he turned in a set whose title track and "It's Not a Crime" rocked heartily, but throughout the record Lofgren's guitar work overwhelmed his songs. As a vocalist, he was more a master of attitude than a skilled singer—*Cry Tough* revealed that weakness. *I Came to Dance* was worse; the title song swings, but the rest of the record is aimless. At his best delivering punchy short numbers, he didn't help matters with a self-indulgent live double album, *Night After Night*.

By penning songs with Lou Reed, Lofgren redeemed himself. *Nils* was nearly as strong as his debut: the lyrics to "No Mercy" were graced with compassion; "Steal Away" was simple and powerful, and the lovely "Shine Silently" was the best song he'd written since "Back It Up."

Both *Night Fades Away* and *Wonderland*, however, were mediocre—again Nils played well, but his songs were formulaic. Enlisted then by Bruce Springsteen as lead guitarist for a round of the Boss's epic tours, he took a break from recording. With *Flip* he recovered some of the energy he always expended in concert (if only haphazardly in the studio)—but he has yet to live up to his early promise. — P.E.

LOGGINS AND MESSINA

★ ★ ★   **Sittin' In (Columbia, 1972)**
★ ★ ½   **Loggins and Messina (Columbia, 1972)**
★ ★   **Full Sail (Columbia, 1973)**
★ ★ ½   **On Stage (Columbia, 1974)**
★ ★   **Motherlode (Columbia, 1974)**
★ ★   **Native Sons (Columbia, 1976)**
★ ★ ½   **The Best of Friends (Columbia, 1976)**

Jim Messina was present at the birth of country rock. He'd worked as an engineer and producer in Los Angeles, joining Buffalo Springfield during its last days. After that seminal group split up, Messina helped found Poco with Richie Furay and pedal-steel player Rusty Young. Bolting from Poco after three albums, Messina hooked up with a folkie singer-songwriter named Kenny Loggins. He quickly put his studio experience to use; country is just another item on Loggins and Messina's mellow pop agenda, along with easy-listening balladry and nostalgic gunk. *Sittin' In* is the duo's most palatable effort by far; "Danny's Song" sports a winning melody and the (relatively) up-tempo "Vahevala" floats along like a breeze. But on "House at Pooh Corner," Loggins strikes a cloying note.

Loggins and Messina offers up a decent

soft-rocker ("Angry Eyes") alongside the egregious "Your Mama Don't Dance." *Full Sail* serves up the Vegas-ready "My Music," adding a touch of John Denver-style contemplation ("Watching the River Run") for, ahem, balance. *On Stage* is the requisite live double album; the hits dried up soon after that. *The Best of Friends* reflects the drop-off; most of the cuts on it come from albums one and two. Jim Messina released a pair of solo albums in the adult romance mode during the early '80s, though he's never come close to matching his ex-partner's ongoing presence on the charts. — M.C.

LONE JUSTICE

★ ★ ★   **Lone Justice (Geffen, 1985)**
★ ★ ★½ **Shelter (Geffen, 1986)**
Originally considered cowpunks because of their interest in country and rockabilly, Lone Justice is actually closer in sound (if not spirit) to U2. That's not to deny its country twang, for *Lone Justice* has more than its share of heartworn laments ("Don't Toss Us Away") and raucous honky-tonk numbers ("Working Late"), all of which showcase Maria McKee's powerhouse voice. But the band's penchant for sweeping gestures and grandiose sentiment tends to overwhelm the rest of the material, making it seem shallow and silly; of its rockers, only "Ways to Be Wicked" bears up under repeated listening. *Shelter* doesn't do much to rectify the problem. Apart from the anthemic "I Found Love," the band still seems unsure of how to deal with its tendency to overstatement, and winds up squandering the potential of tunes like the gentle "Wheels." — J.D.C.

LOOSE ENDS

★ ★ ★   **A Little Spice (MCA, 1985)**
★ ★ ★½ **Zagora (MCA, 1986)**
★ ★ ★½ **The Real Chuckeeboo (MCA, 1988)**
★ ★ ★   **Look How Long (MCA, 1990)**
Loose Ends' synthesized brand of modern R&B isn't completely smoothed-over: there aren't many loose ends on these painstakingly arranged and produced albums, but there is a consistent, satisfying edge. Building on the orchestrated Philly Soul tradition, producer Nick Martinelli and head End Carl "Macca" McIntosh create a lean, high-tech setting for Jane Eugene's sweet-and-sour vocal harmonizing and Steve Nichol's semi-classical keyboard shading. The debut album peaks with "Hanging on a String," perhaps the British trio's most fully realized achievement. But if *Zagora* and *The Real Chuckeeboo* can't quite match that

natural high, each album deepens and prolongs the buzz; this is dance 'n' romance music that actually sounds better when you sit and listen. *Look How Long* found McIntosh working with a variety of session players; while Jane Eugene is sorely missed, Loose Ends' exotic rhythms and original melodies won't be mistaken as computer samples. — M.C.

TRINI LOPEZ

★ ★ **The Best of Trini Lopez (Exact, NA)**
★ ★ **Trini Lopez (Bella Musica, NA)**
★ ★ **25th Anniversary Album (WEA Latina, 1991)**
Trini Lopez is a Texas-born pop-folk singer of Hispanic descent who recorded extensively for Reprise in the '60s and had a Top Ten hit in 1963 with a jaunty version of "If I Had a Hammer." *The Best of Trini Lopez* showcases a number of familiar songs from his early years, but the whole affair is devoid of substance. *Trini Lopez* and *25th Anniversary Album* feature newly recorded versions of "If I Had a Hammer" and "Lemon Tree" (another trademark Lopez song from the early '60s), as well as Latin songs and cover versions of early rock & roll hits such as "La Bamba" and "Kansas City." — D.M.

LOS LOBOS

★ ★ ★ ★   **. . . And a Time to Dance (Slash, 1983)**
★ ★ ★ ★   **How Will the Wolf Survive? (Slash/Warner Bros., 1984)**
★ ★ ★½ **By the Light of the Moon (Slash/Warner Bros., 1987)**
★ ★ ★ ★   **La Bamba (Slash/Warner Bros., 1987)**
★ ★ ★ ★   **La Pistola y El Corazón (Slash/ Warner Bros., 1988)**
★ ★ ★ ★½ **The Neighborhood (Slash/ Warner Bros., 1990)**
★ ★ ★ ★ ★ **Kiko (Slash/Warner Bros., 1992)**
What sets Los Lobos apart from most roots-rock acts isn't that it counts *musica norteño* among its sources, but that it treats that style as just part of the mix, and every bit the equal of R&B or the blues. In other words, they're interested in making music that's as catholic as their own tastes—and, for the most part, it is. . . . *And a Time to Dance* introduces the group with seven sweatily endearing dance tunes, which manage to cover everything from the classic rock & roll of Richie Valens's "Come On Let's Go" to the spirited two-step of "Anselma." Still, it's the accordion-spiked blues, "Let's Say Goodnight," that most clearly defines the band, and that rootsy

eclecticism is what ultimately drives *How Will the Wolf Survive?*. What makes this album so stunning isn't the way Los Lobos leaps easily from the snarling blues-rock of "Don't Worry Baby" to the giddy *norteño* groove of "Corrida #1" to the delicate string-band interplay of "Lil' King of Everything," but the way it maintains its identity in each.

With *By the Light of the Moon*, Los Lobos tries to broaden its lyrical perspective, moving from the realm of everyday romance to more explicitly ethical-political ground. But the writing seems forced for the most part, and the album is generally disappointing—though "One Time One Night" strongly recalls Dave Alvin's later writing for the Blasters, and "River of Fools" is lovely. The album is generally disappointing. Ironically, *By the Light of the Moon* was followed by the group's biggest success, a soundtrack album from the Richie Valens bio-pic, *La Bamba*, that mainly shows how well the group plays oldies; it includes the chart-topping remake of "La Bamba." Los Lobos also provided the film with several Mexican numbers, none of which made it onto the soundtrack album. Perhaps the Mexican traditional tunes collected on *La Pistola y El Corazón* are a sort of compensation; whatever the case, the album is a delight, true both to the spirit of the music and the sound of the group.

Apparently reinvigorated, the group sounds stronger than ever on *The Neighborhood*, its return to rock & roll. Some of that may have to do with the use of studio drummers to shore up Louis Pérez's often shaky time, but mostly it's the material, which finds the band showing all its strengths, whether in the muscular stomp of "Georgia Slop," the gentle strains of "Little John of God" or the giddy, multi-ethnic waltz of "The Giving Tree." *Kiko* is even more eclectic, freeing the band's compositional ideas through imaginative exotic settings that often say as much as any of the words. "Wake Up Delores," for instance, underscores the lyric's aura of mysticism through an eerie, otherworldly gloss on the mabaquanga; likewise "Kiko and the Lavender Moon" reinforces its saga of childhood slumber through a dark, sleepy pulse and ghostly sax harmonies. All told, it's a wonderfully inventive work, easily the band's best. — J.D.C.

LOUNGE LIZARDS
★★★ **The Lounge Lizards (Editions EG, 1981)**
★★½ **Live 79/81 (ROIR, 1985)**
★★★½ **No Pain for Cakes (Antilles, 1987)**
★★★★ **Live in Tokyo—Big Heart (Antilles, 1988)**
★★★½ **Voice of Chunk (1-800-44CHUNK, 1989)**
In their initial incarnation, the Lounge Lizards were a "fake jazz" combo, meaning that the group didn't follow the traditional chord-based discipline of jazz improvisation, but simply made whatever sounds seemed appropriate to the piece being played. Amateurish as the idea sounds, the music made on *The Lounge Lizards* is unexpectedly convincing—although that may have more to do with the direction of producer Teo Macero than with the Lizards themselves. After all, *Live 79/81* (recorded for the most part with the same band) is hardly as cogent.

Still, the lead Lizards—saxophonist John Lurie and his pianist brother Evan—hardly considered the group a joke, and introduced a more cohesive lineup with *No Pain for Cakes*. Good as they sound in the studio, this new ensemble sounds even stronger on *Live in Tokyo*, on which the input of trombonist Curtis Fowlkes and guitarist Marc Ribot seems especially eloquent. Unfortunately, this increase in quality was not greeted by an equivalent expansion in the group's audience, with the end result that *Voice of Chunk*—an album every bit as good as *No Pain for Cakes*—had to be released on the Luries' own label. — J.D.C.

LOVE
★★★½ **Love (Elektra, 1966)**
★★★★ **Da Capo (Elektra, 1967)**
★★★★ **Forever Changes (Elektra, 1968)**
★★★★ **Best of Love (Rhino, 1980)**
With lead singer-guitarist Arthur Lee as the group's weird mastermind, this L.A. quintet made three psychedelicized folk-rock classics in the mid-'60s. *Love* plays like strange, sloppy Byrds: Chiming guitars and dark vocals transmute Burt Bacharach's "My Little Red Book" from fluff into a sly threat; "Hey Joe" is all frenzied jangling; "Signed D.C." is a remarkably candid drug song; and, with titles like "A Message to Pretty" and "My Flash on You," Lee flourishes whimsically hip kiddie lyrics that find parallels only in Donovan or Prince. A critical success, the record engendered a cult that included Robert Plant and the Move; it also introduced, in Lee, a trippy visionary whose singular soul and private humor would preclude any mass acceptance. *Da Capo* is bolder: "7 and 7 Is" outright pounds; "Orange Skies" and "She Comes in Colors" are strange and lovely. Considered Love's *Sgt. Pepper's*, *Forever Changes* lives

up to its hype: horns and strings enliven Lee's best group of songs, and melody reigns, without at all softening the band's surreal power. These three albums are the essential Love: after making them, Lee worked with different players and never quite recaptured the fire. His out-of-print solo album, *Vindicator* (1972), is pretty wild, as such titles as "Ol' Morgue Mouth" and "Love Jumped Through My Window" suggest. — P.E.

LOVERBOY

★ ★ ★   **Loverboy (Columbia, 1980)**
★ ★ ★   **Get Lucky (Columbia, 1981)**
★ ★ ★   **Keep It Up (Columbia, 1983)**
★ ★ ★   **Lovin' Every Minute of It (Columbia, 1985)**
★ ★ ★   **Wildside (Columbia, 1987)**
★ ★ ★½ **Big Ones (Columbia, 1989)**

Compared to Loverboy, Journey seems like a blazingly innovative band and Billy Squier could pass for an idiosyncratic auteur, but that doesn't mean this Canuck quintet is bad. Rather, Loverboy's mega-hit '80s product proves the group to be masters of arena rock, a form within which originality is nearly a dirty word. Consistency, instead, is the measure of success for this genre, and guitarist Paul Dean and vocalist Mike Reno have been nothing but consistent, resourcefully recycling bar-band riffs and horny teen poetics with a true professionalism and a jocky pep.

Big Ones suffices in delivering whatever message these boys (and their medium) can deliver. And it's pretty neat. "Working for the Weekend," "Hot Girls in Love," "The Kid Is Hot Tonite" hit zero on the political-correctness meter, but they do kick efficiently and retain a certain suburban teen charm. The slower stuff, "Turn Me Loose," "Lovin' Every Minute of It" and "For You," is headbanger kitsch for aficionados only. — P.E.

LOVE AND ROCKETS

★ ★½   **Seventh Dream of Teenage Heaven (1985; RCA, 1988)**
★ ★ ★½ **Express (Big Time, 1986)**
★ ★ ★½ **Earth-Sun-Moon (Big Time, 1987)**
★ ★ ★ ★   **Love and Rockets (RCA, 1989)**

There are two pieces of trivia every Love and Rockets fan knows: First, that the group includes three of the four original members of Bauhaus (singer Peter Murphy being odd man out); and, second, that its name was swiped from Jaime and Gilbert Hernandez's award-winning alternative comic. Unfortunately, both factoids are largely irrelevant. Unlike the comic, this

Love and Rockets has nothing to do with Chicano culture, L.A. punk or mythical Central American small towns; and unlike Bauhaus, the group has little use for gothic doom-and-gloom, preferring instead simple, upbeat melodies and neo-psychedelic drones. That formula doesn't quite click on *Seventh Dream of Teenage Heaven*, an album that, for the most part, seems as forced and pretentious as its title. *Express*, however, kicked the band into gear by adding a dollop of dance music by the likes of "Kundalini Express" and "Ball of Confusion," and *Earth-Sun-Moon* further refined the approach by rechanneling that sense of groove into the hypnotic circularity of "Mirror People" and "No New Tale to Tell." Yet it was the harder-edged *Love and Rockets* that gave the band its greatest success, thanks to the Lou Reed–influenced "So Alive" (a Top Five hit in the U.S.), as well as the more gratingly insistent "No Big Deal" and "Motorcycle." — J.D.C.

LYLE LOVETT

★ ★ ★½ **Lyle Lovett (MCA/Curb, 1986)**
★ ★ ★ ★   **Pontiac (MCA/Curb, 1988)**
★ ★ ★   **Lyle Lovett and his Large Band (MCA/Curb, 1989)**
★ ★ ★½ **Joshua Judges Ruth (MCA/Curb, 1992)**

A sly purveyor of ultra-cool, postmodern country music, Lyle Lovett veers, sometimes intriguingly, sometimes puzzlingly, between ironic distancing from, and heartfelt homage to, his less self-conscious predecessors. Ambivalence, however, is his thematic keynote: his are story songs without resolution, sort of like fascinating trailers for odd movies. All the playing on his records is first rate—precise, but lacking in the studio chill of Nashville. As a vocalist, he's kind of a method actor: effectively, he tends less to sing than whisper, mumble and talk. "An Acceptable Level of Ecstasy (The Wedding Song)," "Cowboy Man" and "If I Were the Man You Wanted" are the standouts of his classy 1986 debut, *Lyle Lovett*, which is a more straightforward album than *Pontiac*, delivered the following year. *Pontiac*, however, is his best—"If I Had a Boat," is, among other things, a sweet, surreal tribute to Roy Rogers and Tonto; "Walk Through the Bottomland" is strange, moonlit poetry; "L.A. County" features his best singing and strongest melody. With *Lyle Lovett and His Large Band*, Lovett boosts his horn accompaniment, and experiments with swing. The songs sound great, but, with the exception of a deadpan cover of Tammy

Wynette's "Stand By Your Man," the singer's characteristic humor is muted. *Joshua Judges Ruth* is a wonderful return to form, emphasizing gospel-inspired arrangements and a modern take on biblical themes. — P.E.

THE LOVIN' SPOONFUL
★★★★ **Anthology (Rhino, 1990)**
Taking their band name from a Mississippi John Hurt blues verse, John Sebastian and Zal Yanovsky had been early-'60s New York folkies before founding the Spoonful, and heading toward radio triumph with effervescent pop. Notorious merrymakers onstage, the band settled down in the studio to combine folk and jug-band elements with hooks and melodies that were as accessible as anything the Brill Building had managed. "Did You Ever Have to Make Up Your Mind?" and "You Didn't Have to Be So Nice" were sweet teenage love songs; "Do You Believe in Magic?" remains one of the best—if sunniest—rock & roll anthems. A very casual, somewhat flat-voiced crooner, Sebastian sang with an aw-shucks sincerity that suited the Spoonful's engaging modesty. Finger-picking his guitar, Yanovsky kept the tunes airy and stirring. The fine "Summer in the City," with its effective drill-hammer and car-honk sound effects, was as heavy as the band ever got, its key signature remaining a sense of wistfulness, wonder and deliberate naivete. — P.E.

NICK LOWE
★★★★ **Pure Pop for Now People (Columbia, 1978)**
★★★★ **Labour of Lust (Columbia, 1979)**
★★★ **Nick the Knife (Columbia, 1982)**
★★★ **The Abominable Showman (Columbia, 1983)**
★★★ **Nick Lowe & His Cowboy Outfit (Columbia, 1984)**
★★★ **The Rose of England (Columbia, 1985)**
★★★ **Pinker and Prouder Than Previous (Columbia, 1988)**
★★★★ **Basher: The Best of Nick Lowe (Columbia, 1989)**
★★★★ **Party of One (Reprise, 1990)**
Most traditionalists aren't as articulate, inventive or funny as Nick Lowe. Lowe kept his eyes and ears open during his six-year stint with the pub rockers Brinsley Schwarz. He absorbed some of the oft-missed virtues of country songwriting—especially a fondess for double-edged wordplay—into a distinctly British sensibility. Lowe's acidic tendencies are balanced by revealing flashes of

you-fool-you lucidity. More often than not, Lowe baits the hooks with enough musical and emotional substance to keep listeners snapping for more.

Pure Pop for Now People isn't quite tongue-in-cheek, though it's close. Targeting the plethora of late-'70s rock styles, this survey course scores bull's-eye after bull's-eye, from bubblegum ("Tonight") to Bowie ("I Love the Sound of Breaking Glass") to punk-paced Chuck Berry ("Heart of the City"). Nick Lowe's solo debut asserts a refreshing, eclectic spirit alongside its grasp of authenticity. After producing a couple of albums for like-minded guitarist Dave Edmunds, Lowe joined him in Rockpile (along with second guitarist Billy Bremner and drummer Terry Williams). *Labour of Lust* captures that band's pure pop side; however, Lowe's silly love songs come equipped with memorable little stingers. Listen to the way Edmunds's riff mirrors the payoff line on "Crackin Up"— "I don't think it's funny no more." Or to the way Terry Williams's quick-stepping beat gooses the chorus of "Switchboard Susan." Or to a dozen other telling details. Despite the surface impression, this album cuts further than "Skin Deep." *Labour of Lust* also spawned Lowe's only bona-fide hit, "Cruel to Be Kind."

The '80s proved a rough time for Nick Lowe; his crafted gems started to seem ready-made from *Nick the Knife* onward. Lowe's more pronounced country bent and (relatively) sober take on marriage result in a good heart song (or two) on *Abominable Showman* and *Cowboy Outfit*. The best-of collection, *Basher*, rescues these tracks from Lowe's creeping case of the blahs. *Party of One* indicates that Lowe has shaken off the journeyman's curse, hopefully for good. Produced by Dave Edmunds (after a long estrangement), the overall sound is crisp and forceful. Lowe responds with a batch of sassy, bracing melodies. "All Men Are Liars," a combination of '70s wit and '80s irony, feels like Lowe's truest shot since "Cruel to Be Kind." Of course, in 1990 it just bounced off the wall. Too bad: *Party of One* wouldn't disappoint a larger audience. — M.C.

LTD
★★★ **Classics Volume 27: LTD (Featuring Jeffrey Osborne) (A&M, 1988)**
Cut from the Earth, Wind and Fire cloth, LTD (Love, Togetherness and Devotion) weaves lightweight boogie with the romantic plaints of lead singer Jeffrey Osborne. The

results are pleasant, but nothing more. Osborne is a wily vocal seducer in the Teddy Pendergrass mode, though his material rarely rises to the occasion. "Love Ballad," LTD's 1976 chart breakthrough, also happens to be Osborne's least generic slow moment. The ballad-heavy *Classics* quickly descends to the level of "Make Someone Smile, Today!" LTD's uptempo disco-bound cuts sound a bit cobwebbed now, too. But the soulful mid-tempo strut of "(Every Time I Turn Around) Back in Love Again" and "Holding On (When Love Is Gone)" could still cause a heart flutter or two. Sifting the two bona-fide classics out of this hour-long CD requires some patience, however. — M.C.

L'TRIMM
★ ★ ★ ½ **Grab It! (Atlantic, 1988)**
★ ★ ★ **Drop That Bottom (Atlantic, 1989)**
★ ★ **Groovy (Atlantic, 1991)**
"Grab It," an innuendo-laden answer to Salt-n-Pepa's "Push It," may paint L'Trimm as unrepentant boy toys, but the giggly good nature of the duo's delivery keeps these raps from sounding like mere sexploitation. Campy and cute, but the formula wears pretty thin by *Groovy*.
— J.D.C.

BOB LUMAN
★ ★ **American Originals (Columbia, 1989)**
A Texas lad who seemed fatally fixated on looking and sounding like Elvis Presley, Luman emerged with rockabilly's last gasp and had a Top Ten pop hit in 1960, "Let's Think About Living," before his draft notice arrived and put him on ice for two years. He returned bent on conquering the country market, but always seemed to come up short on compelling material. One song looms large in his semi-legend: "Lonely Women Make Good Lovers," featuring a vocal that was both impassioned and tender. Nothing else here equals that peak moment, but if one song makes an entire album worthwhile, it's this one. — D.M.

FRANKIE LYMON & THE TEENAGERS
★ ★ ★ ★ ★ **Frankie Lymon & the Teenagers: For Collectors Only (Murray Hill, 1986)**
★ ★ ★ ★ ★ **Best of Frankie Lymon & the Teenagers (Rhino, 1989)**
If all you knew of Frankie Lymon was the wonderful performances on the 20-cut Rhino set, you'd come away with a mental picture of a teenage boy whose every sung note celebrated life. Even his more introspective, pained numbers—"Share," "Out in the Cold Again"—communicate a bright optimism. Indeed, when Lymon entered the public arena in 1956 at age 13, rock & roll had never seen anything quite like him. His face was a cherub's, but his eyes radiated an intelligence far beyond his years; his voice was a plaintive, malleable tenor that retained its clarity even when Lymon soared into the upper register; onstage he displayed the suave and charm of a wizened pro; he also developed some dazzling dance moves that had a measurable impact on the styles later developed for Motown artists; and he had a touch of the poet about him, too, possibly having written both sides of his group's first single. One of those songs is among the most famous and most performed in American popular music, "Why Do Fools Fall in Love." Its release in 1956 began an 18-month run of international stardom for Lymon and his friends from Manhattan's Washington Heights section who had changed their name from the Premiers to the Teenagers before their first record's release.

"Why Do Fools Fall in Love," issued on the independent Gee label, was a mammoth hit, peaking at Number Six on the pop charts, and catapulting the group into the upper echelons of entertainment's elite. They appeared on national TV shows, in movies, and performed for royalty in England; more important, Lymon and the Teenagers brought the doo-wop group harmony sound to mainstream America, adding to it a rock & roll beat and irrepressible enthusiasm. In addition to "Fools," the group's next three singles—"I Want You to Be My Girl," "I Promise to Remember" and "The ABCs of Love"—all hit the Top Fifty, a remarkable streak for independent label releases. The group continued producing some fine singles, but none had the chart success of the first four. By late '57, Gee's label executives had decided Lymon should be a solo act; the process of extricating him from the Teenagers was, for all intents and purposes, a career-smashing move. The Teenagers never had a hit without Lymon, and Lymon, who started off strong with the ebullient "Goody Goody," which hit Number 22, soon floundered himself. "Portable on My Shoulder" and "Thumb Thumb" on this set show that Lymon was in a good-rockin' groove in 1958, but his voice had begun to change. His last charted single, a remake of Thurston Harris's 1957 hit, "Little Bitty Pretty One," came in 1960, though Lymon's version had actually been cut two years earlier and released on his *Rock 'N' Roll* album. By 1959, Lymon's voice had lost its elasticity; he couldn't deliver the high, soaring notes, and seemed even to struggle for balance in the lower register. There are performances on the Murray Hill release that sound like anyone *but* Frankie Lymon. Rhino's collection ends with "Little Bitty Pretty One," though Lymon continued to record into 1961 without success. By that time he was battling heroin addiction, and his personal life was spiraling out of control as well, culminating in a mid-'60s arrest for stealing drums from a recording studio to finance his habit. A stint in the U.S. Army seemed to help him get his life together again, and his old label, Roulette (it had been started by Alan Freed as a pop subsidiary of Gee), responded by scheduling a recording session for him in February of 1968, when he was to be discharged from the army. The day before the session Lymon overdosed and died in his grandmother's apartment in New York. He was 25 years old.

The excellent liner notes and the songs on Rhino's *Best of* tell a good chunk of the Lymon story, and *Best of* is the only Lymon collection still in print. In 1986 the now-defunct Murray Hill label released a five-record boxed set containing 23 previously unreleased recordings by Lymon with and without the Teenagers, plus an exhaustive biographical booklet and complete sessionography. It's essential for anyone interested in the evolution of doo-wop into a commercially viable music as well as for its tragic march through the recorded chronicle of Lymon's rise and fall. Questions remain regarding the circumstances of Lymon's death and the authorship of "Why Do Fools Fall in Love" (it's credited to Lymon/Levy, the latter being Roulette's unsavory label boss Morris Levy, who bought the rights to the song from Lymon for $1500 in 1965, when Lymon was desperate for cash after being arrested in California). Highly recommended for its solid reporting on Lymon's latter days and the messy aftermath of a royalty dispute over "Fools" among Lymon's widow and ex-wives is Calvin Trillin's American Chronicles column in the February 25, 1991, issue of *The New Yorker*. Next to Clyde McPhatter, it would be hard to name another artist as gifted and influential as Lymon whose demise was so prolonged and so tragic. — D.M.

LORETTA LYNN

★ ★ ★ ★ ★   **Greatest Hits (MCA, 1968)**
★ ★ ★   **Coal Miner's Daughter (MCA, 1970)**
★ ★ ★ ★½   **Greatest Hits, Volume 2 (MCA, 1974)**
★ ★ ★½   **I Remember Patsy (MCA, 1977)**
★ ★ ★   **20 Greatest Hits (MCA, 1987)**
★ ★ ★ ★ ★   **The Country Music Hall of Fame: Loretta Lynn (MCA, 1991)**

WITH CONWAY TWITTY

★ ★ ★½   **We Only Make Believe (MCA, 1970)**
★ ★ ★ ★   **Lead Me On (MCA, 1971)**
★ ★ ★   **Very Best of Conway Twitty and Loretta Lynn (MCA, 1979)**

Loretta Lynn (née Webb) of Butcher Hollow, Kentucky, was a twenty-five-year-old housewife and mother when she cut her first record in 1960. Released on a tiny Canadian label, "Honky Tonk Girl" got the fledgling singer noticed in Nashville. By the mid-'60s, Lynn had officially arrived on Music Row: performing on the Grand Ole Opry, dueting with Ernest Tubb ("Mr. & Mrs. Used to Be") and, most important, scoring chart singles with weepers like "Success," on which the husband's fast-track career leads to domestic disaster. Something about Lynn's voice—perhaps her unfettered drawl and crystalline high notes—suits this sort of material. She may be waiting at home while her man indulges in "Wine, Women and Song," but Lynn hardly plays the role of understanding wife on her subsequent hits. "Don't Come Home a-Drinkin' (With Lovin' on Your Mind)" (1967) and "You Ain't Woman Enough" (1966) are propelled by her gutsy mixture of humor and indignation. Buttressed by pedal-steel guitar and a clanking railroad-trestle beat, she doesn't suffer fools—whether male ("Drinkin' ") or female ("Woman"). *Greatest Hits* charts her rise, including the tunes already mentioned and "Blue Kentucky Girl." *Greatest Hits, Volume 2* follows Lynn into the early '70s, when she kept the audacious singles coming fast and furious. "Fist City," "Wings Upon Your Horns" and "Your Squaw Is on the Warpath" make good on their comeuppance-threatening metaphors, while "Coal Miner's Daughter" and "You're Looking at Country" offer pungent, revealing slices of autobiography. "One's on the Way" pillories American class distinctions with cutting accuracy, though

Lynn takes the inevitable turn toward countrypolitan corn with "Love Is the Foundation." After *Greatest Hits, Volume 2,* her albums quickly became interchangeable. Maybe that's why they're mostly out of print, save for the stirring Patsy Cline tribute album (*I Remember Patsy*). Loretta Lynn and Conway Twitty recorded a long string of duets throughout the '70s as well; similarly, their earliest efforts are searing, guilt-drenched honky tonk cheating scenarios. *We Only Make Believe* and (especially) *Lead Me On* can still inspire heated are-they-or-aren't-they debates: the (usually) thwarted desire is downright audible in those teasing, frisky voices. Conway and Loretta's later hits sank into formula schmaltz as the decade wore on; the goony 1978 novelty "You're the Reason Our Kids Are Ugly" provides some needed comic relief on their rather spotty duet compilation. Though it's too short, the *Country Music Hall of Fame* album is the best available Lynn primer. Along with the bulk of both greatest-hits albums, you get the amazing 1975 birth-control manifesto "The Pill" and a handful of salvageable items from the mid-'70s. When Lynn identifies herself as the Real Thing on "You're Looking at Country," she's not bragging—just stating a fact.   — M.C.

GLORIA LYNNE
★ ★ I Wish You Love (Collectables, NA)
A jazz singer in the Sarah Vaughan mold, Lynne had a Top Thirty pop hit in 1964 with the melancholy "I Wish You Love," and cut several items that charted lower through 1965. Her husky contralto could imbue ballads with a haunting ambience, but wasn't well-suited to cutting loose on uptempo numbers. Hence an emphasis on ballads in her repertoire, which leads to a certain *ennui* after a while when songs start sounding alike. The 14 cuts on *I Wish You Love* include the title track and three other charted singles, as well as tasteful interpretations of "Try a Little Tenderness," "Perdido" and "Stella by Starlight."   — D.M.

JEFF LYNNE
★ ★ ★ Armchair Theatre (Reprise, 1989)
A modestly pleasing solo album from the driving force behind Electric Light Orchestra, *Armchair Theatre* exemplifies the sleek roots-rock Jeff Lynne perfected through his work with the Traveling Wilburys.   — M.C.

LYNYRD SKYNYRD
★ ★ ★ ★	(pronounced leh-nerd skin-nerd) (MCA, 1973)
★ ★ ★ ★	Second Helping (MCA, 1974)
★ ★ ★½	Nuthin' Fancy (MCA, 1975)
★ ★ ★	Gimme Back My Bullets (MCA, 1976)
★ ★ ★ ★	One More for the Road (MCA, 1976)
★ ★ ★ ★ ★	Street Survivors (MCA, 1977)
★ ★ ★	Skynyrd's First . . . and Last (MCA, 1978)
★ ★ ★ ★ ★	Gold and Platinum (MCA, 1979)
★ ★ ★	Best of the Rest (MCA, 1986)
★ ★ ★	Legend (MCA, 1987)
★ ★ ★	Southern by the Grace of God (MCA, 1988)
★ ★ ★	Skynyrd's Innyrds (MCA, 1989)
★ ★ ★	Lynyrd Skynyrd 1991 (Atlantic)
★ ★ ★ ★	Lynyrd Skynyrd (MCA, 1991)

If the Allman Brothers invented Southern rock at the dawn of the '70s, then Lynyrd Skynyrd perfected it as the decade wore on. These shaggy guitar troopers from Jacksonville, Florida, really weren't the unapologetic rednecks or wasted all-night jammers ("Freeeee Bird!") of popular description. Skynyrd boiled down its potent regional influences—blues, country, soul—into a heady, potentially crippling homebrew. They liked to play; those three lead guitars weren't just for show. But a taut command of rhythm drives even Skynyrd's lengthiest excursions. Overexposed as it might be, the studio version of "Free Bird" (from *[pronounced leh-nerd skin-nerd]*) climbs to a dizzying height.

Guitarists Allen Collins and Gary Rossington formed the nucleus of Skynyrd's frontline. Bassist Leon Wilkeson and guitarist Ed King (formerly of Strawberry Alarm Clock!) rounded out the sound. Lead singer Ronnie Van Zant provided the band's anchor; the gruff authority of his voice is matched by his forthright and forceful way with words. On *pronounced*, his take on Washington politics ("Things Goin' On") is as startlingly fresh as his views on local customs ("Mississippi Kid," "Poison Whiskey"). Producer Al Kooper adds pop keyboard sweetening to the slow-building "Tuesday's Gone" that sounds unnecessary; Skynyrd's tuneful guitar interplay provides just the right touch of sugar—and salt.

Second Helping served up the band's feisty hard-rock twang to a broad national audience. "Sweet Home Alabama" is the consummate Skynyrd platter; while the guitars sigh and sting like a stiff breeze, Ronnie Van Zant draws a line in the dirt. While Neil Young may have wounded his pride, Van Zant hardly sounds like a card-carrying George Wallace supporter on "The Ballad Of Curtis Lowe." Skynyrd's tribute to a black grocery store owner who played the blues underlines the crucial role music plays in kicking down racial barriers. Though songs about rock and life on the road quickly became clichéd in the'70s, Van Zant wrote some of the best, beginning with *Second Helping*'s searing "Workin' for MCA," reflective "Was I Right or Wrong" and cautionary "The Needle and the Spoon."

Nuthin' Fancy kicks off with further proof of Skynyrd's idiosyncracy; "Saturday Night Special," the band's hardest rocker, is also a full-bore assault against handguns. The rest of the album never exactly slacks off, but aside from that opener, Skynyrd seems to be repeating itself on tracks like "On the Hunt" and "Am I Losin.' " And that goes double for *Gimme Back My Bullets*: especially J.J. Cale's too-telling "I Got the Same Old Blues." While Skynyrd's musical strength hasn't diminished on these albums, the pressures of constant touring clearly have an effect on its creativity. That said, live albums don't get much more exciting than *One More From the Road*. With new guitarist Steve Gaines stepping in for Ed King, Skynyrd roars through a set of mostly earlier material and two wholly appropriate covers: Robert Johnson's "Crossroads" (with a touch of Cream) and Jimmie Rodgers's "T for Texas."

Street Survivors is even better than might have been expected. Gaines stimulated

Ronnie Van Zant's songwriting as well as axemen Rossington and Collins's playing. "What's Your Name," "That Smell," "You Got That Right" and "I Never Dreamed" cover familiar Skynyrd territory with a sharpened melodic focus and wide-ranging instrumental reach. What should have been the band's second coming turned out to be its swan song; Ronnie Van Zant, Steve Gaines and backup singer Cassie Gaines (his sister) were killed when the band's private plane crashed in late 1977—just days after *Street Survivors'* release.

Gary Rossington, Allen Collins, Leon Wilkeson and keyboard pounder Billy Powell hooked up with an assertive female vocalist named Dale Krantz a few years later. The Rossington-Collins Band's two albums—*Anytime, Anyplace, Anywhere* (MCA, 1980) and *This Is the Way* (1982)—flash the expected guitar heat, but the original material falls short of Skynyrd's imposingly high standards. Surprisingly, the revamped-for-the-'90s Lynyrd Skynyrd comes much closer to realizing its goal. Though Allen Collins died in 1990, Rossington rounds up Ed King and singer Johnny Van Zant (Ronnie's brother) for a satisfyingly brash boogie session. *Lynyrd Skynyrd 1991* probably won't win Southern rock any new converts, but it's nice to see these guys haven't given up the faith. The various posthumous releases of the original Skynyrd are completely eclipsed by the 1991 boxed set. *Lynyrd Skynyrd* mixes early demos, unreleased tracks, acoustic outtakes, live cuts and acknowledged classics in a swaggering, impressive three-disc package.
— M.C.

M

KIRSTY MacCOLL
★★★   Kite (Charisma, 1990)
★★★½ Electric Landlady (Charisma, 1991)
When Kirsty MacColl released *Kite* in 1990, its skillful, introspective elegance placed her in the line of such other crafty neo-folkers as Tracy Chapman and Suzanne Vega. Its followup, *Electric Landlady*, was considerably more ambitious. Featuring one of Steve Lillywhite's trademark big productions, the set found the singer working with such interesting songwriting collaborators as Marshall Crenshaw and ex-Smiths guitarist Johnny Marr. A crew of studio veterans joined guitarist Elliot Randall and an impressive assortment of Hispanic brass players and percussionists—and the overall sound was complex urban pop with world-beat inflections. MacColl's a strong, distinctive vocalist—and she's proven herself a musician very capable of taking risks.
— P.E.

LONNIE MACK
★★★   The Wham of That Memphis Man!
       (1963; Alligator, 1987)
★★★   Home at Last (Capitol, 1977)
★★★   Strike Like Lightning (Alligator,
       1985)
★★   Second Sight (Alligator, 1986)
★★½ Roadhouses & Dance Halls (Epic,
       1988)
★★   Live! Attack of the Killer V
       (Alligator, 1990)
One of the most influential of the early rock & roll guitarists, Lonnie Mack earned a reputation among pickers that far exceeds his meager showing on the charts (one Top Ten single in 1963, an instrumental version of Chuck Berry's "Memphis"). Mack's 1963 debut album, *The Wham of That Memphis Man!*, reissued by Alligator in 1987, is one of the primers in rugged roadhouse rock that blurs the lines between country and

blues. It also established Mack's distinctive voice—his guitar voice, that is—forever. His trademark axe is a Gibson Flying V, strung with heavy-gauge strings and equipped with a Bigsby whammy bar (it's featured on the cover of *Live! Attack of the Killer V* in all its ancient glory); his style is marked by maximum vibrato and frenetic single-note runs. As wild as he sounds, Mack is always under control. Duane Allman and Dickie Betts clearly picked up some tricks listening to Mack, and in fact the entire school of Southern rock guitarists acknowledges Mack with every stinging solo.

Apart from *The Wham of That Memphis Man!*, the essential Mack album is *Strike Like Lightning*, which teams Mack with one of his acolytes, the late Stevie Ray Vaughan, as co-producers. Vaughan and Mack cook up a thick sludge of roiling blues-rock that remains the most appropriate showcase Mack has had. Vaughan himself is stunning throughout the album, particularly on the final track, "Oreo Cookie Blues," featuring Mack on guitar and vocal, Vaughan on National steel, and Bill McIntosh (Lonnie's brother) on slide guitar. This salacious blues comes by way of Mississippi, and all three players get an opportunity to wrap their own statements around Mack's insinuating vocal. *Second Sight* and *Live! Attack of the Killer V*, are less inspired, but Mack's playing is always interesting.   — D.M.

MADNESS
★★★★   One Step Beyond . . . (Sire, 1979)
★★★★   Absolutely (Sire, 1980)
★★★   7 (Stiff UK, 1981)
★★★★   Complete Madness (Stiff UK,
         1982)
★★★½ Madness Presents the Rise and
         Fall (Stiff UK, 1982)
★★★★½ Madness (Geffen, 1983)
★★★   Keep Moving (Geffen, 1984)
★★½   Mad Not Mad (Geffen, 1985)

★★★★ **Utter Madness (Zarjazz UK, 1986)**
★★ **The Peel Sessions (Strange Fruit UK, 1986)**

In its prime, Madness was one of England's most beloved pop acts, and no wonder; its blend of irrepressible rhythm, insinuatingly catchy choruses and brash music-hall humor all but guaranteed the group a place on the pop charts. Here in the U.S., however, the group's success was limited, in large part due to the fact that Madness's ska-revival roots and Cockney sensibility didn't quite translate to American tastes.

Our loss. From the inspired R&B revelry of *One Step Beyond* to the Kinksian wit of *7*, the group's early albums use the ska beat not as a defining quality but merely as a stylistic starting point; its best singles, like "Baggy Trousers" from *Absolutely*, stand on their own. *Madness* draws from *7* and *The Rise and Fall*, as well as such English singles as "It Must Be Love" and "House of Fun"; it gave the band its biggest Stateside hit—"Our House," an engagingly tuneful number powered by a neo-Motown bass-line—and is perhaps its best overall album. But the ambitious *Keep Moving* is unable to match its predecessor's charm or melodic integrity (though the Caribbean-flavored "Wings of a Dove" has its moments), while *Mad Not Mad* finds the group sinking into unseemly self-reflection. Madness released two English best-ofs, *Complete Madness* and *Utter Madness*; both are good, but neither measures up to *Madness*. As for *The Peel Sessions*, it would take an extraordinary amount of devotion to justify spending good money on 11 minutes of so-so live ska. — J.D.C.

MADONNA

★★★½ **Madonna (Sire, 1983)**
★★★½ **Like a Virgin (Sire, 1984)**
★★★★ **True Blue (Sire, 1986)**
★★½ **Who's That Girl (Sire, 1987)**
★★★★ **You Can Dance (Sire, 1987)**
★★★★½ **Like a Prayer (Sire, 1989)**
★★★½ **I'm Breathless (Sire, 1990)**
★★★★★ **Immaculate Collection (Sire, 1990)**

Because so much of what has been said about Madonna focuses on the non-musical aspects of her career—her sexuality, her ambition, her calculated manipulation of publicity—it's easy to forget that she made some marvelous albums, and even a few great ones. Granted, her artistic reputation hasn't been helped by the fact that she has never been a "rock" star per se, having started in dance music and graduated to pop—two styles held in low esteem by most of the rock press. But just because her albums are accessible doesn't mean they're simple-minded; indeed, her best work is smart, insightful and exquisitely artful in its exploitation of the post-modernist aesthetic.

Mostly, though, it's tuneful and enticing, the sort of music that can be enjoyed without any consideration of underlying intent or intellectual baggage. That's certainly the case with *Madonna*, a dance-pop effort with few pretensions but plenty of melodic appeal. Although much was made at the time of the album's brazen sexuality—"Burning Up," for instance, had the singer proclaiming, "Unlike the others, I'll do anything/I'm not the same/I have no shame"—what seems most remarkable about her debut in retrospect is how uncategorizable it is. Although Madonna's music obviously derives from the New York dance-club scene, she avoids both the soulful exhortations of Hi-NRG and the impassioned artlessness of Latin hip-hop. Instead, her singing is surprisingly subtle; although she is obviously in complete command of the beat, she avoids overt displays of vocal ability, preferring to rely more on personality than virtuosity. And it works, too, emphasizing the wistfulness in "Holiday" and the playfulness in "Lucky Star," while lending a poignancy to "Borderline" that makes it irresistible.

Working with producer Nile Rodgers and the Chic rhythm section on *Like a Virgin* gives her sound more power musically, but she makes her greatest strides conceptually. Her declaration of boy-toy-ism in "Material Girl" is obviously tongue-in-cheek, but there's enough mischief and insinuation in Madonna's delivery to leave the listener wondering. That vampishness carries through much of the album, and adds a delicious ambiguity to the title tune. But as with her first album, Madonna avoids overt statements, preferring to cloak her most controversial content in a beguiling girlishness. It's that implied innocence that makes the "Like" in "Like a Virgin" credible as metaphor, and it has a similar effect elsewhere, turning determination into pluck in "Over and Over" and bringing a Barbie-ish sense of play to "Dress You Up." As such, the only song that rings false is "Love Don't Live Here Anymore," in part because Madonna doesn't quite have the power to pull it off, but mostly because its womanly despair seems woefully out of character.

True Blue is where Madonna first delivers

greatness. It's unimpeachable from a pop standpoint, sashaying through dance tunes, ballads and genre exercises without a single misstep, and cementing her superstar status. Yet what it offered was more than mere singles fodder, as Madonna rounds out the usual assortment of love songs with more dramatic material. Not that the album isn't fun—"Where's the Party" throbs with dance fever, while the title tune is a '50s-style frolic—just that it goes for something more resonant. It attracted controversy, thanks to the teen-in-trouble tune "Papa Don't Preach," which was attacked at the time for its "I'm gonna keep my baby" chorus, though its message has more to do with courage and responsibility than teen sexuality. Courage is also an important component in the ballad "Live to Tell," but this time Madonna relies less on personality than naked emotion, using her lower register to show just how affecting a singer she can be.

After a half-wit soundtrack (*Who's That Girl*, which features four new Madonna tunes and an overload of filler) and a remix compilation (*You Can Dance*), Madonna picks up where "Live to Tell" left off with *Like a Prayer*. Easily the most ambitious album in her catalog, it addresses such frankly personal issues as the dissolution of her marriage, her strained relationship with her father, and ambiguous feelings about sex and religion. To her credit, the album rarely degenerates into the sort of self-indulgence that has marred other rock-star attempts at self-examination. Credit her willingness to take chances for some of that, for *Like a Prayer* boasts some remarkably risky moments, including an arch, arty duet with Prince ("Love Song") and the Catholic in-joke, "Act of Contrition." Mostly, though, it's her unfailing pop sense that carries the album, from the gospel-inflected "Like a Prayer" to the dark, moody Beatle-isms of "Oh, Father."

For all her pop ambition, Madonna maintained her roots in the club scene, even to the point of releasing "Express Yourself" in a synth-heavy house version (by Shep Pettibone) that shares only its vocals with the retro-funk rendition on *Like a Prayer*. "Vogue," from *I'm Breathless*, pushed that approach further, playing another muscular house groove (again provided by Pettibone) as well as the phenomenon of "voguing," a dance craze appropriated from the gay subculture. "Vogue," though, is like nothing else on *I'm Breathless*, as the rest of the album—which, as the cover explains, was "inspired by the film *Dick Tracy*"—tends

more to period pieces and novelty tunes. Vocally, it's stunning, with Madonna revealing unexpected strength and versatility. But there's only so much that can be done with these songs, even when they're as witty as "Hanky Panky" or the Carmen Miranda tribute, "I'm Going Bananas."

But by that point, Madonna had turned her attention to Hollywood, and moved away from pop music. As such, there are only two new tracks on her greatest-hits album, *The Immaculate Collection*: One is a house tune called "Rescue Me" (not the Fontella Bass hit); the other is "Justify My Love," which was more notorious for its kinky video and the controversy over co-writer Lenny Kravitz's input (he was accused of stealing the words from Ingrid Chavez, and the backing loop from Public Enemy) than for any of its heavy-breathing emoting. — J.D.C.

MAGAZINE

★ ★½ **Real Life (Virgin, 1978)**
★ ★½ **Secondhand Daylight (Virgin, 1979)**
★ ★½ **The Correct Use of Soap (Virgin, 1980)**
★ ★ ★ **Play (I.R.S., 1980)**
★ ★½ **Magic, Murder and the Weather (I.R.S., 1981)**
★ ★ ★ **After the Fact (I.R.S., 1982)**
★ ★ ★ **Rays & Hail, 1978–1981 (Virgin, 1987)**

Virtually unrelenting in its mongering of doom 'n' gloom, Magazine was a very professional post-punk outfit led by ex-Buzzcock Howard Devoto. The band's more passionate subscribers claim to discern irony in some of Devoto's lyrics, but it's hard to see the humor. And the lad's dire singing doesn't help. Barry Adamson's great bass playing drives *Real Life*; "Rhythm of Cruelty" and "Permafrost" from *Secondhand Daylight* encapsulate Magazine's thematic despair. A key line from *The Correct Use of Soap*'s "A Song From Under the Floorboards" seems almost a parody of the band's weltschmerz—"My irritability keeps me alive/and kicking"—but, again, Devoto sounds chillingly "sincere." *Rays & Hail* is the depressing "greatest hits." Fine musicianship in service of infuriating angst, Magazine comes off ultimately as posturing. — P.E.

TAJ MAHAL

★ ★ ★½ **Taj Mahal (Columbia, 1967)**
★ ★ ★ ★ **Giant Step/De Ole Folks at Home (Columbia, 1969)**

★★★½ The Natch'l Blues (Columbia, 1969)
★★★ The Real Thing (Columbia, 1971)
★★★ Recycling the Blues (and Other Related Stuff) (Columbia, 1972)
★★★½ Ooh So Good 'n' Blues (Columbia, 1973)
★★★½ Mo' Roots (Columbia, 1974)
★★★★ The Best of Taj Mahal (Columbia, 1980)
★★★½ Like Never Before (Private Music, 1991)

His eclectic, all-embracing approach to the blues fell out of favor for a while, but Taj Mahal is ripe for rediscovery. Though he's an accomplished roots scholar, Taj never comes off as a fussy purist. Amazingly, his musical reach only rarely exceeds his grasp; at various times, Taj has gracefully absorbed folk, rock, reggae and calypso influences into his down-home Mississippi Delta–bred sound. He began by smoothly updating country-blues standards and his own similarly inspired compositions with solid support from guitarist Jesse Ed Davis. If the debut (*Taj Mahal*) is sketchy, the double set *Giant Step/De Ole Folks at Home* presents a telling picture of Taj's multi-instrumental ability and the seductive charm of his relaxed, yet resonant vocal style. *De Ole Folks at Home* finds Taj alone on the front porch, with his guitar, banjo, harp and incredible repertoire for company.

The Natch'l Blues backs away from the rock experimentations of *Giant Step*, while *The Real Thing* (an in-concert offering) makes up for that by including strings and a tuba! Perhaps *Recycling the Blues* does ramble on too long, but *Ooh So Good 'n Blues* is a much more taut, rhythm-driven affair. Taj breathes new life into blues-revival standards like Elmore James's "Dust My Broom" and parries with the Pointer Sisters on "Little Red Hen." *Mo' Roots* sails into Caribbean waters; by putting "Cajun Waltz" to a reggae lilt, Taj underscores a deep musical connection. Subsequent albums in this vein for Columbia and Warner Bros.—all out of print—are slicker and less satisfying. After a quiet spell, Taj added some compelling, bluesy incidental music to the score of *The Hot Spot*. *Like Never Before* finds him blending synths and even turntable scratching into his mix, as well as reworking classics like "Cakewalk Into Town" and "Take a Giant Step." It's a fascinating introduction to a vibrant—and still developing—talent. — M.C.

MAHAVISHNU ORCHESTRA
★★★★ The Inner Mounting Flame (Columbia, 1971)
★★★★ Birds of Fire (Columbia, 1973)
★★★ Between Nothingness and Eternity (Columbia, 1973)
★★ Apocalypse (Columbia, 1974)
★★½ Visions of the Emerald Beyond (Columbia, 1975)
★★★★ Best of Mahavishnu Orchestra (Columbia, 1980)
★★½ Adventures in Radioland (Relativity, 1987)

Forming the Mahavishnu Orchestra when his stint with Tony Williams's Lifetime ended, British guitarist John McLaughlin led the charge of amplified improvisation in the early '70s. *The Inner Mounting Flame* and *Birds of Fire* are far more listenable albums than many non-guitar buffs might expect. McLaughlin assembled a flexible quintet—including violinist Jerry Goodman—that could keep up with his lightning intensity, if not always equal it. On *Between Nothingness and Eternity*, drummer Billy Cobham and keyboardist Jan Hammer slip into the flashy, funkless style of accompaniment that turned many people away from the fusion movement. Not long after the orchestral debacle called *Apocalypse* (gulp), McLaughlin briefly retreated from electric music and recorded an acoustic album with Indian musicians. The brief anthology, *Best of Mahavishnu Orchestra*, sums up the band's '70s career. McLaughlin revived the dusty Mahavishnu concept with a young band of players in the mid-'80s; *Adventures in Radioland* doesn't come close to the electrifying blare of that prime-period Orchestra, however. — M.C.

MAMA CASS
★★ Dream a Little Dream (Dunhill, 1968)
★★ Make Your Own Kind of Music (Dunhill, 1969)
★★ Mama's Big Ones (Dunhill, 1971)

A strong, clear-voiced singer, Cass Elliot was a true power in the Mamas and the Papas, but her likeable persona was such that she was often saddled with the group's trite or novelty numbers. On her own, she delivered nothing but well-crafted fluff. Over-reliant on the slighter efforts of the classic songwriting team of Barry Mann and Cynthia Weil, these albums are nice but insignificant. — P.E.

THE MAMAS AND THE PAPAS
★★★★ If You Can Believe Your Eyes and Ears (Dunhill, 1966)

★ ★½ **The Mamas and the Papas (1966; MCA, 1987)**
★ ★ ★ **The Mamas and the Papas Deliver (1967; MCA, 1987)**
★ ★½ **The Papas and the Mamas Presented by the Mamas and the Papas (Dunhill, 1968)**
★ ★ ★ **Farewell to the First Golden Era (Dunhill, 1968)**
★ ★ **16 of Their Greatest Hits (1969; MCA, 1986)**
★ **A Gathering of Flowers (Dunhill, 1970)**
★ ★ **People Like Us (1971; MCA, 1989)**
★ ★ ★ **Twenty Golden Hits (Dunhill, 1973)**
★ ★ ★ ★ **Creeque Alley: The History of the Mamas and the Papas, Vols. 1 & 2 (MCA, 1991)**

The cover of their debut showed the Mamas and the Papas lounging in teasing, unisex bliss in one big bathtub—four personable hippies, they came on in 1966 like life-style radicals promising hedonistic freedom. Their true gift, though, was compromise: fusing folk-rock urgency with the gloss of highly commercial studio pop. *If You Can Believe Your Eyes and Ears* was a fresh wonder. By far their best record, it boasted the yearning "California Dreamin' "; the free-spirit manifesto, "Go Where You Wanna Go"; a vaudeville take on Lennon-McCartney's "I Call Your Name"; and a nice, breathy cover of Leiber-Stoller's "Spanish Harlem." John Phillips, Denny Doherty, Michelle Phillips and especially Mama Cass were all clear-voiced singers with solid folk backgrounds, but the group's very radio-oriented strength was John's songwriting—coupling a sure melodic sense to a flair for zeitgeist sloganeering, he made music that was hip yet unthreatening. The band's marketability was also boosted by a clearly delineated visual lineup: John, the six-foot-four "genius," Doherty the winsome one, Mama Cass the earth mother and Michelle the mistily gorgeous hippie chick.

The Mamas and the Papas continued in the folk-rock vein with "Trip, Stumble & Fall" and "Dancing Bear," but with the fine "Dedicated to the One I Love" the group began moving toward a more generic pop sound. The autobiographical "Creeque Alley" off *Deliver* showed them already waxing nostalgic about their history. By the time of *Mamas and Papas Presented*, the hippie anthems verged on genial parody ("Meditation Mama," "Gemini Childe"),

and "Dream a Little Dream of Me" is coy, even by pop standards.

As symbols, the group remained significant for a while—John and Michelle, after all, organized the Monterey Pop Festival—but they seemed just as comfortable delivering nice, innocuous tuneful fare. Of their abundant greatest-hits packages, *Creeque Alley* is the strongest. It not only covers essential hits but selects choice bits from their early work (as the Mugwumps) and the four singers' later solo albums. — P.E.

MANDRILL
★ ★ ★ **The Best of Mandrill (Polydor, 1975)**
High-struttin' funk is Mandrill's turf, and this seven-piece Brooklyn outfit holds its own against mighty stiff competition. Mandrill won't be mistaken for innovators or visionaries; this isn't P-Funk, just a dependable and versatile dance band. On Mandrill's sole surviving album, the locked-tight grooves are greased with jazzy horn charts and stinging Latin rhythms. Profound they're not: in fact, the dated, chant-along lyrics verge on nonsense most of the time. "Right on, everybody, right on" (from "Git It All") is one thing; "The Ape is high, and so am I" (from "Ape Is High") is something else entirely. When the music starts to pump and glide, however, you may not have the energy to argue semantics. — M.C.

MANFRED MANN
★ ★ ★ **The Best of Manfred Mann (EMI, 1987)**
★ ★ **Plains Music (Rhythm Safari/Priority, 1991)**
★ ★ ★½ **The Best of Manfred Mann: The Definitive Collection (EMI, 1992)**
Manfred Mann's 1964 version of "Do Wah Diddy Diddy" was trashy fun; "Oh No Not My Baby" (1965) and "Pretty Flamingo" (1966)—although rendered redundant by Rod Stewart's drastically better versions—were neat pop soul, but Manfred Mann soon began veering toward portentousness. Born in Johannesburg as Mike Lubowitz, the Lincoln-bearded Mann was a keyboardist with jazz aspirations whose playing fell short of his contemporaries, Rod Argent and Brian Auger; Paul Jones was a fair belter. Jack Bruce also played bass with Mann, for six months. Like all period bands of an intellectual bent, Manfred Mann was enraptured with Dylan. "With God on Our

Side" is leaden and "Just Like a Woman" is only passable—"The Mighty Quinn" (1968), however, is pretty rollicking.

In the late '60s Jones exited and Mike D'Abo came on board. The writer of the beautiful "Handbags and Gladrags" (also covered much more strongly by Stewart), D'Abo was a class act. Beatles hanger-on Klaus Voorman also entered, on bass—and the group began a period of bewildering personnel changes.

In 1969, the brass-driven Manfred Mann Chapter Three debuted with a cool take on "Shapes of Things," a song Mann's drummer, Mike Hugg, had given to the Yardbirds for their 1966 hit. Three years later, the group transmuted yet again, into Manfred Mann's Earth Band. On their first album and on *Get Your Rocks Off* (both out of print), they kept up the Dylanizing— adding grandiose versions of Randy Newman and John Prine tunes. By 1974, on *The Roaring Silence* (also deleted), they were hard at mining a similar lode, with a melodramatic cover of Springsteen's "Blinded by the Light." The Mann that followed was status quo. Stick to the greatest-hits album for the best Manfred Mann tracks, unless you have new-age leanings, then *Plains Music* may be your cuppa tea. — P.E.

THE MANHATTANS
★★★ **Greatest Hits (Columbia, 1980)**
★★★ **After Midnight (Columbia, 1980)**
★★★ **Dedicated to You: Golden Carnival Classics, Pt. 1 (Collectables, NA)**
★★★ **For You and Yours: Golden Carnival Classics, Pt. 2 (Collectables, NA)**

This veteran vocal quintet hit its stride in the mid-'70s, working with Philadelphia producer Bobby Martin on a string of lushly appointed R&B ballads. Martin's stately arrangements, lead singer Gerald Alston's creamy pleas, baritone singer "Blue" Lovett's spoken love-raps: it all starts to sound automatic after a while. But this proven Philly Soul formula works wonders on several tracks: the crossover hits "Kiss and Say Goodbye" and "Shining Star" (not the Earth, Wind & Fire song) unfold slowly, so that the velvet crush of voices envelopes you in sweet, soulful melancholy. — M.C.

THE MANHATTAN TRANSFER
★½ **Jukin' (Capitol, 1975)**
★★½ **The Manhattan Transfer (Atlantic, 1975)**
★½ **Comin' Out (Atlantic, 1976)**
★★ **Pastiche (Atlantic, 1978)**
★★½ **Extensions (Atlantic, 1979)**
★★★★ **Mecca for Moderns (Atlantic, 1981)**
★★★½ **The Best of Manhattan Transfer (Atlantic, 1981)**
★★★ **Bodies and Souls (Atlantic, 1983)**
★★½ **Bop Doo-Wopp (Atlantic, 1984)**
★★★½ **Vocalese (Atlantic, 1985)**
★★★ **Manhattan Transfer Live (Atlantic, 1987)**
★★ **Brasil (Atlantic, 1987)**
★★★★ **The Offbeat of Avenues (Columbia, 1991)**
★★★★ **Anthology (Rhino, 1992)**

Few pop vocal groups can sing as well as the Manhattan Transfer, particularly when it comes to the sort of close-harmony vocalese popularized by Lambert, Hendricks and Ross. Trouble is, the Transfer— particularly in its early years—often rounds out its be-bop numbers with forays into doo-wop, novelty tunes and campy nostalgia, an approach that may be more rewarding commercially, but doesn't hold up to repeated listenings. From *The Manhattan Transfer* through *The Best of*, the group's taste for gimmicky, recherché material runs at least as strong as its interest in jazz; only *Mecca for Moderns*, which includes the charming "Boy From New York City" as well as a poignant rendition of "A Nightingale Sang in Berkeley Square" is worth enduring from start to finish (though *The Best of*, which also includes "Four Brothers" and the band's zippy take on Weather Report's "Birdland," is also a reasonable buy). Both *Bodies and Souls* and *Bop Doo-Wopp* up the jazz quotient, though maintaining a strong interest in pop marginalia. But *Vocalese*, which includes cameos by Jon Hendricks, Bobby McFerrin and the Four Freshmen, finds the group utterly in its element and trying hard to meet the impossibly high standards set by Lambert, Hendricks and Ross. And though the wonderfully sung *Brasil*, which features English-language versions of songs by Djavan, Gilberto Gil, Ivan Lins and Milton Nascimento, is undercut by its annoyingly inane lyrics, *The Offbeat of Avenues* balances imaginative numbers like the bebop-hip-hop fusion of "What Goes Around Comes Around" with jazz workouts like Jon Hendricks's setting of Miles Davis's "Blues for Pablo." — J.D.C.

BARRY MANILOW
★★ **Barry Manilow (Arista, 1973)**
★★ **Barry Manilow II (Arista, 1974)**
★★ **Tryin' to Get the Feeling (Arista, 1975)**

★½ **This One's for You (Arista, 1976)**
★★ **Live (Arista, 1977)**
★★ **Even Now (Arista, 1978)**
★★½ **Barry Manilow's Greatest Hits (Arista, 1978)**
★½ **One Voice (Arista, 1979)**
★½ **Barry (Arista, 1980)**
★ **If I Should Love Again (Arista, 1981)**
★ **Here Comes the Night (Arista, 1982)**
★½ **Barry Manilow's Greatest Hits, Volume 2 (Arista, 1983)**
★½ **Swing Street (Arista, 1984)**
★★ **2:00 A.M. Paradise Cafe (Arista, 1985)**
★½ **Greatest Hits, Volume 3 (Arista, 1989)**
★½ **Barry Manilow (Arista, 1989)**
★★ **Live on Broadway (Arista, 1990)**
★★½ **Showstoppers (Arista, 1991)**

This middle-of-the-road icon first gained notoriety as Bette Midler's pianist and arranger; Barry Manilow shared the Divine Miss M's fondness for pre-rock pop songcraft, but possessed neither her boom-bastic vocal ability or her campy sense of humor. Alas. Though he's long been a target for ridicule among the rock & roll faithful, it's easy to understand Barry Manilow's tremendous appeal in the mid-'70s. Basically, he's a nice boy from Brooklyn who exudes aw-shucks charm by the bucketful—city folks like a taste of corn too. This didn't stop Manilow from becoming a monumental pain in the neck, of course. For a few years there, his swelling key changes and drippy sentiments were truly impossible to avoid.

More important than his stint with Midler, Manilow's prior experience as a commercial jingle-writer proved to be his secret weapon. Working with studio maven Ron Dante (the voice of the Archies' "Sugar Sugar"), Manilow seeded his easy-listening clouds with cunningly orchestrated hooks. Even if he didn't always write the songs, Manilow delivered them with an unnerving, nerdy bravura—the melodies helped.

"Mandy" (from *Barry Manilow II*) cracked the Top Ten in 1974, touching off a deluge of "beautiful music" or total schmaltz, depending on your tastebuds. Retrospectively, "Could It Be Magic" (from *Barry Manilow*) became a follow-up hit the following year and Manilow turned into something of an icon as well as an easy-listening hit machine. Those strains of Chopin's "Prelude in F Minor" running alongside the gushing feelings of "Magic" are the first signs of Manilow's grandiose bent. While he salted the first pair of albums with abysmal almost-rock knockoffs,

Manilow turned his back on contemporary accommodations around the time of *Tryin' to Get the Feeling* and started working on his live onstage spectacular. "I Write the Songs" reached Number One in 1975, making Manilow an instant household name and something of a self-parody. It's hard to take a man seriously when he claims to have *invented music.*

Even Now figures as Manilow's commercial and creative peak. "Can't Smile Without You" continued his sentimental streak, while "Copacabana" admitted a tiny hint of rhythm. *Live* doesn't contain those last two Top Tenners, but it does communicate Manilow's sincerity and self-deprecating, er, wit.

Barry and "I Made It Through the Rain" mark the end of Manilow's collaboration with Ron Dante and the end of his feel-good reign. Today that abrupt finale seems perfectly natural; this brand of overkill was custom-made for the '70s. Manilow explored his jazz leanings on *Swing Street* and *2:00 A.M. Paradise Cafe.* The latter features cameos from Sarah Vaughan, Mel Torme and Gerry Mulligan—definitely for Barry fans curious about jazz and not the other way around. More successful by far is the *Showstoppers* package of show-tune standards. — M.C.

MANTRONIX
★★★ **Music Madness (Sleeping Bag, 1986)**
★★★½ **In Full Effect (Capitol, 1988)**
★★½ **This Should Move Ya (Capitol, 1990)**
★★★ **The Incredible Sound Machine (Capitol, 1991)**

Mantronix is a hip-hop combo headed by DJ-mixer Curtis Mantronik, a multi-instrumentalist specializing in hypnotic, bass-heavy dance material. As the name—a corruption of "man" and "electronics"—suggests, the Mantronix sound is heavy on technology, which leads to some interesting textures on *Music Madness*, although the accompanying raps (by M.C. Tee) are disappointingly lightweight. *In Full Effect* toughens the verbal attack while similarly boosting the beat, making it the group's leanest and meanest album; *This Should Move Ya*, though, is so overburdened with samples and electronic effects that it almost collapses under its own weight. Shifting gears, *The Incredible Sound Machine* puts its focus on singer Jade Trini with impressive results, particularly on Latin hip-hop workouts like "Don't Go Messin' With My Heart" and "Step to Me (Do Me)." — J.D.C.

THE MARCELS
★★½ **The Best of the Marcels (Rhino, 1990)**
Cornelius Harp was an extraordinary lead singer, Fred Johnson was an incomparable bass man, and the Marcels' incandescent 1961 version of Rodgers and Hart's 1934 love song "Blue Moon" remains one of rock & roll's and group harmony's peak moments. Harp sang as if the world were about to explode in a hot minute, behind him a quartet of vocalists buttressed the attack with pulsating doo-wop call-and-response fills, and Johnson's bass ranged far and wide, coming on like a Greek chorus over and around Harp's perfervid lead. The group followed up with a similar approach on "Heartaches," a remake of a Tin Pan Alley hit dating back to 1931, with Johnson's nonsense bass chanting playing a more prominent role this time. "Blue Moon" topped the charts, "Heartaches" made it into the Top Ten, and that is the story of the Marcels. Never again would the group's special artistry be matched so well with compelling material, and by 1962 the group was disintegrating. The 18 cuts here show that the Marcels, outside of their two moments in the sun, were first-rate vocalists forever in search of direction. One caveat: digital remastering has removed some of the explosiveness of the analog "Blue Moon." Amazing what some good old-fashioned tape hiss could do for a record. — D.M.

BOBBY MARCHAN
★★★ **Golden Classics (Collectables, NA)**
The wonderful lead singer on Huey "Piano" Smith's "Don't You Just Know It" and "Don't You Know Yockomo" had a Top Forty hit on his own in 1960 with "There Is Something On Your Mind," a record that had been a hit a year earlier for Big Jay McNeely and his band. Marchan, a female impersonator (which was something of a second occupation for most members of Smith's group, the Clowns), could sing in a high, feminine voice or a blues shouter's rasp—in either mode he could put across a lyric as fervently as any vocalist of his day. *Golden Classics* offers a broad sweep of Marchan's inventive approaches to his repertoire. After his New Orleans days, Marchan went on to become an original member of Otis Redding's band, and wound up cutting some singles for Stax, two of

which are included on the boxed set, *The Complete Stax/Volt Singles, 1959–1968*. — D.M.

THE MAR-KEYS
★★½ **Mar-Keys (Atlantic, 1961)**
★★★½ **The Great Memphis Sound (1965; Atlantic, 1991)**
★★★½ **Booker T. & The M.G.'s and the Mar-Keys: Back to Back (1967; Atlantic, 1991)**
Horn players Packy Axton, Wayne Jackson and Don Nix delivered the sass for the Mar-Keys on such nifty instrumentals as "Last Night" (1961) and its thematic followups ("The Morning After," "About Noon"), but the subtle, soulful underpinning was provided by guitarist Steve Cropper and bassist Donald "Duck" Dunn. Cropper and Dunn, of course, were also members of the legendary Booker T. and the M.G.'s, the house band that, together with the Mar-Keys, helped create Stax/Volt Records and the sound of Southern soul. Hardly a prolific outfit—their time was taken up backing their Stax labelmates—the Mar-Keys never became stars. But their albums contain gems of bright, efficient rhythm & blues. — P.E.

MARKY MARK & THE FUNKY BUNCH
★★ **Music for the People (Interscope/Atlantic, 1991)**
The brother of Donnie Wahlberg of New Kids on the Block, Bostonian Marky Mark pulled together the all-black Funky Bunch and released an album of innocuous white rap in 1991. The dance jam, "Good Vibrations," was the album's first hit, followed by the social commentary of "Wildside," delivered over a sample from Lou Reed's "Walk on the Wild Side." Unexciting stuff, but harmless. — P.E.

BOB MARLEY AND THE WAILERS
★★★★   **Catch a Fire (1973; Tuff Gong, 1990)**
★★★★   **Burnin' (1973; Tuff Gong, 1990)**
★★★★★ **Natty Dread (1975; Tuff Gong, 1990)**
★★★★   **Live! (1975; Tuff Gong, 1990)**
★★★½ **Rastaman Vibration (1976; Tuff Gong, 1990)**
★★★½ **Exodus (1977; Tuff Gong, 1990)**
★★★½ **Kaya (1978; Tuff Gong, 1990)**
★★★   **Babylon by Bus (1979; Tuff Gong, 1990)**
★★★½ **Survival (1979; Tuff Gong, 1990)**
★★★★   **Uprising (1980; Tuff Gong, 1990)**

★ ★ ★   **Confrontation (1983; Tuff Gong, 1990)**

★ ★ ★ ★ ★   **Legend: The Best of Bob Marley and the Wailers (1984; Tuff Gong, 1990)**

★ ★ ★½   **Rebel Music (1986; Tuff Gong, 1990)**

★ ★ ★½   **Talkin' Blues (Tuff Gong, 1991)**

★ ★ ★ ★   **One Love: Bob Marley and the Wailers at Studio One (Heartbeat, 1991)**

Bob Marley created a vast, resonant body of work in the '70s; his achievement and influence extends far beyond the confines of "reggae" or even "black music." The original Wailers—Marley, Peter (Mackin) Tosh and Neville "Bunny Wailer" Livingston—were a leading Jamaican vocal trio in the '60s, cutting their R&B flavored sides with distinctive island rhythms. The development of the Wailers into a self-contained band mirrors the growth of reggae itself; gradually, the group shook off the derivative singles approach of the early Jamaican studio system and forged an expansive new groove from established local styles like ska, mento and bluebeat.

Emerging as a fiery topical songwriter and spiritually compelling frontman, Marley led the Wailers to international acclaim with the release of two startling albums in 1973. With stalwart bassist Aston "Family Man" Barrett and drummer Carlton Barrett pumping out incendiary "riddims" behind the Wailers' smoky harmonies, *Catch a Fire* is a blazing debut. "Concrete Jungle" and "Slave Driver" crackle with streetwise immediacy, while "Kinky Reggae" and "Stir It Up" (a pop hit for Johnny Nash in '72) revel in this music's vast capacity for sinuous good-time skanking. "400 Years" and "Stop That Train," both written by Peter Tosh, indicate the original Wailers weren't strictly a one-man show. *Burnin'* glows even hotter; "Get Up, Stand Up" backs its activist message with an itchy motivating beat. "I Shot the Sheriff" (covered by Eric Clapton in 1974) and "Small Axe" both show Marley's verbal and melodic skills growing by leaps and bounds; he expertly blends personal testimony with political philosophy to make enduring points about institutionalized racism.

Tosh and Livingston left for solo careers after that album and were effectively replaced by the "I-Threes" trio: Marcia Griffiths, Rita Marley (Mrs. Bob) and Judy Mowatt. *Natty Dread* captures the refurbished Wailers at an ambitious peak. "No Woman No Cry" features Marley's most soulful, touching vocal performance; "Them Belly Full (but We Hungry)" and "Rebel Music (Three O'Clock Roadblock)" articulate the anger of the oppressed and downtrodden while avoiding crippling despair; the title track and "So Jah Seh" posit the tangled web of Rastafarian beliefs without totally slipping into the cosmos. *Live!* documents a thrilling, tight-as-a-drum 1974 London performance of highlights from the first three albums.

On *Rastaman Vibration*, Marley starts to fall back on proven formulas and ganja-stoked rhetoric. The grimly prophetic "War" and the deceptively feel-good "Positive Vibration" stand out, and if it isn't quite another revelation, the rest of the album holds up to repeated listening (and dancing). Marley opted for a lighter touch on *Exodus* and *Kaya*, gradually adding lead guitars to the bass-defined reggae pocket. Again, these albums don't command attention the way the earlier ones do, but either one will grow on a committed fan. Recent converts should begin at the top. *Babylon by Bus* is probably Marley's flattest and least inspiring effort; this live set isn't bad, but the loose readings of Wailers classics can't compare to the marvelously succinct *Live!* Marley ups the political ante on the impassioned *Survival*: "Wake Up and Live" and "Ride Natty Ride" recast familiar messages in fresh musical surroundings, while "Zimbabwe" and "Africa Unite" confidently extend the Wailers' sphere of influence. If Marley hadn't been fatally stricken with cancer in 1980, *Uprising* would probably have ushered in a productive new decade for the world reggae ruler. As it is, the final Wailers album deftly summarizes Marley's revolutionary career. "Coming in From the Cold" strikes a measured note of hope, "Real Situation" acknowledges the reasons for hopelessness, "Could You Be Loved" incorporates a winning taste of commercial funk and "Redemption Song" closes the album with a heart-stopping acoustic plea.

The posthumous Marley releases have maintained a fairly high standard of quality. The double-disc *One Love* covers Marley and the Wailers early days at Studio One. *Confrontation* includes rare tracks and outtakes, most notably the hit "Buffalo Soldier." *Rebel Music* collects some of the Wailers' most overtly radical statements in a listenable agit-pop broadside. *Talkin' Blues* mixes live versions and outtakes from the mid-'70s prime period with telling interview snippets. *Legend* is an indomitable greatest hits set; yet as deep as this sterling single-disc album sounds, it barely scratches the surface. — M.C.

ZIGGY MARLEY AND THE MELODY MAKERS
★ ★   **Time Has Come . . . The Best of Ziggy Marley and the Melody Makers (EMI, 1988)**
★ ★½ **Conscious Party (Virgin, 1988)**
★ ★½ **One Bright Day (Virgin, 1989)**
★ ★ ★½ **Jahmekya (Virgin, 1991)**

The family resemblance is obvious: David "Ziggy" Marley not only looks like his late father, he tries to sing like the reggae patriarch, too. Nothing inherently wrong with that: so did dozens of other Jamaican artists in the early-to-mid-'80s. But Ziggy Marley's two out-of-print albums for EMI (summarized on *Time Has Come*) seem premature—to put it kindly. Tapping on the journeyman instrumental talents of some former Wailers didn't exactly help Ziggy at first; the Melody Makers' spicy, swirling roots-rock points up his glaring lack of seasoning as a performer. Talking Heads Chris Frantz and Tina Weymouth produced the next two albums, bolstering Ziggy's vocal confidence with a clean, breezy mix. Oddly enough, *Conscious Party* and *One Bright Day* never quite get off the ground; the repetitious, judgmental Rastafarian pronouncements on many songs reinforce the music's secondhand feel. "Urb-an Music" (from *One Bright Day*) hints at contemporary redemption, however, and *Jahmekya* makes good on Ziggy Marley's promise. It's not a perfect album: several of the more politicized "message" tunes pump up the usual stock observations and received ideas. But the percolating synth bleeps of current "dancehall reggae" enliven cuts like "Kozmik," and a straightforward soul horn chart converts an African freedom plea ("Namibia") into a universal hook. Finally, Ziggy Marley comes into his own on "So Good So Right"—a chugging, undeniable love song. Ziggy also tackles Bob's joyous "Rainbow Country" on *Jahmekya*, and the result sounds like a cover version, not a nostalgic computer-perfect copy. For 1991, that represents progress. — M.C.

BRANFORD MARSALIS
★ ★ ★ ★   **Scenes in the City (Columbia, 1984)**
★ ★ ★   **Romances for Saxophone (CBS Masterworks, 1986)**
★ ★ ★½ **Renaissance (Columbia, 1987)**
★ ★ ★ ★½ **Random Abstract (Columbia, 1988)**
★ ★ ★ ★ ★   **Trio Jeepy (Columbia, 1989)**
★ ★ ★ ★   **Crazy People Music (Columbia, 1990)**
★ ★ ★ ★½ **The Beautyful Ones Are Not Yet Born (Columbia, 1991)**
★ ★ ★½ **Blue Interlude (Columbia, 1992)**

Branford is the saxophone-playing older brother of Wynton Marsalis, and in many ways the more original of the two. Although pop fans probably know him better as Sting's sax-playing sidekick in *Bring on the Night* (or as Jay Leno's choice to replace Doc Severinsen as the "Tonight Show" band leader), Branford has made solo albums that tend to be straight jazz dates, the one exception being the light-classical pieces collected as *Romances for Saxophone*. Initially displaying a heavy debt to early-'60s Coltrane (just listen to "Solstice," from *Scenes in the City*), he quickly refined his approach into a more distinctive style, one that incorporates the harmonic audacity of Coltrane but leaves room for a Hank Mobley–style lyricism and a personable wit. Energetic, swinging and inspired, *Random Abstract* is the breakthrough album in that regard, and *The Beautyful Ones Are Not Yet Born* boasts some of his strong and incisive solos, particularly on soprano sax. But *Trio Jeepy*, a wonderfully conversational set recorded with bassist Milt Hinton, is perhaps his finest recording to date. — J.D.C.

WYNTON MARSALIS
★ ★½ **Wynton Marsalis (Columbia, 1982)**
★ ★ ★   **Fathers & Sons (Columbia, 1982)**
★ ★ ★ ★   **Trumpet Concertos (CBS Masterworks, 1983)**
★ ★   **Think of One (Columbia, 1983)**
★ ★½ **Hot House Flowers (Columbia, 1984)**
★ ★ ★½ **Black Codes (From the Underground) (Columbia, 1985)**
★ ★ ★   **J Mood (Columbia, 1986)**
★ ★ ★½ **Royal Garden Blues (Columbia, 1986)**
★ ★ ★   **Marsalis Standard Time, Vol. 1 (Columbia, 1987)**
★ ★ ★ ★   **Carnaval (CBS Masterworks, 1987)**
★ ★ ★   **Live at Blues Alley (Columbia, 1988)**
★ ★ ★ ★   **Portrait of Wynton Marsalis (CBS Masterworks, 1988)**
★ ★ ★½ **The Majesty of the Blues (Columbia, 1989)**
★ ★ ★ ★   **Standard Time, Vol. 3: The Resolution of Romance (Columbia, 1990)**

★ ★ ★ ★   **Tune In Tomorrow (Columbia, 1990)**

★ ★ ★½   **Standard Time, Vol. 2: Intimacy Calling (Columbia, 1991)**

★ ★ ★   **Thick In the South: Soul Gestures in Southern Blue, Vol. 1 (Columbia, 1991)**

★ ★ ★   **Uptown Ruler: Soul Gestures in Southern Blue, Vol. 2 (Columbia, 1991)**

★ ★ ★   **Levee Low Moan: Soul Gestures in Southern Blue, Vol. 3 (Columbia, 1991)**

As the leading light of the neo-traditionalist movement in jazz, trumpeter Wynton Marsalis has inspired countless young musicians, encouraged those critics who feared that fusion would be the death of jazz, and brought new glamour to the music he champions. And though it would be hard to imagine a more appropriate hero for the movement—Marsalis, after all, is attractive, intelligent, articulate and accomplished—it would be just as hard to find an artist who better typifies what's wrong with neo-traditional jazz.

That's not to say that Marsalis hasn't made good albums; indeed, he has. But great albums? Sorry. It's bad enough that his attempts to reestablish the jazz styles of the past—to resurrect the sensibilities that were responsible for the classic recordings of Duke Ellington, Miles Davis, Clifford Brown and others—have meant that his own work must be judged against what he apes. Rather, what leaves his work wanting is that Marsalis, even when he finds his own voice and forges his own sound, turns out to have precious little to say.

Perhaps that's why his classical recordings have been his most consistently satisfying. His orchestral debut, a pairing of Haydn and Hummel concertos, offers ample proof of his flawless technique and warm tone; unlike Al Hirt or Doc Severinsen, Marsalis sounds completely at home with the classical repertoire. Half a dozen symphonic recordings followed, highlights of which can be found on *Portrait of Wynton Marsalis*. One, though, is worth seeking on its own: *Carnaval*, a collection of turn-of-the-century cornet favorites recorded with the Eastman Wind Ensemble. As a technical showcase, it's hard to beat, for he whips through such crowd-pleasers as "The Flight of the Bumblebee" and "Moto Perpetuo," as well as giving a flawless reading of Jean-Baptiste Arban's notoriously demanding "Variations sur 'Le Carnaval de Venise.'" But *Carnaval* is also interesting because it finds Marsalis

hearkening back to an earlier age in American music—something his jazz recordings have done from the start.

Marsalis's first Columbia session was with a rhythm section led by Herbie Hancock, portions of which appear on *Wynton Marsalis* (the rest can be found on Hancock's *Quartet*). Along with bassist Ron Carter and drummer Tony Williams, Hancock played in the classic mid-'60s quintet of Miles Davis, and this session found Marsalis working much the same territory Davis pioneered. Except that where Davis's playing was sparse, lyrical and harmonically incisive, Marsalis was brash but mechanical, offering solos that were more technically challenging than Davis's, but considerably less eloquent. Apart from *Fathers and Sons*, a conceptual curiosity split between the Marsalises (Wynton on trumpet, older brother Branford on tenor, and father Ellis on piano) and the Freemans (tenor men Von and Chico), that pattern holds throughout the trumpeter's early albums. With his own quintet, both on *Wynton Marsalis* and *Think of One*, his playing is ambitious but unconvincing; for the most part, it's Branford and pianist Kenny Kirkland who come off as the group's great soloists. But they take a backseat on *Hot House Flowers*, an album of high-class mood music that finds Wynton once again chasing ghosts—in this case, Clifford Brown, whose *With Strings* this lushly orchestrated album emulates.

Black Codes (From the Underground) finally pulls the Marsalis quintet into focus, filling the music with fire. Unfortunately, that fire didn't burn long, as Branford and Kenny Kirkland left soon after to tour with Sting. As a result, *J Mood* was recorded with a quartet featuring pianist Marcus Roberts, a group Marsalis would maintain through *Live at Blues Alley*. But as much as this coolly cerebral lineup suits the trumpeter's conservatism, the performances are mannered and unconvincing. With *The Majesty of the Blues*, however, Marsalis finally latches on to a sense of tradition that is both more forgiving of cliché, and less prone to icy intellectuality. Now working with a sextet, Marsalis emphasizes the collective groove of old-fashioned New Orleans jazz. It isn't vintage jazz, exactly—though his use of banjo and clarinet makes for some very explicit echoes—so much as an attempt to tap what Marsalis sees as an ongoing tradition in African-American music: namely, the blues. It doesn't always work—"Premature

Autopsies (Sermon)," for all its good intentions, seems hokey and unauthentic—but it obviously reinvigorates the trumpeter. *Standard Time, Vol. 3* follows through with a meditation on melody that is midwifed by Ellis Marsalis (filling in for Roberts); the performances may not be earthshaking, but they are wonderfully nuanced. But it's the semi-Ellingtonian sweep of *Tune In Tomorrow* that really shows his ambition. Even if some of it sounds like film scoring (which, in fact, it is), Marsalis's writing has the kind of heart many of his earlier albums lack, making it remarkably easy to love.

It's when Marsalis tries to apply that approach to a less idiomatic style that he runs into trouble. As cultural theory, his three-volume *Soul Gestures in Southern Blue* series is admirably ambitious, but as music, it only occasionally works. Despite a markedly more soulful groove (particularly on *Uptown Ruler* and *Levee Low Moan*), Marsalis and company have trouble pulling these performances out of the theoretical realm, suggesting that his latest notion of "tradition" is as contrived as the one that fed his earlier albums. — J.D.C.

THE MARSHALL TUCKER BAND
★★★★ **The Marshall Tucker Band** (1973; Capricorn/AJK Music, 1988)
★★★½ **A New Life** (1974; Capricorn/AJK Music, 1988)
★★★½ **Where We All Belong** (1974; Capricorn/AJK Music, 1988)
★★★★ **Searchin' for a Rainbow** (1975; Capricorn/AJK Music, 1988)
★★★ **Long, Hard Ride** (1976; Capricorn/AJK Music, 1988)
★★★ **Carolina Dreams** (1977; Capricorn/AJK Music, 1988)
★★½ **Still Holdin' On** (Mercury, 1987)

Hailing from South Carolina, the Marshall Tucker Band wields a command of straight country music that no other Southern rockers can touch. Overshadowed by the combined memory of Lynyrd Skynyrd and the Allman Brothers, this comparatively mellow sextet can still lay claim to some of the best records to come out of the mid-'70s boogie swamp. *The Marshall Tucker Band* introduces the group's signature versatility; reedman Jerry Eubanks adds breathy flute ("Take the Highway") and honking sax ("Ramblin'") where they're appropriate, while guitarist-songwriter Toy Caldwell exhibits a sensitive touch with heartbreak songs ("Losing You," "Can't You See") and tongue-in-cheek stompers ("Hillbilly

Band," "My Jesus Told Me So") alike. Combining a live set with a studio session, *Where We All Belong* proves that Tucker could hold its own in the jamming department ("Everyday [I Have the Blues]"). The country twang becomes overt on *Searchin' for a Rainbow*. Caldwell's quietly evocative vocals and fluid picking illuminate the anthemic title track, while pungent R&B ("Walkin' and Talkin'") and western swing ("Bop Away My Blues") influences come bubbling to the surface. Sweet as this album is, its overall brevity and the reappearance of "Can't You See" (in a live version) drops some ominous hints about Tucker's flagging inspiration. *Carolina Dreams* scored a hit with "Heard It in a Love Song," but the later albums feel like retreads of *Rainbow*. Still searchin', Tucker recorded several (now deleted) albums for Warner Bros. in a more subdued, commercially minded country mode. *Still Holdin' On* finds the group desperately requiring a jolt of that old-time boogie religion. Maybe some long-overdue credit for past achievements—a modest box set?—would light a fire under Marshall Tucker once more. — M.C.

MARTHA AND THE VANDELLAS
★★★★★ **Anthology** (Motown, 1974)
★★★★★ **Super Star Series, Vol II** (Motown, 1981)

With the mid-'60s classics, "Nowhere to Run," "Dancing in the Streets" and "Heat Wave," Martha Reeves and the Vandellas achieved immortality as one of Motown's edgiest outfits. Recipient of some of Holland-Dozier-Holland's toughest production work, the group's best songs are all bass, brass and thunder—the singers have to fight hard just to keep up. The Vandellas hung around longer than their 1963–64 heyday, and Reeves kept recording on her own throughout the '70s, but none of the later work could rekindle the early spark. — P.E.

MARTIKA
★★ **Martika** (Columbia, 1988)

Very much in the Madonna mode, this is synthesizer-crunchy dance fluff. "If You're Tarzan, I'm Jane" does flash a bit of humor, and a cover of Carole King's "I Feel the Earth Move" is peppy, but the rest of the lyrics are clunky or forgettable, and Martika's strong voice in this context sounds generic. — P.E.

JOHN MARTYN

★ ★ ★   **London Conversation (Island, 1968)**
★ ★ ★   **The Tumbler (Island, 1968)**
★ ★ ★   **So Far So Good (Island, 1977)**
★ ★ ★   **One World (Island, 1977)**
★ ★ ★   **Grace and Danger (Island, 1980)**
 ★ ★½ **Sapphire (Island, 1985)**
 ★ ★½ **Piece by Piece (Island, 1986)**
★ ★ ★   **Foundations (Island, 1988)**

With Pentangle bassist Danny Thompson as his chief collaborator, Glasgow guitarist-vocalist John Martyn started out as a tasteful folkie, his late-'60s fare (the out-of-print *London Conversation*) not too dissimilar from Fairport Convention. Turning toward more jazz-inflected material in the following decade, he developed, on *So Far So Good* (also deleted), a style of greater complexity—while sacrificing some of his earlier, clean charm. More recently he's joined the ranks of those ultra-tasteful AOR artists (Steve Winwood, Michael Franks, Phil Collins) whose records are misguided triumphs of style over content. A vocalist of astonishing gifts, Martyn has become a mannerist—he seldom passes up a chance for melodrama. *Foundations* is the better of his later works; a woeful "Johnny Too Bad" gets redeemed by a lovely "Over the Rainbow." — P.E.

THE MARVELETTES

   ★ ★ ★ **Please Mr. Postman (1961; Motown, 1990)**
   ★ ★ ★ **Playboy (1962; Motown, 1990)**
 ★ ★ ★ ★ **Greatest Hits (1966; Motown, 1987)**
 ★ ★ ★ ★ **The Marvelettes (1967; Motown, 1986)**
★ ★ ★ ★ ★ **Anthology (Motown, 1975)**
★ ★ ★ ★ ★ **Compact Command Performances (Motown, 1986)**

While still in her teens, Michigan's Georgeanna Dobbins penned "Please Mr. Postman," managed to get herself and four of her girlfriends signed to Berry Gordy's Motown Records, and delivered the label its first Number One hit. Illness forced her departure soon after, but "Postman" remains the group's signature song—an irresistible upbeat groove, it's a solid smash in the tradition of the Ronettes and the early-'60s girl groups. "Beechwood 4-5789" is nearly its equal in perkiness (and perhaps the best of rock & roll's many "phone number" songs); "Too Many Fish in the Sea" is also prime early Marvelettes—lead singer Gladys Horton exudes good-humored sass.

Toward the end of the '60s, the group went in for a more mature sound—the commanding "The Hunter Gets Captured by the Game" is the classic example—but its pop appeal never wavered. "My Baby Must Be a Magician" and "Here I Am Baby," both released in 1968, marked the waning of their heyday; dizzying personnel changes ultimately were to make the Marvelettes an echo of their former glory. — P.E.

RICHARD MARX

★ ★ ★   **Richard Marx (EMI, 1987)**
 ★½ **Repeat Offender (EMI, 1989)**
★ ★ ★   **Rush Street (Capitol, 1991)**

A pop-rock pro in the best sense of the term, Marx has a strong voice and a good instinct for melody, qualities that may not enhance a performer's artistic reputation but virtually guarantee commercial success. That's not much of a problem with his debut, where the occasional bit of balladic treacle ("Hold On to the Nights," for instance) is offset by catchy, boogie-based rockers like "Don't Mean Nothing" and "Have Mercy." And though *Repeat Offender* finds his writing turning glib—the sappy dramatics of ballads like "Right Here Waiting" and "Angelia" are especially hard to take—the gritty, groove-oriented *Rush Street* finds him comfortably back on course, from the bass-heavy funk of "Hands in Your Pocket" to the bluesy "Keep Coming Back." — J.D.C.

DAVE MASON

★ ★ ★   **Alone Together (Blue Thumb, 1970)**
 ★ ★½ **Headkeeper (1972; MCA 1988)**
★ ★ ★   **It's Like You Never Left (Columbia, 1974)**
★ ★ ★   **Dave Mason (Columbia, 1974)**
★ ★ ★½ **Dave Mason at His Very Best (1975; MCA, 1988)**
 ★ ★½ **Let It Flow (Columbia, 1977)**

Mason's pop contributions "Feelin' Alright," "Hole in My Shoe," "We Can All Join In"—to Traffic's heady classical-jazz-blues mix were a bright, sharp leavening. But gone solo, Mason soon turned soft, and only got softer. The guitarist's way with a hook is apparent throughout his work, but more telling are a middle-brow tastefulness, the limits in range of his tonally strong vocals, an overall sense of caution, and lyrics that too often descend to pop-psych clichés. His big hit, "We Just Disagree," from 1977, was pablum. Backed by Delaney and Bonnie and their excellent group of players, *Alone Together* was crisp and highly successful; *Headkeeper*, part-live, part-studio work, was also well-crafted, if a little bland. With *It's Like You Never Left,* Mason hit a peak, of sorts. Graham Nash's singing is pleasant, as always, but the album's dense instrumentation shows Mason heading toward the glossiness from which, thereafter, he'd seldom depart. Ultimately killing off almost anything interesting by the sheer competence of his approach, Mason won his biggest audience with his most boring material on *Let It Flow.* Released in 1977, the year punk fully erupted, it was sad, dinosaur music from a former innovator, and provided a cautionary tale in the perils of growing comfortable, expert and redundant. — P.E.

MATERIAL

★★½ Temporary Music (Celluloid, 1981)
★★★ Memory Serves (Elektra/Musician, 1982)
★★★★ One Down (Elektra, 1982)
★★★½ Seven Souls (Virgin, 1989)
★★★½ The Third Power (Axiom, 1991)

In its original incarnation, Material was a floating rhythm section built around bassist Bill Laswell, keyboardist Michael Beinhorn and drummer Fred Maher, New York–based musicians whose music freely crossed the boundaries of jazz, rock and the avant-garde. Their earliest efforts, compiled on *Temporary Music,* flirted with the relationship between stasis (as represented by Laswell's repetitious, funk-influenced bass lines) and change (as manifested in most of the other instruments, particularly Beinhorn's keyboards and tapes); its mixture of rhythm and noise is sometimes bracing, but too often self-indulgent. Sometime after these sessions, the group tried to apply its rhythmic strengths to more commercial ends, and cut a fiercely catchy dance single, "Busting Out," with vocalist Nona Hendryx. That experience isn't much reflected in *Memory Serves,* which extends the experimentalist approach of *Temporary Music* through looser song structures and more inventive guest soloists (including guitarists Sonny Sharrock and Fred Frith, trombonist George Lewis and alto saxophonist Henry Threadgill), but *One Down* finds the group—by then minus Maher—returning to a funk-grounded approach. But because Material sees R&B as a means rather than an end, the songs here invariably push the envelope of popular music, with such wonderfully unexpected results as "Take a Chance," an edgily aggressive dance tune again featuring Hendryx, and "Memories," a lovely ballad

which contrasts Archie Shepp's tenor sax howls against Whitney Houston's soulfully assured singing.

It was almost seven years before another album arrived under the Material imprimatur, by which point Beinhorn was also gone. Although funk beats are once again used to tie the music's disparate elements together, the songs on *Seven Souls* play off of a sort of pan-Arabic melodic base; guests include singer Fahiem Dandan, violinists Simon Shaheen and Shankar and narrator William Burroughs. As for *The Third Power,* it's a Material album in name only, with Laswell handling production chores but no playing duties, and an all-star cast—Bootsy Collins, the Jungle Brothers, Bernie Worrell, Sly Dunbar, Robbie Shakespeare—generating the same reggae-funk style featured on Sly & Robbie's Laswell-produced solo albums. — J.D.C.

MATERIAL ISSUE

★★★ International Pop Overthrow (Polygram, 1991)

While Material Issue doesn't quite manage to pull off the *International Pop Overthrow* the title promises, this trio does display a fine grasp of pop essentials. No fewer than four songs on the debut feature girls' names in their hook-lines; the group's guitar work is nice Buffalo Springfield–early Beatles throwback stuff; the anglophile accents are endearing—and none of the tunes is too long. Good summertime fare. — P.E.

JOHNNY MATHIS

★★★★½ Warm/Open Fire, Two Guitars (1959; Columbia, 1975)
★★★★ Heavenly/Faithfully (1959, 1959; Columbia, 1975)
★ Love Story (Columbia, 1971)
★★ Johnny Mathis Sings the Music of Bacharach and Kaempfert (Columbia, 1970)
★★★★½ All-Time Greatest Hits (Columbia, 1972)
★★★ Johnny Mathis in Person (Columbia, 1972)
★★ The First Time Ever I Saw Your Face (Columbia, 1972)
★★ Killing Me Softly With Her Song (Columbia, 1973)
★★ When Will I See You Again (Columbia, 1975)
★ Feelings (Columbia, 1975)
★★ Johnny Mathis & Deniece Williams: That's What Friends Are For (Columbia, 1978)

★ ★　Love Songs (Columbia, 1980)
★ ★ ★½ The First 25 Years: The Silver
　　　Anniversary Album (Columbia,
　　　1981)
　★　Friends in Love (Columbia, 1982)
★ ★ ★　In the Still of the Night (Columbia,
　　　1985)
★ ★ ★　In a Sentimental Mood: Mathis
　　　Sings Ellington (Columbia, 1990)
★ ★ ★　Better Together: The Duet Album
　　　(Columbia, 1991)

If there were an album called *Makeout Classics of the '50s*, it would have to number more than a few Johnny Mathis tracks among its selections. Although his first hit single, "Wonderful! Wonderful!," wasn't released until 1957, he was so dominant a presence on radio and on the sales charts that it seemed he had been around much longer. His original greatest-hits album, the now-deleted *Johnny Mathis' Greatest Hits*, was comprised of his first five singles and some other odd recordings, but it remained on the charts for 490 weeks and was Number One for three weeks upon release in 1958. Mathis's early success was stunning, with four Top Twenty singles coming in 1957, including one Number One in "Chances Are," two others in the Top Ten, and another in the Top Twenty. By the end of that year he and Harry Belafonte effectively ruled the realm of the romantic ballad.

Mathis's style owed little if anything to the black balladeers who preceded him. If anything, Mathis hearkened back to the precise diction and controlled emotion of the Ink Spots' Bill Kenny, with whom Mathis shares a piercing, feminine-sounding falsetto. Mathis's uptempo stylings also betrayed more than passing nods to popular white crooners such as Tony Bennett and Dean Martin. In fact, Mathis seems almost totally a product of Tin Pan Alley, Broadway and Hollywood in both style and sensibility, approaching the sanctity of the song with a mindset more Neapolitan than, say, Memphis or Chicago.

What has happened over the years, though, is that Mathis has developed into a richer vocalist, even as the quality of material available to him has diminished. One hesitates to say they don't write songs like they used to, but in Mathis's case, this old saw is true. Which makes his current in-print catalog disappointing. *Feelings*, *Friends in Love* and *Love Story*, to name three particularly egregious examples, are so rife with bad songs that one must question the deletion of so many of Mathis's

wonderful '50s albums in favor of work so devoid of personality. *Friends in Love* at least has a couple of interesting duets with Dionne Warwick, but that's hardly enough to save it.

The albums to focus on from Mathis's early period are the two-fer repackages of *Warm/Open Fire, Two Guitars* (from 1957 and 1959, respectively) and *Heavenly/Faithfully* (from 1959), as well as, of course, *All-Time Greatest Hits* for those critical '50s and early-'60s singles. Of note among these is *Open Fire, Two Guitars* with its exemplary song selection including "In the Still of the Night" (not the Five Satins song), "I'll Be Seeing You" (an especially compelling version of this '40s standard), "My Funny Valentine" and others, with Mathis in superb form throughout and, as the title suggests, accompanied only by twin electric guitars—an unusual setting that brings out the most measured and probing vocal performances Mathis ever put on record. Apart from these, *Johnny Mathis in Person* is recommended as an engaging live document of the Mathis *oeuvre* and *The First 25 Years* offers an overview of Mathis's work through the years that buttresses the artist's reputation as a first-rate interpreter, but also makes the point about the diminishing quality of his material. — D.M.

KATHY MATTEA
★ ★ ★　Kathy Mattea (Mercury, 1985)
★ ★ ★　From My Heart (Mercury, 1985)
　★ ★½ Walk the Way the Wind Blows
　　　(Mercury, 1986)
★ ★ ★　Untasted Honey (Mercury, 1987)
　★ ★½ Willow in the Wind (Mercury, 1989)
★ ★ ★½ A Collection of Hits (Mercury,
　　　1990)
　★ ★½ Time Passes By (Mercury, 1991)

Although her vocal style and reputation lies in country, there's a lot of folkie in Kathy Mattea, and that (along with some lightly rocking arrangements) helped make both *Kathy Mattea* and *From My Heart* genuinely refreshing albums. Unfortunately, as Mattea's popularity grew, so did her reliance on boilerplate and cliché. That's not a problem on *Untasted Honey*, where the strength of songs like "Eighteen Wheels and a Dozen Roses" and the title tune carried the day, but the other albums are spotty enough to make *A Collection of Hits* the best buy for casual fans. — J.D.C.

IAN MATTHEWS
★★★ **Walking a Changing Line (Windham Hill, 1988)**
★★ **Pure and Crooked (Gold Castle, 1990)**

For two years a member of the original Fairport Convention, Ian Matthews gained from his tenure with those dazzling folk-rock experimentalists a pedigree notable enough to sustain at least a cult following during his early solo career. Certainly, Matthews was a fine, sweet-voiced singer, and his choice of material was resolutely tasteful, but the cautious blandness of most of his output makes his critical success during the '70s now seem baffling. The public, however, rarely embraced him—and it now seems that they were right.

Forming Matthews Southern Comfort in 1969, Matthews released four albums with that lackadaisical country-rock outfit; characterized chiefly by a pastel rendition of Joni Mitchell's "Woodstock," MSC was the essence of "laid back," unredeemed even by the energy of a fine pedal-steel player. On his own, the singer then put out *Tigers Will Survive* (now out of print), one of the best examples of his instrospective original material (an a capella version of the Crystals' "Da Doo Ron Ron" was pretty neat too), before embarking on a series of snoozes. *Some Days You Eat the Bear* (also out of print) encapsulated the Matthews formula—careful covers of good singer-songwriter fare (such as Tom Waits) free of any personal interpretation.

At the end of the '80s, Matthews delivered *Walking a Changing Line*, and in the moody, artful songs of Jules Shear finally discovered a writer who suited him; it was, by far, his best effort. Its successor, *Pure and Crooked*, found Matthews returned to his more representative style—nice guy music of fairly amazing insignificance. A master of that dubious genre, he's rivaled only, perhaps, by Graham Nash. — P.E.

JOHN MAYALL
★★ **John Mayall Plays John Mayall (1965; London, 1988)**
★★★★ **Bluesbreakers—John Mayall With Eric Clapton (London, 1965)**
★★★½ **Bluesbreakers (London, 1965)**
★★★ **Crusade (1967; London, 1987)**
★★ **Raw Blues (1967; London, 1987)**
★★ **The Blues Alone (1967; PolyGram, 1988)**
★★★ **A Hard Road (1967; London, 1987)**
★★★½ **Bare Wires (1968; PolyGram, 1988)**

★★ **Diary of a Band, Vols. 1 and 2 (London, 1968)**
★★★ **Blues From Laurel Canyon (1969; Polydor, 1989)**
★★★★ **Looking Back (1969; PolyGram, 1990)**
★★★½ **The Turning Point (Polydor, 1970)**
★★ **Live in Europe (London, 1970)**
★★★ **Jazz-Blues Fusion (Polydor, 1972)**
★★½ **Thru the Years (London, 1972)**
★★ **Down the Line (London, 1973)**
★★ **New Year, New Band, New Company (ABC, 1975)**
★★ **Notice to Appear (ABC, 1975)**
★★ **A Banquet in Blues (London, 1976)**
★★ **Lots of People (ABC, 1977)**
★★ **A Hard Core Package (ABC, 1977)**
★★★½ **Primal Solos (London, 1977)**
★★ **Last of the British Blues (ABC, 1978)**
★★ **Bottom Line (DJM, 1979)**
★★ **No More Interviews (DJM, 1979)**
★★ **Behind the Iron Curtain (GNP Crescendo, 1986)**
★★ **Chicago Line (Island, 1988)**
★★★½ **Archives to Eighties (Polydor, 1988)**
★★ **A Sense of Place (Island, 1990)**

A bit of an eccentric—in his early days he favored a curious nine-string guitar, and, later, sported a kind of caveman loincloth (on *Blues From Laurel Canyon*)—John Mayall was the great pedagogue of British blues. The bands he led functioned as schools of the form, tutoring young hopefuls in the then-arcane arts of Sonny Boy Williamson and J. B. Lenoir, and their graduates included such luminaries as Eric Clapton, Mick Taylor, Peter Green, Jack Bruce, Aynsley Dunbar, among many others: from Mayall, in fact, came the instrumental stars of some of the best bands in rock & roll. Shifting his personnel constantly—he went through more than nine groups in the years 1963 to 1967 alone—Mayall was a guiding light and obviously a catalyst, but the best playing on his albums remains that of his "sidemen."

John Mayall Plays John Mayall reveals the man's strength as a harmonica player, as well as his very reverent treatment of the blues—even while he wrote many of his songs, in the early days they seldom varied from the classic 12-bar pattern—but it would take Clapton's arrival to make Mayall's music catch fire. On *Bluesbreakers—John Mayall With Eric*

Clapton, it did; the guitarist plays Chicago blues with precocious authority here, and it remains one of Mayall's toughest sets. With *Crusade,* the teenaged Mick Taylor is highlighted—his stinging lead work is an embryonic version of the mastery he'd develop with the Rolling Stones—and Mayall begins experimenting with a horn section. For all but blues purists, *Bare Wires* remains one of the more interesting records: Mayall tries out an early form of jazz-rock fusion; the horns, by Dick Heckstall-Smith and Chris Mercer, add elegance, and Mayall himself—never a very strong singer—finds, in a breathy, whispering style, a haunting delivery that works. Peter Green, who with Mayall veterans John McVie and Mick Fleetwood, would go on to form Fleetwood Mac, enlivens *A Hard Road*; his playing is spare, fierce and supple. On *Blues From Laurel Canyon,* a conceptual album featuring Mayall's musings about L.A., the sound is soft and fluid, jazz-inflected and moody. An entirely acoustic effort, *Turning Point* gave Mayall an FM radio hit in the harp-extravaganza "Room to Move,"; *Jazz-Blues Fusion* showed off the trumpet skills of Blue Mitchell.

While many of his records are now mainly of historical interest, they can provide fascinating glimpses of talents not yet fully developed, and they certainly testify to Mayall's industry and influence. All the work released after *Jazz-Blues,* however, is primarily for the man's fanatics.

Mayall's early London albums remain the most enjoyable. *Looking Back* and *Primal Solos* are good overviews. *From Archives to Eighties* is an intriguing curio: Mayall updates badly mixed tracks featuring Clapton, Taylor and violinist Sugarcane Harris—the new sound is excellent, and the record provides a good intro to the vast Mayall canon. — P.E.

PERCY MAYFIELD
★ ★ ★ ★ **The Best of Percy Mayfield (Specialty, 1970)**
★ ★ ★ **Please Send Me Someone to Love (Intermedia, 1982)**
★ ★ ★ ★ ★ **Percy Mayfield: Poet of the Blues (Specialty, 1990)**
★ ★ ★ ★ **For Collectors Only (Specialty, 1991)**

Among the artists who recorded for Art Rupe's Los Angeles–based Specialty Records label in the 1950s, Little Richard was the most influential, but only Jesse Belvin approached Percy Mayfield in terms of all-around artistry. As a songwriter,

Mayfield evinced a command of language and an understanding of human motives; as a singer, his warm delivery was as comfortable as a warm fire on a cold night; as a performer, he was smooth, assured, witty, electrifying. Apart from his own best-selling R&B singles cut in the 1950s, Mayfield's songs have been often covered by some of the best singers American music has produced; notable among these is Ray Charles, who signed Mayfield to his Tangerine label in the early '60s and then proceeded to cut four of Mayfield's songs, including "Hit the Road, Jack," a song that topped both the pop and R&B charts in 1961.

Fortunately a good sampling of Mayfield's genius remains in print. Specialty has three albums in its catalog, a *Best of* set dating from 1970 and containing a dozen choice cuts, and the more recent 25-song retrospective *Poet of the Blues,* assembled and annotated by Billy Vera. The latter renders the former superfluous now, since it contains everything on *Best of* plus 13 more tracks. You don't have to get too far into *Poet of the Blues* to understand you're in the presence of an enlightened mind. The first track, "Please Send Me Someone to Love," recorded in 1950, has the feel and presentation of a yearning love song until Mayfield hammers home the key lyric: "If the world don't put an end to this damnable sin/Hate will put the world in flame." Mayfield was singing of racial prejudice, a topic virtually ignored at that time by artists seeking popular appeal. And Mayfield's singing equals the task he set out for himself as a writer. In laid-back fashion he twists and turns lyrics to achieve an emotional effect that doubles their impact.

As a live recording, Intermedia's *Please Send Me Someone to Love* owns a hallowed place in the Mayfield catalog. Unfortunately there is no liner information regarding when and where and with whom Mayfield is performing, but the singer's deepened voice indicates the set is from his later years. Nevertheless, Mayfield is in fine shape, joking with the band and the audience, but always taking care to bring the goods home when it's time to sing. *Poet of the Blues* is a must-have, but *Please Send Me Someone to Love* is an important document in rounding out the picture of this great American artist. Mayfield went on to record for Tangerine, RCA and Brunswick, but nothing remains in print from those years. — D.M.

MAZE FEATURING FRANKIE BEVERLY

★★½ Maze (Capitol, 1977)
★★½ Golden Time of Day (Capitol, 1978)
★★½ Inspiration (Capitol, 1979)
★★★ Joy and Pain (Capitol, 1980)
★★★ Live in New Orleans (Capitol, 1981)
★★★ We Are One (Capitol, 1983)
★★★½ Can't Stop the Love (Capitol, 1985)
★★★★ Live in Los Angeles (Capitol, 1986)
★★½ Lifelines Volume One (Capitol, 1989)
★★★½ Silky Soul (Warner Bros., 1989)

Right off the bat, Frankie Beverly established himself as a capable band-leader and vocal frontman with the L.A.-based Maze: he's a pleading tenor with a flair for lush, mid-tempo romance and a major Marvin Gaye fixation. It just took the group's material a while to catch up. Beverly and Maze stuck to their traditional guns throughout the high-tech music revolution of the early '80s, dropping increasingly sleek singles on an adoring audience of black, mostly middle-aged cultists. *Live in New Orleans* pits three concert sides against Maze's strongest studio side so far, yielding the danceable R&B chart smash "Running Away." The bittersweet twist-and-turn of "Before I Let Go" (also from *New Orleans*) is a fave Maze rave; others might point to the jaunty "Back in Stride" from the consistently fine *Can't Stop the Love* as the group's sterling moment.

Live in Los Angeles, another three-concert-sides/one-studio split, should have been Frankie Beverly and Maze's equivalent of *Frampton Comes Alive!*. Well, at least fans got to feast on the funky interplay and streaks of rock guitar that enliven Beverly's immaculate middle-of-the-road repast, even if the pop mainstream missed out on the party. And on *Los Angeles*'s studio portion, Beverly pleads for freedom in "Freedom (South Africa)" without showing the slightest strain. *Lifelines* mars a solid greatest-hits selection with distracting raps and extraneous remixes; try one of the live albums instead. *Silky Soul* finds Maze updating its graceful sound with a subtly bracing touch of synthesized rhythms, but there's not enough electro-whomp to disturb the emotional texture of the music. That title fits. And "Mandela" proves that Beverly isn't ready to close his eyes and go

to sleep just yet—no matter how elegantly mellow the rest of *Silky Soul* may sound.
— M.C.

PAUL McCARTNEY

★★★ McCartney (Apple/Capitol, 1970)
★★★½ Ram (Apple/Capitol, 1971)
★★★ McCartney II (Columbia, 1980)
★★★★ Tug of War (Columbia, 1982)
★★★½ Pipes of Peace (Columbia, 1983)
★★ Give My Regards to Broad Street (Columbia, 1984)
★★½ Press to Play (Capitol, 1986)
★★★½ All the Best! (Capitol, 1987)
★★★★ Choba b CCCP (1988; Capitol, 1991)
★★★½ Flowers in the Dirt (Capitol, 1989)
★★★★ Tripping the Live Fantastic (Capitol, 1990)
★★★½ Unplugged (Capitol, 1991)
★★★ Liverpool Oratorio (EMI Classics, 1991)

An epic howl, John Lennon's *Plastic Ono Band* was his cathartic cry of deliverance from the Beatles; against stripped-down accompaniment, he wailed inside a vast, echoing Phil Spector production, delivering some of the biggest statements in rock history, climaxing in "Don't Believe in Beatles" (or Dylan or Elvis or God, for that matter). All home-studio coziness and love songs, Paul's *McCartney* was a murmur by comparison—but ultimately no less emphatic a declaration of independence from his fabled, insurmountable past. The slight instrumentals, easy pop ("The Lovely Linda," "Every Night") and one strong rocker ("Maybe I'm Amazed") showed Paul downscaling from the Olympian heights he'd achieved as a Beatle; the fact, though, that he played every instrument on the album attested to an odd, fanatic urge to prove his skill. Skill, of course, was something no one had ever questioned about Lennon's partner-rival; on his own and with his band Wings, however, he set about belaboring the point—and in doing so, raised serious questions about his taste. Becoming in time pop music's most ingenious miniaturist, McCartney squandered melodic gifts unrivaled except by Brian Wilson's, remarkable bass playing and a commendable instinct for pleasing the broadest array of listeners on gilded curios—albums that collected either deliberate, charming ditties or that strung such ditties together in bewildering mini-suites. Almost always, he lavished attention on arrangements, whimsical instrumentation, studio wizardry—his songs became too much filigree, and not enough solid form. Virtually never would he attempt lyrics of any significance, but he sang his lyrics with utmost care. His solo output, then, remains a puzzle, alternately impressive and infuriating.

Following up *McCartney*, Paul turned out *Ram*—an album of hollow virtuosity best summed up by the bucketful of recording effects, funny voices, shifting time signatures and general inscrutable effervescence that comprised "Uncle Albert/Admiral Halsey." It seemed that he was attempting a *Sgt. Pepper's* (or more precisely *Magical Mystery Tour*) all on his own—he almost succeeded in crafty sound, but missed the sense by a mile. *Wild Life* found him assembling the components for Wings, a full-blown band that engaged his democratic spirit and his love for team-playing (see separate entry). They went on, of course, to sell oodles of albums throughout the '70s, release one masterpiece (*Band on the Run*), and, with no member's skills even approaching Paul's, predictably collapse under the weight of its leader's talent.

Wings' legacy wasn't so great that any striving for modesty after the band's demise was necessary; nonetheless Paul felt compelled to return to basics on *McCartney II*, the record that initiated his second solo career. Like *McCartney*, it was a nice, do-it-yourself, unspectacular outing; it produced one fine hit in "Coming Up (Live at Glasgow)." Mac's best post-Beatles work after *Band on the Run*, came next: while the album's gorgeous inconsequentiality confirmed that Paul was now terminally content to play the odd role of eccentric genius as AOR-tiste, so smooth, clever and seamless was the music on *Tug of War* (and so engaging its single, "Take It Away") that it proved irresistible to all but die-hard cynics. Ringo Starr, Stevie Wonder, 10cc's Eric Stewart and rockabilly legend Carl Perkins joined in, with Wonder starring on the saccharine "Ebony and Ivory" and the assertive "What's That You're Doing?"— the best and worst of McCartney, circa 1982. Michael Jackson joined Paul for "Say Say Say," a bit of funk-lite that made *Pipes of Peace* a big seller—although the album, in fact, was hardly mainstream stuff; one of Paul's strangest and subtlest, its novel instrumentation (helped out by the presence of stellar jazz bassist Stanley Clarke) sounds at times like extraterrestrial elevator music.

A movie soundtrack, *Give My Regards to Broad Street* was mainly fluff (new versions of McCartney and Beatles hits); and with

Press to Play Paul redefined "forgettable" in customarily expert fashion. *Flowers in the Dirt* paired him with the strongest melody-maker of the postpunk idiom, Elvis Costello: unsurprisingly, it was McCartney's strongest album in years. His most engaging work, however, occurs either when he goes full-bore for high-polish crowd-pleasing—of which the in-concert *Tripping the Live Fantastic* is the stellar example—or resurrects the easy spirit of his early rock & roll: *Choba b CCCP* and *Unplugged* are delightful "official bootleg" albums, on which the legitimate rocker reasserts himself with strong, casual versions of oldies, Beatle faves and his own songs. *The Liverpool Oratorio* found McCartney trying his hand, with customary facility, as a full-bore classical musician.   — P.E.

DELBERT McCLINTON

★ ★ ★	**Keeper of the Flame** (Capricorn, 1979)	
★ ★ ★½	**The Jealous Kind** (Capitol, 1980)	
★ ★ ★ ★	**The Best of Delbert McClinton** (MCA, 1981)	
★ ★ ★	**Plain from the Heart** (Capitol, 1982)	
★ ★ ★	**I'm With You** (Curb, 1990)	
★ ★ ★½	**Best of Delbert McClinton** (Curb, 1991)	
★ ★ ★	**Never Been Rocked Enough** (Curb, 1992)	

An R&B belter with a Texas twang, Delbert McClinton emerged in the early '70s with a series of albums (on ABC, all now deleted) placing him at the forefront of the progressive country movement, complemented with a helping of blue-eyed soul. His songs celebrate the party-boy lifestyle while revealing its desperate edge. *The Best of Delbert McClinton*, on MCA, collects cuts from the early albums; the uptempo grooves ("Let Love Come Between Us," "Turn on Your Lovelight") supply the necessary juice, but none of these blue-eyed soul interpretations hits home like the two country gems "Victim" and "Two More Bottles of Wine." That last song (a hit for Emmylou Harris) gets remade with a punchy horn line on *Keeper of the Flame*. From this point on, McClinton's considerable songwriting ability seems to have dried up. His interpretations are always respectable and often exciting—but never definitive. On *The Jealous Kind*, Muscle Shoals producer and sideman Barry Beckett helps McClinton assemble a tasty platter of horn-laden redneck funk; "Givin' It Up for Your Love" boogied into the Top

Forty in 1980, and McClinton handles the likes of "Take Me to the River" (Al Green) and "Bright Side of the Road" (Van Morrison) with deceptive ease. McClinton's reliance on covers gradually propelled him back to the bar scene—where he can still raise a crowd's temperature. Hopefully, his grainy duet with Bonnie Raitt on her smash *Luck of the Draw* (on Womack and Womack's "Good Man, Good Woman Blues") will jump-start McClinton's stalled career. He sure could teach the young folks a thing or two. — M.C.

CHARLIE McCOY

★ ★   **Charlie McCoy (Monument, 1972)**
★ ★   **The Real McCoy (1972; Monument, 1991**
★ ★   **Good Time Charlie (Monument, 1973)**
★ ★   **The Fastest Harp in the South (1973; Monument, 1988)**
★ ★   **Nashville Hit Man (Monument, 1974)**
★ ★ ½ **Harpin' the Blues (Monument, 1975)**
★ ★   **Play It Again, Charlie (Monument, 1977)**
★ ★   **Country Cookin' (Monument, 1977)**
★ ★ ★ **Greatest Hits (1978; CBS Special Products, 1982)**
★ ★   **Appalachian Fever (Monument, 1979)**

In any role other than accompanist, this brilliant harmonica player is hampered by possessing zero discernable taste. Virtually any harp featured on any '70s Nashville record was McCoy's; he also did fine work for Bob Dylan. But his solo albums are country easy-listening; they're virtually indistinguishable schmaltz. His tribute to Little Walter on *Harpin' the Blues*, for example, shows him almost eerily capable of his mentor's chilling style but the tedious competence of the studio veterans' accompaniment is sad and distracting. On "Shenandoah," off *Greatest Hits*, his playing is pristine and elegant, but it gets trashed by kitschy strings. In sum, McCoy's a remarkable player in search of a sensibility. — P.E.

JIMMY McCRACKLIN

★ ★ ★ **High on the Blues (1971; Stax, 1991)**
A blues pianist-vocalist who had a Top Ten hit in 1958 with "The Walk," which set off a dance craze of the same name, McCracklin cut this propulsive album in 1971 with Memphis producers Al Jackson and Willie Mitchell, the former being the MG's stalwart drummer, the latter the founder of Hi Records and architect of some of soul music's greatest moments as writer-producer for Al Green. Here McCracklin is plopped down into the Memphis soul bag and emerges with a strong album that modulates nicely between the strutting and slow blues he built his reputation on and straight-ahead Southern soul. — D.M.

IAN McCULLOCH

★ ★ ★ ½ **Candleland (Reprise, 1989)**
★ ★ ★ ½ **Mysterio (Sire, 1992)**
Wailing and sighing, Ian McCulloch on his own sounds a whole lot like he did when fronting Liverpool's ace trance-rock outfit, Echo and the Bunnymen. His voice still recalls Jim Morrison; his persona remains that of an ultra-romantic. On guitar, he hasn't the intimidating expertise of Echo's Will Sergeant, nor do his tunes boast the savage density of his former band's. But he's gained in pop power and accessibility—the synthwork throughout is lush and melodic, the occasional string arrangements add elegance without pretension. While his lyrical themes—death, faith, transcendence—prove that he's hardly become a lightweight, McCulloch, on *Candleland*, seems considerably more human than he had before. And that's a victory. His 1992 release continues in the same vein. — P.E.

REBA McENTIRE

★ ★ ½ **Feel the Fire (Mercury, 1980)**
★ ★ ½ **Heart to Heart (Mercury, 1981)**
★ ★ ★ **Unlimited (Mercury, 1982)**
★ ★ ½ **Behind the Scene (Mercury, 1983)**
★ ★ ½ **Just a Little Love (MCA, 1984)**
★ ★ ★ ½ **My Kind of Country (MCA, 1984)**
★ ★ ★ **The Best of Reba McEntire (Mercury, 1985)**
★ ★ ★ ★ **Have I Got a Deal for You (MCA, 1985)**
★ ★ ★ ½ **Whoever's in New England (MCA, 1986)**
★ ★ ★ **What Am I Gonna Do About You (MCA, 1986)**
★ ★ ★ **The Last One to Know (MCA, 1987)**
★ ★ ★ ★ ★ **Reba McEntire's Greatest Hits (MCA, 1987)**
★ ★   **Reba (MCA, 1988)**
★ ★   **Sweet Sixteen (MCA, 1989)**
★ ★   **Live (MCA, 1989)**
★ ★   **Rumor Has It (MCA, 1990)**
★ ★ ★ ½ **For My Broken Heart (MCA, 1991)**

This former rodeo rider from Chockie, Oklahoma, kicked off her musical career with a series of polite countrypolitan-style efforts on Mercury. She found her voice on the 1982 single "Can't Even Get the Blues No More" and the following year's "You're the First Time I've Ever Thought About Leaving" (both included on *The Best of Reba McEntire*), scoring back-to-back Number Ones on the country charts. Switching labels, McEntire positioned herself in the center of the New Traditionalist movement with the rootsy, acoustic-flavored *My Kind of Country*. "How Blue" and "Somebody Should Leave" highlight her unbridled Ozark quaver and her knack for narrative detail, respectively. *Have I Got a Deal for You* is too tempting to refuse. Reba pitches romance (the title track) and depicts heartbreak ("Red Roses [Won't Work Now]," "The Great Divide") with conviction. She even heads back toward MOR territory on "Only in My Mind," with no loss of emotional impact. In fact, the tart orchestration enhances the psychological subtlety of the lyric. "Only in My Mind" is a woman's unflinching response to the question: "Have you ever cheated on me?"

The hit title track of *Whoever's in New England* continues in that vein. This time the tables are turned; the wife is asking questions—and offering to wait for an answer. "Little Rock" catches McEntire in a feistier, take-no-mess mode; the title refers to a discarded wedding ring, not the city in Arkansas. Reba displayed a sure hand with singles ("What Am I Gonna Do About You," "The Last One to Know") for another year or so, but the accompanying albums (*What Am I Gonna Do About You* and *The Last One to Know*) begin to show definite signs of bland-out. *Greatest Hits* accurately traces this country traditionalist's path to superstardom: after two smoochy ballads with strings, the acoustic-based "How Blue" points the way toward the above-mentioned domestic melodramas. A storehouse of vocal resilience and clarity save McEntire from ever succumbing to outright weepiness; though it's brief, *Greatest Hits* follows as she confidently leaps from giddy pinnacles to the absolute pits.

Predictably, Reba dulls her approach after that. Choosing overly formulaic new material, issuing blasé cover versions ("Cathy's Clown," "Respect")—McEntire quickly became another cog in the Nashville machine. She snaps out of it for a while on

Live, especially on her older hits and a Dolly Parton cover. Still, while *For My Broken Heart* could be mistaken for the latest installment in a depressing series of woefully overproduced albums, it's a lot better than that. The musical backing is laid on a bit thick, but McEntire reaches a mature peak as an interpretive singer. She turns some potentially maudlin songs into memorable and affecting character sketches ("Bobby") and vignettes ("All Dressed Up [With Nowhere to Go]"). With leaner accompaniment and a couple of hooks, Reba McEntire might just surpass herself.
— M.C.

BOBBY McFERRIN

★★★ **Bobby McFerrin (Elektra/Musician, 1982)**
★★★ **The Voice (Elektra/Musician, 1984)**
★★★ **Spontaneous Inventions (Blue Note, 1986)**
★★★ **Simple Pleasures (EMI-Manhattan, 1988)**
★★★½ **Medicine Music (EMI-USA, 1990)**

Bobby McFerrin's schtick was arresting when he first tried it out in the mid-'80s—an a capella one-man band, he'd croon, scat and grunt, and thump percussively on his chest, stomach and whatnot. A little of this, however, goes a mighty long way. And while he's far too middlebrow-tasteful ever to come off as a novelty act, he's held back exactly by such tastefulness. His own tunes are sprightly enough, but his Lennon-McCartney covers (on *Spontaneous Inventions* and *Simple Pleasures*) are merely funky Muzak; and, in fact, he rarely interprets a tune—he just re-formats it. *Pleasures* includes the perky "Don't Worry, Be Happy"—a song with the zing of a well-crafted advertising jingle; *Spontaneous* offers the textural relief of Wayne Shorter's sax; *Medicine Music* features McFerrin's best originals ("Soma So De La De Sase" and a version of the 23rd Psalm), but Bobby's weakness is that of so many other instrumental virtuosos—he produces great sounds, but he doesn't have much to say.
— P.E.

THE MC5

★★★ **Kick Out the Jams (Elektra, 1969)**
★★★★ **Back in the USA (1970; Rhino, 1992)**
★★★★ **High Time (1971; Rhino, 1992)**
★★ **Babes in Arms (ROIR, 1983)**

About as ballsy as it gets, the MC5 were Motor City madmen making punk before its time. House band for the radical leftie White Panther Party led by John Sinclair (whom John Lennon championed), the MC5 used the '68 Democratic convention as the riotous backdrop for an early gig; the band's first album presaged 2 Live Crew in its First Amendment testing—screaming "Kick Out the Jams, Motherfuckers!," gravel-voiced Rob Tyner offended delicate sensibilities as well as eardrums. "Rocket Reducer No. 62 (Rama Lama Fa Fa Fa)" revealed the acidhead mindset of counterculturalists in extremis; the guitar-as-God attack of Wayne Kramer and Fred "Sonic" Smith, however, hinted that at heart the MC5 weren't nothing but a party. *Back in the USA* is the essential MC5; combining Little Richard and Chuck Berry with such prophetically slasher-film fare as "The Human Being Lawn-mower" and "High School" (the kind of stoked pop the Ramones would later perfect), the band's second album was unrivalled rock & roll. *High Time* was the desperadoes' most ambitious set; the monster features horns, Bob Seger, a full choir, and players from the Salvation Army—and gives up nothing in its rock righteousness. A neat epitaph, *Babes in Arms* is Kramer's collection of rarities—hits and misses from the MC5 vaults. — P.E.

KATE AND ANNA McGARRIGLE
★ ★ ★ ★   **Kate and Anna McGarrigle (Warner Bros., 1976)**
★ ★ ★ ★   **Dancer With Bruised Knees (Warner Bros., 1977)**
★ ★ ★ ½   **Pronto Monto (Warner Bros., 1978)**
★ ★ ★ ★ ½ **French Record (Hannibal, 1981)**
★ ★ ★ ★   **Love Over and Over (Polydor, 1982)**
★ ★ ★ ★ ½ **Heartbeats Accelerating (Private Music, 1990)**

Specializing in tart, tuneful songs that marry the resonance of folk to the emotional immediacy of everyday life, the McGarrigle sisters are probably the finest singer-songwriter team ever to go ignored by the American public. Well, not entirely ignored; Anna's "Heart Like a Wheel" is certainly well known to Linda Ronstadt fans, as is Kate's "(Talk to Me of) Mendocino." But *Kate and Anna McGarrigle*, the album that contains their versions of these songs, is, like most of their catalog, out-of-print.

Indeed, the only of their albums available at this point are *French Record*, a frankly intoxicating blend of pop smarts and Acadian tradition, and *Heartbeats Accelerating*, a heartbreakingly beautiful meditation on love and family that covers everything from the thrill of infatuation

("Heartbeats Accelerating") to the soul-deadening mundanity of life without romance ("I Eat Dinner"). Still, adventurous listeners would do well to seek out any of the others, especially *Love Over and Over*, which augments its winning originals with a charming French-language version of Bob Seger's "You'll Accompany Me." — J.D.C.

ROGER McGUINN
★ ★ ★ ½ **Roger McGuinn (Columbia, 1973)**
★ ★ ★   **Peace on You (Columbia, 1974)**
★ ★ ★   **Roger McGuinn and Band (Columbia, 1975)**
★ ★ ★ ½ **Cardiff Rose (Columbia, 1976)**
★ ★ ★   **Thunderbyrd (Columbia, 1977)**
★ ★ ★ ★   **Back From Rio (Arista, 1991)**
★ ★ ★ ★   **Born to Rock and Roll (Columbia/ Legacy, 1991)**

As is fitting for a musician of remarkable taste, chief Byrd Roger McGuinn has put out solo albums notable mainly for consistent finesse. Only sometimes does he strive determinedly to echo the Byrds' astonishing harmonies and buoyant strength, but his 12-string guitar and distinctive vocals can't help recalling the pioneering band he once led. Powered by fine playing from L.A. studio stalwarts, McGuinn's debut concentrated on Roger's songwriting collaborations with psychologist Jacques Levy—the record's artful folk rock set the pattern for McGuinn's next few albums.

Due mainly to the participation of ex–Bowie/Mott sideman, Mick Ronson, *Cardiff Rose* was tougher and more rocking; *Thunderbyrd* wasn't quite so assured, but with such standouts as George Jones's "Why Baby Why," a haunting remembrance of San Francisco entitled "Russian Hill" and a great cover of Tom Petty's best Roger McGuinn imitation, "American Girl," the record remains a pleasurable listen.

Back From Rio—which followed a 14-year layoff—is a powerhouse. Elvis Costello, Petty and his Heartbreakers, Michael Penn and ex-Eagle Timothy B. Schmidt join McGuinn in his stunning return to form. While, in the past, a pinched and adenoidal quality sometimes marred his very affecting delivery, McGuinn now sings with absolute command. The most Byrd-like of all his solo work, the record suggests that McGuinn deservedly has come to terms with his legacy—a style so ahead of its time that all the songs on *Rio* sound sharp and up to the minute. *Born to Rock and Roll* is a 20-track collection focusing on the best of

McGuinn's post-Byrds solo work in the '70s. — P.E.

MARIA McKEE
★★★★ **Maria McKee (Geffen, 1989)**
McKee's work with Lone Justice promised quite a bit, but it wasn't until she struck out on her own that she found a workable balance between her powerhouse voice and unrepentently romantic songwriting. — J.D.C.

MALCOLM McLAREN
★★   **Duck Rock (Island, 1983)**
★★★   **Fans (Island, 1984)**
★½   **Swamp Thing (Island, 1985)**
★★   **Waltz Darling (Epic, 1989)**
★★½ **Round the Outside! Round the Outside! (Virgin, 1990)**
The former Sex Pistols manager and boutique owner fashions his "solo" albums from samples, appropriations and contributions from various sessioners and gullible guests. His overweening conceptual presence is obvious, of course, just as his musical input is nebulous, at best. *Duck Rock* jumbles break-dance-era hip-hop from the Bronx's World Famous Supreme Team with source music from Africa and Appalachia. "Buffalo Gals" is an appealing novelty, but Malc's failure to properly credit several South African traditionals landed him in critical hot water. If that's not enough to put you off his dilletantish dabbling, the opera-meets–Donna Summer collision of *Fans* certainly sounds a hell of a lot more entertaining than it reads. *Swamp Thing* is a hellishly self-referential mess, while *Waltz Darling* tries to do for rock and Strauss what *Fans* did for disco 'n' arias—and falls flat. *Round the Outside, Round the Outside* reunites the multicultural bunko artist with the World Famous Supreme Team; the result is an occasionally funky, surprisingly tame take on hip-hop-house fusion. Could it be that Malcolm McLaren has run out of new ideas? — M.C.

JOHN McLAUGHLIN
★★★½ **My Goal's Beyond (1970; Douglas/Rykodisc, 1987)**
★★★★½ **Electric Guitarist (Columbia, 1978)**
★★★★ **Best of John McLaughlin (Columbia, 1980)**
WITH AL DIMEOLA AND PACO DELUCIA
★★★   **Friday Night in San Francisco (Columbia, 1981)**

★★★ **Passion Grace & Fire (Columbia, 1983)**
British-born John McLaughlin brought the speed and precision of traditional jazz playing to the wild 'n' wooly post-Hendrix electric guitar scene. Discovered by Miles Davis, he has a song named for him on the 1969 fusion landmark *Bitches Brew*—quite a tribute. Arguably, McLaughlin's mind-blowing virtuosity peaks on another Miles Davis album; on the *Jack Johnson* soundtrack, from 1970, he ignites a sprawling hard-funk groove with powerchord surges and terse solo snippets. This is the high-water mark of jazz-rock fusion, one of the few times both styles actually merge into a singular, pulsating wall of sound. McLaughlin continued to do yeoman work in drummer Tony Williams's electric band Lifetime; the 1982 Polygram two-fer set *Once in a Lifetime* collects some of McLaughlin's fiercest and most adventurous work; Williams and organist Larry Young push him into the stratosphere. *My Goal's Beyond* reveals McLaughlin's surprisingly tender acoustic side along with his consistent interest in Indian music. A lightly swinging run through Mingus's "Goodbye Pork Pie Hat" reasserts the other side of his roots. Next, McLaughlin founded Mahavishnu Orchestra, with whom he released several albums before bidding adieu to electricity. The result was the acoustic-based album, *Shakti With John McLaughlin*, performed with an Indian ensemble led by violinist L. Shankar.

McLaughlin snapped back with *Electric Guitarist,* an excellent sampler featuring striking collaborations with sympathetic souls and old mates alike. Stinging riffs and tricky rhythms abound, though the highlight is a throbbing, funky trio piece with Jack Bruce and Tony Williams ("Are You the One, Are You the One?"). Although *Best of John McLaughlin* is brief, it is well edited, and neatly covers a varied, inconsistent career. The later albums with Al DiMeola and Paco DeLucia are acoustic showcases, primarily composed of flamenco and Spanish-influenced material. — M.C.

MC LYTE
★★★   **Lyte as a Rock (First Priority/Atlantic, 1988)**
★★★   **Eyes on This (First Priority/Atlantic, 1989)**
★★★½ **Act Like You Know (First Priority/Atlantic, 1991)**
MC Lyte displays the credentials of a hip-hop heavyweight on her very first single.

"I Cram to Understand U (Sam)" takes rap storytelling to a new level. Rather than preach, this Brooklyn teenager fires off a point-blank personal account of a love affair polluted by drugs: turns out that "Sam" is two-timing her with a girl whose name "begins with a 'C' and ends with a 'K.' " On the rest of her debut, Lyte proves she can boast and riddle as well as the male competition—but not much more. With the exception of the surreal "I Am Woman" sample, the other def jams on *Lyte as a Rock* are skeletal at best. *Eyes on This* suffers from the same sketchiness, though this time Lyte kicks in two sharply observed narratives: "Not Wit' a Dealer" and "Cappuccino." *Act Like You Know* is where MC Lyte delivers—and expands—on her promise. "When in Love" and "Eyes Are the Soul" add synth sweetening to the funky beats, and Lyte trains her vision on romance. The day-to-day violence on the streets is never far off, though—the tragic characters portrayed in "Lola From the Copa" and "Poor Georgie" die from AIDS and lung cancer, respectively. Lyte doesn't lecture the sisters on "Like a Virgin"; she offers her own experience as a cautionary tale. And on "2 Young 4 What" she states her sexual preference with Millie Jackson-style sauciness and randy humor. This hour-long CD fills out with some pro forma braggadocio, but the scratchy grooves and inventive sampling keep Lyte and her listeners on their toes most of the time.
— M.C.

JAMES McMURTRY
★ ★ ★ ½ **Too Long in the Wasteland (Columbia, 1989)**
Son of the Texas novelist Larry McMurtry, James writes and sings strong modern folk music, rich in anecdotal detail and precocious wisdom. His effective, dry delivery somewhat recalls Guy Clark, and his flair for short-story detail isn't dissimilar to Billy Joe Shaver's, but he reveals more than enough confidence to stand on his own. "Terry," a great, unsentimental lament for a mixed-up rehab bad boy, the spare, atmospheric "Outskirts" and the lovely, regretful "Angeline" are standouts—but all of McMurtry's work is graced by maturity, intelligence and laconic beauty. — P.E.

BIG JAY McNEELY
★ ★ ★ **Swingin' (Collectables, NA)**
No mere recording artist, Big Jay McNeely had a reputation as one of the premier showmen of rock's early era. The cover photo on this collection of singles cut for the Swingin' label in the late '50s and early '60s tells it all: McNeely flat on his back onstage, blowing away, as kids bop in the aisles. Of the 16 cuts here, five are previously unissued; the one that really counts is an uncut version of McNeely's one substantial R&B hit, "There Is Something on Your Mind," from 1959, featuring band vocalist Little Sonny Warner in a yearning performance. The song was more successful a year later in a cover version by Bobby Marchan, whose single hit the Top Forty. *Swingin'* shows McNeely and his band doing what the title says and mellowing out to good effect as well. It's nothing revolutionary, but for its time it was guaranteed good rocking. — D.M.

CLYDE McPHATTER
★ ★ ★ ★ **Deep Sea Ball: The Best of Clyde McPhatter (Atlantic, 1991)**
To anyone who loved his lead vocals with Billy Ward and the Dominoes and especially with the first incarnation of the Drifters, Clyde McPhatter's solo career is a case of an extraordinary artist forever shy of consistently first-rate material. With the Dominoes, McPhatter sang on some of the decade's outstanding R&B singles ("Have Mercy Baby," "Sixty-Minute Man," "These Foolish Things Remind Me of You") and then entered into legend by forming the Drifters and recording a handful of the '50s most exquisite vocals ("Bells of St. Mary's," "Honey Love," "Money Honey," "Three Thirty Three," "What 'Cha Gonna Do," and a heartbreaking version of "White Christmas") before being drafted into the army in 1954. He began recording solo while on furlough in 1955, and picked up from that point upon his discharge in 1956.

In his solo career McPhatter was regularly in the R&B Top Ten, but his crossover success was more limited—only four Top Thirty singles between 1956 and 1959, when he left Atlantic for Mercury. But as this long-overdue retrospective makes clear, McPhatter had plenty of mesmerizing performances left in him after he came out of the army. Even when he got schlocky, as on "My Island of Dreams," the enormous drama in his quavering, high tenor couldn't be dismissed. And when he got into a good song—"Treasure of Love," "A Lover's Question," "Just to Hold My Hand"—he was completely entrancing. Given a great song—"Without Love (There Is Nothing)"—McPhatter could deliver a performance so resonant with feeling that it brooked favorable comparison to the sweeping artistry of, say, Ray Charles. McPhatter's sad demise in 1972 leaves one fact of his career immutable: By any standard, this was a great singer. — D.M.

MEAT LOAF

★ ★ **Bat Out of Hell (Epic/Cleveland International, 1977)**
Nutrition-free audio lunchmeat. Veteran of both *The Rocky Horror Picture Show* and one of Ted Nugent's marauding mid-'70s road bands, the hefty metal belter known as Meat Loaf came roaring out of leftfield with this inexplicably popular schlock-rock magnum opus. Produced by Todd Rundgren, *Bat Out of Hell* positions Loaf as an unholy cross between Bruce Springsteen and Freddie Mercury. If that sounds at all appealing, or even listenable, you'll probably be amused by the sex spiel of "Paradise by the Dashboard Light" and deeply touched by the tuneless shopping-mall balladry of "Two Out of Three Ain't Bad." *Bat* is also recommended to punk and disco scholars—originally, there really was something to rebel against. — M.C.

MEAT PUPPETS

★½ **Meat Puppets (SST, 1982)**
★ ★½ **Meat Puppets II (SST, 1983)**
★ ★ ★ **Up on the Sun (SST, 1985)**
★ ★½ **Out My Way (EP) (SST, 1986)**
★ ★ ★½ **Mirage (SST, 1987)**
★ ★ ★ ★ **Huevos (SST, 1987)**
★ ★ ★ ★ **Monsters (SST, 1989)**
★ ★ ★ **No Strings Attached (SST, 1990)**
★ ★ ★ ★ **Forbidden Places (London, 1991)**
It's amazing what instrumental competence can add to a band. When this trio roared out of Arizona with *Meat Puppets*, its audacious mix of hardcore and honkytonk was innovative and inspired—but also so gratingly amateurish it was hard to tell if the group's jackrabbit rhythm work was the result of artistic intention or technical limitation. *Meat Puppets II* clears up the confusion somewhat by slowing the pace and adding a semblance of dynamics to the arrangements, although Cris and Curt Kirkwood's vocals are too haphazard to gauge the band's melodic growth. Perhaps that's why the most engaging performances on *Up on the Sun* are instrumentals: "Maiden's Milk," a folk-inflected number that owes not a little to Leo Kottke, and the jazzy "Enchanted Pork Fist." Further refinements are added on the six-song *Out*

My Way as the Puppets work new elements into their decidedly eclectic groove, but the breakneck cover of "Good Golly Miss Molly" is pure gimmickry. *Mirage,* on the other hand, works in an astonishing variety of licks and tricks without ever seeming to show off, as the Puppets Travis-pick their way through the country flourishes of "The Wind and the Rain" and "Get On Down."

So what does the band do for an encore? Why, a ZZ Top tribute, naturally. Granted, there are no cover tunes on *Huevos*, but with songs as wholeheartedly imitative as "Paradise" and "Automatic Mojo," there don't need to be—even Billy Gibbons couldn't write riffs truer to the Top aesthetic than this. In fact, the only musical difference between the two is Gibbons and Dusty Hill can both sing, and the Kirkwoods can't. Still, that doesn't keep the Puppets from inching ever closer to the mainstream on *Monsters*, which not only consolidates the country-folk influences with ZZ Top–style boogie, but wisely depends on group vocals for most songs (sometimes there really is safety in numbers).

After *Monsters*, the Meat Puppets left for London Records; *No Strings Attached*, the group's final SST release, is a career-spanning retrospective that takes ten tracks to reach *Up on the Sun*. But *Forbidden Places* is compensation enough, as it not only builds on the advances made on *Monsters* but suggests that the Kirkwoods may yet learn to sing. — J.D.C.

MEGADETH

★ ★ ★ **Killing Is My Business . . . and Business Is Good (Combat, 1985)**
★ ★ ★ **Peace Sells . . . But Who's Buying? (Capitol, 1986)**
★ ★ ★ **So Far, So Good . . . So What! (Capitol, 1988)**
★ ★ ★½ **Rust in Peace (Capitol, 1990)**
Thrash acts may play at virtuosity, but when push comes to shove most have to fudge, covering their lack of articulation in a blur of angrily buzzing noise. Not Megadeth, though; this group attacks its double-time unison passages and hell-for-leather solos with the note-conscious pride of fusion stars. And while that's not always enough to salvage the low-budget nihilism of frontman Dave Mustaine's material, it does at least put some teeth into the band's apocalyptic worldview.
— J.D.C.

THE MEKONS

★★½ **The Quality of Mercy Is Not Strnen (1979; Blue Plate/Caroline, 1990)** •

★★ **The Mekons (Red Rhino UK, 1980)**

★★ **It Falleth Like Gentle Rain From Heaven—The Mekons Story (CNT UK, 1982)**

★★★ **Fear and Whiskey (Sin UK, 1985)**

★★½ **Crime and Punishment (EP) (Sin UK, 1986)**

★★★½ **The Edge of the World (Sin UK, 1986)**

★★ **Slightly South of the Border (EP) (Sin UK, 1986)**

★★★ **Honky Tonkin' (Twin/Tone, 1987)**

★★★½ **Original Sin (Twin/Tone, 1989)**

★★ **New York (1987; ROIR, 1990)**

★★½ **So Good It Hurts (Twin/Tone, 1988)**

★★★★ **The Mekons Rock 'n' Roll (A&M, 1989)**

★★★ **F.U.N. '90 (EP) (A&M, 1990)**

★★★★ **The Curse of the Mekons (Blast First UK, 1991)**

Adored by rock's intelligentsia and ignored by everyone else, the Mekons are a classic example of punk-rock perseverance. Yet as heartening as the band's struggle has been, and as admirable as its aesthetic stance frequently is, the Mekons' music has, frankly, never been terribly good. Take, as an example, the band's debut, *The Quality of Mercy Is Not Strnen*; for all the wit of the title and cover (which features a photo of a monkey at a typewriter, almost typing Shakespeare), the music is noisy and brittle, an unsuccessful attempt to fuse the sparse eloquence of Wire with the rhythmic agility of Gang of Four. *The Mekons* (a.k.a. *Devils Rats and Piggies a Special Message From Godzilla*) is an unsuccessful stab at pop, so muddled it's hard to tell whether the band is being facetious. Nor is it easy to decode the intentions behind *It Falleth Like Gentle Rain From Heaven*, a collection of outtakes, leftovers and the like that marks both the band's surrender (the Mekons had more or less disbanded at this point) and its refusal to remain silent; on the whole, though, it's a better gesture than an album.

Reinventing themselves as a septet three years later, the Mekons return with a pronounced bent toward country music. But this crew doesn't play the music Nashville-style, nor does it hot-rod its Chet Atkins licks like the cow-punks. Instead, the Mekons take a revisionist approach, retro-fitting the music with ragged punk guitar and a heightened sense of politics. It's an uneven mix, and *Fear and Whiskey* doesn't always make it work, particularly given Jon Langford's vocal limitations, but the passionate commitment evident in "Chivalry" and "Hard to Be Human Again" makes up for the bum notes (the album has since been reissued, with bonus tracks, as *Original Sin*). The *Crime and Punishment* EP refines the Mekons' approach further, and includes a credible Merle Haggard cover ("Deep End"), but it's *The Edge of the World* that brings the band's sound into focus (and, not coincidentally, introduces Sally Timms as the band's second voice). But the sound of *Slightly South of the Border* is overly intellectualized, while *Honky Tonkin'*, despite its well-schooled playing and vigorous politicking, is still too poorly sung to capture the power and pathos of the styles it so dutifully evokes. (*New York* offers a glimpse of this version of the band on tour, but the album's sub-bootleg sound quality makes it an unreliable document.)

Broadening its stylistic base, the band adds reggae and Cajun elements for *So Good It Hurts*, but rather than lend an aura of universality to the Mekons' sound, it only makes them sound like bad-imitation Beausoleil. Not to worry, though—*The Mekons Rock 'n' Roll* not only puts the band back on track, but delivers its most convincing performances, from Langford's rollicking "Only Darkness Has the Power" to the lovely twang of Timms's "I Am Crazy." *F.U.N.* is exactly that, thanks to the band's unexpectedly loose-limbed reading of the Band's "Makes No Difference."

More eclectic than ever, *The Curse of the Mekons* offers a greatly expanded line-up (fourteen players, not counting the occasional horn section) and a gutsy, wide-ranging sound. Yet it isn't the album's stylistic sprawl that astonishes (though the mandolin obbligati on "Wild and Blue" are impressively genuine) so much as the band's vastly increased instrumental competence, which manifests itself in everything from the raging country rock of "The Curse" to the dub-inflected funk groove beneath "Sorcerer." — J.D.C.

JOHN "COUGAR" MELLENCAMP

★ **Chestnut Street Incident (1976, Rhino, 1986)**

½★ **The Kid Inside (1977, Rhino, 1986)**

★½ **Early Years (1976–77, Rhino, 1986)**

★½ **A Biography (Riva UK, 1978)**

★½ **John Cougar (Riva, 1979)**

★ **Nothin' Matters and What If It Did (Riva, 1980)**
★ ★ ★½ **American Fool (Riva, 1982)**
★ ★ ★½ **Uh-huh (Riva, 1983)**
★ ★ ★ ★ **Scarecrow (Riva, 1985)**
★ ★ ★½ **The Lonesome Jubilee (Mercury, 1987)**
★ ★ ★ **Big Daddy (Mercury, 1989)**
★ ★ ★ **Whenever We Wanted (Mercury, 1991)**

If playing rock & roll is as much a matter of attitude as of musical proficiency, it's no wonder John Mellencamp became a star. Although his music is rarely anything special, his understanding of pop mythology and ability to play off of those myths is nothing short of phenomenal. Whether or not that makes him a great rocker depends in part on how much stock you put in such cultural icons as '60s rock, small-town life and the American dream: Mellencamp's albums generally expect his listeners to believe in such things just as fervently as he does.

It takes more than a leap of faith to be excited by his first five or six albums, however. Mellencamp launched his career as "Johnny Cougar," a sobriquet thrust upon him by then-manager Tony DeFries, and *Chestnut Street Incident* and *The Kid Inside* present an artist whose instincts run to recycled Stones riffs and Springsteen-derived braggadocio—an embarrassing combination. *The Early Years* contains highlights (loosely speaking) of both. Switching labels and management but still stuck with the name, he produced the import-only *A Biography*, which swaps Stones-isms for a sound closer to that of the Faces and is noteworthy only for having produced his first hit (in Australia, anyway), "I Need a Lover." *John Cougar*, which did see domestic release, also includes "I Need a Lover." Mellencamp ploughs ever deeper into the Great American Rock Cliché with *Nothin' Matters and What If It Did*, which pushes his I'm-a-rebel posturing to ever more ridiculous heights.

What changed things for Mellencamp was "Jack & Diane," a heartland slice-of-life number from *American Fool*. Although its lyrics rarely get more than ankle deep, the music strikes an impressive balance between anthemic power and down-home intimacy, a combination Mellencamp returned to for much of *Uh-Huh*. Again, it isn't what he has to say that matters, so much as how he says it, as "Pink Houses" couches its small-town jingoism in cleverly distilled Stones licks (note how the introduction recalls

"Tumbling Dice"), while "Authority Song" offers an agreeable update on Eddie Cochran's wild-youth raveups. *Scarecrow* is where he makes the most of this approach, with music so astonishingly eloquent that it easily outweighs the ideological overreach of songs like "Small Town" and the ludicrous "Justice and Independence '85."

Yet rather than refine that sound still further, Mellencamp took a sharp left turn with *The Lonesome Jubilee*, moving from heartland rock to an Appalachian-influenced sound that owed more to *Desire*-era Dylan than any Stones album. That's not to say the album abandons rock—the sound of "Rooty Toot Toot" or sentiments of "Cherry Bomb" are proof enough to the contrary. *Big Daddy* pushes that approach even further, but its folkie flourishes and grand gestures seem to be largely rhetorical, while its songs, apart from the self-serving "Pop Singer," are unmemorable. *Whenever We Wanted* finds the singer returning to the straight-up, Stones-style guitar rock of *Scarecrow* and *Uh-Huh*, and though there's more than enough melodic appeal to the likes of "Love and Happiness" and "Get a Leg Up," the album's attempts at social commentary are overwrought. — J.D.C.

THE MELLO-KINGS
★ ★ **Greatest Hits (Collectables, NA)**
The Mello-Kings are purveyors of one of early rock's prime ballad moments with their 1957 single, "Tonite, Tonite." It's included in this collection, along with some non-charting releases that set the assertive lead vocals of Bob Scholl against the sort of forceful back-up work that would later characterize Dion and the Belmonts' style. — D.M.

HAROLD MELVIN AND THE BLUE NOTES
★ ★ ★ ★ **Wake Up Everybody (Philadelphia International/CBS, 1975)**
★ ★ ★ ★ **Collectors' Item (1976; Philadelphia International/CBS, 1987)**
Lead singer Teddy Pendergrass doesn't really need top billing. His rich, ripe baritone leaps out of this long-running vocal quintet's majestic early-'70s hits—balancing the swanky, tuxedoed end of Philly Soul with earthy conviction. Smoother than the O'Jays, Harold Melvin and the Blue Notes put across Gamble-and-Huff message songs (like the eye-opening "Wake Up Everybody") just as convincingly as the gospel-inspired romantic testimony of "The Love I Lost" and "If You Don't Know Me

By Now." Covering only the bare bones of the group's heyday, *Collectors' Item* leaves even a casual fan hungering for more. *Wake Up Everybody* is the only original Philly-era Harold Melvin and the Blue Notes album still in print; it's fairly consistent (rare for this singles-oriented label) and includes a stunning version of "Don't Leave Me This Way" (later a disco smash for Motown's Thelma Houston). Teddy Pendergrass struck out on his own not long after that record; as a solo artist in the late '70s, he developed—some say perfected—soul music's now-familiar "love man" stance.
— M.C.

MEN AT WORK
★ ★ ★ **Business as Usual (Columbia, 1982)**
★ ★ ★ **Cargo (Columbia, 1982)**
Pleasant, tightly played pub rock distinguished by the woodwinds that drove their big hits, "Who Can It Be Now" and "Down Under," was the extent of this Australian outfit's skills and ambition. But such pleasantries made Men at Work monster successes in 1982; the group's debut album, *Business as Usual*, charted at Number One for 15 weeks. Why? Because the mildly new wave marketing, haircuts and videos of this amiable quintet staved off the encroachments of true punk, while convincing the unhip that they were grooving to something "new." The Men's second effort, *Cargo*, was business as usual: midtempo chuggers fueled by staccato rhythm guitar. It was nice and insubstantial.
— P.E.

JOHNNY MERCER
★ ★ ★ **Two of a Kind: Johnny Mercer/ Billy May & His Orchestra/Bobby Darin (1985; Atlantic, 1990)**
★ ★ ★ ★ ★ **Johnny Mercer Sings Johnny Mercer (Everest, NA)**
★ ★ ★ ★ ★ **Capitol Collectors Series (Capitol, 1989)**
Johnny Mercer is so towering a figure as a songwriter that his lengthy, productive career as a recording artist is easily overlooked. His first chart hit came in 1938 and he remained a constant in the Top Forty into the early '50s. During that time he was writing some of the greatest popular songs in this country's history, co-founding the Capitol Records label, and signing to the label artists who would make their own lasting contributions to American music: Nat "King" Cole, Jo Stafford, Peggy Lee, Margaret Whiting, to name a few. At his death in 1976, Mercer had written, by most

estimates, more than 1,000 songs, many of which had been hits several times over and in different eras ("Goody Goody" was a Number One single for Benny Goodman in 1936, and a Top Twenty single in an entirely new version by Frankie Lymon in 1957; "Fools Rush In (Where Angels Fear to Tread)" was a Number One single for Glenn Miller and His Orchestra in 1940, a Top Thirty single for Brook Benton in 1960, and a Top Twenty single for Ricky Nelson in 1963). Capitol's Collectors Series release, along with its detailed liner notes, is a breathtaking journey for any devotee of the popular song. Oddly, he wrote only eight of the 20 songs, although all of them were hits. Mercer's own compositions range from the novelty "Strip Polka" (yes, strip polka), to three gems co-written with Harold Arlen ("Blues in the Night," which also features Jo Stafford in one of her first recorded vocals, "Ac-Cent-Tchu-Ate the Positive," and the saloon classic "One for My Baby"). Apart from his own songs, Mercer the vocalist, whose friendly voice made up in personality what it lacked in range, assays the same wide spectrum of subject matter he favored as a writer. "Zip-A-Dee-Doo-Dah," "Winter Wonderland" and "Sugar Blues" are all delivered with remarkable sensitivity to mood and texture.

Two of a Kind teamed Mercer with Bobby Darin during one of the latter's forays into pop singing. This is a classic "swinging" affair keyed by a witty collection of mostly lesser-known Tin Pan Alley songs and the two singers' obvious ease with each others' styles, both musical and personal—the feel is informal and jovial throughout. Mercer co-wrote only four of the 12 tracks, with the most familiar being "Bob White."

More difficult to find, but no less essential is Everest's *Johnny Mercer Sings Johnny Mercer*. There's no liner information or dates to indicate when these recordings were made, but the material and the deeper tone of Mercer's voice dates it considerably later than the tracks on the Capitol album (1942-49). The inclusion of "Moon River" and "Days of Wine and Roses" dates this to at least 1962, when the latter was written for the movie of the same name. Of special interest is the jaunty treatment Mercer gives "Moon River." Where other interpreters have found melancholy and longing, Mercer is cocksure in his certainty that better days are waitin' 'round the bend. Apart from these, Mercer also offers his own treatments of "You Must Have Been a Beautiful Baby," "Goody Goody," "That Old Black

Magic," "Tangerine," "Come Rain or Come Shine" and "Satin Doll." Most of the time his approach is surprising, and provides a new perspective on the depth of Mercer's original material. — D.M.

METALLICA

★★★½ **Kill 'Em All (1983; Elektra, 1987)**
★★★★ **Ride the Lightning (Elektra, 1984)**
★★★★ **Master of Puppets (Elektra, 1986)**
★★★½ **The $5.98 EP: Garage Days Re-Revisited (EP) (Elektra, 1987)**
★★★★½ **. . . And Justice for All (Elektra, 1988)**
★★★★★ **Metallica (Elektra, 1991)**

Innovative, incendiary and influential, Metallica almost single-handedly reinvented thrash, transforming it from monochromatic hyperspeed sludge into a music capable of remarkable depth, resonance and beauty. Granted, "beauty" is not an adjective that readily springs to mind when faced with titles like "Creeping Death," "Leper Messiah" or "To Live Is to Die," nor is Metallica's dark vision in any way compatible with conventional notions of rock accessibility. Then again, it isn't intended to be; Metallica's music is to be accepted on its own terms, or not at all.

That much should have been obvious from the moment *Kill 'Em All* first exploded onto the scene. Drawing equally from the gothic complexity of classic Eurometal and the blunt simplicity of proto-thrash acts like Motörhead, the Misfits and Venom, Metallica found a way to increase the music's impact and velocity without decreasing its breadth or majesty. Thus, something like "The Four Horsemen" can switch tempos, juggle riffs or even change moods as it gallops along, and still maintain its blistering intensity. Even better, as the relentlessly propulsive "No Remorse" makes clear, Metallica understands rhythm, and how to place an accent so that a riff can slyly coax you into its flow, or push you headlong into the beat.

Ride the Lightning is even more accomplished, opening with the old acoustic-prettiness-into-amplified-fury gambit on "Fight Fire With Fire" without ever succumbing to cliché. There's plenty of excitement to be had—"Ride the Lightning," about a prisoner condemned to the electric chair, offers an especially exhilarating taste of the band running its

paces—but the album's highlight has to be "The Call of Ktulu," an instrumental featuring bassist Cliff Burton that, despite its near-nine-minute length, never lags for a moment. *Lightning* helped consolidate the band's following, but it was *Master of Puppets* that marked Metallica's real commercial breakthrough, going platinum despite an almost total lack of airplay. Not that the band was in any way radio-friendly; with an average length approaching seven minutes and a sound that is unrelenting in its aggression, the album accommodates no one. Even so, the music's emotional power is undeniable, whether manifested in the growling rage of "The Thing That Should Not Be" or the textural range of "Orion."

Garage Days Re-Revisited, a charmingly low-key collection of covers that pays tribute to some of the band's influences, was fun, but gave no indication of what was to follow: the epic *. . . And Justice for All*. Easily Metallica's most ambitious work, it pushes the band's arranging skills and ensemble playing to their limits. Yet the extended structures hardly weigh these songs down; if anything, the writing seems richer, with the gradually unfolding "One" being the album's dramatic highlight.

Rather than expand further in that direction, *Metallica* finds the band moving away from long-form writing. That's not to say these songs are short-and-snappy—their average length is still better than five minutes—but they are tight and tuneful. In fact, the brooding "Enter Sandman" even seems to verge on pop, and there's considerable melodic appeal to the likes of "The Unforgiven" and "Wherever I May Roam." Moreover, the wider range of texture and tempos suggests that the band is continuing to grow. — J.D.C.

METERS

★★★★ **Good Old Funky Music (Rounder, 1990)**
★★★★ **Look-Ka Py Py (Rounder, 1990)**
★★★★½ **Funky Miracle (Charly U.K., 1991)**
★★★½ **The Meters Jam (Rounder, 1992)**
★★★½ **Uptown Rulers: The Meters Live on the Queen Mary (Rhino, 1992)**

Long the premiere R&B rhythm section in New Orleans, the Meters—guitarist Leo Nocentelli, keyboardist Art Neville, bassist George Porter, Jr., drummer Joseph "Zigaboo" Modeliste and, eventually, percussionist Cyril Neville—worked with producer Allen Toussaint on dozens of sessions, backing Dr. John, LaBelle, Robert

Palmer and others. They also made quite a few records in their own right, recording three albums for Josie between 1968 and '71 before signing with Reprise in 1972. *Good Old Funky Music, Look-Ka Py Py, The Meters Jam* and *Funky Miracle* all draw from this period, in which the Meters went from operating as a funkier version of the MG's to formulating their own synthesis of James Brown funk and New Orleans second-line syncopations. *Look-Ka Py Py* is the funkier effort, although the "Rock 'n' Roll Medley" on *Good Old Funky Music* has its charms, but contains neither "Cissy Strut" or "Sophisticated Cissy," two of the combo's biggest hits.

Unfortunately, the Meters' six albums for Reprise are long out of print. Unlike the all-instrumental albums for Josie, these sessions add vocals in an attempt to enhance the group's pop appeal; while that works well enough on titles like *Rejuvenation* (1974), which included the classic "Hey Pocky a-Way," and *Fire on the Bayou* (1975), it also led to such embarrassments as the foolishly topical "Disco Is the Thing Today" on *Trick Bag*. The Meters performed *Live on the Queen Mary* at a Paul McCartney-hosted 1975 cruise party; judging from the band's set, it's obvious that fun was had by all. — J.D.C.

PAT METHENY

★★★★½ **Bright Size Life (ECM, 1975)**
★★★★½ **Watercolors (ECM, 1977)**
★★★★ **Pat Metheny Group (ECM, 1978)**
★★★½ **American Garage (ECM, 1979)**
★★★★ **New Chautauqua (ECM, 1979)**
★★★★★ **80/81 (ECM, 1980)**
★★★★½ **As Falls Wichita, So Falls Wichita Falls (ECM, 1981)**
★★★★ **Offramp (ECM, 1982)**
★★★½ **Travels (ECM, 1983)**
★★★★½ **First Circle (ECM, 1984)**
★★★★ **ECM Works (ECM, 1984)**
★★★ **The Falcon and the Snowman (Capitol/EMI America, 1985)**
★★★★ **Still Life (Talking) (Geffen, 1987)**
★★★★ **ECM Works II (ECM, 1988)**
★★★½ **Letter From Home (Geffen, 1989)**
★★★★★ **Question and Answer (Geffen, 1990)**

WITH CHARLIE HADEN AND BILLY HIGGINS:

★★★½ **Rejoicing (ECM, 1984)**

WITH ORNETTE COLEMAN:

★★★★★ **Song X (Geffen, 1986)**

A singular presence among fusion musicians, Pat Metheny is one of the very few guitarists of his generation who can be said to have a genuinely individual voice. Avoiding the speed-demon pyrotechnics of most post-McLaughlin jazz guitarists, Metheny's solos are evenly paced and lyrical, while his tone—full-bodied and warm, making exquisite use of chorusing to soften its edges—is unmistakable.

Bright Size Life, recorded when Metheny was 21 and an alumnus of the Gary Burton Quintet, is an astonishingly precocious debut. Featuring bassist Jaco Pastorius and Burton Quintet drummer Bob Moses, its music is airy and conversational, yet with a solidity that spoke of even greater music to come; the trio's version of Ornette Coleman's "Round Trip/Broadway Blues" is particularly stunning. Metheny introduced his own quartet over his next few albums, and these recordings—*Watercolors, Pat Metheny Group* and *American Garage*—expand upon the sound of his debut, most notably through the keyboard colorings of Lyle Mays, who functions less as Metheny's foil than as his co-pilot. *Pat Metheny Group* is the most satisfying of these, thanks in no small measure to the writing, particularly "Jaco" and the stately, shimmering "San Lorenzo."

New Chautauqua finds the guitarist sparring with himself in a lovely series of multitracked guitar pieces. Still, Metheny seemed to relish the challenge of playing with other musicians in other contexts. Hence, *80/81*, on which the young guitarist goes head-to-head with bassist Charlie Haden, drummer Jack DeJohnette and tenor saxophonists Dewey Redman and Michael Brecker—heavy company, indeed. Metheny more than holds his own, and the level of communication is remarkably high, as exemplified by the first of the "Two Folk Songs."

Teaming up with Mays again for *As Falls Wichita, So Falls Wichita Falls*, Metheny moves into a new arena of expression. Although the selections are seemingly structured as duets, with embellishments by Brazilian percussionist Nana Vasconcelos, Vasconcelos actually plays an integral role in the proceedings, fleshing out the colors of the title tune and even providing the melody (vocally) for "Estupenda Grása." *Offramp* introduces a new bass player, Steve Rodby, and Vasconcelos pops up again, adding tremendously to the flavor of "Barcarole." Still, the group's growing reliance on percussion isn't quite as noteworthy as

Metheny's embrace of the guitar synthesizer and synclavier guitar, devices that increase the timbral range available to him, but at some cost, as the guitarist often ends up with the same sounds as a keyboard synth player, but none of the technical advantages. Metheny mostly avoids the synth-guitar for *Rejoicing*, a trio date with Haden and drummer Billy Higgins, but when he does resort to it, the grandiloquent, trumpet-like tone he gets for "The Calling" suggests he sees the added electronics as a sort of arranging tool.

First Circle, which adds percussionist Pedro Aznar to the lineup, confirms that suspicion, opening with the Carla Bley-ish "Forward March" and proceeding through a series of tightly arranged tunes that seem to point as much to Metheny and Mays's compositional sense as to their improvisational skills. It's an approach not unlike that taken by Weather Report (although its sound is utterly dissimilar), and his score for *The Falcon and the Snowman* has no trouble expanding it to cinematic scale. (There's also a vocal by David Bowie on "This Is Not America.") Metheny gets even more ambitious on *Still Life (Talking)*, adding wordless vocals that lend a dreamy, soaring feel to tunes like "Minuano (Six Eight)"; *Letter From Home* relies on more conventional string orchestration for its occasional bits of textural oomph.

Metheny's most exciting recordings remain those in which he surrounds himself with older, more established players. Like *Song X*, a vigorous, challenging collaboration with Ornette Coleman that recalls the bracingly cacophonous recordings Coleman made in the late '60s and early '70s. Or *Question and Answer*, a far more accessible date featuring Metheny in a trio setting, with bassist Dave Holland and drummer Roy Haynes, whose hard-swinging polyrhythms push the guitarist to new heights. — J.D.C.

MIAMI SOUND MACHINE
★★ Eyes of Innocence (Epic, 1984)
★★★½ Primitive Love (Epic, 1985)
Before it was subsumed into Gloria Estefan's solo career, the Miami Sound Machine was a pleasant if predictable Latin pop outfit that would probably have been ignored by the pop mainstream had it not been for the semi-rousing "Dr. Beat," a percussion-powered dance tune from *Eyes of Innocence*. Taking its lead from that

single's success, *Primitive Love* augments sentimental ballads like "Words Get in the Way" with tepid-but-tuneful dance songs like the salsafied "Conga" and the techno-intense title tune. — J.D.C.

GEORGE MICHAEL
★★★½ Faith (Columbia, 1987)
★★★ Listen Without Prejudice Vol. 1 (Columbia, 1990)
Since no one knew what on earth fellow Wham!-mate Andrew Ridgeley was doing during all those years of posing with George, it made sense that Michael went solo in 1987, having broken hearts and sales records with his former band's high-gloss arena-pop. Wham!'s brilliantly empty teen-pop was the best of its kind since Abba. With *Faith*, Michael tried for the obvious: an album to force listeners over 14 to take him seriously, while building on the mass success he'd so prettily sweated for. And he succeeded in spades. Frantically flashing his talents, he revived the grandstanding trick of playing every instrument in sight—the album was, among other things, a daunting testimony to George's control. And it earned our lad six hit singles, wafting him into that stratosphere peopled only by the likes of Michael Jackson and Madonna. "Faith" was cocky neo-rockabilly; "I Want Your Sex" was silk-sheet funk; "One More Try" was a sweet ode to, perhaps, masochism. In "Hand to Mouth," the album even flourished a social conscience.

Such incipient earnestness, however, was pushed to the wall on the follow-up, *Listen Without Prejudice Vol. 1*. "Freedom 90" has a convincing gospel-ish soul; and "Waiting for That Day" finds George wailing with genuine heart. It's a better record than most of its radio contemporaries; it's just that Michael's straining too hard. — P.E.

LEE MICHAELS
★★★½ The Lee Michaels Collection (Rhino, 1992)
Although multi-instrumentalist Michaels (sax, keyboard, trombone) was a competent, if excessive, guitarist, his main gig was liberating '70s rock organ from Keith Emerson-ish passes at classical pretension: Michaels played the thing like some massive rhythm box. Buck-toothed and grinning from behind his keyboard, he wailed out "Do You Know What I Mean," a funky, syncopated 1971 hit, accompanied only by Frosty—a drummer equivalent in girth and

bombast to guitarist Leslie West. *The Lee Michaels Collection* is an anthology drawn from Michaels's six out-of-print albums, *Carnival of Life, Recital, Lee Michaels, Barrell, Fifth,* and *Space and First Takes,* recorded from 1968 to 1972. — P.E.

MICHEL'LE
★ ★ ★ **Michel'le (Ruthless/Atco, 1990)**
Between her little-girl speaking voice and soul-mama singing, Michel'le has the makings of a pretty good gimmick. But what elevates this album from good to great is the deeply soulful production of N.W.A.'s Dr. Dre. His beats, after all, are what give "No More Lies" its urgency, and though his arrangements can't quite make the slow songs swing, at least he's smart enough to stand back and let her emote. — J.D.C.

MICKEY AND SYLVIA
★ ★ ★ ★ **Love Is Strange & Other Hits (RCA, 1989)**
Mickey Baker was one of the most respected guitarists on the New York R&B scene in the 1950s when a little-known R&B singer named Sylvia Vanderpool asked him to teach her how to play the guitar. Teacher and pupil soon became a duo whose second single, "Love Is Strange," released in 1956 on the RCA subsidiary Groove, sold a million-plus copies and was a Top Twenty hit. Produced by Bob Rolontz, "Love Is Strange" has an exotic ambience and is further enlivened by Baker's stinging, angular guitar lines running throughout the song. The spoken bridge—"How do you call your lover boy?"—is firmly entrenched as a classic of its kind in rock history, a bit of salacious repartee between man and woman in which everything is suggested, but nothing is spoken outright. Mickey and Sylvia failed to match the success of their first hit single, although they cut a couple of other mid-level chart entries, "There Oughta Be a Law" and "Baby You're So Fine." They also tried various producers, including Leiber and Stoller, but Rolontz seemed to be the only one who understood that Baker's guitar work was not only a thing of beauty but a drawing card as well. The Rolontz-produced sides almost always feature the guitar in a starring role, and even when the song is mediocre, Baker remains interesting. One of the non-hits in this collection, "No Good Lover," is a jump blues graced by Sylvia's sassiest vocal and some extraordinary six-string commentaries

courtesy of Baker; "Shake It Up" is a guitar instrumental in which Baker employs distortion, twang and red-hot blues runs to make his point most emphatically.

Mickey and Sylvia split up in 1961, the former retreating to Europe before returning to New York, where he opened a guitar school. Sylvia Vanderpool married and became Sylvia Robinson, and had several hits as a solo artist in the '70s ("Pillow Talk" hit Number Three and topped the R&B charts in '73). She also became a central figure in the birth of rap as a commercial enterprise, signing a number of the genre's early standard-bearers to her Sugar Hill label, including the Sugar Hill Gang, Grandmaster Flash and the Furious Five, and Funky Four + One. — D.M.

BETTE MIDLER
★ ★ ★ ★   **The Divine Miss M (Atlantic, 1972)**
★ ★ ★½ **Bette Midler (Atlantic, 1973)**
★ ★½ **Songs for the New Depression (Atlantic, 1976)**
★ ★ ★   **Live at Last (Atlantic, 1977)**
★ ★   **Broken Blossom (Atlantic, 1978)**
★ ★   **Thighs and Whispers (Atlantic, 1979)**
★ ★ ★   **The Rose (Atlantic, 1979)**
★ ★   **Divine Madness (Atlantic, 1980)**
★ ★   **No Frills (Atlantic, 1983)**
★ ★   **Mud Will Be Flung Tonight (Atlantic, 1985)**
★ ★   **Some People's Lives (Atlantic, 1990)**
Bette Midler touched off the '70s nostalgia boom with *The Divine Miss M* and "Boogie Woogie Bugle Boy," but warm 'n' fuzzy tunnel-vision really wasn't her style—at first. Her audaciously theatrical delivery and campy, taste-zapping zest for life can still strike a listener like a cold slap in the face. She could play the bawdy mama act to the hilt, yet Bette Midler also found the emotional center in a dumbfounding variety of songs. Of course, her voice—surprisingly supple and delicate at times—helps quite a bit. A true child of the '60s underneath her tacky period glitz, Midler exults in girl-group melodrama ("Chapel of Love") and singer-songwriter homilies (John Prine's "Hello in There") alike on her debut album. If you can bear the chattering show-biz patter on the first version of "Friends" (this acid-etched soundtrack chestnut appears twice), the shameless delights offered on *The Divine Miss M* will melt even the sternest objections to non-rock. The early Bette Midler falls somewhere between a

traditional cabaret belter and a modern-day performance artist.

Naturally, this made Bette a dynamite live performer—and also an underdeveloped recording artist. *Bette Midler* repeats the scattershot format of the debut, with respectable-enough results. "Twisted" prefigures Joni Mitchell's hit version of this bitter '50s cocktail, and signals Midler's widespread influence. The soul cover versions are another matter; despite her élan, Midler can't do justice to the raw lust of Ann Peebles's "Breaking Up Somebody's Home" or the spiritual uplift of Jackie Wilson's "Higher and Higher." You can't do *everything;* Midler shines on "Da Doo Ron Ron" and "Lullabye of Broadway."

From the strained opener ("Strangers in the Night") onward, *Songs for the New Depression* is where Bette Midler's musically adventurous act lapses into schtick. *The Rose* established Midler as an actress; she credibly portrays a Janis Joplin-esque doomed rock star in this hit melodrama. *The Rose* album is the first of several very successful Midler soundtracks. "Wind Beneath Your Wings," from the 1988 screen weeper *Beaches,* kickstarted Midler's languishing musical career when it charted that year. Up until then, she'd been sadly adrift on record during the '80s. *Live at Last* and the Broadway stage soundtrack *Divine Madness* will more than satisfy fans, however. Ironically, Midler, who started her career singing deceptively witty little ditties, wound up the '80s pumping straight sentimental hokum on *Some People's Lives* and the 1990 smash "From a Distance."

— M.C.

MIDNIGHT OIL
★★½ **Midnight Oil (1978; Columbia, 1990)**
★★★½ **Head Injuries (1979; Columbia, 1990)**
★★★ **Bird Noises (EP) (1980; Columbia, 1990)**
★★★½ **Place Without a Postcard (1981; Columbia, 1990)**
★★★★ **10, 9, 8, 7, 6, 5, 4, 3, 2, 1 (Columbia, 1983)**
★★★★ **Red Sails in the Sunset (Columbia, 1984)**
★★★★ **Species Deceases (EP) (1985; Columbia, 1990)**
★★★★½ **Diesel and Dust (Columbia, 1987)**
★★★★½ **Blue Sky Mining (Columbia, 1990)**
★★★★ **Scream in Blue (Columbia, 1992)**

Midnight Oil is not the most influential band ever to emerge from Australia, nor is it the most original. But it is the most Australian, and not just because the band's lyrics address topics like aboriginal rights or labor disputes in outback asbestos mines. What makes Midnight Oil seem so quintessentially Australian is the way the band combines the pub-hardened instrumental attack expected of club veterans with the sort of intricate, ambitious arrangements that made the likes of Split Enz so exciting. Granted, the formula took some refining before the band got it right. *Midnight Oil,* for instance, is wonderfully tough-minded at times, roaring through the rave-ups of "Powderworks" or building to an impressive climax in "Surfing With a Spoon," but it's hard to have much enthusiasm for the art-rock meanderings of "Nothing Lost, Nothing Gained." Not to worry; there are no such excesses on *Head Injuries,* which puts a sharper edge on rockers like "Cold Cold Change" and "Back On the Borderline."

Midnight Oil didn't actively seek an audience outside Australia until *Place Without a Postcard,* which boasts a fatter sound and more focused songs but still seems the work of a band more suited to the stage than the studio. Not so with *10, 9, 8, 7, 6, 5, 4, 3, 2, 1,* the first Oil album to earn American release; with Nick Launay producing and the band making the most of overdubs and Jim Moginie's synths, the arrangements become rich and varied, as dramatic as any of the early set-pieces but considerably more concise. Even better, this vivid new sound brings with it a corresponding improvement in the lyrics, as the Oils' political acumen gains insight and bite. What makes "Short Memory" so striking isn't hearing Peter Garrett find parallels between recent and ancient history, but the way the music's growing rage reinforces his argument, and the same goes for the rest of the album.

After that breakthrough, Midnight Oil never looked back. *Red Sails in the Sunset,* also recorded with Launay, broadens the band's sound some more, bringing brass ("Best of Both Worlds"), Fairlight ("Who Can Stand in the Way") and even rap-style edits ("When the Generals Talk") to add aural interest. Again, however, the writing carries the album, and the best songs bring a panoramic sense of melody to the band's historical and political commentary.

Incredibly, that still wasn't enough to convince American radio, or even Columbia

Records, which originally passed on the wonderful, pointed *Species Deceases* EP. But *Diesel and Dust* put the band over the top. Blessed with some of the most compelling political pop since *Highway 61 Revisited*, it was also a hit, thanks in large part to the catchy, compelling "Beds Are Burning." *Blue Sky Mining* doesn't offer much that can match the excitement of *Diesel* rockers like "The Dead Heart" or "Warakurna," although "Blue Sky Mine" and the raging, anthemic "Forgotten Years" certainly hold their own. Then again, between the quiet majesty of "Bedlam Bridge" or the steely resolve of "One Country," *Blue Sky Mining* possesses a low-key eloquence unmatched in the band's catalog. Besides, the exuberant edge of *Scream in Blue* should be compensation enough, inasmuch as the eight years of concert recordings collected here convey precisely the sort of fevered excitement that has made this band a legend on the concert circuit. — J.D.C.

MIDNIGHT STAR

★ ★½ **The Beginning (Solar, 1980)**
★ ★½ **Standing Together (Solar, 1981)**
★ ★ ★ **Greatest Hits (Solar/Epic, 1987)**
★ ★½ **Work It Out (Solar/Epic, 1990)**

As its *Greatest Hits* attests, Midnight Star alternates between two very obvious styles—drecky make-out music ("Move Me," "Can't Give You Up") of the glossiest variety, and marginally more effective dance-floor thumpers ("Freak-a-Zoid," "Electricity" and "Wet My Whistle"). Their party anthems aren't bad—once you get past synth-riffs so elementary that they sound like those of a kindergarten Bernie Worrell. — P.E.

MIKE + THE MECHANICS

★ ★ ★ **Mike + the Mechanics (Atlantic, 1985)**
★ ★ ★½ **Living Years (Atlantic, 1988)**
★ ★ **Word of Mouth (Atlantic, 1991)**

After a few forgettable attempts at a do-it-yourself solo career, Genesis bassist-guitarist Mike Rutherford apparently realized that his strengths ran more to writing and playing than singing, and decided to let others do the things he couldn't. Hence Mike + the Mechanics, a part-time quintet which rounds out Rutherford's skills with a capable keyboardist (Adrian Lee), a good drummer (Peter Van Hooke) and two superb singers (Paul Young, formerly of Sad Cafe, and Paul Carrack, once with Ace and Squeeze). *Mike + the Mechanics* immediately

demonstrates the wisdom of the move; not only is the writing sharp and tuneful, but the band is as adept at the dark drama of "Silent Running" as the soulful urgency of "All I Need Is a Miracle." That versatility carries through to *Living Years*, but the album's best moments—particularly the title tune, a solemn-yet-inspiring song about coming to terms with mortality—move beyond mere formula to push the band to its limits. (Of course, the cameos by Rutherford's Genesis mates, Tony Banks and Phil Collins, can't have hurt). But *Word of Mouth*, despite its sparkling production and rhythmic vitality, never quite clicks, offering excellent performances of unmemorable material. — J.D.C.

BUDDY MILES

★ ★½ **Carlos Santana and Buddy Miles Live (Columbia, 1972)**

Thunder, rather than subtlety, characterized Miles's drumming—and he was a belter, not a singer. As a member of the late-'60s supergroup, Electric Flag, he kept things steady; on his own he went bonkers. After playing alongside Jimi Hendrix and bassist Billy Cox in the Band of Gypsies, he hit big in 1970 with "Them Changes," a hard-funk thumper. His 1972 collaboration with Carlos Santana, *Carlos Santana and Buddy Miles Live*, features a frenzied workout of that hit, and an equally heavy take on Santana's "Evil Ways." The endless jam "Free Form Funkafide Filth," with Carlos stomping over-zealously on the wah-wah pedal, is quintessential Buddy: the man will not let up. — P.E.

ROGER MILLER

★ ★ ★½ **Golden Hits of Roger Miller (Smash, 1966)**
★ ★ ★½ **More Golden Hits (Polygram, 1988)**

An artful scalawag, Roger Miller remains famous for a series of hugely successful comic singles he released in the mid-'60s. Moving from Oklahoma to Nashville, he spent time as Faron Young's drummer (although his primary instrument was guitar) and garnered an impressive reputation as a songwriter for such country giants as Ray Price, George Jones and Ernest Tubb. By 1964, he'd gained his own hits with "You Don't Want My Love," "When Two Worlds Collide," "Dang Me" and "Chug-a-Lug"—the latter two setting the pattern for the cornpone classics that made his name.

His lasting achievement was "King of the Road" (1965), a fondly ironic "redneck" version of the kind of hobo anthem Woody

Guthrie had so earnestly delivered. With a short-story writer's flair, Miller summed up the footloose appeal of a genial, shiftless trailer-park rambler. His subsequent work alternated daffy humor ("Do Wacka Do," "You Can't Roller Skate in a Buffalo Herd") and novelties ("England Swings," "One Dyin' and a Buryin' "), with a little hokem thrown in for good measure (Bobby Russell's "Little Green Apples"). Miller can be cloying, but the sassy exhilaration of his vocals generally redeems him—and his best songs are genuine Americana. — P.E.

STEVE MILLER BAND
- ★★★½ Children of the Future (Capitol, 1968)
- ★★★½ Sailor (Capitol, 1968)
- ★★★½ Brave New World (Capitol, 1969)
- ★★★½ Your Saving Grace (Capitol, 1969)
- ★★★½ Number Five (Capitol, 1970)
- ★★★★ Living in the U.S.A. (Capitol, 1971)
- ★★★ Rock Love (Capitol, 1971)
- ★★★ Recall the Beginning . . . A Journey From Eden (Capitol, 1972)
- ★★★★ Anthology (Capitol, 1972)
- ★★★½ The Joker (Capitol, 1973)
- ★★★★ Fly Like an Eagle (Capitol, 1976)
- ★★★★ Book of Dreams (Capitol, 1977)
- ★★★½ Steve Miller Band's Greatest Hits (Capitol, 1978)
- ★★★ Circle of Love (Capitol, 1981)
- ★★½ Abracadabra (Capitol, 1982)
- ★★ Italian X-Rays (Capitol,
- ★★½ Living in the 20th Century (Capitol, 1987)
- ★★★ Born 2 B Blue (Capitol, 1988)

"Take the Money and Run," the winking title of one of Steve Miller's '70s mega-hits, seems to sum up the blithely commercial drive of this genial radio artiste, but his early work was trailblazing—and even his trifles sound great in the car. Forming his first professional outfit in San Francisco in the late '60s, the guitarist-singer deftly sidestepped the flashier excesses of shopworn psychedelia, and concentrated on clean rockers and supple blues. Helped out greatly by Boz Scaggs on vocals and guitar, "Living in the U.S.A.," "Quicksilver Girl," "Dime-A-Dance Romance" and the bulk of *Children of the Future* and *Sailor* are steady, effortless rock & roll—*Living in the U.S.A.* packages the two records together. *Anthology* also is pretty terrific: "Space Cowboy," "Seasons," "I Love You" and "My Dark Hour," an interesting, heavy thumper featuring Paul McCartney, are

melodically astute and very catchy—the collection also renders *Number Five, Rock Love*, and *Recall the Beginning . . . A Journey From Eden* unnecessary.

With its ultra-clean production, and the absolute efficiency of its songs, *The Joker* was a record made for radio success—and it reaped it in spades. The title track has become Miller's signature tune, and it shows his complete mastery of the single—punchy bass, a nifty guitar motif and witty lyrics delivered with laconic assurance. His next two records, *Fly Like an Eagle* and *Book of Dreams*, form, with *The Joker*, the essential big-time Miller trilogy. As Stephen King does with horror stories, so Miller does with Top Forty rock; that is, he delivers, in such hits as "Rock'n Me," "Jet Airliner," and "Jungle Love," sure-fire pleasures, triumphs not of originality, but of craft.

With infinitessimal shifts in tone and style, Miller continued in the vein set by those three albums above. "Abracadabra" was a tasty smash, even if the album that bore its title was fairly perfunctory; only on *Italian X-Rays* did the formula show signs of real exhaustion—a ditty like "Bongo Bongo" sounds like Miller parodying himself. Miller's gift—and it's a subtle one—is in making the familiar sound fresh. — P.E.

MILLI VANILLI
- ★★ Girl You Know It's True (Arista, 1989)
- ★ The Remix Album (Arista, 1990)

Perhaps the only duo in pop music history that's best known for what it didn't sing, Rob Pilatus and Fabrice Morvan of Milli Vanilli made headlines in 1990 when it was revealed that the two never sang a note. According to producer Frank Farian, Pilatus and Morvan were hired only for their looks, which he felt would add street-level credibility to the music. Apparently, the street he had in mind was Sesame St., since only a listener with the approximate intelligence of Big Bird could have fallen for such a contrived attempt at rap and funk. — J.D.C.

THE MILLS BROTHERS
- ★★★ Our Golden Favorites (MCA, 1961)
- ★★★★ The Best of the Mills Brothers (MCA, 1966)
- ★★★ Our Golden Favorites, Vol. II (MCA, 1971)
- ★★★★ 16 Great Performances (MCA, 1975)

The year 1931 saw the first release of a single by a Cincinnati-based vocal trio that specialized in relaxed, jazz-oriented harmony

singing; it would be nearly 40 years later
before the Mills Brothers finished placing
new recordings on the pop charts, an
unparalleled feat among vocal groups in
America. That first single on Brunswick,
"Tiger Rag," topped the charts. Moreover,
the Mills Brothers begat a style that was
widely imitated and proved influential in the
development of group harmony in the
1950s. Rooted in pop and jazz, the Mills
Brothers, unlike most pre-rock black artists,
were played on white radio stations, sold
records to white audiences and dominated
the otherwise lily-white pop charts.

In 1937 the Mills Brothers began a
fruitful 20-year association with Decca
Records, before concluding their recording
career with Dot in the late '60s. MCA's
various hits collections offer a generous taste
of Mills Brothers Decca classics. The two-fer
Best of contains most of the tracks on the
two *Golden Favorites* albums, and then
some, not the least being "Paper Doll,"
"You Always Hurt the One You Love" and
"The Glow-Worm," Number One records
from, respectively, 1943, 1944, and 1952. *16
Great Performances* includes some
well-known Decca sides, and adds three of
the Dot hits, "Yellow Bird" from 1959 and,
from 1968, "Cab Driver" and "My Shy
Violet." Whether it be on a tender, delicate
lyric such as "You Always Hurt the One
You Love," or the resilient, melancholy
blues of "Basin St. Blues," the Mills
Brothers demonstrate versatility, sensitivity
and creativity. Good music is its own calling
card, regardless of the day's trends. — D.M.

RONNIE MILSAP

★ ★ ★ **Plain and Simple (Pickwick, 1975)**
★ ★ ★ **Ronnie Milsap Live (1976; RCA,
1987)**
  ★ ★ **It Was Almost Like a Song (RCA,
1977)**
★ ★ ★ **Greatest Hits (1980; RCA, 1988)**
★ ★ ★ **Out Where the Bright Lights Are
Glowing (RCA, 1981)**
  ★ ★ **Keyed Up (RCA, 1983)**
★ ★ ★ **Greatest Hits, Vol. 2 (RCA, 1985)**
  ★ ★ **Collector's Series (1986; RCA, 1987)**
  ★ ★ **Lost in the Fifties Tonight (RCA,
1986)**
  ★ ★ **Heart and Soul (RCA, 1987)**
★ ★ ★ **Stranger Things Have Happened
(RCA, 1989)**
★ ★ ★ **Back to the Grindstone (RCA, 1991)**
When Ronnie Milsap debuted in 1973,
much was made of his having done session
work with Elvis Presley, less so of his
abiding affection for early rock & roll and

R&B styles. As the years have worn on,
though, Milsap has managed to slip in
reminders of where his heart's at even as he
occupies the safe middle ground among
mainstream balladeers. That's not to excuse
wimpy efforts on the order of "It Was
Almost Like a Song," but rather to point up
the often-conflicted nature of Milsap's work.
He's made his bones with the country
audience but seems forever wanting to break
out into something more incendiary.

Notably instructive in this regard are
Plain and Simple and *Ronnie Milsap Live*,
the former (now out of print) being nine
cuts produced by Huey Meaux (who
produced Freddie Fender, the Sir Douglas
Quintet and Jerry Lee Lewis, among many
others) in the early '70s before Milsap
landed his RCA contract, the latter finding
Milsap at the Grand Ole Opry serving up a
healthy dose of everything he does best from
weepy ballads to propulsive rockers. *Plain
and Simple* shows a Milsap that has
disappeared, with a voice somewhere
between Ray Charles and Charlie Rich and
purveying some gutbucket R&B-styled
tunes, some his own compositions. He may
never have become the star of the
magnitude he is now had he stuck to the
Plain and Simple material, but it's
interesting to ponder where he might have
gone artistically with this compelling
amalgam of R&B and country.

Otherwise, his RCA catalog is a
predictable mix of hit singles and the odd
rock oldie, none of them particularly bad,
but none particularly enthralling. *Out Where
the Bright Lights are Glowing* is Milsap's
tribute album to the late Jim Reeves, and
the match is a good one. Milsap has a
stronger voice than did Reeves, and is able
to summon forth emotions that Reeves
smoothed over. Particularly noteworthy are
his interpretations of "Four Walls" and
"When Two Worlds Collide." The two
greatest-hits albums are safe bets and good
overviews of Milsap's range; *Vol. 2* contains
a truly awesome vocal performance in "She
Keeps the Home Fires Burning" and a
tender interpretation of "Any Day Now."
Stranger Things Have Happened is the
strongest collection of songs Milsap has ever
put on disc, particularly two of its four hit
singles, "Don't You Ever Get Tired (of
Hurting Me)" and "A Woman in Love,"
which Milsap invests with hard-earned
wisdom. His latest, *Back to the Grindstone*,
is more adventurous than most recent
Milsap efforts. The typical Milsap fare
("When the Hurt Comes Down") is

buttressed by an ingratiating take on the Skyliners' 1959 hit, "Since I Don't Have You"; a track featuring the Boys Choir of Harlem ("Spare the Rod [Love the Child]") that mingles dance rhythm tracks with a gospel feel; a spirited duet with Patti Labelle on "Love Certified"; and guest artists Mark Knopfler ("All Is Fair in Love and War") and John Hiatt (on Hiatt's "Old Habits Are Hard to Break") adding their sounds to the mix. The upshot is that Milsap sounds reinvigorated, and ready to break out of the comfortable mold he's settled into.
— D.M.

CHARLES MINGUS

★ ★ ★ ★ The Jazz Experiments of Charles Mingus (1955; Bethlehem, 1984)

★ ★ ★ ★ Mingus at the Bohemia (1955; Fantasy, 1991)

★ ★ ★ ★ The Charles Mingus Quartet Plus Max Roach (1955; Fantasy, 1990)

★ ★ ★ ★ ★ Pithecanthropus Erectus (Atlantic, 1956; Atlantic, 1981)

★ ★ ★ ★ East Coasting (1957; Bethlehem, 1982)

★ ★ ★ ★½ The Clown (1957; Atlantic, 1984)

★ ★ ★ ★½ Blues and Roots (Atlantic, 1958)

★ ★ ★ ★ ★ Mingus Ah-Um (1959; Columbia, 1991)

★ ★ ★ ★ Mingus Revisited (Emarcy, 1960)

★ ★ ★ ★ ★ Mysterious Blues (1961; Candid, 1989)

★ ★ ★ ★ ★ New Tijuana Moods (1962; Bluebird, 1986)

★ ★ ★ ★ ★ The Black Saint and the Sinner Lady (1962; MCA/Impulse, 1986)

★ ★ ★ ★½ Mingus, Mingus, Mingus, Mingus, Mingus (1963; Impulse, 1983)

★ ★ ★½ Mingus Plays Piano (1963; Mobile Fidelity, 1990)

★ ★ ★ ★ ★ The Great Concert of Charles Mingus (Prestige, 1964)

★ ★ ★½ Right Now: Live at the Jazz Workshop (1964; Fantasy, 1990)

★ ★ ★ ★ ★ Town Hall Concert (1964; Jazz Workshop/Fantasy, 1990)

★ ★ ★ ★ ★ Let My Children Hear Music (Columbia, 1971)

★ ★ ★½ Charles Mingus and Friends in Concert (Columbia, 1972)

★ ★ ★½ Mingus Moves (Atlantic, 1974)

★ ★ ★ ★ At Carnegie Hall (Atlantic, 1976)

★ ★ ★ ★ ★ Mingus at Antibes (1976; Atlantic, 1986)

★ ★ ★½ Three or Four Shades of Blues (1977; Atlantic, 1989)

★ ★ ★ ★ Shoes of the Fisherman's Wife (Columbia, 1988)

★ ★ ★ ★ ★ The Complete Debut Recordings (Fantasy, 1990)

★ ★ ★ ★ ★ Epitaph (Columbia, 1990)

While Charles Mingus stands as the best jazz bassist besides Oscar Pettiford, he's remembered more significantly as the idiom's most original composer since Duke Ellington. As the title of his brilliant, if fanciful, stream-of-consciousness 1970 autobiography, *Beneath the Underdog*, suggests, Mingus saw himself as a resolute outsider, an embattled figure of too vast a dimension to be contained by conventional categories. While his consistent inventiveness in some ways proved him right, the blustery promethean was also a past master of the tradition—the entire history of jazz lay easily under his dextrous fingertips. And while his methods were demanding and his persona blunt, Mingus, again like Ellington, is noteworthy in that so much of his music, for all of its innovative force, offers such sheer accessible joy. Since his death, from Lou Gehrig's disease in 1979, Mingus has assumed his rightful place in the jazz pantheon; even non-jazzers, however, stand a good chance of being seduced by his powerful ghost.

Schooled by his stepmother in church music (gospel would remain an abiding influence), Mingus worked for a while with Red Norvo and his "cool jazz" outfit before forming the Debut record label in the early '50s. Fantasy's 12-CD set of 169 selections, *The Complete Debut Recordings*, offers stellar examples of nascent greatness. Mingus truly cut loose, however, with *Mingus Ah-Um* and the rollicking highlight, "Better Git It in Your Soul," that soon became his theme song—and with *Pithecanthropus Erectus*. The latter's title track was an early instance of his compositional approach: a loosely metaphorical "tale" of pride going before a fall, it showed how Mingus often wrote music to illustrate a very specific, often elusive emotional state. And the playing, with its gospel influence, its whoops and hollers, displayed the characteristic Mingus exuberance.

Tijuana Moods (1962) (repackaged and better edited as *New Tijuana Moods*), with the castanet-crazed "Ysabel's Table Dance," continued to demonstrate the man's equal cunning and passion; the record, too, with drummer-soulmate Dannie Richmond and saxophonist Shafi Hadi showed that part of Mingus's greatness lay in his skill in choosing sidemen—Mingus cited *Tijuana* as his own favorite album, but throughout his career, he always picked the most soulful players. From around the same period, *The Black Saint and the Sinner Lady* and *Blues and Roots* solidified his strengths—a fierce swing, a novel voicing of instruments, and a "narrative" sense of composition. While a mere bagatelle in the context of his overall achievement, *Mingus Plays Piano* was interesting: even without his primary instrument, his distinctiveness comes through.

The end of the '60s was hard on Mingus. He wandered the streets for a period of nearly three years, believing himself to be going mad. Recovering himself, he went on to produce exceptional, if inconsistent, music in the '70s—*Let My Children Hear Music* (repackaged, on *Shoes of the Fisherman's Wife*, with selections from a standout 1959 disc, *Mingus Dynasty*) ranks with his triumphs. — P.E.

MINISTRY

★ ★ ★   **With Sympathy (Arista, 1983)**
★ ★ ★   **Twitch (Sire, 1986)**
★ ★ ½   **Twelve Inch Singles (Wax Trax, 1987)**
★ ★ ★ ★   **The Land of Rape and Honey (Sire, 1988)**
★ ★ ★ ½   **A Mind Is a Terrible Thing to Taste (Sire, 1989)**
★ ★ ★ ★   **In Case You Didn't Feel Like Showing Up (Live) (Sire, 1990)**

Originally just a dance music act with attitude, Ministry's first album, *With Sympathy*, offers none of the post-industrial fury that would eventually become the band's calling card. Instead, its songs come across like the work of a tougher, less quirky Soft Cell, and though singer-frontman Alain Jourgensen's blatant Anglophilia gets to be a bit much at points, it's not enough to undo the engaging melodicism of "Effigy (I'm Not An)" or "Revenge."

Still, Jourgensen eventually threw aside such pop niceties. Some evidence of the hardening of Ministry's sound can be found on *Twelve Inch Singles*, a compilation that offers one pre-*Sympathy* single, and three post-*Sympathy* efforts (although, tellingly, the remixed B-sides are invariably the tougher tracks), but it's not until *Twitch*, produced by English noisemaster Adrian Sherwood, that any genuine aural edge enters into the band's sound. Things get even nastier, sonically speaking, with *The Land of Rape and Honey*, an aggressively ugly piece of work that backs Jourgensen's heavily distorted vocals with bursts of ear-crushing automated noise; unabashedly intimidating, it's the most impressive item in the band's catalog.

There's a similar sense of menace to *A Mind Is a Terrible Thing to Taste*, particularly given the way the accelerated tempos push the music closer to thrash without taking away from its synth-based sound. Even so, the songs don't gain much from the added momentum. But if *A Mind* seemed to suggest that Ministry was becoming monochromatic, the concert recordings on *In Case You Didn't Feel Like Showing Up (Live)* display an awesome range of intensity (not to mention an admirable amount of musicianship) without backing off from the music's implied threat. — J.D.C.

LIZA MINNELLI

★ ★ ★ ½   **Liza With a "Z" (Columbia, 1972)**
★ ★   **The Singer (Columbia, 1973)**
★ ★ ★ ½   **Foursider (A&M, 1988)**
★ ★ ★   **Results (Epic, 1989)**
★ ★ ★ ½   **Liza Minnelli at Carnegie Hall (Telarc, 1989)**

Grooving on Liza Minnelli demands not only an appreciation of her somewhat quaint persona—the plucky waif, smiling through tears—but understanding the show-biz tradition of which she and Barbra Streisand are the last heirs. Minnelli's mother, Judy Garland, of course, was the last great, tragic queen of the style—torch-song music of melodrama and technique that's the antithesis of rock & roll. Apparently aware that the genre's glories are period ones, Liza has spent much of her career translating its standards into a modern idiom, with somewhat haphazard success. On *Foursider* and the live *Liza With a "Z"*, she goes in for an ingratiatingly casual approach—her versions of "God Bless the Child," "The Man I Love" and "Bye Bye Blackbird" are approachable and swinging, and she leavens the classic fare with songs by contemporary writers (Randy Newman, Dory Previn). Singing sometimes in intentionally bungled French and tossing off breathless quips, her humor is the very stagey one of swank nightclubs, but it buoys her appeal as a diva with dimples—a singer so at home in the tradition that she can shrug a little under its weight. The orchestration, by such ace arrangers as Peter Matz and Mort Lindsey, is light and elegant; it doesn't adhere too reverently to the sound of another era, but it doesn't pander misguidedly to "younger" audiences (no ersatz rock). *Liza Minnelli at Carnegie Hall*, from 1987, handles the vintage material more straightforwardly—the 47-piece orchestra kicks with real command—and, even if Minnelli never comes across as overbearing (the way Streisand can), she sings with a veteran's strong authority. "Cabaret," of course, is the centerpiece of her live work; the theme to her breakthrough movie, it remains a nifty showstopper; its continental flair also serves to recall the glamour of Edith Piaf and others of the European school of artful entertainment.

While obviously comfortable, then, with classy material, Minnelli can really flounder when it comes to pop. On *The Singer* her choice of material is banal—"I Believe in Music," "Baby Don't Get Hooked on Me," "I'd Love You to Want Me"—and neither her fine, clear voice nor her show-biz savvy can elevate such tripe. Much more interesting is *Results*, a 1989 collaboration with the Pet Shop Boys. David Lynch's favorite composer, Angelo Badalamenti, helps out with orchestration, and Pet Shoppers Neil Tennant and Chris Lowe turn in novel synth takes on Stephen Sondheim's "Losing My Mind" and Tanita Tikaram's "Twist in My Sobriety." They also provide a handful of their characteristically polished originals—tunes whose cleverness parallels the spirit of the music Liza knows best. It may be glitz, but it's smart glitz. — P.E.

KYLIE MINOGUE

★ ★½ **Kylie (Geffen, 1988)**
★ **Enjoy Yourself (Geffen, 1990)**

Judging Kylie Minogue as a pop singer isn't entirely fair. After all, her real claim to fame (in Britain and Australia, anyway) is as a TV actress. And by those standards, she's not half bad; she's no Rick Springfield, to be sure, but a good bit better than Cheryl Ladd. Despite a rendition of "The Loco-Motion" that leaves Little Eva sounding like Aretha Franklin, *Kylie* is okay, thanks to jovial, insistent tunes like "I Should Be So Lucky." But *Enjoy Yourself* turns the Stock-Aitken-Waterman formula of the first album into pre-programmed dance dreck, particularly when she duets with the exquisitely vapid Jason Donovan on "Especially for You." — J.D.C.

MINUTEMEN

★½ **The Punch Line (SST, 1981)**
★ ★ **What Makes a Man Start Fires? (SST, 1982)**
★ ★ ★½ **Buzz or Howl Under the Influence of Heat (SST, 1983)**
★ ★ ★½ **Double Nickels on the Dime (SST, 1984)**
★ ★ ★½ **The Politics of Time (New Alliance, 1984)**
★ ★ ★ **My First Bells 1980–1983 (SST, 1985)**
★ ★ ★ ★ **Project: Mersh (EP) (SST, 1985)**
★ ★ ★ ★ **3-Way Tie (for Last) (SST, 1985)**
★ ★ ★ **Ballot Result (SST, 1987)**
★ ★½ **Post-Mersh, Vol. 1 (SST, 1987)**
★ ★ ★½ **Post-Mersh, Vol. 2 (SST, 1987)**
★ ★ ★ **Post-Mersh, Vol. 3 (SST, 1989)**

One of the few California underground acts with a genuinely distinctive way of making music, the Minutemen—guitarist D. Boon, bassist Mike Watt and drummer George Hurley—eschewed both the mindless conformity of the mainstream and the predictability of punk. In their place, the Minutemen offered a sound that had less to do with notions of style or fashion than with the interplay between the group's members—a chemistry that subverted the usual dynamics of guitar-led power trios. Granted, that approach is still in its nascent stages on *The Punch Line*, on which the band's knotty, bass-driven rhythms are as static and unswinging as its lyrics are strident and humorless. But by *Buzz or Howl Under the Influence of Heat*, the Minutemen correct both shortcomings, loosening the groove on the funk-fueled "I Felt Like a Gringo" and goofing amiably through "The Toe Jam." The 45-song *Double Nickels on the Dime* (truckdriver slang for 55 mph) is testament to the Minutemen's fecundity, but for the most part it's the playing, not the writing, that stands as the band's strength. This changes to some extent with *Project: Mersh*, a bizarre send-up of mainstream rock that is at times bitingly funny (as on the crushingly insincere "Hey Lawdy Mama") but also shows how much the Minutemen could do with conventional song structures when so inclined. Indeed, *3-Way Tie (for Last)* suggests that the group was itself curious to see where intensive songwriting might lead, but before the Minutemen and their fans could find out, Boon was killed in a van accident, abruptly ending the group. (Watt and Hurley eventually regrouped with guitarist Ed Crawford as fIREHOSE.)

Sorting through the raft of Minutemen

anthologies takes some doing, by the way. *My First Bells 1980–1983* is a cassette-only compilation including all of *The Punch Line* and *What Makes a Man Start Fires?* as well as a few EPs and singles. *Post-Mersh, Vol. 1* also compiles *Punch Line* and *What Makes?*, this time on CD; *Post-Mersh, Vol. 2* joins *Buzz or Howl Under the Influence of Heat* with *Project: Mersh*; *Post-Mersh, Vol. 3* includes *The Politics of Time* plus the contents of four EPs. As for *Ballot Result*, it collects live recordings (from air checks, rehearsals and the like) of Minutemen favorites, as chosen by the group's fans. — J.D.C.

MISSION OF BURMA

★ ★ ★½ **Signals, Calls, and Marches (EP) (Ace of Hearts, 1981)**
★ ★ ★ ★ **VS. (Ace of Hearts, 1982)**
★ ★ ★ ★ **The Horrible Truth About Burma (Ace of Hearts, 1985)**
★ ★ ★ **Mission of Burma (EP) (Taang!, 1987)**
★ ★ ★ **Forget (Taang!, 1987)**
★ ★ ★ ★ **Mission of Burma (Rykodisc, 1988)**

Volume has always been a central part of guitar rock's charm, and few bands have ever exploited its ear-crushing cacophony of over-amplified guitars as adroitly as Mission of Burma. Like fellow noise merchants Sonic Youth and Live Skull, this Boston-based band understood how to exploit the ringing overtones and accidental harmonies that arise out of this amplified din. But Mission of Burma parts company with the avant-gardists in applying its eloquent clangor to tuneful, well-constructed pop songs. Like, for example, "That's When I Reach for My Revolver," from *Signals, Calls, and Marches*, which backs its catchy, minor-key chorus with a wall of ringing, wailing guitar. With *VS.*, the band's sound is denser still, thanks to the gloriously sculpted sound of the screaming guitar on "Weatherbox" or the exuberant noise driving "New Nails."

Unfortunately, making all that racket got to be too much for guitarist Roger Miller, who left the band to save his hearing (switching to piano, he and Erik Lindgren formed Birdsongs of the Mesozoic). If that seems an extreme reaction, the band's live album, *The Horrible Truth About Burma*, ought to put things in perspective, as these performances seem deafening even at low volume, although the raucous cover of the Stooges' "1970" and the pulsating wall-of-sound given "Tremelo" are compensation enough.

Both Taang! releases—*Mission of Burma* and *Forget*—consist of outtakes and other arcana, making them for collectors only. The Rykodisc *Mission of Burma*, on the other hand, combines *Signals, Calls, and Marches* with *VS.*, plus a couple of singles and two tracks from *The Horrible Truth*; with an 80-minute playing time, it's one of the most generous CD compilations on the market. — J.D.C.

MR. MISTER

★ ★ **I Wear the Face (1984; RCA, 1986)**
★ ★ **Welcome to the Real World (RCA, 1985)**
★ ★½ **Go On (RCA, 1987)**

All ultra-clean production, competent playing and harmless good looks, Mr. Mister is formula '80s radio rock. Singer-bassist Richard Page comes across visually and vocally as Sting-lite, and the band occasionally indulges in diluted reggae stylings. Mister's big hit, "Kyrie," sounded like contemporary Christian fare with more commercial flair; otherwise everything by Mr. Mister is equally undistinctive and blandly professional. — P.E.

JONI MITCHELL

★ ★ ★ **Joni Mitchell (Reprise, 1968)**
★ ★ ★½ **Clouds (Reprise, 1969)**
★ ★ ★ ★ **Ladies of the Canyon (Reprise, 1970)**
★ ★ ★ ★ ★ **Blue (Reprise, 1971)**
★ ★ ★ ★ **For the Roses (Asylum, 1972)**
★ ★ ★ ★ ★ **Court and Spark (Asylum, 1974)**
★ ★ ★ **Miles of Aisles (Elektra, 1974)**
★ ★ ★½ **The Hissing of Summer Lawns (Asylum, 1975)**
★ ★ ★½ **Hejira (Asylum, 1976)**
★ ★ ★ **Don Juan's Reckless Daughter (Asylum, 1977)**
★ ★ ★ **Mingus (Asylum, 1979)**
★ ★ ★ **Shadows and Light (Asylum, 1980)**
★ ★ ★ **Wild Things Run Fast (Geffen, 1982)**
★ ★ ★½ **Dog Eat Dog (Geffen, 1985)**
★ ★½ **Chalk Mark in a Rainstorm (Geffen, 1988)**
★ ★ ★ ★ **Night Ride Home (Geffen, 1991)**

Joni Mitchell strummed her way out of Canada and into the L.A. music scene in the late '60s. Produced by David Crosby, her sparse debut album reveals a striking, if somewhat fragile, folk singer in the accepted acoustic mode. Mitchell's heart-piercing coldwater vocals and restless, self-questioning persona already separate her from the competition, however. Judy Collins scored a Top Ten hit with Mitchell's "Both Sides Now" in 1968; Joni's more contemplative version sets the older-and-wiser tone of *Clouds*, her much-improved second album. *Ladies of the Canyon* solidifies those songwriting advances. "Woodstock," too self-conscious to be an all-out anthem, is still Mitchell's most outgoing, least analytical moment. "The Circle Game," the album's closer, asserts Mitchell's ability to express complex emotional states in plain language. A supple chorus puts her personalized message across.

Blue raises the autobiographical stakes and intensifies the melodies; arguably, it's Mitchell's masterpiece. She picks memorable vignettes out of the flood of memories and reflections that accompany an extended journey, spinning off songs like "Carey," "California" and "This Flight Tonight." Though the musical backing (by Stephen Stills, James Taylor and others) is kept to a minimum, Joni's vocals grow in nuance and complexity. *Blue* stays under your skin for quite a while.

Starting with *For the Roses*, Mitchell pushes her musical accompaniment to keep pace with her rapidly evolving singing and writing skills. She's not always successful, but few other singer-songwriters extended their quest to include music as well as lyrics. Certainly, the cozy L.A. cowboy-rock studio scene must've beckoned Joni Mitchell with the lure of easy-going hit singles. True to form, she did it her own way with *For the Roses*. Saxophone player and band leader Tom Scott can be a vapid fusion-Muzak meister on his own, but his light jazz coloring underscores the subtle depths of *Roses*. On *Court and Spark*, Mitchell and Scott concoct a resonant pop-jazz sound that accommodates both swooning melodies ("Help Me") and blue reflection ("Same Situation") with ease. The bouyant humor of "Raised on Robbery" and the Lambert-Hendricks-Ross novelty "Twisted" makes this Joni's most appealing album (if not her most profound). Recorded on the tour following that album, *Miles of Aisles* features revamped versions of Mitchell's better-known early songs. It's a convenient sampler, but the progression from album to album—a big part of the picture—gets lost on both this concert album and the 1980 live set *Shadows and Light*.

Naturally, Mitchell pursued her muse into more adventurous territory on the next two albums. Some of the impressionistic snippets on *The Hissing of Summer Lawns* ("The Jungle Line," "The Boho Dance") never

quite register, though the effervescent melancholy of "In France They Kiss on Main Street" and "Don't Interrupt the Sorrow" sinks in deeply over time, as does the hauntingly slow "Shadows and Light." *Hejira* is even more atmospheric—or formless, depending on your attention level. Bassist Jaco Pastorius keeps up with Mitchell's wandering free-form meditations, while the rest of the music—wintry, detached—lulls in the background. No single track leaps out the way *Summer Lawns'* best ones do, but overall *Hejira* leaves the more lasting—if mysteriously vague—impression.

Don Juan's Reckless Daughter seems inevitable now—the double album in search of an editor. This time, a real lack of focus allows the session musicans to hot-dog their way through Mitchell's stilted set-pieces. *Mingus* represents a brave, attempted collaboration with the noted jazz bassist and composer; unfortunately, the results are sketchy at best.

Mitchell didn't retire in the '80s, though her intermittent releases indicate that she'd retreated from the artistic vanguard. *Wild Things Run Fast* is exactly the sort of competent holding-pattern album—complete with cover versions—that Mitchell went out of her way to avoid in the '70s. *Dog Eat Dog*, which came out of left field in 1984, comes closer to being the individualistic challenge fans might expect. Joni confronts producer Thomas Dolby's synthesized sound with feisty vocals and her most pointed set of songs. Rife with withering political opinions and topical insights, this unsettling album is her best of the period. Avoid *Chalk Mark in a Rainstorm*; a torrent of borderline New Age–easy listening blandness washes over even the most thoughtful lyrics.

Night Ride Home isn't a comeback so much as a chance to catch up with a long-lost confidante. There's a slight return to the jazz-tinged sound of the mid-'70s; succinct orchestrations and smokey sax lines curl around Mitchell's most tuneful material since *Court and Spark*. "Ray's Dad's Cadillac" and "Come in From the Cold" offer two very different—and unsentimental—views of adolescence. On "Only Joy in Town" and "Two Grey Rooms," Mitchell faces down a randy mid-life crisis and an uncertain old age, respectively. Like her old pal Neil Young, Joni Mitchell has managed to forge a mature style from the raw material of her youthful follies.   — M.C.

MODERN ENGLISH
★ ★ ★   After the Snow (Sire, 1983)
★ ★¹/₂ Ricochet Days (Sire, 1984)
★ ★   Stop Start (Sire, 1986)
★ ★¹/₂ Pillow Lips (TVT, 1990)

With "I Melt With You," from *After the Snow*, Modern English combines a memorably sturdy melody, an enticingly dynamic rhythm arrangement and a telling sense of acoustic detail into a singularly irresistible pop package. Trouble is, that's the only point in the band's catalog in which those elements come together so convincingly. The rest of *After the Snow* tends toward bland dance pop, while *Ricochet Days* is long on aural interest but short on melody, and *Stop Start* is a half-hearted lurch toward conventional rockism that has a few hooks but little else. A comeback album of sorts, *Pillow Lips* delivers both texture and momentum but neglects to include decent songs—apart, that is, from an empty reprise of "I Melt With You." — J.D.C.

MOLLY HATCHET
★ ★¹/₂ Molly Hatchet (Epic, 1978)
★ ★¹/₂ Flirtin' With Disaster (Epic, 1979)
★ ★   Beatin' the Odds (Epic, 1980)
★ ★   Take No Prisoners (Epic, 1981)
★ ★¹/₂ No Guts . . . No Glory (Epic, 1983)
★ ★   The Deed Is Done (Epic, 1984)
★ ★¹/₂ Double Trouble Live (Epic, 1985)
★ ★ ★   Greatest Hits (Epic, 1990)

Second-generation Southern rock second-hand, some would say Molly Hatchet bears more than a passing resemblance to Lynyrd Skynyrd. The younger Florida sextet mastered those bluesy dueling-guitar leads, and that's exactly its problem: Molly Hatchet never gets past paying tribute. The Allmans-inspired jams on the debut never spark a new fire; granted, that's hard to do on a cover version of the Brothers' classic "Dreams I'll Never See." But most of Molly Hatchet's songs sound like covers. Even an obvious Skynyrd rip like the hit title track from *Flirtin' With Disaster* possesses a certain rough charm, however: lead singer Danny Joe Brown has a pleasing, mellow burr inside his party growl, and hard-rock producer Tom Werman doesn't clean up the guitarists' mess. Brown left the band for a spell after that success, and even though he returned in 1983, Hatchet never regained its commercial momentum. *The Best of Molly Hatchet* offers consistent (if minor) pleasures that just might surprise longtime fans of this genre who passed by the first time. — M.C.

THE MOMENTS
★ ★ ★ The Moments' Greatest Hits (1977; Chess/MCA, 1984)

Greatest Hits sums up a seven-year, second-string run on the R&B charts. The Moments' performances are uniformly solid and soulful across 20 cuts, but the overall sound is a little stiff. Twice, however, this album smartly jumps to attention: on the pop crossover "Love on a Two-Way Street" and the heavy-breathing "Sexy Mama." The latter song, from 1973, offers a male response to producer Sylvia Robinson's own smoothly orchestrated come-hither rap, "Pillow Talk." A few years later, Robinson started the pioneering rap label Sugar Hill; the Moments became Ray, Goodman & Brown and continued harmonizing in classic fashion. — M.C.

EDDIE MONEY
★ ★¹/₂ Eddie Money (Columbia, 1977)
★ ★¹/₂ Life for the Taking (Columbia, 1978)
★ ★   Playing for Keeps (Columbia, 1980)
★ ★¹/₂ No Control (Columbia, 1982)
★ ★   "Where's the Party?" (Columbia, 1984)
★ ★ ★   Can't Hold Back (Columbia, 1986)
★ ★   Nothing to Lose (Columbia, 1988)
★ ★ ★   Greatest Hits: Sound of Money (Columbia, 1989)
★ ★¹/₂ Right Here (Columbia, 1991)

A former New York City cop trainee, Eddie Money parlayed his straining vocals and average-guy stance into a pair of unremarkable but catchy hit singles. "Baby, Hold On" and "Two Tickets to Paradise" (both from the debut) came as a godsend to meat-and-potatoes rockers—and radio programmers—who felt vaguely threatened by the encroaching onslaught of punk and disco. Defiantly retrograde, Eddie Money distilled—some would say diluted—the Seger-Springsteen approach into a pop formula. By his second album, Money was already bluffing and feinting: the jump from the anti-disco roar of "Rock and Roll the Place" to the blatant Miami-sound steals on "Maybe I'm a Fool" tips his hand. Interestingly, *Sound of Money* skips over these minor hits in favor of outright latter-day duds like "Where's the Party?" and "Peace in Our Time."

But that collection is worth hearing, because the baroque early-'80s phase of Album Oriented Radio somehow stimulated Eddie Money to a creative peak. "Think I'm in Love" (from the mistitled *No Control*) fleshes out his foursquare plod with layers and layers of studio-enhanced sound, including the sort of tangy guitar hook that's missing from the earlier hits. After a couple more misfires, Money finally strikes pay dirt with *Can't Hold Back*. Just one line, that's all it took: Ronnie Spector's sexy interjection on "Take Me Home Tonight" ("Be my leetle bay-bee") prods Money into pleading like he really means it. And "I Wanna Go Back" stands as his one genuine moment of surprise. He sets you up for a nostalgic journey home, hazy sax solo and all, only to reveal the bitter truth on the chorus: "But I can't go back, I know."

Right Here represents another return to form for Money, though not necessarily a step forward. Fourteen years later, he's still poking around for "Heaven in the Back Seat" and trying to wolf-whistle when "She Takes My Breath Away." The full production pumps him up a bit, but Money sounds a little long-in-the-tooth for such pursuits. — M.C.

MONIE LOVE
★ ★ ★ ★ **Down to Earth (Warner Bros., 1990)**
The title of her debut conveys the secret of this female rapper's success. MC Monie Love delights in schoolyard romance on the irresistible single "Monie in the Middle," and she also holds her own when the going gets funky on tracks like "I Do as I Please" and "Read Between the Lines." Her feminist principles and no-bullshit priorities are stated straight-up, but with a personalized directness and urgency. Boldly flirting with actual melodies and outright singing, Monie and her producers employ song-samples as departure points—not mere vehicles. She constructs her own groove out of bare materials provided by Cameo (the stinging "R U Single") and the Motown-era Spinners (the cautionary "It's a Shame [My Sister]"). Mixing def jams and pop hooks, ideology and romance, *Down to Earth* avoids the rhythmic single-mindedness that sabotages many rap albums—but just because she's listenable doesn't mean she's easy. — M.C.

THE MONKEES
★ ★ The Monkees (1966; Arista, 1988)
★ ★ More of the Monkees (1967; Arista, 1988)
★ Headquarters (1967; Arista, 1989)
★ Pisces, Aquarius, Capricorn & Jones (1967; Arista, 1989)
★ ★ ★½ Greatest Hits (Arista, 1969)
★ ★ ★½ Forty Timeless Hits (EMI, 1980)
★ ★ ★ More Greatest Hits (Arista, 1982)

★ ★ ★½ Missing Links (Rhino, 1987)
★ ★ ★ Live, 1967 (Rhino, 1987)
★ Pool It! (Rhino, 1987)
★ ★ ★½ Missing Links, Vol. (Rhino, 1990)
★ ★ ★ Listen to the Band (Rhino, 1991)
With any number of punkish bar bands semi-ironically recycling "Stepping Stone" in the late '70s, and a partially reunited Monkees touring and recording in the '80s, there's been a revisionist twist upward in appraising this band's slight canon. Cynically manufactured, of course, by Don Kirshner and a crew of TV producers looking to dilute *A Hard Day's Night* for the boob tube, Davy Jones, Michael Nesmith, Mickey Dolenz and Peter Tork were the fill-in fab four who lip-synched their way through a few seasons of sitcoms and most of their albums (on the later product, they did play on some songs). Tommy Boyce and Bobby Hart, Neil Diamond and Nesmith wrote their 1966–68 hits: "Last Train to Clarksville," "Daydream Believer," "I'm a Believer," "Pleasant Valley Sunday." Clever and tuneful, along the lines of knock-off Turtles, this was teenybop fare that provoked shudders from anyone who took the Beatles at all seriously. Those teenyboppers grew up, and in a frenzy of nostalgia, reclaimed their idols. The first Arista hits package is pleasant—and more than enough Monkees for everyone except cultists. *Pool It!*, the most recent new stuff, is glossy, tired and redundant. The four-CD retrospective, *Listen to the Band*, takes the bunch far too seriously. — P.E.

BILL MONROE
★ ★ ★ Bluegrass Ramble (MCA, 1962)
★ ★ ★ ★ Bluegrass Special (MCA, 1963)
★ ★ ★ ★ Bluegrass Instrumentals (MCA, 1965)
★ ★ ★ ★ ★ The High, Lonesome Sound of Bill Monroe (MCA, 1966)
★ ★ ★ ★ Bill Monroe's Greatest Hits (MCA, 1968)
★ ★ ★ Voice From on High (MCA, 1969)
★ ★ ★ 16 All-Time Greatest Hits (Columbia, 1970)
★ ★ ★ Kentucky Bluegrass (MCA, 1970)
★ ★ ★ Uncle Pen (MCA, 1972)
★ ★ ★ Kentucky Blue Grass (MCA, 1973)
★ ★ ★ ★ Bean Blossom (MCA, 1973)
★ ★ ★ ★ Best of Bill Monroe (MCA, 1975)
★ ★ ★ ★ The Original Bluegrass Band (Rounder Special Series, 1979)
★ ★ ★ Columbia Historic Edition (Columbia, 1987)

★ ★ ★ **Bluegrass '87 (MCA, 1987)**
★ ★ ★ ★ **Southern Flavor (MCA, 1988)**
★ ★ ★ ★ **Bill Monroe: Bluegrass 1959–1969 (Bear Family, 1989)**
★ ★ ★ ★ **Live at the Opry—Celebrating 50 Years on the Grand Ole Opry (MCA, 1989)**
★ ★ ★ ★ **Mule Skinner Blues (RCA, 1991)**
★ ★ ★ **Country Music Hall of Fame Series (MCA, 1991)**

As the first generation of rock & roll artists are revered, so do they, almost without exception, revere Bill Monroe, who in their eyes is one of the most important figures influencing the big beat music that emerged in the '50s. True enough. As Elvis Presley halted a slow version of Monroe's "Blue Moon of Kentucky" in mid-lyric with the words, "That don't move me. Now let's get real gone!", Bill Monroe had much the same thought when he stepped up to the microphone in 1940 to record a bright cover version of Jimmie Rodgers's "Mule Skinner Blues."

Growing up in Kentucky, Monroe had become conversant with blues, traditional country, folk songs and church hymns. His instrument was the mandolin, primarily because his brothers Birch and Charlie were already the family's fiddler and guitarist, respectively. The brothers began playing together on radio shows, building a loyal following and generating offers from other sponsors. After Birch left the band in 1934, Bill and Charlie continued on as a duo, expanding their repertoire and forging a distinctive style from the disparate musics they favored. In 1936 the Monroe Brothers made their first recordings for the Bluebird label and were soon the most popular brother team in the south. Personal differences over matters relating both to business and music split the brothers in 1938, with each forming separate bands. Bill's Bluegrass Boys won an audition for the Grand Ole Opry in 1939, which led to national exposure via WSM radio and ensuing recording contracts with RCA Victor and Columbia.

Working from a traditional foundation, Bill gradually shaped a unique music keyed by his breakneck mandolin runs and a high, lonesome, pinched voice that packed an emotional wallop. A devotee of discipline and style, Monroe made certain that his bands were well rehearsed and well dressed. He prides himself on having the first band to wear white shirts and ties at the Grand Ole Opry almost as much as he does their being the group to break out of the C, D

and G keys that were most common to Opry groups, thus encouraging spontaneity among the instrumentalists and freeing them for a greater range of expressiveness. Central to all of this was Monroe's own sense of where to take his new music. Rather than adhere to accepted notions of tempo and tuning, he blasted away the barriers, bringing what he called "driving time" and the unusual ambience of open tunings to the songs in his repertoire. And yet his music was traditional in feel and in its concern with family, love, hard times, impending doom and fear of God. Through the years Monroe has hewed steadily to what worked so successfully for him in the '40s; the most dramatic change was probably the addition of a banjo player to the fiddle-mandolin-guitar-bass lineup. On the personnel side, apart from Monroe himself, the players most responsible for bringing a sharp focus to the bluegrass style were guitarist Lester Flatt and banjo player Earl Scruggs, who joined the Bluegrass Boys in 1945. Flatt and Scruggs were both forward-thinking instrumentalists, and their ideas freed Monroe to add more new touches to his sound. This fertile period in Monroe's history is documented on the Rounder Special Series release, *The Original Bluegrass Band*.

Monroe's catalog tends to be in a hide-and-seek mode, with out-of-print titles coming back into print and in-print titles going out of print in no discernible pattern. A title unlisted in the MCA catalog, for example, may be stocked in ample quantities with a rack jobber who services department stores and truck stops—these things show up in the darnedest places. Fortunately, what remains in print is a wonderful sample of the scope of Monroe's work past and present. The early, groundbreaking recordings for Bluebird are collected on RCA's *Mule Skinner Blues*, a smart package well-annotated by producer-critic Billy Altman, whose work on the RCA Heritage Series has been exemplary. The reliable Country Music Hall of Fame Series entry on Monroe contains Decca and MCA sides ranging from "New Mule Skinner Blues" (1950) to "Southern Flavor" (1988), with "My Sweet Blue-Eyed Darlin'," a duet with Ricky Skaggs, being one of the highlights. *Best of Bill Monroe* is a good selection of well-known items such as "Uncle Pen" and "Blue Moon of Kentucky," but it is more significant for its inclusion of some of the despairing, autobiographical material he cut—"Memories of Mother and Dad,"

"Highway of Sorrow," "I Live in the Past."
The Decca years are most effectively
documented on the import four-CD Bear
Family box set, *Bill Monroe: Bluegrass
1959–1969*, which also includes seven
previously unissued sides. There's nothing
quite as stimulating as a live bluegrass show,
and *Bean Blossom* presents an outstanding
one recorded in June 1973 at the 7th Annual
Bill Monroe Bluegrass Festival in Bean
Blossom, Indiana, featuring Monroe and his
band along with several other top-notch
bluegrass outfits. *Live at the Opry*, recorded
in 1989 on the occasion of Monroe's 50th
year with the country music institution, is
quite something in its own right. Those who
have seen Monroe in his still-regular Opry
appearances know that even heart surgery
hasn't kept him from breaking into a two-
step on a moment's notice. The
performances are as graceful and moving as
ever. Of special interest is the album's
opener, a live recording of "New Mule
Skinner Blues" dating from 1948 when the
Opry was still in its original location at the
Ryman Auditorium in downtown Nashville.
— D.M.

WES MONTGOMERY

★★★★ The Wes Montgomery Trio
(1959; Riverside, 1987)
★★★★★ The Incredible Jazz Guitar of
Wes Montgomery (1960;
Riverside, 1987)
★★★½ Movin' Along (1960; Riverside,
1988)
★★★★ So Much Guitar! (1961;
Riverside, 1987)
★★★★ Full House (1962; Riverside,
1987)
★★★ Portrait of Wes (1963;
Riverside, 1990)
★★★★ Boss Guitar (1963; Riverside,
1989)
★★★★ Fusion! (1963; Riverside, 1989)
★★★½ Movin' Wes (1964; Verve, 1986)
★★★ Goin' Out of My Head (1965;
Verve, 1986)
★★★ California Dreamin' (1966;
Verve, 1986)
★★★ A Day in the Life (1967; A&M,
1986)
★★½ Down Here on the Ground
(1968; A&M, 1987)
★★½ Road Song (1968; A&M, 1986)
★★★★★ The Silver Collection
(Polygram, 1984)
★★★★★ The Artistry of Wes
Montgomery (Riverside, 1986)

★★★★ Wes Montgomery Plays the Blues
(Verve, 1988)
★★★★ The Alternative Wes Montgomery
(Milestone, 1989)
★★★ Classics (A&M, 1991)

By the early '60s, Wes Montgomery had
become the most successful jazz guitarist
since Charlie Christian. Achieving a very
distinctive, somewhat muted sound by
playing with his thumb, Montgomery was a
dazzling technician, capable of blinding-fast
solos wherein entire octaves took the place
of single notes. None of the ferocity of later,
rock-inflected players (John McLaughlin,
Steve Morse) characterized his playing, but
his style finds echoes in George Benson and
the mellower work of Al Di Meola.
"Mellow," in fact, became synonymous with
"Montgomery" in the popular mind, due
mainly to the best-selling mid-'60s albums
he recorded on Verve and A&M. Awash in
harps and strings, the later Wes horrified
jazz purists—and his fluid licks (in E-Z
form) became the standard repertoire of
lounge guitarists.

The prime Montgomery (1959–1963),
however, is still great jazz. A strong debut,
The Wes Montgomery Trio was followed by
the significantly more challenging *The
Incredible Jazz Guitar of Wes Montgomery*.
Swinging hard on Sonny Rollins's "Airegin"
and elegantly on Dave Brubeck's "In Your
Own Sweet Way," the guitarist was pushed
past the point of mere dexterity by such
smart sidemen as pianist Tommy Flanagan
and the deft brother rhythm section of Percy
and Albert Heath, on bass and drums,
respectively. *Full House* was a standout 1962
live set boosted by the presence of tenor
saxophonist Johnny Griffin and players on
loan from the contemporary Miles Davis
Sextet (Wynton Kelly on piano, Paul
Chambers on bass, Jimmy Cobb on drums).
Sharp compilations, *The Artistry of Wes
Montgomery* and *The Alternative Wes
Montgomery* do a good job of capturing the
essence of the pre-pop period.

While some of the Verve sides represent
Montgomery's soporific nadir, that label
boasts, in the *Silver Collection*, some great
small-group sessions featuring organist
Jimmy Smith and, with Don Sebesky's
arrangement of "Here's That Rainy Day,"
the kind of intelligent orchestration that the
guitarist was rarely fortunate enough to find
later. The prophetic *Fusion!* set the pattern
for the Wes 'n' Strings fare to come. From
this point until his death in 1968 at age 45,
the guitarist took it easy, turning out album
after orchestrated album of unchallenging,

classy background music. For its sweetly blasphemous renderings of Beatles tunes, and for the presence of such strong sidemen as Herbie Hancock and Ron Carter, *A Day in the Life* is interesting—but the fact that this remarkable player saw fit to cover the Association's "Windy" tells all. — P.E.

THE MOODY BLUES

★★★½ **The Magnificent Moodies (1966; London, 1988)**
★★★ **Days of Future Passed (Deram, 1967)**
★½ **In Search of the Lost Chord (Deram, 1968)**
★½ **On the Threshold of a Dream (Deram, 1969)**
★½ **To Our Children's Children's Children (Threshold/Polygram, 1969)**
★½ **A Question of Balance (Threshold/Polygram, 1970)**
★ **Every Good Boy Deserves Favour (Threshold/Polygram, 1971)**
★½ **Seventh Sojourn (Threshold/Polygram, 1972)**
★★½ **This Is the Moody Blues (1974; Threshold/Polygram, 1989)**
★★ **In the Beginning (Deram, 1975)**
★★ **Caught Live Plus Five (London, 1977)**
★★ **Octave (London, 1978)**
★★ **Long Distance Voyager (Threshold/Polygram, 1981)**
★★ **The Present (Threshold/Polygram, 1983)**
★★★ **Voices in the Sky: The Best of the Moody Blues (Threshold/Polygram, 1985)**
★★ **The Other Side of Life (Threshold/Polygram, 1986)**
★★½ **Prelude (Threshold/Polygram, 1987)**
★★½ **Sur La Mer (Threshold/Polygram, 1988)**
★★★ **Legend of a Band (Threshold/Polygram, 1990)**

No major band has so relentlessly parlayed nonsense as have the Moodies; were it not for their titanic success, in fact, they might easily be dismissed as an odd and overlong joke. Ever since coming up with a name that offered sly tribute to the British beer M&B (in hopes for a corporate sponsorship eons before that hideous practice became popular), the Moody Blues have been nothing if not commercial—but it's the artsiness of their symphonic rock that's truly crass, and their self-importance that's offensive. Gods of '70s FM radio, they invented a sort of easy-listening psychedelia that resolutely combined the worst of both

worlds. Long since their heyday, they've continued to produce mild echoes of that stuff.

Ironically, the Moodies started out great. With Denny Laine on vocals, their first smash was the bold and lovely "Go Now," a ballad version of the British Invasion pop they were masters of—when not performing credible Sonny Boy Williamson numbers and R&B fare along the lines of a sweeter Spencer Davis Group. The reissue of *Magnificent Moodies* captures this fine early period well. Laine soon left, however, and pomposity entered. Justin Hayward and Ray Thomas joined founder Mike Pinder to form the Moodies' new core and to pursue a new direction—the fusing of rock and classical music. Recorded with the London Festival Orchestra, *Days of Future Passed* accomplished exactly that; with its theme of the passage of day into night echoing Vivaldi's *The Four Seasons*, the album produced the haunting "Nights in White Satin" and established the band as pioneers in a sub-genre that Procol Harum and, later, E.L.O. would develop much more winningly.

But the record also previewed a pretentiousness that soon became the Moodies' raison d'etre. Appalling, if not hilarious, poetic introductions to the songs were an innovation. Hippie profundities delivered in a voice-of-God manner, these musings introduced *In Search of the Lost Chord*, a bombastic meditation on Timothy Leary, astral planes and mantras; *Children's Children's Children* and *Threshold* were more of the same, their air of high seriousness underscored by the Mellotron, a keyboard capable of producing orchestral sounds. By now the Moodies had found a pattern they'd seldom depart from—a long, portentous intro, followed by a smooth, stirring ersatz rocker and then roughly equal numbers of fast and slow songs all trading in wide-eyed philosophizing.

"Question," "Story in Your Eyes" and "I'm Just a Singer" all were massive hits, tricked out with furiously strummed acoustic guitars ripped off from the Who, and played with absolute, unsmiling professionalism. With *Octave*, synthesizers became dominant, but the song remained basically the same. The '80s albums showed a slight, but very welcome, relaxing of the heavy lyrical content, and the band's one sure strength—melody—came through clearly. But what they'd gained in accessibility they'd lost in distinction; they now just sounded trite. — P.E.

THE MOONGLOWS

★ ★ ★ ★ **Their Greatest Sides (Chess/MCA, 1983)**

One of the earliest and most influential group harmony ensembles, the Moonglows were formed in Louisville in 1951 by Harvey Fuqua, a talented songwriter and arranger who went on to play a key behind-the-scenes role as a producer-arranger-writer in Motown's early history. Alan Freed discovered the Moonglows in Cleveland and helped them land a recording contract with Chess. One of Fuqua's songs, "Sincerely," cracked the Top Thirty in 1955 and established the quintet. Personnel changes became a way of life with the Moonglows, with Fuqua remaining as the constant, and by 1958 the group was being billed as Harvey and the Moonglows. The year 1958 also saw the release of the song that immortalized the Moonglows, "Ten Commandments of Love," the group's last Top Thirty hit. The '59 edition of the Moonglows featured the then-unknown Marvin Gaye. *Their Greatest Sides* documents the style that defined the mellow side of doo-wop.
— D.M.

VAN MORRISON

★ ★ ★½ **Blowin' Your Mind (Bang, 1967)**
★ ★ ★ ★ ★ **Astral Weeks (Warner Bros., 1968)**
★ ★ ★ ★ ★ **Moondance (Warner Bros., 1970)**
★ ★ ★½ **Van Morrison, His Band and the Street Choir (Warner Bros., 1970)**
★ ★ **Best of Van Morrison (Bang, 1970)**
★ ★ ★½ **Tupelo Honey (1971; Warner Bros., 1988)**
★ ★ ★ ★ **St. Dominic's Preview (1972; Warner Bros., 1988)**
★ ★ ★½ **T.B. Sheets (1972; Columbia 1990)**
★ ★ **Hard Nose the Highway (1973; Warner Bros., 1988)**
★ ★ ★ ★ **It's Too Late to Stop Now (1974; Warner Bros., 1988)**
★ ★ ★ **Veedon Fleece (1974; Warner Bros., 1988)**
★ ★ ★ **A Period of Transition (1977; Warner Bros., 1988)**
★ ★ ★½ **Wavelength (1978; Warner Bros., 1988)**
★ ★ ★ ★ **Into the Music (Warner Bros., 1979)**
★ ★½ **Common One (1980; Warner Bros., 1991)**
★ ★½ **Beautiful Vision (Warner Bros., 1982)**
★ **Inarticulate Speech of the Heart (Warner Bros., 1983)**
★ ★ ★½ **A Sense of Wonder (Mercury, 1985)**
★ ★ ★ ★ **Live at the Grand Opera House Belfast (Mercury, 1985)**
★ ★ ★ ★ **No Guru, No Method, No Teacher (Mercury, 1986)**
★ ★ ★ **Poetic Champions Compose (Mercury, 1989)**
★ ★ ★ ★ **Avalon Sunset (Mercury, 1989)**
★ ★ ★½ **Enlightenment (Mercury, 1990)**
★ ★ ★ ★ **The Best of Van Morrison (Polydor, 1990)**
★ ★ ★½ **Bang Masters (Epic, 1991)**
★ ★ ★½ **Hymns to the Silence (Polydor, 1991)**

WITH THEM

★ ★ ★½ **Them (Parrot, 1965)**
★ ★ **Them Again (Parrot, 1966)**

WITH THE CHIEFTAINS

★ ★ ★ **Irish Heartbeat (Mercury, 1988)**

Whether singing R&B, Celtic tunes or gospel, Van Morrison both defines and transcends the genres he mines. It's a rare skill, one he shares with Sinatra, Aretha, George Jones and very few others. As a writer, too, he's singularly gifted; far more influential than his relatively slight sales suggest. Reclusive, visionary and prolific, Morrison is one of the giants of popular music.

Fronting the Irish soulsters, Them, he debuted with Bert Berns's "Here Comes the Night," Big Joe Williams's "Baby Please Don't Go"—and his own "Gloria," a 1966 rocker whose propulsiveness rivals even the Stones' "Satisfaction." A year later, he went solo with the flawless, summer pop of "Brown Eyed Girl." Though not quite as memorable, "Spanish Rose" and "Send Your Mind" were singles of a catchy perfection most bands never achieve. Having mastered the form, he moved on, releasing, in 1968 and 1970, *Astral Weeks* and *Moondance*, two masterpieces from whose differing sensibilities all his later work would flow.

Astral Weeks shattered the constraints of radio rock. Recorded in a 48-hour fever, the record's mood is blue, wise and yearning, its music combining jazz rhythms and freer structures, impressionist strings and woodwinds, and Morrison voicing his lyrics like a misty, Celtic soul singer gifted with a virtuoso sense of drama. The words he alternately declaims, pants or slurs are a kind of Beat poetry and sketches for semi-surreal short stories; the atmosphere also owes psychic debts to Dylan Thomas and Dylan, Bob. One of rock's most introspective records, *Astral Weeks* is dense and complex, rich with private symbolism and cryptic suggestion.

Moondance is a bolder flipside. Countering *Astral Weeks*' trance-state and its wash of song tumbling into song, *Moondance* is a flourish of individual set-pieces—brash soul, jazz bits, ballads. The best of Morrison's more accessible works, it formed the mold for the horn-driven, bass-heavy R&B that Morrison would later employ to balance the orchestral meta-folk music he premiered with *Astral Weeks*. "Into the Mystic," from *Moondance*, merges the two methods—and the complementary sides of Morrison's psyche—more satisfyingly than anything he's done since.

With its snappy single "Domino" and the jaunty "Blue Money," *His Band and the Street Choir*, is a minor *Moondance*. *Tupelo Honey* is as comfortable as Morrison gets; a country-ish record, it's sweet without getting cloying. *St. Dominic's Preview*, with "Listen to the Lion" and "Almost Independence Day" marks a return to a darker intensity; "Jackie Wilson Said (I'm in Heaven When You Smile)" represents the R&B side of the equation. Of Morrison's other '70s albums, *Hard Nose the Highway* is his vaguest and weakest; *T.B. Sheets* is comprised of recordings from *Blowin' Your Mind*, including the harrowing title song; *Veedon Fleece* seems confused; *A Period of Transition* is tentative; *It's Too Late to Stop Now* (a live set) and *Into the Music* are pretty terrific, the latter broadcasting the overt spirituality that would pervade his work in the '80s.

Common One captures the turn toward literary pretentions that dogged Morrison for a while; *Inarticulate Speech of the Heart* is a puzzling about-face—mainly, it's an album of weak jazz-rock instrumentals. From *A Sense of Wonder* to *Hymns to the Silence*, Morrison's music has been, in spirit, if not in letter, gospel music. Morrison is one of rock's rare religious thinkers whose faith is complicated, tense and all-encompassing. Fittingly, the music all streams down from *Astral Weeks*: slow swirlings of sound beyond any common sense. — P.E.

MORRISSEY
★★★★   **Viva Hate (Sire/Reprise, 1988)**
★★★   **Bona Drag (Sire/Reprise, 1990)**
★★½   **Kill Uncle (Sire/Reprise, 1991)**

The Smiths' brooding front person didn't exactly lighten up on his solo debut. *Viva Hate* continues this flamboyant loner's crusade, elaborating on all Morrissey's pet obsessions: youth culture ("Suedehead"), suicide ("Angel, Angel, Down We Go Together"), girl-group pop ("I Don't Mind If You Forget Me"), Britain's Conservative government ("Margaret on the Guillotine"). That last song lashes out with the expected vinegar sting, while the lushly orchestrated "Everyday Is Like Sunday" could be Morrissey's least affected moment—you never want it to end. *Bona Drag*, an odds 'n sods time-filler, proves Morrissey to be a consistent hand with singles. But *Kill Uncle* marks a disturbing development, or perhaps lack of development. Where Morrissey once appeared to be working out his own personal kinks, the smoothed-over sound and calcified stance of *Kill Uncle* make it all seem like an act. Does mope-rock really need its own Ozzy Osbourne? — M.C.

BILL MORRISSEY
★★★   **North (1986; Philo/Rounder, 1991)**
★★★   **Standing Eight (Philo/Rounder, 1989)**
★★★½   **Bill Morrissey (Philo/Rounder, 1991)**
★★★½   **Inside (Philo/Rounder, 1992)**

With his prematurely cracked voice and his sensibility in shift between fatalistic resignation and wry wit, Bill Morrissey resembles a New England version of prime John Prine. A story–song writer with a great gift for the telling detail, he paints snowy, psychic landscapes of the kind Raymond Carver fashioned—his deadend, small-town Northeast is filled with losers and misfits perpetually reaching for the bottle; factory girls who rendezvous with hard-luck cases; old sentimental landmarks that fall victim to the wrecking ball. "Night Shift," "Married Man" and "Fishing a Stream I Once Fished as a Kid" are standouts of his revisionist Americana on *North*; *Bill Morrissey* (a 1991 reissue of his 1984 debut, plus four additional songs) offers the same kinds of elegy and tender reportage, conveyed effectively by simple acoustic guitar melodies, sparsely accompanied. A cello and trumpet add richness on *Standing Eight*, Morrissey's most accomplished record—and vocal assists by folk-renaissance songbirds Suzanne Vega and Shawn Colvin balance with strength and clarity Morrissey's world-weary and offhanded singing. *Inside* is leaner but nearly as strong. — P.E.

JELLY ROLL MORTON

★ ★ ★ ★ **The Immortal Jelly Roll Morton**
 (Milestone, 1967)
★ ★ ★ ★ ★ **Jelly Roll Morton, 1923-24**
 (Milestone, 1974)
★ ★ ★ ★ **New Orleans Rhythm Kings**
 (Milestone, 1974)
★ ★ ★ ★ **The Pearls (Bluebird/RCA, 1988)**
★ ★ ★ ★ ★ **The Jelly Roll Morton Centennial:**
 His Complete Victor Recordings
 1926–1930 (1936; Bluebird/RCA,
 1990)

Robert Jr. Lockwood talks about how all great guitarists get their ideas from listening to other instruments; Little Walter revolutionized the harmonica by emulating saxophone lines and then amplifying it. Jelly Roll Morton, a man who claimed to have invented jazz and stands as one of the music's great composers-bandleaders-arrangers-musicians, said the piano "should always be an imitation of a jazz band." In that one quote he distilled his genius and laid out the challenge to which jazz pianists have attempted to respond since Morton made his first recordings in the early '20s.

Jelly Roll Morton's music closed out the ragtime era, ushered in the Jazz Age, and prefigured the Swing Era, when the principles Morton had established were redefined and expanded. His Red Hot Peppers combo, which recorded between 1926 and 1930, was the first significant jazz combo. As overarching as is his reputation as a composer and musician, Morton is also credited as being the first jazz band leader to blueprint his recording sessions from first note to last and then drill the musicians in advance of the recording on the placement of their solos and the basic arrangements. In the process he proved that careful attention to structure need not diminish the spontaneity of improvisation.

Of Creole extraction, Morton was born Ferdinand Joseph Lemott in 1890 in New Orleans. By his teens he was working clubs in the city's notorious red-light district, Storyville, and acquiring a reputation as a piano player without peer as he absorbed ragtime, stomps, blues and the Spanish and French musics heard all over town. He also acquired an attitude—he made sure everyone knew of his achievements and wrote a song about himself titled "Mr. Jelly Lord" that pretty much said it all—lived ostentatiously, enjoyed the company of many women and sported a diamond in one tooth. He was stricken with wanderlust, but he also left behind remarkable and still-influential recordings made in Chicago,

New York and Richmond, Indiana, with the best musicians of the '20s and '30s. These recordings are to jazz what *The Bristol Sessions* are to country music, what Elvis Presley's Sun sessions are to rock & roll: a look at a music's past being transformed into something new.

Milestone's two-album *Jelly Roll Morton 1923–24* collects the first recordings Morton ever made, including all of the now-legendary solo piano sides cut for the Gennett label in Richmond. These are indispensable documents that find Morton putting into practice his theory about approaching the piano as a jazz band unto itself. Of special note are Bob Greene's detailed liner notes explaining the specific and altogether revolutionary techniques being employed by Morton on various cuts. In addition to four unaccompanied piano solos recorded in Chicago, sides three and four feature Morton's first small band recordings, which not only mark the break with ragtime styles, but also show Morton lending his musical ideas on the piano to other instrumentalists. *The Immortal Jelly Roll Morton* is a 12-song album containing four of the Gennett solos, two trio recordings, and six small band recordings, all available on Milestone's *Jelly Roll Morton 1923–24*.

Milestone's other entry in the Jelly Roll Morton saga is a two-record set of recordings made by the New Orleans Rhythm Kings in Richmond in 1922 and 1923; the band is joined by Morton for eight songs. These sides with Morton were from the first racially mixed jazz recording sessions. Bluebird/RCA's excellent *The Pearls*, now out of print, was rendered superfluous in 1990 when, on the 100th anniversary of Morton's birth the label, issued *The Jelly Roll Morton Centennial: His Complete Victor Recordings*. A monumental five-CD set, it includes Morton's complete Bluebird and Victor sessions, with the exception only of those on which the artist appeared as a vocal accompanist or sideman. These are the mature works of one of America's most important artists, made with one of the greatest bands ever assembled, the Red Hot Peppers, as well as other tracks cut in trio and orchestra settings that included various Peppers; solo piano numbers; and a dozen tracks by Jelly Roll Morton's New Orleans Jazzmen. *Centennial* gives us Morton looking back and looking ahead, inspiring some of the most important names in jazz to peak moments of artistry. In 1941, two years after

the final Victor sessions, Morton died in
obscurity. If anything rights the wrong of
this lonesome death, it is *Centennial*.
— D.M.

MÖTLEY CRÜE

★ ★½ **Too Fast for Love (1981; Elektra, 1982)**
★ ★ **Shout at the Devil (Elektra, 1983)**
★ ★½ **Theatre of Pain (Elektra, 1985)**
★ ★ ★ **Girls, Girls, Girls (Elektra, 1987)**
★ ★ ★ ★ **Dr. Feelgood (Elektra, 1989)**
★ ★ ★ ★ **Decade of Decadence (Elektra, 1991)**

Considering that Mötley Crüe's initial fame
had more to do with its makeup, attitude
and umlauts than with its music, this group
should have run its course in two or three
albums. Instead, the Crüe defied all
reasonable expectations and actually got
better as its audience grew bigger, something
not even a deal with the devil could have
cinched. Granted, the band always did have
more than its share of pop smarts. *Too Fast
for Love*, the group's independently released
debut (Elektra later remixed and reissued
the album), is nowhere near as
ferocious-sounding as the leather-clad crotch
shot on the cover would suggest. Indeed, its
sound borders on the anemic—but there is a
surprising melodic resilience to songs like
"Come On and Dance," "Piece of Your
Action" and "Merry-Go-Round."

Shout at the Devil goes for a heavier tone,
but still doesn't quite get it; as much as the
Crüe tries to cultivate its bad-boy image
with titles like "Bastard" and "God Bless
the Children of the Beast," the music is a
distressingly mild-mannered distillation of
Kiss and Aerosmith clichés. It's much the
same story with *Theatre of Pain*, which,
despite its beefier mix, doesn't get any
tougher than a tepid remake of Brownsville
Station's teen-attitude classic, "Smokin' in
the Boys' Room." But the band's sound
begins to catch up with its image on *Girls,
Girls, Girls*. Though the song titles promise
all the usual teen titillation, rockers like
"Wild Side" and "Bad Boy Boogie" actually
deliver, backing the lyrics with plenty of
muscular guitar and relentlessly driving
rhythm to push the lyrics along.

That's nothing compared to the mighty
roar unleashed by *Dr. Feelgood*. The title
tune—a coolly cynical commentary on the
drug culture, set to a brutally swinging beat
and featuring some of the band's best guitar
work—sets the tone, and the band never lets
up. Although the group remains as indebted
as ever to older acts, its borrowings are

nowhere near as obvious, and from the
breathless surge of "Kickstart My Heart,"
to the insistent swagger of "Same Ol'
Situation (S.O.S.)," there's not a weak
moment to be heard. Even the ballads, as
"Without You" demonstrates, seem
plausible. And though *Decade of Decadence*
spends most of its time summing up past
strengths (with some re-recording), tracks
like "Rock 'n' Roll Junkie" and the
spiritedly profane cover of "Anarchy in the
U.K." suggest that the Crüe will only
continue to improve. — J.D.C.

MOTÖRHEAD

★ ★ ★½ **Motörhead (1977; Roadracer/Revisited, 1990)**
★ ★ ★½ **Overkill (1979; Roadracer/Revisited, 1992)**
★ ★ ★½ **Bomber (1979; Roadracer/Revisited, 1992)**
★ ★ ★½ **Ace of Spades (1980; Roadracer/Revisited, 1992)**
★ ★ ★½ **No Sleep 'Til Hammersmith (1981; Roadracer/Revisited, 1992)**
★ ★ ★½ **Iron Fist (1982; Bronze/Roadracer, 1990)**
★ ★ ★ ★ **No Remorse (1984; Bronze/Roadracer, 1990)**
★ ★ ★ **Orgasmatron (Profile, 1986)**
★ ★ ★ **Rock 'n' Roll (Profile, 1987)**
★ ★ ★ **No Sleep at All (Enigma, 1988)**
★ ★ ★ **The Birthday Party (GWR, 1990)**
★ ★ ★½ **1916 (WTG/Epic, 1991)**

The black-leather soul of Motörhead
emanates from a lanky Brit biker-type
named Ian Kilmister, better known as
Lemmy. A former roadie for Jimi Hendrix,
self-declared speed freak, maniacally
propulsive bass guitarist, carnival barker of
the sharpest lyrics heavy metal has to offer:
Lemmy is quite a character, but his
earthbound perspective and cutting sense of
humor keep this journeyman band's various
incarnations well grounded. With
machine-like regularity, Motörhead's
straight-ahead brand of rant & roll flattens
the competition.

Ah, there is Lemmy's voice to contend
with. Hoarse? About halfway through most
songs, he gives up any semblance of actual
singing and starts to wail; it's the vocal
equivalent of guitar feedback, deafeningly
crude but effective. Available after a long
absence, Motörhead's debut features the
hard-charging psychedelic guitar style of
Larry Wallis. He was replaced by "Fast"
Eddie Clarke not long after the 1975
session, but Wallis helped develop
Motörhead's speedy power-trio approach.

No Remorse culls an hour or so of sustained hysteria from the deleted albums *Overkill* (1979), *Bomber* (1979), *Ace of Spades* (1980), the live in-your-face *No Sleep 'Til Hammersmith* (1981) and the reissued *Iron Fist* (1982). Topping it all off is Motörhead's dread masterpiece: "Killed by Death," which fully lives up to its title. *The Birthday Party* summarizes Motörhead's comparatively sleeker, "high-tech" phase, drawing on the Bill Laswell–produced *Orgasmatron* (1986), *Rock & Roll* (1987) and *No Sleep at All* (1988), another live set. Easier to appreciate, perhaps, it's not quite as urgent as Motörhead's earlier head-banging. *1916* reapplies the sonic grit with a trowel, however; only Lemmy could pull off a breathless tribute called "Ramones" that actually outguns the bros themselves. — M.C.

MOTT THE HOOPLE

★★★ **Mott the Hoople (Atlantic, 1969)**
★★★ **Mad Shadows (Atlantic, 1970)**
★★ **Wildlife (Atlantic, 1971)**
★★★ **Brain Capers (Atlantic, 1972)**
★★★½ **All the Young Dudes (Columbia, 1972)**
★★★★½ **Mott (Columbia, 1973)**
★★★★½ **The Hoople (1974; Columbia, 1990)**
★★★½ **Mott the Hoople Live (1974; Columbia, 1989)**
★ **Drive On (Columbia, 1975)**
★ **Shouting and Pointing (Columbia, 1976)**
★★★½ **Greatest Hits (Columbia, 1976)**
Combining the swagger of a heavier Rolling Stones and the poetic fervor of a less obscure 1966 Bob Dylan sounds like an audacious idea. What's amazing is that Mott the Hoople pulled it off with remarkable consistency. Kicking in with a debut that featured M.C. Escher cover art and tougher takes on the Kinks' "You Really Got Me" and Doug Sahm's "At the Crossroads," Mott served notice that metallic guitar and introspective lyrics weren't antithetical. With its fourth album, *Brain Capers*, the roles of its star players gelled: Mick Ralphs—who would later harvest big bucks and grunge simplicity with Bad Company—would keep the riffs and solos hard and tasty; wordsmith Ian Hunter would provide midtempo rockers like "Sweet Angeline," that, delivered in an Anglicized Dylan drone, mixed tenderness and toughness, irony with compassion.

In the early '70s, David Bowie went slumming with Mott, finding in its rock &

roll faith an outlet for the raw impulses his cannier approach too often squelched. Penning for Mott the crunching ballad "All the Young Dudes," he wrote an anthem not only for the band but a movement—glitter rock, or, as its proponents (Mott, T. Rex, Slade and others) preferred, glam rock. Exhuming the gilded ghost of James Dean, glam meant cavalier posing, wit and pop power—plus a noble fatalism that fitted Mott exactly, given its early, mysterious commercial faltering.

With *Mott*, the group hit full, romping stride. Mick Ralphs added searing melody to his arsenal; Hunter served up road-life sagas ("All the Way From Memphis"), back-alley psychoanalysis ("I Wish I Was Your Mother") and an outlaw's desperate religiosity ("Hymn for the Dudes"). *The Hoople* was nearly as fine; Gus Dudgeon's Phil Spector-ish, wide-screen production lent grandeur to bombastic material like "The Golden Age of Rock 'n' Roll" and suited the theatrical bent of the first rock band to play Broadway. *Mott the Hoople Live* captures the band's propensity for baroque gesturing and crowd-inciting heat that, early on, provoked a riot at London's Albert Hall and a subsequent ban on rock shows at that venue.

By 1975, both Hunter and Ralphs had departed, and Mott, missing its two chief talents, wasn't worth much: *Drive On* and *Shouting and Pointing* (both out of print) are noisy duds. A *Greatest Hits* collection is good, mainly for its inclusion of the elegiac "Saturday Gigs." Underappreciated and still a vital listening experience, Mott remains a primer for smart, hard rock & roll. — P.E.

BOB MOULD

★★★★ **Workbook (Virgin, 1989)**
★★★★ **Black Sheets of Rain (Virgin, 1990)**
After Hüsker Dü fell apart, guitarist-vocalist Bob Mould did the expected and established a solo career. Then he did the unexpected, and released a partially acoustic album. *Workbook* is pretty much what its title suggests, a collection of song sketches and experiments that eloquently express Mould's restless melancholy. Despite its dearth of guitar crunch ("Whichever Way the Wind Blows" being an exception), it boasts a melodic sensibility similar to Hüsker Dü's later albums, and makes excellent use of Jane Scarpantoni's cello. But for the heartsick *Black Sheets of Rain*, Mould once again cranks his amps to the max, an approach that lends itself to thrillingly cacophonous slash-and-burn solos without

compromising the melodic integrity of tunes like "It's Too Late" and "Hear Me Calling." — J.D.C.

MOUNTAIN

★ ★ ★ **Best of Mountain (Columbia, 1973)**
★ ★ **Twin Peaks (Columbia, 1974)**

Mountain lays it on thick—metal just doesn't get any heavier. Along with dozens of other pretenders to Cream's vacant throne, this power trio–plus (droning electric organ) tried to rule through sheer force: the blues influence disappears in the power-chord sludge. Guitarist Leslie West—a gigantic man who later titled a solo album *The Great Fatsby*—pulls a huge, seismic riff out of his tiny Les Paul on the FM classic "Mississippi Queen," while ex–Cream producer Felix Pappalardi pulls off a stone-cold Jack Bruce imitation on bass and vocals. "Theme for an Imaginary Western" (written, in fact, by Bruce) oozes along at an intoxicatingly slow plod—more like a downer ballad than a power ballad. But the bulk of *Best of Mountain* is mired in the rock conventions of its time: there's a Woodstock memoir ("For Yasgur's Farm"), a rocky-road song ("Boys in the Band"), a lead-bottomed Chuck Berry cover ("Roll Over Beethoven") and an epic titled "The Animal Trainer and the Toad." Only headbangers with a historical bent need apply. — M.C.

ALISON MOYET

★ ★ ★½ **Alf (Columbia, 1984)**
★ ★ **Raindancing (Columbia, 1987)**
★ ★ ★ ★ **Hoodoo (Columbia, 1991)**

What Alison Moyet brought to Yaz wasn't just a strong, bluesy voice, but an understanding that there are as many kinds of musical melancholy as there are shades of blue. Moyet is a virtuoso colorist, a singer whose command of the vocal palette is absolute. And while that can add lustre and resonance to strong songs, it also has the unfortunate habit of emphasizing the hollowness and superficiality of weaker ones. Consequently, Moyet's albums are a lot like the girl with the curl; when they're good, they're very, very good, but when they're bad, you're glad for the remote control. *Alf* is typical. Recorded with Tony Swain and Steve Jolley (the production team responsible for Bananarama's early hits), it has some marvelous moments, like "All Cried Out," with its dramatic, minor-key build to a chugging, soulful chorus. But when it falls flat, it lands with a thud, as the bluesy hyperbole of "Steal Me Blind" makes plain. Still, the album is worth hearing if only for "Invisible," a performance that burns with the anguish of romantic betrayal.

There are more missteps on *Raindancing*, and though most can be blamed on the inappropriateness of Jimmy Iovine's formulaic rock-pop production, it must also be said that Moyet's attempts to tone down her sound for mass consumption on "Is This Love?" and "I Grow Weak In the Presence of Beauty" seem spectacularly ill-advised. Fortunately, *Hoodoo* more than makes up for that, affording Moyet plenty of maneuvering room stylistically without ever compromising her musical integrity. When the groove is hot, she shifts into a gospel shout, while on ballads, her voice is naked and emotional. Best of all, the pop numbers never pander; whether playing off melodic momentum like "It Won't Be Long" or riding the rhythm as "Footsteps" does, Moyet is irresistible. — J.D.C.

MARIA MULDAUR

★ ★ ★ ★ **Maria Muldaur (Reprise, 1973)**
★ ★ ★ **Waitress in a Donut Shop (Reprise, 1974)**
★ ★ ★ ★ **Sweet Harmony (Reprise, 1976)**

Originally hidden in the obscurity of the Jim Kweskin Jug Band, Maria Muldaur came out with a remarkable debut album, *Maria Muldaur*, in 1973. The sly swing of "Midnight at the Oasis" provided her a giant hit, but her graceful, blues-inflected singing made every cut on *Maria Muldaur* delightful. It helped, of course, that among her sidemen were such monster players as Clarence White, Ry Cooder, Dave Grisman and Dr. John—but it was in her smart song selection, too, that Muldaur revealed great taste. With numbers by Dolly Parton, Wendy Waldman and Jimmy Rodgers, the record was lovely and polished, an urbane, folk triumph. *Sweet Harmony,* from 1976, was even more crafty, its jazzier grooves displaying real confidence. Oddly, Muldaur's other work is really weak. Jazz legend Benny Carter provides horn arrangements for *Waitress in a Donut Shop*, from 1974, but the singer sounds a little ill at ease; the other records (all out of print) are tepid, glossy funk. — P.E.

EDDIE MURPHY

★ ★ **Eddie Murphy (Columbia, 1982)**
★ ★ **Eddie Murphy: Comedian (Columbia, 1983)**
★ **How Could It Be (Columbia, 1985)**
½ ★ **So Happy (Columbia, 1989)**

Unlike Richard Pryor, his comic hero, or Bill Cosby, his comic nemesis, Eddie Murphy didn't make albums as a means to getting on television or into the movies; for him, recordings are a sideline, a spin-off, an accessory to the fame his stint on *Saturday Night Live* and his work in Hollywood had already earned him. That may explain why there's so little edge to his comedy albums.

It isn't that Murphy shies away from touchy subjects—profanity, gay bashing, woman bashing and the like—on album, just that he rarely does anything creative with the subjects. Instead, his best bits are silly throw-aways, like the talking car routine on *Eddie Murphy* or the James Brown impression on *Comedian*. Of course, impressions were his strong suit on *SNL*, and he fills both comedy albums with wonderfully realized characters that run the gamut from simple gag inserts (the Buckwheat–Little Richard Simmons version of "Enough Is Enough" on *Eddie Murphy*) to rich, revealing tableaux (the withering family portrait in "The Barbecue," from *Comedian*).

Given the vocal virtuosity of his comic routines, you'd think his actual singing would be at least half-decent. But you'd be wrong. Not only does Murphy lack the equipment to carry off his soul-star ambitions, he seems genuinely uncomfortable trying to deliver any but the most basic emotions. Perhaps that's why he so emphasizes musical jokes, an approach that works passably well on "Party All the Time," from the otherwise execrable *How Could It Be*, but wears thin throughout *So Happy*. — J.D.C.

ELLIOTT MURPHY
★★★★ Aquashow (1973; Polydor, 1988)
★★★½ Diamonds by the Yard (Razor & Tie, 1992)

You notice it right away: Elliott Murphy is one '70s singer/songwriter who really earns that "New Dylan" tag. *Aquashow*'s hyper-literate stance and over-familiar harmonica strains aren't the whole story, though. A unique post-hippie sensibility—probing, decadent, obsessed with pop culture—emerges from this young New Yorker's debut album. Opening with a song called "Last of the Rock Stars," *Aquashow* reads like the missing link between glitter and punk—even though it sounds like the stripped-down album Dylan fans were praying for at that time. Murphy must have listened to Lou Reed as closely as he did to Dylan; "Hangin' Out" and "Graveyard

Scrapbook" reflect an unromanticized fascination with self-destruction. If Elliott Murphy relies a little too strongly on his "Poise 'n' Pen," his forthright singing compensates, somehow. He puts a slightly affected tone to devastating affect on "Like a Great Gatsby" and "Marilyn"—that corny line about Monroe dying for our sins becomes haunting, indelible. An expert team of New York and Nashville session players propels *Aquashow* with just the right precision and restraint.

Murphy's subsequent (out-of-print) albums on RCA (*Lost Generation*, *Street Lights*) and Columbia (*Just a Story From America*) never recapture such a spare, sympathetic groove. And unless you're enraptured by it, his overemphasis on literary wit grates after a while. *Diamonds by the Yard*, though, combines 17 of the best Murphy tracks from the '70s.

Murphy moved to Paris in the '80s, and continues to record for labels overseas.
— M.C.

PETER MURPHY
★★★ Love Hysteria (Beggars Banquet/RCA, 1988)
★★★ Deep (Beggars Banquet/RCA, 1989)
★★★ Holy Smoke (Beggar's Banquet/RCA, 1992)

Most Bowie-influenced singers try to emulate the tremulous tension of his upper register, the better to convey the mannered angst of their lyrics. Former Bauhaus frontman Peter Murphy, on the other hand, prefers the resonant depths of Bowie's low notes, no doubt appreciating the weight they add to even the slightest of lyrics. That, in any case, is the voice Murphy conjures up for most of his solo work. When contrasted against the chilly, metallic synths of *Love Hysteria*, Murphy manages to make it sound almost friendly, particularly on the eerie, atmospheric "All Night Long." *Deep*, however, tends more toward guitar-based arrangements, and while that affords Murphy a wider range of expression, from the knife-edged roar of "Shy" to the lean, folkie narrative of "Marlene Dietrich's Favourite Poem," it doesn't diminish the album's melodic strengths, as demonstrated by "Cuts You Up" or the exotic "Seven Veils." And though *Holy Smoke* maintains much of its predecessor's sense of mood, it finds Murphy moving close enough toward pop convention that the title of the album-closing "Hit Song" seems only partly ironic. — J.D.C.

MUSICAL YOUTH

★ ★ ★   **The Youth of Today (MCA, 1982)**
★ ½ **Different Style! (MCA, 1984)**

Springing from the same tradition that gave
us "My Boy Lollipop," Musical Youth
consisted of five young Britons of Jamaican
extraction who enjoyed a short but
successful career in the U.S. and U.K.
singing the reggae equivalent of bubblegum.
The group's biggest hit—in fact, its only
entry in the American Top Forty—was
"Pass the Dutchie," which was a sanitized
version of the Mighty Diamonds' "Pass the
Coochie." ("Dutchie" is Jamaican slang for
a cooking pot, "coochie" a marijuana pipe.)
Even though little else on *The Youth of
Today* is as catchy as the jovial, sing-song
"Pass the Dutchie," it makes for pleasant
enough listening. Unfortunately, the album's
success clearly went to the record company's
head. *Different Style!* is egregiously
overproduced and larded with charming but
incongruous cameos by Stevie Wonder and
Donna Summer. — J.D.C.

MY BLOODY VALENTINE

★ ★ ★   **Isn't Anything (1989; Relativity,
             1991)**
★ ★ ★   **Tremolo (EP) (1990; Sire, 1991)**
★ ★ ★ ½ **Loveless (Sire, 1991)**

Vocalist-guitarists Kevin Shields and Bilinda
Butcher head up this quartet of
noisemakers—a band whose assaultive style
recalls both the Jesus and Mary Chain and
Sonic Youth. The crew sounds tough
enough to make its frenzy seem truly
menacing, but it's too early to tell whether
the group will develop much in the way of
meaning—at this point, they flourish sheer
sonic mastery. — P.E.

THE MYSTICS

★ ★ **16 Golden Classics (Collectables, NA)**

The Mystics are a Brooklyn quintet that
could harmonize like the Belmonts, but
didn't have a lead singer to compare to
Dion. Sixteen songs is a bit too much of a
group so bland and inconsequential. What's
notable here is the much-anthologized Top
Twenty hit "Hushabye," written by Doc
Pomus and Mort Shuman to replace
"Teenager in Love," which the pair had
written for the Mystics only to have the
head of Laurie Records give it instead to
Dion and the Belmonts. Also notable is a
minor Mystics hit from 1960, "All Through
the Night," which features an uncredited
vocalist named Paul Simon. — D.M.

N

NAJMA
★★★½ **Qareeb (Shanachie, 1988)**
★★★★ **Atish (Shanachie, 1990)**
Although Najma Akhtar was born in
Britain, her roots are clearly in the
traditional music of India; her vocals are
flavored with the odd intervals and exotic
ornamentation of the Indian subcontinent.
Even so, she's hardly a traditionalist; synths
and saxophones are as much a part of her
sound as tabla and santur. *Qareeb*, a
collection of Urdu love poems set to music,
is a stunning testament to her vocal abilities,
while *Atish* effectively fuses Najma's keening
vocals with evocative, inventive art-rock
arrangements—then tops the whole thing
with a stunning, straightforward rendition of
"Faithless Love." — J.D.C.

NAPOLEON XIV
★★★½ **They're Coming to Take Me Away,
Ha-Haaa (Rhino, 1986)**
Calling himself "Napoleon XIV," obscure
comedian Jerry Samuels had a fairly big
1966 hit with "They're Coming to Take Me
Away" before fading into the shadows.
Rhino's reissue of his one album proves that
the world of entertainment lost one truly
weird dude. Ever since the '50s, comedians
from Lenny Bruce to Buddy Hackett had
gotten big laughs doing schtick about Freud
and padded cells. Napoleon XIV took the
routine to bonkers levels—with their
pseudo-Joycean wordplay, Spike Jones
sound effects, and trash-rock backing tracks,
cuts like "I'm in Love With My Little Red
Tricycle," "Dr. Psyche, the Cut-rate Head
Shrinker" and "I Live in Split Level Head"
are both hilarious, and just a wee bit
frightening; it really seems like this guy is
unhinged. Samuels was sui generis—nothing
but his own mad, bad self. — P.E.

MILTON NASCIMENTO
★★★ **Travessia (Sigla Brz., 1967)**
★★★ **Courage (1969; A&M, 1989)**
★★★★ **Milton (EMI Brz., 1970)**
★★★★ **Clube da Esquina (EMI Brz.,
1971)**
★★★★½ **Minas (EMI Brz., 1972)**
★★★★★ **Geraes (EMI Brz., 1973)**
★★★★ **Milagre dos Peixes (1973;
Capitol/Intuition, 1988)**
★★★½ **Milagre dos Peixes (Gravado
Ao Vivo) (EMI Brz., 1974)**
★★★★★ **Milton (A&M, 1976)**
★★★½ **Journey to Dawn (A&M, 1979)**
★★★ **Sentinela (1980; Verve, 1990)**
★★★★ **Ănimă (Verve, 1982)**
★★★ **Ao Vivo (1983; Philips, 1989)**
★★★ **Paixăo a Fé (EMI Brz., 1985)**
★★★½ **Encontros e Despedidas
(Polydor, 1985)**
★★★½ **A Barca dos Amantes (Verve,
1986)**
★★★★ **Personalidade (Philips, 1987)**
★★★★ **Yauarête (1987; Columbia,
1988)**
★★★½ **A Arte de Milton Nascimento
(Verve, 1988)**
★★★½ **Miltons (1988; Columbia, 1989)**
★★★★ **Txai (Columbia, 1990)**
One of Brazil's most talented singer-
songwriters, Milton Nascimento is blessed
with one of pop music's most perfect
voices—rich and soulful in its lower register,
angelically pure in falsetto—as well as the
sort of melodic instincts that can exploit
such a voice to its fullest. Understandably,
that combination has made him a superstar
in his homeland, where his recordings are
treated with the fervor and respect
Americans once lavished on Stevie Wonder.
Yet even though numerous attempts have
been made to translate Nascimento's appeal
into American terms, he remains a cult artist
at best in this country, a situation that is
less an indictment of U.S. pop fans than a
reflection of how quintessentially Brazilian
Nascimento's music is.
 That's not to say he's strictly a samba
singer, mind you. Like many Brazilian

musicians who came up under the sway of *tropicalismo,* Nascimento was as in awe of the Beatles as any American rock fan; indeed, the first selection on *Milton* is a version of the Lõ Borges tune "Para Lennon e McCartney." But Nascimento's first American album, *Courage,* gives his songs the same lush backing that had been lavished on similar efforts by samba stars like Antonio Carlos Jobim. Consequently, the album, though listenable enough, fails to offer any real sense of Nascimento's talents.

It would take seven years before he assembled another album for U.S. consumption, but Nascimento's Brazilian output improved steadily, offering a masterful synthesis of Brazilian pop styles, from the childlike cadences of "Ponta de Areia" (from *Minas*) to the hypnotic primitivism of "Promessas do Sol" (from *Geraes*) and the dramatic splendor of "Milagre dos Peixes" (from *Milagre dos Peixes*). In 1975, Nascimento was featured on the Wayne Shorter album *Native Dancer,* and Shorter returned the favor a year later by appearing—along with Herbie Hancock—on *Milton,* his 1976 album for A&M. A wonderfully alluring album, it neither diluted Nascimento's sound nor made it seem in any way foreign, and the versions of "Raca" and "The Call (A Chamada)" rival the Brazilian originals. But *Journey to Dawn,* which backs away from *Milton*'s jazzy insouciance, isn't quite as exciting, and Nascimento's option with A&M was not renewed.

Not that this lack of U.S. success adversely affected his output at home. In fact, *Ãnimã* is one of his most assured efforts, showing with "As Várias Pontas de Uma Estrela" that Nascimento could easily hold his own even against such an eminence as Caetano Veloso. Shorter returns for three cameos on the live *A Barco dos Amantes,* while Pat Metheny adds some delightfully coloristic guitar to "Vidro e Corte" on *Encontros e Despedidas* (although that album's highlight is undoubtedly the Winnie Mandela tribute "Lágrima do Sul"). Nascimento's most inspired pairing, though, is with Paul Simon on *Yauarête,* on which Simon adds an exquisite harmony part to "O Vendedor de Sonhos." Overall, *Yauarête* is Nascimento's most balanced American release since *Milton,* although the winningly exotic *Txai* has its moments, particularly the hauntingly emotional "Yanomami e Nós."
— J.D.C.

GRAHAM NASH
★★★ **Songs for Beginners (Atlantic, 1971)**
★★ **Wild Tales (1973; Atlantic, 1988)**
★★ **Earth and Sky (EMI, 1980)**
★★ **Innocent Eyes (Atlantic, 1986)**

Leader of the Hollies during their early British Invasion glory, and then serving as the weakest (if most charming) link in Crosby, Stills and Nash (and Young), Nash sings in a sweet, high register—and with just enough grit to make him a fine, distinctive addition to any harmony ensemble. On his own, however, he's such a lightweight that even his nice melodic sense and obvious sincerity can't carry him far. His debut is his only strong album; backed up by studio stalwarts and big names (Jerry Garcia, Rita Coolidge, Dave Mason), he delivers an appealing, if slight, set of tuneful meditations on the strains of love (he was then Joni Mitchell's squeeze) and current affairs ("Military Madness" and "Chicago" are nice-guy protest songs). *Wild Tales* is the lesser record—Nash's lyrics are either platitudinous or uncomfortably "poetic"— and the album's mediocrity sets the pattern for those to follow. — P.E.

JOHNNY NASH
★★★ **I Can See Clearly Now (Epic, 1972)**

A Texas-born singer and actor, Johnny Nash discovered the scintillating rhythms of Jamaican pop at the moment when a complex new sound—reggae—began to emerge from the dance-oriented ska and rock-steady styles. Recording on his own label, Johnny Nash had reached the R&B Top Ten with "Let's Move and Groove (Together)" in 1965. He crossed over to the pop charts three years later with an insinuating little hit single—"Hold Me Tight" didn't make a big splash, perhaps, but its ripples were inescapable. The gently irregular beat and lilting vocal sigh on "Hold Me Tight" opened American ears to a realm of possibilities. On the title track of his Epic debut, Johnny Nash tempers the steely optimism of early-'70s soul anthems with reggae's gracefully hesistant lope and his own erotic high tenor voice. "I Can See Clearly Now" went to Number One and stayed four weeks, offering a hopeful alternative to the concurrent pessimism of "Back Stabbers" and "Freddie's Dead." The rest of *I Can See Clearly Now*—Nash's best and sole surviving LP—shuttles between Memphis and Kingston. Nash gives one Bob Marley cover version (the hit "Stir It Up") a percolating, faithful treatment, and then turns another ("Pour Some Sugar On

Me") into a horny Southern soul workout. No longer essential, perhaps, *I Can See Clearly Now* is still an interesting stop along reggae's path. — M.C.

NAZARETH
½ ★ **Razamanaz (A&M, 1973)**
★ **Hair of the Dog (A&M, 1975)**
½ ★ **Close Enough for Rock & Roll (A&M, 1976)**
★ **Hot Tracks (A&M, 1977)**
½ ★ **Expect No Mercy (A&M, 1977)**
Like dozens of other '70s arena-rockers, Nazareth kept on trucking around the country and issuing albums through the decade's end. Diligence is about all this Scottish quintet has to offer besides its ear-piercing metallic version of Boudleaux Bryant's "Love Hurts." That 1976 hit comes from *Hair of the Dog*, though *Hot Tracks* also includes a stupefying cover of Joni Mitchell's "This Flight Tonight." But connoisseurs of heavy rock should be forewarned: Nazareth doesn't come close to equaling Judas Priest's concurrent desecration of "Diamonds and Rust" by Joan Baez. — M.C.

THE NAZZ
★ ★ ★½ **Nazz (1968; Rhino, 1984)**
★ ★ ★ **Nazz Nazz (1969; Rhino, 1984)**
★ ★ **Nazz III (1969; Rhino, 1984)**
★ ★ ★ ★ **Best of Nazz (Rhino, 1984)**
With its cover art aping *Meet the Beatles*, the Nazz's 1968 debut showed a Philadelphia foursome of 20-year-olds on fire for rock & roll greatness. They'd taken their name from a Yardbirds' tune—the Yardbirds themselves had copped the idea from a Lord Buckley routine about Jesus of Naz(areth)—and they behaved from the start like a supergroup. Few fell for such hubris at the time; in recent years, however, the band's three albums have been reevaluated as spotty examples of true pop glory—risky, passionate, and endearingly experimental.

There's no denying "Open My Eyes." Building on a crunching guitar riff lifted from the Move's "Do Ya," the song rises into a swirling concoction of breathless harmonies and Thom Mooney's Keith Moon–tribute drumming. Few records begin so powerfully, and guitarist Todd Rundgren, the Nazz's resident genius, has never since rocked so hard. *Nazz* also introduced "Hello It's Me," the sort of ballad Todd would soon make a career out of endlessly rewriting. The two sides of the Nazz—and Rundgren—personality also found

expression in the Jeff Beck–oid "Lemming Song" and in the string-driven "If That's the Way You Feel." The group's one weakness, Stewkey Antoni's colorless vocals, was also made painfully clear.

By *Nazz Nazz*, the band's ambitions had already extended to the 11 minutes of "A Beautiful Song." "Meridian Leeward" is Beatles-ish fun, and "Hang On Paul" is great Americanized Merseybeat. Due to tensions with Stewkey, Rundgren had already departed when *Nazz III* was released—but, with his slow songs forefronted, it's the most Toddish of their work. There's snarling rock on "How Can You Call That Beautiful" and a cover of "Kicks" is fine, but the rest suffers from the wordiness and monotone meandering of Todd at his most sincere. Power pop, from the Raspberries to Cheap Trick, owes much to the Nazz. The band deserves its cult. — P.E.

YOUSSOU N'DOUR
★ ★ ★ ★ **Immigrés (1984; Earthworks/Virgin, 1989)**
★ ★ ★ ★ **Inédits '84–'85 (Celluloid, 1985)**
★ ★ ★ ★ **Nelson Mandela (Polydor, 1986)**
★ ★ ★½ **The Lion (Virgin, 1989)**
★ ★ ★ ★ **Set (Virgin, 1990)**
★ ★ ★ ★ **Eyes Open (Columbia, 1992)**
Most Americans know Youssou N'Dour, if at all, as Peter Gabriel's duet partner on "In Your Eyes." But in Senegal—indeed, in much of Africa—N'Dour is a superstar, perhaps the most famous singer alive. And no wonder. Blessed with a voice as expressive as it is spectacular, N'Dour manages to combine the soaring lyricism of the griots with the fluttering virtuosity of the great Islamic singers. As a singer, he has no peer. Unfortunately, he also has no obvious entree into the U.S. pop market, something that has befuddled Western record companies since his recordings first made their way to Europe in the mid-'80s. Not only does N'Dour sing almost exclusively in Wolof, his native language, but the mbalax—literally, "rhythmic accompaniment"—sound he has developed seems to the Western ear nowhere near as pop-friendly as Fela's Afrobeat, or the South African mbaqanga Paul Simon co-opted for *Graceland*. Consequently, even though there's much to recommend the recordings N'Dour intended for his African audience—*Inédits* and the wonderfully moving *Immigrés*—the potential for crossover seemed maddeningly elusive. *Nelson Mandela* tried a version of the

Spinners' "The Rubberband Man," but that only underscored the African-ness of his music; *The Lion* augmented the singer's own Étoile de Dakar with members of Peter Gabriel's band (and, on "Shakin' the Tree," Gabriel himself), but this tended only to dilute the music. *Set*, by contrast, fleshed out N'Dour's band with synth sequences and funk licks without crowding its own sound, thereby enlivening the group's indigenous groove while creating the sort of middle ground that would make it easier for Western pop fans to appreciate the marvels of this singular singer. But where N'Dour really makes that crossover work is *Eyes Open*. The album finds him singing in English on some songs; more important, he delivers a genuinely organic fusion between African and American pop styles. As such, he's able to deliver both a track as instantly accessible as "Africa Remembers" while holding onto the rhythmic exoticisms of material like "Yo Le' Le (Fulani Groove)." — J.D.C.

NELSON
★ ★ **After the Rain (Geffen, 1990)**
Rick Nelson's sons Gunnar and Matthew reportedly took two years to record their debut album, and wound up with a substantial hit when all was said and done. However much grooming they required, Nelson *fils* learned their melodic lessons well from their dad, and their pop-metal, slick as it is, achieves a certain emotional grandeur. Hard to figure, though, if their commitment to music will ever be on a scale comparable to the effort they put into primping and strutting. By the time we know the answer, they'll probably be too rich to care what anyone thinks. — D.M.

RICK NELSON
  ★ ★ ★ **Rick Nelson Sings "For You" (1963; MCA, 1990)**
★ ★ ★ ★ **Garden Party (MCA, 1972)**
★ ★ ★ ★ **Rick Nelson in Concert: The Troubadour, 1969 (1973; MCA, 1990)**
  ★ ★ **Intakes (Epic, 1977)**
  ★ ★ ★ **Playing to Win (Capitol, 1981)**
  ★ ★ ★ **Rick Nelson: The Decca Years (MCA, 1982)**
★ ★ ★ ★ **Greatest Hits (Rhino, 1984)**
  ★ ★ ★ **All My Best (1985; MCA, 1986)**
★ ★ ★ ★ **The Memphis Sessions (Epic, 1986)**
★ ★ ★ ★ **The Best of Rick Nelson (EMI, 1987)**
  ★ ★ ★ **Live 1983–1985 (1986; Rhino, 1989)**

★ ★ ★ **The Best of Rick Nelson 1963–1975 (MCA, 1990)**
★ ★ ★ ★ ★ **Ricky Nelson (Volume One): The Legendary Masters Series (EMI, 1990)**
★ ★ ★ ★ ★ **The Best of Rick Nelson, Vol. 2 (EMI, 1991)**
If he had to die young and in circumstances over which he had no control, then at least Rick Nelson went to his grave knowing he had won the respect he had sought in the years following his comeback in 1970. At the time of his death Nelson had been acknowledged as an important artist whose work in the late '50s and early '60s was a vital entry on the pop side of rock & roll. Nelson wasn't blessed with a great voice, but by choosing material carefully he was able to employ his smooth, almost monotone tenor in ways that communicated a broad spectrum of emotions.

Marketed as a teen idol, given a springboard to national recognition through his weekly appearances on his parents' sitcom, "The Adventures of Ozzie and Harriet," Nelson could have coasted all the way to the bank. He chose instead to make good music. Even after some fallow years in the late '60s, he made his return to the public arena by insisting on an opportunity to demonstrate the degree to which he had grown as an artist—a concession an oldies crowd was unwilling to grant him in 1971 when he appeared at a revival concert at Madison Square Garden and was booed by fans who resented his contemporary look and sound. That experience, however, provided the impetus for his final, productive years, and immediately produced a Top Ten hit in "Garden Party." It would be his last appearance in the Top Forty, but Nelson went on to produce a number of outstanding records before perishing in a plane crash on New Year's Eve 1985.

For those who prefer to think of the early Rick Nelson as the essential Rick Nelson, opportunities abound to collect the original recordings on one or two discs. For annotation and song selection, EMI's two-volume *The Best of Rick Nelson* covers the waterfront from his first Number One, "Poor Little Fool," to "It's Up to You" (1962) with interesting stops along the way.

EMI's first volume in its Legendary Masters Series entry on Nelson has a good sampling of lesser-known hits mixed in with "Stood Up," "Lonesome Town," "Never Be Anyone Else but You," "It's Late" and other hits. *The Best of Rick Nelson 1963–1975* spotlights the close of the teen-idol era—"String Along," "Fools Rush In," "For You," and "The Very Thought of You"—and the beginning of the Stone Canyon Band era that produced "She Belongs to Me" and "Garden Party," which are also included. An abridged version of this album is available as *Rick Nelson: The Decca Years*. Rhino's *Greatest Hits* is exactly that: 14 tracks, all of them choice. *All My Best* and *Live: 1983–1985*, live albums both, are in essence greatest-hits sets, both well done. *Rick Nelson Sings "For You"* is a re-release of the artist's 1963 album, complete with original cover art and liner notes.

Nelson's comeback is documented in two albums, *In Concert: The Troubadour, 1969* and *Garden Party*. For the Troubadour set, the material ranges from the Gene Pitney–penned Nelson classic "Hello Mary Lou, Goodbye Heart" to Nelson's self-penned epic, "Who Cares About Tomorrow—Promises," from Doug Kershaw's Cajun-rock chestnut, "Louisiana Man," to three Bob Dylan songs, including "She Belongs to Me." He extended this approach on *Garden Party*, which underscored his growing facility as a songwriter on the title track and five other originals, prominent among them the touching "A Flower Opens Gently."

While "Garden Party" marked the end of his chart days, Nelson wasn't finished by a long shot. *Intakes*, like *Garden Party*, was produced by Nelson himself and continues the blend of lighthearted rockers and introspective, self-revealing songs Nelson favored at this juncture. In '81 Nelson released *Playing to Win*—yet another worthy addition to his catalog—which includes a terrific cover version of John Fogerty's "Almost Saturday Night," nice touches on Graham Parker's "Back to Schooldays" and John Hiatt's "It Hasn't Happened Yet," and two more top-notch originals in "The Loser Babe Is You" and "Call It What You Want."

The final and most moving document is *The Memphis Sessions*. These tracks, cut in 1978, were intended for release as an album (a few showed up on an EP), but remained in the can until a year after Nelson's death. This is a taste of an artist going back to his roots, covering "That's Alright (Mama)," "Dream Lover," "Rave On" and "True Love Ways" as well as more current material. Of all the tracks, none matches the tenderness of "Lay Back in the Arms of Someone You Love." The song affords Nelson an opportunity for a vocal performance that is as strong as it is gentle. In every respect it's a fitting grace note to cap the legacy of a dignified man. — D.M.

WILLIE NELSON

★★★½ The Best of Willie Nelson (EMI Manhattan, 1973)
★★★½ Shotgun Willie (1973; Atlantic, 1987)
★★★★ Phases and Stages (1974; Atlantic, 1991)
★★★★ Red Headed Stranger (Columbia, 1975)
★★★ The Sound in Your Mind (Columbia, 1976)
★★★★ To Lefty From Willie (Columbia, 1977)
★★★★ Stardust (Columbia, 1978)
★★★ Willie Sings Kris Kristofferson (Columbia, 1979)
★★½ The Electric Horseman (Columbia, 1979)
★★★ Honeysuckle Rose (Columbia, 1980)
★★★ Somewhere Over the Rainbow (Columbia, 1981)
★★★★ Greatest Hits (and Some That Will Be) (Columbia, 1981)
★★★ Always on My Mind (Columbia, 1982)
★★½ Tougher Than Leather (Columbia, 1983)
★★ Without a Song (Columbia, 1983)
★★ City of New Orleans (Columbia, 1984)
★★ Angel Eyes (Columbia, 1984)
★★ Music From Songwriter (Columbia, 1984)
★★★ Half Nelson (Columbia, 1985)
★★★★ Me and Paul (Columbia, 1985)
★★ Partners (Columbia, 1986)
★★ The Promiseland (Columbia, 1986)
★★ Island in the Sea (Columbia, 1987)
★★ What a Wonderful World (Columbia, 1988)
★★★ All-Time Greatest Hits, Vol. 1 (RCA, 1988)
★★★ A Horse Called Music (Columbia, 1989)
★★★★ Nite Life: Greatest Hits and Rare Tracks 1959–71 (Rhino, 1990)
★★½ Born for Trouble (Columbia, 1990)
★★★★ Who Will Buy My Memories? (Sony Music Special Products, 1991)

WITH LEON RUSSELL

★★★ One for the Road (Columbia, 1978)

WITH RAY PRICE
★ ★ ★ ★ **San Antonio Rose (Columbia, 1980)**
WITH WEBB PIERCE
★ ★ ★ ★ **In the Jailhouse Now (Columbia, 1982)**
WITH FARON YOUNG
★ ★ ★ **Funny How Time Slips Away (Columbia, 1984)**
WITH HANK SNOW
★ ★ ★ ★ **Brand on My Heart (Columbia, 1985)**

This native Texan earned a solid behind-the-scenes reputation as a hot Nashville composer in the '60s. Willie Nelson wrote the hits "Crazy" for Patsy Cline, "Hello Walls" for Faron Young and "Night Life" for Ray Price—just to mention the acknowledged standards. His own versions didn't quite fit the conventional notion of country singing, at first. With time, Nelson's somewhat talky delivery grew more musical; between his bluesy phrasing and cadenced drawl, Nelson puts across his deceptively simple melodies better than anybody. Before leading the outlaw movement away from Music Row in the '70s, Nelson tried recording within the Nashville system in the '60s. The strength of the material, as well as the growing confidence in Nelson's mellow growl, overcomes the occasional intrusions by string sections and the Anita Kerr Singers. The Rhino anthology *The Best of Willie Nelson 1959–71* offers a generous and superior selection from this period; sweet but far shorter, the EMI *Best of* gets the job done at a budget price.

Nelson escaped the grind by moving to Austin, Texas, in the early '70s; he checked out the hippie scene, let his hair grow out and expanded his musical consciousness in various, far-ranging directions. His last album for RCA, the deleted *Yesterday's Wine*, from 1971, is the first of his bold, conceptual departures from country's hits-plus-filler norm. Rather than tack rock guitar riffs onto modern honky-tonk sagas, Nelson absorbed the innovations of Bob Dylan and the singer-songwriters into his own distinct style. Even if the narrative concepts don't always hold together, Willie hangs his most ambitious albums on some of his catchiest tunes. "Me and Paul," a highlight from *Yesterday's Wine*, rounds out the Rhino collection. Produced by Arif Mardin and Jerry Wexler, *Shotgun Willie* blends Memphis horns and western swing with mixed results—it alternately sounds too loose and somewhat forced. On *Phases and Stages*, Nelson gets to do his own thing.

Progressive country, or the Outlaw sound, begins here. The haunting and spare "Phases and Stages" theme—just Willie and his Mexican-flavored guitar picking—unites the seemingly unrelated songs into an ultimately cohesive whole. The breakup of an itinerant musician's marriage is documented from both the man and woman's points of view, the fiddle and steel guitars echoing the overall tone of dirty realism. Ending with the gracefully whacked-out anthem "Pick Up the Tempo," *Phases and Stages* is just about perfect.

Moving to Columbia Records, Nelson followed up with another narrative concept album. *Red Headed Stranger* is pared down even further in terms of accompaniment, while the storyline is considerably more ambiguous than the last album's. A cowboy catches his lover with the aforementioned stranger; "wild in his sorrow," he shoots them both and then hits the road, taking listeners along for the ride. Nelson wanders out toward the cosmos near the end of *Stranger*, but it's easy enough to drift along with his flow. And the beautiful hit single "Blue Eyes Crying in the Rain" would make sense in any context.

Compared to those records, *The Sound in Your Mind* comes off as slapdash—even a bit lazy. Tellingly, a Nelson oldie ("Healing Hands of Time") and a gem by Austin songwriter Steve Fromholz ("I'd Have to Be Crazy") are the only real standouts. *To Lefty From Willie* sparks an extended period of roots exploration for Nelson. This tribute to hardluck crooner Lefty Frizzell digs deep into the melancholy essence of '50s honky-tonk, though Willie's cover versions retrieve some of Lefty's devil-may-care high spirits too. Reaching all the way back to Tin Pan Alley and beyond, Nelson achieves another effortless peak on *Stardust*. With Booker T. Jones producing Nelson's roughhewn road band, these familiar chesnuts swing in a gentle rhythmic breeze: from "On the Sunny Side of the Street" to "September Song," from "All of Me" to "Georgia on My Mind." *Stardust* made Willie Nelson a superstar, and he's certainly a prolific one. His subsequent work remains eclectic—but nowhere near so artistically risky or groundbreaking as those '70s albums. Unless you consider a duet with Julio Iglesias ("To All the Girls I've Loved Before," from 1984) to be some sort of subversive experiment.

Greatest Hits (and Some That Will Be) does a better-than-acceptable job of summing up Nelson's ascent, building up to the jauntily definitive "On the Road Again" (from the *Honeysuckle Rose* soundtrack, from 1980). Willie hit a slack patch after *Somewhere Over the Rainbow* (a less-than-brilliant *Stardust* redux) and the easy-listening smash *Always on My Mind*. His best work of the '80s lies on the duet albums he cut with a distinguished quartet of country veterans. *San Antonio Rose* places super-smooth Ray Price in a frisky western swing setting. Gutsy honky-tonker Webb Pierce provides staunch company on *In the Jailhouse Now. Funny How Time Slips Away* echoes the Ray Price album, though '60s crooner Faron Young isn't quite as distinct a singer. *Brand on My Heart* proves that the opposite is true of Hank Snow; the "Yodeling Ranger" still sounds like nobody else. Nelson puts each of these legends at ease and manages to get his two cents in without hogging the spotlight. A nice reminder that, apart from everything else, Nelson is a great country singer.

And after listening to *Half Nelson*—a package of Willie's pop duets, including his superstudly showdown with Julio—you may need such a reminder. After shuffling along blandly for several years, Nelson showed signs of renewed interest on *A Horse Called Music*. Aside from a couple of orchestrated misfires, "Nothing I Can Do About It Now" is the best shoulder-shrugging hook he's come up with in years. Unfortunately, it took the Internal Revenue Service to really inspire Willie Nelson. The 1991 clearance-sale album *Who Will Buy My Memories* (available only through mail-order TV ads) is his most striking and satisfying release in years. Outtakes and demos, some well-worn tunes and some unknown grabbers, just Willie and that beat-up guitar: Perhaps this scaled-back approach can re-iginite his songwriting flame. — M.C.

MICHAEL NESMITH
★ ★   **The Wichita Train Whistle Sings (1968; Pacific Arts, 1978)**
★ ★½   **And the Hits Just Keep on Comin' (1972; Pacific Arts, 1977)**
★ ★ ★   **Pretty Much Your Standard Ranch Stash (1973; Pacific Arts, 1977)**
★ ★½   **The Prison (Pacific Arts, 1975)**
★ ★ ★   **From a Radio Engine to a Photon Wing (Pacific Arts, 1977)**
★ ★½   **Live at the Palais (Pacific Arts, 1978)**
★ ★ ★   **Compilation (Pacific Arts, 1978)**
★ ★ ★   **Infinite Rider on the Big Dogma (Pacific Arts, 1979)**
★ ★ ★   **Elephant Parts (Pacific Arts, 1980)**
★ ★ ★½ **The Newer Stuff (Rhino, 1989)**
★ ★ ★ ★ **The Older Stuff: The Best of the Early Years (Rhino, 1991)**
WITH THE FIRST NATIONAL BAND
★ ★ ★   **Magnetic South (RCA, 1970)**
★ ★ ★   **Loose Salute (RCA, 1970)**
★ ★ ★   **Nevada Fighter (RCA, 1971)**
WITH THE SECOND NATIONAL BAND
★ ★½   **Tantamount to Treason, Vol. 1 (RCA, 1972)**

Singer-guitarist Michael Nesmith came to fame as the Monkee with integrity—the only member of the manufactured moptops who was longer on talent than looks, and the only one who betrayed obvious discomfort with their contrived teen-idol status. During his tenure as a *Tiger Beat* cover boy, Nesmith released an odd solo album; *The Wichita Train Whistle Sings* certainly didn't sound like Boyce and Hart pop—instead it featured instrumentals that now come off as Muzak. Departing from the Monkees, he formed the First National Band and put out a trio of country albums (*Magnetic South, Loose Salute, Nevada Fighter*), that for all the rootsy expertise of the fine pedal-steel player, Red Rhodes, remain pleasant exactly because Nesmith didn't strain too hard for authenticity.

Personnel shifts resulted in the Second National Band and more of the same affable ersatz cowboy fare. The solo *Pretty Much Your Standard Ranch Stash*, with one of Nesmith's best songs, "Some of Shelley's Blues," ended the singer's country phase. An ambitious failure, *The Prison* marked his venture into concept-album overreaching (the record came complete with a book); he followed it with *Infinite Rider on the Big Dogma*, an album whose best tunes ("Magic," "Cruisin' ") were smart radio pop (that never found much actual success on the airwaves) and whose filler sounded like Bob Welch.

The strongest Nesmith is *The Newer Stuff*, a collection of his post-country work. While a capable singer, he's best at songwriting, particularly in a humorous vein. Some of his tunes have the dark zing of Warren Zevon at his most perversely winsome; everything else on the record is, at the very least, a flourish of craft. *Compilation* gathers his early work; it, too, has its dependable delights, but Rhino's *The Older Stuff* is the better choice with its excellent song selection, including "Joanne" and "Different Drum," and liner notes. — P.E.

ROBBIE NEVIL

★★½ **Robbie Nevil (Manhattan/Capitol, 1986)**
★★½ **A Place Like This (EMI/Manhattan, 1988)**

AOR in street-kid disguise. With his leather jacket and curling locks, Nevil comes on like a rocker, but his music is actually late-'80s state-of-the-art program fodder for very safe radio stations. Aiming for the surefire mix of studio gloss and soullike vocalizing, he's a bit like Michael Bolton or Paul Young—but he's considerably less distinctive a singer. All keyboard textures and catchy rhythms, his songs are slight on melody and even slighter on verbal interest—everything sounds "good," nothing is memorable. He sings about wanting to go on vacation and about the "Simple Life"; he wails about love and self-pity. And all with a bogus air of importance that recalls such past middlebrow artistes as Gino Vannelli or Michael Franks. — P.E.

AARON NEVILLE

★★★ **Orchid in the Storm (EP) (1985; Rhino, 1990)**
★★½ **Greatest Hits (Curb, 1990)**
★★★½ **My Greatest Gift (Rounder, 1990)**
★★★½ **Tell It Like It Is (Curb, 1991)**
★★★½ **Warm Your Heart (A&M, 1991)**

"Tell It Like It Is," Aaron Neville's 1966 hit single, is arguably the greatest New Orleans R&B ballad ever, and Neville has every right to reprise the song at any and every opportunity. Unfortunately, a lot of what he recorded up to that point is fairly forgettable, which is why *Tell It Like It Is* seems to have less meat than filler. Still, the New Orleans flavor of its material at least seems a bit more genuine than the second-hand Memphis soul and imitation Bacharach-David material included among the late-'60s singles on the obviously mistitled *Greatest Hits* (although that album, like *Tell It Like It Is*, takes care to include "Tell It Like It Is" and "Over You").

There's a different version of "Tell It Like It Is" on *My Greatest Gift*, but the bulk of these '70s-vintage tracks find Neville working with producer Allen Toussaint, a combination that produces memorably funky results on the likes of "Hercules" and "Mojo Hannah." Astonishingly, there isn't a version of "Tell It Like It Is" on *Orchid in the Storm*, but this 1985 ballad session (produced by Joel Dorn) does offer sterling renditions of oldies like the Johnny Ace hit "Pledging My Love" and Jerry Butler's "For Your Precious Love."

Yet it wasn't until *Warm Your Heart*—produced by Linda Ronstadt, with whom he'd recorded a set of Grammy-winning duets in 1990—that Neville had his first Top Forty success since "Tell It Like It Is." Again, there are a fair number of oldies here, with "Everybody Plays the Fool" being the standout, but as the more contemporary sound of "Angola Bound" makes plain, Neville is not just an oldie, but a goodie. — J.D.C.

NEVILLE BROTHERS

★★½ **The Neville Brothers (Capitol, 1978)**
★★★★ **Fiyo on the Bayou (A&M, 1981)**
★★★★ **Neville-ization (Black Top, 1984)**
★★★ **Live at Tipitina's (Spindletop, 1985)**
★½ **Uptown (EMI America, 1987)**
★★★★½ **Treacherous: A History of the Neville Brothers (Rhino, 1988)**
★★★★ **Yellow Moon (A&M, 1989)**
★★★½ **Treacherous Too! (Rhino, 1991)**
★★★★½ **Legacy: A History of the Nevilles (Charly, 1990)**
★★★★ **Brother's Keeper (A&M, 1990)**

In a just world, great bands would make great albums, bad bands would make bad ones, and the pop charts would mark the difference. And in such a world, the Neville Brothers would all but own the hit parade. Unfortunately, life doesn't quite work that way, which may be why the Nevilles—despite having a fearsomely soulful lead singer, flawless harmony vocals and the finest rhythm section in New Orleans—have never achieved a level of success commensurate with their talent. Although the four Neville brothers—Aaron, Art, Charles and Cyril—had been kicking around the New Orleans music scene since the mid-'50s, when Aaron and Art were members of the Hawketts, the Neville Brothers as such didn't come together as a band until after the quartet had united behind the Wild Tchoupitoulas. What made the Tchoupitoulas album so exciting was the ease with which the group meshed contemporary funk licks with traditional Mardi Gras parade rhythms. But there's almost no sign of that sound on *The Neville Brothers*, on which the group wastes its time on such calculated attempts at R&B currency as "Dancin' Jones" (an insipid paean to the Rolling Stones) and "Vieux Carré Rouge" (a pleasant-but-pedestrian soul ballad). Only "All Nights, All Right" and a version of John Hiatt's "Washable Ink" save the album from irrelevancy.

Fiyo on the Bayou puts the band back on

track. Some of the added punch can be attributed to the addition of guitarist Leo Nocentelli (who'd played in the Meters with Art and Cyril) to the rhythm section, but the real secret to this album's success is the shift in focus away from the R&B charts and toward the Crescent City. Apart from "Mona Lisa" and "The Ten Commandments of Love," a pair of oldies included to frame Aaron's otherworldly tenor, the songs are mostly traditional, lending the album a rootsy richness. Yet despite rave reviews, *Fiyo on the Bayou* was barely a blip on the pop charts; likewise, the stunning *Neville-ization*, which documents the group's legendary live act, failed to reach beyond the faithful. (*Live at Tipitina's* offers additional material from the same concert). Perhaps that explains the desperation of *Uptown*, an ill-advised attempt at mainstream respectability that not only downplays the New Orleans elements, but actually stiffens the groove with sequencers and electronic percussion.

By this point, the Nevilles' past appeared far more promising than their future—hence the intoxicating nostalgia of *Treacherous*, which mixes early solo singles by Art, Aaron and Cyril with selections from *The Wild Tchoupitoulas*, *The Neville Brothers* and *Fiyo on the Bayou*. *Treacherous Too!* continues in that vein, with more solo stuff and excerpts from *Neville-ization*, while Charly's *Legacy* takes a pre–Neville Brothers approach, augmenting its Art and Aaron tracks with tunes by the Meters. But just when it seemed the Nevilles would never find a way to reconcile their sound with the modern pop market, the group went into the studio with producer Daniel Lanois, emerging with the triumphant *Yellow Moon*, an album that manages to find room for such contemporary touches as rap ("Sister Rosa," a tribute to civil-rights figure Rosa Parks) without compromising or corrupting the Nevilles' identity. Having found their formula, the Nevilles went back for more on *Brother's Keeper*, which may lack the eerie atmospherics of *Yellow Moon* but otherwise maintains its musical balance, thanks to touches like the low-key funk of "Witness" or the thick, dark harmonies of "Brother Blood." — J.D.C.

THE NEW CHRISTY MINSTRELS
★ ★ ★ **Greatest Hits (Columbia, 1966)**
We will excuse for a moment that this group, named for one of the most famous minstrel shows of the 19th century, begat one Kenny Rogers, who joined them in 1966. At that time the group had been two

years without a hit, and had no others before breaking up in the late '60s. Formed in 1962 by Randy Sparks, the Minstrels rode a folk revival to chart success in '63 and '64. Barry McGuire's big bear of a voice helped propel "Green Green" and "Saturday Night" to hit status in '63; he left the group in '65 for a solo career that started promisingly with his ferocious, albeit somewhat comical, reading of P.F. Sloan's apocalyptic "Eve of Destruction." The group's last hit was in '64, with the Sparks-penned "Today," one of the decade's most affecting love songs. Sparks's smooth, soft tenor was the ideal complement to lyrics replete with graceful references to nature, beauty, devotion to the existential life, and savoring the joy of the moment. It deserved its popularity. *Greatest Hits* contains all three hits, and also surveys the group's intelligent interpretation of Leadbelly's folk classic "Cotton Fields" and rousing renditions of Sparks's "The Drinkin' Gourd" (which tells of the underground railway that carried many slaves to freedom during the Civil War) and "Mighty Mississippi." On the down side, there's also a pointless version of "Downtown." Fans of this type of folk-pop will want to look for the Minstrels' out-of-print *Today* album as well. — D.M.

NEW EDITION
★ ★ ★   **Candy Girl (Streetwise, 1983)**
★ ★ ★½   **New Edition (MCA, 1984)**
★ ★ ½   **All for Love (MCA, 1985)**
★ ★   **Christmas All Over the World (MCA, 1985)**
★ ★   **Under the Blue Moon (MCA, 1986)**
★ ★ ½   **Heart Break (MCA, 1988)**
★ ★ ★ ★ **Greatest Hits (MCA, 1991)**
Originally assembled by songwriter-producer Maurice Starr in the hopes of creating a latter-day Jackson 5, New Edition went from teen idols to hip-hop godfathers in less than a decade. The New Edition of *Candy Girl* is endearing but ragged, a bit unsure in its high notes and none-too-close in its harmonies. That's not to say the album doesn't work—indeed, "Candy Girl" is a near-perfect gloss on the Jackson 5's "ABC," while "Is This the End" does an admirable job of rewriting "I'll Be There." By the time of *New Edition*, the group had moved into the mainstream, dumping Starr as its manager and working with top-flight L.A. studio talent. It paid off, too, thanks to insinuatingly tuneful material like "Cool It Now," which worked rap-style exchanges around Ralph Tresvant's boyish lead, and

the calculatedly innocent "Mr. Telephone Man." *All for Love* repeats that approach, with less success; "Count Me Out" comes across as a "Cool It Now" retread, and ballads like "Whispers in Bed" find the group in over its head. Even so, "A Little Bit of Love (Is All It Takes)" boasts one of the Edition's most memorable choruses, while "School" shows how much the quintet has learned about rap.

New Edition suffered its first defection at this point, when Bobby Brown left for a solo career that would eventually turn his taste for hip-hop into massive crossover success. Meanwhile, the group's remaining members went in the opposite direction, turning in an album's worth of doo-wop oldies on *Under the Blue Moon*. It was a cute idea, but a big mistake. Adding Johnny Gill to its lineup, New Edition began to play catch-up. Produced by Jimmy Jam and Terry Lewis, *Heart Break* updates the group's rhythmic base and incorporates many of the same ideas Brown used on his breakthrough album, *Don't Be Cruel*. Still, not even songs as winning as "If It Isn't Love" or "Boys to Men" are enough to overcome the clunky conceptualism of the album's let's-pretend-this-is-a-concert presentation. Ironically, though, the album's failure to restore New Edition to its former glory ended up working to the group's advantage, as subsequent solo albums by Gill and Bell Biv DeVoe (that is, Ricky Bell, Michael "Biv" Bivins and Ronnie DeVoe) made the now-splintered New Edition hotter than it had been in years. — J.D.C.

NEW KIDS ON THE BLOCK

★★½ New Kids on the Block (Columbia, 1986)
★★½ Hangin' Tough (Columbia, 1988)
★★★ Step by Step (Columbia, 1990)
★★ No More Games:The Remix Album (Columbia, 1990)

Having won radio triumph with New Edition and that group's cuddly, Jackson Five–wannabe R&B, producer-packager Maurice Starr made megastars of New Kids on the Block by cynically rehashing the old Sam Phillips/Elvis strategy—doing black music in white face. Aiming his quintet of toothsome Boston teen idols expressly at the bubblegum crowd whose parents grooved on the Archies, Menudo or the Bay City Rollers, Starr penned cheery dance confections and drippy ballads for the group's debut, *New Kids on the Block*—a record remarkable only for the singers' charmingly clunky aspirations to rap and

B-boy posing ("Are You Down?"). However slight, *New Kids on the Block* hit big in 1986, serving unwittingly to open the ears of mainstream America to hip-hop; all noise, bad attitude and zealous imitation of hardcore rap, the Beastie Boys may have turned high school heavy-metalers on to a tougher groove—NKOTB gave up squeaky-clean funk for fifth graders. *Hangin' Tough,* with Starr again writing all the tunes and, this time, playing every instrument, slickly reprised the first album: "Cover Girl" was catchy, after the manner of the 1910 Fruitgum Company; "Please Don't Go Girl" was breathlessly "sincere." By then gods in fanzines, the Kids inched tentatively away from their trademark swooning slow songs for the ersatz heaviness of "Hangin' Tough" and its riff that recalled Joan Jett's "I Love Rock 'n' Roll." They continued reaping, in equal measure, squealing preteen adulation and critical opprobrium from everyone else.

After learning to shave, the boys delivered *Step by Step* and a bid for maturity—one that came close to succeeding. The title track was their most assured single, and "Tonight" was one odd curio: carried by a "Penny Lane"–style trumpet, the song waxed nostalgic for the band's "history" (elegiac quotes from past hits, and an air of grandeur)—it's a strange, dumb tune, but it's mighty catchy. "Games" thudded along with a surprising swagger; the slower numbers weren't quite so dull as past heartbreakers; and despite the embarrassing overreaching of the plastic reggae "Stay With Me Baby," the record showed the group at least expanding its formula (they even played on a few songs).

With its 900-number hotline info, its accompanying videos and Coke ads, *Step by Step* vehemently underlined the fact that NKOTB remained chiefly a textbook lesson in merchandising—but also that the product could be a fairly hummable one. — P.E.

RANDY NEWMAN

★★★ Randy Newman (Reprise, 1968)
★★★★★ 12 Songs (Reprise, 1970)
★★★★ Sail Away (Reprise, 1972)
★★★★★ Good Old Boys (Reprise, 1974)
★★★ Little Criminals (Warner Bros., 1977)
★★★½ Born Again (Warner Bros., 1979)
★★★½ Trouble in Paradise (Warner Bros., 1983)
★★★ Land of Dreams (Reprise, 1988)

Randy Newman gets lumped in with the singer-songwriter movement, mostly due to his plainspoken delivery. He rarely wrote about himself; musically, he was first inspired by Tin Pan Alley and movie soundtracks (two of his uncles were Hollywood composers) rather than Bob Dylan and the Beatles. Newman uses songs to create settings for his stories and character sketches, shifting from piano-and-voice to a full orchestra as the situation demands. Specializing in perverse Americana and black humor, Newman rarely lapses into mere cleverness or smug putdowns on his best albums.

Slightly tentative, his 1968 debut album (*Randy Newman*) is out of print. On *12 Songs* Newman's attack coalesces into a unique approach. With Ry Cooder accompanying on slide guitar, this is Newman's bluesiest and most cutting work. "My Old Kentucky Home" flows along with deceptive laziness, "Let's Burn Down the Cornfield" hisses out inflammatory passion, while the sad tales of "Rosemary," "Lucinda" and "Suzanne" linger long after the disc stops playing. *Sail Away* reveals the tear in Newman's musical cloth: the headbanging irony of "Political Science" ("Let's drop the big one now") and "God's Song (That's Why I Love Mankind)" seems painfully obvious next to the title track—a stunning indictment of the slave trade that gains strength from its subtlety. Two earlier Newman gems ("Dayton, Ohio—1903," "Simon Smith & the Amazing Dancing Bear") round out an album that's by no means disappointing, despite its flaws.

Cohesive without being "conceptual," *Good Old Boys* surveys the American South through a variety of first-person monologues and narrative tales. History and current events tangle in a complex stream. The mix of revulsion and identification reveals Newman's roots in New Orleans (he moved to California as a child); "Rednecks" and "Birmingham" mock the hypocrisy of Northern liberals as well as the ignorant attitudes the songs themselves proclaim. And "Louisiana 1927," perhaps the most memorable of Newman's songs, mirrors a terse description of a flood with a creeping, inevitable melody.

Little Criminals spawned the dubious "Short People"—Newman's crudest joke, naturally, became a fluke hit single, and his weakest album to that point followed suit. Experimenting with string textures and dallying with various Eagles on "Rider in the Rain," Newman appears to be giving the lyrics short shrift. Oh, it sounds all right, but even the catchiest tracks— "Baltimore" and "Kathleen (Catholicism Made Easier)"—feel overly familiar. *Born Again* is more pointed: "It's Money That I Love" and the straightfaced ELO parody "The Story of a Rock & Roll Band" score bull's-eyes. But "They Just Got Married" is somewhat condescending, and "Half a Man" overtly homophobic.

It's difficult to maintain a satirical edge without turning bitter. The '80s certainly handed Randy Newman plenty of potential material; he responds in kind with the less-than-sunny *Trouble in Paradise*. A few too many glossy supersession riffs are deployed, but "I Love L.A." and "Christmas in Cape Town" pack some bite. *Land of Dreams* is the spottiest Newman album so far, however. Perhaps his ongoing movie soundtrack work—he's scored *Avalon*, *Awakenings* and *Parenthood*, among others—is tapping into his creative energy. *Land of Dreams* features a limp rap sendup ("Masterman & Baby J") as well as several tepid love songs. Still, fans shouldn't completely rule this one out: The album opens with some mildly surprising autobiographical numbers ("Dixie Flyer," "New Orleans Wins the War") and concludes with two well-aimed jabs at the Reaganite mentality. "It's Money That Matters" and "I Want You to Hurt Like I Do" both suggest that the pop scene could use Randy Newman's dark, yet clarifying vision. — M.C.

THUNDERCLAP NEWMAN
★★★ **Hollywood Dream (1970; PolyGram, 1991)**

A small, quirky wonder. Produced by Pete Townshend, Thunderclap Newman's 1969 hit "Something in the Air" was a strange, cheery ode to anarchy ("We've got to get together sooner or later/Because the revolution's here") that, with its eerie, falsetto vocal, heavy drums and swirling strings, captured the time's madcap spirit. Ingeniously employed in *The Magic Christian*—a loopy, amoral comedy, starring Peter Sellers and Ringo Starr—it was the masterstroke of the band's one album. With personnel as odd as its songs, the band—consisting of singer (and ex–John Mayall roadie) Speedy Keen, 16-year-old guitarist Jimmy McCulloch and jazz pianist Andy Newman—had the potential to continue the artful pop its record displayed. Internal turmoil, however, jettisoned

the project, leaving in its wake a single overlooked pearl, *Hollywood Dream*.
— P.E.

NEW ORDER
★★★ **Movement (1981; Qwest 1986)**
★★★★ **1981–82 (EP) (Factory, 1982)**
★★★ **Power, Corruption and Lies (1983; Qwest 1986)**
★★★★ **Low-life (Qwest, 1985)**
★★★★ **Brotherhood (Qwest, 1986)**
★★★★ **Substance (Qwest, 1987)**
★★★ **Technique (Qwest, 1989)**
Bassist Peter Hook, drummer Steven Morris and guitarist Bernard Sumner founded New Order on the ashes of their previous band, Joy Division. After the suicide of lead singer Ian Curtis in 1980, the three surviving members added keyboardist Gillian Gilbert—though Curtis's true replacement was a decidedly post-punk emphasis on music itself. *Movement* stakes New Order's claim: the guitar sound is subdued yet richer, the melodic bass lines are even more pronounced, the synth washes are refreshing and astringent, the steady beat creeps ever closer to the dance floor. The singing sounds tentative, but it wasn't long until Sumner discovered his modest gift: an affecting, here-goes-nothing vocal technique.

The 1982 single "Temptation" reverberates from the murky depths of an all-consuming finding sweet release in the soaring synths and crisp rhythms. This eminently danceable track seethes with raw emotion; the overworked term "cathartic" actually applies—"Temptation" can leave a listener feeling positively cleansed. The *1981-82* EP brackets "Temptation" with earlier sketchy-sounding singles and can almost be heard as a suite. On the subsequent 12-inch releases "Blue Monday" and "Confusion," New Order edges closer still to the pulsing electronic heart of disco. Dreamy, repetitious and slightly lazy-sounding, *Power, Corruption and Lies* fuels the notion that New Order is a natural singles band stuck in the unforgiving album format.

Low-life extinguishes those doubts, deepening the group's trademark sound with a driving, heartfelt anti-war vignette ("Love Vigilantes") as well as a flat-out pretty love song ("The Perfect Kiss"). *Brotherhood* couples a stirring return to the Velvets-guitar crunch of Joy Division with this group's strongest set of songs—the album is highly recommended to alternative rockers who feel New Order is somehow

tainted by its disco associations. The brittle, impassive *Technique* basically supports that crowd's worst suspicions, however. *Substance* collects taut remixes of the standout tracks already mentioned (save for "Love Vigilantes"), and that's all most people will ever need to know about New Order. But, somehow, these seemingly breezy, offhand ditties continue to sound more substantial the second, third or fourth time around. — M.C.

NEW RIDERS OF THE PURPLE SAGE
★★★ **New Riders of the Purple Sage (Columbia, 1971)**
★★★ **The Adventures of Panama Red (Columbia, 1973)**
★ **Best of New Riders of the Purple Sage (Columbia, 1976)**
Besides giving Jerry Garcia a chance to practice pedal-steel guitar, these zonked-out bogus saddle pals served little purpose. A spinoff of the Grateful Dead, the New Riders in their earliest incarnation featured Garcia, Mickey Hart and Phil Lesh and their debut sounds like *American Beauty* outtakes, minus the vision. Neither Riders John Dawson nor David Nelson could really sing, and such fare as "Last Lonely Eagle" and "Louisiana Lady" were country rock of the most trite stripe. By the second album Garcia was gone, and the Riders devolved into mojo cowboy schtick that unintentionally mocked the legitimate neo-country of bands like the Flying Burrito Brothers, as well as the intriguing druggie-redneck fusion of David Allan Coe. *Panama Red* summed up the band's uncertain appeal. They were oddly popular during their early-'70s moment, due to the Dead connection and a zeitgeist that embraced fake western schlock (Commander Cody, Michael Murphy), but whatever the New Riders released that wasn't outright offensive now sounds merely bland. — P.E.

JUICE NEWTON
★★ **Quiet Lies (Capitol, 1982)**
★★ **Greatest Hits (Capitol, 1987)**
★★ **Emotion (Capitol, 1987)**
★★ **Can't Wait All Night (RCA, NA)**
★★ **Old Flame (RCA, 1988)**
★★ **Ain't Gonna Cry (RCA, 1989)**
This Virginia-born country-pop singer knocked around without much success in the mid-to-late '70s before cutting a hit single, a cover version of the Merrilee Rush hit "Angel of the Morning," in 1981. A succession of catchy singles followed, as did a label change as her fortunes began to wear

thin in the late '80s. She returned to her original label RCA, but this time the results proved more fruitful. Working with producer Richard Landis, Newton has revived her career by mining the MOR country field. Landis knows what he's doing in the studio, and his work in finding the proper milieu for Newton's thin vocals is the most interesting aspect of the artist's records. Otherwise there's very little meat on these bones. — D.M.

THE NEW YORK DOLLS

★ ★ ★ ★   New York Dolls (1973; Mercury, 1987)
★ ★ ★ ★   Too Much Too Soon (1974; Mercury, 1988)
★ ★ ★ ★½ Night of the Living Dolls (Mercury, 1985)

High heels, stuffed pants and bad attitude, the Dolls were glamsters who anticipated punk. With David Johansen as a campier Jagger and Johnny Thunders playing Keith Richards, the band's debut was an in-your-face party, a randy twist on '50s rock and cartoon R&B. "Trash," "Pills" and "Personality Crisis" summed up the Dolls' obsessions; big guitar was the basis—played zippier and more crudely than heavy metal, but borrowing that genre's full-out volume. Producer Todd Rundgren, though, didn't help matters; going for clean, mid-'70s gloss, he nearly tamed the beast.

Too Much Too Soon better replicated the Dolls' raw power, and a mix of such stompers as "Chatterbox" and "Puss 'n' Boots," alongside Sonny Boy Williamson and Gamble-Huff tunes, showed off the band's engaging mix of rock & roll parody and true belief. A crash 'n' burn outfit, the Dolls died fast. Their influence, however, outweighs their moment—the Sex Pistols fostered punk's appreciation of these merry predecessors, and such lipstick rowdies as Guns n' Roses owe loads to the Dolls. — P.E.

THE NICE

★ Keith Emerson With the Nice (Mercury, 1970)

It's touching to think people once had the patience for this. Before Emerson, Lake and Palmer, keyboard-Frankenstein Keith Emerson honed his kitsch with the Nice—thrusting knives into Hammond organs while butchering the classics. It's not that he couldn't play; he just never let you forget it. Along with weak vocalist Lee Jackson, drummer Brian Davison and guitarist David O'List, Emerson led the way

for '70s "progressive" music that, deeply embarrassed by rock & roll, thought that stirring in classical gas might help save pop from itself. Genuine fanatics, the Nice tackled the real thing—Tchaikovsky, Sibelius and a supposedly inflammatory version of Bernstein and Sondheim's "America." *Keith Emerson With the Nice* collects more Nice than you'll ever need: the trio's last two albums, with Emerson's endless "Five Bridges Suite" and an odd copy of Dylan's "My Back Pages." — P.E.

STEVIE NICKS

★ ★ ★   Bella Donna (Modern, 1981)
★ ★ ★   The Wild Heart (Modern, 1983)
★ ★ ★   Rock a Little (Modern, 1985)
★ ★½ Other Side of the Mirror (Modern, 1988)
★ ★ ★ ★ Timespace: The Best of Stevie Nicks (Modern, 1991)

Either you find the act bewitching or too precious for words: Stevie Nicks leaves no middle ground. But give her this much credit: the Fleetwood Mac thrush turned her "Rhiannon" character into an enduring solo persona. Nicks fashioned a visual image to go along with her mystical variations on L.A. cowboy rock. There's no self-conscious distance with Stevie, however. She inhabits those gauzy videoscapes; her husky voice grasps onto the most tangled lyrical conceits as if they were lifelines.

Her individual albums attract—and perhaps require—the devotion of cultists and camp followers. But the singles collected on *Timespace* speak to a much broader audience. Nicks asserts herself in duets with Tom Petty ("Stop Draggin' My Heart Around") and Don Henley ("Leather and Lace"), and then lets the world know exactly what it's like to be a "wild winged dove" hovering on the "Edge of Seventeen." (All those songs are from *Bella Donna*.) Beginning with the remarkable "Stand Back" in 1983 and continuing with the singles from *Rock a Little*, Nicks skillfully folds sythesizers into her AOR mix without curdling the formula. If *Other Side of the Mirror* starts to sound a little overbaked even by Stevie's standards, the freshly recorded tracks on *Timespace* come out lean and mean. She belts out contemporary hard-rock schlock anthems by Jon Bon Jovi ("Sometimes It's a Bitch") and Poison's Bret Michaels ("Love's a Hard Game to Play") like the ready-made lyrics actually mean something, teaching her benefactors a thing or two in the process. — M.C.

NICO
★★ Chelsea Girl (Verve, 1967)
★★★½ The Marble Index (Elektra, 1969)
★★★ Desert Shore (Reprise, 1969)
★★★ The End (Island, 1974)
★★★ Do or Die! Nico in Europe, 1982 Diary (Roir, 1982)
★★½ The Peel Sessions (Strange Fruit, 1988)

Crypt-voiced chanteuse and resident femme fatale of the Velvet Underground, Nico turned even darker and stranger on her own. Before hurling to her death off her bicycle in 1988, the spectral beauty would emerge periodically from demimonde obscurity and the recesses of her high European angst to record another set of notes from underground. Debuting with *Chelsea Girl*, Nico tried out songs by a then 16-year-old Jackson Browne, such as "These Days." Her own style came with *The Marble Index*. The quintessential Nico record, this is demanding music—occasionally infuriatingly so. Chanting above John Cale's ultra-art arrangements of harmonium, celesta and various, ofttimes dissonant, atmospheric textures, Nico comes on like an orphic poet, every bit as doomed and obscure as such German symbolists as Rilke or Holderlin. "Lawns of Dawns," "Frozen Warnings" and "Julius Caesar (Memento Hodie)" exert the bleak fascination of a long night with a bottle of absinthe—these tone poems are uncompromisingly highbrow stuff, sometimes heady, sometimes a headache. *Desert Shore* (out of print) is a stripped-down version of more of the same. Perhaps even more fearsomely death-obsessed than Jim Morrison, Nico makes the Doors' "The End" the centerpiece of her next record—it features Cale, Eno and Roxy Music's Phil Manzanera. And as an example of Nico's gothic strain at its most chilling, there's a version of "Deutschland über Alles."

Although the sound of the live recordings isn't too hot, *Do or Die!* is a fair overview: she "rocks" in a jagged manner on early Velvets work like "Waiting for the Man" and on Bowie's "Heroes"—and her own songs, such anti-pop as "Janitor of Lunacy," "Abschied" and "No One Is There" are treated with her customary cold, cold grace. *The Peel Sessions* is a less satisfactory live set from 1971. — P.E.

NIGHT RANGER
★★ Dawn Patrol (Boardwalk/MCA, 1982)
★★½ Midnight Madness (MCA, 1983)
★★½ 7 Wishes (MCA/Camel, 1985)
★★★ Greatest Hits (MCA, 1989)
★★★½ Live in Japan (MCA, 1990)

Night Ranger deserves *some* credit; hey, it took nerve to record "(You Can Still) Rock in America" back in the early days of the Brit-pop video boom. This clean-cut Bay Area quintet met the alien invaders head-on. They placed the keyboard bank right up next to the twin guitars in the mix, emphasized bassist Jack Blades's sweaty flair for slow numbers over the usual shows of instrumental prowess, permed their shoulder-length hair and posed in vaguely futuristic jumpsuits. In many respects, Night Ranger pioneered the streamlined pop-metal sound. "Sister Christian" is the very model of a power ballad, except the slow-building chorus of this 1984 hit actually achieves the soaring melodramatic *bang* that eludes most of the light-metal brigade. That sad, cautionary hook is unforgettable. The followup, *7 Wishes*, calmly xeroxes the breakout *Midnight Madness* to the letter: "(You Can Still) Rock in America" becomes "This Boy Needs to Rock" while "Sister Christian" begets "Sentimental Street" and "Four in the Morning." Of course, you barely notice the difference. Only Night Ranger's faithful will enjoy the professional exuberance displayed on *Live In Japan*, but *Greatest Hits* provides a pure, unadulterated rush of guilty pleasure, the musical equivalent of a junk-food binge. — M.C.

WILLIE NILE
★★★½ Willie Nile (Arista, 1980)
★★½ Golden Down (Arista, 1981)
★★★½ Places I Have Never Been (Columbia, 1991)

Willie Nile proved himself one of the better of the endless line of pseudo-Dylans with his 1980 debut, *Willie Nile*. Side one had the juice; songs like "Vagabond Moon" and "Across the River" found Nile fusing bright Everly Brothers–like rock & roll to lyrics recalling not only *Highway 61*–period Dylan but such Bob predecessors as the French Symbolist poets Rimbaud and Verlaine. *Golden Down* attempted a similar punch, but, the second time around, it came off as bombastic and shopworn.

Ten silent years passed before *Places I Have Never Been*. The record shows Nile gathering such impressive cohorts as Loudon Wainwright III, a couple of Roches and Richard Thompson. "Café Memphis," with its name-dropping of Plato and Descartes, recalls Dylan's "Desolation Row" in its ironic homage to dead, great

minds. On "Rite of Spring," with Roger McGuinn on 12-string, Nile sounds like the Byrds; "Don't Die" could pass for top-notch Tom Petty. Obviously, he can't be accused of flaming originality, but the wells from which he draws his water are deep and sweet—and his sheer exuberance is fetching.
— P.E.

HARRY NILSSON

★★★ **The Pandemonium Shadow Show (RCA, 1967)**
★★★½ **Aerial Ballet (1968; RCA/Camden, 1980)**
★★★ **Harry (RCA, 1969)**
★★★★ **Nilsson Sings Newman (RCA, 1970)**
★★★ **The Point! (RCA, 1970)**
★★★★ **Nilsson Schmilsson (RCA, 1971)**
★★★ **Son of Schmilsson (RCA, 1972)**
★★ **A Little Touch of Schmilsson in the Night (RCA, 1973)**
★★★★ **Pussy Cats (RCA, 1974)**
★★★½ **Nilsson's Greatest Music (RCA, 1978)**

Nilsson added his voice—slight, yet very distinctive—to the outer fringes of the singer-songwriter movement. His early writing and singing hinted at a close familiarity with the work of Burt Bacharach and Hal David as well as Bob Dylan. "Everybody's Talkin' " (used in the film *Midnight Cowboy*) and "One" (a hit for Three Dog Night) are the catchiest examples of his orchestrated folk-rock; both are included on *Aerial Ballet*. Along with the now-deleted late-'60s records *Pandemonium Shadow Show* and *Harry*, this album earned Nilsson a cult following and a variety of well-placed fans. *The Point!*, the soundtrack for an animated television special, positions seven sweetly melodic little song snatches between installments of a hippie-era children's fable.

Somewhere in between the underrated *Nilsson Sings Newman* and his 1971 breakthrough, Harry Nilsson discovered rock & roll. Perhaps exposure to Newman's acute cynicism and corrosive insights toughened Nilsson's artistic stance. Many Newman fanciers insist that Nilsson gently waters down the impact of these songs, though his polished vocal style puts Newman's point across with unaccustomed subtlety. *Nilsson Sings Newman* offers a fine introduction to either artist.

The juiced-up charge that illuminates *Nilsson Schmilsson* quickly turns into a hangover on subsequent followups. But what a party! A guest list of studio-session

heavies brings in the rock element, while producer Richard Perry harnesses Nilsson's diffuse genius to a variety of musical settings. "Without You" could be a Perry Como outtake, "Jump Into the Fire" throbs like a funkier Humble Pie or James Gang. In between those extremes, cuts like "Down" and "Gotta Get Up" temper the melodic ache of Nilsson's older work with exuberance and humor. *Son of Schmilsson* lays on the sloppy charm with a trowel. Though several cuts—most notably "Spacemen"—could hold their own on *Schmilsson*, the album's title isn't as ironic as Nilsson obviously intends. *A Little Touch of Schmilsson in the Night* finds Nilsson reaching for pre-rock elegance; despite the presence of Sinatra arranger Gordon Jenkins, it winds up sounding like self-conscious Muzak. The out-of-print *Pussy Cats* is a dark companion piece to John Lennon's *Rock & Roll*; produced and accompanied by the former Beatle, Nilsson barrels through soul-baring cover versions of sacred cows like Dylan's "Subterranean Homesick Blues." Unsettling stuff, but fans of Neil Young's *Tonight's the Night* or Bryan Ferry's *These Foolish Things* should be intrigued by *Pussy Cats*—if they can find it.

Harry Nilsson continued releasing albums after that, to little notice or effect. Save for a couple of tracks on the now-deleted *That's the Way It Is* (including a revelatory cover of America's "I Need You"!), from 1976, his lost years probably aren't worth rediscovering. But as Nilsson's best work proves, even the friendliest clown routines often possess a fascinating, tragic dimension.
— M.C.

NINE INCH NAILS

★★★ **Pretty Hate Machine (TVT, 1989)**
Programming his electronics with a fair catchiness, Trent Reznor is Nine Inch Nails' one-man band—and, as a lyricist, he's a late-'80s version of an adolescent angster. He sings (in a nice warble) essentially about forms of romantic agony; he's obsessed about heartbreak in, to use his phrase, "this world of piss." His petulant preoccupation with God is kind of interesting; his gift for melody suggests that he's at heart a popster; and once you get past his portentousness, his music (especially the lovely ballad "something i can never have") is appealing. For some reason, this album spawned a cult. Certainly Reznor is intense enough, in a narcissistic way, to qualify as promising—*Pretty Hate Machine*, however, isn't quite earth-shaking. — P.E.

NIRVANA

★ ★ ★½ Bleach (Sub Pop, 1989)
★ ★ ★   Nirvana (EP) (Sub Pop, 1990)
★ ★ ★ ★ Nevermind (DGC, 1991)

Stylistically, this Seattle trio mines a vein of metal-edged punk that's not too distant from the edgy roar of bands like Soul Asylum or early Soundgarden; its lyrics are as much a product of teen dispirit as any Replacements song. On a melodic level, though, the group stands head and shoulders above the rest, thanks to songs that are catchy, insistent and instantly memorable—attributes that make Nirvana's best work nothing less than heavenly.

Admittedly, it takes a few listens to find those qualities in *Bleach*. Although much of the blame for that belongs with the album's low-budget production, it's also true that Kurt Cobain's songs tend to rely as much on metallic riffage as on melodic invention. Still, that hardly hurts numbers like "Blew" or "Negative Creep."

Cobain's writing sharpens some with "Sliver," one of two new songs on the *Nirvana* EP (its other two tracks are concert recordings), but doesn't come into full flower until *Nevermind*. It isn't just that the band's leap to the majors provides it with the means to a meaty, muscular sound (though that helps); the music is also much improved, boasting strong hooks and vocal lines sturdy enough to catapult the churning, infectious "Smells Like Teen Spirit" into the Top Ten. This newfound accessibility doesn't mellow the group's attitude, which seems even more jaded and biting than before, but that hardly undercuts the album's appeal. If anything, it merely adds resonance to the songs, which at their best—"Breed," "Lithium," "Something in the Way"—typify the low-key passion of post-MTV youth. — J.D.C.

NITTY GRITTY DIRT BAND

★ ★ ★ ★ Will the Circle Be Unbroken (United Artists, 1972)
★ ★½   Stars and Stripes Forever (United Artists, 1974)
★ ★½   Twenty Years of Dirt: The Best of the Nitty Gritty Dirt Band (Warner Bros., 1986)
★ ★ ★   Hold On (Warner Bros., 1987)
★ ★ ★½ Workin' Band (Warner Bros., 1988)
★ ★½   More Great Dirt (Warner Bros., 1989)
★ ★ ★½ The Rest of the Dream (MCA, 1990)
★ ★ ★ ★ Will the Circle Be Unbroken, Vol. 2 (MCA, 1990)

Three stages comprise this California band's career—an early attempt to extend beyond its jug-band roots and fashion a synthesis of traditional country and rock & roll; a commercial heyday achieved by a string of tasteful, bland pop and modern country albums; and a late resurgence in authenticity and verve. With guitarist-singer Jeff Hanna and multi-instrumentalist John McEuen (fiddle, banjo, guitar) at the helm, the Dirt Band found mild success with its first album and the single, "Buy for Me the Rain," but then languished in obscurity until the breakthrough *Uncle Charlie*, now out of print. Jerry Jeff Walker's "Mr. Bojangles" was that record's massive hit; along with Mike Nesmith's "Some of Shelley's Blues" and Kenny Loggins's "House at Pooh Corner," it set the pattern for the group's pleasant covers of easy folk pop. *All the Good Times*, now deleted, found the Dirt Band asserting its country side with Hank Williams's "Jambalaya"—and the group followed through with the impressive *Will the Circle Be Unbroken*. Gathering together such country stalwarts as Merle Travis, Roy Acuff, Jimmy Martin and the Scruggs Family, this was the NGDB at its best—modestly allowing the spotlight to fall on the old masters, and gracefully encouraging a union of the hard-country and pop music worlds.

Hold On showed signs of vitality, and *Workin' Band*, with its rootsy instrumentation (accordion, mandolin, jaw harp) was truly fine. So was *The Rest of the Dream*. The boys had recaptured the twang in their singing, and sounded snappier, more casual—and fresher than ever. — P.E.

MOJO NIXON & SKID ROPER

★½   Mojo Nixon and Skid Roper (1985; I.R.S., 1991)
★ ★½   Frenzy (1986, I.R.S., 1991)
★ ★½   Get Out of My Way! (1986; I.R.S., 1991)
★ ★½   Bo-Day-Shus!!! (1987; I.R.S., 1991)
★ ★ ★ ★ Root Hog or Die (1989; I.R.S., 1991)

MOJO NIXON

★ ★½   Otis (1990; I.R.S., 1991)

As with most musical comedians, it's usually funnier to hear about Mojo Nixon than actually listen to him. That's not to say this singer-guitarist isn't amusing at times—heck, he can be quite a hoot when his material works—just that his batting average isn't particularly high. As such, forget *Mojo Nixon and Skid Roper*, and take *Frenzy* in limited doses (e.g., the Martha Quinn lust-opus "Stuffin' Martha's Muffin"). *Get Out of My Way!* recaps a couple of tunes from the first two albums along with some Christmas-oriented material (suggesting that Mojo, like most in the industry, is not above a bit of seasonal exploitation), and thus is also fairly expendable, while *Bo-Day-Shus!!!* truly sizzles only when Mojo addresses the Elvis question in "Elvis Is Everywhere."

Surprisingly, *Root Hog or Die* actually delivers on the promise of its titles, from the not-so-sly sexual innuendo of "Louisiana Liplock" and "She's Vibrator Dependent" to the all-out lunacy of "Debbie Gibson Is Pregnant with My Two Headed Love Child." But *Otis* finds Nixon kicking around the same sort of half-baked witticisms as before, meaning that unless a title like "Destroy All Lawyers" has you in stitches, it's best to fast-forward past this one.
— J.D.C.

NOTTING HILLBILLIES
★★½ **Missing . . . Presumed Having a Good Time (Warner Bros., 1990)**
Country music, English-style—well-intentioned, impeccably played and utterly lifeless, despite the combined talents of Guy Fletcher, Brendan Croker and Mark Knopfler. Now you know why the Wilburys kept traveling. — J.D.C.

NRBQ
★★★½ **Scraps (1972; Red Rooster/Rounder, 1982)**
★★★ **Workshop (1973; Red Rooster/Rounder, 1982)**
★★★ **All Hopped Up (Red Rooster/Rounder, 1977)**
★★★½ **At Yankee Stadium (1978; Mercury, 1988**
★★★½ **Kick Me Hard (1979; Red Rooster/Rounder, 1990)**
★★★ **Grooves in Orbit (1983; Bearsville/Rhino, 1990)**
★★★ **Tapdancin' Bats (1983; Red Rooster/Rhino, 1990)**
★★★ **God Bless Us All (Rounder, 1988)**
★★★ **Wild Weekend (Virgin, 1989)**
★★★★ **Peek-a-Boo: The Best of NRBQ 1969–89 (Rhino, 1990)**
New Rhythm and Blues Quartet is what it stands for, though these venerable virtuosos cheerfully toss jazz and country strains into their chunky rock & roll stew. Eclectic to a fault, NRBQ started recording in 1969; though the group's early albums are out of print, the first two tracks on *Scraps* perfectly illustrate its considerable strengths—and its

crippling weaknesses. Guitarist Al Anderson and pianist Terry Adams are unusually subtle instrumental wizards, not given to flashy solo intrusions. Listen to the way Anderson effortlessly grafts a chicken-scratching funk riff onto the joke-rock opener ("Howard Johnson's Got His HoJo Workin' "), and then marvel at how Adams weaves a cool blue bebop piano run throughout the mid-tempo shuffle ("Magnet") that follows—these fellows sure can play. But the strained humor of the former and the wimpy vocals of the latter sort of get in the way, don't you think? If not, welcome to the cult.

Bassist Joey Spampinato assumed the vocal chores after that (singer Frank Gadler made it a quintet for a while); however, the advent of current drummer Tom Ardolino on *All Hopped Up,* followed by *At Yankee Stadium* (not a live album), from 1978, makes much more of an appreciable difference. The spaced-out boyish charm starts to grate on the later albums, especially the major-label-at-last (again) *Wild Weekend*—the fact that the musicianship is as quick and surefooted as ever underscores the affected singing and offhanded songwriting. Over the course of two well-chosen CDs, *Peek-A-Boo: The Best of NRBQ 1969–89* sifts the golden nuggets from a deep, pebble-filled stream. It's all you need to know. — M.C.

TED NUGENT
★★★ **Ted Nugent (Epic, 1975)**
★★★ **Free-for-All (Epic, 1976)**
★★★★ **Cat Scratch Fever (Epic, 1977)**
★★★½ **Double Live Gonzo! (Epic, 1978)**
★★½ **Weekend Warriors (Epic, 1978)**
★★½ **State of Shock (Epic, 1979)**
★★½ **Scream Dream (Epic, 1980)**
★★½ **Intensities in Ten Cities (Epic, 1981)**
★★★★ **Great Gonzos: The Best of Ted Nugent (Epic, 1981)**
★★ **Nugent (Atlantic, 1982)**
★★ **Penetrator (Atlantic, 1984)**
★★ **Little Miss Dangerous (Atlantic, 1986)**
★★ **If You Can't Lick 'Em . . . Lick 'Em (Atlantic, 1988)**
TED NUGENT AND THE AMBOY DUKES
★★★½ **Ted Nugent and the Amboy Dukes (1968; DCC Classics, 1987)**
★★★½ **The Best of the Original Amboy Dukes (Mainstream, 1969)**
★★★ **Survival of the Fittest (Polydor, 1971)**

★ ★½ **Call of the Wild (1975; Enigma Retro, 1988)**
★ ★ ★ **Tooth, Fang and Claw (1975; Enigma Retro, 1988)**

Ted Nugent has asserted his maniac presence since the 1965 start of the Amboy Dukes'. "Journey to the Center of the Mind" (1968) would be just another pleasant psychedelic excursion without that lead guitar: Nugent makes the instrument snarl and stutter like a Harley-Davidson in low gear, shifting into a high-pressure whoosh on the solo breaks. Along with Motor City peers like the MC5, Nugent and the Amboy Dukes built a bridge between the scruffy garage-rock of the late '60s and the gargantuan structures of '70s heavy metal. The Mainstream *Best of* captures this transition, splitting the difference between acid-laced pop songs and Nugent's full-bore instrumental frenzy. The Amboy Dukes recorded several disappointing albums for Polydor (all now deleted), with varying lineups. The muddled opus *Marriage on the Rocks/Rock Bottom* (1971) offers vivid and frightening evidence of Nugent's secret art-rock bent—his Bartok interpretation doesn't come off any better than Emerson, Lake and Palmer's Mussorgsky.

Nugent's solo career really begins with *Tooth, Fang and Claw*; the taut, rangy guitar workouts on "Hibernation" and "Great White Buffalo" can floor an unsuspecting listener. Nugent worked the arena circuit hard in the mid- '70s, cultivating a flamboyant stage persona to accompany his bag of riffs. Sporting a loincloth, shaking his torrents of dirty-blond hair, wielding a massive hollow-body Gibson like it was a shotgun: he was an act you couldn't ignore. Producer Tom Werman effectively reins in the Neanderthal on his early Epic albums, placing his stream of banshee peals and power chords in an ever-shifting group format. (An up-and-comer named Meat Loaf provides lead vocals on *Free-for-All*.)

Cat Scratch Fever is the catchiest and most fevered entry in the Nugent catalog. Hot-dog guitar licks and slobbering choruses push the sexist swill of "Wang Dang Sweet Poontang" and "Cat Scratch Fever" into the comedy zone. "Live It Up" draws up a blueprint for the Bon Jovi school of pop-metal; "Fist Fightin' Son of a Gun" declares Ted's allegiance with Skynyrd-style Southern boogie; "Death by Misadventure" skids into a wall of granite guitars about halfway through.

A welcome relief at first, Nugent's caveman schtick doesn't exactly make for an enduring formula. He quickly became a caricature. The first live album (*Double Live Gonzo!*) and the *Great Gonzos* collection document Terrible Ted's carnivorous peak; the later albums are mostly comprised of fat and gristle. As his current sideman position in the "supergroup" Damn Yankees suggests, Nugent's limitations as singer and songwriter eventually killed off his solo career. Even in heavy metal, that stuff matters. — M.C.

NU SHOOZ
★ ★ ★ **Poolside (Atlantic, 1986)**
★½ **Told U So (Atlantic, 1988)**

Whether or not American lives have second acts we'll leave to Fitzgerald, but many American bands clearly do not have second albums. That doesn't keep them from releasing those sophomore albums, though—just look at Nu Shooz. This Portland, Oregon, duo did spectacularly well with an offbeat-but-irresistible club single called "I Can't Wait," which was fleshed out with some serviceable (though unremarkable) dance tracks and released as *Poolside*. For the followup, the duo returns with a slicker sound, a handful of high-priced sidemen—and no hits. — J.D.C.

THE NUTMEGS
★ ★ **Greatest Hits (Collectables, NA)**

This quintet from New Haven, Connecticut, had one major R&B hit in 1955 with lead singer Leroy Griffin's "Story Untold," which is remarkable both for Griffin's carefully measured vocal, which put across anguish in an otherwise smooth love ballad, and for being an a capella recording, one of the few in the history of popular music to achieve hit status on any chart. A followup, "Ship of Love," was the group's only other charting single. Most of the selections here are pretty much in-the-pocket, mid-'50s mainstream R&B, with an emphasis on love ballads that are easy on the ear, but hardly compelling. — D.M.

N.W.A
★ ★ ★ **N.W.A and the Posse (1987; Ruthless/Priority, 1989)**
★ ★ ★ ★ **Straight Outta Compton (Ruthless/Priority, 1988)**
★ **100 Miles and Runnin' (EP) (Ruthless/Priority, 1990)**
★ **Efil4zaggin (Ruthless/Priority, 1991)**

N.W.A may not have invented gangsta rap—credit for that undoubtedly belongs with Schoolly D and "PSK: What Does It Mean?"—but they had no trouble installing themselves as its prime practitioners. That they did so while laughing all the way to the bank is less a tribute to their ingenuity than an indictment of how rap is perceived and exploited by the mass-market. Assembled by rap impresario Eric "Eazy-E" Wright, N.W.A takes pains to come on like a collection of self-styled gangsters. Those initials, they remind us, stand for "Niggaz with Attitude," and that attitude is in full effect on *N.W.A and the Posse*, even if the group itself isn't (they perform just four of the album's 11 raps). Yet for all their tough-talking, street-level lyrics, there's nothing menacing about the early N.W.A; the indolent lassitude of Eazy-E's solo track, "Boys-n-the Hood," seems far more chilling than the splattered profanity of "Dope Man" and "A Bitch Iz a Bitch."

Straight Outta Compton makes up for that in a hurry. It isn't just the unrepentant violence described in the title track and elsewhere; it's the fact that N.W.A is able to back that threat with savagely insistent beats and an equally intense delivery. Naturally, the beat takes precedence much of the time, particularly when the basic tracks are as insistently funky as "Gangsta Gangsta" or "Express Yourself," but the shock value of the lyrics was what earned the group the bulk of its notoriety. "Fuck tha Police," in fact, is trenchant enough social commentary to have earned the group's label a threatening letter from the FBI (a record industry first).

But the ready-to-revolt African Americans imagined by the FBI didn't exist. In fact, an awful lot of N.W.A's audience turned out to be thrill-seeking whites who cherished the chance to experience Compton street violence from the safety of their own bedrooms, and N.W.A was more than happy to meet the demand for vicarious thrills. Unfortunately, three things complicated this formula for success: One, Ice Cube, perhaps the group's most gifted writer, left the group after *Straight Outta Compton*; two, the number of gangsta rap acts had grown to near mafia size; and three, the obscenity conviction of 2 Live Crew considerably upped the ante for rap raunch.

Undaunted, N.W.A charged ahead. The EP *100 Miles and Runnin'* was a stopgap release, and sounds it; "Sa Prize (Part 2)" nicely updates "Fuck tha Police," but "Just Don't Bite It" is an appallingly limp blow-job opus. Still, it at least had the advantage of brevity, something which *Efil4zaggin* ("Niggaz4life" spelled backward)

lacked, along with wit, subtlety, discretion and decency. It isn't the rampant profanity, ceaseless violence and outright misogyny of these raps that offends, it's the utter dehumanization of the group and its milieu. By this point, the members of N.W.A have happily transformed themselves into cartoons—gun-toting, bitch-killing, money-making muthafuckas—and reduced their world to unreality. Despite the fact that the musical production, by Dr. Dre and Yella, is soulful and sophisticated, the album as a whole is simply unconscionable. — J.D.C.

THE NYLONS

★ **One Size Fits All (Open Air, 1982)**
★ **Seamless (1984; Open Air, 1986)**
★ **Happy Together (Open Air, 1987)**
★ **Rockapella (Windham Hill, 1989)**
★ **Four on the Floor (Scotti Bros., 1991)**

Sure, this Canadian quartet knows how to sing. What it doesn't know how to do is rock, which is why its "rockapella" approach—a capella harmonies backed by drum machine—comes across like Muzak with an attitude. Their hit, in case it turns up as a trivia question, was a remake of Steam's "Kiss Him Goodbye," and can be found on *Happy Together*. — J.D.C.

LAURA NYRO

★★★½ **Eli and the Thirteenth Confession (Columbia, 1968)**
★★★ **New York Tendaberry (Columbia, 1969)**
★★½ **Christmas and the Beads of Sweat (Columbia, 1970)**
★★★½ **Gonna Take a Miracle (Columbia, 1971)**
★★★½ **The First Songs (Columbia, 1973)**
★★★ **Smile (Columbia, 1975)**
★★★ **Live at the Bottom Line (Cypress Music, 1989)**

Laura Nyro was just a couple of years ahead of her time. Her late-'60s heyday as composer-of-the-moment helped pave the way for the female singer-songwriters of the '70s. Strong R&B influences and a dash of Tin Pan Alley reveal Nyro's New York roots; she definitely departs from the Joan Baez–Judy Collins school, in terms of both songs and singing. Nyro's whoops and sighs often cross the line into screechiness; her ruminative and intensely personal lyrics can easily slip into obscurity. As the hit cover versions of her very best songs suggest, however, Nyro can also bait a melodic hook with the confidence of a Brill Building pro. Three Dog Night ("Eli's Coming") and

Blood, Sweat and Tears ("And When I Die") reaped the benefits, while the Fifth Dimension served as her personal messengers: the pop-soul harmony group scored hit singles with Nyro's "Wedding Bell Blues," "Stoned Soul Picnic" and "Sweet Blindness." Nyro's original versions of all these songs—contained on *Eli and the Thirteenth Confession* and *The First Songs*— bristle with an electrifying confessional charge. She turns overfamiliar golden oldies into searing testimony. *Eli* was Nyro's second album and breakthrough; it's a more honest portrayal of her stark sound than the slightly pop-ified Verve/Forecast debut (later reissued as *The First Songs*), but many listeners may find the reined-in Nyro easier to take. *New York Tendaberry* and (especially) *Christmas and the Beads of Sweat* dissolve into alternating currents of free-floating anxiety and preciousness.

Gonna Take a Miracle comes close to pulling a miracle off. Fronting the post-Bluebelles/pre-glitter LaBelle, Nyro kicks up her heels on a survey of vintage Motown ("Jimmy Mack") and girl-group ("I Met Him on a Sunday") covers. What could have been an eardrum-rattling Battle of the Songbirds turns out to be a pleasant session of nostalgic harmonizing. "Monkey Time" and "Dancing in the Street" work up a respectable rhythmic punch, but the title track sounds a little too pristine and perfectly sung. *Smile* continues in this affable pop-soul vein, though the cover versions also continue to be more compelling than the originals. Though Nyro kept making records through the end of the '70s, it would seem as though her songwriting muse never fully returned. If her voice hasn't aged too terribly on *Live at the Bottom Line*, the four new tracks are quickly forgotten once Nyro starts to boogaloo down Bleecker Street on a few of her signature folk-soul ravers. — M.C.

OAK RIDGE BOYS

★ ★ ★ **Old Fashioned, Down Home, Hand Clappin', Foot Stompin', Southern Style, Gospel Quartet Music (Columbia, 1976)**

★ ★ ★ **Y'all Come Back Saloon (MCA, 1977)**

★ ★ **Room Service (MCA, 1978)**

★ ★ ★ **The Best of the Oak Ridge Boys (Columbia, 1978)**

★ ★ ★ **The Oak Ridge Boys Have Arrived (MCA, 1979)**

★ ★ ★ **The Oak Ridge Boys Have Arrived/Y'all Come Back Saloon (1979, 1977; MCA, 1983)**

★ ★ **Together (MCA, 1980)**

★ ★ ★ **Greatest Hits (MCA, 1980)**

★ ★ ★ **Fancy Free (MCA, 1981)**

★ ★ **Bobbie Sue (MCA, 1982)**

★ ★ **Oak Ridge Boys' Christmas (MCA, 1982)**

★ ★ **American Made (MCA, 1983)**

★ ★ **Deliver (MCA, 1984)**

★ ★ ★ **Greatest Hits, Vol. 2 (MCA, 1984)**

★ ★ **Step on Out (MCA, 1985)**

★ ★ **Bobbie Sue/Step On Out (1982, 1985; MCA, 1985)**

★ ★ **Seasons (MCA, 1986)**

★ ★ ★ ★ **Christmas Again (MCA, 1986)**

★ ★ **Where the Fast Lane Ends (MCA, 1987)**

★ ★ **Heartbeat (MCA, 1987)**

★ ★ ★ **Monongahela (MCA, 1988)**

★ ★ ★ **Greatest Hits, Volume Three (MCA, 1989)**

★ ★ ★ **American Dreams (MCA, 1989)**

★ ★ ★ **Unstoppable (MCA, 1991)**

The gospel quartet tradition in country music finds its contemporary voice in the Oak Ridge Boys, who have been around in name for several decades, but in their current configuration for less than a decade. The longest-standing members of the group are Richard Sterban, Duane Allen and Joe Bonsall; for years their fourth member was William Lee Golden, who left in 1987 amid allegations of personality clashes with the other Oaks. His replacement, Steve Sanders has a sandpaper-rough voice, with a bluesy edge, which stands out from the plain-faced pop stylings of the other Oaks (the lone exception being bass singer Sterban, who is used more as a novelty).

Apart from its gospel roots, which the current Oaks abandoned years ago (check *Old Fashioned, Down Home, Hand Clappin', Foot Stompin', Southern Style, Gospel Quartet Music*), the quartet has established itself as a solid mainstream group, always good for a rousing hit or two or three off every album, playing up to unquestioned values like God, country and family, and polishing its act to a Las Vegas sheen. Their music has long ceased being challenging, and the occasional glimpses of, say, Joe Bonsall's roots in doo-wop have all but disappeared. As examples of mainstream country music, though, their albums are well done. They have had long, productive associations with two ace producers in Ron Chancey and Jimmy Bowen, who also must be given credit for the group's ascension. A recent label change to RCA re-teamed them with Chancey, and the Oaks never missed a beat. Their 1991 album, *Unstoppable*, reasserted the quartet's primacy in the marketplace.

Given that the Oaks are best represented by their greatest-hits albums—and there are many—what should an interested fan look for in their catalog? From the William Lee Golden era, *Y'all Come Back Saloon* has an insouciance about it that seems missing from later efforts, as well as the ingratiating title song, which has become something of a trademark. This album is also available in a two-fer cassette that's a good buy, teamed as it is with *The Oak Ridge Boys Have Arrived*, which contains the group's hit interpretation of an excellent Rodney

Crowell song, "Leaving Louisiana in the Broad Daylight." *Fancy Free* is a solid effort that includes among its cuts the version of Dallas Frazier's "Elvira" that was a major hit. A Christmas album, *Christmas Again*, is set up conceptually, with traditional carols leading into original songs, including two fine efforts by Bonsall, "First Christmas Day" and "It's Christmas Time." *Monongahela* finds the quartet in a bluesy mood, never more so than on the massive hit single, "Gonna Take a Lot of River (Mississippi, Monongahela, Ohio)," with its soaring harmonies and hard-rocking instrumental support. Sentimental as it is, the song "I Can Count on You" is an incredible Oaks track, with smooth, bracing harmonies, honest emotions, and some stinging electric guitar work. It's easy to write off the Oaks as commercial hacks, but the evidence indicates the presence of some collective conscience that summons forth sincere performances at the very point when the quartet seems to have exhausted whatever emotional reserve it had left. As problematic as their work has been of late, the Oak Ridge Boys still know how to look into their hearts and move us with what they find. — D.M.

RIC OCASEK

★ ★½ **Beatitude (Geffen, 1983)**
★ ★½ **This Side of Paradise (Geffen, 1987)**
★ ★ ★ **Fireball Zone (Reprise, 1991)**

In his solo career, Ric Ocasek hasn't veered too far off the Cars' road. *Beatitude* and *This Side of Paradise* both comment on that band's concurrent progress. Recorded while the hits were still comin', *Beatitude* taps a cast of new wave contributors (whose records Ocasek had produced), emphasizing the arty, emotionally stark side of the Cars. *This Side of Paradise* surfaced during the group's fall from grace, and it shows. Immaculate production and inspired performances from the other Cars only highlight the oversimplified, eager-to-please songwriting. Long after most listeners stopped caring, Ocasek came in with a winner. *Fireball Zone* regains the Cars' sleek melodic momentum, while expressing a newfound vulnerability and warmth. No longer alienated, Ocasek strikes a reassuring tone. "Keep That Dream" acknowledges his own tenuous position: poised between comeback and oblivion, striving to avoid nostalgia. — M.C.

BILLY OCEAN

★ ★½ **Nights (Feel Like Getting Down) (Epic, 1981)**
★ ★ ★ **Suddenly (Jive, 1984)**
★ ★½ **Love Zone (Epic, 1986)**
★ ★½ **Tear Down These Walls (Jive, 1988)**
★ ★ ★½ **Greatest Hits (Jive, 1989)**

Born in Trinidad, Billy Ocean (Leslie Charles) got his start as a session voice in London. His sweet tenor lifts the debut album's title track, applying just a touch of Island lilt to its breezy disco groove. "Night (Feel Like Getting Down)" reached the R&B Top Ten in 1981. The remainder of the *Nights* album isn't nearly as striking, however, and Ocean quickly receded from public view. Ocean came crashing back with the fleet *Thriller*-soundalike "Caribbean Queen (No More Love on the Run)" in mid-'84. "Caribbean Queen" is openly derivative; it's also well crafted and articulate. As pop-soul singers go, Ocean has consistently proven to be a lightweight album artist. However, he has the habit of sinking a hook into his singles when you least expect it. "When the Going Gets Tough, the Tough Get Going" (from the 1985 *Jewel of the Nile* soundtrack) and "Get Outta My Dreams, Get Into My Car" (from *Tear Down These Walls*): even the chugging machine rhythms and glossy over-production can't hold him back. The newly recorded cuts on the surprisingly spotty *Greatest Hits*—including a rote guest rap from the Fresh Prince—suggest that Ocean is experiencing artistic confusion. — M.C.

PHIL OCHS

★ ★ ★ ★ **All the News That's Fit to Sing (1964; Carthage, 1986)**
★ ★ ★ ★ **I Ain't a'Marchin' Anymore (1965; Carthage, 1986)**
★ ★ ★ ★ **Phil Ochs in Concert (Elektra, 1966)**
★ ★ ★ ★ **Pleasures of the Harbor (A&M, 1967)**
★ ★ ★ ★ **Tape From California (A&M, 1968)**
★ ★ ★ ★ **Rehearsals for Retirement (A&M, 1969)**
★ ★ ★ ★ **Greatest Hits (A&M, 1970)**
★ ★ **Gunfight at Carnegie Hall (A&M, 1971)**
★ ★ ★ ★ **Chords of Fame (A&M, 1976)**
★ ★ ★ ★ **The War Is Over: The Best of Phil Ochs (A&M, 1988)**
★ ★ ★ ★ **There but for Fortune (Elektra, 1989)**
★ ★ ★ **A Toast to Those Who Are Gone (Archives Alive, 1986)**
★ ★ ★ **The Broadside Tapes: 1 (Folkways, 1989)**
★ ★ ★½ **There and Now: Live in Vancouver (Rhino, 1991)**

Of all the major figures of the early-'60s folk boom, Phil Ochs adhered longest to the Woody Guthrie spirit of message music—songs fired by social activism. Dylan moved on to a more idiosyncratic poetry; Eric Andersen and others shifted their emphasis toward love songs and the softer sensibility that would come to characterize '70s singer-songwriters; Joan Baez kept pace with Ochs in terms of political engagement, but the material she chose to cover lacked the edge of topicality that sharpened the typical Ochs protest song. Like Guthrie himself, a patriot of the most optimistic kind, his righteousness fueled by a populist faith, Ochs in time became a tragic hero—a seer ignored, his idealism shaken by the long agony of Vietnam and America's internal dissension. Not long before his 1976 suicide at age 35, Ochs was attacked mysteriously while traveling in Africa, and with bizarre, metaphoric appropriateness, his vocals cords were damaged. He sang again, but his spirit was shot. He remains emblematic then, of the voice of conscience largely unheeded, the prophet crying in the wilderness. *All the News That's Fit to Sing, I Ain't a'Marchin' Anymore* and *In Concert* are the definitive protest music of Phil Ochs. Lean, graceful acoustic guitar carries the simple melodies, and Ochs's voice is strong, his delivery sharp, witty and precise. "Talking Cuban Crisis," "The Ballad of Oxford (Jimmy Meredith)," "A.M.A. Song," "Draft Dodger Rag," point up the specificity of his targets, and he assails them with zest and sardonic wit. With "There but for Fortune," he begins crafting statements of a more suggestive universality, a turn that helps prepare his listeners for the subtler music to come.

Pleasures of the Harbor is introspective Ochs. No longer relying upon the three-chord melodies of classic folk, the orchestrated song arrangements on *Pleasures* recall 19th-century impressionism. Always an impressive lyricist, Ochs was now writing music of a complexity that matched his verbal dexterity. "Cross My Heart," "I've Had Her" and the title track are brooding elegies; Ochs fuses the personal and political more overtly on "Crucifixion," a remarkable treatise on martyrdom; and satire holds on in "The Party" and "Small Circle of Friends."

With Van Dyke Parks turning in an atypically straightforward production, *Tape From California* stands as Ochs's most solid set, even if, at the time, it continued to mark his descent into relative obscurity. "When in Rome" masterfully delineates

American history as an epic of conquest; "The War Is Over" is strange, bitter and moving; the title track is almost pop. While the songcraft reaches new levels of skill, however, the record betrays a tone of melancholy and defeat that will come to overpower its followup, *Rehearsals for Retirement*. "My Life" is only the most chilling of *Rehearsal*'s farewells; that the album's music is basic, energetic rock & roll only makes more sadly ironic its songs of merciless self-scrutiny.

Greatest Hits has always been derided by fans of the singer's activist music, but it sounds riveting today. Van Dyke Parks provides strange, almost saccharine string arrangements and the nostalgic material they embellish grips with the force of embarrassing revelation. "Jim Dean of Indiana," "Chords of Fame," "No More Songs" and "One Way Ticket Home" are almost schmaltzy—but their poignancy is that of a profound soul in anquish. With its cover showing the singer tricked out in gold lamé in some inscrutable Elvis homage-parody, *Gunfight at Carnegie Hall* ends the story on a painful note of confusion—covering "Okie from Muskogee," oldies, and his own "best hits," Ochs reveals nothing but desperation.

The Ochs compilations are intelligent: *There but for Fortune* and *Chords of Fame* generously cover the entire career; *The War Is Over* concentrates on the more difficult, later period. *A Toast to Those Who Are Gone* presents strong material recorded before 1964. — P.E.

SINÉAD O'CONNOR
★ ★ ★ ★   **The Lion and the Cobra (Chrysalis, 1987)**
★ ★ ★ ½ **I Do Not Want What I Haven't Got (Chrysalis, 1990)**

Rock & roll idealizes adolescence as a matter of course, but rarely does it produce a performer as utterly adolescent as Sinéad O'Connor. Gifted but headstrong, blessed more with conviction than self-restraint, O'Connor can seem full of wisdom, full of passion, or simply full of shit—and in some songs, all of the above. Yet even at her most maddening, the innate musicality of her work bears hearing out.

From the first, it was clear that O'Connor was an artist of unusual precocity. Not only was her achingly personal debut, *The Lion and the Cobra*, entirely self-produced, but it moves through its mix of arty ballads, post-punk ravers and slick, synth-smart dance tunes with an ease that would elude many established stars. Yet as striking as the songs often are—the ululating mystery of "Mandinka," for instance, or the insinuating heat of "I Want Your (Hands On Me)"—it's O'Connor's voice that ultimately carries the album. When the protagonist of "Jackie" rages against the sea that took her lover, you can hear the rage in O'Connor's voice, just as there's genuine tenderness in "Jerusalem." And when she assumes the role of the betrayed lover in "Troy," her fearsome, flamboyant performance would be the envy of any Medea.

O'Connor's ability to convey emotion through her singing paid off on her second album, *I Do Not Want What I Haven't Got*, which produced the chart-topping single, "Nothing Compares 2 U." Although written by Prince for a Time spinoff called the Family, O'Connor virtually reinvents the song, homing in on its implications of listlessness and loss to turn in a performance that perfectly captured what it feels like to be on the losing end of an infatuation. O'Connor touches on similarly strong emotions elsewhere on the album—"Feel So Different," for example—but rarely with the same intensity; the emphasis this time seems more on the music. Not that there's anything wrong with that, since her ideas are often interesting, as the collision between the Celtic fiddle and James Brown drum loop on "I Am Stretched on Your Grave" bears out. But without that emotional edge, the occasional childishness of O'Connor's material (as in the crabby "The Emperor's New Clothes") is somehow less forgivable. — J.D.C.

OHIO PLAYERS
★★★★ **Ohio Players Gold** (Mercury, 1976)
The Dayton-based Ohio Players stirred a lumpy Funkadelic-derived stew for years on Detroit's Westbound label—with only limited returns. The septet signed to Mercury in '74 and cut its recipe back to the basics; soon, salty concoctions like "Fire" and "Love Rollercoaster" would leave entire dance floors slavering for more. Notorious for its silly S&M album jackets, Ohio Players back up the salacious cartoon flash of vocalist Leroy "Sugar" Bonner with a spare, supple groove. The surging melodies and roaming horn lines on these mid-'70s singles strongly recall Sly Stone. If *Gold* doesn't come close to the ecstatic peaks of Earth, Wind & Fire's roughly concurrent *Greatest Hits Volume 1*, at least it never strays into the dreaded Valley of the Commodores. Even "Sweet Sticky Thing"

leaves the peppery aftertaste of bass-heavy, finger-poppin' funk. When you just can't get enough of that stuff, well, all you need is *Gold*. — M.C.

OINGO BOINGO
★★★   **Only a Lad** (A&M, 1981)
  ★½ **Nothing to Fear** (A&M, 1982)
  ★½ **Good for Your Soul** (A&M, 1983)
★★★   **Dead Man's Party** (MCA, 1985)
  ★½ **BOI-NGO** (MCA, 1987)
★★½ **Boingo Alive** (MCA, 1988)
★★   **Skeletons In the Closet** (A&M, 1989)
  ★   **Dark at the End of the Tunnel** (MCA, 1990)
★★½ **Best O' Boingo** (MCA, 1991)
On one level, it's easy to be impressed by Oingo Boingo. A big band—eight pieces—its sound is never cluttered or ponderous, but full of instrumental color and powered by a rhythm section that cuts straight to the heart of a groove, be it upscale new wave funk or brash, athletic ska. Even better, the Boingos have in composer Danny Elfman a craftsman capable of writing arrangements ingenious enough to make even the thinnest melodic ideas seem substantial. On the other hand, it's just as easy to be frustrated or even bored by the Boingos. Despite its obvious talent, the band doesn't have more than two albums of solid material to its credit; trouble is, the Boingos have stretched that two-albums-worth into a nine-album career.

Things start off promisingly enough with *Only a Lad*. Though it's sometimes too gimmicky for its own good, when the band hits its stride, as it does with "On the Outside," "Little Girls" and the title tune, its wicked wit and brazen virtuosity shine bright. *Nothing to Fear* reprises the formula, but fails to match the first album's level of songwriting. "Wild Sex (In the Working Class)" is entertaining in spite of its excesses, and "Nothing to Fear (But Fear Itself)" has its moments, but most of the album is dross, and much the same holds true for *Good for Your Soul*. With *Dead Man's Party*, however, the Boingos are at their peak. Not only is the catchy, grotesque and irresistibly danceable title tune by far the best thing in the band's catalog, but the rest of the album manages to keep pace; "Weird Science," in particular, is wonderfully deranged.

Unfortunately, the Boingos pretty much blew their wad with that album, for the rest of the band's output is repetitious, predictable and easily ignored. *Boingo Alive* offers a good overview since it reprises a fair amount of the band's pre-MCA catalog, but the performance—recorded live, but sounding canned—leaves much to be desired. As for the best-ofs, *Skeletons in the Closet* only covers the band up to *Good for Your Soul*, meaning no "Dead Man's Party," while *Best O' Boingo* deals with the early material by refloating the tepid renditions on *Boingo Alive*. Consumer discretion is advised. — J.D.C.

THE O'JAYS

★★★★½ **Back Stabbers (Philadelphia International/CBS, 1972)**
★★★★ **Ship Ahoy (Philadelphia International/CBS, 1973)**
★★★ **Survival (Philadelphia International/CBS, 1975)**
★★★½ **Family (Philadelphia International/CBS, 1975)**
★★★★ **Collectors' Item (Philadelphia International/CBS, 1977)**
★★★ **Let Me Touch You (EMI America, 1987)**
★★½ **Seriously (EMI America, 1989)**
★★★½ **Emotionally Yours (EMI, 1990)**

"What they do: They smile in your face/all the time they want to take your place"—the O'Jays' warning is well-taken. "Back Stabbers" identifies a creeping, pervasive sense of paranoia that's still with us, 20 years later. In 1972, this danceable message song struck like a thunderbolt. The O'Jays' breakthrough hit also propelled the sleek Sound of Philadelphia into the Top Ten where it ruled for the next several years, eventually spawning disco.

Producers Kenny Gamble and Leon Huff found a perfect vehicle in this vocal power trio. Buoyed by the smooth harmonies of Walter Williams and William Powell, lead singer Eddie Levert's growling authority pushes the O'Jays through the trickiest Gamble and Huff soundscapes. Along with the Spinners' concurrent self-titled debut, *Back Stabbers* is the pinnacle of Philly Soul. (Both albums are out of print!) Though the beauty of the title track is the way it opens personal travails to wider interpretation, the feel-good followup single is much more typical of Gamble and Huff's philosophy. Still, "Love Train" barrels over any objections: the way that jazzy guitar line cuts through the layered vocals and swelling orchestration is so hypnotizing, so right.

Ship Ahoy is an angrier, ambitious followup. "For the Love of Money" matches that base motivation with a frank, funky groove. If "Don't Call Me Brother"

edges toward hostility, the epic title cut depicts the slave passage with impassioned clarity all the more devastating because so few artists have tried to tell this shameful story.

Social commentary takes a backseat after that. "Living for the Weekend" and "I Love Music" from *Family Reunion* sum up the O'Jays' later period: simple sentiments elevated by those towering voices and majestic productions. "Stairway to Heaven" (no, not Zep's) captures the group at its most gospel-flavored, but the Philly formula was already beginning to stagnate. The O'Jays didn't notice, and continued to supply pleasant singles (from "Use ta Be My Girl" in 1978 to "Put Our Heads Together" in 1983) long after the albums became routine.

Let Me Touch You marked the O'Jays return to Philadelphia: reuniting with Gamble and Huff again and teaming up with Thom Bell for the first time. It's gratifying, if a little flat. Eddie Levert is in good voice, and the arrangements leap out of the speakers like the old days. But with just-passable material, the expected chemistry never does take hold. *Seriously* attempts a cross-generational fusion with some help from Eddie's sons Sean and Gerald and their group Levert; it's a nice idea, though this time the younger generation's skittery hip-hop beats don't mesh with the old man's rock-solid R&B foundation. *Emotionally Yours* comes closer to accomplishing that fusion with the smoking, politically charged "Something for Nothing." And the two versions of the title track—an obscure late-Dylan number taken out dancing and then escorted to church—indicate that the O'Jays' blazing voices can still strike like lightning. — M.C.

THE OLYMPICS

★★★ **The Olympics Meet the Marathons (Collectables, NA)**

Fine examples of Los Angeles–style group harmony, which departed from its East Coast counterpart in being more pop-oriented and less dependent on a single lead tenor carrying the vocal load, the Olympics consistently placed records on the charts between 1958 and 1966, with the most popular being their debut single, "Western Movies." Oddly, that track isn't on this collection, but several other Olympics chart entries are, including the rousing "Big Boy Pete," "(Baby) Hully Gully (Pts. 1 and 2)," "Shimmy Like Kate," "Little Pedro" and "The Slop." The Marathons took the novelty approach on most of their recordings, and a novel approach to business—they also recorded as the Jayhawks (and had a Top Twenty hit in 1956 with "Stranded in the Jungle") and the Vibrations (and had a Top Thirty hit in 1961 with "The Watusi"). They were still under contract, as the Vibrations, to Checker Records when they moonlighted as the Marathons, signed to Arvee Records and cut a tasty ode called "Peanut Butter" that hit the Top Twenty. To no one's surprise, Checker objected and eventually obtained the rights to the recording. "Peanut Butter" is here in all its double-entendre glory ("Open up your jar now/spread it on your cracker"), along with other zany items such as "Oink Jones," "C. Percy Mercy of Scotland Yard," "Chicken Spaceman" and "Tight Sweater." — D.M.

ALEXANDER O'NEAL

★ ★ ★　　Alexander O'Neal (Tabu/Epic, 1985)
★ ★ ★½ Hearsay (Tabu/Epic, 1987)
★ ★ ★½ All Mixed Up (Tabu/Epic, 1989)
★ ★ ★ ★　All True Man (Tabu/Epic, 1991)

This Minneapolis soul crooner sparks his love-man agenda with a fiery up-tempo side. Thanks mostly to a stunning Jimmy Jam and Terry Lewis production, *Alexander O'Neal* connected with an adoring audience by way of funky electro-plaints like "Innocent." But it was on a hit duet with disco thrush Cherrelle—the lusciously overwrought "Saturday Love," from her 1986 album, *High Priority*—that Alexander O'Neal found his voice: "strong but sensitive," as he put it a couple years later. Jam and Lewis, hot off Janet Jackson's *Control*, supply O'Neal's next album with more assured songwriting and an expanded sonic pallette. *Hearsay* matches O'Neal's growing emotional range with a seamless blend of musical elements, from down-and-dirty rock guitar to upwardly mobile string sections. "Fake," "Criticize" and the title cut exhibit O'Neal's chesty prowess, while "Never Knew Love Like This" (also featuring Cherrelle) and "The Lovers" reveal his command of vocal intimacy. Deploying songs around conversational sound-bites, *Hearsay* ambitiously tried to chart the effects of loose talk on relationships. As disco concept albums go, it's suprisingly concise and coherent.

All Mixed Up is an even rarer phenomenon: a remixed collection of previous hits that actually improves on the originals. Spicing up the overall impact without obscuring the originals, *All Mixed Up* serves as a catch-up for listeners who have enjoyed a snatch of Alexander O'Neal on the radio. It could also double as a melodic refresher course for jaded, beat-crazed dance-floor mavens. *All True Man* ups the ante even further; it may well be the best pop album released in 1991. O'Neal sounds inflamed about matters in the bedroom ("The Morning After") and out on the streets ("Time Is Running Out"), filling in each situation with sharp details and thoughtful vocal coloring. On haunting mid-tempo tunes like "Midnight Run," Jam and Lewis weave a complex, striking fabric: bittersweet keyboard melodies tangle up in bold rhythm patterns. "Used" crosses the line into foursquare hard rock, and O'Neal definitely holds his own. The quiet, faintly bluesy "Shame on Me" closes *All True Man* on a most encouraging note. — M.C.

100 PROOF AGED IN SOUL

★ ★ ★ ★ Greatest Hits (HDH/Fantasy, 1990)

Not exactly the best-known act on the Invictus/Hot Wax label, 100 Proof Aged in Soul certainly made the most of Holland-Dozier-Holland's post-Motown hit factory. With layers of psychedelicized sound stacked on top of that classic auto-motivating beat, Holland-Dozier-Holland's early-'70s product soon became cluttered, baroque. But 100 Proof Aged in Soul's *Greatest Hits* is lean and mean, thanks to lead singer Steve Mancha's dry intensity and some truly inspired formula songwriting. The 1970 pop Top Ten "Somebody's Been Sleeping in My Bed" breathlessly accumulates a pile of damning evidence ("cigarettes in the ashtray and I don't even smoke"), while Mancha breathes life and soul into the pounding metaphor-hooks favored by H-D-H's staff writers: "One Man's Leftovers (Is Another Man's Feast)," but then again "Too Many Cooks (Spoil the Soup)." Complaining about a lover's cruel "90 Day Freeze" or worrying about those cars parked in her "Driveway," 100 Proof Aged in Soul gets its point across—and then some. — M.C.

THE ONLY ONES

★ ★ ★ ★ Special View (Epic, 1979)
★ ★ ★ Baby's Got a Gun (Epic, 1980)
★ ★ ★ The Peel Sessions (Strange Fruit, 1989)

The only word to describe Peter Perrett's voice is reedy; it drips pathos and sarcasm. The Only Ones articulate his bleak romantic visions in driving guitar rave-ups that owe as much to Neil Young and Crazy Horse as to the Sex Pistols. Eschewing punk primitivism, the Only Ones (along with more commercial peers like the Pretenders) tried to realign rock tradition with the new wave, and largely succeeded. *Special View* reveals a doom 'n' gloom singer-songwriter who also traffics in rocket-powered riffs and tightly wound hooks. This introspective wall of sound may be an acquired taste, but it's a subtle and enduring one. Drawing from two import-only albums (*The Only Ones* and *Even Serpents Shine*), the band's American debut is unusually well-paced and consistent. The out-of-print *Baby's Got a Gun* falls off into brooding murk, unsurprisingly; the group broke up shortly after its release and Perrett hasn't been heard from since. — M.C.

YOKO ONO

★ ★ ★ ★ ½ **Onobox (Rykodisc, 1992)**
★ ★ ★ ★   **Walking on Thin Ice (Rykodisc, 1992)**

Gathered together on the six-CD *Onobox*, the early work of Yoko Ono—by now well established as a seminal influence on punk and alternative bands from the late '70s to the present—attains a charged, hypnotic power. Her later, more pop-oriented material is somewhat less distinctive, though more "listenable" in conventional terms. While Lennon plays on some of the tracks on *Onobox*, the collection focuses exclusively on Ono's solo work—including *A Story*, a previously unreleased album she completed while she and Lennon were separated in the mid-'70s. *Walking on Thin Ice* is the one-CD sampler drawn from tracks on *Onobox*; it's fine on its own terms, but lacks the substantiality of the longer collection. — P.E.

ORCHESTRAL MANOEUVRES IN THE DARK

★ ★ ★   **Orchestral Manoeuvres in the Dark (1980; Virgin 1987)**
★ ★ ★   **Organization (1980; Virgin, 1987)**
★ ★ ★ ½ **O.M.D. (Virgin/Epic, 1981)**
★ ★ ★   **Architecture and Morality (Virgin/Epic, 1981)**
  ★ ★ ½ **Dazzle Ships (Virgin, 1983)**
★ ★ ★ ½ **Junk Culture (Virgin/A&M, 1984)**
★ ★ ★ ½ **Crush (Virgin/A&M, 1985)**
  ★ ★ ½ **The Pacific Age (Virgin/A&M, 1986)**
★ ★ ★ ★   **The Best of OMD (Virgin/A&M, 1988)**
★ ★ ★   **Sugar Tax (Virgin, 1991)**

An English synth duo with brains under their sleek haircuts and hooks aplenty programmed into their keyboards, OMD are the best of their genre—while seldom forgoing the dance-floor punch of electronic pop, the band revs beyond the form's limits by stressing experiment over formula, melody over beat. Compiling their first two British outings, *O.M.D.* features Liverpool's Paul Humphreys and Andy McCluskey—and the beginnings of an ever-shifting cast of players—feverishly joining inventive sound-textures and odd themes ("Electricity," "Enola Gay") to infectious melodic riffs. With *Architecture and Morality*, OMD is straining for seriousness—and finding it in a tribute to "Joan of Arc," the tough thud of "The New Stone Age" and the langour of "She's Leaving." Spacey instrumental passages mar the record, but a live drummer compensates. *Dazzle Ships* is about as recherché as mainstream music gets; a postmodern critique-celebration of technology, the concept album percolates with sound effects, treated vocals and the occasional slice of strange loveliness. *Junk Culture* goes in for scratching and a more boomy sound; "Tesla Girls" finds OMD back on the boulevard to catchiness, a destination they reach on *Crush*. Disowned (of course) by the band's cult, *Crush* is OMD at its most purely pop—"So in Love" and "Secret" are flawless singles. *The Pacific Age* finds the lads running out of ideas, or coming up with bonkers ones: excerpting Dr. King's speeches, penning ethereal odes to "The Dead Girls." *The Best of OMD* is solid pop.

By 1991, Humphreys had split. And on *Sugar Tax*, McCluskey plays it pretty safe—but "Pandora's Box," "Walk Tall" and nearly all of the album's 12 mechano-ditties make for dance-floor wonder. — P.E.

O POSITIVE

★ ★ ★ **ToyBoatToyBoatToyBoat (Epic, 1990)**
Obviously influenced by R.E.M., these young Bostonians build their sound from dark drones, shifting instrumental textures and unexpected bursts of upbeat melody. What keeps them from coming across as mere clones, however, are Dave Herlihy's fondness for narrative (you really can tell what the songs are about) and the sheer ambition of the band's richly layered soundscapes. Not necessarily the stuff of rock & roll greatness, but certainly worth hearing. — J.D.C.

ROY ORBISON

★ ★ ★ ★ ★ **The All-Time Greatest Hits of Roy Orbison (Monument, 1972)**
   ★ ★ ★ **In Dreams: The Greatest Hits (Virgin, 1987)**
★ ★ ★ ★ ★ **For the Lonely: A Roy Orbison Anthology, 1956–1964 (Rhino, 1988)**
  ★ ★ ★ ★ **For the Lonely: 18 Greatest Hits (Rhino, 1988)**
   ★ ★ ★ **The Sun Years (Rhino, 1989)**
   ★ ★ ★ **Mystery Girl (Virgin, 1989)**
   ★ ★ ★ **The Classic Roy Orbison (1965–1968) (Rhino, 1989)**
  ★ ★ ★ ★ **Roy Orbison and Friends: A Black and White Night Live (Virgin, 1989)**
    ★ ★ **The RCA Days (RCA, 1989)**
    ★ ★ **Little Richard/Roy Orbison (RCA, 1990)**
★ ★ ★ ★ ★ **The Legendary Roy Orbison (CBS Special Products, 1990)**

Death is always untimely, but rarely more so than in the case of Roy Orbison, who succumbed to a heart attack in 1988 as his career was moving into high gear for the first time since his glory days in the '60s. In 1986 film director David Lynch, entranced by the dark beauty of Orbison's 1963 hit "In Dreams," featured the song in a key scene in his oddball mystery *Blue Velvet*, sparking renewed interest in Orbison's early sides. A flurry of activity ensued. Orbison signed with Virgin and rushed out a set of newly recorded versions of his '60s hits, *In Dreams: The Greatest Hits.* He then hooked up with some top contemporary artists—Bruce Springsteen, Tom Waits, Bonnie Raitt, k.d. lang and Jackson Browne, among them—for a concert filmed by HBO and aired as *A Black and White Night Live,* which produced the album of the same title. The concert and album were unqualified successes, with Orbison showing that his powerful voice had lost little over the years. Moreover, he introduced two songs he had recorded for a new studio album, one a strong interpretation of Elvis Costello's "The Comedians" and the other a tepid rocker called "(All I Can Do Is) Dream You." He had been touring all along, rebuilding his following; he'd also cut one splendid album with Tom Petty, Bob Dylan, Jeff Lynne and George Harrison in a loose configuration called the Traveling Wilburys. Everything was in place for a full-fledged comeback when he died.

Released in early '89, *Mystery Girl* immediately yielded a hit single in the Jeff Lynne–produced "You Got It." Written by Orbison, Lynne and Petty, the song proved a perfect showcase for the vocal brilliance Orbison had retained. Lynne's other productions are ham-handed and ill-considered, but tracks produced by T-Bone Burnette ("The Comedians" and "[All I Can Do Is] Dream You"), by Orbison and Heartbreaker Mike Campbell (notably "The Only One"), and especially by U2's Bono bring out the best of Orbison's interpretive skills. The one to build on would have been the Bono-produced track, "She's a Mystery to Me," written by Bono and his U2 mate the Edge. Rather than big production numbers, Bono opts for a stark approach, discarding orchestral arrangements for stripped-down support provided by guitars, drum and piano, and he lets Orbison breathe life into a song about obsessive, blind love and its attendant pain. Bono had it right all along: keep the voice out there, give it a good song, and let it play.

This is hardly revelation. Bono took his cue from Fred Foster, who employed the same philosophy in cutting the '60s sides that earned Orbison legendary status, and can be heard on the original Monument double album *The All-Time Greatest Hits,* Rhino's *For the Lonely* collection (*18 Greatest Hits* is an abridged version of *Anthology,* with identical liner notes) and on the essential four-CD boxed set, *The Legendary Roy Orbison.* Foster believed in big productions—nothing about Orbison's Monument recordings can be considered "stripped-down," and the Monument sessions were among the first Nashville dates to use large string sections—but the voice was always hot in the mix; Orbison never battled the arrangements, as he must so often on *Mystery Girl.* Rather, the voice established the mood, and the arrangements were crafted to heighten the tension and mirror the fevered atmosphere of Orbison's stories. Teamed with Joe Melson in the early '60s and Bill Dees in the late '60s, Orbison delivered songs that broke the standard songwriting formula and came on instead like mini-operas of a grandness that matched the tortured emotions the lyrics described. Paranoia, dread and fatalistic anticipation were the dominant moods of the early-'60s gems—"Running Scared," "Only the Lonely (Know How I Feel)," "Crying," "In Dreams," "It's Over," "Leah"—but there were also moments of tenderness in "Blue Angel," "Blue Bayou" and "Dream Baby." And of course Orbison could rock: witness his treatment of "Mean

Woman Blues" and, from 1964, "Oh, Pretty Woman," his last Number One single. Clearly, Orbison's voice was one of the most remarkable instruments in rock, and he used it to full capacity, most effectively on "In Dreams," when his full-bodied tenor rose from a strong, straightforward delivery to a plaintive wail, followed by a piercing falsetto shriek. Rarely have a producer, an artist and their material been so ideally matched.

In 1965, following two mediocre followups to the mammoth "Oh, Pretty Woman," Orbison signed with MGM. *The Classic Roy Orbison 1965–1968* documents this ill-fated association that saw Orbison disappear from the charts altogether. Orbison continued to cut some good records that disappeared quickly. Only the most hard-core Orbison fans will be interested in the '70s albums. *Regeneration* brought Orbison back to Monument and Fred Foster in 1977, but without the old spark. The voice is there, but the songs are mediocre, save for Tony Joe White's "(I'm a) Southern Man." *Laminar Flow* has three Orbison collaborations among its songs, but these and the other tracks are dead in the water. The one great Orbison track from the '70s is available on the *Roadie* soundtrack in the form of a duet with Emmylou Harris on a gentle rocker, "That Loving You Feelin' Again." The two voices blend beautifully, the arrangement is spare, the production unobtrusive, the song warm and tender.

Before Orbison arrived at Monument in 1960 he had put in time at two other labels, Sun and RCA, without notable success. As *The Sun Years* indicates, Sun didn't quite get what Orbison was about. "Oh, Pretty Woman" notwithstanding, Orbison was hardly a great rock & roll singer; at Sun his vocal style was in stark contrast to the wild, unfettered exuberance of Presley, Perkins and Lewis. His first Sun single, "Ooby Dooby," sold 250,000 copies, but that was as close to a hit as Orbison had with the Memphis label. At RCA Orbison was teamed with producer Chet Atkins, and the evidence on *The RCA Days* and the *Rock Legends* entry suggest someone had an idea Orbison could be a pop singer and thus sweetened up the arrangements with jazzy guitars, saxophones, and close harmonizing background singers. Again, nothing, but the Boudleaux Bryant love song, "Seems to Me," approaches the style that would propel Orbison's Monument recordings.

Ultimately *The Legendary Roy Orbison* box set overshadows all the other Orbison

releases. For a concise overview of an important career, it's hard to beat, covering the Sun years through the Mercury years, and adding some songs Orbison wrote for films but didn't record on his own albums. The set stands as a worthy coda to a compelling career. — D.M.

JEFFREY OSBORNE
★★★ **Jeffrey Osborne (A&M, 1982)**
★★★★ **Stay With Me Tonight (A&M, 1983)**
★★★ **Don't Stop (A&M, 1984)**
★★ **Emotional (A&M, 1986)**
★★ **One Love-One Dream (A&M, 1988)**
★★★ **Only Human (Arista, 1990)**

"Sensitive, that's what I am/Make no mistake about it," sings Jeffrey Osborne on his *Only Human* album, and no more accurate statement about the man could be extrapolated from his music. After ten years with L.T.D., Osborne went solo in 1982 and proceeded to develop a style that incorporated both the funk rhythms his previous group had traded on and mainstream rock flourishes in the arrangements. Love is the name of the game for Osborne, and with producer George Duke he carved out what seemed an unassailable niche as a sensitive balladeer with a big heart. Unafraid to bare his emotions, Osborne was equally forceful on uptempo workouts such as "Stay With Me Tonight" (from *Jeffrey Osborne*) and "The Borderlines" (from *Don't Stop*). But inspiration fled after *Don't Stop*, and Osborne's subsequent A&M efforts were hurting in the credibility department. What sounded natural and heartfelt at the outset of his solo career had turned mechanical. A label change to Arista proved fruitful. *Only Human*, from 1990, is slick, to be sure, but Osborne sounds committed again, and the material's the best he's written since *Stay With Me Tonight*. No less than five producers are credited (including Osborne himself), and that's usually a sign of trouble. But the end result shows depth of feeling ("If My Brother's in Trouble"), tenderness ("Lay Your Head") and ebullience ("Baby Wait a Minute"). — D.M.

OZZY OSBOURNE
★★½ **Blizzard of Ozz (Jet/Epic, 1981)**
★★★ **Diary of a Madman (Jet/Epic, 1981)**
★★½ **Speak of the Devil (Jet/Epic, 1982)**
★★ **Bark at the Moon (CBS Associated, 1983)**

★ ★   **The Ultimate Sin (CBS Associated, 1986)**
★ ★ ★½ **Tribute (CBS Associated, 1987)**
★ ★   **No Rest for the Wicked (CBS Associated, 1988)**
★ ★   **Just Say Ozzy (CBS Associated, 1990)**
★ ★ ★ **No More Tears (Epic, 1991)**

Emmissary of the devil or derivative heavy-metal panderer? The former Black Sabbath frontman fits both descriptions. Cranking out cartoon Satanism over the roar of overripe power chords, Ozzy Osbourne supplies a sort of avuncular presence on the headbanging scene. Unfortunately, precious little of that goofy charm translates onto record. Ozzy's first backing band was capable of genuine excitement, primarily due to the late guitar virtuoso Randy Rhoads. His disciplined attack—flashy but fleet—is best sampled on the posthumous *Tribute* from 1987. On that recording of a 1982 concert, Rhoads buoys Ozzy's apocalyptic schtick with his arsenal of distorted chords and machine-gun solo outbursts. There's a strong note of empathy running through Osbourne's horrific metal melodrama: "Suicide Solution," "Crazy Train" and "Flying High Again" are nowhere near as exploitive as their titles might sound. A definitive live album, from the geek godfather of the heavy-rock genre. After Rhoads died in a plane accident while on tour in 1982, Osbourne slowly began to descend into self-parody. Guitarist Zakk Wylde is no Randy Rhoads. *No More Tears* briefly postpones the inevitable conclusion to Ozzy's saga—extinction. Several taut tracks, co-written by Lemmy Kilmister of Motörhead, achieve the bleak tarpit density of primeval metal. But sooner or later, even the most fixated kids will outgrow their fascination with dinosaurs. — M.C.

K.T. OSLIN
★ ★ ★ **'80s Ladies (RCA, 1987)**
★ ★ ★½ **This Woman (RCA, 1988)**
★ ★ ★½ **Love in a Small Town (RCA, 1990)**

Born in Arkansas and bred in Alabama, Kay Toinette Oslin paid dues in New York before conquering Nashville in the late '80s. You can hear that range of experience in the worldly twang of her singing and songwriting. A pedal steel–pumping New Traditionalist she's not: K.T. Oslin's sound is flavored with a dash of Dire Straits–ish guitar, a hint of rhythm and plenty of sweet keyboards and synths. The smooth backing does have a subtle kick to it, though, one that matches Oslin's sly way with words. A breakthrough hit in 1987, " '80s Ladies," is hardly the nostalgic anthem it first appears to be; Oslin's tendency to overgeneralize is more than balanced by her eye for personal detail and vivid characterization. Her best songs don't tell stories so much as plunk you down in the midst of a sticky romantic situation as it unravels. And though Oslin's white soul vocal style occasionally wanders, more often it allows her to mix sexiness and independence.

Even the more conventional songs on her debut reflect Oslin's imaginative fire: she compares her ramblin' ways to a boomerang on "I'll Always Come Back," trains a painful inquisition on both her lover and herself on "Do Ya." *This Woman* features two unforgettable singles: "Hey Bobby" (a crusading feminist's sexual memoir) and "Hold Me" (an exquisitely accurate break-up-make-up saga). And the filler cuts like "Where Is a Woman to Go" and "She Don't Talk Like Us No More" simply put to shame the competition's best shots. If *Love in a Small Town* doesn't quite hit the twin peaks of "Hold Me" and "Hey Bobby," it definitely maintains a high level across all the songs. K.T. Oslin's finely observed slices of modern life—the blinkered expectations of "Mary and Willi," the eye-opening remembrances of "Momma Was a Dancer"—will be around when all the cowboy-hatted country revivalists have bitten the dust. But why wait? — M.C.

JOHNNY OTIS
★ ★ ★ ★ **The Capitol Years (Capitol, 1989)**
★ ★ ★ ★ **The Complete Savoy Recordings with Johnny Otis (Savoy, NA)**
★ ★ ★ **The New Johnny Otis Show (Alligator, 1981)**

Johnny Otis is one of the true oddities in rock & roll history. For one, he had the talent to be a major artist in his own right (his Top Ten hit from 1958, "Willie and the Hand Jive," remains one of the classic early rock & roll records), and indeed, he recorded prolifically for Savoy and Capitol and was a major name on the R&B circuit. As a songwriter he has cut a wide swath: he wrote all of Little Esther's early hits on Savoy, as well as "Dance With Me Henry" for Etta James, "Every Beat of My Heart" for Gladys Knight and "So Fine" for the Fiestas. He's also credited with producing Big Mama Thornton's early version of "Hound Dog," written by Jerry Leiber and Mike Stoller.

But Otis was as zealous in promoting

other artists' careers as he was his own. He was among the first, if not *the* first, to package blues and R&B artists and take them on the road as a traveling all-star show. Otis was also a smart judge of artistry, and his revues were certain to feature some unknown singer bound for glory. Little Esther Phillips, Hank Ballard, Jackie Wilson, Little Willie John, Etta James and Big Mama Thornton were only a few of the names with whom Otis was associated in the '50s.

Otis's early recordings, available on Savoy and Capitol, represent some of the best examples of early rhythm & blues. Otis himself is a wild, personable singer, and his records are almost all party-hearty affairs informed as much by the rambunctious spirit of New Orleans as they are by the smoother sounds that were evolving in the L.A. R&B scene. *The Capitol Years* contains "Willie and the Hand Jive" and Otis's late-'50s rocking efforts, but the Savoy collection is richer.

Otis has recorded sporadically since the late '60s. The only one of these records remaining in print is the 1981 Alligator release, *The New Johnny Otis Show*, which features Shuggie Otis—Shuggie being Otis's then-*wunderkind* guitar-wizard offspring. While the vocalists in this version of the show are a couple of cuts below the wondrous artists Otis worked with in the '50s, there is still plenty of fire and feeling in these grooves. — D.M.

THE OUTFIELD
★★★ **Play Deep (Columbia, 1985)**
★★★ **Bangin' (Columbia, 1987)**
★★★½ **Voices of Babylon (Columbia, 1989)**
★★★ **Diamond Days (MCA, 1990)**
The Outfield generated expert, faceless rock packed mainly with the pleasures of high professionalism, efficient hooks, sharp playing, zero mistakes and an ambition no more complicated than to sound like a monster on the radio. And it does. The London power trio artfully echos '70s rock and adds new wave flourishes—bassist-vocalist Tony Lewis, for example, sounds like Styx's Dennis De Young with Sting's phrasing; guitarist John Spinks alternates power chords with filigrees that recall U2's the Edge. These tactics play best on *Voices of Babylon*; the band doesn't really have much to say, but sounds crafty and assured. With *Diamond Days*, the Outfield pared down to a duo, but the song remains the same—"For You" is a smooth audience

pleaser, and "John Lennon" shows good spirit. — P.E.

THE OUTSIDERS
★★ **The Best of the Outsiders (Rhino, 1986)**
Mid-'60s Cleveland radio popsters, complete with white hip-huggers and double-breasted blazers, the Outsiders scored big in 1966 with the horn-snappy "Time Won't Let Me." It sounded exactly like Paul Revere and the Raiders and almost exactly like the Buckinghams. Industrious journeymen, the band was hardly a trendsetter; instead the Outsiders' sound exactly reflected the high school zeitgeist, circa 1966. "I'll Give You Time (to Think It Over)" and "Gotta Leave Us Alone" don't quite capture Tommy James and the Shondells; "Girl in Love" tries hard to be the Bee Gees' "Massachusetts"; the band also was, alternately, Rascals and Hollies wannabes. A fairly weak singer, a good bassist—the Outsiders were purely generic. — P.E.

BUCK OWENS
★★ **Love Don't Make the Bars (Capitol, 1981)**
★★★ **Hot Dog (Capitol, 1988)**
★★★½ **Act Naturally (Capitol, 1988)**
★★★½ **Buck Owens and the Buckeroos: Live at Carnegie Hall (Country Music Foundation, 1988)**
★★★ **All-Time Greatest Hits, Vol. 1 (Curb, 1990)**
★★★★ **The Buck Owens Collection 1959–1990 (Rhino, 1992)**
Buck Owens is the prototypical country music careerist—he's written a ton of hits, played expert guitar and developed a style that's been influential among the New Traditionalists, particularly Dwight Yoakam. Texas-born son of a sharecropper, he moved to Bakersfield, California, in the '50s and helped establish that town as a talent center. Owens's albums are genial and well played; his best compositions have fared well when covered by others (Ringo Starr comes to mind). *Hot Dog* features a good duet with Yoakam, and some borderline rock & roll. (Buck isn't up to the outrage of Eddie Cochran's "Summertime Blues," but he doesn't do badly with Chuck Berry's "Memphis Tennessee.") *Act Naturally* presents Buck and Ringo chumming it up on the title tune, and Emmylou Harris brings out Buck's best harmonizing on "Crying Time." Vintage Owens is better than his current output, though: Rhino's *The Buck Owens Collection*, a three-CD boxed set that Owens

participated in compiling, is an outstanding anthology, featuring 63 classic tracks, 20 of which were Number One hits. *Live at Carnegie Hall* features his crack band, the Buckeroos, in their 1966 prime. — P.E.

OZARK MOUNTAIN DAREDEVILS
★ ★ ★ The Best (1981; A&M, 1988)

Every region had a band or two like this in the '70s: a shaggy tribe of hippie pickers and strummers that blended folk and bluegrass elements into laid-back rock. The Ozark Mountain Daredevils hailed from the Missouri-Arkansas hills, though their sound falls closer to mellow L.A. The Daredevils released a half-dozen (deleted) albums on A&M; *The Best of* primarily draws from the three earliest (and best). "Jackie Blue," from *It'll Shine When it Shines* (1974), is the band's purest pop shot, and only Top Ten hit. *Best of*'s only other keepers are two bluesy Little Feat knockoffs: "If You Wanna Get to Heaven" (from the 1973 *Ozark Mountain Daredevils* debut) and "Keep on Churnin' " (from the 1975 album, *The Car Over the Lake*). — M.C.

P

JIMMY PAGE
★★★½ **Outrider (Geffen, 1988)**
By no means a ground-breaker, Jimmy
Page's only official post-Zep solo effort
proves he's still the master of earth-moving
hard rock. Jason Bonham fills in his father's
trademark rhythms, while blooze-belters
John Miles and Chris Farlowe rasp out their
molten Plant-isms (you barely notice when
Robert himself pops up on "The Only
One"). But Page's guitar wizardry, as darkly
evocative and richly textured as ever, is
what lifts these mundane cock-walks above
the mindless standard of '80s metal.
"Wanna Make Love" repeats a shivery riff
until it hypnotizes, and the slow scorcher
"Prison Blues" indicates that Page hasn't
lost his knack for pulling intricate, melodic
solos out of hot air. Instrumental workouts
like "Liquid Mercury" and "Blues Anthem"
come as something of a relief after the
screeching vocal tracks. (Page's turgid,
mostly instrumental soundtrack album for
the 1982 film *Death Wish II* is out of print.)
— M.C.

ROBERT PALMER
★★★   **Sneakin' Sally Through the Alley**
        (Island, 1974)
 ★★   **Pressure Drop (Island, 1975)**
 ★★   **Some People Can Do What They**
        Like (Island, 1976)
 ★★   **Double Fun (Island, 1978)**
★★½ **Secrets (Island, 1979)**
 ★★   **Clues (Island, 1980)**
 ★★   **Maybe It's Live (Island, 1982)**
 ★★   **Pride (Island, 1983)**
★★½ **Riptide (Island, 1986)**
 ★★   **Heavy Nova (EMI Manhattan,**
        1988)
★★★ **Addictions Volume One (Island,**
        1989)
 ★★   **Don't Explain (EMI, 1990)**
Impeccable good taste, impressive stylistic
range and an immediately identifiable voice
don't necessarily equal soul. Robert Palmer
has exhibited all those qualities save the last
during his career. A cool blue sterility
pervades his New Orleans stopover
(*Sneakin' Sally Through the Alley*), his
various reggae trips (*Pressure Drop, Some
People Can Do What They Like*), his
macho-rock fling (*Secrets*), his half-serious
new-wave jaunt (*Clues*), his dance-pop
excursion (*Pride*), his soft-core model-rock
adventures (*Riptide* and *Heavy Nova*) and
his soporific jack-of-all-trades demonstration
spiel (*Don't Explain*). Which pretty much
leaves *Addictions Volume One*. It's Robert
Palmer's greatest hits, more or less, heavy
on the synthed-up '80s video habit-formers,
light on the reggae-flavored '70s cult
favorites. "Addicted to Love" (originally
from *Riptide*) never fails to get under your
skin, while Palmer ably handles some astute
R&B cover versions like the System's "You
Are in My System" (*Pride*) and Cherrelle's
"I Didn't Mean to Turn You On" (*Riptide*).
On the other hand, "Simply Irresistible"
(*Heavy Nova*) is a brazen, callow rewrite of
"Addicted to Love" that naturally proved to
be just as popular. Jumping around from
Marvin Gaye to Mose Allison to Bob Dylan
to Rodgers and Hammerstein and beyond,
Palmer just sounds like an accomplished
showoff on *Don't Explain*. Record buyers
weren't impressed with the pop chameleon
act, either, as the album fell off the charts
rather abruptly. — M.C.

THE PARAGONS
★★★ **Best of the Paragons (Collectables,**
    NA)
This is a good sampling of tunes from a
group whose popularity was almost totally
restricted to the New York City area. Lead
singer Julian McMichael's velvet touch with
a lyric still remains one of doo-wop's
treasures. The group had two minor chart
entries with "Florence," from 1957, and

"If," from 1961. Despite their lack of national stature, the Paragons are central to one of the few classic album moments in doo-wop history, *The Paragons Meet the Jesters*, a sing-off between two of the most highly regarded New York groups of their time. Of course the album is long out of print, but remains highly recommended should a stray copy turn up. — D.M.

MICA PARIS
★★ **So Good** (Island, 1989)
★★★ **Contribution** (Island, 1991)
On a technical level, this British-born thrush has the makings of a great soul singer—power, control, a wonderfully warm tone and a great sense of rhythm. What she doesn't have, however, is the sort of material that would give those strengths the necessary context to seem convincing. *So Good* is an ambitious debut, and smartly plays Paris's singing off against the powerhouse tenor sax of Courtney Pine on the album-opening "Like Dreamers Do." Trouble is, that tune—like most of the album—is a forgettable pop ditty, the sort of fluff not even Aretha Franklin could redeem. And though it's perversely funny to hear Paris insist on one song that "Nothing Hits Your Heart Like Soul Music," none of this pseudo-soul hits the heart at all.
Contribution comes closer, but still pulls up short. With remixes by Curtis Mantronik and D-Mob's Dancin' Danny D, the groove is definitely there, but Paris seems oddly disinclined to take advantage of it. Maybe it's the post–Soul II Soul cool of "If I Love U 2 Nite" and the title tune that keeps her in check, but Paris rarely gets beyond a simmer. Still, between the brash exuberance of "Just to Be with You" and the atmospheric embellishments of "Deep Afrika," the promise of her voice remains tantalizing. — J.D.C.

CHARLIE PARKER
★★★★ **At Storyville** (1953; Blue Note, 1988)
★★★★★ **Jazz at Massey Hall** (1953; Fantasy OJC, 1986)
★★★ **One Night in Washington** (1953; Elektra/Musician, 1982)
★★★½ **Now's the Time** (Verve, 1957)
★★★★ **The Verve Years (1948–50)** (Verve, 1976)
★★★★ **The Verve Years (1950–51)** (Verve, 1976)
★★★½ **Bird with Strings** (Columbia, 1977)
★★★★ **Charlie Parker** (Prestige, NA)

★★★★★ **Charlie Parker** (Warner Bros., 1977)
★★★ **Bird & Pres, Carnegie Hall 1949** (Verve, 1977)
★★★ **One Night in Birdland** (Columbia, 1977)
★★★★ **Original Bird: Best on Savoy** (Savoy, NA)
★★★ **Summit Meeting at Birdland** (Columbia, 1977)
★★★½ **The Verve Years (1952–54)** (Verve, 1977)
★★★★ **Bird at St. Nick's** (Fantasy OJC, 1983)
★★★½ **Bird on 52nd Street** (Fantasy OJC, 1984)
★★★★★ **Bird: The Savoy Recordings (Master Takes, 1944–48)** (Savoy, 1986)
★★★★ **Charlie Parker** (Verve Compact Jazz, 1987)
★★★★★ **Bird: The Complete Charlie Parker on Verve** (Verve, 1988)
★★★½ **BeBop & Bird, Vol. 1** (Hipsville/Rhino, 1988)
★★★½ **BeBop & Bird, Vol. 2** (Hipsville/Rhino, 1988)
★★★★ **Bird: The Original Recordings of Charlie Parker** (Verve, 1988)
★★★★★ **The Complete Charlie Parker Savoy Studio Sessions** (Savoy Jazz, 1988)
★★★★★ **The Legendary Dial Masters, Vol. 1** (Stash, 1989)
★★★★★ **The Legendary Dial Masters, Vol. 2** (Stash, 1989)
★★★½ **Charlie Parker Jam Session** (Verve, 1990)
★★★½ **The Cole Porter Songbook** (Verve, 1991)
★★★½ **The Complete Dean Benedetti Recordings of Charlie Parker** (Mosaic, 1991)
★★★★ **With Strings** (Verve, NA)
WITH DIZZY GILLESPIE
★★★★ **Bird and Diz** (1950; Verve, 1986)
Bebop was the beginning of modern jazz, a turning point that marked its transistion from dance pop to art music, and though many musicians contributed to this transformation, none galvanized this new style the way Charlie Parker did. It wasn't just that he was a brilliant improvisor, whose quicksilver solos suggested a world of rhythmic and harmonic possibilities; Parker's status as a jazz legend also owes more than a little to the disparity between his astonishing creativity and his dissolute personal life. Indeed, for some fans, the

myth matters almost as much as the music, and their hunger for pieces of that myth—especially outtakes, live recordings, even fragments of solos—has filled the Parker discography with albums of dubious origin, fidelity and worth. Complicating matters further is the fact that Parker's studio recordings have been issued and reissued in various permutations over the years, with one major chunk—his recordings for the long-defunct Dial label—frequently out of print. As such, his discography is constantly in flux, as sub-bootleg quality concert albums drift on and off the market and his studio output goes through periodic repackaging. So rather than take a strict chronological approach, this entry will break down Parker's recorded legacy into four pieces: The Savoy recordings; the Dial recordings; the Verve recordings; and a general look at air checks, concert recordings and other arcana.

As with most jazz musicians, Parker made his initial recordings as a sideman, first as a member of the Jay McShann band in 1940 and then, in 1944, as part of a quintet fronted by guitarist and vocalist Tiny Grimes. He also recorded a handful of seminal bebop sides—including performances of "Groovin' High," "Salt Peanuts" and "Hot House"—with Dizzy Gillespie, but these were all issued under Gillespie's name, and can currently be found on *Groovin' High* (Musicraft, 1986). But the first recordings to be credited to Parker himself were a handful of tunes for Savoy by Charlie Parker's Ree Boppers, in 1945. Like most of Parker's output, these tracks—along with others recorded for Savoy in 1947–48, are available in two packages: *The Savoy Recordings (Master Takes 1944–1948)* and *The Complete Savoy Studio Sessions*. What's the difference? With the former, what you get are the singles originally released by Savoy, including "Now's the Time," "Donna Lee," "Koko" and "Ah-Leu-Cha." But with *The Complete Charlie Parker Savoy Studio Sessions*, you get all that plus the alternate takes, fragments and false starts; moreover, there is similarly exhaustive coverage offered of Parker's sideman dates with Tiny Grimes and Miles Davis. However they're packaged, though, the Savoy recordings represent some of Parker's most consistent work—rich, bluesy and inventive, it finds him playing from strengths both in terms of his ideas and his technique. Nor are the players in his bands anything to scoff at, particularly trumpeter Miles Davis, whose harmonic

agility is impressive even at this early stage.

Four months after his first Savoy session, Parker was in California recording for Ross Russell's newly formed Dial label. These include some of Parker's most assured performances, as well as some of his most troubled. Parker was deeply into drugs, and turned up at his second Dial session stoked to the gills; the results, including a wobbly "Lover Man" and a disjointed, almost out-of-time reading of "The Gypsy," are deeply depressing. Tracks recorded at other Dial sessions, like "Ornithology," "Moose the Mooche," "Drifting on a Reed" and—especially—"Relaxin' at Camarillo," are truly wondrous to hear, however. Unfortunately, the complete Dial recordings (which include important 1948 New York sessions) were last in print in the late '70s, when Warner Bros. released them as *Charlie Parker*, a six-LP box set in anticipation of a Parker bio-flick starring Richard Pryor (the film, "Bird," was eventually made with Forest Whitaker in the title role). Highlights of the Dial dates (including the tracks mentioned above) can be found on *The Legendary Dial Masters, Vol. 1* and *Vol. 2*; an odd assortment of Dial sessions have been mixed in with the live recordings on the two-volume *Bebop & Bird*. But used copies of *Charlie Parker* are well worth seeking until another complete edition is issued.

Overall, though, Parker's largest and most diverse recordings are on Norman Granz's Verve label. These range from the freewheeling *Jazz at the Philharmonic* jams to combo dates, and from "cubop" big-band recordings with Machito and his Orchestra to the lushly arranged *Bird With Strings* sessions. For a brief introduction, it's hard to beat *The Original Recordings of Charlie Parker*, a single CD which manages to offer samplings of all sides of his Verve output. Other recommended single albums from this period would include the stirring *With Strings* (Verve), and the flashy-but-fun *Bird and Diz*, while the three-volume *Verve Years* sets (on LP and cassette only) cover all the highlights in chronological order. Still, serious listeners owe it to themselves to hear *The Complete Charlie Parker* on Verve, a ten-CD set with surprisingly little flab and a wealth of previously unreleased material; it's especially fascinating to hear failed experiments like the Gil Evans–arranged session in 1953 that found Bird accompanied by strings and mixed chorus (including Dave Lambert and Annie Ross).

From there, we move to the dicey realm

of concert recordings. Buying a Charlie Parker live album is often like making a deal with the devil—you may hear some incredible playing, but you pay for the privilege in bad sound and dubious credits. Perhaps the most legendary of these are compiled as *The Complete Dean Benedetti Recordings of Charlie Parker*. Recorded in extreme lo-fi by a dedicated Parker acolyte, these recordings focus almost exclusively on Parker's improvisations; spread across seven CDs, these often brilliant fragments are a goldmine for students and jazz historians, but a trial for almost any other listener.

Bad sound is almost a given on these recordings, though. *Jazz at Massey Hall* is the only exception, and this quintet recording—featuring Gillespie, Bud Powell, Charles Mingus, Max Roach and Parker, billed for contractual reasons as "Charlie Chan"—is one of the very best; *At Storyville* is also relatively well-recorded, though the playing isn't quite as sparkling. But the *Bird on 52nd Street* and *Bird at St. Nick's* (which are combined on the Prestige two-fer *Charlie Parker*) offer stalwart performances with abysmal sound; there's heavy distortion throughout the "Live at Birdland" portions of *Bebop & Bird*; the sound on *One Night in Birdland* is maddeningly spotty. — J.D.C.

GRAHAM PARKER

   ★★★★   Howlin' Wind (Mercury, 1976)
   ★★★½   Heat Treatment (Mercury, 1976)
   ★★★   Stick to Me (Mercury, 1977)
   ★★½   The Parkerilla (Mercury, 1978)
★★★★★   Squeezing Out Sparks (Arista, 1979)
   ★★★   The Up Escalator (Arista, 1980)
   ★★★   Another Grey Area (Arista, 1982)
   ★★★   The Real Macaw (Arista, 1983)
   ★★½   Steady Nerves (Elektra, 1985)
  ★★★½   The Mona Lisa's Sister (RCA, 1988)
  ★★★½   Human Soul (RCA, 1989)
   ★★½   Live! Alone in America (RCA, 1989)
  ★★★½   Struck by Lightning (RCA, 1991)
   ★★★   Burning Questions (Capitol, 1992)

Though he's widely perceived as a progenitor of punk and new wave, Graham Parker came on like a younger, more angst-ridden version of Van Morrison right from the start. *Howlin' Wind*, his volcanic Nick Lowe–produced debut album, anchors personal explorations worthy of the best singer-songwriters in rock-solid updated white R&B. Assured enough to wrestle with reggae rhythms (the title track), rockabilly ("Back to Schooldays") and his own pessimistic nature ("Don't Ask Me Questions") as well as horn-peppered blue-eyed soul, Parker possesses the talent—and the backing band—necessary to pull it all off. Led by guitarist Brinsley Schwarz, the assembled pub-rock vets known as the Rumour provide bristling support for Parker's pointed eruptions. *Heat Treatment* is a slightly disappointing follow-up; the energy level registers high, but only "Turned Up Too Late" and "Fools Gold" deliver the unaffected, haunting resonance of *Howlin' Wind*. Muddy production and even more lackluster songwriting make *Stick to Me* sound like a rush job; Mercury dropped a shoddy live quickie (*The Parkerilla*) when Parker switched labels. Aggressively clear-headed and laden with pissed-off hooks, *Squeezing Out Sparks* is a triumphant turnaround for Parker. His spleen-venting ("Local Girls") is balanced by romantic conviction ("Passion Is No Ordinary Word"), his feelings of dislocation ("Discovering Japan") offset by a moral center ("You Can't Be Too Strong"). You don't have to agree with that last song's anti-abortion message to be affected by its strength.

Puzzlingly, after attaining that confident peak, Parker lapsed into mercurial inconsistency and outright grouchiness. Hesitant, frustrated and frustrating, full of coulda-been-a-contender bitterness, his subsequent albums will exhaust the patience of all but the most committed fans. There are moments when his muse peeks out, of course—usually when he's not trying too damn hard to be deep. *The Up Escalator* and (especially) *Another Grey Area* suffer from acute symptoms of Springsteen-itis: gusty overwrought vocals, clunking ham-fisted arrangements. *The Real Macaw* is an admirable, if only half-convincing, attempt at a mellowed-out celebration of monogamy: "You Can't Take Love for Granted" hits its target like nothing since *Squeezing Out Sparks*. After bottoming out with the blandly gruff *Steady Nerves*, Parker re-emerged for round three in 1988. His singing is febrile and fired-up on *The Mona Lisa's Sister*, co-producer Brinsley Schwarz sparks the gratifyingly spare accompaniment with spikey guitar lines, but the songs themselves either strain after significance ("OK Hieronymous") or settle for sarcasm

("The Girl Isn't Ready"). *Human Soul* is better; Parker manages to graft some of the old R&B pizzazz onto his family-man profile, with hummable results ("Big Man on Paper," "Call Me Your Doctor"). If Parker sounds a little too relaxed and pleased with his circumstances at the acoustic outset of *Struck by Lightning*, eventually the bolt of inspiration finds him. "A Brand New Book" and "Ten Girls Ago" update and embellish the pub-rock strut and stutter rather than merely echoing it. "Children and Dogs" is so warm and funny you may believe Parker's assertions of hard-won maturity, though the first side of *Lightning* is so laid-back and satisfied many listeners won't make it that far. When it comes to rock & roll, even the "adult" variety, a little pent-up fury never hurts. — M.C.

JUNIOR PARKER

★ ★ ★ ★ **The Best of Junior Parker (MCA, 1973)**

Mississippi-born Herman "Junior" Parker joined Howlin' Wolf's band while still in his teens and in two years was fronting the band after Wolf went into a brief retirement. His recording career began in 1952 for Modern, but it was a move to Memphis's Sun label in 1953 that got things going full throttle. He scored a major R&B hit that year in "Feelin' Good," and a minor hit with "Mystery Train," the latter now better known in its cover version by Elvis Presley, though Parker's own rendition has scarifying urgency to recommend it. In '54 Parker moved to Duke Records and began a fruitful four-year association that found him lighting the transitional path from R&B to rock & roll, both in his bluesy, swaggering vocal style and in the work of his guitarist Pat Hare, who was then experimenting with distortion as a creative tool. Many of Parker's best Duke sides are available on this *Best of*, including three Top Ten R&B hits: "Next Time You See Me" (1957), "Annie Get Your Yo-Yo" (1962) and the towering "Driving Wheel" (1961). Of note as well is Parker's "Stand by Me," which in feel and sentiment would seem to have been the inspiration for the like-titled Ben E. King classic from 1961. Parker continued recording into 1971, when he died after surgery for a brain tumor. Though his post-Duke recordings are now out of print, vinyl versions pop up from time to time and are worthwhile investments. — D.M.

MACEO PARKER

★ ★ ★½ **For All the King's Men (EP) (4th & B'way, 1990)**
★ ★ ★ ★ **Roots Revisited (Verve, 1990)**
★ ★ ★ ★ **Mo' Roots (Verve, 1991)**

Because he's an alumnus of the great James Brown funk machines as well as George Clinton's P-Funk conglomerate, you might think Maceo Parker's own albums would be rhythm workouts all the way. And you'd be right if you were only speaking of his work with the JBs or spin-offs like Maceo & the Macks, remnants of which can be found on *James Brown's Funky People* and *James Brown's Funky People (Part 2)*, or of *For All the King's Men*, a funky, Free-James-Brown! throwaway cut with Bootsy Collins, Fred Wesley and Bobby Byrd.

But Parker's serious solo albums aren't R&B at all—they're old-fashioned, organ-backed soul jazz sides, just like Houston Person or Jimmy Forrest used to make. *Roots Revisited* is big on blues and has the benefit of Don Pullen on organ; *Mo' Roots* is more conventionally soulful, and offers Parker singing Otis Redding's "Fa Fa Fa (Sad Song)" with Kym Mazelle adding a solid Carla Thomas impression. — J.D.C.

RAY PARKER, JR.

★ ★ ★ ★ **Greatest Hits (Arista, 1982)**
★ ★ ★ **Chartbusters (Arista, 1984)**
★ ★½ **I Love You Like You Are (MCA, 1991)**

With the group Raydio and then on his own, Ray Parker, Jr. released some of the most seductive, soulful singles of the late '70s. This Detroit native works the same lush romantic territory as the Thom Bell–era Spinners, though with a slightly randier spin. On "You Can't Change That," "Jack and Jill" and "A Woman Needs Love (Just Like You Do)," Parker melts your resistance with striking melodies and warm, reassuring vocals. *Greatest Hits* proves he could pump up the funk on cuts like "Bad Boy" and "For Those Who Like to Groove." Oddly enough, Parker scored his biggest hit with the theme from "Ghostbusters," which was irresistible in a very different way, to say the least. *Chartbusters* maps his slight, but crucial mid-'80s decline by including the regrettable "Jamie" ("I taught her everything . . . ") alongside the enlightened oldie "A Woman Needs Love (Just Like You Do)." *I Love You Like You Are* finds Parker integrating a graceful touch of rapping and hip-hop rhythms into his patented sound. Besides sampling his earlier hits, however, he's also recycling their melodies and outdated sexual notions. Offers to out-freak the competition aren't exactly what contemporary women want to hear. — M.C.

VAN DYKE PARKS

★ ★ ★   Song Cycle (Warner Bros., 1968)
★ ★ ★   Discover America (Warner Bros., 1972)
★ ★ ★½ The Clang of the Yankee Reaper (Warner Bros., 1975)
  ★ ★   Jump! (Warner Bros., 1984)
★ ★ ★   Tokyo Rose (Warner Bros., 1989)

The work of Van Dyke Parks illustrates the charms and irritations of eccentricity—imagine some mad cross of Stephen Sondheim, Burt Bacharach, Cole Porter and Randy Newman, and you come close to imagining Parks's odd contribution to American pop. Cult figure of all cult figures, the arranger-composer-producer solidified his mini-mythic status when he collaborated with Brian Wilson on the Beach Boys' legendary, unreleased *Smile*—some of the stuff later surfaced on *Surf's Up* and it was beautiful but baffling, all hyper-artistic instrumentation and cryptic poetry. It recalled, in fact, nothing so closely as it did Parks's own 1968 debut and triumph of inscrutability, *Song Cycle*. Taking four years to make, the album employed, it seems, half of L.A. on violins and brasses, along with such redoubtable studio cats as Jim Gordon. Parks's way with a catchy lyric went something like, "Inasmuch as you are touched to have withstood by the very old search for the truth within the bound of toxicity" ("Palm Beach"), and the music was all art-song chord changes, fractured rhythms and ungrounded "atmosphere." Still, the thing cast a strange enchantment.

Next up was *Discover America*, notable for Parks's growing obsession with Trinidadian steel-drum music and for lyrics celebrating arcane Americana; the album features a calypso version of "Stars and Stripes Forever." *The Clang of the Yankee Reaper* seemed almost like Top Forty compared to the first two; resembling the score to some surreal TV documentary on "the development of American popular song," it offered his gorgeous convolutions in their most accessible form—along with a version of Pachebel's "Canon" that sounded like a marching band bumping into steel-drum players with jazz-rock fusionists occasionally joining in.

Then came *Jump!* Boldly unconcerned with political correctness, Parks used, of all things, the Uncle Remus tales of Joel Chandler Harris (complete with all manner of "dat" and "wif" dialect) to spin off a libretto for a sort of pop opera. Southern-born, the composer may indeed have grasped that Harris's work reflected the Atlanta writer's love of period Southern culture—but exhuming Tar Baby still wasn't cool. Not that the music—an adept mix of Gershwinisms and Schubert-lite—was all that compelling either.

Tokyo Rose finds Parks meditating, one supposes, on East-West relations. The music, as is often the case with Van, is delightful; the lyrics are lapidary. — P.E.

PARLIAMENT

★ ★ ★ ★   Up for the Down Stroke (Casablanca, 1974)
  ★ ★ ★   Chocolate City (Casablanca, 1975)
★ ★ ★ ★   Mothership Connection (Casablanca, 1976)
★ ★ ★ ★   The Clones of Dr. Funkenstein (Casablanca, 1976)
★ ★ ★½ Parliament Live—P. Funk Earth Tour (Casablanca, 1977)
★ ★ ★ ★   Funkentelechy Vs. the Placebo System (Casablanca, 1977)
★ ★ ★ ★   Motor-Booty Affair (Casablanca, 1978)
  ★ ★ ★   Gloryhallastoopid or Pin the Tale on the Funky (Casablanca, 1979)
  ★ ★ ★   Trombipulation (Casablanca, 1981)
★ ★ ★ ★½ Parliament's Greatest Hits (Casablanca, 1984)

The Parliaments began as a doo-wop quintet in Plainfield, New Jersey. Former barber George Clinton and crew—Fuzzy Haskins, Calvin Simon, Grady Thomas, Ray Davis—moved to Detroit in the mid-'60s. They snagged a Motown contract, only to wind up on the overtalented label's bench. The group finally got a single out on Revilot Records; "(I Wanna) Testify" hit on the R&B and pop charts in 1967, but lousy distribution and an ensuing contractual dispute prevented an effective followup. In the meantime, Clinton was busy: immersing himself in Sly and Jimi, studying the Beatles and Bob Dylan. Once he discovered the transportational power lurking in those big amplifiers, soul—and rock—would never sound quite the same again.

Unable to use the "Parliaments" name, Clinton labelled the quintet's backup musicians Funkadelic and developed a whole 'nother thang with the same core of players. The rechristened Parliament emerged in 1970, with the long-lost *Osmium* on Holland-Dozier-Holland's Invictus label.

Up for the Down Stroke positions Parliament as the lighter side of P-Funk: the sexy R&B ying to Funkadelic's skanky metal yang. In general, Parliament plays up the danceable harmony chants and cuts back on the guitar-stoked freakouts. Veteran James Brown sidemen like bassist Bootsy Collins and the newly named Horny Horns (Maceo Parker, Fred Wesley) pump up the beat, while an ever-shifting cast of singers dispense party tips, sci-fi fantasy trips, seduction raps, social commentary, scathing satire and tales for tots. Throughout it all, you always feel the "Presence of a Brain," as one *Down Stroke* track insists.

Chocolate City reveals the downside of Clinton's exploratory high-energy approach: even killer riffs turn into repetitious vamps and the most pointed raps can evaporate into hot air when left untended. Parliament snaps back with sharp hooks and a walloping multimedia concept on *Mothership Connection*. The cosmic theatrics are actually supported by music that resembles nothing else on earth. "Tear the Roof Off the Sucker (Give Up the Funk)" is a downright irresistible command; that drumbeat hits your reflex center like a doctor's mallet. Gary Shider's mellifluous rap on the title track—"put a glide in your stride and a dip in your hip and come aboard the mothership"—dodges horn lines and blends into keyboardist Bernie Worrell's exquisitely synthesized fade-out.

The Clones Of Dr. Funkenstein doesn't possess an all-out anthem like "Give Up the Funk," though it may well be the most consistently tuneful of all the Parliament albums. Despite the mad-scientist jive, horn-laden love stomps like "Your Sexy Body" define the albums deliciously warped romantic mood. *Funkentelechy Vs. the Placebo System* lays on the space-bass: it's denser, more bottom-heavy, even more wigged-out than before. "Flash Light" brilliantly epitomizes Bootsy's thumb-plucking propulsion, while "Bop Gun" leaves a deeply lingering sting. *Motor-Booty Affair* has to be the first—and only—free-flow aquafunk cartoon song cycle. Amid imaginative synth squiggles (from Worrell and Walter "Junie" Morrison) and goofy underwater giggles, light-fingered tracks like "One of Those Funky Things" and "Liquid Sunshine" strike some of Parliament's most complex and satisfying grooves. This album (along with Funkadelic's concurrent *One Nation Under a Groove*) represents Clinton's empire at its dizzying creative peak.

But the expansionist P-Funk soon got over-extended. Off-shoots and side-trips such as Bootsy's Rubber Band, Brides of Funkenstein and Parlet started to sap too much juice from the Mothership's source. (The Brides' deleted 1980 Atlantic LP, *Never Buy Texas From a Cowboy*, is worth digging up, however.) *Gloryhallastoopid* and *Trombipulation* have the obvious acid-flash beat but not the underlying mind-funk capability of classic Parliament. Stretched to the limit, Parliament dispersed (along with Funkadelic) in the early '80s. *Greatest Hits* taps all the Casablanca albums save the last; it's a handy introduction or summary. However, true funkateers will insist that such fat-trimming also kills the indescribable flavor of Parliament's original LPs. Just be forewarned: the uncut P-Funk—"The Bomb"—is definitely habit-forming.
— M.C.

GRAM PARSONS

★ ★ ★ ★½ **Gram Parsons/Safe at Home (1968; Shiloh, 1987)**
★ ★ ★ ★½ **G.P. (Reprise, 1973)**
★ ★ ★½ **Gram Parsons and the Fallen Angels Live, 1973 (Sierra, 1982)**
★ ★ ★ ★ ★ **Grievous Angel (Reprise, 1974)**
★ ★ ★ ★ **Sleepless Nights (A&M, 1976)**
★ ★ ★½ **Gram Parsons: The Early Years 1963–65 (Sierra, 1979)**
★ ★ ★ ★ ★ **G.P. / Grievous Angel (Reprise, 1990)**

Gram Parsons didn't completely master country music in his brief life, but he had a much firmer grasp on it than any other rock & roller. Although Parsons virtually invented country rock during his stints with the International Submarine Band and the Flying Burrito Brothers, his actual sound barely resembles the subsequent, often half-formed fruit of that particular union (when transformed into MOR by bands like the Eagles). It was an outlandish, even radical idea at first: Parsons concocted his notion of "country soul," or "Cosmic American Music," after first pursuing folk as a teenager with the Shilohs (on *The Early Years*). Parsons then formed possibly the first country-rock (rock as in R&B) aggregation, the International Submarine Band, who recorded an album that was promptly ignored (now available from Sierra). The Byrds was Parsons's next stop, but by the time people began to accept the band's country turn on *Sweetheart of the Rodeo*, he had already ended his brief, influential tenure. Soon joined by Byrds bassist Chris Hillman, Parsons went further down the country road with his new band, the Flying Burrito Brothers, and stayed long enough to contribute to two albums. Material from this period, along with later solo recordings, make up *Sleepless Nights.*

Parsons continued in a pure country direction for his abbreviated solo career. (He died in 1973, just after the completion of his second solo album.) He didn't cast off the rock influence so much as outgrow it. On *GP*, Parsons finds a soulmate in backup singer Emmylou Harris. The album's melancholy edge cuts deep on songs like "Streets of Baltimore" and "New Soft Shoe," though *GP* could stand a touch of the Burritos' warped humor. That dolorous charge is what cultists have come to idolize about Parsons, of course. *Grievous Angel* displays the full range of his talents. Emmylou Harris is front and center, singing pristine harmony to Parsons's quavery lead—a far cry from the salty "he said, she said" duets of early-'70s mainstream country. This space cowboy–earth mother duo works wonders on familiar material ("Love Hurts") and their own neo-traditionals ("In My Hour of Darkness"). On "Brass Buttons" and "$1000 Wedding," Parsons pinpoints the telling details of a heartbreak with surgical precision. And a cover of Tom T. Hall's raucous "I Can't Dance" adds a welcome, what-the-hell dash of spirit to an otherwise sombre—but never depressing—album. Paired together on a single CD, *GP/Grievous Angel* is a monumental reissue. Parsons paved the way for country's New Traditionalist movement in the mid-'80s. It just took a while for his influence to really sink in. — M.C.

DOLLY PARTON

★ ★ ★ ★ ★   **The Best of Dolly Parton (RCA, 1970)**
★ ★ ★ ★   **Coat of Many Colors (RCA, 1971)**
★ ★ ★   **The World of Dolly Parton Volume One (1972; CBS Special Products, 1988)**
★ ★ ★   **The World of Dolly Parton Volume Two (1972; CBS Special Products, 1988)**
★ ★ ★ ★   **My Tennessee Mountain Home (RCA, 1973)**
★ ★ ★½   **Jolene (RCA, 1974)**
★ ★ ★ ★ ★   **The Best of Dolly Parton (RCA, 1975)**
★ ★   **Here You Come Again (RCA, 1977)**
★ ★ ★½   **9 to 5 (and Other Odd Jobs) (RCA, 1980)**
★ ★   **Greatest Hits (RCA, 1982)**

★ ★ ★   **Dolly Parton Collector's Series (RCA, 1985)**
★ ★   **The Best There Is (RCA, 1987)**
★ ★   **Rainbow (Columbia, 1987)**
★ ★½   **White Limozeen (Columbia, 1989)**
★ ★½   **Eagle When She Flies (Columbia, 1991)**

Born in the Blue Ridge Mountains of Tennessee, Dolly Parton made her radio singing debut at age 10. Her first Nashville sides, cut a decade later for the Monument label in the mid-'60s, are compiled on the two *World of Dolly Parton* albums. Signs of an indomitable singing and writing talent leap out right away, especially on *Volume One;* "Dumb Blonde" is exactly what she ain't. Teaming up with veteran singer Porter Wagoner after that, the bubbly Parton quickly stole the spotlight from her poker-faced benefactor. Between their hit duets and syndicated television variety show, Dolly and Porter ruled the country roost at the turn of the '70s. On *The Best of Dolly Parton* (1970) she starts to shine with a singular, disarming brilliance. Her version of Jimmie Rodgers's "Blue Yodel #8" skips and soars with effortless grace; deep-running bluegrass and folk roots inform Dolly's lyrics as well as her singing. She addresses traditional subject matter—often dark or morbid reflections on life's cruel inconsistencies—in a convincing modern context. "My Blue Ridge Mountain Boy" and "In the Good Old Days (When Times Were Bad)" examine the consequences of leaving the simple life behind, administering an unexpected dose of realism. She wouldn't go back if they paid her, Dolly rightly concludes on "Good Old Days." (The magnificent *The Best of Porter Wagoner and Dolly Parton*, from 1970, now out of print, contains the similarly themed "Daddy Was an Old-Time Preacher Man.") Her gift for empathetic narrative comes to the fore on "Down From Dover" (a pregnant teen's sad awakening) and "Daddy Come and Get Me" (from a padded cell!), while "Just Because I'm a Woman" lays down a sharply worded proto-feminist manifesto.

Parton took advantage of her superstar clout at first, cutting two loosely conceptual albums in the early '70s. Autobiographical but not overly sentimental, *Coat of Many Colors* (childhood inspiration) and *My Tennessee Mountain Home* (music biz aspirations) contain some of Parton's strongest work. The title tracks of both albums provided unforgettable hits, as did the haunting title tracks of *Jolene* and the deleted *Bargain Store* (1975). Though it's brief, *The Best of Dolly Parton*

(1975) captures her dizzying peak. The aforementioned singles are included, along with the unbearably sexy "Touch Your Woman," the guilt-wracked "Lonely Comin' Down" and the randy "Travelin' Man." The dream of a pop crossover, always present, becomes explicit on the icky, string-laden "Love Is Like a Butterfly." By the time Parton achieved that goal a couple of years later, she'd left the distinctive musical approach behind. Her 1977 pop hit "Here You Come Again" could just as easily have been recorded by Helen Reddy. Despite its peppy title hit, however, *9 to 5 (And Other Odd Jobs)* marks a refreshing (and underrated) return to country for Dolly. After years of ever-blander releases, it's a pleasure to hear her pure mountain warble latch onto Woody Guthrie's "Deportee," among others. "In the Stream," Dolly's 1983 duet with Kenny Rogers, is an inexhaustible source of guilty pleasure. But otherwise, *Greatest Hits* is a grim, glitzy testament to the soul-sapping power of media celebrityhood.

Apparently sparked by the success of *The Trio* (with Linda Ronstadt and Emmylou Harris, 1987), Dolly returned to making records in Nashville. Unfortunately, her country comeback has yet to kick into high gear. Ricky Skaggs produced *White Limozeen* though it's a shame he couldn't bring more of a calming bluegrass influence to bear on the post-Hollywood Parton. She sounds nervous and breathy on "Why'd You Come in Here Lookin' Like That," a fidgety uptempo strut. *Eagle When She Flies* is a good deal more confident and assured, though Parton still doesn't quite connect with these polished countrypolitan love songs—even the ones she co-wrote. Perhaps you really can't go home again. — M.C.

THE PASADENAS
★ ★ ★ **To Whom It May Concern (Columbia, 1989)**

English soul revivalists with a '60s sense of harmony but a '70s notion of groove, the Pasadenas were precursors of pop revisionists like Lenny Kravitz, acts whose work echoed the past without openly aping it. And though some of the music seems too mannered to be convincing, the best tracks, like the driving, Philly groove "Riding On a Train" or the neo-Motown "Tribute (Right On)," have all the familiarity of a half-remembered hit. — J.D.C.

CHARLEY PATTON
★ ★ ★ ★ ★ **Founder of the Delta Blues: 1929–34 (1988; Yazoo, 1991)**

★ ★ ★ ★ ★ **King of the Delta Blues (Yazoo, 1991)**
★ ★ ★ ★ ★ **Master of the Delta Blues: The Friends of Charlie Patton (Yazoo, 1991)**

Robert Johnson gets all the headlines, but it was Charley (also spelled "Charlie") Patton who established so many of the stylistic standards of Delta blues as to rightfully deserve the title of "founder" and "king." Among the prominent Delta bluesmen of his time, Patton was the ultimate individualist: Though he spent his childhood working with his family on white-owned plantations, in his adult life his work for whites was pretty much restricted to playing dances or other social engagements; his home was wherever the four winds blew him, and changed when the first strong wind—or jealous husband or boyfriend—came along.

He left behind choice sides that continue to startle in their rhythmic complexity and structural innovation. Singing in a gruff voice that became harsher after his throat was slashed at a dance, Patton employed his voice as a percussive instrument, making his lyrics difficult to understand. Yet the emotion came through undampened and even enhanced when Patton used his slide to echo his vocal. The rhythmic devices he used have been traced back to West African drumming; Patton further complicated his sound by adhering to no set pattern of rhythmic structure. As well, he often disdained the standard eight-bar and 16-bar blues formula, working instead in 13-and-a-half-bar verses, harkening back to a 19th-century folk drumming style.

Though less bedeviled than Johnson, Patton nonetheless crafted some of the most harrowing accounts of Delta life—"Pony Blues," "Tom Rushen Blues," the two-part "High Water Everywhere," "Moon Going Down" and "Bird Nest Bound" are Delta classics, songs that inspired succeeding generations of bluesmen. The tracks on *Founder of the Delta Blues* represent many of Patton's classic blues recordings—some have been lost—but almost without exception these are the most important. In addition to his gut-wrenching blues, another side of Patton—the performer of gospel and pre-blues songs and country tunes—is presented on *King of the Delta Blues*. *Masters of the Delta Blues* is an anthology of recordings by Patton's friends and pupils (Son House, Tommy Johnson and Bertha Lee, among others), all under the sway of Patton's style and themes. The three Yazoo albums together represent "the finest introduction to pre–Robert Johnson Delta blues imaginable," according to Robert Palmer, author of *Deep Blues*. — D.M.

BILLY PAUL

★ ★ ★ **360 Degrees of Billy Paul (Philadelphia International/CBS, 1972)**

Turns out to be about 180 degrees too many. "Me and Mrs. Jones" defines the lush romantic end of Philly Soul: the succinct orchestration delineates the stream of guilt in Billy Paul's onrushing confession of delicious, illicit pleasure. It's still a startling thing to hear, this near-perfect Number One from early '73—too bad the accompanying album typifies the Gamble and Huff team's limitations. "Am I Black Enough for You" tartly contrasts with the breakthrough hit, but mismatched cover versions ("Your Song" is a travesty) and Billy Paul's overriding fondness for genteel cocktail-lounge voice-play reduce *360 Degrees* to a proven formula. Hits plus filler equals quick, inconsistent album. For all their 45 rpm expansions on the Motown Method, Gamble and Huff never did quite surmount this basic obstacle. — M.C.

LES PAUL & MARY FORD

★ ★ **The Fabulous Les Paul and Mary Ford (Columbia, 1965)**
★ ★ ★ ★ **Les Paul: The Legend & the Legacy (Capitol, 1991)**
WITH CHET ATKINS
★ ★ ★ **Chester and Lester (RCA, 1976)**

Though they made some of the liveliest pop records of the 1950s, Les Paul and Mary Ford are destined to be forever overshadowed by Paul's technological innovations of multitrack recording, the solid-body guitar and prototypical synthesizers. Ford (Paul's wife) sang in a pleasant if bland voice, which sounded like the Andrews Sisters when multitracked. Behind her Paul worked out some astonishing harmonic runs and unusual chord progressions, many of them accomplished via tape trickery. Nevertheless, his smooth touch, flawless command and dextrous playing have elevated him to a status among guitarists nearly as legendary as his standing among electronics freaks.

The duo's most productive years were spent on Capitol, which has now honored them with a four-CD box set retrospective containing 34 previously unreleased masters, track-by-track commentary by Paul himself, samples from radio shows and commercials featuring Ford and Paul (a bit much), and most important, all the Capitol hits (24 Top Forty records between 1950 and 1961—two

more on Columbia), including two Number One singles, "How High the Moon" (1951) and "Vaya Con Dios" (1953). *The Fabulous Les Paul and Mary Ford* surveys the post-Capitol years, which found the hits coming less frequently, and finally ending in 1961 with the Top Forty single, "Juva (I Swear I Love You)." Paul's playing is never less than exhilarating, but inspiration was running thin (and music changing radically) by the time he and Ford hit Columbia in 1958. This one is for die-hards only. *Chester and Lester* is a lively teaming of two top instrumentalists, with Chet Atkins joining Paul on an album that has an improvised feel. — D.M.

JOHNNY PAYCHECK

★ ★ ★ ★ **Biggest Hits (Epic, 1982)**

"Take This Job and Shove It" rocketed this plainspoken honky-tonk hero, formerly Donald Lytle of Greenville, Ohio, to national attention in 1978. At that point, Johnny Paycheck had been kicking around the country scene for close to twenty years. A songwriter and ex-sideman for Faron Young and Ray Price, he changed his name and went solo after Tammy Wynette scored a hit with his "Apartment #9." Johnny Paycheck exuded the musically lean aura of an "outlaw" before it became a trend; sadly, his definitive recordings on the defunct Little Darlin' label have all but disappeared. Epic house producer Billy Sherrill softens Paycheck's brooding, sardonic tone without completely losing it: their first hit, "She's All I Got" packs a foolproof iron-fist/velvet-glove hook. The brief *Biggest Hits* album includes that 1971 breakthrough, skips over some of the mushier followups (like "Mr. Lovemaker") and concentrates on Johnny's disco-era heyday. The bluesy, hungover "11 Months and 29 Days" refers to the stretch of time he spent in a Navy brig, while "Colorado Cool Aid" depicts a violence-prone individual with the disarming, casual intensity of a gangster rap. "Take This Job and Shove It" works as both a fantasy anthem and a self-mocking hoot; Paycheck toys with the rabble-rousing urge instead of taking it seriously. He's not the most versatile singer, but "Yesterday's News Just Hit Home Today" asserts his understated command of slow, sad ones. On the down side, "Friend, Lover, Wife" and "The Outlaw's Prayer" reveal his weakness for sentiment and overkill.

All of Johnny Paycheck's original Epic albums have gone out of print; *11 Months and 29 Days Slide Off of Your Satin Sheets* and *Take This Job and Shove It* are well worth scouting for. — M.C.

FREDA PAYNE

★ ★ ★ **Greatest Hits (HDH/Fantasy, 1991)**
Forthright and crystal-clear, Freda Payne's
voice animates the 1970 hit "Band of Gold"
—she turns a stock situation into a juicy
morning-after rap session: "Last night on
our honeymoon, we stayed in separate
rooms." Though "Band of Gold" is one of
the very best Invictus/Hot Wax releases,
Holland-Dozier-Holland's post-Motown
priorities—trendy psychedelic touches and
densely packed rhythms—didn't really gibe
with Freda Payne's tasteful background in
jazz and show tunes. "Deeper and Deeper"
and "You Brought the Joy" are pleasant,
nothing more. But Freda Payne's 1971 pop
crossover, "Bring the Boys Home," lends
Greatest Hits even further significance.
— M.C.

PEARL JAM

★ ★ ★ ★ **Ten (Epic, 1991)**
Blessed with the best bloodline on the
Seattle scene, Pearl Jam is perhaps the most
accessible (and certainly the most
conventional) of the city's grunge rockers.
Guitarist Stone Gossard (who also writes
most of the music) and bassist Jess Ament
were originally half of the seminal Seattle
sludge combo Green River; when the rest of
the band split to form Mudhoney, Gossard
and Ament got together a group of their
own, dubbed Mother Love Bone. But MLB
called it quits when singer Andrew Wood
died of a heroin OD shortly after the band
completed its only album, the much
underrated *Apple* (Polydor, 1990).

Gossard and Ament stayed together and
soon regrouped as Pearl Jam. Although the
new band's approach is similar in form to
what MLB did on *Apple*, Pearl Jam's
execution is something else again. Not only
is Gossard's writing more tuneful and direct
than MLB's, but guitarist Mike McCready's
incisive leads eliminate much of the
instrumental clutter that bogged down the
old band, lending the Jam's music a clear,
commercial sound, but it's the emotional
intensity of Eddie Vedder's vocals that
ultimately puts the band over, giving an
immediacy to songs like "Even Flow" and
"Alive" that goes well beyond the melodic
potency of the hooks. (Members of Pearl
Jam and Soundgarden recorded an album
for A&M, *Temple of the Dog,* as a memorial
for Andrew Wood.) — J.D.C.

PEBBLES

★ ★ ★   **Pebbles (MCA, 1987)**
★ ★ ½ **Always (MCA, 1990)**
The former Perri McKissack is the most
personable exponent of the sleek, super-
tooled dance sound perfected by Atlanta-
based producers L.A. (Reid) and Babyface.
That's meant as a compliment, since Pebbles
definitely has musical talent as well as video
pizzazz. And it's also an indictment, since
most LaFace jobs tend to be rather faceless.
Pebbles triumphs pretty much on the
strength of two zinging, heartfelt teen-love
scenarios: "Girlfriend" and the irresistible
"Mercedes Boy." *Always* represents a leap
into premature "maturity": more consistent
and accomplished overall, it sure could use a
giggly hit single or two.   — M.C.

TEDDY PENDERGRASS

★ ★ ★ ½ **Teddy Pendergrass (Philadelphia**
International, 1977)
★ ★ ★ ½ **Life Is a Song Worth Singing**
(Philadelphia International, 1978)
★ ★ ★ ½ **Teddy (Philadelphia International,**
1979)
★ ★ ½ **Teddy Live! Coast to Coast**
(Philadelphia International, 1979)
★ ★ ★ ★ **TP (Philadelphia International,**
1980)
★ ★ ★   **It's Time for Love (Philadelphia**
International, 1981)
★ ★ ★ ★ **Greatest Hits (Philadelphia**
International, 1984)
★ ★ ½ **Love Language (Asylum, 1984)**
★ ★ ★ **Workin' It Back (Asylum, 1985)**
★ ★ ★ **Joy (Asylum, 1988)**
★ ★ ★ ½ **Truly Blessed (Elektra, 1991)**
After he left Harold Melvin and the Blue
Notes, lead singer Teddy Pendergrass
invented the soulful loveman stance that's
now become commonplace. On *Teddy
Pendergrass,* he smoothly negotiates the
up-tempo, Blue Notes–style struts like "This
Whole Town's Laughing at Me" and "I
Don't Love You Anymore." But the
elegantly sensual ballads are where he takes
command. Beginning with "Close the Door"
(from *Life Is a Song Worth Singing*),
Pendergrass issued a series of intimately
suggestive singles that proved impossible to
resist. On *Teddy,* "Come Go With Me"
leads to "Turn Out the Lights" (but not
before the hot oil rubdown). Rather than
flash his vocal prowess with mock-operatic
gigolo flourishes, Pendergrass testifies with a
gospel singer's sincerity. When it's time, he
vividly states his case without resorting to
macho hyperbole. Gamble and Huff wield a
seductive power of their own, though
Teddy's musical boudoir tends to floral
overdecoration at times. Hence, the
relatively lean and bluesy *TP* is his best
shot: Womack and Womack's "Love TKO"

is a perfect match-up. A crippling auto accident sidelined his matinee-idol career in 1982, but Pendergrass eventually reemerged with his magnificent voice intact on the Asylum albums. *Truly Blessed* puts him right back in the thick of things. Pendergrass swings with synthesized groove on the "Slam Side," but guess what? The "Slow Jam" side is an absolute scorcher. It's so hot it should give nightmares to all his lovemen imitators. — M.C.

THE PENGUINS

★★★ **Golden Classics (Collectables, NA)**
This L.A. quartet with a powerful lead tenor in Cleve Duncan cut several interesting group-harmony sides for the DooTone label in the mid-'50s, but achieved immortality on the basis of one inspired performance— "Earth Angel," from 1954, a bona-fide group harmony classic that ranks with the Moonglows' "Sincerely," the Crows' "Gee" and the Chords' "Sh-Boom" as the key entries in doo-wop annals in the years '54–'55; in '56 the Five Satins would come along and distill all the best elements of these important recordings into their own monumental statement, "In the Still of the Night." Apart from "Earth Angel," the Penguins' recordings here are pretty much standard-issue fare, in spite of Duncan's always-pleasing efforts to reach for something more than the material offered. — D.M.

MICHAEL PENN

★★★½ **March (RCA, 1989)**
Being the brother of actor (and former Madonna spouse) Sean Penn might have earned Michael Penn a momentary flicker of fame, but his songwriting is what makes his work worth hearing, thanks to his acrid wordplay (the song title "Cupid's Got a Brand New Gun" is fair indication) and effortless way with melody. In fact, the album-opening "No Myth" is a near-perfect pop song, establishing a standard the rest of *March* comes close to meeting. — J.D.C.

PENTANGLE

★★★ **The Pentangle (Reprise, 1968)**
★★★★ **Sweet Child (Reprise, 1969)**
★★★ **Basket of Light (1970; Transatlantic, 1988)**
★★★ **Cruel Sister (Reprise, 1971)**
★★★ **Reflection (Reprise, 1971)**
★★★ **Solomon's Seal (Reprise, 1972)**
★★★ **Open the Door (Varrick, 1985)**
★★★ **In the Round (Varrick, 1986)**
★★★½ **A Maid That's Deep in Love (Shanachie, 1989)**

★★★ **So Early in the Spring (Green Linnet, 1990)**
Along with Alexis Korner alumni double-bassist Danny Thompson and percussionist Terry Cox, guitar virtuosos Bert Jansch and John Renbourn formed Pentangle in 1967 to fashion acoustic versions of traditional Celtic folk. Singer Jacqui McShee added her remarkable, bell-like delivery to the sturdy vocals of Jansch and Renbourn, making the outfit an ensemble of singularly precise talents. Their debut helped kick off a trad boom that soon swelled to contain Fairport Convention, Steeleye Span and others. Painstaking in their reconstruction of tunes dating back to the Middle Ages, the band was dogged from the start by their almost academic style (they were a lot more impressive than fun), but McShee's jazzy maneuvers on a cover of the Staple Singers' "Hear My Call" added a measure of mild swing.

The second record, *Sweet Child*, was the group's triumph. The jazz material was both more plentiful and more assured— Thompson soloed on Mingus's "Haitian Fight Song," Jansch-Renbourn dueled on Mingus's tribute to Lester Young, "Goodbye Pork-Pie Hat"; and McShee's singing (particularly on the a capella "So Early in the Spring") was breathtaking enough that the traditional ballads didn't suffer too greatly from over-reverence. One live side, one studio set, the album remains a chaste wonder. *Basket of Light*, nearly the aesthetic equal of *Sweet Child*, surpassed the previous album commercially—and for a while Pentangle was surprisingly popular in the U.K. (they never caught on stateside). *Cruel Sister* found the group taking up electric guitars (with little appreciable effect, however); *Reflection* featured more original material but, again, the essential song remained the same. *Solomon's Seal* was predictably expert but, by then, the band's jazz influence had long faded into the backdrop, and the olde musick sounded played out.

Going their separate ways in the middle '70s, the members reunited a decade later—and their Varrick albums neatly recapture their traditional-music strengths. The Shanachie best-of, *A Maid That's Deep in Love*, concentrates wholly on that side of Pentangle. However lovely, its music refutes the efforts of the band at its eclectic best. Stick with *Sweet Child*. — P.E.

PERE UBU

★★★★ **The Modern Dance (1977; Blank/ Rough Trade, 1981)**

★ ★ ★ ★½ **Dub Housing (Chrysalis, 1978)**
★ ★ ★½ **New Picnic Time (Chrysalis import, 1979)**
★ ★ ★ **The Art of Walking (Rough Trade, 1980)**
★ ★ ★ **Song of the Bailing Man (Rough Trade, 1982)**
★ ★ ★ ★ **Terminal Tower: An Archival Collection (Twin/Tone, 1985)**
★ ★ ★½ **The Tenement Year (Enigma, 1988)**
★ ★ ★½ **Cloudland (Fontana, 1989)**
★ ★ ★½ **Worlds in Collision (Fontana, 1991)**

Pere Ubu prefigured the punk revolution; this maverick band was spawned by Cleveland's infamous Velvets-obsessed rock underground during the bone-dry mid-'70s. Founded by guitarist/critic Peter Laughner and singer David Thomas (aka Crocus Behemoth), the original Ubu mixed post-hippie psychedelia and bargain-basement surrealism into a dense, scarifying hard-rock sound. As the group's early propaganda proudly announced, Pere Ubu's music could only have been produced in an "avant garage." The "30 Seconds Over Tokyo"/"Heart of Darkness" single, released in 1975 on the Hearthan label, helped usher in the heyday of independent recording. Those cuts and the 1976 follow-up "Final Solution" alone make the *Terminal Tower* restrospective essential listening for any student of punk and new wave.

By the time of Pere Ubu's debut album, Laughner's fluid Hendrix-isms had been replaced by Allen Ravenstine's shockingly electronic vocabulary of synthesizer rattles, hums and screeches. *The Modern Dance* introduces rock to the concept of "industrial music." But unlike today's brutal clang-banging dance brigades, Pere Ubu's horrible noise and urbanized teen angst are tempered by the infusion of humanity: Tom Herman's curtly strummed rhythm guitar, Tony Maimone's probing bass and, above all else, David Thomas's quirky, passionate vocal eruptions.

Pere Ubu cuts loose from its rock grounding on *Dub Housing*, and the music takes off into uncharted territory that's alternately beautiful and grim. The group's discipline and implicit sense of structure separate it from raving new wavers and noodling art rockers alike; even the abstract electronic splashes and chattering tape splices on "Codex" congeal into fascinating patterns. There's always a purpose behind Pere Ubu's perverse humor and perplexing logic, and an eerie sense of reality pervades

even the wildest sonic forays on *Dub Housing*.

New Picnic Time feels much looser; the band reaches for a semi-improvised experimental groove, and nails it more often than not. Guitarist Mayo Thompson replaces Tom Herman on the next two albums, and the overall sound slips into arid, arty repose. Most of the familiar elements are present on *The Art of Walking* and *Song of the Bailing Man*, but David Thomas no longer exudes the warped, wonderful essence that so enlivens Pere Ubu's groundbreaking earlier work. Pere Ubu broke up after a sour 1982 tour; 1987 saw the band's reunion with the satisfying album *The Tenement Year*, an un-nostalgic blast of the old alchemy. "We've got the technology!" Thomas croaks and sputters with reactivated glee over the outmoded din of Allen Ravenstine's EML synthesizers. Characteristically, Pere Ubu didn't remain long at the juncture. *Cloudland* and *Worlds in Collision* confront traditional song structures and melodies head on. Sounding more confident than compromised, the middle-aged Pere Ubu just might pull off its commercial coup. Now that would be surreal. — M.C.

CARL PERKINS
★ ★ ★ ★ **Original Sun Greatest Hits (Rhino, 1986)**
★ ★ ★ ★ ★ **Up Through the Years 1954–1957 (Bear Family, 1986)**
★ ★ ★ **Born to Rock (Universal/MCA, 1989)**
★ ★ ★ **Honky Tonk Gal (Rounder, 1989)**
★ ★ ★ ★ ★ **The Classic Carl Perkins (Bear Family, 1990)**
★ ★ ★ ★ **Jive After Five: The Best of Carl Perkins (1958–1978) (Rhino, 1990)**

Carl Perkins will forever be linked to his 1956 classic, "Blue Suede Shoes," and well he should be. In one fell swoop, this Tennessee sharecropper's son gave voice to emerging language, symbols and attitudes, capturing the spirit of rock & roll's first generation and of the 1950s as well. The first song to become a hit on the pop, country and R&B charts simultaneously, it seemed to herald the start of an important career. But at the moment of his greatest triumph, Perkins found the rug pulled out from under him when he was seriously injured in a car wreck while traveling to New York to appear on *The Perry Como Show*. At the time of the accident "Blue Suede Shoes" was jockeying at the top of the chart with "Heartbreak Hotel," the first RCA single by Perkins's friend and former Sun labelmate Elvis Presley. A month later

Presley released his own cover of "Blue Suede Shoes" and, although Perkins's original outsold Presley's, the song became identified with the King.

"Blue Suede Shoes" casts such an immense shadow that it nearly obscures the wealth of music Perkins recorded both during and since the Sun years. Moreover, Perkins overshadowed all the Sun artists as a picker; combining blues, country and boogie, his forceful, economical lead style, unusual progressions and impeccable timing made a profound impression on succeeding generations of guitarists. Both Eric Clapton and George Harrison have pointed to Perkins as one of the players who influenced their styles.

As well, Perkins has carved out a solid history as a songwriter. The Beatles covered three of his songs—"Matchbox," "Everybody's Trying to Be My Baby" and "Honey Don't"; Patsy Cline had a hit with "So Wrong"; Johnny Cash had one of the biggest country singles of the '60s with "Daddy Sang Bass"; and in '91 Mark O'Connor's New Nashville Cats charted with an updated version of "Restless," and Dolly Parton scored with her tender "Silver and Gold," written by Perkins and his sons. When he gets down to looking at his life Perkins becomes a great writer: "Blue Suede Shoes" was inspired by an incident he witnessed at a dance, when a boy upbraided his date for stepping on his blue suede shoes. Even more dramatic are songs reflecting the habits and privations of the rural environment in which Perkins grew up. His first single, "Movie Magg" (issued on Sam Phillips's Flip label), is an account of dating mores in backwoods Tennessee; "That's Right" expresses a jealous man's feelings toward a woman whose infidelities are only imagined; "Dixie Fried," his greatest Sun side, is a dark recounting of the violent, whiskey-soaked nights Perkins observed in the honky-tonks where he plied his trade. In his post-Sun years Perkins has turned inward for material, producing sides notable for self-revelation and eloquence: "Just for You," "A Love I'll Never Win," "Someday, Somewhere, Someone Waits for Me."

Perkins and his brothers Jay and Clayton, along with drummer W.S. Holland, had been playing in the honky-tonks around Jackson, Tennessee, when they signed to Sun in 1954. The Perkins brothers had grown up in Lake County, Tennessee, where theirs was the only white family on a sharecropper's farm. From the black farmhands Carl learned to play blues guitar; from the radio on Saturday night, he learned of traditional country and bluegrass by way of the Grand Ole Opry. When the Perkins Brothers Band began playing dances around Lake County, Carl was already working out a more rhythmically driving style of music that was neither country nor blues, but had elements of both. Hearing Presley's "That's All Right (Mama)" on the radio in 1954 convinced Carl that Sun was the place to be. Indeed, Sam Phillips understood what Perkins was doing, but he already had Elvis doing the same thing, so after signing the Perkins brothers he directed them to country music. Heavily indebted to Hank Williams, Perkins delivered with songs such as "Honky Tonk Gal," "Turn Around," and "Let the Jukebox Keep on Playing." After Presley left Sun for RCA, Perkins has given the go-ahead to cut uptempo material. "Blue Suede Shoes" was the upshot.

After his wreck, Perkins made some of the best music of his life, but failed to approach the success of "Blue Suede Shoes." Along with Cash, he signed with Columbia in 1958. By this time Perkins was deep in the throes of alcoholism. Most of his Columbia efforts were tepid country affairs that met with little enthusiasm, although a couple showed some of the old spark. Signed to Decca in 1963, Perkins got it together long enough to make some startling, pure country records. A ten-year stint with Johnny Cash's revue was part of a regrouping process that saw Perkins kick his alcohol habit and regain his confidence. Signed to Mercury in 1973, he cut a brilliant country album, *My Kind of Country*, notable both for the honesty of its songs and the palpable feeling in Perkins's performances. When yet another generation of British rockers rediscovered rockabilly, Perkins responded with a first-rate return to his roots in *Ol' Blue Suede's Back* (1978).

Again, sustained success on record proved elusive, but Perkins, backed by a band that included his sons Stan and Greg, worked steadily through the '80s. Signed to the new Universal label in 1989, Perkins released *Born to Rock*, an album that comes down strong on his rockabilly heritage ("Born to Rock," "Charlene," "Don't Let Go") even as it attempts to establish a contemporary country foundation. It's hardly Perkins's strongest effort, and his vocals, particularly on the slower songs, sound forced at times.

Of the in-print recordings, Bear Family's five-CD *Classic Carl Perkins* offers all the Sun sides as well as Perkins's early Columbia and Decca recordings. It's pricey, but it sheds light on some years undocumented on other available releases. *Jive After Five* offers a broad sweep of post-Sun recordings; among its more important tracks are the solo guitar entry, "Just Coastin'," from an album Perkins recorded with NRBQ, *Boppin' the Blues* (1970); "I'm in Love Again," from *Ol' Blue Suede's Back*; and three tracks from *My Kind of Country*. Both *Up Through the Years* and *Original Sun Greatest Hits* summarize the best of the Sun sides, with the former offering 24 tracks to the latter's 16. Being comprised of rare and previously unissued Sun masters otherwise available only on the Perkins box, Rounder's *Honky Tonk Gal* serves as a complementary disc to the Sun hits collections. — D.M.

STEVE PERRY

★★½ **Street Talk (Columbia, 1984)**
Steve Perry of Journey helped shape the power ballad mold with his 1984 solo hit, "Oh Sherrie," and that is *Street Talk*'s primary recommendation. — M.C.

THE PERSUASIONS

★★★½ **A Capella (1968; Enigma/Retro, 1989)**
★★½ **We Came to Play (Capitol, 1971)**
★★★ **Street Corner Symphony (Capitol, 1972)**
★★★½ **Spread the Word (Capitol, 1972)**
★★★½ **We Still Ain't Got No Band (MCA, 1973)**
★★½ **More Than Before (A&M, 1974)**
★★½ **I Just Want to Sing With My Friends (A&M, 1974)**
★★★★ **Chirpin' (Elektra, 1977)**
★★★ **Comin' at Ya (Flying Fish, 1979)**
★★½ **Good News (Rounder, 1983)**
★★★ **No Frills (Rounder, 1986)**

Formed in 1962, the Persuasions continue to find success—through smart song selection, hard touring and sheer perseverance—performing doo-wop. Coming together in Brooklyn, New York, they began early to formulate the mix of R&B and gospel standards that remains their selling card. These days, bass singer Jimmy Hayes is still their ace, but it's the grit in baritone Jerry Lawson's delivery that saves the quartet from devolving into the funky barber-shopping doo-wop can become.

Such recent work as *No Frills* (1986) finds them in classic form, taking elegant turns on "Under the Boardwalk" and "I Wonder Do You Love the Lord Like I Do." *Chirpin'* is

the definitive Persuasions, featuring the genre's signature tune, "Lookin' for an Echo." Consistency marks their catalog, almost all of which is worthwhile. Their gospel standout is *Spread the Word*, their funkiest, *We Still Ain't Got No Band*.
— P.E.

PETER, PAUL AND MARY

★★★ **Peter, Paul and Mary (Warner Bros., 1962)**
★★ **Moving (1963; Warner Bros., 1989)**
★★★ **In the Wind (Warner Bros., 1963)**
★★★½ **Peter, Paul and Mary in Concert (Warner Bros., 1964)**
★★★ **A Song Will Rise (1965; Warner Bros., 1990)**
★★★ **See What Tomorrow Brings (Warner Bros., 1965)**
★★★ **The Peter, Paul and Mary Album (1966; Warner Bros., 1991)**
★★★½ **Album 1700 (Warner Bros., 1967)**
★★ **Late Again (Warner Bros., 1968)**
★★ **Peter, Paul and Mommy (Warner Bros., 1969)**
★★★½ **The Best of Peter, Paul and Mary (Ten Years Together) (Warner Bros., 1970)**
★★ **Reunion (Warner Bros., 1978)**
★★½ **No Easy Walk to Freedom (Gold Castle, 1986)**
★★½ **A Holiday Celebration (Gold Castle, 1988)**
★★★ **Flowers and Stones (Gold Castle, 1990)**

Carefully enunciating their lyrics while radiating an intelligent, unthreatening hipness, Peter Yarrow, Paul Stookey and Mary Travers were folk popularizers whose early gift was teasing a mainstream audience slightly leftward into music more rootsy than AM radio and indirectly into politics of an earnest liberal stripe. Engaging, very careful performers—the blonde Travers looked bohemian but freshly scrubbed, the boys kept their goatees trimmed—PP&M helped gain exposure for Dylan and Eric Andersen, for traditional folk and blues. Very successful in their heyday, they now seem mainly of pedagogical interest—although almost all of their records are pleasant.

The trio's first record inspired countless college singers with its easy folk standards ("500 Miles," "If I Had a Hammer") and smooth versions of Pete Seeger's "Where Have All the Flowers Gone," Will Holt's "Lemon Tree" and the Rev. Gary Davis's "If I Had My Way." *Moving* was slighter, although it gave PP&M a giant hit in "Puff,

the Magic Dragon"—at the time, some
hysterics considered the sweet ditty an
encoded marijuana manifesto. The 1964 live
set perhaps best captures their early
moment—Dylan's "The Times They Are
a'Changin' " is emblematic of PP&M's
gently prophetic role; "Le Deserteur"
reveals their more artful inclinations; "Oh,
Rock My Soul" reflects their interest in
spirituals; "Single Girl" is almost pop; and
the 12 minutes of Paul's comedy routine,
while only mildly amusing, underscores the
group's indefatigable insistence on
entertaining. Their reverent intro to Dylan's
"Blowin' in the Wind" now seems quaint; at
the time, it may well have been stirring.

With a nice take on "Motherless Child,"
A Song Will Rise helped introduce future
Peace Corps volunteers to the blues; and
with help from Paul Butterfield, Paul Winter
and Harvey Brooks, *Album 1700*
emancipated PP&M from the guitars-only
purism of their early work. The latter
album's John Denver song, "Leaving on a
Jet Plane" was the first PP&M hit that
sounded deliberately commercial; Yarrow's
"Weep for Jamie" and Stookey's "No Other
Name" were two of their finer originals; and
while "I Dig Rock and Roll Music" hardly
sounded like Gene Vincent, its spirit was
appreciated.

The rest of the PP&M catalog is skillful,
undemanding folk pop. Of their later
reunion efforts, *Flowers and Stones* is
actually quite strong, with good versions of
Dylan's "I Shall Be Released" and "The
Last Thing On My Mind." — P.E.

PET SHOP BOYS
★ ★ ★   **Please (EMI/America, 1986)**
★ ★½   **Disco (EMI/America, 1986)**
★ ★ ★   **Actually (1987;EMI/Manhattan, 1988)**
★ ★ ★½   **Introspective (EMI/Manhattan, 1988)**
★ ★ ★ ★   **Behavior (EMI, 1990)**
★ ★ ★ ★   **The Pet Shop Boys Discography: The Complete Singles Collection (EMI, 1991)**

When "West End Girls" became a hit in
1986, this London-based pair of disco
fanatics already seemed destined for the
one-hit wonder bin. Intentionally so,
perhaps: the combination of vocalist Neil
Tennant's arch, high-nasal delivery and his
background as a rock journalist smacked of
overly self-conscious manipulation.
Surprisingly, *Please* expands on the wry
hookiness of that breakthrough, and the Pet
Shop Boys haven't looked back since. Each

successive album sounds broader and more
sure of itself. *Actually* deepens the droll,
subversive tone of the debut on ditties like
"Rent," though the dream duet with Dusty
Springfield ("What Have I Done to Deserve
This") clearly opens new melodic horizons
for both Tennant and keyboard-and-tape
man Chris Lowe. *Introspective* is an
ambitious sampler of dance-floor trends;
Lowe mixes hot Latin hip-hop, high-energy
camp and the ominous bass-blur of house,
while Tennant screws up his courage and
actually sings the politically charged club hit
"It's Alright." His cover version isn't half as
soulful as the original by Blaze, but it's a
satisfying album closer nonetheless.

Behavior leaves the dance floor behind;
Lowe fashions a richly synthesized backdrop
from swatches of adult-contemporary pop,
old film scores and even classical music.
Tennant's singing continues to improve,
though the newfound breadth of his
songwriting is what makes *Behavior* such a
keeper. Ruminative cuts like "Being Boring"
and "This Must Be the Place" evoke
suburban adolescence and its discontents
with a fond, unsparing eye: zeroing in on
personal revelations, these complex and
sophisticated songs also offer insight on
universal concerns. *The Pet Shop Boys
Discography* illustrates how the duo have
gone from commenting on pop's inherent
limitations to stretching its boundaries.
— M.C.

TOM PETTY AND THE HEARTBREAKERS
★ ★ ★   **Tom Petty and the Heartbreakers (Shelter, 1976)**
★ ★ ★   **You're Gonna Get It (Shelter, 1978)**
★ ★ ★ ★   **Damn the Torpedoes (Backstreet/MCA, 1979)**
★ ★ ★½   **Hard Promises (Backstreet/MCA, 1981)**
★ ★ ★½   **Long After Dark (Backstreet/MCA, 1982)**
★ ★ ★ ★½   **Southern Accents (MCA, 1985)**
★ ★ ★½   **Pack Up the Plantation: Live! (MCA, 1985)**
★ ★ ★½   **"Let Me Up (I've Had Enough)" (MCA, 1987)**
★ ★ ★½   **Into the Great Wide Open (MCA, 1991)**

TOM PETTY SOLO
★ ★ ★ ★   **Full Moon Fever (MCA, 1989)**

A rocker of major stature, Florida's Tom
Petty gains richness by adhering to two
traditions—for power, he returns to the rock
& roll fundamentalism of the Rolling

Stones; for grace, the Byrds' folk rock. While R.E.M. and many others have since mined the style of McGuinn and company, Petty and the Heartbreakers were the earliest of the revivalists. An extremely fertile influence, McGuinn provided not only a trademark 12-string elegance but the moving, nasal vocal style Petty sometimes almost eerily mimics—through the Byrds, too, Petty reaches back to their precursors, Dylan and the Beatles. On occasion, his later work has echoed the bluesy grit of Southern rock, and there have been country overtones as well, but Petty is distinctive primarily for holding with fierce faith to his early inspirations and forming from them music that's very much his own.

With co-writer/guitarist Mike Campbell providing precise leads and Benmont Tench updating *Blonde on Blonde*'s keyboards, the Heartbreakers' debut laid the foundation for the Petty sound, the record's standouts being the Stones-ish "Breakdown" and the Byrds-like "American Girl." *You're Gonna Get It* wasn't quite so confident, but on only their third time out, the band achieved a near masterpiece in *Damn the Torpedoes*. All of Petty's albums begin with a flourish: the trio of "Refugee," "Here Comes My Girl" and "Even the Losers" is the best example. A new sense of compassion enlivens the lyrics; "Louisiana Rain" is an early example of the big, atmospheric ballad Petty soon would perfect; and aggressive self-confidence pervades the record.

Hard Promises didn't have *Torpedoes'* cohesiveness but, in "The Waiting," "A Woman in Love (It's Not Me)" and "The Insider" (a duet with Stevie Nicks), it featured some very fine songs. *Long After Dark* continued in the same vein, with the band proving its strong consistency. With *Southern Accents* came a breakthrough. Petty's best record, this adamant statement of Southern identity was backed up with rock & roll of nearly the sweep and ease of the Stones' *Exile on Main Street*. Seldom had a horn section been employed so effectively in a basic rock context, and a number of songs showed new stylistic range—the fine country-ish "Spike," the passable funk of "It Ain't Nothin' to Me" and the sweeping balladry of "The Best of Everything."

Looser and easier, *Let Me Up* revealed a band now secure enough to assemble a set of smart and varied songs that rocked with a casual, jamming power. A pair of love songs tinged with regret and bitterness, "Think About Me" and "It'll All Work

Out," were the most affecting numbers. While it still featured Campbell and, to a lesser degree, Tench, *Full Moon Fever* was Petty's solo album—and the pop influence of ex–E.L.O. leader (and Beatle fanatic) Jeff Lynne was apparent. A year before its release, Petty and Lynne had banded together with Dylan, George Harrison, and Roy Orbison in the ad hoc supergroup, the Traveling Wilburys—and Petty-Lynne became a songwriting team. Petty's best single, "Free Fallin' " kicks off the record, and while its spare beauty recalls vintage Heartbreakers, much of the rest of the material has a lightness the band's work does not possess. "Zombie Zoo" is downright whimsical, and the lullaby "Alright for Now" just misses sounding cute, but overall *Moon* sounds both fresh and commanding. Reunited with the Heartbreakers on *Into the Great Wide Open*, Petty brought Lynne aboard—along with some of the buoyancy that enlivens their partnership. With acoustic guitars to the fore, and a new air of ease, this was Petty at his most relaxed—and sounding no less immediate for all his ripened assurance. — P.E.

P FUNK ALL STARS
★★★★ **Urban Dancefloor Guerrillas (Uncle Jam/CBS Associated, 1983)**
It looks like a quickie, but don't be fooled. What probably began as yet another cosmic jam session winds up as a radiant statement of purpose—"a declaration of interdependence," in the words of auteur d'funk George Clinton. He knows how to get the best out of his dependents, too: Bootsy Collins, Walter "Junie" Morrison, Gary Shider, Eddie Hazel, Michael Hampton, Fred Wesley and Maceo Parker all contribute to the groove. Clinton even lights a fire under Sly Stone's butt. Their effervescent collaboration "Catch a Keeper" sinks its synthesized hooks in deep. On the second half, the entire crew stretches out and gets busy: "Pumpin' It Up," slowly coolin' it down, and then "Pumpin' It Up" to a climax. Former Spinners lead voice Philipe Wynne powers "Hydraulic Pump"; it turned out to be one of his last recordings, but that's the only sad note on *Urban Dancefloor Guerrillas*. — M.C.

ESTHER PHILLIPS
★★★ **From a Whisper to a Scream (Kudu/CBS, 1972)**
★★★ **What a Diff'rence a Day Makes (Kudu/CBS, 1975)**
★★★★ **Confessin' the Blues (Atlantic, 1976)**

★ ★ ★ **The Best of Esther Phillips**
(Kudu/CBS, NA)
★ ★ ★ **The Complete Savoy Recordings with**
Johnny Otis (Savoy, NA)

A versatile stylist rooted in blues and classic pop, Esther Phillips achieved her first acclaim as Little Esther while working with Johnny Otis's troupe in the early '50s. Still in her teens when she recorded with Otis and Mel Walker, Phillips notched eight Top Ten R&B hits between 1950 and 1952, the career-launcher being "Double Crossing Blues," a Number One single in 1950. Illness forced her into retirement, though, in 1954; when she returned to performing and recording, she cut some interesting sides for Atlantic before being waylaid by heroin addiction and undergoing treatment.

Her second comeback, in the '70s, found her recording for Kudu Records, where one of the best records in her long career, a cover of Gil Scott-Heron's antidrug screed, "Home Is Where the Hatred Is," hit the Top Forty of the R&B charts. She finally returned to the pop charts in 1975 with a quavering, stark reading of the classic "What a Diff'rence a Day Makes" that was a major disco hit and rose to Number 20 on the pop chart. *Best of* is the definitive Phillips sampling from these years, although *From a Whisper to a Scream* and *What a Diff'rence a Day Makes* have virtues. These albums, as well as her late-'70s sides for Mercury (now out of print) are in a more commercial jazz-pop vein, but Phillips's edgy attack keeps everything from sliding into mush.

A 1976 Atlantic release, *Confessin' the Blues*, is the single most complete overview of Phillips's many moods. Comprised of one side of new studio takes and one live side from the artist's 1970 Atlantic album *Burnin'*, *Confessin'* takes Phillips through 12-bar blues, jazz, and pop in a series of performances that are by turns amusing, bittersweet and heart-rending. — D.M.

WILSON PICKETT
★ ★ ★ ★ **The Best of Wilson Pickett**
(Atlantic, 1984)
★ ★ ★½ **American Soul Man (Motown,**
1987)
★ ★ ★ ★ **Greatest Hits (Atlantic, 1987)**
★ ★ ★ ★ ★ **A Man and a Half: The Best of**
Wilson Pickett (Rhino/Atlantic,
1992)

Wilson Pickett's R&B wasn't the blowtorch burst of almost surreal funk that James Brown invented, nor did it boast Otis Redding's gorgeous melodicism, but it was the most insistently earthy of all soul music.

Flourishing the persona of an ultra-stud, "The Wicked Pickett" coaxed fierce energy out of the great Muscle Shoals players, and "In the Midnight Hour," "Land of 1,000 Dances," "Mustang Sally," "Funky Broadway" and "I'm a Midnight Mover" remain some of the most urgent singles ever released. Staccato horn parts and surging bass lines were key to the sound, but it was Pickett's growling style that made the records hot—every note he sang was propulsive. "Hey Jude" proved that Pickett could tackle ballads, too. For a while in the mid-'70s, he sounded confused, but at the end of the decade, he reemerged with at least some of his trademark fury. *The Best of* and *Greatest Hits* provide his essential music, but for the ultimate anthology of Pickett's explosive work, *A Man and a Half* is crucial. — P.E.

WEBB PIERCE
★ ★ ★ **The Best of Webb Pierce (1968;**
MCA, 1987)
★ ★ **C&W (Plantation, 1976)**
★ ★ **Golden Hits (Plantation, 1976)**
★ ★ **Golden Hits, Vol. 2 (Plantation,**
1976)
★ ★ ★ ★ **The Wondering Boy, 1951–1958**
(Bear Family, 1989)

One of the most popular of all country singers in the 1950s, Webb Pierce influenced the sound of modern country music by being the first to use a pedal steel guitar in his songs, and also ennobled the literature of country music with his own observations on drinkin', cheatin', lovin' and runnin' afoul of the law. "I Ain't Never," "I'm in the Jailhouse Now," "Tupelo County Jail," "I Don't Care," "There Stands the Glass," "Back Street Affair" and other Pierce recordings from the '50s are no-compromise classics of the genre. A dedicated honky-tonk artist, Pierce steered clear of production gloss for the most part and stayed true to the hard-edged sound that best suited his style. Even though its songs are remakes of the originals, the MCA *Best of Webb Pierce* contains the essential songs by which Pierce will be remembered. Pierce devotees, though, will prefer the Bear Family four-CD box set, *The Wondering Boy, 1951–1958*, containing 114 songs, including duets with the Wilburn Brothers, Kitty Wells and Red Sovine, and carrying a hefty price tag. — D.M.

PINK FAIRIES
★ ★ ★½ **Kings of Oblivion (Polydor, 1973)**

The Pink Fairies thrash out a distinctly British variant on the loud, high-energy sound of Detroit rock & roll on the long-forgotten romp, *Kings of Oblivion*. Predecessor to Motörhead, the Pink Fairies will entice unreconstructed punks and thrash fans alike.

PINK FLOYD

★★★★	**The Piper at the Gates of Dawn** (Capitol, 1967)	
★★★	**A Saucerful of Secrets** (Capitol, 1968)	
★★★½	**Ummagumma** (Capitol, 1969)	
★★	**More** (Capitol, 1969)	
★★	**Atom Heart Mother** (Capitol, 1970)	
★★★½	**Meddle** (Capitol, 1971)	
★★★½	**Relics** (Capitol, 1971)	
★★	**Obscured by Clouds** (Capitol, 1972)	
★★★★★	**Dark Side of the Moon** (Capitol, 1973)	
★★★★★	**Wish You Were Here** (Columbia, 1975)	
★★★	**Animals** (Columbia, 1977)	
★★★★	**The Wall** (Columbia, 1979)	
★★★★	**A Collection of Great Dance Songs** (Columbia, 1981)	
★★★	**Works** (Capitol, 1983)	
★★★	**The Final Cut** (Columbia, 1983)	
★★½	**A Momentary Lapse of Reason** (Columbia, 1987)	
★★	**Delicate Sound of Thunder** (Columbia, 1988)	

Pink Floyd emerged in 1965, comprising Great Britain's answer to the San Franciscan psychedelic revolution. This quartet could fill a ballroom with swirling atmospheric feedback, no question, though lead guitarist and singer Syd Barrett's lysergic explorations stem from folk and pop roots rather than the blues. Instead of jamming like its American peers, Pink Floyd seems to lose it on *The Piper at the Gates of Dawn*'s adventuresome tracks. "Astronomy Domine" and "Interstellar Overdrive" slip off into free-floating noiseplay, dramatically cohering again at just the right moment. Barrett exhibits a knack for writing pretty little ditties that can turn into unhinged sonic ruminations when you least expect it. *Piper's* slightly addled air of inspiration is genuine; the singularly talented Barrett became rock's most notorious chemical casualty not long after its release. Recruiting guitarist David Gilmour, the remainder of the band (bassist Roger Waters, keyboardist Rick Wright, drummer Nick Mason) carried on after Barrett's departure.

A Saucerful of Secrets continues the freakouts, though Waters's emergent songwriting voice surfaces on the eerie "Set the Controls for the Heart of the Sun." Gradually, David Gilmour asserts a fresh musical personality into Floyd's mix: his probing solos and coherent tone are a far cry indeed from Barrett's hyperkinetic, unpredictable outbursts. On the rambling double album *Ummagumma*, Pink Floyd assembles the raw material from which *Dark Side of the Moon* will later emerge. Sound-effect collages here, brooding elongated versions of early material there: it took Pink Floyd a while to reduce these elements into a readily accessible blend. *Atom Heart Mother* is an orchestrated, conventional art-rock mess—Pink Floyd's only trip down this dead-end road. The two soundtrack albums (*More* and *Obscured by Clouds*) are failed attempts to soften the Floyd attack with folk-rock influences.

Meddle is far more hard-edged and (slightly) more song-oriented than *Ummagumma*. It revolves around "Echoes," a slow-building, side-long psychedelic set-piece. Even without a lightshow, this epic still wields considerable transportative powers. The concert movie *Pink Floyd at Pompeii* was shot around this time; that version of "Echoes" captures Floyd at its trippiest. *Relics* is a surprisingly packed odds 'n' sods collection that includes two Barrett-era gems: the British hit single "See Emily Play" and the proto-glitter ode "Arnold Layne."

Dark Side of the Moon is Pink Floyd's commercial-meets-conceptual equinox. All the extra-musical weirdness gets reduced into a strong, orderly set of songs. Cunning little details like the cash-register ring on "Money" or the alarm-clock buzz on "Time" actually enhance their surroundings. That's indicative of Floyd's newfound focus and discipline; so are the catchy chorus and Waters's pointed lyrics. Even the spare, distinctive packaging reflects the clarity and precision of the music. A certain distance— and chill—results, too. There's a faint above-it-all air to the sound of this masterpiece, and to the substance of Waters's pronouncements about humanity. Arguably, *Wish You Were Here* is warmer and more approachable than *Dark Side*. The previous record's dynamic contrasts are smoothed out in a suite ("Shine On You Crazy Diamond") interrupted by related songs. The band confidently moves through space rock and lite jazz-fusion sections, the haunting central theme never far out of consciousness. "Welcome to the Machine" introduces Waters's fascination with pessimistic sci-fi views of the future. There lies Pink Floyd's future, too.

The Orwell-inspired allegory of *Animals* isn't nearly as involving, though the music sighs and surges exactly according to plan. David Gilmour's relaxed guitar lines—lyrical and stinging—come to dominate the Floyd horizon at this point. Ironically, *The Wall* is where Roger Waters virtually assumes control of the group. This double-album narrative spawned Pink Floyd's biggest hit ("Another Brick in the Wall"); many people hear it as the fulfillment of previous ambitions. If you're not inclined to listen with the indecipherable liner notes in hands, however, you may wish this convoluted story included a couple more guitar-baited hooks like "Comfortably Numb."

The Final Cut articulates Waters's anti-war theme well enough, but at this point Floyd's studious high-tech approach begins to sound antiseptic and hidebound. Waters then left—the parting was acrimonious—but the remaining trio valiantly carried on with *A Momentary Lapse of Reason* and the live *Delicate Sound of Thunder*. They shouldn't have bothered. Even though Waters's presence had become overbearing, his absence reduces Pink Floyd to an FM rock oldies act (at best) or a lumbering self-parody (at worst). The group remains a cash cow, of course. The conceptual tilt of Pink Floyd's best work makes compilation a tough job; Capitol's *Works* is woefully spotty, but Columbia's *A Collection of Great Dance Songs* (with "Money" and "Another Brick") makes for one great driving album. — M.C.

GENE PITNEY
★ ★ ★ ★ **Anthology (1961–1968) (Rhino, 1986)**

Along with Johnnie Ray and Roy Orbison, Gene Pitney was one of pop's great sufferers: almost his entire, vast canon consists of weeping and wailing. But if Orbison's melodramatic hurt was grand and earned, and Ray's pathological and forced, the cute Pitney's lush pain seemed almost winsome, a theatrical sobbing for strange, sheerly musical effect. Its emotionalism laid on with a trowel, his voice is pretty intriguing and eccentrically pretty.

Debuting during the early-'60s rock & roll hiatus that came after early Elvis and before the Beatles, Pitney careened wildly between pathos and bathos. He never hit the smarmy lows of the period's worst exemplar, Bobby Vinton; yet he was miles away, too, from the swagger of its minor monarch, Bobby Darin. Collaborating in turn with Phil Spector and Burt Bacharach, Pitney staked

out his own wounded ground: sweeping, orchestral singles that forefronted the baroque quiver of his trebly, sometimes falsetto, pleading.

With his 1961 debut single, "(I Wanna) Love My Life Away," the then–college student wrote the song himself, multitracked his voice 12 times and played all the instruments in the arrangement. A trademark style soon evolved and whether tricked out in the ersatz Western trappings of "(The Man Who Shot) Liberty Valance" and "Town Without Pity" or the mariachi theater of "24 Hours From Tulsa," the effect was of B-grade, queasily moving, cinematic excess. In 1964 the Rolling Stones gave "That Girl Belongs to Yesterday" to Pitney when they discovered that some of the Beatles' big money came from writing originals: the first Jagger-Richard song ever to hit the U.S. charts, it's a not-bad Spector-ish tidbit. Later that same year, Pitney unleashed Mann-Weill's "I'm Gonna Be Strong"—it's definitive, heartbreakingly Pitney.

More curiosities soon followed. Driven by apt instinct toward the hammy glory of operatic bel canto, Pitney began recording in Italian; these albums are out of print, as is the rest of Pitney's original recordings. Searching around for an actual C&W collaborator, he unerringly teamed up with moody extremist George Jones on *Famous Country Duets* and *It's Country Time*; both albums are worth searching for. The masterful Rhino *Anthology* includes all the singles listed above; it's a heady, if somewhat guilty, pleasure. What's up with Pitney now is uncertain although his genius would provide soundtrack shudders for a John Waters flick. — P.E.

THE PIXIES
★ ★ ★ **Come on Pilgrim (EP) (4AD/Rough Trade, 1987)**
★ ★ ★ **Surfer Rosa (4AD/Rough Trade, 1988)**
★ ★ ★½ **Doolittle (4AD/Elektra, 1989)**
★ ★ ★½ **Bossanova (4AD/Elektra, 1990)**
★ ★ ★ **Trompe Le Monde (4AD/Elektra, 1991)**

The Pixies are college rock personified. This Boston quartet built a rep on the late-'80s alternative circuit with its tuneful blend of cheerfully incoherent lyrics and cheezy, distorted guitar riffs. The Pixies shuffle fuzzy power chords and textural strumming around itchy ditties and halting melodies. *Surfer Rosa* brings the noise; the subsequent, far more coherent Pixies albums don't commercialize so much as clarify the band's foggy notions. *Doolittle* sharpens the guitars' impact without sacrificing the loopy edge of lead screamer Black Francis. Drummer David Lovering supplies the Pixies with a stronger four-on-the-floor than most of the competing pack, and bassist Kim Deal's vocal implants lend a refreshing breeze to "Here Comes Your Man." The catchy mayhem ("Gouge Away") and cryptic fury sound insular after a while, though. The crinkly, sunburned buzz of *Bossanova* seems like a step in the right direction: it's anti-surf music, the Walkman soundtrack for a pale-faced, black-clad bohemian's day at the beach. *Trompe Le Monde* moves backward into fields of Velvet guitar-grunge—either a bold return to form or a distressing retrenchment, depending on your point of view. These big-time fringe-rock avatars resemble a late-'70s heavy-metal outfit: okay, but nowhere near as dangerous—or as bad—as they're supposed to be. — M.C.

ROBERT PLANT
★★★½ **Pictures at 11 (Swan Song, 1982)**
★★★½ **The Principle of Moments (Es Paranza, 1983)**
★★★½ **Shaken 'n' Stirred (Es Paranza, 1985)**
★★★ **Now and Zen (Es Paranza, 1988)**
★★★½ **Manic Nirvana (Es Paranza, 1990)**
WITH THE HONEYDRIPPERS
★★★ **Volume One (EP) (Es Paranza, 1984)**

Though guitarist Jimmy Page is widely credited as the brains behind Led Zeppelin, brawny vocalist Robert Plant has proven to be a far more reliable solo artist. Plant runs a taut ship, steering his bands into fresh territory without ever losing sight of his past. In fact, his most Zeppelin-heavy solo album (*Now and Zen*) is the weakest of the lot. Fans of that band will find a feast on the early-'80s albums, however. *Pictures at 11* boasts two cavernous crushers; on "Burning Down One Side" and "Worse Than Detroit," guitarist Robbie Blunt pierces Plant's molten lava cries with peels of thunder. *The Principle of Moments* spawned two hits in 1983; the floating art rock of "Big Log" and the warm R&B nostalgia of "In the Mood" neatly represent Plant's diverse interests. As Album Oriented Radio began to fade in the mid-'80s, Plant opted for his eclectic mode. *Shaken 'n' Stirred* mixes strong doses of hip-hop beats and world rhythms into Plant's rock cocktails on tracks like "Hip to Hoo,"

"Kallalou" and "Too Loud." Even the familiar-sounding rockers ("Little by Little," "Easily Lead") benefit from the judicious addition of sythesizers to the guitar-led strut. The Honeydrippers' *Volume One* is a one-off EP of vintage soul and R&B covers; excessive orchestrations distract from Plant's restrained interpretations, while the guest hotshots (Jimmy Page, Jeff Beck, Nile Rodgers) are underutilized.

Quoting Led Zep throughout and featuring a crisp Page solo on "Tall Cool One," *Now and Zen* is the only time Robert Plant appears to be treading water. (Sampling your own records doesn't count as innovation.) Thankfully, his next album suggests that Plant merely had to break in a new band. On *Manic Nirvana*, he confidently skips from jumpin' boogie ("Hurting Kind [I've Got My Eyes on You]") to brutal funk metal ("Nirvana"), to sardonic psychedelia ("Tie Die on the Highway") and to gale-force blooze wailing ("Your Ma Said You Cried in Your Sleep Last Night"), and the young players keep up. Too bad Plant's legions of imitators haven't copied his adventurous spirit. — M.C.

THE PLATTERS
★★★★ **The Platters: Anthology (Rhino, 1986)**
★★★★★ **The Magic Touch: Platters Anthology (Polygram, 1991)**

In the end the story of the Platters comes down to two dominant personalities, lead singer Tony Williams, and the group's manager-songwriter-producer, Buck Ram. The four original male members of the group were working as parking lot attendants when Ram, a successful songwriter, began using them to record demos of his material. One of those demos, a song called "Only You (and You Alone)," landed the group a recording contract with Mercury in 1955. Shortly thereafter the Platters, as the quartet (soon to be a quintet with the addition of female vocalist Zola Taylor) was dubbed, had a Top Ten hit, the first in a career that remained commercially viable into the late '60s. Recording consistently between 1955 and 1961, the Platters placed 20 records in the Top Forty during this period, and saw four of those top the pop chart.

Williams's soaring, melodramatic tenor leads defined the Platters. Stylistically he was beholden to the Ink Spots' Bill Kenny and the Ravens' two outstanding tenors, Maithe Marshall and Joe Van Loan, taking from Kenny an unerring sense of the dramatic and from Marshall and Van Loan great instincts for control-and-release. Kenny can also be seen as Williams's forebear in terms of the great dignity with which he delivered a lyric, but one might justifiably point to two superior R&B vocalists of the early '50s, Billy Eckstine and Bobby "Blue" Bland, as having informed Williams's approach as well. As rougher-edged R&B gained a greater foothold among young white rock & roll fans and evolved into soul in the '60s, Williams's style of vocalist fell out of favor. Still, Williams and the Platters did help kick open pop music charts that had been racially segregated, and their broad-based appeal was yet another signal in the '50s that a change was gonna come.

Like many of the vocal groups of their time, the Platters combined original material (mostly written by Ram) with popular songs from decades past. Back-to-back Number One singles in 1958 were "Twilight Time," a Top Twenty hit for the Three Suns in 1944, and "Smoke Gets in Your Eyes," a Jerome Kern tune that had been a Number One single in 1933 for Paul Whiteman and His Orchestra. "Harbor Lights," a Top Ten single for the Platters in 1960, dates back to 1937, when it was also a Top Ten single for Frances Langford. It's a measure of Ram's artistry that his own songs compare favorably to these classic American pop entries. The first three songs Ram wrote for the Platters in 1955–56 display a sophistication in both lyric and melody and were well in advanced of most of the romantic pablum then directed at teenagers. One of those Ram efforts, "The Great Pretender" was a Number One single, while the other two, "Only You" and "The Magic Touch," peaked at Number Five and Number Four, respectively.

Just as Ram and Williams represent the twin poles of the Platters' success, so do they represent the dissolution of that success. Williams went solo in 1960 and never had a hit on his own; the Platters continued recording but failed to enter the Top Ten again, although several singles featuring Sonny Turner as lead singer made the Top Forty, the last one coming in 1967, "With This Ring." In the '70s Ram and Williams opposed each other in a legal action over the rights to the group's name. Ram won the case, and after that both he and Williams put groups out on the road bearing the Platters name, thus soiling the group's proud history.

Anthology hits the high points of the Platters' career, but the *Magic Touch* two-CD set offers a more comprehensive overview (with complete annotation) and chronicles the Platters' history from beginning to end, including a Tony Williams solo track. To call it an overwhelming emotional experience is to trivialize it; to say it is simply great music is to best appreciate the magnitude of the Platters' achievement.
— D.M.

POCO

★ ★ ★ **Pickin' Up the Pieces (Epic, 1969)**
★ ★ ★ **Poco (Epic, 1970)**
★ ★½ **Deliverin' (Epic, 1971)**
★ ★½ **From the Inside (Epic, 1971)**
★ ★ ★ **A Good Feelin' to Know (Epic, 1972)**
★ ★½ **Crazy Eyes (Epic, 1973)**
★ ★ **Seven (Epic, 1974)**
★ ★ **Cantamos (Epic, 1974)**
★ ★ ★ **The Very Best of Poco (Epic, 1975)**
★ ★ **Head Over Heels (ABC, 1975)**
★ ★ **Indian Summer (ABC, 1977)**
★ ★½ **Legend (ABC, 1978)**
★ ★ **Under the Gun (MCA, 1980)**
★ ★½ **Crazy Loving: The Best of Poco 1975–1982 (MCA, 1989)**
★ **Legacy (RCA, 1989)**
★ ★ ★½ **Poco: The Forgotten Trail 1969–74 (Epic/Legacy, 1990)**

Guitarist Richie Furay and bassist Jim Messina followed their country longings after Buffalo Springfield split up in 1968. With pedal-steel guitarist Rusty Young in tow, they formed Poco. *Pickin' Up the Pieces*, now out of print, sets their agenda: high-end harmonies cut from the CSN cloth, a concentration on upbeat love songs and let's-get-mellow rallying cries rather than hard-core honky-tonk heartbreak and tales of everyday life. The members of Poco are competent-plus pickers and singers, but their take on country music is superficial, at best. Mostly, Poco deploys country implements at a crisp rock pace: adding an extra twang to folkish melodies of varying quality. The early albums all sport a gentle hook or two—snagging listeners with a mellow soft spot. Messina left for greener pastures after *Deliverin'*, a stop-gap live album with a couple of lively tracks. Furay departed following *A Good Feeling to Know*; despite the gush of its lyrics, that soaring title track is probably Poco's most spirited performance. Rusty Young soldiered Poco through the mid- 70's. Subsequent albums for Epic (*Crazy Eyes*, *Cantamos* and *Seven*, all deleted), ABC and MCA have little to recommend them. Poco scored a pop hit with "Crazy Love" in 1979. Otherwise, the group's latter-day obscurity is richly deserved.

However, Poco's Epic anthology (*The Forgotten Trail*) marks a minor rediscovery. Two CDs cover this journeyman band's breadth and length without overdoing it: focusing on the fruitful first half of the '70s, separating the wheat from the chaff. Maybe *The Forgotten Trail* can erase the stale taste of *Legacy*—this 1989 reunion of the 1969 lineup centers around a Richard Marx–penned power ballad. — M.C.

THE POGUES

★★½ **Red Roses for Me (1984; Enigma, 1986)**
★★★½ **Rum, Sodomy & the Lash (MCA, 1985)**
★★ **Poguetry in Motion (EP) (MCA, 1986)**
★★★ **If I Should Fall From Grace With God (Island, 1988)**
★★½ **Peace and Love (Island, 1989)**
★½ **Yeah, Yeah, Yeah, Yeah, Yeah (EP) (Island, 1990)**
★★★ **Hell's Ditch (Island, 1990)**
★★ **Essential Pogues (Island, 1991)**

Sounding like a cross between the Clancy Brothers and the Clash, the Pogues are a rollicking, rowdy, drunken brawl of a band. At its best, the group is a marvel, matching the tuneful spirit of traditional Irish folk with near-poetic lyrics and a straight-to-hell punk attitude. More often, though, the group comes across as loutish buffoons, a sort of musical Pat and Mike routine portraying Irish culture as little more than drunken dissolution.

There's more than a hint of that on *Red Roses for Me*, particularly on Shane McGowan's self-satisfied "Streams of Whiskey" and "The Boys From County Hell." But the traditional tunes—raucous ravers like "Waxie's Dargle"—tip the balance in the band's favor, showing off the fervor that gave the band its name (shortened from the Gaelic "poguemahone," or "kiss my ass") and reputation. But it's the Elvis Costello–produced *Rum, Sodomy and the Lash* that proves there's more to the Pogues than a bad reputation. Granted, the album's best songs are both covers (Ewan MacColl's lovely "Dirty Old Town" and Eric Bogle's chilling, anti-war tune "And the Band Played Waltzing Mathilda"), and McGowan still at times comes across as a second-rate Tom Waits. But when he hits his mark, as on the swirling "The Sick Bed

of Cuchulainn," it's worth indulging his excesses.

After *Poguetry in Motion*, an EP more noteworthy for its title than its music, the Pogues began self-mythologizing in earnest with *If I Should Fall From Grace with God*. That the cover photo uses trick editing to slip James Joyce into their ranks should tell you something of the Pogues' ambition; it's doubtful, though, that Joyce would have resorted to lyrics like "You scumbag/You maggot/You cheap lousy faggot." Still, "Turkish Song of the Damned" makes an interesting connection between Turkish tunes and Irish reels, but even that bit of experimentalism comes a cropper on *Peace and Love*, on which the band attempts to augment its Irish groove with unconvincing stabs at jazz, Caribbean and other non-Irish styles. *Yeah, Yeah, Yeah, Yeah, Yeah* is a lurch toward straight rock that's every bit as silly as the psychedelic title tune suggests, but *Hell's Ditch* is, if not a return to form, a reminder at least of the strengths that made the Pogues worth hearing in the first place. Indeed, should McGowan manage to write an album's worth of songs as good as "The Ghost of a Smile" or "The Sunny Side of the Street," this band might finally deliver on its potential. — J.D.C.

POI DOG PONDERING

★★ **Poi Dog Pondering (Columbia, 1989)**
★½ **Wishing Like a Mountain and Thinking Like the Sea (Columbia, 1990)**
★★★ **Volo Volo (Columbia, 1992)**

Hailing from Hawaii but based in Austin, Texas, Poi Dog Pondering gives new meaning to the term "sophomoric." Although the theory behind this combo—that the best way to avoid rock clichés is to mix your musical sources—seems sound enough, the actual music produced is annoyingly diffuse. *Poi Dog Pondering*, which combines the group's two indie EPs, has some memorable hooks, like the perky tin whistle melody that introduces "Living With the Dreaming Body," but more often than not the group hasn't a clue what to do with them. Worse, the lyrics are insufferably inane, a situation that actually gets worse with *Wishing Like a Mountain and Thinking Like the Sea*. On that album, the Poi Dogs put the "dip" in "hippie-dippy" through such peace-and-love piffle as "U-Li-La-Lu" and "Big Walk."

Fortunately, there's enough discipline to *Volo Volo* to ensure that the band's melodic instincts actually overcome its self-indulgence. And though the songs still seem silly at times, the best among them—"Jack Ass Ginger," for instance—should make most listeners excuse the band's mistakes. — J.D.C.

THE POINTER SISTERS

- ★ ★ ★   The Pointer Sisters (Blue Thumb/MCA, 1973)
- ★ ★ ★   Steppin' (Blue Thumb/MCA, 1975)
- ★ ★ ★ ★   Best of the Pointer Sisters (Blue Thumb/MCA, 1976)
- ★ ★ ★½   Energy (Planet, 1978)
- ★ ★ ★½   Special Things (Planet, 1980)
- ★ ★ ★½   Black & White (Planet, 1981)
- ★ ★ ★½   Break Out (Planet, 1984)
- ★ ★ ★   Contact (RCA, 1985)
- ★ ★ ★ ★   Greatest Hits (RCA, 1989)
- ★ ★½   Right Rhythm (Motown, 1990)

Bonnie, Ruth and Anita Pointer started off working as backup singers for various rock and soul groups in the late '60s. When younger sister June joined the group in '71, the Pointers headed off in a decidedly unique direction. Mixing jazzy scats and Andrews Sisters jive into funkified pop confections, the Pointer Sisters delighted hippies and squares alike. There's a solid musical foundation underneath the outrageous period costumes and campy feel."Yes We Can Can," from the debut album, reshuffles the New Orleans beat of Lee Dorsey's 1970 R&B hit without losing its essential, off-center kick. The Pointer Sisters' time-tripping experiments weren't always as successful, of course; the original Blue Thumb LPs are inconsistent. "How Long (Betcha' Got a Chick on the Side)," a hit from the deleted *Steppin'*, tosses the Pointers' flexible harmonies against an elastic, bass-plucking funk pulse. Also out of print, *The Best of the Pointer Sisters* (Blue Thumb, 1976) convincingly recaps Part One of the saga. Bonnie left the group in 1978, recording a solo album for Motown (*Bonnie Pointer*). The remaining sisters hooked up with producer Richard Perry—and vaulted into the present with a snazzy new sound.

The albums with Perry at the helm are even spottier than before; yet each one of these deleted items spawned an absolute killer single. *Energy* has a striking version of Bruce Springsteen's "Fire"; *Special Things* (1980) holds the radiant "He's So Shy"; *Black and White* contains the creeping "Slow Hand." *Break Out* disrupts that hits-plus-filler pattern; it's stuffed with vibrant dance grooves and stinging vocal performances. On "Jump (for My Love)," "I'm So Excited," and "Neutron Dance," the Pointer Sisters vie with a pinging electro-beat and emerge victorious. The sultry "Automatic" alone proves that machine-enhanced grooves don't have to neuter a song's romantic intent. *Break Out* is a surprisingly listenable blockbuster.

Subsequent efforts—both with Perry (the deleted *Contact*) and without him (*Right Rhythm*)—have been competent, but unremarkable. *Greatest Hits* tabulates the Pointers' modern period with special care; it's a consistent eye-opener. For once, the occasional remix heightens the impact of a familiar track, rather than deadening it. — M.C.

POISON

- ★   Look What the Cat Dragged In (Capitol, 1986)
- ★   Open Up and Say . . . Ahh! (Enigma/Capitol, 1988)
- ★ ★½   Flesh and Blood (Enigma/Capitol, 1990)
- ★ ★ ★   Swallow This Live (Capitol, 1991)

Poison's debut missed its targets—on "Play Dirty," the band couldn't quite clone AC/DC; "Let Me Go to the Show" lacked the buoyancy of Sweet. MTV made hits of *Open Up*'s "Fallen Angel," a pale lament about the perils of stardom, and "Every Rose Has Its Thorn," a fatuous, acoustic ballad. With *Flesh and Blood*, however, Poison masters its plastic form. "Something to Believe In" is Poison scaling heights of dim-wit portentousness. — P.E.

THE POLICE

- ★ ★ ★   Outlandos d'Amour (A&M, 1979)
- ★ ★ ★ ★   Reggatta de Blanc (A&M, 1979)
- ★ ★ ★ ★ ★   Zenyatta Mondatta (A&M, 1980)
- ★ ★ ★ ★½   Ghost In the Machine (A&M, 1981)
- ★ ★ ★ ★ ★   Synchronicity (A&M, 1983)
- ★ ★ ★ ★   Every Breath You Take: The Singles (A&M, 1986)

Unlike most aspiring punk rockers, who spent albums working their way up to basic instrumental competence, the Police came in at the other end of the spectrum. Founder Stewart Copeland, for instance, had previously drummed with the art-rock combo Curved Air, while guitarist Andy Summers was an alumnus of the jazzy progressive band Soft Machine; even bassist-vocalist Sting, though a provincial unknown, had cut his teeth in fusion bands. But because punk had more interest in passion than technical prowess, that kind of ability was useless to the band. So the Police traded overt flash for a sort of covert virtuosity, burying its talent within intricate rhythm arrangements and quietly complex reggae grooves.

What that led to still wasn't punk, of course, but neither was it like anything else in rock. *Outlandos d'Amour* merely hints at the possibilities, mixing jazzy reggae workouts like "Masoko Tanga" with predictable punk fare along the lines of "Born in the 50's." Nor is the band's pop potential fully manifest, though "Roxanne" (a Top Forty single), "So Lonely" and "Can't Stand Losing You" are obvious indicators of what was to come. Even so, it's not the melodic appeal of "The Bed's Too Big Without You" or "Message In a Bottle" that powers *Reggatta de Blanc*; it's the playing. Instead of the normal power-trio approach, in which the guitar provides the bulk of the sound while the drums and bass add rhythmic support, the Police invert the formula, letting Copeland's swirling polyrhythms lead the way while Sting's bass grounds the pulse and Summers's phased-and-flanged guitar adds color.

This sly twist on tradition put most of the band's energy into the groove, and that pays off big-time with *Zenyatta Mondatta*. It isn't just that this emphasis on rhythmic intensity made the band's songs catchier, though as "Voices Inside My Head" shows, the band certainly knew how to work a vamp; rather, it's the way the band's sense of rhythmic dynamics adds punch to its material. Just listen to the way the groove's ebb and flow underscores the dramatic tension in "Don't Stand So Close to Me"—good as the lyric is, it's the music that brings the story to life. *Ghost in the Machine* augments the band's instrumentation with keyboards and even a little saxophone, but otherwise maintains its predecessor's approach through catchy, well-modulated singles like "Every Little Thing She Does Is Magic" and "Spirits in the Material World" (though the most interesting and entrancing rhythmic ideas are lavished on non-pop numbers, like the funky "Too Much Information" or the relentless "Demolition Man").

Synchronicity is the band's strongest statement, and also its swan song. As clearly collaborative as the playing is—and the band is at its most supple and inspiring, from the percolating exoticism of "Walking in Your Footsteps" to the full-throttle fury of "Synchronicity I," to the slow boil of "Every Breath You Take"—the fact that Sting's writing so conspicuously dominated the band's songbook began to grate on the others, whose input amounted to one song each on this album (Copeland's wry "Miss Gradenko" and Summers's irritating "Mother"). Consequently, the band fell apart soon after *Synchronicity*, reuniting only long enough to manage an unimpressive update of "Don't Stand So Close to Me" for the best-of package *Every Breath You Take: The Singles.*
— J.D.C.

IGGY POP

★★★★   **The Idiot (1977; Virgin, 1990)**
★★★★   **Lust for Life (1977; Virgin, 1990)**
★★   **TV Eye Live (RCA, 1978)**
★★★½   **New Values (Arista, 1979)**
★★★½   **Soldier (Arista, 1980)**
★★   **Party (Arista, 1981)**
★★   **Zombie Birdhouse (Animal, 1982)**
★★★★½   **Choice Cuts (RCA, 1984)**
★★★½   **Blah Blah Blah (A&M, 1986)**
★★   **Instinct (A&M, 1988)**
★★★½   **Brick By Brick (Virgin, 1990)**

"I'm just a modern guy/Of course I've had it in the ear before." Tongue in cheek, Iggy Pop put his decadent past behind him with *The Idiot* and *Lust for Life*, but not too far. That quote from "Lust for Life" sums up the former Stooge's solo attitude: a cutting, ironic distance replaces the self-lacerating edge of his legendary early-'70s performances. Producer David Bowie modernizes the dense psychedelic blare of the Stooges, substituting synth moans for guitar wails and keeping the jackhammer beat largely intact. This stark electronic sheen alienated more than a few old Pop fans, but the Bowie association and the advent of new wave brought Iggy to a much larger audience.

A unique sensibility inhabits the crunching rockers and burnt-out torch songs on these two albums: brooding, sardonic, restless, outraged, perceptive, funny as hell, slightly bitter. *The Idiot* knowingly pokes through the residue of hedonism-run-amuck on "Funtime" and "Nightclubbing," while *Lust for Life* highlights like the title cut and "The Passenger" portray Iggy Pop as a punk survivor. He's battle-scarred, but still searching.

Reuniting with later-day Stooges guitarist James Williamson, Iggy cooks up a lean, keyboard-enhanced hard-rock sound on

New Values. If he doesn't quite consummate the title track's ambitious quest, Iggy does find strength in the old verities. "Endless Sea" perfects his post-Doors romantic doomsayer stance, and sets the stage for hundreds of mopey underground sensations to come. This initial stage of Iggy's career wields a tremendous influence over the '80s; he translated the glittery innovations of Bowie and Roxy Music into a streetwise argot any art-school dropout could understand.

After that, however, the dreaded roadshow syndrome sets in. Through the '80s, each successive Iggy album sounds more dispiriting and uninspired than the last. It's hard to decide which A&M album is worse: The slick Bowie reunion (*Blah Blah Blah*) mysteriously fails to spark either participant's batteries, while the numbing dinosaur-rock return (*Instinct*) stumbles into the tar pits. Ever the phoenix, Iggy stumbles halfway back from artistic oblivion with the surprisingly consistent *Brick By Brick*. This self-consciously "mature" effort offends the faithful, but Iggy curls his lip and lets his delightfully twisted mind roam the contemporary media landscape. — M.C.

THE POWER STATION
★ ★ **The Power Station (Capitol, 1985)**
Meltdown time already? The fury over this Duran Duran splinter group didn't last long. Truth be told, guitarist Andy Taylor was always too much of a closet rocker for that glam video troupe; after Power Station, he never did rejoin the fold. And we know John Taylor wasn't the most adored Duran because of his bass playing—heh, heh. All Robert Palmer and Chic drummer Tony Thompson had to do here was show up. They did, and this mismatched supersession spawned a pair of serviceable funk-rock chuggers: "Some Like It Hot" and a cover of Marc Bolan's "Get It On." Palmer managed to rechannel that zap back into his flagging solo career, but the Taylors flayed their reputation by touring without him. If recording with Palmer indicates where these third-generation Brit-poppers came from, replacing him with the perennial second-string moaner Michael Des Barres says something about where *The Power Station* will end up—the dumper. If you're so inclined, Duran Duran's albums are a much safer bet. — M.C.

PREFAB SPROUT
★ ★ ★ **Swoon (Kitchenware/Epic, 1984)**
★ ★ ★½ **Two Wheels Good**
    (Kitchenware/Epic, 1985)
★ ★ ★ ★ **From Langley Park to Memphis**
    (Kitchenware/Epic, 1988)
★ ★ ★ ★ **Jordan the Comeback (Epic, 1990)**
If the world knew Brian Wilson only from his intricate post-surf music song suites, Paul McCartney only from his more eccentric pop experiments or Stevie Wonder only from *The Secret Life of Plants*, each of those titans might be in the same position that Paddy McAloon is in now—that of a cult figure with decent sales, virtually no air play and truckloads of critical raves.

A low-profile Brit hooksmith, singer-guitarist-keyboardist McAloon makes pop bagatelles with the care Mozart lavished on symphonies. Together with brother Martin on bass and vocalist Wendy Smith, he fashioned Prefab Sprout into one of the most eclectic and idiosyncratic outfits of the '80s. Musically encyclopedic (the band draws on every sound from jazz to advertising jingles), the Sprouts are masters, above all, of nuance—the Prefab mood is one of refined impressionism: intelligent, clever, bittersweet, romantic.

Swoon was a jazzy tour de force debut, introducing the group's breathy vocals, intimidating musicianship and occasionally cryptic sense of humor. With Thomas Dolby as producer, *Two Wheels Good* (the English title is wittier: *Steve McQueen*), Prefab shucked some of its preciousness and delivered melodic pop, complex but irresistible: "When Love Breaks Down," "Bonny" and "Faron" were the standouts.

By the time of *From Langley Park to Memphis*, the Sprouts had hit full stride. Stevie Wonder, Pete Townshend and the Andrae Crouch Singers played on the album, but it was irrefutably McAloon's masterpiece—"Venus of the Soup Kitchen," "The King of Rock 'n' Roll" and "Hey Manhattan" flourished his gift for pastiche (he cops riffs from such high-end schlock-meisters as Burt Bacharach and Jimmy Webb, favors glossy intros that recall the hokiest of Philly soul ballads, and achieves a sort of genius Muzak).

The semi-concept album, *Jordan the Comeback*, came next—if anything, it bested even *Langley Park*. A tribute, of sorts, to Elvis, it celebrated also such diverse heroes as Frank and Jesse James, Abba's lead singer, Fred Astaire and Harlem doo-woppers. One song features the Almighty as crooner ("Hi, this is God here") and yet manages a strange, heartfelt reverence; another conflates two mythic figures, a Delta bluesman and a guerilla fighter. Hyper-literate, and exerting a strange fascination, Prefab Sprout, for all its

influence-pillaging, remains sui generis—this
is gorgeous stuff. — P.E.

ELVIS PRESLEY
★★★★★ Elvis Presley (RCA, 1956)
★★★★★ Elvis (RCA, 1956)
★★★★ Lovin' You (RCA, 1957)
★★★★★ Elvis' Christmas Album (RCA, 1957)
★★★★ King Creole (RCA, 1958)
★★★★★ Elvis' Golden Records, Vol. 1 (RCA, 1958)
★★★★★ For LP Fans Only (RCA, 1959)
★★★★★ A Date With Elvis (RCA, 1959)
★★★ G.I. Blues (RCA, 1960)
★★★★ Elvis Is Back! (RCA, 1960)
★★★★★ His Hand in Mine (RCA, 1960)
★★★★★ 50,000,000 Elvis Fans Can't Be Wrong: Elvis' Golden Records, Vol. 2 (RCA, 1960)
★★★ Something for Everybody (RCA, 1961)
★★★ Blue Hawaii (RCA, 1961)
★★★ Pot Luck (RCA, 1962)
★★★ Girls! Girls! Girls! (RCA, 1962)
★★ Fun in Acapulco (RCA, 1963)
★★★★ Elvis' Golden Records, Vol. 3 (RCA, 1963)
★★★★ It Happened at the World's Fair (RCA, 1963)
★★★ Kissin' Cousins (RCA, 1963)
★★ Roustabout (RCA, 1964)
★★★ Elvis for Everyone (RCA, 1965)
★★ Girl Happy (RCA, 1965)
★★ Harum Scarum (RCA, 1965)
★★ Frankie and Johnny (RCA, 1966)
★★ Paradise, Hawaiian Style (RCA, 1966)
★★★★ Spinout (RCA, 1966)
★★ Double Trouble (RCA, 1967)
★★★★★ How Great Thou Art (RCA, 1967)
★★★★ Clambake (RCA, 1967)
★★★ Speedway (RCA, 1968)
★★★★★ Elvis (TV Special) (RCA, 1968)
★★★★ Elvis' Golden Records, Vol. 4 (RCA, 1968)
★★★★★ From Elvis in Memphis (RCA, 1969)
★★★ Elvis Sings "Flaming Star" and Other Hits from His Movies (RCA Camden, 1969)
★★★ Elvis Sings Hits from His Movies (RCA Camden, 1969)
★★★★ From Memphis to Vegas (RCA, 1969)
★★★★ Back in Memphis (RCA, 1970)
★★★ That's the Way It Is (RCA, 1970)
★★ Almost in Love (RCA Camden, 1970)
★★★★ On Stage—February, 1970 (RCA, 1970)

★★★★ Elvis in Person at the International Hotel, Las Vegas, Nevada (RCA, 1970)
★★★★★ World Wide 50 Gold Award Hits, Vol. 1, No. 1 (RCA, 1970)
★★★★★ World Wide 50 Gold Award Hits, Vol. 1, No. 2 (RCA, 1971)
★★★★ World Wide 50 Gold Award Hits, Vol. 1, No. 3 (RCA, 1971)
★★★★ World Wide 50 Gold Award Hits, Vol. 1, No. 4 (RCA, 1971)
★★ I Got Lucky (RCA Camden, 1971)
★★★★ You'll Never Walk Alone (RCA Camden, 1971)
★★★ Love Letters From Elvis (RCA, 1971)
★★★ C'mon Everybody (RCA Camden, 1971)
★★★★★ Elvis Country (RCA, 1971)
★★★ Elvis (RCA, 1971)
★★★★ Elvis Sings the Wonderful World of Christmas (RCA, 1971)
★★★★ Burning Love (RCA Camden, 1972)
★★★★★ He Touched Me (RCA, 1972)
★★ As Recorded at Madison Square Garden (RCA, 1972)
★★★ Elvis Now (RCA, 1972)
★★★★ Separate Ways (RCA Camden, 1973)
★★★ Elvis Raised on Rock/For Ol' Times Sake (RCA, 1973)
★★★ Aloha from Hawaii (Via Satellite) (RCA, 1973)
★★★★ A Legendary Performer: Volume 1 (RCA, 1974)
★★ Recorded Live on Stage in Memphis (RCA, 1974)
★ Having Fun With Elvis on Stage (RCA, 1974)
★★ Good Times (RCA, 1974)
★★★ Let's Be Friends (RCA Camden, 1975)
★★★ Promised Land (RCA, 1975)
★★ Today (RCA, 1975)
★★★ Pure Gold (RCA, 1975)
★★★★ A Legendary Performer: Volume 2 (RCA, 1976)
★★ From Elvis Presley Boulevard, Memphis, Tennessee (RCA, 1976)
★★★ Welcome to My World (RCA, 1977)
★★★ Moody Blue (RCA, 1977)
★★ Elvis in Concert (RCA, 1977)
★★★ The Elvis Tapes (Redwood, 1977)
★★ Elvis on Stage (RCA, 1977)
★ Interviews and Memories of: The Sun Years (Sun, 1977)
★★★★ A Legendary Performer: Volume 3 (RCA, 1978)

★ ★ ★ He Walks Beside Me (RCA, 1978)
★ ★ ★ ★ From Memphis to Vegas/From Vegas to Memphis (RCA, 1978)
★ ★ ★ A Canadian Tribute (RCA, 1978)
★ ★ ★ Elvis Sings for Children and Grownups Too! (RCA, 1978)
★ ★ Our Memories of Elvis (RCA, 1979)
★ ★ Our Memories of Elvis, Vol. 2 (RCA, 1979)
★ ★ Guitar Man (RCA, 1980)
★ ★ ★ Elvis Aron Presley (RCA, 1980)
★ ★ ★ ★ This is Elvis (RCA, 1981)
★ ★ ★ ★ Elvis: The Hillbilly Cat (The Music Works, 1982)
★ ★ ★ ★ Elvis: The First Live Recordings (The Music Works, 1982)
★ ★ ★ ★ Memories of Christmas (RCA, 1982)
★ ★ ★ ★ A Legendary Performer: Volume 4 (RCA, 1983)
★ I Was the One (RCA, 1983)
★ ★ ★ ★ ★ Rocker (RCA, 1984)
★ ★ ★ ★ Elvis' Gold Records, Vol. 5 (RCA, 1984)
★ ★ The Elvis Presley Interview Record: An Audio Self-Portrait (RCA, 1984)
★ ★ ★ ★ Elvis—A Golden Celebration (RCA, 1984)
★ ★ ★ ★ ★ Reconsider Baby (RCA, 1985)
★ ★ ★ ★ A Valentine Gift for You (RCA, 1985)
★ ★ ★ ★ Always On My Mind (RCA, 1985)
★ ★ ★ ★ ★ Return of the Rocker (RCA, 1986)
★ ★ ★ ★ ★ The Complete Sun Sessions (RCA, 1987)
★ ★ ★ ★ ★ The Sun Sessions CD (RCA, 1987)
★ ★ ★ ★ ★ The Number One Hits (RCA, 1987)
★ ★ ★ ★ ★ The Memphis Record (RCA, 1987)
★ ★ ★ ★ ★ Essential Elvis (RCA, 1988)
★ ★ ★ ★ ★ Stereo '57 (Essential Elvis Volume 2) (RCA, 1988)
★ ★ ★ ★ ★ 50 World Wide Gold Award Hits, Volume 1, Part 1 (RCA, 1988)
★ ★ ★ ★ ★ 50 World Wide Gold Award Hits, Volume 1, Part 2 (RCA, 1988)
★ ★ ★ ★ The Top Ten Hits (RCA, 1988)
★ ★ Elvis Country (RCA, 1988)
★ ★ ★ ★ Elvis in Nashville (RCA, 1988)
★ ★ ★ ★ The Alternate Aloha (RCA, 1988)
★ ★ ★ ★ ★ Known Only to Him: Elvis Gospel, 1957–1971 (RCA, 1989)
★ ★ ★ ★ The Million Dollar Quartet (RCA, 1990)
★ ★ ★ ★ The Great Performances (RCA, 1990)
★ ★ ★ ★ The Essential Elvis, Vol. 3 (RCA, 1991)

★ ★ ★ ★ Collector's Gold (RCA, 1991)
★ ★ ★ ★ ★ Elvis Presley Sings Leiber & Stoller (RCA, 1991)
★ ★ ★ The Lost Album (RCA, 1991)
★ ★ ★ ★ ★ Elvis—the King of Rock & Roll: The Complete '50s Masters (RCA, 1992)

There was no model for Elvis Presley's success; what Sam Phillips sensed was something in the air, an inevitable outgrowth of all the country and blues he was recording at his Union Avenue studio. Enter Presley in 1954, and with him a musical vocabulary rich in country blues, gospel, inspirational music, bluegrass, traditional country and popular music—as well as a host of emotional needs that found their most eloquent expression in song. And his timing was impeccable: emerging in the first blush of America's postwar ebullience, Presley captured the spirit of a country flexing its industrial muscle, of a generation unburdened by the concerns of war, more mobile, more affluent and better educated than any that had come before.

The Sun recordings thus take on a degree of importance unmatched by Presley's later records. Here are the first salvos in an undeclared war on segregated radio stations nationwide. Overnight, it seemed, "race music," as the music industry had labeled the work of black artists, became a thing of the past, as did "hillbilly" music. Suddenly, Elvis Presley could be heard following Ray Charles or Al Hibbler, who might follow Ernest Tubb, who might follow Jo Stafford or Tony Bennett.

The Complete Sun Sessions two-album set contains all the essential Sun recordings, as well as one side of outtakes and one side of alternate takes (three of "I Love You Because," six of "I'm Left, You're Right, She's Gone"); *The Sun Sessions CD* contains the same master takes and outtakes, but five fewer alternate takes. No matter: in the history of rock & roll, there is no more important document than this. Presley evinces an energy, rawness and vitality other rock artists have long sought, sometimes approached, but never equaled. The two Music Works titles are comprised of early live performances from Presley's 1955–56 appearances on the Louisiana Hayride radio show emanating from Shreveport, Louisiana. Poorly recorded on a mono, one-track machine, these show Presley in raw form, getting low down and bluesy as he blazes his way through "That's All Right (Mama)," and several other Sun tracks—the performance of "Good Rockin' Tonight" and "I Wanna Play House With You" are extraordinary—in addition to offering a tough version of "Hound Dog." Despite the poor sound, the urgency of Presley's performance cuts through, unlike anything else on record from this time. Finding both *The Hillbilly Cat* and *The First Live Recordings* is difficult now, but well worth the effort. The famed *Million Dollar Quartet* is not a quartet at all, but a trio—the mythical assembling of Presley, Jerry Lee Lewis, Carl Perkins and Johnny Cash in the Sun studio on December 4, 1956 is indeed mythical. Cash may have come by for a couple of songs, but his voice is nowhere to be heard on these tracks. Presley, Perkins and Lewis are joined now and then by other Sun musicians of little note, but primarily it's the trio doing all the work. Most of the 41 songs listed are performed only in part, but nothing is less than tantalizing, and history students will appreciate the display of rock & roll's deep roots represented by the song selection. Each artist contributes something relating to his most direct influences, and in doing so summons forth nearly 30 years of American music.

The early RCA albums are virtually of a piece with *The Sun Sessions*, displaying the wide-ranging reach Presley exhibited in his choice of material and all the fervor of the Sun performances. Sadly, the CD reissues of the first two albums (*Elvis Presley* and *Elvis*) omit songwriter credits. The production values, of course, are a bit advanced over those at Sun, but the edges remain sharp. Also, on *Elvis*'s "First in Line" we hear the beginning of the awesome presence—tender, searching, vulnerable, but forthright—he would bring to ballad material in his later years. *A Date With Elvis* and *For LP Fans Only* are mixtures of Sun and RCA material released during Elvis's army years and are exemplary in every respect.

In 1957 Presley recorded *Elvis' Christmas Album*, a Yuletide issue challenged only by Phil Spector's for the title of all-time greatest rock & roll Christmas album. As a result of RCA's ambitious reissue program in the '80s, which restored Presley's early albums to their original mono sound, this title is again available in its original gatefold package. *The Elvis Tapes* is a Canadian release containing a complete backstage press conference held in Vancouver prior to a 1957 concert. The mood is informal, the questions fairly routine, but in his answers you sense the seriousness with which Presley regarded the roots of his music.

One of the best-kept secrets of Presley's enduring appeal is that he was an indisputably great singer, apart from being an icon. The proof is in the soundtrack albums, on which he manages to make lackluster material memorable. On the other hand, he's also given some of the worst songs ever written. Still there are moments when Presley gets hold of a good song and takes it into the ionosphere. The best sustained efforts are on *Lovin' You* and *King Creole*, thanks to Jerry Leiber and Mike Stoller's uniformly outstanding material, along with Presley's inspired interpretations of Claude Demetrius's "Mean Woman Blues" and "Hard Headed Woman," Ivory Joe Hunter's "I Need You So," and Fred "Wise-Ben" Weisman's "As Long as I Have You." *It Happened at the World's Fair* is one of the stronger early-'60s efforts, with tracks including "They Remind Me Too Much of You," "I'm Falling in Love Tonight" and the great single "One Broken Heart for Sale." *Spinout* includes a fine version of Dylan's "Tomorrow Is a Long Time" and the original recording of "I'll Remember You." One of the most forgettable of Presley's movies, *Clambake*, produced one of his best soundtracks, although five of the cuts weren't even in the movie. Nevertheless, "Big Boss Man," "Guitar Man," "How Can You Lose What You Never Had" and "You Don't Know Me" are all first-rate performances. Among the otherwise-forgettable tracks on *Girls! Girls! Girls!* is one of Presley's best '60s singles, "Return to Sender." The awful docu-drama *This is Elvis* provides a soundtrack that happens to be one of the most complete career overviews of Presley contained on one disc or tape. Ranging from "That's All Right (Mama)" to early RCA tracks, to soundtrack items, to Christmas and gospel songs, to concert recordings, to one of his last singles, "Moody Blue," the set encapsules the sweep of Presley's work over the years.

Like the soundtracks, Elvis's '60s studio albums contain gems among a certain amount of dross. All are worthwhile, but *Elvis is Back!*, his first post-army recording, has a vibrancy missing from some of the later releases. It also has the best collection of songs since the first two RCA albums, among them devastating versions of "Fever" and Lowell Fulsom's "Reconsider Baby," and rousing takes of "The Girl of My Best Friend," Otis Blackwell's "Make Me Know It" and Leiber-Stoller's "Dirty, Dirty Feeling." One of Presley's most dependable and blues-oriented songwriters, Doc Pomus, is represented with five tracks on *Pot Luck*, four of them written with his long-time partner Mort Shuman. These include the hit single "Kiss Me Quick," and two minor classics in the Presley repertoire, "Suspicion" and "Night Rider."

On *The Elvis Tapes* a reporter asks Presley if he knows a lot of gospel songs, and Presley responds: "I think I know every gospel song that's ever been written." Gospel pervaded Presley's character and was a defining influence, more so than any other music he heard and sang as a youngster. Even near the end of his life, when stumbling through concerts in a daze, he delivered the goods when he got to "How Great Thou Art." The only mediocre effort among his gospel albums is *He Walks Beside Me*. Subtitled *Favorite Songs of Faith and Inspiration*, the album is a collection of various gospel tracks and topical material such as "If I Can Dream." Otherwise all the gospel outings (*His Hand in Mine, How Great Thou Art, You'll Never Walk Alone, He Touched Me, Known Only to Him*) are highly recommended. *How Great Thou Art* features the original version of "Peace in the Valley," as well as the title song, the stirring "In the Garden" and "Crying in the Chapel." The extraordinary *He Touched Me* contains the best examples of gospel quartet harmonizing on any of these entries, with "Bosom of Abraham" ranking as one of the most overpowering performances of Presley's career. *His Hand in Mine* was recorded in a single all-night session and covers a wider range of gospel styles than the other releases. *Known Only to Him* offers a well-considered survey of Presley's key gospel tracks from 1957 through 1971.

At the moment he was in danger of becoming a rock relic, Presley bid adieu to Hollywood and made the decision to return to live performing. In his first step back, a 1968 television special, Presley's face filled the screen, the eyes set in a serious glare, and he sang: "If you're looking for trouble, you came to the right place." Tough and unequivocal, "Trouble" set the tone for an evening in which Presley reasserted his primacy as a rock & roll artist. His ammo is blues, gospel and powerhouse rock & roll; in the special's most memorable sequence he plays in the round to a small audience, accompanied by his former band members Scotty Moore on guitar and drummer D.J. Fontana, all of them rocking out on some of the '50s songs that Elvis made famous. Elsewhere, he displays the control and

nuance of a great stylist on gentle, evocative readings of "Memories" and "Love Me Tender." Throw in a seasonal touch via "Blue Christmas," and a moving performance of the topical "If I Can Dream" and you have a performance of emotional grandeur and historical resonance. Here was Presley refusing to be discarded by the music he helped create, seizing his moment with a fury that remains astonishing to this day. In its own way, *Elvis (TV Special)* is as critical to our understanding of this extraordinary artist as is *The Sun Sessions*.

Before the triumph of the TV special had worn off, Presley delivered one of the finest studio albums of his career in *From Elvis in Memphis*. Recorded in January of 1969 at Memphis's famed American studios, Presley produced 21 usable tracks in less than a week, with another 14 tracks cut in six nights a month later, from which were culled the songs comprising the studio side (*Back in Memphis*) of the wonderful *From Memphis to Vegas/From Vegas to Memphis* release. It was the first time he'd recorded in Memphis since 1955, and as his producer he'd enlisted Chips Moman, whose own history in the Bluff City dated back to the formation of Stax Records. With a house band that included some of the city's best players (including a large horn section and female background chorus), Moman fashioned recordings that hold together conceptually and aesthetically, integrating strings and other flourishes seamlessly with the rock-solid core provided by a basic Southern soul band. *From Elvis in Memphis* finds the artist moving gracefully from a version of Jerry Butler's "Only the Strong Survive" to John Hartford's "Gentle on My Mind," and he goes on to assay in compelling fashion Hank Snow's "I'm Movin' On," Johnny Tillotson's "It Keeps Right on a-Hurtin," Chuck Jackson's version of "Any Day Now" before closing with Mac Davis's "In the Ghetto." *The Memphis Record* is a complete account of the Memphis sessions, and its detailed liner notes by Peter Guralnick elevate it to the essential category. But there's nothing quite like hearing *From Elvis in Memphis* and *From Memphis to Vegas/From Vegas to Memphis* in the original incarnations, either.

As his comeback had mirrored his arrival nearly two decades earlier, so did the live albums of the '70s approximate the movie years of the '60s—that is, wildly uneven, often uninspired, but with startling, penetrating performances on occasion. On the road Presley expanded the sound Moman had crafted in the Memphis sessions, adding a full orchestra to blast over a crack band whose members included the estimable James Burton on guitar, Ronnie Tutt on drums, Glen D. Hardin on piano and Jerry Scheff on bass. In addition, he employed both a male gospel quartet (J.D. Sumner and the Stamps) and a female gospel trio (the Blossoms). *On Stage* and *Elvis in Person* are indicative of the hard edge common to those early-'70s shows— coming off his TV special Elvis was lean and hungry, pouring everything into every moment of the concerts. Acceptance wasn't yet assured, and he was playing to win. (*Elvis in Person* is also one disc of the *From Memphis to Vegas/From Vegas to Memphis* set.) By 1972, though, the concerts had become ritual annointings and the music was spotty. Still, Presley cut some great singles in the '70s, and in concert songs such as "Suspicious Minds" and "Burning Love" commanded his full attention. *Aloha From Hawaii* contains his best self-defining treatment of Mickey Newbury's "American Trilogy." Newbury's weaving together of "All My Trials," "The Battle Hymn of the Republic" and "Dixie" spoke to Presley's Southern pride and to his own sense of mortality, the two feelings clashing in a bombastic finale that becomes a showcase for a bone-chilling display of vocal muscle on Presley's part. *The Alternate Aloha* is the fiery dress rehearsal done two days before the concert proper, showing a looser Presley at work before only 5,000 fans. Anyone who questions the quality of the band during these years is advised to check out the hot playing here, particularly that of Burton and Tutt, who push their leader to ever-more-searing vocals—the blistering workout on James Taylor's "Steamroller Blues" is awe-inspiring. The other live sets are uneven, reflecting Presley's diminishing interest in the concert routine. Must to avoid: *Having Fun With Elvis On Stage*, an album consisting of nothing more than the star's onstage wisecracks.

In the '70s Presley got it together for some great tracks right up until his death— "Suspicious Minds," "Burning Love," "Steamroller Blues," "My Way" and "Moody Blue" are only a few of the exceptional performances from this time. But one or two tracks does not an album make, and great care is advised in navigating his '70s studio albums. There are high points, though. One of the best albums of Presley's career came in 1971 with *Elvis*

Country (not to be confused with a like-titled collection released on RCA's budget line in 1988). Subtitled "I'm 10,000 Years Old" after a song of the same title that is heard in snippets between tracks (the complete song is available on *Elvis Now*), the album is, along with *Promised Land*, the most introspective of Presley's career. Its cover shows a now-famous baby photo of Elvis, with an inset of an old photo of the Presley family. The song selection leans heavily toward country and toward songs of loss and longing: "Tomorrow Never Comes," written by Johnny Bond and Ernest Tubb; the Bill Monroe–Lester Flatt gem, "Little Cabin on the Hill"; Willie Nelson's "Funny How Time Slips Away"; Bob Wills's "Faded Love"; Hank Cochran's "Make the World Go Away." It's by far the strangest and most beautiful album Presley ever recorded, and you don't have to be a fan to find it unsettling. Also recommended is *Elvis*, originally released in 1971 as *Fool*, after the title single, another of Presley's better efforts from this period. In a confessional mode, *Elvis* is graced by insightful treatments of Gordon Lightfoot's "(That's What You Get) For Lovin' Me" and Bob Dylan's "Don't Think Twice, It's Alright." Not the least of the '70s albums is another Christmas effort, *Elvis Sings the Wonderful World of Christmas*.

The titles of Elvis's various greatest-hits packages pretty much tell the whole story. Anyone desiring the cream of the crop will find it in abundance in any number of collections, particulary those beginning with *Rocker*, the first of an RCA reissue series that lumps tracks together by theme and concept—thus, the excellent blues overview, *Reconsider Baby*; the ballads of *A Valentine Gift for You*; the important singles collected on *The Essential Elvis* and *Stereo '57*; the flat-out, no-holds-barred raveups on *Rocker* and *Return of the Rocker*; and the 21 tracks comprising the classic Leiber and Stoller songs plus a previously unreleased (in the U.S.) duet with Ann-Margret, "You're the Boss," recorded in 1963 for *Viva Las Vegas*. Another of these selections, *Always on My Mind*, assembles some of the best tracks from Presley's later years, including the title song. Of special note: *The Great Performances Vol. 2* contains "My Happiness," reputed to be the recording Elvis made for his mother's birthday present the first time he visited the Sun studio. Abomination: *I Was the One*, some great tracks given new instrumental backing. Avoid it at all costs.

Treachery is afoot on the various

posthumous Elvis releases, and the buyer better beware. *Interviews and Memories of: The Sun Years* is a shameless and overpriced attempt to capitalize on Presley's death with an album containing only a few bars of music here and there, and some totally inconsequential reminiscences of Elvis, along with portions of a few Presley interviews. Both *Guitar Man* and *Our Memories of Elvis* are based on the conceit that Presley is best heard minus strings and orchestral backings, and so the producers have stripped away all but the most basic accompaniment. The problem is that Presley played off his band and we miss such interplay here. In the end, these are little more than glorified hits collections. *A Canadian Tribute* contains portions of the interview released as *The Elvis Tapes*, along with several songs composed by Canadian writers (Buffy Ste. Marie, Gordon Lightfoot, Hank Snow, Paul Anka), all available on other albums. *Memories of Christmas* is a greatest Christmas hits album comprised of tracks (alternate takes and previously unreleased versions) from Presley's two Christmas albums, with the addition of a personal message from Elvis tacked onto the end. The *Interview Record* is a rare, non-commercial release sent out to radio stations for use in specials honoring Presley's 50th birthday. Interviews included date from 1956, and 1960–61, but there's not much meat to chew on: Presley's comments are sound bites, generally less than a minute in length. *The Lost Album* collects songs listed as "bonus tracks" on Presley's soundtrack albums, which were in fact recorded in two sessions in 1963 for release on a single album followup to *Pot Luck*. RCA changed its strategy, though, when it discovered *Pot Luck* and other Presley soundtrack LPs were selling well. So, instead, the label began including a track here and there to flesh out succeeding soundtrack releases. Among the essential tracks here are the poignant Pomus-Shuman meditation "Long Lonely Highway," a terrific "Devil in Disguise," and two strong tearjerkers "It Hurts Me" and "Ask Me." *Elvis in Nashville* is an extremely valuable release, which contains several gospel numbers and some of Presley's better folk and country recordings ("Early Mornin' Rain," "Little Cabin Home on the Hill"). Well-annotated, this overview displays great care in representing the scope of Presley's work during a period when he recorded over 250 songs in Music City.

The two out-of-print box sets (*Elvis Aron Presley* and *Elvis—A Golden Celebration*)

contain a wealth of valuable Presley material unavailable elsewhere, which goes far toward fleshing out the man's career with alternate takes, live performances, singles that never made it onto albums, solo performances and other collector's items. Of the two, *A Golden Celebration* has the most familiar material, but it also has two discs' worth of live performances from the Mississippi-Alabama State Fair in 1956 and some demo tapes Presley cut alone at Graceland. *Elvis Aron Presley*, a limited-edition, eight-volume collection honoring the King's 25th year in the music business (even though he'd been dead three years by the time of the release) is full of small treasures. Both sets may fall into the category of "for completists only," and, given their scarcity, both are no doubt wildly overpriced at this juncture. In 1992 RCA gave Elvis the ultimate boxed-set treatment he deserves. *Elvis—the King of Rock & Roll: The Complete '50s Masters* superbly compiles all of Presley's '50s recordings, just as they were originally made, including his very first demos and previously unreleased tracks. The label plans to give the same treatment to Elvis's '60s and '70s material. — D.M.

BILLY PRESTON
★★½ **The Best** (A&M, 1982)
An experienced session keyboardist and former gospel prodigy, Billy Preston became a name after his appearance in the Beatles' *Let It Be*. His electric piano enhances the charm of "Get Back," without question. But as a solo artist, Preston's resources proved limited. It's hard to remember which sounded more annoying on the radio: the novelty-funk instrumentals ("Outa-Space," "Space Race") or the mindless, cheery vocal hooks ("Will It Go Round in Circles," "Nothing From Nothing"). However, those four singles all reached the Top Five during the mid-70s. They're all included on *The Best*. A smattering of also-rans rounds out the package: "I Wrote a Simple Song" sums up Preston's appeal—unintentionally. After returning to the church, Preston resurfaced for a plush duet with Motown vet Syreeta Wright. A Top Ten hit in 1979, "With You I'm Born Again" really does make Preston sound like a new man. This long-lost one-shot qualifies as a minor miracle; it's available on several Motown compilations. — M.C.

THE PRETENDERS
★★★★★ **Pretenders** (Sire, 1980)
★★★½ **Extended Play (EP)** (Sire, 1981)

★ ★ ★   **Pretenders II** (Sire, 1981)
★ ★ ★ ★ ★   **Learning to Crawl** (Sire, 1983)
★ ★ ★ ★   **Get Close** (Sire, 1986)
★ ★ ★ ★½ **The Singles** (Sire, 1987)
★ ★½ **packed!** (Sire, 1990)

It might be tempting to decide that the Pretenders are a front for Chrissie Hynde—who, after all, not only sings and writes the majority of the band's songs, but is also the sole Pretender to have appeared on every album. It's a neat theory, but all it takes is a single listen to *Pretenders* to punch significant holes in it. This is a band album, and the character of the songs isn't determined by who wrote them, but who's playing. Indeed, the only track on the album that seems wholly Hynde's is "Stop Your Sobbing"—a Kinks song that, ironically enough, is the album's only cover. Elsewhere, the music is a group effort, from the way Hynde's wry delivery plays off the churning, odd-metered guitar riffs of "Tattooed Love Boys" to the perfectly locked rhythm work propelling "The Wait" from chorus to chorus. That's not to dismiss the album's way with a tune, for Hynde's material is memorably melodic, from the emotional vulnerability of "Kid" to the sassy "Brass in Pocket." But what makes those songs work is the way the band backs her, adding soul to the sentimentality of "Kid" or putting bounce in each step of "Brass in Pocket."

Likewise, the band is to blame for the relative disappointment of *Extended Play* and *Pretenders II*. Sure, the players acquit themselves admirably through "Message of Love" and "Talk of the Town." But instead of adding the necessary edge to "The Adultress" or putting some bite into "Jealous Dogs," the group merely goes through the motions, playing with minimal energy and conviction.

This version of the Pretenders fell apart when bassist Pete Farndon left in early 1982, and guitarist James Honeyman Scott died of a drug overdose soon after. Surviving Pretenders Hynde and Martin Chambers then recorded "Back on the Chain Gang" and "My City Was Gone" with ex–Rockpile guitarist Billy Bremner and bassist Tony Butler before completing *Learning to Crawl* with guitarist Robbie McIntosh and bassist Malcolm Foster. Though this game of musical chairs affects the sound of the album, it doesn't undermine the group's identity. If anything, songs like "Time the Avenger," "Watching the Clothes" and "I Hurt You" sound more like the original Pretenders than most of *II*.

So Hynde really is the key, then? Not on the evidence of *Get Close*. As with the transition from *II* to *Learning to Crawl*, the Pretenders are down two members, leaving only Hynde and McIntosh. But the mood of the music is radically different, trading the aggressive rhythms of "Middle of the Road" and "Thumbelina" for the airy arabesques of "Tradition of Love" and the gentle bop of "Don't Get Me Wrong." Obviously, some of the shift has to do with Hynde's own change in attitude, for the tenor of the songs is warm and tender in ways *Learning to Crawl* never was, but at the same time, the music's feel is so markedly different that it's impossible to discount the band's input. That seems equally the case with *packed!*, on which the arrangements take on a low-key confidence that's halfway between the gentleness of *Get Close* and the cool maturity of *Learning to Crawl*. But as much as this seems yet another "band" sound, it's worth noting that the only Pretender pictured anywhere on the album is Hynde. Then again, given the generally lax quality of the songs on *packed!*, it's just as possible that none of the backing musicians wanted to own up to their involvement. —J.D.C.

LLOYD PRICE

★ ★ ★   **Lloyd Price** (Specialty, 1986)
★ ★   **Personality Plus** (Specialty, 1986)
★ ★   **Walkin' the Track** (Specialty, 1986)
★ ★ ★ ★ **Lawdy!** (Specialty, 1991)

Lloyd Price's best-known hits—"Stagger Lee," "Personality," "I'm Gonna Get Married," "Where Were You on Our Wedding Day"—came after he left Specialty for ABC-Paramount Records following a stint in the army in 1956. At Specialty, though, he cut a raft of rocking R&B-oriented sides in the early '50s in his native New Orleans backed by some of the Crescent City's finest musicians. One of these, "Lawdy Miss Clawdy," hit the top of the R&B chart in 1952, logged some crossover action (unusual for an independent label in those pre–rock & roll days), and was covered by Elvis Presley on the latter's first RCA album.

Specialty's 1991 set, *Lawdy!*, another entry in the label's Legends of Specialty series, showcases Price's work from 1952 through 1956, including a number of alternate and previously unissued takes. Those familiar with Price only from the above-mentioned hits will hear a young artist with distinctive gifts as a writer, and a singer who could deliver a rollicking good time in an uptempo mode, or dip into himself for some compelling emotion and grittier deliveries on more personal lyrics of the sort to be found on, say, the blues ballad "All Alone."

Among Price's other albums, both *Lloyd Price* and *Personality* offer tracks unavailable on *Lawdy!*: *Personality* mixes in the title song, "Stagger Lee," and "Where Were You on Our Wedding Day" with a handful of the artist's better Specialty sides (including "Lawdy Miss Clawdy") and some previously unreleased tracks; *Lloyd Price* collects a number of early recordings, both familiar ("Lawdy Miss Clawdy," "Mailman Blues," "Where You At") and otherwise unavailable. *Walkin' the Track* is comprised of unreleased and alternate takes from Price's Specialty sessions and is a must set for completists. — D.M.

SAM PRICE
★ ★ ★ ★ **Rib Joint** (Savoy, 1979)
Issued as part of Savoy's "Roots of Rock" series, Sam Price's *Rib Joint* is a two-record set of breathtaking scope and feverish playing. Price is a piano player who cannot be pigeonholed—on the four sides of this album he surveys practically every rhythmic and riff pattern common to rock & roll in its broadest definition, and plays them all as if he invented them. The Texas-born Price made his first recordings in Dallas in 1929, gravitated to New York in 1937 and settled in at Decca Records, where he proceeded to accompany all manner of artists, ranging from pop balladeers to gospel singers. In 1956 he began recording for Savoy with his own group, playing uptempo blues. One of those tracks, "Rib Joint," was an R&B hit. Sides one and two of this collection feature Price's 1956 band, and at least a couple of the names ought to alert listeners as to what was going on here: Price's sax player was King Curtis, his guitarist Mickey Baker. Though less heralded, Leonard Gaskin on bass and Bobby Donaldson on drums were a dependable rhythm section who belonged in this league. Sides three and four are from Price's 1959 Savoy sessions, minus Curtis, but with Baker and Al Casey on guitars, Al Lucas on bass and the well-traveled Panama Francis on drums.

The '56 sessions include two takes of the rollicking "Rib Joint," as well as another spicy, food-oriented tune, "Bar-B-Q Sauce," and some bluesier efforts that have a real midnight feel about them. On the '59 sessions, Price explores a variety of styles, from boogie-woogie ("Kansas City Boogie") to blues ("Sammy Sings the Blues") to a taste of traditional country on "Chicken

Strut." *Rib Joint* rocks the room every which way; that it also happens to be an entertaining history lesson is our gain. — D.M.

CHARLEY PRIDE
★ ★ ★ **The Best of Charley Pride** (1969; RCA, 1979)
★ ★ ★ **The Best of Charley Pride, Vol. II** (1972; RCA, 1988)
★ ★ **Greatest Hits** (RCA, 1980)
★ **Greatest Hits, Vol. 2** (RCA, 1985)
★ ★ **Christmas in My Old Home Town** (RCA, 1970)
★ ★ ★ **Best of Charley Pride** (Curb, 1991)
One of the most consistently successful country singers of the '70s, Charley Pride happens to be black. He first recorded under the name "Country Charley Pride" in the '60s, but nobody could mistake Pride's voice for a blues or soul instrument. If his black characteristics get buried in that warm baritone, Pride certainly doesn't strain to sound like something he's not. His best performances flow naturally, projecting a low-key vulnerability that deepens over time. The two *Best of* sets are equally divided between quietly convincing heart songs and more formulaic numbers. Overproduced fluff surrounds the meat on these albums, but the leanest cuts—"Does My Ring Hurt Your Finger" and "The Snakes Crawl at Night" from *Best of*; "Kiss an Angel Good Morning" and "Is Anybody Going to San Antone?" from *Best of, Vol. II*—provide plenty of down-home nourishment. Pride's tastefulness and reserve eventually get the better of him; after the autobiographical "Mississippi Cotton Pickin' Town" on *Greatest Hits*, the treadmill takes over. Charley Pride recorded dozens of original albums for RCA that have all fallen out of print; his recent efforts on Nashville's tiny 16th Coast label sleepily drift off into the easy-listening zone. And somehow, "Adult Contemporary" Charlie Pride doesn't have the same ring. — M.C.

MAXI PRIEST
★ ★½ **You're Safe** (1985; Charisma, 1992)
★ ★½ **Intentions** (1986; Charisma, 1992)
★ ★½ **Maxi** (Virgin, 1988)
★ ★ ★ **Bona Fide** (Charisma, 1990)
★ ★ ★½ **Best of Me** (Charisma, 1991)
A pleasant-voiced pop reggae singer, Maxi Priest managed to parlay Jamaican success into a berth on the U.K. pop charts through the tuneful understatement of *You're Safe* and *Intentions*, and finally topped the

American singles chart in 1990 with "Close to You" (from *Bona Fide*), and all without appreciably changing his approach. It helps, of course, that his vocal style has more in common with soul crooners like Jeffrey Osborne than with reggae stylists like Gregory Isaacs, but the slick accessibility of Maxi has as much to do with the pop-oriented material (including fine covers of "Wild World" and "Some Guys Have All the Luck") and production (Sly and Robbie at their grooviest) as with Priest's singing. *Bona Fide* broadens that approach somewhat, drawing from Soul II Soul's bass-driven sound for "Close to You" and other tracks, but never quite compromises the singer's reggae roots. *Best of Me* compiles his most successful singles.

— J.D.C.

THE PRIMITIVES

★ ★ **Lazy 86–88 (Lazy UK, 1989)**
★ ★ ★ **Lovely (RCA, 1988)**
★ ★ ★ **Pure (RCA, 1989)**

Madonna may have had blonde ambition, but the Primitives had Blondie ambition—that is, the group wanted nothing better than to recreate the ironic pop innocence of the early Blondie records. It's not as if the band started out as a Blondie tribute act; in fact, the early recordings collected on *Lazy 86–88* owe as much to the clangorous formalism of the Jesus and Mary Chain. But with the thin-voiced, platinum-haired Tracy (the only name she admitted to) out front and the band's arsenal of early-punk mannerisms in back, the Blondie tag seemed inescapable. *Lovely* has fun with it, cheerfully doling out peroxide pop from the breathlessly hooky "Crash" to the wry Spectorisms of "I'll Stick With You" (although, to be fair, guitarist-songwriter Paul Court sings lead on a few tunes). *Pure* finds the Primitives rinsing Blondie out of their sound, though, with the best songs—like the swirling, circular "Sick of It" or the bouncy "Can't Bring Me Down"—broadening the band's pop vocabulary. Then again, given the Velvet Underground adulation implicit in "All the Way Down" and as the cover of "I'll Be Your Mirror" make plain, it could be that the Primitives have simply switched role models. — J.D.C.

PRINCE

★ ★ ★   **For You (Warner Bros., 1978)**
★ ★ ★½ **Prince (Warner Bros., 1979)**
★ ★ ★ ★½ **Dirty Mind (Warner Bros., 1980)**
★ ★ ★½ **Controversy (Warner Bros., 1981)**

★ ★ ★ ★½ **1999 (Warner Bros., 1982)**
★ ★ ★ ★ ★ **Purple Rain (Warner Bros., 1984)**
★ ★ ★   **Around the World in a Day (Paisley Park, 1985)**
★ ★   **Parade (Paisley Park, 1986)**
★ ★ ★ ★ **Sign O' the Times (Paisley Park, 1987)**
★ ★ ★½ **Lovesexy (Paisley Park, 1988)**
★ ★ ★ ★ **Batman (Warner Bros., 1989)**
★ ★   **Music From "Graffiti Bridge" (Paisley Park, 1990)**
★ ★ ★   **Diamonds and Pearls (Paisley Park, 1991)**

Prince is a true musical polymath. Equally adept on guitar, keyboards, bass and drums, he (like Stevie Wonder) is a totally self-contained unit; he produced all 13 of his albums, and plays everything himself on at least six of them. Moreover, he has overseen or contributed to dozens of albums by other artists. As remarkable as his musicianship obviously is, his music can be maddeningly erratic, swinging from intoxicatingly accessible funk rock to self-obsessed psychedelia. At times, his astonishing proficiency seems more a curse than a blessing, for Prince's ability to realize almost any musical idea has led to more than one stylistic dead-end. Yet even at his most obtuse, it's hard to dismiss his work entirely; there's always at least one gem hidden amidst the mistakes.

Prince's first album, *For You*, offers mostly conventional R&B, like the falsetto lovesong "Baby," but with a few twists, like the gorgeous, multi tracked chorale on the title tune, or the jazzy synth breakdown at the end of "Just As Long As We're Together." Its single, the mildly lubricious "Soft and Wet," did passably on the R&B charts, but Prince didn't have a real hit until "I Wanna Be Your Lover," from *Prince*. What sets this tune apart from its predecessor isn't its slightly more explicit sexuality but its obvious rock influence. *Prince* is a guitar album, and though its overall sound still leans toward R&B, songs like "When We're Dancing Close and Slow" or "Bambi" defy categorization.

Dirty Mind breaks almost completely with Prince's R&B sound. Although some of the songs are certainly danceable, only "Head" sounds anything like conventional funk; the rest of the album seems to owe more to new wave, from the Cars-like rhythm arrangement of "When You Were Mine" to the itchy, synth-spiked groove of "Partyup." But it wasn't Prince's stylistic shift that got this album noticed, so much as the frankly sexual nature of the songs, from "Head" to the incest-endorsing "Sister" to the intimations of bisexuality in "Uptown." All of which served as the focus for Prince's next album, *Controversy*, which played coy in the title tune, then went on to include such titles as "Sexuality" and "Jack U Off." More telling is the music, which, though seldom as catchy as on *Dirty Mind*, shows the full range of Prince's ambition, including nods to synth pop ("Sexuality"), new wave ("Annie Christian"), even boogie-woogie of a sort (the stylized, parodic "Jack U Off" and "Ronnie, Talk to Russia"). Only "Do Me Baby," a fairly conventional love-me-all-night R&B ballad, hearkens back to Prince's initial instincts.

To this point, Prince had been something of a cult artist, in part because of the provocative nature of his lyrics but mostly because he had yet to hit upon a sound that would seduce the mainstream. *1999* changed that. Despite its double-album sprawl and some decidedly kinky material ("Lady Cabdriver," for instance), *1999* emphasizes his strengths, from the apocalyptic dance pulse of "1999" to the smirking lover-man moves of "International Lover." It also included "Little Red Corvette," which not only proved that Prince could write rock & roll as well as anyone, but gave him his first Top Ten hit. In fact, *1999* would probably have been an even bigger hit had Prince trimmed some of its more indulgent moments and left the album as lean and purposeful as *Purple Rain*.

Instead, it was *Purple Rain* that put Prince on a par with Springsteen and Madonna, and suggested that even Michael Jackson might have something to fear. Granted, some of that had to do with the simultaneous success of the *Purple Rain* film, but there's no denying the strength of these songs, from the gospel-tinged "Let's Go Crazy" and "I Would Die 4 U" to the haunting pathos of "When Doves Cry."

No sooner had Prince found his métier than he tossed it away. *Around the World in a Day*, the first release on his own Paisley Park imprint, is a curiously wholehearted embrace of pop mysticism which surrounds its few pop-friendly moments—most notably "Pop Life" and the wistful "Raspberry Beret"—with impenetrable symbol songs like "Paisley Park" and "The Ladder." *Parade* pushes even further in this direction; although the album seems tangentially related to Prince's second feature film, *Under the Cherry Moon*, it's hard to see how exactly these songs fit in.

Clearly, Prince is trying to articulate a belief system in which the notions of sex and God are somehow intertwined, but just what he's getting at is harder to see with each successive album. The double album *Sign O' the Times* finds him dropping even further down the rabbit hole and runs the gamut from the flat-out brilliant—"I Could Never Take the Place of Your Man," "U Got the Look"—to the virtually self-parodic. But it's easier to cope with the clubland clichés of "Housequake" than the strange psycho-sexual turns of "If I Was Your Girlfriend" and "It." But Prince's struggles with sex and salvation are too strange to shrug off. Indeed, his next album was originally supposed to be *The Black Album*, a sex-drenched collection including such numbers as "Bob George," an odd nod to rap braggadocio, and "Cindy C," a lust-letter to model Cindy Crawford. Yet at the last minute, Prince decided that *The Black Album* put sex before love and was therefore immoral. Warner Bros. never issued the album, although it was widely bootlegged. In its place came *Lovesexy*, a morality play of sorts. As theology, it's a muddle, particularly when Prince rambles on about characters like "Spooky Electric," but as pop, it has its moments, thanks to the quirky "Alphabet Street" and the ballad "When 2 R in Love" (a leftover from *The Black Album*).

This good-evil, sex-love duality also carried through Prince's soundtrack projects, *Batman* and *Music From "Graffiti Bridge"*— although in both cases taking a secondary role to the plot. *Batman* was apparently composed on the spur of the moment, and though the songs aren't all that consistent, the best—"Electric Chair," "Partyman," "Batdance"—sizzle. But *Graffiti Bridge*, the much-ballyhooed sequel to *Purple Rain*, is an embarrassment. Even though the film again pits Prince's band, the New Power Generation, against Morris Day and the Time, there's no sense of conflict or tension; the Time sounds stiff, guest shots by Mavis Staples and George Clinton seem wasted, and Prince's songs are flat and pedantic. Only Tevin Campbell's Michael Jackson-ish rendition of "Round and Round" keeps the album from total disaster.

With *Diamonds and Pearls*, Prince finally puts his spiritual theories aside and gets down to music. It's not terribly imaginative music—"Thunder" is a half-hearted rewrite of "Let's Go Crazy," "Cream" cops licks from T. Rex's "Bang a Gong," while "Jughead" is a simple-minded rap

rip-off—but it does seem to open a new, less conceptual chapter in the Prince saga.
— J.D.C.

JOHN PRINE

★ ★ ★ ★ ★   John Prine (Atlantic, 1971)
  ★ ★ ★½ Diamonds in the Rough (Atlantic, 1972)
  ★ ★ ★½ Sweet Revenge (Atlantic, 1973)
  ★ ★ ★½ Common Sense (Atlantic, 1975)
  ★ ★ ★   Prime Prine (Atlantic, 1976)
  ★ ★ ★   Bruised Orange (Asylum, 1978)
  ★ ★ ★½ Pink Cadillac (Asylum, 1979)
  ★ ★ ★½ Storm Windows (Asylum, 1980)
  ★ ★ ★   Aimless Love (Oh Boy, 1984)
  ★ ★ ★   German Afternoons (Oh Boy, 1985)
 ★ ★ ★ ★   The Missing Years (Oh Boy, 1991)

With a wicked tongue and a sharp eye, John Prine introduced an unforgettable cast of characters on his 1971 debut, *John Prine.* There's an OD-bound Vietnam vet ("Sam Stone"), a pair of loveless lovers ("Donald and Lydia") and several neglected elderly people who can still speak their minds ("Angel From Montgomery," "Hello in There"). And who's John Prine? That guy with the "Illegal Smile" over there, the one "digesting the *Reader's Digest* in the back of the dirty bookstore." Prine's deep, reedy voice takes some getting used to, but he manages to turn his croak into an affecting country twang at times. The generous amounts of pedal-steel guitar help quite a bit, coaxing melody out of Prine's tightly constructed sketches and reveries. That twang comes to the fore on the raucous "Yes I Guess They Ought to Name a Drink After You" (from *Diamonds in the Rough*). But the rest of this followup reworks the debut's themes—Vietnam, Jesus—in less striking fashion. The remainder of Prine's career continues under the "Difficult, but Rewarding" banner. He loves throwing curve balls and boomerangs. Though it's laden with more tart country influences, *Sweet Revenge* is actually somewhat bitter; the tersely observed "Christmas in Prison" and "Grandpa Was a Carpenter" both meet Prine's high standard, though. *Common Sense* administers a moody rock thrashing to what are probably sensible-enough songs; the words get swallowed up in the melancholoy blur. The best-of format (*Prime Prine*) hardly suits this mercurial artist—even Prine's fans can't agree on what his best tracks are. *Bruised Orange*, which features a collaboration with Phil Spector ("If You Don't Want My Love"), is a

subdued, quietly sung outing. *Pink Cadillac* is the polar opposite; muddy-sounding, insanely raucous rockabilly recorded at the source, Sun Studios in Memphis. Prine's vocal control—never faultless—seemed to waver a bit on his self-produced, lo-fi albums of the '80s. But *The Missing Years* artfully fills in the gaps, with subtle assists from various friends and the most graspable set of Prine originals since the '70s. "It's a Big Old Goofy World" will lead you right into his uniquely skewed corner of the universe. — M.C.

PROCLAIMERS

  ★ ★   This Is the Story (Chrysalis, 1987)
  ★ ★ ★ Sunshine On Leith (Chrysalis, 1988)

When Craig and Charlie Reid wrap their voices around a song as insinuatingly melodic as "Letter from America," it's easy to forgive their thick Scots burrs and folkie stubbornness. Unfortunately, songs like that are rare on *This Is the Story* (although, in an act of compensation, "Letter from America" appears twice), but *Sunshine On Leith* is far more consistent. It's also better produced and slightly slicker, but as much as those qualities might make it more listenable, what makes it worth hearing are songs like the catchy, exuberant "I'm Gonna Be (500 Miles)." — J.D.C.

PROCOL HARUM

  ★ ★ ★ ★ Procol Harum (Deram, 1967)
  ★ ★ ★ ★ Shine on Brightly (A&M, 1968)
  ★ ★ ★ ★ A Salty Dog (A&M, 1969)
  ★ ★ ★½ Home (A&M, 1970)
  ★ ★ ★½ Broken Barricades (A&M, 1971)
  ★ ★ ★½ Live in Concert (A&M, 1972)
  ★ ★ ★ ★ The Best of Procol Harum (1972; A&M, 1987)
  ★ ★½ Grand Hotel (Chrysalis, 1973)
  ★ ★ ★ Exotic Birds and Fruit (Chrysalis, 1974)
  ★ ★   Procol Ninth (Chrysalis, 1975)
  ★ ★   Something Magic (Chrysalis, 1977)
  ★ ★ ★ ★ Classics (A&M, 1987)
  ★ ★ ★ The Chrysalis Years (1973–77) (Chrysalis, 1989)
  ★ ★   The Prodigal Stranger (Zoo, 1991)

Ever since Paul McCartney underscored the melody of "Eleanor Rigby" with a string quartet, many pop players have attempted a fusion of rock and classical music. The Moody Blues and Emerson, Lake and Palmer came up with grandiose versions, E.L.O contrived a much more pleasant mix—but the band that pulled off the idea with absolute mastery was Procol Harum. United by tremendous ambition, all of the musicians were adept soloists—pianist Gary Brooker's voice was not only a first-rate blues vehicle, but was graced with the command to handle Procol's oft-times stentorian lyrics; Matthew Fisher played organ with rare subtlety; B.J. Wilson was a drummer as unique in his way as Keith Moon or John Bonham; Robin Trower flourished not only technique but sheer rock power. And in Keith Reid, a literary figure who wrote the words to their songs, Procol found a lyricist whose odd, vaguely surreal lyrics matched their own very distinctive vision.

Even if Trower and Wilson were brought on board only after its release, the staggering "Whiter Shade of Pale" provided the blueprint for Procol's early glory. Based on Bach's "Suite No. 3 in D Major," this was music of a haunting resonance—and the single remains the centerpiece of the group's impressive debut. The two-keyboard approach, heard first on Dylan's *Highway 61 Revisited* and *Blonde on Blonde*, was employed with a fresh majesty, and Brooker's singing had all the urgency of a prime R&B vocalist's. *Shine on Brightly* developed the sound, with "Shine on Brightly" having nearly the power of "Pale." With *A Salty Dog* and such standout cuts as the title track, "Wreck of the Hesperus" and "Boredom," Procol purveyed spacious, crafty epics. Brooker favored classical progressions; virtually never did he limit himself to the standard three chords of rock & roll—and, while the playing was always first-rate, the group seldom came off as self-indulgent.

Matthew Fisher, however, then departed—the first of Procol's significant personnel losses. *Broken Barricades* showed the group going in for a heavier, less leisurely style, especially on the full-out attack of "Simple Sister"; with "Whiskey Train," off *Home*, Procol proved it could rock with undeniable credibility. Trower, the only true rocker of the group, then left, however, and the band developed signs that it had lost the creative tension that initially inspired it. *Grand Hotel* was capable, with Brooker going in for Tchaikovsky-like stylings on the title track; *Exotic Birds and Fruit* demonstrated a strong, if short-lived return to form; and the group's last two albums were unnecessary. *Ninth*, produced by the ace songwriting team of Leiber/Stoller, jettisons almost all of Procol's classical music leanings; *Something*

Magic just sounds exhausted. The 1991 comeback, *The Prodigal Stranger*, was deeply uninspired.

Of the compilations, *The Best of* and *Classics* are interchangeable and excellent; also of note is the outstanding 1972 live album that produced a great symphonic reworking of "Conquistador," a classic from the debut. — P.E.

PROFESSOR GRIFF
★★½ **Pawns in the Game (Luke Records, 1990)**
★★★ **Kao's II Wiz*7*Dome (Luke Records, 1991)**

Originally a member of Public Enemy's "Security of the First World" troupe, Professor Griff (born Richard Griffin) made headlines before he made rap records. In 1989, Griff—Public Enemy's Minister of Information—gave an interview in which he insisted that the Jews were responsible for "the majority of wickedness" in the world and were chiefly responsible for the slave trade that brought blacks to America. A storm of protest broke out. Griff was eventually forced out of the group, and signed a solo deal with Luther Campbell.

Pawns in the Game isn't a bad start, with enough hard beats built into the backing tracks to cover for Griff's sometimes shaky delivery, but his fondness for strident, humorless harangues like "The Verdict" makes the album hard to take. *Kao's II Wiz*7*Dome* ("chaos to wisdom"), although no less singleminded in its agenda, is considerably funkier, thanks to its adroit samples and insistent grooves. Still, Griff's increasing sense of martyrdom suggests an inability to distinguish "wisdom" from "paranoia." — J.D.C.

PROFESSOR LONGHAIR
★★★★★ **New Orleans Piano (Blues Originals, Vol. 2) (1953; Atlantic, 1989)**
★★★★ **Rock 'n' Roll Gumbo (1974; Dancing Cat, 1985)**
★★★ **Live on the Queen Mary (Harvest, 1978)**
★★★ **Crawfish Fiesta (Alligator, 1980)**
★★★★★ **Mardi Gras in New Orleans (Nighthawk, 1981)**
★★★★ **The Last Mardi Gras (Atlantic, 1982)**
★★★ **Houseparty New Orleans Style (Rounder, 1987)**

As Jelly Roll Morton was to New Orleans music in particular and jazz in general at the turn of the century, so was Henry Roeland

Byrd, aka Professor Longhair, to the singular gumbo that was the Crescent City's contribution to R&B and rock & roll. Simply put, the New Orleans school of rock & roll is inconceivable without Longhair's sweeping, profound technique. Longhair perfected the synthesis of rhumba and boogie-woogie rhythms that has come to be a trademark of New Orleans music, working out these black and Latin influences with his left hand while with his right hand he conjured all manner of syncopated magic in the melody lines. Add a fondness for blues and calypso, and you have Longhair's singular mix.

Apart from his instrumental prowess, Longhair was a versatile singer, whose influence is less obvious because in a city full of idiosyncratic singers, he may have been the most idiosyncratic of them all. Yelps, yodels and whistles were part of his trick bag, but that's not to dismiss the warmth or personality evident in his stylish vocalizing. Having a sense of humor helped, too. His rocking interpretation of Hank Williams's "Jambalaya" finds him singing one verse in a Fats Domino voice; likewise, on "Got My Mojo Working" he affects an Elvis Presley sound when he slurs some lyrics. The sound effects, the irresistible rhythmic assault and the unexpected vocal flourishes make a case for Longhair as the greatest one-man band of all time.

Nighthawk's *Mardi Gras in New Orleans* and Atlantic's *New Orleans Piano* collect Longhair's most important late-'40s and early-'50s recordings, including "She Ain't Got No Hair," "Mardi Gras in New Orleans," "Professor Longhair's Boogie" and "Tipitina." From 1964 to 1971 Longhair dropped out of music and worked as a manual laborer in New Orleans, until a talent scout for the New Orleans Jazz and Heritage Festival persuaded him to perform again. He continued to play and record until his death in 1980, and the remainder of the albums listed date from this later period. *Crawfish Fiesta*, his final studio album, and *The Last Mardi Gras*, his final live album (recorded in 1978 at the Tipitina Club), show no diminution in the master's touch nor in his jubilant approach to his material. *Live on the Queen Mary* was the first live recording of Longhair's career, from a 1975 party hosted by Paul McCartney aboard the Queen Mary in Long Beach, CA. *Houseparty New Orleans Style* was Longhair's first postretirement recording, and it's notable for including more than the

evergreens dotting most of Longhair's releases. "Tipitina" is included, but so is "She Walk Right In" and "Cherry Pie," to name a couple of interesting tracks. *Rock 'n' Roll Gumbo*, originally issued in France in 1974 and released Stateside in 1985 on George Winston's Dancing Cat label, teams the Professor with Louisiana blues master Clarence "Gatemouth" Brown, who plays guitar throughout and adds some frenetic fiddling to buttress Longhair on "Jambalaya." — D.M.

PRONG

★ ★½ **Primitive Origins (Spigot, 1987)**
★ ★½ **Force Fed (1987; In-Effect, 1991)**
★ ★ ★ **Beg to Differ (Epic, 1990)**
★ ★ ★½ **Prove You Wrong (Epic, 1991)**

As much as there is to admire about the tightly-coiled intensity of Prong's instrumental attack, it's hard to get past the fact that both *Primitive Origins* and *Force Fed* offer few variations on the basic thrash-and-churn of metalcore. That changes some with *Beg to Differ*, as the band begins to move away from the usual lock-step rhythm work, particularly on the title tune, in which the backbeat shows intimations of funk. But it's not spelled out until *Prove You Wrong*, on which Prong's stylistic repertoire expands to include material like the funky, drum-driven "Shouldn't Have Bothered" and the itchy, dissonant "Prove You Wrong," which sounds as if it could as easily have been a Minutemen number. Well worth hearing. — J.D.C.

PSYCHEDELIC FURS

★ ★ ★ ★ **The Psychedelic Furs (Columbia, 1980)**
★ ★ ★ ★ **Talk Talk Talk (Columbia, 1981)**
★ ★ ★ **Forever Now (Columbia, 1982)**
★ ★ ★ **Mirror Moves (Columbia, 1984)**
★ ★½ **Midnight to Midnight (Columbia, 1987)**
★ ★ ★ ★ **All of This and Nothing (Columbia, 1988)**
★ ★½ **Book of Days (Columbia, 1989)**
★ ★½ **World Outside (Columbia, 1991)**

The Psychedelic Furs represents a major step forward in the evolution of punk. The energy level is relentless, and lead snarler Richard Butler lets the invective fly; he's got Johnny Rotten down cold, plus a few gutter moves all his own. Doubling the guitars and dropping in a saxophone, this British sextet raised punk's musical consciousness without sacrificing its defiant spirit. The debut album expands on the inward gaze and rich, mystical guitar sound of Siouxsie and the Banshees's groundbreaking *Scream* from the year before (the Furs' first manager was a former Banshees roadie), adding Butler's more volatile sense of melody and the band's propulsive arrangements to the bubbling turmoil. *Talk Talk Talk* varies the musical and emotional tone, moving away from sheer anger and making explicit the band's debts to Roxy Music and David Bowie. Butler suavely croaks his way through the definitive "Pretty in Pink," exhumes the '60s on the stinging "Dumb Waiters" and offers sex as the surefire cure for alienation on the pile-driving "Into You Like a Train." These two albums attempt to meet the punk-shy American mass audiences halfway; most AOR stations didn't cotton to something called a Psychedelic Fur, needless to say, so the group never did escape the new wave ghetto.

Through the mid-'80s, Richard Butler turned the Furs into his personal vehicle. Like too many Todd Rundgren productions, *Forever Now* recalls a promising arranged date that never quite gets off the ground. The richly synthesized single "Love My Way" introduces Butler's stark, bracing ballad style: slow dance time at the local disco Videodrome. And while the first half of *Mirror Moves* keeps those moody hooks coming, producer Keith Forsey eventually sweeps away Butler's rough edges in his superclean video-rock jetstream. The band's original members reconvened after the disastrously bland *Midnight to Midnight*; sadly, the latter-day albums are well-intentioned downers, all drone and no drive, every classic element in place except the *passion*. The Furs' greatest hits—half-true, anyway—are collected on the worthy *All of This and Nothing*. — M.C.

PUBLIC ENEMY

★ ★ ★ ½ **Yo! Bum Rush the Show (Def Jam, 1987)**
★ ★ ★ ★ ½ **It Takes a Nation of Millions to Hold Us Back (Def Jam, 1988)**
★ ★ ★ ★ ★ **Fear of a Black Planet (Def Jam, 1990)**
★ ★ ★ ★ ★ **Apocalypse 91 . . . The Enemy Strikes Black (Def Jam, 1991)**

As tempting as it is to praise Public Enemy for its politics or point of view, what the group has to say doesn't have half the impact of how it sounds. Don't take that as a dismissal; even when Public Enemy hedges its bets, the fact that its music sparks debate and encourages its listeners to think makes

the group both admirable and influential. But the truth is, that message wouldn't be half as impressive without Chuck D's booming delivery, Flavor Flav's comic counterpoint or Terminator X's turntable slice-and-dice.

That emphasis on sound has been obvious from the first. With its lean, hard sound, alternating conventionally funky samples with exhilarating bursts of noise, *Yo! Bum Rush the Show* sounded like nothing else on the scene at the time. And no wonder; hearing it now, the album seems like nothing so much as a musical workshop in which the PE production team ran through a variety of stylistic devices, from a funkier version of Run-D.M.C.'s "Rock Box" crunch on "Sophisticated Bitch" (check the Vernon Reid guitar solo) to the acrobatic scratch of "Rightstarter (Message to a Black Man)," to the simple bass-driven beats of "Yo! Bum Rush the Show."

With *It Takes a Nation of Millions to Hold Us Back* Public Enemy truly comes into being. Credit the group's ideological growth for some of that, as raps like "Prophets of Rage," "Black Steel in the Hour of Chaos" and "Bring the Noise" develop the black-power rhetoric of "Rightstarter" into a more fully articulated political stance. But the album's sound does most of the work, from the air-raid siren intro to "Countdown to Armageddon" to the dense, noise-splattering samples churning behind the likes of "She Watch Channel Zero?!," "Rebel Without a Pause" and—especially—"Bring the Noise." It isn't just a matter of sonic impact, though, as if this were merely dance music; it's the emotional energy that puts the album over, as with "Black Steel," on which the anxious quiet of the piano vamp underscores the rage in Chuck D's delivery.

That rage, combined with the group's obvious intelligence, made Public Enemy scary to many in the media, and *Fear of a Black Planet* artfully plays off that apprehension. Opening with an aural collage peppered with sound bites culled from coverage of the Professor Griff controversy (Griff, a member of Public Enemy's security force-cum-dance group, had been quoted as blaming Jews for "the majority of wickedness" in the world; he eventually left to pursue a solo career), the album establishes PE as a group under siege, then immediately assumes control of the situation with "Brothers Gonna Work It Out." Public Enemy plays off its public image throughout the album, whether through the personal commentary of "Welcome to the Terrordome" or the call to arms of "War at 33⅓." The group remains on the offensive for most of the album, challenging the portrayal of blacks in movies ("Burn Hollywood Burn"), the inadequate response of most urban rescue squads ("911 Is a Joke") and the Eurocentrism of American culture ("Fight the Power"). And as always, the music is more provocative than the wordplay, thanks to the chances taken by tracks like "Leave This Off Your Fu*kin Charts" or "Pollywanacraka."

By *Apocalypse 91 . . . The Enemy Strikes Black*, Public Enemy's strategy was fairly familiar, but that hardly diminishes the album's impact. Topically, the album adjusts its focus to the role the black community plays in its own destruction, be it by tolerating drug dealers ("Nighttrain"), listening to radio stations that care more for demographics than for people ("How to Kill a Radio Consultant") or by buying and drinking malt liquor ("1 Million Bottlebags"). Musically, though, this album's sound is even richer than its predecessors, thanks to production that delivers everything from the stone soul of "I Don't Wanna Be Called Yo Niga" to the full-blown frenzy of "Nighttrain." Add in the thrash-rap fusion of "Bring the Noise" (performed with Anthrax), and Public Enemy once again proves why it is the most influential and imitated rap act of its day.
— J.D.C.

PUBLIC IMAGE LTD.
★★★ **Public Image (Virgin, 1978)**
★★★★ **Second Edition (Island, 1980)**
★★ **The Flowers of Romance (Warner Bros., 1981)**
★★½ **This Is What You Want . . . This Is What You Get (Elektra, 1984)**
★★½ **Album (Elektra, 1986)**
★★ **Live in Tokyo (Elektra, 1986)**
★★½ **Happy? (Virgin, 1987)**
★★½ **9 (Virgin, 1989)**
★★★½ **The Greatest Hits, So Far (Virgin, 1990)**
★★½ **That What Is Not (Virgin, 1992)**
The Sex Pistols didn't leave much room for an encore. *Public Image* reflects the confusion of John Lydon (né Johnny Rotten) as he gropes for a new attack mode. The title rant is both the most convincing and most traditionally oriented track on the album. *Second Edition* is anything but tentative—or traditional. Originally released as three EPs inside a round container (*Metal

Box), the contents of PiL's double-album opus retain a remarkable degree of freshness. After more than a decade on the shelf, Lydon's postpunk (and postrock) musical vision still fascinates and disturbs. His bitter diatribes and cautionary mantras are propelled by a wildly imaginative pair of sidemen. Guitarist Keith Levene spews forth near-psychedelic outbursts and oddly lyrical Middle Eastern asides, while bassist Jah Wobble plies a slippery reggae-flavored space beat.

On *The Flowers of Romance*, Lydon already seems to have run out of ideas. Pseudo-ethnic percussion and free-ranging spleen don't add up to much of a statement—let alone an antidote to boredom. Bored is exactly how Lydon sounds on *This Is What You Want . . . This Is What You Get*. From this point on, his albums are sleekly produced walk-throughs: the former Rotten one does his scattershot thing to state-of-the-art "alternative rock" accompaniment. Oh, he gets off a zinger now and then: "This Is Not a Love Song" from *What You Want*, "Rise" from *Album*, "Seattle" from *Happy*. "Anger is an energy" Lydon dutifully snarls on "Rise," over a churning Siouxsie and the Banshees imitation. But it comes across as an easy one-liner, not a defiant statement of purpose. Lydon reaches his cynical nadir on the best-of collection, though. "Don't Ask Me" is pure stand-up schtick. "Don't blame me, I told you so," he declares at the end of a snide ecological rap. It's a long way from "No future" to the optimistically titled *Greatest Hits, So Far*. Or is it?
— M.C.

GARY PUCKETT AND THE UNION GAP
★★ **Greatest Hits (Columbia, 1970)**
Tricked out inanely in Billy Yank garb, San Diego's Union Gap scored in the late '60s with "Woman, Woman," "Young Girl," "This Girl Is a Woman Now" and "Lady Willpower." Virtually identical to each other, the hits were leering, lounge-rock monstrosities, with Puckett offering oily love instruction to ingenues, and investing the word "woman" with unctuous pseudo-reverence. A barrel-voiced singer resembling a cut-rate David Clayton Thomas in his macho skill, Puckett led a band whose songwriter ended up singing backup on "The Tonight Show." 'Nuff said.
— P.E.

PURE PRAIRIE LEAGUE
★ ★ ★ **Bustin' Out (RCA, 1975)**
★ ★ ★ **Two Lane Highway (RCA, 1975)**
★ ★ ★ **If the Shoe Fits (RCA, 1976)**
★ ★ ★ **Live! Takin' the Stage (1977; RCA, 1988)**
★ ★ ★ **"Amie" and Other Hits (RCA, 1990)**

This Cincinnati-based band's debut album interprets country rock as singer-songwriter musings laced with a little pedal-steel. Lead singer Craig Fuller's earnest melancholy may seem a bit wispy today, but in the early '70s, "Amie" massaged the weary sensibilities of many an FM radio listener. Pure Prairie League found an audience, and the group continued to prosper after Fuller's early departure. *Two Lane Highway* and *If the Shoe Fits* are slightly more downhome in focus. *Two Lane Highway* glances at traditional country subject matter, albeit through a gauze of hippie sentimentality, on satisfying tracks like "Kentucky Moonshine" and "Kansas City Southern." *If the Shoe Fits* hinges on a not-bad Buddy Holly cover ("That'll Be the Day") and "Early Morning Riser," a pretty-going-on-sappy ballad that just about equals "Amie." Craig Fuller resurfaced in the late '80s as lead singer of the revived Little Feat, replacing the late Lowell George. — M.C.

THE PURSUIT OF HAPPINESS
★ ★ ★ ½ **Love Junk (Chrysalis, 1988)**
★ ★ ★ ★ **One-Sided Story (Chrysalis, 1990)**

Where the Pursuit of Happiness parts company with most male-led rock bands is sex. Songwriters in other bands write about girls, but TPOH's Moe Berg writes about women—actual adult females—and that makes a world of difference. Never mind that he still calls them "girls," or sometimes entertains sexist thoughts; his songs aren't about politics or theory, but the way real people think and feel. And it's the humanity of his music—along with a good deal of wit and affection—that gives these albums their heart. Surprisingly, the band does all this with a sound that's loud and simple, drawing heavily from mainstream rock without succumbing to its clichés. Berg and the band even manage to have fun with the ordinariness of their sound; one of *Love Junk*'s best songs is the jocular, witheringly honest "I'm an Adult Now." Yet for all its knowing wit, very little of the album is played for irony; as a result, it's easy for any (aging male) rock fan to identify with the likes of "Looking for Girls" or "Hard to Laugh." But it's *One-Sided Story* that finds TPOH truly coming into its own;

there's added depth and power to relationship songs like "Two Girls in One" or "Something Physical," an impressive maturity to "Shave Your Legs" and "All I Want." Not to mention the wonderfully affectionate—and utterly hilarious—metaphors piled on in "Food." — J.D.C.

PUSSY GALORE
★ ★ **Right Now! (Caroline, 1987)**
★ ★ **Dial 'M' for Motherfucker (Caroline, 1989)**
★ ★ ½ **Historia de la Musica Rock (Caroline, 1990)**

Everything about the Washington, D.C., quartet Pussy Galore is guaranteed to offend. Available only on import, *Groovy Hate Fuck*, from 1987, compiles the "greatest hits" from their notorious early days, but the more recent fare isn't much different—three guitars (no bass), this is noise music, deliberately ugly and wrongheadedly provocative. Dissonance and shock value are hardly radical concepts, of course: punk thrived on outrage, Zappa and Beefheart were granddaddies of dada rock, and Ornette Coleman's free jazz fractured many an unsympathetic eardrum. But the Pussies are notable for the relentless stupidity of their assault—from *Dial 'M*,' "Eat Me," "Penetration of the Centerfold" and "Adolescent Wet Dream" may be some cretin's (or twisted intellectual's) idea of an emancipatory gesture, but unlistenable songs ultimately have no impact whatsoever. Among the album's 20 cuts are sound-bite snatches of found dialogue and random electronic squawking—the kind of thing that rendered Lou Reed's *Metal Machine Music* dismissable eons ago. *Historia de la Musica Rock*, presumably a "deconstruction" of the artform, is more endurable—the takeoff on Jagger's version of "Little Red Rooster," for example, does flash a sick wit—but the album's trashing of rock & roll clichés gets old real fast. — P.E.

PYLON
★ ★ ½ **Gyrate (DB, 1980)**
★ ★ ★ ½ **Chomp (DB, 1983)**
★ ★ ★ ★ **Hits (DB, 1988)**
★ ★ ½ **Chain (Sky, 1990)**

This charmingly amateurish Athens, Georgia, quartet was in many ways the missing link between the B-52's and R.E.M., both in terms of chronology (*Gyrate* arrived one year after the B-52's made their major-label debut and one year before R.E.M. recorded "Radio Free Europe") and style. Granted, Pylon's blend of guitar-band jangle and dance-pop groove didn't always work, and much of *Gyrate* sounds like bad-imitation Gang of Four. *Chomp*, on the other hand, finds Pylon coming into its own musically, and tracks like "Beep," "Yo-Yo" and "Crazy" rank among the band's best.

Pylon called it quits not long after that album; *Hits* compiles most of *Gyrate*, some of *Chomp* and both of the band's non-LP single tracks, while the so-so *Chain* introduces a brief (and unsuccessful) reunion attempt. — J.D.C.

Q

QUEEN

- ★ ★ **Queen (1973; Hollywood, 1991)**
- ★ ★½ **Queen II (1974; Hollywood, 1991)**
- ★ ★ ★ **Sheer Heart Attack (1974; Hollywood, 1991)**
- ★ ★ ★ **A Night at the Opera (1975; Hollywood, 1991)**
- ★ ★ **A Day at the Races (1977; Hollywood, 1991)**
- ★ ★½ **News of the World (1977; Hollywood, 1991)**
- ★ ★ **Jazz (1978; Hollywood, 1991)**
- ★ ★ **Live Killers (1979; Hollywood, 1991)**
- ★ ★ ★ **The Game (1980; Hollywood, 1991)**
- ★ ★ **Flash Gordon (1980; Hollywood, 1991)**
- ★ ★ ★½ **Greatest Hits (1981; Hollywood, 1991)**
- ★ ★ **Hot Space (1982; Hollywood, 1991)**
- ★ ★ **The Works (Capitol, 1984)**
- ★ ★ **A Kind of Magic (Capitol, 1986)**
- ★ ★ **The Miracle (Capitol, 1989)**
- ★ ★ ★ **Innuendo (Hollywood, 1991)**
- ★ ★ ★ **Classic Queen (Hollywood, 1992)**
- ★ ★½ **Live at Wembley (Hollywood, 1992)**

Excessive, decadent, theatrical, androgynous, tasteless, mocking, ironic, self-conscious: Queen lived up to its moniker with a gleeful abandon. It could only have happened in the '70s. In fact, this British quartet's popularity in the States fell off—I mean plummeted—immediately after the career peak of *The Game* in 1980. With good reason, too; the font of crafty hooks had suddenly dried up. But in the group's prime, guitarist Brian May and irrepressible lead singer Freddie Mercury provide a steady flow of bombastically catchy shlock-rock hits. Mercury's outrageous stage presence and mock-operatic vocal range established Queen as a ranking concert draw, ruling at the very peak of the arena-circuit scene.

The group began as a somewhat crude glam-metal outfit, with arty underpinnings.

Gradually, the members' college backgrounds and musical chops start to emerge. On *Sheer Heart Attack*, "Killer Queen" and "Stone Cold Crazy" weld Mercury's creamy falsetto strut to propulsive, tightly wound arrangments. You can get winded just listening to all those multitracked Freddies singing rings around each other. That's nothing compared to "Bohemian Rhapsody," of course: the notorious six-minute-plus centerpiece of *A Night at the Opera* is either a progressive-rock benchmark or the most convoluted novelty song ever recorded. This over-the-top approach is precisely what makes Mercury and company so endearing, but it's also responsible for Queen's eventual downfall. A little too predictably, *A Day at the Races* is a quickie sequel to *Night at the Opera*—minus a surefire hit single. *News of the World* sports two of those; however, the jackboot jock-rock pomp stomp of "We Are the Champions" and "We Will Rock You" may be one of Queen's most dubious chart achievements—mindlessly catchy. *Jazz* is utter jive; *The Game* finds the group back at the top of theirs. The snazzy ersatz rockabilly groove on "Crazy Little Thing Called Love" isn't any more authentic than the thumping bass riff (swiped from Chic) on "Another Ones Bites the Dust," yet those songs proved to be the first consistently listenable Queen opuses.

Poised for further success as a stylishly derivative singles machine, Queen promptly marched down the road to genial self-parody. After the rococco indulgences of the tuneless *Flash Gordon* soundtrack, the group seemed to lose its popwise footing—and knack for killer riffs. All pomp and no rock makes Queen a rather stale proposition. Freddie Mercury wowed the masses at Live Aid in 1985, but the subsequent comeback bid (*A Kind of Magic*) rings hollow at the core. *Innuendo*, Queen's 1991 reemergence, is a remarkably enthusiastic, letter-perfect recreation of the group's past glories. Yet in an era of rampant nostalgia, when even Donny Osmond has been rehabilitated, these '70s superstars couldn't get arrested; *Innuendo* flopped big time. Queen's catalog is now available on CD for those faithful fans who require replacement parts. Everyone else should proceed with caution: these albums are so emblematic of their time that even *Greatest Hits* sounds dated. Unfortunately, the sad death of Freddy Mercury in 1991 assures that Queen will never have the opportunity to bring its sound into the present. — M.C.

QUEEN LATIFAH
★ ★ ★ ★ **All Hail the Queen (Tommy Boy, 1989)**
   ★ ★ ★ **Nature of a Sista' (Tommy Boy, 1991)**

Formerly Dana Owens of East Orange, New Jersey, distaff rapper Queen Latifah earns that Afrocentric crown with her debut album. *All Hail the Queen* is a masterful sampler package, a state-of-the-dance-floor tour of hip-hop at the dawn of its second decade. Working with sympathetic producers (Daddy-O from Stetsasonic, the members of De La Soul, KRS-One of Boogie Down Productions, DJ Mark, the 45 King), Latifah displays an uncommon versatility, especially for an up-and-comer. She moves comfortably from soul-music roots to house-music echoes, from spacious dub-reggae to cosmic funk, from feminist insistence to convincing romance: even without a surefire hit single, this is one of the most consistently listenable—and inspired—rap albums ever assembled. Latifah even introduces British rapper Monie Love on an insistently sharp duet called "Ladies First." Latifah is somewhat overwhelmed by *Nature of a Sista*'s various producers and their tradition-bound musical outlook. The disco elegance of "Give Me Your Love" and "How Do I Love Thee" is a turnaround from the no-nonsense groove on earlier tracks like "Ladies First" or "Mama Gave Birth to the Soul Children."
— M.C.

QUEENSRŸCHE
   ★½ **Queensrÿche (EMI, 1983)**
   ★½ **The Warning (EMI, 1984)**
  ★ ★½ **Rage for Order (EMI USA, 1986)**
★ ★ ★ **Operation Mindcrime (EMI Manhattan, 1988)**
★ ★ ★½ **Empire (EMI USA, 1990)**
★ ★ ★ **Operation Livecrime (EMI, 1991)**

Most of Queensrÿche's early output is standard-issue metal, with more than a little owed to the sound of Judas Priest (particularly Geoff Tate's vocals). With "Roads to Madness" (from *The Warning*), the band begins to take an artier approach that expands the basic crunch-and-stomp of metal without losing its gut-level impact. *Rage for Order* has it moments, but the songs don't always differentiate between aural embellishment ("Screaming in Digital") and musical ambition ("I Will Remember").

Still, it sets the stage for *Operation Mindcrime*, a full-blown concept album that spins Reagan-era media manipulation into a nightmarish vision of the future. The album is smart enough to rely more on character songs than straight narrative, which may slow the plot but makes the action more involving; musically, the band does a wonderful job of building tension with "Spreading the Disease" and "Breaking the Silence," but relies too much on stock devices like the ominous choir in "Electric Requiem." (*Operation Livecrime* merely reprises the album in concert, an exercise that makes more sense on video.) Perhaps that's why *Empire*, though it lacks the unity of its predecessor, is a more fulfilling album, for these songs make the most of their music, whether through the muscular throb of "Jet City Woman" or the quietly shifting dynamics of "Silent Lucidity." — J.D.C.

? AND THE MYSTERIANS
★ ★ ★ ★ **The Dallas Reunion Tapes: 96 Tears Forever (ROIR, 1985)**

Since ? and the Mysterians' original Cameo issues of the mid-'60s are nearly impossible to find, it's a blessing that *The Dallas Reunion Tapes* is such a terrific collection. It makes the most of the Michigan outfit's signature tune—the immortal "96 Tears," from 1966—and the great Farfisa organ noodling that would be resurrected much later by Blondie and Elvis Costello, but it's hardly a one-hit-and-filler recording. In all its Tex-Mex trash-rock glory, the band sounds startlingly fresh. Keyboardist Frank Rodriguez nearly steals the show, but the real action remains that of vocalist, ? himself (who used the name Rudy Martinez to collect royalties, but never let his real name be known). An R&B growler after the fashion of Mitch Ryder or Mick Jagger, ? leers and incites—this was the author, after all, of a tune he safely entitled "Girl, You Captivate Me" but cleverly, in concert, insisted on rendering as "Girl, You

Masturbate Me." Punks ahead of their time, the Mysterians were shunted aside by psychedelia, and wouldn't have stood a chance in the singer-songwriter era of the early '70s. That they crashed and burned after only two albums, then, was unsurprising. Their one-shot return, however, brings them back very much alive; it's just a drag that they didn't continue the comeback. — P.E.

QUICKSILVER MESSENGER SERVICE
- ★★★ **Quicksilver Messenger Service (Capitol, 1968)**
- ★★★½ **Happy Trails (Capitol, 1969)**
- ★★★ **Shady Grove (Capitol, 1970)**
- ★★ **Just for Love (Capitol, 1970)**
- ★★ **What About Me (Capitol, 1971)**
- ★★ **Quicksilver (Capitol, 1971)**
- ★★ **Comin' Thru (Capitol, 1972)**
- ★★★½ **Anthology (Capitol, 1973)**
- ★★★★ **Sons of Mercury: The Best of Quicksilver Messenger Service, 1968-1975 (Rhino, 1991)**

The quintessence of San Francisco jamming, the Quicksilver Messenger Service had, in John Cipollina, a guitarist capable of noodling away with some skill, but the band's long, loping, free-form excursions haven't aged well. LSD may have helped contemporary listeners groove through the 12 minutes of "The Fool" on the band's 1968 debut; now this sort of thing is untranslatable. Cipollina and bassist David Freiberg were colorless singers, and even the group's big moment—the endless reworking of "Who Do You Love" and "Mona" on *Happy Trails*—suffers from the aimlessness of most acid rock. Where anything by Bo Diddley should fiercely pound, these versions drift. (All these tracks are on

Rhino's anthology, *Sons of Mercury*.) In 1969 Quicksilver brought aboard Stones session pianist Nicky Hopkins. He, too, took on their coloring; the same musician who'd played toughly and efficiently on, say, "Sympathy for the Devil," was given, on Quicksilver's "Edward (the Mad Shirt Grinder)," endless time for free expression. He took it, to the point of tedium. "Fresh Air" provided the band with a middling hit in 1970; it's competently played, but sounds like a very long commercial. — P.E.

QUIET RIOT
- ★★½ **Metal Health (Pasha, 1983)**
- ★★ **Condition Critical (Pasha, 1984)**
- ★ **QR III (Pasha, 1986)**
- ★ **Quiet Riot (Pasha, 1988)**

Quiet Riot has two claims to fame, neither of which seems to have done it any good. Take, for instance, the fact that this was the band that gave guitarist Randy Rhoads his start. A nice point of pride, except that Rhoads was long gone by the time Quiet Riot recorded these albums; in truth, it was Ozzy Osbourne who gave Rhoads the exposure who that made him a guitar hero. Then there's the fact that Quiet Riot had greater U.S. success with Slade's "Cum On Feel the Noize" than Slade did. True, "Cum On Feel the Noize" did push *Metal Health* all the way to the top of the charts, but it was pretty much downhill from there. *Condition Critical* is just a cheap copy of *Metal Health*, right down to its de rigueur Slade cover, "Mama Weer All Crazee Now," while *QR III* isn't even that good. Singer Kevin DuBrow bailed out thereafter, and *Quiet Riot* is forgettably generic hard rock. — J.D.C.

R

EDDIE RABBITT
★★ The Best of Eddie Rabbit (Elektra, 1979)
★★ Step by Step (1981; Capitol Nashville, 1990)
★★ Radio Romance (1982; Capitol, 1990)
★★ The Best of Eddie Rabbit/Greatest Hits, Volume II (1979; WB, 1983)
★★ The Best Year of My Life (Warner Bros., 1984)
★★ Jersey Boy (Capitol Nashville, 1990)
★★ Ten Years of Greatest Hits (Capitol Nashville, 1990)
★★ Classics Collection (Capitol Nashville, 1991)
★★ Ten Rounds (Capitol Nashville, 1991)

Predictable country-pop with occasional rockabilly and western swing overtones has earned Eddie Rabbitt a host of best-selling singles and albums. But this is all assembly-line, formula record-making designed to get the cash registers ringing and nothing more. Like Kenny Rogers, Rabbitt is a businessman who happens to sing, and not very convincingly at that. Rabbitt's finest hour came as a songwriter, when Elvis Presley recorded a powerful version of "Kentucky Rain" (which Rabbitt co-wrote with Dick Heard) and Ronnie Milsap gave one of his trademark aggressive interpretations to "Pure Love." Presley's and Milsap's vocal presence and emotional commitment are qualities that have eluded the composer whenever he's turned performer. — D.M.

RADIATORS
★★★½ Law of the Fish (Epic, 1987)
★★★½ Zigzagging Through Ghostland (Epic, 1989)
★★★½ Total Evaporation (Epic, 1991)

Together for a decade before their major-label debut, the Radiators honed their craft in the smoke and sizzle of New Orleans bars. The years of silencing drunks and delighting dancers obviously paid off—this six-piece outfit cooks with real efficiency. Fond of Little Feat–like syncopations, they derive their core power from updating the swing and assurance of mid-'60s soul (Stax and Atlantic, rather than Motown). Keyboardist Ed Volker is the band's mainstay. A powerful singer, but never an excessive one, he shines on "Red Dress" and "Hardcore" (off *Zigzagging Through Ghostland*, from 1989), and turns tender on the marvelous "I Want to Go Where the Green Arrow Goes," the best slow song on *Total Evaporation*. Produced by Jim Dickinson and featuring the Memphis Horns, *Evaporation* is the group's most varied album, but all the Radiators' records are tasty—timeless, bluesy rock & roll. — P.E.

GERRY RAFFERTY
★★½ Right Down the Line: The Best of Gerry Rafferty (EMI, 1991)

Gerry Rafferty's hit "Baker Street" sticks to the middle of the road; this 1978 Number One epitomizes the cooled-out, post-rock "adult" love song. The hook—a warm, sprawling sax line (by studio player Raphael Ravenscroft)—also supplies "Baker Street" with its lingering, bittersweet emotional tone: Rafferty's vocals are pleasantly homogenous, at best. "Right Down the Line" gets pulled along in the powerful slipstream of "Baker Street," but the '80s-dominated *Best of Gerry Rafferty* comes to a smooth standstill after that. More interesting by far would be a compilation that tapped Rafferty's folk-rock debut (*Can I Have My Money Back?*, from 1971) and his early-'70s group, Stealer's Wheel ("Stuck in the Middle With You"). — M.C.

RAINDOGS
★★½ Lost Souls (Atco, 1990)
★★★ Border Drive-In Theatre (Atco, 1991)

Second-string alternative circuit veterans team up with Irish folk fiddler and go roots-cruising: a predictable journey, you might think. The Raindogs' debut doesn't depart from the straight-and-narrow, either. *Lost Souls* is a perfectly unremarkable example of foursquare folk-rock traditionalism. Deviating only slightly, *Border Drive-In Theatre* nonetheless constitutes a leap forward. Mark Cutler's singing and Johnny Cunningham's fiddling ring out, more confident and evocative than before; perhaps the newfound synthesizers and surprising rhythmic accents have allowed them room to breathe. Producer Don Gehman is best known for whittling John Mellencamp's big sound down to the bone, and he keeps the Raindogs' experiments in steady check. A subtle funk edge underlies some up-tempo cuts ("Carry Your Cross"), while deft strings and keyboards sweeten the slower ones ("Stop Shakin' Me Down"). Iggy Pop adds a demonic rap to the streetwise "Dance of the Freaks," and Wilbert Harrison's R&B classic "Let's Work Together" throbs with an appropriately fresh beat half-way between hard rock and hip-hop. — M.C.

MA RAINEY

★ ★ ★ ★ ★ **Ma Rainey (Milestone, 1974)**
★ ★ ★ ★ **The Immortal Ma Rainey (Milestone, 1975)**
★ ★ ★ ★ **Ma Rainey's Black Bottom (Yazoo, 1990)**

Billed on stage and records as "The Mother of the Blues," Ma Rainey (née Gertrude Pridgett) is an artist for whom extravagant claims are justified. For example, at the turn of the century, when she was touring the South with a popular minstrel show, she heard a girl in a small town in Missouri perform a song bemoaning her faithless lover. Rainey was so moved by the song that she incorporated it into her act, much to her audience's delight. Blues at this time was still rural folk music, but Rainey, when asked what kind of song it was that she had added to her repertoire, replied, "It's the blues." As Alan Freed would do decades later in taking a term that had been in widespread use in the black community for years and attaching it to the big-beat music emerging in the '50s, Rainey in effect liberated "blues"—the word and the music—from the fields and backwoods of rural black America and made it an accepted form of professional entertainment.

That's the least of her accomplishments. In terms of phrasing, attitude and showmanship, "The Mother of the Blues" had an impact on virtually every female blues singer—Bessie Smith, who may have been Rainey's protégée, and Billie Holiday being two of the most prominent examples. A flamboyant onstage presence, Rainey was given to adorning herself with headbands, feather boas, tiaras, dangling earrings, necklaces of gold and diamonds, dresses cut from expensive material; her teeth, as photos prove, were literally lined with gold. Her popularity so transcended that of other artists of her time that she became the pacesetter on the minstrel circuit.

Between 1923 and 1929 she cut over 90 sides for the Paramount label in Grafton, Wisconsin. Thirty-two of the best performances are on the two-record *Ma Rainey* set, which has the added bonus of authoritative liner notes by Dan Morgenstern. Rainey was always accompanied by outstanding musicians, and so it is on side one that she is joined by Louis Armstrong, Coleman Hawkins and Fletcher Henderson, among others; Armstrong's replies to Rainey's low-down vocalizing are a delight, especially on "See See Rider Blues." It's a subjective call, but the performances on side four, when Rainey is accompanied only by guitarist Tampa Red and pianist Georgia Tom Dorsey, are among the most moving blues performances ever recorded. There are moments on this side when Rainey seems to be singing a cappella, so overpowering are her vocals. Dorsey has said "she had that cry in her voice," and you can hear it here on wrenching tunes like "Tough Luck Blues" and "Sweet, Rough Man." *The Immortal Ma Rainey* and *Ma Rainey's Black Bottom* duplicate some of the material from the *Ma Rainey* set, but the bulk of the material on those two albums is unavailable elsewhere. Milestone has deleted two Rainey albums from its catalogue, *Blame It on the Blues* and *Down in the Basement*, and at present has no plans to reissue them. Collectors should be alert for two albums on the Biograph label, *Oh My Babe Blues* and *Queen of the Blues*, which will be reissued on CD. — D.M.

RAIN PARADE

★ ★½ **Emergency Third Rail Power Trip (Enigma, 1983)**
★ ★ ★½ **Beyond the Sunset (Restless/Enigma, 1985)**
★ ★ ★½ **Crashing Dream (Island, 1986)**

While capable singers and players, Rain Parade overdosed on too many psychedelic clichés (sitar, mixing-board daffiness) on its 1983 debut, *Emergency Third Rail Power Trip*, to come off as anything more than cute. The live *Beyond the Sunrise* was a considerable improvement: this time Will Glenn's violin seemed more like an instrument than a prop, the Buffalo Springfield–derived guitar playing had gained in looseness and credibility, and the songs were surer. Back in the studio, the sound coalesced for *Crashing Dream*: smart rock-pop that, for all its California '60s influence, is fresh, direct and sometimes exhilarating. — P.E.

BONNIE RAITT

★★★ **Bonnie Raitt (Warner Bros., 1971)**
★★★★ **Give It Up (Warner Bros., 1972)**
★★★★ **Takin My Time (Warner Bros., 1973)**
★★★ **Streetlights (Warner Bros., 1974)**
★★ **Home Plate (Warner Bros., 1975)**
★★ **Sweet Forgiveness (Warner Bros., 1977)**
★★★ **The Glow (Warner Bros., 1979)**
★★★ **Green Light (Warner Bros., 1982)**
★★★ **Nine Lives (Warner Bros., 1986)**
★★★★ **Nick of Time (Capitol, 1989)**
★★★★ **The Bonnie Raitt Collection (Warner Bros., 1990)**
★★★★ **Luck of the Draw (Capitol, 1991)**

When Bonnie Raitt picked up four Grammys for her 1989 album *Nick of Time*, she wasn't earning long-overdue credit. Rather the Grammys were testimony to the wisdom of hewing to a course that the artist knew to be right for her. Time and tide finally brought her to producer Don Was for *Nick of Time*. Which is not to suggest that Raitt's previous producers were hacks. Of the many with whom she has worked, only Paul Rothchild (whose credits include the Doors, Paul Butterfield Blues Band, Janis Joplin) misfired wildly, attempting to convert Raitt into a country-rock chanteuse on *Home Plate* and *Sweet Forgiveness*. Peter Asher, who produced *The Glow*, moved Raitt closer to the grit of her early albums even as he put a pop sheen on the proceedings. Looking back over Raitt's career leads one to the inescapable conclusion that the problem lay not in the producers but in the star. Simply put, it took a long time for Bonnie Raitt to grow up. As an artist she's always had the right idea—sliding in the blues she loves amongst a smattering of tough-rocking originals and smart outside material written by many of the best and brightest of her generation—but she hasn't always had undeniable

presence. It's there sporadically on all of her Warners albums, and produces some exhilarating moments. *Give It Up* is first-rate, with electrifying performances of Jackson Browne's "Under the Falling Sky" and Eric Kaz's tormented "Love Has No Pride," as well as her own forthright "Give It Up or Let Me Go." Thoughtful interpretations of songs by Kaz ("Cry Like a Rainstorm"), Browne ("I Thought I Was a Child") and Randy Newman ("Guilty") enliven *Takin My Time*, with Mississippi Fred McDowell's "Write Me a Few of Your Lines/Kokomo Blues" adding a raw-nerve edge to the proceedings. On the otherwise muddled *Sweet Forgiveness* she delivers a delicate take on Paul Seibel's enigmatic "Louise" that approaches both Seibel's own definitive version and the subdued but stirring treatment given the song by Leo Kottke on his *Greenhouse* album. But even her best work seemed too eclectic for its own good. Finally, she appeared too polished to be completely convincing as a blues singer, too gritty to be a pop singer, too restrained to be an out-and-out rocker.

By the time Raitt reached Don Was, she was ready to make a statement. Was provided the rock-steady focus—crisp, stripped-down, bottom-heavy arrangements with Raitt's voice riding strong over everything, her slide guitar lines mixed hot and played tasty and soulful—and Raitt responded with one well-modulated performance after another. Where her singing had often been an example of studied casualness, she emerges with a voice easy, confident, free, robust and alive. The uptempo material—notably the hit single "Thing Called Love" (written by John Hiatt)—cooks righteously, and Raitt sounds utterly absorbed in its emotion. On meditative numbers such as the title song and Michael Ruff's "Cry on My Shoulder" she works from knowledge learned the hard way.

So it is that she builds on these strengths on *Luck of the Draw*, which sounds of a piece with *Nick of Time*. Co-produced by Was and Raitt, the album serves up Raitt's forthright originals—"I ain't lookin' for the kind of man/Can't stand a little shaky ground/He'll give me fire and tenderness/And got the guts to stick around," she sings on "Come to Me"—and outside material that speaks most directly to her newfound assurance. Everything she touches reflects a gemlike luster. When she gets down with Delbert McClinton on "Good Man, Good Woman," their

ebullience is infectious; by contrast, her yearning on "I Can't Make You Love Me" is profound and real, a serious turn inward to unburden the heart of sadness born of love gone wrong. A variety of moods, a variety of settings, and regardless of the context, Raitt's choices are impeccable.
— D.M.

RAMONES

★ ★ ★ ★ **Ramones (Sire, 1976)**
★ ★ ★ ★ **Leave Home (Sire, 1977)**
★ ★ ★ ★ ½ **Rocket to Russia (Sire, 1977)**
★ ★ ★ ★ **Road to Ruin (Sire, 1979)**
  ★ ★ ★ **End of the Century (Sire, 1980)**
  ★ ★ ★ **Pleasant Dreams (Sire, 1981)**
  ★ ★ ★ **Subterranean Jungle (Sire, 1983)**
★ ★ ★ ★ **Too Tough to Die (Sire, 1984)**
  ★ ★ ★ **Animal Boy (Sire, 1986)**
  ★ ★ ½ **Halfway to Sanity (Sire, 1987)**
★ ★ ★ ★ **Ramones Mania (Sire, 1988)**
  ★ ★ ½ **Brain Drain (Sire, 1989)**
★ ★ ★ ★ ½ **All the Stuff (And More), Volume One (Sire, 1990)**
★ ★ ★ ★ ½ **All the Stuff (And More), Volume Two (Sire, 1991)**

You call this a revolution? Four scruffy ex-juvenile delinquents from Queens, New York—identically clad in ripped denims and biker leathers—hurtle through simple two- and three-minute odes to brain damage as if their lives depended on it. Well, why not? The Ramones really did kick-start punk, and went on to permanently alter the overall rock landscape with their accelerated urban surf music. Now that the original controversies have faded, and slam-dancing seems about as rebellious as a hula-hoop contest, the Ramones' magnificent first four albums can be appreciated for what they are: an indefatigable source of gross-out humor, geeky compassion, grabby chants and glaring attitude. A guaranteed good time, in other words.

Tommy lays down the breathless beat, Dee Dee plunks away on bass, Johnny slashes at power chords, Joey ennunciates in a peculiarly expressive Noo Yawk drawl. *Ramones* goes by fast—14 songs in 30 minutes. But the bruddahs' hooks have a sneaky way of getting stuck in listeners' craws: from the opening achtung of "Blitzkrieg Bop" ("Hey! Ho! Let's Go!") on to statements of purpose like "Beat on the Brat," "Now I Wanna Sniff Some Glue" and a metallized "Let's Dance." *Leave Home* doesn't let up on that energy level. "Sheena Is a Punk Rocker" and "Suzy Is a Headbanger" find the Ramones celebrating their nascent audience without a trace of

condescension, while "Gimme Gimme Shock Treatment" expresses punk's utter contempt for the cultural heritage of the preceding decade. Another key track on *Leave Home*, "Pinhead" points out the empathetic credo behind the Ramones' occasionally sick humor: "D-U-M-B. EVERYONE'S ACCUSIN' ME . . . gabba, gabba, we accept you, we accept you." On the other hand, the Nazi jokes on "Commando" are a misfire. Most of the time, however, the Ramones' aim stays remarkably sharp. For two more albums, anyway.

Rocket to Russia fortifies the quartet's sonic attack, staying well clear of any unwanted refinement or embellishment. They're getting better in spite of their primal mandate. "Rockaway Beach," "Teenage Lobotomy," "We're a Happy Family" and "Cretin Hop" address familiar situations with increased musical dexterity. Though it's not a historical document along the lines of the Sex Pistols' debut, the Ramones' third album is still one of the most immediately likable punk-rock artifacts.

Tommy Ramone (né Erdelyi) left his trapset for a studio career behind the mixing boards; former Voidoids drummer Marc Bell became Marky Ramone in time for *Road to Ruin*. The previous album's confident air is maintained, even furthered; Joey handles a Merseybeat cover ("Needles and Pins") and a virtual ballad ("Questioningly") with the same aplomb he administers to "I Wanna Be Sedated," while Johnny pulls off an actual guitar solo (!) on "Go Mental." The much-hyped matchup between Phil Spector and the boys results in *End of the Century*'s cluttered uncertainty. One man's wall of sound is another man's splitting headache—and vice versa. Rote songwriting from the Ramones doesn't help matters any. For the first time, Joey and crew wax nostalgic on the bombast-laden "Do You Remember Rock 'n' Roll Radio" —a complete turnaround from the unrelentingly crude realism of those early albums. "We Want the Airwaves," from *Pleasant Dreams*, is a far more satisfying mix of punk protest and AOR capitulation. That album and *Subterranean Jungle* add some attractive options to the Ramones' basic four-on-the-floor drive: touches of '70s metal and '60s psychedelia underline the bruddahs' "roots," so to speak, but the professional gleam of these not-bad-at-all records just can't hold a candle to the incandesent amatuerism of *Ramones* and *Leave Home*. Sometimes, less really is more.

Richie Ramone stepped in for Marky just

before *Too Tough to Die*; with a new drummer in tow and original drummer Tommy Erdelyi producing, the band reasserted itself as a viable force in 1984. "Mama's Boy" blends metal leanings into a punchy postpunk screed; "Howling at the Moon" (produced by Eurythmic Dave Stewart) is the Ramones' truest pop shot. Joey's singing seems to have improved by leaps and bounds, while Dee Dee weighs in with two barking, hilarious hardcore-style rants. *Animal Boy* veers back into heavy-plodding territory, however; "Bonzo Goes to Bitburg" and "Somebody Put Something in My Drink" indicate the Ramones are still capable of surprises in the lyrics department, but the music is strictly pro forma pogo rock. On *Halfway to Sanity* and *Brain Drain*, the boys sound exhausted and somewhat bitter. Dee Dee left the band on bad terms right after *Brain Drain*, releasing a "rap" solo album in 1989. (Dee Dee King's clueless *Standing in the Spotlight* makes Vanilla Ice look like Ice Cube—'nuff said.) Even Ramones are only human: what's amazing is how long they were able to keep up the pace—and our spirits. *Ramones Mania* culls the best tracks from the '80s albums, adding a questionable selection of '70s goodies. Stick with *All the Stuff (And More)*: Volume One puts *Ramones* and *Leave Home* on one disc, Volume Two holds *Rocket to Russia* and *Road to Ruin*. — M.C.

THE RASCALS

★★★ The Young Rascals (1966; Rhino, 1988)
★★★ Groovin' (1967; Rhino, 1988)
★★★★ Collections (Atlantic, 1967; Rhino, 1988)
★★★★ The Rascals' Greatest Hits/Time-Peace (Atlantic, 1968)
★★★ Once Upon a Dream (1968; Rhino, 1988)
★★★ Freedom Suite (1968; Rhino, 1988)
★★½ See (Atlantic, 1969)
★★ Search and Nearness (Atlantic, 1971)
★★ Peaceful World (Columbia, 1971)
★★ The Island of Real (Columbia, 1972)
★★★★½ The Rascals Anthology (1965–1972) (Rhino, 1992)

No matter how silly they looked in their Brit-aping stage gear of knickers and Fauntleroy collars, New Jersey's Young Rascals (the "Young" was dropped after three LPs) were one soulful unit, desperate to copy their Stax and Motown idols. Singer-organist Felix Cavaliere handled the rawer fare, and Eddie Brigati crooned the pop—such radio cookers as "Ain't Gonna Eat Out My Heart Anymore" and "Good Lovin' " (from the debut) and "Groovin' " (from *Groovin'*). Making keg-party "blue-eyed soul" before the term was coined, Cavaliere-Brigati enjoyed the sort of tough-tender exchange that furthered the Lennon-McCartney partnership, a freer vocal delivery than that of later white R&B singers, plus the secret weapon of Dino Danelli's stop-on-a-dime drum style. From definitive covers of R&B bar-band classics ("In the Midnight Hour," "Mustang Sally") to love songs and feel-good pop ("How Can I Be Sure," "A Beautiful Morning"), they brought class and punch to all their hits.

Not content with Top Forty brilliance, the boys tried their hand at pseudo-jazz on *Peaceful World* (now out of print), and, long after their mid-'60s heyday, Cavaliere returned with a decent comeback. But it was their brief summertime moment that made this band great: a funky-sweet alternative to the British Invasion. The highlights of the band's entire career can be found on the excellent *Anthology*. — P.E.

RASPBERRIES

★★½ Raspberries (Capitol, 1972)
★★½ Fresh (Capitol, 1972)
★★ Side 3 (Capitol, 1973)
★★★½ Starting Over (Capitol, 1974)
★★★½ Raspberries' Best Featuring Eric Carmen (Capitol, 1976)
★★★½ Collectors Series (Capitol, 1991)

The Raspberries' are either underrated or overrated. Just as progressive rock reached its zenith, this Cleveland quartet donned matching suits and zealously pursued the Top Forty teen-dream of the '60s. Several years before the rise of power-pop, lead singer-songwriter Eric Carmen brazenly appropriated ideas from the Beatles and Beach Boys, updating their innocence with frank '70s sexuality. "Go All the Way," "I Wanna Be With You" and "Tonight" shout the unspoken theme of so many classic rock & roll songs: should we or shouldn't we?

The accompanying albums (*Rasperries*, *Fresh* and *Side 3*, respectively) bottom out quickly after the singles. And a penchant for saccharine balladry—Eric Carmen's tragic flaw—surfaces on cuts like "Don't Want to Say Goodbye." After a personnel reshuffle, *Starting Over* deepens the band's focus without discarding its "Rose Coloured Glasses." Compare the easy momentum of

"Cruisin' Music" to the sputtering, uncertain "Driving Around" from *Fresh*: the latter tune sounds like a Beach Boys parody. "Overnight Sensation," a complex and deeply ironic ode to commercial calculation, sums up the Raspberries' evolution. It's catchy, all right, but it sounds better on headphones than on a car radio. Combining the hits and near-misses with representative filler from each album, *Collectors Series* provides all the Raspberries anybody really needs. The succinct (and out-of-print) *Best* also satisfies. — M.C.

RATT

★ ★   **Ratt (Time Coast, 1983)**
★ ★½   **Out of the Cellar (Atlantic, 1984)**
★ ★½   **Invasion of Your Privacy (Atlantic, 1985)**
★ ★½   **Dancing Undercover (Atlantic, 1986)**
★ ★ ★   **Reach for the Sky (Atlantic, 1988)**
★ ★ ★½ **Detonator (Atlantic, 1990)**

Ratt purveys very competent arena rock. The limits of this genre, of course, are obvious—the words are insipid, the guitar riffing is an exercise in recycling, the singing ranges from a shout to a scream. But Ratt knows its trade, and the sheer craft the band displays is formidable. "Round and Round," from *Out of the Cellar*, was Ratt's first big hit—basically a retread of David Lee Roth-period Van Halen, it was punchy yet melodic, with Stephen Pearcy yowling engagingly and guitarist Warren De Martini managing very precise pyrotechnical turns. And, unlike so many pop-metal bands, Ratt has only gotten better as its career has progressed. While bringing in songwriting's Mr. Fixit, Desmond Child, seems like cheating, his efforts help make *Detonator* a strong record. Glossy but thunderous, this may not be art, but for the genre, it's state-of-the-art. — P.E.

THE RAVENS

★ ★ ★ ★ **The Greatest Group of Them All (Savoy, 1978)**

The Ravens had few competitors when it came to the heart, skill and versatility its members brought to their music. Their distinction of being the first popular group named after a bird pales in comparison to the long shadow the Ravens cast over early R&B and rock & roll group-harmony styles. Maithe Marshall had as sweet a falsetto tenor as anyone recording in the late '50s, but he was challenged by fellow tenor Leonard Puzey and baritone Warren Suttles, each of whom could carry a song on their own (though Suttles was never given a lead).

These three then had to contend with the greatest voice in the group, bass singer Jimmy Ricks, who had so delicate a touch with lyrics that he sang lead rather than background on many Ravens singles.

The Greatest Group of Them All collects three sides of essential Ravens recordings from the group's productive years on the National label, before the original configuration of singers began splitting up. Of these many remarkable recordings, several stand out, including "Write Me a Letter," superior readings of Irving Berlin's "Always" and Kurt Weill's "September Song," a version of "Deep Purple" that features Ricks's bass at its most searching, and two Christmas songs, "White Christmas" and "Silent Night." Two of the Ravens' most influential recordings are missing from this collection, "Old Man River" from 1946, and "Count Every Star," a 1950 track with a vocal arrangement that was quintessential doo-wop before anyone knew doo-wop existed; however, side four offsets this omission with the inclusion of eight previously unissued recordings. Two other Savoy titles, *Old Man River* and *Ravens Rarities*, are now out of print, but are no less critical to a complete understanding of the Ravens' legacy than *The Greatest Group of Them All*, though this is an excellent overview. — D.M.

LOU RAWLS

★ ★ ★   **Stormy Monday (1962; Blue Note, 1990)**
★ ★ ★   **Lou Rawls Live (1966; Capitol, 1988)**
★ ★ ★½ **The Best of Lou Rawls: The Capitol/Blue Note Years (Capitol, 1968)**
★ ★ ★½ **All Things in Time (Philadelphia International, 1976)**
★ ★ ★½ **Unmistakably Lou (Philadephia International, 1977)**
★ ★ ★½ **At Last (Blue Note, 1989)**
★ ★ ★½ **Greatest Hits (Curb, 1990)**

Gifted with a remarkable voice, deep, rich and slightly wearied, Lou Rawls has for years purveyed a sophisticated soul style that owes as much to Nat "King" Cole and jazz-lite vocalists as it does to that of classic R&B. He hit biggest in the mid-'70s with Gamble and Huff's "You'll Never Find Another Love Like Mine," a song whose Philly Soul smoothness encapsulated his appeal. Hardly a visionary, the singer instead is a dependable craftsman: rarely does he catch real fire, even less often does he turn in a weak performance. Capitol's

Best Of, with "Dead End Street" and "Tobacco Road," remains his strongest set. — P.E.

JAMES RAY
★ ★ **Golden Classics (Collectables, NA)**
A Washington, D.C., soul singer with a strong, smooth voice (at times resembling Chuck Jackson and Brenton Wood), James Ray cut one terrific record in 1961, "If You Gotta Make a Fool of Somebody," which went Top Thirty. Despite the forcefulness of his gutsy, heartfelt style, Ray's followup, "Itty Bitty Pieces," barely dented the charts, and he entered the golden realm of one-hit wonders. *Golden Classics* offers the one, true golden classic in Ray's history and a host of lesser numbers. — D.M.

JOHNNIE RAY
★ ★ **Johnnie Ray—An American Legend (Columbia, 1978)**
Encouraged by LaVern Baker and shaped by Mitch Miller, Johnnie Ray became one of the most popular male recording artists of the early '50s on the strength of his overwrought vocal style and flamboyant personal appearances. As emotional as Ray could get on record, he could truly whip himself into a frenzy in concert. The point at which he wound up on the stage floor crying to the heavens marks the point at which American popular music took on a decidedly different cast from that of the staid postures of Ray's contemporaries. Elvis Presley eclipsed Ray both in emotional fervor and in vocal prowess, but Ray must be credited with giving audiences a preview of things to come.

Although he had a few hits in the mid-'50s, Ray's productive years were 1951 through 1954, when he landed nearly two dozen singles in the Top Forty; his debut on the Okeh label, "Cry," became his signature song—and well it should: it was Number One for 11 weeks in 1951. He moved to Columbia after "Cry" and came under the guidance of Mitch Miller, who smoothed out some of Ray's rough edges but also cut some good sides with the partially deaf singer, including "Please Mr. Sun," "Here I Am, Broken-Hearted" and "Walkin' My Baby Back Home." *An American Legend* is an apt summary of Ray's most popular sides. — D.M.

CHRIS REA
★ ★ ★ **New Light Through Old Windows (Atco, 1988)**
★ ★ ★ ★ **The Road to Hell (Atco, 1989)**
★ ★ ★ ★ **Auberge (Atco, 1991)**

With his rough, dark voice and lazily assured way with the blues, Chris Rea sounds like a cross between Robbie Robertson and Mark Knopfler—in theory a terrifically commercial sound, but not in practice. Although many of Rea's 13 albums have been available at one time or another in this country, only *Whatever Happened to Benny Santini?*, which produced the 1978 Top Twenty single "Fool (If You Think It's Over)," made any lasting impression on the charts. That song, along with most of most of Rea's U.K. hits, can be found on *New Light Through Old Windows*. But Rea's most interesting work doesn't begin until *The Road to Hell*, a moody, malevolent album that uses the sound of the blues to throw new and disturbing light on modern life and the American dream. It's a riveting album, and so stunning that almost any followup would seem a disappointment; yet despite a couple of minor missteps, *Auberge* maintains its predecessor's pace with admirable grace and imagination. — J.D.C.

OTIS REDDING
★ ★ ★ ★ **Pain in My Heart (1965; Atlantic, 1991)**
★ ★ ★ ★ **The Great Otis Redding Sings Soul Ballads (1965; Atlantic 1991)**
★ ★ ★ ★ ★ **Otis Blue—Otis Redding Sings Soul (1965; Atlantic, 1991)**
★ ★ ★ ★ **The Otis Redding Dictionary of Soul (1966; Atlantic, 1991)**
★ ★ ★ ★ ★ **The Soul Album (1966; Atlantic, 1991)**
★ ★ ★ ★ **Live in Europe (1967; Atlantic, 1991)**
★ ★ ★ ★½ **The Dock of the Bay (1968; Atlantic, 1991)**
★ ★ ★ ★ ★ **The Immortal Otis Redding (1968; Atlantic, 1991)**
★ ★ ★ ★ ★ **History of Otis Redding (Atco, 1968)**
★ ★ ★ ★ ★ **In Person at the Whisky-a-Go-Go (1968; Rhino/Atlantic, 1992)**
★ ★ ★ ★ **Love Man (1969; Rhino/Atlantic, 1992)**
★ ★ ★ ★ **Tell the Truth (1970; Rhino/Atlantic, 1992)**
★ ★ ★ ★ **Otis Redding/Jimi Hendrix Experience: Historic Performances Recorded at the Monterey International Pop Festival (Reprise, 1970)**
★ ★ ★ ★ **The Best of Otis Redding (1972; Atlantic, 1985)**
★ ★ ★ ★ **Recorded Live (1982; Atlantic, 1992)**

★★★★ **The Legend of Otis Redding**
   (Pair/Atlantic, 1986)
★★★★★ **The Otis Redding Story (Atlantic,**
   1987)
WITH CARLA THOMAS
   ★★★★ **King & Queen (1967; Atlantic,**
   1991)

Otis Redding was the premier Southern soul singer. Providing counterpoint to Motown, the Memphis-based sound Redding defined made the '60s R&B renaissance a glorious tension of complementary styles. While Motown, as Peter Guralnick explains in *Sweet Soul Music*, was string-laden, melodic and tended toward pop, Stax/Volt/Atlantic, adhering more closely to gospel and blues roots, was horn-driven and primarily rhythmic, its fierceness the product of stellar solo vocalists and a lean rhythm section. Otis Redding remains its quintessence. In league with the Stax/Volt studio players—Booker T. Jones (organ), Steve Cropper (guitar), Donald "Duck" Dunn (bass) and Al Jackson (drums)—Redding tested to the limits his quick musical intelligence. His horn parts alone were radically innovative—by employing trumpets as exclamation points, for example, he altered forever the syntax of the brass section in popular music, and his use of difficult, unexpected key signatures added density to the simple melodic lines his horn parts accompanied. Co-writing many of his hits with Cropper, Otis pared R&B down to its lean core—in Stax/Volt no note was redundant. All of Redding's technique, however, served emotion—and that emotion, celebratory or anguished, was conveyed by the absolute urgency of his remarkable voice.

The title track to *Pain in My Heart* set the pattern for all his ballads to come—Otis triumphed at rendering agony. Signs of the singer's virtuosity are already apparent in the almost teasing way he lingers over some lyrics and spits out others; virtually never would he sing a line the same way twice. *The Great Otis Redding Sings Soul Ballads* continues his rapid development as a style-setter: "Mr. Pitiful" sums up his persona as a tortured romantic. "That's How Strong My Love Is" demonstrates his skill at transforming gospel witnessing into erotic testifying. With *Otis Blue*, he achieves his first masterwork. "Respect" becomes not only a soul standard but a black-pride anthem; "I've Been Loving You Too Long (to Stop Now)" may be Otis's strongest ballad; the assertiveness of B.B. King's "Rock Me Baby" and Sam Cooke's

"Shake" finds him as at home with blues and rockers as he is with ballads. His furious cover of the Stones' "(I Can't Get No) Satisfaction" is prescient—suggesting the spirit of such later R&B-rock fusions as Hendrix's, Sly Stone's and Prince's. "Chain Gang" and the moody swing of "Cigarettes and Coffee" highlight *The Soul Album*. By the time of *Dictionary of Soul*, Otis had arrived at another plateau. "Try a Little Tenderness," first recorded by Bing Crosby, is Stax/Volt at its most sophisticated; in an elegant, almost jazzy setting, Redding, for all his customary fervor, delivers one of his most mature performances, smoky and at times almost langorous. "Fa-Fa-Fa-Fa-Fa (Sad Song)" is more typical Southern soul—hard, precise but swinging. *In Person at the Whiskey-a-Go-Go* is dependably intense. From *King & Queen*, his duet with Carla Thomas, "Tramp" offers a rare display of Otis's sassy humor; their cover of Steve Cropper and Eddie Floyd's "Knock on Wood" is almost assaultive in its drive. By 1967, the singer had reached a point of such assurance that he seemed riper for even more ranging explorations of style, new shifts in tone. But even his record company didn't quite know what to do with the latest product of his impatient creativity—a soft, acoustic-guitar ballad, "(Sittin' On) The Dock of the Bay." The first soul singer to absorb the influence of Bob Dylan turns out a folk melody of indelible, simple force, his lyrics have all the immediacy of conversation—but he sings the line with an undertone of yearning that makes the record unmistakably soul music, and the final triumph of his deep, swift career. By the end of the year, the singer had died in a plane crash; given the potential suggested by *The Dock of the Bay*, as well as the consistent, challenging beauty of all the music he'd made up until that record's release, Otis Redding's loss remains immeasurable. Because of its thoroughness and its excellent notes, the three-CD *The Otis Redding Story* is the strongest compilation. All of the live sets are good; the best are *Live in Europe* and *In Person at the Whisky-a-Go-Go*.
— P.E.

RED HOT CHILI PEPPERS
   ★★½ **The Red Hot Chili Peppers (EMI**
   America, 1984)
★★★ **Freaky Styley (EMI America, 1985)**
   ★★ **The Uplift Mofo Party Plan (EMI**
   America, 1987)
★★★ **The Abbey Road EP (EMI America,**
   1988)

★ ★ **Mother's Milk (EMI America, 1989)**
★ ★½ **BloodSugarSexMagik (Warner Bros., 1991)**
The idea of hardcore punks giving up the funk is damn enticing. Five albums down the line, however, this pioneering L.A. quartet is still head-banging against a brick wall. The Red Hot Chili Peppers huff and puff, flail and wail—but the barrier remains. Maybe slam-dancing and polyrhythms just don't mix.

At first, the clumsy backbeat and eruptions of untutored guitar overkill seemed like traits the Peppers would outgrow. *Freaky Styley* benefits from George Clinton's production: a jagged horn chart jump-starts a Bootsy-esque cartoon jam called "Brothers Cup," and for once, the Peppers ride a groove home instead of running it aground. *The Uplift Mofo Party Plan* pummels listeners with harsh, pseudopsychedelic fretwork and hoarsely barked party-chant choruses. The chaotic in-your-face charge of the group's live shows doesn't exactly translate to recording, and the lyrics regularly sink to the lockerroom-humor level ("Party on Your Pussy"). After the death of guitarist Hillel Slovek in 1988, bassist Flea and lead singer Anthony Kiedis regrouped the Peppers on *Mother's Milk*. The new band is more metallic and even less tuneful, unfortunately. Producer Rick Rubin clarifies the group's thrust on *BloodSugarSexMagik*, but it's much ado about nothing. All his sonic embellishments and stylistic asides just point out the absence of a single killer riff—let alone a coherent song. — M.C.

JERRY REED
★ ★ ★½ **The Best of Jerry Reed (RCA, 1971)**
★ ★ ★ **When You're Hot, You're Hot (RCA, 1976)**
★ ★ ★ **Both Barrels (RCA, 1976)**
★ ★ ★ **East Bound and Down (RCA, 1977)**
★ ★½ **The Bird (RCA, 1983)**
★ ★ ★ **Collector's Series (RCA, 1985)**
★ ★½ **Lookin' at You (Capitol, 1986)**
For all but hard-core country audiences, Jerry Reed's wily redneck persona, displayed in Burt Reynolds's *Smokey and the Bandit* movies, has tended to obscure his musical gifts. And, however erratically displayed, they are considerable. Starting off as a songwriter (he gave Gene Vincent a 1956 hit with "Crazy Legs"), Reed worked throughout the early '60s as a Nashville studio player, honing his dexterous guitar skills. Lightning picking distinguished his

playing, though he never developed a truly personal approach. With his songwriting he did manage a trademark style—Elvis scored big with "Guitar Man" and "U.S. Male," and for a while Reed concentrated on hyperdriven rockers that were country only in their outlaw swagger. His real strength, however, was made apparent in the '70s with a series of sassy comic singles— "Tupelo Mississippi Flash," the swamp-rock "Amos Moses" and "When You're Hot, You're Hot." For a while he capitalized on the CB-radio-trucker craze (*East Bound and Down* is chockful of big-rig ditties), and he had consistent success on the country charts throughout the decade. Reed's ballads, however, were mawkish—and on almost all of his albums, every snappy redneck rocker finds its counterpart in a soupy slow song. While dogged by the overearnest "Georgia Sunshine" and "Today Is Mine," *The Best of* remains Reed's strongest collection. *When You're Hot, You're Hot* and *Both Barrels*, though out of print, are worth checking out if you can find them. — P.E.

JIMMY REED
★ ★ ★ ★ ★ **Jimmy Reed at Carnegie Hall (Vee Jay, 1962)**
★ ★ ★ **I'm Jimmy Reed (Vee Jay, 1963)**
★ ★ ★ ★ **Jimmy Reed: The Legend, the Man (Vee Jay, NA)**
★ ★ ★ **Now Appearing (Vee Jay, NA)**
★ ★ ★ **Rockin' with Reed (Vee Jay, NA)**
★ ★ ★ **Jimmy Reed at Soul City (Vee Jay, NA)**
★ ★ ★ ★ ★ **The Best of Jimmy Reed (GNP Crescendo, 1974)**
★ ★ ★ ★ **Bright Lights, Big City (Chameleon, 1988)**
Raised in the Mississippi Delta on Delta blues, Jimmy Reed made the exodus to Chicago in 1953, and two years later had a national hit with "You Don't Have to Go." He continued to produce hits—and to make a dent on the pop charts as well—in to the early '60s, by which time a generation of young British rockers had come to make his songs a part of their repertoires. Like Bo Diddley, Reed found a groove and stuck with it. His was a lazy but relentless shuffle. Reed spiced it with elemental blues progressions, crying harmonica and a vocal style that was personable and mellow. His music was insidious: the groove kept coming and coming, and pretty soon it was in your system. He was medium cool and like nobody else in the way he contained his fire.

Once he got started, Reed was on a roll. He followed his 1955 hit a year later with

"Ain't That Lovin' You Baby," "Honest I Do" in 1957, and "Baby What You Want Me to Do" in 1960. In 1961 he delivered two transcendent singles in "Big Boss Man" and "Bright Lights, Big City." Each one of these has earned the accolade "classic."

Reed recorded for the Chicago-based Vee Jay label, and several of his albums remain in print. Reed packages also show up on other labels from time to time, as licensed from Vee Jay. Hence, the essential Chameleon *Bright Lights, Big City* collection of greatest hits as recorded for Vee Jay, as well as GNP Crescendo's double album *The Best of Jimmy Reed*. *At Carnegie Hall* is essentially another greatest-hits collection, but how much, if any, of it is live is another question. There's nary a clap, whistle, cheer, cough, shout or scream to be heard on what sounds like a series of studio performances. Which doesn't make the songs any less wonderful. *Jimmy Reed at Soul City* is also supposed to be a live album, and indeed one can hear people talking and glasses clinking in the background. Not once does Reed acknowledge the audience's presence, though, and the applause is identical from track to track. It's a puzzlement, but again, the music is worthwile even if the setting is contrived. — D.M.

LOU REED

★ ★ ★½   **Lou Reed** (RCA, 1972)
★ ★ ★ ★   **Transformer** (RCA, 1972)
★ ★ ★   **Berlin** (RCA, 1973)
★ ★ ★ ★   **Rock 'n' Roll Animal** (RCA, 1974)
★ ★ ★½   **Sally Can't Dance** (RCA, 1974)
★   **Metal Machine Music** (RCA, 1975)
★ ★ ★   **Lou Reed Live** (RCA, 1975)
★ ★ ★ ★   **Coney Island Baby** (RCA, 1976)
★ ★   **Rock and Roll Heart** (Arista, 1976)
★ ★ ★ ★   **Walk on the Wild Side—The Best of Lou Reed** (RCA, 1977)
★ ★ ★½   **Street Hassle** (Arista, 1978)
★ ★   **Take No Prisoners—Live** (Arista, 1978)
★ ★ ★ ★   **The Bells** (Arista, 1979)
★ ★ ★   **Growing up in Public** (Arista, 1980)
★ ★ ★   **Rock and Roll Diary 1967-1980** (Arista, 1980)
★ ★ ★ ★   **The Blue Mask** (RCA, 1982)
★ ★ ★½   **Legendary Hearts** (RCA, 1983)
★ ★ ★ ★   **New Sensations** (RCA, 1984)
★ ★ ★   **Mistrial** (RCA, 1986)
★ ★ ★½   **New York** (Sire, 1989)
★ ★ ★ ★   **Magic and Loss** (Sire, 1992)

★ ★ ★ ★   **Between Thought and Expression: The Lou Reed Anthology** (RCA, 1992)
WITH JOHN CALE
★ ★ ★ ★   **Songs for Drella** (Sire, 1990)

Don't come here looking for the focused, glowering brilliance of the Velvet Underground; you'll be disappointed. What makes Lou Reed's solo career so fascinating is his volatile unpredictabilty. In the '70s Reed's sense of direction often seemed downright perverse; he cultivated an outrageously decadent image, lurched from style to style, released masterful albums and quickie rip-offs back to back. Even as he returned to the Velvets' terse rhythm guitar strum in the '80s, Reed's songwriting continued to take unexpected turns. *New York* proves that the happily married, mellowed-out Reed can still raise a few hackles with his patented brand of provocative, street-smart rock & roll.

Lou Reed sounds a bit tentative coming after the Velvets' *Loaded*, though Lou regains his sea legs on the kicky, articulate "Wild Child" and the other tracks sink in over time. Many of these songs were Velvet Underground outtakes, later released on *VU*. Next to that album, *Lou Reed*'s genteel art-rock treatment (courtesy of Rick Wakeman and others) seems beside the point. Co-produced by David Bowie, *Transformer* casts Reed in the role of androgynous glam rocker—sort of like Ziggy Stardust's earthier, sexually brazen older brother. "Walk on the Wild Side" strolled out of left field onto the pop charts in 1973; "Shaved her legs and then he was a she" actually co-existed with the Carpenters and Donny Osmond. Of course, Reed's startling reminiscenses of those infamous Warhol superstars come cloaked in billowy sax strains and an ironic, catchy background chorus. Though *Transformer* is one of Reed's best-known and most popular albums, overall it's uneven; the affected, campy tone (as well as Bowie's production) grows thin and brittle after a while. But the good bits are great: that snarling guitar riff on "Vicious," the halting beauty of "Satellite of Love," every last "do-do-do" of "Walk on the Wild Side."

Berlin, Reed's conceptual glory shot, is a bomb. With its majestic backdrop provided by heavy-metal producer Bob Ezrin and a wizardly cast of rock pros, this rambling, morose tale of drug-crossed lovers goes nowhere. Apparently relieved of any musical duties, Reed does what his critics have always accused him of—talks in a flat Noo

Yawk monotone rather than make any attempt at singing. He has to yell just to be heard on *Rock 'n' Roll Animal*; however, that's a definite improvement. On this live set, a crack band led by guitarists Steve Hunter and Dick Wagner blasts its way though the supercharged renditions of "Sweet Jane," "Heroin" and "White Light/White Heat." Lou's fiery performance lacks the nuance of the Velvets originals, of course, but it's the perfect topper to this high-octane arena-rock party album. *Lou Reed Live* offers more of that same tour, though it's far less compelling.

Sally Can't Dance offers a snapshot of Lou Reed at his trashiest and most sarcastic; it's messy, but interesting. Over surprisingly funky horn lines and taut lead guitar lines, he dishes up the obvious dirt ("Kill Your Sons," "Sally Can't Dance") and slips in one of his most affecting ballads ("Billy") amid the glittery malevolence. *Metal Machine Music* is Reed's two-record amplifier noise opus—a gigantic "fuck you" disguised as a groundbreaking experiment. *Coney Island Baby* couches some of Reed's most revelatory and sensitive lyrics in a deceptively slight soft-rock package; on the astounding title track, the former rock & roll animal recalls wanting to "play football for the coach."

Switching record labels, Reed released the eminently forgettable *Rock and Roll Heart* that same year. The pro-Onan thumper "Banging on My Drum" pretty much sums it up. Ballyhooed as an artistic triumph, *Street Hassle* is a somewhat stiff restatement of Lou's career up to that point. The guitar-driven nastiness of "Dirt" and "Real Good Time Together" has a welcome, bracing affect, but the orchestral title epic is hardly the sweeping tour de force it's intended to be. *Take No Prisoners—Live* is a middling concert set ruined by endless between-song banter. As a stand-up comedian, Lou Reed makes a great rhythm guitar player. On the other hand, *The Bells* just may be his most ambitious work. Returning to *Coney Island Baby*'s confessional mode and incorporating a subtle jazz influence, Reed makes one of his strongest musical statements. Reed's razor-edge frankness is riveting throughout. The appropriately titled *Growing up in Public* finds Lou contemplating marriage and middle age to the tune of galumphing FM-radio rock. Clearly a transition.

Walk on the Wild Side presents a succinct overview of the RCA years, and is preferable to the overreaching *Rock & Roll*

Diary. (Including the Velvets' classics next to a spotty selection of solo Lou does neither act a favor.) Landing back on his old label and strapping on his guitar again, Reed finally wheels out the album many long-suffering fans had been waiting for. Still, *The Blue Mask* takes some getting used to. While the emphasis on six-string interplay and crisp rhythms revitalizes Reed as a writer, he now strikes a more personal tone; his new, almost-journalistic voice is a far cry from his earlier stance as poet of the demimonde. Guitarist Robert Quine and bassist Fernando Saunders prod Lou Reed beyond his previous achievements; he makes you believe that "writing, my motorcycle and my wife" now mean as much as the speed freaks and drag queens of yore.

With the addition of drummer Fred Maher on the solid follow-up *Legendary Hearts*, this unit functioned as an actual band rather than a hotshot backup group. (Then they broke up.) Reed's fresh songwriting approach crystallizes on *New Sensations*' haunting title track; this sober look at aging is bolstered by a quietly resilient melody. There's a casual, me-and-my-guitar feel to this album, but the offhand valentines ("I Love You Suzanne") and video-game sendups ("My Red Joy Stick") all pack a hidden punch. *Mistrial* is the only album on which Reed sounds like he's trying to keep abreast of the changing times; the drum machine tracks really aren't up his alley, while the rote three-chord rant "Video Violence" feels crotchety and strained.

New York starts out strong; tracks like "Romeo Had Juliet," "Dirty Boulevard" and "Halloween Parade" indicate that Reed's observational powers and one-of-a-kind delivery are intact, while his ongoing duels with guitarist Mike Rathke bristle and sting. By the time Lou gets around to "Good Evening Mr. Waldheim" and "Last Great American Whale," though, he starts to sound like that seemingly smart guy at the local bar who always turns open discussions into opinionated diatribes. The elegantly understated "Dime Store Mystery," a tribute to Andy Warhol that also appears on *Songs for Drella*, the 1990 elegiac collaboration with John Cale, serves as a soothing closer to the occasionally overheated *New York*. *Magic and Loss*, one of Reed's strongest efforts, is an unblinking—but beautifully executed—look at death and sorrow. Given the erratic nature of his '70's career, *Between Thought and Expression* is far more consistent than any Lou Reed boxed set has a right to be. The first of these four CDs has lots of *Berlin*-era decadence—six grueling cuts' worth—but the warmth and vigor of Reed's '80s renaissance supplies a healthy balance. — M.C.

JIM REEVES
- ★★★ **Pure Gold, Volume 1 (1978; RCA, 1988)**
  - ★ **Jim Reeves & Patsy Cline: Greatest Hits (RCA, 1981)**
  - ★★ **Collector's Series (1984; RCA, 1988)**
- ★★★ **Collector's Series (RCA, 1985)**
- ★★★★ **Live at the Grand Ole Opry (Country Music Foundation, 1986)**
  - ★★ **Pure Gold, Volume 1 (RCA, 1987)**
  - ★★ **The Best of Jim Reeves (RCA, 1988)**
  - ★★ **He'll Have to Go and Other Hits (RCA, 1990)**

Along with Eddy Arnold, the late Jim Reeves is most closely identified with the development of the lush Nashville Sound; like Arnold he had a warm, smooth vocal delivery well-suited to what Arnold's and Reeves's producer, Chet Atkins, was after in those days: his style was sort of pop, sort of country, and easily accessible by lovers of either genre. So in the midst of his success as a country artist, Reeves also notched four Top Forty singles, including one, "He'll Have to Go," that peaked at Number Two in 1960. After his death in a plane crash in 1964, Reeves's popularity grew with each passing year, and more and more posthumous releases began showing up, mostly available by mail order only and largely under the supervision of Reeves's widow. So much material was being released that by the early '80s it was easy to believe that Reeves, not Elvis, had faked his death and was actually secreted away in a studio somewhere pumping out product.

Reeves's remaining RCA catalogue consists of various packages of his best-known songs in the countrypolitan vein. But Reeves had a harder side that largely disappeared on record after he was signed to RCA and the hits started coming. He had begun recording for an independent label in his native Texas, Abbot Records, and one of his early efforts, "Mexican Joe," hit Number One on the country charts in 1953. British RCA once released two volumes of Reeves's Abbot recordings, but these are now out of print. Vestiges of Reeves's harder side show up, however, on the essential *Live at the Grand Ole Opry*, on the Country Music Foundation label. These previously unreleased performances date from the singer's initial appearance on the Opry in 1953, when he performed "Mexican Joe," to December of 1960, and include moving versions of many of his best-known songs, including "Four Walls," "He'll Have to Go" and the beautiful "Anna Marie," as well as several spiritual numbers. If there is one Jim Reeves record to own, it's this one.

Among the hits collections, the most inclusive now available would be the CD version of *Pure Gold, Volume One*, and the 16-track version of *Collector's Series*, which has the same packaging as the other *Collector's Series* album, but eight more tracks and the entire song selection listed on the front of the cassette. The must-to-avoid is the Reeves-Patsy Cline hits collection, which has remastered takes of familiar songs ("Crazy," "Four Walls," "I Fall to Pieces," "He'll Have to Go") and a duet conjured up via studio wizardry long after each artist's death. Enough already. — D.M.

TERRY REID
- ★★★ **Bang Bang You're Terry Reid (Epic, 1968)**
  - ★★½ **Terry Reid (Epic, 1969)**
  - ★★½ **River (Atlantic, 1973)**
- ★★★ **Seed of Memory (ABC, 1976)**

On his first two records, Reid came on strong as a great, slashing electric guitarist and an urgent, hoarse-voiced singer (his power was such that he was able to make even Sonny and Cher's "Bang, Bang" sound ominous). Then, in an almost schizophrenic turnabout, he became a folkie. *River* doesn't really work, but *Seed of Memory* does—after an odd Tim Hardin-meets-Nick Drake fashion. — P.E.

R.E.M.
- ★★★½ **Chronic Town (EP) (I.R.S., 1982)**
- ★★★★★ **Murmur (I.R.S., 1983)**
- ★★★½ **Reckoning (I.R.S., 1984)**
- ★★★★ **Fables of the Reconstruction (I.R.S., 1985)**
- ★★★★½ **Life's Rich Pageant (I.R.S., 1986)**
- ★★★★★ **Document (I.R.S., 1987)**
- ★★★ **Dead Letter Office (I.R.S., 1987)**
- ★★★ **Eponymous (I.R.S., 1988)**
- ★★★★ **Green (Warner Bros., 1988)**
- ★★★★½ **Out of Time (Warner Bros., 1991)**

Progenitors of the New Southern Rock and easily the most popular American alternative act of the late '80s, R.E.M. has never been the likeliest of revolutionaries. After all, the group's recordings espoused no discernible ideology and played off no recognizable trends; its lyrics are oblique to the point of incomprehensibility, while its members, though not without charisma, studiously avoid any pretensions to rock-star presence.

R.E.M.'s sound, however, is another matter. Instead of taking an obvious course and emulating the Beatle-isms of the dB's or the post-punk thrash of hardcore, the approach R.E.M. comes up with on *Chronic Town* is strikingly idiosyncratic, surrounding Michael Stipe's tart, sonorous baritone with interlocking layers of arpeggiated guitar and insistently tuneful bass, all driven by smart, supple drumming. And despite inscrutable titles like "Wolves, Lower" or "1,000,000," the songs are instantly likeable, making up in melodic appeal what the lyrics lack in accessibility.

With *Murmur*, the band's sound becomes more intricately detailed, as R.E.M. augments its four-piece arrangements with keyboards, sound effects and extra instrumentation (some of which is played by Mitch Easter, one of the album's producers). More significantly, the writing is unexpectedly mature and mesmerizingly tuneful, from the semiacoustic melancholy of "Talk About the Passion" to the dark, driving cadences of "Catapult." It's a tough act to follow, and *Reckoning* doesn't always rise to the challenge, although "So. Central Rain" and the countryish "(Don't Go Back to) Rockville" show how capably the band subverts traditional songforms.

Rather than settling into predictability, *Fables of the Reconstruction* finds R.E.M. confident enough of its direction to freely experiment with its sound. As such, the album includes not only the pop-friendly "Driver 8" and "Can't Get There From Here" but also the edgy dissonance of "Feeling Gravity's Pull" and the anxious throb of "Old Man Kensey." *Life's Rich Pageant* is where the band's chance-taking truly pays off, however, as the group's sonic daring reinforces the music's unerring melodic instincts, from the out-of-character crunch of Peter Buck's guitar in "Begin the Begin" to the Top Forty pep of Mike Mills's vocal on "Superman." Incredibly, *Document* actually expands on that achievement, moving easily from the muscular strains of "Finest Worksong" to the breathless verbiage of "It's the End of the World As We Know It (and I Feel Fine)" to the ominous grind of "Oddfellows Local 151," and still finding room for a ballad as sly and beautiful as "The One I Love."

R.E.M. finished out its I.R.S. contract with two compilations: *Dead Letter Office*, a collection of covers, B sides and other ephemera (which, on CD, also includes the whole of *Chronic Town*); and *Eponymous*, a more-or-less greatest-hits album (which features the original version of "Radio Free Europe"). By this point, the band had a large enough audience to be considered a mainstream act, something the band (in typically oblique fashion) pokes fun at on *Green* with the noisy deadpan of "Pop Song 89." Of course, "pop" is hardly an accurate description; although the songs here are consistently catchy, from the curiously chipper "Stand" to the melancholy of "World Leader Pretend," it would be misleading to suggest that R.E.M. has made any concessions to its (now) mass audience.

In the long run, that's perhaps the most revolutionary thing about this group. Like few bands since the Beatles, R.E.M. has been able to keep growing artistically while somehow continuing to broaden its audience. And the uniformly excellent *Out of Time*, with its unorthodox instrumentation (the mandolin that carries the haunting choruses of "Losing My Religion," the horns and strings that frame the gentle "Endgame") and ever-widening stylistic base (which even includes a nod to rap in "Radio Song"), suggests that R.E.M. is only just beginning to hit its stride.

— J.D.C.

JOHN RENBOURN

★★★½ **Sir John—A Lot of Merre Englandes Musik Thynge and Ye Grene Knyghte (1969; Shanachie, 1992)**

★★★ **The Lady and the Unicorn (1970; Shanachie, 1992)**

★★★ **John Renbourn (Reprise, 1972)**

★★★★ **Faro Annie (Reprise, 1972)**

★★★½ **The Nine Maidens (Flying Fish, 1986)**

★★★½ **John Renbourn's Ship of Fools (Flying Fish, 1988)**

★★★ **The Black Balloon (Shanachie, 1989)**

★★★ **The Enchanted Garden (Shanachie, 1990)**

★ ★ ★ **Live in America (Flying Fish, 1991)**
★ ★ ★½ **The Solo Years (The Essential Collection, Vol. 1) (Transatlantic, NA)**

WITH STEFAN GROSSMAN

★ ★ ★½ **Snap a Little Owl (Shanachie, 1989)**
★ ★ ★½ **Live (Shanachie, 1990)**
★ ★ ★ ★ **The Three Kingdoms (Shanachie, 1991)**

After serving with Bert Jansch as one of the two instrumental pillars of Pentangle, John Renbourn holed up at his Welsh farm and delved even deeper into traditional Scots-Irish folk. Emerging periodically for trips to the studio, he began a solo career that consisted of gemlike, primarily instrumental recordings—each one an example of understated virtuosity. Sir John established medieval music as his essential repertoire, although he'd continue to make occasional forays into jazz. *Faro Annie* remains his best-known work, but *The Nine Maidens*, featuring recorder and drum accompaniment, is also outstanding, and Maggie Boyle's vocals on *Ship of Fools* add dimension. Recorded with guitarist Stefan Grossman, *The Three Kingdoms* features some of his best jazz work on " 'Round About Midnight" and "Farewell to Mr. Mingus." — P.E.

REO SPEEDWAGON

★ ★ ★½ **REO Speedwagon (Epic, 1971)**
★ ★ ★½ **R.E.O./T.W.O. (Epic, 1972)**
★ ★ ★½ **Ridin' the Storm Out (Epic, 1973)**
★ ★ **Lost in a Dream (Epic, 1974)**
★ ★ **"This Time We Mean It" (Epic, 1975)**
★ ★ **R.E.O. (Epic, 1976)**
★ ★½ **Live: You Get What You Play For (Epic, 1977)**
★ ★½ **You Can Tune a Piano, but You Can't Tuna Fish (Epic, 1978)**
★ ★ **Nine Lives (Epic, 1979)**
★ ★½ **Hi Infidelity (Epic, 1980)**
★ ★½ **A Decade of Rock & Roll: 1970 to 1980 (Epic, 1980)**
★ ★ **Good Trouble (Epic, 1982)**
★ ★ **Wheels Are Turnin' (Epic, 1985)**
★ ★ **Life as We Know It (Epic, 1987)**
★ ★ ★ **The Hits (Epic, 1988)**
★ **The Earth, a Small Man, His Dog and a Chicken (Epic, 1990)**
★ ★ **The Second Decade of Rock & Roll (Epic, 1991)**

Perseverance paid off in buckets for this Illinois-based outfit. REO Speedwagon barreled out of the college town of Champaign-Urbana in the early '70s, carrying a hefty load of generic bar-band boogie. The first three albums register at a slightly higher octane than you might expect, though they contain nothing that the house combo down at the local gin mill couldn't kick out of a Saturday night. *Ridin' the Storm Out* features lead singer Mike Murphy, a temporary (and indistinguishable) replacement for squeaky-clean longtime frontman Kevin Cronin. When Cronin rejoined the group on *R.E.O.*, the band slid into a stretch of mediocre records relieved only by ceaseless touring. *Live: You Get What You Play For* managed to trade on some of that collected good will, but *REO Comes Alive* it ain't. Finally, *Hi Infidelity* put this journeyman quintet on the the the chart map in 1980; the album sat at Number One for 15 excruciating weeks. Soft-rocking hits like "Keep On Loving You" emphasized Cronin's numbingly earnest "regular dude" stance over guitarist Gary Richrath's tattered sack of Berry-derived riffs, but docked a notch or two for begetting the power ballad in all its mock-sensitive glory. After *Hi Infidelity*, the follow-ups to REO's out-of-nowhere blockbuster become increasingly less tuneful (and successful), until cofounder Richrath left the band in 1989. As for the continuing saga, well, running on empty probably won't stop REO Speedwagon from releasing albums well into the next century. — M.C.

THE REPLACEMENTS

★ ★½ **Sorry Ma, Forgot to Take Out the Trash (Twin/Tone, 1981)**
★ ★ **The Replacements Stink (EP) (Twin/Tone, 1982)**
★ ★ ★½ **Hootenanny (Twin/Tone, 1983)**
★ ★ ★ ★ ★ **Let It Be (Twin/Tone, 1984)**
★½ **The Shit Hits the Fans (Twin/Tone, 1985)**
★ ★ ★ ★ **Tim (Sire, 1985)**
★ ★ ★ ★ ★ **Pleased to Meet Me (Sire, 1987)**
★ ★ ★ **Don't Tell a Soul (Sire, 1989)**
★ ★ ★½ **All Shook Down (Sire, 1990)**

According to the myth, what made the Replacements so great was that they were so terrible. Ragged, raucous and rowdy, this Minneapolis foursome not only epitomized the fuck-you attitude of post-punk middle American youth, but found a way of converting that attitude into gloriously tuneful three-chord rock. In fact, there are even those among the faithful who will swear that what ultimately brought the band to ruin was frontman Paul Westerberg's efforts to clean up their act—that without the drunken craziness, the Replacements just weren't the Replacements anymore.

Which is complete crap. However much the Replacements' gleeful incompetence added to its performance, the bottom line for this band has always been the songs—Westerberg's songs, to be exact. That much is obvious even on the abysmally recorded *Sorry Ma, Forgot to Take Out the Trash*. Part of the appeal is the band's amiably warped sense of humor; "I Hate Music," for instance, builds its chorus around the thrash-fueled couplet "I hate music/It's got too many notes." But the music truly soars when the songs play off Westerberg's irrepressible sense of melody, as on "I Bought a Headache" or "Otto." That's not much of a factor on *The Replacements Stink*, which adds acceleration but otherwise coasts on cheap yuks. *Hootenanny*, however, shows impressive growth as Westerberg moves away from three-chord rants and toward ambitiously melodic material like "Color Me Impressed" or his synth-and-drum-machine solo number, "Within Your Reach."

With *Let It Be*, the Replacements finally reach musical maturity. That's not to say they shed their youthful exuberance entirely—the album does include such titles as "Tommy Gets His Tonsils Out" and "Gary's Got a Boner"—but the band's energies are better focused, whether exploiting the pop potential of "I Will Dare" or giving in to the trash-rock aesthetic of "Black Diamond" (yes, it is the Kiss classic). *Let It Be* was also the band's last recording as an indie act (apart from the hard-to-find, harder-to-listen-to live cassette, *The Shit Hits the Fans*), but all that the move to major-label status changed was the band's recording budget. As a result, *Tim* benefits from the expertise and perspective of a producer (former Ramone Tommy Erdelyi) who clarifies the band's sound and reins in its self-indulgence, a bit of discipline that brings out the humor in "Kiss Me on the Bus" while enhancing the hooks in "Left of the Dial" and "Bastards of Young."

Pleased to Meet Me is perhaps the band's finest moment. Westerberg's writing is irresistible throughout, whether showing off his pop smarts on the impossibly catchy choruses to "Alex Chilton" or "Can't Hardly Wait," or poking fun at the group's not-quite-underground, not-quite-mainstream status in songs like "I Don't

Know." *Don't Tell a Soul* finds the band pulling back a bit, and though its introspective mood adds quite a bit to tunes like "Achin' to Be," the album as a whole feels more like a Westerberg solo project than the next logical step from *Pleased to Meet Me*. Things get back on track with *All Shook Down*, thanks to typically tuneful rockers like "Merry Go Round" and "When It Began," but by this point, Westerberg dominates things so totally that the Replacements seem a band in name only. — J.D.C.

THE RESIDENTS

★★★½ Meet the Residents (Ralph, 1974)
★★★½ The Residents Present the Third Reich & Roll (Ralph, 1975)
★★★ Fingerprince (Ralph, 1976)
★★★½ Not Available (Ralph, 1978)
★★★★ Duck Stab/Buster & Glen (Ralph, 1978)
★★★ Eskimo (Ralph, 1979)
★★★ The Residents Commercial Album (Ralph, 1980)
★★★ Mark of the Mole (Ralph, 1981)
★★ The Tunes of Two Cities (Ralph, 1982)
★★ Residue of the Residents (Ralph, 1983)
★★★ George & James (Ralph, 1984)
★★ Whatever Happened to Vileness Fats? (Ralph, 1984)
★★ The Big Bubble (Ralph, 1985)
★★★ Heaven? (Rykodisc, 1986)
★★★ Hell! (Rykodisc, 1986)
★★ Stars & Hank Forever (Ralph, 1986)
★★ 13th Anniversary Show—Live in Japan (Ralph, 1986)
★★ God in Three Persons (Rykodisc, 1988)
★★ God in 3 Persons: Original Soundtrack Recording (Rykodisc, 1988)
★★ The King and Eye (Enigma, 1989)
★★★ Stranger than Supper (UWEB Special Products, 1990)

These anonymous San Francisco parodists have been deconstructing pop music with gleefully atonal results since the mid-'70s. The earliest Residents records take the Frank Zappa–Captain Beefheart approach to rock and run it through an garbage compactor. The result? Churning post-LSD musique concrete that never quite settles into solid forms. The earliest records are probably the most gripping—and shocking, if that was the intent. *Third Reich 'n' Roll* grinds various deserving '60s classics—"In-a

Gadda-Da-Vida" and the like—under the jackboot of technology. The mauled version of the Stones' "(I Can't Get No) Satisfaction" gains its sting from the late guitarist Phil "Snakefinger" Lithman's incredibly tangled lines. *Duck Stab/Buster & Glen*, originally released as two EPs, compiles a series of short, song-like outbursts that are probably the Residents' most approachable and light-hearted moments. *Commercial Album* fires off a machine-gun round of 60-second spots—these people were sampling and sound-biting before either activity had a name. *Eskimo* is a dreary and dank concept album about . . . oh, you guessed! *The Mark of the Mole*—the first installment of an ongoing suite, or something—ushers in a more ambitious era of Residence. The group's American Composer Series begins with George & James; Gershwin gets his unjust desserts on one side, the Godfather of Soul on the other. Further honorees-victims include Hank Williams and John Phillp Sousa (*Stars & Hank Forever*) and that most hackneyed of satirical targets, Elvis Presley (*The King and Eye*). If you're wondering why anyone wouldn't just be satisfied with listening to the rich achievements of those artists (save Sousa), well, the Residents aren't for you. A generalized, elitist contempt for popular culture would appear to be the point of entry. *Heaven?* and *Hell!* summarize the group's voluminous, daunting output. Tellingly, the fan-club release *Stranger Than Supper* offers a more succint, pointed display of the Residents' bizarre—and infamous—sonic reduction. — M.C.

REVENGE
★★½ **One True Passion (Capitol, 1990)**
New Order bassist Peter Hook's solo project isolates his contributions to NO, though his immediately recognizable bass playing sounds limited when thrown into relief. — M.C.

PAUL REVERE AND THE RAIDERS
★★★   **Greatest Hits (Columbia, 1967)**
★★★½ **All-Time Greatest Hits (Columbia, 1972)**
★★★½ **The Legend of Paul Revere (Columbia, 1990)**
Tricked out in silly Revolutionary War frock coats and gaiters, keyboardist and ultra-ham Paul Revere, together with darling ponytailed front man Mark Lindsay, reigned supreme on Dick Clark's mid-'60s afternoon TV show, *Where the Action Is*.

Given this nifty platform from which to deliver their product, the Raiders capitalized on the exposure, scoring massively with "Hungry," "Just Like Me," "Him or Me—What's It Gonna Be?" and Barry Mann and Cynthia Weill's antidrug number, "Kicks." All these hits were slick pop-craft; Lindsay's breathy, well-trained voice was made for radio; and the frenzy the studio dance floor displayed made the songs seem like rock & roll. But the band's "We're just entertainers" spirit was even then apparent, and it became more so as the gig got tired. Revere himself, however, is still at it—touring maniacally with a new crew, whose synchronized dance steps and general foolery are kitsch beyond parody. *All Time Greatest Hits* is probably enough Raiders for anyone. *The Legend of Paul Revere* is baffingly comprehensive: 55 songs presented with enough brouhaha to convince the unsuspecting that this was a significant band. Don't be fooled. — P.E.

RHINOCEROS
★ **Rhinoceros (Elektra, 1968)**
★ **Satin Chicken (Elektra, 1969)**
★ **Better Times Are Coming (Elektra, 1970)**
Lumbering and graceless, this seven-piece band, it seems, wasn't being ironic when it named itself. Former bit players in such big-name outfits as Buffalo Springfield, the Mothers of Invention, Electric Flag and Iron Butterfly, Rhinoceros played pompous blues-derived rock—the band's guitar playing poorly aped Mike Bloomfield's, and the two lead vocalists' singing was overblown mock-soul. No doubt it's wishful thinking to presume that Alan Gerber and John Finley knew they couldn't sing, but "Apricot Brandy," the minor hit off *Rhinoceros*, from 1968, was a heavy funky instrumental—and, on the opening cut, the vocals are so oddly recorded that they sound like they're coming from some other planet. Sadly, Rhinoceros didn't follow through with this technique; the rest of the band's work is gratingly bad. — P.E.

CHARLIE RICH
★★★★ **Lonely Weekends (1960; Sun, 1969)**
  ★★★ **Original Charlie Rich (Sun, NA)**
  ★★★ **A Time for Tears (Sun, 1970)**
  ★★★ **20 Golden Hits (Sun, NA)**
  ★★★ **Best of Charlie Rich (1972; Epic, 1986)**
  ★★★ **Behind Closed Doors (Epic, 1973)**
  ★★★ **Greatest Hits (Epic, 1976)**
★★★★ **Silver Linings (Epic, 1976)**
★★★★ **Pictures and Paintings (Sire, 1992)**

A once-bloated catalogue that only deranged completists could appreciate or desire has now been whittled down to the essence of Charlie Rich's best work. A man whose reputation has always exceeded his popular appeal (save for a brief stretch in the early '70s, when his country singles were consistent Top Twenty items), Rich was a second-generation Sun rock artist who was equally at home with rock & roll, blues, jazz and country music. Being so eclectic, Rich was something of an enigma to Sun founder Sam Phillips, who never quite figured out in which direction to channel the artist's talents. Rich became Sun's house pianist in the late '50s and began cutting his own records in between sessions. Nothing clicked until 1960, when "Lonely Weekends" hit the Top Thirty. Three years passed with Rich unable to duplicate that success. Thus began a long march from label to label that found him recording for Groove, Smash (where he hit with another Top Thirty single, "Mohair Sam"), Hi, and finally, in 1967, Epic. With the guidance of producer Billy Sherrill, Rich hit it big in 1973 with "Behind Closed Doors," a languid love song featuring an irresistible vocal from Rich. Rich followed the Top Twenty success of "Behind Closed Doors" with an even bigger record, "The Most Beautiful Girl," which hit Number One on the pop and country charts. But "The Most Beautiful Girl" was also the beginning of another end for Rich; three more Top Thirty singles followed in '74 and '75, but the material was second-rate country-pop fodder. Rich's 1976 *Greatest Hits* album documents the high points as well as the dissolution of his career at Epic, while Sun's *Lonely Weekends* summarizes his best work in the '50s. An out-of-print Epic album from 1976, *Silver Linings*, is the best work he did for the label, although there wasn't a single hit on the album. Rather, this is Rich performing classic gospel songs. One has only to hear the stirring treatments of "Were You There," "Sometimes I Feel Like a Motherless Child" and "Down by the Riverside" to understand why Rich's peers tend to be in awe of his gifts. Rich returned in fine form with *Pictures and Paintings,* a jazz-inflected, moody work highlighted by his remake of the classic "Feel Like Going Home."
— D.M.

KEITH RICHARDS

★ ★ ★½ Talk Is Cheap (Virgin, 1988)
★ ★ ★ ★ Live at the Hollywood Palladium, December 12, 1988 (Virgin, 1991)

Reportedly, Keith Richards has years of studio jams stored in vaults; no doubt, by the year 2010, they'll all come out in box sets. For now, apart from a late-'70s single that reworked Jimmy Cliff's "The Harder They Come" and Chuck Berry's "Run, Run Rudolph," his 1988 *Talk Is Cheap* will have to do. And it does fine. This collaboration with funksters (Bernie Worrell) and L.A. rock pros (Waddy Wachtel) is one strong set. "How I Wish" has swagger; most of the other rockers are torrid one-riff jobs. An Al Green-ish thumper featuring Sarah Dash is a nice beauty-and-the-beast duet and "Locked Away" is a good Richards ballad. Keith proudly mixes his relatively on-key vocals a bit high—and it's arguable that "better" singing makes him more expressive. The Richards guitar, however, is in top form—unflanged, unwah-wahed and irresistible. *Live at the Hollywood Palladium* is a rambunctious live set recorded by the X-Pensive Winos in 1988. — P.E.

JONATHAN RICHMAN

★ ★ ★ ★ ★ The Modern Lovers (1976; Berserkley/Rhino, 1986)
★ ★ ★ Jonathan Richman & the Modern Lovers (1977; Beserkley/Rhino, 1986)
★ ★ Rock n' Roll With the Modern Lovers (1977; Beserkley/Rhino, 1986)
★ ★½ Back in Your Life (1979; Beserkeley/Rhino, 1986)
★ ★½ Jonathan Sings! (Sire, 1983)
★ ★ Rockin' and Romance (Twin/Tone, 1985)
★ ★ It's Time for Jonathan Richman and the Modern Lovers (Upside, 1986)
★ ★ ★ The Beserkley Years: the Best of Jonathan Richman and the Modern Lovers (Berserkley/Rhino, 1987)
★ ★ Modern Lovers 88 (Rounder, 1988)
★ ★ Jonathan Richman (Rounder, 1989)
★ Jonathan Goes Country (Rounder, 1990)

The most notorious case of arrested development in the history of rock, Jonathan Richman came cruising out of Boston at the helm of the Modern Lovers in the early '70s. Boldly copping riffs from the Velvet Underground and applying his own clearheaded post-hippie vision to Lou Reed's deadpan poet-outlaw stance, Richman tapped a vein of musical exploration that's still flowing today. Recorded for the most part in 1971 and released five years later, *The Modern Lovers* was at least that far ahead of its time. Future Talking Head Jerry Harrison lays down swirling organ fills over Richman's choppy rhythm guitar and half-spoken vocals, while bassist Ernie Brooks and future Cars drummer David Robinson provide a terse, throbbingly simple beat. The oft-covered statement-of-purpose "Roadrunner"—driving all-night with the radio ON—is justifiably famous, but there simply isn't a weak cut on this album.

While it would be unfair to insist that Richman stay fixated at that point, his loopy devolution is hard—if not impossible—to fathom. *Jonathan Richman & the Modern Lovers*—recorded with a new, mostly acoustic unit—spells out the dilemma in stereo. Why would anyone who could write and sing (in a manner of speaking) the heart-tearing ballad "Important in Your Life" even bother with banalities like "Abominable Snowman in the Market" or "Hey There Little Insect"? Why would a presumed fan of the genre attach the name *Rock & Roll With the Modern Lovers* to an album of ersatz children's ditties like "Ice Cream Man" and "Dodge Veg-O-Matic"? Could actual kids even stomach this stuff?

Richman returns to more-or-less adult fare on his '80s albums, though he unfortunately retains that cloying, quavering, terminally self-conscious delivery. His cult followers identify *Jonathan Sings!* and *Modern Lovers 88* as confident returns-to-form, however. It sure doesn't take an expert to recognize the absurdly patronizing tilt of *Jonathan Goes Country*: apparently, Richman thinks Nashville popcorn is even sillier than his own cotton-candy repertoire. *The Berserkley Years: The Best of Jonathan Richman and the Modern Lovers* patches over his happy-go-lucky downslide about as well as can be expected. Sad, if not downright tragic. — M.C.

THE RIGHTEOUS BROTHERS
- ★★★ **Greatest Hits (Verve, 1967)**
- ★★★★★ **Anthology (1962–1974) (Rhino, 1989)**
- ★★★½ **Best of the Righteous Brothers (Curb, 1990)**
- ★★★★ **Unchained Melody: The Very Best of the Righteous Brothers (Polygram, 1990)**
- ★★★★ **The Moonglow Years (Polygram, 1991)**

With Bill Medley moaning low and Bobby Hatfield wailing high over the grandest Wall of Sound production Phil Spector ever achieved, "You've Lost That Lovin' Feelin'," from 1964, may be the most dramatic ballad single ever released. All echos, kettledrums and surging strings, the instrumental track is wonderful, ersatz Wagner, but it's the vocal duel, mounting from resignation to longing to hysteria, that provokes the chills and the erotic/divine madness. It's odd then, that this California duo's 1963 debut, "Little Latin Lupe Lu," was such a dud. Medley actually wrote the sassy rocker, but it was left to Mitch Ryder to fire it up; the Brothers, in fact, with the exception of the nifty Little Richard-like "Justine" (1965), never could rock convincingly at any speed past mid-tempo—their artform was rhapsodic ballads. Dark and Lincolnesque, Medley was the baritone and brains behind the operation, and his stellar moments were many: he tends to dominate such glories as "(You're My) Soul and Inspiration" and "Hung on You." A small, blond ex-jock, Hatfield was the more tender deliverer—it's his warm elegance that carries "Unchained Melody," the 1965 hit that, recycled, got Demi Moore and Patrick Swayze all hot and bothered in *Ghost*. No fools, the pair spent much of their career attempting reruns of "You've Lost That Lovin' Feelin'," either by working with Spector or covering Mann-Weill songs. Only "See That Girl" bordered on self-parody, however, and while "Ebb Tide" and "The White Cliffs of Dover" were sappy clunkers, most of the Brothers' hits carried a rare dignity, especially considering the ultraromantic songs they covered.

Rhino's brilliant two-CD *Anthology* collects all the best Righteous Brothers performances—and these epics remain riveting. *Unchained Melody*, not quite as comprehensive or well-packaged, runs a close second. *The Moonglow Years* is a good representation of the duo's early days. Each time out, the boys go for broke, overpowering the listener with feeling. — P.E.

LEE RITENOUR
- ★★ **First Choice (Epic, 1976)**
- ★★ **Captain Fingers (Epic, 1977)**
- ★★★ **Rio (1979; GRP, 1985)**
- ★★ **Best of Lee Ritenour (Epic, 1980)**
- ★★ **Rit (Elektra, 1981)**
- ★★ **Rit 2 (Elektra, 1982)**
- ★★ **On the Line (GRP, 1985)**

★ ★ **Earthly Run (GRP, 1986)**
★ ★ **Portrait (GRP, 1987)**
★ ★ ★ **Festival (GRP, 1988)**
★ ★ ★ **Color Rit (GRP, 1989)**
★ ★ ★ **Stolen Moments (GRP, 1990)**
★ ★ ★ **Collection (GRP, 1991)**

An acolyte of Wes Montgomery and student of Joe Pass and Howard Roberts, Lee Ritenour has taken his intelligent guitar stylings and explored various fusions of pop, jazz and tropical rhythms. He's also been aggressive in his embrace of new recording technology and electronic instruments. But unlike so many techno-geeks whose music winds up brilliantly recorded but emotionally sterile, Ritenour has by and large kept his eye square on the heart of the song and let the technology do its thing without intruding on the intended spirit of the work. All of his albums have their virtues, but the most consistently pleasing ones feature Ritenour mostly on acoustic guitar and in a distinctively South American mode (*Rio*, *Festival*, and *Color Rit*). Notable among these is *Festival*, which features one of Brazil's most influential musicians, Caetano Veloso, whose "Vocee e Linda" (or "Linda," as it's titled here) is a moment of supreme beauty, with Veloso's vocal supported with grace and sensitivity by Ritenour and a first-rate band. Breaking out of the mold a bit on *Color Rit*, Ritenour offers a commendable interpretation of the Isley Brothers' "I Can't Let Go." Apart from that, those seeking the essential Lee Ritenour should check out *Collection*, which offers 13 examples of the guitarist's varied excursions into fusion music dating back to 1981. — D.M.

TEX RITTER

★ ★ ★ **Tex Ritter: Country Music Hall of Fame Series (MCA, 1991)**

This celebrated movie cowboy actually got his start in show business in the legitimate theater in New York City, where he gravitated in 1928 after studying at the University of Texas at Austin. As his acting career took off, Ritter began performing cowboy songs on WINS radio in New York and was signed to Decca Records in 1935. The 16 cuts on this Country Music Hall of Fame Series entry are culled from Decca sessions between 1935 and 1939 and show the singer delivering both traditional cowboy material and more folk-based songs of the sort he was performing in his Broadway roles. As well, there are several tracks Ritter recorded for his early westerns. His rich baritone is emotionally contained

but still compelling, despite its relative drabness, owing largely to the feelings it gives up on occasion. Gene Autry may have been the more celebrated of moviedom's cowboys, but Ritter's was the voice that sounded like a lonely wind blowing across a landscape populated only by tumbleweeds, rattlesnakes and human vermin. There's nothing citified about it. One listen to "(Take Me Back to My) Boots and Saddles" and you will have learned something about the pull of the prairie. After leaving Decca, Ritter recorded extensively for Capitol Records, and in 1953 won an Oscar for his performance of the theme song for *High Noon*. All of Ritter's Capitol recordings are out of print. — D.M.

JOHNNY RIVERS

★ ★ ★ **The Very Best of Johnny Rivers (EMI-Manhattan, 1975)**
★ ★ ★ **The Best of Johnny Rivers (EMI America, 1987)**
★ ★ ★ ★ **Johnny Rivers: Anthology (1964-1977) (Rhino, 1964)**

From his roost at L.A.'s Whisky-A-Go-Go club, Johnny Rivers generated a stream of mid-'60s hits—covers of Chuck Berry's "Memphis" and "Maybellene," Willie Dixon's "Seventh Son" and Harold Dorman's "Mountain of Love." All of them were engaging, and at the time served to expose black music to white audiences—but Rivers remained less an interpreter than a popularizer. Certainly funkier than Pat Boone, he played his cover material with straightforward enthusiasm and added no schmaltz—but his singing and guitar work were never more than competent, and his records were no more revealing than the sets of a very good bar band with an impeccable song list. Ultimately a hip show-biz entertainer rather than a genuine rocker, Rivers released the cool and campy "Secret Agent Man" in 1966—a TV show theme song that captured his essence: that of an industry vet who would follow trends smartly and rack up hits with deft assurance. A pro rather than a hack, Rivers never condescended to his material; his instincts were sharp enough that he never made an embarrassing record; and his greatest-hits compilations (of which Rhino's two-CD set is the most complete) remain enjoyable. — P.E.

THE RIVINGTONS

★ ★ ★ **The Liberty Years (EMI, 1991)**

One of doo-wop's last commercial gasps, the Rivingtons are remembered primarily for the driving nonsense song, "Papa-Oom-Mow-Mow," which peaked at Number 48 in 1962. Some might remember a lesser single, "The Bird's the Word" (1963), which became the model later that year for the Trashmen's Top Five single, "Surfin' Bird." *The Liberty Years* shows the group had a lot going for it in the way of soul. "Deep Water" is a gospel-inspired song of trouble and strife, and "Standing in the Love Line" is a rousing number from 1962. Not a major group, the Rivingtons were more interesting than would be indicated by their brief fling with fame. — D.M.

ROACHFORD

★ ★ Roachford (Columbia, 1988)
Hot on the heels of Terence Trent D'Arby, a young man named Andrew Roachford ascended to England's vacant pop-soul throne with this 1988 debut. He's not a half-bad singer: that warm, casual delivery goes down better than some of D'Arby's melodramatic flash. But in terms of content, Roachford is an empty set. Unlike such distinguished Brit predecessors as the Imaginations' Lee John and Hot Chocolate's Errol Brown, Roachford lacks the unifying musical vision required of any true genre-breaker. Even his strongest hook—"Cuddly Toy (Feel for Me)"—gets stuck between power-chord pummel and a funky strut, as if he can't decide which radio market to court. — M.C.

ROB BASE AND D.J. E-Z ROCK

★ ★ ★½ It Takes Two (Profile, 1988)
★ ★½ The Incredible Base (Profile, 1990)
With the cockiness characteristic of his genre, this feisty rapper alters the lyrics of the Motown classic "Ain't Nothing Like the Real Thing," to "Ain't Nothing Like the Rob Base" on his second album; its title, too, *The Incredible Base*, gives up nothing in the way of false modesty. Actually, he could have voiced his outrageous claims almost convincingly with his debut: *It Takes Two*, from 1988, really kicked, especially the title track—a tough, quick rap set atop a James Brown sample. Base was among the leaders of the rap pack in moving the form beyond "talking only" purism. "Get Up and Have a Good Time" is the highlight of *The Incredible Base*; spun off from Redbone's "Come and Get Your Love," the track is snappy and melodic; the rest of the record sounds a bit halfhearted. — P.E.

MARTY ROBBINS

★ ★ ★ ★ Marty Robbins' Greatest Hits (Columbia, 1959)
★ ★ ★ ★ More Greatest Hits (Columbia, 1961)
★ ★ ★ ★ Marty Robbins' Greatest Hits (1962; Columbia, 1991)
★ ★ ★ ★ Gunfighter Ballads & Trail Songs/My Woman, My Woman, My Wife (1959; Columbia, 1970)
★ ★ ★ ★ More Gunfighter Ballads & Trail Songs (Columbia, 1961)
★ ★ ★ What God Has Done (Columbia, 1966)
★ ★ ★ ★ El Paso (Columbia, 1970)
★ ★ ★ ★ The World of Marty Robbins (Columbia, 1971)
★ ★ ★ Greatest Hits—Volume III (Columbia, 1971)
★ ★ ★ ★ All-Time Greatest Hits (Columbia, 1972)
★ ★ ★ El Paso City (Columbia, 1976)
★ ★ ★ Greatest Hits, Volume IV (Columbia, 1978)
★ ★ ★ What God Has Done (Columbia, 1978)
★ ★ ★ ★ All Around Cowboy (Columbia, 1979)
★ ★ ★ Encore (Columbia, 1981)
★ ★ ★ Come Back to Me (Columbia, 1982)
★ ★ ★ Some Memories Just Won't Die (Columbia, 1982)
★ ★ ★ Biggest Hits (Columbia, 1982)
★ ★ ★ ★ ★ The Marty Robbins Files, Vols. 1–5 (Bear Family, 1983)
★ ★ ★ ★ A Lifetime of Song, 1951–1982 (Columbia, 1983)
★ ★ ★ ★ Long, Long Ago (Columbia, 1984)
★ ★ ★ ★ ★ Rockin' Rollin' Robbins, Vols. 1–5 (Bear Family, 1985)
★ ★ ★ ★ The Essential Marty Robbins (Columbia/Legacy, 1991)
At the time of his death in 1982, Marty Robbins had one of the most extensive and most interesting catalogues of any CBS artist. Nearly a decade later, the phases of his career have been blurred by repackagings of songs connected only by theme rather than by style or concept. Worse still, once-extensive liner notes and sessionographies have disappeared. This is shameful treatment of an artist who was a resourceful vocalist; a songwriter who extended the tradition of the western song into the modern era; a historian who explored his interest in the old west over the course of four concept albums, only two of which remain in print; an all-around threat in the studio who worked with producers

both great (Bob Johnston, Don Law) and controversial (Mitch Miller, Billy Sherrill) and became his own best producer. In short, Marty Robbins was in control of his art and shaped it to suit his vision.

Among the currently available titles, the best place to start is *A Lifetime of Song*. A posthumous release, *Lifetime* attempts to summarize a 31-year career in 20 cuts; this is not an impossible task, but the title is misleading. The greatest hits are on hand, but this artist's lifetime of song encompassed a broader spectrum of music than this album suggests. Nevertheless, if it's the familiar and famous Marty Robbins you're after, this is a must. The first seven cuts represent Robbins's transition from rockabilly to rock & roll and include the two songs that put him on the map with hip teens in the '50s, "A White Sport Coat" and "The Story of My Life," both from '57 and both produced, ironically, by Mitch Miller. There follows a nice selection of his western songs, including the Number One Robbins-penned hit from 1959, "El Paso," as well as "The Hanging Tree" and "Big Iron." The end of the El Paso saga is stirringly documented in the 1976 hit "El Paso City," in which Robbins's modern-day narrator, flying over the west Texas city of the title, experiences déjà vu and portents of death, all as the Spanish guitar, horns and marimba familiar from "El Paso" swirl around the vocal. In his later years Robbins gravitated toward the soft center of the country-pop mainstream, not always to great effect. Some of his tougher mainstream efforts appear, including one of his last and most sensitive readings, "Some Memories Just Won't Die," from 1982, which marries Robbins's quavering vocal to a lyric that is halfway between heartbreak and hope. Say this about *Lifetime*: anyone who is introduced to Robbins through this disc will want more.

Beyond this, the albums most essential to the Robbins legend would be the two remaining concept albums, *Gunfighter Ballads & Trail Songs*, from 1959 (now packaged as a two-fer with the 1970 LP, *My Woman, My Woman, My Wife*, interesting primarily for Robbins's touching interpretations of two songs that for all intents and purposes belong to Elvis Presley, "Can't Help Falling in Love" and "Love Me Tender") and *More Gunfighter Ballads & Trail Songs*, from 1961. No one ever wrote a better western song than did Bob Nolan, and Robbins honors the poet laureate of the genre on both these records with sturdy

interpretations of Nolan's blissful "Cool Water" and the lesser-known Nolan gem, "Song of the Bandit." To these Robbins added his own compositions, which stand head-to-head with Nolan's in their understanding of the cowboy's mystical ties to land and nature. *More Gunfighter Ballads* also includes one of Robbins's most devastating accounts of faithless love, "She Was Young and She Was Pretty." The 1959 album, by the way, contains both "El Paso" and "Big Iron" as its hit attractions.

In addition to these, both *El Paso City* and *All Around Cowboy* are also built around western themes, and both include a Bob Nolan song ("Way Out There" and "Tumbling Tumbleweeds," respectively) amid the Robbins originals. Of note on *El Paso City* is "Among My Souvenirs," a pop hit dating from 1928. This is indicative of Robbins's wide-ranging tastes and underlines his skill at adapting all manner of song to his distinctive style. *Long, Long Ago* bears witness to this fact, as Robbins leavens the cowboy tales with his interpretation of Stephen Foster's "Beautiful Dreamer" and the gospel standard, "Where Could I Go (But to the Lord)." Equally interesting, half of the 20 cuts feature Robbins accompanied only by an acoustic guitar. Spanning a period from 1960 to 1968, *Long, Long Ago* shows Robbins in peak form, addressing both the western songs he loved and laying the groundwork for his later forays into pop. Also recommended is the gospel album *What God Has Done*.

At this point you're pretty much into various hits packages, although all are not labeled as such. *The World of Marty Robbins* and *Marty Robbins' All-Time Greatest Hits* offer the biggest bang for the buck, both being two-record sets that touch on some of the highlights of the deleted catalogue. The out-of-print albums to search for are *Return of the Gunfighter* and *The Drifter*. The latter is of special interest because it includes the chronological center of the El Paso saga, "Feleena (From El Paso)." Also worth searching for is Robbins's last full-bore blast of rock & roll, *Devil Woman*, from 1962, which features the Top Twenty title song.

As the Bear Family imports suggest, Marty Robbins is an artist worthy of the boxed-set treatment as a way of consolidating the various phases of his career into an authoritative historical statement that might lead listeners deeper into the catalog. Unfortunately, *The*

Essential Marty Robbins is little more than a greatest-hits package, leaving the definitive overview still to come. — D.M.

ROBBIE ROBERTSON

★★★★ **Robbie Robertson (Geffen, 1987)**
★★★★½ **Storyville (Geffen, 1991)**
More than ten years after achieving greatness as the guitarist and songwriter for the Band, Robbie Robertson released a 1987 solo album (*Robbie Robertson*) whose songs sounded very little like the music he'd crafted for the most instrumentally accomplished group in American rock history. From the Band, only bassist Rick Danko and keyboardist Garth Hudson joined him on the new project; perhaps the most telling sign of a shift in direction was Robertson's choice of drummer—instead of the Band's Levon Helm, a player of absolute instinct, he chose Zappa-Berlin percussionist Terry Bozzio and studio craftsman Manu Katché, both ultratechnicians. Plainly, Robertson wanted an atmosphere much different than the Band's trademark air of cabin fever and backwoods ecstasy—he found it with help from producer Daniel Lanois, by all means a roots-music enthusiast, but one of a decidedly artful kind. And Robertson employed a virtual army of guest stars: Peter Gabriel, U2, Neil Young and the Gil Evans horn section. So commanding is Robertson, however, that he wasn't overwhelmed by his collaborators. Instead, he accomplished a very personal masterpiece: such songs as "Sweet Fire of Love," "Broken Arrow" and "Somewhere Down the Crazy River" found him at the peak of his powers, turning out music diverse, artful and satisfying.

In Robertson's case, however, masterpieces seem to take time. He waited until 1991 for his followup, *Storyville*—and topped even *Robbie Robertson*. Primarily, the new record was a triumph of focus—in concentrating on New Orleans music, he found thematic unity (and so rich is the sound of the Crescent City that there still was stylistic variety aplenty). Enlisting the services of a reunited Meters, members of the Neville Brothers and the Zion Harmonizers, he crafted music deriving from blues, R&B and gospel without sacrificing anything in the way of his own vision. Neil Young and Bruce Hornsby joined in, as well—but the triumph, spiritual, lyrical and musical—was unmistakably that of this ever-resourceful composer. — P.E.

THE ROBINS

★★★ **Best of the Robins (GNP/Crescendo, 1974)**
The original Robins featured one of R&B's great vocal comics in lead singer Carl Gardner, whose artistry was put to good use when the group teamed up with songwriters-producers Jerry Leiber and Mike Stoller in 1954 to cut "Smokey Joe's Cafe" and "Riot in Cell Block No. 9" on Leiber and Stoller's Spark label. Both were R&B hits. In 1955 Atlantic Records' new Atco subsidiary bought the Spark label, a move that brought Leiber and Stoller into the Atlantic fold, but split the Robins. While Gardner and bass singer Bobby Nunn wanted to make the move, the other Robins declined. Gardner and Nunn went on to form the Coasters and become one of the most successful crossover R&B groups of the '50s. H. B. Barnum then joined the remaining Robins, who signed with the Whippet label in Los Angeles and out of the box had a hit single with "Cherry Lips." This is the group represented on *Best of*, which shows the band staying firmly in an uptempo R&B and ballad groove, and heading for the middle of the road in covering standards such as "That Old Black Magic" and "Blues in the Night." Barnum has a high, plaintive tenor similar in timbre to Clyde McPhatter's and a graceful way with a song even at his most possessed. The Robins are hardly legendary, but that's not to say their music isn't worthwhile. — D.M.

SMOKEY ROBINSON AND THE MIRACLES

★★★★ **Doin' Mickey's Monkey (1963; Motown, 1986)**
★★★½ **Miracles Going to a Go-Go (1964; Motown, 1989)**
★★★★ **The Miracles Greatest Hits From the Beginning (1965; Motown, 1989)**
★★★½ **Away We a Go-Go (1966; Motown, 1989)**
★★★★ **The Miracles Greatest Hits, Vol. 2 (Tamla, 1966)**
★★★½ **The Tears of a Clown (1970; Motown, 1991)**
★★★ **Time Out for Smokey Robinson and the Miracles (1970; Motown, 1989)**
★★★★ **Whatlovehasjoinedtogether (1970; Motown, 1990)**
★★★ **One Dozen Roses (Tamla, 1971)**
★★★ **Flying High Together (Tamla, 1972)**
★★★★★ **Anthology (Motown, 1986)**

★★★★ **Smokey Robinson and the Miracles Greatest Hits, Vol. 2 (Motown, 1991)**
THE MIRACLES
  ★★½ **Renaissance (Tamla, 1973)**
  ★★★ **Do It, Baby (Tamla, 1974)**
  ★★½ **Don't Cha Love It (Tamla, 1975)**
  ★★★ **City of Angels (Tamla, 1975)**
  ★★★ **Power of the Music (Tamla, 1975)**
  ★★★½ **The Miracles Greatest Hits (Tamla, 1977)**
SMOKEY ROBINSON
  ★★★ **Smokey (Tamla, 1973)**
  ★★★ **Pure Smokey (Tamla, 1974)**
  ★★★★ **A Quiet Storm (1975; Motown, 1991)**
  ★★★ **Smokey's Family Robinson (Tamla, 1975)**
  ★★★ **Deep in My Soul (Tamla, 1977)**
  ★★★ **Love Breeze (Tamla, 1978)**
  ★★★ **Smokin' (Tamla, 1979)**
  ★★★★ **Where There's Smoke (1979; Motown, 1989)**
  ★★★★ **Warm Thoughts (Tamla, 1980)**
  ★★★★ **Being With You (1981; Motown, 1989)**
  ★★½ **Yes It's You Lady (Tamla, 1982)**
  ★★★½ **Touch the Sky (Tamla, 1983)**
  ★★★½ **Blame It on Love and All the Greatest Hits (1983; Motown, 1991)**
  ★★★½ **Essar (Tamla, 1984)**
  ★★★½ **Smoke Signals (Motown, 1986)**
  ★★★★ **One Heartbeat (Motown, 1987)**
  ★★★½ **Love, Smokey (Motown, 1990)**
  ★★★½ **Double Good Everything (SBK, 1991)**

Not only is "The Tears of a Clown" (1970) the definitive song for Smokey Robinson and the Miracles, but it's one of pop's few perfect singles. Kicked off by a sprightly flute and oboe interchange, soon followed by sassy trombone, and featuring an ingenious jew's harp twanging exactly as the chorus's key line arrives, the arrangement is audacious—it's pure pop frosting piled atop Motown's customarily delicious bass and drums. Smokey sings in his unerring falsetto, and his lyrics justify Bob Dylan's only half-outrageous claim that Robinson qualifies as America's greatest living poet. Master of supple half-rhymes ("public" and "subject") and of virtuosic language games (Robinson works in the name of the classic Italian clown "Pagliacci" without sounding at all arch), the songwriter delivers his tour-de-force.

And "Tears" remains only one of a barrage of Miracles classics. Along with the Temptations, the Four Tops and the Supremes, the Detroit quartet defined Motown—and cinched its ingenious wedding of R&B's depth and physicality to pop's airy melodicism. Robinson, however, as composer and producer, was arguably Motown's most significant creative force besides owner Berry Gordy: nearly all of the label's acts were lucky recipients of his songs. While Smokey's "Got a Job" (1958)—an answer to the Silhouette's "Get a Job"—was little more than (very capable) doo-wop, the band's followup, "Bad Girl" hinted at the Miracles' later greatness; for one thing, it properly forefronted Smokey's lead vocals, for another, it featured in embryo the glossy instrumentation that would stamp the group's ballads.

Throughout the '60s, the Miracles alternated between great rave-ups and elegant love songs. Particulary fetching were the crowd-noise intros to "Mickey's Monkey" and "Going to a Go-Go"—while Motown 45s became known as ultra-tight productions, Smokey's dance fare often began with the tape rolling as the musicians casually led off, only to kick in with absolute assurance. "Ooo Baby Baby" (1965) was the first great slow song, notable primarily for Robinson's tender singing; that same year also saw the release of the staggering "The Tracks of My Tears," a triumph of the songwriter's gift for metaphor. With Marvin Tarplin on guitar, the group continued to produce epic radio fare up until the early '70s, climaxing in "Tears of a Clown." With Robinson departing in 1972, the Miracles continued successfully for another six years; "Do It Baby" (1974) and "Love Machine (Part 1)" (1975) remain their finest moments, even if none of their singles managed to reproduce Smokey's panache.

On his own, Robinson managed to do what few Motown artists, with the notable exception of Marvin Gaye and Stevie Wonder, were able to accomplish—continue to make vital music after the label's '60s heyday. His solo work lacks some of the obvious freshness of his early Miracles' efforts; instead, it's been an exercise in seamless expertise. The obvious shift has been in his records' arrangements; he's concentrated on developing albums as much as singles, and where the best Miracles songs often featured melodic motifs and instrumentation that borrowed from classical music, Smokey's later style is jazzier, its rhythms often langorous, and its ambience sometimes recalling that of such classic pop writers as Cole Porter and the

Gershwins. While never conceding totally to the predominant R&B genres of the late '70s and early '80s—disco and funk—he still engaged them, while concentrating primarily on the romantic ballad. At the art of the love song he remains a master—he does "mellow" better than just about any pop composer.

With such standouts as "Sweet Harmony and "Just My Soul Responding," *Smokey* ushered in the mature Robinson, and a series of fine, subtle albums that met with a bewildering lack of commercial success. The singer's older audience kept faith—the elegant sexiness of Smokey's material found favor, too, with critics—but younger R&B fans seemed to prefer the blatant flash of Rick James or the cartoon sensuality of Barry White. Six years after his solo debut, Smokey's style coalesced on *Where There's Smoke*, with a great single ("Cruisin' "), high-gloss production, and some of the singer's most assertive vocals in years. *Warm Thoughts* (1980) was an equally fluid masterwork, and one of his strongest collections of love songs. *Being With You* (1981) rounded out a now-classic trio, confirming that solo Smokey had finally lived up to the promise of his own early legacy. His next records wouldn't quite approach this sort of excellence, but such triumphs as "Just to See Her" (1987) off *One Heartbeat* have continued to prove his staying power. — P.E.

THE ROCHES

★★★★　The Roches (Warner Bros., 1979)
★★★　Nurds (Warner Bros., 1980)
★★★½　Keep on Doing (Warner Bros., 1982)
★★　Another World (Warner Bros., 1985)
★★　No Trespassing (Rhino, 1986)
★★★½　Speak (MCA, 1989)
★★★½　We Three Kings (MCA/Paradox, 1990)
★★★½　A Dove (MCA, 1992)

The Roches are not for everybody, to say the least. But the post-folkie acoustic pop stylings of this Manhattan-based sisters act offer definite charms. On the debut album, producer Robert Fripp weaves a hypnotic ambient lull through the quirky, yet grounded harmonies of Maggie, Terre and Suzzy Roche. From such beguiling (and mysteriously opaque) songs as "Hammond Song," *The Roches* envelops a listener in a stunning pure sound. Fans of the group swear by their songwriting, but a tendency toward precious humor and blinkering

self-consciousness deep-sixes the less musically adventurous follow-up (*Nurds*). That title is a tip-off. If you're already in their camp, these plucky and independent women regain some oddball focus from another oddball Fripp treatment on *Keep on Doing*. After two rock-slanted misfires (*Another World* and *No Trespassing*), the Roches concocted an electro-organic landscape of their own on the confident, if largely unheard *Speak*.

We Three Kings finds the group returning to its (true) roots as seasonal carolers in Greenwich Village; this collection of radiantly sung traditionals makes a winning addition to any Christmas album shelf. — M.C.

ROCKIN' DOPSIE

★★★　Hold On (GNP, 1983)
★★★　Big Bad Zydeco (GNP, 1982)
★★★½　Good Rockin' (GNP, 1984)
★★★　Saturday Night Zydeco (Maison de Soul, 1988)

A zesty singer and an exuberant accordionist, Rockin' Dopsie serves up absolutely authentic zydeco. Cajun party music that combines the bounce of the polka and the grit of the blues, his albums are consistently entertaining—but the Cajun-French-language takes on such New Orleans standards as "I'm Walkin' " and "I Hear You Knockin' " make *Good Rockin'* the standout. Recorded with a cast of zydeco all-stars rather than his usual Cajun Twisters, *Saturday Night* is Dopsie at his most technically accomplished—the raw charm of the earlier records, however, provides the more enduring pleasure. — P.E.

ROCKPILE

★★★½　Seconds of Pleasure (Columbia, 1980)

Rockpile earned its reputation onstage and on the solo records by founding members Nick Lowe and Dave Edmunds. The exemplary roots-rock quartet's only proper release, *Seconds of Pleasure*, underwhelmed many fans' expectations when it came out. And Rockpile spilt up—acrimoniously—not long after. In retrospect, *Seconds* is a worthy, integrated group effort: for the first and last time, Rockpile rocked consistently. Guitarist Edmunds flashes his rockabilly edge, and Nick Lowe exhibits his bent pop sensibility, while second guitarist Billy Bremner holds the spotlight with a pair of solid vocal performances and drummer Terry Williams seems to be everywhere at once. *Seconds of Pleasure* contains 40 minutes worth of traditional, prepsychedelic rock & roll, played with conviction and joie de vivre. The CD includes acoustic cover versions of four heartbreakingly sweet Everly Brothers songs—for once, bonus tracks that constitute an actual bonus!

— M.C.

JIMMIE RODGERS

★ ★ ★ ★ ★ **First Sessions, 1927-1928 (Rounder, 1991)**

★ ★ ★ ★ ★ **The Early Years, 1928–1929 (Rounder, 1991)**

★ ★ ★ ★ ★ **On the Way Up, 1929 (Rounder, 1991)**

★ ★ ★ ★ ★ **Riding High, 1929–1930 (Rounder, 1991)**

★ ★ ★ ★ ★ **America's Blue Yodeler, 1930-1931 (Rounder, 1991)**

★ ★ ★ ★ ★ **Down the Old Road, 1931–1932 (Rounder, 1991)**

★ ★ ★ ★ ★ **No Hard Times, 1932 (Rounder, 1991)**

★ ★ ★ ★ ★ **Last Sessions, 1933 (Rounder, 1991)**

When Jimmie Rodgers cut his first sides for Victor talent scout Ralph Peer in Bristol, Tennessee, in 1927, there was virtually no market, as we understand the term, for country, or "hillbilly," music. Rodgers's recordings, along with those of the Carter Family, created the market, and he and they became its first significant artists. That's all business stuff, though. Rodgers and the Carters ushered in modern country music, a stylistic departure from the string band music that was standard hillbilly fare before they showed up for the Bristol sessions. The irony is that while Rodgers may have been pigeonholed as a hillbilly artist, his music was far broader-based than that of the Carters, who drew on Southern folk and spiritual traditions that could be traced back to European (Scottish and Irish) styles; Rodgers's first love was blues, which he had heard constantly while working for the railroad as a water carrier—the job usually held only by black workers, was the only one available to Rodgers, who, afflicted by tuberculosis, was too frail to hold down more physically demanding positions on the line. In fact, at his Bristol sessions, Peer was critical of Rodgers for singing black blues, and through the years counseled Rodgers on the advisability of downplaying his Southern roots in order to reach a broader audience.

As it happened, it was no problem for Rodgers to shift gears musically, because, like A. P. Carter, he could take any type of song, whether written by himself, composed by other writers for him, or snatched from the public domain, and adapt it to a style that bridged black and white tastes. Where black blues singers employed guttural moans and shouts as dramatic devices in their songs, Rodgers took to yodeling—"blue" yodeling he called it, not the clear, bright, ululating sound we stereotype as Swiss style, but something darker and more evocative of trouble in mind.

More than his singing style, even more than his songs, Rodgers's most valuable contribution to country music—indeed, to popular music in general—was in expanding its boundaries. In addition to solo and traditional string band dates, Rodgers recorded with an orchestra as early as 1929. That Hawaiian music is intrinsically related to country (or vice versa) should be obvious by now, but wasn't so in 1930 when Rodgers cut several sides in a Hollywood, California, studio backed by Lani McIntire's Hawaiians, which brought new dimension to the high, lonesome sound. In 1930 Rodgers engaged in a summit meeting of note, when he recorded "Blue Yodel No. 9" with Louis Armstrong on trumpet and Louis's wife Lillian on piano. On this outing Rodgers made explicit an emotional link between jazz, blues and country. A year after the Armstrong session, Rodgers went against form again and recorded in Louisville with a black jug band.

This eclectic approach isn't at all surprising, given Rodgers's background. Born in 1897 in Meridian, Mississippi, he grew up in a region where he was surrounded by blues and country music. His mother died of TB when he was four, and since his father worked on the railroad and was often away from home, the young Rodgers spent much of his childhood with relatives in Mississippi and Alabama. Traveling and listening to the radio broadened his musical vocabulary.

Rodgers's catalogue has been in disarray for years, but Rounder, through an agreement with the German Bear Family label and RCA, is correcting the problem by reissuing all of the Singing Brakeman's recordings on CD with accompanying annotation by Rodgers's biographer, Nolan Porterfield. Each disc is essential as a means of showing the ways in which this towering figure shaped and reshaped his music through the years. *First Sessions* is largely Rodgers accompanying himself on guitar (the two original Bristol sides are here), and incorporating additional stringed instruments in the 1928 sessions. *The Early*

Years and *On The Way Up* show him expanding his repertoire and working with different combinations of instrumentalists. *The Early Years* includes tracks cut with an orchestra as well as three of the most famous recordings of Rodgers's career: "Waiting for a Train," "My Little Lady" and "Daddy and Home." *On the Way Up* includes two of Rodgers's choice blues performances, "Jimmie's Texas Blues" and "Train Whistle Blues." On these he is accompanied by a group of Texas musicians who went on to cut several important sides with him. One of these musicians, Joe Kaipo, a steel guitarist of Hawaiian extraction, stands out on these two cuts. The group also included 17-year-old guitarist Billy Burkes, who became a regular and outstanding accompanist with Rodgers in later years. *Riding High* charts Rodgers at a time when he was one of the most popular recording artists in the country; he'd even made a short film for Columbia Pictures. These sides take the artist from an Atlanta recording studio to Hollywood, where he delivered some of his most outstanding performances. Lani McIntire's Hawaiians are on two cuts, as well as Bob Sawyer's Jazz Band, a contingent comprised of piano, cornet, clarinet, banjo and tuba, on "My Blue-Eyed Jane." Commercially speaking, *America's Blue Yodeler* represents a pinnacle for Rodgers, as it collects tracks recorded in 1930 and 1931 that are among the his best-known, including the classic "Blue Yodel No. 8," or "Mule Skinner Blues." Included among these sides is the Armstrong track, "Blue Yodel No. 9," which finds Louis tentative at first but finally warming up and delivering a strutting solo. Lani McIntire's Hawaiians are featured prominently on three lovely pop-oriented songs; and Rodgers duets with Sara Carter (with Maybelle on guitar) on two tracks, including the powerful gospel tune, "The Wonderful City." In keeping with blues tradition, Rodgers had a bawdy streak that surfaced on occasion, as in "Let Me Be Your Side Track" and "The Mystery of Number Five." *Down the Old Road* is both forward-thinking and static. Rodgers is treading water on many of the tunes, but in sessions with the Louisville Jug Band, he suggested connections that Bob Wills and other western swing pioneers would seize on nearly two decades later. *No Hard Times* and *Last Sessions* conclude the Rodgers legacy. Even with death approaching (he cut "Old Love Letters" while propped up on a cot, only two days before he died), Rodgers

was still looking ahead to the next breakthrough. — D.M.

JIMMIE RODGERS
★ ★ ★ **The Best of Jimmie Rodgers (Rhino, 1990)**

A first-rate folk singer sold as a rock & roll star, Jimmie Rodgers scored his first hit in 1957 with "Honeycomb" and his last chart entry occurred ten years later with "Child of Clay." In between he turned out one good record after another, all characterized by catchy lyrics and strong melodies. Whether backed by a band or an orchestra, Rodgers's performances are intelligent, even challenging. This *Best of* set provides a generous overview of an artist whose work was informed by folk and blues as much as by pop. In addition to his best-known early hits "Honeycomb," "Kisses Sweeter Than Wine," "Oh-Oh, I'm Falling in Love Again," and "Secretly," the album shows Rodgers's growth as a songwriter later in his career with the buoyant folk tale, "Woman From Liberia," and "It's Over," which uses a simple acoustic guitar line to drive home a lacerating account of lost love. His last hit, "Child of Clay," expresses a growing social conscience in a story about the devastations of street life and society's abandonment of those most in need. Shortly after "Child of Clay" hit the charts, Rodgers suffered severe head injuries in a beating at the hands of an off-duty Los Angeles policeman who claimed he had stopped the artist to question him about his erratic driving. The incident remains mysterious to this day; regardless, Rodgers was never the same afterward, has recorded infrequently since then and has had no further hits. The only critical track missing from this collection is "The World I Used to Know," from 1964, possibly his most heartfelt performance and a song whose title alone pretty much says it all about the latter-day Jimmie Rodgers. One of rock's saddest stories. — D.M.

TOMMY ROE
★ ½ **The Best of Tommy Roe (Curb/MCA, 1990)**

Coming out of the Atlanta mid-'60s scene that produced, in Joe South, a true giant, and in Billy Joe Royal, a fairly funky warbler, Tommy Roe was strictly for teenyboppers. Unctuous and cute, Roe basically rewrote Buddy Holly's "Peggy Sue" for his own "Sheila" (a smash in '62) and then went on to score with other bubblegum ditties—"Dizzy," "Hooray for Hazel" and the oh-so-naughty "Jam Up

Jelly Tight." The Curb collection captures the classic kitsch—and some more recent songs that haven't even the saccharine charm of his hits. — P.E.

KENNY ROGERS AND THE FIRST EDITION
- ★ Hits & Pieces (MCA, 1985)
- ★ Greatest Hits (MCA, 1986)

KENNY ROGERS
- ★ Daytime Friends (EMI, 1977)
- ★ Ten Years of Gold (EMI, 1978)
- ★★ The Gambler (EMI, 1978)
- ★★ Greatest Hits (EMI, 1980)
- ★ Love Will Turn You Around (EMI, 1982)
- ★ We've Got Tonight (EMI, 1983)
- ★ Twenty Greatest Hits (EMI, 1983)
- ★ Eyes That See in the Dark (RCA, 1983)
- ★ Duets with Kim Carnes, Sheena Easton & Dottie West (EMI, 1984)
- ★ What About Me? (RCA, 1984)
- ★ The Heart of the Matter (RCA, 1985)
- ★ They Don't Make Them Like They Used To (RCA, 1986)
- ★ 25 Greatest Hits (EMI, 1987)
- ★ I Prefer the Moonlight (RCA, 1987)
- ★ Greatest Hits (RCA, 1988)
- ★ Something Inside So Strong (Reprise, 1989)
- ★ Love Is Strange (Reprise, 1990)

So much music, so little substance: Is there any artist who matches Kenny Rogers for sustained, predictable mediocrity? Even his first hit, the pseudo-psychedelic "Just Dropped In to See What Condition My Condition Was In," cut in 1968 with the First Edition, is aging gracelessly, its appeal as a novelty now outstripped by its shallowness. Rogers seems an agreeable enough personality, but as a singer his emotional and technical range is so limited that his songs blur into one another, to the point where little more than "The Gambler" stands apart from the crowd, owing to its menacing authority and its ongoing life as the basis for a series of forgettable TV movies starring Rogers in the title role. Nominally a country artist, he's achieved enormous pop success by crafting records that consciously straddle those genres without landing firmly in either camp; Rogers has also done a good job of injecting little of his own personality into his material, so it's impossible to state definitively what he stands for. If necessary, opt for the 1980 *Greatest Hits* album on EMI, which at least has "The Gambler" and a couple of other noteworthy singles, "Lucille" and Mel Tillis's "Ruby, Don't

Take Your Love to Town"; the CD remote control comes in handy for bailing out of the cloying ballads. It's hard to believe Rogers actually sang a song called "You Decorated My Life." Forget life—what about the house? — D.M.

THE ROLLING STONES
- ★★★★★ The Rolling Stones: England's Newest Hit Makers (1964; Abkco, 1986)
- ★★★★★ 12 X 5 (1964; Abkco, 1986)
- ★★★★★ The Rolling Stones, Now! (1965; Abkco, 1986)
- ★★★½ Out of Our Heads (1965; Abkco, 1986)
- ★★★★★ December's Children (and Everybody's) (1965; Abkco, 1986)
- ★★★★★ Big Hits/High Tide and Green Grass (1966; Abkco, 1986)
- ★★★★★ Aftermath (1966; Abkco, 1986)
- ★★★ Got Live if You Want It! (1966; Abkco, 1986)
- ★★★½ Between the Buttons (1967; Abkco, 1986)
- ★★★ Flowers (1967; Abkco, 1986)
- ★★½ Their Satanic Majesty's Request (1967; Abkco, 1986)
- ★★★★★ Beggars Banquet (1968; Abkco, 1986)
- ★★★★★ Through the Past, Darkly (Big Hits, Vol.2) (1969; Abkco, 1986)
- ★★★★★ Let It Bleed (1969; Abkco, 1986)
- ★★★★★ Get Yer Ya-Ya's Out! (1970; Abkco, 1986)
- ★★★★★ Sticky Fingers (Rolling Stones, 1971)
- ★★★★★ Hot Rocks 1964–71 (1972; Abkco, 1986)
- ★★★★★ Exile on Main Street (Rolling Stones, 1972)
- ★★★★★ More Hot Rocks: Big Hits and Fazed Cookies (1973; Abkco, 1986)
- ★★★½ Goats Head Soup (Rolling Stones, 1973)
- ★★★½ It's Only Rock 'n' Roll (Rolling Stones, 1974)
- ★★★½ Made in the Shade (Rolling Stones, 1975)
- ★★★★ Black and Blue (Rolling Stones, 1976)
- ★★★ Love You Live (Rolling Stones, 1977)
- ★★★★ Some Girls (Rolling Stones, 1978)

★ ★   **Emotional Rescue (Rolling Stones, 1980)**
★ ★ ★ ★   **Sucking in the Seventies (Rolling Stones, 1981)**
★ ★ ★ ★   **Tattoo You (Rolling Stones, 1981)**
★ ★½   **Still Life (Rolling Stones, 1982)**
★ ★½   **Undercover (Rolling Stones, 1983)**
★ ★ ★ ★   **Rewind (1971–1984) (Rolling Stones, 1984)**
★ ★ ★   **Dirty Work (Rolling Stones, 1986)**
★ ★ ★ ★ ★   **The Singles Collection (Abkco, 1989)**
★ ★ ★½   **Steel Wheels (Rolling Stones, 1989)**
★ ★ ★ ★   **Flashpoint (Rolling Stones, 1991)**

The Rolling Stones confirmed four basic rock & roll truths: attitude is (nearly) everything; rock's original sources (black and country music) remain its most fertile ones; Chuck Berry–derived rhythm guitar is rock's essential sonic vehicle; and lyrics are most evocative when just short of indecipherable. Insisting, against the example of other '60s legends, that rock & roll is foremost a live music, Mick Jagger and Keith Richards evolved an onstage partnership of frontman and sidekick that spawned successors ranging from Led Zep's Page-Plant to the Sex Pistols' Rotten-Vicious; as songwriters, the Glimmer Twins range in influence alongside Lennon-McCartney and Bob Dylan. But if the Beatles' music and Dylan's words constituted victories of innovation, the Stones championed fidelity—seldom straying from its roots, they preserved rock & roll. The classic Rolling Stones provided the standard for all trad rock to come.

Mixing Rufus Thomas and Buddy Holly, Willie Dixon, Marvin Gaye and Sam Cooke, the Stones' first three albums were black music primers of raw force; the blues appeal of *Now!* makes it the strongest of the trio, but each was a revelation to white U.S. and U.K. teens. While a lesser album as a whole, *Out of Our Heads* provided the breakthrough "(I Can't Get No) Satisfaction." Not only did the hit forecast Keith's mastery of the art of the riff, but in "I can't get no satisfaction," the band found its central theme.

"Get Off My Cloud" and "As Tears Go By" from *December's Children* showed Jagger-Richards capable of writing equally effective rockers and ballads; and with *High Tide and Green Grass*, the band produced

the best greatest-hits record of the mid '60s. *High Tide*'s 12 cuts remain the triumph of a perfect rhythm section: Charlie Watts's backbeat—casual, unerring and swinging—by then was unrivaled; Bill Wyman's bass lines fused exactly with Watts's drumming; and Richards' guitar was unabashed body music.

With *Aftermath*, Brian Jones and Mick Jagger came into their own. In the early days the band's reigning sex symbol, blues purist and de facto leader, Jones now branched out musically—adding sitar to "Paint It Black," marimba to "Under My Thumb," dulcimer to "Lady Jane." A passionate elegance informed a number of the songs' arrangements; and while the sound remained intense, it wasn't pop but a new way of rocking. On *Aftermath*, too, Jagger revealed his essential gift: assuming a range of personae, he became the rock & roll actor non pareil. The touching, if inexpert mimicry of R&B stars that stamped his early singing gave way to a new, ironic virtuosity. Cockiness, in fact, would come to characterize all his postures, even if the posing hadn't hardened as yet. What the growing expertise of his role playing did confirm, however, was that the rebel authenticity of Keith Richards's character had found a sophisticated, distancing counterpart—and if Keith would soon stand for the Stones' go-for-broke power, Mick's cunning would ensure that they wouldn't burn out like doomed artists, but endure like pros.

Between the Buttons and its near-repeat, *Flowers*, continued the advances begun by *Aftermath*. "Let's Spend the Night Together" was one more bad-boy manifesto, and in "Ruby Tuesday," with its lovely flute passages, Jagger-Richard's melodic flair rivaled McCartney's. The Stones' one "experimental" album, a response to *Sgt. Pepper's*, was predictably shakey: on *Their Satanic Majesties Request*, the best work was done by outsiders—Nicky Hopkins' brilliant piano on "She's a Rainbow," John Paul Jones's orchestration of "2,000 Light Years From Home"—and the neatest thing about the record remains its original campy 3-D cover art.

Returning with a vengeance to roots rocking, the Stones of *Beggars Banquet* had become the Stones of legend. Outlaw anthems ("Street Fighting Man," "Sympathy for the Devil," "Stray Cat Blues") alternated with acoustic numbers of a country or country-blues turn ("Prodigal Son," "Factory Girl" and "Salt of the

Earth"), and the album contained Jagger's best lyrics. Including "Honky Tonk Women," the *Through the Past, Darkly* compilation offered a review of the Stones' obsessions—sex and power, along with the tenderness of the outsider and an impulse toward fervent romanticism. The end of the decade brought *Let It Bleed*, a summing up of the '60s Stones. (Brian Jones had died while the album was being recorded, to be replaced by Mick Taylor.) Keith's guitar work on "Monkey Man" and "Midnight Rambler" flashed exuberant assurance; on "Love in Vain" and "Country Honk," he reasserted the band's blues and country sides; and on "You Got the Silver" he tried out a kind of Dylanesque vocalizing whose stark emotiveness contrasted with Jagger's increasing mannerism. On "Gimme Shelter," "You Can't Always Get What You Want" and "Live With Me," however, Jagger still sounded absolutely compelling.

With their best live set, *Get Yer Ya-Ya's Out!*, the Stones embarked upon an exceptional five-year period of work with Taylor. A graduate of John Mayall's Bluesbreakers, Taylor was an ace technician, his style somewhat recalling Eric Clapton's. Grafted onto the rhythm machine of the Stones, his playing produced iffy results—on *Sticky Fingers*, his work on "Moonlight Mile" helped lift the song into a majesty the group had never before achieved; but on the second half of "Can't You Hear Me Knocking," Taylor's jazzy runs made a great rocker descend into Santana-like lounge rock. The record, however, stands as the classic "decadent" Stones' album—Jagger's singing on "Dead Flowers," "Sister Morphine" and "Wild Horses" finds few equals in its chronicling of exhaustion.

The Stones' final masterpiece, *Exile on Main Street*, remains the best double album in rock & roll history. Astonishing primarily for the guitar interplay—on "Tumbling Dice" Keith elevates riffing into grandeur, and Taylor's blues work was passionate throughout—the record was a triumph less of stellar moments than of relentless intensity. Sprung from a core of hyperdriven Chuck Berry–style rockers ("Rocks Off," "Rip This Joint," "Casino Boogie"), *Exile* plunged into a soulful re-examination of the ethnic music that created the Stones. By now, however, they'd so completely absorbed the essence of the blues, Stax/Volt and country that songs like "Sweet Black Angel" and "Loving Cup" no longer pay tribute to their roots, but extend beyond

them. This music is more knowing, more complex and ambivalent, sometimes more skillful and occasionally even more driven than its primal models. The Stones would never again sound so confident.

Only one year later, *Goats Head Soup* found them drained of energy. Skill replaces fire; this was primarily Jagger's record, and his ballad work ("Angie," "Winter") was excellent, a little theatrical but not the parody singing he'd soon assume. Mick Taylor's swan song, *It's Only Rock 'n' Roll* was dogged by some of his most excessive playing ("Time Waits for No One"); and while its faster numbers offer dependable kicks, the album was the Stones marking time as "the world's greatest rock & roll band." With *Black and Blue*'s "Memory Motel" the band delivered its fondest and most anecdotal road epic; otherwise, the reggae tunes are good and crude, Jagger's singing achieved absolute finesse—and the record debuted new guitarist Ron Wood. Formerly of the Faces (essentially a cheerier Stones soundalike), Woody brought along none of Taylor's skill; but the Keith lookalike turned out to be more of a Stone than Taylor ever was, his devil-may-care rowdiness a cartoon version of their bad-boy pose.

By the time of *Some Girls*, Wood found his role—he'd fuse with Richards, the two guitarists becoming a rhythm juggernaut, their lead work a casual, conversational trade-off. With the album, too, the Stones came to terms with more contemporary black music; "Miss You" was disco, but they played it with more aggression than its "genuine" purveyors did, and the rest of the album's funk was tougher and more fluid than the kind they'd been working ever since *Goats Head Soup*. With few exceptions, however, the late-model R&B they drew from lacked the subtlety of its '60s precursors—and the Stones rarely overcame the weakness of their sources. But "Shattered" rocked mercilessly, "Beast of Burden" swung steadily, and Keith's "Before They Make Me Run" was his last convincing outlaw anthem.

Weakly echoing *Some Girls*, *Emotional Rescue* was the first Stones record that was absolutely bland, not even distinguished by the professionalism that came to stamp their later work. It was exactly that professionalism, however, that provoked the derision of their former fanatics—even though in other genres (blues, country, etc.), such honorable work is considered "carrying on the tradition." In the '80s, the veteran

Stones indeed proved cautious, but their alternate strategies—recycling the raucous sound of their glory days, or guardedly experimenting—sometimes delivered real pleasure. In their rawer style, *Tattoo You* was absolutely accomplished rock & roll; *Dirty Work* faltered under the weight of its self-conscious primitivism. *Undercover*, with its strange, showy guitar work and odd political consciousness, was a misguided attempt to keep current; *Steel Wheels* was all glossiness and craft, but craft of a very high order. Remarkably, *Flashpoint*, from 1991, featured their best live work since *Ya-Ya's*—and if its richest pleasures were also its most predictable ones ("Satisfaction," "Jumpin' Jack Flash"), the ferocity of the playing proved that the Stones—onstage, at least—still sounded nothing like a nostalgia act.

While their classic individual records, of course, are essential to any understanding of rock & roll, the Stones' best-of collections aren't throwaways. The band has always been less album-oriented than its peers—and hearing the hits in different sequences robs them of none of their power. *Hot Rocks, More Hot Rocks* and *Rewind* are the best of the compilations. *The Singles Collection* is magnificent. The weakest live set is *Still Life*; and while the blues numbers on *Love You Live* are good, sloppy fun, the rockers offer few surprises. — P.E.

SONNY ROLLINS

★★★ Sonny Rollins With the Modern Jazz Quartet (1953; Prestige, 1988)
★★★ Movin' Out (1954; Prestige, 1987)
★★★★ Worktime (1955; Prestige, 1982))
★★★★½ Tenor Madness (1956; Prestige, 1987)
★★★★★ Saxophone Colossus (1956; Prestige, 1987)
★★★★ Plus Four (1956; Prestige, 1987)
★★★½ Sonny Boy (1956; Prestige, 1989)
★★★½ Rollins Plays for Bird (1956; Prestige, 1986)
★★★★ Way Out West (1957; Contemporary, 1988)
★★★★ Tour de Force (1957; Prestige, 1984)
★★★★ The Sound of Sonny (1957; Riverside, 1987)
★★★★½ A Night at the Village Vanguard, Vol. 1 (1957; Blue Note, 1987

★★★★★ A Night at the Village Vanguard, Vol. 2 (1957; Blue Note, 1987)
★★★★½ Sonny Rollins and the Contemporary Leaders (1958; Contemporary, 1988)
★★★★★ Newk's Time (1958; Blue Note, 1990)
★★★★★ Freedom Suite (1958; Riverside, 1989)
★★★★ Sonny Rollins on Impulse (1965; MCA/Impulse, 1986)
★★★★ Alfie (1965; MCA/Impulse 1988)
★★★½ The Standard Sonny Rollins (RCA, 1965)
★★★★ Sonny Rollins' Next Album (1972; Milestone, 1987)
★★★ Horn Culture (1973; Milestone, 1987)
★★★★ The Cutting Edge (1974; Milestone, 1990)
★★★ Nucleus (1975; Milestone, 1991)
★★★½ Easy Living (Milestone, 1977)
★★★★ Don't Stop the Carnival (1978; Milestone, 1989)
★★★★½ Sunny Days, Starry Nights (Milestone, 1984)
★★★★½ The Solo Album (Milestone, 1985)
★★★★ Sonny Rollins, Vol. 1 (Blue Note, 1985)
★★★★½ Sonny Rollins, Vol. 2 (Blue Note, 1985)
★★★★ Alternate Takes (Contemporary, 1986)
★★★★½ The Quartets (Bluebird, 1986)
★★★★ G-Man (Milestone, 1987)
★★★ Dancing in the Dark (Milestone, 1988)
★★★★½ The Best of Sonny Rollins (Blue Note, 1989)
★★★★★ The Essential Sonny Rollins on Riverside (Riverside, 1986)
★★★★½ All the Things You Are (1963–1964) (Bluebird, 1990)
★★★★ Falling in Love With Jazz (Milestone, 1990)
★★★★ Here's to the People (Milestone, 1991)

Combining some of the melodic intricacy and flat-out attack of Charlie Parker and the bop pioneers with the assured swing and round, full tone of the tenor sax's original genius, Coleman Hawkins, Sonny Rollins was among that instrument's toughest players when he began recording in the early 1950s. While he achieved his peak during a brief period of dazzling inventiveness (1956–1957), he continued to make exciting jazz into the mid-'60s. His work since then has been uneven, although in the late '80s he showed signs of a renewed vigor.

The staggering *Saxophone Colossus* remains his milestone. Playing with the superb backing of drummer Max Roach, pianist Tommy Flanagan and bassist Doug Watkins, Rollins not only flourishes the tonal power that's apparent also on such standouts as *Worktime* and *Tenor Madness*, but on the minor blues, "Blue Seven," debuts a style of improvisation that, rather than simply taking off from the piece's chord changes, works endlessly cunning variations on its central theme. Confirming Rollins's status as an instrumentalist of indisputable power, the record also suggests his promise as a creative force.

The saxophonist's graceful playing on such albums as *Plus Four* and *Way Out West*, influenced by the elegance of Lester Young, destroyed hasty assessments of his style as exclusively that of the hard bopper who'd smoked through such assaultive music as *Worktime*—he proved himself capable of shimmering melody lines. In 1958, the title track to *Freedom Suite* showed Rollins reaching for a freer, more abstract form of extended improvisation; the demanding set, again with Roach on drums, and with Oscar Pettiford on bass, stands as some of Rollins's most challenging work. Other examples of Rollins's mid-'50s strength can be found on the Blue Note reissue, *Sonny Rollins, Vol. 2*: the colossus is joined by such giants as Thelonious Monk and Horace Silver.

Retiring briefly from the music scene, Rollins holed up from 1959–1961, practicing his horn on the Williamsburg Bridge above New York's East River. Returning in 1961, he came on, in the company of guitarist Jim Hall, with a subtler, more fluid approach (Bluebird's *The Quartets*, which includes his 1962 breakthrough track, "The Bridge," compiles the best of this period). In the early '60s, as well, Rollins seized the chance to play with his early idol, Coleman Hawkins, and with such up-and-comers as pianist Herbie Hancock (hear the results on Bluebird's fine *All the Things You Are*).

After another spell of seclusion came Rollins's lighter work. He asserts himself on the live Montreaux performance of *The Cutting Edge*, with of all things a duet with bagpipe on "Swing Low, Sweet Chariot," but many of his '70s recordings feature fusion fare that's way beneath his talents. By the middle of the next decade, though, he'd reemerged—*Sunny Days, Starry Nights*

marks a return to grace; *The Solo Album* is astonishing in terms of sheer propulsion; *Falling in Love With Jazz* is a lovely set that includes fine accompanying work by Branford Marsalis and Jack DeJohnette.

In sum, Sonny Rollins has proved himself a composer of only occasional brilliance, but a player of the very highest stature.   — P.E.

THE ROMANTICS

★ ★ ★   **The Romantics (Nemperor/Epic, 1980)**
★ ★½   **National Breakout (Nemperor/Epic, 1980)**
★ ★   **Strictly Personal (Nemperor/Epic, 1981)**
★ ★½   **In Heat (Nemperor/CBS, 1983)**
★ ★ ★½   **What I Like About You (and Other Romantic Hits) (Epic, 1990)**

Along with dozens of other new wave bands, the Romantics displayed a winning knack for Beatlesque power pop. What set this Detroit quartet apart from the turn-of-the-decade competition was a strong command of roots. Yes, the Romantics *did* wear skinny ties and shiny suits on their album covers, but they also tipped their caps to the blues and R&B greats behind Merseybeat. Having a stalwart drummer helped that cause mightily; Jimmy Marinos makes that immobile 4/4 really jump, and he sings most of the Romantics' best songs with a raggedy-assed vulnerability that can be quite affecting. Once power pop started to fizzle, the Romantics inched closer and closer to arena rock. (*Strictly Personal* is a botched Loverboy album.) Two years later, the reformed group hit the rebound when "Talking in Your Sleep" became an early MTV staple. The rest of *In Heat* pales in comparison to that love-it-or-loathe-it single, though it's the only original Romantics LP still in print. Collecting half of *In Heat* and a handful of earlier gems like the title track, *What I Like About You* contains a perfect dose of the Romantics: almost 40 minutes worth of rock & roll songs played short, sweet and straight to the point.   — M.C.

LINDA RONSTADT

★ ★½   **Don't Cry Now (Asylum, 1973)**
★ ★½   **Different Drum (Capitol, 1974)**
★ ★ ★ ★ ★   **Heart Like a Wheel (Capitol, 1974)**
★ ★ ★   **Prisoner in Disguise (Asylum, 1975)**
★ ★ ★   **Hasten Down the Wind (Asylum, 1976)**
★ ★ ★ ★   **Greatest Hits (Asylum, 1976)**

★★★½ **A Retrospective (Capitol, 1977)**
★★★★ **Simple Dreams (Asylum, 1977)**
★★★ **Living in the U.S.A. (Asylum, 1978)**
★★★½ **Mad Love (Asylum, 1980)**
★★★ **Greatest Hits, Volume II (Asylum, 1980)**
★★ **Get Closer (Asylum, 1982)**
★★★ **What's New (Asylum, 1983)**
★★★ **Lush Life (Asylum, 1984)**
★★★ **Sentimental Reasons (Asylum, 1986)**
★★★ **'Round Midnight (Asylum, 1986)**
★★★ **Canciones de Mi Padre (Elektra, 1987)**
★★★½ **Cry Like a Rainstorm, Howl Like the Wind (Elektra, 1989)**
★★★ **Mas Canciones (Elektra, 1991)**

The dulcet purity—and sheer power—of her voice stands out right from the start, though it took Linda Ronstadt several years to corral her talents. "Different Drum," her 1967 folk-rock hit with the Stone Poneys, hinges on that sweet lonesome wail. In the '70s, Ronstadt rose to prominence as a keen, often definitive interpreter of young singer-songwriters. Her early, deleted Capitol albums (*Hand Sown . . . Home Grown, Silk Purse* and *Linda Rondstadt*) and *Don't Cry Now* are somewhat tentative, exploratory efforts. On *Heart Like a Wheel*, producer Peter Asher and the cream of L.A.'s session-playing crop provide impeccable backing; more importantly, Ronstadt finds the material her voice had been crying out for. She leaps out of the Southern rock–flavored guitar mesh on "You're No Good" and "When Will I Be Loved"; tackles contemporary material both well-known (James Taylor's "You Can Close Your Eyes") and undiscovered (Anna McGarrigle's title track); asserts a natural command of country roots (with an assist from backup singer Emmylou Harris) on Hank Williams's "I Can't Help It (If I'm Still in Love With You"). Deservedly, *Heart Like a Wheel* made Ronstadt a superstar. Her subsequent pop success with lightweight cover versions of rock & roll classics soon came to overshadow her vital connection to country and folk—too bad. The further Ronstadt ventures from *Heart Like a Wheel*'s comfortable mix, the more inconsistent her albums become. Some of her biggest hits completely miss the mark.

Two Motown nuggets carry *Prisoner in Disguise*: her peppy readings of "Heatwave" and "Tracks of My Tears" neither subtract nor add much to the originals. *Hasten Down the Wind* centers on a trilogy of lovelorn,

somewhat lugubrious songs by Karla Bonoff: "If He's Ever Near," "Lose Again" and "Someone to Lay Down Beside Me." However, *Simple Dreams* pulls off this eclectic old-new-borrowed-blue approach. Ronstadt's strident treatment of Roy Orbison's "Blue Bayou" and the Stones' "Tumbling Dice" will sound like sacrilege to some listeners. But her acoustically spare, heart-piercing takes on "I Never Will Marry" (a Dolly Parton oldie) and the traditional "Old Paint" seem just right. Then-fledgling songwriter Warren Zevon benefits from Ronstadt's patronage here, and vice versa: she concocts a nearly convincing "wild side" for "Carmelita" and "Poor Poor Pitiful Me."

Living in the U.S.A.—a.k.a. "Rollerskates"—is where Ronstadt coasts into neutral. Retooled classics by Chuck Berry and Smokey Robinson fall flat, while more adventurous covers of Zevon ("Mohammed's Radio") and Elvis Costello ("Alison") never quite connect. Her chart momentum unabated, Ronstadt drops her first bomb at the dawn of a new decade. *Mad Love* is her new-wave fashion travesty—every artist of this period should be allowed one, anyway. Amid the herky-jerky tempos and three uncertain Costello covers, Ronstadt sounds downright relieved when she gets to Neil Young's pretty "Look Out for My Love." Penned by future "Like a Virgin" co-writer Billy Steinberg, "How Do I Make You" proves that Ronstadt can still bait a hook quite alluringly. The bulk of *Mad Love*, however, suggests that the foremost female singer of the '70s is rapidly losing touch with the pop marketplace. On *Get Closer* she no longer wields the attention-grabbing power of old; for the first time in ten years, Ronstadt appears totally out of the loop.

Starring in Gilbert & Sullivan's *Pirates of Penzance* on Broadway during the early '80s, Ronstadt apparently got bitten by the prerock pop bug. She released three albums of orchestrated standards with former Frank Sinatra arranger and conductor Nelson Riddle: every perfect note in place, *What's New, Lush Life* and *Sentimental Reasons* (issued together in the set *'Round Midnight*) are tasteful to the point of seeming dispassionate. Those torch songs were meant to smolder, spark and glow. Ronstadt's two albums of Spanish-language traditionals are far warmer—and more involving. Growing up in Arizona, Ronstadt obviously developed an ear for Mexican folk melodies and Spanish phrasing. *Canciones de Mi*

Padre and *Mas Canciones* are enjoyable
side-trips, though hardly transcendent.
Ronstadt returned to the pop field in 1989;
Cry Like a Rainstorm, Howl Like the Wind
hinges on the elegant hit single "Don't
Know Much," a duet with the
shivery-voiced New Orleans giant Aaron
Neville. Believe it or not, the one-time
Queen of Bombast gives her guest room to
soar this time. The rest of *Cry* is pleasant, if
slightly pedestrian adult-contemporary fare.
The first *Greatest Hits* on Asylum combines
Ronstadt's breakthrough singles with some
Stone Poneys and Capitol tracks. Her
individual albums—for all their highs and
lows—offer a more accurate, telling portrait.
— M.C.

TIM ROSE
★ ★ ★ ★ **Morning Dew (1967; Demon/Edsel,
1988)**

Sixties folkie Tim Rose wasn't prolific, and
all but one of his handful of albums are, as
of this writing, out of print. But his debut,
reissued as *Morning Dew* in 1988, features
fine, sturdy, introspective performances.
Excellent playing from session drummer
Bernard Purdie, bassist Felix Pappalardi and
guitarist Hugh McCracken nicely
emphasized Rose's gritty voice, and he
delivered his one classic, the gorgeous
ballad, "Morning Dew" (of its numerous
cover versions, the best remains the Jeff
Beck Group's). Rose also reworked a
traditional folk song, "Hey Joe"—with
which Jimi Hendrix later made history.
— P.E.

DIANA ROSS
★ ★ ★ **Diana Ross (Motown, 1970)**
★ ★ ★ **Everything Is Everything (Motown,
1970)**
★ ★ ★½ **Lady Sings the Blues (Motown,
1972)**
★ ★ ★ **Touch Me in the Morning (Motown,
1973)**
★ ★ ★½ **Diana and Marvin (Motown, 1973)**
★ ★ ★ **Diana Ross Live at Caesar's Palace
(Motown, 1974)**
★ ★½ **Mahogany (Motown, 1975)**
★ ★ ★½ **Diana Ross (Motown, 1976)**
★ ★ ★½ **Diana Ross' Greatest Hits (Motown,
1976)**
★ ★ ★½ **An Evening With Diana Ross
(Motown, 1977)**
★ ★ ★ **Baby It's Me (Motown, 1977)**
★ ★ ★ **Ross (Motown, 1978)**
★ ★ ★ **The Boss (Motown, 1979)**
★ ★ ★½ **Diana (Motown, 1980)**
★ ★ ★ **To Love Again (Motown, 1981)**

★ ★ ★½ **All the Greatest Hits (Motown,
1981)**
★ ★ ★ **Why Do Fools Fall in Love? (RCA,
1981)**
★ ★½ **Silk Electric (RCA, 1982)**
★ ★ ★ **Diana Ross Anthology (Motown,
1983)**
★ ★½ **Swept Away (RCA, 1984)**
★ ★½ **Eaten Alive (RCA, 1985)**
★ ★ ★ **Red Hot Rhythm and Blues (RCA,
1987)**
★ ★½ **Workin' Overtime (Motown, 1989)**
★ ★½ **The Force Behind the Power
(Motown, 1991)**

Leaving the Supremes in 1970—three years
after the departure of Motown's songwriting
team, Holland-Dozier-Holland—Diana Ross
embarked on a pellmell pursuit of
superstardom. With Motown investing
$100,000 in her stage act, and with her own
show-biz instincts honed to a razor's edge
during her years as the Supremes' only
high-profile singer, she soon achieved that
goal. But at considerable aesthetic cost.
Holding on only fitfully to her R&B
credibility, she came across alternately as an
ingratiating Vegas showstopper and an
ebony Streisand; sheer professionalism
remains her signal "virtue"—by the end of
the '80s, she had become an out-of-touch
diva, her success gained only by her dogged
following of obvious trends.

With the exception of her movie
soundtracks—*Lady Sings the Blues*, and its
flashy renditions of Billie Holiday standards,
and the much less interesting
Mahogany—Ross's early-'70s albums mixed
predictably strong hits and an
overabundance of filler. Ashford-Simpson's
"Reach Out and Touch (Somebody's
Hand)" and "Ain't No Mountain High
Enough" made *Diana Ross* a credible
glossy-soul debut; soon, however, she began
working with weaker writers, and such slick
pablum as "Touch Me in the Morning" and
"Last Time I Saw Him" was the sad result.
Her duets with Marvin Gaye, *Diana and
Marvin*, displayed her comfortable expertise,
but by mid-decade Ross was lost in
disco-land; her endless dance epic, "Love
Hangover," was a smash, but the fact that it
sounded like Donna Summer suggested that
Diana was in need of new direction.

She chose, however, to coast. The inflated
double album *An Evening With Diana Ross*
epitomized her Vegas period. Chic's Nile
Rodgers and Bernard Edwards came to the
rescue with *Diana*, the ace producers
providing streamlined designer-funk. *Why
Do Fools Fall in Love?* was a diluted version

of the same sort of dance-pop, with "Work That Body" generating a frenzy in aerobics classes. Capitalizing on that single's success, Ross then released Michael Jackson's shameless "Muscles," off *Silk Electric. Silk*'s Warhol cover art summed up Ross's fully realized upward mobility—she'd reached a safe pinnacle from which she'd rarely descend. Even Jeff Beck couldn't enliven *Swept Away* and its AOR "rock"; *Eaten Alive* found Ross, fairly late in the game, aping Barbra Streisand's *Guilty*—the record was a typical Barry Gibb affair: smooth, competent and cautious. *Red Hot Rhythm and Blues* didn't live up to its title, but it at least showed the singer moving onto the right track. — P.E.

DAVID LEE ROTH

★ ★ ★½ Crazy From the Heat (EP) (Warner Bros., 1985)
★ ★   Eat 'Em and Smile (Warner Bros., 1986)
★ ★   Skyscraper (Warner Bros., 1987)
★ ★½ A Little Ain't Enough (Warner Bros., 1991)

When David Lee Roth was Van Halen's vocalist, his ribald wit and unabashed showmanship were the perfect counterpoints to the inventive anarchy of Edward and Alex Van Halen. On his own, though, Roth more often than not comes across as a self-impressed boor, the kind of not-funny clown most of us try to avoid at parties. *Crazy From the Heat*, recorded before Roth's split with Van Halen, is the best of his solo efforts; he may not have the voice for "California Girls," and "Just a Gigolo" may go a little heavy on the borscht-belt shtick, but overall the EP is entertaining and energetic. With *Eat 'Em and Smile* and *Skyscraper*, though, Roth forgoes such indulgences, relying instead on an ersatz Van Halen built around Steve Vai, a guitarist whose earliest claim to fame was a transcription of Edward Van Halen's "Eruption" solo, and Billy Sheehan, who had previously been known as the "Eddie Van Halen of bass." Instrumental firepower is no substitute for songs, though, and apart from "Just Like Paradise" (from *Skyscraper*), Roth had little in the way of memorable melodies. *A Little Ain't Enough*, recorded after Vai and Sheehan had departed, recaptured a little of Roth's early vitality, but not enough to make the album matter. — J.D.C.

ROXETTE

★ ★   Pearls of Passion (EMI Sweden, 1986)
★ ★ ★   Look Sharp! (EMI, 1988)
★ ★ ★½ Joyride (EMI, 1991)

Tempting as it might be to lump this Swedish pop phenomenon in with Abba, such a comparison overlooks one important difference between the two: namely, that Abba was purely pop, whereas Roxette's sound derives entirely from rock & roll. Granted, that distinction doesn't exactly help *Pearls of Passion* much, since its best moments are spirited but derivative genre exercises like "Soul Deep" (later remixed and re-released on *Joyride*). With *Look Sharp!*, though, Roxette really came into its own, churning out classic Beatlesque rockers ("The Look"), stirring power-ballads ("Listen to Your Heart") and snappy dance pop ("Dressed for Success"). *Joyride* merely refined the formula, expanding the group's dynamic range from the quiet balladry of "Watercolours in the Rain" to the full-throttle rock of "Hotblooded." — J.D.C.

ROXY MUSIC

★ ★ ★ ★   Roxy Music (1972; Reprise, 1989)
★ ★ ★½ For Your Pleasure (1973; Reprise, 1989)
★ ★ ★ ★   Stranded (1974; Reprise, 1989)
★ ★ ★½ Country Life (1974; Reprise, 1989)
★ ★ ★ ★ ★ Siren (1975; Reprise, 1989)
★ ★ ★½ Viva! Roxy Music (1976; Reprise, 1989)
★ ★ ★ ★   Manifesto (1979; Reprise, 1989)
★ ★ ★   Flesh + Blood (1980; Reprise, 1989)
★ ★ ★ ★½ Avalon (Warner Bros., 1982)
★ ★ ★½ The High Road (EP) (Warner Bros., 1983)
★ ★ ★ ★   The Atlantic Years (Atco, 1983)
★ ★ ★ ★   Street Life—20 Greatest Hits (Reprise, 1989)
★ ★ ★½ Heart Still Beating (Warner Bros., 1990)

"Looking for love in a looking-glass world is pretty hard to do." So concludes Roxy Music's lead singer, Bryan Ferry, on "Mother of Pearl," the immaculately jaded centerpiece of the group's third album. Ferry went right ahead with his search anyway. Often lumped together, Ferry and David Bowie do share certain arty fascinations and vocal inflections—but only on the surface. Because Roxy Music really was a working band, Ferry's quest is more firmly grounded—both in music and emotion—than Bowie's multimedia sensation-seeking. Roxy Music's albums don't combust with the visually enhanced bang of *Ziggy Stardust* or *Station to Station*. Instead, this group's patented web of intricate riffs, unexpected influences and obsessive lyrics unfolds at its own pace, either pulling listeners in or putting them off totally. If you enjoy the first taste of Roxy Music, well, dig in: these albums comprise a remarkably consistent body of work.

The debut album signals a radical shift in rock's overall perspective; from the opening track ("Remake/Remodel") onward, *Roxy Music* manages to look forward and backward at the same time. Juggling a fondness for historical kitsch with a bold sense of experimentation, Roxy keeps its pretensions aloft with a strong rhythmic pulse. Rather than attempt the usual botched classical surgery, Roxy keyboardist Brian Eno pioneered a nonmusicianly approach to electronics: he took delight in the rude "natural" sounds of synthesizers, the bleeps and crackles and screams and random giggles that all erupt from a button. Eno constructs lush, repetitious backgrounds behind Bryan Ferry's crooning fits, lays barrages of taped noise on top of guitarist Phil Manzanera's compact solos, and redirects Andy Mackay's honking sax lines. His sensibility pervades the first two Roxy Music albums, though Ferry provides the group's focus and introspective direction.

Eno's "treatments" and Ferry's bleak tone slow the second half of *For Your Pleasure* down to a crawl. But the album's first half still can leave you breathless. Between its breakneck pace and ironic spin, "Do the Strand" helped introduce the punk sound and stance: "A danceable solution to teenage revolution." And "In Every Dream Home a Heartache" vividly conveys Roxy's double-edged decadance: this deadpan tale of a proto-yuppie bungalow owner and his pneumatic companion is funny, of course, but it's also affecting in some unsettling way.

Stranded replaces Eno with Eddie Jobson, a more traditional keyboardsman and violinist. The overall sound is less experimental and abrupt, but it's still challenging. Roxy's newly expanded musical range is matched by more assured songwriting—and singing—from Ferry. "Mother of Pearl" measures the group's development; it begins with towering waves of hard-rock guitar, and then boom! The fury crests around Ferry's heartbroken soliloquy. The effect is like slowly opening your eyes after a doomed-from-the-start affair finally dies. *Country Life* continues in this mode, mixing riff-driven uptempo rockers with moody, complex set pieces in a carefully wrapped package. On *Siren* Roxy perfects its suave attack. "Love Is the Drug" captures the funky allure of the singles scene, while "Just Another High" pinpoints the regrets of one ex-swinger. And in "Sentimental Fool," a breathtaking arrangement sets off the emotional resolve behind Ferry's weary façade: "I've seen what love can do/And I don't regret it."

Roxy Music drifted apart for a while in the late '70s, while Ferry pursued his solo career. On *Manifesto*, the regrouped Roxy seems better for the rest: deftly blending fresh rhythms into its signature sound, shortening the instrumental passages and concentrating more on songcraft. But the follow-up, *Flesh + Blood*, is the group's thinnest effort; the line between Roxy and Ferry's solo work blurs at this point. However, *Viva!*, *The High Road* and *Heart Still Beating* aptly document Roxy's considerable live chops.

Roxy Music resurfaced after another break with *Avalon*; this austere, beautiful set of songs represents a mature peak. The controlled chaotic edge of the early albums is completely gone, and cofounders Manzanera and Mackay provide only skeletal guitar and sax lines. Ferry fills in the details, creating layered synth landscapes around his tragic scenarios and melodic ruminations. *Avalon*'s pervasive influence on the British pop scene of the '80s can't be overstated. Roxy Music's stature is even further enhanced by the absence of a latter-day comeback album. So far, anyway.
— M.C.

BILLY JOE ROYAL

  ★★   **Looking Ahead (Atlantic, 1986)**
★★★   **The Royal Treatment (Atlantic, 1987)**
★★★½ **Greatest Hits (Columbia, 1989)**
★★★   **Tell It Like It Is (Atlantic, 1989)**
★★★   **Out of the Shadows (Atlantic, 1990)**
★★★½ **The Best of Billy Joe Royal (Atlantic, 1991)**

A protégé of Bill Lowery, the Atlanta promoter whose haphazard tastes led to the discovery of the commendable Joe South, but also such schlocksters as Ray Stevens, Dennis Yost and Tommy Roe, Royal hit it big in 1965 with "Down in the Boondocks."

A punchy, poor-boy lament written by South, the song was pretty groovy, and it introduced a singer whose trebly warble placed him in the stylistic company of such vocal eccentrics as Robin Gibb and Johnny Ray. Gaining minor smashes with the poppy funk of "Hush," the Buckinghams-like "Cherry Hill Park" and standard tearjerkers like "Tell It Like It Is" and "Save the Last Dance for Me," Royal's AM hour was a tasty one and it's captured well on *Greatest Hits*.

In the '80s, Royal came back countrified. He's no George Jones, but his Atlantic country-hits collection has its snappy moments, particularly in the vibrato fest of "Till I Can't Take It Anymore." — P.E.

ROYAL CRESCENT MOB

★★½ **Land of Sugar (EP) (No Other, 1986)**
★★ **Omerta (Moving Target, 1987)**
★★★ **Something New, Old and Borrowed (Moving Target, 1988)**
★★★½ **Spin the World (Sire, 1989)**
★★½ **Midnight Rose's (Sire, 1991)**

Specializing in heartfelt if uneven white funk, the Royal Crescent Mob almost single-handedly raised the Ohio Players to new wave hipdom with *Land of Sugar*, an engagingly ragged funk-rock effort that, in keeping with the title's tribute to Players' guitarist Leroy "Sugar" Bonner, includes a snappy cover of "Love Rollercoaster." They continue in a similar vein with *Omerta* (this time covering "Fire"), but the Mob's limits as groove merchants are more pronounced; things tighten up on *Something New, Old and Borrowed*, however, which augments two solid studio numbers with a smattering of live tracks and all of *Land of Sugar*.

Spin the World, the Mob's major-label debut, finds the band in its glory. Not only is the playing more polished and assured, but the writing—particularly tuneful efforts like "Big Show" and "Nanana"—shows strong pop instincts. Unfortunately, *Midnight Rose's* is unable to capitalize on that advance, as the material degenerates into wry, gimmicky vignettes that stress clever lyrics over appealing melodies. — J.D.C.

THE ROYAL TEENS

★ **Short Shorts (Collectables, NA)**

One big hit, the insipid "Short Shorts" from 1958, and two notations in rock history: the New Jersey group's original piano player and one of its writers was Bob Gaudio, who later joined the Four Seasons and wrote some of the truly great teen rock epics of

the '60s; its bass player was Al Kooper, who went on to become Al Kooper in many guises. Otherwise, not much to hang your hat on here. — D.M.

DAVID RUFFIN

★★★★ **My Whole World Ended (1969; Motown, 1981)**
★★½ **Feelin' Good (Motown, 1969)**
★★½ **David Ruffin (Motown, 1973)**
★★ **Me 'n' Rock 'n' Roll Are Here to Stay (Motown, 1974)**
★★ **Who Am I? (Motown, 1975)**
★★ **Everything's Coming Up Love (Motown, 1976)**
★★ **In My Stride (Motown, 1977)**
★★★½ **David Ruffin at His Best (Motown, 1978)**
★ **So Soon We Change (Warner Bros., 1979)**
★★ **Gentleman Ruffin (Warner Bros., 1980)**
★★★ **David Ruffin and Eddie Kendricks (RCA, 1987)**

One of Motown's finest singers, David Ruffin sang lead for the Temptations during their early glory years, 1964 to 1968, his distinctively gruff tone buffered by his elegant phrasing and a capacity for easy swing. Departing in 1969, he continued with Motown on his own—and didn't fare well. "My Whole World Ended (the Moment You Left Me)," his first single (and biggest solo hit), suggested that he'd follow squarely in the style of the Temps' graceful pathos, but Ruffin's uncertain choice of material and his long bouts with drug abuse meant that his records were only periodically inspired. Switching labels at the end of the '70s didn't help. His voice continued to offer delight (rejoining the Temptations for their 1982 *Reunion* album, he sounded as strong as ever), but too often it was a brilliant gem in a shoddy setting. *David Ruffin at His Best* is a serviceable compilation, containing both his Temps highlights and the better work of his early solo career. — P.E.

RUFUS

★★★★ **Rags to Rufus (1974; MCA, 1990)**
★★★½ **Rufusized (1974; MCA, 1990)**
★★★½ **Rufus Featuring Chaka Khan (1975; MCA, 1990)**
★★½ **Ask Rufus (ABC, 1977)**
★★½ **Streetplayer (ABC, 1978)**
★★½ **Masterjam (MCA, 1979)**

Rufus was a racially integrated unit hailing from Chicago, and its debut, *Rags to Rufus*, blends a touch of jazz-rock fusion jamming into an otherwise danceable sound. Apart from a few dated keyboard squiggles, it's an enjoyable, varied album, from "Smoking Room" to "Swing Down, Chariot." On "Tell Me Something Good," Chaka Khan proves women can be bad, too. Written by Stevie Wonder, the tune is almost unbearably sexy. "You Got the Love," the group's follow-up, burns with an equal glow.

Truth be told, that remains Chaka Khan's crowning album achievement. She wields a sure hand with singles, both with Rufus and later on her solo recordings, but the subsequent albums are all plagued by inconsistency. Rufus landed in a muddle, caught between fusion and disco. *Rufusized* continues the hot *Rags to Rufus* groove; "Once You Get Started" reveals Kahn's voluptuously smooth romantic mode. *Rufus Featuring Chaka Khan* is the point at which Khan's interest in jazz interpretation and pre-rock tradition begins to predominate, though Rufus revs its funky motor on "Sweet Thing." The group seemed to lose its knack right after that; only a single or two—"Do You Love What you Feel" from *Masterjam*—is worth retrieving from the bland later albums. Chaka Khan left the band in the late '70s; Rufus's post-Chaka efforts are all out of print. — M.C.

THE RUNAWAYS
★★   The Runaways (Mercury, 1976)
★★   Queens of Noise (Mercury, 1977)
★★   Waitin' for the Night (Mercury, 1977)
★★   Little Lost Girls (Rhino, 1981)
★★½ Best of the Runaways (1982; Mercury, 1987)

Hype dies hard. The Runaways helped pave the way for female punkers, perhaps, but that sure doesn't render this shrieky L.A. fivesome's inept metal albums any more listenable. "Cherry Bomb," from the debut, detonates its trashy hook with youthful glee—and that's it. Shclockmeister-producer Kim Fowley wields a tuneless, overweening hand at the controls, so guitarist Joan Jett gets lost in the bright plastic din; no wonder she titled her first solo album *Bad Reputation*. (Lead guitarist Lita Ford's subsequent career as a metal vixen is a different story altogether.) You'd never figure the Runaways for a launching pad on the basis of these records; even *Best of the Runaways* fails to deliver the expected quota of escapist fun. — M.C.

TODD RUNDGREN
★★★½ Runt (1970; Bearsville/Rhino, 1987)
★★★★ The Ballad of Todd Rundgren (1971; Bearsville/Rhino, 1987)
★★★★★ Something/Anything? (1972; Bearsville/Rhino, 1987)
★★★½ A Wizard/A True Star (1973; Bearsville/Rhino, 1987)
★★½ Todd (1974; Bearsville/Rhino, 1987)
★★   Initiation (1975; Bearsville/Rhino, 1987)
★★★½ Faithful (1976; Bearsville/Rhino, 1987)
★★★½ Hermit of Mink Hollow (1978; Bearsville/Rhino, 1987)
★★★ Back to the Bars (1978; Bearsville/Rhino, 1987)
★★   Healing (1981; Bearsville/Rhino, 1987)
★★   Todd Rundgren Presents the Ever Popular Tortured Artist Effect (1983; Bearsville/Rhino, 1987)
★★   A Cappella (Rhino, 1988)
★★★★ Anthology (Rhino, 1989)
★★★½ Nearly Human (Warner Bros., 1989)
★★   2nd Wind (Warner Bros., 1991)
★★★½ An Elpee's Worth of Productions (Rhino, 1992)

TODD RUNDGREN'S UTOPIA
★★   Todd Rundgren's Utopia (1974; Bearsville/Rhino, 1987)
★★½ Another Live (1975; Bearsville/Rhino, 1987)
★★½ RA (1977; Bearsville/Rhino, 1987)
★★★ Oops! Wrong Planet (1978; Bearsville/Rhino, 1987)
★★★ Adventures in Utopia (1980; Bearsville/Rhino, 1987)
★★½ Deface the Music (1980; Bearsville/Rhino, 1987)
★★   Swing to the Right (1982; Bearsville/Rhino, 1987)
★★½ Utopia (1983; Bearsville/Rhino, 1987)
★★★ Anthology (Rhino, 1989)

Bouyed by an uncanny skill in the studio and a well-developed ego, Todd Rundgren floated between two extremes during the '70s: sainted pure-pop balladeer (his solo albums) and bedeviled hippie technocrat (Utopia). Of course, there's plenty of spillover, too. Despite the public indifference to some of his more ambitious projects, this self-confessed "tortured artist" is still pitching curve balls after 20 years. Suffer along with him, and you'll discover some lasting treasures amid the cosmic debris and failed experiments. Patience and a sense of humor are definitely required.

Rundgren learned his way around a recording studio while leading Nazz in the late '60s. That Philadelphia quartet's debt to the Beatles is obvious from the first three notes of "Open My Eyes" (1968), but Rundgren also had an ear cocked toward his hometown R&B scene. And his taste for scorchingly ironic hard rock rises to the top of *Runt*, though the vulnerable hook of "We Gotta Get You a Woman"—poor "Leroy boy"—is what attracted mainstream interest. Except for one crazed raveup ("Parole"), *The Ballad of Todd Rundgren* is exclusively devoted to melodic heartbreak scenarios: beautiful three-minute songs that hark back to various '60s styles without directly quoting or mimicking. Rundgren truly "does it all" on the one-man-opus *Something/Anything?*, and damn near everything works: the irresistibly sweet hit singles ("I Saw the Light" and "Hello It's Me"), the ominous metal hunk ("Black Mariah"), the taut psychedelically enhanced rocker ("Couldn't I Just Tell You"). Even the jokey nostalgia ("Wolfman Jack") holds up, and the tracks on which Todd and pals run amok in the studio have their unforgettable moments, too.

His songwriting is a big part of what makes *Something/Anything?* so appealing, but Rundgren grew bored with the pop format almost as soon as he seemed to master it. *A Wizard/A True Star* tries to cram too much stylistic diversity into its grooves: three fully realized songs ("Sometimes I Don't Know What to Feel," "International Feel," "Just One Victory") get swamped by all the half-baked sonic decoration. Too loose and largely tuneless, the rambling double-album *Todd* finds Rundgren playing the self-indulgent cult hero role to the hilt. It's the polar opposite of *Something/Anything?*

You want unpredictable? How about a celestial multikeyboard art-rock band playing long, trippy instrumentals? In 1974! *Todd Rundgren's Utopia* and *Another Live* are rather hellish, actually—jazz-rock fusion minus the funky rhythms (save for a ringing cover of the Move's "Do Ya" on *Live*). *Initiation* sneaks in a gratifyingly organic chorus ("Real Man") amid depressing fare like "The Death of Rock and Roll" and "A Treatise on Cosmic Fire." *Faithful* matches a side of letter-perfect late-'60s covers with like-minded Rundgren originals—the first "classic rock" block! After visiting the pyramids on *RA*, Utopia abruptly transforms into a straightahead (for Rundrgren) rock & roll band on *Oops! Wrong Planet*. Add "Love in Action" to Todd's pop canon; the rest is a definite,

unexpected improvement over the previous space twaddle. Similarly, *Hermit of Mink Hollow* returns to earth, reassuring Todd's melodic knack and stylistic command, though the advent of punk and new wave does make his '60s fixations seem terribly hidebound all of a sudden. The live *Back to the Bars* offers a decent—not definitive—retrospective.

Adventures in Utopia supplies a pair of middling AOR hits ("Set Me Free" and "The Very Last Time"), and then Rundgren begins to listlessly repeat himself: flat Beatles tribute-parody (*Deface the Music*), fussbudget virtuoso showcase (*Healing*), failed synth-pop move (*Swing to the Right*), failed returns-to-previous-form (*The Ever Popular Tortured Artist Effect*). The alien *A Cappella* shrieks for itself. After a quiet spell, Todd rebounded on a new label with *Nearly Human*—his tightest and most tuneful outing in years, from the subtly haunting "Parallel Lines" to several synthed-up Philly Soul salutes. *2nd Wind* is a melodramatic, overreaching attempt at fusing elements of Broadway theater and rock. Geniuses never learn. *An Elpee's Worth of Productions* showcases Rundgren's career as a producer from 1973–1990: highlights include cuts by Fanny and the New York Dolls. — M.C.

RUN-D.M.C.

★★★★ **Run-D.M.C. (Profile, 1984)**
★★★★ **King of Rock (Profile, 1985)**
★★★★★ **Raising Hell (Profile, 1986)**
★★★★ **Tougher Than Leather (Profile, 1988)**
★★★ **Back From Hell (Profile, 1990)**
★★★★★ **Together Forever: Greatest Hits 1983–1991 (Profile, 1991)**

Even if it had never cut another record after "It's Like That" b/w "Sucker M.C.'s," this trio would still deserve its place in pop history, for with that single Run-D.M.C. invented rap as we know it. This was the first taste of rap's hard-core to make it to vinyl, and from the bruising insistence of their rhymes to the brutal simplicity of the backing tracks (no band, just drum machine and turntable scratch), Run-D.M.C. had the B-Boy aesthetic in full effect. To its credit, *Run-D.M.C.* doesn't opt for the easy out of single-plus-filler; although neither "Hollis Crew" nor "Wake Up" are classics, "Rock Box" actually ups the ante, using a grinding, heavy-metal guitar hook for extra punch. *King of Rock* pushes that idea to its logical conclusion with "King of Rock" itself, although "Can You Rock It Like This," with its intricate layers of synth, guitar and drum machine actually hits harder.

But it's with *Raising Hell* that Run-D.M.C. truly realizes its potential. Sure, bringing in Aerosmith's Steve Tyler and Joe Perry for "Walk This Way" was a brilliant move, since it furthered the guitar-rap trend while scoring a massive crossover hit. But even without the tune, *Raising Hell* would be a killer, for this is where Run-D.M.C. brings its vision into focus. It isn't just a matter of sneakers and slang, although both "My Adidas" and "You Be Illin' " tapped into a deep vein of street culture; what *Raising Hell* really captures is the depth and immediacy of hip-hop, from the simple assertion of "Proud to Be Black" to the classic scratches in "Peter Piper." *Tougher Than Leather* tried the same moves, but suffered commercially from a contractual dispute that held up the album's release for more than a year. Too bad; although the pop moves of "Mary, Mary" (based on the Monkees hit) may seem obvious, "Run's House" and "Beats to the Rhyme" hit as hard as anything in the group's catalog.

Run-D.M.C. had lost the moment, though, and *Back From Hell* finds the group in the unfortunate position of playing catch-up. Forget the braggadocio of "Sucker D.J.'s"—when this crew locks into the pumping beat of "Pause" or "The Ave.," currency is beside the point. Still, those unwilling to sift through the individual albums ought to enjoy *Together Forever*, a greatest-hits package including all the expected tracks from the first five albums, as well as live versions of "Here We Go" and "Together Forever" and the charming, non-LP "Christmas In Hollis." — J.D.C.

RUSH
★ ★   **Rush (Mercury, 1974)**
★ ★   **Fly by Night (Mercury, 1975)**
★ ★   **Caress of Steel (Mercury, 1975)**
★ ★½ **2112 (Mercury, 1976)**
★ ★½ **All the World's a Stage (Mercury, 1976)**
★ ★½ **A Farewell to Kings (Mercury, 1977)**
★ ★½ **Hemispheres (Mercury, 1978)**
★ ★ ★½ **Permanent Waves (Mercury, 1980)**
★ ★ ★½ **Moving Pictures (Mercury, 1981)**
★ ★ ★ **Exit . . . Stage Left (Mercury, 1981)**
★ ★ ★ **Signals (Mercury, 1982)**
★ ★½ **Grace Under Pressure (Mercury, 1984)**
★ ★½ **Power Windows (Mercury, 1985)**
★ ★   **Hold Your Fire (Mercury, 1987)**
★ ★   **A Show of Hands (Mercury, 1989)**
★ ★   **Presto (Atlantic, 1989)**
★ ★ ★½ **Chronicles (Mercury, 1990)**
★ ★½ **Roll the Bones (Atlantic, 1991)**

At least Rush pumps out a more approachable and human brand of sci-fi fusionoid pomposity than, say, lofty elitists like Pink Floyd or King Crimson. That vague populist bent suits this musicianly Canadian power trio, and hints at its preconceptual roots as dull, perennially second-billed metal plotzers. Drummer Neil Peart, guitarist Alex Lifeson and bassist Geddy Lee have all developed some fearsome chops on their instruments over the years; their love of tricky time signatures and busy solos is what hypnotizes fans and bores everybody else. Lyricist Peart's mystifying cosmic bent and lead singer Lee's clawing banshee howl inspire similiar love-it-or-loathe it debates. *2112* and *All the World's a Stage* mark the end of Rush's muddy space-plowboy phase; with *Permanent Waves* ("Spirit of the Radio," "Jacob's Ladder") and *Moving Pictures* ("Limelight," "Tom Sawyer") the group sculpts a more tuneful, AOR-friendly approach without forsaking its trademarks—middlebrow philosophizing and flashy instrumental trappings. After *Signals* and "New World Man," popular tastes took a shift away from the '70s-identified progressive-rock sound—of course, Rush has continued to follow its quest, regardless of trends. *Chronicles* gives a definitive overview of Rush's first 15 years, graphically charting the band's gradual development over two hour-long discs—the impeccable sense of chronological detail will either be informative or excruciating, depending on your taste. After that, you're on your own. Rush is in it for the long haul. — M.C.

OTIS RUSH
★ ★ ★ ★½ **Tops (Blind Pig, 1988)**
★ ★ ★ ★½ **Lost in the Blues (Alligator, 1991)**

A classic Chicago bluesman, Otis Rush remains largely unknown—except to musicians. Players as diverse as Jeff Beck, Carlos Santana and Eric Clapton have gushed over his stinging guitar style and impassioned vocals, and both are impressively in evidence on Blind Pig's live *Tops*. The master tears through "Right Place, Wrong Time" the title cut of his 1976 masterpiece (on the Bulldog label, it's currently out of print), and proves himself equally the master of fast shuffles and slower blues. *Lost in the Blues* is just as strong; a version of Willie Dixon's "Little Red Rooster" may be the standout, but every performance is clean, sharp and trenchant. — P.E.

TOM RUSH

★ ★ ★   **Blues, Songs, and Ballads (1963; Fantasy 1989)**
★ ★ ★   **Tom Rush (Elektra, 1965)**
★ ★ ★   **Take a Little Walk with Me (Elektra, 1966)**
★ ★ ★ ★   **The Circle Game (Elektra, 1968)**
★ ★ ★   **Tom Rush (1970; Columbia, 1990)**
★ ★ ★ ½   **Classic Rush (Elektra, 1971)**
★ ★   **Tom Rush (Fantasy, 1972)**
★ ★ ★   **The Best of Tom Rush (Columbia, 1976)**

A Harvard B.A., Rush began as a folkie of the Library of Congress archival school, gigging around Cambridge and releasing forthright, strong-voiced versions of such traditional fare as "Joe Turner," "Cocaine" and "Drop Down Mama." Fantasy's *Blues, Songs, and Ballads* compiles two of his 1963 albums of likeable, earnest material. By mid-decade, Rush began rocking (mildly): *Take a Little Walk With Me* (now out of print) finds him handling Buddy Holly competently, although Bo Diddley is beyond his grasp ("Who Do You Love" is a minstrel-show embarrassment). Hip to Joni Mitchell, James Taylor and Jackson Browne well before most of the folk-pop pack were, he peaked with *The Circle Game* a songwriters' showcase with arrangements boosted by artful strings.

Classic Rush is a nice greatest-hits collection, containing some gems off *The Circle Game*, and avoiding the mellow insignificance of his later work. Sort of a Jim Croce without the vocal mannerisms, or a Jimmy Buffet without the Floridian mythology, Rush works the high end of an undemanding genre, MOR folk. — P.E.

JIMMY RUSHING

★ ★ ★ ★   **The Essential Jimmy Rushing (Vanguard, 1978)**
★ ★ ★ ★   **Mister Five by Five (Columbia, 1980)**
★ ★ ★   **The Classic Count (Intermedia, 1982)**
★ ★ ★ ★   **The You and Me That Used to Be (RCA, 1988)**

Born in Oklahoma City and raised in his home town's melting pot of Texas blues, Western swing and traditional jazz, Jimmy Rushing honed his unique style during the late '20s, when he spent hard, physically demanding years playing Southwestern theaters, dance halls and roadhouses with a traveling band called the Blue Devils, who included such extraordinary players as Count Basie, Lester Young, Hot Lips Page, Buster Smith and Eddie Durham, among others. By the time Rushing settled in with Bennie Moten's band in Kansas City in the early '30s, he had fashioned a distinctive disposition as a vocalist: forever ebullient, perennially optimistic, the brightest shade of blue this side of the sky. A big man nicknamed "Mister Five by Five" (a reference to his height and width), Rushing could deliver the saddest blues with a warm, soothing tone that implied better days ahead; he was ennobled, rather than diminished, by misfortune.

When Moten died in 1935, Basie formed his own group, with Rushing as its lead singer; the association, productive and prolific, lasted until 1950, when Basie broke up the band. Rushing made an effort to assemble his own band, couldn't deal with the scope of the administrative duties, and ended that experiment in 1952. Producer John Hammond, a longtime fan of Rushing's, produced for the Vanguard label in the mid-'50s a series of albums that teamed the singer with some of his mates from the Basie days. The late '50s and early '60s found Rushing in a variety of interesting settings while signed to Columbia and being produced by Irving Townsend and Teo Macero. In 1971, working with producer Don Schlitten and a small band that included Zoot Sims and Al Cohn on tenor saxophones, Budd Johnson on soprano saxophone, David Frishberg on piano, Milt Hinton on bass, Ray Nance on cornet and violin and Mel Lewis on drums, Rushing cut ten sides for RCA that turned out to be his last recordings before his death in 1972. Through the decades, at every label stop, Rushing produced exemplary performances: what he has left behind is entertaining, exhilarating, instructive.

With Basie, Rushing established a style of singing that epitomized swing: he created a wonderful tension between band and vocalist by singing ahead of or behind the beat and generally toyed with the rhythm, stretching songs in new directions. He was at once a blues singer and a jazz singer, and his ability to work within both frameworks had an incalculable influence on succeeding generations of jazz and popular music vocalists.

Classic Count collects ten recordings from the vintage Basie band of the 1940s, including some live performances; four tracks feature the young Rushing in readings of "Blue Skies," "I Never Knew," "Please Don't Talk About Me" and "Tain't Me." Unfortunately there are no specific dates or personnel listings, and the brief liner notes are uninformative. *The Essential Jimmy Rushing* is a 14-track compilation of Vanguard highlights, and there isn't a bad cut among them. While his legend rests on his ability as a singer, Rushing developed into quite a good songwriter. Some of his better efforts are included, including several collaborations with Basie; a smoky, after-hours blues co-written with boogie-woogie catalyst Sam Price (and featuring Price on piano); and that buoyant model of prevarication, "Sometimes I Do," penned by Rushing alone. The deleted *Mister Five by Five* is, like the Vanguard album, selected highlights, these being from Columbia's Rushing vaults; and like all of Rushing's remaining in-print albums save the RCA release, it's devoid of or at least annoyingly vague about dates. The music is another matter entirely. Here Rushing is heard fronting big bands, quartets, and, in one of the most remarkable moments of a remarkable career, a trio that includes Rushing on piano with support from bassist Walter Page and drummer Jo Jones. Three must-hear selections date from a 1960 reunion with Helen Humes, Rushing's female counterpart in the Basie band. Fronting a quartet of instrumentalists, these two extraordinary singers complement each other in grand style, Hume's sensuality being a soothing match for Rushing's earthy exuberance.

Finally, there is Rushing's last testament, *The You and Me That Used to Be*. The title song and several others—"My Last Affair," "When I Grow Too Old to Dream," "Fine and Mellow," "Linger Awhile"—have an endgame theme, but Rushing delivers them brightly. The last song sums up Rushing's point of view: "Thanks a Million" is sung with the gripping sincerity of a man taking stock. It's Rushing's most introspective moment on record, and a touching coda to a monumental career. — D.M.

LEON RUSSELL
★★★ Leon Russell (1970; DCC, 1989)
★★★½ Leon Russell and the Shelter People (1971; DCC, 1989)
★★½ Carney (1972; DCC, 1989)
★★★ Leon Live! (1973; DCC, 1990)
★★★ Hank Wilson's Back (1973; DCC, 1990)
★★ Stop All That Jazz (1974; DCC, 1990)
★★ Will O' the Wisp (1975; DCC, 1990)
★★★½ Best of Leon (1976; DCC, 1990)
★★½ Anything Can Happen (Virgin, 1992)

A veteran of some epochal Phil Spector sessions in the '60s, this Oklahoma-born pianist piloted Joe Cocker's Mad Dogs & Englishmen carnival during its successful early-'70s run. On his own, Leon Russell concocts an agreeably rough-hewn brand of mock-apocalyptic swamp-rock: qauvering, drawled vocals, pounding gospel piano chords, Southern-fried boogie beat. *Leon Russell and the Shelter People* contains his best work; originals like the backwoods sci-fi prediction "Stranger in a Strange Land" and some rollicking Dylan covers—redolent of the times, to say the least. *Carney* takes on a disturbingly mawkish—and regrettably catchy—tack with the likes of "Tightrope" ("one side's hate and one is hope") and the faux Tin Pan Alley ballad "This Masquerade." *Best of Leon* accentuates this turn, contrasting his questionable sentimental streak ("Hummingbird") with his solid-as-a-rock instincts ("Roll Away the Stone"). Russell veers all over the stylistic map on his 1992 comeback album, produced by Bruce Hornsby. Unfortunately the various world-music motifs and exotic keyboards on *Anything Can Happen* never take off. Maybe Russell should try New Orleans music next time. — M.C.

MITCH RYDER
★★★★ Detroit (1971; Paramount, 1988)
★★★ How I Spent My Vacation (Seeds & Stems, 1978)
★★★ Naked But Not Dead (Seeds & Stems, 1979)
★★★ Never Kick a Sleeping Dog (Riva, 1983)
★★★★★ Rev Up: The Best of Mitch Ryder and the Detroit Wheels (Rhino, 1989)

The rubber-scorching Motor City quintet Mitch Ryder and the Detroit Wheels laid down a definitive patch of white soul in 1966 and '67. Mitch Ryder (formerly Billy Levise) led the Wheels (formerly the Rivieras) with his frayed, feverish wail. Guitarist Jim McCarty supplies clenched solo snippets, while drummer John Badanjek anchors the groove with a piston-pumping backbeat and teeth-rattling rapid-fire outbreaks. "Jenny Take a Ride," "Sock It to Me, Baby" and "Devil With a Blue Dress On/Good Golly Miss Molly" all reached the pop Top Ten, leaving a trail of sweat and exhaust fumes behind. These tightly wound hits not only put Ryder on the map, they also eastablished the rhythmic groundwork for the then-emergent "high energy" sound of Detroit rock & rollers like Bob Seger, Ted Nugent, the MC5 and the Stooges. However, producer Bob Crewe did his best to undermine the Detroit Wheels R&B intensity; with the release of Ryder's infamous strings 'n' things solo album (*What Now My Love*) in late '67, he succeeded. Barely out of the starting gate, the Wheels broke up not long after that debacle.

Rev Up: The Best of Mitch Ryder and the Detroit Wheels is a high-octane summary of the group's brief heyday, including some dynamite B-side rarities and vintage cover versions. *Rev Up* also touches on some of Ryder's subsequent, unjustly ignored solo work: "Joy" gives a tasty sample of the long-lost *Detroit-Memphis Experiment* (1969), along with two tracks from the better-known *Detroit* session ("Rock and Roll," "Long Neck Goose"). With Badanjek and guitar discovery Steve Hunter in tow,

Ryder updates the Wheels' sound with an expertly deployed hard-rock wallop. He blows a gusty blast of boogie fever into Lou Reed's "Rock and Roll," while "Long Neck Goose" grafts a loping slide riff onto a supercharged rhythm track. Unfortunately, this unflashy-but-talented aggregation never recorded another album after its classic debut. Ryder retired after that, returning in the late '70s with two albums released on his own label. *How I Spent My Vacation* and *Naked But Not Dead* resemble psychotherapy sessions set to somewhat generic rock arrangements: these dark, tortured, muddy-sounding ruminations on failed rock-stardom hold some interest, though Ryder's voice is obviously worse for the wear. His John Mellencamp–produced major-label shot from 1983, *Never Kick a Sleeping Dog*, is considerably better, especially when Ryder attacks Prince's "When You Were Mine" with head-on assurance. The album failed to attract a new audience, and it soon disappeared. Ryder has recorded a half-dozen albums for the German Line label since then, none of which comes close to matching the manic spark of *Rev Up* and *Detroit*. — M.C.

S

SADE

★★★½ Diamond Life (Portrait, 1985)
★★★ Promise (Portrait, 1986)
★★★ Stronger Than Pride (Portrait, 1988)

Born Helen Folasade Adu in Lagos, Nigeria, Sade turned a fascination for Nina Simone and Billie Holiday into mid-'80s success with "Smooth Operator" and "Sweetest Taboo," both from *Diamond Life*. These smoky faux-jazz hits were rendered with bright sophistication by her excellent sax-spicy British band. Limited both in range and tone, Sade as a vocalist may be more interesting in concept than execution—but *Diamond Life* and *Promise* are victories of attitude; she projects a wised-up sensuality, and the records neither creak with the revivalism of Harry Connick nor the sterility of Simply Red, to name but two of Sade's neo-cocktail rivals. While more fascinating when working her ice-queen persona, Sade also musters vulnerability and compassion: "Maureen," off *Promise*, is a graceful valentine to a female friend. *Stronger Than Pride* is the same record as Sade's other two, but milder. — P.E.

DOUG SAHM (THE SIR DOUGLAS QUINTET)

★★ The Best of the Sir Douglas Quintet (Tribe, 1965)
★★★ Honkey Blues (Smash, 1968)
★★★½ Mendocino (Smash, 1969)
★★★½ Together After Five (Smash, 1970)
★★★½ 1+1+1 = 4 (Philips, 1970)
★★ The Return of Doug Saldana (Philips, 1971)
★ Doug Sahm and Band (Atlantic, 1973)
★★ Rough Edges (Mercury, 1973)
★★★ Texas Tornado (Atlantic, 1973)
★★★ Groovers Paradise (Warner Bros., 1976)
★★★ Texas Rock for Country Rollers (ABC/Dot, 1976)
★★★ Hell of a Spell (Takoma, 1979)
★★★★ Border Wave (Takoma, 1981)
★★★★ Juke Box Music (Antone's, 1988)
★★★★ Best of the Sir Douglas Quintet (Mercury, 1990)
★★★ Texas Tornado: The Best of Doug Sahm's Atlantic Sessions (Rhino. 1992)

With a jukebox mind under his ten-gallon hat, Doug Sahm has ranged from psychedelia to country to horn-heavy blues, and, even, at the start of his career, to a unique mix of garage funkiness and Merseybeat. The Sir Douglas Quintet's "She's About a Mover" started the trip. The 1965 hit laid a mop-top catchiness atop Augie Meyer's Farfisa organ syncopations and revealed a gift for eccentric fusions that would stamp the band's subsequent efforts. *Honkey Blues* was James Brown-ish horns overlaid with San Francisco guitar noodling; *Together* was Latino swagger meeting the blues meeting C&W. *Mendocino* produced another hit in the flower-power title track; "At the Crossroads" was Doug doing Dylan.

Through the years, Sahm has faltered (*Doug Sahm and Band*, *Hell of a Spell*); his guitar sounds better when he reins it in; and earnestness remains his singing's greatest virtue—but his musical imagination has paid off consistently in happy, novel ways. *Groovers Paradise* united him with Creedence Clearwater's rhythm section for a satisfying, casual set; *Texas Rock for Country Rollers* was country enough for pedal steel; *Border Wave* saw him back with the Quintet and tending more toward rootsy good timing than the experimentalism of his earlier work. The 1992 Rhino anthology collects the best of Sahm's two Atlantic albums, including his brilliant version of Dylan's "Wallflower." — P.E.

BUFFY SAINTE-MARIE

★ ★ ★   It's My Way (Vanguard, 1964)
★ ★½   Many a Mile (Vanguard, 1965)
★ ★½   Little Wheel Spin and Spin
         (Vanguard, 1966)
★ ★½   Fire and Fleet and Candlelight
         (Vanguard, 1967)
★ ★½   I'm Gonna Be a Country Girl Again
         (Vanguard, 1968)
★ ★   Illuminations (Vanguard, 1969)
★ ★ ★½   The Best of Buffy Sainte-Marie
         (1970; Vanguard, 1987)
★ ★ ★   The Best of Buffy Sainte-Marie,
         Vol. 2 (Vanguard, 1971)
★ ★ ★   She Used to Wanna Be a Ballerina
         (Vanguard, 1971)
★   Moonshot (Vanguard, 1972)
★ ★½   Quiet Places (Vanguard, 1973)
★ ★½   Native North American Child (An
         Odyssey) (Vanguard, 1974)
★ ★½   Sweet America (ABC, 1976)

Her most distinctive feature, Buffy Sainte-Marie's voice is an odd wonder—compelling, if wholly uncommercial, it ranges with gruff sweetness in and out of key, and Buffy wails and keens as often as she sings. Starting off as an early-'60s folkie, she wrote the protest classic "Universal Soldier" for her debut album, but moved on to embrace a wide range of influences—notably, orchestral styles, as well as song patterns based on the Native American music that formed part of her own Cree heritage. A haphazard performer, she was better at conceiving songs than albums. A bid for radio success, *Moonshot* was her slightest record; her most consistent was *Ballerina*, with its backup by Ry Cooder and Crazy Horse. Her first greatest-hits package captures her variety—"Summer Boy," with its orchestration by Peter Schickele (P.D.Q. Bach) is lovely and intense; her versions of songs by Leonard Cohen and Patrick Sky are very original treatments; and her own material holds up well. — P.E.

THE SAINTS

★ ★ ★½   (I'm) Stranded (Sire, 1977)
★ ★ ★½   Eternally Yours (Sire, 1978)
★ ★ ★½   All Fools Day (TVT, 1987)
★ ★ ★   Prodigal Son (TVT, 1988)

Records like this Australian punk quartet's breathless debut (*[I'm] Stranded*) are what made 1977 such a miraculous year in rock. Misfit groups from all over the world seemed to have arrived at the same point simultaneously; the Saints' tunefully aggressive three-chord raveups ("[I'm] Stranded," "Wild About You," even Elvis's

"Kissin' Cousins"!) could've just as easily come barking out of the London or Lower Manhattan scenes. Saints guitarist Ed Kuepper lets his ambition show on "Story of Love," however, when he drops a loping guitar solo and some crude Dylan-esque musing into the bash-ahead mix. Both he and lead singer Chris Bailey were interested in developing as musicians, it turns out. *Eternally Yours* (1978) is marked by sophisticated songwriting leaps—and the intrusion of pseudo-soul horn lines that will quickly separate true believers from casual observers. Still, "Know Your Product" stands as the sharpest—and catchiest—punk denouncement of the established music biz. The original band split up after this album; Kuepper formed a band called Laughing Clowns while Chris Bailey kept the Saints extant in various guises. The Bailey-dominated Saints reappeared on the American scene with *All Fools Day* in 1988. Hard to believe it's the same singer who barked out "[I'm] Stranded." However mellowed-out, Bailey's grainy roughshod vocals fit the dreamy, offhand feel of the lyrics and the lush acoustic-electric folk-rock groove. *All Fools Day* is sure to please fans of '80s alternative janglers like the mid-period R.E.M. *Prodigal Son* is an obvious and altogether less striking followup. — M.C.

STEVIE SALAS

★ ★ ★   Stevie Salas Colorcode (Island, 1990)

Salas's guitar playing is Hendrixian in the best sense of the term, moving beyond the usual funk-and-metal clichés to a similar degree of inventiveness. Like Hendrix, Salas is also pretty good at transfiguring the blues, as "Two Bullets and a Gun" and "Indian Chief" make plain. Well worth hearing. — J.D.C.

WALTER SALAS-HUMARA

★ ★ ★½   Lagartija (Record Collect, 1988)

Featuring a style not dissimilar from that of the Silos, his New York–based neo-country-rock band, guitarist Walter Salas-Humara's *Lagartija* is subtle, smart mood music. A clear-voiced singer and assertive instrumentalist, he forgoes any gimmickry and concentrates on his songs, of which "Cuba" and "About Her Steps" are the most assured. — P.E.

SALT-N-PEPA

★ ★ ★ ★   Hot, Cool & Vicious (Next Plateau,
         1986)

★★★½ A Salt With a Deadly Pepa (Next
      Plateau, 1988)
★★★ Blacks' Magic (Next Plateau, 1990)
Like many early female rappers, Salt-n-Pepa
(Cheryl "Salt" James, Sandy "Pepa"
Denton and DJ Dee Dee "Spinderella"
Roper) began their career with a back-at-ya
answer record to a macho rapper's hit. "The
Showstopper," the group's first record, was
a response to "The Show" by Slick Rick
and Doug E. Fresh. Changing their name
from Supernature to Salt-n-Pepa when they
hooked up with producer Hurby "Luv Bug"
Azor, the group forges its own sassy,
distinct musical identity on Hot, Cool &
Vicious. "Tramp" skillfully plays off the
Otis Redding-Carla Thomas duet, arriving
at the (half-serious) conclusion that all men
are bums. The irresistibly sexy jams "Push
It" and "My Mike Sounds Nice" suggest
that these independent women—while no
pushovers—are willing to make the best of
that situation. Salt-n-Pepa continue to rap
rings around each other on A Salt With a
Deadly Pepa, alternating and then
combining their rich, throaty voices. They
try to sing a bit this time as well; if the
cover of the Isley Brothers' "Twist and
Shout" doesn't get over, the sputtering
chorus of "I Gotcha" by Joe Tex perfectly
lends itself to hip-hopping interpretation.
Backed by the powerhouse go-go band EU
(of "Da Butt" fame) as well as Spinderella,
Salt-n-Pepa put a feminist spin on another
Isleys stomper ("It's Your Thing"). While
the rappers turn the tables ("It's my
thing!"), Spinderella splices the male voices
from the original version in between
Salt-n-Pepa's declaration of sexual
independence. "Do what you wanna do,"
the Isleys seem to tell them, and they do it
till you're satisfied. The samples and verbal
sallies on Blacks' Magic aren't quite as
inspired, though "Let's Talk About Sex"
provided an articulate and funny dose of
frankness on the pop charts in 1991.
— M.C.

SAM AND DAVE
★★★ Sam and Dave (Roulette, 1966)
★★★★ Hold On, I'm Comin' (1966;
       Atlantic, 1991)
★★★ Double Dynamite (1966; Atlantic,
       1991)
★★★½ Soul Men (1967; Atlantic, 1992)
★★★ I Thank You (1968;
       Rhino/Atlantic, 1992)
★★★★ Best of Sam and Dave (1969;
       Atlantic, 1985)
★★ Back Atcha (United Artists, 1975)

In terms either of emotional depth or
stylistic innovation, Sam and Dave fall far
short of Otis Redding, the giant with whom
they helped create '60s Southern soul. But
the propulsiveness of their hits makes them
irresistible. Precision of attack was this
duo's trademark: Very few bands kick into
their material with the immediacy and
confidence Sam and Dave managed, and the
pair also never let the energy flag. Between
1966 and 1968 they released a catalog of
bass- and horn-driven soul smashes—"You
Don't Know Like I Know," "Hold On, I'm
Comin'," "Soul Man" and "I Thank You,"
among others—that have lost none of their
immediacy over the years. As craftsmen,
then, if not visionaries, they remain
significant—their sound informing virtually
every R&B bar band that followed in their
wake. — P.E.

SAM THE SHAM AND THE
PHAROAHS
★★★ Pharaohization: The Best of Sam the
      Sham and the Pharoahs (Rhino, 1985)
As immortal trash rock goes, Sam the
Sham's "Wooly Bully" beats hell out of
"Louie, Louie" because the Pharoahs could
play and the Kingsmen couldn't. It also
beats the Surfaris' "Wipeout" because there
are words. Borrowing—at least
indirectly—from Screamin' Jay Hawkins a
flair for costumery and the yen for thrills
and chills that enlivened his first single,
"Haunted House," as well as such later fare
as "Ju Ju Hand" and "Medicine Man,"
Sam fashioned mid-'60s Tex-Mex rock that
was fun and funky. Oddly echoing drums
and Farfisa syncopations kept the beat
infectious—and Sam's nonsense lyrics, sung
tauntingly or yelped, made the mix
distinctive. The band's nutsy nursery
rhymes, "Lil' Red Riding Hood" and
"Black Sheep," weren't quite so catchy as
the "Wooly Bully" soundalikes, and the
entire Pharoahs shtick lasted only two years.
Solo, Sam wasn't quite so gassy a trip.
— P.E.

DAVID SANBORN
★★★ Taking Off (Warner Bros., 1975)
★★★ David Sanborn (Warner Bros.,
      1976)
★★★½ Heart to Heart (Warner Bros.,
      1978)
★★★ Hideaway (Warner Bros., 1980)
★★★ Voyeur (Warner Bros., 1981)
★★★½ As We Speak (Warner Bros.,
      1982)
★★★ Backstreet (Warner Bros., 1983)

★ ★ ★ ★   Straight to the Heart (Warner Bros., 1984)

★ ★ ★   A Change of Heart (Warner Bros., 1987)

★ ★ ★   Close-Up (Reprise/Warner Bros., 1988)

★ ★ ★ ★   Another Hand (Elektra, 1991)

★ ★ ★½   Upfront (Elektra, 1992)

David Sanborn possesses one of the most distinctive saxophone sounds in popular music, and he uses it to make records that are almost indistinguishable from one another. It isn't that he has nothing to say, for given the proper setting he shines as a soloist; nor is it that he lacks leadership ability, for his albums are packed with top sidemen and first-rate arrangements. It isn't even a question of quality, for Sanborn's jazz fusion avoids most of the usual clichés, never plays down to the listener, and is enjoyable despite its maddening consistency.

So why the rut? Because Sanborn is essentially a groove player, and tends to settle in the same groove from album to album, year to year. It rarely wears thin, in part because Sanborn has impeccable taste in rhythm sections, but mostly because he's one of the few saxophonists around who understands how to translate a soul singer's sense of time and line to jazz. As such, it hardly matters whether he's working a wah-wah pedal in "Butterfat" from *Taking Off*, squawking through the funk of "I Told U So" from *Backstreet* or soaring against the refrain of "You Are Everything" from *Close-Up*; his playing is equally solid, every time.

Granted, things to tend to improve when he makes changes or takes chances. *Heart to Heart*, for instance, augments the usual pop-fusion rhythm section with horns, at one point including the Gil Evans Orchestra (Sanborn is an Evans alumnus); *As We Speak* doesn't alter the backing tracks but switches Sanborn from alto to soprano for several tunes; and *Straight to the Heart* uses a live-in-the-studio strategy to add extra fire to the instrumental interplay.

Overall, only *Another Hand* stands out as a complete departure—and for good reason. Instead of his usual fusion sidemen, this album matches Sanborn with an odd mix of new music types like guitarists Bill Frisell and Marc Ribot as well as mainstream jazz heavyweights like bassist Charlie Haden and drummer Jack DeJohnette. The result is some of the most inspired playing Sanborn has offered in fifteen years, and a much-needed break in his musical routine. Unsurprisingly, he returns to form with the funk-laced *Upfront*. — J.D.C.

PHAROAH SANDERS

★ ★ ★½   Karma (Impulse, 1969)

★ ★ ★½   Thembi (1971; MCA/Impulse,1987)

★ ★ ★   Love Will Find a Way (Arista, 1978)

★ ★ ★   The Heart Is a Melody (Theresa, 1982)

★ ★ ★   Shukuru (Theresa, 1987)

★ ★ ★½   Oh Lord, Let Me Do No Wrong (Dr. Jazz, 1987)

★ ★ ★   Africa (Timeless, 1988)

★ ★ ★   Moon Child (Timeless, 1990)

★ ★ ★   Welcome to Love (Timeless, 1991)

WITH NORMAN CONNORS

★ ★ ★½   Beyond a Dream (Arista, 1981)

While primarily a tenor saxophonist, Pharoah Sanders blows alto and soprano with equal power—his tone rich and sometimes raw, his blues-based delivery sometimes almost assaultively dynamic. In the mid-'60s he played on John Coltrane's landmark, *Ascension*, and also worked with others among the cream of the avant-garde jazz crop—including Don Cherry and Alice Coltrane. His own aggregations of the late '60s and early '70s reflected his interest in non-Western idioms, free-form soloing and highly charged atmospheres; like Coltrane, Sanders embraced music as a vehicle for a highly personal mystic communication, even while the physicality of his style was abundantly apparent. Unfortunately, such examples of Sanders at his toughest as *Summun Bukmun Umyun* (Impulse, 1972), a bold outing with Lonnie Liston Smith, and *Love in Us All* (Impulse, 1974), with its 20-minute powerhouse title cut, are out of print. *Karma*, *Thembi* and *Love Will Find a Way* all found surprising commercial success; *Love* is interesting primarily for its scope—24 players are featured. In the late '70s and early '80s, however, many critics attacked Sanders for going soft; the live set with drummer Norman Connors, *Beyond a Dream*, counters that charge with muscular performances. More recently, he's moved closer to traditional jazz, as evidenced by his ballad work on *Welcome to Love*. — P.E.

MONGO SANTAMARIA

★ ★ ★ ★   Afro Roots (Prestige, 1972)

★ ★ ★ ★   Skins (Milestone, 1976)

★ ★ ★ ★   Summertime (Pablo, 1981)

★ ★ ★ ★   Mongo's Greatest Hits (Fantasy, 1987)

★ ★ ★   Mongo Y Su Charanga (Fantasy, 1987)

★ ★ ★ ★   Soca Me Nice (Concord Picante, 1988)

★ ★ ★   Olé Ola (Concord Picante, 1989)

If anyone's music is ripe for a revival it is that of conga drummer Ramon "Mongo" Santamaria. His lone Top Ten hit, "Watermelon Man," from 1963, was an irresistible fusion of blues, jazz and Santamaria's Afro-Latin rhythms. It suggested new directions for popular music.

Born in Cuba, Santamaria worked with bands in Mexico City before venturing to America in 1949. His first jobs were with the Perez Prado and Tito Puente orchestras. In 1958 he joined a group led by vibraphonist Cal Tjader that featured Al McKibbon on bass and Vince Guaraldi on piano, and he followed that stint by forming his own group, a traditional Latin *charanga* band. This evolved into the Mongo Santamaria Afro-Latin Group, which numbered among its members saxophonist and Sun Ra alum Pat Patrick and an up-and-coming keyboard player named Armando Corea, nicknamed "Chick." The group's first album, *Go, Mongo!* (now packaged with the band's final Riverside album as *Skins*), featured some profound ethnic material (Santamaria's own composition "Carmela" being a standout) that would have been suitable on any of the specialty labels serving Latin communities in the States, but was practically revolutionary released on a nationally distributed jazz label like Riverside.

This small but significant event was followed by an even larger moment of consequence. In 1963 Santamaria recorded "Watermelon Man." The song had been written by a then-unknown piano player named Herbie Hancock, and to its blues structure Santamaria added his own Afro-Latin rhythmic flourishes. Well ahead of its time, "Watermelon Man" today can be seen as one of the signposts pointing toward soul and funk, in addition to being many Americans' first exposure to a world beat sensibility.

Pop success has since eluded Santamaria, but his ensuing albums—many have gone out of print, unfortunately—find him always supported by standout musicians and exploring an interesting range of material. As mentioned, *Skins* is a packaging of Santamaria's first and final albums for the Riverside label, and defines the astonishing growth in Santamaria's music between 1962 and 1964. One of Santamaria's most ruthlessly rhythmic outings can be heard on *Summertime*, on which his band is joined by Dizzy Gillespie and Toots Thielemans. Of the four extended jams here, the group's reinterpretation of the title track is notably ingratiating. *Soca Me Nice* is an interesting

primer, circa 1988, in soca, or soul calypso, a West Indian music gaining increasing popularity in the States. Santamaria also uses this album to jazz up Lennon-McCartney's "Day Tripper" with some Afro-Cuban rhythms. The least interesting of the albums is Columbia's *Greatest Hits*, a selection of would-be "Watermelon Man" clones; on the other hand, Fantasy's *Mongo's Greatest Hits* is a must-have featuring the original "Watermelon Man" as well as other influential recordings. One of Santamaria's best small-label recordings, now technically out of print, is *Afro-Indio* (1975) on the Vaya label, which teamed him with the extraordinary Colombian saxophonist and flautist Justo Almario. *Afro Roots* is essential for anyone desiring a greater understanding of Santamaria's history and the introduction of Afro-Cuban music in the American marketplace. This two-record set contains 22 sides recorded in 1958–59, Santamaria's first sessions as a band leader. Always a magnet for top-flight musicians, Santamaria is joined on these tracks by the likes of Willie Bobo, Armando Peraza, Paul Horn, Pablo Mozo, Cal Tjader, Al McKibbon, Carlos Vidal, Vince Guaraldi, and others. — D.M.

SANTANA
★★★★ Santana (Columbia, 1969)
★★★★ Santana: Abraxas (Columbia, 1970)
★★★★ Santana 3 (Columbia, 1971)
★★★★ Caravanserai (Columbia, 1972)
★★★½ Welcome (Columbia, 1973)
★★★★★ Santana's Greatest Hits (Columbia, 1974)
★★★½ Borboletta (Columbia, 1974)
★★★★★ Lotus (1974; Columbia, 1991)
★★★★ Amigos (Columbia, 1976)
★★★ Festival (Columbia, 1977)
★★★ Moonflower (Columbia, 1977)
★★ Inner Secrets (Columbia, 1979)
★★ Marathon (Columbia, 1979)
★★ Zebop! (Columbia, 1981)
★★ Shangó (Columbia, 1983)
★★ Beyond Appearances (Columbia, 1985)
★★½ Freedom (Columbia, 1987)
★★★★ Viva Santana! (Columbia, 1988)
★★★ Spirits Dancing in the Flesh (Columbia, 1990)
CARLOS SANTANA SOLO
★½ Carlos Santana and Buddy Miles Live (Columbia, 1972)
★★★ Love, Devotion, Surrender (Columbia, 1973)
★★½ Illuminations (Columbia, 1974)
★★½ Oneness (Columbia, 1979)

★ ★ ★   **Silver Dreams—Golden Reality** (Columbia, 1979)
★ ★ ½   **The Swing of Delight** (Columbia, 1980)
★ ★ ★   **Havana Moon** (Columbia, 1988)
★ ★ ★ ★   **Blues for Salvador** (Columbia, 1988)
★ ★ ★ ½   **Milagro** (Polydor, 1992)

A compelling 22-song live set, *Lotus* best captures Santana's considerable appeal. Formed in San Francisco in 1967, the band fed that scene's appetite for long open-air jams with an athletic mixture of blazing guitar and frenetic percussion. Santana's novelty lay in employing the jam format for Latin music—leader-guitarist Carlos Santana, drummer Michael Shrieve and percussionist Jose "Chepito" Areas were the band's anchors; fusing Hispanic dance-forms and bluesy rock, they achieved a synthesis that combined the familiar and the exotic. *Lotus* finds Santana at its peak; throughout its history, the band was marked by frequent personnel changes, and this lineup is its strongest—with Leon Patillo, they'd enlisted a singer markedly more soulful than either original vocalist Greg Rolie or later mainstay Alex Ligertwood, and the entire eight-member unit achieves a remarkable, instinctive symbiosis. Charging through early hits (Fleetwood Mac's "Black Magic Woman," Tito Puente's "Oye Como Va"), this outfit is both fiery and fluid, and with Airto Moreira's "Xibaba (She-Ba-Ba)" and Richard Kermode's "Yours Is the Light" the group suggests its coming direction— jazz-rock fusion and flights into the mystic.

Because its rhythmic basis was so strong and the music itself a solid mix of genres, Santana's jazz-fusion was of a less irritating variety than most (the band drew heavily on Miles Davis' *Bitches Brew* period aggressiveness and rarely stooped to jazz-lite). But at the late-'70s height of its experimenting with complex chord structures and aimless "atmosphere" (*Moonflower*, *Inner Secrets*) Santana had become something unimaginable for so passionate an ensemble: boring. After the jazz foray, then, came the pop one, starting with *Zebop!* and continuing ever since—and Santana began bordering on trite.

Santana's first albums remain the strongest, and they hold up very well. World-beat ahead of the time, Santana riveted Woodstock audiences with one of the most exciting stage acts of the festival—and Carlos's playing continued, throughout the band's career, to offer delight, even when squandered on inferior material.

On his own, Santana flexed his guitar in a number of settings. An instantly recognizable musician—with an intense B.B. King-style clarity of tone, he achieves long, fluid lead lines that resemble a violinist's—Carlos sounds best when he's juxtaposed against heavy percussion. Becoming a devotee of Indian guru Sri Chinmoy in the early '70s (and in the process, taking the name Devadip: "light of the lamp of the Supreme"), he recorded the drifty *Love, Devotion, Surrender* with fellow disciple and guitar wizard John McLaughlin in 1974, and the driftier *Illuminations* a year later with another Chinmoy adherent, jazz composer Alice Coltrane. *Havana Moon*, despite the presence of such big-name (if unlikely) collaborators as Willie Nelson, the Fabulous Thunderbirds and Booker T. Jones, is fairly bland; *Blues for Salvador* remains his strongest solo effort. — P.E.

JOE SATRIANI

★ ★ ★   **Not of This Earth** (1986; Relativity, 1988)
★ ★ ★ ★   **Surfing With the Alien** (Relativity, 1987)
★ ★ ★   **Dreaming #11** (EP) (Relativity, 1988)
★ ★ ★ ½   **Flying In a Blue Dream** (Relativity, 1989)

What sets Satriani above almost every other post–Van Halen guitar virtuoso isn't that he has cleaner chops (which he does) or better tricks (ditto); it's that he's more interested in making music than in strutting his stuff. Unlike the work of other axe heroes, Satriani's compositions aren't just riff-a-rama launching pads for fleet-fingered solos; they're actual songs, with a strong sense of structure and a gift for melody. In that sense, Satriani is a throwback to the days of Duane Eddy and Lonnie Mack, guitar instrumentalists who understood that you didn't need words to make an interesting album. *Not of This Earth* establishes his sound early, offering a surprisingly mature and inventive set of compositions that only rarely degenerate into fretboard pyrotechnics. It's *Surfing with the Alien*, though, that really put Satriani on the map. Beautifully played and well-paced, it manages to capture all the icy fire of fusion jazz without losing any of the visceral power of rock & roll, whether he's playing a full-tilt rocker like "Satch Boogie" or sketching the softer lines of a ballad like "Always with Me, Always with You." Though the three live tracks on *Dreaming #11* show how well Satriani works with a

live rhythm section (featuring bassist Stu Hamm), the EP adds little to the sound of *Surfing*. But *Flying in a Blue Dream* adds an unexpected wrinkle: vocals. Predictably, Satriani's guitar is far more eloquent than his voice, but the overall sound of the album suggests that Satriani's interest in songcraft is continuing to develop.
— J.D.C.

BOZ SCAGGS

★ ★ ★ ½ **Boz Scaggs (Atlantic, 1971)**
★ ★ ★ **Moments (Columbia, 1971)**
★ ★ ★ ½ **Boz Scaggs and Band (Columbia, 1971)**
★ ★ ★ **My Time (Columbia, 1972)**
★ ★ ½ **Slow Dancer (Columbia, 1974)**
★ ★ ★ ★ **Silk Degrees (Columbia, 1976)**
★ ★ ½ **Down Two Then Left (Columbia, 1977)**
★ ★ ★ **Middle Man (Columbia, 1980)**
★ ★ ★ ½ **Hits (Columbia, 1980)**
★ ★ ½ **Other Roads (Columbia, 1988)**

Boz Scaggs first gained notice as a rhythm guitarist and occasional singer in the Steve Miller Band; Scaggs and Miller had been playing together since their college days in Wisconsin. You can hear his soul and R&B vent start to emerge on a sizzling track called "Overdrive," from the Miller Band's 1968 *Sailor* album. But Scaggs's solo debut marks a bold, confident departure from the psychedelic sound of San Francisco (his adopted home). Recorded at the legendary Muscle Shoals studio (and produced by ROLLING STONE editor Jann S. Wenner), *Boz Scaggs* centers on a searing slow blues called "Loan Me a Dime." Scaggs and guitarist Duane Allman engage in a deliciously down-and-out voice-and-guitar duet; it's a · highlight of both of their careers.

Though it was unfashionable in the early '70s, Scaggs set out to fuse sleek romantic soul and mellow rock. The process wasn't realized until 1976 with *Silk Degrees*, but there are some interesting stops along the way. *Boz Scaggs and Band* cooks up a consistently spicey, yet thoroughly digestible, horn-encrusted ensemble sound. The inconsistent *My Time* sports two sharp-hooked FM rockers ("Dinah Flo," "Full-Lock Power Slide"), while bland loveman ballads dominate *Slow Dancer*. On *Silk Degrees*, Scaggs pulls all these strands together in a comfortably taut groove: the Top Five hit "Lowdown," especially, mixes bluesy grit and string-section elegance with an unaffected grace. That offhand feel and an absence of catchy tunes makes the followup albums sound a bit distanced,

however. When he doesn't have compelling material to work with, Scaggs comes off as several degrees too smooth for his own good. *Hits* tips the balance toward his disappointing later work; *Silk Degrees* and one of the earlier albums—try the debut or *Boz Scaggs and Band*—represent a safer, sounder investment for most pop-soul fans. *Other Roads*, a surprisingly directionless comeback attempt, just isn't worth the bother. — M.C.

SCANDAL

★ ★ ½ **Scandal (EP)(Columbia, 1982)**
★ ★ **The Warrior (Columbia, 1984)**

Scandal's sound, a perky blend of guitar-based melodies and post-punk attitude, is so typical of new-wave pop as to verge on the generic. Two things prevent that: Patty Smyth, whose voice boasts all the power of Pat Benatar's but none of the mannerisms; and "Goodbye to You," a sassy kiss-off song that immediately lifts the *Scandal* EP out of anonymity. Unfortunately, one song does not a career make, and the colorless writing on *The Warrior* squanders both Smyth's voice and the band's momentum. Smyth, unsurprisingly, went solo soon after that album's failure. — J.D.C.

SCHOOLLY D

★ ★ ★ **Saturday Night—The Album (Jive, 1987)**
★ ★ ★ **The Adventures of Schoolly D (Rykodisc, 1987)**
★ ★ **Smoke Some Kill (Jive, 1988)**
★ ★ **Am I Black Enough for You? (Jive, 1989)**
★ ★ **How a Black Man Feels (Capitol, 1991)**

This Philadelphia rapper paved the way for gangsta-rap with a shockingly matter-of-fact depiction of street warfare, "PSK—What Does It Mean?" (It stands for Park Side Killers, a real-life gang in Philly). While that cut and the rest of his deleted independent 1986 debut (*Schoolly D*) gain a certain veracity from the bone-chilling delivery and DJ Code Money's forcefully simple scratches, Schoolly D has been stuck in the same crude confrontational rut ever since. While Ice-T steps back from even his most hopeless scenarios to make some sort of larger point, Schoolly D plays his interchangeable street-crime tales for cheap melodrama and intimidation value. He wields his dick like an Uzi, and vice versa, so pity the sucker or bitch who gets in the way. "I Don't Like Rock 'n' Roll," also from the debut, offers a clue about the audience he presumably scares (and attracts); Schoolly D also happens to be one of the few hip-hop acts to have actually played at "alternative" rock clubs. *The Adventures of Schoolly D* combines the debut and its photocopy sequel (*Saturday Night!—The Album*). The addition of Black Nationalist rhetoric and more creative sampling on *Am I Black Enough for You?* can't disguise Schoolly's inherent shortcomings as a rapper; he's so taken with his subject matter that he will often lose the beat of his clumsy rhymes and just start to talk. Or yell. Similarly, while the musical backing on *How a Black Man Feels* is the most compelling he's been afforded, Schoolly makes little or no use of the dynamic reggae ("Original Gangster") and soul ("Where'd You Get That Funk From") breaks; he's at his absolute slackest on the supposedly devastating title track. And his idea of a conciliatory gesture is a plodding chorus chant that goes "Peace to the motherfucking nation!" After a while, it seems like the only appropriate response to all this grim posturing is a yawn. — M.C.

GIL SCOTT-HERON

★★★ Small Talk at 125th and Lenox (Flying Dutchman, 1972)
★★★ Free Will (Flying Dutchman, 1972)
★★★ Pieces of a Man (Flying Dutchman, 1973)
★★★½ The Revolution Will Not Be Televised (Flying Dutchman, 1974)
★★★ The First Minute of a New Day (Arista, 1974)
★★★½ From South Africa to South Carolina (Arista, 1975)
★★★ It's Your World (Arista, 1976)
★★★ Bridges (Arista, 1977)
★★★ Secrets (Arista, 1978)
★★★½ The Mind of Gil Scott-Heron (Arista, 1978)
★★★½ 1980 (Arista, 1980)
★★★ Real Eyes (Arista, 1980)
★★★ Reflections (Arista, 1981)
★★★½ Moving Target (Arista, 1982)
★★★★ The Best of Gil Scott-Heron (1984; Arista, 1991)

Gil Scott-Heron's '70s albums were jazzy funk of an intelligence notably lacking in the Age of Disco—and his political wordplay anticipated rap. As a novelist (*The Vulture*, *The Nigger Factory*), poet and pianist, Scott-Heron achieved an arresting synthesis of laid-back soul music—with jazz-fusion embellishments borrowed from

Bitches Brew–period Miles Davis—and class-struggle sermonizing. As evidenced by the title track and "Whitey on the Moon" from *The Revolution Will Not Be Televised*, the singer often leavened his heavy messages with crafty wit, but at his most direct ("Home Is Where the Hatred Is") he could come on with all of the significant fury—if little of the furious noise—of Public Enemy or the Clash.

"Johannesburg," off *From South Africa to South Carolina*, gave him FM-radio airplay, but Scott-Heron has generally remained only a critical success. Playing with expert musicians (Bernard Purdie, Ron Carter, David Spinozza), he's made extremely competent records—but his vocals have lacked distinction, and an over-reliance on the glossy flute work of both Hubert Laws and collaborator Brian Jackson has sometimes blunted the rhythmic edge of his songs. "Re-Ron," a biting anti-Reagan panegyric off *The Best of* shows him working with a tougher sound, courtesy of Material's Bill Laswell—and his '80s work, as a whole, gained in force. But it's as an early influence on urban message-music that he's most noteworthy. Ahead of his time in a decade when most funk was escapism, Scott-Heron prophesied while others just partied. — P.E.

SCRITTI POLITTI

★★½ Songs to Remember (Rough Trade, 1982)
★★★½ Cupid & Psyche 85 (Warner Bros., 1985)
★★½ Provision (Warner Bros., 1988)

A mere description of Scritti Politti sounds unbelievable, and potentially unbearable: yet another synth-pop outfit, this one fronted by Green Gartside, a Brit falsetto who name-drops French literary critics and looks fabulous in a tailored suit. *Songs to Remember* is a collection of catchy tunes performed by this originally conceptualist trio from Leeds. For *Cupid & Psyche 85*, Green Gartside moved to America and, minus his bandmates, actually pulls off his tuneful pop deconstruction; "Absolute" and "Wood Beez (Pray Like Aretha Franklin)" kick in like car-radio classics, and you can read everything (or nothing) into the spiraling, cross-referenced lines of "The Word Girl" and "Hypnotized." Parts of this album could be mistaken for Wham! in a blindfold test, and that's part of the joke.

Provision leaps forward on a purely musical level. David Gamson deftly synthesizes a supple cushion of sound, fluffing up the rap-derived beats with lush electronic melodies. Miles Davis donates a muted squiggle on "Oh, Patti," and his trumpet fits right in. But Gartside sounds flat and disengaged, as if he's impatient with these straightforward love songs. "Tell us what you really mean, Green," coo the back-up singers at one point. Scritti Politti is a lot more convincing when Gartside avoids that question entirely. — M.C.

SON SEALS
★★★★ **The Son Seals Blues Band (Alligator, 1973)**
★★★★ **Midnight Son (Alligator, 1977)**
★★★★ **Live and Burning (Alligator, 1978)**
★★★½ **Bad Axe (Alligator, 1985)**
★★★½ **Living in the Danger Zone (Alligator, 1991)**

The Arkansas native learned the blues while hanging around the backwoods roadhouse that his father owned. Starting off his professional career on the drums, Seals made a name for himself in Albert King's late-'60s band (he appears on King's 1968 Stax LP *Live Wire/Blues Power*). Guitar turned out to be his forte, however; Seals was a quick study, blending elements of King's solo style into his own lightning-fingered attack when he moved to Chicago and went solo. Rough as a slug of rotgut, *The Son Seals Blues Band* established him as the most distinctive stylist of the Windy City's second (or third) blues generation. The instrumental "Hot Sauce" delivers a fiery kick, while the festering pain of the vocal on "Your Love Is Like a Cancer" will haunt you for days. *Midnight Son* adds a soulful horn section and more diverse material, from the joyful noise of "Four Full Seasons of Love" to the desolate wails of "Strung Out Woman." *Live and Burning* captures a seasoned club performer on a hot night. Live work sustained Seals through most of the '80s, though the 1984 check-in, *Bad Axe*, finds him singing with newfound subtlety. Cheery Memphis-soul horn lines and clever wordplay can't disguise the undercurrents of despair of *Living in the Danger Zone*; Seals knows this territory like the back of his calloused hands. Here's hoping he resumes recording on at least a semiregular basis. — M.C.

THE SEARCHERS
★★★ **The Searchers (Sire, 1979)**
★★★ **Love Melodies (Sire, 1981)**
★★★★ **Greatest Hits (Rhino, 1988)**

Like their Liverpool betters (and pals), the Searchers were mad about Buddy Holly and the Everly Brothers, served time in Hamburg's Star Club, joined fresh harmonies to chiming guitars—and in their 1964 covers of Sonny Bono's "Needles and Pins" and Jackie DeShannon's "When You Walk in the Room," actually managed to make Merseybeat nearly as fine as the early Beatles. Pure pop—the brilliant 12-string attack of "Room" is about as heavy as they get—the Searchers were melody freaks and sweet vocalists whose happy covers made them unthreatening, winsome and polite. It was the sincerity, though, of their nice-guyism that carried them—that, and excellent playing, lifted such boppy fare as "Sweets for My Sweet" and "Sugar And Spice" beyond fluff, into a fresh, charming ozone. Their early-'60s moment was gone in a flash, but the lads carried on—from bar to supper-club to revivalist tours. And then, miraculously, they returned for two albums that recaptured their glory days. — P.E.

JOHN SEBASTIAN
★★★ **The Best of John Sebastian (Rhino, 1989)**

The tripping embodiment of the blissful hippie thing, John Sebastian wouldn't give the grinning a rest. After smiling through the Lovin' Spoonful's short but memorable career, he returned, aggressively tie-dyed, in the '70s. His debut, *John B. Sebastian* (1970), was his only real success, featuring his back-porch vocals and offhand guitar backed up by Stephen Stills and David Crosby. A celebrator of pastel states of mind—wistfulness, melancholy, nostalgia—he purveyed, through "Magical Connection," "You're a Big Boy Now" and "She's a Lady," the greeting-card philosophizing Harry Chapin and Jim Croce also specialized in. *Welcome Back*, with its title-track sit-com theme, *The Four of Us* and *Tarzana Kid* continued along these laid-back lines: tentative, tasteful, soporific. — P.E.

NEIL SEDAKA
★★★ **Neil Sedaka Sings His Greatest Hits (RCA, 1975)**
★★★★ **All-Time Greatest Hits (1975; RCA, 1988)**
★★ **Superbird (Quicksilver, 1982)**
★★★ **Me and My Friends (Polydor, 1986)**
★★ **"Oh! Carol" & Other Hits (RCA, 1990)**
★★★ **All-Time Greatest Hits (RCA, 1991)**

Born and raised in Brooklyn, Neil Sedaka came from a family with a long history as musicians. Sedaka began studying classical piano while he was in grade school, but his interest turned increasingly toward pop music. In high school he teamed with a friend named Howard Greenfield, who began writing lyrics for Sedaka's melodies. While on scholarship to the Juilliard School, Sedaka and Greenfield sold a song to Connie Francis. "Stupid Cupid" peaked at Number 14 on the singles chart in 1958, and the duo turned their attention to songwriting on a full-time basis. Encouraged by music publishers Al Nevins and Don Kirshner, Sedaka cut a demo and was signed to RCA as a solo artist. When Little Anthony and the Imperials delayed releasing their version of Sedaka-Greenfield's "The Diary," Sedaka cut it himself as his first single and had a Top Twenty hit. Less than a year later Sedaka and Greenfield wrote an uptempo love song inspired by Sedaka's affections for a neighborhood friend named Carole King, who grew up to become a songwriter of note herself. "Oh! Carol" hit the Top Ten and initiated a four-year run of Top Twenty singles for Sedaka, whose songs tapped into the passion and pain of teenage love. Distinguished by strong, syncopated rhythms, beautiful melodies, and doo-wop-style vocal embellishments supporting Sedaka's boyish, double-tracked voice, Sedaka cut five successive singles in the early '60s—"Calendar Girl," "Little Devil," "Happy Birthday, Sweet Sixteen," "Breaking Up Is Hard to Do" and "Next Door to an Angel"—that remain among the strongest pop rock produced by any American artist. By the end of '63 Sedaka's appeal had waned. It would be ten years before he returned to the charts, but he did so with flair. After signing with Elton John's Rocket label in 1974, Sedaka had a Number One single out of the box with the languorous "Laughter in the Rain." He followed that with another Number One, a rocker titled "Bad Blood" that featured Sedaka trading frenetic choruses with John. His final Top Ten hit came in 1975—a shameless emasculation of one of his best songs, "Breaking Up Is Hard to Do," done at a slower tempo for the cocktail-lounge crowd. A couple of minor singles later and Sedaka was once again put out to pasture as a recording artist, though he has never stopped performing.

Sedaka's Rocket albums are all out of print, but the key songs from his mid-'70s period are collected on Polydor's *Me and My Friends*, which is dedicated to Greenfield, who died in 1986. Of the three extant RCA albums, *All-Time Greatest Hits* contains his essential first 12 hits, plus two other noncharting items. The other two albums are greatest-hits collections. *Neil Sedaka Sings His Greatest Hits* is preferable, as it contains 12 essential tracks; *"Oh! Carol" & Other Hits* has only eight songs. *Superbird* (1982) finds Sedaka in good voice but purveying weak material. — D.M.

THE SEEDS
★★★ **Future (GNP, 1967)**
★★½ **Raw & Alive: Merlin's Music Box (GNP, 1968)**
★★ **A Full Spoon of Seedy Blues (GNP, 1969)**
★★★ **Fallin' Off the Edge (1977; GNP, 1987)**
★★★½ **The Seeds (GNP, 1987)**

Even if this bizarre West Coast foursome had released only *Future*, the Seeds would still qualify as the definitive trash-rock auteurs. Intended as an epic psychedelic mini-opera, the record is now absolutely hilarious. Along with the grab-bag instrumentation (cello, flügelhorn, "weather" and "whips") that comes with any *Sgt. Pepper's* knock-off, there's the singing of Sky Saxon at its truly strangest. On "March of the Flower Children," "Flower Lady and Her Assistant" and "Where Is the Entrance Way to Play," the Seeds' resident genius goes for broke—his thin voice alternately a growling and a campy wonder. Described on *Future*'s liner notes as "a perfect being," Saxon was indeed one of rock's more appealing eccentrics. His fellow Seeds, particularly the fumble-fingered Ray Manzarek imitator, Daryl Hooper, played the way Sky sang—ineptly, but with a certain druggy charm. *The Seeds* compiles the band's landmark 1966 recordings—*The Seeds* and *Web of Sound*—and it's a real hoot, featuring not only the band's one hit ("Pushin' Too Hard") but such great reefer madness as "Tripmaker," "Mr. Farmer" and the 14-minute ode to "balling," "Up in Her Room." *A Full Spoon of Seedy Blues*, credited to "The Sky Saxon Blues Band," is the group's attempt to get down with the blooze—a form whose severity unfortunately precludes the wacky experimentalism in which the Seeds specialized. *Merlin's Music Box* is the obligatory live set, interesting primarily for the thrilling "900 Million People Daily All Making Love." *Fallin' Off the Edge* is mainly discards and repeats, but still loads of fun. Compared to the Seeds, the Mothers of Invention seem labored, Arthur Lee comes across as a logician, and the Troggs sound tame. The band virtually defines the term "guilty pleasure." — P.E.

PETE SEEGER

★★★ Talking Union & Other Union Songs (Folkways, 1941)

★★★ Songs of the Civil War, Vol. 1 (Folkways, 1943)

★★★ Darling Corey (Folkways, 1950)

★★★ Lonesome Valley (Folkways, 1951)

★★ Songs to Grow On (Folkways, 1951)

★★★ American Folksongs for Children (Folkways, 1953)

★★ A Pete Seeger Concert (Stinson, 1953)

★★ Birds, Beasts, Bugs & Little Fishes (Folkways, 1954)

★★★ Frontier Ballads, Vol. I (Folkways, 1954)

★★★ Frontier Ballads, Vol. II (Folkways, 1954)

★★ Goofing-Off Suite (Folkways, 1954)

★★ How to Play the Five-string Banjo (Folkways, 1954)

★★★★ Bantu Choral Folk Songs (Folkways, 1955)

★★★ Folk Songs of Four Continents (Folkways, 1955)

★★ Love Songs for Friends and Foes (Folkways, 1956)

★★★ With Voices Together We Sing (Folkways, 1956)

★★ American Industrial Ballads (Folkways, 1956)

★★ American Ballads (Folkways, 1957)

★★ American Favorite Ballads, Vol. I (Folkways, 1957)

★★ Abiyoyo and Other Story Songs for Children (1958; Folkways/Rounder, 1989)

★★★ Pete Seeger & Sonny Terry at Carnegie Hall (Folkways, 1958)

★★★ Folk Songs for Young People (Folkways, 1959)

★★ American Playparties (Folkways, 1959)

★★ Camp Songs (Folkways, 1959)

★★ American Favorite Ballads, Vol. II (Folkways, 1959)

★★★ Old Time Fiddle Tunes (Folkways, 1960)

★★ Rainbow Quest (Folkways, 1960)

★★ Champlain Valley Songs (Folkways, 1960)

★★★ With Memphis Slim & Willie Dixon at the Village Gate (Folkways, 1960)

★★ American Favorite Ballads, Vol. III (Folkways, 1960)

★★★ American History in Ballad and Song, Vols. 1 (Folkways, 1960)

★★★ American History in Ballad and Song, Vols. 2 (Folkways, 1961)

★★ American Favorite Ballads, Vol. IV (Folkways, 1961)

★★ At the Village Gate (Folkways, 1962)

★★ American Game and Activity Songs for Children (Folkways, 1962)

★★★ Pete! Folk Songs and Ballads (Stinson, 1962)

★★ American Favorite Ballads, Vol. V (Folkways, 1962)

★★ The Nativity (Folkways, 1963)

★★★ Broadside Ballads, Vol. 1 (Folkways, 1963)

★★★★ We Shall Overcome (Columbia, 1963)

★★★★ Songs of Struggle and Protest: 1930–1950 (Folkways, 1964)

★★★ Broadside Ballads, Vol. 2 (Folkways, 1965)

★★★★ WNEW's Songs of Selma (Folkways, 1965)

★★★ Traditional Christmas Carols (Folkways, 1967)

★★★★ Waist Deep in the Big Muddy (Columbia, 1967)

★★ Sings & Answers Questions at Ford Hall Forum in Boston (Broadside, 1968)

★★★ Sings Woody Guthrie (Folkways, 1967)

★★★ Pete Seeger's Greatest Hits (Columbia, 1967)

★★★ Sings Leadbelly (Folkways, 1968)

★★ Young vs. Old (Columbia, 1969)

★★★ The World of Pete Seeger (Columbia, 1972)

★★ Banks of Marble (Folkways, 1974)

★★★ Pete Seeger & Arlo Guthrie in Concert Together (Warner Bros., 1975)

★★★★ The Essential Pete Seeger (Vanguard, 1978)

★★★ Circles and Seasons (Warner Bros., 1979)

★★★ Precious Friend: Arlo Guthrie and Pete Seeger (Warner Bros., 1982)

★★★★½ We Shall Overcome: The Complete Carnegie Hall Concert (Columbia, 1989)

★★ 20 Golden Pieces of Pete Seeger (Bulldog, NA)

★★★ Children's Concert at Town Hall (Columbia, 1990)

★★★½ Pete Seeger Singalong: Sanders Theater, 1980 (Smithsonian/Folkways/ Rounder, 1991)

As we look to Jelly Roll Morton, Muddy Waters, Louis Armstrong and Elvis Presley as artists who synthesized the past and created something new and lasting out of it, so, too, must we regard Pete Seeger with the same deep respect. Seeger's standing, however, rests not on innovation, but on conscience and commitment. Born in New York City in 1919 to parents who were faculty members at the Juilliard School of Music, Seeger found his calling at age 16 when he attended a folk festival in Asheville, North Carolina. After dropping out of Harvard in 1938, Seeger began wandering the country, banjo in hand, eventually hooking up with Woody Guthrie; along the way he absorbed hundreds of songs and learned to write his own. He studied and developed an abiding faith in humanitarian socialism as a cure for society's ills; as his personal political views crystallized, Seeger became more vocal in his support of workers and labor unions and was quick to advance their point of view in his music. In 1940 he set out to do this in explicit terms by forming the Almanac Singers with Lee Hays and Millard Lampell and recording two albums, *Songs for John Doe* and *Talking Union and Other Union Songs*. (Guthrie was also an informal member of the Almanac Singers, but the two albums he made with the group curiously lack much political orientation.)

Through it all Seeger remained fixed on the idea of the song as a source of information, as a link between the past and the present, as a window into other worlds. In addition to workers' songs, he plumbed the folk songs of other countries and other cultures, became a master storyteller and a master synthesist, weaving contemporary ideas and attitudes into ballads centuries old. He became a repository of traditional American songs of all types; and, being a bit of a musicologist (his father's profession), Seeger tracked down the stories behind the old songs he was digging up and used this background to bring dimension, historical sweep, to his concerts. And while he could be contentious and sanctimonious, he delivered his scholarly anecdotes with the eagerness and joy of a child finding buried treasure.

The folk revival of the '50s and '60s officially began in 1948, when Seeger, Hays, Ronnie Gilbert and Fred Hellerman joined together as the Weavers and continued the work the Almanac Singers had begun earlier in the decade. But accused of being Communists during the '50s Red Scare, the Weavers—one of the most popular groups in the country—were forced to disband (but made a triumphant 1955 comeback), and

Seeger was blacklisted by television and radio. He continued recording for Columbia, though, remaining an active recording artist apart from the Weavers as he had since 1940. The Weaver's reunion in '55 was the beginning of the next phase of Seeger's career, one that would find him again on the front lines supporting the civil-rights movement and, in the '60s, raising his voice in protest against the Vietnam War.

Seeger's chosen medium for reaching people was by touring, constantly and globally. How many people first heard Bob Dylan's songs at a Pete Seeger concert is impossible to calculate, as is the number whom Seeger introduced to the music of Jimmie Rodgers, Leadbelly, Woody Guthrie and other great American artists. Seeger's historic 1963 Carnegie Hall concert, issued in its entirety on Columbia's *We Shall Overcome*, is representative of a prime Seeger performance. Seeger has recorded almost without interruption since 1940, and a good deal of his work remains in print. Even a cursory listen to his catalog is akin to taking a journey into the history of song. He must be genuinely amused by the current interest in African music, since his recording of *Bantu Choral Folk Songs* dates from 1955. And when Ken Burns's powerful *Civil War* series made the War Between the States fashionable again in 1990, Seeger could look back to 1943, when he recorded his first album of Civil War songs. There's no end to this. Pick a Pete Seeger album, and there's usually something of interest impossible to find anywhere else. There are children's albums, how-to albums (*How to Play the Five-String Banjo*, from 1954; another how-to on Leadbelly's 12-string guitar technique is out of print), blues-folk summit meetings, work songs, protest songs, nature songs, and numerous tributes to other artists. Seeger has also cut two fine live albums with Arlo Guthrie, both of them offering a capsule history of 20th Century American popular music. Seeger's 1979 studio album, *Circles and Seasons*, illustrates in its song selection Seeger's gentle approach to consciousness-raising, this time relative to environmental issues. Without becoming strident, the songs "Garbage," "Maple Syrup Time" and "Garden Song" emphasize the need for humans to live in harmony with the earth. This album re-teams Seeger with fellow Weaver Fred Hellerman, who produced and contributed background vocals. Remarkable and of unassailable integrity, Seeger's music renews the spirit as it feeds the mind. *Pete Seeger Singalong*, recorded live in Cambridge, Massachusetts, in 1980, contains 41 tracks documenting the eclecticism, good humor and great humanity the man brings to his in-person appearances. Seeger's own extensive liner notes provide much in the way of informative background on the folk history behind the song selection. — D.M.

THE SEEKERS
★ **The Best of the Seekers (Capitol, 1967)**
The Seekers delivered the breathy theme for "Georgy Girl, " Lynn Redgrave's breakout movie. They also made a brief career of truly awful folk Muzak. They broke up and came back, as the New Seekers, to sing the Coke commercial, "I'd Like to Teach the World to Sing." — P.E.

BOB SEGER
★ ★ ★	**Ramblin' Gamblin' Man (Capitol, 1969)**
★ ★ ★	**Noah (Capitol, 1969)**
★ ★ ★	**Mongrel (Capitol, 1970)**
★ ★ ★	**Smokin' O.P.'s (1972; Capitol, 1977)**
★ ★ ★	**Back in '72 (Reprise, 1973)**
★ ★ ★½	**Seven (Capitol, 1974)**
★ ★ ★½	**Beautiful Loser (Capitol, 1975)**
★ ★ ★ ★	**Live Bullet (Capitol, 1976)**
★ ★ ★ ★	**Night Moves (Capitol, 1976)**
★ ★ ★ ★	**Stranger in Town (Capitol, 1978)**
★ ★ ★½	**Against the Wind (Capitol, 1980)**
★ ★ ★	**Nine Tonight (Capitol, 1981)**
★ ★ ★ ★	**The Distance (Capitol, 1982)**
★ ★ ★½	**Like a Rock (Capitol, 1986)**
★ ★ ★	**The Fire Inside (Capitol, 1991)**

Whether gigging in long, tireless obscurity in the journeyman bars and clubs of his native Michigan or gliding through his late-'70s success, Bob Seger remained in spirit a working-class hero. Gruff-voiced and dramatic, he's a premier rock & roll singer, and his best songs render with dignity and empathy the hard victories and close defeats of ordinary lives. A sort of John Fogerty with more of a naturalist approach than that expressed by Creedence's ruralist myths, or a Springsteen without the vast sweep of the Boss's vision, Seger balances romance and realism—for all its inspirational verve, his work mainly is honest, solid and strong.

Heavy rock along the lines of Free or Cream, *Ramblin' Gamblin' Man* boasts a great, Mitch Ryder-ish title track and very tough, bluesy stompers driven home with raw assurance. *Mongrel* hasn't quite the same crude, lean power—a remake of Ike

and Tina Turner's "River Deep, Mountain High" betrays Seger's occasional tendency toward bombast—but with "Big River," the record sees the singer debuting the kind of confident midtempo ballad writing he'd later perfect with such hits as "You'll Accomp'ny Me" and "Against the Wind." A grab bag of covers as oddly diverse as Stephen Stills's "Love the One You're With" and Chuck Berry's "Let It Rock," *Smokin' O.P.'s* features "Heavy Music," its swagger recalling Spencer Davis's "Gimme Some Lovin' " and a reading of Tim Hardin's "If I Were a Carpenter" that shows Seger capable, as ever, of fierce conviction, if not yet of much restraint. "Get Out of Denver," off *Seven*, is Seger at his fast-rocking finest; "U.M.C. (Upper Middle Class)" shows him flourishing a political conscience—and the album introduces the Silver Bullet Band, whose no-frills dependability makes possible a gaining confidence in the singer that soon will pay off in a new refinement that sacrifices little of his earlier energy.

Beautiful Loser's stately title track and its punchy cover of Tina Turner's "Nutbush City Limits" begin Seger's mature period. The trilogy that follows, *Live Bullet, Night Moves* and *Stranger in Town* is remarkable—"Night Moves" is not only Seger's best song, but one of rock's most moving exercises in elegy, and the vigor of the fast songs testifies not only to the pleasures of craft, but the rewards of keeping faith with fundamental rock & roll. Seger's glory moment, these three records sum up his strengths—clarity, endurance and heart.

While "The Horizontal Bop" and "Betty Lou's Gettin' Out Tonight" rock with the offhand assurance Seger had unassailably gained by then, *Against the Wind*'s ballads betray strain and a certain softness. *Nine Tonight* is expert but unecessary. *The Distance* marks a return to form in its moody remake of Rodney Crowell's "Shame on the Moon" and in Seger's Detroit valedictory, "Makin' Thunderbirds"—but the note of nostalgia he'd first sounded with *Stranger in Town*'s "Old Time Rock 'n' Roll" is beginning to seem perfunctory. *Like A Rock*, however, testifies to Seger's survivalist courage. While the breakthrough intensity of his best work is missing, this is wise and confident music. A cover of Fogerty's "Fortunate Son" truly kicks, and in "The Ring" and its lament for an exhausted love, the veteran is doing what he—and few others—can do with frankness and focus: make rock & roll for full-grown men and women. *The Fire Inside* carries on the good fight. — P.E.

THE SELECTER
★ ★ ★   Too Much Pressure (Chrysalis, 1980)
★ ★½   Celebrate the Bullet (Chrysalis, 1981)

One of the better British ska acts, the Selecter didn't mess much with the genre's formula—brittle new wave melodies, brisk skanking afterbeats, and edgy, anxious vocals—choosing instead to make its mark through sure-footed playing and solid songwriting. And *Too Much Pressure* is packed with both, thanks to such tuneful, efficient numbers as "Missing Words," "Murder" and a terrific tribute to the power of hit singles entitled "Three Minute Hero." Too bad the band couldn't maintain that momentum; although *Celebrate the Bullet* makes the most of Pauline Black's vocal power, the playing is less focused (perhaps due to personnel changes), and the songs lack the spark of the first album. — J.D.C.

SEX PISTOLS
★ ★ ★ ★ ★   Never Mind the Bollocks Here's the Sex Pistols (Warner Bros., 1977)
★ ★ ★   The Great Rock 'n' Roll Swindle (Virgin import, 1979)

The Sex Pistols fired a shot heard 'round the world; too bad it turned out to be a blank. Or was that part of the plan? For a strange couple of weeks in 1978, anyway, the avatars of British punk made a significant dent in the American media landscape. Then the group promptly broke up—at the end of an abbreviated U.S. tour, before its music and general attitude had a chance to infect the mainstream here. And truth be told, *Never Mind the Bollocks* is just too raw and corrosive to qualify as any kind of pop. Thousands of lousy imitations have dulled punk's jagged edge over the years, but the Pistols' recorded legacy still cuts deep into the heart of rock & roll—and still draws blood.

Here are the nihilistic singles that brought an empire to its knees during 1976–77 ("Anarchy in the U.K.," "God Save the Queen"), alongside the scornful anthems that shocked a previous generation of rebels ("Pretty Vacant," "No Feelings"). Steve Jones rips blaring antiriffs out of his guitar, while Johnny Rotten taunts us with alternating flashes of wild insight and utter rudeness. The astounding cuts "Bodies" and "Holidays in the Sun" suggest that the once

(and future) John Lydon sensed something basic about the sanctity of human life, as well as the rotten way human beings have come to live it.

The Great Rock 'n' Roll Swindle is a soundtrack compilation, documenting the Sex Pistols' dissolution in more detail than necessary. Rotten is long gone by this point, and the concepts of manager Malcolm McLaren loom large over the proceedings: choral foreign-language versions of the hits, Steve Jones and drummer Paul Cook's tasteless match-up with Great Train Robber Ronald Biggs, and so on. *Swindle*'s only essential moment is a poignant mauling of "My Way" by the late Sid Vicious. — M.C.

CHARLIE SEXTON
★½   Pictures for Pleasure (MCA, 1985)
★ ★½   Charlie Sexton (MCA, 1989)

Despite his high cheekbones, Bowie-ish croon and guitar-hero chops, Charlie Sexton has yet to make an album that justifies his reputation as a rock wunderkind. Then again, considering that he made his name playing roots-rock guitar but makes records peddling slick, quasi-new-wave pop rock, it's no wonder. *Pictures for Pleasure* starts things off on exactly the wrong footing: it ignores the fact that Sexton sounds more at home with the classic lines of "Hold Me" and instead emphasizes his own material, which sounds like nothing so much as rejected Cars demos (though "Beat's So Lonely" ended up an AOR hit anyway). Sexton's second album merely intensifies the efforts of his first; thanks to a higher class of collaborator—including Steve Earle, Tonio K. and Scott Wilk—the songs are far more workmanlike, but his sound is essentially unchanged. Still, the sheer momentum of his performances, particularly on tunes like "Blowing Up Detroit" and "For All We Know," keeps the album from seeming a complete failure. — J.D.C.

SHALAMAR
★ ★½   Uptown Festival (Solar/Soul Train, 1977)
★ ★½   Disco Gardens (Solar/RCA, 1978)
★ ★ ★   Big Fun (Solar/RCA, 1979)
★ ★ ★½   Three for Love (Solar/RCA, 1981)
★ ★ ★ ★   Go for It (Solar/RCA, 1981)
★ ★ ★½   Friends (Solar/Elektra, 1982)
★ ★ ★½   Shalamar's Greatest Hits (Solar/RCA, 1982)
★ ★ ★½   The Look (Solar/Elektra, 1983)
★ ★½   Heartbreak (Solar/Elektra, 1984)
★ ★   Circumstantial Evidence (Solar/Capitol, 1987)
★ ★   Wake Up (Solar/Sony, 1990)

Shalamar was put together by mellow-rapping *Soul Train* host Don Cornelius; Jeffrey Daniels and Jody Watley had both been dancers on the program. Gerald Brown wasn't the most distinctive lead singer, but the trio scored an R&B chart hit with a glitzy Motown medley called "Uptown Festival." Replacing Brown with Howard Hewett, Shalamar moved to the fledging Solar (Sounds Of Los Angeles Records) in 1978. Dick Griffey wanted to make his label the '80s successor to Philadelphia International, and Shalamar must have looked like the perfect vehicle. Working with producer Leon Sylvers, the group became the prime exponent of the Solar sound: synthesizers, dynamic jump-out-of-the-radio arrangements, a funky bottom, even the occasional rock guitar line. Shalamar was one of the label's few success stories. Solar's hot streak didn't last all that long, but the music itself still glows—brilliantly, at times.

"Take That to the Bank" (from *Disco Gardens*) and "The Second Time Around" (from *Big Fun*) established Shalamar's knack with high-stepping fare and romantic melodrama, respectively. On *Three for Love* the group comes into its own: wrapping complex three-part harmonies around a taut groove ("Make That Move"), turning a routine ballad ("This Is for the Lover in You") into a seductive tour de force. Jeffrey Daniels steps forward on *Go for It*, producing and co-writing several cuts on this forgotten gem. From the shimmering title track to the closing "Rocker," from Watley's irresistible "Appeal" to the disarming "Final Analysis," *Go for It* is a remarkably wide-ranging pop album.

The material on *Friends* seems formulaic in comparison, though the performances are strong. Watley continues to assert her vocal presence, especially on the hit "A Night to Remember." Shalamar goes New Wave on *The Look*. A nervous synth-beat and nagging guitar solo ignite "Dead Giveaway," but some of the more rock-influenced tracks sound cluttered and busy. Watley and Daniels left the group in 1984. Howard Hewett carried on with near-clones Delisa Davis and Micki Free for one more album (the weak *Heartbreak*), and then took off on his own solo flight. With lead singer Sidney Justin, Shalamar has released a pair of faceless albums, one of which, *Circumstantial Evidence*, was produced by L.A. Reid and Babyface. Whether anyone will admit it or not, the Shalamar franchise belongs to Hewett, Watley and Daniels. *Greatest Hits* is a brief, breathless overview. — M.C.

SHANGRI-LAS

★ ★ ★ **Remember . . . The Shangri-Las at Their Best (Collectables, NA)**
This girl-group foursome had all the earmarks of a novelty act: two of them were twins, they once released a record under the name of the Beatlelettes, and their heavy Queens accents sounded wonderfully kitschy. Breathless sincerity, however, remains the strongest of their considerable charms: only in high school when they began recording, the girls tried so damn hard to be the Ronettes that they're quite endearing. "Leader of the Pack," that great 1964 anthem for juvenile delinquents, is still their most winning moment, but "Remember (Walking in the Sand)" is excellent fake Phil Spector, too. "Out in the Streets" and "I Can Never Go Home Anymore" (with its fine, drippy spoken confessional) round out an impressive quartet of hits. A real-life version of *Grease*, these gal wonders are lots of fun. — P.E.

DEL SHANNON

★ ★ ★ ★ **Little Town Flirt (1963; Bug/Rhino, 1990)**
★ ★ **Del Shannon Sings Hank Williams: Your Cheatin' Heart (1965; Bug/Rhino, 1990)**
★ ★ ★ ★ ★ **Greatest Hits (Bug/Rhino, 1990)**
★ **The Liberty Years (EMI, 1991)**
★ ★ ★ **Rock On! (Bug/MCA, 1991)**
The notion that the late '50s and pre-Beatles '60s was a fallow period for rock & roll can be disputed on several fronts, one of the strongest being the music erupting from Del Shannon's angst-ridden sensibility. "Runaway," "Little Town Flirt," "Hats off to Larry," "Keep Searchin' "—these are tough, aggressive epistles informed by the extreme emotions of teen life. A nasal sneer rife with heartbreak and rage; stinging top-strings guitar lines; Max Crook's cheesy, insinuating Musitron riffs; and minor-to-major key modulations (a trick Shannon learned from listening to Hank Williams) were the dominant features of Shannon's towering singles, all of them so perfect that they evoke the spirit of their time without sounding like period pieces.

Unlike many of his contemporaries, Shannon wasn't rent asunder by the British Invasion. One of his best singles, the desperate "Keep Searchin'," hit the Top Ten in late '64 when Beatlemania was at a fever pitch, and a year later Peter and Gordon had a Top Ten single with Shannon's "I Go to Pieces." Shannon also holds the distinction of being the first American artist to cover a Lennon-McCartney song; his 1963 version of "From Me to You" preceded the Beatles' by two months and charted higher than the Fab Four's single.

Shannon's creative well ran dry in '65, even though he had a Top Forty single that year in the paranoid-drenched "Stranger in Town." Changing labels and producers failed to produce anything of note. Comebacks always seemed to be in the offing as the '60s and '70s wore on, but alas, Shannon's career foundered. A fine live album, *Del Shannon Live in England*, gained little attention Stateside upon its release in 1973. A Tom Petty–produced album, *Drop Down and Get Me*, released in 1981, captured Shannon's spirit and paid homage to his country roots, but so-so material doomed it. Saddest of all, in 1990 Shannon teamed up with producer Jeff Lynne and several of Petty's Heartbreakers for an album all thought would bring Shannon back to the charts. He died under mysterious circumstances before its release. But *Rock On* is yet another disappointment.

On the plus side, *Greatest Hits* and *Little Town Flirt* are quintessential American pop-rock, and represent Shannon's finest moments as a songwriter and performer. The *Hank Williams* album, originally released in 1965, finds Shannon running through a dozen familiar songs in a strict country format and adhering to Williams's phrasing as best he can. It's interesting as a curiosity. *The Liberty Years* is for hard-core Shannon fans only, as it shows the artist short of inspiration and finally resorting to rewriting his greatest song as "Runaway '67" in a failed attempt to crack the charts again. — D.M.

ROXANNE SHANTÉ
★★★★ **Bad Sister (Cold Chillin', 1989)**
Fifteen-year-old Lolita Gooden of Queens, New York, cut a scorching, definitive answer record to "Roxanne, Roxanne," the 1985 rap hit by U.T.F.O. "Roxanne's Revenge" (included on *Bad Sister*) rolls out a funky tongue-lashing with verbal relish and saucy beats. No one-hit wonder, Roxanne Shanté ups the ante with two saltier-still singles: "Have a Nice Day" and "Go on Girl" are further pumped by ripping lyrics (from Big Daddy Kane) and raw, scratched-up jams (from producer Marly Marl). After a delay that stretched several years, Shanté delivered a debut album that matched the impact of those

classic in-your-face performances. Even the sole "message" track on *Bad Sister*, "Independent Woman," is gripped with the same indomitable do-it-yourself spirit that guides randy raps like "Fatal Attraction," "Feelin' Kinda Horny" and "Knockin' Hiney." — M.C.

SHEILA E
★★★ **The Glamorous Life (Warner Bros., 1984)**
★★★★ **Romance 1600 (Paisley Park, 1985)**
★★ **Sheila E (Paisley Park, 1987)**
★★½ **Sex Cymbal (Warner Bros., 1991)**
Even though Sheila E had a recording career—making Latin jazz albums with her father, percussionist Pete Escovedo—before being "discovered" by Prince, the Royal One's musical sensibility has most shaped her solo career. *The Glamorous Life*, for instance, is a Prince album in all but name; her voice and percussion may carry most of the musical weight, but his aesthetic is what provides the direction, from the whimsical flavor of "Oliver's House" to the jazzy angularity of the title tune. And when his actual input is diminished, as on *Romance 1600*, its impact seems that much stronger. After all, it's the gloriously funky "A Love Bizarre" (co-written and co-produced by Prince) that gives *Romance 1600* its kick, turning the album from a slick, jazz-inflected R&B workout into something far meatier.

It's when the singer-percussionist tries for a more individual sound that her albums begin to weary. *Sheila E* is flat and mechanical, boasting some rhythmic flash but not enough melody to make it worthwhile, and though *Sex Cymbal* has its moments—the hi-tech funk of the title tune, the salsa-style workout on "Family Affair" —its overall lack of focus robs the album of any real zip. — J.D.C.

ARCHIE SHEPP
★★★★ **Four for Trane (Impulse, 1965)**
★★★★ **Fire Music (Impulse, 1965)**
★★★★½ **Mama Too Tight (Impulse, 1967)**
★★★½ **The Magic of Ju-Ju (Impulse, 1967)**
★★★ **Attica Blues (1972; MCA/Impulse, 1981)**
★★★ **Montreux One (Arista/Freedom, 1975)**
★★★½ **There's a Trumpet in My Soul (Arista, 1975)**
★★★½ **Green Dolphin Street (Denon, 1977)**

★ ★ ★½ **Trouble in Mind (Steeplechase, 1980)**
★ ★ ★ ★ **Looking at Bird (Steeplechase, 1980)**

Archie Shepp's records aren't easy to find—except for *Fire Music*, his trailblazing early work is out of print—but they're worth searching for. Playing alto and soprano, but chiefly tenor sax, Shepp came to the fore in the '60s alongside John Coltrane, Don Cherry, Cecil Taylor and other representatives of a new, freer jazz that soared beyond the rhythmic and melodic tropes of the tradition. Influenced, in the breadth of his tone, by Sonny Rollins, Shepp played with abundant energy—his style was marked, however, with an occasional idiosyncratic, delicate romanticism. *Fire Music* found him exploring Ellington; *Mama Too Tight* incorporated R&B maneuvers; the drum-crazed *The Magic of Ju-Ju* mined African music and revealed a wicked sense of humor—all of these albums flourished Shepp's dazzlingly eclectic approach. Adamantly political, he examined, using the orchestral idiom, the Attica prison riots in *Attica Blues*; with Semenya McCord on vocals, *There's a Trumpet in My Soul* continued to reflect Shepp's world-music interests—he tackles sambas and other Brazilian forms. More recently, he's turned his attention back to earlier jazz and bop; the import *Looking at Bird* is an excellent Charlie Parker set.   — P.E.

ALLAN SHERMAN

★ ★ **Best of Allan Sherman (Rhino, 1979)**
★ ★ **A Gift of Laughter: The Best of Allan Sherman, Vol. 2 (Rhino, 1986)**
★ ★ ★ **My Son, the Greatest: The Best of Allan Sherman (Rhino, 1988)**

The late Allan Sherman's G-rated song parodies may seem quaint by today's standards, but one also hopes that contemporary audiences still have the capacity to laugh at humor as self-effacing, topical and inspired as this. Sherman, who began his career in show business as a comedy writer for Jackie Gleason (and went on to create the long-running TV quiz show "I've Got a Secret"), was adept at reconfiguring pop and folk tunes with lyrics that referenced the everyday travails of commonfolk young and old. His first hit, 1963's "Hello Muddah, Hello Fadduh," described a young boy's first camp experience and the passage from cowering fear to utter independence in little over two minutes. The song went to Number Two,

and thrust Sherman into a national spotlight he was ill-equipped to handle. Despite off-stage troubles, he remained prolific, producing three consecutive Number One albums, *My Son, the Folk Singer* (1962), *My Son, the Celebrity*, and *My Son, the Nut* (both from 1963). Sherman's great gift was sharp but compassionate wit and an ability to express his ethnicity in universal terms. All of Shermans' Warner Bros. albums are out of print, but the Rhino packages, particulary the 19-cut CD *My Son, the Greatest*, offer a representative sampling of the breadth of the artist's humor. The *Best of* cassettes largely duplicate the material on the CD, with a couple of notable exceptions, such as Volume 1's love song to a Martian beauty ("Eight Foot Two, Solid Blue") and Volume 2's "Grow, Mrs. Goldfarb." Of the out-of-print albums, the three *My Son . . .* LPs are keepers, as is the underappreciated *For Swinging Livers Only*, a 1964 release.   — D.M.

BOBBY SHERMAN

★ **The Very Best of Bobby Sherman (Restless, 1991)**

The kind of dimpled teen-idol who adorned an album (*With Love, Bobby*) with his baby pictures, Bobby Sherman was a singer so blithely robotic and contrived that he made Shawn Cassidy seem like Robert Johnson. "Julie, Do Ya Love Me" and "Easy Come, Easy Go" were his big early-'70s hits—showbiz fluff that doesn't even hold up as kitsch.   — P.E.

SHINEHEAD

★ ★ ★½ **Unity (Elektra, 1988)**
★ ★ ★ **The Real Rock (Elektra, 1990)**

Jamaican-born and Bronx-bred, Edmund Carl Aiken—a.k.a. Shinehead—deploys both sets of musical roots in a smooth, fiery rap-reggae blend. He hips and hops between the two styles on *Unity*, blending them on the should-have-been-a-hit "Chain Gang Rap." Grafting a humorous urban monologue onto a rhythmic revision of the Sam Cooke oldie "Chain Gang," Shinehead projects a low-key personal charm along with a taut command of the groove. On the rest of his debut, Shinehead fields def beats on several cuts produced by Jam Master Jay of Run-D.M.C. and keeps pace with the smoking Jamaican session band known as Roots Radics. A promising start, *Unity*'s ambitious scope also leaves Shinehead plenty of room to grow. Of course, the dreaded second album syndrome—a sudden paucity of fresh material—can strike even the most talented young artist. *The Real Rock* offers no gross disappointments and no surefire hooks, either—just a formulaic retread of Sly's "Family Affair" and some rather preachy attempts ("Strive") to put more of a message in the music. — M.C.

JOHNNY SHINES
★ ★ ★ ★ **Hey Ba-Ba-Re-Bop (Rounder, 1978)**
★ ★ ★ **Hangin' On (Rounder, 1980)**
★ ★ ★ **Mr. Blues Is Back to Stay (Rounder, 1981)**
★ ★ ★ **Traditional Delta Blues (Biograph, 1991)**

Born outside of Memphis and taught guitar by Howlin' Wolf, the exemplary Delta bluesman Johnny Shines traveled extensively with Robert Johnson and developed a solid, stirring repertoire of traditional Delta blues before electrifying his music to rousing effect. A live album recorded in 1974, *Hey Ba-Ba-Re-Bop*, catches a powerful Shines solo performance, his propulsive slide guitar lines providing stirring counterpoint to troubled tales of bad luck, bad women, and the search for spiritual redemption. As usual, Shines throws in a few Johnson songs—"Kind Hearted Woman," "Terraplane Blues"—and delivers moving versions of each. *Hangin' On* and *Mr. Blues Is Back to Stay* team Shines with fellow Delta bluesman and Johnson stepson Robert Jr. Lockwood, and the duo proceeds to take the blues in all sorts of directions. Theirs is a forward-thinking approach that would appear to have had some impact on the eclectic but blues-rooted style that has earned critical hosannahs for Robert Cray. — D.M.

THE SHIRELLES
★ ★ ★ ★ **The Shirelles Anthology (1959–1967) (Rhino, 1984)**
★ ★ ★ ★ **The Shirelles Anthology (1959–1964) (Rhino, 1986)**

In 1958 four young ladies from Passaic, New Jersey, joined together as a vocal quartet and adopted a name they thought had a feminine sound like that of the Chantels, the first of the great female groups in rock history. But the Shirelles were like the Chantels in more than name: when it came to delivering a lyric with passion, power and yearning, lead singer Shirley Alston gave little ground to the Chantels' Arlene Smith. And in the area of songs, Alston and her three friends had it all over the Chantels, whose chart run was as brief as it was brilliant. From 1958 through 1963 the Shirelles were mainstays on the pop

charts, rarely out of the Top Forty, and often in the Top Ten. Two singles, "Will You Love Me Tomorrow" (1960), written by Gerry Goffin and Carole King, and "Soldier Boy" (1962) went to Number One. Alston had a husky, sensuous voice and a sly delivery that gave the impression of someone telling a story in a disinterested manner, until she would burrow into a key lyric and let loose with all the pent-up passion in her heart. "Will You Love Me Tomorrow," "Mama Said" (1961) and "Foolish Little Girl" (1963) rank among the finest vocal performances of their time. The 1986 *Anthology* collects all the critical Shirelles tracks; the harder-to-find 1984 double album configuration also includes a number of B sides and unsuccessful singles, as well as oddities. — D.M.

SHIRLEY AND COMPANY
★ ★ ★ ½ **Shame Shame Shame (Vibration, 1975)**

Not to be confused with Evelyn "Champagne" King's sleek 1978 hit, "Shame," Shirley and Company's "Shame, Shame, Shame" boogied out of left field and onto the pop charts two years earlier. One of the first disco crossovers, "Shame, Shame, Shame" fits in the same pocket as the best-known records on Miami's T.K. label (KC's hits, George McCrae's "Rock Your Baby")—halfway between Jamaican reggae and New Orleans funk. Shirley Goodman interrupts male lead Jesus Alvarez's fly-guy spiel with piercing, gleeful admonishments: "Shame on you, if you can't dance, too." Her breathy tone is as captivating here as it is on Shirley & Lee's early-'60s New Orleans sides; maybe "Let the Good Times Roll" is the original disco song? Shirley and Company's long-lost debut album is a classic disco quickie, complete with cocktail-lounge instrumental versions of "Shame, Shame, Shame" and its soundalike follow-up "Cry, Cry, Cry." Producer Sylvia Robinson—of Mickey and Sylvia, "Pillow Talk" and Sugar Hill Records fame—drapes Shirley's seductive buzz in slinky, sweet soul on oddly compelling cuts like "Love Is" and "I Gotta Get Next to You." "Shame, Shame, Shame" is a true pop artifact, right down to its crude-but-effective cover illustration: "Disco Shirley" wagging her finger at Richard Milhous Nixon. — M.C.

SHIRLEY & LEE
★ ★ ★ ½ **Shirley & Lee: The Legendary Masters Series (EMI, 1990)**

Aided by a steady-rolling New Orleans beat supplied by ace drummer Earl Palmer, tenor saxophonist Lee Allen, guitarists Justin Adams and Ernest McLean, upright bassist Frank Fields and pianist Edward Frank, the sassy and often sensuous duets recorded by the New Orleans duo of Shirley & Lee were a mainstay on the R&B charts in the mid-'50s and rose into the Top Forty of the pop charts twice. Dubbed "The Sweethearts of the Blues," Shirley Goodman and Leonard Lee began their recording career in 1952 with "I'm Gone," a slow blues written by Lee and produced by New Orleans legend Dave Bartholomew. It rose to Number Two on the R&B charts and began a six-year run of Shirley & Lee hits on the Aladdin label, 20 of which are included on this set. Compared to the other great male singers working in New Orleans at that time, Lee's voice was average at best, but he made up in enthusiasm and energy what he lacked in technical facility; Shirley, on the other hand, overcame her own limitations with an insinuating, tinny voice and a sassy delivery. Lee became quite a prolific songwriter over the years—all but five of the tracks represented here are his originals—and penned two enduring rock & roll classics in "Feel So Good," from 1955, and the eternal watchword, "Let the Good Times Roll," from 1956. Bartholomew was the steady hand behind the board on all of the tracks here, which can be seen as laying the groundwork for the spate of male-female duos that infiltrated rock & roll as the '50s wore on. — D.M.

MICHELLE SHOCKED

★½ **The Texas Campfire Tapes (Mercury, 1986)**
★ **Short Sharp Shocked (Mercury, 1988)**
★ **Captain Swing (Mercury, 1989)**
★★½ **Arkansas Traveler (Mercury, 1992)**

In many ways the perfect modern folksinger, Michelle Shocked has more attitude than talent, and better schtick than songs. And while that combination has done much for her reputation on the folk circuit, it makes for pretty thin listening. *The Texas Campfire Tapes* captures her in the raw, so to speak, giving an impromptu performance by an actual campfire, and is her least affected recording. But both *Short Sharp Shocked* and *Captain Swing* are so full of musical posturing and ideological hectoring that it's hard to imagine anyone mistaking them for entertainment, much less art.

Fortunately, the ambitious *Arkansas Traveler* is more bearable than its

predecessors. Granted, that's not quite the same thing as saying the album is successful: Although her avowed intention is to illuminate the tradition of minstrelsy in American popular music, Shocked's songs as usual tell us more about her than her subject—but its 14 songs are fleshed out with such top-drawer talent (including Taj Mahal, Doc Watson, Pop Staples and the Red Clay Ramblers) that not even her ideological grandstanding can spoil the music. — J.D.C.

SHOES

★★★★ **Black Vinyl Shoes (1977; PVC, 1978)**
★★★ **Present Tense (Elektra, 1979)**
★★★★ **Tongue Twister (Elektra, 1981)**
★★★½ **Boomerang (1982; Black Vinyl, 1990)**
★★★½ **Silhouette (1984; Black Vinyl, 1991)**
★★★★ **Shoes Best (Black Vinyl, 1987)**
★★★★ **Present Tense/Tongue Twister (Black Vinyl, 1988)**
★★★½ **Stolen Wishes (Black Vinyl, 1989)**

This Zion, Illinois, quartet first attracted attention with a homemade album in 1977. Despite its crude living-room sound quality, *Black Vinyl Shoes* puts most of the subsequent power-pop bands to shame. That low-fi buzz gives the guitar lines a distinct melancholic character. Even in its earliest stages, the group juggles sweet vocal hooks and salty guitar riffs with aplomb. Though the Shoes' choice of subject matter rarely strays from the suburban single guy heartbreak blues, the presence of three strong writing and singing voices lends some needed variety. Bassist John Murphy and guitarists Jeff Murphy and Gary Klebe each contribute winning tracks to all of the Shoes' albums. If *Present Tense* suffers from the expected major-label upgrading, *Tongue Twister* leaps out of the speakers with full-bodied authority—the metallic finishing on "She Satisfies" definitely does the trick. *Boomerang* leans on the band's pensive and blue side, with keyboards and synths filling out the careful arrangements. Dropped by its American label, the Shoes released *Silhouette*—more pretty keyboards and sad songs—in England and Europe. After a protracted silence, the Shoes released *Stolen Wishes* on its own Black Vinyl label. Benefiting from the clarity of CD sound, the group's creamy harmonies, propulsive three-chord riffing and yearning choruses cut as deep as ever. — M.C.

THE SHOWMEN
★★ It Will Stand—Golden Classics
  (Collectables, NA)
It was one hit and out for this quintet in
1961 with the release of "It Will Stand," an
anthem in praise of rock & roll. This
16-track album is comprised of the title song
and various issued and unissued takes of
material cut for the Minit label in New
Orleans. Lead singer Norman Johnson has a
penetrating vocal style—bright, vigorous,
crisp—and the harmony singers work
themselves into some interesting
combinations, but there's nothing as
outstanding as "It Will Stand" in the rest of
the repertoire. Johnson later left the group
and formed the Chairmen of the Board,
singing lead on that group's 1970 hit, "Give
Me Just a Little More Time." — D.M.

JANE SIBERRY
★★★   No Borders Here (Open Air, 1983)
★★★   The Speckless Sky (Duke
        Street/Open Air, 1985)
  ★★½ The Walking (Duke Street/Reprise,
        1987)
★★★½ Bound by the Beauty (Duke
        Street/Reprise, 1989)
Graceful, literate and technically impressive,
Jane Siberry's first two records, *No Borders
Here* and *The Speckless Sky*, were knowing
variations on singer-songwriter themes—
love, isolation, nature—all put across in a
very careful style. *The Walking* was slight,
but with her fourth album, the Canadian
chanteuse achieved an understated triumph.
Bound by the Beauty is gorgeous music,
softly jazz-tinged at times, and on the title
track, "Hockey" and "Half Angel Half
Eagle" Siberry displays real poetic gifts. Her
tendency toward whimsy ("Everything
Reminds Me of My Dog") can get cloying;
otherwise, she's a writer of fine, closely
observed vignettes. — P.E.

THE SIDEWINDERS
★★★ Witchdoctor (RCA, 1989)
★★★ Auntie Ramos' Pool Hall (RCA, 1990)
Echoes of Paul Revere and the Raiders,
early Alice Cooper, the Clash, and Lou
Reed abound in the promising debut from a
Tuscon-based band. The point of view tends
to be insular and self-reliant—codified on a
morose, Zeppelin-like assault on Neil
Diamond's "Solitary Man"—with the world
viewed through a glass darkly. Songwriter-
guitarist Dave Slutes weighs in with a
growling, bluesy vocal style that adds
precisely the right touch of menace to the
grim proceedings herein. — D.M.

THE SILENCERS
★★★ A Letter From St. Paul (RCA, 1987)
★★★ A Blues for Buddha (RCA, 1989)
★★★ Dance to the Holy Man (RCA, 1991)
Brisk, tuneful and intense, this Glasgow
foursome makes very intelligent pop rock.
Vocalist/guitarist Jimme O'Neill and
guitarist Cha Burns come up with supple
melodies, often based on lean acoustic
figures, and then drive them home with
grace. Their album titles and such songs as
"God's Gift," off *A Letter From St. Paul*
and "John the Revelator" off *Dance to the
Holy Man* suggest that these boys are
indeed fired by some prophetic spirit—but
their lyrics are often as angry as they are
inspirational. Less literal about their fervor
than U2, they still share with that band a
sensibility of high passion. — P.E.

SILLY WIZARD
★★★½ So Many Partings (Shanachie, 1985)
★★★½ Wild and Beautiful (Shanachie,
        1986)
★★★   Kiss the Tears Away (Shanachie,
        1987)
★★★½ The Best of Silly Wizard
        (Shanachie, 1987)
★★★   Caledonia's Hardy Sons (Shanachie,
        1989)
Masters of classic Scottish folk, this quartet
turns out trad fare and original tunes that
make the most of Phil Cunningham's
fleet-fingered accordion work and Andy
Stewart's high, strong voice. Occasionally
they'll augment their banjo-and-guitar
energy with synthesized string ensembles
and electric piano, but their sound remains
direct and uncluttered; they achieve a fierce
loveliness. Consistently expert in its choice
of material, Silly Wizard hasn't made a bad
album: *Wild and Beautiful* and *So Many
Partings* may be the best, but all the discs
feature highland delights. — P.E.

THE SILOS
★★★   About Her Steps (Record Collect,
        1985)
★★★   Cuba (Record Collect, 1987)
★★★½ The Silos (RCA, 1990)
Guitarists and singers Walter Salas-Humara
and Bob Rupe led this subtle New York
quintet, whose spare, smart updating of
folk-rock styles is immediately enjoyable and
wears very well. When the band rocks, they
sound a bit like Crazy Horse; their slower
material features unemphatic but insinuating
melodies—they're ballads that are built to
last. Both singers favor casual, plain-spoken
deliveries; neither of them is a flashy player,

and their emphasis is placed squarely on the songs.

On *About Her Steps*, the standouts are "4 Wanted Signs," with its engaging pedal steel, and the moody "Start the Clock." "Going Round," off *Cuba*, features a great string arrangement, as do some of the standouts on *The Silos*, the band's major-label debut. From the elegant "Pictures of Helen" to the Keith Richards–like kick of "Don't Talk This Way," *The Silos* is confident music, and the group's best record. — P.E.

CARLY SIMON

★★ Carly Simon (Elektra, 1970)
★★½ Anticipation (Elektra, 1971)
★★★½ No Secrets (Elektra, 1972)
★★ Hotcakes (Elektra, 1974)
★★ Playing Possum (Elektra, 1975)
★★★½ The Best of Carly Simon (Elektra, 1975)
★★★ Another Passenger (Elektra, 1976)
★★★ Boys in the Trees (Elektra, 1978)
★★★ Spy (Warner Bros., 1979)
★★½ Come Upstairs (Warner Bros., 1980)
★★½ Torch (Warner Brothers, 1981)
★★★ Hello Big Man (Warner Bros., 1983)
★★ Spoiled Girl (Epic, 1985)
★★½ Coming Around Again (Arista, 1987)
★★★ Greatest Hits Live (Arista, 1989)
★★½ My Romance (Arista, 1990)
★★★ Have You Seen Me Lately (Arista, 1990)

Long on atmosphere and short on vocal precision, Carly Simon's first few hits left a deep impression nevertheless. "That's the Way I've Always Heard It Should Be" (from *Carly Simon*) hangs in the air like an unfinished argument; Simon's postadolescent discovery—that many marriages are empty façades—echoes amid a hushed, somewhat melodramatic setting. This confessional approach can sound unbearably self-conscious when Simon doesn't have a catchy chorus at her disposal, which is most of the time on the debut. *Anticipation*'s title track and "Legend in Your Own Time" both match the lush, musing tone of "That's the Way I Always Heard It Should Be" sigh for sigh, positioning Carly as a natural singles artist and a (mild) feminist presence on the pop charts.

Hooking up with producer Richard Perry seemed to bolster Simon's confidence as a singer and writer. On the 1972 Number One "You're So Vain," Simon (with backup singer and lookalike Mick Jagger) lacerates a self-satisfied playboy with a double-edged hook: "You probably think this song is about you, don't you?" The rest of *No Secrets* integrates Simon's tell-all assertiveness with Perry's post-folkie popcraft, while Carly's marriage to James Taylor is celebrated on "The Right Thing to Do." Both those sources of inspiration soon ran dry, however. *Hotcakes* (home of the squawky duet "Mockingbird") is James and Carly's attempt to open a mom & pop record franchise; in this case, the couple that played together didn't stay together. On *Playing Possum* Perry and Simon's collaboration starts to go sour; the disco-EST groove on "Attitude Dancing" comes off as glib and irritating. In fact, *The Best of Carly Simon* gets sabatoged by the unavoidable inclusion of the later hits. Her best is a very mixed bag.

Another Passenger resembles the typical L.A. supersession of the period, but Simon's strengthened voice is more than up to the task of covering the Doobie Brothers ("It Keeps You Runnin' ") and Little Feat ("One Love Stand"). *Boys in the Trees* reemphasizes Simon's own relationship songs and moody set pieces, though "You Belong to Me" (co-written by Doobie Michael McDonald) projects a pop-soul warmth that's quite unlike her previous work. *Spy* contains a couple of her most incisive lyrics since "You're So Vain" ("Vengeance," "We're So Close"), while "Jesse" (from the otherwise lackluster *Come Upstairs*) reached the Number 11 in 1980. *Hello Big Man* is a much more relaxed and sexy effort; even the reggae-flavored collaborations with Sly and Robbie work better than you'd expect. *Torch* (1981) and *My Romance* (1990) find Simon negotiating prerock balladry with surprisingly stiff results. She's better at interpreting her own words.

Carly Simon reached a nadir on *Spoiled Girl*, as too many meddling producers spoiled her always-distinctive soup. Her late-'80s comeback got off to a slow start with the tepid 'n' tasteful *Coming Around Again*, but *Have You Seen Me Lately* is up to speed. The music moves along at a stately—almost New Age–influenced—pace, which suits the somewhat ponderous tone of "Didn't I" and "Life Is Eternal." And on "Happy Birthday," Carly Simon commits a grown-up-and-sober anthem that sounds as clear and unsentimental as her warbly, weathered voice. — M.C.

JOE SIMON

★ ★ ★½ **Drowning in a Sea of Love (Ace, 1972)**

★ ★½ **Get Down (Ace, 1975)**

★ ★ ★ **Lookin' Back: The Best of Joe Simon (Charly/Ripete, 1989)**

In the late '60s, Joe Simon recorded a clutch of heartbreakers—most notably "The Chokin' Kind" (1969)—that established him as an intelligent, understated deliverer of lush ballads. Teaming up with Gumble and Huff, Simon then recorded "Drowning in a Sea of Love," a magnificent portrayal of erotic obsession—the singer's strong voice loses its ususal cool as the instrumentation swirls toward crescendo. While Simon never achieved the high-profile fame of R&B's legends, his work remains memorable: check out the early gems on *Lookin' Back.* — P.E.

PAUL SIMON

★ ★ ★ ★½ **Paul Simon (1972; Warner Bros., 1988)**

★ ★ ★ ★ **There Goes Rhymin' Simon (1973; Warner Bros., 1988)**

★ ★ ★½ **Live Rhymin' (1974; Warner Bros., 1988)**

★ ★ ★ ★ ★ **Still Crazy After All These Years (1975; Warner Bros., 1988)**

★ ★ ★½ **One-Trick Pony (Warner Bros., 1980)**

★ ★ ★ **Hearts and Bones (Warner Bros., 1983)**

★ ★ ★ ★ ★ **Graceland (Warner Bros., 1986)**

★ ★ ★ ★ **Negotiations and Love Songs (Warner Bros., 1988)**

★ ★ ★ ★ ★ **The Rhythm of the Saints (Warner Bros., 1990)**

★ ★ ★ ★ **Paul Simon's Concert in the Park (Warner Bros., 1991)**

When he was half of Simon & Garfunkel, part of what earned Paul Simon his reputation was the near-literary quality of his wordplay in telling social sketches like "The Dangling Conversation" or picaresque epics like "America." But when Simon set out on his own, what set his work apart from that of other singer-songwriters was the music. That's not to say he downplays his words, of course, but as *Paul Simon* makes plain, his lyrics are only part of the picture. After all, no matter how much the words might add to the story of "Me and Julio Down by the Schoolyard," what ultimately sets the tone for the song is the breathless strum of the calypso-flavored arrangement—just as the mournful Andean pipes in "Duncan" underscore its plaintive longing, or the reggae rhythms beneath "Mother and Child Reunion" shore up its irrepressible optimism.

Simon's stylistic diversity is equally apparent in *There Goes Rhymin' Simon*, even if the music he draws from isn't quite so foreign. Instead of continuing the Third World eclecticism of its predecessor, *Rhymin'* is almost self-consciously American in its focus. "Loves Me Like a Rock," for instance, draws from the gospel quartets of the '40s; "Take Me to the Mardi Gras" (which boasts exquisite vocal counterpoint by the Rev. Claude Jeter) not only evokes the sound of New Orleans but even leaves room for a chorus or two from the Onward Brass Band, while Simon's "American Tune" sets its view of the American dream to a stately, hymn-like melody that could as easily have come from *The Bay Psalm Book*. Yet as exciting as his wide-ranging approach was, it did have its liabilities, as the concert recording *Live Rhymin'* shows. On that album Simon sidesteps the Latin undercurrents of "Me and Julio," treats musical guests Urubamba and the Jessy Dixon singers as special effects rather than parts of a unified band, and reduces "Mother and Child Reunion" and "Loves Me Like a Rock" to their common ingredients.

Perhaps that's why Simon's next few albums avoid the exotic, tending instead toward singer-songwriter conventionality. Not that his listeners lost out on the deal; his first album in this vein, *Still Crazy After All These Years*, is one of his very best. Working with jazz- or R&B-oriented session players, Simon gets a highly crafted, but in no way slick or sterile, sound. Songs like "My Little Town" (a reunion of sorts for Simon & Garfunkel), "50 Ways to Leave Your Lover" and "I Do It for Your Love" use their polish to bring out the emotional undertones in Simon's singing. By contrast, the songs on *One-Trick Pony* sound somewhat stilted—but then, this is not just an album but a soundtrack, meaning that these pieces do double duty as musical set-pieces and plot expediters. It's not a comfortable mix, and apart from moments like "Ace in the Hole" or "Late in the Evening," which let Simon's band show its stuff, the album is one of Simon's least involving works. Still, *One-Trick Pony* is at least musically coherent, which is more than can be said for *Hearts and Bones*. On that album, Simon pursues the same course as he did on *Still Crazy*, but the match between his songs and their settings is maddeningly uneven; some songs, like "Hearts and

Bones" or "Train in the Distance," seem under-supported by the backing tracks, while others—"Think Too Much (a)" or "Cars Are Cars"—are almost overwhelmed by the rhythm tracks.

Simon shifted gears for his next project and returned to the globe-trotting approach of *Paul Simon* for *Graceland*. Although this album is probably best known for its use of South African mbaqanga and mbube idioms, the truth is that apart from a tune like "I Know What I Know," which essentially finds Simon singing over a track originally recorded by General M.D. Shirinda and the Gaza Sisters, the songs merely fuse South African elements with Western pop. To that extent, Simon's real genius is in understanding what South African musicians like guitarist Ray Phiri, bassist Baghiti Khumalo and the mbube choir Ladysmith Black Mambazo could add to his songs, and working in collaboration with them. At root, the real appeal of "You Can Call Me Al," "The Boy in the Bubble" or "Graceland" itself is the way the African influences enhance the singer's melodic ideas. (*Negotiations and Love Songs*, which followed, is a best-of meant to update and replace Columbia's long-deleted 1977 album, *Greatest Hits, Etc.*).

The Rhythm of the Saints applies the same strategy with similar success. This time around, though, Simon's starting point is the music of Brazil, but rather than take the usual samba-style approach of American pop artists, he develops a sound that's far more unique, balancing the cool, percussive chatter of Uakti against J.J. Cale's blues guitar on "Can't Run But," or using his acoustic guitar to play off the rhythmic throb of the Olodum drum band. And unlike the problems with *Live Rhymin'*, Simon's genre-blending this time around proved far more easily translated to the concert arena; in fact, the Afro-Brazilian-American band featured on *Paul Simon's Concert in the Park* not only sails through the songs from *Graceland* and *Rhythm of the Saints*, but brings new life to the likes of "Me and Julio," "Late in the Evening" and even "Bridge Over Troubled Water." — J.D.C.

SIMON AND GARFUNKEL

★★ **Wednesday Morning, 3 A.M. (Columbia, 1966)**

★★★ **Sounds of Silence (Columbia, 1966)**

★★★★ **Parsley, Sage, Rosemary and Thyme (Columbia, 1966)**

★★★½ **The Graduate (Columbia, 1968)**

★★★½ **Bookends (Columbia, 1968)**

★★★★★ **Bridge Over Troubled Water (Columbia, 1970)**

★★★★★ **Greatest Hits (Columbia, 1972)**

★★★ **The Concert in Central Park (Warner Bros., 1982)**

★★★★½ **Collected Works (Columbia, 1990)**

Although Simon and Garfunkel made their name as America's most accessible folk act, in truth the duo's success represented something altogether different—acoustic pop's transition from the singalong simplicity of folk music to the commercially savvy craft of the singer-songwriters. Ironically, it was a role the duo fell into almost by accident, having split up after releasing a fairly conventional folk album entitled *Wednesday Morning, 3 A.M.* But "The Sounds of Silence" became a massive hit after producer Tom Wilson dubbed electric guitar and drums onto that album's acoustic arrangement, and they reunited to record an album of similarly flavored folk-rock. In addition to the revamped version of its title tune, *Sounds of Silence* also includes "Richard Cory" and "I Am a Rock," but for the most part, the album downplays its pop ambitions, sticking close to understated guitar-and-voice arrangements.

With *Parsley, Sage, Rosemary and Thyme,* the duo's break with folkie convention becomes more pronounced. Although the album-opening "Scarborough Fair/Canticle" maintains Simon and Garfunkel's attachment to tradition, the music's point of reference shifts from the coffeehouse to the drawing room, as Simon's songwriting moves toward the increasingly personal perspective of songs like "The Dangling Conversation" and "For Emily, Whenever I May Find Her." Of course, as the Dylan-savaging "A Simple Desultory Philippic" makes plain, there's a world of difference between the personal and the solipsistic, and Simon's buoyant sense of melody ensures that these songs are pop-friendly; indeed, "Homeward Bound" was a Top Five single. *Bookends* continues that progression, with a wider range of songs and even more ambitious arrangements than its predecessor. Yet its strength has less to do with the uncluttered appeal of songs like "Mrs. Robinson" or "A Hazy Shade of Winter" than the way the duo managed to make the rambling melodies of "Fakin' It" and "America" seem just as straightforward.

From there, it's an easy leap past the soundtrack album from *The Graduate* (which merely reiterated tracks from *Sounds of Silence*, *Bookends* and *Parsley, Sage, Rosemary and Thyme*) to *Bridge Over Troubled Water*, the pair's final and most successful studio album. A stunning piece of popcraft, it finds hooks in the most unlikely places—the Peruvian folk tune that was the basis for "El Condor Pasa," say, or the way Garfunkel's angelic tenor contrasted against the gospel piano of "Bridge Over Troubled Water," or the bass harmonica groove that fires up the last verse of "The Boxer"—and remains one of the most irresistibly tuneful albums of its day. It, along with all of *Bookends, Parsley, Sage, Rosemary and Thyme, Sounds of Silence* and *Wednesday Morning, 3 A.M.*, is included in the set *Collected Works*.

Simon and Garfunkel never cut another album's worth of new material, but they did record together after *Bridge Over Troubled Water*. Unfortunately, their first post-breakup hit, "My Little Town," is not included on Simon and Garfunkel's *Greatest Hits*, but can be found on Simon's *Still Crazy After All These Years* and Garfunkel's *Breakaway*. "Wake Up Little Susie" is one of the few non-nostalgic moments on *The Concert in Central Park*, which documents Simon and Garfunkel's 1981 reunion show. — J.D.C.

NINA SIMONE
★ ★ ★½ Silk and Soul (RCA, 1967)
★ ★ ★½ 'Nuff Said (RCA, 1968)
★ ★ ★½ Black Gold (RCA, 1970)
★ ★ ★½ Emergency Ward (RCA, 1972)
★ ★ ★½ It Is Finished (RCA, 1972)
★ ★ ★ ★ The Best of Nina Simone (Phillips, 1969)
★ ★ ★ ★ The Best of Nina Simone (RCA, 1970)
★ ★ ★½ Here Comes the Sun (RCA, 1971)
★ ★ ★½ Baltimore (CTI, 1978)
★ ★ ★½ Let It Be Me (Verve, 1987)
★ ★ ★ ★ Don't Let Me Be Misunderstood (Mercury, 1988)
★ ★ ★½ Live (Zeta, 1990)
★ ★ ★ ★ The Blues (Novus/RCA, 1991)

Dubbed "The High Priestess of Soul," Nina Simone isn't so much an R&B singer as a highly artful interpreter of all kinds of music—jazz, traditional ballads and African songs, folk and pop. A skillful, understated pianist, she's also an inventive arranger; virtually all of her covers transform the original songs into music more elegant, leaner, more haunting. As a vocalist, Simone

swings with a nearly austere finesse—her trademark is authority. Many of her individual albums are hard to find, but she's been served well by compilations. The Phillips *Best of* concentrates on her mid-'60s material (she had hits with "I Put a Spell on You" and "Don't Let Me Be Misunderstood"); the RCA collection of later work features outstanding takes on material by Gershwin, Dylan, Leonard Cohen and Jimmy Webb. The concert sets, *Live* and *Let It Be Me*, are also exceptional, with Simone's gruff-graceful delivery taking on a more assertive edge in concert. The best intro to her work, though, is probably Novus's *The Blues*: with such ace musicians as drummer Bernard Purdie and guitarist Eric Gale, she takes on Dylan's "I Shall Be Released" and Hoyt Axton's "The Pusher," sets Langston Hughes's "Backlash Blues" to music and, accompanied only by herself on piano, delivers one of the strongest of her own compositions, "Nobody's Fault but Mine." Nothing Simone ever did lacked class, however, so all her albums are worth checking out. — P.E.

SIMPLE MINDS
★ ★ Life in a Day (1979; Virgin, 1987)
★ ★ Real to Real Cacophony (1980; Virgin, 1982)
★ ★ Empires and Dance (1980; Virgin, 1982)
★ ★ ★ Sons and Fascination/Sister Feelings Call (Virgin, 1981)
★ ★ ★ Sister Feelings Call (1981; Virgin, 1987)
★ ★ Celebration (Virgin, 1982)
★ ★½ Themes for Great Cities (Stiff, 1982)
★ ★ ★ New Gold Dream (81-82-83-84) (1982; Virgin/A&M, 1987)
★ ★ ★ Sparkle in the Rain (A&M, 1984)
★ ★ ★½ Once Upon a Time (A&M, 1985)
★ ★ ★ Simple Minds Live: In the City of Light (A&M, 1987)
★ ★½ Street Fighting Years (A&M, 1989)
★ ★ ★ Real Life (A&M, 1991)

It's a thin line between pretension and profundity, but Scotland's Simple Minds have made quite a career of walking that tightrope. Attaching the grand designs of art-rock to a mechanical postdisco beat, the early albums sound overstretched and a bit hollow. (*Life in a Day* and *Real to Real Cacophony* remain in print, if people care to re-create the peculiar ambience of early-'80s "new-wave disco" in their living rooms.) The pieces fall into place on *Sister Feelings Call* (originally released with *Sons and*

Fascination): singer Jim Kerr's passion, guitarist Charlie Burchill's subtle eruptions, keyboardist Michael McNeil's rich synthesizer palate. "The American" and "20th Century Promised Land" stake a solid claim next to U2's anthemic turf. *New Gold Dream* heightens that sensation by applying layers and layers of quiet synthesizers. Even though the overall sound is more ethereal and less propulsive, "Promised You a Miracle" kicks in with a deft melodic thrust—and yes, a pop hook. Thus begins Simple Minds' decline, at least in the minds of its cult. Mainstream American audiences felt differently. *Sparkle in the Rain* begins the group's love-hate affair with R.O.C.K. in the U.S.A, striking an unlikely balance between headphone rumination and stadium boogie. The breakthrough hit "Don't You (Forget About Me)," from the soundtrack of *The Breakfast Club*, dangerously flirts with Billy Idol-atry, but Simple Minds are too sharp for the panderer's trap. *Once Upon a Time* makes the most of that opening; Kerr brings a newfound directness to more firmly ground material. On songs like "Sanctify Yourself" and "Alive and Kicking," Simple Minds realizes its lofty ambitions.

Live: In the City of Light captures the band at its peak, spurred on by drummer Mel Gaynor and back-up singer Robin Clark. *Street Fighting Years* finds Simple Minds adrift in a sea of foggy synth washes and half-baked politics, however. Alienating new converts in the States, *Years* perversely re-established Simple Minds as British superstars. Just as unexpectedly, *Real Life* snaps back with confidence and grace. "See the Lights" and the title track rank with the group's most affecting work. — M.C.

SIMPLY RED

★★★ **Picture Book (Elektra, 1986)**
★★★ **Men and Women (Elektra, 1987)**
★★½ **A New Flame (Elektra, 1989)**
★★★½ **Stars (EastWest, 1991)**
With breezy confidence, singer Mick Hucknall staked a firm claim on pop-soul territory with Simply Red's debut album. The 1986 Number One "Holding Back the Year" established his deft, understated way with a ballad. *Picture Book*'s other standout track is a cover of the Valentine Brothers' funky protest "Money's Too Tight (to Mention)." No individual cut on *Men and Women* strikes as deep, but the band's musical attack is fortified and expanded. Hucknall co-writes with Motown veteran Lamont Dozier ("Infidelity," "Suffer"),

covers Bunny Wailer ("Love Fire") and Sly Stone ("Let Me Have It All"), tries his own hand at writing topically informed love songs ("Move On Out"), and respectfully tackles Cole Porter ("Ev'ry Time We Say Goodbye"). The results are mixed, though the overall effect is stimulating.

Rather abruptly, *A New Flame* swerves toward the middle of the road. Luxuriant cocktail-jazz noodling and Hucknall's flaccid Teddy Pendergrass imitation on the hit version of "If You Don't Know Me By Now" point Simply Red straight toward adult-contemporary, VH-1 limbo status. So *Stars* couldn't come as more of a surprise—or relief. The fourth Simply Red album is a stripped-down set of originals, superbly sung without a trace of rootsy nostalgia or gross crossover ambition. On *Stars* Simply Red's true colors shine.
— M.C.

FRANK SINATRA

★★★★★ **Songs for Young Lovers (Capitol, 1954)**
★★★★ **Swing Easy (Capitol, 1955)**
★★★★★ **In the Wee Small Hours (Capitol, 1955)**
★★★★★ **Songs for Swingin' Lovers (Capitol, 1956)**
★★★½ **Close to You (Capitol, 1956)**
★★★★★ **A Swingin' Affair! (Capitol, 1957)**
★★★★★ **Where Are You (Capitol, 1957)**
★★★★★ **Come Fly With Me (Capitol, 1958)**
★★★★★ **Only the Lonely (Capitol, 1958)**
★★★★★ **Come Dance With Me (Capitol, 1959)**
★★★★ **The Rare Sinatra (Capitol, 1959)**
★★★★ **No One Cares (Capitol, 1959)**
★★★★★ **Nice 'n' Easy (Capitol, 1960)**
★★★½ **All the Way (Capitol, 1960)**
★★★★½ **Sinatra's Swingin' Session (Capitol, 1961)**
★★★½ **Ring-a-Ding Ding! (Reprise, 1961)**
★★ **Come Swing With Me! (Capitol, 1961)**
★★★★★ **Frank Sinatra—20 Golden Greats (Capitol, 1961)**
★★★½ **Sinatra Swings (Reprise, 1961)**
★★★½ **I Remember Tommy (Reprise, 1961)**
★★½ **Sinatra and Strings (Reprise, 1962)**
★★½ **Sinatra and Swingin' Brass (Reprise, 1962)**

640 • Frank Sinatra

★ ★ ★   Sinatra Sings of Love and
Things! (Capitol, 1962)

★ ★½ Point of No Return (Capitol,
1962)

★ ★½ Sinatra Sings Great Songs from
Great Britain (Reprise, 1962)

★ ★ ★ ★ Sinatra and Basie (Reprise,
1962)

★ ★ ★½ Sinatra's Sinatra (Reprise,
1963)

★ ★   Days of Wine and Roses, Moon
River and Other Academy
Award Winners (Reprise,
1964)

★ ★   It Might as Well Be Swing
(Reprise, 1964)

★ ★   Softly as I Leave You (Reprise,
1964)

★ ★   Sinatra for the Sophisticated
(Capitol, 1965)

★ ★ ★ ★ ★ September of My Years
(Reprise, 1965)

★ ★ ★ Moonlight Sinatra (Reprise,
1965)

★ ★ ★ ★ ★ Sinatra—A Man and his Music
(Reprise, 1965)

★ ★ ★ Strangers in the Night (Reprise,
1966)

★ ★½ Sinatra at the Sands (with
Count Basie and his Orchestra)
(Reprise, 1966)

★ ★ ★ ★ Francis Albert Sinatra and
Antonio Carlos Jobim (Reprise,
1967)

★ ★ ★ ★ Francis A. Sinatra and Edward
K. Ellington (Reprise, 1967)

★ ★½ Frank Sinatra and the World
We Knew (Reprise, 1967)

★ ★   Cycles (Reprise, 1968)

★ ★   My Way (Reprise, 1969)

★ ★   A Man Alone (Reprise, 1969)

★ ★   Watertown (Reprise, 1970)

★ ★   Sinatra and Company (Reprise,
1971)

★ ★ ★ Frank Sinatra's Greatest Hits,
Vol. 2 (Reprise, 1972)

★ ★ ★½ Ol' Blue Eyes Is Back (Reprise,
1973)

★ ★½ Some Nice Things I've Missed
(Reprise, 1974)

★ ★ ★½ Frank (Reprise, 1973)

★ ★   Sinatra—The Main Event Live
(Reprise, 1974)

★ ★ ★ ★ Sinatra—The Reprise Years
(Reprise, 1975)

★ ★ ★½ Portrait of Sinatra (400 Songs
From the Life of a Man)
(Reprise, 1977)

★ ★ ★ ★ Trilogy: Past, Present and
Future (Reprise, 1980)

★ ★ ★ She Shot Me Down (Reprise,
1981)

★ ★ ★ ★½ The Dorsey/Sinatra Sessions,
Vol. 1 (1940) (RCA, 1982)

★ ★ ★ ★½ The Dorsey/Sinatra Sessions,
Vol. 2 (1940-1) (RCA, 1982)

★ ★ ★ ★½ The Dorsey/Sinatra Sessions,
Vol. 3 (1941-2) (RCA, 1982)

★ ★ ★ ★½ The Dorsey/Sinatra Radio
Years (RCA, 1983)

★ ★ ★ L.A. is My Lady (Reprise,
1984)

★ ★ ★ ★ All-Time Classics (Pair, 1986)

★ ★ ★ ★ ★ The Voice: The Columbia Years
(1943-1952) (Columbia, 1986)

★ ★ ★ ★½ Tommy Dorsey/Frank Sinatra,
All-Time Greatest Hits. Vol 1
(RCA, 1988)

★ ★ ★ ★½ Tommy Dorsey/Frank Sinatra,
All-Time Greatest Hits. Vol 2
(RCA, 1988)

★ ★ ★ ★½ Tommy Dorsey/Frank Sinatra,
All-Time Greatest Hits, Vol. 3
(RCA, 1989)

★ ★ ★ ★½ Tommy Dorsey/Frank Sinatra,
All-Time Greatest Hits Vol. 4
(RCA, 1990)

★ ★ ★ ★ ★ The Capitol Years (Capitol,
1990)

★ ★ ★ ★ ★ The Reprise Collection (Reprise,
1990)

Combining a jazz player's technique, an
actor's sense of language, and the
instinctual, provocative style of a natural
star, Frank Sinatra transformed American
pop culture. For a very long time, almost all
of his maneuvers were oracular. At first
merely the special attraction of Tommy
Dorsey's orchestra, he so outdistanced his
horn-playing mentors and peers that he
speeded the end of the big-band era that
had brought him to prominence; after
Sinatra (who patterned his phrasing on
Dorsey's trombone), no instrumentalist
would rival a singer as the essential player
in pop music. While learning much from the
melodic qualities of bel canto and from Bing
Crosby's crooning (both forms emphasizing
the sound of lyrics rather than their sense),
Sinatra sang with a sure understanding of
American speech—Crosby deployed words
as mellifluous syllables; Sinatra interpreted
them, and in doing so, not only made
language matter in a way it had mattered
only in blues, folk and country music, but,
however unconsciously, paved the way for
Dylan and the language-experiments of '60s
songwriters. Sinatra's colloquialism, too,
helped make American music the world's
primary popular form; before him, the style

of mainstream singers had derived from music hall and light opera—ultimately, from European, classical sources. Sinatra learned his vernacular approach from jazz and blues singers—he maintained that his greatest influence was Billie Holiday—and in turning to jazz, he was again prophetic; Elvis would follow, drawing from the blues inspiration that caused the century's other great pop upheaval. Finally, through his movies, his raffish fashion sense, and his tense charismatic combination of hurt romanticism and gangster swagger, Sinatra defined a certain kind of American male—a Bogart with a microphone, a guy tough enough to be tender.

A good place to begin considering Sinatra's voluminous recording history is with four brilliant, very different compilations. A three-album set, *The Dorsey-Sinatra Sessions* features the voice that drove crowds of early-'40's bobby-soxers crazy at New York's Paramount Theatre. Dorsey's swing band soars, and Sinatra's approach is that of a prodigy: he vocalizes with an almost eerie, sure purity—it's the sound of a singer surprising himself with his skill. The often-sappy material is cuddle-up music at its sweetest ("Head on My Pillow," "Shake Down the Stars"); the youth idol identifies completely with his audience, a following to whom he will soon refuse to condescend but, instead, grow with (his later career longevity is a product of Sinatra's ongoing creative impatience; he would become one of pop's few stars to embrace aging, to wrench from the fact of mortality an eloquent pathos). In 1942 Sinatra left Dorsey, and *The Columbia Years* records his next decade. Alex Stordahl becomes his arranger-conductor and, by piling up the strings and harps, crafts lush, heady backdrops. This is Sinatra at his most romantic (and, at times, his least effective), but already he's inching ahead of the game—the first singer to manipulate the microphone as other players work their trumpets or saxes, he whispers, strains and "talks" while he sings, and the effective combat of Stordahl's orchestral classicism and Sinatra's saloon smarts creates stirring, subtextual tension.

The Capitol Years is Sinatra coming into his own. Three arrangers—Nelson Riddle, Gordon Jenkins and Billy May—freed him not only to swing but to get serious by treating lyrics with an unprecedented attention. On Riddle's *In the Wee Small Hours*, the happy-go-lucky crooner has been replaced by the ruminative cosmopolitan;

Sinatra comes across harder and bluer than he ever has before. Gordon Jenkins's *Where Are You* is Sinatra as pop existentialist, anxious and intense. With Billy May's *Come Fly With Me*, Frank's high humor and casual zest come to the fore; as cocky as his trademark snap-brimmed hat, the songs swing with risky exhilaration. *The Capitol Years* covers the hits, but also necessary are *Songs for Young Lovers, Songs for Swingin' Lovers, Only the Lonely, A Swingin' Affair, Come Dance With Me* and *Nice 'n' Easy*.

Founding Reprise Records in 1961, Sinatra spent the decade working with a remarkable spectrum of arrangers (Riddle, May, Jenkins, Sy Oliver, Don Costa, Neal Hefti, Quincy Jones) and genre giants (jazz legends Duke Ellington and Count Basie, bossa nova artist Antonio Carlos Jobim and Latin music maestro Eumi Deodato). It could be argued that the ascendancy of rock & roll indirectly encouraged Sinatra to react and evolve—whatever the source of his impressive restlessness, its results were fascinating. Sometimes he faltered when trying out newer songwriters (Joni Mitchell, Rod McKuen, John Hartford)—*Cycles*, from 1968, is a representative lowpoint—sometimes he triumphed (Jenkins's *September of My Years*). From the standpoint of musical technique, Sinatra's '60s work lacks the assurance of some of his previous work; if read, however, like a great psychological novel, this stretch of time is infinitely richer—in equal measure tentative, defensive and courageous, he fights the onslaught of a newer popular music, and, on occasion, cagily concedes to it; at times, he gives in to self-parody, at others, he rises to sing with a new, wounded wisdom. In the '60s, it's not so much Sinatra the Musician but Sinatra the Myth that provides excitement—his romance with Ava Gardner, the allegations of Mafia involvement, the Vegas hijinks of the Rat Pack, the brawls with reporters and his odd, compelling pose as both bully and underdog make Sinatra less of an artist (or show-biz commodity) than an American legend—a character study of a fighter cornered both by the passage of time and his own demons. *The Reprise Collection* is hardly exhaustive in its study of the period, but it's a very capable sampler: its contents comprise a riveting autobiography. Among Sinatra's essential individual albums of the time are *Francis A. Sinatra and Edward K. Ellington, Francis Albert Sinatra and Antonio Carlos Jobim*, and *Sinatra and Basie*.

In 1980 Sinatra released his last epic,

Trilogy. Don Costa's arrangement of "Theme From New York, New York," gave the singer another signature tune to stand alongside "Nancy With the Laughing Face," "It Was a Very Good Year," "Strangers in the Night" and "My Way." Gordon Jenkins provided embarrassing, inflated "Ol'-Blues-Eyes-Is-God" stuff; and Billy May resurrected the swinging '50s. A valorous attempt to prove Sinatra's staying power, it succeeded triumphantly—the man's voice sometimes betrayed itself, but the spirit remained indomitable. — P.E.

NANCY SINATRA
★★ **Nancy and Lee (Rhino, 1986)**
★★ **The Hit Years (Rhino, 1986)**
★★ **All-Time Hits (Rhino, 1986)**
Part snarl, part fashion statement, Nancy's 1966 "These Boots Are Made for Walkin' " was an ultracommercial variant of the "in-your-face" message song all '60s acts included. Soon after, she released "Sugar Town," a nice, flirtatious tidbit. Finally, with "Somethin' Stupid," she made room for Daddy (Frank, of course, dominates the jingle). Even though these records contained all Nancy had to "say," she kept on going—like a trouper. A certain period charm may adhere to her fluff, but anything else is disastrous—country: the duet with moose-voiced Lee Hazlewood on the Johnny Cash–June Carter theme song "Jackson"; soundtrack epics: "You Only Live Twice"; lush balladry: "Summer Wine." Most of her songs were penned by Hazlewood, Duane Eddy's chief writer, and they're inflated formula schlock. — P.E.

SIOUXSIE AND THE BANSHEES
★★★★ **The Scream (1978; Geffen, 1984)**
★★½ **Join Hands (1979; Geffen, 1984)**
★★★ **Kaleidoscope (1980; Geffen, 1984)**
★★★ **Ju Ju (1981; Geffen, 1984)**
★★★★ **Once Upon a Time/The Singles (1981; Geffen, 1984)**
★★★ **A Kiss in the Dreamhouse (1982; Geffen, 1984)**
★★★ **Nocturne (Geffen, 1983)**
★★★ **Hyaena (Geffen, 1984)**
★★★½ **Tinderbox (Geffen, 1986)**
★★½ **Through the Looking Glass (Geffen, 1987)**
★★½ **Peep Show (Geffen, 1988)**
★★★ **Superstition (Geffen, 1991)**
Along with Billy Idol and Sid Vicious, Siouxsie Sioux (formerly Susan Dallion) first gained notoriety as a highly visible and vociferous early Sex Pistols fan. She started her own band in short order; Siouxsie and

the Banshees' debut performance in late '76 consisted of one number, an epic desecration of the Lord's Prayer. Cohering around bassist Steve Severin and guitarist John McKay, the Banshees later forged a unique, introspective strain of punk rock. Even if you can't figure out exactly what makes Siouxsie wail the way she does, *The Scream* creates a rich, claustrophobic maelstrom of crude sound and half-submerged feelings. Though Siouxsie & Co. never quote the '60s directly, their debut draws a vital connection between punk and psychedelia. The Cure and the Psychedelic Furs—just for starters—were directly inspired by *The Scream.* Bless her or blame her, Siouxsie is the Godmother of Mope.

The atypical single "Hong Kong Garden," a British hit in 1978, evinces the Banshees' flair for melody and hooky exotica. *Join Hands,* however, indicates just how easily the brooding trance music can slip into dankness. With guitarist John McGeoch and drummer Budgie, *Kaleidoscope* and *Juju* refine the Banshees' attack, diversifying the sound without losing its swirling impact. *Once Upon a Time/The Singles* neatly documents the group's development; at its catchiest and most direct, Siouxsie's stylized gothic weirdness is surprisingly inviting.

A Kiss in the Dreamhouse hurls the Banshees back into the simmering postpsychedelic pea soup, with only marginally captivating results. And then Robert Smith of the Cure jumped on board for a spell during the tour documented on *Nocturne.* His suprisingly disciplined influence can be felt on *Hyaena*'s best cuts: the liquid-mercury "Dazzle," the sparse "Swimming Horses," a lushly appointed cover of the Beatles' "Dear Prudence." But *Tinderbox,* recorded with a virtual Smith clone named John Valentine Carruthers on guitar, is just as good. "Cities in Dust" sports a knockout chorus and Siouxsie's most confident vocals to date. If she's not exactly warm, well, she certainly sounds inflamed about something.

Through the Looking Glass presents overpolished covers of the group's obvious influences: Roxy Music, Bowie-era Iggy Pop, Television. *Tinderbox* integrates synthesizers and a lighter pop touch with the Banshees' trademark howl, but it lacks spark. The similarly inclined *Superstition* has a great single; "Kiss Them for Me" weaves a bewitching electronic stitch through Siouxsie's familiar cloth. Too bad the overwhelming fullness and texture of this tune is totally lost on a rock video soundtrack, the only place most people will hear it.   — M.C.

SIR MIX-A-LOT

★ ★½ Swass (Nastymix, 1988)
★ ★ ★   Seminar (Nastymix, 1989)
★ ★ ★½ Mack Daddy (Def American, 1992)

Sir Mix-a-Lot may hail from Seattle, but *Swass* is pure Miami—it has the same sing-song raps and thumping, 808 grooves as Miami Bass acts like the 2 Live Crew and Gucci Crew. That was the sound that gave him his first hit, "Posse On Broadway," but it was the metal-rap fusion of "Iron Man" (recorded with Seattle thrash legends Metal Church) that set him apart from the pack. Even so, Mix-a-Lot's music doesn't really mature until *Seminar*, which not only upgrades his musical approach—check the Prince "Batdance" sample that flavors "Beepers"—but adds an angry political edge to his material, as "National Anthem" makes plain. Mix-a-Lot continues to grow with *Mack Daddy*, grounding his aggressive delivery with deeply funky rhythm beds like the clavinet-driven loop beneath "One Time's Got No Cause." Yet as hard as these rhymes are, Mix-a-Lot avoids most gangsta rap clichés, and relies more on humor (as in "Swap Meet Louie" and the big-butt tribute "Baby Got Back") than on violence. — J.D.C.

SISTER SLEDGE

★ ★   Circle of Love (Atco, 1975)
★ ★   Together (Cotillion, 1977)
★ ★ ★   We Are Family (Cotillion, 1979)
★ ★   Love Somebody Today (Cotillion, 1980)
★ ★   All American Girls (Cotillion, 1981)
★ ★ ★½ The Best of Sister Sledge (Rhino, 1992)

Capable singers, these four siblings always sounded good, but it was the Chic Organization Ltd. (producers Nile Rodgers and Bernard Edwards) who provided the fluid propulsion that gave their songs elegance. "He's the Greatest Dancer" and the title track of *We Are Family* are carried along by nifty percussive guitars and great thumping bass lines. The rest of their catalogue is generic dance fluff. Rhino's anthology gathers the sisters' best material on one very danceable album. — P.E.

RICKY SKAGGS

★ ★ ★ ★ Sweet Temptation (Sugar Hill, 1979)
★ ★ ★   Waiting for the Sun to Shine (Epic, 1981)
★ ★ ★½ Highways and Heartaches (Epic, 1982)
★ ★ ★ ★   Don't Cheat in Our Hometown (Epic, 1983)
★ ★ ★½ Country Boy (Epic, 1984)
★ ★ ★ ★   Favorite Country Songs (Epic, 1985)
★ ★ ★½ Live in London (Epic, 1985)
★ ★ ★ ★   Family and Friends (Rounder, 1986)
★ ★ ★½ Love's Gonna Get Ya! (Epic, 1987)
★ ★ ★   Comin' Home to Stay (Epic, 1988)
★ ★ ★½ Kentucky Thunder (Epic, 1989)
★ ★ ★½ My Father's Son (Epic, 1991)

Kentucky-born Ricky Skaggs is one of the most successful of country's neo-traditionalists—young singers who have sidestepped the rowdy "outlaw" style of Waylon, Willie and Billy Joe Shavers, and generally ignored the pop crossover attempts of such '70s stars as Dolly Parton and the Oak Ridge Boys. Skaggs turns back, instead, to country music's finest hour—'60s Nashville and the earlier music that formed it. Born to the tradition, Skaggs learned hill music from his parents, played concerts with Flatt and Scruggs by the time he was seven, and had joined the Ralph Stanley Band while still in his teens. After honing his skills on guitar, mandolin and fiddle with Emmylou Harris's Hot Band, he released his first solo album, *Sweet Temptation*, with help from Harris and guitarist Albert Lee.

Instantly taken up by listeners tired of diluted or compromised country, Skaggs began turning out albums distinguished by expert playing and very careful (sometimes overcautious) song selection. *Live in London* or the 1985 compilation, *Favorite Country Songs*, provide a good intro—while contemporary material broadens their scope (and helps win a wider audience), the sets concentrate on standards by Bill Monroe and Johnny Bond. The live rendition of Flatt and Scruggs's "Don't Get Above Your Raising"—Skaggs's first hit, off *Sweet Temptation*—encapsulates the singer's appeal: his high, pure singing gently swings, and his apostolic reading of the song's "traditional values" message is sweet and convincing, rather than defensive.

A consistent artist, Skaggs hasn't made a bad record. *Country Boy* and *Don't Cheat in Our Hometown* are two of his best—the latter features a fine collaboration with Dolly Parton on "A Vision of Mother." Married to Sharon White of the notable country-music family the Whites, Skaggs often employs their excellent ensemble singing—the most moving examples can be found on *Family and Friends*. A lovely revival of pure hill music, of dobros, banjos and mandolin, the record's standouts are its hymns—"River of Jordan" and a moving a capella "Talk About Sufferin'." — P.E.

SKATALITES
★ ★ ★ **Scattered Lights (Alligator, 1984)**
★ ★ ★ ★ **Stretching Out (ROIR, 1986)**
Before reggae, came ska—relentlessly upbeat, syncopated Jamaican dance fare. In the early '60s, the Skatalites were the music's masters, incredibly assured instrumentalists who, over an endless, pumping beat, wailed wildly melodic jazz riffs. Two tenor saxophonists, Tommy McCook and Roland Alphonso, were the band's twin powers, engaged in happy honking wars. *Scattered Lights* is a strong 1984 studio set, and *Stretching Out* is a tuneful marvel: 90 minutes of a live reunion, it captures the fire of the band's nine players (and three guest horns) as they blaze through "Confucius," "Lee Harvey Oswald," "Fidel Castro" and 14 other ska delights. — P.E.

SKID ROW
★ ★½ **Skid Row (Atlantic, 1989)**
★ ★ ★ **Slave to the Grind (Atlantic, 1991)**
It's a typical tale of the times. This metal quintet earned its rowdy rep opening shows for Bon Jovi, but Skid Row's debut album succeeded on the strength of "I Remember You." Lead singer Sebastian Bach pierces hearts and eardrums alike on this wailing, grandiose power ballad. That snail-paced hit single gives scant preparation for the sheer velocity of Skid Row's second album; "Quicksand Jesus" and "Mudkicker" suggest these hirsute hard rockers may have dabbled in hardcore punk during their garage days. Shrewdly ditching pop-metal gloss in favor of bloozy grit, *Slave to the Grind* twists and shouts convincingly. Maybe a little too convincingly on "Get the Fuck Out": the only shocking thing about this ugly, violent put-down of a groupie is the fact that we're supposed to laugh at it. Skid Row has come quite a way in terms of musical brawn, but brains? That may take a while. — M.C.

THE SKYLINERS
★ ★½ **Greatest Hits (Original Sound, 1986)**
In Jimmy Beaumont the Skyliners had one of the most distinctive pop voices of the '50s, a husky, plaintive tenor that made up in expressiveness what it lacked in swagger. Dion, a contemporary of Beaumont's and

the singer Beaumont resembles most, had a harder edge and altogether better material; but Beaumont coulda been a contender. The Skyliners' first two big hits, "Since I Don't Have You" and "This I Swear" (both in 1959), allowed Beaumont to advance an almost Zen acceptance of love and its potentially dire consequences, but he was not without feeling. Where Dion would rage, Beaumont opted for a subtler approach: angst roiled beneath his surface equanimity, but this was apparent only as the songs built to explosive conclusions. It was a technique Roy Orbison would use to great effect. The Skyliners were tapped out by 1960, though, done in by weak songs and a disastrous move toward sugar-coated pop, best demonstrated on this set by the group's last hit, "Pennies From Heaven." This collection also includes interesting liner notes describing the origins of each song by Joe Rock, the Skyliners' manager and co-writer (with Beaumont) of most of the group's original material, including the big hits. — D.M.

SLAM SLAM
★ ★ ★½ **Free Your Feelings (MCA, 1991)**
Wisely, Paul Weller, founder of the Jam and the Style Council, let his wife take center stage after the breakup of the latter band. He does provides the songs, the accompaniment, the arrangements and the production on Slam Slam's debut, however. The unhurried intensity of Dee C. Lee's voice connects with every one of the gratifyingly sparse electro-grooves on *Free Your Feelings*. This is satisfying, if not exactly wall-shaking, dance music. And who would have thought that angry young Paul Weller would ever be associated with something so sweet? — M.C.

SLAUGHTER
★½ **Stick It to Ya (Chrysalis, 1990)**
Pretty-boy arena metal. Mark Slaughter has mastered the screeching castrato vocals of the genre. Tim Kelly musters some great raw thunder from his guitar—but then, in this kind of music, who doesn't? Purely generic. — P.E.

SLAVE
★ ★½ **Slave (Cotillion, 1977)**
★ ★½ **The Hardness of the World (Cotillion, 1977)**
★ ★½ **The Concept (Cotillion, 1978)**
★ ★ ★ **Just a Touch of Love (Cotillion, 1979)**
★ ★ ★ **Stone Jam (Cotillion, 1980)**

★ ★ ★½ **Show Time (Cotillion, 1981)**
★ ★½ **Visions of the Lite (Cotillion, 1982)**
★ ★½ **Bad Enuff (Cotillion, 1983)**
★ ★ ★ ★ **Best of Slave (Cotillion, 1984)**
★ ★½ **'88 (Ichiban, 1988)**

Like many bands in the P-Funk mold, Slave functions as a democracy: male and female singers trade sassy lines, sweet synths mingle with squealing rock guitars, a bass-heavy rhythm stutter *demands* equal time. Membership fluctuated in this Dayton, Ohio–based troupe; its albums cluster into three distinct phases. Lead singer and multi-instrumentalist Stephen Washington steers the early records; the R&B hit "Slide" (from the debut) eases into the pocket, but overextended party chants predominate. Singers Starleana Young and Steve Arrington first step foward on *The Concept;* the title track from *Just a Touch of Love* blends their voices in subtle, sensual contrast. Steve Washington left after the newly solidified *Stone Jam* LP just as Arrington began to display leadership potential to match his warm, unassuming vocal prowess. *Show Time* brings improved songwriting into the mix, deepening Slave's complex, all-encompassing funk bottom. "Snap Shot" edges closer still to rock, though Arrington's subsequent departure signals a final return to just-adequate gutbucket jamming. *The Best of Slave* picks the ripest plums from each branch of an almost-forgotten career. Sustaining this kind of funky forward momentum isn't quite as easy as Slave makes it sound. — M.C.

SLAYER
★ ★ **Reign in Blood (Def Jam, 1986)**
★ **Live Undead (Metal Blade/Enigma, 1987)**
★ **Hell Awaits (Metal Blade/Restless, 1988)**
★ ★ **South of Heaven (Def American, 1988)**
★ **Seasons in the Abyss (Def American, 1990)**
★ ★ **Show No Mercy (Metal Blade/Restless, 1990)**
★ ★ **Decade of Aggression Live (Def American, 1991)**

Thrash metal of an ugliness extreme even for the genre, Slayer is Tipper Gore's proper nightmare. They flourish song titles like "Mandatory Suicide," "Necrophobic" and "Reign in Blood." Bassist Tom Araya is, of course, a tuneless shouter. Guitarists Kerry King and Jeff Hanneman blaze away with the furious, misguided technique that distinguishes thrash from punk's engaging sloppiness. The house metal band of rap-meister Rick Rubin, this is amazingly depressing stuff. Nasty, brutish and endless. — P.E.

PERCY SLEDGE
★ ★ ★ **The Best of Percy Sledge (Atlantic, 1969)**
★ ★ **I'll Be Your Everything (Capricorn, 1974)**
★ ★ **Percy! (Monument, 1983)**
★ ★ ★ ★ **The Ultimate Collection, Percy Sledge: When a Man Loves a Woman (Atlantic, 1987)**
★ ★ ★ ★½ **It Tears Me Up: The Best of Percy Sledge (Rhino/Atlantic, 1992)**

Spooner Oldham's haunting Farfisa organ sets the mood, the Stax rhythm section kicks in, Percy wails and the song climaxes with a great horn-section ostinato—released in 1966, "When a Man Loves a Woman" is one of the great soul ballads, its message of sacrifice and surrender remaining timelessly romantic. Coarse-voiced and absolutely passionate, Sledge hadn't the endurance or distinctiveness to be one of R&B's premier figures, but he's one of the most heartfelt—his delivery is rich in its equal capacity for transcendence and sheer physical force. "When a Man Loves a Woman" is clearly the standout, but any number of Sledge's songs hit with devastating force. Working with great Southern songwriters like Dan Penn and Eddie Hinton, Sledge is best when he wails about suffering, as on "Dark End of the Street." The 1992 anthology, *It Tears Me Up*, is a wonderful summation of Sledge's career highlights, including material recorded from 1966 to 1971. — P.E.

GRACE SLICK
★ ★½ **Grace Slick & the Great Society Collector's Item (Columbia, 1990)**

Along with the recorded output of Hot Tuna, Jorma Kaukonen, Marty Balin and Jefferson Starship, Grace Slick's solo albums (now out of print) prove that the greatness of Jefferson Airplane was a matter of synergy—together, its members sparked great collisions of creativity; on their own, they touch off merely a slight bang.

While chiefly of documental interest, *Collector's Item* is kind of intriguing—gathering together two albums (*Conspicuous Only in Its Absence, How It Was*) of pre-Airplane work with a nondescript crew called the Great Society, the CD features the original versions of "Somebody to

Love" (very lame drumming drags it down) and "White Rabbit" (the Society jams for four and a half minutes with an inscrutable woodwind wailing along, and Slick then finally sings). More fun is the strange meditation from Rex Reed, reprinted from a 1970 *Stereo Review*. While chuckling your way through Rex's arch, baffled prose, you'll learn that the singer's real name is Grace Wing, and that she's nuts about "Peer Gynt," Irving Berlin and Miles Davis's *Sketches of Spain*. — P.E.

SLICK RICK

★ ★ ★   **The Great Adventures of Slick Rick (Def Jam/CBS, 1988)**
  ★ ★½ **The Ruler's Back (Def Jam/Sony, 1991)**

Between its wiggy trumpet hook and liquid rhymes, "The Ruler" establishes Slick Rick as a rapper with his own style. However, the supposed humor of "Treat Her Like a Prostitute" (also from his debut) just furthered hip-hop's ugly, know-nothing tradition of misogyny. *Pretty Woman*–style pampering isn't what he's got in mind. Recorded in three weeks while Rick was out of jail on bail, *The Ruler's Back* sounds just about as hurried as you'd expect. The jazzy groove starts off strong, but the offhand spin of the raps quickly becomes tired. "I Shouldn't Have Done It" teases with the promise of autobiographical detail; Rick faced a three-to-ten-year sentence for attempted murder. The song turns out to be a reluctant father's grudging acceptance of responsibility; it's not bad, but like the rest of *The Ruler's Back*, it's too little, too late. — M.C.

P.F. SLOAN

★ **Precious Times: The Best of P.F. Sloan (Rhino, 1986)**

Primarily a songwriter for such soft '60s popsters as Johnny Rivers, Herman's Hermits, the Grass Roots and the Searchers, Sloan sang lead on Jan & Dean's "The Little Old Lady from Pasadena" and then careened into significance penning "Eve of Destruction" (1965) for Barry McGuire. A ham-fisted protest song that attempted to rhyme words like "coagulatin'," "Eve" was an unintentional parody of the political Dylan. Cursed with earnestness, Sloan went on to tackle "alienation" on "The Sins of a Family," and self-actualization on "Take Me for What I'm Worth," and to blithely defend the motherland on "When the Wind Changes." His love songs ("Here's Where You Belong"), easing up a tad on the

seriousness, weren't half so bad—but everything P.F. tried was, ultimately, milky Dylan. — P.E.

SLY AND THE FAMILY STONE

★ ★ ★ ★ ★ **Stand! (Epic, 1969)**
★ ★ ★ ★ ★ **Greatest Hits (Epic, 1970)**
★ ★ ★ ★ ★ **There's a Riot Going On (Epic, 1971)**
  ★ ★ ★ ★ **Fresh (Epic, 1973)**
  ★ ★ ★ ★ **Anthology (Epic, 1981)**

"Different strokes for different folks." The tag line of "Everyday People," from *Stand!* sums up both Sly and the Family Stone's musical philosophy and the group's magnetic appeal. Sylvester Stewart, a former San Francisco DJ, forged an ecumenical rock & soul sound on the Family Stone's three earlier, out-of-print Epic albums: *A Whole New Thing*, *Life* and *Dance to the Music*. That last album's title track, "I Want to Take You Higher" and "Everyday People" (both of which can be found on *Greatest Hits*) got over as hippie anthems and hit singles; an uplifting vibe carried Sly's message to the masses, though he never sugarcoated the counterculture's dark side—quite the opposite. *Stand!* is balanced by "Don't Call Me Nigger, Whitey" and the instrumental throb of the 15-minute "Sex Machine." *Greatest Hits* adds the sweat-dripping "Thank You (Falletinme Be Mice Elf Agin)" and the breezy "Hot Fun in the Summertime" to Sly's string of jewels.

There's a Riot Going On drops the hopeful dance-party rhetoric and turns the band's musical reach inward. Sly concocts a brooding, lethal funk setting for his dark and dissolute musings on the state of the nation—from Woodstock to Watts. "Family Affair" and "Runnin' Away" couch bleak scenarios in hauntingly light tunes; even at rock-bottom, Sly can nail a catchy hook when it suits his mood. Cancelled shows and erratic performances plagued Sly and the Family Stone at this point, adding to the air of dread surrounding *Riot*. However, Sly rebounded with the playful, sharp *Fresh* in 1973. "If You Want Me to Stay" became the Family Stone's last Top Twenty single; if that sounds a bit coy coming from Sly, "Thankful 'n' Thoughtful" and the acid-drenched "Que Sera, Sera" carry the expected sting, along with a newfound mellow glow. That grace period turned out to be cruelly short-lived, though. Sly's subsequent releases probably deserve to remain out-of-print: the sound of such a brilliant inventor turning imitative of his followers is just too much to bear. Surfacing on Funkadelic's *Electric Spanking of War Babies* and the *P-Funk All-Stars* album in the early '80s, Sly convincingly kicked out a few jams and then promptly faded from view. — M.C.

SLY AND ROBBIE

★★★½ **Sly and Robbie Present Taxi (Mango, 1981)**
★★★ **Sixties, Seventies + Eighties = Taxi (Mango, 1981)**
★★★ **Raiders of the Lost Dub (Mango, 1981)**
★★★½ **Crucial Reggae Driven by Sly & Robbie (Mango, 1982)**
★★★ **A Dub Experience (Mango, 1985)**
★★★½ **Reggae Greats (Mango, 1985)**
★★★ **Language Barrier (Island, 1985)**
★★★ **Taxi Fare (Heartbeat, 1986)**
★★★★★ **Rhythm Killers (Island, 1987)**
★★★½ **Silent Assassin (Island, 1989)**

Drummer Sly Dunbar and bassist Robbie Shakespeare were premiere Kingston sessionmen who struck up a creative partnership at the tail end of the '70s. At first, they produced and accompanied a broad variety of Jamaican artists, from the politically charged trio Black Uhuru to "lovers' rock" crooners like Gregory Isaacs and Dennis Brown. Laying bare the bedrock bass lines, trimming away the keyboard and guitar excesses, allowing room for cosmic dub effects and ricocheting syndrums, Sly and Robbie brought roots reggae skanking into the '80s. They branched off into pop with immediately satisfying results: rehabilitating Grace Jones's credibility with three strong albums and supplying several tracks for Bob Dylan, among other projects. Under their own names, Sly and Robbie began releasing singles compilations culled from their *Taxi* label at home. The first cut is the deepest: *Sly and Robbie Present Taxi* effortlessly veers from soothing romance ("My Woman's Love" by Jimmy Riley) to teeth-gnashing protest ("Fort Augustus" by Junior Delgado) to DJ rap-toasting ("Drunken Master" by General Echo) to a simply irresistible Police cover ("The Bed's Too Big Without You" by Shelia Hynton). It's compelling and sexy as hell, all in a very low-key way: proof that reggae didn't roll over when Bob Marley died.

None of the subsequent Taxi packages come close to hitting that mark; *Crucial Reggae* mixes lesser cuts by various crooners and vocal groups, while *Sixties, Seventies + Eighties* and the dub albums are recommended only to aficionados of that

hallucinatory instrumental style. The first Taxi album is preferable to the spotty *Reggae Greats* collection, as well. Sly and Robbie moved toward a more conceptual, ensemble-oriented approach on *Language Barrier*; though this Bill Laswell–produced jumble of world music influences and guest appearances never quite gels, it's clearly the start of something. *Rhythm Killers* is so coherent and smooth that you could mistake it for a suite if it wasn't also so thoroughly down and dirty. Progressive hip-hopper Shinehead and P-Funkateer Bootsy Collins, among others, all do their respective thangs while riding that impeccable bottom-heavy groove. *Silent Assassin* taps the talents of a younger crew in a similar strategy; though well-intentioned, the patois raps by KRS One and Queen Latifah come off as stiff and didactic compared to Shinehead's natural eruptions on *Rhythm Killers*. — M.C.

SLY FOX

★★★½ **Let's Go All the Way (Capitol, 1985)**

Sly Fox scored on its first album, and then promptly disappeared. But, oh, what a night! Impossible to resist, the title track was a refreshing one-shot smash in 1985. "Let's Go All the Way" welds the metallic edge of synth-pop to a flexible, funky vocal-group sound, and cuts to the bone. Lead singer Gary "Mudbone" Cooper was a charter member of Bootsy's Rubber Band during the late '70s; in Sly Fox he casually updated and pop-ified the P-Funk approach without compromising its spirit. If the rest of the album doesn't quite outshine that fireball of a single, "If Push Comes to a Shove" and "Merry-Go-Round" certainly sustain the temperature. Out of hundreds of one-hit wonders, precious few can claim a debut album as consistent and confident as *Let's Go All the Way*. — M.C.

THE SMALL FACES

★★★½ **There Are But Four Small Faces (1967; Immediate, 1991)**
★★★★ **Ogden's Nut Gone Flake (1968; Immediate, 1991)**

Cute and tiny and flashing a giddy, soaring arrogance, the Small Faces, circa 1966, had the mod pose down better even than fellow-Londoners the Who. And they were tunesmiths, too. Frontman (and former kiddie actor) Steve Marriott, organist Ian McLagan, drummer Kenney Jones and bassist Ronnie Lane made jaunty R&B-ish rock & roll that highlighted Marriott's onstage dramatics, bluesy guitar and patented scratchy vocal stylings he'd later parody gratingly with Humble Pie. "Itchycoo Park," from *There Are But Four Small Faces*, was a great flower-power single whose outsized influence reaches down to the Raspberries and Prince. *Ogden's Nut Gone Flake* may be the best contemporary *Sgt. Pepper's* clone: everything about it was nicely quirky—a round record sleeve, a sweet mix of psychedelia and R&B, and the charm of "Afterglow." When Marriott left in 1969 for Humble Pie, Ron Wood and Rod Stewart joined up, and the band became the Faces. — P.E.

BESSIE SMITH

★★★★★ Any Woman's Blues (Columbia, 1970)
★★★★★ The World's Greatest Blues Singer (Columbia, 1971)
★★★★★ Empty Bed Blues (Columbia, 1971)
★★★★★ The Empress (Columbia, 1971)
★★★★★ Nobody's Blues But Mine (Columbia, 1972)
★★★★★ Bessie Smith—The Collection (Columbia, 1989)
★★★★★ The Complete Recordings, Vol. 1 (Columbia/Legacy, 1991)
★★★★★ The Complete Recordings, Vol. 2 (Columbia/Legacy, 1991)

Columbia has done right by one of the most influential singers in this country's history. In 1970, under the aegis of the late John Hammond, the label began releasing double-album sets of her work, and by 1972 everything the Empress of the Blues had recorded was back on the market. Yet another reissue program began with the 1989 release of *The Collection*, a well-annotated overview of Smith's decade-long recording history; a more ambitious project began in 1991 with the sets, *The Complete Recordings, Vol. 1* and *Vol. 2*, which helps to bring Smith's complete works to compact disc.

Born in Chattanooga, Tennessee, in 1895, Smith began performing on the streets for money, and by her late teens was a local star on the strength of her performances in amateur shows around town. In 1912 her brother Clarence, who had left town to perform with a minstrel troupe, came through town as a member of the Moses Stokes minstrel show, whose featured vocalist, Ma Rainey, had given her music the name "blues" and was on her way to being the most popular black artist of her day. Smith joined the Moses troupe, but Rainey's influence on the young singer

remains debatable. Musicians who were around at that time assert that Smith had already developed a distinctive style that needed no further grooming; if anything, it appears Rainey may have been of most help in educating Smith to the sometimes nefarious ways of showbiz types.

Smith's recording career began in 1923, when Frank Walker, head of Columbia's race records division, produced her first sessions, out of which came the single "Downhearted Blues," a song written and previously recorded by Alberta Hunter. Smith's version sold 780,000 copies in its first six months of release, catapulted her to headliner status, and expanded her touring schedule to include dates in Chicago, Detroit and Cleveland, a rarity at a time when black revues toured rigorously, but only in the South.

Smith's singing was fueled by rage and anger. A woman of overpowering passions, she had a reputation as a hard drinker whose temper was of the hair-trigger variety that would sometimes result in physical attacks, the most memorable being the occasion when she learned of her husband's infidelity and proceeded to trash both their hotel room and him. One can hear in her dark, powerful voice the brooding intensity of someone who has been deeply wounded and sees no light ahead.

Throughout the '20s Smith recorded with the best musicians of the era, but it was a fleeting session with Louis Armstrong that has justifiably entered into legend. In 1925, with pianist Fred Longshaw the only other musician on the date, they recorded five songs—including a staggering performance of "St. Louis Blues"—and challenged each other in ways geniuses need to be challenged. Theirs is one of the great conversations in blues history, preserved on *The Empress* and *The Collection*, and on Volume 2 of *The Complete Recordings*.

The Depression in effect ended Smith's career, although she continued to record into the early '30s; *The Collection* includes two of sides she cut in 1933 in what proved to be her final recording session. Her legend endured, darkly, after she died in a car wreck in 1937. Her recordings, of course, live on. Resonant, stirring, troubling, electrifying, the art of Bessie Smith is a national treasure. — D.M.

DARDEN SMITH

★★★ Darden Smith (Epic, 1988)
★★★½ Trouble No More (Columbia, 1990)

Not quite rock, not entirely country, Darden Smith exemplifies the strengths of the Southwestern music scene. Like Nanci Griffith, he understands how to fold the immediacy of rock into the intimacy of folk; like James McMurtry, he's able to pull poetry from the language of country music; and like Joe Ely, he makes music that's as simple as it is deep. *Darden Smith* makes a modest introduction, playing close enough to country conventions to sound like old Austin, but cut with a sly sophistication that raises the likes of "Two Dollar Novels" and "God's Will" above the merely conventional. But it's *Trouble No More* that truly shows his strengths, offering insightful writing, sprightly melodies and wonderfully understated performances. Written in part with Boo Hewerdine (with whom Smith cut the engagingly offhand duo album, *Evidence*), the songs range from the jazzy wit of "Frankie & Sue" to the neo-Nashville melancholy of "Fall Apart at the Seams." Well worth hearing. — J.D.C.

HUEY "PIANO" SMITH & THE CLOWNS
★ ★ ★ **Serious Clownin'—The History of Huey "Piano" Smith and the Clowns (Rhino, 1986)**

After working with Guitar Slim, Lloyd Price, Smiley Lewis and Little Richard, Huey Smith assembled one of New Orleans' most accomplished R&B outfits, the Clowns. In addition to backing some of the Crescent City's most popular artists in the '50s, the group cut some lively singles on its own with the estimable Bobby Marchan as lead singer. Pianist Smith had been influenced by the dexterous style of Jelly Roll Morton and the steady rolling approach of Fats Domino, but it was less his playing than his eye for talent that distinguished his career. The Clowns could groove with the best New Orleans had to offer, as the variety of cuts on *Serious Clownin'* indicates. In addition to the group's Smith-penned hits—"Rockin' Pneumonia and the Boogie Woogie Flu" (1957), "Don't You Just Know It" (1958) and "Don't You Know Yockomo" (1959)—the album also includes Smith and the Clowns backing Jimmy Clanton on his 1958 hit, "Just a Dream," and, a year later, Frankie Ford on "Sea Cruise." Other New Orleans musicians may have cut a higher profile, but few were as important as Smith to the development of the city's distinctive brand of R&B. — D.M.

PATTI SMITH
★ ★ ★ ★ ★ **Horses (Arista, 1975)**
★ ★ ★½ **Radio Ethiopia (Arista, 1976)**
★ ★ ★½ **Easter (Arista, 1978)**
★ ★ ★ **Wave (Arista, 1979)**
★ ★ ★ **Dream of Life (Arista, 1988)**

With the very first utterance of her debut album, Patti Smith declares war on the musical complacency of the mid-'70s: "Jesus died for somebody's sins but not mine." *Horses* defies the reigning rock conventions of its time, and deflates a few current notions, too. Smith's idiosyncratic mix of Beat poetry and the big beat still has the power to either entice or offend. Teeming with ambition, primitivism, anybody-can-do-this chutzpah and casual androgyny, *Horses* demands a reaction. On the basis of attitude alone, Smith inspired every punk and new-wave artist who followed in her wake. After a while, she even learned how to sing!

Admitedly, singing wasn't Smith's first priority. A published poet and rock critic, she began reciting her Beat-tribute "Babelogues" over fellow writer Lenny Kaye's guitar accompaniment in the early '70s. On *Horses*, her visionary metaphors and verbal riffs collide with the inviting din of late-'60s-style garage-band rock. The title track refers both to stallions as a psychosexual image and to "doin' the pony." Smith expands the words of oldies like "Gloria" and "Land of 1,000 Dances," although the band's furious pounding never obscures the power of those three mighty chords. Quieter, reflective tracks like "Kimberly" and "Elegie" underline the passionate romanticism in her voice. *Radio Ethiopia* boasts the Patti Smith Group's growing power as a band, broadcasting a gritty, hard-rocking rhythm guitar sound. "Pumping (My Heart)" and "Ask the Angels" ring out like anthems, but the grueling title cut reveals the Achilles' heel among Patti's pretensions: her squalling guitar-feedback orgies never reach beyond the annoyance level.

On *Easter*, producer Jimmy Iovine makes good on Smith's professed rebel stance by moving her sound even closer to solid, meat-and-potatoes mainstream rock. You can hear the newfound confidence in her singing, and the more traditionally structured approach doesn't dull the jagged conviction of "25th Floor," "Space Monkey" and "Till Victory." Maybe Bruce Springsteen did Smith a big favor on their hit songwriting collaboration from this album, finally rendering her skittery energy accessible. But another way of hearing "Because the Night" suggests that this so-called punk priestess breathes a much-needed air of subtlety into the Boss's lofty anthemic construct.

Wave continues that melodic roll with "Dancing Barefoot," and "Frederick," though for the rest of the album Smith sounds uncharacteristically fuzzy, even disengaged. Once the Patti Smith Group had completed its most successful tour to date in 1979, Smith abruptly retired from the music scene. Though some manner of stardom seemed to beckon, perhaps her mission felt complete. After eight subsequent years of marriage (to Detroit rocker Fred "Sonic" Smith) and two children, Smith quietly resurfaced in perhaps the only low-profile comeback of the late '80s. Overproduced by Iovine (with Fred Smith) this time, *Dream of Life*'s net effect underwhelms most expectations. Oddly, it sounds a bit out of time—more 1983 than 1977, of all things. Not that Smith needs to monitor current trends: when her rekindled vision clicks into overdrive beside Fred Smith's zinging guitar lines on "Up There Down There," "Where Duty Calls" or "People Have the Power," *Dream of Life* sounds timeless. — M.C.

THE SMITHEREENS
★ ★ ★   **Beauty and Sadness (EP) (1983; Enigma, 1988)**
★ ★ ★½ **Especially for You (Enigma, 1987)**
★ ★ ★   **The Smithereens (EP) (Restless/Enigma, 1987)**
★ ★ ★½ **Green Thoughts (Enigma/Capitol, 1988)**
★ ★ ★½ **The Smithereens 11 (Capitol, 1989)**
★ ★ ★½ **Blow Up (Capitol, 1991)**

Expert at mining some jukebox version of the collective unconscious, front man-guitarist Pat DiNizio writes great pop songs that recall Brit mod glory, but don't sound at all cute or slavishly recycled. *Especially for You* is clean, tough and snappy—the four-piece group doesn't mess with DiNizio's hooks, which, fortunately, overpower the so-so quality of his singing. With *Green Thoughts*, the players get subtler, their style verging in places on the mid-tempo numbers of Elvis Costello. *Smithereens 11* is heavier; while "William Wilson" (its title taken from Poe's short story) recalls the Kinks, the record's thick guitar tones sound more '70s than '60s. "Maria Elena" (a song for Buddy Holly's widow) is smart and tender, proving that DiNizio's skill at ballads rivals his flair for

ravers. *Blow Up* finds the Smithereens still honest and tough. Solid and sharp, this band makes genuine rock & roll. — P.E.

THE SMITHS
★ ★ ★   **The Smiths (Sire, 1984)**
★ ★ ★½ **Hatful of Hollow (Rough Trade Import, 1984)**
★ ★   **Meat Is Murder (Sire, 1985)**
★ ★ ★ ★ **The Queen Is Dead (Sire, 1986)**
★ ★ ★ ★ **Louder Than Bombs (Sire, 1987)**
★ ★½ **Strangeways, Here We Come (Sire, 1987)**
★ ★ ★   **Rank (Sire, 1988)**

Hypersensitive, painfully shy, aggressively vegetarian, supposedly celibate, verbally unfettered, incurably tuneless: the Smiths' Morrissey isn't your run-of-the-mill lead singer. A lot of people who might otherwise have celebrated this British quartet's succinct rock & roll approach were utterly repelled by the brooding, obsessive persona of the band's bard-in-residence. The debut album lays everything on the table: endless potential and glaring pretensions, side by side. The songwriting chemistry between Morrissey and guitarist Johnny Marr is readily apparent; sparks fly on "This Charming Man" and "Hand in Glove." More often, Marr's ringing rhythm patterns and fleet arrangements sustain and nourish Morrissey's lingering bouts of depression.

The Smiths achieved a good deal of pop chart success at home; arguably, a single is just the right dose of Morrissey's decidedly British wit and wisdom. *Hatful of Hollow* improves the debut by culling its best tracks and adding some good non-LP fare such as "How Soon Is Now?" Pretentious and murderously slow, *Meat Is Murder* drops all of Morrissey's rotten eggs in one basket. Maybe he got something out of his system: *The Queen Is Dead* varies the musical attack, matching Morrissey's expanded focus. He scores quivering bull's-eyes on nearly every topic he targets, and this time the ponderous moments *unfold* rather than blurt out. *Louder Than Bombs* detonates a hefty segment of the Smiths' singles file, and hits definitely outnumber misses. *Strangeways* maps the band's (inevitable?) descent into obscurely personal, sonically overwrought formula: Morrissey floats rudderless in producer Stephen Street's string-happy arrangements of his increasingly morbid meditations. *Rank* captures some, but not all, of the Smiths' surprising live capacity. — M.C.

PATTY SMYTH
★ ★ **Never Enough (Columbia, 1987)**
A well-sung but inconsequential solo effort
from Scandal's former lead singer, this is
worth hearing only if you've ever wondered
what a female Eddie Money would have
sounded like. — J.D.C.

HANK SNOW
★ ★ ★ **Collector's Series, Vol. 2 (RCA, 1990)**
★ ★ ★ ★½ **I'm Movin' On and Other Great Country Hits (RCA, 1990)**
Today a grandfatherly presence on the
Grand Ole Opry and slowed by failing
health, Hank Snow stands as an artist who
brought a wide-ranging sensibility to
traditional country music in the early 1950s.
In exerting considerable influence over his
peers, Snow opened the country genre to
more sophisticated rhythmic patterns and
lyric possibilities, and also made a name for
himself as an adventurous guitarist. He
topped this off with a distinctive singing
style—a nasally baritone and clipped
diction—that was influenced by Jimmie
Rodgers, but sounded like no one else.
Considered altogether, Snow's early
recordings bespeak a groundbreaking
approach that can be seen as yet another
link between country and rockabilly.
   Born in Nova Scotia in 1914, Snow
experienced a harsh childhood, his parents
divorcing when he was eight, his mother
remarrying later to a man who expressed his
dislike for Hank in physical terms. By the
time he was 12 Snow had left this abusive
environment and was earning a living as a
cabin boy and fisherman; at 16 he heard
Jimmie Rodgers and decided to devote his
life to music. His popularity bolstered by
frequent radio appearances, Snow landed a
recording contract with RCA in Canada by
the time he was 22 and quickly became the
best-selling C&W artist in his native land.
He came to the United States in 1944 and
again used radio exposure to establish a
name for himself in country-music circles.
His first U.S. recording session was in
March 1949, and over the next five years he
produced a remarkable series of sides, many
self-penned, that form the foundation of his
legend. Notable among these are "I'm
Movin' On," from 1950, one of many
first-rate train songs (another bow to the
Rodgers influence) in Snow's repertoire.
"I'm Movin' On" is also marked by
instrumentation that would help define the
uptempo side of Snow's sound: a stark,
stinging guitar, a chugging beat, and

relentless drive courtesy of the fiddle and
steel guitar—most unusual in country music
at that time. Another 1950 cut, "Rhumba
Boogie," is similarly propulsive, featuring a
well-turned boogie guitar solo by Snow and
some tongue-twisting lyrics that again were
altogether different than anything that was
nominally considered country at the turn of
the decade. In "Rhumba Boogie" and "The
Golden Rocket," also from 1950, one hears
startling similarities to the arrangement that
would surface four years later in "Mystery
Train" as sung by Elvis Presley for Sun
Records. Listening to Snow's early
recordings, it's apparent that Presley's
guitarist, Scotty Moore, was eating up
everything Hank Snow had to offer.
   *I'm Moving On and Other Great Country
Hits*, out of print as of this writing, collects
the essential Hank Snow in 20 cuts. Missing
is his sentimental version of "(Now and
Then) There's a Fool Such As I," which
would later become a hit for Presley, as well
as a couple of interesting early-'60s outings,
"Miller's Cave" and "I've Been
Everywhere." Otherwise this disc, with its
detailed liner notes, puts Snow in proper
perspective. In addition to the
groundbreaking songs noted above, and
other influential sides such as "Music
Makin' Momma from Memphis" and
"Unwanted Sign Upon Your Heart," *I'm
Moving On* shows the surprising depth of
Snow's deceptively smooth voice and his
intelligent approach to a lyric. *Collector's
Series* has only eight cuts, including Snow's
gentle interpretation of a Bob Nolan
cowboy classic, "Tumbling Tumbleweeds,"
and "I'm Moving On." In addition, Snow
delivers a remarkable performance with his
warm, worried, low-down blues vocal on
Ivory Joe Hunter's "I Almost Lost My
Mind," and even assays Buddy Knox's
gently swinging 1957 hit, "Hula Love,"
which is marked by the same type of verbal
wordplay for which Snow himself was
noted. "A Fool Such As I" is here as well,
but only in instrumental form, as Snow uses
it as background for a recitation of his early
life and hard times. This is hardly the most
satisfying Snow title extant, but there's
nothing else left in print of his
once-formidable catalog. — D.M.

PHOEBE SNOW
★ ★ ★ ★ **Phoebe Snow (1974; DCC, 1989)**
★ ★ ★½ **Second Childhood (Columbia, 1976)**
★ ★ ★½ **It Looks Like Snow (Columbia, 1976)**

★★★ Never Letting Go (Columbia, 1977)
★★★ Against the Grain (Columbia, 1978)
★★★★ The Best of Phoebe Snow
(Columbia, 1981)
★★★ Something Real (Elektra, 1990)
A bluesy and assured alto voice sets Phoebe
Snow apart from the mass of other
singer-songwriters right from the start of her
debut album, *Phoebe Snow*. The indelible
intro of the hit "Poetry Man"—when she
soars over a spare acoustic guitar—gives
you some idea of her astounding range and
emotional control. Actually, that isn't the
strongest performance on the album:
"Harpo's Blues" epitomizes her high-flying
(and high-strung) approach to singing and
writing. Snow opts for a fuller, jazz-flavored
sound on *Second Childhood*, accompanying
a set of psychologically subtle lyrics. The
overall effect is a little underwhelming after
the quiet rush of the debut, though she
breathes immediacy into the lines about
"dying on the vine in suburbia" (from
"Two-Fisted Love")—among other telling
moments. *It Looks Like Snow* casts her in
an appealing, uptown-R&B light with covers
of "Shakey Ground" (Temptations), "Don't
Let Me Down" (Beatles) and "Teach Me
Tonight" (Dinah Washington). *Never
Letting Go* and *Against the Grain* are slicker
and less satisfying, but *The Best of Phoebe
Snow* offers a highly listenable—if
abbreviated—recap of her career. Phoebe
Snow quietly resurfaced in 1990 with
Something Real, echoing the somber
folk-pop sound of Joan Armatrading on
songs like "Mr. Wonderful" and "Touch
Your Soul." — M.C.

SOCIAL DISTORTION
★★★ Mommy's Little Monster (1983;
Triple X, 1990)
★★★ L.A. Prison Bound (Restless,
1988)
★★★½ Social Distortion (Epic, 1990)
★★★★ Between Heaven and Hell (Epic,
1992)
Rock classicists in spite of their L.A. punk
origins, Social Distortion frontman Mike
Ness and his bandmates have always taken
a tough-but-tuneful approach to their music,
a tack that produces fairly predictable
results on the punkish *Mommy's Little
Monster* but begins to pay dividends with
L.A. Prison Bound. With that album, the
group develops an interest in country
music—not the sweet, Gram Parsons-ish
country rock you'd expect of Stones fans
like this crew, but a sound more akin to the
brusque, edgy tone of Johnny Cash's Sun
recordings. This change shifts the band's

focus slightly, moving its emphasis away
from the guitars and toward Ness's
rough-hewn vocals, a shift that adds
emphasis to "Like an Outlaw (For You)"
and "No Pain No Gain."
    Social Distortion plays down the country
influence (though it does include a cover of
"Ring of Fire") and generally toughens the
group's attack, but maintains many of the
same musical values, as "Ball and Chain"
and "It Coulda Been Me" make plain. As
such, the only change offered by *Between
Heaven and Hell* is a slight increase in guitar
noise and a marked strengthening of the
songwriting—both of which serve only to
enhance Social Distortion's sound and
reputation. — J.D.C.

SOFT BOYS
★★★ Live at the Portland Arms (1978;
Glass Fish UK, 1987)
★★★½ A Can of Bees (1979; Rykodisc,
1992)
★★★★ Underwater Moonlight (1980;
Rykodisc, 1992)
★★★ Two Halves for the Price of One
(1981; Glass Fish UK, 1990)
★★★ Invisible Hits (1983; Rykodisc,
1992)
Seriously strange and terrifically tuneful, the
Soft Boys were perhaps the most engagingly
deranged act to have washed up with the
English new wave. Between the deadpan
insanity of singer-guitarist Robyn Hitchcock
and the pure-pop virtuosity of lead guitarist
Kimberley Rew, the Soft Boys had a rock-
solid front line, while the rhythm section—
drummer Morris Windsor and bassists Andy
Metcalfe or Matthew Seligman—was as
supple as it was expert. But what really
made the Soft Boys sizzle were the songs—
delightfully droll numbers like "Sandra's
Having Her Brain Out" or "Do the Chisel."
Both appear on *A Can of Bees*, along with
such should-have-been hits as "Leppo & the
Jooves" and "The Pigworker." The only
thing that keeps these entertainingly played
and exceedingly melodic songs from being
career highlights is that the stuff on
Underwater Moonlight is even better. Of
course, it's hard to argue with any album
that can slip from something called "I
Wanna Destroy You" into "Kingdom of
Love," but the Boys manage that transition
with aplomb, then outdo it later on as they
move from the triumphant Beatle-isms of
"Tonight" into the spacy, Pink Floyd-ian
"You'll Have to Go Sideways."
    Invisible Hits is a bit of a disappointment,
being merely terrific when its predecessors
are absolutely marvelous, but the presence

of "Let Me Put It Next to You," "Have a Heart, Betty (I'm Not Fireproof)" and "Rock 'n' Roll Toilet" is more than enough to recommend it. The all-acoustic *Live at the Portland Arms* is quite fun but given to such unexpected selections as "I Like Bananas (Because They Have No Bones)" and an all-vocal rendition of Glenn Miller's "In the Mood." As for *Two Halves for the Price of One*, it's mostly given over to outtakes and oddities—which, given the likes of this crew, is saying something. — J.D.C.

SOFT CELL

  ★ ★ ★   **Non-Stop Erotic Cabaret (Sire, 1981)**

  ★ ★½   **Non-Stop Ecstatic Dancing (Sire, 1982)**

  ★ ★   **The Art of Falling Apart (Sire, 1983)**

  ★½   **Soul Inside (EP) (Sire, 1983)**

  ★   **This Last Night in Sodom (Sire, 1984)**

★ ★ ★ ★   **Memorabilia: The Singles (Mercury, 1991)**

Few groups took as much pleasure in perversity as Soft Cell. It wasn't just the way this campy act reveled in the kinky sex described in *Non-Stop Erotic Cabaret* or gleefully entitled its farewell album *This Last Night in Sodom*; Soft Cell got as much pleasure from assaulting rock & roll notions of decency—that is, respect for such classics as Gloria Jones's "Tainted Love" or Jimi Hendrix's "Purple Haze."

Still, a little of this stuff goes a long way, and *Erotic Cabaret* probably goes as far as most pop fans will want to follow. A strange conceptual salute to the sex industry, it makes the most both of Marc Almond's mannered tenor and David Ball's electronic soundscapes; in context, the exaggerated sense of shame lent "Tainted Love" seems almost like comic relief. As its title indicates, *Non-Stop Ecstatic Dancing* is a jokingly cynical attempt by the group to cash in its unexpected pop currency, but only "Memorabilia" actually repays the effort.

The Art of Falling Apart is an amazingly earnest effort, but that doesn't always work in the group's benefit—the charming domesticity of "Kitchen Sink Drama," for instance, is undercut by Almond's resolute refusal to stay on pitch, while the warts-and-all portrayal of prostitution in "Baby Doll" ends up sounding more vicious than realistic. Even so, it's worth enduring such excesses if only to hear the deliriously goofy "Hendrix Medley" offered as a bonus track. It's hard, however, to have the same enthusiasm for

Soul Inside, while *This Last Night in Sodom* is a noisy, overburdened attempt at art that proves conclusively that these two were better off going for camp. *Memorabilia: The Singles* is a surprisingly enduring collection, showing the group's strengths while avoiding its weaknesses. — J.D.C.

SOFT MACHINE

★ ★ ★½   **The Soft Machine (Probe, 1968)**

★ ★ ★½   **Volume 2 (Columbia, 1968)**

★ ★ ★½   **Third (Columbia, 1970)**

★ ★ ★   **Fourth (Columbia,1971)**

★ ★ ★   **Six (Columbia, 1973)**

  ★ ★½   **Seven (Columbia, 1974)**

★ ★ ★   **The Peel Sessions (Strange Fruit, 1990)**

While virtually every form of late-'60s Brit rock, from psychedelia to folk to "progressive," has enjoyed a revival—Brit fusion has not. And that's largely due to the fact that this stuff was so dense. Graham Bond helped initiate the subtrend, but its major proponents were a Canterbury outfit that dubbed itself Soft Machine after a William Burroughs novel and that, soon after its third album, became synonymous with the term "critical darlings." Personnel shifts and a general air of facelessness helped keep the band from gaining any significant popular following—the strongest members were drummer Robert Wyatt and keyboardist Mike Ratledge—but what really relegated the group to underground status was the intimidating quality of its music.

Free-form improvisation, massed, squawking horns, epic-long compositions, the Softs were primarily jazzers, burying whatever rock inclinations they occasionally flourished under layers of artful noise. *Third* stands as their strongest set. The others represent a valiant attempt to make uncompromising music—and they make for difficult listening. — P.E.

SONIC YOUTH

  ★ ★½   **Sonic Youth (EP) (1982; SST, 1987)**

  ★ ★½   **Confusion Is Sex (1983; SST, 1987)**

  ★ ★   **Sonic Death (1984; SST, 1988)**

  ★ ★ ★   **Bad Moon Rising (Homestead, 1985)**

★ ★ ★ ★   **EVOL (SST, 1986)**

★ ★ ★ ★½   **Sister (SST, 1987)**

  ★ ★ ★   **Master = Dik Beat On the Brat (EP) (SST, 1987)**

★ ★ ★ ★ ★   **Daydream Nation (Enigma/Blast First, 1988)**

★ ★ ★ ★½   **Goo (DGC, 1990)**

★ ★ ★ ★½   **Dirty (DGC, 1992)**

CICCONE YOUTH
★ ★ ★ ★ **The Whitey Album (Blast First, 1988)**
Protégés of composer Glenn Branca, Sonic Youth was an art band originally (and, to some extent, still is), and at first more interested in guitar noise as a matter of harmonic structure than as a means to rock out. As such, the band's early recordings can be slow going. *Sonic Death*, a collection of early odds and ends, is poorly recorded and moves at such an excruciatingly slow pace that only the most devoted fans will have the patience to wade through its rambling workouts. Focus is not a problem with *Sonic Youth*, which, though hardly pop-friendly, at least offers songs; trouble is, the focus of these pieces isn't on any kind of melody but the ringing harmonics and richly textured feedback that guitarists Thurston Moore and Lee Ranaldo stretch across these static rhythmic structures. If that makes the album sound like egghead fare, well . . . yeah, egghead fare about says it. And despite its fragmented cover of the Stooges' "I Wanna Be Your Dog," *Confusion Is Sex* isn't a whole lot grittier; if anything, this crew plays the Stooges as if they like the idea of rocking out better than the act.

That begins to change with *Bad Moon Rising*, on which "Society Is a Hole" uses its guitar clangor more to frame the vocal than the other way around, while "Death Valley '69" (recorded with Lydia Lunch) triples its intensity by tying the harmonic momentum of the rhythm guitars to the steadily intensifying pulse of the rhythm section. Brainy, sure, but exciting as hell. There's even more of that sort of thing on *EVOL*, but the most interesting development isn't the pummelling physicality of "Expressway to Yr. Skull" but the understated menace of the whispered "Shadow of a Doubt."

From there, it's not far to the near-conventional song structures on *Sister*—although the Youth, as might be expected, make sure to wrap the most melodic elements of songs like "(I Got a) Catholic Block" in snarling swirls of noise. But even the band's noise had become by this point eloquent enough to be considered a hook, and the same goes for the dense, dark sprawl of *Daydream Nation*, the Youth's most successful subversion of pop appeal to this point. From the light, Lou Reed–ish melody in "Teen Age Riot" to the whirling soundstorms within "Eric's Trip" and the ineluctable energy of "Silver Rocket," Sonic Youth achieves a perfect balance between melody and noise, accessibility and ugliness.

Around this point, the Youth also began to flirt with genre parodies. *Master = Dik Beat on the Brat* is only a so-so rap send-up, but *The Whitey Album*, credited to Ciccone Youth though actually the work of Sonic Youth plus fIREHOSE bassist Mike Watt, is far more successful, pushing the Youth's Madonna fixation to an amusing extreme with "Into the Groovey" and wittily deconstructing Robert Palmer's "Addicted to Love."

Such shenanigans didn't change the band's overall direction, however, which is why the only rap overtone on *Goo* is a Chuck D cameo on "Kool Thing." But the writing is even stronger than it was on *Daydream Nation*, meaning that not only are songs like "Dirty Boots," "Titanium Exposé" and "My Friend Goo" blessed with sharper melodies and more tightly constructed soundscapes, but the lyrics are often ingeniously affecting, as with "Tunic (Song for Karen)," a surprisingly sympathetic treatment of Karen Carpenter's life and hard times. There's little sympathy to be had on *Dirty*; though most of what the Youth serve up here is pure unadulterated rage, from the screaming soundstorm of "Swimsuit Issue" to the pointedly political rant of "Youth Against Fascism," trouble is it's all heat but no warmth, meaning that only a handful of the songs—the carefully drawn "Shoot," for instance, or the growling, garagey "100%"—come across as convincingly as the best of *Daydream Nation*. — J.D.C.

SONNY AND CHER
★ ★ ★ **The Beat Goes On—The Best of Sonny & Cher (Atlantic, 1991)**
This anthology collects the duo's sub-Spector, pre-variety-show trash classics, such as "Baby Don't Go," "I Got You Babe" and the title cut. — M.C.

S.O.S. BAND
★ ★½ **The S.O.S. Band (Tabu/Epic 1980)**
★ ★½ **Too (Tabu/Epic, 1981)**
★ ★ ★ **On the Rise (Tabu/Epic, 1983)**
★ ★ ★ **Just the Way You Like It (Tabu/Epic, 1984)**
★ ★ ★ **Sands of Time (Tabu/Epic, 1986)**
★ ★ **Diamonds in the Raw (Tabu/Epic, 1987)**
★ ★ ★½ **The Way You Like It (CBS Special Products, 1988)**
★ ★ ★ **One of Many Nights (A&M, 1991)**
The S.O.S. Band transmits on two frequencies. Mostly, this long-running Atlanta dance band provides dependable,

medium-watt grooves. With ex-Time members Jimmy Jam and Terry Lewis producing, it's a different story: S.O.S. singer Mary Davis's voice shines like a beacon through the pulsing, synthesized storm. Through the mid-'80s, Jam and Lewis sculpted a series of leisurely, exquisite disco singles with Davis and the S.O.S. Band. Songs like "Just Be Good to Me," "Tell Me If You Still Care, "Just the Way You Like It," "No One's Gonna Love You" and "The Finest" (and all their endless remixes) helped update R&B for the computer age. Tempering the modern techno feel of Minneapolis with a taste of Southern soul's drawling intensity, Jam and Lewis found a challenging outlet for their ambitions: the S.O.S. Band's enticing blend of funk, pop and rock still sounds fresh.

This group's legacy is not well served by the album format. *On the Rise*, *Just the Way You Like It* and *Sands of Time* include the above-mentioned hits alongside material that suffers by comparison. Though it misses a few gems, the budget-line sampler *The Way You Like It* captures some of the S.O.S. Band's urgency and elegance. — M.C.

SOUL ASYLUM
- ★★ **Say What You Will . . . (Twin/ Tone, 1984)**
- ★★★ **Made to Be Broken (Twin/Tone, 1986)**
- ★½ **Time's Incinerator (Twin/Tone, 1986)**
- ★★★ **While You Were Out (Twin/Tone, 1986)**
- ★★★★ **Hang Time (A&M, 1988)**
- ★★★ **Clam Dip & Other Delights (Twin/Tone, 1988)**
- ★★★½ **And the Horse They Rode In On (A&M, 1990)**

Heavily indebted to Hüsker Dü, Soul Asylum roared out of Minneapolis with a sound that was piquantly melodic, brutally loud and subtly eclectic. Traces of these qualities can be heard beneath the bargain-basement sound of *Say What You Will . . .* , but the group doesn't come into focus until *Made to Be Broken*, on which songs like "Ship of Fools" and "Made to Be Broken" make the most of the band's innate tunefulness and fondness for country and jazz licks. (The cassette-only *Time's Incinerator* compiles outtakes from those sessions plus other collectors-only arcana). Apart from slightly sharper melodies (as in the ragingly infectious "Crashing Down"), not much changes with *While You Were Out*, but *Hang Time* is a significant step forward,

thanks to the knotty riffs and muscular attack of "Down on up to Me," "Ode" and "Little Too Clean." Boasting a cover that parodies Herb Alpert's *Whipped Cream and Other Delights* (apparently an in-joke over the band's relationship with A&M, which Alpert owned), *Clam Dip and Other Delights* is a pleasant-but-short collection of oddities that's worth hearing mostly for the jokey folk number "P-9." But then it's back to form with *And the Horse They Rode In On*, which alternates raucous rockers like "Easy Street" with quietly dynamic numbers like "Nice Guys (Don't Get Paid)." — J.D.C.

THE SOUL STIRRERS
- ★★★★★ **The Original Soul Stirrers Featuring Sam Cooke (Specialty, 1959)**
- ★★★★★ **The Soul Stirrers Featuring Sam Cooke (Specialty, 1970)**
- ★★★ **Going Back to the Lord Again (Specialty, 1972)**
- ★★★ **Tribute to Sam Cooke (Chess/MCA, 1986)**
- ★★★ **Resting Easy (Chess/MCA, 1986)**
- ★★★★★ **Sam Cooke With the Soul Stirrers (Specialty, 1991)**

Creators of the modern gospel quartet sound, the Soul Stirrers have been blessed with some of the most important lead singers in gospel history—singers whose shadow looms over not only gospel but rock and soul as well. Sam Cooke is only the best known in this honored line of frontmen, but the finest of them all was R. H. Harris; Johnnie Taylor, who like Cooke went on to success in the secular world, Paul Foster, Willie Rogers, James Medlock, and Leroy Taylor were eyeball-to-eyeball with Cooke, although none possessed Cooke's charisma, nor did all have the benefit, as Cooke did, of Harris's counsel to help them develop their abilities as showmen. But it was Harris who was the consummate stylist, often imitated, never equaled, with a flair for phrasing and emotional control other singers could only envy. Cooke attempted, but failed, to emulate Harris's style, but in the process developed his own approach that incorporated cool sensuality, intense commitment and signature vocal filigrees that served him well when he left gospel to lay the foundation for modern soul music.

The current in-print catalogue of Soul Stirrers titles includes little of Harris's work, unfortunately. *The Soul Stirrers Featuring Sam Cooke*, *The Original Soul Stirrers Featuring Sam Cooke* and *Sam Cooke With the Soul Stirrers* all contain "By and By," an extraordinary performance featuring Harris and Paul Foster that leaves you desiring more. Cooke's performances on these two albums are overwhelming; his voice is fully developed and all the nuances that would prove so affecting on his secular recordings are in evidence: the Harris-taught diction, the modulated timbre and the delicate "whoa-whoa-oa-o" that became a trademark Cooke device are employed to stirring effect on "Wonderful," in a vibrant double lead with Foster on "He'll Welcome Me" and especially on "Touch the Hem of His Garment," wherein the twists and turns of Cooke's phrasing create a shattering impact. Taylor is heard performing "The Love of God" in a style reminiscent of Cooke's, but with telltale signs of the gritty delivery he developed on his Stax recordings in the '60s.

Going Back to the Lord Again, Resting Easy and *Tribute to Sam Cooke* are latter-day Soul Stirrers. Lead singers Richard Miles and Martin Jacox are powerful in their own right, but the material isn't as consistently moving as the group's earlier repertoire. Still, the Soul Stirrers were one of the first groups to adapt to modern instrumental backing, and these later albums are full-blown productions betraying a Memphis influence in their arrangements. *Resting Easy* might have been titled *Tribute to Sam Cooke, Vol. 2*, so close is it in style to Cooke's music, in addition to being graced by lead singers Willie Rogers and Martin Jacox, whose voices and technique are similar to Cooke's. This aside, both albums, as well as *Going Back to the Lord*, are worthy additions to the Soul Stirrers' legacy. — D.M.

SOUL SURVIVORS

★ ★ ★½ **When the Whistle Blows, Anything Goes (Collectables, NA)**

Gamble and Huff's "Expressway to Your Heart" (1967) was this Northeastern sextet's only big hit, but it was snappy, surefire R&B—as was everything else this highly energetic bunch attempted. Resembling a cruder version of the Young Rascals, the Survivors had the great nerve to take on James Brown and almost pull it off (their version of "Please, Please, Please" really kicks) and the hip humor to fashion a funky cover of Donovan's "Hey Gyp." Holding up much better than some of their more famous contemporaries, Soul Survivors sound strong even now. — P.E.

SOUL II SOUL

★ ★ ★ ★ **Keep on Movin' (Virgin, 1989)**
★ ★ ★½ **Vol. II 1990—A New Decade (Virgin, 1990)**

Soul II Soul started out as a sound system—a sort of roving disco setup—and never completely coalesced into a band. Even so, when this English outfit hit the airwaves in 1989, it turned the R&B world on its ear. Much of Soul II Soul's success stemmed from its ability to fold rumbling, hypnotic reggae bass lines into snappy, swaggering hip-hop drum patterns for a pulse that seemed at once languorous and urgent. Yet as much as that unmistakable groove made the group's singles stand out, what ultimately made them hits were the singers Soulsters Jazzie B and Nellee Hooper found for each song: Caron Wheeler ("Keep on Movin' " and "Back to Life," from *Keep on Movin'*), Victoria Wilson-James ("A Dream's a Dream," from *A New Decade*) and Kym Mazelle ("Missing You," from *A New Decade*). — J.D.C.

SOUNDGARDEN

★ ★½ **Screaming Life/Fopp (1987, 1988; Sub Pop, 1990)**
★ ★ ★ **Ultramega OK (SST, 1988)**
★ ★ ★ ★ **Louder Than Love (A&M, 1989)**
★ ★ ★ ★ **Badmotorfinger (A&M, 1991)**

Like other alumni of Seattle's Sub Pop stable, Soundgarden appropriates the sound and fury of heavy metal without falling prey to its stylistic excesses. Of course, none of that much mattered before the band's songwriting matured. *Screaming Life/Fopp* (which compiles two late-'80s EPs) is far less interesting when the group performs its own tunes than when it covers the Ohio Players ("Fopp"), while *Ultramega OK*, despite its texturally adventurous use of feedback and multitracking, squanders the band's fevered intensity on forgettable, post-Sabbath riff rockers.

But *Louder Than Love* upgrades the band's melodic content and better exploits the contrast between Chris Cornell's keening vocals and Kim Thayil's slab-o-metal guitar grind; as such, there's an almost Zeppelinesque majesty to "Hands All Over," and a dizzying, hypnotic power to "Loud Love." *Badmotorfinger* continues to build on that foundation, from the relentless momentum of "Rusty Cage" to the savage psychedelia of "Searching with My Good Eye Closed." — J.D.C.

SOUP DRAGONS

★½ **Hang Ten! (Sire, 1987)**
★½ **This Is Our Art (Sire, 1988)**
★½ **Love God (Big Life/Mercury, 1990)**

What's most depressing about the Soup Dragons isn't the fact that this Scots quartet will switch styles every time the musical fashion changes; given the intensely trend-conscious nature of the U.K. pop scene, that kind of attitude was probably inevitable. Rather, what makes hearing the Soup Dragons such a joyless experience is the group's almost total lack of conviction, a deep-seated shallowness that makes even its best work seem cheap and tawdry.

When the group first made it to vinyl, the big rage in Britain was for what critic Simon Frith described as "shambling" music. Naturally, the Soup Dragons fit right in, thanks to the amiably raucous sound of *Hang Ten!*, which finds the Dragons trying to emulate the more endearing sounds of the Shop Assistants and the Woodentops. When shambling fell out of fashion the Dragons were at a loss; *This Is Our Art* reflects that confusion in its astonishingly pointless stylistic range. After sitting out the acid-house craze, the group emerged in 1990 with *Love God*, an album of Manchester-derived dance pop that included a dumb-but-catchy remake of the Rolling Stones' "I'm Free."
— J.D.C.

JOE SOUTH

★★★½ **Joe South's Greatest Hits (Capitol, 1970)**
★★★½ **The Best of Joe South (Rhino, 1990)**

Before country or crossover were cool, Joe South made redneck rock & roll with verve, wit and a dab of folksy poetry. Session guitarist for everyone from Bob Dylan and Aretha Franklin to Conway Twitty and Wilson Pickett, South took off solo in 1968 with three hit singles, "Games People Play," "Birds of a Feather" and "These Are Not My People." With material covered by artists as diverse as Mel Torme and Deep Purple, South was fully established as a songwriter. He deserves that reputation, but it limits his achievement—his own records are punchy and memorable, driven by his tough guitar and amiable, deep-voiced twang. In spirit, South foretold the arrival of much bigger-selling outlaws. — P.E.

SOUTHSIDE JOHNNY AND THE ASBURY JUKES

★★★½ **I Don't Want to Go Home (Epic, 1976)**
★★★ **This Time It's for Real (Epic, 1977)**
★★★★ **Hearts of Stone (Epic, 1978)**
★★★★ **Havin' a Party With Southside Johnny and the Asbury Jukes (Epic, 1979)**
★★ **The Jukes (Mercury, 1979)**
★★ **Love Is a Sacrifice (Mercury, 1980)**
★★★★ **Reach Up and Touch the Sky: Southside Johnny and the Asbury Jukes Live! (Mercury, 1981)**
★★★★ **Better Days (Impact, 1991)**

SOUTHSIDE JOHNNY SOLO

★★★ **Slow Dance (Cypress, 1988)**

Sweat, more than polish, marked the approach of these R&B revivalists, but it was righteous sweat—Southside Johnny Lyon and the Asbury Jukes were a bar band made in heaven. Fittingly, their quintessential set is the live one, *Reach Up and Touch the Sky*. With its 15 numbers taxing the limits of the band's terrific horn section, and guitarists Billy Rush and Joe Gramolini trading riffs with blazing efficiency, Johnny cuts loose—his vocals echoing the urgency of Otis Redding, Wilson Pickett and Eric Burdon. On this album, the group is as truly a rock & roll band—Chuck Berry's "Back in the U.S.A." really kicks—as a soul revue, and the highlights include rollicking takes on Sam Cooke's "Having a Party," as well as the band's signature tunes, Bruce Springsteen's "The Fever" and Steve Van Zandt's "I Don't Want to Go Home."

With Springsteen first their fan and then, for a while, a casual mentor, the Jukes grew from house-band status at Asbury Park's famed Stone Pony nightclub to headliners, by reviving the greatness of the music Southside, Springsteen, and Van Zandt grew up on—muscular soul and early-'60s rock. Ronnie Spector and Lee Dorsey sat in on their very accomplished 1976 debut, *I Don't Want to Go Home*, and the band's next three records showed no slackening in skill or zest (Springsteen's title track and "Talk to Me" make *Hearts of Stone* the standout).

Billy Rush took over as chief songwriter on *The Jukes* and *Love Is a Sacrifice*; his tunes, particularly the rockers, were capable, but he couldn't match Van Zandt. On *Sacrifice*, Southside was less fevered than he'd been before. As its title suggests, *Slow Dance* features Johnny dealing in a softer sort of soul; he sounds fine, if a bit muted. *Better Days*, produced by Little Steven Van Zandt, constituted a powerful comeback.
— P.E.

SPANDAU BALLET

★½   Journeys to Glory (Chrysalis, 1981)
★   Diamond (1982; Chrysalis, 1986)
★★★ True (Chrysalis, 1983)
★★   Parade (Chrysalis, 1984)
★★½ The Singles Collection (Chrysalis, 1985)
★½   Through the Barricades (Epic, 1986)

Eyebrows arched and strutting gamely, London's Spandau Ballet joined Duran Duran in initiating the New Romantic fad—a bombastic fusion of frilly shirts and neo-disco. Spandau's debut sounded an awful lot like Duran Duran and contained only one decent cut, the single "To Cut a Long Story Short." The rest, featuring songs with such portentous titles as "Musclebound" and "Reformation," sounded thin and monotonous; the band's appeal wasn't helped by its air of vaguely fascist snobbery. *Diamond* was more of the same; its offhand attempts at experimentalism didn't help.

With *True*, however, the band found a style. Tony Hadley developed a way of vocalizing that joined the heavy dramatics of Bryan Ferry to the lounge-act "feeling" of a Gary Puckett or a bad Bobby Darin. And guitarist Gary Kemp, with "Gold" and "True," provided Hadley perfect songs for hamming it up: lush MOR that would've been clever if it had been intended ironically. Guitarist-percussionist Steve Norman switched over to sax, and added fittingly smarmy fills. *Parade* was a lesser *True*, but with *Through the Barricades*, Spandau took a bizarre turn toward arena rock and power ballads. *The Singles Collection* is an all-right greatest-hits package; *True*, however, remains creepily fascinating. Incidentally, Kemp and his bassist brother, Martin, starred in the gangster movie *The Krays* and were brilliant. Perhaps, after all, their years of posing paid off. — P.E.

SPANKY AND OUR GANG

★ The Best Of Spanky and Our Gang (Rhino, 1986)

"Sunday Will Never Be the Same" was a slight 1967 Mamas and Papas soundalike. The rest of the Spanky oeuvre was dreadful mid-'60s dreck. Spanky McFarlane's voice is cute, but forcing it to try Hoagy Carmichael's "Stardust" or the Depression lament "Brother Can You Spare a Dime" was cruel. "Lazy Day," the sunny sextet's second hit, was more typically Spanky—a breezy la-la-la tailormade for a jingle.
— P.E.

OTIS SPANN

★★★½ The Blues Never Die! (1965; Prestige, 1990)

In his brief, influential career (he died at age 40 in 1971), Mississippi-born pianist Otis Spann managed to help define the hard, urban blues sound as a member of Muddy Waters's powerhouse band in the '50s and '60s. The blues revival of the late '60s introduced him to the young rock audience and to the standard-setting young white blues players of that time, notably Paul Butterfield and Mike Bloomfield, who joined Spann and Waters on the latter's wonderful *Fathers and Sons* album. On his own, Spann displayed a smooth voice with a dollop of grit that underscored his real-life experiences with the blues. Most of his solo recordings are now out of print, but the little that remains available is first-rate. Prestige's *The Blues Never Die!* features Spann on piano throughout its 11 cuts, and on vocals on five tracks. There's not a missed step here, as the blues delivered by Spann and his estimable cohorts—who include James Cotton on harmonica and vocals and a guitarist whose *nom de disc* of "Dirty Rivers" does little to disguise the source of the distinctive, stinging lines that crop up—blow red hot and blue through some Cotton originals, Elmore James's "Dust My Broom" and Willie Dixon's "I'm Ready." — D.M.

SPARKS

★ The Best of Sparks: Music You Can Dance To (Curb/MCA, 1990)
★★½ Profile: The Ultimate Sparks Collection (Rhino, 1991)

Does the following prospect sound enticing? A long-running cult band that combines the vocal tone of Bryan Ferry at his most adenoidal—make that a falsetto Bryan Ferry—with the music-hall indulgences of Queen at its most rococco, a group whose career spans more than half a dozen record labels and more than a dozen (deleted) albums. Well, brothers Ron and Russell Mael are your men. *Profile: The Ultimate Sparks Collection* follows the demented art-rock duo through its various phases, culling representative tracks from myriad sources. Chronologically, in excruciating detail: Todd Rundgren–produced proto-punk (*Sparks*, *A Woofer in Tweeter's Clothing*), expatriate British glam-pop (*Kimono My House*, *Propaganda*, *Indiscreet*), hollow metal bombast (*Big Beat*, *Introducing Sparks*), Giorgio Moroder-produced epic disco (*No. 1 in Heaven*), blood-curdling operatic synth-pop (*Angst in My Pants*), four more out-of-print albums and off into the sunset. *The Best of Sparks: Music You Can Dance To* is a deceptively labeled reissue of a similiarly titled 1985 album. Docked a notch for inspiring the grossest excesses of both the late-'70s skinny-tie new-wave school and the early-'80s haircut pop movement. Talk about a double whammy! — M.C.

SPECIALS

★ ★ ★½   The Specials (Two Tone/Chrysalis, 1979)
★ ★ ★   More Specials (Two Tone/Chrysalis, 1980)
★ ★ ★ ★   The Singles Collection (Chrysalis, 1991)

SPECIAL AKA

★ ★ ★½   In the Studio (Two Tone/Chrysalis, 1984)

The British ska revival of the early '80s had quite a bit going for it. Dubbed the Two Tone movement after a record label and the racially integrated bands (Specials, Madness, the Beat, Selecter) on its roster, this loose conglomeration of groups mined the rapid-fire rhythms of prereggae Jamaican pop. Problem is, that particular vein couldn't sustain much more than a dance fad: Jamaican ska was a rough-edged, transitional style that didn't really lend itself to updating or expansion. *The Specials* is about as good as the British variant gets. "Message to You Rudy" and "Gangsters" deploy ska's fidgety beat and fluid horn charts in service of socially concerned hooks. While the nervous new-wave pace feels dated now, the group's energy level and audible commitment are still quite refreshing. And danceable, even without the requisite skinny tie and porkpie hat. *More Specials* is a somewhat sloppy second helping, though "Rat Race" holds up favorably with the debut's highlights. Keyboardist and Two Tone majordomo Jerry Dammers takes the Specials in an even more politicized direction after that. "Ghost Town," originally released on a 1981 EP and included on *The Singles Collection*, offers a gripping and tuneful acount of the Brixton riots and their chilling effect on British society. When several group members bailed out and formed Fun Boy Three, Dammers bounced back with the Special AKA. Solid jazz and soul influences buoy the somewhat didactic songwriting on *In the Studio*; however, the centerpiece, "Free Nelson Mandela," is a gracefully assured, genuinely catchy plea for the South African leader's release. Three years in the making, *In the Studio* seems to be Jerry Dammers's swan song. *The Singles Collection* offers resounding proof that the Specials were more than another trend-hopping English dance band. — M.C.

PHIL SPECTOR

★ ★ ★ ★ ★   Back to Mono (1958–1969) (Abkco, 1991)

Finally, after all the legends and scandals die, we will be left with the music as the measure of the man. And it is here, four CDs worth of grand, glorious, visionary pop productions aimed directly at the heart of every teenager who has ever felt the explosions—hormonal, emotional, whatever—that make adolescence the best and worst of times. In the process Phil Spector refined and redefined the concept of record producer as *auteur*, which he had learned as a protégé of Jerry Leiber and Mike Stoller. But Spector took rock production far beyond anything Leiber and Stoller—or anyone else at that time—ever envisioned. Layer upon layer of guitars, drums, pianos, strings and a couple of warehouses worth of percussion mesh into a solid roar behind some of the best pop, rock and soul singers of the era, creating an aural extravaganza that has no parallel in popular music—though, in Spector's estimation, there may be a parallel in opera. He spoke of his "Wagnerian approach to rock & roll," and somewhere along the way it became "the Wall of Sound." Maybe we should leave it at that.

Spector was born and raised in the Bronx, New York, but moved to Los Angeles with his mother after his father died. In high school he took up guitar and piano, and befriended another aspiring musician, Marshall Lieb. With another friend, Annette Kleinbard, they formed a group called the Teddy Bears and recorded a song Spector had written, "To Know Him Is to Love Him," the title sentiment taken from the inscription on Spector's father's tombstone. Produced by the 17-year-old Spector for the Doré label, the single hit Number One in October 1958 and remained there for three weeks.

The Teddy Bears failed to deliver a successful followup and disbanded in 1959. By that time Spector had begun to shuttle between New York and L.A., producing or assisting whenever the opportunity arose. In L.A. he struck up a friendship with two producers, Lester Sill and Lee Hazelwood, who had a number of independent labels and plenty of work for the ambitious

660 • The Spinners

Spector. In 1959 and '60 Spector formed another trio, Spector's Three, with Annette Merar (later Spector's first wife) and Russ Titelman, who would go on to be one of the top producers at Warner Bros. Spector's Three were much in the mold of the Fleetwoods—soft, close harmony with a smooth, bland lead voice. Two singles failed, but one of them, "Mr. Robin," features a faint, echoed vocal that would become a familiar element of Spector's later productions. In 1960 Spector produced a Clyde McPhatter–style singer named Kell Osborne. The A side of the single was "The Bells of St. Mary's," a song McPhatter had cut with the Drifters. The B side has become more significant, though: "That's Alright Baby" finds Osborne supported by twanging guitars, pounding tom toms, and a faceless but wailing background chorus. It is the first, faint stirrings of "a Wagnerian approach."

Spector went back to New York to apprentice with Leiber and Stoller, and one of his early successes came when he co-wrote Ben E. King's "Spanish Harlem" (1961) with Leiber. Another trio then figured prominently in Spector's story. With the Paris Sisters Spector cut a single, "I Love How You Love Me," upon which he lavished hours of studio time refining every detail; this focus on control and perfection would become part of the Spector method, much to the exasperation of those around him. But he got results: in New York in '61 and '62 he produced some of his first and best pop sides in Curtis Lee's "Pretty Little Angel Eyes," Ray Peterson's "Corinna, Corinna" and the extraordinary "Every Breath I Take."

The year 1962 was notable for another event in Spector's life: fed up with working for independent labels, he teamed up with his first mentor, Lester Sill, and formed Philles Records, and shortly thereafter bought out Sill and took complete control of the label. For material he drew from the deep well of the era's greatest pop and rock songwriters: Goffin-King, Barry-Greenwich, Mann-Weill, Gene Pitney and, of course, Phil Spector. For musicians, he used virtually anyone who was anyone in Los Angeles. For artists he found the best of the second generation of girl groups in the Crystals and the Ronettes; used the overpowering vocal style of session singer Darlene Love both on solo recordings and with the Crystals (Love's is the only voice on the Crystals classic, "He's a Rebel") and Bob B. Soxx and the Blue Jeans; and

uncovered the prototypical blue-eyed soul aggregate in the Righteous Brothers. He also worked with Ike and Tina Turner, whose 1966 Spector-produced single and album, "River Deep–Mountain High," is the apotheosis of the Wall of Sound.

Back to Mono focuses primarily on the best-known Spector recordings between '58 and '69, but does offer a healthy dose of otherwise-rare Ronettes album tracks and several top-flight Darlene Love solo sides. One of the rarest tracks is the Crystals' 1962 recording of Goffin-King's "He Hit Me (It Felt Like a Kiss)," which was withdrawn by Spector shortly after release for fear that the lyrics were too controversial for pop radio. A special treat is the inclusion of the great *A Christmas Gift to You*, Spector's 1963 Christmas album with all of the Philles stars on board. Only Elvis's first Christmas album approaches this one in terms of melding rock with the Yuletide spirit. Some of the earliest Spector tracks—those by Kell Osborne and Spector's Three—aren't included on *Back to Mono* but can be found on an out-of-print Rhino Records title, *The Early Productions 1958-1961*. Spector completists will want to track down the *sine qua non* of the producer's work, the six-volume *Phil Spector Wall of Sound* series issued in the mid-'70s by the Phil Spector International label. The set includes two volumes of Rare Masters, including tracks by April Stevens, Betty Willis and Bonnie and the Treasures. Other volumes include a hits album (*Yesterday's Hits Today*), and individual titles devoted to the Crystals, the Ronettes and Bob B. Soxx and the Blue Jeans.

Back to Mono is indeed in glorious mono, and it comes with a Back to Mono button and a book with song lyrics, sessionography, personnel listings, a 1965 profile on Spector by Tom Wolfe and an appreciation by writer David Hinckley. — D.M.

THE SPINNERS

★ ★ ★ ★½ Spinners (Atlantic, 1973)
★ ★ ★ ★   Mighty Love (Atlantic, 1974)
★ ★ ★   New and Improved (Atlantic, 1974)
★ ★ ★ ★½ Pick of the Litter (Atlantic, 1975)
★ ★ ★   Happiness Is Being With the Spinners (Atlantic, 1976)
★ ★½ Yesterday, Today and Tomorrow (Atlantic, 1977)
★ ★ ★ ★½ Best of the Spinners (Atlantic, 1978)
★ ★   Motown Superstar Series, Vol. 9 (Motown, 1981)

★ ★ **Best of the Spinners (Motown, 1981)**

★ ★ ★ ★ ★ **A One of a Kind Love Affair: The Anthology (Atlantic, 1991)**

The liner notes for *Mighty Love* say it best: "Whenever Thom wants a hit he simply has to keep still long enough to hear it coming. Riding on the wings of the wind. Thom has a lot to say to the world and much of it is said through the Spinners. So Talk On Thom Bell—With Your Bad Self." For a stretch in the early '70s, it really did seem as though this Philadelphia producer had the magic touch. Using the same studios and many of the same musicians as crosstown rivals Kenny Gamble and Leon Huff, Thom Bell carved out a distinct niche in the emerging Philly Soul spectrum. He worked well with falsetto-drenched harmony groups like the Delfonics and Stylistics, but his subtle dynamics clicked into place with the Spinners: second-string Motown vets with an unproven lead singer.

Philippé Wynne quickly asserted himself as a different kind of soul man: sensitive (but never hesitant), thoughtful (not impulsive), ever ready to throw down when the rhythm section kicks in. His warm tenor embraces listeners in a conversational tone; Wynne never lets emotion or his ample technique overwhelm the message. *The Spinners* is also a shining example of Thom Bell's pop art. The simple, stunning arrangements isolate each voice—human and instrumental—and then gently weave the diverse strands into an indelible melody. "I'll Be Around" leads the charge, but follow-ups like "One of a Kind Love Affair," "Could It Be I'm Falling In Love" and "Ghetto Child" aren't too far behind. "How Could I Let You Get Away" establishes Wynne's devastating ballad prowess and elevates a sterling collection of singles to classic album status.

The 1991 two-CD Atlantic anthology, *A One of a Kind Love Affair*, superbly summarizes the Spinners' brilliant career, from 1961 ("That's What Girls Are Made For") to 1982 (Willie Nelson's "Funny How Time Slips Away." Also included are "Mighty Love," the Dionne Warwick duet "Then Came You," the boogie-down epic "The Rubberband Man" and, of course, *Pick of the Litter*'s "Games People Play." That song may be Thom Bell's masterpiece: immediately catchy and emotionally complex, you can hum along with "Games People Play" dozens—even hundreds—of times before the profundity of Wynne's disarming interior monologue really sinks in.

Then you're hooked. There's not a wasted note or expendable breath on *Pick of the Litter*, but Thom Bell's increasingly grand orchestral designs inevitably begin to overshadow the Spinners' mellow virtuosity. Wynne left after the disappointing *Yesterday, Today and Tomorrow*, and the Spinners achieved only one more undeniable hit with replacement John Edwards: "Workin' My Way Back to You" (from the out-of-print 1979 album, *Dancin' and Lovin'*), also included on the Atlantic anthology. Wynne toured and recorded intermittently with the P-Funk clan until his death in 1984, while Thom Bell's singular productions have become less and less frequent during the last ten years. — M.C.

SPIRIT

★ ★ ★½ **Spirit (Ode, 1968)**

★ ★ ★½ **The Family That Plays Together (Ode, 1968)**

★ ★ ★ **Clear Spirit (Ode, 1969)**

★ ★ ★ ★ **The Twelve Dreams of Dr. Sardonicus (Epic, 1970)**

★ **Feedback (Epic, 1971)**

★ ★ ★ **The Best of Spirit (Epic, 1973)**

★ **Spirit of 76 (Mercury, 1975)**

★ **Son of Spirit (Mercury, 1976)**

★ **Farther Along (Mercury, 1976)**

★ **Future Games (A Magical Kahauna Dream) (Mercury, 1977)**

★ ★ **Journey to Potatoland (Beggar's Banquet/Rhino, 1981)**

★ ★ **Spirit of '84 (Mercury, 1984)**

★ ★ **Rapture in the Chambers (I.R.S., 1989)**

★ ★ **Tent of Miracles (Dolphin, 1990)**

★ ★ ★ ★ **Time Circle (1968–1972) (Epic/Legacy, 1991)**

Originally calling themselves Spirits Rebellious after a book by Kahlil Gibran, and boasting, in middle-aged drummer Ed Cassidy, with his shaved head, a visual focus of a decidedly curious sort, this California band was a group of hippie mystics—and makers of some of the most intriguing music of the late '60s. A classically trained Hendrix disciple, Randy California joined Cassidy, keyboardist John Locke, vocalist Jay Ferguson and bassist Mark Andes in 1967, and the group soon achieved an idiosyncratic synthesis of jazz and mildly psychedelic rock, augmented by inventive orchestral arrangements. While there are echoes of the Who's harmonies on "Uncle Jack," and "Topanga Canyon" recalls Neil Young's Buffalo Springfield work, Spirit's material doesn't really sound like any other music of the time. This was a band who released as its first single a strange meditation on death ("Mechanical World"), toyed intriguingly with wordplay ("The Great Canyon Fire in General," "Fresh Garbage")—and seemed hellbent on achieving a resolutely uncommercial cult status. Their first album certainly gained them that. With its infectious riff and dazzling guitar solo, "I Got a Line On You," from *The Family That Plays Together*, however, made them accessible to a broader audience—even if the jazz flair of "Sherozode" and the ethereal grace of "Dream Within a Dream" were hardly easy radio fodder.

Clear Spirit showed a tougher side of the band—the guitar on "Dark-Eyed Woman" kicks and crunches, and an assertive single, "1984," gave Spirit its second hit. "I'm Truckin' " and "New Dope in Town" now hold only period interest, but the instrumental finesse of "Ice" remains impressive. *Twelve Dreams of Dr. Sardonicus* was the masterwork; a mix of kettle drums, cowbell and acoustic guitar made "Nature's Way" one of the band's most memorable singles, and with "Mr. Skin" and "Morning Will Come" Spirit proved that it could deliver not only characteristically eccentric material but straightforward songs. On *Feedback,* only Cassidy remained of the original members, so it's not really Spirit and it's not very good.

Randy California rejoined for a series of albums on Mercury, and there have been other attempts to re-create the band's early glory. None has panned out. Spirit's first five records all are worth having; *Time Circle,* supplanting *The Best of Spirit,* is an excellent compilation. — P.E.

SPOOKY TOOTH
★ ★ ★ ½ **Spooky Two (A&M, 1969)**
This British quintet is survived by its second—and best—album. Mixing keyboardist Gary Wright's mid-range grumble with guitarist Mike Harrison's blood-curdling falsetto, Spooky Tooth carved out its own niche in rock's newly erected wall of solid metal. The wooden beat and hammerhead guitar riffs are leavened, in this case, by Wright's organ washes and warm vocal tone. Melodic dirges like "That Was Only Yesterday" and "Hangman Hang My Shell On a Tree" bring a touch of neo-Californian folk-rock to Spooky's proceedings, though "Evil Woman"—all nine whomping minutes of it—should satisfy even the most deranged fuzztone fanatic. Gary Wright left Spooky

Tooth a year after *Two,* returning to the fold for the bloozier (and now-deleted) *You Broke My Heart So I Busted Your Jaw.* That 1973 album also features a young Mick Jones on guitar; in retrospect, the seeds of Foreigner's later pop-metal hybrid can be unearthed on *Spooky Two.* Gary Wright's solo career—peaking with the featherweight debut hit "Dreamweaver" in 1975—is another story altogether. — M.C.

DUSTY SPRINGFIELD
★ ★ ★ ★ **Dusty Springfield's Golden Hits (1966; Polydor, 1985)**
★ ★ ★ ★ **Dusty in Memphis (1969; Rhino, 1992)**
★ ★ ★ **A Brand New Me (1970; Rhino, 1992)**
★ ★ **White Heat (Casablanca, 1982)**
After flirting with Peter, Paul and Mary–style folk and scoring big with "Silver Threads and Golden Needles" (1962), Dusty Springfield left a band she'd formed with her brother (and titled, obviously enough, the Springfields) to triumph with "I Only Want to Be With You" in 1963. Heavily influenced by Motown, the single's rhythmic drive and sure melody freed the singer to flourish one of the best (and huskiest) voices English pop ever delivered. "Wishin' and Hopin' " and "I Just Don't Know What to Do With Myself," both by Bacharach-David, came next, establishing her as a star. Finally, "You Don't Have to Say You Love Me" (1966) made her Britain's queen of the dramatic ballad.

In 1969, she released her finest effort, *Dusty in Memphis.* Produced by Jerry Wexler and featuring Atlantic's crack soul players, it was commanding R&B, including a phenomenal version of "Son of a Preacher Man." (This LP and its Atlantic follow-up, *A Brand New Me,* were both reissued on CD by Rhino in 1992.) Floundering throughout the '70s (during which she was reduced for a while to singing backup for Anne Murray), Springfield unsuccessfully attempted a comeback at the end of the decade with *White Heat* (now out of print). As a late-in-the-game disco diva, she came off sounding strained. In 1987, she turned in a great guest performance on the Pet Shop Boys' "What Have I Done to Deserve This"—but no Springfield revival seemed in sight. — P.E.

RICK SPRINGFIELD
★ ★ **Working Class Dog (RCA, 1980)**
★ ★ **Success Hasn't Spoiled Me Yet (RCA, 1982)**

★½ Living in Oz (RCA, 1983)
★½ Hard to Hold (RCA, 1984)
★ Tao (RCA, 1985)
★ Rock of Life (RCA, 1988)
★★½ Rick Springfield's Greatest Hits (RCA, 1989)

Because he's a good-looking guy who has augmented his singing career with a stint in soap operas, it's very easy to write Rick Springfield off as just another pretty face selling empty, derivative rock & roll. But that's not entirely fair—Springfield's music would seem empty and derivative even if he were bone-ugly.

Music was actually Springfield's first career choice; he hit the big-time in his native Australia as a member of Zoot, and released three albums in the U.S. before pursuing a career in TV: The sappy, Beatle-ish *Beginnings* (1972); the slightly harder-rocking *Comic Book Heroes* (1973); and the oddly elaborate *Wait for the Night* (1976), which at times suggests an unholy alliance between Elton John and Queen. All are mercifully out of print.

Springfield decided to have another go at the pop life in 1980, with *Working Class Dog*, which offers a tunefully sanitized approximation of Springsteen-Mellencamp prole rock, with then-fashionable new wave overtones. As typified by the earnest, hook-filled "Jessie's Girl," it was an eminently marketable sound, and Springfield's added visibility as "Dr. Noah Drake" on the soap opera *General Hospital* all but guaranteed the album's sales. *Success Hasn't Spoiled Me Yet* offers more of the same, although downplaying the guitar-rock aspect of his sound in favor of a lighter, love-song-oriented approach; *Living in Oz* works a bit of bleached-out reggae into the mix, but otherwise sticks to the same, predictable slop as its immediate predecessors.

With the soundtrack album *Hard to Hold*, Springfield combines his two careers in a single burst of audience exploitation; a more apt title would have been *Hard to Stomach*. But by this point, Springfield-mania had pretty much reached its zenith, and rather than become yesterday's pin-up, he changed styles for *Tao* and *Rock of Life*, beefing up the beat and upping the synth-quotient in an attempt to sound modern. It didn't work. *Greatest Hits* compiles Springfield's most listenable efforts. —J.D.C.

BRUCE SPRINGSTEEN

★★★½ Greetings From Asbury Park, New Jersey (Columbia, 1973)

★★★★★ The Wild, the Innocent and the E Street Shuffle (Columbia, 1973)
★★★★★ Born to Run (Columbia, 1975)
★★★★ Darkness at the Edge of Town (Columbia, 1978)
★★★★ The River (Columbia, 1980)
★★★★½ Nebraska (Columbia, 1982)
★★★★★ Born in the U.S.A. (Columbia, 1984)
★★★★ Live, 1975–1985 (Columbia, 1986)
★★★★★ Tunnel of Love (Columbia, 1987)
★★★★½ Human Touch (Columbia, 1992)
★★★½ Lucky Town (Columbia, 1992)

Bruce Springsteen is the last of the great rock & roll true believers—and with work of remarkable consistency, range and power, he demands the same seriousness of attention that rock's older masters require. By the time of Springsteen's advent, a wholly original rocker was a contradiction in terms; the music had simply been around too long. The Beatles and Stones had absorbed and transmuted the sounds of early rock & roll, blues and R&B; Dylan had concentrated on folk, gospel and country. Springsteen saturated himself, then, with the music of two past generations—his gift remains the astonishing one of achieving an original synthesis of all these strains. Alternately, he recalls the hope and hard vernacular of Woody Guthrie, the operatic darkness of Roy Orbison, the zest of British Invasion pop, the drama of Motown and the punch of Stax/Volt. In time, each of these influences became less studied, and Springsteen grew in ease and stature; he was no longer only the passionate fan of these styles but their inheritor. With his mature work, he began making songs that were vehemently his own, their strength only the deeper from being draped in the glories of the past.

With *Greetings From Asbury Park*, Springsteen's obvious reference is Dylan. Way too wordy and sabotaged by thin production, the songs still bespeak a remarkable debut. "Blinded by the Light" and "For You" are strong and smart, and Springsteen's epic ambition is immediately apparent. *The Wild, the Innocent, and the E Street Shuffle* is a masterpiece—and it's only his second time out. Cinematic in its sweep, the record collects vignettes of urban dreams and adolescent restlessness; crammed with poetic detail, "4th of July, Asbury Park (Sandy)" and "Rosalita (Come Out Tonight)" are affecting short stories, and

Springsteen's themes of loyalty, courage, the sheer joy of rock & roll, and the aching need to live up to the future's promise, get their first full treatment. Having assembled a cast of ace musicians, he taxes them to the uttermost: the horn riffs, tempo changes and stylistic shifts come fast and furious within almost all of the (long) songs—the thrill comes in listening to the players go for broke.

With *Born to Run*, Springsteen declares himself a rocker. Shearing his style of the admittedly impressive fanciness of *The Wild, the Innocent*, he aims for music with as big a sound as Phil Spector's and as much kick as the early Elvis—and he delivers. Theatricality still adheres to his approach, and the record's majesty is still self-conscious—but "Thunder Road," "Backstreets" and "She's the One" are absolutely heartfelt drama. Springsteen's lyrics have gained in precision; the poetry is more colloquial, hence more deeply moving. By this time, Springsteen had assembled an actual band—the E Street Band—and a lovely camaraderie helps sustain his new power; he's playing with the benign equivalent of a kick-ass gang.

If *Born to Run* is fueled by youthful optimism and a sense of release, *Darkness* is a hard-eyed coming of age. "Adam Raised a Cain" and "Promised Land" live up to the biblical resonance of their titles; Springsteen's anger and yearning seem universal, archetypal. Howling almost like John Lennon and playing blistering guitar, he rocks tougher than ever before (or since); on the slower numbers, however, he retains his signal gift for empathy. The songs' settings—dead-end small towns, vast stretches of highway—highlight Springsteen's revisionist Americana; on *Darkness*, he's coming on like Thomas Wolfe or John Steinbeck, writers whose passionate love of their homelands concedes nothing in the way of pathos, loss and regret.

A giant four-sided set, *The River* is Springsteen's most generous album. In terms of the lyrics, there's nothing quite so stirring as the songs off *Born to Run*; *Darkness*'s hurt is also missing. But what comes through is assurance: The E Streeters sound lean and relaxed, Springsteen's voice is strong but unstrained. And the songs—dazzling variations, mainly, on fundamental three-chord rock—are more efficient than anything he'd done before. "Cadillac Ranch" swaggers like Duane Eddy; "I Want to Marry You" is soulfully direct; "Wreck on the Highway" is a chilling

snapshot; "The Ties That Bind" speaks with a new, unforced seriousness. "Hungry Heart" is the crowd pleaser, and it worked—*The River* made Springsteen a household name.

In a willful turn, Springsteen then made his starkest record, one with the black-and-white power of a Walker Evans photograph. *Nebraska*'s "Mansion on the Hill" and "My Father's House" are genuine folk music, sung by a man who sounds almost paralyzed by feeling. Throughout the record, he punctuates his songs with the word "sir"—it's a brilliant touch; his songwriting persona here sounds like a worker, not a star. A solo album, the sound of *Nebraska* is stripped down and essential; everything on the record resounds.

Having witheringly downscaled mass-audience expectations, Springsteen then reversed himself and put out his most varied and solid music on *Born in the U.S.A.* "Dancing in the Dark" was a big, superficially simple single; its infectiousness and the accompanying all-smiles video won over a following of Beatlemaniac proportions. *U.S.A.* made Bruce as big as Coca-Cola. Especially intriguing was the vast misreading of the title track; while Springsteen had intended its message to be just short of despairing, many of his new fans simply read the big drums and the shouted chorus as patriotic sloganeering. To what degree an artist is responsible for the quality of his audience remains debatable, but *U.S.A.*'s honest and beautiful songs ("Glory Days," "My Hometown," "I'm on Fire") hardly seem pandering.

What had become genuinely problematic, however, were Bruce's shows. Each one aiming to be a tour de force, the three-hour extravaganzas were overwhelming. And as the E Streeters bashed through yet another brilliant Springsteen song or wonderful cover, the enterprise took on an inflated air of almost surreal giganticism. Why were these guys trying so hard? Releasing a 40-song live album of a decade's worth of material, Springsteen followed the ultrasuccess of *U.S.A.* with an instant Number One hit. The record is breathtaking, but the sheer glorious immodesty of it is a bit off-putting; Springsteen sounds bigger than the stadiums. Subtle and powerful, *Tunnel of Love* redeems him. Its title song and "Brilliant Disguise" are some of Springsteen's best songs ever, and the record reveals the full, mature development of his vision.

In 1992, after five years without releasing

an album, Springsteen emerged with two: *Human Touch* and *Lucky Town*. Except for redoubtable keyboardist Roy Bittan, gone was the E Street Band, Springsteen replacing them with studio vets (Gary Mallabar, Jeff Porcaro) and handling a lot of the instruments himself. The sound, though, was close to his vintage style and a number of the songs came across like ready-made classics—the albums' title tracks, "The Big Muddy," "Souls of the Departed." In the main, the lyrics focused on hard-won maturity, family life, broken dreams, loss and survival. It was subject matter arguably more complex than his young-man blues, and grappling with that complexity took courage. Sacrificing flash to a subtle simmering has never been the classic rock & roll route, but with Springsteen's growing older we see a chance that we missed with Elvis—that of a great American rocker confronting age with grace. — P.E.

SPYRO GYRA

★ ★   **Spyro Gyra (MCA, 1978)**
★ ★½   **Morning Dance (MCA, 1979)**
★ ★   **Catching the Sun (MCA, 1980)**
★ ★   **Carnaval (MCA, 1980)**
★ ★   **Freetime (MCA, 1981)**
★½   **Incognito (MCA, 1982)**
★½   **City Kids (MCA, 1983)**
★ ★   **Access All Areas (MCA, 1984)**
★ ★   **Alternating Currents (MCA, 1985)**
★½   **Breakout (MCA, 1986)**
★ ★   **Stories Without Words (MCA, 1987)**
★½   **Rites of Summer (MCA, 1988)**
★½   **Point of View (MCA, 1989)**
★ ★   **Fast Forward (GRP, 1990)**
★ ★ ★   **Collection (GRP, 1991)**
★ ★   **Three Wishes (GRP, 1992)**

Spyro Gyra has been remarkably consistent over the years, churning out album after album of pleasant-but-indistinguishable instrumental pop. Although the group's lineup shifts constantly—only saxophonist Jay Beckenstein, keyboardist Tom Schuman and mallet-percussionist Dave Samuels have stuck it out for all 15 titles—the Spyro Gyra sound offers only the slightest variations: *Freetime* leans somewhat to funk, *Stories Without Words* has a Caribbean bent, *Fast Forward* is more openly influenced by Afro-Cuban grooves, and so on. Otherwise, almost any Spyro Gyra album will offer the same slick fusion grooves, polished ensemble playing and effortless, jazz-like solos.

So why bother? It depends on what you expect from the group. Although Spyro Gyra is a waste of time if what you want is the inspired serendipity of jazz, it does make

excellent easy-listening fare. After all, the music is tuneful (particularly the pop-friendly *Morning Dance*), perky, unobtrusive and infinitely hipper than the Living Strings. — J.D.C.

SQUEEZE

★ ★½   **U.K. Squeeze (A&M, 1978)**
★ ★ ★½ **Cool for Cats (A&M, 1979)**
★ ★ ★ ★ **Argybargy (A&M, 1981)**
★ ★ ★ ★ **East Side Story (A&M, 1981)**
★ ★ ★½ **Sweets From a Stranger (A&M, 1982)**
★ ★ ★ ★½ **Singles—45's and Under (A&M, 1982)**
★ ★ ★   **Cosi Fan Tutti Frutti (A&M, 1985)**
★ ★ ★   **Babylon and On (A&M, 1987)**
★ ★ ★½ **Frank (A&M, 1989)**
★ ★½   **A Round and a Bout (I.R.S., 1990)**
★ ★   **Play (Warner Bros., 1991)**

A writers' band in the most literal sense, Squeeze is essentially the creature of its principal songwriters, Chris Difford and Glenn Tilbrook. Squeeze bubbled up at about the same time as Elvis Costello and Joe Jackson, but the band's allegiance to the new wave was more a matter of instrumental color than musical attitude, although its John Cale–produced debut, *U.K. Squeeze*, does include such game efforts as "Sex Master" and "Wild Sewerage Tickles Brazil." *Cool for Cats* is much closer to what the band is about. Despite such period touches as the sequenced synths on "Slap & Tickle," these songs make their point through a deft combination of melody and characterization, and with the wicked wit of keyboardist Jools Holland acting in counterpoint to Difford and Tilbrook's songcraft, the group serves up several gems, including the breathless "Goodbye Girl" and the gorgeous "Up the Junction."

With *Argybargy* and *East Side Story*, Squeeze truly hits its stride. *Argybargy* starts off strong with the endearing "Pulling Mussels (From the Shell)" and builds from there, with songs that range from the personal ("Another Nail in My Heart") to the picaresque ("Misadventure"). *East Side Story* fleshes out the band's approach further, adding a country feel to "Labelled with Love" and—with the aid of new keyboardist Paul Carrack—a bit of blue-eyed soul to "Tempted," perhaps the group's most memorable single.

From there it's a slow slide downhill. *Sweets From a Stranger*, recorded with yet another new keyboardist, has its moments (particularly "Black Coffee in Bed") but lacks the sparkle of its predecessors. No wonder; the band was falling apart, and in fact disbanded right before releasing *Singles—45's and Under*, a best-of with one new song, "Annie Get Your Gun."

Difford and Tilbrook recorded a solo album, but it lacked the Squeeze chemistry, and eventually the group reorganized, with Holland back in the fold. Strangely, *Cosi Fan Tutti Frutti* didn't really have either that Squeeze chemistry either, and it wasn't until *Babylon and On* that the group regained its footing. "Hourglass," a tuneful trifle, is the album's standout track, but "Trust Me to Open My Mouth" and "853-5937" are equally charming. Charm, though, is about as much as the band has to offer by this point, and though *Frank* is well-crafted, it's only occasionally involving, while the live *A Round and a Bout* will be of interest only to completists. Still, that's not quite as alarming as *Play*, on which Difford and Tilbrook's cleverness takes on a self-satisfied cast. — J.D.C.

BILLY SQUIER
★★★ The Tale of the Tape (Capitol, 1980)
★★★ Don't Say No (Capitol, 1981)
★★½ Emotions in Motion (Capitol, 1982)
★★ Signs of Life (Capitol, 1984)
★★ Hear & Now (Capitol, 1989)
★★ Creatures of Habit (Capitol, 1991)

With his sliced-up Zep riffs and shag haircut, Boston rocker Billy Squier appeared to be a rather ordinary metal craftsman in the early '80s. History has proven him to be remarkably influential, believe it or not. "The Big Beat," from *The Tale of the Tape*, was cited early on by DJ Jam Master Jay of Run-D.M.C. as a crucial hip-hop sample. You can hear that funky kick in "The Big Beat" even more clearly now. The genesis of the late-'80s pop-metal hybrid can be found on the rest of *The Tale of the Tape*; Squier lays a fine gloss over his churning gut rhythms and me-so-horny wordplay, providing a model for the Bon Jovi–led generation to come. "The Stroke," from the followup *Don't Say No*, is another burning hunk of metalized semifunk that stands as Squier's one undeniable moment; conveniently, it's been his biggest and best hit. Just three years later, however, Squier already appears woefully out-of-touch on *Signs of Life*. In video-saturated 1984, his chest-thumping single "Rock Me Tonite" could've passed for an outtake from the then-current parody *Spinal Tap*. Since then, Squier has slipped even further into clichéd

macho cocksmanship: without the saving grace of hooky riffs or catchy choruses, rote come-ons like "Facts of Life," "(Love) Four Letter Word" and (mmm-hm) "She Goes Down" (all from *Creatures of Habit*) just sound strained—even a little desperate.
— M.C.

JO STAFFORD
★★★ G.I. Jo (Corinthian, 1987)
★★★★ Jo + Jazz (Corinthian, 1987)
★★★★½ Greatest Hits (Corinthian, 1990)

Discovered by Tommy Dorsey, Jo Stafford sang with Dorsey both solo and as a member of the acclaimed vocal group the Pied Pipers. Stafford is one of the most ingratiating voices in the history of American popular music. Blessed with a rich, slightly husky contralto, Stafford had an uncanny way of caressing a lyric, of turning a phrase with a light touch that peeled away layers of emotion. Her intense involvement in a song was the sort of passion that wins artists devoted followers who find in her affirmation of their own feelings. Like her peerless contemporary (and fellow Dorsey discovery) Frank Sinatra, Stafford projected attitude and style to listeners, consummate musicianship to other artists.

Stafford was a regular entry on the pop charts beginning in 1944 and continuing through the '50s. During this time she recorded material ranging from traditional popular songs, to Broadway show tunes, to movie songs, to country songs, to Christmas carols, to jazz songs. Of her four Number One singles, "You Belong to Me" (1952) occupied the top spot for 12 weeks and sold nearly two million copies; another chart-topper, "My Darling, My Darling" (1948), was a duet with Gordon McRae. On most of her recordings she was accompanied with great simpatico by her husband Paul Weston and his Orchestra.

Stafford, who recorded for Capitol and Columbia, can now be found exclusively on the Beverly Hills–based Corinthian label, which is run by Weston. Several titles once available on vinyl have been discontinued, with three CDs now representing the sum total of Stafford's enormous recorded legacy. Of this in-print material, the bulk is from the '40s and early '50s, with virtually nothing remaining of Stafford's later productive years. Still, what's out there is choice, beginning with, of course, *Greatest Hits*, an essential album. "You Belong to Me" is included, as well as another Number One single from 1954, "Make Love to Me," based on a 1923 jazz instrumental called "Tin Roof Blues." For excellent examples of Stafford's versatility, check out "Jambalaya" and "St. Louis Blues." A gentle treatment of "Stardust" is a breathtaking journey through tenderness and longing, very nearly as compelling as Stafford's ethereal treatment of "I'll Be Seeing You." *Jo + Jazz* teams the singer with some first-rate players of her day, including tenor saxophonist Ben Webster, legendary alto saxophonist Johnny Hodges, trumpeter Ray Nance, former Billie Holiday pianist Jimmy Rowles, drummer Mel Lewis and others, with the superlative songwriter Johnny Mandel serving as arranger and conductor. The interpretations given "What Can I Say After I Say I'm Sorry" and "You'd Be So Nice to Come Home To" are remarkable musical moments, among many on this album. *G.I. Jo* is a collection of songs that were popular during World War II, including "You'll Never Know," "We Mustn't Say Goodbye," "I'll Remember April" and the enduring "I'll Be Seeing You." — D.M.

CHRIS STAMEY

★ ★ ★½ It's a Wonderful Life (DB, 1982)
★ ★ ★ Instant Excitement (EP) (Coyote, 1984)
★ ★ ★ Christmas Time (Coyote, 1985)
★ ★ ★ ★ It's Alright (Coyote/A&M, 1987)
★ ★ ★ ★ Fireworks (RNA, 1991)

After Chris Stamey left the dB's, that band's pop sense grew more conventional while his moved in the opposite direction. That's not to say there aren't hooks on *It's a Wonderful Life*, but they're not the tuneful tidbits that might have been expected, tending instead toward wittily subtle touches like the guitar skronk in "Brush Fire in Hoboken" or the snatch of Nat Adderley's "Work Song" Stamey hums in "Get a Job." There's not quite as much experimenting on *Instant Excitement*, but the song selection (which includes a cover of John Lennon's "Instant Karma") is too hodge-podge to be convincing. *It's Alright* brings Stamey's pop instincts back to the fore, particularly on showy production numbers like the deliciously lush "When We're Alone." And though the sound of *Fireworks* isn't quite as exquisite, the writing is sharper, particularly when Stamey applies himself to melancholy love songs like "Glorious Delusion" or "Perfect Time." — J.D.C.

THE STANDELLS

★ ★ The Best of the Standells (1966–1968) (Rhino, 1987)

The Standells' "Sometimes Good Guys Don't Wear White" was a good, snarling defense of teenage misfits, and "Try It" was banned for suggestive lyrics by right-wing radio stations—but nothing this L.A. outfit did ever measured up to the sludge-rock power of their 1966 smash, "Dirty Water." Written by producer Ed Cobb and sung by drummer Dick Dodd, the song remains a trashy monolith. — P.E.

LISA STANSFIELD

★ ★ ★½ Affection (Arista, 1990)
★ ★ ★½ Real Love (Arista, 1991)

"All Around the World" goes all the way. This lilting dance-floor ballad reasserts the power of melody over mechanical rhythms, while Lisa Stansfield brings a sweet burn to its tasteful Top Forty glow. Rather than quote the orchestrated grooves of Thom Bell or Barry White, Stansfield and her producers emulate their methods: broad instrumentation, bold arrangements, a subtly insistent beat. The rest of *Affection* creeps up on a listener unawares, much like the soulful tear in this young Brit's voice. "This Is the Right Time" mixes electronic throb with R&B emotion until they gel perfectly; "Sincerity," "Live Together" and "Poison" end up being as memorable as that breakthrough single. *Real Love* doesn't quite scale the heights of *Affection*. Still, Stansfield's voice and arrangements carry the day. — M.C.

THE STAPLE SINGERS

★ ★ ★½ Soul Folk in Action (1968; Stax/Fantasy, 1992)
★ ★ ★½ Bealtitude: Respect Yourself (Stax, 1972)
★ ★ ★ Be What You Are (Stax, 1973)
★ ★ ★ ★½ The Best of the Staple Singers (Stax, 1975)
★ ★ ★½ This Time Around (1969; Stax, 1981)
★ ★ ★½ Great Day (Milestone, 1975)
★ ★ ★ We'll Get Over (Stax, 1982)
★ ★ ★ Turning Point (Private I, 1984)
★ ★ ★ Are You Ready (Private I, 1985)
★ ★ ★ ★ Freedom Highway (Columbia Legacy, 1991)

MAVIS STAPLES

★ ★ ★ Time Waits for No One (Paisley Park, 1989)

The Staple Singers recorded folk songs and secular cover versions for various labels in the '60s, but never left religion too far behind. Landing on Stax/Volt right before the '70s dawned, Roebuck "Pop" Staples and his daughters—Cleotha, Yvonne and the mighty Mavis—found a supportive home for their pop missionary work. "Heavy Makes You Happy," "Respect Yourself," "I'll Take You There," "If You're Ready (Come Go With Me)" and "Touch a Hand, Make a Friend": The Staples' inspirational hits issued forth like funky bulletins from somewhere up above. Combining the politicized urgency of late-period soul music with the warm assurance of gospel faith, the Staples connected with a newly receptive mainstream audience. The taut, horn-laden Memphis sound accentuates the group's genetic strengths on those singles; Pop's weathered vocals and gnarly guitar lines alternate with Mavis's assertive, sexy contralto voice, while the family's easy-flowing harmonies turn each chorus into a rockin' revival meeting. Even though *The Best Of The Staple Singers* dips into occasional feel-good-about-yourself clichés, the unshakable conviction behind these golden oldies doesn't sound a bit strained or dated.

The Staples' top-shelf releases rank as soul classics, but the individual Stax albums are patchy, burdened with fair-to-middling material from the house songmill. *Bealtitude* kicks off the group's string of hits, and it's probably the best of the lot. However, *This Time Around* is a low-key odds 'n' sods repackage that outshines some of the official albums; try Mavis's fevered rendition of Rance Allen's "I Got to Be Myself" for starters. *We'll Get Over* glances at the group's earliest Memphis sessions, with folk and rock leanings much more in evidence. The *Great Day* collection covers a broad swatch of the Staples' '60s work, including righteous traditionals as well as topical covers of Bob Dylan and Pete Seeger. *Freedom Highway* offers a more tightly focused overview of this same period, and comes highly recommended to fans of the Staples' best-known work.

The Staples charted one last time with "Let's Do It Again" in 1975; this glossy, mismatched Curtis Mayfield production signals a rough spell for the group's pop-gospel crossover dreams. Mavis released several uneven solo albums during the disco years, including the Mayfield-produced *A Piece Of the Action* (1977) and *Oh, What a Feeling* (1979). The Staples reemerged with the encouraging comeback attempt *Turning Point*, which updates the sound subtlely. A

cover of Talking Heads' "Slippery People" proves the Staples have kept their ears to the ground. *Are You Ready* continues the stylistic search, though it could use a grabby single or two. On her much-anticipated Paisley Park solo album, Mavis drowns in Princely pomp and circumstance. Competently funky and no more, *Time Waits for No One* would qualify as an event if it came from one of Prince's talented underlings. Coming from such a distinctive singer, it's a mystifying anticlimax. — M.C.

EDWIN STARR
★ ★ ★ **25 Miles (1969; Motown, 1986)**
★ ★ ★ **War and Peace (1970; Motown, 1986)**
In the mid-'60s, gruff-voiced Edwin Starr scored a few hits for Detroit's tiny Ric-Tic label, and then moved on to the mothership, Motown. There, he's chiefly remembered as an early proponent of message music— "War" (1970) became a Number One pop hit and was later covered by Bruce Springsteen; its followup, "Stop the War Now," reached Number 26 on the pop charts. Both of his in-print albums are sturdy soul music, not the work of a true trailblazer, but certainly the commendable product of an ace craftsman. — P.E.

RINGO STARR
★ ★½ **Sentimental Journey (Capitol, 1970)**
★ ★ **Beaucoups of Blues (Capitol, 1970)**
★ ★ ★ **Ringo (Capitol, 1973)**
★ ★ **Goodnight Vienna (Capitol, 1974)**
★ ★ ★ **Blast From Your Past (Capitol, 1975)**
★ ★ **Ringo's Rotogravure (Atco, 1976)**
★ ★ **Ringo the 4th (Atco, 1977)**
★ ★ **Bad Boy (Epic, 1977)**
★ ★ **Old Wave (RCA Canada, 1983)**
★ ★ **Stop and Smell the Roses (Boardwalk, 1981)**
★ ★ ★ **Starr Struck: Best of Ringo Starr, Vol. 2 (Rhino, 1989)**
★ ★ ★ **Ringo Starr and His All-Starr Band (Rykodisc, 1990)**
★ ★ ★ **Time Takes Time (Private Music, 1992)**

Blast from Your Past and *Starr Struck* contain all the necessary Ringo. *Blast* mines mainly his early records: his best single, the punchy "It Don't Come Easy"; the tolerably silly "You're Sixteen"; the plodding "Photograph"; Hoyt Axton's novelty number, "No No Song"; and his reminiscence of the Beatles' demise, "Early 1970" (it's cute, not maudlin). Aside from reprising numbers from *Beaucoups of Blues*,

the affable country album Ringo made with Nashville session legend Pete Drake, *Starr Struck* covers the later stuff, emphasizing McCartney's tuneful tidbits from *Stop and Smell the Roses* and oldies off a Canadian LP, *Old Wave* (peppy takes on Doug Sahm's "She's About a Mover" and Leiber and Stoller's "I Keep Forgettin' "). Trading on the clownish sweetness he'd developed in his Beatle role, Ringo's solo output is cheerful fluff, aided greatly by crack sidemen (Gary Brooker, Dr. John, Joe Walsh, not to mention John, Paul and George). His drumming remains unspectacular but unerring (none of his own records demand the flashes of brilliance he'd displayed with the Beatles), and his vocalizing makes feckless hit-or-miss passes at singing. A collection of Tin Pan Alley standards dripping with strings, *Sentimental Journey*, is Ringo's oddest album (and maybe his most interesting). Ringo made a comeback of sorts in 1990 with his All-Starr Band roadshow, recorded for posterity on the Rykodisc LP. The upswing continued in 1992 with his most consistent, energetic album since *Ringo* in 1974. Ringo was assisted in the studio by top producers Don Was, Phil Ramone, Peter Asher and Jeff Lynne, and the result included such catchy pop songs as "Weight of the World."
— P.E.

STEEL PULSE

★ ★ ★ ★   **Handsworth Revolution (Mango, 1978)**
★ ★ ★½   **Tribute to the Martyrs (Mango, 1979)**
★ ★ ★   **Caught You (Mango, 1980)**
★ ★ ★   **True Democracy (Elektra, 1982)**
★ ★ ★½   **Earth Crisis (Elektra, 1983)**
★ ★ ★ ★   **Reggae Greats (Mango, 1984)**
  ★ ★½   **Babylon the Bandit (Elektra, 1986)**
    ★ ★   **State of . . . Emergency (MCA, 1988)**
    ★ ★   **Victims (MCA, 1991)**

One of Britain's premier reggae units, Steel Pulse inspired a slew of younger bands in its hometown of Birmingham, including UB40 and the English Beat. Led by singer and guitarist David Hinds, Steel Pulse picked up on the crossover-era (mid-'70s) sound of Bob Marley and the Wailers. Keyboardist Selwyn Brown lends a sweetening touch with both voice and hands, while Hinds blends aggressive rock lead guitar lines into politicized musings. Loose-limbed and accessible, the Steel Pulse groove is further strengthened by saucy horn lines and dub echoes on *Handsworth Revolution*. The title track, "Soldiers" and "Ku Klux Klan" all contrast pointed messages with giving rhythms; the lighthearted melodies underline, rather than obscure, the all-too-realistic lyrics. *Tribute to the Martyrs* is a worthy follow-up; the title track haunts, while "Sound System" pumps up an irresistible party-time buzz. Originally released as *Reggae Fever* in the United States, *Caught You* (the British title) leans a little too heavily on Steel Pulse's poppier side. "Reggae Fever" itself simply sounds like a rote self-celebration, and the romantic motif of "Caught You Dancing" doesn't subtly elbow you the way the slice-of-life tale in "Drug Squad" does. Perhaps *True Democracy* dips too far in the opposite direction; for the first time, Hinds sinks in a sea of incomprehensible Rasta ideology, and even the band's light-fingered touch can't save him. However, *Earth Crisis* goes a long way toward striking a balance between commercial aspirations and Armageddon. After a slow start, Steel Pulse kicks into comfortable high gear on the album's second half: the title track, "Bodyguard," "Grab Education" and "Wild Goose Chase" mix harmonies with a fresh array of tuneful synths and crisp beats.

Reggae Greats draws heavily on *Handsworth* and glances at the subsequent Mango albums, including the early single "Prodigal Son"; this is a choice introduction to Steel Pulse. On the MCA albums, the group strives for an American black-pop crossover with surprisingly stiff results. Even the presence of guest producers like the Family Stand ("Soul of My Soul") and former Madonna henchman Steven Bray ("Can't Get You [Out of My System]") doesn't enliven the sodden mush. Adjusting to the lightweight dance grooves on those tracks seems to take a toll on Steel Pulse, because the more familiar reggae protest numbers (like the title track and "Gang Warfare") don't catch fire, either. — M.C.

STEELY DAN

  ★ ★ ★ ★   **Can't Buy a Thrill (MCA, 1972)**
  ★ ★ ★ ★½   **Countdown to Ecstasy (MCA, 1973)**
★ ★ ★ ★ ★   **Pretzel Logic (MCA, 1974)**
  ★ ★ ★ ★   **Katy Lied (MCA, 1975)**
    ★ ★ ★   **The Royal Scam (MCA, 1976)**
  ★ ★ ★ ★   **Aja (MCA, 1977)**
    ★ ★½   **Greatest Hits (MCA, 1978)**
    ★ ★½   **Gaucho (MCA, 1980)**
    ★ ★ ★   **Gold (MCA, 1982)**

★ ★ ★ **A Decade of Steely Dan (MCA, 1989)**
★ ★ ★ **Gold, Extended Edition (MCA, 1991)**
The strange saga of Steely Dan only could
have occurred in the '70s. Mixing verbal
idiosyncracy and slick musicianship in
measured doses, songwriters Donald Fagen
and Walter Becker distilled their love of bebop and Beat poetry into an impeccable
series of dense, yet approachable four-
minute FM opuses. Rarely has pop music
this complex actually been popular.

Can't Buy a Thrill introduces the basic
pattern: durable melodies underlie spiraling
guitar solos, twisted lyrics and jazzy beats.
The hit "Do it Again" establishes Fagen's
voice: wry and ruminative, equally capable
of withering scorn and surprising
compassion. You hear that voice throughout
Thrill, even when oblivious lead singer
David Palmer blares away—a problem
quickly solved on the follow-up, *Countdown
to Ecstasy*, recorded minus Palmer. Fagen's
obsessions have layers and levels, it turn
out, and the music grows even more
nuanced without losing its immediacy. By
the time of *Pretzel Logic* and the hit "Rikki
Don't Lose That Number," Steely Dan had
stopped touring and taken up exclusive
residence in the studios of Los Angeles. At
first, that move seemed to shore up Fagen
and Becker's vision. *Pretzel Logic* captures
Steely Dan at a creative and commercial
peak: from the first sad piano chord
onward, "Rikki Don't Lose that Number"
projects an intriguing, almost unbearable
sense of romantic uncertainty.

Katy Lied taps a growing circle of session
pros; the pop hooks gleam sharp as ever,
though, and harmony vocals from future
Doobie Brother Michael McDonald help
leaven the increasing doses of irony and
black humor. *The Royal Scam* broods on
the bleakest aspects of the '60s legacy: these
bitter tales of drug burns and emotional bail
outs can leave a harsh aftertaste. For the
first time, the tasteful backing starts to
resemble the jazz-rock fusion many of Steely
Dan's hired hands plied elsewhere:
accomplished, cold, brittle. *Aja* tips the
balance toward extended instrumental
arrangements, but that seems to give Fagen
and Becker some needed room. The title
track, "Peg" and especially "Deacon Blues"
exude a newfound warmth and insight. If
some of the fire is gone, the embers still
glow and sputter unexpectedly. With one
notable exception (the tragic May-December
love of "Hey 19"), the blandly competent
performances and sketchy compositions on
Gaucho barely register. By this time, of

course, the '70s were fading fast. And
during their peak period, nobody ever
accused Fagen and Becker of sounding
unformed or wishy-washy. Whether you
revere Steely Dan or retch at the very idea
of the band, those early records have a
sneaky way of getting under your skin—and
staying there. — M.C.

STEPPENWOLF
★ ★½ **Early Steppenwolf (1969; MCA, 1990)**
★ ★ **Monster (1970; MCA, 1988)**
★ ★ **Steppenwolf Seven (1970; MCA, 1989)**
★ ★ ★½ **Steppenwolf Gold (Dunhill, 1971)**
★ ★ **For Ladies Only (1971; MCA, 1989)**
★ ★ ★ ★ **16 Greatest Hits (Dunhill, 1973)**
★ **16 Great Performances (Dunhill, 1975)**
★ ★ ★ **Skullduggery: The ABC Collection (Dunhill, 1976)**
★ **Hour of the Wolf (Epic, 1975)**
★ **Reborn to Be Wild (Epic, 1977)**
★ **Wolf Tracks (Nautilus, 1982)**
★ ★½ **Rise and Shine (I.R.S., 1990)**
★ ★ ★ ★ **Born to Be Wild: A Retrospective (1966–1990) (MCA, 1991)**
"Born to Be Wild" and "Magic Carpet
Ride" are great, punchy tunes—John Kay
sings with bad-boy zest and Goldy
McJohn's snappy organ provides a graceful
note rare in heavy rock—but so are "Hey
Lawdy Mama," "Rock Me," "Sookie,
Sookie" and "Move Over." In fact, nearly
all of the albums by this outfit feature a
couple of choice cuts of bluesy
biker-rock—surrounded, unfortunately, by
embarrassing stabs at significance.

With their intellectual pretensions made
apparent by their name, the members of
Steppenwolf were an unusual bunch of
black-leather boys who believed in leavening
their music with messages. Though they
were hardly the Clash, their obvious
sincerity and prole identification at least
rivaled the much more highly regarded
MC5. German-born Kay actually once ran
for a city council post, and the crew took
politics seriously. Both "The Pusher" and
"Snowblind Friend" were effective antidrug
songs, mainly because Steppenwolf's
toughness suggested that they knew the
perils of which they spoke.

A weakness for concept albums, however,
resulted in some true, if commendable,
failures. Intended as a blow against the
empire, *Monster* tried for a revisionist look
at the entire history of America, from the

slaughter of Indians to the Vietnam war. It now sounds like the earnest musings of high-school dropouts, but the "America" section of the title-track suite is kinda stirring. *For Ladies Only* was the bizarre attempt of the biker mentality to grapple with feminism; it's awful, but, in a period way, intriguing.

With Steppenwolf, the obvious way to go is with a best-of collection: MCA's 1991 anthology, *Born to Be Wild,* is far and above the best, running the gamut of the band's career and hitting all the high points. — P.E.

STETSASONIC

★ ★ ★ **On Fire (Tommy Boy, 1986)**
★ ★ ★ ★ **In Full Gear (Tommy Boy, 1988)**
★ ★ ★ ★ **Blood Sweat & No Tears (Tommy Boy, 1991)**

One of the few late-'80s rap bands to incorporate live instruments in its act, Stetsasonic has always maintained a strong sense of tradition in its music. How the group conveys that varies from album to album; for instance, though "Rock De La Stet" (from *On Fire*) covers much the same territory Run-D.M.C. opened with "Rock Box," the heavy guitar Stetsasonic pumps isn't generic metal but Hendrix-style grunge. *In Full Gear* pushes that a step further as it goes from the realm of tribute, with its sweet, sassy rap remake of the Floaters' "Float On" (cut with the Force M.D.'s) to a sort of practical music criticism with "Talkin' All That Jazz," which explains both musically and culturally how rap fits in the development of African-American music. But it also balances such talk with dope beats like those mixmaster Prince Paul slips into such tracks as the title tune and "Music for the Stetfully Insane." *Blood, Sweat & No Tears* picks up from there, continuing the group's consciousness raising with raps like the infectious "Free South Africa" and the brutal "Ghetto Is the World," while maintaining its entertainment value through the likes of "Speaking of a Girl Named Suzy." — J.D.C.

CAT STEVENS

★ ★ ★ **Matthew and Son/New Masters (1967, 1968; London, 1971)**
★ ★ ★ **Mona Bone Jakon (A&M, 1970)**
★ ★ ★ **Tea for the Tillerman (A&M, 1971)**
★ ★ ★ **Teaser and the Firecat (A&M, 1971)**
★ ★½ **Catch Bull at Four (A&M, 1972)**
★ ★ **Foreigner (A&M, 1973)**
★ **Buddah and the Chocolate Box (A&M, 1974)**

★ ★ ★ **Greatest Hits (A&M, 1975)**
★ **Izitso (A&M, 1977)**
★ ★ **Cat's Cradle (London, 1977)**
★ **Back to Earth (A&M, 1979)**
★ ★ ★ **Classics Volume 24 (A&M, 1988)**

Cat Stevens was a British folkie who scored a Top Ten pop hit at home with "Matthew and Son" in 1967. Sidelined by tuberculosis for several years, he emerged on the American scene several years later. *Mona Bone Jakon* fit right into the emerging singer-songwriter movement: Stevens delivers his romantic sentiments, simplistic homilies and hokey hippie mysticism with an affecting, gentle acoustic touch. *Tea for the Tillerman* and the likably underwrought hit "Wild World" established Stevens as a more reserved British version of James Taylor. *Teaser and the Firecat* continued working this vein, yielding two more U.S. hits: the chug-chug-chugging "Peace Train" and the pretty-verging-on-precious "Morning Has Broken." With *Catch Bull at Four,* Stevens began to lard his approach with strings, horns, guitar-led rock arrangements—anything and everything that came to mind, it seems. His delicate melodies and mewling voice all but collapse under the weight, though. Either *Greatest Hits* or the slightly longer *Classics Volume 24* redeem what few catchy choruses poke through the growing fog ("Sitting" from *Catch Bull,* "Oh Very Young" from *Buddah and the Chocolate Box*). Stevens converted to Islam in the late '70s, leaving his pop career behind. — M.C.

RAY STEVENS

★ ★ **The Best of Ray Stevens (Mercury, 1970)**
★ ★ ★ **Greatest Hits (RCA, 1983)**
★ ★ **He Thinks He's Ray Stevens (MCA, 1984)**
★ **I Have Returned (MCA, 1985)**
★ **Collector's Series (RCA, 1985)**
★ **Collector's Series (RCA, 1986)**
★ ★ **Surely You Joust (MCA, 1986)**
★ ★ **Greatest Hits, Vol. II (MCA, 1987)**
★ ★ **Beside Myself (MCA, 1989)**
★ ★ **Everything Is Beautiful & Other Hits (RCA, 1990)**

Not exactly an artist whose career has been on an upward curve, Ray Stevens has been on the pop and/or country charts steadily since 1961, has had two Number One singles ("Everything Is Beautiful" in 1970 and "The Streak" in 1974), four Top Ten singles, and very little that is truly memorable. He began his career singing rock novelty songs, one of which remains among his best-known and

best records, "Ahab the Arab," from 1962. Since then he has reworked the "Ahab" formula countless times in addressing a variety of topics, but none of the other novelties match the original's manic brilliance. In the late '60s and early '70s he got serious and topical and dull: the muddy philosophy of "Everything Is Beautiful" hasn't worn well with age, and an otherwise sharp attack on materialism, "Mr. Businessman," is undercut by Stevens's strident delivery. About the time he seemed a lost cause, Stevens came up with a winner: the country version of "Misty"—graceful, delicate, tasteful—that hit the Top Twenty in 1975. He continues to alternate between novelties and serious numbers without much chart success. Caveat emptor: the original version of "Ahab the Arab" is no longer available on any of Stevens's albums. He recorded the song for Mercury, but the version on *The Best of Ray Stevens* is a live take, and a perfunctory one at that; RCA's *Greatest Hits* album also has a live version of "Ahab" (although the audience applause and laughter sounds canned) that is nowhere near the quality of the studio version. Also note that RCA has two albums out titled *Collector's Series*. Much of the material is duplicated from one album to the next, but the tracks are not identical throughout.
— D.M.

STEVIE B
★ ★ ★   Party Your Body (LMR/RCA, 1988)
★ ★ ½ In My Eyes (LMR/RCA, 1988)
★ ★ ★ ½ Love & Emotion (LMR/RCA, 1990)

Although it was a ballad—"Because I Love You (The Postman Song)"—that broke Stevie B in the pop market, his albums tend more toward Latin hip-hop. *Party Your Body*, in fact, is all dance music, with beats ranging from the Miami synth groove of "I Need You" to the slippery funk of "Day n' Night." But given the nature of Stevie's soft, crooning vocals, a move to more ballad-oriented material is only natural, and *In My Eyes* makes that leap with two slow songs—the dreamy "Love Me for Life" and the sappy "Children of Tomorrow." Even so, the dance tunes dominate, with Stevie making the most of the slicker sound of rhythm-driven numbers like "I Came to Rock Your Body" and "I Wanna Be the One."

With *Love & Emotion*, the emphasis shifts from mood to melody, and that makes a world of difference. In addition to providing better ballads—not just "Because I Love

You," but also the lachrymose "Broken Hearted"—the groove tunes are stronger, as songs like "Facts of Love" and "Forever More" offer enough melodic interest to make the rhythm seem almost secondary.
— J.D.C.

STEVIE V
★ ★ ★ Adventures of Stevie V (Mercury, 1990)

Not to be confused with synth-popper Stevie B, Stevie V is a New York–based house producer whose frugally funky "Dirty Cash" was a club hit in Britain and America. To his credit, Stevie V goes for a more organic feel than most house artists, while singer Melody Washington is soulful, making this album listenable even when the writing lacks the immediacy of "Dirty Cash." — J.D.C.

AL STEWART
★ ★ ½ Past, Present and Future (1974; Rhino, 1992)
★ ★ ½ Modern Times (1975; Rhino, 1992)
★ ★ ½ Year of the Cat (Arista, 1976)
★ ★ ½ Time Passages (Arista, 1978)
★ ★ ★   The Best of Al Stewart (Arista, 1986)
★ ★   Last Days of the Century (Engima, 1988)

This Scottish singer-songwriter possesses a weird, whispering burl of a voice and an uncommon historical bent. Produced by Alan Parsons (of *Dark Side of the Moon* fame), the Top Ten hits "Year of the Cat" (1977) and "Time Passages" ('78) frame Stewart's vague musings and featherweight melodies in a crystalline art-pop setting. They're both catchy in a mewling sort of way, but the accompanying albums (*Year of the Cat* and *Time Passages*) are padded with pristine high-grade filler. *The Best of Al Stewart* collects those hits, along with the equally catchy "Nostradamus," from the concept album *Past, Present and Future*. Predictably, Stewart's sci-fi concepts and gently bubbling synth arrangements make *Last Days of the Century* sound dated.
— M.C.

BILLY STEWART
★ ★ ★ The Greatest Sides (MCA/Chess, 1984)
★ ★ ★ ★ One More Time (MCA/Chess, 1988)

One of the most distinctive vocalists in the Chess stable, the late Billy Stewart is best-remembered for his frenetic interpretation of George Gershwin's

"Summertime," a Top Ten hit in 1966. But the hefty Stewart was a dynamic song interpreter who put an individual spin on any song he touched, and could work in a variety of styles. Given an opportunity to record for Chess after playing piano in Bo Diddley's band, Stewart debuted in 1956 with a robust, self-penned R&B raveup instrumental called "Billy's Blues," which featured Diddley on guitar and Diddley's sidekick, Jerome Green, on maracas; on the flipside, "Billy's Blues, Part Two" (included on *One More Time*), he made a stirring entrance as a vocalist and in essence never looked back. He scored a Top Twenty R&B hit in 1962 with "Reap What You Sow," and three years later broke into the pop market with a tender ballad, "I Do Love You." The twin poles of "Summertime" and "I Do Love You" define the broad range of Stewart's approach: he could roar and swing with the best of R&B belters, or caress a lyric as gently as any crooner around. Equally informed by gospel, jazz, and R&B, Stewart's style bespeaks a remarkable artist whose influence cannot be measured by mere chart success.

Both Stewart albums contain the essential hit tracks, but *One More Time* is the more complete historical overview, containing "Billy's Blues, Part Two," all the hits, some heretofore-unavailable '60s tracks and an informative biographical sketch by Adam White, along with notes detailing session personnel and recording and release dates. For noncompletists, *The Greatest Sides* will do fine. Don't be surprised if you wind up wanting more, though. — D.M.

DAVE STEWART

★ ★½ Lily Was Here (Arista, 1989)
★ ★ Dave Stewart and the Spiritual
       Cowboys (Arista, 1990)

As David A. Stewart, the instrumental half of the Eurythmics scored a fairly obscure film called *Lily Was Here*; most of the music is expectably forgettable background material, but a few tracks—particularly the title theme, recorded with Dutch saxophonist Candy Dulfer, and a lovely string-quartet rearrangement of "Here Comes the Rain Again," with Annie Lennox—are listenable enough to make the album worth hearing. A year later, as mere Dave Stewart, he uncorked *Dave Stewart and the Spiritual Cowboys*, a pompous, overwrought solo album on which the former Eurythmic shows off his Bowie impression, to no discernible advantage. Only the album's obviously high degree of

musicianship keeps it from being a total waste of time. — J.D.C.

GARY STEWART

★ ★ ★ ★½ Out of Hand (1975;
         RCA/HighTone, 1991)
   ★ ★ ★ Brand New (HighTone, 1988)
   ★ ★ ★ Battleground (HighTone, 1990)
★ ★ ★ ★ ★ Gary's Greatest (HighTone,
         1991)

Prime period (mid-'70s) Gary Stewart is powerful stuff. This Kentucky-bred singer examines the traditional subject matter—cheating, drinking, hell-raising and more drinking—with a mercilessly sharp eye and ear on his 1975 breakthrough, *Out of Hand*. There's a soulful crack in Stewart's voice that matches the full-on barroom frankness of both the words and the music. "She's Actin' Single (I'm Drinkin' Doubles)" actually has a chilling effect; Stewart forces you to laugh along with a self-pitying fool, the pedal steel mocking and sighing in the background. The title track paints a realistic, less than idyllic picture of extramarital activity; Stewart's rueful and brave moan on the chorus eventually collapses under all the weight of those unanticipated complications. Stewart put out another solid album (*Your Place Or Mine*, 1977) and several mediocre ones, all out of print. Hard living and a half-successful fling with Southern rock eventually caught up to Stewart in the early '80s, when he stopped recording for a spell. *Gary's Greatest* boils down his inconsistent career into a compellingly messy glob of hell-raising high times ("Your Place or Mine," "Whiskey Trip") and hellish lows ("Quits, "Ten Years of This"). Stewart reemerged with *Brand New* in 1988; his spirit seems willing ("Brand New Whiskey," "An Empty Glass") but the voice has weakened a bit. Still, *Gary's Greatest* offers the chance to catch up with one of Nashville's best-kept secrets, whether you're a recent convert or one of the many bona fide country fans who missed Gary Stewart the first time around. — M.C.

ROD STEWART

★ ★ ★ ★½ The Rod Stewart Album
         (Mercury, 1969)
★ ★ ★ ★½ Gasoline Alley (Mercury, 1970)
★ ★ ★ ★ ★ Every Picture Tells a Story
         (Mercury, 1971)
   ★ ★ ★ ★ Never a Dull Moment (Mercury,
         1972)
     ★ ★ ★ Sing It Again, Rod (Mercury,
         1973)

★ ★   **Smiler (Mercury, 1974)**
★ ★ ★   **Atlantic Crossing (Warner Bros., 1975)**
★ ★ ★½ **A Night on the Town (Warner Bros., 1976)**
★ ★ ★   **The Best of Rod Stewart (Mercury, 1976)**
★ ★ ★   **The Best of Rod Stewart, Vol. 2 (Mercury, 1977)**
★ ★ ★   **Foot Loose and Fancy Free (Warner Bros., 1977)**
★ ★½   **Blondes Have More Fun (Warner Bros., 1978)**
★ ★ ★ ★ **Rod Stewart Greatest Hits, Vol. I (Warner Bros., 1979)**
★ ★½   **Tonight I'm Yours (Warner Bros., 1981)**
★ ★ ★   **Absolutely Live (Warner Bros., 1982)**
★ ★½   **Body Wishes (Warner Bros., 1982)**
★ ★ ★   **Camouflage (Warner Bros., 1984)**
★ ★ ★   **Out of Order (Warner Bros., 1988)**
★ ★ ★ ★ ★ **Storyteller: The Complete Anthology: 1964–1990 (Warner Bros., 1990)**
★ ★ ★   **Downtown Train (Selections From Storyteller) (Warner Bros., 1990)**
★ ★ ★ ★ **Vagabond Heart (Warner Bros., 1991)**

An object lesson in the perils of pandering, Stewart's career proves that "selling out" wasn't just some thought-crime dreamed up by '60s idealists. For a golden hour, Rod the Mod was one of rock's finest singers, with a lock on, of all things, sincerity, taste and self-mocking humor. In the much longer period since then, exactly those values have been sacrificed, as, rushing headlong after megabucks and artistic bankruptcy, the working-class Scot became the Hollywood tart, the definitive parody, the saddest poseur. He continues to get it up for brilliant bits, and even his worst echoes a truly remarkable voice—it's only that, given his promise, the bulk of his product radiates pathos and a certain shame.

In the late '60s, no one rocked harder. Paired with ex-Yardbird Jeff Beck in the Jeff Beck Group, Stewart debuted the proto-metal Led Zep would later perfect; heavy blooze, "You Shook Me" and scorchers like "Let Me Love You" made *Truth* and *Beck-Ola* exercises in brilliant bombast. Two talents this huge, however, weren't easy roommates, and Stewart moved on to replace Steve Marriott as frontman of the (Small) Faces and thrive on the giggly fraternity of that band. In the interim, he'd put out an astonishing solo debut. Keith Emerson (on Mike D'Abo's "Handbags and Gladrags"), guitarist Ronnie Wood at his most ambitious, and the sloppy thunder of drummer Mick Waller provided much of the album's pleasure—but the star was Stewart, revealed as a highly original interpreter whose skill at selecting material encompassed the Stones' "Street Fighting Man" and Ewan MacColl's lovely "Dirty Old Town." Even better, Rod's songs "Cindy's Lament," "Man of Constant Sorrow" and "An Old Raincoat Won't Ever Let You Down" ushered in a writer capable of startlingly bare emotion and compassion for the hard-hit strivers, misfits and survivors who peopled his songs.

Gasoline Alley was equally strong. With Stewart's folk heart thumping, the dignifed empathy of "Only a Hobo" saw him beginning a minicareer of covering Dylan consistently better than anyone else; "Gasoline Alley" marked the cementing of the Stewart-Wood alliance. The blending of slide guitar and hoarse-voiced yearning is a thing of rare beauty, and when the duo elsewhere kicks it up on homages to the Stones and Eddie Cochran, rock seldom sounds freer or more fun. "Maggie May" and the title track of *Every Picture Tells a Story* made for Rod and Ron's finest hour—happy lads wearing their hearts on their sleeves. *Never a Dull Moment* was still strong, raw and honest, Stewart refreshing his narrative skills with the lusty travelogue "Italian Girls," and paying his debt to Sam Cooke on "Twistin' the Night Away."

With *Smiler*, danger signals began to flash. Dylan's "Girl From the North Country" was fine, but Chuck Berry's "Sweet Little Rock 'n' Roller" was far too obvious, and trans-sexing Aretha, on "(You Make Me Feel Like) A Natural Man," was shockingly misguided. Also, a fatal tendency toward hokum reared its head. *A Night on the Town*, with an excellent take on Cat Stevens's "The First Cut Is the Deepest" and a gallant nod toward Stewart's gay following ("The Killing of Georgie [Part I and II]"), was Rod's last cohesive and respectable set for quite some time. Subsequent albums—*Foolish Behaviour*, *Blondes Have More Fun* (Stewart reaches his nadir on "Do Ya Think I'm Sexy"), and *Body Wishes*—spell out his disastrous turn toward stadium-mediocrity and soft-porn eroticism.

Throughout the '80s, Stewart's

singles—for example, "Lost in You" and "Forever Young," from *Out of Order*—have been competent hitcraft. And hope springs eternal—*Vagabond Heart* was Stewart's best in years. While hardly a full return to his early form, a Tina Turner duet, material by Robbie Robertson and help from the Stylistics show a singer beginning at last to think again—and perhaps (it would take a miracle) to reemerge.

Storyteller collects a ton of the better Rod, and it's fine. Even better, get the first four records of his shining moment—and honor an incredible singer by forgoing his tripe. — P.E.

STEPHEN STILLS

★ ★ ★½ **Stephen Stills (Atlantic, 1970)**
★ ★ ★½ **Stephen Stills 2 (Atlantic, 1971)**
★ ★ **Down the Road (Atlantic, 1972)**
★ **Stephen Stills Live (Atlantic, 1975)**
★ **Stephen Stills (Columbia, 1975)**
★ ★½ **Still Stills (Atlantic, 1976)**
★ **Illegal Stills (Columbia, 1976)**

After failing an audition to become one of the Monkees, Stephen Stills formed, with Neil Young, one of America's best bands, Buffalo Springfield. While Young provided the greater depth, Stills proved himself a force to be reckoned with—his guitar playing was smart and inventive, his melodic sense expert, his hoarse-voiced singing often affecting. While working with Crosby, Stills, Nash and Young, he also put out solo albums featuring casts of big-name sidemen; on the whole, the records are surprisingly uninspired. Stills's debut, however, is an exception. Jimi Hendrix, Eric Clapton, Booker T., David Crosby and Graham Nash make their considerable presences felt, and on the driving "Love the One You're With" and the assured "We Are Not Helpless," his power-of-positive-thinking retort to Neil Young's "Helpless," Stills sounds convincing and at ease. The waltz-like "Change Partners" is the standout from his strong second record, and there's good guitar work by Clapton on *Still Stills*—a best-of compilation. With former Byrd and Flying Burrito Brother Chris Hillman, Stills in the early '70s founded Manassas, a crew of high-calibre players who squandered their talents on Stills's increasingly perfunctory material (in concert, however, the outfit was truly impressive). Stills's range of musical interests—straight rock, country, Latin and an occasional nod toward funkier rhythms—is commendable, and he's such a veteran player that he never descends beneath competence. But he seems

to need prodding (usually in the person of Neil Young) to bring out the best in him.
— P.E.

STING

★ ★ ★ ★ **The Dream of the Blue Turtles (A&M, 1985)**
★ ★ ★ ★ **Bring On the Night (A&M, 1986)**
★ ★ ★ ★½ **. . . Nothing Like the Sun (A&M, 1987)**
★ ★ ★½ **Nada Como el Sol (A&M, 1988)**
★ ★ ★ ★ **The Soul Cages (A&M, 1991)**

Having been a jazz bassist before he became a pop star, it was only natural that Sting's first post-Police band would be built around young jazz stars like Branford Marsalis and Kenny Kirkland. But his writing style remained essentially unchanged, and it's the balance between the pop appeal of his songs and the improvisational fire of his band that gives *The Dream of the Blue Turtles* its distinctive character. How that works varies somewhat from song to song, but for the most part it's a matter of mood in which the arrangements set the emotional context for each song, like the chilly anxiety of "Russians" or the jazzy melancholy of "Moon Over Bourbon Street." The approach is not without its risks—his remake of the Police tune "Consider Me Gone" says more about the band than the song—but when the playing manages to bring the song into focus, as with the soulful "If You Love Somebody Set Them Free," its success is stunning.

A concert album, *Bring on the Night* simply pushes that dynamic to another level. Impressively, the band is tighter while the playing seems looser, and Sting seems more than happy merely to ride herd over his sidemen; the oddly perfunctory Police covers are the only drawback. With . . . *Nothing Like the Sun*, Sting shifts gears slightly. For one thing, his band is no longer a jazz outfit, for despite the continued input of Kirkland and Marsalis, the addition of drummer Manu Katché (who powered Peter Gabriel's *So*) pulls the groove in an entirely new direction; for another, the songs on this album are more word-centered than their predecessors. Fortunately, that never seems to get in the way of the melody, allowing Sting the luxury of his elaborate imagery without compromising the music's allure. Some of that, admittedly, is simply a matter of his vocal phrasing, as in "Be Still My Beating Heart," where Sting's polysyllabic melody dances around the metronomic pulse of Katché's drumming. But the most accessible songs—the jovial "Englishman In

New York" or the danceable "We'll Be Together"—simply repeat the strengths of Sting's previous efforts. (His Gil Evans–arranged cover of "Little Wing," though, is sumptuously solemn.) *Nada Como el Sol* sprang out of "They Dance Alone (Cueca Solo)," a song about the "disappeared" in Chile from . . . *Nothing Like the Sun*. Sting offers a version of the song in Spanish along with translations of "We'll Be Together" (rendered as "Si Estamos Juntos"), "Little Wing" ("Mariposa Libre") and "Fragile" ("Frágilidad"), plus a version of "Fragile" in Portuguese.

The Soul Cages is in some ways the most difficult of Sting's albums. Not that it's especially obtuse or abstract; "All This Time" is as tuneful and accessible as anything in Sting's songbook. But between the music's low-key complexity and the lyrics' heavy metaphors and autobiographical references, getting a handle on the album requires quite a few listenings. On the whole, though, it's worth it. As before, the band is first-rate, augmenting . . . *Nothing Like the Sun*'s line-up with guitarist Dominic Miller and keyboardist David Sancious, and the rich, layered arrangements add an extra layer of interest to songs like "Why Should I Cry for You?" or "Mad About You." — J.D.C.

THE STONE ROSES
★★★½ **The Stone Roses (Silvertone/RCA, 1989)**

With their "action painting" album art, Small Faces' haircuts and Gretsch and Rickenbacker guitars, the Stone Roses have got their '60s pose down cold. More impressively, their sound also rivals the ambitiousness of the period they idolize—every one of their songs features smart playing, lyrical cunning and great hooks. His dark delivery somewhat recalling Echo and the Bunnyman's Ian McCulloch, Ian Brown sings with precocious confidence, and his lyrics to "(Song for My) Sugar Spun Sister," "She Bangs the Drums" and "I Am the Resurrection" reveal a gift for pop poetry. Guitarist John Squire draws upon an arsenal of effects—wah-wah, fuzztone, studio trickery—to create a heavy, swirling sound, and the rhythm section shines not only on the more melodic numbers but also on the ten-minute funk workout, "Fools Gold." The band's influences may be daunting ones—the Move, the Velvet Underground's "Heroin"—but the boys respond convincingly to the challenge of the past. They make trance-rock sound fresh. — P.E.

THE STOOGES
★★★½ **The Stooges (Elektra, 1969)**
★★★★★ **Fun House (Elektra, 1970)**
★★★★ **Raw Power (Columbia, 1972)**
★★ **Metallic K.O. (1976; Fan Club/New Rose import, 1987)**
★★★½ **Rubber Legs (Fan Club/New Rose import, 1987)**

During the Stooges' brutal and brief career, more people heard about the antics of singer Iggy Pop than ever heard the band's music. His lizard charisma still is undeniable, but these albums have endured beyond all expectations. Punk, glitter, shock-rock, thrash-metal: this is where it begins—and ends up.

Produced by John Cale just after he left the Velvet Underground, *The Stooges* gleefully defies the idea of progressive rock. This is regressive rock: three chords pumping like pistons, oil-can-banging rhythms, some bored loser howling "I Wanna Be Your Dog." Even when he's trying to act dumb, though, Iggy emits a feral intelligence. Guitarist Ron Asheton drenches every solo in feedback and wah-wah effects, yet he also demonstrates a subtle command of sonic overkill: there's a finely honed metal edge to the Stooges' Motor City psychedelia that keeps it from sounding dated.

From Iggy's introductory scream on "Down in the Street" to the cataclysmic shut-down of "L.A. Blues," *Fun House* is a scarifying trip through the All-American freak show. Iggy goads Asheton's wailing guitar and guest Steve Mackay's saxophone a little higher on each successive cut, but the foundation of *Fun House* rests on drummer Scott Asheton's ample shoulders. His slightly off-center rhythms are so tightly wound it's frightening: for all its pounding heft, this heavy music swings, too. That integral feature of Detroit rock & roll—the Motown-influenced beat—is something the Stooges' legions of inheritors have largely ignored.

David Bowie resurrected the group after a year's lay-off; Ron Asheton switched to bass and the more traditional lead guitarist James Williamson became Iggy's songwriting partner. *Raw Power* is marred by the Bowie-influenced watery production, but the utterly enthralling performances more than compensate. After that debacle, Iggy spiraled off into self-destruction, dragging the band down in flames. *Metallic K.O.* documents the Stooges' final (1974) concert, down to the last hurled bottle; you had to be there, but be glad you weren't. Reams of bootlegged sessions from the group's final days are available on import; *Rubber Legs* is the best, gathering some nonalbum material that stands up to *Raw Power*. Meanwhile, the curious career of Iggy Pop continues—albeit on a completely different plane. But deep in his heart, Iggy must realize that he'll never top the Stooges. — M.C.

GEORGE STRAIT

★★★★ Strait Country (MCA, 1981)
★★★ Strait From the Heart (MCA, 1982)
★★★ Right or Wrong (MCA, 1983)
★★★★ Does Fort Worth Ever Cross Your Mind? (MCA, 1984)
★★ Something Special (MCA, 1985)
★★★★ Greatest Hits (MCA, 1985)
★★★ George Strait #7 (MCA, 1986)
★★★ Strait Country/Strait from the Heart (1981, 1982; MCA, 1986)
★★★ Merry Christmas Strait to You (MCA, 1986)
★★★★ Ocean Front Property (MCA, 1987)
★★★★ Greatest Hits, Volume Two (MCA, 1987)
★★★ If You Ain't Lovin', You Ain't Livin' (MCA, 1988)
★★★ Beyond the Blue Neon (MCA, 1989)
★★ Livin' It Up (MCA, 1990)
★★★★ Chill of an Early Fall (MCA, 1991)
★★★★ 10 Strait Hits (MCA, 1992)

Having been a dominant figure in country music virtually since his 1981 debut, George Strait enters his second decade as a recording artist with an imposing history of solid music behind him. It's too easy to suggest that Strait has profited tremendously from his clean-cut good looks and Sensitive Hunk image; Strait, working with producer Jimmy Bowen, really hasn't cut a bad record—uneven ones, yes—and therein lies the secret of his success.

With Bowen, Strait has developed a musical palette that incorporates elements of honky-tonk, western swing, country blues, rock & roll and pop in service to songs that are literate, witty and self-deprecating, and sometimes poignant and heart-rending. Material and production aside, Strait gets inside his songs in a profound way to make the lyrics come alive. A sly twist of phrase, an attenuated word, a catch in the throat, and Strait creates a world full of pain and joy. Strait is forever beset by ex-wives ("All My Ex's Live in Texas"), duplicity ("Ocean Front Property"), a sense of time passing and opportunities fading ("The Chill of an Early Fall") and his own irreversible failings ("Her Only Bad Habit Is Me"). Vocally he's the great amalgamator, incorporating some of the phrasing techniques of Lefty Frizzell

and George Jones in a sturdy timbre that sometimes has a Conway Twitty feel and at other times has the warmth and sincerity of early Merle Haggard. On a more troublesome note, his 1991 album, *Chill of an Early Fall*, finds Strait dipping into Garth Brooks's bag of calculated low moans.

Strait's two *Greatest Hits* albums collect his most popular singles and are highly recommended. Among the other albums, his debut, *Strait Country*, is his strongest blast of honky-tonk; *Does Fort Worth Ever Cross Your Mind?* and *Ocean Front Property* arguably have the strongest song selections; *Beyond the Blue Neon* is the most melancholy (it includes "Baby's Gotten Good at Goodbye"); and *The Chill of an Early Fall* has that season's burnished feel about it. When he came on the scene in '81, Strait was nominally part of the New Traditionalist movement, owing to his embrace of harder sounds and roots music. That these elements remain evident in his work, polished as it's become, speaks well of the man. — D.M.

STRANGLERS

★★ IV Rattus Norvegicus (A&M, 1977)
★★ No More Heroes (A&M, 1977)
★½ Black and White (A&M, 1978)
★½ Live (X Cert) (U.A. UK, 1979)
★ The Raven (1979; EMI America, 1985)
★ IV (I.R.S., 1980)
★ The Meninblack (EMI America, 1981)
★ La Folie (EMI America, 1981)
★★ The Collection 1977–1982 (Liberty UK, 1982)
★ Feline (Epic, 1982)
★ Aural Sculpture (Epic, 1985)
★ Off the Beaten Track (Liberty UK, 1986)
½★ Dreamtime (Epic, 1986)
½★ All Live and All of the Night (Epic, 1988)
½★ 10 (Epic, 1990)
★ Greatest Hits 1977–1990 (Epic, 1991)

Repulsive even by punk standards, the Stranglers' early albums represent rock & roll at its most thuggish and base, as the band uses an assumed attitude of yob oafishness to excuse the gratuitous sexism of songs like "Peaches" (*Rattus Norvegicus*) and "Bring on the Nubiles" (*No More Heroes*). But as punk became yesterday's news, the ever-insincere Stranglers changed their sound in a hurry. Hence, *The Meninblack* puts Dave Greenfield's Doors-like keyboard in the band's frontline, a move which raises it from the level of minor annoyance to major irritation. Eventually, the band slipped into full-blown synth-pop pretentiousness, filling *Meninblack* and *La Folie* with all sorts of pseudoartistic posturing. (*The Collection* and *Off the Beaten Track* collect the singles and B sides, respectively, from this period; why anyone would want to bother with them is another issue entirely).

Moving to Epic with *Feline*, the Stranglers continue to bloat their sound, until by *Dreamtime* it sounds like bad-imitation Midge Ure. Obviously without a clue at this point, the band slips into revisionism, padding the not-these-songs-again concert recording *All Live and All of the Night* with a thoroughly unimaginative Kinks cover ("All Day and All of the Night"), while *10* similarly bludgeons ? and the Mysterians' "96 Tears." As for the band's *Greatest Hits*, don't you have better things to do with your money? — J.D.C.

SYD STRAW

★★★ **Surprise (Virgin, 1989)**

A talented singer with an understated but utterly affecting delivery, Straw came to prominence through her association with Anton Fier's all-star pickup band, the Golden Palominos. *Surprise* is aggressively eclectic, hustling from astringent guitar pop (an airy take on the dB's "Think Too Hard") to arty Americana (a remake of Stephen Foster's "Hard Times") to coy technorock (the arch, burbling "Crazy American"). But as much as the album showcases Straw's versatility, its emphasis on range tends to undercut her attempts at depth, leaving her with an album that's far more impressive than it is involving. — J.D.C.

STRAY CATS

★★★ **Built for Speed (EMI America, 1982)**
★★★ **Rant n' Rave With the Stray Cats (EMI America, 1983)**
★★ **Rock Therapy (EMI America, 1984)**
★★ **Blast Off (EMI, 1989)**
★★★ **Best of the Stray Cats—Rock This Town (EMI, 1990)**

This rockabilly revivalist trio from Long Island came on in '81 with the right look, a classic Sun sound and a batch of hard-pumping original songs. Working with producer Dave Edmunds, the Cats seemed to have all the pieces in place and indeed found a willing audience, initially in England and then in the States. Their first two albums, released in America as *Built for Speed* and *Rant n' Rave with the Stray Cats*, yielded three Top Ten singles. Their ace in the pocket was frontman Brian Setzer, who had the boyish, blonde good looks of Eddie Cochran and a plaintive voice that seemed to have come from another era. He also played a wicked guitar—snarling, serpentine lines and ringing chords.

Where to take this music proved a problem for the Cats, though, and the trio's third and fourth albums show the strain of fading inspiration. *Best of the Stray Cats* is a well-considered overview of the Cats' best work, with heavy emphasis on tracks from the first two albums and no liner information. However quick their fortunes may have faded, the Stray Cats impressed upon its audience the continuing pull of this most rebellious form of '50s rock & roll. — D.M.

BARBRA STREISAND

★★★★ **The Barbra Streisand Album (Columbia, 1963)**
★★★★ **The Second Barbra Streisand Album (Columbia, 1963)**
★★★½ **The Third Album (Columbia, 1964)**
★★★½ **Funny Girl (Original Cast) (Capitol, 1964)**
★★★★ **People (Columbia, 1965)**
★★½ **My Name Is Barbra (Columbia, 1965)**
★★½ **My Name Is Barbra, Two (Columbia, 1966)**
★★½ **Color Me Barbra (Columbia, 1966)**
★★★ **Je m'appelle Barbra (Columbia, 1966)**
★★★★ **Simply Streisand (Columbia, 1967)**
★★ **A Christmas Album (Columbia, 1967)**
★★★½ **A Happening in Central Park (Columbia, 1967)**
★★★½ **What About Today (Columbia, 1967)**
★★★ **Funny Girl (Original Soundtrack) (Columbia, 1968)**
★★★★ **Barbra Streisand's Greatest Hits (Columbia, 1970)**
★★★★ **Stoney End (Columbia, 1971)**
★★★★ **Barbra Joan Streisand (Columbia, 1972)**
★★★★ **Live Concert at the Forum (Columbia, 1972)**
★★★ **Barbra Streisand . . . and Other Musical Instruments (Columbia, 1973)**

★ ★ ★   **The Way We Were (Columbia, 1974)**

★ ★   **ButterFly (Columbia, 1974)**

★ ★ ★   **Classical Barbra (Columbia, 1976)**

★ ★ ★   **Lazy Afternoon (Columbia, 1975)**

★   **A Star Is Born (Columbia,1976)**

★ ★ ★ ★   **Streisand Superman (Columbia, 1977)**

★ ★ ★   **Songbird (Columbia, 1978)**

★ ★ ★ ★   **Barbra Streisand's Greatest Hits, Vol. 2 (Columbia, 1978)**

★ ★ ★   **Wet (Columbia, 1979)**

★ ★ ★ ★   **Guilty (Columbia, 1980)**

★ ★ ★ ★   **Memories (Columbia, 1981)**

★ ★   **Yentl (Columbia, 1983)**

★ ★ ★   **Emotion (Columbia, 1984)**

★ ★ ★ ★   **The Broadway Album (Columbia, 1985)**

★ ★ ★ ★   **One Voice (Columbia, 1987)**

★ ★ ★ ½   **Till I Loved You (Columbia, 1988)**

★ ★ ★ ½   **A Collection . . . Greatest Hits and More (Columbia, 1989)**

★ ★ ★ ★   **Just for the Record (Columbia, 1991)**

Basically ignoring contemporary pop throughout most of the '60s, Brooklyn-born Barbra Streisand established herself as keeper of the flame of the American show-biz tradition. The songs she relied on were Broadway ballads and nightclub standards—sophisticated music that reached back to Gershwin and Noel Coward, and achieved its acme in the work of Hoagy Carmichael, Jerome Kern, Sammy Cahn, Rodgers and Hart and a handful of other extremely crafty songwriters. Irony, airiness, worldly wisdom, technique and subtlety were among the genre's values, and Streisand's commanding singing on her first three albums was that of a precocious veteran—she understood this music completely, and yet her youth brought freshness to the artfully orchestrated material; her interpretations were often casual or irreverent, and they were very much her own.

Streisand's stunning self-titled first album and her Broadway triumph in *Funny Girl* introduced a performer of the classic kind—patrician, confident, already larger than life. On her TV-special soundtrack albums, *My Name Is Barbra, My Name Is Barbra, Two* and *Color Me Barbra*, she cultivated also the persona of the waif, the ugly duckling about to flourish. Like Judy Garland's, then, Streisand's appeal was based on a tension of self-assurance and vulnerablity—she'd descend from an almost light-operatic delivery to a Brooklyn-girl chumminess, provoking both adoration and

sympathy. The *My Name* and *Color Me* albums now sound quaint in their old-style insistence on "entertaining," but they helped mightily to make Streisand a star.

After *Je m'appelle Barbra*, a glittering set of French composer Michel Legrand's airy love songs, a return to her vintage style on *Simply Streisand* and the gushy *The Way We Were*, Streisand finally confronted music of a more modern idiom. Laura Nyro's title track to *Stoney End* provided her a breakthrough—she still enunciated more properly than any other pop singer, but with producer Richard Perry and an all-star cast of studio players she was able to swing with new colloquial flair. *Barbra Joan Streisand* continued in this vein, with strong versions of Becker-Fagen, Bacharach-David and Carole King songs—remarkably, Streisand's remake of John Lennon's "Mother" was a credible one. The surreality of David Bowie's "Life on Mars," from *ButterFly*, however, eluded her grasp, and Tom Scott's arrangements of such bizarrely diverse material as "Let the Good Times Roll," Buck Owens's "Cryin' Time" and Bill Withers's "Grandma's Hands," were inscrutable. An interesting experiment, *Classical Barbra* found Streisand tackling such heady composers as Hugo Wolf and Gabriel Fauré. Recorded with the Columbia Symphony Orchestra, it suggested a rich direction Streisand never again pursued.

Streisand Superman, Songbird and *Wet* were highly professional pop, but Streisand's records were beginning to sound formulaic. Bee Gee Barry Gibb provided exactly the right new start. Glossy and melodramatic, disco was in some ways much closer in spirit, if not in sound or lyrical richness, to the prerock pop Streisand excelled at—and in *Guilty*, she turned in a performance alternately langorous, delicate and impassioned. "Woman in Love" was the standout, but the Gibb duets, "Guilty" and "What Kind of Fool," were very classy confections. A strong compilation, *Memories* included duets with Donna Summer ("No More Tears") and Neil Diamond ("You Don't Bring Me Flowers")—and with "Evergreen," "New York State of Mind" and "Memory" it reasserted Streisand's preeminence.

Material by inappropriate writers (Jim Steinman, and a John Cougar Mellencamp–Streisand collaboration) marred the otherwise capable *Emotion*, but Streisand's return to her roots on *The Broadway Album* was a predictable tour de force. *One Voice*, her first concert album in two decades, served as a more vital retrospective than *Collection*, and *Till I Loved You* (despite an embarrassing duet with then-boyfriend Don Johnson) was satisfying—alongside string arrangements, the record's techno-pop synthesizers made for textural richness, and Streisand sounded, as always, very much in control. Streisand's four-CD retrospective, *For the Record*, a predictably lavish set, smoothly concentrates on the '60s gems and omits the stodgier of the newer songs. — P.E.

JOE STRUMMER

★ ★½ **Walker (Virgin, 1987)**
★ ★ **Earthquake Weather (Epic, 1989)**
In front of the Clash, Joe Strummer seemed the ideal rock & roller—intelligent, impassioned and ebullient, full of good humor and great ideas. Unfortunately, none of those qualities seem to have followed him into his post-Clash solo career. It isn't for lack of trying; his 1986 single "Love Kills," from the soundtrack to *Sid and Nancy*, manages to recall both the raucous charm of "Train In Vain" and punchy guitars of "Clash City Rockers." But Strummer's next venture into film music, the score to *Walker*, is a disappointment, whether taken as a rock album (which it isn't) or as an exercise in approximating Central American folk idioms (which it tries in vain to do).

Apparently star-struck, Strummer returned to Hollywood yet again, to bestow the *Permanent Record* soundtrack (Epic, 1988) with four forgettable performances by his band, the Latino Rockabilly War. *Earthquake Weather*, his first noncinematic solo album, arrived a year later; empty and enervated, it's an embarrassment. — J.D.C.

STRYPER

★ **The Yellow and Black Attack (1984; Hollywood, 1991)**
★ ★ **Soldiers Under Command (1985; Hollywood, 1991)**
★ ★½ **To Hell with the Devil (1986; Hollywood, 1991)**
★ ★½ **In God We Trust (1988; Hollywood, 1991)**
★ ★½ **Against the Law (Hollywood, 1990)**
★ ★ ★ **Can't Stop the Rock: The Stryper Collection, 1984–1991 (Hollywood, 1991)**
What elevates these California stadium rockers at least to novelty-act status is the fact that they're born-again Christians. And, taking their name from Isaiah 53:5 ("and with his stripes we are healed"), they're resolutely apostolic. Tipper Gore may find

ramrod guitars and the gospel message antithetical; but the credible fury these boys muster disproves her. The limitations of their genre, of course, mean that little this band has done is anything more than high-tech boogie or power balladry, but Michael Sweet is a zesty belter, and Oz Fox manages a mean Eddie Van Halen imitation. Over the course of their seven-year career, the band members have become better players, but their albums are almost interchangeable. The greatest-hits collection, however, is solid—and if these guys come across as wimps when set against, say, Slayer, they still serve an instructional purpose in suggesting that power rock needn't confine itself to such subject matter as raping corpses. — P.E.

THE STYLE COUNCIL

★ ★½ **My Ever Changing Moods (Geffen, 1984)**
★ ★ ★½ **Internationalists (Geffen, 1985)**
★ ★ **Home & Abroad (Geffen, 1986)**
★ ★ **The Cost of Loving (Polydor, 1987)**
★½ **Confessions of a Pop Group (Polydor, 1988)**
★ ★ ★ **The Singular Adventures of the Style Council (Polydor, 1989)**
After the Jam dissolved in 1982, Paul Weller dabbled with cocktail-lounge eclecticism on the Style Council's initial releases. The title track of *My Ever Changing Moods*—the U.S. debut that absorbs some U.K. singles and a previous EP—is the only really coherent thing to be found amid the demi-jazz tinkling and half-baked orchestrations. Reactivating his politicized bent, Weller turned in a much more convincing follow-up, *Internationalists*. With a soulful assist from backup singer (and future wife) Dee C. Lee, he wraps those somewhat rusty pipes around fervent neo-'70s funk anthems like "Shout to the Top" and "Walls Come Tumbling Down!" It might not be the British *Superfly*, but it's not bad. And "Come to Milton Keynes" is Weller's most closely observed bit of Kinks-style sociology since the Jam's late heyday. *Home & Abroad* is a sterile live album taken from post-*Internationalists* tours. Awkward lyrics and klutzy rhythms sink *The Cost of Loving*, while *Confessions of a Pop Group* marks a bitter, frustrated return to the rambling experimentation of the debut. The Style Council's abrupt skid into muddy indulgence is reflected in the spotty quality of *The Singular Adventures of the Style Council*. — M.C.

STYX

★ **Styx II (RCA, 1973)**
★ **Serpent Is Rising (RCA, 1973)**
★ **Man of Miracles (1974; RCA, 1990)**
★ **Equinox (A&M, 1975)**
★ **Crystal Ball (A&M, 1976)**
★★ **Best of Styx (1977; RCA, 1980)**
★★ **The Grand Illusion (A&M, 1977)**
★★ **Pieces of Eight (A&M, 1978)**
★★ **Cornerstone (A&M, 1979)**
★★½ **Paradise Theater (A&M, 1980)**
★★ **Kilroy Was Here (A&M, 1983)**
★★ **Caught in the Act/Live (A&M, 1984)**
★★½ **Classics Volume 15 (A&M, 1987)**

Abandon hope all ye who enter here. Even when compared to such midwestern brethren as Kansas and REO Speedwagon, Styx is dire stuff indeed. The Chicago art-rock quintet centered on two songwriters: keyboardist Dennis DeYoung and lead guitarist Tommy Shaw, who possesses a lethal falsetto voice. His superhuman yelps distinguish the band's handful of catchy songs—and render them virtually unlistenable. "Lady," a galloping pomp-rocker from *Styx II*, broke out as a hit single two years after the album's release. Styx managed to score another pop crossover with "Come Sail Away" and *The Grand Illusion* in 1977. But it was "Babe," a nauseatingly sweet proto–power ballad from *Cornerstone*, that first took Styx to the very top of the singles chart in 1979. *Paradise Theater* topped the album charts in the next year; this nostalgic concept album is also the group's strongest musical effort. An actual spark of passion—rather than the usual bombast—enlivens the de facto unemployment anthem "Too Much Time on My Hands." After *Kilroy Was Here* and the herky-jerky "Mr. Roboto" in 1983, Styx rapidly trickled out of the public consciousness. Rock video made the elaborate escapist fantasies of art-rock—even the watered-down pop variety—seem awfully redundant. — M.C.

THE SUGARCUBES

★★★★ **Life's Too Good (Elektra, 1988)**
★★★ **Here Today, Tomorrow Next Week! (Elektra, 1989)**
★★★½ **Stick Around for Joy (Elektra, 1992)**

It doesn't take long to realize that the focus of this Icelandic sextet is its singers, Björk Gudmundsdottir and Einar Örn; all it takes is one listen to the intriguing, infectious "Motorcrash," from *Life's Too Good*, to get the sense that these two would enliven any band. Even so, the group's real strength is

its rhythm section, which manages to infuse standard-issue alternative rock riffs with a surprisingly supple grace. Its spacey, jazz-inflected interplay lends "Birthday" an otherworldly quality (though the vocal effects by Björk are a help), while Einar's wiseguy ruminations in "Deus" would ring hollow were it not for the zing put into the music surrounding them. And though the playing is just as good on *Here Today*, the writing isn't; apart from admirable efforts like "Regina" or "Hot Meat," the album is pedestrian. Fortunately, *Stick Around for Joy* is far more consistent, downplaying Einar's irritating interjections while emphasizing the band's instrumental strengths. Thus, as much as Bjork's vocals might add to "Hit," "Chihuahua" or "Gold," it's the churning interplay of guitarist Thor Eldon and the rhythm section that ultimately carries the album. — J.D.C.

SUICIDAL TENDENCIES

★★½ **Suicidal Tendencies (Frontier, 1983)**
★★★ **Join the Army (Caroline, 1987)**
★★★ **How Will I Laugh Tomorrow When I Can't Even Smile Today (Epic, 1988)**
★★ **Controlled by Hatred/Feel Like Shit . . . Déjà-Vu (Epic, 1989)**
★★★½ **Lights . . . Camera . . . Revolution (Epic, 1990)**

It would be hard to imagine a band better attuned to teen anxieties—or, more accurately, what parents fear about those feelings—than Suicidal Tendencies. All it takes is a quick scan of the titles on *Suicidal Tendencies* to get the drift: "I Want More," "Institutionalized" and the immortal "Suicide's an Alternative/You'll Be Sorry." But as vividly as singer Mike Muir expresses the raging despair of adolescent nihilism, there's nothing so distinctive about the music's pro forma hardcore rave-ups. Muir recruits two new members for *Join the Army* and updates the band's sound impressively, meeting genre expectations with "Possessed to Skate" but surpassing them through the imaginative dynamism of "Join the Army" and "A Little Each Day."

Readjusting the lineup once again, Muir and the Tendencies add a touch of metallic brawn to *How Will I Laugh Tomorrow When I Can't Even Smile Today*, which makes the most of the chant-along choruses to "Pledge Your Allegiance" and "Suicyco Mania" without diluting the mosh-pit intensity of "Surf and Slam." But by *Controlled By Hatred/Feel Like Shit . . . Déjà-Vu*, the heavy-metal influence is pushed to the point of meltdown through the predictable hypercrunch of "Just Another Love Song" and "Controlled By Hatred." Thankfully, that's downplayed on *Lights . . . Camera . . . Revolution*, in part by the band's muscular momentum, but mostly through ferociously melodic material like "Alone" and "Emotion No. 13."

Muir and musical collaborator Robert Trujillo later developed a side project called the Infectious Grooves, which produced an album's worth of energetic but unconvincing thrash funk entitled *The Plague That Makes Your Booty Move . . . It's the Infectious Grooves* (Epic, 1991). — J.D.C.

SUICIDE

★ ★ ★   Suicide (Red Star, 1977)
★ ★ ★   Alan Vega and Martin Rev: Suicide (Ze, 1980)
★ ★ ★½ 1/2 Alive (ROIR, 1981)
★ ★ ★½ Ghost Riders (ROIR, 1986)
★ ★ ★   A Way of Life (Wax Trax, 1989)

Perhaps the most influential and least accessible group to emerge from the New York punk scene, Suicide pioneered everything from synth-pop to industrialized disco with its low-rent electronic angst-fests. Alan Vega acts out the most confrontational street-poet routine this side of Iggy Pop, riding roughshod over the whirring, ricocheting blare of Martin Rev's homemade synths. *Suicide* includes the group's apocalyptic epic "Frankie Teardrop" and the brooding punch-out "Rocket USA," while the Ric Ocasek–produced *Alan Vega and Martin Rev: Suicide* is (relatively) easier to swallow—and forget. "Dream Baby Dream," released as a 1980 12-inch single, stands as the group's most perversely beautiful—and listenable—moment; pity it's unavailable. *1/2 Alive* collects outtakes and live tapes in realistic low-fi, providing what is probably the most accurate portrait of a hard-to-document force of nature. Lester Bangs's liner notes place Suicide in its proper historical context: the filthy, loud subway-station heart of New York City. *A Way of Life* finds Suicide in a revealing modern context, even though it's not a completely successful return. Wax Trax Records—from flagship act Ministry on down—simply wouldn't exist if it hadn't been for these two brave souls. Nice to know they endured all that audience abuse—check out the live *Ghost Riders*—for a reason. — M.C.

DONNA SUMMER

★ ★ ★½   Love to Love You Baby (Oasis, 1975)
★ ★   A Love Trilogy (Casablanca, 1976)
★ ★   Four Seasons of Love (EP) (Casablanca, 1976)
★ ★ ★   I Remember Yesterday (Casablanca, 1977)
★ ★ ★   Once Upon a Time . . . (Casablanca, 1977)
★ ★   Live and More (Casablanca, 1978)
★ ★ ★ ★ Bad Girls (Casablanca, 1979)
★ ★ ★ ★ ★ On the Radio: Greatest Hits Volumes I & II (Casablanca, 1979)
★ ★ ★ ★ The Wanderer (Geffen, 1980)
★ ★ ★   Donna Summer (Geffen, 1982)
★ ★ ★½   She Works Hard for the Money (Mercury, 1983)
★ ★   Cats Without Claws (Geffen, 1984)
★ ★ ★   The Summer Collection (Mercury, 1985)
★ ★   All Systems Go (Geffen, 1987)
★ ★ ★   The Dance Collection (Casablanca, 1987)
★ ★ ½   Another Place and Time (Atlantic, 1989)
★ ★ ★   Mistaken Identity (Atlantic, 1991)

"Love to Love You Baby" sounds like a pure novelty record at first: a sultry, disembodied woman's voice shudders and sighs in the throes of passion, while a fluid dance groove provides water-bed support. With its seamless orchestration and brazen sensuality, however, this 1975 Top Ten hit heralded the dawn of disco. And from such humble beginnings sprang Donna Summer, who went on to rule this oft-maligned musical province. A Boston-born singer who'd performed in European productions of *Hair* and *Godspell*, Summer met up with producer Giorgio Moroder in Germany. Moroder and songwriting parter Pete Belotte crafted a sleek, propulsive, orchestrated backdrop—Eurodisco—for Summer's heart-piercing (and occasionally ear-piercing) vocal workouts. The full-length album version of "Love to Love You Baby," more than fifteen minutes of it, is a hugely influential piece of work. Moroder incorporates the mix-moves of a club DJ into a record; over a stalwart bass line, Summer's moans float endlessly around symphonic variations and a startling, Kraftwerk-style electronic intrusion.

A series of failed quasi-autobiographical

concept albums followed—Eurodisco is big on concepts—*A Love Trilogy, Four Seasons of Love* and *I Remember Yesterday*. That last album spawned a masterfully synthesized Top Ten hit, "I Feel Love," in 1977. *Once Upon a Time* is a slighty more successful opus, while Summer's studio-bound sound falls predictably flat on *Live and More*. And then Donna Summer came into her own. On *Bad Girls*, the addition of soaring lead guitar lines and tighter, earthier songwriting took everybody—especially dance fans—by surprise. "Bad Girls" and "Hot Stuff" took this disco-rock fusion to the top of the pop charts, while slow-dancers like "Dim All the Lights" tapped into Summers's sweet side. Her *On the Radio—Greatest Hits Volume I & II* belongs on your shelf, right next to Chic's greatest hits. Even if you don't dance: disco doesn't get any more listenable than this.

The Wanderer continues, and deepens, the rock influence while hueing to a still-danceable Eurobeat. Quincy Jones produced the mega-ambitious *Donna Summer* for the new Geffen label; to put it mildly, not everything works. There is a lot to choose from: a Bruce Springsteen cover ("Protection"), a bona-fide hit single ("Love Is in Control [Finger on the Trigger]"), a new-age choral nightmare epic ("State of Independence"). *She Works Hard for the Money* serves up another winning, seemingly effortless vocal hook (the hit title track), amid plenty of pleasantly unambitious tunes. Summer hit a rough patch after that; even Stock-Aitken-Waterman's machine-tooled dance fluff (on *Another Place and Time*) can't seem to get her motivated again. *Mistaken Identity* is not a full-fledged comeback, but it's quite encouraging. In between the misguided opener ("Get Ethnic") and the strained closer ("Let There Be Peace") lies striking evidence of Summer's enduring talent. Something about her voice hits home, whether she's aiming for the heart ("Work That Magic"), the soul ("Say a Little Prayer") or the feet ("Fred Astaire").
— M.C.

ANDY SUMMERS
★ ★ **XYZ (MCA, 1987)**
★ ★ ★ **Mysterious Barricades (Private Music, 1988)**
★ ★ ★ ★ **The Golden Wire (Private Music, 1989)**
★ ★ ★ ★ **Charming Snakes (Private Music, 1990)**

★ ★½ **World Gone Strange (Private Music, 1991)**
Before joining the Police, guitarist Andy Summers worked in an unusually wide range of bands, playing everything from classic blues rock with the Animals to arty experiments with Kevin Ayers and the Soft Machine. So it's no wonder that Summers's post-Police output should be so varied. Granted, his far-flung interests don't always pan out; the semitraditional rock format of *XYZ*, for instance, is a near-total washout, while the low-key fusion instrumentals of *World Gone Strange* miss as often as they hit. But the quiet guitar-and-keyboard duets of *Mysterious Barricades* are intimately expressive, conveying many of the strengths apparent in his collaborations with Robert Fripp; the luscious exoticisms of *The Golden Wire* are atmospheric and evocative, especially when Najma Akhtar sings on "Piya Tose"; and the jazz-inflected tunes on *Charming Snakes*, particularly the Sting-powered title tune, bring out his skills as an improvisor. — J.D.C.

SUN RA
★ ★ ★ ★ **Sun Song (1956; Delmark, 1990)**
★ ★ ★ ★ ★ **The Heliocentric Worlds of Sun Ra, I (ESP, 1965)**
★ ★ ★ ★½ **The Heliocentric Worlds of Sun Ra, II (ESP, 1966)**
★ ★ ★ **Pictures of Infinity (Black Lion, 1971)**
★ ★ ★½ **Live at Montreux (Inner City, 1976)**
★ ★ ★ **Solo Piano, Vol. 1 (Improvising Artists, 1977)**
★ ★ ★ ★ **Sunrise in Different Dimensions (Hat Hut, 1981)**
★ ★ ★ ★½ **Blue Delight (A&M, 1989)**
The fact that venerable composer-pianist Sun Ra lists the planet Saturn as his birthplace is only one of the obvious indicators of his lifelong commitment to eccentricity—his mad, joyous jazz is the more profound index of his 70-year pursuit of idiosyncratic, aesthetic freedom. While Ra's head is adamantly in the clouds, his insistence on the work ethic is hardly extraterrestrial—whether he's dubbed his outfits the Solar Arkestra, the Myth-Science Arkestra, the Band from Outer Space, or the Astro-Intergalactic-Infinity Arkestra, Ra has pulled off the incredible feat of keeping a working big band together for decades.

An innovator, back in the '50s, on electric keyboards (*Sun Song*), Ra has managed to work his own subtle twists on Ellington-derived big-band jazz, incorporate the rhythmic whimsy of Thelonious Monk, and collaborate with McCoy Tyner, Quincy Jones, Mongo Santamaria and Art Blakey, all the while furthering the product of his own muse. A deft and often subtle pianist, his work builds on the stride tradition, his sidemen are always crack musicians—and, in ways unheard-of in "serious jazz," he's always insisted that live performance incorporate theater (outlandish African-Martian costumery, percussion marathons, huge ritual gestures).

The bulk of Ra's recordings are on his own Saturn label, and they're nearly impossible to find except at his (many) concerts. His other albums are on import or obscure labels: the seminal set remains the two volumes of *The Heliocentric Worlds of Sun Ra*, a pathfinding work of atmospheric "free" jazz. So assured, however, is the rhythmic sense of any Arkestra Ra has fashioned that his music is rarely inaccessible—the term "joyful noise" suits Sun Ra perfectly. Novices might start with *Blue Delight*, which shows just how engagingly bonkers a big band can be. Even better, the curious should catch Ra in concert: long before Beefheart, Zappa, John Zorn or any of a number of other exponents of musical surreality, Ra had the act down.
— P.E.

SUPERTRAMP

★★   Supertramp (A&M, 1970)
★★★   Crime of the Century (A&M, 1974)
★★½   Crisis? What Crisis? (A&M, 1975)
★★   Even in the Quietest Moments . . . (A&M, 1977)
★★★   Breakfast in America (A&M, 1979)
★★   Paris (A&M, 1980)
★★   "famous last words" (A&M, 1982)
★   Brother Where You Bound (A&M, 1985)
★   Free as a Bird (A&M, 1987)
★★★   Classics Volume 9 (A&M, 1987)

These second-string British art-rockers finally sprung some pop hooks in the mid-'70s, after years of flailing away in a tuneless fog. Whether you find Supertramp to be winsome or whiny, intricate ditties like "Bloody Well Right" and sentimental set pieces like "Dreamer" (both from *Crime of the Century*) helped pave the way for Genesis's eventual rehabilitation as a mega-platinum singles mill. Supertramp itself crossed over to the big time in '79, briefly, with *Breakfast in America*; "The Logical Song" and "Goodbye Stranger" coasted into the Top Ten that summer, but

Rodger Hodgson's cloyingly polite vocal tone and a general air of preciousness convert these catchy choruses into stomach-turning contrivances. The 1982 album *"famous last words"* delivers another hit ("It's Raining Again") in that genteel mode, amid soft mountains of audiophile fluff. When Rodger Hodgson left Supertramp the year after that, however, the group had already returned to the depths of semiobscurity—deservedly so. — M.C.

THE SUPREMES

★★½   Meet the Supremes (Motown, 1963)
★★½   A Bit of Liverpool (1964; Motown, 1989)
★★★½   Where Did Our Love Go (1965; Motown, 1991)
★★½   The Supremes at the Copa (1965; Motown, 1991)
★★★½   More Hits by the Supremes (Motown, 1965)
★★★   I Hear a Symphony (1966; Motown, 1991)
★★½   Supremes a Go Go (Motown, 1966)
★★★   The Supremes Sing Holland, Dozier, Holland (Motown, 1967)
★★   The Supremes Sing Rodgers & Hart (Motown, 1967)
★★★★   Diana Ross and the Supremes Greatest Hits, Vol. 1 (1967; Motown, 1989)
★★★★   Diana Ross and the Supremes Greatest Hits, Vol. 2 (Motown, 1967)
★★★   Reflections (1968; Motown, 1991)
★★★   Love Child (1968; Motown, 1989)
★★★   Diana Ross and the Supremes Join the Temptations (Motown, 1968)
★★½   T.C.B. (With the Temptations) (Motown, 1968)
★★   Let the Sunshine In (Motown, 1969)
★★   Cream of the Crop (1969; Motown, 1986)
★★★   Diana Ross and the Supremes Greatest Hits, Vol. 3 (Motown, 1969)
★★★   Farewell (Motown, 1970)
★★★★★   Anthology (Motown, 1974)
★★★   Right On (Motown, 1970)
★★★   New Ways, But Love Stays (1970; Motown, 1991)
★★½   Floy Joy (Motown, 1972)
★★   High Energy (Motown, 1976)

★ ★ ★ **Supremes at Their Best (Motown, 1978)**
WITH THE FOUR TOPS
★ ★ ★ **The Magnificent 7 (Motown, 1970)**
★ ★ **Dynamite (Motown, 1971)**
Although it was Florence Ballard who first led the girl group that went on to rival the Temptations as Motown's most successful act, Diana Ross very soon took over. With Ross at the helm—a figure with a commanding stage presence and a singular voice (a tense balance of the cool and the flirtatious)—the Supremes ruled soul radio in the mid-'60s by turning out a prodigious series of hits. Holland-Dozier-Holland assembled overpowering, finger-snapping, bass-thumping backing tracks for the singers—and the group delivered an awesome five-in-a-row clutch of Number One smashes: "Where Did Our Love Go," "Baby Love," Come See About Me," "Stop! In the Name of Love" and "Back in My Arms Again." As certainly pop records as they were R&B ones, these 45s made soul music safe for white audiences—without costing Motown any of its massive black following. And had the Supremes retired in, say, 1967, their achievement would've been mythic—sweet, short and perfect.

As it was, they moved on—to the Copa, internal dissension, glitz and confusion. After Ross departed in 1970 (Jean Terrell took over on lead), they put out arguably only one magnificent single, "Stoned Love," and descended, as did most of their Motown label-mates, into mere professionalism. The length of their discography shouldn't trick anyone into thinking that all of their albums were significant—even more of a singles band than most Motown acts, they're best represented on compilations. *Anthology* should do the trick. — P.E.

AL B. SURE!
★ ★ ★ **In Effect Mode (Warner Bros., 1988)**
★ ★½ **Private Times . . . and the Whole 9 (Warner Bros., 1990)**
Coupling the romantic allure of falsetto balladry to the rangy machine-beats of New Jack Swing, 19-year-old Al B. Sure! connected with two sizzling singles from his debut: "Nite and Day" and "Off on Your Own (Girl)." Forceful and clear, Sure's voice rises to a heavenly register with ease. Unfortunately, he doesn't have a vocal group like the Stylistics or the Chi-Lites to highlight his accomplished singing and occasionally thin songwriting and producing. *In Effect Mode* draws heat from the early-'70s soul references, but Sure displays inconsistent taste by covering Roberta Flack's dirgelike "Killing Me Softly." That's nothing: on *Private Times*, he begins by crawling through the Eagles' "Hotel California." By the end, Al B. Sure! still hasn't quite regained his original stride. Give him time. — M.C.

SURFACE
★ ★ **Surface (Columbia, 1987)**
★ ★ ★½ **2nd Wave (Columbia, 1988)**
★ ★ ★ **3 Deep (Columbia, 1990)**
★ ★ ★ **The Best of Surface . . . A Nice Time 4 Lovin' (Columbia, 1991)**
If Keith Sweat is the Marvin Gaye of new jack swing, then this trio is its Chi-Lites, a group whose satin-smooth sound and tastefully understated grooves mask a surprisingly tough-minded approach to R&B. Admittedly, that toughness isn't terribly obvious on *Surface*, a musical marshmallow that offers a pleasant blur of synth textures and soul harmony singing, but little substance. Astonishingly, though much of *2nd Wave* is as low-key as its predecessor, it packs twice the punch. It helps that the rhythm arrangements behind "I Missed" and the new-wavy "Black Shades" state what the first album merely implied—that the group has strong roots in new jack swing—but it doesn't hurt that the melodic interest is similarly enlivened. Indeed, "Shower Me with Your Love" and "Closer Than Friends" make the most of Bernard Jackson's romantic, insinuating delivery. From there, *3 Deep* refines the formula, improving the instrumental textures but changing little else, which adds power to ballads like "Never Gonna Let You Down" without pushing the groove tunes into overdrive. Even so, *The Best of Surface* isn't quite what it claims; although it offers a representative overview of the group's singles (plus a couple of extra tracks), its ballad-heavy song list loses some of the other albums' balance. — J.D.C.

BILLY SWAN
★ ★ ★ ★ **Billy Swan's Best (1978; CBS Special Products, 1990)**
He's not exactly an overpowering singer, but Billy Swan's latter-day rockabilly packs a knockout punch. His skinny voice gets over on sheer force of personality and a great beat. "I Can Help" epitomizes his wry, decidedly unmacho approach to music, and life: "If your child needs a daddy, I can help." A shimmering, fully electrified reminder of Sun-era Memphis, "I Can

Help" went from left field to Number One in 1974. "I Can Help" was also Billy Swan's only hit, though this remarkably consistent package would suggest otherwise. Placing quirky originals like "You Just Woman-Handled My Mind" next to boldly reshuffled oldies such as "Shake, Rattle & Roll" and "Don't Be Cruel," *Billy Swan's Best* stakes a fresh claim on some familiar territory. This budget-line album duplicates a 1978 Monument LP called *At His Best*, drawing from three solid albums Swan cut for that defunct Southern label (later reissued by Columbia). Those records *I Can Help*, *Rock & Roll Moon*, *Billy Swan* have all fallen out of print, along with Swan's disappointing later efforts for CBS and A&M. At his best, Billy Swan updates a hybrid style by adding new elements, everything from Motown to pop psychology. — M.C.

SWANS

    ★   **Greed (PVC, 1986)**
    ★½   **Holy Money (PVC, 1986)**
    ★½   **Children of God (Caroline, 1987)**
  ★ ★   **Love Will Tear Us Apart (EP) (Caroline, 1988)**
  ★ ★ ★ **The Burning World (Uni-MCA, 1989)**
    ★½   **Filth (1982–83) (Young God, 1990)**
  ★ ★   **White Light From the Mouth of Infinity (Young God, 1991)**
  ★ ★   **Love of Life (Sky, 1992)**

Rock, as a rule, tends to be fairly hedonistic, rarely deviating from the philosophy of "If it feels good, do it." To appreciate the Swans' aesthetic, however, it's helpful to consider the maxim "It can't be good for you if it doesn't hurt." Indeed, this ensemble's recorded output seems almost to go out of its way to be unbearable, filling its albums with dirges so bloated and depressing that listening to them seems at times the aural equivalent of self-flagellation. *Filth* is loud and bottom heavy, but not quite as lugubrious as *Greed* or *Holy Money*, both of which are so slow and bassy that the vinyl versions almost have to beg the listener not to switch the speed to 45; *Holy Money* also includes "A Screw (Holy Money)," which with its slow-but-insistent beat sounds like dance music for the extremely weary. There's also a bit more rhythm on *Children of God*, but the big news is that the Swans have begun to shift dynamics occasionally, making it easier to tell the songs apart, but no easier to listen to them.

Still, there are signs of a growing pop consciousness in the group. For instance, *Children* is followed by *Love Will Tear Us Apart*, an EP built around a cover of the Joy Division classic, although Michael R. Gira's groaning rendition makes Ian Curtis's performance on the original seem positively cheery. And *The Burning World* not only picks up the pace from the band's usual death-march to a tired trot, but has Jarboe offer a lovely, low-key reading of Blind Faith's "Can't Find My Way Home." Credit producer Bill Laswell for the album's increased accessibility, and try not to be disappointed as *White Light From the Mouth of Infinity* and *Love of Life* return the band to the droning pretension of its earlier output. — J.D.C.

SWAN SILVERTONES

★ ★ ★ ★ ★ **Get Right With the Swan Silvertones (Rhino, 1986)**
★ ★ ★ ★ ★ **Love Lifted Me/My Rock (Specialty, 1991)**

In lead singer Claude Jeter the Swan Silvertones had one of the most important vocalists in modern gospel quartet history. Where the Sensational Nightingales' Julius Cheeks roused congregations with his rough-and-tumble hortatory style, Jeter caressed them into submission with a gentle voice that soared into a delicate, soul-piercing falsetto. Jeter's style made its way into secular music, and profoundly so, by way of Clyde McPhatter, Sam Cooke, David Ruffin, Curtis Mayfield and, most significant of all, Al Green.

But Jeter was only one of the Swans' strengths. In the Rev. Robert Crenshaw they had a gravel-throated screamer without peer; Solomon J. Womack brought hard-driving rhythm in his co-lead role with Jeter; and a later edition of the Swans featured Paul Owens, who had come over after stints with the Dixie Hummingbirds and the Sensational Nightingales. Ira Tucker, the Hummingbirds' outstanding lead vocalist, has called Owens the fastest-thinking singer he ever heard, but it was his ear for popular music that had the most far-reaching effect on the Swan Silvertones. Owens, an expert arranger, shaped the Swans by incorporating pop rhythmic patterns and tighter harmonies.

Specialty has reissued two critical Swans albums on a single disc. Chief among the cuts here is one of the title songs, "My Rock," and "How I Got Over," the latter a monumental entry in gospel's annals. *Get Right With the Swan Silvertones* is from the group's late-'50s period with Vee Jay, when

Owens was exerting his full influence. Johnson, Owens and Jeter made their crowning statement on "Saviour Pass Me Not." By the end of the song Jeter is wrapping his sweet, ad-libbed lines around Johnson's gruff cries in a soul-baring explosion of religious passion. This overpowering performance is only a degree or two cooler than that delivered on "Mary Don't You Weep." Extraordinary on every level. — D.M.

KEITH SWEAT
★★★ **Make It Last Forever** (Vintertainment/Elektra, 1987)
★★★½ **I'll Give All My Love to You** (Vintertainment/Elektra, 1990)
★★★½ **Keep It Comin'** (Elektra, 1991)

Keith Sweat's first single helped lay the foundation for New Jack Swing, which came to dominate black music in the late '80s. "I Want Her" pairs the drawling desire of Sweat's vocal with one of Teddy Riley's lighter-than-air rhythm tracks—and sparks fly. Even though Sweat is credited with producing his debut album, *Make It Last Forever* more closely resembles a drawing-board version of the sound Riley later perfected with his group Guy. A winning cover version of the Dramatics' evocative "In the Rain" points out Sweat's future direction, however. His second album sounds like he produced it. Rather than angling for Riley's pop thrust, "I'll Give All My Love to You" mines a more traditional R&B groove: luxuriously synthesized, mid-tempo romantic testimony. Backing off a bit on the funky inflections, Sweat proves an adept leading man; he caresses "Love to Love You" until those over-used words open up with fresh possibility. "Make You Sweat" high-steps back into New Jack territory, but for the most part, *I'll Give All My Love to You* confidently roams the area beween ecstasy and heartbreak. Though not quite as consistent as *I'll Give All, Keep It Comin'* is more of the same. — M.C.

SWEET
★★★ **Desolation Boulevard** (Capitol, 1975)

The term "affected" doesn't begin to describe Sweet. "Ballroom Blitz" kicks off *Desolation Boulevard* with a winking, fey introduction of the band members; actually, this British quartet provided a vehicle for the producing-songwriting team of Nicky Chinn and Mike Chapman. They pretty much had one idea, though it was a brilliant one: enhancing the flavor of bubblegum with the power-chord zap of heavy metal.

Early Sweet singles like the rockin' British hit "Blockbuster" and the irritating U.S. hit "Little Willy" were released on the defunct Bell label; *Desolation Boulevard* picks up the string in late '73. The Bowiesque decadence of "A.C.D.C." and "The Sixteens" sounds a bit put on, but the car-radio chorales of "Fox on the Run" and "Solid Gold Brass" boom like cannons. Sweet veered toward the metal end of this equation on the mundane follow-up, *Give Us A Wink*, from 1976, and then went the opposite direction for one last hit, "Love Is Like Oxygen," from 1978. Sweet's earlier hits come closer to nitrous oxide. — M.C.

MATTHEW SWEET
★★★½ **Inside** (Columbia, 1986)
★★★ **Earth** (A&M, 1988)
★★★½ **Girlfriend** (Zoo/BMG, 1991)

Formerly the guitarist for cult faves Oh-OK and Buzz of Delight, Matthew Sweet makes terrific pop music. On *Inside*, he's joined by members of the Bangles, Tom Petty's Heartbreakers and the dB's, as well as such interestingly paired playmates as Valerie Simpson and Anton Fier. The tunes, however, don't sound at all like guest-star jams—they come across like the snappy work of a brainy Tommy James or a looser Dwight Twilley. Sweet's songwriting remains impressive on *Earth*, but aside from great guest guitar work by Robert Quine and Richard Lloyd, the album suffers from synth-itis. Much stronger is *Girlfriend*: again Lloyd and Quine help out, along with Lloyd Cole, as Sweet meditates on love supreme ("Divine Intervention," "Holy War") and love fleshly ("Winona" is a fine mash note to actress Winona Ryder). With Sweet's players sounding not unlike Crazy Horse, the album is smart rock-pop. And if radio had any imagination, this hooksmith would be a star. — P.E.

RACHEL SWEET
★★★ **Fool Around: The Best of Rachel Sweet** (Rhino, 1992)

Her first album arriving in 1978 with a punchy version of "B-A-B-Y," an old Carla Thomas hit, 15-year-old Rachel Sweet was marketed first by the British underground label, Stiff, as the teen queen of the Akron scene—the unlikely birthplace for such early new-wavers as Devo and the Waitresses. But given great catchy material and backed by veterans of the Brit pub-rock scene, Sweet's best work was always pure pop. Her voice has a great cartoon power, and she sounds best when she's belting—either on a snappy version (with teen idol Rex Smith) of "Everlasting Love" or the theme to John Waters' *Hairspray*. — P.E.

SWEET HONEY IN THE ROCK
★★★ Sweet Honey in the Rock (Flying Fish, 1975)
★★★ B'lieve I'll Run On . . . See What the End's Gonna Be (Redwood, 1978)
★★★★ Good News (Flying Fish, 1980)
★★★ We All . . . Everyone of Us (Flying Fish, 1980)
★★★ The Other Side (Flying Fish, 1983)
★★★★ Sweet Honey in the Rock at Carnegie Hall (Flying Fish, 1988)
★★★★ Breaths (Flying Fish, 1988)

This sextet raises its stirring voice in defense of individual liberty and women's rights and in support of the idea that freedom is found ultimately in a deep and abiding faith in God. The group's harmonies compellingly summon hope, fury, sorrow and rage. There's not a bad record in this bunch, nor is there any single one that stands tall above all the others. *Breaths* is a good introduction, being a sort of greatest-hits live album whose song selection covers the range of issues Sweet Honey addresses in its music. *At Carnegie Hall* and *Good News*, both live albums, feature material unavailable on other albums. *We All . . . Everyone of Us* lives up to the theme in a set of songs dealing with the ideas of peace and freedom. Sweet Honey's is not the only voice thundering in the night, but it is one of the most valuable. — D.M.

SWIMMING POOL Q'S
★★ The Deep End (DB Recs, 1981)
★★★ The Swimming Pool Q's (A&M, 1984)
★★★½ Blue Tomorrow (A&M, 1986)

With Bob Elsey, this Atlanta quintet boasts a truly fine guitarist, capable of brittle, lean riffs recalling Athens, Georgia's Pylon, a full-out power that harks back to bands like Big Country, or Elsey's own soaring neopsychedelia. And guitarist-vocalist Jeff Calder is one smart writer—his slows songs are elegant; on the rockers he often flashes a wicked wit. But the Q's' secret weapon was singer Anne Richmond Boston. On their first A&M record, *The Swimming Pool Q's*, from 1984, Boston's power on such numbers as "She's Bringing Down the Poison" and "Silver Slippers" transcends the rest of the material; on *Blue Tomorrow*, from 1986, whether dueting with Calder on the country-ish title tune or gliding through his best midtempo number, "Pretty on the Inside," she recalls the dignity of Sandy Denny, the passion of an early Grace Slick. Boosted by a fine production, *Blue Tomorrow* is the Q's' most accomplished album—Calder comes on particularly strong, and Elsey's encyclopedic style adds to the varied nature of the material. After *Tomorrow*, Boston went solo. The Q's remain, as they have been since the late '70s, a commendable bastion of Atlanta's alternative-rock scene. — P.E.

DAVID SYLVIAN
★★★½ Brilliant Trees/Words with the Shaman (1984, 1985; Caroline, 1991)
★★ Alchemy—An Index of Possibilities (Virgin U.K., 1985)
★★★ Gone to Earth (Virgin, 1986)
★★★ Secrets of the Beehive (Virgin, 1987)
★★★½ Weatherbox (Virgin, 1989)
WITH HOLGER CZUKAY
★★ Plight & Premonition (Venture, 1988)
★★ Flux + Mutability (Venture, 1989)

On the surface, *Brilliant Trees*—David Sylvian's first full-length solo effort, which has since been repackaged with *Words With the Shaman*—sounds very much like a Japan album. After all, not only is here Sylvian's voice, warbling as warmly as it did with his old band, but Richard Barbieri's exotic synth colorings and Steve Jansen's lean, supple percussion can be heard as well. And even though bassist Mick Karn is among the missing, Wayne Braithwaite offers a pretty good impression on the haunting "Red Guitar."

But if you listen past the echoes, it's obvious that Sylvian is eager to move beyond the sound he helped establish with Japan. You can hear it in the jazzy overtones to "The Ink in the Well" or the otherworldly thrum of Jon Hassell's trumpet on "Brilliant Trees" itself. And, indeed, *Brilliant Trees* would prove the last album on which Sylvian could be accused of Japanning his sound.

Unfortunately, that doesn't always work to his advantage. *Words With the Shaman*, though pleasant enough, relies more on colorisms than composition and as such sometimes seems like little more than high-concept background music. Still, that's better than *Alchemy—An Index of Possibilities*, which augments "Words With the Shaman" with atmospheric instrumentals that, despite a cast of players including Hassell, Can alum Holger Czukay and guitarist Robert Fripp, could easily be used in place of a prescription soporific. Things aren't quite so snoozy on the double-length *Gone to Earth*, on which the "pop" half offers enough melodic interest on numbers like "Taking the Veil" to break the tedium of the album's instrumental side. But not even the presence of vocals is enough to guarantee a degree of liveliness, as the wonderfully detailed but utterly enervated songs on *Secrets of the Beehive* make plain. (*Weatherbox* combines all of the above in a deluxe CD package). Sylvian also recorded two albums of meticulous but largely unfocused instrumentals with Czukay; *Flux + Mutability* is probably the more interesting of the two, but why anyone would bother making such a distinction is hard to say, given the generally vacuous nature of the music. — J.D.C.

T

TACKHEAD
★ ★ ★　**Tackhead Sound System (Nettwerk, 1987)**
★ ★ ★½ **Friendly as a Hand Grenade (TVT, 1989)**
　★ ★　**Strange Things (SBK, 1990)**
Tackhead isn't a band in the traditional sense of the term, but a collaborative arrangement that combines the talents of Skip McDonald, Doug Wimbish and Keith LeBlanc—who played guitar, bass and drums, respectively, on dozens of rap hits as members of the legendary Sugar Hill house band—and mixmaster-engineer Adrian Sherwood, who alters and treats the basic tracks produced by his bandmates. Although all four worked together on LeBlanc's (now deleted) solo album, *Major Malfunction*, their first release as Tackhead was *Tackhead Sound System*, which features the rhyming rants and dub-influenced remixes of Gary Clail. With a sound that's dense almost to the point of being cluttered, the album offers a dizzying blend of hip-hop, reggae and rock styles, but relatively limited melodic content. That changes somewhat with *Friendly as a Hand Grenade*, on which Bernard Fowler's vocals add a more conventional sense of song structure. Even so, Sherwood's samples and the rhythm section's muscular groove are ultimately what put an edge on tunes like "Airborn Ranger." Apparently, though, edge wasn't enough for Tackhead, and *Strange Things* finds the group moving half-heartedly toward the mainstream. Still, not even cameos by Melle Mel, Lisa Fischer and Mick Jagger (on harmonica) are enough to salvage the prefab funk licks proffered here. — J.D.C.

TACO
★ **After Eight (RCA, 1982)**
You might think that a song like Irving Berlin's "Puttin' On the Ritz" would be too staid and established to be the stuff of novelty records. But in the hands of Taco Ockerse, that's pretty much what it is—high-tech nostalgia, a campy collision between Taco's Rudy Vallee–style croon and its cheesily synthesized backing. Unfortunately, the joke wears thin in a hurry; unless you're dying to hear how he handles "La vie en rose," give this a wide berth. — J.D.C.

TAKE 6
★ ★ **Take 6 (Reprise, 1988)**
★ ★ ★ **So Much 2 Say (Reprise, 1990)**
Nothing much about Take 6 makes sense. A sextet of black males living and recording in Nashville, Tennesssee, singing jazz-based gospel music (largely a cappella), Take 6 would be right at home in Rockefeller Center's Rainbow Room. Imagining them in a church is a stretch, but that's exactly the point. Simply put, Take 6 has revolutionized the pop vocal group tradition by using it as a vehicle for communicating its deep and abiding faith in God.

But no matter how dazzling the medium, it never supersedes the message, which gains momentum with each song. As you listen, the passion of the voices cuts through, particularly when the men dig into great old hymns such as "Mary" and "Get Away, Jordan" (from the group's debut album) and reinvigorate the songs with their fresh approach. *So Much 2 Say* updates the sound slightly, and has better material than its predecessor. Notable among the new songs are "Something Within Me," which is done close to traditional gospel style; "Sunday's on the Way," for a street version of the Crucifixion; and "Where Do the Children Play?," which implores us to focus on the needs of children. Powerful stuff, but it goes down easy, and leaves you thinking. — D.M.

TALKING HEADS

★★★★ **Talking Heads 77 (Sire, 1977)**
★★★★★ **More Songs About Buildings and Food (Sire, 1978)**
★★★½ **Fear of Music (Sire, 1979)**
★★★★½ **Remain in Light (Sire, 1980)**
★★★½ **The Name of this Band Is Talking Heads (Sire, 1982)**
★★★★ **Speaking in Tongues (Sire, 1983)**
★★★★ **Stop Making Sense (Sire, 1984)**
★★★★ **Little Creatures (Sire, 1985)**
★★★ **True Stories (Sire, 1986)**
★★★ **Naked (Sire, 1988)**

Talking Heads 77 applied a series of brief shocks to rock & roll's bloated system. This New York quartet's debut sounds just as minimal and direct as *The Ramones*; only the art-schooled members of Talking Heads took in a wider swath of source material—from funk to bubblegum—than most of their CBGB's peers. When Heads lead singer David Byrne expressed admiration for the Carpenters in an early interview, he wasn't being completely ironic. There's a bright tunefulness to the group's early work, despite the skewed rhythms and Byrne's nerdy, nervy edge. Behind his arty utilitarian facade lies a reservoir of conflicting reactions and observations; from the infamous "Psycho Killer" on down, the seemingly innocent little ditties on *77* are stocked with hair-raising tension and emotional depth.

Talking Heads (especially David Byrne) found a soulmate in producer Brian Eno—perhaps too kindred, after a while. Eno's organic electronic sounds and nontraditional approach to recording provided a solid framework for the group's rapidly expanding interplay on *More Songs About Buildings and Food*. Bassist Tina Weymouth and drummer Chris Frantz pump up an increasingly complex rhythmic pulse while utility man Jerry Harrison fills in guitar and keyboard details. A triumphantly assured cover of Al Green's "Take Me to the River" rounds a weirdly eloquent set of originals. Striking a perfect balance between art-rock and pop commerce, *More Songs* captures this resourceful band at a hypercreative, yet extremely accessible, peak.

Opening with the shivery chant "I Zimbra," *Fear of Music* conjures flashes of the polyrhythmic volcano that's waiting to erupt on future Heads albums. Along with one of the group's best-loved songs ("Life During Wartime"), *Music* also documents its first lapse into experimental filler. Byrne

and Eno became fascinated with African music around this time, resulting in their own somewhat stiff fusion attempt *My Life in the Bush of Ghosts*, and the Heads' altogether more successful *Remain in Light*. The band locks into the flowing African groove, underlining the James Brown connection with a spacey P-Funk synthesized air. *Remain in Light* doesn't rock so much as it rolls like a muddy summer river, dense and inevitable. Searching for a sense of purpose behind this quest, Byrne discovers something on "Once in a Lifetime."

In retrospect, it also seems obvious that solo projects began to sap the band's collective energy during the '80s. However, *Speaking in Tongues* does benefit greatly from some key additions to the lineup. P-Funk keyboardist Bernie Worrell and former LaBelle vocal warrior Nona Hendryx deepen the futuristic dance-rock of "Slippery People" and "Moon Rocks." A dynamic and deservedly legendary live band, this expanded Talking Heads crew is best encountered in the movie *Stop Making Sense*, though the earlier live double LP (*The Name of This Band Is Talking Heads*) offers a more satisfying overview than the later soundtrack album. *Little Creatures* marks the emergence of the older-and-wiser Heads. Returning home to a more simple attack, the group avoids punk nostalgia by encountering current reality head-on: "Up All Night" is one of a few rock children's songs that works. Not the most adventurous Heads album, but a rewarding one.

After that, the group seems to have drifted apart. The next album connects some *Little Creatures* outtakes to the sketchy, anecdotal story line of David Byrne's self-conscious shaggy-dog tale *True Stories*. It only takes hold about half the time, unfortunately. And Talking Heads' tenth album hardly bodes well. *Naked* reflects the transglobal boogie of *Remain in Light*, but in a gutless, studio-perfect mix. Contributions from accomplished African musicians and British guitarist Johnny Marr reduce the other Heads to session players. *Naked* emanates the same sympathetic, sterilizing precision as Byrne's recent solo albums and none of the Heads' original collaborative wallop. — M.C.

TALK TALK

★½ **Talk Talk (EP) (EMI Manhattan, 1982)**
★ **The Party's Over (EMI Manhattan, 1982)**
★ **It's My Life (EMI Manhattan, 1984)**

★ **The Colour of Spring (EMI Manhattan, 1986)**
★ **Spirit of Eden (EMI Manhattan, 1988)**
★½ **Natural History: The Very Best of Talk Talk (EMI, 1990)**
★ **History Revisited: The Remixes (EMI, 1991)**
★ ★ **Laughing Stock (Polydor, 1991)**

Good bands usually improve over time, while bad bands generally just fall apart. But Talk Talk took a different approach with its musical growth; instead of getting better or worse, this band simply grew more pretentious with each passing year. On "Talk Talk," from the *Talk Talk* EP (which was absorbed into *The Party's Over*), the group sounds like an artier Duran Duran, while *It's My Life* finds it bumbling along like an ersatz Japan, all exotic color and tremulous vocal mannerisms. Finally, by *Spirit of Eden*, Mark Hollis's Pete Townshend–on–Dramamine vocals have been pushed aside by the band's pointless noodling. — J.D.C.

TANGERINE DREAM
★ ★ ★ **Phaedra (Virgin, 1974)**
★ ★ ★ **Rubycon (Virgin, 1975)**
★ ★ **Ricochet (Virgin, 1975)**
★ ★ ★½ **Stratosfear (Virgin, 1977)**
★ ★ **Encore—Tangerine Dream Live (Virgin, 1977)**
★ ★ **Cyclone (Virgin, 1978)**
★ ★ **Force Majeure (Virgin, 1979)**
★ ★ **Tangerine Dream (Virgin, 1980)**
★ ★ **Exit (Elektra, 1981)**
★ ★ **Poland (Jive/Electro, 1984)**
★ ★ **Le Parc (Relativity, 1985)**
★ ★ ★ **Tangerine Dream—In the Beginning (Relativity, 1985)**

Tangerine Dream represents the sombre, meditative end of the pioneering German electronic space-rock void, a hippie scene that ranged from the robotic blip-bop of Kraftwerk to the psychedelic explorations of Can. A trio of synthesizer alchemists— Edgar Froese, Christophe Franke and Peter Baumann—compose Tangerine Dream's peak-period (mid-'70s) lineup. *Phaedra* and *Rubycon* both reached the upper registers of the British charts when they were released, and Tangerine Dream's subsequent influence on the synth-dominated sound of '80s Brit-pop is significant. Short on rhythmic pulse and long on ambient atmospheric shifts, these albums also predict Tangerine Dream's evolution into a supplier of sleek, vaguely futuristic-sounding movie and television soundtracks. (The group's '80s screen credits include *Thief, Risky Business, Firestarter* and *Flashpoint*.) After Baumann left for a solo career in 1981, Tangerine Dream added a drummer (Klaus Krieger) for two disappointing "rock" albums and then retreated into the background on later releases. *In the Beginning* is a box set comprised of five earlier albums; it traces the group's development from Pink Floyd–like freefall jamming to scientific instrumental probing (*Alpha Centauri* and *Zeit*) to the orderly trance-programming of its triple-keyboard lineup (*Atem*). Guaranteed to slake the most desperate Tangerine Dream thirst. — M.C.

TAVARES
★ ★ ★½ **The Best of Tavares (1977; Capitol, 1986)**

This family act released more than a dozen albums during a ten-year run on Capitol; only this brutally abridged 1977 greatest-hits edition remains in print. The Tavares brothers release cooling gusts of close harmony amid ornate protodisco arrangements: the crossover hits "It Only Takes a Minute" and "Heaven Must Be Missing an Angel" yearn with a bracing eloquence. When "More Than a Woman" appeared in *Saturday Night Fever* (1978), Tavares capped a solid run of R&B singles with another sleek and soulful pop hit. That high-profile moment overshadows the group's later efforts; *The Best of Tavares* traces the ascent to that point. Whether it's a sampler or a summation, this taste of Tavares lingers for quite a spell. — M.C.

CECIL TAYLOR
★ ★ ★½ **Jazz Advance (Transition, 1956)**
★ ★ ★½ **Looking Ahead (Contemporary, 1958; Contemporary, 1990)**
★ ★ ★½ **The World of Cecil Taylor (Candid, 1960)**
★ ★ ★ ★ **Nefertite—Beautiful One (Freedom, 1962)**
★ ★ ★ ★ ★ **Conquistador! (Blue Note, 1965)**
★ ★ ★ ★ ★ **Unit Structures (Blue Note, 1966)**
★ ★ ★ ★ **Cecil Taylor and the Jazz Composer's Orchestra (1968; ECM, 1990)**
★ ★ ★ ★ **The Great Concert of Cecil Taylor (Prestige, 1969)**
★ ★ ★ ★ ★ **Silent Tongues (Freedom, 1974)**
★ ★ ★ ★ **In Transition (Blue Note, 1975)**
★ ★ ★½ **Dark to Themselves (Enja, 1976)**
★ ★ ★½ **3 Phasis (New World, 1979)**

★★★½ **The Cecil Taylor Unit (New World, 1978)**
★★★★★ **In Florescence (A&M, 1990)**

Declaiming lines of hermetic poetry as he introduces such cryptic compositions as "Anast in Crisis Mouthful of Fresh Cut Flowers" and "Chal Chuiatlichue Goddess of Green Flowing Waters" on *In Florescence*, Cecil Taylor sounds like a high priest of some private cult—then, with equally high ceremony, he lays into the piano, dropping down scattershot clusters of notes like intermittent, dancing rain. For the neophyte listener, this is baffling, intimidating stuff; to make matters more difficult, the percussionist and bassist function hardly at all like a conventional rhythm section—instead, they provide strange punctuation and odd embellishments for Taylor's intriguing, expressively free-form musical statements. After a while, though—and with the paying of necessary, close attention—the listener enters a rarefied zone of elusive beauty; this is dense, compelling music.

But Taylor's style has proved so demanding that *In Florescence* was his first American release in more than ten years; domestic companies have been daunted by his high jazz—it sounds like choirs of aliens compared to someone like Kenny G—so most of his recordings are on hard-to-find import labels. There's poetic justice, however perverse, in this state of affairs. Taylor has been, for a long time, as much of a "world musician" as a jazzer; early on, he synthesized the off-beat innovations of Thelonious Monk with the European classical influences explored by Dave Brubeck, becoming a kind of musical impressionist. His first, late-'50s work—*In Transition*, *Jazz Advance* and *Looking Ahead!*—swung in a recognizable manner, but by the time of *Nefertite—Beautiful One*, he'd soared, with Jimmy Lyons on sax, far beyond any of traditional jazz's rhythmic tropes. *Unit Structures*, *The Great Concert of 1969* and his work on *Jazz Composer's Orchestra* found him stepping further out into uncharted territory—these albums are gorgeous, but again, difficult.
— P.E.

JAMES TAYLOR

★★★½ **James Taylor (1969; Capitol, 1991)**
★★★★★ **Sweet Baby James (Warner Bros., 1970)**
★★★ **Mud Slide Slim and the Blue Horizon (Warner Bros., 1971)**
★★ **One Man Dog (Warner Bros., 1972)**
★★ **Walking Man (Warner Bros., 1973)**
★★★ **Gorilla (Warner Bros., 1975)**
★★ **In the Pocket (Warner Bros., 1976)**
★★★½ **Greatest Hits (Warner Bros., 1976)**
★★★½ **JT (Columbia, 1977)**
★★ **Flag (Columbia, 1979)**
★★ **Dad Loves His Work (Columbia, 1981)**
★★ **That's Why I'm Here (Columbia, 1985)**
★★ **Never Die Young (Columbia, 1988)**
★★★½ **New Moon Shine (Columbia, 1991)**

James Taylor's 1969 debut, *James Taylor*, reissued in 1991, was one of the first releases on the Beatles' Apple label; highlights like the kicky "Knocking 'Round the Zoo" and the winsome "Something in the Way She Moves" (re-recorded on the 1976 *Greatest Hits*) point out the path he'd pursue in the next decade. *Sweet Baby James*, Taylor's landmark second release, heralds the arrival of pop music's sensitive phase. "Fire and Rain" epitomizes the singer-songwriter stance: acoustic-based autobiography, where the arresting musical spareness puts Taylor's gentle melodies and warm, unassuming vocals in full relief. On "Steamroller Blues," he effectively mocks the straining pomposity of then-current white bluesmen—though Taylor became entrapped by his own laid-back image soon enough.

It's easy to hear Taylor's reflective bent as self-satisfaction; he's never really pushed himself musically (in the way, for example, Joni Mitchell has). The fact that Taylor actually improved in the role of MOR crooner is the saving grace of his recording career. In the long run, he turned out to be a more dependable singer than songwriter. *Mud Slide Slim and the Blue Horizon* cemented Taylor's superstar status. But the hit reading of Carole King's "You've Got a Friend" drops some strong hints about the inherent flaccidity of this mellow troubadour approach. It's sappy, and the rest of *Mudslide* isn't much better (save for "Long Ago and Faraway," with Joni Mitchell's backing vocals). Taylor spent the next few years casting around for a broader-based sound; *One Man Dog* is so wispy it nearly evaporates, while *Walking Man* sums up the confusion of this period with its near-stationary title track. (The less said about James and Carly Simon's hit version of "Mockingbird," the better.) Despite an unforgivably clunky cover of Marvin Gaye's "How Sweet It Is (to Be Loved by You)," *Gorilla* is where Taylor regains his balance. "Mexico" introduces a welcome strain of humor, the title track is a natural children's song and "You Make It Easy" positions Sweet Baby James as a post-hippie torch singer.

In the Pocket misses the mark, and *Greatest Hits* mostly marks a record-label move. (*Sweet Baby James* and *Gorilla* combined is the safest investment.) *JT* ranks right up there, however. Taylor reaches back for another R&B classic, and nails down "Handy Man" with his strongest vocal performance to date. A slight rock influence sparks the rest of *JT*, though the goofy blues-rap "Traffic Jam" and the relaxed pace of "Your Smiling Face" feel as familiar as faded denim. Subsequent albums repeat the formula with diminishing results. *Dad Loves His Work* spawned Taylor's last hit, a duet with L.A. songwriter J. D. Souther called "Her Town Too." Instead of fading into the sunset, though, Taylor reemerged in 1991 with his most focused—and tuneful—album in more than ten years. *New Moon Shine* doesn't exactly pick up where *JT* left off, either. The most memorable songs, such as "Slap Leather" and "Native Son," target current events with surprising accuracy: Taylor provides some rather affecting takes on the human cost of the Persian Gulf war. — M.C.

JOHNNIE TAYLOR

★★★★   **Wanted: One Soul Singer (1967; Atlantic, 1991)**
★★★★   **Who's Making Love . . . (Stax, 1968)**
★★★½ **Taylored in Silk (Stax, 1973)**
★★★★ **Raw Blues (1981; Stax, 1987)**
★★★★½ **Chronicle—The 20 Greatest Hits (1977; Stax, 1989)**
★★★   **Eargasm (Columbia, 1976)**
★★★   **In Control (Malaco, 1989)**
★★★   **Little Bluebird (Stax, 1990)**
★★★   **Crazy 'Bout You (Malaco, 1990)**
★★★   **I Know It's Wrong, But I . . . Just Can't Do Right (Malaco, 1991)**

If you're looking for an underappreciated soul giant, Johnnie Taylor fits the bill. Born near Memphis in Crawfordsville, Arkansas, Taylor's roots in blues and gospel make him a natural candidate. (Little Johnny Taylor, of "Part Time Love" fame, is an unrelated blues singer.) Barely out of his teens, Johnnie Taylor added his voice to several gospel groups in the early '60s: first the Highway QC's, and then the Soul Stirrers, in which he replaced his idol Sam Cooke. Early R&B singles for Cooke's SAR label didn't fly, but Taylor immediately took to the signature sound of his next record company—Stax/Volt.

Though *Wanted: One Soul Singer* was slightly overshadowed by the likes of Aretha and Otis in the late '60s, Taylor certainly measures up to the title's specifications. He displays a solid grasp of the basics on Isaac Hayes–David Porter nuggets like "Toe Hold" and "Outside Love," though his gruff conversational tone blossoms on a series of unexpected cover versions. Backed by Booker T. and MG's, Taylor transforms Herbie Hancock's "Watermelon Man," the prerock standard "Blues in the Night" and Tennessee Ernie Ford's "16 Tons" into Memphis dynamite.

Who's Making Love . . . put across Taylor's straight-talking soul-brother persona to the general public. Balancing upbeat imprecations ("Take Care of Your Homework") against bluesy heartbreak sagas ("Woman Across the River"), it's another remarkably well-rounded album. The hit title track provides a model for an entire sequence of funky advice songs, all driven home by Taylor's disarming baritone and snazzy musical backing. "Who's Making Love" led to the cautionary topical metaphor of "Hijackin' Love," the jazzy what-the-hell attitude of "Cheaper to Keep Her" and two songs documenting the exploits of a near-mythic back door man: "Standing in for Jody" and "Jody's Got Your Girl and Gone."

Chronicle pulls together a mightily impressive string of R&B chart singles, arguing that Taylor was the preeminent soul singer of the early '70s—after Al Green, of course. The sweetening influence of string sections creeps into some of the later *Chronicle* entries, and Taylor leapt right into the dance-floor fray in 1976 with "Disco Lady." His first Top Ten single since "Who's Making Love," it's a pleasantly lightweight novelty with just a touch of gruff sexuality. Otherwise, the accompanying album, *Eargasm*, sticks to mild pop-soul excursions rather than pursuing the great demon disco any further. The songwriting is nowhere near as punchy or pointed as on the Stax records; however, Taylor throws down some heavy gospel-style testimony. Taylor floundered in a sea of rhythmic confusion on several subsequent Columbia (and RCA) efforts, now deleted. His latter-day Malaco albums are a big improvement, in perfect keeping with that label's rootsy integrity. But truth be told, some of the grit and fire in Taylor's voice has subsided. Of the Stax reissues, *Raw Blues* captures the man in top form.
— M.C.

TEARS FOR FEARS

★★½ **The Hurting (Mercury, 1983)**
★★★ **Songs From the Big Chair (Mercury, 1985)**
★★★★ **The Seeds of Love (Mercury, 1989)**

After the fairly extraordinary *The Seeds of Love*, it was hard to remember that Tears for Fears had begun as run-of-the-mill English synthsters. Indeed, starting out as teen-angst mongerers, taking their "philosophy" from Arthur Janov's primal scream therapy and their haircuts from the Shop of Cute, Tears seemed especially hard to take. With its liner notes capitalizing the word "Pain," *The Hurting* was big-echo sighing and wailing—but there were hints of intelligence. A title like "Ideas as Opiates," for example, suggested thought, and the melodic sense behind even such lyrical embarrassments as "Watch Me Bleed" was strong.

Two years later, *Songs From the Big Chair* showed uncanny progress. The hits, "Shout" and "Everybody Wants to Rule the World," were intriguingly textured and memorable. The playing, especially by guest saxophonist Mel Collins, was at times spine-tingling—and the boys' self-pity had expanded to include the larger, outraged hurt of "The Working Hour." Plus, Curt Smith and Roland Orzabal began emerging as singers whose warbled pain 'n' suffering paid off in sonic loveliness.

But *The Seeds of Love* was something else. Helped out by drummer Manu Katché and bassist Pino Palladino, and by the remarkable trumpet of Jon Hassell and gorgeous vocals and piano of Oleta Adams, the record was a sophisticated pop masterpiece. Social consciousness came on strong with "Woman in Chains"; the title track wittily reprised "I Am the Walrus"; and "Famous Last Words" was a minisymphony—gorgeous, strong and deep. — P.E.

TECHNOTRONIC

★★★½ **Pump Up the Jam: The Album (SBK, 1989)**
★★★ **Trip On This: The Remixes (SBK, 1990)**

What set this Belgian studio team apart from other house outfits wasn't its way with a beat, but its talent for melody. That much was clear from the first notes of "Pump Up the Jam," the single that launched the group; even though the melodic components were minimal, producer Jo "Thomas DeQuincey" Bogaert made every note count, whether in the synth arrangement or the half-sung vocal by rapper Ya Kid K. *Pump Up the Jam: The Album* extends that formula and produced two similarly tuneful dance hits: "Get Yo! (Before the Night Is Over)" and "This Beat Is Technotronic." But even the songs that didn't cut it on the dance floor hold up well on the album, particularly dark, hooky numbers like "Tough" and "Come On." *Trip On This: The Remixes* sacrifices the melodic focus of the original album for a stronger groove—a reasonable trade-off if dancing is your main interest, but a loss if all you want to do is listen. It does, however, include a version of "Spin That Wheel," which was originally released under the group name Hi Tek 3. — J.D.C.

TEENA MARIE

★★★½ **Wild and Peaceful (Gordy, 1979)**
★★★ **Lady T (Gordy, 1980)**
★★★ **Irons in the Fire (Gordy, 1980)**
★★★★ **It Must Be Magic (Gordy, 1981)**
★★★½ **Robbery (Epic, 1983)**
★★★★½ **Starchild (Epic, 1984)**
★★★★ **Greatest Hits (Motown, 1985)**
★★★½ **Emerald City (Epic, 1986)**
★★★½ **Naked to the World (Epic, 1988)**
★★★★ **Ivory (Epic, 1990)**
★★★★½ **Greatest Hits (Epic, 1991)**

Like Prince, Teena Marie is a singer/songwriter/multi-instrumentalist whose work is often as brilliant as it is quirky, combining a jazz-inflected vocal style with strongly soulful melodies and a sure sense of funk. Her first album, *Wild and Peaceful*, presents her as a Rick James protégé, which, as "I'm a Sucker for Your Love" indicates, was a fair match. But her talents soon outstripped those of the Gordy production staff; as *It Must be Magic* makes plain, not only could she handle the writing and production chores herself, but she understood R&B styles well enough to move effortlessly from the rap-tinged pop of "Square Biz" to the sultry balladry of "Portuguese Love."

Still, she didn't really come into her own until her move to Epic. It wasn't just the freedom to write, produce and play as she saw fit that made this move pay off, but the freedom she was afforded to move from style to style with each new album. Thus, *Starchild* finds her grooving with abandon, scoring one of her most memorable R&B performances with "Lovergirl," while *Emerald City* presents a more convincing funk-rock fusion than anything Prince managed at the time, slipping easily from the slow burn of "You So Heavy," with its searing Stevie Ray Vaughan solo, to the jazzy eclecticism of the percussion-powered "Batucada Suite." Yet as adventurous as her albums sometimes got, she never lost sight of her core audience. Indeed, *Ivory* updates her arrangements to the latest hip-hop standards (including a touch of Soul II Soul groove on the Jazzie B-produced "Since Day One") without diluting the distinctive flavor of her music. — J.D.C.

TEENAGE FANCLUB
★★★ A Catholic Education (Matador, 1990)
★★★★ Bandwagonesque (DCG, 1991)
Hastily recorded on a shoestring budget, this Scottish quartet's first effort, *A Catholic Education*, boasted powerful guitar riffing (à la Dinosaur Jr) and muffled but melodic vocals. Beneath the growling garage-grunge surface, there definitely lurked the soul of a pop band. *Bandwagonesque*, Teenage Fanclub's major-label debut, left behind the murky, rushed sound of the previous album and highlighted the band's Big Star–derived pop harmonies and catchy tunecraft, with such winning songs as "The Concept," "December," "Metal Baby" and "Star Sign." — P.E.

TELEVISION
★★★★★ Marquee Moon (Elektra, 1977)
★★★★ Adventure (Elektra, 1978)
★★★ The Blow-Up (ROIR, 1982)
At its frequent best, Television lifted psychedelia to an even higher plane. Lead guitarist Tom Verlaine plugged his Fender into the wet socket of New York City, charging his solos with searing urban energy and deadly logic. Television was the first of the new breed of bands to play at CBGB in 1974, with founding bass player Richard Hell, though the group's fiercely detailed rave-ups had almost nothing in common with the primitive efforts of the Ramones, Blondie and Talking Heads. Like Verlaine's compadre Patti Smith, Television made a lot of early punks uncomfortable. In fact, Smith and Verlaine are both diehard hippie iconoclasts who didn't find their poetic voices until long after the revolution had ended.

Marquee Moon is a solid set of angst-ridden songs, but searching guitar interplay and a sharp, unsettling tone renders the whole indelible. Richard Lloyd proves to be a sensitive rhythm guitarist, keeping one eye on Verlaine's trajectory and the other on the crossfire between

drummer Billy Ficca and new bassist Fred Smith. Verlaine's brittle tenor voice often breaks under the strain of his articulate passion, but the music buoys his sagging spirits time and again. The title track truly is a tour de force: "Marquee Moon" forges a spiritual connection between Allman Brothers–style virtuosity and Velvet Underground–style introspection. There's nothing else in rock quite like it.

Adventure is slick and overproduced; "The Fire" nearly smothers the otherwise-smokin' second half. But the concluding track ("The Dream's Dream") stands as one of Verlaine's most lyrical excursions, rockers like "Glory" and "Foxhole" score bull's-eyes and Richard Lloyd weighs in with an achingly wistful ballad called "Days."

Television broke up in 1978, and the still-booming New York scene suddenly lost its guiding lights. *The Blow-Up* offers crude but convincing evidence of the group's legendary live detonation—recorded at CBGB, of course. In early 1992 Television reunited and returned to the studio to record an album for Capitol. — M.C.

THE TEMPTATIONS
★★★★½ Meet the Temptations (1964; Motown, 1991)
★★★★★ The Temptations Sing Smokey (1965; Motown, 1991)
★★★½ Temptin' Temptations (1965; Motown, 1991)
★★★★ Gettin' Ready (1966; Motown, 1991)
★★★★½ The Temptations Greatest Hits (1966; Motown, 1988)
★★½ Temptations Live! (Motown, 1967)
★★★ With a Lot o' Soul (1967; Motown, 1989)
★★ In a Mellow Mood (Motown, 1967)
★★★ The Temptations Wish It Would Rain (Motown, 1968)
★★★ Live at the Copa (1968; Motown, 1989)
★★★½ I Wish It Would Rain (1968; Motown, 1986)
★★★ Cloud Nine (1969; Motown, 1991)
★★★ Puzzle People (1970; Motown, 1989)
★★★ Psychedelic Shack (1970; Motown, 1991)
★★★★ Temptations Greatest Hits, Vol. 2 (1970; Motown, 1988)

★★ **The Temptations Christmas Card** (Motown, 1970)
★★★ **Sky's the Limit** (1971; Motown, 1990)
★★ **Solid Rock** (1972; Motown, 1990)
★★★★ **All Directions** (1972; Motown, 1989)
★★★ **Masterpiece** (1974; Motown, 1991)
★★★★★ **Anthology 64–73** (1973; Motown, 1986)
★★ **1990** (Gordy, 1974)
★★ **A Song for You** (1974; Motown, 1986)
★★ **House Party** (Gordy, 1975)
★★ **Wings of Love** (Gordy, 1976)
★★ **The Temptations Do the Temptations** (Gordy, 1976)
★★ **Hear to Tempt You** (Atlantic, 1977)
★★ **Bare Back** (Atlantic, 1978)
★★ **Power** (Gordy, 1980)
★ **Give Love at Christmas** (Gordy, 1980)
★½ **The Temptations** (Gordy, 1981)
★★★★ **All the Million-Sellers** (Gordy, 1981)
★★★½ **Reunion** (Gordy, 1982)
★★ **Surface Thrills** (Gordy, 1983)
★★★★ **The Temptations** (Gordy, 1983)
★★ **Back to Basics** (Gordy, 1983)
★★★ **Truly for You** (Gordy, 1984)
★★★ **Touch Me** (Gordy, 1985)
★★★★ **The Temptations 25th Anniversary** (Motown, 1986)
★★½ **To Be Continued** (Gordy, 1986)
★★★ **Together Again** (Gordy, 1987)
★★★ **In a Mellow Mood** (Motown, 1991)

At their early-'60s prime, the Temptations boasted a lineup of singers whose individual talents and skillful ensemble work has rarely been equalled in pop history. With three leads (gritty tenor David Ruffin, supple, high tenor Eddie Kendricks, assured baritone Paul Williams) and two backup vocalists (baritone Otis Williams, bass Melvin Franklin), the group became the Motown flagship, finding, primarily in the songs of Smokey Robinson and the blend of R&B assertiveness and pop melodies, a formula for radio greatness. Smokey's "The Way You Do the Things You Do" and "My Girl" began a remarkable series of tight, perfectly arranged singles that only slowed down as the '60s waned. The Norman Whitfield–produced songs "Ain't Too Proud to Beg," "(I Know) I'm Losing You" and "I Wish It Would Rain" were

also among the standouts of a style whose fluid grace provided counterpoint to the tortured soul of Otis Redding and Stax-Atlantic soul. The Temptations' impact was enormous, influencing not only native soulsters but priming the emulation of the Stones, Beatles and other British rhythm & blues fanatics; highly choreographed and ultraprecise, the Temps' stage show embodied the music's pristine efficiency—and yet, under the tuxedos, the singers worked up a righteous sweat.

At the end of the decade, the Temps (with new lead singer Dennis Edwards) turned funkward. Influenced both by Sly Stone's rock-inflected jams and by Marvin Gaye's explorations of concept material, their songs got longer, roomier, edgier. When the newer material worked—"I Can't Get Next to You," "Psychedelic Shack," "Papa Was a Rollin' Stone," "Ball of Confusion (That's What the World Is Today)"—the group achieved a new gritty realism that nearly compensated for its abandonment of its trademark violins-and-love-lyrics grace (and the departure, as well, of Eddie Kendricks). Often, however, the Temps seemed to be overreaching; long gone was their early, remarkable concision.

As a whole, the Temptations' '70s and '80s work was haphazard. Sly, P-Funk and, later, Prince had captured R&B's harder, more experimental edge—and the Temps, however occasionally impressive, seemed retrograde. Years of performing meant that the band could be counted on for extremely professional product, but their best moments came when they worked hardest at recapturing the sound of their earliest glory.
— P.E.

10CC

★★½ **The Original Soundtrack** (1975; Mercury, 1990)
★★ **How Dare You** (1976; Mercury, 1990)
★★ **Deceptive Bends** (1977; Mercury, 1990)

GODLEY AND CREME

★★ **Freeze Frame** (1979; Polydor, 1987)
★★ **The History Mix Volume I** (Polydor, 1985)

Bassist Graham Gouldman and guitarist Eric Stewart formed 10cc after leaving the Mindbenders. Working with guitarist-keyboardist Lol Creme and drummer Kevin Godley, they inflated sweet Merseybeat harmony-pop to monstrous art-rock proportions. 10cc's earliest albums, now out of print, didn't make much of an impression in the States, though the bouncy British hit

"Rubber Bullets" became a cult favorite in late '73. "I'm Not in Love" (from *The Original Soundtrack*) insinuated its way to the top of the charts, almost; this slow-creeping single—a creamy orchestrated string of ironic denials—stalled at Number Two for three weeks in '75. It's the most palatable thing on the album by far; Creme and Godley's "witty" eclectic impulses run amok on smirking, labored pastiches like "Un Nuit in Paris" and "Life Is a Minestrone." Godley and Creme split off in 1976; 10cc scored another Beatlesque hit in '77 with "The Things We Do for Love" (*Deceptive Bends*) and then faded from view. Godley and Creme pursued their peculiar muse on the (mercifully) deleted *Consequences* (1977)—a murky three-LP rock opera centering on the deployment of a guitar device called the Gizmo. *Freeze Frame* is the only surviving remnant of the more song-oriented albums that followed: imagine a British Frank Zappa with an arid sense of humor and far less instrumental ability. Ever the masters of high-tech gimmickry, Godley and Creme hit with an arresting, innovative video clip ("Cry") in 1985. As music, however, the mushy synth-pop of "Cry" barely registers, and *The History Mix Volume One* reworks a repertoire that wasn't exactly stacked with hooks to begin with. — M.C.

10,000 MANIACS

★★½ **Human Conflict Number Five (EP) (Christian Burial, 1982)**
★★★ **Secrets of the I Ching (Christian Burial, 1983)**
★★★★ **The Wishing Chair (Elektra, 1985)**
★★★★★ **In My Tribe (Elektra, 1987)**
★★★★ **Blind Man's Zoo (Elektra, 1989)**
★★★ **Hope Chest (Elektra, 1990)**

Sounding nothing like their name, 10,000 Maniacs emerged from tiny Jamestown, New York, with a sound that was complex and distinctive—and, at first, not entirely focused. Indeed, *Human Conflict Number Five*, the sextet's first release, offers an awkward mix of folk-tinged new wave ("Orange") and odd, reggae-flavored rock ("Planned Obsolescence") that often seems to emphasize guitarist Robert Buck at the expense of singer Natalie Merchant. Fortunately, things improve considerably with *Secrets of the I Ching*; from the album-opening notes of "Grey Victory," it's obvious that the Maniacs have not only reined in their few excesses but have taken

pains to hone their material. And though the reggae influences are still there (in "Death of Manolete," for example), they're one of several elements in the band's sound. (Both *Human Conflict Number Five* and *Secrets of the I Ching* are combined on *Hope Chest*.)

With *The Wishing Chair*, the Maniacs make their move to the majors. Although the album repeats two songs from *Secrets of the I Ching* (three on the CD version), the band's sound has evolved a full step beyond its first album, exuding a confident eclecticism that at its best recalls the Band. Still, that wasn't enough to give the group the mass audience it deserved, and so the Maniacs moved from Joe Boyd, who produced *The Wishing Chair*, to Peter Asher, who handled *In My Tribe*. The album's success didn't quite come as expected, as an ill-advised cover of Cat Stevens's "Peace Train" flopped, while idiosyncratic originals like "What's the Matter Here?" and "Like the Weather" found an audience. And no wonder, for the band's arrangements were leaner (as was its lineup, after the departure of guitarist John Lombardo) and its sound more melody-intense. But best of all was the writing, which made the most of Merchant's luscious melodies and subtle narrative cadences.

Blind Man's Zoo isn't quite as cheerful, but given its issue-oriented focus, it's hard to imagine how it could be. Yet no matter how pointed the lyrics become, Merchant and her bandmates never turn the songs into a social-commentary bully pulpit, keeping the focus personal and the melodies perky on songs like "Eat for Two" and "Poison in the Well." — J.D.C.

TEN YEARS AFTER

★★½ **Ten Years After (1967; Polydor, 1988)**
★★½ **Undead (1968; Polydor, 1988)**
★★ **Stonedhenge (Deram, 1969)**
★★½ **Ssssh (1969; Chrysalis, 1975)**
★★★ **Cricklewood Green (1970; Chrysalis, 1975)**
★★½ **Watt (Deram, 1970)**
★★½ **A Space in Time (1971; Chrysalis, 1987))**
★★½ **Rock and Roll Music to the World (1972; Chrysalis, 1987)**
★ **Alvin Lee and Company (1972; Deram, 1990)**
★★★ **Recorded Live (1973; Chyrsalis, 1987)**
★ **Positive Vibrations (1974; Chrysalis, 1987)**

★ ★½ **Goin' Home: Their Greatest Hits (Deram, 1975)**
★ ★½ **The Classic Performances of Ten Years After (Columbia, 1976)**
★ ★ ★ **Universal (Chrysalis, 1987)**
★ ★½ **About Time (Chryalis, 1989)**

Charisma and blinding speed made guitarist-singer Alvin Lee a standout at Woodstock—especially in that tie-dyed context, the boogie fever and early rock & roll swagger of all thirteen minutes of "I'm Going Home" were mightily refreshing. But while Lee and organist Chick Churchill were better players than, say, Savoy Brown, TYA now sounds like one more middling English blues band, lacking even the crude distinctiveness of Humble Pie.

Not a strong vocalist, Lee never developed an interesting style of nonsinging, either—and while the faster, grittier Ten Years After is punchy, few of the ballads work, and the group's blues numbers are wearisome. "I'd Love to Change the World," Ten Years After's big hit off *A Space in Time*, is melodic, but its lyrics creak with an odd mixture of grumpy conservatism and hippie defeat. *Cricklewood Green* stands as TYA's most cohesive album—again, though, it's really only Lee's guitar that smokes. Unfortunately, none of the greatest-hits albums features intelligent song selection, although *Universal* comes closest: ravers such as "Good Morning Little School Girl" and "Going Back to Birmingham," plus the entire epic of "I'm Going Home," are included. — P.E.

TERMINATOR X
★ ★ ★ ★ **Terminator X and the Valley of the Jeep Beets (Columbia, 1991)**

As the title suggests, this solo effort by Public Enemy's DJ is based on bass, precisely the sort of percussive, propulsive rumble the group referred to in the opening line of "Bring the Noise"—to wit, "How low can you go?" And because that booming groove speaks more directly to the energies of the hip-hop nation than any rhyme ever could, the best parts of this album leave Terminator X sounding like PE's most articulate member. — J.D.C.

TESLA
★½ **Mechanical Resonance (Geffen, 1986)**
★ ★ ★ **The Great Radio Controversy (Geffen, 1989)**
★ ★ **Five Man Acoustical Jam (Geffen, 1990)**
★ ★ ★½ **Psychotic Supper (Geffen, 1991)**

Named for the eccentric electronics genius Nikola Tesla (he discovered AC current, among other things), this Sacramento quintet plays with the heartfelt passion of true cornballs, a condition that has its advantages. After all, it's the group's faith in hoary rock clichés that enables it to get away with reviving an oldie like the hippy-dippy "Signs" (*Five Man Acoustical Jam*) or lyrics as hokey as "We're the younger generation/And we're here to face the day/Heard all across the nation/And we got something to say" ("Change In the Weather," from *Psychotic Supper*).

On the other hand, that same lunkheaded devotion to rock cant is also responsible for the undigested clichés of *Mechanical Resonance*, a semimetal debut that's well played but utterly lacking in originality. Not so with *The Great Radio Controversy*, on which the band comes up with songs solid enough to make the most of its instrumental ability, and though the sentiments expressed in numbers like "Lazy Days, Crazy Nights" aren't exactly novel, Tesla keeps things tuneful enough to keep us from minding.

As the title suggests, *Five Man Acoustical Jam* swaps the band's hi-watt grunge for a less-amplified sound. Despite a song list that draws heavily from the band's first two albums, the oldies set the tone, from a straight-up rendition of "Truckin' " to "Signs." It's impressive, but only if you're too young to remember how ridiculous the originals were. Fortunately, *Psychotic Supper* brings the decibel level back up with a set of solidly melodic, boogie-based rockers. Good stuff, provided you pay no attention to the lyrics. — J.D.C.

JOE TEX
★ ★ ★ **Best of Joe Tex (Atlantic, 1985)**
★ ★ ★ ★ **I Believe I'm Gonna Make It: The Best of Joe Tex, 1964–1972 (Rhino, 1988)**

A prime R&B belter, Tex never developed a highly personalized style of the kind that makes James Brown the idiosyncratic genius of the genre, but at his toughest, he rivaled Wilson Pickett. And it's as the sly grunter of such novelty hits as "Skinny Legs and All" (1967) and the bass-driven "I Gotcha" (1972) that he's mainly remembered. But Tex had more range—from a growl to a sweet near-falsetto—than those sweaty hits suggest: "Don't Make Your Children Pay," "Grandma Mary" and "I Believe I'm Gonna Make It" are grassroots homilies. A fundamentalist minister who later became a Muslim, Tex preached with a straightforward power; his story songs are instructional fables delivered in vernacular poetry. Cynics may find his sermonizing tiresome; the sheer gorgeousness of his voice might overcome their quibbles. While his best work was recorded for Atlantic, Tex's style is close to Stax/Volt's—rhythm outdistances melody, fervor is all. *I Believe I'm Gonna Make It* is masterful: slow, gospel-like love songs, ultrafunk and essential soul. — P.E.

TEXAS TORNADOS
★ ★ ★½ **Texas Tornados (Warner Bros., 1990)**
★ ★ ★ ★ **Zone of Our Own (Warner Bros., 1991)**

A true roots-rock supergroup, the Texas Tornados unite guitarist Doug Sahm and organist Augie Meyers of the great '60s Tex-Mex pioneers, the Sir Douglas Quintet, with legendary Latino accordionist Flaco Jiminez and the wonderfully lugubrious Freddy ("Before the Next Teardrop Falls") Fender. Whether on the Spanish-language debut album or on its Spanish-English successor, Fender's voice is all gush and heartache—and the band absolutely kicks. Swagger this assured takes years to muster; that these gray-hairs also sound like unleashed joyous thunder takes heart. Among *Zone*'s standout cuts: Freddy's "Oh Holy One" and a fierce, fresh reworking of the Sir Doug classic, "Is Anybody Goin' to San Antone." — P.E.

THAT PETROL EMOTION
★ ★ ★ **Manic Pop Thrill (Demon, 1986)**
★ ★ ★ ★ **Babble (Polydor, 1987)**
★ ★ ½ **End of the Milennium Psychosis Blues (Polygram, 1988)**
★ ★ ★ **Chemicrazy (Virgin, 1990)**

Clanging and catchy at the same time, That Petrol Emotion translate classic punk aggression into accessible, contemporary musical terms. On *Manic Pop Thrill*, guitarist Seán O'Neill and his bass-playing brother Damian pick up where they'd left off with the Undertones a few years before: the spot at which Merseybeat melody and back-alley clamor coincide. In the meantime, Seán O'Neill and fellow guitarist Reáman O'Gormáin developed a more complex, meticulously frenzied attack. *Babble* harnesses their abrasive impact behind barb-wire hooks and mechanical rhythms: the points on "Chester Burnette" and "Creeping Toward the Cross" about Irish racism and Irish religion, respectively,

couldn't be any sharper. Athletically inclined listeners can even dance to the whirring techno-bop of "Big Decision." *Babble* towers above the mid-'80s "alternative" competition; That Petrol Emotion does much more than just bring the noise.

That said, *End of the Milennium Psychosis Blues* could stand an extra blast of six-string insanity. The groove shifts from fierce industrialized disco to slightly tinny funk. Lead singer Steve Mack possesses an angelic art-rock tenor, and given half a chance, he leads this band seriously astray. Slivers of the original six-string fire light up *Chemicrazy*, but for every electric high-wire drone like "Abandon," there's a crawling, formulaic rock number like "Sweet Shiver Burn." *Babble* maintains a compelling, delicate balance between those two opposing forces. Perhaps that high-pressure feat has contributed to That Petrol Emotion's current schizophrenia. — M.C.

THE THE
★ ★ **Soul Mining (Epic, 1983)**
★ ★ ★ **Infected (Epic, 1986)**
★ ★ ½ **Mind Bomb (Columbia, 1989)**

Basically, The The is Matt Johnson—and he's one excitable boy. *Soul Mining* was merely passable pop, but *Infected* has a dense, hyper-driven power. A skillful texturalist on synth, Johnson crafts mini-epics that often suffer from verbal overreaching, but do manage to work on a level of funky atmosphere. He's infatuated with dread, alienation, remorse and the usual stock in trade of postpunk artists, and his vocals verge on the melodramatic, but his canny deployment of a host of guest players (Neneh Cherry, Bashiri Johnson, a squad of brass and string players) makes for a varied and ambitious album. *Mind Bomb* is less slick, more assaultive and less interesting. — P.E.

THEY MIGHT BE GIANTS
★ ★ ★ **They Might Be Giants (Bar/None, 1986)**
★ ★ ★ ★ **Lincoln (Restless/Bar/None, 1988)**
★ ★ ★ ★ **Flood (Elektra, 1990)**
★ ★ ★ **Miscellaneous T (Restless, 1991)**
★ ★ ½ **Apollo 18 (Elektra, 1992)**

Sounding at times like jingle writers run amok, John Flansburgh and John Linnell—the guys who Might Be Giants—specialize in songs that are relentlessly catchy and hopelessly cheesy, full of giddy non sequiturs, cartoonish combinations of instruments and hooks that leave you feeling like a freshly landed trout.

Although a fair amount of *They Might Be Giants* is given over to novelty tunes and marginalia, the best material—"Don't Let's Start," "Put Your Hand Inside the Puppet Head," "(She Was a) Hotel Detective"—is almost insanely tuneful, avoiding any pretense to deeper meaning (or even surface meaning) in its headlong pursuit of melody. *Lincoln* maintains that standard even as it unleashes puns of cosmic awfulness.

Flood, however, finds the Giants taking a few tentative steps toward pop convention, with arrangements that flirt with commercial competence, and even a couple of songs that dare to have a message. As always, though, what drives the album is the duo's melodic impetuousness, whether manifested in pop-rock moves like "Birdhouse in Your Soul" or genre spoofs like "Istanbul (Not Constantinople)." There's even more ambition evident in the sound of *Apollo 18*, which finds the Giants not only rounding out their sound with a host of guest musicians, but actually concocting a cantata of sorts on "Fingertips." Impressive, sure, but not much fun—a fatal flaw for a band so dependent on whimsy. As for *Miscellaneous T*, it's pretty much what its title suggests, compiling remixes and B sides, although "Hey Mr. DJ, I Thought You Said We Had a Deal" is a semihit in its own right. — J.D.C.

THIN LIZZY
★★ **Thin Lizzy (Mercury, 1972)**
★★ **Shades of a Blue Orphanage (Mercury, 1973)**
★★½ **Night Life (Mercury, 1974)**
★★½ **Fighting (Mercury, 1975)**
★★★★ **Jailbreak (Mercury, 1975)**
★★½ **Johnny the Fox (Mercury, 1976)**
★★½ **Bad Reputation (Mercury, 1977)**
★★★½ **Live and Dangerous (Warner Bros., 1978)**
★★★★½ **Dedication: The Very Best of Thin Lizzy (Polygram, 1991)**
PHIL LYNOTT
★★★ **Solo in Soho (Warner Bros., 1980)**
The melancholy tear in Phil Lynott's rich voice sets Thin Lizzy far apart from the braying mid-'70s metal pack. Projecting a dissolute sensitivity above dueling lead guitars, this black Irish bass player chiseled out a distinct niche for his long-running quartet: lyrical hard rock. There's a slight formulaic sameness to Thin Lizzy's approach; unsurprisingly, the group's only hit album (*Jailbreak*) is also its only consistent one. "The Boys Are Back in Town," a lingering hit single in 1976, set the

tone: celebratory riffs cut by bittersweet reflection. Though Lynott gets caught up in macho adventures like *Jailbreak*'s definitive "Cowboy Song," the band's spacious arrangements and propulsive rhythms usually carry him forward. Thin Lizzy's taut discipline and drive are in evidence on *Live and Dangerous*, though filler sinks most of the Mercury albums (as well as the other, out-of-print Warner Bros. albums). The seamless best-of compilation (*Dedication*) successfully taps each stage of the band's bumpy decade-plus career, serving Thin Lizzy's memory well.

On the long-lost *Solo in Soho*, Lynott stretches his musical boundaries with typically uneven, though often compelling results. The disco attempts sound suitably atrocious, but the rock-reggae experiments and the unprecedented "Ode to a Black Man" reveal hidden depths. Lynott succumbed to a drug overdose in 1986. — M.C.

3RD BASS
★★★ **The Cactus Album (Def Jam/Columbia, 1989)**
★★½ **The Cactus Revisted: 3rd Bass Remixes (DefJam/Columbia, 1990)**
★★★ **Derelicts of Dialect (Def Jam/Columbia, 1991)**
Sure, these white rappers wax funkier than Vanilla Ice—but so did Neil Diamond. Actually, 3rd Bass has quite a lot on the ball: MC Serch and Prime Minister Pete Nice trade social observations and locker-room talk with the ease of two long-standing homeboys, while DJ Richie Rich (who departed the group in 1991) flexes an imaginative hand at the sampler and turntables. But while *Licensed to Ill* captures the hip-hop spirit by flaunting the Beastie Boys' nasal Caucasian whining, Serch and Pete Nice try to appropriate the black vernacular as their own. These resourceful young men are most compelling when they deal with the inherent contradictions of their color-blind stance, on sharp cuts such as "Product of the Environment," from *The Cactus Album*, and "No Master Plan, No Master Race," from *Derelicts of Dialect*. If 3rd Bass sounds too tough to be mistaken for wannabes, this meticulous and studied approach to such a combustible art form guarantees that the group will never be regarded as innovators, either. And including two labored anti–Vanilla Ice raps on *Derelicts* indicates a crippling lack of imagination; why bother lampooning such a witless self-parody? For

all the painfully elongated joke tracks on both albums, 3rd Bass's righteous rapping too often seems humorless. — M.C.

.38 SPECIAL

★ ★   .38 Special (A&M, 1977)
★ ★   Special Delivery (A&M, 1978)
★ ★½ Rockin' Into the Night (A&M, 1979)
★ ★½ Wild Eyed Southern Boys (A&M, 1981)
★ ★½ Special Forces (A&M, 1982)
★ ★ ★   Tour de Force (A&M, 1983)
★ ★   Strength in Numbers (A&M, 1986)
★ ★ ★ ★ Flashback (A&M, 1987)
★ ★   Rock & Roll Strategy (A&M, 1988)
★ ★   Bone Against Steel (Charisma, 1991)

Strictly hit-or-miss, the *Flashback* collection isn't quite the bummer you'd expect from these second-generation Southern boogie specialists. .38 Special packs a pair of smoking singles—"Caught Up in You" and "If I'd Been the One"—that found their mark in the early '80s. Album Oriented Rock doesn't get any better than this. Working with producer Rodney Mills, the group harnesses its roaring mutiple-guitar horsepower behind the high-gloss grittiness of singer Donnie Van Zant (brother of Lynyrd Skynyrd's late Ronnie). Those two singles sport vocal hooks that the craftsmen in Squeeze or Foreigner might envy; "Hold On Loosely," "Back Where You Belong" and even the mindlessly exuberant "Rockin' into the Night" aren't too far behind. But bland latter-day soundtrack anthems fill out *Flashback*, and there are only a few minor delights (such as "You Keep Runnin' Away," from *Special Forces*) lurking amid the numb gut-crunch on .38 Special's original albums. Founding guitarist and songwriter Don Barnes sits out the 1991 comeback attempt—wisely. The creaky-sounding *Bone Against Steel* suggests this once-refreshing well has already run dry. — M.C.

CARLA THOMAS

★ ★ ★½ Carla Thomas (1966; Atlantic, 1991)
★ ★ ★½ Comfort Me (1966; Atlantic, 1991)
★ ★ ★½ The Queen Alone (1967; Rhino/Atlantic, 1992)

Daughter and labelmate of Stax novelty hitmaker Rufus Thomas, Carla Thomas delivered the first hit for the legendary Memphis record company in "Gee Whiz" (1960), a song she'd written when she was

16. A sweet, doo-wop love song, the ballad was distinguished only by Carla's precociously adept singing—a warm delivery that would strengthen to power as Thomas and Stax Records matured. Thomas enjoys a deserved cult following among R&B insiders, but despite a star turn with Otis Redding on "Tramp" (1967) she never achieved a lasting success. *Carla Thomas*, *Comfort Me* and *The Queen Alone* are strong, representative albums: the R&B numbers are assured, and the singer lends assurance to her 1966 hit "B-A-B-Y" (*Carla Thomas*) and grace to such oft-covered standards as "Let It Be Me" and "What the World Needs Now" (*Comfort Me*). — P.E.

CHRIS THOMAS

★ ★ ★ Cry of the Prophets (Sire/Hightone/Reprise, 1990)

Bathed in the blood and the blues, Chris Thomas lays out his spiritual vision in music that is tough-minded about the need for spiritual renewal without being preachy. Echoes of Jimi Hendrix, Jimmy Page, Steve Cropper and Stevie Ray Vaughan resonate in Thomas's fluid guitar lines, which complement the assertive lyrics. With titles such as "Dance to the Music Till My Savior Comes," "Alpha-Omega," "Cry of the Prophets" and "Help Us, Somebody," it's no secret where Thomas is coming from. Whatever one thinks of Thomas's message, the most important voice belongs to the guitar. Thomas makes it talk, and what it says is profound. — D.M.

DAVID THOMAS AND THE PEDESTRIANS

★ ★ ★ The Sound of the Sand and Other Songs of the Pedestrians (Rough Trade, 1981)
★ ★ ★ Variations on a Theme (Rough Trade, 1983)
★ ★ ★ More Places Forever (Twin/Tone, 1985)

DAVID THOMAS AND THE WOODEN BIRDS

★ ★ ★ Monster Walks the Winter Lake (Twin/Tone, 1986)
★ ★ ★ Blame the Messenger (Twin/Tone, 1987)

Pere Ubu vocalist David Thomas's childlike, playful side dominates his solo work. *The Sound of the Sand* and *Variations on a Theme* feature astringent guitar work by Richard Thompson that never quite connects with Thomas's rambling whimsicality. *More Places Forever* begins a gradual return to more aggressive, Ubu-style instrumentation; it's a trend that intermittently continues across the next two Twin/Tone albums. However, Thomas's naïve delivery and preferred subject matter—he's big on geographical trivia and the travails of birds and fish—will probably bore the pants off most listeners over the age of ten. — M.C.

IRMA THOMAS

★★★ **Soul Queen of New Orleans (Maison De Soul, 1978)**
★★★½ **The Best of Irma Thomas: Breakaway (EMI America, 1986)**
★★★★ **The New Rules (Rounder, 1986)**
★★★★ **The Way I Feel (Rounder, 1988)**
★★★ **Something Good: The Muscle Shoals Sessions (Chess, 1990)**
★★★★½ **"Live: Simply the Best" (Rounder, 1991)**

Summing up 30 years in soul music, Irma Thomas's *Simply the Best*, is one of the great live R&B recordings. A scorching "Time Is on My Side" makes even prime Jagger sound feeble; an Otis Redding medley honors the master; Crescent City classics like "Iko Iko" never were zestier; and Allen Toussaint's "It's Raining" is balladry of a heart-stopping order.

Debuting in 1958 with the swaggering "You Can Have My Husband (but Please Don't Mess With My Man)," this powerhouse from Ponchatoula, Louisiana, went Top Twenty nationwide in 1964 with "Wish Someone Would Care." The consistent big-time eluded her, however, and Thomas retreated to the congenial intimacies of New Orleans nightclubs. There, she reigns. Both *The Way I Feel* and *The New Rules* are excellent recent Thomas. But *Simply the Best* is essential, nearly in a class with vintage Aretha. — P.E.

RUFUS THOMAS

★★★½ **Walking the Dog (1964; Atlantic, 1991)**
★★★ **That Woman Is Poison (Alligator, 1988)**

Clown prince of rhythm & blues, Rufus Thomas was already a legend in Memphis when the fledgling Stax label recorded him in 1960; he'd had a 1953 Sun Records hit with "Bear Cat" (a song spun off Big Mama Thornton's "Hound Dog"), and as a sly, jive-talking DJ, he'd gained a massive local following. For Stax, he put the humor to music: "Walking the Dog" (1963) became his signature tune; the single is party music with a slightly ribald twist. In the early '70s,

the gruff-voiced Thomas scored with "Do the Funky Chicken" and the mildly naughty "(Do the) Push and Pull, Part 1" two prime examples of his novelty funk. Alligator's *That Woman Is Poison* finds the veteran in sturdy form, sassing up on such grunt-and-wink fare as "Big Fine Hunk of Woman" and "The Walk." — P.E.

HANK THOMPSON

★★★★ **Collectors Series (Capitol, 1989)**
★★ **Best of the Best of Hank Thompson (Gusto, NA)**
★★★ **All-Time Greatest Hits (Curb, 1990)**

One of the last veteran practitioners of small-band-variety western swing, Hank Thompson had a prolific run of hit singles spanning the years 1946 to 1958. Without benefit of new material, he has continued to work steadily and draw appreciative audiences to his good-time music. Bob Wills reached for poetry; Thompson's songs are low humor, and proudly so. It takes quite a man to write and perform "Waiting in the Lobby of Your Heart" and "The Blackboard of My Heart"—and what about "Squaws Along the Yukon"?—with a crooked smile and jaunty manner, and still be taken seriously. Beloved as these songs are, Thompson created one genuine classic in "The Wild Side of Life" (1952), which spawned an answer record—one of the most important recordings in country music history—in Kitty Wells's "It Wasn't God Who Made Honky Tonk Angels." However off-center his songs, Thompson and his band, the Brazos Valley Boys, have always been a proficient outfit. The *Collectors Series* album contains the most essential of Thompson's early tracks; the shabbily packaged Gusto album is for die-hards only. — D.M.

LINDA THOMPSON

★★★½ **One Clear Moment (Warner Bros., 1985)**

Linda Thompson's post–Richard & Linda solo debut may have its angry moments—there's plenty of edge, for instance, to the wronged-woman rocker "Telling Me Lies"—but it's nowhere near as vituperative as her ex-husband's divorce album, *Hand of Kindness*. Instead, it focuses on the lustrous splendor of her voice, and while that may sometimes lead to bland embarrassments like "Best of Friends," it also affords her the range to try anything, from the reel-rock of "Can't Stop the Girl" to the quiet beauty of Ravel's "Les trois beaux oiseaux du paradis." — J.D.C.

RICHARD THOMPSON

★ ★ ★ **Starring as Henry the Human Fly!**
(1972; Hannibal/Rykodisc, 1991)
★ ★ ★½ **Strict Tempo! (Hannibal, 1983)**
★ ★ ★ **(Guitar, Vocal) (1976;**
Hannibal/Rykodisc, 1991)
★ ★ ★ ★ **Hand of Kindness (1983;**
Hannibal/Rykodisc, 1991)
★ ★ ★½ **Small Town Romance (Hannibal,**
1984)
★ ★ ★½ **Across a Crowded Room (Polydor,**
1985)
★ ★ ★ ★½ **Daring Adventures (Polydor,**
1986)
★ ★ ★½ **Amnesia (Capitol, 1988)**
★ ★ ★ ★½ **Rumor and Sigh (Capitol, 1991)**
★ ★ ★ **Sweet Talker (Capitol, 1992)**

Although Richard Thompson released his
first solo album in 1972, his solo career
really doesn't properly begin until 1983 and
Hand of Kindness. In large part that's
because after recording *Henry the Human
Fly,* Thompson married singer Linda Peters
(who sings backup on that first album), and
the two began touring and recording as
Richard and Linda Thompson; as such,
Thompson had no real solo career until the
marriage failed and the duo fell apart.

Besides which, *Henry the Human Fly*
sounds less like a genuine solo effort than
an ersatz Fairport Convention album.
Granted, the album comes by that honestly,
since Thompson (himself a Fairport alum) is
backed by several ex-Conventioneers,
including singers Sandy Denny and Ashley
Hutchings. Moreover, the material is in the
same vein as Fairport's fusion of rock and
Celtic folk, from the mournful drone of
"Wheely Down" to the self-explanatory
"Roll Over Vaughn Williams." *Strict
Tempo!,* though recorded without Linda or
anyone else but drummer Dave Mattacks
(and even then only on a few tracks), is also
not typical of his subsequent albums,
consisting entirely of instrumental
treatments of traditional-style tunes. And
despite the fact that *(Guitar, Vocal)* is listed
under his name, its contents actually consist
of Fairport Convention B sides augmented
by Richard and Linda outtakes, making it
interesting, but hardly essential.

Then, in 1983, *Hand of Kindness* picks up
where Richard and Linda's *Shoot Out the
Lights* left off—almost literally. Although
it's probably a mistake to read these
broken-love songs as commentary on the
demise of the Thompsons' marriage, it's
hard not to notice the vitriol in tunes like
"Tear Stained Letter" or "A Poisoned Heart
and a Twisted Memory." But nastiness

becomes Thompson, and the angrier his
lyrics get, the stronger the performances
seem to be, adding a gleeful edge to the
Celtic-style melodies. *Small Town Romance*
has a completely different feel, but then, it
was recorded under dissimilar circumstances.
Unlike the full-band *Hand of Kindness,* this
album features Thompson in an acoustic
setting (it was recorded live in New York)
and alternates between witty folk-style songs
like "Woman or a Man?" and solo versions
of Richard and Linda tunes, including "The
Great Valerio," "For Shame of Doing
Wrong" and "A Heart Needs a Home."

Thompson is back with his band for
Across a Crowded Room, which finds him
returning to the subject of romantic
recrimination ("She Twists the Knife
Again," "When the Spell Is Broken"), but
this time with a greater sense of wit (the
biting "You Don't Say") and poetry ("Love
in a Faithless Country"). But it's *Daring
Adventures* on which he hits his stride,
thanks to songs as tuneful and assured as
"How Will I Ever Be Simple Again" or the
wickedly biting "A Bone Through Her
Nose." Thompson widens his scope even
further with *Amnesia,* but as ambitious as
the lyrics often are, the music is
maddeningly uneven. *Rumor and Sigh* more
than compensates, however, as Thompson
excels both in character songs, like the
wickedly funny "Read About Love" and the
frighteningly intense "I Feel So Good," and
wonderfully evocative sketches like "1952
Vincent Black Lightning" and "Mystery
Wind." As for *Sweet Talker,* this mostly
instrumental soundtrack is likely to be of
great interest only to guitar buffs, although
songs like "Boomtown" do have their
moments.   — J.D.C.

RICHARD AND LINDA THOMPSON

★ ★ ★ ★½ **I Want to See the Bright Lights**
Tonight (1974; Hannibal/
Rykodisc, 1991)
★ ★ ★ ★ **Hokey Pokey (1974; Hannibal/**
Rykodisc, 1991)
★ ★ ★ ★ **Pour Down Like Silver (1975;**
Hannibal/Rykodisc, 1991)
★ ★ ★½ **First Light (1978; Rykodisc,**
1992)
★ ★ ★ **Sunnyvista (1979; Rykodisc,**
1992)
★ ★ ★ ★ ★ **Shoot Out the Lights (1982;**
Hannibal/Rykodisc, 1991)

Fairport Convention may have originally
come up with the idea of marrying rock &
roll to Celtic folk styles, but it was Richard
and Linda Thompson who perfected the

approach. Granted, it helped that Richard was one of Fairport's founding fathers and had several albums' seasoning before hooking up with Linda (then Linda Peters, who sang backup on the Bunch's *Rock On*). But the difference between the two groups isn't simply a matter of experience, for what sets this duo apart from Fairport is that instead of trying to merge two disparate styles, the Thompsons simply ignored any notion of boundaries, writing and playing as if rock and folk were all part of the same sound.

Richard's is the first voice heard on *I Want to See the Bright Lights Tonight*—which was originally released in this country as half of the now-deleted *Live (More or Less)*—but Linda's is by far the most resonant, and that's not simply because she delivers the album's best songs. His singing tends to build off the mood of the music itself (as in "The Calvary Cross"), while hers sets the tone on its own, filling the plain melodic lines of "The Great Valerio" with revealing layers of nuance or fleshing out the wry wit of "The Little Beggar Girl." Add in some slashing guitar fills like those Richard adds to the title tune and the Thompsons are already beating Fairport at its own game.

With *Hokey Pokey*, they refine their sound further, thanks to knowingly revisionist trad-style tunes like "Smiffy's Glass Eye" and the ice cream–mania number "Hokey Pokey." But *Pour Down Like Silver*, recorded after their conversion to Sufism, replaces its predecessors' whimsy with a somber solemnity that shines brilliantly through songs like "For Shame of Doing Wrong" and the wonderfully elegiac "Night Comes In" (which also boasts some of Richard's most memorable guitar playing). *First Light* doesn't change the duo's mood much, but it does increase the music's energy, particularly on the rollicking "Layla" (not the Eric Clapton tune). Mood, though, doesn't really seem to be the answer. After all, *Sunnyvista* is almost oppressively cheerful, but that doesn't make its music any better. Indeed, the duo's approach on that album seems at times almost a parody of pop ambition, as songs like "Why Do You Turn Your Back?" and "Lonely Hearts" are given arrangements that leave them seeming absurdly overdressed. Still, performances like "Sisters," which finds Linda's voice supported by the warm harmonies of Kate and Anna McGarrigle, keep the album from being a complete loss.

Shoot Out the Lights, on the other hand,

is absolutely perfect, an album for which even five stars seems not enough. Between the vividly emotional writing and the stirringly impassioned playing, the album would be a winner even if neither Thompson sang a note. But sing they do, exquisitely, from the gentle resignation of "Walking on a Wire" to the gleeful snarl of "Back Street Slide" to the electric energy of "Shoot Out the Lights." Unfortunately, the Thompsons separated—personally and professionally—soon after, with both pursuing solo careers.
— J.D.C.

THOMPSON TWINS

★★½ **In the Name of Love (Arista, 1982)**
★★½ **Side Kicks (Arista, 1983)**
★★★ **Into the Gap (Arista, 1984)**
★★½ **Here's to Future Days (Arista, 1985)**
★½ **Close to the Bone (Arista, 1987)**
★★★ **Greatest Mixes: The Best of the Thompson Twins (Arista, 1988)**
★★★½ **Big Trash (Warner Bros/Reprise, 1989)**
★★½ **Queer (Warner Bros., 1991)**

Along with dozens of other British post-punk bands, Thompson Twins got its start by frankly emulating the funky twitch of Talking Heads. "In the Name of Love" was a last-minute addition to the group's arty debut album, but a crucial one: that bouncy, chant-along chorus propelled Thompson Twins' vague funk onto urban dance floors and playlists in 1982. Even though the obvious followup "Love on Your Side" and the even-springier "Lies" ply their hooks with enough cunning to make up for Tom Bailey's thin voice, the rest of *Side Kicks* is puffy synth-pop filler. Trimming down to the photogenic core trio of Bailey, Alannah Currie and Joe Leeway, Thompson Twins helped detonate the video-pop explosion with its next album. "Hold Me Now" pumps a wonderfully simple three-note melody, while Tom Bailey works out his exasperation with an angry lover—this time his quavering tone comes across as reassuringly human, rather than wimpy. "You Take Me Up," "Doctor, Doctor" and "Day After Day" forsake the dance floor for the video-set, though the melodramatic, hooky choruses compensate for the loss of disco momentum. *Into the Gap* stands up as a surprisingly consistent effort from a hot singles group; on the other hand, *Here's to Future Days* strives to be a rock album—right down to its respectful cover of the Beatles' "Revolution"—and only half succeeds. After one outright bomb,

Close to the Bone, Tom Bailey and Alannah Currie found a comfortable niche in 1989; the universally ignored *Big Trash* backs up the old catchiness with deeper, more confident grooves. Maybe the Thompson Twins will fare better—commercially—when the mid-'80s revival begins in a few years, but at present there's a suprising amount of musical life in this former new-wave cartoon. — M.C.

BIG MAMA THORNTON
★★★★ **Ball N' Chain (Arhoolie, 1968)**
★★★ **Jail (Vanguard, 1975)**
Blues belter Willie Mae "Big Mama" Thornton remains indelibly linked to rock history as the artist who recorded the original growling version of Leiber and Stoller's "Hound Dog" and her own "Ball N' Chain," the latter being the number with which Janis Joplin slayed a generation at Monterey in 1967. Cut from the Ma Rainey–Bessie Smith mold of big-boned, big-voiced, free-spirited blues women, Thornton cuts an engaging presence on record, especially on the live album, *Jail*, which finds her sassy, bawdy and flirtatious. Thornton's in-print albums were all recorded after her rediscovery in the mid-'60s, when she enjoyed one last fling in the spotlight after laboring for years in obscurity on the chitlin' circuit following her initial success in the early '50s. The Arhoolie album is 16 tracks worth of vintage Thornton sessions dating from '65 through '68, recorded in London, San Francisco and Hollywood with some of the stellar bluesmen on the planet. Five cuts find her fronting a band that includes Buddy Guy on guitar, Little Walter Horton on harmonica, Fred Below on drums, Eddie Boyd on piano and organ and Jimmy Lee Robinson on bass. They push Thornton—or she pushes them—to some effusive performances, but none comparing to the intensity evident on six tracks with Muddy Waters's blues band, which includes Waters, James Cotton, Otis Spann, Samuel Lawhon, Luther Johnson and Francis Clay. On these tracks Waters, Cotton and Spann rock the joint with their soloing and filigrees, and Thornton sounds mightily possessed. The two tracks recorded in Hollywood feature a low-profile band that is more in-the-pocket rock & roll than the others, but Thornton rolls on undeterred. The two transcendent tracks here feature only Thornton and Mississippi Fred McDowell on two dark, deep Delta blues numbers that they co-wrote, "School Boy" and the scary "My Heavy Load."

Thornton's raw testifying has an immediacy and urgency lacking on the other fine tracks, perhaps as a result of McDowell's ragged-but-right percussive slide guitar support. He's clearly pushing the envelope on his solos, sometimes getting so carried away that he's doing little more than flailing the strings as he sets up Thornton's next sortie.

Jail, recorded live at Monroe State Prison in Monroe, Washington, and the Oregon State Reformatory in Eugene in 1975, is a little more than 30 minutes long and showcases good performances of "Hound Dog," "Ball N' Chain," and "Little Red Rooster" and one scorching rendition of "Rock Me Baby." The show ends with a version of Edwin Hawkins's "Oh Happy Day" that reveals a contemplative side of Thornton that rarely turned up on disc. — D.M.

GEORGE THOROGOOD AND THE DESTROYERS
★★★ **George Thorogood and the Destroyers (Rounder, 1977)**
★★★ **Move It on Over (Rounder, 1978)**
★★ **Better Than the Rest (MCA, 1979)**
★★ **More George Thorogood and the Destroyers (Rounder, 1980)**
★★★ **Bad to the Bone (EMI Manhattan, 1982)**
★★ **Maverick (EMI Manhattan, 1985)**
★★½ **Live (EMI Manhattan, 1986)**
★★ **Born to Be Bad (EMI Manhattan, 1988)**
★★ **Boogie People (EMI, 1991)**
Nothing wrong with a raucous party album—now and then. This Delaware blues mauler gets over on sheer enthusiasm, but over the years his raggedy-ass good-timin' approach sure hasn't developed much. Moving from a joyously raspy "One Bourbon, One Scotch, One Beer" on his debut to a resigned "I Drink Alone" on *Maverick* to a desperate "If You Don't Start Drinkin' (I'm Gonna Leave)" on *Boogie People* isn't a healthy progression. Thorogood slicked up his foursquare barroom shuffles just a notch on *Bad to the Bone*, with major results; the title track's stuttering lead-guitar riff quickly became a favorite soundbite on sports broadcasts (and commercials, of course). Signing off that album with an uncharacteristically sober reading of Bob Dylan's "Wanted Man," Thorogood almost sounds ready to move on. The subsequent albums—dominated by pro forma blooze and flat cover versions—squash that notion with a leaden vengeance. — M.C.

THREE DOG NIGHT

★★½ **Captured Live at the Forum (Dunhill/MCA, 1969)**
★★½ **Cyan (Dunhill/MCA, 1973)**
★★½ **Hard Labor (Dunhill/MCA, 1974)**
★★★ **Joy to the World (Greatest Hits) (1974; MCA, 1989)**
★★★ **The Best of Three Dog Night (Dunhill/MCA, 1989)**

By the late '60s, "show bands" could be found anywhere from the local Holiday Inn cocktail lounge to Las Vegas. Three Dog Night epitomizes the formula: three versatile lead singers (Danny Hutton, Cory Wells and Chuck Negron) fronting a well-schooled cover band that could mix and match the current styles. What set this L.A. outfit apart was its material; whoever selected Three Dog Night's songs had surprising taste. The group's string of Top Ten singles introduced a young mainstream audience to singer-songwriters Harry Nilsson ("One"), Laura Nyro ("Eli's Coming"), Randy Newman ("Mama Told Me Not to Come"), Hoyt Axton ("Never Been to Spain") and, it must be noted, Paul Williams ("Just an Old-Fashioned Love Song"). Three Dog Night's emphasis on sharp vocal hooks and soft-rock backing began to take on a nagging quality, though. The mindless "messages" of the 1972 hits "Black and White" and "Family of Man" rang out hollow next to the Staple Singers and O'Jays on the radio, and today the falsetto oom-pah-pah melodrama of "The Show Must Go On" (1974) is quite painful to hear. *The Best of Three Dog Night* gets the nod over *Joy to the World*, though both albums include a few telling, leaden misfires along with those singalong singles. Either one will bring your next nostalgia binge to a screeching, embarrassed halt. — M.C.

3 MUSTAPHAS 3

★★★ **Shopping (1987; Shanachie, 1988)**
★★★★ **Heart of Uncle (Rykodisc, 1989)**
★★★★ **Soup of the Century (Rykodisc, 1990)**

Worldbeat wiseguys claiming to come from an obscure Balkan backwater called Szegerely, 3 Mustaphas 3 is a joke band that's worth taking seriously. An amiable goulash of Mediterranean, Middle-Eastern, Eastern European, African and Asian folk styles, the group's sound is at once authentic and eclectic, demonstrating a genuine love for each style it appropriates even as it abandons all notions of context. Although the least of the group's efforts, *Shopping* offers a quick introduction to its method, with "Selver" matching a Turkish dance

tune with ju-ju drumming, while "Xamenh Evtexia/Fiz'n" works in bits of klezmer, hillbilly, rai and go-go. *Heart of Uncle*, though just as eclectic, shifts its emphasis away from the jokiness of its predecessor and toward more telling juxtapositions, as on "Taxi Driver," which draws an unexpected parallel between Calypso, Nigerian ju-ju and Hawaiian folk styles. But the biggest change is the addition of Lavra, a female vocalist proficient in a dozen languages and as many vocal styles; with her aboard, the Mustaphas enlarge their musical vocabulary to include several new dialects, giving both *Heart of Uncle* and *Soup of the Century* a larger stage on which to work their magic. — J.D.C.

THE THREE O'CLOCK

★★★ **Sixteen Tambourines (Frontier, 1983)**
★★★ **Arrive Without Travelling (I.R.S., 1985)**
★★★ **Ever After (I.R.S., 1986)**
★★★½ **Vermillion (Paisley Park, 1988)**

Dripping with sweetness and charm, this quartet of choirboy types released a retropop minimasterpiece in their 1985 debut album, *Sixteen Tambourines*. Imagine some spirited blend of the Hollies, Sparks and Tommy James and the Shondells and you get the drift—coy, clever lyrics ("Stupid Einstein," "A Day in Erotica"), harpsichords, punchy guitars, and ersatz English accents. *Arrive Without Travelling* and *Ever After* were more of the same— what the band lost in conceptual freshness, it gained in instrumental edge. The makings of a big break came when Prince discovered the group at the end of the '80s. He signed the Clock to Paisley Park, pseudonymously contributed a nifty song ("Neon Telephone") to *Vermillion* and hoped to boost the band's profile. The strategy didn't pay off—*Vermillion* sank like a stone. — P.E.

THROWING MUSES

★★★★ **Throwing Muses (4AD, 1986)**
★★★ **Chains Changed (EP) (4AD, 1987)**
★★★½ **The Fat Skier (EP) (Sire, 1987)**
★★½ **House Tornado (Sire, 1988)**
★★★½ **Hunkpapa (Sire, 1989)**
★★★ **The Real Ramona (Sire, 1991)**

Even as rock & roll matures, its ability to embody the drama and anxieties of adolescence is hard to ignore. Consider, for instance, *Throwing Muses*, which turns the disquieting passion of troubled youth into smart, engaging music. Instead of taking the usual approach into self-revealing songwriting, Kristin Hersh relies more on metaphor and delivery to convey her swirl of emotional distress, and that—coupled with the surprising sophistication of the band's minimal arrangements—makes tracks like "Hate My Way" or "Rabbits Dying" devastatingly effective.

House Tornado isn't quite as stunning, mostly because the Muses squandered their better songs on two EPs, *Chains Changed* and *The Fat Skier*, which boasts the hypnotic "Garoux des Larmes." There's a stronger sense of groove on *Hunkpapa*, which makes its better songs—the irrepressible "Dizzy," for instance—all the more enticing. By *The Real Ramona*, the fun of trying to decode the Muses' enigmatic lyrics had worn thin, but the increasingly vigorous music is fair compensation, thanks to danceably endearing tunes like "Counting Backwards." — J.D.C.

JOHNNY THUNDERS

- ★★★★ So Alone (Real, 1978)
- ★★★ New Too Much Junkie Business (ROIR, 1983)
- ★★★ Que Sera, Sera (Jungle, 1985)
- ★★★ Stations of the Cross (ROIR, 1987)

HEARTBREAKERS

- ★★★ L.A.M.F. (1977; Jungle, 1984)
- ★★★ Live at Max's Kansas City (Max's Kansas City, 1979)
- ★★½ D.T.K.—Live at the Speakeasy (Jungle, 1982)
- ★★★★ D.T.K. L.A.M.F. (Jungle, 1984)
- ★★ Live at the Lyceum Ballroom (ABC, 1984)

In a perversely brilliant casting maneuver, filmmaker Lech Kowalski picked Johnny Thunders to play Jesus in a 1982 documentary on New York junkie life. In actuality, Thunders was a Jesus noir, a trashy Jean Genet saint, his hard-fated life a furious, unfocused rebellion. Never more than a cult figure, he died in 1991, readymade for myth—the last of the hellbent rock & roll true believers. Even when Thunders started out in the '70s, that faith was anachronistic—in the New York Dolls, playing Keith Richards to David Johansen's Jagger, the guitarist was trapped between two forms of parody: glitter (which inflated basic rock & roll) and punk (which deflated it). Thunders was instrumental in making the waters semisafe for the Sex Pistols, the Dead Boys and the like, but his own playing, however sloppy, contained no irony: he rocked

straight out of Chuck Berry. The zeitgeist, though, demanded caricature—and Thunders soon became a pathetic one, a kamikaze sadder than Sid Vicious, because Thunders had real talent.

When the Dolls predictably imploded, he just as predictably continued—and his records have all the power of an apocalyptic party, a stumbling dance toward annihilation. *So Alone*, with help from ex-Pistols Paul Cook and Steve Jones, the underrated Only Ones, Steve Marriott and Phil Lynott, remains his most cohesive set, and it's terrific, dangerous music. With the Heartbreakers (guitarist Walter Lure, ex-Doll Jerry Nolan on drums, ex-Television bassist Richard Hell) his work was shakier, but *D.T.K. L.A.M.F.* kicks with a desperate power. The first side (with Billy Rath, who replaced Hell) features savage live versions of the band's anthems— "Chinese Rocks," "Born To(o) Lo(o)se"; the second reissues the Heartbreakers' ragged debut.

Que Sera, Sera is surprisingly tidy Stones-ish rock, lacking only an imaginative drummer. *New Too Much Junkie Business*, despite the presence of veteran Stones' producer Jimmy Miller, suffers from wretched sound; it's worth checking out, however, for Thunders's elegy for Sid Vicious, "Sad Vacation." *Stations of the Cross*, music originally intended for the Kowalski documentary, isn't a bad intro to Thunders—the live release collects almost all his "greatest hits." — P.E.

TIFFANY

- ★★½ Tiffany (MCA, 1987)
- ★½ Hold an Old Friend's Hand (MCA, 1988)
- ★ New Inside (MCA, 1990)

While her precocious peer and competitor Debbie Gibson often seemed transparently calculated, Tiffany gushed and gestured with the huffy exuberance of a true-life 15-year-old on her 1987 debut. *Tiffany* was propelled to success in part by the budding artist's promotional tour of shopping malls—a wonderful bit. It's possible to hear Tiff's too-cute version of "I Saw Him (Her) Standing There" as a deconstruction of the Beatles hit, though *denatured* is closer to the truth: that halftime-show sax riff and diet-soda-fueled pep rally beat are downright gruesome. She renders this classic giddy teen come-on absolutely sexless—much like the sterile teen-idol pop the Beatles replaced. However obnoxious, undeniable hooks like that one or "Could've Been Me" are conspicuously missing on the unctuous *Hold an Old Friend's Hand* and the disastrously "mature" *New Inside*. As her fans grew up and discovered the illicit thrills offered by the likes of Skid Row and Nirvana, Tiffany's fresh-faced hormone pop faded into the background. — M.C.

TANITA TIKARAM

★★½ **Ancient Heart (Reprise, 1988)**
★★ **The Sweet Keeper (Reprise, 1990)**
★½ **Everybody's Angel (Reprise, 1991)**

Part-Malayan, part-Fijian, born in Germany and maturing in England, the exotic Tikaram is a cosmopolitan folkie who radiates class. Perhaps a little too much class, given that her records have gotten slicker each time out. Pensive and mildly Celtic in spirit, *Ancient Heart* made her name, with "Twist in My Sobriety" becoming a New Age-y classic covered by 17 other singers, including Liza Minnelli. Precociously worldly-wise, Tikaram had the dark voice to carry off the role and help from sophisticated arrangements by ex-Zombie great Rod Argent. The moody numbers carried her on *The Sweet Keeper*, but she sounded a bit glib. *Everybody's Angel* continued that trend—toward professionalism, range and (very fine) orchestral settings. She remains a smart talent; it just would be nice to hear her cut loose. — P.E.

SONNY TIL AND THE ORIOLES

★★★ **Greatest Hits (Collectables, NA)**

While critics and fans continue to disagree on what was the first rock & roll record, the identity of the first R&B vocal group of stature has pretty much been established. The Orioles, led by Sonny Til's plaintive lead tenor, took the close harmony style of the Ink Spots and Ravens and added to it a stronger rhythmic pulse and more inventive use of backing vocals—particularly bass fills and falsetto wails—and established a pattern that would be emulated by the Five Keys, the Platters, the Moonglows, the Flamingos and just about every other significant vocal group of the '50s.

As the Vibranaires, the quintet had achieved some local fame in the late '40s in its native Baltimore when a local songwriter named Deborah Chessler gave the group a new song she had written, "It's Too Soon to Know." Chessler soon became the group's manager and booker, convinced the group to change its name to the Orioles, and landed a recording deal with Natural

Records. "It's Too Soon to Know" was the Orioles' first single release. The record hit the Top Ten of the R&B chart, and the Orioles moved to the Jubilee label, where they would make their most important records between 1949 and 1953. The most enduring of these is "Crying in the Chapel," an R&B chart-topper in 1953 and a Number Three pop hit 12 years later in a cover version by Elvis Presley. The most important, though, in terms of far-reaching influence, was a 1949 single, "Tell Me So," that featured a soaring falsetto moan in the background, which was soon incorporated by other vocal groups—check out the Flamingos' "Would I Be Crying" for an excellent example of this technique—seeking a more mournful edge on their ballads.

Unfortunately, *Greatest Hits* omits "Tell Me So," but hits most of the group's other recorded highlights, including "Crying in the Chapel," "Chapel in the Moonlight," "Back to the Chapel Again" (never let it be said that the Orioles didn't know a good thing when they found it), "It's Too Soon to Know," "What Are You Doing New Year's Eve" and a wonderful R&B Christmas song, "Lonely Christmas." Dock the collection one star for the absence of any liner notes or session information and bad mixes on a couple of songs. — D.M.

'TIL TUESDAY

★★½ **Voices Carry (Epic, 1985)**
★★★ **Welcome Home (Epic, 1986)**
★★★★ **Everything's Different Now (Epic, 1988)**

Between the band's quiet competence and Aimee Mann's ability to spin melancholia into hummable hooks, it's no surprise that 'Til Tuesday made it into the Top Forty on its first try. Granted, the Cars-like "Voices Carry" is by far the strongest song on *Voices Carry*, but Mann and company more than make up for that inconsistency with *Welcome Home*, on which the achingly lovely "What About Love" (another Top Forty hit) is matched by such richly melodic material as "Lovers' Day" and the Simon and Garfunkel–ish "On Sunday." So why is it that the group's best album, *Everything Is Different Now*, had the least commercial success? Maybe it's because the subject matter—the end of Mann's affair with songwriter Jules Shear—seemed too emotionally loaded for some listeners. Or perhaps the fact that these two mourn their lost love by writing songs for one another struck people as a trifle weird. But whatever their inspiration or circumstance, songs like

"Everything's Different Now," " 'J' for Jules" and "Crash and Burn" are too emotionally vibrant and melodically memorable to be denied. — J.D.C.

THE TIME

★★½ **The Time (Warner Bros., 1981)**
★★★★½ **What Time Is It? (Warner Bros., 1982)**
★★★ **Ice Cream Castle (Warner Bros., 1984)**
★★★½ **Pandemonium (Reprise, 1990)**

Forget Prince and the Revolution; back in the early '80s, this was Minneapolis's best funk band. Maybe its best band, period. Back then, the Time had it all: good material, a great image, incredible chops, an amazing stage show. Everything, in fact, except the recording career it deserved—and for that, we only have Prince to blame.

How so? Start with *The Time*. Even though the original lineup—Morris Day, Jesse Johnson, Monte Moir, Jimmy Jam, Terry Lewis and Jellybean Johnson—is credited on the cover, the album was actually recorded by Day (who does the singing) and Prince (who does everything else). Prince, it is said, assembled the album in exchange for a song (reputedly, Day had written "Partyup," which Prince took as his own for the album *Dirty Mind*). Once the studio stuff was done, Prince convinced another Twin Cities funk act, Flyte Time, to ditch singer Alexander O'Neal and back Day as the Time.

It may have begun as a marriage of convenience, but as *What Time Is It?* makes plain, it turned into a truly soulful affair. Alternately cock-sure and comical, Day pushed the R&B sex machine image almost to the point of self-parody, yet at the same time never forgot to have a heart. As a result, he could seem as self-mockingly crass as the skirt-chasing pop star in "Wild and Loose" and still pull some pathos from a ballad like "Gigolos Get Lonely Too." Even better, the band could walk it just the way he talked it, making this a more convincing commentary on sex and love than anything Prince ever managed.

Unfortunately, that magic didn't last. Jam and Lewis were forced out of the group by Prince, ostensibly for missing concert dates but more likely because they were building a reputation as producers; Moir left soon after. Thus, even though *Ice Cream Castle* had its moments, including the guitar-fueled "Jungle Love" and a dance-craze parody called "The Bird," it fell well short of its predecessor, and what was left of the band quickly fell apart.

Six years later, the Time got back together to record *Pandemonium*, but by then styles had changed and so had the band. Instead of the mostly organic funk that powered *What Time Is It?*, the reunion album relied on electronics for much of its groove, and while that was enough to bring its sound up to contemporary standards, it recaptured little of the original magic. — J.D.C.

TOM TOM CLUB

★★★½ **Tom Tom Club (Sire, 1981)**
★★½ **Close to the Bone (Sire, 1983)**
★★½ **Boom Boom Chi Boom Boom (Sire, 1989)**

Tom Tom Club is where drummer Chris Frantz and bassist Tina Weymouth occupy themselves during Talking Heads' between-album lulls. The debut sounds like a delightful accident; funky beats collide with dub reggae keyboards, rap ("Wordy Rappinghood") bumps into new wave ("Genius of Love") on the dance floor. Like a vacation trip on which everything clicks into place, this insouciant groove seems impossible to duplicate. "Pleasure of Love" is about as close as the follow-up comes. By the time of the forced, hollow-sounding *Boom Boom Chi Boom Boom* Tom Tom Club couldn't help but reflect some of Frantz and Weymouth's frustration with the uncertain status of their old band. Ironically, Tom Tom Club's sense of wonder (and humor) is exactly what's missing from David Byrne's recent work. Tom Tom Club's intermittent career winds up proving an old rock & roll adage: breaking up is hard to do. — M.C.

TONE LŌC

★★★ **Lōc-ed After Dark (Delicious Vinyl/Island, 1989)**
★★ **Cool Hand Lōc (Delicious Vinyl/Island, 1991)**

Though he's not the most inventive rapper around, Tone Lōc's place in hip-hop history is assured with the popularity of his 1988 single "Wild Thing," which helped to propel *Lōc-ed After Dark* to Number One on the pop charts—the first black rap LP to accomplish that feat. The follow-up single, "Funky Cold Medina," strikes an even deeper chord. *Lōc-ed After Dark* surrounds those two classic singles with studio-crafted padding. The tough-talking title track doesn't quite wash, and the pothead rap ("Cheeba Cheeba") should be left to Cheech and Chong, but somehow Lōc's oblivious high spirits pull him through. The first album appears to have been a flash in the pan, however. *Cool Hand Lōc* came on like a lead balloon, with the single "All Through the Night" failing to crack the Top Twenty. — M.C.

TONES ON TAIL
★ ★½ **Pop (Beggars Banquet, 1984)**
★ ★ ★½ **Tones on Tail (Beggars Banquet, 1990)**

That Tones On Tail occupies a middle ground between the gothic gloom of Bauhaus and the skewed pop sensibility of Love and Rockets should hardly come as a surprise, since this was where guitarist Daniel Ash and drummer Kevin Haskins made music between their stints in Bauhaus and L&R. *Pop*, though it has its tuneful moments (in particular, the oddly swinging "Happiness"), is mostly given to noisy, antipop exercises like "Slender Fungus" or the rumbling, dub-influenced "The Never Never (Is Forever)." An interesting curiosity, but offering little that Public Image Ltd. didn't do better. *Tones on Tail* includes nearly all of *Pop* as well as several of the group's singles, and is not only a better overview but a more fulfilling album, since it augments the group's aural experiments with such sturdily melodic fare as "Lions," the feedback-seared "Christian Says" and the brutally propulsive "Go!" — J.D.C.

TONY! TONI! TONÉ!
★ ★ ★ **Who? (Polygram, 1988)**
★ ★ ★½ **The Revival (Polygram, 1990)**

"Little Walter"—a sweet gospel-tinged ballad that turns out to be about a casual street murder, not the blues harp player—brought this Oakland funk trio to national attention in 1988. *The Revival* delivers on the debut album's vague promises; title aside, Tony! Toni! Toné! isn't a nostalgia act. Rather than merely sample the historic jams of Sly Stone or Parliament, Tony incorporates some of that loose magic into its own loping, hip-hoppity "Oakland Stroke." Dwayne Wiggins, Raphael Wiggins and Tim Christian blend their voices into a convivial mix, moving from the rap mode to straight singing with ease on uptempo cuts like "The Blues" and "Those Were the Days." Over the gruelling course of a CD-length album, Toni's inspiration does start to sound a little musty, though. "Skin Tight" isn't funky enough to dispel the burning strains of the Ohio Players' "Skin Tight," while the hit ballad "It Never Rains (in Southern California)"—of course—rips off its title from a mush-mellow '70s soft-rock "classic." Toné's best songs suggest the

group could make a taut, centered album; all it needs is time—or maybe a little less of it. — M.C.

TOO MUCH JOY
★ ★½ **Son of Sam I Am (1988; Giant/Warner Bros., 1990)**
★ ★ ★½ **Cereal Killers (Giant/Warner Bros., 1991)**

Amusingly spoiled brats from New York's posh Westchester County, the members of TMJ were cast in 1990 as unlikely free-speech heroes—a jury took 12 minutes to drop obscenity charges against them for serving up 2 Live Crew covers at a Florida concert. Hip. On *Son of Sam I Am*, they'd played around with outrage, and turned out a respectable version of L.L. Cool J's "That's a Lie." But with *Cereal Killers* they became more than just a good joke. A 15-song extravaganza, this is crashing guitar pop about as booze-soaked as the early Replacements—funny, tuneful, smart-idiotic. It's also a nifty celebration of wacko Americana, with song titles like "William Holden Caulfield" and "Thanksgiving in Reno." — P.E.

TOO SHORT
★ ★½ **Life is . . . Too Short (Dangerous Music/RCA, 1988)**
★ ★ **Born to Mack (Dangerous Music/Jive, 1989)**
★ ★ ★ **Short Dog's in the House (Jive, 1990)**

A surfeit of crass pimp 'n' ho routines ruins the first two albums by this Oakland, California, rapper. The side of *Life Is . . . Too Short* that isn't X-rated does show some promise, especially on a streetwise tale called "City of Dope." Too Short may not be as flashy as his southern counterparts in N.W.A, but his matter-of-fact drawl suits his cautionary tone. *Short Dog's in the House* balances the requisite "Pimpology" with some very unsensationalized glimpses of life under King Crack. Ice Cube also guests here, on a wickedly funny anticensorship novelty called "Ain't Nothin' but a Word to Me." The single "So You Want to Be a Gangster?," released in early 1992, sounds like Too Short's hardest scared-straight story yet. A tough-talker with a human touch, hopefully he will grow. — M.C.

TOOTS AND THE MAYTALS
★ ★ ★ ★ ★ **Funky Kingston (Island, 1973)**
★ ★ ★½ **Reggae Got Soul (Island, 1976)**
★ ★ ★½ **Pass the Pipe (Mango, 1979)**
★ ★ ★ **Just Like That (Mango, 1980)**
★ ★ ★ **Toots Live (Mango, 1980)**

★ ★ ★ ★ ★ **Reggae Greats: Toots and the**
Maytals (Mango, 1984)
  ★ ★ ★ ★ **Toots in Memphis (Mango, 1988)**
The title of Toots and the Maytals'
American debut says it all; *Funky Kingston*
forges a rock-solid connection between the
spiritual lilt of reggae and the gutbucket
roar of Memphis soul. Toots Hibbert is
clearly an admirer of Otis Redding, though
he brings his own light touch to the
proceedings. The Maytals pump up a sparse
yet bottom-heavy groove that drops hints of
New Orleans, too. *Funky Kingston* collects
the singles that made Toots a Jamaican
superstar: "Pressure Drop" (which also
appears on the soundtrack to *The Harder*
They Come) and "Time Tough" ring out
with humble streetwise urgency, while the
radical versions of "Louie Louie" and John
Denver's "Country Road" just couldn't
sound any more natural or unforced.
Reggae Got Soul and *Pass the Pipe* push this
proposed merger a little harder than the
somewhat hackneyed material can bear,
though each album contains three or four
rock-solid vocal workouts. *Just Like That* is
a bit skimpy in comparison, while some
excessive audience-pleasing maneuvers mar
the otherwise-fine *Toots Live*. Along with
the expected hits, *Reggae Greats* includes the
definitive "54-46"—an ex-con's stunning
anthem that got left off *Funky Kingston*.
Another revealing title brings Toots
Hibbert's career full-circle: *Toots in*
Memphis is an exultant set of Stax/Volt
covers, featuring many songs Toots had
performed live for years, though never
recorded. His affectionate mastery of soul
music is obvious, while the shifting riddims
(supplied by Sly and Robbie) are anything
but. — M.C.

PETER TOSH
★ ★ ★ ★   **Legalize It (Columbia, 1976)**
★ ★ ★ ★   **Equal Rights (Columbia, 1977)**
  ★ ★ ★ ½ **Bush Doctor (Rolling Stones,**
           1978)
    ★ ★ ½ **Mystic Man (Rolling Stones,**
           1979)
  ★ ★ ★   **No Nuclear War (EMI America,**
           1987)
  ★ ★ ★ ½ **The Toughest (Capitol, 1988)**
His voice is probably the weakest of the
three original Wailers; Peter Tosh can't
match Bob Marley's graceful authority or
Bunny Wailer's stinging subtlety. After the
original Wailers broke up, however, it was
Tosh who quickly asserted himself as a
reggae force. *Legalize It* and *Equal Rights*
spread the Rastafarian word to a receptive

American audience; Tosh and a crack studio
band concoct a delicious bass-heavy stew
leavened only slightly by an occasional
guitar lead. These records are considerably
less crossover-oriented than some of
Marley's later albums. Tosh's rumbling
baritone voice intoxicates on the lightheaded
Legalize It, but on *Equal Rights* he hurls fire
and brimstone with deadly aim. "Equal
Rights," "Downpressor Man," "Stepping
Razor," "African" and the remade "Get Up
Stand Up" all exude the trademark
Jamiacan musical buzz, but the messages
and aggressive stance could easily fit into
some of today's more politicized rap.
  The Toughest collects the best tracks from
Tosh's out-of-print albums for the Rolling
Stones label and EMI; tellingly, it sticks to
the earlier albums for soulful grooves like
"Don't Look Back" (a duet with Mick
Jagger from *Bush Doctor*). Even though
Tosh's voice sounds strained around the
edges on *No Nuclear War*, his indignation
powers the title cut and there are signs of
life throughout. Sadly, this inconclusive, but
encouraging album stands as his last
testament; Peter Tosh was murdered in
1987. — M.C.

TOTO
★ ½   **Toto (Columbia, 1978)**
★   **Hydra (Columbia, 1979)**
★   **Turn Back (Columbia, 1981)**
★ ★   **Toto IV (Columbia, 1982)**
★   **Isolation (Columbia, 1984)**
★   **Fahrenheit (Columbia, 1986)**
★   **The Seventh One (Columbia, 1988)**
★ ★   **Toto Past to Present (Columbia, 1990)**
Without Toto, today's adult-contemporary
radio format wouldn't exist. This L.A.-based
band of studio pros offended legions of
high-energy rock & rollers when its studied,
tunefully inoffensive debut album conquered
the airwaves in late '78. Over the course of
an entire album, Toto's meek hooks and
trebly lead vocals can quickly become as
grating as the most clueless, caterwauling
punk band. But any one of the group's
committee-designed singles can grab a
listener unawares: the airy synth line from
"Africa" or the hokey barbershop chorus of
"Rosanna" (both on *IV*) snagged me, but
that nagging solo guitar on "Hold the Line"
or Cheryl Lynn's creamy vocals on the
unlikely R&B hit "Georgy Porgy" (both on
Toto) might creep up on you. Toto could be
wellserved by a brief greatest-hits package:
Past to Present decidedly ain't it. If the
tuneless 1990 efforts are any indication, this
pop machine is obsolete. — M.C.

TOWER OF POWER

★ ★ ★½ **Tower of Power (Warner Bros., 1973)**
★ ★ ★½ **Back to Oakland (Warner Bros., 1974)**
★ ★ ★½ **Urban Renewal (Warner Bros., 1975)**
★ ★ ★   **Live and in Living Color (Warner Bros., 1976)**
  ★ ★½ **Ain't No Stoppin' Us Now (Columbia, 1976)**
  ★ ★½ **We Came to Play (Columbia, 1978)**
  ★ ★½ **Monster on a Leash (Epic, 1991)**

Masters of the brass-laden "Oakland Stroke," Tower of Power boasts a mighty five-man horn section led by Emilio Castillo. On its first three albums, an excellent soul singer named Lenny Williams holds his own against the often overbearing horn charts. Williams handles uptempo sass (*Tower of Power*'s "What Is Hip?") and lovelorn balladry (*Back to Oakland*'s "Man From the Past") with equal finesse. "Only So Much Oil in the Ground," from *Urban Renewal*, still rings true—both thematically and rhythmically. The temperature rises to the expected boiling point on *Live and in Living Color*, but the absence of Williams takes away the group's focus. "Knock Yourself Out" becomes an end in itself. The Tower of Power nucleus continues to record sporadically, in between hundreds of session appearances. Castillo and company have never found another singer to match Williams, though. *Monster on a Leash*'s too-polite title track is yet another sober adulthood anthem; it's funkier than Huey Lewis's "Hip to Be Square," but not much. — M.C.

PETE TOWNSHEND

  ★ ★ ★   **Who Came First (MCA, 1972)**
  ★ ★ ★½ **Rough Mix (1977; Atco, 1983)**
  ★ ★ ★ ★ **Empty Glass (Atco, 1980)**
    ★ ★   **All the Best Cowboys Have Chinese Eyes (Atco, 1982)**
  ★ ★ ★½ **Scoop (Atco, 1983)**
  ★ ★ ★   **White City—A Novel (Atco, 1985)**
  ★ ★ ★   **Pete Townshend's Deep End Live! (Atco, 1986)**
  ★ ★ ★½ **Another Scoop (Atco, 1987)**
    ★ ★½ **The Iron Man (Atco, 1989)**

Spiritually and intellectually striving, Pete Townshend remains one of the most appealing figures in rock & roll. As the Who's driving force, he wrote mainly about struggle: youth's hard quest for identity, the urge of the soul and the demands of the world. On his own, he extends from those themes—many of his songs chronicle a mid-life crisis nearly as public as John Lennon's—and continues to experiment with new musical textures and approaches to his lyrics. Fighting hard, and generally succeeding, at not becoming a dinosaur, he remains open to influence, while resolutely proud of his own history.

With Townshend singing and playing almost everything on the record, *Who Came First* is a valentine to his guru, Meher Baba; six minutes of the prayer "Parvardigar" may leave cynics scoffing, as they might also at the sweet version of one of Baba's favorite Jim Reeves tunes, but the album's verve and home-studio easiness is winning. The takes on the Who's "Nothing Is Everything (Let's See Action)" and "Pure and Easy" are strong, and "Evolution," written and sung by Townshend's longtime pal (and Faces' bassist) Ronnie Lane, is charming. Townshend and Lane collaborate on *Rough Mix*, along with Eric Clapton and Charlie Watts. The record's intimate, casual pleasures are those of big names relaxing—while "Street in the City" is orchestral Townshend, and as sweeping as almost anything off the Who's *Quadrophenia*—the rest is folksy, immediate and smart.

Empty Glass is Pete's solo breakthrough and his best record. The jaunty "Let My Love Open the Door" was properly a hit, but it's the lovely keyboard work on "And I Moved" that's breathtaking. Dedicating the rocker "Rough Boys" to his children and the Sex Pistols, Townshend reiterates his solidarity with youth. Mark Brzezicki and Tony Butler, later to form Big Country, provide strong rhythm backup, and Townshend's singing sounds stronger than ever. *All the Best Cowboys Have Chinese Eyes* lives up to its title by featuring bafflingly obscure lyrics—plainly trying hard for poetry, many of the songs are indecipherable, and the music suffers, too, from inscrutable ambition. "Stardom in Action" is pretty tough, and "Uniforms" is another interesting youth-cult study, but the record ultimately fails to cohere.

While essential for Who fans, *Scoop* and *Another Scoop* are fascinating listening for anyone interested in the creative process. Outtakes, demos and experiments, the fifty-two pieces collected on both albums chronicle Townshend's songwriting history in sketchbook form. Even in their skeletal state "Behind Blue Eyes," "Pictures of Lily" and "Substitute" sound powerful; synthesizer noodlings and jazz guitar bits offer glimpses of roads not taken; and the records' stylistic range underscores not only Townshend's industry but the fertile impatience of his musical imagination.

A mini *Tommy* or *Quadrophenia*, *White City—A Novel* is the soundtrack to a longform video about urban alienation and street survival, two of Townshend's trademark themes. The narrative structure doesn't really hold up, but "Face to Face" is a sharp, propulsive single, and a horn section enlivens some very fine numbers. *The Iron Man*, a musical based on a fable by England's poet laureate, Ted Hughes, however, doesn't really work. Its big-name cast features Nina Simone, Roger Daltrey and John Lee Hooker—they all sound uncomfortable, and while the orchestral settings are competent, the music suffers by adhering too literally to the story line. *Deep End Live!* finds Townshend back on much more familiar ground; with fresh, casual versions of Who songs and R&B numbers ("Barefootin'," "I Put a Spell on You"), the record is an easy delight. — P.E.

TRAFFIC
   ★ ★ ★½ **Mr. Fantasy (1968; Island, 1989)**
   ★ ★ ★½ **Traffic (1968; Island, 1989)**
   ★ ★ ★ **Last Exit (1969; Island, 1988)**
   ★ ★ ★ ★ **The Best of Traffic (United Artists, 1970)**
   ★ ★ ★ ★ **John Barleycorn Must Die (1970; Island, 1989)**
   ★ ★ ★ **Welcome to the Canteen (1971; Island, 1988)**
   ★ ★ ★ **The Low Spark of High Heeled Boys (1971; Island, 1989)**
   ★ ★ ★ **Shoot Out at the Fantasy Factory (Island, 1973)**
   ★ ★ **Traffic on the Road (Island, 1974)**
   ★ ★½ **When the Eagle Flies (Asylum, 1974)**
   ★ ★ ★ **Heavy Traffic (United Artists, 1975)**
   ★ ★½ **More Heavy Traffic (United Artists, 1975)**
   ★ ★ ★ ★ **Smiling Phases (Island, 1991)**

Traffic boasted the reedy, soulful vocals, cerebral keyboards and guitar of Stevie Winwood, the sharp grace of lyricist Jim Capaldi's drumming, the elegance of Chris Wood's flute and sax and Dave Mason's way with melody. Copping ideas from a range of genres—jazz, classical and Eastern—for a kind of embryonic world music, Traffic epitomized the ambitious impulse of the best British late-'60s artrock. *Mr. Fantasy* is psychedelia for brain people: Dave Mason's sitar lifts "Paper Sun"

toward sonic majesty; "Hole in My Shoe" is clever; "Dear Mr. Fantasy" is that rarity, an epic pop song that (almost) justifies its length. *Traffic*, with Mason's insistent "Feelin' Alright" and Winwood sounding otherworldly on "Forty Thousand Headmen" and "Who Knows What Tomorrow May Bring" is the band's strongest—an album of dense, swirling musicality. After Mason left to pursue a mediocre solo career of caution and craft, Traffic turned jazzy with *John Barleycorn Must Die*. The band would later push jamming to the point of exhaustion on *The Low Spark of High Heeled Boys*, but on *Barleycorn*, the extended flourishes of instrumental virtuosity are exhilarating—leavened with the folk-poetry of the lyrics and Winwood's freest singing, the title song and "Freedom Rider" reveal dazzling playing that never obscures sheer melody.

Mason rejoined briefly on *Welcome to the Canteen*, on which the African percussion of Reebop Kwaku Baah adds zest to the Traffic style. Endless personnel shifts and exhaustion led to the band's mid-'70s demise, but in its wake came a load of fairly good compilations culminating in the excellent two-CD set *Smiling Phases*. — P.E.

THE TRAMMPS
   ★ ★½ **Disco Inferno (Atlantic, 1977)**
   ★ ★ ★½ **The Best of The Trammps (Atlantic, 1978)**

The Trammps posed a musical question in 1975: "Where Do We Go From Here?" The answer came three years later, on the inescapable *Saturday Night Fever* soundtrack: "Disco Inferno." It's not that far a leap. "Where Do We Go" and the other R&B hits contained on the long-deleted *The Legendary Zing Album* (Buddah) and *The Trammps* (Golden Fleece) really stretch those orchestrated rhythm breaks. Emphasizing playful harmonies over dramatic balladry, the Trammps (and producers such as Norman Harris) point the Sound of Philadelphia toward the dancefloor. *The Best of the Trammps* smartly packages two marathon boogie sessions ("Disco Inferno" and "Disco Party") alongside a half-dozen more compact party songs. Succinct and jumpy, cuts like "The Night the Lights Went Out" and "That's Where the Happy People Go" offer three minutes of intense pleasure after a teasing build-up. Unlike many disco groups, the Trammps deliver even after you've abandoned the dancefloor for your living room. — M.C.

TRANSVISION VAMP
★½ **Pop Art (Uni, 1988)**
★½ **Velveteen (Uni, 1989)**
★½ **Little Magnets Vs. the Bubble of Babble (MCA, 1991)**

Noisy, semituneful Brit-rock owing more than a little to the sound and look of Blondie, Transvision Vamp is a big hit in Britain, but a nonentity on this side of the Atlantic. Although Wendy James, the group's pouty, pulchritudinous lead singer, makes a charismatic frontwoman, the sad truth is that she doesn't have much to front, for the T.V. sound is just slickly produced guitar noise, exploiting the most obvious pop aspects of punk without capturing either its rage or irony. *Pop Art* features a so-so cover of Holly & the Italians' "Tell That Girl to Shut Up," and *Little Magnets* includes an inadvertently funny reading of Dylan's "Please Crawl Out Your Window," but on the whole the band relies on too much vamp and not enough vision.
— J.D.C.

TRAVELING WILBURYS
★★★½ **Traveling Wilburys, Volume One (Wilbury/Warner Bros., 1988)**
★★★ **Vol. 3 (Wilbury/Warner Bros., 1990)**

The Ruttles-ish humor and determined casualness of the Traveling Wilburys counters understandable fears for this "band" of '60s gods (Bob Dylan, George Harrison), the '50s idol they dug (Roy Orbison) and the aging pups who worshipped them, Tom Petty and ELO's Jeff Lynne. Giddy with the freedom of their winking "anonymity," these significant figures doff their crowns and get down to effortless and remarkably fresh rocking. Dylan sings better, on the first Wilburys, than he has in years; Harrison again proves that he's best when surrounded by real talents, not sidemen; Orbison's "Not Alone Any More" is a weeper (almost) up there with his classics. With Roy departed, the second try isn't quite so fine. But Lynne again turns in expensive garage production, Petty matches his mentors, and Dylan's ease is infectious. — P.E.

MERLE TRAVIS
★★★★ **The Best of Merle Travis (Rhino, 1990)**

Several generations of guitar players know Merle Travis as the man who popularized a finger-picking technique he learned growing up in Kentucky; several generations of popular music fans may know him as the man who wrote Tennessee Ernie Ford's mammoth 1955 hit, "Sixteen Tons." *The Best of Merle Travis* shows that the measure of the man cannot be taken by two achievements alone. Travis was a superior songwriter whose lyrics resonate with sympathy for and understanding of the plight of the working class in this country. In addition to "Sixteen Tons," Travis's "Dark as a Dungeon" painted a grim portrait of life in the coal mine and remains a haunting evocation of despair and helplessness. His adaptation of the hymn "I Am a Pilgrim" effectively explores the sense of spiritual dislocation he observed in his home state. But Travis was also a fellow whose own life was tortured—pills and alcohol were his long-standing demons—and he could easily relate to the quiet desperation he saw around him. Still, his songs are replete with earthy good humor, poking fun at himself and at the women who crossed his path. And always, his guitar playing is a wonder of concision, precision and extreme good taste.

The Best of Merle Travis chronicles the most fertile period of Travis's recording career, beginning with "Cincinnati Lou" in 1946 and concluding with an instrumental track from 1968, "Cannon Ball Rag." "Sixteen Tons," "Dark as a Dungeon" and "I Am a Pilgrim" are included, culled from Travis's long-out-of-print *Folk Songs of the Hills* (1947), as well as his version of "Steel Guitar Rag." "So Round, So Firm, So Fully Packed," "Fat Gal," "I Like My Chicken Fryin' Size" and "When My Baby Double Talks to Me" are appreciations of the female of the species. Apart from his undeveloped feminist consciousness, Travis nonetheless left behind a remarkable body of work that is witty, literate and involved in the real world to a degree uncommon to many of the country artists of his day.
— D.M.

RANDY TRAVIS
★★ **Storms of Life (Warner Bros., 1986)**
★★★ **Always and Forever (Warner Bros., 1987)**
★★★★ **Old 8x10 (Warner Bros., 1988)**
★★★ **An Old Time Christmas (Warner Bros., 1989)**
★★★ **No Holdin' Back (Warner Bros., 1989)**

★ ★ ★ **Heroes and Friends (Warner Bros., 1990)**
★ ★ ★ **High Lonesome (Warner Bros., 1991)**
Because his reputation rests largely on his skill as an interpreter rather than a songwriter, it's easy to dismiss Randy Travis as perhaps the least important of the so-called New Traditionalist country artists whose passion for a rawer sound and disdain of pop flourishes is seen as injecting the genre with a breath of fresh air. Travis, however, cannot be dismissed aesthetically anymore than can Elvis Presley, Jo Stafford, Rosemary Clooney, Tony Bennett, Frank Sinatra or any of the great interpreters in other genres. He fills the bill more than adequately when it comes to finding that point at which another writer's lyrics move his heart and then being able to express those feelings dramatically in his singing.

Thematically Travis's work is fairly simple. Love is the name of the game, and apart from a few poignant reminscences about childhood heroes ("He Walked on Water," from *No Holdin' Back*, and "Heroes and Friends" from the like-titled album), this artist shows little inclination to do anything but plumb that deep well. Two early albums, *Always and Forever* and *Old 8x10*, are stirring collections of wide-ranging observations on the ways of the heart. Some of these are downbeat, and the truth cuts like a razor ("The Truth is Lyin' Next to You," from *Always and Forever*, "It's Out of My Hands," from *Old 8x10*); others take a humorous slant ("What'll You Do About Me"); and still others are simply joyous exaltations and affirmations of everlasting love ("Deeper Than a Holler," from *Old 8x10*, "Forever and Ever, Amen," from *Always and Forever*).

No Holdin' Back, despite a wonderful single in "Hard Rock Bottom of Your Heart," sounds static, as if Travis were desiring some kind of change in direction, but was unsure of where to go next. He may have found part of the answer in his 1990 album of duets, *Heroes and Friends*. Here, in addition to teaming up with some simpatico country legends (Dolly Parton, Merle Haggard, Willie Nelson, Roy Rogers and especially George Jones, among others), Travis also hooks up with B.B. King on "Waiting for the Light to Change." For King the leap is unsurprising, but Travis's reaching out to King indicated a willingness to accept the challenges posed by other types of music. He chose not to follow those directions on his 1991 release, *High Lonesome*, but he showed continued growth

as a songwriter (Alan Jackson and Don Schlitz being his estimable co-writers this time around), and his singing was as potent as ever. — D.M.

RALPH TRESVANT
★ ★½ **Ralph Tresvant (MCA, 1990)**
The last of New Edition's members to deliver a solo album, Tresvant put forth an effort that is neither as innovative as the Bell Biv DeVoe album, as pop-savvy as Bobby Brown's breakthrough, or as soulful as Johnny Gill's post-Edition outing. That doesn't mean it's without merit—rap numbers like "Rated R" may not work, but Tresvant's boyish tenor soars through ballads like "Love Hurts" and rides the title tune's new jack groove with assurance—just that it lacks sparkle. — J.D.C.

T. REX
★ ★ ★ ★ **Electric Warrior (Reprise, 1971)**
★ ★ **The Essential Collection (Relativity, 1991)**
Tyrannosaurus Rex was a hippie-dippie British folk duo of the late '60s. Marc Bolan and sidekick Mickey Finn mixed mostly acoustic ingredients in a rather precious psychedelic stew. Somewhere between "She Was Born to Be My Unicorn" and "Ride a White Swan," Bolan picked up an electric guitar and cultivated a singular, spooky vocal tone. Reemerging as T. Rex in the '70s, Bolan's vehicle evolved from an Incredible String Band ripoff to a glittery, decadent pop beast. Glam or glitter rock was the first of many English music trends that never quite took hold in the States. Bolan became a teen idol in Britain, while "Bang a Gong (Get It On)" (from *Electric Warrior*) was perceived as a novelty hit by most Americans. Novel or no, it casts an unforgettable spell. A distended guitar riff buzzes and broods with Bolan strutting his stuff over a quirky, sprung rhythm. *Electric Warrior* offers more of the same; it's definitely a groove album, long on unique sonic atmosphere and lacking any stylistic variation at all. "Rip Off," "Jeepster" and "Mambo Sun" all sport deeply twisted hooks and cosmic goofball wordplay, though: Marc Bolan possessed a rocker's edge behind his mascara-ed pop pose. Now out of print, *The Slider* (1972) surpassed *Electric Warrior* on the U.S. album charts, though the material is nowhere near as weirdly memorable as those jagged early hits. His star status finally slipping at home, Bolan was in the process of reinventing his sound when he died in a 1977 auto wreck.

Frankly, what's missing from *The Essential Collection* makes a mockery of its title. No "Bang a Gong (Get It On)" is bad enough, but this hastily assembled three-CD set skips T. Rex's fascinating preglam transition period in favor of Bolan's far weaker mid-'70s work. *Electric Warrior* remains the essential T. Rex album. — M.C.

A TRIBE CALLED QUEST
★ ★ ★ ★ **People's Instinctive Travels and the Paths of Rhythm (Jive, 1990)**
★ ★ ★ ★ **The Low End Theory (Jive, 1991)**
Like De La Soul and the Jungle Brothers, A Tribe Called Quest is part of rap's reaction against the aggressive, in-your-face style of old school and hardcore rappers; the Tribe's delivery is low-key and relaxed and its rhymes tend to flow in loose, rolling cadences instead of a stiff staccato. Not that this laid-back approach diminishes the group's intensity; from the dense overlays of "After Hours" to the insinuating repetitions of "Bonita Applebaum," there's no shortage of fascinating rhythms on *People's Instinctive Travels and the Paths of Rhythm*. But even that seems obvious and old-fashioned when compared to the cool, bass-heavy beats that drive *The Low End Theory*, on which the group incorporates jazz samples, acoustic bass (courtesy of Ron Carter) and slyly insistent drum patterns into the mix, a sound that's the perfect complement to the Tribe's incisive, intelligent wordplay. — J.D.C.

TRIO: DOLLY PARTON, LINDA RONSTADT, EMMYLOU HARRIS
★ ★ ★ ★ ★ **Trio (Warner Bros., 1987)**
Dolly Parton runs the show at this country-pop summit meeting, but she gives her soul sisters plenty of room to shine. *Trio* is the best thing any of these inconsistently brilliant singers had done in years. Linda Ronstadt limits herself to unshowy harmonizing, thankfully; she and Emmylou Harris follow Dolly's expert lead into traditional mountain-ballad territory on "My Dear Companion," "Rosewood Casket" and "Farther Along." Sparsely produced, and simply devastating. Add a couple of soft-rock ("To Know Her [Him] Is to Love Her [Him]") and light-country ("Wildflowers") ringers for contemporary tastes, and you've got a supersession that actually lives up to its billing. — M.C.

TRIUMPH
★ **Rock 'n' Roll Machine (1979; MCA, 1986)**
★ **Just a Game (1979; MCA, 1986)**
★ **Progressions of Power (1980; MCA, 1986)**
★ **Allied Forces (RCA, 1981)**
★ **The Sport of Kings (MCA, 1986)**
★ **Stages (MCA, 1986)**
★ ★ **Never Surrender (MCA, 1987)**
★ ★ **Surveillance (MCA, 1988)**
★ ★ **Thunder Seven (MCA, 1984)**
★ ★ **Triumph Classics (MCA, 1989)**
From the school of Rush or the more theatrical Styx, Triumph is a Canadian power trio that favors clean, technically adept arena rock—the group is loud without being raucous. And Triumph has intellectual aspirations (the liner notes to *Never Surrender* quote Matthew Arnold and Alexander Pope). With the advent of thrash (Metallica) and death metal (Slayer), Triumph now seems tame and '70s-ish—and its reliance on concept-album pretentiousness doesn't help in terms of hipness. Rik Emmett remains a fast, precise guitarist, and his screeching vocals are about standard for the genre. That every one of Triumph's albums sounds the same probably isn't a criticism; dependablity, after all, is a crucial virtue in hard rock. Lyrics ridden with self-help clichés or pseudo-mysticism help make Triumph a band for unthreatening headbangers—at least they're not Satanists, but they're pretty bland. — P.E.

THE TROGGS
★ ★ ★ **The Best of the Troggs (Rhino, 1984)**
★ ★ ★ **Athens Andover (Rhino, 1992)**
With its leering vocal, its goose-stepping rhythm stomping the life out of even the merest suggestion of swing and—oddest of all—its naïvely graceful out-of-tune ocarina solo, "Wild Thing," from 1966, was a trash-rock classic of a decidedly wacky stripe. The Troggs' only other Top Ten hit, "Love Is All Around" (1968), was pale Brit Invasion stuff, but the rest of this foursome's catalogue nearly outdistanced "Wild Thing"—not in crude rock power, but in sheer strangeness. "I Can't Control Myself" and "Give It to Me," both banned by the BBC, were lecherous little numbers played poorly enough to achieve a primitive fascination. "Cousin Jane," a brief, breathy ballad, was downright creepy—sort of like the perverse "Uncle Ernie" bit off the Who's *Tommy*. Ozzy Osbourne and other metal minds claim to be influenced by the Troggs, and you can believe it: Reg Presley was one bent nonsinger and his "vision" remains a warped one. The oddly infectious *Athens Andover* pairs Presley and the Troggs with

members of R.E.M. to amazingly listenable results. — P.E.

TROUBLE FUNK

★★★★ **Drop the Bomb (Sugar Hill, 1982)**
★★★ **Saturday Night Live From Washington, D.C. (Island, 1985)**
★★½ **Trouble Over Here/Trouble Over There (Island, 1987)**

Despite massive hype, the funky go-go sound of Washington, D.C., failed to take the nation by storm in the mid-'80s. Above all else, go-go is a live event: drums and assorted percussion cook up itchy polyrhythmic jams, spiced by floating JB-style horn riffs, spare keyboard washes, call-and-response vocals and the occasional rap. Audience participation is key, and, unlike the early hip-hop scene, so is traditional musicianship. Go-go bands like Trouble Funk, E.U. or Chuck Brown and the Soul Searchers could indeed play their instruments, and loved to prove it all night.

Released on the pioneering rap label Sugar Hill, Trouble Funk's debut is probably the most accurate and exciting transcription of the go-go experience. The antinuke title track and the aerobics workout "Pump It Up" qualify as bona fide songs, but it's breathless, refreshing rhythms that establish *Drop the Bomb* as a classic groove album, a perfect party-peak explosion. Trouble Funk's major-label debut, *Live From D.C.* actually split the difference, combining a representative live set with stiff, overproduced studio tracks. *Trouble Over Here, Trouble Over There* gets mired in clichéd R&B moves. Having failed as both revolutionaries and crossover ambassadors, Trouble Funk returned to the Washington, D.C., scene that nurtured it, where the group continues to drop the bomb on its longstanding audience with deadly accuracy. — M.C.

ROBIN TROWER

★★★ **Twice Removed From Yesterday (Chrysalis, 1973)**
★★★½ **Bridge of Sighs (Chrysalis, 1974)**
★★★ **For Earth Below (Chrysalis, 1975)**
★★★ **Long Misty Days (Chrysalis, 1976)**
★★½ **In City Dreams (Chrysalis, 1977)**
★★★★ **Robin Trower—Live! (Chrysalis, 1977)**
★★½ **Caravan to Midnight (Chrysalis, 1978)**
★★★ **Victims of the Fury (Chrysalis, 1980)**
★★★ **B.L.T. (Chrysalis, 1981)**

★★½ **Truce (Chrysalis, 1982)**
★★★ **Back It Up (Chrysalis, 1983)**
★★★ **Take What You Need (Atlantic, 1988)**
★★★ **No Stopping Anytime (Chrysalis, 1989)**
★★½ **In the Line of Fire (Atlantic, 1990)**

Few guitarists come on as heavy as Robin Trower; what makes him truly distinctive, however, is that he delivers his blues-based pyrotechnics with a grace almost unheard of in hard rock. A master of effects—wah-wah crunch, vibrato sheets of sound, rich, spacey atmosphere—Trower has remained throughout his long career the ace Hendrix disciple (one particularly influenced by Jimi's *Electric Ladyland* period). Yet unlike countless other acolytes, Trower learned subtlety as well as power from his idol.

While enlivening Procol Harum's early work, Trower's rock urgency (at the time resembling Eric Clapton's) soon proved unsuitable for that band's symphonic aspirations. Procol's lyricist, Keith Reid, later helped Trower co-write some of his solo material, and Matthew Fisher, Procol's organist, produced the first few albums—but Trower on his own sounded nothing like the band he'd left. Instead, his first four albums were rock of an unabated intensity—the spirit of Hendrix rules, especially on the best of the quartet, *Bridge of Sighs*. Utilizing the power-trio format of the Jimi Hendrix Experience and Cream, Trower kept the sound clean and focused; in the underappreciated bassist/singer James Dewar he found a vocalist whose gritty appeal recalled Free's Paul Rodgers. *Live!* encapsulated Trower's early strength; the record stands as one of the best live hard-rock albums ever made.

With *In City Dreams* and *Caravan to Midnight*, Trower took a turn toward a relatively easier sound. Some of the longer instrumental passages are much more jazz-rock fusion than rock; a glossy production softens things up, and while the playing is reliable, some of the fire is missing. Dewar's vocals, in fact, are the real strength of these albums; he's matured into a fairly supple stylist. *Victims of the Fury* and *Back It Up* marked a smart return to heaviness, yet while they echo Trower's vintage work, they don't have the freshness. *B.L.T.*, *Truce* and *Back It Up* (*No Stopping* compiles the latter two albums) were products of a collaboration with the great Cream bassist, Jack Bruce. The starkest of Trower's albums, they rock righteously— even if Bruce's singing lacked the finesse of his vocals with Cream. Replacing James Dewar with the less-distinctive Davey Pattison on vocals, *Take What You Need*, too, lacks a really strong singer; otherwise the record sounds very much the way Trower has always sounded—sharp, consistent, assured. — P.E.

ERNEST TUBB

   ★ ★ ★ **The Ernest Tubb Story (1959; MCA, 1980)**

   ★ ★ ★ **Golden Favorites (1961; MCA, 1973)**

★ ★ ★ ★ **Ernest Tubb's Greatest Hits (1968; MCA, 1971)**

   ★ ★ ★ **Greatest Hits Vol. 2 (MCA, 1973)**

★ ★ ★ ★ **Honky-Tonk Classics (Rounder, 1982)**

★ ★ ★ ★ **Live 1965 (Rhino, 1990)**

★ ★ ★ ★ **Ernest Tubb: Country Music Hall of Fame Series (MCA, 1991)**

Hard to believe, but a tonsillectomy performed on Ernest Tubb has proven to be one of the key events in country music history. For several years before going under the knife, Texas native Tubb had toured and recorded as a surrogate version of his idol, Jimmie Rodgers, who had passed away from tuberculosis in 1933. But after his tonsils were removed, Tubb had to abandon his Rodgers-style singing (which can be heard on a rare album on the Golden Country label, *Ernest Tubb Sings Jimmie Rodgers*) because he was unable to yodel any longer. One of his first post-op sessions in 1941 produced Tubb's first major hit, "Walking the Floor Over You," and for the remainder of the decade into the early '50s Tubb's rough-hewn honky-tonk music was among the most popular and influential of any musician of his generation. Hank Williams, for one, had more than a little Ernest Tubb in him, as did the major proponents of the Bakersfield sound, Buck Owens and Merle Haggard, and modern-day studs such as Dwight Yoakam and George Strait owe Tubb a tip of their broad-brimmed Resistols.

Tubb and Merle Travis helped popularize the electric guitar in country music in the early '40s, and Tubb's enormous audience appeal was a key factor in the Grand Ole Opry's decision to lift its ban on electric instruments. In 1947 Tubb took country music to the city by headlining the first country concert at Carnegie Hall. Even today his Ernest Tubb Record Shop remains a prime outlet for contemporary and rare country music recordings, and the Shop's Saturday night post-Opry "Midnight Jamboree" concert is as much of an institution as the Opry itself.

The Country Music Hall of Fame's 16-track Tubb entry contains many of the recordings that established his primacy in the field during the years 1941 to 1953, as well as some later songs that have earned a proper place in the Tubb pantheon. Tubb wasn't even close to having a good voice in the traditional sense—he rarely started a song on key, and pretty much spent a lifetime looking for the right note—but the stark, untutored nature of his delivery had undeniable impact. The original, unaltered versions of "Walking the Floor Over You," "You Nearly Lose Your Mind," "Soldier's Last Letter," "Have You Ever Been Lonely (Have You Ever Been Blue)" and "Thanks a Lot" are among the best country records ever made, and they're included on the CMF set.

MCA's various greatest-hits packages are troublesome owing to the number of re-recordings of songs and duplications of material. *The Ernest Tubb Story*, for example, contains '60s re-recordings of songs cut initially in the '40s and early '50s, with new instrumentation and, on some cuts, a disembodied background chorus. *Greatest Hits* contains six new cuts recorded between 1958 and 1963, when Tubb's voice had become deeper and his delivery more assured and casual. *Greatest Hits Vol. 2* is half remakes and half originals.

Two of the more interesting Tubb titles are Rounder's *Honky-Tonk Classics* and Rhino's more recent *Live 1965*, the only live album extant of Tubb and his Troubadours. The Rounder album consists of lesser-known recordings from 1940–54, including some that are making their first appearance on a domestic release. *Live 1965*, recorded at the Magic Castle Ballroom in Seattle, captures the band and Tubb in good form on a wide range of songs dating back to the early '40s. Apart from the albums listed, fans should look for any of the artist's albums on the Vocalion and Coral labels. These contain the original versions of Tubb's recordings. Finding them is another matter entirely. — D.M.

MAUREEN "MOE" TUCKER

   ★ ★ ★   **Playin' Possum (EP) (Trash, 1981)**

   ★ ★ ★   **MoeJadKateBarry (EP) (50 Skidillion Watts, 1987)**

★ ★ ★½ **Life in Exile After Abdication (50 Skidillion Watts, 1989)**

★ ★ ★½ **I Spent a Week There the Other Night (Rough Trade, 1991)**

Crude but somehow soulful, Maureen Tucker's super-simple drumbeat pulse supplied the Velvet Underground's backbone—and a lot of its heart, too. Still, her late-blooming solo career may be the least anticipated aspect of that groundbreaking band's enduring legacy. Tucker reemerged in 1981 with a homemade-and-sounding-like-it one-woman show. Strapping on a guitar and wailing over her own thudding beat, she negotiated oldies like "Slippin' and Slidin' " and "Bo Diddley" with abrasive Velveteen grace. After another long silence, Tucker took time out from her full-time gig as a single parent to cut some (slightly) more "professional" records. Members of such Velvets-influenced bands as the Violent Femmes and Sonic Youth lend sympathetic support on *Life in Exile After Abdication* and *I Spent a Week There One Night*. Godfather Lou Reed even weighs in with some guitar snarls on *Life in Exile*, but it's the raw, cutting tone of Tucker originals like "Hey Mersh!" and "Spam Again" that distinguish this album from the '80s college-rock milieu. Not too many current-day alternative pathfinders can write from such a mature ground-level perspective. The presence of Reed, John Cale and long-retired Velvets guitarist Sterling Morrison practically makes the import-only *I Spent a Week There* an unofficial reunion album. "Waitin' for the Man" gets a rough-handed revival, and Cale laces "Then He Kissed Me" with eerie viola. Yet, again, Tucker's slightly bitter, brutally frank originals ("I'm Not") are what make this album truly notable. Moe Tucker isn't making a nostalgic grab for the past with her mid-life punk rock; she's groping after her own voice, and finding it within that familiar sonic roar. — M.C.

TANYA TUCKER

★★★★   Greatest Hits (Columbia, 1975)
  ★★★   Greatest Hits (MCA, 1979)
    ★★   Girls Like Me (Capitol, 1986)
  ★★½ Love Me Like You Used To (Capitol, 1987)
  ★★½ Strong Enough to Bend (Capitol, 1988)
    ★★   Tennessee Woman (Capitol, 1989)
  ★★★   Greatest Hits (Capitol, 1990)
    ★★   Greatest Hits—Encore (Capitol, 1990)
★★★½ What Do I Do With Me (Capitol, 1991)

In 1972, a year before Helen Reddy took it to the top of the pop charts, "Delta Dawn" made 14-year old Tanya Tucker a country-music sensation. And that tale of creeping insanity is nothing compared to her subsequent country hits: She calmly watches her father commit murder in "Blood Red and Goin' Down," cruelly sizes up "The Man That Turned My Mama On" and delivers the ultraseductive "Would You Lay With Me (in a Field Of Stone)" with eager innocence. On these records, producer Billy Sherrill's full orchestrations are entirely appropriate to the melodramatic tilt of the material. In the words of critic John Morthland, the Columbia *Greatest Hits* represents nothing less than "American Gothic's last stand in country music." Tucker's later work on MCA and Capitol grows increasingly more "adult" and routine. Some of the initial MCA singles (like "Lizzie and the Rainman," from 1975, included on the second *Greatest Hits*) are involving, but after she married Glen Campbell, Tanya Tucker became part of the bland album-a-year Nashville establishment. Some of her late-'80s Capitol singles exude a certain brassy charm: "Strong Enough to Bend" and "If It Don't Come Easy" steamrolled their hooks across country radio in 1988. But only her 1987 heart song "Love Me Like You Used To" sinks in slowly—the way Tanya Tucker's earlier *Greatest Hits* used to, and still do. Sparser and twangier than recent outings, the musical backing on *What Do I Do With Me* throws Tanya's husky, nuanced voice into clear relief. Incorporating brief flashes of rock and pop in its solid country base, the album proves that mainstream Nashville doesn't have to mean watered-down.
— M.C.

IKE & TINA TURNER

★★★★ River Deep—Mountain High (A&M, 1969)
  ★★★ Golden Classics (Collectables, NA)
  ★★★ It's Gonna Work Out Fine (Collectables, NA)
★★★★ Proud Mary: The Best of Ike and Tina Turner (EMI, 1991)

Having made a name for himself as a disc jockey, band leader, session player and talent scout working in and around Memphis, Ike Turner and his band the Kings of Rhythm were joined in 1956 by a young female vocalist from Tennessee named Annie Mae Bullock. Annie Mae became Tina Turner as per Ike's rechristening (and Mrs. Turner, without benefit of a marriage license), and as Ike and Tina Turner they landed a recording contract with Sue Records. Their first single,

"A Fool in Love," became a Top Thirty pop hit and peaked at Number Two on the R&B chart. It set the pattern for a succession of hit singles on Sue in the early '60s: Tina's gravel-throated blues shouts and cries set against a churning, muddy sound, with occasional spoken double-entendre-laden byplay between Ike and Tina.

A 1969 tour with the Rolling Stones proved to be the beginning of the end for Ike and Tina. On the plus side, it brought them more attention than they'd ever received—and justifiably so—and reinvigorated their recording career. But after their Top Ten cover version of "Proud Mary" in 1971, the group faltered commercially and didn't get back to the Top Thirty until 1973 with an autobiographical song written by Tina, "Nutbush City Limits." Their failure to achieve any consistency in the studio mirrored the decline in their live performances. In 1975 the group cut a cover version of Pete Townshend's "Acid Queen" that took Tina out of her R&B base and pointed her in the pop-soul direction she would explore so successfully in the next decade.

Ike and Tina's tenure with Sue is well represented by the two Collectables albums, which are testimonials to the power of the analog sludge mix. The vintage photographs of Ike and Tina are priceless, too. *River Deep—Mountain High* is a legendary anomaly in this catalogue. The celebrated 1966 title track was produced by Phil Spector, who had expectations of it being the jewel in his crown. But despite its grandeur—both in production and in Tina's urgent vocal—the single bombed in the U.S. after being a Top Ten hit in England, and Spector went into seclusion for three years. The ensuing album, partly produced by Spector, partly by Ike Turner, reveals that Spector's Wall of Sound was a most inappropriate vehicle for Tina's voice, which was harsh and bluesy and demanded the starker setting provided by Ike's productions, which are barely updated from what he was doing at Sue earlier in the decade. EMI's *The Best of* is a well-rounded retrospective of Ike and Tina's time together, beginning with "A Fool in Love" and systematically rolling through the years before concluding with "Acid Queen." Its liner notes provide a good thumbnail sketch of the duo's recording history as well.

— D.M.

JOE TURNER

★★★★★ The Boss of the Blues (1956; Atlantic, 1981)
★★★★ Big Joe Rides Again (1960; Atlantic, 1987)
★★★ Nobody in Mind (Pablo, 1976)
★★★ Things That I Used to Do (Pablo, 1977)
★★★ The Midnight Special (Pablo, 1980)
★★★★ The Best of Joe Turner (1980; Pablo, 1987)
★★★ Have No Fear Joe Turner Is Here (Pablo, 1981)
★★ Boss Blues (Intermedia, 1982)
★★ The Very Best of Joe Turner (Intermedia, 1982)
★★ Roll Me Baby (Intermedia, 1982)
★★ Rock This Joint (Intermedia, 1982)
★★★ Life Ain't Easy (Pablo, 1983)
★★★★ Blues Train (Muse, 1983)
★★★★ Kansas City Here I Come (Pablo, 1984)
★★★ Patcha, Patcha All Night Long: Joe Turner Meets Jimmy Witherspoon (Pablo, 1985)
★★★★★ Big Joe Turner Memorial Album: Rhythm & Blues Years (Atlantic, 1986)
★★★★★ Big Joe Turner: Greatest Hits (Atlantic, 1987)
★★★ Flip, Flop & Fly (Pablo, 1989)

"Boss of the Blues" Joe Turner owns the distinction of laying legitimate claim to being one of the founding fathers of both rhythm & blues and rock & roll; this in addition to being regarded as one of the most powerful blues singers in history, a physically imposing man with a huge voice and a singing style unadorned by gimmickry. The very straightforwardness of his approach was its own recommendation: Whether shouting it out or getting into what passed for a gentle mode, Turner's voice remained a stately instrument, dynamic without being ostentatious, long on legato, short on melisma, always believable, always moving.

Turner's career dates to the mid-'20s, when he landed a job tending bar in his native Kansas City; as an extracurricular activity he took up shouting the blues with pianist Pete Johnson. Turner, Johnson, Sam Price and Jay McShann became the key figures in a vital Kansas City music scene that merged blues and jazz into boogie-woogie, which swept the country after Turner's appearance at New York's Carnegie Hall in 1938. Turner remained in

New York, ensconced at Cafe Society and recording under his own name and with other prominent jazz and blues artists. A 1956 Atlantic release, *Boss of the Blues*, re-creates the fertile Kansas City period of Turner's career, reuniting him with the estimable Johnson and other first-rate players on the tunes that secured Turner's early acclaim: "Cherry Red" and "Roll 'Em Pete," written by Turner and Johnson; "I Want a Little Girl"; "Wee Baby Blues" and "Low Down Dog," both Turner originals. In their original recordings, these sides and others that Turner cut in the late '40s constituted a new sound that would evolve into rhythm & blues, spurred in no small measure by Turner's own voluminous 1950s recordings for Atlantic. It wasn't a long leap from Turner's style of R&B to rock & roll, as evidenced by the success of Turner's "Shake, Rattle and Roll" in a sanitized cover version by Bill Haley and His Comets. Other of Turner's sides remain important genre-busting entries that are considered rock & roll by some, R&B by others: of these the most prominent are "Flip, Flop and Fly," "Honey Hush," "Corrine, Corrina" and "Sweet Sixteen." This fruitful era is well documented on both *Big Joe Turner's Greatest Hits* and *Big Joe Turner Memorial Album: Rhythm and Blues Years*. A 1960 Atlantic release, *Big Joe Rides Again*, shows the ease with which this masterful singer could adapt material to suit his personal style. Here he rolls through great popular ballads ("Until the Real Thing Comes Along," "I Get the Blues When It Rains," "Pennies From Heaven") and uptempo blues ("Switchin' in the Kitchen"), and drops in a soulful meditation in blues, "When I Was Young."

Turner continued to record sporadically through the '60s, then found his career in high gear again come the '70s, thanks to producer Norman Granz, who teamed Turner with jazz giants Count Basie, Milt Jackson, Roy Eldridge and others on several recordings for the Pablo label. Age hardly diminished the authority of Turner's singing; moreover, his stellar accompanists inspired him to fine performances. Of note here are *Flip, Flop & Fly*, with the Count Basie Orchestra (recorded in 1972); *Nobody in Mind*, with Milt Jackson, Roy Eldridge and Pee Wee Clayton among the supporting cast; and *In the Evening*, a moody set featuring Turner's swaggering, laconic take on George Gershwin's "Summertime."

In 1983 Turner got together with the great songwriter Doc Pomus to co-write a new tune, "Blues Train," that became the centerpiece of Turner's final album. Coproduced by Pomus (who had been inspired to become a singer and songwriter after hearing Turner's recording of "Piney Brown Blues" in 1941) and Bob Porter, *Blues Train* rumbles and roars mightily, with Turner backed by Roomful of Blues and Dr. John on nine cuts that take him all the way back to Kansas City and bring him forward into the present. It was the last great testament of a great singer. Turner died in 1985, but oh how those melodies linger on. — D.M.

TINA TURNER

★★★★ **Private Dancer (Capitol, 1984)**
★★★ **Break Every Rule (Capitol, 1986)**
★★★ **Tina Live in Europe (Capitol, 1988)**
★★★½ **Foreign Affair (Capitol, 1989)**
★★★½ **Simply the Best (Capitol, 1991)**

After an unproductive solo stint with United Artists in the late '70s, after escaping from the abusive Ike Turner, a wiser and harder Tina Turner emerged in 1984, having forsaken R&B entirely in favor of a high-gloss, high-tech, hard-rock sound heavy on electronic drum programs and synthesizers. In one fell swoop, *Private Dancer* captured the zeitgeist of the Me Decade with its cynicism and its solipsism. It made Tina Turner an international star on her own merits. The song that did it was "What's Love Got to Do With It." A second hit single off the album, "Private Dancer," was sung from the disengaged viewpoint of an erotic dancer whose only pleasure is in the money men give her; she can neither feel nor envision any other future.

Notwithstanding "Private Dancer" and "What's Love Got to Do With It," few seemed to notice the real pain Turner was now expressing in her harsh, pinched voice. It should have been obvious from the first song, "I Might Have Been Queen," when she sang of "searching through the wreckage/for some recollection/that I might have been queen." Compelling interpretations of Al Green's "Let's Stay Together" and Lennon-McCartney's "Help" might have made the point as well. It was left for her autobiography, *I, Tina*, written with Kurt Loder, to cut away the scar tissue left by her impoverished childhood and the wrenching years with Ike, allowing Turner to come out whole on the other side and enjoy her newfound solo acclaim.

Through the '80s she built up an

enormous reservoir of good will among fans and critics who saw in her life a genuine triumph over forces that would overwhelm most folks. She toured incessantly after *Private Dancer* broke big, so it was unsurprising that *Break Every Rule* sounded a bit rote, and failed to generate the excitement or sales of its predecessor. *Foreign Affair* (1989) is closer to the bone. Featuring a number of songs by swamp rocker Tony Joe White, who also contributes some typical grungy guitar licks, the album is more rooted in blues than anything Turner had done in years, but its sound is grounded in contemporary rock. Her singing is more ebullient, her throaty moans deeply felt and sincere. *Simply the Best* sums up Turner's '80s work, but also takes a broader overview by including the towering Ike and Tina single, "River Deep—Mountain High," remastered by producer Phil Spector, as well as "the '90s version" of Ike and Tina's 1973 hit, "Nutbush City Limits." — D.M.

THE TURTLES

★ ★½ It Ain't Me Babe (1965; Rhino, 1986)
★ ★ ★ Happy Together (1967; Rhino, 1983)
★ ★ ★ 20 Greatest Hits (Rhino, 1982)
★ ★ ★½ The Best of the Turtles (Rhino, 1987)
★ ★ ★½ Turtle Wax: The Best of the Turtles, Vol. 2 (Rhino, 1988)

While hitting the Top Ten in 1965 with Bob Dylan's "It Ain't Me Babe" and releasing a number of P.F. "Eve of Destruction" Sloan songs, this L.A. band proved too gigglesome an outfit for the philosophical strainings of folk rock; they moved on to infectious and exuberantly slight radio fluff. With Howard Kaylan and Mark Volman, the Turtles possessed two strong lead singers—of a visual mold riotously at odds with rock-star stereotypes—and their combination of careful song selection and self-mocking humor made them successful and endearing. "Happy Together" (1967) remains their most memorable track; released the same year, "You Know What I Mean" and "She'd Rather Be With Me" were also crafty rock candy. With the same eccentricity that later found Volman and Kaylan recording with Frank Zappa and, as "Flo and Eddie," singing back-up for T. Rex, the Turtles expressed a laudable, if occasional, discontent with their limited role as hitmakers. They flexed this urge not only on the concept album, *The Turtles Present the Battle of the Bands* (now out of print,

the album has the group doing send-ups of a vast range of styles), but in an artful choice of songwriters, Harry Nilsson and Warren Zevon, among them. Rhino's *20 Greatest Hits* exhaustively covers the straighter Turtles; *Turtle Wax* does the same for the bent. — P.E.

24-7 SPYZ

★ ★½ Harder Than You (In-Effect, 1989)
★ ★ ★ Gumbo Millennium (In-Effect, 1990)
★ ★ ★ This Is . . . 24-7 Spyz! (EP) (East-West, 1991)

Like Primus, 24-7 Spyz juggles elements of thrash and funk within its sound, although in the Spyz' case, the thrash side usually wins out. That's certainly the case with *Harder Than You*, on which even relatively funky numbers like "Spyz Dope" and the cover of Kool & the Gang's "Jungle Boogie" take on an unexpectedly brittle edge. With *Gumbo Millennium*, the Spyz loosen up considerably; as much as the band likes to rock out, there's a relaxed, fluid groove to tunes like "Valdez 27 Million?" or the rap-flavored "Don't Push Me." *This Is . . . 24-7 Spyz!* introduces a new singer and drummer, but doesn't change the band's sound, as even the most adventurous moments (like the jazzy intro to "Peace & Love") are simply extensions of ideas broached on *Gumbo Millennium*. — J.D.C.

TWISTED SISTER

★ You Can't Stop Rock and Roll (Atlantic, 1983)
★ ★ Stay Hungry (Atlantic, 1985)
★ Come Out and Play (Atlantic, 1985)
★ Love Is for Suckers (Atlantic, 1987)

Just when everybody thought the '70s were over for good, this veteran Long Island bar band finally reached the charts with an Alice Cooper–style metal rebellion fantasy called "We're Not Gonna Take It" in 1984. Propelled by a classroom-trashing video clip, "We're Not Gonna Take It" (from *Stay Hungry*) is one of the earliest examples of a telegenic hit single—a mediocre song with a strong visual hook. Take away the mascaraed clown routine of lead singer Dee Snider—please—and you're left with a pretty flimsy reshuffling of several vintage anthems by the Who and Alice Cooper. Success proved to be a mixed blessing for Snider and his long-toiling journeymen crew, however; after releasing sodden (and commercially stiff) follow-ups, *Come Out and Play* and *Love Is for Suckers*, Twisted Sister called it quits. Even though "We're Not Gonna Take It" helped usher in the pop '80s, Twisted Sister can be heard as the last, dying gasp of the preceding era. Ahhh. — M.C.

CONWAY TWITTY

★ ★ **Hello Darlin' (MCA, 1970)**
★ ★ **Greatest Hits, Vol. I (MCA, 1972)**
★ ★ ★ **Greatest Hits, Vol. II (MCA, 1976)**
★ ★ ★ ★ **The Very Best of Conway Twitty (MCA, 1978)**
★ ★ **Number Ones (MCA, 1982)**
★ ★ ★ **Classic Conway (MCA, 1983)**
★ ★ **Conway's Latest Greatest Hits Volume 1 (Warner Bros., 1984)**
★ ★ **A Night With Conway Twitty (MCA, 1986)**
★ ★ ★ **Borderline (MCA, 1987)**
★ ★ ★ **20 Greatest Hits (MCA, 1987)**
★ ★ **Still in Your Dreams (MCA, 1988)**
★ ★ ★ **Conway Twitty Number Ones: The Warner Bros. Years (Warner Bros., 1988)**
★ ★ ★ **House on Old Lonesome Road (MCA, 1989)**
★ ★ ★ **Crazy in Love (MCA, 1990)**
★ ★ ★ ★ **Silver Anniversary Collection (MCA, 1990)**
★ ★ **Greatest Hits, Vol. III (MCA, 1990)**

For someone who's not generally regarded as hip, Conway Twitty (né Harold Jenkins) has done his share to push the boundaries of propriety in mainstream country music. Perhaps this rebellious streak can be traced back to Twitty's roots as a first-generation rock & roll artist, whose Presley-inspired weeper, "It's Only Make Believe," topped the pop charts in 1958. Whatever its source, Twitty has cultivated it assiduously over the years since retooling himself as a country artist in the late '60s after rock & roll passed him by. And it's worked: Published reports claim he's had more Number One records than any artist in history, and his total record sales since 1968 (when he scored his first C&W Number One single, "Next in Line") are off the board.

Thematically, Twitty's concerns aren't all that different from those of other mainstream country artists, particularly when it comes to songs with sexual themes (and, of course, feelings of guilt, shame and anxiety). He loves thinking about it ("Tight Fittin' Jeans," "I'd Love to Lay You Down," "I've Already Loved You in My Mind"), he loves doing it ("You've Never Been This Far Before"), he loves the games people play in its behalf ("I Want to Know You Before We Make Love").

This suggests Twitty's a one-note artist,

but that's not quite accurate. He's also explored love's more tender avenues (a good cover version of "The Rose") and even pokes fun at himself on occasion. His has not been a monumental career in terms of artistic achievement, but he has proven to be a reliable and durable artist capable of surprising anyone who writes him off as a nondescript commercial hack.

Obviously Twitty has been recording longer and more prolifically than is indicated by his current catalogue. A number of his MCA albums are technically out of print, but will probably be available again in time. Still, there's a great deal of material out there from MCA, and two greatest-hits packages from his short stint at Warner Bros. Among the MCA titles, check out *The Very Best of Conway Twitty* for his earliest recordings for the label, all produced by Owen Bradley; and *Greatest Hits Vol. II* for a wider variety of subject matter. More recent albums, *Crazy in Love* and *House on Old Lonesome Road*, team with the new breed of Nashville session players and sound fresher, as does Twitty, than his stolid work in the mid-'80s. If any of Twitty's albums could be considered essential it would be the 25-cut *Silver Anniversary Album*, which is bookended by a minor mid-'60s single, "Guess My Eyes Were Bigger Than My Heart" and one of his best performances of late, "She's Got a Single Thing in Mind," from 1989. — D.M.

THE 2 LIVE CREW

★½ **2 Live Crew "Is What We Are" (1986; Luke/Atlantic, 1990)**
★ ★½ **Move Somethin' (1988; Luke/Atlantic, 1990)**
★½ **As Nasty As They Wanna Be (1989; Luke/Atlantic, 1990)**
★ **As Clean As They Wanna Be (1989; Luke/Atlantic, 1990)**
★ ★ **Live In Concert (Effect, 1990)**
★ ★ ★ **Sports Weekend (As Nasty As They Wanna Be Part II) (Luke/Atlantic, 1991)**
★½ **Sports Weekend (As Clean As They Wanna Be Part II) (Luke/Atlantic, 1991)**

After *As Nasty As They Wanna Be* was declared obscene by a Broward County, Florida, judge in 1990, the 2 Live Crew ascended to a level of notoriety beyond anything the Rolling Stones or Sex Pistols ever imagined. Almost immediately, the group became synonymous with pop music depravity, even as other rap groups (N.W.A., the Geto Boys) did their best to outstrip the Crew in sexual explicitness. At the same time, the 2 Live Crew became a symbol of just how fragile the right to free speech had become for pop performers in general—a situation that saw the Crew defended by everyone from Bruce Springsteen to Sinéad O'Connor to Mötley Crüe.

Ironically, had it not been for the Broward County obscenity ruling, it's doubtful that the 2 Live Crew would ever have been as well known as it is today. Musically, the Crew stands as fairly pedestrian proponents of the Miami bass sound, while its sex-centered lyrics derive from a party-record tradition running from Rudy Ray Moore to Blow Fly, a combination that earned the Crew a solid regional following through the South and Southwest, but no real national audience. And no wonder. "*Is What We Are*" (recorded before Luther "Luke Skyywalker" Campbell became a full member of the group) is so awkward and amateurish that "We Want Some Pussy" stands out more for its exuberance than for its explicitness.

Things get a little funkier with *Move Somethin'*, which augments the tinny 808-beat of "*Is What We Are*" with heavy scratching and more elaborate sampling, while the rapping becomes more intense and inventive. Granted, it's still fairly bush-league, thanks to juvenile bad-boy stuff like "P-A-N," but the title tune kicks, and the Crew's incorporation of rock licks on "Do Wah Diddy" and the Kinks-inspired "One and One" adds much-needed variety.

As Nasty As They Wanna Be squanders that progress. Musically, it adds little to the 2 Live repertoire, apart from the arrestingly tuneful "Me So Horny," built around an ingenious sample from the film *Full Metal Jacket*, and the insistently percussive "Get the Fuck Out of My House." Lyrically, it pushes the group's sexual braggadocio to uncomfortable extremes in tracks like "Put Her In the Buck" and "Dick Almighty." But the real problem with this album isn't that it's obsessed with fucking so much as it's fucking boring. And though it's tempting to blame the 80-minute playing time for part of that, *As Clean As They Wanna Be* is even less compelling, though barely half as long. (It does, however, included several non-*Nasty* tracks, including the 2 Live version of "Pretty Woman.")

Given the fact that few rap acts really shine in concert, it seems reasonable to expect *Live in Concert* to disappoint. Yet as insubstantial as it often is, it does reinforce the group's identity as a party band. Hearing the audience reaction to "Banned in the U.S.A." (from Campbell's solo album, *Banned in the U.S.A.*) is inspiring, but the album's real energy stems from call-and-response numbers that have the crowd enthusiastically completing the Crew's rhymes. That spirit carries over to *Sports Weekend*, both versions of which are packed with silly audience-response numbers. As before, the clean version is something of a gyp, being shorter and musically less satisfying. But despite its jejune jokes, the nasty *Weekend* not only captures the spirit of those old party albums, but actually adds an aura of responsibility, thanks to an AIDS-awareness rap called "Who's Fuckin' Who." — J.D.C.

U

UB40

- ★★★ **Signing Off (Graduate UK, 1980)**
- ★★½ **The Singles Album (Graduate UK, 1980)**
- ★★★½ **Present Arms (DEP UK, 1981)**
- ★★★ **Present Arms in Dub (DEP UK, 1981)**
- ★★★★ **UB44 (DEP UK, 1982)**
- ★★★ **Live (DEP UK, 1983)**
- ★★★★ **1980–83 (A&M, 1983)**
- ★★★★½ **Labour of Love (A&M, 1983)**
- ★★★★ **Geffery Morgan (A&M, 1984)**
- ★★★ **The UB40 File (Graduate UK, 1985)**
- ★★★★ **Baggariddim (DEP UK, 1985)**
- ★★★½ **Little Baggariddim (A&M EP, 1985)**
- ★★★½ **Rat in the Kitchen (A&M, 1986)**
- ★★★ **CCCP—Live In Moscow (A&M, 1987)**
- ★★★★ **The Best of UB40 Vol. One (DEP UK, 1987)**
- ★★★★ **UB40 (A&M, 1988)**
- ★★★½ **Labour of Love II (A&M, 1989)**

UB40 has maintained its status as Britain's most popular reggae act not because the group is racially mixed or homegrown, but because it has consistently taken a pop-friendly approach to the music. That's not to denigrate UB40's way with a groove, for the group neither dilutes nor whitewashes its riddim-driven pulse. But between Ali Campbell's warm tenor and the group's melody-centered songwriting, UB40's sound is accessible without ever seeming condescending.

Although its earliest material (that is, the Graduate recordings, which include *Signing Off* and the compilations *The Singles Album* and *The UB40 File*) is fairly traditional reggae fare, the group's sound becomes progressively funky and dub-wise through *Present Arms* (which features the throbbing "One in Ten") and *UB44* (which boasts the soulful, rhythmically vibrant "So Here I

Am"). The compilation album *1980–83* introduced the band to American audiences, with no noticeable reaction, but U.S. interest picked up with *Labour of Love*, a collection of cover tunes that reprises many of the band's favorite early reggae hits. Campbell's vocals are particularly expressive, and the album eventually became a hit on the strength of the chart-topping single "Red Red Wine." Trouble is, it took four years, during which time UB40 had long since moved on. Indeed, *Geffery Morgan* picks up where *UB44* left off, adding more dub effects and continuing to play off the resilience of the rhythm section. There's also a growing eloquence to the songs' social content, for even though UB40—whose name derives from the standard U.K. unemployment compensation form—always had a political edge, songs like "Riddle Me" and "As Always You Were Wrong Again" expertly articulate anti-Thatcherite class resentment.

UB40's next album, *Baggariddim*, wasn't released in its entirety in this country. In the U.K., the album combines an EP featuring a charming "I Got You Babe" cut with Chrissie Hynde, with an album of dub remakes of tracks from *Labour of Love* and *Geffery Morgan*; in the U.S., *Little Baggariddim* delivers the EP plus a couple of dubs for a less-satisfying package. Nor does *Rat in the Kitchen* entirely return the band to strength, for despite the urgently percolating pulse of "All I Want to Do" and the engaging groove behind the title tune, songs like "Don't Blame Me" and "The Elevator" seem forced.

With *UB40*, the band's pop instincts return to full working order. Hynde makes another guest appearance, this time covering the Sheila Hylton hit "Breakfast in Bed," but the band hardly needs the help, as the songs are wonderfully strong, from the relentless "Dance With the Devil" to the insinuating "I Would Do It for You." *Labour of Love II* isn't quite as appealing as its predecessor, despite the soul-cum-reggae groove of the Al Green tune "Here I Am (Come and Take Me)" and a slinky remake of the Temptations' "The Way You Do the Things You Do." — J.D.C.

JAMES BLOOD ULMER

★ ★ ★ ★½ Tales of Captain Black (Artists House, 1979)
★ ★ ★ ★　Are You Glad to Be in America (Artists House, 1981)
　★ ★ ★½ Free Lancing (Columbia, 1981)
★ ★ ★ ★　Black Rock (Columbia, 1982)
★ ★ ★ ★½ Odyssey (Columbia, 1983)
★ ★ ★ ★　Part Time (Rough Trade, 1984)
★ ★ ★ ★　Live at the Caravan of Dreams (Caravan of Dreams, 1986)
　★ ★ ★½ America—Do You Remember the Love? (Blue Note, 1987)

Like drummer Ronald Shannon Jackson and bassist Jamaaladeen Tacuma, guitarist James Blood Ulmer is a disciple of Ornette Coleman and an exponent of the "harmolodic" funk Coleman introduced with his Prime Time band. *Tales of Captain Black* (which credits Ulmer as "James Blood") in fact features Coleman as well as Tacuma, and is thrilling to hear, though it is perhaps the guitarist's most demanding album. With *Are You Glad to Be in America*, Ulmer moves to a slightly more pop-oriented sound, working more off backbeat-grounded grooves on some tunes, as well as singing on a few numbers. Unfortunately, the disparity between selections like the R&B-oriented title tune and the free-blowing "Revelation March" may be a bit much for some listeners.

Moving from the indies to the majors, Ulmer consolidates his focus, and tones down the more experimental elements of his sound for *Free Lancing*; he even brings in back-up singers for one track. Ulmer's attempt to find a middle ground between rock accessibility and harmolodic freedom falters until *Odyssey*, on which he abandons the multiband format of *Black Rock* for a bass-less trio featuring violinist Charles Burnham. The sound is deeply blues-inflected yet freed from the usual level of cliché; unfortunately, the band did not find the audience it deserved and was back in the minors for the concert albums *Part Time* and *Live at the Caravan of Dreams*. Despite a few sterling moments, *America—Do You Remember the Love?* is yet another half-hearted attempt at crossover acceptability, this time recorded

under the aegis of the ubiquitous Bill Laswell. — J.D.C.

ULTRA VIVID SCENE

★ ★ ★　Ultra Vivid Scene (4AD/Rough Trade, 1988)
★ ★ ★½ Joy 1967–1990 (4AD/Columbia, 1990)

An intense, low-profile outfit led by songwriter Kurt Ralske, Ultra Vivid Scene crafts irresistibly melodic tunes and then piles on the synths and Frippertronic guitars. So well constructed are the songs, however, that they hardly groan under the weight of the furious instrumentation— instead the brooding vocals ease slyly through a glade of hooks. Ultraefficient postmodern rock. — P.E.

URIAH HEEP

★　Uriah Heep (Mercury, 1970)
★　Salisbury (Mercury, 1971)
★ ★　Look at Yourself (Mercury, 1972)
★ ★　Demons and Wizards (Mercury, 1972)
★　The Magician's Birthday (Mercury, 1972)
★ ★　Sweet Freedom (1973; Warner Bros., 1991)
★½　Wonderworld (1974; Warner Bros., 1991)
★ ★½ The Best of Uriah Heep (Mercury, 1976)

It seems reasonably certain that Uriah Heep is the real-life Spinal Tap. Perhaps the most damning bit of evidence rests on *The Magician's Birthday* and *The Best of Uriah Heep*. Today "Bird of Prey" sounds like a parody of the lacey-sleeved, decadent school of heavy metal: "oh-ah!" pipes falsetto-bound singer David Byron as the power chords plod through the mud. Uriah Heep harnesses Ken Hensley's "progressive" keyboard squiggles to a thumping, party-down boogie beat. A couple of years later, Queen refined this approach and took it to the bank. *The Best of Uriah Heep* achieves a crude, campy tunefulness on stompers like "Easy Livin'," but the arty flourishes on the second half aren't even funny. This band's one good song, "Stealin'," appears on the guitar-dominated *Sweet Freedom*. And echoes of the modern power ballad definitely occur throughout the last two Uriah Heep albums. But be forewarned: Nothing this unmourned band ever recorded comes close to matching Bon Jovi's faux-'70's classics "Dead or Alive" and "Living on a Prayer." So much for authenticity. — M.C.

U.T.F.O.

★ ★ ★ **UTFO (Select, 1985)**
★ ★ **Skeezer Pleezer (Select, 1986)**
★ ★ ★ **Lethal (Select, 1987)**
★ ★ **Doin' It (Select, 1989)**
★ ★ **Bag It and Bone It (Jive, 1990)**

The UnTouchable Force Organization—Doctor Ice, the Kangol Kid and the Educated Rapper—created a citywide stir in New York with its second single, included on *UTFO*. On "Roxanne, Roxanne," the hip-hop trio disses an uncooperative, foxy female in rhyme, their enthusiastic insults buoyed by a thundering rhythm cascade on the chorus. The Brooklyn-based Full Force production team provides the juice on this and later U.T.F.O. records, zapping the group's resolutely ordinary boasts and toasts with soul samples and original synth riffs. A series of female answer records (including zingers from Roxanne Shanté and the Full Force–backed Real Roxanne) cemented the song's status as a phenomenon. U.T.F.O. had trouble following up this history-making break, however. The attempts at singing on *Skeezer Pleezer* are flat-out disasters, and the expanded horizions on *Lethal* (Anthrax metal and gangsta rap) feel like something imposed on their clueless charges. Similiarly, the reggae and New Jack moves on the recent albums get overshadowed by crude 'n' lewd dunce raps of the "Bag It and Bone It" ilk. — M.C.

U2

★ ★ ★ ★ **Boy (Island, 1980)**
★ ★ ★ **October (Island, 1981)**
★ ★ ★ ★½ **War (Island, 1983)**
★ ★ ★ **Under a Blood Red Sky (EP) (Island, 1983)**
★ ★ ★ ★½ **The Unforgettable Fire (Island, 1984)**
★ ★ ★ **Wide Awake in America (EP) (Island, 1985)**
★ ★ ★ ★ ★ **The Joshua Tree (Island, 1987)**
★ ★ ★ ★ **Rattle and Hum (Island, 1988)**
★ ★ ★ ★ ★ **Achtung Baby (Island, 1991)**

Because U2's music had a grandiose sound long before its lyrics had anything especially grand to say, some listeners immediately assumed that this Irish quartet was self-impressed and shallow. And, to be honest, there is some truth in that. But despite the occasional eloquence of issue songs like "Sunday Bloody Sunday" or "Pride (In the Name of Love)," most U2 songs emphasize the sound of the band over the sense of the lyrics, an approach that, at its best, lends a certain naïve majesty to the group's albums.

That's certainly the case with *Boy,* U2's debut. It helps, of course, that the ten tunes are sturdily constructed and winningly melodic, from the rousing refrain of "I Will Follow" to the elegiac quiet of "The Ocean." But by far the most arresting thing about the band is its sound. U2's instrumental approach is fairly minimal, but the band parts company with its contemporaries by making sure that every part in its stripped-down arrangements is played for maximum impact. Obviously, the ringing ostinatos and colorful chording provided by the Edge's echo-laden guitar play a large part in this, but he hardly carries all the melodic weight. Adam Clayton's bass line in "Twilight," for instance, doesn't just shore up the beat, but supplies a secondary melodic line; likewise, Larry Mullen's drums in "Stories for Boys" don't just keep time, but provide musical cues to underscore the song's inner drama. Thus, the band's instrumental voices manage an almost greater eloquence than Bono's amiably heroic vocals.

The same principle holds for *October,* though not for the same reasons. Although the band as a whole suffers from sophomore slump here, Bono seems particularly at a loss, making an impressive noise but precious little sense in "Gloria," "With a Shout" and "I Threw a Brick Through a Window." But *War* more than makes up for that. Not only is the writing more tightly focused, but the band leaps nimbly between the personal ("New Year's Day," "Two Hearts Beat as One") and the political ("Sunday Bloody Sunday") without a single misstep. Even better, the instrumental palette is richer and more varied, finding room for everything from the martial funk of "Sunday Bloody Sunday" to the shimmering acoustic touches of "Drowning Man."

Under a Blood Red Sky offers a hint of how this translated in concert, but the vivid, bristling presence producer Jimmy Iovine gets for that EP is worlds away from the rich, atmospheric aura producers Brian Eno and Daniel Lanois give the music on *The Unforgettable Fire.* On that album, the instrumental sound is blurred, giving the band a warmer, more intimate sound, one that brings out the emotional immediacy in "Bad" and adds soul to the insistent thrust of "Pride." But that isn't the only change introduced by *The Unforgettable Fire,* for with this album Bono begins to explore his obsession with America. The intensely personal *The Joshua Tree* album doesn't entirely avoid the political—how could it, with songs like "Mothers of the Disappeared"—but such concerns seem secondary to the quest for love and identity described in songs like "With or Without You" or "I Still Haven't Found What I'm Looking For." Yet as vivid as the album's wordplay may be, it's still the music that carries these songs, from the itchy throb of "Bullet the Blue Sky" to the racing pulse of "Where the Streets Have No Name."

At this point, the next logical move for U2 would have been a live album, but the semilive soundtrack album *Rattle and Hum* isn't quite what fans expected. Sure, it includes concert versions of hit singles like "Pride" and "I Still Haven't Found What I'm Looking For," but those are accompanied by cover material like "Helter Skelter" and "All Along the Watchtower." Moreover, not all of the album is live; indeed, some of the strongest performances, like the Bo Diddley–style "Desire" or the bluesy "When Love Comes to Town," are studio recordings. Granted, those inclined to nitpick will find plenty to niggle over, but as usual, it's wiser to pay less attention to the words than the notes.

And that goes double for *Achtung Baby*. Thanks to the sound-shaping technology applied to the Edge's guitar and Larry Mullen's drums, the band's sound is more intricate and articulate than ever, affording the album a stylistic range that runs from the techno grunge of "Zoo Station" to the hip-hop-inflected groove of "Mysterious Ways." That's not to say the lyrics don't deserve attention, for some—like "So Cruel" —are as vividly evocative as the music they adorn. But just as his conspiratorial whisper inflames the desperate clangor of "The Fly," Bono's delivery often says more than the words themselves, proving once again that U2's sound is invariably more eloquent than its lyrics. — J.D.C.

V

RITCHIE VALENS

★★★★ **Ritchie Valens (1959; Del-Fi/Rhino, 1981)**
★★★ **Ritchie (1959; Del-Fi/Rhino, 1981)**
★★★★ **The Best of Ritchie Valens (Del-Fi/Rhino, 1986)**
★★★★ **Ritchie Valens in Concert at Pacoima Jr. High (1960; Del-Fi/Rhino, 1981)**
★★★★★ **The History of Ritchie Valens (Del-Fi/Rhino, 1981)**
★ **La Bamba '87 and Other Great Rock n' Roll Classics (Original Sound, 1987)**

Unlike Buddy Holly, with whom Ritchie Valens is forever linked by virtue of the 1959 plane crash that claimed their lives and that of the Big Bopper, Valens didn't leave behind a treasure trove of unreleased recordings; like Holly, though, what Valens did leave gives only a tantalizing hint of where he might have taken his music. While Holly may well have become the quintessential American pop artist and a producer of note, Valens seemed headed for more exotic turf, where he would have made explicit the links between Afro-Cuban and Mexican song forms and rhythms and those of the then-nascent style called rock & roll.

Born of Mexican Indian–American parents, Valens (né Richard Stephen Valenzuela) cherished the tradition of the Mexican song and honored it. His most enduring hit, "La Bamba," is based on an old wedding *huapango*, and is sung with the original Spanish lyrics Valens learned as a child. From this starting point, we can go to side two of *In Concert at Pacoima Jr. High*, where we find a selection of songs Valens had intended to finish after returning from the Holly tour. On one track we hear Valens working out a guitar piece that incorporates the African rhythms he had heard Bo Diddley playing when they shared a concert bill in New York.

What remains are two studio albums of mostly original work; the fascinating live recording made shortly before Valens's death (he was only 17 when his life ended); the side of partially completed studio work; and a greatest-hits package. The latter, *The Best of Ritchie Valens*, will suffice for those whose interest is limited to Valens's best-known commercial recordings. "La Bamba," of course, leads off the 16-track package, which also includes the lovely "Donna," "Come On, Let's Go," "Ooh! My Head" and other inspired but more obscure selections. Valens sang in a keening, emotional tenor, and his supporting guitar work was concise and often explosive.

Completists will opt for the three-record box set, *The History of Ritchie Valens*. Here, on Valens's two studio albums, *Ritchie Valens* and *Ritchie*, are all the tracks contained on *Best of*, in addition to nonsingle sides unavailable elsewhere. The third album in the *History* box is *In Concert at Pacoima Jr. High*. The concert, contained on side one, sounds sedate and measured; Valens's singing and playing are thin, but that may have as much to do with the lack of sophisticated recording technology as it does with the actual performance. Certainly the artist's ingratiating but cheesy guitar cuts through, and on the first song, "Come On, Let's Go," we get a good example of how Valens toyed with lyrics.

The real curiosity—or is that atrocity?—is Original Sound's *La Bamba '87*, which purports to be a sampling of what Valens might have done had he lived. What this boils down to are four versions of "La Bamba" newly transfigured with an eye towards the contemporary dance market. These include a Latino Power Mix and a Hi-Tone Rock Box Mix. Unbelievable, right? Yes. You can put all manner of maracas, horns, and sampled vocals on a disc and tell us "this is a vision of how 'La

Bamba' would have sounded had Ritchie Valens lived to record it today," and the question remains: Sez who? — D.M.

LUTHER VANDROSS

★ ★ ★½ **Never Too Much (Epic, 1981)**
★ ★ ★ **Forever, for Always, for Love (Epic, 1982)**
★ ★ ★½ **Busy Body (Epic, 1983)**
★ ★ ★ ★ **The Night I Fell in Love (Epic, 1985)**
★ ★ ★½ **Give Me the Reason (Epic, 1986)**
★ ★ ★½ **Any Love (Epic, 1988)**
★ ★ ★ ★ ★ **The Best of Luther Vandross . . . The Best Of Love (Epic, 1989)**
★ ★ ★ ★ **Power of Love (Epic, 1991)**

Diehard fans of sweat-drenched late-'60s soul probably won't be swayed by Luther Vandross and his fully appointed romantic fantasies. It's their loss: the consummate loveman of modern R&B is also one of the most consistent—and challenging—pop singers to emerge during the '80s. Neither a chesty seducer nor a wimp, Vandross girds his towering vocal constructs on a rock-solid emotional base. For all his awesome technique and intensity, he almost never lapses into self-indulgence or schmaltz. *Never Too Much* not only established this former session star's solo career in 1981, it laid down his artistic credo as well.

The debut sets a distinctive mold for future albums: an uptempo strut or two, several gradations of heartbreak ballad, one pull-out-the-stops cover version, an expertly juxtaposed medley or a male-female duet for variety. Refining this approach rather than rethinking each record, Vandross can be accused of making the same album over and over. It does get better over time, though. *The Night I Fell in Love* reaches a new level of musical depth and emotional sophistication: the songs contrast and complement each other, cohering into an elegant, revealing documentary of a nascent love affair. His subsequent albums prove that he doesn't work in a hothouse. *Give Me the Reason* and *Any Love* deftly infuse the Vandross sound with fresh rhythms, replacing the string sections with synths as appropriate. *The Best of Luther Vandross* doesn't miss a trick; stretching from his early performances to his later pop crossovers ("Here and Now," from 1989), *The Best* captures the full range of Vandross's communicative powers. Nobody but Vandross could follow that title with *Power of Love*—and actually best himself in

the process. He continues to explore new avenues without any loss of direction. "The Rush" pits the singer against an itchy electro-funk pulse, which Vandross scratches in all the right places. Tellingly, he's stretching even on the familiar set-ups: the medley ("Power of Love/Love Power") is resonant, while the diva duet ("I Who Have Nothing" with Martha Wash) stays bouyant. This streak of inspiration should continue through the '90s; Vandross isn't about to run out of material for his finely tailored love songs. — M.C.

VANGELIS

★½ **L'Apocalypse des Animaux (Polydor, 1973)**
★½ **Earth (Polydor, 1974)**
★ ★½ **Heaven and Hell (RCA, 1975)**
★½ **Albedo 0.39 (RCA, 1976)**
★ ★ **La Fête Sauvage (Barclay)**
★½ **Spiral (RCA, 1977)**
★½ **Ignacio (Barclay, 1977)**
★ ★ **Beauborg (RCA, 1978)**
★ ★ **Opera Sauvage (Polydor, 1979)**
★ ★½ **China (Polydor, 1979)**
★ ★ ★ **Chariots of Fire (Polydor, 1981)**
★ ★ **To the Unknown Man (RCA, 1982)**
★ ★ **Soil Festivities (Polydor, 1984)**
★ **The Mask (Polydor, 1985)**
★ ★ ★ **Themes (Polydor, 1989)**
★ ★ ★ **The City (Atlantic, 1990)**

Born Evangelos Papathanassiou, Vangelis is a multi-instrumentalist and composer whose theme for the film *Chariots of Fire* topped the U.S. charts in 1982. Taken from David Puttnam's film about English runners, "Chariots of Fire" is everything a synth-and-keyboards instrumental ought to be—stately, melodic, symphonic in its sweep yet intimate in its sense of dynamics. It is also, sad to say, atypical of Vangelis's work. His first solo albums, recorded while he was still a member of the windy progressive-rock outfit Aphrodite's Child, are for the most part typical '70s synth efforts, ambitious in their reach but hobbled by the limited timbral range of the relatively primitive electronics. *L'Apocalypse des Animaux* and *La Fête Sauvage* try to compensate with soundtrack-style African percussion, *Albedo 0.39* makes a stab at fusion jazz and *Beauborg* dabbles in clangorous electronic abstractions, but the majority of his early albums are simply earwash—sometimes pleasant, sometimes pretentious, but invariably forgettable.

Only *Heaven and Hell* offers a hint of what is to come, as "Heaven and Hell (Part One)" closes with a solemn, majestic theme that seems a precursor to "Chariots of Fire." At this point, Vangelis's recordings seem less mechanical, although whether that's due to his musical maturity or the ongoing improvement in synthesizer technology is hard to say. For whatever reason, *China* is a thoroughly impressive piece of work, evocative without seeming derivative, and full of sonic detail. In fact, the only real difference between *China* and *Chariots of Fire* is that the former tries to be true to its Eastern idiom, while the latter has the commercial advantages of a hit film and predictably English melodies.

To his credit, Vangelis didn't try to cash in on his new-found fame (although RCA did, releasing *To the Unknown Man*, an uneven, early-'70s sampler with a runner misleadingly pictured on the cover). He recorded three albums—*Short Stories*, *Friends of Mr. Cairo* and *Private Collection* —with Yes singer Jon Anderson, but that was as close as he ventured to pop stardom again. *Soil Festivities*, though interesting enough sonically, is too short on melody to make for enduring listening, and the bombastic *Mask* is bad imitation Carl Orff, but *The City*, with its bits of aural drama sprinkled through the electronic soundscape, is fascinatingly vivid. Still, his only post-*Chariots* album with anything resembling pop appeal is *Themes*, a best-of collection that reprises the hit and includes selections from *China*, *Opera Sauvage* and his soundtrack to *Bladerunner*. — J.D.C.

VAN HALEN

★ ★ ★½ Van Halen (Warner Bros., 1978)
★ ★ ★ Van Halen II (Warner Bros., 1979)
★ ★ ★ Women and Children First (Warner Bros., 1980)
★ ★ ★½ Fair Warning (Warner Bros., 1981)
★ ★ ★½ Diver Down (Warner Bros., 1982)
★ ★ ★ ★ 1984 (MCMLXXXIV) (Warner Bros., 1983)
★ ★ ★ ★½ 5150 (Warner Bros., 1986)
★ ★ ★ ★ OU812 (Warner Bros., 1988)
★ ★ ★½ For Unlawful Carnal Knowledge (Warner Bros., 1991)

Van Halen blew onto the scene with all the goals expected of a hard-rock party band: To be larger than life, louder than hell and cool as shit. And the band was, too, thanks in large part to the incredible charisma (and considerable smarts) of singer David Lee Roth. Not only was the band almost instantly successful, but by the time of *Women and Children First*, Van Halen was almost as well-known for its attitude as for its solid-platinum sales or spectacular stage shows. But Roth had nothing to do with making Van Halen more than just another party-hearty heavy rock act; credit for that lies with guitarist Edward Van Halen, the musical brains behind this band. Unlike virtually every rock guitarist before him, he didn't simply build upon the electric-blues vocabulary of Clapton, Beck, Page and Hendrix—he created a whole new language, one that replaced the bluesy string bends and stinging sustain of old with screeching tremolo dive-bombs and lightning-fast hammer-ons and pull-offs. As far as guitarists were concerned, it was as if the wheel had been reinvented, and set-pieces like "Eruption" (from *Van Halen*) assumed the status of holy writ among the fretboard set. Without his example, it would be hard to imagine the sound of Randy Rhoads, Steve Vai or Adrian Vandenberg.

But Edward mattered more to Van Halen as a composer than as a player, something that became increasingly obvious after *Diver Down*. In addition to pop-conscious cover material like "(Oh) Pretty Woman" and a techno-pop take on "Dancing in the Streets," that album significantly expanded the band's audience and instrumental approach. *1984*, in turn, blew things wide open, giving the group its first No. 1 single, "Jump" (which, ironically, found Edward playing more synthesizer than guitar) and establishing Van Halen as a mainstream powerhouse. Roth left in 1985 to pursue a career in self-parody, and was replaced by Sammy Hagar, a singer-guitarist with little of Roth's wit, charm or intelligence, but considerably more vocal ability. That was precisely what the band needed, though, and *5150* (police code for "escaped lunatic") was a leap forward musically, proving Van Halen to be as adept at ballads as balls-out rockers. And despite their snickeringly stupid titles, both the pop-savvy *OU812* and the harder-rocking *For Unlawful Carnal Knowledge* produced further refinements in Van Halen's sound. — J.D.C.

VANILLA FUDGE

★ ★½ Vanilla Fudge (Atco, 1967)
★ The Beat Goes On (Atco, 1968)
★ Renaissance (Atco, 1968)
★ Near the Beginning (Atco, 1969)
★ Rock & Roll (Atco, 1969)
★ ★½ The Best of Vanilla Fudge (Atco, 1982)

Specializing in bombast, this New York band parlayed extremely self-important

versions of tried-and-true pop songs—
almost all of them clocking in at around six
minutes. What saves the group, however, is
its sheer heaviness—bassist Tim Bogert and
drummer Carmine Appice are truly sweaty
players. Seven minutes of the Supremes'
"You Keep Me Hanging On," tricked out
with baroque organ and ponderous
vocalizing, gained the Fudge a hit in 1968,
and the band followed that formula on such
other mini-epics as "Ticket to Ride," Sonny
and Cher's "Bang, Bang," and, most
amusingly, Donovan's "Season of the
Witch." The Fudge's first album is its only
(relatively) cohesive one; *Greatest Hits* is
interesting only for including "Witch" and
the neat "Where Is My Mind"—a number
that could pass for the Fudge's theme song.
— P.E.

VANILLA ICE
★ ★   To the Extreme (SBK, 1990)
★½ Extremely Live (SBK, 1991)
Off Vanilla Ice's 1990 breakthrough, *To The
Extreme*, "Ice Ice Baby" gained this Miami
instant-idol a horde of mall-rat fans, and
provoked the ire of hard-core rappers. In
rap, of course, image is crucial—and Ice's
made for an easy target. With his *GQ*
jawline and Duran Duran fashion sense, this
very white boy hardly came on like a
gangsta, and his tales, in interviews, of a
bad-boy past sure sounded bogus. The song
itself was snappy—but only because the
sampled bass line from Bowie and Queen's
"Under Pressure" sounded terrific, not
because Ice's rhymes were clever. The rest of
the album was substandard rap-lite,
suggesting that, ultimately, the most
offensive thing about Ice is his blandness.
Top-volume screaming groupies provide
secondhand excitement on *Extremely Live*—
due exclusively to that frenzied ambience,
the record is interesting. At crowd control,
the boy's an expert, but his thin, whining
version of the Stones' "Satisfaction" betrays
his limitations. He doesn't have anything
new to say, and when he grapples with
clichés, he doesn't even have the savvy to do
so with conviction. — P.E.

VANITY
★ Wild Animal (Motown, 1984)
★ Skin On Skin (Motown, 1986)
After leaving the Prince empire and Vanity
6 and before beginning her career as a
B-movie bimbo, Vanity made two eminently
forgettable solo albums, in which she
moaned and cooed, delivered double
entendres, and sang . . . after a fashion.

Wild Animal, recorded with Bill Wolfer, is
straight synth funk, and memorable mostly
for "Such a Pretty Mess," perhaps the first
song in rock history in which a woman
applauds premature ejaculation. Despite a
high calibre of collaborators (including Skip
Drinkwater and Robbie Nevil), *Skin on Skin*
is no better than its predecessor; although
"Under the Influence" masks her vocal
limitations enough to seem listenable, her
mewling on "Confidential" suggests that
moving on to movies was not such a bad
idea. — J.D.C.

VANITY 6
★ ★½ Vanity 6 (Warner Bros., 1982)
Campy, vampy and not without wit, this
Prince-produced girl group may not have
been able to sing, but they panted with the
best of them. Still, when Vanity insists over
the sinuous groove of "Nasty Girl" that she
needs "at least seven inches," it's worth
pondering whether she's thinking of her
boyfriend or wondering if the single has
12-inch potential. — J.D.C.

GINO VANNELLI
½ ★ Crazy Life (A&M, 1973)
★ Powerful People (A&M, 1974)
★ Storm at Sunup (A&M, 1975)
½ ★ The Gist of the Gemini (A&M, 1976)
½ ★ A Pauper in Paradise (A&M, 1977)
½ ★ Brother to Brother (A&M, 1978)
★ The Best of Gino Vannelli (A&M, 1980)
½ ★ Nightwalker (Arista, 1981)
★ ★ Black Cars (Columbia, 1985)
★ ★ Big Dreamers Never Sleep (Columbia, 1987)
★ Classics (A&M, 1987)
Perhaps Vannelli reached his nadir by
wailing the ludicrous lyric, "I'm just a male
Caucasian," to overblown synthesizer
accompaniment on *Storm at Sunup*. But for
this shlockmeister, "nadir" is a relative
term. Virtually his entire career has been a
progression from valley to gulley, and he
qualifies as an absolute Il Duce of bad taste.
With his brother helping out on synth
arrangements, Vannelli concocted pap arias
that combined pretensions to classical music,
the worst of jazz-fusion posturing and an
operatic singing style that conveyed bogus
sensitivity and all the sexiness of an obscene
phone call. Flashing his chest hair and the
bulge in his pants, Vannelli was a Tom
Jones for the '70s—although completely
lacking in Tom's sense of fun.
Improvements in studio and synthesizer
technology marked the textural clotting that
increased from album to album—by the

time of *Gist of the Gemini*, Vanelli was strangling in lushness—but all of his first half-dozen records sound alike. Again and again, he whispers and bellows; all his songs are crescendos going nowhere. Interchangeable, *The Best of* and *Classics* capture this period—and they are music that is deeply offensive.

Miraculously, Vanelli's Columbia albums aren't. Switching over to pop, he retains all of his previous format's mechanics, but he tones down the vocals, rids his tunes of the artsy augmented chords that had been his trademark and comes off merely as ultraprofessional and bland. Thank God. — P.E.

DAVE VAN RONK
★★ **Black Mountain Blues (Folkways, 1959)**
★★★ **Inside Dave Van Ronk (Prestige, 1962)**
★★★ **Folksinger (Prestige, 1962)**
★★★½ **Inside Dave Van Ronk (Fantasy, 1989)**

Former merchant marine and pope of Greenwich Village's folk scene, Dave Van Ronk is an American original. Around since the late '50s, he's made many records—almost all of them clean, but not reverent, readings of traditional blues and folk. Fantasy's 1989 CD, *Inside Dave Van Ronk* (along with *Black Mountain Blues,* the only Van Ronk LP in print) combines the 1962 album of the same name with *Folksinger* (also from 1962) for a representative sampler of his finest work. "Cocaine Blues" is deadpan and chilling; "Talking Cancer Blues" brandishes a gallows humor; and "Poor Lazarus" is awesome—grit enters Van Ronk's voice, thrusting it past its usual carefulness, and he's seldom sounded more engaged or intense. *In the Tradition* is Dave doing Louis Armstrong and Rev. Gary Davis material, backed by the Red Onion Jazz Band. *Van Ronk* finds him interpreting Randy Newman and Leonard Cohen, with a lush accompaniment leagues away from his standard, intimate acoustic guitar. *Sunday Street* is also good nonpurist Van Ronk. But his strength remains lean versions of archival fare, which he saves from sounding nice by the zest of his attack. — P.E.

LITTLE STEVEN VAN ZANDT
★★★½ **Men Without Women (EMI, 1982)**
★★★ **Voice of America (EMI, 1984)**
★★★ **Freedom—No Compromise (EMI-Manhattan, 1987)**

Steve Van Zandt contributed much to the drama of Bruce Springsteen's early albums before departing the E Street Band in 1984, and his writing and production for Southside Johnny and the Asbury Jukes helped elevate them to something more than merely the best bar band in the country. Absolutely committed to classic rock & roll in the Rolling Stones tradition, Little Steven, with his gypsy head-rag and flamboyant stage presence, then came on convincingly as a frontman—*Men Without Women* was a scorching debut, and it seemed, for a short while, that the Disciples of Soul might stand as a Great Last Hope for rock undiluted either by postpunk irony or revivalist overreverence. But neither *Men* nor its two capable successors (both of which revved up Steven's streetwise political activism) found much of an audience. America lost its chance to embrace a kind of homegrown Clash, but Steven continued his admirable apostolic work in the late '80s as one of the guiding lights behind Artists United Against Apartheid. — P.E.

TOWNES VAN ZANDT
★★½ **Delta Momma Blues (1978; Tomato, 1989)**
★★★ **Townes Van Zandt (1978; Tomato, 1989)**
★★★½ **Our Mother, the Mountain (1978; Tomato, 1989)**
★★★ **Flying Shoes (1979; Tomato, 1989)**
★★★ **At My Window (Tomato, 1989)**
★★★½ **The Great Tomato Blues Package (Tomato, 1989)**
★★★ **Live and Obscure (Sugar Hill, 1990)**

Texas singer-songwriter Townes Van Zandt never gained much more than a long-lasting cult following for his well-crafted, mildly country folk-pop, but his best record, *Our Mother, the Mountain* remains powerful—and he deserves a revival. He hasn't the fine voice that Eric Andersen had circa Andersen's classic *Blue River* (1972), but he shares some of the same sensibility—he writes well about loss and yearning, and conveys subtle emotions through telling images. Willie Nelson and Merle Haggard scored a country hit with his "Poncho and Lefty," a song with pervasive, dark nostalgia that encapsulates Van Zandt's approach. A deft finger-picking guitarist and a careful lyricist, he has delivered work that stands the test of time. — P.E.

SARAH VAUGHAN

★ ★ ★	In the Land of Hi-Fi (Mercury, 1956)
★ ★ ★	Sarah Vaughan's Golden Hits (Mercury, 1967)
★ ★ ★ ★ ★	Recorded Live (EmArcy/ Polygram, 1977)
★ ★ ★ ★	Billie, Ella, Lena, Sarah! (Columbia, 1980)
★ ★ ★ ★	A Celebration of Duke (1980; Pablo Today, 1990)
★ ★ ★½	Duke Ellington Songbook, Vol. 1 (1980; Pablo, 1987)
★ ★ ★½	Duke Ellington Songbook, Vol. 2 (1980; Pablo, 1987)
★	Songs of the Beatles (Atlantic, 1981)
★ ★ ★	Sarah Vaughan and the Count Basie Orchestra: Send in the Clowns (1981; Pablo Today, 1989)
★ ★ ★	The Best of Sarah Vaughan (1983; Pablo, 1990)
★ ★ ★ ★	Sarah Vaughan & Billy Eckstine: The Irving Berlin Songbook (EmArcy/Polygram, 1984)
★ ★ ★ ★ ★	The Complete Sarah Vaughan on Mercury, Vol. 1: Great Jazz Years, 1954–1956 (Polygram, 1986)
★ ★ ★ ★ ★	The Complete Sarah Vaughan on Mercury, Vol. 2: Sings Great American Songs, 1956–1957 (Polygram, 1986)
★ ★ ★ ★ ★	The Complete Sarah Vaughan on Mercury, Vol. 3: Great Show on Stage, 1957–1963 (Polygram, 1986)
★ ★ ★ ★ ★	The Complete Sarah Vaughan on Mercury, Vol. 4: 1963–1967 (Polygram, 1987)
★ ★ ★	Sassy Swings the Tivol (EmArcy/Polygram, 1987)
★ ★ ★ ★	Copacabana (1981; Pablo Today, 1988)
★ ★ ★	George Gershwin Songbook, Vol. 1 (EmArcy/Polygram, 1990)
★ ★ ★	A Time in My Life (Mainstream, 1991)
★ ★ ★	The Singles Sessions (Capitol/ Blue Note, 1991)
★ ★ ★	Sassy Swings Again (Mercury, NA)
★ ★ ★	Rodgers and Hart Songbook (Mercury, NA)
★ ★ ★ ★	Sarah Vaughan Compact Jazz Live! (Mercury, NA)

Acknowledged as the most important female jazz singer apart from Ella Fitzgerald, the late Sarah Vaughan possessed a voice of such supreme majesty and dimension that to compare her to anyone else is a waste of time. Her vocal signatures were so distinctively her own that she became a genre unto herself. While many singers could match the husky, sensuous timbre of her voice, Vaughan had no peers when it came to controlling mood, melody and phrasing. Blessed with impeccable command of dynamics, she developed a stylistic quirk—swooping from a warm alto to a cool soprano (she had a three-octave range) and hitting the notes dead-on—that remains one of the sweetest sounds in American music. A flawless improvisor who improved with age, she accommodated with little strain the harmonic innovations Charlie Parker and Dizzy Gillespie were introducing in the '40s, and indeed, Parker and Gillespie, who were in Earl "Fatha" Hines's band when Vaughan joined it in 1943, came to be among her most ardent supporters.

Born in Newark, New Jersey, in 1924, she began playing organ for and singing in her church choir when she was a young girl. In 1942, when she was 18, she won an Amateur Night contest at Harlem's Apollo Theater, which led to her discovery by Billy Eckstine, then a featured vocalist with Hines's band. On Eckstine's recommendation, Hines hired Vaughan; a year later Eckstine formed his own band and was joined by Vaughan, Gillespie and Parker (the band also included, at times, Fats Navarro, Miles Davis, Art Blakey and Dexter Gordon).

In the '50s Vaughan was crossing over to the pop charts with some regularity—nine Top Forty singles between 1954 and 1959—but her greatest achievements were as an interpreter of jazz and classic popular songs. One of the priceless moments in her catalogue is a teaming with Eckstine on *The Irving Berlin Songbook*; the two singers bring new dimension to even the most well-worn of Berlin's great songs. Duke Ellington was a particular favorite of Vaughan's, and the obvious affection she had for the challenges his material posed made her Ellington's foremost interpreter. Of the three strong latter-day examples listed here, *A Celebration of Duke* comes most highly recommended, owing to the greater sympatico Vaughan exhibits with her small combo here. But anyone who passes up the two *Duke Ellington* albums does so at risk.

The Best of Sarah Vaughan numbers ten

tracks of Vaughan backed by small combos and studio orchestras, and serves as a fine, focused collage of styles and disparate settings. The best of Vaughan's not always superior pop singles are found on *Sarah Vaughan's Golden Hits*. Here she is too often drowned in strings and leaden arrangements, and whoever multitracked her voice at the end of "How Important Can It Be" ended up making her sound like Patti Page. Still, some of these stand up as lively fare. The only must to avoid is, sad to say, *Songs of the Beatles*.

Recorded Live presents four sides of Vaughan in her prime, recorded in concert settings in Copenhagen (1963) and Chicago (1957 and 1958). For historical perspective, try Columbia's *Billie, Ella, Lena, Sarah!*, a collection of tracks by four of the greatest voices in jazz history. Vaughan's four—"Nice Work If You Can Get It," "East of the Sun (West of the Moon)," "Ain't Misbehavin'," "Goodnight, My Love"—are from 1950, when she was backed by George Treadwell (whom she married) and His All Stars, whose members included Miles Davis, Budd Johnson, Billy Taylor, J. C. Heard and others. Again, the alchemy of superb, sensitive work in front of sympathetic and inspired accompaniment produces art as memorable as it is durable. — D.M.

STEVIE RAY VAUGHAN

   ★ ★ ★ **Texas Flood (Epic, 1983)**
   ★ ★ ★ **Couldn't Stand the Weather (Epic, 1984)**
★ ★ ★ ★ **Soul to Soul (Epic,1985)**
★ ★ ★ ★ **Live Alive (Epic, 1986)**
   ★ ★ ★ **In Step (Epic, 1989)**
★ ★ ★ ★ **The Sky Is Crying (Epic, 1991)**

Among the generation of blues guitarists who came of age in the early '80s, only Robert Cray approaches Stevie Ray Vaughan's skill and influence, with Vaughan's brother Jimmie probably sneaking in there as well on the strength of his powerful work with the Fabulous Thunderbirds. To be sure, though, Vaughan kicked the latest blues revival into high gear with his first two albums, *Texas Flood* and *Couldn't Stand the Weather*, which came out of nowhere to become best-sellers in the midst of a rock world being consumed by techno-pop.

Texas Flood pays its debts to traditional Texas blues and R&B, sounding a tad muddy, the better to experience the slice-and-dice solos Vaughan delivers. Stylistically, Vaughan was a true eclectic whose hard-driving, steely sound achieved

individuality while incorporating quotes from Hubert Sumlin, Buddy Guy, T-Bone Walker, Lonnie Mack, Albert Collins, B.B. King and Jimi Hendrix. That's a broad palette, but it also shows how Vaughan built on the best influences to express the emotional extremes of his songs.

Couldn't Stand the Weather finds Vaughan broadening out a bit beyond R&B to include a stirring rendition of Hendrix's "Voodoo Child" and a Charlie Christian–Kenny Burrell flavor on the jazz-tinged "Stang's Swang." *Soul to Soul* represents Vaughan's and Double Trouble's great leap forward. First the addition of keyboardist Reese Wynans expands the sound, adding textural possibilities. Wynans makes his presence felt most dramatically on a version of Hank Ballard's "Look at Little Sister." Vaughan shows more facility with melody in his songwriting, producing his first outstanding ballad in "Life Without Love." Vaughan had a tender side that he could express effectively with either a delicate vocal or pained guitar solo. *Live Alive* sums up the first part of Vaughan's career in a rousing live set recorded at the Montreux Jazz Festival and in Austin and Dallas. Of note is Jimmie Vaughan's special guest appearance on four tracks cut in Austin. *In Step*, Vaughan's last studio album, collects more well-turned Vaughan originals, along with a tasty selection of Howlin' Wolf, Buddy Guy and Willie Dixon covers. Vaughan's "Crossfire" is one of his peak solo turns in a pure, gut-wrenching style.

The lovingly assembled posthumous album, *The Sky Is Crying*, contains ten studio performances recorded between 1984 and 1989, with only one track, "Empty Arms," having appeared on a previous Vaughan album (*Soul to Soul*), and that in a different version. Whether by design or accident the tunes offer a good overview of Vaughan's stylistic range. Most pronounced are the nods to Albert King, but there are also touches of Kenny Burrell (whose "Chitlins Con Carne" is covered), Hubert Sumlin, Lonnie Mack ("Wham," a Mack classic) and of course Hendrix ("Little Wing"). A somber note closes the album, "Life by the Drop," Vaughan's first recorded acoustic solo. It's a moment you don't want to end. But it does. — D.M.

THE VAUGHAN BROTHERS
★ ★ ★ ★ **Family Style (Epic, 1990)**

The album that blues guitar fans, Texas branch, had been waiting years to hear was finally realized in 1990, but came clouded in the tragedy of Stevie Ray Vaughan's death shortly before its release. Apart from his family's considerable loss, modern blues was stripped of a giant, who perished on the eve of a professional triumph. *Family Style* provides bold displays of both the fire and the tenderness that marked the brothers' approach as influential instrumentalists and underrated vocalists.

Produced by Nile Rodgers, who keeps a hard sheen on the proceedings, *Family Style* shows off the Vaughans' guitars in tandem (a rousing twin-guitar workout on "D/FW") and apart, but also showcases each brother's affecting vocal style on several cuts. A particular treat is Jimmie's laconic vocal over a steadily percolating rhythm track on "Good Texan." By the same token, Stevie Ray delivers a powerful blue-eyed soul plea for peace and understanding on "Tick Tock," his voice all smoky-gray and a model of controlled urgency.

Guitar enthusiasts will hardly be disappointed, though. The brothers come on strong—Jimmie tough and economical, Stevie Ray robust and razor-edged—on a couple of blues-rock steamers, "Long Way from Home" and "Telephone Song." On "Brothers" they make the connection clear: the distinction between the two disappears as one angular solo blends into another. This is blood on blood, a fitting final gesture. — D.M.

BOBBY VEE

- ★ **Bobby Vee Meets the Crickets (1962; EMI, 1991)**
- ★ **Merry Christmas from Bobby Vee (1962; EMI, 1990)**
- ★★★ **Nothin' Like a Sunny Day (UA, 1972)**
- ★★★ **The Best of Bobby Vee (EMI Manhattan, 1987)**
- ★★★★ **The Legendary Masters Series (EMI, 1990)**

Too long regarded as a shameless Buddy Holly imitator who cashed in on the singer's death to get his start, Fargo, North Dakota, native Robert Thomas Velline—Bobby Vee—was one of the few early-'60s teen-idol types whose music had some class and believable feeling. It's true that Vee and his band, the Shadows, replaced Holly at a concert in Mason City, Iowa, days after Holly's plane crash, and that Vee's first self-penned single, "Suzie Baby," is shameless in its vocal references to Holly. Vee always had the Holly hiccup in his voice, but as his career developed he evolved a style of singing that was smoother and

even more pop-oriented. Working with producer Snuff Garrett (a friend of Holly's from Lubbock, Texas), Vee became one of the dominant pop-rock vocalists in the business between 1960 and 1963, during which time he had 11 Top Forty hits, with "Take Good Care of My Baby" (1961) perching at Number One.

Vee was blessed with first-rate material throughout his early career. Gerry Goffin and Carole King contributed four of Vee's most literate songs ("How Many Tears," "Take Good Care of My Baby," "Sharing You," "Walkin' With My Angel"), but he also benefited from contributions made by Crickets Sonny Curtis and Jerry Allison ("More Than I Can Say"), Burt Bacharach and Hal David ("Be True to Yourself") and John D. Loudermilk ("Stayin' In"). Garrett enveloped Vee's singing in strings and lush orchestration, and made sure he had a good rhythm section behind him. Although he hit a dry period after '63, Vee came back strong in '67 with "Come Back When You Grow Up." His last chart hit came in '68 with a medley of "My Girl" and "My Guy."

EMI's *Legendary Master Series* entry on Vee covers his most important '60s singles. From the adolescent yearnings of "Suzie Baby" to the unsentimental declarations of "Come Back When You Grow Up," this collection also works as something of a primer on the development of a particular strain of '60s pop-rock. The re-release of Vee's 1962 album, *Bobby Vee Meets the Crickets*, is an underwhelming moment. For one, only two of the three Crickets actually play on the tracks, and considering the all-star stature of the other musicians on board, one must ask, what's the point of meeting the Crickets if you can't distinguish their work? Moreover, Vee simply could not handle material that cries out for a blast of full-bore rock & roll—songs such as "Lucille," "Bo Diddley," and "Sweet Little Sixteen." *Merry Christmas from Bobby Vee* sounds neither merry nor inspired.

Vee continued recording into the early '70s without any significant success. He did, however, produce one terrific album in 1972, *Nothin' Like a Sunny Day*, now out of print. Reverting to his real name on the cover, Vee/Velline's bearded, solemn visage on the cover is not that of a teen idol, while the introspective songs (all but two written by Velline) are the logical progression of the artist's mindset. This is a mature work wherein Velline seems to question every aspect of his life and career. — D.M.

SUZANNE VEGA
★ ★ ★　　Suzanne Vega (A&M, 1985)
★ ★ ★½　Solitude Standing (A&M, 1987)
★ ★ ★ ★　Days of Open Hand (A&M, 1990)
Almost dauntingly intelligent, Vega's third album, *Days of Open Hand*, is her finest—its cryptic lyrics, sophisticated melodies and complex, crack jazz playing revealing a breathtaking progression from her impressive debut just five years before. Starting off as a folkie, Vega hit big with "Luka," a haunting, cinema verité portrait of domestic violence. Taken from her second album, *Solitude Standing*, the single was surrounded by equally strong material—the jaunty, a capella "Tom's Diner" showed that a writer capable of songs akin to Leonard Cohen's high-flown poetics could also encompass the street smarts of Lou Reed. Vega is her own woman, though. Compassion, hope and mystery are themes not very subtly handled in pop music: Vega delves into them with an almost philosophical acuity. And she sings like an earth angel. — P.E.

CAETANO VELOSO
★ ★ ★　　Muito (1978; Verve, 1991)
★ ★ ★ ★　Cores Nomes (1982; Verve, 1990)
★ ★ ★ ★½　Caetano Veloso (Nonesuch, 1986)
★ ★ ★½　Totalmente Demais (1986, Verve, 1987)
★ ★ ★ ★　Caetano (Philips, 1987)
★ ★ ★½　Personalidade (Philips, 1987)
★ ★ ★½　A Arte de Caetano Veloso (Philips, 1988)
★ ★ ★ ★　Estrangeiro (Elektra/Musician, 1989)
★ ★ ★ ★　Sem Lenço Sem Documento (Verve, 1990)
★ ★ ★ ★　Circuladô (Elektra, 1992)
WITH CHICO BUARQUE
★ ★ ★　　Juntos E Ao Vivo (Philips, 1988)
Along with Gilberto Gil, Caetano Veloso was one of the founders of *tropicalismo,* the anything-goes Brazilian pop movement that expanded the music's stylistic base from the samba and bossa nova until it included pretty much anything that struck the performer's fancy. And in the case of Veloso, that was quite a lot, from the high-tech synths of *Caetano* to the screaming guitar and rock-like dynamics of some tracks from *A Arte de Caetano Veloso*, to *Caetano Veloso*'s stunning guitar-and-voice medley of the Brazilian tune "Nega Maluca," Michael Jackson's "Billie Jean" and the Beatles' "Eleanor Rigby."

Veloso's recording career in Brazil dates back to the mid-'60s, but few of those early albums are widely available in this country. Indeed, the earliest of his material in print here—*Muito* and *Cores Nomes*—seems almost to have been released in response to the David Byrne–curated collection *Beleza Tropical*; *Muito* opens with "Terra" (the last track on *Beleza Tropical*) and *Cores Nomes* includes "Um Canto De Afoxé Para O Bloco Do Ilê" (one of *Beleza Tropical*'s most charming selections). *Personalidade, A Arte de* and *Sem Lenço Sem* are all best-of collections, with *Sem Lenço* being the most consistent and *A Arte De* the most rock-oriented and adventurous (and also the album with the most songs in English). *Juntos E Ao Vivo* and *Totalmente Demais* are both concert recordings, with the latter showing more wit while the former suffers from too-low fidelity and too-high audience enthusiasm.

But *Caetano Veloso, Estrangeiro* and *Circuladô*, his most American albums, are perhaps the best place for novice listeners to start. The first is an all-acoustic album that finds the singer reprising many of his best-known songs in classic singer-songwriter fashion. By contrast, *Estrangeiro* is edgy and electric, as Veloso augments his usual Brazilian backup with performances by Arto Lindsay, Bill Frisell, Marc Ribot and Peter Scherer; the sound of *Circuladô* is just as daring, but its cast ranges even farther afield, with contributions from Gilberto Gil to Melvin Gibbs to Ryuichi Sakamoto. Scary and audacious, they're not quite as easy to listen to as *Caetano Veloso*, but just as emotionally powerful. — J.D.C.

VELVET UNDERGROUND
★ ★ ★ ★ ★　The Velvet Underground and Nico (1967; Verve/Polygram, 1985)
★ ★ ★ ★　White Light/White Heat (1968; Verve/Polygram, 1985)
★ ★ ★ ★　The Velvet Underground (1969; Verve/Polygram, 1985)
★ ★ ★ ★ ★　Loaded (Cotillion, 1970)
★ ★ ★　　Live at Max's Kansas City (Cotillion, 1972)
★ ★ ★ ★½　1969 Live (Mercury, 1974)
★ ★ ★ ★　V.U. (Polygram, 1984)
★ ★ ★½　Another View (Polygram, 1986)
The most influential rock & roll band of the last 20 years? This one—no contest. However, the Velvet Underground wasn't really "ahead of its time." These records offer a clarifying, bracing vision; Lou Reed trained his acute songwriter's eye on the world around him. Specifically, the streets and demimonde of New York City. While

San Francisco groups benignly celebrated the Summer of Love, *The Velvet Underground and Nico* documented the side effects of drug experimentation and sexual freedom on chilling tracks like "Heroin" and "Waiting for the Man." A former student of avant-garde classical music, bassist John Cale tempers the Velvets' dense guitar onslaught with stark, jarring viola cries. Reed and Sterling Morrison had been playing guitar together since the early '60s; they took the steady, rhythmic strumming of folk and gradually distorted it into a crude, propulsive electric blur. But Reed also displays a finely honed pop sense on the achingly insightful love songs "Femme Fatale" and "I'll Be Your Mirror." Nico's artfully murmured vocals on these two tracks are a matter of taste; certainly, her efforts pale in comparison to Reed's deadpan mastery of talk-singing.

By the second album, Nico was gone and the Velvet Underground's association with Andy Warhol was winding down. *White Light/White Heat* taps into the group's brilliant, blinding musical essence: the 17-minute "Sister Ray"—a minimalist tour de force—hurtles along like an amphetamine rush, bypassing the usual psychedelic detours in a headlong charge. Yet in the end, underneath the guitar mesh and trance-inducing organ, Maureen Tucker's nervous-but-steady drum pulse just may be what renders "Sister Ray" so hypnotic. Just as confidently, *The Velvet Underground* bolts off in the opposite direction. With Cale departed for a solo career, Reed really starts to deepen his songwriting. "Pale Blue Eyes" and "Beginning to See the Light" reveal the compassion and insight behind his skeptical, world-weary stance, while "What Goes On" indicates the Velvets can still push your stereo's readout dials well into the red zone.

Reed reaches his songwriting zenith on *Loaded*, and the band's wall-of-raunch crystalizes into instantly recognizable song structures. "Sweet Jane" and "Rock & Roll" deserve their status as anthems; those invigorating three-chord heartbeat riffs underscore the stirring, evocative details in the lyrics. Singing about suburban Jenny, whose "life was saved by rock & roll," Reed struck a resonant chord with a new, disaffected generation of rock & rollers. Never a best-seller, this landmark album is now out of print.

Of course, the Velvet Underground broke up before its influence began to be felt. Reed left the group right after *Loaded*, and embarked on a mercurial solo career a

couple of years later. (Sterling Morrison retired from music and became an English professor; Maureen Tucker resurfaced in the '80s with a pair of independent-label solo projects.) The *Live at Max's* set records some of the group's legendary last stand during the summer of '70; the muddy, bootleg-quality sound gets rough, but the rearranged final version of "Sweet Jane" is well worth hearing. Released at the height of punk's gestation period, *1969 Live* captures the Velvet Underground at an absolutely incandescent peak: even the between-songs patter fascinates. Recorded between the third album and *Loaded*, the posthumously released *V.U.* displays more of Lou Reed's frank sensitivity and ironic humor along with the expected devastations of "Ocean" and "Foggy Notion." *Another View* scrapes against the bottom of the Velvets barrel, but even this group's instrumentals and outtakes emit a weird, enveloping buzz that's never quite been duplicated. Maybe in another 20. — M.C.

THE VENTURES
★★★ **The Best of the Ventures (EMI America, 1987)**
★★★ **Walk, Don't Run: The Best of the Ventures (EMI, 1990)**
★★★ **Greatest Hits (Curb, 1990)**

An entire army of '60s high-school guitarists learned their licks off Ventures' records— and while that lends this California instrumental quartet historical interest and quaint charm, it doesn't mean their records hold up. "Walk Don't Run," their signature tune, is truly tasty—a twangy, sinuous lead guitar line wraps neatly around propulsive drumming—but their other hits, "Perfidia," "Hawaii Five-O" and "Ram-Bunk-Shush," now seem bland and campy. Duane Eddy, they weren't. — P.E.

BILLY VERA
★★★ **By Request (The Best of Billy Vera & the Beaters) (Rhino, 1986)**
★ **Retro Nuevo (Capitol, 1988)**

A man with deep roots in soul and R&B music, Billy Vera began his recording career in the late '60s on Atlantic, had his songs recorded by the likes of Rick Nelson and Fats Domino, and in the past decade or so has parlayed his passion into a long-standing career as one of L.A.'s most popular club attractions. "At This Moment," a song Vera recorded for Alfa Records in the early '80s, gained a second life when used in the TV show "Family Ties" and went to Number One in 1987. Unfortunately, on record Vera sounds more like a student of the form than a person possessed by it. Of the two albums in print, *By Request* (which includes "At This Moment") is the best bet, it being a mostly live album (two tracks were recorded at Muscle Shoals Sound and coproduced by Jerry Wexler) recorded in 1981 on a night when Vera and his band the Beaters were playing it fast and loose. *Retro Nuevo* is a nice try, but it is stiff and unsatisfying. — D.M.

TOM VERLAINE

★★★★ **Tom Verlaine (Elektra, 1979)**
★★★ **Dreamtime (Warner Bros., 1981)**
★★★ **Words From the Front (Warner Bros., 1982)**
★★★★ **Cover (Warner Bros., 1984)**
★★★★ **Flashlight (I.R.S., 1987)**
★★★ **Warm and Cool (Rykodisc, 1992)**

Not long after Television's sudden breakup in 1978, daredevil guitarist Tom Verlaine bounced back with a balanced, assured solo debut. *Tom Verlaine* offers a stronger set of songs than did TV's swan song (*Adventure*), although it's similarly wired. A hired studio crew can't provide the same communicative spark as a longstanding band, of course, but Verlaine pushes himself to the outer limits anyway on the angular rocker "Breakin' in My Heart." Always an imaginative (if occasionally impenetrable) songwriter, Verlaine clarifies his impassioned talk-singing and flaunts his melodic bent on slow-building cuts like "Flash Lightning" and "Souvenir From a Dream." The successive efforts *Dreamtime* and especially *Words From the Front* wander off into the ethereal—crossing the line from downright beautiful to merely pretty. However, "Postcard From Waterloo" (from the latter album) is a stunner: it crystalizes Verlaine's solo approach, pointing toward the pop direction of his next album.

Cover is hardly a sell-out (none of these out-of-print albums have exactly been commercial bonanzas), but Verlaine does an extraordinary job of integrating synthesized keyboards and high-tech rhythmic quirks into his low-tech, guitar-based signature. Rather than pursue that path any further, Verlaine heats up his vintage Fender again on *Flashlight*. The sturdy, luminescent I.R.S. album does continue *Cover*'s catchy streak, though; some of Verlaine's tangled interior monologues—most notably the observant "A Town Called Walker"—won't sink in until that pleasant ringing in your ears finally subsides. — M.C.

THE VIBRATORS

★★★★ **Pure Mania (Columbia, 1977)**
Older and slightly less pissed off than most British punks, the Vibrators could also play instruments and sing, after a fashion. Maybe that's cheating, but *Pure Mania* delivers the expected jolt of rude energy—along with a flood of nonstop hooky choruses: "Keep It Clean" (antidrugs), "Whips & Furs" (pro-S&M), "No Heart" (about being stuck with one). The quartet puts its modicum of self-control to good use, deftly arranging the violent guitar outbursts and bombshell drumbeats so their impact is maximized. At the time of its release, the Vibrators' debut was hailed as a comfortable introduction to rock's abrasive new offspring; today it's one of the few original punk artifacts that still sound urgent—and necessary. — M.C.

VILLAGE PEOPLE

★★½ **Greatest Hits (Rhino, 1988)**
Absolute scourges of the disco era, assembled by producer Jacques Morali, the Village People trooped through a succession of mildly homoerotic novelty hits in the late '70s. The winking in-jokes—what kind of "Macho Man" works up so much enthusiasm for a stay at the "YMCA," pray tell?—seem corny and obvious now. But the Village People themselves, with their overt role-playing and campy humor, managed to inject a minute element of gay sensibility into the mainstream. Despite its social import, the music itself doesn't really bear further investigation: the martial beats and robot chants sound awfully dated, more so than many dance-floor remnants of the same period. *Greatest Hits* documents the Village People's moment in the sun and their swift decline into formula, including a taste of the infamous "New Romantic" comeback ("Ready for the '80s"). — M.C.

GENE VINCENT

★★★★ **Capitol Collectors Series (Capitol, 1990)**
Until some enterprising soul decides to assemble a box set, most of Gene Vincent's music will remain available only on import albums. His fleeting Stateside stardom aside, Vincent recorded prolifically from the time of his first hit in 1956 (the immortal "Be-Bop-a-Lula") up to his death in 1971 at the age of 36 (injured in the car wreck that killed Eddie Cochran, Vincent's health suffered further thereafter as he became increasingly dependent on alcohol). While only a smidgen of his prolific output is as inspired as his early work, at least Vincent

stayed on the rock & roll course to the end: he always favored black leather and the big beat. He wasn't as primitive as Link Wray, but he shared with Wray an unswerving commitment to keep on rocking when other stars of their generation were attempting to transform themselves into country or MOR singers.

Domestically, the Capitol Collectors Series disc at least makes clear what all the fuss was about back in '56. Vincent combined Presley's sensuality with Johnnie Ray's hypersensitivity, added some echo, and created a distinctive vocal identity. "Be-Bop-a-Lula" remains one of the very best rock & roll moments, driven by a throbbing beat, fevered ambience and Vincent's inflamed passion. Its flip side, "Woman Love," was banned in some parts of the country. "Lotta Lovin'," "Dance to the Bop," "Git It" and "Race with the Devil" are all first-rate tracks featuring Vincent and his solid band, the Blue Caps, rocking furiously. — D.M.

BOBBY VINTON

★★★ **Bobby Vinton's Greatest Hits (Epic, 1964)**
★★★ **Bobby Vinton's Greatest Hits/Bobby Vinton's Greatest Hits of Love (1964, 1969; Epic, 1972)**
★★ **More of Bobby Vinton's Greatest Hits (Epic, 1966)**
★★★ **Bobby Vinton's All-Time Greatest Hits (Epic, 1972)**
★★ **Timeless (Curb, 1988)**
★★ **Greatest Hits (Curb, 1990)**
★★ **Greatest Polka Hits of All Time (Curb, 1991)**
★★ **16 Most Requested Songs (Epic, 1991)**

In the early to mid-'60s, Bobby Vinton emerged as a successor to the throne previously occupied by Pat Boone, that being the lily-white balladeer singing songs of love and loss. But Vinton had it all over Boone as a vocalist, and while his recordings may not stand as the greatest aesthetic achievements in rock & roll history, they were embraced by a young audience reeling from the turbulence caused by raging hormones. For this audience, Vinton's nasally warbling, sincere posture and yearning romanticism were right on target. Their response was profound and long-lasting: Vinton notched four Number One singles between 1962 and 1964, all but one having multiple-week runs at the top; between '62 and '69 he was consistently in the Top Forty. His career was revived in the early '70s with a label change to ABC and a

more adult approach in his song selection, resulting in a Number Three single in '72, "My Melody of Love," which played on Vinton's Polish heritage (its refrain was sung in Polish).

Vinton's productive years on Epic are well chronicled in the various hits collections. Depending on one's tolerance for schmaltz, *Bobby Vinton's Greatest Hits* will serve as the essence of this artist's career. "Roses Are Red (My Love)," "Blue on Blue," "Blue Velvet," "There! I've Said It Again," "My Heart Belongs to Only You" and "Mr. Lonely" are all included, representing the core of Vinton's legacy. Try *All-Time Greatest Hits* (1972) for a compendium of the top chart entries and some lesser singles, as well. Vinton's ABC material has long since fallen out of print, but some of it, including "My Melody of Love," finds its way onto the Curb *Greatest Hits* album. — D.M.

VIOLENT FEMMES

★★★ **Violent Femmes (Slash/Warner Bros., 1983)**
★★ **Hallowed Ground (Slash/Warner Bros., 1984)**
★★★½ **The Blind Leading the Naked (Slash/Warner Bros., 1986)**
★★½ **3 (Slash/Warner Bros., 1989)**
★★ **Why Do Birds Sing? (Slash/Warner Bros., 1991)**

This Milwaukee trio took punk's revenge-of-the-nerds aspect to heart; clean-cut choirboy Gordon Gano gleefully wheeled out his tales of sexual frustration and impending psychosis, while bassist Brian Ritchie and stand-up drummer Victor DeLorenzo both slammed away on acoustic instruments. The Violent Femmes really stood out on the fledgling alternative circuit, and the group capitalized on its bare-bones mobility by playing impromptu street-corner gigs—talk about punk pragmatism! The debut album gets over mostly on that loose ensemble feel; strumming and haranguing, Gano works up a convincing (if not compelling) neurotic fury on three-chord throbbers like "Add It Up." Like most Lou Reed disciples, however, he tends to sound unpleasantly nasal on the inevitable, talky mid-tempo melodramas. That tendency peaks on *Hallowed Ground*'s pointlessly overwrought "Country Death Song"; between its shallow roots excavations and sarcastic fits, Violent Femmes' second album is nearly unlistenable. Producer Jerry Harrison (of Talking Heads) turns things around on *The Blind Leading the Naked*, focusing some of the group's manic energy and filling in some of the gaps in their technique. Gano responds with a far more considered set of songs, even looking out beyond his own cracked world: "Mother Reagan" stands as one of the best politico-rockers of the '80s, and the cover version of Marc Bolan's "Children of the Revolution" is actually less ironic than the glittery T. Rex original. The Violent Femmes began to draw a younger, much-enthused audience around this time, and the prospect of MTV-fueled teen idolatry must've frightened the group. *3* is a jumbled stylistic grab bag, reflecting the members' various solo projects. (Gano has a gospel band called Mercy Seat, and Brian Ritchie records for the independent SST label.) The acoustic return of *Why Do Birds Sing?* makes a sad, brazen play for the early-'80s nostalgia market—too bad the Violent Femmes' tuneless take on Culture Club's "Do You Really Want to Hurt Me?" actually makes you pine for Boy George. Not quite the intended effect. — M.C.

THE VOGUES
★ **The Vogues Greatest Hits (Rhino, 1988)**
"Five O'Clock World" was a fairly catchy mid-'60s single—a sort of Brit Invasion soundalike by these natives of Turtle Creek, Pennsylvania. But nothing else the Vogues did measured up, and they soon betrayed their true show-biz soul by doing covers of stuff like "The Impossible Dream." — P.E.

ANDREAS VOLLENWEIDER
- ★ **Behind the Gardens, Behind the Walls, Under the Tree (CBS, 1981)**
- ★ **Caverna Magica (CBS, 1983)**
- ★ **White Winds (Seeker's Journey) (CBS, 1985)**
- ★ **Down to the Moon (CBS, 1986)**
- ★ **Dancing With the Lion (Columbia, 1989)**
- ★ **The Trilogy (Columbia, 1990)**
- ★★ **Book of Roses (Columbia, 1991)**
Taken simply on the basis of craft, Vollenweider's music is impressive stuff. Not only does this Swiss new age harpist incorporate everything from light jazz to Chinese classical influences in his playing, but his sense of orchestration allows him to create richly detailed soundscapes with just a handful of players. On an artistic level, well . . . suffice it to say that the only thing separating Vollenweider's output with that of most mood-music purveyors is its level of pretension. Vollenweider doesn't write songs, he composes suites, each with its own set of thematic ideas—and, in the case of *White Winds*, zodiac signs—all of which are set out in his screamingly obvious song titles. As for his sidemen, they're billed as providing not "percussion" or "backing vocals" but "rhythmanatomic acousticolors" and "moonvoice—snakevoice." And they play like it.

Behind the Gardens, *Caverna Magica* and *White Winds* are apparently a trilogy, and are also packaged together as *The Trilogy*, along with two earlier works; *Down to the Moon* and the almost-lively *Dancing With the Lion* must be purchased separately. Each is wonderfully soporific, and unlike prescription sedatives are definitely not habit-forming. But *Book of Roses*, though just as compositionally vacuous as its predecessors, does at least wrap its empty calories in an interesting array of world-beat flavorings. — J.D.C.

THE VULGAR BOATMEN
★★★½ **You and Your Sister (Record Collect, 1989)**
★★★½ **Please Panic (Caroline, 1992)**
Accordion adds surprise to a few of the numbers on the Vulgar Boatmen's debut, but the sound is essentially that of a smart postmodern folk-rock. Frontman (and day-job English professor) Robert Ray is good at aphoristic lyrics—often about anomie, frustration or other indeterminate states of mind—and the rest of this Florida crew are skilled players. Produced by Walter Salas-Humara, lynch-pin of the fine New York mind-rockers the Silos, *You and Your Sister* has a clean, gorgeous spareness that highlights the sturdiness of the Boatmen's melodies—and the resonant suggestiveness of such standout numbers as "Margaret Says" and "Change the World All Around." *Please Panic* continues the Boatmen's obsession with lovely, drifting melodies and nervous rhythms. — P.E.

BUNNY WAILER

★★★★★ **Blackheart Man (Island, 1976)**
★★★ **Protest (Island, 1977)**
★★★★½ **Bunny Wailer Sings the Wailers (Island, 1980)**
★★★★ **Time Will Tell: A Tribute to Bob Marley (1981; Solomonic/ Shanachie, 1990)**
★★★★ **Roots Radics Rockers Reggae (Shanachie, 1983)**
★★★ **Marketplace (Shanachie, 1986)**
★★★★ **Rootsman Skanking (Shanachie, 1987)**
★★★ **Rule Dance Hall (Shanachie, 1988)**
★★★ **Liberation (Shanachie, 1989)**
★★★ **Gumption (Shanachie, 1991)**

The ethereally sweet tenor third of the original Wailers, blessed with seductive phrasing ability and a nimble intensity, Bunny Wailer (Neville Livingston) could well be the most gifted reggae singer currently practicing. Only Toots Hibbert comes close. And while the Maytals' fiery frontman is a strict disciple of Otis Redding, Bunny Wailer resembles a Rasta Marvin Gaye. He's nowhere near as mercurial as Gaye, though his peak performances radiate a similiar, enveloping spiritual buzz. *Blackheart Man* updates the hard-strutting sound of the Wailers with a funky edge, digging into the gutbucket rhythms rather than glancing at rock or pop accents. Peter Tosh contributes guitar and vocals, there's a flexibly tight Jamaican studio band in tow, and Bunny comfortably soars from "Dream Land" to "Amagideon (Armageddon)" to points off the map. His version of the standard reggae traditional "This Train" is damn near definitive. *Blackheart Man* holds its own against the best Bob Marley and the Wailers records.

Bunny Wailer pays a wonderful tribute to his late bandmate on the two memorial albums. *Bunny Wailer Sings the Wailers*

recasts the group's crudely recorded '60s hits in the crisp, pulsating style of Sly (Dunbar) and Robbie (Shakespeare). It's one of this influential rhythm section-production team's signature efforts; the muscular bottom anchors Wailer, while the dubwise spaces give him room to stretch the tightly wound three-minute songs into new shapes. The Marley-Tosh compositions "Walk the Proud Land" and "Burial" are highlights of a stellar set. *Time Will Tell* covers the more familiar later material—including many post-Bunny favorites—in a more reverent fashion. Not a replacement for the originals, it's a fascinating footnote.

A tendency toward didactic politics and the more obscure vagaries of Rastafarianism first surfaces on *Protest*, the comparatively stolid followup to *Blackheart Man*. The most satisfying Bunny Wailer outings of the '80s have been the singles compilations *Roots Radics Rockers Reggae* ("Rockers," "Rockin' Time") and *Rootsman Skanking* ("Cool Runnings," "Jammins"). *Liberation*, from 1988, deftly makes a stinging point about South Africa ("Botha the Mosquito"), but sermons like "Food" and "Serious Thing" could use a dose of humor—or a more supportive rhythm. Surprisingly, Bunny Wailer's stabs at current trends in New York (*Marketplace*) and Kingston (*Rule Dance Hall*) sound somewhat heavy-handed and grasping, as well. While the title of *Gumption* accurately describes the enduring quality of Bunny Wailer's vocals, those programmed drums aren't really his speed.
— M.C.

WAITRESSES
★★★ **Wasn't Tomorrow Wonderful? (ZE-Polydor, 1982)**
★★½ **I Could Rule the World If . . . I Could Only Get the Parts (EP) (ZE-Polydor, 1982)**

★★½ **Bruiseology (Polydor, 1983)**
★★★ **Best of the Waitresses (Polydor, 1990)**
How can a feminist pop group be fronted
by a woman but masterminded by a man?
How honest can a song called "I Know
What Boys Like" or "A Girl's Gotta Do"
be when the "girl" in question is only
reading lines written by a guy? The answer
to both questions ought to be "not very,"
yet somehow the Waitresses make a strong
case for the contrary view. Of course, it
helps that the most convincing element in
the group's chemistry is singer Patty
Donohue, whose winningly amateurish
delivery injects enough personality into these
songs to bring even the most exaggerated of
songwriter Chris Butler's constructs to life.
Over the jangly, new-wave funk of *Wasn't
Tomorrow Wonderful?*, Donohue brings
depth and credibility to character songs like
"No Guilt" and "It's My Car," and slips
enough deadpan wit into "I Know What
Boys Like" to bring its nyah-nyah choruses
to life (though even she can't quite make
"Pussy Strut" work).

I Could Rule the World may be just an
EP, but it boasts two of the group's best
numbers—the catchy "Square Pegs" theme
and "Christmas Wrapping," perhaps the
most affecting character sketch in the
Waitress's repertoire. *Bruiseology*, on the
other hand, is a mixed bag. The music is
great, effortlessly weaving together jazz,
funk and new wave, but the writing is
unfocussed and unfunny, with Donohue just
going through the motions. — J.D.C.

TOM WAITS
★★★   **Closing Time (Asylum, 1973)**
★★★   **The Heart of Saturday Night
(Asylum, 1974)**
★★★   **Nighthawks at the Diner (Asylum,
1975)**
★★★½ **Small Change (Asylum, 1976)**
★★★½ **Foreign Affairs (Asylum, 1977)**
★★★   **Blue Valentine (Asylum, 1978)**
★★★   **Heartattack and Vine (Asylum,
1980)**
★★★★ **Swordfishtrombones (Island, 1983)**
★★★★ **Rain Dogs (Island, 1985)**
★★★½ **Anthology of Tom Waits (Asylum,
1985)**
★★★   **Frank's Wild Years (Island, 1987)**
★★★   **Big Time (Island, 1988)**
★★★   **The Early Years (Bizarre/
Straight, 1991)**
Rasping his way through comic-nostalgic
cocktail jazz and garrulous streams of
Beat-derived wordplay, Tom Waits rose
from the seamy side of Los Angeles in the

'70s. Some of his first recordings from 1971
are on the 1991 release, *The Early Years*.
Lingering like a bad hangover, he eventually
developed a musical approach to match
both his devil-may-care wit and bluesy sense
of despair. Waits's early albums are
dreadfully uneven, thanks mostly to his
parched voice and well-lubricated point of
view: he sounds like he's had a bottle in
front of him and a frontal lobotomy for
quite some time. The less he tends to
marinate his tales of floozies and loosers in
alcoholic sentiment, the better his albums
get. *Small Change* is where his half-mad
maundering style gels into something more
than a hip novelty act. The slippery-sly
evasions of "The Piano Has Been Drinking
(Not Me)" and the amphetamine pitchman
spiel of "Step Right Up" hold up to close
and repeated inspections—more than you
can say for many spoken comedy albums.
Singing might not be an accurate description
of what he does on *Foreign Affairs*, but
Waits does expand his somewhat rigidly
defined boundaries, dueting with Bette
Midler on "I Never Talk to Strangers" and
offering the disquieting "Burma Shave" amid
the expected bleary reveries. After releasing
two comparatively rote thumb-twiddlers
(*Blue Valentine* and *Heartattack and Vine*),
Waits jumped labels and opted for a
challenging, clear-headed approach on
Swordfishtrombones and *Rain Dogs*. The
down-and-out subject matter remains the
same, but Waits seems to be in full control
of his voice—writing and croaking—now.
Stellar session crews on both albums flesh
out the compositions with abrasive rock and
schizzy jazz motifs. More substantial than
his early albums could ever have suggested,
it's still not what you'd call easy to digest.
Naturally attracted to the theater, Waits
followed his triumphant reemergence with
the sketchy *Frank's Wild Years* (excerpts
from a musical play) and the even-vaguer
soundtrack *Big Time* (drawn mostly
from its predecessor and *Rain Dogs*).
— M.C.

JERRY JEFF WALKER
★★★   **Jerry Jeff Walker (MCA, 1973)**
★★★   **Viva Terlingua (MCA, 1973)**
★★★½ **Ridin' High (MCA, 1975)**
★★★½ **A Man Must Carry On (MCA,
1977)**
★★★½ **The Best of Jerry Jeff Walker
(MCA, 1980)**
★★   **Navajo Rug (1987; Rykodisc, 1991)**
★★★   **Driftin' Way of Life (Vanguard,
1987)**

★ ★ ★   **Live at Gruene Hall (Rykodisc, 1989)**
★ ★   **Gypsy Songman (Rykodisc, 1990)**
★ ★ ★½ **Great Gonzos (MCA, 1991)**

Paul Crosby migrated to Texas from upstate New York in the late '60s, and was reborn Jerry Jeff Walker—legendary Gonzo troubadour and unrepentent hippie boozer. Calling him a singer-songwriter might be exaggerating a bit: even Walker's cult followers don't make claims for his talky rasp of a voice, and "Mr. Bojangles" supplied Walker with his first and only hit composition when the Nitty Gritty Dirt Band covered it in 1970. A depressing atmopshere of looseness-verging-on-sloth dogs all of Jerry Jeff's albums, though *Ridin' High* includes some surprisingly lucid song choices: Guy Clark's "Like a Coat From the Cold," Willie Nelson's "Pick Up the Tempo," Jesse Winchester's "Mississippi You're on My Mind" and Walker's own philosophical "Pissin' in the Wind." Either that album or *A Man Must Carry On*, comprised of live cuts and outtakes, offers the best introduction to Walker's intermittent bursts of inspiration. All the boisterous good times surveyed on *The Best of Jerry Jeff Walker* and the even-lengthier *Great Gonzos* start to fade into a lump. After a protracted layoff, *Live at Gruene Hall* finds Walker in front of a friendly, fired-up audience—his natural habitat. Unfortunately, his subsequent Rykodisc albums lack that rowdy charge, as well as anything resembling memorable new material. For diehards only, but then all Walker fans are diehards by definition. — M.C.

JUNIOR WALKER AND THE ALL STARS

★ ★ ★ ★   **Shotgun (1965; Motown, 1989)**
★ ★ ★ ★   **Road Runner (1966; Motown 1989)**
★ ★ ★½ **Live! (1967; Motown, 1990)**
★ ★ ★ ★   **Greatest Hits (1967; Motown, 1991)**
★ ★ ★ ★½ **Anthology (Motown, 1974)**
★½ **Whopper Bopper Show Stopper (Soul, 1976)**
★½ **Smooth Soul (Soul, 1978)**
★ ★ ★ ★   **Superstar Series, Vol. 5 (Motown, 1981)**
★ ★ ★ ★   **Compact Command Performances (Motown, 1986)**

Whether it's Bobby Keys, David Sanborn or Clarence Clemons, every time a pop sax player starts to blow, it's hard not to hear echoes of Junior Walker. With his specialty being a passionate, sweet growl, he made great hard soul music in the mid-'60s; such fun cuts as "(I'm a) Road Runner," "Pucker Up Buttercup," "Hip City—Pts. 1 & 2" and his trademark "Shotgun," are now classics. He sang tough, too, with a scratchy, swinging delivery. The later work got swamped in glossy arrangements, but any of his best-of records still sounds tough. By now "Junior Walker" is a style in itself, one that Foreigner deployed excellently, on "Urgent," by getting the man himself to sit in. — P.E.

T-BONE WALKER

★ ★ ★ ★   **T-Bone Blues (1960; Atlantic, 1989)**
★ ★ ★   **I Want a Little Girl (Delmark, 1973)**
★ ★ ★ ★   **The Complete Recordings of T-Bone Walker, 1940–1954 (Mosaic, 1990)**
★ ★ ★ ★ ★ **The Complete Imperial Recordings, 1950–1954 (EMI, 1991)**

The one-string-at-a-time guitar solo pioneered by Lonnie Johnson and personalized by B.B. King had no greater proponent than Texas-born Aaron Thibeaux (T-Bone) Walker, whose influence ranges across the entire spectrum of American popular music since the 1930s. Walker began playing guitar at age 13; Leroy Carr and Scrapper Blackwell were early influences on him, but it was Lonnie Johnson and Blind Lemon Jefferson who held Walker in their sway. (Jefferson's visits to Dallas would find Walker leading him around the streets as he played for money.) In the late '20s he began touring with carnivals and medicine shows and supplemented his income by playing on street corners, at parties and at dances. His first recordings were made in 1929 for Columbia under the name Oak Cliff T-Bone, but they didn't sell, and Walker didn't record again for another decade. Work went on, though, as Walker toured throughout the southwest as a member of the Lawson Brook Band; when he left in 1935, he turned over his spot to Charlie Christian, who along with Walker and a few others would later pioneer the use of amplified guitars.

Walker's career moved into high gear when he joined Les Hite's band in the late '30s and recorded "T-Bone Blues," his first national hit. For the next 15 years Walker produced groundbreaking, often spectacular, always provocative blues, showcasing his fluid, emotional attack as well as his strong, personable singing voice. On these recordings, made for the Black & White (later acquired by and released on Capitol), Comet and Imperial labels, rests the legend of an important artist whose work continues to exert its influence. The Mosaic and EMI sets capture this critical body of work and provide extensive annotation and session information. Mosaic's six-CD set, available by mail order only, is somewhat muddy sounding, but does offer the big picture of Walker's most productive years. EMI's two-CD set focuses strictly on the Imperial years, but is no less essential or rewarding than the Mosaic set; also, EMI's remastering process has produced a clear, crisp sound that brings out all the subtleties of Walker's technique.

In three separate sessions over the years 1955–59 Walker cut 15 sides for Atlantic with producers Jerry Wexler, Ahmet Ertegun and Nesuhi Ertegun. Most of these, issued in 1960 as *T-Bone Blues*, are Walker compositions. *T-Bone Blues* led to Walker's rediscovery by young blues fans at the same time he was being acknowledged as an important jazz instrumentalist. Walker underscored his affinity for both musics on his final album, *I Want a Little Girl*, a swinging affair on which Walker gives his sound some air, compressing solos into a few well-chosen notes, and allowing the superb tenor-sax man Hal "Cornbread" Singer ample room for his own pertinent observations. The album's after-hours, small-club feel, heightened by Walker's relaxed singing, makes for pleasant listening.
— D.M.

FATS WALLER
    ★ ★ ★ **A Legendary Performer (RCA, 1978)**
★ ★ ★ ★ ★ **Fine Arabian Stuff (Muse, 1979)**
★ ★ ★ ★ ★ **Fats Waller in London (1979; Disques Swing, 1984)**
    ★ ★ ★ ★ **20 Golden Pieces of Fats Waller (Bulldog, 1981)**
★ ★ ★ ★ ★ **The Complete Fats Waller, Vol. 1 (Bluebird/RCA, 1981)**
★ ★ ★ ★ ★ **The Complete Fats Waller, Vol. 2 (Bluebird/RCA, 1981)**
★ ★ ★ ★ ★ **The Complete Fats Waller, Vol. 3 (Bluebird/RCA, 1981)**
★ ★ ★ ★ ★ **The Complete Fats Waller, Vol. 4 (Bluebird/RCA, 1987)**
    ★ ★ ★ ★ **The Joint is Jumpin' (Bluebird/RCA, 1988)**
★ ★ ★ ★ ★ **The Fats Waller Piano Solos: Turn on the Heat (Bluebird/RCA, 1991)**

What Memphis was to rock & roll, so was the Harlem of the '20s to jazz piano. James P. Johnson was the most important pianist to come out of the fertile upper Manhattan jazz scene. As the link between the formalism of ragtime and the friskiness of stride, Johnson found his style quickly emulated by Harlem pianists, who included Thomas "Fats" Waller. As Johnson was an incalculable influence on the young Waller, so does Waller show up in the styles of immortals who followed him, such as Count Basie, Art Tatum, Erroll Garner, Jaki Byard and Joe Turner, to name the most prominent. Time has only enhanced Waller's reputation as one of the greatest of all jazz pianists.

When he took up piano and organ in his early teens, Waller's passions were gospel music and ragtime. In 1920, at age 16, he was discovered by Johnson, who in short order became Waller's teacher and surrogate father. Two years later Waller began a recording career that was frantic and productive until his death at age 39 in 1943. In that time Waller not only became a musician much admired by his peers and the general public alike, but also proved himself an engaging entertainer whose popularity spread well beyond America's borders. And yet Waller's ebullient, fun-loving personality and gift for comedy were also his curse, for when he signed with RCA a clause in his contract required him to record songs provided by a staff A&R man. Invariably these proved to be novelty items intended to enhance Waller's image as a jovial, joking entertainer, with the music a secondary feature. That he constructed a legacy admired for its musical integrity is testimony to his genius.

Waller's repertoire wasn't entirely fed to him. He wrote a good deal of his own material. His elegant, yearning "Ain't Misbehavin' " (from the Broadway musical *Hot Chocolates*, written in part by Waller) is one of the best-loved songs in American popular music, but "Honeysuckle Rose," "The Joint Is Jumpin' " and "Your Feets Too Big" are hardly obscure. Waller's recordings were omnipresent on the pop charts from the time "Ain't Misbehavin' " landed in the Top Twenty in 1929 until his final charted single, "Your Socks Don't Match," reached the Top Thirty in 1943.

The four-volume *Complete Fats Waller* set is an obvious starting point for anyone interested in the broad sweep of Waller's artistry, although Volume IV concludes in 1936, leaving another seven years' worth of recordings for another, as-yet-unreleased volume. The two-CD set *The Fats Waller Piano Solos: Turn on the Heat* and *The Joint is Jumpin'* collect some of the later sides, along with a nice balance of well- and lesser-known Waller tracks. Waller alone at the piano is the focus, and the effect of journeying along on recordings dating from 1927 to 1941 is a capsule lesson in the evolution of stride piano.

Fine Arabian Stuff and *Fats Waller in London* fill in some of the gaps in the late-'30s releases, although neither album contains any of the Victor hits. What they do contain is even better: Waller on the pipe organ, his favorite instrument and one over which he exerted supreme mastery. *Fine Arabian Stuff* is from a single session recorded in 1939 and includes gospel, folk and turn-of-the-century popular songs. The *London* album is comprised of two sessions recorded nearly a year apart, in 1938 and 1939. Here the tune stack runs from original gems such as "Ain't Misbehavin' " (two versions), to organ instrumentals of four gospel songs, concluding with an ambitious suite of songs depicting Waller's musical impressions of six different London neighborhoods. There is so much to admire about Waller, and his work is of such consistent high quality, that picking out highlights becomes frustrating, and in the end impossible. Waller's entire career is a highlight, one of this century's grand moments in music. — D.M.

JOE WALSH

★★★ **Barnstorm (1972; Mobile Fidelity, 1990)**
★★★ **The Smoker You Drink, the Player You Get (MCA, 1973)**
★★★ **So What? (MCA, 1974)**
★★ **You Can't Argue With a Sick Mind—Live (MCA, 1976)**
★★★ **But Seriously, Folks . . . (Asylum, 1978)**
★★★½ **The Best of Joe Walsh (MCA, 1978)**
★★ **There Goes the Neighborhood (Asylum, 1981)**
★★ **The Confessor (Warner Bros., 1985)**
★★½ **Ordinary Average Guy (Epic, 1991)**

Calling his backup band Barnstorm, Joe Walsh pursued his folkie streak after leaving the James Gang in 1971. The Cleveland guitar hero didn't forswear his trademark stutter-funk riffs and searing slidework; he tempered the thick-stringed rave-ups with gentle country-rock. Not the strongest singer on the block, Walsh hangs his nasal voice on hooky riffs and an agreeably goony sense of humor. Agreeable at first, anyway. Walsh's breakthrough, *The Smoker You Drink, the Player You Get*, fully displays his rowdy charm and his acoustic-tinged sensitive side. "Rocky Mountain Way" sets a pastoral idyll amid the echoing roar of a primal power chord slam—metal mellow! Tracks like "Meadows" bolster their bucolic acoustic melodies with rippling electric choruses. *So What?* is probably a stronger album overall, though it lacks a classic-rock nugget like "Rocky Mountain Way." "Turn to Stone" comes close: Walsh weaves a droning, hypnotic bottleneck throughout the sure-footed beat. With vocal backups from various Eagles, easy-rocking tracks like "Help Me Through the Night" and "Time Out" foreshadow Walsh's next move. Recorded while Walsh was in the Eagles and sounding like it, *But Seriously Folks . . .* is where his jokey party-boy side starts to dominate. "Life's Been Good," which hit Number 12 in 1978, is either an exposé of the whole bloated rock-star image or a smug, nose-thumbing insult to the record-buying public. You decide.

Walsh's recording career has been extremely spotty ever since. *The Best of Joe Walsh* packs the catchiest early-'70s cuts with a couple of James Gang ringers: it's the only truly necessary Joe Walsh album. *You Can't Argue With a Sick Mind* is a snoozy, holding-pattern concert album. Out-of-print items like *You Bought It, You Name It* and *Got Any Gum?* are only worth searching for if the titles sound like the soul of wit to you. Walsh tries for a more sober, "adult" perspective on *Average Ordinary Guy*, but he seems out of touch. The title track and "I'm Actin' Different" strut Huey Lewis–style populist wisdom on weatherbeaten choruses. — M.C.

WAR

★★½ **War (1971; Rhino, 1992)**
★★★½ **All Day Music (1971; Rhino, 1992)**
★★★½ **The World Is a Ghetto (1972; Rhino, 1992)**
★★★½ **Deliver the Word (1973; Rhino, 1992)**
★★½ **War Live! (1974; Rhino, 1992)**
★★★ **Why Can't We Be Friends? (1975; Rhino, 1992)**
★★★★★ **War's Greatest Hits (United Artists, 1976)**
★★½ **Platinum Jazz (Blue Note, 1977)**
★★★ **Galaxy (United Artists, 1977)**

★ ★ ★ **The Best of War . . . and More**
(Avenue, 1987)

As soon as this Los Angeles–bred funk band shook free of Eric Burdon, it was in business. You can hear traces of War's jazzy dance groove on "Spill the Wine," its 1971 hit with the ex-Animal. The two acts parted ways after the unfortunately titled *The Black Man's Burdon*, and the band recorded *War*. With the release of *All Day Music*, War became an impeccable source of earth-moving singles. Lee Oskar's wide-ranging harmonica dances around chanted vocals, snazzy horn charts and a Latin-tinged bottom; War cuts its ominous rhythmic power with beguiling melodies. "All Day Music" displays the group's lush, seductive side, while the equally atmospheric "Slippin' Into Darkness" administers an unflinching shot of social realism.

War's exploratory impulses often lead from fusion into Muzak, making for inconsistent-at-best albums. The vocal highpoints outweigh the instrumental valleys on *The World Is a Ghetto* (title track, "Cisco Kid"), *Deliver the Word* ("Gypsy Man," "Me and Baby Brother") and the slightly sweeter *Why Can't We Be Friends?* (title track, "Low Rider"). But *War's Greatest Hits*, including "Summer," is a nonstop party platter with strong progressive undercurrents. Conversely, *The Best of War . . . and More* lacks key hits by the band and includes questionable new material and remixes, including a poorly edited version of "Spill the Wine." *Platinum Jazz* surveys War's jazz-fusion excursions—the group's Achilles' heel revealed. *Galaxy* softens and simplifies the tone. Like many preeminent funk bands, War seemed to be shaken by the rise of disco, unsure of how to proceed; the group drifted off into a sea of rudderless, MOR-friendly albums. However, hip-hop samplers and rappers are just starting to discover War's catchy and complex early '70s classics. Don't miss the originals, though; Rhino has recently reissued these hugely influential albums.
— M.C.

JENNIFER WARNES

★ ★ **The Best of Jennifer Warnes**
(Arista, 1982)
★ ★ ★½ **Famous Blue Raincoat (Cypress,**
1986)

Warnes is an interesting pop songstress with a warm voice and a delicate touch with lyrics. She probably belongs to another time, however, or at least would be better served by material from the great masters of American popular song than by contemporary writers with their ears tuned to commercial radio. While *Best of* contains two Top Twenty hits ("Right Time of the Night," from 1977, and "I Know a Heartache When I See One," from 1979), the most interesting performances and gutsiest lyrics are on Warnes's own "I'm Restless" and "Shot Through the Heart." *Famous Blue Raincoat*, a haunting collection of Leonard Cohen songs, was a step in the right direction—its moody ambience brought an element of intrigue to Warnes's music. — D.M.

WARRANT

★ ★ ★ **Dirty Rotten Filthy Stinking Rich**
(Columbia, 1988)
★ ★ ★ **Cherry Pie (Columbia, 1990)**

One reason these heavy metallers caught so much flack over their soft-porn "Cherry Pie" video clip is their music. "Cherry Pie" is a devilishly catchy slice of cartoon lust. Of course, a recipe that combines the essence of the Runaways' "Cherry Bomb," a heaping helping of Joan Jett's "I Love Rock 'N Roll" and a splash of Queen's "We Are the Champions" would be hard to botch. Warrant brings just the right touch of shamelessness to the proceedings, too: lead howler Jani Lane's horny chuckle-and-jive sends *Cherry Pie* completely over the top. As the market stipulates, Warrant deploys its raised-fist anthems alongside thunderous, turgid power ballads; you can sense Lane's total devastation on "I Saw Red" because he sings—rather than shrieks—the first and second choruses. Awesome. Nothing on Warrant's debut quite reaches the "Cherry Pie" level of mindless inspiration, though "So Damn Pretty (Should Be Against the Law)" and "Sometimes She Cries" contain satisfying elements of the group's later hits. Warrant is more fun than Winger, White Lion and Whitesnake combined—whatever that's worth. — M.C.

DIONNE WARWICK

★ ★ ★½ **Presenting Dionne Warwick**
(Scepter, 1962)
★ ★ ★½ **The Sensitive Sound of Dionne**
Warwick (Scepter, 1965)
★ ★ ★½ **Here I Am (Scepter, 1966)**
★ ★ ★ **Here Where There Is Love (Scepter,**
1967)
★ ★ ★ **The Windows of the World (Scepter,**
1967)
★ ★ ★ **On Stage and in the Movies**
(Scepter, 1968)
★ ★ ★½ **Dionne Warwick's Golden Hits,**
Part One (Scepter, 1968)
★ ★ ★ **Valley of the Dolls (Scepter, 1968)**

Dinah Washington • 749

★ ★ ★   Promises, Promises (Scepter, 1969)
★ ★ ★   Soulful (Scepter, 1969)
★ ★ ★   Dionne Warwick's Greatest Motion Picture Hits (Scepter, 1969)
★ ★ ★½ Dionne Warwick's Golden Hits, Part Two (Scepter, 1969)
★ ★ ★ ★ The Dionne Warwicke Story (Scepter, 1971)
★ ★ ★   Dionne (Warner Bros., 1972)
★ ★   Just Being Myself (Warner Bros., 1973)
★ ★ ★½ Then Came You (Warner Bros., 1975)
★ ★½ Track of the Cat (Warner Bros., 1975)
★ ★ ★   A Man and a Woman (Hot Buttered Soul, 1977)
★ ★½ Only Love Can Break a Heart (Musicorp, 1977)
★ ★½ Love at First Sight (Warner Bros., 1977)
★ ★½ Dionne (Arista, 1979)
★ ★½ No Night So Long (Arista, 1980)
★ ★ ★   Hot! Live and Otherwise (Arista, 1981)
★ ★ ★   Friends in Love (Arista, 1982)
★ ★ ★   Heartbreaker (Arista, 1982)
★ ★½ How Many Times Can We Say Goodbye (Arista, 1983)
★ ★ ★   Finder of Lost Loves (Arista, 1985)
★ ★ ★   Friends (Arista, 1985)
★ ★ ★   Reservations for Two (Arista, 1987)
★ ★ ★ ★ ★ The Dionne Warwick Collection/Her All Time Greatest Hits (Rhino, 1989)
★ ★ ★ ★ Hidden Gems (Rhino, 1992)

Starting out in the very early '60s with the Gospelaires—a quintet whose superabundance of talent included her aunt Cissy Houston, sister Dee Dee and their friend Doris Troy—Dionne Warwick caught the attention of composer Burt Bacharach. With Warwick, the ace songwriting team of Bacharach-David found their perfect vehicle, and the trio went on to make pop hits whose crafty complexity and disarming effervescence has rarely been equalled. Not only was Warwick's range astonishing, but her delivery—cool, swinging and unerring—was one of effortless grace. Particularly fetching in rendering David's busy, staccato lyrics, her voice projecting a sassy elegance. Beginning with *Presenting Dionne Warwick* and concluding with the live double-album *The Dionne Warwicke Story* (Warwick briefly added an *e* to her last name), the singer thrived; while contemporary R&B and rock audiences were chary of her music's classiness, its sleek arrangements and absolute lack of funk, she hit big on MOR radio, and the songs hold up extremely well. Almost all her '60s albums contain gems, and each of the 24 cuts on Rhino's *Her All Time Greatest Hits*—from "Walk on By," "Message to Michael" and "I Say a Little Prayer" to "Do You Know the Way to San Jose" and "Promises, Promises"—is a marvel of craft. For a reprise of her great stuff, turn to *Hidden Gems*, a gallery of exhumed Bacharach-David rarities.

After Bacharach-David's bitter split, Warwick floundered. She recovered slightly with "Then Came You," a 1975 duet with the Spinners that hit Number One, but her post-'60s output didn't live up to her glory days. Basically, Warwick never found material as strong as Bacharach-David's and, especially in the disco '70s, her particular finesse was out of style. Her Arista records have been slightly duet-crazed—she's been paired with Luther Vandross, Johnny Mathis, Barry Manilow and Stevie Wonder—and her distinctiveness has suffered. Calling in Barry Gibb for *Heartbreaker*—an album of slick love songs of the kind Gibb provided for Streisand's *Guilty* and, later, for Diana Ross's *Eaten Alive*—she managed a solid pop album in a more modern idiom, and none of her recent records has been embarrassing. The title track of *Friends* deserves mention as a commendable AIDS-research benefit song at a time when many musicians still hadn't contributed much to that cause. Still, Warwick remains a staggering talent in search of direction. — P.E.

DINAH WASHINGTON

★ ★ ★ ★ Dinah Jams (1954; EmArcy/Polygram, 1990)
★ ★ ★ ★ ★ In the Land of Hi-Fi (1956, EmArcy/Polygram)
★ ★ ★ The Bessie Smith Songbook (1958; EmArcy/Polygram, 1986)
★ ★ ★ What a Difference a Day Makes! (1959; Mercury, 1984)
★ ★ ★ ★ Dinah Washington's Greatest Hits (Mercury, 1963)
★ ★ ★ Dinah '63 (1963; Roulette Jazz, 1990)
★ ★ ★ ★ The Jazz Sides (EmArcy/Polygram, 1976)
★ ★ ★ ★ ★ A Slick Chick (On the Mellow Side) (EmArcy/Polygram, 1983)

★ ★ ★ **Dinah Washington Sings the Blues**
(Mercury, 1987)
★ ★ ★ ★ ★ **The Complete Dinah Washington**
on Mercury, Vol. 1 1946–1949
(Mercury, 1987)
★ ★ ★ ★ ★ **The Complete Dinah Washington**
on Mercury, Vol. 2 1950–1952
(Mercury, 1987)
★ ★ ★ ★ ★ **The Complete Dinah Washington**
on Mercury, Vol. 3 1952–1954
(Mercury, 1988)
★ ★ ★ ★ ★ **The Complete Dinah Washington**
on Mercury, Vol. 4 1954–1956
(Mercury, 1988)
★ ★ ★ ★ ★ **The Complete Dinah Washington**
on Mercury, Vol. 5 1956–1958
(Mercury, 1989)
★ ★ ★ ★ ★ **The Complete Dinah Washington**
on Mercury, Vol. 6 1958–1960
(Mercury, 1989)
★ ★ ★ ★ ★ **The Complete Dinah Washington**
on Mercury, Vol. 7 1961
(Mercury, 1989)
★ ★ ★ **Golden Classics (Collectables,**
NA)

It's almost enough to assert that the late
Dinah Washington was simply a great singer
who could handle everything from gospel to
pop, and leave it at that. But the immediacy
and emotional sweep of her vocals demand
more: how could a person come on so sassy
and tough one minute, so demure and
vulnerable the next? After you have
marveled at her extraordinary
technique—the three-octave alto voice, clear
and bright, working behind the beat,
heightening the tension; the final notes of a
lyric being bitten off sharply, giving her
reading a stylish twist; the precise phrasing,
sometimes taut, sometimes airy, in perfect
sync with the intended mood—you are left
with the heart that informs it. Dinah
Washington had a big heart and an appetite
for life lived hard.

Born Ruth Lee Jones in Tuscaloosa,
Alabama, she was raised singing in church
choirs, although her earliest vocal
inspirations were Bessie Smith and Ethel
Waters. By age 16 she was touring with
gospel legend Sallie Martin in Martin's
seminal female gospel group, the Sallie
Martin Colored Ladies Quartet. She quickly
set out to serve God and Mammon both,
though, developing a taste for men, alcohol
and nightlife. A year after joining Martin,
she began her professional career singing in
Chicago nightclubs, where she teamed up
with Fats Waller, then with Lionel
Hampton's band. Even at this stage she
drew attention for the assurance she brought

to ballads and blues songs, early evidence of
the versatility that was to mark her work in
succeeding years.

As reported by various biographers,
Washington's offstage exploits were
legendary. At last count she was reported to
have had nine husbands in her 39 years,
though how many of them were legally
betrothed to her remains in doubt. She had
a reputation for suffering hecklers during a
show, then meeting them afterward and
beating them up. Club owners who
attempted to shortchange Washington
learned what it was like to look down the
barrel of her pistol.

In 1945 Washington made her first
recordings, cutting a dozen mostly blues
sides for the Apollo label. Signed to
Mercury in 1946, she embarked on a 15-year
association that would produce some of the
most moving and memorable records made
by any singer of her era. Early on she was
dubbed the Queen of the Blues, and so it
was that in the late '40s and early '50s,
Washington was dominant on the R&B
charts. Also in the early '50s, Mercury
attempted to transform her into a pop artist
by broadening her repertoire (fine by
Washington, who once stated: "I can sing
anything. Anything at all.") to include pop
standards. White radio stations refused to
play the records, but that didn't stop
Washington from delivering some of the
classic pop albums of the '50s, one of which,
In the Land of Hi-Fi, remains in print in its
original configuration. A less successful
effort, *The Bessie Smith Songbook* (1958), at
least showed Washington in good form,
even if her accompanists were not quite
attuned to the her moods. Pop success came
at last in 1959 with a Top Ten single,
"What a Diff'rence a Day Makes."

Attempts to duplicate her 1959 success
failed. However, her best subsequent records
hearkened back to her roots in gospel and
blues instead of addressing a pop world that
quickly lost interest in her overproduced
ballads. In 1960 she returned to the pop
Top Ten via two duets with Brook Benton,
"Baby (You've Got What It Takes)" and
"A Rockin' Good Way (to Mess Around
and Fall in Love)." A 1963 album, *Back to
the Blues*, featured some of her most
possessed vocals; it turned out to be the last
album released in her lifetime.

Although some of her great '50s albums
are now out of print, the recordings
themselves remain available on Mercury's
awesome seven-volume *The Complete Dinah
Washington on Mercury* CD collection. This

represents everything Washington recorded for Mercury, including some newly discovered, previously unreleased tracks and some rare singles. The annotation is first-rate—each set contains a booklet describing Washington's life and work during the corresponding time frame and also includes complete lyrics to each song.

Those looking for lower-priced investments in the Washington oeuvre are directed to the self-explanatory *A Slick Chick (On the Mellow Side)* and *The Jazz Sides*, both titles containing nearly 90 minutes of music. The latter comes highly recommended, both for its 1955 Quincy Jones–arranged jam sessions and for the inclusion of Washington's only live recordings, two tracks from the 1958 Newport Jazz Festival. A 1954 album, *Dinah Jams*, documents a classic session teaming the singer with a band whose towering players include Clifford Brown, Clark Terry, Junior Mance and Max Roach. A quick listen to them jamming on Mercer-Arlen's "Come Rain or Come Shine" and Cole Porter's "I've Got You Under My Skin" will bring new appreciation for the depth of this material. Though death came too soon for Dinah Washington, her music lives on and grows richer in ways she could hardly have envisioned. — D.M.

WALTER "WOLFMAN" WASHINGTON
   ★ ★ ★ **Wolf Tracks (Rounder, 1987)**
   ★ ★ ★ **Out of the Dark (Rounder, 1988)**
   ★ ★ ★ ★ **Wolf at the Door (Rounder, 1991)**
When not sitting in with New Orleans' great soul singer Johnny Adams, Washington makes his own first-rate R&B. Heading up the Roadmasters, a tough six-man crew of nightclub vets, Washington plays guitar with some of the sting and crispness of Albert King—and he sings with a swinging, casual power. Chiefly because of the Doc Pomus–Dr. John ballad, "Hello Stranger," and the easiest, jazziest vocal performances Wolfman has mustered, *Wolf at the Door* is his strongest album—the brass arrangements, in particular, are stunning—but the man seems incapable of making music lacking in either kick or class.
   — P.E.

WAS (NOT WAS)
   ★ ★ ★ **Was (Not Was) (ZE/Island, 1981)**
   ★ ★ ★ **Born to Laugh at Tornadoes (ZE/Geffen, 1983)**
   ★ ★ ★ **What Up, Dog? (Chrysalis, 1988)**
   ★ ★ **Are You Okay? (Chrysalis, 1990)**

David (Weiss) Was and Don (Fagenson) Was have periodically released oddball and near-uncategorizable albums that are equal parts rock, funk, soul, and aural collage. In their more inspired moments—as on the cut "Tell Me That I'm Dreaming" from the duo's now-deleted 1981 debut LP, *Was (Not Was)*—they come off as politically incisive commentators; at too many other times their efforts sound vapid and smug. However, their loose confederation of musicians includes two outstanding vocalists in Sir Harry Bowens and, especially, Sweet Pea Atkinson. When these two get a solid number to work on, the results are often stirring. Check out the tender treatment Bowens gives "Somewhere in America There's a Street Named After My Dad" on *What Up, Dog?* On the same album, Atkinson burns mightily on "Spy in the House of Love" and roars with conviction on his cover of Otis Redding's "I Can't Turn You Loose." Otherwise, there's much silliness and several top-notch but inconsequential dance tunes to recommend the albums listed, which sound more like notes on a work in progress than fully realized visions. (Note: Don Was is now better known and justifiably celebrated for his sterling production work for Bonnie Raitt, the B-52's and others.) — D.M.

W.A.S.P.
   ½ ★ **W.A.S.P. (Capitol, 1984)**
   ½ ★ **The Last Command (Capitol, 1985)**
   ½ ★ **Live . . . in the Raw (Capitol, 1987)**
   ½ ★ **Inside the Electric Circus (Capitol, 1988)**
   ★ ½ **The Headless Children (Capitol, 1989)**
Having been replaced by 2 Live Crew as the PMRC's most bloodied whipping boys, W.A.S.P. no longer serves its marginally necessary political purpose, and we're left with Blackie Lawless and his music. Alice Cooper makeup and songs like "Ballcrusher," "Harder, Faster" and a slavish cover of Humble Pie's cover of Ashford & Simpson's "I Don't Need No Doctor" catch the drift—awful plod-metal of the sex-apocalypse school. *The Headless Children* is the group's "best"—"The Real Me" (from the Who's *Quadrophenia*) is neat, and, in "Forever Free," W.A.S.P. masters the gothic big ballad all metalheads employ when aping sincerity. — P.E.

THE WATERBOYS
   ★ ★ ★ ★ **The Waterboys (Chrysalis, 1983)**
   ★ ★ ★ **A Pagan Place (Chrysalis, 1984)**
   ★ ★ ★ ½ **This Is the Sea (Chrysalis, 1985)**

★★★½ **Fisherman's Blues (Chrysalis, 1988)**
★★★½ **Room to Roam (Chrysalis, 1991)**
★★★★ **The Best of the Waterboys (Chrysalis, 1991)**

With its arresting cover art—a photo of Sitting Bull and a pre-Raphaelite portrait of main man Mike Scott—the Waterboys' debut was immediately intriguing. Its contents were even more so. With surging acoustic guitars, hyperpoetic lyrics and the sinuous saxophone of Anthony Thistlethwaite, this was music of a high, obscure intensity, its mood recalling Van Morrison's *Astral Weeks* or the tortuous, lovely art songs of Tim Buckley. Plainly, Mike Scott was coming on like a visionary—in "December," he ambivalently celebrated Christ's incarnation; "It Should Have Been You" was a portait in bitterness of nearly the power of Dylan's "Positively Fourth Street"; "Savage Earth Heart" was a manifesto demanding the same sort of spiritual deliverance William Blake once entreated. A fusion of fanatic Celtic soul and rock power along the lines of early Patti Smith, the record sounded the arrival of a genuine, if idiosyncratic, artist.

"Church Not Made With Hands," "The Big Music," and the title track off *A Pagan Place* continued Scott's journey into the mystic. With "Red Army Blues," a strange, cinematic narrative about Stalinism, he broadened his writing, and with "Somebody Might Wave Back" and "All the Things She Gave Me" he tried out a new and affecting vernacular approach. A powerful record—some of the horn parts sound like Springsteen's arrangements—*Pagan* wasn't the breakthrough the first album was, but it was passionate enough. *This Is the Sea* was yet one more epic. "Spirit" was its ode to transcendence; "The Whole of the Moon" recalled the imagery and ideas of Nick Drake, albeit more fervently; Scott's saturation in myth came out clearly in "The Pan Within"; and the insistent piano riff of "Old England" was the most interesting musical touch. By now it was apparent that Scott's congenital posture was that of swooning—the lad was simply overcome by feeling, and only the most fevered listeners could keep up.

Taking a break from ecstasy, Scott then released *Fisherman's Blues*. The most likeable Waterboys album, it pairs the group with traditional Irish musicians, and offers the pleasures of Van Morrison's "Sweet Thing" and a poem by Yeats set to music by Scott. Rich and relaxed, it's very fine—but it lacks the overheated, Orphic power of Scott's earlier work. *Room to Roam* continues in the same vein, with less impressive songs. The 1991 best-of album showcases the Waterboys diverse catalogue.
— P.E.

ETHEL WATERS
★★★ **Ethel Waters' Greatest Years (Columbia, 1972)**
★★★★ **Ethel Waters on Stage and Screen 1925–40 (Columbia, 1989)**
★★★ **Miss Ethel Waters (Monmouth Evergreen, NA)**

Dignified and majestic, Ethel Waters surmounted a troubled childhood on the streets of a red-light district in Philadelphia—she was a petty thief, a gang leader at age 10, a wife at age 13, and a divorcée at age 14—to become the first black pop singer to gain widespread acceptance by black and white audiences alike. She parlayed her success as a singer into a long-standing career as an actress acclaimed for her work in Broadway plays and in movies, and in her later years appeared regularly in evangelist Billy Graham's Crusades. Shortly after her marriage failed, she found religion, and for the remainder of her life (she died in 1976 at age 80) her unwavering faith dictated her style and course of action. Apart from the sheer power of her voice, Waters eschewed any stylistic technique that might characterize her as a blues singer, blues being a music and a state of mind she had abandoned. Her diction was precise and crisp, unaccompanied by any grunts, shouts, purrs or other suggestive flourishes she associated with blues singers.

While her conservatism no doubt eased Waters's passage into white society, it didn't diminish her ability to move listeners of all races. Between 1921 and 1938 she cut 26 Top Forty singles, the earliest sides recorded with Fletcher Henderson, the later ones featuring Benny Goodman. Her biggest hit came in 1933, when her original and still definitive version of "Stormy Weather" remained Number One for three weeks. This followed by four years her first Number One, a mesmerizing rendition of "Am I Blue?" that topped the charts for two weeks. However accidental, she was a pioneer among black musical artists, and her success broadened the crossover opportunities for black artists in show business. Among Waters's most immediate beneficiaries would be Louis Armstrong, Billie Holiday and Lena Horne.

Her most famous movie role came in 1943, when she joined an all-black cast in director Vincente Minnelli's first movie, *Cabin in the Sky*. Teamed with Horne, Armstrong, Duke Ellington and others, Waters came on with two powerhouse performances, "Taking a Chance on Love" and "Happiness Is Just a Thing Called Joe." With the advent of television in the '50s, Waters became the first black actress to star in her own network series, *Beulah*, and she went on to appear in many of that decade's most popular dramatic shows. By then her most important work had already been done. In her later years she recorded some spiritual albums centered on the Southern gospel songs she favored in the Billy Graham crusades, but these are all out of print.

Ethel Waters On Stage and Screen contains cuts spanning from 1925 to 1940, and is the one essential disc here. Its songs include the original versions of "Stormy Weather," "Am I Blue" and "Taking a Chance on Love." *Ethel Waters' Greatest Years* collects material from the '30s, but also includes her 1925 hit single, "Sweet Georgia Brown." For a sampling of the live Ethel Waters, *Miss Ethel Waters* contains concert performances from the '50s, including a terrific version of "St. Louis Blues." The definitive Ethel Waters disc—which should include a sampling of her gospel years as well as the secular material—remains unissued and sorely needed. — D.M.

MUDDY WATERS

★★★★★ The Best of Muddy Waters (1958; Chess/MCA, 1987)
★★★★★ Muddy Waters at Newport, 1960 (1960; Chess/MCA, 1986)
★★★ Muddy Waters Sings Big Bill Broonzy (1960; Chess/MCA, 1986)
★★★★ Folk Singer (1964; Chess/MCA, 1987)
★★★★ Muddy Waters Sings Big Bill Broonzy/Folk Singer (1960, 1964; Chess/MCA, 1987)
★★★★★ Down on Stovall's Plantation (Testament, 1966)
★★★ The Real Folk Blues (1966; Chess/MCA, 1987)
★ Muddy, Brass and the Blues (1966; Chess/MCA, 1989)
★★★ More Real Folk Blues (1967; Chess/MCA, 1988)
★★★ Mud in Your Ear (1967; Muse, 1989)

★★★ Fathers and Sons (Chess, 1969)
★★★★ They Call Me Muddy Waters (1971; Chess/MCA, 1990)
★★★ The London Muddy Waters Sessions (1972; Chess/MCA, 1989)
★★★ Can't Get No Grindin' (1973; Chess/MCA, 1990)
★★ The Muddy Waters Woodstock Album (Chess, 1975)
★★★★ Hard Again (Blue Sky, 1977)
★★★½ I'm Ready (Blue Sky, 1978)
★★★★ Muddy "Mississippi" Waters Live (Blue Sky, 1979)
★★★★ King Bee (Blue Sky, 1981)
★★★½ Muddy & the Wolf (1982; Chess/MCA, 1986)
★★★½ Rolling Stone (1982; Chess/MCA, 1984)
★★ Sweet Home Chicago (Quicksilver/Intermedia, 1982)
★★★★ Rare and Unissued (1982; Chess/MCA, 1991)
★★★★★ Trouble No More (Singles, 1955–1959) (Chess/MCA, 1989)
★★★★★ The Chess Box (Chess/MCA, 1989)

Muddy Waters stands in a select group of American musical artists whose work altered the landscape, reaching across the years to mark everything that has come in its wake. It is well-known at this juncture how one of his songs, "Rollin' Stone," became the name of one of the most important rock bands in history, as well as an inspiration for what many consider Bob Dylan's finest song. His 1950s recordings for Chicago-based Chess Records transformed his native Delta blues into a music with widespread popular appeal both here and abroad, thereby laying a huge chunk of rock & roll's foundation. Waters also brought the blues into the modern age by giving it a new shape crafted via electric instruments and amplification, introduced a stop-time riff that has since become one of the most familiar sounds in blues and rock, and, unschooled though he was, brought historical dimension in eloquent lyrics rooted in the folklore and traditions of African-Americans. Moreover, musicians who played in Waters's bands always profited from his rigorous discipline, many of them going on to form their own bands and make important records.

At his death in 1983 Waters left behind a substantial body of recordings, many of which remain in print. Most indispensable, of course, are the Chess albums; what's remarkable, though, is that Waters was still going strong in the late '70s. It's impossible to point to one or two compilations and pronounce them definitive, although *The Chess Box* approaches such distinction. However, Waters is best appreciated by dipping into other titles apart from the *Box*.

Had Waters never made it out of the Delta, *Down on Stovall's Plantation* would show only the raw beginnings of an artist much admired in his own region, whose reputation for brewing the best moonshine whiskey in Coahoma County was on a par with his standing as a musician. Born McKinley Morganfield in 1915 in Rolling Fork, Mississippi, Waters grew up in Clarksdale, raised by his grandmother, who gave him the nickname Muddy. He was 17 when he started playing guitar. Taught by a friend, Waters was most influenced by Charley Patton, Son House and Robert Johnson; House, in particular, was the model for Waters's bottleneck guitar style. A neighbor owned a record player, as did Muddy's grandmother, and so he was exposed to Blind Lemon Jefferson, Lonnie Johnson, Tampa Red, Leroy Carr and other seminal blues artists, further broadening his musical vocabulary. In between "plowin' mules, choppin' cotton, and drawin' water," as he described his duties on Stovall Plantation, he began to make a name locally by converting his one-room log-cabin home into a juke joint on weekends and providing music, drink and gambling for the attending revelers.

Folklorist Alan Lomax, heading up a field recording team for the Library of Congress, came to Clarksdale in 1941 looking for Robert Johnson, unaware he had been dead for nearly three years. Told that the man on Stovall's played a lot like Johnson, Lomax went out to the plantation and recorded Waters performing two songs; a year later he came back and recorded more sides, some with Waters playing solo in a distinctly Johnson vein; some with Waters and a primitive string band, the Son Sims Four; some with Waters and Sims on twin guitars; some with Waters and guitarist Charles Berry. Thirteen sides in all, these recordings, cut in Waters's cabin, are raw, moving and suggestive of things to come. One of the 1941 tracks, "Country Blues, No. 1," is descended musically and lyrically from House's "My Black Mama" and Johnson's "Walkin' Blues." Thus a pattern emerged: Over the course of his career Waters would make frequent figurative forays back to the Delta for material, building new songs out of folk tales and fragments of choruses he had absorbed in his youth, adding new and sometimes bolder

lyrics to material otherwise decades old. As for thematic focus, Waters's songs were in the Delta tradition of brooding ruminations on death and faithless love, aptly summarized in titles such as "You're Gonna Miss Me When I'm Dead and Gone," "You Got to Take Sick and Die Some of These Days" and "Why Don't You Live So God Can Use You?" Vocally he displays mastery of the nuances of Delta blues singing, but while the stark authority of his voice is commanding, he's not yet the overpowering presence he would become a few years later after relocating to Chicago.

In 1943, Waters he packed his belongings in a suitcase and boarded the Illinois Central railroad, joining the mass exodus of black people out of Mississippi to greater opportunity in the north, in this case, Chicago. In the mid-'40s he got his first electric guitar and began working with various combinations of musicians headed by an older Delta-born bluesman, Sunnyland Slim. With Slim and bassist Big Crawford he recorded some unsuccessful sides for the Columbia and Aristocrat labels, the latter a Chicago-based label run by brothers Phil and Leonard Chess.

In 1948, Waters cut for Aristocrat two sides in the Delta bottleneck style, "I Can't Be Satisfied" b/w "(I Feel Like) Going Home," which sold rapidly in Chicago and in the South. By this time Waters was working the clubs with a band that included Claude Smith on guitar, Jimmy Rogers doubling on guitar and harmonica, Baby Face Leroy on guitar and drums, and Little Walter Jacobs also doubling on guitar and harmonica. This configuration, which later included Elgin Evans on drums, began recording in 1950 and developed the hard-driving sound of modern Chicago blues on "Louisiana Blues," "She Moves Me,""Honey Bee," "Still a Fool" and "Long Distance Call," all heard (along with the early Aristocrat sides) on disc one of the three-CD *Chess Box*. "Louisiana Blues" was a significant track in that it was Waters's first recording to feature the amplified harmonica of Little Walter and his first national R&B hit; it was also the single that established the Chess label, which had been formed in early 1950 after the Chess brothers bought out their partner in Aristocrat.

Leonard Chess was producing Waters in these days, and his lack of musical training worked in his and Waters's favor. Like Waters, Chess went on instinct and feel. He close-miked Waters's voice, so that it was bold and out front of the raging band; ditto for Little Walter's amplified harp, which was virtually a second voice, searing and ruthless. In 1954, bassist Willie Dixon, who had been playing sessions for Chess, penned three songs for Waters that became major R&B hits and, as subsequent years have shown, blues masterpieces—"Hoochie Coochie Man," "Just Make Love to Me," and "I'm Ready." In 1954, pianist Otis Spann and drummer Francis Clay (replacing Elgin Evans) joined Waters, and the band developed such rhythmic innovations as stop-time patterns and driving backbeat, which were quickly emulated by other artists. Disc one and the first half of disc two in *The Chess Box* document the groundbreaking period from 1947 through 1956 and demonstrate most emphatically Waters's growing confidence in his artistry. He was surrounded by great musicians, and in Dixon and Chess he had the support and advice of two studio-smart, blues-wise artist-technicians who understood where this music was headed and knew how to get it there.

Come 1956 (and the second half of the *Chess Box*'s second disc), Waters's band was undergoing change. Late in the year Little Walter left to form his own band, and was replaced by James Cotton; in early '57 Rogers left and was replaced by Pat Hare. This combination proved even more incendiary than Waters's first band. These late-'50s sides, as critic Robert Palmer notes in his essay accompanying the box set, represent Waters's most explicit use of gospel vocal techniques that had then become a common element of both Ray Charles's and Sam Cooke's work. Check out "Evil," "Diamonds at Your Feet," "Take the Bitter with the Sweet," and particularly "Good News" for examples of how Waters brought gospel-derived elements into the secular world of the blues.

In 1958, Waters and Spann toured England with great success, which led to a booking at the Newport Jazz Festival of 1960. The live album from that date, *Muddy Waters at Newport, 1960*, was a substantial hit in England, where it had enormous impact on the then-emerging generation of young white blues musicians. That album remains available and should be heard, if only for the sake of Pat Hare's revelatory guitar work. It is Waters's work to this point, sealed by the Newport album, that so inflamed the young musicians who formed the Rolling Stones, the Animals and the Yardbirds.

The early '60s brought new personnel into the band, including guitarists Buddy Guy,

Sammy Lawhorn and Pee Wee Madison and drummers Willie Smith and S. P. Leary. It was a time of experiments, with Waters cutting an album on which horns were later overdubbed (to mediocre effect), *Muddy, Brass and the Blues. The London Muddy Waters Sessions* united Waters with some of his British acolytes (Georgie Fame, pre–Blind Faith Rick Grech, pre-Hendrix Mitch Mitchell). In 1969, a group of young American blues artists got together with Waters for their own salute to the master on the *Fathers and Sons* album. Two alternate takes from that album are featured on disc three of the *Chess Box*, with Waters and Spann accompanied by Paul Butterfield, Michael Bloomfield, "Duck" Dunn, and Phil Upchurch, among others.

Other titles offer fascinating glimpses into aspects of Waters's artistry. *Folk Singer* is a return to the Delta blues, an all-acoustic session with Waters and Buddy Guy on guitars and Willie Dixon on bass. *The Best of Muddy Waters* is an excellent sampling of early tracks from 1948 ("I Can't Be Satisfied") through 1954, including the most crucial of the 1951–54 sides. *Rare and Unissued* is recommended as an adjunct to *The Chess Box*, as most of its sides cannot be found elsewhere. Beware the cassette version, though: It has no liner information. *Mud in Your Ear* is one of the best recordings from the late-'60s band, with the underrated Lawhorn and Spann in notably fine fettle throughout. Despite the presence of the Band's Levon Helm and Garth Hudson, plus Paul Butterfield, Waters's final Chess album, *The Muddy Waters Woodstock Album*, released in 1975, is an uninspired effort, with the musicians trudging through their paces and Waters straining to get something out of half-baked material. *Sweet Home Chicago* contains some of the early-'50s tracks available elsewhere, as well as the rare "Goin' Home," a blues done gospel style, with Waters backed by a female chorus. *Muddy & the Wolf* is a compilation of tracks from the Waters and Howlin' Wolf *London Sessions* albums.

After the disappointment of the Woodstock album, Waters came back two years later, with Johnny Winter providing the sensitive production touch otherwise lacking on his early-'70s recordings. Old hands James Cotton and Bob Margolin, among others, are back on board; Jimmy Rogers shows up for *I'm Ready*, as does Walter Horton. Each of these albums comes recommended: Waters is fully in command again, inspired and roaring as the players fall under his spell. The live album demonstrates what everyone who saw Waters in the late '70s learned: On any given night the man could cut any other artist who stepped on the stage. The version of "Mannish Boy" on *Muddy "Mississippi" Waters Live* starts slow and grinds its way to an explosive climax with Waters and Winter pushing each other to greater emotional peaks. *King Bee* is a fitting final testament, with Waters mixing in some stirring originals ("Too Young to Know," "Sad Sad Day") with covers of Slim Harpo's "I'm a King Bee" and Arthur Crudup's "Mean Old Frisco Blues." The cover photo shows Waters smiling benignly, sitting comfortably in an ornate chair that is topped by a king's crown, which rests right above Waters's head. It looks like a good fit. — D.M.

ROGER WATERS

★ ★ **The Pros and Cons of Hitchhiking (Columbia, 1984)**
★ ★ ★ **Radio KAOS (Columbia, 1987)**
★ ★ **The Wall—Live in Berlin (Mercury, 1990)**

Bassist Roger Waters left Pink Floyd in 1983, taking his concepts and lead vocals along with him. Assembling a weighty studio crew for his first solo venture, Waters ponders *The Pros and Cons of Hitchhiking*. Eric Clapton drips rivulets of blues guitar in between the floating story segments, somewhat incongruously, but Waters's wandering tale doesn't amount to much without a tune or three to hang it on. And even the full-blown chorus on the climactic title track can't quite pull that out of hot air. *Radio KAOS* is a more sucessful attempt at constructing an art-rock-enhanced narrative. Resolutely unswinging rhythms and mellow voice-overs from archetypal FM DJ Jim Ladd enhance Waters's depiction of a wheelchair-bound computer genius: a saintly hacker and phone freak who zaps the nuclear "Powers That Be." Despite the stiffened beat and occasional horn lines, *Radio KAOS* sounds exactly like a transmission from another time. That's a large part of its appeal, too. Waters commemorated the fall of communism by re-creating Pink Floyd's 1979 concept rock opus at Berlin's Wall with an all-star cast: Bryan Adams, Joni Mitchell, Cyndi Lauper, Sinéad O'Connor and the Scorpions all joined in the fun. — M.C.

JODY WATLEY

★ ★ ★½ **Jody Watley (MCA, 1987)**
★ ★ ★ **Larger Than Life (MCA, 1989)**
★ ★ ★ **Affairs of the Heart (MCA, 1991)**

Jody Watley got tagged with Janet Jackson comparisons when her dancey debut album went megaplatinum; frankly, she deserves better. The former Shalamar member and *Soul Train* dancer may not be a virtuoso singer, but she has the power to cast spells over a walloping electronic beat. Producer André Cymone lays down a glossy Minneapolis funk-strut on Watley's breakthrough single, "Looking for a New Love." Chic-man Bernard Edwards provides a more human pulse on the next Top Ten hit, "Don't You Want Me." The album balances its hard core of Princely electro-boogie (Cymone) with some slightly rock-tinged songs (Edwards). "Learn to Say No," the album-closing duet with George Michael, even approaches a certain level of steaminess.

Despite its title, *Larger Than Life* is pretty much a run-of-the-mill dance-pop package. "Real Love" turned out to be a successful sequel to "Looking for a New Love," though the ballad "Everything" offers a more vivid picture of Watley's talents. On *Affairs of the Heart*, she strives to broaden those parameters, an admirable effort that yields mixed results. "Commitment of Love" and "It All Begins With You" enroll Watley in the Whitney Houston school of slo-mo emoting—not exactly her ideal career path. And "I'm the One You Need" gets overwhelmed by its own house-music blur. However, the cuts produced by Cymone place Watley back on comfortably funky, mid-tempo ground. — M.C.

WEATHER REPORT

★ ★ ★ **Weather Report (Columbia, 1971)**
★ ★ ★ **I Sing the Body Electric (Columbia, 1972)**
★ ★ ★½ **Mysterious Traveller (Columbia, 1974)**
★ ★ ★ **Black Market (Columbia, 1976)**
★ ★ ★ **Heavy Weather (Columbia, 1977)**
★ ★½ **Mr. Gone (Columbia, 1978)**
★ ★ **Night Passages (Columbia, 1980)**

Weather Report was one of several fusion groups that spun off from the epochal 1969 sessions for Miles Davis's jazz-rock landmark *Bitches Brew*. Saxophonist Wayne Shorter had been a key player in the groundbreaking Davis Quintet of the '60s, while keyboardist Joe Zawinul made his mark on Davis's *In a Silent Way*, the hauntingly sparse precursor to the volcanic *Bitches Brew*. The earliest Weather Report albums resemble a somewhat cleaner, guitarless version of Davis's electro-cosmic funkadelic sprawl; Zawinul's layered synth textures and skeletal electric piano lines are tangled around Shorter's floating soprano and all manner of exotic percussion. There are moments of drama and beauty on *Weather Report* and *I Sing the Body Electric*, but both albums suffer from a distracting lack of thematic structure—and memorable tunes. This is especially disappointing when you consider Shorter's pedigree as a composer as well as player. Recruiting funk bassist Alphonso Johnson, Weather Report anchors *Mysterious Traveller* in a firm, bottom-heavy groove. Direct and accessible, it also features the group's sharpest, most adventuruous ensemble playing on record. Not its catchiest, however. That comes with the advent of bassist Jaco Pastorius on the 1977 commercial breakthrough *Heavy Weather*; his crowd-pleasing virtuoso style—flashy finger-pops and fluid progessions—serves as the hook; insidious melodic snippets like the instrumental hit "Birdland" provide the bait. Though Weather Report continued successfully in this languid showboating mode for several years, its simplified approach reduced the subsequent albums to accomplished background music: proto–New Age atmospherics for the discerning listener. — M.C.

THE WEAVERS

* ★ ★ ★ ★ **The Weavers at Carnegie Hall (1961; Vanguard, 1988)**
* ★ ★ ★ **Reunion at Carnegie Hall, 1963 (1963; Vanguard, 1987)**
* ★ ★ ★ ★ **The Weavers at Carnegie Hall, Vol. 2 (Vanguard, 1963)**
* ★ ★ ★ ★ ★ **The Weavers' Greatest Hits (1971; Vanguard, 1986)**
* ★ **The Best of the Weavers (MCA, 1983)**
* ★ ★ ★ ★ **The Weavers on Tour (Vanguard, 1985)**
* ★ ★ ★ ★ **Weavers Classics (Vanguard, 1987)**
* ★ ★ ★ **Reunion at Carnegie Hall, Part 2 (Vanguard, 1987)**

The Weavers would have recoiled at being termed a great American institution, but that they were, in the best sense of the word. It honors their restless quest to find and to write songs that spoke to our common humanity; to recover songs from antiquity that had wisdom relevant to contemporary issues; to fulfill the purpose they described in Weavers' Lee Hays and Pete Seeger's beloved song, "If I Had a Hammer"—"sing about danger, sing about a warning, sing about love between all of my brothers all over this land."

The spiritual center of the folk revival of the '50s and '60s, the Weavers—Hays, Seeger,

Ronnie Gilbert, Fred Hellerman—came together on an informal basis in 1948, singing in Seeger's Greenwich Village apartment and eventually making appearances in neighborhood clubs and on New York City radio shows. Seeger and Hays had formed the Almanac Singers in the '40s, and both had been involved in People's Songs, an organization dedicated to using folk songs to help labor unions and activist groups achieve political goals. Their history took an unfortunate turn in 1952 when they were blacklisted after an FBI informant testified at the McCarthy hearings that the Weavers were Communists. Though unproven, the accusation forced the quartet to disband. Three years later they reassembled for what proved to be a triumphant Christmas concert at Carnegie Hall, captured on the essential *The Weavers at Carnegie Hall* disc.

The individual members' varied interests in other cultures and song forms produced a repertoire of wide scope and breathtaking depth, encompassing traditional American tunes and a great number of international folk songs. So Woody Guthrie's "Reuben James," a ballad about the first American ship sunk by Nazi submarines, might follow Blind Blake's "Run, Come, See Jerusalem," and then by the Indonesian folk song "Suliram," or an African chant, "Wimoweh," or a sprightly Israeli tale, "Tzena, Tzena." Appropriately enough, the Weavers didn't dazzle with the quality of their voices: they were fairly plainspoken people, and their harmonies were sometimes ragged. What they were blessed with was infectious spirit and absolute dedication to the integrity of their material. Hence the one star for MCA's *The Best of the Weavers*, wherein we find that someone has tried to turn them into a pop vocal group.

Apart from the MCA album, all the remaining in-print Weavers albums are concert recordings, which show the group at its best. The reunion albums find the original quartet expanded to include Erik Darling, Bernie Krause and Frank Hamilton, all of whom had been Weavers at various times; this lineup is somewhat unwieldy, but the result remains satisfactory. Whether they number four or seven, the Weavers offer music of dignity and purpose that reaches across the years to touch hearts and move souls. — D.M.

BOB WEIR

* ★ ★ ★ **Ace (1972; Grateful Dead, 1988)**
* ★ ★ ★ **Heaven Help the Fool (1978; Arista, 1988)**

★ ★ ★½ **Bobby and the Midnights (1981; Arista, 1988)**

Rhythm guitarist and singer for the Grateful Dead, Weir doesn't stray far from that band's sound and spirit on his debut, *Ace*. His bandmates provide backup, and the record is smooth, clean and unsurprising. Undercut by Keith Olsen's overglossy production and the busy drumming of Nigel Olsen and Mike Baird, *Heaven Help the Fool* is more distinctive, but it's a weaker album. In very clear voice, and deftly assisted by session vet Waddy Wachtel on guitar, Weir delivers accomplished midtempo numbers—some so slick, and burdened with a backup choir, that they verge on passages of high-end MOR. Much tougher, *Bobby and the Midnights* joins Weir with the late Dead keyboardist Brent Mydland and jazz drummer Billy Cobham. The highlights from Weir's best set include the reggae-ish "Book of Rules," the graceful "Carry Me," and a neat, bluesy shuffle, "Josephine." — P.E.

KITTY WELLS

★ ★ ★ **Dust on the Bible (MCA, 1959)**
★ ★ ★ **The Kitty Wells Story (1963; MCA, 1982)**
★ ★ **Greatest Hits (MCA, 1968)**
★ ★ ★ ★ **The Golden Years (MCA, 1982; Rounder, 1988)**
★ ★ ★ ★ ★ **Country Music Hall of Fame Series (MCA, 1991)**

Other women had preceded her in country music, and a few—one thinks of Mother Maybelle Carter, primarily—even made a difference; but when Kitty Wells cut an answer record to Hank Thompson's "The Wild Side of Life" and dared to advance a distinctively female point of view regarding the real villain in the cheating game, she was mapping virgin territory. Even if she had retired after releasing "It Wasn't God Who Made Honky Tonk Angels" in 1952, she would be remembered today as a trailblazer. Wells never made another record as important as that first one, but rarely did she cut a bad record either—songs such as "Making Believe," "I Heard the Jukebox Playing" and "Dust on the Bible" remain immensely satisfying. Wells's voice was a limited but powerful instrument, less expressive than, say, Patsy Cline's, but in its simple, unadorned state well able to drive home the hurt so explicit in the material Wells sang. Wells's prototype was emulated by Loretta Lynn, Wanda Jackson, Patsy Cline and every other strong-willed female country singer.

The Country Music Hall of Fame series album is the most accurate representation of Wells's development as an artist, since it includes the original recordings of many of her hits as well as slicker productions from the '60s. In particular, the early tracks have Wells backed with a basic lineup of rhythm guitars, bass, steel guitar and fiddle, which lends a stark, mesmerizing quality to these tales of deception and adulterous treachery. *The Kitty Wells Story* is likewise a wonderful survey of Wells's oeuvre, but these are re-recordings that find Wells fully embracing the Nashville Sound, with strings and vocal choruses supplanting the basic band as the dominant texture. Purists will opt for the former release, but both are deeply satisfying (*Story* has 24 cuts to the CMHF's 16, but the latter is extensively annotated, for those who care about such things).

Rounder's *The Golden Years* is an interesting addendum to the Wells catalogue. Its dozen cuts include duets with Red Foley, Roy Acuff, Webb Pierce and Johnnie & Jack (Johnnie Wright being Wells's husband and musical mentor) and feature Wells fronting the small combo that provided such sympathetic accompaniment on her early sessions. Covering the years 1953 to 1958, this album helps fill in the picture of Wells's formative years. *Greatest Hits* has been rendered superfluous over time; *Dust on the Bible* is a stirring collection of gospel numbers. — D.M.

MARY WELLS

★ ★ ★ **Bye Bye Baby (Motown, 1961)**
★ ★ ★ **The One Who Really Loves You (Motown, 1962)**
★ ★ ★ **Two Lovers (1962; Motown, 1991)**
★ ★ ★ ★ **Mary Wells' Greatest Hits (Motown, 1964)**
★ ★ ★½ **Together (with Marvin Gaye) (Motown, 1964)**
★ ★ ★ **My Guy (1964; Motown, 1991)**
★ ★ ★ ★ **Compact Command Performance (Motown, 1986)**
★ ★ ★½ **Bye Bye Baby/The One Who Really Loves You (Motown, 1987)**
★ ★ ★½ **Greatest Hits (Motown, 1987)**
★ ★ ★ **Mary Wells (Quality, 1990)**

Motown's reigning diva until the arrival of Diana Ross, Mary Wells began making hits at 16 with "Bye Bye Baby," which she wrote herself, and went on to release a stirring round of singles, generally co-written with the label's in-house genius, Smokey Robinson. Her light, airy approach stamped her as more of a '50s-style doo-wopper

than a soul singer, and her trademark songs—"My Guy," "You Beat Me to the Punch," "The One Who Really Loves You" —were more snappy than fervent. With Marvin Gaye, however ("What's the Matter With You Baby," "Once Upon a Time"), she swung with more confidence. Holland-Dozier-Holland produced her one exceptional go-for-broke number, "You Lost the Sweetest Boy," and it remains a fine treatise on agonized romance. The 22 cuts on *Compact Command Performance* cover the essential Wells; the 1990 comeback, *Mary Wells*, is respectable.
— P.E.

WENDY AND LISA

★ ★ ★½ **Wendy and Lisa (Columbia, 1987)**
★ ★ ★   **Fruit at the Bottom (Columbia, 1989)**
★ ★ ★½ **Eroica (Virgin, 1990)**

Perhaps the two best-known alumnae of the Revolution, Prince's *Purple Rain*–era band, Wendy Melvoin and Lisa Coleman specialize in a sort of soul psychedelia that may be too low-key for the Top Forty, but is generally rich enough to reward close listening. *Wendy and Lisa* finds the duo playing nearly all of the instruments (Wendy's brother Jonathan drums on some tracks, and Tom Scott sits in for an instrumental), and ranges from the dreamy dance pulse of "Honeymoon Express" to the Joni Mitchell–like quiet of "The Life."

With the quirky and ambitious *Fruit at the Bottom*, Wendy and Lisa become a full band (among the new members is Wendy's sister Susannah, who had been in the Family before this). On a textural level, the songs are fascinating, with rich, interlocking layers of vocals and instruments on songs like the Princely "Lolly Lolly" or the slippery "Everyday," though the melodies rarely sparkle. Fortunately, that's not a problem with *Eroica*, which is as aurally interesting as *Fruit* but much more tuneful, from the insinuating soul whisper of "Rainbow Lake" to the acid overtones and Eastern undercurrents of "Why Wait for Heaven." — J.D.C.

WET WILLIE

★ ★ ★ ★ **Greatest Hits (1977; Polydor, 1988)**

If this is Southern rock, where are the guitar solos? Wet Willie mines the soulful side of the South's musical heritage—territory ignored by many of the band's jam-happy Capricorn labelmates. Actually, guitarist Ricky Hirsch unfurls a burner on "Dixie Rock," but most of the time he carves out chunky chord patterns behind lead singer Jimmy Hall's straightforward R&B shouting. *Greatest Hits* saves ten jumpin' tracks from oblivion, drawing from seven deleted Capricorn albums. The closest thing to a big hit here is the hopeful shuffle "Keep On Smilin'," a pleasing Top Ten single in 1974. Wet Willie doesn't overwhelm you with original ideas (as the Allmans and Skynyrd often do), but the players' tight grasp always feels comfortable—whether they're flash-frying covers of Otis Redding ("Shout Bamalama") and Little Milton ("Grits Ain't Groceries") or simmering a jazz-flavored pop song ("Everything That'cha Do") in its own juices. Ricky Hirsch left the band after the 1977 album *Left Coast Live*. The deleted Epic album *Manorisms* offers a far more enticing view of Wet Willie's final period than the bland, over-produced last album, *Which One's Willie* (also deleted). The fluid, funky combo groove captured on *Greatest Hits* provides the answer to that query. — M.C.

WHAM!

★ ★   **Fantastic (Columbia, 1983)**
★ ★ ★½ **Make It Big (Columbia, 1984)**
★ ★ ★   **Music From the Edge of Heaven (Columbia, 1986)**

An instant U.K. success in 1983, Wham! (the music) provided nearly superfluous aural backgrounding for Wham! (the pinups). Both were delivered by two twee haircut wonders, the greyhound-elegant Andrew Ridgeley and a drippy Adonis named George Michael (formerly Georgios Panayiotou). *Fantastic* was mainly high-gloss, forgettable dance pop, but "Bad Boys" was a witty anthem for preening brats, and "Young Guns (Go for It!)" flourished a social conscience of a kind; it warned its teen audience against premature wedlock. With Michael sighing breathily, the record heralded the arrival of a postmodern Tom Jones. Much snappier, *Make It Big* found the lads discovering melody. "Freedom" was great fluff, its arch, baroque chord changes putting it in the league of Abba's orchestral efforts (or the Toys' "I Hear a Symphony"). "Credit Card Baby" summed up yuppie romance; "Everything She Wants" and "Careless Whisper" were oily, massage-parlor ballads that suggested that Wham! had the hubris not to let Prince go it alone on that turf. "Wake Me Up Before You Go Go," the album's big single, was silliness at its almost transcendent extreme.

With *Music From the Edge of Heaven*,

maturity began infecting the boys. Hip-hopping into trendy significance and claiming, on "Wham! Rap '86," to possess "street credibility" (!), they released a record whose "Hot Side" featured a funny slap at answering machines ("Battlestations"), and whose "Cool Side" had Michael wailing with real loveliness ("A Different Corner"). But a lot of Wham!'s cotton-candy appeal was M.I.A. Michael wrote and played most everything on the album, preparing himself for his solo career and the vault into seriousness that beckoned just around the corner. — P.E.

THE WHISPERS
★ ★ ★ **More of the Night (Solar/Capitol, 1990)**

Borrowing a little from Prince, a lot from Luther Vandross and Al B. Sure, and nodding toward classic Philly soul of the Gamble-Huff variety, the veteran Whispers wrap the urgent lead vocals of Leaveil Degree and the smooth-as-silk background provided by his four cohorts around a bevy of drum programs and electronic noodlings to come up with a sound that's correct for the New Jack '90s. However fevered the singing, though, the material is a bit on the bland side, and hardly up to the more classic soul stylings on some of the group's late-'70s albums. This Capitol-distributed album is the Whispers' only Solar title remaining in print, but *Best of the Whispers* (1982) is worth searching out as a first-rate example of '70s group soul, Los Angeles variety. — D.M.

BARRY WHITE
★ ★ ★ ★½ **Greatest Hits, Volume 1 (Polygram, 1975)**
★ ★ ★½ **Greatest Hits, Volume 2 (Polygram, 1981)**
★ ★ ½ **The Man Is Back (A&M, 1988)**
★ ★ ½ **The Right Night (A&M, 1989)**
★ ★ ★½ **Put Me in Your Mix (A&M, 1991)**

The image of Barry White at his peak remains indelible: The Man himself, looming over his gold grand piano, decked out in tux, tails and cape, flanked by the full Love Unlimited Orchestra—who could forget those female back-up singers, statuesque doesn't even begin to . . . too much, *whew*, you givin' your love to me babe is just too much. White revels in excess, no question about that. But he also made some of the sharpest, most satisfying music of the disco era. Behind his velvet bedroom raps and penchant for lush orchestration, White

wields the sure, steady hand of a naturally gifted musican. His arrangements are lean and rhythmically compelling, while his melodies are simply put and consistent. White picked up on the innovations of the Philly Sound producers, applying his own outrageous pleasure principle to their meticulous studio-soul blueprints. Of course, the fact that most Barry White songs revolve around sex—offering "hands on" experience and play-by-play commentary at times—may have something to do with the platinum success of *Greatest Hits, Volume 1*. He's not Al Green, but his crushed velvet baritone rumbles through seduction preambles ("You're the First, the Last, My Everything") and straight ballads ("I've Got So Much to Give") with equal aplomb. Overkill isn't his style; not even on "Love Serenade," all seven heavy-breathing minutes of it. This prolonged slow-motion stab of audio erotica makes Prince's *Dirty Mind* sound like bathroom graffiti.

Greatest Hits, Volume 2 doesn't document a decline so much as a leveling off; the late-'70s disco boom that *Volume 1* helped inspire soon rendered White's approach hopelessly square. As the almighty Beat came to dominate dance music, White kept right on doin' it, impeccably: "It's Ecstasy When You Lay Down Next to Me," because "Your Sweetness Is My Weakness," so turn out the lights and "Let the Music Play." After an extended break, White reemerged just as a new strain of dance music—rap—began to reach mainstream audiences. On *Put Me in Your Mix*, Barry White laces the title track with his signature strings and soulful moans. "I'll make your toenails curl," he declares and then proceeds to do so. In general, though, the A&M albums occupy an uncertain position between old and new, as though White couldn't decide whether to preserve or update his signature sound. — M.C.

BUKKA WHITE
★ ★ ★ ★ **Sky Songs (1963; Arhoolie, 1990)**
★ ★ ★ ★ **Legacy of the Blues: Bukka White (GNP/Crescendo, 1976)**

Born just west of the Mississippi Delta, inspired by the towering Charley Patton, bedeviled by the hard times and the misfortunes that often greet men of limited means (he served time in Mississippi's notorious Parchman Farm prison for shooting another man), Booker T. Washington White's sparse musical legacy cannot diminish the power and authority of the man's alternately tormented and ebullient view of the world as expressed in his songs. The GNP/Crescendo *Legacy of the Blues* is a definitive personal statement straight from the Delta, and its darkest moments play like a deep, disturbing cry of the soul. Recorded in 1963 in Memphis by blues enthusiasts Ed Denson and John Fahey (yes, the guitar virtuoso), who had succeeded in tracking down the then-forgotten White in his hometown of Aberdeen, Mississippi, this group of 11 songs marked White's first recordings in 24 years; and as Samuel Charters observes accurately in his liner notes, White sings like a man who'd been bottling up nearly two-and-a-half decades of pain and abuse. Following this, White went on to work steadily as a musician before appreciative audiences until his death in 1977. *Legacy* finds White delivering a number of songs he had recorded years earlier, but the textures in his voice and the ornamentation in his percussive slide guitar style had deepened, becoming richer, and certainly sadder. To hear his lamentations in "Baby Please Don't Go," "Parchman Farm Blues" and "Poor Boy a Long Ways From Home," is to hear a man with hellhounds on his trail. This is a stirring, important document.

The 60-plus minutes of music contained in seven lengthy story-songs on Arhoolie's *Sky Songs* are vintage examples of White's ability at improvisation, both oral and instrumental. On two cuts, "Bald Eagle Train" and "Alabama Blues," White's propulsive slide guitar is buttressed by his buddy Big Willie Wayne's go-for-broke support on washboard. These songs have a looser, more upbeat feel than the more probing material on *Legacy of the Blues* and reveal White's gift for striking imagery and powerful storytelling. — D.M.

KARYN WHITE
★★½ **Karyn White (Warner Bros., 1988)**
★★½ **Ritual of Love (Warner Bros., 1991)**
An accomplished studio backing voice, Karyn White slid into the dance-floor spotlight with a 1988 solo debut. "The Way That You Love Me" fared quite well in the post-Madonna sweepstakes; compared to Paula Abdul's efforts, say, White's breakthrough hit evinces soul and a modicum of personality. Unsurprisingly, the rest of her album falls short of that. *Ritual of Love* sounds brighter. Producers Jimmy Jam and Terry Lewis splash around synthesized color patterns and solid beats, filling the space around White's somewhat washed-out entreaties and regrets. Shifting

producers for several cuts near the end of the album, White makes a regrettable—and revealing—move toward showtune-style bombast. Madonna emulation has its pleasant side-effects, but one Whitney Houston is plenty. — M.C.

WHITE LION
★★★ **Fight to Survive (Grand Slamm, 1985)**
★★½ **Pride (Atlantic, 1987)**
★★★★ **Big Game (Atlantic, 1989)**
★★★½ **Mane Attraction (Atlantic, 1991)**
White Lion, Whitesnake, Great White—is it any wonder today's heavy-metal fans look so confused? Remembering which of these bands is which must be a full-time occupation. Here's the trick: Whitesnake is the one with the singer that does a good Robert Plant impression, Great White is the one with a singer who does a bad Robert Plant impression, and White Lion is the one whose singer does no Robert Plant impression at all.

Instead, what White Lion has going for it is songs, pure and simple. That's true of the band's low-budget debut, *Fight to Survive*, which kicks hard through the likes of "Cherokee" and "Fight to Survive," and of *Pride*, which moves easily from the fist-pumping insistence of "All You Need Is Rock n Roll" to the tuneful balladry of "Wait." *Big Game*, though, is where the band really shows its stuff, stressing its songwriting strengths from catchy hard-rockers like "Dirty Woman" to chorus-savoring slow songs like "Baby Be Mine" and "Little Fighter." And though the writing on *Mane Attraction* isn't quite as impressive, the arrangements are so well polished—particularly on the likes of "Lights and Thunder" and "Warsong"— that it almost makes up the difference. — J.D.C.

WHITESNAKE
★½ **Snakebite (1978; Geffen, 1988)**
★½ **Trouble (1978; Geffen, 1988)**
★★ **Love Hunter (1979; Geffen, 1988)**
★★★½ **Live . . . In the Heart of the City (1980; Geffen, 1988)**
★½ **Come an' Get It (1981; Geffen, 1988)**
★ **Saints & Sinners (1982; Geffen, 1988)**
★★ **Slide It In (1984; Geffen, 1988)**
★★★ **Whitesnake (Geffen, 1987)**
★½ **Slip of the Tongue (Geffen, 1989)**
Formed by one-time Deep Purple singer David Coverdale, Whitesnake started out as

a defiant rebuff to punk rock and ended up as a derivative dinosaur playing to the inbred conservatism of album-rock radio. Not the most inspiring story, but then, it's not the most inspiring band.

Chronologically, *Snakebite* is the band's debut, but it's actually a four-song EP repackaged with a handful of pre-Whitesnake demos. Not bad, particularly on the bluesy "Ain't No Love in the Heart of the City," if a bit on the skimpy side. *Trouble* finds the band settling into a strong post-Purple groove, a shift abetted by the addition of keyboardist Jon Lord; musically, it's not bad, but lyrics like "Lie down, I think I love you" push the 'Snakes deep into Spinal Tap territory. There are some equally ludicrous moments on *Love Hunter*, but the playing is as good as on any early-'70s Deep Purple album, while *Live . . . In the Heart of the City* suggests that this crew (particularly slide guitarist Micky Moody) could be a brilliant blues-rock band.

But as *Come an' Get It* makes plain, there was far more money to be made playing slick-and-predictable hard rock. That's not to say the album is a complete waste of time, thanks to catchy numbers like "Hot Stuff" and "Hit an' Run," but *Saints & Sinners* certainly is. Coverdale and company get back on track with *Slide It In*, an album that's only marginally more inspired than its predecessors, but considerably more commercial, and finally hit the jackpot with *Whitesnake*—mostly by retrofitting Led Zeppelin riffs into "Still of the Night," although the genuine pop smarts of "Here I Go Again" mitigates the album's lack of originality. Success didn't come cheap for Coverdale, who lost or fired all his Whitesnake sidemen before recording *Slip of the Tongue*; unfortunately, because the new guys (particularly lead guitarist Steve Vai) have more technique than soul, *Slip* ends up an unusually empty-sounding album, even by Whitesnake standards. — J.D.C.

CHRIS WHITLEY

★ ★ ★ ★ **Living With the Law (Columbia, 1991)**

With spooky Southern gothic lyrics and deft National steel guitar playing, Whitley's *Living With the Law* was a remarkable debut. Helped out by producer Daniel Lanois, the album has the aural shimmer of Lanois's own *Acadie*—and some of that record's novel arrangements (*Law* mixes viola and electric guitar, acoustic finger-picking and full-out feedback). While an energetic singer, Whitley shines brightest as a writer—his songs are minidramas, blues set-pieces that crackle with vitality and set him up as an intriguing explorer of the dark side of the American myth. — P.E.

KEITH WHITLEY

    ★ ★ ★   **A Hard Act to Follow (RCA, 1984)**

    ★ ★ ★   **L.A. to Miami (RCA, 1985)**

    ★ ★ ★ ★   **Don't Close Your Eyes (RCA, 1988)**

  ★ ★ ★ ★ ★   **I Wonder Do You Think of Me (RCA, 1989)**

    ★ ★ ★ ★   **Greatest Hits (RCA, 1990)**

WITH RICKY SKAGGS

  ★ ★ ★½ **Second Generation Bluegrass (1973; Rebel Records, 1990)**

WITH J. D. CROWE AND THE NEW SOUTH

    ★ ★ ★   **Somewhere Between (Rounder, 1982)**

Because his roots ran so deep, Keith Whitley towered above the so-called new traditionalist movement in country music. Unfortunately, his career can be examined in its totality; Keith Whitley died of an alcohol overdose shortly after completing *I Wonder Do You Think of Me* in 1989. If that tragedy ensures Whitley's legendary status, his unflinching music cuts though the sentimental hype. Just two years before his death, though, Whitley appeared to be a perennial bridesmaid. He'd been around: He began extensive touring and recording with Ralph Stanley and the Clinch Mountain Boys at 15, released *Second Generation Bluegrass* with his boyhood friend Ricky Skaggs just a year later. Joining J. D. Crowe and the New South in 1979, Whitley became the group's lead singer and started gravitating toward his true calling: honky-tonk, and its songs of big-city displacement, whiskey and sin. The transitional *Somewhere Between* kicks off with a cover of Lefty Frizzell's "I Never Go Around Mirrors," squarely placing Whitley's heartbreaking baritone in the barroom tradition. When he returned to this song on *Don't Close Your Eyes*, however, Whitley carved out a niche of his own.

That took some doing. *A Hard Act to Follow* and *L.A. to Miami* find Whitley slightly at odds with the countrypolitan leanings of his Nashville producers; the latter album includes flawed-but-heartfelt versions of "On the Other Hand" (later a hit for Randy Travis) and "Nobody in His Right Mind Would've Left Her" (later a hit for George Strait). A subsequent album was recorded and canned, and then Keith found a kindred spirit in producer Garth Fundis. On *Don't Close Your Eyes*, Whitley's voice leaps out with fresh confidence—and country radio responded. The hit singles—"No Stranger to the Rain," "Don't Close Your Eyes," "When You Say Nothing at All"—skillfully balance pop accessibility and emotional purity. Fearlessly, *I Wonder Do You Think of Me* ups the ante even further; Whitley faces up to his relationship with Jack Daniels' on subtly devastating tunes like "Tennessee Courage," "Brother Jukebox" and "I'm Over You." *I Wonder Do You Think of Me* proved what fans and insiders suspected all along. His timing was lousy, but Keith Whitley's music already is timeless. — M.C.

THE WHO

★ ★ ★ ★	The Who Sing My Generation (MCA, 1966)
★ ★ ★½	Happy Jack (MCA, 1967)
★ ★ ★½	The Who Sell Out (MCA, 1967)
★ ★½	Magic Bus—The Who on Tour (MCA, 1968)
★ ★ ★ ★ ★	Tommy (MCA, 1969)
★ ★ ★ ★ ★	The Who Live at Leeds (MCA, 1970)
★ ★ ★ ★ ★	Who's Next (MCA, 1971)
★ ★ ★ ★ ★	Meaty, Beaty, Big and Bouncy (MCA, 1971)
★ ★ ★ ★	Quadrophenia (MCA, 1973)
★ ★ ★	Odds and Sods (MCA, 1974)
★ ★ ★½	The Who By Numbers (MCA, 1975)
★ ★ ★	Who Are You (MCA, 1978)
★ ★ ★ ★ ★	The Kids Are Alright (MCA, 1979)
★ ★ ★	Quadrophenia (Polydor, 1979)
★ ★ ★½	Face Dances (1981; MCA, 1989)
★ ★ ★	Hooligans (MCA, 1981)
★ ★ ★½	It's Hard (1982; MCA, 1989)
★ ★ ★½	Who's Missing (MCA, 1985)
★ ★ ★ ★	Who's Better Who's Best (MCA, 1989)
★ ★ ★ ★	Join Together (MCA, 1990)

Ranking just below the Beatles and the Rolling Stones in the great triumvirate of British rock, the Who achieved an absolutely distinctive sound by fusing melody and raw percussive power; expanding far beyond the structural limitations of early rock & roll, the members of the Who proved themselves consistent pioneers. And yet, through a combination of internal tension, earnest ambition and an appetite for the exhilaration of risk, their trailblazing always seemed haphazard—a game of breaking rules, never a precious or self-important experiment.

Each of the players was an innovator. Not only an early master of assault guitar, his Gibson an arsenal of feedback fury and power chords, Pete Townshend also developed a technique of lightning strumming—resembling a revved-up flamenco style—that became his trademark. Keith Moon on drums was an eloquent banshee; even in the earliest days, he boasted a 16-piece set, and by eschewing the use of the hi-hat cymbal and concentrating on fluid, thunderous around-the-kit rolls, he managed an idiosyncratic synthesis that incorporated the kettledrum power of classical music, the speedy glide of the Surfaris' "Wipeout" and the elegant density of such jazz drummers as Elvin Jones. Bassist John Entwistle favored complex melody lines; virtually never did he resort to the traditional blues figures almost all rock players rely on. And, while his delivery coalesced only after the Who's songs became epics, Roger Daltrey ultimately sang rock & roll with a street-opera grandeur.

The Who gained early notoriety by giving voice to the Mods—a Brit teen cult of motorbike and Motown fanatics, of sharp dressers and thrill-seekers. A single like "Anyway, Anyhow, Anywhere" captured their exuberance; "I Can't Explain" summed up, with equal empathy, their inchoate urge toward self-expression. In a brilliant inspiration, Daltrey stuttered the lyrics of "My Generation," an anthem for these knock-kneed searchers; and with "The Kids Are Alright," the band asserted an identity with its following that became almost unique in rock history—The Who and its (almost exclusively male) teen fans were one. The delightful *Meaty, Beaty, Big and Bouncy* collects the early singles, and the album is wonderful.

With the Who's first album, *The Who Sings My Generation*, Pete Townshend showed himself a writer capable of acknowledging Daltrey's tough-guy bravado and accommodating Keith Moon's love for surf music—soon Pete, Roger and John would produce great ensemble harmonies, inspired somewhat by the Beach Boys. Entwistle tried out his French horn embellishments; they'd later be thoroughly employed when Townshend began incorporating classical music elements more fully. The record's James Brown covers are credible enough, but the Who would soon leave any R&B influence behind. *Happy Jack* showed the band trying hard for stylistic range. Entwistle, with "Boris the Spider" and "Whiskey Man," debuted as a songwriter—his material would henceforth tend toward the macabre. "See My Way" and "So Sad About Us" were early examples of the Who's intriguing combination of grace and power. The nine-minute "A Quick One While He's Away" was Townshend's first miniopera; while a patchwork attempt, energetic but clumsy, the suite featured a coda, based on the lyric "You are forgiven," whose celestial sound and spiritual message hinted at the *Tommy* glory to come. And with "Happy Jack," Townshend firmed up his skill at writing, with some irony and a lot of charm, about the kind of misfit kid who provided his surest inspiration.

Joke commercials and fake announcements made *Sell Out* a parody of Top Forty radio. These conceptual trappings now seem a bit quaint, but they hardly obscure the transcendent single "I Can See for Miles"; a crashing, swirling anthem about deceit, revenge and the urge for release, it remains the Who's best song. "Rael" was another *Tommy* preview, a busy bite-size opera. *Magic Bus* was spotty, but its Bo Diddley beat made the title track an in-concert fave, and "Pictures of Lily," a touching ode to masturbation, again displayed Townshend's talent for rendering adolescent longing.

Nearly as important as *Sgt. Pepper's*, *Tommy* was the opera that tapped Townshend's resources to their limit. A fable of an emblematic "deaf, dumb and blind kid" who finds ecstasy through pinball, the album fused Townshend's uncontestable pop sense with his spiritual yearning. Not only a personal triumph for the Who, the record remains one of the rare fusions of classical music and rock that works. "Pinball Wizard" was a completely efficient single; "See Me, Feel Me" was one of Townshend's simplest and most resonant melodies.

After pulling off their bid for artful glory, the Who reasserted its rock force with *Live at Leeds*. One of the handful of essential in-concert records, the album celebrated the majesty of noise. "My Generation" took on new, more desperate life when played by the older, wised-up Who; but it was the relentless attack of "Substitute" and a string of early rock revamps, "Young Man Blues," "Summertime Blues" and "Shakin' All Over" that proved overwhelming.

Who's Next, fashioned from material taken from the aborted *Life House*, an attempt to craft a follow-up to *Tommy*, was the next studio album, and—alongside the Stones' *Let It Bleed*—it is rock & roll's most assured record. A pristine production captured the band's textural richness; Townshend had discovered the synthesizer and, employing it for staccato, hypnotic passages, he became one of its most intelligent players—using it less for sci-fi effect than as deliberately mechanical counterpoint to his slashing guitar. "Won't Get Fooled Again" and "Baba O'Reilly" were two classic anthems about disaffection and deliverance—and "Bargain" and "Song Is Over" featured Townshend's writing and Daltrey's singing at their prime.

By the time of *Quadrophenia*—a Mod elegy and an attempt to render in music the characters of the Who's four members—the band found itself in a state of overdrive. Plainly, the foursome had conquered entire new worlds in rock & roll, but their ambition would not let up. Horns and orchestral adornments sometimes threatened to overcome Townshend's most complicated set of melodies and lyrical ideas—but on a song like "The Real Me," the group flourished its mastery of the baroque gesture, the operatic stance.

If *Quadrophenia* sounded a nostalgic note with the symphonic air of a last hurrah, the Who's next records mix were redolent of memory and exhaustion. The self-mocking modesty of its title proved true to the grab-bag, retrospective quality of *Odds and Sods*—a compilation whose standouts were fine *Life House*-period outtakes ("Pure and Easy," "Long Live Rock," "Naked Eyes") and a very early Mod theme song, "I'm the Face." *The Who by Numbers* reflected Townshend's mid-life crisis—so charged were the individual personalities of the band's members that their collisions had always been fertile; but strain had begun showing, and Townshend, too, felt threatened by the idea that the Who was becoming a dinosaur. The man who had, in "My Generation," written, "Hope I die before I get old," was now confronted with aging—and he panicked. "However Much I Booze" and "Blue Red and Grey" attested with pathos to Pete's struggle; the slight novelty number "Squeeze Box" seemed a deliberate exercise in downscaling the Olympian expectations the Who had always provoked.

With Keith Moon dying shortly after *Who Are You*'s release, the album served as an epitaph for the original Who. The title track was stirring enough, even if Daltrey's vocals sounded hectoring, and "Guitar and Pen" and Entwistle's "Trick of the Light" were assured compositions, but the album as a whole sounds more professional than inspired. *Face Dances*, with ex-Faces drummer Kenney Jones wisely attempting not to copy Moon, was stronger. "Don't Let Go the Coat" and "You Better You Bet" were powerful but tuneful; Entwistle's "The Quiet One" was an intriguing autobiography; and while "Cache Cache" came off as cynical, "Daily Records" reaffirmed Pete's rock & roll faith. *It's Hard*, however, ended things with a relative whimper—the record was competent, but the energy and vision were gone.

Aside from *Meaty, Beaty, Big and Bouncy*, *The Kids Are Alright* is the standout of the Who's compilations and special packages—the soundtrack for a documentary film, it's a treasure trove of rare bits and live numbers. *Who's Missing* collects previously unreleased gems from 1965 though 1972; *Join Together* is a fine record of the 1989 reunion tour. *Who's Better, Who's Best* is a good greatest hits, but with a band of this stature, no best-of suffices. — P.E.

WHODINI
★ ★   **Whodini (Jive/Arista, 1983)**
★ ★ ★   **Escape (Jive/Arista, 1984)**
★ ★ ★½ **Back in Black (Jive/Arista, 1986)**
★ ★ ★   **Open Sesame (Jive/Arista, 1987)**
★ ★ ★½ **Bag-a-Trix (MCA, 1991)**
From the beginning, Whodini has anchored its hip-hop in the song-oriented tradition of soul and R&B. Those roots must have taken hold; this Brooklyn trio is still rapping and scratching while most of the original competition has fallen by the wayside. Producer Larry Smith couples Grandmaster Dee's def beats with melodic synth lines on the Jive albums, prefiguring the New Jack Swing sound by several years. The debut's humorous raps come across as crowd-pleasing novelties ("Haunted House of Rock" was the breakthrough hit), but the subsequent albums make the most of hip-hop's unique relationship with its audience. Like all the groundbreaking old-school rappers, Jalil and Ecstasy address their peers—asserting their manly prowess, offering brotherly advice and thinking about women all the damn time. *Escape* and *Back in Black* are hit-and-miss affairs, but the spirited high points carry the slack tracks: "Freaks Come Out at Night" and the insightful "Friends" on the former, "Funky Beat" and the devastating "The Good Part"

on the latter. *Open Sesame* sounds more consistent—and less exciting; Whodini trades jibes with Millie Jackson and drops a heartfelt "Early Mother's Day Card," but by this time rap music was moving onto Public Enemy's turf. *Bag-a-Trix* is defiantly—triumphantly—out of place on the 1991 rap scene.

Whodini hasn't changed with the times, but Jalil and Ecstasy have mastered their anecdotal style of delivery—and changed their tune. No more boasts about "tag-team sex" (see "I'm a Ho" on *Back in Black*); now these two studs get their come-uppance on "Judy" and the sizzling hot "Bag-a-Trix." Deftly mixing romantic funk (courtesy of Midnight Star) with hip-hop's high-energy rhythms, *Bag-a-Trix* indicates that Whodini is playing for keeps. — M.C.

JANE WIEDLIN
★ ★½ **Jane Wiedlin (IRS, 1985)**
★ ★   **Fur (EMI Manhattan, 1988)**
★ ★   **Tangled (EMI, 1990)**
Although Wiedlin is obviously a better writer than the other ex-Go-Go's, she isn't much of a singer. Consequently, many of the best songs on *Jane Wiedlin*—the catchy "Sometimes You Really Get on My Nerves," for instance, or "Modern Romance"—are undercut by her reedy delivery. *Fur* works around her vocal limitations whenever possible, putting the perky "Rush Hour" in a low enough key to keep Wiedlin from whining, but never quite achieves its pop ambitions. No wonder, then, that *Tangled* resorts to the desperation strategy of massed guitars and multitracked vocals in an attempt to put some muscle behind Wiedlin's waifish vocals; apart from the tepid "World On Fire," it's a wasted effort. — J.D.C.

WEBB WILDER
★ ★ ★ **Hybrid Vigor (Island, 1989)**
★ ★ ★ **Doo Dad (Praxis/BMG, 1991)**
In-the-pocket roots rock with a hard, contemporary edge and a sense of humor. Echoes of the Stones, Georgia Satellites, ZZ Top abound, and Wilder delivers the lyrics in a voice just a notch above a personable growl. Mississippi-born Wilder is well known around the Austin rock circuit; indeed, Wilder, the LeRoi Brothers and Omar and the Howlers often swap personnel—the names change, but the rock-solid drive remains the same. *Hybrid Vigor* crunches along, sounds great on a home system, awesome in a live setting. The cut "Human Cannonball" cries out to be played

loud, and repeatedly. *Doo Dad* represents an uncompromising step forward for the eccentric Wilder in a collection of rocking, witty and often moving sagas with a Southern motif. — D.M

WILD TCHOUPITOULAS

★ ★ ★ ★ ★ **Wild Tchoupitoulas (Antilles, 1976)**
The Wild Tchoupitoulas were Mardi Gras "Indians"—that is, a "tribe" of creoles who dressed in elaborate, stylized Indian costumes to march and compete in Mardi Gras parades—fronted by George "Big Chief Jolly" Landry. Like many Mardi Gras Indians, the Wild Tchoupitoulas performed musical routines as part of their act—hence, *Wild Tchoupitoulas*. But because Landry happened to have a few nephews named Neville, the Wild Tchoupitoulas were able to recruit the Meters as their rhythm section, something which lends their Indian numbers a solid grounding in New Orleans funk. As such, the album sounds as festive as a Mardi Gras album should; not only are the Tchoupitoulas' songs solidly soulful (particularly Landry's "Meet De Boys On the Battle Front"), but the album also includes a few songs from the Meters' repertoire, including "Hey Pocky A-Way" and the stirring "Brother John." *Wild Tchoupitoulas* is also the first recording to feature Meters Charles and Cyril Neville harmonizing with their brothers, Art and Aaron, a temporary combination which eventually (and without the Indians) became a full-time band: The Neville Brothers. — J.D.C.

DENIECE WILLIAMS

★ ★ ★ ½ This Is Niecy (Columbia, 1976)
★ ★ ★ ★ My Melody (Columbia/ARC, 1981)
★ ★ ★ ★ Niecy (Columbia/ARC, 1982)
★ ★ ★ I'm So Proud (Columbia, 1983)
★ ★ ★ ½ Let's Hear It for the Boy (Columbia, 1984)
★ ★ ★ As Good As It Gets (Columbia, 1988)

Whitney Houston is related to a couple of great soul singers: her mother Cissy Houston and her cousin Dionne Warwick. But her strongest stylistic forebearer may well be Deniece Williams. Like Whitney, "Niecy" combines a startling, dulcet clarity with the emotional command of gospel. Even Williams's upper-register flights are firmly grounded; she never chirps. When producer Maurice White replicates his Earth, Wind and Fire groove on her debut ("Free" and "It's Important To Me"),

Williams confidently steps into Philip Bailey's shoes. But "That's What Friends Are For"—definitely not the song Whitney made famous—fully demonstrates her sensitive touch with a slow ballad.

After the easy-listening hit "Too Much, Too Little, Too Late" (a duet with Johnny Mathis), Williams met her musical match. Philadelphia producer Thom Bell had been lying low for several years, but Williams's graceful range and careful phrasing must have been just what he was waiting for. *My Melody* steers clear of any Philly-style disco rhythms, but between Williams's singing and Bell's simple, striking orchestrations, you certainly don't miss the dance floor. *Niecy* revs up the beat slightly, without diluting that lush, enveloping tone. These two albums are the last, sweet gasps of '70s-style pop-soul. After parting ways with Bell, Williams scored her biggest hit with the insouciant, charming "Let's Hear It for the Boy" in 1984. But her subsequent albums never quite clicked; after *As Good As It Gets*, Williams, whose roots had always been visible, went back to singing gospel. — M.C.

HANK WILLIAMS

★ ★ ★ Wanderin' Around (Polydor, NA)
★ ★ ★ Greatest Hits (Polydor, 1963)
★ ★ ★ Beyond the Sunset (Polydor, 1963)
★ ★ The Very Best of Hank Williams (Polydor, 1963)
★ ★ ★ ★ Wait for the Light to Shine (Polydor, 1963)
★ ★ 24 Greatest Hits (Polydor, 1976)
★ ★ 24 Greatest Hits, Volume 2 (Polydor, 1977)
★ ★ ★ Hank Williams Live at the Grand Ole Opry (MGM, 1976)
★ ★ ★ ★ 40 Greatest Hits (1978; Polydor, 1988)
★ ★ ★ ★ Rare Takes and Radio Cuts (Polydor, 1984)
★ ★ ★ ★ On the Air (Polydor, 1985)
★ ★ ★ ★ ★ Hank Williams: I Ain't Got Nothin' But Time, December 1946–August 1947 (Polydor, 1985)
★ ★ ★ ★ ★ Hank Williams: Lovesick Blues, August 1947–December 1948 (Polydor, 1985)
★ ★ ★ ★ ★ Hank Williams: Lost Highway, December 1948–March 1949 (Polydor, 1986)
★ ★ ★ ★ ★ Hank Williams: I'm So Lonesome I Could Cry, March 1949–August 1949 (Polydor, 1986)
★ ★ ★ ★ ★ Hank Williams: Long Gone Lonesome Blues, August 1949–December 1950 (Polydor, 1987)

★ ★ ★ ★ ★ **Hank Williams: Hey, Good Lookin', December 1950–July 1951 (Polydor, 1987)**
★ ★ ★ ★ ★ **Hank Williams: Let's Turn Back the Years, July 1951–June 1952 (Polydor, 1987)**
★ ★ ★ ★ ★ **Hank Williams: I Won't Be Home No More, June 1952–September 1952 (Polydor, 1987)**
★ ★ ★ ★ **Rare Demos First to Last (Country Music Foundation, 1990)**
★ ★ ★ ★ **The Original Singles Collection (Polydor, 1991)**

Born in Mount Olive, Alabama, in 1923, Hank Williams had a youth that coincided with the modern era of country music. By the time he made his first recordings in 1946, he'd absorbed styles ranging from Appalachian folk music to blues to honky tonk. By the time of his death in 1953, Williams, though not completely accepted by the country music establishment, had effected sweeping changes in country songwriting by personalizing his own material to a painful degree; and in the instrumental attack of his later sides, his music presaged the advent of rockabilly.

The focus, though, must remain clearly on the songs. Williams's music, though well played by his band the Drifting Cowboys with assistance in the studio from some of Nashville's top hands, wasn't notably innovative in structure or style. What Williams had in abundance was an ability to render his own travails in plainspoken lyrics that also spoke to the times and conditions his Southern audience knew well. There was both defiance and dignity in his approach, as well as a strong spiritual base that expressed itself in near-mystical terms, particularly on his many gospel recordings. Moreover, Williams embodied his songs to a degree country music hadn't seen before; his tumultuous marriage to Audrey Sheppard Guy was a classic love-hate affair, explicitly described in some of Williams's greatest songs ("Cold, Cold Heart," "I Can't Escape From You," "Your Cheatin' Heart").

Yet Williams spoke to an audience far beyond the bounds of country. A measure of his eloquence is in the number of cover versions of his songs that have been recorded over the years by artists spanning the popular music spectrum. Williams himself had six Top Thirty singles between '49 and '53, one of the few country artists to enjoy such distinction at that time.

In recent years Williams's catalog has been restored to respectability from its once-pathetic shambles. There's no longer any justification for owning the overdubbed versions of his classic songs found on *24 of Hank Williams' Greatest Hits* and *24 Greatest Hits, Volume 2*, when you can hear the tracks in their pure band format on other collections. Moreover, an ambitious reissue program undertaken in the mid-'80s by Polygram has restored virtually everything Williams recorded, with a major helping hand provided by the Country Music Foundation's *Rare Demos First to Last* issue, which has 24 songs in their earliest form performed by Williams accompanying himself on guitar (*Rare Demos* combines into one set recordings from two previous releases, *Just Me and My Guitar* and *The First Recordings*). An overview of the most commercial sides is available via the three-CD release, *The Original Singles Collection*, comprised of every single released during Williams's lifetime, and the excellent *40 Greatest Hits*, mastered from the original mono tapes. A different sort of greatest hits perspective is provided by *On the Air* and *Rare Takes and Radio Cuts*. The former is a compilation of radio show appearances from 1949–1952, and features well-known songs such as "I'm So Lonesome I Could Cry" and "I Can't Help It (If I'm Still in Love With You)" along with minor gems such as " 'Neath a Cold Gray Tomb of Stone" and "A Mansion on the Hill." In addition to the rare tracks (including a version of "Honky Tonkin' " from his second session for Sterling Records, pre-MGM), *Rare Takes and Radio Cuts* includes five radio performances that demonstrate the subtle changes Williams worked on his material over repeated performances.

Williams recorded many spiritual songs, and some of the best are collected on *Wait for the Light to Shine*. Two other releases, *Beyond the Sunset* and *Wanderin' Around*, are not spiritual albums by definition, but limn a man's spiritual journey; the latter, in songs such as "Nobody's Lonesome for Me," "Take These Chains From My Heart" and "You're Gonna Change (or I'm Gonna Leave)," is most explicitly about Williams's marriage. Ultimately, though, the *ne plus ultra* of Williams collections is Polydor's eight-volume *Hank Williams* series presenting his MGM recordings in chronological order and original undubbed mono. — D.M.

HANK WILLIAMS JR.
★ ★ ★ ★ **Live at Cobo Hall, Detroit (Polydor, 1969)**

★ ★ Eleven Roses (Polydor, 1972)
★ ★ ★ ★ ★ Hank Williams, Jr. & Friends
(1975; MGM, 1987)
★ ★ ★ 14 Greatest Hits (Polydor, 1976)
★ ★ ★ One Night Stands (Warner/Curb,
1977)
★ ★ ★ ★ The New South (Warner Bros.,
1978)
★ ★ ★ ★ Family Tradition (Elektra/Curb,
1979)
★ ★ ★ ★ Whiskey Bent and Hell Bound
(Elektra, 1979)
★ ★ ★ Habits Old and New (Elektra,
1980)
★ ★ ★ Rowdy (Warner Bros./Curb, 1981)
★ ★ ★ High Notes (Warner Bros./Curb,
1982)
★ ★ ★ ★ Hank Williams Jr.'s Greatest Hits
(Warner Bros./Curb, 1982)
★ ★ ★ Man of Steel (Warner Bros./Curb,
1983)
★ ★ ★ Strong Stuff (Warner Bros./Curb,
1983)
★ ★ ★ Major Moves (Warner
Bros./Curb, 1985)
★ ★ ★ Five-O (Warner Bros./Curb, 1985)
★ ★ ★ ★ Greatest Hits, Vol. 2
(Warner/Curb, 1985)
★ ★ ★ ★ The Early Years 1976–78
(Warner/Curb, 1986)
★ ★ ★ ★ Montana Cafe (Warner/Curb,
1986)
★ ★ ★ ★ Born to Boogie (Warner/Curb,
1987)
★ ★ ★ ★ Standing in the Shadows (Polydor,
1988)
★ ★ ★ ★ Wild Streak (Warner Bros., 1988)
★ ★ ★ ★ Greatest Hits III (Warner/Curb,
1989)
★ ★ Lone Wolf (Warner/Curb, 1990)
★ America (The Way I See It)
(Warner/Curb, 1990)
★ ★ ★ ★ Again: Hank Williams–Hank
Williams Jr. (MGM, NA)
★ ★ ★ ★ Father and Son (MGM, NA)
★ ★ ★ ★ Songs My Father Left Me
(MGM, NA)

Once cast as the heir to his father's legacy, Hank Williams Jr. found his own voice only after he embraced the spirit of that legacy rather than fighting it. Williams's music is like his father's only in that it is honest, speaks to its own time, reflects the man's values and is informed by styles other than country even as it is identifiably country. Managed by his mother, Williams began performing professionally when he was eight years old, singing his father's songs for audiences interested solely in genuflecting at the altar of Hank Sr.'s memory. The burden of this was rarely revealed to the adoring public, but it seeped through. In his first Number One country single (and the first song he wrote himself), "Standing in the Shadows" (1965), the 16-year-old artist sings, "It's hard to live in the shadow of a very famous man." In fact, Williams's early career, when he was signed to MGM, is respectful of country music traditions from A to Z. Most of his albums, some now available on Mercury, are foursquare Nashville Sound productions, weighted with syrupy strings and songs of lost love. Both *14 Greatest Hits* and *Eleven Roses* chart this period, or rather, this aspect of this period; that there was something else going on in Williams's head is more evident elsewhere. *Live at Cobo Hall, Detroit*, from 1969, slips in "Detroit City" and a tough version of Joe South's "Games People Play" amidst the Hank Sr.'s songs; and stripped of lush production, Williams's voice proves a strong instrument. Three other albums are revelatory as well: on *Father and Son* and *Again: Hank Williams–Hank Williams Jr.*, Jr. and Sr. are brought together, via editing, for duets on the latter's songs. Jr. is right at home in this raw setting, and his performances are believable, passionate and well-considered. On *Songs My Father Left Me*, Williams's adds melodies to some of his father's unfinished songs. Again the setting is traditional, and the performances meaningful.

It's important to remember that in 1969, when he recorded *Live at Cobo Hall*, Hank Jr. was only 20 years old. Regardless of whether he played it, he grew up with rock & roll, and he understood its roots. In early 1975, fed up with himself and his career, Williams decided to take charge. He called together a group of young musicians steeped equally in country and rock—Toy Caldwell, Chuck Leavell, Charlie Daniels, Pete Carr, Lenny LeBlanc, et al.—and went to Muscle Shoals, Macon and Nashville recording *Hank Williams, Jr. & Friends*, a collection of mostly original songs that addressed his life and his philosophy in acoustic-based music elevated to a high-lonesome plateau by Carr's Southern lead guitar lines and by mournful pedal-steel solos courtesy of Caldwell and Gary Boggs. In August of that year he left most of his face on the side of a Montana mountain after falling 500 feet down its side while on a hunting trip; that he lived was a miracle, but he required extensive plastic surgery to reconstruct his features. While he was recovering from his injuries, MGM released *Hank Williams, Jr.*

& Friends. Hailed as a landmark, the album stands as one of the seminal documents of the outlaw movement that swept country in the late '70s, and for sheer emotional power and inspired playing ranks with the best records of the decade. The exquisite imagery of "Montana Song" bespeaks a man cut off from feeling, abandoned by his lover, and seeking solace in nature. Standing on the Great Divide, where he can "look out on America and feel so free inside," Williams tells a painful truth about his life. That he isn't entirely free is indicated by references to his lineage on "Living Proof" and "Stoned at the Jukebox." Still, Hank Jr. came out whole on the other side. From this point forward, he has crystallized his image as a rough and rowdy fellow, made no apologies for his macho posturing or his fast-lane lifestyle, been a tireless champion of young, rock-influenced country bands ("Young Country" on *Born to Boogie*), and continued to provide running commentary on his father's pull on his life. Unfortunately, *Hank Williams, Jr. & Friends* is available only on cassette, but two of its tracks are included on the Polydor retrospective, *Standing in the Shadows.*

Cut loose from the restraints of the past, Williams moved to Warner Bros., where he has remained except for a brief fling with Elektra Records. His first album post-accident, *The New South*, is indicative of an experimental bent Williams has taken since *Friends.* The mix here includes one of his father's songs, Bill Monroe's bluegrass standard "Uncle Pen," a down and dirty honky-tonk tune "How's My Ex Treating You" and the now-standard tribute to the South in the title song. In the title song from his 1979 album, *Family Tradition*, Williams disavows all responsibility for his vices, ascribing his penchant for drink and smoke as being "a family tradition." The album also contains one of Williams's early blasts of political extremism in "I've Got Rights." Railing against a system that freed ("on a technicality") a man who killed his wife and son, the narrator of Williams's song vows revenge ("there won't be no damn lawyer and system to protect you"), and at song's end the killer is "on his knees beggin' for his life."

This aspect of Williams's evolution is troubling because, for one, he knows better, and two, it undercuts what is, on balance, music of admirable depth. So a terrific bit of comedic, separatist fantasy such as *Wild Streak*'s "If the South Woulda Won" (which proposes national holidays honoring Patsy Cline, Elvis Presley and Lynyrd Skynyrd, and suggests Hank Williams Sr.'s picture be put on $100 bills) is enjoyed or loathed depending on the listener's political and geographical orientation. Which is not to suggest Williams hasn't gone too far on occasion. *America (The Way I See It)* came on the heels of Charlie Daniels's descent into right-wing radicalism on "Simple Man" and gained new momentum during the war with Iraq, when the militaristic "Don't Give Us a Reason" and the jingoistic "The American Way" played into the warmongering characterizing the Desert Storm PR campaign. To hammer home his point, Williams includes "I've Got Rights" as well as his tale of urban horror and revenge, "A Country Boy Can Survive."

Anyone who can get by his bluster will find numerous rewards in Williams's catalog. The greatest-hits albums provide bang for the buck, because Williams's singles tend to be prime cuts. *Whiskey Bent and Hell Bound* is Williams in a dark mood, mean and nasty; *Montana Cafe* includes a nice change of pace in its medley of "Harvest Moon" and "St. Louis Blues"; *Born to Boogie* and *Wild Streak* are two flat-out, unrelenting rock & roll albums, the title song of the latter being notably scalding. Hank Jr. is a formidable artist, but as these albums indicate, he's more compelling when he casts aside his politics.
— D.M.

LARRY WILLIAMS
★★★ **Here's Larry Williams (Specialty, 1959)**
★★ **Unreleased Larry Williams (Specialty, 1986)**
★★ **Hocus Pocus (Specialty, 1986)**
★★★★ **Bad Boy (Specialty, 1990)**

New Orleans–born Larry Williams got his chance to record after Lloyd Price, for whom Williams had been playing piano (and by some accounts serving as valet), left the label after a stint in the Army. In 1957 he responded with two Top Twenty singles: "Short Fat Fannie" and "Bony Moronie." Subsequent singles failed to generate much chart action, and Williams's career soon hit the skids commercially. As an artist, though, Williams was growing, and his later sides showed a skilled lyricist developing, as well as a singer capable of more subtle textures than he had demonstrated on his rocking sides. In 1959, though, he was arrested for narcotics possession and subsequently dropped by Specialty. He wound up at Chess, to ill fortune, then moved over to

Okeh as a producer. His name reemerged in the mid-'60s thanks to the Beatles, who covered three of his songs ("Bad Boy," "Dizzy Miss Lizzy" and "Slow Down"). In the late '60s Williams teamed up with Johnny "Guitar" Watson on a minor hit, a version of Cannonball Adderley's "Mercy, Mercy, Mercy" to which the duo added their own lyrics, and followed that with an underrated, rocking album, *Two for the Price of One*. In January of 1980 Williams was found dead in his apartment, apparently a suicide.

Specialty's *Bad Boy* release is pretty much the definitive Larry Williams. Its 23 tracks include his most prominent singles and other inspired moments. His red-hot version of "Heeby-Jeebies" stands up to Little Richard's own smoking version; "Hocus Pocus" has an enthralling groove; "Iko Iko a.k.a. Jockomo" hearkens back to the singer's New Orleans roots. *Here's Larry Williams* is Williams's first album, with its packaging unchanged since its release in 1959, complete with his three famous singles. *Unreleased Larry Williams* is a fine complement to *Bad Boy*, containing alternative versions of "High School Dance," "Slow Down," "Bad Boy" and "Just Because," in addition to unreleased versions of songs still unavailable elsewhere. *Hocus Pocus*, with liner notes by Little Walter, is another treasure of unreleased material, notable among the titles being "Hey Now Hey Now," a new interpretation of "Iko Iko"; a stirring ballad, "I Was a Fool"; a Latin-flavored version of "Bad Boy" called "Bad Boy Cha Cha"; and "Make a Little Love," minus the background voices that had been supplied by Sonny Bono. — D.M.

LUCINDA WILLIAMS

   ★★   **Ramblin' on My Mind (1979; Rounder, 1991)**
  ★★★ **Happy Woman Blues (1980; Rounder, 1991))**
★★★★ **Lucinda Williams (1988; Chameleon, 1992)**
  ★★★ **Passionate Kisses (EP) (1989; Chameleon, 1992)**
 ★★★½ **Sweet Old World (Chameleon, 1992)**

Born in Louisiana and based in Austin, Texas, where her music first took shape, Lucinda Williams honed her style in Houston, in a fertile local scene where Nanci Griffith and Lyle Lovett were working their own intriguing variations on music rooted in country, western swing,

blues and folk. Williams's college-professor father was a Hank Williams fan, and the family's home often resonated with all manner of country and folk music. Williams financed two albums released on the Smithsonian/Folkways label (which were reissued on Rounder in 1991), then held out for creative control when major labels began bidding for her services. She then signed with Rough Trade, who soon after declared bankruptcy, temporarily rendering *Passionate Kisses* and *Lucinda Williams* out of print.

Of the two earlier albums, *Ramblin' on My Mind* is the less satisfying. Interpreting songs by Robert Johnson, Memphis Minnie, Hank Williams, A.P. Carter and others, Williams sounds like the product of academia she is, approaching the material as if it were too fragile to reshape. Williams is totally defeated by the three Johnson songs, and her stilted phrasing sounds learned rather than felt. That is, until she gets to "The Great Speckled Bird," the strange quasi-hymn indelibly linked with Roy Acuff. In Williams's hands, the song sounds vital and mesmerizing as her crystalline, keening voice evokes the unsettling mystery of larger forces shaping our lives. As the one honest, deeply felt performance on the album, it points the way to *Happy Woman Blues*.

Having paid respects to her influences on *Ramblin'*, Williams comes back with a collection of original songs more representative of her own life and better suited to her style. "Lafayette" and "Louisiana Man" are loving reminiscences of places and people in her home state. Otherwise, Williams appears ambiguous and compelling in recounting some dangerous and ill-fated liaisons. *Lucinda Williams* is such a startling advance over her first two releases that it seems to be have been done by a different artist. The writing is sharp and tough with plenty of tender moments rendered in a heartfelt manner. She's moved foursquare into rock & roll, with conviction and assurance. "I Just Wanna See You So Bad," the album's opener, comes out of the Springsteen school, but the rest of the album hews closer to country-rock and folk-rock arrangements. Williams hasn't resolved her ambiguous feelings regarding commitment and love—expressed with devastating clarity in "Side of the Road," when she implores, "I wanna know you're there, but I wanna be alone"—but the search becomes more interesting as she spills blood on the tracks. There's not a false step, and the depth of feeling is powerful:

Williams's original songs reveal new layers of meaning with each listening. *Passionate Kisses* is a bit of a holding pattern, with two of its tracks, including the title song, having appeared on *Lucinda Williams*, and the other three being covers. — D.M.

MARION WILLIAMS
★ ★ ★ ★ ★ **I've Come So Far (SpiritFeel, 1986)**
★ ★ ★ ★ ★ **Born to Sing the Gospel (SpiritFeel, 1988)**
★ ★ ★ ★ ★ **Surely God Is Able (SpiritFeel, 1989)**
★ ★ ★ ★ ★ **Strong Again (SpiritFeel, 1991)**

In her lifetime Marion Williams has been hailed, justifiably, as the greatest living gospel singer; as one of the greatest of all gospel singers ever; as one of the greatest singers in any genre, period. One can be overwhelmed by the accolades, and suspicious, too; but one will come away from her recordings believing she was nothing less than . . . the greatest singer ever. Flawless on every front, Williams's choice of material is impeccable; her own songs or adaptions of songs are in a contemporary mode even while reflecting ages-old gospel traditions; and her command of color, tone, nuance, meter and the dramatic elements of gospel singing are simply beyond criticism, let alone comprehension. And there's the rub: Like all great singers, Williams renders personal experience in terms universally understood and felt, thus abrogating sustained, dispassionate aesthetic judgment of her work. Rather, the listener becomes one with the singer, feeling the same pain born of personal spiritual failings, reveling in the shared joy found in her gospel's promises of forgiveness, redemption and renewal. So compelling is her testimony that anyone who enters her sanctuary becomes a devout member of her flock.

This being the case, judging Williams's recordings becomes a simple matter. They are as good as gospel gets, for all the reasons enumerated above, each one in its own way essential. *Born to Sing the Gospel* is of special note, because one side is recorded live in a Philadelphia church. Its closing seven-minutes-plus sermon-in-song, "I've Come So Far," is a masterful performance detailing how the singer got over in spite of her enemies' temptations—an exercise in spiritual discipline of the first order. *I've Come So Far* is one of her strongest outings with a contemporary gospel-soul feel; but then

after taking us through a mesmerizing set done in a commercial vein, she yanks us back to the source on the album's last cut, "The Man I'm Looking For" (the man of the title being Jesus, lest anyone be confused). Performed a cappella, it finds Williams employing every emotive device in her arsenal in order to express the extreme urgency of her quest. At the song's close she is so consumed by feeling that she sounds as if she's struggling to express the inexpressible, which is exactly the point.

But then how to judge *Surely God Is Able*, with its powerful re-recording of the title track, one of her early hits when she was a member of the Clara Ward Singers in the late '40s through the mid-'50s? There's also an astonishing a cappella rendition of that old warhorse "Amazing Grace," given some interesting new twists. *Strong Again* includes "Prayer List," a powerful commentary enumerating social ills ranging from "AIDS and arthritis" to homelessness to child abuse, as well as moving versions of "O Happy Day," Julius Cheeks's "The New Burying Ground" and a reading of "Sometimes I Feel Like a Motherless Child" that brings tears.

Some of Williams's early recorded work with the Clara Ward Singers can be found on the infrequently available Savoy set, *The Best of the Famous Ward Singers of Philadelphia*. *Blessed Assurance* and *Prayer Changes Things*, two out-of-print solo albums recorded for Atlantic in the mid-'70s, are must-haves, as well. — D.M.

MAURICE WILLIAMS & THE ZODIACS
★ ★ ★ ★ **The Best of Maurice Williams & the Zodiacs (Collectables, 1982)**

The cover photo shows six young men, but Maurice Williams & the Zodiacs were, in fact, a quartet from South Carolina powered by Williams's earnest tenor leads as well as his considerable skill as a songwriter. Recording as the Gladiolas in 1955, the group cut a Williams song called "Little Darlin'" that failed to stir up much interest on the pop side but turned into a royalty bonanza for Williams two years later when a cover version by the Diamonds had an eight-week run at Number Two on the chart and sold over a million copies. It would be another three years before Williams & the Zodiacs had their moment of fame with a percussive Williams-penned plea, "Stay," that made it to Number One and has since spawned numerous cover versions. Succeeding singles "Come Along," "We're Lovers," "I Remember" and "Come and

Get It" didn't do much for the group's fortunes, but feature uniformly outstanding performances by Williams and his mates. All the singles are here, as well as lesser-known gems such as "Someday," featuring a Williams vocal that is a marvel of controlled yearning and breathless agonizing, and "High Blood Pressure," a rocker enhanced by the sort of studio party atmosphere that would later be used to juice up the ambience of Gary "U.S." Bonds's hits. — D.M.

OTIS WILLIAMS AND HIS CHARMS
★ ★ ★ **Otis Williams and His Charms (King/Gusto, 1978)**

A Cincinnati quintet, Otis Williams and His Charms had a string of hits in the mid-'50s that were among the finest examples of group harmony at a time when the charts were full of fine examples of group harmony. Williams was the smooth lead tenor with the right amount of grit in his voice to lend the Charms' material a rough, bluesy edge. This collection contains the group's three Top Thirty pop hits—"Hearts of Stone" (from 1954, and revived in 1973 by John Fogerty's one-man band, the Blue Ridge Rangers), "Ling Ting Tong" (1955) and "Ivory Tower" (1956)—and includes lower-charting items such as "That's Your Mistake." After leaving the Charms, Williams recorded solo for Okeh and cut some country sides for Stop Records, but all of these are now out of print. — D.M.

TONY WILLIAMS
★ ★ ★	**Life Time (1964; Blue Note, 1987)**
★ ★ ★	**Spring (1965; Blue Note, 1987)**
★ ★ ★ ★½	**Emergency! (1969; Polydor, 1991)**
★ ★ ★½	**Turn It Over (Polydor, 1970)**
★ ★ ★	**Ego (Polydor, 1971)**
★ ★ ★	**The Old Bum's Rush (Polydor, 1973)**
★ ★ ★ ★	**Believe It (Columbia, 1975)**
★ ★ ★½	**Million Dollar Legs (Columbia, 1976)**
★ ★ ★	**The Joy of Flying (Columbia, 1979)**
★ ★ ★½	**Foreign Intrigue (Blue Note, 1986)**
★ ★ ★	**Civilization (Blue Note, 1987)**
★ ★ ★	**Angel Street (Blue Note, 1988)**
★ ★ ★½	**Native Heart (Blue Note, 1990)**
★ ★ ★½	**The Story of Neptune (Blue Note, 1992)**

Miles Davis may have gotten the credit for it, but jazz-rock was actually Tony Williams's idea. It was Williams (who was drumming for Davis at the time) who introduced the trumpeter to guitarist John McLaughlin, and though Davis got into the studio with McLaughlin first (for the lovely, reflective *In a Silent Way*), it was Williams's band Lifetime that first afforded McLaughlin the opportunity to merge rock with jazz, on *Emergency!* Fusion starts there.

Williams's recording career, however, does not. A child prodigy, he was well known in Boston jazz circles while still in his teens, and led his first sessions—for the fiercely avant-garde *Life Time*—at the ripe old age of 19. He didn't start experimenting with electric music, though, until the late '60s, when he formed Lifetime with McLaughlin and organist Larry Young (a.k.a. Khalid Yasin). Although the instrumentation recalls the organ trios led by the likes of Jimmy McGriff or Richard "Groove" Holmes, the music is something else again, gleefully indulging in volume and distortion, and coloring jazz's usual swing with the furious intensity of acid rock (although, to be honest, the playing is miles beyond the misdirected flailings of most psychedelic-era rock acts). Yet apart from "Spectrum," the songs don't "rock out" in any conventional sense of the term; indeed, it isn't until "Vuelta Abajo" from *Turn It Over* (which brings Cream bassist Jack Bruce aboard) that Williams and Lifetime latch onto the sort of riff-based structures necessary for rock-style repetition. (Williams also sings at points, though the less said about that, the better).

McLaughlin and Bruce left before Williams recorded *Ego* (though Bruce can be heard in an uncredited vocal on "Two Worlds"). Not that their presence would have made that much difference, since a fair amount of *Ego* is given over to drum numbers like "Clap City" or "Piskow's Filigree," but there's still plenty of fire in Ted Dunbar's guitar playing, particularly on the moody "There Comes a Time." Williams introduces an entirely new line-up with *The Old Bum's Rush*, which finds the group moving more toward a conventional jazz-funk sound, thanks to the soulful vocals of *Tequila*, yet he doesn't fully attempt to cash in on the fusion craze he helped launch until *Believe It* and *Million Dollar Legs*. Using guitarist Allan Holdsworth as his foil, Williams emulates the rock-based sound of McLaughlin's Mahavishnu Orchestra and the later Return to Forever, but manages to avoid the technique-conscious wankery that made most fusion so stultifying. Both are excellent albums, but the band broke up after it was unable to attract the arena-sized audience the music deserved. Taking one last stab at fusion, Williams cut *The Joy of Flying* with a variety of fusion stars, including Jan Hammer, George Benson, Tom Scott, Stanley Clarke and even a quartet featuring rockers Ronnie Montrose, Brian Auger and Mario Cipollina, but the album's most intriguing collaboration is with pianist Cecil Taylor on "Morgan's Motion"—and that wasn't fusoid in the slightest! Since then, Williams has focused on more traditional jazz fare, fronting a combo including trumpeter Wallace Roney and pianist Mulgrew Miller; all of their albums are excellent, but *Foreign Intrigue* and *Native Heart* are the standouts.

— J.D.C.

SONNY BOY WILLIAMSON (RICE MILLER)

- ★★★★ **Down and Out Blues (1959; Chess/MCA, 1987)**
- ★★★★ **The Real Folk Blues (1966; Chess/MCA, 1987)**
- ★★★★ **More Real Folk Blues (1967; Chess/MCA, 1988)**
- ★★★ **In Paris: Sonny Boy Williamson & Memphis Slim (GNP Crescendo, 1973)**
- ★★★★ **One Way Out (MCA, 1976)**
- ★★★★★ **King Biscuit Time (Arhoolie, 1989)**
- ★★★★ **Clownin' with the World: Sonny Boy Williamson and Willie Love (Acoustic Archives/Trumpet Records, 1992)**
- ★★★★ **Goin' in Your Direction (Trumpet Records, 1992)**

A man fond of myth and mythmaking, Rice Miller, the younger of two Delta blues musicians to take the name Sonny Boy Williamson, at least left a legacy that justifies his tall tales and eccentricities. Born around the turn of the century in Glendora, Mississippi, Miller began teaching himself to play harmonica at age eight. By 14 he was performing around the Delta and hooking up with other traveling bluesman, including Robert Jr. Lockwood, Robert Johnson (one of Miller's tales is that he was present at Johnson's death), Elmore James and Howlin' Wolf. After Miller adopted the name of the first Sonny Boy Williamson (who had been recording for Bluebird), his career took a quantum leap, with bookings all over the South and, beginning in 1941, a steady gig on the King Biscuit Time show on KFFA radio in Helena, Arkansas. When Lillian McMurry launched her now-revered Trumpet label, Miller was one of the first artists she approached about recording.

Early sessions proved unproductive, but Miller finally found his groove in 1951 and laid down some of the strongest Delta blues sides extant.

A peerless instrumentalist whose most noted acolyte was Little Walter Jacobs, Miller exhibited superior command of the harp's tonal possibilities to where it did not merely accompany his vocals, but in essence became a second singing voice. Without any help, though, Miller was a first-rate singer who could invest a gruff, half-spoken lyric with a moving immediacy born of the hard life of which he wrote in his songs. The Trumpet recordings, now available on the Arhoolie CD, *King Biscuit Time*, encompass many of Miller's most important songs—"West Memphis Blues," "Mr. Downchild," "Eyesight to the Blind," "Pontiac Blues"—and stand as one of the key documents in Delta blues history. The CD also includes a live, four-song set from one of Miller's appearances on the King Biscuit radio show.

In the mid-'50s Miller joined other Delta bluesmen in the migration to Chicago and was signed to Chess Records' Checker subsidiary. His first single, "Don't Start Me Talkin'," climbed into the R&B Top Ten, beginning an eight-year run in which Miller became one of the label's most productive and popular artists, his fame taking on an international dimension when he toured Europe in 1963 and dazzled the locals with his music and his dapper attire. *One Way Out* is comprised of Miller's early Chess sides, many featuring him accompanied by Muddy Waters, Otis Spann, Willie Dixon, Jimmy Rogers, Robert Jr. Lockwood and Fred Below. The title track became one of the Allman Brothers' signature songs. In order, *Down and Out Blues*, *Real Folk Blues* and *More Real Folk Blues* pick up where *One Way Out* ends, taking Miller through the remainder of his Chess years, when he often worked at peak proficiency. Taken as a whole, these sides constitute one of the saddest portraits any bluesman has ever painted of himself. Miller moans his way through "Sad to Be Alone," "Your Funeral and My Trial," "Nine Below Zero" and "Somebody Help Me." *In Paris* is a rousing live set recorded in 1963, when Miller was touring Europe accompanied by Memphis Slim on piano. Before a respectful audience, Miller bares his soul, easing into a pain-wracked take on Elmore James's "The Skies are Crying"—the title is slightly amended—with Slim providing sensitive accompaniment, before commanding the stage solo for powerful performances of "Your Funeral and My Trial" and "Explain Yourself to Me." While in England, Miller also recorded a live set at London's Crawdaddy Club, with the Yardbirds (and Eric Clapton). Released as *The Yardbirds with Sonny Boy Williamson* and repackaged over the years under variations on its original title, it stands as a seminal document in the fusion of blues and rock.

The legacy of Miller's pre-Chess years is rounded out by two early '92 releases encompassing a number of the exceptional sides Miller recorded in Mississippi for the Trumpet label before heading north to Chicago and Chess Records. *Clownin' with the World* features a side each of Williamson and the underrated pianist Willie Love with their respective bands (Love also plays on four of Williamson's tracks cut in a Houston studio in 1953). *Goin' in Your Direction* offers a survey of Williamson tracks cut for Trumpet between 1951 and 1954, including two cuts with Arthur "Big Boy" Crudup on guitar, and another track, "From the Bottom," with the sweet sound of B.B. King's guitar. All in all, an entertaining and vital lesson in blues history is here for those inclined to get to it.
— D.M.

SONNY BOY WILLIAMSON (JOHN LEE WILLIAMSON)

★ ★ ★ **Blues Classics by Sonny Boy Williamson** (Blues Classics, NA)

★ ★ ★ **Blues Classics by Sonny Boy Williamson, Vol. 2** (Blues Classics, NA)

★ ★ ★ **Blues Classics by Sonny Boy Williamson, Vol. 3** (Blues Classics, NA)

★ ★ ★ ★ ★ **Blues in the Mississippi Night** (1959; Rykodisc, 1990)

History has not been so kind to the original Sonny Boy Williamson as it has been to his like-named Delta acolyte, a.k.a. Rice Miller. Little Walter, James Cotton, Big Walter Horton and certainly Miller himself were deeply indebted to Williamson, who transformed the harmonica from an accompanying instrument into a powerful solo voice and was a major draw on the Chicago blues circuit from the time of his arrival there in 1934. Born in Jackson, Tennessee, Williamson honed his chops touring the South with Sleepy John Estes before migrating to the Windy City where he became one of the most frequently recorded and most popular blues artists of the day. His unusual technique was to rapidly alternate between vocal and

instrumental, to the point where his colleague Big Bill Broonzy once described Williamson's style as singing and playing at the same time. Without question, Williamson is best remembered for his groundbreaking work as a harp player, and rightly so, since it became a hallmark of the Chicago blues sound; but he was also one of the deepest deep-blues singers of his time, every note carrying in its plaintive tone the weight of the black man's burden in the Delta. Of the many songs bearing Williamson's name as composer, the best known today is probably "Good Morning Little Schoolgirl," a touchstone for countless American and British blues bands.

Unfortunately, Williamson's recordings are largely out of print domestically. The Blues Classics titles are well worth seeking out for an overview of this neglected but significant artist. The newest title available on Williamson is Rykodisc's essential *Blues in the Mississippi Night*. In 1946 folklorist Alan Lomax traveled to Chicago to record Williamson's, Broonzy's and Memphis Slim's Delta reminiscences of the roots of the blues, of their own tortured personal histories and those of the blacks in Mississippi. So brutal were the details of these oral histories that Lomax was warned by a newspaper editor in Greenville, Mississippi, to lock the tapes in his trunk and leave the state before certain people discovered them. The artists recorded asked that their names not be revealed when the discs were released, for fear of reprisals against their families and friends. Hence the raw nature of the dialogues herein, interspersed with examples of each artist's work, as well as field chants and work songs common to the people in the Delta. Also included is an extensive booklet with a background essay by Lomax on the recording sessions, transcriptions of some of the dialogue, and brief biographies of each artist. Anyone who wishes to understand the blues should own this disc. — D.M.

CHUCK WILLIS

★ ★ ★ ★ ½ **His Greatest Recordings** (Atlantic, 1971)

★ ★ ★ ★ ½ **Chuck Willis—My Story** (Columbia, 1980)

Loaded with talent as a performer and singer, Chuck Willis lived out the quintessential hard-luck rock & roll saga. Recording for Columbia's Okeh subsidiary in 1952, his first record, "Caldonia," backed by a Willis original, "My Story," was one of the top-selling R&B records of the year. Five years later, having failed to produce any more significant hits on Okeh, Willis moved to Atlantic, and in less than a year had cut loose with one of his finest vocal performances on an updated version of an ages-old black blues song written and originally recorded by Ma Rainey, "C.C. Rider." A popular new dance called the Stroll emerged about the same time, with Willis's "C.C. Rider" its signature song. Crowned "The King of the Stroll," Willis took to wearing a turban onstage, along with flashy suits, and became something of a fashion plate in the eyes of his young fans. Couture aside, he was, not incidentally, one of his generation's finest vocalists, with a sweet but strong voice that served him well on blues ballads such as "That Train Is Gone," as well as harder-edged, uptempo material along the lines of "Thunder and Lightning."

Just as his star was ascending, though, Willis was struck down—he died in 1958 of a stomach ulcer, six weeks after his thirtieth birthday, one week before his new single, "Hang Up My Rock and Roll Shoes," entered the charts. The irony of the title is almost too much to handle, given that the song features one of Willis's most forceful readings. Both the Atlantic and Columbia sets offer enough compelling evidence to rank Willis among the best artists of his time, however brief that time was. The Columbia set contains 14 of his Okeh sides, which spotlight Willis's strong writing and remarkable growth as a singer. An Atlantic retrospective, which is unfortunately out of print, collects the hits and other sides that might well have become hits had the artist lived. These show Willis writing and singing in a variety of modes, and offer a moving epitaph for an artist who had much more to offer than he was allowed to exhibit.

— D.M.

BOB WILLS AND HIS TEXAS PLAYBOYS

★★★ **The Best of Bob Wills (MCA, 1973)**

★★★★ **The Bob Wills Anthology (Columbia, 1973)**

★★★ **The Best of Bob Wills, Vol. 2 (MCA, 1975)**

★★★ **Remembering . . . The Greatest Hits of Bob Wills (Columbia, 1976)**

★★★ **In Concert (Capitol, 1976)**

★★★ **24 Great Hits by Bob Wills and His Texas Playboys (Polydor, 1977)**

★★★★★ **The Tiffany Transcriptions 1946 & 1947 Vol. 1 (Kaleidoscope, 1982)**

★★★★★ **Best of the Tiffanys: The Tiffany Transcriptions 1946 & 1947 Vol. 2 (Kaleidoscope, 1984)**

★★★★★ **Basin Street Blues: The Tiffany Transcriptions 1946 & 1947 Vol. 3 (Kaleidoscope, 1984)**

★★★★★ **You're From Texas: The Tiffany Transcriptions 1946 & 1947 Vol. 4 (Kaleidoscope, 1985)**

★★★★★ **The Tiffany Transcriptions 1946 & 1947 Vol. 5 (Kaleidoscope, 1986)**

★★★★★ **Sally Goodin: The Tiffany Transcriptions 1946 & 1947 Vol. 6 (Kaleidoscope, 1987)**

★★★★★ **Keep Knockin': The Tiffany Transcriptions 1946 & 1947 Vol. 7 (Kaleidoscope, 1987)**

★★★★ **Fiddle (Country Music Foundation, 1987)**

★★★★ **The Golden Era (Columbia, 1987)**

★★★★★ **More of the Best: The Tiffany Transcriptions 1946 & 1947 Vol. 8 (Kaleidoscope, 1988)**

★★★★★ **In the Mood: The Tiffany Transcriptions 1946 & 1947 Vol. 9 (Kaleidoscope, 1990)**

★★★ **Columbia Historic Edition (Columbia, 1987)**

★★★★★ **Anthology 1935–1973 (Rhino, 1991)**

Bob Wills was not the father of western swing—several prominent bands were playing it well ahead of Wills's emergence—but he quickly became its most famous practitioner, its reigning visionary and its conscience; in the end his music so dwarfed all the western swing that came before him that Wills *seemed* to have created this country offshoot out of the many varieties of music he heard growing up in west Texas.

A fiddler in the traditional style, as was his father, Wills *fils et pere* played west Texas house parties together, with the son moving on to work with medicine shows touring the region. The roots of Wills's style can be traced to several influences. The fiddle and guitar duets of virtuoso jazz players Eddie Lang and Joe Venuti were popular with musicians in the southwest, Wills among them. But the young fiddler also had a taste for blues, Dixieland jazz, Mariachi, Cajun music and the native dance music of the central European immigrants who had settled in the Lone Star state. One of the first important influences in the development of Wills's personal style was Emmett Miller, a blackface singer popular in the 1920s and '30s whose rhythm section included a drummer—a instrument conspicuous by its absence from that era's country bands—and whose music was jazz-influenced. Miller also employed a number of unusual flourishes in his singing style, including yodels and witty asides to spur on his musicians, later appropriated by Wills.

In 1930 a trio consisting of Wills, guitarist Herman Arnspiger and vocalist Milton Brown landed a steady gig as the Light Crust Doughboys plugging Light Crust Flour on a Fort Worth radio station. Brown left in 1932 to form his own band, and Wills followed suit a year later with his banjo-playing brother Johnnie Lee in tow, along with a versatile singer named Tommy Duncan. Rechristening his group the Texas Playboys, Wills relocated to Tulsa, Oklahoma, abandoned the traditional country band lineup and concentrated on assembling a large group to play dance halls. Adding a drummer and, later, horns and electric instruments to his lineup was a revolutionary step for a country artist, but it made perfect sense to Wills. Nevertheless, in this "big band" approach to country music Wills maintained the fiddles as a focal point of his sound and the signature of what has variously been called country jazz and western swing. Always, Wills attracted stellar musicians, among them many who are now considered among the most important in country music history: apart from Wills himself, Duncan and Arnspiger, the list would include guitarist Eldon Shamblin, unpredictable piano player Al Stricklin, steel guitarist Leon McAuliffe, electric mandolin player Tiny Moore and fiddlers Jesse Ashlock and Joe Holley.

From the time of his first sessions in 1935 through his last productive sessions in the early '60s, Wills was about change and movement, his band shrinking and expanding, his music taking on different hues and textures that reflected his drive to keep it fresh, his influence growing throughout the South, Southwest and West Coast as tours brought western swing to new audiences. Disdaining the commonly accepted wisdom about what constituted country music enabled Wills to redefine and broaden conventional boundaries. His influence on country music is profound. If he had written only "New San Antonio Rose," "Faded Love" and "Take Me Back to Tulsa," he would be significant. That his grasp was equal to his considerable reach marks him as one of the most important musical artists of the 20th Century.

Wills's catalog is accessible from a number of vantage points. Those desiring the hits and other familiar tracks would do well to start with Rhino's two-CD set, *Anthology 1935–1973*, which kicks off with "Maiden's Prayer," an evocative instrumental cut at Wills's first session, and ends with two tracks from the now-deleted tribute album *For the Last Time*, a reunion of Wills and several former Playboys, along with contemporary disciples such as Merle Haggard. *Anthology*'s 32 well-chosen cuts show the band's remarkable range in its execution of variegated material—check out Wills's own bluesy vocal on "Corrina, Corrina"—as well as the evolution of Wills's sound with different configurations of Playboys. Similarly, *The Bob Wills Anthology* and *The Golden Era* on Columbia chronicle the first rich period in Wills's recording history, from 1935 through the late '40s. On these tracks it's possible to form a picture of Wills's aggressive pursuit of new ideas as the years progressed. An early track, "Spanish Two-Step," is equal parts swing and traditional western music. *Golden Era* finds him taking on Liszt's "Liebestraum" in a fiddle-less arrangement driven by horns and a quicksilver solo from McAuliffe on pedal steel, all but the last being in a big-band bag that would have been right at home on a Glenn Miller record; on the same disc he offers up a version of Rossini's "William Tell Overture" that comes right out of the Jelly Roll Morton era, although one wonders if even Morton could have delivered a piano solo as wacky but totally appropriate as Stricklin's. As the Columbia sides indicate, Wills's guitarists brought their own styles to bear. Arnspiger played in a traditional country manner, while his replacement, Eldon Shamblin, could cut and run like a jazz player; conversely, Shamblin's replacement, Lester Barnard, was the most basic of the three and the one most rooted in deep blues. That Wills adapted his music to accommodate each of these distinctive stylists' individual voices speaks volumes about his wisdom as a bandleader. He seemed to sense that in change lay continuity, and simply provided a solid framework—drums, fiddles, piano—on which to build a living, breathing legacy.

Columbia Historic Edition and *Remembering . . .* both offer abridged but sensible samplings of Wills's '40s recordings, some well known, some not. The Country Music Foundation's entry in the Wills catalog is the interesting *Fiddle* album, with seven previously unreleased recordings among its 20 all-instrumental tracks. This, too, is an example of how adept an alchemist Wills was in incorporating blues and jazz into his traditional fiddle style.

For Wills completists, Kaleidoscope's nine-volume *Tiffany Transcriptions* set is the Holy Grail. In 1946–47 Wills and the Playboys recorded some 370 sides (more than he recorded for any label) on 16-inch acetate discs that were sent to radio stations with an accompanying script to be read by DJs between songs. The Tiffany Music Company had been formed in 1945 by Wills, songwriter Cliff Sundlin and radio personality Clifton Johnson as a radio syndication vehicle for Wills's shows. Sundlin, the money man behind the project, was also a songwriter hoping to interest Wills in recording some of his material, hence his willingness to back the project. Only a few of the recordings had been released before the company dissolved; the transcriptions and related promotional material were then stored in Sundlin's house, unplayed and for all intents and purposes nonexistent until after Sundlin's death in 1981, when his granddaughter made them available to Kaleidoscope.

It's fair to say that Wills and the Playboys functioned at their highest level on the Tiffany shows—for sustained excellence *The Tiffany Transcriptions* has few parallels in American music. Since these were designed to be shows, Wills didn't rehearse his band beforehand. The musicians set up in a San Francisco studio and played as if they were working a dance. Thus we hear some of the finest instrumentalists of their day playing off the cuff, as it were, nothing prearranged, Wills calling out solos according to his fancy. The staggering range of the music on these discs is indicated by subtitles such as *Basin Street Blues* and *You're from Texas*. Virtually no genre goes untouched. Those who want the tried and true Wills should opt for Volume 2, which contains "Faded Love," "San Antonio Rose," "Cotton Eyed Joe," "Time Changes Everything" and other Wills standards; those who want great music should purchase each volume. — D.M.

JACKIE WILSON

★★★★½ **The Jackie Wilson Story (Epic, 1983)**
★★★★½ **The Jackie Wilson Story, Vol. 2 (Epic, 1985)**
★★★ **Through the Years (Rhino, 1987)**
★★★★★ **Mr. Excitement! (Rhino, 1992)**
Influenced heavily by Roy Brown and Clyde McPhatter, Detroit native Jackie Wilson

broke into the music business in 1953 as McPhatter's replacement in Billy Ward's Dominoes. Three indifferent years produced only one minor hit, "St. Therese of the Roses," before Wilson went solo and cut a Top Twenty R&B hit out of the box, "Reet Petite," written by Berry Gordy, then a struggling songwriter, later the founder of Motown Records. The next year produced a Top Thirty pop hit, "To Be Loved," and ended with Wilson in the Top Ten with the enduring "Lonely Teardrops." From that point through 1968 Wilson was found regularly in the Top Forty. Among his hits are a couple of early soul classics in "Baby Workout" and "Higher and Higher," as well as a raft of powerful performances of both uptempo and ballad material. His appeal was further bolstered by frenetic live performances, with Wilson using his athlete's grace and physical command (he had been a Golden Gloves champion) to whip his audiences into a frenzy. Spins, splits and slides were all part of his repertoire, as was the one-footed dance. Wilson had all the tools.

Wilson's entire recording career was spent with the now-defunct Brunswick label. Rhino's three-CD, 72-track anthology *Mr. Excitement!* renders the out-of-print *Jackie Wilson Story Vol. 1* and *2* and *Through the Years* obsolete. The collection includes the most vital tracks from "Reet Petite" through the '60s, up to the Top Thirty R&B single "You Got Me Walking" (1972), written by the Chi-Lites' Eugene Record. Wilson aficionados will find some interesting previously out-of-print album tracks and singles, such as a steamy duet with LaVern Baker, "Think Twice," and a foray into country-pop, "Right Now" (1958). *Mr. Excitement!* adds dimension and perspective to the work of an important and still underappreciated artist. — D.M.

WILSON PHILLIPS

★★½ **Wilson Phillips (SBK, 1990)**
★★½ **Shadows and Light (SBK, 1992)**
It would be hard to imagine a purer California rock bloodline than this—Carnie and Wendy Wilson are the daughters of Beach Boy Brian Wilson, while Chynna Phillips had Michelle and John Phillips as Mama and Papa. But these three aren't just second-generation rockers; they're also children of the California culture that rock produced, and that plays as large a part in their approach as any musical tradition. Granted, the group's ability to harmonize had a lot more to do with its radio success

than any lyrical concept, but it would be hard to imagine songs like "Hold On" or "You're In Love" (from *Wilson Phillips*) having the same placid pace were it not for their "I'm OK, You're OK" underpinnings. But rather than add depth to the music, the group's rehashed pop psychology—particularly when applied to the famous-family troubles addressed in "Where Are You" and "Flesh and Blood," on *Shadows and Light*—merely reinforces the sense that Wilson Phillips' songs are as shallow as they are pretty.   — J.D.C.

THE WINANS
★★ **Let My People Go (Qwest/WB, 1985)**
★★ **Decisions (Qwest/WB, 1987)**
★★ **Return (Qwest/WB, 1990)**
★★ **Long Time Comin' (Light, NA)**
★★ **Tomorrow (Light, NA)**
The Winans make gospel music that would serve God and Mammon too. The four Winans brothers from Detroit are steeped in the Word and the world, their music informed by the pop-gospel stylings of Andrae Crouch, their sensibility by the evening news that shows a civilization in decline. Their message is relentlessly upbeat and can get preachy, but their sincerity seems real. Unfortunately, this contemporary gospel music has no relation to the great work of the gospel giants of the '40s and '50s, whose testimony was forged from rugged personal experience and fear of the Lord's vengeance. What the Winans purvey is Lite Gospel—Michael McDonald sings on one cut on *Decisions* and Kenny G shows up on *Return*. There's no question the Winans believe in the power of their message, but is this any way to save a soul?   — D.M.

WINGER
★★ **Winger (Atlantic, 1988)**
★★½ **In the Heart of the Young (Atlantic, 1990)**
Had there been no MTV, or had Kip Winger not been so good looking, it's still possible that this conventionally melodic hard-rock act would have been a hit. But between MTV's market power and the singer's videogenic appearance, the band's ascendence was all but guaranteed. If that makes it sound as if Winger's music played only a minor role in the band's success story, well, what can I say? "Headed for a Heartbreak," from *Winger*, is fairly imaginative for a power ballad, with interesting harmonies and a pleasantly

dramatic chorus, but the rest of the album is club-circuit dreck, from the Van Halen-ish "Hangin' On" to the guitar overkill of Hendrix's "Purple Haze." And though the band doesn't improve much with *In the Heart of the Young*, it has at least learned from its initial success; not only are the rockers less given to excess, offering fewer guitar solos and more vocal harmonies, but the album's ballad quotient has gone up significantly.   — J.D.C.

WINGS
★★½ **Wild Life (1971; Capitol, 1989)**
★★ **Red Rose Speedway (1973; Capitol, 1988)**
★★★★ **Band on the Run (1973; Capitol, 1987)**
★★★½ **Venus and Mars (Capitol, 1975)**
★★★ **Wings at the Speed of Sound (Capitol, 1976)**
★★★★ **Wings Over America (Capitol, 1977)**
★★★ **London Town (Capitol, 1978)**
★★★★ **Greatest (Capitol, 1978)**
★★½ **Back to the Egg (1978; Capitol, 1989)**
After he left the Beatles, Paul McCartney's best and worst tendencies came to the fore—his flawless technique and brilliant pop instincts continued to make him a musician impossible to dismiss; uncorked, his compulsive cuteness too often gushed like a geyser. Demonstrating his commendable adaptability, love of team spirit and faith in the creative mechanics of a working band, he alone of the former Fab Four founded an actual group—in Wings, Paul was joined by ex–Moody Blues-er Denny Laine on guitar, bass and vocals, sessionman Denny Seiwell on drums, and McCartney's wife, Linda (much to subsequent ridicule) on keyboards and backup vocals. Almost from the start, the outfit was a commercial success— McCartney's production skills, his gift for pouring forth radio-ready hits, and the loyalty of Beatle fans ensured that Wings would've had to release abysmal music in order to flop.

During their career, however, they often came close to doing just that. After their bland, reggae-inflected debut, *Wild Life*, Wings added ex–Joe Cocker guitarist Henry McCullogh, put out *Red Rose Speedway*, and nearly confirmed suspicions that McCartney was little more than the world's best jingle writer. In terms of its lyrics, "My Love" was certainly the worst single Paul had ever penned. However, even on such piffle, McCartney's bass playing was remarkable, and, throughout the album, his overall musicianship was so obviously apparent that he could only be dismissed by the hardiest of cynics.

Proving that any announcement of his creative demise was premature, he answered his critics with *Band on the Run*. Siewell and McCullogh had flown the coop, making the album basically an all-Paul triumph—the best post-Beatles music he's ever produced. "Helen Wheels," "Jet" and the title track were pop at its most artful; the album demonstrated that McCartney's skill was still intact.

The followup, *Venus and Mars*, was no masterpiece, but it wasn't bad. With new drummer Joe English and guitarist Jimmy McCulloch, the group scored hits with "Listen to What the Man Said" and "Crossroads," and prepared for a massive world tour. *Wings at the Speed of Sound* featured mediocre lead vocals by each of the band members (Paul, proving true, however misguidedly, to his democratic ideal), but it was McCartney's songs that sold the record—the affable "Let Me In," and the defensive "Silly Love Songs." The 30-song tour documentary, *Wings Over America*, established the band's credibility as a highly skilled live outfit; the record's five Beatles songs also proved that McCartney's higher ambitions were indeed a thing of the past. *London Town* and its hit, "With a Little Luck," was Paul at his cuddliest; *Back to the Egg* was singularly uninspired, and in 1981, Wings called it quits. Wings' *Greatest*, demonstrating Paul's attention to the art of the single, is better than any individual album the group did except *Band on the Run*. — P.E.

GEORGE WINSTON
   ★   **Ballads and Blues (1973, Dancing Cat, 1992)**
  ★★   **Autumn (Windham Hill, 1980)**
  ★★   **Winter Into Spring (Windham Hill, 1982)**
  ★★   **December (Windham Hill, 1982)**
★★★½ **Summer (Windham Hill, 1991)**
WITH MERYL STREEP
 ★★½ **The Velveteen Rabbit (Dancing Cat, 1985)**
One of the first new age artists to achieve any sort of commercial success, George Winston specializes in what he has called "folk piano." Indeed, his first album, *Ballads and Blues*, was originally released on Takoma Records, and offered rambling,

repetitious performances not unlike—but not quite as imaginative as—John Fahey's guitar albums. With *Autumn*, Winston began a sequence of seasonally oriented recordings that rely less on the blues and more on circular themes and episodic song structures, an approach that at its best sounds like dumbed-down Keith Jarrett; *December*, which features his interpretations of several Christmas carols as well as a near-interminable "Variations on the Kanon by Johann Pachelbel," is typical. But *Summer*, recorded after a nine-year hiatus, finds Winston's playing far more focussd, supplying solos of substance instead of mere mood music. — J.D.C.

EDGAR WINTER
  ★★★   **Edgar Winter's White Trash (Epic, 1971)**
 ★★★½ **Roadwork (Epic, 1972)**
★★★★ **They Only Come out at Night (Epic, 1972)**
  ★★½ **Shock Treatment (Epic, 1974)**
  ★★½ **Jasmine Nightdreams (Blue Sky, 1975)**
The younger sibling of blues-guitar whiz Johnny Winter, Edgar is a musical switch-hitter who juggles sax, keyboards and vocals. He debuted with the now-deleted *Entrance* in 1970. After that jazz-rock fiasco, Edgar Winter found his voice on *White Trash*: a slightly nasal take on roadhouse R&B, bolstered by a hot and horny backing band. "Keep on Playing That Rock 'n' Roll" pretty much sets the agenda. Recorded live, *Roadwork* captures the group in its natural environment; brother Johnny strolls in for an incendiary "Rock & Roll Hootchie Koo."

They Only Come Out at Night is an entirely different propositon. Trimming his band down to a quartet, Winter gets hard-rock underpinning from guitarist Ronnie Montrose and much-needed pop focus from bassist-songwriter Dan Hartman. "Free Ride" and "Frankenstein" provide the hitbound hooks, while touches like the country twang of "Round and Round" add variety and depth. It's not exactly a deathless classic, but *They Only Come Out at Night* offers suprisingly consistent thrills and chills. *Shock Treatment* and the deleted *Jasmine Nightdreams* (1975) attempt to replicate that success, with lukewarm results. — M.C.

JOHNNY WINTER
★★★★ **Johnny Winter (Columbia, 1969)**
 ★★★ **Second Winter (Columbia, 1969)**

★★★★   Johnny Winter And (Columbia, 1970)
★★★   Johnny Winter And Live! (Columbia, 1971)
★★★½ Still Alive and Well (Columbia, 1973)
★★★   John Dawson Winter III (Blue Sky, 1974)
★★★   Saints and Sinners (Columbia, 1974)
★★★   Captured Live (Blue Sky, 1976)
★★★½ Nothin' but the Blues (Blue Sky, 1977)
★★★½ Guitar Slinger (Alligator, 1984)
★★★   Serious Business (Alligator, 1985)
★★★   3rd Degree (Alligator, 1986)
★★½ The Winter of 88 (MCA/Voyager, 1988)
★★★½ Let Me In (Point Blank/Charisma, 1991)

Johnny Winter emerged from Texas as a full-formed white bluesman in the late '60s; he was met with thundering media acclaim and a juicy contract from Columbia Records. The fact that Winter is an albino just added to the hype, but what really set him apart was his guitar playing. While most of his peers indulged themselves with lengthy solos, Winter planned his terse, stinging breaks into thought-out arrangements—he never loses sight of the song at hand. Having spent most of the '60s woodshedding in his blues-saturated native state, Winter also developed one febrile howl of a singing voice. Not exactly pop-ish or soulful (like his brother Edgar's could be), his distinctive second instrument perfectly suits Winter-ized standards like Sonny Boy Williamson's "Good Morning Little School Girl." *Second Winter* dishes up a messier second serving of the same Chicago and country-blues fare. Moving toward hard rock with the superb *Johnny Winter And*, Winter formed a versatile (and underrated) band with ex-McCoys guitarist Rick Derringer. The album comfortably ranges from the Southern-fried boogie of "Rock & Roll Hoochie Koo" to the haunting pop-psychedelia of "No Time to Love."

Winter bounced back from a bout with hard drugs on the snarlingly sober *Still Alive and Well*—the title track and "Too Much Seconal" apply a stinging cold slap in the face. *Saints and Sinners* and *John Dawson Winter III* tip the balance a shade too close to heavy metal, though. Producing the triumphant *Hard Again* for Muddy Waters in 1977 must've stimulated Winter's own deep-seated feel for the blues; *Nothin'*

but the Blues is a gratifying return to early form. Riding out the '70s with some unremarkable and out-of-print albums, Winter lay low until the mid-'80s. Reentering the traditional blues market with the splashy *Guitar Slinger*, he doesn't really get his mojo working again until *Let Me In*. Cranking up his National Steel guitar, covering forebears like T-Bone Walker and Jimmy Reed, Winter comes close to rocking that door off its hinges. — M.C.

STEVE WINWOOD

★★★½ Steve Winwood (Island, 1977)
★★★★   Arc of a Diver (Island, 1980)
★★★   Talking Back to the Night (Island, 1982)
★★★½ Back in the High Life (Island, 1986)
★★★★   Chronicles (Island, 1987)
★★★   Roll With It (Virgin, 1988)
★★★½ Refugees of the Heart (Virgin, 1990)

Boy wonder of British blues, Winwood powered through "Gimme Some Lovin'" (1966) and "I'm a Man" (1967) for the Spencer Davis Group, his Hammond organ being played with banshee intensity and his soaring vocals sounding like a mod Ray Charles. The brain behind the bluesy elegance of Traffic, Winwood took dazzling guitar solos and edged rock further into harmonic complexity without capitulating to the crass synthesis of jazz-rock fusion. After dominating Blind Faith, the brilliant but strife-ridden supergroup he'd formed with Eric Clapton and Ginger Baker, Winwood became for a while a virtual hermit.

His return was impressive. "Vacant Chair" and "Time Is Running Out" display his trademark classiness—even if he sounds a little tentative in places throughout *Steve Winwood*, whose atmosphere is one of restraint and careful polish. With *Arc of a Diver*, however, Winwood takes total control. With poetically suggestive lyrics by, of all people, Viv Stanshall, formerly head of the loopy comedy troupe Bonzo Dog Band, the album's title track and "While You See a Chance" are pop of a brilliant calibre: Winwood's keyboards concoct gorgeous sound-tapestries, through which his keening vocals shimmer coolly—and then take off. Winwood's best, this is the kind of mature pop that proves "AOR" needn't be read as a mild obscenity: while played with intimidating craft, the songs demonstrate no lack of passion.

A one-man band on *Talking Back to the Night*, Winwood seems slightly exhausted;

the record is, of course, accomplished, but the singer's moves are beginning to sound calculated, and the material trades more heavily on skill than heart. *Back in the High Life* is absolute gloss. "Higher Love" sounds amazing at first listen, and, if you forget the beer commercial it eventually became, so does the title track—but this is yuppie soul music, a triumph only of artful design. *Roll With It* is even blander, particularly when, as on the boring title tune, it tries for funk. With *Refugees of the Heart*, Winwood edges tentatively back toward music fired by more than fearsomely intelligent technique: "I Will Be Here" and "In the Light of Day" are ballads that mark a return to grace, but the fully dimensional art Winwood had achieved in the past remains missing in action. Aside from *Arc of a Diver*, the *Chronicles* hit collection contains the only essential music. — P.E.

WIRE

★ ★ ★ ★½ **Pink Flag (1977; Restless Retro, 1989)**

★ ★ ★ ★½ **Chairs Missing (1978; Restless Retro, 1989)**

★ ★ ★ ★½ **154 (1979; Restless Retro, 1989)**

★ ★ ★ ★½ **On Returning (1977–79; Restless Retro, 1989)**

   ★ ★½ **The Peel Sessions (1978–79) (EP) (1989; Dutch East India, 1991)**

   ★ ★ **Document and Eyewitness (1981; Mute, 1991)**

   ★ ★ ★½ **Snakedrill (EP) (Mute/Enigma, 1986)**

★ ★ ★ ★½ **The Ideal Copy (1987; Restless Mute, 1991)**

   ★ ★½ **Ahead (EP) (Mute/Enigma, 1987)**

   ★ ★ **A Bell Is a Cup Until It Is Struck (1988; Restless Mute, 1991)**

   ★ ★ **Kidney Bingos (EP) (Mute/Enigma, 1988)**

   ★ ★ **Silk Skin Paws (EP) (Mute, 1988)**

   ★ ★ ★ **It's Beginning to and Back Again (1989; Restless Mute, 1991)**

   ★ ★½ **Manscape (1990; Restless Mute, 1991)**

   ★½ **The Drill (EP) (Mute/Elektra, 1991)**

WIR

   ★ ★½ **The First Letter (Mute/Elektra, 1991)**

Most English punk acts were minimalists only to the extent that their approach rejected rock's unnecessary excess: the solos, the sweetening, the show-biz. Wire, though, didn't just trim away the fat, but distilled the music to its essence. On *Pink Flag*, for instance, the songs rarely offer more than just a simple riff, a basic beat and enough vocal to put the melody across. Once the point has been made, the song ends—a process that usually takes just a couple minutes (or, in the case of "Field Day for the Sundays," a mere 28 seconds). On a formal level, it's an astonishing achievement, pulling punk away from the rock revivalism of the Sex Pistols and Clash without sacrificing its energy or gut-level impact. Indeed, these songs are enormously expressive and offer much to the listener, from the streamlined melody of "Brazil" to the ominous, dissonant drama of "Reuters."

Having established its sound, Wire expands upon it with *Chairs Missing*. In addition to longer songs (one, "Mercy," lingers for almost six minutes!), the arrangements are fleshed out with layered vocals and occasional keyboard fills by producer Mike Thorne. These pop-like touches add tremendously to tunes like "I Am the Fly," "Another the Letter" and "I Feel Mysterious Today." From there, it's but a short hop to the richer textures of *154*, with its exotic instrumentation ("A Mutual Friend," for instance, brings in an English horn for added color) and savvy use of the studio (note how "I Should Have Known Better" cannily manipulates the music's mood through a mix that initially buries the pulse while highlighting the vocal and feedback guitar). Even more impressive, though, is the album's melodic resilience, which in songs like "The 15th" and "Map Ref. 41°N 93°W" manages to pull memorable hooks even from the most angular ideas.

After *154*, Wire announced an indefinite suspension of recording, and singer Colin Newman pursued a solo career while guitarist Bruce Gilbert and bassist Graham Lewis worked as a duo (under the name Dome), and the only new Wire material released during the early '80s came in the form of live recordings: *The Peel Sessions*, a collection of generally enigmatic performances recorded for English disc jockey John Peel's BBC show; and *Document and Eyewitness*, a none-too-accessible live album. (*On Returning* compiles highlights from *Pink Flag*, *Chairs Missing* and *154*, but given the quality of each, *On Returning* should be considered only by those on a budget.)

In 1986, Wire returned, first with a four-song EP called *Snakedrill*, then with a full album, *The Ideal Copy* (which, on CD, also includes all of *Snakedrill* plus three live tracks). Amazingly, the band picked up pretty much where it left off, using synthesizer technology to update the specifics of its sound but offering an otherwise similar approach, as the likes of "Ahead" and the stark, morose "Feed Me" make plain. Still, there are some new wrinkles, the most notable being the fondness for mechanical repetition manifest in "Drill." That techno-drone technique recurs through *Ahead* and *Kidney Bingos*, although the songs in each case are strong enough to keep either EP from seeming like mere experiments. Even so, *A Bell Is a Cup Until It Is Struck* is a disappointment, as the songs—apart from "Kidney Bingos," "Silk Skin Paws" and "The Queen of Ur and the King of Um"—seem to exist more as a means to demonstrate the band's mastery of form. Things improve somewhat with *It's Beginning To and Back Again* (or *IBTABA*), thanks to the oddly appealing "Eardrum Buzz," but as its title hints, the album as a whole focuses on reconfiguring previously recorded material like *A Bell Is a Cup*'s "Finest Drops" and "Boiling Boy." (Even "Eardrum Buzz" itself is offered in two versions.)

With *Manscape*, Wire's experimental side becomes somewhat less reductive, even as the band's increasing technophilia—as evidenced by the abundant use of sequencers, samplers and drum machines—threatens to transform the group into a compositional workshop. *The Drill* attempts to have it both ways, presenting nine variations on the song "Drill," ranging from the ultraremixed "(A Berlin) Drill," in which the band itself becomes a sort of manipulated datum, to "(A Chicago) Drill," a concert recording which grinds away at the song's central riff for 12 excruciating minutes. Apparently, that was too much even for drummer Robert Gotobed, who left (muttering about his technology-induced redundancy) after *The Drill*. His bandmates acknowledged his departure by dropping the final letter from the group's name; their first album as Wir, *The First Letter* continues in the same vein as *Manscape*, with a greater emphasis on instrumental texture and a similar lack of melodic interest. — J.D.C.

WISHBONE ASH
★ ★½ Wishbone Ash (MCA, 1970)
★ ★ Pilgrimage (MCA, 1971)
★ ★ ★ Argus (MCA, 1972)
★ ★½ Wishbone Four (MCA, 1973)
★ ★ ★ Live Dates (MCA, 1973)
★ ★ Here to Here (I.R.S., 1989)

Dual lead guitars (Andy Powell and Ted Turner) and bassist-lyricist Martin Turner's folkloric bent are what distinguishes this journeyman British quartet from the boogie hordes of the early '70s. The debut album and *Pilgrimage* pound along like Grand Funk with an English accent—and no hooks save for the occasional pungent riff. *Argus* is an improvement; the acoustic element adds some drama to the inevitable crunchathons, and the muddled concept—maidens, warriors, a sylvan glade, that sort of thing—actually makes for consistency.

Wishbone Ash thrived on the concert circuit; the band was a classic second- or third-billed act of the time. References to the rocky road abound on *Wishbone Four*, and it's only fitting that the likes of "Rock 'n' Roll Widow" and earlier "hits" sound more forceful on *Live Dates*. That album captures a minor band at its peak; the next half-dozen Wishbone Ash albums—all mercifully out of print—are complete washouts. Tellingly, the group reunited in the late '80s to pursue an instrumental path bordering on New Age; *Here to Here* exemplifies the band's new leanings.
— M.C.

BILL WITHERS
★ ★ ★ ★ Just As I Am (1972; Sussex/Columbia, 1985)
★ ★ ★ ★ Still Bill (1972; Sussex/Columbia, 1985)
★ ★ ★ Greatest Hits (Columbia, 1981)
Bill Withers was already in his thirties when his debut album caught on, and his voice conveys an unfazed assurance. Produced by Booker T. Jones, *Just As I Am* accentuates Withers's folk-flavored songwriting with spare arrangements and subtle, funky support. "Ain't No Sunshine" is the single that rocketed Withers into the national spotlight, while tracks like "Harlem" and "Grandma's Hands" indicate he's more than another golden throat. *Still Bill* is a followup effort that repeated the debut's success—artistically and commercially. The gospel-tinged "Lean On Me" and the scintillating "Use Me" broadened his range, but Bill Withers seemed to back off from that challenge a little more with each successive album. After he got to Columbia in the mid-'70s, Withers discreetly stepped over to the middle of the road. His quiet-storm collaborations with Grover Washington Jr. ("Just the Two of Us") and the Crusaders ("Soul Shadows") create a pleasing background haze, but they're a bit

frustrating. That voice is clearly capable of more than supper-club soul. —M.C.

PETER WOLF

★ ★ ★½ **Lights Out (EMI America, 1984)**
★ ★ ★   **Come As You Are (EMI America, 1987)**
★ ★ ★   **Up to No Good (MCA, 1990)**

After leaving seminal R&B partiers the J. Geils Band, lead singer Peter Wolf released the solo album *Lights Out* in 1984. Boston hip-hop maven Michael Jonzun helped concoct a rangy, comfortable electro-wallop that suited the blues-belting rocker a lot better than you'd think. Unfortunately, Wolf plays it much safer on his subsequent solo albums; after *Lights Out*, he seemed to lose that manic, magic spark. —M.C.

BOBBY WOMACK

★ ★ ★ **Communication (U.A., 1971)**
★ ★ ★ **Understanding (U.A., 1972)**
★ ★ ★ **Facts of Life (U.A., 1973)**
★ ★ ★ **Safety Zone (U.A., 1976)**
★ ★   **Womagic (MCA, 1986)**
★ ★   **The Last Soul Man (MCA, 1987)**

A man of considerable talent with little to show for it in the way of in-print albums, Bobby Womack seems a man whose potential is forever in need of being realized. His career began in the '50s, when he and his brothers formed a gospel group, the Womack Brothers, who were transformed into the Valentinos after Sam Cooke signed them to his Sar label. There they proceeded to cut two R&B classics, "It's All Over Now" and "Lookin' for a Love," which were later covered by the Rolling Stones and J. Geils, respectively. Following Cooke's death, the Valentinos disbanded, and Bobby turned to session work, in short order becoming one of the most in-demand guitarists in the business. After beginning his solo career in the late '60s on the Minit label, he moved to United Artists and cut a string of flawed but compelling albums (now out of print), one being *Facts of Life*, a stirring collection of soul ballads and uptempo numbers done in a style reminiscent of Cooke's. The U.A. period, though, is erratic, despite Womack's obvious strength as a singer and songwriter (admirably displayed on *Communication* and *Understanding*). His final U.A. album, *Safety Zone*, has the grit of Womack's early work, owing to producer David Rubinson's intelligent production. Late-'70s albums for Columbia and Arista are half-baked self-productions burying some strong songs in pointless, overblown arrangements.

The pattern continued at MCA. *Womagic* teamed Womack with Memphis-based producer Chips Moman. Bobby Womack in Memphis sounds like a good idea, but *Womagic* is a schizoid effort, at times properly restrained and supportive of Womack's forceful vocals, but for the most part overblown beyond all reason. So Womack went back to producing himself on *The Last Soul Man*, with disastrous results. Someday Bobby Womack will make a great record. It's been a long time coming. —D.M.

WOMACK AND WOMACK

★ ★ ★ **Love Wars (Elektra, 1983)**
★ ★ ★ **Radio M.U.S.C. Man (Elektra, 1985)**
★ ★   **Conscience (Island, 1988)**
★ ★   **Family Spirit (RCA, 1991)**

Brother of Bobby Womack, daughter of Sam Cooke, Cecil and Linda Womack went right to the heart of the matter in the '80s in a series of albums whose songs echoed the temper of the times in households all across the land. The Womacks undertook to explore the disintegration of love. The result was three of the strangest records of the decade. The large themes the Womacks addressed included domestic violence, abandonment, infidelity, duplicity . . . you get the drift. And so we'd know where their own hearts were at, each album closed with a song meant to convey their belief in tomorrow. Still, it's tough to sit through *Radio M.U.S.C. Man* and hear them sing lyrics on the order of "I'm leavin', we're not compatible" ("No Relief"); "I'm gonna bury my fantasies / In the deep, dark sea / So the emotional stress of love / Won't cause no misery" ("Maze"); "Time has changed our voices / We no longer blend / The guilt is in the air / We got secrets everywhere" ("Strange and Funny"); and then be confronted at album's end with George Harrison's "Here Comes the Sun."

But that's not nearly as extreme as *Conscience*. The songs are less explicit than those on *Love Wars* (where the title song makes reference to the woman hitting the man "upside his head") and *Radio M.U.S.C. Man*, but a lyric booklet offers an explanation of the characters' motives in each song. So we are told that a song about people failing to understand the meaning of friendship, "Friends (So Called)," underscores how "the end results have reflected a breakdown in mans' [sic] progress." Or this by way of informing us that the female character is determined to get on with her life after her man has gone:

"Her hurtness shines through the teardrops that drip on the dance floor as she tries to party her blues away." And then there's the happy-face ending, "Celebrate the World," a plea for world peace and unity through music, because "musical words and melodies of song have the power to bring together people of different beliefs, languages and nationalities, under one common groove."

Family Spirit finds the duo more hangdog in their view of the world than we might have expected coming off "Celebrate the World." Without belaboring the point, it sounds as if all those love wars have taken a toll, and now there's little left to ponder save the fine mess we're in. And yet, there's that glimmer, faint but visible off in the distance: "Keep on Climbing," redolent of the gospel tradition with which both artists are conversant, rendered in moving, proud voices, saying—in words more eloquent than any they've mustered since *Love Wars*—stay strong; the struggle continues, but love, pride, and dignity will out in the end. Perhaps. — D.M.

STEVIE WONDER

★ ★½ **The Jazz Soul of Little Stevie (Motown, 1963)**
★ ★ ★ **The 12 Year Old Genius (Motown, 1963)**
★ ★ **Tribute to Uncle Ray (Motown, 1963)**
★ ★ **With a Song in My Heart (Motown, 1963)**
★ ★ ★ **Up-Tight (Motown, 1966)**
★ ★½ **Down to Earth (1966; Motown, 1986)**
★ ★ ★½ **I Was Made to Love Her (Motown, 1967)**
★ ★ ★½ **Greatest Hits (Motown, 1968)**
★ ★ ★ **Alfie (Motown, 1968)**
★ ★ ★½ **For Once in My Life (Motown, 1968)**
★ ★ ★ **My Cherie Amour (Motown, 1969)**
★ ★ ★ **Signed Sealed & Delivered (Motown, 1970)**
★ ★ ★ ★ **Where I'm Coming From (Motown, 1971)**
★ ★ ★ ★ **Stevie Wonder's Greatest Hits Vol. 2 (Tamla, 1971)**
★ ★ ★ ★ **Music of My Mind (Motown, 1972)**
★ ★ ★ ★ ★ **Talking Book (Tamla, 1972)**
★ ★ ★ ★ ★ **Innervisions (Motown, 1973)**
★ ★ ★ ★ **Fulfillingness' First Finale (Motown, 1974)**
★ ★ ★ ★ ★ **Songs in the Key of Life (Motown, 1976)**
★ ★ ★ ★½ **Looking Back (Motown, 1978)**
★ ★ ★ ★ **Journey Through the Secret Life of Plants (Tamla, 1979)**
★ ★ ★ ★ **Hotter Than July (Tamla, 1980)**
★ ★ ★ ★ **Stevie Wonder's Original Musiquarium I (Tamla, 1982)**
★ ★ ★ **The Woman in Red (Motown, 1984)**
★ ★ ★ **In Square Circle (Tamla, 1985)**
★ ★ ★½ **Characters (Motown, 1987)**
★ ★ ★½ **Jungle Fever (Motown, 1991)**

Perhaps the most singular talent ever to grace the Motown roster, Stevie Wonder began his recording career at age 11. At his peak, he scored five Number One singles in six years, and was a perennial favorite at award shows like the Grammys. Even more amazing is the fact that Wonder did so entirely on his own terms, building a catalog of songs that managed to retain the harmonic sophistication of prerock pop while remaining completely up-to-date rhythmically. It would be an exaggeration, though, to suggest that the scope of Wonder's potential was evident from the first. True, his second album did bill him as *The 12 Year Old Genius*, but "prodigy" would have been a more appropriate term. His debut, *The Jazz Soul of Little Stevie*, is an instrumental album featuring Wonder on piano, organ, harmonica, drums and bongos, and while it's impressive from a technical standpoint, musically it sounds too much like the work of an 11-year-old. Fortunately, one track from that album, a bongo number called "Fingertips," is transformed into an absolutely incandescent harmonica showcase on *The 12 Year Old Genius*, a concert recording that became Wonder's fist chart-topping single. But it's the only real bright point on Wonder's first four albums; *A Tribute to Uncle Ray* finds the young singer reprising some of Ray Charles's better-known hits, while *With a Song in My Heart* is an appallingly earnest attempt at MOR ballad-singing.

Wonder doesn't get a proper Motown sound until *Up-Tight*, which even kicks off with a Motown-tribute tune, "Love a Go Go." Still, his commitment to the style is far from absolute, as *Up-Tight* finds room for a version of "Blowin' in the Wind," while *Down to Earth* has him handling such seemingly inappropriate material as "Bang Bang (My Baby Shot Me Down)" and "Sixteen Tons." *I Was Made to Love Her* has much better taste in cover material, tending more toward classic soul tunes like "My Girl" and "Can I Get a Witness" (although Wonder doesn't quite know what to do with James Brown's "Please Please Please"). But it's the title tune, with its incredible James Jamerson bass line, that makes this album—or the subsequent *Greatest Hits Vol. 1*—worth owning.

And yet he continued to yo-yo stylistically, swinging from the innocuous instrumentals of *Alfie* to the jazz-tinged soul of *For Once in My Life* to the sentimental balladry of *My Cherie Amour* to the straight-up soul of *Signed Sealed & Delivered*. The latter was the first album Wonder produced on his own, but he doesn't truly begin to take control of his music until *Where I'm Coming From*, an album in which he uses his multi-instrumental virtuosity to provide nearly all the parts himself. It sounds dated today, but that's more a function of technology (primitive synths and the like) than the music itself, which is often striking. Wonder's *Greatest Hits Vol. 2* covers most of the period's big singles, but a far better overview (if you can find it) is the now-deleted *Looking Back*, which not only highlights his albums to this point, but includes a number of non-LP singles.

With *Music of My Mind*, Wonder's albums turn a corner. His albums from this point find him working as a self-sufficient, completely independent recording entity, handling the writing, production and most of the instrumental chores himself—an unprecedented move for a Motown artist at that time. Unlike *Where I'm Coming From*, *Music of My Mind* arrives fully realized, with a resonant sound and songwriting that pushes his melodic instincts in unexpected directions. Yet as "Superwoman (Where Were You When I Needed You)" makes plain, this change of approach hasn't hurt his pop appeal. *Talking Book*, for instance, is a pop tour de force, with Wonder's work running the gamut from the blissful romanticism of "You Are the Sunshine of My Life" to the melodic exuberance of "I Believe (When I Fall in Love It Will Be Forever)" to the snaky funk of "Superstition," and *Innervisions* continues in kind, thanks to songs as accessible and inspired as the jazzy "Don't You Worry 'Bout a Thing" or the deliciously melancholy "All in Love Is Fair." *Innervisions* also finds Wonder addressing deeper issues, as "Living for the City" dramatizes the injustice of black urban life while "Higher Ground" and "Jesus Children of America" evoke a sense of spiritual struggle. Those topics crop up again on *Fulfillingness' First Finale*, and, indeed,

spark one of its highlights, the bitingly anti-Nixon "You Haven't Done Nothin'." Still, Wonder's playful side dominates, and it's a pleasure to hear his almost bashful profession of lust in "Boogie on Reggae Woman."

By *Songs in the Key of Life*, Wonder is clearly at his peak, effortlessly sustaining the focus required of a double album while demonstrating an almost frightening capacity for hit singles. Even better, he's able to deal with an astonishing range of material, writing memorably about anything from childhood ("I Wish") to childbirth ("Isn't She Lovely"), and from ardent love ("Knocks Me Off My Feet") to fervent fandom ("Sir Duke"). But rather than try to top that album, Wonder went off in an entirely different direction, spending three years on *The Secret Life of Plants*. Although ridiculed at the time for its lack of commerciality, the album doesn't entirely deserve its reputation as a pop-star boondoggle, for not only does this atmospheric soundtrack succeed on its own terms, but it manages to do everything expected of a new age album without succumbing to the usual directionless noodling. And it does have its share of pop elements, including "Send One Your Love" and the insinuatingly rhythmic "Race Babbling."

Even so, Wonder wasn't forgiven until he delivered the buoyantly tuneful *Hotter Than July*, an album most fans considered a return to form. To the extent that it produced two Top Twenty singles ("I Ain't Gonna Stand for It" and "Master Blaster [Jammin']") as well as the shoulda-been hit "Happy Birthday" (a Martin Luther King tribute), that's a fair assessment. Wonder's methods are different this time around, though, as many tracks are recorded with either an all-star backing choir, a full rhythm section, or both, while "Do I Do," one of the four new numbers for the greatest-hits package *Stevie Wonder's Original Musiquarium I*, actually finds him jamming with a live band (and guest soloist Dizzy Gillespie).

From there, Wonder's output becomes maddeningly unpredictable. His soundtrack album from *The Woman in Red* has some astonishingly lovely melodies, including "Love Light in Flight" and a charming collaboration with Dionne Warwick entitled "Moments Aren't Moments," but it also presents Wonder at his schlockiest in "I Just Called to Say I Love You." *In Square Circle* is even more uneven, as Wonder backs lusciously melodic songs like "Part-Time Lover" and "Stranger on the Shore of Love" with gratingly mechanical rhythm programs, while *Characters* undercuts its obvious ambition with a near-complete lack of musical edge. The dearth of great new Stevie Wonder material guaranteed his lightweight-but-likeable soundtrack to *Jungle Fever* a far more enthusiastic reception than it would have received ten years earlier. — J.D.C.

BRENTON WOOD
★ ★ ★ **The Best of Brenton Wood (Rhino, 1986)**
While hardly an R&B heavy hitter, Brenton Wood was so sure and engaging a singer that he gained two big mid-'60s hits in "Gimme Little Sign" and the novelty favorite, "Oogum Boogum Song." Tight playing characterizes the songs, and Wood's voice—a supple, deft wonder—makes each of them unerring examples of prime Top Forty. A catalogue of benign clothes fetishism, "Oogum Boogum" lists the charms of a miniskirted object of Wood's desire; the singer ogles, but he doesn't leer. Including a nifty verion of "Psychotic Reaction," Wood's *Best of* is unchallenging but consistently entertaining. — P.E.

RON WOOD
★ ★ ★ **I've Got My Own Album to Do (Warner Bros., 1974)**
★ ★ ★ **Now Look (Warner Bros., 1975)**
★ ★ ½ **Gimme Some Neck (Columbia, 1979)**
★ ★ ★ ½ **1234 (Columbia, 1981)**
From his rooster haircut and eternal cigarette to his passionately ragged Chuck Berry guitar style, Ron Wood seemed like Keith Richards's kid brother even before he joined the Stones. The leap from Rod Stewart's Faces to Mick 'n' Keith came by way of *I've Got My Own Album to Do*, an engaging mess of rock and funk; "Crotch Music" captures the spirit of superstar sessions that featured Jagger and Richards joining in with Wood's scratchy guitar and scratchier vocals. Round two, *Now Look*, was punchier and more precise; Bobby Womack added a more authentic soulfulness, and a tough take on the R&B classic "I Can't Stand the Rain" was convincing. Curiously, Wood's least interesting solo effort, *Gimme Some Neck*, is his only album currently in print. Wood's solo best was *1234*, a sort of Dylan-meets-Faces workout. Wood's records, basically, are party music—and

indeed the boy does bring merriment to the proceedings. His best playing, though, is on Rod Stewart's original solo albums; not only does he rock with a fierceness gained from his early tenure on bass with Jeff Beck, but his acoustic and slide work is clever, lean and inspiring. — P.E.

WOODENTOPS
★ ★ ★ ★ **Well Well Well . . . (Upside, 1985)**
★ ★ ★ ★ ½ **Giant (Columbia, 1986)**
★ ★ ★ ½ **Hypno-Beat (Upside, 1987)**
★ ★ ★ ★ **Wooden Foot Cops on the Highway (Columbia, 1988)**
The Woodentops' sound emphasized the innocence implicit in punk's do-it-yourself aesthetic. Their instrumentation was simple (guitars, bass, minimal drums, Casio keyboard), their playing was fast (a mid-tempo gallop being about as slow as it got), and their songwriting was resolutely melodic—all qualities that made *Well Well Well . . .* (a compilation including several of the 'Tops' early singles plus the *Straight Eight Bushwalker* EP) an engaging debut.

Giant refines the band's sound, fleshing out the arrangements with occasional splashes of color like the marimba on "Good Thing" or the trumpet on "Good Time," but never messes with its essential energies. It's the writing that carries the album, though, thanks to infectious numbers like "Love Train," "History" and "Love Affair with Everyday Living"—many of which are repeated on the adrenalized live album *Hypno-Beat*. There's a bit more ambition in the sound of *Wooden Foot Cops on the Highway*, however. With the assistance of top-scale studio players like Fred Maher, Bernie Worrell and Doug Wimbish, the Woodentops not only vary their rhythmic ideas but add breadth to the music's sense of mood, changes that allow the band to pull off anything from the slow-burning dance groove of "Wheels Turning" to the intriguing nuances of "You Make Me Feel." — J.D.C.

WORLD PARTY
★ ★ ★ **Private Revolution (Chrysalis, 1986)**
★ ★ ★ ½ **Goodbye Jumbo (Chrysalis, 1990)**
★ ★ ★ ½ **Thank You World (EP) (Chrysalis, 1991)**
An ex-member of the Waterboys, World Party mainman Karl Wallinger carries over some of the highflown Celtic romanticism of his former group, but he tricks it out in '60s pop clothing. *Private Revolution* is a striking debut—with Dylan as its guiding light

(there's a great version of "All I Really Want to Do") and hooks aplenty, its music sounds like neat revivalist folk rock with a few psychedelic embellishments. But Wallinger's woozily utopian lyrics make it more than crafty—the revolution he so breathlessly espouses is obviously a Green one ("World," for Wallinger, is a kind of sanctified, neo-pagan concept: Mother Earth as God, or something like that), and he's fervent, too, about New Age self-reliance. Plainly, he's working out some sort of vision—though his "ideas" are about as concrete as Donovan's or Arthur Lee's. *Goodbye Jumbo* mixes in some fine love ballads—with Sinéad O'Connor on backing vocals, "Sweet Soul Dream" is particularly moving—along with Wallinger's usual cosmic consciousness, and the record's Beatle quotes and strong melodies find him developing as a songwriter. Better yet, his words treat the concerns of soul and flesh with just as poetic a passion as his first album did—but he's gained, too, in toughness. His version of John Lennon's "Happiness Is a Warm Gun" (from *Thank You World*) is faithful, but not overreverent, and the fact that he chose that Beatles oldie to cover, rather than, say, "Across the Universe," is reassuring. Wonder, however, remains Wallinger's forte—and amid the professionalism (or mere cynical campiness) of most postmodern pop, the presence of a dreamer is welcome. — P.E.

GARY WRIGHT
★ ★ ★ **The Dream Weaver (Warner Bros., 1975)**
Formerly of the proto-metal unit Spooky Tooth, keyboardist and singer Gary Wright helped pave the way for synth-pop with this 1975 album—unwittingly, perhaps. The gushy title ballad luxuriates in tuneful electronic frippery, while the peppy "My Love Is Alive" cops a half-funky strut: both tracks reached Number Two in 1976. Subsequent Gary Wright albums, all out of print, repeated the formula but failed to duplicate that success. As historical footnotes go, however, *The Dream Weaver* possesses some discrete charms, even if it is less than spellbinding. — M.C.

ROBERT WYATT
★ ★ ★½ **Rock Bottom (1974; Blue Plate, 1990)**
★ ★ ★½ **Ruth Is Stranger Than Richard (1975; Blue Plate, 1990)**
★ ★ ★½ **Nothing Can Stop Us (1981; Gramavision, 1986)**
★ ★ ★½ **Old Rottenhat (Gramavision, 1985)**
★ ★ ★½ **Compilation (Gramavision, 1990)**
★ ★ ★ **Dondestan (Gramavision, 1992)**
Brit drummer-keyboardist-vocalist Robert Wyatt combines technical virtuosity, a fragile, lovely ballad-singer's vocal style, interesting, if intellectualized, jazz inclinations, and enormous personal courage (he's made music from a wheelchair ever since he fell out a window in the early '70s) in ways that make him the quintessential cult figure. Alternately admirable, inscrutable and infuriating, his records are an acquired taste.

Starting off with late-'60s jazz-rock fusionists Soft Machine, Wyatt headed up the short-lived Marxist jazz ensemble Matching Mole before putting out his solo breakthrough, *Rock Bottom* (his debut, *The End of an Ear*, had only a U.K. release). Produced by Pink Floyd's Nick Mason, *Rock Bottom* was art-rock with a vengeance: obscurantist, impressionistic and sporadically lovely. Then came *Ruth Is Stranger Than Richard*, a marginally more accessible work. Featuring four variations on "Muddy Mouse," including a ditty he penned with avant-garde guitarist Fred Frith and a piece spun off from a melody by Offenbach, this was no one's idea of Top Forty, however—and it confirmed Wyatt's highbrow reputation.

Compilation draws together the best of Wyatt's '80s work: *Nothing Can Stop Us* and *Old Rottenhat*. With such songs as "The Red Flag," the 1940s leftist rouser "Stalin Wasn't Stallin' " and the Cuban revolutionary anthem "Caimanera," combat fatigue sets in but the anthology has its gems: Elvis Costello's composition ("Shipbuilding"). *Dondestan* is minimalist atmospherics galore. — P.E.

TAMMY WYNETTE
★ ★ ★ **Your Good Girl's Gonna Go Bad (Epic, 1967)**
★ ★ ★½ **D-I-V-O-R-C-E (Epic, 1968)**
★ ★ ★½ **Stand by Your Man (Epic, 1969)**
★ ★ ★ **Inspiration (Epic, 1969)**
★ ★ ★ ★ ★ **Tammy's Greatest Hits (Epic, 1969)**
★ ★ ★ **The First Lady (Epic, 1970)**
★ ★ ★ ★ **Tammy's Greatest Hits, Vol. 2 (Epic, 1971)**
★ ★ ★ **Bedtime Story (Epic, 1972)**
★ ★½ **My Man (Epic, 1972)**
★ ★ ★ **First Songs of the First Lady (Epic, 1973)**

★ ★½ **Kids Say the Darndest Things (Epic, 1973)**
★ ★½ **Woman to Woman (Epic, 1974)**
★ ★ ★ **Another Lonely Song (Epic, 1974)**
★ ★ ★½ **Tammy's Greatest Hits, Vol. 3 (Epic, 1975)**
★ ★ ★ **I Still Believe in Fairy Tales (Epic, 1975)**
★ ★ ★ **Till I Can Make It on My Own (Epic, 1976)**
★ ★ ★ **You and Me (Epic, 1976)**
★ ★ **Let's Get Together (Epic, 1977)**
★ ★ ★ **One of a Kind (Epic, 1977)**
★ ★ ★½ **Womanhood (Epic, 1978)**
★ ★ ★ **Tammy's Greatest Hits, Vol. 4 (Epic, 1978)**
★ ★ ★ **Just Tammy (Epic, 1979)**
★ ★ ★ **Only Lonely Sometimes (Epic, 1980)**
★ ★ ★ **You Brought Me Back (Epic, 1981)**
★ ★ ★ ★ **Biggest Hits (1982; Epic, 1991)**
★ ★ ★½ **Higher Ground (Epic, 1987)**
★ ★ ★ ★ **Anniversary: 20 Years of Hits (Epic, 1988)**
★ ★½ **Next to You (Epic, 1989)**
★ ★ ★ **Heart Over Mind (Epic, 1990)**
★ ★ ★½ **Best Loved Hits (Epic, 1991)**

While Tammy Wynette continued to pile up sales in the decades following the late '60s, her groundbreaking work was accomplished during that Nashville heyday—the most passionate of all women country singers, she established herself as a riveting musical force, and patented her problematic persona as the antifeminist.

In hindsight, the perception of her as the C&W equivalent of Phyllis Schlafly, however, seems condescending and facile—while it's true that she parlayed more than her share of long-suffering wife apologias, not only do such songs as "Your Good Girl's Gonna Go Bad," "The Only Time I'm Really Me," "I Stayed Long Enough" and "Don't Come Home a Drinkin' (With Lovin' on Your Mind)" counter her perceived submissiveness, but the dismissal of Wynette specifically reads like the more general loathing of white Southern life that afflicted many critics of the time. Basically, Wynette, a former beautician, embodied the sensibility of a certain culture; Bobbie Ann Mason and Andre Dubus would later write stories about the kind of character she represented—Wynette, however, sang directly from inside the scene, and she gave it authentic, soulful expression.

While her first Epic single, "Apartment #9," didn't fare well (Keith Richards later covered it with the New Barbarians), the title track of *Stand By Your Man* made Tammy a star—and provoked the early trashing of her as slavish wifey. In actuality the song was both tougher and more compassionate than its opponents averred; it also set the pattern for the very affecting approach Wynette would deploy on many of her ballads—she begins singing with a dramatic hesitancy and then builds to a startling intensity. Produced by Billy Sherrill (and co-written by Wynette and Sherrill in about 20 minutes), the single has a melodramatic force, and while the album's uptempo numbers were capable, it's the songs of agony that remain riveting. Understandably, Wynette concentrated on heartache for the rest of her career, with either formulaic results (*Bedtime Story*) or impressive ones (*Womanhood*). In the '80s, Wynette's sound, courtesy of Chips Moman (the great Stax/Volt producer), had progressed past the gooey arrangements Sherrill provided, but the results were iffy—she no longer came across as quaint, but her records occasionally suffered from glossiness. Her first greatest-hits album remains her strongest, by far; *Anniversary* is a fair career overview; and, of the more recent work, *Higher Ground* (an album primarily of duets with Ricky Van Shelton and other contemporary country faves), is a strong example. — P.E.

STEVE WYNN

★ ★ ★½ **Kerosene Man (RNA/Rhino, 1990)**
★ ★ ★ ★½ **Dazzling Display (RNA/Rhino, 1992)**

As director of the Dream Syndicate, Wynn wasn't an especially convincing songwriter, relying too much on self-consciously literary lyrics and not enough on melodic ingenuity. But he was a hell of a band leader, with a connoisseur's taste in guitar grunge. Those interested in highlights should seek out *The Best of the Dream Syndicate* (Rhino, 1992), which boasts a smattering of memorable songs ("Tell Me When It's Over," "Burn") but generally presents guitarist Karl Precoda to better effect than Wynn. Fortunately, Wynn's writing has grown considerably since then, to the point that most of *Kerosene Man* offers accompaniment so lean it's barely noticeable. And though Wynn still tends to ramble, that hardly undoes the quiet charm of "Carolyn" or "Here on Earth as Well." *Dazzling Display* rocks much harder, at times even outdoing the mighty guitar roar of the Dream Syndicate (most notably on "A Dazzling Display"). Yet as much as the album shows off Wynn's stylistic diversity, thanks to arrangements that run from the neopsychedelia of "Tuesday" to the Dylanesque swirl of "Dandy in Disguise," it makes an even stronger case for his strengths as a writer, whether through the sly wordplay of "When She Comes Around" or the dramatic narrative in "Bonnie & Clyde" (sung in duet with Concrete Blonde's Johnette Napolitano). — J.D.C.

X

★ ★ ★½ **Los Angeles (Slash, 1980)**
★ ★ ★ ★ **Wild Gift (Slash, 1981)**
★ ★ ★ **Under the Big Black Sun (Elektra, 1982)**
★ ★ ★ ★ **More Fun in the New World (Elektra, 1983)**
★ ★ ★ **Ain't Love Grand (Elektra, 1985)**
★ ★ ★½ **See How We Are (Elektra, 1987)**
★ ★ ★ **Live at the Whisky a Go-Go on the Fabulous Sunset Strip (Elektra, 1988)**

X was hardly the first punk band to make the scene in Los Angeles, but it was definitely the first one that mattered. Naturally, some of that had to do with the fact that X didn't merely ape the approach of New York or London acts but perfected a metal-edged, rockabilly-based sound unique to L.A. But mostly it was because the songs on *Los Angeles* are so obviously and audaciously intelligent, with verses that read more like poetry than punk doggerel. Trouble is, between their minimal melodies and Exene Cervenka's almost complete inability to sing on pitch, these songs generally look better on the lyric sheet than they sound coming out of the stereo. *Wild Gift* improves things somewhat by emphasizing Billy Zoom's eloquently twangy guitar and giving a slightly larger share of the vocals to bassist John Doe. Still, it's hard not to admire the band's range, which stretches from tuneful shuffles like "In This House That I Call Home" to the chaotic ferocity of "We're Desperate."

X moved up to the majors with *Under the Big Black Sun*, which boasts an even beefier sound—note the punch of the tom-toms rumbling beneath "The Hungry Wolf"—but doesn't begin writing major-label songs until *More Fun in the New World* and the instantly familiar "The New World." Thus, *Ain't Love Grand* should have been X's breakthrough album, yet despite some of the band's best writing, including "Burning House of Love," "My Soul Cries Your Name" and the gleefully nasty "What's Wrong with Me . . . ," the music seems too self-conscious to be convincing. Zoom bailed out at this point, and is replaced by Tony Gilkyson for *See How We Are*. Unfortunately, it's all too obvious how they are—confused, exhausted and directionless. X called it quits after *Live at the Whisky a Go-Go*, but announced its reunion in 1991.
— J.D.C.

XTC

★ ★ ★½ **White Music (1978; Geffen, 1984)**
★ ★ ★ **Go 2 (1978; Geffen, 1984)**
★ ★ ★ ★ **Drums and Wires (1979; Geffen, 1984)**
★ ★ ★ **Black Sea (1980; Geffen, 1984)**
★ ★ ★ **English Settlement (1982; Geffen, 1984)**
★ ★ ★ **Mummer (Geffen, 1984)**
★ ★ ★ ★ **Waxworks: Some Singles 1977–82 (Geffen, 1984)**
★ ★ ★ **The Big Express (Geffen, 1984)**
★ ★ ★ ★ **Skylarking (Geffen, 1986)**
★ ★ ★ **Oranges & Lemons (Geffen, 1989)**
★ ★ ★ **Rag & Bone Buffet (Geffen, 1991)**
★ ★ ★½ **Nonsuch (Geffen, 1992)**

DUKES OF STATOSPHEAR

★ ★ ★ **25 O'Clock (Virgin, 1985)**
★ ★ ★ **Psonic Psunspot (Geffen, 1987)**
★ ★ ★½ **Chips From the Chocolate Fireball (1987; Geffen, 1988)**

This British combo took it upon itself to blend art-rock experimentation with factory-stamped pop hooks. At the height of punk, no less. Robot beats collide with short-circuited electronics on *White Music*; guitarist Andy Partridge gulps his way through shifty, intricate ditties like "Radios in Motion" and "This Is Pop." The latter title is sincere, or at least more so than "Dance Band." XTC flashes a real knack for crafty choruses on the nagging refrains of "Spinning Top" and "Statue of Liberty." Partridge and bassist Colin Moulding share songwriting chores; early on, Moulding's less-frequent work tends to be more precious and less compelling, though he eventually catches up. Keyboardist Barry Andrews swamps *Go 2* in a sea of synthesized effluvia; only the telegraphic "Are You Receiving Me?" reaches dry land. With second guitarist Dave Gregory replacing Andrews, XTC tightens up its high-strung sonic constitution—almost to the breaking point—on *Drums and Wires*. A delicious tension results: rather than busily herky-jerking around the room, the carefully packed sound pulls you into the group's cleverly skewed perspective. The songwriting is sharpened up, too; Moulding weighs in with two arresting uptempo highlights: "Life Begins at the Hop" and "Making Plans for Nigel." If *Drums and Wires* is all just a "Complicated Game," as Partridge insists with particular urgency and eloquence at one point, then it's an endlessly fascinating one.

XTC steps back from the pop-fashion rat race after that; beginning with *Black Sea*, the influence of the psychedelic Beatles and the nostalgic Kinks looms imposingly large over the proceedings. Somewhat turgid, *Black Sea* finally gets over on the strength of politically charged observations like "Towers of London" and "Generals and Majors." The next three albums are cluttered and fussy affairs, however, with only the occasional hook rising from the intellectualized din: "Senses Working Overtime" on *English Settlement* holds up to the sterling standard of *Waxworks: Some Singles 1977–82*, but Partridge sounds woefully cynical (and nasal) on *Mummer*'s

"Funky Pop a Roll." After *Mummer*, XTC retired from live performing. With "The Everyday Story of Smalltown," from *The Big Express*, XTC nails one of its attempted Ray Davies–style set pieces and points the way toward a more approachable form of studio wizardry.

Producer Todd Rundgren sweeps up the loose ends on *Skylarking*—far and away the most immediately likable XTC music. Under his watchful eye, the group takes some of the failed motifs from the previous albums (espcially the rustic acoustic touches of *Mummer*) and applies them to less self-involved, more traditonal song forms. Both songwriters reveal a far warmer side than ever before; Moulding on the sly and sexy "Grass," Partridge on the hopeful "Earn Enough for Us." The acoustic-meets-electric epic "Dear God" posits XTC as the Great Lost Classic Rock Band; in a world in which Moral Majority boycotts didn't exist, this cutting agnostic diatribe might've even become the group's first hit. Ah, wishful thinking: see what '60s-fixated rock albums from the '80s, even definitive ones like *Skylarking*, can do to your thought processes? In keeping with that authentic spirit, perhaps, the next XTC album (*Oranges and Lemons*) is a rambling, full-barreled return to witty indulgence. *Rag & Bone Buffet* delivers a groaning board of "rare cuts and leftovers"—either a treasure trove or slow torture, depending on your taste. Dukes of Stratosphear is XTC in acid-soaked hippie disguise; *Chips from the Chocolate Fireball* collects all the cheerfully sloppy derivations from two previous releases: *25 O'Clock* and *Psonic Psunspot*.
— M.C.

YARDBIRDS

★ ★ ★   **Five Live Yardbirds (1964; Rhino, 1988)**

★ ★ ★ ★ ★   **Roger the Engineer (1966; Edsel UK, 1986)**

★ ★ ★   **Little Games (1967; EMI UK, 1991)**

★ ★ ★ ★   **Greatest Hits, Vol. 1 (1964–66) Rhino, 1986)**

★ ★ ★ ★   **The Yardbirds, Vol. 1: Smokestack Lightning (Sony Special Products, 1991)**

★ ★ ★ ★ ★½   **The Yardbirds, Vol. 2: Blues, Backtracks and Shapes of Things (Sony Special Products, 1991)**

Although other English blues bands tried to play R&B the American way, with the emphasis on the singing or the groove, or both, the Yardbirds saw it as a means of showcasing guitar playing. That this should be the case hardly seems surprising in retrospect, particularly given the quality of guitarist the band favored; this, after all, was where both Eric Clapton and Jeff Beck made their names, and where Jimmy Page laid the foundation for what would become Led Zeppelin. But at the time, the Yardbirds' approach to blues and R&B transformed rock & roll, making the music harder and more exciting than before, while in the process setting the groundwork for what would become acid rock and heavy metal.

What made the Yardbirds distinctive is almost immediately apparent in the raucous interplay of *Five Live Yardbirds*. Despite Keith Relf's lackluster vocals and a set list entirely given over to cover material, the Yardbirds nonetheless set themselves apart from their peers, both through the quality of the guitar playing and the feral energy of the ensemble. Just listen to the way these five rip through the Isley Brothers' "Respectable"; not only do the Yardbirds make the original sound tame, but their

rhythm work converts the Isley's breathless backbeat into something far more insistent than swinging. This music doesn't roll—it just rocks.

As much as that added excitement to their sound, it didn't do much for the Yardbirds' authority with the blues, a point made embarrassingly clear by the group's live recordings with Sonny Boy Williamson (included on *The Yardbirds, Vol. 2*). But its studio work is another matter entirely. As *The Yardbirds, Vol. 1* and *Greatest Hits, Vol. 1* demonstrate, the Yardbirds had little trouble exploiting the heavy-riff potential of cover tunes like John Lee Hooker's "Boom Boom" or Howlin' Wolf's "Smokestack Lightning," and when that edgy aggression was applied to a more conventional pop format, as on "For Your Love," the Yardbirds' sound almost sparkled.

Unfortunately, "For Your Love" was a tad too pop for Clapton, who left the group in disgust. But his replacement, Jeff Beck, was more than happy to try other colors, and the singles he played on—"Heart Full of Soul," "Shapes of Things," "The Train Kept a Rollin' "—find the Yardbirds breaking significant new ground (even more so in the alternate takes included on *The Yardbirds, Vol. 2*). As such, *Roger the Engineer* stands as the Yardbirds' crowning achievement, an album that, through the likes of "Over, Under, Sideways, Down" and "Jeff's Boogie," pushes the band well into the psychedelic era without betraying its sound or roots.

Bassist Paul Samwell-Smith left the group shortly after *Roger*, and was replaced by Page, who later moved over to co-lead (and, eventually, sole lead) guitar. Both Page and Beck are heard on the dramatic "Happenings 10 Years Time Ago" (originally a single, but now included on *Roger the Engineer*), as well as "Stroll On," a none-too-subtle rewrite of "The Train Kept a Rollin' " that the group cut for the

Michelangelo Antonioni film *Blow Up* (and which is included on *The Yardbirds, Vol. 2*). That, though, was the Yardbirds' last bit of greatness, for the group fell apart after cutting *Little Games*, a disastrous attempt at conventional pop.

Although five album's worth of Yardbirds material was released in the U.S. during the band's prime, at this writing, only *Five Live Yardbirds* remains on the American market as a distinct album. That's not entirely a disadvantage; *The Yardbirds, Vol. 1* includes much of *Five Live Yardbirds* as well as most of the studio tracks originally offered on *For Your Love* and *Having a Rave Up*, while *Vol. 2* includes the rest of the pre-1966 singles, all of the Sonny Boy Williamson material and notable outtakes. Hard-core collectors, though, should seek out *Second Helping*, if only to hear "Baby What's Wrong," a rare, pre-Clapton recording with Anthony "Top" Topham playing lead.
— J.D.C.

YAZ

★★★ **Upstairs at Eric's (Sire, 1982)**
★★★★ **You and Me Both (Sire, 1983)**
This unique British duo got lost in all the brouhaha surrounding synth-pop. A founding member of Depeche Mode, Vince Clarke left that group after one album, casting his lot with a robust-voiced young woman known as "Alf"—Alison Moyet. She achieves a grainy soulfulness without affecting an American twang; Moyet's vocals glow with an earned passion. Clarke's clattering machine-beats mesh with simple, airy melodies; when the parts click into place, Yaz brings a human touch to push-button dance music. A couple of stolid collage pieces disfigure the debut, but *You and Me Both* strikes a richer, more varied tone—and sustains it. "No, I don't want to be just another page," Moyet declares in "Nobody's Diary." She goes on to assert her identity in a variety of tuneful situations, from the slightly desperate "Good Times" to the downright joyful "Walk Away From Love." Yaz found success on urban dancefloors in 1983, only to break up just as the new Brit-pop invasion loomed on the horizon. Clarke still pursues a similar musical path with Erasure, while Moyet's intermittent solo career moves ever closer to mainstream pop. Now that the band's more fashionable peers have been long forgotten (or become household names), Yaz is ripe for rediscovery. — M.C.

YES

★★½ **Yes (Atlantic, 1969)**
★★½ **Time and a Word (Atlantic, 1970)**
★★★½ **The Yes Album (Atlantic, 1971)**
★★★★ **Fragile (Atlantic, 1972)**
★★½ **Close to the Edge (Atlantic, 1972)**
★★★ **Yessongs (Atlantic, 1973)**
★ **Tales From Topographic Oceans (Atlantic, 1974)**
★★ **Relayer (Atlantic, 1974)**
★★ **Yesterdays (Atlantic, 1975)**
★★½ **Going for the One (Atlantic, 1977)**
★★ **Tormato (Atlantic, 1978)**
★ **Drama (Atlantic, 1980)**
★ **Yesshows (Atlantic, 1980)**
★★★ **90125 (Atlantic, 1983)**
★ **9012 Live—The Solos (Atlantic, 1985)**
★★ **Big Generator (Atco, 1987)**
★ **Union (Arista, 1990)**
★★★½ **Yesyears (Atco, 1991)**

Pointlessly intricate guitar and bass solos, caterwauling keyboards, quasi-mystical lyrics proclaimed in alien falsetto, acid-dipped album-cover illustrations: this British group wrote the book on art-rock excess. Compared to King Crimson's genre-defining debut album, however, *Yes* and *Time and a Word* hardly sound like the birth of a genre. Jon Anderson's piercing tenor vocals put across the cover versions well enough; a punchy run-through of the Beatles' "Every Little Thing" highlights the debut. But the long minutes of instrumental probing—classically trained psychedelic exploration—never quite catch hold. When guitarist Steve Howe replaces Peter Banks on *The Yes Album*, the group's approach gels around a much-improved set of originals. "I've Seen All Good People" integrates the melodic highpoints of the previous albums into a focused song structure, while Howe ignites the epic excursions ("Starship Trooper," "Yours Is No Disgrace") with a well-stocked arsenal of complex electric and acoustic riffs. Bassist Chris Squire and drummer Bill Bruford respond with crisp, flexible accompaniment—there's little sign of the cosmic discursiveness yet to come. Keyboardist Tony Kaye is probably the weakest link in the Yes chain at this point, but his low-key synth and organ coloring would soon seem like subtlety.

Kaye was replaced by Rick Wakeman on *Fragile*, the album that established Yes (and art-rock in general) as a cultural force. His classical conceits and fits of bombast add surface flash, though the grabby vocal hooks of "Roundabout," "Heart of the Sunrise" and "Long Distance Runaround" are really propelled by Howe's fevered picking and the disciplined stomp of the rhythm section. Even at their most accessible and coherent, however, Jon Anderson's lyrics creep toward the deep end: "In and around the lake . . . mountains come out of the sky . . . they stand there." Wow. "Roundabout" is so catchy that you can hum along with Anderson's spacey non sequiturs—or ignore them. Chris Squire's extended bass solo ("The Fish") provides a welcome breather on *Fragile*, but it proves to be a chilling omen of Yes's next, fatal step.

Close to the Edge has its moments, but most of this hotly anticipated follow-up is a monumental snore, a dubious hot-air suite whipped up around a handful of promising song fragments ("I Get Up I Get Down," "And You and I"). Still, it's a masterwork compared to *Tales From Topographic Oceans*, an endless set in which Yes drowns in tuneless, noodling shows of individual skill. It was all too much for Rick Wakeman, who opted for a solo career when *Tales* sank like a stone. His instrumental concept LPs (*The Six Wives of Henry The VIII, Journey to the Centre of the Earth, The Myths and Legends of King Arthur and the Knights of the Round Table*) found a ready audience among teen eggheads in the mid-'70s, though this synthesized symphonic approach sounds absurd in today's high-tech musical climate. Those albums are out of print.

Yes held on to its core audience on the road, but fumbled each successive record. *Relayer* dips into the jazz-fusion stewpot with alarming results; Howe produces some downright ugly noises with a guitar-synthesizer. After a blah streak, *Going for the One* shows definite signs of life—not to mention half a melody here and there. A refreshingly out-of-character slide guitar riff distinguishes the title track, while "Wonderous Stories" pleasantly bleats along in the manner of "All Good People." *Tormato* marks a return to the tempest-in-a-teapot turbulence of yore, and Jon Anderson abandoned ship in its wake.

For all his high-pitched overkill, *Drama* lacks that identifying note; it could be a Yes copy-band. Ex-Buggles Trevor Horn and Geoff Downes attempt to replicate Anderson's voice, but their new-wave sensibility never meshes with the Yes aesthetic. The return of Anderson and "Owner of a Lonely Heart"—the strongest Yes song since "Roundabout"—heralded a retooled future for these venerable art-rockers. *90125* could use another hook

like that one, however. And the subsequent live album *9012 Live—The Solos* could use a truckload of 'em. Anderson left again after the chilly *Big Generator*, amid fighting over rights to the group's name. *Union* takes a stab at reconciliation; everyone reconverges for an eight-man blowout. A nice idea, but it comes about ten years too late.

The *Yesyears* box is generous to a fault, stuffing four CDs to the brim. But discs one and two chart the bounding development—and inevitable stagnation—of a trailblazing band. Discs three and four are where the path gets hopelessly tangled. *Yessongs* is a quaint throwback to the heyday of live concerts; the fact that the Yesmen really could play this way was a key part of their appeal. Go figure. — M.C.

DWIGHT YOAKAM

★★★ **Guitars, Cadillacs, Etc., Etc. (Reprise, 1986)**
★★★ **Hillbilly Deluxe ((Reprise, 1987)**
★★★★ **Buenas Noches from a Lonely Room (Reprise, 1988)**
★★★★ **Just Lookin' for a Hit (Reprise, 1989)**
★★★★ **If There Was a Way (Reprise, 1990)**

Coming out of Los Angeles by way of Pikeville, Kentucky, Dwight Yoakam made a statement when he kicked off his first major-label release with a cover version of Johnny Horton's "Honky Tonk Man." (Yoakam had cut an EP in 1984 for the Oak label that features songs re-recorded for his Reprise debut.) Everything he's done in the intervening years has paid testimony to his diligent pursuit of a roots sound and unsentimental point of view. Nominally a country artist, Yoakam has no truck with Nashville, nor it with him. Yoakam and his producer and guitarist, Pete Anderson, keep things lean and mean with a basic band supplemented by fiddles, mandolins, steel guitars and dobros, with little regard for mainstream country niceties. Yoakam is pretty much of an outcast as a country artist, never honored by the Country Music Association, hardly a staple on country radio, even his videos are seldom seen on TNN and CMT.

Ultimately the path leads to California, where Yoakam resides, and specifically to Bakersfield, where in the '60s Buck Owens and Merle Haggard came on with a searing blast of rock- and blues-informed country that wilted the sanitized, string-laden efforts being packaged as the Nashville Sound. It was Yoakam, in fact, who lured Owens out of retirement and back into a recording studio for a rocking remake of Owens's paranoiac classic, "Streets of Bakersfield." Yoakam writes often of family, dislocation (both spiritual and physical) and love wars. *Guitars, Cadillacs* and *Hillbilly Deluxe* deal most directly with reminiscences of his early life ("South of Cincinnati," "Readin', Rightin', Rt. 23," "Johnson's Love") and his family ("Miner's Prayer"), but the overriding theme of his music is the difficulty in finding true love. This all comes to a head on *Buenas Noches from a Lonely Room*, which sounds torn from the deepest part of a man who's utterly bereft of friends and lovers. In the title song he tells of a woman who bore him a child, then ran off with the baby, and of how he hunted her down and blew out her brains. Even the cover choices are telling: "Streets of Bakersfield," Johnny Cash's "Home of the Blues" and Hank Locklin's "Send Me the Pillow."

After a respite for the best-of collection, *Just Lookin' for a Hit*, Yoakam returned with another first-rate effort, *If There Was a Way*. Less tortured than *Buenas Noches*, *If There Was a Way* is nonetheless almost totally about loss and self-recrimination. Yet there's tenderness in "If There Was a Way" and in "Send a Message to My Heart." Ending with a cover of Wilbert Harrison's "Let's Work Together" bespeaks an optimism foreign to Yoakam's bleak sensibility, but he makes it work. For good measure, throw in a touch of Duane Eddy twang at the end of "The Distance Between You and Me" and quotes from Link Wray's "Rumble" in "If There Was a Way," and you get a sense that this album represents a summing up of the past and present that finds light, albeit faint, illuminating a path once enveloped in darkness and pain.
— D.M.

JESSE COLIN YOUNG

★★ **Together (Warner Bros., 1972)**
★★ **Song for Juli (Warner Bros., 1973)**
★★ **The Soul of a City Boy (Capitol, 1974)**
★★ **Light Shine (Warner Bros., 1974)**
★★ **Songbird (Warner Bros., 1975)**
★★ **On the Road (Warner Bros., 1976)**
★★ **Love on the Wing (Warner Bros., 1977)**
★★ **American Dreams (Warner Bros., 1978)**
★★★ **The Best of Jesse Colin Young: The Solo Years (Rhino, 1991)**

As main man for the Youngbloods, this sweet-tempered singer occasionally exerted himself to reach beyond mellow melodicism and come up with something gripping and stark—"Darkness, Darkness," for example, was truly haunting. On his own, however, he wallows in sunshine. Often accompanied by his wife on vocals, and playing invariably with a tasteful, nondescript band, he makes music so evenly inoffensive that it gets irritating. His records are interchangeable— nostalgic, glossed-up folk Muzak for former hippies. — P.E.

NEIL YOUNG

★★★½ **Neil Young (Reprise, 1969)**
★★★★ **Everybody Knows This Is Nowhere (Reprise, 1969)**
★★★★★ **After the Gold Rush (Reprise, 1970)**
★★★★ **Harvest (Reprise, 1972)**
★★ **Journey Through the Past (Reprise, 1972)**
★★★ **Time Fades Away (Reprise, 1973)**
★★★ **On the Beach (Reprise, 1974)**
★★★★★ **Tonight's the Night (Reprise, 1975)**
★★★★ **Zuma (Reprise, 1975)**
★★★★★ **Decade (Reprise, 1976)**
★★★ **American Stars 'n Bars (Reprise, 1977)**
★★½ **Comes a Time (Reprise, 1978)**
★★★★★ **Rust Never Sleeps (Reprise, 1979)**
★★★★½ **Live Rust (Reprise, 1979)**
★★★½ **Hawks & Doves (Reprise, 1980)**
★★★ **Re-ac-tor (Reprise, 1981)**
★★½ **Trans (Geffen, 1982)**
★★½ **Everybody's Rockin' (Geffen, 1983)**
★★½ **Old Ways (Geffen, 1985)**
★★½ **Landing on Water (Geffen, 1986)**
★★★ **Life (Geffen, 1987)**
★★★ **This Note's for You (Reprise, 1987)**
★★★½ **Freedom (Reprise, 1989)**
★★★★ **Ragged Glory (Reprise, 1990)**
★★★★ **Weld (Reprise, 1991)**
★★½ **Arc (Reprise, 1991)**

Whether helping to invent California folk rock with Buffalo Springfield, rocking with inspired abandon with Crazy Horse, experimenting with lush orchestral arrangements or going solo with acoustic guitar, Neil Young sounds like no one else. Fierce, free, dark or lovely, his songs are keyed to a note of wonder; Young remains a singularly fresh visionary—his art is one of absolute emotion. As an electric guitarist, Young plays like an abstract expressionist;

turning his amazing technical skill against itself, he achieves a visceral grace. His voice, however, is his essential instrument—high, thin, careless of meter or key signature, capable of confessional immediacy or laconic humor, it's tinged with loss and longing. Young sings like a misfit, knowing child. With the pioneering Buffalo Springfield, he'd ranged from propulsive rock ("Mr. Soul") to naïve balladry ("I Am a Child") to idiosyncratic, often string-laden longer songs ("Nowadays Clancy Can't Even Sing," "Broken Arrow"). *Neil Young* employed all three styles, but tended toward a muted, elegiac mood—its love songs ("If I Could Have Her Tonight," "I've Been Waiting for You") were bittersweet, and with its choirs, violins and ruminative lyrics, the record displayed new subtlety, though some of the Springfield drive was missing. *Everybody Knows This Is Nowhere* hit hard, however; "Cinnamon Girl" managed to be both heavy and catchy, and with "Down by the River" and "Cowgirl in the Sand," Young sketched in the pattern for all his later extended guitar workouts. Filled with jagged edges and twisted runs, his solos built upon the expansive West Coast–style rock he'd helped to create. Neither blues-based nor tricked out with the spacey effects of psychedelia, however, his own instrumental passages came closer in spirit, if not in sound, to free jazz; deliberate ugliness colliding with grace, they were brooding, tortuous and risky. With *Everybody Knows*, Young had hooked up, too, with Crazy Horse. Guitarist Danny Whitten, bassist Billy Talbot and drummer Ralph Molina were fitful, intuitive players; with them, Young would consistently seek out an inspired sloppiness, a freedom beyond technique.

His first masterpiece, *After the Gold Rush,* found him succeeding at a highly charged simplicity. The haunting "Southern Man" was another electric guitar epic, but the rest of the album derived from the style of "Helpless," the lovely ballad he'd contributed a half-year before to Crosby, Stills, Nash and Young's *Déjà Vu.* CSN&Y was a hodgepodge enterprise, but in "Helpless," with its spare piano and lyrics evoking dream landscapes from Young's Canadian boyhood, he'd come up with the fusion of clear melody and imagistic poetry that would characterize all his best slow songs. "After the Goldrush," "Don't Let It Bring You Down" and "Till the Morning Comes" were fluid, suggestive pieces, immediate, yet memorable. And the album

drew together Young's obsessions—his romance with a mythic Wild West, as well as his preoccupation with love, hope and the hardships of basic emotional survival.

Young then faltered a while. "The Needle and the Damage Done" movingly lamented Whitten's fatal drug overdose, but most of *Harvest* reduced the lean power of *Gold Rush* to elementary formulas: "Heart of Gold" and "Old Man" weren't poems, they were sentimental jingles. The soundtrack for a lame experimental film, *Journey Through the Past* was intended also as a career retrospective, but it sounded aimless and confused. Things picked up with the live *Time Fades Away,* its savage country rock played by an L.A. studio band calling itself the Stray Gators, but *On the Beach* was again unsatisfying. Perhaps trying to free himself from the "hitmaker" expectations that dogged him ever since the commercial success of *Harvest,* Young retreated into dissonance and strangeness.

Tonight's the Night redeemed him. A true "dark night of the soul," it mourned Whitten's loss and that of roadie Bruce Berry. It then extended from personal pain to chronicle the slow exhaustion of the American Sixties—with "Come On Baby Let's Go Downtown" offering some release, if only in the power of its primal, cathartic rock & roll. One of Young's staggering achievements, it remains his most darkly honest record. Then, with "Don't Cry No Tears," "Cortez the Killer" and "Danger Bird" as standouts, the lyrics of *Zuma* alternated a poetry of fantasy with the directness of *Tonight*—and Young again turned loose his raw guitar.

American Stars 'n Bars featured "Like a Hurricane," Young's best long song since "Southern Man." *Comes a Time* showed him returning to folk rock with pleasant, if slight, duets with Nicolette Larson. The six-sided *Decade* was a best-of album, and it stands as one of the strongest in rock. Fourteen albums, however, have followed that monumental release, and at least four are masterworks. Virtually alone among the musicians who matured during the West Coast singer-songwriter renaissance, Young not only consistently returned to purist country-folk for inspiration, but also confronted (and supported) the punk revolt that reviled everything California music stood for: ruralist fantasy, laid-back charm, fatalism, instrumental accomplishment. Responding with *Rust Never Sleeps* and *Live Rust,* Young and Crazy Horse delivered acoustic songs whose spare beauty and total absence of schmaltz defended the spirit of *After the Gold Rush*; they revived, also, the primitive kick of *Tonight's the Night* by countering with angry, exhilarating rockers ("Hey Hey, My My [Into the Black]," "Powderfinger"). It would take Young another ten years to muster this sort of command, but with *Freedom* and its anthemic "Rockin' in the Free World," he did. A year later, *Ragged Glory* repeated his revival, with Crazy Horse coming on as crude and compelling as ever.

In the time between landmarks, Young experimented. *Trans* was a strange, Kraftwerk-like synthesizer record, complete with sci-fi musings and awful digitalized vocals; its polar opposite, *Old Ways*, found Young singing sentimental duets with Waylon Jennings. *This Note's for You* clumsily tried out R&B horns; *Everybody's Rockin'* was nifty, if puzzling, rockabilly. *Life* and *Landing on Water* rocked along blandly; *Hawks & Doves* and *Re-ac-tor* showed him turning from the subject matter he handles brilliantly (love and myth) to irony and political commentary—his voice and guitar sounded great, but they signified confusion. The feedback catharsis of the live recording *Weld* (as well as the instrumental *Arc*, also recorded during Young's 1991 concert tour) show the veteran in unapologizing form.

Young's career, then, has been a fitful one, full of detours and retreats. But when he breaks through—and his epiphanies have been many and various—he makes brilliant American music.   — P.E.

PAUL YOUNG

★ ★ ★ ★   No Parlez (Columbia, 1983)
★ ★ ★   The Secret of Association (Columbia, 1985)
★ ★   Between Two Fires (Columbia, 1986)
★ ★ ★   Other Voices (Columbia, 1990)
★ ★ ★½   From Time to Time/The Singles Collection (Columbia, 1991)

At his best a singularly convincing British blue-eyed soulster, Young earns credibility with the maturity of his tenor delivery and inventive repetoire. While a fair songwriter himself, he's strongest at lending dignified heat to material as diverse as Joy Division's "Love Will Tear Us Apart" (on *No Parlez*), Tom Waits's "Soldier's Things" (from *The Secret of Association*) and the Chi-Lites' "Oh Girl" (on *Other Voices*).

Helped by Laurie Latham's echoey, percussion-happy production, Young's first album is his most eclectic and best. Marvin

Gaye's "Wherever I Lay My Hat (That's My Home)" gets a supple rendering; Young's strongest original, "Broken Man," is a breathtaking near-sobber, backed by elegant strings. His next album produced Young's mega-hit, "Everytime You Go Away"—a deserved success. Packed with his own compostions, *Between Two Fires* is Young's weakest set, showing a tendency toward slickness. *Other Voices* is more of a return to form; it also features Young's toughest rock & roll, an ultratight take on Free's "A Little Bit of Love."   — P.E.

THE YOUNGBLOODS

★ ★ ★   Youngbloods (RCA, 1967)
★ ★ ★½   Elephant Mountain (RCA, 1969; Mobile Fidelity, 1989)
★ ★ ★   The Best of the Youngbloods (RCA, 1970)
★ ★ ★   This Is the Youngbloods (RCA, 1972)

Upon its 1969 release, this East Coast band's *Elephant Mountain* was hailed for greatness. The haunting, underplayed "Darkness, Darkness" remains the finest song written by Jesse Colin Young; "Quick Sand" is also subtle and spooky, and "Double Sunlight" is a good love song. But the rest now sounds weak: strained folksiness, plodding electric piano passes at jazz. "Get Together," for all its earnestness, was one tight performance—and the band's big hit. Most of the rest of the Youngbloods' work retains only period interest.   — P.E.

YOUNG MC

★ ★ ★½   Stone Cold Rhymin' (Delicious Vinyl/Island, 1989)
★ ★½   Brainstorm (Capitol, 1991)

Marvin Young didn't forget about New York City when he went away to college in California. By writing rhymes for the lovably indolent Tone Lōc and then rapping on his own as Young MC, this former Queens resident helped cement rap's presence in the mainstream. If Young MC's average-Joe stance and bass-heavy throb can't quite compete with L.L. Cool J's aggressive verbal dexterity (let alone Public Enemy's expansive musical vocabulary), the basic funk factor is never in question. He's a popularizer, not an innovator, but Young MC gets the job done with flair and humor, as his Top Ten breakthrough, "Bust a Move," proves.

Reacting too predictably to hip-hop fashion, Young MC grows "serious" on the followup and the beats follow suit.

Brainstorm quickly turns into a migraine. The closest he comes to that familiar carefree groove is "That's the Way Love Goes." His rap glances off a swooping female vocal track on that song, and then he slips into a jive superstar pout about all the women slavering after his crossover booty. Most of the time, though, he intones against the easy temptations of sex ("Keep It in Your Pants"), idleness ("After School") and so on. It's all very well-intentioned, but boring. — M.C.

FRANK ZAPPA

★★★★ Freak Out (1966; Rykodisc, 1985)

★★★ Absolutely Free (1967; Rykodisc, 1988)

★★★★★ We're Only in It for the Money (Verve, 1967)

★★★½ Lumpy Gravy (Verve, 1967)

★★★½ Cruisin' With Ruben and the Jets (1968; Rykodisc, 1985)

★★ Mothermania (Verve, 1969)

★★ The Worst of the Mothers (Verve, 1969)

★★★★★ Uncle Meat (1969; Rykodisc, 1987)

★★★★ Weasels Ripped My Flesh (1970; Rykodisc, 1990)

★★★★ Chunga's Revenge (1970; Rykodisc, 1990)

★★★★ Hot Rats (1970; Rykodisc, 1987)

★★★★ Burnt Weeny Sandwich (1970; Rykodisc, 1991)

★★ Mothers Live at the Fillmore East—June, 1971 (1971; Rykodisc, 1990)

★★ Just Another Band from L.A. (1972; Rykodisc, 1990)

★★ 200 Motels (United Artists, 1972)

★★★★ The Grand Wazoo (1972; Rykodisc, 1986)

★★★★ Waka Jawaka (1972; Rykodisc, 1988)

★★★ Overnite Sensation (Discreet, 1973)

★★★ Apostrophe (Discreet, 1974)

★★★ The Roxy and Elsewhere (Discreet, 1974)

★★★½ One Size Fits All (1975; Rykodisc, 1988)

★★★ Bongo Fury (1975; Rykodisc, 1989)

★★★ Zoot Allures (1976; Rykodisc, 1990)

★★★ In New York (Discreet, 1978)

★★★ Studio Tan (Discreet, 1978)

★★★ Sleep Dirt (Discreet, 1979)

★★★ Orchestral Favorites (Discreet, 1979)

★★½ Sheik Yerbouti (1979; Rykodisc, 1990)

★★★ Joe's Garage, Act I (Zappa, 1980)

★★★ Joe's Garage, Acts II and III (Zappa, 1980)

★★★½ Tinseltown Rebellion (1981; Rykodisc, 1990)

★★★½ You Are What You Is (1981; Rykodisc, 1990)

★★★★ Shut Up 'n Play Yer Guitar (Barking Pumpkin, 1981)

★★★★ Shut Up 'n Play Yer Guitar Some More (Barking Pumpkin, 1981)

★★★★ Return of the Son of Shut Up 'n Play Yer Guitar (Barking Pumpkin, 1981)

★★★ Ship Arriving Too Late to Save a Drowning Witch (Barking Pumpkin, 1982)

★★★★ London Symphony Orchestra (Barking Pumpkin/Rykodisc, 1983)

★★★½ Thing-Fish (Barking Pumpkin/Rykodisc, 1984)

★★★ Apostrophe/Overnite Sensation (Rykodisc, 1986)

★★★ Them or Us (Barking Pumpkin/Rykodisc, 1986)

★★★★★ We're Only In It for the Money/Lumpy Gravy (Rykodisc, 1986)

★★★★ Shut Up 'n Play Yer Guitar (Complete Set) (Rykodisc, 1986)

★★★★ Jazz From Hell (Barking Pumpkin/Rykodisc, 1986)

★★★½ Meets the Mothers of Prevention (Barking Pumpkin/Rykodisc, 1986)

★★★ Joe's Garage, Acts I, II, & III
(Rykodisc, 1987)
★★★★ Guitar (Barking
Pumpkin/Rykodisc, 1988)
★★★★½ You Can't Do That on Stage
Anymore Vol.1 (Barking
Pumpkin/Rykodisc, 1988)
★★★★½ You Can't Do That on Stage
Anymore Vol. 2 (Barking
Pumpkin/ Rykodisc, 1988)
★★★★½ You Can't do That on Stage
Anymore Vol. 3 (Barking
Pumpkin/ Rykodisc, 1988)
★★★ Broadway the Hard Way (Barking
Pumpkin/Rykodisc, 1989)
★★★★½ You Can't Do That on Stage
Anymore Vol. 4 (Barking
Pumpkin/Rykodisc, 1991)
★★★★ Beat the Boot, #2 (Rhino, 1992)

Relentlessly experimental, Frank Zappa
defies categorization. In a sly manner that
recalls Warhol's odd fusion of parody and
homage, he has worked at virtually all kinds
of music—and, whether it's guised as a
satirical rocker, jazz-rock fusionist, guitar
virtuoso, electronics wizard or orchestral
innovator, his eccentric genius is undeniable.
Cross Dion and the Belmonts with Harry
Partch, and you get some idea of Zappa's
musical sensibility; as a humorist—and
humor is crucial to Zappa—he comes on
like a hybrid of Lenny Bruce and the Three
Stooges. Elusive, indulgent, at times
inscrutable, Zappa's tone and intention are
often hard to determine—it seems calculated
to provoke equal measures of fury, awe and
giggling. An early crusader against rock
censorship, he has always been political—if
sometimes perplexingly so—but his ultimate
significance resides in his music. Brandishing
as his motto a quote from his idol, the
French avant-gardiste Edgar Varese, "The
present-day composer refuses to die!,"
Zappa is indeed as much a modern classical
composer as he is a rock legend—and the
erasure of the lines between high and pop
art that he premiered with his first band, the
Mothers of Invention, remains one of the
emancipatory gestures of the '60s.

With a riff aping the Stones'
"Satisfaction," "Hungry Freaks, Daddy"
provided the anthemic intro to Freak Out.
Lyrically, the record's antilove songs and
daft non sequiturs raised the rebel flag for
the misfit clowns and underdogs Zappa and
the Mothers would henceforth champion;
the music was both a triumph and mockery
of psychedelia, folk rock, blooze and
doo-wop. Considerably more demanding,
Absolutely Free pushed the envelope even

further—composed of fragmentary jazz
allusions, vibraphone noodlings, chanting
and operatic vocals, its determined messiness
seemed totally mad. On "Plastic People," a
"Louie, Louie" guitar motif disintegrates
into freeform swinging, all in service of a
poke at LBJ and American suburbia. And,
with We're Only in It for the Money, with its
mock–Sgt. Pepper's cover art, orchestral
segments and general ferocity, the Mothers
had already achieved their masterpiece.

The prototype of the technically brilliant
aggregations upon which Zappa would come
to insist, the Mothers of 1967 were basically
a crack rock outfit with woodwind
capability. Money was, of course, in large
part the musicians' work, but the vision was
assuredly Zappa's. "Who Needs the Peace
Corps?," "Flower Punk" and "Harry
You're a Beast" were early exercises of his
trademark themes—paranoia, political and
sexual; hatred for the bourgeoisie; and a
utopian insistence on completely free
expression. In search of that goal, Zappa
detoured from the Mothers that same year
by putting out Lumpy Gravy, his first solo
work. Recorded with a 50-piece orchestra,
this difficult and sometimes suprisingly
lovely record of John Cage–ish modern
music paved the way for the Mothers'
second major set, Uncle Meat. A pastiche of
31 sound bites—either in the form of tape
edits, nonsense phone conversations,
"songs," or instrumental passages—Meat
was an inspired monstrosity. There are
lyrics, but they're secondary to the assault
of glorious noise. A kind of musical version
of William Burroughs's "cut-up" method of
literary construction—the insertion of
random passages within an otherwise
narrative text—Meat reinvented pop music.
The only problem was that this kind of
zonked brilliance could never be
"popular"—and Meat marked the
coalescence of one of Zappa's characteristic
stances, the cryptic prophet howling in the
wilderness.

The quartet of Weasels Ripped My Flesh,
Chunga's Revenge, Hot Rats and Burnt
Weeny Sandwich was a high point of a
consistency Zappa never again achieved.
While members of the Mothers would
resurface throughout his career, the band as
such was kaput—and Zappa began working
with a bewildering array of talents (Little
Feat's Lowell George, violinist Don
"Sugarcane" Harris, drummer Aynsley
Dunbar, keyboardist George Duke). While
there were vocals on all these albums, it was
the music that mattered. Propulsive neo-jazz

alternated with gorgeous, classically derived pieces that flourished the grace or power of soundtracks for dreams. A collaboration with Captain Beefheart resulted in *Hot Rats'* nifty standout "Willie the Pimp." And in "Peaches en Regalia," from *Rats* as well, Zappa had found a music of majesty.

In comparison, the next Mothers records, *Live* and *Just Another Band*, sounded lame or silly—adding ex-Turtles singers Howard Kaylan and Mark Volman only increased the yuks factor—and while the *200 Motels* soundtrack was fairly ambitious, the movie that accompanied it was mere weirdness. *Grand Wazoo* (jazz-rock fusion recalling *Bitches Brew*–period Miles or the Mahavishnu Orchestra), *Waka Jawaka*, and *One Size Fits All* made for an impressive clutch of Mothers-less outings; *Overnite Sensation* and *Apostrophe* (despite good work by ex-Cream bassist Jack Bruce), however, were squawking, predictable and only desperately "hilarious."

Although Zappa's approach resists generalization, it became apparent by the mid-'70s that those albums that concentrated on humor would be the least satisfying; the musical experiments would be the ones to watch out for. The records that balanced both approaches varied: *Bongo Fury* was a stronger Beefheart performance than a Zappa one; *Zoot Allures* was comparatively bland—but the "funny" *Sheik Yerbouti*, with its disco parody and churlishness ("Broken Hearts are for Assholes") was much less impressive than the three *Shut Up* sets, wherein Zappa simply turned loose his astonishing guitar playing. By the time of *Joe's Garage, Act I,* and such fare as "Why Does It Hurt When I Pee?" the sophomoric smuttiness of Zappa's humor had gotten very old (sexism remained this freethinker's egregious blind spot)—and his turn strictly toward music was welcome. *You Are What You Is,* however, found the naughty lad reclaiming the stand-up stage. But this time, the musical parodies were varied enough to carry the day. Mock versions of reggae, ska, Journey-style power ballads and country music, and a hilarious takeoff on the Doors, produced the most inventive comedy he'd attempted in years.

More recently the joke-predominant albums (*Tinseltown, Broadway, Them or Us*) have been fairly tasty, especially the rock send-up, *Them or Us,* but the real excitement has been elsewhere. *London Symphony Orchestra* finally found Zappa in an all-orchestral setting, with impressive

results; *Jazz From Hell,* with Zappa executing virtually all the pieces on synclavier, displayed his longtime mastery of music tech. His most ambitious releases, however, were retrospectives—*Guitar,* a sequel to the *Shut Up* series, that featured 32 live solos recorded between 1979 and 1984; and the staggering eight-CD *You Can't Do That* package. Twenty years in the making, the set presents previously unreleased live work from 1968 to 1988. Obviously intended for Zappaddicts, it's hardly the best place for a neophyte to start. But, undeniably, it's monumental. Absolute Frankophiles will want to check out *Beat the Boot, #2.* Seven CDs of live work from 1968–1977 presents the Mothers at their fiercest and sometimes most inspired. The set includes a massive scrapbook that loosely chronicles Zappa's career from high school through his scrape with the PMRC.
— P.E.

ZEBRA

★ ★ **Zebra (Atlantic, 1986)**
★ ★ **3.V (Atlantic, 1987)**
★ ★ **Zebra Live (Atlantic, 1990)**

Pro forma pop metal. Randy Jackson wails sometimes like Geddy Lee, sometimes like Robert Plant. His guitar work is of the ultracompetent variety characteristic of this kind of power trio—the bassist and drummer also would probably amaze the judges at some bad radio station's "Battle of the Bands." On *3.V,* Zebra curiously resurrects saxist Stan Bronstein of Elephant's Memory—otherwise, there's virtually nothing distinctive about this crew. If you must, check out *Live:* stripped of studio-production varnish, Zebra sounds vital enough to recall the glory days of—oh, say—Angel or Styx. — P.E.

WARREN ZEVON

★ ★ ★ ★ ★   **Warren Zevon (Asylum, 1976)**
★ ★ ★ ★   **Excitable Boy (Asylum, 1978)**
★ ★ ★   **Bad Luck Streak in Dancing School (Asylum, 1980)**
★ ★ ★ ★   **Stand in the Fire (Asylum, 1980)**
★ ★ ★ ½   **The Envoy (Asylum, 1982)**
★ ★ ★ ★ ½   **A Quiet Normal Life: The Best Of Warren Zevon (Asylum, 1986)**
★ ★ ★ ½   **Sentimental Hygiene (Virgin, 1987)**
★ ★ ★ ★   **Transverse City (Virgin, 1989)**
★ ★ ★   **Mr. Bad Example (Giant/ Reprise, 1991)**

Warren Zevon openly defies the *muy sensitivo* stereotype of the L.A. singer-songwriter. Literate, satiric, violence-obsessed, funny as hell, piano-pounding, equally capable of deranged rock-outs and beautifully sustained melodies: gee, you'd never guess that *Warren Zevon*, his first Asylum album (his debut was the now-deleted *Wanted—Dead or Alive* on Imperial in 1969), was produced by Jackson Browne! "Desperadoes Under the Eaves" brilliantly skewers the self-deluded "Life in the Fast Lane" pose. "Today I'm angry at the sun," sneers Zevon's protagonist—and then a fully orchestrated, Randy Newman–esque finale clears the air. Zevon's terse, dynamic readings of "Carmelita," "Poor Poor Pitiful Me" and "Mohammed's Radio" put Linda Ronstadt's better-known cover versions in their proper perspective. *Excitable Boy* established Zevon as a commercial comer; his deadpan, finger-on-the-trigger delivery drives home the sardonic hooks on "Werewolves of London" and the title track. "Roland the Headless Thompson Gunner" and "Lawyers, Guns and Money" define his probing geo-political mode. Though *Excitable Boy* remains Zevon's biggest chart success and best-known work, its middling second half renders *Warren Zevon* his overall best.

Bad Luck Streak in Dancing School lands a flat follow-up blow, especially coming after such a stunning one-two punch. Between the obvious retreads ("Jeannie Needs a Shooter") and failed experiments ("Jungle Work"), the ever-mercurial Zevon sounds overextended. No rest, however: *Stand in the Fire* is a galvanizing live album. Rather than appear with the expected slew of studio pros, Zevon leads a band of nobodies through a riveting set of fiery uptempo material that loses none of its original nuance. *The Envoy* is where he steps back from the edge. At first the move feels tentative, but the loved-and-learned message of "Looking for the Next Best Thing"—and its melody—really sink in over time. Reassuringly, the title track asserts Zevon's (over)active imagination, while "Ain't That Pretty at All" flaunts his remaining wild hair. After a quiet spell, Zevon comes out sober and swinging on *Sentimental Hygeine*. "Detox Mansion" and "Trouble Waiting to Happen" look at both sides of the rehab process with a pitiless, unsentimental eye. Musically supported by three-quarters of R.E.M., Zevon turns his perceptive gaze to the boxing ring ("Boom Boom Mancini") and Springsteen-Mellencamp territory ("The Factory") with tuneful results.

Even the most loyal Zevon followers got thrown for a loop by *Transverse City*. It's a sci-fi concept album, of all things. With a headful of ideas lifted from "cyber-punk" paperbacks and an imposing synthesizer arsenal, Zevon sets out to do for art rock what he once did for the singer-songwriter movement—kick it in the ass. By and large, he succeeds by matching his new complex, multilayered sound with observant lyrics that consider the current "Turbulence" in Russia as well as the local action ("Down in the Mall"). Overall, *Transverse City* is an unmitigated downer—its mood is summed up by a heart-opening closer called "Nobody's in Love This Year." But given some time, Zevon's bleak (and realistic) future projection will definitely grow on you. *Mr. Bad Example* takes a giant leap backward. Vitriolic spurts like "Finishing Touches" sound like answers to a long-unanswered, nagging question: "Hey, Warren, couldn't you do another one like that excitable werewolves number, you know, the one that goes woo-woo-woo, like that." For the first time, Zevon comes across as cynical and nasty; the note of hope lurking behind those cathartic rants of old is now long gone. Only the country-tinged "Heartache Spoken Here" hints at the emotional depth that was once Zevon's signature as a singer and songwriter. Pray that he doesn't take *Mr. Bad Example* to heart. — M.C.

THE ZOMBIES
★ ★ ★½ **Odyssey and Oracle (1968; Rhino, 1987)**
★ ★ ★½ **Greatest Hits (DCC, 1990)**
Propelled by Rod Argent's jazzy keyboards, the Zombies were the most musically intriguing of the British Invasion bands. Hauntingly catchy, "She's Not There" served as a blueprint for their sharper work—pop that wrestled the genre's limits, yet still triumphed on radio. Colin Blunstone's sexy choirboy vocals on "Time of the Season" made the group sound like few of its peers; Blunstone insinuated rather than shouted—his elegance suiting a band that swung more than it rocked. *Odyssey and Oracle* is the Zombies' best, a sort of concept album including mildly precious musings on World War I and faded love.

After the Zombies, Rod Argent formed Argent, a progressive rock outfit; Blunstone released a few albums, the standout being *One Year*. For all its string-laden gushiness, it contains passages of sheer, lovely grace.
— P.E.

JOHN ZORN

★ ★ ★½ **The Big Gundown (Icon/Nonesuch, 1986)**
★ ★ ★½ **Spillane (Nonesuch/Elektra, 1987)**
★ ★ ★½ **News for Lulu (Hatart, 1988)**
★ ★ ★½ **Naked City (Nonesuch/Elektra, 1990)**

Something of a cult god in New York City's East Village, alto saxophonist John Zorn mixes heavy influence (Ornette Coleman, modern classical music) with a playful postmodern sensibility to come up with records sounding like scores to dream film noir. The Lounge Lizards and James White and the Blacks tried to do jazz-for-punks in the late '70s; Zorn's is the more credible version.

Zorn gets gritty, indeed—but with no sacrifice of skill. On *The Big Gundown* he collects a host of downtown talents—guitarists Arto Lindsay, Robert Quine, Vernon Reid, Fred Frith, as well as a host of other neo-jazz experts—and turns them loose on smart reworkings of Ennio Morricone's spaghetti-western oeuvre. *Spillane*, notable especially for the blinding-fast time changes Zorn favors, combines film-noir atmospherics, funk and R&B. *News for Lulu* joins him with trombonist George Lewis and guitarists Bill Frisell for an expert bop set. *Naked City* mixes Ornette and Morricone remakes and brash reworkings of the *Batman* and James Bond themes alongside Zorn originals—again, it's dense, smart, exhilarating.

What makes Zorn street-credible is neither coyness, crassness or ease (some of his pieces are furiously demanding). Instead, he's managed to infuse the sensibility of classic, hip jazz with his own fresher hipness—and combine the best of both underworlds. — P.E.

ZZ TOP

★ ★ **ZZ Top's First Album (1970; Warner Bros., 1979)**
★ ★ **Rio Grande Mud (1972; Warner Bros., 1979)**
★ ★ **Tres Hombres (1973; Warner Bros., 1979)**
★ ★½ **Fandango! (1975; Warner Bros., 1979)**
★ ★½ **Tejas (1976; Warner Bros., 1979)**
★ ★ ★½ **The Best of ZZ Top (1977; Warner Bros., 1979)**
★ ★ ★ ★ **Deguello (Warner Bros., 1979)**
★ ★ ★½ **El Loco (Warner Bros., 1981)**
★ ★ ★½ **Eliminator (Warner Bros., 1983)**
★ ★ ★ **Afterburner (Warner Bros., 1985)**
★ ★ ★ **Recycler (Warner Bros., 1990)**

This Texas trio slogged around the arena circuit for years, bashing out metalized boogie 'n' blooze that never quite survived the transition to record. Except for the apocalyptic quiver of "Jesus Just Left Chicago" (from *Tres Hombres*), the early recorded efforts of guitarist Billy Gibbons, bassist Dusty Hill and drummer Frank Beard form a largely undifferentiated mass—a parched riverbed, if you will. By the mid-'70s, ZZ Top began to sprout a juicy hook here and there: first the incongruous lingo of "Tush" (from the half-live *Fandango!*), and then the sober slide of "Arrested for Driving While Blind" (from *Tejas*). All the roadwork paid off, both financially and artistically. *The Best of ZZ Top* dryly contradicts the band's previous cartoon status, and after a three-year layoff, *Deguello* proves these old boys really are capable of more than barbecuing a few borrowed riffs. From the steely pulse of "I'm Bad, I'm Nationwide" to the kicking version of "Dust My Broom," this is a superior white blues album. *El Loco* isn't too far behind, but ZZ Top takes another sharp left turn with *Eliminator*. Video-friendly and synthesizer-enhanced, the Top's retooled image takes some getting used to. The hit single "Legs" provided the opportunity; while the thematic, ah, thrust is a little primitive, the sight of these bearded gents on MTV was extremely gratifying in 1984. As was the sound of Billy Gibbons leaning—head on—into a taut, drawling solo during the Top Forty countdown. But that winning formula already starts to wear thin on *Afterburner* ("Sleeping Bag," "Velcro Fly"). *Recycler* is one of the least propitious titles in recent memory; ZZ Top continue to pack 'em in on the road, though. — M.C.

ANTHOLOGIES

ATLANTIC RHYTHM & BLUES
1947–1974 (Atlantic, 1985)
★★★★★ **Volume 1: 1947–1952**
★★★★★ **Volume 2: 1952–1955**
★★★★★ **Volume 3: 1955–1958**
★★★★★ **Volume 4: 1958–1962**
★★★★★ **Volume 5: 1962–1966**
★★★★★ **Volume 6: 1966–1969**
★★★★ **Volume 7: 1969–1974**

What to say beyond that this collection offers a capsule history of the evolution of modern black music styles? *Volume 1* focuses on urban blues, group harmony, and New Orleans jump blues; over the course of the succeeding volumes we hear Ray Charles evolving soul out of rhythm & blues, Chuck Willis bringing rock & roll and R&B together, Solomon Burke and Aretha Franklin bringing the church into their secular music, the rise of southern soul in sessions cut in Memphis and Muscle Shoals with Franklin, Otis Redding, Percy Sledge and others, early New Orleans pop in Barbara Lewis's first recordings, and in *Volume 7*, the last gasp of traditional soul via the great Tyrone Davis and Clarence Carter and the first stirrings of the soft black pop that dominated the mainstream in the early '70s and led directly to modern-day Love Men such as Luther Vandross and Freddie Jackson. In addition to the obvious hits and classic tracks contained in this set, the first three volumes in particular include songs by some artists who may not be in the pantheon but whose contributions were important: the Cardinals' "Wheel of Fortune," Harry Van Walls's "Tee-Nah-Nah," Joe Morris's "Applejack," the two Ivory Joe Hunter tracks on *Volume 3*, and the Cookies, as well. All in all, an extraordinary history of a once-great label whose artists, even the minor ones, had a spirit and style that remains invigorating and instructive to this day. — D.M.

★★★★ THE BEST OF CHESS VOCAL
GROUPS (MCA/Chess, 1988)

Though widely known for its pioneering role as a blues and rock & roll label, Chicago's Chess Records also had a long and illustrious history recording vocal groups in the 1950s and 1960s. Some of the very best came through Phil and Leonard Chess's door during that time and left behind some wonderful sides before moving on to greater success elsewhere; some inspired one-hit wonders came through as well before disappearing altogether.

Chess didn't specialize in any single area of group harmony vocalizing; rather, the Chess brothers made their decisions based on what they thought would sell, without regard to stylistic consistency. *The Best of Chess Vocal Groups* shows an impressive range of group harmony approaches that serve as portents of the split that would occur in black music in the '60s, with Motown cornering the market on pop soul, while Stax purveyed a tougher, more blues-based brew. These considerations aside, the set also represents one of the last, best gasps of doo-wop, which faded into obscurity as the '50s ended.

Of special interest are a couple of moments that are significant in light of what came after. The Four Tops, for example, offer a tender rendition of "I Wish You Would" (recorded in 1956 and previously unissued) that couldn't be farther from the tough, spectacular records the group recorded a decade later for Motown. Similarly, the O'Jays close the album with a 1969 cut, "One Night Affair," an early Gamble and Huff production in which the production flourishes—especially the lush, zinging strings and close-miked drums—clearly presage the disco sound the duo would trade on in the following decade. At the opposite end of the spectrum were the Ravens, the dominant vocal group of the late '40s and early '50s, whose style influenced many of the groups included. Pretty much finished and lacking any of their original personnel in 1956, the group pulled it together for one spectacular moment, "(Give Me) A Simple Prayer," on which lead tenor Joe Van Loan hits a falsetto note that must be heard to be believed.

Elsewhere amid familiar items such as Lee Andrews & the Hearts' "Long Lonely Nights," the Marathons' "Peanut Butter" and the Dells' "There Is" are some vital but lesser-known recordings. The Students justify their immortal ranking among doo-wop fanatics with the driving "Every Day of the Week," while the Sensations' "(Put Another Nickel In) Music, Music, Music" and the Gems' "Dear One" showcase two outstanding female vocalists in Yvonne Baker and Vandine Harris, respectively. The Knight Brothers offer a soaring interpretation of "Temptation 'Bout to Get Me" that brooks comparison to Billy Stewart's original *tour de force*. — D.M.

★★★ **THE BEST OF THE CHICAGO BLUES (Vanguard, 1986)**
Best of the Chicago Blues is an anthology featuring Otis Spann piano instrumentals, including "Spann's Stomp," along with selections by James Cotton, Junior Wells, Buddy Guy, J. B. Hutto and Homesick James. — D.M.

★★★ ½ **THE BEST OF COOL YULE (Rhino, 1988)**
A first-rate survey of Christmas visions from artists of varying stripes. Brenda Lee kicks off the set with a jaunty "Papa Noel"; from this peak the song selection maintains a high standard through another 17 tracks. Of special note is Solomon Burke's testifying on "Presents for Christmas," a plea for peace and prosperity for every man, woman and child on the planet. In the midst of all this wishful thinking, Burke is moved to pronounce: "I'm fat enough to be the world's biggest Santa Claus!" On the opposite end from Burke's righteous declaiming is the Drifters' tender rendition of "White Christmas," featuring a lead vocal by Clyde McPhatter. The Ventures are here with a track from their classic long-player, *The Ventures' Christmas Album*. The must-have selection is a version of Leroy Anderson's "Sleigh Ride" that starts out as "Walk Don't Run" before segueing neatly into Anderson's Yule standard. James Brown gets in on the action with a message

from 1968, "Santa Claus, Santa Claus"; Huey "Piano" Smith and the Clowns do New Orleans proud on "Silent Night," which features an inspired vocal by Bobby Marchan; and Tina Turner burns with lusty fervor on her and Ike's reading of the Charles Brown standard, "Merry Christmas, Baby." Lesser lights such as Dodie Stevens, the Marquees and the Sonics occupy an honored place for their inspired efforts in service to the season. — D.M.

THE DISCO YEARS
★★★★★ Volume 1: Turn the Beat Around 1974–78 (Rhino, 1990)
★★★★½ Volume 2: On the Beat 1979–82 (Rhino, 1990)
★★★★ Volume 3: Boogie Fever (Rhino, 1992)
★★★★ Volume 4: Lost in Music (Rhino, 1992)
★★★★ Volume 5: Must Be the Music (Rhino, 1992)
Late-night television is chockful of ads proclaiming one quickie disco compilation or another, but these five deftly programmed sets are a true bargain. *The Disco Years, Volumes 1–5* completes the cornerstone of any dance-music collection: alongside the *Saturday Night Fever* soundtrack, *On the Radio—Donna Summer's Greatest Hits* and Chic's greatest-hits albums. Chronologically precise yet smoothly paced, *The Disco Years* refutes the old "disco sucks" argument with irresistible rhythms, sly horniness, sinfully rich string sections and all manner of (mostly female) singers—from heavenly divas to breathy sweet-nothing whisperers. *Volume 1 (1974–78)* traces disco's rise, from the gay and black underground clubs in the big city to surburban shopping malls and the top of the pop charts, in just four short years. Gauzy Miami funk with R&B overtones (KC & the Sunshine Band, Shirley & Co.) gives way to gushing orchestrated decadance (Van McCoy's "The Hustle," "More More, More" by the Andrea True Connection). Disco was always a singles medium, where hokey novelties vastly outnumbered brilliant one-shots: miraculously, the Rhino albums include just the right amount of camp. One Village People track ("YMCA" on *Volume 2*) communicates their cartoon appeal—and the giggly side of disco—quite well. *Turn the Beat Around* reaches a coronary-inducing romantic peak when "Love Hangover" by Diana Ross segues into the immortal "Don't Leave Me This Way" by Thelma Houston—both songs wrap seductive vocals around

explosive, soaraway rhythmic breaks.
Volume 2 (*1978–82*) captures the heyday of
disco, when its influence spread to new wave
(Blondie's "Heart of Glass"), synth-pop
(Lipps, Inc.'s "Funkytown"), traditional
R&B (McFadden & Whitehead's "Ain't No
Stoppin' Us Now") and harder-edged funk
(Chic's "I Want Your Love"). Rather than
map the backlash against disco and its
inevitable decline, *On the Beat* retrieves
some delicious rock and rap-flavored
obscurities from the early-'80s New York
dance scene, like the B.B. & Q. band's
bounding title track and Indeep's haunting
"Last Night a DJ Saved My Life." Three
more volumes, released in 1992, provide
enough danceable hits to make your next
disco party last till dawn. Equipped with
these collections, even an ordinary record-
spinner can work miracles. — M.C.

★★★★ **THE BEST OF DOO WOP**
UPTEMPO (Rhino, 1989)
★★★★ **THE BEST OF DOO WOP**
BALLADS, VOLS. 1 & 2 (Rhino,
1989)
Two splendid surveys of the tender and the
boisterous sides of doo-wop show off some
of the best voices in the genre's history.
Uptempo's 18 cuts begin and end with the
best of the Dell-Vikings ("Whispering Bells"
and "Come Go With Me"), which bookend
a rich variety of the various styles of
doo-wop extant between 1954 (represented
here by the Crows' jazz-inflected "Gee") and
1963 (Randy and the Rainbows' propulsive
"Denise"). Those into reprogramming CDs
are likely to become orgasmic over the
options here. This combination is highly
recommended: the Marcels' "Blue Moon" to
Dion and the Belmonts' "I Wonder Why"
to Randy and the Rainbows' "Denise" to
the Silhouettes' "Get a Job" to the
Dell-Vikings' "Whispering Bells" to the
Mystics' "Hushabye" to the Elegants'
"Little Star." Wonderful. And we haven't
even touched Frankie Lymon yet!

Like *Uptempo, Ballads* is mostly familiar
ground as far as the tune stack is concerned:
"In the Still of the Night," "Sincerely,"
"Daddy's Home," and so on. Still, these
songs always seem fresh, owing to
sometimes transcendent, often
extraordinary, always deeply felt vocalizing.
Thirty years after the release of the Jive
Five's "My True Story," to cite one
example, Eugene Pitt's lead vocal remains a
mesmerizing display of nuance and phrasing
in service of lyrics that would have made O.
Henry proud. Lesser-heard gems such as

"Lover's Island" by the Blue Jays and
"Been So Long" by the Pastels are nice
touches in a package that otherwise offers a
Murderer's Row of doo-wop's heavy hitters.
— D.M.

★★★ **THE BEST OF THE GIRL**
GROUPS, VOLUMES 1 & 2
(Rhino, 1990)
Girl Groups promulgates an adolescent
world view that is often expressed in
Hallmark simplicities. Okay. The first blush
of love (be it puppy or true) is an experience
that ought to be full of sweetness and light.
Here it is, about as sweet and light as it can
get, what with the Murmaids ("Popsicles
and Icicles," written by David Gates, who
would continue to purvey sweetness and
light with Bread), the Paris Sisters
(produced by Phil Spector), the Honeys (the
prototype for Wilson Phillips, produced by
Brian Wilson and featuring his wife as lead
singer) and Robin Ward ("Wonderful
Summer") on hand. There's grittier turf
explored as well, courtesy of the Cookies
("Don't Say Nothin' Bad [About My
Baby]"), the Chiffons ("Sweet Talkin'
Guy"), the Jaynetts (the atmospheric,
inscrutable "Sally Go 'Round the Roses")
and, on Vol. 2, two superb Ellie Greenwich
tracks, the Raindrops' "The Kind of Boy
You Can't Forget" and her solo turn, "You
Don't Know." As a collection *Girl Groups*
lacks backbone, but it's got a great big
heart. That'll work. — D.M.

THE BEST OF NEW ORLEANS
RHYTHM & BLUES (Rhino, 1988)
★★★★ **Volume One**
★★★★ **Volume Two**
Rhino's *Best of New Orleans Rhythm &*
Blues two-volume anthology duplicates
many of the highlights on its three-volume
History of New Orleans series, while adding
interesting cuts by the likes of Roy Montrell
("[Every Time I Hear] That Mellow
Saxophone," since covered by the Stray
Cats and Dr. John) and the estimable Roy
Brown ("Let the Four Winds Blow").
Thorough annotation by critic and author
Jeff Hannusch further recommends this
collection. — D.M.

★★★★ **BILLBOARD GREATEST**
CHRISTMAS HITS
(1955–PRESENT) (Rhino, 1988)
A first-rate sampling of R&B and pop
Christmas singles from the sublime (Harry
Belafonte's delicate "Mary's Boy Child,"
from 1956, and the Drifters' "White

Christmas," from 1954, featuring Clyde McPhatter's startling lead vocal) to the ridiculous (Elmo 'N Patsy's "Grandma Got Run Over by a Reindeer"). Whether your taste runs to rock & roll, MOR or R&B, there's something that's worthwhile. Of note: The Harry Simeone Chorale's version of "Little Drummer Boy" is a re-recording of the 1958 hit, although the two versions sound the same, and Charles Brown, whose best-known Christmas single is "Merry Christmas, Baby," is represented by another pain-wracked Yuletide plea dating from 1961, "Please Come Home for Christmas." Toss in Bobby Helms's "Jingle Bell Rock," Brenda Lee's "Rockin' Around the Christmas Tree" and Elvis Presley's "Blue Christmas"—three acknowledged classics of this underappreciated genre—and you have a minor gem. — D.M.

BILLBOARD'S TOP R&B HITS (Rhino, 1989)

★★★★ 1955
★★★★ 1956
★★★ 1957
★★★ 1958
★★★★ 1959
★★★ 1960
★★★★ 1961
★★★ 1962
★★★★ 1963
★★★★ 1964
★★★★ 1965
★★★ 1966
★★★★ 1967
★★★ 1968
★★★ 1969
★★★ 1970
★★★ 1971
★★★★ 1972
★★★★ 1973
★★★ 1974

Top R&B Hits is a marvelous exercise in geneology. There's a link between the style and sensibility of Johnny Ace's 1955 testimonial "Pledging My Love" and Al Green's soul flight on "Livin' for You," from the 1974 volume, that is without parallel on *Billboard*'s *Rock 'N' Roll* set, which covers the same years. The nascent disco of Eddie Kendricks ("Keep on Truckin'," 1973) and Kool and the Gang ("Hollywood Swinging," 1974) has roots in some of the powerhouse R&B stylings on the Fifties discs and most definitely in the grooves of James Brown, who is represented profusely herein. From disc one to disc twenty this collection offers a profound history lesson in the degree to which doo-

wop, rhythm & blues, urban blues and gospel evolved, but remained everpresent in black music throughout the decades. In doing so it also offers first-rate performances, cut to cut, year to year, and becomes an essential addition to any serious music library. — D.M.

BILLBOARD'S TOP ROCK 'N' ROLL HITS 1955–1974 (1988; Rhino, 1989)

★★★ 1955
★★★ 1956
★★★★ 1957
★★★ 1958
★★★ 1959
★★★★ 1960
★★★★ 1961
★★★★ 1962
★★★★ 1963
★★★ 1964
★★★★ 1965
★★★★ 1966
★★★ 1967
★★★ 1968
★★★ 1969
★ 1970
★ 1971
★★ 1972
★★ 1973
★★ 1974

Compiled by *Billboard*'s indefatigable chart researcher Joel Whitburn, this 20-volume series offers an interesting overview of the development of the pop music market from the beginning of the rock & roll era to the dawn of disco and attempts to provide some historical context in liner notes that summarize the year's key events. Since each volume purveys top chart hits, the artists represented are fairly predictable and well heard. *Rock 'N' Roll Hits* is missing any cuts by the Beatles and Rolling Stones (a disclaimer in the liner notes indicates that some licenses were unavailable), but otherwise rolls out the big AM radio guns of the years in question. It is also an incredibly depressing set: as stimulating, inventive and clever as the music is on all of the '50s and many of the '60s discs, so is it contrived and flaccid in the later years. That AM radio went right into the toilet in the 1970s is a brutal fact borne out here with sledgehammer force. In 1970, for example, seven of the ten hits are fluff by the Partridge Family, the Shocking Blue, the Jaggerz, the Ides of March, Three Dog Night, Norman Greenbaum and Sugarloaf—bad to the bone, no?—leaving only Edwin Starr ("War"), Smokey and the Miracles ("Tears of a Clown") and the

Jackson Five ("I Want You Back") to deliver music with some heart. The volumes '72, '73, and '74 rate two stars on the basis of each disc containing one killer track ('72—"Back Stabbers," the O'Jays; '73—"Let's Get It On," Marvin Gaye; '74—"Come and Get Your Love," Redbone); otherwise, the decline is apparent as early as '68 and '69, both of which slouch towards assembly-line pop with the inclusion of the Ohio Express, the Archies and Steam. — D.M.

THE BLUES
★ ★ ★ ★ **Volume 1 (1963; MCA, 1986)**
★ ★ ★ ★ **Volume 2 (1963; MCA, 1987)**
★ ★ ★ ★ **Volume 3 (1964; MCA, 1988)**
★ ★ ★ ★ ★ **Volume 4 (1965; MCA, 1988)**
★ ★ ★ ★ ★ **Volume 5 (1966; MCA, 1990)**
The roots of rock & roll and soul are found in these first-rate collections of urban and country blues, boogie, and seminal R&B originally released by Chess in the '60s as samplers of the label's extensive blues catalog. All of the big names are present and accounted for, as well as lesser-knowns whose importance shouldn't be discounted. *Volume 5* stands out, not only for the powerful Howlin' Wolf track "How Many More Years," but also for top-flight performances by Percy Mayfield ("Double Dealing"), Willie Mabon ("Seventh Son") and Memphis Minnie, one of the great female blues singers, who's represented by the naughty "Me and My Chauffeur." There's a good sampling of blues classics here—"Spoonful," by Howlin' Wolf, Muddy Waters's "Rollin' Stone," Little Walter's "My Babe," and others—mixed in with some nice surprises (the Berry selections are not the hits, but some of the blues sides he cut for albums) to make each volume a winner. — D.M.

★ ★ ★ ½ **THE BRIDGE: A TRIBUTE TO NEIL YOUNG (Caroline, 1989)**
Of all the mainstream music coming out of California in the '70s, the only artist who didn't repulse the up-and-coming generation of punks and noise artistes was Neil Young. They grooved on his mondo distorto guitar work, his ragtag stage gear and adamantly unrehearsed vocals, and the cryptic poetry of his lyrics. It helped, too, that Young hadn't stood in the way of change: on *Rust Never Sleeps* and *Live Rust*, he embraced the Sex Pistols, and on *Trans*, he'd tried his hand at Kraftwerk-styled synth-pop.
The Bridge gathers 14 (12 on cassette) wildly diverse late-'80s bands to revive,

deconstruct or otherwise genially fuck with Young's hits and oddments. Sonic Youth charges through "Computer Age"; Nick Cave transforms "Helpless" into a hard, elegant mid-tempo number that recalls John Cale. The Pixies and Loop play things relatively straight with "Cinnamon Girl" and "Winterlong," respectively; Psychic TV adds insinuating violin to "Only Love Can Break Your Heart." Bongwater goes in for pastiche, mixing sampled Young vocals and the band's own guitars on "Mr. Soul," and Henry Kaiser turns in a strong medley of "The Needle and The Damage Done" and "Tonight's The Night." Only Dinosaur Jr's "Lotta Love" seems less than imaginative. This is one sharp album—and it proves Young's strength as one of American music's most consistently provocative songwriters. — P.E.

★ ★ ★ ★ ★ **THE BRISTOL SESSIONS (Country Music Foundation, 1987)**
This collection documents the beginning of modern country music as it evolved from a string band, instrumental form to a vocal form. Recorded in 1927 in Bristol, located on the Tennessee-Virginia border, by Victor talent scout Ralph Peer, the sessions drew musicians of all stripes, representing the many different strands of country music—folk songs, ballads, gospel, blues. Most critical were the first recordings of the Carter Family (five tracks) and Jimmie Rodgers (two tracks), who went on to change the music forever. But in addition to these giants, Peer also recorded the Stoneman family, whose surviving members have carried on the tradition and still appear on country shows; Blind Alfred Reed, a protest singer whose songs have retained their resonance; the extraordinary gospel singer Alfred Karnes; and several fiddle bands playing what was then the dominant style of country music. This is a rare moment when a window of history opens for us and we are witness to the first stirrings of a revolution that would change country music forever. — D.M.

THE BRITISH INVASION: A HISTORY OF BRITISH ROCK
★ ★ ★½ **Vol. 1 (Rhino, 1988)**
★ ★ ★½ **Vol. 2 (Rhino, 1988)**
★ ★ ★½ **Vol. 3 (Rhino, 1988)**
★ ★ ★½ **Vol. 4 (Rhino, 1988)**
★ ★ ★½ **Vol. 5 (Rhino, 1991)**
★ ★ ★½ **Vol. 6 (Rhino, 1991)**
★ ★ ★½ **Vol. 7 (Rhino, 1991)**

★ ★ ★½ **Vol. 8 (Rhino, 1991)**
★ ★ ★½ **Vol. 9 (Rhino, 1991)**
With its final volume extending into 1972,
Rhino's excellent, exhaustive nine-CD
history actually soars beyond the British
Invasion's acknowledged '64-'65 heyday and
stops just short of heavy metal, prog-rock
and nascent glam. And, with 20 songs per
volume, virtually no '60s pop obscurity of
any consequence is ignored. While it
features big names aplenty (Kinks, Faces,
Animals, Beatles, Cream), the collection is
especially helpful in gathering up the hits of
lesser-knowns—hard-to-find wonders like
the Swinging Blue Jeans' "Hippy Hippy
Shake," Los Bravos's "Black Is Black" and
Jonathan King's "Everyone's Gone to the
Moon."

With their selections a neat balance of
greatness and schlock, the series is
consistent; no volume is inessential. And
while concentrating on the gems of Britain's
first-wave acts would certainly have resulted
in, say, four five-star records, the presence
of occasional clunkers (Flying Machine's
"Smile a Little Smile for Me," Tommy
Quickly's "Tip of My Tongue") adds
contextual richness—and pumps up the
guilty-pleasure factor.

With so generous a compilation, it's
impossible (and wrongheaded) to attempt
any summarizing definition of the period's
strengths—other than that of the delightful
zeitgeist energy that powers almost every
song on *British Invasion*. From the blues
power of Eric Burdon to the jazzy elegance
of the Zombies to the coy charm of Lulu
and the trippy folksiness of Donovan, what
these acts had in common was a sense of
renaissance—an exhiliration at remaking the
world of the pop song in their new image.
— P.E.

COLLECTABLES PRESENTS: THE
HISTORY OF ROCK (Collectables, NA)
★ ★ ★ ★ **Volume 1**
★ ★ ★ ★ **Volume 2**
★ ★ ★ ★ **Volume 3**
★ ★ ★ ★ **Volume 4**
★ ★ ★ ★ **Volume 5**
★ ★ ★ ★ **Volume 6**
★ ★ ★ ★ **Volume 7**
★ ★ ★ ★ **Volume 8**
★ ★ ★ ★ **Volume 9**
★ ★ ★ ★ **Volume 10**
A splendid if chronologically schizoid
overview of virtually every style of rock &
roll from glorious '50s doo-wop to inane
'70s pop in ten volumes. There's no rhyme
or reason to the song selection from album

to album—the Soul Survivors followed by
Chuck Berry is about par for the
course—but there are few tracks that aren't
genuinely rocking good songs. Overall the
emphasis is on the R&B side, but the
pop-rockers, especially girl groups and solo
female artists, are given their just due as
well. Songs are mostly familiar oldie entries,
but it's the rare volume that doesn't include
one lesser-programmed gem along the lines
of the Paradons' "Diamonds & Pearls," Sue
Thompson's "Sad Movies (Make Me Cry)"
and Gogi Grant's "The Wayward Wind."
— D.M.

★ ★ ★ ★ ★ **THE COMPLETE**
STAX/VOLT SINGLES
1959–1968 (Atlantic, 1991)
A nine-volume collection gathering nearly
250 cuts of the toughest R&B ever made,
the *Stax/Volt Singles* set is a wonder. Not
only are the hits and experiments of the
label's stars, from Otis Redding to Johnnie
Taylor, fully represented, but the vast
assemblage of knockout songs by
lesser-knowns makes the compilation
indispensable. There are enough so-so tracks
to ground the Stax/Volt achievement in
some kind of recognizable human reality
(and to allow the gems to shine even more
brightly), but the undiminished visceral
immediacy of most of this music lends the
label an almost eerie luminosity—it seems
uncanny that so strong a sound was
developed in so short a time, by so few a
number of central players. Outmanned and
out-monied, Stax never quite matched
Motown in terms of sales, but compared to
Motown's brilliant, irresistible pop-soul,
Stax's R&B cut straight to the bone—
technically simpler, at its best it was music
of a disturbing emotional depth; Motown
pleased, Stax demanded. Quintessentially
Southern, the Memphis-based label reflected
the hard grandeur of America's most
conflicted and most poetic region—and the
fact that its ownership and a significant
handful of its key musicians were white
Southerners added to the creative tension.

White banker Jim Stewart and his sister,
Estelle Axton, founded the label; some of its
greatest writing and producing talent (Chips
Moman, Spooner Oldham) were country
boys; one half of its peerless house band
(guitarist Steve Cropper, bassist Donald
"Duck" Dunn) wouldn't have looked out of
place in Buck Owens's Buckeroos. But the
'60s R&B Stax produced drew consistently
from the gospel and blues roots of the
genre; the songs were the colloquial poetry

of African-American experience; and the stars were black. Otis Redding, Sam and Dave, Booker T. Jones, Isaac Hayes, Eddie Floyd and Rufus Thomas were Stax's legends; close behind came Rufus's daughter Carla (among the Stax set's treasures are cuts that reveal this singer's neglected greatness; the same holds true for Mabel Thomas), William Bell, Johnnie Taylor and Barbara Stephens. An instrumental powerhouse, Stax presented, in the Mar-Keys, a truly fearsome horn section (most imaginatively deployed by Redding) and boasted soul music's answer to rock & roll's Charlie Watts in the essentialist drumming of Al Jackson—even the acoustics of the studio itself (a refashioned theater) were magic, helping to deliver a mono sound stretched as tight as Jackson's snare drumhead.

The Stax set includes all the standards by Otis Redding (in moods ranging from "I Can't Turn You Loose" to "Try a Little Tenderness"), Booker T. & the MG's ("Green Onions," "Hip Hug-Her"), Sam and Dave ("Soul Man"); it ranges from stone blues (Albert King) to the high, weird humor of Rufus Thomas, from doo-wop to nascent funk. It's an epic collection. — P.E.

★★★ CONCERTS FOR THE PEOPLE OF KAMPUCHEA (Atlantic, 1981)

A benefit to try to undo some of the damage wreaked upon Cambodia (a.k.a. Kampuchea) by Pol Pot's Khmer Rouge, the Concerts for the People of Kampuchea was a sort of transitional charity event, halfway between the well-meaning ineptitude of the Concert for Bangladesh and the epochal achievement of Live Aid. Musically, it was all over the map, ranging from the overblown (like Queen or Paul McCartney's ridiculous all-star Rockestra) to the pedestrian (Wings and the Kenney Jones–era Who). But the stand-out moments are well worth hearing, particularly the Pretenders' edgy reading of "Precious," Ian Dury & the Blockheads' knife-edged "Hit Me with Your Rhythm Stick" and an exquisitely off-hand rendition of "Little Sister" by Rockpile and Robert Plant. — J.D.C.

CRUISIN' (1970–1973; Increase, 1987–1988)
★★★★ 1955
★★★★ 1956
★★★★ 1957
★★★ 1958
★★★ 1959
★★★★ 1960
★★★★ 1961
★★★★ 1962
★★★★ 1963
★★★★ 1964
★★★★ 1965
★★★★ 1966
★★★★ 1967
★★★ 1968
★★ 1969

In its original form, released in the early '70s, the volumes that make up the *Cruisin'* series comprised a classic capsule history of rock & roll music, rock & roll radio and rock & roll culture. In the late '80s the series was reconfigured for compact disc, resulting in some songs being dropped and others substituted to accommodate the CD's time limitations. It remains a singular effort, worthy of its four-star rating, but some of the programming changes have been made at the expense of continuity and excitement.

The great virtue of the series is that each volume purports to be a radio show from the year in question, featuring a disc jockey doing his shtick as well as commercials that were aired at the time. So in addition to tracing the progression of AM rock & roll radio in its heyday, the *Cruisin'* volumes also showcase the work of some pioneer disc jockeys whose flamboyance was part and parcel of the attitudes and ideas favored by their audiences. Some of these are priceless performances: 1961 features Boston's Arnie "Woo Woo" Ginsberg, "old achin' adenoids" himself, who was notable for his self-deprecating humor and use of sound effects; New York City's B. Mitchell Reed, one of the original WMCA "Good Guys," is all controlled chaos on the 1963 volume, speaking so rapidly it's a wonder he can enunciate at all, and cutting loose with bells, whistles and all manner of weird noises whenever the mood strikes, which is often. The 1967 disc features Atlanta's Dr. Donald D. Rose, whose introductions are small masterpieces of precision comic timing. The '50s jocks are less flamboyant than their '60s counterparts, but there is in the frenetic deliveries of, say, "Jumping" George Oxford of KSAN in San Francisco (1955) and Hunter Hancock of KGFJ in Los Angeles (1959) the roots of the maniac styles of '60s AM jocks.

Packaging is a point of interest here as well. Inside the CD sleeves are brief but informative biographies of the artists on each disc as well as background on the featured jock. Of special note are the covers by California-based artist Mike Royer. These tell single-panel stories about the circuitous relationship of Peg and Eddie, who represent the prototypical couple of the time. And there is music of unsurprising variety. One might quarrel with the song selection, particularly when it excludes artists of great stature such as Little Willie John, who is nowhere to be found on the 1956 disc after once being represented by his swaggering version of "Fever." Virtually every album has been altered in some way from its original incarnation, not always to good effect. The 1961 volume, for example, had a searing opening that began with "Woo Woo" Ginsberg's wild theme and segued immediately into the Marcels' "Blue Moon," and from there went to the Jive Five's "My True Story." The Marcels aren't on the CD version; Chuck Berry's "Nadine" opens the set on a less explosive note, after a clumsy edit of Ginsberg's theme. Obviously, newcomers to the *Cruisin'* series won't have a problem here. "Can't lose what you never had" is the way Muddy Waters once put it, but those familiar with this otherwise exemplary effort might prefer to stick with the original releases rather than upgrading to CD. — D.M.

★ ★ ★ ½ **DEADICATED (Arista, 1991)**
Although the Grateful Dead's following is one of the largest and longest lasting in rock history, it remans a cult—for noninitiates, the gushing of Deadheads continues to provoke either consternation or bemusement. The advantage of *Deadicated*, then, is that this album of Garcia-Hunter and Weir-Barlow covers entices the curious to venture past the patchouli-and-incense mystique of the band and discover some very engaging songs. Dead purists may find Midnight Oil's brooding version of "Wharf Rat" heretical, or balk at the throbbing "Ripple" delivered by Jane's Addiction—but part of the fun of *Deadicated* is that it features a good many bands whose own styles seem antithetical to "hippie music." Elvis Costello makes "Ship of Fools" an epic beauty; Suzanne Vega does "China Doll" and "Cassidy" with characteristic artfulness. An ad-hoc "super-group" of members of the Georgia Satellites and Tom Petty's Heartbreakers rock "U.S. Blues" significantly harder than the original; Burning Spear transforms "Estimated Prophet" into credible reggae. In fact, it's the more faithful remakes, by Los Lobos, Bruce Hornsby and the Indigo Girls, that comprise the album's less satisfying moments—on each of these cuts, Garcia's guitar is sorely missed. Dwight Yoakam,

Warren Zevon, Lyle Lovett and the Cowboy Junkies round out the list of contributors; their strong performances may not send neophytes out to grab *Workingman's Dead* or *American Beauty,* but they offer convincing proof that the Dead's best ideas aren't confined to endless jams. — P.E.

DIDN'T IT BLOW YOUR MIND!: SOUL HITS OF THE '70's (Rhino, 1991)
★ ★ ★½ Volume 1
★ ★ ★½ Volume 2
★ ★ ★ ★ Volume 3
★ ★ ★½ Volume 4
★ ★ ★ ★ Volume 5
★ ★ ★½ Volume 6
★ ★ ★½ Volume 7
★ ★ ★ ★ Volume 8
★ ★ ★ ★ Volume 9
★ ★ ★ ★ Volume 10
★ ★ ★½ Volume 11
★ ★ ★ Volume 12
★ ★ ★ Volume 13
★ ★ ★ ★ Volume 14
★ ★ ★ Volume 15

Didn't It Blow Your Mind documents a brilliant moment in pop history, when listening to the radio could be exciting and entertaining, informative and inspiring—for hours at a stretch. Though the early '70s are generally perceived as a hangover from the highs of the '60s, this set extends soul music's peak through 1972. That year, mind-blowing Top Ten hits like "Back Stabbers," "Freddie's Dead," "I'll Take You There," "Lean On Me"—included on Volumes *8* and *9*—crossed over without a trace of compromise. Musically bold and frankly topical, most of these golden oldies still pack a mighty wallop. The early volumes establish a comfortable mix: sweet Southern grit from studios in Memphis and Muscle Shoals, soaring Philly slickness from producers Thom Bell and Gamble and Huff, psychedelic post-Motown from the Holland-Dozier-Holland team, and some truly wonderful one-shots. *Volume 3* collects two Motown gems (the Spinners' "It's a Shame" and "War" by Edwin Starr), along with Charles Wright's funky "Express Yourself." *Volume 5* adds reggae to the blend, while addressing racial paranoia ("Smiling Faces Sometimes" by the Undisputed Truth) and the rise of feminism (Jean Knight's "Mr. Big Stuff"; "Treat Her Like a Lady" by Cornelius Brothers & Sister Rose).

The Sound of Philadelpia exerts its dominance on the later albums; you can hear how those concise orchestrations, gripping arrangements and life-affirming harmonies overwhelmed—and influenced—the competition. The Staple Singers, Curtis Mayfield and Bill Withers do more than hold their own on the breathtaking eighth and ninth volumes, though. *Volume 10* captures the emergence of a sexier, rhythm-based groove, making room for Sylvia's "Pillow Talk" amid the pessimism of Mayfield's "Superfly" and War's "The World Is a Ghetto." Taking its name from the idiosyncratic producer Thom Bell's first hit single—"Didn't I (Blow Your Mind This Time)," by the Delfonics—and signing off with his last gasp before disco—"I'm Doin' Fine Now," by New York City—the first ten volumes of *Didn't It Blow Your Mind* feel reasonably complete. And unlike most various-artists compilations, it's remarkably coherent and clear-headed.

Strains in the fabric of the soul coalition begin to show during the final installment of the series. In the mid-70s, black music split off into discrete subgroups like funk, disco and "quiet storm" classicism. Volumes 11 through 14 compile one-shots rather than serve as a definitive guide. There are some classic tracks, but that unifying buzz ever-present through *Volume 10* completely slips away by the scattershot *Volume 15*. Barry White ("I'm Gonna Love You Just a Little More Baby") and his underlings Love Unlimited ("Walkin' in the Rain With the One I Love") kicks off *Volume 11* in elegantly orchestrated style, but the subsequent leaps seem abrupt: from soulful R&B throwbacks (the Devils' "Give Your Baby a Standing Ovation" and Ann Peebles's "I Can't Stand the Rain") to kicking straight-up groove jams (Eddie Kendricks's "Keep On Truckin' " and Fred Wesley and the JBs' "Doing It to Death") to eclectic pop crossovers (Gladys Knight and the Pips' "Midnight Train to Georgia," the Pointer Sisters' "Yes We Can Can"). It never quite adds up.

Volume 12 centers on some solid vocal nuggets that are best enjoyed on the respective groups' greatest-hits albums: Harold Melvin and the Blue Notes' "The Love I Lost, Part 1," the O'Jays' "Love Train" and the Chi-Lites' Philly-by-way-of-Chicago "Stoned out of My Mind." Al Wilson's winning "Show and Tell" and William DeVaughn's low-riding "Be Thankful for What You Got" are invaluable rarities; Joe Simon's "Theme From Cleopatra Jones" and Bobby Womack's "Lookin' for a Love" prove that even the

expansive '70s soul sound had its formulaic moments. "Rock the Boat" by the Hues Corporation and "Rock Your Baby" by George McCrae open *Volume 13* with another smoothly satisfying predisco salvo, but uneven stylistic shifts mar the rest of the album. Foward-looking funksters like Kool and the Gang ("Hollywood Swinging") and Rufus ("Tell Me Something Good") bump rumps with old-school soul acts like Blue Magic ("Sideshow") and the Impressions ("Finally Got Myself Together [I'm a Changed Man]"). Corny pop trifles from Billy Preston ("Nothing From Nothing") and Carl Carlton ("Everlasting Love") tip the set in the wrong direction.

A fairly consistent pulse is sustained throughout *Volume 14*; from the hot Ohio Players ("Fire") to the sultry LaBelle ("Lady Marmalade") with a little full-fledged dance mania from Shirley and Company ("Shame, Shame, Shame") and Gloria Gaynor ("Never Can Say Goodbye"). The "dooby dooby dooby" chorus of the Tymes' "You Little Trustmaker" alone justifies the price of admission. Several veterans' disco misfires deflate *Volume 15*: "Supernatural Thing—Part 1" by Ben E. King, Joe Simon's "Get Down, Get Down (Get on the Floor" and "Let's Do It Again" by the Staple Singers—each one stumbles. And Minnie Riperton's annoying "Lovin' You" belongs on a collection of novelty hits even if it was produced by Stevie Wonder. Gwen McCrae's swaying "Rockin' Chair" can be sampled on Rhino's own *The Best of T.K. Records* collection (along with the aforementioned George McCrae gem and others). For that matter, Tavares' "It Only Takes a Minute" probably belongs on one of Rhino's sterling *Disco Years* compilations. If you can swing with the rhythm, those albums pick up where the earlier versions of *Didn't It Blow Your Mind* leave off. — M.C.

★ ★ ½ **ELVIRA PRESENTS HAUNTED HITS (Rhino, 1988)**
Spanning the years of one of rock's curious subgenres, horror songs, *Elvira Presents Haunted Hits* trades on the buxom TV hostess's name and image in offering a 17-track CD and 23-track cassette/LP sampling of purportedly spooky songs. Some classics are included: Vic Mizzy's "Addams Family" theme, Bobby "Boris" Pickett's venerable "Monster Mash," Gene Simmons's "Haunted House," the Marketts' "Out of Limits," Sheb Wooley's "Purple

People Eater," and Screamin' Jay Hawkins's transcendent "I Put a Spell on You"—but there's much dross here as well, including Elvira's own "Full Moon." That this genre is pretty much played out is demonstrated by the strained contributions of contemporary artists such as Dave Edmunds, Ray Parker Jr. and Oingo Boingo, although the latter's Danny Elfman–penned "Dead Man's Party" reminds us that Elfman's music is its own kind of horror. Two gems: LaVern Baker's fiery reading of "Voodoo Voodoo" and Lambert, Hendricks and Ross's "Halloween Spooks," in which Annie Ross's banshee wail clearly prefigures the vocal style of Lene Lovich. — D.M.

★★★★★ **FATHER AND SONS (Spirit Feel, 1987)**

For anyone curious about gospel music's influence on R&B, doo-wop, soul and rock & roll singing styles, this album stands as an essential primer. Side one features eight towering performances by the original Soul Stirrers, as headed by R. H. Harris, an innovator and stylist virtually without peer in American music. Side two is evenly divided between performances by the Five Blind Boys of Mississippi, with their redoubtable lead singer Archie Brownlee, a disciple of the Harris style; and the Sensational Nightingales, whose Julius Cheeks delivered his messages in a raucous baritone that influenced the macho school of soul epitomized by Wilson Pickett, Levi Stubbs and, certainly, James Brown. Cheeks, who joined the Soul Stirrers in one of their post-Harris incarnations, also had a hand in pushing Sam Cooke, one of Harris's luminous successors, to add a harder edge to his sweet vocalizing. If Harris is widely regarded as the most important male singer in gospel history, Brownlee and Cheeks are close behind. Harris is credited with creating the gospel quartet tradition. In doing so he laid the groundwork for the earliest forms of rock & roll. To gospel he introduced the technique of ad-libbing, chanting background repetition, singing in delayed time; his voice was light and clear and charged with emotion on every lyric; and he could swoop up into a falsetto that was a chilling exhortation to a higher power. Side one's eight cuts, recorded between 1939 and 1948, amply demonstrate Harris's singular approach. The force of the Soul Stirrers' testimony is an overwhelming emotional experience that almost renders analysis moot. Music so perfect and so honestly felt begs to be left alone to work its magic on your heart.

Not that side two's featured artists give much ground to the Soul Stirrers. The Five Blind Boys' Archie Brownlee had a lustier voice than Harris, and his version of the Harris falsetto had the effect of a rather frightening series of shrieks, at once terrifying and beautiful expressions of the spirit moving. A 1952 track, "Will Jesus Be Waiting," one of the Blind Boys' most explosive performances, is a potent example of Brownlee's intricate interaction with his fellow singers. The Sensational Nightingales were the vehicle for Julius Cheeks's forceful leads, which were often buttressed by spot-perfect baritone counterpoint courtesy of Paul Owens. *Father and Sons* features Cheeks and Owens on only one cut, "Vacant Room in Glory," and a later configuration of the Nightingales minus Owens on three other cuts. The latter group is heard on the album's most relentless report, the yearning "Somewhere to Lay My Head." When this tape is over, everything is over. Turn out the lights, lay there in silence and try to grasp what you've heard.
— D.M.

★★★★ **FOLKWAYS: A VISION SHARED—A TRIBUTE TO WOODY GUTHRIE AND LEADBELLY (Columbia, 1988)**
★★★★ **FOLKWAYS: THE ORIGINAL VISION (Smithsonian/Folkways, 1989)**

Giants and friends, Woody Guthrie and Huddie Ledbetter were the twin pillars of American folk. They solidified its plainspoken singing style, asserted the acoustic guitar as its primary instrument and grounded its psychic force in grassroots politics and populist Christianity. *Folkways: A Vision Shared* gathers more than a dozen diverse artists to pay tribute to the pair—and it's a brilliant collection. The key to the album's vitality is the producers' decision to let the performers interpret the songs as freely as they wish: Arlo Guthrie's, Bob Dylan's and Bruce Springsteen's versions of Woody, then, derive very closely from the lean force of the originals, but Brian Wilson virtually reinvents Leadbelly's "Good Night Irene" as a Phil Spector-ish production, and, backed by Fishbone, Little Richard makes Leadbelly's "Rock Island Line" a screamer of his frenzied own. Of the other Guthrie homages, the strongest are a blistering "Jesus Christ" by U2, a swinging, fiddle-driven "Do Re Mi" by John

Mellencamp and a stirring "This Land Is
Your Land" done by Guthrie's old comrade
in arms, Pete Seeger, and an accompanying
school choir. Sweet Honey in the Rock does
Leadbelly with a cappella gospel fire, and
Taj Mahal's take on "Bourgeois Blues" is
gruff and knowing.

Folkways: The Original Vision compiles
the original Guthrie and Leadbelly
recordings, plus six additional songs.
Needless to say, it's a remarkable
album—and a fine (if obviously insufficient)
introduction to the two trailblazers. — P.E.

★★★★ **FRAT ROCK!: THE GREATEST**
ROCK 'N' ROLL PARTY TUNES
OF ALL TIME, VOLUMES 1–4
(1987; Rhino, 1988)
★★★★ **FRAT ROCK! (Rhino, 1987)**
★★★★ **SON OF FRAT ROCK! (Rhino,**
1988)

For those who exhibit an aversion to
fraternities, the advice in this case is to
ignore the title of these collections if it's the
power of the big beat you're looking for to
enliven a party, a dull evening at home or a
long drive. *Frat Rock!* purports to be
nothing more than the good-time music that
the first generation raised on rock swung to
in its college days. That's a nice hook for a
collection, but in fact these songs were
speaking to a broader audience than college
students—let's say this music belongs to all
of us, and leave it at that. The difference
between the various *Frat Rock!* collections is
that *Frat Rock!* and the 18-track *Son of Frat
Rock!* are, with few exceptions, distillations
of the four-volume set into two CDs.
Whichever you choose, you won't go wrong.

The four volumes are well thought-out in
their programming selections. Otherwise,
there's not too much in the way of surprises.
Volume 1 does offer the seldom-heard
Righteous Brothers groover "Little Latin
Lupe Lu" (written by Brother Bill Medley
and notable for being the duo's first hit, in
1963). That song was later covered by the
Kingsmen, who are represented on *Frat
Rock!* with—what else?—"Louie Louie,"
and on *Volume 3* with the vegetable
call-and-response classic, "Jolly Green
Giant." *Volume 3* also supplants Bobby
Freeman's original version of "Do You
Wanna Dance" with a storming cover by
Del Shannon; the Midniters are likely to
cause a power outage at least with their
rompin', stompin', slashing guitar attack on
"Whittier Blvd." Paul Revere and the
Raiders are heavily represented, and
justifiably so, with two cuts on *Frat Rock!*

("Hungry" and "Just Like Me") and "Just
Like Me" on *Volume 2. Volume 4* offers an
especially sweat-inducing side two featuring,
in succession, Ernie Maresca's "Shout Shout
(Knock Yourself Out)," the Rivieras'
"California Sun," Roger Miller's loopy
"Chug-a-Lug," the Fireballs' paean to
inebriation, "Bottle of Wine," with the Isley
Brothers bringing the whole affair to an
incendiary close with "Shout—Parts 1 & 2."
— D.M.

★★★★ **GO GO CRANKIN' (Island, 1985)**
Island Records tried to drum up a go-go
breakthrough in 1985, with releases by the
Washington, D.C., group Trouble Funk and
this compilation, but the albums couldn't
quite communicate the urgency and fun of
those sweaty concerts. The *Go Go Crankin'*
compilation, featuring Chuck Brown, E.U.
and T-Funk, along with others, does work
up a head of steam. "Let's Get Small," one
of two Trouble Funk cuts, sports a
major-league hook along with simmering
beats. — M.C.

★★★★★ **THE GOSPEL SOUND OF**
SPIRIT FEEL (Spirit Feel, 1991)
Anyone feeling 'buked and scorned is
advised to partake of a full-bore immersion
in *The Gospel Sound of Spirit Feel*, a 27-cut,
90-minute-plus journey to spiritual
redemption through song. Twenty-two of
the tracks are from gospel's golden era of
1946 through 1960 and afford listeners an
overview of a time of tremendous stylistic
innovation, when artists such as R. H.
Harris, the Soul Stirrers' magnificent lead
singer; Archie Brownlee (a Harris acolyte)
of the Five Blind Boys of Mississippi; Sister
Rosetta Tharpe; and others altered gospel's
course, and in the process laid the
foundation for doo-wop, R&B, soul, and
rock & roll. Even the pop sound of early
girl groups such as the Chantels has its
roots in the sassy harmonies of the Gospel
All Stars backing Professor Charles Taylor
on a 1956 track, "New Born Soul."

While the thread of history is woven
deeply into the fabric of this album—Clara
Ward begat Aretha Franklin; Julius Cheeks
begat Wilson Pickett; R. H. Harris begat
Sam Cooke—the sheer power of the
testifying herein overwhelms all other
virtues. Certainly there is nothing in
contemporary music to prepare one for the
way Cheeks scorches "Sinner Man" with a
fierceness and conviction that bespeak
terrifying knowledge of the wages of sin. At
the opposite end of the spectrum, Harris's

gentle ebullience at the beginning of the Soul Stirrers' "Canaan" gives way to a frenetic ad-libbing style (which would later become standard procedure for gospel quartets) that culminates in an overpowering display of joyous anticipation in the repeated chanting of "I'm worthy," as six voices soar heavenward. Elsewhere Mahalia Jackson and Marion Williams are given two cuts each that they turn into mesmerizing statements, the former being all classic, stately grandeur, the latter all sanctified, blues-tinged testimony to the power of faith.

The secular world creeps into the act in sly ways, too. "99 1/2" opens the album on a swinging note more common to R&B than to gospel at that time; it also pits Katie Bell's languid singing style against the younger Sister Rosetta Tharpe's highly rhythmic approach to a lyric (a harbinger of change in the gospel world when it was recorded in 1949); a 1953 track, "No Room at the Hotel," finds Sister Jessie Mae Renfro employing her most penetrating blues gospel voice to inveigh against prejudice and management while adopting a pro labor stance on the eve of the civil-rights movement.

Such examples abound—someone influenced someone else; someone anticipated a trend, indeed a movement, well ahead of its time. Ultimately, though, this music isn't so much about history as it is about the often-conflicting emotions we seek to control even as they control us. To anyone willing to embrace its bolstering spirit, *The Gospel Sound of Spirit Feel* reaches across the years to provide meaning, to provide solace, perhaps even to provide answers where once there were none.

— D.M.

★ ★ ★ ★ ★ GOSPEL WARRIORS (Spirit Feel, 1987)

A companion volume to Spirit Feel's essential *Father and Sons* collection, *Gospel Warriors* brings into sharp focus the influential styles and quite different attributes of the female solo vocalists working in gospel music. As Spirit Feel label founder and gospel authority Anthony Heilbut points out in his excellent liner notes to this set, the gospel soloist occupied a world free of the musical restraints placed on vocalists within a group or choir setting; consequently, Heilbut asserts, these soloists "may be the freest of all performers." The eight female artists represented here bear out this fact. Each of the singers is represented by two songs, all chosen for a

purpose. The oldest track, for example, shows the Georgia Peach (née Clara Hudman) captured in a tentative, unpolished performance from 1931, "Lordy, Won't You Come By Here"; she is heard again in 1960 in more assured form on "Lord Have Mercy," where she closes out her moving performance with a quietly spoken "Yes Lord" that indicates her own surprise at the transporting quality of the moment.

Sister Rosetta Tharpe's two selections raise issues regarding the gospel soloist's forays between the sacred and secular world. In the late '30s she was one of the biggest names on the gospel circuit and had several hit records with rousing versions of hymns by the great Thomas A. Dorsey. Tharpe was a gifted entertainer, who could be swept away by the passion of her material, then snap to with a smart quip, raising the roof with laughter as much as she did with spirit. No wonder big-band leaders like Cab Calloway, Benny Goodman and Lucky Millinder employed her at times: she was a natural. She also happened to be an inventive blues guitarist, another instance where the secular was brought to bear upon the sacred in her work. Heilbut credits her with inventing pop gospel, and it would appear that she did so in 1941, on one of the two cuts featured here, the Sallie Martin standard, "Just a Closer Walk With Thee," where Sister Tharpe's bouncing vocal and bluesy guitar accompaniment blur the distinction between gospel and blues; or maybe she did it in 1939, on "Savior Don't Pass Me By," when she used a vocal technique that employed both speaking and singing on what sounds for all the world like a pop song, no matter the lyrical content.

Where *Father and Sons* took us into the '50s, *Gospel Warriors* shows a progression of styles from the '30s into the '80s, the latter decade being represented by the powerful Marion Williams and the less-heralded but no less compelling Frances Steadman, whose wordless version of "Amazing Grace," titled "Moan Frances," must be heard to be believed. One might quibble at the exclusion of the obvious giant, Mahalia Jackson, but we get instead Mary Johnson Davis, perhaps the most profound influence on Jackson's style. This overview then shows a certain continuity within the disparity of styles over the years and points up how few concessions the music has made—has needed to make, more properly—to the modern age. Like *Father and Sons*, though,

Gospel Warriors both begs for historical examination and at the same time demands only that we allow the spirit to wash over us. This is a glorious sound. — D.M.

GREAT GROUPS OF THE FIFTIES
(Collectables, NA)
★ ★ ★ **Volume I**
★ ★ ★ **Volume II**
★ ★ ★ **Volume III**
A good primer in East Coast–style doo-wop as purveyed mostly by the second-string groups that fell a tad short of the Olympian status of the Five Satins, Flamingos and Spaniels, who are among the name groups represented. *Volume I* contains a previously unreleased track by the Veltones, "A Fool Was I," as does *Volume II* in the Capris' "Milk and Gin" and the Skylarks' "Never Let Her Go." Always interesting, this collection, if not always moving. — D.M.

HARLEM HOLIDAY: NEW YORK RHYTHM AND BLUES (Collectables, NA)
★ ★ ★ **Volume One**
★ ★ ★ **Volume Two**
★ ★ ★ **Volume Three**
★ ★ ★ ★ **Volume Four**
★ ★ ★ **Volume Five**
★ ★ ★ **Volume Six**
★ ★ ★ ★ **Volume Seven**
First-rate survey of New York doo-wop graced with group harmony talismans such as the Bop Chords' "Castles in the Sky" (Volume One is a virtual Bop Chords greatest hits album), the Turbans' "When You Dance," the Five Satins' "In the Still of the Night," Maurice Williams & the Zodiacs' "Stay," the Mello-Kings' "Tonight Tonight" and the Silhouettes' "Get a Job." Along the way, though, there's plenty of minor classics on the order of Lewis Lymon & the Teenchords' "Please Tell the Angels" and the Loungers' "Remember the Night." Volume Four is highly recommended, it being a virtual Paragons vs. Jesters rematch, a dream bill for doo-wop aficionados. — D.M.

★ ★ ★ ★ HARLEM NY: THE DOO-WOP ERA (Collectables, NA)
A must-have double-album set that zeroes in on some of doo-wop's best hits by its major artists and some important sides by the B teamers. The Students' magnificent "Every Day of the Week"—as essential a doo-wop single as exists—kicks off the set, and along the way there are sterling contributions from the Videos ("Trickle Trickle"), the Bop Chords ("So Why"), the Edsels ("Rama

Lama Ding Dong"), and the Eternals (the immortal "Babalu's Wedding Day"). Lewis Lymon & the Teenchords check in for three first-rate tracks, the Dells come on with a rare track in "Time Makes You Change" and the Continentals work it out on "Fine Fine Frame." There's real poetry coming through on some of these sides, much of it tender and romantic, some of it bragadocious, all of it sharp. The vocal pyrotechnics and heartfelt performances on display made people crazy about doo-wop. Listen, and prepare to be dazzled and moved. — D.M.

A HISTORY OF NEW ORLEANS RHYTHM & BLUES (Rhino, 1987)
★ ★ ★ ★ **Volume 1: 1950–1958**
★ ★ ★ ★ **Volume 2: 1959–1962**
★ ★ ★ ★ **Volume 3: 1962–1970**
The three-volume Rhino set *A History of New Orleans Rhythm & Blues* is the most important of the New Orleans overviews. Not only does the collection sprinkle inspired obscurities (Aaron Neville's "Over You," with its themes of murder and betrayal) among its enduring hits, it also spans the years 1950 to 1970, indicating the wide swath cut by New Orleans music. And Lord knows, the succeeding years have hardly been dry ones—the Neville Brothers, for one, link the '70s with the '90s, and are the subject of their own Rhino appreciation, *Treacherous*, that might suffice as *History*'s Volume 4. The point is that New Orleans has remained a vital center for traditional musics without selling out or compromising its sound to accommodate passing fancies in the commercial marketplace. For those who care about such things, *Volume 2* offers the best selection of radio and retail hits, but the lesser-known tracks in this set are rife with such endearing performances that their lack of commercial success can only be attributed to nonmusical factors. — D.M.

★ ★ ★ ★ THE HISTORY OF ROCK INSTRUMENTALS, Volumes 1 and 2 (Rhino, 1987)
These two volumes give a listener a good feel for the variety of rock instrumentals produced in the late '50s and early '60s, and *Volume 2* in particular is an especially compelling showcase of highly idiosyncratic guitar styles that continue to influence aspiring axemen of all ages. *Volume 1* surveys a wider variety of instrumental styles than its companion volume, particularly in the realm of drumming. Here is the Surfaris' "Wipe Out," Sandy Nelson's

"Let There Be Drums" and Preston Epps's "Bongo Rock," each of which, for all intents and purposes, uses drums as the lead instrument. In "Wipe Out," drummer Ron Wilson lets loose with an athletic display of drum rolls that has few parallels in popular music; guitarist Jim Fuller checks in with some pungent power chording, as well. Similarly, Nelson's kit work dwarfs the instruments in his band, but it's less flamboyant, if no less propulsive, than Wilson's star turn two years later. Epps is notable for being the only artist in history to have writ his name in the history books with a hit featuring bongo drums.

Otherwise, *Volume 1* gives us two rare and evocative appearances by French horns, on the Marketts' "Out of Limits" and, most dramatically, on Jack Nitzsche's grandiose, melodramatic surfing classic, "The Lonely Surfer," while roller-rink organ is featured on Dave "Baby" Cortez's "Happy Organ." Not that guitarists get short shrift in *Volume 1*, though. The Ventures are represented twice, with guitarist Nokie Edwards getting a better chance to shine on "Walk—Don't Run" than on "Hawaii Five-O." On the aforementioned "The Lonely Surfer," Jack Nitzsche plays the melody entirely on the bass strings of the guitar, certainly an unusual ploy. And Santo and Johnny are here with their plaintive "Sleep Walk," although this version is a different take than the one usually programmed on radio, with the guitars mixed lower, the bass up, and an organ added as unsatisfying and distracting augmentation.

Volume 2 goes nuclear with two of Duane Eddy's quintessential twangy workouts in "Rebel Rouser" and "Because They're Young," the latter an evocative movie theme that has the big-sky ambience of *The Magnificent Seven* theme; Lonnie Mack, whose influence extends to the modern era in the playing of the late Stevie Ray Vaughan, among others, is on board with two of the instrumentals that launched his legend, "Memphis" and "Wham." Where Eddy influenced rock and country artists and Mack influenced blues and rock artists, the godfather of the punks would have to be unreconstructed primitive Link Wray. Wray's "Raw-Hide" and "Rumble" struck the sort of desolate ambience the punks reveled in. It didn't hurt that he was often clad entirely in black leather, spared no grease on his jet-black hair and hid his eyes behind dark sunglasses, adding visual menace to his aural appeal.

Would any survey of rock instrumentals be complete without the saxophone in a starring role? *Volume 2* also weighs in strong here. Alvin Cash and the Crawlers offer a splendid model of King Curtis–style stuttering sax in "Twine Time," while the Viscounts offer Lester Young–style grace on the bluesy, sensual "Harlem Nocturne." Though its once-privileged perch in the rock world has been eroded, the instrumental has played a vital role in the music's evolution. Whatever the form's fate in the years ahead, *The History of Rock Instrumentals* offers compelling witness to a rich vein of music that has spoken volumes without speaking a word. — D.M.

★ ★ ★ ★ ★ **HITS FROM THE LEGENDARY VEE JAY RECORDS (Motown, 1986)**
The Dells' initial '50s hits are included on this great Vee Jay compilation along with Jerry Butler's solo breakthrough, Betty Everett's original "You're No Good" and two dozen other roots revelations from this seminal Chicago label. — M.C.

★ ★ ★ **I SHALL BE UNRELEASED: THE SONGS OF BOB DYLAN (Rhino, 1991)**
Bob Dylan himself hadn't commercially released the 18 songs on this collection when its artists recorded them over a period ranging from 1965 to 1988, but Dylan properly dominates *I Shall Be Unreleased*. Rod Stewart's "Only a Hobo" and Ron Wood's "Seven Days" are the strongest cuts, largely because they stick closest to the Dylan spirit; such novelties as Jah Malla's reggae version of "Ain't No Man Righteous, Not No One" and the Hollies' rockabilly treatment of "Quit Your Low Down Ways" are interesting chiefly for proving that truly sturdy songs often remain effective no matter what the treatment. And the songs on this CD primarily are Dylan's craftsmanlike work, rather than his idiosyncratic personal statements. Instead, the artists, from Manfred Mann to Dream Syndicate, Johnny Cash to the Staple Singers, bear witness to Dylan's gifts as a formalist—all of the songs remain sound. — P.E.

★ ★ ★ ★ **LAY THAT NEW ORLEANS ROCK 'N' ROLL DOWN (Specialty, 1988)**
Specialty's 14-track New Orleans anthology, *Lay That New Orleans Rock 'N' Roll Down*, is of particular interest owing to the

inclusion of several previously unreleased tracks by significant New Orleans artists such as Ernie K-Doe, Bobby Marchan, Larry Williams and Lloyd Price. The latter's "Doomed to End This Way," from 1956, betrays little of the New Orleans influence in its ambience, but the sax and guitar work complementing Williams's haunted performance are irrefutably Crescent City. In addition to these stalwarts, the record includes other cuts seeing the light of day for the first time. Big Boy Myles and the Shaw Wees are represented by three tracks, two of them previously unreleased, all of them splendid examples of Professor Longhair–style arrangements and vocals. Roy Montrell shows up with a previously unreleased alternate take of "Oooh-Wow!," a barn-burner from 1956. History buffs will also delight in a rare solo track from Edgar Blanchard (better known as the guitarist on such great records of the '50s as Roy Brown's "Good Rockin' Tonight" and Little Richard's "Long Tall Sally" and "Rip It Up"), who checks in with a New Orleans–style update of "Sweet Sue," a bouncy pop song dating back to 1928.
— D.M.

★★★★ LOST IN THE STARS: THE MUSIC OF KURT WEILL (A&M, 1985)

"Single artist interpretations" is what producer Hal Wilner calls his ongoing series of eclectic all-star tribute albums. These records enshrine a deliberate, personalized approach to making music; they're hard to pin down—by definition. This celebration of Kurt Weill is the most successful to date. Though he'd worked with many jazz artists on previous tributes to Thelonious Monk and composer Nino Rota, Wilner displays a shrewd, intuitive feel for rock on Lost in the Stars. However they were achieved, most of these marriages bear fruit. Weill composed music for the theater, collaborating with playwright Bertolt Brecht in Berlin and a variety of writers on Broadway. Marianne Faithfull, Lou Reed, Tom Waits, Todd Rundgren and Sting all have a theatrical bent, and each of their contributions sounds totally in character. Sting's disquieting "The Ballad of Mack the Knife" and Lou Reed's sentimental "September Song" are the real standouts, but the instrumental pieces by Van Dyke Parks, Carla Bley and the Armadillo String Quartet point out the strength and invention of Kurt Weill's melodies. He even withstands the squeaks and whistles of avant-garde sax technician

John Zorn for five long minutes. The other 55 make up for that lapse. — M.C.

★★★ METAL AGE: THE ROOTS OF METAL (Rhino, 1992)

This catch-all '70s compilation should rightly be called The Reign of Metal; the true roots of metal lie in the late-'60s roar of Steppenwolf, Blue Cheer, the MC5 and the Stooges. Metal Age taps a wide variety of groups that, arguably, were merely influenced by heavy metal: bloozey power-slurpers like Beck, Bogert and Appice and Ten Years After, heavy crossovers like Bachman-Turner Overdrive and Cheap Trick, psychedelic throwbacks like Robin Trower and Hawkwind, protopunks like the Runaways and Blue Oyster Cult, forgotten arena soldiers like Angel and Wishbone Ash. It's only about as coherent as the average late-night TV mail-order special: it's a hastily assembled heavy mess, in other words. — M.C.

NUGGETS
★★★★ Nuggets, Vol. 1: The Hits (Rhino, 1984)
★★★★ Nuggets (Rhino, 1986)
★★★ Nuggets, Vol. 9: Acid Rock (Rhino, 1987)
★★★ More Nuggets (Rhino, 1987)
★★ Even More Nuggets (Rhino, 1989)

These albums are all descendants of the original Nuggets, a two-album set compiled by critic-guitarist Lenny Kaye. That collection focused on mid-Sixties garage rock by the likes of the Amboy Dukes, the Vagrants, the Shadows of Knight, Count Five and others. Though long out of print, it's a classic.

In the early Eighties, the people at Rhino took the concept—and the name—and ran with it. They eventually released nine volumes on vinyl and cassette. Only the first and the last—focusing on the hits (the Leaves' version of "Hey Joe," the Electric Prunes' "I Had Too Much to Dream [Last Night]," "Dirty Water" by the Standells) and on acid rock—remain in print.

Depending on your zest for schtick, Nuggets, Vol. One is pretty fun, kind of like K-tel repackaged by smart guys. While the singing is almost invariably lame (aping genuine styles, either Brit or black) and the playing varies crazily, these one-hit wonders are not only nifty in their own right, but provide perspective on the contemporary work of more significant talents. With "I Had Too Much to Dream Last Night," the

Electric Prunes fuse the exoticism of the Stones' "Paint It Black" and the Yardbirds at their dervish best; the Standells' "Dirty Water" anticipates punk; Blue Cheer's "Summertime Blues" gleefully destroys Eddie Cochran. Creaky studio wizardry, and sensibilities varying from power pop to bubblegum to psychedelia enliven such transistor classics as The Nazz's "Open My Eyes," the Count Five's "Psychotic Reaction," and the Blues Magoos' "We Ain't Got Nothin' Yet."

Vol. 9 goes in for heavy. There's glory in this acid-rock collection: The Byrds' "Eight Miles High," the Chambers Brothers' "Time Has Come Today," Steppenwolf's "Magic Carpet Ride" and the Young Rascal's "It's Wonderful." There's also tripe: the Strawberry Alarm Clock's "Incense and Peppermints," the First Edition's "Just Dropped in to See What Condition My Condition Was In," and—oh, god—Iron Butterfly's "In-A-Gadda-Da-Vida."

The nine-volume vinyl and cassette series has been boiled down to three CDs—*Nuggets, More Nuggets* and *Even More Nuggets*. They are equally exhaustive. — P.E.

OLDIES BUT GOODIES (Original Sound, 1987)

★★★★ Vol. 1
★★★ Vol. 2
★★★★ Vol. 3
★★★★ Vol. 4
★★★★ Vol. 5
★★★★ Vol. 6
★★★★ Vol. 7
★★★★ Vol. 8
★★★★ Vol. 9
★★★★ Vol. 10
★★★★ Vol. 11
★★★★ Vol. 12
★★★ Vol. 14
★★★ Vol. 15

The first and still-venerable oldies anthology offers its share of pleasures for listeners unconcerned with matters such as context, discographies, liner notes, artist photos and so on. Each disc contains between 15 and 17 songs selected in haphazard fashion—they're not from the same year, they're not all Number One records, they're not connected thematically or stylistically and all are given the Original Sound treatment of being faded out at the end, whether the originals were or not. What the various volumes do have in common is a wealth of wonderful old rock & roll—could this be a concept?— encompassing all the styles and eccentricities

that fall under the genre's broad definition. In terms of programming, there's little that's surprising, but taken as a whole, the collection offers a wide sampling of the wondrous variety of music made by rock artists of all races over the years and takes on the aspect of a good oldies station by integrating the work of important artists with the fleeting contributions made by one-hit wonders. It's also unique in that it has no Vol. 13—superstition rears its head.

As a rule, the Original Sound series is not the place to look for the obscure or unfamiliar; an exception would be *Volume 3*, which offers the Penguins' rarely heard regional hit from 1963, "Memories of El Monte." A tribute to El Monte Stadium, site of some of the first rock & roll shows presented in Los Angeles, the song incorporates snippets of several group harmony hits from the mid-'50s, including the Penguins' own immortal "Earth Angel." Rock trivia fans take note: "Memories of El Monte" was co-written by Frank Zappa. Unfortunately, *Volume 3* also includes Tony Orlando and Dawn's execrable rendering of "Tie a Yellow Ribbon 'Round the Old Oak Tree," a plague upon our land.

On the other hand, *Volume 5* showcases an interesting array of black music styles that gained popular favor over the years, from the Dominoes hit "Sixty Minute Man" (1951) to Jean Knight's 1971 in-your-face romp, "Mr. Big Stuff," with stops for Shep and the Limelites' "Daddy's Home," the Paradons' elegant "Diamonds and Pearls," Johnnie Taylor's "Who's Makin' Love" and others. *Volume 10* has at its center a knockout triple play comprised of Johnny Ace's "Pledging My Love," the heart-rending Jerry Butler–Betty Everett duet "Let It Be Me," and Jimmy Reed's down-and-dirty blues-rock, "Bright Lights, Big City." What becomes of the brokenhearted? They put on *Volume 14* and get on the catharsis express that rolls through Brenda Lee's "I'm Sorry," the Platters' "Smoke Gets in Your Eyes," Dinah Washington's delicate "Unforgettable" and Jackie DeShannon's "What the World Needs Now Is Love."

So it goes. Music to fit every mood, memory and taste; all you need is a remote control so you can quickly bail out of less palpable cuts (to wit, anything by Tony Orlando and Dawn). Don't be misled by the plain packaging: *Oldies but Goodies* may not be sexy or glamorous, but it has proven itself a reliable and trustworthy series. Good bang for the buck. — D.M.

★★★★ **RADIO CLASSICS OF THE '50S (Columbia, 1989)**

There was a time when radio was really something, a true melting pot that exposed virtually every kind of music being recorded in this country. Pop coexisted peacefully with R&B; rock & roll shared air time with folk-oriented material; country & western and urban blues were not-so-strange bedfellows. *Radio Classics of the '50s* offers a glimpse of this scintillating melange in 14 cuts ranging far and wide in both style and content. Some of these have remained staples of oldies radio through the years—Johnny Mathis's "Chances Are," a Number One single in 1957; Marty Robbins's western melodrama, "El Paso," another Number One from 1959; Johnny Horton's rousing history lesson set to a big beat, "The Battle of New Orleans," the second biggest-selling record of 1959—while others have receded into history, no less compelling, only less programmed. Here is a powerful Tony Bennett performance of "Rags to Riches," the hyperkinetic Johnnie Ray's tortured reading of "Cry," the Brothers Four's high-tone folk rendition of "Greenfields," Frankie Laine's melodramatic interpretation of the *High Noon* theme, Guy Mitchell's pop-cum-country treatment of "Singing the Blues," the Four Lads' exercise in soaring, close group harmony on the treacly "Moments to Remember." This thoroughly enjoyable record isn't a complete overview of commercial radio in the '50s, but it does deliver a broad enough spectrum of material to make one want more and to wonder if radio will ever again be so all-inclusive. — D.M.

★★★★ **RCA VICTOR BLUES & RHYTHM REVUE (RCA, 1988)**

A terrific overview of various blues and rhythm & blues styles of the 1940s and 1950s, *RCA Victor Blues & Rhythm Revue* makes its points via some relatively rare cuts by some relatively well-known artists and throws in a few other brilliant obscurities along the way. The artist lineup is representative of the myriad R&B tributaries, including pure blues (e.g., Mr. Sad Head), blues ballads (Lil Green, Little Richard in an early incarnation), big-band blues (the immortal Jimmy Rushing fronting the Count Basie Orchestra on "Hey, Pretty Baby") and group harmony (the Delta Rhythm Boys, Du Droppers). Of the 26 cuts, the oldest are the first two on the CD, both being Lil Green tracks from 1940 and

1941; the disc concludes in 1956 with a roiling instrumental blast courtesy of King Curtis ("Open Up") and with the Isley Brothers infusing their R&B with the big beat of rock & roll ("Shout") as a new era begins. Of particular historical import: the Delta Rhythm Boys, whose smooth harmony style presaged the influential sound of the Ravens, offering two mellow delights, "Dry Bones" and "Take the 'A' Train"; Little Richard coming on like blues shouter Roy Brown on "Get Rich Quick" and sounding a bit like Sam Cooke on the blues ballad "Thinkin' 'Bout My Mother," tracks dating from 1951 and 1952, respectively; and the Du Droppers rocking and rolling their way through an early Leiber-Stoller gem, "Bam Balam." This one's a first-rate package, with complete personnel listings and recording dates and some music that can't be beat. — D.M.

★★★½ **REBEL ROUSERS SOUTHERN ROCK CLASSICS (Rhino, 1992)**

A perfect starter kit for anyone who missed this central '70s movement. *Rebel Rousers* balances the requisite blues ("Statesboro Blues" by the Allman Brothers) and boogie (Lynyrd Skynyrd's live "Free Bird") with a handful of deep-fried pop crossovers like Elvin Bishop's "Fooled Around and Fell in Love" and "Jackie Blue" by the Ozark Mountain Daredevils. And .38 Special's resonant FM hit "Caught up in You" brings the reign of *Southern Rock Classics* up to 1982, anyway. If this genre's not exactly thriving, the music still sounds gritty and vital. Appropriately wild-eyed liner notes by discophile and former Brownsville Station guitarist Cub Koda round out this learned introduction. — M.C.

★★★½ **RED HOT & BLUE: A BENEFIT FOR AIDS RESEARCH AND RELIEF (Chrysalis, 1990)**

Cole Porter's songs brim with a show-biz wit and urbane sophistication that would seem alien to rock & roll. But this hour-long tribute album works more often than not; only Tom Waits's contribution is downright grating, and it's over soon enough. The Brit-pop contingent—Fine Young Cannibals, Erasure, Thompson Twins, Annie Lennox, Lisa Stansfield and especially Neneh Cherry—are the ones who best capture Porter's wry sensitivity. "Don't Fence Me In" certainly does David Byrne a world of good. He hasn't sounded so loose and agreeable in years. *Red Hot & Blue*

provides plenty of thought-provoking
listening, along with some essential reading
matter: an accompanying booklet explains
in clear, well-researched terms exactly what
this disease is—and isn't.   — M.C.

★★★ A RHYTHM & BLUES
      CHRISTMAS (Collectables, NA)
How blue can you get? Check out the
heartbreaking tenor lead vocal on the Blue
Notes' "Oh Holy Night," or Sonny Til's
pain-wracked lead on "Lonely Christmas."
The emphasis here is on the blue side of the
R&B Christmas equation, and a number of
sad tracks make the point that all is not
merry and bright during the Yuletide.
Unless you're Lightnin' Hopkins comin' on
like a back-door Santa in "Santa."
Elsewhere, Chuck Berry gets into a
blues-guitar workout on Charles Brown's
"Merry Christmas, Baby," and the
Moonglows offer both a group harmony
tearjerker in "Just a Lonely Christmas" and
a Louis Jordan–style jump-blues revel on
"Hey Santa Claus." A good set, with Til
and the Moonglows supplying the
transcendent moments.   — D.M.

★★★ RISQUÉ RHYTHM: NASTY 50s
      R&B (Rhino, 1991)
Serving as a reminder that "rock & roll"
itself was originally slang for "the wild
thing," Risqué Rhythm returns to the early
'50s and exhumes bump 'n' grind treasures
and truly blue blues. Actually, in the post–2
Live Crew era, this raunchy stuff is pretty
genial fare—broad double entendres, rather
than smut. There's Dinah Washington
singing about a trombonist and his "Big
Long Slidin' Thing" and Moose Jackson
bragging about his "Big Ten-Inch Record"
(a ditty that inspired Aerosmith to fashion a
sly miniclassic of their own). Wynonie
Harris, of "Good Rockin' Tonight" fame,
contributes "Keep on Churnin' " and
"Wasn't That Good"; the Toppers turn in
the most brazen title, "(I Love to Play Your
Piano) Let Me Bang Your Box." All
nudging saxes, boom-boom drums and
leering vocals, the playing is that of
standard (i.e., very good) early R&B—and
it's a kick to note that quite a few of these
numbers were massive sellers in their day.
The ultimate impression these songs give,
however, is that of a loopy charm and
blushing innocence—they're actually a form,
no matter how marginal, of Americana, a
nostalgic look back at a time when it was
possible to be shocked.   — P.E.

SOUL SHOTS (Rhino, 1987, 1988)
★★★★★ Volume 1: Dance Party
★★★★★ Volume 2: Sweet Soul
  ★★★★ Volume 3: Soul Instrumentals
★★★★★ Volume 4: Screamin' Soul Sisters
★★★★★ Volume 5: Soul Ballads
  ★★★★ Volume 6: Blue-Eyed Soul
★★★★★ Volume 7: Urban Blues
  ★★★★ Volume 8: Sweet Soul Sisters
  ★★★★ Volume 9: More Dance Party
★★★★★ Volume 10: More Sweet Soul
  ★★★★ Volume 11: More Ballads
James Brown, Aretha Franklin and the
Stax/Volt gang may have ruled supreme,
but a number of less famous names made
substantial contributions to the dictionary of
'60s soul. That's the basis for this
outstanding anthology series: there are
plenty of big-time hits, but they are
buttressed by other powerful performances
that deserve to be called classic tracks. In
essence, Soul Shots is an unabridged version
of Epic's first-rate Lost Soul series of the
early '80s that showcases not only artists but
disparate styles within the category of soul
music. The scope is amazing in its
inclusiveness—no base is left untouched,
from blues to instrumentals to both the
mellow and the boisterous sides of the male
and female points of view; even some real
gone palefaces get their just due in Blue
Eyed Soul (nice to hear the underestimated
Roy Head again). The highlights are too
numerous too mention, except to say that
each cassette is a bona fide classic, one
highlight after another. You can't go wrong
with this one, and you'll be a better person
for having listened to the complete series.
  — D.M.

SOUL SHOTS: A COLLECTION OF
SIXTIES SOUL CLASSICS (Rhino, 1988,
1989)
★★★★★ Volume 1
★★★★★ Volume 2
★★★★★ Volume 3
★★★★★ Volume 4
On the surface this appears to be an
abridged version of the Soul Shots
11-volume cassette series; on closer
inspection, this four-CD set does indeed
reprise some of the highlights of its epic
ancestor, but it also contains several tracks
unavailable on the original collection. The
blues set, Volume 4, is especially strong,
with Albert Collins, Z.Z. Hill, and Roscoe
Gordon joining the lineup, and Little
Richard being represented by one of the
tracks cut when Jimi Hendrix was his
guitarist. Also note on Volume 1 the

presence of James Brown, unrepresented on the previous *Soul Shots* anthology but in top form here on two cuts, "Night Train" and "I Got You." Add in the minor gems that make life worth living, and you get, again, a classic collection. — D.M.

★ ★ ★ ½ STAY AWAKE (A&M, 1988)
Having produced a trio of oddly fascinating tribute albums to Nino Rota, Thelonious Monk and Kurt Weill that feature a dazzling diversity of musicians, offbeat conceptualist Hal Willner pulls off a coup of sorts by getting Sun Ra, the Replacements and Sinéad O'Connor, among others, to turn in takes on "hits" from Walt Disney chestnuts. By turns bizarre and whimsical, *Stay Awake* comes across as a high-art kiddie album when Suzanne Vega performs a ditty from *Mary Poppins* or Harry Nilsson assays "Zip-a-Dee-Doo-Dah"; as a novelty record when NRBQ rocks "Whistle While You Work"; and like an acid trip when Yma Sumac operatically wails "I Wonder" from *Sleeping Beauty*. Among the stranger highlights are Tom Waits turning "Heigh Ho" into a bit of Captain Beefheart-ish surrealism; Natalie Merchant, Michael Stipe and the Roches making like a preschool choir on a theme from *Bambi*; and Buster Poindexter camping up a *Babes in Toyland* song. Betty Carter's contribution is strong, straightforward jazz; Bonnie Raitt, with Was (Not Was), converts "Baby Mine," from *Dumbo*, into a neat R&B ballad. James Taylor's *Peter Pan* selection sounds exactly like one of his (better) MOR offerings, and Ringo Starr's "When You Wish Upon a Star" is predictably cute. While the album is definitely a curio, it's a good curio—and its pleasures are more lasting than you might think. — P.E.

TROUBADOURS OF THE FOLK ERA (Rhino, 1992)
★ ★ ★ Volume 1
★ ★ ★½ Volume 2
★ ★ ★½ Volume 3: The Groups
From the spare loveliness of Joan Baez to the elegant experimentalism of Tim Buckley, the three volumes of *Troubadours of the Folk Era* comprehensively celebrate the energy, commitment and, above all, earnestness of the early-'60s American folk revival. Keyed in with a growing enthusiasm for black culture spawned by the civil-rights movement, an urgent antiwar activism and a distaste for the saccharine pop of the day, the young coffeehouse folkies turned to the Walt Whitman–inspired poetry of the Beats

and the Scots-Irish folk music tradition first politicized by Woody Guthrie. These records gather the big names (Phil Ochs, Tim Hardin, Judy Collins, Joni Mitchell, Pete Seeger, Ian and Sylvia) of the genre, as well as some strong lesser lights (Fred Neil, Hamilton Camp, Judy Henske). While some of the selections sound dated, the good work remains exhilarating. These were artists singing about things of substance. — P.E.

THE SUGAR HILL STORY (Sugar Hill, 1990)
★ ★ ★ ★ Volume 1
★ ★ ★ ★ ★ Volume 2
Founded by R&B singer Sylvia Robinson (of "Pillow Talk" fame), Sugar Hill was the most important of the pioneering rap labels, having produced the genre's first hit, the Sugarhill Gang's "Rapper's Delight." These recordings weren't entirely representative of what was going on in rap clubs, though. Because Sugar Hill wanted to avoid the copyright complications of having a DJ scratch beats and break tracks in the studio, most Sugar Hill singles were recorded with a live rhythm section, featuring bassist Doug Wimbish and drummer Keith LeBlanc (both of whom eventually wound up in Tackhead). Even so, the Sugar Hill sound defined an era in rap, thanks to such touchstones as "The Message" by Grandmaster Flash & the Furious Five, "Disco Dream" by the Mean Machine and "Let's Dance" by the West Street Mob. All three tracks appear on *Volume Two* of the series, along with "Rapper's Delight" and Trouble Funk's go-go jam "Hey Fellas." *Volume One* is somewhat less hit-intense, although it does include Melle Mel's anticocaine "White Lines (Don't Do It)" and Grandmaster Flash's turntable masterpiece, "The Adventures of Grandmaster Flash on the Wheels of Steel." — J.D.C.

★ ★ ★ ★ SUMMER & SUN (Rhino, 1989)
This superb Rhino collection offers 18 lazy, hazy, crazy tracks, most of them classics of their kind, that call up, in splended fashion, the most langorous and carefree time of the year. Grizzled veterans will revel in the seminal summer classics from 1958, the Jamies' immortal "Summertime, Summertime" and Eddie Cochran's "Summertime Blues"; punks will point to the Ramones' "Rockaway Beach" and Blondie's "In the Sun." Sixties fugitives have a host of selections to jar their

memories, including tracks by the Rivieras ("California Sun"), the Lovin' Spoonful ("Summer in the City"), Chad & Jeremy ("A Summer Song") and the Beach Boys ("Girls on the Beach" and "All Summer Long"). Sly and the Family Stone close out the '60s with "Hot Fun in the Summertime" and War gently brings in the first summer of the '70s with "Summer." The surprising, but smart, inclusion of the Sandals' evocative "Theme From Endless Summer" and Lesley Gore's lilting take on "California Nights" round out a package that is sheer delight—no heavy messages, only great escapism back to a time when the world was simpler, we thought, and the ozone layer was largely intact. In this setting, even Annette Funicello's wooden reading of "Beach Party" comes out a winner. — D.M.

SUN RECORDS

★ ★ ★ ★ ★ The Sun Story (Rhino, 1987)
★ ★ ★ ★ ★ Blue Flames: A Sun Blues
    Collection (Rhino, 1990)
    ★ ★ ★ ★ Memphis Ramble: A Sun Country
    Collection (Rhino, 1990)

Today, more than 40 years after Sam Phillips opened the Memphis Recording Service at 706 Union Avenue, the very fact that a Sun Records actually existed once in this country's history remains remarkable. While it is forever linked with the birth of rock & roll, Phillips's creation was considerably more broad-based. Long before Elvis Presley stepped up to the microphone in 1954, Phillips was recording some of the most important blues artists in the South and leasing the masters out to other independent labels such as Chess and Modern; in time, some of the region's most interesting and eccentric country artists came around as well. And after 1954, of course, Sun was the lodestar of rock & roll, drawing a group of artists whose naïve genius created a body of work that has been an enduring influence on succeeding generations of musicians.

The three albums of Sun material now available from Rhino (the import Charly label released a voluminous collection of Sun material in the mid-'70s, and the German Bear Family label has an 11-LP boxed set, *The Sun Country Years*, for completists only) are all essential to understanding what happened to popular music in America in the 1950s. Foremost among these is *The Sun Story*, which documents Sun's legacy from 1953 through 1959, when the label's fortunes waned (by that time Elvis Presley was on RCA, Johnny

Cash and Carl Perkins had moved to Columbia, Jerry Lee Lewis's career had been submarined by his marriage to his 13-year-old cousin and Roy Orbison was headed for Nashville, Monument Records and legendary status). Many of the tracks here are familiar—Presley's "Good Rockin' Tonight" and "That's All Right (Mama)" Jerry Lee's "Whole Lotta Shakin' Going On," Cash's "I Walk the Line," Perkins's "Blue Suede Shoes," Charlie Rich's "Lonely Weekends," Billy Lee Riley's shot in the spotlight, "Flying Saucers Rock 'N' Roll"—but hearing them back-to-back on one disc is an experience that defies explanation (as John Sebastian wrote, "It's like trying to tell a stranger 'bout rock & roll"). Beyond this, *The Sun Story* flat out *rocks*. Apart from the familiar titles listed above, Junior Parker gets on board with his 1953 track, "Mystery Train," and we all know what Presley did with that song; lesser but no less inspired Sun artists such as Carl Mann ("Mona Lisa") and Warren Smith ("Ubangi Stomp") are also represented, as is Bill Justis, with one of rock's first great instrumentals, "Raunchy."

Blue Flames proves that Phillips's chops for spotting talent were developed well ahead of Presley's arrival. His Memphis Recording Service became a clearing house for the music made by some of Memphis's and Mississippi's most important blues artists, which Phillips then leased out to other labels prior to forming Sun in 1952 after one of his recordings leased to Chess, Jackie Brenston's "Rocket 88," topped the R&B charts. Brenston was a session player backed by Ike Turner and his Kings of Rhythm, and "Rocket 88" (which kicks off *Blue Flames*) was, according to Turner, a knocked-off item done solely for gas money. It is also a wild, incendiary romp that is often cited as the first rock & roll recording. The cuts on *Blue Flames* chronicle Phillips's work from 1951 through 1954, primarily, and showcase a wide variety of blues styles, and even one gospel number, "Forgive Me Lord," by the Southern Jubilee Singers. In B.B. King's "B.B. Blues" and James Cotton's "Cotton Crop Blues," you hear the roots of the urban blues and R&B styles these gifted artists helped pioneer; Rufus Thomas's "Bear Cat," an answer record to Big Mama Thornton's "Hound Dog," is a 1953 cut that fuses R&B and gutbucket blues shouting; "Terra Mae" features the legendary one-man band Doctor Ross in a stripped-down blues with accompaniment by Reuben Martin on washboard. Also notable is the inclusion of guitarist Pat Hare's "I'm Gonna Murder My Baby," a 1954 track. Hare, who was in essence a Sun session player (he can be heard to searing effect on the aforementioned "Cotton Crop Blues" with James Cotton), was an early, though probably unconscious, proponent of distortion; his blistering sound is instantly identifiable not only on Sun Records, but in the work of any number of '60s guitar heroes. Hare went on to play in Junior Parker's band and to contribute some extraordinary lead guitar work on Muddy Waters's *At Newport* album. But true to his word, in 1962 Hare did indeed murder his baby—his girlfriend, that is—and spent the last 16 years of his life in prison.

Country wasn't Phillips's first love, but he understood something about the point at which country music, bluegrass and blues met. It's fair to say that the country artists that came to Sun would have been given no quarter in slick, conservative Nashville, but felt welcomed at Sun. Certainly they were encouraged to do their thing, and Phillips was smart enough to get out of the way and let the music happen. *Memphis Ramble* is rife with signposts of things to come. Two takes of Warren Smith's "So Long I'm Gone," one leading off the disc, the other closing it, show Smith picking up the tempo on the latter and turning a weepy country ballad into a rockabilly raveup. "My Kind of Carryin' On" by Doug Poindexter & the Starlite Wranglers is an unremarkable record in most respects—Poindexter was only an average singer, and the song itself is mundane—but the man punctuating the verses with brief guitar solos happens to be Scotty Moore, whose stylistic signature would later flourish when he became part of Elvis Presley's band along with his fellow Starlite Wrangler, bassist Bill Black. Rockabilly wild man Charlie Feathers is on hand as well, with "Man in Love," a more sedate track and more of a straight-ahead country effort than Feathers would attempt in later years as one of Sun's most promising rockabilly artists. There's also a rare track from one of music's true primitive artists, and a man who could only have wound up at Sun, Harmonica Frank Floyd, who had perfected the technique of singing out of one side of his mouth while playing the harmonica with the other side all the while accompanying himself on guitar. His bare-bones "Swamp Root" workout must be heard to be believed. Three of Sun's bright, shining stars are included as well, with Johnny Cash ("Train of Love"), Carl

Perkins ("Y.O.U.") and Jerry Lee Lewis ("I'm the Guilty One") all showing in their contributions the country strains they helped reconfigure as rough-and-tumble rockabilly.
— D.M.

HAVE A NICE DAY: SUPER HITS OF THE SEVENTIES (Rhino, 1990)

★ ★ ★	Volume 1
★ ★ ★	Volume 2
★ ★ ★	Volume 3
★ ★ ★½	Volume 4
★ ★ ★ ★	Volume 5
★ ★½	Volume 6
★ ★	Volume 7
★ ★½	Volume 8
★ ★½	Volume 9
★ ★½	Volume 10
★	Volume 11
★ ★	Volume 12
★ ★ ★	Volume 13
★ ★ ★	Volume 14
★ ★ ★	Volume 15

At first, this elongated series seems to fulfill the premise put forward in *Billboard* writer Paul Grein's liner notes: namely, that the early '70s really is a peculiar and fascinating stretch of pop history. The techniques of post–*Sgt. Pepper's* progressive rock began to trickle down to hack Top Forty at this point, and Volumes 1–5 bottle the results: dozens of sappy, innovative hit singles by faceless artists with clunky handles like the Tee Set ("Ma Belle Amie," from *Volume 2*) or Hamilton, Joe, Frank and Reynolds ("Don't Pull Your Love," from *Volume 5*). The third volume unearths a genuine find (Alive & Kicking's "Tighter, Tighter") along with a taste for hopeless novelties. R. Dean Taylor's "Indiana Wants Me" is a trashy hoot, but those garbage hits by Bobby Sherman and the Partridge Family barely raise a chuckle. *Volume 4* places countrypolitan smoothies like Lynn Anderson and Ray Price next to some highly enjoyable back-to-the-earth hippie anthems, while *Volume 5* summarizes *Have a Nice Day*'s sunny attitude: horny fake R&B ("Chick-a-Boom") meets squeaky-clean, Beatle-ized harmonies ("Here Comes That Rainy Day Feeling Again"). This could only happen in the crazed, democratic environs of AM radio, and it didn't last long.

Spotty selection dogs the middle five albums; some noticeably hookless followups and coulda-beens drag down the stronger cuts on *Volumes 6, 7* and *9*. Even though *Volume 8* throws in FM-rock ringers from Commander Cody, Jo Jo Gunne and

Argent, the collection's limitations emerge as the mindless good times wear on. At its campiest, *Have a Nice Day* creates a somewhat phony, sterile context for this vibrant music: songs that sounded great in between "Back Stabbers" and "Layla" and "Take It Easy" and "Lean On Me" can't be expected to prosper in hot-house isolation. However, the DeFranco Family ("Heartbeat—It's a Lovebeat," *Volume 10*) seem to have aged better than the Partridges.

"Playground in My Mind," "Dueling Banjos," "Daisy a Day," Deodato's disco "Also Sprach Zarathustra"—*Volume 11* explains why car radios come equipped with push buttons. *Volume 12* cries out for judicious scanning; a couple of cute instrumental novelties ruin the grungy mood generated by the likes of "Rock On" and "Rock and Roll, Hoochie Koo." Andy Kim's "Rock Me Gently" sets the tone for the remaining albums: still Top Forty, but decidedly post-hippie. Nostalgia becomes an important factor at this point, and that can be off-putting. The campy strains of shclock-epics like "Billy, Don't Be a Hero" and "The Night Chicago Died" (from *Volume 13*) immediately conjure up memories of the summer of '74, but maybe you had to be there. *Volumes 14* and *15* ride out on an unassuming mix of prefab funk, dreamy housewife pop, mellow country-flavored rock and, of course, those darn novelty songs. There's a huge gulf separating Hot Chocolate's divinely funky "You Sexy Thing" and C. W. McCall's corny CB ode "Convoy" (from *Volume 15*). *Super Hits of the Seventies* deliriously pretends that gulf does not exist. — M.C.

★★★★ **SURFIN' HITS (Rhino, 1989)**
Rhino once had a multivolume *History of Surf Music* series in its catalogue; this has now been compressed into 18 essential tracks by the major players of the subgenre's first and only golden era, omitting the newer surf bands who have energy and little else to recommend them. In addition to some expected classics—the Surfaris' "Wipeout," Jan and Dean's "Ride the Wild Surf," Dick Dale's "Miserlou" and, of course, the Beach Boys' tracks—lesser gods make rousing appearances as well: the Trashmen ("Surfin' Bird"), the Lively Ones ("Surf Rider"), the Pyramids ("Penetration") and the Belairs ("Mr. Moto"). Of special note are Jack Nitzsche's one big solo blast, the elegiac "The Lonely Surfer," and the Trade Winds' "New York's a Lonely Town," one of the last big surf hits, from 1965. Guitar fans are treated to two Dick Dale selections, though the King of Surf Guitar had much more to offer than is indicated by even the two excellent sides on this disc. Can't go wrong, though, with *Surfin' Hits* as a concise overview before moving on to individual titles by the featured artists. — D.M.

★★ **TEENAGE TRAGEDY (Rhino, 1984)**
Most of the signal works of the teenage death song subgenre are here—Jody Reynolds's "Endless Sleep," Mark Dinning's ne plus ultra "Teen Angel," J. Frank Wilson & the Cavaliers' "Last Kiss," the Shangri-Las' "Leader of the Pack" and Dickey Lee's "Patches"—with Pat Boone's "Moody River" being the only significant omission. Characterized by melodramatic and portentous arrangements supporting ominous, pain-wracked vocalizing, the death songs were rather amusing at the time of their release.

This Rhino package comes complete with one unnerving, disturbing note by way of a re-recorded live version of Jan and Dean's "Dead Man's Curve." Jan Berry suffered aphasia as a result of severe head injuries sustained in a near-fatal car wreck in 1966. It was another six years before he could even remember song lyrics. Despite the duo's making a return to live performing in the late '70s, Berry could barely carry a tune and had problems pronouncing, much less singing, most of his lyrics. In its original version, "Dead Man's Curve" is a great rock production. However, the "Dead Man's Curve" on this set is an unbelievable horror. One can only wonder about the reasons for including a newer version that finds Berry struggling to recite (he makes no attempt to sing) the lyrics in a voice so tuneless as to be painful. Given the context of *Teenage Tragedy*, it appears someone thought it would send a covert message to listeners, that this is what happens when these songs come true. Either that, or someone has a cruel sense of humor. — D.M.

★★ **TEEN IDOLS (Rhino, 1987)**
Teen Idols demonstrates that Del Shannon, Dion, Bobby Vee and Johnny Tillotson really had some intellect and feeling going for them, while Tab Hunter, Fabian, Frankie Avalon, Troy Shondell (Troy Shondell?) and the dreaded Paul Anka had none. The first four artists partially redeem this package (and offer evidence that rock & roll wasn't a wasteland after Elvis went into

the army and before the Beatles arrived), but all were more than one-hit wonders whose work is best appreciated in their own greatest-hits collections. — D.M.

THIS IS THE ERA OF MEMORABLE SONG HITS (RCA, 1972)
★ ★ ★ **The Decade of the '30s**
★ ★ ★ **The Decade of the '40s**
★ ★ ★ ★ **The Decade of the '50s**
There was a time in recent history when RCA's artists dominated the Hit Parade. And while the term Hit Parade invariably suggests blandness, RCA's roster was replete with variety and talent. These three twin-pack cassettes state the case most eloquently and also provide the listener with a good understanding of the breadth of the Hit Parade's spectrum—there were forgettable moments to be sure (Tommy Leonetti's tortured rendition of the Lloyd Price hit "Personality" on the '50s set answers the question as to why you never heard of him), but there's much to write home about as well. This is the mainstream before and during the inception of the rock & roll era, and a fine, diverse mainstream it is. Phil Harris has a couple of memorable turns, with a swinging version of the chestnut "Is It True What They Say About Dixie" (*'30s*) and the inspired novelty item, "The Thing" (*'50s*). Also on the novelty front, Spike Jones checks in with his frenzied social commentary masquerading as "Cocktails for Two" (*'40s*). Cuba native Perez Prado contributes Spanish-influenced sounds with the rumba "Peanut Vendor" (*'30s*) and his Number One pop hit from '55, "Cherry Pink and Apple Blossom White" (*'50s*); Glenn Miller and Tommy Dorsey (the latter with Frank Sinatra on the *'40s* set) are worthy ambassadors for the big bands; Domenico Modugno brings "Volare" from Italy (*'50s*); the Ames Brothers (represented in all decades) showcase the style of pop-based vocal harmony that would remain popular into the '50s and influence countless groups; the Sons of the Pioneers carry the banner for western songs (*'30s* and *'40s*); Lena Horne (*'30s*) offers a sensual, lilting blues in "Let's Put Out the Lights and Go to Sleep"; Harry Belafonte introduces the Caribbean beat into the mix with "Day-O" (*'50s*); the Browns and Eddy Arnold (the latter represented with tougher tracks than are available on his remaining in-print albums) display, respectively, the sentimentality and the grit of country music (*'50s*); Perry Como, one of the most dependable and distinctive stylists in

American pop, produces object lessons in the school of cool with two popular performances on the *'50s* album; the Glahe Musette Orchestra delivers a rousing polka (*'30s*); not least of all, Sam Cooke closes out side one of the *'50s* with a sensual and yearning rendition of "Cry Me a River."

All that's missing is some detailed liner notes. Release dates; chart history; thumbnail artist bios; instrumental soloists; producer and studio identifications—even the most minimal background info would add needed perspective. That omission cost a star for an anthology that is in all other respects well-considered. — D.M.

U.S.A. FOR AFRICA
★ ★½ **We Are the World (Columbia, 1985)**
Apart from the all-star sentimentality of the title track, the "previously unreleased songs" used to flesh out this album constitute rock's first attempt to save the world through leftovers. — J.D.C.

WCBS-FM 101 HISTORY OF ROCK: THE DOO WOP ERA (Collectables, 1988)
★ ★ ★ ★ **Part One**
★ ★ ★ ★ **Part Two**
This four-record set is notable for disdaining chart hits in favor of first-rate records that helped define the doo-wop genre but had little or no impact at the sales counter. So in this case familiar and well-worn entries such as Dion and the Belmonts' "I Wonder Why," the Edsels' "Rama Lama Ding Dong" and the Mystics' "Hushabye" serve only to represent the commercial high end; the real show-stoppers, from a historical vantagepoint, are rare items such as the Eternals' bass-fired workout on "Babalu's Wedding Day"; the Bob Chords' spirited street-corner harmony on "Castles in the Sky"; and the Frankie Lymon–soundalike lead singer of the Students delivering a tender reading of the seldom-heard tearjerker "I'm So Young." *Part One* has the Students', and one of doo-wop's, finest hours in "Every Day of the Week," a remarkable melding of powerhouse bass vocal, four-part harmony and soaring lead tenor work that has entered into legend among doo-wop aficionados. If distinctions must be made, *Part One* contains more minor doo-wop classics, while *Part Two* mixes in a high number of songs that would be familiar to anyone who listens to oldies radio on a regular basis. Most anthologies bearing a radio station's imprimatur are usually chart-bound to a fault, as if consumers wouldn't dare accept anything

that smacked of the unknown or obscure. However, in its programming choices New York City's WCBS-FM demonstrates a commitment to deepening its listeners' understanding of the varied musical styles, in and out of the mainstream, that fall under the broad banner of rock & roll. With its mixture of the familiar and the forgotten, *The Doo Wop Era* exemplifies an intelligent approach and honors a radio station that dares to take its audience seriously. — D.M.

★★★★ WONDER WOMEN: THE HISTORY OF THE GIRL GROUP SOUND (Rhino, 1986)

In an age when date rape and violence against women are widespread, it's a bit unsettling to hear Joanie Sommers plead with her boyfriend to show his love by getting angry, and then add, "I want a brave man/I want a cave man/Johnny, show me that you care, really care for me." But then when Sommers sings "Johnny Get Angry," on *Wonder Women*, she opens a window on a world long vanished. Hers is an extreme point of view, however. The Angels ("My Boyfriend's Back") may look to their men for retribution, but the other artists here are in pursuit of love on an even plane. Contrary to the popular perception of these females, their starry-eyed aspects should not be misread as subservience.

Wonder Women offers some bold music. For one, the Shirelles ("Mama Said," "Soldier Boy," "Tonight's the Night") feature the husky, sensuous lead vocals of Shirley Alston, who's cut from the irrepressible mold of earthy R&B singers like LaVern Baker. Similarly, Barbara Lewis and Betty Everett bring a depth of experience to their work that makes it revelatory as personal statement. Lumping Dionne Warwick with the girl-group sound is a bit off the track, but so what? She rides roughshod over the rest of the compilation with two ferocious performances, "Don't Make Me Over" and "This Empty Place." On the former she strikes a blow for reality that is singular among her contemporaries when she sings, "Just love me with all my faults/The way that I love you." In "This Empty Place," Warwick surveys the ruins of a broken heart in a voice so mournful and tenuous as to render her distress palpable. Operating from a consciousness well advanced beyond that of her companions here, Warwick stands as the most precious jewel in a crown studded with many gems. — D.M.

SOUNDTRACKS

★ ★ ★ **BACK TO THE BEACH (Columbia, 1987)**
Whether or not the collision of '60s California beach culture (in the person of Frankie Avalon and Annette Funicello) and '80s California beach culture (or as close to it as Hollywood would dare get) strikes you as the stuff of cinematic comedy, this soundtrack is well worth hearing. Granted, having Annette try to keep pace with Fishbone is funny in ways the producers never intended, but Pee-wee Herman's take on "Surfin' Bird" is everything anyone could have hoped, while the guitar shoot-out between Dick Dale and Stevie Ray Vaughan on "Pipeline" should not be missed. — J.D.C.

★ ½ **BEACHES (Atlantic, 1988)**
Shameless sentimentality and cheap, campy humor are the hallmarks of this Bette Midler soundtrack. Her Grammy-winning rendition of "Wind Beneath My Wings"—a classic piece of self-serving show-biz tripe—should be reason enough to give it a wide berth. — J.D.C.

★ ★ ★ **BEAT STREET (Atlantic, 1984)**
★ ★ ★ ½ **BEAT STREET, Vol. 2 (Atlantic, 1984)**
As a film, this hip-hop-graffiti-breakdancing musical had its problems, but none of them involved the soundtrack. Granted, some of the tracks on *Beat Street* were tarted up for the more mainstream listener, placing lush love themes alongside hip-hop offerings like Afrika Bambaataa's "Frantic Situation," Arthur Baker's "Breaker's Revenge" and "Beat Street Breakdown," one of Melle Mel's first post–Grandmaster Flash efforts. But *Beat Street, Vol. 2* plays to the purists, and includes a number of gems. — J.D.C.

★ ★ ★ ½ **THE BIG CHILL (Motown, 1983)**
★ ★ **THE BIG CHILL (More Songs From the Original Soundtrack) (Motown, 1984)**
Lawrence Kasdan's soap opera about former flower children struggling with mortality and materialism didn't just give America yet another nickname for baby-boomers, it also helped define an aesthetic—or, at least, a radio format. Kasdan's characters still worship the music of their youth (when Kevin Kline's Harold is asked if he has any other music, he snaps, "There is no other music, not in my house!"), and the mostly Motown soundtrack reflects that adoration, although without the film's irony.

As oldies albums, this multiplatinum soundtrack and its let's-cash-in supplement are certainly listenable enough, since Kasdan augments the usual assortment of Miracles, Temptations and Marvin Gaye singles with such Top Forty fodder as Three Dog Night's "Joy to the World" (*Big Chill*) and Creedence Clearwater Revival's "Bad Moon Rising" (*More Songs*). And from a historical standpoint, the albums are worth noting if only for having anticipated the "classic rock" radio boom of the late '80s. But as cultural statements, well . . . would you want your generation summarized by what amounts to a high-concept K-Tel compilation? — J.D.C.

★ ★ **THE BREAKFAST CLUB (A&M, 1985)**
Singles by Simple Minds and Wang Chung, along with Keith Forsey's new wave-ish score, lend a certain youth-culture credibility to this soundtrack, but not enough to let it stand on its own. — J.D.C.

★★★ COAL MINER'S DAUGHTER
(MCA, 1980)

In this film version of Loretta Lynn's autobiography, Sissy Spacek not only acts the role, but sings it as well. With Owen Bradley's production know-how behind her, Spacek (who later cut an album of country songs on her own) does an admirable job of imitating Lynn; Beverly D'Angelo is somewhat less credible as Patsy Cline, Lynn's best buddy in the biz. Anyone interested in Lynn's career would obviously do better with the original recordings, but this album has its pleasures, the greatest of which is hearing Levon Helm (as Lynn's father) sing "Blue Moon of Kentucky." — J.D.C.

★★★ ½ COLORS (Warner Bros., 1988)

As a film, *Colors* was just another cop opera; as an album, it made a pretty impressive rap compilation. Ironically, though the film focuses on L.A. gang violence, most of the musical talent—Big Daddy Kane, Salt-N-Pepa, Eric B. & Rakim, Roxanne Shanté—hails from New York. But it's Ice-T's gangsta rap title tune that sets the mood and ultimately sells the album. — J.D.C.

★★½ DIRTY DANCING (RCA, 1987)
★★★ MORE DIRTY DANCING (RCA, 1988)

As with the mega-hit soundtrack to *Grease*, the popular appeal of these albums has less to do with the music offered than with the spectacle the music recalls. That's not to say these albums aren't worth listening to, just that their merit hardly explains their massive sales. Never mind the plot, in which a shy, socially awkward girl from a good family finds fun, romance and truth with a group of working-class dance instructors at a Catskills resort in the early '60s; the songs on *Dirty Dancing* are set-pieces more interested in evoking mood than conveying information. And apart from the oldies, most are utter schlock, too, tending to such stock soundtrack devices as limp balladry like Eric Carmen's "Hungry Eyes" and overexcited instrumentals. (Star Patrick Swayze is even allowed a song.) Only "(I've Had) The Time of My Life," a sort of Righteous Brother and Sister duet between Bill Medley and Jennifer Warnes, manages to capture both the period feel and the plot's romantic uplift. *More Dirty Dancing*, though it relies almost entirely on oldies and scene-setting incidental music, actually conveys more of the film's mood. Then

again, with tracks by Otis Redding, the Contours and Solomon Burke, you'd expect it to have an edge over the likes of Carmen and Swayze. — J.D.C.

★★★½ DO THE RIGHT THING
(Motown, 1989)
★★½ DO THE RIGHT THING
(Columbia, 1989)

The smarts and charm of Spike Lee's *She's Gotta Have It* heralded the arrival of a real force in American filmmaking, but *Do the Right Thing* really broke things open. Lee's unflinching study of urban racism was political cinema of a pop power that made it irresistibly watchable; this was a message movie so "action-packed," and at times so expertly comic, that Lee's skill could not be denied. And that skill was a subversive one—rather than preach with a documentary-styled earnestness, Lee got over by besting mainstream directors at their own game. *Do the Right Thing* brought realpolitik into the escapist sanctums of the mall cineplexes.

Its music boosted its appeal. Motown's soundtrack is the songs of *Do The Right Thing*, and it's dominated by Public Enemy's "Fight the Power." Ruben Blades, Take 6, Teddy Riley and EU also help make the record a primer of smart late-'80s soul; the record stands as a great funk-rap sampler. Columbia's companion album is the orchestral score. Composed by the director's father, Bill Lee, it's smoky, atmospheric stuff—alluding at times to Ellington, at others, to Gershwin—though less compelling than the Motown set. — P.E.

★★★ ½ FALLING FROM GRACE
(Mercury, 1992)

For the soundtrack to *Falling From Grace*, his debut as a film director, John Mellencamp called on a number of friends to help delineate his story of a successful recording artist who returns to a problematic life in his small hometown. Nanci Griffith ("Cradle of the Interstate") and John Prine ("All the Best") contribute strong songs, while Mellencamp's former guitarist Larry Crane weighs in with four tunes and his violinist Lisa Germano chips in with two. Meanwhile, Mellencamp, Prine, Dwight Yoakam, Joe Ely and James McMurtry team up as the Buzzin' Cousins on "Sweet Suzanne." The result is a soundtrack that perfectly suits the movie and seems of a piece with Mellencamp's best work—and that's saying something. — P.E.

★ ½ **FAME (RSO, 1980)**
Despite its synth-heavy arrangements and
semihip rock rhythms, *Fame* is really just an
old-fashioned movie musical—and sounds it.
Apart from the title tune, which launched
Irene Cara's brief career, there's little of
note here. — J.D.C.

★★ **FLASHDANCE (Casablanca, 1983)**
Set in some imaginary Pittsburgh where lady
ironworkers spend their evenings mounting
elaborate dance extravaganzas in
working-class bars, *Flashdance* the film is
about as divorced from reality as the
average rock video. Except that rock videos
at least have the music as an excuse,
whereas this soundtrack is listenable exactly
twice: During Irene Cara's album-opening
"Flashdance . . . What a Feeling" and again
during the last song, Michael Sembello's
urgently electronic "Maniac." All else
should be ignored. — J.D.C.

★★★ **FOOTLOOSE (Columbia, 1984)**
As a film, *Footloose* concerns a young man's
efforts to encourage other teens to
dance—an astonishing premise for any
movie with a Kenny Loggins title song, but
that's Hollywood. As a soundtrack, though,
Footloose contains some surprisingly
credible dance pop, including Deniece
Williams's irrepressible "Let's Hear It for
the Boy" and Shalamar's slinky, insinuating
"Dancing in the Sheets," as well as the
surprisingly palatable power-ballad "Almost
Paradise" (bellowed by Mike Reno and Ann
Wilson). The rest, though, is overproduced
dreck, including Loggins's cliché-addled,
rhythmically inert title tune. — J.D.C.

★★★ **THE GOOD, THE BAD AND THE
    UGLY (1968; EMI Manhattan, 1985)**
Ennio Morricone went on to make more
elevated film scores—notably the gorgeous
pan-pipe and massed strings triumph of the
Jeremy Irons–Robert DeNiro epic, *The
Mission*—but *The Good, the Bad and the
Ugly* was the pop triumph of his pastiche
style. Perfectly suiting the existentialist
Western it served, the music combined
chanted choruses, a trademark ocarina
passage, twang-bar guitar worthy of Duane
Eddy and a canyon of echo. The movie
itself, despite its period clothing, reflected a
'60s rock & roll sensibility. Rail-thin, very
young, and nearly mute, Clint Eastwood
stalked through melodramatic scenery, his
head in a cloud of cheroot smoke; he was a
Dylanesque gunslinger, an iconic, disaffected
sort who, without the high-art straining,

paralleled Sam Shepard's Presleyesque
cowboys.
   Neo-jazzer John Zorn remains one of
Morricone's biggest fans (he's reworked the
Italian composer's oeuvre into feverish
nightclub music), but Adam Ant, various
rappers and others have borrowed from the
sound of *The Good, the Bad and the Ugly*,
and it remains very listenable pop art.
— P.E.

½ ★ **HAIR (Original Cast) (1968; RCA,
      1988)**
½ ★ **HAIR (Soundtrack) (RCA, 1979)**
A tremendously big deal at its time, this
1968 "American Tribal Love-Rock Musical"
was the brainstorm of actors Gerome Ragni
and James Rado, along with composer Galt
MacDermot. They put together this
manipulative celebration, which, according
to its riotously dated *Original Cast* liner
notes, championed the "pro-drugs, pro-sex
and anti-establishment tribe, who in the
course of the action, attend be-ins, scare
tourists, protest at induction centers,
re-create a war or two, smoke pot, take off
their clothes, sing in the streets, make love
and otherwise amuse themselves . . . " The
pale fare of "Aquarius" provided a hit for
the Fifth Dimension—which should have
been notice enough that *Hair* wasn't the real
thing. In 1979, Milos Forman made *Hair*,
the movie. Why? — P.E.

★★★★★ **THE HARDER THEY COME
        (1972; Mango, 1973)**
This mesmerizing reggae collection (and the
accompanying low-budget film) spread the
World Music gospel among a generation of
young Americans. Nearly 20 years later,
these deceptively simple tunes remain quite
potent: next to Bob Marley, there's no
better introduction to the intoxicating sound
of Trenchtown. *The Harder They Come* is a
haphazard and very revealing selection of
Jamaican singles from the late '60s and early
'70s—a time when reggae asserted its slower,
more complex rhythms over ska and
blue-beat. On the soundtrack, the soulful
strut of Toots and the Maytals and
Desmond Dekker's socially conscious
shimmy-beat demonstrate reggae's musical
origins, while the Melodians' "Rivers of
Babylon" and Jimmy Cliff's uplifting,
pop-conscious anthems ("The Harder They
Come" and "You Can Get It If You Really
Want") reveal its spiritual center. The
Slickers' "Johnny Too Bad" could hold its
own against today's toughest gangster
rappers, and for that matter, Scotty's wild

"Draw Your Brakes" offers an inescapable parallel between reggae's dub style and hip-hop. One small quibble: the title track and "You Can Get It If You Really Want" repeat at the end of *The Harder They Come*—but by then, you'll probably be ready to hear them again. — M.C.

★ ★ ★ ★ **LA BAMBA (Slash/WB, 1987)**
The film biography of the late Ritchie Valens's life stands alone among its kind both in conception and in execution. Written and directed by Luis Valdez, *La Bamba* gave its audience a compassionate portrait of the gifted but doomed Valens and his Hispanic-American family's struggle to escape a stultifying life picking oranges in southern California. For Valens, that escape came through music. The movie soundtrack is remarkable on several levels. Performing Valens's songs, Los Lobos give an inspired performance. It's easy to say that since they share Valens's heritage, they bring a depth of understanding to their interpretations that might elude others. More than that, they bring the intangible quality of spirit. Their playing is by turns raucous and tender; the vocals by Cesar Rosas and David Hidalgo are wonders of feeling and nuance. One regrets only that the traditional folk version of "La Bamba," which we hear during the film's Mexico segment, was not included in its entirely on the disc.

Los Lobos is the reason to own this record, but the other performers featured on the soundtrack all turn in fine outings as well. Howard Huntsberry comes out of nowhere to do a splendid Jackie Wilson take on "Lonely Teardrops," Brian Setzer is at his retro best delivering a rousing version of Eddie Cochran's "Summertime Blues," and Marshall Crenshaw offers an urgent reading of Buddy Holly's "Crying, Waiting, Hoping." Leave it to the gunslinger himself, Bo Diddley, to reduce these fine performances to ashes with a version of "Who Do You Love" that threatened to burn holes in screens the world over. Diddley enters, slashing away over his familiar beat, then proceeds to growl the lyrics in a voice that is menace personified. It's worth the price of admission alone to hear Diddley announce, "I'm an older woman's wish, and a young woman's dream." You can almost hear him chuckling as the song fades out. — D.M.

★ ★ ★ ★ **LESS THAN ZERO (Columbia, 1987)**
Arguably the best idea producer Rick Rubin ever had, this soundtrack has almost nothing to do with the lamentable movie version of Brett Easton Ellis' teen-ennui novel of the same name. Instead, it celebrates two realizations: First, that Slayer and Public Enemy can exist side-by-side on one album; and second, that the musical roots of pop postmodernism are in the shallow commerciality of the '70s, not the earnest idealism of the '60s. Thus, Slayer demolishes Iron Butterfly's "In-A-Gadda-Da-Vida" while Poison consecrates Kiss's "Rock and Roll All Nite," the Black Flames evoke the Chi-Lites, and Aerosmith remakes "Rockin' Pneumonia and the Boogie Woogie Flu" as if Johnny Rivers's version were the original. Add in the Bangles' surprisingly beefy "Hazy Shade of Winter" and Public Enemy's epochal "Bring the Noise," and *Less Than Zero* looks more and more like a classic. — J.D.C.

★ ★ ★ **MIAMI VICE (MCA, 1985)**
★ ★½ **MIAMI VICE II (MCA, 1986)**
Although the show was built around then–NBC exec Brandon Tartikoff's immortal phrase, "MTV cops," there's little on these soundtrack albums that reflects the adventurous eclecticism of the show itself. Instead, what we get is Top Forty predictability and a heavy emphasis on MCA recording artists. As a result, the best things about these albums aren't the rock-star tracks, but Jan Hammer's edgy, adrenalized instrumentals, the best of which can be found on the first volume. — J.D.C.

★ ★ ★ ½ **PERFORMANCE (Warner Bros., 1970)**
With Mick Jagger, in his best movie role, typecast as Turner, a decadent, kimono-clad, ex–rock star junkie, and with an on-set ambience so unsettling that it sent the brilliant James Fox off to a religious retreat, Nicolas Roeg's *Performance* took an intriguing look at the London drugs 'n' thugs underworld. Arranged by Jack Nitzsche and conducted by Randy Newman, the *Performance* soundtrack remains a fascinating curio; Jagger's at his ripest and most dramatic singing "Memo From Turner"; Ry Cooder contributes some great bottleneck solos; "Wake Up, Niggers" features the Last Poets and their prescient Afro protorap; and, with a great version of Nitzsche's "Gone Dead Train," which later was covered ably by Crazy Horse, Randy Newman—astonishingly—rocks out. — P.E.

★★★ ½ **PUMP UP THE VOLUME (MCA, 1990)**

Incredibly, the soundtrack to this film about a teen-run pirate radio station actually manages to include a lot of the sort of music a hip and alienated teen might play. Among the better moments: Sonic Youth's ear-searing "Titanium Expose," the Bad Brains' rethink of "Kick Out the Jams" and Liquid Jesus's revision of Sly and the Family Stone's "Stand." — J.D.C.

½ ★ **SGT. PEPPER'S LONELY HEARTS CLUB BAND (RSO/Polygram, 1978)**

Declared the worst album of all time when it came out, this moldy curio doesn't even cut it as camp entertainment anymore. It's just a boring, absolutely directionless ego trip. How could the Bee Gees, perhaps the most skillful Beatles imitators ever, commit such clueless cover versions to record? Why did Beatles producer George Martin dirty his hands with this? What was Peter Frampton thinking about while he purred an Andy Gibb–style interpretation of "The Long and Winding Road"? Who the hell was Frankie Howerd, anyway? These questions may never be fully answered. And since Earth, Wind and Fire's "Got to Get You Into My Life" and Aerosmith's "Come Together" are available elsewhere, there's no reason on earth to reopen this can of worms. — M.C.

★★★★★ **SATURDAY NIGHT FEVER (RSO, 1977)**

The Bee Gees' "Stayin' Alive" not only provides the disco pulse of this blockbuster album, it also communicates the spirit of the film: corny, but somehow deeply resonant. And the Bee Gees' falsetto harmony wails still project an arresting, almost painful innocence. *Saturday Night Fever* brought a largely urban movement to the rock-saturated hinterlands, and millions of middle Americans didn't have to think twice about hustling on board. Collecting the best of the Gibb brothers' born-again funk phase (like the itchy "Jive Talkin' ") and some authentic dance-floor jams (like the Trammps' blazing "Disco Inferno"), *Saturday Night Fever* deserves its preeminent status. Unlike 90 percent of the rip-offs that followed, you can *still* dance to it. — M.C.

★ **THE SIMPSONS (Geffen, 1990)**

Marketing gone mad. Along with "Roseanne" and "Married . . . With Children," the Simpsons—first a tidbit on a 1987 Tracey Ullman show, then a half-hour cartoon starting in 1990—recast the American sitcom family as blue-collar, manic and frothily dysfunctional. Creator Matt Groening's Anti-Beaver and Superbrat, Bart, became a school-locker pin-up, his playground Jimmy Dean retorts—"Don't have a cow, man" and "Eat my shorts"—being quoted with the fervor the Red Guards had mustered for Chairman Mao's little red book. With his dad a dumbo, asleep at the wheel while at a nuclear power plant, his mom a hovering ditz, and sister Lisa a strange, bright child with a yen for Muddy Waters, Bart was a kind of hip-hop Huck Finn—and an instant youth hero (especially for black kids). Done by actress Nancy Cartwright, Bart's voice was his sly, whining signature tune.

Bart key chains, bubble gum, T-shirts were inevitable—so, it seems, was this album. "Do the Bartman" was the obvious rap hommage (or parody), basically just a booming backtrack with Bart squealing atop. Other bits were odder: Bart backing away from Joe Walsh's guitar on a version of Chuck Berry's "School Days," B.B. King earnestly grinding out "Born Under a Bad Sign" while Bart's dad mumbles along. Even with Buster Poindexter and Dr. John as part of the cast, the record was about what you'd expect—the Chipmunks, Part II. — P.E.

★★★★ **SOMETHING WILD (MCA, 1986)**

An easily overlooked gem, the soundtrack to Jonathan Demme's *Something Wild* is wonderfully exotic, willfully perverse and thoroughly engaging. As might be expected, there's plenty of name-brand new wave on hand—New Order, Jerry Harrison, Oingo Boingo, even Fine Young Cannibals debuting "Ever Fallen In Love"—but the tracks that stretch beyond the expected make this worth hearing. Like, for instance, "Loco de Amor," a David Byrne salsa duet with Celia Cruz that presaged *Rei Momo* by three years; an all-too-short taste of juju from Sonny Okosun; and a sublime reggae version of the Troggs' "Wild Thing" by Sister Carol. Don't read the book, don't see the movie—hear the album. — J.D.C.

★★★★½ **SUPERFLY (1972; RSO-Polygram, 1988)**
★★ **RETURN OF SUPERFLY (Capitol, 1990)**

Curtis Mayfield brought soul music to a sophisticated peak with the original *Superfly* soundtrack. "Successfully arranged and orchestrated from the original dictations of Curtis Mayfield by Johnny Pate," read the credits, and for once they're accurate. Those full-blown orchestrations complement Mayfield's sweet melodies, adding detail and breadth to his shattering vision. The Top Ten hits "Freddie's Dead" and "Superfly" both glow and pulsate with the funk, even as they impart their morals about drugs and prostitution. *Superfly* offers social commentary that's challenging—and danceable. The zoot-suit fashion excesses popularized by the film are considered high camp in the '90s, but the music and (unfortunately) the message of *Superfly* haven't aged a whit.

Return of Superfly attempts to re-create that immediacy: a mission doomed to failure. The sequel is a merely acceptable rap sampler, spanning from Tone Lōc's trashy-but-fun pot ode ("Cheeba Cheeba") to typically sexist garbage from N.W.A's Eazy E ("Eazy Street"). A couple of okay Mayfield cuts really stand out in this crowd, though he fares much better on another *Superfly*-inspired soundtrack: *I'm Gonna Get You Sucka*. An affectionate parody of the blaxploitation genre, that package reflects a bit of *Superfly*'s low-budget illumination. — M.C.

★ **TEENAGE MUTANT NINJA TURTLES (The Original Motion Picture Soundtrack) (SBK, 1990)**
★ **TEENAGE MUTANT NINJA TURTLES II (The Secret of the Ooze) (SBK, 1991)**
Proving themselves capable of an almost frightening identification with the mindset of the American nine-year-old, Turtles creators Kevin Eastman and Peter Laird assembled their comic-book gang of good-guy rowdies out of the stuff of preteen obsessions. Every skinny fifth grader is afraid he's a misfit, nurtures revenge fantasies about the junior-high kid who picks on him, harbors guilty nostalgia for the Disney-fied or Hensonized animals of his preschool years and aspires to the perceived power and freedom of adolescence. He also wants to be cool. His perfect dream idols, then? Pizza-chomping crusaders who spout surf-talk ("Cowabunga!"), male-bond like crazy, come in the guise of growth-spurt Muppets, and vanguish the neighborhood bully. First a cartoon, then two "major motion pictures," the Turtles escalated upward like genuine stars. Music, of course, went along with the marketing—and it's a tribute to the hipness of Eastman/Laird that it's not ersatz rock, but a softcore version of the rap that's finally conquered the malls. Each soundtrack features a big-star cameo—

Vanilla Ice's bit on *Turtles II* is better than M.C. Hammer's on *I*, probably because Ice is the more genuinely juvenile performer—some funk lite by Dan Hartman, and assorted instrumental filler enlivened only by periodic bursts of Turtles' sloganeering ("Excellent!" "Radical, dude!"). Obviously for kiddies only. — P.E.

★★★★ **THANK GOD IT'S FRIDAY (Casablanca, 1978)**
The movie itself is an exploitative quickie, but this soundtrack compilation goes a long way toward explaining disco's phenomenal breakout in the late '70s. While the *Saturday Night Fever* album blurs the distinction between workaday dance music and the Bee Gees' cosmopolitan pop, *Thank God It's Friday* magnifies the heartbeat pulse beyond all previous proportion. Oh, there are songs here, including Donna Summer's magnificient "Last Dance." But those goddamn rhythms really are inescapable: sometimes hundreds of percussive voices, sometimes one thick bass-heavy vibration, always itching, insisting that you get out on the floor and shake it like a fool. Listen to those hyperventilating singers, the corny orchestral swoons, the obviously fake exotic touches: Paul Jabara ("Trapped in a Stairway"), Sunshine ("Take It to the Zoo") and the Wright Brothers Flying Machine ("Leatherman's Theme") aren't worried about embarrassing themselves out there. So why should anybody else care? Like a hedonistic blowout at the end of a tough week, *Thank God It's Friday* provides therapeutic release. — M.C.

★★★ **TOMMY: As Performed by the London Symphony Orchestra and Chambre Choir with Guest Soloists (Ode, 1972)**
★★★ **TOMMY (The Motion Picture Soundtrack) (Polydor, 1975)**
The story line to the Who's rock opera may be a shaky one, but by drawing together all of his obsessions—teenage angst, alienation, spiritual release—Pete Townshend's tale of the deaf, dumb and blind boy who achieves transcendence through a combination of pinball and cosmic enlightenment serves just fine as dramatic underpinning for his band's greatest work. With *Tommy*, Townshend flourished the sheer ambition of his band at its most daunting—and he crafted some of his most notable melodies.

Given over to the London Symphony Orchestra and soloists ranging from Steve Winwood to Rod Stewart to Ringo Starr to

Maggie Bell, *Tommy* sounds less like a rock opera than a rock musical. Less bombastic, but also more pretentious than the Who's, this version is a victory for middlebrows. *Tommy III* came into being with Ken Russell's campy movie. The flick was fun and flashy. The album, with starring roles taken by Tina Turner, Ann-Margret and Elton John, is merely flashy. Stick with the Who. — P.E.

★ ★ **TWIN PEAKS (Warner Bros., 1990)**
Even if David Lynch is middle America's Fellini (he's not), and Angelo Badalamenti its Nino Rota (ditto), it would still take the devotion of a *Twin Peaks* zealot to find any lasting value in this cheesy homage to twangy guitar soundtracks and junior-college art music. — J.D.C.

★ ★ ★ ★ **UNTIL THE END OF THE WORLD (Warner Bros., 1991)**
It's a tribute to director Wim Wenders that such stellar artists as U2, R.E.M., Lou Reed, Talking Heads, Daniel Lanois and Patti Smith all consented to contribute songs to *Until the End of the World*, Wenders's penetrating, and characteristically sweet, look at the potentially apocalyptic future. Despite the strong personal visions of the individual artists, this album is a seamless whole—the rare soundtrack that fully stands as an intriguing complement to the movie that spawned it. — P.E.

WOODSTOCK
★ ★ ★½ Woodstock (Cotillion, 1970)
★ Woodstock II (Cotillion, 1971)
Revving up with John Sebastian's spacey "I Had a Dream" and the sweet ruralist fantasy of Canned Heat's "Going up the Country," then crashing marvelously with

13 minutes of Hendrix freaking out on "Star Spangled Banner" and "Purple Haze," the Woodstock soundtrack faithfully time-capsules the Age of Aquarius. Half a million attended the three-day love-in; the record's ragged power transcends the fest's joyous, muddy moment—you didn't have to be there to be moved.

Encyclopedic in cataloging late-'60s styles, Woodstock captures tie-dyed folk rock in Crosby, Stills and Nash's shaky "Suite: Judy Blue Eyes," acid-rock revolt in a slashing "Volunteers" by the Jefferson Airplane, and boogie madness in Ten Years After's "I'm Going Home." There's also period politics aplenty: Country Joe's antiwar black humor and Joan Baez's old-school leftism in a purist version of the union hymn "Joe Hill." Sly Stone serves up manic R&B; the funk frenzy of his attack shaking the dopers out of pie-eyed lethargy. A nod toward '50s revivalism comes by dimwitted way of Sha-Na-Na. British rock power is underrepresented, although the Who is at its fiercest in a *Tommy* excerpt, and the ghost of Lennon-McCartney wafts through Joe Cocker's baroque take on "With a Little Help From My Friends." A creaky documentary approach—overgenerous amounts of recorded "Rainstorm, Crowd Sounds, Announcements & General Hysteria"—messes up the album and stresses too hard Woodstock's sociological import, but, given the moment's admitted glory, you can't blame the producers for trying to get it all down on tape. *Woodstock II*, however, like most sequels, is redundant. Again, the Hendrix material is vital, and Mountain delivers incipient heavy metal, but the album is mainly bell-bottom nostalgia. — P.E.